STANDARD

SPANISH - ENGLISH
AND
ENGLISH - SPANISH

DICTIONARY

COMPLETELY REVISED BY
CARLOS FRANCISCO DURAN

*Giving the spelling, pronunciation, and meaning
of over 65,000 words in both languages.*

DICCIONARIO MODELO
ESPAÑOL - INGLÉS
e
INGLÉS - ESPAÑOL

COMPLETAMENTE REVISADO POR
CARLOS FRANCISCO DURAN

Más de 65,000 palabras en ambas lenguas

THE WORLD PUBLISHING COMPANY
CLEVELAND, OHIO　　　　　　　　　　**NEW YORK, N. Y.**

Table of Contents

Spanish-English

English-Spanish

Tabla de Materias

Español-Inglés

Inglés-Español

Clave para la pronunciación de la lengua inglesa
(Key to the Pronunciation of the English Language)

å se pronuncia como *e* en *ébano, hé.*

ǎ " " " *a* " *ala.*

ã sonido propio de la lengua inglesa, participando de *a* y *o*, muy parecido al sonido de *por.*

a̐ se pronuncia como *a* en *ana*, pero breve y de golpe.

ė " " " *i* " *ídolo, mí.*

ĕ " " " *e* " *editor, escampar*, pero breve y de golpe.

ī " " " *ai* " *aislar, maizal*, pero pronunciando ambas letras aun más unidas.

ĭ " " " *i* " *igual*, breve y de golpe.

ȯ " " " *o* " *cobre, mote.*

ŏ " " " *u* " *ubre, único.*

o̐ " " " *o* " *por*, pero más participando de *o* que en castellano.

ô " " " *o* " *dado*, breve y de golpe.

ú " " " *iu* " *viuda*, pero de golpe.

û sonido propio de la lengua inglesa, muy parecido al de *eu* en la lengua francesa, pero siempre breve y de golpe.

ŭ se pronuncia como la *u* española, pero breve y de golpe.

oė, oĭ se pronuncian como *oy* en *hoy*, pero pronunciando ambas letras aun más unidas.

o̐a̐ se pronuncia como *au* en *aula.*

j " " · " *ch* " *chapa*, pero así como si estuviera escrita esta voz: *dzchapa.*

sh " " " *ch* " francés.

th " " alguna vez como *z* muy suave (*th*): *youth*; otra vez (*th*) como *s* silbada: *father, that, there.*

Los sonidos *j, sh, th*, propios de la lengua inglesa, requieren la viva voz, por no hallarse análogos en el idioma castellano.

Key to the Spanish Pronunciation
(Clave para la pronunciación de la lengua espanola)

å sounds as *a* in *paper, tame.*

ã " " *a* " *far, lark.*

ē " " *e* " *here, we.*

ĕ " " *e* " *hell, tell.*

ẽ " " *i* " *kill, big.*

ȯ " " *o* " *globe, pope.*

ŏ " " *o* " *not, spot.*

ū " " *u* " *rule, true.*

ŭ " " *u* " *bull, full.*

y (as vowel) sounds as *ē.*

c (before *e* and *i*) sounds as *th* in *thank.*

d' is to be pronounced very much lisped, as if followed by *h*; similar to *dh* in Gaelic *dhû.*

j sounds as *h* very harshly aspirated.

h if heard at all, is to be pronounced with a very slight aspiration.

'h is to be pronounced very harshly aspirated.

z sounds as *th* in *thank.*

Abbreviations used in this Dictionary
(Abreviaturas usadas en este diccionario)

a. = adjective, *adjetivo*.
ad. = adverb, *adverbio*.
am. = Americanism, *americanismo*.
ar. = arithmetic, *aritmética*.
art. = article, *artículo*.
bot. = botany, *botánica*.
c. = conjunction, *conjunción*.
cant = cant term, *jerigonza*.
chem. = chemistry, *química*.
com. = commerce, *comercio*.
fam. = familarly, *familiarmente*.
fig. = figuratively, *metafóricamente*.
gr. = grammatically, *gramática*.
in comp. = in compounds, *usado en palabras compuestas*.
law = law term, *jurisprudencia*.
mar. = marine, *marina*.
med. = medicine, *arte médica*.

mil. = military art, *milicia, guerra*.
mus. = music, *música*.
p. = participle, *participio*.
pl. = plural number, *plural*.
poet. = poetical word, *poéticamente*.
pn. = pronoun, *pronombre*.
pr. = preposition, *preposición*.
rail. = railway, *ferrocarril*.
sf. = feminine substantive, *sustantivo femenino*.
sm. = masculine substantive, *sustantivo [masculino]*.
v. a. = verb active, *verbo activo*.
v. def. = verb defective, *verbo defectivo*.
v. imp. = verb impersonal, *verbo impersonal*.
v. n. = verb neuter, *verbo neutro*.
v. r. = verb reflective, *verbo recíproco*.
vulg. = vulgarly, *vulgarmente*.

SPANISH AND ENGLISH.

A.

á, ǎ, pr. to, in, at, according to, on, by, for, of.

ababa, ăbǎ'bǎ, sf. red poppy, corn-rose.

abacería, –thěrē'ǎ, sf. grocery.

abacero, –thā'rŏ, sm. grocer.

abacial, –thǐǎl', a. abbatial.

ábaco, ǎ'bǎkŏ, sm. abacus (of a column); multiplication-table.

abad, ǎbǎd'', sm. abbot.

abada, ǎbǎ'dǎ, sf. female rhinoceros.

abadejo, –dā'h'ŏ, sm. codfish; yellow wren; Spanish fly.

abadengo, ga, –děn'gŏ, a. abbatial.

abades, ǎbǎ'děs, sm. pl. cantharides.

abadesa, –dā'sǎ, sf. abbess.

abadía, –dē'ǎ, sf. abbey; abbacy.

abajo, ǎbǎ'h'ŏ, ad. under, underneath; below.

abalanzar, –lǎnthǎr', v. a. to balance, to counterpoise; to dart; to impel; –, v. n. to rush on with impetuosity; to venture.

abalear, –lěǎr', v. a. to fan or winnow corn.

abalorio, –lŏ'rǐŏ, sm. glass-bead.

aballestar, –lyěstǎr', v. a. (mar.) to haul a cable.

abanderado, ǎbǎnděrǎ'dŏ, sm. (mil.) ensign; standard-bearer.

abanderizador, ra, –rǐthǎdŏr', sm. ringleader, complotter.

abanderizar, –rǐthǎr', v. a. to band together.

abandonamiento, ǎbǎndŏnǎměn'tŏ, sm. abandonment.

abandonar, –nǎr', v. a. to abandon; –se, to despond, to despair; to give one's self up to.

abandono, ǎbǎndŏ'nŏ, sm. abandonment; forlornness; debauchery.

abanicar, ǎbǎnǐkǎr', v. a. to fan.

abanico, –nē'kŏ, sm. fan.

abaniquero, –nǐkā'rŏ, sm. fan-maker.

abanto, ǎbǎn'tŏ, sm. dwarf-hawk.

abaratar, ǎbǎrǎtǎr', v. a. to abate the price.

abarca, ǎbǎr'kǎ, sf. shoe of coarse leather, worn by Spanish peasants.

abarcadura, –dŏ'rǎ, sf. abarcamiento, –měn'tŏ**, sm. embrace.

abarcar, ǎbǎrkǎr', v. a. to a clasp, to embrace; to contain.

abarcón, –kŏn', sm. iron ring, hoop.

abarquillar, –kǐlyǎr', v. a. to shape like a boat; –se, to curl up; to be cocked.

abarracarse, ǎbǎrrǎkǎr'sě, v. r. to withdraw into barracks.

abarraganamiento, ǎbǎrrǎgǎnǎměn'tŏ, sm. concubinage.

abarraganarse, –nǎr'sě, v. r. to live in

abarrancadero, ǎbǎrrǎnkǎdā'rŏ, sm. boggy place; precipice; difficult business.

abarrancamiento, –měn'tŏ, sm. fall into a pit or trap; embarrassment.

abarrancar, –kǎr', v. a. to dig holes; –se, to become embarrassed.

abarrotar, ǎbǎrrŏtǎr', v. a. to tie down; (mar.) to stow the cargo.

abarrote, –rŏ'tě, sm. (mar.) small stowage.

abastecedor, ra, ǎbǎstěthědŏr', sm. & f. purveyor, caterer.

abastecer, –thěr', v. a. to purvey.

abastecimiento, –thěměn'tŏ, sm. provision; provisions, pl.

abastionar, ǎbǎstǐŏnǎr', v. a. to fortify with bastions.

abasto, ǎbǎs'tŏ, sm. supply of provisions.

abatanar, ǎbǎtǎnǎr', v. a. to full cloth.

abate, ǎbǎ'tě, sm. abbé.

ábate, ǎ'bǎtě, I take care!

abatido, da, ǎbǎtē'dŏ, a. dejected, low-spirited, faint; abject, mean.

abatimiento, –měn'tŏ, sm. low spirits, depression.

abatir, –tēr', v. a. to throw down; to humble; –, v. n. to descend, to stoop.

abdicación, ǎbdǐkǎthǐŏn', sf. abdication.

abdicar, –dǐkǎr', v. a. to abdicate.

abdomen, ǎbdŏ'měn, sm. abdomen.

abdominal, ǎbdŏmǐnǎl', a. abdominal, abdominous.

abecé, ǎběthā', sm. alphabet.

abecedario, –thědǎ'rǐŏ, sm. spelling-book, primer.

abedul, ǎbědǔl', sm. birch-tree.

abeja, ǎbā'h'ǎ, sf. bee; — maestra ó madre, queen-bee.

abejar, ǎbā'hǎr', sm. bee-hive.

abejarrón, ǎbā'hǎrrŏn', sm. horse-fly.

abejero, ǎbā'hā'rŏ, sm. bee-master.

abejón, ǎbā'hŏn', sm. drone; hornet.

abellacarse, ǎbělyǎkǎr'sě, v. r. to degrade one's self.

aberración, ǎběrrǎthǐŏn', sf. aberration.

abertal, ǎběrtǎl', a. full of clefts.

abertura, –tŏ'rǎ, sf. aperture, chink, cleft; (fig.) plain dealing; (mus.) overture.

abestiar, ǎběstǐǎr', v. a. to stupefy.

abeto, ǎbā'tŏ, sm. fir-tree.

abetunado, da, ǎbětǔnǎ'dŏ, a. bituminous.

abierto, ta, ǎbǐěr'tŏ, a. open; sincere; frank.

abigarrar, *abigărrăr',* v. a. to variegate, to dapple, to chequer; to diversify.

abigeato, *abigéă'tō,* sm. cattle-theft.

abigeo, *abigé'ō,* sm. cattle-thief.

abigotado, da, *abigōtă'dō,* a. (person) wearing long whiskers.

ab intestato, *ab intestă'tō,* a. intestate.

abismal, *abismăl',* a. abysmal; —es, s. pl. clasp-nails.

abismar,—*măr',* v.a. to depress, to humble

abismo, *abis'mō,* sm. abyss; gulf; hell.

abitaque, *abită'kĕ,* sm. rafter. [like.

abizcochado,da, *abiskōtshă'dō,* a. biscuit-

abjuración, *abhŭrăthiōn',* sf. abjuration.

abjurar, —*hŭrăr',* v. a. to abjure, to recant upon oath. [lification.

ablandamiento, *ablăndămiēn'tō,*sm. mol-

ablandar, —*dăr',* v. a. & n. to mollify.

ablandativo, —*dătē'vō,* a. mollificative.

ablativo, *ablătē'vō,* sm. (gr.) ablative.

ablución, *ablŭthiōn',* sf. ablution, lotion.

abnegación, *abnegăthiōn',* sf. abnegation.

abnegar, —*dăr',* v. a. to renounce.

abobado, da, *abobă'dō,* a. stultified, silly.

abobamiento, —*miēn'tō,* sm. stupefaction.

abobar, —*băr',* v. a. to stupefy.

abocado, da, *abōkă'dō,* a. light (wine).

abocamiento, —*miēn'tō,* sm. meeting, interview.

abocar, —*kăr',* v. a. to seize with the mouth; —se, to meet by agreement.

abocardado,da, —*dă'dō* a. wide-mouthed.

abocinado, da, *abōthină'dō,* a. trumpet-like. [face.

abocinar, —*năr',* v. n. to fall upon one's

abochornar, *abōtshōrnăr',* v.a. to swelter; to provoke; —se, to be angry with; to blush.

abofellar, —*fĕlyăr',* v. n. to puff, to pant.

abofetear, *abōfĕtĕăr',* v. a. to slap or box someone's ears.

abogacía,—*găthē'ă,* sf. advocateship.

abogada,—*gă'dă,* sf. mediatrix.

abogado,—*dō,* sm. advocate; mediator.

abogar, *abōgăr',* v. n. to advocate; to intercede. [swollen.

abohetado, da, —*hĕtă'dō,* a. inflated,

abolengo, —*lēn'gō,* sm. ancestry; inheritance from ancestors. [tion.

abolición, —*lĭthiōn',* sf. abolition, abroga-

abolir, —*lĭr',* v. a. to abolish.

abolorio, —*lō'riō,* sm. ancestry.

abolsado, da, *abōlsă'dō,* a. puckered.

abolladura, *abōlyădŭ'ră,* sf. indent; relief.

abollar, —*lyăr',* v. a. to emboss; to confound; to tire, to bore.

abollonar, —*lyōnăr',* v. a. to emboss.

abominable, —*mină'blĕ,* a. abominable, cursed. [tion, cursedness.

abominación, —*mĭnăthiōn',* sf. abomina-

abominar, —*năr',* v. a. to detest.

abonado, da, *abōnă'dō,* a. creditable, rich; fit for. [bail for another.

abonador, —*dōr',* sm. & f. person who is

abonamiento, —*miēn'tō,* sm. surety, bail.

abonanzar, *abōnănthăr',* v. n. to clear up.

abonar, *abōnăr',* v. a. to bail; to insure; to improve; to make good an assertion; to manure; to give one credit; —se, to subscribe to; —, v. n. to clear up.

abonaré, *abōnărē',* sm. (com.) cheque.

abono, *abō'nō,* sm. approbation; subscription; surety, bail; dung, manure; —de pasaje, (rail.) season-ticket. [truder.

abordador, *abōrdădōr',* sm. boarder; in-

abordaje, *abōrdă'hĕ,*sm. act of boarding a ship.

abordar, —*dăr',* v. a. (mar.) to board.

abordo, —*dō,* sm. act of boarding a ship.

aborrachado, da, *abōrrătshă'dō,* a. high coloured. [stormy; to get tipsy.

aborrascarse, *abōrrăskăr'sĕ,* v. r. to grow

aborrecer, *abōrrĕthĕr',* v. a. to hate, to abhor; to desert (of birds). [able.

aborrecible, —*thē'blĕ,* a. hateful, detest-

aborrecimiento, *abōrrĕthĭmiēn'tō,* sm. abhorrence, hatred. [tion.

abortamiento, *abōrtămiēn'tō,* sm. abor-

abortar, —*tăr',* v. n. to miscarry, to have an abortion.

abortivo, va, —*tē'vō,* a. abortive.

aborto, —*tō,* sm. abortion; monster.

abortón, —*tōn',* sm. abortion of a quadruped. [up.

aborujarse,*abōrŭhăr'sĕ,*v.r. to be muffled

abotagarse, —*tăgăr'sĕ,* v. r. to be swollen.

abotinado, da, —*tină'dō,* a. in the form of Bluchers, half-boots. [to button.

abotonador, —*tōnădōr',* sm. a. to button; —v. n. to vault.

abovedar, —*vĕdăr',* v. a. to arch, to vault.

aboyar, —*yăr',* v. a. (mar.) to lay down buoys. [mountain-canyon.

abra, *ă'bră,* sf. bay; mountain-gorge.

abracijo,—*thĭ'hō,* sm. embrace, hug.

abrasador, r..., *abrăsădōr',* sm.&f. burner.

abrasamiento, —*sămiēn'tō,* sm. burning.

abrasar, —*săr',* v. a. to burn; to parch the ground; to squander; —se, to be agitated by a violent passion.

abrasilado, —*silă'dō,* a. of the colour of Brazil-wood.

abrazadera,*abrăthădĕ'ră,* sf. cramp-iron, clasp, hasp, ferule. [thief-taker.

abrazador, ra, —*dōr',* sm. & f. embracer;

abrazamiento, —*miēn'tō,* sm. embracing.

abrazar, —*thăr',* v. a. to embrace; to surround; to give into; to contain.

abrazo, —*thō,* sm. embrace.

ábrego, *ă'brĕgō,* sm. south-west wind.

abrevadero, *abrĕvădĕ'rō,* sm. watering-place for cattle.

abrevar, —*văr',* v. a. to water cattle.

abreviación, *abrĕviăthiōn',* sf. abbreviation, abridgment; shortening.

abreviador, ra, —*dōr',* sm. & f. abridger.

abreviar, —*viăr',* v. a. to abridge, to cut short; to accelerate. [abbreviature.

abreviatura, —*viătŭ'ra,* sf. abbreviation,

abribonarse, *abrĭbōnăr'sĕ,* v. r. to act the scoundrel. [peach.

abridero, —*dĕ'rō,* sm. nectarine, hasty

abridor, —*dōr',* sm. nectarine-tree; opener; plaiting-iron; —de láminas, engraver; —en hueco, die-sinker.

abrigar, —*găr',* v. a. to shelter; to protect; —se, to take shelter; (mar.) to becalm.

abrigo, *ăbrē'gŏ*, sm. shelter; protection, aid;
abril, *ăbrēl'*, sm. April. [mantle.
abrillantador, *ăbrĭlyāntădŏr'*, sm. diamond-cutter. [mond into facets.
abrillantar, *—tăr'*, v. a. to cut a diamond into facets.
abrimiento, *ăbrĭmĭĕn'tŏ*, sm. opening.
abrir, *ăbrĭr'*, v. a. to open; to unlock; to be open; to disclose a secret. [hook.
abrochador, *ăbrŏtshădŏr'*, sm. buttonhook.
abrochar, *—tshăr'*, v. a. to button on, to clasp on.
abrogación, *ăbrŏgăthĭŏn'*, sf. abrogation.
abrogar, *—găr'*, v. a. to abrogate.
abrojo, *ăbrō'hŏ*, sm. (bot.) caltrop; **—s,** pl. dangerous cliffs.
abromado, da, *ăbrŏmă'dŏ*, a. hazy, foggy.
abromarse, —se, *—sĕ*, v. r. (mar.) to be worm-eaten.
abroquelarse, *ăbrŏkĕlăr'sĕ*, v. r. to interpose shield or buckler; to use defensive weapons. [wood.
abrótano, *ăbrŏ'tănŏ*, sm. (bot.) southernwood.
abrumador, ra, *ăbrŭmădŏr'*, a. troublesome, annoying. [cause trouble.
abrumar, *—măr'*, v. a. to overwhelm; to
abrutado, da, *ăbrŭtă'dŏ*, a. brutish.
absceso, *ăbsthĕ'sŏ*, sm. abscess.
absolución, *ăbsŏlŭthĭŏn'*, sf. forgiveness; absolution.
absoluto, ta, *ăbsŏlŭ'tŏ*, a. absolute, independent; unconditional; imperious.
absolutorio, *—tŏ'rĭŏ*, a. absolutory.
absolver, *ăbsŏlvĕr'*, v. a. to absolve.
absorbencia, *ăbsŏrbĕn'thĭă*, sf. absorption. [sorbent.
absorbente, *—tĕ*, sm. & a. (med.) absorbent.
absorber, *ăbsŏrbĕr'*, v. a. to absorb; (also fig.); **—se,** v. r. to be astonished.
absorto, *ăbsŏr'tŏ*, a. amazed.
abstenerse, *ăbstĕnĕr'sĕ*, v. r. to abstain.
abstinencia, *ăbstĭnĕn'thĭă*, sf. abstinence.
abstinente, *—tĕ*, a. abstinent, abstemious.
abstracción, *ăbstrăkthĭŏn'*, sf. abstraction; retirement.
abstractivo, va, *—tĕ'vŏ*, a. abstractive.
abstracto, ta, *—tŏ*, a. abstract.
abstraer, *ăbstrăĕr'*, v. a. to abstract; to pass over in silence; to become lost in thought.
abstraído, *ăbstrăē'dŏ*, a. retired.
abstruso, sa, *ăbstrŏ'sŏ*, a. abstruse.
absurdidad, *ăbsŭrdĭdăd'*, sf., **absurdo,** *—sŭr'dŏ*, sm. absurdity.
absurdo, da, *—sŭr'dŏ*, a. absurd.
abubilla, *ăbŭbēl'yă*, sf. hoopoop.
abuela, *ăbwĕ'lă*, sf. grandmother.
abuelo, *—lŏ*, sm. grandfather; ancestor.
abultado, da, *ăbŭltă'dŏ*, a. bulky, large, massive. [—, v. n. to be bulky.
abultar, *—tăr'*, v. a. to increase, to enlarge.
abundancia, *ăbŭndăn'thĭă*, sf. abundance.
abundante, *—tĕ*, a. abundant, copious.
abundar, *ăbŭndăr'*, v. n. to abound.
aburrido, da, *ăbŭrrē'dŏ*, a. weary.
aburrimiento, *—mĭĕn'tŏ*, sm. tediousness.
aburrir, *—rĭr'*, v. a. to vex, to weary; to hazard; to relinquish. [heap together.
aburujar, *ăbŭrŭhăr'*, v. a. to press or

aburujonarse, *—hŏnăr'sĕ*, v. r. to clot.
abusar, *ăbŭsăr'*, v. a. to abuse.
abusivo, va, *ăbŭsē'vŏ*, a. abusive.
abuso, *ăbŭ'sŏ*, sm. ill-usage, misuse.
abyección, *ăbyĕkthĭŏn'*, sf. abjectness.
acá, *ăkă'*, ad. here, hither. [plished; old.
acabado, da, *ăkăbă'dŏ*, a. perfect, accomplished.
acabalar, *—bălăr'*, v. a. to complete.
acaballadero, *—bălyădĕr'ŏ*, sm. covering-season, covering-place of horses and mares.
acaballar, *—bălyăr'*, v. a. to cover a mare. [manlike.
acaballerado, da, *—bălyĕră'dŏ*, a. gentle-
acaballerar, *—bălyĕrăr'*, v. a. to render genteel.
acabar, *—băr'*, v. a. & n. to finish, to complete; to achieve; to terminate in anything; to die, to expire; **—se,** to grow feeble.
acabildar, *—bĭldăr'*, v. a. to put to the vote.
acacia, *ăkă'thĭă*, sf. acacia.
academia, *—dă'mĭă*, sf. academy; literary society. [—, a. academical.
académico, ca, *—dă'mĭkŏ*, sm. academician;
acaecedero, ra, *—ĕthĕdĕr'ŏ*, a. incidental.
acaecer, *—ĕthĕr'*, v. n. to happen.
acaecimiento, *—ĕthĭmĭĕn'tŏ*, sm. event, incident.
acal, *ăkăl'*, sm. canoe.
acalenturarse, *ăkălĕntŭrăr'sĕ*, v. r. to be feverish.
acalia, *ăkă'lĭă*, sf. (bot.) marsh-mallows.
acallar, *ăkălyăr'*, v. a. to quiet, to hush; to soften, to assuage, to appease.
acamado, da, *ăkămă'dŏ*, a. laid flat (of corn). [encampment.
acampamento, *ăkămpămĕn'tŏ*, sm. (mil.)
acampar, *—păr'*, v. a. (mil.) to encamp.
acampo, *—pŏ*, sm. common pasture.
acanalado, da, *ăkănălă'dŏ*, a. striated, fluted.
acanalador, *—dŏr'*, sm. chamfering-plane.
acanalar, *—lăr'*, v. a. to make a channel; to flute, to chamfer.
acandilado, da, *ăkăndĭlă'dŏ*, a. peaked, pointed (of hats). [mon colour.
acanelado, da, *ăkănĕlă'dŏ*, a. of a cinna-
acanillado, da, *ăkănĭlyă'dŏ*, a. ribbed (applied to cloth). [the quart.
acantarar, *ăkăntărăr'*, v. a. to measure by
acanto, *—tŏ*, sm. (bot.) brankursine.
acantonamiento, *ăkăntŏnămĭĕn'tŏ*, sm. cantonment. [into cantons.
acantonar, *—năr'*, v. a. (mil.) to divide
acañonear, *ăkănyŏnĕăr'*, v. a. to cannonade. [peras coloured.
acaparrosado, da, *ăkăpărrŏsă'dŏ*, a. cop-
acaponado, da, *—pŏnă'dŏ*, a. capon-like; effeminate.
acardenalar, *ăkărdĕnălăr'*, v. a. to beat black and blue; **—se,** to be covered with livid spots. [caress.
acariciar, *ăkărĭthĭăr'*, v. a. to fondle, to
ácaro, *ă'kărŏ*, sm. cheese-mite.
acarreador, *ăkărrĕădŏr'*, sm. carrier.
acarrear, *—rĕăr'*, v. a. to convey in a cart; to occasion.
acarreo, *—rĕ'ŏ*, sm. carriage, portage.
acaso, *ăkă'sŏ*, sm. chance, hap, hazard; **—,** ad. by chance.

1*

acastorado, da, ăkăstŏră dŏ, a. beavered.
acatarrarse, ăkătărrăr sĕ, v. r. to catch
   cold.   [wealthy.
acaudalado, da, ăkădălă dŏ, a. rich,
acaudalar, —lăr´, v.a. to hoard up riches.
acaudillador, ăkădălyădŏr´, sm. commander of troops.   [troops.
acaudillar, —lyăr´, v. a. to command
acayoiba, ăkăyŏ´ĭbă, sf. mahogany.
acceder, ăkthĕdĕr´, v. n. to accede.
accesible, ăkthĕs´blĕ, a. attainable; of
   easy access.   [munication.
acceso, ăkthĕs´ŏ, sm. access; carnal com-
accesorias, —sŏ´rĭăs, sf. pl. out-buildings.
accesorio, ria, —sŏ´rĭŏ, a. accessory, additional.   [casual.
accidental, ăkthĭdĕntăl´, a. accidental.
accidentarse, —tăr´sĕ, v. r. to have a fit.
accidente, ăkthĭdĕn´tĕ, sm. accident; hap-
   hazard.
acción, ăkthĭŏn´, sf. action, operation;
   battle; position, posture; (com.) share.
accionar, ăkthĭŏnăr´, v. n. to gesticulate.
accionista, —ĭs´tă, sm. actionary, share-
acebo, ăthĕ´bŏ, sm. holly-tree.   [holder.
acebuche, ăthĕbōŏsh´ĕ, sm. wild olive-tree.
acebuchina, —tshĕ´nă, sf. wild olive.
acechador, ăthĕtshădŏr´, sm. listener.
acechar, ăthĕtshăr´, v. a. to lie in ambush, to lurk.
aceche, ăthĕtsh´ĕ, sm. copperas.
acecho, ăthĕtsh´ŏ, sm. lying in ambush,
   waylaying.
acecinar, ăthĕthĭnăr´, v. a. to salt meat
   and smoke it; —sĕ, to wither.
acedar, ăthĕdăr´, v. a. to sour; to displease, to disquiet.
acedera, —dĕ´ră, sf. (bot.) sorrel.
acedía, —dĕ´ă, sf. acidity; squeamishness;
   roughness; asperity of address.
acedo, da, ăthĕ´dŏ, a. acid, acetous.
aceitar, ăthĕĭtăr´, v. a. to oil.
aceite, ăthĕ´ĭtĕ, sm. oil.
aceitera, ăthĕĭtĕ´ră, sf. oil-cruet.
aceitería, —tĕrĕ´ă, sf. oilshop; oil-mill.
aceitero, —tĕ´rŏ, sm. oil-seller; oil-cruet.
aceitoso, sa, —tŏ´sŏ, a. oily.
aceitunado, da, —tūnă´dŏ, a. olive-green.
aceitunero, —tūnĕ´rŏ, sm. olive-seller.
aceituno, —tŏ´—´, sm. olive-tree.   [tion.
aceleración, uthĕlĕrăthĭŏn´, s. accelera-
aceleradamente, —dămĕn´tĕ, ad. swiftly,
   hastily.   [hurry.
acelerar, —răr´, v. a. to accelerate; to
acelga, ăthĕl´gă, sf. (bot.) beet.
acémila, ăthĕ´mĭlă, sf. beast of burden.
acemilar, —mĭlăr´, a. belonging to mules
   and muleteers.
acemilería, —mĭlĕrĕ´ă, sf. mule-stable.
acemilero, —mĭlĕ´rŏ, sm. muleteer.
acemita, —mĭt´ă, sf. Graham bread.
acemite, ăthĕmĭt´ĕ, sm. fine bran; grits.
acendrar, ăthĕndrăr´, v. a. to refine metals; to free from blemish.
acensuar, ăthĕnsūăr´, v. a. to impose a tax.
acento, ăthĕn´tŏ, sm. accent.   [tion.
acentuación, ăthĕntăăthĭŏn´, sf. accentua-
acentuar, —tăăr´, v. a. to accentuate.

aceña, ăthĕn´yă, sf. water-mill.
aceñero, ăthĕnyă´rŏ, sm. keeper of a
   water-mill.
acepar, ăthĕpăr´, v. n. to take root.
acepción, ăthĕpthĭŏn´, sf. acceptation.
acepilladura, ăthĕpĭlyădŏ´ră, sf. smoothing with a plane; chips, pl.
acepillar, —ăr´, v. a. to plane; to brush.
aceptable, ăthĕptă´blĕ, a. acceptable;
   worthy of acceptance.
aceptación, —tăthĭŏn´, sf. acceptation;
   approbation; acceptance (of a bill).
aceptador, ra, —tădŏr´, s. acceptor.
aceptar, —tăr´, v. a. to accept, to admit.
acepto, to, ăthĕp´tŏ, a. agreeable.
acequia, ăthĕ´kĭă, sf. canal, channel,
   drain; mill-trench.   [drains or cisterns.
acequiar, —kĭăr´, v. a. to construct canals.
acequiero, —kĭĕ´rŏ, sm. inspector of
   canals.   [(am.) side-walk.
acera, ăthă´ră, sf. flag-way, pavement;
acerado, da, ăthĕră´dŏ, a. steeled, made
acerar, ăthĕrăr´, v. a. to steel.   [of steel.
acerbidad, —bĭdăd´, sf. acerbity, rigour.
acerbo, ba, ăthĕr´bŏ, a. rigorous, harsh,
   rude; cruel.
acerca, ăthĕr´kă, pr. about, relating to.
acercar, —kăr´, v. a. to approach; —se,
   to accost.
acerico, ăthĕrĕ´kŏ, acerillo, —rĭl´yŏ, sm.
   pin-cushion; small bed-pillow.
acerino, na, —rĕ´nŏ, a. made of steel.
acero, ăthă´rŏ, sm. steel; edged small arms;
   (fig.) courage.   [uous, very vigorous,
acérrimc, ma, ăthĕr´rĭmŏ, a. most stren-
acertado, da, ăthĕrtă´dŏ, a. fit, proper;
   prudent.   [true prophet.
acertador, ra, —tădŏr´, sm. & f. dead-shot,
acertajo, —tă´hŏ, sm. riddle.
acertar, —tăr´, v. a. to hit the mark; to
   conjecture right; to turn out true; —, v. n.
   to happen unexpectedly; to take root.
acertijo, —tĭ´hŏ, sm. riddle.
aceruelo, ăthĕră´lŏ, sm. small pack-
   saddle for riding.
acervar, —văr´, v. a. to accumulate.
acervo, ăthĕr´vŏ, sm. heap, pile; totality
   of tithes.   [measure.
acetábulo, ăthĕtă´bălŏ, sm. apothecary's
acetato, —tŏ, sm. (chem.) acetate.
acetosa, ăthĕtŏ´să, sf. (bot.) sorrel.
acetre, ăthă´trĕ, sm. small bucket; holy-
   water-fount.
aciago, ga, ăthĭă´gŏ, a. unlucky, ominous.
acial, ăthĭăl´, sm. barnacle.
aciano, ăthĭă´nŏ, sm. corn-flower.
acíbar, ăthĕ´băr, sm. aloes-tree; (fig.) bitterness, displeasure.
acibarar, —bărăr´, v. a. to add juice of
   aloes; to gall; to imbitter.
acicalador, ăthĭkălădŏr´, sm. polisher;
   burnisher, burnishing-stick.
acicaladura, —dŏ´ră, sf., acicalamiento,
   —mĭĕn´tŏ, sm. burnishing.
acicalar, —lăr´, v. n. to polish, to furbish;
   —se, to dress in style; to paint one's face.
acidez, ăthĭdĕth´, sf. acidity.   [sour.
ácido, a´thĭdŏ, sm. acid; —, da, a. acid,

acidular, –dälär', v. a. to acidulate.

acidulo, a, äthĕ dŭlŏ, a. acidulous.

acierto, äthiër'tŏ, sm. act and effect of hitting; dexterity, chance, casualty.

acijado, da, –hä'dŏ, a. copperas coloured.

acije, äthĭ'k'ĕ, sm. copperas.

acimboga, äthĭmbŏ'gä, sf. citron-tree.

ación, äthĭŏn', sf. stirrup-leather.

acipado, a, –hä'pä'dŏ, a. well milled (of broadcloth). [boundaries].

acirate, –rä'tĕ, sm. landmark (to show acitara, –tä'rä, s. rails of a bridge; partition-wall.

acitrón, –trŏn', sm. candied lemon.

aclamación, äklämäthĭŏn', sf. acclamation.

aclamar, –mär', v. a. to applaud, to huzza; to cry up.

aclarar, äklärär',v.a. to clear; to brighten; to explain; to clarify; –se, to clear up.

aclimatar, äklĭmätär', v. a. to acclimatize.

aclocarse, äklŏkär'sĕ, v. r. to brood.

acobardar, äkŏbärdär', v. a. to intimidate.

acoceador, ra, äkŏthĕädŏr', sm. & f. kicking horse. [of horses].

acocear, –thĕär', v. a. to kick, to wince

acocharse, –tshär'sĕ, v. r. to squat, to stoop down. [to injure sorely.

acochinar, –tshĭnär', v. a. to assassinate;

acodar, –där', v. a. to lean the elbow upon; to lay layers of vines. [angle.

acodillar, –dĭlyär', v. a. to bend at an

acodo, äkŏ'dŏ, sm. (bot.) layer, scion, shoot.

acogedizo, za, äkŏ'hĕdĕ'thŏ, a. gathered promiscuously.

acogedor, ra, –'hĕdŏr', sm.&f. harbourer.

acoger, –'hĕr', v. a. to receive; to protect; to harbour; –se, to resort to.

acogida, –'hĭd'ä, sf. reception; asylum; confluence.

acogimiento, –'hĭmĭĕn'tŏ, sm. asylum.

acogollar, –gŏlyär', v. a. to cover delicate plants with straw; –se, to cabbage.

acogombrar, –gŏmbrär', v. a. to dig up the ground about plants; to cover plants with earth. [on the head.

acogotar, –gŏtär', v. a. to kill by a blow

acolchar, äkŏltshär', v. a. to quilt; to cotton.

acólito, äkŏ'lĭtŏ, sm. acolyte; assistant.

acollarar, äkŏlyärär', v. a. to yoke horses &c.; to couple hounds. [gressor.

acometedor, ra, äkŏmĕtĕdŏr', sm.&f. ag-

acometer, –tĕr', v. a. to attack; to undertake; to overtake; to steal over one (sleep).

acometida, –tĭd'ä, sf., acometimiento, äkŏmĕtĭmĭĕn'tŏ, sm. attack, assault.

acomodadizo, äkŏmŏdädĭ'thŏ, a. accommodable.

acomodado, da, –dä'dŏ, a. commodious; suitable, convenient, fit; wealthy.

acomodamiento, –mĭĕn'tŏ, sm. accommodation.

acomodar, –där', v. a. to accommodate, to arrange; –, v. n. to fit, to suit; –se, to condescend, to comply.

acomodaticio, cia, –dätĕ'thĭŏ, a. figurative, metaphorical.

acomodo, –mŏ'dŏ, sm. accommodation; employment.

acompañador,ra,äkŏmpänyädŏr', sm.&f. companion; (mus.) accompanist.

acompañamiento, –mĭĕn'tŏ, sm. attendance; (mus.) accompaniment.

acompañar, –nyär', v. a. to accompany; to join; (mus.) to accompany; –se, to consult with others.

acompasado, da, äkŏmpäsä'dŏ, a. measured by the compass; well-proportioned.

acomplexionado, da, –plĕksĭŏnä'dŏ, a. of a (good or bad) complexion.

aconchar, äkŏntshär', v. a. to accommodate; (mar.) to embay.

acondicionado, da, äkŏndĭthĭŏnä'dŏ, a. conditioned, of a (good or bad) disposition.

acondicionar, –thĭŏnär', v. a. to dispose; –se, to acquire a certain position.

acongojar, äkŏngŏ'här', v. a. to oppress, to afflict. [monk's hood.

acónito, äkŏ'nĭtŏ, sm. (bot.) aconite.

aconsejable, äkŏnsĕ'hä'blĕ, a. advisable.

aconsejador, ra, –'hädŏr', sm. adviser, counsellor. [to take advice.

aconsejar, –'här', v. a. to advise; –se,

aconsonantar, äkŏnsŏnäntär', v. a. to use false rhymes.

acontecedero, ra, äkŏntĕthĕdĕ'rŏ, a. that which may happen.

acontecer, –thĕr', v. imp. to happen.

acontecimiento, –thĭmĭĕn'tŏ, sm. event, incident. [bell-shaped.

acopado, da, äkŏpä'dŏ, a. cup-shaped,

acopar, –pär', v. n. (mar.) to bend or arch boards.

acopiamiento, –pĭämĭĕn'tŏ, acopio, äkŏ'pĭŏ, sm. gathering, storing.

acopiar, –pĭär', v. a. to gather, to store up.

acoplar, –plär', v. a. to couple; to adjust or fit pieces of timber-work.

acoquinar, –kĭnär', v. a. to intimidate.

acorazonado, –räthŏnä'dŏ, a. heartshaped. [shrivel (of fruits).

acorcharse, –tshär'sĕ, v. r. to dry up and

acordado, da, äkŏrdä'dŏ, a. deliberate.

acordar, –där', v. a. to concert; to tune musical instruments; –, v. n. to agree; –se, to come to an agreement; to remember. [–, s. accord.

acorde, äkŏr'dĕ,a. conformable, accordant;

acordonar, äkŏrdŏnär', v. a. (mil.) to form a cordon. [horns.

acornear, –nĕär', v. a. to gore with the

ácoro, ä'kŏrŏ, sm. (bot.) sweet cane, sweet grass.

acorralar, äkŏrrälär', v. a. to shut up cattle or sheep in pens; to intimidate.

acorrucarse, äkŏrrükär'sĕ, v. r. to squat.

acortar, äkŏrtär', v. a. to abridge, to shorten; –se, to be perplexed.

acorullar, äkŏrŭlyär', v. a. to ship oars.

acosar, äkŏsär', v. a. to pursue close; to molest. [down; accosted.

acostado, da, äkŏstä'dŏ, a. stretched, laid

acostar, –stär', v. a. to put to bed; –se, to incline to one side (of buildings); (mar.) to lie along.

acostumbradamente, *ăkŏstŭmbrădă-*
měn'tě. ad. customarily.

acostumbrar, *-brar'*, v. a. to accustom;
—, v. n. to be accustomed.

acotación, *ăkŏtăthŏn'*, sf. setting bounds;
quotation in the margin.

acotar, *-tar'*, v. a. to set bounds; to quote;
—se, to take to one's heels.

acotillo, *-tĭl'yŏ*, sm. large sledge-hammer.

acoyundar, *-yŭndar'*, v. a. to inspan oxen.

acre, *ă'krě, s.* acid; sharp; —, s. acre.

acrecencia, *ăkrěthěn'thĭă,* sf., acrecentamiento, *-tămĭěn'tŏ,* sm. increase, augmentation, augment.

acrecentar, *-tar'*, acrecer, *ăkrěthěr'*,
v. a. to increase, to augment.

acreditar, *ăkrědĭtar'*, v. a. to assure, to
affirm; to give credit; —se, to gain credit.

acreedor, *ăkrěēdŏr'*, sm. creditor.

acribadura, *ăkrĭbădŏ'ră*, sf. sifting.

acribar, *-bar'*, v. a. to sift; to pierce like
a sieve.   [sieve; to molest; to torment.

acribillar, *-bĭlyar'*, v. a. to pierce like a

acriminación, *ăkrĭmĭnăthĭŏn'*, sf. crimination.

acriminador, ra, *-dŏr'*, sm. & f. accuser.

acriminar, *-nar'*, v. a. to exaggerate a
fault; to accuse.   [ity.

acrimonia, *-mŏ'nĭă*, sf. acrimony; asper-

acrisolar, *-sŏlar'*, v. a. to refine, to purify.

acristianar, *-stĭanar'*, v. a. to christen, to
baptize.

acritud, *ăkrĭtŭd''*, sf. acrimony.

acromático, ca, *ăkrŏmă'tĭkŏ,* a. achromatic.

acta, *ăk'tă,* sf. act; —s, pl. acts, records, pl.

actitud, *ăktĭtŭd''*, sf. attitude, posture.

actividad, *ăktĭvĭdăd''*, sf. activity; liveliness.

activo, va, *ăktĭ'vŏ,* a. active, diligent.

acto, *ăk'tŏ,* sm. act, action; act of a play;
thesis; carnal communication.   [ney.

actor, *ăktŏr'*, sm. player, comedian; attor-

Actos, *ăk'tŏs,* spl. Acts of the Apostles.

actriz, *ăktrĭth'*, sf. actress.   [tion.

actuación, *ăktŭăthĭŏn'*, sf. actuation, opera-

actuado, da, *-tŭă'dŏ,* a. actuated; experien-

actual, *ăktŭăl'*, a. actual, present.   [ced.

actualidad, *ăktŭălĭdăd''*, sf. actuality.

actuante, *ăktŭăn'tě,* a. college-exponent.

actuar, *ăktŭar'*, v. a. to digest; to proceed;
to support a thesis; —se, to instruct one's

actuario, *ăktŭă'rĭŏ,* sm. actuary.   [self.

acuario, *ăkŭă'rĭŏ,* sm. tank.

Acuario, —, sm. Aquarius, Waterman (sign
of the zodiac).   [quartering of troops.

acuartelamiento, *ăkŭărtělămĭěn'tŏ,* sm.

acuartelar, *-lar'*, v. a. (mil.) to quarter
troops; (mar.) to furl sails.

acuartillar, *ăkŭărtĭlyar'*, v. n. to knock
or bend one's knees in walking; to interfere (of horses).

acuático, ca, *ăkŭă'tĭkŏ,* a. aquatic.

acuátil, *-tĭl,* a. aquatic.

acubado, da, *ăkŭbă'dŏ,* a. resembling a
pail or bucket.

acucharado, da, *-tshără'dŏ,* a. spoonlike.

acuchillado, da, *-tshĭlyă'dŏ,* a. experienced, skilful.   [some person, bully.

acuchillador, ra, *-tshĭlyădŏr'*, s. quarrel-

acuchillar, *-tshĭlyar'*, v. a. to cut with a
sabre; —se, to fight with knives.

acudimiento, *-dĭmĭěn'tŏ,* sm. aid, assistance.   [to be docile.

acudir, *-dĭr'*, v. n. to assist, to succour;

acueducto, *ăkŭědŭk'tŏ,* sm. aqueduct.

ácueo, ea, *ă'kŭěŏ,* a. watery.

acuerdo, *ăkŭěr'dŏ,* sm. deliberation; resolution; tribunal; consent; de —, unanimously.

aculebrar, *ăkŭlěbrar'*, v. n. to meander.

acullá, *ăkŭlyă'*, ad. on the other side,
yonder.   [to heap together; to impute.

acumular, *ăkŭmŭlar'*, v. a. to accumulate.

acumulativamente, *-mŭlătĭvăměn'tě,*ad.
(law) by way of precaution; jointly.

acuñación, *ăkŭnyăthĭŏn'*, sf. coining.

acuñador, *-dŏr'*, sm. coiner, minter.

acuñar, *-yar'*, v. a. to coin, to mint; to
wedge in, to fasten with wedges.

acuosidad, *ăkŭŏsĭdăd''*, sf. wateriness.

acuoso, sa, *ăkŭŏ'sŏ,* a. watery.

acurrucarse, *ăkŭrrŭkar'sě,* v. r. to muffle
one's self up; to squat.

acusación, *ăkŭsăthĭŏn'*, sf. accusation.

acusador, ra, *-dŏr'*, sm. & f. accuser.

acusar, *ăkŭsar'*, v. a. to accuse; to reproach; —se, to acknowledge sins to a
confessor.

acusativo, *ăkŭsătĭ'vŏ,* sm. (gr.)accusative.

acusatorio, ria, *-tŏ'rĭŏ,* a. accusatory.

acuse, *ăkŭ'sě,* sm. declaring (at cards).

acústica, *ăkŭs'tĭkă,* sf. acoustics, pl.

acústico, ca, *-ŏ,* a. acoustic.

acutángulo, *ăkŭtăn'gŭlŏ,* sm. acute angle.

achacar, *ătshăkar'*, v. a. to impute.

achacoso, sa, *-kŏ'sŏ,* a. sickly, unhealthy.

achaparrarse, *-părrar'sě,* v. r. to grow
stunted.

achaque, *ătshă'kě,* sm. habitual indisposition; monthly courses; excuse; vice;
subject, matter.

achaquiento, ta, *-kĭěn'tŏ,* a. sickly.

acharolar, *-rŏlar'*, v. a. to japan.

achicado, da, *ătshĭkă'dŏ,* a. childish.

achicador, *-kădŏr'*, sm. scoop for baling
boats.   [duction.

achicadura, *-kădŏ'ră,* sf. diminution, re-

achicar, *ătshĭkar'*, v. a. to diminish; to
bale a boat.   [too much; to over-heat.

achicharrar, *ătshĭtshărrar'*, v. a. to fry meat

achicoria, *-kŏ'rĭă,* sf. (bot.) succory.

achinar, *-nar'*, v. a. to intimidate.

achisparse, *-spăr'sě,* v. r. to get tipsy.

achocar, *ătshŏkar'*, v. a. to knock asunder;
to hoard money; —se, to become a dotard.

achuchar, *ătshŭtshar'*, v. a. to crush with
a blow.   [frolicsome.

achulado, da, *ătshŭlă'dŏ,* a. waggish,

adagio, *ădă'hĭŏ,* sm. adage, proverb;
(mus.) adagio.

adala, *-lă,* sf. (mar.) pump-dale.

adalid, *ădălĭd'*, sm. chief, commander.

adamado, —, *-mă'dŏ,* a. girl-like; effeminate.

adamantino, na, -mántĭnŏ, a. adamantine; adamantean. [like.

adamascado, na, -máskă dŏ, a. damask-

adaptable, ădáptă blĕ, a. adaptable.

adaptar, -tár', v. a. to adapt.

adaraja, ădárá'k'ă, sf. projecting-stones left to continue a wall.

adarga, ădár'gă, sf. oval shield.

adargar, -gár', v. a. to shield.

adarve, ădár've, sm. flat top of a wall.

adatar, ădátár', v. a. to book an expense.

adecenar, ădĕthĕnár', v. a. to divide troops into companies of ten.

adecuación, ădĕkŭáthĭŏn', sf. fitness.

adecuado, da, -kŭă'dŏ, a. adequate, fit.

adecuar, -kŭár', v. a. to fit, to accommodate, to proportion.

adefesio, -fē'sĭŏ, sm. folly, nonsense.

adefueras, -fŭĕ'răs, sf. pl. suburbs.

adehala, ădĕ'lă, sf. gratuity.

adehesar, -ĕsár', v. a. to convert land into pasture. [pated; onward, bold.

adelantado, da, ădĕlántă'dŏ, a. antici-

adelantamiento, -mĭĕn'tŏ, sm. progress, improvement, advancement.

adelantar, -tár', v. a. & n. to advance, to accelerate; to pay beforehand; to ameliorate, to improve; -se, to take the lead; to outdo. [ward; hence-forth.

adelante, ădĕlán'tŏ, ad. farther off; on-

adelfa, ădĕl'fă, sf. (bot.) rose-bay.

adelgazar, ădĕlgăthár', v. a. to make thin or slender; to discuss with subtlety.

ademán, ădĕmán', sm. gesture; attitude.

ademar, -már', v. a. to line the sides of mines with planks.

además, -más', ad. moreover, besides.

adentellar, ădĕntĕlyár', v. a. to bite; to indent; - una pared, to leave bricks to continue a wall.

adentro, ădĕn'trŏ, ad. within; inwardly.

aderezar, ădĕrĕthár', v. a. to dress, to adorn; to prepare; to clean, to repair.

aderezo, -rĕ'thŏ, sm. adorning; finery; arrangement; - de caballo, trappings.

ad(i)estrador, ăd(ĭ)ĕstrădŏr', sm. & f. instructor, teacher.

ad(i)estrar, -trár', v. a. to guide; to teach, to instruct; -se, to practise.

adeudado, da, ădĕŭdá'dŏ, a. indebted.

adeudar, -dár', v. a. to pay duty; to contract debts; -se, to be indebted.

adeudo, ădĕŭ'dŏ, s. duty; (rail.) freight.

adherencia, ădhĕrĕn'thĭă, sf. adhesion, cohesion; alliance, kindred.

adherente, -tĕ, a. adherent, cohesive.

adherir, -rĭr', v. n. to adhere to a sect; to espouse a cause; - v.n. to hold; to cling.

adhesión, ădĕsĭŏn', sf. adhesion; cohesion.

adiado, da, ădĭá'dŏ, a. día -, sm. the day appointed. [mantine.

adiamantado, da, -mántă'dŏ, a. ada-

adición, ădĭthĭŏn', sf. addition; (law) entry into an inheritance. [tions.

adicionar, -thĭŏnár', v. a. to make addi-

adicto, ta, ădĭk'tŏ, a. addicted, devoted to.

adietar, ădĭĕtár', v. a. to put on a diet.

adinerado, da, ădĭnĕrá'dŏ, a. moneyed, rich. [rich.

adir, ădĭr', v. a. to inherit a legacy.

aditamento, ădĭtámĕn'tŏ, sm. addition.

adiva, ădĭvă, sf., **adive,** -vĕ, sm. jackal.

adivinación, ădĭvĭnáthĭŏn', sf. divination.

adivinador, ra, -dŏr', sm. & f. diviner, soothsayer. [tion.

adivinanza, -nán'thă, sf. enigma; divina-

adivinar, -nár', v. a. to foretell; to conjecture. [sayer; fortune-teller.

adivino, na, -vē'nŏ, sm. & f. diviner, sooth-

adjetivar, ăd'hĕtĭvár', v. a. to make the adjective agree with the substantive.

adjetivo, -tē'vŏ, sm. adjective. [cation.

adjudicación, ăd'hŭdĭkáthĭŏn', sf. adjudi-

adjudicar, -kár', v. a. to adjudge; -se, to appropriate to one's self.

adjunta, ăd'hŭn'tă, sf. enclosure.

adjunto, ta, -tŏ, a. united, joined, annexed; -, s. annex; (gr.) adjective.

adminículo, -nĭkŭlŏ, sm. legal proof or evidence.

administración, ădmĭnĭstráthĭŏn', sf. administration. [ministrator.

administrador, ra, -dŏr', sm. & f. ad-

administrar, -trár', v. a. to administer.

administrativo, va, -trăĭ'vŏ, a. administrative. [vellous.

admirable, ădmĭră'blĕ, a. admirable, mar-

admiración, ădmĭráthĭŏn', sf. admiration; wonder; (gr.) note of exclamation.

admirar, -rár', v. a. to admire; to cause admiration.

admisible, ădmĭsĭ'blĕ, a. admissible.

admisión, ădmĭsĭŏn', sf. admission, acceptance. [to concede; to permit.

admitir, ădmĭtĭr', v. a. to receive, to let in;

adobado, ădŏbá'dŏ, sm. pickled pork.

adobar, -bár', v. a. to dress; to pickle; to stew; to tan hides. [tomer.

adobasillas, -básĭl'yăs, sm. chair-bot-

adobe, ădŏ'bĕ, sm. adobe, sun-dried brick.

adobería, ădŏbĕr'ĕ ă, sf. brick-field; tanyard.

adobo, ădŏ'bŏ, sm. repairing; mending; pickle-sauce; paint for ladies; ingredients for dressing leather or cloth.

adocenado, da, ădŏthĕná'dŏ, a. very common, ordinary; by the dozen.

adocenar, -nár', v. a. to count, sell or make by dozens; to despise. [fillness.

adolecer, ădŏlĕthĕr', v. n. to be seized with

adolescencia, ădŏlĕsĕn'thĭă, sf. adolescence.

adolescente, -tĕ, a. adolescent, young. [ship.

¿adónde? ădŏn'dĕ, ad. whither?; where?

adopción, ădŏpthĭŏn', sf. adoption.

adoptador, ra, -tádŏr', sm. & f. adopter.

adoptar, -tár', v. a. to adopt.

adoptivo, va, -tē'vŏ, a. adoptive. [ship.

adoración, ădŏráthĭŏn', sf. adoration, wor-

adorador, ra, -dŏr', sm. & f. adorer.

adorar, -rár', v. a. to adore; to love exceedingly. [(in America).

adoratorio, -tŏ'rĭŏ, sm. temple of idols

adormecer, ădŏrmĕthĕr', v.r.t. to fall asleep.

adormecimiento, -thĭmĭĕn'tŏ, sm. drowsiness, sleepiness.

adormidera, -mĭdd'rā, sf. (bot.) poppy.

adornar, -năr', v. a. to embellish, to ornament. [ments.

adornista, -nĭs'tā, sm. painter of ornament, decoration.

adorno, ădŏr'nŏ, sm. adornment; ornament, decoration.

adquirir, ādkŭrĭr', v. a. to acquire.

adquisición, ādkĭsĭthĭŏn', sf. acquisition.

adra, ā'drā, sf. turn, successive order.

adragante, ādrăgăn'tē, sm. gum tragacanth.

adrales, ădră'lĕs, sm. pl. cart-rack.

adredo, ădrē'dĕ, ad. purposely.

adscribir, ădskrĭbĭr', v. a. to appoint a person to a post.

aduana, ădŭā'nā, sf. custom-house.

aduanar, -năr', v. a. to enter goods at the custom-house; to pay duty.

aduanero, -nē'rŏ, sm. custom-house officer. [Arabs; borde of gypsies.

aduar, ădŭăr', sm. nomadic village of

aduendado, da, ădŭĕndā'dŏ, a. ghostly.

adufe, ădŭ'fĕ, sm. tambourine.

adufero, -fē'rŏ, sm. tambourine-player.

aduja, ădŭ'hā, sf. (mar.) coiled cable.

adujar, -hăr', v. a. (mar.) to coil a cable.

adulación, ădŭlāthĭŏn', sf. adulation.

adulador, ra, -dŏr', s. flatterer; fawner.

adular, -lăr', v. a. to flatter; to fawn.

adulear, -lĕăr', v. n. to bawl, to cry out.

adulero, -lē'rŏ, sm. keeper of horses (or mules). [terate; to commit adultery.

adulterar, ădŭltĕrăr', v. a. & n. to adulterino, na, -rē'nŏ, a. begotten in adultery; misborn; falsified.

adulterio, -dŭl'tē'rŏ, sm. adultery [adulteress.

adúltero, ra, ădŭl'tĕrŏ, sm. & f. adulterer.

adulto, ta, ădŭl'tŏ, a. adult, grown-up.

adunar, ădŭnăr', v. a. to unite, to join.

adustión, ădŭstĭŏn', sf. (med.) burning.

adusto, ta, ădŭ'stŏ, a. gloomy, intractable.

advenedizo, za, ădvĕnĕdē'thŏ, a. exotic, foreign.

advenimiento, -mĭĕn'tŏ, sm. arrival.

adventicio, cia, ădvĕntē'thĭŏ, a. adventitious; accidental.

adverbio, ădvĕr'bĭŏ, sm. adverb.

adversario, -sā'rĭŏ, sm. adversary; antagonist. [lamity.

adversidad, -sĭdăd', sf. adversity, calamity.

adverso, sa, ădvĕr'sŏ, a. adverse, calamitous. [attention to; advice.

advertencia, -tĕn'thĭā, sf. advertence.

advertido, da, -tē'dŏ, a. skilful, intelligent.

advertir, -tĭr', v. a. to advert, to take notice of; to give heed; to mark.

Adviento, ădvĭĕn'tŏ, sm. Advent.

adyacente, ădyăthĕn'tē, a. adjacent.

aechar, ăĕchăr', v. a. to winnow, to sift.

aecho, ăĕ'tshŏ, sm. winnowing.

aéreo, rea, āĕ'rĕŏ, a. aerial; airy, fantastic.

aeronauta, āĕrŏnă'ŭtā, sm. aeronaut.

aerostática, -stā'tĭkā, sf. aerostatics.

afabilidad, āfăbĭlĭdăd', sf. affability.

afable, ā'ā'blĕ, a. affable, complacent.

afaca, ā'ā'kā, sf. yellow vetch.

afán, ăfăn', sm. anxiety, solicitude.

afanar, -ăr', v. n. & r. to toil; to be over-solicitous. [taking.

afanoso, sa, -nŏ'sŏ, a. solicitous; pains-taking.

afascalar, ăfăskălăr', v. a. to build ricks of corn, to stack corn.

afear, ăfĕăr', v. a. to deform, to misshape.

afección, ăfĕkthĭŏn', sf. affection; fondness, attachment.

afectación, -tāthĭŏn', sf. affectation.

afectadamente, -tădămĕn'tē, ad. affectedly, for appearance's sake.

afectar, -tăr', v. a. to affect, to feign.

afectivo, va, -tē'vŏ, a. fond, tender.

afecto, ăfĕk'tŏ, sm. affection; passion; disease; -, ta, a. affectionate; disposed; reserved. [moving, tender.

afectuoso, sa, -tŭŏ'sŏ, a. affectionate.

afeitar, ăfĕĭtăr', v. a. to shave; to paint

afeite, ăfĕ'ĭtĕ, sm. paint, rouge. [the face.

afelpado, da, ăfĕlpā'dŏ, a. shaggy.

afeminado, da, ăfĕmĭnā'dŏ, a. effeminate.

afeminar, -năr', v. a. to effeminate.

aferrar, ăfĕrrăr', v. a. to grapple, to grasp, to seize. [wavy pattern.

afestonado, ăfĕstŏnā'dŏ, a. worked in a

afianzar, ăfĭănthăr', v. a. to bail, to guarantee; to prop. [ing.

afición, ăfĭthĭŏn', sf. affection; fancy, lik-aficionado, da, -nā'dŏ, sm. & f. lover, devotee.

aficionar, -năr', v. a. to inspire affection; -se, to give one's mind to.

afijo, ja, ăfē'k'ŏ, a. (gr.) affix.

afiladera, ăfĭlădē'rā, sf. whetstone.

afilado, da, ăfĭlā'dŏ, a. sharp.

afilar, -lăr', v. a. to whet, to sharpen, to grind. [like.

afiligranado, da, -lĭgrănā'dŏ, a. filigree-afilón, -lŏn', sm. whetstone.

afilosofado, -lŏsŏfā'dŏ, sm. person who plays the philosopher.

afín, ăfēn', sm. relation by affinity.

afinación, ăfĭnāthĭŏn', sf. completion; refining, tuning of instruments.

afinar, ăfĭnăr', v. a. to complete; to tune musical instruments; to refine.

afinidad, -nĭdăd', sf. affinity; analogy.

afirmación, -māthĭŏn', sf. affirmation.

afirmado, -mā'dŏ, sm. macadamization.

afirmar, -măr', v. a. to secure, to fasten; to affirm, to assure.

afirmativa, -mătē'vā, sf. affirmation.

afirmativo, va, -tē'vŏ, a. affirmative.

aflicción, ăflĭkthĭŏn', sf. affliction, grief, heart-ache, painfulness.

aflictivo, va, -tē'vŏ, a. afflictive.

afligir, ăflĭhĭr', v. a. to afflict, to grieve, to torment. [incombustible.

aflogisticar, ăflŏhĭstĭkăr', v. a. to render

aflojar, ăflŏhăr', v. a. to loosen, to slacken, to relax; to relent; -, v. n. to grow weak; to abate; to grow cool in fervour.

afluente, ăflŭĕn'tē, a. affluent, abundant; loquacious.

afollar, ăfŏlyăr', v. a. to blow with bellows.

afondar, ăfŏndăr', v. a. to put under water; (mar.) to sink; -, v. n. to go to the bottom.

aforar, *afŏrár*, v.a. to gauge; to measure; to calculate the duty on goods.

aforismo, *afŏrísmŏ*, sm. aphorism.

aforístico, ca, *– rís tíkŏ*, a. aphoristical.

aforo, *afŏ'rŏ*, sm. gauging; custom-house examination of goods or luggage.

aforrar, *afŏrrár*, v.a. to line (clothes); (mar.) to sheathe.

aforro, *afŏrrŏ*, sm. lining; sheathing.

afortunado, da, *afŏrtŭná dŏ*, a. fortunate, happy. [one's self.

afosarse, *afŏsár sĕ*, v.r. (mil.) to entrench

afrancesar, *afrănthĕsár*, v.a. to frenchify.

afrenta, *afrĕn'tă*, sf. outrage; insult; infamy. [insult.

afrentar, *afrĕntár*, v.a. to affront; to

afrentoso, sa, *–tŏ'sŏ*, a. ignominious; insulting. [free from wood-worms.

afretar, *afrĕtár*, v.a. (mar.) to scour; to

afrontar, *afrŏntár*, v.a. to confront; to reproach one to one's face with a crime.

afuera, *afŭĕ'ră*, ad. abroad; outward; besides, moreover; [–I stand out of the way!

afueras, *–s*, sm. pl. environs of a place.

afufar(se), *afŭfár (sĕ)*, v.n. & r. to run away, to escape.

afuste, *afŭs'tĕ*, sm. gun-carriage. [fied.

agabachado, da, *agăbătshá dŏ*, a. frenchi-

agachadiza, *–tshă diʼthă*, sf. snipe.

agacharse, *–tshár sĕ*, v.r. to stoop, to squat.

agalla, *agăl'yă*, sf. gall-nut; –s, pl. glands of the throat; wind-galls of horses; gills of fishes. [fustian of galls.

agallado, da, *–lyá dŏ*, a. steeped in an in-

agallón, *–lyŏn'*, sm. large gall-nut; –es, pl. strings of large silver beads; wooden beads used for rosaries. [coloured.

agamuzado, da, *agămŭthá dŏ*, a. chamois

agarbanzar, *agárbănthár*, v.n. to bud.

agarbarse, *–bár sĕ*, v.r. to cower, to squat.

agárico, *agá rĭkŏ*, sm.(bot.) agaric (fungous excrescence on the trunks of trees).

agarradero, *agárrădĕ'rŏ*, sm. anchoring-ground; hold, haft.

agarrado, da, *–rá dŏ*, a. miserable, stingy.

agarrafar, *–ráfár*, v.a. to grapple hard in a scuffle. [to gripe.

agarrar, *agárrár*, v.a. to grasp, to seize,

agarro, *agár'rŏ*, sm. grasp

agarrotar, *agárrŏtár*, v.a. to tie down.

agasajador, ra, *agăsă'hădŏr*, a. officious, complacent.

agasajar, *–hár*, v.a. to receive and treat kindly; to regale.

agasajo, *agăsá'hŏ*, sm. graceful reception; kindness; friendly present.

ágata, *á gătă*, sf. agate.

agavillar, *agăvĭlyár*, v.a. to tie up corn in sheaves; –se, to associate with a gang of sharpers.

agazapar, *–thăpár*, v.a. to catch a person; –se, to hide one's self.

agencia, *a'hĕn'thă*, sf. agency.

agenciar, *–thĭár*, v.a. to solicit, to endeavour, to obtain a thing.

agencioso, sa, *–thĭŏ'sŏ*, a. diligent, active; officious. [torney.

agente, *a'hĕn'tĕ*, sm. agent; actor; attorney.

agestado, da, *a'hĕstá'dŏ*, **(bien ó mal–),** good- or bad-looking. [industry.

agibilibus, *a'hĭbĭ'lĭbŭs*, sm. application.

agilidad, *a'hĭlĭdád*, sf. agility, nimble-ness. [make active.

agilitar, *–tár*, v.a. to render nimble, to

agio, *a'hĭŏ*, sm. agio.

agiotador, *–tádŏr*, **agiotista,** *–tĭs'tă*, sm. money-changer, bill-broker, stock-broker.

agiotaje, *–tá'h'ĕ*, sm. stock-jobbing.

agitación, *a'hĭtăthĭŏn'*, sf. agitation.

agitanado, da, *–tăná dŏ*, a. gipsy-like.

agitar, *–tár*, v.a. to agitate, to move.

aglomerar, *ăglŏmĕrár*, v.a. to agglome-rate, to conglomerate.

agnación, *ăgnăthĭŏn'*, sf. consanguinity.

agnado, da, *–ná'dŏ*, **agnaticio, cia,** *–nătĭ'thĭă*, a. consanguineous. [nition.

agnición, *ăgnĭthĭŏn'*, sf. agnition, recog-

agobiar, *ăgŏbĭár*, v.a. to bend down to the ground; to oppress. [crowds.

agolparse, *ăgŏlpár sĕ*, v.a. to assemble in

agone, *ăgŏ'nĕ* **(in –),** ad. in the struggle

agonía, *ăgŏnĭ'ă*, sf. agony. [of death.

agonizar, *–nĭthár*, v.a. to assist dying persons; –, v.n. to be in the agony of death, to agonise.

agorar, *ăgŏrár*, v.a. to divine; to augur.

agorero, *ăgŏrĕ'rŏ*, sm. augurer; diviner.

agorgojarse, *ăgŏrgŏ'hár sĕ*, v.r. to be destroyed by grubs (corn).

agostar, *ăgŏstár*, v.a. to be parched with heat; –, v.n. to pasture cattle on stubbles in summer.

agostero, *–tĕ'rŏ*, sm. harvester; religious mendicant (who begs corn in August).

agostizo, za, *–tĭ thă*, a. born in August.

agosto, *ăgŏs'tŏ*, sm. August (month); harvest-time. [haust.

agotar, *ăgŏtár*, v.a. to misspend; to ex-

agoticado, *–tĭkă dŏ*, a. Gothic. [genteel.

agraciado, da, *ăgrăthĭá dŏ*, a. graceful,

agraciar, *–thĭár*, v.a. to embellish; to grace; to give an employment.

agradable, *–dá blĕ*, a. agreeable; lovely.

agradar, *–dár*, v.a. to please, to gratify.

agradecer, *–dĕthĕr*, v.a. to acknowledge a favour.

agradecido, da, *–thĕ dŏ*, a. thankful.

agradecimiento, *–thĭmĭĕn'tŏ*, sm. grati-tude, gratefulness, thankfulness.

agrado, *ăgrá'dŏ*, sm. agreeableness, court-eousness; will, pleasure; liking.

agramadera, *ăgrămădĕ'ră*, sf. brake (for dressing flax or hemp).

agramar, *–már*, v.a. to dress flax or hemp with a brake. [fuse of hemp.

agramiza, *–mĭ'thă*, sf. stalk of hemp; re-

agrandar, *ăgrăndár*, v.a. to enlarge, to extend; to aggrandize.

agranujado, da, *ăgrănŭ'hă dŏ*, a. grained.

agrario, ria, *ăgrá rĭă*, a. agrarian.

agravación, *ăgrăvăthĭŏn'*, sf. aggravation.

agravar, *ăgrăvăr'*, v. a. to oppress; to aggrieve; to aggravate; to exaggerate.

agravatorio, ria, *—văt͡o'ri͡o*, a. compulsory, aggravating.   [fender.

agraviador, ra, *—vĭădŏr'*, s. injurer, of-

agraviar, *—vĭăr'*, v. a. to wrong, to injure; *—se,* to be aggrieved; to be piqued.

agravio, *ăgră'vĭo,* sm. offence, injury.

agraz, *ăgrăth'*, sm. verjuice; unripe grape; **en —,** unseasonably.   [gooseberry bush.

agrazón, *ăgrăthŏn',* sm. wild grape;

agregación, *ăgrĕgăthĭon',* sf. aggregation.

agregado, *—gă'dŏ,* sm. aggregate.

agregar, *—găr'*, v. a. to aggregate, to heap together; to collate; to muster.

agresión, *ăgrĕsĭon',* sf. aggression, attack.

agresor, *ăgrĕsŏr'*, sm. aggressor, assaulter.

agreste, *ăgrĕs'tĕ,* a. rustic; produced by nature without cultivation.

agrete, *ăgrĕ'tĕ,* a. a bitter-sweet.

agriar, *ăgrĭăr'*, v. a. to sour, to acidify; to exasperate.

agricultura, *—kŭltŭ'ră,* sf. agriculture.

agridulce, *—dŭl'thĕ,* a. half sweet and half sour.   [the taste.

agrillo, lla, *ăgrĭl'yŏ,* a. sourish, sharp to

agrimensor, *ăgrĭmĕnsŏr'*, sm. land-surveyor, surveyor.

agrimensura, *—sŏ'ră,* sf. land-surveying.

agrimonia, *ăgrĭmŏ'nĭă,* sf. (bot.) agrimony.

agrio, *ă'grĭo,* a. sour, acrid; rough, craggy; sharp, rude, unpleasant; *—,* sm. acidity of the juice of certain fruits.

agrumarse, *ăgrŭmăr'sĕ,* v. r. to clog.

agrupar, *—păr'*, v. a. to group (in a picture); to cluster, to crowd.

agrura, *ăgrŏ'ră,* sf. acidity.

agua, *ă'gwă,* sf. water; lustre of diamonds; **— llovediza,** rain-water; **—fuerte,** aqua fortis; **— bendita,** holy water; **—s,** pl. mineral waters; cloudings in silk.

aguacero, *—thă'rŏ,* sm. short heavy shower of rain.

aguachirle, *—tshĭr'lĕ,* sf. slip-slop.

aguada, *ăgwă'dă,* sf. fresh-water hold or supply on board ship; water-colour; painting in water-colours.

aguaderas, *ăgwădĕ'răs,* sf. pl. wooden framework for the carriage of jars of water by mules.   [cattle, horse-pond.

aguadero, *—dă'rŏ,* sm. watering-place for

aguado, *ăgwă'dŏ,* sm. water-drinker.

aguador, *—dŏr'*, sm. water-carrier.

aguaje, *ăgwă'h͡ĕ,* sm. rapid current of sea-water; (mar.) spring-tide.

aguamanil, *ăgwămănĭl'*, sm. earthen or metal water-jug for the wash-hand stand.

aguamanos, *—mă'nŏs,* sm. water for washing the hands.   [(precious stone).

aguamarina, *—mărē'nă,* sf. aqua marina

aguamiel, *—mĭĕl'*, sf. hydromel.

aguanieve, *—nĭĕ'vĕ,* sf. sleet; lap-wing.

aguanoso, sa, *—nŏ'sŏ,* a. aqueous.

aguantar, *ăgwăntăr'*, v. a. to sustain, to suffer.

aguante, *ăgwăn'tĕ,* sm. firmness; patience.

aguapié, *ăgwăpĭĕ',* sm. small wine.

aguar, *ăgwăr'*, v. a. to mix water with wine; *—se,* to be submerged.

aguardar, *ăgwărdăr'*, v. a. to expect, to wait for; to grant time.   [shop.

aguardentería, *—dĕntĕrē'ă,* sf. brandy-

aguardentero, *—dĕntĕ'rŏ,* sm. keeper of a liquor-shop.

aguardiente, *—dĭĕn'tĕ,* sm. brandy.

aguardo, *ăgwăr'dŏ,* sm. place where a sportsman waits to fire at the game, stand.

aguarrás, *—răs',* sf. spirit of turpentine.

aguatocha, *ăgwătŏtsh'ă,* sf. fire-engine.

aguaza, *ăgwă'thă,* sf. juice extracted from trees by incision.   [boggy or marshy.

aguazarse, *—thăr'sĕ,* v. r. to become

aguazo, *ăgwă'thŏ,* sm. painting in gouache.

agudeza, *ăgŭdĕ'thă,* sf. keenness, sharpness; acuteness; acidity; smartness.

agudo, da, *ăgŏ'dŏ,* a. sharp-pointed; keen-edged; smart; fine; acute, witty; brisk.

aguijada, *ăg͡ĭhă'dă,* sf. spur, goad.

aguijar, *—hăr'*, v. a. to prick, to spur, to goad; to stimulate.   [&c.; stimulation.

aguijón, *—hŏn'*, sm. sting of a bee, wasp,

aguijonear, *ăg͡ĭhŏnĕăr'*, v. a. to prick, to spur; to stimulate.

águila, *ă'gĭlă,* sf. eagle; a gold coin.

aguileño, ña, *ăg͡ĭlĕn'yŏ,* a. aquiline; hawk-nosed.

aguilucho, *—lŏ'tshŏ,* sm. eaglet.

aguinaldo, *—năl'dŏ,* sm. Christmas-box.

aguja, *ăgŏ'hă,* sf. needle; bodkin; magnetic needle; (rail.) switch, siding; **— de coser,** sewing-needle; **— de marear,** mariner's compass; **— de hacer media,** knitting-needle.

agujar, *—hăr'*, v. a. to prick with a needle; to sew, to stitch; to knit.

agujazo, *—hă'thŏ,* sm. prick with a needle.

agujerear, *—hĕrĕăr'*, v. a. to pierce, to bore.

agujero, *—hă'rŏ,* sm. hole in clothes; needle-maker; needle-seller.

agujeta, *—hă'tă,* sf. leather-strap; lace; *—s,* pl. pour-boire given to post-boys; pains from fatigue.   [shop.

agujetería, *—hĕtĕrē'ă,* sf. haberdasher's

aguosidad, *ăgwŏsĭdăd',* sf. lymph.

aguoso, sa, *ăgwŏ'sŏ,* a. aqueous.

agusanarse, *ăgŭsănăr'sĕ,* v. r. to be worm-eaten.

agustiniano, *ăgŭstĭnĭă'nŏ,* **agustino,** *ăgŭstē'nŏ,* sm. monk of the order of St. Augustin.

aguzadera, *ăgŭthădĕ'ră,* sf. whetstone.

aguzanieve, *—nĭă'vĕ,* sf. wagtail.

aguzar, *ăgŭthăr'*, v. a. to whet, to sharpen; to stimulate.   [for irons.

aherrojar, *ăĕrrŏ'hăr'*, v. a. to put in chains

ahí, *ăē',* ad. there.   [like, noble.

ahidalgado, da, *ăĭdălgă'dŏ,* a. gentleman-

ahijada, *ăĭhă'dă,* sf. goddaughter.

ahijado, *—dŏ,* sm. godson.

ahijar, *ăĭhăr'*, v. a. to adopt as one's child; *—,* v. n. to bring forth young; to bud.

ahilarse, *ăĭlăr'sĕ,* v. r. to grow faint for want of nourishment; to grow ropy (of wine).

ahilo, *ăĕ´lŏ,* sm. faintness for want of food, inanition.

ahinco, *ăĭn´kŏ,* sm. earnestness, eagerness.

ahitar, *ătĭăr´,* y. a. to surfeit; to cloy.

ahogar, *ăhŏgăr´,* v. a. to throttle, to smother; to drown, to suffocate; to oppress; to quench.

ahogo, *ăhŏ´gŏ,* sm. anguish, pain.

ahojar, *ăŏhăr´,* v. n. to eat the leaves of trees.

ahondar, *ăhŏndăr´,* v.a. to sink, to deepen; —, v. n. to penetrate far into a thing.

ahora, *ăhŏ´ră,* ad. now, at present; — —, just now; —, c. whether, or.

ahorcajarse, *ăhŏrkăhăr´sĕ,* v. r. to sit astride.

ahorcar, *—kăr´,* v. a. to hang; —se, to be very angry.

ahormar, *—măr´,* v. a. to fit or adjust a form.

ahorquillado, da, *—kĭlyă´dŏ,* a. forked.

ahorquillar, *—kĭlyăr´,* v. a. to prop up with forks.

ahorrar, *ăhŏrrăr´,* v. a. to enfranchise, to emancipate; to economize; to shun labour.

ahorrativo, va, *ăhŏrrătĭvŏ´,* a. frugal, thrifty, saving; niggardly, stingy.

ahorro, *ăhŏr´rŏ,* sm. parsimony; saving; thrift.

ahoyar, *ăhŏyăr´,* v. a. to dig holes for trees.

ahuchar, *ăhŭtshăr´,* v. a. to hoard up.

ahuecar, *ăhŭĕkăr´,* v. a. to hollow, to scoop out; —se, to grow haughty.

ahumar, *ăhŭmăr´,* v. a. to smoke, to cure in smoke.

ahusar, *ăhŭsăr´,* v. a. to make a thing as slender as a spindle; —se, to taper.

ahuyentar, *ăhŭyĕntăr´,* v. a. to put to flight.

aijada, *ăĭhă´dă,* sf. goad; pungency.

airarse, *ătrăr´sĕ,* v. r. to grow angry.

airazo, *ătră´thŏ,* sm. violent gust of wind.

aire, *ă´ĭrĕ,* sm. air; wind; gracefulness of manners; aspect, countenance; musical composition; en —, in a good humour.

airearse, *ătrĕăr´sĕ,* v. a. to take the air.

airón, *ătrŏn´,* sm. violent gale.

airoso, sa, *ătrŏ´sŏ,* a. airy; windy; graceful, genteel; successful.

aislado, da, *ăĭslă´dŏ,* a. insulated, isolated.

aislar, *ăĭslăr´,* v. a. to surround with water; to isolate.

ajar, *ăhăr´,* sm. garlic-field; —, v. a. to spoil, to tarnish; to abuse.

aje, *ă´hĕ,* sm. habitual complaint.

ajedrez, *ăhĕdrĕth´,* sm. chess (game); netting, grating.

ajedrezado, da, *—thă´dŏ,* a. chequered.

ajenabe, *ăhĕnă´bĕ,* sm. wild mustard.

ajenjo, *ăhĕn´hŏ,* sm. wormwood, absinthium.

ajeno, na, *ăhĕ´nŏ,* a. foreign, strange; insane; contrary to; ignorant; improper.

ajenuz, *ăhĕnŭth´,* sm. fennel-flower.

ajetrearse, *ăhĕtrĕăr´sĕ,* v.a. to exert one's self; to bustle; to toil; to fidget.

ajetreo, *ăhĕtrĕ´ŏ,* sm. activity; bustling disposition.

aji, *ă´hĕ,* sm. red Indian dwarf-pepper.

ajicola, *—kŏ´lă,* sf. glue made of scraps of leather boiled with garlic.

ajimez, *—mĕth´,* sm. arched window with a pillar in the centre to support it.

ajipuerro, *—pŭĕr´rŏ,* sm. (bot.) leek.

ajo, *ă´hŏ,* sm. garlic; garlic-sauce; paint for ladies; discreditable transaction taken part in by several persons.

ajobar, *ăhŏbăr´,* v. a. to carry heavy loads upon one's back.

ajolio, *ă´hŏ´lĭŏ,* sm. sauce made of oil and garlic.

ajonje, *ă´hŏn´hĕ,* sm. bird-lime.

ajoqueso, *ă´hŏkă´sŏ,* sm. dish made of garlic and cheese.

ajorca, *ăhŏr´kă,* sf. gold and silver anklets worn by Moorish women.

ajordar, *—dăr´,* v. a. to bawl, to cry out.

ajornalar, *—nălăr´,* v. a. to hire by the day.

ajuar, *ăhŭăr´,* sm. household furniture.

ajudiado, da, *ă´hŭdĭă´dŏ,* a. jewish.

ajuiciado, da, *ă´hŭĭthĭă´dŏ,* a. judicious, prudent, sensible.

ajustar, *ă´hŭstăr´,* v. a. to regulate, to adjust; to concert; to settle a balance.

ajuste, *—tĕ,* sm. agreement pact; accommodation.

ajusticiar, *—tĭthĭăr´,* v. a. to execute a malefactor.

al, *ăl,* art. for á el.

ala, *ă´lă,* sf. wing; aisle; row, file; brim of the hat; auricle; —s, pl. (mar.) upper-studding sails; protection.

alabandina, *ălăbăndĕ´nă,* sf. manganese.

alabanza, *—thă,* sf. praise, applause.

alabar, *ălăbăr´,* v. a. to praise, to applaud.

alabarda, *—dă´,* sf. halberd.

alabardero, *—dă´rŏ,* sm. halberdier.

alabastrado, da, *ălăbăstră´dŏ,* a. resembling alabaster.

alabastrino, na, *—trĕ´nŏ,* a. of alabaster.

alabastro, *—trŏ,* sm. alabaster; gypsum.

álabe, *ă´lăbĕ,* sm. drooping branch of an olive-tree; flier of a water-mill; fan-wheel.

alabearse, *ălăbĕăr´sĕ,* v. r. to warp.

alabeo, *—bĕ´ŏ,* sm. warp, warping.

alacena, *—thĕ´nă,* sf. cupboard, small cupboard in the wall; wainscot-chest.

alacrán, *—krăn´,* sm. scorpion; ring of the mouth-piece of a bridle; stop, hook.

alacranado, da, *—nă´dŏ,* a. bitten by a scorpion; infected.

alada, *ălă´dă,* sf. fluttering of the wings.

aladares, *—dă´rĕs,* sm. pl. love-curls.

alado, da, *—dŏ,* a. winged.

álaga, *ă´lăgă,* sf. (bot.) spelt.

alama, *ălă´mă,* sf. gold or silver cloth.

alambicado, da, *ălămbĭkă´dŏ,* a. given sparingly, grudgingly.

alambicar, *—kăr´,* v. a. to distil; to investigate closely.

alambique, *—bĕ´kĕ,* sm. alambic; still.

alambre, *ălăm´brĕ,* sm. copper; copper-wire; sheep-bells.

alambrera, *—bră´ră,* sf. wire-cage.

alameda, *ălămĕ´dă,* sf. poplar-avenue.

álamo, *ă´lămŏ,* sm. poplar, poplar-tree; — temblón, aspen-tree.

alamparse, *ălămpăr´sĕ,* v. r. to long, to wish earnestly.

alamud, *ălămŭd´´,* sm. door-bolt; bar of

alancear, ălănthĕăr', v. a. to dart, to spear; to wound with a lance.

alano, ălă'nŏ, sm. boar-hound.

alar, ălăr', sm. birdsnare, noose.

alarbe, –bĕ, sm. Arabian; unmannerly person. [–, to boast.

alarde, –dĕ, sm. military review; hacer

alargar, ălărgăr', v. a. to lengthen; to ex- [tend.

alarida, ălărē'dă, sf. hue and cry.

alarido, –dŏ, sm. outcry, shout; dar –s,

alarife, ălărē'fĕ, sm. architect. [to howl.

alarma, ălăr'mă, sf. (mil.) alarm.

alarmar, –măr', v. a. to alarm, to call to

alarmista, –mĭs'tă, sm. alarmist. [arms.

alatón, ălătŏn', sm. latten, brass.

alazán,ana, –ăn', a. sorrel-coloured (of horses).

alazo, ălă'thŏ, sm. blow with the wings.

alba, ăl'bă, sf. dawn of day, dayspring; alb, surplice. [cutor.

albacea, –thĕ'ă, sm. testamentary exe-

albaceazgo, –thĕăth'gŏ, sm. office of a testamentary executor.

albada, –dă, sf. morning-serenade.

albahaca, –ă'kă, sf. (bot.) sweet basil.

albalá, ălbălă', sm. & f. quittance, certi- ficate. [passport.

albanega, –nĕ'gă, sf. hair-net.

albañal, –nyăl', albañar, –nyăr', sm. common sewer; gully-hole.

albañil, –nyĭl', sm. mason, bricklayer.

albañilería, –nyĭlĕrē'ă, sf. masonry.

albar, ălbăr', a. white, whitish.

albarán, ălbărăn', sm. bill or placard for letting a house.

albarazado, da, ălbărăthă'dŏ, a. affected with the white leprosy; pallid, pale.

albarazo, –thŏ, sm. white leprosy.

albarooquero, ălbărkŏkĕ'rŏ, sm. apricot- tree. [beasts of burden; slice of bacon.

albarda, ălbăr'dă, sf. pack-saddle for

albardar, –dăr', v. a. to saddle with a pack-saddle.

albardilla, –dĭl'yă, sf. small pack-saddle; coping; ridge; mother-wool.

albaricoque, ălbărēkŏ'kĕ, sm. apricot.

albaricoquero, –kŏkĕ'rŏ, sm. apricot-tree.

albarillo, ălbărĭl'yŏ, sm. country-dance tune for the guitar; small kind of apricot.

albarrada, ălbărră'dă, sf. dry wall; trench

albayalde, ălbăyăl'dĕ, sm. white-lead, ceruse. [nut colour.

albazano, na, –thă'nŏ, a. of a dark chest-

albear, ălbĕăr', v. a. to whiten.

albedrío, –drē'ŏ, sm. free-will, freedom of will; arbitrament. [surgeon.

albéitar, ălbĕ'ĭtăr, sm. farrier, veterinary

albeitería, ălbĕĭtĕrē'ă, sf. farriery.

albengala, ălbĕngă'lă, sf. muslin.

albentola, –tŏ'lă, sf. fine bag-net.

alberca, ălbĕr'kă, sf. reservoir, cistern.

albérchiga, –tshĭgă, sf. peach.

albergar, –găr', v. a. to lodge, to har- bour; –se, to take a lodging.

albergue, –gĕ, sm. lodging-house, har- bour; charity-school for orphans.

albina, ălbē'nă, sf. marshy ground inun- dated with sea-water.

albo, ba, ăl'bŏ, a. white.

albogue, ălbŏ'gĕ, sm. bagpipe; cymbal.

albohol, ălbŏŏl', sm. bind-weed; poppy.

albóndiga, ălbŏn'dēgă, sf. forcemeat-ball.

albor, ălbŏr', sm. (poet.) dawn.

alborada, ălbŏră'dă, sf. first dawn of day; (mil.) action fought at the dawn of day; morning-watch.

alborear, ălbŏrĕăr', v. n. to dawn.

alborga, ălbŏr'gă, sf. mat-weed sandal.

albornía, ălbŏrnē'ă, sf. large glazed jug.

albornoz, –nŏth', sm. coarse woollen stuff; moorish cloak. [clusion of a bargain.

alboroque, ălbŏrŏ'kĕ, sm. treat at the con-

alborotadizo, za, –tădē'thŏ, alboro- tado, da, ălbŏrŏtă'dŏ, a. restless, turbu- lent.

alborotapueblos, –pŭĕ'blŏs, s. disturber.

alborotar, ălbŏrŏtăr', v. a. to make a dis- turbance. [tumult, riot.

alboroto, –rŏ'tŏ, sm. noise, disturbance.

alborozar, –rŏthăr', v. a. to exhilarate.

alborozo, –rŏ'thŏ, sm. joy, gaiety.

albricias, ălbrē'thĭăs, sf. pl. reward given for good news; ¡–! joy! joy!

albufera, ălbŏfĕ'ră, sf. lagoon. [nous.

albugíneo, nea, ălbŏ'hē'nĕŏ, a. albumi-

albugo, ălbŏ'gŏ, sm. albugo (eye-disease).

albur, ălbŏr', sm. dace (pez).

albura, ălbŏ'ră, sf. whiteness.

alcabala, ălkăbă'lă, sf. commerce-excise.

alcacel, –thĕl', alcacer, –thĕr', sm. meslin, maslin, mash.

alcachofa, –tshŏ'fă, sf. artichoke.

alcahaz, –ăth', sm. large bird-cage.

alcahazar, –thăr', v. a. to cage birds.

alcahuete, ta, –hŭĕ'tĕ, sm. & f. pimp, bawd.

alcahuetear, –hŭĕtĕăr', v. a. to bawd.

alcahuetería, –hŭĕtĕrē'ă, sf. bawdry.

alcaide, ălkă'ĭdĕ, sm. governor of a castle; jailor, warden. [nor or jailor.

alcaidesa, ălkăĭdĕ'să, sf. wife of a gover-

alcaidía, –dē'ă, sf. governorship; gover- nor's district. [ringleader.

alcalde, ălkăl'dĕ, sm. justice of the peace;

alcaldía, –dē'ă, sf. office and jurisdiction of an alcalde.

alcalino, na, ălkălē'nŏ, a. alkaline.

alcamonías, –mŏnē'ăs, sf.pl. various kinds of aromatic seeds.

alcance, ălkăn'thĕ, sm. balance of an ac- count; arm's length; range of fire-arms; capacity, ability; fathom; hit; compass.

alcancía, –thē'ă, sf. money-box; (mil.) hand-grenade.

alcanfor, –fŏr', sm. camphor.

alcanforado, da, –fŏră'dŏ, a. camphorated.

alcantarilla, –tărĭl'yă, sm. small bridge; drain; conduit under ground.

alcanzado, da, –thă'dŏ, a. necessitous, wanting.

alcanzar, –thăr', v. a. to overtake, to come up with, to reach; to get, to obtain; to be a creditor; – v. n. to suffice; to reach.

alcaparra, ălkăpăr'ră, sf., alcaparro, –rŏ, sm. caper-bush; caper.

alcaraván, ălkărăvăn', sm. bittern.
alcaravea, -vă'ă, sf. caraway-seed.
alcartaz, ălkărtăth', sm. paper-bag.
alcatifa, ălkătĭ'fă, sf. fine carpet.
alcatraz, -trăth', sm. pelican. [staple.
alcayata, -yă'tă, sf. hook; clothes-hook;
alcázar, -thăr', sm. castle, fortress.
alcazuz, -thŭth', sm. liquorice.
aloe, ăl'thĕ, sm. the cut (at cards).
alcedón, ălthĕdŏn', alción, -thĭŏn', sm.
alcoba, -kŏ'bă, sf. alcove. [halcyon.
alcohol, -kŏŏl', sm. antimony; alcohol.
alcoholar, -kŏŏlăr', v. a. to paint with antimony; to rectify spirits, to reduce to an impalpable powder.
alcorán, -kŏrăn', sm. Alcoran, Koran.
alcoranista, -ĭs'tă, sm. expounder of the Koran. [son of uncouth manners.
alcornoque, -kŏrnŏ'kĕ, sm. cork-tree; per-
alcrebite, -krĕbĕ'tĕ, sm. sulphur, brimstone.
alcribis, -krĕ'bĭs, sm. tewel, tewel-iron.
alcuza, -kŏŏ'thă, sf. oil-bottle. [bar.
aldaba, -dă'bă, sf. knocker; clapper; cross-
aldabada, -dă, sf. rap with a knocker; sudden fear. [knocker.
aldabazo, -thŏ, sm. violent rap with the
aldabear, ăldăbĕăr', v. n. to knock at the door with the knocker.
aldea, ăldĕ'ă, sf. hamlet; large farm.
aldeana, ăldĕă'nă, sf. countrywoman; lass.
aldeano, -nŏ, sm. villager; -, a. rustic.
aleación, ălĕăthĭŏn', sf. art of alloying metals. [alloy.
alear, -ăr', v. n. to flutter; -, v. a. to
alegación, ălĕgăthĭŏn', sf. allegation.
alegar, -găr', v. a. to allege, to quote.
alegato, -gă'tŏ, sm. allegation; (law) plaintiff's deposition.
alegoría, -gŏrĕ'ă, sf. allegory.
alegórico, ca, -gŏ'rĭkŏ, a. allegorical.
alegorizar, -gŏrĭthăr', v. a. to allegorise.
alegrar, -grăr', v.a. to gladden; to lighten; to exhilarate; to enliven; to beautify; -se, to rejoice; to grow merry with drinking. [- de cascos, tipsy.
alegre, ălĕ'grĕ, a. merry, joyful, content;
alegría, ălĕgrĕ'ă, sf. mirth, gaiety; (bot.) oily-grain; public festivals, pl.
alegro, ălĕ'grŏ, sm. (mus.) allegro.
alegrón, -grŏn', sm. sudden joy; sudden flicker. [removal.
alejamiento, -hămĭĕn'tŏ, sm. elongation.
alejar, -hăr', v. a. to remove to a greater distance.
alelarse, -lăr'sĕ, v. r. to become stupid.
alelí, -lĭ', sm. (bot.) winter gilliflower.
aleluya, -lŏ'yă, sf. allelujah; easter-time.
alemán, ălĕmăn', sm. German language.
alemana, ălĕmă'nă, sf. (old) Spanish dance.
alentar, ălĕntăr', v.n. to respire, to breathe; -, v. a. to animate.
alepín, ălĕpĭn', sm. a kind of bombasine.
alerce, ălĕr'thĕ, sm. larch-tree.
alero, ălĕ'rŏ, sm. gable-end; eaves.
alerta, ălĕr'tă, sf. (mil.) watch-word.
alerta, -, alertamente, -mĕn'tĕ, ad. vigilantly, attentively, on the watch.

alertar, ălĕrtăr', v. a. to render vigilant.
alesna, ălĕs'nă, sf. awl.
alesnado, da, -nă'dŏ, a. awl-shaped.
aleta, ăld'tă, sf. fin.
aletargarse, -lĕtărgăr'sĕ, v. r. to fall into a lethargic state; to sink to sleep.
aletazo, -tă'thŏ, sm. blow from a wing.
aletear, ălĕtĕăr', v. n. to flutter, to flit, to flicker. [tering.
aleteo, -tĕ'ŏ, sm. flapping of wings; flut-
aleve, ălĕ'vĕ, a. treacherous, perfidious.
alevosía, ălĕvŏsĕ'ă, sf. treachery, perfidy.
alevoso, sa, -vŏ'sŏ, a. treacherous, perfidious. [alphabetically.
alfabéticamente, ălfăbĕ'tĭkămĕn'tĕ, ad.
alfabético, ca, -tĭkŏ, a. alphabetical.
alfabeto, -tŏ, sm. alphabet; abecedary.
alfahaya, ălfăhă'yă, sf. floss-silk.
alfajor, -hŏr', sm. gingerbread.
alfalfa, ălfăl'fă, sf. (bot.) lucern.
alfanjazo, -hă'thŏ, sm. cutlass-wound.
alfanje, ălfăn'hĕ, sm. hanger, cutlass.
alfaquí, ălfăkĭ', sm. fakir.
alfar, -făr', sm. pottery; potter's clay.
alfarería, -fărĕrĕ'ă, sf. potter's art.
alfarero, -ră'rŏ, sm. potter. [cate.
alfeñicado, ălfĕnĭkă'dŏ, a. sugared; deli-
alfeñique, -kĕ, sm. sugar-paste; weakling.
alferecía, ălfĕrĕthĕ'ă, sf. epilepsy.
alfil, -fĭl', sm. bishop (at chess).
alfiler, -fĭlĕr', sm. pin (to fasten clothes); pl. pin-money.
alfilerazo, -fĭlĕră'thŏ, sm. prick of a pin.
alfolí, -fŏlĭ', sm. granary; salt warehouse.
alfoli(n)ero, -fŏlĭ(n)ĕ'rŏ, sm. keeper of a granary or magazine.
alfombra, -fŏm'bră, sf. carpet; (poet.) field adorned with flowers.
alfombrar, -fŏmbrăr', v. a. to carpet.
alfombrero, -fŏmbrĕ'rŏ, sm. carpet-maker.
alfombrilla, -fŏmbrĭl'yă, sf. small carpet; (med.) scarlatina. [or nut).
alfóncigo, -fŏn'thĭgŏ, sm. pistachio (tree
alforja, -fŏr'hă, sf. saddle-bag, knapsack.
alforjero, -fŏrhă'rŏ, sm. maker or seller of saddle-bags.
alga, -gă, sf. (bot.) sea-weed.
algaida, -găĭ'dă, sf. sand-dune.
algalia, -gă'lĭă, sf. civet; civet-cat.
algarabía, -gărăbĕ'ă, sf. Arabic tongue; gabble, gibberish.
algarada, -gără'dă, sf. loud cry.
algarroba, -gărrŏ'bă, sf. (bot.) carob.
algarrobera, -gărrŏbĕ'ră sf., alga-rrobo, -gărrŏ'bŏ, sm. (bot.) carob-tree.
algazara, -găthă'ră, sf. buzza (cry of Moors); hubbub of a multitude.
álgebra, ăl'hĕbră, sf. algebra.
algebrista, ăl'hĕbrĭs'tă, sm. algebraist.
algo, ăl'gŏ, pn. somewhat, something, ought; -, ad. somewhat.
algodón, ălgŏdŏn', sm. cotton; cotton-plant; cotton-wool. [cotton.
algodonado, da, -dŏnă'dŏ, a. filled with
algodonal, -dŏnăl', sm. cotton-plantation.
algodonero, -dŏnĕ'rŏ, sm. cotton-plant; dealer in cotton, cotton-broker.

algoso, sa, *algŏ'sŏ,* a. full of sea-weed.
alguacil, *algwăthĕl',* sm. bum-bailiff; market-clerk; high constable; watchman.
alguien, *ăl'gĭĕn,* pn. somebody.
algún, na, *-gŏn',* a. anyone; - *poco ó tanto,* ad. a little, rather.
alhaja, *ălă'hă,* sf. furniture; jewel.
alhajar, *-ă'hăr',* v. a. to supply with furniture. [tion.
alharaca, *-ără'kă,* sf. clamour, vocifera-
alheña, *ălĕn'yă,* sf. (bot.) common privet, dogwood; corn-blight.
alhoja, *-ŏ'hă,* sf. lark.
alhóndiga, *-ŏn'dĭgă,* sf. public granary.
alhondiguero, *-ŏndĭgă'rŏ,* sm. keeper of a public granary.
alhucema, *ălŭthă'mă,* sf. lavender.
aliacanado, da, *ălăkănă'dŏ,* a. jaundiced.
aliado, da, *ălă'dŏ,* a. allied. [diced.
alianza, *ălĭăn'thă,* sf. alliance, league.
aliarse, *ălĭăr'sĕ,* v. r. to be allied.
alias, *ă'lĭăs,* ad. otherwise.
alicaído, da, *ălĭkă'ĕdŏ,* a. lame-winged; weak, extenuated; uncocked.
alicantina, *-kăntē'nă,* st. artifice, stratagem, cunning.
alicates, *-kă'tĕs,* sm. pl. pincers, nippers.
aliciente, *-thĭĕn'tĕ,* sm. attraction, incitement. [ber).
alícuanta, *-kăăn'tă,* a. f. aliquant (num-
alícuota, *-kŏ'tă,* a. f. aliquot (quantity).
aliento, *ălĭĕn'tŏ,* sm. breath, respiration; courageousness.
alifafe, *ălĭă'fĕ,* sm. tumour (on a horse's hock); habitual ailment.
aligación, *-găthĭŏn',* sf. allegation.
aligador, *-gădŏr',* sm. alligator.
aligar, *ăgăr',* v. a. to tie, to unite.
aligeramiento, *-hĕrămĭĕn'tŏ,* sm. alleviation. [viate; to hasten.
aligerar, *-hĕrăr',* v. a. to lighten, to alle-
alijador, *-hădŏr',* sm. (mar.) lighter.
alijar, *-hăr',* v. a. (mar.) to lighten, to lighter; -, sm. uncultivated ground.
alijo, *ălĭ'hŏ,* sm. lightening of a ship; alleviation.
alimentación, *ălĭmĕntăthĭŏn',* sf. alimentation, maintenance, nourishment.
alimentar, *-tăr',* v. a. to feed, to nourish.
alimenticio, cia, *-tĕ'thĭŏ,* a. nutritious, nutritive. [sioner.
alimentista, *-tĭs'tă,* sm. boarder, pen-
alimento, *ălĭmĕn'tŏ,* sm. aliment, food; -s, s. pl. alimony. [delimitate.
alindar, *ălĭndăr',* v. a. to fix limits; to
alineación, *ălĭnĕăthĭŏn',* sm. delimitation.
alinear, *-nĕăr',* v. a. to measure by line, to arrange in line.
aliñar, *ălĭnyăr',* v. a. to adorn; to season.
aliño, *ălĭn'yŏ,* sm. dress, ornament, decoration; apparatus. [feet; swift-footed.
alípede, *ălĭ'pĕdĕ,* a. (poet.) with winged
aliquebrado, da, *-kĕbră'dŏ,* a. broken-winged; dejected, low-spirited.
alisadura, *-săă'ră,* sf. planing, smoothing, polishing; -s, s. pl. shavings, cuttings.

alisar, *ălĭsăr',* v. a. to plane, to polish; to smoothe; to mangle.
aliseda, *ălĭsă'dă,* sf. plantation of alder-
aliso, *ălĭ'sŏ,* sm. alder-tree. [trees.
alistado, da, *ălĭstă'dŏ,* a. striped.
alistador, *-dŏr',* sm. accountant; one who enlists. [conscription, levy.
alistamiento, *-mĭĕn'tŏ,* sm. enrolment,
alistar, *ălĭstăr',* v. a. to enlist, to enrol.
aliviador, ra, *ălĭvĭădŏr',* sm. assistant.
aliviar, *-vĭăr',* v. a. to lighten; to ease, to relieve, to mollify. [comfort.
alivio, *ălĭ'vĭŏ,* sm. alleviation, mitigation;
aljaba, *ăl'hă'bă,* sf. quiver.
aljez, *-hĕth',* crude gypsum.
aljibe, *-hĕ'bĕ,* sm. cistern.
aljofaina, *-hŏfă'ĕnă,* sf. earthen jug; wash-hand basin.
aljofar, *-hŏfăr',* sm. misshapen pearl; (poet.) drop of dew; tear. [pearls.
aljofarar, *-hŏfărăr',* v. a. to adorn with
aljor, *-hŏr',* sm. crude gypsum.
aljuba, *ăl'hŏ'bă,* sf. a moorish garment.
alma, *ăl'mă,* sf. - soul; human being; principal part of a thing; conscience; energy; mould for casting statues.
almacén, *ălmăthĕn',* sm. warehouse, store, magazine. [rent; housage.
almacenaje, *-thĕnă'h'ĕ,* sm. warehouse
almacenar, *-thĕnăr',* v. a. to store, to lay up. [keeper.
almacenero, *-thĕnă'rŏ,* sm. warehouse-
almáciga, *ălmă'thĭgă,* sf. mastich; nursery.
almadén, *ălmădĕn',* sm. mine.
almadía, *ălmădĭ'ă,* sf. Indian canoe; raft.
almadraba, *-dră'bă,* sf. tunny-fishery.
almadreña, *-drĕn'yă,* sf. wooden shoe.
almaganeta, *-gănĕ'tă,* sf. sledge-hammer.
almagrar, *ălmăgrăr',* v. a. to tinge with red ochre, to ruddle.
almagre, *ălmă'grĕ,* sm. red ochre, ruddle.
almanaque, *ălmănă'kĕ,* sm. almanac.
almanaquero, *-kă'rŏ,* almanaquista, *-kĭs'tă,* sm. maker or vender of almanacs.
almáraco, *ălmă'răkŏ,* sm. (bot.) marjoram.
almargo, *ălmăr'gŏ,* sm. (bot.) glass-wort.
almarjal, *ălmăr'hăl',* sm. plantation of glass-wort; low marshy ground. [shalter.
almártaga, *-tăgă,* sf. litharge; a sort of
almástiga, *ălmă'stĭgă,* sf. mastich.
almastigado, da, *-gă'dŏ,* a. containing mastich.
almazara, *ălmăthă'ră,* sf. oil-mill.
almazarero, *-thără'rŏ,* sm. oil-miller.
almazarrón, *-thărrŏn',* sm. ruddle.
almena, *ălmă'nă,* sf. battlement.
almenado, da, *-nă'dŏ,* a. embattled.
almenaje, *-nă'hĕ,* sm. series of turrets around a rampart. [with battlements.
almenar, *-năr',* v. a. to crown a rampart
almendra, *ălmĕn'dră,* sf. almond.
almendrada, *-dră'dă,* sf. almond-milk;
almendrado, da, *-dră'dŏ,* a. almond-like; -, sm. macaroon.
almendrera, *ălmĕndră'ră,* sf. almen-
drero, -ŏ, **almendro,** *ălmĕn'drŏ,* sm. green almond.
almez(o), *ălmă'th(ŏ),* sm. nettle-tree, lotus-

almeza, –thǎ, sf. lotus-berry.

almiar, ǎlmēǎr′, sm. stack of hay.

almíbar, ǎlmē′bǎr, sm. syrup; treacle; –es, pl. preserved fruit.

almibarar, ǎlmēbǎrǎr′, v. a. to preserve fruit in sugar; to conciliate with soft and endearing words.

almidón, –dōn′, sm. starch.

almidonado, da, –dōnǎ′dō, a. starched; affected; spruce.

almidonar, –dōnǎr′, v. a. to starch.

almilla, ǎlmēl′yǎ, sf. under waistcoat; short military jacket; pork-chop.

alminar, ǎlmēnǎr′, sm. minaret.

almiranta, ǎlmērǎn′tǎ, sf. flag-ship; the admiral's wife. [admiral's dues.

almirantazgo, –tǎth′gō, sm. admiralty.

almirante, ǎlmērǎn′tē, sm. admiral; swimming-master.

almirez, ǎlmērĕth′, sm. brass mortar.

almizclar, ǎlmǐthklǎr′, v. a. to musk.

almizcle, ǎlmǐth′klĕ, sm. musk.

almizcleña, –klĕn′yǎ, sf. grape-hyacinth.

almizcleño, ña, –ō, a, musky.

almizclera, ǎlmǐthklĕ′rǎ, sf. musk-rat.

almo, ma, ǎl′mō, a. supporting; nourishing; (poet.) venerable, holy. [hoe.

almocafre, ǎlmōkǎ′frĕ, sm. gardener's

almodrote, –drō′tĕ, sm. sauce for mad-apples; hodge-podge.

almofía, –fē′ǎ, sf. wash-hand basin.

almofrej, –frĕh′, sm. pillow-case.

almohada, –ǎ′dǎ, sf. pillow, bolster; coach-box; cushion. [working-case.

almohadilla, –ǎdēl′yǎ, sf. small pillow;

almohadón, –ǎdōn′, sm. large cushion.

almohaza, –ǎ′thǎ, sf. curry-comb.

almohazador, –ǎthǎdōr′, sm. groom, stable-boy, ostler.

almohazar, –ǎthǎr′, v. a. to curry.

almojábana, –hǎ′bǎnǎ, sf. cheese-cake.

almoneda, –nǎ′dǎ, sf. auction.

almonedear, –nĕdĕǎr′, v. a. to sell by auction. [joram.

almoradují, ǎlmōrǎdǔ′h′, sm. sweet mar-

almorí, ǎlmōrē′, sm. sweetmeat-cake.

almorranas, ǎlmōrrǎ′nǎs, sf. pl. hemorrhoids. [floor.

almorrefa, ǎlmōrrĕ′fǎ, sf. mosaic-tile

almorta, ǎlmōr′tǎ, sf. chickling vetch.

almorzada, –thǎ′dǎ, sf. double-handful of grain &c. [fasted.

almorzado, da, –dō, a. one who has break-

almorzar, ǎlmōrthǎr′, v. a. to breakfast.

almotacén, ǎlmōtǎthĕn′, sm. inspector of weights and measures.

almotacenazgo, –nǎth′gō, sm. office of an inspector of weights and measures.

almozárabe, ǎlmōthǎ′rǎbĕ, sm. christian who lived under the Moors.

almud, ǎlmǔd′, sm. measure of grain (the twelfth part of a fanega).

almudada, ǎlmǔdǎ′dǎ, sf. piece of ground which it takes half a fanega of grain to sow. [of grain, fruits &c.).

almuerza, ǎlmǔĕr′thǎ, sf. double-handful

almuerzo, –ō, sm. breakfast; cupboard.

alobadado, da, ǎlōbǎdǎ′dō, a. bitten by a wolf; plague-sore (of animals).

alobunado, da, –bǔnǎ′dō, a. wolf-coloured.

alocado, da, –kǎ′dō, a. crack-brained; foolish, inconsiderate.

alocución, –kǔthiōn′, sf. allocution.

alodio, ǎlō′diō, sm. allodium.

áloe, ǎ′lŏĕ, sm. (bot.) aloes.

aloja, ǎlō′hǎ, sf. metheglin.

alojamiento, ǎlō′hǎmiĕn′tō, sm. lodging; (mar.) steerage. [side in lodgings.

alojar, –hǎr′, v. a. to lodge; –se, to re-

alojería, –hĕrē′ǎ, sf. place where metheglin is prepared and sold.

alojero, –hĕ′rō, sm. seller of metheglin; box near the pit in some theatres of Spain.

alomado, da, –mǎ′dō, a. crook-backed (of horses).

alomar, –mǎr′, v. a. to distribute equally the strength of a horse; –, v. n. to grow strong and vigorous.

alón, ǎlōn′, sm. wing of a bird stripped of its feathers; ¡–! let us go!

alondra, ǎlōn′drǎ, sf. lark. [opium.

alopiado, da, ǎlōpiǎ′dō, a. composed of

aloque, ǎlō′kĕ, a. light-red (wine).

alosa, ǎlō′sǎ, sf. shad (pez).

alpañata, ǎlpǎnyǎ′tǎ, sf. piece of leather for smoothing pottery.

alpargata, ǎlpǎrgǎ′tǎ, sf. hempen shoe.

alpargatar, –tǎr′, v. a. to make hempen shoes. [hempen shoes.

alpargatero, –tĕ′rō, sm. manufacturer of

alpargatilla, –tēl′yǎ, sm. crafty fellow, wheedler.

alpiste, ǎlpǐs′tĕ, sm. canary-seed.

alpistela, ǎlpǐstĕ′lǎ, alpistera, –rǎ, sf. cake made of flour, eggs, sesamum and honey. [canary-seed.

alpistero, –tĕ′rō, sm. sieve for sifting

alquería, ǎlkĕrē′ǎ, sf. grange, farm-house.

alquifol, ǎlkēfōl′, sm. alquifou, potter's ore.

alquiladizo, za, ǎlkēlǎdē′thō, a. for hire.

alquilador, ra, –lǎdōr′, sm. (& f.) hirer, tenant.

alquilar, –lǎr′, v. a. to let, to hire. [rent.

alquiler, –lĕr′, sm. wages, hire; house-

alquimia, ǎlkē′miǎ, sf. alchemy.

alquímico, ca, –mǐkō, a. alchemical.

alquimista, –mǐs′tǎ, sm. alchemist.

alquitara, –tǎ′rǎ, sf. alembic.

alquitarar, –tǎrǎr′, v. a. to distil.

alquitrán, –trǎn′, sm. tar, liquid pitch.

alquitranado, –trǎnǎ′dō, sm. (mar.) tarpaulin.

alquitranar, –trǎnǎr′, v. a. to tar.

alrededor, ǎlrĕdĕdōr′, ad. around.

alrededores, –ĕs, sm. pl. environs.

alta, ǎl′tǎ, sf. (mil.) discharge-ticket from hospital.

altanería, ǎltǎnĕrē′ǎ, sf. haughtiness.

altanero, ra, ǎltǎnĕ′rō, a. haughty, arrogant, vain, proud.

altar, ǎltǎr′, sm. altar; – de ánima, altar of indulgence; – mayor, high-altar.

altarero, ǎltǎrĕ′rō, sm. decorator of altars for festivals.

altea, *ălŭ'ă,* sf. (bot.) marsh-mallow.

alterabilidad, *ăltĕrăbĭlĭdăd'',* sf. alterableness; mutability.

alterable, *-rā'blĕ,* a. alterable, mutable.

alteración, *-thĭŏn',* sf. alteration, mutation; strong emotion; disturbance, tumult.

alterar, *ăltĕrăr',* v. a. to alter, to change; to disturb; **—se,** to fling.

altercación, *ăltĕrkăthĭŏn',* sf., **altercado,** *ăltĕrkă'dŏ,* sm. altercation, controversy; quarrel, contest, strife.

altercador, ra, *-kăr',* sm. (& f.) wrangler.

altercar, *-kăr',* v. a. to dispute, to altercate, to quarrel.

alternación, *ăltĕrnăthĭŏn',* sf. alternation.

alternar, *ăltĕrnăr',* v. a. & n. to alternate.

alternativa, *ăltĕrnătĕvă,* sf. alternative.

alternativo, *-vŏ,* a. alternate.

alteza, *ăltĕ'thă,* sf. height, elevation.

Alteza, *—'',* sf. Highness (title).

altibajo, *ăltĭbă'hŏ,* sm. downright blow in fencing; uneven ground; **—s,** pl. vicissitudes of human affairs, ups and downs.

altillo, *ăltĭl'yŏ,* sm. hillock.

altísimo, ma, *ăltĭs'ĭmŏ,* a. extremely high, highmost; **—,** sm. the Most High, God.

altisonante, *ăltĭsŏnăn'tĕ,* altísono, na, *ăltĭs'ŏnŏ,* a. high-sounding, pompous, fustian. [ing, high-sounding.

altitonante, *-tŏnăn'tĕ,* a. (poet.) thunder-

altivez, *ăltĭvĕth',* sf. haughtiness, huff.

altivo, va, *ăltĭ'vŏ,* a. haughty, proud, high-flown.

alto, ta, *ăl'tŏ,* a. high, elevated; arduous, difficult; eminent; enormous, atrocious; **—,** sm. height; storey; highland; (mil.) halt; (mus.) tenor, tenor-notes; **| —! |,** *——,* **ahí !** stop there ! **— de aquí !** move off !

altramuz, *ăltrămŭth',* sm. (bot.) lupine.

altura, *ăltŭ'ră,* sf. height; highness; mountain summit; altitude; **—s,** pl. the heavens.

alubia, *ălŭ'bĭă,* sf. kidney-bean.

alucinación, *ălŭthĭnăthĭŏn',* sf., **alucinamiento,** *-mămĭĕn'tŏ,* sm. hallucination.

alucinar, *-năr',* v. a. to blind, to deceive; **—se,** to deceive oneself, to labour under a delusion.

aludir, *ălŭdĭr',* v. n. to allude.

alumbrado, da, *ălŭmbră'dŏ,* a. aluminous; a little tipsy; **—,** sm. illumination; **— por el gas,** gas-lighting.

alumbramiento, *-mĭĕn'tŏ,* sm. illumination; illusion, deceit; child-birth.

alumbrar, *ălŭmbrăr',* v. a. to light; to enlighten, to instruct; to soak in alum-water; **—se,** to be intoxicated.

alumbre, *ălŭm'brĕ,* sm. alum.

alumbrera, *-bră'ră,* sf. alum-mine.

aluminado, da, *ălŭmĭ'nă'dŏ,* a. impregnated with alum.

aluminio, *ălŭmĕ'nĭŏ,* sm. aluminium.

aluminoso, sa, *-nŏ'să,* a. aluminous.

alumno, na, *ălŭm'nŏ,* sm. foster-child; disciple, pupil. [modic; long-tusked.

alunado, da, *ălŭnă'dŏ,* a. lunatic; spas-

alusión, *ălŭsĭŏn',* sf. allusion, hint.

alusivo, va, *ălŭsĕ'vŏ,* a. allusive.

alustrar, *ălŭstrăr',* v. a. to give lustre, to polish. [brought to light by washing.

alutación, *ălŭtăthĭŏn',* sf. grains of gold.

aluvión, *ălŭvĭŏn',* sf. alluvion.

álveo, *ăl'vĕŏ,* sm. bed of a river.

alvéolo, *ălvă'ŏlŏ,* sm. socket of a tooth; cell of a honey-comb. [ware.

alvidriar, *ălvĭdrĭăr',* v. a. to glaze earthen-

alvitana, *ălvĭtă'nă,* sf. shelter.

alza, *ăl'thă,* sf. advance in price; lift.

alzacuello, *-kŭĕl'yŏ,* sm. gorget; pad.

alzadamente, *-dămĕn'tĕ,* ad. wholesale.

alzado, da, *ălthă'dŏ,* sm. plan of a building showing front elevation; **—s,** pl. spare stores; **—,** da, a. fraudulent (of a bank-

alzadura, *-dŏ'ră,* sf. elevation. [rupt).

alzamiento, *-mĭĕn'tŏ,* sm. raise; elevation; higher bid.

alzaprima, *-prĕ'mă,* sf. lever.

alzaprimar, *-prĭmăr',* v. a. to lever; (fig.) to excite. [of a mute servant.

alzapuertas, *-pŭĕr'tăs,* sm. part or rôle

alzar, *ălthăr',* v. a. to raise, to lift up, to heave; to construct, to build; to hide; to lock up; to cut cards; to plough for the first time; **—se,** to rise in rebellion; **—se á mayores,** to be petulant; **—se con algo,** to encroach.

allá, *ălyă',* ad. there; thither; in other times.

allanar, *ălyănăr',* v. a. to level, to flatten; to overcome difficulties; to pacify; to subdue; **—se,** to submit; to tumble down.

allegadizo, za, *ălyĕgădĭ'thŏ,* a. swept or scraped together. [conjunct, follower.

allegado, da, *ălyĕgă'dŏ,* a. near, proximate.

allegar, *ălyĕgăr',* v. a. to collect, to gather; to approach.

allende, *ălyĕn'dĕ,* ad. on the other side.

allí, *ălyĕ',* ad. there, in that place.

alloza, *ălyŏ'thă,* sf. green almond.

allozo, *ălyŏ'thŏ,* sm. wild almond-tree.

ama, *ă'mă,* sf. mistress, house-wife; **— de llaves,** house-keeper; **— de leche,** nurse.

amabilidad, *ămăbĭlĭdăd'',* sf. amiability, loveliness.

amable, *ămă'blĕ,* a. amiable, lovely.

amador, ra, *ămădŏr',* sm. & f. lover, sweetheart. [berry-like.

amadroñado, da, *-drŏnyă'dŏ,* a. straw-

amaestrado, da, *-ĕstră'dŏ,* a. taught; artfuly contrived. [struct.

amaestrar, *-ĕstrăr',* v. a. to teach, to in-

amagar, *-găr',* v. a. to threaten; to shake one's fist. [symptom.

amago, *ămă'gŏ,* sm. threat; indication;

amainar, *ămăĭnăr',* v. a. (mar.) to lower a sail; to give up, to withdraw from.

amajadar, *ămă'hădăr',* v. n. to pen sheep.

amalgama, *ămălgă'mă,* sf. amalgam.

amalgamación, *ămălgămăthĭŏn',* sf. amalgamation. [gamate.

amalgamar, *ămălgămăr',* v. a. to amal-

amamantar, *ămămăntăr',* v. a. to suckle.

amancebamiento, *ămănthĕbămĭĕn'tŏ,* sm. concubinage. [cubinage.

amancebarse. *-băr'sĕ,* v. r. to live in con-

amancillar, *ămănsĭlyăr´,* v. a. to stain, to defile; to injure; to tarnish one's reputation. [—, at day-break.

amanecer, *ămănĕthĕr´,* v. n. to dawn; al

amanojar, *ămănŏ´hăr´,* v. a. to gather by handfuls. [tamer, subduer; soother.

emansador, ra, *ămănsădŏr´,* sm. & f.

amansamiento, *—mĭen´tŏ,* sm. taming.

amansar, *ămănsăr´,* v. a. to tame, to domesticate; to soften, to meeken.

amantar, *ămăntăr´,* v. a. to cover with a

amante, *ămăn´tĕ,* sm. lover.   [blanket.

amanuense, *ămănŭĕn´sĕ,* sm. amanuensis, clerk, copyist.

amañar, *ămănyăr´,* v. a. to do a thing cleverly; -se, to accustom one's self to do things cleverly.

amaño, *ămăn´yŏ,* sm. skill, dexterity; -s, s. pl. tools; implements; intrigue.

amapola, *ămăpŏ´lă,* sf. (bot.) poppy.

amar, *ămăr´,* v. a. to love; to fancy.

amaranto, *ămărăn´tŏ,* sm. (bot.) amaranth.

amargar, *ămărgăr´,* v. a. to make bitter; to exasperate; -, v. n. to be bitter.

amargo, ga, *ămăr´gŏ,* a. bitter, acrid; painful; -, sm. bitterness; sweet-meat made of bitter almonds; -, s. pl. bitters.

amargón, *ămărgŏn´,* sm. (bot.) dandelion.

amargor, *—gŏr´,* sm. bitterness; sorrow, vexation, distress.

amargoso, sa, *—gŏ´sŏ,* a. bitter.

amargura, *—gŏ´ră,* sf. bitterness; sorrow.

amaricado, da, *ămărĭkă´dŏ,* a. effeminate.

amarillazo, za, *ămărĭlyă´thŏ,* a. pale yellow.

amarillear, *—yĕăr´,* v. n. to turn yellow.

amarillejo, ja, *ămărĭlyĕ´hŏ,* amarillento, ta, *—yĕn´tŏ,* a. yellowish.

amarillez, *—yĕth´,* sf. yellowness of the skin.   [sm. jaundice.

amarillo, lla, *ămărĭl´yŏ,* a. yellow; —,

amarinar, *ămărĭnăr´,* v. a. (mar.) to man, to equip.

amarra, *ămăr´ră,* sf. cable; martingale.

amarradero, *—dĕ´rŏ,* sm. a post to make fast to; (mar.) mooring-berth.

amarrar, *ămărrăr´,* v. a. to tie, to fasten.

amarrazones, *ămărrăthŏ´nĕs,* sm. pl. (mar.) ground-tackle.

amartelar, *ămărtĕlăr´,* v. a. to court, to make love; -se, to fall in love with.

amartillar, *—tĭlyăr´,* v. a. to hammer; to cock a gun or pistol.   [trough.

amasadera, *ămăsădă´ră,* sf. kneading-

amasadijo, *—dĕ´hŏ,* sm. bread-dough.

amasadura, *—dŏ´ră,* sf. kneading.

amasar, *ămăsăr´,* v. a. to knead; (fig.) to arrange, to prepare, to settle.

amasijo, *ămăsĭ´hŏ,* sm. dough; mixed mortar; bread-dough; medley.

amatista, *ămătĭs´tă,* sf. amethyst.

amatorio, ria, *—tŏ´rĭŏ,* a. relating to love.

amazona, *ămăthŏ´nă,* sf. amazon; masculine woman.   [line woman.

ámbar, *ăm´băr,* sm. amber.

ambarino, na, *ămbărĭ´nŏ,* a. amber.

ambición, *ămbĭthĭŏn´,* sf. ambition; coverousness.   [to covet.

ambicionar, *ămbĭthĭŏnăr´,* v. a. to crave,

ambicioso, sa, *—thĭŏ´sŏ,* a. ambitious.

ambiente, *ămbĭen´tĕ,* sm. surrounding atmosphere.

ambigú, *ămbĭgŏ´,* sm. ambigu.

ambigüedad, *—gŭĕdăd´,* sf. ambiguity.

ambiguo, gua, *ămbĭ´gŏ,* a. ambiguous, doubtful, equivocal.

ámbito, *ăm´bĭtŏ,* sm. circuit, circumference.

ambo, *ăm´bŏ,* sm. double lottery prize.

ambos, bas, *ăm´bŏs,* pn. both.

ambrosia, *ămbrŏ´sĭă,* sf. ambrosia; any delicious liquor; (bot.) buck-thorn.

ambulante, *ămbŭlăn´tĕ,* a. ambulatory; -s, sm. pl. railway post-office.

ambulativo, va, *—lătĭ´vŏ,* a. of a roving disposition.   [to terrify, to intimidate.

amedrentar, *ămĕdrĕntăr´,* v. a. to frighten,

amelga, *ămĕl´gă,* sf. ridge between two furrows.   [the plough.

amelgar, *—găr´,* v. a. to open furrows with

amelonado, da, *ămĕlŏnă´dŏ,* a. melonshaped.

amen, *ămĕn´,* sm. amen, so be it; **sacristán de —,** one who blindly adheres to the opinion of another; -de, besides; except.

amenaza, *ămĕnă´thă,* sf. threat, menace.

amenazar, *—thăr´,* v. a. to threaten, to menace.   [apt; to adorn a speech.

amenizar, *ămĕnĭthăr´,* v. a. to render pleas-

ameno, na, *ămĕ´nŏ,* a. pleasant, delicious; flowery (of language).   [spoken.

amerengado, *ămĕrĕngă´dŏ,* a. (fig.) fair.

ametalado, da, *ămĕtălă´dŏ,* a. brasscoloured.

amicísimo, *ămĭthĭ´sĭmŏ,* a. most friendly.

amiento, *ămĭen´tŏ,* sm. stay of a helmet.

amiga, *ămĭ´gă,* sf. female friend; concubine; school-mistress.   [suitable.

amigable, *ămĭgă´blĕ,* a. amicable, friendly,

amigo, *ămĭ´gŏ,* sm. friend; comrade; lover; -, ga, a. friendly.   [terrify.

amilanar, *ămĭlănăr´,* v. a. to frighten, to

amillaramiento, *ămĭlyărămĭen´tŏ,* sm. tax-assessment.

amillarar, *ămĭlyărăr´,* v. a. to assess a tax.

amillonado, da, *ămĭlyŏnă´dŏ,* a. liable to pay a certain tax, called millones.

amistad, *ămĭstăd´,* sf. friendship; juncture; gallantry; civility, favour; desire.

amistar, *ămĭstăr´,* v. a. & r. to reconcile.

amistoso, sa, *ămĭstŏ´sŏ,* a. friendly, cordial.

amito, *ămĭ´tŏ,* sm. amice.   [dial.

amnistia, *ămnĭstĭ´ă,* sf. amnesty.

amo, *ă´mŏ,* sm. master of a house; proprietor, owner; foster-father; overseer.

amoblar, *ămŏblăr´,* v. a. to furnish.

amodorrarse, *ămŏdŏrrăr´sĕ,* v. r. to grow sleepy.   [mouldy.

amohecerse, *—ĕthĕr´sĕ,* v. r. to grow

amohinar, *—ĭnăr´,* v. a. to put out of humour.   [gre.

amojamado, da, *—´hămă´dŏ,* a. dry, mea-

amojonar, *—hŏnăr´,* v. a. to set landmarks.

amoladera, *—lădă´ră,* sf. whetstone, grindstone.   [coachman; unskilful artist.

amolador, *—lădŏr´,* sm. grinder; unskilful

amoladura, *—lădŏ´ră,* sf. whetting, grinding, sharpening.

amolar, –lár´, v. a. to whet, to grind, to sharpen.

amoldar, ămŏldár´, v.a. to mould; to one to his duty. [shaped.

amolletado, da, ămŏllyĕtä´dŏ, a. loaf-shaped.

amomo, ămŏ´mŏ, sm. (bot.) Guinea-grains.

amonedar, ămŏnĕdär´, v. a. to coin.

amonestación, ămŏnĕstäthiŏn´, sf. advice, admonition; publication of marriage-bans.

amonestar, –nĕstär´, v. a. to advise, to admonish; to publish bans of marriage.

amoníaco, ămŏnĭ´ăkŏ, sm. ammoniac.

amontarse, ămŏntär´sĕ, v. r. to take to the woods. [to accumulate.

amontonar, –tŏnär´, v.a. to heap together,

amor, ămŏr´, sm. love; fancy; flame; the object of love; – mío, mis –es, my love; por – de Dios, for God's sake; – propio, self-love; –es, pl. gallantry; amours, criminal love.

amoratado, da, ămŏrätä´dŏ, a. livid.

amorcillo, –thĭl´yŏ, sm. flirtation.

amoroso, sa, –rŏ´sŏ, a. affectionate, loving; lovely. [head.

amorrar, ămŏrrär´, v. n. to hang one's

amorronar, –rŏnär´, v. a. to hoist or fly a flag. [corpse.

amortajar, –tä´här´, v. a. to shroud a

amortecén, –tĕthĕn´, sm. pay-master.

amortiguar, –tĭgwär´, v. a. to mortify, to deaden; to temper.

amortización, –tĭthäthiŏn´, sf. mortmain.

amortizar, –tĭthär´, v. a. to entail an estate, to render it inalienable; to pay, to liquidate, to discharge a debt.

amoscar, ămŏskär´, v. a. to whisk flies; –se, to drive off flies with the tail (of animals); to fly into a passion at nothing.

amostachado, ămŏstätshä´dŏ, a. moustachioed.

amotinador, ămŏtĭnädŏr´, a. mutineer.

amotinamiento, –nämiĕn´tŏ, sm. mutiny.

amotinar, ămŏtĭnär´, v. a. to excite rebellion; –se, to mutiny.

amovible, ămŏvĕ´blĕ, a. removable.

ampara, ämpä´rä, sf. (law) distraint.

amparar, ämpärär´, v. a. to shelter, to favour, to protect; to sequestrate; –se, to claim protection.

amparo, ämpä´rŏ, sm. protection, help, support; sequestration; refuge, asylum.

ampelita, ämpĕlĭ´tä, sf. cannel-coal.

ampliación, ämpliäthiŏn´, sf. amplification, enlargement.

ampliar, ämpliär´, v. a. to amplify, to enlarge, to extend, to expand. [ing.

ampliativo, va, ämpliätĭ´vŏ, a. amplify-

amplificar, ämplĭfĭkär´, v. a. to amplify.

amplio, lia, äm´pliŏ, a. ample, extensive.

amplitud, ämplĭtüd´, sf. amplitude, extension, largeness.

ampo (de la nieve), äm´pŏ, sm. whiteness.

ampolla, ämpŏl´yä, sf. blister (on the cuticle); phial, cruet.

ampollar, ämpŏlyär´, v.a. to raise blisters; –se, to rise in bubbles; –, a. bubble-shaped.

ampolleta, –yä´tä, sf. small phial; hour-glass, – de arena, powder-box.

amprar, ämprär´, v. n. to borrow. [tion.

amputación, ämpŭtäthiŏn´, sf. amputa·

amputar, ämpŭtär´, v. n. to amputate.

amuchachado, da, ämŭtshätshä´dŏ, a. boyish, childish.

amueblar, ämŭĕblär´, v. a. to furnish.

amugronar, ämŭgrŏnär´, v.a. to provine.

amujerado, da, ämŭ´hĕrä´dŏ, a. effeminate. [nate.

amuleto, ämŭlĕ´tŏ, sm. amulet.

amunicionar, ämŭnĭthiŏnär´, v. a. to supply with ammunition. [with walls.

amurallar, ämŭräl´yär´, v. a. to surround

amurcar, ämŭrkär´, v. a. to gore.

amurco, ämŭr´kŏ, sm. blow with the horns.

amusco, ämŭs´kŏ, a. dark-brown.

amusgar, ämŭsgär´, v. a. to lay back the ears; to half-close one's eyes to see better.

ana, ä´nä, sf. ell, (-measure).

anabaptista, änäbäptĭs´tä, sm. anabaptist.

anacoreta, –kŏrĕ´tä, sm. anchorite, hermit.

anacorético, ca, –kŏrĕ´tĭkŏ, a. relating to a hermit. [nism.

anacronismo, –krŏnĭs´mŏ, sm. anachro-

ánade, ä´nädĕ, sm. & f. duck.

anadear, änädĕär´, v. n. to waddle.

anadeja, –dä´hä, sf. duckling.

anadino, na, –dĕ´nŏ, sm. & f. young duck.

anadón, –dŏn´, sm. & f. duck.

anafaya, –fä´yä, sf. thick-corded silk-stuff.

anafe, änä´fĕ, sm. portable stove.

anagálida, –gä´lĭdä, sf. (bot.) pimpernel.

anagrama, –grä´mä, sf. anagram.

anales, änä´lĕs, sm. pl. annals.

análisis, änä´lĭsĭs, sf. analysis.

analista, änälĭs´tä, sm. writer of annals.

analítico, ca, –lĭ´tĭkŏ, a. analytical.

analizar, –lĭthär´, v. a. to analyse.

analogía, –lŏ´hĭ´ä, sf. analogy.

analógico, ca, –lŏ´hĭkŏ, **análogo, ga,** änä´lŏgŏ, a. analogous.

anana, änä´nä, sm. pine-apple.

anaquel, –kĕl´, sm. shelf in a book-case.

anaranjado, da, –rän´hä´dŏ, a. orange-coloured.

anarquía, änärkĕ´ä, sf. anarchy.

anárquico, ca, änär´kĭkŏ, a. anarchical, confused.

anascote, änäskŏ´tĕ, sm. serge.

anata, änä´tä, sf. annats.

anatema, –tä´mä, sf. anathema.

anatematizar, –tĕmätĭthär´, **v. a. to ana**-thematize.

anatomía, –tŏmĕ´ä, sf. anatomy.

anatómico, ca, –tŏ´mĭkŏ, a. anatomical.

anatomista, –tŏmĭs´tä, sm. anatomist.

anatomizar, –tŏmĭthär´, v. a. to anatomize, to dissect.

anca, än´kä, sf. buttocks of a horse.

ancianar, änthiänär´, v. n. (poet.) to grow old. [antiquity.

ancianidad, änthiänĭdäd´, sf. old age;

anciano, na, änthiä´nŏ, a. old, stricken in years. [sheet-anchor.

ancla, än´klä, sf.anchor; – de esperanza,

anclaje, änklä´hĕ, sm. act of anchoring; anchor-ground; anchorage.

anclar, ánklâr, v. n. to anchor. [nel.
anclote, ánklô tê, sm. stream-anchor, grapanco, ân'kô, sm. roof made of lead.
ancón, ânkôn', sm. anconada, ânkônâdâ, sf. bay. [ground.
ancorage, ânkôrâ'hê, sm. anchoring
ancorar, ânkôrâr', v. a. to cast anchor.
ancorero, ânkôrâ'rô, sm. anchor-smith.
ancho, cha, ân'tshô, a. broad, wide, large;
—, sm. breadth, width.
anchoa, ântshô'â, sf. anchovy.
anchura, ântshô'râ, sf. width, breadth.
andadero, ra, ândâdê'rô, a. accessible.
andado, ândâ'dô, sm. step-son; —, da, a.
beaten, much frequented; threadbare.
andador, —dôr', sm. stroller; leading
string; alley or small walk in a garden;
—, ra, a. fast-going.
andadura, —dô'râ, sf. walk; pace; amble.
andana, ândâ'nâ, sf. row, rank, line; tier
of guns; volley; (mar.) broadside; llamarse —, to unsay, to retract.
andanada, —nâ'dâ, sf. (mar.) broadside.
andaniño, —nîn'yô, sm. go-cart in which
children learn to walk.
andar, ândâr', v. n. to go, to walk; to fare;
to act, to proceed, to behave, to transact;
to elapse; to move (machines); ¡—! well I
never mind!
andaraje, ândârâ'hê, sm. wheel of a well.
andarín, ândârîn', sm. fast walker.
andas, ân'dâs, sf. pl. hand-barrow, bier
with shafts.
andén, ândên', sm. shelf; pavement; (am.)
side-walk; (rail.) platform; horse-path
round the draw-well. [building.
andito, ân'dîtô, sm. gallery around a
andorrear, ândôrrêâr', v. a. to stroll.
andorrera, —rô'râ, sf. street-walker.
andrajo, ândrâ'hô, sm. rag (of worn
clothes).
andrajoso, sa, —hô'sô, a. ragged. [dite.
andrógino, ândrô'hinô, sm. hermaphroandrómina, —mînâ, sf. trick, fraud, artifice. [timbrel.
andullo, ândûl'yô, sm. roll of tobacco;
andurriales, ândûrriâ'lês, sm. pl. byways.
aneaje, ânêâ'hê, sm. alnage, ell-measure.
anear, ânêâr', v. a. to measure by the ell.
aneblar, ânêblâr', v. a. to cloud, to darken.
anécdota, ânêk'dôtâ, sf. anecdote.
anegadizo, za, ânêgâdî'thô, a. easily inundated. [merge.
anegar, ânêgâr', v. a. to inundate, to subanexar, ânêksâr', v. a. to annex, to join.
anexidades, —sîdâ'dês, sf. pl. appertinent
rights.
anexión, ânêksîôn', sf. annexation.
anexo, xa, ânêk'sô, a. annexed.
anfibio, bia, ânfî'bîô, a. amphibious; —,
sm. amphibium. [double meaning.
anfibologia, ânfîbôlô'hîâ, sf. words of
anfión, ânfîôn', sm. opium.
anfiteatro, ânfîtêâ'trô, sm. amphitheatre.
angarillas, ângârîl'yâs, sf. pl. handbarrow; cruet-stand.

ángaro, ân'gârô, sm. signal-smoke.
angel, ân'hêl, sm. angel; barshot.
angelical, ân'hêlîkâl', a. angelical, heavenborn.
angelote, ân'hêlô'tê, sm. large figure of
an angel (on altars); fat, goodnatured child.
angina, ân'hê'nâ, sf. quinsy.
angla, ân'glâ, sf. cape.
anglicismo, ânglîthîs'mô, sm. anglicism.
angostar, ângôstâr', v. a. to narrow, to
contract. [strait.
angosto, ta, ângôs'tô, a. narrow, close,
angostura, ângôstô'râ, sf. narrowness;
narrow passage.
angra, ân'grâ, sf. small bay.
anguarina, ângwârê'nâ, sf. loose coat
hanging down to the knees.
anguila, ângê'lâ, sf. eel.
angular, ângûlâr', a. angular; piedra —,
sf. corner-stone. [fulsome flattery.
angulema, —lê'mâ, sf. tow-linen; —s, pl.
ángulo, ân'gûlô, sm. angle, corner.
anguloso, sa, —lô'sô, a. angled, cornered.
angustia, ângûs'tîâ, sf. anguish; heart-ache.
angustiar, ângûstîâr', v. a. to cause
anguish. [ficulty; to wish eagerly.
anhelar, ânêlâr', v. n. to breathe with difanhelo, ânê'lô, sm. vehement desire, longing. [rous.
anheloso, sa, ânêlô'sô, a. very desianidar, ânîdâr', v. n. to nestle, to make a
nest; to dwell, to inhabit.
anillo, ânîl'yô, sm. gold or silver ring.
ánima, â'nîmâ, sf. soul; diameter of the
chase of a gun; —s, pl. bell-ringing at
sunset; á las —s, at sunset.
animal, ânîmâl', sm. & a. animal.
animalazo, —â'thô, sm. big animal.
animalejo, —â'hô, sm. small animal,
animalcule. [animal.
animalucho, —âtsh'ô, sm. ugly, hideous
animar, ânîmâr', v. a. to animate, to enliven, to abet, to comfort, to revive.
ánimo, â'nîmô, sm. soul; courage; mind,
intention, meaning, will; thought; ¡—!
come on! [rage; boldness.
animosidad, ânîmôsîdâd', sf. valour, couanimoso, sa, ânîmô'sô, a. courageous,
spirited. [ish manner.
aniñarse, ânînyâr'sê, v. r. to act in a childaniquilar, ânîkîlâr', v. a. to annihilate,
to destroy; —se, to decline, to decay; to
humble; to consume.
anis, ânîs', sm. (bot.) anise.
anisar, ânîsâr', v. a. to tincture with anise.
anisete, —sê'tê, sm. anisette.
aniversario, ria, ânîvêrsâ'rîô, a. annual;
ano, â'nô, sm. anus. [—, sm. anniversary.
anoche, ânôtsh'ê, ad. last night.
anochecer, ânôtshêthêr', v. n. to grow dark.
anodinar, ânôdînâr', v. a. to apply an
anodyne.
anodino, na, —dî'nô, a. (med.) anodyne.
anomalia, ânômâlî'â, sf. anomaly.
anómalo, la, ânô'mâlô, a. anomalous.
anonadar, ânônâdâr', v. a. to annihilate;
to lessen; —se, to humble one's self.
anónimo, ma, ânô'nîmô, a. anonymous.

anotación, *ănŏtăthĭŏn'*, sf. annotation, note.

anotar, *ănŏtăr'*, v. a. to comment, to note.

ánsar, *ăn'săr*, sm. goose. [are reared.

ansarería, *ănsărĕrē'ă*, sf. place where geese

ansarero, *ănsărĕ'rŏ*, sm. goose-herd.

ansia, *ăn'sĭă*, sf. anxiety, eagerness, hanker- [ingly.

ansiar, *ănsĭăr'*, v. a. to desire exceed-

ansioso, *sa*, *ănsĭŏ'sŏ*, a. anxious, eager.

anta, *ăn'tă*, sf. tapir; antes (pillar).

antagonista, *ăntăgŏnĭs'tă*, sm. antagonist.

antaño, *ăntăn'yŏ*, ad. last year.

antártico, *ca*, *ăntăr'tĭkŏ*, a. antarctic.

ante, *ăn'tĕ*, sm. dressed buffalo skin; first course of dishes; —, pr. before; in the presence of.

anteado, *da*, *ăntĕă'dŏ*, a. buff-coloured.

anteanteanoche, *—ăntĕănŏtsh'ĕ*, ad. three nights ago. [ago.

anteanteayer, *—ăntĕăyĕr'*, ad. three days

antebrazo, *—bră'thŏ*, sm. fore-arm.

antecama, *—kă'mă*, sf. bed-carpet.

antecámara, *—kăm'ără*, sf. antechamber.

antecamarilla, *—kămărĭl'yă*, sf. room leading to the king's antechamber.

antecedente, *—thĕdĕn'tĕ*, sm. & a. ante-cedent. [forego.

anteceder, *—thĕdĕr'*, v. a. to precede, to

antecesor, *ra*, *—thĕsŏr'*, sm. & f. prede-cessor; forefather.

antecoger, *—kŏ'hĕr'*, v. a. to bring any person or thing before one; to gather in fruit before the due time.

antecristo, *—krĭs'tŏ*, sm. antichrist.

antedata, *—dă'tă*, sf. antedate.

antedatar, *—dătăr'*, v. a. to antedate.

antediluviano, *na*, *—dĭlŭvĭă'nŏ*, a. ante-diluvian.

anteespolón, *—ĕspŏlŏn'*, sm. ice-breaker.

antelación, *—lăthĭŏn'*, sf. preference.

antemano, *—mă'nŏ*, ad. de —, beforehand.

antemeridiano, *na*, *—mĕrĭdĭă'nŏ*, a. ante-meridional. [fortress-wall.

antemural, *—mŭrăl'*, sm. (mil.) outworks.

antemuralla, *—mŭrăl'yă*, sf. antemuro, *—mŏ'rŏ*, sm. (mil.) rampart, parapet.

antena, *ăntă'nă*, sf. feeler, antenna.

antenallas, *ănĕnăl'yăs*, sf. pl. pincers.

antenoche, *—nŏtsh'ĕ*, ad. the night before last.

antenombre, *—nŏm'brĕ*, sm. title prefixed to a proper name (as **Don, San,** &c.).

anteojo, *—ŏ'hŏ*, sm. spy-glass; eye-glass; — de larga vista, telescope; — de puño, opera-glass; —s, pl. spectacles.

antepagar, *—păgăr'*, v. a. to pay in advance.

antepasado, *aa*, *—păsă'dŏ*, a. passed, elapsed; —s, sm. pl. ancestors.

antepecho, *—pĕtsh'ŏ*, sm. (mil.) breastwork, parapet; footstep of a coach; harness.

antepenúltimo, *ma*, *—pĕnŭl'tĭmŏ*, a. ante-penultimate.

anteponer, *—pŏnĕr'*, v. a. to prefer.

antepuerta, *—pŭĕr'tă*, sf. door-hangings.

antera, *ăntă'ră*, sf. (bot.) anther.

anterior, *ăntĕrĭŏr'*, a. anterior, fore, former.

anterioridad, *ăntĕrĭŏrĭdăd'*, sf. anterio-rity, priority; preference.

antes, *ăn'tĕs*, pr. before; —, ad. first, rather, better.

antesala, *ăntĕsă'lă*, sf. antechamber; hacer —, to wait in an antechamber.

antestatura, *ăntĕstătŏ'ră*, sf. light, hasty entrenchment of palisades and sand-bags.

antevíspera, *ăntĕvĭs'pĕră*, sf. day before yesterday. [tion.

anticipación, *ăntĭthĭpăthĭŏn'*, sf. anticipa-

anticipar, *—thĭpăr'*, v. a. to anticipate; to forestall.

anticuado, *da*, *ăntĭkŭă'dŏ*, a. antiquated.

anticuar, *ăntĭkŭăr'*, v. a. to antiquate, to outdate. [antiquarian.

anticuario, *ăntĭkŭă'rĭŏ*, sm. antiquary, antiquarian.

antídoto, *ăntĭ'dŏtŏ*, sm. antidote.

antífona, *ăntĭ'fŏnă*, sf. antiphony, anthem.

antigualla, *ăntĭgŭăl'yă*, sf. monument of antiquity; antique. [ly, of old.

antiguamente, *ăntĭgŭămĕn'tĕ*, ad. ancient-

antigüedad, *ăntĭgŭĕdăd'*, sf. antiquity, oldness; the times of yore; the ancients.

antiguo, *gua*, *ăntĭ'gŭŏ*, a. antique, old, ancient; —, sm. senior. [antimonarchic.

antimonárquico, *ca*, *ăntĭmŏnăr'kĭkŏ*, a.

antimonio, *—mŏ'nĭŏ*, sm. antimony.

antinacional, *—năthĭŏnăl'*, a. antinational.

antipapa, *—pă'pă*, sm. anti-pope.

antípara, *—pă'ră*, sf. screen; gaiter.

antipatía, *—pătĭ'ă*, sf. antipathy.

antipático, *ca*, *—pă'tĭkŏ*, a. antipathetical.

antípodas, *—pŏ'dăs*, sm. pl. antipodes.

antítesis, *ăntĭ'tĕsĭs*, sf. (gr.) antithesis.

antojadizo, *za*, *ăntŏ'hădĭ'thŏ*, a. capri-cious, fanciful. [earnestly; to itch.

antojarse, *—'hăr'sĕ*, v. r. to long, to desire

antojera, *—'hă'ră*, sf. spectacle-case; blinker (of horses).

antojo, *ăntŏ'h'ŏ*, sm. whim; longing, fancy.

antor, *ăntŏr'*, sm. seller of stolen goods.

antorcha, *ăntŏr'tshă*, sf. torch, taper.

antro, *ăn'trŏ*, sm. (poet.) cavern, den, grotto.

antropófago, *ăntrŏpŏ'făgŏ*, sm. man-eater, cannibal. [logy.

antropología, *—pŏlŏ'h'ă*, sf. anthropo-

antruejar, *ăntrŭĕ'hăr'*, v. a. to wet with water, or play some joke at a carnival.

antruejo, *ăntrŭĕ'h'ŏ*, sm. the three days of the carnival. [attack.

antuvión, *ăntŭvĭŏn'*, sm. sudden stroke or [rence.

anual, *ănŭăl'*, a. annual.

anualidad, *ănŭălĭdăd'*, sf. yearly recur-

anubarrado, *da*, *ănŭbărră'dŏ*, a. clouded (of linens and silks).

anublar, *ănŭblăr'*, v. a. to cloud, to obscure; -se, to become clouded; to miscarry.

anudar, *ănŭdăr'*, v. a. to knot, to join; -se, to waste away. [compliance.

anuencia, *ănŭĕn'thĭă*, sf. condescension.

anuente, *ănŭĕn'tĕ*, a. condescending, cour-teous.

anulación, *ănŭlăthĭŏn'*, sf. abrogation.

anular, *ănŭlăr'*, v. a. to annul; —, a. annular.

anulativo, *va*, *ănŭlătĭ'vŏ*, a. derogatory.

anunciar, *ănŭnthĭăr'*, v. a. to announce.

anuncio, *—thĭŏ*, sm. advertisement.

anverso, *ănvĕr'sŏ*, sm. obverse (in coins).

anzuelo, *ănthŭĕ'lŏ*, sm. fish-hook; allurement; kind of fritters.

aña, *ăn'yă*, sf. stink-fox.

añadidura, *ănyădĭdŏ'ră*, sf. addition.

añadir, *ănyădĭr'*, v. a. to add.

añafea, *–fĕ'ă*, sf. brown paper.

añafil, *–fĭl'*, sm. Moorish trumpet.

añagaza, *–găthă*, sf. bird-call.

añal, *ănyăl'*, a. annual.   [manac.

añalejo, *–lĕ'h'ŏ*, sm. ecclesiastical almanac.

añascar, *ănyăskăr'*, v. a. to collect lumber *or* odds and ends.

añejar, *ănyĕhăr'*, v. a. to make old; –se, to grow old; to become stale.

añejo, ja, *ănyĕ'hŏ*, a. old, stale, musty.

añicos, *ănyĕ'kŏs*, sm. pl. bits, small pieces; hacerse –, to overheat one's self.

añil, *ănĭl'*, sm. indigo plant; indigo.

añino, *ănyĕ'nŏ*, sm. yearling lamb; fleece of a yearling lamb.

año, *ăn'yŏ*, sm. year; –s, pl. birth-day.

añojal, *ănyŏhăl'*, sm. fallow land.

añojo, *ănyŏ'h'ŏ*, sm. a yearling calf.

añudar, *ănyŭdăr'*, v. a. to make fast; to unite.   [to fascinate.

aojar, *ăŏ'hăr'*, v. a. to charm, to bewitch.

aojo, *ăŏ'h'ŏ*, sm. witchery, fascination.

aorta, *ăŏ'rtă*, sf. aorta (the great artery).

aovar, *ăŏvăr'*, v. a. to lay eggs.

apabilar, *ăpăbĭlăr'*, v. a. to prepare the wick of a wax-candle; –se, to expire.

apacentadero, *ăpăthĕntădĕ'rŏ*, sm. pasture, grazing-ground.   [cattle.

apacentar, *–tăr'*, v. a. to tend grazing

apacible, *ăpăthĕ'blĕ*, a. affable, gentle, placid, quiet,   [to pacify, to calm.

apaciguar, *ăpăthĕgŭăr'*, v. a. to appease, to pacify, to calm.

apacheta, *ăpăthĕ'tă*, sf. mile-stone.

apadrinar, *ăpădrĭnăr'*, v. a. to support, to favour, to patronise.   [fire-engine.

apagaincendios, *ăpăgăĭnthĕn'dĭŏs*, sm.

apagar, *ăpăgăr'*, v. a. to quench, to extinguish; to damp; to destroy; to soften.

apalabrar, *ăpălăbrăr'*, v. a. to appoint a meeting; to bespeak.   [lever.

apalancar, *ăpălănkăr'*, v. a. to lift with a

apalear, *ăpălĕăr'*, v. a. to cane, to drub; to shovel grain (to prevent its being spoiled).

apancora, *ăpănkŏ'ră*, sf. common crab.

apandillar, *ăpăndĭlyăr'*, v. a. to form a faction.   [of stagnant water.

apantanar, *ăpăntănăr'*, v. a. to make a pool

apantuflado, da, *ăpăntŭflă'dŏ*, a. slipper-like.

apañado, da, *ăpănyă'dŏ*, a. cloth-like.

apañar, *ăpănyăr'*, v. a. to grasp; to pilfer; to patch; –se, to get ready.

apaño, *ăpăn'yŏ*, sm. grasp; seizure; patch.

apañuscar, *ăpănyŭskăr'*, v. a. to rumple; to crush.   [like.

apapagayado,da, *ăpăpăgăyă'dŏ*, a. parrot-

aparador, *ăpărădŏr'*, sm. buffet, sideboard; workshop of an artizan; estar de –, to be dressed for receiving visitors.

aparar, *ăpărăr'*, v. a. to stretch out the bands *or* skirts of clothes for catching any-

thing thrown by another; to dig and heap the earth round plants.

aparato, *ăpără'tŏ*, sm. apparatus; preparation; ostentation; show, circumstance.

aparcería, *ăpărthĕrĕ'ă*, sf. partnership in a farm (*or* other business).

aparcero, *–thĕ'rŏ*, sm. partner; associate.

aparear, *ăpărĕăr'*, v. a. to match; to accouple; –se, to be paired off by twos.

aparecer, *ăpărĕthĕr'*, v. n. to appear.

aparecido, *–thĕ'dŏ*, sm. ghost.

aparejar, *ăpărĕhăr'*, v. a. to prepare; to harness horses; to rig a ship.

aparejo, *ăpărĕ'h'ŏ*, sm. preparation; harness, gear; sizing of a piece of linen on which something is to be painted; (mar.) tackle, rigging; –s, pl. tools, implements.

aparentar, *ăpărĕntăr'*, v. a. to make a false show; to pretend, to deceive.

aparente, *–rĕn'tĕ*, a. apparent; convenient.

aparición, *ăpărĭthĭŏn'*, sf. apparition.

apariencia, *ăpărĭĕn'thĭă*, sf. appearance, outside.   [to trees and plants].

aparrado,da, *ăpărră'dŏ*, a. crooked(applied

aparroquiar, *ăpărrŏkĭăr'*, v. a. to bring customers to a shop.

apartadero, *ăpărtădĕ'rŏ*, sm. parting-place, siding, cross-roads.

apartadijo, *–dĭ'h'ŏ*, sm. small part; adjoining closet.   [apartment.

apartado, *–tă'dŏ*, sm. detached or private

apartar, *ăpărtăr'*, v. a. to separate, to divide, to dissuade; to remove; to sort; –se, to withdraw; to be divorced; to desist.

aparte, *ăpăr'tĕ*, sm. break in a line; –, ad. apart, separately; aside on the stage.

aparvar, *ăpărvăr'*, v. a. to arrange the corn for being threshed.

apasionado, da, *ăpăsĭŏnă'dŏ*, a. passionate; suffering, devoted to; fond.

apasionar, *–năr'*, v. a. to excite a passion.

apatía, *ăpătĭ'ă*, sf. apathy.   [different.

apático, ca, *ăpă'tĭkŏ*, a. apathetic, inapea, *ăpĕ'ă*, sf. tether.

apeadero, *ăpĕădĕ'rŏ*, sm. horse-block; house of accommodation.

apeador, *–dŏr'*, sm. land-surveyor.

apear, *ăpĕăr'*, v. a. to dismount; to measure lands; to take a thing; to dissuade.

apechugar, *ăpĕtshŭgăr'*, v. a. to push with the breast; to undertake a thing with spirit and boldness.

apedreado, da, *ăpĕdrĕă'dŏ*, a. pelted; cara –a, a face pitted with the small-pox.

apedrear, *–drĕăr'*, v. a. to throw stones; to lapidate; –, v. n. to hail; to talk in a rude, uncouth manner.

apego, *ăpĕ'gŏ*, sm. attachment, fondness.

apelación, *ăpĕlăthĭŏn'*, sf. appeal.

apelado, da, *–dŏ*, a. of the same colour.

apelambrar, *ăpĕlămbrăr'*, v. a. to steep hides in pits of lime-water.

apelante, *ăpĕlăn'tĕ*, sm. appellant.

apelar, *ăpĕlăr'*, v. n. to appeal; to have recourse to; to be of the same colour.

apelativo, *ăpĕlătĭ'vŏ*, a. (gr.) nombre –, sm. generic name.

apelmazar, *ăpĕlmăthăr*, v. a. to compress.
apellar, *ăpĕlyăr*, v. a. to dress leather.
apellidar, *ăpĕlyĕdăr*, v. a. to call by name; to proclaim.   [name; epithet.
apellido, *ăpĕlyēdŏ*, sm. surname; family-name.
apenas, *ăpā′năs*, ad. scarcely, hardly.
apendice, *ăpen′dĭthĕ*, sm. appendix, supplement.   [to crush.
apeñuscar, *ăpĕnyŭskăr*, v. a. to rumple.
apeo, *ăpā′ŏ*, sm. survey, mensuration of land; props and stays for underpinning a building.
apeonar, —*năr*, v. a. to run swiftly.
aperador, *ăpĕrădŏr*, sm. wheel-wright.
aperar, *ăpĕrăr*, v. a. to carry on the trade of a cartwright.   [ready.
apercibido, da, *ăpĕrthĭbĭ dŏ*, a. provided;
apercibir, —*thĭbĭr*, v. a. to prepare; to provide; to warn, to advise.
apercollar, —*kŏlyăr*, v. a. to seize by the collar; to snatch away secretly; to assassinate.   [toasted.
aperdigado, da, —*dĭgā′dŏ*, a. broiled,
apernar, —*năr*, v. a. to seize by the hough or ham.   [ments; sheep-fold.
apero, *ăpā′rŏ*, sm. agricultural implement.
aperreado, da, *ăpĕrrēā dŏ*, a. harassed, dog-weary.
aperrear, —*rēăr*, v. a. to throw to the dogs to be torn to pieces; to molest; —se, to worry one's self to death.
apertura, —*tŏ′ră*, sf. aperture, opening, chink, cleft.
apesadumbrar, *ăpĕsădŭmbrăr*, v. a. to cause trouble and affliction.
apesgar, *ăpĕsgăr*, v. a. to overload, to press down.
apestar, *ăpĕstăr*, v. a. to infect with the pestilence; to produce an offensive smell.
apetecer, *ăpĕtĕthĕr*, v. a. to long, to hanker.
apetecible, —*thĕ′ blĕ*, a. desirable.
apetitivo, va, *ăpĕtĭtē′ vŏ*, a. appetising.
apetito, *ăpĕtē′tŏ*, sm. appetite; that which excites desire.   [taste, appetising.
apetitoso, sa, —*tō′ sŏ*, a. pleasing to the
apezuñar, *ăpĕthŏnyăr*, v. n. to tread heavily (of horses).   [knavish.
apicarado, da, *ăpĭkărā′dŏ*, a. roguish.
apice, *ă′pĭthĕ*, sm. summit, point; smallest part of a thing.
apilar, *ăpĭlăr*, v. a. to pile up.
apimpollarse, *ăpĭmpŏlyăr sĕ*, v. r. to shoot, to germinate.   [pine-shaped.
apiñado, da, *ăpĭnyā dŏ*, a. pyramidal;
apiñar, —*nyăr*, v. a. to press things close together; —se, to clog, to crowd.
apio, *ă′pĭŏ*, sm. (bot.) celery.
apiolar, *ăpĭŏlăr*, v. a. to gyve a hawk; to seize; to kill.   [earth.
apisonar, *ăpĭsŏnăr*, v. a. to ram down
apitonar, *ăpĭtŏnăr*, v. n. to put forth shoots; to bud; —v. a. to pick (as hens do their eggs); —se, to rail at each other.
aplacable, *ăplăkă′ blĕ*, a. appeasable.
aplacar, *ăplăkăr*, v. a. to appease, to pacify.

aplanadera, *ăplănădā′ră*, sf. roller for levelling the ground.
aplanar, *ăplănăr*, v. a. to level, to flatten; to astonish; —se, to fall to the ground.
aplanchado, da, *ăplănshā dŏ*, a. ironed, smoothed; —, sm. parcel of linen to be ironed; ironing linen.
aplanchadora, —*dŏ′ră*, sf. ironer.
aplanchar, —*tshăr*, v. a. to iron linen.
aplantillar, *ăplăntĭlyăr*, v. a. to adjust or fit a stone, a piece of timber or a board, according to model.
aplastar, *ăplăstăr*, v. a. to flatten, to crush; to confound.   [extol.
aplaudir, *ăplăudĭr*, v. a. to applaud; to
aplauso, *ăplău′ sŏ*, sm. applause; approbation, praise.   [to invest; to regulate.
aplazar, *ăplăthăr*, v. a. to call together;
aplicable, *ăplĭkă blĕ*, a. applicable.
aplicacion, *ăplĭkăthĭŏn*, sf. application, attention.   [dustrious.
aplicado, da, —*kā′dŏ*, a. studious, in-
aplicar, *ăplĭkăr*, v. a. to apply; to clasp; to attribute; —se, to devote one's self to anything; to earn a living.
aplomado, da, *ăplŏmā′dŏ*, a. lead-coloured; leaden; heavy, dull.
aplomar, —*măr*, v. n. to plumb; —se, to tumble, to fall to the ground.
apocado, da, *ăpŏkā′dŏ*, a. pusillanimous; narrow-hoofed.
Apocalipsis, *ăpŏkălĭp′ sĭs*, sm. Apocalypse.
apocar, *ăpŏkăr*, v. a. to lessen, to diminish; to contract.   [fabulous.
apócrifo, fa, *ăpŏ′ krĭfŏ*, a. apocryphal;
apodar, *ăpŏdăr*, v. a. to give nick-names.
apoderado, da, —*dĕrā′dŏ*, a. powerful; —, sm. proxy, attorney.
apoderarse, —*dĕrăr′ sĕ*, v. r. to take possession of a thing.   [cal.
apodictico, ca, *ăpŏdĭk′ tĭkŏ*, a. apodicti-
apodo, *ăpŏ′ dŏ*, sm. nick-name, sobriquet.
apolillar, *ăpŏlĭlyăr*, v. a. to gnaw or eat clothes; —se, to be moth-eaten.
apologia, *ăpŏlŏ·hĭ′ă*, sf. apology.
apoltronarse, *ăpŏltrŏnăr′ sĕ*, v. r. to grow lazy, to loiter.
apomazar, *ăpŏmăthăr*, v. a. to glaze printed linens with pumice-stone.
apoplejia, —*plĕ′hĕ′ă*, sf. apoplexy.
apoplético, ca, —*plĕ′tĭkŏ*, a. apoplectic.
aporcar, *ăpŏrkăr*, v. a. to cover plants with earth.
aporrar, *ăpŏrrăr*, v. n. to stand mute, to remain silent; —se, to become importunate.
aporrear, *ăpŏrrēăr*, v. a. to cudgel, to knock; —se, to have a fight; to drudge.
aportadera, *ăpŏrtădā′ră*, sf. provision-chest for portage by mules.
aportadero, —*rŏ*, sm. landing-place.
aportar, *ăpŏrtăr*, v. n. to arrive at a port.
aportillar, —*tĭlyăr*, v. a. to make a breach in a wall; to break down, to break open.
aposentar, *ăpŏsĕntăr*, v. a. to harbour; to house.
aposento, *ăpŏsĕn′tŏ*, sm. room, apartment; inn; a temporary habitation; opera-box.

aposesionar, *ăpŏsĕsĭŏnăr'*, v. a. to give possession.

aposición, *ăpŏsĭthĭŏn'*, sf. (gr.) apposition.

apósito, *ăpŏ'sĭtŏ*, sm. external medicinal application.

aposta, *ăpŏs'tä*, ad. on purpose.

apostadero, *–dā'rŏ*, sm. stand, station; (mar.) station; dock-yard.

apostar, *ăpŏstär'*, v. a. to bet, to lay a wager; to post soldiers.

apostasía, *ăpŏstäsē'ä*, sf. apostasy.

apóstata, *ăpŏs'tätä*, sm. apostate.

apostatar, *–tär'*, v. n. to apostatize.

apostema, *ăpŏstā'mä*, sf. abscess, tumor.

apostilla, *ăpŏstĭl'yä*, sf. marginal note; postscript.

apóstol, *ăpŏs'tŏl*, sm. apostle.

apostolado, *–lä'dŏ*, sm. apostleship.

apostólico, ca, *–tŏ'lĭkŏ*, a. apostolical.

apostrofar, *ăpŏstrŏfär'*, v. a. to apostrophise.

apóstrofe, *ăpŏs'trŏfĕ*, sf. apostrophe.

apóstrofo, *ăpŏs'trŏfŏ*, sm. (gr.) apostrophe.

apoteosis, *ăpŏtĕŏ'sĭs*, sf. apotheosis.

apoyar, *ăpŏyär'*, v. a. to favour, to patronise; to support; to found; –, v. n. to rest on; to lie; **–se,** to lean upon.

apoyo, *–yŏ*, sm. prop, stay, support; protection.   [valuable, respectable.

apreciable, *ăprĕthĭä'blĕ*, a. appreciable,

apreciar, *–thĭär'*, v. a. to appreciate, to estimate, to value.

aprecio, *–thĭŏ*, sm. appreciation; esteem.

aprehender, *ăprĕĕndĕr'*, v. a. to apprehend, to seize; to fancy, to conceive.

aprehensión, *–ĕnsĭŏn'*, sf. apprehension, seizure; perception; ready and witty saying.   [sive, quick to understand; fearful.

aprehensivo, va, *–ĕnsē'vŏ*, a. apprehen-

apremiar, *ăprĕmĭär'*, v. a. to press; to compel.   [tion; judicial compulsion.

apremio, *ăprā'mĭŏ*, sm. pressure, constric-

aprender, *ăprĕndĕr'*, v. a. to learn; **– de memoria,** to learn by heart.

aprendiz, *–dĭth'*, sm. apprentice.

aprendizaje, *–thä'hĕ*, sm. apprenticeship.

aprensar, *ăprĕnsär'*, v. a. to press, to calender.   [to capture an enemy's ship.

apresar, *ăprĕsär'*, v. a. to seize, to grasp;

aprestar, *ăprĕstär'*, v. a. to prepare, to make ready.

apresto, *ăprĕs'tŏ*, sm. preparation.

apresurar, *ăprĕsŭrär'*, v. a. to accelerate, to hasten, to expedite.

apretadillo, lla, *ăprĕtädēl'yä*, a. somewhat constrained, rather hard put to it.

apretado, da, *ăprĕtä'dŏ*, a. mean, miserable, closehanded, hard, difficult.

apretadura, *–dū'rä*, sf. compression.

apretar, *–tär'*, v. a. to compress, to tighten; to constrain; to distress; to urge

apretón, *–tŏn'*, sm. pressure.   [earnestly

apretura, *–tō'rä*, sf. crowd.

apriesa, *ăprĭā'sä*, ad. in a hurry.

aprieto, *ăprĭā'tŏ*, sm. crowd; conflict; exigence.

aprisa, *ăprē'sä*, ad. swiftly, promptly.

aprisco, *ăprĭs'kŏ*, sm. sheep-fold, sheep-cot.

aprisionar, *ăprĭsĭŏnär'*, v. a. to imprison.

aproar, *ăprŏär'*, v. n. (mar.) to bring a ship's head to the wind.

aprobación, *ăprŏbäthĭŏn'*, sf. approbation.

aprobar, *–bär'*, v. a. to approve.

aproches, *ăprŏtshĕs*, sm. pl. approaches.

aprontar, *ăprŏntär'*, v. a. to prepare hastily, to get ready.   [paration.

apronto, *ăprŏn'tŏ*, sm. expeditious pre-

apropiación, *ăprŏpĭäthĭŏn'*, sf. appropriation, assumption.

apropiar, *–pĭär'*, v. a. to appropriate.

aprovechable, *ăprŏvĕtshä'blĕ*, a. profitable.   [utility; progress.

aprovechamiento, *–mĭĕn'tŏ*, sm. profit,

aprovechar, *–tshär'*, v. n. to make progress; **–,** v. a. to profit by a thing.

aproximar, *ăprŏksĭmär'*, v. a. to approach.

aptitud, *ăptĭtŭd'*, sf. aptitude, fitness, ability.

apto, ta, *ăp'tŏ*, a. apt, fit, able; clever.

apuesta, *ăpŭĕs'tä*, sf. bet, wager.

apulgarar, *ăpŭlgärär'*, v. a. to press with the thumb.   [musical note; aim.

apuntación, *ăpŭnfäthĭŏn'*, sf. annotation;

apuntado, da, *–tä'dŏ*, a. pointed.

apuntador, *–tädŏr'*, sm. prompter; billiard-marker.   [to shore a vessel.

apuntalar, *–tälär'*, v. a. to prop; (mar.)

apuntar, *ăpŭntär'*, v. a. to aim; to level, to point out; to mark, to begin to appear *or* show itself; to prompt (theatre); **–se,** to begin to turn, to be pricked (of wine).

apunte, *ăpŭn'tĕ*, sm. annotation; stage-prompting.   [the fist.

apuñetear, *ăpŭnyĕtĕär'*, v. a. to strike with

apurado, da, *ăpŭrä'dŏ*, a. poor, destitute of means, exhausted.

apurar, *ăpŭrär'*, v. a. to purify, to clear up, to verify; to exhaust; to tense and perplex,   [affliction.

apuro, *ăpŭ'rŏ*, sm. want, indigence; pain,

aquejar, *ăkĕhär'*, v. a. to fatigue, to afflict.

aquel, *ăkĕl'*, **– la,** *–lyä*, **– lo,** *–lyŏ*, pn. that; he, she; **– los,** **– las,** pl. those.

aquerenciarse, *ăkĕrĕnthĭär'sĕ*, v. r. to be fond of a place (applied to cattle).

aquese, sa, so, *ăkä'sĕ*, pn. that.

aqueste, ta, to, *ăkĕs'tĕ*, pn. this, that.

aquí, *ăkē'*, ad. here, in this place; **¡ – de Dios !** God help me!

aquiescencia, *ăkĭĕsthĕn'thĭä*, sf. consent.

aquietar, *ăkĭĕtär'*, v. a. to quiet, to appease, to lull.   [and silver.

aquilatar, *ăkĭlätär'*, v. a. to assay gold

aquilea, *ăkĭlä'ä*, sf. (bot.) milfoil.

aquilino, na, *–lē'nŏ*, a. aquiline.

aquilón, *ăkĭlŏn'*, sm. north wind.

ara, *ä'rä*, sf. altar.

arabesco, *äräbĕs'kŏ*, sm. arabesque.

arado, *ärä'dŏ*, sm. plough.

arador, *ärädŏr'*, sm. plough-man.

arancel, *äränthĕl'*, sm. fixed price *or* provisions; tariff.   [berry.

arándano, *ärän'dänŏ*, sm. bilberry, cran-

arandela, *ărăndā´lă*, sf. pan of the socket of a candlestick; ruffles of shirts.

aranzada, *ărănthă´dă*, sf. a measure of land. [chandelier, lustre.

araña, *ărăn´yă*, sf. spider; sea-spider;

arañar, *ărănyăr´*, v. a. to scratch; to scrape; to corrode.

araño, *ărăn´yŏ*, sm. scratch, slight wound.

arar, *ărăr´*, v. a. to plough the land.

arbellón, *ărbĕlyŏn´*, sm. gutter.

arbitrar, *ărbītrăr´*, v. a. to arbitrate.

arbitrariedad, *ărbītrărīĕdăd´*, sf. arbitrariness. [va, –trăr´vŏ, a. arbitrary.

arbitrario, ria, *–trā´rīŏ*, arbitrativo,

arbitrio, *ărbī´trĕ*, sm. free-will; means, expedient, way; arbitration, arbitrament; compromise. [jector, contriver.

arbitrista, *ărbītrīs´tă*, sm. schemer, pro-

árbitro, *ăr´bītrŏ*, sm. arbiter, arbitrator.

árbol, *ăr´bŏl*, sm. tree; (mar.) mast.

arbolado, da, *ărbŏlă´dŏ*, a. forested; wooded; –, sm. wood-land.

arboladura, *–dō´ră*, sf. masting, masts.

arbolar, *ărbŏlăr´*, v. a. to hoist, to set upright. [fastening lime-twigs.

arbolete, *–lĕ´tĕ*, sm. branch of a tree for

arbolista, *–lĭs´tă*, sm. arborist.

arbollón, *ărbŏlyŏn´*, sm. flood-gate, sluice.

arbóreo, rea, *ărbŏ´rĕŏ*, a. arboreous.

arbusto, *ărbŭs´tŏ*, sm. shrub.

arca, *ăr´kă*, sf. chest, wooden box; sepulchral urn; — del Testamento — fĕderis, ark of the Covenant.

arcabucería, *–băthĕrē´ă*, sf. number of cross-bows; manufactory of arquebuses.

arcabucero, *–băthā´rŏ*, sm. arquebusier, gunsmith.

arcabuz, *–băth´*, sm. arquebuse.

arcada, *ărkă´dă*, sf. rising of the stomach before vomiting; arcade.

arcaduz, *–dŭth´*, sm. conduit or pipe for conveying water; draw-well bucket.

arcaísmo, *ărkăĭs´mŏ*, sm. archaism.

arcángel, *ărkăn´hĕl*, sm. archangel.

arcano, *ărkă´nŏ*, sm. arcanum.

arce, *ăr´thĕ*, sm. maple-tree.

arcilla, *ărthĭl´yă*, sf. argil, clay.

arcilloso, sa, *ărthĭlyŏ´sŏ*, a. clayey, argillaceous.

arcipreste, *ărthĭprĕs´tĕ*, sm. archpriest.

arco, *ăr´kŏ*, sm. arc, arch; fiddle-bow; hoop; – del cielo, rainbow.

archiducado, *ărtshĭdŭkă´dŏ*, sm. archdukedom.

archiducal, *–dŭkăl´*, a. archducal.

archiduque, *–dō´kĕ*, sm. archduke.

archiduquesa, *–dŭkā´să*, sf. archduchess.

archipiélago, *–pĭā´lăgŏ*, sm. archipelago.

archivar, *–văr´*, v. a. to deposit among archives. [sm. keeper of the records.

archivero, *–vā´rŏ*, archivista, *–vĭs´tă*,

archivo, *ărtshē´vŏ*, sm. archives.

arder, *ărdĕr´*, v. n. to burn, to blaze.

ardid, *ărdĭd´*, sm. stratagem, artifice, cunning.

ardido, da, *ărdē´dŏ*, a. heated (of grain, tobacco, &c.); in a state of fermentation.

ardiente, *ărdĭĕn´tĕ*, a. ardent, flagrant, burning, passionate; active, fervid, fiery.

ardilla, *ărdĭl´yă*, sf. squirrel.

ardor, *ărdŏr´*, sm. great heat; valour, vivacity, fieriness, fervour.

ardoroso, sa, *ărdŏrŏ´sŏ*, a. fiery, restless.

arduo, dua, *ăr´dŭŏ*, a. arduous, difficult; high.

área, *ā´rĕă*, sf. area (of a building).

arena, *ărā´nă*, sf. sand; grit; arena.

arenal, *ărĕnăl´*, sm. sandy ground.

arenga, *ărĕn´gă*, sf. harangue, speech.

arengar, *–găr´*, v. n. to harangue.

arenisco, ca, *ărĕnĭs´kŏ*, arenoso, sa, *ărĕnŏ´sŏ*, a. sandy; arenaceous.

arenque, *ărĕn´kĕ*, sm. herring; – ahumado, red-herring.

areómetro, *ărĕŏ´mĕtrŏ*, sm. aerometer.

argadijo, *–mănd´h´ŏ*, sm. small cleaning-implements. [building.

argamasa, *–mă´să*, sf. mortar, cement for

argamasar, *–măsăr´*, v. a. to make mortar.

árgana, *ăr´gănă*, sf. crane (machine); –s, pl. horse-baskets, paniers.

argentado, da, *ărhĕntă´dŏ*, a. silver-like.

argentar, *–tăr´*, v. a. to silverplate; to colour. [broidery.

argentería, *–tĕrē´ă*, sf. gold or silver em-

argentura, *–tō´ră*, sf. whiteness of silver.

argolla, *ărgŏl´yă*, sf. large iron-ring, pillory.

argüe, *ăr´gŭĕ*, sm. windlass. [to oppose.

argüir, *ărgŭĭr´*, v. n. to argue, to dispute,

argumentación, *ărgŭmĕntăthĭŏn´*, sf. argumentation. [pute; to conclude.

argumentar, *–tăr´*, v. n. to argue, to dis-

argumento, *ărgŭmĕn´tŏ*, sm. argument.

aria, *ă´rĭă*, sf. (mus.) aria, tune, air.

aridez, *ărĭdĕth´*, sf. drought, want of rain.

árido, da, *ă´rĭdŏ*, a. dry; barren.

Aries, *ă´rĭĕs*, sm. Aries, the Ram (sign of the zodiac).

ariete, *ărĭĕ´tĕ*, sm. battering-ram.

arijo, ja, *ărĭh´ŏ*, a. easily tilled (applied to soil).

arillo, *ărĭl´yŏ*, sm. a small hoop; ear-ring.

arimez, *ărĭmĕth´*, sf. projecting part of a building. [tractable.

arisco, ca, *ărĭs´kŏ*, a. fierce, rude, untractable.

aristarco, *ărĭstăr´kŏ*, sm. severe censurer of another's writings.

aristocracia, *ărĭstŏkră´thĭă*, sf. aristocracy.

aristócrata, *ărĭstŏ´krătă*, sm. aristocrat.

aristocrático, ca, *–krā´tĭkŏ*, a. aristocratical.

aritmética, *ărĭtmā´tĭkă*, sf. arithmetic.

aritmético, ca, *–tĭkŏ*, a. arithmetical.

arlequín, *ărlĕkīn´*, sm. harlequin, buffoon.

arma, *ăr´mă*, sf. weapon, arms; – falsa, false alarm.

armada, *ărmă´dă*, sf. fleet, armada.

armadía, *ărmădē´ă*, sf. raft.

armador, *–dŏr´*, sm. ship-owner; privateer, cruiser; jacket, jerkin.

armadura, –dŏ'rä, sf. armour; roof-frame.

armamento, –měn'tō, sm. warlike preparation, armament.

-armar, ärmär', v. a. to furnish with arms; to man; to arm; to fit up; – la, to cheat at cards.	[board.

armario, ärmä'rĕō, sm. clothes-press; cupboard.

armatoste, ärmätŏs'tĕ, sm. hulk; lumber; frame.	[hulk of a ship; fishing-tackle.

armazón, ärmäthōn', sf. wooden frame;

armelina, ärmĕlē'nä, sf. ermine-skin.

armería, ärmĕrē'ä, sf. arsenal; heraldry; art of armour-making.	[of arms.

armero, ärmě'rō, sm. armourer; keeper

armilla, ärmēl'yä, sf. bracelet.

armiño, ärmēn'yō, sm. ermine.

armipotente, ärmĭpŏtěn'tĕ, a. (poet.) mighty in war.

armisticio, –stē'thēō, sm. armistice.

armonía, ärmŏnē'ä, sf. harmony.

armónico, ca, ärmŏ'nĭkō, a. harmonical.

armonioso, sa, ärmŏnĭō'sō, a. harmonious.

arna, är'nä, sf. bee-hive.

arnés, ärněs', sm. harness; gear, trapping.

arnilla, ärnēl'yä, sf. small bee-hive.

aro, ä'rō, sm. hoop of wood; iron-staple.

aroca, ärŏ'kä, sf. Portuguese linen.

aroma, ärŏ'mä, sm. & f. aroma; fragrance.

aromático, ca, ärŏmä'tĭkō, a. aromatic.

aromatizar, –tēthär', v. a. to aromatize, to perfume.

arpa, är'pä, sf. harp.

arpado, da, ärpä'dō, a. serrated, toothed.

arpar, ärpär', v. a. to tear to pieces, to rend.

arpegio, ärpě'h'tō, sm. (mus.) arpeggio.

arpeo, ärpě'ō, sm. grappling-iron.

arpía, ärpě'ä, sf. (poet.) harpy.

arpillera, ärpĭlyě'rä, sf. sack-cloth.

arpista, ärpĭs'tä, sm. harper.

arpón, ärpōn', sm. harpoon.	[poon.

arponado, a, ärpŏnä'dō, a. like a har-

arponar, ärpŏnär', v. a. to harpoon.

arponero, ärpŏně'rō, sm. harpooner.

arqueada, ärkě'ädä, sf. (mus.) stroke or movement of the violin-bow.

arqueado, da, –dō, a. arched, vaulted.

arquear, ärkě'är', v. a. to arch; to gauge the dimensions of ships.	[a ship.

arqueo, ärkě'ō, sm. arcuation; gauging of

arqueología, ärkěŏlŏ'hē'ä, sf. archæology.

arquería, ärkěr'ē'ä, sf. arcade.

arquero, ärkě'rō, sm. hoop-maker; cashier.

arqueta, –tä, sf. small trunk.

arquilla, ärkēl'yä, sf. little chest.

arquitecto, ärkĭtěk'tō, sm. architect.

arquitectónico, ca, –těktŏ'nĭkō, a. architectonic.

arquitectura, –těktŏ'rä, sf. architecture.

arquitrabe, –trä'bě, sm. architrave.

arrabalero, ärräbälě'rō, sm. suburban; very common person, churl.

arrabio, ärrä'bĭō, sm. cast-iron.

arracada, ärrä'kä'dä, sf. ear-ring.

arracimarse, ärräthĭmär'sě, v. r. to cluster.	[ship.

arráez, ärrä'ěth, sm. captain of a Moorish

arraigar, ärräĭgär', v. n. to fix the root; to establish.

arraigo, ärrä'ĭgō, sm. landed property.

arramblar, ärrämblär', v. a. to cover with sand (of torrents); to sweep away.

arrancadera, ärränkädě'rä, sf. bell of the bell-wether.

arrancar, ärränkär', v. a. to pull up by the roots; to force out; to wrest; to draw out a tooth.

arrancasiega, ärränkäsĭě'gä, sf. mowing of stunted corn; altercation, dispute.

arranque, ärrän'kě, sm. extirpation; sudden and violent fit of passion.

arrapiezo, ärräpĭě'thō, arrapo, ärrä'pō, sm. tatter, rag.

arras, är'räs, sf. pl. dowry; earnest-money.

arrasar, ärräsär', v. a. to demolish, to destroy; –, v. n. to clear up.

arrastrado, da, ärrästrä'dō, a. miserable, painstaking.

arrastrar, –rär', v. a. & n. to creep, to crawl; to drag along the ground; to lead a trump at cards.

arrastre, ärräs'trě, sm. lead of a trump at cards; knocking-mill.

arrayán, ärräyän', sm. myrtle.

¡arre! ärrě, gee!, geho!, go on!

arrear, ärrěär', v. a. to drive horses, mules &c.	[gether, to pick up.

arrebañar, ärrěbänyär', v. a. to scrape to-

arrebata, –bä'tä, sf. violent attack.

arrebatado, da, –bätä'dō, a. rapid, violent, impetuous; rash, inconsiderate.

arrebatar, –bätär', v. a. to carry off, to snatch with hurry and precipitation; to enrapture; to dry up.

arrebatiña, –bätĭn'yä, sf. carrying off a thing precipitately out of a crowd.

arrebato, –bä'tō, sm. surprise.

arrebol, ärrěbōl', sm. red appearance of the sky; rouge.	[rouge.

arrebolar, –bōlär', v. a. to paint red; to

arrebozarse, –bōthär'sě, v. r. to swarm (of bees, &c.).	[wrap up.

arrebujar, –bŏhär', v. a. to crumple; to

arrecafe, –kä'fě, sm. (bot.) cardoon; share-wort.

arrecife, –thě'fě, sm. causeway; reef.

arrecirse, ärrěthĭr'sě, v. r. to grow stiff with cold.	[greater distance; to terrify.

arredrar, –drär', v. a. to remove to a

arredro, ärrě'drō, ad. backwards.

arregazado, da, –gäthä'dō, a. turned up; cocked.	[tuck up the skirts of clothes.

arregazar, –gäthär', v. a. to truss, to

arreglado, da, ärrěglä'dō, a. regular, moderate.	[adjust.

arreglar, ärrěglär', v. a. to regulate; to

arreglo, ärrě'glō, sm. rule, order; con – á, according to.

arregostarse, ärrěgōstär'sě, v. r. to relish.

arrejacar, ärrě'häkär', v. a. to weed out.

arrejaco, ärrě'hä'kō, sm. swift martlet (ave).	[fork, trident.

arrejaque, ärrě'hä'kě, sm. three-pronged

arrellanarse, ärrělyänär'sě, v. r. to sit at ease; to make one's self comfortable.

arremangar, ärrěmängär', v. a. to tuck up one's sleeves or petticoats.

arremango, *ărrĕmän'gŏ,* sm. tucking up of clothes. [tack; to seize suddenly.

arremeter, *–mĕtĕr',* v. a. to assail, to attack.

arremetida, *–mĕtē'dä,* sf. attack, assault.

arrendadero, *ărrĕndädā'rŏ,* sm. stablering for tying horses.

arrendado, da, *–dä'dŏ,* a. manageable, tractable (of horses).

arrendador, *–dädŏr',* sm. tenant, lessee; lessor, hirer. [mimic, buffoon.

arrendajo, *ărrĕndä'hŏ,* sm. mocking-bird.

arrendamiento, *–dämĭĕn'tŏ,* sm. lease.

arrendar, *ărrĕndär',* v. a. to rent, to let out, to lease; to tie a horse by the reins; to imitate. [tenant; lessee; farmer.

arrendatario, ria, *–dätä'rĭŏ,* sm. & f.

arreo, *ărrā'ŏ,* sm. dress, ornament; –s, pl. dependencies; *ad.* successively; uninterruptedly. [for bun.

arrepápalo, *ărrĕp'äpälŏ,* sm. sort of fritter

arrepentido, da, *–pĕntē'dŏ,* a. repentant.

arrepentimiento, *–pĕntĭmĭĕn'tŏ,* sm. repentance, penitence.

arrepentirse, *–pĕntēr'sĕ,* v. r. to repent.

arrepistar, *–pĭstär',* v. a. to grind or pound rags into a fine pulp (in papermills).

arrequives, *–kē'vĕs,* sm. pl. ornaments; circumstances of a case; requisites.

arrestado, da, *ărrĕstä'dŏ,* a. intrepid, bold.

arrestar, *–tär',* v. a. to arrest, to imprison; –se, to be bold and enterprising.

arresto, *ărrĕs'tŏ,* sm. boldness in undertaking an enterprise; prison, arrest.

arrezafe, *ărrĕthä'fĕ,* sm. place full of thistles, brushwood, and brambles.

arriada, *ărrĭä'dä,* sf. flood, overflowing.

arriar, *ărrĭär',* v. a. (mar.) to lower, to strike.

arriata, *ărrĭä'tä,* sf., **arriate,** *ărrĭä'tĕ,* sm. hot-bed, shelving-bed; causeway.

arriba, *ărrē'bä,* ad. above, over, up, high, on high, overhead; aloft.

arribada, *–bä'dä,* sf. arrival of a vessel in port. [harbour; to fall off to leeward.

arribar, *ărrēbär',* v. n. (mar.) to put into a

arribo, *ărrē'bŏ,* sm. arrival.

arricete, *ărrēthĕ'tĕ,* sm. shoal, sand-bank.

arriendo, *ărrĭĕn'dŏ,* sm. lease, farm rent.

arriería, *ărrēĕrē'ä,* sf. mule-driver's trade.

arriero, *ărrĭĕ'rŏ,* sm. muleteer.

arriesgar, *ărrĭĕsgär',* v. a. to risk, to hazard, to expose to danger.

arrimadero, *ărrēmädā'rŏ,* sm. scaffold; stick or support to lean upon.

arrimadillo, *–mädĭl'yŏ,* sm. silk wainscoting, pannelling.

arrimadizo, *–mädē'thŏ,* a. sustaining, sustainable; –, sm. parasite, sponger.

arrimador, *–mädŏr',* sm. back-log in a fire-place.

arrimar, *ărrēmär',* v. a. to approach, to draw near; (mar.) to stow the cargo; to lay aside; to give up a command; to displace, to dismiss.

arrinconar, *ărrēnkŏnär',* v. a. to put a thing in a corner; to lay aside; to drive from office; –se, to retire, to withdraw.

arriscado, da, *ărrĭskä'dŏ,* a. forward, bold, audacious, impudent; brisk.

arriscador, *–kädŏr',* sm. olive gleaner.

arrizar, *ărrēthär',* v. a. (mar.) to reef; to tie or lash.

arroba, *ărrŏ'bä,* sf. weight of twenty-five pounds; measure (thirty-two pints); por –s, by wholesale. [ecstasy.

arrobadizo, za, *–bädē'thŏ,* a. feigning

arrobamiento, *–mĭĕn'tŏ,* sm. rapture; amazement, rapturous admiration.

arrobarse, *ărrŏbär'sĕ,* v. r. to be intensely amazed, to be out of one's senses.

arrocero, *ărrŏthā'rŏ,* sm. rice-grower; rice-merchant.

arrocinado, da, *–thĭnä'dŏ,* a. stupid, asinine; ass-like (applied to horses).

arrocinarse, *–thĭnär'sĕ,* v. r. to become dull and stupid. [knee; –se, to kneel.

arrodillar, *–dĭlyär',* v. n. to bend the

arrodrigar, *–drĭgär',* **arrodrigonar,** *–drĭgŏnär',* v. a. to prop vines.

arrogación, *ărrŏgäthĭŏn',* sf. arrogation; adoption. [haughtiness.

arrogancia, *ărrŏgän'thĭä,* sf. arrogance,

arrogante, *–gän'tĕ,* a. haughty, proud, assuming; valiant, stout; **caballo –,** mettlesome, spirited horse.

arrogar, *ărrŏgär',* v. a. to arrogate; to appropriate to one's self. [or thrown.

arrojadizo, za, *–hädē'thŏ,* a. easily cast

arrojado, da, *–hä'dŏ,* a. rash, inconsiderate; bold, fearless.

arrojar, *–här',* v. a. to dart, to fling, to jet; to dash; to shed a fragrance; to emit light; to shoot, to sprout. [fearlessness.

arrojo, *ărrŏ'hŏ,* sm. boldness, intrepidity, to revolve, to enwrap; to sweep away; to confound an opponent. [catch cold.

arrollar, *ărrŏlyär',* v. a. to roll up, to revolve, to enwrap; to sweep away; to confound an opponent. [catch cold.

arromadizarse, *–mädĭthär'sĕ,* v. r. to

arromar, *ărrŏmär',* v. a. to blunt.

arrompido, *ărrŏmpē'dŏ,* sm. broken ground.

arropar, *ărrŏpär',* v. a. to clothe, to dress.

arrope, *ărrŏ'pĕ,* sm. must (new wine boiled until it is as dense as a syrup).

arropea, *–pā'ä,* sf. irons, fetters, pl.

arrostrar, *ărrŏsträr',* v. a. to perform in a cheerful manner; to encounter dangers.

arroyada, *ărrŏyä'dä,* sf. torrent.

arroyar, *ărrŏyär',* v. a. to overflow sown ground.

arroyo, *ărrŏ'yŏ,* sm. rivulet. [ground.

arroz, *ărrŏth',* sm. rice.

arrozal, *ărrŏthäl',* sm. rice-field. [boar.

arruar, *ărrŭär',* v. n. to grunt like a wild

arrufar, *ărrŭfär',* v. a. to incurvate.

arrufianado, da, *ărrŭfĭänä'dŏ,* a. impudent; like a ruffian.

arruga, *ărrŭ'gä,* sf. wrinkle; rumple.

arrugar, *ărrŭgär',* v. a. to wrinkle; to rumple, to fold; **–la frente,** to knit the brow; **–se,** to shrivel; to die.

arruinar, *ărrŭĭnär',* v. a. to demolish; to ruin. [cajoling.

arrullador, ra, *ărrŭlyädŏr',* a. flattering,

arrullar, *ărrŭlyär',* v. a. to lull to rest; to court, to bill and coo. [lullaby.

arrullo, *ărrŭl'yŏ,* sm. cooing of pigeons;

arrumaco, *ărrŭmă´kŏ,* sm. caress; curl of the lips.

arrumaje, *–mă´hĕ̆,* sm. cargo-stowage.

arrumar, *ărrŭmă´r,* v. a. to stow cargo.

arrumazón, *–măthŏ´n,* sm. (mar.) stowing; cloudy horizon.

arrumbar, *ărrŭmbă´r,* v. a. to set aside as useless lumber; to refute or silence in conversation; to decant wine; **–se,** (mar.) to steer the proper course.

arrunflarse, *ărrŭnflăr´sĕ̆,* v. r. to have a "flush" at cards.

arsenal, *ărsĕnă´l,* sm. arsenal; dock-yard.

arsénico, *ărsĕ´nĭkŏ,* sm. arsenic.

arte, *ăr´tĕ̆,* sm. & f. art; skill; artfulness; rudiments of grammar.

artefacto, *ărtĕfă´ktŏ,* sm. manufacture.

artejo, *ărtĕ´hŏ,* sm. finger-joint.

arteria, *ărtĕ´rĭă,* sf. artery.   [artful.

artero, ra, *ărtĕ´rŏ,* a. dexterous, cunning,

artesa, *ărtĕ´să,* sf. kneading-trough;   wooden bowl.   [man.

artesano, *ărtĕsă´nŏ,* sm. artisan, work-

artótico, ca, *ărtŏ´tĭkŏ,* a. arthritical, gouty.

ártico, ca, *ăr´tĭkŏ,* a. arctic, northern.

articulación, *ărtĭkŭlăthĭŏn,* sf. articulation, clear and distinct pronunciation.

articular, *ărtĭkŭlăr,* v. a. to articulate, to pronounce distinctly.

artículo, *ărtĭ´kŭlŏ,* sm. article; clause; point; (gr.) article; condition.

artifice, *ărtĭ´fĭthĕ̆,* sm. artisan; artist.

artificial, *ărtĭfĭthĭă´l,* a. artificial.

artificio, *ărtĭfĭ´thĭŏ,* sm. workmanship, craft; artifice, cunning, trick.

artificioso, sa, *–thĭŏ´sŏ,* a. skilful, ingenious; artful, cunning.

artillar, *ărtĭllyăr,* v. a. to mount cannon.

artillería, *ărtĭllyĕrĭ´ă,* sf. gunnery; artillery.

artillero, *ărtĭllyĕ´rŏ,* sm. artillery-man.

artista, *ărtĭ´stă,* sm. artist; craftsman.

arúspice, *ărŭ´spĭthĕ̆,* sm. augurer, soothsayer.

arveja, *ărvĕ´hă,* sf. (bot.) vetch.   [sayer.

arvejo, *–ŏ,* sm. (bot.) bastard chick-pea.

arzobispado, *ărthŏbĭspă´dŏ,* sm. archbishopric.

arzobispal, *–bĭspă´l,* a. archiepiscopal.

arzobispo, *–bĭ´spŏ,* sm. archbishop.

arzón, *ărthŏn,* sm. bow of a saddle.

as, *ăs,* sm. ace; roman copper coin.

asa, *ă´să,* sf. handle, haft, hold.

asado, *ăsă´dŏ,* sm. roast-meat.

asador, *ăsădŏr,* sm. turn-spit.

asadura, *–dŏ´ră,* sf. chitterlings; toll paid for cattle.   [eatiny.

asaetinado, da, *ăsăĕtĭnă´dŏ,* a. silky,

asalariar, *ăsălărĭăr,* v. a. to give a fixed salary.   [to assail, to fall upon.

asaltar, *ăsăltă´r,* v. a. to storm a position;

asalto, *ăsă´ltŏ,* sm. assault, storm against a place.   [ing.

asamblea, *ăsămblĕ´ă,* sf. assembly, meeting.

asar, *ăsăr,* v. a. to roast.

asargado, da, *ăsărgă´dŏ,* a. serge-like.

asativo, va, *ăsătĭ´vŏ,* a. boiled in its own juice.

asbestino, na. *ăsbĕstĭ´nŏ,* a. asbestine.

asbesto, *ăsbĕ´stŏ,* sm. asbestos.

ascalonia, *ăskălŏ´nĭă,* sf. (bot.) shallot.

ascendencia, *ăsthĕndĕn´thĭă,* sf. ascending line; line of descent.

ascendente, *–dĕn´tĕ̆,* a. ascending; (rail.) **tren –,** s. up-train.

ascender, *–dĕr,* v. n. to be promoted to a higher dignity.

ascendiente, *–dĭĕn´tĕ̆,* sm. ascendant, forefather; influence.

Ascensión, *–sĭŏn,* sf. feast of Ascension.

ascenso, *ăsthĕn´sŏ,* sm. promotion to a higher dignity or station.

ascensor, *–sŏr,* sm. lift.

asceta, *ăsthĕ´tă,* sm. ascetic.

ascético, ca, *ăsthĕ´tĭkŏ,* a. ascetic.

asco, *ăs´kŏ,* sm. nausea, loathing.

ascua, *ăs´kŭă,* sf. red hot coal.

¡ascuas! –s, how it hurts! good heavens!

aseado, da, *ăsĕă´dŏ,* a. clean, elegant, neat.

asear, *ăsĕăr,* v. a. to set off, to adorn.

asedado, da, *ăsĕdă´dŏ,* a. silky.

asediar, *ăsĕdĭăr,* v. a. to besiege.

asedio, *ăsĕ´dĭŏ,* sm. siege.   [one's self.

aseglararse, *ăsĕglărăr´sĕ̆,* v. r. to secularize

asegundar, *–gŭndăr,* v. a. to repeat.

aseguración, *–gŭrăthĭŏn,* sf. insurance.

asegurador, *–gŭrădŏr,* sm. insurer.

asegurar, *–gŭrăr,* v. a. to secure; to insure; to affirm; to bail.

asemejar, *ăsĕmĕ´hăr,* v. a. to assimilate, to make alike.   [to force one's way.

asenderear, *ăsĕndĕrĕăr,* v. a. to persecute;

asenso, *ăsĕn´sŏ,* sm. assent, consent.

asentaderas, *ăsĕntădĕ´răs,* sf. pl. buttocks.

asentadillas, *–dĭ´lyăs,* ad. (á –) sitting on horseback like a woman.

asentar, *–tăr,* v. a. to place on a chair or other seat; to suppose; to affirm, to assure; to adjust; to note; **–,** v. n. to sit down; to settle; to sit (of clothes); **–se,** to settle (of liquids).   [concede.

asentir, *ăsĕntĭr,* v. n. to acquiesce, to

asentista, *–tĭs´tă,* sm. purveyor, contractor.

aseo, *ăsĕ´ŏ,* sm. cleanliness, neatness.

asequible, *ăsĕkĭ´blĕ̆,* a. attainable, obtainable.   [mation.

aserción, *ăsĕrthĭŏn,* sf. assertion, affirmation.

aserradero, *ăsĕrrădĕ´rŏ,* sm. saw-mill.

aserraduras, *–dŏ´răs,* sf. pl. saw-dust.

aserrar, *ăsĕrrăr,* v. a. to saw; to scrape (upon a fiddle).

asertivo, va, *ăsĕrtĭ´vŏ,* a. affirmative.

asesar, *ăsĕsăr,* v. n. to become prudent.

asesinar, *–sĭnăr,* v. a. to assassinate.

asesinato, *–sĭnă´tŏ,* sm. assassination.

asesino, *–sĕ´nŏ,* sm. assassin; impostor, cheat

asesor, *ăsĕsŏr,* sm. counsellor, assessor.

asesorarse, *–sŏrăr´sĕ̆,* v. r. to employ counsel.

asestar, *ăsĕstăr,* v. a. to aim, to point.

aseverar, *ăsĕvĕrăr,* v. a. to asseverate, to solemnly affirm.

asfalto, *ăsfă´ltŏ,* sm. asphaltum.

así, *ăsĭ´,* ad. so, thus, in this manner; therefore, so that; also; **– bien,** as well; **– que,** so that, therefore; así, así, so, so;

middling; – que –, whether this or that
way; como –, even so, just so.

asidero, ăsĭdā′dŏ, sm. handle; hold; occasion, pretext. [tached.

asido, da, ăsē′dŏ, a. fastened, tied, at-

asiduo, dua, ăsē′dŭŏ, a. assiduous.

asiento, ăsĭĕn′tŏ, sm. chair, bench, stool; seat; contract; entry; residence; – común, privy. [destination.

asignación, ăsĭgnăthĭŏn′, sf. assignation;

asignar, ăsĭgnăr′, v. a. to assign; to attribute.

asignatura, ăsĭgnătū′ră, sf. catalogue of university lectures for one year.

asilla, ăsĭl′yă, sf. small handle; slight pretext; clavicle.

asilo, ăsē′lŏ, sm. asylum, refuge.

asimilar, ăsĭmĭlăr′, v. n. to resemble; –, v. a. to assimilate. [same manner.

asimismo, ăsĭmĭs′mŏ, ad. similarly, in the

asimplado, da, ăsĭmplā′dŏ, a. silly.

asir, ăsēr′, v. a. & n. to grasp, to seize; to hold, to grip, to take root.

asistencia, ăsĭstĕn′thĭă, sf. actual presence; assistance; help; – de Sevilla, magistracy of Seville. [maid at court.

asistenta, –tĕn′tă, sf. hand-maid; servant-

asistente, –tĕn′tĕ, sm. assistant, helper; chief officer of justice at Seville; officer's servant, orderly.

asistir, ăsĭstēr′, v. n. to be present, to assist; –, v. a. to help, to minister, to further; to attend a sick person.

asma, ăs′mă, sf. asthma.

asmático, ca, ăsmā′tĭkŏ, a. asthmatic.

asna, ăs′nă, sf. she-ass, jenny-ass.

asnada, ăsnā′dă, sf. foolish action.

asnal, ăsnăl′, a. asinine.

asnallo, ăsnăl′yŏ, sm. worm-seed.

asnazo, ăsnā′thŏ, sm. a large jack-ass.

asnería, ăsnĕrē′ă, sf. stud of asses; egregious blunder. [andiron.

ásnico, ca, ăsnē′kŏ, sm. & f. little ass.

asnillo, lla, ăsnĭl′yŏ, sm. & f. little ass; grass-hopper; field-cricket.

asno, ăs′nŏ, sm. ass; stupid fellow.

asobarcar, ăsŏbărkăr′, v. a. to pick up and put under one's arm. [crafty.

asocarronado, ăsŏkărrŏnā′dŏ, a. waggish.

asociación, ăsŏthĭăthĭŏn′, sf. association; co-partnership.

asociado, –thĭā′dŏ, sm. associate.

asociar, –thĭăr′, v. a. to associate.

asolanar, ăsŏlănăr′, v. a. to parch, to dry up (of easterly winds).

asolar, ăsŏlăr′, v. a. to destroy, to devastate; –se, to settle, to clear (of liquids).

asolear, ăsŏlĕăr′, v. a. to expose to the sun; –se, to be sun-burnt.

asolvarse, ăsŏlvăr′sĕ, v. r. to be stopped (of pipes, canals). [apparition.

asomada, ăsŏmā′dă, sf. sudden appearance.

asomar, ăsŏmăr′, v. n. to begin to appear; –se, to be flustered with wine.

asombradizo, za, ăsŏmbrădē′thŏ, a. fearful, timid, easily frightened.

asombrar, ăsŏmbrăr′, v. a. to frighten, to

amaze; to astonish; (poet.) to obscure, to overshadow. [tonishment.

asombro, ăsŏm′brŏ, sm. dread, terror; astonishment.

asombroso, sa, –brŏ′sŏ, a. astonishing, marvellous. [tion; conjecture.

asomo, ăsŏ′mŏ, sm. mark, token, indication; conjecture.

asonancia, ăsŏnăn′thĭă, sf. assonance; harmony.

asortir, ăsŏrtēr′, v. a. to assort.

asotanar, ăsŏtănăr′, v. a. to build arched cellars.

aspa, ăs′pă, sf. reel. [cellars.

aspar, ăspăr′, v. a. to reel; to crucify; to vex, to mortify; –se á gritos, to cry out loudly, to yell. [ment; exclamation.

aspaviento, ăspăvĭĕn′tŏ, sm. astonishment; exclamation.

aspecto, ăspĕk′tŏ, sm. appearance, aspect.

aspereza, ăspĕrā′thă, sf. asperity, acerbity.

asperges, ăspĕr′hĕs, sm. sprinkling with holy-water; quedarse –, to be disappointed. [ripe fruit.

asperillo, ăspĕrĭl′yŏ, sm. bitterness of unripe fruit.

áspero, ra, ăs′pĕrŏ, a. rough, rugged; craggy, hirsute, knotty; horrid; harsh, hard; crabbed; severe, austere, gruff.

asperón, ăspĕrŏn′, sm. grindstone.

aspersión, ăspĕrsĭŏn′, sf. aspersion, sprinkling.

aspersorio, –sŏ′rĭŏ, sm. water-sprinkler.

áspid, ăs′pĭd, sm. aspic. [inspiration.

aspiración, ăspĭrăthĭŏn′, sf. aspiration;

aspirante, –rănt′ĕ, sm. aspirant, aspirer.

aspirar, ăspĭrăr′, v. a. to inspire the air; to aspire; (gr.) to aspirate. [squeamish.

asqueroso, sa, ăskĕrŏ′sŏ, a. loathsome, squeamish.

asta, ăs′tă, sf. lance; horn; handle of a pencil, brush.

astaco, ăstā′kŏ, sm. lobster.

asterisco, ăstĕrĭs′kŏ, sm. asterisk.

asterismo, –rĭs′mŏ, sm. constellation.

astil, ăstĭl′, sm. handle, shaft.

astilla, ăstĭl′yă, sf. chip of wood, splinter of timber.

astillar, ăstĭlyăr′, v. a. to chip.

astillazo, –yā′thŏ, sm. crack (produced by a splinter being torn from a block); damage which results from an enterprise to those who have not been its principal authors.

astillero, –yā′rŏ, sm. holdfast for soldiers' arms; dockyard, ship-wright's yard.

astral, ăstrăl′, a. astral.

astricción, ăstrĭkthĭŏn′, sf. astriction.

astrictivo, va, –tē′vŏ, a. astrictive, styptic.

astricto, ta, ăstrĭk′tŏ, a. contracted, compressed.

astringente, ăstrĭn′hĕn′tĕ, a. astringent.

astringir, –hēr′, a. to astringe, to constringe. [tract.

astro, ăs′trŏ, sm. star. [tract.

astrología, ăstrŏlŏhē′ă, sf. astrology.

astrológico, ca, ăstrŏlŏ′hĭkŏ, a. astrological.

astrólogo, ăstrŏ′lŏgŏ, sm. astrologer.

astronomía, ăstrŏnŏmē′ă, sf. astronomy.

astronómico, ca, ăstrŏnŏ′mĭkŏ, a. astronomical.

astrónomo, ăstrŏ′nŏmŏ, sm. astronomer.

astroso, sa, ăstrŏ′sŏ, a. indecent, sordid.

astucia, ăstŏ′thĭă, sf. cunning, slyness.

asturión, ăstŭrĭŏ́n', sm. pony.

astuto, ta, ăstŏ́tŏ́, a. cunning, sly, astute.

asueto, ăsŭ́ĕtŏ́, sm. holidays; vacation.

Asunción, ăsŭnthĭŏn', sf. ascent of the Holy Virgin to heaven.

asunto, ăsŭn'tŏ́, sm. subject, matter treated upon; affair, business.

asurarse, ăsŭrăr'sĕ, v. r. to be burnt in cooking (applied to meat).

asurcar, ăsŭrkăr', v. a. to furrow sown land for the purpose of rooting out the weeds.   [to be frightened.

asustar, ăsŭstăr', v. a. to frighten; -se,

atabacado, da, ătăbăkắdŏ́, a. tobacco-coloured.

atabal, ătăbăl', sm. kettle-drum.

atabalear, -ĕăr', v. n. to make a noise like kettle-drums.

atabalero, -ĕ'rŏ́, sm. kettle-drummer.

atabe, ătắbĕ́, sm. small vent left in water-pipes.   [taverns.

atabernado, da, -bĕrnắdŏ́, a. retailed in

atabladera, -blădĕ́rắ, sf. roller to level land sown with corn.   [with corn.

atablar, ătăblăr', v. a. to level land sown

atacado, da, ătăkắdŏ́, a. irresolute; narrow-minded.   [poniard.

atacador, -kădŏ́r', sm. aggressor; ramrod;

atacar, -kăr', v. a. to fit clothes tight to the body; to force the charge into fire-arms with a ramrod; to attack; to onset.

atado, ătắdŏ́, sm. bundle, parcel; -, da, a. pusillanimous, easily embarrassed; attached.

atador, -dŏr', sm. sheaves-binder.

atafagar, -făgăr', v. a. to stupefy; to take away one's breath; to tease.

atafetanado, da, -fĕtănắdŏ́, a. resembling tiffany.   [pack-saddle.

ataharre, ătăắr'rĕ́, sm. broad crupper of a

ataharma, ătăr'mắ, sf. osprey (ave).

ataire, ătắĭrĕ́, sm. moulding in the pannels and frames of doors and windows.

atajadizo, ătắhădĕ́thŏ́, sm. partition-wall.

atajar, ătắhăr', v. a. to cut off part of the road; to intercept; to stop, to obstruct; -se, to be confounded with dread.

atajasolaces, -hăsŏlắthĕs, sm. kill-joy.

atajea, -hĕ́ắ, atajía, -hĕ́ắ, sf. sewer.

atajo, ătắh'ŏ́, sm. cross-path, by-path.

atalaya, -lắyắ, sf. watch-tower; -, sm. guard in a watch-tower.

atalayar, -lăyăr', v. a. to overlook the country and sea-coast from a watch-tower; to spy into the action of others.   [silk.

atanquía, ătănkĕ́ắ, sf. depilatory; refuse of

ataque, ătắkĕ́, sm. attack; trenches; fit of the palsy, &c.; verbal dispute.

ataquizar, -kĭthăr', v. a. to provine.

atar, ătăr', v. a. to tie, to bind, to fasten; to stop; -se, to be embarrassed or perplexed.   [work.

ataracea, ătărăthĕ́ắ, sf. marquetry, checker-

ataracear, -thĕăr', v. a. to checker, to inlay.   [tarantula; surprised, amazed.

atarantado, da, ătărăntắdŏ́, a. bitten by a

atarazana, ătărăthắnắ, sf. arsenal; shed in rope-walks.

atarazar, -thăr', v. a. to bite.

atarear, ătărĕăr', v. a. to impose a task; -se, to overdo one's self.

atarjea, ătăr'hĕ́ắ, sf. protecting vault over the pipes of an aqueduct; small drain.

atarquinar, -kĭnăr', v. a. to bemire.

atarugar, ătărŭgăr', v. a. to wedge; to silence; -se, to be perplexed.

atasajar, ătăsăhăr', v. a. to cut meat into small pieces, and dry it in the sun.

atascar, ătăskăr', v. a. to stop a leak; to throw an obstacle in the way; -se, to become bogged.

ataúd, ătăŭ́d', sm. coffin.

ataujía, ătăŭhĕ́ắ, sf. damaskeen.

ataujiado, da, -hĭắdŏ́, a. worked in a damaskeen fashion.   [to adorn.

ataviar, ătăvĭăr', v. a. to dress out, to trim, to deck.

atavío, -vĕ́ŏ́, sm. dress, ornament, finery.

atediar, ătĕdĭăr', v. a. to disgust; -se, to be tired.

ateísmo, ătĕĭ́smŏ́, sm. atheism.

ateísta, ătĕĭ́stắ, sm. atheist.

atemorizar, ătĕmŏrĭthăr', v. a. to strike with terror, to daunt.   [tion.

atemperación, ătĕmpĕrăthĭŏn', sf. modera-

atemperar, -pĕrăr', v. a. to temper, to soften, to assuage; to accommodate.

atenaze(a)r, ătĕnăthĕ(ă)r', v. a. to tear off the flesh with pincers.

atención, ătĕnthĭŏn', sf. attention, heedfulness; civility, complaisance; observance, consideration; en -, attending; in consideration of; as regards.

atender, -dĕr', v. n. to be attentive; to heed, to hearken, to expect, to wait for; to look at.

atentado, da, -tắdŏ́, a. discreet, prudent, moderate; noiseless; -, sm. attempt, transgression, offence.

atentar, -tăr', v. a. to attempt crime; to go about a thing deliberately.

atento, ta, ătĕn'tŏ́, a. attentive; heedful; observing; mindful; polite, courteous, mannerly; compliant; notable; -, pr. in consideration.   [maceration.

atenuación, ătĕnŭăthĭŏn', sf. attenuation

atenuar, ătĕnŭăr', v. a. to diminish, to macerate, to mince.

atercianado, da, ătĕrthĭănắdŏ́, a. afflicted with the tertian fever.

aterciopelado, da, -thĭŏpĕlắdŏ́, a. velvet-like.   [cold.

aterirse, ătĕrĭr'sĕ, v. r. to grow stiff with aternerado, da, ătĕrnĕrắdŏ́, a. calf-like.

aterrar, ătĕrrăr', v. a. to prostrate; to terrify; -se, to be terrified.

aterronar, ătĕrrŏnăr', v. a. to clod, to coagulate.   [to terrify.

aterrorizar, ătĕrrŏrĭthăr', v. a. to frighten;

atesorar, ătĕsŏrăr', v. a. to treasure or hoard up riches.   [dence.

atestación, ătĕstăthĭŏn', sf. testimony, evi-

atestado, da, -tắdŏ́, a. stubborn; -, sm. certificate.

atestar, -tăr', v. a. to cram, to stuff; to

overstock; to attest, to witness; **—se**, to overeat one's self. [attest.

atestiguar, *—tĭgăr'*, v. a. to witness, to

atetado, da, *ătĕtă'dō*, a. mammiform.

atetar, *ătĕtăr'*, v. a. to suckle.

atetillar, *—tĭlyăr'*, v. a. to lay bare the roots of trees.

atezado, da, *—thă'dō*, a. black.

atezar, *—thăr'*, v. a. to blacken; **—se**, to grow black. [wool, &c.; to eat one's fill.

atiborrar, *ătĭborrăr'*, v. a. to stuff with

aticismo, *—thĭs'mō*, sm. atticism.

atigrado, da, *—gră'dō*, a. tiger-coloured.

atildar, *ătĭldăr'*, v. a. to punctuate, to underline; to censure; to deck, to dress, to adorn.

atinar, *ătĭnăr'*, v. n. to touch the mark, to reach the point; to hit; to guess.

atiriciarse, *ătĭrĭthĭăr'sĕ*, v. r. to grow jaundiced, to get the jaundice.

atisbadero, *ătĭsbădĕ'rō*, sm. peep-hole.

atisbar, *ătĭsbăr'*, v. a. to pry, to examine closely.

atisuado, da, *ătĭsŭă'dō*, a. tissue-like.

atizar, *ătĭthăr'*, v. a. to stir the fire with a poker; to stir up.

atizonar, *ătĭthŏnăr'*, v. a. to fill up the chinks in a wall; **—se**, to be smutted.

atlantico, ca, *ătlăn'tĭkŏ*, adj. atlantic.

atlas, *ăt'lăs*, sm. atlas (collection of maps); kind of rich silk.

atleta, *ătlĕ'tă*, sm. wrestler.

atlético, ca, *ătlĕ'tĭkŏ*, a. athletic.

atmósfera, *ătmŏs'fĕră*, sf. atmosphere.

atmosférico, ca, *ătmŏsfĕ'rĭkŏ*, a. atmospherical.

atoar, *ătŏăr'*, v. a. to tow a vessel.

atocinar, *ătŏthĭnăr'*, v. a. to cut up a pig for salting. [gorse.

atocha, *ătŏth'ă*, sf. (bot.) broom, furze,

atolondramiento, *ătŏlŏndrămĭĕn'tō*, sm. stupefaction, consternation.

atolondrar, *—drăr'*, v. a. to stun, to stupefy; **—se**, to be stupefied.

atolladero, *ătŏlyădă'rō*, sm. bog; obstacle; impediment.

atollar, *—lyăr'*, v. n. to stick in the mire.

atomismo, *ătŏmĭs'mō*, sm. atomical philosophy.

atomo, *ă'tŏmŏ*, sm. atom; mote. [sophy.

atondar, *ătŏndăr'*, v. a. to spur a horse.

atonía, *ătŏnĭ'ă*, sf. (med.) weakness, debility.

atónito, ta, *ătŏ'nĭtŏ*, a. astonished, amazed.

atontar, *ătŏntăr'*, v. a. to stun, to stupefy; **—se**, to grow stupid.

atorarse, *ătŏrăr'sĕ*, v. r. to stick in the mire.

atormentadamente, *ătŏrmĕntădămĕn'tĕ*, ad. anxiously. [to give pain.

atormentar, *—mĕntăr'*, v. a. to torment,

atorozonarse, *ătŏrŏthŏnăr'sĕ*, v. r. to suffer from gripes or colic.

atortolar, *ătŏrtŏlăr'*, v. a. to intimidate.

atosigar, *ătŏsĭgăr'*, v. a. to poison; to harass, to oppress.

atrabancar, *ătrăbănkăr'*, v. a. to huddle.

atracadero, *—kădă'rō*, sm. landing-place.

atracar, *ătrăkăr'*, v. a. to overhaul a ship; to glut, to pamper.

atracción, *ătrăkthĭŏn'*, sf. attraction.

atractivo, va, *—tĕ'vō*, a. attractive; magnetic; **—**, sm. charm, grace.

atraer, *ătrăĕr'*, v. a. to attract, to allure.

atrafagado, da, *ătrăfăgă'dō*, a. over-busy, overworked. [self.

atrafagar, *—făgăr'*, v. n. to exhaust one's

atragantarse, *—găntăr'sĕ*, v. r. to stick in the throat, to choke; to stick fast in conversation. [ous.

atraidorado, da, *ătrăĭdŏră'dō*, a. treacher-

atraillar, *ătrăĭlyăr'*, v. a. to leash.

atramparse, *ătrămpăr'sĕ*, v. r. to be caught in a snare; to be stopped or blocked up; to be involved in difficulties.

atrancar, *ătrănkăr'*, v. a. to bar a door; to take long steps; to read so fast as to skip over passages. [to deceive.

atrapar, *ătrăpăr'*, v. a. to overtake, to nab;

atrás, *ătrăs'*, ad. backwards; past; **hacia —**, quite the contrary.

atrasado, da, *ătrăsă'dō*, a. in arrear.

atrasar, *ătrăsăr'*, v. a. to outstrip, to leave behind; to hinder another's fortune; to postpone; **— el reloj**, to put back a watch. [fortune; arrears of money.

atraso, *ătră'sō*, sm. backwardness; loss of

atravesado, da, *ătrăvĕsă'dō*, a. squint-eyed; oblique; cross-grained, perverse; mongrel, degenerate.

atravesaño, *—săn'yŏ*, sm. cross-timber.

atravesar, *—săr'*, v. a. to lay a beam of timber across a place; to run through with a sword, to cross; to pass over; to trump a trick; **—se**, to get in the way; to thwart one's purpose.

atreguado, *ătrĕgŭă'dō*, a. rash, precipitate.

atresnalar, *ătrĕsnălăr'*, v. a. to collect sheaves of corn into heaps. [ture.

atreverse, *ătrĕvĕr'sĕ*, v. r. to dare, to ven-

atrevido, da, *—vĕ'dō*, a. bold, audacious, daring. [audacity.

atrevimiento, *—vĭmĭĕn'tō*, sm. boldness,

atribución, *ătrĭbŭthĭŏn'*, sf. attribution, imputation. [ascribe; to impute.

atribuir, *ătrĭbŭĭr'*, v. a. to attribute, to

atribular, *—bŭlăr'*, v. a. to vex, to afflict.

atributivo, va, *—bŭtĕ'vō*, a. attributive.

atributo, *—bŏ'tō*, sm. attribute.

atrición, *—thĭŏn'*, sf. attrition.

atril, *ătrĭl'*, sm. mass-book desk.

atrincheramiento, *ătrĭntshĕrămĭĕn'tō*, sm. (mil.) intrenchment.

atrincherar, *—tshĕrăr'*, v. a. to intrench.

atrio, *ă'trĭŏ*, sm. porch; portico.

atrito, ta, *ătrĭ'tŏ*, a. contrite, penitent.

atro, ra, *ă'trŏ*, a. (poet.) black.

atrocidad, *ătrŏthĭdăd'*, sf. atrocity.

atrochar, *ătrŏtshăr'*, v. n. to take by-paths.

atrochemoche, *ătrŏtshĕmŏtsh'ĕ*, ad. criss-cross.

atrofia, *ătrŏfĭ'ă*, sf. atrophy; body.

atrófico, ca, *ătrŏ'fĭkŏ*, a. affected with atrophy. [pet-like.

atrompetado, da, *ătrŏmpĕtă'dō*, a. trum-

atronado, da, *ătrŏnă'dō*, a. unadvised, thoughtless, rash. [struck.

atronarse, *—năr'sĕ*, v. r. to be thunder-

atronerar, –*něrär',* v. a. to make embrasures in a wall.

atropado, da, –*pä' dŏ,* a. grouped, clumped.

atropar, –*pär',* v. a. to assemble in groups.

atropellado, da, –*pělyä' dŏ,* a. hasty, precipitate.

atropellar, –*pělyär',* v. a. to trample; to run down; to hurry, to flurry; –se, to hurry one's self too much.

atroz, *ätrŏth',* a. atrocious, heinous, cruel.

atrozar, *ätrŏthär',* v. a. to truss a yard to the mast.

atufar, *ätŭfär',* v. a. to vex, to plague; –se, to be on the fret (applied to wine).

atún, *ätŭn',* sm. tunny-fish.

atunara, *ätŭnä' rä,* sf. tunny-fishery.

aturdido, da, *ätŭrdē' dŏ,* a. hare-brained.

aturdimiento, *ätŭrdēmēěn' tŏ,* sm. stupefaction; astonishment; dulness.

aturdir, –*dēr',* v. a. to perturbate, to confuse; to stupefy.

atusar, *ätŭsär',* v. a. to cut the hair; to shear.

auca, *ä' kä,* sf. goose.

audacia, *ädä' thēä,* sf. audacity, boldness.

audaz, *ädäth',* a. audacious, bold.

audiencia, *ädēěn' thēä,* sf. audience; audience-chamber; a court of oyer and terminer.

auditivo, va, *ädētē' vŏ,* a. auditive, auditory.

auditorio, –*tō' rēŏ,* sm. auditory.

auge, *ä' hě,* sm. the pinnacle of power; apogee of a planet.

augur, *ägŭr',* sm. augurer.

augusto, ta, *ägŭs' tŏ,* a. august, majestic.

aula, *ä' ŭlä,* sf. auditory, lecture-room.

aullar, *ädlyär',* v. n. to howl.

aullido, –*yě' dŏ,* aullo, *ädl' yŏ,* sm. howling.

aumentar, *ädměntär',* v. a. to augment, to increase; –, v. n. to grow larger.

aumentativo, va, –*tätē' vŏ,* a. increasing, enlarging.

aumento, *ädměn' tŏ,* sm. augmentation, increase; promotion, advancement.

aun, *äŭn',* ad. yet, as yet, nevertheless; still, farther, even, further.

aunar, *äŭnär',* v. a. to unite, to assemble.

aunque, *äŭn'kě,* ad. though, notwithstanding.

¡aupa! *äŭ' pä,* up, up!

aura, *ä' rä,* sf. gentle breeze; –popular, popularity.

áureo, rea, *ä' rěŏ,* a. golden, gilt; –, sm. doubloon; apothecary's weight of 4 scruples.

auréola, *ädrě' ŏlä,* sf. glory; nimbus.

aurícula, *ädrē' kŭlä,* sf. (bot.) bear's-ear.

auricular, –*kŭlär',* a. within hearing.

aurífero, ra, *ädrē' fěrŏ,* a. (poet.) containing gold.

aurora, *ädrŏ' rä,* sf. first dawn of day; (poet.) origin or first appearance of a thing; – boreal, north-light.

aurragado, da, *ädrrägä' dŏ,* a. badly tilled.

ausencia, *ädsěn' thēä,* sf. absence.

ausentarse, –*tär' sě,* v. r. to absent one's self.

ausente, *ädsěn' tě,* a. absent.

auspicio, *ädspē' thēŏ,* sm. auspice; prediction; protection.

austero, ra, *ädstě' rŏ,* a. austere, severe;

austral, *ädsträl',* **austrino, na,** –*trē' nŏ,* a. austral, southern.

austro, *ädš' trŏ,* sm. south wind.

auténtica, *ädtěn' tĭkä,* sf. certificate.

autenticar, –*tĭkär',* v. a. to authenticate.

autenticidad, –*tĭthĭdäd',* sf. authenticity.

auténtico, ca, *ädtěn' tĭkŏ,* a. authentic.

autillo, *ädtē' yŏ,* sm. horned owl; secret auto-da-fe.

auto, *ä' tŏ,* sm. judicial sentence; warrant, edict, ordinance; – de fe, auto-da-fe, sentence given by the Inquisition.

autocracia, *ädtŏkrä' thēä,* sf. autocracy.

autócrata, *ädtŏ'krä' tä,* sm. autocrat.

autógrafo, *ädtō' gräfŏ,* sm. autograph.

autómata, –*mätŏ,* sm. automaton.

autonomía, *ädtŏnŏmē' ä,* sf. autonomy.

autopsia, –*psē' ä,* sf. autopsy.

autor, *ädtŏr',* sm. author; maker; writer.

autora, *ädtō' rä,* sf. authoress.

autorcillo, *ädtŏrthēl' yŏ,* sm. bad writer.

autoría, *ädtŏrē' ä,* sf. managership of a theatre.

autoridad, *ädtŏrēdäd',* sf. authority.

autoritativo, va, –*tätē' vŏ,* a. authoritative.

autorización, *ädtŏrēthäthēŏn',* sf. authorisation.

autorizar, –*thär',* v. a. to authorise.

autorzuelo, *ädtŏrthŭě' lŏ,* sm. scribbler.

auxiliar, *ädksēlēär',* v. a. to aid, to help, to assist; to attend a dying person; –, a. auxiliary.

auxilio, *ädksē' lēŏ,* sm. aid, help, assistance.

avadarse, *ävädär' sě,* v. r. to become fordable.

avalentado, da, *ävälěntä' dŏ,* a. bragging, vainly boasting.

avalo, *ävä' lŏ,* sm. slight shock; earthquake.

avalorar, *ävälŏrär',* v. a. to estimate, to value; to heighten the value of a thing; to inspirit, to animate.

avambrazo, *ävämbrä' thŏ,* sm. fore-arm.

avance, *ävän' thě,* sm. (mil.) advance, attack.

avantrén, *ävänträn',* sm. (mil.) limbers of a gun-carriage.

avanzada, –*thä' dä,* sf. (mil.) vanguard.

avanzar, –*thär',* v. a. & n. to advance.

avanzo, *ävän' thŏ,* sm. (com.) balance.

avaricia, *ävärē' thēä,* sf. avarice.

avariento, ta, –*rēěn' tŏ,* a. avaricious, covetous.

avaro, ra, *ävä' rŏ,* a. avaricious, miserly.

avasallar, *äväsälyär',* v. a. to subdue, to enslave.

ave, *ä' vě,* sf. bird; fowl.

avechucho, –*tshŭtsh' ŏ,* sm. sparrow-hawk, ragamuffin.

aveoindar, *ävěthēndär',* v. a. to admit to the privileges of a citizen; –se, to approach, to join; than one's age.

avejentar, –*hěntär',* v. a. to look more.

avejigar, –*hēgär',* v. a. to blister.

avellana, *ävělyä' nä,* sf. filbert, hazel-nut.

avellanar, *ävělyänär',* sm. plantation of hazels.

avellanarse, –*när' sě,* v. r. to shrivel, to grow dry as a nut.

avellano, *ävělyä' nŏ,* sm. hazel-nut tree.

Ave María, *ävě märē' ä,* sf. Ave, the angel's salutation of the Holy Virgin.

avena, ăvḗnă, sf. oats.

avenamiento, –mĭen'tŏ, sm. drainage.

avenar, ăvĕnăr', v. a. to drain or draw off

avenate, –nă'tĕ, sm. water-gruel. [water.

avenencia, –nĕn'thĭă, sf. agreement, bargain ; union, concord.

aveniceo, cea, –nĕ'thĕŏ, a. oaten.

avenida, ăvĕnḗ dă, sf. flood, inundation ; concurrence of several things.

avenido, da, –nĕ'dŏ, a. agreed.

avenir, –nĭr', v. a. to reconcile ; to accommodate ; to get reconciled ; to join, to consent. [fire-fan.

aventador, ăvĕntădŏr', sm. winnower ; fan ;

aventadura, –dŏ'ră, sf. wind-gall.

aventajado, da, –'hă'dŏ, a. advantageous, profitable ; beautiful, excellent.

aventajar, –'hăr', v. a. to surpass, to excel. [to be puffed up.

aventar, ăvĕntăr', v. a. to fan ; to expel ; –se,

aventura, –tŏ'ră, sf. adventure, event, incident ; chance. [risk.

aventurar, –tŏrăr', v. a. to venture, to

aventurero, ra, –tŏrĕ'rŏ, a. adventurous.

avergonzar, ăvĕrgŏnthăr', v. a. to shame, to abash ; –se, to be ashamed.

avería, ăvĕrḗ ă, sf. (mar.) average, damage by sea ; aviary. [sea-water.

averiado, da, ăvĕrĭă'dŏ, a. damaged by

averiarse, ăvĕrĭăr' sĕ, v. r. to suffer damage at sea. [gation.

averiguación, ăvĕrĭgŭăthĭŏn', sf. investi-

averiguar, –gŭăr', v. a. to inquire, to investigate, to explore. [of birds.

averío, ăvĕrḗ ŏ, sm. beast of burden ; flight

averno, ăvĕr'nŏ, sm. (poet.) hell.

aversión, ăvĕrsĭŏn', sf. aversion, dislike ; abhorrence.

avestruz, ăvĕstrŭth', sm. ostrich.

aviar, ăvĭăr', v. a. to provision, to provide for a journey ; to accoutre ; to hasten the execution of a thing ; –se, to get ready.

avidez, ăvĭdĕth', sf. covetousness. [ous.

ávido, da, ă'vĭdŏ, a. (poet.) greedy, covet-

aviejarse, ăvĭĕ'păr' sĕ, v. r. to grow old.

aviento, ăvĭĕn'tŏ, sm. winnowing-fork.

avieso, sa, ăvĭĕ'sŏ, a. irregular, out of the way ; mischievous, perverse.

avigorar, ăvĭgŏrăr', v. a. to inspire with vigour and spirit. [ness.

avilantez, –lăntĕth', sf. forwardness, bold-

avillanado, da, ăvĭlyănă'dŏ, a. a clownish, mean, vile, base. [debase.

avillanar, –yănăr', v. a. to villanise, to

avinado, da, ăvĭnă'dŏ, a. tasting or smelling of wine. [peevish, bad-tempered.

avinagrado, da, –gră'dŏ, a. crabbed,

avinagrar, –grăr', v. a. to acidify.

avío, ăvḗ ŏ, sm. preparation, provision.

avión, ăvĭŏn', sm. house-swallow.

avisado, da, ăvĭsă'dŏ, a. prudent, cautious ; sagacious, skilful ; **mal –**, ill advised, injudicious. [notice ; to admonish.

avisar, –săr', v. a. to inform, to give

aviso, ăvḗ sŏ, sm. information, intelligence, notice ; warning, hint ; prudence ; care ; [counsel.

avispa, ăvĭs'pă, sf. wasp.

avispado, da, –pă'dŏ, a. lively, brisk, vivacious. [peevish.

avispar, –păr', v. a. to spur ; –se, to be

avispero, –pĕ'rŏ, sm. wasps' nest.

avispón, –pŏn', sm. hornet.

avistar, ăvĭstăr', v. a. to descry at a distance ; to have an interview, to transact business. [victual.

avituallar, ăvĭtŭălyăr', v. a. (mil.) to

avivar, ăvĭvăr', v. a. to quicken, to enliven, to encourage. [narrowly.

avizorar, ăvĭthŏrăr', v. a. to spy, to search

avocar, ăvŏkăr', v. a. to carry a law-suit into a superior court.

avucasta, ăvŭkăs'tă, sf. widgeon (ave).

avutarda, –tăr'dă, sf. bustard, wild turkey.

axioma, ăksĭŏ'mă, sm. axiom, maxim.

¡ay ! , äï, alas ! ; – **de mi !** alas ! poor me !

aya, ä'yă, sf. governess, instructress.

ayer, ăyĕr', ad. yesterday ; lately.

ayo, ä'yŏ, sm. tutor, governor.

ayuda, ăyŏ'dă, sf. help, aid ; support ; syringe ; –, sm. deputy, assistant.

ayudante, ăyŭdăn'tĕ, sm. (mil.) adjutant, aid-de-camp. [sist, to further.

ayudar, –dăr', v. a. to toaid, to help, to as-

ayunar, –năr', v. a. to fast, to abstain from food. [out knowledge.

ayunas, ăyŏ'năs, (en), ad. fastingly ; with-

ayuno, ăyŏ'nŏ, sm. fast, abstinence from food ; –, na, a. fasting.

ayunque, ăyŭn'kĕ, sm. anvil.

ayuntamiento, ăyŭntămĭen'tŏ, sm. Spanish town-council.

ayustar, ăyŭstăr', v. a. (mar.) to bend two ends of a cable. [black.

azabachado, da, ăthăbătchă'dŏ, a. jet-

azabache, –bătch'ĕ, sm. jet.

azacán, –kăn', sm. water-carrier.

azacaya, –kă'yă, sf. water-pipe.

azada, ăthă'dă, sf. spade, hoe.

azadón, –dŏn', sm. pick-axe, grub-axe.

azafata, –fă'tă, sf. queen's waiting-woman.

azafrán, –frăn', sm. saffron.

azafranar, –frănăr', v. a. to dye with saffron.

azagador, –gădŏr', sm. cattle-path.

azahar, –hăr', sm. orange or lemon flower.

azainadamente, ăthăĭnădămĕn'tĕ, ad. perfidiously ; viciously.

azar, ăthăr', sm. unforeseen disaster, unexpected accident ; unfortunate card or throw at dice ; disappointment ; impediment.

azarbe, ăthăr'bĕ, sm. irrigation-trench.

azaria, ăthăr'hă, sf. silk-reel.

azaroso, sa, –rŏ'sŏ, a. unlucky, ominous.

azaya, ăthă'yă, sf. silk-reel.

aznallo, ăthnăl'yŏ, sm. Scotch fir.

azoe, ăthŏ'ĕ, sm. (chem.) nitrogen.

azófar, ăthŏ'făr, sm. latten-brass.

azogadamente, ăthŏgădămĕn'tĕ, ad. in a quick and restless manner

azogar, ăthŏgăr', v. a. to overlay with quick-silver ; **– la cal,** to slake lime ; –se, to suffer from quick-silver poisoning ; to be in a state of agitation.

azogue, *ăthŏ'gã*, sm. quick-silver; -s, pl. ships which carry quick-silver. [works.

azoguería, *—gĕrĭ'ă*, sf. amalgamating-

azolar, *ăthŏlăr'*, v. a. to cut timber with a hatchet.

azor, *ăthŏr'*, sm. goshawk. [be agitated.

azorar, *—răr'*, v. a. to frighten, to terrify; to

azorrarse, *ăthŏrrăr'sĕ*, v. r. to feel a heaviness in the head.

azotacalles, *—tăkăl'yĕs*, sm. lounger, loafer; (am.) bummer. [flogging.

azotaina, *—tă'ĭnă*, sf. drubbing, sound

azotar, *—tăr'*, v. a. to whip, to lash; to horsewhip. [a whip; calamity.

azote, *ăthŏ'tĕ*, sm. whip, lash given with

azotea, *ăthŏtă'ă*, sf. platform, flat roof of a house.

azúcar, *ăthŏ'kăr*, sm. sugar; — de pilón, loaf-sugar; — piedra ó cande, sugar-candy; — terciado ó moreno, brown sugar. [sugary.

azucarado, da, *ăthŭkără'dŏ*, a. sugared;

azucarar, *—kărăr'*, v. a. to sugar, to sweeten. [fectioner.

azucarero, *—kără'rŏ*, sm. sugar-basin; con-

azucena, *ăthŭthă'na*, sf. white lily.

azud, *ăthŭd"*, sf. dam with a sluice or flood-gate. [tion.

azuda, *ăthŏ'dă*, sf. water-works for irriga-

azuela, *ăthŏlă'lă*, sf. chip-axe.

azufaifa, *ăthăfă'ĭfă*, sf. jujube.

azufaifo, *—fŏ*, sm. jujube-tree.

azufrado, da, *ăthăfră'dŏ*, a. whitened with sulphur; sulphurous. [phur.

azufrar, *—frăr'*, v. a. to fumigate with sul-

azufre, *ăthŏ'frĕ*, sm. sulphur, brimstone.

azufroso, sa, *—frŏ'sŏ*, a. sulphureous.

azul, *ăthŭl'*, a. blue; — celeste, sky blue; — subido, bright blue; — turquí, Turkish or deep blue.

azulado, da, *—lă'dŏ*, a. azure, bluish.

azular, *—lăr'*, v. a. to dye blue.

azulear, *—lĕăr'*, v. n. to have a bluish tint.

azulejo, *—lĕ'hŏ*, sm. Dutch glazed tile painted with various colours.

azulenco, *—lĕn'kŏ*, a. bluish.

azumbre, *ăthăm'brĕ*, sf. liquid measure (half a galion).

azutero, *ăthŭtă'rŏ*, sm. sluice-master.

azuzador, ra, *—thădŏr'*, sm. & f. instigator.

azuzar, *—thăr'*, v. a. to set on dogs; to irritate, to stir up.

B.

baba, *bă'bă*, sf. drivel, slaver.

babada, *băbă'dă*, sf. thigh-bone.

babadero, *—dă'rŏ*, babador, *băbădŏr'*, sm. bib, chin-cloth. [from the mouth.

babaza, *băbă'thă*, sf. slime; foam or froth

babear, *băbăăr'*, v. n. to drivel, to slaver.

babera, *bă'ră*, sf. chin-piece of a helmet; foolish, silly fellow.

babero, *—rŏ*, sm. bib, chin-cloth.

babia, *bă'bĭă*, sf. estar en —, to be absent-minded or dreaming. [fellow.

babieca, *băbĭĕ'kă*, sm. ignorant, stupid

babilonia, *băbĭlŏ'nĭă*, sf. es una —, it is all uproar and confusion.

babosa, *băbŏ'să*, sf. slug.

babosear, *băbŏsăr'*, v. a. to beslaver.

baboso, sa, *băbŏ'sŏ*, a. drivelling, slavering.

babucha, *băbŏtsh'ă*, sf. oriental slipper.

bacallao, *băkălyă'ŏ*, sm. ling, poor jack, cod-fish.

bacanales, *băkănă'lĕs*, sf. pl. bacchanals.

bacante, *băkăn'tĕ*, sf. bacchant.

bacía, *băthĭ'ă*, sf. basin; barber's basin.

bacinica, *băthĭnĭ'kă*, sf. chamber-pot for children.

báculo, *bă'kŭlŏ*, sm. walking-stick; support; — pastoral, bishop's crosier.

bachiller, *bătshĭlyĕr'*, sm. bachelor; —, a. garrulous, loquacious. [to prattle.

bachillerear, *bătshĭlyĕrăr'*, v.n. to babble,

badajo, *bădă'hŏ*, sm. clapper of a bell.

badana, *bădă'nă*, sf. dressed sheep-skin.

badil, *bădĭl'*, badila, *bădĭ'lă*, sf. fire-shovel.

badulaque, *bădŭlă'kĕ*, sm. stupid fellow.

bagaje, *băgă'hĕ*, sm. beast of burden; army-baggage. [burden.

bagajero, *—hă'rŏ*, sm. driver of beasts of

bagatela, *—tă'lă*, sf. bagatelle, trifle.

bagazo, *băgă'thŏ*, sm. sediment of grapes.

bahía, *bă-ĭ'ă*, sf. bay. [olives, palms, &c.

bailador, ra, *băĭlădŏr'*, sm. & f. dancer.

bailar, *—lăr'*, v. n. to dance.

bailarín, ina, *—lărĭn'*, sm. & f. dancer.

baile, *bă'ĭlĕ*, sm. dance, ball; bailiff.

baja, *bă'hă*, sm. bashaw, pacha.

baja, *bă'h'ă*, sf. fall, diminution; (mil.) ticket of admission into a regiment; (mil.) head of casualties in a muster-roll.

bajada, *bă'hă'dă*, sf. descent; inclination.

bajamar, *bă'hămăr'*, sf. low water.

bajar, *bă'hăr'*, v. a. to lower, to let down; to abate (the price); to lessen; to humble; to bend downwards; —, v. n. to descend; to grow less; -se, v. n. to crouch; to lessen.

bajel, *bă'hĕl'*, sm. vessel, ship. [master.

bajelero, *—lă'rŏ*, sm. ship-owner, ship-

bajete, *bă'hă'tĕ*, sm. (mus.) barytone.

bajeza, *bă'hă'thă*, sf. meanness, abject ness; littleness; lowliness, fawningness.

bajío, *bă'hĭ'ŏ*, sm. shoal, sand-bank; decline.

bajo, ja, *bă'h'ŏ*, a. low; abject, despicable; faint; common; dull (of colours); bent; —, pr. under, underneath, below; —, ad. low (of the voice); —, sm. (mus.) base; low place; -s, pl. under-petticoats of women.

bajón, *bă'hŏn'*, sm. bassoon. [women.

bajonero, *bă'hŏnă'rŏ*, sm. player on the bassoon.

bala, *bă'lă*, sf. ball, bullet, shot; bale of paper; printer's inking-ball. [less.

baladí, *—dĭ'*, a. mean, despicable, worth-

baladre, *bălă'drĕ*, sm. rose-bay.

baladrón, *—drŏn'*, sm. boaster, bully.

baladronada, *—drŏnă'dă*, sf. boast, brag, bravado.

baladronear, –dronĕăr', v. n. to boast, to brag.

bálago, bă'lăgŏ, sm. hay-rick; soap-suds.

balance, bălăn'thĕ, sm. fluctuation; equipoise; balance of accounts; rolling of a ship.

balancear, –thĕăr', v. a. & n. to balance; to roll; to hold in equipoise; to waver.

balancilla, –thĭl'yă, sf. gold-weights.

balancín, –thĭn', sm. swing-bar of a cart; minting-mill; rope-dancer's pole.

balandra, bălăn'dră, sf. (mar.) bilander, sloop. [comparative estimate.

balanza, –thă, sf. scale; pair of scales;

balanzario, –thă'rĭŏ, sm. balancer.

balar, bălăr', v. n. to bleat as a sheep.

balaustrada, bălăŭstră'dă, sf. balustrade.

balaustre, bălăŭs'trĕ, sm. baluster.

balazo, bălă'thŏ, sm. shot. [stuttering.

balbuciente, bălbŭthĭĕn'tĕ, a. stammering,

balcón, bălkŏn', sm. balcony. [conies.

balconaje, –kŏnă'hĕ, sm. range of balconies.

baldar, –dăr', v. a. to cripple.

balde, băl'dĕ, sm. bucket; de –, ad. gratis, for nothing; en –, in vain.

baldés, băldĕs', sm. piece of dressed skin.

baldío, día, –dĕ'ŏ, a. untilled, uncultivated.

baldón, –dŏn', sm. reproach, insult.

baldosa, –dŏ'să, sf. fine square tile.

balería, bălĕrĕ'ă, sf. pile of balls or bullets.

balido, bălĭ'dŏ, sm. bleating, bleat,

balija, bălĭ'hă, sm. portmanteau; mail; post. [postman.

balijero, –'hă'rŏ, sm. country or local postman.

balín, bălĭn', sm. buck-shot. [goods.

balón, bălŏn', sm. large foot-ball; bale of

baloncita, bălŏnthĭ'tă, sf. save-all.

balota, bălŏ'tă, sf. ballot.

balotada, –tă'dă, sf. ballotade (leap of a horse in which he shows the shoes of his hinder feet).

balsa, băl'să, sf. pool; raft, float; ferry.

balsámico, ca, bălsă'mĭkŏ, a. balmy.

bálsamo, băl'sămŏ, sm. balsam, balm.

balsear, bălsĕăr', v. a. to cross rivers on ferries or floats.

balsero, bălsĕ'rŏ, sm. ferry-man.

balsopeto, bălsŏpĕ'tŏ, sm. large pouch carried near the breast; bosom.

baluarte, bălŭăr'tĕ, sm. bastion; bulwark.

balumbo, bălŭm'bŏ, sm. bulk of things heaped together.

ballena, bălyĕ'nă, sf. whale; whale-bone.

ballenato, –nă'tŏ, sm. cub of a whale.

ballenero, bălyĕnĕ'rŏ, sm. (mar.) whaler.

ballesta, bălyĕs'tă, sf. cross-bow; á tiro de –, at a great distance. [bow.

ballestada, –tă'dă, sf. shot from a crossbow.

ballestear, –tĕăr', v. a. to shoot with a crossbow. [hole.

ballestera, bălyĕstĕ'ră, sf. (mil.) loop-

ballestería, –tĕrĕ'ă, sf. archery; crossbows; crossbow-men.

ballestero, –tĕ'rŏ, sm. archer; crossbow-maker; king's armourer. [bow.

ballestilla, bălyĕstĭl'yă, sf. small cross-

bamba, băm'bă, sf. riding-chair.

bambalina, –lĕ'nă, sf. soffits of a theatre.

bambolear, bămbŏlĕăr', v. n. to reel.

bamboleo, –lĕ'ŏ, sm. reeling, staggering.

bambolla, bămbŏl'yă, sf. ostentation, vain show. [boo.

bambú, bămbŏŏ', **bambuc,** –k', sm. bam-

banana, bănă'nă, sf. banana, plantain.

banano, bănă'nŏ, sm. plantain-tree.

banasta, bănăs'tă, sf. large basket.

banastero, –tĕ'rŏ, sm. basket-maker.

banasto, bănăs'tŏ, sm. large round basket.

banca, băn'kă, sf. bench; washing-box.

bancal, bănkăl', sm. garden-bed, parterre; carpet.

bancarrota, bănkărrŏ'tă, sf. bankruptcy.

banco, băn'kŏ, sm. bench; carpenter's bench; bench of rowers; bank.

banda, băn'dă, sf. sash; ribbon; band of troops; party; gang; crew; covey; bank,

bandada, –dă'dă, sf. covey. [border.

bandearse, –dĕ'ăr'sĕ, v. r. to shift for one's

bandeja, –dĕ'hă, sf. salver. [self.

bandera, –dĕ'ră, sf. banner, standard; flag.

banderilla, bănderĭl'yă, sf. small decorated dart used at a bull-fight.

banderillear, –rĭlyĕăr', v. a. to plant banderillas in a bull's neck or shoulder.

banderillero, –rĭlyĕ'rŏ, sm. thrower of banderillas.

banderín, –rĭn', sm. cockade.

banderizo, za, –rĕ'thŏ, a. factious.

banderola, –rŏ'lă, sf. bannerol. [man.

bandido, băndĭ'dŏ, sm. bandit, highway-

bando, băn'dŏ, sm. faction, party.

bandolera, –lĕ'ră, sf. bandeleer.

bandolero, –lĕ'rŏ, sm. highwayman.

bandolín, –lĭn', sm. (mus.) mandolin.

bandullo, băndŭl'yŏ, sm. belly.

bandurria, –dŭr'rĭă, sf. bandore (musical instrument resembling a fiddle).

banquero, –kĕ'rŏ, sm. banker.

banqueta, –kĕ'tă, sf. three-legged stool.

banquete, –kĕ'tĕ, sm. banquet.

baña, băn'yă, sf., **bañadero,** –dĕ'rŏ, sm. pool, puddle (in which wild boars wallow).

bañar, bănyăr', v. a. to bathe; to tub; to water, to irrigate; to candy; to wash over a painting with a second coat of transparent colours.

bañero, –yĕ'rŏ, sm. bath-keeper.

baño, băn'yŏ, sm. bath; bathing-place; bathing-tub; varnish; crust of sugar; coat of paint put over another.

baqueta, băkĕ'tă, sf. ramrod, gun-stick; drumstick; (mil.) gantlet. [falling body.

baquetazo, –tă'thŏ, sm. heavy thud of a

baqueteado, da, –tĕă'dŏ, a. inured, habituated.

báquico, ca, bă'kĭkŏ, a. bacchanal.

baraja, bără'h'ă, sf. complete pack of cards.

barajadura, –dŏ'ră, sf. shuffling of cards.

barajar, bără'hăr', v. a. to shuffle cards; to entangle. [trade, small railing.

barandilla, bărăndĭl'yă, sf. small balus-

baratero, bărătĕ'rŏ, sm. card-sharper, black-leg.

baratijas, –tĕ'hăs, sf. pl. trifles, toys.

baratillero, –tĭlyĕ'rŏ, sm. fripperer.

baratillo, –tíl'yō, sm. frippery.

barato, ta, bārā'tō, a. cheap; de –, gratis; –, sm. cheapness, low price; money given by the winners at a gaming-table to the by-standers as part of the gain.

baratura, –tō'rā, sf. cheapness.

baraúnda, bārāūn'dā, sf. noise, hurly-burly.

barba, bār'bā, sf. chin; beard; – á –, face to face; –, sm. actor who personates old men.

barbacana, –kā'nā, sf. (mil.) barbican.

barbada, –bā'dā, sf. beard of a horse; dab (fish).

barbar, bārbār', v. n. to grow a beard; to rear or keep bees; to take root.

barbaridad, –rīdād', sf. barbarity, barbarism; rashness; rudeness.

barbarie, –rē, sf. barbarism; rusticity.

barbarismo, –rīs'mō, sm. barbarism (form of speech); (poet.) crowd of barbarians.

bárbaro, ra, bār'bārō, a. barbarous; rash, bold, daring; rude, unpolished.

barbechar, bārbētshār', v. a. to plough.

barbechera, –tshē'rā, sf. series of successive ploughings. [fallow.

barbecho, bārbētsh'ō, sm. first ploughing.

barbería, bārbērē'ā, sf. barber's shop.

barbero, –bā'rō, sm. barber. [rope.

barbeta, –bā'tā, sf. (mar.) rackline; rope.

barbiblanco, ca, bārbīblān'kō, a. white-bearded.

barbicano, na, –kā'nō, a. grey-beard.

barbihecho, –ētsh'ō, a. fresh shaved.

barbilampiño, ña, –lāmpīn'yō, a. thin bearded.

barbilucio, cia, –lō'thīō, a. pretty, genteel.

barbilla, bārbīl'yā, sf. chin-point.

barbinegro, gra, bārbīnā'grō, a. black-bearded.

barbirrubio, bia, –rō'bīō, a. red-bearded.

barbo, bār'bō, sm. barbel. [strong beard.

barbón, bārbōn', sm. man with a thick, beard.

barbosa, bārbō'sā, sf. layer, provine.

barbote, bārbō'tē, sm. chin-cloth.

barbudo, da, bārbō'dā, a. long-bearded.

barbulla, bā.bōl'yā, sf. confused noise.

barbullar, –lyār', v. a. to paint badly; to dirty; to talk confusedly and disorderly.

barbullón, ona, –lyōn', a. loud talking; babel of tongues.

barca, bār'kā, sf. boat, barge.

barcada, bārkā'dā, sf. passage in a ferry-boat; boat full of persons or goods.

barcaje, bārkāh'ē, sm. fare.

barco, bār'kō, sm. boat, barge; bark.

barda, bār'dā, sf. bard.

bardal, bārdāl', sm. mud-wall, covered at the top with straw, brush or fence-wood.

bardana, bārdā'nā, sf. common burdock.

bardar, bārdār', v. a. to cover the top of walls with straw or brushwood.

barga, bār'gā, sf. steepest part of a declivity.

baritono, bārī'tōnō, sm. (mus.) baritone.

barloar, bārlōār', v. n. (mar.) to grapple for the purpose of boarding.

barloventear, bārlōvēntār', v. n. (mar.) to tack, to tack about. [gage.

barlovento, –vēn'tō, sm. (mar.) weather-

barniz, bārnīth', sm. varnish; Japan paint; printer's ink.

barnizar, –nīthār', v. a. to varnish.

barómetro, bārō'mētrō, sm. barometer.

barón, bārōn', sm. baron.

baronesa, bārōnēs'ā, sf. baroness.

baronía, bārōnē'ā, sf. barony; baronage.

barquear, bārkēār', v. n. to cross in a boat.

barquero, bārkā'rō, sm. bargeman.

barquilla, bārkīl'yā, sf. (mar.) log; thin boat-formed pastry-cake.

barquillero, –yā'rō, sm. wafer-baker.

barquillo, –yō, sm. wafer.

barquín, bārkīn', sm. large bellows for furnaces. [body.

barquinazo, –ā'thō, sm. thud of a falling

barquino, bārkī'nō, sm. wine-bag.

barra, bār'rā, sm. crowbar. lever; ingot of gold, silver, &c.; rock, sandbank; de – á –, from place to place. [trigue.

barrabasada, –bāsā'dā, sf. trick, plot, in-

barraca, bārrā'kā, sf. hut (for soldiers or for fishermen). [timber.

barraganete, bārrāgānā'tē, sm. top-

barranca, bārrān'kā, sf. deep break made by mountain-floods; cleft, glen.

barranco, –rān'kō, sm. gill; (fig.) great difficulty, embarrassment.

barrancoso, sa, bārrānkō'sō, a. full of breaks and holes.

barrar, bārrār', **barrear**, bārrēār', v. a. to barricade, to fortify. [turn-pike.

barreda, bārrā'dā, **barrera**, bārrā'rā, sf.

barredero, –dā'rō, sm. mop.

barreduras, bārrēdō'rās, s. pl. sweepings; remains, residue.

barrena, bārrā'nā, sf. borer, gimlet, auger.

barrenar, –nār', v. a. to bore; (fig.) to frustrate one's designs. [dust-man.

barrendero, bārrēndā'rō, sm. sweeper.

barreno, bārrā'nō, sm. large borer; hole made with a borer or auger.

barreño, bārrēn'yō, sm. earthen pan; tub.

barrer, bārrēr', v. a. to sweep; to carry off the whole. [turn-pike.

barrera, bārrā'rā, sf. clay-pit; barrier;

barrero, –rā'rō, sm. potter; clay-pit;

barretear, –tār', v. a. to bar; to line the inside of shoes.

barretero, bārrētā'rō, sm. one who works with a crowbar, wedge or pick (in mines).

barriada, bārrīā'dā, sf. suburb, ward of a city.

barrica, bārrē'kā, sf. keg, small barrel.

barricada, –kā'dā, sf. barricade.

barrido, –rē'dō, sm. sweep.

barriga, –rē'gā, sf. abdomen, belly; pregnancy; (mar.) middle part of a vessel.

barrigudo, da, –gō'dō, a. big-bellied.

barril, bārrīl', sm. barrel; jar.

barrilame, bārrīlā'mē, sm., **barrilería**, bārrīlērē'ā, sf. number of barrels collected in one place.

barrilero, bārrīlā'rō, sm. cooper.

barrilete, –ā'tē, sm. (mar.) mouse; keg; holdfast. [rrilla.

barrilla, –rīl'yā, sf. (bot.) salt-wort, ba-

barrillar, –yār', sm. barrilla-pits.

barrillón, *-yŏn'*, sm. brine-prover.
barrio, *băr'rĕ*, sm. district of a town.
barrizal, *bărrĭthăl'*, sm. clay-pit.
barro, *băr'rŏ*, sm. clay, mud.
barroso, sa, *băr'rŏ s̄ŏ*, a. muddy.
barrote, *băr̄rŏ'tĕ*, sm. iron-work of doors, windows, tables; ledge of timber.
barrueco, *bărrŭă'kŏ*, sm. pearl of irregular shape.
barruntador, *bărrŭntădŏr'*, sm. conjecturer.
barruntamiento, *-mĭĕn'tŏ*, sm. conjecture, guess.   [jecture.
barruntar, *-tăr'*, v. a. to foresee, to conjecture.   [ness.
barrunto, *-rŭn'tŏ*, sm. conjecture, business.
bártulos, *băr'tŭlŏs*, sm. pl. affairs, business.
barzón, *bărthŏn'*, sm. idle walk.
barzonear, *bărthŏneăr'*, v. n. to loiter.
basa, *bă'să*, sf. basis ; base.
basada, *băsă'dă*, sf. crane, derrick.
basalto, *băsăl'tŏ*, sm. basalt, basaltes.
basca, *băs'kă*, sf. squeamishness, nausea.
bascosidad, *băskŏsĭdăd"*, sf. nastiness, filth.
base, *bă'sĕ*, sf. base, basis.
basílica, *băsĕ'lĭkă*, sf. basilica (cathedral).
basilisco, *băsĭlĭs'kŏ*, sm. basilisk, cockatrice.
basquear, *băskĕăr'*, v. n. to be squeamish.
basquiña, *băskĭn'yă*, sf. upper petticoat worn by Spanish women.
basta, *băs'tă*, sf. basting.
bastante, *băstăn'tĕ*, a. sufficient, enough.
bastar, *băstăr'*, v. n. to suffice, to be proportioned to something, to be enough.
bastarda, *băstăr'dă*, sf. bastard-file; italic (type).   [bastardize.
bastardear, *-dĕăr'*, v. n. to degenerate; to
bastardía, *-dĕ'ă*, sf. bastardy; meanness.
bastardo, da, *-tăr'dŏ*, a. bastard, spurious; —, sm. bastard.   [sew slightly.
bastear, *băstĕăr'*, v. a. to stitch loosely, to
bastero, *băstĕ'rŏ*, sm. maker and seller of pack-saddles.
bastidor, *băstĭdŏr'*, sm. embroidery-frame; side-scene; **-es,** pl. scenery (on the stage).
bastilla, *băstĭl'yă*, sf. hem, seam.
bastimentar, *băstĭmĕntăr'*, v. a. to supply with provisions.
bastimentero, *-tĕ'rŏ*, sm. purveyor.
bastimento, *-mĕn'tŏ*, sm. supply of provisions; (mar.) vessel.
bastión, *băstĭŏn'*, sm. (mil.) bastion.
basto, *băs'tŏ*, sm. pack-saddle for beasts of burden; —, ta, a. coarse, rude, unpolished.
bastón, *băstŏn'*, sm. cane, stick; truncheon; staff of command; military command.
bastonazo, *băstŏnă'thŏ*, sm. bastinado.
bastoncillo, *-thĭl'yŏ*, sm. narrow lace.
bastonear, *-nĕăr'*, v. a. to stir must with a stick to prevent its becoming ropy.
batonero, *-nĕ'rŏ*, sm. marshal or manager of a ball; steward of a feast; assistant jail-keeper.   [four suits at cards.
bastos, *băs'tŏs*, sm. pl. clubs, one of the
basura, *băsŏ'ră*, sf. sweepings; dung, ordure.
basurero, *-rĕ'rŏ*, sm. dustman; dung-hill.
bata, *bă'tă*, sf. morning-gown; refuse of silk.

batacazo, *-kă'thŏ*, sm. noise of a fall.
batahola, bataola, *-ŏ'lă*, sf. hurly-burly, bustle.   [agitation of the mind.
batalla, *bătăl'yă*, sf. battle, combat, fight;
batallador, *bătălyădŏr'*, sm. combatant, warrior.   [to fence with foils; to dispute.
batallar, *-yăr'*, v. n. to battle, to fight;
batallón, *-yŏn'*, sm. (mil.) battalion.
batán, *bătăn'*, sm. fulling-mill.
batanar, *-năr'*, v. a. to full cloth.
batanear, *-nĕăr'*, v. a. to beat, to handle roughly.
batanero, *-nă'rŏ*, sm. fuller.   [roughly.
batata, *bătă'tă*, sf. Spanish potato.
batea, *bătĕ'ă*, sf. painted tray or hamper of japanned wood; washing-trough.
batería, *bătĕrĕ'ă*, sf. battery; impression made on the mind or body.
batera, *bătĕ'ră*, sf. mantua-maker.
batida, *bătĕ'dă*, sf. battue (chase).
batidera, *bătĭdĕ'ră*, sf. beater (instrument for beating and mixing mortar).
batidero, *-dĕ'rŏ*, sm. clashing of one thing against another; collision; uneven ground.
batido, da, *bătĕ'dŏ*, a. changeable (applied to silks); beaten (as roads); —, sm. batter of flour and water for making the host; wafers, biscuits.
batidor, *-dŏr'*, sm. scout; ranger; outrider; one of the life-guards, who rides before a royal coach; **- de oro,** gold-beater.
batiente, *bătĭĕn'tĕ*, sm. jamb or post of a door.
batihoja, *bătĭŏ'h'ă*, sm. gold-beater; artisan who works iron and other metal into sheets; warp of cloth.
batir, *bătĭr'*, v. a. to beat, to dash; to clash, to clap; to demolish; to move in a violent manner; to strike (of the sun).
batista, *bătĭs'tă*, sf. batiste, cambric.
baturrillo, *bătŭrrĭl'yŏ*, sm. hotch-potch, salmagundi.
baúl, *băŭl'*, sm. trunk; belly.
bauprés, *băŭprĕs'*, sm. (mar.) bow-sprit.
bausán, ana, *băŭsăn'*, sm. & f. guy; fool; idiot.
bautismal, *băŭtĭsmăl'*, a. baptismal.
bautismo, *băŭtĭs'mŏ*, sm. baptism.
bautisterio, *-tĕ'rĭŏ*, sm. baptistery.
bautizar, *băŭtĭthăr'*, v. a. to baptise, to christen.
bautizo, *băŭtĭ'thŏ*, sm. baptism.
baya, *bă'yă*, sf. berry; husk, cod.
bayeta, *băyĕ'tă*, sf. baize (kind of cloth).
bayetón, *-tŏn'*, sm. coating.
bayo, ya, *bă'yŏ*, a. bay (of a horse).
bayoneta, *băyŏnĕ'tă*, sf. bayonet.
bayonetazo, *-nĕtă'thŏ*, sm. thrust with a bayonet.
baza, *bă'thă*, sf. card-trick.
bazo, *bă'thŏ*, sm. spleen, milt.   [wash.
bazofia, *băthŏ'fĭă*, sf. offal; refuse; hogwash.
bazucar, *băthŭkăr'*, v. a. to stir liquids by shaking.   [by shaking.
bazuqueo, *-kĕ'ŏ*, sm. stirring of liquids
be, *bĕ*, baa (cry of sheep).   [methodist.
beata, *bĕă'tă*, sf. sister of charity; rank
beatería, *bĕătĕrĕ'ă*, sf. bigotry.

beaterio, –*tä´riŏ,* sm. house of sisters of charity. [tion.

beatificación, –*fĭkäthĭŏn´,* sf. beatifica-

beatificar, –*tĭfĭkär´,* v. a. to beatify; to hallow, to sanctify, to make blessed.

beatífico, ca, –*tĕ´fĭkŏ,* a. beatific.

beatilla, –*tĭl´yä,* sf. French lawn.

beatísimo, ma, –*tĭs´ĭmŏ,* a. most holy; –**padre,** sm. most holy father (the pope).

beatitud, –*tĭtŭd´,* sf. beatitude, blessedness.

beato, ta, *bĕä´tŏ,* a. happy, blessed; devout; –, sm. religionist; pious person.

bebedero, *bĕbĕdä´rŏ,* sm. drinking-trough; place where birds resort to drink.

bebedizo, za, –*dĕ´thŏ,* a. drinkable.

bebedizo, –, sm. love-potion.

bebedor, ra, *bĕbĕdŏr´,* sm. & f. tippler.

beber, *bĕbĕr´,* v. a. to drink. [drunkard.

bebida, *bĕbĕ´dä,* sf. drink, beverage.

bebido, da, –*dŏ,* bien –, drunk.

bebistrajo, *bĕbĭsträ´hŏ,* sm. bad drink; cat-lap, washy stuff, water bewitched.

beborretear, *bĕbŏrrĕtĕär´,* v. a. to sip.

beca, *bĕ´kä,* sf. part of a collegian's dress in the shape of an oar, which is worn over the gown; fellowship; allowance, scholarship; –s, pl. strips of velvet, &c. with which the forepart of cloaks is lined by way of ornament.

bacabunga, –*bŭn´gä,* sf. (bot.) brook-lime.

bocada, *bĕkä´dä,* sf. wood-cock.

becafigo, –*fĕ´gŏ,* sm. fig-pecker.

becerra, *bĕthĕr´rä,* sm. (bot.) snap-dragon.

becerrillo, –*rĭl´yŏ,* sm. calf; dressed calf-skin.

becerro, –*thĕr´rŏ,* sm. yearling calf; calf-skin; register in which are entered the privileges and appurtenances of cathedral churches and convents; the Golden Book of the Castilian nobility at Simancas; – **marino,** sea-calf.

bedel, *bĕdĕl´,* sm. beadle.

bedelía, *bĕdĕlĕ´ä,* sf. beadleship.

bederre, *bĕdĕr´rĕ,* sm. (cant) hangman.

bedija, *bĕdĕ´hä,* sf. flock of wool.

bedilla, *bĕdĕl´yä,* sf. woollen bed-cloth.

befa, *bĕ´fä,* sf. jeer, scoff, mock; garland.

befar, *bĕfär´,* v. a. to mock, to ridicule.

befo, fa, *bä´fä,* a. blubber-lipped.

bejucal, *bĕhŭkäl´,* sm. reed-plot, reed-bank. [India).

bejuco, –*hŏ´kŏ,* sm. reed (growing in

bejuquillo, –*hăkĭl´yŏ,* sm. small gold chain.

beldad, *bĕldäd´,* sf. beauty. [chain.

beleño, *bĕlĕn´yŏ,* sm. (bot.) hen-bane.

bélico, ca, *bä´lĭkŏ,* a. warlike, martial.

belicoso, sa, –*kŏ´sŏ,* a. martial, pugnacious.

beligerante, –*hĕrän´tĕ,* a. belligerant.

bellacamente, *bĕlyäkämĕn´tĕ,* ad. knavishly, roguishly. [ning, roguish.

bellaco, ca, –*yä´kŏ,* a. artful, sly; cun-

belladama, –*dä´mä,* belladona, –*dŏ´nä,* sf. (bot.) deadly night-shade.

bellaquear, –*kĕär´,* v. a. to cheat, to play roguish tricks.

bellaquería, –*kĕrĕ´ä,* sf. knavery, roguery.

belleza, *bĕlyä´thä,* sf. beauty.

bello, lla, *bĕl´yŏ,* a. beautiful, handsome, fair, fine; perfect.

bellota, *bĕlyŏ´tä,* sf. acorn; smelling-bottle (in the shape of an acorn).

bellote, –*tĕ,* sm. large round-headed nail.

bellotear, –*tĕär´,* v. n. to feed on acorns (applied to swine).

bellotera, –*tä´rä,* sf. acorn season.

bemol, *bĕmŏl´,* sm. (mus.) b-flat.

bendecir, *bĕndĕthĭr´,* v. a. to consecrate; to praise, to exalt.

bendición, –*dĭthĭŏn´,* sf. benediction.

bendito, ta, –*dĕ´tŏ,* a. saint, blessed; simple, silly.

benedícite, *bĕnĕdĕ´thĭtĕ,* sm. grace at meals; clergyman's leave of absence.

benedictino, *bĕnĕdĭktĕ´nŏ,* benito, *bĕnĕ´tŏ,* sm. Benedictine.

beneficencia, –*fĭthĕn´thĭä,* sf. beneficence.

beneficiado, –*fĭthĭä´dŏ,* sm. incumbent of a benefice; beneficiary.

beneficiador, –*fĭthĭädŏr´,* sm. benefactor; improver; careful administrator.

beneficiar, –*fĭthĭär´,* v. a. to benefit; to work and improve mines.

beneficiario, –*fĭthĭä´rĭŏ,* sm. beneficiary.

beneficio, –*fĕ´thĭŏ,* sm. benefit, favour, kindness; labour; culture; profit; benefit-night; – curado, benefice to which a curacy is attached.

benéfico, ca, *bĕnä´fĭkŏ,* a. beneficent, kind.

benemérito, ta, *bĕnĕmä´rĭtŏ,* a. meritorious. [approbation.

beneplácito, –*plä´thĭtŏ,* sm. good-will.

benevolencia, –*vlĕn´thĭä,* sf. benevolence, well-wishing.

benévolo, la, *bĕnä´vŏlŏ,* a. benevolent, favourable, kind-hearted.

benignidad, *bĕnĭgnĭdäd´,* sf. benignity; mildness of the weather. [mild.

benigno, na, *bĕnĭg´nŏ,* a. benign; kind; beodo, da, *bĕŏ´dŏ,* a. drunk, drunken.

berberís, *bĕrbĕrĕs´,* sm. barberry, berberry.

Bercebú, *bĕrthĕbŏ´,* sm. (fam.) the devil.

bergamota, –*gämŏ´tä,* sf. bergamot (sort of pear). [mŏ´tŏ, sm. bergamot-tree.

bergamote, –*gämŏ´tĕ,* bergamoto, –*gä-*

bergante, –*gän´tĕ,* sm. brazen-faced villain, ruffian.

bergantín, –*gäntĭn´,* sm. (mar.) brig.

beril, *bĕrĭl´,* sm. beryl, a precious stone.

berlina, –*lĕ´nä,* sf. landau, berlin.

bermejear, –*mĕhĕär´,* v. n. to incline to red.

bermejizo, za, –*mĕhĕ´thŏ,* a. reddish.

bermejo, ja, –*mĕ´hŏ,* a. crimson.

bermejura, –*mĕhŏ´rä,* sf. crimson.

bermellón, –*mĕlyŏn´,* sm. vermilion.

bernardinas, –*närdĕ´näs,* sf. pl. fanfaronade, false boasts.

bernardo, –*när´dŏ,* sm. Bernardine monk.

berra, *bĕr´rä,* sf. coarse water-cress plant.

berrear, –*rĕär´,* v. n. to low, to bellow.

berrenchín, –*rĕntshĭn´,* sm. crying of angry children. [different colours.

berrendo, da, –*rĕn´dŏ,* a. tinged with two

berrido, –*rĕ´dŏ,* sm. bellowing of a calf.

berrin, –*rĭn´,* sm. child in a violent passion.

berrinche, –rin'tshĕ, sm. anger, passion, sulkiness (applied to children)

berrizal, –rĭthăl', sm. place full of water-cress. [cress.

berro, băr'rŏ, sm. water-cress.

berroqueño, ña, berrŏken'yŏ, a. granite-like; **piedra – a,** granite.

berruga, bĕrrŏ'gă, sf. wart.

berza, –thă, sf. cabbage.

besamanos, bĕsămā'nŏs, sm. kissing of hands; levee; court-day.

besar, bĕsăr', v. a. to kiss; to knock up against one another; **–se,** to knock one's head against another's.

beso, bă'sŏ, sm. kiss; collision of persons on things. [idiot.

beslia, bĕs'tĭă, sf. beast; animal; dunce,

bestiaje, bĕstĭă'h'ĕ, sm. herd of beasts of burden.

bestial, bĕstĭăl', a. bestial, brutal.

bestialidad, –lĭdăd'', sf. bestiality.

besugo, bĕsŏ'gŏ, sm. sea-bream.

besuqueo, bĕsŏkĕ'ŏ, sm. repeated kisses.

betún, bĕtŏn', sm. bitumen.

bezar, bĕthăr', sf. bezoar (stone).

bezo, bă'thŏ, sm. blubber-lip; proud flesh in a wound.

biazas, bĭă'thăs, sf. pl. leather-saddlebags.

Biblia, bĕ'blĭă, sf. Bible.

bíblico, ca, bĕ'blĭkŏ, a. biblical. [worm.

bibliófilo, bĭblĭŏ'fĭlŏ, sm. book-lover, book-

bibliografía, bĭblĭŏgrăfĕ'ă, sf. bibliography. [graphical.

bibliográfico, ca, –grā'fĭkŏ, a. biblio-

bibliógrafo, bĭblĭŏ'grăfŏ, sm. biblio-grapher.

bibliomanía, na, –mănĕ'ă, a. bibliomaniac.

biblioteca, –tă'kă, sf. library.

bibliotecario, –tĕkă'rĭŏ, sm. librarian.

bicoca, bĭkŏ'kă, sf. sentry-box; small borough or village; thing of little value.

bicho, bĭtsh'ŏ, sm. vermin; hop o' my thumb; **mal –,** mischievous urchin.

bichón, bĭtshŏn', sm. lap-dog.

bielda, bĭĕl'dă, sf. pitchfork with six or seven prongs.

bieldar, –dăr', v. a. to winnow corn.

bieldo, bĭĕl'dŏ, **bielgo,** bĭĕl'gŏ, sm. winnowing-fork.

bien, bĭĕn', sm. good, utility, benefit; welfare; **–es,** pl. property, riches, land; –, ad. well, right; very; willingly, heartily; **– que,** although; **– está,** very well.

bienal, bĭĕnăl', a. biennial. [ity, success.

bienandanza, bĭĕnăndăn'thă, sf. prosper-

bienaventurado, da, –ăvĕntŏră'dŏ, a. blessed, happy, fortunate; simple, silly.

bienaventuranza, –ăvĕntŏrăn'thă, sf. beatitude; prosperity; **–s,** pl. the eight beatitudes of heaven mentioned in the Scriptures.

bienestar, –ĕstăr', sm. well-being.

bienhablado, da, –ăblă'dŏ, a. well and civilly spoken.

bienhadado, da, –ădă'dŏ, a. lucky, happy.

bienhecho, cha, –ĕtsh'ŏ, a. well-shaped.

bienhechor, ra, –ĕtshŏr', sm. & f. benefactor.

bienio, bĭĕ'nĭŏ, sm. space of two years.

bienquisto, ta, bĭĕnkĭs'tŏ, a. generally esteemed and beloved.

bienvenida, –vĕn'dă, sf. welcome.

bigamia, bĭgă'mĭă, sf. bigamy.

bígamo, bĕ'gămŏ, sm. bigamist. [tiously.

bigardear, bĭgărdĕăr', v. n. to live licen-

bigardía, –dĕ'ă, sf. dissoluteness; trick, turn, jest. [morals; lubber.

bigardo, bĭgăr'dŏ, sm. friar of loose

bigornia, bĭgŏr'nĭă, sf. anvil.

bigote, bĭgŏ'tĕ, sm. whisker, mustachio; **tener –s,** to be firm and undaunted.

bilioso, sa, bĭlĭŏ'sŏ, a. bilious.

bilis, bĕ'lĭs, sf. bile.

bilorta, bĭlŏr'tă, sm. ring of twisted willow; cricket (among country people).

billar, bĭlyăr', sm. billiards, pl.

billear, bĭlyĕăr', v. a. to make cannons (at billiards).

billero, bĭlyĕ'rŏ, sm. billiard-player.

billete, bĭlyĕ'tĕ, sm. billet, label, esquela; (rail.) ticket, railway-ticket; **– directo,** through-ticket; **– de ida y vuelta,** return-ticket.

bimestre, bĭmĕs'trĕ, a. of two months' duration; **–,** sm. two months leave of absence. [ground for the second time.

binar, bĭnăr', v. a. to plough a piece of

binario, bĭnă'rĭŏ, sm. binary.

binazón, bĭnăthŏn', sf. ploughing.

binóculo, bĭnŏ'kŭlŏ, sm. opera-glass.

biografía, bĭŏgrăfĕ'ă, sf. biography.

biógrafo, bĭŏ'grăfŏ, sm. biographer.

biombo, bĭŏm'bŏ, sm. screen.

bípedo, bĕ'pĕdŏ, sm. biped.

biricú, bĭrĭkŏ', sm. sword-belt.

birla, bĭr'lă, sf. bowl for playing.

birlar, –lăr', v. a. to knock down at one blow (at nine-pins); to dispossess.

birlocha, –lŏtsh'ă, sf. paper-kite.

birlocho, –lŏtsh'ŏ, sm. barouche.

birreta, bĭrrĕ'tă, sf. cardinal's red cap.

birretina, bĭrrĕtĕ'nă, sf. grenadier's cap.

bisabuela, bĭsăbŏĕ'lă, sf. great-grand-mother. [father.

bisabuelo, –săbŏĕ'lŏ, sm. great-grand-

bisagra, –ă'gră, sf. hinge; shoemaker's polisher. [year.

bisiesto, bĭsĭĕs'tŏ, a. bissextile; **año –,** leap-

bisojo, ja, bĭsŏ'h'ŏ, a. squint-eyed.

bisoñada, bĭsŏnyă'dă, **bisoñería,** –yĕrĕ'ă, sf. inconsiderate speech or action.

bisoño, ña, bĭsŏn'yŏ, a. raw, undisciplined; [novice.

bisonte, bĭsŏn'tĕ, sm. bison. [nous.

bitor, bĭtŏr', sm. rail, king of the quails (ave.)

bituminoso, sa, bĭtŭmĭnŏ'sŏ, a. bitumi-

bivac, bĭvăk', sm. (mil.) bivouac.

bivacar, bĭvăkăr', v. a. (mil.) to bivouac.

bizarramente, bĭthărrămĕn'tĕ, ad. courageously, gallantly. [and gallant manner.

bizarrear, –rĕăr', v. n. to act in a spirited

bizarría, –rĕ'ă, sf. gallantry, valour; liberality, generosity.

bizarro, rra, bĭthăr'rŏ, a. brave, gallant; high-spirited; generous.

bizco, ca, bĭth'kŏ, a. squint-eyed,

bizcochero, *bĭthkŏtshā'rŏ*, sm. biscuit-cask; maker or seller of biscuits.

bizcocho, *bĭthkŏtsh'ŏ*, sm. biscuit, sea-biscuit, whiting.

bizma, *bĭth'mä*, sf. cataplasm, poultice.

bizmar, *–mä'r*, v. a. to apply a poultice.

biznieta, *–nĕä'tä*, sf. great-granddaughter.

biznieto, *–nĕä'tŏ*, sm. great-grandson.

bizquear, *–kĕär'*, v. n. to squint.

blanca, *blän'kä*, sf. half a maravedi; (mus.) minim; magpie.

blanco, ca, *–kŏ*, a. white, blank; –, sm. first form, prime (printing); blank, mark (to shoot at); – a ropa, linen, linen-cloth; en –, in vain.

blancura, *blänkŏ'rä*, sf. whiteness; hoariness.

blandear, *bländĕär'*, v. n. to soften; to make one change his opinion; –, v. n. to yield; –se, to sway, to waver.

blandir, *–dĭr'*, v. a. to brandish a sword, lance, &c.; –se, to quiver.

blando, da, *blän'dŏ*, soft, smooth; cotton-like; mellowy; lithe; mild, gentle.

blandón, *–dŏn'*, sm. wax-taper; church-candlestick. [loose, insecure

blanducho, cha, *–dŭtsh'ä*, a. flabby,

blandura, *–dŏ'rä*, sf. softness; daintiness, delicacy; gentleness of temper; mild temperature. [bleacher.

blanqueador, ra, *blänkĕädŏr'*, sm. & f.

blanqueadura, *–dŏ'rä*, sf. bleaching; whitening.

blanquear, *blänkĕär'*, v. a. to bleach; to whitewash; to give coarse wax to bees in winter; –, v. n. to show whiteness.

blanquecer, *–kĕthĕr'*, v. a. to blanch metal.

blanquecino, na, *–thĕ'nŏ*, a. whitish.

blanqueo, *–kĕ'ŏ*, sm. whitening; white-wash.

blanquete, *–kĕ'tĕ*, sm. white rouge.

blanquición, *blänkĭthĭŏn'*, sf. blanching (of metals). [liquid.

blanquimiento, *–mĕĕn'tŏ*, sm. bleaching

blanquizco, ca, *blänkĭth'kŏ*, a. whitish.

blasfemable, *bläsfĕmä'blĕ*, a. blamable.

blasfemador, ra, *–mädŏr'*, sm. & f. blasphemer. [phemously.

blasfemamente, *–mämĕn'tĕ*, ad. blas-

blasfemar, *bläsfĕmär'*, v. n. to blaspheme.

blasfematorio, ria, *bläsfĕmätŏ'rĕŏ*, a. blasphemous. [verbal insult.

blasfemia, *bläsfĕ'mĕä*, sf. blasphemy; gross

blasfemo, ma, *–mŏ*, a. blasphemous; –, sm. blasphemer. [honour, glory.

blasón, *bläsŏn'*, sm. heraldry, blazonry;

blasonador, ra, *bläsŏnädŏr'*, sm. & f. boaster, braggart.

blasonar, *bläsŏnär'*, v. a. to blazon; to blow one's own trumpet.

bledo, *blä'dŏ*, sm. (bot.) wild amaranth; no me importa un –, I don't care a straw.

blonda, *blŏn'dä*, sf. lace; blonde.

blondo, da, *–dŏ*, a. light-haired; fair.

bloquear, *blŏkĕär'*, v. a. to blockade.

bloqueo, *blŏkĕ'ŏ*, sm. blockade. [show.

boato, *bŏä'tŏ*, sm. ostentation, pompous

bobada, *bŏbä'dä*, sf. folly, foolishness.

bobático, ca, *bŏbä'tĭkŏ*, a. silly, stupid.

bobear, *bŏbĕär'*, v. a. to act or talk in a stupid manner; to dally; to loiter about.

bobería, *bŏbĕrĕ'ä*, sf. folly, foolishness.

bobills, *bŏ'bĭlĭs*, ad. de –, without more bobinas, *bŏbĕ'näs*, sf. pl. bobbins. [ado.

bobo, ba, *bŏ'bŏ*, sm. & f. dunce; stage-buffoon; –, ba, a. stupid, silly; large, ample.

boca, *bŏ'kä*, sf. mouth; entrance, opening; mouth of a river; – á –, ad. by word of mouth; á pedir de –, to one's heart's content. [buckram.

bocací, *bŏkäthĕ'*, bocacín, *bŏkäthĕn'*,sm.

bocadillo, *–dĭl'yŏ*, sm. luncheon given to labourers in the field.

bocado, *–kä'dŏ*, sm. morsel, mouthful.

bocaje, *bŏkä'hĕ*, sm. boscage.

bocal, *bŏkäl'*, sm. pitcher; mouth-piece of a trumpet.

bocamanga, *bŏkämän'gä*, sf. sleeve-wrist.

bocanada, *–nä'dä*, sf. mouthful of liquor.

bocarte, *bŏkär'tĕ*, sm. crushing-mill.

bocatejas, *bŏkätĕ'häs*, sf. pl. ridge-tiles.

bocel, *bŏthĕl'*, sm. fluting-plane.

bocina, *bŏthĕ'nä*, sf. bugle-horn; speaking-trumpet.

bocinero, *bŏthĕnĕ'rŏ*, sm. horn-blower.

bocón, *bŏkŏn'*, sm. wide-mouthed person; braggart. [scorching heat; blush.

bochorno, *bŏtshŏr'nŏ*, sm. sultry weather,

bochornoso, sa, *bŏtshŏrnŏ'sŏ*, a. shameful, reproachful.

boda, *bŏ'dä*, sf. nuptials, pl.

bodega, *bŏdĕ'gä*, sf. wine-cellar; growth of wine; warehouse.

bodegón, *bŏdĕgŏn'*, sm. chop-house, eating-house; tippling-house.

bodegonear, *–gŏnĕär'*, v. a. to frequent mean eating-houses. [keeper.

bodegonero, *–gŏnĕ'rŏ*, sm. eating-house

bodigo, *bŏdĕ'gŏ*, sm. small loaf of finest flour.

bodijo, *bŏdĕ'hŏ*, sm. hedge-marriage.

bodoque, *bŏdŏ'kĕ*, sm. pellet; dunce, idiot.

bodoquero, *bŏdŏkĕ'rŏ*, sm. (am.) smuggler.

bodorrio, *bŏdŏr'rĕŏ*, sm. hedge-marriage.

bodrio, *bŏ'drĕŏ*, sm. poor soup made of leavings; hodge-podge.

bofes, *bŏ'fĕs*, sm. pl. lungs, lights.

bofetada, *bŏfĕtä'dä*, sf. slap, box on the ear.

bofetón, *–tŏn'*, sm. box on the ear; folding-doors on the stage.

boga, *bŏ'gä*, sf. ox-eyed cackerel; rowing; rower; estar en –, to be fashionable.

bogada, *bŏgä'dä*, sf. stroke at rowing.

bogador, *–dŏr'*, sm. rower.

bogar, *bŏgär'*, v. n. to row, to paddle.

bohemio, *bŏä'mĕŏ*, sm. short cloak formerly worn by the guard of archers; gipsy.

boj, *bŏh'*, sm. box, box-tree.

boja, *bŏ'hä*, sf. mug-wood, southern-wood.

bojar, *bŏ'här'*, bojear, *bŏ'hĕär'*, v. a. to sail round an island or cape, and measure the coast-line thereof; to scrape off the rough integuments of leather; –, v. n. to measure around. [trees.

bojedal, *bŏ'hĕdäl'*, sf. plantation of box-

bojeo, *bŏ·hắ'ŏ*, sm. circumnavigation; doubling of a cape.

bola, *bŏ'lă*, sf. ball; globe; bolus; game of bowls; (fam.) lie, fib; escurrir la —, to take French leave, to run away.

bolazo, *bŏlä'thŏ*, sm. blow of a bowl.

bolear, *bŏlĕăr'*, v. n. to knock the balls about (billiards); to throw wooden balls for a wager.

boleo, *bŏlĕ'ŏ*, sm. Spanish dance; bowling-green.

bolero, *bŏlĕ'rŏ*, sm. Spanish dancer; runaway child.

boleta, *bŏlĕ'tă*, sf. entrance-ticket; soldier's billet.

boletero, *-tĕ'rŏ*, sm. ticket-collector.

boletin, *-tin'*, sm. warrant given for the payment of money; ticket for the quartering of soldiers; bulletin.

boliche, *bŏlītshĕ*, sm. king-ball at bowls; small fish caught in a drag-net near the shore; drag-net; hole table.

bolichero, *-tshĕ'rŏ*, sm. keeper of a pigeon-hole table.

bolillo, *bŏlīl'yŏ*, sm. small bowl; bobbin; starching-frame; **-s**, pl. starched cuffs worn by counsellors of state; paste-nuts.

bolina, *bŏlĕ'nă*, sf. noise, scuffle; (mar.) bowline; **ir á la —**, to sail on a wind.

bolo, *bŏ'lŏ*, sm. one of the nine-pins; notch-board of a winding-staircase.

bolsa, *bŏl'să*, sf. purse; purse-net; money; exchange; richest vein of gold in a gold-mine.

bolsería, *-sĕrĭ'ă*, sf. purse-manufactory.

bolsillo, *-sīl'yŏ*, sm. pocket; money; fortune; the king's private purse.

bolsista, *-sts'tă*, sm. speculator on change.

bolso, *bŏl'sŏ*, sm. purse of money.

boisor, *bŏīsŏr'*, sm. key-stone.

bollero, *bŏlyĕ'rŏ*, sm. pastry-cook.

bollo, *bŏl'yŏ*, sm. small Spanish cake.

bollón, *bŏlyŏn'*, sm. brass-headed nail.

bollonado, da, *bŏlyŏnă'dŏ*, a. adorned with brass-headed nails.

bomba, *bŏm'bă*, sf. pump; bomb; **dar á la —**, to pump; **— de fuego ó de vaho**, steam-engine; **— de apagar incendios**, fire-engine.

bombarda, *bŏmbăr'dă*, sf. bomb-ketch.

bombardear, *bŏmbărdĕăr'*, v. a. to bombard.

bombardeo, *-dĕ'ŏ*, sm. bombardment.

bombardero, *-dĕ'rŏ*, sm. bombardier.

bombasí, *bŏmbăsĕ'*, sm. bombasine, dimity.

bombazo, *bŏmbă'thŏ*, sm. report of a bursting bomb.

bombo, *bŏm'bŏ*, sm. large drum.

bonachón, *bŏnătshŏn'*, sm. good-natured person.

bonancible, *bŏnănthĕ'blĕ*, a. calm, fair, serene (applied to the weather at sea).

bonanza, *bŏnăn'thă*, sf. fair weather at sea; prosperity; kind.

bonazo, za, *bŏnă'thŏ*, a. good-natured.

bondad, *bŏndăd'*, sf. goodness; suavity; kindness, courtesy; excellence, healthfulness.

bondadoso, sa, *bŏndădŏ'sŏ*, a. bountiful.

bonetada, *bŏnĕtă'dă*, sf. salutation made by raising the hat.

bonete, *bŏnĕ'tĕ*, sm. clerical hat; college-cap; secular clergyman.

bonetería, *bŏnĕtĕrĭ'ă*, sf. hatter.

bonetero, *-tĕ'rŏ*, sm. cap-maker.

bonico, ca, *bŏnĕ'kŏ*, a. pretty good, passable; **andar á las bonicas**, to take things easily.

bonito, ta, *bŏnĕ'tŏ*, a. pretty good, passable; affecting elegance and neatness; graceful, minion; effeminate.

boñiga, *bŏnyĕ'gă*, sf. cow-dung.

boqueada, *bŏkĕă'dă*, sf. act of opening the mouth; **la última —**, the last gasp.

boquear, *-ăr'*, v. n. to gape, to gasp; to breathe one's last; **—**, v. a. to pronounce, to utter a word.

boquera, *bŏkĕ'ră*, sf. sluice in an irrigating canal; eruption at the corners of the mouth; hole.

boquerón, *-kĕrŏn'*, sm. anchovy; large gap, narrow entrance.

boquete, *bŏkĕ'tĕ*, sm. gap, narrow entrance.

boquiabierto, ta, *bŏkĭăbĭĕr'tŏ*, a. with the mouth open; gaping.

boquiancho, cha, *-ăn'tshŏ*, a. wide-mouthed.

boquiangosto, ta, *-ăngŏs'tŏ*, a. narrow-mouthed.

boquiduro, ra, *-dŭ'rŏ*, a. hard-mouthed (of horses); (applied to horses).

boquifresco, ca, *-frĕs'kŏ*, a. fresh-mouthed (of horses).

boquifruncido, da, *-frŭnthĕ'dŏ*, a. having the mouth contracted.

boquihundido, da, *-hŭndĕ'dŏ*, a. having the mouth sunk in from age or want of teeth.

boquilla, *bŏkĕl'yă*, sf. little mouth; mouth-piece of a musical instrument *or* a pipe.

boquirroto, ta, *bŏkĭrrŏ'tŏ*, a. loquacious, garrulous; easily imposed upon.

boquirrubio, bia, *-rŏ'bĭŏ*, a. (fig.) simple, dry-mouthed.

boquiseco, ca, *-sĕk'ŏ*, a. dry-mouthed.

boquituerto, ta, *-tŭĕr'tŏ*, a. wry-mouthed.

borbollar, *bŏrbŏlyăr'*, v. n. to bubble out.

borbollon, *-lyŏn'*, borbotón, *-tŏn'*, sm. bubbling; **á borbollones**, in hurry and confusion; boot.

borcegui, *bŏrthĕgĭ'*, sm. buskin, half-boot.

borda, *bŏr'dă*, sf. (mar.) board; hut.

bordado, *bŏrdă'dŏ*, sm. embroidery.

bordadora, *-dŏ'ră*, sf. embroiderer.

bordadura, *-dŏ'ră*, sf. embroidery.

bordaje, *bŏrdă'hĕ*, sm. side-planks of a ship; anything artistically.

bordar, *bŏrdăr'*, v. a. to embroider; to do.

borde, *bŏr'dĕ*, sm. border; margin; (mar.) board; windward.

bordear, *bŏrdĕăr'*, v. n. (mar.) to ply to windward.

bordo, *bŏr'dŏ*, sm. board of a ship.

bordón, *bŏrdŏn'*, sm. pilgrim's staff; base of a stringed musical instrument.

bordura, *bŏrdŏ'ră*, sf. embroidery.

boreal, *bŏrĕăl'*, a. boreal, northern.

Boreas, *bŏ'rĕăs*, sm. Boreas, north-wind.

borgoña, *bŏrgŏ'nyă*, sf. Burgundy wine.

borla, *bŏr'lă*, sf. tassel; tuft; doctor's bonnet; twist.

bornear, *bŏrnĕăr'*, v. a. to bend, to turn or

borní, *bŏr̄nē'*, sm. merlin, dwarf-falcon.

borona, *bŏr̄ō'nȧ*, sf. millet; maize.

borra, *bŏr̄'r̄ȧ*, sf. yearling ewe; goat's hair; nap raised on cloth by shearers; hairy wool. [wine.

borracha, *bŏr̄r̄ȧtsh'ȧ*, sf. leather-bag for

borrachear, *–tshēār'*, v. n. to be drunk; to get drunk habitually.

borrachera, *–tshā'r̄ȧ*, sf. drunkenness; hard-drinking; revelry; madness.

borrachez, *–tshĕth'*, sf. intoxication.

borracho, cha, *bŏr̄r̄ȧtsh'ō*, a. drunk, intoxicated; inflamed by passion. [tippler.

borrachón, *–tshōn'*, sm. great drinker.

borrachuela, *–tshȧȧ'lȧ*, sf. (bot.)ray-grass.

borrador, *–dŏr'*, sm. foul copy; wastebook, blotting-book.

borraja, *bŏr̄r̄ȧ'h'ȧ*, sf. (bot.) borage.

borrajear, *–hēār'*, v. a. to scribble.

borrar, *bŏr̄r̄ȧr'*, v. a. to blot or efface a writing; to blur; to cloud, to obscure.

borrasca, *bŏr̄r̄ȧs'kȧ*, sf. storm, violent squall of wind; hazard, danger.

borrascoso, sa, *–kō'sō*, a. stormy.

borrasquero, *–kȧ'r̄ō*, sm. reveller.

borregada, *bŏr̄r̄ēgȧ'dȧ*, sf. large flock of sheep or lambs. [simpleton, blockhead.

borrego, ga, *bŏr̄r̄ā'gō*, sm. yearling lamb;

borreguero, *–rēgȧ'r̄ō*, sm. shepherd who tends lambs.

borrén, *bŏr̄r̄ēn'*, sm. panel of a saddle.

borrica, *bŏr̄r̄ē'kȧ*, sf. she-ass, jenny-ass;

borricada, *–kȧ'dȧ*, sf. drove of asses; cavalcade on asses; foolish action.

borrico, *bŏr̄r̄ē'kō*, sm. ass, jack-ass; blockhead. [fruit.

borrilla, *bŏr̄r̄ēl'yȧ*, sf. down or bloom on

borriqueño, ña, *bŏr̄r̄ēkēn'yō*, a. asinine.

borriquero, *–kȧ'r̄ō*, sm. ass-driver.

borro, *bŏr̄'r̄ō*, sm. wether under two years old; dolt.

borrón, *bŏr̄r̄ōn'*, sm. ink-blot, blur; rough draft of a writing; first sketch of a painting; stain, tarnish; unworthy action.

borronear, *–ār'*, v. a. to sketch.

boscaje, *bŏskȧ'h'ē*, sm. boscage; landscape (in painting).

bosque, *bŏs'kē*, sm. forest, grove.

bosquejar, *bŏskē'hȧr'*, v. a. to make a sketch of a painting; to explain a thought rather obscurely; to make a rough model of a figure. [ing; unfinished work.

bosquejo, *bŏskē'h'ō*, sm. sketch of a painting.

bostezar, *bŏstēhȧr'*, v. n. to yawn; to gape.

bostezo, *–thā'thō*, sm. yawn, yawning.

bota, *bō'tȧ*, sf. wine-bag; boat.

botabala, *–bȧ'lȧ*, sf. ramrod, gun-stick.

botador, *–dŏr'*, sm. driver; punch (tool); crow's bill.

botafuego, *–fēȧ'gō*, sm. linstock.

botana, *bŏtȧ'nȧ*, sf. plug, stopple.

botánica, *bŏtȧ'nĭkȧ*, sf. botany.

botánico, ca, *–nĭkō*, a. botanic. [nist.

botánico, *—*, botanista, *–nĭs'tȧ*, sm. botanist.

botar, *bŏtȧr'*, v. a. to cast, to fling, to launch. [person.

botarate, *–rȧ'tē*, sm. mad-cap, blustering

botarga, *bŏtȧr'gȧ*, sf. gaskins; harlequin's costume; harlequin; motley dress of a harlequin; buffoon.

botasilla, *bŏtȧsĭl'yȧ*, sf. (mil.) signal given with a trumpet for the cavalry to saddle.

botavante, *–vȧn'tē*, sm. (mar.) grappling-iron. [boat.

bote, *bō'tē*, sm. thrust with a pike or lance;

botecillo, *–thĭl'yō*, sm. small colour-pan;

botella, *bŏtēl'yȧ*, sf. bottle, flask. [skiff.

botequin, *bŏtēkĭn'*, sm. small boat.

botica, *bŏtē'kȧ*, sf. apothecary's shop.

boticario, *–kȧ'r̄iō*, sm. apothecary.

botiga, *bŏtē'gȧ*, sf. shop.

botija, *bŏtē'h'ȧ*, sf. earthen jar with a short and narrow neck. [little child.

botijo, *–ō*, botijón, *bŏtē'hōn'*, sm. plump child.

botilla, *bŏtĭl'yȧ*, sf. small wine-bag.

botillería, *–yēr̄ē'ȧ*, sf. ice-house.

botillero, *–tĭl'r̄ō*, sm. preparer or seller of iced liquors. [dash; gaiter; booty.

botín, *bŏtĭn'*, sm. buskin, half-boot; spatter-

botinero, *bŏtĭnȧ'r̄ō*, sm. (mil.) booty guard; one who makes or sells gaiters. [chest.

botiquín, *bŏtĭkĭn'*, sm. travelling medicine-

botivoleo, *–vōlā'ō*, sm. catching of a ball at the rebound.

botón, *bŏtōn'*, sm. button; (bot.) bud.

botonadura, *bŏtōnȧdō'r̄ȧ*, sf. set of buttons for a suit of clothes. [a foil.

botonazo, *–nȧ'thō*, sm. thrust given with a button.

botonero, ra, *–nȧ'r̄ō*, sm. & f. button-maker; button-seller.

bóveda, *bō'vēdȧ*, sf. arch, vault; crypt.

boya, *bō'yȧ*, sf. (mar.) buoy; piece of cork fastened to a fishing-net.

boyada, *bōyȧ'dȧ*, sf. drove of oxen.

boyante, *–yȧn'tē*, p. & a. buoyant, floating; sailing well; fortunate, successful.

boyar, *bōyȧr'*, v. n. (fig.) to buoy, to be afloat.

boyardo, *–dō*, sm. boyar.

boyera, *bōyā'r̄ȧ*, boyeriza, *bōyēr̄ē'thȧ*, sf. ox-stall, cow-house.

boyero, *bōyā'r̄ō*, sm. ox-herd.

boyezuelo, *bōyēthȧ̆'lō*, sm. young ox.

boyuno, na, *bōyō'nō*, a. belonging to cattle.

bozal, *bŏthȧl'*, sm. muzzle; –, a. novice, inexperienced in business.

bozo, *bō'thō*, sm. down which precedes the beard; headstall of a horse.

brabante, *brȧbȧn'tē*, sm. Brabant linen.

braceada, *brȧthēȧ'dȧ*, sf. violent movement of the arms. [money.

braceaje, *–ā'h'ē*, sm. coinage; coining of

bracear, *–ār'*, v. n. to swing the arms; –, v. a. (mar.) to brace.

bracero, *brȧthā'r̄ō*, sm. day-labourer; strong-armed man.

bracman, *brȧkmȧn'*, sm. Brahmin.

braco, ca, *brȧ'kō*, a. flat-nosed; –, s. pointer (dog). [breeches.

braga, *brȧ'gȧ*, sf. child's clout; –s, pl.

bragadura, *–dŏr'ȧ*, sf. fork of the body; fork of a pair of breeches.

bragazas, *brȧgȧ'thȧs*, sf.pl. wide breeches; –, sm. one who is easily persuaded.

braguero, *brȧgȧ'r̄ō*, sm. truss, braces.

bragueta, -tā, sf. cod-piece.

braguillas, brāgīl'yās, sm. child breeched for the first time; dwarfish person.

brama, brā'mā, sf. rut.

bramadera, -dā'rā, sf. rattle.

bramadero, -dā'rō, sm. rutting-place.

bramante, brāmān'tē, sm. pack-thread; bramant linen; roaring.

bramar, brāmār', v. n. to roar, to bellow; to storm, to bluster; to be in a passion.

bramido, brāmī'dō, sm. cry uttered by wild beasts; clamour of persons enraged; roaring of the elements.

brancada, brānkā'dā, sf. drag-net, sweep-net.

brasa, brā'sā, sf. live coal; estar hecho unas -s, to be all in a blaze.

brasero, brāsā'rō, sm. brazier.

brasil, brāsīl', sm. Brazil-wood; rouge.

brasilado, da, -lā'dō, a. ruddy.

brasilete, -lā'tē, sm. Jamaica-wood, braziletto.

bravamente, brāvāmēn'tē, ad. bravely, gallantly, cruelly; finely, extremely well.

bravata, brāvā'tā, sf. bravado, boast, braggadocio.

bravear, -vār', v. n. to bully, to hector.

braveador, ra, brāvēādōr', sm. & f. bully.

braveza, brāvā'thā, sf. fury of the elements.

bravío, vía, brāvī'ō, a. ferocious, savage, wild; coarse; -, sm. fierceness, savageness.

bravo, va, brā'vō, a. brave, valiant; bullying; savage, fierce; rude, unpolished; sumptuous; excellent, fine; I—I bravo!

bravura, brāvū'rā, sf. ferocity; courage; bravado, boast.

braza, brā'thā, sf. fathom.

brazada, -thā'dā, sf. extension of the arms; arm-full.

brazado, -thā'dō, sm. arm-full.

brazaje, -thā'hĕ, sm. (mar.) number of fathoms, depth of water.

brazal, brāthāl', sm. bracer (piece of armour); biceps; arm pad of wood or leather (at ball-play).

brazalete, brāthālā'tē, sm. bracelet.

brazo, brā'thō, sm. arm; branch of a tree; valour, strength, power; - & -, man to man; & - partido, locked in each other's arms.

brazuelo, brāthwā'lō, sm. small arm; foreleg of beasts; branch of the mouth-bit of a bridle.

brea, brā'ā, sf. pitch; tar; coarse canvas for wrapping up wares.

brear, brār', v. a. to pitch; to tar; to vex, to plague; to play a joke upon.

brebaje, brābā'hĕ, sm. beverage.

brecha, brātsh'ā, sf. (mil.) breach; impression made upon the mind; batir en —, (mil.) to make a breach; to persecute.

brega, brā'gā, sf. strife, contest; pun, jest, trick.

bregar, brāgār', v. n. to contend, to struggle; to struggle with difficulties; —, v. a. to work up dough on a board with a rolling-pin; full of brakes and brambles.

breña, brān'yā, sf. craggy, broken ground

breñal, brānyāl', breñar, -yār', sm. briars, underwood.

breñoso, sa, -yō'sō, a. craggy and brambled.

brete, brā'tē, sm. fetters, shackles; (fig.) perplexity; difficulties, pl.

bretel, brātĕl', sm. brace (for trowsers).

breva, brā'vā, sf. early-fig; early large acorn.

breval, brāvāl', sm. early fig-tree.

breve, brā'vē, sm. apostolic brief; (mus.) brief; —, a. brief, short; en —, shortly.

brevedad, -dād', sf. brevity, shortness, conciseness.

breviario, brāvīā'rīō, sm. breviary; brevier (small letter used in printing).

brezal, brāthāl', sm. heath.

brezo, brā'thō, sm. (bot.) heath, heather, ling.

briaga, brīā'gā, sf. rope made of bass-weed.

briba, brē'bā, sf. truancy, idleness.

bribón, ona, brībōn', a. vagrant; knavish, rascally.

bribonada, -nā'dā, sf. knavery, mischievous trick.

bribonear, bribōnēār', v. n. to rove; to lead a vagabond's life; beggar's trade.

bribonería, -nērē'ā, sf. life of a vagabond; bricho, brītsh'ō, sm. spangle.

brida, brē'dā, sf. bridle; horsemanship; (fig.) restraint, check, curb.

bridar, -dār', v. a. to bridle; to curb.

brigada, brīgā'dā, sf. brigade.

brigadier, -dīēr', sm. brigadier; diant.

brillador, ra, brīlyādōr', a. brilliant, radiant.

brillante, -yān'tē, a. brilliant; bright, shining; —, sm. brilliant.

brillar, brīlyār', v. n. to shine; to sparkle, to glisten; to outshine in talents or merits.

brillo, brīl'yō, sm. brilliancy, brightness.

brincador, ra, brīnkādōr', sm. & f. jumper, leaper.

brincar, -kār', v. n. to leap, to jump, to gambol; to omit something; to fly into a passion; gambol.

brinco, brīn'kō, sm. leap, jump, bounce;

brindar, brīndār', v. n. to drink one's health, to toast; —, v. a. to invite; to allure.

brindis, brīn'dīs, sm. health, toast.

brío, brē'ō, sm. strength, vigour; spirit, courage; courageously.

briosamente, brīōsāmēn'tē, ad. spiritedly.

brioso, sa, brīō'sō, a. vigorous, full of spirit; courageous, lively.

brisa, brē'sā, sf. breeze.

brisca, brīs'kā, sf. a game at cards.

briscar, -kār', v. a. to embroider with gold or silver twist mixed with silk.

broca, brō'kā, sf. reel for twist; drill; shoemaker's tack.

brocado, brōkā'dō, sm. gold or silver brocade; —, da, a. embroidered, like brocade.

brocal, brōkāl', sm. kerb-stone; metal rim of the scabbard of a sword; and silk.

brocatel, -tĕl', sm. stuff made of hemp

bróculi, brō'kūlī, sm. broccoli.

brocha, brōtsh'ā, sf. painter's brush, pencil.

brochada, -tshā'dā, sf. stroke with a pencil.

brochado, da, -tshā'dō, a. figured (of stuffs); decoration worked into cloth.

brochadura, -tshādō'rā, sf. ornaments or cloth.

broche, brōtsh'ē, sm. clasp; brooch.

brochón, -tshōn', sm. large brush; plasterers' brush; jest.

broma, brō'mā, sf. clatter, noise; joke,

bromear, *-měǎr'*, v. n. to jest; to bore with dull talking. [companion.

bromista, *-mǐs'tǎ*, sm. merry fellow; jolly

bronce, *brǒn'thě*, sm. bronze, brass; (poet.) trumpet.

bronceado, *-thěǎ'dǒ*, sm. bronzing.

broncear, *-thěǎr'*, v. a. to bronze. [ware.

broncería, *-thěrě'ǎ*, sf. brass-works; brass-

broncista, *-thǐs'tǎ*, sm. worker in bronze.

bronco, ca, *brǒn'kǒ*, a. rough, coarse; crusty; crabbed; rude, hoarse; harsh (to the ear). [ners; unmalleability.

bronquedad, *-kědǎd'*, sf. rudeness of man-

broquel, *brǒkěl'*, sm. shield, buckler; (fig.) support, protection; **rajar −es,** to bully, to swagger.

brotadura, *brǒtǎdǒ'rǎ*, sf. budding.

brotar, *brǒtǎr'*, v. n. to bud, to germinate; to gush, to rush out; to break out, to appear (applied to the small-pox, &c.).

broza, *brǒ'thǎ*, sf. bark; vegetable rubbish; brush-wood; farrago; printer's brush.

brozar, *brǒthǎr'*, v. a. to brush type.

brucero, *brǔthě'rǒ*, sm. brush-maker.

bruces, *brǒ'thěs*, sf. pl. lips; **á −, de −,** face downwards.

brueta, *brǔě'tǎ*, sf. wheel-barrow.

bruja, *brǒ'hǎ*, sf. witch, hag. [craft.

brujear, *-hěǎr'*, v. n. to practise witch-

brujería, *-hěrě'ǎ*, sf. witchcraft.

brujidor, *brǔhǐdǒr'*, sm. glaziers' nippers.

brujir, *-hǐr'*, v. a. to pare off the corners and edges of panes of glass.

brujo, *brǒ'hǒ*, sm. sorcerer.

brújula, *brǒ'hǔlǎ*, sf. sea-compass.

brujulear, *-hǔlěǎr'*, v. a. to turn up one card after another; to discover by deduction; to conjecture.

brujuleo, *-hǔlě'ǒ*, sm. exposure of cards (at card games); close examination; con-

brulote, *brǔlǒ'tě*, sm. fire-ship. [jecture.

bruma, *brǔ'mǎ*, sf. (mar.) haziness.

brumal, *brǔmǎl'*, a. wintry.

brunella, *brǔněl'ǎ*, sf. prunello.

bruñido, *brǔnyǐ'dǒ*, sm. polish, burnish.

bruñidor, *-yǐdǒr'*, sm. burnisher (person and instrument). [to put on rouge.

bruñir, *-yǐr'*, v. a. to burnish; to polish;

bruñola, *-yǒ'lǎ*, sf. prunello. [ward.

brusco, ca, *brǔs'kǒ*, a. rude, peevish, for-

brutal, *brǔtǎl'*, a. brutal, brutish; − sm. brute, rude person. [brutal action.

brutalidad, *brǔtǎlǐdǎd'*, sf. brutality;

bruto, *brǒ'tǒ*, sm. brute; rude, immoral person; **−, ta,** a. coarse, unpolished, in a rough state. [children into silence.

bu, *bǒ*, sm. word used by nurses to frighten

buba, *bǒ'bǎ*, sf. pustule; **−s,** pl. venereal disease. [the venereal disease.

bubático, ca, *bǔbǎ'tǐkǒ*, a. infected with

bubón, *bǔbǒn'*, sm. large morbid tumour, full of matter. [pustules.

buboso, sa, *bǔbǒ'sǒ*, a. afflicted with

bucear, *bǔthěǎr'*, v. n. to dive.

buceo, *bǔthě'ǒ*, sm. diving. [to a hound).

bucero, *bǔthě'rǒ*, a. black-nosed (applied

bucle, *bǒ'klě*, sm. curl. [(fam.) food.

bucólica, *bǔkǒ'lǐkǎ*, sf. pastoral poetry;

buchada, *bǔtshǎ'dǎ*, sf. draught or mouthful of liquor.

buche, *bǔtshě'*, sm. craw, crop, stomach of quadrupeds; mouthful; sucking ass; pucker or crease in clothes; (fig.) girl's bosom.

buchete, *bǔtshě'tě*, sm. blown-out cheek.

buen, *bǒěn'*, a. good. [modiously.

buenamente, *bǒěnǎměn'tě*, ad. easily, com-

buenaventura, *-věntǒ'rǎ*, sf. fortune, good luck.

bueno, na, *bǒě'nǒ*, a. good, perfect; fair, plain; fit, proper; sociable, agreeable; strong; sound, healthy; useful; **¿ de dónde −?** where do you come from? **de buenas á buenas,** freely, willingly; **−,** ad. enough, sufficiently; **− está,** enough, no more. [subsistence.

buenpasar, *bǒěnpǎsǎr'*, sm. comfortable

buey, *bǒě'ǐ*, sm. ox, bullock.

¡ buf ! *bǔf*, pooh, pooh !

bufa, *bǒ'fǎ*, sf. jeer, scoff, taunt, mock.

búfala, *bǒ'fǎlǎ*, sf. female buffalo.

bufalino, na, *bǔfǎlǐ'nǒ*, a. belonging to

búfalo, *bǒ'fǎlǒ*, sm. buffalo. [buffaloes.

bufar, *bǔfǎr'*, v. n. to choke with anger; to huff; to snort.

bufete, *bǔfě'tě*, sm. desk, writing-table.

bufido, *bǔfǐ'dǒ*, sm. blowing of an animal; snorting of a horse; huff.

bufo, *bǒ'fǒ*, sm. buffoon on the stage; **−, fa,** a. comic; **ópera −a,** sf. comic opera.

bufón, *bǔfǒn'*, sm. buffoon, merry Andrew; jester; **−, ona,** a. funny, comical.

bufonada, *-nǎ'dǎ*, sf. buffoonery; raillery, sarcastic taunt. [make fun of.

bufonearse, *-něǎr'sě*, v. r. to jest, to

bufonería, *-něrě'ǎ*, sf. buffoonery.

buhera, *bǔě'rǎ*, sf. embrasure, loop-hole.

buhero, *-rǒ*, sm. owl-keeper.

buho, *bǒ'ǒ*, sm. owl; an unsocial man.

buhonería, *bǔǒněrě'ǎ*, sf. pedlar's box.

buhonero, *-ně'rǒ*, sm. pedlar, hawker.

buitre, *bǔě'trě*, sm. vulture.

buitrero, *bǔǐtrě'rǒ*, sm. vulture-fowler; **−, ra,** a. vulturine.

bujarrón, *bǔhǎrrǒn'*, sm. Sodomite.

bujería, *bǔhěrě'ǎ*, sf. gewgaw, bauble, knick-knack. [perfume-box.

bujeta, *bǔhě'tǎ*, sf. box made of box-wood;

bujía, *bǔhě'ǎ*, sf. wax-candle.

bula, *bǒ'lǎ*, sf. papal bull.

bulbo, *bǔl'bǒ*, sm. (bot.) bulb.

bulboso, sa, *bǔlbǒ'sǒ*, a. bulbous.

bulero, *bǔlě'rǒ*, sm. one who is charged with distributing bulls of crusades, and collecting the alms of charity given for

buleto, *-tǒ*, sm. apostolic letter. [them.

bulto, *bǔl'tǒ*, sm. bulk; tumour, swelling; bust; luggage; (am.) baggage; **−s á la mano,** pl. (rail.) small luggage; **á −,** indistinctly, confusedly; **en −,** by the lump.

bulla, *bǔl'yǎ*, sf. confused noise, clatter; crowd; **meter −,** to make a noise.

bullaje, *bǔlyǎ'hě*, sm. crowd.

bullanguero, *bǔlyǎngǎ'rǒ*, sm. rioter.

bullebulle, *bǔlyěbǔl'yě*, sm. busy body.

bullicio, *bŭlyĕ́thĭŏ,* sm. bustle; tumult, uproar.

bullicioso, sa, *–thĕ́ŏsŏ,* a. lively, restless, noisy, clamorous, busy; turbulent; boisterous.

bullidor, ra, *bŭlyĭdŏr,* a. noisy, turbulent.

bullir, *bŭlyĭr,* v.n. to boil; (fig.) to bustle, to fluster; –, v. a. to manage a business.

bullón, *bŭlyŏn,* sm. making of a decoction; dyeing-mixture.

buñolero, ra, *bŭnyŏlĕ́rŏ,* sm. & f. maker or seller of buns. [fritter.

buñuelo, *bŭnyŭĕ́lŏ,* sm. bun; pan-cake,

buque, *bŏ́kĕ,* sm. bulk, capacity of a ship; hull of a ship; vessel, ship.

burdel, *bŭrdĕl,* sm. brothel.

burdo, da, *bŭr'dŏ,* a. coarse (of stuffs).

bureo, *bŏrĕ́ŏ,* sm. amusement, diversion.

burocracia, *bŭrĕŏkrắthĭă,* sf. bureaucracy.

burocrático, *–krắtĭkŏ,* a. bureaucratic.

burga, *bŭr'gă,* sf. thermal waters, pl.

burgomaestre, *bŭrgŏmăĕs'trĕ,* sm. burgomaster. [master.

buril, *bŭrĭl,* sm. burine, graver. [master.

burilada, *bŭrĭlắdă,* sf. stroke of a burine.

buriladura, *–dŏ́ră,* sf. engraving.

burilar, *bŭrĭlăr,* v. a. to engrave.

burla, *bŭr'lă,* sf. scoff, mockery, sneer; trick, slight deceit; hoax; **de –s,** in jest.

burlar, *bŭrlăr,* v. a. to mock, to scoff; to hoax, to abuse, to play tricks, to deceive; to frustrate; **–se,** to jest, to laugh at.

burlesco, ca, *–lĕs'kŏ,* a. burlesque, comical, funny. [ad. de –, in jest.

burlicas, *bŭrlĭkăs,* **burlitas,** *bŭrlĭ'tăs,*

burlón, ona, *bŭrlŏn',* sm. & f. great wag, joker. [Jack-pudding.

burra, *bŭr'ră,* sf. she-ass.

burrada, *bŭrrắdă,* sf. drove of asses; stupid action. [fuel.

burrajo, *–rắh'ŏ,* sm. dry stable-dung for

burrero, *bŭrrĕ́rŏ,* sm. ass-keeper who sells asses' milk.

burro, *bŭr'rŏ,* sm. ass, donkey; stupid fellow; jack, saw-horse. [olives.

burujo, *bŭrŭh'ŏ,* sm. dregs of pressed

busca, *bŭs'kă,* sf. search, examination.

buscada, *bŭskắdă,* sf. research, inquiry.

buscador, ra, *–dŏr,* sm. & f. searcher, investigator.

buscapiés, *–pĭĕ́,* sm. (fig.) feeler.

buscapiés, *–,* sm. crackers (fireworks).

buscar, *bŭskăr,* v. a. to seek, to search; to look for or after; to hunt after.

buscarruidos, *bŭskărrŭ́ĕ dŏs,* sm. quarrelsome fellow. [spy, busybody.

buscavidas, *–vĕ́dăs,* sm. prying person,

buscón, *bŭskŏn',* sm. searcher; cheat, pilferer, petty robber.

busilis, *bŭsĕ́lĭs,* sm. point in question; main point of an argument.

busola, *bŭsŏ́lă,* sf. sea-compass.

busto, *bŭs'tŏ,* sm. bust.

butifarra, *bŭtĭfăr'ră,* sf. sausage made in Catalonia; gaskins. [or pay respect to.

buz, *bŭth,* sm. **hacer el –,** to do homage

buzo, *bŏ́thŏ,* sm. diver.

buzón, *bŭthŏn',* sm. conduit, canal; letter-box; post-box (am.); cover of a cistern, pond, jar, &c.

C.

cabal, *kăbăl',* a. just, exact; perfect, complete, accomplished. [intrigue.

cábala, *kắbălă,* sf. cabala (mystical science)

cabalgada, *kăbălgắdă,* sf. horseback excursion; cavalcade; (mil.) foray.

cabalgador, *–dŏr,* sm. rider; horseman.

cabalgadura, *–dŏ́ră,* sf. sumpter-mule, sumpter-horse, beast of burden.

cabalgar, *kăbălgăr,* v. n. to parade on horseback; to take part in a cavalcade; to spring to horse.

cabalista, *kăbălĭs'tă,* sm. cabalist.

cabalístico, ca, *–lĭs'tĭkŏ,* a. cabalistic.

caballa, *kăbăl'yă,* sf. horse-mackerel (fish).

caballaje, *–lyă'h'ĕ,* sm. place where mares and she-asses are served by stallions; money paid for that service.

caballar, *–lyăr,* a. belonging to or resembling horses.

caballejo, *–lyĕ́h'ŏ,* sm. trave, wooden frame for shoeing unruly horses.

caballerear, *–lyĕrĕăr,* v. n. to set up for a gentleman. [chivalrous.

caballeresco, ca, *–lyĕrĕs'kŏ,* a. knightly,

caballerete, *–lyĕrắtĕ,* sm. spruce young gentleman.

caballería, *–lyĕrĭ́ă,* sf. cavalry; cavalry-horse; chivalry; knighthood; knight-errantry.

caballeriza, *–lyĕrĭ́thă,* sf. stable; number of horses, mules, &c. standing in a stable.

caballerizo, *–lyĕrĭ́thŏ,* sm. head-groom of a stable.

caballero, *–lyĕrŏ,* sm. knight; cavalier; gentleman; rider; horseman; horse-soldier; **– andante,** knight-errant.

caballeroso, sa, *–lyĕrŏ́sŏ,* a. noble, gentlemanlike. [polished gentleman.

caballerote, *–lyĕrắtĕ,* sm. graceless, un-

caballete, *–lyă'tĕ,* sm. ridge of a house forming an acute angle; horse (instrument of torture); painter's easel; hemp-brake; trestle. [ing-horse.

caballico, *–lyă'kŏ,* sm. hobby-horse, rock-

caballo, *kăbăl'yŏ,* sm. horse; (at chess) knight; **á –,** on horseback. [torture.

caballote, *–lyŏ'tĕ,* sm. wooden horse (for

caballuno, na, *–lyŏ́nŏ,* a. belonging to a horse.

cabaña, *kăbăn'yă,* sf. shepherd's hut, cottage; hovel; flock of ewes; drove of asses for carrying corn; line drawn on a billiard-table, within which the players must play.

cabañal, *kăbănyăl',* sm. mule or sheep track (of travelling or migratory herds).

cabañero, *–yă'rŏ,* a. belonging to the droves of travelling mules and asses.

cabañil, *–yĭl',* sm. keeper of asses for carrying corn.

cabecear, *kăbăthăăr,* v. n. to nod with sleep; to shake one's head; (mar.) to pitch.

cabeceo, *–thă'ŏ,* sm. nod, shaking of the head. [bed-pillow; vignette.

cabecera, *–thă'ră,* sf. upper end of a hall;

cabecilla, _–thǐl'yǎ,_ sm. ringleader.

cabecita, _–thǐ'ǎ,_ sf. wrong-headed person.

cabellera, _kǎbělyǎ'rǎ,_ sf. long hair spread over the shoulders; wig; tail of a comet.

cabello, _kǎbĕl'yŏ,_ sm. hair of the head.

cabelludo, da, _–lyŏ'dŏ,_ a. hairy, overgrown with hair. [contain; to include.

caber, _kǎběr',_ v. a. & n. to comprehend; to

cabestraje, _kǎběstrǎ'h'ā,_ sm. halter; bridle-money; money paid to a driver for conducting cattle to market.

cabestrar, _–trǎr',_ v. a. to halter; _–,_ v. n. to fowl with a stalking-ox.

cabestrear, _–trěǎr',_ v. n. to be led easily by the halter.

cabestrillo, _–trǐl'yŏ,_ sm. sling, splint; necklace; gold chain.

cabestro, _kǎběs'trŏ,_ sm. halter; bell-ox.

cabeza, _kǎbā'thǎ,_ sf. head; top; end; chief; leader; beginning of a thing.

cabezada, _kǎbāthǎ'dǎ,_ sf. head-shake; head-stall of a bridle; head-band of a book; instep of a boot. [post of a door.

cabezal, _–thǎl',_ sm. pillow; compress;

cabezo, _kǎbā'thŏ,_ sm. summit of a hill.

cabezón, _–thŏn',_ sm. collar of a shirt; opening in a garment for the passage of the head; nose-band. [tioned head.

cabezorro, _–thŏr'rŏ,_ sm. large disproportioned head.

cabezudo, da, _–thŏ'dŏ,_ a. large-headed; thick-headed; head-strong, obstinate.

cabezuela, _–thwā'lǎ,_ sf. small head; simpleton; coarse flour; rose-bud.

cabida, _kǎbē'dǎ,_ sf. content, capacity; **tener – con una persona,** to be in high favour with one.

cabildada, _kǎbǐldǎ'dǎ,_ sf. hasty, illgrounded resolution of a chapter or council.

cabildo, _kǎbǐl'dŏ,_ sm. chapter of a cathedral or collegiate church); meeting of a chapter; corporation of a town.

cabizbajo, ja, _kǎbǐthbǎ'h'ŏ,_ **cabizcaído, da,** _–kǎ-ē'dŏ,_ a. crestfallen; pensive; thoughtful. [hypocritical.

cabiztuerto, ta, _–tūěr'tŏ,_ a. wry-headed;

cable, _kǎ'blě,_ sm. (mar.) cable.

cabo, _kǎ'bŏ,_ sm. extremity; cape, head-land.

cabotaje, _–tǎ'h'ā,_ sm. coasting-trade; pilot-

cabra, _kǎ'brǎ,_ sf. goat. [age.

cabrahigo, _–hē'gŏ,_ sm. wild fig-tree.

cabrería, _kǎbrěrē'ǎ,_ sf. place where goats' milk is sold.

cabrero, _kǎbrā'rŏ,_ sm. goat-herd. [stan.

cabrestante, _kǎbrěstǎn'tā,_ sm. (mar.) cap-

cabrilla, _kǎbrǐl'yǎ,_ sf. prawn; _–s,_ pl. Pleiades (constellation); heat-marks on the legs. [chevron.

cabrio, _kǎ'brǐŏ,_ sm. rafter, roof-spar;

cabrío, _kǎbrē'ŏ,_ sm. flock of goats.

cabriola, _kǎbrǐŏ'lǎ,_ sf. caper; gambol.

cabriol(e)ar, _–l(ě)ǎr',_ v. n. to cut capers; to curvet.

cabriolé, _–lā',_ sm. cabriolet, gig.

cabrita, _kǎbrē'tǎ,_ sf. small female kid; kid-skin. [seller of kid-skins.

cabritero, _kǎbrǐtā'rŏ,_ sm. dealer in kids;

cabritilla, _kǎbrǐtǐl'yǎ,_ sf. dressed kid-skin.

cabrito, _kǎbrē'tŏ,_ sm. kid.

cabrón, _kǎbrŏn',_ sm. buck, he-goat; one who consents to the adultery of his wife.

cabronada, _–ǎ'dǎ,_ sf. infamous action which a man permits against his own honour. [tutes his own wife.

cabronazo, _–ǎ'thŏ,_ sm. one who prosti-

cabroncillo, _–thǐl'yŏ,_ sm. easy husband.

cabruno, na, _kǎbrŏ'nŏ,_ a. goatish.

cacahual, _kǎkǎhwǎl',_ **cacaotal,** _kǎkǎŏtǎl',_ sm. plantation of chocolate-trees.

cacao, _kǎkǎ'ŏ,_ sm. (bot.) smooth-leaved chocolate nut-tree; cocoa.

cacareador, ra, _kǎkǎrěǎdŏr',_ sm. & f. crowing cock; cackling hen; cackler; braggart. [to brag, to boast.

cacarear, _–rěǎr',_ v. n. to crow, to cackle;

cacareo, _–rā'ŏ,_ sm. crowing of a cock, cackling of a hen; boast, brag.

cacera, _kǎthā'rǎ,_ sf. canal, channel, conduit.

cacería, _kǎthěrē'ǎ,_ sf. hunting-party.

cacerina, _–rē'nǎ,_ sf. cartridge-box.

cacerola, _–rŏ'lǎ,_ sf. stewing-pan.

caceta, _kǎthā'tǎ,_ sf. small pan used by apothecaries.

cacique, _kǎthē'kě,_ sm. Cazique (prince or nobleman among the Indians).

caco, _kǎ'kŏ,_ sm. pickpocket; coward.

cacofonía, _–fŏnē'ǎ,_ sf. harsh unharmonious sound.

cacha, _kǎtsh'ǎ,_ sf. handle of a knife.

cachalote, _–lŏ'tā,_ sm. sperm-whale.

cachamarín, _–mǎrēn',_ sm. (mar.) lugger.

cachar, _kǎtshǎr',_ v. a. to break in pieces.

cacharpalla, _kǎtshǎrpǎl'yǎ,_ sf. (am.) farewell-dinner.

cacharro, _kǎtshǎr'rŏ,_ sm. coarse earthen pot; sherd. [ness.

cachaza, _kǎtshǎ'thǎ,_ sf. inactivity, tardi-

cachemira, _kǎtshěmē'rǎ,_ sf. cashmere.

cachera, _kǎtshā'rǎ,_ sf. coarse, shaggy cloth. [the fist.

cachete, _kǎtshā'tā,_ sm. check; blow with

cachetero, _–tā'rŏ,_ sm. short, broad, sharp-pointed knife; bull-fighter who kills the bulls with the cachetero.

cachetudo, da, _–tŏ'dŏ,_ a. chubby-cheeked.

cachicán, _kǎtshǐkǎn',_ sm. farm-overseer.

cachidiablo, _–dǐǎ'blŏ,_ sm. hobgoblin.

cachigordete, _–gŏrdā'tā,_ a. thick and dumpy. [short.

cachiporra, _–pŏr'rǎ,_ sf. cudgel.

cachivache, _–vǎtsh'ā,_ sm. broken crockery-ware, old trumpery; despicable fellow.

cacho, _kǎtsh'ŏ,_ sm. slice, piece (applied to lemons, oranges, &c.); game of chance at cards. [(of female beasts).

cachonda, _kǎtshŏn'dǎ,_ a. ruttish, proud

cachorrillo, _kǎtshŏrrǐl'yŏ,_ sm. pocket-pistol.

cachorro, ra, _kǎtshŏr'rŏ,_ sm. & f. grown whelp or puppy; cub (of any animal).

cachucha, _kǎtshǔtsh'ǎ,_ sf. Spanish dance and its tune.

cachuela, _kǎtshwā'lǎ,_ sf. fricassee made of the livers and lights of rabbits.

cachupín, _kǎtshǔpēn',_ sm. Spanish settler in America.

cada, _kǎ'dǎ,_ pn. every; every one; **each.**

cadalso, _kǎdǎl'sŏ,_ sm. scaffold.

cadarzo, *kādär'thŏ*, sm. floss-silk.
cadáver, *kādä'vĕr*, sm. corpse, cadaver.
cadavérico, ca, *kādävä'rïkŏ*, a. cadaverous.
cadena, *kādē'nä*, sf. chain; series, link.
cadencia, *kādĕn'thïä*, sf. cadence.
cadente, *—tĕ*, a. declining; harmonious, mellifluous (of declamation).
cadera, *kādē'rä*, sf. hip.
caderillas, *kādĕrïl'yäs*, sf. pl. crinoline.
cadete, *kādē'tĕ*, sm. (mil.) cadet.
caducar, *kādūkär'*, v. n. to dote; to lapse (of a legacy, etc.).
caduceo, *kādūthē'ŏ*, sm. caduceus; herald's staff.
caducidad, *kādūthïdäd'*, sf. caducity; decrepitude.
caduco, ca, *kādū'kŏ*, a. worn out; enfeebled by age, decrepit; perishable; mal —, sm. epilepsy.
caedizo, za, *kāēdï'thŏ*, a. tottering, frail.
caedura, *—dū'rä*, sf. loose threads dropping from the loom in weaving.
caer, *kāer'*, v. n. to fall; to tumble down; to lapse; to befall, to happen, to come to pass; to die.
café, *kāfē'*, sm. coffee-tree; coffee; coffee-house.
cafetera, *kāfētē'rä*, sf. coffee-pot.
cafetero, *—rŏ*, sm. coffee-tree; coffee-house keeper, coffee-man.
cáfila, *kā'fïlä*, sm. multitude of people, animals or other things; caravan.
cafre, *kā'frĕ*, a. savage, inhuman; rude, uncivil.
cagaflerro, *kägäfïer'rŏ*, sm. scoria, dross of iron.
cagajón, *—hŏn'*, sm. horse-dung.
cagalar, *—lär'*, sm. rectum.
cagalera, *—lē'rä*, sf. looseness, diarrhœa.
cagarruta, *—rrŏ'tä*, sf. dung of sheep, goats and mice.
cagatinta, *—tïn'tä*, sm. term of contempt for attorney's clerks.
cagón, ona, *kägŏn'*, sm. & f. person afflicted with diarrhœa; cowardly person.
cahiz, *kāïth'*, sm. measure of corn (about 12 English bushels).
cahizada, *kāïthä'dä*, sf. tract of land which requires about one cahiz of grain to be properly sown.
caída, *kāï'dä*, sf. fall, falling; declivity; descent.
caídos, *—dŏs*, sm. pl. rents due but unpaid; arrears of taxes.
caimán, *kāïmän'*, sm. caiman, alligator; cunning man.
caimiento, *—mïen'tŏ*, sm. low spirits; languidness; fall.
caja, *kā'hä*, sf. box, case, coffin; chest in which money is kept; libro de —, cash-book.
cajero, *kāhē'rŏ*, sm. cashier, cash-keeper.
cajeta, *kāhē'tä*, sf. snuff-box; poor-box.
cajetín, *kāhētïn'*, sm. very small box.
cajista, *kāhïs'tä*, sm. compositor, composer.
cajón, *kāhŏn'*, sm. chest of drawers; locker; book-case.
cal, *kāl*, sf. burnt lime-stone; — viva, quick lime.
cala, *kā'lä*, sf. creek, small bay; small piece of melon, &c.; hole made in a wall to judge of its thickness.

calabacera, *—bāthä'rä*, sf. pumpkin.
calabacero, *—bāthä'rŏ*, sm. retailer of pumpkins. [tender pumpkin.
calabacín, *—bāthïn'*, sm. small, young.
calabacino, *—bāthä'nŏ*, sm. wine-gourd.
calabaza, *—bä'thä*, sf. pumpkin or gourd; — vinatera, bottle-calabash. [head.
calabazada, *—bāthä'dä*, sf. blow with the calabazate, *—bāthä'tĕ*, sm. preserved pumpkin.
calabozo, *—bŏ'thŏ*, sm. dungeon. [kin.
calada, *kālä'dä*, sf. rapid flight of birds of prey. [wood or linen.
calado, *kālä'dŏ*, sm. open work in metal, calador, *—dŏr'*, sm. probe (surgeon's instrument).
calafate, *—fä'tĕ*, sm. (mar.) calker.
calafatear, *—fätēär'*, v. a. (mar.) to calk.
calafateo, *—fätē'ŏ*, sm. (mar.) calking.
calafatería, *—fätērï'ä*, sf. (mar.) calking.
calambre, *käläm'brĕ*, sm. spasm, cramp.
calamidad, *kälämïdäd'*, sf. misfortune, calamity, misery. [fortunate.
calamitoso, sa, *—tŏ'sŏ*, a. calamitous, uncálamo, *kä'lämŏ*, sm. (bot.) sweet flag; pen; shepherd's flute; currente —, offhand. [be somewhat fuddled.
calamocano, *—kä'nŏ*, a. estar ó ir —, to calandrajo, *käländrä'hŏ*, sm. rag hanging down from a garment; ragamuffin.
calandria, *kälän'drïä*, sf. calendar-lark.
calaña, *kälän'yä*, sf. character, quality.
calar, *kälär'*, v. a. to penetrate, to pierce; to discover a design; to put, to place; — las cubas, to gage a barrel; —se, to introduce one's self; to insinuate one's self into; to stoop. [fellow.
calavera, *kälävä'rä*, sf. skull; hot-brained calaverada, *—värä'dä*, sf. ridiculous, foolish action.
calaverear, *—vērēär'*, v. n. to act foolishly.
calcañar, *kälkänyär'*, sm. heel-bone.
calcar, *kälkär'*, v. a. to counter-draw; to trample on.
calcáreo, rea, *kälkä'rēŏ*, a. calcareous.
calce, *käl'thĕ*, sm. tire of a wheel.
calceta, *kälthē'tä*, sf. under-stocking.
calcetería, *—tērē'ä*, sf. trade of a hosier.
calcetero, ra, *—tē'rŏ*, sm. one who makes, mends or sells thread-stockings; knitter.
calcillas, *kälthïl'yäs*, sm. little coward.
calcina, *kälthē'nä*, sf. mortar.
calcinar, *kälthïnär'*, v. a. to calcine.
calco, *käl'kŏ*, sm. counter-drawing.
calcografía, *—grä'fï'ä*, sf. art of engraving.
calculable, *kälkülä'blĕ*, a. calculable.
calculación, *—läthïŏn'*, sf. calculation, computation. [puter.
calculador, *—lädŏr'*, sm. calculator, comcalcular, *—lär'*, v. a. to calculate, to reckon, to compute.
cálculo, *käl'külŏ*, sm. calcule, calculation, computation; (med.) gravel.
calda, *käl'dä*, sf. warmth, heat; warming or heating; —s, pl. hot baths.
caldear, *käldēär'*, v. a. to weld iron; to warm, to heat.
caldera, *käldē'rä*, sf. caldron, kettle, boiler; las —s de Pero Botero, (fam.) hell.

calderada, -rä´dä, sf. a caldron-full.

calderería, -rēr´ä, sf. brazier's shop.

calderero, -rä´rõ, sm. brazier, copper-smith.

caldereta, -rä´tä, sf. small caldron; — de agua bendita, holy-water fount.

calderilla, -rīl´yä, sf. holy water fount; copper-coin. [dron.

caldero, käl´dõ, sm. bucket-shaped cal-

calderón, käldãrõn´, sm. copper, large caldron; paragraph; (mus.) fermata-sign.

calderuela, käldãrä´lä, sf. dark lantern (used by sportsmen to drive partridges into the net). [liquors.

caldo, käl´dõ, sm. broth; -s, pl. spirituous

caldoso, sa, käldõ´sõ, a. having too much broth or gravy. [day of every month.

calendas, kälōn´däs, sf. pl. calends, first

calendario, -dä´riõ, sm. almanac, calendar. [large, clumsy watch.

calentador, -tädõr´, sm. warming-pan;

calentar, -tär´, v. a. to warm; to heat; to be ruttish or proud (of beasts); -se, to grow hot, to dispute warmly.

calentura, kälōntõ´rä, sf. fever.

calenturiento, ta, -tūrīōn´tõ, a. fever-ish; fever-sick.

calera, kälã´rä, sf. lime-kiln.

calería, -rä´ä, sf. lime-kiln.

calero, kälã´rõ, sm. lime-burner.

calesa, kälã´ä, sf. calash, cab. [cabman.

calesero, kälãsã´rõ, sm. driver of a calash.

calesín, kälãsín´, sm. single horse-chaise.

caletre, kälã´trã, sm. understanding, judg-ment, discernment. [kind.

calibre, kälē´brã, sm. calibre; (fig.) sort,

calidad, kälīdäd´, sf. quality, condition, character; kind.

cálido, da, kä´līdõ, a. hot, calid.

caliente, kälīōn´tã, a. hot, calid; fiery, ve-hemently; en —, on the spot, immediately.

califa, kälē´fä, sm. caliph.

califato, -fä´tõ, sm. caliphate.

calificación, kälīfīkäthõn´, sf. qualifica-tion; judgment, censure; proof.

calificar, -fīkär´, v. a. to qualify; to au-thorise; to attest; to ennoble; -se, to prove one's noble birth.

caligrafía, kälīgräfē´ä, sf. calligraphy.

calígrafo, kälē´gräfõ, sm. one who writes a beautiful hand.

cáliz, kä´līth, sm. chalice; flower-cup.

calizo, za, kälē´thõ, a. calcareous. [sea.

calma, käl´mä, sf. calm; calmness, smooth

calmante, kälmän´tã, sm. (med.) anodyne.

calmar, kälmär´, v. a. to calm, to quiet, to pacify; -, v. n. to be becalmed.

calmoso, sa, kälmõ´sõ, a. calm; tranquil.

calofriarse, kälõfrīär´sã, v. r. to shiver with cold.

calofrío, -frē´õ, sm. shivering with cold.

calor, kälõr´, sm. heat, hotness, ardour, fieriness.

calórico, kälõ´rīkõ, sm. caloric.

calumnia, kälũm´nīä, sf. calumny.

calumniador, ra, -nīädõr´, sm. & f. ca-lumniator, slanderer. [to slander.

calumniar, -nīär´, v. a. to calumniate.

calumnioso, sa, -nīõ´sõ, a. calumnious, slanderous. [lively.

caluroso, sa, kälũrõ´sõ, a. warm, hot;

calva, käl´vä, sf. bald pate; a children's game played with stones. [calva).

calvar, kälvär´, v. a. to hit a stone (at

calvario, kälvä´riõ, sm. Calvary; (fig.) debts. [(of the whole head).

calvatrueno, kälvätrũã´nõ, sm. baldness

calvicie, kälvē´thē, sf. baldness.

calvinismo, kälvīnīs´mõ, sm. Calvinism.

calvinista, -nīs´tä, sm. Calvinist.

calvo, va, käl´võ, a. bald; barren. [pl.

calza, käl´thä, sf. trousers, pl.; stockings,

calzada, kälthä´dä, sf. causeway, highway.

calzado, -dõ, sm. any kind of shoe or foot-covering.

calzador, kälthädõr´, sm. shoeing-horn.

calzadura, kälthädũ´rä, sf. putting on of shoes; felloe of a cart-wheel.

calzar, kälthär´, v. a. to put on shoes; to strengthen with iron or wood; to stop a wheel; to carry a ball of a certain size (of fire-arms).

calzón, kälthõn´, sm. breeches, pl.

calzonazo, kälthõnä´thõ, sm. big pair of breeches; es un —, he is a weak fellow.

calzoncillos, -thīl´yõs, sm. pl. drawers.

calla callando, käl´yä kälyän´dõ, ad. pri-vately, secretly.

callada, kälyä´dä, sf. dish of tripe; de —, á las -s, ad. without noise, privately.

callado, da, -yä´dõ, a. silent, reserved, noiseless. [voice; silently.

callandico, -kälyändē´kõ, ad. in a low

callar, kälyär´, v. n. to keep silence, to be silent, to hold one's tongue; to conceal, to hush.

calle, käl´yã, sf. street; lane; alley; 1—1 strange! wonderful!; mightily!

callear, kälyãär´, v. a. to clear the walks in a vineyard of loose branches.

calleja, kälyã´hä, sf. lane, narrow passage.

callejear, -hãär´, v. a. to loiter about the streets. [bling.

callejero, ra, -hã´rõ, a. loitering, ram-

callejón, -hõn´, sm. narrow pass.

callejuela, -´hũã´lä, sf. lane, narrow pas-sage; subterfuge, shift. [pl. tripe.

callo, käl´yõ, sm. corn; wen; callus; -s,

callosidad, kälyõsīdäd´, sf. callosity.

calloso, sa, kälyõ´sõ, a. callous; horny.

cama, kä´mä, sf. bed, couch; litter; hacer la —, to make up the bed.

camachuelo, -tshũã´lõ, sm. linnet.

camada, kämä´dä, sf. brood of young ani-mals; de ladrones, nest of rogues.

camafeo, -fã´õ, sm. cameo.

camal, kämäl´, sm. halter.

camaleón, kämälãõn´, sm. chameleon.

camaleopardo, kämälãõpär´dõ, sm. came-leopard.

camamila, kämämē´lä, sf. camomile.

camándula, kämän´dũlä, sf. rosary of one or three decades.

camandulería, kämändũlãr´ä, sf. hypo-crisy, insincerity, dissimulation.

camandulero, *–lā′rŏ*, a. full of tricks, hypocritical.

cámara, *kăm′ără*, sf. hall; chamber; [king's court.

camarada, *–rä′dă*, sm. comrade, companion.

camaranchón, *–răntshŏn′*, sm. garret.

camarera, *–rā′ră*, sf. head waiting-maid in great houses.

camarero, *–rā′rŏ*, sm. valet de chambre.

camariento, ta, *–rĭen′tŏ*, a. troubled with diarrhœa. [advisers of the king.

camarilla, *–rĭl′yă*, sf. coterie of private

camarín, *–rĭn′*, sm. shrine behind an altar where the images are kept with their ornaments; closet.

camarista, *–rĭs′tă*, sm. a member of the supreme council of **la Cámara**; –, sf. maid of honour of the queen of Spain.

camarlengo, *kămărlĕn′gŏ*, sm. lord of the bed-chamber of the king.

camarote, *kămărŏ′tĕ*, sm. berth, cabin.

camasquince, *kămăskĭn′thĕ*, sm. nickname jocularly applied to a meddlesome person. [low.

camastrón, *kămăstrŏn′*, sm. cunning fellow.

cambalache, *kămbălă′tshĕ*, sm. traffic by exchange, barter.

cambalachear, *–tshĕăr′*, v. a. to barter.

cambalachero, *–tshă′rŏ*, sm. barterer.

cambiable, *kămbiă′blĕ*, a. fit to be exchanged.

cambiar, *kămbiăr′*, v. a. to barter, to exchange; to change; to alter; to give or take money on bills.

cambija, *kămbĭ′hă*, sf. basin of water.

cambio, *kăm′bĭŏ*, sm. barter, exchange; course of exchange; bank; alteration, change.

cambista, *kămbĭs′tă*, sm. banker.

cambray, *kămbrăĭ′*, sm. cambric, fine linen. [horn.

cambrón, *kămbrŏn′*, sm. common buck-

cambronal, *–năl′*, sm. thicket of briers, brambles and thorns.

cambronera, *–nŏ′ră*, sf. box-thorn.

camella, *kămĕl′yă*, sf. she-camel; milk-pail. [camels.

camellero, *kămĕlyă′rŏ*, sm. driver of

camello, *kămĕl′yŏ*, sm. camel.

camellón, *kămĕlyŏn′*, sm. ridge turned up by the plough; flower-bed.

camilla, *kămĭl′yă*, sf. pallet; bed for women after child-birth; clothes-horse.

caminador, *kămĭnădŏr′*, sm. good walker.

caminante, *–năn′tĕ*, sm. traveller, walker.

caminar, *–năr′*, v. n. to travel; to walk, to march.

caminata, *–nă′tă*, sf. long walk.

camino, *kămĕ′nŏ*, sm. highroad; way; – **real**, highway; **de –**, in one's way, going along.

camisa, *kămĕ′să*, sf. shirt; shift, chemise.

camisola, *kămĭsŏ′lă*, sf. ruffled shirt.

camisolín, *kămĭsŏlĭn′*, sm. shirt-front.

camisote, *kămĭsŏ′tĕ*, sm. coat of mail.

camorra, *kămŏr′ră*, sf. quarrel, dispute.

camorrista, *kămŏrrĭs′tă*, sm. & f. quarrelsome person.

campamento, *kămpămĕn′tŏ*, sm. (mil.) encampment, camp, lager.

campana, *kămpă′nă*, sf. bell; **– de chimenea**, funnel of a chimney.

campanada, *–nă′dă*, sf. sound of a bell; (fig.) scandal.

campanario, *–rĭ′ŏ*, sm. belfry.

campanear, *–nĕăr′*, v. a. to ring the bell frequently; to divulge.

campanela, *kămpănā′lă*, sf. rapid rotation upon one foot in a Spanish dance.

campaneo, *–nā′ŏ*, sm. bell-ringing, chime; affected manner of walking.

campanero, *–nā′rŏ*, sm. bell-founder; bell-man. [uvula.

campanilla, *kămpănĭl′yă*, sf. hand-bell.

campanillazo, *–lyă′thŏ*, sm. signal given with a bell. [small bell often.

campanillear, *–lyĕăr′*, v. a. to ring a

campante, *kămpăn′tĕ*, p. & a. excelling, surpassing.

campanudo, da, *kămpănŏ′dŏ*, a. wide, puffed up; pompous, high-sounding.

campánula, *kămpă′nŭlă*, sf. bell-flower.

campaña, *kămpă′nyă*, sf. campaign, level country; (mil.) campaign.

campar, *kămpăr′*, v.n. to encamp; to excel.

campeador, *kămpĕădŏr′*, sm. warrior; surname of the Cid.

campear, *kămpĕăr′*, v. n. to be in the field; to frisk about in the fields; to excel.

campeche, *kămpĕtsh′ĕ*, sm. Campeachy-wood, camwood.

campeón, *kămpĕŏn′*, sm. champion.

campesino, na, *kămpĕsĕ′nŏ*, **campestre**, *kămpĕs′trĕ*, a. rural. [land, campaign.

campiña, *kămpĭn′yă*, sf. flat tract of arable

campo, *kăm′pŏ*, sm. country; field; camp;

camuesa, *kămŭĕ′să*, sf. pippin. [ground.

camueso, *–sŏ*, sm. pippin-tree; simpleton.

can, *kăn′*, sm. dog; (poet.) dog-star.

cana, *kă′nă*, sf. measure (= two ells); **–s**, pl. grey hair; **peinar –s**, to grow old.

canal, *kănăl′*, sm. channel, canal.

canalizar, *kănălĭthăr′*, v. a. to canalise.

canalizo, *kănălĕ′thŏ*, sm. narrow channel, strait.

canalón, *kănălŏn′*, sm. large gutter.

canalla, *kănăl′yă*, sf. mob, rabble; populace. [lace.

canana, *kănă′nă*, sf. cartridge-box.

canapé, *kănăpĕ′*, sf. canopy, sofa.

canario, *kănă′rĭŏ*, sm. canary-bird.

canasta, *kănăs′tă*, sf. basket, hamper.

canastilla, *kănăstĭl′yă*, sf. small basket.

canasto, *kănăs′tŏ*, sm. large basket.

cancamusa, *kănkămŏ′să*, sf. trick, fraud.

cancel, *kănthĕl′*, sm. screen (at church-doors); royal box in the castle-church.

cancelación, *kănthĕlăthĭŏn′*, sf. cancellation, erasion.

canceladura, *–dŏ′ră*, sf. cancellation, erasion.

cancelar, *–lăr′*, v. a. to cancel, to expunge; to efface from the memory.

cancelaría, *–lără′ă*, sf. papal chancery, place where grants and licences are expedited.

cancelario, *–lă′rĭŏ*, sm. chancellor.

cáncer, *kăn′thĕr*, sm. cancer (ulcer).

Cáncer, —, sm. Cancer, Crab (sign of the zodiac). [flicted with a cancer.
cancerarse, *kánthĕrár sĕ*, v. r. to be af-
canceroso, sa, *kánthĕrō sŏ*, a. cancerous.
canciller, *kánthĭlyĕr'*, sm. chancellor.
canción, *kánthĕón'*, sf. song.
cancionero, *kánthĕŏnĕ'rŏ*, sm. song-book.
candado, *kándá dŏ*, sm. padlock.
candela, *kándā'lā*, sf. candle.
candelabro, *kándĕlá'brŏ*, sm. candlestick.
Candelaria, *—lā'rĭä*, sf. Candlemas.
candelero, *—lĕ'rŏ*, sm. candlestick; chan-delier. [brails.
candelizas, *kándĕlē'thás*, sf. pl. (mar.)
candente, *kándĕn'tĕ*, a. red-hot.
candidato, *kándĭdá'tŏ*, sm. candidate.
cándido, da, *kán'dĭdŏ*, a. white, snowy; candid; simple. [lamp.
candil, *kándĭl'*, sm. kitchen- or stable-
candilada, *kándĭlá dá*, sf. oil or grease spot.
candileja, *kándĭlē'há*, sf. (bot.) willow.
candonga, *kándŏn'gá*, sf. servile civility (intended to deceive); old mule no longer fit for service. [ing.
candongo, ga, *—dŏn'gŏ*, a. cajoling, fawn-
candonguear, *—gĕár'*, v.a. to jeer, to sneer.
candor, *kándŏr'*, sm. candour, ingenuous-ness. [ness.
canela, *kánĕ'lä*, sf. cinnamon.
canelo, *kánĕ'lŏ*, sm. cinnamon-tree.
canelón, *kánĕlŏn'*, sm. icicle (hanging from the eaves); sugar-stick with a slice of cin-namon. [sail.
cangreja, *kángrĕ'há*, sf. brig-sail, gaff-
cangrejo, *—ŏ*, sm. craw-fish, crab.
cangrena, *kángrá'ná*, sf. gangrene.
cangrenarse, *—nár'sĕ*, v. r. to be afflicted with gangrene.
cangrenoso, sa, *—nŏ'sŏ*, a. gangrenous.
canguro, *kángŭ'rŏ*, sm. kangaroo.
canibal, *kánĭ'bäl*, sm. cannibal, man-eater.
canicula, *kánĭ kŭlä*, sf. dog-days.
canijo, ja, *kánĭ'k'ŏ*, a. weak, sickly.
canilla, *kánĭl'yä*, sf. shin-bone; tap of a cask; spool.
caninez, *kánĭnĕth'*, sf. canine appetite.
canino, na, *kánĭ'nŏ*, a. canine; **hambre —a,** sf. canine appetite.
caniquí, *kánĭkĭ'*, sf. fine muslin (from the East Indies). [prisoners of war.
canje, *kán'hĕ*, sm. (mil.) exchange of
canjear, *kán'hĕár'*, v. a. (mil.) to exchange prisoners of war.
canjilón, *kán'hĭlŏn'*, sm. earthen pitcher.
cano, na, *kä'nŏ*, a. hoary, gray-headed
canoa, *kánŏ'ä*, sf. canoe. [canoe.
canoero, *kánŏĕ'rŏ*, sm. one who steers a
canon, *kä'nŏn*, sm. canon; catalogue, list; canon, a large sort of type; (mus.) canon; **—es,** pl. canonical law.
canonesa, *kánŏnĕ'sä*, sf. canoness.
canongia, *kánŏn'hĕ'ä*, sf. canonry; **canonicato,** *kánŏntká'tŏ*, sm. canonry; canonicate.
canónico, ca, *kánŏ'nĭkŏ*, a. canonical.
canónigo, *—nĭgŏ*, sm. canon, prebendary.
canonista, *—nĭs'tä*, sm. canonist.
canonización, *kánŏnĭtháthĭŏn'*, sf. cano-nisation.

canonizar, *—thär'*, v. a. to canonise.
canoro, ra, *kánŏ'rŏ*, a. canorous, tuneful.
canoso, sa, *kánŏ'sŏ*, a. hoary, gray-headed.
cansado, da, *kánsá'dŏ*, a. weary, wearied, tired; tedious, tiresome. [fatigue.
cansancio, *kánsán'thŏ*, sm. lassitude,
cansar, *kánsár'*, v. a. to weary, to fatigue; to harass, to molest; **—se,** to grow weary.
cantable, *kántá blĕ*, a. tunable.
cantada, *—dä*, sf. (mus.) cantata.
cantaleta, *—lĕ'tä*, sf. pun, jest, joke.
cantar, *kántár'*, sm. song; **—es,** pl. Solo-mon's Song; —, v. a. to sing; to creak; (at cards) to call out the score.
cántara, *kän'tärä*, sf. pitcher; wine-measure (containing about 32 pints). [cantharis.
cantárida, *kántá'rĭdä*, sf. Spanish fly.
cantarín, *kántárĭn'*, sm. opera-singer; fellow who is always singing.
cantarina, *—rē'nä*, sf. opera-singer.
cántaro, *kán'tärŏ*, sm. pitcher; ballot-box; **llover á —s,** to rain heavily, to pour.
cantatriz, *kántátrĭth'*, sf. songstress.
cantera, *kántĕ'rä*, sf. quarry.
cantería, *—rē'ä*, sf. trade of a stone-cutter.
cantero, *kántĕ'rŏ*, sm. stone-cutter.
cántico, *kán'tĭkŏ*, sm. canticle; **— de los —s,** the song of Solomon.
cantidad, *—ĭdád'*, sf. quantity; number.
cantimplora, *—tĭmplŏ'rä*, sf. syphon; vessel for cooling liquors.
cantina, *—tē'nä*, sf. cellar; canteen.
cantinela, *—tĭnĕ'lä*, sf. short song; irk; some repetition of a subject.
cantinero, *—nĕ'rŏ*, sm. butler.
cantizal, *—tĭthál'*, sm. stony ground.
canto, *kän'tŏ*, sm. stone; singing; edge; canto (poet.).
cantón, *kántŏn'*, sm. corner; canton.
cantonearse, *kántŏnĕár'sĕ*, v. r. to walk affectedly.
cantonera, *kántŏnĕ'rä*, sf. corner-clips.
cantor, ra, *kántŏr'*, sm. & f. singer; song-stress. [stones.
cantorral, *kántŏrrál'*, sm. place full of
canturia, *kántŭr'ĕ'ä*, sf. vocal music.
canutillo, *kánŭtĭl'yŏ*, sm. stalk of a straw.
caña, *kän'yä*, sf. cane, reed; stalk; — dulce, sugar-cane.
cañada, *kányá'dä*, sf. dale (between two mountains); sheep-walk.
cañal, *kányál'*, sm. pond-grate; fish-garth.
cañamar, *kányámár'*, sm. hemp-field.
cañamiel, *—mĭĕl'*, sf. sugar-cane. [cloth.
cañamo, *kän'yámŏ*, sm. hemp; hempen
cañamón, *—mŏn'*, sm. hemp-seed.
cañavera, *—vĕ'rä*, sf. common reed-grass.
cañaveral, *—vĕrál'*, sm. reed-plot, reed-bank.
cañazo, *kányá'thŏ*, sm. blow with a cane.
cañería, *kányĕrĕ'ä*, sf. conduit of water, water-pipe. [limbed (of horses).
cañilavado, da, *kányĭlává'dŏ*, a. small
cañiza, *kányĕ'zä*, sf. kind of coarse linen.
cañizo, *—thŏ*, sm. hurdle.
caño, *kän'yŏ*, sm. tube, pipe; sewer.
cañón, *kányŏn'*, sm. tube, pipe; cannon.

cañonazo, –*nã̃′thõ*, sm. cannon-shot.

cañonear, –*neãr′*, v. a. to cannonade.

cañoneo, –*nã′õ*, sm. cannonade.

cañonera, –*nõ′rã*, sf. embrasure.

cañonería, –*rẽ′ã*, sf. pipes of an organ.

cañutillo, *kãnyŭtĭl′yõ*, sm. bugle (small glass tubes). [phalange ; pipe, tube.

cañuto, *kãnỹŭ′tõ*, sm. internode of a cane.

caoba, *kã̃õ′pã*, sf. mahogany-tree.

caos, *kã′õs*, sm. chaos ; confusion.

capa, *kã′pã*, sf. cloak ; mantle ; layer, stratum ; cover ; pretext ; **de — y gorra,** in a plain manner.

capacidad, –*thĭdãd′*, sf. capacity ; extent ; talent.

capachero, –*tʃhã′rõ*, sm. basket-maker.

capacho, *kãpãtʃh′õ*, sm. hamper ; frail ; bricklayer's-hod ; barn-owl.

capada, *kãpã′dã*, sf. anything portable in a person's cloak. [whistle.

capador, –*dõr′*, sm. sow-gelder ; gelder's

capadura, –*dõ′rã*, sf. castration, gelding.

capar, *kãpãr′*, v. a. to geld ; (fig.) to castrate, to curtail.

caparazón, *kãpãrãthõn′*, sm. caparison.

caparra, *kãpã′rã*, sf. earnest-money.

caparrosa, *kãpãrrõ′sã*, s. copperas.

capataz, *kãpãtãth′*, sm. overseer ; warden of the mint.

capaz, *kãpãth′*, a. capacious, capable, spacious, roomy ; fit, apt ; ingenious, clever.

capazo, *kãpã′thõ*, sm. rush-basket, frail.

capcionar, *kãpthĭõnãr′*, v. a. to seize, to arrest.

capcioso, sa, *kãpthĭõ′sõ*, a. captious.

capeador, *kãpẽãdõr′*, sm. a cloak-stealer.

capear, *kãpẽãr′*, v. a. to rob a passenger of his cloak ; to flourish one's cloak before a bull ; –, v. n. (mar.) to try or lay to.

capelo, *kãpẽ′lõ*, sm. dues received in ancient times by bishops from their clergy ; red hat (of a cardinal). [shoe.

capellada, *kãpẽlyã′dã*, sf. toe-piece of a

capellán, *kãpẽlyãn′*, sm. chaplain ; almoner.

capellanía, *kãpẽlyãnẽ′ã*, sf. chaplainship.

capellar, *kãpẽlyãr′*, sm. moorish cloak.

capellina, *kãpẽlyẽ′nã*, sf. (mil.) spike-helmet ; hood worn by country-people.

capeo, *kãpẽ′õ*, sm. challenging of a bull with a cloak.

capero, *kãpẽ′rõ*, sm. priest who carries the cope or pluvial in churches.

caperuza, –*rõõ′thã*, sf. hood.

capialzado, *kãpĭãlthã′dõ*, a sloping on the outside and indented on the inside.

capiello, *kãpĭẽl′yõ*, sm. biggin.

capigorrista, *kãpĭgõrrĭs′tã*, capigorrón, –*gõrrõn′*, sm. vagabond ; parasite.

capilar, *kãpĭlãr′*, a. capillary.

capilla, *kãpĭl′yã*, sf. hood ; cowl ; chapel.

capilleja, *kãpĭlyẽ′hã*, sf. small chapel.

capillejo, –*õ*, sm. small hood ; skein of silk for sewing. [warden.

capiller(o), –*lyẽ′r(õ)*, sm. sexton, church-

capillo, *kãpĭl′yõ*, sm. child's cap ; hood of a hawk. [a monk's cowl.

zapilludo, da, *kãpĭlyõ′dõ*, a. resembling

capirotada, *kãpĭrõtã′dã*, sf. American paste made up of herbs, eggs, garlic and

capirotazo, –*tã′thõ*, sm. fillip. [spice.

capirote, *kãpĭrõ′tẽ*, sm. hood.

capisayo, *kãpĭsã′yõ*, sm. garment which serves both as a cloak and riding-coat.

capiscol, *kãpĭskõl′*, sm. precentor.

capitación, *kãpĭtãthõn′*, sf. poll-tax.

capital, *kãpĭtãl′*, sm. stock ; sum of money put out at interest ; fortune of a husband at the time of his marriage ; capital-stock of a merchant ; –, sf. capital, metropolis ; –, a. capital ; principal.

capitalista, *kãpĭtãlĭs′tã*, sm. capitalist.

capitalizar, *kãpĭtãlĭthãr′*, v. a. to capitalize.

capitán, *kãpĭtãn′*, sm. captain. [talize.

capitana, –*tã′nã*, sf. admiral's ship.

capitanazo, –*nã′thõ*, sm. able general.

capitanear, *kãpĭtãnẽãr′*, v. a. to have the command in chief of an army ; to head a troop of people. [captainry.

capitanía, *kãpĭtãnẽ′ã*, sf. captainship.

capitel, *kãpĭtẽl′*, sm. spire over the dome of a church ; capital (of a column).

capitolio, *kãpĭtõ′lĭõ*, sm. capitol.

capitón, *kãpĭtõn′*, sm. pollard, chub.

capítula, *kãpẽ′tŭlã*, sf. part of the prayers read at divine service.

capitulación, *kãpĭtŭlãthõn′*, sf. capitulation ; agreement ; **—ones,** pl. matrimonial contract.

capitular, –*lãr′*, v. a. to conclude an agreement ; (mil.) to capitulate ; to accuse by public authority ; –, v. n. to sing prayers at divine service ; –, sm. capitular ; –, a. capitulary. [antiphoner.

capitulario, *kãpĭtŭlã′rĭõ*, sm. antiphonal.

capítulo, *kãpẽ′tŭlõ*, sm. chapter of a cathedral ; assembly of the prelates of religious orders ; chapter (section of a book).

capolar, *kãpõlãr′*, v. a. to mince ; to behead.

capón, *kãpõn′*, sm. eunuch ; gelding ; capon ; anchor-stopper.

caponar, *kãpõnãr′*, v. a. to geld ; to curtail ; to tie up vine-branches.

caponera, *kãpõnẽ′rã*, sf. coop (for capons).

caporal, *kãpõrãl′*, sm. chief, ringleader ; (mil.) corporal. [thistle.

capota, *kãpõ′tã*, sf. head of the fuller's

capote, –*tẽ*, sm. rain-cloak ; austere look or mien.

capotillo, *kãpõtĭl′yõ*, sm. mantelet.

capotón, *kãpõtõn′*, sm. large wide coat.

capotudo, da, *kãpõtõ′dõ*, a. frowning.

capricornio, *kãprĭkõr′nĭõ*, sm. wood-bob, wood-beetle ; cuckold. [the zodiac).

Capricornio, —, sm. Capricorn (sign of

capricho, *kãprĭtʃh′õ*, sm. caprice, whim, fancy ; (mus.) irregular but pleasing composition. [whimsical ; obstinate.

caprichoso, sa, *kãprĭtʃh′õsõ*, a. capricious,

caprichudo, da, –*tʃhõ′dõ*, a. stubborn, capricious.

caprino, na, *kãprẽ′nõ*, a. goatish.

cápsula, *kãp′sŭlã*, sf. (bot.) capsule.

capsular, –*lãr′*, a. capsular, capsulary.

captar, *kãptãr′*, v. a. to captivate.

captura, *kăpto͞o'ră,* sf. capture, seizure.

capucha, *kăpŭtsh'ă,* sf. circumflex; cap, fur-cap, cowl hood of a woman's cloak; monk's hood.

capuchina, *kăpŭtshĕ'nă,* sf. Capuchin nun; (bot.) great Indian cress.

capuchino, *—tshĕ'no,* sm. Capuchin monk; **na,** a. appertaining to Capuchin friars or nuns.

capucho, *kăpŭtsh'o,* sm. cowl or hood forming part of a monk's dress.

capullo, *kăpŭl'yo,* sm. pod of a silk-worm; rose-bud; coarse stuff made of spun silk.

cara, *kă'ră,* sf. face, visage; á —, face to face.

carabina, *kărăbĕ'nă,* sf. carbine, carabine.

carabinero, *—bĕnĕ'ro,* sm. carabinier.

cárabo, *kă'răbo,* sm. horned owl; earth-beetle; chub.   [case.

caracol, *kărăkŏl',* sm. snail; winding stair-case.

caracolear, *—kŏlĕăr',* v. n. to caracole.

carácter, *kărăk'tĕr,* sm. character; quality; condition; hand-writing.   [acteristical.

característico, ca, *—kĕrĕs'tĭkŏ,* a. a char-

caracterizar, *kărăktĕrĭthăr',* v. a. to characterize.

caramanchón, *kărămăntshŏn',* sm. garret.

carámbano, *kărăm'băno,* sm. icicle; flake of ice.   [billiards); trick.

carambola, *kărămbŏ'lă,* sf. cannon (at

carambolear, *—bŏlĕăr',* v. n. to cannon (at billiards).

caramelo, *kărămĕ'lo,* sm. caramel.

caramente, *—mĕn'tĕ,* ad. dearly.

caramillo, *—mĭl'yo,* sm. small flute; tale-carrying.   [mask.

carantamaula, *kărăntămă'ŭlă,* sf. hideous

carantoña, *kărăntŏn'yă,* sf. hideous mask; vulgar old woman who paints and dresses stylishly or gaudily; —s, pl. caresses.

carantoñero, *kărăntŏnyĕ'ro,* sm. wheedler, cajoler.   [histrionic art.

carátula, *kără'tŭlă,* sf. pasteboard-mask.

caratulero, *—tŭlĕ'ro,* sm. dealer in masks.

caravana, *kărăvă'nă,* sf. caravan.

caravanera, *—vănĕ'ră,* sf. caravansary.

caray, *kără'ĭ,* sm. tortoise-shell.

carbón, *kărbŏn',* sm. charcoal.

carbonada, *kărbŏnă'dă,* sf. grillade; kind of pancake.

carboncillo, *—thĭl'yo,* sm. charcoal-pencil.

carbonear, *—nĕăr',* v. n. to make coal out of wood.

carbonera, *—nĕ'ră,* sf. coal-pit, coal-mine.

carbonería, *—nĕrĕ'ă,* sf. coal-yard; coal-shed; coal-mine.   [collier.

carbonero, *—nĕ'ro,* sm. charcoal-burner;

carbónico, ca, *kărbŏ'nĭkŏ,* a. carbonic.

carbonilla, *kărbŏnĭl'yă,* sf. coal-dust.

carbonizar, *kărbŏnĭthăr',* v. a. to carbonise.

carbono, *kărbŏ'no,* sm. (chem.) carbon.

carbunclo, *kărbŭn'klŏ,* carbunco, *kăr-bŭn'kŏ,* sm. carbuncle; red pustule.

carcaj, *kărkăh',* sm. quiver.

carcajada, *kărkăhă'dă,* sf. horse-laugh.

carcamal, *kărkămăl',* sm. nick-name for old people.

carcaño, *kărkăn'yo,* sm. heel-bone; screw clamp, vice.

cárcel, *kăr'thĕl,* sf. prison; gaol, jail.

carcelaje, *—lă'hĕ,* sm. prison-fees.

carcelería, *—lĕrĕ'ă,* sf. imprisonment.

carcelero, *—lĕ'ro,* sm. jailor.

cárcola, *kăr'kŏlă,* sf. treadle.

carcoma, *kărkŏ'mă,* sf. wood-louse; dust made by the wood-louse; grief; anxious concern.

carcomer, *—mĕr',* v. a. to gnaw, to corrode; -se, to grow worm-eaten.

carcomido, da, *—mĕ'dŏ,* a. worm-eaten.

carda, *kăr'dă,* sf. teazel, teasel; card; severe reprimand, wigging, jobation.

cardador, *—dŏr',* sm. carder, comber.

cardadura, *—dŏ'ră,* sf. carding.

cardar, *—dăr',* v. a. to card wool; to raise the wool on cloth with a teasel.

cardenal, *kărdĕnăl',* sm. cardinal; Virginian nightingale; livid tumour.

cardenalato, *—lă'tŏ,* sm. cardinalate.

cardenalicio, cia, *—lĕ'thĭŏ,* a. belonging to a cardinal.   [comb.

cardencha, *kărdĕn'tshă,* sf. teasel; card,

cardenillo, *kărdĕnĭl'yo,* sm. rust of copper; verdigris.

cárdeno, na, *kăr'dĕnŏ,* a. livid.

cardero, *kărdĕ'ro,* sm. card-maker.

cardico, *kărdĕ'kŏ,* sm. small thistle.

cardillo, *kărdĭl'yŏ,* sm. golden thistle.

cardinal, *kărdĭnăl',* a. cardinal, principal.

cardo, *kăr'dŏ,* sm. thistle.

cardón, *kărdŏn',* sm. (bot.) teasel.

carducha, *kărdŭtsh'ă,* sf. large iron comb for combing wool.

carduzador, *kărdŭthădŏr',* sm. carder.

carduzar, *—thăr',* v. a. to card or comb wool.

carear, *kărĕăr',* v. a. to confront criminals; to compare; to tend a drove of cattle; -se, to assemble for business.

carecer, *kărĕthĕr',* v. n. to want.

carena, *kărĕ'nă,* sf. careening; careen; ship.

carenar, *—năr',* v. a. to careen a ship.

careo, *kărĕ'o,* sm. (law) confrontation.

carero, ra, *kărĕ'ro,* a. in the habit of selling things dear.

carestía, *kărĕstĕ'ă,* sf. scarcity; want; famine; dearness.

careta, *kărĕ'tă,* sf. pasteboard-mask.

careto, ta, *—tŏ,* a. blazed (applied to horses).

carga, *kăr'gă,* sf. load, freight, pack; cargo; charge (of a fire-arm); impost, tax; (fig.) burden of the mind, heaviness.

cargadas, *kărgă'dăs,* sf. pl. a game at cards.

cargadero, *—dĕ'ro,* sm. loading-place.

cargadilla, *—dĭl'yă,* sf. increase of a debt newly contracted.   [rammer.

cargador, *—dŏr',* sm. freighter; loader;

cargamento, *—mĕn'tŏ,* sm. (mar.) cargo.

cargar, *kărgăr',* v. a. to load, to burden, to freight; to attack the enemy; to charge a gun; to clog; to impose taxes; to impeach.   [heaviness of the head.

cargazón, *kărgăthŏn',* sf. cargo (of a ship);

cargo, *kär´gŏ,* sm. burden, loading; employment, dignity; office; charge; care; obligation; accusation. [dize.

carguío, *kärgē´ŏ,* sm. cargo of merchandise.

cariaguileño, ña, *kärïägïlēn´yŏ,* a. long-faced and crook-nosed.

carialegre, *–älē´grĕ,* a. pleased-looking.

cariampollado, *–ämpŏlyä´dŏ,* a. round-faced. [chubby.

cariancho, cha, *–än´tshŏ,* a. broad-faced.

cariarse, *kärïär´sĕ,* v. r. to grow carious.

caribe, *kär´bĕ,* sm. cannibal.

caricatura, *kärïkätŏ´rä,* sf. caricature.

caricia, *kär´thïä,* sf. caress. [ing.

caricioso, sa, *–thïŏ´sŏ,* a. fondling, caress-

caricuerdo, da, *–kŭēr´dŏ,* a. having a composed look. [alms, pl.

caridad, *–däd´,* sf. charity; benevolence;

caridoliente, *–dŏlïen´tĕ,* a. sad-faced.

caries, *kä´rïĕs,* sf. caries, cariosity.

cariescrito, *kärïĕskrï´tŏ,* a. corrugated, shrivelled. [a wrinkled face.

carifruncido, da, *–frŭnthï´dŏ,* a. having

carigordo, da, *–gŏr´dŏ,* a. full-faced.

carilargo, ga, *–lär´gŏ,* a. long-visaged.

carilucio, cia, *–lŏ´thïŏ,* a. smooth-faced.

carilla, *kärïl´yä,* sf. little face; mask used by bee-keepers.

carilleno, na, *kärïlyē´nŏ,* a. full-faced.

carinegro, gra, *kärïnē´grŏ,* a. swarthy-complexioned. [endearing manner.

cariño, *kärïn´yŏ,* sm. fondness, tenderness;

cariñoso, sa, *–yŏ´sŏ,* a. affectionate, endearing; loving.

cariota, *kärïŏ´tä,* sf. wild carrot.

carirraído, da, *–rä´ï´dŏ,* a. brazen-faced, impudent. [faced.

carirredondo, da, *–rēdŏn´dŏ,* a. round-

carita, *kärï´tä,* sf. lovely face of a woman.

caritativo, va, *–tätï´vŏ,* a. charitable.

carlán, *kärlän´,* sm. justice of the peace, J.P.

carlanca, *kärlän´kä,* sf. training-collar.

carlancón, *–kŏn´,* sm. sly-boots, dodger.

carlina, *kärmē´nä,* sf. paco-wool.

carmelita, *–lē´tä,* sf. Carmelite.

carmen, *kär´mĕn,* sm. country-house; Carmelite order.

carmenador, *kärmĕnädŏr´,* sm. teaser.

carmenar, *–när´,* v. a. to card wool; to pull out the hair of the head; to cheat at

carmes, *kär´mĕs,* sm. kermes. [play.

carmesí, *kärmĕsï´,* sm. cochineal powder; crimson; purple.

carmín, *kärmïn´,* sm. & a. carmine.

carnada, *kärnä´dä,* sf. bait, lure.

carnaje, *–ä´hĕ,* sm. salt beef.

carnal, *kärnäl´,* a. carnal, fleshy; sensual; — sm. time of the year in which meat may be eaten. [liness.

carnalidad, *–lïdäd´,* sf. lustfulness, flesh-

carnaval, *kärnäväl´,* sm. carnival.

carnaza, *kärnä´thä,* sf. fleshy part of a hide; abundance of meat.

carne, *kär´nĕ,* sf. flesh; meat; pulp (of fruit). [runcle.

carnecilla, *–thïl´yä,* sf. carnosity, ca-

carnerada, *–rä´dä,* sf. flock of sheep.

carneraje, *–rä´h´ĕ,* sm. tax laid on sheep.

carnerear, *–rēär´,* v. a. to fine the proprietor of sheep which have done damage.

carnerero, *–nä´rŏ,* sm. shepherd.

carnoril, *–rïl´,* sm. sheep-walk.

carnero, *kärnā´rŏ,* sm. sheep, mutton; family-vault. [sheep.

carneruno, na, *–rŏ´nŏ,* a. belonging to

carnestolendas, *kärnĕstŏlĕn´däs,* sf. pl. shrovetide, shrove-Tuesday.

carnicería, *kärnïthĕrē´ä,* sf. shambles, slaughter-house; carnage, slaughter.

carnicero, *–thä´rŏ,* sm. butcher; —, ra, a. carnivorous. [animals.

carnicol, *–kŏl´,* sm. hoof of cloven-footed

carnificarse, *–fïkär´sĕ,* v. r. to carnify, to breed flesh.

carnívoro, ra, *kärnē´vŏrŏ,* a. carnivorous.

carniza, *kärnï´thä,* sf. refuse of meat.

carnosidad, *kärnŏsïdäd´,* sf. proud flesh; fatness; fleshiness.

carnoso, sa, *kärnŏ´sŏ,* **carnudo,** *–nŏ´dŏ,* a. fleshy; marrowy; pulpous.

caro, ra, *kä´rŏ,* a. dear, costly; beloved, affectionate; —, ad. dearly.

caroca, *kärŏ´kä,* sm. caress.

carocha, *–rŏtsh´ä,* sf. eggs of cloven-footed.

carochar, *–rŏtshär´,* v. a. to lay and hatch eggs (applied to the queen-bee).

caromomia, *kärŏmŏ´mïä,* sf. dry flesh of a mummy.

carona, *kärŏ´nä,* sf. padding of a saddle; part of the animal's back on which the

caroña, *kärŏn´yä,* sf. jade. [saddle lies.

caroquero, *kärŏkä´rŏ,* sm. wheedler, flatterer.

carótida, *kärŏ´tïdä,* sf. the carotid artery.

carozo, *kärŏ´thŏ,* sm. core of a pomegranate.

carpa, *kär´pä,* sf. carp (fish); part torn off a bunch of grapes. [folio.

carpeta, *kärpä´tä,* sf. table-carpet; port-

carpintear, *kärpïntäär´,* v. a. to carpenter.

carpintería, *–rē´ä,* sf. carpentry; carpenter's shop.

carpintero, *–tä´rŏ,* sm. carpenter; – de blanco, joiner; – de carretas, cartwright; – de obras de afuera, carpenter who timbers or roofs houses; – de ribera, ship-wright.

carpo, *kär´pŏ,* sm. wrist, carpus.

carraca, *kärä´kä,* sf. carack (ship); rattle.

carral, *käräl´,* sm. barrel, butt, vat.

carraleja, *–lē´h´ä,* sf. black-beetle.

carralero, *–lä´rŏ,* sm. cooper.

carrasca, *kärräs´kä,* sf. **carrasco,** *–kŏ,* sm. evergreen oak. [wine.

carraspada, *kärräspä´dä,* sf. negus, mulled

carraspante, *–pän´tĕ,* a. acrid, strong (of wine).

carraspera, *–pä´rä,* sf. hoarseness.

carrasqueño, ña, *–kēn´yŏ,* a. harsh, sharp; belonging to the evergreen oak.

carrera, *kärä´rä,* sf. career, course, race; race-ground; high-road; alley; row, line; course of life; á – abierta, at full speed.

carreta, *kärä´tä,* sf. long narrow cart.

carretada, *kärrä´dä,* sf. cart-load; great quantity; á –s, in abundance.

carretaje, -tā'h'ĕ, sm. cartage.

carrote, kărrŏ'tĕ, sm. small reel for winding off silk, &c.; fishing-pulley.

carretear, -tēăr', v. a. to cart; to drive a cart; —se, to draw unevenly.

carretela, -tĕ'lă, sf. light coach.

carretera, -tĕ'ră, sf. high-road.

carretería, -tĕrĕ'ă, sf. number of carts; trade of a carman; cart-wright's yard.

carretero, -tĕ'rŏ, sm. cart-wright; carman.

carretilla, -tĕl'yă, sf. go-cart; squib, cracker; wheel-barrow.

carretón, -tŏn', sm. go-cart (for children).

carriego, kărrĭĕ'gŏ, sm. osier fish-basket.

carril, kărrĭl', sm. cart-way; cart-rut; furrow. [box on the ears.

carrillada, kărrĭlyă'dă, sf. hog's cheek;

carrillo, kărrĭl'yŏ, sm. cheek; tackle.

carrilludo, da, -yŏ'dŏ, a. chub-cheeked.

carriola, kărrĭŏ'lă, sf. truckle-bed; small chariot; curricle.

carrizo, kărrĕ'thŏ, sm. common reed-grass.

carro, kăr'rŏ, sm. cart.

Carro, –, sm. Charles' Wain.

carrocín, kărrŏthĕn', sm. chaise, curricle.

carromatero, -mătĕ'rŏ, sm. charioteer, carman. [cart.

carromato, -mă'tŏ, sm. two-wheeled tilted

carroña, kărrŏn'yă, sf. carrion.

carroñar, kărrŏnyăr', v.a. to infect sheep with the scab.

carroño, ña, kărrŏn'yŏ, a. putrid, rotten.

carroza, kărrŏ'thă, sf. state-coach; (mar.) awning. [riages or vehicles.

carruaje, kărruā'h'ĕ, sm. all sorts of car-

carruatero, -'hă'rŏ, sm. carrier, carter, waggoner. [mountainous countries.

carruco, kărrŏ'kŏ, sm. small cart used in

carta, kăr'tă, sf. letter; map; —blanca, carte-blanche; —credencial ó de creencia, credentials, pl.; —certificada, registered letter; —de vuelta, dead letter; —en lista, letter "to be kept till called for", letter addressed "Post-Office"; —con valores declarados, money-letter.

cartabón, -bŏn', sm. square (tool).

cartapacio, -pă'thĭŏ, sm. memorandum-book; scholar's portfolio. [party.

cartapartida, -părtĕ'dă, sf. (mar.) charter-

cartazo, -thŏ, sm. insulting, accusing letter.

cartear, kărtĕăr', v. n. to play low cards; to see how the cards lie; —se, to keep up a correspondence by letter.

cartel, kărtĕl', sm. placard; hand-bill; —de comedia, play-bill.

cartela, kărtĕ'lă, sf. slip of paper; cornice.

cartera, -ră, sf. portfolio, pocket-book; letter-case; flap of a pocket.

cartero, -rŏ, sm. letter-carrier, postman.

cartilaginoso, sa, kărtĭlă'hĭnŏ'sŏ, a. cartilaginous.

cartílago, kărtĕ'lăgŏ, sm. cartilage.

cartilla, kărtĕl'yă, sf. short letter; primer.

cartón, kărtŏn', sm. pasteboard; metal ornament; cartoon. [maker.

cartonero, kărtŏnĕ'rŏ, sm. pasteboard-

cartuchera, kărtŏtshĕ'ră, sf. (mil.) cartridge-box; cartridge-pouch.

cartucho, kărtŏtsh'ŏ, sm. cartouch.

cartuja, kărtŭ'h'ă, sf. Carthusian order.

cartujo, -ŏ, sm. Carthusian monk.

cartulario, kărtŭlă'rĭŏ, sm. cartulary.

cartulina, -lĕ'nă, sf. card, visiting-card.

carúncula, kărŭn'kŭlă, sf. caruncle.

carvi, kăr'vĕ, sm. common caraway.

casa, kă'să, sf. house; home; —de campo, country-house; —de locos, mad-house; —de moneda, mint; —de posada, lodging-house.

casaca, kăsă'kă, sf. coat.

casación, -thĭŏn', sf. abrogation.

casadero, ra, -dĕ'rŏ, a. marriageable.

casamata, -mă'tă, sf. (mil.) casemate.

casamentero; ra, -mĕntĕ'rŏ, sm. & f. marriage-maker. [made on cards.

casamiento, -mĭĕn'tŏ, sm. marriage; bet

casapuerta, -pŭĕr'tă, sf. porch.

casaquilla, -kĭl'yă, sf. short and loose jacket.

casar, kăsăr', v. a. to marry; to consort; to couple; to adjust; to abrogate; to annul; —se, to marry. [shop.

casatienda, kăsătĭĕn'dă, sf. tradesman's

casca, kăs'kă, sf. husks of grapes; bark for tanning leather. [bell; rattle-snake.

cascabel, kăskăbĕl', sm. rattle, little round

cascabelada, -lă'dă, sf. jingling of small bells; inconsiderate speech or action.

cascabelear, -lĕăr', v. a. to feed one with vain hopes; —v. n. to act with levity.

cascaciruelas, kăskăthĭrŭĕ'lăs, sm. mean, despicable fellow.

cascada, -kă'dă, sf. cascade, water-fall.

cascajal, -kă'hăl', sm. place full of pebbles.

cascajo, -kă'h'ŏ, sm. gravel; fragments of broken vessels; rubbish; copper coin.

cascajoso, sa, -'hŏ'sŏ, a. gravelly.

cascamajar, -mă'hăr', v. a. to pound a thing to bits.

cascanuez, kăskănŭĕth', sm. nut-cracker.

cascanueces, -nŭĕ'thĕs, sm. nut-cracker.

cascapiñones, -pĭnyŏ'nĕs, sm. (fig.) poor wretch.

cascar, kăskăr', v. a. to crack, to break into pieces; to lick, to beat; —se, to be broken open.

cáscara, kăs'kără, sf. rind, peel, husk; bark.

¡cáscaras! -s, zounds! [Jesuit's bark.

cascarilla, kăskărĭl'yă, sf. Peruvian bark.

cascarón, -rŏn', sm. egg-shell; niche for the sacrament. [rude.

cascarrón, na, kăskărrŏn', a. rough, harsh,

cascarudo, da, kăskărŭ'dŏ, a. thick-skinned, thick-peeled.

casco, kăs'kŏ, sm. skull, cranium; fragments of a pot; helmet; hulk of a ship; crown of a hat; hoof of a horse.

cascote, kăskŏ'tĕ, sm. rubbish, fragments of material used in building.

cascudo, da, kăskŏ'dŏ, a. large-hoofed.

caseoso, sa, kăsĕŏ'sŏ, a. caseous, cheesy.

casera, kăsĕ'ră, sf. bachelor's housekeeper.

casería, kăsĕrĕ'ă, sf. messuage; economical management of a house.

caserío, -ŏ, sm. series of houses; village.

caserna, kăsĕr'nă, sf. (mil.) barracks.

casero, *kăs͞e'rŏ*, sm. landlord; –, ra, a, domestic; familiar; house-keeping.

casi, *kă'sĭ*, ad. almost, nearly; – que, – –, very nearly.

casia, *kă'sĭă*, sf. bastard cinnamon.

casillas, *kăstl'yăs*, sf. pl. place where backgammon is played; checkers (for backgammon).

casiller, *kăstlyer'*, sm. cleanser of the close-stools in the royal palace.

casillo, *kăstl'yŏ*, sm. trifling cause.

casimiro, *kăsĭmē'rŏ*, sm. kerseymere.

casino, *kăsĭ'nŏ*, sm. club, club-house.

caso, *kă'sŏ*, sm. case, occurrence, event; hap, casualty; occasion; (gr.) case; en – de eso, in that case; en todo –, at all events; – que, in case; –, sa, a. null and void.   [riage.

casorio, *kăsŏ'rĭŏ*, sm. inconsiderate marriage.

caspa, *kăs'pă*, sf. dandriff; scurf.

¡ cáspita ! *kăs'pĭtă*, wonderful!

casquetazo, *kăskĕtă'thŏ*, sm. blow with the head.   [cataplasm.

casquete, *kăskĕ'tĕ*, sm. helmet, casque;

casquiblando, da, *kăskĭblăn'dŏ*, a. soft-hoofed.   [wide-hoofed.

casquiderramado, da, *–derrămă'dŏ*, a.

casquijo, *kăskĭ'h'ŏ*, sm. gravel.

casquilucio, cia, *kăskĭlū'thĭŏ*, a. gay, frolicsome.   [bee.

casquila, *kăskĭl'yă*, sf. cell of the queen-

casquillo, *kăskĭl'yŏ*, sm. iron socket with which a spear is shod; point of an arrow.

casquimuleño, ña, *–mūlĕn'yŏ*, a. narrow-hoofed (like mules).   [kind, quality.

casta, *kăs'tă*, sf. cast, race, lineage; breed;

castaña, *kăstăn'yă*, sf. chestnut; jug in the shape of a chestnut; club of hair; – pilonga, dried chestnut.

castañal, *kăstănyăl'*, castañar, *–yăr'*, sm. chestnut-grove.

castañeta, *kăstănyĕ'tă*, sf. castanet.

castañetear, *kăstănyĕtĕăr'*, v. n. to rattle the castanets in dancing.

castaño, *kăstăn'yŏ*, sm. chestnut-tree; –, ña, a. hazelly.

castañuela, *–yŭĕ'lă*, sf. castanet.

castañuelo, la, *–lŏ*, a. chestnut-coloured.

castellán, *kăstĕlyăn'*, sm. governor of a castle.   [district belonging to a castle.

castellania, *kăstĕlyănĭ'ă*, sf. castellany.

castellano, *kăstĕlyă'nŏ*, sm. Castilian language, Spanish.

castidad, *kăstĭdăd'*, sf. chastity.

castigar, *–găr'*, v. a. to chastise, to punish; to afflict.   [ishment; correction.

castigo, *kăstĭ'gŏ*, sm. chastisement, pun-

castillejo, *kăstĭlyĕ'h'ŏ*, sm. castlet; go-cart (for little children).

castillete, *–yĕ'tĕ*, sm. small castle.

castillo, *kăstĭl'yŏ*, sm. castle; cell of the queen-bee.   [scent; pure, uncorrupt.

castizo, za, *kăstĭ'thŏ*, a. of a noble de-

casto, ta, *kăs'tŏ*, a. pure, chaste.

castor, *kăstŏr'*, sm. beaver.

castoreo, *kăstŏ'rĕŏ*, sm. castoreum.

castra, *kăs'tră*, sf. pruning of plants and trees.

castradera, *–dă'ră*, sf. knife for cutting the hives.

castrar, *kăstrăr'*, v. a. to geld, to castrate; to prune; to cut the honey-combs out of bee-hives.   [combs out of hives.

castrazón, *kăstrăthŏn'*, sf. cutting honey-

casual, *kăsŭăl'*, a. casual, accidental.

casualidad, *kăsŭălĭdăd''*, sf. casualty, accident.

casucha, *kăsŭtsh'ă*, sf. miserable hut.

casuista, *kăsŭĭs'tă*, sm. casuist.

casulla, *kăsŭl'yă*, sf. chasuble.

cata, *kă'tă*, sf. tasting.

catábulo, *kătă'bŭlŏ*, sm. stable.

catacumbas, *–kŭm'băs*, sf. pl. catacombs.

catadura, *–dŏ'ră*, sf. face, countenance.

catafalco, *–făl'kŏ*, sm. funeral canopy over a bier.

catalejo, *–lĕh'ŏ*, sm. telescope.

catálogo, *kătă'lŏgŏ*, sm. catalogue.

cataplasma, *–plăs'mă*, sf. cataplasm, poultice.

catapulta, *–pŭl'tă*, sf. catapult.

catar, *kătăr'*, v. a. to taste; to inspect, to examine; to judge; to esteem.

catarata, *kătără'tă*, sf. cataract (disease of the eye); water-fall, cascade.

catarral, *kătărrăl'*, a. catarrhal.

catarriento, ta, *kătărrĭĕn'tă*, a. catarrhal.

catarro, *kătăr'rŏ*, sm. catarrh.

catarroso, sa, *kătărrŏ'sŏ*, a. catarrhal, catarrhous.   [purging.

catártico, ca, *kătăr'tĭkŏ*, a. cathartic.

catastro, *kătăs'trŏ*, sm. general tax on land.

catástrofe, *kătăs'trŏfĕ*, sf. catastrophe.

catavino, *kătăvĭ'nŏ*, sm. small cup for tasting wine; –s, sm. wine-taster; tippler.

catecismo, *kătĕthĭs'mŏ*, sm. catechism.

cátedra, *kă'tĕdră*, sf. professor's chair.

catedral, *kătĕdrăl'*, a. & sf. cathedral.

catedrático, *–dră'tĭkŏ*, sm. professor of a university.

categoria, *–gŏrĭ'ă*, sf. category; rank.

categórico, ca, *–gŏ'rĭkŏ*, a. categorical, decisive.

catequismo, *–kĭs'mŏ*, sm. catechism.

catequista, *–kĭs'tă*, sm. catechist.

catequizar, *–kĭthăr'*, v. a. to catechise.

caterva, *kătĕr'vă*, sf. mob.

cato, *kă'tŏ*, sm. Japan earth.   [cism.

catolicismo, *kătŏlĭthĭs'mŏ*, sm. catholi-

católico, ca, *kătŏ'lĭkŏ*, a. & sm. catholic.

catorcena, *kătŏrthĕ'nă*, sf. conjunction of fourteen unities.

catorceno, na, *–nŏ*, a. fourteenth.

catre, *kă'trĕ*, sm. field-bed.

catricofre, *kătrĭkŏ'frĕ*, sm. bed-closet.

cauce, *kă'ŭthĕ*, sm. drain.   [guaranty.

caución, *kăŭthŏn'*, sf. caution, security,

caucionar, *–thĭŏnăr'*, v. a. to guarantee.

caucho, *kă'ŭtshŏ*, sm. (am.) caoutchouc.

cauda, *kă'ŭdă*, sf. train of a bishop's robe.

caudal, *kăŭdăl'*, sm. property, fortune, wealth; fund, stock; plenty.

caudaloso, sa, *kăŭdălŏ'sŏ*, a. carrying much water (speaking of rivers).

caudatario, *–tă'rĭŏ*, sm. train-bearer of a cardinal.

causa, kŭ˙ŭsä, sf. cause; occasion; motive, reason; law-suit; á – de, considering.
causal, kä˙sŭl', a. causal. [because of.
causante, kä˙sŏn'tē, sm. constituent.
causar, kä˙sŭr', v. a. to cause, to produce; to occasion. [law-suits.
causídico, ca, kä˙sē˙dĭkō, a. belonging to
causón, kä˙sŏn', sm. burning fever which lasts only some hours.
cáustico, kä˙ŭstĭkō, sm. (med.) caustic; –, ca, a. caustic. [heedfulness.
cautela, kä˙ŭtē˙lä, sf. caution, prudence.
cautelar, –tēlär', v. a. to take necessary precautions. [ful.
cauteloso, sa, –lō˙sō, a. cautious, heed-
cauterio, kä˙ŭtē˙rĭō, sm. cautery.
cauterizar, –rēthär', v. a. to cauterize; to reproach with severity.
cautivar, kä˙ŭtēvär', v. a. to take prisoner in war; to captivate, to charm.
cautiverio, –vē˙rĭō, sm. captivity; confinement.
cautivo, va, kä˙ŭtē˙vō, sm. & f. captive.
canto, ta, kä˙ŭtō, a. cautious, wary.
cava, kä˙vä, sf. digging and earthing of vines; wine-cellar.
cavar, kävär', v. a. to dig up, to excavate; –, v. n. to penetrate far into a thing; to think profoundly (to paw of horses).
caverna, kävēr'nä, sf. cavern, cave.
cavernoso, sa, kävērnō˙sō, a. cavernous.
cavidad, kävēdäd', sf. cavity, hollow.
cavilación, kävĭläthĭōn', sf. cavillation.
cavilar, –lär', v. a. to cavil.
caviloso, sa, –lō˙sō, a. captious, cavillous.
cayada, käyä˙dä, sf., cayado, –dō, sm. shepherd's hook.
cayo, kä˙yō, sm. rock, shoal.
caz, käth, sm. canal, trench.
-caza, kä˙thä, sf. chase; game.
cazadero, käthädä˙rō, sm. hunting-ground.
cazador, –dōr', sm. hunter, huntsman; –, furtivo, poacher.
cazamoscas, –mŏs˙käs, sm. fly-catcher, gnat-snapper (bird).
cazar, käthär', v. a. to chase, to hunt.
cazcalear, käthkälēär', v. n. to fidget. [pl.
cazcarria, –kär˙rĭä, sf. splashings of dirt.
cazo, kä˙thō, sm. copper saucepan with an iron handle; ladle.
cazolero, ra, –lē˙rō, a. too officious.
cazudo, da, käthō˙dō, a. thick-backed (of knives).
cazuela, käthä˙lä, sf. stewing-pan.
cazumbrón, käthämbrōn', sm. cooper.
cazurro, rra, käthär˙rō, a. silent, taciturn.
¡ce! thā, hark!, come hither!
cea, thā˙ä, sf. thigh-bone.
ceática, thā˙ĭkä, sf. (med.) sciatica.
ceba, thā˙bä, sf. sea-weed.
cebada, thēbä˙dä, sf. barley.
cebadazo, za, –dä˙thō, a. of barley.
cebadera, –dä˙rä, sf. fodder-bag; nose-bag (for horses).
cebadura, –dō˙rä, sf. feeding fowls.

cebar, thēbär', v. a. & n. to feed animals, to fatten; to keep up a fire; to grapple; to prime; to let off a rocket. [skin.
cebellina, thēbĕlyē˙nä, sf. sable; sable-
cebo, thä˙bō, sm. food; bait, lure; priming.
cebolla, thēbŏl˙yä, sf. onion; bulb of the onion.
cebolleta, –yē˙tä, sf. tender onion.
cebollino, –yē˙nō, sm. onion-seed.
cebolludo, da, –yē˙dō, a. bulbous.
cebón, thēbŏn', sm. fat bullock or hog.
cebra, thä˙brä, sf. zebra.
cebruno, thē˙brō˙nō, a. reddish brown.
cecear, thēthēär', v. a. to pronounce the s in the same manner as the c; to call one by ,,ce-ce''; to lisp.
cecial, thēthĭäl', sm. cod (fish).
cecilia, thēthē˙lĭä, sm. blind-worm.
cecina, –nä, sf. hung beef, salt beef.
cedacero, thēdäthä˙rō, sm. sieve-maker.
cedazo, thēdä˙thō, sm. hair-sieve, strainer.
ceder, thēdär', v. a. to grant, to resign, to yield, to give up; –, v. n. to submit, to comply, to give in; to abate, to grow less.
cedrella, thēdrēl˙yä, sf. cedar-wood.
cedrino, na, thēdrē˙nō, a. cedrine.
cedro, thä˙drō, sm. cedar.
cedronela, thēdrŏnä˙lä, sf. cider.
cédula, thä˙dŭlä, sf. slip of paper; bill; decree; schedule; – de cambio, bill of exchange.
céfalo, thä˙fälō, sm. mullet.
céfiro, thä˙fĭrō, sm. zephyr.
cegar, thēgär', v. n. to grow blind; –, v. a. to deprive of sight; to darken; to shut.
cegarrita, thēgär˙rō, sm. short-sighted person; á – s, with shut eyes.
cegarro, thēgär˙rō, cegato, ta, thēgä˙tō, a. short-sighted
ceguedad, thēgēdäd'', sf. blindness.
ceja, thā˙hä, sf. eye-brow; edging of clothes; (mus.) bridge of a stringed instrument; summit of a mountain.
cejar, thēhär', v. n. to go backward; to slacken, to give in.
cejo, thā˙hō, sm. thick mist or fog which usually arises from rivers.
celada, thēlä˙dä, sf. Burgundy helmet; ambush; artful trick.
celaje, thēlä˙hē, sm. colour of the clouds.
celar, thēlär', v. n. & a. to fulfil the duties of an office with care; to watch over; to conceal; to engrave.
celda, thēl˙dä, sf. cell.
celdilla, thēldĭl˙yä, sf. cellule.
celebérrimo, ma, thēlēbēr˙rĭmō, a. most celebrated. [praise.
celebración, thēlēbräthĭōn', sf. celebration.
celebrar, –brär', v. a. to celebrate; to praise; – misa, to say mass.
célebre, thä˙lēbrē, a. famous, renowned; gay; agreeable in conversation. [fame.
celebridad, thēlēbrĭdäd', sf. celebrity.
celebro, thä˙brō, sm. skull; brain; fancy.
celemín, thēlēmĭn', sm. dry measure (the 12th part of a fanega). [locity.
celeridad, thēlērĭdäd', sf. celerity, ve-
celeste, thēlĕs˙tē, a. heavenly; sky-blue.

celestial, *thĕlĕstĭăl'*, a. heavenly; perfect; excellent.

celibato, *thĕlĭbă'tŏ*, sm. celibacy.

célibe, *thă'lĭbĕ*, sm. bachelor.

celo, *thā'lŏ*, sm. zeal; rut (in animals).

celosía, *thĕlŏsē'ă*, sf. lattice of a window.

celoso, *sa*, *thĕlō'sŏ*, a. zealous; jealous.

célula, *thă'lŭlă*, sf. cellule.

celular, *thĕlŭlăr'*, a. cellular.

cementar, *thĕmĕntăr'*, v. a. to cement.

cena, *thā'nă*, sf. supper.

cenáculo, —*nă'kŭlŏ*, sm. cenatory hall in which our Lord administered the last supper to his disciples.

cenacho, *thĕnăch'ŏ*, sm. market-basket.

cenador, —*dŏr'*, sm. one who sups; arbour.

cenagal, —*găl'*, sm. quagmire.

cenagoso, *sa*, —*gō'sŏ*, a. miry, marshy.

cenar, *thĕnăr'*, v. a. to sup; [slender.

cenceño, *ña*, *thĕnthĕn'yŏ*, a. lean, thin,

cencerrada, *thĕnthĕrră'dă*, sf. rough music, hubbub, clatter, Dutch concert.

cencerrear, —*rĕăr'*, v. n. to jingle continually; to play badly; to make a dreadful noise.

cencerro, *thĕnthĕr'rŏ*, sm. bell worn by the leading-mule; ill-tuned guitar; á —s tapados, privately, by stealth.

cencerrón, —*rŏn'*, sm. grape which remains after the vintage.

cendal, *thĕndăl'*, sm. crape; furbelow; (poet.) garter. [potash for cleaning silver.

cendra, *thĕn'dră*, sf. paste made of boiled

cenefa, *thĕnĕ'fă*, sf. picture-frame; fringes, pl.; (poet.) bank of a river, brim of a pond.

cenicero, *thĕnĭthĕ'rŏ*, sm. ash-hole.

ceniciento, *ta*, —*thĭĕn'tŏ*, a. ash-coloured.

cenit, *thĕnĭt'*, sm. zenith.

ceniza, *thĕnē'thă*, sf. ashes, pl.; miércoles de —, Ash-Wednesday.

cenojil, *thĕnŏ-hĭl'*, sm. garter.

censatario, *thĕnsătă'rĭŏ*, sm. copyholder.

censo, *thĕn'sŏ*, sm. quit-rent; censual roll; poll-tax. [critic; censorious person.

censor, *thĕnsŏr'*, sm. censor, reviewer.

censual, *thĕnsŭăl'*, a. belonging to a quit-rent. [copyholder.

censualista, —*lĭs'tă*, sm. life-annuitant;

censura, —*sō'ră*, sf. critical review; censure, blame.

censurar, —*sŭrăr'*, v. a. to review, to criticise; to censure, to blame.

centauro, *thĕntă'drŏ*, sm. Centaur.

centella, —*tĕl'yă*, sf. lightning; spark,

centellar, —*tĕlyăr'*, centellear, —*tĕlyĕăr'*, v. n. to sparkle.

centena, —*tă'nă*, sf. hundred. [dreds.

centenadas, —*tĕnă'dăs*, ad. á —, by hun-

centenal, —*tĕnăl'*, sm. field sown with rye. [secular; —, sm. centennial.

centenario, *ia*, —*nă'rĭŏ*, a. centenary,

centeno, —*tă'nŏ*, sm. common rye; —, á. hundredth. [hundredth.

centésimo, *ma*, —*tă'sĭmŏ*, a. centesimal,

céntimo, *thĕn'tĭmŏ*, sm. French copper coin.

centinela, —*tĭnĕ'lă*, sf. sentry, sentinel; — avanzada, advanced guard; — perdida, forlorn hope; — á caballo, vedette.

centón, —*tŏn'*, sm. cento (literary composition formed by joining scraps from other authors). [central, centric.

central, —*trăl'*, centrical, —*trĭkăl'*, a.

centralizar, —*trălthăr'*, v. a. to centralize.

céntrico, *thĕn'trĭkŏ*, a. focal. [fugal.

centrifugo, *ga*, *thĕntrē'fŭgŏ*, a. centri-

centripeto, *ta*, —*pĕtŏ*, a. centripetal.

centro, *thĕn'trŏ*, sm. centre; principal object. [cate.

centuplicar, —*tăplĭkăr'*, v. a. to centupli-

céntuplo, *pla*, *thĕn'tŭplŏ*, a. centuple, hundredfold.

centuria, —*tŭ'rĭă*, sf. century.

cenzalo, —*thā'lŏ*, sm. gnat.

ceñido, *da*, *thĕnyē'dŏ*, a. moderate; encircled with rings.

ceñidor, *thĕnyĭdŏr'*, sm. belt, girdle.

ceñir, *thĕnyĭr'*, v. n. to gird, to surround, to circle; to environ; to reduce, to abbreviate, to abridge.

ceño, *thĕn'yŏ*, sm. frown; ferrule.

ceñudo, *da*, *thĕnyō'dŏ*, a. frowning, grimly.

cepa, *thă'pă*, sf. stock of a vine; origin of a family.

cepacaballo, —*kăbăl'yŏ*, sm. cardoon.

cepejón, *thĕpĕ-hŏn'*, sm. largest branch of a tree torn from the trunk. [shavings.

cepilladuras, *thĕpĭlyădō'răs*, sf. pl. wood-

cepillo, *thĕpĭl'yŏ*, sm. plane; brush.

cepo, *thă'pŏ*, sm. block; trap, snare; poor-box; (fig.) entanglement.

ceporro, *thĕpŏr'rŏ*, sm. old vine.

cequi, *sĕkĭ'*, cequin, *sĕkĭn'*, sm. Venetian gold coin of about 9s.

cera, *thă'ră*, sf. wax; wax-taper, wax-candle; side-walk; —s, pl. the cells of wax and honey formed by bees.

cerafolio, *thĕrăfŏ'lĭŏ*, sm. (bot.) common

cerato, *thĕră'tŏ*, sm. cerate. [chervil.

cerbatana, *thĕrbătă'nă*, sf. pea-shooter; acoustic trumpet.

cerca, *thĕr'kă*, sf. inclosure; fence; —s, pl. objects placed in the foreground of a painting; —, ad. near, at hand, close by; — de, close, near.

cercano, *na*, *thĕrkă'nŏ*, a. near, close by, neighbour, adjoining.

cercar, —*kăr'*, v. a. to inclose, to environ, to circle; to fence.

cercenar, —*thĕnăr'*, v. a. to pare; to retrench, to clip; to lop off; to reduce, to lessen; to curtail, to cut away; to abridge.

cercera, —*thă'ră*, sf. air-tube.

cerceta, —*tă'*, sf. widgeon.

cercillo, —*thĭl'yŏ*, sm. tendril of the vine.

cerciorar, *thĕrthĭŏrăr'*, v. a. to assure, to ascertain, to affirm. [circle.

cerco, *thĕr'kŏ*, sm. blocade of a place;

cerda, *thĕr'dă*, sf. strong hair growing in a horse's tail or mane; bristle.

cerdear, —*dĕăr'*, v. n. to be weak in the fore-quarter; to emit a harsh sound; to decline a request by subterfuges.

cerdo, *thĕr'dŏ*, sm. hog, pig.

cerdoso, *sa*, —*dō'sŏ*, cerdudo, *da*, —*dā'dŏ*, a. bristly. [brain.

cerebelo, *thĕrĕbă'lŏ*, sm. cerebel, the little

ceremonia, *—mó'nĭä*, sf. ceremony.
ceremonial, *—móntäl'*, a. &sm, ceremonial.
ceremonioso, sa, *—mónió só*, a. ceremonious.
cerería, *thĕrĕ'ä*, sf. wax-chandler's shop.
cerero, *thĕró'ró*, sm. wax-chandler; idle [vagrant.
cereza, *thĕrĕ'thä*, sf. cherry.
cerezo, *—thó*, sm. cherry-tree.
cerilla, *thĕrĕ'lyä*, sf. wax-light; wax-tablet; ear-wax; —s, pl. matches, safety-matches.
cerillera, *thĕrĭlyä'rä*, sf. little candlestick.
cermeña, *thĕrmēn'yä*, sf. muscadine pear.
cernada, *—nä'dä*, sf. leached ashes.
cerneja, *—nä'hä*, sf. fetlock.
cerner, *thĕrner'*, v. a. to sift, to bolt; —, v. n. to bud and blossom; to drizzle; —se, to waddle.
ceraído, *—nä'dó*, sm. sifting.
cernidura, *—nĭdó'rä*, sf. siftings, pl.
cero, *thá'ró*, sm. zero.
cerollo, lla, *thĕrŏl'yŏ*, a. (applied to grain) reaped rather green and soft.
cerón, *thĕrón'*, sm. dregs of pressed wax formed into a cake.
ceroso, *thĕró'só*, a. waxy. [panic, fear.
cerote, *thĕró'tĕ*, sm. shoemaker's wax; (fig.)
ceroto, *—tó*, sm. soft cerate. [monk.
cerquillo, *thĕrkĭl'yŏ*, sm. tonsure of a
cerquita, *—kĕ'tä*, ad. at a small distance.
cerrada, *thĕrrä'dä*, sf. backbone-hide of an animal.
cerradero, *—dä'ró*, sm. staple of a lock; —, ra, a. serving for locking. [be locked.
cerradizo, za, *—dĕ'thó*, a. that which may
cerrado, da, *—dó*, a. close, reserved; concealed; thick-grown.
cerradura, *—dó'rä*, sf. locking-up; lock; — de golpe, spring-lock.
cerrajear, *thĕrrä'hĕär'*, v. n. to do locksmith's work. [smith; locksmith's shop.
cerrajería, *—'hĕrĕ'ä*, sf. trade of a lock-
cerrajero, *thĕrrä'hĕró*, sm. locksmith.
cerramiento, *—mĕĕn'tó*, sm. stopping-up; inclosure; finishing of the roof of a building; (rail.) — de vía, block-up.
cerrar, *thĕrrär'*, v. a. & n. to close, to shut; to obstruct a passage; to lock; to engage the enemy; — la cuenta, to close an account; —se, to be shut up; to cicatrized; to grow dark.
cerrazón, *thĕrräthón'*, sf. dark and cloudy weather which precedes tempests.
cerrero, ra, *thĕrrä'ró*, a. running wild from one hill or eminence to another; caballo —, an unbroken horse.
cerril, *thĕrrĕl'*, a. mountainous, rough, wild, untamed.
cerrión, *thĕrrĭón'*, sm. icicle.
cerro, *thĕr'ró*, sm. hill; neck of an animal; backbone; combed flax or hemp; en —, nakedly, barely.
cerrojo, *thĕrró'hŏ*, sm. bolt of a door.
certamen, *thĕrtä'mĕn*, sm. literary controversy. [shot.
certero, ra, *thĕrtä'ró*, a. an excellent
certeza, *thĕrtä'thä*, certidumbre, *thĕrtĭdóm'brĕ*, sf. certainty.

certificación, *thĕrtĭfĭkäthĭón'*, sf. certificate; return of a writ.
certificado, *—fĭkä'dó*, sm. certificate; — da, a. registered (of a letter).
certificar, *—fĭkär'*, v.a. to certify, to affirm.
certificatorio, ria, *—fĭkätó'rĭó*, a. authenticating. [blue.
cerúleo, lea, *thĕró'lĕŏ*, a. ceruleous, sky-
cerval, *thĕrväl'*, cervuno, ria, *thĕrvä'rĭó*, a. belonging to a deer or resembling it.
cervatillo, *thĕrvätĭl'yŏ*, sm. small deer.
cervato, *—vä'tó*, sm. fawn. [brewery.
cervecería, *thĕrvĕthĕrĕ'ä*, sf. brew-house,
cervecero, *—thä'ró*, sm. brewer.
cerveza, *thĕrvĕ'thä*, sm. beer, ale.
cervicabra, *thĕrvĭkä'brä*, sf. gazelle.
cerviguillo, *—gĕl'yŏ*, sm. big nape.
cerviz, *thĕrvĭth'*, sf. nape.
cervuno, na, *thĕrvó'nä*, a. deer-coloured.
cesación, *thĕsäthĭón'*, sf. cessation, ceasing, pause, discontinuation.
cesar, *thĕsär'*, v. n. to cease, to desist.
César, *thĕ'sär*, sm. Roman emperor.
cesáreo, rea, *thĕsä'rĕó*, a. imperial.
cesible, *thĕsĕ'blĕ*, a. that which may be ceded.
cesión, *thĕsĭón'*, sf. cession, transfer.
cesionario, *thĕsĭónä'rĭó*, sm. cessionary.
césped, *thĕs'pĕd*, sm. sod, turf covered with grass; grass-plot. [sods are cut.
cespedera, *—dä'rä*, sf. field where green
cesta, *thĕs'tä*, sf. basket, pannier.
cestada, *thĕstä'dä*, sf. basket-full.
cestería, *thĕstĕrĕ'ä*, sf. basket-shop; basket-stand.
cestero, *thĕstä'ró*, sm. basket-maker.
cesto, *thĕs'tó*, sm. hand-basket, hutch.
cetrino, na, *thĕtrĕ'nó*, a. a citrine, lemon-coloured; jaundiced, melancholic.
cetro, *thä'tró*, sm. sceptre.
cía, *thĕ'ä*, sf. hip-bone.
ciar, *thĭär'*, v. a. to rein back; (mar.) to backwater; (fig.) to slacken in the pursuit of an affair.
ciática, *thĭä'tĭkä*, sf. sciatica, hip-gout.
ciático, ca, *—tĭkó*, a. sciatical.
cibera, *thĭbĕ'rä*, sf. mill-hopper; grist put at once in the hopper; all seeds or grains; husks, grounds.
cibla, *thĕ'blä*, sf. shooting at a popinjay.
cicatear, *thĭkätĕär'*, v. n. to be niggardly.
cicatería, *—tĕrĕ'ä*, sf. niggardliness.
cicatero, ra, *—tä'ró*, a. niggardly, sordid.
cicatriz, *thĭkätrĕth'*, sf. cicatrice; gash.
cicatrizar, *—trĭthär'*, v. a. to cicatrise.
ciclo, *thĕ'klŏ*, sm. cycle. [Cyclops.
cíclope, *thĕ'klŏpĕ*, cíclope, *thĕklŏ'pĕ*, sm.
cicuta, *thĭkó'tä*, sf. (bot.) hemlock.
cidra, *thĕ'drä*, sf. citron.
cidro, *—dró*, sm. citron-tree.
ciegamente, *thĭĕgämĕn'tĕ*, ad. blindly.
ciego, ga, *thĭĕ'gŏ*, a. blind.
cielo, *thĕ'lŏ*, sm. heaven; atmosphere, climate; — de la cama, tester of a bed; — de coche, roof of a coach; — de la boca, roof of the palate.
cien, *thĭĕn'*, a. one hundred.

ciencia, *thiĕn'thiă*, sf. science.
cieno, *thiă'nō*, sm. mud, mire.
científico, ca, *thiĕntĕ'fĭkō*, a. scientific.
ciento, *thiĕn'tō*, a. one hundred; —, sm. a hundred; juego de los —s, piquet (game at cards) [louse, centipede.
cientopiés, —*piĕs'*, sm. wood-louse, hog-louse.
cierna, *thiĕr'nă*, sf. blossom of vines, corn, &c. [to be in its infancy.
cierne, —*nĕ*, en—, in blossom; estar en—.
¡ Cierra España ! *thiĕr'ră ĕspăn'yă*, the war-whoop of the ancient Spaniards.
cierro, *thiĕr'rō*, sm. enclosure.
cierto, ta, *thiĕr'tō*, a. certain, doubtless; por —, certainly.
cierva, *thiĕr'vă*, sf. hind.
ciervo, *thiĕr'vō*, sm. deer, hart, stag; — volante, stag-beetle.
cierzo, *thiĕr'thō*, sm. cold northerly wind.
cifra, *thē'fră*, sf. cipher; abbreviation.
cifrar, *thĭfrăr'*, v. a. to write in ciphers; to abridge.
cigarra, *thĭgăr'ră*, sf. grass-hopper.
cigarro, —*rō*, sm. cigar.
cigarrero, —*răr'rō*, sm. cigar-seller.
cigarrista, —*rĭs'tă*, sm. one who smokes many cigars.
cigarrillo, —*rĭl'yō*, cigarrito, —*rē'tō*, sm. cigarette. [well.
cigoñal, *thĭgōnyăl'*, sm. swipe of a draw-
ciguato, ta, *thĭgwă'tō*, a. jaundiced.
cigüeña, *thĭgŭĕn'yă*, sf. stork; crank of a
cigüeño, —*yō*, sm. male stork. [bell.
cilicio, *thĭlē'thĭō*, sm. hair-shirt.
cilíndrico, ca, *thĭlĭn'drĭkō*, a. cylindric.
cilindro, —*drō*, sm. cylinder.
cilla, *thĭl'yă*, sf. granary.
cillazgo, *thĭlyăth'gō*, sm. store-house fees paid for the tithes kept in a granary.
cillerero, *thĭlyĕrĕ'rō*, sm. cellarist, butler.
cilleriza, —*rē'thă*, sf. stewardess in a nun-nery. [granary.
cillero, *thĭlyĕ'rō*, sm. keeper of a granary.
cima, *thē'mă*, sf. summit; nap; top of trees.
cimballillo, *thĭmbăl'yō*, sm. small bell.
címbalo, *thĭm'bălō*, sm. cymbal.
cimbel, —*bĕl'*, sm. decoy-pigeon.
cimborio, —*bōr'ĭō*, cimborrio, —*bōr'rĭō*, sm. cupola.
cimbra, *thĭm'bră*, sf. centring of an arch.
cimbrado, —*bră'dō*, sm. quick movement in a Spanish dance.
cimbr(e)ar, —*br(ĕ)ăr'*, v. a. to brandish a rod or wand; — á alguno, to give one a drubbing; —, v. n. to bend, to vibrate.
cimbreño, ña, —*brĕn'yō*, a. pliant, flexible.
cimbronazo, —*brōnă'thō*, sm. thrust of a foil. [gold.
cimentado, *thĭmĕntă'dō*, sm. refinement of
cimentar, —*tăr'*, v. a. to lay the foundation of a building; to ground; to establish the fundamental principles of religion, morals and sciences; to refine metals.
cimenterio, —*tĕr'ĭō*, sm. cemetery, church-yard.
cimiento, *thĭmĕn'tō*, sm. cement. [yard.

cimero, ra, —*rō*, a. uppermost; at the very top. [of a building; basis, origin.
cimiento, *thĭmĕn'tō*, sm. ground-work
cimitarra, *thĭmĭtăr'ră*, sf. cimeter, falchion.
cimorra, *thĭmōr'ră*, sf. glanders, pl.
cinabrio, *thĭnă'brĭō*, sm. cinnabar; ver-milion.
cinamomo, —*mō'mō*, sm. bead-tree.
cinca, *thĭn'kă*, sf. hacer —, to gain five points in the game of nine-pins.
cincel, *thĭnthĕl'*, sm. chisel. [tor.
cincelador, —*thĕlădōr'*, sm. engraver, sculp-
cincelar, —*thĕlăr'*, v. a. to chisel, engrave.
cinco, *thĭn'kō*, a. & sm. five.
cincuenta, *thĭnkwĕn'tă*, sm. fifty.
cincuenteno, na, —*tĕ'nō*, a. fiftieth.
cincha, *thĭn'chă*, sf. girth, cingle.
cinchar, —*chăr'*, v. a. to girth.
cinchera, —*chĕ'ră*, sf. girth-place.
cincho, *thĭn'chō*, sm. belt used by labourers to keep their bodies warm.
cíngaro, ra, *thĭn'gărō*, s. gipsy.
cíngulo, —*gŭlō*, sm. girdle; band, wreath.
cínico, ca, *thĕ'nĭkō*, a. cynical.
Cinosura, *thĭnōsŭ'ră*, sf. Cynosure, the Lesser Bear.
cinqueño, *thĭnkĕn'yō*, cinquillo, —*kĭl'yō*, sm. game at cards played among five per-sons. [be with child.
cinta, *thĭn'tă*, sf. ribbon; estar en —, to
cintadero, —*tădĕ'rō*, sm. notch in the crossbow to which the string is fastened.
cintagorda, —*gōr'dă*, sf. coarse hempen net for the tunny-fishery. [ribands.
cinteado, da, *thĭntĕă'dō*, a. adorned with
cintero, *thĭntĕ'rō*, sm. riband-weaver.
cintillo, *thĭntĭl'yō*, sm. hat-band.
cinto, *thĭn'tō*, sm. belt, girdle; (poet.)zodiac.
cintura, *thĭntŭ'ră*, sf. girdle; waist.
cinturón, —*tŭrōn'*, sm. broad-sword belt.
ciprés, *thĭprĕs'*, sm. cypress-tree.
cipresal, *thĭprĕsăl'*, sm. grove of cypress-trees. [belonging to cypress.
cipresino, na, —*sē'nō*, a. resembling or
circo, *thĭr'kō*, sm. circus. [circle.
circuir, *thĭrkŭĭr'*, v. a. to surround, to en-
circuito, *thĭrkŭē'tō*, sm. circuit; circum-ference. [currency.
circulación, *thĭrkŭlăthĭōn'*, sf. circulation;
circular, —*kŭlăr'*, a. circular, circulatory; —, v. n. to circulate.
círculo, *thĭr'kŭlō*, sm. circle; circumfe-rence; district; orb; compasses. [pole.
circumpolar, *thĭrkŭmpōlăr'*, a. near the
circuncidar, *thĭrkŭnthĭdăr'*, v. a. to cir-cumcise.
circuncisión, —*thĭsĭōn'*, sf. circumcision.
circundar, —*dăr'*, v. a. to surround, to encircle. [ference.
circunferencia, —*fĕrĕn'thĭă*, sf. circum-
circunferencial, —*fĕrĕnthĭăl'*, a. circum-ferential, surrounding.
circunflejo, ja, —*flĕ'hō*, a. acento —, sm. circumflex.
circunloquio, —*lō'kĭō*, sm. circumlocution.
circunscribir, —*skrĭbĭr'*, v. a. to circum-scribe. [scription.
circunscripción, —*skrĭpthĭōn'*, sf. circum-

circunspección, *–spĕkthĕŏn'*, sf. circumspection. [spect, cautious.
circunspecto, ta, *–spĕk'tŏ*, a. circumstance.
circunstancia, *–stăn'thiă*, sf. circumstance. [circumstantial, minute.
circunstanciado, da, *–stĕnthiă'dŏ*, a.
circunstantes, *–stăn'tĕs*, sm. pl. bystanders. [to circumvallate.
circunvalar, *–vălăr'*, v. a. to surround;
circunvecino, na, *–vĕthē'nŏ*, a. neighbouring, adjacent.
cirial, *thiriăl'*, sm. large candlestick.
cirineo, *thirinē'ŏ*, sm. mate, assistant.
cirio, *thē'riŏ*, sm. wax-candle.
cirro, *thir'rŏ*, sm. indurated gland; tuft of horse-mane.
ciruela, *thirŭĕ'lă*, sf. plum, prune.
ciruelo, *–lŏ*, sm. plum-tree.
cirugía, *thirŭhē'ă*, sf. surgery.
cirujano, *–hă'nŏ*, sm. surgeon.
ciscar, *thiskăr'*, v. a. to make dirty; –se, to ease nature.
cisco, *this'kŏ*, sm. coal-dust.
cisión, *thisiŏn'*, sf. incision.
cisma, *this'mă*, sm. & f. schism; disturbance.
cismático, ca, *–mă'tikŏ*, a. schismatic.
cisne, *this'nĕ*, sm. swan; (fig.) an eminent musician.
cisquero, *thiskĕ'rŏ*, sm. pouncing-bag.
cister, *thistĕr'*, sm. Cistertian order.
cisterna, *thistĕr'nă*, sf. cistern.
cisura, *thisū'ră*, sf. incisure, incision.
cita, *thē'tă*, sf. citation, quotation; rendezvous. [mons.
citación, *thiăthiŏn'*, sf. quotation; summons.
citano, *thitā'nŏ*, sm. such a one.
citar, *thităr'*, v. a. to make an appointment to meet a person; to convoke; to cite; to quote; to summon; to give judicial notice.
cítara, *thē'tără*, sf. (mus.) cithern; partition-wall of the thickness of a common brick.
citarista, *–ris'tă*, s. cithern-player.
citatorio, ria, *thiătō'riŏ*, a. (law) citatory.
citerior, *thitĕriŏr'*, ad. hither, nearer.
cito, *thē'tŏ*, s. word used to call dogs.
citola, *thē'tŏlă*, sf. mill-clapper.
ciudad, *thiŭdăd'*, sf. city; civic body.
ciudadano, *–dădă'nŏ*, sm. citizen; –, na, a. civil; citizen-like.
ciudadela, *–dădē'lă*, sf. citadel.
cívico, ca, *thē'vikŏ*, a. civic.
civil, *thivĭl'*, a. civil; polite, courteous; (law) not criminal. [tion.
civilización, *thivĭlĭthăthiŏn'*, sf. civilisation.
civilizar, *–thăr'*, v. a. to civilise.
civismo, *thivĭs'mŏ*, sm. patriotism.
cizalla, *thithăl'yă*, sf. fragments or filings of gold, silver or other metal.
cizallar, *–yăr'*, v. a. to clip money.
clamar, *klămăr'*, v. a. to cry out in a mournful tone; to show a want of something.
clamor, *klămŏr'*, sm. clamour, outcry; exclamation; peal of passing-bells.
clamorear, *klămŏrĕăr'*, v. a. to clamour; –, v. n. to toll the passing-bell.
clamoreo, *–rē'ŏ*, sm. knell.

clamoroso, sa, *–rŏ'sŏ*, a. clamorous.
clandestino, na, *klăndĕstē'nŏ*, a. clandestine, secret, concealed.
clara, *klă'ră*, sf. short interval of fair weather on a rainy day; white of an egg.
claraboya, *–bŏ'yă*, sf. sky-light.
clarea, *klă'rĕă*, sf. mulled wine.
clarear, *–rĕăr'*, v. n. to dawn; –se, to be transparent; to clear up.
clarete, *klă'rē'tă*, a. vino –, sm. claret.
claridad, *klăridăd'*, sf. brightness, clearness. [clarify.
clarificar, *klărĭfikăr'*, v. a. to brighten; to
clarificativo, va, *–fikătĕ'vŏ*, a. purificatory, clarifying.
clarín, *klărĭn'*, sm. trumpet; trumpeter.
clarinero, *–nĕ'rŏ*, sm. trumpeter.
clarinete, *–nĕ'tĕ*, sm. clarinet; player on the clarinet.
claro, ra, *klă'rŏ*, a. clear, bright; intelligible; evident, manifest; –, sm. skylight; opening or space between the columns of a building. [(in painting).
claroscuro, *klărŏskŏ'rŏ*, a. light and shade
clase, *klă'sĕ*, sf. class, rank; order.
clásico, ca, *klă'sikŏ*, a. classical.
clasificación, *klăsĭfikăthiŏn'*, sf. classification.
clasificar, *–fikăr'*, v. a. to classify.
claudicar, *klăŭdikăr'*, v. n. to halt, to limp.
claustral, *klăŭstrăl'*, a. claustral.
claustro, *klăŭs'trŏ*, sm. cloister; assembly of the principal members of a university; womb, uterus.
cláusula, *klă'ŭsŭlă*, sf. period; clause.
clausular, *klăŭsŭlăr'*, v. a. to close a period.
clausura, *klăŭsŏ'ră*, sf. clausure, confinement. [scupper-hole.
clava, *klă'vă*, sf. club, heavy stick; (mar.)
clavado, da, *klăvă'dŏ*, a. exact, precise; furnished with nails.
clavar, *klăvăr'*, v. a. to nail; to fasten in, to force in; to drive into; to drive a wedge; (fig.) to cheat, to deceive; –se, to run one's self through.
clavazón, *klăvăthŏn'*, sf. set of nails.
clave, *klă'vĕ*, sf. key-stone; (mus.) clef.
clavecín, *–thĭn'*, sm. harpsichord, pianoforte.
clavel, *klăvĕl'*, sm. (bot.) common pink.
clavera, *klăvĕ'ră*, sf. mould for nail-heads; hole in a horse-shoe.
clavero, *–rŏ*, sm. aromatic clove-tree.
clavetear, *klăvĕtĕăr'*, v. a. to garnish with nails.
clavicordio, *klăvikŏr'diŏ*, sm. harpsichord.
clavícula, *klăvē'kŭlă*, sf. clavicle.
clavija, *klăvē'hă*, sf. pin, peg. [clove.
clavo, *klă'vŏ*, sm. nail; corn (on the feet);
clemencia, *klĕmĕn'thiă*, sf. clemency.
clemente, *klĕmĕn'tĕ*, a. clement, merciful.
clerecía, *klĕrĕthē'ă*, sf. clergy.
clerical, *klĕrikăl'*, a. clergical.
clericato, *–kă'tŏ*, sm. state and dignity of a clergyman. [tempt).
clerigalla, *–găl'yă*, sf. priesthood (in contempt).
clérigo, *klĕ'rigŏ*, sm. clergyman.
clero, *klă'rŏ*, sm. clergy.
cliente, *kliĕn'tĕ*, sm. client.

clientela, *klĭĕntĕ´lǎ,* sf. clientship.

clima, *klĭ´mǎ,* sm. climate.

clin, *klĭn,* sf. mane (of a horse). [hospital.

clinica, *klĭ´nĭkǎ,* sf. clinical surgery *or*

clinico, ca, *–nĭkŏ,* a. clinical.

clisaje, *klĭsǎ´h´ĕ,* sm. stereotyping.

clisar, *klĭsǎr,* v. a. to stereotype.

clister, *klĭstĕr,* sm. clyster.

clivoso, za, *klĭvŏ´sŏ,* a. (poet.) declivous.

clo-clo, *klŏ´klŏ,* sm. clucking of a hen.

cloaca, *klŏǎ´kǎ,* sf. sewer.

cloque, *klŏ´kĕ,* sm. grapnel; harpoon.

cloquear, *klŏkĕǎr,* v. a. to cluck.

cloqueo, *klŏkǎ´ŏ,* sm. chuck.

cloquera, *klŏkǎ´rǎ,* sf. hatching of fowls; brooding-time.   [fishery.

cloquero, *–rŏ,* sm. harpooner in the tunny-

clorosis, *klŏrŏ´sĭs,* sf. green-sickness.

clueca, *klŭĕ´kǎ,* a. clucking and hatching

clueco, ca, *–kŏ,* a. decrepit.   [(of a hen).

coacción, *kŏǎkthĭŏn´,* sf. coaction, compulsion.

coactivo, va, *–tĭ´vŏ,* a. coactive, coer-

coadjutor *kŏǎd´hŭtŏr´,* sm. coadjutor, [helper, assistant.

coadyuvador, *–yŭvǎdŏr´,* sm. fellow-

coadyuvar, *–yŭvǎr´,* v.a. to help, to assist.

coagular, *kŏǎgŭlǎr´,* v. a. to coagulate, to curd.

coágulo, *kŏǎ´gŭlŏ,* sm. coagulated blood.

coalición, *kŏǎlĭthĭŏn´,* sf. coalition, confederacy.

coarrendador, *kŏǎrrĕndǎdŏr´,* sm. joint partner in the rent of a property; co-lessor.

coartación, *kŏǎrthǎthĭŏn´,* sf. obligation of the holder of a benefice, *or* its recipient, to receive ordination.

coartada, *–tǎ´dǎ,* sf. (law) alibi.

coartar, *–tǎr´,* v. a. to limit, to restrict,

cobalto, *kŏbǎl´tŏ,* sm. cobalt. [to restrain.

cobanillo, *kŏbǎnĭl´yŏ,* sm. basket for vintage.

cobarde, *kŏbǎr´dĕ,* a. coward, timid.

cobardía, *–dĕ´ǎ,* sf. cowardice.

cobertera, *kŏbĕrtĕ´rǎ,* sf.pot-lid; procuress.

cobertizo, *–tĕ´thŏ,* sm. small shed; hovel.

cobertura, *–tŭ´rǎ,* sf. coverlet; coverele; prerogative of the Spanish grandees to appear with covered head before their sovereign.

cobija, *kŏbĭ´h´ǎ,* sf. gutter-tile.

cobijar, *kŏbĭ´hǎr´,* v. a. to cover, to shelter.

cobradero,ra, *kŏbrǎdĕ´rŏ,* a. recoverable.

cobrador, *–dŏr´,* sm. collector of rents.

cobranza, *kŏbrǎn´thǎ,* sf. recovery or collection of money.   [to come to one's self.

cobrar, *kŏbrǎr´,* v. a. to recover; –se,

cobre, *kŏ´brĕ,* sm.copper; kitchen-furniture.

cobrizo, za, *kŏbrĭ´thŏ,* a. coppery.

cobro, *kŏ´brŏ,* sm. encashment.   [coax.

cocar, *kŏkǎr´,* v. a. to make grimaces; to

cocarar, *kŏkǎrǎr´,* v. a. to gather.

coccíneo, nea, *kŏkthĕ´nĕŏ,* a. of a purple colour.

cocción, *kŏkthĭŏn´,* sf. coction, concoction.

coceador, ra, *kŏthĕǎdŏr´,* a. kicking. (of horses).

cocear, *kŏthĕǎr´,* v. a. to kick, to fling out; (fig.) to repugn, to resist.

cocedero, ra, *kŏthĕdĕ´rŏ,* a. easily cooked; –, sm. bake-house.

cocedizo, za, *–dĕ´thŏ,* a. easily boiled.

cocer, *kŏthĕr´,* v. a. to boil; to bake (bricks, &c.); to digest; –, v. n. to boil; to ferment; –se, to suffer intense pain.

cocido, da, *kŏthĭ´dŏ,* a. boiled; (fig.) skilled, experienced; –, sm oglio, a dish made of boiled meat and vegetables.

cocimiento, *–mĭĕn´tŏ,* sm. decoction; dyer's bath.

cocina, *kŏthĕ´nǎ,* sf. kitchen.

cocinar, *kŏthĭnǎr´,* v. a. to cook.

cocinera, *–nĕ´rǎ,* sf. cook-maid, female

cocinero, *–rŏ,* sm. cook.   [cook.

cocle, *kŏ´klĕ,* sm. grapnel.

cóclea, *kŏ´klĕǎ,* sf. endless screw.

coclear, *kŏklĕǎr´,* v. a. to catch with a harpoon; –, v. n. to cluck.   [bug-bear.

coco, *kŏ´kŏ,* sm. cocoa-tree; cocoa-nut;

cocodrilo, *kŏkŏdrĭ´lŏ,* sm. crocodile; (fig.) false, faithless person.

cocoso, sa, *kŏkŏ´sŏ,* a. worm-eaten.

cochambre, *kŏtshǎm´brĕ,* sm. dirty, stinking object.   [and filthy objects.

cochambrería, *–brĕrĭ´ǎ,* sf. heap of nasty

cochambroso, sa, *–brŏ´sŏ,* a. nasty,filthy, stinking.

cocharro, *kŏtshǎr´rŏ,* sm. wooden cup.

cochastro, *kŏtshǎs´trŏ,* sm. little sucking wild boar.   [– cama, sleeping-car.

coche, *kŏtsh´ĕ,* sm. coach, carriage; (rail.)

cochear, *kŏtshĕǎr´,* v. n. to drive a coach.

cochera, *kŏtshĕ´rǎ,* sf. coach-house.

cocheril, *–rĭl´,* a. belonging to coachmen.

cochero, *kŏtshĕ´rŏ,* sm. coachman.

cochifrito, *kŏtshĭfrĕ´tŏ,* sm. fricassee.

cochina, *kŏtshĕ´nǎ,* sf. sow.

cochinería, *–nĕrĭ´ǎ,* sf. dirtiness, foulness.

cochinilla, *kŏtshĭnĭl´yǎ,* sf. wood-louse; cochineal.   [filthy; –, sm. pig.

cochino, na, *kŏtshĕ´nŏ,* a. dirty, nasty,

cochiquera, *kŏtshĭkĕ´rǎ,* sf. pig-sty.

codaste, *kŏdǎs´tĕ,* sm. (mar.) stern-post.

codazo, *kŏdǎ´thŏ,* sm. blow given with the

codear, *kŏdĕǎr´,* v. a. to elbow.   [elbow.

códice, *kŏ´dĭthĕ,* sm. old manuscript.

codicia, *kŏdĭ´thĭǎ,* sm. covetousness, cupidity, greediness.

codiciable, *–thĭǎ´blĕ,* a. covetable.

codiciar, *–thĭǎr´,* v. a. to covet, to desire eagerly.   [codicil.

codicilar, *–thĭlǎr´,* a. pertaining to a

codicilo, *–thĕ´lŏ,* sm. (law) codicil.

codicioso, sa, *–thĭ´ŏsŏ,* a. greedy, covetous; diligent, laborious.

código, *kŏ´dĭgŏ,* sm. code of laws.

codillo, *kŏdĭl´yŏ,* sm. knee of horses and other quadrupeds; angle; crotch of a tree; codille, a terin at hombre.

codo, *kŏ´dŏ,* sm. elbow.

codoña, *kŏdŏn´yǎ,* sf. quince.

codoñero, *kŏdŏnyĕ´rŏ,* sm. quince-tree.

codorniz, *kŏdŏrnĭth´,* sf. quail.

coerción, *kŏĕrthĭŏn´,* sf. coercion,restraint.

coercitivo, va, *–thĭtĭ´vŏ,* a. coercive.

coetáneo, nea, *kŏĕtā′nĕŏ,* a. contemporary.

coeterno, na, *kŏĕtēr′nŏ,* a. coeternal.

coevo, va, *kŏĕ′vŏ,* a. coeval. [tence.

coexistencia, *kŏĕksĭstĕn′thĭā,* sf. coexis-

coexistente, *–tĕ,* a. coexistent.

coexistir, *kŏĕksĭstīr′,* v. n. to coexist.

cofia, *kŏ′fĭā,* sf. coif; silken hair-net; head-gear.

cofín, *kŏfīn′,* sm. small basket for fruit.

cofrade, *kŏfrā′dĕ,* sm. colleague.

cofradía, *kŏfrādē′ā,* sf. confraternity.

cofre, *kŏf′rĕ,* sm. trunk.

cofrero, *kŏfrē′rŏ,* sm. trunk-maker.

cogedera, *kŏ′hĕdā′rā,* sf. hive used to gather an escaped swarm of bees.

cogedizo, za, *–dē′thŏ,* a. gatherable.

cogedor, *–dōr′,* sm. collector, gatherer; dust-box.

cogedura, *kŏğ′rā,* sf. gathering.

coger, *kŏ′hĕr′,* v. a. to catch, to lay hold of, to occupy, to take up; to surprise.

cogitabundo, da, *kŏ′hĭtābŭn′dŏ,* a. pensive, thoughtful. [tate.

cogitar, *–tār′,* v. a. to reflect, to medi-

cogite, *kŏ′hē′tĕ,* (fam.) I have caught you.

cognoscitivo, va, *kŏgnŏsthĭtē′vŏ,* a. cognitive. [cabbage, &c.; shoot of a plant.

cogollo, *kŏğŏl′yŏ,* sm. heart of a lettuce,

cogote, *kŏğŏ′tĕ,* sm. occiput.

cogujada, *kŏğŭhā′dā,* sf. crested lark.

cogujón, *–hŏn′,* sm. corner of a mattress or bolster.

cogulla, *kŏğŭl′yā,* sf. cowl, monk's hood.

cohabitar, *kŏābĭtār′,* v. n. to cohabit, to live together. [suborn.

cohechar, *kŏĕtshār′,* v. a. to bribe, to

cohecho, *kŏĕtsh′ŏ,* sm. bribery; season for ploughing the ground.

coheredera, *kŏĕrĕdē′rā,* sf. co-heiress.

coheredero, *–rŏ,* sm. co-heir, joint-heir.

coherencia, *kŏĕrĕn′thĭā,* sf. coherence.

coherente, *–tĕ,* a. coherent, cohesive.

cohete, *kŏē′tĕ,* sm. sky-rocket.

cohetero, *–tē′rŏ,* sm. rocket-maker.

cohibir, *kŏībīr′,* v. a. to prohibit, to restrain. [cidence.

cohombral, *kŏŏmbrāl′,* sm. cucumber-bed.

cohombro, *kŏŏm′brŏ,* sm. cucumber.

cohonestar, *kŏŏnĕstār′,* v. a. to give an honest appearance to an action.

cohorte, *kŏŏr′tĕ,* sm. cohort. [cidence.

coincidencia, *kŏĭnthĭdĕn′thĭā,* sf. coin-

coincidente, *–tĕ,* a. coincident.

coincidir, *kŏĭnthĭdīr′,* v. n. to coincide.

coito, *kŏ′ĭtŏ,* sm. coition, cohabitation.

cojear, *kŏ′hĕār′,* v. n. to halt, to hobble; to deviate from virtue.

cojera, *kŏ′hĕ′rā,* sf. lameness, halting.

cojijoso, sa, *kŏ′hĭ′hŏ′sŏ,* a. peevish, irritable.

cojín, *kŏ′hĭn′,* sm. cushion. [table.

cojo, ja, *kŏ′h′ŏ,* a. lame, cripple, halt.

cojudo, da, *kŏ′hŏ′dā,* a. entire, not castrated.

col, *kŏl,* sf. cabbage. [not castrated.

cola, *kŏ′lā,* sf. tail; train (of a gown); glue; de la —, behind, backwards.

colación, *kŏlāthĭŏn′,* sf. collation (luncheon); collation (bestowing an ecclesiastical benefice).

colacionar, *–thĭŏnār′,* v. a. to collate, to compare.

colada, *kŏlā′dā,* sf. bucking of linen with lie made of ashes; linen itself thus bucked.

coladera, *–dē′rā,* sf. strainer, colander.

coladero, *–rŏ,* sm. colander; narrow passage. [sage.

colador, *–dŏr′,* sm. colander.

coladura, *dŏ′rā,* sf. straining, filtering.

colanilla, *–nēl′yā,* sf. small bolt.

colapez, *–pĕth′,* colapiscis, *–pĭs′thĭs,* sf. isinglass.

colar, *kŏlār′,* v. á. & n. to strain, to filter; to confer ecclesiastical benefices; to pass through a strait place; to drink wine; —se, to be filtered.

colateral, *kŏlātĕrāl′,* a. collateral.

colcha, *kŏl′tshā,* sf. coverlet, counterpane.

colchadura, *–dŏ′rā,* sf. quilting.

colchar, *kŏltshār′,* v. a. to quilt.

colchero, *kŏltshĕ′rŏ,* sm. quilt-maker.

colchón, *kŏltshŏn′,* sm. mattress. [maker.

colchonero, *kŏltshŏnĕ′rŏ,* sm. mattress-

coleada, *kŏlĕā′dā,* sf. wagging of an animal's tail.

colear, *kŏlĕār′,* v. n. to wag the tail.

colección, *kŏlĕkthĭŏn′,* sf. collection.

colecta, *kŏlĕk′tā,* sf. distribution of a tax levied on a town; collect (an oration of the mass).

colectar, *–tār′,* v. a. to collect taxes.

colecticio, cia, *–tē′thĭŏ,* a. collectitious, assembled together without discipline (of troops).

colectivo, va, *–tē′vŏ,* a. collective.

colector, *–tŏr′,* sm. collector, gatherer.

colega, *kŏlē′gā,* sm. colleague. [gatary.

colegatario, ria, *–tā′rĭŏ,* sm. & f. colle-

colegial, *kŏlĕ′hĭāl′,* sm. collegian; —, a. collegial; iglesia —, sf. collegiate church.

colegiala, *kŏlĕ′hĭā′lā,* sf. female member of a seminary or college.

colegiata, *–tā,* sf. collegiate church.

colegio, *kŏlē′hĭŏ,* sm. college.

colegir, *kŏlĕ′hĭr′,* v. a. to collect, to deduce; to infer.

cólera, *kŏ′lĕrā,* sf. bile; anger, fury, rage.

coléricamente, *kŏlĕrĭkāmĕn′tĕ,* ad. in a rage. [sionate.

colérico, ca, *kŏlĕ′rĭkŏ,* a. choleric; pas-

coleta, *kŏlĕ′tā,* sf. cue; short addition to a discourse or writing. [maker.

coletero, *kŏlĕtē′rŏ,* sm. buff-breeches-

coleto, *kŏlĕ′tŏ,* sm. doublet, jacket.

colgadero, *kŏlgādē′rŏ,* sm. hook to hang things upon; —, ra, a. fit to be hung up.

colgadizo, *–dē′thŏ,* sm. shed; —, za, a. pendent, suspended. [niture.

colgadura, *–dŏ′rā,* sf. tapestry; bed-fur-

colgajo, *kŏlgā′h′ŏ,* sm. tatter, rag.

colgar, *kŏlgār′,* v. a. to hang; to suspend; to adorn with tapestry; —, v. n. to be suspended. [bri.

colibrí, *kŏlĭbrē′,* sm. humming-bird, coli-

cólica, *kŏ′lĭkā,* sf. colic. [hair in the tail.

colicano, na, *kŏlĭkā′nŏ,* a. having grey

cólico, *kŏ′lĭkŏ,* sm. colic.

colicorto, *kŏlĭkŏr′tŏ,* a. short-tailed (of animals).

colicuar, *kōlĭkwăr'*, v. a. to colliquate, to melt, to dissolve; –se, to become liquid.

coliflor, *kōlĭflŏr'*, sm. cauliflower.

coligación, *kōlĭgăthĭōn'*, sf. connexion, union, alliance.

colilla, *kōlĭl'yă*, sf. end *or* stump of a cigar.

colina, *kōlĕ'nă*, sf. hill, hillock.

colinabo, *kōlĭnă'bō*, sm. turnip.

coliseo, *kōlĭsĕ'ō*, sm. opera-house, theatre.

colisión, *kōlĭsĭōn'*, sf. collision; friction.

colitigante, *kōlĭtĭgăn'tĕ*, sm. litigant; party to a law-suit.

colmar, *kōlmăr'*, v. a. to heap up.

colmena, *kōlmĕ'nă*, sf. hive, bee-hive.

colmenar, *–năr'*, sm. bee-hive stand, bee-house.

colmenero, *–nĕ'rō*, sm. bee-master.

colmenilla, *–nĭl'yă*, sf. morel, moril (mushroom).

colmillo, *kōlmĭl'yō*, sm. eye-tooth.

colmilludo, da, *–yō'dō*, a. having eye-teeth; (fig.) sagacious, quick-sighted.

colmo, *kōl'mō*, sm. heap; completion, crown; full; height; á –, plentifully.

colocación, *kōlōkăthĭōn'*, sf. employment; arrangement; situation.

colocar, *kōlōkăr'*, v. a. to arrange, to place; to provide with an employment.

colodra, *kōlō'dră*, sf. milking-pail; wooden can with which wine is measured. [head.

colodrillo, *kōlōdrĭl'yō*, sm. back of the

colofonia, *kōlōfō'nĭă*, sm. colophony.

colon, *kō'lōn*, sm. (gr.) two points (:); colon, the largest of the intestines.

colonia, *kōlō'nĭă*, sf. colony; silk ribbon two fingers' wide.

colonial, *kōlōnĭăl'*, a. colonial.

colonizar, *kōlōnĭthăr'*, v. a. to colonise.

colono, *kōlō'nō*, sm. colonist; farmer.

coloquio, *kōlō'kĭō*, sm. colloquy.

color, *kōlōr'*, sm. colour, hue, dye; rouge; pretext; so –, on pretence, under pretext.

coloración, *kōlōrăthĭōn'*, sf. colouring, coloration.

colorado, da, *kōlōră'dō*, a. ruddy.

colorar, *kōlōrăr'*, v. a. to colour; to make plausible; –, v. n. to blush with shame.

colorativo, va, *kōlōrătē'vō*, a. colorific.

colorear, *kōlōrĕăr'*, v. a. to colour; to palliate, to excuse; –, v. n. to grow red.

colorete, *kōlōrĕ'tĕ*, sm. rouge (paint).

–lorido, *kōlōrĕ'dō*, sm. colouring; pretext, pretence.

colorín, *kōlōrĭn'*, sm. linnet; vivid colour.

colorir, *kōlōrĭr'*, v. a. to colour.

colorista, *kōlōrĭs'tă*, sm. colourist.

colosal, *kōlōsăl'*, a. colossal.

coloso, *kōlō'sō*, sm. colossus.

columbrar, *kōlŭmbrăr'*, v. a. to discern at a distance; to guess.

columna, *kōlŭm'nă*, sf. column.

columnata, *–nă'tă*, sf. colonnade. [ro.

columpiar, *–păr'*, v. a. to swing to and

columpio, *kōlŭm'pĭō*, sm. swing, see-saw.

coluna, *kōlō'nă*, sf. column.

colusión, *kōlŭsĭōn'*, sf. collusion.

colusorio, ria, *kōlŭsō'rĭō*, a. collusive.

colza, *kōl'thă*, sf. rape, rape-seed.

collado, *kōlyă'dō*, sm. hill.

collar, *kōlyăr'*, sm. necklace, necklet.

collera, *kōlyă'ră*, sf. collar; gang of convicts chained together.

collón, *kōlyōn'*, sm. coward.

collonería, *kōlyōnĕrē'ă*, sf. cowardice.

coma, *kō'mă*, sf. (gr.) comma. [mother.

comadre, *kōmă'drĕ*, sf. midwife; god-

comadreja, *–drĕ'hă*, sf. weasel.

comadrería, *–drĕrē'ă*, sf. gossiping.

comadrero, ra, *–drĕ'rō*, a. idle and gossiping.

comadrón, *–drōn'*, sm. man-midwife.

comadrona, *kōmădrō'nă*, sf. mid-wife.

comandancia, *kōmăndăn'thĭă*, sf. command.

comandante, *–dăn'tĕ*, sm. commander.

comandar, *kōmăndăr'*, v. a. to command.

comarca, *kōmăr'kă*, sf. territory, district; boundary, limit. [bordering upon.

comarcano, na, *–kă'nō*, a. neighbouring,

comarcar, *–kăr'*, v. a. to plant trees in a straight line; –, v. n. to border, to confine upon.

comaya, *kōmă'yă*, sf. large basket, pannier.

comba, *kōm'bă*, sf. curvature (of timber when warped); convexity. [warp.

combar, *kōmbăr'*, v. a. to bend; –se, to

combate, *kōmbă'tĕ*, sm. combat, conflict; fighting; – singular, duel.

combatidor, *–tĭdŏr'*, sm. combatant.

combatir, *kōmbătĭr'*, v. a. & n. to combat, to fight; to attack; to contradict. [tion.

combinación, *kōmbĭnăthĭōn'*, sf. combina-

combinar, *kōmbĭnăr'*, v. n. to combine.

combo, ba, *kōm'bō*, a. bent, crooked, warped; –s, sm. pl. stand for casks; gawn-tree. [–, sm. combustible; fuel.

combustible, *kōmbŭstē'blĕ*, a. combustible;

comedero, *kōmĕdĕ'rō*, sm. dining-room.

comedero, ra, *–rō*, a. eatable.

comedia, *kōmĕ'dĭă*, sf. comedy.

comediante, *–dĭăn'tĕ*, sm. player, actor, comedian. [shares.

comediar, *–dĭăr'*, v. a. to divide into equal

comedido, da, *–dĕ'dō*, a. polite, gentle.

comedir, *–dĭr'*, v. a. to commit; –se, to govern one's self. [–, sm. dining-room.

comedor, ra, *–dŏr'*, sm. & f. eater; feeder.

comendador, *kōmĕndădŏr'*, sm. knight commander of a military order.

comendadora, *–dŏ'ră*, sf. mother superior of a nunnery.

comendaticio, cia, *–tĕ'thĭō*, comendatorio, ria, *–tō'rĭō*, a. recommending, introductory (of letters). [expound.

comentar, *kōmĕntăr'*, v. a. to comment, to

comentario, *kōmĕntă'rĭō*, sm. comment.

comento, *kōmĕn'tō*, sm. comment. [tary.

comenzar, *kōmĕnthăr'*, v. n. to commence, to begin.

comer, *kōmĕr'*, v. a. to eat, to chew; to dine; to consume; to take a piece at chess.

comerciable, *kōmĕrthĭă'blĕ*, a. marketable; sociable.

comercial, *–thĭăl'*, a. commercial.

comerciante, *–thĭăn'tĕ*, sm. trader, merchant, tradesman.

comerciar, –thiár', v. a. to trade, to commerce; to have intercourse with.

comercio, kõmér'thiõ, sm. trade, commerce; communication, intercourse; company of merchants.

comestible, kõmèstī'blĕ, a. eatable; –s, pl. all sorts of provisions.

cometa, kõmé'tä, sm. comet; –, sf. kite.

cometer, kõmètér', v. a. to commit, to charge; to intrust; to attempt.

comezón –thõn', sf. itch; ardent desire.

cómica, kõ'mĭkä, sf. actress.

cómico, ca, –mĭkõ, a. comic, comical.

comida, kõmé'dä, sf. eating, food; dinner.

comilón, ona, kõmílõn', sm. & f. great eater, glutton.

comino, kõmé'nõ, sm. cumin (plant or seed).

comisaria, kõmïsäré'ä, sf. comissaryship; commissariat.

comisario, kõmĭsä'rĭõ, sm. commissary.

comisión, kõmĭsĭõn', sf. trust, commission; mandate; committee.

comisionado, kõmĭsĭõnä'dõ, sm. commissionary; commissioner. [sion, to depute.

comisionar, kõmĭsĭõnär', v. a. to commission.

comisionista, kõmĭsĭõnĭs'tä, sm. commissioner.

comiso, kõmé'sõ, sm. confiscation.

comistrajo, kõmĭsträ'hõ, sm. hodge-podge.

comitiva, kõmĭté'vä, sf. suite, retinue, followers. [a galley.

cómitre, kõ'mĭtrĕ, sm. boatswain on board

como, kõ'mõ, ad. how, in what manner; as; why; in such a manner; in what manner; like; –quiera, however.

cómoda, kõ'mõdä, sf. chest of drawers.

comodatario, –dätä'rĭõ, sm. (law) borrower; pawn-broker.

comodato, –dä'tõ, sm. (law) loan.

comodidad, kõmõdĭdäd'', sf. comfort; convenience; profit, interest; –es, pl. wealth, estate.

cómodo, da, kõ'mõdõ, a. convenient, commodious; comfortable; –, sm. utility, profit, benefit. [dense.

compacto, ta, kõmpäk'tõ, a. compact, close.

compadecerse, –pädĕthér'sĕ, v. r. to pity; to agree with each other.

compadrar, –pädrär', v. n. to become a godfather. [ship.

compadrazgo, –pädräth'gõ, sm. godfather-

compadre, –pä'drĕ, sm. godfather; compeer, friend.

compadrería, –pädrĕré'ä, sf. friendly intercourse between friends or companions.

compaginar, –pä'hĭnär', v. a. to join, to couple.

compañero, ra, –pänyé'rõ, sm. & f. companion, friend; compeer, comrade; partner.

compañía, –pänyé'ä, sf. company, society; partnership. [conference, conferring.

comparación, –päräthĭõn', sf. comparison.

comparar, –pärär', v. a. to compare, to confront. [rative.

comparativo, va, –pärätĭ'võ, a. comparative.

comparecer, –pärĕthér', v. n. to appear before a judge.

comparendo, –pärĕn'dõ, sm. summons.

comparición, –päríthĭõn', sf. (law) appearance.

comparsa, –pär'sä, sm. & f. super.

comparte, –pär'tĕ, sm. joint party in a law-suit. [equal parts.

compartir, –pärtĭr', v. a. to divide into

compás, –pás', sm. pair of compasses; (mus.) measure; rule of life; pattern.

compasar, –päsär', v. a. to measure with a compass. [miseration.

compasión, –päsĭõn', sf. compassion, commiseration.

compasivo, va, –päsĭ'võ, a. compassionate. [sistent with.

compatible, –pätĭ'blĕ, a. compatible, consistent with.

compatriota, –pätrĭõ'tä, sm. & f. countryman; countrywoman; fellow-citizen.

compeler, –pĕlér', v. a. to compel, to constrain. [to abridge.

compendiar, –pĕndĭär', v. a. to epitomize,

compendio, –pĕn'dĭõ, sm. epitome, abridgment, summary.

compendioso, sa, –pĕndĭõ'sõ, a. brief, abridged, compendious.

compensación, –pĕnsäthĭõn', sf. compensation; recompense.

compensar, –pĕnsär', v. a. & n. to compensate; to make amends; to recompense.

competencia, –pĕtén'thĭä, sf. competition, rivalry; competence. [ficient.

competente, –pĕtén'tĕ, a. competent, sufficient.

competer, –pĕtér', v. n. to be one's due.

competición, –pĕtĭthĭõn', sf. competition.

competidor, –pĕtĭdõr', sm. competitor, rival. [with, to rival.

competir, –pĕtĭr', v. n. to vie; to compete

compilación, –pĭläthĭõn', sf. compilation.

compilador, –pĭlädõr', sm. compiler.

compilar, –pĭlär', v. a. to compile.

compinche, –pĭn'chĕ, sm. comrade, confidant, crony. [compliance.

complacencia, –pläthén'thĭä, sf. pleasure;

complacer, –pläthér', v. a. to please another; –se, to be pleased with.

complaciente, –pläthĭén'tĕ, a. pleasing.

complemento, –plĕmén'tõ, sm. complement, completion.

completar, –plĕtär', v. a. to complete.

completo, ta, –plé'tõ, a. complete, perfect.

complexión, –plĕksĭõn', sf. complexion, temperature of the body.

complexionado, da, –plĕksĭõnä'dõ, a. complexioned; bien ó mal –, of a good or bad complexion.

complejo, –plé'hõ, sm. complex.

complicar, –plĭkär', v. a. to complicate.

cómplice, kõm'plĭthĕ, sm. & f. accomplice.

complicidad, –plĭthĭdäd', sf. complicity.

complotar, –plõtär', v. a. to conspire, to plot. [author; compositor.

componedor, –põnĕdõr', sm. composer,

componer, –põnér', v. a. to compose; to compound; to construct; to mend, to repair; to strengthen, to restore; to garnish; to adjust; to reconcile; to compose, to calm.

comportable, –põrtä'blĕ, a. supportable, tolerable, sufferable.

comportar, –põrtär', v. a. to suffer, to

tolerate; **—se**, to comport, to behave one's self.

composición, —pŏsĭthĭŏn', sf. composition; composure, making; adjustment; agreement; musical *or* literary composition; modest appearance. [compositor.

compositor, —pŏsĭtŏr', sm. composer.

compostura, —pŏstŏŏ'rä, sf. composition, composure, mending, repairing; neatness of dress; accommodation, adjustment; modesty, demureness.

compota, —pŏ'tä, sf. conserve of fruit.

compotera, —pŏtā'rä, sf. vessel in which jams are served.

compra, kŏm'prä, sf. purchase; necessaries bought for the daily use of the house.   [buyer; caterer.

comprador, ra, kŏmprädŏr', sm. & f.

comprar, kŏmprär', v. a. to buy, to purchase.

comprender, kŏmprĕndĕr', v. a. to include, to contain; to comprehend; to understand.   [sible.

comprensible, —prĕnsē'blĕ, a. comprehensible.

comprensión, —prĕnsĭŏn', s. comprehension, understanding.   [prehensive.

comprensivo, va, —prĕnsē'vŏ, a. comprehensible, —prĕs'blĕ, a. compressible.

compresión, —prĕsĭŏn', s. compression, compressure.   [sive.

compresivo, va, —prĕsē'vŏ, a. compressive.

comprimir, —prĭmĭr', v. a. to compress; to repress; to restrain; **—se**, to subdue one's passion.   [confirm; to prove.

comprobar, —prŏbär', v. a. to verify, to

comprometer, —prŏmĕtĕr', v. a. to compromise; to render one answerable for; to put in danger.   [trator, umpire.

compromisario, —prŏmĭsä'rĭŏ, sm. arbitrator.

compromiso, —prŏmē'sŏ, sm. compromise.

compuerta, —pŭĕr'tä, sf. half door; sluice.

compuesto, —pŭĕs'tŏ, sm. compound; **—, ta**, a. composed, compounded; made up.

compulsa, —pŭl'sä, sf. attested copy of an instrument.   [authentic copy.

compulsar, —pŭlsär', v. a. to make an

compulsivo, va, —pŭlsē'vŏ, a. compulsive.

compulsorio, ria, —pŭlsŏ'rĭŏ, a. compulsory; ordering an authentic copy to be made.   [contrition.

compunción, —pŭnthĭŏn', sf. compunction.

compungirse, —pŭnhĭr'sĕ, v. r. to feel compunction.

compungivo, va, —pŭnhē'vŏ, a. pricking, stimulating.   [tion.

computación, —pŭtäthĭŏn', sf. computation.

computar, —pŭtär', v. a. to compute.

cómputo, kŏm'pŭtŏ, sm. compute, calculation.

comulgar, kŏmŭlgär', v. a. & n. to administer the sacrament; to communicate.

común, kŏmŭn', a. common, usual, general, **—, sm.** community, public: **en —**, conjointly.

comunal, kŏmŭnäl', sm. commonalty.

comunero, ra, kŏmŭnā'rŏ, a. popular; **—, sm.** joint holder of a tenure of lands.

comunicación, kŏmŭnĭkäthĭŏn', sf. communication.

comunicar, kŏmŭnĭkär', v. a. to communicate; **—se**, to have intercourse; to correspond; to be united.

comunicativo va, kŏmŭnĭkätē'vŏ, a. communicative.

comunidad, kŏmŭnĭdäd', sf. commonness; commonally; community.

comunión, kŏmŭnĭŏn', sf. communion; fellowship; common possession.

comuña, kŏmŭ'nyä, s. meslin; **—s**, pl. stores.   [fore.

con, kŏn, pr. with; by; **—que**, then, thereconato, kŏnä'tŏ, sm. endeavour, effort; crime attempted but not executed.

cóncava, kŏn'kävä, concavidad, kŏnkävĭdäd', sf. concavity.

cóncavo, va, kŏn'kävŏ, a. concave.

concebir, kŏnthĕbĭr', v. a. & n. to conceive; to become pregnant.

conceder, —thĕdĕr', v. a. to give; to grant; to concede, to allow.   [council.

concejal, —thĕhäl', sm. member of a

concejil, —thĕhĭl', a. relating to public boards.

concejo, —thĕ'n'ŏ, sm. civic body of a small town; town-hall.   [centration.

concentración, —thĕnträthĭŏn', sf. concentrar, —thĕnträr', v. a. to concentrate.

concéntrico, ca, —thĕn'trĭkŏ, a. concentric.

concepción, —thĕpthĭŏn', sf. conception; idea, conceit.   [witty sayings.

conceptear, —thĕptĕär', v. n. to abound in

conceptible, —thĕptē'blĕ, a. conceivable.

conceptista, —thĕptĭs'tä, sm. man of genius, wit.   [judgment, opinion.

concepto, —thĕp'tŏ, sm. conceit, thought;

conceptuar, —thĕptŭär', v. a. to conceive, to judge, to think.

conceptuoso, sa, —thĕptŭŏ'sŏ, a. sharp, witty; sententious.   [relating.

concerniente, —thĕrnĭĕn'tĕ, a. concerning,

concernir, —thĕrnĭr', v. imp. to regard, to concern.

concertar, —thĕrtär', v. a. to concert, to settle; to adjust; to conclude an agreement; to compose differences; **—, v. n.** to agree, to accord.

concesión, —thĕsĭŏn', sf. concession.

conciencia, —thĭĕn'thĭä, sf. conscience.

concierto, —thĭĕr'tŏ, sm. concert; agreement; accommodation; (mus.) concert; **de —**, according to agreement.

conciliación, —thĭlĭäthĭŏn', sf. conciliation, reconciliation.

conciliar, —thĭlĭär', v. a. to conciliate, to reconcile; **—**, a. belonging to councils.

conciliativo, va, —thĭlĭätē'vŏ, a. conciliatory;   [of bishops.

concilio, —thē'lĭŏ, sm. council; assembly

concinidad, —thĭnĭdäd', sf. harmony.

concisión, —thĭsĭŏn', sf. conciseness.

conciso, sa, —thē'sŏ, a. concise, brief.

concitar, —thĭtär', v. a. to excite; to stir up commotions.

concidadanía, —thĭŭdädän'ĕ, sf. joint-citizenship; the burgesses.

concidadano, —thĭŭdädä'nŏ, sm. fellow-citizen; countryman.

cónclave, *kŏn'klăvĕ*, **conclave**, *kŏn-klā'vĕ*, sm. conclave.

concluir, *kŏnklŭŕr'*, v. a. to conclude, to end, to complete; to convince; to infer, to deduce; to disarm an adversary by grasping the hilt of his sword.

conclusión, *-klŭsŏn'*, sf. conclusion, end; consequence. [conclusive.

concluyente, *-klŭyĕn'tĕ*, a. concludent.

concolega, *-kŏlā'gă*, sm. fellow-collegian.

concomerse, *-kŏmĕr'sĕ*, v. r. to shrug the shoulders, to give a shrug.

concomitante, *-kŏmĭtăn'tĕ*, a. concomitant, accompanying.

concordancia, *-kŏrdăn'thĭă*, sf. concordance, concord; harmony.

concordar, *-kŏrdăr'*, v. a. to accord; v. a. to agree, to concord.

concordato, *-kŏrdā'tŏ*, sm. concordate.

concorde, *-kŏr'dĕ*, a. concordant, agreeing.

concordia, *-kŏr'dĭă*, sf. conformity, union, harmony; de –, by common consent.

concreción, *-krĕthŏn'*, sf. concretion.

concretar, *-krĕtăr'*, v. a. to combine, to concrete.

concreto, ta, *-krā'tŏ*, a. concrete. [tress.

concubina, *-kŭbī'nă*, sf. concubine, mistress.

concubinato, *-kŭbĭnā'tŏ*, sm. concubinage.

concubito, *-kō'bĭtŏ*, sm. coition.

conculcar, *-kŭlkăr'*, v. a. to trample under foot. [cupiscence, lust.

concupiscencia, *-kŭpĭsthĕn'thĭă*, sf. con-

concurrencia, *-kŭrrĕn'thĭă*, sf. convention of persons; concurrence; coincidence; confluence.

concurrir, *-kŭrrĭr'*, v.n. to concur; to contribute; to coincide; to convent; to fall in.

concurso, *-kŭr'sŏ*, sm. concourse; crowd.

concusión, *-kŭsŏn'*, sf. concussion; shaking. [tortoise-shell.

concha, *kŏn'tshă*, sf. shell; conch; oyster;

conchabanza, *kŏntshăbăn'thă*, sf. the making of one's self easy and comfortable; plotting, conspiracy.

conchabar, *-băr'*, v. a. to join, to unite; –se, to plot, to conspire.

conchado, da, *kŏntshā'dŏ*, a. scaly, covered with shells.

conchil, *kŏntshĭl'*, sm. rock-shell.

conchudo, da, *kŏntshŭ'dŏ*, a. scaly, crustaceous; cunning, crafty.

condado, *kŏndā'dŏ*, sm. earldom, county.

condal, *kŏndăl'*, a. relating to an earl.

conde, *kŏn'dĕ*, sm. earl, count; chief of gypsies. [fit, proper.

condecente, *kŏndĕthĕn'tĕ*, a. convenient,

condecorar, *-dĕkŏrăr'*, v. a. to adorn, to embellish.

condenable, *-dĕnā'blĕ*, a. damnable.

condenación, *-dĕnăthŏn'*, **condena**, *-dā'nă*, sf. condemnation.

condenar, *-dĕnăr'*, v. a. to condemn; to refute; to disapprove; –se, to condemn or blame one's self. [demnatory.

condenatorio, ria, *-dĕnātō'rĭŏ*, a. con-

condensación, *-dĕnsăthŏn'*, sf. condensation.

condensar, *-dĕnsăr'*, v. a. to condense, to thicken. [densible, condensive.

condensativo, va, *-dĕnsātī'vŏ*, a. con-

condesa, *-dĕs'ă*, sf. countess.

condesado, *-dĕsā'dŏ*, sm. earldom.

condescendencia, *-dĕsthĕndĕn'thĭă*, sf. condescendence, condescension, compliance. [descend, to yield, to comply.

condescender, *-dĕsthĕndĕr'*, v. a. to con-

condestable, *-dĕstā'blĕ*, sm. constable. [ship.

condestablía, *-dĕstāblĭ'ă*, sf. constable-

condición, *-dĭthĭŏn'*, sf. condition, quality; state, footing; rank; clause, stipulation. [ditioned.

condicionado, da, *-dĭthĭŏnā'dŏ*, a. con-

condicional, *-dĭthĭŏnăl'*, a. conditional, not absolute. [to accord, to condition.

condicionar, *-dĭthĭŏnăr'*, v. n. to agree,

condignidad, *-dĭgnĭdăd''*, sf. condignness; condignity.

condigno, *-dĭg'nŏ*, a. condign.

condimentar, *-dĭmĕntăr'*, v. a. to condite, to season. [seasoning.

condimento, *-dĭmĕn'tŏ*, sm. condiment,

condiscípulo, *-dĭsthĕ'pŭlŏ*, sm. fellow-disciple, fellow-scholar.

condolecerse, *-dŏlĕthĕr'sĕ*, **condolerse**, *-dŏlĕr'sĕ*, v. r. to condole. [forgiving.

condonación, *-dŏnāthŏn'*, sf. pardoning,

condonar, *-dŏnăr'*, v. a. to pardon, to forgive.

conducción, *-dŭkthŏn'*, sf. conveyance; carriage (the act); conduct; payment for conducting. [factory.

conducente, *-dŭthĕn'tĕ*, a. suitable, satis-

conducir, *-dŭthĭr'*, v. a. & n. to convey, to conduct; –, v. n. to be serviceable; –se, to conduct one's self.

conducta, *-dŭk'tă*, sf. conduct; behaviour; conveyance. [conductory.

conductivo, va, *-dŭktĭ'vŏ*, a. conducive,

conducto, *-dŭk'tŏ*, sm. conduit, sewer, drain.

conductor, *-dŭktŏr'*, sm. conductor, guide; (rail.) guard, conductor.

conejal, *kŏnĕ'hăl*, **conejar**, *kŏnĕ'hăr*, sm. rabbit-warren.

conejera, *kŏnĕ'hā'ră*, sf. warren, coney-burrow; cavern inhabited by poor people.

conejero, –ro, sm. warrener; –, ra, a. trained to hunt rabbits.

conejo, ja, *kŏnĕ'hŏ*, sm. & f. rabbit.

conejuna, *kŏnĕ'hŭ'nă*, sf. rabbit fur.

conejuno, na, *-nŏ*, a. belonging to rabbits; rabbit-like.

conexidades, *kŏnĕksĭdā'dĕs*, sf. pl. (law) all matters pertinent to the principal subject. [junction.

conexión, *kŏnĕksŏn'*, sf. connection, con-

conexo, xa, *kŏnĕk'sŏ*, a. connected, united.

confabular, *kŏnfăbŭlăr'*, v. a. to confabulate. [standard.

confalón, *-fălŏn'*, sm. gonfalon, banner,

confección, *-fĕkthŏn'*, sf. electuary.

confeccionador, *-fĕksĭŏnādŏr'*, sm. confectioner. [up into conserves.

confeccionar, *-fĕkthĭŏnăr'*, v. a. to make

confederación, *-fĕdĕráthŏn',* sf. confederacy.

confederado, da, *-fĕdĕrá dŏ,* a. confederate.

confederar, *-fĕdĕrár',* v. a. **-se,** to confederate.

conferencia, *-fĕrĕn'thĭă,* sf. conference.

conferenciar, *-fĕrĕnthĭár',* v. a. to hold a conference.

conferir, *-fĕrír',* v. a. to confer.

confesado, da, *-fĕsá dŏ,* a. penitent.

confesar, *-fĕsár',* v. a. to confess; to avow.

confesión, *-fĕsĭŏn',* sf. confession, avowal.

confesionario, *-fĕsĭŏnă'rĭŏ,* sm. treatise on hearing confessions; confessional.

confesionista, *-fĕsĭŏnĭs'tă,* sm. Lutheran.

confeso, sa, *-fĕs'ŏ,* a. (law) confessed.

confesonario, *-fĕsŏnă'rĭŏ,* s. m. confessional.

confesor, *-fĕsŏr',* sm. confessor.

confiado, da, *-fĭá dŏ,* a. confident; arrogant, forward.

confiador, *-fĭădŏr',* sm. (law) joint surety.

confianza, *-fĭán'thă,* sf. confidence, boldness; assurance; **en -,** confidential; **traje de -,** sm. undress.

confiar, *-fĭár',* v. a. & n. to confide, to trust in; to feed with hope.

confidencia, *-fĭdĕn'thĭă,* sf. confidence.

confidencial, *-fĭdĕnthĭăl',* a. confidential.

confidente, *-fĭdĕn'tĕ,* sm. confidant; **-,** a. true, faithful, trusty.

configurar, *-fĭgŭrár',* v. a. to configure.

confín, *-fĭn',* sm. limit, boundary.

confinar, *-fĭnár',* v. a. & n. to exile; to confine; to border upon.

confirmación, *-fĭrmáthŏn',* sf. confirmation.

confirmar, *-fĭrmár',* v. a. to confirm; to corroborate.

confiscación, *-fĭskáthŏn',* sf. confiscation, forfeiture.

confiscar, *-fĭskár',* v. a. to confiscate.

confitar, *-fĭtár',* v. a. to confect; to preserve; to candy.

confite, *-fĭ'tĕ,* sm. comfit, confect; **-s,** pl. whipping given to children.

confitera, *-fĭtĕ'ră,* sf. sugar-plum box.

confitería, *-fĭtĕrĕ'ă,* s. confectioner's shop.

confitero, *-fĭtĕ'rŏ,* sm. confectioner.

confitura, *-fĭtŭ'ră,* sf. preserved or potted fruit; jam.

conflación, *-fláthŏn',* sf. melting metals.

conflagración, *-flágráthŏn',* sf. conflagration.

conflicto, *-flĭk'tŏ,* sm. conflict.

confluencia, *-flŭĕn'thĭă,* sf. confluence.

confluir, *-flŭír',* v. n. to join (applied to rivers and sea-currents).

conformar, *-fŏrmár',* v. a. to conform, to fit; **-,** v. n. to suit, to fit; **-se,** to submit, to accommodate.

conforme, *-fŏr'mĕ,* a. conformable, suitable; **-,** ad. according to.

conformidad, *-fŏrmĭdăd',* sf. conformity, patience, resignation; **de -,** by common consent, in company; **-,** consolation.

confortación, *-fŏrtáthŏn',* sf. comfort.

confortar, *-fŏrtár',* v. a. to comfort; to strengthen; to console.

confortativo, va, *-fŏrtátē vŏ,* a. comfortable, cordial.

confracción, *-frákthŏn',* sf. fraction.

confraternidad, *-fráternĭdăd',* sf. confraternity.

confrontación, *-frŏntáthŏn',* sf. confrontation.

confrontar, *-frŏntár',* v. a. to confront.

confundir, *-fŭndír',* v. a. to confound, to jumble; to perplex; to huddle; to throw into confusion.

confusamente, *-fŭsámĕn'tĕ,* ad. confusedly.

confusión, *-fŭsĭŏn',* sf. confusion, disorder; tumultuous medley; perplexity, perturbation; obscurity; humiliation.

confuso, sa, *-fŭ'sŏ,* a. confused, confounded; obscure; perplexed.

confutación, *-fŭtáthŏn',* sf. confutation, conviction.

confutar, *-fŭtár',* v. a. to confute.

congelación, *-hĕláthŏn',* sf. congelation.

congelar, *-hĕlár',* v. a. to congeal.

congeniar, *-hĕnĭár',* v. n. to be congenial.

congerie, *-hĕ'rĭĕ,* sf. congeries.

congestión, *-hĕstĭŏn',* sf. (med.) congestion.

conglutinar, *-glŭtĭnár',* v. a. to conglutinate; to flatter.

congoja, *-gŏ'hă,* sf. anguish, pang, heart-breaking.

congojoso, sa, *-gŏ'hŏ sŏ,* a. afflictive, painful.

congraciar, *-grăthĭár',* v. a. to ingratiate.

congratulación, *-grătŭláthŏn',* sf. congratulation.

congratular, *-grătŭlár',* v. a. to congratulate.

congregación, *-grĕgáthŏn',* sf. congregation, assembly.

congregar, *-grĕgár',* v. a. to assemble, to collect; to meet.

congreso, *-grĕ'sŏ,* sm. congress.

congrua, *kŏn'grŭă,* sf. a competent sustenance for a priest.

congruamente, *kŏngrŭámĕn'tĕ,* ad. conveniently, becomingly.

congruencia, *-grŭĕn'thĭă,* sf. convenience, opportunity, congruency.

congruente, *-grŭĕn'tĕ,* a. congruent; corresponding; convenient, suitable.

congruo, ua, *kŏn'grŭŏ,* a. congruous, convenient.

cónico, ca, *kŏ'nĭkŏ,* a. conical.

conjetura, *kŏn'hĕtŭ'ră,* sf. conjecture.

conjetural, *-hĕtŭrál',* a. conjectural.

conjeturar, *-hĕtŭrár',* v. a. to conjecture.

conjugación, *-'hŭgáthŏn',* sf. (gr.) conjugation.

conjugar, *-'hŭgár',* v. a. (gr.) to conjugate.

conjunción, *-'hŭnthŏn',* sf. conjunction.

conjuntamente, *-'hŭntámĕn'tĕ,* ad. together.

conjunto, ta, *-'hŭn'tŏ,* a. united, conjunct; allied by kindred; **-,** sm. conjunctness, gross.

conjuración, *-'hŭráthŏn',* sf. conspiracy, plot.

conjurado, *-'hŭrá dŏ,* sm. conspirator.

conjurador, *-'hŭrádŏr',* sm. conjurer; exorcist.

conjuramentar, *-'hŭrámĕntár',* v. a. to bind by an oath; to administer an oath.

conjurar, *-'hŭrár',* v. n. to conjure; to conspire, to plot; to exorcism.

conjuro, *-'hŏ'rŏ,* sm. conjuration, ex-

conmemoración, –memŏrăthiŏn', sf. remembrance; commemoration; requiem.

conmemorar, –memŏrăr', v. a. to commemorate. [messmate.

commensal, –mensăl', sm. commensal,

conmensuración, –mensŭrăthiŏn', sf. commensuration. [mensurate.

conmensurar, –mensŭrăr', v. a. to commensurate.

conmigo, –mēgŏ, pn. with me, with myself. [fellow-soldier.

conmilitón, –milĭtŏn', sm. comrade.

conminación, –minăthiŏn', sf. commination, threat.

conminar, –minăr', v. a. to threaten; to threaten a criminal with punishment.

conminatorio, ria, –minătŏrĭŏ, a. comminatory, threatening.

conmiseración, –misĕrăthiŏn', sf. commiseration, pity, compassion.

conmoción, –mŏthiŏn', sf. commotion; concussion; fretting; tumult, disturbance.

conmover, –mŏvĕr', v. a. to move; to disturb. [tion, exchange.

conmutación, –mŭtăthiŏn', sf. commutation.

conmutar, –mŭtăr', v. a. to commute; to barter, to exchange. [cording to nature.

connatural, –nătŭrăl', a. natural; according to nature.

connaturalizar, –nătŭrălĭthăr', v. a. to naturalise; –se, to accustom one's self to.

connivencia, –nĭvĕn'thĭă, sf. connivance.

connotación, –nŏtăthiŏn', sf. connection; distant relation.

connotado, –nŏtā'dŏ, sm. relationship.

connotar, –nŏtăr', v. a. to imply.

connubio, –nŭ'bĭŏ, sm. (poet.) matrimony, cono, kŏ'nŏ, sm. cone. [wedlock.

conocedor, ra, kŏnŏthĕdŏr', sm. & f. connoisseur.

conocer, kŏnŏthĕr', v. a. to know, to understand; –se, to know one another.

conocido, da, kŏnŏthĭ'dŏ, sm. & f. acquaintance, acquaintant.

conocimiento, –thĭmĭen'tŏ, sm. knowledge, understanding; connoisseurship; cognition; acquaintance; (mar.) bill of landing.

conque, kŏnkĕ', sm. condition. [tion.

conquista, –kĭs'tă, sf. conquest; acquisition.

conquistador, –kĭstădŏr', sm. conqueror.

conquistar, –kĭstăr', v. a. to conquer.

conreinar, –rĕĭnăr', v. n. to reign at the same time with another.

consabido, da, –săbĭ'dŏ, a. already known; above-mentioned. [tion.

consagración, –săgrăthiŏn', sf. consecration.

consagrar, –săgrăr', v. a. to consecrate.

consanguíneo, nea, –săngŭĭ'nĕŏ, a. consanguineous. [sanguinity.

consanguinidad, –săngŭĭnĭdăd', sf. consanguinity.

conscripto, –skrĭp'tŏ, a. conscript.

consecución, –sĕkŭthiŏn', sf. attainment.

consecuencia, –sĕkŭĕn'thĭă, sf. consequence; conclusion; por –, therefore.

consecuente, –sĕkŭĕn'tĕ, sm. consequent, consequence.

consecutivo, va, –sĕkŭtĭ'vŏ, a. consecutive; consequential. [to obtain.

conseguir, –sĕgĭr', v. a. to attain, to get,

conseja, –sĕ'hă, sf. fable, feigned story.

consejero, –sĕhĕrŏ, sm. counsellor.

consejil, –sĕhĭl', sf. (cant) public woman.

consejo, –sĕh'ŏ, sm. counsel, advice; council; council-house; (cant) crafty sharper. [children].

consentido, –sĕntĭ'dŏ, a. spoiled (of children).

consentir, –sĕntĭr', v. a. to consent, to agree; to comply, to acquiesce; to rely.

conserje, –sĕr'hĕ, sm. warden of a royal castle.

conserva, –sĕr'vă, sf. conserve. [castle.

conservación, –sĕrvăthiŏn', sf. conservation. [guard; candy fruit.

conservar, –sĕrvăr', v. a. to conserve; to candy fruit.

conservativo, va, –sĕrvătĭ'vŏ, a. conservative.

conservatorio, –sĕrvătŏrĭŏ, sm. conservatory; –, ria, a. conservatory, preservative. [great, large.

considerable, –sĭdĕrā'blĕ, a. considerable, large.

consideración, –sĭdĕrăthiŏn', sf. consideration, notice, sake, account; reflection.

consideradamente, –sĭdĕrădămĕn'tĕ, ad. considerately. [siderate.

considerado, –sĭdĕrā'dŏ, a. prudent, considerate.

considerar, –sĭdĕrăr', v. a. to consider.

consigna, –sĭg'nă, sf. (mil.) watch-word.

consignación, –sĭgnăthiŏn', sf. consignation; consignment.

consignador, –sĭgnădŏr', sm. one who consigns goods to a foreign correspondent.

consignar, –sĭgnăr', v. a. to consign; to deposit; to forward goods to a correspondent, to be sold for account of the consigners. [consignee.

consignatario, –sĭgnătā'rĭŏ, sm. trustee; consignee.

consigo, –sĕ'gŏ, pn. with one's self.

consiguiente, –sĭgĭĕn'tĕ, a. consequent, consecutive. [stability; solidity.

consistencia, –sĭstĕn'thĭă, sf. consistence, stability; solidity.

consistente, –sĭstĕn'tĕ, a. consistent, firm, solid. [contained; to be composed.

consistir, –sĭstĭr', v. n. to consist; to be contained; to be composed.

consistorio, –sĭstŏ'rĭŏ, sm. consistory; town-house. [nion.

consocio, –sŏ'thĭŏ, sm. partner, companion.

consolación, –sŏlăthiŏn', sf. consolatory.

consolador, ra, –sŏlădŏr', a. consolatory, comfortable. [fort, to cheer.

consolar, –sŏlăr', v. a. to console, to comfort, to cheer.

consolidar, –sŏlĭdăr', a. a. to consolidate; –se, (law) to tie up interest with principal.

consolidativo, va, –sŏlĭdătĭ'vŏ, a. consolidant, healing. [congruence.

consonancia, –sŏnăn'thĭă, sf. consonance; congruence.

consonante, –sŏnăn'tĕ, sm. rhyme; –, sf. (gr.) consonant; –, a. consonant, conformable. [ciety.

consorcio, –sŏr'thĭŏ, sm. partnership, society.

consorte, –sŏr'tĕ, sm. consort, companion, partner; accomplice. [plot.

conspiración, –spĭrăthiŏn', sf. conspiracy, plot.

conspirador, –spĭrădŏr', sm. conspirator, plotter. [plot.

conspirar, –spĭrăr', v. n. to conspire, to plot.

constancia, –stăn'thĭă, sf. constancy, steadiness, immutability. [alterable.

constante, –stăn'tĕ, a. constant, firm, un-

constar, –stär', v. imp. to be evident, certain; to be composed of, to consist of.

constelación, –stĕlāthȳŏn', sf. constellation. [nation.

consternación, –stĕrnāthȳŏn', sf. consternation.

consternar, –stĕrnär', v. a. to strike with amazement, to confound; [tiveness.

constipación, –stĭpāthȳŏn', sf. cold; costiveness.

constipar, –stĭpär', v. a. to cause a cold; to constipate. [(in all senses).

constitución, –stĭtāthȳŏn', sf. constitution

constitucional, –stĭtāthȳŏnäl', a. constitutional. [establish; to appoint.

constituir, –stĭtūĭr', v. a. to constitute; to

constitutivo, va, –stĭtūtȳvŏ, a. constitutive, essential. [stituent.

constituyente, –stĭtūyĕn'tĕ, sm. constituent.

constreñimiento, –strĕnyĭmȳĕn'tŏ, sm. constraint.

constreñir, –strĕnyĭr', v. a. to constrain, to force; (med.) to constipate.

constricción, –strĭkthȳŏn', sf. constriction, contraction. [gent.

constrictivo, va, –strĭktĭvŏ, a. astringent.

construcción, –strūkthȳŏn', sf. construction. [to construct; to construe.

construir, –strūĭr', v. a. to form, to build,

constuprar, –strūpär', v. a. to deflour.

consuegro, gra, –sūĕ grŏ, sm. & f. parents of two children who marry; fathers or mothers who marry their children together. [fort; joy, merriment.

consuelo, –sūĕ'lŏ, sm. consolation, comfort; joy, merriment.

cónsul, kŏn'sŭl, sm. consul; member of the tribunal of commerce.

consulado, –sŭlä'dŏ, sm. consulate; tribunal of commerce.

consular, –sŭlär', a. consular.

consulta, –sŭl'tä, sf. consult, consultation.

consultación, –sŭltāthȳŏn', sf. consultation.. [advice; to give advice.

consultar, –sŭltär', v. a. to consult, to ask

consultivo, va, –sŭltĭvŏ, a. consultative.

consultor, ra, –sŭltŏr', sm. & f. adviser, counsel.

consumación, –sūmāthȳŏn', sf. consummation, perfection, finishing.

consumado, da, –sūmä'dŏ, a. consummate, complete, perfect, accomplished, exquisite; –, sm. jelly-broth.

consumar, –sūmär', v. a. to consummate, to finish, to perfect.

consumir, –sūmĭr', v. a. to consume, to destroy; to waste, to exhaust; –se, to waste away, to languish.

consumo, –sū'mŏ, sm. consumption of provisions and merchandise.

consunción, –sūnthȳŏn', sf. (med.) consumption; wasting. [stancial.

consustancial, –sŭstänthȳäl', a. consubstantial. [tability; to account; book-keeping.

contabilidad, –tābĭlĭdäd', sf. accounts; book-keeping.

contacto, –täk'tŏ, sm. contact.

contadero, ra, –tādā'rŏ, a. countable.

contado, da, –tä'dŏ, a. scarce, rare; de –, instantly; in hand; al –, cash, ready money.

contador, –tādŏr', a. computer, reckoner; accountant; counter (table); counter (for games).

contaduría, –tādārē'ä, sf. accountant's office at the exchequer; auditorship.

contagiar, –tähȳär', v. a. to infect.

contagio, –tä'hȳŏ, sm. contagion.

contagioso, sa, –tähȳŏ'sŏ, a. contagious.

contaminación, –tämĭnāthȳŏn', sf. contamination, pollution.

contaminar, –tämĭnär', v. a. to contaminate; to infect by contagion; to corrupt.

contante, –tän'tĕ, sm. ready money.

contar, –tär', v. a. to count, to reckon, to compute, to calculate; –con, to rely upon.

contemplación, –tĕmplāthȳŏn', sf. contemplation.

contemplar, –tĕmplär', v. a. to contemplate, to consider, to study; to meditate; to flatter; to condescend. [templative.

contemplativo, va, –tĕmplätĭvŏ, a. contemporáneo, nea, –tĕmpŏrä'nĕŏ, a. contemporary, coeval. [temporise.

contemporizar, –tĕmpŏrĭthär', v. n. to temporise.

contencioso, sa, –tĕnthȳŏ'sŏ, a. contentious; quarrelsome.

contender, –tĕndĕr', v. n. to contend, to strive; to contest, to debate.

contendiente, –tĕndĭĕn'tĕ, sm. competitor.

contener, –tĕnĕr', v. a. to contain, to comprehend; to refrain; to repress.

contenido, da, –tĕnĭ'dŏ, a. moderate, temperate, modest; –, sm. tenour, contents.

contentadizo, za, –tĕntädĭ'thŏ, a. bien –, easily contented; mal –, hard to please.

contentar, –tĕntär', v. a. to content, to satisfy, to please; –se, to be pleased or satisfied.

contento, ta, –tĕn'tŏ, a. glad; pleased; content; –, sm. contentment; receipt.

contestación, –tĕstāthȳŏn', sf. answer, reply; debate, disputation.

contestar, –tĕstär', v. a. to prove, to attest; to answer, to reply; –, v. n. to agree; to accord. [dence of another.

conteste, –tĕs'tĕ, a. confirming the evidence of another.

contexto, –tĕks'tŏ, sm. intertexture.

contienda, –tĭĕn'dä, sf. contest, dispute. [debate.

contigo, –tĭ'gŏ, pp. with thee.

contigüidad, –tĭgŭĭdäd', sf. contiguity.

contiguo, gua, –tĭ'gŭŏ, a. contiguous, close. [abstinence, moderation.

continencia, –tĭnĕn'thȳä, sf. continence, continental, –tĭnĕntäl', a. continental.

continente, –tĭnĕn'tĕ, sm. abstinence; countenance; continent, mainland; –, a. abstinent, moderate.

contingencia, –tĭnhĕn'thȳä, sf. accidental possibility; contingent.

contingente, –tĭnhĕn'tĕ, a. fortuitous, accidental; –, sm. contingent.

continuación, –tĭnūāthȳŏn', sf. continuation, lengthening; continuity.

continuar, –tĭnūär', v. a. & n. to continue.

continuo, nua, –tĭnŭŏ, a. continuous, ceaseless. [an affected manner.

contonearse, –tŏnĕär'sĕ, v. r. to walk in

contoneo, –tŏnĕ'ŏ, sm. affected manner of walking.

contorno, -tŏr'nŏ, sm. environs, pl.; contour, outline; en -, round about.

contorsión, -tŏrsiŏn', sf. contortion, wry motion.   [opposite to.

contra, kŏn'trä, pr. against, contrary to,

contrabajo, -bä'hŏ, sm. counter-bass; bass-viol.   [counterbalance.

contrabalanzear, -bälänthäär', v. a. to

contrabandista, -bändis'tä, sm. smuggler, contrabandist.   [trade, smuggling.

contrabando, -bän'dŏ, sm. contraband

contrabatería, -bäterï'ä, sf. (mil.) counter-battery.

contracambio, -käm'biŏ, sm. re-exchange.

contracarril. -kärril', sm. (rail.) counter-rail.   [tion.

contracción, kŏnträkthiŏn', sf. contrac-

contradanza, kŏnträdän'thä, sf. country-dance.   [to gainsay.

contradecir, -dethïr', v. a. to contradict,

contradicción, -dikthiŏn', sf. contra-diction verbal opposition.

contradictorio, ria, -diktŏ'riŏ, a. contra-dictory, opposite to.

contradique, -dï'ke, sm. counter-dike.

contraer, kŏnträër', v. a. & n. to contract, to shrink; to make a bargain; -se, to shrink up.   [counter-scarp.

contraescarpa, kŏnträëskär'pä, sf. (mil.)

contraescritura, -ëskrïtü'rä, sf. counter-deed.   [a countermanding decree.

contrafirmar, -firmär', v.a. (law) to obtain

contrafoso, -fŏ'sŏ, sm. outer ditch of a fortress.   [privilege.

contrafuero, -füë'rŏ, sm. violation of a

contrafuerte, -füër'te, sm. counter-fort.

contraguardia, -gwär'diä, sf. counter-guard.

contrahacer, -äthër', v. a. to counterfeit, to falsify; to pirate the works of an author.

contrahaz, -äth', sm. wrong side of cloth.

contrahecho, cha, -ëtsh'ŏ, a. deformed, miscreated; counterfeited, feint.

contralor, kŏnträlŏr', sm. controller, in-spector.

contralto, kŏnträl'tŏ, sm. (mus.) contralto.

contramaestre, -kŏnträmäës'tre, sm. (mar.) boatswain; overseer of a manu-factory.   [catching fish.

contramalla, -mäl'yä, sf. double net for

contramallar, -mälyär', v.a. to make nets with double meshes.   [mand.

contramandar, -mändär', v.a. to counter-

contramarca, -mär'kä, sf. countermark; customs stamp duty.

contramarco, -mär'kŏ, sm. counter-frame of a glass window.   [march.

contramarcha, -mär'tshä, sf. counter-

contramarchar, -märtshär', v. a. to counter-march.   [tide, spring-tide.

contramarea, -märë'ä, sf. (mar.) counter-

contramesana, -mësä'nä, sf. mizen-mast.

contramina, -mē'nä, sf. countermine.

contraminar, -mïnär', v. a. to counter-mine; to counter-work.   [braye.

contramuralla, -märäl'yä, sf. fausse-

contramuro, -mü'rŏ, sm. countermure.

contraorden, -ŏr'den, sm. countermand.

contraordenar, -ŏrdenär', v.a. to counter-mand.   [opposing party.

contrapasar, -päsär', v. n. to join the opposite party.

contrapaso, -pä'sŏ, sm. back step.

contrapechar, -pëtshär', v. a. to strike breast against breast (applied to horses in tournaments).

contrapelo, -pä'lŏ, ad. against the grain.

contrapesar, -pësär', v.n. to counterpoise.

contrapeso, -pä'sŏ, sm. counterpoise; rope-dancer's pole.   [pilaster.

contrapilastra, -pïläs'trä, sf. counter-

contraponer, -pŏnër', v. a. to compare, to oppose.

contraposición, -pŏsithiŏn', sf. counter-view, contrast; clair-obscure.

contraprueba, -prüä'bä, sf. counterproof.

contrapuerta, -püër'tä, sf. inner hall-door of a house.

contrapuntearse, -püntëär'se, v. r. to quarrel with abusive language.   [point.

contrapunto, -pün'tŏ, sm. (mus.) counter-

contrapunzón, -pünthŏn', sm. counter-punch; gunsmith's counter-mark.

contraquilla, -kïl'yä, sf. (mar.) false keel.

contrariar, kŏnträriär', v. a. to contra-dict, to oppose, to counteract.

contrariedad, -träriedäd', sf. contrariety, opposition.

contrario, -trä'riŏ, sm. opponent, anta-gonist; contrary; -, ria, a. contrary, opposite; adverse, abhorrent; por el -, on the contrary; en -, against.

contrarrestar, kŏnträrrëstär', v. a. to strike back a ball; (fig.) to resist, to oppose.

contrarresto, -rës'tŏ, sm. player who is to strike back the ball; opposition, con-tradiction.   [counter-revolution.

contrarrevolución, -rrevŏlüthiŏn', sf.

contrarronda, -rŏn'dä, sf. (mil.) counter-round.   [organ.

contras, kŏn'träs, sf. pl. bass-pipes of an

contrasellar, -sëlyär', v. a. to counterseal.

contraseña, -sën'yä, sf. countersign; (mil.) watch-word.

contrastar, kŏnträstär', v. a. to contrast, to oppose; to resist, to contradict; to assay metals; to examine measures and weights.

contraste, kŏnträs'te, sm. assayer of the mint; assayer's office; assayer of weights and measures; contrast; opposition, strife; (mar.) sudden change of the wind.

contrata, kŏnträ'tä, sf. contract.   [merce.

contratación, -trätäthiŏn', sf. trade, com-

contratante, -trätän'te, sm. contractor; trader.   [fig.; to contract, to stipulate.

contratar, -trätär', v. a. to trade, to traf-

contratiempo, -trätiëm'pŏ, sm. disap-pointment, misfortune..

contratista, -trätis'tä, sm. conventionist.

contrato, -trä'tŏ, sm. contract, pact.

contratreta, kŏnträtrë'tä, s. counterplot.

contratrinchera, -trïntshä'rä, s. counter-trench.   [of contravallation.

contravalar, -välär', v. a. to form a line

contravención, -venthiŏn', sf. contra-vention.

contraveneno, *–věnd' nŏ*, sm. counter-poison.

contravenir, *–věnir'*, v. n. to contravene, to transgress; to oppose. [shutter.

contraventana, *–věntd' nd，*, sf. window-

contraventor, ra, *–věntŏr'*, sm. & f. offender, transgressor.

contravidriera, *–vidrié' rd*, sf. second glass window. [bution; tax.

contribución, *kŏntrĭbūthiŏn'*, sf. contri-

contribuir, *–trĭbūir'*, v. a. to contribute.

contributario, *–trĭbūtd' riŏ*, sm. contributor, payer of taxes.

contribuyente, *–trĭbūyěn' tě*, v. a. contributing; contributory. [tence.

contrición, *–trĭthiŏn'*, sf. contrition, penitence.

contrincante, *–trĭnkán' tě*, sm. competitor.

contristar, *–trĭstár'*, v. a. to afflict, to sadden.

contrito, ta, *–trē' tŏ*, a. contrite, penitent.

controversia, *–tŏ věr' siä*, sf. controversy, dispute. [versialist.

controversista, *–trŏ věrsĭs' tä*, sm. contro-

controvertir, *–trŏ věrtir'*, v. a. to controvert, to dispute.

contumacia, *–tūmá' thiä*, sf. obstinacy, stubbornness; (law) contumacy.

contumaz, *–tūmáth'*, a. obstinate, stubborn (law) contumacious. [abuse.

contumelia, *–tūmé' liä*, sf. contumely.

contumelioso, sa, *–tūmělĭŏ' sŏ*, a. contumelious.

contundir, *–tūndir'*, v. a. to beat together; to bruise; to cause a contusion.

conturbación, *–tūrbáthiŏn'*, sf. perturbation. [to disquiet.

conturbar, *–tūrbár'*, v. a. to perturbate.

contusión, *–tūsiŏn'*, sf. contusion.

convalecencia, *–válěthěn' thiä*, sf. convalescence, recovery from disease.

convalecer, *–válěthěr'*, v. n. to recover from sickness; to recover lost prosperity or power. [ing.

convecino, na, *–věthē' nŏ*, a. neighbour-

convencer, *–věnthěr'*, v. a. to convince.

convencimiento, *–věnthĭmiěn' tŏ*, sm. conviction. [pact.

convención, *–věnthiŏn'*, sf. convention.

convencional, *–věnthiŏnál'*, a. conventional, agreed upon by compact.

conveniencia, *–věniěn' thiä*, sf. utility, profit; convenience; ease, commodity.

conveniente, *–věniěn' tě*, a. useful, convenable, conformable.

convenio, *–vě' niŏ*, sm. convention, contract, accordance.

convenir, *–věnir'*, v. n. to agree, to coincide; to compromise; to fit, to suit, to correspond; to assemble.

conventículo, *–věntī' kūlŏ*, sm. conventicle.

convento, *–věn' tŏ*, sm. convent, monastery, nunnery.

conventual, *–věntūál'*, a. monastic.

convergencia, *–věr'hěn' thiä*, sf. convergence. [sociable.

conversable, *–věrsä' blě*, a. conversable.

conversación, *–věrsáthiŏn'*, sf. conversation, easy talk; communication.

conversar, *–věrsár'*, v. n. to converse; to live together. [change.

conversión, *–věrsiŏn'*, sf. conversion.

converso, *–věr' sŏ*, sm. convert. [vert.

convertir, *–věrtir'*, v. a. –se, v. r. to con-

convexidad, *–věksĭdád'*, sf. convexity.

convexo, xa, *–věk' sŏ*, a. convex.

convicción, *–vĭkthiŏn'*, sf. conviction.

convicto, ta, *–vĭk' tŏ*, a. convicted (found guilty).

convidar, *–vĭdár'*, v. a. to invite, to bid; to allure, to persuade; –se, to offer one's service spontaneously.

convincente, *–vĭnthěn' tě*, a. convincing.

convite, *–vē' tě*, sm. invitation; feast to which persons are invited. [semble.

convocar, *–vŏkár'*, v. a. to convoke, to as-

convocatorio, ria, *–vŏkätŏ' riŏ*, a. that which convokes. [vulus.

convólvulo, *–vŏl' vūlŏ*, sm. (bot.) convol-

convoy, *–vŏi'*, sm. convoy, conduct, escort, retinue, suit. [escort.

convoyar, *–vŏyár'*, v. a. to convoy, to

convulsión, *–vūlsiŏn'*, sf. convulsion.

convulsivo, va, *–vūlsē' vŏ*, a. convulsive.

conyugal, *–yūgál'*, a. conjugal, connubial.

cónyuges, *kŏn' yū hěs*, sm. pl. married couple, husband and wife. [tion.

cooperación, *kŏŏpěráthiŏn'*, sf. coopera-

cooperador, ra, *–dŏr'*, sm. & f. cooperator.

cooperar, *kŏŏpěrár'*, v. a. to cooperate.

cooperativa, va, *kŏŏpěrätē' vŏ*, a. cooperative.

coopositor, *kŏŏpŏsĭtŏr'*, sm. competitor.

coordinar, *kŏŏrdĭnár'*, v. a. to arrange, to classify.

copa, *kŏ' pä*, sf. cup; top of a tree; crown of a hat; brazier; –s, pl. hearts (at cards).

copado, da, *kŏpä' dŏ*, a. tufted, copped.

copera, *kŏpě' rä*, sf. cupboard.

copero, *–rŏ*, sm. cup-bearer.

copete, *–tě*, sm. toupee; crown-work of a looking-glass frame; top of a shoe; top, summit.

copetudo, da, *–tŏ' dŏ*, a. copped; supercilious on account of one's noble descent.

copia, *kŏ' piä*, sf. plenty, abundance; copy, transcript; portrait taken from original design; copy of a picture; (gr.) list of nouns and verbs. [libro – copy-book.

copiador, *kŏpiádŏr*, sm. copyist; copier;

copiar, *kŏpiár'*, v. a. to copy; to imitate, to draw from life; (poct.) to describe, to depict. [dant, plentiful.

copioso, sa, *kŏpiŏ' sŏ*, a. copious, abun-

copista, *kŏpĭs' tä*, sm. copyist. [mark.

copla, *kŏ' plä*, sf. couplet; sarcastic re-

coplear, *kŏplěár'*, v. n. to make couplets.

coplero, *kŏplě' rŏ*, sm. poetaster; ballad-seller.

copo, *kŏ' pŏ*, sm. small bundle of cotton, flax &c., put on the distaff to be spun; flake of snow. [Catholic churches]

copón, *kŏpŏn'*, sm. cibary (cup used in

copudo, *kŏpŏ' dŏ*, a. tufted, tufty, bushy.

cópula, *kŏ' pūlä*, sf. joining of two things together; cupola; (gr.) copula.

copulativo, va, *kōpŭlătĭ vŏ*, a. copulative.

coqueta, *kōkĕ'tă*, sf. coquette, flirt.

coquetear, —*tĕăr*, v. n. to coquet.

coquetería,—*tĕrĕ ă*, sf. coquetry, flirtation.

coquillo, *kōkĭ'yŏ*, sm. cocoa-nut (of the Indian palm-tree).   [amuse children.

coquito, *kōkĭ'tŏ*, sm. grimace made to

coracero, *kōrăthē'rŏ*, sm. cuirassier.

corcha, *kōrŭtsh'ă*, sf. leather sack, used for the transport of cocoa, tobacco, &c., from America.   [sion.

coraje, *kōrä'h'ĕ*, sm, courage; anger, passion.

corajudo, da, —*hŏ'dŏ*, a. angry, passionate.   [of corals; —, a. choral.

coral, *kōrăl'*, sm. coral; —es, pl. strings

coralero, *kōrălē'rŏ*, sm. worker or dealer in corals.

coralina, *kōrălē'nă*, sf. sea-coralline.

corambre, *kōrăm'brĕ*, sf. all hides and skins of animals, dressed or undressed.

corambrero,—*brē'rŏ*, sm. dealer in hides.

coramvobis,—*vŏ'bĭs*, sm. outward appearance, gravity.

coraza, *kōrä'thä*, sf. cuirass; cuirassier.

corazón, *kōräthŏn'*, sm. heart; core; benevolence; courage; centre; pith of a tree; de —, heartily.

corazonada, *kōräthŏnä'dă*, sf. inspiration; quick decision; presentiment.

corbachada, *kōrbätshä'dă*, sf. lash given with a hunting-crop.

corbacho, *kōrbätsh'ŏ*, sm. hunting-crop.

corbato, *kōrbă'tă*, sf. cravat, neckerchief.

corbatín, —*tĭn'*, sm. cravat with a clasp.

corbato, *kōrbä'tŏ*, sm. cooler.

corbeta, *kōrbĕ'tă*, sf. corvet (light vessel with three masts and square sails).

corcel, *kōrthĕl'*, sm. steady horse, charger.

corcino, *kōrthē'nŏ*, sm. small deer.

corcova, *kōrkō'vă*, sf. hump; protuberance.   [backed, crooked.

corcovado, da, *kōrkŏvä'dŏ*, a. hump-

corcovear,—*vĕăr'*, v. n. to curvet, to cut capers.

corcovo, *kōrkō'vŏ*, sm. curvet; caper.

corchea, *kōrtshē'ă*, sf. (mus.) crotchet.

corchera, *kōrtshĕ'ră*, sf. vessel made of pitched cork to cool liquor.

corcheta, —*tă*, sf. eye of a hook or clasp.

corchete, —*tĕ*, sm. clasp; locket; catchpoll; bench-hook of a carpenter's bench.

corcho, *kōrtsh'ŏ*, sm. cork; bee-hive; cork-stopple.

cordaje, *kōrdä'h'ĕ*, sm. (mar.) cordage.

cordal, *kōrdăl'*, sm. double-tooth.

cordel, *kōrdĕl'*, sm. cord, rope; (mar.) line.

cordelazo, *kōrdĕlä'thŏ*, sm. lash given with a rope.

cordelería, —*lĕrĕ ă*, sf. rope-walk.

cordelero, —*lĕ'rŏ*, sm. rope-maker.

corderillo, *kōrdĕrĭl'yŏ*, sm. dressed lamb-skin.   [lamb-skin; meek, gentle man.

cordero, *kōrdĕ'rŏ*, sm. lamb; dressed

cordial, *kōrdiăl'*, a. cordial, affectionate; —, sm. cordial.

cordialidad, *kōrdiălĭdäd'*, sf. cordiality.

cordillera, *kōrdĭlyĕ'ră*, sf. range of mountains.

cordobán, *kōrŭbŏăn'*, sm. cordovan, cord-wain.   [lace; military cordon.

cordón, *kōrdŏn'*, sm. cord, string; twisted

cordonería, *kōrdŏnĕrĕ'ă*, sf. lace-making.

cordonero, —*nĕ'rŏ*, sm. lace-maker; rope-maker.   [wisdom; judgment.

cordura, *kōrdŭ'ră*, sf. prudence, practical

coreo, *kōrĕ'ŏ*, sm. harmonious melting of musical chords.   [small leather hide.

corezuelo, *kōrĕthŭĕ'lŏ*, sm. sucking-pig;

corifeo, *kōrĭfĕ'ŏ*, sm. coryphoeus.

corista, *kōrĭs'tă*, sm. chorister.

coriza, *kōrĭ'thă*, sf. coryza, dry catarrh; peasant's strap-shoe.

corladura, *kōrlädŭ'ră*, sf. gold-varnish.

cornada, *kōrnä'dă*, sf. thrust with a bull's horn.

cornadura, *kōrnädŭ'ră*, sf. horns, pl.

cornamenta, —*mĕn'tă*, sf. horns of an animal, pl.   [of rustic flute.

cornamusa, —*mū'să*, sf. cornemuse; sort

córnea, *kŏr'nĕă*, sf. cornea (second integument of the eye).   [horns.

cornear, —*nĕăr'*, v. n. to butt with the

corneja, *kōrnĕ'h'ă*, sf. crow.

córneo, ea, *kŏr'nĕŏ*, a. horny.

cornerina, —*nĕrē nă*, sf. onyx.

corneta, —*nĕ'tă*, sf. cornet; hunting-horn; cornet (ensign).   [bleeding horses.

cornezuelo, *kōrnĕthŭĕ'lŏ*, sm. instrument for

cornijal, —*g'hăl'*, sm. corner of a building.   [ing.

cornisa, —*nē'să*, sf. cornice.

corno, *kŏr'nŏ*, sm, cornelian cherry-tree.

cornucopia, —*nŭkŏ'piă*, sf. cornucopia, horn of plenty; branched candlestick.

cornudo, da, —*nŏ'dŏ*, a. horned.

coro, *kō'rŏ*, sm. choir, quire; chorus; (poet.) summer solstitial wind.

corógrafo, *kōrŏ'grăfŏ*, sm. chorographer.

corolario, *kōrŏlä'rĭŏ*, sm. corollary.

corona, *kōrō'nă*, sf. crown; coronet; top of the head; clerical tonsure; crown (English silver coin); regal power; monarchy; honour, splendour, decoration; halo.

coronación, *kōrŏnäthĭŏn'*, sf. coronation.

coronar, *ndr'*, v. a. to crown; to complete, to perfect; to ornament the top of a building.   [crown; (bot.) coronary.

coronario, ria, —*nä'riŏ*, a. relating to a

coronel, —*nĕl'*, sm. (mil.) colonel.

coronela, *kōrŏnĕ'lă*, sf. colonel's lady.

coronilla, —*nĭl'yă*, sf. crown of the head.

coroza, *kōrō'thă*, sf. coronet of pasteboard, worn as a mark of infamy.

corozo, —*thŏ*, sm. bactris (a palm-tree).

corpanchón, *kōrpänshŏn'*, sm. huge carcass.

corpezuelo, *kōrpĕthŭĕ'lŏ*, sm. corpiño, *kōrpĭn'yŏ*, sm. waistcoat; bodice.

corporación, *kōrpŏräthĭŏn'*, sf. corporation, guild.   [altar linen.

corporal, *kōrpŏräl'*, a. corporal; —es, s.pl.

corporalidad, —*rălĭdăd'*, sf. corporality, corporeity.

corpóreo, rea, *kōrpŏ'rĕŏ*, a. corporeal.

corporificar, *kōrpŏrĭfĭkăr'*, v. a. to embody.

corpudo, da, —*kŏrpŏ'dŏ*, a. corpulent, bulky.

corpulencia, *kŏrpŭlĕn'thĭă,* sf. corpulence.

corpulento, ta, *-tŏ,* a. corpulent, bulky.

Corpus, *kŏr'pŭs,* sm. Corpus-Christi day.

corpúsculo, *kŏrpŭs'kŭlŏ,* sm. corpuscle.

corral, *kŏrrăl',* sm. yard; a poultry-yard; play-house; blank space in notebooks of students who have neglected a lecture.

corralero, *-lā'rŏ,* sm. keeper of a dung-yard.   [flexibility.

correa, *kŏrrā'ă,* sf. leather strap, thong;

correaje, *-ā'hĕ,* sm. heap of leather straps.

correar, *kŏrrĕăr',* v. a. to draw out wool and prepare it for use.

corrección, *kŏrrĕkthĭŏn',* sf. correction; reprehension; amendment.

correctivo, va, *-tĭ'vŏ,* a. corrective.

correcto, ta, *kŏrrĕk'tŏ,* a. exact, correct.

corrector, *-tŏr',* sm. corrector; proof-reader.   [upper grinding-stone.

corredera, *kŏrrĕdā'ră,* sf. race-ground;

corredizo, za, *-dĭ'thŏ,* a. easy to be untied.

corredor, *-dŏr',* sm. runner; race-horse; corridor; broker; -a, sf. procuress.

corredura, *-dŏ'ră,* sf. liquor which flows over the brim of a vessel.   [brokerage.

correduría, *-dŭrē'ă,* sf. trade of a broker;

correería, *-ĕrē'ă,* sf. trade of a strap-maker.

correero, *-ā'rŏ,* sm. strap-maker.

corregencia, *kŏrrĕhĕn'thĭă,* sf. coregency.

corregente, *-rĕhĕn'tĕ,* sm. coregent.

corregidor, *-hĭdŏr',* sm. corregidor (Spanish magistrate).   [regidor.

corregidora, *-hĭdō'ră,* sf. wife of a corregidor.

corregir, *-hĭr',* v. a. to correct, to amend; to reprehend; to mitigate.

correjel, *-hĕl',* sm. English sole-leather.

correlación, *kŏrrĕlăthĭŏn',* sf. correlation.

correlativo, va, *-rĕlătĭ'vŏ,* a. correlative.

correncia, *-rĕn'thĭă,* sf. looseness of the belly.

correo, *-rā'ŏ,* sm. express, courier; post-boy; post-office; bag of letters; (law) accomplice; **á vuelta de —,** by return of post; **en la casa de -s,** "Post-Office," to be kept till called for (applied to letters arrived).   [leathery.

correoso, sa, *-rā'ŏsŏ,* a. ductile, flexible,

correr, *kŏrrĕr',* v. a. & n. to run; to flow; to blow (applied to the wind); to pass away; to take the proper course; to act heedlessly; **-se,** to be ashamed; to fly into a passion.   [strap.

correría, *-rĕrē'ă,* sf. incursion; [leather

correspondencia, *-rĕspŏndĕn'thĭă,* sf. correspondence; relation; intercourse, reciprocal intelligence; proportion.

corresponder, *-rĕspŏndĕr',* v. a. to make a suitable return; to correspond, to answer; to regard; to agree; to be congruent; **-se,** to correspond; to esteem one another.

correspondiente, *-rĕspŏndĭĕn'tĕ,* a. correspondent, conformable, suitable; -, sm. correspondent.   [dent.

corresponsal, *-rĕspŏnsăl',* sm. correspon-

corretaje, *-rĕtă'hĕ,* sm. brokerage; money paid to a pimp.

corretear, *-rĕtĕăr',* v. a. to rove, to ramble.

correvedile, *-rĕvĕdē'lĕ,* sm. tale-bearer; procurer, pimp.   [at full speed.

corrida, *-rē'dă,* sf. course, race; **de —,**

corrido, da, *-rē'dŏ,* a. expert; artful; ashamed.

corriente, *-rĭĕn'tĕ,* sf. course of rivers; current; course, progression; **- alternativa ó inversa,** alternative or inverse electric fluid; -, a. current; easy; generally received; common, general; fluent; running; marketable.

corrillero, *-rĭlyĕ'rŏ,* sm. braggadocio.

corrillo, *-rĭl'yŏ,* sm. circle of persons; **-s,** pl. town-talk.

corro, *kŏr'rŏ,* sm. circle formed by people who meet to talk or see a show; round (a dance).   [rate, to strengthen.

corroborar, *-rŏbŏrăr',* v. a. to corrobo-

corroer, *-rŏĕr',* v. a. to corrode.

corromper, *-rŏmpĕr',* v. a. to corrupt; to alter the form of a thing; to seduce a woman; to bribe, to suborn; -, v. n. to stink; **-se,** to rot, to putrify.

corrosión, *-rŏsĭŏn',* sf. corrosion.

corrosivo, va, *-rŏsē'vŏ,* a. corrosive.

corrupción, *-rŭpthĭŏn',* sf. corruption, putrefaction; spurious alteration in a book or writing; depravity.   [abuse.

corruptela, *-rŭptĕ'lă,* sf. corruption; (law)

corruptible, *-rŭptē'blĕ,* a. susceptible of corruption.

corruptivo, va, *-rŭptē'vŏ,* a. corruptive.

corrupto, ta, *-rŭp'tŏ,* a. corrupted, corrupt.

corruptor, *-rŭptŏr',* sm. corruptor, misleader.

corrusco, *-rŭs'kŏ,* sm. offal, broken bread.

corsario, *kŏrsā'rĭŏ,* sm. corsair, privateer; -, ria, a. cruising.

corsé, *kŏrsā',* sf. corset, bodice, stays.

corta, *kŏr'tă,* sf. felling of wood.

cortabolsas, *-bŏl'săs,* sm. pick-pocket.

cortadera, *-dā'ră,* sf. chisel for cutting hot iron; knife for extracting honey-combs.

contadillo, *-dĭl'yŏ,* sm. small drinking-glass; **echar -s,** to speak in an affected manner; to drink wine.

cortador, *-dŏr',* sm. butcher; **-es,** pl. incisors; -, ra, a. cutting.

cortadura, *-dŏ'ră,* sf. cut; cutting; incision; fissure; **-s,** pl. shreds, cuttings, parings.   [cold iron.

cortafrio, *-frē'ŏ,* sm. chisel for cutting

cortafuego, *-fŭā'gŏ,* sm. fire-proof wall.

cortapicos y callares, *-pē'kŏs ĭ kălyă'rĕs,* hold your tongue!   [legs in fencing.

cortapiés, *-pĭĕs',* sm. thrust made at the

cortaplumas, *-plŏ'măs,* sm. pen-knife.

cortar, *kŏrtăr',* v. a. to cut, to cut off, to curtail; to separate, to hew, to chop; (mil.) to cut off part of the enemy's army; to cut (at cards); to interrupt; to abridge; **-se,** to be ashamed or confounded; to coagulate.

corte, *kŏr'tĕ,* sm. edge of knife, &c.; abscission, cutting; cut; felling of trees; expedient; -, sf. court, residence town; the tribunal of chancery; retinue, suits; yard; courtship, flattery; **-s,** sf. pl. cortes, assembly of the states of the realm in Spain.

cortedad, *kŏrtĕdăd',* sf. smallness, little-ness; stupidity; pusillanimity.

cortejante, *-hăn'tĕ,* a. courtier, gallant.

cortejar, *-hăr',* v. a. to make love; to court; to accompany.

cortejo, *-tĕ'h'ŏ,* sm. homage; courtship; gift, present; gallant; wooer.

cortés, *kŏrtĕs',* a. courteous, genteel, polite.

cortesana, *-tĕsă'nă,* sf. courtesan.

cortesanazo, za, *-nă'thŏ,* a. awkwardly civil. [ness.

cortesanía, *-nĕ'ă,* sf. courtesy, polite-

cortesano, na, *-să'nŏ,* a. courtier-like; courteous, gentle.

cortesano, *-,* sm. courtier, courtling.

cortesía, *kŏrtĕsĕ'ă,* sf. courtesy, good manners, pl.; polite form of speech in a letter.

corteza, *kŏrtĕ'thă,* sf. bark; peel; crust; outward appearance; rusticity.

cortezudo, da, *kŏrtĕthŏ'dŏ,* a. barky; rustic, unmannerly.

cortina, *kŏrtĕ'nă,* sf. curtain. [a house.

cortinaje, *-tĭnă'h'ĕ,* sm. set of curtains for

corto, ta, *kŏr'tŏ,* a. short; scanty, narrow, small, little; stupid; pusillanimous, fearful; concise; defective; **á la -a ó á la larga,** sooner or later. [mouse.

cortón, *kŏrtŏn',* sm. ring-worm; field-

corusco, ca, *kŏrŭs'kŏ,* a. (poet.) brilliant.

corva, *kŏr'vă,* sf. ham; curb (disease in horses' knees). [of an arch.

corvadura, *-dŭ'ră,* sf. curvature; bend

corvaza, *kŏrvă'thă,* sf. curb (disease).

corvejón, *kŏrvĕh'ŏn',* sm. hough; spur of a cock.

corveta, *kŏrvĕ'tă,* sf. curvet, bound of a horse; (mar.) corvet, sloop of war.

corvetear, *-vĕtĕăr',* v. n. to curvet.

corvo, va, *kŏr'vŏ,* a. bent, crooked.

corzo, za, *kŏr'thŏ,* sm. & f. roe-deer, fallow-deer.

corzuelo, *kŏrthŭĕ'lŏ,* sm. wheat which has been left in the husks by the thrashers.

cosa, *kŏ'să,* sf. thing; **- de entidad,** important thing; **no es -,** it does not matter; **no hay tal -,** no such thing; **-,** ad. about, little more or less.

cosaco, *kŏsă'kŏ,* sm. cossack. [shoulders.

coscarse, *kŏskăr'sĕ,* v. r. to shrug the

coscoja, *-kŏ'h'ă,* sf. scarlet-oak; dry leaves of the kermes-oak; knob on the cross-bit of a bridle.

coscojo, *-kŏ'h'ŏ,* sm. kermes-grain.

cosecha, *-sĕ'chă,* sf. harvest; harvest-time; **de su -,** of one's own invention.

cosechar, *kŏsĕchăr',* v. a. to crop, to reap.

cosechero, *kŏsĕchĕ'rŏ,* sm. husbandman; vintager. [woman.

cosedera, *kŏsĕdĕ'ră,* sf. seamstress, needle-

coser, *kŏsĕr',* v. a. to sew; to join.

cosicosa, *kŏsĭkŏ'să,* sf. riddle.

cosido, *kŏsĕ'dŏ,* sm. stitching, sewing; clothes for the wash; **- de cama,** quilts and blankets of a bed.

cosmético, *kŏsmĕ'tĭkŏ,* sm. cosmetic.

cosmopolita, *-mŏpŏlĕ'tă,* sm. cosmopolite, cosmopolitan. [agitation; inquietude.

cosquillas, *-kĭl'yăs,* sf. pl. tickling; (fig.)

cosquilloso, sa, *-kĭlyŏ'sŏ,* a. ticklish; easily offended.

costa, *kŏs'tă,* sf. cost, price; charge, expense; fatigue, labour; coast, shore; **á toda -,** at all events. [side of a ship.

costado, *kŏstă'dŏ,* sm. side; (mil.) flank;

costal, *kŏstăl',* sm. sack, large bag, rammer, beetle. [ground.

costalada, *kŏstălă'dă,* sf. fall flat on the

costalero, *-lĕ'rŏ,* sm. porter (who carries goods). [pl.

costaneras, *-nă'răs,* sf. pl. rafters, timbers,

costanero, ra, *-nă'rŏ,* a. declivous.

costar, *kŏstăr',* v. n. to cost; to suffer detriment or loss. [tas, at first cost.

coste, *kŏs'tĕ,* sm. cost, expense; **á - y cos-**

costear, *kŏstĕăr',* v. a. to pay the cost; **-,** v. n. to sail along the coast.

costera, *kŏstĕ'ră,* sf. side of a bale of goods; fisherman's basket; outside quire of a ream of paper. [ing.

costero, ra, *-rŏ,* a. outward; (mar.) coast-

costilla, *kŏstĕl'yă,* sf. rib; (fig.) wife; stave; wealth; **-s,** pl. ribs of a ship.

costillaje, *-yă'h'ĕ,* **costillar,** *-yăr',* sm. human ribs.

costo, *kŏs'tŏ,* sm. cost, price, expense.

costoso, sa, *kŏstŏ'sŏ,* a. costly, dear, expensive. [given to the galley-slaves.

costra, *kŏs'tră,* sf. crust; broken biscuit

costrada, *kŏstră'dă,* sf. Spanish seed-cake.

costroso, sa, *kŏstrŏ'sŏ,* a. crusty.

costumbre, *kŏstŭm'brĕ,* sf. custom, habit; established manner. [splicing of a rope.

costura, *kŏstŏ'ră,* sf. seam; needle-work;

costurera, *kŏstŏrĕ'ră,* sf. seamstress.

cota, *kŏ'tă,* sf. coat of mail. [woman.

cotarrera, *kŏtărrĕ'ră,* sf. a gadding

cotarro, *kŏtăr'rŏ,* sm. charity-hut for the reception of beggars. [front.

cotejar, *kŏtĕhăr',* v. a. to compare, to con-

cotejo, *-tĕ'h'ŏ,* sm. comparison, collation.

cotí, *kŏtĕ',* sm. ticking used for mattresses.

cotidiano, na, *kŏtĭdĭă'nŏ,* a. daily.

cotilla, *kŏtĕl'yă,* sf. stays, pl.

cotillero, *-yă'rŏ,* sm. stay-maker.

cotillón, *kŏtĕl'yŏn,* sm. cotillon (dance).

coto, *kŏ'tŏ,* sm. inclosure of pasture-grounds; district; land-mark.

cotón, *kŏtŏn',* sm. printed cotton.

cotonada, *kŏtŏnă'dă,* sf. calico, print, printed calico, prints.

cotonía, *kŏtŏnĕ'ă,* sf. dimity.

cotorra, *kŏtŏr'ră,* sf. magpie; small parrot; loquacious woman.

cotorrera, *kŏtŏrrĕ'ră,* sf. hen-parrot; prattling woman.

cotorrería, *-rĕrĕ'ă,* sf. loquacity.

coturno, *kŏtŭr'nŏ,* sm. cothurnus; buskin.

covacha, *kŏvă't'hă,* sf. small cave, grotto.

covachuela, *-tshŭĕ'lă,* sf. office of secretary of state.

covachuelista, *-tshŭĕlĭs'tă,* sm. clerk in the secretary of state's office.

cavanillo, *kŏvănĭl'yŏ,* sm. basket for gathering grapes.

coyunda, *-yŭn'dă,* sf. strap with which oxen are tied to the yoke.

coyuntura, -yántŏ´rä, sf. joint, articulation; conjuncture.

coz, kŏth, sf. kick; recoil of a gun; flowing pack of a flood. **A coces,** by dint of [kicking.

crabrón, krabrŏn´, sm. hornet.

cráneo, krä´nĕŏ, sm. skull, head-pan.

crápula, krä´pŭlä, sf. intoxication.

crasitad, krásitäd´´, sf. grease, fat; corpulency.

craso, sa, krás´ŏ, a. fat, greasy, thick.

cráter, k´äter, sm. **cratera,** krätĕ´rä, sf. crater of a volcano.

creación, krĕäthĭŏn´, sf. creation.

creador, -ŏr´, sm. the Creator, God.

crear, krĕär´, v. a. to create, to make; to establish. [to raise the price.

crecer, krĕthér´, v. n. to grow, to increase; [to raise the price.

creces, krĕ´thĕs, sf. pl. augmentation, increase, additional quantity of corn paid by a farmer to a public granary, besides what he borrowed from it.

crecida, krĕthĭ´dä, sf. swell of rivers.

crecido, da, -dŏ, a. grown, increased; grave, important; -s, sm. pl. widening stitches in knitting.

creciente, krĕthĭén´tĕ, sf. swell; leaven; crescent (moon); (mar.) flood-tide.

crecimiento, -mĭén´tŏ, sm. increase; increase of the price. [an altar.

credencia, krĕdén´thĭä, sf. side-board or credence. [an altar.

credencial, -thĭäl´, a. credential.

credibilidad, krĕdĭbĭlĭdäd´, sf. credibility.

creditiva, -dĭt´ĭvä, sf. credentials, pl.

crédito, krĕ´dĭtŏ, sm. credit: belief, faith; reputation; note, bill.

credo, krĕ´dŏ, sm. creed.

credulidad, krĕdŭlĭdäd´, sf. credulity.

crédulo, la, -dŭlŏ, a. credulous.

creencia, krĕén´thĭä, sf. credence, belief; persuasion. [credit.

creer, krĕér´, v. a. to believe; to think; to [credit.

creible, krĕ´ĭblĕ, a. credible, believable.

crema, krĕ´mä, sf. cream; custard; (gr.)

crémor, krĕ´mŏr, sm. cremor. [diæresis.

crencha, krén´tshä, f. parting of the hair.

crepúsculo, -pŭs´kŭlŏ, sm. crepuscule, [twilight.

cresa, krĕ´sä, sf. maggot. [twilight.

crespo, pa, krés´pŏ, a. crisp, curled; obscure and bombastic; angry, displeased.

crespón, krĕspŏn´, sm. crape. [some birds.

cresta, krés´tä, sf. cock's-comb; crest of [some birds.

crestado, da, -tä´dŏ, a. crested.

crestón, -tŏn´, sm. crest of a helmet.

creta, krĕ´tä, sf. chalk.

cria, krĕ´ä, sf. breed or brood of animals; hatch; suckling; child reared by a nurse.

criada, krĭä´dä, sf. maid-servant, handmaid.

criadero, -dä´rŏ, sm. nursery for trees; breeding-place; -, ra, a. fruitful, prolific.

criadilla, -dĭl´yä, sf. testicle; small loaf in the form of a testicle; truffle.

criado, krĭä´dŏ, sm. servant; -, da, a. educated, instructed, bred.

criador, -dŏr´, sm. Creator; breeder; -, ra, a. fruitful, fecund.

crianza, krĭän´thä, sf. breeding, education.

criar, krĭär´, v. a. to create, to produce;

to breed, to procreate; to nurse; to suckle; to foster. [significations).

criatura, krĭätŏ´rä, sf. creature (in all its [significations).

criba, krĭ´bä, sf. sieve; riddle.

cribadero, krĭbädä´rŏ, sm. sieve-maker.

cribar, krĭbär´, v. a. to sift.

cribo, krĕ´bŏ, sm. sieve.

crimen, krĕ´mĕn, sm. crime, guilt.

criminal, krĭmĭnäl´, a. criminal.

criminalidad, -däd´, sf. criminality.

criminalista, -lĭs´tä, sm. author who has written on criminal matters.

orin, krĭn, sf. mane, horse-hair.

criollo, lla, krĭŏl´yŏ, sm. & f. Creole.

cripta, krĭp´tä, sf. crypt.

crisis, krĕ´sĭs, sf. crisis; (med.) acme; judgment passed after a mature deliberation.

crisma, krĭs´mä, sm. & f. chrism.

crismera, -mĕ´rä, sf. chrismatory.

crisol, krĭsŏl´, sm. crucible; cruset.

crisolada, krĭsŏlä´dä, sf. crucible full of metal.

cristal, krĭstäl´, sm. crystal; crystal-glass; looking-glass; (poet.) water.

cristalino, na, krĭstälĭ´nŏ, a. crystalline.

cristalización, -thäthĭŏn´, sf. crystallisation. [lise.

cristalizar, krĭstälĭthär´, v. a. to crystal- [lise.

cristiandad, krĭstĭändäd´, sf. christianity; observance of the law of Christ.

cristianismo, -nĭs´mŏ, sm. Christianism, Christendom. [tianize.

cristianizar, -nĭ´thär´, v. a. to chris- [tianize.

cristiano, na, krĭstĭä´nŏ, a. & sm. & f.

Cristo, krĭs´tŏ, sm. Christ. [Christian.

cristus, krĭs´tŭs, sm. criss-cross-row, alphabet. [phabet.

criterio, krĭtĕ´rĭŏ, sm. criterion. [phabet.

critica, krĭ´tĭkä, sf. critic.

criticador, -dŏr´, sm. critic, censurer.

criticar, -kär´, v. a. to criticise.

critico, krĭ´tĭkŏ, sm. critic, censurer; affected refiner of style and language; -, ca, a. critical.

crónica, krŏ´nĭkä, sf. chronicle. [ness.

cronicidad, krŏnĭthĭdäd´, sf. chronical- [ness.

crónico, ca, krŏ´nĭkŏ, a. chronic, chronical.

cronista, krŏnĭs´tä, sm. chronicler.

cronología, krŏnŏlŏ´hĕ´ä, sf. chronology.

cronológico, ca, -lŏ´hĭkŏ, a. chronological. [meter.

cronómetro, krŏnŏ´mĕtrŏ, sm. chronometer. [meter.

cruce de trenes, krŏthĕ dĕ trä´nĕs, sm. (rail.) crossing of trains.

crucera, krŏthĕ´rä, sf. withers of a horse.

crucero, -rŏ, sm. cross-vault of a church under the dome; cross-bearer; piece of timber which lies across the rafters in a building; crick of a mill; (mar.) cruising-station; cruiser; Cross (southern constellation). [to molest, to torment.

crucificar, krŏthĭfĭkär´, v. a. to crucify.

crucifijo, krŏthĭfĭ´h´ŏ, sm. crucifix.

crudeza, krŏdä´thä, sf. unripeness; rudeness; cruelty; vain boasting; indigestion.

crudo, da, krŏ´dŏ, a. raw, crude; green, unripe; rude, cruel; unfinished, immature; hard of digestion; blustering, boasting; immature (of tumours).

cruel, *krāĕl′,* a. cruel; (fig.) insufferable; severe, hard; bloody, violent.

crueldad, *-dăd′,* sf. cruelty, inhumanity; savageness.

cruento, ta, *krāĕn′tŏ,* a. bloody, cruel.

crujido, *krā′hī′dŏ,* sm. crack, creak, clash, crackling.

crujir, *krā′hīr′,* v. n. to crackle, to rustle.

crustáceo, cea, *krāstā′thĕŏ,* a. crustaceous.

cruz, *krūth,* sf. cross (as instrument, order, ensign of the Christian religion, line); (fig.) trial of patience, &c.

cruzada, *krāthā′dă,* sf. crusade; indulgences granted to those who support the crusade.

cruzado, *-dŏ,* sm. cruzado (old Spanish coin); crusader; –, da, a. cruel, transverse.

cruzamiento, *-mĭĕn′tŏ,* sm. crossing; – de nivel, (rail.) crossing-road; – de vía, (rail.) junction.

cruzar, *krāthār′,* v. a. to cross; to cross a road; (mar.) to cruise; –se, to be knighted; to cross and trip, to stumble along (of horses).

cuácaro, ra, *kwā′kărŏ,* sm. & f. quaker.

cuaderna, *kwādĕr′nă,* sf. fourth part; (mar.) timber-work forming the ribs of a ship. [of paper; log (of a vessel).

cuadernillo, *-dĕrnī′yŏ,* sm. small parcel

cuaderno, *-dĕr′nŏ,* sm. parcel of paper stitched together; small memorandum book; four pages of printed matter; punishment of students. [stable.

cuadra, *kā′drā,* sf. hall; drawing-room;

cuadrado, da, *kāādrā′dŏ,* a. square, quadrate; perfect; –, sm. square, quadrate; clock (in stockings); gusset of a shirt sleeve; de –, in front, face to face; squared.

cuadragenario, ria, *-hĕnā′rĭŏ,* a. forty years old. [gesimal, lenten.

cuadragesimal, *-′hĕstmăl′,* a. quadra-

cuadragésimo, ma, *-′hĕ′sĭmŏ,* a. fortieth. [gular, fourcornered.

cuadrangular, *-drăngūlăr′,* a. quadran-

cuadrángulo, *-drăn′gūlŏ,* sm. quadrangle.

cuadrante, *-drăn′tĕ,* sm. quadrant; dialplate of a sun-dial; square board put up in churches, pointing out the order of masses to be celebrated.

cuadrar, *kwādrār′,* v. a. & n. to square; to square timbers; to multiply a number by itself; to fit, to suit, to correspond.

cuadratura, *-drātū′ră,* sf. quadrature.

cuadricular, *-drĭkūlăr′,* v. a. to copy by means of squares.

cuadriforme, *-fŏr′mĕ,* a. fourfaced.

cuadrilátero, ra, *-lā′tĕrŏ,* a. quadrilateral. [lar, oblong.

cuadrilongo, ga, *-lŏn′gŏ,* a. quadrangu-

cuadrilla, *kwādrĭl′yă,* sf. gang, crew, troop; any one of the four divisions of sheep-masters which form the board of Mesta; band of armed men, sent in pursuit of highwaymen.

cuadrillero, *-yā′rŏ,* sm. member of the court of La Santa Hermandad; com-

mander of an armed band employed by that court. [fold.

cuádriple, *kwā′drĭplĕ,* a. quadruple, four-

cuadriplicado, da, *-drĭplĭkā′dŏ,* a. quadrupled. [syllabic.

cuadrisílabo, ba, *-drĭsĭ′lăbŏ,* a. quadri-

cuadriyugo, *-drĭyŏ′gŏ,* sm. cart with four horses.

cuadro, *kwā′drŏ,* sm. square; picture; picture-frame; window-frame; parterre in a garden; (mil.) square body of troops.

cuadrúpedo, da, *kwāārŏ′pĕdŏ,* a. quadruped. [quadruplicate.

cuadruplicar, *kwādrŭplĭkăr′,* v. a. to

cuádruplo, pla, *kwā′drŭplŏ,* a. quadruple, fourfold.

cuaj-da, *kwā′hā′dă,* sf. butter, curd, coagulated fat. [goose-grass.

cuajaleche, *-lĕtsh′ĕ,* sf. (bot.) yellow

cuajamiento, *-mĭĕn′tŏ,* sm. coagulation.

cuajar, *kwā′hăr′,* sm. runnet-bag (of ruminants).

cuajar, –, v. a. to coagulate; to ornament too much; –, v. n. to succeed; to please; –se, to coagulate, to curdle.

cuajarón, *kwā′hărŏn′,* sm. grume, clot, gore. [coagulation.

cuajo, *kwā′hŏ,* sm. runnet, rennet;

cual, *kwăl,* a. which; he who; same, like, such; one, other, partly; –, ad. as; how.

cualidad, *kwălĭdăd′,* sf. quality.

cualquier, *kwălkĕr′,* a. anyone.

cualquiera, *-ă,* a. anyone, someone, anybody, somebody. [nouns).

cuan, kwăn, ad. how, as (used only before

cuando, *kwăn′dŏ,* ad. when; in case that; if; although; even; sometimes; de – en–, from time to time; –más, –mucho, at most, at best; –menos, at least; ¿ de cuándo acá ? since when ? [tinction.

cuantía, *kwăntī′ă,* sf. quantity; rank, dis-

cuantidad, *kwăntĭdăd′,* sf. quantity.

cuantioso, sa, *-tĭŏ′sŏ,* a. numerous, copious.

cuantitativo, va, *-tĭtā′vŏ,* a. quantitive.

cuanto, ta, *kwăn′tŏ,* a. containing, consisting of; as many as, as much as, all, whatever; ¿ cuánto ? how much ? ¿ cuántos ? how many ? –, ad. respecting, whilst; –más, moreover, the more as; en – á, with regard to; in the mean time; por –, inasmuch as.

cuarenta, *kwărĕn′tă,* a. forty.

cuarentena, *-tĕ′nă,* sf. space of forty days; Lent; (mar.) quarantine.

cuaresma, *kwărĕs′mă,* sf. Lent; collection of Lent sermons.

cuaresmal, *kwărĕsmăl′,* a. lenten.

cuarta, *kwăr′tă,* sf. quarter; sequence of four cards in the game of piquet; quadrant (of a circle); (mar.) quarter (point of the compass). [quarter (dry measure).

cuartal, *kwărtăl′,* sm. quartern loaf;

cuartana, *-tā′nă,* sf. (med.) quartan.

cuartanal, *-tănăl′,* a. intermittent (of fever). [under a quartan.

cuartanario, ria, *-tănā′rĭŏ,* a. labouring

cuartear, *kwărtĕăr′,* v. a. to quarter, to

divide into four parts; to bid a fourth more at public sales; to make a fourth person at a game; **-se,** to split into pieces.

cuartel, *kwärtĕl'*, sm. quarter, fourth part; district of a city; place where soldiers are lodged; duty imposed on villages for the quartering of soldiers; dwelling, home; (mar.) hatch.

cuartelero, *-tĕlā'rō*, sm. soldier in each company who keeps their apartment clean.

cuarterón, *-tĕrōn'*, sm. quarterer, quarter; upper part of windows, quarteroon.

cuarteta, *-tā'tä*, sf. (poet.) quatrain.

cuartilla, *-tîl'yä*, sf. fourth part of an arroba, *or* sixteenth part of a quintal; fourth part of a sheet of paper; pastern of horses.

cuartillo, *-tîl'yō*, sf. pint; fourth part of a peck in grain; fourth part of a real.

cuarto, *kwär'tō*, sm. fourth part; quarter; dwelling, room, apartment; copper coin worth four maravedis; pedigree; **-s,** pl. cash money; **-, ta,** a. fourth.

cuartón, *-tōn'*, sm. large joist.

cuarzo, *kwär'thō*, sm. quartz.

cuasi, *kwä'sî*, ad. almost, nearly.

Cuasimodo, *-mō'dō*, sm. first Sunday after Easter.　　　　[white feet (horses).

cuatralbo, ba, *kwäträ'bō*, a. having four white feet.

cuatrero, *-trä'rō*, sm. horse-thief.

cuatrinca, *-trĭn'kä*, sf. union of four persons *or* things; four cards of the same suit.　　　　[four; (mus.) quartet.

cuatro, *kwät'rō*, a. four; **-,** sm. figure four.

cuatrocientos, tas, *kwätrōthĭĕn'tōs*, a. four hundred.

cuatropea, *-pā'ä*, sf. horse-tax.

cuatropeado, *-pĕä'dō*, sm. step in dancing.

cuatropear, *-pĕär'*, v. n. to run on all fours.

cuatrotanto, *-tän'tō*, sm. fine amounting to four times the value of the sum *or* object embezzled.　　　　[tub.

cuba, *kō'bä*, sf. task; (fig.) toper, drunkard; **cubero,** *kåbā'rō*, sm. cooper.

cubertura, *kåbĕrtō'rä*, sf. cover, covering.

cubeta, *kåbā'tä*, sf. small barrel; bucket.

cubeto, *-tō*, sm. small barrel.

cubicar, *kåbîkär'*, v. a. to cube a number.

cúbico, ca, *kō'bîkä*, a. cubic.

cubierta, *kåbĭĕr'tä*, sf. cover, covert; pretext; deck of a ship.

cubierto, *-tō*, sm. dish-cover; shelter; allowance of a soldier in a house; course of dishes.

cubil, *kåbîl'*, sm. lair of wild beasts.

cubilete, *kåbîlā'tĕ*, sm. copper pan for baking pies &c.; tumbler; dice-box; small pie stuffed with mince meat.

cubito, *kō'bîtō*, sm. ulna.　　　[nave.

cubo, *kō'bō*, sm. cube; pail; mill-pool.

cubrepán, *kåbrēpän'*, sm. fire-shovel, used by shepherds.

cubrir, *kåbrîr'*, v. a. to cover; to palliate; to disguise; to cover a post; to roof a building; to cover a mare; **-se,** to put on one's hat.　　　　[wicked person.

cuca, *kō'kä*, sf. edible cyperus; mala **-,**

cucaña, *kåkän'yä*, sf. any thing acquired with little trouble and at other people's expense.

cucañero, *-yā'rō*, sm. parasite.

cucaracha, *-rätsh'ä*, sf. wood-louse.

cucarda, *kåkär'dä*, sf. cockade.

cuclillas, (en —,) *kåklîl'yäs*, ad. in a cowering manner.　　　　[cuckold.

cuclillo, *kåklîl'yō*, sm. cuckoo; (fig.)

cucurucho, *kåkårūtsh'ō*, sm. paper-cornet.

cuchara, *kåtshä'rä*, sf. spoon.

cucharada, *-rä'dä*, sf. spoonful, ladleful.

cucharón, *-rōn'*, sm. ladle; large spoon.

cuchichear, *kåtshĭtshĕär'*, v. n. to whisper.

cuchicheo, *-tshā'ō*, sm. whispering.

cuchichero, ra, *kåtshĭtshā'rō*, sm. & f. whisperer.

cuchilla, *kåtshĭl'yä*, sf. large kitchen-knife; chopping-knife; ancient poniard; (poet.) sword; bookbinder's knife.

cuchillada, *-yä'dä*, sf. cut with a knife; gash; **-s,** pl. wrangles, quarrels.

cuchillería, *-yĕrĕ'ä*, sf. cutler's shop; place (*or* street) where there are many cutlers' shops.

cuchillero, *-yā'rō*, sm. cutler.

cuchillo, *kåtshîl'yō*, sm. knife; triangular gore, gusset of a garment.

cuchufleta, *kåtshōflā'tä*, sf. joke, jest, fun.

cuelga, *kåĕl'gä*, sf. cluster of grapes hung up for use; birth-day present.

cuello, *kåĕl'yō*, sm. neck; neck of a bottle; collar of a priest's garment; small end of a wax-candle; shirt-collar.　　　[of the eye.

cuenca, *kåĕn'kä*, sm. earthen bowl; socket

cuenco, *-kō*, sm. earthen bowl.

cuenta, *kåĕn'tä*, sf. computation, calculation; account; narrative; bead of a rosary; reason, satisfaction.

cuentagarbanzos, *kåĕntägärbän'thōs*, sm. niggardly person.

cuentista, *kåĕntîs'tä*, sm. tale-bearer.

cuento, *kåĕn'tō*, sm. a million; butt-end of a spear, &c.; prop, support; fable; tale, story, narrative.

cuerda, *kåĕr'dä*, sf. cord; string for musical instruments; match for firing a gun; chain of a watch *or* clock; Spanish measure of about 8 ells.　　　[in his senses.

cuerdo, da, *kåĕr'dō*, a. prudent, judicious;

cuerna, *kåĕr'nä*, sf. horn vessel into which cows &c. are milked; stag's horn; hunting-horn.

cuerno, *-nō*, sm. horn; corn.

cuero, *kåä'rō*, sm. hide, skin, leather; (fig.) great drinker.

cuerpo, *kåĕr'pō*, sm. body; cadaver, corpse.

cuerva, *kåĕr'vä*, sf. crow.

cuervo, *-vō*, sm. raven.

cuesco, *kåĕs'kō*, sm. kernel; stone (of fruits); mill-stone of an oil-mill.

cuesta, *kåĕs'tä*, sf. hill; rising ground with a slope; quest, charity; **ir — abajo,** to go down hill; **— arriba,** with great trouble and difficulty.

cuestión, *kåĕstĭōn'*, sf. question; dispute; quarrel; problem.　　　[able, problematical.

cuestionable, *kåĕstĭōnä'blĕ*, a. question-

cuestionar, *kŭĕstiŏnăr'*, v. a. to question, to dispute. [gatherer.

cuestor, *kŭĕstŏr'*, sm. questor; alms-

cuestura, *kŭĕstŏ'rā*, sf. questorship.

cueva, *kā̆d'vā*, sf. cave, grotto, den.

cuévano, *kā̆d'vănŏ*, sm. great basket for carrying grapes to the wine-press.

cuezo, *kā̆d'thŏ*, sm. hod.

cugujada, *kŭgŭ'hă'dā*, sf. sky-lark.

cugulla, *kŭgŭl'yā*, sf. cowl, monk's hood.

cuidado, *kŭidā'dŏ*, sm. care, heed, solicitude; fear; custody, charge.

cuidadoso, **sa**, *-dŏ'sŏ*, a. careful, heedful, vigilant. [mind, to look after.

cuidar, *kŭidăr'*, v. a. to heed, to care; to

cuita, *kŭĭ'tā*, sf. grief, affliction, trouble.

cuitado, **da**, *kŭitā'dŏ*, a. anxious, wretched, miserable; timid.

cuja, *kŭ'h'ā*, sf. leather bag.

culada, *kŭlā'dā*, sf. fall on one's backside; -s, pl. rolling of a ship.

culantrillo, *kŭlăntril'yŏ*, sm.(bot.) maidenhair, fern.

culantro, *kŭlān'trŏ*, sm. (bot.) coriander.

culata, *kŭlā'tā*, sf. breech of a gun; screwpin; back part of any thing.

culousido, *kŭlkŭst'dŏ*, sm. botch-work.

culebra, *kŭlā'brā*, sf. snake.

culebrear, *kŭlĕbrĕăr'*, v. n. to crankle.

culebrina, *-brē'nā*, sf. (mil.) culverin.

culera, *kŭlā'rā*, sf. stain of urine in the swaddling-clothes of children.

culero, *-rŏ*, sm. clout; disease in birds; -, **ra**, a. slothful, lazy.

culo, *kŏ'lŏ*, sm. breech, backside; bottom, socket. [ableness; guilt.

culpa, *kŭl'pā*, sf. misdemeanour, culp-

culpable, *kŭlpā'blĕ*, a. culpable; guilty.

culpado, **da**, *-dŏ*, sm. & f. transgressor.

culpar, *kŭlpăr'*, v. a. to accuse, to blame.

cultivación, *kŭltĭvăthĭŏn'*, sf. cultivation, culture.

cultivador, *-dŏr'*, sm. cultivator.

cultivar, *kŭltĭvăr'*, v. a. to cultivate.

cultivo, *kŭltĭ'vŏ*, sm. cultivation; improvement; culture of the mind and manners.

culto, **ta**, *kŭl'tŏ*, a. pure, elegant, correct; polished; enlightened, civilised; -, sm. culture; worship. [style.

cultura, *kŭltŏ'rā*, sf. culture; elegance of

cumbre, *kŭm'brĕ*, sf. top, summit; greatest height of favour, fortune, &c.

cumpleaños, *kŭmplĕăn'yŏs*, sm. birth-day.

cumplido, **da**, *kŭmplī'dŏ*, a. large, plentiful; faultless; polished, polite, courteous; -, sm. compliment. [compliment.

cumplimentar, *kŭmplĭmĕntăr'*, v. a. to

cumplimentero, **ra**, *-tā'rŏ*, a. full of compliments; complaisant.

cumplimiento, *kŭmplĭmĭĕn'tŏ*, sm. compliment; accomplishment; perfection; abundance.

cumplir, *kŭmplĭr'*, v. a. to execute; to provide; to fulfil; -, v. n. to be convenient; to suffice; -se, to be realized.

cumquibus, *kŭmkŭ'bŭs*, sm. (fam.) money.

cúmulo, *kŏ'mŭlŏ*, sm. heap, pile; (fig.) press of business.

cuna, *kŏ'nā*, sf. cradle; (fig.) native country; family, lineage; origin; - **de viento**, hanging cradle.

cundir, *kŭndĭr'*, v. n. to spread (of stains); to grow, to increase; to propagate.

cuña, *kŭn'yā*, sf. wedge; (fig.) artifice, slyness.

cuñado, **da**, *kŭnyā'dŏ*, sm. & f. brother- or sister-in-law.

cuño, *kŭn'yŏ*, sm. die for coining money; impression made by the die.

cuociente, *kŭŏthĭĕn'tĕ*, sm. (ar.) quotient.

cuota, *kŭŏ'tā*, sf. quote.

cupé, *kŭpĕ'*, sm. landau. [ticket.

cupo, *kŏ'pŏ*, **cupón**, *kŭpŏn'*, sm. interest-

cúpula, *kŏ'pŭlā*, sf. cupola, dome.

cupulino, *kŭpŭlī'nŏ*, sm. lantern (small cupola raised upon another). [fretter.

cuquillo, *kŭkīl'yŏ*, sm. cuckoo; vine-

cura, *kŏ'rā*, sm. parson; -, sf. care, healing.

curable, *kŭrā'blĕ*, a. curable, healable.

curación, *-thĭŏn'*, sf. cure, healing.

curador, *-dŏr'*, sm. overseer; guardian; curator, administrator.

curadora, *-dŏ'rā*, sf. female guardian.

curaduría, *kŭrădŭrī'ā*, sf. guardianship.

curandero, *kŭrăndā'rŏ*, sm. quack, medicaster.

curar, *kŭrăr'*, v. a. to cure, to heal; to prescribe the regimen of a patient.

curatela, *kŭrātĕ'lā*, sf. tutorship.

curativo, **va**, *-tē'vŏ*, a. a curative, healing.

curato, *kŭrā'tŏ*, sm. rectory, parsonage; parish; - **anejo**, chapel at ease.

cureña, *kŭrĕn'yā*, sf. gun-carriage; stay of a cross-bow; **á** - **rasa**, (mil.) without a breast-work (applied to a barbet-battery); without shelter.

curia, *kŏ'rĭā*, sf. ecclesiastical court where church affairs are examined and decided in Rome; care and skill.

curial, *kŭrĭāl'*, a. belonging to the Roman curia; -, sm. member of the Roman curia; subaltern in the courts of justice.

curiosidad, *kŭrĭŏsĭdăd'*, sf. curiosity; neatness; object of curiosity, rarity.

curioso, **sa**, *kŭrĭŏ'sŏ*, a. a curious; neat, fine, beautiful; careful, attentive, diligent.

curruca, *kŭrrŏ'kā*, sf. babbling warbler.

currutaco, *-tā'kŏ*, sm. beau, fop; -, a. beauish; affected.

cursado, **da**, *kŭrsā'dŏ*, a. skilled; versed.

cursante, *kŭrsăn'tĕ*, a. frequenting; assiduous; -, sm. student, scholar.

cursar, *kŭrsăr'*, v. a. to frequent a place; to do a thing often.

cursillo, *kŭrsĭl'yŏ*, sm. short course of lectures (in a university).

cursivo, **va**, *kŭrsē'vŏ*, a. italic (type).

curso, *kŭr'sŏ*, sm. course, direction; course of lectures. [dresser.

curtidor, *kŭrtĭdŏr'*, sm. tanner, leather-

curtidos, *kŭrtĭ'dŏs*, sm. pl. tanned leather.

curtiduría, *-dŭrī'ā*, sf. tan-yard.

curtir, *kŭrtĭr'*, v. a. to tan leather; to sunbrown; to inure to hardships.

curva, *kŭr'vā*, sf. curved line; (mar.) knee.

curvatura, *-tō'rā*, sf. curvature, of any piece of timber employed in ship-building.

curvilíneo, nea, *kŭrvēlē'nĕō*, a. curvi-
curvo, va, *kŭr'vŏ*, curved, bent. [linear.
cuscurro, *kŭskŭr'rŏ*, sm. little crust of
cúspide, *kŭs'pīdĕ*, sf. cuspis. [bread.
custodia, *kŭstŏ'dīā*, sf. custody, keeping,
hold ; guard, escort ; monstrance ; reliquary
in Catholic churches. [man.
custodio, *—dīŏ*, sm. guard, keeper, watch-
cutáneo, nea, *kŭtā'nĕō*, a. cutaneous.
cúter, *kŏ'tĕr*, sm. (mar.) cutter.
cuti, *kŭtī'*, sm. ticking, tick.
cutícula, *kŭtē'kŭlă*, sf. cuticle.
cutir, *kŭtīr'*, v. a. to knock one thing
against another.
cutis, *kŏ'tĭs*, sm. & f. skin.
cuyo, ya, *kŭy'ŏ*, pn. of which, of whom,
whose, whereof.

Ch.

cha, *tshă*, sf. tea (in Mexico).
chabacanada, *tshăbăkănă'dă*, sf. very
vulgar word or observation.
chabacano, na, *—kā'nŏ*, a. coarse, unpolished ; bungling.
chabeta, *tshăbĕ'tă*, sf. forelock-key ;
perder la —, to lose one's senses.
chacolí, *tshăkŏlī'*, sm. light red wine of a
sourish taste.
chacota, *tshăkŏ'tă*, sf. noisy mirth.
chacotear, *—kŏtĕăr'*, v. n. to indulge in
noisy mirth [ing the merry-Andrew.
chacotero, ra, *—kŏtā'rŏ*, a. waggish, act-
cháchara, *tshă'tshără*, sf. chit-chat, chatter, idle talk. [purpose.
chacharear, *—rĕăr'*, v. n. to talk to no
chacharería, *—rĕrĕ'ă*, sf. verbiage, garrulity.
chacharero, *—ră'rŏ*, sm. prater.
chacho, *tshătsh'ŏ*, sm. stake at the game
of hombre. [ment.
chafaldita, *tshăfăldē'tă*, sf. teasing, merri-
chafalditero, *—făldītā'rŏ*, sm. teaser.
chafallar, *—făl'yăr'*, v. a. to botch, to mend.
chafallo, *—făl'yŏ*, sm. coarse patch.
chafallón, ona, *—fălyŏn'*, sm. & f. botcher.
chafar, *—făr'*, v. a. to mat down the pile
of velvet ; to cut one short in his discourse.
chafarote, *—fărŏ'tĕ*, sm. short broad
Turkish sword. [in clothes &c.
chafarrinada, *—fărrēnă'dă*, sf. blot or stain
chafarrinar, *—fărrēnăr'*, v. a. to blot, to
stain.
chafarrinón, *—fărrēnŏn'*, sm. blot, stain.
chaflán, *tshăflăn'*, sm. blaze of a horse ;
chal, *tshăl*, sm. shawl. [slope.
chalán, *tshălăn'*, sm. hawker, huckster ;
who is very clever in selling things ;
horse-dealer. [fully ; to deal in horses.
chalanear, *—năr'*, v. a. to sell things art-
chalanería, *—nĕrĕ'ă*, sf. artifice and cunning used by dealers in buying and selling.
chaleco, *tshălĕ'kŏ*, sm. waistcoat.
chalote, *tshălŏ'tĕ*, sm. shallot-garlic.
chalupa, *tshălŭ'pă*, sf. (mar.) sloop.
chamarra, *tshămăr'ră*, sf. garment made
of sheep-skins or of very coarse frieze.

chamarreta, *—mărrĕ'tă*, sf. short loose
jacket [uncocked (applied to a hat).
chambergo, ga, *tshămbĕr'gŏ*, a. slouched,
chambón, *—bŏn'*, sm. unskilful person or
gamester. [gown.
chambra, *tshăm'bră*, sf. woman's night-
chamelote, *tshămĕlŏ'tĕ*, sm. camlot.
chamorra, *tshămŏr'ră*, sf. shorn head.
chamorro, *—mŏr'rŏ*, sm. (bot.) beardless
wheat. [liquors ; to speak gibberish.
champurrar, *tshămpŭrrăr'*, v. a. to mix
chamuscado, da, *tshămŭskă'dŏ*, a. tipsy,
flustered with wine ; addicted to some vice.
chamuscar, *—mŭskăr'*, v. a. to singe, to
scorch. [(fig.) scolding, wrangling.
chamusquina, *—mŭskē'nă*, sf. scorching ;
chancero, ra, *tshănthā'rŏ*, a. jocose,
sportive, merry ; —, sm. (cant) young thief.
chanciller, *tshĭlyĕr*, sm. chancellor.
chancillería, *—thĭlyĕrē'ă*, sf. chancery.
chancleta, *tshănklĕ'tă*, sf. slipper.
chanclo, *tshăn'klŏ*, sm. patten, clog, galosh.
chanfaina, *tshănfī'nă*, sf. ragout of livers
and lights ; worthless thing.
chanflón, ona, *—flŏn'*, a. made in a bungling
manner ; —, sm. money beaten out to appear larger.
chantre, *tshăn'trĕ*, sm. precentor.
chantría, *—trē'ă*, sf. office of a precentor.
chanza, *tshăn'thă*, sf. joke, jest, fun.
chanzoneta, *—thŏnĕ'tă*, sf. joke, jest ;
merry chansonnette.
chapa, *tshă'pă*, sf. thin metal plate which
serves to strengthen or adorn the work it
covers ; rouge. [roof.
chaparra, *tshăpăr'ră*, sf. coach with a low
chaparro, *—rŏ*, sm. evergreen oak-tree.
chaparrón, *—rŏn'*, sm. violent shower of
rain. [metal plates.
chapear, *tshăpĕăr'*, v. a. to garnish with
chapería, *tshăpĕrĕ'ă*, sf. ornament consisting of a number of metal plates.
chapín, *tshăpēn'*, sm. clog with a cork-sole
lined with morocco leather.
chapitel, *tshăpītĕl'*, sm. capital of a column ;
graver, tool used in
engraving. [branches of trees.
chaple, *tshă'plĕ*, sm.
chapodar, *tshăpŏdăr'*, v. a. to lop off the
chapotear, *—tĕăr'*, v. a. to wet with a
spunge ; —, v. n. to paddle in the water ;
to dab. [to bungle.
chapucear, *tshăpŭthĕăr'*, v. a. to botch,
chapucería, *—thĕrē'ă*, sf. clumsy performance, bungling work.
chapucero, *—thă'rŏ*, sm. blacksmith ;
nailer ; bungler ; —, ra, a. clumsy, rude.
chapurrar, *tshăpŭrrăr'*, v. a. to speak
gibberish ; to mix liquors.
chapuz, *tshăpŭth'*, sm. act of ducking or
sousing. [to dive ; to souse.
chapuzar, *tshăpŭthăr'*, v. a. & r. to duck
chaqueta, *tshăkĕ'tă*, sf. jacket.
chaquete, *—tĕ*, sm. game resembling backgammon. [icing.
charca, *tshăr'kă*, sf. pool of water for
charco, *—kŏ*, sm. pool of standing water.
charla, *tshăr'lă*, sf. idle chit-chat, prattle.

bharlador, ra, *tshărlădŏr'*, sm. & f. prater, garrulous person.

charladuría, *–dūrě'ă*, sf. garrulity, gossip.

charlatín, *–tín'*, sm. mean prattler.

charlar, *–lăr'*, v. n. to prattle, to chatter.

charlatán, *tshărlătăn'*, sm. prater, idle talker; quack, mountebank. [quackery.

charlatanería, *–tănĕrĕ'ă*, sf. garrulity;

charnela, *tshărně'lă*, sf. hinge, joint.

charol, *tshărŏl'*, sm. varnish; Japan.

charolar, tehărŏlăr', v. a. to varnish; to japan. [japanner.

charolista, *tshărŏlĭs'tă*, sm. varnisher, japanner.

charpa, *tshăr'pă*, sf. holster.

charrada, *tshărră'dă*, sf. speech or action of a clown; a dance; any work made in a tasteless manner; tinsel, tawdriness.

charretera, *tshărrětĕ'ră*, sf. epaulet.

charro, *tshăr'rŏ*, sm. churl; **–, rra, a.** gaudy.

chasco, *tshăs'kŏ*, sm. fun, joke, jest; lash.

chasquear, *tshăskĕăr'*, v. a. to crack a whip; **–,** v. n. to play tricks; to disappoint; to cheat. [runner (in Peru).

chasqui, *tshăskĭ'*, sm. foot-messenger.

chasquido, *–kĕ'dŏ*, sm. crack of a whip; crack. [playing tricks.

chasquista, *–kĭs'tă*, sm. person fond of

chata, *tshă'tă*, sf. flat-bottomed boat.

chato, ta, *–tŏ*, a. flat, flattish; flatnosed.

chaza, *tshă'thă*, sf. point where the ball is driven back or stops, in a game at balls; berth on board ship.

chazador, *tshăthădŏr'*, sm. person employed to stop the ball and mark the game.

chazar, *tshăthăr'*, v.a. to stop the ball before it reaches the winning point; to mark the point whence the ball was driven back.

chelín, *tshělín'*, sm. shilling.

chiba, *tshě'bă*, sf. kid.

chibalete, *–lě'tě*, sm. chest of drawers with a desk for writing.

chibato, *–bă'tŏ*, sm. kid between six and twelve months old; he-goat.

chibetero, *tshĭbětě'rŏ*, sm. fold for kids.

chibo, *tshě'bŏ*, sm. kid.

chibor, *–bŏr'*, sm. baboon.

chicada, *tshĭkă'dă*, sf. herd of sickly kids.

chicarrero, *–kărrě'rŏ*, sm. shoemaker who makes pumps.

chico, ca, *tshě'kŏ*, a. little, small; **–,** sm. little boy. [gallantry.

chicolear, *–kŏlěăr'*, v. a. to joke, to jest in

chicoleo, *–kŏlě'ŏ*, sm. jest in gallantry, joke. [(applied to children).

chicoorrotín, *–kŏrrŏtín'*, a. very small

chicote, *tshĭkŏ'tě*, sm. end of a cable.

chicha, *tshĭtsh'ă*, sf. meat (used only in speaking to children). [vest-fly.

chicharra, *tshăr'ră*, sf. froth-worm, harvest-fly.

chicharrero, *–tshărră'rŏ*, sm. hot place or climate. [fish; horse-mackerel.

chicharro, *–tshăr'rŏ*, sm. young tunny.

chicharrón, *–tshărrŏn'*, sm. crackling, morsel of fried lard left in the pan.

chichisvear, *–tshĭsvěăr'*, v. a. to woo, to court.

chichisveo, *–tshĭsvě'ŏ*, sm. attendance paid to a lady; gallant, attendant on a lady. [occasioned by a blow.

chichón, *–tshŏn'*, sm. lump on the head

chichonera, *–tshŏně'ră*, sf. tumbling-cap (for children).

chifla, *tshě'flă*, sf. whistle; paring-knife.

chifladera, *–flădě'ră*, sf. whistle.

chiflar, *–flăr'*, v. n. to whistle; to mock, to jest; to tipple.

chifle, *tshě'flě*, sm. whistle, call.

chiflete, *–flě'tě*, **chiflo,** *tshě'flŏ*, sm. whistle.

chiflido, *–flě'dŏ*, sm. sound of a whistle.

chilindrina, *tshĭlĭndrě'nă*, sf. trifle.

chilindrón, *–lĭndrŏn'*, sm. game at cards; cut in the head.

chilla, *tshĭl'yă*, sf. call for foxes, &c.; **clavo de –,** tack; **tablas de –,** thin boards.

chillar, *–yăr'*, v. n. to scream, to shriek; to crackle, to creak; to hiss in frying.

chillido, *–yě'dŏ*, sm. squeak, shriek.

chillón, *–yŏn'*, sm. bawler; common crier; nail, tack.

chimenea, *tshĭmĕně'ă*, sf. chimney.

china, *tshě'nă*, sf. pebble; porcelain; chinaware; china silk.

chinarro, *–năr'rŏ*, sm. large pebble.

chinazo, *–nă'thŏ*, sm. blow with a pebble.

chincharrazo, *tshĭntshărră'thŏ*, sm. thrust with a sword in an affray.

chincharrero, *–tshărrě'rŏ*, sm. nasty place infested by vermin.

chinche, *tshĭn'tshě*, sf. bug.

chinchorrería, *–tshŏrrěrě'ă*, sf. mischievous tale. [drag-net.

chinchorro, *–tshŏr'rŏ*, sm. fishing-boat;

chinchoso, sa, *–tshŏ'sŏ*, a. peevish, fastidious.

chinela, *tshĭně'lă*, sf. slipper.

chingarse, *tshĭngăr'sě*, v.r. to get drunk; to cut one's self.

chino, *tshě'nŏ*, sm. chinese language.

chiquero, *tshĭkě'rŏ*, sm. hog-sty.

chiquichaque, *tshĭkĭtshă'kě*, sm. sawyer; noise made by things rubbing against each other.

chiquirritín, *–kĭrrĭtín'*, sm. little boy.

chiribitil, *tshĭrĭbĭtíl'*, sm. crib; small room. [clarion-player.

chirimía, *tshĭrĭmě'ă*, sf. clarion; **–,** sm.

chirinola, *–rĭnŏ'lă*, sf. game played by boys; trifle.

chiripa, *tshĭrě'pă*, sf. fortunate chance.

chiripear, *–rĭpěăr'*, v. a. to be fortunate in a game, in spite of not understanding it well. [at games of chance.

chiripero, *–rĭpě'rŏ*, sm. one who is lucky

chirivía, *–rěvě'ă*, sf. (bot.) parsnip; wagtail. [tail.

chirla, *tshĭr'lă*, sf. sm. mussel.

chirlador, ra, *–dŏr'*, sm. & f. clamorous prattler.

chirlar, *tshĭrlăr'*, v. n. to prattle.

chirlo, *tshĭr'lŏ*, sm. large wound in the face.

chirriar, *tshĭrrĭăr'*, v. n. to hiss; to creak; to chirp.

chirrido, *tshĭrrě'dŏ*, sm. chirping of birds.

chirrio, *tshirrĕ'ŏ,* sm. creaking noise made by the wheels of a cart. [(on a violin).

chirrión, *tshirriŏn',* sm. tumbrel; scraper

chirrionero, *tshirriŏnĕ'rŏ,* sm. scavenger.

ckirumbela, *tshĭrŭmbĕ'lä,* sf. shawm, cornet. [swords or other arms.

chis-chás, *tshĭstshäs',* sm. clashing of

chisgarabis, *tshĭsgärä'bĭs',* sm. superficial meddler. [of wine.

chisguete, *tshĭsgä'tĕ,* sm. small draught

chisme, *tshĭs'mĕ,* sm. misreport; lumber.

chismear, *—mĕär',* v. a. to tattle, to carry tales, to misreport. [bearing.

chismoso, sa, *—mŏ'sŏ,* a. tattling, tale-

chispa, *tshĭs'pä,* sf. spark; very small diamond; short gun; small particle; slight intoxication; ¡—s ! fire and tow!

chispazo, *—pä'thŏ,* sm. the flying off of a spark from the fire, and the damage it does; tale mischievously circulated.

chispear, *—pĕär',* v. n. to sparkle; to drizzle. [ber of sparks.

chispero, ra, *—pĕ'rŏ,* a. emitting a num-

chisporrotear, *—pŏrrŏtĕär',* v. n. to sparkle, to hiss (of liquids).

chisposo, sa, *—pŏ'sŏ,* a. sparkling.

chistar, *—tär',* v. a. to mumble, to mutter.

chiste, *tshĭs'tĕ,* sm. fine witty saying; joke, jest. [funny.

chistoso, sa, *—tŏ'sŏ,* a. gay, cheerful; ¡chite ! *tshĭt'ĕ,* silence! hush!

chiticalla, *tshĭtĭkäl'yä,* sm. discreet and silent person. [not to make a noise.

chiticallar, *—yär',* v. a. to keep silence; ¡chito ! *tshĭ'tŏ,* ¡chitón ! *tshĭtŏn',* hush! mum! mum!

¡cho! *tshŏ,* word used by the drivers of mules or horses to make them stop.

chocar, *tshŏkär',* v. n. to strike, to knock; to encounter, to rush against each other; to fight, to combat; —, v. a. to provoke.

chocarrear, *tshŏkärrĕär',* v. n. to act the buffoon.

chocarrería, *—rĕrĕ'ä,* sf. buffoonery.

chocarrero, *—rä'rŏ,* sm. buffoon; —, ra, a. scurrilous, buffoon-like.

chocolate, *tshŏkŏlä'tĕ,* sm. chocolate.

chocolatera, *—tä'rä,* sf. chocolate-pot.

chocolatero, *—rŏ,* sm. chocolate-manufacturer.

chochear, *tshŏtshĕär',* v. n. to dote.

chocho, *tshŏ'tshŏ,* a. doting.

chofes, *tshŏ'fĕs,* sm.pl. lungs,pl.

chofeta, *tshŏfĕ'tä,* sf. chafing-dish.

chofista, *—fĭs'tä,* sm. a 'poor fellow' who lives upon livers and lights.

cholla, *tshŏl'yä,* sf. skull; (fig.) powers of the mind, judgment.

chopo, *tshŏ'pŏ,* sm. black poplar-tree.

choque, *—kĕ,* sm. shock, collision; (mil.) skirmish; dispute, contest; jar.

choquezuela, *tshŏkĕthŭĕ'lä,* sf. knee-pan, patella, rotula. [maker or -seller.

choricero, *tshŏrĭthĕ'rŏ,* sm. sausage-

chorizo, *tshŏrĕ'thŏ,* sm. pork-sausage.

chorlito, *tshŏrlĕ'tŏ,* sm. curlew, gray plover.

chorrear, *tshŏrrĕär',* v. n. to drop from a spout, to gush, to drip; to come successively.

chorrera, *tshŏrrä'rä,* sf. spout or place from whence liquids drop; mark left by water or other liquids; frill of the breast of a shirt. [liquid) rushing from a spout.

chorretada, *—tä'dä,* sf. water (or other

chorrillo, *tshŏrrĭl'yŏ,* sm. the continual coming-in and out-going of money.

chorro, *tshŏr'rŏ,* sm. gush; á -s, abundantly.

chorrón, *tshŏrrŏn',* sm. dressed hemp.

chotacabras, *tshŏtäkä'bräs,* sf. goat-sucker.

choto, *tshŏ'tŏ,* sm. sucking-kid. [sucker.

chotuno, na, *tshŏtŏ'nŏ,* a. sucking.

choya, *tshŏ'yä,* sf. jack-daw

choza, *tshŏ'thä,* sf. hut, shepherd's cottage.

chozil, *tshŏthĭl',* sm. hut, hovel.

chozuela, *—thŭĕ'lä,* sf. small hut.

chubasco, *tshŭbäs'kŏ,* sm. squall.

chucero, *—thä'rŏ,* sm. (mil.) pikeman.

chuchear, *tshŭtshĕär',* v. a. to fowl with calls, gins and nets; to whisper. [toy.

chuchería, *—tshĕrĕ'ä,* sf. gewgaw, bauble;

chuchero, *—tshĕ'rŏ,* sm. bird catcher.

chucho, *tshŭtsh'ŏ,* sm. dog; whip, scourge (in Cuba); word used to call a dog.

chuchumeco, *tshŭtshŭmä'kŏ,* sm. a sorry, contemptible little fellow. [to pound.

chuchurrar, *—tshŭrrär',* v. a. to bruise,

chuecazo, *tshŭĕkä'thŏ,* sm. stroke (at ball play)

chufeta, *tshŭfä'tä,* sf. jest, joke; coal-pan.

chufleta, *—flä'tä,* sf. taunt, jeer.

chufletear, *—flĕtĕär',* v. n. to sneer, to taunt. [sneering.

chufletero, ra, *—flĕtä'rŏ,* a. taunting

chulada, *tshŭlä'dä,* sf. droll speech or action.

chulear, *—lĕär',* v. a. to jest, to joke.

chuleta, *—lä'tä,* sf. chop, steak.

chulo, la, *tshŏ'lŏ,* sm. & f. punster, jester, merry-Andrew; bull-fighter's assistant.

chunga, *tshŭn'gä,* sf. jest, joke; estar de —, to be in good humour. [humour.

chunguear, *—gĕär',* v. n. to be in good

chupa, *tshŏ'pä,* sf. waistcoat; jacket.

chupadero, ra, *tshŭpädĕ'rŏ,* a. sucking.

chupador, *—dŏr',* sm. sucking-bottle.

chupar, *tshŭpär',* v. a. to suck; (fig.) to sponge upon.

chupetear, *—pĕtĕär',* v. a. to suck gently.

chupetín, *—pĕtĭn',* sm. doublet.

chupón, *—pŏn',* sm. sucker (twig); —, ona, sm. & f. swindler, sponger.

chupona, *tshŭpŏ'nä,* sf. mean, bloodsucking strumpet.

chardón, *tshärdŏn',* sm. raspberry-jam.

churre, *tshŏr'rĕ,* sm. thick dirty grease.

churriburri, *tshŏrrĭbŏ'rĭ,* sm. low-fellow; rabble.

churriento, ta, *—ĕn'tŏ,* a. greasy.

churro, *tshŏr'rŏ,* a. applied to sheep that have coarse wool. [scorched.

churruscarse, *tshŏrrŭskär'sĕ,* v. r. to be

churrusco, *tshŏrrŭs'kŏ,* sm. over-toasted bread.

churumbela, *tshŏrŭmbä'lä,* sf. shawm.

chuscada, *tshŭskä'dä,* sf. pleasantry, drollery.

chusco, ca, *tshŭs'kŏ,* a. pleasant, droll.
chusma, —má, sf. rabble, mob.   [merry.
chus ni mus, *tshŭs nĭ mŭs,* ad. (fam.)
(no decir —), not to say a word.
chuzo, *tshŏ'thŏ,* sm. little spear or pike;
llover á —s, to pour heavily.

D.

dable, *dǎ'blĕ,* a. easy, possible.
dádiva, *dǎ'dĭvǎ,* sf. gift, present.
dadivoso, sa, *dǎdĭvŏ'sǎ,* a. generous,
open-handed.
dado, *dǎ'dŏ,* sm. die (pl. dice).
daga, *dǎ'gǎ,* sf. dagger.
dala, *dǎ'lǎ,* sf. pump-dale of a ship.
¡ **dale !** *dǎ'lĕ,* word used to express displeasure at another's obstinacy.
dalmática, *dǎlmǎ'tǐkǎ,* sf. dalmatica,
vestment worn by the deacons of the Roman Catholic church in the performance
of divine service.
dallador, *dǎlyǎdŏr',* sm. mower.
dallar, —yǎr', v. a. to mow grass.
dalle, *dǎl'yĕ,* sm. scythe.
dama, *dǎ'mǎ,* sf. lady, gentlewoman; mistress; queen (in the game of draughts);
actress who performs the principal parts.
damascado, da, *dǎmǎskǎ'dŏ,* a. damask-
like.   [damson (plum).
damasco, *dǎmǎs'kŏ,* sm. damask (stuff).
damasina, *dǎmǎsē'nǎ,* sf. light silk stuff
resembling damask.   [maskeened.
damasquino, na, *dǎmǎskē'nŏ,* a. da-
damería, *dǎmĕrē'ǎ,* sf. prudery; scruples.
damero, *dǎmě'rŏ,* sm. draught-board.
damisela, *dǎmĭsē'ǎ,* sf. young gentlewoman; girl about town.
damnificar, *dǎmnĭfĭkǎr',* v. a. to hurt,
to damage, to injure.
danza, *dǎn'thǎ,* sf. dance.
danzador, ra, *dǎnthǎdŏr',* sm. & f. dancer.
danzante, *dǎnthǎn'tĕ,* sm. dancer; fickle,
airy person.
danzar, *dǎnthǎr',* v. n. to dance; to meddle;
sacar á —, to engage a lady to dance.
danzarín, *dǎnthǎrēn',* sm. fine dancer;
meddling person.   [to injure.
dañar, *dǎnyǎr',* v. a. to hurt, to damage;
dañino, na, *dǎnyē'nŏ,* a. noxious; mischievous.
daño, *dǎn'yŏ,* sm. damage, prejudice, loss.
dañoso, sa, *dǎnŏ'sŏ,* a. hurtful, noxious.
dar, *dǎr',* v. a. to give; to supply, to minister,
to afford; to deliver; to bestow; to strike;
to beat, to knock; to communicate; —se,
to conform to the will of another; to give
one's self up to; —se priesa, to make
haste.
dardo, *dǎr'dŏ,* sm. dart.   [haste.
data, *dǎ'tǎ,* sf. date; article put down in
an account; condition, quality.
datar, *dǎtǎr',* v. a. to date.
dataria, *dǎtǎrē'ǎ,* sf. Datary (office where
the pope's bulls are expedited).
datario, *dǎtǎ'rǐŏ,* sm. principal officer of
the Datary.
dátil, *dǎ'tǐl,* sm. (bot.) date.   [the Datary.

datilado, da, *dǎtǐlǎ'dŏ,* a. resembling a
dative. [date.
dativo, *dǎtǐ'vŏ,* sm. (gr.) dative.
dato, *dǎ'tŏ,* sm. datum.
dauco, *dǎ'ŭkŏ,* sm. carrot.
de, *dĕ,* pr. of; from; for; by; on; to; with.
deán, *dĕǎn',* sm. dean.
deanato, *dĕǎnǎ'tŏ,* sm. deanship.
debajo, *dĕbǎ'h'ŏ,* a. under, underneath,
below.   [contest, altercation.
debate, *dĕbǎ'tĕ,* sm. debate, discussion,
debatir, *dĕbǎtǐr',* v. a. to debate, to argue,
to discuss.   [debit and credit.
debe, *dĕ'bĕ,* sm. (com.) debit; — y haber.
deber, *dĕbĕr',* sm. obligation, duty; debt;
—, v. a. to owe; to be obliged.
debidamente, *dĕbĭdǎmĕn'tĕ,* ad. justly;
duly, exactly, perfectly.
débil, *dǎ'bĭl,* a. feeble, weak; sickly;
frail; pusillanimous.
debilidad, *dĕbĭlĭdǎd',* sf. debility, weakness.   [weaken.
debilitar, —tǎr', v. a. to debilitate, to
débito, *dǎ'bĭtŏ,* sm. debt; duty.
década, *dǎ'kǎdǎ,* sf. decade. [cline.
decadencia, *dĕkǎdĕn'thĭǎ,* sf. decay, de-
decaer, *dĕkǎĕr',* v. n. to decay, to decline,
to fade.   [decline.
decaimiento, *dĕkǎĭmĭĕn'tŏ,* sm. decay.
decálogo, *dĕkǎ'lŏgŏ,* sm. the Decalogue.
decampar, *dĕkǎmpǎr',* v. n. to decamp.
decanato, *dĕkǎnǎ'tŏ,* sm. seniority.
decano, *dĕkǎ'nŏ,* sm. senior. [to decant.
decantar, *dĕkǎntǎr',* v. a. to cry up, to puff;
decapitación, *dĕkǎpĭtǎthĭŏn',* sf. decapitation, beheading.
decapitar, —tǎr', v. a. to behead.
decena, *dĕthĕ'nǎ,* sf. denary.
decenal, *dĕthĕnǎl',* a. decennial.
decenario, ria, *dĕthĕnǎ'rĭŏ,* a. decennary.
decencia, *dĕthĕn'thĭǎ,* sf. decency.
deceno, na, *dĕthĕ'nŏ,* a. tenth.
decentar, *dĕthĕntǎr',* v. a. to use for the
first time; —se, to injure the skin or body.
decente, *dĕthĕn'tĕ,* a. a decent, honest.
decible, *dĕthĕ'blĕ,* a. expressible.
decidir, *dĕthĭdĭr',* v. a. to decide, to determine.   [stanza of ten verses; tithe.
décima, *dǎ'thĭmǎ,* sf. (poet.) a Spanish
decimal, *dĕthĭmǎl',* a. (decimal; belonging
to tithes.
décimo, ma, *dǎ'thĭmŏ,* a. tenth.
décimoctavo, va, *dǎthĭmŏktǎ'vŏ,* decio-
cheno, na, *dǎthĭtshǎ'nŏ,* a. eighteenth.
décimocuarto, ta,—kwǎr'tŏ, a. fourteenth.
décimonono, na, —nŏ'nŏ, a. nineteenth.
décimoquinto, ta,—kĭn'tŏ, a. fifteen 2.
décimoséptimo, ma,—sĕp'tĭmŏ, seventeenth.
décimosexto, to, —sĕks'tŏ, a. sixteenth.
décimotercio, cia,—tĕr'thĕŏ, a. thirteenth.
decir, *dĕthĭr',* v. a. to say, to tell, to speak;
to name; — de repente, to make im-
promptu verses; — de sí, to affirm any
thing.   [mination, resolution; sentence.
decisión, *dĕthĭsĭŏn',* sf. decision, deter-
decisivo, va, —sē'vŏ, a. decisive, final.

declamación, dĕklămäthĭŏn', sf. declamation, discourse, oration; oratorical invective; declamatory style of reading.

declamador, ra, –dŏr', sm. & f. declaimer. [harangue.

declamar, dĕklämär', v. n. to declaim, to

declaración, dĕklärăthĭŏn', sf. declaration, explanation; interpretation; manifest; (law) deposition.

declarar, dĕklärär', v. a. to declare, to manifest; to expound; to explain; (law) to decide; –se, to declare one's opinion.

declaratorio, ria, dĕklärätŏ'rĭŏ, a. declaratory, explanatory.

declinable, dĕklĭnä'blĕ, a. (gr.) declinable.

declinación, –thĭŏn', sf. declination, descent; decline; (gr.) declination.

declinar, dĕklĭnär', v. n. to decline; to decay, to degenerate; –, v. a. (gr.) to decline.

declinatoria, dĕklĭnätŏ'rĭä, sf. plea which attacks the competency of a judge.

declive, dĕklĭ'vĕ, sm. declivity.

decocción, dĕkŏkthĭŏn', sf. decoction.

decomiso, sa, dĕkŏmĭ'sŏ, a. confiscate.

decoración, dĕkŏräthĭŏn', sf. decoration.

decorar, dĕkŏrär', v. a. to decorate; to adorn; to illustrate.

decoro, dĕkŏ'rŏ, sm. honour, respect; circumspection; honesty; decency.

decoroso, sa, dĕkŏrŏ'sŏ, a. decorous, decent. [diminution.

decremento, dĕkrĕmĕn'tŏ, sm. decrease,

decrepitar, dĕkrĕpĭtär', v. n. to decrepitate; to crackle in the fire.

decrépito, ta, dĕkrĕ'pĭtŏ, a. decrepit, crazy, worn out with age.

decrepitud, dĕkrĕpĭtŭd', sf. decrepitude.

decretal, dĕkrĕtäl', sf. letter of the pope which decides a question of ecclesiastical law; –, a. decretal.

decretar, dĕkrĕtär', v. a. to decree, to determine; to give a decree in a suit.

decreto, dĕkrĕ'tŏ, sm. decree, decision; judicial decree.

décuplo, pla, dä'kŭplŏ, a. decuple, tenfold.

decuria, dĕkŏ'rĭä, sf. ten Roman soldiers under a decurion; assembly of ten students to take their lessons.

decurión, dĕkŭrĭŏn', sm. decurion; student who has the care of ten other students.

decursas, dĕkŭr'säs, sf. pl. arrears of rent.

decurso, –sŏ, sm. course of time.

dechado, dĕtshä'dŏ, sm. sample, pattern; sampler; model of virtue and perfection.

dedada, dĕdä'dä, sf. a pinch (of anything), a finger-full. [drinking-glass.

dedal, dĕdäl', sm. thimble; very small

dedalera, dĕdälĕ'rä, sf. (bot.) fox-glove.

dedicación, dĕdĭkäthĭŏn', sf. dedication; consecration.

dedicar, dĕdĭkär', v. a. to dedicate, to devote, to consecrate; –se, to apply one's self to.

dedicatoria, dĕdĭkätŏrä, sf. dedication.

dedo, dä'dŏ, sm. finger; toe; the forty-eighth part of a Spanish yard; hand of a clock; finger's breadth, small bit; – meñique,

little finger; – pulgar, thumb; – del corazón, middle-finger; – anular, ring-finger. [derivation, consequence.

deducción, dĕdŭkthĭŏn', sf. deduction.

deducir, dĕdŭthĭr', v. a. to deduce, to infer; to allege in pleading; to subtract.

defección, dĕfĕkthĭŏn', sf. defection, apostasy.

defectible, –tĭ'blĕ, a. imperfect, deficient.

defectivo, va, –tĭ'vŏ, a. defective.

defecto, dĕfĕk'tŏ, sm. defect, defectiveness; maimedness. [perfect, faulty.

defectuoso, sa, –tŭŏ'sŏ, a. defective, im-

defender, dĕfĕndĕr', v. a. to defend, to protect; to justify, to assert, to maintain; to prohibit, to forbid; to resist, to oppose.

defensa, dĕfĕn'sä, sf. defence, justification, apology; guard, shelter, protection, fence; (mil.) flanking defences.

defensiva, –sĭ'vä, sf. defensive.

defensivo, –sĭ'vŏ, sm. defence, safeguard; –, va, a. defensive.

defensor, ra, dĕfĕnsŏr', sm. & f. defender, protector; lawyer, counsel. [yielding.

deferente, dĕfĕrĕn'tĕ, a. pliant, docile,

deferir, dĕfĕrĭr', v. n. to defer; to yield to another's opinion; –, v. a. to communicate.

definición, dĕfĭnĭthĭŏn', sf. definition; decision.

definir, dĕfĭnĭr', v. a. to define, to describe, to explain; to decide. [positive.

definitivo, va, dĕfĭnĭtĭ'vŏ, a. definitive.

deforme, dĕfŏr'mĕ, a. deformed, ugly.

deformidad, dĕfŏrmĭdäd', sf. deformity, ugliness; gross error. [usurpation.

defraudación, dĕfräŭdäthĭŏn', sf. fraud,

defraudador, –dädŏr', sm. defrauder, usurper.

defraudar, dĕfräŭdär', v. a. to defraud, to cheat; to usurp; to disturb. [wardly.

defuera, dĕfŭĕ'rä, ad. externally, out-

defunción, dĕfŭnthĭŏn', sf. death; funeral.

degeneración, dĕhĕnĕräthĭŏn', sf. degeneracy.

degenerar, dĕhĕnĕrär', v. n. to degenerate.

degollación, dĕgŏlyäthĭŏn', sf. decollation, beheading.

degolladero, –dä'rŏ, sm. throttle; abattoir; seat near the orchestra (in theatres).

degollador, –dŏr', sm. headsman, executioner. [destroy; to ruin.

degollar, dĕgŏlyär', v. a. to behead; to

degradación, dĕgrädäthĭŏn', sf. degradation.

degradar, dĕgrädär', v. a. to degrade; –se, to degrade or demean one's self.

degüello, dĕgŭĕ'lyŏ, sm. decollation; neck of a bottle.

degustar, dĕgŭstär', v. a. to taste liquors.

dehesa, dĕhĕ'sä, sf. pasture-ground.

dehesar, dĕhĕsär', v. a. to turn arable land into pasture-ground.

dehesero, dĕhĕsĕ'rŏ, sm. keeper of a pasture-ground. [Christ.

deicidio, dĕĭthĭ'dĭŏ, sm. deicide, murder of

deidad, dĕĭdäd', sf. deity, divinity; goddess

deificación, –fĭkäthĭŏn', sf. deification.

deificar, -fikár', v. a. to deify.
deifico, deī'fikō, a. divine.
deismo, dēs'mō, sm. deism.
deista, dēīs'tä, sm. deist.
dejadez, dě'hädéth', s. slovenliness, neglect, lassitude. [dolent; dejected.
dejado, da, dě'hä'dō, a. slovenly, idle, indojar, dě'här', v. a. to leave, to let, to quit; to omit; to permit, to allow; to leave, to forsake; to bequeath; to pardon; —se, to abandon one's self (to).
dejo, dě'hō, sm. end, termination; negligence, laziness; after-taste, tang; effect of a passion; particular accentuation on the last syllable of words.
del, děl, a. of the (contraction of de el).
delación, dělähthōn', sf. accusation, impeachment.
delantal, děläntäl', sm. apron.
delante, dělän'tě, ad. before (in the front of; preceding in time; in preference to).
delantera, -tě'rä, sf. forefront, forepart of something; advantage.
delantero, ra, -tě'rō, a. foremost; —, sm. one who takes the lead; out-rider.
delastrar, dělästrär', v. a. to unballast.
delatable, dělätä'blě, a. accusable, blamable. [nounce.
delatar, dělätär', v. a. to accuse, to delator, -tōr', sm. accuser, informer, denouncer, delator.
delectación, dělěktähthōn', sf. pleasure, delight; —morosa, deliberate indulgence of some sensual pleasure, that is contrary to good manners. [substitution.
delegación, dělěgähthōn', sf. delegation, delegado, dělěgä'dō, sm. delegate, deputy.
delegar, dělěgär', v. a. to delegate, to substitute.
deleitable, dělěītä'blě, a. delightful.
deleitar, dělěītär', v. a. to delight.
deleite, dělěī'tě, sm. pleasure, delight, lust. [ful.
deleitoso, sa, -tō'sō, a. pleasing, delightdeletrear, dělětrěär', v. a. to spell; to examine; to conjecture.
delfin, dělfīn', sm. dolphin; dauphin.
delgado, da, dělgä'dō, a. thin, delicate, light; slender, lean; acute, fine, ingenious; little, scanty; —, sm. strait place.
deliberación, dělīběrähthōn', sf. deliberation; resolution. [liberately.
deliberadamente, -dämen'tě, ad. dedeliberar, dělīběrär', v. n. to consider, to deliberate; to consult. [tive.
deliberativo, va, -rätī'vō, a. deliberadelicadeza, dělīkädě'thä, sf. tenderness, softness; exquisiteness; delicacy, daintiness; subtlety.
delicado, da, dělīkä'dō, a. delicate, tender; faint; finical, minion; exquisite; delicious, dainty; slender, subtle.
delicia, dělī'thiä, sf. delight, pleasure.
delicioso, sa, -thiō'sō, a. delicious, delinquent.
delincuente, dělinkūěn'tě, sm. delinquent.
delineación, děliněähthōn', sf. delineation, sketch.

delinear, děliněär', v. a. to delineate, to sketch; to describe.
delinquir, dělinkīr', v. n. to transgress the law. [to talk nonsense.
delirar, dělīrär', v. n. to delirate, to rave; delirio, dělī'riō, sm. delirium; dotage; nonsense. [crime.
delito, dělī'tō, sm. transgression of a law, della, delle, děl'yä, děl'yě, contractions of the words de ella, de ello, of her, of it.
demagogia, děmägō'hiä, sf. demagogy.
demagogo, děmägō'gō, sm. demagogue.
demanda, děmän'dä, sf. demand, claim; pretension, complaint; challenge; request; charity-box; — y respuestas, haggling between sellers and buyers before they come to a price.
demandadero, ra, -dädě'rō, sm. & f. servant of a nunnery, or a jail. [ant.
demandado, da, -dä'dō, sm. & f. defenddemandador, -dädōr', sm. petitioner for charity for pious uses; plaintiff, demandant; claimant; suitor, wooer.
demandar, -där', v. a. to demand, to ask, to petition; to claim; to covet.
demarcación, děmärkähthōn', sf. demarcation; boundary-line.
demarcar, -kär', v. a. to mark out limits.
demás, děmäs', a. the rest, the others; y así de lo —, and so on; estar —, to be over and above; to be useless or superfluous; por —, in vain, to no purpose.
demasía, děmäsī'ä, sf. excess in the price; overmuch; arduous enterprise; rudeness; want of respect; abundance, plenty; en —, excessively.
demasiado, da, -sīä'dō, a. excessive, overmuch; bold, daring; useless; —, ad. enough, too.
demencia, děměn'thiä, sf. madness.
demente, děměn'tě, a. mad, insane.
demérito, děmě'ritō, sm. demerit.
demeritorio, ria, děměritō'riō, a. without merit.
democracia, děmōkrä'thiä, sf. democracy.
demócrata, děmō'krätä, sm. democrat.
democrático, ca, -krä'tikō, a. democratical. [destroy.
demoler, děmōlěr', v. a. to demolish; to demolición, děmōlīthōn', sf. demolition.
demonio, děmō'niō, sm. demon.
demora, děmō'rä, sf. delay; demurrage.
demorar, děmōrär', v. n. to remain.
demostrable, děmōsträ'blě, a. demonstrable. [tion; manifestation.
demostración, -thōn', sf. demonstrademostrar, děmōsträr', v. a. to prove, to demonstrate, to manifest. [monstrative.
demostrativo, va, děmōsträtī'vō, a. dedenegación, děněgähthōn', sf. denial, refusal.
denegar, děněgär', v. a. to deny, to refuse.
dengue, děn'gě, sm. prudery; short veil.
denigración, děnigrähthōn', sf. defamation, stigma, disgrace.
denigrar, děnigrär', v. a. to blacken; to calumniate.

denodado, da, *děnŏdă′dŏ,* a. bold, intrepid, audacious.

denominación, *děnŏmĭnăthĭŏn′,* sf. denomination, distinct appellation

denominar, *děnŏmĭnăr′,* v. a. to surname.

denotar, *děnŏtăr′,* v. a. to denote, to express. [ity.

densidad, *děnsĭdăd′,* sf. density; obscurity.

denso, sa, *děn′sŏ,* a. dense, thick; compact. [indented.

dentado, da, *děntă′dŏ,* a. dentated, toothed;

dentadura, *děntădoo′ră,* sf. set of teeth.

dental, *děntăl′,* sm. plough-share bed; dentist's pelican; wooden fork.

dentar, *děntăr′,* v. a. & n. to tooth; to indent; to teeth, to cut teeth.

dentellada, *děntělyă′dă,* sf. gnashing of the teeth; nip; pinch with the teeth; á –s, snappishly, peevishly.

dentellado, da, *–yă′dŏ,* a. denticulated.

dentellear, *–yăr′,* v. a. to bite.

dentera, *děntě′ră,* sf. setting on edge of teeth; (fig.) jealousy. [ing.

dentición, *děntĭthĭŏn′,* sf. dentition, teething.

denticular, *děntĭkŭlăr′,* a. like teeth, toothed.

dentista, *děntĭs′tă,* sm. dentist.

dentro, *děn′trŏ,* ad. within.

dentudo, da, *děntoo′dŏ,* a. uneven-toothed.

denuedo, *děnooĕ′dŏ,* sm. boldness, intrepidity.

denuesto, *děnooĕs′tŏ,* sm. affront, insult.

denuncia, *děnoon′thĭă,* sf. denunciation.

denunciable, *–thĭă′blĕ,* a. capable of being denounced. [tion.

denunciación, *–thĭăthĭŏn′,* sf. denunciation

denunciador, *–thĭădŏr′,* sm. denunciator, accuser. [nounce; to prognosticate.

denunciar, *–thĭăr′,* v. a. to advise; to denunciatory, ria, *–thĭă′rĭŏ,* a. denunciatory. [sent.

deparar, *děpărăr′,* v. a. to offer, to present.

departamento, *děpărtămĕn′tŏ,* sm. department; (rail.)compartment.

dependencia, *děpĕndĕn′thĭă,* sf. dependency, relation, affinity; business, affair.

depender, *děpĕndĕr′,* v. n. to depend, to be dependent on.

dependiente, *děpĕndĭĕn′tĕ,* sm.dependant, client, follower; hanger-on; clerk.

deplorable, *děplŏră′blĕ,* a. deplorable, lamentable.

deplorar, *děplŏrăr′,* v. a. to deplore.

deponer, *děpŏnĕr′,* v. a. to depose, to declare; to displace; to deposit. [tion.

deportación, *děpŏrtăthĭŏn′,* sf. deportation.

deportar, *děpŏrtăr′,* v. a. to transport.

deposición, *děpŏsĭthĭŏn′,* sf. deposition; assertion, affirmation; (law) deposition upon oath.

depositar, *–tăr′,* v. a. to deposit, to confide; to put in any place to be kept safe.

depositaría, *–tărĕ′ă,* sf. depository.

depositario, *–tă′rĭŏ,* sm. depositary.

depósito, *děpŏ′sĭtŏ,* sm. deposit; trustee.

depravación, *děprăvăthĭŏn′,* sf. depravity.

depravar, *děprăvăr′,* v. a. to deprave, to vitiate, to corrupt. [earnest entreaty.

deprecación, *děprěkăthĭŏn′,* sf. petition;

depresión, *děprěsĭŏn′,* sf. depression, abasement. [humble, to deject.

deprimir, *děprĭmĭr′,* v. a. to depress, to

depuración, *děpoorăthĭŏn′,* sf. purification.

depurar, *děpoorăr′,* v. a. to cleanse, to purify, to filter.

derecha, *děrĕtsh′ă,* sf. right hand, right side; á –s, right; well done.

derechamente, *–mĕn′tĕ,* ad. directly, straight; rightly, prudently.

derechera, *děrětshě′ră,* sf. direct road.

derecho, cha, *děrĕtsh′ŏ,* a. right; straight; just; perfect; certain; –, sm. right, justice, law; just claim; tax, duty; fee.

derechura, *děrětshoo′ră,* sf. rectitude, right way. [source; origin.

derivación, *děrĭvăthĭŏn′,* sf. derivation;

derivar, *děrĭvăr′,* v. a. & n. to derive; (mar.) to deflect from the course.

derivativo, va, *–vătĭ′vŏ,* a. derivative.

derogación, *děrŏgăthĭŏn′,* sf. derogation, abolition; deterioration; diminution.

derogar, *–găr′,* v. a. to derogate, to abolish; to reform.

derogatorio, ria, *–gătŏ′rĭŏ,* a. derogatory.

derrama, *děrră′mă,* sf. assessment of a tax or impost. [thrift.

derramador, *–dŏr′,* sm. prodigal, spendthrift.

derramamiento, *–mĭĕn′tŏ,* sm. effusion, waste; dispersion.

derramar, *děrrămăr′,* v. a. to drain off water; to spread; to spill, to scatter, to waste, to shed; –se, to be spread, to fly abroad. [marjoy.

derramasolaces, *děrrămăsŏlă′thĕs,* sm.

derrame, *děrră′mĕ,* sm. loss in measuring; leakage.

derredor, *děrrĕdŏr′,* sm. circumference, circuit; al –, en –, round about.

derrengado, da, *děrrĕngă′dŏ,* a. bent, crooked. [to abominate, to detest.

derrengar, *–găr′,* v. a. to sprain the hip;

derretimiento, *děrrĕtĭmĭĕn′tŏ,* sm. liquefaction, fusion.

derretir, *–tĭr′,* v. n. to melt; to consume, to expend; –se, to fall in love very easily; to be melted.

derribar, *děrrĭbăr′,* v. a. to demolish; to flatten; –se, to throw one's self down on the ground. [a demolished building.

derribo, *děrrĭ′bŏ,* sm. demolition; ruins of

derrocar, *děrrŏkăr′,* v. a. to pull down, to demolish.

derrochador, *děrrŏtshădŏr′,* sm. prodigal.

derrochar, *–tshăr′,* v. a. to dissipate.

derrota, *děrrŏ′tă,* sf. ship's course; road, path; defeat of an army.

derrotar, *děrrŏtăr′,* v. a. (mar.) to cause to fall off; to destroy; to defeat.

derrotero, *–tě′rŏ,* sm. collection of sea-charts; ship's course; (fig.) course, way.

derruir, *děrrooĭr′,* v. a. to demolish.

derrumbadero, *děrroombădě′rŏ,* sm.precipice; thorny or arduous affair; risk.

derrumbar, *–băr′,* v. a. to precipitate.

desabarrancar, *děsăbărrănkăr',* v. a. to drag; to extricate from difficulties.

desabastecer, *—ăbăstěthěr',* v. a. to cut off supplies from.

desabillé, *—ăbĭlyā',* sm. dishabille, undress.

desabollar, *—ăbŏlyăr',* v. a. to take bulges out of pewter dishes, &c.

desabonarse, *—ăbŏnăr'ěs,* v. r. to withdraw one's subscription.

desabotonar, *—ăbŏtŏnăr',* v. a. to unbutton; **—se,** to blossom. [sipid; peevish.

desabrido, da, *—ăbrē'dŏ,* a. tasteless, in-

desabrigado, da, *—ăbrĭgă'dŏ,* a. uncovered; shelterless.

desabrigar, *—ăbrĭgăr',* v. a. to uncover, to deprive of clothes or shelter.

desabrigo, *—ăbrē'gŏ,* sm. nakedness; destitution.

desabrimiento, *—ăbrĭmĭēn'tŏ,* sm. insipidity; asperity of temper; dejection.

desabrir, *—ăbrēr',* v. a. to vex, to plague; to harass; **—se,** to be angry.

desabrochar, *—ăbrŏtchăr',* v. a. to unclasp; **—se,** to unbosom.

desacabalar, *—ăkăbălăr',* v. a. to pilfer.

desacalorarse, *—ăkălŏrăr'sĕ,* v. r. to take the fresh air; to cool one's self. [respect.

desacatamiento, *—ăkătămĭēn'tŏ,* sm. dis-

desacatar, *—ăkătăr',* v. a. to treat in a disrespectful manner.

desacato, *—ăkă'tŏ,* sm, disrespect, incivility.

desacertado, da, *—ăthěrtă'dŏ,* a. inconsiderate. [mit a mistake.

desacertar, *—ăthěrtăr',* v. a. to err, to com-

desacierto, *—ăthĭěr'tŏ,* sm. error, gross mistake, blunder. [spire courage.

desacobardar, *—ăkŏbărdăr',* v. a. to in-

desacomodado, da, *—ăkŏmŏdă'dŏ,* a. destitute of the conveniences of life; out of service; incommodious.

desacomodamiento, *—ăkŏmŏdămĭēn'tŏ,* sm. incommodity, trouble.

desacomodar, *—ăkŏmŏdăr',* v. a. to incommode, to molest; **—se,** to lose one's place. [tŏ sm. want of company.

desacompañamiento, *—ăkŏmpănyămĭēn'*

desacompañar, *—ăkŏmpănyăr',* v. a. to leave the company.

desaconsejado, da, *—ăkŏnsĕhă'dŏ,* a. inconsiderate, ill-advised.

desacordado, da, *—ăkŏrdă'dŏ,* a. discordant (applied to colours).

desacordar, *—ăkŏrdăr',* v. a. to untune; **—se,** to be forgetful; to be at variance.

desacorde, *—ăkŏr'dĕ,* a. discordant.

desacorralar, *—ăkŏrrălăr',* v. a. to let the flock or cattle out of the penfold.

desacostumbrado, da, *—ăkŏstŭmbră'dŏ,* a. unusual. [disuse.

desacostumbrar, *—ăkŏstŭmbrăr',* v. a. to

desacotar, *—ăkŏtăr',* v. a. to lay open a pasture-ground; to withdraw a prohibition.

desacreditar, *—ăkrĕdĭtăr',* v. a. to discredit.

desacuerdo, *—ăkŭĕr'dŏ,* sm. derangement of mental faculties; discordance, disagreement, disunion. [to disorder.

desaderezar, *—ăděrěthăr',* v. a. to undress;

desadeudar, *—ădĕŭdăr',* v. a. to pay one's debts, to get out of debt.

desadorar, *—ădŏrăr',* v. a. to cease to love.

desadormecer, *—ădŏrmĕthěr',* v. a. to wake, to rouse from sleep; to rouse from mental stupor.

desadornar, *—ădŏrnăr',* v. a. to divest of ornaments or decorations.

desadorno, *—ădŏr'nŏ,* sm. want of embellishments or charms. [affectedness.

desafecto, *—ăfěk'tŏ,* sm. disaffection, dis-

desaferrar, *—ăfěrrăr',* v.a. to weigh anchor; to loosen; **—se,** to let go one's hold; to give up.

desafiador, *—ăfĭădŏr',* sm. challenger.

desafiar, *—ăfĭăr',* v. a. to challenge, to call out (to fight a duel).

desaficionar, *—ăfĭthĭŏnăr',* v.a. to destroy one's affection for anything.

desafinar, *—ăfĭnăr',* v. a. to untune.

desafío, *—ăfē'ŏ,* sm. challenge; struggle, contest, combat.

desaforado, da, *—ăfŏră'dŏ,* a. huge; disorderly, lawless, impudent.

desaforar, *—ăfŏrăr',* v. a. to encroach upon one's rights; (mil.) to cashier; **—se,** to relinquish one's rights; to be outrageous.

desaforrar, *—ăfŏrrăr',* v. a. to take the lining from anything.

desafortunado, da, *—ăfŏrtŭnă'dŏ,* a. unfortunate, unlucky. [excess.

desafuero, *—ăfŭĕ'rŏ,* sm. act of injustice;

desagarrar, *—ăgărrăr',* v. a. to release.

desagraciado, da, *—ăgrăthĭă'dŏ,* a. ungraceful, inelegant. [to disfigure.

desagraciar, *—ăgrăthĭăr',* v. a. to deform.

desagradable, *—ăgrădă'blĕ,* a. disagreeable, unpleasant.

desagradar, *—ăgrădăr',* v. a. to displease.

desagradecido, da, *—ăgrădĕthĭ'dŏ,* a. ungrateful. [sm. ingratitude.

desagradecimiento, *—ăgrădĕthĭmĭēn'tŏ,*

desagrado, *—ăgră'dŏ,* sm. asperity, harshness; displeasure.

desagraviar, *—ăgrăvĭăr',* v. a. to make amends for an injury. [faction.

desagravio, *—ăgră'vĭŏ,* sm. relief, satis-

desagregar, *—ăgrĕgăr',* v. a. to disjoin, to separate. [drain.

desaguadero, *—ăgŭădĕ'rŏ,* sm. channel,

desaguador, *—ăgŭădŏr',* sm. channel for carrying off water.

desaguar, *—ăgŭăr',* v. a. to draw off water; **—,** v. n. to empty or to flow into the sea.

desaguazar, *—ăgŭăthăr',* v. a. to drain or draw off the water from a thing.

desagüe, *—ăgŭ'ĕ,* sm. channel, drain; extraordinary expense.

desahijar, *—ăĭhăr',* v. a. to wean; **—se,** to swarm (of bees).

desahitarse, *—ăĭtăr'sĕ,* v. r. to relieve indigestion. [impudent.

desahogado, da, *—ăŏgă'dŏ,* a. petulant,

desahogar, *—ăŏgăr',* v. a. to ease pain; **—se,** to recover; to unbosom.

desahogo, *—ăŏ'gŏ,* sm. ease, alleviation from pain; freedom of speech.

desahuciar, –*ăhŭthĭăr'*, v. a. to despair; to give up; to dismiss a tenant.

desahucio, –*ăhŏ'thĭŏ*, sm. dismissing of a tenant *or* driving away cattle from a pasture-ground (at the expiration of the stipulated time). [smoke.

desahumar, –*ăhŭmăr'*, v. a. to free from

desairado, da, –*ăvră'dŏ*, a. disregarded, slighted. [take no notice.

desairar, –*ăvrăr'*, v. a. to disregard, to

desaire, –*ă'ĭră*, sm. disdain, disrespect; frown of fortune.

desajustar, –*ă'hŭstăr'*, v. a. to disproportion; –se, to withdraw from an agreement.

desajuste, –*ă'hŭs'tĕ*, sm. disturbance of proper *or* regular conditions.

desalar, –*ălăr'*, v. a. to cut off the wings; to take the salt out of fish, salt meat, &c. by steeping it in fresh water; –se, to run to meet someone with open arms.

desalentar, –*ălĕntăr'*, v. a. to put out of breath; to discourage. [carpet.

desalfombrar, –*ălfŏmbrăr'*, v. a. to un-

desaliento, –*ălĭĕn'tŏ*, sm. dismay, desertion of mind.

desalinar, –*ălĭnăr'*, v. a. to discompose.

desalino, –*ălĭn'yŏ*, sm. slovenliness; carelessness. [human, impious.

desalmado, da, –*ălmă'dŏ*, a. cruel, in-

desalmarse, –*ălmăr'sĕ*, v. r. to desire very ardently. [turrets.

desalmenado, da, –*ălmĕnă'dŏ*, a. without

desalojar, –*ălŏ'hăr'*, v. a. to dislodge the enemy's troops; –, v. n. to move to other lodgings. [assuage, to settle.

desalterar, –*ăltĕrăr'*, v. a. to allay, to

desalumbrado, da, –*ălŭmbră'dŏ*, a. dazzled; groping in the dark.

desamarrar, –*ămărrăr'*, v. a. to unmoor a ship; to untie; to remove.

desamoldar, –*ămŏldăr'*, v. a. to unmould; to change the proportion *or* symmetry of anything. [dull, silent person talk.

desamorrar, –*ămŏrrăr'*, v. a. to make a

desamotinarse, –*ămŏtĭnăr'sĕ*, v. r. to withdraw from mutiny.

desamparar, –*ămpărăr'*, v. a. to forsake, to abandon, to relinquish; to desist.

desamparo, –*ămpă'rŏ*, sm. abandonment; helplessness; dereliction. [furnish.

desamueblar, –*ămŏĕblăr'*, v. a. to un-

desancorar, –*ănkŏrăr'*, v. a. (mar.) to weigh anchor.

desandar, –*ăndăr'*, v. a. to retrograde, to go back the same road by which one came.

desandrajado, da, –*ăndră'hă'dŏ*, a. ragged, in tatters.

desangrar, –*dĕsăngrăr'*, v.a. to bleed one to excess; to drain a pond; (fig.) to exhaust one's means.

desanidar, –*ănĭdăr'*, v. n. to forsake the nest; –, v. a. to dislodge from a post.

desanimar, –*ănĭmăr'*, v. a. to discourage.

desanudar, –*ănŭdăr'*, v. a. to untie; to extricate, to disentangle.

desapacibilidad, –*ăpăthĭbĭlĭdăd'*, sf. rudeness, churlishness, peevishness.

desapacible, –*ăpăthĕ'blĕ*, a. disagreeable, unpleasant, harsh. [prove, to contradict.

desapadrinar, –*ăpădrĭnăr'*, v. a. to dis-

desaparear, –*ăpărĕăr'*, v. a. to unmatch.

desaparecer, –*ăpărĕthĕr'*, v. a. to remove out of sight; –, v. n. –se, to disappear.

desaparejar, –*ăpărĕ'hăr'*, v. a. to unharness beasts; (mar.) to unrig a ship.

desapasionar, –*ăpăsĭŏnăr'*, v. a. to root out a passion.

desapego, –*ăpĕ'gŏ*, sm. alienation of affection; coolness; disinterestedness.

desapercibido, da, –*ăpĕrthĭbĭ'dŏ*, a. unprovided. [sm. unpreparedness.

desapercibimiento, –*ăpĕrthĭbĭmĭĕn'tŏ*,

desapestar, –*ăpĕstăr'*, v.a. to cure persons infected with the plague. [merciless.

desapiadado, da, –*ăpĭădă'dŏ*, a. impious,

desaplicación, –*ăplĭkăthĭŏn'*, sf. want of application. [careless, neglectful.

desaplicado, da, –*ăplĭkă'dŏ*, a. indolent,

desapoderar, –*ăpŏdĕrăr'*, v. a. to dispossess; to repeal a power of attorney.

desapolillar, –*ăpŏlĭlyăr'*, v. a. to free from moths; –se, to take the air when it is cold and sharp.

desaposentar, –*ăpŏsĕntăr'*, v. a. to turn someone out of his lodgings.

desaposesionar, –*ăpŏsĕsĭŏnăr'*, v. a. to dispossess.

desapoyar, –*ăpŏyăr'*, v. a. to cut the ground from beneath one's feet.

desapreciar, –*ăprĕthĭăr'*, v. a. to depreciate, to undervalue.

desaprender, –*ăprĕndĕr'*, v. a. to unlearn. [to loosen.

desapretar, –*ăprĕtăr'*, v. a. to slacken,

desaprisionar, –*ăprĭsĭŏnăr'*, v. a. to release from confinement; –se, to extricate one's self from difficulties.

desaprobación, –*ăprŏbăthĭŏn'*, sf. disapprobation. [prove, to reprove.

desaprobar, –*ăprŏbăr'*, v. a. to disap-

desapropiamiento, –*ăprŏpĭămĭĕn'tŏ*, sm. alienation. [alienate.

desapropiarse, –*ăprŏpĭăr'sĕ*, v. r. to

desaprovechado, da, –*ăprŏvĕthă'dŏ*, a. useless, unprofitable; backward.

desaprovechamiento, –*ăprŏvĕthămĭĕn'tŏ*, sm. backwardness.

desaprovechar, –*ăprŏvĕthăr'*, v. a. to misspend, to turn to a bad use.

desapuntalar, –*ăpŭntălăr'*, v. a. to take away the props.

desapuntar, –*ăpŭntăr'*, v. a. to unstitch; to lose one's aim, to aim fire-arms badly.

desarbolar, –*ărbŏlăr'*, v. a. to unmast a ship; to lay up a ship in ordinary.

desarbolo, –*ărbŏ'lŏ*, sm. unmasting a ship.

desarenar, –*ărĕnăr'*, v. a. to clear a place of sand.

desarmadura, –*ărmădŏ'ră*, sf. disarming.

desarmar, –*ărmăr'*, v. a. to disarm; to disband troops; to dismount (a cross-bow, a cannon); (fig.) to pacify.

desarme, –*ăr'mĕ*, sm. disarmament of ships; breaking up of an army.

desarraigar, *–árráĭgár',* v. a. to root out; to extirpate.

desarraigo, *–árrá'ĭgŏ,* sm. eradication.

desarrapado, da, *–árrápá'dŏ,* a. ragged.

desarrebozar, *–árrĕbŏthár',* v. a. to unmuffle; to manifest, to discover.

desarrebujar, *–árrĕbŭhár',* v. a. to unfold, to spread out. [ad. disorderly.

desarregladamente, *–árrĕgládámĕn'tĕ,*

desarreglado, da, *–árrĕglá'dŏ,* a. immoderate in eating, drinking, &c.

desarreglar, *–árrĕglár',* v. a. to disorder, to derange.

desarreglo, *–árrĕ'glŏ,* sm. disorder, derangement; licentiousness. [to dissuade.

desarrimar, *–árrĭmár',* v. a. to remove;

desarrollar, *–árrŏlyár',* v. a. to unroll, to unfold; **–se,** to be unfolded, to open.

desarropar, *–árrŏpár',* v. a. to undress.

desarrugar, *–árrŭgár',* v. a. to take out wrinkles. [a ship.

desarrumar, *–árrŭmár',* v. a. to unload

desasear, *–ásĕár',* v. a. to make dirty; to discompose.

desaseo, *–ásĕ'ŏ,* sm. disorder.

desasimiento, *–ásĭmĭĕn'tŏ,* sm. letting loose; disinterestedness.

desasir, *–ásĭr',* v. a. to loosen, to disentangle; **–se,** to extricate one's self.

desasnar, *–ásnár',* v. a. (fig.) to polish one's manners. [quiet, to disturb.

desasosegar, *–ásŏsĕgár',* v. a. to dis

desasosiego, *–ásŏsĭĕ'gŏ,* sm. restlessness, feverishness. [miserable; ragged.

desastrado, da, *–ástrá'dŏ,* a. wretched,

desastre, *–ás'trĕ,* sm. disaster; misfortune.

desatacar, *–átákár',* v. a. to loosen, to untie; **– una escopeta,** to draw the charge out of a gun.

desatar, *–átár',* v. a. to untie, to loose; to separate; to unriddle; **–se,** to give rein to one's tongue; to lose all reserve.

desatascar, *–átáskár',* v. a. to draw out of the mire; to extricate one from difficulties.

desataviar, *–átávĭár',* v. a. to strip off decorations. [ness in dress.

desatavio, *–átávĭ'ŏ,* sm. want of neat

desatención, *–átĕnthĭŏn',* sf. want of attention, absence of mind; want of politeness.

desatender, *–átĕndĕr',* v. a. to pay no attention; to disregard, to contemn.

desatentado, da, *–átĕntá'dŏ,* a. inconsiderate; thoughtless; excessive.

desatento, ta, *–átĕn'tŏ,* a. inattentive, careless; rude, uncivil. [treasure.

desatesorar, *–átĕsŏrár',* v. a. to spend a

desatinado, *–átĭná'dŏ,* a. extravagant; **–,** sm. fool, madman.

desatinar, *–átĭnár',* v. a. & n. to derange one's mind; to throw into a violent passion; to talk nonsense; to reel, to stagger.

desatino, *–átĭ'nŏ,* sm. extravagance; staggering; nonsense. [the mire.

desatollar, *–átŏlyár',* v. a. to pull out of

desatolondrar, *–átŏlŏndrár',* v. a. to

bring someone to himself; **–se,** to recover one's senses, to come to one's self.

desatontarse, *–átŏntár'sĕ,* v. r. to come to one's self (from a faint, &c.)

desatracar, *–átrákár',* v. a. (mar.) to sheer off. [to clean a well.

desatrancar, *–átránkár',* v. a. to unbar;

desatufarse, *–átŭfár'sĕ,* v. a. to grow calm.

desaturdir, *–átŭrdĭr',* v. a. to rouse from a state of dizziness or stupor. [authorise.

desautorizar, *–áŭtŏrĭthár',* v. a. to dis

desavecindado, da, *–ávĕthĭndá'dŏ,* a. deserted, unpeopled.

desavecindarse, *–ávĕthĭndár'sĕ,* v. r. to change one's domicile. [disagreement.

desavenencia, *–ávĕnĕn'thĭá,* sf. discord.

desavenido, da, *–ávĕnĭ'dŏ,* a. discordant, disagreeing.

desavenir, *–ávĕnĭr',* v. a. to discompose, to disconcert; **–,** v. n. to quarrel.

desaventajado, da, *–ávĕntáhá'dŏ,* a. disadvantageous, unprofitable.

desaviar, *–ávĭár',* v. a. to deviate from the high road; to strip of necessaries.

desavío, *–ávĭ'ŏ,* sm. going astray; want of the necessary means.

desavisado, da, *–ávĭsá'dŏ,* a. ill-advised.

desavisar, *–ávĭsár',* v. a. to countermand.

desayunar, *–áyŭnár',* v. a. to give the first intelligence of news; **–se,** to breakfast. [fast.

desayuno, *–áyŭ'nŏ,* sm. breakfast.

desazogar, *–áthŏgár',* v. a. to take off the quicksilver from a looking-glass.

desazón, *–áthŏn',* sf. insipidity; disgust; uneasiness; unfitness of a soil for agricultural purposes.

desazonado, da, *–áthŏná'dŏ,* a. ill-adapted; ill-humoured.

desazonar, *–áthŏnár',* v. a. to render tasteless; to disgust; **–se,** to become indisposed. [portmanteau or its contents.

desbalijar, *–bálĭhár',* v. a. to steal a

desbancar, *–bánkár',* v. a. to clear a room of the benches; to break the bank (in gambling); (fig.) to supplant.

desbandarse, *–bándár'sĕ,* v. r. to disband.

desbaratado, da, *–bárátá'dŏ,* a. debauched, lewd.

desbaratar, *–bárátár',* v. a. to destroy; to defeat an army; to dissipate; **– la paz,** to break the peace; **–,** v. n. to talk nonsense; **–se,** to be confounded. [tion.

desbarato, *–bárá'tŏ,* sm. defeat; dissipa

desbarbado, *–bárbá'dŏ,* a. beardless.

desbarbillar, *–bárbĭlyár',* v. a. to prune the roots of young vines.

desbardar, *–bárdár',* v. a. to uncover a wall or fence. [beyond limits.

desbarrar, *–bárrár',* v. n. to slip, to go

desbarretar, *–bárrĕtár',* v. a. to unbar, to unbolt, to take off the bars and bolts.

desbarrigado, da, *–bárrĭgá'dŏ,* a. little-bellied. [to open the belly.

desbarrigar, *–bárrĭgár',* v. a. to rip up,

desbarro, *–bár'rŏ,* sm. slipping; (fig.) nonsense, extravagance; frenzy.

desbastar, *–bástár',* v. a. to smooth; to polish; to waste; to purify one's morals and manners.

desbaste, –*băs' tě,* sm. hewing, smoothing.

desbastecido, da, –*băstěthě' dŏ,* a. without sufficient provisions.

desbautizarse, –*băŭtĭthăr' sě,* v. r. (fig.) to be irritated.

desbecerrar, –*běthěrrăr',* v. a. to wean [animals].

desblanquecido, da, –*blănkěthě' dŏ,* a. blanched.

desbocado, da, –*bŏkă' dŏ,* a. open-mouthed (applied to a cannon); wild (applied to a horse); foul-mouthed, indecent.

desbocar, –*bŏkăr',* v. a. to break the brim of a jar or other vessel; –, v. n. to disembogue; –**se,** to be insensible of the bridle; to use abusive language.

desboquillar, –*bŏkĭl' yăr',* v. a. to break the mouth of a vessel.

desborrar, –*bŏrrăr',* v. a. to cut off the loose threads of stuff, when it comes out of the loom; to lop off.

desbragado, da, –*brăgă' dŏ,* a. without breeches.

desbraguetado, da, –*brăgětă' dŏ,* a. having the forepart of the breeches unbuttoned.

desbrevarse, –*brěvăr' sě,* v. r. to evaporate.

desbrozar, –*brŏthăr',* v. a. to clear away rubbish.

desbrozo, –*brŏ' thŏ,* sm. clearing away rubbish.

desbuchar, –*bŭtshăr',* v. a. to disclose one's secrets; to ease the stomach (applied to birds of prey).

descabal, –*kăbăl',* a. incomplete.

descabalar, –*kăbălăr',* v. a. to make incomplete, to unmatch; to pilfer; to impair.

descabalgar, –*kăbălgăr',* v. n. to alight from a horse; –, v. a. to dismount.

descabellado, da, –*kăbělyă' dŏ,* a. dishevelled; disorderly; wild, unrestrained; disproportional; violent.

descabellar, –*kăbělyăr',* v. a. to disorder the hair.

descabezado, da, –*kăběthă' dŏ,* a. beheaded; lightheaded, giddy.

descabezar, –*kăběthăr',* v. a. to behead; to lop off; –**se,** to puzzle one's brains.

descabullirse, –*kăbŭlyĭr' sě,* v. r. to steal away, to scamper; to elude difficulties cleverly.

descaderar, –*kăděrăr',* v. a. to sprain the hip.

descaecer, –*kăěthěr',* v. n. to decline, to decay.

descaecimiento, –*kăěthĭmĭěn' tŏ,* sm. weakness; languor.

descalabazarse, –*kălăbăthăr' sě,* v. r. to puzzle one's brains.

descalabrado, da, –*kălăbră' dŏ,* a. wounded on the head; imprudent.

descalabradura, –*kălăbră'dŏ'ră,* sf. contusion or wound in the head.

descalabrar, –*kălăbrăr',* v. a. to break or wound the head; to attack one's character.

descalabro, –*kălă'brŏ,* sm. calamitous event, considerable loss.

descalcez, –*kălthěth',* sf. nudity of the feet; barefootedness of monks.

descalificar, –*kălĭfĭkăr',* v. a. to disqualify.

descalzar, –*kălthăr',* v. a. –**se,** to pull off the shoes and stockings.

descalzo, za, –*kăl'thŏ,* a. barefooted.

descaminar, –*kămĭnăr',* v. a. to misguide, to lead astray. [less; very poor.

descamisado, da, –*kămĭsă' dŏ,* a. shirtless; very poor.

descampado, da, –*kămpă' dŏ,* a. disengaged, free, open. [working.

descampar, –*kămpăr',* v. n. to leave off working.

descansado, da, –*kănsă' dŏ,* a. reposing, rested, refreshed; quiet.

descansar, –*kănsăr',* v. n. to rest from labour and fatigue; to pause in the execution of a thing; to repose, to sleep; – **las tierras,** to lie fallow or at rest.

descanso, –*kăn' sŏ,* sm. rest, repose.

descanterar, –*kăntěrăr',* v. a. to cut the crust of bread. [to lessen.

descantillar, –*kăntĭlyăr',* v. a. to pare off; to lessen.

descañonar, –*kănyŏnăr',* v. a. to pluck out the feathers; (fig.) to trick one out of his money. [cover the head.

descaperuzar, –*kăpěrŭthăr',* v. a. to uncover the head.

descapillar, –*kăpĭlyăr',* v. a. to take off the hood. [the hood.

descapirotar, –*kăpĭrŏtăr',* v. a. to take off the hood.

descarado, da, –*kără' dŏ,* a. impudent, barefaced. [solently.

descararse, –*kărăr' sě,* v. r. to behave insolently.

descarga, –*kăr' gă,* sf. disburdening, unloading; volley, discharge.

descargadero, –*kărgădě' rŏ,* sm. wharf.

descargador, –*kărgădŏr',* sm. unloader.

descargar, –*kărgăr',* v. a. to unload, to discharge; –**se,** to give a plea to an accusation. [justification.

descargo, –*kăr' gŏ,* sm. discharge, acquittal, justification.

descargue, –*kăr' gě,* sm. alleviation from any burden. [of affection.

descariño, –*kărĭn' yŏ,* sm. coolness, loss of affection.

descarnar, –*kărnăr',* v. a. to strip off the flesh; to clean away the flesh from; –**se,** to dissipate, to squander one's wealth.

descaro, –*kă' rŏ,* sm. impudence.

descarriar, –*kărrĭăr',* v. a. to lead astray; to separate cattle from one another; –**se,** to deviate from justice or reason.

descarrilamiento, –*kărrĭlămĭěn' tŏ,* sm. (rail.) running off the rails.

descarrilar, –*kărrĭlăr',* v. n. (rail.) to leave or run off the rails. [way.

descarrillar, –*kărrĭlyăr',* v. a. to tear the jaws asunder.

descarrío, –*kărrě' ŏ,* sm. losing of one's way.

descartar, –*kărtăr',* v. a. to discard; to dismiss; –**se,** to excuse one's self.

descarte, –*kăr' tě,* sm. cards discarded; discarding; evasion, subterfuge.

descasar, –*kăsăr',* v. a. to separate a husband and wife.

descascarar, –*kăskărăr',* v. a. to decorticate, to husk; –**se,** to fall off.

descaspar, –*kăspăr',* v. a. to remove dandriff from the head.

descasque, –*kăs' kě,* sm. decortication.

descastado, da, –*kăstă' dŏ,* a. degenerate; ungrateful. [arms.

descebar, –*thěbăr',* v. a. to unprime firearms.

descendencia, –*thěnděn' thĭă,* sf. descent, offspring.

descendente, –*thĕndĕn'tĕ,* a. descending; (rail.) **tren –,** sm. down-train.

descender, –*thĕndĕr',* v. n. to descend, to walk downward; to flow; to be derived from. [cending; descendant.

descendiente, –*thĕndĕn'tĕ,* a. & sm. descending. [tion.

descensión, –*thĕnsiŏn',* sf. descent, descending.

descenso, –*thĕn'sŏ,* sm. descent; degradation.

desceñir, –*thĕnyir',* v. a. to ungird.

descepar, –*thĕpär',* v. a. to uproot, to root up; to clear a wood.

descerar, –*thĕrär',* v. a. to take the empty combs from a bee-hive. [fortified.

descercado, da, –*thĕrkä'dŏ,* a. open, unfortified.

descercar, –*thĕrkär',* v. a. to destroy or pull down a wall.

descerrajar, –*thĕrrä-här',* v. a. to take off the lock of a door, &c.; to discharge fire-arms. [unravel.

descifrar, –*thĭfrär',* v. f to decipher; to unravel.

descinchar, –*thĭntshär',* v. a. to ungirth a horse. [claw-hammer.

desclavador, –*klävädŏr',* sm. nail-claw.

desclavar, –*klävär',* v. a. to draw out nails. [solve.

descoagular, –*kŏägülär',* v. a. to dissolve.

descobajar, –*kŏbä'här',* v. a. to pull the stem from a grape.

descobijar, –*kŏbĭ'här',* v. a. to uncover, to undress. [pudent.

descocado, da, –*kŏkä'dŏ,* a. bold, impudent.

descocar, –*kŏkär',* v. a. to free trees from insects; **–se,** to be impudent. [ness.

descoco, –*kŏ'kŏ,* sm. impudence, sauciness.

descoger, –*kŏ'hĕr',* v. a. to unfold, to expand. [plants.

descogollar, –*kŏgŏlyär',* v. n. to prune plants.

descogotado, da, –*kŏgŏtä'dŏ,* a. barenecked.

descogotar, –*kŏgŏtär',* v. a. to knock off the horns of a stag at one blow.

descolar, –*kŏlär',* v. a. to dock.

descolchar, –*kŏltshär',* v. a. to untwist a cable.

descolgar, –*kŏlgär',* v. a. to unhang; **–se,** to come down gently; to glide; to run (of streams). [out the eye-teeth.

descolmillar, –*kŏlmĭlyär',* v. a. to draw out the eye-teeth.

descolorar, –*kŏlŏrär',* v. a. to discolour.

descolorido, da, –*kŏlŏrĭ'dŏ,* a. pale, colourless. [excel, to surpass.

descollar, –*kŏlyär',* v. n. to overtop, to surpass.

descomedido, da, –*kŏmĕdĭ'dŏ,* a. impudent, insolent; huge.

descomedirse, –*kŏmĕdĭr'sĕ,* v. r. to be rude or disrespectful.

descompasado, da, –*kŏmpäsä'dŏ,* a. excessive; disproportionate.

descompasarse, –*kŏmpäsär'sĕ,* v. r. to exceed all rule and measure.

descomponer, –*kŏmpŏnĕr',* v. a. to discompose, to set at odds, to disconcert; (chem.) to decompose; **–,** v. n. to be out of temper; to be indisposed; **to change for the worse** (of the weather).

descomposición, –*kŏmpŏsĭthĭŏn',* sf. disagreement, discomposure; decomposition.

descompostura, –*kŏmpŏstŏ'rä,* sf. disagreement; disorder, confusion; want of modesty.

descompuesto, ta, –*kŏmpŭĕs'tŏ,* a. impudent, insolent.

descomunal, –*kŏmŭnäl',* a. uncommon; beyond all measure. [discredit.

desconceptuar, –*kŏnthĕptŭär',* v. a. to discredit.

desconcertado, da, –*kŏnthĕrtä'dŏ,* a. disorderly, slovenly.

desconcertar, –*kŏnthĕrtär',* v. a. to disturb; to confound; to disconcert; **–se,** to disagree; to exceed the limits of prudence and judgment; to be indisposed with a looseness of the body; to be out of joint.

desconchar, –*kŏntshär',* v. a. to unscale.

desconcierto, –*kŏnthĭĕr'tŏ,* sm. discomposure; disorder, confusion; indolence, negligence; sprain.

desconfiado, da, –*kŏnfĭä'dŏ,* a. diffident, mistrustful. [jealousy.

desconfianza, –*kŏnfĭän'thä,* sf. diffidence; jealousy.

desconfiar, –*kŏnfĭär',* v. n. to mistrust, to suspect. [contrary; unequal, unlike.

desconforme, –*kŏnfŏr'mĕ,* a. discordant.

desconformidad, –*kŏnfŏrmĭdäd',* sf. disagreement, opposition; inequality, unlikeness, dissimilitude.

desconocer, –*kŏnŏthĕr',* v. a. to disown, to disavow; to be totally ignorant of a thing; not to know a person; not to acknowledge (a favour received).

desconocido, da, –*kŏnŏthĭ'dŏ,* a. ungrateful; disguised; unknown.

desconsiderado, da, –*kŏnsĭdĕrä'dŏ,* a. inconsiderate, imprudent.

desconsolado, da, –*kŏnsŏlä'dŏ,* a. comfortless, painful; sick with indigestion.

desconsolar, –*kŏnsŏlär',* v. a. to afflict.

desconsuelo, –*kŏnsŭĕ'lŏ,* sm. affliction, trouble; disorder of the digestive organs.

descontar, –*kŏntär',* v. a. to discount; to abate, to diminish.

descontentadizo, za, –*kŏntĕntädĭ'thŏ,* a. squeamish, easily disgusted.

descontentar, –*kŏntĕntär',* v. a. to discontent, to displease. [tion, disgust.

descontento, –*kŏntĕn'tŏ,* sm. dissatisfaction, disgust.

desconvenible, –*kŏnvĕnĭ'blĕ,* a. discordant, disagreeing, dissimilar.

desconveniencia, –*kŏnvĕnĭĕn'thĭä,* sf. incommodity, inconvenience; discord, disunion; dissimilitude.

desconveniente, –*kŏnvĕnĭĕn'tĕ,* a. inconvenient; incongruous. [not to suit.

desconvenir, –*kŏnvĕnĭr',* v. n. to disagree; not to suit.

descopar, –*kŏpär',* v. a. to lop off the branches of a tree.

descorazonar, –*kŏräthŏnär',* v. a. to pull out the heart; to dishearten, to discourage; to smite with love.

descorchar, –*kŏrtshär',* v. a. to strip off the bark; to break a bee hive to steal the honey; to break open a chest or trunk.

descordar, –*kŏrdär',* v. a. to unstring an instrument. [horns of an animal.

descornar, –*kŏrnär',* v. a. to knock off the

descorrear, –kŏrrĕār′, v. n. to loosen the skin that covers the tenderlings of a deer.

descorrer, –kŏrrĕr′, v. n. to run, to flow; —, v. a. to retrograde; **– la cortina,** to draw the curtain.

descortés, –kŏrtĕth′, a. impolite, uncivil.

descortesía, –kŏrtĕsē′ā, sf. incivility, want of politeness.

descortezar, –kŏrtĕthār′, v. a. to descorticate; to flay; (fig.) to polish. [a seam.

descosedura, –kŏsĕdō′rā, sf. unseaming

descoser, –kŏsĕr′, v. a. to unseam; to separate; **–se,** to give rein to one's tongue.

descosido, –kŏsē′dŏ, sm. idle talker.

descostillar, –kŏstĭlyār′, v. a. to break the ribs; **–se,** to fall with great violence on one's back. [off.

descostrarse, –kŏstrār′ĕs, v. r. to scale

descotar, –kŏtār′, v. a. to remove the restrictions against the use of a path or road.

descoyuntamiento, –kŏyŭntāmĭĕn′tŏ, sm. dislocation; pain from overexertion.

descoyuntar, –kŏyŭntār′, v. a. to lux or disjoint bones; to vex, to molest.

descrédito, –krĕ′dĭtŏ, sm. discredit.

descreer, –krĕĕr′, v. a. to disbelieve.

describir, –dĕskrĭbīr′, v. a. to draw, to delineate; to describe.

descripción, dĕskrĭpthĭŏn′, sf. delineation; description; inventory. [tive.

descriptivo, va, dĕskrĭptē′vŏ, a. descriptive.

descruzar, –krūthār′, v. a. to uncross.

descuadernar, –kŭādĕrnār′, v. a. to unbind; to disorder.

descuajar, –kŭāhār′, v. a. to dissolve, to liquefy; to pluck up weeds; to frighten.

descuajo, –kŭā′hŏ, sm. eradication.

descuartizar, –kŭārtĭthār′, v. a. to quarter (to divide the body into four parts); to carve. [nition; á la—, openly, clearly.

descubierta, –kŭbĭĕr′tā, sf. (mil.) recognition; á la—, openly, clearly.

descubierto, –tŏ, sm. solemn exposition of the sacrament; deficit.

descubridor, ra, dĕskŭbrĭdŏr′, sm. & f. discoverer, descrier; investigator; (mil.) scout; vessel on a voyage of discovery.

descubrimiento, –kŭbrĭmĭĕn′tŏ, sm. discovery, country lately discovered.

descubrir, –kŭbrīr′, v. a. to discover, to disclose; to uncover; to reveal; (mil.) to overlook any place in a fortification.

descuello, –kŭĕl′yŏ, sm. excessive stature; pre-eminence; haughtiness.

descuento, –kŭĕn′tŏ, sm. sum paid in part payment of a debt; discount; satisfaction; diminution, decrease.

descuerno, –kŭĕr′nŏ, sm. contempt; affront. [negligent.

descuidado, da, –kŭĭdā′dŏ, a. careless, negligent.

descuidar, –kŭĭdār′, v. a. & n. to neglect, to relieve from care; to render careless.

descuido, –kŭĭ′dŏ, sm. indolence, carelessness, negligence, forgetfulness; want of attention, incivility; improper action; **al —,** affectedly careless.

descular, –kŭlār′, v. a. to break the bottom or end of a thing.

desde, dĕs′dĕ, pr. since, after, from; **— luego,** thereupon; **— entonces,** since then.

desdecir, –dĕthĭr′, v. a. to disavow; —, v. n. to degenerate; to differ, to disagree; to tumble down; **–se,** to gainsay; to retract. [tempt; al —, affectedly careless.

desdén, –dĕn′, sm. disdain, scorn, contempt; al —, affectedly careless.

desdentado, da, –dĕntā′dŏ, a. toothless.

desdentar, –dĕntār′, v. a. to draw out teeth. [despicable.

desdeñable, –dĕnyā′blĕ, a. contemptible, despicable.

desdeñar, –dĕnyār′, v. a. to disdain, to scorn; **–se,** to be disdainful.

desdeñoso, sa, –dĕnyō′sŏ, a. disdainful; contemptuous. [a clew.

desdevanar, –dĕvānār′, v. a. to develop a clew.

desdicha, –dĭtsh′ā, sf. misfortune, calamity; great poverty.

desdichado, da, –dĭtshā′dŏ, a. unfortunate, wretched, miserable.

desdoblar, –dŏblār′, v. a. to unfold, to spread open.

desdorar, –dŏrār′, v. a. to take off the gilding; to tarnish one's reputation.

desdoro, –dō′rŏ, sm. dishonour, blot on one's reputation.

deseable, dĕsĕā′blĕ, a. desirable.

desear, dĕsĕār′, v. a. to desire, to wish; to require, to demand.

desecación, dĕsĕkāthĭŏn′, sf. desiccation.

desecar, dĕsĕkār′, v. a. to dry.

desechar, dĕsĕtshār′, v. a. to depreciate; to reject, to reprove; to refuse; to exclude, to reprobate; to lay aside.

desecho, dĕsĕtsh′ŏ, sm. residue, remainder; refuse, offal; contempt.

desedificar, dĕsĕdĭfĭkār′, v. a. to scandalise.

desejecutar, dĕ′hĕkūtār′, v. a. (law) to raise a sequestration.

desellar, dĕsĕlyār′, v. a. to unseal.

desembalar, –ĕmbālār′, v. a. to unpack.

desembanastar, –ĕmbānāstār′, v. a. to take out of a basket; to talk at random; **–se,** to break out (of a person confined).

desembarazar, –ĕmbārāthār′, v. a. to disembarrass; to clear; to disencumber; **–se,** to be extricated from difficulties.

desembarazo, –ĕmbārā′thŏ, sm. disembarrassment; liberty to do a thing.

desembarcadero, –ĕmbārkādĕ′rŏ, sm. landing-place.

desembarcar, –ĕmbārkār′, v. a. to unship, to disembark; —, v. n. to disembark, to land.

desembarco, –ĕmbār′kŏ, sm. landing; unshipment; landing of stairs; descent, hostile landing. [an embargo.

desembargar, –ĕmbārgār′, v. a. to raise an embargo.

desembargo, –ĕmbār′gŏ, sm. (law) raising an embargo.

desembarque, –ĕmbār′kĕ, sm. landing.

desembaular, –ĕmbāŭlār′, v. a. to empty a trunk; to disclose one's secret thoughts.

desembelesarse, –ĕmbĕlĕsār′ĕs, v. r. to recover from amazement.

desembocadero, –ĕmbŏkādĕ′rŏ, sm. mouth of a river or canal.

desembocar, *–émbŏkắr*, v. n. to disembogue.

desembojar, *–émbŏ'hắr*, v. a. to remove the silk-pods from the southern-wood.

desembolsar, *–émbŏlsắr*, v. a. to empty a purse; to disburse.

desembolso, *–émbŏl'sŏ*, sm. disbursement, expenditure.

desemborrachar, *–émbŏrrắtshắr*, v. a. to sober; –, v. n. to grow sober.

desembocarse, *–émbŏkắr'sé*, v. r. to get out of the woods; to get clear of an ambuscade. [muffle.

desembozar, *–émbŏthắr*, v. a. to undesembozo, *–émbŏ'thŏ*, sm. uncovering of the face. [tame, to domesticate.

desembravecer, *–émbrăvéthér*, v. a. to

desembriagar, *–émbriăgắr*, v. a. & r. to sober; to recover from drunkenness.

desembrollar, *–émbrŏlyắr*, v. a. to disentangle, to disembroil.

desembuchar, *–émbŭtshắr*, v. a. to disgorge; to unbosom. [different.

desemejante, *désémé'hắn'té*, a. dissimilar,

desemejanza, *–thă*, sf. dissimilitude, unlikeness. [similar.

desemejar, *désémé'hắr*, v. n. to be dis-

desempalagar, *–émpălăgắr*, v. a. to clean one's palate, to restore the appetite; to clear a mill of stagnant water.

desempañar, *–émpănyắr*, v. a. to unswathe; to clean a tarnished looking-glass.

desempapelar, *–émpăpélắr*, v. a. to unwrap. [unpack.

desempaquetar, *–émpăkétắr*, v. a. to un-

desemparejar, *–émpăré'hắr*, v. a. to unmatch. [the thrashed corn in heaps.

desemparvar, *–émpărvắr*, v. a. to pile

desempatar, *–émpătắr*, v. a. to make unequal. [pave.

desempedrar, *–émpédrắr*, v. a. to un-

desempeñar, *–émpényắr*, v. a. to redeem; to extricate from debt; to fulfil any duty or promise; to acquit.

desempeño, *–émpén'yŏ*, sm. redeeming a pledge; proof of an account; performance of an obligation; perfection, completion.

desemperezar, *–émpéréthắr*, v. n. to relinquish habits of laziness and indolence.

desempolvorar, *–émpŏlvŏrắr*, v. a. to free from dust.

desemponzoñar, *–émpŏnthŏnyắr*, v. a. to expel poison; to cure a disordinate passion. [a bow.

desempulgar, *–émpŭlgắr*, v. a. to unbend

desenalbardar, *–énălbărdắr*, v. a. to take off a pack-saddle. [love.

desenamorar, *–énămŏrắr*, v. a. to destroy

desencabalgar, *–énkăbălgắr*, v. a. (mil.) to dismount cannon.

desencabestrar, *–énkăbéstrắr*, v. a. to disentangle a beast from the halter.

desencadenar, *–énkădénắr*, v. a. to unchain; to dissolve all connection or obligation. [thing out of its place.

desencajar, *–énkă'hắr*, v. a. to take a

desencajonar, *–énkă'hŏnắr*, v. a. to take out of a box.

desencalabrinar, *–énkălăbrĭnắr*, v. a. to remove dizziness. [stranded vessel.

desencallar, *–énkălyắr*, v. a. to float a

desencaminar, *–énkămĭnắr*, v. a. to lose one's way, to go astray. [chant.

desencantar, *–énkăntắr*, v. a. to disen-

desencantarar, *–énkăntărắr*, v. a. to draw by lot the names of persons for office. [ment.

desencanto, *–énkăn'tŏ*, sm. disenchant-

desencapotar, *–énkăpŏtắr*, v. a. to strip of one's cloak; to uncover; to make manifest; to raise and keep up the head of a horse; –se, to put on a pleasing expression. [dissuade from prejudice.

desencaprichar, *–énkăprĭtshắr*, v. a. to

desencerrar, *–énthérrắr*, v. a. to free from confinement; to open, to unclose.

desenclavar, *–énklăvắr*, v. a. to draw out nails; to tear from its place.

desenclavijar, *–énklăvĭ'hắr*, v. a. to take out the pegs of a musical instrument.

desencoger, *–énkŏ'hér*, v. a. to unfold; –se, to grow bold.

desencolar, *–énkŏlắr*, v. a. to unglue.

desencolerizarse, *–énkŏlérĭthăr'sé*, v. r. to grow calm or appeased.

desenconar, *–énkŏnắr*, v. a. to cure an inflammation; to appease one's passion; –se, to become milder.

desencono, *–énkŏ'nŏ*, sm. cooling of anger or passion. [string.

desencordar, *–énkŏrdắr*, v. a. to un-

desencordelar, *–énkŏrdélắr*, v. a. to untie, to take away ropes. [straighten.

desencorvar, *–énkŏrvắr*, v. a. to

desendemoniar, *–éndémŏnĭắr*, **desendiablar**, *–éndĭăblắr*, v. a. to exorcise.

desenfadado, da, *–énfădă'dŏ*, a. free, unembarrassed; gay; wide, spacious.

desenfadar, *–énfădắr*, v. a. to assuage anger; to appease passion.

desenfado, *–énfă'dŏ*, sm. ease; facility; calmness, relaxation.

desenfaldar, *–énfăldắr*, v. a. to let fall the train of a gown.

desenfangar, *–énfăngắr*, v. a. to clear from mud or filth.

desenfardar, *–énfărdắr*, **desenfardelar**, *–énfărdélắr*, v. a. to open bales of goods. [the monastic life.

desenfrailar, *–énfrăĭlắr*, v. n. to leave

desenfrenado, da, *–énfrénă'dŏ*, a. outrageous; ungovernable.

desenfrenar, *–énfrénắr*, v. a. to unbridle; –se, to give full play to one's passions; to fly into a violent passion.

desenfreno, *–énfré'nŏ*, sm. licentiousness.

desenfundar, *–énfŭndắr*, v. a. to take out of a bag, pillow-case.

desenfurecerse, *–énfŭréthér'sé*, v. r. to grow calm; to lay aside anger and passion. [hook.

desenganchar, *–éngănchắr*, v. a. to un-

desengañado, da, *–éngănyă'dŏ*, a. undeceived; despicable, ill-executed.

desengañar, –*ēngānyār'*, |v. a. to undeceive, to free from error, to disabuse, to free from a mistake, to set right.

desengaño, –*ēngān'yŏ*, sm. undeception; naked truth; reproach, upbraiding.

desengarzar, –*ēngārthār'*, v.a. to unravel.

desengastar, –*ēngāstār'*, v.a. to take a diamond out of a ring, [out the grease.

desengrasar, –*ēngrāsār'*, v. a. to take

desengrosar, –*ēngrōsār'*, v. a. to extenuate, to make lean. [off the paste.

desengrudar, –*ēngrūdār'*, v. a. to scrape

desenhebrar, –*ēnhēbrār'*, v. a. to unthread; to unravel. [harness horses.

desenjaezar, –*ēn'hāēthār'*, v. a. to un-

desenjalmar, –*ēn'hālmār'*, v. a. to take off a pack-saddle from a beast of burden.

desenjaular, –*ēnjāūlār'*, v. a. to let loose out of a cage. [chain, to unlink.

desenlabonar, –*ēnlābōnār'*, v. a. to un-

desenlace, –*ēnlā'thē*, sm. climax of a dramatic poem; end of an affair.

desenladrillar, –*ēnlādrīlyār'*, v.a. to take up floor-tiles. [to distinguish.

desenlazar, –*ēnlāthār'*, v. a. to unlace;

desenlosar, –*ēnlōsār'*, v. a. to unpave.

desenlutar, –*ēnlūtār'*, v. a. to leave off mourning; to banish sorrow.

desenmarañar, –*ēnmārānyār'*, v. a. to disentangle.

desenmudecer, –*ēnmūdēthēr'*, v. a. to remove an impediment of speech; to break a long silence.

desenojar, –*ēnō'hār'*, v. a. to appease; –se, to amuse one's self. [anger.

desenojo, –*ēnō'hŏ*, sm. abatement of

desenredar, –*ēnrēdār'*, v.a. to disentangle; –se, to extricate one's self.

desenrizar, –*ēnrīthār'*, v. a. to uncurl.

desenrollar, –*ēnrōlyār'*, v. a. to unroll.

desenroscar, –*ēnrōskār'*, v. a. to untwist, to unroll. [to unravel.

desensartar, –*ēnsārtār'*, v.a. to unthread.

desensillar, –*ēnsīlyār'*, v. a. to unsaddle.

desensoberbecerse, –*ēnsōbērbēthēr'sē*, v. r. to moderate one's pride. [of joint.

desensortijado, da, –*ēnsōrtī'hā'dŏ*, a. out

desentablar, –*ēntāblār'*, v. a. to rip off planks; to disturb; to embroil; to interrupt a friendly intercourse.

desentenderse, –*ēntēndēr'sē*, v. r. to feign not to understand; to pass by without noticing. [disinterment.

desenterramiento, –*ēntērrāmīēn'tŏ*, sm.

desenterrar, –*ēntērrār'*, v. a. to disinter, to unbury; to recall to memory things forgotten.

desentoldar, –*ēntōldār'*, v. a. to take away an awning; to strip a thing of its ornaments. [nance.

desentonación, –*ēntōnāthīōn'*, sf. dissonance.

desentonar, –*ēntōnār'*, v.a.&n.to humble; to be out of tune; –se, to raise the voice disrespectfully. [screw.

desentono, –*ēntō'nŏ*, sm. disharmony; rude tone of voice.

desentornillar, –*ēntōrnīlyār'*, v.a. to un-

desentorpecer, –*ēntōrpēthēr'*, v. a. to free

from torpor; –se, to become lively, smart or pert.

desentrañar, –*ēntrānyār'*, v. a. to gut, to eviscerate; to go into a matter very deeply; –se, to give away all one's fortune for love.

desentristecer, –*ēntrīstēthēr'*, v. a. to banish sadness and grief.

desentronizar, –*ēntrōnīthār'*, v. a. to dethrone; to deprive of authority.

desentumecer, –*ēntūmēthēr'*, v. a. to restore motion to torpid limbs.

desenvainar, –*ēnvāīnār'*, v. a. to unsheath; to bring to light; to stretch out the claws. [from poison.

desenvenenar, –*ēnvēnēnār'*, v. a. to cure

desenvergar, –*ēnvērgār'*, v. a. to unbend a sail.

desenvoltura, –*ēnvŏltŏ'rā*, sf. sprightliness; cheerfulness; impudence, boldness; lewd posture or gesture; graceful, easy delivery of one's sentiments and thoughts.

desenvolver, –*ēnvŏlvēr'*, v. a. to unfold, to unroll; to decipher, to unravel; –se, to be forward. [licentious.

desenvuelto, ta, –*ēnvŭēl'tŏ*, a. forward;

deseo, *dēsē'ŏ*, sm. desire, wish.

deseoso, sa, *dēsē'ŏsō*, a. desirous.

deserción, *dēsērthīōn'*, sf. desertion.

desertar, *dēsērtār'*, v. a. to desert, to forsake one's colours or post; (law) to abandon a cause.

desertor, *dēsērtŏr'*, sm. deserter, fugitive.

deservicio, *dēsērvē'thīŏ*, sm. disservice.

deservir, *dēsērvēr'*, v. a. to disserve, not to perform one's duty.

deseslabonar, *dēsēslābōnār'*, v. a. to cut the links of a chain.

desesperación, *dēsēspērāthīōn'*, sf. despair, desperation; anger, fury. [hopeless.

desesperado, da, *dēsēspērā'dŏ*, a. desperate,

desesperanzar, *dēsēspērānthār'*, v. a. to deprive of hope; to make desperate.

desesperar, *dēsēspērār'*, v. n. to despair; –, v. a. to make desperate.

desesterar, *dēsēstērār'*, v. a. to take away the mats from a room.

desestimación, *dēsēstīmāthīōn'*, sf. disesteem, crying down. [to contemn.

desestimar, *dēsēstīmār'*, v. a. to disregard,

desfajar, *dēsfā'hār'*, v. a. to ungird.

desfalcar, *dēsfālkār'*, v. a. to cut off, to lop off; to dissuade from an undertaking.

desfalco, *dēsfāl'kŏ*, sm. diminution, deduction. [fall away; –, v. n. to weaken.

desfallecer, *dēsfālyēthēr'*, v. n. to pine, to

desfallecimiento, *dēsfālyēthīmīēn'tŏ*, sm. languor, fainting.

desfavorecer, *dēsfāvōrēthēr'*, v. a. to disfavour; to contemn; to injure, to hurt; to contradict, to oppose.

desfigurar, *dēsfīgūrār'*, v. a. to disfigure, to deform; to disguise; –se, to be disfigured by passion. [move.

desfijar, *dēsfī'hār'*, v. a. to unsettle, to re-

desfilar, *dēsfīlār'*, v. n. (mil.) to defile.

desflemar, *dēsflēmār'*, v. a. to clear from phlegm.

desfloración, *dēsflōrāthīōn'*, sf. defloration

desflorar, *—flōrár',* v. a. to pull or pluck the flowers in a garden; to deflower; to tarnish.

desflorecer, *—flōréthér',* v. n. to wither.

desfogar, *—fōgár',* v. a. to make an opening for the fire; to give vent to the violence of passion; to moderate passion or desire; **—se,** to give vent to one's passion or anger.

desfogue, *—fō'gĕ,* sm. venting of one's passion.

desfondar, *—fóndár',* v. a. to break the bottom of any vessel; to penetrate the bottom of a ship.

desfortalecer, *—fōrtáléthér',* v. a. to demolish the works of a fortress.

desgajar, *—gáhár',* v. a. to lop off the branches of trees; to break in pieces; **—se,** to be separated; to be torn in pieces.

desgalgadero, *—gálgádē'rō,* sm. rugged declivitous place.

desgalgar, *—gálgár',* v. a. to precipitate.

desgana, *—gá'ná,* sf. disgust, want of appetite; aversion, reluctance.

desganar, *—gánár',* v. a. to deprive of the pleasure of doing something; **—se,** to lose all pleasure in doing a thing; to lose one's appetite. [branches of trees.

esganchar, *—gántshár',* v. a. to lop off

desgañifarse, *—gányifár'sĕ,* **desgañitarse,** *—tár'sĕ,* v. r. to scream, to bawl.

desgargantarse, *—gárgántár'sĕ,* v. r. to become hoarse by bawling.

desgargolar, *—gárgōlár',* v. a. to shed the seed. [the course.

desgaritar, *—gáritár',* v. n. (mar.) to lose

desgarrado, da, *—gárrá'dō,* a. licentious, dissolute.

desgarrar, *—gárrár',* v. a. to rend, to tear; **—se,** to withdraw, to retire.

desgarro, *—gár'rō,* sm. rent, breach; impudence; idle boast; ogling.

desgarrón, *—gárrōn',* sm. large rent; piece of cloth torn off.

desgastar, *—gástár',* v. a. to consume, to waste; to corrode; **—se,** to weaken one's self. [scream.

desgaznatarse, *—gáthnátár'sĕ,* v. r. to

desglosar, *—glōsár',* v. a. to scratch out MS. notes or remarks. [comment.

desglose, *—glō'sĕ,* sm. erasure of a note or

desgobernar, *—gōbérnár',* v. a. to disturb the order of government; to misgovern; to dislocate; to bar a vein on a horse's leg; to steer an unsteady course; **—se,** to affect ridiculous motions in dancing.

desgobierno, *—gōbiér'nō,* sm. misgovernment, mismanagement.

desgonzar, *—gónthár',* v. a. to separate; to unhinge; to disjoint.

desgoznar, *—gōthnár',* v. a. to unhinge; **—se,** to distort the body with violent motions. [grace; enmity; unpleasantness.

desgracia, *—grá'thiá,* sf. misfortune, disgrace; enmity; unpleasantness.

desgraciado, da, *—gráthiá'dō,* a. unfortunate, unhappy, miserable; out of favour; disagreeable; ungrateful.

desgraciarse, *—gráthiár'sĕ,* v. r. to fall out with; to be out of order; to degenerate.

desgramar, *—grámár',* v. a. to pluck up grasses; to husk.

desgranar, *—gránár',* v. a. to shake out the grain from the ears of corn; to scatter about; **—se,** to wear away (of the touchhole of a fire-arm). [hair; to disorder.

desgreñar, *—grényár',* v. a. to dishevel the

desguarnecer, *—guárnéthér',* v. a. to strip clothes or trimmings and other ornaments; to deprive a thing of its strength; to disgarnish. [timber.

desguazar, *—guáthár',* v. a. to cut asunder

desguindar, *—gindár',* v. a. (mar.) to take and bring down; **—se,** to slide down by a rope. [in paper-mills.

desguinzar, *—ginthár',* v. a. to cut rags

deshabitado, da, *—ábitá'dō,* a. deserted, uninhabited, desolate.

deshabitar, *—ábitár',* v. a. to quit one's habitation; to unpeople.

deshabituar, *—ábituár',* v. a. to disaccustom. [vios, avenger of injuries.

deshacedor, *—áthédōr',* sm. **— de agra-**

deshacer, *—áthér',* v. a. to undo, to destroy; to cancel; to efface; to rout an army; to spend profusely; to melt; to cut up, to divide; to dissolve in a liquid; to violate a treaty; to diminish; to disband troops; **—se,** to grieve, to mourn; to excuse one's self; to disappear; to do a thing with vehemence; to mollify; to grow feeble or meagre.

deshalajar, *—álá'hár',* v. a. to unfurnish

desharrapado, da, *—árrápá'dō,* a. shabby, ragged, in tatters.

deshebillar, *—ébilyár',* v. a. to unbuckle.

deshebrar, *—ébrár',* v. a. to unthread; to divide into filaments; (fig.) to shed a flood of tears.

deshecha, *—étshá,* sf. simulation, fiction; genteel farewell; burden of a song.

deshechizar, *—étshithár',* v. a. to disenchant. [ment.

deshechizo, *—étshi'thō,* sm. disenchant-

deshecho, cha, *—étsh'ō,* a. undone, destroyed, wasted; melted, in pieces; perfectly mixed (of colours): borrasca **—,** a violent tempest. [thaw, to melt.

deshelar, *—élár',* v. a. to thaw; **—se,** to

desherbar, *—érbár',* v. a. to weed.

desheredamiento, *—érédámién'tō,* sm. disinheriting. [**—se,** to degenerate.

desheredar, *—érédár',* v. a. to disinherit;

deshermanar, *—érmánár',* v. a. to remove the likeness or similarity of things; **—se,** to fall out or quarrel with one's brother.

desherrar, *—érrár',* v. a. to unchain; to rip off the shoes of horses.

deshielo, *—iá'lō,* sm. thaw. [unweave.

deshilachar, *—ilátshár',* v. a. to ravel, to

deshilado, *—ilá'dō,* sm. open-work; **—da,** a marching in file.

deshilar, *—ilár',* v. a. to ravel; to convert into lint; to distract bees in order to get them into a new hive.

deshilo, *—ási'lō,* sm. obstructing the communication of bees, to get them into a new hive.

deshincar, –ĭnkär', v. a. to draw out a nail; to tear up what is nailed fast.

deshinchar, –ĭnshär', v. a. to reduce a swelling; to explain the cause of one's displeasure; –se, to be removed (applied to a swelling); to abate presumption.

deshojar, –ō'här', v. a. to strip off the leaves. [pare.

deshollejar, –ōlyĕ'här', v. a. to peel, to

deshollinador, –ōlyĭnädō', sm. chimney-sweeper, sweep; scraper for sweeping chimneys; (fig.) a careful examiner.

deshollinar, –ōlyĭnär', v. a. to sweep chimneys; to clean what is dirty; to change clothes; to view and examine with careful attention.

deshonestidad, –ōnestĭdäd', sf. immodesty, indecency; lewdness.

deshonesto, ta, –ōnĕs'tō, a. immodest; lewd; unreasonable.

deshonor, –ōnō', sm. dishonour; insult.

deshonorar, –ōnōrär', v. a. to deprive of an office or employ. [tion of a woman.

deshonra, –ōnrä', sf. dishonour; seduc-

deshonrabuenos, –ōnräbädˈnōs, sm. calumniator, libeller; he who degenerates from his ancestors.

deshonrar, –ōnrär', v. a. to affront, to insult, to defame; to dishonour; to deflower a woman. [able, indecent.

deshonroso, sa, –ōnrō'sō, a. dishonour-

deshora, dĕsō'rä, sf. unseasonable time.

deshuesar, –hŭĕsär', v. a. to rid of bones.

deshumedecer, –ŭmĕdĕthĕr', v. a. to deprive of humidity; –se, to grow dry.

desidia, dĕsĭ'dĭä, sf. idleness, indolence.

desidioso, sa, –sĭdĭō'sō, a. lazy, idle.

desierto, ta, dĕsĭĕr'tō, a. deserted, solitary; –, sm. desert, wilderness. [tion.

designación, –sĭgnäthĭōn', sf. designa-

designar, –sĭgnär', v. a. to design, to intend; to appoint; to express, to name.

designio, dĕsĭg'nĭō, sm. design, purpose; road, course. [uneven, craggy, cliffy.

desigual, dĕsĭgŭäl', a. unequal, unlike;

desigualar, –gŭälär', v. a. to make unequal or dissimilar; –se, to excel, to surpass.

desigualdad, –ĭgŭäldäd', sf. inequality, dissimilitude; inconstancy; knottiness, unevenness. [undeceive.

desimpresionar, –ĭmprĕsĭōnär', v. a. to

desinclinar, –ĭnklĭnär', v.a. to desincline.

desinfección, –ĭnfĕkthĭōn', sf. disinfection. [infect.

desinficionar, –ĭnfĭthĭōnär', v. a. to dis-

desinflamar, –ĭnflämär', v. a. to cure an inflammation. [ness.

desinterés, –ĭntĕrĕs', sm. disinterested-

desinteresado, da, –ĭntĕrĕsä'dō, a. disinterested.

desistir, dĕsĭstĭr', v. n. to desist, to cease.

desjarretadera, dĕs'härrĕtädĕ'rä, sf. hooked knife for houghing cattle.

desjarretar, –härrĕtär', v. a. to hough, to hamstring; to deprive one of the means of making a fortune; to bleed to excess.

deslamar, –lämär', v. a. to clear of mud.

deslastrar, –lästrär', v. a. to unballast a ship. [barefaced.

deslavado, da, –lävä'dō, a. impudent,

deslavadura, –lävädō'rä, sf. washing.

deslavar, –lävär', v. a. to wash superficially.

deslazar, –läthär', v. a. to unlace.

desleal, –lĕäl', a. disloyal; perfidious.

deslealtad, –lĕältäd', sf. disloyalty, breach of faith. [the branches of vines.

deslechugar, –lĕshŭgär', v. a. to prune

desleir, –lĕĭr', v. a. to dilute, to dissolve.

deslenguado, da, –lĕngŭä'dō, a. foul-mouthed, free-tongued.

deslenguar, –lĕngŭär', v. a. to cut out the tongue; –se, to slander.

desliar, –lĭär', v. a. to untie.

desligar, –lĭgär', v. a. to loosen, to unbind; (fig.) to explain. [limits.

deslindar, –lĭndär', v. a. to mark the

deslinde, –lĭn'dĕ, sm. demarcation.

desliz, –lĭth', sm. slip, sliding; (fig.) slip, weakness. [place.

deslizadero, –lĭthädĕ'rō, sm. slippery

deslizadizo, za, –lĭthädĭˈthō, a. slippery, slippy, glib; lubricous.

deslizar, –lĭthär', v. n. to slip, to slide; to speak carelessly, to go too far in conversation.

deslomar, –lōmär', v. a. to break the back, to distort the loins, to chine.

deslucimiento, –lŭthĭmĭĕn'tō, sm. disgrace, dishonour.

deslucir, –lŭthĭr', v. a. to tarnish the lustre; to obscure one's merit.

deslumbramiento, –lŭmbrämĭĕn'tō, sm. overpowering lustre; dazzling. [to puzzle.

deslumbre, –lŭm'brĕ, sm. overpower-

deslumbrar, –lŭmbrär', v. a. to dazzle;

deslustrar, –lŭsträr', v. a. to tarnish; to obscure; to blast one's reputation.

deslustre, dĕslŭs'trĕ, sm. spot which obscures the lustre; disgrace, ignominy.

deslustroso, sa, –lŭstrō'sō, a. unbecoming, ugly. [sm. languishment.

desmadejamiento, –mädĕhämĭĕn'tō,

desmadejar, –mädĕ'här', v. a. to enervate, to produce languor. [misconduct.

desmán, dĕsmän', sm. misfortune, disaster;

desmandar, –mändär', v. a. to countermand; to revoke a legacy; –se, to disband; to stray from the flock.

desmangar, –mängär', v. a. to take off the handle of any thing.

desmanotado, da, –mänōtä'dō, a. unhandy, awkward. [ruinous, dilapidated.

desmantelado, da, –mäntĕlä'dō, a.

desmantelar, –mäntĕlär', v. a. to dismantle; to abandon, to forsake; (mar.) to unmast. [tangle.

desmarañar, –märänyär', v. a. to disen-

desmayado, da, –mäyä'dō, a. pale, wan; dismayed, appalled.

desmayar, –mäyär', v. n. to be dispirited or faint-hearted; –, v. a. to dismay, to dispirit; –se, to faint.

desmayo, —mā'yō, sm. swoon; dismay.

desmedido, da, —mĕdĭ'dō, a. unpropor-
tionable. [all measure.

desmedirse, —mĕdĭr'sĕ, v. r. to be beyond

desmedrar, —mĕdrār', v. n. to decrease,
to decay; —, v. a. to deteriorate.

desmejorar, —mĕ'hōrār', v. a. to debase,
to make worse.

desmelenar, —mĕlĕnār', v. a. to dishevel.

desmembración, —mĕmbrăthĭōn', sf.
dismemberment.

desmembrar, —mĕmbrār', v. a. to dismember; to curtail; to separate.

desmentida, —mĕntĭ'dā, sf. giving the lie.

desmentir, —mĕntĭr', v. a. to give the lie.

desmenuzar, —mĕnŭthār', v.a. to crumble,
to chip, to fritter; to examine minutely.

desmeollar, —mĕōlyār', v. a. to take out
the marrow.

desmerecer, —mĕrĕthĕr', v.a. to demerit.

desmerecimiento, —mĕrĕthĭmĭĕn'tō, sm.
demerit, ill desert.

desmesurada, da, —mĕsŭrā'dō, a. excessive; huge; immeasurable.

desmesurar, —mĕsŭrār', v. a. to perturbate, to put out; to put out of order;
—se, to talk impudently, to forget one's
self. [to break into bits.

desmigajar, —mĭgā'hār', v.a. to crumble.

desmigar, —mĭgār', v. a. to crumble bread
into small pieces. [mutilate.

desmochar, —mōtshār', v. a. to lop; to

desmoche, —mōtsh'ĕ, sm. mutilation.

desmontar, —mōntār', v. a. to cut down
wood; to remove a heap of rubbish; to
uncock fire-arms; to dismount a troop of
horse; to dismount cannon; —, v. n. to
dismount, to alight from a horse, &c.

desmonte, —mōn'tĕ, sm. felling; clearing
a wood. [demoralisation.

desmoralización, —mŏrălĭthăthĭōn', sf.

desmoralizar, —mŏrălĭthār', v. a. to de-
moralise.

desmoronadizo, za, —mŏrōnădē'thō, a.
delapidated, ruinous, rickety.

desmoronar, —mŏrōnār', v.a. to destroy
little by little.

desmullir, —mŭlyĭr', v. a. to press together a loose object. [less.

desnarigado, da, —nārĭgā'dō, a. nose-

desnarigar, —nārĭgār', v. a. to cut off
the nose. [to take the choicest part.

desnatar, —nātār', v. a. to skim milk;

desnaturalizar, —nātŭrălĭthār', v. a. to
divest of naturalisation rights; —se, to
forsake one's country. [solve.

desnevar, —nĕvār', v. a. to thaw, to dis-

desnivel, —nĭvĕl', sm. unevenness of the
ground. [neck.

desnucar, —nŭkār', v. a. to break one's

desnudar, —nŭdār', v. a. to denude, to
strip of clothes; to discover, to reveal;
—se, to undress.

desnudez, —nŭdĕth', sf. nakedness.

desnudo, da, —nō'dō, a. naked, bare, uncovered; ill clothed; (fig.) plain, evident.

desobedecer, —ŏbĕdĕthĕr', v. a. to disobey.

desobediencia, —ŏbĕdĭĕn'thĭā, sf. disobedience; insubordination.

desobediente, —ŏbĕdĭĕn'tĕ, a. disobedient.

desocupación, —sŏkŭpāthĭōn', sf. leisure,
want of occupation.

desocupar, —sŏkŭpār', v. a. to quit, to
empty; —se, to retire from a business;
to withdraw from an arrangement.

desoír, —sōĭr', v. a. to pretend not to hear.

desojar, —sō'hār', v. a. to break the eye of
a needle &c.; —se, to strain the sight by
looking steadfastly at a thing.

desolación, —dĕsŏlăthĭōn', sf. destruction;
affliction. [consolate.

desolado, da, —sŏlā'dō, a. desolate, dis-

desolar, —sŏlār', v. a. to lay waste; to
harass.

desoldar, —sōldār', v. a. to unsolder.

desollada, —sŏlyā'dā, sf. strumpet.

desolladero, —sŏlyādĕ'rō, sm. slaughter-
house. [insolent, saucy.

desollado, da, —sŏlyā'dō, a. impudent,

desollar, —sŏlyār', v. a. to flay, to skin;
(fig.) to extort an immoderate price.

desorden, —dĕsōr'dĕn, sm. disorder, confusion. [orderly, disordinate.

desordenado, da, —ōrdĕnā'dō, a. dis-

desordenar, —ōrdĕnār', v. a. to disorder;
—se, to get out of order.

desorejar, —ōrĕ'hār', v. a. to crop the ears.

desorganización, —ōrgănĭthăthĭōn', sf.
disorganization. [organize.

desorganizar, —ōrgănĭthār', v. a. to dis-

desorillar, —ōrĭlyār', v. a. to cut off the
selvage of cloth.

desovar, —ōvār', v. n. to spawn.

desove, dĕsō'vĕ, sm. spawning; spawn.

desovillar, —ŏvĭlyār', v. a. to follow or
develop a clew. [snuffers.

despabiladeras, dĕspābĭlādĕ'răs, sf. pl.

despabilado, da, —pābĭlā'dō, a. watchful, vigilant (in the time for sleeping).

despabilador, —pābĭlādōr', sm. candle-
snuffer. [the candle.

despabiladura, —pābĭlādū'rā, sf. snuff of

despabilar, —pābĭlār', v. a. to snuff a
candle; (fig.) to despatch briefly; —se, to
rouse.

despacio, dĕspā'thĭō, ad. slowly, leisurely;
little by little. [—! softly! gently!

despacito, —pāthē'tō, ad. gently, leisurely;
[—! wait a bit!

despachaderas, —pātshādĕ'răs, sf. pl.
surly words in answer.

despachar, —pātshār', v. a. to despatch;
to expedite; —se, to make haste.

despacho, dĕspā'tshō, sm. despatch, expedition; cabinet; office; counting-house;
commission; warrant, patent; expedient;
a smart answer.

despachurrar, —tshārrār', v.a. to squash,
to crush; to mangle a speech.

despaldillar, dĕspāldĭlyār', v. a. to dislocate the shoulder. [robber.

despalmante, —pālmān'tĕ, sm. (cant)

despalmar, —pālmār', v. a. to clean and
calk the bottoms of ships; to pare off a
horse's hoof.

despampanar, *–pămpănăr'*, v. a. to prune the shoots of vines; (fig.) to unbosom.

desparejar, *–părĕhăr'*, v. a. to make unequal *or* uneven.

desparpajar, *–părpă'hăr'*, v. a. to undo in a disorderly manner; to prattle at random.   [speech *or* action.

desparpajo, *–părpă'h'ŏ*, sm. pertness of

desparramar, *–părămăr'*, v. a. to disseminate, to overspread; to squander, to lavish; –se, to be dissipated.

despartir, *–părtir'*, v. a. to divide; to conciliate.

desparvar, *–părvăr'*, v. a. to take the sheaves of corn out of the stack to be thrashed.

despatarrarse, *–pătărăr'sĕ*, v. r. to fall on the ground with the legs wide spread.

despavesar, *–păvĕsăr'*, v. a. to snuff the candle.

despavorido, *–păvŏr'ĭd'ŏ*, a. frightened.

despeadura, *–pĕădŏ'ră*, sf. foundering.

despear, *–pĕăr'*, v. a. to founder; –, v. n. to surbate.

despechar, *–pĕtshăr'*, v. a. to enrage, to excite indignation; to overwhelm with taxes; –se, to despair.

despecho, *–pĕtsh'ŏ*, sm. indignation, displeasure; wrath; harshness of temper; despite, spite; dismay, despair; disrespect, insolence; deceit; derision, scorn; á –, in spite of.

despechugar, *–pĕtshŏgăr'*, v. a. to cut off the breast of a fowl; –se, to uncover the breast; to walk with the breast open.

despedazar, *–pĕdăthăr'*, v. a. to tear into pieces, to cut asunder; to mangle; –se de risa, to burst into fits of laughter.

despedida, *–pĕd'ĭd'ă*, sf. farewell.

despedir, *–pĕdir'*, v. a. to discharge, to dart; to dismiss from office; –se, to take leave.   [sour of temper.

despegado, da, *–pĕgă'd'ŏ*, a. rough, sullen,

despegar, *–pĕgăr'*, v. a. to unglue; –se, to withdraw one's affection.

despego, *–pĕp'ŏ gŏ*, sm. asperity; want of love, coolness.   [hair.

despeinar, *–pĕĭnăr'*, v. a. to entangle the

despejado, *–pĕ'hă'd'ŏ*, a. sprightly, quick, sagacious; clear.

despejar, *–pĕ'hăr'*, v. a. to clear away obstructions; –se, to cheer up; to amuse one's self; to become clear weather.

despejo, *–pĕp'h'ŏ*, sm. removal of obstacles; sprightliness; grace.

despelazar, *–pĕlăthăr'*, v. a. to make the hair stand on end; –se, to stand erect.

despellejar, *–pĕlyĕhăr'*, v. a. to skin.

despensa, *–pĕn'să*, sf. pantry, larder; provisions, pl.

despensero, ra, *–pĕnsă'rŏ*, sm. & f. butler, caterer; steward on board ship; distributer.

despeñadero, *–pĕnyădă'rŏ*, sm. precipice; (fig.) bold and dangerous undertaking.

despeñar, *–pĕnyăr'*, v. a. to precipitate; –se, to throw one's self headlong.

despeño, *–pĕpĕn'yŏ*, sm. precipitate fall; flux of the belly.

despepitarse, *–pĕpĭtăr'sĕ*, v. r. to vociferate; to act imprudently.

desperdiciador, ra, *–pĕrdĭthĭăd'ŏr'*, sm. & f. spendthrift, squanderer.   [squander.

desperdiciar, *–pĕrdĭthĭăr'*, v. a. to

desperdicio, *–pĕrdĭthĭŏ*, sm. prodigality, profusion; residuum, remains.

desperdigar, *–pĕrdĭgăr'*, v. a. to separate, to scatter.

desperezarse, *–pĕrĕthăr'sĕ*, v. r. to stretch oneself on being roused from sleep.

despernado, *dă, –pĕrnă'd'ŏ*, a. weary, tired.   [legs.

despernar, *–pĕrnăr'*, v. a. to break one's

despertar, *–pĕrtăr'*, v. a. to awaken, to rouse from sleep; to excite; –, v. n. to wake up; to grow lively *or* sprightly.

despierto, ta, *dĕsp'ĭĕr'tŏ*, a. awake; vigilant; fierce; brisk, sprightly.

despilfarrar, *–pĭlfărăr'*, v. a. to waste through slovenliness.

despilfarro, *–pĭlfăr'rŏ*, sm. slovenliness; waste; mismanagement.

despintar, *–pĭntăr'*, v. a. to efface a painting; to obscure things; to mislead; –, v. n. to degenerate; –se, to be deceived by mistaking one card for another.

despinzar, *–pĭnthăr'*, v. a. to nap cloth.

despinzas, *dĕspĭn'thăs*, sf. pl. tweezers, pincers.   [to relieve from misery.

despiojar, *–pĭŏ'hăr'*, v. a. to louse; (fig.)

despique, *dăspĕ kĕ*, sm. vengeance, revenge.

desplantar, *–plăntăr'*, v. a. to eradicate; to transplant; –se, to lose one's erect posture (in fencing *or* dancing).

desplante, *dĕsplăn'tĕ*, sm. oblique posture in fencing.   [tion, unfolding.

desplegadura, *–plĕgădŏ'ră*, sf. explica-

desplegar, *–plĕgăr'*, v. a. to unfold, to display; to explain; to elucidate; (mar.) to unfurl; –se, to blow, to open.

desplomar, *–plŏmăr'*, v. a. to make a wall bulge out; –se, to bulge out; to fall flat to the ground.   [wall.

desplomo, *dĕsplŏ'mŏ*, sm. jutting out of a

desplumar, *–plŭmăr'*, v. a. to deplume, to strip off feathers; (fig.) to despoil of one's property.   [lation.

despoblación, *–pŏblăthĭŏn'*, sf. depopu-

despoblado, *–pŏblă'd'ŏ*, sm. desert.

despoblar, *–pŏblăr'*, v. a. to depopulate; to desolate; –se, to become depopulated.

despojar, *–pŏ'hăr'*, v. a. to despoil; to deprive of; –se, to undress.

despojo, *dĕspŏ'h'ŏ*, sm. spoliation; plunder; slough; –s, pl. giblets, wings, neck, heart, and gizzard of fowls; remains; offal.

despolvar, *–pŏlvăr'*, v. a. to dust.

despolvorear, *–pŏlvŏrĕăr'*, v. a. to brush, to dust, to beat (carpets, etc.).

desportillar, *–pŏrtĭlyăr'*, v. a. to break the neck of a bottle, pot.

desposado, da, *–pŏsă'd'ŏ*, a. hand-cuffed.

desposar, *–pŏsăr'*, v. a. to marry, to betroth; –se, to be betrothed *or* married.

desposeer, *–pŏsĕĕr'*, v. a. to dispossess.

desposeimiento, *–nŏsĕmĭĕn'tŏ*, sm. dispossession.

desposorio, –*pŏsō'rĭŏ,* sm. mutual promise to contract marriage.

déspota, *dĕs'pŏtä,* sm. despot.

despotado, *dĕspŏtä'dŏ,* sm. despotic government. [despotical.

despótico, ca, *dĕspŏ'tĭkŏ,* a. despotic,

despotismo, *dĕspŏtĭs'mŏ,* sm. despotism.

despreciable, –*prĕthä'blĕ,* a. contemptible, despicable. [to despise.

despreciar, –*prĕthär',* v. a. to depreciate,

desprecio, –*prä'thĭŏ,* sm. scorn, contempt.

desprender, –*prĕndĕr',* v. a. to unfasten, to loosen, to separate; –se, to give way, to fall down; to extricate oneself.

desprendimiento, –*prĕndĭmĭĕn'tŏ,* sm. alienation, disinterestedness.

despreocupar, –*prĕŏkŭpär',* v. a. to free from prejudice.

desprevenido, da, –*prĕvĕnĭ'dŏ,* a. unprovided, unprepared.

desproporción, –*prŏpŏrthĭŏn',* sf. disproportion. [a. to disproportion.

desproporcionar, –*prŏpŏrthĭŏnär',* v.

despropósito, –*prŏpŏ'sĭtŏ,* sm. absurdity.

desproveer, –*prŏvĕĕr',* v. a. to deprive of provisions; (mil.) to deprive of ammunition.

desprovisto, ta, –*prŏvĭs'tŏ,* a. unprovided.

después, *dĕspŭĕs',* ad. after, afterwards.

despumar, –*pŭmär',* v. a. to skim.

despuntar, –*pŭntär',* v. a. to blunt; (mar.) to double a cape; –, v. n. to manifest wit and genius; **al – del día,** at break of day. [discompose, to disorder.

desquiciar, –*kĭthĭär',* v. a. to unhinge; to

desquijarar, –*kĭ'härär',* v. a. to break the jaws.

desquitar, –*kĭtär',* v. a. to retrieve a loss; –se, to win one's money back again; to return by giving like for like; to take revenge. [revenge, retaliation.

desquite, –*kĕ'tĕ,* sm. recovery of a loss;

desreglado, da, –*rĕglä'dŏ,* a. disorderly, irregular. [lar, to be ungovernable.

desreglarse, –*rĕglär'sĕ,* v. r. to be irregu-

desrizar, –*rĭthär',* v. a. to uncurl.

destacamento, –*täkämĕn'tŏ,* sm. (mil.) detachment. [body of troops].

destacar, –*täkär',* v. a. (mil.) to detach (a

destajar, –*tä'här',* v. a. to hire or undertake work by the piece or job, to do taskwork.

destajero, –*tä'hä'rŏ,* sm. task-worker, one who undertakes work by the job.

destajo, –*tä'hŏ,* sm. job, undertaking work by the job. [horses' hoofs.

destalonar, –*tälŏnär',* v. a. to level

destapar, –*täpär',* v. a. to uncover; –se, to be uncovered. [mud-walls.

destapiar, –*täpĭär',* v. a. to pull down

destaponar, –*täpŏnär',* v. a. to uncork a bottle.

destazar, –*täthär',* v. a. to cut to pieces.

deste, ta, to, *dĕs'tĕ,* pn. contraction for de este, de esta, de esto.

destejer, –*tĕ'här',* v. a. to untile; to leave a thing defenceless. [ravel.

destejer, –*tĕ'här',* v. a. to unweave, to

---

destello, *dĕstĕl'yŏ,* sm. flowing out drop by drop; sparkle.

destemplado, da, –*tĕmplä'dŏ,* a. inharmonious, incongruous (applied to paintings); intemperate.

destemplanza, –*tĕmplän'thä,* sf. intemperateness; unsteadiness of the weather; disorder; alteration in the pulse.

destemplar, –*tĕmplär',* v. a. to distemper, to alter, to disconcert; to dissolve; to untune; –se, to be ruffled; to be ill with a fever; to grow blunt; to act improperly.

destemple, –*tĕm'plĕ,* sm. discordancy; disorder; intemperance, distemper.

desteñir, –*tĕnyĭr',* v. a. to discolour.

desterrar, –*tĕrrär',* v. a. to banish; to expel, to drive away. [wilderness.

desterradero, –*tĕrrädĕ'rŏ,* sm. desert,

desterronar, –*tĕrrŏnär',* v. a. to break the clods in the fields with a harrow or spade. [tate.

destetar, –*tĕtär',* v. a. to wean, to ablac-

destete, –*tä'tĕ,* sm. ablactation.

destierro, –*tĭĕr'rŏ,* sm. exile, banishment.

destilación, *dĕstĭläthĭŏn',* sf. distillation.

destiladera, *dĕstĭlädĕ'rä,* sf. still, alembic;

destilador, *dĕstĭlädŏr',* sm. distiller; filtering-stone; alembic.

destilar, *dĕstĭlär',* v. a. & n. to distil.

destilatorio, *dĕstĭlätŏ'rĭŏ,* sm. distillery; alembic. [intend for.

destinar, *dĕstĭnär',* v. a. to destine for, to

destino, *dĕstĭ'nŏ,* sm. destiny; fate, doom; destination; office. [abandonment.

destitución, *dĕstĭtŭthĭŏn',* sf. destitution.

destituir, *dĕstĭtŭĭr',* v. a. to deprive.

destocar, –*tŏkär',* v. a. to uncoif; to uncover the head.

destorcer, –*tŏrthĕr',* v. a. to untwist; to uncurl; (fig.) to arrange, to put in order; –se, (mar.) to deviate from one's course.

destornillador, –*tŏrnĭlyädŏr',* sm. screwdriver. [(fig.) to act or speak rashly.

destornillar, –*tŏrnĭlyär',* v. a. to unscrew;

destrabar, –*träbär',* v. a. to unfetter; (fig.) to separate.

destramar, –*trämär',* v. a. to unweave; to break off an intrigue. [tress of hair.

destrenzar, –*trĕnthär',* v. a. to undo a

destreza, *dĕstrĕ'thä,* sf. dexterity, cleverness, cunning, expertness, skill.

destripar, –*trĭpär',* v. a. to unbowel; to disembowel; to trample.

destripaterrones, –*trĭpätĕrrŏ'nĕs,* sm. day-labourer, harrower, clod-beater.

destripular, –*trĭpŭlär',* v. a. to unrig a ship. [all the trumps at cards.

destriunfar, –*trĭŭnfär',* v. a. to extract

destrocar, –*trŏkär',* v. a. to return a thing bartered.

destrón, *dĕstrŏn',* sm. blind man's guide.

destronamiento, –*trŏnämĭĕn'tŏ,* sm. dethronement.

destronar, –*trŏnär',* v. a. to dethrone.

destroncar, –*trŏnkär',* v. a. to lop, to cut short; to maim, to cut to pieces; (fig.) to ruin, to frustrate.

destrozar, –*trŏthär',* v. a. to destroy, to break into pieces; (mil.) to defeat.

destrozo, *–tró' tho*, sm. destruction; (mil.) defeat, massacre. [ruin.

destrucción, *–trŭkthĭŏn'*, sf. destruction.

destructivo,va, *–trŭktĭ' vŏ*, a. destructive.

destrueque, *–trŭĕ' kĕ*, sm. mutual restitution of things bartered *or* exchanged.

destruir, *–trŭĭr'*, v. a. to destroy.

desuellacaras, *dĕsŭĕlyăkă' răs*, sm. impudent, wicked person.

desuello, *–sŭĕl' yŏ*, sm. (fam.) flaying; impudence; exorbitant price.

desuncir, *dĕsŭnthĭr'*, v. a. to unyoke.

desunión, *–ŭnĭŏn'*, sf. separation, disjunction; discord, dissension.

desunir, *–ŭnĭr'*, v. a. to separate, to disunite; to occasion discord.

desurdir, *–ŭrdĭr'*, v. a. to unweave cloth.

desusar, *–ŭsăr'*, v. a. to disuse.

desuso, *–dĕsŭ' sŏ*, sm. disuse; obsoleteness.

desvahar, *–văăr'*, v. a. to trim off the withered part of a plant. [less.

desvaído, da, *–văĭ' dŏ*, a. tall and graceful.

desvalido, da, *–vălĭ' dŏ*, a. helpless, destitute.

desván, *dĕsvăn'*, sm. garret. [stitute.

desvanecer, *–vănĕthĕr'*, v. n. to divide into imperceptible parts; to cause to vanish; to undo, to remove; to swell with pride; **–se**, to grow vapid, to become insipid; to vanish; to be affected with giddiness.

desvanecido, *–vănĕthĭ' dŏ*, a. giddy; proud.

desvanecimiento, *–vănĕthĕmĭĕn'tŏ*, sm. pride, haughtiness; giddiness; swoon.

desvarío, *–vărĭ' ŏ*, sm. delirium; giddiness; inconstancy, caprice; extravagance.

desvedar, *–vĕdăr'*, v. a. to revoke a prohibition against a thing.

desvelar, *–vĕlăr'*, v. a. to keep awake; **–se**, to be watchful. [watchfulness.

desvelo, *dĕsvĕ' lŏ*, sm. want of sleep;

desvenar, *–vĕnăr'*, v. a. to clear the veins of flesh; to extract from the veins of mines.

desvencijar, *–vĕnthĭ' hăr'*, v. a. to disunite, to weaken, to divide; **–se**, to be ruptured; to be relaxed. [bandage.

desvendar, *–vĕndăr'*, v. a. to take off a bandage.

desventaja, *–vĕntă' hă*, sf. disadvantage, damage. [calamity.

desventura, *–vĕntŏ' ră*, sf. misfortune,

desventurado, da, *–vĕntŭră' dŏ*, a. unfortunate, calamitous.

desvergonzado, da, *–vĕrgŏnthă' dŏ*, a. impudent, shameless.

desvergonzarse, *–vĕrgŏnthăr' sĕ*, v. r. to speak in an impudent manner.

desvergüenza, *–vĕrgŭĕn' thă*, sf. impudence; shameless word.

desviar, *–vĭăr'*, v. a. to divert from the right way; to dissuade; to parry (at fencing).

desvío, *dĕsvĭ' ŏ*, sm. turning away, going astray; aversion; disdain; indifference.

desvirtuar, *–vĭrtŭăr'*, v. a. to pare off the superfluous part of a sole.

desvirtuar, *–vĭrtŭăr'*, v. a. to rob of virtue *or* strength.

detal, *dĕtăl'*, (en –), ad. in detail; minutely.

detallar, *dătălyăr'*, v. a. to detail, to relate minutely.

detalle, *dĕtăl' yĕ*, sm. detail.

detallista, *–vĭt' tă*, sm. retailer. [detain.

detención, *dĕtĕnthĭŏn'*, sf. detention;

detener, *dĕtĕnĕr'*, v. a. to stop, to detain; to arrest; to keep back; to reserve; to withhold; **–se**, to tarry, to stay.

detenido, da, *dĕtĕnĭ' dŏ*, a. sparing, niggardly; slow, inactive.

detentar, *dĕtĕntăr'*, v. a. to detain.

deterioración, *dĕtĕrĭŏrăthĭŏn'*, sf. deterioration, damage.

deteriorar, *dĕtĕrĭŏrăr'*, v. a. to deteriorate,

deterioro, *dĕtĕrĭŏ' rŏ*, sm. deterioration.

determinación, *dĕtĕrmĭnăthĭŏn'*, sf. determination, resolution; boldness.

determinado, da, *–nă' dŏ*, a. determinate; resolute. [mine.

determinar, *dĕtĕrmĭnăr'*, v. a. to determine.

determinativo, va, *–nătĭ' vŏ*, a. determinative. [crable.

detestable, *dĕtĕstă' blĕ*, a. detestable, execrable.

detestación, *dĕtĕstăthĭŏn'*, sf. detestation, abomination. [hor.

detestar, *dĕtĕstăr'*, v. a. to detest, to abhor.

detonación, *dĕtŏnăthĭŏn'*, sf. detonation.

detractar, *dĕtrăktăr'*, v. a. to detract, to defame, to slander.

detractor, *–tŏr'*, sm. slanderer, detracter.

detractora, *–tŏ' ră*, sf. detractress.

detrás, *dĕtrăs'*, ad. behind; behind one's back, in the absence of.

detrimento, *dĕtrĭmĕn' tŏ*, sm. detriment, damage, loss.

deuda, *dĕ' ŭdă*, sf. debt; fault; offence.

deudo, da, *dĕ' ŭdŏ*, a. parent; kindred.

deudor, ra, *dĕŭdŏr'*, sm. & f. debtor.

Deuteronomio, *dĕŭtĕrŏnŏ' mĭŏ*, sm. Deuteronomy.

devanadera, *dĕvănădă' ră*, sf. reel; movable decoration on the stage.

devanador, ra, *–dŏr'*, sm. & f. winder; quill, bit of paper or other thing, on which yarn is wound into a clew. [up.

devanar, *dĕvănăr'*, v. a. to reel; to wrap

devanear, *dĕvănĕăr'*, v. n. to rave, to talk nonsense; to dote. [pursuit.

devaneo, *dĕvănĕ' ŏ*, sm. delirium; idle pursuit.

devantal, *dĕvăntăl'*, sm. apron.

devastación, *dĕvăstăthĭŏn'*, sf. devastation, desolation.

devastador, *–dŏr'*, a. desolater, devastator, harasser, spoiler. [waste.

devastar, *dĕvăstăr'*, v. a. to desolate, to waste.

devengar, *dĕvĕngăr'*, v. a. to deserve.

devoción, *dĕvŏthĭŏn'*, sf. devotion, piety; strong affection, ardent love. [book.

devocionario, *dĕvŏthĭŏnă' rĭŏ*, sm. prayer-book.

devolución, *dĕvŏlŭthĭŏn'*, sf. (law) devolution. [devolutive.

devolutivo, *–tĭ' vŏ*, a. (law) transferable,

devolver, *dĕvŏlvĕr'*, v. a. (law) to return a cause to an inferior court to be tried anew; to restore a thing to its former possessor.

devorar, *dĕvŏrăr*, v. a. to devour, to swallow up.

devotero, *-tĕrŏ*, sm. pilgrim.

devoto, ta, *dĕvŏ'tŏ*, a. devout, pious, devotional; strongly attached.

dezmar, *dĕthmăr*, v. a. to tithe.

día, *dĕ'ă*, sm. day; - de años, birth-day.

diabla (á la -), *dĕ'ă blă*, ad. carelessly; rudely.   [man.

diablillo, *dĕăblĭl'yŏ*, sm. acute, clever

diablo, *dĕă'blŏ*, sm. devil, Satan; person of a perverse temper; ugly, cunning or subtle person.   [taking; devilishness.

diablura, *dĕăblŭ'ră*, sf. diabolical under-

diabólico, ca, *dĕăbŏ'lĭkŏ*, a. diabolical, devilish.   [served in sugar.

diacitrón, *-thĭtrŏn'*, sm. lemon-peel pre-

diaconato, *dĕăkŏnă'tŏ*, sm. deaconship.

diaconisa, *dĕăkŏnĭ'să*, sm. deaconess.

diácono, *dĕ'ăkŏnŏ*, sm. deacon.   [halo.

diadema, *dĕădĕ'mă*, sm. & f. diadem;

diafanidad, *-fănĭdăd'*, sf. transparency, pellucidness.

diáfano, na, *dĕ'ăfănŏ*, a. diaphanous, transparent, pellucid.   [mid-riff.

diafragma, *dĕăfrăg'mă*, sm. diaphragm,

diagnóstico, *dĕăgnŏs'tĭkŏ*, sm. diagnosis; -, ca, a. diagnostic.

diagonal, *dĕăgŏnăl'*, a. diagonal.

dialéctica, *dĕălĕk'tĭkă*, sf. logic, dialectic.

dialéctico, *dĕălĕk'tĭkŏ*, sm. logician; -, ca, a. dialectical, logical.

dialecto, *dĕălĕk'tŏ*, sm. dialect.

dialogismo, *-lŏ'hĭs'mŏ*, sm. dialogism.

diálogo, *dĕă'lŏgŏ*, sm. dialogue.

diamante, *dĕămăn'tĕ*, sm. diamond; hardness, resistance; - tabla, diamond-cut into angles.

diamantino, na, *-măntĭ'nŏ*, a. adamantine.

diamantista, *-măntĭs'tă*, sm. lapidary.

diametral, *dĕămĕtrăl'*, a. diametrical, diametral.

diámetro, *dĕă'mĕtrŏ*, sm. diameter.

diana, *dĕă'nă*, sf. (mil.) reveille, the beating of the drum at day-break.

diantre, *dĕăn'trĕ*, sm. the deuce, devil.

diapasón, *dĕăpăsŏn'*, sm. (mus.) diapason, octave.

diario, *dĕă'rĭŏ*, sm. journal, diary; daily newspaper; daily expense; -, ria, a. daily.

diarista, *-rĭs'tă*, sm. journalist.

diarrea, *dĕărrĕ'ă*, sf. diarrhœa.

diatónico, *dĕătŏ'nĭkŏ*, a. (mus.) diatonic.

diatriba, *dĕătrĭ'bă*, sf. diatribe.

dibujador, *-hădŏr'*, a. designer.

dibujar, *-hăr'*, v. a. to draw, to design; to paint any passion of the mind.

dibujo, *dĕbŭ'hŏ*, sm. drawing, sketch, draught; description.   [pression.

dicción, *dĭkthĭŏn'*, sf. diction, style, ex-

diccionario, *dĭkthĭŏnă'rĭŏ*, sm. dictionary.

diciembre, *dĭthĭĕm'brĕ*, sm. December.

dictado, *dĭktă'dŏ*, sm. a title of dignity or honour.

dictador, *dĭktădŏr'*, sm. dictator.

dictadura, *-dŏ'ră*, sf. dictatorship.

dictamen, *dĭktă'mĕn*, sm. opinion, notion; suggestion, insinuation.

dictar, *dĭktăr'*, v. a. to dictate.   [insult.

dicterio, *dĭktĕ'rĭŏ*, sm. sarcasm, taunt,

dicha, *dĭtsh'ă*, sf. happiness, good fortune; por -, á -, by chance.   [sion.

dicharacho, *-rătsh'ŏ*, sm. vulgar expres-

dicho, *dĭtsh'ŏ*, sm. saying, sentence; declaration; promise of marriage; -, cha, a. said.   [ous.

dichoso, sa, *dĭtshŏ'sŏ*, a. happy, prosperous.

diente, *dĭĕn'tĕ*, sm. tooth; fang, tusk; jag.

diestra, *dĭĕs'tră*, sf. right hand; (fig.) favour, support, protection.

diestro, tra, *dĭĕs'trŏ*, a. right; dexterous, skilful, clever; sagacious, prudent; sly, cunning; favourable, propitious; -, sm. skilful fencer; halter, bridle.

dieta, *dĭĕ'tă*, sf. diet, regimen; diet, assembly; daily salary of judges; -s, pl. cattle put on board a fleet to furnish fresh provisions for the sick.

diez, *dĭĕth'*, a. & sm. ten; - de rosario, each tenth bead of a rosary.

diezmar, *dĭĕthmăr'*, v. a. to decimate; to tithe; to take the tenth.

diezmero, *-mĕ'rŏ*, sm. tithe-payer.   [old.

diezmesino, na, *-mĕsĭ'nŏ*, a. ten months

diezmo, *dĭĕth'mŏ*, sm. tithe; -, ma, a. tenth.

difamación, *dĭfămăthĭŏn'*, sf. defamation.

difamar, *dĭfămăr'*, v. a. to defame, to libel.

difamatorio, ria, *dĭfămătŏ'rĭŏ*, a. defamatory, calumnious.

diferencia, *dĭfĕrĕn'thĭă*, sf. difference; á -, with the difference; -s, pl. controversies, disputes.   [ent.

diferencial, *-thĭăl'*, a. differential, differ-

diferenciar, *-thĭăr'*, v. a. to differ, to differenciate; -se, to differ, to distinguish oneself.

diferente, *dĭfĕrĕn'tĕ*, a. different, unlike.

diferir, *dĭfĕrĭr'*, v. a. to defer, to put off; to differ.   [to differ.

difícil, *dĭfĭ'thĭl*, a. difficult.

dificultad, *dĭfĭkŭltăd'*, sf. difficulty.

dificultar, *-kŭltăr'*, v. a. to raise difficulties; to render difficult.   [painful.

dificultoso, sa, *-kŭltŏ'sŏ*, a. difficult;

difidencia, *dĭfĭdĕn'thĭă*, sf. diffidence.

difidente, *-tĕ*, a. diffident, disloyal.

difundir, *dĭfŭndĭr'*, v. a. to diffuse, to outspread; to divulge.   [late.

difunto, ta, *dĭfŭn'tŏ*, a. dead, deceased.

difusión, *dĭfŭsĭŏn'*, sf. diffusion.

difusivo, va, *dĭfŭsĭ'vŏ*, a. diffusive.

difuso, sa, *dĭfŭ'sŏ*, a. diffusive, copious; large; prolix, circumstantial.

digerible, *dĭhĕrĭ'blĕ*, a. digestible.

digerir, *dĭhĕrĭr'*, v. a. to digest; to bear with patience; to adjust; to arrange; (chem.) to digest.

digestible, *dĭhĕstĭ'blĕ*, a. digestible.

digestión, *dĭhĕstĭŏn'*, sf. digestion, concoction.

digestivo, va, *dĭhĕstĭ'vŏ*, a. digestive.

dignación, *dĭgnăthĭŏn'*, sf. condescension.

dignarse, *dĭgnăr'sĕ*, v. r. to condescend, to deign.

7 *

dignidad, *dignidád'*, sf. dignity, rank; grandeur of mien; prebend of a cathedral superior to a simple canonry, and the dignitary who possesses it.

digno, na, *dig'nó*, a. meritorious, worthy; suitable, correspondent.

digresión, *digresión'*, sf. digression; departure of a planet from the equinoctial line.

dij, *dī'h*, **dije**, *dī'Ñé*, sm. relic; trinket fastened to children's clothes; —es, pl. toys.

dilacerar, *dilāthérár'*, v. a. to dilacerate.

dilación, *dilāthión'*, sf. delay.

dilapidar, *dilāpidár'*, v. a. to dilapidate.

dilatable, *dilātā'blé*, a. dilatable.

dilatación, *dilātāthión'*, sf. dilatation, extension; greatness of mind; calmness.

dilatado, da, *dilātā'dó*, a. large, numerous; prolix; spacious, extensive.

dilatar, *dilātár'*, v. a. to dilate, to expand; to spread out; to defer, to protract; to comfort, to cheer up; —se, to expatiate; to speak largely and copiously. [dilates.

dilatativo, va, *—tātī'vó*, a. that which dilates.

dilatorio, ria, *—tō'rió*, a. dilatory.

dilección, *dilékthión'*, sf. dilection, love, affection, good will.

dilecto, to, *dilék'tó*, a. loved, beloved.

dilema, *dilē'mā*, sm. dilemma.

diligencia, *dilī'hén'thiá*, sf. diligence; affair, business; call to ease nature; stagecoach. [self, to endeavour.

diligenciar, *—thiár'*, v. a. to exert oneself.

diligenciero, *—thié'ró*, sm. agent; apparitor. [prompt, swift.

diligente, *dilī'hén'té*, a. diligent, assiduous.

dilucidación, *dilūthidāthión'*, sf. explanation, illustration. [plain.

dilucidar, *—dár'*, v. a. to elucidate, to explain.

dilucidario, *—dā'rió*, sm. explanatory writing.

diluviano, *dilūviā'nó*, a. diluvian.

diluviar, *dilūviár'*, v. n. imp. to rain like a deluge. [vast abundance.

diluvio, *dilū'vió*, sm. deluge, inundation; dimanación, *dimānāthión'*, sf. emanation.

dimanar, *dimānár'*, v. n. to spring from; to originate, to flow.

dimensión, *dimensión'*, sf. dimension; dimensity, extent, capacity, bulk.

dimes, *dē'més*, sm. pl. andar en — y diretes, to use ifs and ands, to contend.

diminución, *diminūthión'*, sf. diminution; contraction of the diameter of a column as it ascends. [tively; by retail.

diminutamente, *—tāmén'té*, ad. diminutively.

diminutivo, va, *—tī'vó*, a. a diminutive.

diminuto, ta, *diminō'tó*, a. defective, faulty, small.

dimisión, *dimisión'*, sf. dimission.

dimisorias, *dimisō'riás*, sf. pl. dimissory letters. [dicate.

dimitir, *dimitír'*, v. a. to give up, to abdinámica, *dinā'mikā*, sf. dynamics.

dínamo, *dinā'mó*, sm. dynamo (electric dinastía, *dināstī'ā*, sf. dynasty. [engine).

dineral, *dinerál'*, sm. large sum of money.

dinero, *dinē'ró*, sm. coin, money, coinage.

---

dingolondangos, *dingólóndán'gós*, sm. pl. showy ornaments on women.

diocesano, na, *diothésā'nó*, a. diocesan.

diócesis, *diō'thesīs*, sf. diocese.

Dios, *diós'*, sm. God; any person or thing passionately beloved or adored; á —, farewell, adieu; á — y á ventura, at all risks.

diosa, *diō'sā*, sf. goddess. [risks.

diploma, *diplō'mā*, sm. diploma, patent.

diplomacia, *diplōmā'thiā*, sf. diplomática, *diplōmā'tikā*, sf. diplomacy.

diplomático, ca, *—mā'tikó*, a. diplomatic.

diplomatizar, *—mātithár'*, v. a. to act the diplomatist.

diptongo, *diptón'gó*, sm. diphthong.

diputación, *diputāthión'*, sf. deputation; object of a deputation.

diputado, *—tā'dó*, sm. deputy. [stitute.

diputar, *diputár'*, v. a. to depute; to condique, *dī'ké*, sm. dike, dam, mole.

dirección, *dirékthión'*, sf. direction; guidance, administration.

directivo, va, *—tī'vó*, a. directive.

directo, ta, *dirék'tó*, a. direct, straight; apparent, evident.

director, *diréktór'*, sm. director; conductor; president; manager.

directora, *—tō'rā*, sf. directress, governess.

directorio, ria, *—tō'rió*, a. directive, directorial; —, sm. directory.

dirigir, *dirīhír'*, v. a. to direct; to conduct; to dedicate a work; to regulate, to govern; —se, to address oneself.

dirimente, *dirimén'té*, a. breaking off, dissolving.

dirimir, *dirīmír'*, v. a. to dissolve, to separate; to accommodate differences.

discernimiento, *disthérnimién'tó*, sm. discernment; appointment of a guardian by the proper magistrates.

discernir, *disthérnír'*, v. a. to discern, to distinguish; to appoint a guardian.

disciplina, *disthiplī'nā*, sf. discipline.

disciplinante, *—plinán'té*, sm. flagellator.

disciplinar, *—plinár'*, v. a. to discipline.

discípulo, *disthī'pūló*, sm. disciple, scholar.

disco, *dis'kó*, sm. disk; face of the sun or moon; lens of a telescope; (rail.) disk, signal-disk. [peevish.

díscolo, la, *dis'kóló*, a. ungovernable;

discordancia, *diskórdán'thiā*, sf. disagreement, discordance. [cordant.

discordante, *—dán'té*, a. dissonant, dis-

discordar, *—kórdár'*, v. n. to discord, to disagree. [dissonant.

discorde, *diskór'dé*, a. discordant; (mus.)

discordia, *—kór'diā*, sf. discord, disagreement; contrariety of opinion.

discreción, *—krethión'*, sf. discretion; acuteness of mind, sharpness of wit; á —, at the will of another.

discrepar, *—krepár'*, v. n. to differ.

discreto, ta, *diskrē'tó*, a. discreet; ingenious, witty, eloquent.

disculpa, *—kūl'pā*, sf. apology, excuse.

disculpar, *—kūlpár'*, v. a. to exculpate, to excuse, to acquit, to absolve.

discurrir, *-kŭrrir'* v. n. to ramble about, to run to and fro; to discourse upon a subject; to discuss; —, v. a. to invent, to contrive; to meditate. [contemplative.

discursivo, *-kŭr sē'vō*, a. discursive.

discurso, *-kūr sō*, sm. discourse; ratiocination; discourse, conversation; dissertation; space of time.

discusión, *diskūsēōn'*, sf. discussion.

discutir, *-kūtir'*, v. a. to discuss.

disecar, *disēkar'*, v. a. to dissect. [tomy.

disección, *-sēkthōn'*, sf. dissection, anatomy.

disector, *-sēktōr'*, sm. dissector, anatomist.

diseminar, *disēminar'*, v. a. to scatter as seed; to disseminate, to propagate.

disensión, *disensōn'*, sf. dissension, misunderstanding, contest, strife; cause of dissension.

disentería, *disēntērē'ā*, sf. dysentery.

disentimiento, *disēntimiēn'tō*, sm. dissent, disagreement. [agree.

disentir, *disentir'*, v. n. to dissent, to disdiseñador, *disēnyādōr'*, sm. designer.

diseñar, *disēnyar'*, v. a. to draw, to design.

diseño, *disēn'yō*, sm. design, draught; description; picture. [discussion.

disertación, *disērtāthōn'*, sf. dissertation.

disertar, *disērtar'*, v. a. to dispute, to debate, to argue. [favour.

disfavor, *-favōr'*, sm. disregard, want of

disforme, *-fō ̄r'mē*, a. ugly, monstrous, formless; huge. [querade; dissimulation.

disfraz, *-frāth'*, sm. mask, disguise; mas-

disfrazar, *-frāthar'*, v. a. to disguise, to conceal; to cloak, to dissemble.

disfrutar, *-frŭtar'*, v. a. to enjoy.

disfrute, *-frō'tē*, sm. enjoyment.

disgustar, *-gŭstar'*, v. a. to disgust; to offend; —se, to be displeased, to fall out.

disgusto, *disgŭs'tō*, sm. disgust, aversion; ill-humour; grief, sorrow; á —, in spite of.

disidente, *disidēn'tē*, a. & s. dissident, dissenter. [lation; hypocrisy.

disimulación, *disimŭlāthōn'*, sf. dissimulation

disimulado, *da*, *-mŭlā'dō*, a. reserved, dissembled; á lo —, dissemblingly; reservedly. [cloak; to hide; to tolerate.

disimular, *-mŭlar'*, v. a. to dissemble; to

disimulo, *disimŭ'lō*, sm. dissimulation.

disipación, *disipāthōn'*, sf. dissipation; (chem.) resolution into component parts; resolution into vapour.

disipado, *da*, *-pā'dō*, a. prodigal, lavish.

disipador, *ra*, *-pādōr'*, sm. & f. spendthrift. [perse; to scatter; to lavish.

disipar, *disipar'*, v. a. to dissipate, to dis-

dislate, *dislā'tē*, sm. nonsense, absurdity.

dislocación, *-lōkāthōn'*, sf. dislocation.

dislocarse, *-lōkar'sē*, v. r. to be dislocated or put out of joint.

disminuir, *-minŭir'*, v. a. to diminish.

disoluble, *-sōlŭ'blē*, a. dissoluble.

disolución, *-sōlŭthōn'*, sf. dissolution; lewdness, licentiousness.

disolutivo, *va*, *-sōlŭtē'vō*, a. dissolvent.

disoluto, *ta*, *-sōlŭ'tō*, a. dissolute, licentious, lewd.

disolver, *-sōlvēr'*, v. a. to loosen, to untie; to dissolve, to disunite; to melt, to liquefy; to interrupt. [disagreement, discord.

disonancia, *-sōnān'thiā*, sf. dissonance.

disonante, *-sōnān'tē*, a. dissonant, inharmonious; (fig.) discordant.

disonar, *-sōnar'*, v. n. to disagree in sound; to disagree; to be repugnant.

disono, *na*, *dē'sōnō*, a. dissonant.

dispar, *dispar'*, a. unlike, unequal, different

disparador, *-pārādōr'*, sm. shooter; trigger of a gun-lock.

disparar, *-pārar'*, v. a. & n. to shoot, to discharge, to fire; to let off; to throw with violence; to talk nonsense; —se, to run headlong; to stoop, to dart down upon a prey. [sistent, absurd, extravagant.

disparatado, *da*, *-pārātā'dō*, a. incon-

disparatar, *-pārātar'*, v. a. to extravagate; to talk nonsense. [dity, extravagance.

disparate, *-pār ā'tē*, sm. nonsense, absur-

disparidad, *-pāridād'*, sf. disparity, inequality.

disparo, *-pā'rō*, sm. discharge, explosion.

dispasto(s), *-pās'tō(s)*, sm. pulley, tackle-block.

dispendio, *-pēn'diō*, sm. extravagant expense; voluntary loss of life, honour or fame.

dispendioso, *sa*, *-pēndiō'sō*, a. costly, expensive. [granting a dispensation.

dispensa, *-pēn'sā*, sf. dispense; diploma

dispensable, *-pēnsā'blē*, a. dispensable.

dispensación, *-pēnsāthōn'*, sf. dispensation, exemption. [distributer.

dispensador, *-pēnsādōr'*, sm. dispenser;

dispensar, *-pēnsar'*, v. a. to dispense; to excuse, to dispense with; to distribute.

dispersión, *-pērsōn'*, sf. dispersion.

disperso, *sa*, *dispēr'sō*, a. dispersed.

displicencia, *-plithēn'thiā*, sf. displeasure, dislike. [offensive; angry, fretful.

displicente, *-plithēn'tē*, a. displeasing,

disponer, *-pōnēr'*, v. a. & n. to arrange; to dispose, to prepare; to dispose of; to resolve.

disponible, *-pōn'blē*, a. disposable.

disposición, *-pōsithōn'*, sf. disposition, ordering; proportion; resolution; command; power, authority.

dispositivo, *va*, *-pōstē'vō*, a. dispositive.

dispuesto, *ta*, *dispūēs'tō*, a. disposed, fit, ready; bien —, quite well; mal —, indisposed, ill.

disputa, *dispō'tā*, sf. dispute, controversy.

disputable, *-pūtā'blē*, a. disputable, controvertible.

disputador, *-dōr'*, sm. disputant, disputer.

disputar, *dispūtar'*, v. a. & n. to dispute, to controvert, to question; to debate, to argue.

distancia, *distān'thiā*, sf. distance, interval; difference.

distante, *distān'tē*, a. distant, far off.

distar, *distar'*, v. n. to be distant; to be different.

dístico, *dis'tikō*, sm. distich. [different.

distinción, *distinthōn'*, sf. distinction; difference; prerogative; á —, in contradistinction.

distinguido, da, *–tĭng´dŏ,* a. distinguished, conspicuous.

distinguir, *–tĭngĭr´,* v. a. to distinguish; to see clearly and at a distance; to discern, to set a peculiar value on things. or persons; *–se,* to distinguish oneself.

distintivo, *–tĭnt´vŏ,* sm. distinctive mark; particular attribute.   [clear.

distinto, ta, *–tĭn´tŏ,* a. distinct, different; want of attention.

distracción, *–tràkthĭŏn´,* sf. distraction, want of attention.

distraer, *–tràĕr´,* v. a. to distract; *–se,* to be absent-minded, to be inattentive.

distraído, da, *–tràĭ´dŏ,* a. absent, inattentive; dissolute, licentious.

distribución, *–trĭbūthĭŏn´,* sf. distribution, division, separation; arrangement.

distribuidor, *–trĭbūĭdŏr´,* sm. distributer.

distribuir, *–trĭbūĭr´,* v. a. to distribute, to dispose; to distribute type.   [tive.

distributivo, va, *–trĭbūtĭ´vŏ,* a. distributive.

distrito, *distrĭ´tŏ,* sm. district; territory.

disturbar, *–tūrbàr´,* v. a. to disturb, to interrupt.   [interruption.

disturbio, *–tūr´bĭŏ,* sm. disturbance.

disuadir, *dĭsūàdĭr´,* v. a. to dissuade.

disuasión, *dĭsūàsĭŏn´,* sf. dissuasion.

disyunción, *–yūnthĭŏn´,* sf. disjunction; (gr.) disjunctive particle.   [key.

disyunta, *–yūn´tà,* sf. (mus.) change of key.

disyuntivo, va, *–yūntĭ´vŏ,* a. disjunctive.

diurno, na, *dĭūr´nŏ,* a. diurnal; daily; *–,* sm. prayer-book.

diuturnidad, *dĭūtūrnĭdàd´,* sf. diuturnity.   [ing.

diuturno, na, *–tūr´nŏ,* a. diturnal, lasting.

diva, *dē´và,* sf. a celebrated songstress.

diván, *dĭvàn´,* sm. Divan (supreme council among the Turks).   [gence.

divergencia, *dĭvĕrhĕn´thĭà,* sf. divergence.

divergente, *–´hĕn´tĕ,* a. divergent.

diversidad, *–vĕrsĭdàd´,* sf. diversity, variety of things.   [sify, to vary.

diversificar, *–sĭfĭkàr´,* v. a. to diversify.

diversión, *–vĕrsĭŏn´,* sf. diversion; sport, amusement; (mil.) diversion.

diverso, sa, *–vĕr´sŏ,* a. diverse, different; several, sundry.   [ing.

divertido, da, *–tĭ´dŏ,* a. amused; amusing.

divertimiento, *–tĭmĭĕn´tŏ,* sm. diversion, amusement, pastime, sport.

divertir, *dĭvĕrtĭr´,* v. a. to divert (the attention); to amuse, to entertain; (mil.) to draw the enemy off from some design; *–se,* to sport, to dally.   [dividend.

dividendo, *dĭvĭdĕn´dŏ,* sm. (ar. & com.) dividend.

dividir, *dĭvĭdĭr´,* v. a. to divide, to disunite, to separate; *–se,* to break up a friendship.

divieso, *dĭvĭĕ´sŏ,* sm. (med.) furuncle.

divinidad, *–vĭnĭdàd´,* sf. divinity; Supreme Being; false god; woman of exquisite beauty.   [sanctify.

divinizar, *–nĭthàr´,* v. a. to deify; to sanctify.

divino, na, *dĭvē´nŏ,* a. divine, heavenly, excellent.

divisa, *dĭvē´sà,* sf. posy, motto, device.

divisar, *dĭvĭsàr´,* v. a. to perceive indistinctly; to vary.

divisible, *–sĭ´blĕ,* a. divisible.

división, *–sĭŏn´,* sf. division; partition; separation; difference; (gr.) hyphen.

divisor, *–sŏr´,* sm. (ar.) divisor.

divisorio, ria, *–sŏ´rĭŏ,* a. divisive.

divorciar, *dĭvŏrthĭàr´,* v. a. to pronounce a sentence of divorce; to divorce, to separate; *–se,* to be divorced.

divorcio, *dĭvŏr´thĭŏ,* sm. divorce; separation, disunion.   [tion, publication.

divulgación, *dĭvūlgàthĭŏn´,* sf. divulgation.

divulgar, *–gàr´,* v. a. to publish, to divulge.   [divulge.

dobela, *dŏbē´là,* sf. key-stone.

dobladillo, lla, *dŏblàdĭl´yŏ,* a. squat and broad; *–,* sm. hem.

doblado, *dŏblà´dŏ,* sm. measure of the fold in cloth; *–, da,* a. robust, thickset; deceitful, dissembling.

dobladura, *dŏrà´dà,* sf. fold.

doblar, *dŏblàr´,* v. a. & n. to double, to fold; to bend; to ring the passing-bell; *–se,* to bend, to bow, to submit.

doble, *dŏ´blĕ,* a. double; thick and short, robust; artful, deceitful; al *–,* doubly; *–,* sm. passing-bell.   [curvate.

doblegar, *dŏblĕgàr´,* v. a. to bend, to indoblete.

doblete, *dŏblē´tĕ,* a. false jewel; double taffety.   [& f. duplicity.

doblez, *dŏblĕth´,* sm. crease; fold; *–,* sm.

doblón, *dŏblŏn´,* sm. doubloon.

doce, *dŏ´thĕ,* a. & sm. twelve.

docena, *dŏthē´nà,* sf. dozen.

docenal, *dŏthĕnàl´,* a. sold by the dozen.

doceno, na, *dŏthē´nŏ,* a. twelfth.

dócil, *dŏth´ĭl,* a. docile, tractable.

docilidad, *dŏthĭlĭdàd´,* sf. docility, compliance, gentleness.

docto, ta, *dŏk´tŏ,* a. learned.

doctor, *dŏktŏr´,* sm. doctor; physician.

doctora, *–tŏ´rà,* sf. doctoress; wife of a physician or doctor.   [ship.

doctorado, *–rà´dŏ,* sm. doctorate, doctorship.

doctoral, *–ràl´,* a. doctoral; *–,* sf. canonry called doctoral in the Spanish cathedrals; *–,* sm. canon of the doctoral.

doctorando, *–ràn´dŏ,* sm. one who is on the point of taking out his degrees as doctor.   [doctor.

doctorear, *dŏktŏrĕàr´,* v. n. to play the doctor.

doctrina, *dŏktrē´nà,* sf. doctrine, instruction; science; discourse on the tenets of the Christian faith.   [doctrinal.

doctrinal, *–trĭnàl´,* sm. catechism; *–,* a.

doctrinar, *–trĭnàr´,* v. a. to teach, to instruct.   [muniment, record.

documento, *dŏkūmĕn´tŏ,* sm. document; muniment, record.

dogal, *dŏgàl´,* sm. rope tied round the neck of asses, mules, &c.

dogma, *dŏg´mà,* sm. dogma.

dogmático, ca, *dŏgmà´tĭkŏ,* a. dogmatical.

dogmatista, *–tĭs´tà,* sm. dogmatist.

dogmatizador, *–tĭthàdŏr´,* dogmatizante, *–tĭthàn´tĕ,* sm. dogmatizer. dogmatist.

dogmatizar, *–tĭthàr´,* v. a. to dogmatize.

dogo, *dŏ´gŏ,* sm. terrier.

dolencia, *dōlĕn'thĭă,* sf. disease, affliction.

doler, *dōlĕr',* v. a. to feel pain; to ache; to be repugnant; to be sorry; to repent; to feel for the sufferings of others; to complain. [ful.

doliente, *dōlĭĕn'tĕ,* a. suffering; sorrow-

dolo, *dō'lō,* sm. fraud, deceit. [filiction.

dolor, *dōlōr',* sm. pain, aching; ache; af-

dolorido, da, *dōlōrē'dō,* a. afflicted, painful, heart-sick; —, sm. chief mourner, the nearest relation of a person deceased.

doloroso, sa, *dōlōrō'so,* a. sorrowful, afflicted, dolorous, dismal; painful.

doloso, sa, *dōlō'sō,* a. deceitful, knavish.

domable, *dōmä'blĕ,* a. tameable.

domador, ra, *dōmädōr',* sm. & f. tamer; subduer; horsebreaker.

domadura, *dōmädō'ră,* sf. taming, subduing.

domar, *dōmär',* v. a. to tame; to subdue, to master. [able, to tame.

domeñar, *dōmĕnyär',* v. a. to make tract-

domesticable, *dōmĕstĭkä'blĕ,* a. tameable.

domesticar, *-tĭkär',* v. a. to domesticate.

domesticidad, *-tĭthĭdäd',* sf. domesticity; affability; servants, domestics, pl.

doméstico, ca, *dōmĕs'tĭkō,* a. domestical; —, sm. domestic, menial. [filiated.

domiciliado, *dōmĭthĭlĭä'dō,* a. domi-

domiciliarse, *-lĭär'sĕ,* v. r. to establish oneself in a residence.

domicilio, *dōmĭthĭ'lĭō,* sm. habitation, domicile, home, abode.

dominación, *dōmĭnäthĭōn',* sf. dominion, authority, power; —ones, pl. dominations (some angelic beings).

dominador, *-nädōr',* sm. dominator.

dominante, *-nän'tĕ,* a. dominant, domineering. [moderate one's passions.

dominar, *dōmĭnär',* v. a. to domineer; to

dómine, *dō'mĭnĕ,* sm. grammarian.

domingo, *dōmĭn'gō,* sm. Sunday.

dominguero, ra, *-gä'rō,* a. done or worn on Sunday.

dominguillo, *-gēl'yō,* sm. figure of a boy made of straw, and used at bull-fights to frighten the bulls.

dominica, *dōmĭnĭ'kä,* sf. Sunday (in ecclesiastical language).

dominical, *-nĭkäl',* a. manorial; dominical. [of Saint Dominic.

dominico, ca, *-nĭ'kō,* sm. friar of the order

dominio, *dōmĭ'nĭō,* sm. dominion, domination, power, authority; domain.

dominó, *dōmĭnō',* sm. domino (a masquerade garment). [gentleman.)

Don, *dōn,* sm. Don (the Spanish title for a

donación, *dōnäthĭōn',* sf. donation, gift.

donado, *dōnä'dō,* sm. & f. lay-brother; lay-sister. [stower, giver.

donador, ra, *-dōr',* sm. & f. donor, be-

donaire, *dōnä'rĕ,* sm. grace, elegance; witty saying.

donar, *dōnär',* v. a. to make free gifts, to bestow. [pient.

donatario, *dōnätä'rĭō,* sm. donee, reci-

donativo, *-tē'vō,* sm. free contribution.

doncel, *dōnthĕl',* sm. king's page.

doncella, *-thĕl'yä,* sf. virgin, maiden; lady's-maid. [maidenhood.

doncelles, *-thĕlyĕth',* sf. virginity.

donde, *dōn'dĕ,* ad. where; — quiera, anywhere; ¿de dónde? whence? ¿por dónde? by what way? for what reason?

dondiego de noche, *dōndĭĕgō dĕ nōtsh'ĕ,* sm. (bot.) jalap.

donillero, *dōnĭlyä'rō,* sm. swindler, sharper; cheat. [comely.

donoso, sa, *dōnō'sō,* a. gay, witty; pleasant,

doña, *dōn'yä,* sf. lady, mistress.

doquier, *dōkĭĕr',* doquiera, *dōkĭä'rä,* ad. anywhere.

dorada, *dōrä'dä,* doradilla, *-dīl'yä,* sf. gilt-head, gilt-poll (fish).

doradillo, *-dīl'yō,* sm. fine brass wire; wagtail.

dorado, da, *dōrä'dō,* a. gilt; —, sm. gilding.

dorador, *-dōr',* sm. gilder.

doradura, *-dō'rä,* sf. gilding.

dorar, *dōrär',* v. a. to gild; (fig.) to palliate.

dórico, ca, *dō'rĭkō,* a. Doric.

dormidero, ca, *dōrmĭdä'rō,* a. sleepy, soporific; —, sm. place where cattle repose.

dormidor, *-dōr',* sm. great sleeper.

dormilón, ona, *-lōn',* sm. dull, sleepy person. [fall asleep.

dormir, *dōrmēr',* v. n. to sleep; -se, to

dormitar, *dōrmĭtär',* v. n. to doze, to be half asleep.

dormitorio, *-tō'rĭō,* sm. dormitory.

dorsal, *dōrsäl',* a. dorsal.

dorso, *dōr'sō,* sm. back.

dos, *dōs,* a. & sm. two. [hundred.

doscientos, tas, *dōsthĭĕn'tōs,* a. pl. two

dosel, *dōsĕl',* sm. canopy.

doselera, *dōsĕlä'rä,* sf. valance.

dosis, *dō'sĭs,* sf. dose, dosis.

dospuntos, *dōspūn'tōs,* sm. (gr.) colon.

dotación, *dōtäthĭōn',* sf. dotation, endowment. [donor; institutor.

dotador, ra, *-dōr',* sm. one who endows;

dotal, *dōtäl',* a. dotal. [to gift.

dotar, *dōtär',* v. a. to endow with a fortune,

dote, *dō'tĕ,* sm. & f. dower, dowry; —s, pl. gifts of nature; endowments. [curves.

dovelar, *dōvĕlär',* v. a. to hew a stone in

dovelas, *dōvĕ'läs,* sf. pl. curved sides of the key-stone of an arch.

dozavo, va, *dōthä'vō,* sm. twelfth part.

dracma, *drä'kmä,* sf. drachm.

drago, *drä'gō,* sm. dragon-tree.

dragón, *drägōn',* sm. a dragon; (mil.) dragoon; white spots in the pupils of horses' eyes. [dragon.

dragona, *drägō'nä,* sf. shoulder-knot; female

drama, *drä'mä,* sm. drama.

dramática, *drämä'tĭkä,* sf. dramatic art.

dramático, ca, *-tĭkō,* a. dramatic.

dramatizar, *-tĭzär',* v. a. to dramatize.

dríada, *drē'ädä,* dríade, *-ädĕ,* sf. dryad.

droga, *drō'gä,* sf. drug; stratagem, artifice, deceit. [drug-trade.

droguería, *drōgĕr'ē'ä,* sf. druggist's shop;

droguero, *drōgĕr'ō,* sm. druggist.

droguista, *drōgĭs'tä,* sm. druggist; cheat, impostor.

dromedario, *drŏmĕdåʹrĭŏ,* sm. dromedary.

drops, *drŏps,* sm. (rail.) dead level.

dubitativo, va, *dŭbĭtătĕʹvŏ,* a. doubtful, dubious (applied to conjunctions).

ducado, *dŭkåʹdŏ,* sm. duchy, dukedom; ducat.

ducal, *dŭkåʹl,* a. ducal.   [customed.

ducho, cha, *dŭtshʹŏ,* a. dexterous; accustomed.

ducientos, tas, *dŭthĕnʹtŏs,* a. two hundred.   [tion.

duda, *dŏʹdă,* sf. doubt, suspense, hesitation.

dudable, *dŭdåʹblĕ,* a. dubitable, dubious.

dudar, *dŭdåʹr,* v. a. to doubt.   [doubtful.

dudoso, sa, *dŭdŏʹsŏ,* a. doubtful, dubious.

duela, *dŭĕʹlă,* sf. stave.   [uncertain.

duelista, *dŭĕlĕsʹtă,* sm. duellist, dueller; quarreller.

duelo, *dŭĕʹlŏ,* sm. duel; grief; affliction; mourning, funeral; **—s,** pl. troubles; afflictions.

duende, *dŭĕnʹdĕ,* sm. elf, hobgoblin.

dueña, *dŭĕnʹyă,* sf. married lady; single woman who has lost her virginity.

dueño, *dŭĕnʹyŏ,* sm. owner; master.

dulce, *dŭlʹthĕ* a. sweet; pleasing to the taste; mild, soft, gentle, meek; **—,** sm. comfiture; sweetness.

dulcificante, *dŭlthĭfĭkănʹtĕ,* a. sweetening.

dulcificar, *-fĭkår,* v. a. to sweeten.

dulzaina, *dŭlthăʹnă,* sf. German flute.

dulzaino, *-nŏ,* a. excessively sweet.

dulzura, *dŭlthŏʹră,* sf. sweetness; gentleness, graciousness; pleasant manner in speaking or writing.   [corate.

dulzurar, *-răr,* v. a. (chem.) to edulcorate.

dúo, *dŏʹŏ,* sm. (mus.) duo, duet.

duodécimo, *dŭŏdĕthĭmŏ,* a. twenth.

duplicación, *dŭplĭkăthĭŏnʹ,* sf. duplication.   [tion.

duplicado, *-kåʹdŏ,* sm. duplicate.

duplicar, *-kår,* v. a. to double, to duplicate; to repeat.   [ness.

duplicidad, *-thĭdăʹd,* sf. duplicity; falseness.

duplo, *dŭʹplŏ,* sm. double.

duque, *dŭʹkĕ,* sm. duke.

duquesa, *dŭkĕʹsă,* sf. duchess.

dura, *dŏʹră,* sf. duration, continuance.

durable, *dŭrăʹblĕ,* a. durable, lasting.

duración, *-thĭŏnʹ,* sf. duration.

duradero, ra, *-dĕʹrŏ,* a. lasting, durable.

durante, *dŭrănʹtĕ,* p. & a. during.

durar, *dŭrårʹ,* v. n. to last, to continue.

durazno, *dŭråthʹnŏ,* sm. peach.

durazno, —, duraznero, *dŭråthnăʹrŏ,* sm. peach-tree.

dureza, *dŭrĕʹthă,* sf. hardness, solidity, firmness; acerbity; steadiness; want of softness in paintings; tumour, callosity; **— de vientre,** costiveness; **— de oido,** hardness of bearing.

durillo, *dŭrĭʹyŏ,* a. rather hard.

durin, *dŭrĭnʹ,* sm. (cant) sbirro, bailiff, constable.

durmiente, *dŭrmĭĕnʹtĕ,* p. & a. sleeping; **—,** sm. dormer, dormant; **—s,** pl. (mar.) clamps, sleepers.

duro, ra, *dŏʹrŏ,* a. hard, solid; unjust; oppressive, rigorous, cruel; stubborn; avaricious; rude, harsh, peevish, rough; **—,** sm. dollar.

duunvir, *dŭănvĭrʹ,* sm. one of the duumviri.

duunvirato, *-vĭråʹtŏ,* sm. duumvirate.

dux, *dŭks,* sm. doge (of Venice and Genoa).

E.

é, ĕ, c. and.

ea, *ĕʹă,* a kind of aspiration used to awaken attention; **¡— pues!** well then! let us see!   [ebonist.

ebanista, *ĕbănĕsʹtă,* sm. cabinet-maker, ebonist.

ébano, *ĕʹbănŏ,* sm. ebony.

ebullición, *ĕbŭlyĭthĭŏnʹ,* sf. ebullition, boiling over.

Eccehomo, *ĕkthĕŏʹmŏ,* sm. Ecce Homo.

eclesiástico, *ĕklĕsĭăsʹtĭkŏ,* sm. clergyman, ecclesiastic; **—, ca,** a. ecclesiastical.

Eclesiástico, —, sm. Ecclesiasticus.

eclipsable, *ĕklĭpsăʹblĕ,* a. that may be eclipsed.   [shine.

eclipsar, *ĕklĭpsårʹ,* v. a. to eclipse, to outshine.

eclipse, *ĕklĭpʹsĕ,* sm. eclipse.

eclíptica, *ĕklĭpʹtĭkă,* sf. ecliptic.

eco, *ĕkʹŏ,* sm. echo.

economía, *ĕkŏnŏmĕʹă,* sf. economy.

económico, ca, *-nŏʹmĭkŏ,* a. economical; avaricious.

económo, *ĕkŏʹnŏmŏ,* sm. economist.

ecuación, *ĕkŭăthĭŏnʹ,* sf. equation.

ecuador, *ĕkŭădŏrʹ,* sm. equator.

ecuestre, *ĕkŭĕsʹtrĕ,* a. equestrian.

eculeo, *ĕkŭlĕʹŏ,* sm. wooden horse (for torture).   [cal, universal.

ecuménico, ca, *ĕkămĕʹnĭkŏ,* a. œcumenical.

echadizo, za, *ĕtshădĕʹthŏ,* a. fit to be thrown away; suborned to pry into other people's actions; supposititious; **—,** sm. foundling.

echar, *ĕtshårʹ,* v. a. to cast, to throw, to dart, to jet; to cast away; to shoot, to bud; to impose a tax; **—se,** to lie, to rest, to stretch oneself at full length.

edad, *ĕdăʹd,* sf. age.

edecán, *ĕdĕkănʹ,* sm. (mil.) aide-de-camp.

edición, *ĕdĭthĭŏnʹ,* sf. edition; published book.   [book.

edicto, *ĕdĭkʹtŏ,* sm. edict.

edificación, *ĕdĭfĭkăthĭŏnʹ,* sf. construction; (fig.) good example.

edificar, *-fĭkărʹ,* v. a. to build; to fabricate; to construct a building; to set a good example.   [instructive.

edificativo, va, *-kătĕʹvŏ,* a. exemplary, instructive.

edificio, *ĕdĭfĕʹthĭŏ,* sm. building, structure.

editor, *ĕdĭtŏrʹ,* sm. editor, publisher.

educación, *ĕdŭkăthĭŏnʹ,* sf. education.

educador, ra, *ĕdŭkădŏrʹ,* sm. & f. instructor, educator.   [scholar.

educando, da, *-kănʹdŏ,* sm. & f. pupil, scholar.

educar, *ĕdŭkărʹ,* v.a. to educate, to instruct.

educción, *ĕdŭkthĭŏnʹ,* sf. drawing forth, eduction, extraction.   [to bring out.

educir, *ĕdŭthĭrʹ,* v. a. to educe, to extract.

efectivamente, *ĕfĕktĭvămĕnʹtĕ,* ad. effectually, powerfully; certainly.

efectivo, va, –tĕ'vŏ, a. effective. true, certain.

efecto, ĕfĕk'tŏ, sm. effect; consequence; purpose; –s, pl. effects, goods; en –, in fact, in truth.

efectuar, –tŭăr', v. a. to effectuate.

efemérides, ĕfĕmĕ'r dĕs, sf. ephemeris.

efervescencia, ĕfĕrvĕsthĕn'thĭă, sf. effervescence, ebullition.

eficacia, ĕfĭkă'thĭă, sf. efficacy.

eficaz, –kăth', a. efficacious, effective.

eficiente, ĕfĭthĭĕn'tĕ, a. efficient, effective.

efigie, ĕfĭ'h'ĕ, sf. effigy, image.

efímero, ra, ĕfĭ'mĕrŏ, a. ephemeral.

efluvio, ĕflŏŏ'vĭŏ, sm. effluvium.

efugio, ĕfŏŏ'hĭŏ, sm. subterfuge.

efusión, ĕfŭsiŏn', sf. effusion.

égida, d'hĭdă, sf. (fig.) protection.

égloga, ĕ'glŏgă, sf. eclogue.

egoísmo, ĕgŏ-ĭs'mŏ, sm. selfishness.

egoísta, –ĭs'tă, sm. self-seeker.

egregio, gia, ĕgrĕ'hĭŏ, a. egregious, eminent, remarkable.

eje, ĕ'h'ĕ, sm. axle-tree.

ejecución, ĕ'hĕkŭthiŏn', sf. execution.

ejecutable, –tă'blĕ, a. performable.

ejecutar, –tăr', v. a. to execute, to perform; to put to death; (law) to distrain, to seize.

ejecutivo, va, –tĕ'vŏ, a. executive.

ejecutor, ra, –tŏr', sm. & f. executor; (law) distrainer.

ejecutoria, –tŏ'rĭă, sf. (law) writ of execution.

ejecutorial, –tŏrĭăl', a. applied to the execution of the sentence of an ecclesiastical tribunal.

ejecutoriar, ria, –tŏ'rĭŏ, a. (law) executory.

ejemplar, ĕ'hĕmplăr', sm. exemplar; example; –, a. exemplary.

ejemplificar, ĕ'hĕmplĭfĭkăr', v. a. to exemplify.

ejemplo, ĕ'hĕm'plŏ, sm. example; comparison; pattern, copy; por –, for instance.

ejercer, ĕ'hĕrthĕr', v. a. to exercise.

ejercicio, –thĕ'thĭŏ, sm. exercise.

ejercitación, –thĭtăthiŏn', sf. exercise, practice.

ejercitar, –thĭtăr', v. a. to exercise; –se, to apply oneself to the functions of an office.

ejército, ĕ'hĕr'thĭtŏ, sm. army.

el, ĕl, art. m. the.

él, ĕl', ella, – yă, ello, –yŏ, pn. he, she, it.

elaboración, ĕlăbŏrăthiŏn', sf. elaboration.

elaborado, da, –ră'dŏ, a. elaborate.

elaborar, ĕlăbŏrăr', v. a. to elaborate.

elamí, ĕlămĭ', sf. the sixth ascending note in the scale of music.

elasticidad, ĕlăstĭthĭdăd', sf. elasticity.

elástico, ca, ĕlăs'tĭkŏ, a. elastic.

elección, ĕlĕkthiŏn', sf. election, discernment, choice.

electivo, va, –tĕ'vŏ, a. elective.

electo, ĕlĕk'tŏ, sm. elect.

elector, ĕlĕktŏr', sm. elector.

electorado, –tŏră'dŏ, sm. electorate.

electoral, –tŏrăl', a. electoral.

electricidad, –trĭthĭdăd', sf. electricity.

eléctrico, ca, ĕlĕk'trĭkŏ, a. electric, electrical.

electrización, –trĭthăthiŏn', sf. electrification.

electrizar, –trĭthăr', v. a. to electrify.

electuario, –tŭă'rĭŏ, sm. electuary.

elefante, ĕlĕfăn'tĕ, sm. elephant.

elegancia, ĕlĕgăn'thĭă, sf. elegance.

elegante, –găn'tĕ, a. elegant, fine.

elegía, ĕlĕhĭ'ă, sf. elegy.

elegible, ĕlĕhĭ'blĕ, a. eligible.

elegidos, –hĕ'dŏs, sm. pl. the elect, the blessed.

elegir, ĕlĕhĭr', v. a. to choose, to elect.

elemental, ĕlĕmĕntăl', a. elemental.

elemento, –mĕn'tŏ, sm. element; –s, pl. elements, rudiments, first principles.

elevación, –văthiŏn', sf. elevation; highness; exaltation, dignity; ecstasy, rapture; haughtiness, pride, height; altitude.

elevar, –văr', v. a. to raise; to elevate; to heave; –se, to be enraptured; to be puffed up, to be conceited.

élice, ĕ'lĭthĕ, sf. screw.

elidir, ĕlĭdĭr', v. a. to weaken, to enervate; eclipse, ĕlĭp'sĕ, sf. (geom.) ellipse.

elipsis, ĕlĭp'sĭs, sf. (gr.) ellipsis.

Eliseo, ĕlĭsĕ'ŏ, Elisio, –sĭŏ, sm. Elysian fields, pl.

elixir, ĕlĭksĭr', sm. elixir.

elocución, ĕlŏkŭthiŏn', sf. elocution.

elocuencia, ĕlŏkŭĕn'thĭă, sf. eloquence.

elocuente, –tĕ, a. eloquent.

elogiador, ĕlŏ'hĭădŏr', sm. eulogist, praiser.

elogiar, ĕlŏ'hĭăr', v. a. to praise, to eulogise.

elogio, ĕlŏ'hĭŏ, sm. eulogy, praise.

elucidación, ĕlŭthĭdăthiŏn', sf. elucidation, explanation.

eludir, ĕlŭdĭr', v. a. to elude, to escape by stratagem.

emanación, ĕmănăthiŏn', sf. emanation.

emanar, ĕmănăr', v. n. to emanate.

emancipación, ĕmănthĭpăthiŏn', sf. emancipation.

emancipar, –thĭpăr', v. a. to emancipate, to set free.

embadurnar, ĕmbădŭrnăr', v. a. to besmear, to bedaub.

embajada, ĕmbă'hă'dă, sf. embassy.

embajador, ĕmbă'hădŏr', sm. ambassador.

embalaje, ĕmbălă'h'ĕ, sm. packing, package.

embalar, ĕmbălăr', v. a. to bale, to pack in bales.

embaldosado, ĕmbăldŏsă'dŏ, sm. tile-floor.

embaldosar, –săr', v. a. to pave with flags.

embalijar, ĕmbălĭhăr', v. a. to pack into a portmanteau.

emballestarse, ĕmbăllĕstăr'sĕ, v. r. to be on the point of discharging a cross-bow.

embalsadero, ĕmbălsădĕ'rŏ, sm. pool of stagnant rain-water.

embalsamador, –mădŏr', sm. embalmer.

embalsamar, –măr', v. a. to embalm.

embanastar, ĕmbănăstăr', v. a. to put into a basket.

embarazada, ĕmbărăthă'dă, sf. woman with child.

embarazar, –thăr', v. a. to embarrass; –se, to become intricate.

embarazo, ĕmbără'thŏ, sm. embarrassment; obstacle, pregnancy.

embarazoso, sa, –*thă'sŏ*, a. difficult, intricate, entangled.

embarbecer, *ĕmbărbĕthĕr'*, v. n. to appear, to begin to show (of one's beard); to be getting a beard.

embarcación, *ĕmbărkăthiŏn'*, sf. embarkation; navigation; any vessel or ship.

embarcadero, –*dā'rŏ*, sm. quay, wharf; port; harbour.

embarcar, *ĕmbărkăr'*, v. a. to embark; –se, to go on shipboard; (fig.) to engage in any affair. [embarkment.

embarco, *ĕmbăr'kŏ*, sm. embarkation.

embargar, *ĕmbărgăr'*, v. a. to lay on an embargo; to impede, to restrain.

embargo, *ĕmbăr'gŏ*, sm. embargo on shipping, sequestration; sin –, notwithstanding.

embarnizador, –*nĭthădŏr'*, sm. varnisher.

embarnizadura, –*nĭthădŏ'rā*, sf. varnishing. [(fig.) to set off.

embarnizar, –*nĭthăr'*, v. a. to varnish

embarque, *ĕmbăr'kĕ*, sm. embarkation.

embarrador, *ĕmbărrădŏr'*, sm. plasterer.

embarradura, –*dŏ'rā*, sf. plastering (of walls, etc.), laying on of mortar.

embarrancarse, *ĕmbărrănkăr'sĕ*, v. r. to bemire oneself.

embarrar, *ĕmbărrăr'*, v. a. to overlay with plaster; to parget; –se, to take to the trees (of frightened birds, etc.).

embarrilar, *ĕmbărrĭlăr'*, v. a. to pack in barrels. [sew roughly.

embastar, *ĕmbăstăr'*, v. a. to baste, to

embate, *ĕmbă'tĕ*, sm. breakers, pl., surf, surge; impetuous attack. [impostor.

embaucador, *ĕmbăŭkădŏr'*, sm. sharper.

embaucamiento, –*miĕn'tŏ*, sm. deception, illusion. [pose upon.

embaucar, –*kăr'*, v. a. to deceive, to im-

embaular, *ĕmbăŭlăr'*, v. a. to pack up in a trunk; to cram, to fill with food beyond satiety.

embazar, *ĕmbăthăr'*, v. a. to tinge, to shade; (fig.) to astonish; to impede, to stop, to check; –, v. n. to be amazed; –se, to become tired; to be ashamed.

embebecer, *ĕmbĕbĕthĕr'*, v. a. to astonish, to stupefy; to amuse; –se, to be struck with amazement.

embebecimiento, *ĕmbĕbĕthĭmiĕn'tŏ*, sm. amazement, astonishment.

embeber, *ĕmbĕbĕr'*, v. a. to imbibe; to soak; to case, to include; to squeeze, to press; –, v. n. to shrink; –se, to be enraptured; to retain firmly in the mind.

embelecar, *ĕmbĕlĕkăr'*, v. a. to impose upon, to deceive.

embeleco, *ĕmbĕlĕ'kŏ*, sm. fraud, delusion, imposition. [rapture.

embelesamiento, *ĕmbĕlĕsămiĕn'tŏ*, sm.

embelesar, –*săr'*, v. a. to amaze, to astonish. [ravishment.

embeleso, *ĕmbĕlĕ'sŏ*, sm. amazement,

embellecer, *ĕmbĕlyĕthĕr'*, v. a. to embellish, to adorn.

emberrincharse, *ĕmbĕrrĭntshăr'sĕ*, v. r. to fly into a violent passion (of children).

embestida, *ĕmbĕstĭ'dā*, sf. assault, violent attack. [tack.

embestir, *ĕmbĕstĭr'*, v. a. to assail, to at-

embetunar, *ĕmbĕtŭnăr'*, v. a. to cover with gum-resin or bitumen.

emblanquecer, *ĕmblănkĕthĕr'*, v. a. to whiten; –se, to grow white. [enamel.

emblema, *ĕmblĕ'mā*, sm, emblem; inlay,

embobamiento, *ĕmbŏbămiĕn'tŏ*, sm. astonishment; stupefaction.

embobar, *ĕmbŏbăr'*, v. a. to amuse, to divert from, to distract; –se, to be in suspense, to stand gaping.

embobecer, *ĕmbŏbĕthĕr'*, v. a. to stultify, to stupefy; –se, to become stupefied or stultified. [faction.

embobecimiento, –*thĭmiĕn'tŏ*, sm. stupe-

embocadero, *ĕmbŏkădā'rŏ*, sm. mouth of a channel or of a river.

embocadura, –*dŏ'rā*, sf. mouth-piece.

embocar, *ĕmbŏkăr'*, v. a. to put into one's mouth; to put one's mouth to; to swallow in haste; to enter by a pass; (fig.) to take hold of, to seize upon; to deceive.

embodegar, –*bŏdĕgăr'*, v. a. to warehouse.

embolar, –*bŏlăr'*, v. a. to put balls on the ends of bull's horns.

embolismador, ra, –*bŏlĭsmădŏr'*, sm. & f. detracter, reviler.

embolismar, –*bŏlĭsmăr'*, v. a. to propagate malicious rumours.

embolismo, –*bŏlĭs'mŏ*, sm. imbroglio; confusion. [a pump.

émbolo, *ĕm'bŏlŏ*, sm. embolus, sucker of

embolsar, –*bŏlsăr'*, v. a. to put money into a purse; to reimburse.

embolso, –*bŏl'sŏ*, sm. putting of money into a purse, repayment.

emboque, –*bŏ'kĕ*, sm. passage of a ball through a ring, etc. (at games).

emborrachar, –*ĕmbŏrrătshăr'*, v. a. to intoxicate, to inebriate.

emborrar, –*bŏrrăr'*, v. a. to stuff with goat's hair; to comb the wool a second time; to swallow victuals hastily, to cram.

emborrascar, –*bŏrrăskăr'*, v. a. to provoke, to enrage. [stupefied.

emborricarse, –*bŏrrĭkăr'sĕ*, v. r. to be

emborrizar, –*bŏrrĭthăr'*, v. a. to give the first combing to wool. [(mil.) ambush.

emboscada, –*bŏskā'dā*, sf. ambuscade;

emboscar, –*bŏskăr'*, v. a. (mil.) to post in ambush; –se, to retire into the thickest part of a forest; (mil.) to lie in ambush.

embotadura, –*bŏtădŏ'rā*, sf. bluntness.

embotar, –*bŏtăr'*, v. a. to blunt; (fig.) to enervate, to debilitate. [wine.

embotellar, –*bŏtĕlyăr'*, v. a. to embottle

embotijar, –*bŏtĭhăr'*, v. a. to lay a stratum of small earthen jars, before the flooring is put down, to keep out the damp; –se, to swell; to be in a passion.

embozado, da, –*bŏthā'dŏ*, a. covered; involved

embozar, –*bŏthăr'*, v. a. to muffle the greater part of the face; (fig.) to cloak, to dissemble.

embozo, -bŏ'thŏ, sm. part of a cloak, veil or any other thing with which the face is muffled: muffling of one's face.

embravecer, -brăvěthăr', v. a. to enrage, to irritate; -, v. n. to grow strong and healthy (of plants).

embravecimiento, -brăvěthămĭěn'tŏ, sm. fury, rage, passion. [shield.

embrazar, -brăthăr', v. a. to clasp a

embreadura, -brěădŏ'ră, sf. pitching or tarring of a ship.

embrear, -brěăr', v. a. to pitch a ship.

embriagar, -brĭăgăr', v. a. to intoxicate, to inebriate; to transport, to enrapture.

embriaguez, -brĭăgěth', sf. intoxication, drunkenness; rapture, transport of mind.

embridar, -brĭdăr', v. a. to bridle.

embrión, ěmbrĭŏn', sm. embryo.

embrocar, -brŏkăr', v. a. to pour out of one vessel into another, to decanter.

embrollador, ra, -brŏlyădŏr', sm. & f. entangler, confounder. [embroil.

embrollar, -brŏlyăr', v. a. to entangle, to

embrollo, -brŏl'yŏ, sm. imposture; embroiling. [bearer, impostor; entangler.

embrollón, ona, -brŏlyŏn', sm. & f. tale-

embromado, da, -brŏmă'dŏ, a. misty, hazy, foggy; chaffed. [wheedle.

embromar, -brŏmăr', v. a. to cajole, to

embrujar, -brŏŏhăr', v. a. to bewitch.

embrutecer, -brŏŏtěthăr', v. a. to stupefy.

embuchado, -bŏŏchă'dŏ, sm. large sausages made of pork, minced very small.

embuchar, -bŏŏchăr', v. a. to cram the maw of animals; to swallow victuals without chewing them.

embudar, -bŏŏdăr', v. a. to put through a funnel; to insnare. [ice.

embudo, ěmbŏŏ'dŏ, sm. funnel; fraud, artifice.

embuste, ěmbŏŏs'tě, sm. fraud, imposition; pleasing quibble of children; -s, pl. gewgaws, trinkets. [cheat.

embustero, ra, -tě'rŏ, sm. & f. impostor,

embutido, ěmbŏŏtě'dŏ, sm. inlaid work.

embutir, -tĭr', v. a. to inlay; to enchase one thing in another; to mix confusedly; to cram, to eat too much.

emendar, ěměndăr', v. a. to correct, to amend.

emérito, ěmă'rĭtŏ, a. emerited. [amend.

emético, ca, ěmă'tĭkŏ, a. emetic.

emigración, ěmĭgrăthĭŏn', sf. emigration, migration. [emigrant (m. & f.).

emigrado, da, -gră'dŏ, a. & s. emigrated;

emigrar, -grăr', v. n. to emigrate.

eminencia, -něn'thĭă, sf. eminence.

eminente, -něn'tě, a. eminent, high; excellent, conspicuous.

emisario, -să'rĭŏ, sm. emissary.

emitir, ěmĭtĭr', v. a. to emit, to send forth; to let go, to let fly. [ing.

emoliente, ěmŏlĭěn'tě, a. emollient, softening.

emolumento, ěmŏlŏměn'tŏ, sm. emolument, fee, profit, advantage.

empachar, ěmpăchăr', v. a. to impede, to embarrass; to cram, to surfeit; -se, to be ashamed, to be confounded.

empacho, ěmpă'chŏ, sm. bashfulness, timidity; embarrassment.

empachoso, sa, -chŏ'sŏ, a. embarrassing; bashful, timid.

empadronamiento, ěmpădrŏnămĭěn'tŏ, sm. register of excisable persons.

empadronar, -pădrŏnăr', v. a. to enter in a register the names of those who are liable to pay certain taxes.

empalagamiento, -păl̆ăgămĭěn'tŏ, sm. surfeiting, surfeit. [disgust; to trouble.

empalagar, -păl̆ăgăr', v. a. to loathe; to

empalago, -păl̆ă'gŏ, sm. disgust, nausea.

empalagoso, -gŏ'sŏ, a. squeamish, loathsome; fastidious, troublesome.

empalar, ěmpăl̆ăr', v. a. to empale.

empalizada, -păl̆ĭthă'dă, sf. (mil.) palisade or palisado.

empalizar, -păl̆ĭthăr', v. a. to palisade.

empalmadura, -păl̆mădŏ'ră, sf. joining of two pieces of wood; welding of metals.

empalmar, -păl̆măr', v. a. to join the ends of two pieces of timber.

empalme, -păl̆'mě, sm. (rail.) junction.

empanada, -pănă'dă, sf. meat-pie.

empanar, -pănăr', v. a. to cover with paste.

empantanar, -păntănăr', v. a. to submerge; to drag in the mire; to complicate a matter. [of children.

empañadura, -pănyădŏ'ră, sf. swaddling

empañar, -pănyăr', v. a. to swaddle, to swathe; to tarnish a glass with one's breath; to impeach one's reputation; -se, to grow dull.

empapar, -păpăr', v. a. to imbibe; -se, to imbibe; to go deeply into a matter.

empapelar, -păpěl̆ăr', v. a. to wrap up in paper. [into bales.

empaquetar, -păkětăr', v. a. to pack goods

emparedamiento, -părědămĭěn'tŏ, sm. confinement; cloister. [immure.

emparedar, -dăr', v. a. to confine, to

emparejadura, -hădŏ'ră, sf. equalisation. [match, to fit, to equalise.

emparejar, -hăr', v. a. to level; to

emparentar, ěmpărěntăr', v. n. to be related by marriage.

emparrado, -pără'dŏ, sm. vine-arbour.

emparrar, -părăr', v. a. to embower.

emparvar, -părvăr', v. a. to put grain in order to be thrashed.

empastar, -păstăr', v. a. to paste; to cover plentifully with colours. [pension.

empastadera, -păstădă'ră, sf. check; suspension.

empatar, -pătăr', v. a. to equal; to check, to suspend; to cut short a speech.

empate, ěmpă'tě, sm. equality of votes; stop, suspension.

empavesar, -păvěsăr', v. a. to deck out with flags; (mar.) to dress a ship.

empecatado, (da,) -pěkătă'dŏ, a. turbulent.

empedernir, -pěděrnĭr', v. a. to harden; -se, to petrify; to be inflexible.

empedrado, -pědră'dŏ, sm. pavement.

empedrador, -pědrădŏr', sm. paver, pavier, pavior.

empedrar, -pědrăr', v. a. to pave.

empega, *émpé'gä*, sf. varnish of pitch; mark of pitch.

empegado, *-pégä'dŏ*, sm. (mar.) tarpaulin.

empegadura, *-pégädŏ'rä*, sf. varnish of pitch put on vessels.

empegar, *-pégär'*, v. a. to pitch.

empeine, *-pä'ïnë*, sm. groin; instep; hoof of a beast. [with skins.

empellejar, *-pélyëhär'*, v. a. to cover [with plumes.

empellón, *-pélyŏn'*, sm. push, heavy blow; á –ones, rudely. [with plumes.

empenachar, *-pénätshär'*, v. a. to adorn

empeñar, *-pényär'*, v. a. to pawn, to pledge; to engage, to oblige; –se, to bind oneself to pay debts contracted; to persist in a resolution; to intercede.

empeño, *-pén'yŏ*, sm. obligation; engagement; courage; perseverance; protection.

empeorar, *-péŏrär'*, v. a. to make worse; –, v. n. to grow worse.

emperador, *-pérädŏr'*, sm. emperor.

emperatriz, *-pérätrëth'*, sf. empress.

emperejilar, *-pérë'hïlär'*, v. a. to trick out. [or indolent.

emperezar, *-pérëthär'*, v. n. & r. to be lazy

emperifollarse, *-pérïfŏlyär'së*, v. a. to overdress oneself.

empero, *émpë'rŏ*, c. yet, however.

emperrarse, *-pérrär'së*, v. r. to grow mad.

empezar, *-péthär'*, v. a. to begin, to commence. [alted, raised to a high dignity.

empinado, da, *-pënä'dŏ, ä*, a. elevated, exempinadura, *-pënädŏ'rä*, sf. elevation, raising.

empinar, *-pïnär'*, v. a. to raise; to exalt; to drink much; –se, to stand on tiptoe; to rise high. [of hawks with jesses.

empiolar, *-pïŏlär'*, v. a. to tie the legs

empíreo, *émpï'rëŏ*, sm. empyrean (the highest heaven); –, rea, a. celestial.

empírico, *-pë'rïkŏ*, sm. quack, empiric; –, ca, a. empirical.

empirismo, *-pïrïs'mŏ*, sm. empiricism.

empizarrado, *-pïthärrä'dŏ*, sm. slate-roofing. [to roof with slate.

empizarrar, *-pïthärrär'*, v. a. to slate,

emplastadura, *-plästädŏ'rä*, sf. plastering.

emplastar, *-plästär'*, v. a. to apply plasters; to paint the face; to check the course of an affair; –se, to bedaub one's hands or feet.

emplasto, *-pläs'tŏ*, sm. plaster.

emplazador, *-pläthädŏr'*, sm. (law) summoner, apparitor. [mons, citation.

emplazamiento, *-pläthämïen'tŏ*, sm. summemplazar, *-pläthär'*, v. a. to summon.

empleado, *-plëä'dŏ*, sm. official.

emplear, *-plëär'*, v. a. to employ; to occupy; to commission. [occupation.

empleo, *émplë'ŏ*, sm. employ, employment.

emplomador, *-plŏmädŏr'*, sm. plumber.

emplomar, *-plŏmär'*, v. a. to lead.

emplumar, *-plŏmär'*, v. a. to adorn with feathers; –se, to get feathers.

emplumecer, *-plŏmëthër'*, v. n. to begin to get feathers.

empobrecer, *-pŏbrëthër'*, v. a. to reduce to poverty; –, v. n. to become poor.

empobrecimiento, *-pŏbrëthïmïen'tŏ*, sm. impoverishing. [–, v. n. to putrify.

empodrecer, *-pŏdrëthër'*, v. a. to corrupt;

empolvar, *-pŏlvär'*, v. a. to powder, to sprinkle powder.

empolladura, *-pŏlyädŏ'rä*, sf. brood, hatch, covey (of birds); brood (of bees).

empollar, *-pŏlyär'*, v. a. to brook, to hatch.

emponzoñador, ra, *-pŏnthŏnyädŏr'*, sm. & f. poisoner. [ing.

emponzoñamiento, *-mïen'tŏ*, sm. poison-

emponzoñar, *-pŏnthŏnyär'*, v. a. to poison; to taint, to corrupt.

emporcar, *-pŏrkär'*, v. a. to soil, to dirty.

emporio, *émpŏ'rïŏ*, sm. emporium.

empotrar, *-pŏträr'*, v. a. to join with a mortise; to scarf, to splice.

emprendedor, *-prëndëdŏr'*, sm. enterpriser; undertaker. [to undertake.

emprender, *-prëndër'*, v. a. to enterprise.

empreñar, *-prënyär'*, v. a. to impregnate; –se, to beget.

empresa, *émprë'sä*, sf. symbol, motto; enterprise, undertaking; design, purpose.

empresario, *-presä'rïŏ*, sm. manager of a theatre. [loan.

empréstito, *-prës'tïtŏ*, sm. lending money;

empringar, *-prïngär'*, v. a. to grease.

empujar, *-pŏhär'*, v. a. to push, to press forward. [pulse, pushing.

empuje, *émpŏ'hë*, sm. impulsion, inempujón, *-pŏhŏn'*, sm. impulse, push; á –ones, pushingly, rudely. [sword.

empuñadura, *-pŏnyädŏ'rä*, sf. hilt of a empuñar, *-pŏnyär'*, v. a. to clinch, to clutch, to gripe with the fist.

emulación, *émŏläthïŏn'*, sf. emulation, corrivalship.

emular, *émŏlär'*, v. a. to emulate, to rival.

émulo, *ä'mŏlŏ*, sm. competitor, rival.

emulsión, *émŏlsïŏn'*, sf. emulsion.

en, *ën*, pr. in; for; on, upon.

enaguas, *ënä'gŭäs*, sf. pl. petticoat.

enajenación, *-ä'hënäthïŏn'*, sf. alienation; absence of mind.

enajenamiento, *-mïen'tŏ*, sm. change of affection; rapture, astonishment.

enajenar, *-ä'hënär'*, v. a. to alienate; to rapture; se, to fall out.

enalbardar, *-älbärdär'*, v. a. to lay a pack-saddle on beasts of burden; to cover with a batter of eggs, flour, and sugar.

enamoradamente, *-ämŏrädämën'të*, ad. lovingly. [to love.

enamoradizo, za, *-ämŏrädï'thŏ,ä.* inclined

enamorado, da, *-ämŏrä'dŏ*, a. in love, enamoured, lovesick. [wooer.

enamorador, *-ämŏrädŏr'*, sm. lover,

enamoramiento, *-ämŏrämïen'tŏ*, sm. enamouring, love-suit.

enamorar, *-ämŏrär'*, v. a. to inspire love; –se, to fall in love. [slightly in love.

enamoricarse, *-ämŏrïkär'së*, v. r. to be

enano, na, *ënä'nŏ*, a. dwarfish; –, sm. dwarf. [high.

enarbolar, *-ärbŏlär'*, v. a. to hoist, to raise

enardecer, –ārdĕthĕr', v. a. to fire with passion, to inflame.

enarenar, –ărĕnār', v. a. to fill with sand.

enarrar, ĕnărrār', v. a. to narrate.

enastar, ĕnăstār', v. a. to put a handle to.

encabalgar, –kăbălgār', v. a. to provide horses, to horse.

encabestrar, –kăbĕstrār', v. a. to guide by a halter; **–se,** to be entangled in the halter.

encabezamiento, –kăbĕthămĭĕn'tō, sm. register of persons liable to pay a tax; tax, tribute.

encabezar, –kăbĕthār', v. a. to make up the tax-roll; **–se,** to compound for taxes.

encabritarse, –kăbrĭtār'sĕ, v. r. to rear (of horses). [nails).

encachar, –kă'chār', v. a. to drive in (of

encadenamiento, –kădĕnămĭĕn'tō, sm. linking together, chaining.

encadenar, –kădĕnār', v. a. to chain, to link together; to connect, to unite.

encajador, –kă'hădōr', sm. enchasing-tool.

encajadura, –kă'hădū'rā, sf. enchasing.

encajar, –kă'hār', v. a. to enchase, to drive in, to foist; to introduce something with craft and cunning; **–se,** to thrust oneself into some narrow place.

encaje, ĕnkă'h'ĕ, sm. enchasing; joining together; lace; inlaid work.

encajera, –kă'hĕrā, sf. lacewoman.

encajonado, –kă'hōnă'dō, sm. mud-wall supported by pillars of bricks.

encajonamiento, –mĭĕn'tō, sm. packing into boxes, etc.

encajonar, –kă'hōnār', v. a. to pack up in a box, to lay in a chest.

encalabrinar, –kălăbrĭnār', v. a. to make confused; **–se,** to become obstinate.

encaladura, –kălădō'rā, sf. whitening, whitewash.

encalar, –kălār', v. a. to whitewash.

encallar, kălyār', v. n. (mar.) to run aground; to be checked in the progress of some enterprise.

encallecer, –kălyĕthĕr', v. n. to get corns.

encamarse, –kămār'sĕ, v. r. to lie abed or **–se,** to go to bed.

encaminar, –kămĭnār', v. a. to guide, to show the way; **–se,** to take a road.

encandecer, –kăndĕthĕr', v. a. to heat to a white heat. [to grow old.

encanecer, –kănĕthĕr', v. n. to grow grey.

encanillar, –kănĭlyār', v. a. to wind silk, wool or linen on a quill of cane.

encantador, –kăntădōr', sm. enchanter, sorcerer, magician. [chantress.

encantadora, –dō'rā, sf. sorceress, enchantress.

encantamiento, –mĭĕn'tō, sm. enchantment, charming. [charm.

encantar, –kăntār', v. a. to enchant, to charm.

encantarar, –kăntărār', v. a. to put into a jar or a pitcher. [charm.

encanto, ĕnkăn'tō, sm. enchantment, spell.

encañado, –kănyă'dō, sm. conduit of water; hedge of canes or reeds.

encañar, –kănyār', v. a. to enclose with a hedge of cane; to convey water through conduits.

encañizada, –kănyĭthă'dā, sf. weir made of cane and reeds for catching mullets.

encañonar, –kănyōnār', v. a. & n. to begin to grow fledged; to plait, to fold; to introduce. [plait.

encañutar, –kănyŭtār', v. a. to flute; to plait.

encapado, da, –kăpă'dō, a. cloaked.

encaperuzarse, –kăpĕrŭthār'sĕ, v. r. to cover one's head with a hood.

encapillar, –kăpĭlyār', v. a. to cover the head-with a hood, &c.

encapotar, –kăpōtār', v. a. to cover with a cloak; **–se,** to be clouded; to look sullen.

encapricharse, –kăprĭchār'sĕ, v. r. to become stubborn.

encapuchar, –kăpŭchār', v. a. to cover any thing with a hood. [exfol.

encaramar, –kărămār', v. a. to raise; to

encarar, –kărār', v. a. to face, to come face to face. [ceration.

encaracelación, –kărthĕlāthĭōn', sf. incar-

encarcelar, –kărthĕlār', v. a. to imprison.

encarecer, –kărĕthĕr', v. a. to raise the price; (fig.) to enhance, to exaggerate.

encarecimiento, –thĭmĭĕn'tō, sm. enhancement; exaggeration; **con–,** ardently.

encargar, –kărgār', v. a. to charge, to commission. [office, employ.

encargo, ĕnkăr'gō, sm. charge, commission;

encarnación, –kărnăthĭōn', sf. incarnation; carnation.

encarnado, da, –kărnă'dō, a. incarnate, dyed flesh-colour; **–,** sm. flesh-colour.

encarnamiento, –mĭĕn'tō, sm. (med.) incarnation.

encarnar, –kărnār', v. n. to incarnate, to breed flesh; **–,** v. a. to give a flesh-colour to pieces of sculpture; to pierce the flesh; **–se,** to incorporate one thing with another.

encarnativo, –kărnătĕ'yō, a. incarnative.

encarnizado, da, –kărnĭthă'dō, a. fleshed; blood-shot, inflamed.

encarnizar, –kărnĭthār', v. a. to satiate with flesh; to provoke, to irritate; **–se,** to be glutted with flesh; to be cruelly minded towards. [lawry, proscription.

encartamiento, –kărtămĭĕn'tō, sm. out-

encartar, –kărtār', v. a. to proscribe; to involve in an unpleasant affair; to enter in the register of taxes; **–se,** to receive a card which spoils a game.

encarte, ĕnkăr'tĕ, sm. cards laid out.

encasquetar, –kăskĕtār', v. a. to cram a hat on to one's head; (fig.) to induce one to adopt or espouse an opinion; **–se,** to be headstrong.

encastar, –kăstār', v. a. to improve a race of animals; to procreate, to generate.

encastillar, –kăstĭlyār', v. a. to fortify with castles; **–,** v. n. to make the cell of the queen-bee; **–se,** to shut oneself up for defence in a castle; to be heady.

encebadar, –thĕbădār', v. a. to surfeit with oats and water drunk immediately after (applied to horses); **–se,** to be surfeited by drinking water immediately after eating oats.

encebollado, –*thĕbŏlyă'dŏ,* sm. fricassee of beef or mutton and onions, seasoned with spice.   [cheese in a wattle.

encellar, –*thĕlyăr',* v. a. to mould curds or cheese in a wattle.

encenagada, da, –*thĕnăgă'dŏ, a.* mixed with mud.   [ing in dirt or mire.

encenagamiento, –*mĭen'tŏ,* sm. wallow-

encenagar, v. a., –se, –*thĕnăgar',* to wallow in dirt or mire; (fig.) to wallow in vices.

encender, –*thĕndĕr',* v. a. to kindle, to light, to set on fire; to inflame, to incite; to foment a party; **–se,** to fire, to take fire; to fly into a passion.   [coloured.

encendido, da, –*dĕ'dŏ, a.* inflamed; high

encendimiento, –*dĭmĭen'tŏ,* sm. inflamation; glow.   [blind; sticking-plaster.

encerado, –*thĕră'dŏ,* sm. oil-cloth; window-

encerar, –*thĕrăr',* v. a. to wax; to fill or stiffen with wax.

encerotar, –*thĕrŏtăr',* v. a. to wax thread.

encerrar, –*thĕrrăr',* v. a. to shut up, to confine; to contain; **–se,** to withdraw from the world.

encespedar, –*thĕspĕdăr',* v. a. to turf.

encia, *ĕnthĕ'ă,* sf. gum (of the teeth).

enciclica, *ĕnthĕ'klĭkă,* sf. encyclical epistle.

enciclopedia, –*thĭklŏpĕ'dĭă,* sf. cyclopædia, encyclopedia.   [clopedian.

enciclopédico, ca, –*thĭklŏpĕ'dĭkŏ, a.* ency-

encierro, –*thĭĕr'rŏ,* sm. confinement, enclosure; cloister; prison; driving bulls into the pen-fold for the bull-feasts.

encima, –*thĕ'mă, ad.* above, over; at the top; over and above, besides.

encina, –*thĕ'nă,* sf. evergreen oak.

encinar, –*thĕnăr',* sm. evergreen oak-wood; evergreen oak-grove.   [ribbons.

encintar, –*thĭntăr',* v. a. to garnish with

enclaustrado, da, –*klăŏstră'dŏ, a.* shut up in cloisters.

enclavadura, –*klăvădŏ'ră,* sf. groove.

enclavar, –*klăvăr',* v. a. to nail.

enclavijar, –*klăvĭhăr',* v.a. to join closely; to put pegs in a musical instrument.

enclenque, –*klĕn'kĕ,* sm. weakling.

encobertado, –*kŏbĕrtă'dŏ, a.* wrapped up.

encoger, –*kŏ'hĕr',* v. a. to contract, to shorten; to shrink; **–se,** to be low spirited; to humble oneself.

encogidamente, –*kŏ'hĭdămĕn'tĕ,ad.* meanly, abjectly.   [timid, narrow-minded.

encogido, da, –*kŏ'hĭ'dŏ, a.* pusillanimous,

encogimiento, –*kŏ'hĭmĭen'tŏ,* sm. contraction; constriction; pusillanimity.

encohetar, –*kŏĕtăr',* v. a. to throw squibs at bulls (at bull-fights).

encojar, –*kŏ'hăr',* v. a. to cripple, to lame; **–se,** to grow lame; to feign sickness.

encoladura, –*pŏlădŏ'ră,* sf. gluing.

encolar, –*kŏlăr',* v. a. to glue.

encolerizar, –*kŏlĕrĭthăr',* v. a. to provoke, to irritate.

encomendar, –*kŏmĕndăr',* v. a. to recommend; **–se,** to commit oneself to another's protection.

encomienda, –*kŏmĭen'dă,* sm. commission, charge; message; (mil.) commandery; patronage, protection; **–s,** pl. compliments.   [commendation.

encomio, *ĕnkŏ'mĭŏ,* sm. encomium, praise.

enconar, –*kŏnăr',* v.a. to inflame, to irritate.

encono, *ĕnkŏ'nŏ,* sm. malevolence, rancour.

enconoso, sa, –*kŏnŏ'sŏ, a.* hurtful, prejudicial; malevolent.

encontradizo, za, –*kŏntrădĕ'thŏ, a.* that which may be met on the way.   [in front.

encontrado, da, –*kŏntră'dŏ, a.* opposite.

encontrar, –*kŏntrăr',* v. a. & n. to meet, to encounter; to assemble, to come together; **–se,** to encounter in an hostile manner, to clash; to be of contrary opinions.   [tuous, boastful.

encopetado, da, –*kŏpĕtă'dŏ, a.* presump-

encorajar, –*kŏ'ră'hăr',* v.a. to give courage; to inflame; **–se,** to be in a rage.

encorchar, –*kŏrt'shăr',* v. a. to hive bees.

encordar, –*kŏrdăr',* v. a. to chord musical instruments.   [cords; to cord a bed.

encordelar, –*kŏrdĕlăr',* v. a. to tie with

encorvadura, –*kŏrvădŏ'ră,* sf. act of bending; crookedness.

encorvar, –*kŏrvăr',* v. a. to bend, to crook.

encostrar, –*kŏstrăr',* v. a. to crust, to incrust; to rough-cast.

encrespar, –*krĕspăr',* v. a. to curl, to frizzle; **–se,** to become boisterous; to be involved in quarrels.   [haughty, lofty.

encrestado, da, –*krĕstă'dŏ, a.* (fig.)

encrestarse, –*krĕstăr'sĕ,* v. r. to get the crest (applied to a young cock).

encrucijada, –*krŭthĕ'hă'dă,* sf. cross-way.

encrudecer, –*krŭdĕthĕr',* v. a. to make a wound worse; to exasperate, to irritate.

encuadernación, –*kŭădĕrnăthĕon',* sf. binding books.   [binder.

encuadernador, –*kŭădĕrnădŏr',* sm. book-

encuadernar, –*kŭădĕrnăr',* v. a. to bind books; to reconcile.   [casks.

encubar, –*kŏbăr',* v. a. to put liquids into

encubiertamente, –*kŭbĭertămĕn'tĕ,* ad. secretly; deceitfully.   [cealed.

encubierto, ta, –*kŭbĭer'tŏ,* a. hidden, con-

encubridor, ra, –*kŭbrĭdŏr',* sm. & f. concealer, harbourer; receiver of stolen goods.

encubrimiento, –*mĭen'tŏ,* sm. concealment, hiding.   [ceal.

encubrir, –*kŭbrĭr',* v. a. to hide, to con-

encuentro, –*kŭen'trŏ,* sm. chock, justle; encounter.   [elevated.

encumbrado, da, –*kŭmbră'dŏ, a.* high, elevated.

encumbramiento, –*mĭen'tŏ,* sm. elevating; height.

encumbrar, –*kŭmbrăr',* v. a. to raise, to elevate; to mount, to ascend a height; **–se,** to be raised.

encureñado, da, –*kŭrĕnyă'dŏ, a.* put into the carriage or stock.   [for vinegar.

encurtir, –*kŭrtĭr',* v. a. to souse in pickle

enchapar, –*tshăpăr',* v. a. to veneer.

encharcarse, –*tshărkăr'sĕ,* v. r. to be inundated.

endeble, *ĕndă'blĕ, a.* feeble, weak.

endecasílabo, ba, –*dĕkăsĕ'lăbŏ, a.* consisting of eleven syllables.

endecha, –*dĕtsh'ă,* sf. dirge.

endechar, –*dětshär*, v. a. to sing funeral songs in honour and praise of the dead; –se, to grieve, to mourn.

endemoniado, da, –*děmōniä'dŏ*, a. possessed with the devil; devilish.

endemoniar, –*děmōniär'*, v. a. to possess with the devil; to irritate, to provoke.

enderezadamente, –*děrěthädämě̈n'tě*, ad. justly, rightly; directly.

enderezamiento, –*miěn'tŏ*, sm. guidance, direction.

enderezar, –*děrěthär'*, v. a. to rectify, to set right; to address; –se, to stand upright.

endiablada, –*diäblä'dä*, sf. mummery.

endiablado, da, –*diäblä'dŏ*, a. devilish, diabolical; ugly.

endiosar, –*diōsär'*, v. a. to deify; –se, to be puffed up with pride.

endosante, –*dōsän'tě*, sm. endorser.

endosar, –*dōsär'*, v. a. to endorse a bill of exchange.

endosatario, –*dōsätä'riŏ*, sm. endorsee.

endoso, *ěndō'sŏ*, sm. endorsement of a bill of exchange.

endrina, –*drě'nä*, sf. sloe.

endrino, –*drě'nŏ*, sm. black-thorn, sloe-tree.

endulzar, –*dŭlthär'*, v. a. to sweeten; to soften.

endurecer, –*dŭrěthěr'*, v. a. to harden, to indurate; –se, to become cruel, to grow hard.

endurecidamente, *ěndŭrěthidämě̈n'tě*, ad. pertinaciously.

endurecimiento, –*thimiěn'tŏ*, sm. hardness; obstinacy; hardness of heart.

enebro, *ěně'brŏ*, sm. (bot.) common juniper.

enemigo, ga, *ěně̈mě'gŏ*, a. inimical, hostile; –, sm. fiend.

enemistad, –*mistäd'*, sf. enmity, hatred.

enemistar, –*mistär'*, v. a. to make an enemy; –, v. n. to become an enemy.

energía, *ěněr'hě'ä*, sf. energy, power, vigour; strength of will.

enérgico, ca, *ěněr'hikŏ*, a. energetic; expressive.

energúmeno, na, *ěněrgŏ'měnŏ*, sm. & f. demoniac, one possessed.

enero, *ěně'rŏ*, sm. January.

enervar, *ěněrvär'*, v. a. to enervate.

enfadadizo, za, *ěnfädädě'thŏ*, a. irritable, irascible.

enfadar, –*fädär'*, v. a. to vex, to molest, to trouble.

enfado, –*fä'dŏ*, sm. trouble, vexation.

enfadoso, sa, –*fädō'sŏ*, a. vexatious, troublesome.

enfaldar, –*fäldär'*, v. a. to lop off the lower branches of trees; –se, to tuck up one's clothes.

enfardar, –*färdär'*, v. a. to pack, to bale goods.

enfardelar, –*färdělär'*, v. a. to make up into bales.

énfasis, *ěn'fäsis*, sm. & f. emphasis.

enfático, ca, *ěnfä'tikŏ*, a. emphatic.

enfermar, –*fěrmär'*, v. n. to fall ill; –, v. a. to make sick; to weaken.

enfermedad, –*fěrmědäd'*, sf. indisposition, illness.

enfermería, –*fěrměrě'ä*, sf. infirmary.

enfermero, ra, –*fěrmě'rŏ*, sm. & f. sick-nurse; hospital nurse or attendant.

enfermizo, za, –*fěrmě'thŏ*, a. infirm, sickly; indisposed.

enfermo, ma, *ěnfěr'mŏ*, a. sick, diseased, indisposed.

enfervorizar, –*fěrvōrithär'*, v. a. to heat, to inflame, to incite.

enfeudar, –*fěüdär'*, v. a. to enfeoff.

enfilar, –*filär'*, v. a. to put in a row; (mil.) to put in closed ranks; to enfilade.

enfitéusis, –*fte'üsis*, sf. emphyteusis, copyhold, alienation of the usufruct.

enfiteuta, –*ftě'ütä*, sm. emphyteuta, copyholder.

enfitéutico, ca, –*ftě'ütikŏ*, a. emphyteutic.

enflaquecer, –*fläkěthěr'*, v. a. to weaken, to thin; –se, to fall away.

enflaquecimiento, –*thimiěn'tŏ*, sm. extenuation, maceration.

enfoscado, da, *ěnfōskä'dŏ*, a. brow-beaten; confused, entangled.

enfoscarse, –*fōskär'sě*, v. r. to be troubled or perplexed; to be immersed in business; to be cloudy.

enfrascar, –*fräskär'*, v. a. to pour liquid into a flask; –se, to be entangled in brambles and briers; to be involved in difficulties.

enfrenar, –*frěnär'*, v. a. to bridle; to curb, to restrain.

enfrente, –*frěn'tě*, ad. over against, opposite, in front of the house.

enfriadera, –*friädě'rä*, sf. cooler, refrigerator.

enfriamiento, –*friämiěn'tŏ*, sm. refrigeration.

enfriar, –*friär'*, v. a. to cool, to refrigerate; –se, to cool down.

enfurecer, –*fürěthěr'*, v. a. to irritate, to enrage; –se, to grow boisterous or furious (of the wind and sea); to become furious or enraged.

enfurruñarse, –*fürrünyär'sě*, v. r. to grow angry, to frown.

engalanar, –*gälänär'*, v. a. to adorn, to deck.

engallado, da, –*gälyä'dŏ*, a. erect, upright.

engalladura, –*gälyädŭ'rä*, sf. tread, the cock's sperm in the egg.

engallarse, –*gälyär'sě*, v. r. to carry it high.

enganchador, –*gäntshädŏr'*, sm. (mil.) recruiter.

enganchar, –*gäntshär'*, v. a. to hook, to accroach; to ensnare; to decoy into the military service; to entrap.

engañabobos, –*gänyäbō'bōs*, sm. impostor, fooltrap.

engañadizo, za, –*gänyädě'thŏ*, a. deceivable, easily deceived.

engañador, –*gänyädŏr'*, sm. cheat, impostor, deceiver.

engañar, –*gänyär'*, v. a. to deceive, to cheat; –se, to be deceived; to make a mistake.

engañifa, –*gänyě'fä*, sf. deceit, trick.

engaño, *ěngän'yŏ*, sm. mistake, misunderstanding, deceit, fraud; artful, false.

engañoso, sa, –*gänyō'sŏ*, a. deceitful, deceiving.

engarabatar, –*gäräbätär'*, v. a. to hook; –se, to grow crooked.

engarabitarse, –*gäräbitär'sě*, v. r. to climb, to mount.

engaritar, –*gäritär'*, v. a. to place sentry-boxes; to deceive in a dexterous manner.

engarzar, –gârthâr´, v. a. to enchain, to link; to curl.

engastar, –gâstâr´, v. a. to enchase.

engaste, ḗngâs´tĕ, sm. enchasing.

engastrimismo, –gâstrĭmĭs´mō, sm. ventriloquism. [loquist.

engastrimita, –gâstrĭmē´tâ, sm. ventri-

engatar, –gâtâr´, v. a. to cheat in a dexterous manner. [a cramp-iron.

engatillar, –gâtĭlyâr´, v. a. to bind with

engatusamiento, –gâtŭsâmĭḗn´tō, sm. deception, cheat, coaxing.

engatusar, –gâtŭsâr´, v. a. to coax.

engazar, –gâthâr´, v. a. to enchain, to link; to splice an end of a rope in a circular form about a block; to dye cloth in the piece. [engender, to produce.

engendrar, –hḗndrâr´, v. a. to beget, to

engendro, ĕn´hĕn´drō, sm. fœtus, embryo; mal—, low breed; a perverse youth.

engolfar, –gōlfâr´, v. n. to enter a gulf; –se, to be engaged in arduous undertakings or difficult affairs.

engolillado, –gōlĭlyâ´dō, a. wearing the collar which is worn by lawyers in Spain.

engolosinar, –gōlōsĭnâr´, v. a. to give a taste for; –se, to find delight in.

engomadura, –gōmâdō´râ, sf. gumming.

engomar, –gōmâr´, v. a. to gum.

engordar, –gōrdâr´, v. a. to fatten; –se, to grow fat; to grow rich.

engorro, ĕngōr´rō, sm. (fam.) embarrassment, obstacle. [cumbrous.

engorroso, sa, –gōrrō´sō, a. troublesome,

engrandecer, –grândĕthḗr´, v. a. to augment, to aggrandize; to exaggerate.

engrandecimiento, –thĭmĭḗn´tō, sm. increase, aggrandisement; exaggeration.

engrasar, ĕngrâsâr´, v. a. to grease, to oil, to fat. [sumption, vanity.

engreimiento, –grḗimĭḗn´tō, sm. presumption, vanity.

engreir, –grḗir´, v. a. to make proud; –se, to grow proud.

engrescar, –grĕskâr´, v. a. & n. to goad into quarrelling or fighting. [displeased.

engrifarse, –grĭfâr´sĕ, v. r. to tiff, to be

engrosar, –grōsâr´, v. a. to make fat; –, v. n. to increase in bulk. [ing; gluing.

engrudamiento, –grŭdâmĭḗn´tō, sm. pasting.

engrudar, –grŭdâr´, v. a. to paste.

engrudo, ĕngrō´dō, sm. paste.

engualdrapar, –gŭâldrâpâr´, v. a. to caparison a horse. [with pebbles.

enguijarrar, –gĭhârrâr´, v. a. to pave

engullidor, ra, –gŭlyĭdōr´, sm. & f. devourer; gobbler. [gobble, to glut.

engullir, –gŭlyir´, v. a. to swallow, to

enharinar, –ârĭnâr´, v. a. to cover or besprinkle with flour. [rows in a quiver.

enhastillar, –âstĭlyâr´, v. a. to put ar-

enhebrar, –ĕbrâr´, v. a. to put a needle.

enhestar, –ĕstâr´, v. a. to erect, to set up-

enhilar, –ilâr´, v. a. to thread. [right.

enhorabuena, –ōrâbōĕ´nâ, sf. congratulation; felicitation; —, ad. well and good.

enhoramala, –mâ´lâ, ad. in an evil hour.

enigma, ĕnĭg´mâ, sm. enigma, riddle.

enigmático, ca, ĕnĭgmâ´tĭkō, a. enigmatical, dark, obscure. [ing.

enjabonadura, ĕn´hâbōnâdō´râ, sf. soap-

enjabonar, –´hâbōnâr´, v. a. to soap; to insult with foul language and blows.

enjaezar, –´hâĕthâr´, v. a. to caparison a horse.

enjalbegar, –´hâlbĕgâr´, v. a. to whitewash the walls of a building.

enjalma, ĕn´hâl´mâ, sf. pack-saddle.

enjalmero, –´hâlmĕ´rō, sm. pack-saddle maker.

enjambradero, ´hâmbrâdĕ´rō, sm. place where bees swarm to form their hives.

enjambrar, –´hâmbrâr´, v. a. to gather a scattered swarm of bees; –, v. n. to swarm; to multiply. [ing of bees.

enjambrazón, –´hâmbrâthōn´, sf. swarm-

enjambre, –´hâm´brĕ, sm. swarm of bees; crowd, multitude. [cage; to imprison.

enjaular, –´hâŭlâr´, v. a. to shut up in a

enjebar, –hĕbâr´, v. a. to steep in lye.

enjebe, –hâ´bĕ, sm. lye-steeping; bucking.

enjergar, –hĕrgâr´, v. a. to set about a business. [trees.

enjertal, –hĕrtâl´, sm. nursery of grafted

enjoyar, –hōyâr´, v. a. to adorn with jewels; to set a ring with precious stones; to heighten the brilliancy of a thing.

enjuagadura, –hŭâgâdō´râ, sf. rinsing of the mouth.

enjuagar, –hŭâgâr´, v. a. to rinse the mouth and teeth; to rinse clothes.

enjuague, ĕn´hŭâ´gĕ, sm. water used to rinse the mouth; intrigue.

enjugador, ra, –hŭâgâdōr´, sm. & f. one who dries; clothes-horse.

enjugar, –hŭgâr´, v. a. to dry; to wipe off; –se, to dry up; to grow lean.

enjuiciar, –hŭithĭâr´, v. a. to prepare a law-suit for judgment; to pass judgment.

enjuncar, –hŭnkâr´, v. a. to tie with rush ropes. [of fowls.

enjundia, ĕn´hŭn´dĭâ, sf. fat in the inside

enjutar, –hŭtâr´, v. a. to dry.

enjutez, –hŭtĕth´, sf. dryness.

enjuto, ta, –hŭ´tō, a. dried.

enlace, ĕnlâ´thĕ, sm. connection, coherence; link; kindred, affinity; flourish.

enladrillado, –lâdrĭlyâ´dō, sm. pavement of bricks. [layer.

enladrillador, –lâdrĭlyâdōr´, sm. bricklayer.

enladrillar, –lâdrĭlyâr´, v. a. to pave a floor with bricks. [grease, to baste.

enlardar, –lârdâr´, v. a. to rub with

enlazable, –lâthâ´blĕ, a. which can be fastened together. [knit, to lace.

enlazar, –lâthâr´, v. a. to join, to unite; to

enlodar, –lōdâr´, v. a. to bemire.

enloquecer, –lōkĕthḗr´, v. a. to madden, to make mad.

enloquecimiento, –lōkĕthĭmĭḗn´tō, sm. enraging, maddening. [flags.

enlosar, –lōsâr´, v. a. to lay a floor with

enlozanarse, –lōthânâr´sĕ, v. r. to boast of one's dexterity or strength.

enlutar, –lŭtâr´, v. a. to put into mourning; –se, to go into mourning.

enmaderar, –mădĕrăr′, v. a. to roof a house with timber.

enmarañar, –mărănyăr′, v. a. to entangle, to involve in difficulties; to puzzle.

enmarillecerse, –mărllyĕthĕr′sĕ, v. r. to become pale or yellow.

enmaromar, –mărōmăr′, v. a. to tie with a rope.

enmascarar, –măskărăr′, v. a. to mask; –se, to go in disguise, to masquerade.

enmendación, –mĕndăthĭōn′, sf. emendation, correction.

enmendar, ĕnmĕndăr′, v. a. to correct, to reform; to repair; to compensate; to abrogate.

enmienda, ĕnmĭĕn′dă, sf. correction, amendment; emendation; reward; compensation; parliamentary amendment.

enmohecer, –mōĕthĕr′, v. a. to mould, to must; –se, to grow mouldy or musty; to rust.

enmudecer, –mŭdĕthĕr′, v. n. to grow dumb; to be silent; –, v. a. to impose silence.

ennegrecer, –nĕgrĕthĕr′, v. a. to darken, to obscure.

ennoblecer, –nōblĕthĕr′, v. a. to blacken; to ennoble.

ennoblecimiento, –thĭmĭĕn′tō, sm. ennoblement, nobilitation.

enojadizo, za, ĕnō′hădĭ′thō, a. fretful; peevish.

enojar, ĕnō′hăr′, v. a. to irritate, to make angry; to tease; to molest; to offend; –se, to be boisterous.

enojo, ĕnō′h′ō, sm. peevishness, anger, choler, passion.

enojoso, sa, –hō′sō, a. offensive, vexatious; horrible; wicked beyond measure.

enorme, ĕnōr′mĕ, a. enormous, vast, huge; horrible.

enormidad, ĕnōrmĭdăd′, sf. enormity, monstruosity.

enramada, –rămă′dă, sf. hut covered with the branches of trees; shed; pent-house; ramification; branches of trees.

enramar, –rămăr′, v. a. to cover with the branches.

enranciarse, –rănthĭăr′sĕ, v. r. to grow rancid; rarefy.

enrarecer, –rărĕthĕr′, v. a. to thin, to rarefy.

enredadera, –rĕdădĕ′ră, sf. climbing plant; bind-weed.

enredador, ra, –dōr′, sm. & f. entangler; tattler, tale-bearer; busybody.

enredar, ĕnrĕdăr′, v. a. to entangle, to ensnare, to confound, to perplex; to puzzle; to sow discord; –se, to fall in love (of unlawful love).

enredo, ĕnrĕ′dō, sm. entanglement, perplexity, embarrassment; imposition; mischievous lie; plot of a play.

enredoso, sa, –rĕdō′sō, a. full of snares and difficulties; open-work embroidery.

enrejado, –rĕ′hă′dō, sm. trellis-work; lattice.

enrejar, –rĕ′hăr′, v. a. to fix a grating to a window; to grate; to lattice.

enriar, –rĭăr′, v. a. to steep hemp and flax in water.

enriquecer, –rĭkĕthĕr′, v. a. to enrich; to adorn; –, v. n. to grow rich.

enriscada, da, –rĭskă′dō, a. mountainous, craggy.

enriscamiento, –mĭĕn′tō, sm. taking refuge among rocks.

enriscar, ĕnrĭskăr′, v. a. to place on the top of mountains or rocks; –se, to take refuge among rocks.

enristrar, –rĭstrăr′, v. a. to couch the lance; to range, to file; (fig.) to meet a difficulty.

enristre, ĕnrĭs′trĕ, sm. couching a lance.

enrizar, –rĭthăr′, v. a. to curl.

enrobustecer, –ĕnrōbŭstĕthĕr′, v. a. to make robust; wheel.

enrodar, –rōdăr′, v. a. to break on the wheel.

enrodrigonar, –rōdrĭgōnăr′, v. a. to prop vines with stakes; hot.

enrojecer, –rō′hĕthĕr′, v. a. to make red-hot.

enronquecer, –rōnkĕthĕr′, v. a. to make hoarse; –, v. n. to grow hoarse.

enroscadura, –rōskădō′ră, sf. act of twisting; to curl or roll up.

enroscar, –rōskăr′, v. a. to twist; –se, to curl or roll up.

ensalada, –sălă′dă, sf. salad; hodge-podge, medley.

ensaladera, –ldĕ′ră, sf. salad-bowl.

ensalmar, ĕnsălmăr′, v. a. to set dislocated bones; to heal by spells.

ensalmo, ĕnsăl′mō, sm. enchantment, spell.

ensalobrarse, –sălōbrăr′sĕ, v. r. to become putrid, to stagnant water.

ensalzar, –sălthăr′, v. a. to exalt, to aggrandize; to exaggerate; –se, to boast.

ensamblador, –sămblădōr′, sm. joiner.

ensanchar, –sănthăr′, v. a. to widen, to extend, to enlarge; –se, to assume an air of importance.

ensanche, ĕnsăn′tshĕ, sm. dilation, augmentation; widening; gear.

ensangrentar, –săngrĕntăr′, v. a. to stain with blood; –se, to be overzealous in the pursuit of a thing; to proceed in a cruel and barbarous manner.

ensañado, –sănyă′dō, a. courageous.

ensañar, –sănyăr′, v. a. to irritate, to enrage.

ensartar, –sărtăr′, v. a. to string (beads, etc.) (fig.) to go through a long story.

ensayar, –săyăr′, v. a. to assay precious metals; to rehearse; to examine, to prove; –se, to exercise oneself.

ensayo, ĕnsă′yō, sm. assay, trial, proof; rehearsal of a play.

ensebar, –sĕbăr′, v. a. to grease.

ensenada, –sĕnă′dă, sf. creek.

enseña, ĕnsĕn′yă, sf. colours, pl., standard.

enseñanza, –yănthă, sf. teaching, instruction.

enseñar, ĕnsĕnyăr′, v. a. to teach, to instruct; –se, to accustom oneself.

enserar, –sĕrăr′, v. a. to cover with bass-weed.

enseres, –sĕ′rĕs, sm.pl. chattels, pl.

ensillado, da, –sĭlyă′dō, a. hollow-backed.

ensilladura, –dō′ră, sf. saddle of a horse's or mule's back.

ensillar, ĕnsĭlyăr′, v. a. to saddle.

ensoberbecer, –sōbĕrbĕthĕr′, v. a. to make proud; –se, to become proud; to become boisterous.

ensordecer, –sōrdĕthĕr′, v. a. to deafen; –, v. n. to grow deaf; to become silent.

ensordecimiento, –thĭmĭĕn′tō, sm. deafness.

ensortijamiento, *–sŏrtĭ´hämĭĕn´tŏ*, sm. curling the hair.

ensortijar, *–sŏrtĭ´här´*, v. a. to form into a ring; to curl.

ensuciar, *–sŭthĭär´*, v. a. to stain, to soil; to pollute with vicious habits; –se, to dirty one's bed, &c.; to allow oneself to be bribed by presents.

entablado, *–täblä´dŏ*, sm. floor made of boards.

entablar, *–täblär´*, v. a. to cover or floor with boards.

entablillar, *–täblĭlyär´*, v.a. to secure with small boards.

entallador, *–tälyädŏr´*, sm. sculptor; engraver.

entalladura, *–dŏ´rä*, sf. sculpture; engraving.

entallar, *–tälyär´*, v. a. to sculpture, to carve; to engrave; –, v. n. to cut or shape a thing so as to fit it to the body.

entallecer, *–tälyĕthĕr´*, v. n. to shoot, to sprout (of plants).

entapizar, *–täpĭthär´*, v. a. to hang with tapestry.

entarimar, *–tärĭmär´*, v. a. to cover a floor with boards.

ente, *ĕn´tĕ*, sm. entity, being; ridiculous man.

entenada, *–tĕnä´dä*, sf. daughter by a former marriage.

entenado, *–tĕnä´dŏ*, sm. son by a former marriage.

entendederas, *–tĕndĕdĕ´räs*, sf.pl. understanding, judgment.

entender, *–tĕndĕr´*, v. a. & n. to understand, to comprehend; to remark, to take notice of; to reason, to think; á mi –, in my opinion; –se, to understand each other.

entendido, da, *–tĕndĭ´dŏ*, a. wise, learned, prudent, knowing.

entendimiento, *–dĭmĭĕn´tŏ*, sm. understanding, knowledge, judgment.

enteramente, *–tĕrämĕn´tĕ*, ad. entirely, completely.

enterar, *–tĕrär´*, v.a. to inform thoroughly; to instruct.

entereza, *–tĕrä´thä*, sf. entireness, integrity; uprightness; perfection; firmness of mind.

enterizo, za, *–tĕrĭ´thŏ*, a. entire, complete.

enternecer, *–tĕrnĕthĕr´*, v. a. to soften; to move to compassion; –, v. n. to pity, to commiserate.

enternecimiento, *–thĭmĭĕn´tŏ*, sm. compassion, pity, melting.

entero, ra, *ĕntĕ´rŏ*, a. entire; perfect, complete; sound; just, right; pure, uncorrupted; strong, robust; uncastrated; por –, entirely, completely.

enterrador, *–tĕrrädŏr´*, sm. grave-digger.

enterrar, *–tĕrrär´*, v. a. to inter, to bury.

entibiar, *–tĭbĭär´*, v. a. to cool.

entidad, *–tĭdäd´*, sf. entity, real being; (fig.) consideration, importance.

entierro, *ĕntĭĕr´rŏ*, sm. burial; tomb, grave.

entimema, *–tĭmä´mä*, sf. enthymem.

entiznar, *–tĭthnär´*, v. a. to revile, to defame, to slander.

entoldar, *–tŏldär´*, v. a. to cover with an awning; to hang the walls with clothes; –se, to dress pompously.

entonación, *–tŏnäthŏn´*, sf. modulation; intonation; blowing of the bellows of an organ; (fig.) presumption, pride.

entonador, *–dŏr´*, sm. organ-blower; player of the first verse of a psalm.

entonar, *–tŏnär´*, v. a. to tune, to intonate; to blow the bellows of an organ; –se, to be puffed up with pride.

entonces, *ĕntŏn´thĕs*, ad. then, at that time.

entonelar, *–tŏnĕlär´*, v. a. to barrel.

entontecer, *–tŏntĕthĕr´*, v. a. to mope, to fool; –, v. n., –se, to grow stupid.

entontecimiento, *–thĭmĭĕn´tŏ*, sm. growing stupid.

entorchado, *–tŏrtshä´dŏ*, sm. twisted cord which serves for embroideries.

entorchar, *–tŏrtshär´*, v. a. to twist a cord; to cover cords for musical instruments with wire.

entornar, *–tŏrnär´*, v. a. to turn.

entornillar, *–tŏrnĭlyär´*, v. a. to make anything in the form of a screw or ring.

entorpecer, *–tŏrpĕthĕr´*, v. a. to benumb; to stupefy.

entorpecimiento, *–thĭmĭĕn´tŏ*, sm. torpor, numbness, stupefaction.

entortar, *–tŏrtär´*, v. a. to bend; to pull out an eye.

entrada, *ĕnträ´dä*, sf. entrance, entry; –s, pl. temporal angles, pl.

entrambos, bas, *ĕnträm´bŏs*, pn. pl. both.

entrampar, *–trämpär´*, v. a. to entrap, to ensnare; to involve in difficulties; to deceive; to encumber an estate with debts; –se, to become indebted.

entrañable, *–tränyä´blĕ*, a. intimate, affectionate.

entrañas, *ĕnträn´yäs*, sf. pl. entrails, intestines, pl.

entrar, *ĕnträr´*, v. a. & n. to enter, to go in; to commence.

entre, *ĕn´trĕ*, pr. between; in; – año, in the course of the year; –manos, in hand.

entreabrir, *–äbrĭr´*, v. a. to half open a door, to leave it ajar.

entrecano, na, *–kä´nŏ*, a. grey-black, greyish.

entrecejo, *–thĕ´hŏ*, sm. the space between the eye-brows; frowning supercilious look.

entrecoger, *–kŏ´hĕr´*, v. a. to catch, to intercept.

entrecubiertas, *–kŭbĭĕr´täs*, sf.pl. (mar.) between-decks.

entredicho, *–dĭtsh´ŏ*, sm. prohibition; ecclesiastical interdict, and fine.

entrefino, na, *–fĕ´nŏ*, a. between coarse and fine.

entrega, *ĕnträ´gä*, sf. delivery; conveyance.

entregar, *ĕntrĕgär´*, v. a. to deliver; to restore; –se, to deliver oneself up into the hands of another; to abandon oneself to vice.

entrelazar, *–läthär´*, v. a. to interlace.

entrelistado, da, *–lĭstä´dŏ*, a. striped, variegated.

entremedias, *–mĕd´dĭäs*, ad. in the mean time.

entremés, *–mĕs´*, sm. interlude.

entremeter, *–mĕtĕr´*, v. a. to put one thing between others; to intermeddle; to unswathe children.

entremetido, *–mĕtĭ´dŏ*, sm. meddler, obtruder; –, da, a. meddling.

entremetimiento, *–mĕtĭmĭĕn´tŏ*, sm. interposition; meddling.

entreoir, *–ŏĭr´*, v. a. to hear without perfectly understanding what is said.

entrepalmadura, *-pálmădŏ´rā*, sf. disease in horses' hoofs.

entrepaño, *-pán´yŏ*, sm. panel.

entrepiernas, *-pĭĕr´năs*, sf. pl. opening between the legs; pieces put into the fork of a pair of breeches.

entrepuentes, *-pŭĕn´tĕs*, sm. pl. (mar.) between-decks. [sf. interlinea] note.

entrerrenglonadura, *-rĕnglŏnădŏ´rā*,

entrerrenglonar, *-rĕnglŏnár´*, v. a. to write between lings.

entresaca, *-sā´kā*, sf. cutting down trees, in order to thin a wood. [to separate.

entresacar, *-săkár´*, v. a. to garble, to sift.

entresuelo, *-sŭĕ´lŏ*, sm. entresol.

entretalladura, *-tălyădŏ´rā*, sf. sculpture in bass-relief.

entretallar, *-tălyár´*, v. a. to sculpture in bass-relief; to slash, to mangle.

entretejer, *-tĕhĕr´*, v. a. to tissue, to interweave. [strong linen.

entretela, *-tĕ´lā*, sf. buckram, stiff or strong linen.

entretelar, *-tĕlár´*, v. a. to put buckram or strong linen between the lining and cloth.

entretener, *-tĕnĕr´*, v. a. to amuse; to entertain; to divert; to allay pain; -se, to amuse oneself.

entretenido, da, *-tĕnĭ´dŏ*, a. pleasant, amusing; doing business in an office, in hopes of obtaining a place.

entretenimiento, *-tĕnĭmĭĕn´tŏ*, sm. amusement, entertainment.

entrever, *-vĕr´*, v. a. to have a glimpse of, to see imperfectly.

entreverado, da, *-vĕrā´dŏ*, a. interlined with fat and lean. [mix together.

entreverar, *-vĕrár´*, v. a. to intermix, to

entrevista, *-vĭs´tā*, sf. interview.

entripado, da, *-trĭpā´dŏ*, a. contained in the entrails. [to afflict.

entristecer, *-trĭstĕthĕr´*, v. a. to sadden,

entrojar, *-trŏhár´*, v. a. to put up grain in barns. [the same family.

entroncar, *-trŏnkár´*, v. n. to belong to

entronización, *-trŏnĭthăthĭŏn´*, sf. elevation to a throne.

entronizar, *-trŏnĭthár´*, v. a. to enthrone.

entronque, *-trŏn´kĕ*, sm. relationship with the chief of a family.

entruchada, *-trŭtchā´dā*, sf. clandestine operation, underhand business.

entruchar, *-trŭtchár´*, v. a. to decoy, to lure into a snare.

entumecer, *-tŭmĕthĕr´*, v. a. to swell; to benumb; -, v. n. to swell, to surge.

entumecimiento, *-thĭmĭĕn´tŏ*, sm. swelling; torpor.

enturbiar, *-tŭrbĭár´*, v. a. to make turbid; to obscure, to confound; -se, to disorder or derange any thing.

entusiasmar, *-tŭsĭăsmár´*, v. a. to transport, to enrapture.

entusiasmo, *-tŭsĭăs´mŏ*, sm. enthusiasm.

entusiasta, *-tŭsĭăs´tā*, sm. enthusiast.

enumeración, *ĕnŭmĕrăthĭŏn´*, sf. enumeration, counting over.

enumerar, *ĕnŭmĕrár´*, v. a. to enumerate.

enunciación, *ĕnŭnthĭăthĭŏn´*, sf. enunciation, declaration. [declare.

enunciar, *ĕnŭnthĭár´*, v. a. to enunciate, to

enunciativo, va, *ĕnŭnthĭătĭ´vŏ*, a. enunciative. [sheath.

envainar, *ĕnvāĭnár´*, v. a. to sheathe, to

envalentonar, *-vălĕntŏnár´*, v. a. to encourage, to inspirit.

envanecer, *-vănĕthĕr´*, v. a. to make vain; to swell with pride; -se, to become proud. [ness, numbness.

envaramiento, *-vărămĭĕn´tŏ*, sm. stiffness,

envarar, *-vărár´*, v. a. to benumb.

envasador, *-văsădŏr´*, sm. funnel.

envasar, *-văsár´*, v. a. to tun, to barrel; to drink to excess.

envejecer, *-vĕhĕthĕr´*, v. a. to make old; -, v. n. to grow old.

envejecido, da, *-vĕhĕthĭ´dŏ*, a. grown old; looking old. [poisoner.

envenenador, ra, *-vĕnĕnădŏr´*, sm. & f.

envenenar, *-vĕnĕnár´*, v. a. to envenom, to poison, to despatch. [ing.

envenenamiento, *-mĭĕn´tŏ*, sm. poisoning.

envestidura, *-vĕstĭdŏ´rā*, sf. investiture.

envestir, *-vĕstĭr´*, v. a. to invest; to illuminate, to enlighten; to cover; -se, to accustom oneself.

enviado, *-vĭā´dŏ*, sm. envoy, messenger.

enviar, *-vĭár´*, v. a. to send, to transmit, to convey, to despatch.

enviciar, *-vĭthĭár´*, v. a. to vitiate, to corrupt; -se, to be excessively fond of.

envidar, *-vĭdár´*, v. a. to open the game by staking a certain sum.

envidia, *ĕnvĭ´dĭa*, sf. envy; emulation.

envidiable, *-vĭdĭā´blĕ*, a. enviable.

envidiar, *-vĭdĭár´*, v. n. to envy, to grudge. [ydious, jealous.

envidioso, sa, *-vĭdĭŏ´sŏ*, a. envious; in-

envilecer, *-vĭlĕthĕr´*, v. a. to vilify, to debase; -se, to degrade oneself.

envinagrar, *-vĭnăgrár´*, v. a. to put vinegar into anything. [goods.

envío, *ĕnvĭ´ŏ*, sm. (com.) remittance of

envirar, *-vĭrár´*, v. a. to clasp together cork-wood to form a bee-hive.

enviscar, *-vĭskár´*, v. a. to glue; to irritate, to anger; -se, to be glued with bird-lime.

envite, *ĕnvĭ´tĕ*, sm. opening the game by staking a certain sum; invitation.

enviudar, *-vĭŭdár´*, v. n. to become a widower or widow. [clothes.

envoltorio, *-vŏltŏ´rĭŏ*, sm. bundle of

envolturas, *-tŏ´răs*, sf. pl. swaddling- or swathing-clothes, pl.

envolver, *-vŏlvĕr´*, v. a. to involve; to wrap up; -se, to be implicated in an affair. [with gypsum.

enyesadura, *-yĕsădŏ´rā*, sf. plastering

enyesar, *-yĕsár´*, v. a. to plaster, to parget.

enyugar, *-yŭgár´*, v. a. to yoke cattle.

enzainarse, *-thăĭnár´sĕ*, v. r. to squint, to have a cast in one's eye.

enzamarrado, da, *-thămărrā´dŏ*, a. dressed in a shepherd's great-coat made of sheep-skins, with the wool on.

enzarzado, da, _–thárthá'dó,_ a. curled, matted.

enzarzar, _–thárthár',_ v. a. to throw among brambles and briers; to sow discord; **–se,** to be entangled among brambles and briers; to be involved in difficulties.

epacta, _épák'tá,_ sf. epact.

epactilla, _épáktíl'yá,_ sf. small calendar for the performance of divine service.

épico, ca, _é'píkó,_ a. epic.

epicúreo, rea, _épíkú'réó,_ a. epicurean.

epidemia, _épídá'míá,_ sf. epidemic disease.

epidémico, ca, _épídá'míkó,_ a. epidemic.

epidermis, _épídár'mís,_ sf. epidermis, cuticle.

Epifanía, _épífáné'á,_ sf. Epiphany.

epígrafe, _épígrá'fé,_ sf. epigraph, inscription; motto, device, posy.

epigrama, _épígrá'má,_ sm. epigram.

epilepsia, _épílép'síá,_ sf. epilepsy.

epilogar, _épílógár',_ v. a. to recapitulate, to sum up.

epílogo, _épí'lógó,_ sm. epilogue.

epiqueya, _épíké'yá,_ sf. mild and prudent interpretation of the law.   [bishopric.

episcopado, _épískópá'dó,_ sm. episcopacy;

episcopal, _–pál',_ a. episcopal.

episódico, ca, _épísó'díkó,_ a. episodical.

episodio, _–só'díó,_ sm. episode.

epístola, _épís'tólá,_ sf. epistle, letter; sub-deaconship.

epistolar, _épístólár',_ a. epistolary.

epistolario, _–lá'ríó,_ sm. collection of epistles which are read or sung at mass; guide for letter-writing.

epitafio, _építá'fíó,_ sm. epitaph.

epitalamio, _építálá'míó,_ sm. nuptial song.

epíteto, _épé'tétó,_ sm. epithet.

epitomar, _építómár',_ v. a. to epitomize.

epítome, _épé'tómé,_ sm. epitome, compendium.

época, _é'pókú,_ sf. epoch.   [dium.

epopeya, _épópá'yá,_ sf. epopee.

equidad, _ékídád',_ sf. equity, honesty; cheapness; impartiality, justice.

equidistar, _ékídístár',_ v.n. to be equidistant.

equilátero, ra, _–lá'téró,_ a. equilateral, having all sides equal.

equilibrar, _–líbrár',_ v. a. to equilibrate; to counterpoise, to counterbalance.

equilibrio, _lé'bríó,_ sm. equilibrium.

equinoccial, _–nókthíál',_ a. equinoctial.

equinoccio, _–nók'thíó,_ sm. equinox.

equipaje, _–pá'hé,_ sm. luggage; equipment; (mar.) crew of a ship; **–s,** pl. (rail.) luggage-office.

equipar, _–pár',_ v. a. to fit out, to equip, to furnish, to accoutre.

equitación, _–táthíón',_ sf. horsemanship.

equitativo, _va,_ _–tá'tíbó,_ a. equitable; just.

equivalencia, _–válén'thíá,_ sf. equivalence, compensation.

equivalente, _–válén'té,_ a. equivalent.

equivaler, _–válér',_ v. n. to be of equal value.   [error, misunderstanding.

equivocación, _–vókáthíón',_ sf. mistake,

equivocar, _–vókár',_ v. a. to mistake, to misconceive, to misunderstand.

equívoco, _ékí'vókó,_ a. equivocal, ambiguous; **–,** sm. equivocation, quibble.

era, _á'rá,_ sf. era, æra; thrashing-floor; plot in a garden.

eral, _érál',_ sm. two-year old ox.

erario, _érá'ríó,_ sm. Exchequer, public treasury, fisc.

erección, _érékthíón',_ sf. foundation, establishment; erection, elevation. [solitary.

eremítico, ca, _érémé'tíkó,_ a. hermitlike,

ergotear, _érgótár',_ v. n. to argue, to debate without reason.

erguir, _érgír',_ v. a. to erect, to raise up, straight; **–se,** to be elated with pride.

erial, _érál',_ a. untilled, uncultivated.

erigir, _érí'hír',_ v. a. to erect, to raise, to build; to establish.

erisipela, _érísípé'lá,_ sf. (med.) erysipelas.

erisipelar, _–pélár',_ v. a. to cause erysipelas.   [on end (of hair, etc.).

erizamiento, _éríthámién'tó,_ sm. standing

erizar, _éríthár',_ v. a. & r. to bristle.

erizo, _éré'thó,_ sm. hedgehog.

ermita, _érmí'tá,_ sf. hermitage.

ermitaño, _–táñ'yó,_ sm. hermit.

erradizo, za, _érrádé'thó,_ a. wandering to and fro.   [roving.

errante, _érrán'té,_ p. & a. errant, erring,

errar, _érrár',_ v. a. to err, to commit errors; to mistake; **–,** v. n. to go astray.

errata, _érrá'tá,_ sf. error in printing.

erre, _ér'ré,_ **– que –,** ad. pertinaciously, obstinately.

erróneo, nea, _érró'néó,_ a. erroneous.

error, _érrór',_ sm. error, mistake, fault.

eructar, _éráktár',_ v.n. to belch, to eructate.

eructo, _érák'tó,_ sm. belch, eructation.

erudición, _érúdíthíón',_ sf. erudition, learning.

erudito, ta, _–dí'tó,_ a. learned, lettered.

erupción, _érúpthíón',_ sf. eruption, outbreak.   [belching.

eructación, _érúktáthíón',_ sf. eructation,

esbelto, ta, _ésbél'tó,_ a. tall, genteel, well-shaped.

esbirro, _ésbír'ró,_ sm. bailiff, apparitor.

escabechar, _éskábéchár',_ v. a. to souse, to pickle.   [pickled fish.

escabeche, _–bé'ché,_ sm. souse, pickle;

escabel, _éskábél',_ sm. foot-stool.

escabrosidad, _–brósídád',_ sf. unevenness, roughness; asperity.

escabroso, sa, _–bró'só,_ a. rough, uneven; craggy, crabbed; rude, unpolished.

escabullirse, _–búlyír'sé,_ r. to escape, to evade; to slip through one's fingers.

escala, _éská'lá,_ sf. ladder; (mus.) scale.

escalada, _éskálá'dá,_ sf. scalade, escalade; **– á escala vista,** a day-light escalade.

escalador, _–dór',_ sm. climber, he who scales walls.   [suspicious, wary.

escaldado, da, _éskáldá'dó,_ a. cautious,

escaldar, _–dár',_ v. a. to scald.

escalera, _éskálé'rá,_ sf. staircase; ladder.

escalfador, _éskálfádór',_ sm. barber's pan for keeping water warm; chafing-dish.

escalfar, *-fär',* v. a. to boil eggs; to scorch. [degree of dignity.

escalón, *ĕskălōn',* sm. step of a stair;

escama, *ĕskä'mä,* sf. fish-scale.

escamado, da, *ĕskämä'dŏ,* a. tutored by experience. [broidery.

escamadura, *-dŏ'rä,* sf. scale-like embroidery.

escamar, *ĕskämär',* v. a. to take off the scales; —, v. n. to embroider scale or shell fashion; —se, to resent, to take ill.

escamoso, sa, *ĕskämŏ'sŏ,* a. scaly.

escamotar, *-mŏtär',* v. a. to make a thing disappear from one's hands (in conjuring).

escampar, *ĕskämpär',* v. a. to cease raining; —, v. a. to clean a place.

escanciador, ra, *ĕskänthĭädŏr',* sm. & f. cup-bearer.

escanciar, *-thĭär',* v. a. to pour wine from one vessel into another to drink.

escanda, *ĕskän'dä,* sf. (bot.) spelt-wheat.

escandalizador, *-dälĭthädŏr',* sm. scandal-monger. [-se, to be scandalised.

escandalizar, *-lĭthär',* v. a. to scandalise;

escándalo, *ĕskän'dälŏ,* sm. scandal.

escandaloso, sa, *-dälŏ'sŏ,* a. scandalous; turbulent.

escaño, *ĕskän'yŏ,* sm. bench with a back.

escapada, *ĕskäpä'dä,* sf. escape, flight.

escapar, *ĕskäpär',* v. a. to liberate from danger; to slip one's memory; —, v. n. to escape. [cupboard (in Havannah).

escaparate, *ĕskäpärä'tĕ,* sm. shop-front;

escapatoria, *-tŏ'rĭä,* sf. escape, flight; excuse.

escape, *ĕskä'pĕ,* sm. escape, flight; escapement (part of a watch); á todo —, with the utmost velocity.

escapulario, *ĕskäpŭlä'rĭŏ,* sm. scapulary.

escarabajear, *ĕskäräbähĕär',* v.n. to crawl to and fro like insects; to scribble; to sting, to give pain. [short, ill-shaped person.

escarabajo, *ĕskäräbä'hŏ,* sm. black-beetle;

escaramuza, *-mŏ'thä,* sf. skirmish; dispute, quarrel. [misher; disputer.

escaramuzador, *-mŭthädŏr',* sm. skir-

escaramuzar, *-mŭthär',* v. a. to skirmish.

escarapela, *-pä'lä,* sf. cockade.

escarbadientes, *ĕskärbädĭĕn'tĕs,* sm. tooth-pick. [scratching.

escarbadura, *-dŏ'rä,* sf. act and effect of

escarbaorejas, *-ŏrĕ'häs,* sm. ear-pick.

escarbar, *ĕskärbär',* v. a. to scratch the earth (as fowls do); to inquire minutely into.

escarcha, *ĕskär'tshä,* sf. white frost.

escarchar, *-tshär',* v. n. to be frozen.

escardadera, *-dädĕ'rä,* sf. woman employed to clear corn-fields of weeds.

escardador, *-dŏr',* sm. weeder.

escardar, *-där',* v. a. to weed. [hook.

escardillo, *-dĕl'yŏ,* sm. small weeding-

escarlata, *-lä'tä,* sf. scarlet (colour); scarlet (cloth); kermes.

escarlatín, *-tĭn',* sm. coarse kind of scarlet.

escarlatina, *-tĕ'nä,* sf. scarlet-fever, scarlatina. [pick wool.

escarmenar, *-mĕnär',* v. a. to comb, to

escarmentar, *-mĕntär',* v. n. to be tutored by experience; to take warning; —, v. a. to punish severely.

escarmiento, *-mĭĕn'tŏ,* sm. warning, caution; chastisement. [to ridicule.

escarnecer, *ĕskärnĕthĕr',* v. a. to mock,

escarnio, *ĕskär'nĭŏ,* sm. scoff, contemptuous ridicule. [frill round the neck.

escarola, *ĕskärŏ'lä,* sf. (bot.) endive; plaited

escarolado, da, *-lä'dŏ,* a. of the colour of endive, pale yellowish; curly.

escarpa, *ĕskär'pä,* sf. declivity; scarp.

escarpado, da, *-pä'dŏ,* a. sloped, craggy.

escarpar, *-pär',* v. a. to scarf timbers; (mil.) to escarp, to slope down.

escarpia, *ĕskär'pĭä,* sf. tenter.

escarpidor, *-pĭdŏr',* sm. wide, large-toothed comb.

escarpín, *-pĭn',* sm. sock; pump (shoe).

escasear, *ĕskäsĕär',* v. a. to give sparingly and with reluctance; to spare; —, v. n. to grow less, to decrease. [liness.

escasez, *ĕskäsĕth',* sf. scantiness, niggard-

escaso, sa, *ĕskä'sŏ,* a. small, short, little; sparing, niggardly; scanty, defective.

escatimar, *ĕskätĭmär',* v. a. to curtail, to lessen; to haggle; to corrupt the sense and meaning of words.

escena, *ĕsthĕ'nä,* sf. stage; scene; bed and shepherd's hut made of branches.

escénico, ca, *ĕsthĕ'nĭkŏ,* a. scenic. [cism.

escepticismo, *ĕsthĕptĭthĭs'mŏ,* sm. scepti-

escéptico, ca, *ĕsthĕp'tĭkŏ,* a. sceptic, scep-schelin, *ĕstshĕlĭn',* sm. shilling. [tical.

esclarecer, *ĕsklärĕthĕr',* v. a. to lighten; to illuminate; to illustrate; —, v. n. to dawn. [noble.

esclarecido, da, *-thĕ'dŏ,* a. illustrious,

esclarecimiento, *-thĭmĭĕn'tŏ,* sm. dawn; illustriousness.

esclavina, *ĕsklävĕ'nä,* sf. pilgrim's pall; collar worn by priests in Spain; pelerine, fur-cape.

esclavitud, *-vĭtŏd',* sf. slavery; servitude.

esclavo, va, *ĕsklä'vŏ,* sm. & f. slave, captive.

esclusa, *ĕsklŏ'sä,* sf. sluice, flood-gate.

escoba, *ĕskŏ'bä,* sf. broom, besom.

escobada, *ĕskŏbä'dä,* sf. sweeping slightly.

escobajo, *-bä'hŏ,* sm. remains of an old broom; stalk of a bunch of grapes (without the fruit). [broom.

escobazo, *-bä'thŏ,* sm. blow given with a

escobilla, *-bĭl'yä,* sf. brush; small broom.

escobillón, *-yŏn',* sm. artillery-sponge.

escocer, *ĕskŏthĕr',* v. a. to cause a sharp lively pain; to irritate; to provoke; —se, to smart. [of gauze, &c.

escofieta, *-fĭĕ'tä,* sf. women's head-dress

escofina, *-fĕ'nä,* sf. rasp.

escofinar, *-fĕnär',* v. a. to rasp.

escoger, *-hĕr',* v. a. to choose, to select.

escogidamente, *-hĭdämĕn'tĕ,* ad. choicely, selectly. [scholastic.

escolar, *ĕskŏlär',* sm. scholar, student; —, a.

escolástico, ca, *-läs'tĭkŏ,* a. scholastic; —, sm. professor of theology.

escolio, *ĕskŏ'lĭŏ,* sm. scholion, comment.

escollo, *ĕskŏl'yŏ,* sm. sunken rocks, pl.

escolta, *ĕskŏl'tă,* sf. (mil.) escort, convoy.

escoltar, *-tăr',* v. a. to escort.

escombrar, *ĕskŏmbrăr',* v. a. to remove obstacles; to purify. [mackerel.

escombro, *ĕskŏm'brŏ,* sm. rubbish.

esconce, *ĕskŏn'thĕ,* sm. corner, angle.

escondedero, *-dĕ'rŏ,* sm. lurking-place.

esconder, *ĕskŏndĕr',* v. a. to hide, to conceal; to dissemble; to contain; **-se,** to lie hid.

escondidas, *-dē'dăs,* **escondidillas,** *-dēl'yăs* (à -), nd, in a secret manner.

escondite, *-dē'tĕ,* sm. concealment; hiding; **juego de -,** hide and seek.

escondrijo, *-drē'h'ŏ,* sm. hiding-place.

esconzado, da, *-thă'dŏ,* a. oblique, wry.

escopeta, *-tă'thŏ,* sf. firelock, gun; **á tira de -,** within gun-shot.

escopetazo, *-tă'thŏ,* sm. gun-shot; gun-shot wound.

escopetear, *-tĕăr',* v. a. to discharge a gun repeatedly; **-se,** to discharge firelocks at each other; to insult each other with foul language. [arms.

escopeteo, *-tĕ'ŏ,* sm. discharge of firearms.

escopetero, *-tĕ'rŏ,* sm. musketeer.

escopleadura, *-plĕădŏ'ră,* sf. mortise-hole made in timber.

escoplear, *-plĕăr',* v. a. to chisel out.

escoplo, *ĕskŏ'plŏ,* sm. chisel.

escorbútico, ca, *ĕskŏrbŏ'tĭkŏ,* a. scorbutic.

escorbuto, *-bŏ'tŏ,* sm. scurvy. [thing.

escoria, *ĕskŏ'rĭă,* sf. dross; lee; worthless

escoriación, *ĕskŏrĭăthĭŏn',* sf. incrustation.

escorial, *ĕskŏrĭăl',* sm. dross-heap.

Escorial, -, sm. Escurial, pleasure-seat near Madrid.

escoriarse, *-rĭăr'sĕ,* v. r. to get skinned.

Escorpio, *ĕskŏr'pĭŏ,* sm. Scorpio, Scorpion (sign of the zodiac).

escorpión, *ĕskŏrpĭŏn',* sm. scorpion.

escorzonera, *-thŏnĕ'ră,* sf. viper-grass.

escotadura, *ĕskŏtădŏ'ră,* sf. curve of a jacket or corset.

escotar, *-tăr',* v. a. to cut out a garment about the neck; to slope; to pay one's share of scot and taxes.

escote, *ĕskŏ'tĕ,* sm. slope of a garment; tucker; one's share of a reckoning at a club.

escotero, ra, *-tĕ'rŏ,* a. free, disengaged.

escotilla, *-tĭl'yă,* sf. (mar.) hatchway.

escotillón, *-tĭlyŏn',* sm. trap-door; drop, slot (in theatres).

escozor, *-thŏr',* sm. smart pungent pain; lively sensation or perception of the mind.

escriba, *ĕskrē'bă,* sm. scribe (among the Hebrews). [notary; escritoire.

escribanía, *ĕskrĭbănē'ă,* sf. office of a

escribano, *-bă'nŏ,* sm. notary, scrivener.

escribiente, *-bĭĕn'tĕ,* sm. amanuensis.

escribir, *ĕskrĭbēr',* v. a. to write; to compose literary works. [(law) libel.

escrito, *ĕskrē'tŏ,* sm. literary composition.

escritor, *-tŏr',* sm. writer, author.

escritorio, *-tŏ'rĭŏ,* sm. cupboard adorned with inlaid ivory; counting-house; escritoire, writing-desk; office, study. [ture.

escritura, *-tŏ'ră,* sf. writing; deed; Scrip-

escriturar, *-tŭrăr',* v. a. to bind oneself legally. [lous.

escrofuloso, sa, *ĕskrŏfŭlŏ'sŏ,* a. scrofulous.

escrupulizar, *ĕskrăpŭlĭhăr',* v. n. to scruple, to doubt.

escrúpulo, *ĕskrŏ'pŭlŏ,* sm. doubt, scruple, scrupulousness; minute on a graduated sphere. [losity.

escrupulosidad, *-lŏsĭdăd'',* sf. scrupu-

escrupuloso, sa, *-lŏ'sŏ,* a. scrupulous; exact. [quiry.

escrutinio, *ĕskrŭtē'nĭŏ,* sm. scrutiny, en-

escrutiñador, *-tăr',* sm. scrutiniser, enquirer.

escuadra, *ĕskŭă'dră,* sf. square; squadron.

escuadrar, *ĕskŭădrăr',* v. a. to square.

escuadrón, *-drŏn',* sm. squadron, troop of horse. [in squadrons.

escuadronar, *-drŏnăr',* v. a. to form troops

escuadronista, *-drŏnĭs'tă,* sm. clever cavalry leader. [scout.

escucha, *ĕskŭ'chă,* sf. sentinel, sentry;

escuchar, *-chăr',* v. a. to listen, to hearken.

escudar, *ĕskŭdăr',* v. a. to shield; to guard from danger; **-se,** to depend on some means of evading danger. [office.

escudería, *-dĕrē'ă,* sf. shield-bearer's

escuderil, *-dĕrĭl',* a. belonging to the office of a shield-bearer. [page.

escudero, *-dĕ'rŏ,* sm. shield-bearer; lady's

escudilla, *-dĭl'yă,* sf. porringer.

escudillar, *-yăr',* v. a. to pour out broth into porringers.

escudo, *ĕskŭ'dŏ,* sm. shield, buckler; scutcheon of a lock; Crown (gold coin).

escudriñamiento, *ĕskŭdrĭnyămĭĕn'tŏ,* sm. investigation, scrutiny.

escudriñar, *-yăr',* v. a. to search, to pry into; to examine into.

escuela, *ĕskŭĕ'lă,* sf. school.

esculpir, *ĕskŭlpēr',* v. a. to sculpture.

escultor, *-tŏr',* sm. sculptor, carver.

escultura, *-tŏ'ră,* sf. sculpture; work of a sculptor.

escupidera, *ĕskŭpĭdĕ'ră,* sf. spittoon.

escupidero, *-dĕ'rŏ,* sm. spitting-place.

escupidura, *-dŏ'ră,* sf. spittle.

escupir, *ĕskŭpēr',* v. a. to spit. [flees.

escurriduras, *ĕskŭrrĭdŏ'răs,* sf. pl. dregs,

escurrir, *ĕskŭrrēr',* v. a. to drain to the dregs; **-,** v. n. to drop; to slip, to slide; to glide slowly; **-se,** to slip away.

esdrújulo, *ĕsdrŭ'h'ŭlŏ,* sm. a Spanish word of more than two syllables, the last two of which are short; **- la,** a. belonging to the words called esdrújulos.

ese | *ĕ'sĕ,* | **esa** | *ĕ'să,* eso, *ĕ'sŏ,* that.

esencia, *ĕsĕn'thĭă,* sf. essence.

esencial, *-thĭăl',* a. essential; principal.

esfera, *ĕsfĕ'ră,* sf. sphere; globe.

esférico, ca, *ĕsfĕ'rĭkŏ,* a. spherical.

esferoide, *ĕsfĕrŏĭ'dĕ,* sm. spheroid.

esfinge, *ĕsfĭn'hĕ,* sm. sphinx.

esforzado, da, *ĕsfŏrthă'dŏ,* a. strong, vigorous, valiant.

esforzar, *-thăr',* v. a. to strengthen; **-se,**

to exert oneself, **to make an effort**; to be confident. [vigour; effort.

esfuerzo, *ĕsfŭĕr'thŏ*, sm. courage, spirit.

esgrima, *ĕsgrē'mă*, sf. fencing; maestro de —, fencing-master. [fencing-master.

esgrimador, *ĕsgrēmădŏr'*, sm. fencer;

esgrimir, *ĕsgrēmĭr'*, v. a. to fence.

eslabón, *ĕslăbŏn'*, sm. link of a chain; steel for striking fire.

eslabonar, *ĕslăbŏnăr'*, v. a. to link; to unite.

esmaltador, *ĕsmăltădŏr'*, sm. enameller.

esmaltar, *ĕsmăltăr'*, v. a. to enamel.

esmalte, *ĕsmăl'tĕ*, sm. enamel.

esmerado, da, *ĕsmĕră'dŏ*, a. high-finished.

esmeralda, *–răl'dă*, sm. emerald. [nice.

esmerar, *–răr'*, v. a. to polish; –se, to endeavour to attain eminence or superior excellence.

esmeril, *–rĭl'*, sm. emery. [emery.

esmerilar, *–rĭlăr'*, v. a. to polish with an

esmero, *ĕsmĕ'rŏ*, sm. careful attention, elaborate effort.

esófago, *ĕsŏ'făgŏ*, sm. gullet; throat.

esotro, tra, *ĕsŏ'tră*, p. this or that other.

espabiladeras, *ĕspăbĭlădĕ'răs*, sf. pl. snuffers, pl.; candle-snuffer.

espabilar, *–bĭlăr'*, v. a. to snuff a candle.

espaciar, *–thĭăr'*, v. a. to extend, to dilate, to spread; to insert spaces (print.); –se, to walk to and fro; to cheer up.

espacio, *ĕspă'thĭŏ*, sm. space, capacity; distance; slowness. [ness, capacity.

espaciosidad, *–thĭŏsĭdăd'*, sf. spaciousness, capacity.

espacioso, sa, *–thĭŏ'sŏ*, a. spacious, roomy; slow.

espada, *ĕspă'dă*, sf. sword; ace of spades; —, m. bull-fighter.

espadachín, *–dăthĭn'*, sm. bully. [tail.

espadaña, *–dăn'yă*, sf. (bot.) great cat's-

espadar, *–dăr'*, v. a. to break hemp or flax with a swing-staff.

espadería, *–dĕrē'ă*, sf. sword-cutler's shop.

espadero, *–dĕ'rŏ*, sm. sword-cutler.

espadilla, *–dĭl'yă*, sf. scotching-handle; ace of spades.

espadín, *–dĭn'*, sm. small short sword.

espalda, *ĕspăl'dă*, sf. shoulder; shoulder of a bastion; back, back-part.

espaldar, *–dăr'*, sm. back-piece of a suit of armour; back-board; espalier in gardens.

espaldilla, *–dĭl'yă*, sf. shoulder-blade.

espalmar, *–măr'*, v. a. to pare a horse's hoof for shoeing.

espantable, *ĕspăntă'blĕ*, a. frightful, horrid, terrible; marvellous, wonderful.

espantadizo, za, *–tădĭ'thŏ*, a. timid, easily frightened. [bear.

espantajo, *–tă'hŏ*, sm. scarecrow; bug-

espantar, *–tăr'*, v. a. to frighten, to daunt; to chase or drive away.

espanto, *ĕspăn'tŏ*, sm. fright; menace, threat; wonder, surprise.

espantoso, sa, *–tŏ'sŏ*, a. frightful, dreadful; wonderful.

español, *ĕspănyŏl'*, sm. Spanish language.

españoleta, *–yŏlĕ'tă*, sf. ancient Spanish dance.

esparaván, *ĕspărăvăn'*, sm. malanders, pl.; sparrow-hawk.

esparavel, *–vĕl'*, sm. casting-net, drag-net.

esparcir, *ĕspărthĭr'*, v. a. to scatter; to divulge; –se, to amuse oneself.

espartería, *ĕspărtĕrē'ă*, sf. place where mats of esparto are made or sold.

espartero, *–tĕ'rŏ*, sm. maker and seller of esparto-work. [feather-grass.

esparto, *ĕspăr'tŏ*, sm. (bot.) esparto,

espárrago, *ĕspăr'răgŏ*, sm. asparagus.

espasmo, *ĕspăs'mŏ*, sm. spasm.

espátula, *ĕspă'tŭlă*, sf. spatula.

especería, *ĕspĕthĕrē'ă*, sf. grocer's shop, grocery; spices. [cinal drugs.

especia, *ĕspĕ'thĭă*, sf. spice; –s, pl. medicinal drugs.

especial, *ĕspĕthĭăl'*, a. special, particular; en –, specially.

especialidad, *–lĭdăd''*, sf. speciality.

especie, *ĕspĕ'thĭĕ*, sf. species; matter; motive.

especiero, *ĕspĕthĭĕ'rŏ*, sm. dealer in spices and aromatic drugs. [tion.

especificación, *–fĭkăthĭŏn'*, sf. specifica-

especificar, *–fĭkăr'*, v. a. to specify.

específico, ca, *ĕspĕthē'fĭkŏ*, a. specific, specifical.

espacioso, sa, *–thĭŏ'sŏ*, a. neat, beautiful, finished with care; specious.

espectáculo, *ĕspĕktă'kŭlŏ*, sm. spectacle.

espectador, *–dŏr'*, sm. spectator.

espectro, *ĕspĕk'trŏ*, sm. spectre, phantom, ghost, apparition.

especulación, *ĕspĕkŭlăthĭŏn'*, sf. speculation, contemplation; commercial scheme.

especulador, ra, *–dŏr'*, sm. & f. speculator.

especular, *ĕspĕkŭlăr'*, v. a. to speculate.

especulativa, *ĕspĕkŭlătē'vă*, sf. faculty of speculating. [thoughtful.

especulativo, va, *–tē'vŏ*, a. speculative;

espejismo, *ĕspĕhĭs'mŏ*, sm. mirage.

espejo, *ĕspĕ'hŏ*, sm. looking-glass, mirror.

espera, *ĕspĕ'ră*, sf. stay, waiting; (law) respite, adjournment, delay.

esperanza, *ĕspĕrăn'thă*, sf. hope; (mar.) áncora de –, sheet-anchor.

esperanzar, *–thăr'*, v. a. to give hope.

esperar, *ĕspĕrăr'*, v. a. to hope; to expect, to wait for.

esperma, *ĕspĕr'mă*, sf. sperm.

espermático, *–mă'tĭkŏ*, a. spermatic.

espernancado, *–nănkă'dŏ*, a. with widespread legs.

espesar, *ĕspĕsăr'*, v. a. to thicken, to condense; –se, to grow thick, to solidify.

espeso, sa, *ĕspĕ'sŏ*, a. thick, dense.

espesor, *ĕspĕsŏr'*, sm. thickness.

espesura, *–sŏ'ră*, sf. thickness, density, solidity.

espetar, *ĕspĕtăr'*, v. a. to spit; to transfix; –se, to be stiff and stately.

espetera, *–tĕ'ră*, sf. kitchen-furniture.

espetón, *ĕspĕtŏn'*, sm. spit; large pin.

espía, *ĕspē'ă*, sm. & f. spy. [sea-pike.

espiar, *ĕspĭăr'*, v. a. to spy, to lurk.

espiga, *espī́gă,* sf. ear (of corn); fusee of a bomb; sail of a galley.

espigadora, *espīgădō'ră,* sf. gleaner.

espigar, *espīgăr',* v. n. to shoot into ears; to grow, to increase; —, v. a. to glean. apigón,—*gōn',* sm. ear of corn; sting.

espina, *espī́nă,* sf. thorn; fish-bone; woolly-cotton thistle.

espinaca, *espīnă'kă,* sf. (bot.) spinage.

espinar,—*năr',* v. a. to prick with thorns; —, sm. place full of thorn-bushes, brambles &c.; arduous undertaking.

espinazo,—*nă'thō,* sm. spine, back-bone.

espingarda, *espīngăr'dă,* sf. small piece of ordnance.

espinilla, *espīnī́'yă,* sf. shin-bone.

espino, *espī́nō,* sm. thorn, prickly tree.

espinoso, sa, *espīnō'sō,* a. thorny, arduous, dangerous.

espión, *espīōn',* sm. spy.

espiral, *espīrăl',* a. spiral; —, sf. spiral line.

espirar, *espīrăr',* v. a. to exhale.

espiritar, *espīrītăr',* v. a. to possess with the devil; to wish someone to the devil; to irritate, to agitate; —se, to be possessed with an evil spirit.

espíritu, *espī́rītū,* sm. spirit, soul; genius; ardour, courage; el — Santo, the Holy Ghost; —s, pl. demons, hobgoblins, mpl.

espiritual, *espīrītū̆ăl',* a. spiritual; ghostly.

espiritualidad, *espīrītū̆ălĭdăd',* sf. spirituality; principle and effect of what is spiritual.

espiritualizar,—*thăr',* v. a. to spiritualize, to refine the intellect.

espirituoso, sa, *espīrītū̆ō'sō,* a. spirituous; vivid, lively.

espitar, *espītăr',* v. a. to put a faucet in a tub.

esplendente, *esplendēn'tĕ,* pa.(poet.) shining, resplendent.

esplendidez,—*dĭdĕth',* sf. splendour, magnificence.

espléndido, da, *esplēn'dĭdō,* a. splendid, magnificent; brilliant.

esplendor,—*dŏr',* sm. splendour.

espliego, *esplīĕ'gō,* sm. (bot.) lavender.

espolazo, *espōlă'thō,* sm. violent prick with a spur.

espolear,—*lĕăr',* v. a. to spur, to instigate, to incite.

espoleta,—*lĕ'tă,* sf. fusee of a bomb.

espolín,—*lĭn',* sm. small spool for raising flowers on stuff; running footman.

espolique, *espŏlī́'kĕ,* **espolista,**—*stă,* sm.

espolón, *espōlōn',* sm. spur of a cock; ice-breaker; (mar.) beakhead of a galley; (mil.) salient angle of a fortification; chilblain, kibe.

espondeo, *espŏn'dĕō,* sm. spondee.

esponja, *espŏn'hʼă,* sf. sponge.

esponjadura,—*dū'ră,* sf. act of sponging.

esponjar, *espŏn'hăr',* v. a. to sponge; —se, to be puffed up with pride.

esponjoso, sa,—*hō'sō,* a. spongy.

esponsales,—*să'lĕs,* sm. pl. espousals, pl.

espontaneidad, *espŏntănĕĭdăd',* sf. spontaneity.

espontáneo, nea,—*tă'nĕō,* a. spontaneous.

esportillero, *espŏrtīlyĕ'rō,* sm. porter.

esportillo,—*tī́l'yō,* sm. pannier, market basket.

esposas, *espō'săs,* sf. pl. manacles, handcuffs, pl.

esposo,—*sō,* sm. husband.

espuela, *espū̆ĕ'lă,* sf. spur; stimulus; (bot.) larkspur.

espuerta, *espū̆ĕr'tă,* sf. pannier, basket.

espulgar, *espŭlgăr',* v. a. to louse; to flea; to examine closely.

espulgo, *espŭl'gō,* sm. cleaning from lice or fleas.

espuma, *espū́mă,* sf. froth, spume.

espumadera, *espūmădē'ră,* sf. skimmer.

espumajear,—*hĕăr',* v. n. to froth at the mouth.

espumajoso, sa,—*hō'sō,* a. foamy, frothy, full of spume.

espumar, *espūmăr',* v. a. to skim, to take off the scum; (from the mouth).

espumarajo,—*mără'h'ō,* sm. foam, froth.

espumoso, sa,—*mō'sō,* a. spumous, frothy, foamy.

espurio, ria, *espū́rĭō,* a. spurious; adulterated, corrupted.

espurrir, *espŭrrĭr',* v. n. to stretch out the legs.

esputo, *espū́tō,* sm. spittle, saliva.

esquela, *eskĕ'lă,* sf. billet, note, slip of paper.

esqueleto, *eskĕlē'tō,* sm. skeleton.

esquife, *eskī́'fĕ,* sm. skiff, small boat.

esquilador, *eskīlădŏr',* sm. sheep-shearer.

esquilar,—*lăr',* v. a. to shear sheep.

esquileo,—*lĕ'ō,* sm. sheep-shearing.

esquilmar, *eskīlmăr',* v. a. to gather and get in the harvest.

esquilmo, *eskīl'mō,* sm. harvest-corn inned; produce of vines, cattle.

esquilón, *eskīlōn',* sm. small bell, bell worn by cattle.

esquina, *eskī́'nă,* sf. corner, angle.

esquinado, da, *eskīnă'dō,* a. cornered, angled.

esquinar,—*năr',* v. a. to form into an angle.

esquinazo,—*nă'thō,* sm. corner, angle.

esquivar, *eskīvăr',* v. a. to shun, to avoid, to evade; —se, to disdain, to scorn.

esquivez, *eskīvĕth',* sf. disdain, scorn.

esquivo, va, *eskī́'vō,* a. scornful; shy, reserved.

estabilidad, *estăbīlĭdăd',* sf. stability.

estable, *estă'blĕ,* a. stable.

establecer, *estăblĕthĕr',* v. a. to establish.

establo, *estă'blō,* sm. stable.

estaca, *estă'kă,* sf. stake; stick, cudgel.

estacada,—*kă'dă,* sf. (mil.) palisade; paling.

estacar,—*kăr',* v. a. to enclose with stakes.

estacazo,—*kă'thō,* sm. blow given with a stake.

estación, *estăthĭōn',* sf. state; situation; season of the year; station; railway-station, terminus; seasons.

estacional,—*năl',* a. belonging to the seasons.

estacionario, ria,—*nă'rĭō,* a. stationary.

estadio, *estă'dĭō,* sm. race-course; furlong.

estadista,—*dĭs'tă,* sm. statesman.

estadística,—*dĭs'tĭkă,* sf. statistics.

estadístico, ca,—*dĭs'tĭkō,* a. statistical.

estado, *estă'dō,* sm. state, condition.

estafa,—*fă,* sf. trick, imposition.

estafador,—*fădŏr',* sm. impostor, swindler.

estafar, -fär', v. a. to deceive, to defraud.

estafermo, -fér'mō, sm. wooden movable figure of an armed man; idle fellow who affects dignity and importance.

estafeta, -fā'tä, sf. courier, express; general post-office for letters.

estafetero, -fā'tró, sm. post-master.

estallar, estălyär', v. n. to crack, to burst; to break out into fury.

estallido, -yē'dō, sm. crack, crackling.

estambre, estăm'bré, sm. fine wool; stamen of flowers.

estamento, estămén'tō, sm. name given to each of the three estates of Spain, composing the Cortes.

estameña, -mén'yä, sf. serge.

estampa, estăm'pä, sf. print, stamp; pattern, model.

estampador, -dōr', sm. printer.

estampar, estămpär', v. a. to print.

estampería, -pérē'ä, sf. office for printing or selling prints.

estampero, -pé'rō, sm. he who makes or sells stamps.

estampido, -pē'dō, sm. report of a gun, &c.; crack.

estampilla, -pēl'yä, sf. signet.

estancar, estănkär', v. a. to check a current; to monopolise; to prohibit, to suspend.

estancia, estăn'thiä, sf. stay, sojourn; mansion; (am.) cattle-ranche; bed-room; (poet.) stanza.

estanco, estăn'kō, sm. forestalling, monopoly; place where only monopoly goods are sold; —, ca, a. water-fast.

estandarte, -där'té, sm. banner, standard.

estanque, estăn'ké, sm. pond, basin.

estanquillero, -kēlyé'rō, sm. tobacconist.

estanquillo, -kēl'yō, sm. tobacconist's shop. [pl. props of the cross-beams.

estante, estăn'té, sm. shelf (for books); —s,

estañador, estănyädōr', sm. tinman.

estañadura, -dō'rä, sf. tinning.

estañar, estănyär', v. a. to tin.

estaño, estăn'yō, sm. tin.

estar, estär', v. n. to be; to be in a place.

estática, estä'tikä, sf. statics.

estatua, estä'tuä, sf. statue.

estatuario, -tuä'rió, sm. statuary.

estatura, -tō'rä, sf. stature.

estatuto, -tō'tō, sm. statute, law.

este, ĕs'té, sm. east; —, ta, to, pn. this.

estera, estä'rä, sf. mat.

esterar, estärär', v. a. to cover with mats.

estercoladura, estěrkōlädō'rä, sf. stercoration.

estercolar, -lär', v. a. to dung, to manure; —, v. n. to void the excrements.

estercolero, -lé'rō, sm. dung-hill; dung-pit, lay-stall. [type.

estereotipar, estěrěōtipär', v. a. to stereotype.

estereotipia, -tē'piä, sf. stereotypography.

esterero, estěrä'rō, sm. mat-maker.

estéril, estä'ril, a. sterile, barren.

esterilidad, -lidäd', sf. sterility, barrenness. [gold or silver.

esterilla, -uä, sf. ferret lace made of

esterlino, na, -tě'nō, a. sterling, genuine, lawful. [stick.

esteva, estä'vä, sf. plough-handle; long

estevado, da, estävä'dō, a. bow-legged; hump-backed.

estiércol, estiēr'kōl, sm. dung; excrement.

estigio, gia, estē'hiō, a. Stygian.

estilar, estilär', v. a. & n. to use, to be accustomed.

estilo, estē'lō, sm. style; use, custom.

estima, estē'mä, sf. esteem. [of esteem.

estimable, estimä'blé, a. estimable, worthy

estimación, -mäthión', sf. estimation, valuation, account.

estimar, -mär', v. a. to estimate, to value; to esteem; to judge; to thank, to acknowledge. [stimulate, to excite, to goad.

estimular, -mulär', v. a. to sting, to

estímulo, estē'mulō, sm. sting, stimulus.

estío, estē'ō, sm. summer. [diary.

estipendiario, estipendiä'rió, sm. stipendiary.

estipendio, -pén'dió, sm. stipend, salary.

estipulación, -pläthión', sf. stipulation.

estipular, -pulär', v. a. to stipulate.

estirar, -rär', v. a. to dilate, to stretch out; to extend a discourse.

estirón, -rōn', sm. pulling; hauling; dar un —, to grow rapidly.

estirpe, estēr'pé, sf. race, origin, stock.

estocada, estōkä'dä, sf. stab.

estofa, estō'fä, sf. quilted stuff; quality.

estofado, da, estōfä'dō, a. quilted; stewed.

estofar, -fär', v. a. to quilt; to stew meat.

estola, estō'lä, sf. stole.

estolidez, estōlidéth', sf. stupidity.

estólido, da, estō'lidō, a. stupid.

estomacal, estōmäkäl', a. stomachic.

estomagar, -mägär', v. a. to stomach, to resent; to enrage.

estómago, estō'mägō, sm. stomach.

estopa, estō'pä, sf. tow.

estopilla, estōpil'yä, sf. fine spinning-flax; long-lawn (tissue).

estopín, -pin', sm. quick-match.

estopón, -pōn', sm. coarse tow.

estoposo, sa, -pō'sō, a. filamentous.

estoque, estō'ké, sm. tuck (long narrow sword). [ment.

estorbo, estōr'bō, sm. hindrance, impedi-

estornudar, -nüdär', v. n. to sneeze.

estornudo, -nō'dō, sm. sternutation, sneeze. [otro, this other.

estotro, tra, estō'tró, contraction for este

estrada, esträ'dä, sf. causeway.

estrado, -dō, sm. drawing-room; —s, pl. law-court.

estrafalario, ria, -fälä'rió, a. slovenly, uncleanly dressed; extravagant. [rupt.

estragar, -gär', v. a. to deprave, to cor-

estrago, esträ'gō, sm. ravage; havoc.

estrambótico, ca, estrămbō'tikō, a. extravagant, irregular. [trick.

estratagema, estrătä'hä'mä, sf. stratagem;

estrategia, -tä'hiä, sf. strategy.

estratégico, ca, -tä'hikō, a. strategical.

estraza, esträ'thä, sf. rag; papel de —, brown paper.

estrechar, estrétshär', v. a. to tighten; to

contract, to constringe; to compress;
—se, to bind oneself strictly; to reduce
one's expenses; to communicate in confidence; to be intimate with.

estrechez, *-tchéth'*, sf. straitness, narrowness; intimate union; poverty.

estrecho, *Estrēsh'ō*, sm. strait; narrow
passage between two mountains: —, cha,
a. narrow, close; strait, tight; intimate;
rigid, austere; exact; poor, indigent.

estregadura, *-gādō'rā*, sf. friction, rubbing.   [against another.

estregar, *-gr'*, v. a. to rub one thing

estrella, *Estrēl'yā*, sf. star.

estrellado, da, *-yā'dō*, a. starry; **huevos
—s,** poached eggs.   [to make ashamed.

estrellar, *-yr'*, v. a. to dash to pieces;
to make tremble; —se, to shake, to tremble.

estremecimiento, *-thimĭen'tō*, sm. trembling, shaking.   [Year's gift; handsel.

estrena, estrenas, *Estrē'nā(s)*, sf. New-

estrenar, *Estrēnār'*, v. a. to handsel; to
regale; —se, to use for the first time; to
begin.   [tion; costiveness.

estreñimiento, *-yĭmĭen'tō*, sm. obstruc-

estreñir, *-yr'*, v. a. to restrain; —se, to
restrain oneself.

estrépito, *Estrē'pĭtō*, sm. noise, clamour,
bustle, noisiness, obstreperousness.

estrepitoso, sa, *Estrēpĭtō'sō*, a. noisy.

estribar, *Estrĭbār'*, v. n. to prop; to found;
to be supported.

estribillo, *-bĭl'yō*, sm. burden of a song.

estribo, *Estrē'bō*, sm. buttress; stirrup;
step on the side of a coach; **perder los
—s,** to lose courage.   [severe.

estricto, ta, *Estrĭk'tō*, a. strict; exact;

estrofa, *Estrō'fā*, sf. strophe.

estropajear, *Estrōpā'hēār'*, v. a. to clean
a wall with a dry brush.

estropajo, *-pā'hō*, sm. dish-clout.

estropajoso, sa, *-pā'hō'sō*, a. ragged;
despicable; mean; stammering.

estropear, *-pēār'*, v. a. to maim, to cripple.

estructura, *Estrūktō'rā*, sf. structure.

estruendo, *-ēn'dō*, sm. clamour, noise;
confusion, bustle; pomp, ostentation.

estrujadura, *-hādō'rā*, sf. pressure,
compressing.

estrujar, *-hār'*, v. a. to press, to squeeze.

estrujón, *-hōn'*, sm. last pressing of
grapes; pressing, squeezing.

estuche, *Estūsh'ē*, sm. case (for scissors,
&c.); etui; (fig.) a clever fellow.

estudiante, *Estūdĭan'tē*, sm. scholar,
student.   [the manner of students.

estudiantina, *-tē'nā*, (á la —,), ad. in

estudiar, *Estūdĭār'*, v. a. to study.

estudio, *Estū'dĭō*, sm. study; (also as
apartment); **— general,** university.

estudioso, sa, *Estūdĭō'sō*, a. studious.

estufa, *Estū'fā*, sf. stove; hot-house.

estufador, *Estūfādōr'*, sm. stewing-pan.

estufero, *-fē'rō*, sm. stove-maker.

estufilla, *-fēl'yā*, sf. muff; small brasier.

estupefacción, *Estūpēfākthĭōn'*, sf. stupefaction.

estupefacto, *-fāk'tō*, a. petrified with
astonishment; stupefied.

estupendo, da, *-pēn'dō*, a. stupendous,
marvellous.

estupidez, *-pĭdēth'*, sf. stupidity.

estúpido, da, *Estū'pĭdō*, a. stupid.

estupor, *Estūpōr'*, sm. stupor; astonishment.   [flourer.

estuprador, *-prādōr'*, sm. ravisher, de-

estuprar, *-prār'*, v. a. to violate, to deflour.

estupro, *Estū'prō*, sm. ravishment, rape.

etapa, *Etā'pā*, sf. (mil.) rations.   [on.

etcétera, *Etthē'tērā*, adv. et cetera, and so

éter, *ē'tēr*, sm. ether.

etéreo, rea, *Etē'rēō*, a. ethereal.

eternidad, *Etērnĭdād'*, sf. eternity, everlasting.   [perpetuate.

eternizar, *-thār'*, v. a. to eternalize, to

eterno, na, *Etēr'nō*, a. eternal.

ética, *ē'tĭkā*, sf. ethics.

ético, ca, *ē'tĭkō*, a. ethical, moral.

etimología, *Etĭmōlō'hĭā*, sf. etymology.

etimológico, ca, *-lō'hĭkō*, a. etymological.

etiqueta, *Etĭkē'tā*, sf. etiquette, formality.

Eucaristía, *Eūkārĭstē'ā*, sf. Lord's Supper.

eucarístico, ca, *-rĭs'tĭkō*, a. eucharistical.

eufonía, *Eūfōnē'ā*, sf. euphony.

eufónico, ca, *Eūfō'nĭkō*, a. euphonious.

Euro, *Eū'rō*, sm. Eurus, the east-wind.

evacuación, *Evākūāthĭōn'*, sf. evacuation;
issue.   [empty.

evacuar, *-kūār'*, v. a. to evacuate, to

evadir, *Evādīr'*, v. a. to evade, to escape.

evangélico, ca, *Evān'hē'lĭkō*, a. evange-
lical.   [lical.

evangelio, *-hā'lĭō*, sm. gospel.

evangelista, *-hēlĭs'tā*, sm. evangelist;
gospeller.   [gelize.

evangelizar, *-hēlĭthār'*, v. a. to evan-

evaporar, *Evāpōrār'*, v. a. to evaporate;
—, n. to pass away; to grow vapid.

evasión, *Evāsĭōn'*, sf. evasion, escape;
subterfuge, poor excuse.

eventual, *Eventūāl'*, a. eventual, fortuitous.

evidencia, *Evĭden'thĭā*, sf. evidence, manifestation.   [fest.

evidente, *-den'tē*, a. evident, clear, mani-

evitable, *Evĭtā'blē*, a. avoidable.

evitar, *Evĭtār'*, v. a. to avoid.

evocación, *Evōkāthĭōn'*, sf. evocation;
pagan invocation.

evocar, *Evōkār'*, v. a. to call out; to invoke.

evolución, *Evōlūthĭōn'*, sf. (mil.) evolution.

exacción, *Eksākthĭōn'*, sf. exaction; impost; contribution.   [to irritate.

exacerbar, *-thērbār'*, v. a. to exasperate,

exactitud, *-tĭtūd'*, sf. exactness, exactitude.   [assiduous.

exacto, ta, *Eksāk'tō*, a. exact, punctual,

exageración, *-ā'hērāthĭōn'*, sf. exaggeration.   [one that exaggerates.

exagerador, ra, *-dōr'*, sm. & f. amplifier,

exagerar, *-ā'hērār'*, v. a. to exaggerate,
to amplify.   [elevation.

exaltación, *-āltāthĭōn'*, sf. exaltation,

exaltar, *-āltār'*, v. a. to exalt, to elevate;
to praise, to extol; **—se la cólera,** to
worry oneself, to get angry.

examen, ĕksă'mĕn, sm. examen, examination, trial, inquiry.

exámetro, ĕksă'mĕtrŏ, sm. hexameter (verse). [nation.

examinación, ĕksămĭnăthĭŏn', sf. exami-

examinador, -dŏr', sm. examiner.

examinando, -năn'dŏ, sm. examinant.

examinar, -ăṗĭnăr', v. a. to examine.

exánime, ĕksă'nĭmĕ, a. a spiritless, weak, dead. [ration.

exasperación, -ăspĕrăthĭŏn', sf. exaspe-

exasperar, -ăspĕrăr', v. a. to exasperate, to irritate.

excavación, -kăvăthĭŏn', sf. excavation.

excavar, -kăvăr', v. a. to excavate, to dig out. [ceeding.

excedente, -thĕdĕn'tĕ, a. excessive, ex-

exceder, -thĕdĕr', v. a. to exceed, to surpass, to excel, to outdo.

excelencia, -thĕlĕn'thĭă, sf. excellence.

Excelencia, -thĕlĕn'thĭă, sf. Excellency (title).

excelente, -lĕn'tĕ, a. excellent.

excelso, sa, ĕksthĕl'sŏ, a. elevated, sublime, lofty. [tricity.

excentricidad, -thĕntrĭthĭdăd', sf. eccen-

excéntrico, ca, -thĕn'trĭkŏ, a. eccentric.

excepción, -thĕpthĭŏn', sf. exception.

excepto, ĕksthĕp'tŏ, ad. except that, excepting. [sempt.

exceptuar, -tăăr', v. a. to except, to

excesivo, va, -thĕsĭ'vŏ, a. excessive.

exceso, ĕksthĕ'sŏ, sm. excess.

excitar, -thĭtăr', v. a. to excite. [tion.

exclamación, -klămăthĭŏn', sf. exclama-

exclamar, -klămăr', v. a. to exclaim, to exclaim. [cry out.

excluir, -klŭĭr', v. a. to exclude.

exclusión, -klŭsĭŏn', sf. exclusion.

exclusivamente, -klŭsĭvămĕn'tĕ, **exclusive**, -klŭsĭ'vŏ, ad. exclusively.

exclusivo, va, -sĭ'vŏ, a. exclusive.

excogitable, -kŏ'hĭtăblĕ, a. imaginable.

excogitar, -kŏ'hĭtăr', v. a. to excogitate, to strike out by thinking. [municate.

excomulgar, -kŏmŭlgăr', v. a. to excom-

excomunión, -kŏmŭnĭŏn', sf. excommunication. [tion, flaying.

excoriación, -kŏrĭăthĭŏn', sf. excoria-

excoriar, -kŏrĭăr', v. a. to excoriate, to flay.

excremento, -krĕmĕn'tŏ, sm. excrement.

excursión, -kŭrsĭŏn', sf. excursion; liquidation of the estate of a debtor for paying off his debts.

excusa, ĕkskŭ'să, sf. excuse, apology, plea.

excusable, -kŭsă'blĕ, a. excusable.

excusado, da, -kŭsă'dŏ, a. superfluous, useless; preserved; exempted, privileged; —, sm. subsidy from the clergy of Spain for carrying on the war against the infidels; privy, water-closet, W. C.

excusalí, -kŭsălĭ', sm. apron, pinafore.

excusar, -kŭsăr', v. a. to excuse; to exempt from taxes; to shun, to avoid; —se, to decline a request.

execrable, -ĕkră'blĕ, a. execrable, accursed. [curse.

execración, -ĕkrăthĭŏn', sf. execration,

execrar, -ĕkrăr', v. a. to execrate, to curse.

exención, -ĕnthĭŏn', sf. exemption, immunity, privilege. [vilege.

exentar, -ĕntăr', v. a. to exempt, to pri-

exento, ta, ĕksĕn'tŏ, a. exempt, free; —, sm. officer in the Spanish life-guards who holds the rank and brevet of a colonel in the army. [obsequies.

exequias, ĕksĕ'kĭăs, sf. pl. funeral rites,

exhalación, -ălăthĭŏn', sf. exhalation; velocity. [to evaporate.

exhalar, -ălăr', v. a. to exhale; —se,

exhausto, ta, -hăŭs'tŏ, a. exhausted.

exhibición, -ĭbĭthĭŏn', sf. exhibition.

exhibir, -ĭbĭr', v. a. to exhibit.

exhortación, -ŏrtăthĭŏn', sf. exhortation.

exhortar, -ŏrtăr', v. a. to exhort.

exhorto, ĕksŏr'tŏ, sm. letters requisitorial sent by one judge to another.

exhumación, -ŭmăthĭŏn', sf. exhumation.

exhumar, -ŭmăr', v. a. to disinter, to unbury. [want.

exigencia, -ĭhĕn'thĭă, sf. exigence,

exigible, -ĭhĭ'blĕ, a. requirable.

exigir, -ĭhĭr', v. a. to demand, to require.

exiguo, gua, ĕksĭ'gŭŏ, a. exiguous, small.

eximio, mia, ĕksĭ'mĭŏ, a. eximious, famous, very eminent. [vilege.

eximir, -ĭmĭr', v. a. to exempt, to pri-

existencia, -ĭstĕn'thĭă, sf. existence, existency, being.

existente, -tĕn'tĕ, a. existing, existent.

existir, -ĭstĭr', v. n. to exist, to be.

éxito, ĕksĭ'tŏ, sm. end, termination, issue.

Éxodo, ĕksŏ'dŏ, sm. Exodus. [tion.

exoneración, -ŏnĕrăthĭŏn', sf. exonera-

exonerar, -ŏnĕrăr', v. a. to exonerate, to unload. [ance.

exorbitancia, -ŏrbĭtăn'thĭă, sf. exorbit-

exorbitante, -ŏrbĭtăn'tĕ, a. exorbitant, excessive, immoderate.

exorcismo, -ŏrthĭs'mŏ, sm. exorcism.

exorcista, -ŏrthĭs'tă, sm. exorciser, exorcist.

exorcizar, -ŏrthĭthăr', v. a. to exorcise.

exordio, ĕksŏr'dĭŏ, sm. exordium.

exótico, ca, ĕksŏ'tĭkŏ, a. exotic. [tension.

expansión, -pănsĭŏn', sf. expansion, ex-

expansivo, va, -pănsĭ'vŏ, a. expansive.

expatriarse, -pătrĭăr'sĕ, v. r. to be exiled; to emigrate. [tion.

expectación, -pĕktăthĭŏn', sf. expecta-

expectativa, -tăĭ'vă, sf. right or claim respecting some future thing; hope of obtaining a reward.

expectoración, -pĕktŏrăthĭŏn', sf. expectoration. [rate.

expectorar, -tŏrăr', v. a. to expecto-

expedición, -pĕdĭthĭŏn', sf. expedition; speed, activity. [peditionary.

expedicionario, -thĭŏnă'rĭŏ, a. ex-

expediente, -pĕdĭĕn'tĕ, sm. affair of easy discussion and despatch; expedient; pretext; provision. [patch.

expedir, -pĕdĭr', v. a. to expedite, to des-

expeditivo, va, -dĭtĭ'vŏ, a. expeditive, expeditious. [titious, speedy.

expedito, ta, -dĭ'tŏ, a. prompt, expedi-

expeler, *-pēlĕr*, v. a. to expel. [out.
expender, *-pĕndĕr*, v. a. to spend, to lay
expensas, *ĕkspĕn'sâs*, sf. pl. expenses,
  charges. [trial.
experiencia, *-pĕrĭĕn'thĭâ*, sf. experience;
experimentado, da, *-pĕrĭmĕn'dŏ*, a.
  experienced, expert.
experimental, *-mĕntâl'*, a. experimental.
experimentar, *-mĕntâr'*, v. a. to experience; to experiment. [trial.
experimento, *-mĕn'tŏ*, sm. experiment.
experto, ta, *ĕkspĕr'tŏ*, a. expert, experienced. [purification.
expiación, *-pĭăthĭŏn'*, sf. expiation;
expiar, *ĕkspĭâr'*, v. a. to atone for; to
  purify.
expiatorio, ria, *-pĭătŏ'rĭŏ*, a. expiatory.
expirar, *ĕkspĭrâr'*, v. n. to expire, to
  breathe the last.
explanada, *-plâ̌nâ'dâ*, sf. esplanade.
explanar, *-plâ̌nâr'*, v. a. to explain.
explayar, *-plâ̌yâr'*, v. a. to extend, to
  dilate. [tion, explication.
explicación, *-plĭkăthĭŏn'*, sf. explana-
explicaderas, *-dĕ'râs*, sf. pl. manner
  in which anything is explained; facility
  of explaining.
explicar, *-plĭkâr'*, v. a. to explain, to
  expound; **-se**, to speak plainly; to explain oneself. [clear, distinct.
explícito, ta, *ĕksplĭ'thĭtŏ*, a. explicit,
exploración, *-plŏrăthĭŏn'*, sf. exploration. [plorer.
explorador, ra, *-râdŏr'*, sm. & f. ex-
explorar, *-plŏrâr'*, v. a. to explore.
explosión, *-plŏsĭŏn'*, sf. explosion.
exponente, *-pŏnĕn'tĕ*, sm. (ar.) exponent.
exponer, *-pŏnĕr'*, v. a. to expose; to explain.
exposición, *-pŏsĭthĭŏn'*, sf. exposition.
expósito, ta, *ĕkspŏ'sĭtŏ*, a. exposed.
expresar, *-prĕsâr'*, v. a. to express.
expresión, *-prĕsĭŏn'*, sf. expression.
expresivo, va, *-sĕ'vŏ*, a. expressive;
  energetic.
expreso, sa, *-prĕs'ŏ*, a. expressed; express, clear, manifest, not dubious; **-**, sm.
  express, courier.
express, *-prĕs'*, m. (rail.) express-train.
exprimir, *-prĭmĭr'*, v. a. to squeeze out;
  to express. [purpose.
ex profeso, *-prŏ'fĕsŏ*, ad. avowedly, on
expuesto, ta, *-pŭĕs'tŏ*, a. exposed. [out.
expulsar, *-pŭlsâr'*, v. a. to expel, to drive
expulsión, *-sĭŏn'*, sf. expulsion.
expulso, sa, *ĕkspŭl'sŏ*, a. expelled; outcast. [tion, purification.
expurgación, *-pŭrgăthĭŏn'*, sf. expurga-
expurgar, *-pŭrgâr'*, v. a. to expurge, to
  purify. [summate, excellent.
exquisito, ta, *-kĭsĭ'tŏ*, a. exquisite, con-
éxtasi, éxtasis, *ĕks'tâsĭs*, sm. ecstasy,
  enthusiasm.
extático, ca, *ĕkstâ'tĭkŏ*, a. ecstatical.
extender, *-tĕndĕr'*, v. a. to extend, to
  stretch out; **-se**, to be extended; to increase in bulk; to swell; to be elated with
  pride.

extensión, *-sĭŏn'*, sf. extension; extent.
extensivo, va, *-sĕ'vŏ*, a. extensive.
extenso, sa, *ĕkstĕn'sŏ*, a. extensive.
extenuación, *-tĕnŭăthĭŏn'*, sf. extenuation, feebleness, debility.
extenuar, *-tĕnŭâr'*, v. a. to extenuate, to
  debilitate.
exterior, *ĕkstĕrĭŏr'*, a. exterior, external;
  -, sm. exterior, outward appearance.
exterioridad, *-rĭdâd'*, sf. exteriority;
  outward appearance; outside; superficies;
  pomp, ostentation.
exteriormente, *-mĕn'tĕ*, ad. externally.
exterminador, *-tĕrmĭnâdŏr'*, sm. ex-
  terminator. [to root out.
exterminar, *-nâr'*, v. a. to exterminate,
exterminio, *-mĕ'nĭŏ*, sm. extermination,
  extirpation. [ward; foreign.
externo, na, *ĕkstĕr'nŏ*, a. external, out-
ex testamento, *ĕks tĕstâmĕn'tŏ*, ad. by
  will or testament.
extinción, *ĕkstĭnthĭŏn'*, sf. extinction.
extinguible, *-gĕ'blĕ*, a. extinguishable.
extinguir, *-gĭr'*, v. a. to quench; to extinguish.
extirpación, *-tĭrpăthĭŏn'*, sf. extirpation,
  extermination.
extirpar, *-pâr'*, v. a. to extirpate, to root
extorsión, *-tŏrsĭŏn'*, sf. extortion. [out.
extra, *ĕks'trâ*, pr. out, without, besides.
extracción, *-trâkthĭŏn'*, sf. exportation;
  extraction.
extractar, *-târ'*, v. n. to extract, to abridge.
extracto, *-trâk'tŏ*, sm. extract. [por.
extraer, *ĕkstrâĕr'*, v. a. to extract; to ex-
extrajudicial, *-'hŭdĭthĭâl'*, a. extrajudicial. [walls.
extramuros, *-mŏ'rŏs*, a. without the
extranjero, ra, *ĕkstrân'hâ'rŏ*, sm. & f.
  stranger, foreigner; **-**, a. foreign, outlandish.
extrañar, *ĕkstrânyâr'*, v. a. to alienate; to
  admire; to reprimand.
extraño, ña, *ĕkstrân'yŏ*, a. foreign; rare;
  singular, strange, odd.
extraordinario, ria, *-ŏrdĭnâ'rĭŏ*, a.
  extraordinary, uncommon, odd.
extratémpora, *-tĕm'pŏrâ*, sf. dispensation for receiving orders out of the time
  specified by the church.
extravagancia, *-vâgân'thĭâ*, sf. extravagance.
extravagante, *-vâgân'tĕ*, a. & f. extravagant. [to lose one's way.
extraviar, *-vĭâr'*, v. a. to mislead; **-se**,
extravío, *-vĕ'ŏ*, sm. deviation; irregularity; misguidance.
extremado, da, *ĕkstrĕmâ'dŏ*, a. extreme;
  accomplished.
extremaunción, *-ânthĭŏn'*, sf. extreme
  unction. [brim of any thing.
extremidad, *ĕkstrĕmĭdâd'*, sf. extremity;
extremo, ma, *ĕkstrĕ'mŏ*, a. extreme, last;
  -, sm. extreme, highest degree; **en -**,
  por -, extremely. [external.
extrínseco, ca, *ĕkstrĭnsĕ'kŏ*, a. extrinsic,
exuberancia, *-ŭbĕrân'thĭâ*, sf. exuberance;
  luxuriance.

F.

fábrica, *fă brē' ă,* sf. fabrication; fabric.

fabricante, *făbrĭkăn' tĕ,* sm. fabricator, manufacturer.

fabricar, *–kăr',* v. a. to build, to construct; to fabricate, to manufacture.

fabril, *făbrīl',* a. belonging to manufacturers or workmen.

fabuco, *făbō' kō,* sm. beech-nut.

fábula, *fă' bŭlă,* sf. fable; fiction; rumour, common talk.

fabulista, *făbŭlĭs' tă,* sm. fabulist.

fabuloso, sa, *–lō' sō,* a. fabulous, fictitious.

facción, *făkthĭōn',* sf. military exploit; faction; feature.

faccioso, sa, *–thĭō' sō,* a. factious, turbulent.

facie ecclesiae, (in –), *fāthĭĕ ĕklā' sĭĕ,* a. legally married.

fácil, *fă' thĭl,* a. facile, easy.

facilidad, *făthĭlĭdăd',* sf. facility, easiness.

facilitar, *–tăr',* v. a. to facilitate.

facineroso, *–nĕrō' sō,* a. wicked, detestably bad.

facistol, *–stōl',* sm. chorister's desk.

factible, *făktē' blĕ,* a. feasible, practicable.

facticio, cia, *făktĭ' thĭō,* a. factitious.

factor, *făktōr',* sm. performer; (ar.) factor; (com.) factor, agent.

factoría, *–rē' ă,* sf. factory; factorage.

factura, *făktō' ră,* sf. invoice.

facultad, *făkŭltăd',* sf. faculty.

facultativo, va, *–tē' vă,* a. optional; –, sm. master of a science or art.

facha, *fătsh' ă,* sf. appearance, aspect, mien.

fachada, *fătshă' dă,* sf. façade, face, front.

fachenda, *fătshĕn' dă,* a. vain, ostentatious; –, sm. busybody.

fachendear, *–dĕăr',* v. a. to pretend to have important business on hand.

faena, *fă ĕ' nă,* sf. work, labour, fatigue; work on shipboard.

fagina, *fă hē' nă,* sf. fascine; fagot.

faja, *fă' hă,* sf. band, fillet; border (line); **bajo –,** by book-post, under open cover.

fajar, *fă' hăr',* v. a. to swathe; to fillet.

fajero, *fă' hĕ' rō,* sm. knitted swaddling-band for children.

falacia, *fălă' thĭă,* sf. fallacy, fraud.

falange, *fălăn' hĕ,* sf. phalanx.

falaz, *fălăth',* a. deceitful, fraudulent; fallacious.

falda, *făl' dă,* sf. skirt; lap; flap; train; brow of a hill; **perrillo de –,** lap-dog.

faldellín, *–dĕlyĭn',* sm. short under-petticoat.

faldero, ra, *–dĕ' rō,* a. belonging to the lap; fond of being constantly among women; **perrillo –,** lap-dog.

faldillas, *–dēl' yăs,* sf. pl. small skirts of a jacket.

faldón, *–dōn',* sm. long flowing skirt.

falible, *fălē' blĕ,* a. fallible.

falsamente, *fălsămĕn' tĕ,* ad. falsely.

falsario, ria, *fălsă' rĭō,* a. falsifying, forging; accustomed to tell falsehoods.

falsear, *fălsĕăr',* v. a. to falsify, to counter-

feit; –, v. n. to slacken; not to agree in sound.

falsedad, *–dăd',* sf. falsehood; untruth, fib.

falsete, *fălsĕ' tĕ,* sm. spigot.

falsificación, *fălsĭfĭkăthĭōn',* sf. falsification.

falsificador, *–kădōr',* sm. falsifier.

falsificar, *–kăr',* v. a. to falsify, to forge, to counterfeit.

falso, sa, *făl' sō,* a. false, untrue; faint.

falta, *făl' tă,* sf. fault, defect, want; slight crime, failure, flaw.

faltar, *făltăr',* v. n. to be wanting; to fail; not to fulfil one's promise; to need; to die.

falto, ta, *făl' tō,* a. wanting, defective; jejune; miserable, wretched; mad.

faltriquera, *făltrĭkĕ' ră,* sf. pocket.

falúa, *fălō' ă,* sf. (mar.) felucca.

fallar, *fălyăr',* v. a. to give sentence, to judge; to trump (at cards).

fallecer, *fălyĕthĕr',* v. n. to die; to decay.

fallecimiento, *–thĭmĭĕn' tō,* sm. decease, death.

fallido, da, *fălyē' dō,* a. disappointed, frustrated; bankrupt; nonplused (at cards).

fallo, *făl' yō,* sm. judgment, sentence; renounce (at cards).

fama, *fă' mă,* sf. fame; reputation, name.

familia, *fămē' lĭă,* sf. family.

familiar, *fămĭlĭăr',* a. familiar, domestic; frequent; agreeable; –, sm. domestic; college-servant.

familiaridad, *–dăd',* sf. familiarity.

familiarizar, *–thăr',* v. a. to familiarise; –se, to become familiar.

famoso, sa, *fămō' sō,* a. famous, renowned; noted.

fámulo, *fă' mŭlō,* sm. servant of a college.

fanal, *fănăl',* sm. poop-lantern of a commodore's ship.

fanático, ca, *fănă' tĭkō,* a. fanatical; enthusiastic.

fandango, *făndăn' gō,* sm. fandango (lively Spanish dance).

fanega, *fănĕ' gă,* sf. a dry measure of about an English bushel.

fanfarria, *fănfăr' rĭă,* sf. empty brag.

fanfarrón, *–rōn',* sm. bully, hector.

fanfarronada, *–nă' dă,* sf. fanfaronade, boast, brag.

fanfarronear, *–nĕăr',* v. n. to bully, to brag.

fanfarronería, *–nĕrē' ă,* sf. fanfaronade.

fango, *făn' gō,* sm. mire, mud.

fangoso, sa, *făngō' sō,* a. muddy, miry.

fantasía, *făntăsē' ă,* sf. fancy; phantasy; caprice; presumption.

fantasma, *făntăs' mă,* sf. phantom.

fantasmagoría, *–gōrē' ă,* sf. phantasmagoria; whimsical; presumptuous.

fantástico, ca, *făntăs' tĭkō,* a. fantastic, whimsical.

faquín, *făkĭn',* sm. porter, carrier.

faramalla, *fărămăl' yă,* sf. imposition, artful trick; prattling; –, sm. treacherous man.

faramallón, *–yōn',* sm. tattling, deceitful man.

farándula, *fărăn' dŭlă,* sf. profession of a low comedian; artful trick.

farandulero, *–lĕ' rō,* sm. actor; player; idle tattler, deceitful talker.

faraón, *fărăōn',* sm. game at cards.

faraute, *fără ō' tĕ,* sm. messenger; interpreter; principal manager; meddling fellow.

fardel, *fărdĕl'*, sm. fardel, bag, knapsack.

fardo, *fär dŏ*, sm. bale of goods, parcel.

farfantón, *fărfăntōn'*, sm. boasting babbler.

farfantonada, *–tōnā dă*, sf. idle boast.

farfulla, *fărfŭl'yă*, sm. stammering person.

farfullar, *–yär'*, v. a. to talk stammeringly; to do in a hurry and confusion.

farisaico, ca, *fărĭsā'ĭkŏ*, a. pharisaical.

farisaismo, *–sā'ĭs mŏ*, sm. pharisaism.

fariseo, *fărĭsē'ŏ*, sm. pharisee; very tall, ugly person. [maceutical.

farmacéutico, ca, *fărmăthā'ūĭtkŏ*, a. pharmaca, *fărmā'thĭă*, sf. pharmacy.

faro, *fä'rŏ*, sm. (mar.) light-house.

farol, *fărŏl'*, sm. lantern. [body.

farolear, *fărŏlĕăr'*, v. n. to act the busy-

farolero, *–lā'rŏ*, sm. lantern-maker; lamplighter.

fárrago, *fär'răgŏ*, sm. farrago, medley.

farsa, *fär'să*, sf. farce; company of players.

farsante, *fărsän'tĕ*, sm. actor, player; mountebank. [ad. justly or unjustly.

fas (por) ó por nefas, *făs ŏ pŏr nē'făs*,

fascinación, *făsthĭnăthĭŏn'*, sf. fascination; imposition, deceit.

fascinar, *–năr'*, v. a. to fascinate; to enchant; to deceive. [planet.

fase, *fä'sĕ*, sf. phasis (of the moon or

fastidiar, *făstĭdĭăr'*, v. a. to excite disgust; to grate, to offend. [gust.

fastidio, *făstĭ'dĭŏ*, sm. squeamishness; dis-

fastidioso, sa, *–dĭ'ŏsŏ*, a. fastidious; nauseous; tedious.

fastoso, sa, *făstŏ'sŏ*, a. proud, ostentatious.

fatal, *fătăl'*, a. fatal; mortal; unfortunate.

fatalidad, *fătălĭdăd'*, sf. fatality, mischance, ill luck.

fatalismo, *fătălĭs'mŏ*, sm. fatalism.

fatalista, *fătălĭs'tă*, sm. fatalist.

fatiga, *fătĭ'gă*, sf. toil, fatigue. [harass.

fatigar, *fătĭgär'*, v. a. to fatigue, to tire, to

fatigoso, sa, *–gŏ'sŏ*, a. tiresome, troublesome. [ness, silliness.

fatuidad, *fătŭĭdăd'*, sf. fatuity, foolish-

fatuo, tua, *fä'tŭŏ*, a. fatuous, stupid, foolish, silly, trifling.

fauces, *fä'ŭthĕs*, sf. pl. fauces, gullet.

fausto, *fä'ŭstŏ*, a. happy, fortunate;

–, sm. splendour, pomp. [ostentatious.

faustoso, sa, *–tŏ'sŏ*, a. fastuous, haughty,

fautor, *fäŭtŏr'*, sm. fautor.

fautora, *–tŏ'ră*, sf. fautress.

favor, *făvŏr'*, sm. favour, favor, protection, good graces. [geous, propitious.

favorable, *–ā'blĕ*, a. favourable, advanta-

favorecer, *–rĕthĕr'*, v. a. to favour, to protect. [loved.

favorito, ta, *făvŏrĭ'tŏ*, a. favourite. be-

faz, *făth*, sf. face. [my honour.

fe, *fă*, sf. faith, belief; **á – mía,** upon

fealdad, *fĕăldăd'*, sf. ugliness; turpitude, dishonesty.

Febo, *fĕ'bŏ*, sm. (poet.) Phœbus (the sun).

febrero, *fĕbrā'rŏ*, sm. February.

febril, *fĕbrĭl'*, a. febrile.

fecal, *fĕkăl'*, a. feculent.

fecundar, *fĕkŭndăr'*, v. a. to fertilise.

fecundidad, *–dĭdăd'*, sf. fecundity, fertility.

fecundo, da, *fĕkŭn'dŏ*, a. fruitful, fertile.

fecha, *fĕtch'ă*, sf. date (of a letter, &c.); **larga–,** great age.

fechar, *fĕtchär'*, v. a. to date.

fechoría, *fĕtchŏrē'ă*, sf. action, exploit.

felicidad, *fĕlĭthĭdăd'*, sf. felicity, happiness. [to felicitate.

felicitar, *–thĭtär'*, v. a. to congratulate,

feligrés, esa, *–grĕs'*, sm. & f. parishioner.

feligresía, *–grĕsē'ă*, sf. district of a parish.

feliz, *fĕlĭth'*, a. happy, fortunate.

felonía, *fĕlŏnē'ă*, sf. treachery, felony.

felpa, *fĕl'pă*, sf. plush; a good drubbing.

felpilla, *–pĭl'yă*, sf. corded silk for embroidering.

felpudo, da, *–pŭ'dŏ*, a. shaggy.

femenil, *fĕmĕnĭl'*, a. feminine, womanly.

femenino, na, *–nē'nŏ*, a. feminine, female.

fementido, da, *fĕmĕntĭ'dŏ*, a. false, unfaithful. [clude.

fenecer, *fĕnĕthĕr'*, v. a. to finish, to con-

fenecimiento, *–thĭmĭĕn'tŏ*, sm. termination, end.

fenómeno, *fĕnŏ'mĕnŏ*, sm. phenomenon.

feo, ea, *fĕ'ŏ*, a. ugly, deformed.

feracidad, *fĕrăthĭdăd'*, sf. feracity, fertility. [lity.

feraz, *fĕrăth'*, a. fertile, fruitful.

féretro, *fĕ'rĕtrŏ*, sm. bier, coffin, hearse.

feria, *fĕ'rĭă*, sf. week-day (not Saturday or Sunday); fair, market-day.

ferial, *fĕrĭăl'*, a. ferial.

feriar, *fĕrĭăr'*, v. a. to sell, to buy; to give fairings; to suspend. [tation.

fermentación, *fĕrmĕntăthĭŏn'*, sf. fermen-

fermentar, *–tär'*, v. n. to ferment.

fermento, *fĕrmĕn'tŏ*, sm. ferment; leaven.

ferocidad, *fĕrŏthĭdăd'*, sf. ferocity, wildness; cruelty.

feroz, *fĕrŏth'*, a. ferocious, cruel, savage.

ferruginoso, sa, *fĕrrŭhĭnŏ'sŏ*, a. ferruginous.

fértil, *fĕr'tĭl*, a. fertile, fruitful. [ous.

fertilidad, *fĕrtĭlĭdăd'*, sf. fertility, fecundity, fruitfulness.

fertilizar, *–thär'*, v. a. to fertilise.

férula, *fĕ'rŭlă*, sf. ferula, ferule.

ferviente, *fĕrvĭĕn'tĕ*, a. fervent, ardent.

fervor, *fĕrvŏr'*, sm. fervour, zeal, ardour.

fervoroso, sa, *–rŏ'sŏ*, a. fervent, ardent, fervid, passionate. [to woo.

festejar, *fĕstĕhär'*, v. a. to feast; to court,

festejo, *fĕstĕ'hŏ*, sm. courtship; feast.

festín, *fĕstĭn'*, sm. feast.

festividad, *fĕstĭvĭdăd'*, sf. festivity; solemnization of some occurrence.

festivo, va, *–tĕ'vŏ*, a. a festive, gay, merry; **día –,** holiday.

festón, *fĕstŏn'*, sm. garland; festoon.

festonear, *fĕstŏnĕăr'*, v. a. to ornament with festoons.

fétido, da, *fĕ'tĭdŏ*, a. fetid, stinking.

feto, *fĕ'tŏ*, sm. fœtus.

feudal, *fĕŭdăl'*, a. feudal.

feudalidad, *–dăd'*, sf. feudality.

feudatario, *–tā'rĭŏ*, sm. & a. feudatary.

feudo, *fĕ'ŭdŏ*, sm. fief; tribute paid to a feudal lord.

fiado, da, *fiā'dŏ,* a. confident; **al —,** upon trust; **en —,** upon bail.

fiador, fiadŏr, sm. surety (person); loop of a cloak; (fam.) backside; dog of a musket-lock; staple which supports a gutter.

fiambre, *fiām'brĕ,* a. cold (applied to meat).

fiambrera, —brā'rā, sf. pannier (for carrying cold meat).

fianza, *fiān'thā,* sf. caution, security.

fiar, *fiār',* v. a. to bail; to sell on trust; to commit to another, to credit; —, v. n. to confide.

fiat, *fĕ'ăt,* sm. consent; (law) fiat.

fibra, *fĕ'brā,* sf. fibre.

fibroso, sa, *fĕbrŏ'sŏ,* a. fibrous.

ficción, *fĭkthĭŏn',* sf. fiction.

ficticio, cia, *fĭktĭ'thĭŏ,* a. fictitious, fictive.

ficha, *fĕsh'ā,* sf. counter (at games).

fidedigno, na, *fĭdĕdĭg'nŏ,* a. worthy of credit, deserving of belief. [trustee.

fideicomisario, *fĭdĕĭkŏmĭsā'rĭŏ,* sm. feoffment in trust. [punctuality.

fideicomiso, *fĭdĕĭkŏmĭ'sŏ,* sf. feoffment in trust.

fidelidad, *fĭdĕlĭdād',* sf. fidelity; loyalty; [punctuality.

fideos, *fĭdĕ'ŏs,* sm. pl. vermicelli.

fiebre, *fĭĕ'brĕ,* sf. fever.

fiel, *fĭĕl',* a. faithful, loyal; —, sm. clerk of the market; needle of a balance.

fielazgo, *fĭĕlăth'gŏ,* sm. office of the town-clerk.

fieltro, *fĭĕl'trŏ,* sm. felt; rain-cloak.

fiera, *fĭĕ'rā,* sf. wild beast.

fierabrás, *fĭĕrābrăs',* sm. bully, braggart.

fiereza, —rā'thā, sf. fierceness, cruelty, ferocity. [rough, rude.

fiero, ra, *fĭĕ'rŏ,* a. fierce, cruel, ferocious;

fiesta, *fĭĕs'tā,* sf. feast; festivity; —s, pl. holidays, vacations.

figón, *fĭgŏn',* sm. eating-house, chop-house.

figonero, —nŏ'rŏ, sm. eating-house keeper.

figura, *fĭgŏ'rā,* sf. figure, shape.

figurable, *fĭgŏrā'blĕ,* a. figurable, that which may be figured.

figurado, da, —rā'dŏ, a. figurative.

figurar, —rār', v. a. to figure; —se, to fancy, to imagine.

figurativo, va, —rātĕ'vŏ, a. figurative.

figurero, —rā'rŏ, sm. mimic, ludicrous imitator.

figurilla, —rĕl'yā, sf. ridiculous little figure.

figurón, —rŏn', sm. low-bred person assuming an air of dignity and importance.

fijacarteles, *fĭ'hākārtĕ'lĕs,* sm. bill-sticker.

fijar, *fĭhār',* v. a. to fix, to fasten; —se, to fix or settle itself in a place.

fijo, *fĭ'hŏ,* a. a fixed, firm; settled, permanent; attentive. [in a line, in a row.

fila, *fĕ'lā,* sf. row, line of soldiers; en —, [in a line, in a row.

filamento, *fĭlāmĕn'tŏ,* sf. filament.

filantropía, *fĭlāntrŏpĕ'ā,* sf. philanthropy, good-nature. [—s, pl. burdock.

filántropo, *fĭlăn'trŏpŏ,* sm. philanthropist;

filete, *fĭlĕ'tĕ,* sm. fillet; hem; small roasting-spit. [fillets.

filetear, *fĭlĕtĕăr',* v. a. to adorn with

filiación, *fĭlĭāthĭŏn',* sf. filiation; regimental register of a soldier's height, age, [&c.

filial, *fĭlĭăl',* a. filial.

filiar, *fĭlĭār',* v. n. to prove one's descent.

filibustero, *fĭlĭbŏstĕ'rŏ,* sm. freebooter.

filigrana, —grā'nā, sf. filigree.

filisteo, tea, —stĕ'ŏ, a. tall, gigantic.

filo, *fĕ'lŏ,* sm. edge (of a sword, &c.).

filología, *fĭlŏlŏ'hĕ'ā,* sf. philology.

filológico, ca, —lŏ'hĭkŏ, a. philological.

filólogo, *fĭlŏ'lŏgŏ,* sm. philologist.

filosofar, *fĭlŏsŏfār',* v. a. to philosophize.

filosofía, —sŏfĕ'ā, sf. philosophy.

filosófico, ca, —sŏ'fĭkŏ, a. philosophical.

filosofismo, —sŏfĭs'mŏ, sm. philosophism.

filósofo, *fĭlŏ'sŏfŏ,* sm. philosopher.

filtración, *fĭltrāthĭŏn',* sf. filtration.

filtrar, *fĭltrār',* v. a. to filter, to strain.

filtro, *fĕl'trŏ,* sm. filter; love-potion.

fin, *fĭn,* sm. end, termination, conclusion; **al —,** at last; **en —, por —,** finally, lastly.

final, *fĭnăl',* a. final; —, sm. end, termination, conclusion.

finalizar, *fĭnālĭthār',* v. a. to finish, to conclude; —, v. n. to be finished.

finalmente, —mĕn'tĕ, ad. finally, at last.

finca, *fĭn'kā,* sf. land or house property.

fineza, *fĭnĕ'thā,* sf. fineness, perfection; expression of love; delicacy, beauty; friendly zeal; small, friendly gift.

fingido, da, *fĭn'hĕ'dŏ,* a. feigned, dissembled, sham.

fingimiento, *fĭn'hĕmĭĕn'tŏ,* sm. simulation, pretence, false appearance.

fingir, *fĭn'hĭr',* v. a. to feign, to dissemble; to imitate.

finiquito, *fĭnĭkĕ'tŏ,* sm. close of an account; final receipt or discharge.

finito, ta, *fĭnĕ'tŏ,* a. finite, limited, bounded.

fino, na, *fĕ'nŏ,* a. fine, perfect, pure; delicate, nice; acute, sagacious.

finura, *fĕnŏ'rā,* sf. fineness.

firma, *fĭr'mā,* sf. signature, subscription;

firmamento, *fĭrmāmĕn'tŏ,* sm. firmament, sky, heaven.

firmar, *fĭrmār',* v. a. to sign, to subscribe.

firme, *fĭr'mĕ,* a. firm, stable, strong, secure; constant, resolute.

firmeza, *fĭrmĕth'ā,* sf. firmness, stability, constancy. [prosecutor; fiscal.

fiscal, *fĭskăl',* sm. attorney-general; public

fiscalía, *fĭskălĕ'ā,* sf. office and business of the fiscal. [criminal offence.

fiscalizar, —lĭthār', v. a. to accuse of a

fisco, *fĭs'kŏ,* sm. fisc, fiscal, exchequer.

fisga, *fĭs'gā,* sf. three-pronged harpoon; grimace; raillery, scoff. [jeer.

fisgar, *fĭsgār',* v. a. to mock, to scoff, to

fisgón, *fĭsgŏn',* sm. punster, buffoon.

física, *fĕ'sĭkā,* sf. physics.

físico, ca, *fĕ'sĭkŏ,* a. physical; real; —, sm. physician.

fisonomía, *fĭsŏnŏmĕ'ā,* sf. physiognomy.

fisonomista, —mĭs'tā, sm. physiognomist.

fístola, *fĕs'tŏlā,* sf. fistula. [languid.

flaco, ca, *flā'kŏ,* a. lean, meagre; feeble,

flacura, *flākŏ'rā,* sf. meagreness.

flagelación, *flā'hēl̄ăthǐŏn'*, sf. flagellation.
flagelante, *flā'hēlăn'tē*, sm. flagellant.
flagrante, *flāgrăn'tē*, a. flagrant; en —, in the act, red-handed.
flagrar, *flāgrăr'*, v. n. to glow, to flame.
flamante, *flāmăn'tē*, a. flaming, bright; (quite new.
flanco, *flăn'kō*, sm. flank.
flanquear, *flănkēăr'*, v. a. (mil.) to flank.
flaquear, *flākēăr'*, v. n. to flag; to grow spiritless; to slacken.
flaqueza, *flākā'thā*, sf. leanness, extenuation, meagreness, feebleness, weakness.
flato, *flā'tō*, sm. flatulency; gust of wind.
flatulento, ta, *flātūlēn'tō*, a. flatulent.
flauta, *flāū'tā*, sf. (mus.) flute.
flautado, da, *flāū'tā'dō*, a. resembling a flute; —, sm. stop of an organ.
flautero, —tā'rō, sm. flute-maker.
flautista, —tēs'tā, sm. flute-player, flutist.
flecha, *flāsh'ā*, sf. arrow.
flechero, *flāshā'rō*, sm. archer, bowman; (maker.
flema, *flāmă*, sf. phlegm. [bow-maker.
flemático, ca, *flāmā'tīkō*, a. phlegmatic.
flemón, *flāmōn'*, sm. furuncle; ulcer in the gums.
flemoso, sa, *flāmō'sō*, a. pituitous.
flemudo, da, *flāmō'dō*, a. dull, sluggish.
fletar, *flātār'*, v. a. to freight a ship.
flete, *flā'tē*, sm. (mar.) freight. [ity.
flexibilidad, *flěksēbǐlǐdăd'*, sf. flexibility.
flexible, *flěksē'blě*, a. flexible, pliant; docile. [laziness, negligence.
flojedad, *flōhēdăd'*, sf. feebleness, laxity.
flojo, ja, *flō'hō*, a. flexible, lax, slack; insipid, feeble; lazy. [ficial flowers.
flor, *flōr'*, sf. flower; —es de mano, artiflorear, *flōrēăr'*, v. a. to adorn with flowers; to flourish (of swords); (mus.) to flourish.
florecer, *flōrēthěr'*, v. n. to blossom.
florero, *flōrā'rō*, sm. flower-pot.
floresta, *flōrēs'tā*, sf. forest, thicket, grove; fine delightful place.
florete, *flōrā'tē*, sm. fencing-foil.
floretista, *flōrētēs'tā*, sm. fencer.
florido, da, *flōrē'dō*, a. florid; choice, excellent.
florín, *flōrēn'*, sm. florin. [cellent.
florista, *flōrēs'tā*, sm. florist.
florón, *flōrōn'*, sm. flower-work.
flota, *flō'tā*, sf. fleet. [with the hand.
flotadura, *flōtādō'rā*, sf. gentle rubbing
flotante, *flōtăn'tē*, a. floating.
flotar, *flōtār'*, v. n. to float.
flote, *flō'tē*, sm. floating; á —, buoyant.
flotilla, *flōtēl'yā*, sf. small fleet, flotilla.
fluctuación, *flūktūăthǐŏn'*, sf. fluctuation; uncertainty. [irresolute.
fluctuar, *flūktūăr'*, v. n. to fluctuate; to be fluidez, *flūǐděth'*, sf. fluidity, liquidness.
fluido, da, *flūē'dō*, a. fluid; (fig.) fluent.
fluir, *flūǐr'*, v. n. to flow. [—, sm. fluid.
flujo, *flū'hō*, sm. (med.) flux; flowing; — de vientre, diarrhœa.
fluvial, *flūvǐăl'*, a. fluviatic.
fluxión, *flūksǐŏn'*, sf. flowing, fluction.
foco, *fō'kō*, sm. focus; centre; flash of fire-arms; mortise; (mar.) main-sail of a bilander.

fofo, fa, *fō'fō*, a. spongy, soft, bland.
fogata, *fōgā'tā*, sf. blaze; heat caused by the fumes of wine. [a gun.
fogón, *fōgōn'*, sm. hearth; touch-hole of a fogonazo, *fōgōnā'thō*, sm. flame of the priming of a gun. [city, fieriness.
fogosidad, *fōgōsǐdăd'*, sf. excessive vivafogoso, sa, *fōgō'sō*, a. fiery, ardent, fervent; impetuous, boisterous.
foguear, *fōgēăr'*, v. a. to accustom soldiers or horses to stand fire; to clean fire-arms by firing off a small quantity of gunpowder in them. [books).
foliación, *fōlǐăthǐŏn'*, sf. pagination (of foliar, *fōlǐăr'*, v. a. to page.
foliatura, *fōlǐătō'rā*, sf. numbering the pages of a book; pagination.
follados, *fōlyā'dōs*, sm. pl. old-fashioned trunk-hose.
follaje, *fōlyā'hě*, sm. foliage.
follero, *fōlyā'rō*, sm. one who makes or sells bellows.
folletista, *fōlyětēs'tā*, sm. pamphleteer.
folleto, *fōlyā'tō*, sm. pamphlet; small manuscript newspaper. [tation.
fomentación, *fōměntăthǐŏn'*, sf. fomenfomentar, —tăr', v. a. to foment; to patronise; to excite. [patronage.
fomento, *fōměn'tō*, sm. fomentation; fuel; fonda, *fōn'dā*, sf. hotel, inn, lodging-house.
fondeadero, *fōndēădā'rō*, sm. anchoringground, anchorage.
fondear, *fōndēăr'*, v. a. to sound; to search a ship; —, v. n. to cast anchor.
fondista, *fōndēs'tā*, sm. innkeeper.
fondo, *fōn'dō*, sm. bottom; ground; space occupied by files of soldiers; —s, pl. intrinsic brilliancy of a diamond; stock, fund, capital; dar —, to cast anchor; á —, perfectly, completely; —, da, a. profound.
fontanería, *fōntănērē'ā*, sf. art of making water-works; conduit-pipes, water-duct.
fontanero, —nā'rō, sm. conduit-maker, turncock.
forajido, da, *fōrā'hē'dō*, a. highway robbing; wicked, villanous (also used substantively). [of a country.
foral, *fōrăl'*, a. belonging to the statute law
forastero, ra, *fōrăstā'rō*, a. strange, exotic; —, sm. stranger.
forcejar, *fōrthěhăr'*, v. n. to struggle, to strive, to oppose.
forcejudo, da, —hō'dō, a. strong, robust.
forense, *fōrěn'sě*, a. forensic.
forjador, *fōrhădōr'*, sm. framer, forger.
forjadura, —dō'rā, sf. forging.
forjar, *fōrhăr'*, v. a. to forge; to frame; to invent.
forma, *fōr'mā*, sf. form, shape, fashion; handwriting; host to be consecrated by a priest; de — que, in such a manner that.
formación, *fōrmăthǐŏn'*, sf. formation; form, figure; twisted cord of silk, gold, silver, &c. used by embroiderers.
formal, *fōrmăl'*, a. formal; proper, genuine, serious, grave.
formalidad, *fōrmălǐdăd'*, sf. formality; punctuality; gravity.

formalizar, _–lithār´_, v. a. to form; **–se**, to grow formal, to affect gravity.

formar, _fōrmār´_, v. a. to form, to shape.

formero, _fōrmā´rō_, sm. centring of an arch.

formidable, _fōrmĭdā´blĕ_, a. formidable, dreadful, terrific.

formón, _fōrmōn´_, sm.paring-chisel; punch.

fórmula, _fōr´mŭlă_, sf. formula.

formulario, _fōrmŭlā´rĭō_, sm. formulary.

fornicación, _fōrnĭkāthĭōn´_, sf. fornication.

fornicador, _–dōr´_, sm. fornicator.

fornicar, _fōrnĭkār´_, v. n. to commit fornication. [fornication.

fornicario, **ria**, _–kā´rĭō_, a. relating to

fornitura, _fōrnĭtŭ´ră_, sf. leather straps worn by soldiers. [ground of the stage.

foro, _fō´rŏ_, sm. court of justice; bar; back-

forradora, _fōrrădō´ră_, sf. lining (of clothes).

forraje, _fōrrā´hĕ_, sm. forage.

forrajeador, _–hĕădōr´_, sm. forager.

forrajear, _fōrrăhĕār´_, v. a. to forage.

forrar, _fōrrār´_, v. a. to line.

forro, _fōr´rŏ_, sm. lining.

fortalecer, _fōrtălĕthĕr´_, v. a. to fortify, to strengthen, to encourage.

fortaleza, _–lĕth´ă_, sf. fortitude, valour, courage; strength, vigour; (mil.) fortress, stronghold.

fortepiano, _fōrtĕpĭā´nŏ_, sm. piano-forte.

fortificación, _fōrtĭfĭkāthĭōn´_, sf. fortification. [comfort; to fortify a place.

fortificar, _–kār´_, v. a. to strengthen, to

fortín, _fōrtēn´_, sm. (mil.) small fort.

fortuito, **ta**, _fōrtŭ´ĭtŏ_, a. fortuitous.

fortuna, _fōrtŏ´nă_, sf. fortune.

forzado, _fōrthā´dŏ_, sm. criminal sentenced to the galleys.

forzar, _fōrthār´_, v. a. to force.

forzosa, _fōrthō´să_, sf. decisive move at the game of draughts; necessity.

forzoso, **sa**, _–thō´sŏ_, a. indispensable, necessary.

forzudo, **da**, _–thŏ´dŏ_, a. strong, vigorous.

fosfórico, **ca**, _fōsfō´rĭkŏ_, a. phosphoric.

fósforo, _fōs´fŏrŏ_, sm. phosphorus; –s, pl. matches.

fósil, _fōs´ĭl_, a. & sm. fossil. [matches.

foso, _fō´sŏ_, sm. pit; moat, ditch, fosse.

frac, _frāk_, sm. evening-coat, dress-coat.

fracasar, _frākăsār´_, v. n. to crumble, to break into pieces. [struction.

fracaso, _–kā´sŏ_, sm. downfall, ruin, de-

fracción, _frākthĭōn´_, sf. fraction.

fractura, _–tŏ´ră_, sf. fracture.

fracturar, _–tărār´_, v. a. to break a bone.

fragancia, _frăgān´thĭă_, sf. fragrance, sweetness of smell.

fragante, _–gān´tĕ_, a. fragrant, odoriferous; **en –**, in the act itself, red-handed.

fragata, _frăgā´tă_, sf. (mar.) frigate.

frágil, _frā´hĭl_, a. brittle, frail.

fragilidad, _–lĭdăd´_, sf. fragility, brittle-ness; infirmity.

fragmento, _frăgmĕn´tŏ_, sm. fragment.

fragosidad, _frăgŏsĭdăd´_, sf. roughness of a road; imperviousness of a forest.

fragoso, **sa**, _frăgō´sŏ_, a. craggy, rough, uneven. [(fig.) reputation for virtue.

fragrancia, _frăgrăn´thĭă_, sf. fragrance.

fragrante, _–grān´tĕ_, a. fragrant, odori-

fragua, _frā´gŭă_, sf. forge. [ferous.

fraguar, _frăgŭār´_, v. a. to forge; to con-trive; **–**, v. n. to solidify, to harden (of mortar, clay, &c.).

fraile, _frā´ĭlĕ_, sm. friar, monk.

framasón, _frămăsōn´_, sm. freemason.

frambuesa, _frămbŭā´să_, sf. raspberry.

frambueso, _–ā´sŏ_, sm. raspberry-bramble.

francachela, _frănkăthā´lă_, sf. frankly.

francés, _frănthĕs´_, sm. French language.

francesilla, _frănthĕsĕ´lyă_, sf. (bot.) com-mon yard crow-foot.

franco, _frăn´kŏ_, sm. frank (coin); **–**, **ca**, a. frank; generous, liberal.

francolín, _frănkŏlēn´_, sm. Indian partridge.

franela, _frănĕ´lă_, sf. flannel.

franja, _frăn´hă_, sf. fringe.

franquear, _frănkĕār´_, v. a. to exempt; to franchise; to disengage; to stamp letters; **–se**, to give oneself up to the service of others; to unbosom oneself.

franqueza, _frănkĕ´ă_, sf.freedom, liberty; generosity. [taxes.

franquicia, _frănkē´thĭă_, sf.immunity from taxes.

frasco, _frăs´kŏ_, sm. flask; powder-horn.

frase, _frā´sĕ_, sf. phrase. [case.

frasquera, _frăskā´ră_, sf. bottle-case, liquor-case.

frasqueta, _frăskĕ´tă_, sf. frisket of a printing-press.

fraternal, _frătĕrnăl´_, a. fraternal, brotherly.

fraternidad, _–nĭdăd´_, sf. fraternity, brotherhood. [(murderer of a brother)

fratricida, _frătrĭthē´dă_, sm. & f. fratricide

fratricidio, _–thē´dĭō_, sm.fratricide (murder of a brother).

fraude, _frā´ŭdĕ_, sm. fraud; deceit, cheat.

fraudulento, **ta**, _–dŭlĕn´tŏ_, a. fraudulent, deceitful.

frecuencia, _frĕkŭĕn´thĭă_, sf. frequency.

frecuentación, _–tāthĭōn´_, sf. frequen-tation.

frecuentar, _–tār´_, v. a. to frequent.

frecuente, _frĕkŭĕn´tĕ_, a. frequent.

fregadero, _frĕgădā´rŏ_, sm. scullery.

fregado, _frĕgā´dŏ_, sm. scouring of kitchen utensils; (fig.) intrigue; underhand work.

fregador, _–dōr´_, sm. dish-clout. [scour.

fregar, _frĕgār´_, v. a. to rub; to cleanse, to

fregona, _frĕgō´nă_, sf. kitchen-maid.

freidura, _frĕ´ĭdŭră_, sf. frying.

freir, _frĕēr´_, v. a. to fry. [caprice.

frenesí, _frĕnĕsē´_, sm. frenzy; extravagant

frenético, **ca**, _frĕnĕ´tĭkŏ_, a. mad, lunatic, insane. [tongue.

frenillo, _frĕnē´lyŏ_, sm. impediment of the

freno, _frĕ´nŏ_, sm. bridle; (rail.) brake.

frente, _frĕn´tĕ_, sf. front; face; **– á –**, face to face; **en –**, opposite; (mil.) front rank of a body of troops.

fresa, _frĕ´să_, sf. strawberry.

fresal, _frĕsăl´_, sm.strawberry-plant; ground bearing strawberry plants.

frescachón, **ona**, _frĕskătshōn´_, a. good looking and stout.

fresco, **ca**, _frĕs´kŏ_, a. fresh, coolish; new; recent; plump, ruddy; brisk, gay; **–**, sm. refreshing air.

frescura, *fresko'rá*, sf. freshness; frankness; smart repartee; carelessness.

fresno, *fres'no*, sm. ash-tree.

frialdad, *frialdád'*, sf. frigidity, coldness; indifference.

fricación, *frikathión'*, sf. friction.

fricandó, *frikandó'*, sm. Scotch collop.

fricción, *frikthión'*, sf. friction.

friega, *frie'gá*, sf. friction with flannel.

frigido, da, *fri'hido*, a. (poet.) cold.

frio, fria, *frio'*, a. cold, frigid; indifferent; —, sm. cold; fresh air; shivering.

friolento, ta, *friolen'to*, a. chilly.

friolera, —*lá'rá*, sf. trifle.   [or shagging.

frisadura, *frisadó'rá*, sf. act of frizzling

frisar, *frisár'*, v. a. to frizzle; to rub against the grain; —, v. n. to resemble; to approach.

friso, *fri'so*, sm. frieze; wainscot.

frisón, *frisón'*, sm. large draught-horse.

fritada, *fritá'dá*, sf. dish of fried meat or [fish.

frito, ta, *fri'to*, p. & a. fried.

frivolidad, *frivolidád'*, sf. frivolity.

frívolo, la, *fri'volo*, a. frivolous, trifling.

frondosidad, *frondosidád'*, sf. foliage, tuft of leaves.   [ing with leaves.

frondoso, sa, *frondó'so*, a. leafy, abound-

frontal, *frontál'*, sm. front-ornament of an altar.

frontera, *frontá'rá*, sf. frontier.

fronterizo, za, *fronteri'tho*, a. limita-neous; opposite, over-against.

frontis, *fron'tis*, sm. face, façade.   [piece.

frontispicio, *frontispi'thio*, sm. frontis-

frontón, *frontón'*, sm. wall for playing at fives.

frotación, *frotathión'*, frotadura, *frotá-dó'rá*, sf. friction, rubbing.

frotar, *frotár'*, v. a. to rub.   [fruitful.

fructífero, ra, *frúktí'fero*, a. fructiferous,

fructificar, *frúktifikár'*, v. a. to fructify, to fertilize.

fructuoso, sa, *frúktuó'so*, a. fruitful; useful.

frugal, *frugál'*, a. frugal, sparing.

frugalidad, *frugalidád'*, sf. frugality, parsimony.

fruncidor, *frúnthidór'*, sm. plaiter, folder.

fruncimiento, —*mien'to*, sm. wrinkling, corrugation; imposture.

fruncir, *frúnthír'*, v. a. to plait; to knit; to reduce to a smaller size; to conceal the truth; — las cejas, to knit the eyebrows; — los labios, to curl the lips.

frusleria, *frúsleri'á*, sf. trifle, futility.

frustrar, *frústrár'*, v. a. to frustrate; to disappoint; —se, to miscarry

fruta, *frú'tá*, sf. fruit; — del tiempo, fruit in season.   [fresh fruit.

frutal, *frutál'*, sm. fruit-tree.

frutera, *frutá'rá*, sf. fruit-woman.

frutero, —*ró*, sm. fruiterer; fruit-basket.

frutilla, *frúti'yá*, sf. strawberry in Peru; round shell of which rosaries are made.

fruto, *frú'to*, sm. fruit; benefit, profit.

¡fu! *fú*, fy! shame! faugh!

fuego, *fué'go*, sm. fire; ¡—! fire! ¡—! bless me! what is this!

fuelle, *fué'lye*, sm. bellows; tale-bearer.

fuente, *fúen'te*, sf. fountain; original, first principle; source; issue, fontanel.

fuera, *fúé'rá*, ad. without; from outward; over and above; ¡—! out of the way!

fuero, —*ró*, sm. statute-law of a country; jurisdiction; privileges granted to a pro-vince.

fuerte, *fúer'te*, sm. fortification, fort; —, a. vigorous, stout; strong; —, ad. strongly.

fuerza, *fúer'thá*, sf. force, strength, vigour; valour, courage; violence, coercion; & — de, by dint of; —s, pl. troops.

fuga, *fú'gá*, sf. flight, escape.

fugarse, *fugár'se*, v. r. to escape, to fly.

fugaz, *fugáth'*, a. fugitive; volatile; per-ishable.   [fugitive.

fugitivo, va, *fú'hiti'vo*, a. & sm. & f such a one.

fulano, na, *fúlá'no*, sm. & f. such a one.

fulgente, *fúl'hén'te*, a. (poet.) brilliant

fulgurar, *fúlgurár'*, v. n. to emit flashes of light.   [sharping; cogging, fallacy.

fullería, *fúlyeri'á*, sf. cheating, card-

fullero, *fúlyá'ró*, sm. card-sharper, cheat.

fulminación, *fúlminathión'*, sf. flash; re-port; thundering.   [n. to rave.

fulminar, —*nár'*, v. a. to fulminate; —, v.

fumada, *fúmá'dá*, sf. whiff.

fumadero, —*dá'ró*, sm. smoking-room.

fumar, *fúmár'*, v. a. & n. to smoke.

fumarada, *fúmará'dá*, sf. blast of smoke; a pipeful of tobacco.

fumigación, *fúmigáthión'*, sf. fumigation.

fumigatorio, ria, —*ógtó'rió*, a. fumigatory.

fumosidad, *fúmosidád'*, sf. smokiness.

fumoso, sa, *fúmó'so*, a. full of smoke or fume, fumid, smoky.

funámbulo, *fúnám'búlo*, sm. rope-dancer.

función, *fúnthión'*, sf. function; solemnity, festival; fight, battle.

funda, *fún'dá*, sf. case, sheath; — de al-mohada, pillow-case.   [groundwork.

fundación, *fúndáthión'*, sf. foundation;

fundador, —*dór'*, sm. founder.

fundamental, —*mentál'*, a. fundamental.

fundamento, —*men'to*, sm. foundation, groundwork; reason, cause.

fundar, *fún'dár'*, v. a. to found; to estab-lish, to ground.

fundible, *fúndí'ble*, a. fusible.

fundición, *fúndithión'*, sf. fusion; foundry.

fundidor, —*dór'*, sm. founder.

fundir, *fúndír'*, v. a. to melt metals.

fúnebre, *fú'nébré*, a. mournful, sad; funeral.

funeral, *fúnérál'*, a. funeral; á la —, manner in which soldiers carry arms dur-ing the holy week and at funerals; —es, sm. pl. funeral, obsequies.

funerario, ria, —*rá'rió*, a. funeral, funereal.

funesto, ta, *fúnés'to*, a. funereal, mourn-ful, sad, dismal.

furia, *fú'riá*, sf. fury, rage; á toda —, ad. with the utmost speed.   [furylike.

furibundo, da, *fúribún'do*, a. furious

furioso, sa, *fúrió'so*, a. furious.

furor, *fúrór'*, sm. fury.

furrier, *fúrriér'*, sm. quarter-master.

furtivamente, *fŭrtĭvámĕn'tā,* ad. by stealth.

furtivo, va, *–tē'vō,* a. furtive.

fusil, *fŭsēl',* sm. fusil, firelock; **— que se carga por la recámara,** breech-loader.

fusilazo, *–lä'thō,* sm. musket-shot.

fusilería, *–lē'rē'ā,* sf. body of fusileers.

fusilero, *–lā'rō,* sm. fusileer.

fusión, *fūsēŏn',* sf. fusion.

fusique, *fūsē'kē,* sm. kind of snuff-box.

fuste, *fūs'tā,* sm. tree and bows of a saddle; shaft of a lance; fust of a column.

fútil, *fō'tĭl,* a. futile, trifling.

futilidad, *fūtĭlĭdád',* sf. futility.

futuro, ra, *fūtō'rō,* a. & sm. future.

G.

gabacho, cha, *gäbätsh'ō,* a. applied to the natives of some places at the foot of the Pyrenees; used also in derision to the French. [verano, dust-coat.

gabán, *gäbän',* sm. great-coat; sack; —de

gabardina, *gäbärdē'nä,* sf. cassock.

gabarra, *gäbär'rä,* sf. (mar.) lighter (boat).

gabela, *gäbē'lä,* sf. gabel, tax, duty.

gabinete, *gäbĭnē'tā,* sm. cabinet.

gaceta, *gäthē'tä,* sf. newspaper.

gacetero, *gäthēt'rō,* sm. gazetteer, news-writer; newsvender.

gacetilla, *–tēl'yä,* sf. news, tidings.

gacetista, *–tēs'tä,* sm. newsmonger.

gachas, *gätsh'äs,* sf. pl. any sort of soft pap; **á—,** on all fours; **¡ánimo á las —!** cheer up! courage! go ahead!

gacho, cha, *gätsh'ō,* a. curvated, bent downwards. [tacles.

gafa, *gä'fä,* sf. kind of hook; **—s,** pl. spec-

gaita, *gä'tä,* sf. bagpipe; flageolet; corne-muse.

gaitería, *gätērē'ä,* sf. gay and gaudy dress.

gaitero, *–tē'rō,* sm. bag-piper, bag-pipe player; **—, ra,** a. gay, gaudy, showy.

gaje, *gä'hē,* sm. salary, wages; **—s,** pl. fees.

gajo, *gä'hō,* sm. branch of a tree broken off; part torn off a bunch of grapes.

gala, *gä'lä,* sf. court-dress; **día de —,** court-day; holiday; graceful, pleasing address; parade; **hacer —,** to glory in having done a thing. [ning rogue.

galafate, *gäläfä'tā,* sm. artful thief; cun-

galán, *gälän',* sm. gallant, gentleman in full dress; courtier; lover; actors who perform serious characters in plays, are distinguished in order as first, second, &c.

galán; —, ana, a. gallant, fine, neat, elegant.

galante, *gälän'tā,* a. gallant, courtly; brave, generous, liberal; elegant.

galanteador, *–tēädōr',* sm. wooer, lover.

galantear, *–tēär',* v. a. to court, to woo.

galanteo, *–tē'ō,* sm. gallantry, courtship.

galantería, *–tērē'ä,* sf. gallantry, elegance; liberality, generosity.

galápago, *gälä'pägō,* sm. fresh-water tor-

toise; (fig.) cunning man; **—s,** pl. (mar.) cleats, pl. [pense.

galardón, *gälärdōn',* sm. reward, recom-

galardonar, *–dōnär',* v. a. to reward, to recompense. [indolence.

galbana, *gälbä'nä,* sf. laziness, idleness,

galbanero, ra, *–nā'rō,* a. lazy, indolent.

galenismo, *gälēnĭs'mō,* sm. doctrine of Galen.

galeón, *gälēŏn',* sm. (mar.) galleon.

galeota, *gälēŏ'tä,* sf. (mar.) galliot.

galeote, *gälēŏ'tē,* sm. galley-slave.

galera, *gälē'rä,* sf. (mar.) galley; wagon; gally, type-gally; reformatory for lewd women.

galería, *gälērē'ä,* sf. gallery.

galga, *gäl'gä,* sf. greyhound bitch.

galgo, *gäl'gō,* sm. greyhound.

gálico, *gä'lĭkō,* sm. venereal disease.

galicoso, sa, *gälĭkō'sä,* a. syphilitic.

galocha, *gälŏtsh'ä,* sf. clog, golosh.

galón, *gälŏn',* sm. galloon; gallon.

galoneadura, *–nēädō'rä,* sf. garnishing with galloons.

galonear, *gälōnēär',* v. a. to lace.

galope, *gälō'pē,* sm. gallop; hasty execution of a thing.

galopear, *gälōpēär',* v. n. to gallop.

galopín, *–pĭn',* sm. swabber; cabin-boy; scullion; boy meanly dressed.

galvánico, ca, *gälvä'nĭkō,* a. galvanic.

galvanismo, *gälvänĭs'mō,* sm. galvanism.

galladura, *gälyädō'rä,* sf. tread (in an egg).

gallarda, *gälyär'dä,* sf. a Spanish dance.

gallardear, *–dēär',* v. n. to do anything gracefully or elegantly. [streamer.

gallardete, *–dē'tē,* sm. (mar.) pendant,

gallardía, *–dē'ä,* sf. genteelness, elegance, gracefulness; activity, briskness; liberality.

gallardo, da, *gälyär'dō,* a. gay, graceful, elegant, genteel; magnanimous; generous, brave, daring.

gallear, *gälyēär',* v. a. to tread (as birds); to assume an air of importance; **—, v. n.** to raise the voice menacingly.

galleta, *gälyē'tä,* sf. sea-biscuit.

gallillo, *–yēl'yō,* sm. uvula.

gallina, *gälyē'nä,* sf. hen; (fig.) coward; **— ciega,** blindman's buff.

gallinaza, *–yĭnä'thä,* sf. hen-dung.

gallinero, ra, *–yĭnā'rō,* a. preying or feeding upon fowls; **—,** sm. poulterer; cock-loft, hen-roost; women's gallery of a Spanish theatre.

gallineta, *–yĭnē'tä,* sf. sand-piper (bird).

gallipavo, *–pä'vō,* sm. turkey.

gallito, *gälyē'tō,* sm. beau, coxcomb.

gallo, *gäl'yō,* sm. cock; chief of a village.

gama, *gä'mä,* sf. (mus.) gamut; doe, she-deer. [dancing.

gambeta, *gämbē'tä,* sf. cross-caper in

gamella, *gämēl'lä,* sf. hamper, dosser.

gamella, *gämēl'yä,* sf. yoke for oxen and mules; large wooden trough.

gamo, *gä'mō,* sm. buck of the fallow deer.

gana, *gä'nä,* sf. appetite; healthy disposition; desire, mind, list; **de buena —,**

with pleasure, voluntarily; **de mala —,** unwillingly, with reluctance.

ganadería, *gănădēr'ă*, sf. breeding or feeding of cattle. [in cattle.

ganadero, *-dē'rō*, sm. cattle-owner; dealer

ganado, *gănă'dō*, sm. cattle; **— mayor,** black-cattle, mules; **— menor,** sheep, asses; **— merino,** merino sheep; **— de cerda,** swine. [lucre.

ganancia, *gănăn'thĭă*, sf. gain, profit.

ganancial, *-thĭăl'*, a. lucrative.

ganancioso, sa, *-thĭō'sō*, a. gainful.

ganapán, *gănăpăn'*, sm. porter, carrier.

ganar, *gănăr'*, v. a. to gain, to win.

gancho, *găn'tshō*, sm. hook; crook.

ganga, *găn'gă*, sf. little pin-tailed grouse; gangue, bed of minerals; any valuable thing or profit acquired with little trouble or ado.

gangoso, sa, *găngō'sō*, a. snuffling.

gangrena, *găngră'nă*, sf. gangrene.

gangrenarse, *-năr'sĕ*, v. r. to become gangrenous.

gangrenoso, sa, *-nō'sō*, a. gangrenous.

ganguear, *găngĕăr'*, v. n. to snuffle, to speak through the nose.

gangueo, *găngĕ'ō*, sm. snuffling.

gansarón, *gănsărōn'*, sm. gosling; tall, thin man. [tall slender person.

ganso, sa, *găn'sō*, sm. & f. gander; goose.

gañote, *gănyō'tĕ*, sm. wind-pipe; kind of fritters.

garabatear, *gărăbătĕăr'*, v. a. to catch with a hook; to scrawl, to scribble.

garabato, *-bă'tō*, sm. pot-hook; attractive deportment; **—s,** pl. scrawling letters or characters; improper gestures or movements of the hands and fingers.

garante, *gărăn'tĕ*, sm. guarantee.

garantía, *-tĭ'ă*, sf. warranty, guaranty.

garantir, *-tĭr'*, v. a. to guarantee.

garañón, *gărănyōn'*, sm. jack-ass.

garapiña, *gărăpĭn'yă*, sf. ice, ice-cream; the congealed particles of any liquid; kind of black lace.

garapiñar, *-pĭnyăr'*, v. a. to ice.

garapiñera, *-pĭnyĕ'ră*, sf. ice-safe.

garbanzal, *gărbănthăl'*, sm. piece of ground sown with chick-peas.

garbanzo, *-băn'thō*, sm. chick-pea.

garbanzuelo, *-thŭĕ'lō*, sm. spavin (foot-disease in horses).

garbear, *gărbĕăr'*, v. n. to affect elegance or fineness. [(sieve).

garbillo,, *-bĭl'yō*, sm. riddle (coarse

garbo, *găr'bō*, sm. gracefulness, elegance of manner; generosity; cleverness.

garboso, sa, *-bō'sō*, a. genteel, graceful; liberal, generous. [marten.

garduña, *gărdŭn'yă*, sf. pole-cat, house-

garfiña, *gărfĭn'yă*, sf. (cant) stealth.

garfiñar, *-yăr'*, v. a. to steal. [spit.

gargajear, *gărgă'hĕăr'*, v. n. to spawl, to

gargajo, *gărgă'hō*, sm. phlegm, spittle.

garganta, *gărgăn'tă*, sf. throat, gullet; instep; mountain-flood, torrent; narrow pass between mountains or rivers.

gargantilla, *-tĭl'yă*, sf. women's necklace.

gárgara, *găr'gără*, sf. noise made by gargling. [gargle.

gargarismo, *-rĭs'mō*, sm. gargling.

gargarizar, *-rĭthăr'*, v. a. to gargle.

garguero, *gărgŭĕ'rō*, sm. gullet; wind-pipe. [line-keeper's lodge.

garita, *gărĭ'tă*, sf. (mil.) sentry-box; (rail.)

garitero, *-tĕ'rō*, sm. master of a gaming-house; gamester.

garlito, *gărlĭ'tō*, sm. weel; snare.

garnacha, *gărnăt'shă*, sf. counsellor's robe.

garra, *găr'ră*, sf. claw, talon, paw; clutch; hand (in contempt).

garrafa, *gărră'fă*, sf. decanter.

garrafal, *-făl'*, a. great, vast, huge.

garrapata, *-pă'tă*, sf. tick (insect); bum-bailiff. [to scrawl.

garrapatear, *-pătĕăr'*, v. n. to scribble,

garrapato, *-pă'tō*, sm. clothes-moth; **—s,** pl. pot-hooks. [herd's prick.

garrocha, *gărrōt'shă*, sf. drover's or neat-

garrotazo, *gărrōtă'thō*, sm. blow with a cudgel.

garrote, *gărrō'tĕ*, sm. cudgel; capital punishment in Spain, performed by strangling with an iron collar.

garrotillo, *-tĭl'yō*, sm. quinsy.

garrucha, *gărrŭt'shă*, sf. pulley.

gárrulo, la, *găr'rŭlō*, a. chirping; chattering, prattling.

garulla, *gărŭl'yă*, sf. ripe grapes which remain in the basket; (fig.) rabble.

garza, *găr'thă*, sf. heron (bird).

garzo, *găr'thō*, sm. agaric; **—, sa,** a. blue-eyed. [lage, crest of a helmet.

garzota, *gărthō'tă*, sf. night-heron; plum-

gas, *găs*, sm. gas.

gasa, *gă'să*, sf. gauze.

gasconada, *găskōnă'dă*, sf. gasconade.

gasómetro, *găsō'mĕtrō*, sm. gasometer.

gastador, *găstădōr'*, sm. spendthrift, prodigal; corrupter; (mil.) pioneer.

gastar, *găstăr'*, v. a. to expend; to waste; to plunder; to digest; **—se,** to become gasto; *găs'tō*, sm. expense, cost. [rotten.

gastronomía, *găstrōnōmĕ'ă*, sf. gastronomy. [fours.

gata, *gă'tă*, sf. she-cat; **á —s,** on all

gatada, *gătă'dă*, sf. clawing; robbery effected in an artful manner; artful action.

gatear, *gătĕăr'*, v. n. to climb up; **—,** v. a. to scratch or claw; to steal.

gatera, *gătĕ'ră*, sf. cat's hole.

gatesco, ca, *gătĕs'kō*, a. feline, catlike.

gatillazo, *gătĭlyă'thō*, sm. click of the trigger in firing. [of a gun.

gatillo, *gătĭl'yō*, sm. tooth-pincer; trigger

gato, *gă'tō*, sm. cat; hand-screw; cat-algalia, civet-cat.

gatuno, na, *gătŭ'nă*, a. catlike, feline.

gaudeamus, *găudĕă'mŭs*, sm. feast, entertainment, merry-making. [flocker.

gaveta, *găvĕ'tă*, sf. drawer of a desk,

gavia, *gă'vĭă*, sf. (mar.) top, crow's-nest; pit into which a tree is transplanted with its roots; cell for mad persons; —s, pl. top-sails of the main and fore-mast. [(ave).

gavilán, *gávilăn'*, sm. sparrow-hawk

gavilla, *gávĭl'yă'*, sf. sheaf of corn; gang of suspicious persons.

gavota, *gávŏ'tă'*, sf. gavotte (French dance).

gazapera, *găthăpĕ'ră*, sf. warren.

gazapo, *găthă'pŏ*, sm. young rabbit; artful knave; great lie.

gazmoñada, *găthmŏnyă'dă*, **gazmoñeria,** —nyĕrĕ'ă, sf. prudery; hypocrisy.

gazmoñero, ra, —mŏnyĕ'rŏ, **gazmoño, na,** —mŏn'yŏ, a, hypocritical; [throttle.

gaznatada, —nătă'dă, sf. blow on the **gaznate,** —nă'tĕ, sm. throttle, wind-pipe.

gazpacho, —pătsh'ŏ, sm. a Spanish refreshing dish for labourers.

gazuza, *găthŏ'thă*, sf. keenness of stomach.

gemelo, la, *hĕmă'lŏ*, sm. & f. twin.

gemido, *hĕmĭ'dŏ*, sm. groan, moan, howl.

Géminis, *hĕ'mĭnĭs*, sm. Gemini, Twins (sign of the zodiac).

gemir, *hĕmĭr'*, v. n. to groan, to moan.

genciana, *hĕnthĭă'nă*, sf. (bot.) gentian.

gendarma, *hĕndăr'mă*, sm. gendarme.

gendarmería, —mĕrĕ'ă, sf. gendarmery.

genealogía, *hĕnĕălŏhĕ'ă*, sf. genealogy.

genealógico, ca, —lŏ'hĭkŏ, a. genealogical.

generación, *hĕnĕrăthĭŏn'*, sf. generation; progeny, race.

general, *hĕnĕrăl'*, sm. general; —, a. general; **en** —, generally, in general.

generala, —ră'lă, sf. (mil.) general (a beat of the drum).

generalato, —ră'lă'tŏ, sm. generalship.

generalidad, —rălĭdăd', sf. generality.

generalísimo, —răl'ĭ'mŏ, sm. generalisimo.

generalizar, —răl'ĭthăr', v. a. to generalize.

genérico, ca, *hĕnĕ'rĭkŏ*, a. generic.

género, *hĕn'ĕrŏ*, sm. genus; sex, gender; —s, pl. goods, commodities.

generosidad, —sĭdăd', sf. generosity.

generoso, sa, —rŏ'sŏ, a. noble, generous.

Génesis, *hĕ'nĕsĭs*, sf. Genesis, first book of the Pentateuch.

genial, *hĕnĭăl'*, a. genial.

genio, *hă'nĭŏ*, sm. genius. [tals.

genital, *hĕnĭtăl'*, a. genital; —es, pl. genitals.

genitivo, —tĭ'vŏ, sm. (gr.) genitive case.

genízaro, ra, *hĕnĕ'thărŏ*, a. begotten by parents of different nations; composed of different species; —, sm. janizary.

gente, *hĕn'tĕ*, sf. people; nation; family; army, troops.

gentecilla, —thĕl'yă, sf. mob, rabble.

gentil, *hĕntĭl'*, sm. pagan, heathen; —, a. genteel, elegant, excellent.

gentileza, —lĕ'thă, sf. genteelness, elegance of behaviour; politeness.

gentilhombre, —ŏm'brĕ, sm. gentleman.

gentílico, ca, *hĕntĭ'lĭkŏ*, a. -pagan, heathenish.

gentilidad, *hĕntĭlĭdăd'*, sf. & **gentilismo,** *hĕntĭlĭs'mŏ*, sm. heathenism.

gentío, *hĕntĭ'ŏ*, sm. crowd, multitude.

gentualla, —tŏăl'yă, sf. rabble, mob.

genuflexión, *hĕnŏflĕksĭŏn'*, sf. genuflection.

genuino, na, *hĕnŏĭ'nŏ*, a. genuine, pure.

geografía, *hĕŏgrăfĕ'ă*, sf. geography.

geográfico, ca, —grăf'ĭkŏ, a. geographical.

geógrafo, *hĕŏ'grăfŏ*, sm. geographer.

geología, *hĕŏlŏhĕ'ă*, sf. geology.

geómetra, *hĕŏmĕtră*, sm. geometrician.

geometría, *hĕŏmĕtrĕ'ă*, sf. geometry.

geométrico, ca, —mĕ'trĭkŏ, a. geometrical, geometric.

geranio, *hĕră'nĭŏ*, sm. (bot.) crane's bill.

germen, *hĕr'mĕn*, sm. germ, bud; source, original cause. [to bud.

germinar, *hĕrmĭnăr'*, v. n. to germinate.

gerundio, *hĕrŏn'dĭŏ*, sm. (gr.) gerund.

gesolreut, *hĕsŏlrĕŭt'*, sm. (mus.) the first sign or clef to music.

gesticular, *hĕstĭkŭlăr'*, v. a. to gesticulate.

gesto, *hĕs'tŏ*, sm. face, visage; grimace; aspect, appearance; resemblance.

giganta, *hĭgăn'tă*, sf. giantess.

gigante, —tĕ, sm. giant; —, a. gigantic.

gigantesco, ca, —tĕs'kŏ, a. gigantic, giant.

gigantilla, —tĭl'yă, sf. figure made of paste or pasteboard, with a very large head. [corpulence.

gijas, *hĕ'hăs*, sf. pl. strength; vigour;

gimnasio, *hĭmnă'sĭŏ*, sm. gymnasium; school, academy.

gimnástica, —năs'tĭkă, sf. gymnastics.

gimnástico, ca, —năs'tĭkŏ, a. gymnastic.

ginebra, *hĭnĕ'bră*, sf. rattle; gin, Geneva.

gineta, *hĭnĕ'tă*, sf. genet (kind of weasel).

girafa, *hĭră'fă*, sf. cameloparad.

giralda, *hĭrăl'dă*, sf. weathercock in the form of a statue.

girándula, *hĭrăn'dŭlă*, sf. girandole.

girar, *hĭrăr'*, v. n. to turn round; to remit by bills of exchange from one place to another. [other.

girasol, *hĭrăsŏl'*, sm. sun-flower.

giro, *hĕ'rŏ*, sm. turning round; circulation of bills of exchange. [rag.

girón, *hĭrŏn'*, sm. facing of a garment;

gitanada, *hĭtănă'dă*, sf. wheedling (like gipsies). [wheedle.

gitanear, *hĭtănĕăr'*, v. a. to flatter, to

gitanería, —rĕ'ă, sf. wheedling, flattery.

gitanesco, ca, —nĕs'kŏ, a. gipsy-like.

gitano, na, *hĭtă'nŏ*, sm. & f. gipsy; sly fellow; person of a genteel, pleasing address. [dress.

glacial, *glăthĭăl'*, a. icy.

glacis, *glă'thĭs*, sm. sloping bank, glacis.

gladiador, *glădĭădŏr'*, sm. gladiator, prize-fighter.

glándula, *glăn'dŭlă*, sf. gland. [fighter.

glanduloso, sa, —lŏ'sŏ, a. glandulous.

globo, *glŏ'bŏ*, sm. globe; sphere; orb; **en** —, by the lump; — **aerostático,** air-balloon.

globoso, sa, *glŏbŏ'sŏ*, a. globular.

glóbulo, *glŏ'bŭlŏ*, sm. globule. [taffety.

gloria, *glŏ'rĭă*, sf. glory; sort of light thin

gloriarse, *glŏrĭăr'sĕ*, v. r. to glory, to pride in; to take delight in.

glorieta, *glŏrĭĕ'tă*, sf. bower, arbour.

glorificación, —fĭkăthĭŏn', sf. glorification; praise.

glorificador, –dŏr', sm. glorifier.
glorificar, –kăr', v. a. to glorify; **–se**, to boast.
glorioso, **sa**, glŏrĭŏ'sŏ, a. glorious.
glosa, glŏs'ä, sf. gloss. [glosser.
glosador, glŏsädŏr', sm. commentator.
glosar, glŏsär', v. a. to gloss.
glotón, **ona**, glŏtŏn', sm. & f. glutton.
glotonería, glŏtŏnĕrĕ'ä, sf. gluttony.
glutinoso, **sa**, glūtĭnŏ'sŏ, a. glutinous, viscous. [ment.
gobernación, gŏbĕrnäthĕŏn', sf. government.
gobernador, –dŏr', sm. governor.
gobernalle, –nä'lyĕ, sm. rudder, helm.
gobernar, –när', v. a. to govern; to regulate; to direct.
gobierno, gŏbĭer'nŏ, sm. government.
goce, gŏ'thĕ, sm. enjoyment, fruition; possession. [session.
goleta, gŏlä'tä, sf. schooner.
golfo, gŏl'fŏ, sm. gulf, bay.
golilla, gŏlĭl'yä, sf. Spanish collar; magistrate who wears the golilla.
golondrina, gŏlŏndrē'nä, sf. swallow.
golosina, gŏlŏsē'nä, sf. dainty, titbit; cupidity, desire. [tonous.
goloso, **sa**, gŏlŏ'sŏ, a. lickerish; gluttonous.
golpe, gŏl'pĕ, sm. blow, stroke, hit; knock; unfortunate accident; **de –**, all at once.
golpear, gŏlpĕär', v. a. to beat, to knock; to give blows; to bruise.
goma, gŏ'mä, sf. gum. [viscosity.
gomosidad, gŏmŏsĭdäd', sf. gumminess.
gomoso, **sa**, gŏmŏ'sŏ, a. gummy, viscous.
góndola, gŏn'dŏlä, sf. gondola.
gondolero, gŏndŏlĕ'rŏ, sm. gondolier.
gordiflón, **ona**, gŏrdĭflŏn', sm. & f. very corpulent person. [big-bellied.
gordo, **da**, gŏr'dŏ, a. fat, corpulent, plump.
gordura, gŏrdŏ'rä, sf. grease; fatness, corpulence, obesity.
gorgojo, gŏrgŏ'hŏ, sm. grub, weevil.
gorgojoso, **sa**, gŏrgŏ'hŏsŏ, a. full of grubs or weevils.
gorgorita, –rē'tä, sf. bubble formed on water by the fall of rain.
gorgoritear, –rĭtĕär', v. n. to warble, to quiver the voice. [voice.
gorgoritos, –rē'tŏs, sm. pl. quivers of the
gorigori, gŏrĭgŏ'rĭ, sm. song with which children mimic the clerk's chant at funerals.
gorjear, gŏr'hĕär', v. n. to warble; (mus.) to trill, to quaver, to shake. [chirping.
gorjeo, gŏr'hĕŏ, sm. trilling; quaver;
gorra, gŏr'rä, sf. cap, bonnet.
gorrión, gŏrrĭŏn', sm. sparrow.
gorrista, gŏrrĭs'tä, sm. parasite, sponger.
gorro, gŏr'rŏ, sm. round cap.
gota, gŏ'tä, sf. drop; **– coral ó caduca**, falling-sickness; **– serena**, amaurosis.
gotear, gŏtĕär', v. a. to fall drop by drop.
gotera, gŏtĕ'rä, sf. gutter; fringe of bed-hangings.
gótico, **ca**, gŏ'tĭkŏ, a. Gothic.
gotoso, **sa**, gŏtŏ'sŏ, a. gouty.
gozar, gŏthär', v. a. to enjoy, to have possession or fruition of; **–se**, to rejoice.

gozne, gŏth'nĕ, sm. hinge.
gozo, gŏ'thŏ, sm. joy, pleasure.
gozoso, **sa**, gŏthŏ'sŏ, a. joyful, cheerful, content, glad, merry, pleased.
grabado, gräbä'dŏ, sm. engraving.
grabador, –dŏr', sm. engraver.
grabar, gräbär', v. a. to engrave; **– al agua fuerte**, to etch.
gracejo, gräthĕ'hŏ, sm. joke, jest, mirth; graceful deliverance.
gracia, grä'thĭä, sf. grace; favour; affability; benevolence; pardon.
graciosidad, –thĭŏsĭdäd', sf. gracefulness, beauty, perfection.
gracioso, **sa**, –thĭŏ'sŏ, a. graceful, beautiful; funny, pleasing; benevolent; gratuitous; **–**, sm. merry-Andrew, buffoon.
grada, grä'dä, sf. step of a staircase; harrow; gradual; **–s**, pl. (law) bar; seats of an amphitheatre. [steps.
gradería, grädĕrē'ä, sf. series of seats or gradas.
gradilla, grädĭl'yä, sf. tile-mould.
grado, grä'dŏ, sm. step; degree; will, pleasure. [(mil.) rank.
graduación, grädŏäthĭŏn', sf. graduation;
gradual, grädäl', a. gradual; **–**, sm. a gradual, a text read between the epistle and gospel at the celebration of mass.
graduando, grädäŏn'dŏ, sm. graduate, candidate for academical degrees.
graduar, grädäär', v. a. to graduate.
graja, grä'h'ä, sf. jay (bird).
grajo, grä'h'ŏ, sm. jack-daw (bird).
grama, grä'mä, sf. dog's grass.
gramática, grämä'tĭkä, sf. grammar.
gramatical, –tĭkäl', a. grammatical.
gramático, grämä'tĭkŏ, sm. grammarian.
gran, grän, a. for grande, great.
grana, grä'nä, sf. grain; cochineal; scarlet grain; fine scarlet cloth. [granate.
granada, gränä'dä, sf. (mil.) grenade; pomegranate.
granadero, –dĕ'rŏ, sm. (mil.) grenadier.
granadilla, –dĭl'yä, sf. passion-flower.
granado, **da**, gränä'dŏ, a. large, remarkable; illustrious; **–**, sm. pomegranate tree.
granar, gränär', v. a. to run to seed.
granate, gränä'tĕ, sm. garnet (precious stone).
granazón, –thŏn', sf. seeding. [stone).
grande, grän'dĕ, a. great; **–**, sm. grandee (Spanish nobleman).
grandeza, gründä'thä, sf. greatness; grandeur; grandeeship; body of grandees.
grandiosidad, gründĭŏsĭdäd', sf. greatness, grandeur; magnificence. [ficent.
grandioso, **sa**, –dĭŏ'sŏ, a. grand, magnificent.
grandor, gründŏr', sm. size, bigness, extent, magnitude.
granear, gränĕär', v. a. to sow grain in the earth; to engrave; to grain leather.
granero, gränĕ'rŏ, sm. granary.
granito, gränē'tŏ, sm. granite.
granizada, gränĭthä'dä, sf. copious fall of hail; multitude of things which fall in abundance.
granizar, –thär', v. n. to hail. [eyes.
granizo, gränĕ'thŏ, sm. hail; web in the

granja, *grăn'h'ă,* sf. farm; summer resort.

grano, *grā'nŏ,* sm. grain.

granoso, sa, *—nŏ'sŏ,* a. grainy; granulary.

grasa, sa, *grās'ă,* sf. suet, fat; grease.

grasiento, ta, *grăsĭen'tŏ,* a. greasy; rusty, filthy. [gum sandarach.

grasilla, *grăsĭl'yă,* sf. powder made of

gratificación, *grătĭfĭkăthĭŏn',* sf. gratification, recompense.

gratificar, *—fĭkăr',* v. a. to gratify, to reward, to recompense.

gratis, *grā'tĭs,* a. gratis, for nothing.

gratitud, *grătĭtūd',* sf. gratitude, grate-

grato, ta, *grā'tŏ,* a. grateful. [fulness.

gratuito, ta, *grătū'ĭtŏ,* a. gratuitous.

gravamen, *grăvā'men,* sm. charge, obligation; nuisance. [press, to molest.

gravar, *grăvăr',* v. a. to burden, to oppress.

grave, *grā'vĕ,* a. weighty, heavy; grave, important; haughty; troublesome, grievous. [vanity, pride.

gravedad, *—dăd',* sf. gravity; graveness.

gravemente, *—men'tĕ,* ad. gravely, seriously. [tion.

gravitación, *grăvĭtăthĭŏn',* sf. gravita-

gravitar, *grăvĭtăr',* v. a. to gravitate; to weigh down. [able.

gravoso, sa, *grăvŏ'sŏ,* a. onerous, unbear-

graznar, *grăthnăr',* v. n. to croak; to cackle; to gaggle.

graznido, *—nĭ'dŏ,* sm. croak, cackle.

greda, *grā'dă,* sf. chalk, marl.

gregueria, *grĕgĕrē'ă,* sf. outcry, confused clamour. [pany, guild, corporation.

gremio, *grā'mĭŏ,* sm. lap; society; com-

greña, *grĕn'yă,* sf. entangled, clotted hair.

greñudo, da, *grĕnyŏ'dŏ,* a. dishevelled.

gresca, *grĕs'kă,* sf. clatter, tumult, outcry, confusion; wrangle, quarrel.

grey, *grā'ĭ,* sf. flock (of sheep and goats); congregation of the faithful. [fire.

griego, ga, *grĭā'gŏ,* a. **fuego —,** grecian

grieta, *grĭā'tă,* sf. crevice, crack, chink.

grifo, *grē'fŏ,* sm. griffin.

grifón, *grĭfŏn',* sm. cock for water.

grilletes, *grĭlyā'tĕs,* sm. pl. shackles, fetters. [irons.

grillo, *grĭl'yŏ,* sm. cricket; **—s,** pl. fetters,

grima, *grē'mă,* sf. fright, horror.

gris, *grĭs,* sm. grizzle, gray; meniver (russian squirrel); cold sharp air *or* weather. [bawler.

gritador, ra, *grĭtădŏr',* sm. & f. clamourer,

gritar, *grĭtăr',* v. n. to cry out, to clamour, to bawl. [confused cry of many voices.

griteria, *grĭtĕrē'ă,* sf. outcry, clamour.

grito, *grē'tŏ,* sm. cry, scream; **á — herido,** with a clamorous cry. [currant.

grosella, *grŏsĕl'yă,* sf. fruit of the red

grosellero, *grŏsĕlyā'rŏ,* sm. currant-bush.

groseria, *grŏsĕrē'ă,* sf. coarseness, illbreeding. [polished.

grosero, ra, *grŏsā'rŏ,* a. coarse, rude, un-

grosura, *grŏsū'ră,* sf. suet, tallow.

grotesco, ca, *grŏtĕs'kŏ,* a. grotesque.

grúa, *grŏ'ă,* sf. crane (machine).

gruesa, *grŏă'să,* sf. gross (twelve dozen); chief part of a prebend.

grueso, sa, *—sŏ,* a. bulky, gross; large; coarse; **—,** sm. corpulence.

grulla, *grŏl'yă,* sf. crane (bird).

grumo, *grŏ'mŏ,* sm. clod; curd; cluster, bunch; pith of trees.

grumoso, sa, *grŏmŏ'sŏ,* a. clotted.

gruñido, *grŏnyĭ'dŏ,* sm. grunt, grunting; growl. [mumbler.

gruñidor, ra, *—dŏr',* sm. & f. grunter,

gruñir, *grŏnyĭr',* v. n. to grunt; to creak (of hinges, &c.).

grupa, *grŏ'pă,* sf. crupper, buttock.

grupera, *grŏpā'ră,* sf. crupper.

grupo, *grŏ'pŏ,* sm. group.

gruta, *grŏ'tă,* sf. grotto, grot.

grutesco, *grŏtĕs'kŏ,* a. sm. grotesque.

guadaña, *gŭădăn'yă,* sf. scythe.

guadañero, *—yā'rŏ,* sm. mower.

gualderas, *gŭăldā'răs,* sf.pl. sides; cheeks *or* brackets of a gun-carriage.

gualdrapa, *gŭăldrā'pă,* sf. horse-cloth; tatter, rag.

guantada, *gŭăntā'dă,* sf. slap given with the palm of the hand. [boire.

guante, *gŭăn'tĕ,* sm. glove; **—s,** pl. pour-

guanteria, *—rē'ă,* sf. glover's shop; glover's

guantero, *gŭăntā'rŏ,* sm. glover. [art.

guapear, *gŭăpăr',* v. n. to boast of one's courage; to take a pride in fine dress.

guapeza, *gŭăpā'thă,* sf. courage; ostentation in dress.

guapo, pa, *gŭā'pŏ,* a. stout, courageous; valiant, bold; spruce, neat; ostentatious; gay, sprightly.

guarda, *gŭăr'dă,* sm. & f. guard, keeper; **—,** sf. custody, wardship, keeping.

guardaaguja, *—ăgŭ'h'ă,* sm. (rail.) switchman, pointsman. [keeper.

guardaalmacén, *—ălmăthĕn',* sm. store-

guardabarreras, *—bărrā'răs,* sm. (rail.) line-keeper. [forest.

guardabosque, *—bŏs'kĕ,* sm. keeper of a

guardacantón, *—kăntŏn',* sf. corner-stone.

guardacostas, *—kŏs'tăs,* sm. guard-ship, cruiser.

guardafuegos, *—fŭĕ'gŏs,* sm. fender.

guardamonte, *—mŏn'tĕ,* sm. guard of a gunlock, sword, &c. [petticoat.

guardapiés, *—pĭĕs',* sm. women's black

guardapolvo, *—pŏl'vŏ,* sm. any cloth *or* leather article worn on account of the dust; dust-coat; piece of leather attached to the instep of spatterdashes.

guardar, *gŭărdăr',* v. a. to keep, to preserve; to guard; **—se,** to be upon one's guard, to avoid, to abstain from.

guardarropa, *—gŭărdărŏ'pă,* sf. wardrobe; **—,** sm. keeper of a wardrobe.

guardasellos, *—sĕl'yŏs,* sm. Keeper of the Seal; **— del rey,** Lord Privy-Seal.

guardavía, *—vē'ă,* sm. (rail.) line-keeper.

guardia, *gŭăr'dĭă,* sf. guard; (mar.) watch; **—,** sm. guardsman (soldier).

guardián, ana, *gŭărdĭăn',* sm.&f. keeper; guardian. [ship.

guardianía, *gŭărdĭănē'ă,* sf. guardian-

guardilla, *gŭărdĭl'yă,* sf. garret; skylight.

guarecer, *găăr-ĕthĕr'*, v. a. to aid, to succour; to guard; to cure; —se, to take refuge.

guarida, *găără-dă*, sf. den, couch of a wild beast; shelter; lurking-place.

guarismo, *găărĭs-mŏ*, sm. cipher.

guarnecer, *găărnĕthĕr'*, v. a. to garnish; to set (in gold, &c.); to adorn.

guarnición, *găărnĭthĭŏn'*, sf. flounce, furbelow; gold setting; sword-guard; garniture; (mil.) garrison.   [maker.

guarnicionero, *—nĕ'rŏ*, sm. harnessmaker.

guasón, *găăsŏn'*, sm. joker, jester.

guedeja, *gĕdĕ'k'ă*, sf. ear-lock; lion's mane.

guerra, *gĕr'ră*, sf. war; hostility.

guerreador, ra, *gĕrrĕădŏr'*, a. warlike.

guerrear, *gĕrrĕăr'*, v. a. to war, to wage war.   [martial, warlike.

guerrero, *gĕrră'rŏ*, sm. warrior; —, ra, a.

guerrilla, *—Rĭl'yă*, sf. war of partisans; body of skirmishers or light horsemen.

guia, *gĕ'ă*, sm. & f. guide.

guiar, *gĕăr'*, v. a. to guide.

guija, *gĭ'k'ă*, sf. pebble, pebble-stone.

guijarral, *gĭ'hărrăl'*, sm. place abounding in pebbles.   [pebble.

guijarrazo, *—ră'thŏ*, sm. blow with a

guijarro, *gĭ'hăr'rŏ*, sm. pebble.

guijarroso, sa, *—rŏ'sŏ*, a. pebbly.

guillotina, *gĭlyŏtĭ'nă*, sf. guillotine.

guillotinar, *gĭlyŏtĭnăr'*, v. a. to guillotine.

guinda, *gĭn'dă*, sf. cherry.

guindal, *gĭndăl'*, sm. cherry-tree.

guindilla, *gĭndĭl'yă*, sf. capsicum; nickname of the Spanish police established in 1843.

guinea, *gĭnĕ'ă*, sf. guinea (gold coin).

guiñada, *gĭnyă'dă*, sf. wink, hint.

guiñapo, *—yă'pŏ*, sm. tatter, rag.

guiñar, *—yăr'*, v. a. to wink, to hint.

guión, *gĭŏn'*, sm. royal standard; hyphen (in writing);   [language.

guirigay, *gĭrĭgăĭ'*, sm. gibberish, confused

guirindola, *gĭrĭndŏ'lă*, sf. frill.

guirnalda, *gĭrnăl'dă*, sf. garland, wreath.

guisado, *gĭsă'dŏ*, sm. ragout, fricassee.

guisandero, ra, *gĭsăndĕ'rŏ*, sm. & f. cook.

guisante, *gĭsăn'tĕ*, sm. (bot.) pea.

guisar, *gĭsăr'*, v. a. to dress victuals.

guiso, *gĕ'sŏ*, sm. seasoning of a dish; condiment.   [country-fashion.

guisote, *gĭsŏ'tĕ*, sm. dish of meat dressed

guitarra, *gĭtăr'ră*, sf. guitar.

guitarrero, *—ră'rŏ*, sm. guitar-maker; guitar-player.

guitarrista, *—rĭs'tă*, sm. guitar-player.

gula, *gŏ'lă*, sf. gluttony.

gusano, *găsă'nŏ*, sm. maggot, worm.

gusarapo, *găsără'pŏ*, sm. water-worm.

gustar, *găstăr'*, v. a. to taste, to gust; to like, to love; to experience, to examine; to take pleasure or delight in a thing.

gusto, *găs'tŏ*, sm. taste; gust, pleasure, delight; liking, mind; election, choice.

gustosamente, *găstŏsămĕn'tĕ*, ad. tastefully; very desirously.

gustoso, sa, *găstŏ'sŏ*, a. gustable, dainty, lickerish; tasty.

gutagamba, *gătăgăm'bă*, sf. gamboge.

gutural, *gătŭrăl'*, a. guttural.

H.

¡**ha**! *ă*, ¡ha! ah! alas!

haba, *ă'bă*, sf. (bot.) bean.

haber, *ăbĕr'*, v. a. to have; to possess; —, v. imp. to happen; to exist; to fall out, to befall; —se, to behave; —, sm. possepepty, goods and chattels; (com.) credit.

habichuela, *ăbĭchŏĕ'lă*, sf. kidney-bean.

hábil, *ă'bĭl*, a. able, clever, skilful, dexterous, apt.

habilidad, *ăbĭlĭdăd'*, sf. ability, ableness, dexterity, aptitude.   [qualification.

habilitación, *—tăthĭŏn'*, sf. habilitation.

habilitado, *—tă'dŏ*, sm. officer who is charged in every Spanish regiment with the agency of his regiment.   [enable.

habilitar, *ăbĭlĭtăr'*, v. a. to qualify, to habilitate, to enable.

habitable, *ăbĭtă'blĕ*, a. habitable, lodgeable.

habitación, *—thĭŏn'*, sf. habitation, abode, lodging, dwelling, residence.   [dweller.

habitante, *ăbĭtăn'tĕ*, sm. inhabitant.

habitar, *ăbĭtăr'*, v. a. to inhabit, to reside.

hábito, *ă'bĭtŏ*, sm. dress, habit; habitude, customariness, custom.

habitual, *ăbĭtŏăl'*, a. habitual, customary.

habituar, *ăbĭtŏăr'*, v. a. to accustom; —se, to accustom oneself.

habitud, *ăbĭtŭd'*, sf. habitude.

habla, *ă'blă*, sf. speech; language; discourse; talk, conversation.

hablador, ra, *ăblădŏr'*, sm. & f. prattler.

habladuría, *—dŭrĕ'ă*, sf. impertinent speech.

hablar, *ăblăr'*, v. a. to speak; to talk; to reason, to converse; to harangue.

habilla, *ăbĭl'yă*, sf. rumour, report; little tale.   [ticable.

hacedero, ra, *ăthĕdĕ'rŏ*, a. feasible, practicable.

hacedor, ra, *—dŏr'*, sm. & f. maker, author; factor; able performer.

hacendado, *ăthĕndă'dŏ*, sm. man of property; —, da, a. landed.

hacer, *ăthĕr'*, v. a. & n. to make, to do, to practise; to perform; to effect; to correspond; to matter; to fit, to suit; —se, to become.   [hitherward.

hacia, *ă'thĕ̆ă*, ad. towards; about; — acá,

hacienda, *ăthĕndă'*, sf. landed property; estate, fortune, wealth; domestic work.

hacina, *ăthĕ'nă*, sf. stack, rick.   [maker.

hacinador, ra, *ăthĕnădŏr'*, sm. & f stackmaker.

hacinar, *ăthĕnăr'*, v. a. to stack or pile up sheaves of corn; to hoard.

hacha, *ătsh'ă*, sf. large taper; axe, hatchet; — de viento, flambeau.

hachazo, *ătshă'thŏ*, sm. blow with an axe.

hachero, *ătshă'rŏ*, sm. torch-stand; (mil.) pioneer.   [bass and pitch.

hachón, *ătshŏn'*, sm. large torch made of

hado, *ă'dŏ*, sm. fate, destiny.

halagar, *ălăgăr'*, v. a. to cajole, to flatter;

halago, ălă'gŏ, sm. cajolery, caress.
halagüeño, ña, ălăgüēn'yŏ, a. attractive,
halcón, ălkŏn', sm. falcon. [flattering.
halconero, ălkŏnē'rŏ, sm. falconer.
hálito, ă'lĭtŏ, sm. breath; gentle breeze.
hallar, ălyăr', v. a. to find; to meet with;
to discover; to mean; —se, to happen to
find; to be pleased with a place; to find
himself, to be.
hallazgo, ălyăth'gŏ, sm. finding, discovery; reward given for finding.
hambre, ăm'brĕ, sf. hunger; famine; eagerness, desire, greediness.
hambrear, ămbrĕăr', v. n. to be hungry.
hambriento, ta, ămbrĭēn'tŏ, a. hungry;
starved; greedy, eager. [loiterer.
haragán, ana, ărăgăn', sm. & f. idler,
haraganear, ărăgănĕăr', v. n. to lead an
idle life, to loiter. [ness.
haraganería, —nĕrē'ă, sf. idleness, lazi-
harapo, ără'pŏ, sm. rag, tatter.
haraposo, ărăpō'sŏ, a. ragged.
harina, ărē'nă, sf. flour; powder, dust.
harinero, ărĭnē'rŏ, sm. meal-man; meal-
box; —, ra, a. made of flour.
harinoso, sa, ărĭnō'sŏ, a. mealy.
harnero, ărnē'rŏ, sm. sieve. [disgust.
hartar, ărtăr', v. a. to cloy, to satiate; to
harto, ta, ăr'tŏ, a. satiated; sufficient; —,
ad. enough. [dance.
hartura, ărtū'ră, sf. satiety; plenty, abun-
hasta, ăs'tă, ad. until, as far as; also, even.
hastío, ăstī'ŏ, sm. loathing, disgust.
hatajo, ătă'h'ŏ, sm. small herd of cattle;
assemblage, collection.
hato, ă'tŏ, sm. clothes, wearing-apparel;
herd of cattle, flock of sheep; provisions
for shepherds; heap, cluster; crowd, mul-
haya, ăy'ă, sf. beech-tree. [titude.
haz, ăth, sm. fagot, bundle of brush-wood;
—, sf. right side of cloth; surface of the
ground.
hazaña, ăthăn'yă, sf. exploit, achievement.
hazmerreír, ăthmĕrrēīr', sm. ridiculous
person, laughing-stock.
he, ē, ad. behold, look here.
hebilla, ēbĭl'yă, sf. buckle. [buckles.
hebillaje, ēbĭlyă'hĕ, sm. collection of
hebra, ē'bră, sf. needleful; vein of minerals
or metals; filament. [Hebrews.
hebraico, ca, ēbră'ĭkŏ, a. belonging to the
hebraísmo, ēbră's'mŏ, sm. Hebraism.
hebreo, ēbrē'ŏ, sm. Hebrew; Hebrew
language; (fig.) merchant; — ea, a.
Hebraic, Judaical. [charm.
hechicería, ĕtshĭthĕrē'ă, sf. witchcraft.
hechicero, ra, —thē'rŏ, a. charming, be-
witching. [enchant; to charm.
hechizar, —thăr', v. a. to bewitch; to
hechizo, ĕtshē'thŏ, sm. bewitchment, enchantment; —, za, a. done on purpose.
hecho, cha, ĕtsh'ŏ, a. made, done; accustomed; —, sm. action; act, feat; point
contested.
hechura, ĕtshō'ră, sf. form, shape, fashion;
making; workmanship; creature; client.
heder, ēdĕr', v. a. to stink, to smell badly.
hediondez, ēdĭŏndĕth', sf. strong stench.

hediondo, da, ēdĭŏn'dŏ, u. ʼetid, stinking.
hedor, ēdŏr', sm. stench, stink.
helada, ēlă'dă, sf. frost; nip.
helado, da, —dŏ, a. frozen; glacial, icy;
astonished; astounded; —, sm. ice-cream.
helar, ēlăr', v. a. & n. to congeal; to freeze;
to astonish, to amaze; —se, to be frozen;
to turn into ice; to congeal.
hélice, ā'lĭthĕ, sf. helix, helical line.
Hélice, —. sf. Great Bear (constellation).
hembra, ēm'bră, sf. female.
hemina, ēmē'nă, sf. measure containing
the third part of a fanega.
hemisferio, ēmĭsfā'rĭŏ, sm. hemisphere.
hemorragia, ēmŏrră'hĕă, sf. hemorrhage.
henchir, ĕntshĭr', v. a. to fill up; —se,
to fill or gorge oneself. [crevice.
hendedura, ĕndĕdō'ră, sf. fissure, chink.
hender, ĕndĕr', v. a. to chink, to split; to
go through; to open a passage.
heno, ā'nŏ, sm. hay.
heraldo, ĕrăl'dŏ, sm. herald.
herbaje, ĕrbă'hĕ, sm. herbage, pasture.
herbolario, ĕrbŏlă'rĭŏ, sm. herbalist;
ridiculous, extravagant man.
herborizar, —rĭthăr', v. n. to botanise.
heredad, ĕrēdăd', sf. patrimony, inherited
property; fruitful ground.
heredar, ĕrēdăr', v. a. to inherit.
heredera, ĕrēdē'ră, sf. heiress.
heredero, ĕrēdē'rŏ, sm. heir.
hereditario, ria, ĕrēdĭtă'rĭŏ, a. hereditary.
hereje, ĕrē'hĕ, sm. & f. heretic.
herejía, ĕrē'hē'ă, sf. heresy.
herencia, ĕrēn'thĭă, sf. inheritance, heri-
tage, hereditament; heirship.
herida, ĕrē'dă, sf. wound, hurt.
herido, da, ĕrē'dŏ, a. wounded, hurt.
herir, ĕrīr', v. a. to wound, to hurt; to
affect, to touch, to move; to offend.
hermafrodita, ĕrmăfrŏdē'tă, sm. herma-
phrodite, androgyne.
hermana, ĕrmă'nă, sf. sister; — de la
caridad, sister of charity.
hermanar, —năr', v. a. to match, to suit,
to acknowledge as a brother; —, v. n. to
fraternise. [half-sister.
hermanastra, —năs'tră, sf. step-sister,
hermanastro, —trŏ, sm. step-brother,
half-brother. [conformity; brotherhood.
hermandad, ĕrmăndăd', sf. fraternity,
hermano, ĕrmă'nŏ, sm. brother; —, na, a.
matched; resembling. [chemical.
hermético, ca, ĕrmā'tĭkŏ, a. hermetical,
hermosear, ĕrmōsĕăr', v. a. to beautify,
to embellish, to adorn. [some.
hermoso, sa, ĕrmŏ'sŏ, a. beautiful, hand-
hermosura, ĕrmōsō'ră, sf. beauty.
hernia, ĕr'nĭă, sf. hernia, rupture.
héroe, ā'rŏē, sm. hero.
heroicidad, ĕrŏĭkĭdăd', sf. heroism,
heroic courage or virtue.
heroico, ca, ĕrŏ'ĭkŏ, a. heroic.
heroína, ĕrŏ'ĭnă, sf. heroine.
heroísmo, ĕrŏĭs'mŏ, sm. heroism.
herpe, ĕr'pĕ, sm. herpes, tetters, pl.
herrada, ĕrră'dă, sf. well-bucket.
herrador, ĕrrădŏr', sm. farrier.

herradura, ĕrrădŏ'ră, sf. horse-shoe.

herraje, ĕrră̄Wĕ, sm. iron-work.

herramienta, –mĕn'tă, sf. set of tools for workmen; iron-work; (fig.) teeth, grinders.

herrar, ĕrrăr', v. a. to shoe horses.

herrería, ĕrrĕr'ă̄, sf. iron-works; forge; clamour, confused noise.

herrero, ĕrră'ŏ, sm. smith. [quantity.

hervidero, ĕrvĭdĕ'rŏ, sm. ebullition; great

hervir, ĕrvĭr', v. n. to boil; to be fervent.

hervor, ĕrvŏr', sm. ebullition.

heterogeneidad, ĕtĕrŏ̄hĕnā̆dăd', sf. heterogeneousness. [neous.

heterogéneo, nea, –hā'nĕŏ, a. heteroge-

hética, ā'tĭkă, sf. phthisis, hectic.

hético, ca, ā'tĭkŏ, a. hectic, hectical.

hexámetro, ĕksā'mĕtrŏ, sm. hexameter.

hez, ĕth, sf. lee, dregs; dross.

hidalgo, ga, ĭdăl'gŏ, sm. & f. hidalgo; hidalga (nobleman or noblewoman).

hidalguía, ĭdălgĭ'ă̄, sf. nobility.

hidra, ĭ'dră, sf. hydra.

hidráulica, ĭdră̄ŭlĭkă, sf. hydraulics.

hidráulico, ca, –ŭlĭkŏ, a. hydraulic.

hidrofobia, ĭdrŏfŏ'bĭă, sf. hydrophobia.

hidrógeno, ĭdrŏ'hĕnŏ, sm. (chem.) hydrogen.

hidropesía, ĭdrŏpĕsĭ'ă̄, sf. dropsy.

hidrópico, ca, ĭdrŏ'pĭkŏ, a. hydropical.

hiedra, ĭā'dră, sf. ivy.

hiel, ĭĕl, sf. gall, bile.

hielo, ĭā'lŏ, sm. frost, ice.

hiena, ĭā'nă, sf. hyæna.

hierro, ĭĕr'rŏ, sm. iron; –s, pl. irons, [fetters.

hígado, ĭ'gădŏ, sm. liver; (fig.) courage, [valour.

higo, ĭ'gŏ, sm. fig. [valour.

higuera, ĭgĕr'ă, sf. fig-tree.

hijastro, tra, ĭ'hăs'trŏ, sm. & f. step-child.

hijo, ja, ĭ'hŏ, sm. & f. son; daughter; child; young of animals.

hijodalgo, ĭ'hŏdăl'gŏ, sm. nobleman.

hijuela, ĭ'hŭā'lă, sf. patch; eking-piece; a small drain; inventory of the distributive shares of a succession; rural postman.

hila, ĭ'lă, sf. row, line; lint to lay on sores.

hilacha, ĭlătsh'ă̄, sf. filament or threads ravelled out of cloth. [riband.

hiladillo, –dĭl'yŏ, sm. ferret silk; narrow

hilado, ĭlă'dŏ, sm. spun flax, wool, &c.

hilador, ra, –dŏr', sm. & f. spinner; spinster. [ning-room.

hilandero, ĭlăndā'rŏ, sm. spinner; spin-

hilar, ĭlăr', v. a. to spin.

hilera, ĭlā'ră, sf. row, line, file.

hilo, ĭ'lŏ, sm. thread; wire.

hilván, ĭlvăn', sm. basting.

hilvanar, ĭlvănăr', v. a. to baste, to sew slightly; to perform in a hurry.

himeneo, ĭmĕnā'ŏ, sm. (poet.) marriage.

himno, ĭm'nŏ, sm. hymn.

hin, ĭn, sm. neighing. [one's foot.

hincapié, ĭnkăpĭĕ', sm. firm planting of

hincar, ĭnkăr', v. a. to thrust in, to drive into. [arrogant.

hinchado, da, ĭntshă'dŏ, a. swollen; vain,

hinchar, ĭntshăr', v. a. to swell; –se, to swell; to be elated with arrogance.

hinchazón, ĭntshăthŏn', sf. swelling, tumid inflammation; ostentation, vanity.

hinojo, ĭnŏ'hŏ, sm. knee; (bot.) fennel.

hipar, ĭpăr', v. n. to hiccough; to pant.

hipérbola, ĭpĕr'bŏlă, sf. hyperbola, section of a cone. [tion.

hipérbole, –bŏlĕ, sf. hyperbole, exaggera-

hiperbólico, ca, ĭpĕrbŏ'lĭkŏ, a. hyperbolical. [Virgin Mary.

hiperdulía, –dŭlĭ'ă̄, sf. worship of the

hipo, ĭ'pŏ, sm. hiccough. [dria.

hipocondría, ĭpŏkŏndrĭ'ă̄, sf. hypochon-

hipocóndrico, ca, –kŏn'drĭkŏ, a. hypochondriac.

hipocresía, –krĕsĭ'ă̄, sf. hypocrisy.

hipócrita, ĭpŏ'krĭtă, a. & sm. hypocritical; hypocrite. [circus.

hipódromo, –drŏmŏ, sm. hippodrome,

hipopótamo, ĭpŏpŏ'tămŏ, sm. hippopotamus. [cal.

hipostático, ca, –stā'tĭkŏ, a. hypostati-

hipoteca, –tā'kă, sf. mortgage.

hipotecar, –tēkăr', v. a. to mortgage.

hipotecario, ria, –tēkā'rĭŏ, a. belonging to a mortgage.

hipótesis, ĭpŏ'tĕsĭs, sf. hypothesis.

hipotético, ca, ĭpŏtā'tĭkŏ, a. hypothetical.

hisopear, ĭsŏpĕăr', v. a. to sprinkle water about with a water-sprinkler. [sprinkler.

hisopo, ĭsŏ'pŏ, sm. (bot.) hyssop; water-

hispano, na, ĭspă'nŏ, a. (poet.) Spanish.

histérico, ca, ĭstā'rĭkŏ, sm. hysterics; –ca, a. hysterical.

historia, ĭstŏ'rĭă, sf. history; tale, story.

historiador, ora, ĭstŏrĭădŏr', sm. & f. historian, historiographer.

historiar, –rĭăr', v. a. to record in history; to represent historical events in painting. [toric; – sm. historian.

histórico, ca, ĭstŏ'rĭkŏ, a. historical, his-

historieta, ĭstŏrĭā'tă, sf. short story, short novel. [to shoot at; á –, fixedly.

hito, ĭ'tŏ, sm. landmark; guide-post; mark

hocicar, ŏthĭkăr', v. a. to break up the ground with the snout; –, v. n. to fall headlong with the face to the ground.

hocico, ŏthĭ'kŏ, sm. snout; flap-mouthed man; (fig.) face; meter el– en todo, to meddle in everything.

hocicudo, da, ŏthĭkŏ'dŏ, a. long-snouted; blubber-lipped; flap-mouthed.

hogar, ŏgăr', sm. hearth, fire-place; (fig.) house, residence, home. [bread.

hogaza, ŏgă'thă̄, sf. large loaf of household

hoguera, ŏgā'ră, sf. bonfire; blaze.

hoja, ŏ'hă, sf. leaf; blade of a sword; half of each of the principal parts of a coat, &c.; – de lata, tin.

hojalatero, ŏ'hălătā'rŏ, sm. tin-man.

hojaldrar, ŏ'hăldrăr', v. a. to make a pastry of puff-paste.

hojaldre, ŏ'hăl'drĕ, sf. puff-paste.

hojaldrista, –drĭs'tă, sm. pastry-cook.

hojarasca, ŏ'hărăs'kă, sf. redundancy of leaves; foliage; useless trifles. [a book.

hojear, ŏ'hĕăr', v. a. to turn the leaves of

hojuela, ŏ'hŭā'lă, sf. puff-paste; skins of olives after pressing.

¡hola! *ŏl'ă,* holla!

holgado, da, *ŏlgă'dŏ,* a. loose, wide, broad at leisure; in easy circumstances.

holganza, *ŏlgăn'thă,* sf. ease, tranquillity of mind; recreation, amusement.

holgar, *ŏlgăr',* v. n. to rest; —se, to sport, to be pleased with. [loiterer, vagabond.

holgazán, ana, *ŏlgăthăn',* sm. & f. idler,

holgazanear, *—neăr',* v. n. to idle, to loiter, to lounge. [dolence.

holgazanería, *—nerē'ă,* sf. idleness, in-

holgura, *ŏlgō'ră,* sf. country-feast; width, breadth; ease, repose.

hollejo, *ŏlyĕ'hŏ,* sm. pellicle, peel.

hollín, *ŏlyīn',* sm. soot.

holliniento, ta, *ŏlyĭnēĕn'tŏ,* a. sooty.

holocausto, *ŏlŏkăŭs'tŏ,* sm. holocaust.

hombre, *ŏm'brĕ,* sm. man; human being; ombre (game at cards).

hombrera, *ŏmbrĕ'ră,* sf. piece of ancient armour for the shoulders.

hombría de bien, *ŏmbrē'ă dĕ bēĕn',* sf.

hombro, *ŏm'brŏ,* sm. shoulder. [probity.

hombruno, na, *ŏmbrō'nŏ,* a. manlike, virile, manly.

homenaje, *ŏmĕnă'hĕ,* sm. homage.

homicida, *ŏmĭthĕ'dă,* sm. & f. murderer; —, a. homicidal, murderous.

homicidio, *—thĕ'dĭŏ,* sm. murder.

homilía, *ŏmĭlē'ă,* sf. homily. [geneity.

homogeneidad, *ŏmŏ'hĕnĕĭdăd',* sf. homo-

homogéneo, nea, *—'hĕ'nĕŏ,* a. a homoge- neous. [synonymous.

homólogo, ga, *ŏmŏ'lŏgŏ,* a. homologous;

honda, *ŏn'dă,* sf. sling. [sling.

hondazo, *ŏndă'thŏ,* sm. throw with a

hondero, *ŏndĕ'rŏ,* sm. slinger.

hondillo, *ŏndēl'yŏ,* sm. any of the pieces of cloth which form the seats of breeches.

hondo, da, *ŏn'dŏ,* a. profound, deep; dif-

bondonada, *ŏndŏnă'dă,* sf. dale. [ficult.

hondura, *ŏndō'ră,* sf. depth, profundity.

honestidad, *ŏnĕstĭdăd',* sf. honesty, modesty; urbanity.

honesto, ta, *ŏnĕs'tŏ,* a. honest; modest.

hongo, *ŏn'gŏ,* sm. mushroom; fungus.

honor, *ŏnŏr',* sm. honour.

honorable, *ŏnŏră'blĕ,* a. honourable.

honorario, ria, *—ră'rĭŏ,* a. honorary; —, sm. salary. [honourable.

honorífico, ca, *—rē'fĭkŏ,* a. creditable,

honra, *ŏn'ră,* sf. honour, reverence; repu- tation; chastity (in women); —s, pl. funeral honours.

honradez, *ŏnrădĕth',* sf. honesty, probity.

honrado, da, *ŏnră'dŏ,* a. honest, honour- able, reputable. [to caress.

honrar, *ŏnrăr',* v. a. to honour; to cajole,

honrilla, *ŏnrēl'yă,* sf. nice point of honour.

honroso, sa, *ŏnrŏ'sŏ,* a. honourable; honest.

hopalanda, *ŏpălăn'dă,* sf. fur cloak.

hora, *ŏ'ră,* sf. hour; —s, pl. canonical hours; devotional book, prayer-book.

horadar, *ŏrădăr',* v. a. to bore from side to side.

horario, ria, *ŏră'rĭŏ,* a. horary, horal.

horca, *ŏr'kă,* sf. gallows; pitchfork.

horcajadas, *ŏrkă'hă' dăs,* horcajadillas, *—hădēl'yăs,* (á —), ad. astride.

horcajadura, *—hădŏ'ră,* sf. fork formed by the two thighs.

horchata, *ŏrtshă'tă,* sf. orgeat.

horizontal, *ŏrĭthŏntăl',* a. horizontal.

horizonte, *ŏrĭthŏn'tĕ,* sm. horizon.

horma, *ŏr'mă,* sf. mould.

hormero, *ŏrmă'rŏ,* sm. last-maker.

hormiga, *ŏrmē'gă,* sf. ant, pismire.

hormigueamiento, *ŏrmĭgwĕămēĕn'tŏ,* sm. formication. [about like ants.

hormiguear, *—gĕăr',* v. n. to itch; to run

hormiguero, *—gă'rŏ,* sm. ant-hill; place where there is a crowd of people moving.

hormiguillo, *—gēl'yŏ,* sm. scarf of the hoof; work-people ranged in line, who pass the working materials from hand to hand.

hornacho, *ŏrnătsh'ŏ,* sm. shaft of a mine.

hornada, *ŏrnă'dă,* sf. batch.

hornaza, *—nă'thă,* sf. goldsmith's furnace.

hornazo, *ŏrnă'thŏ,* sm. Easter-cake.

hornero, *ŏrnă'rŏ,* sm. baker.

hornilla, *ŏrnēl'yă,* sf. stew-hole.

horno, *ŏr'nŏ,* sm. oven; furnace.

horóscopo, *ŏrŏs'kŏpŏ,* sm. horoscope.

horquilla, *ŏrkēl'yă,* sf. forked stick.

horrendo, da, *ŏrrĕn'dŏ,* a. horrible; extra-

hórreo, *ŏr'rĕŏ,* sm. granary. [ordinary.

horrible, *ŏrrē'blĕ,* a. horrid, horrible.

horrísono, na, *ŏrrē'sŏnŏ,* a. (poet.) dread- ful-sounding.

horror, *ŏrrŏr',* sm. horror, fright.

horrorizar, *ŏrrŏrĭhăr',* v. a. to cause horror; —se, to be terrified. [frightful.

horroroso, sa, *—rŏ'sŏ,* a. horrid, hideous, [pot-herbs.

hortaliza, *ŏrtălē'thă,* sf. garden-stuff,

hortelano, *ŏrtĕlă'nŏ,* sm. gardener, horti- culturist; ortolan (bird).

hortera, *ŏrtă'ră,* sf. wooden bowl; —, sm. nickname of shop-boys in Madrid.

hospedador, ra, *ŏspĕdă'dŏr,* sm. & f. one who kindly receives and entertains guests and strangers, entertainer.

hospedaje, *—dă'hĕ,* sm. kind reception of guests and strangers.

hospedar, *—dăr',* v. a. to lodge and enter- tain strangers and travellers.

hospedería, *—dĕrē'ă,* sf. a hospitium.

hospedero, *—dă'rŏ,* sm. one who kindly receives guests and strangers; hospitaller.

hospicio, *ŏspē'thĭŏ,* sm. house of charity.

hospital, *ŏspĭtăl',* sm. hospital.

hospitalario, ria, *ŏspĭtălă'rĭŏ,* a. applied to the religious communities which keep hospitals.

hospitalero, ra, *—lă'rŏ,* sm. & f. warden of a hospital. [sity.

hospitalidad, *ŏspĭtălĭdăd',* sf. hospital-

hostería, *ŏstĕrē'ă,* sf. inn, tavern, hostelry.

hostia, *ŏs'tĭă,* sf. host; wafer.

hostiario, *ŏstĭă'rĭŏ,* sm. wafer-box.

hostigar, *ŏstĭgăr',* v. a. to trouble, to molest, to gall, to tire.

hostil, *ŏstēl',* a. hostile, adverse.

hostilidad, ŏstĭlĭdåd', sf. hostility.

hostilizar, —thär', v. n. to commit hostilities.

hoy, ŏ'ĭ, ad. to-day, this day; **de — en adelante**, henceforth, henceforward.

hoya, ŏ'yå, sf. hole, pit; sepulture.

hoyo, ŏ'yŏ, sm. hole, pit, excavation.

hoyoso, **sa**, ŏyŏ'sŏ, a. full of holes.

hoz, ŏth, sf. sickle, reaping-hook.

hozar, ŏthår', v. a. to grub.

hucha, ŭtsh'å, sf. large chest in which labouring people keep their clothes, money, and other valuable articles; money-box.

huebra, ŏĕ'brå, sf. day's work; extent of ground which a yoke of oxen can plough in a day; pair of mules with a plough-man let out for a day's work. [a spindle.

hueca, ŏĕ'kå, sf. notch at the small end of

hueco, **ca**, ŏĕ'kŏ, a. hollow, concave; empty, vain, ostentatious; —, sm. interval; gap, hole; office vacant, vacancy.

huelga, ŏĕl'gå, sf. rest, repose; recreation; fallow ground; strike of workmen; lock-out of employers.

huella, ŏĕl'yå, sf. track, footstep.

huérfano, **na**, ŏĕr'fånŏ, sm. & f. & a. orphan.

huero, **ra**, ŏĕ'rŏ, a. empty, addle.

huerta, ŏĕr'tå, sf. orchard, kitchen-garden.

huerto, ŏĕr'tŏ, sm. walled garden, kitchen-garden.

huesa, ŏĕ'så, sf. grave, sepulture.

hueso, ŏĕ'sŏ, sm. bone; stone, core.

huesoso, **sa**, ŏĕsŏ'sŏ, a. bony.

huésped, **da**, ŏĕs'pĕd, sm. & f. guest, lodger; inn-keeper; stranger.

hueste, ŏĕs'tĕ, sf. army in campaign.

huesudo, **da**, ŏĕsŏ'dŏ, a. bony.

huevar, ŏĕvår', v. n. to lay eggs.

huevera, ŏĕvĕ'rå, sf. ovary of birds; egg-stand; egg-cup.

huevero, **ra**, —rŏ, sm. & f. dealer in eggs.

huevo, ŏĕ'vŏ, sm. egg; spawn.

huída, ŏĕ'då, sf. flight, escape.

huir, ŏĕr', v. n. to fly, to escape.

hule, ŏ'lĕ, sm. oil-cloth.

humanarse, ŏmånår'sĕ, v. r. to become man (applied to the Son of God); to become humane or meek.

humanidad, ŏmånĭdåd', sf. humanity; benevolence; corpulence; —es, pl. humanities, pl. human learning. [kind.

humano, **na**, ŏmå'nŏ, a. human; humane.

humareda, —rå'då, sf. great deal of smoke; confusion, perplexity.

humeante, ŏmĕån'tĕ, a. smoking, steaming (of blood, &c.).

humear, ŏmĕår', v. n. to smoke.

humedad, ŏmĕdåd', sf. humidity, moisture, wetness. [wet, to soak.

humedecer, —dĕthĕr', v. a. to moisten, to

húmedo, **da**, ŏ'mĕdŏ, a. humid, wet, moist, damp. [shaft of a chimney.

humero, ŏmĕ'rŏ, sm. tunnel, funnel.

humildad, ŏmĭldåd', sf. humility, humbleness; meanness; submission.

humilde, ŏmĭl'dĕ, a. humble.

humillación, ŏmĭlyåthĭŏn', sf. humiliation, submission.

humilladero, —då'rŏ, sm. small chapel in the roads and near the villages.

humillar, ŏmĭlyår', v. a. to humble; to subdue; —se, to humble oneself.

humo, ŏ'mŏ, sm. smoke; fume.

humor, ŏmŏr', sm. humor, humour.

humorada, —rå'då, sf. graceful sprightliness. [well- or ill-disposed.

humorado, **da**, —dŏ, a. full of humours;

humoroso, **sa**, ŏmŏr'ŏsŏ, a. humorous.

humoso, **sa**, ŏmŏ'sŏ, a. smoky.

hundir, ŏndĭr', v. n. to submerge; to sink, to overwhelm; to confound; —se, to sink, to go the bottom; to hide, to lie hid.

huracán, ŏråkån', sm. hurricane.

hurgar, ŏrgår', v. a. to stir; to excite quarrels. [quarrels.

hurón, ŏrŏn', sm. ferret; ferreter.

huronear, ŏrŏnĕår', v. a. to ferret.

huronera, ŏrŏnĕ'rå, sf. ferret-hole; lurking-place. [ing-place.

hurraca, ŏrrå'kå, sf. magpie.

hurtadillas, **(á)**, ŏrtådĭl'yås, ad. by stealth.

hurtar, ŏrtår', v. a. to steal, to rob.

hurto, ŏr'tŏ, sm. theft, robbery.

husar, ŏsår', sm. husar. [drains.

husillo, ŏsĭl'yŏ, sm. clamp-screw; —s, pl.

husma, ŏs'må, andar á la —, to pry into a thing, to spy out a secret. [to peep.

husmear, ŏsmĕår', v. a. to scent; to pry,

huso, ŏ'sŏ, sm. spindle.

huta, ŏt'å, sf. hut.

I.

ictericia, ĭktĕrĭthĭå, sf. jaundice.

ida, ĭ'då, sf. departure; sally; —s, pl. frequent visits; —s y venidas, coming and going. [going.

idea, ĭdĕ'å, sf. idea; scheme.

ideal, ĭdĕål', a. ideal.

idealmente, —mĕn'tĕ, ad. ideally.

idear, ĭdĕår', v. a. to conceive; to think, to contrive.

ídem, ĭ'dĕm, pn. item, the same.

idéntico, **ca**, ĭdĕn'tĭkŏ, a. identical.

identidad, ĭdĕntĭdåd', sf. identity.

identificar, —fĭkår', v. a. to identify.

idilio, ĭdĭ'lĭŏ, sm. idyl.

idioma, ĭdĭŏ'må, sm. idiom. [syncrasy.

idiosincrasia, ĭdĭŏsĭnkrå'stå, sf. idiosyncrasy. [ance.

idiota, ĭdĭŏ'tå, sm. idiot. [tance.

idiotismo, —ĭs'mŏ, sm. idiotism; ignorance.

idólatra, ĭdŏ'låtrå, sm. idolater.

idolatrar, ĭdŏlåtrår', v. a. to idolize; to love with excessive fondness.

idolatría, —trĭ'å, sf. idolatry.

ídolo, ĭ'dŏlŏ, sm. idol.

idoneidad, ĭdŏnĕĭdåd', sf. aptitude, fitness. [suitable.

idóneo, **nea**, ĭdŏ'nĕŏ, a. idoneous, fit,

iglesia, ĭglĕ'sĭå, sf. church.

ignominia, ĭgnŏmĭ'nĭå, sf. ignomy, infamy. [nious.

ignominioso, **sa**, —mĭnĭŏ'sŏ, a. ignomi-

ignorancia, *ignŏrăn'thĭā*, sf. ignorance.
ignorante, *–răn'tĕ*, a. ignorant, stupid.
ignorar, *–răr'*, v. a. to be ignorant of, not to know.
igual, *ĭgdăl'*, a. equal, similar; al —, [equally.
igualar, *ĭgŭălăr'*, v. a. to equalize, to equal; to match; —, v. n. to be equal; –se, to level; to agree.
igualdad, *–dăd'*, sf. equality.
igualmente, *–mĕn'tĕ*, ad. equally.
ijada, *ĭ'hă'dă*, sf. flank; side of pork or bacon; pork. [pitate.
ijadear, *ĭ'hădĕăr'*, v. n. to pant, to pal-
ijar, *ĭ'hăr'*, sm. flanks, pl.
ilación, *ĭlăthĭon'*, sf. inference, deduction.
ilegal, *ĭlĕgăl'*, a. illegal, unlawful.
ilegalidad, *ĭlĕgălĭdăd'*, sf. illegality.
ilegitimar, *ĭlĕhĭtĭmăr'*, v. a. to render illegitimate.
ilegitimidad, *–mĭdăd'*, sf. illegitimacy.
ilegítimo, ma, *–'hĭ'tĭmŏ*, a. illegal; illegitimate.
ileso, sa, *ĭlĕ'sŏ*, a. unhurt.
ilícito, ta, *ĭlĭ'thĭtŏ*, a. illicit, unlawful.
ilimitado, da, *ĭlĭmĭtă'dŏ*, a. unlimited.
iluminación, *ĭlŭmĭnăthĭon'*, sf. illumination. [illuminate, to enlighten.
iluminar, *–năr'*, v. a. to illumine, to
ilusión, *ĭlŭsĭon'*, sf. illusion.
ilusivo, va, *ĭlŭsĕ'vŏ*, a. illusive.
iluso, sa, *ĭlŭ'sŏ*, a. deceived; fanatical;
visionary.
ilusorio, ria, *ĭlŭsŏ'rĭŏ*, a. illusory.
ilustración, *ĭlŭstrăthĭon'*, sf. illustration;
explication. [spire.
ilustrar, *–trăr'*, v. a. to illustrate; to in-
ilustre, *ĭlŭs'trĕ*, a. illustrious, celebrated.
imagen, *ĭmă'hĕn*, sf. image.
imaginable, *ĭmă'hĭnă'blĕ*, a. imaginable.
imaginación, *–năthĭon'*, sf. imagination,
fancy; conceit, idea.
imaginar, *–'hĭnăr'*, v. n. to imagine.
imaginaria, *–nă'rĭă*, sf. (mil.) reserve
guard.
imán, *ĭmăn'*, sm. loadstone, magnet.
imbécil, *ĭmbĕ'thĭl*, a. weak, feeble, imbecile.
imbecilidad, *–thĭlĭdăd'*, sf. imbecility.
imbuir, *ĭmbŭĭr'*, v. a. to imbue, to infuse
into the mind.
imitable, *ĭmĭtă'blĕ*, a. imitable.
imitación, *–tăthĭon'*, sf. imitation; a —,
in imitation of.
imitador, ra, *–tădŏr'*, sm. & f. imitator.
imitar, *ĭmĭtăr'*, v. a. to imitate, to copy;
to counterfeit. [tience.
impaciencia, *ĭmpăthĭĕn'thĭā*, sf. impa-
impacientar, *–thĭĕntăr'*, v. a. to put one
out of all patience.
impaciente, *–thĭĕn'tĕ*, a. impatient.
impar, *ĭmpăr'*, a. unequal, odd; uneven.
imparcial, *ĭmpărthĭăl'*, a. impartial.
imparcialidad, *–lĭdăd'*, sf. impartiality.
impasibilidad, *ĭmpăsĭbĭlĭdăd'*, sf. impassibility.
impasible, *–sĭ'blĕ*, a. impassible.
impavidez, *ĭmpăvĭdĕth'*, sf. intrepidity.

impávido, da, *ĭmpă'vĭdŏ*, a. dauntless,
intrepid. [ment, obstacle.
impedimento, *ĭmpĕdĭmĕn'tŏ*, sm. impedi-
impedir, *–pĕdĭr'*, v. a. to impede, to
hinder. [to stimulate.
impeler, *–pĕlĕr'*, v. a. to impel; to incite,
impenetrable, *–pĕnĕtră'blĕ*, a. impenetrable, impervious; incomprehensible.
impenitencia, *–pĕnĭtĕn'thĭā*, sf. impenitence.
impenitente, *–tĕn'tĕ*, a. impenitent.
impensado, da, *–pĕnsă'dŏ*, a. unexpected, unforeseen. [perative.
imperativo, va, *–pĕrătĭ'vŏ*, a. & sm. im-
imperatorio, ria, *–tŏ'rĭŏ*, a. imperial.
imperceptible, *–pĕrthĕptĭ'blĕ*, a. imperceptible. [fection.
imperfección, *–pĕrfĕkthĭon'*, sf. imper-
imperfecto, ta, *ĭmpĕrfĕk'tŏ*, a. imperfect.
imperial, *ĭmpĕrĭăl'*, sm. roof of a coach;
—, a. imperial. [rience.
impericia, *–pĕrĭ'thĭā*, sf. want of expe-
imperio, *ĭmpĕ'rĭŏ*, sm. empire.
imperioso, sa, *–pĕrĭŏ'sŏ*, a. imperious;
arrogant, haughty. [skilled.
imperito, ta, *–pĕrĭ'tŏ*, a. unlearned, un-
impermeable, *–pĕrmĕă'blĕ*, a. impermeable.
impermutable, *–pĕrmŭtă'blĕ*, a. immutable.
impersonal, *–pĕrsŏnăl'*, a. impersonal.
impertérrito, ta, *ĭmpĕrtĕ'rrĭtŏ*, a. intrepid, unterrified.
impertinencia, *–tĭnĕn'thĭā*, sf. impertinence; troublesomeness.
impertinente, *–tĭnĕn'tĕ*, a. impertinent,
importunate. [turbable.
imperturbable, *–tŭrbă'blĕ*, a. imper-
impetración, *ĭmpĕtrăthĭon'*, sf. impetra-
tion.
impetrar, *–trăr'*, v. a. to impetrate.
impetu, *ĭm'pĕtŭ*, sm. impetus; impetuosity.
impetuoso, sa, *–pĕtŭŏ'sŏ*, a. impetuous.
impiedad, *–pĭĕdăd'*, sf. impiety; cruelty.
impío, pía, *ĭmpĕ'ŏ*, a. impious.
implacable, *–plăkă'blĕ*, a. implacable,
inexorable.
implicación, *–plĭkăthĭon'*, sf. implication.
implicar, *–plĭkăr'*, v. a. to implicate, to
involve; to entangle.
implícito, ta, *–plĕ'thĭtŏ*, a. implicit.
implorar, *–plŏrăr'*, v. a. to implore.
impolítica, *ĭmpŏlĭ'tĭkă*, sf. incivility; im-
policy. [polite.
impolítico, ca, *–tĭkŏ*, a. impolitic; im-
imponderable, *ĭmpŏndĕră'bl...*, a. inexpressible, unutterable.
imponer, *–pŏnĕr'*, v. a. to impose a tax;
to impute falsely; to advise, to impose
upon. [tion.
importación, *–pŏrtăthĭon'*, sf. importa-
importancia, *–pŏrtăn'thĭā*, sf. importance,
import. [siderable.
importante, *–pŏrtăn'tĕ*, a. important, con-
importar, *–pŏrtăr'*, v. imp. to be important, to matter. [amount, value.
importe, *ĭmpŏr'tĕ*, sm. amount or gross

importunación, *-tŭnăthĭŏn',* sf. impor-tunity.
importunar, *-tŭnăr',* v. a. to importune.
importunidad, *-tŭnĭdăd',* sf. impor-tunity, annoyance. [unreasonable.
importuno, na, *-tō'nŏ,* a. importunate;
imposibilidad, *ĭmpŏsĭbĭlĭdă',* sf. im-possibility. [possible.
imposibilitar, *-tăr',* v. a. to render im-
imposible, *ĭmpŏsē'blĕ,* a. impossible; ex-tremely difficult. [impost.
imposición, *-pŏsĭthĭŏn',* sf. imposition.
impostor, *-pŏstŏr',* sm. impostor, cheater.
impostura, *-pŏstō'ră,* sf. false imputation; imposture, deceit, cheat.
impotencia, *-pŏtĕn'tĭă,* sf. impotence.
impotente, *-pŏtĕn'tĕ,* a. impotent.
impracticable, *-prăktĭkă'blĕ,* a. imprac-ticable, unfeasible. [tion, curse.
imprecación, *-prĕkăthĭŏn',* sf. impreca-
imprecar, *-prĕkăr',* v. a. to imprecate, to curse.
imprecatorio, ria, *-prĕkătŏ'rĭŏ,* a. con-taining curses, full of evil wishes.
impregnarse, *-prĕgnăr'sĕ,* v. r. to be im-pregnated. [office.
imprenta, *-prĕn'tă,* sf. printing; printing-
imprescindible, *-prĕsthĭndē'blĕ,* a. that which cannot be prescinded or put aside.
imprescriptible, *-prĕskrĭptē'blĕ,* a. im-prescriptible.
impresión, *-prĕsĭŏn',* sf. impression; stamp; print; impression, edition; effica-cious agency, influence.
impresionar, *-prĕsĭŏnăr',* v. a. to im-print, to fix on the mind. [treatise.
impreso, *-prĕ'sŏ,* sm. small book, short
impresor, *-prĕsŏr',* sm. printer.
imprevisto, ta, *-prĕvĭs'tŏ* a. unforeseen; unprovided against. [print; to stamp.
imprimir, *-prĭmĭr',* v. a. to print; to im-
improbable, *-prŏbă'blĕ,* a. improbable, unlikely. [laborious, painful.
improbo, ba, *ĭm'prŏbŏ,* a. corrupt, wicked;
improperar, *-prŏpĕrăr',* v. a. to upbraid, to taunt, to chide, to abuse.
improperio, *-prŏpĕ'rĭŏ,* sm. contemp-tuous reproach, injurious censure.
impropiedad, *-prŏpĭĕdăd',* sf. impro-priety. [unfit; misbecoming.
impropio, pia, *ĭmprŏ'pĭŏ,* a. improper;
improrrogable, *-prŏrrŏgă'blĕ,* a. that which cannot be prorogued.
improvisar, *-prŏvĭsăr',* v. a. to extem-porize, to improvise.
improviso, sa, *-prŏvē'sŏ,* a. improvised, unforeseen; not provided against; de —, unexpectedly. [dence.
imprudencia, *-prŭdĕn'thĭă,* sf. impru-
imprudente, *-prŭdĕn'tĕ,* a. imprudent.
impudencia, *-pŭdĕn'thĭă,* sf. impudence.
impudente, *-pŭdĕn'tĕ,* a. impudent, shame-less, descarado, desfachatado.
impúdico, ca, *-pŏ'dĭkŏ,* a. unchaste; shameless, brazen-faced.
impuesto, *-pŭĕs'tŏ,* sm. tax, impost, duty.
impugnación, *-pŭgnăthĭŏn',* sf. opposi-tion, contradiction.

impugnar, *-pŭgnăr',* v. a. to impugn, to oppose.
impulsivo, va, *-pŭlsē'vŏ,* a. impulsive.
impulso, *-pŭl'sŏ,* sm. impulsion.
impune, *ĭmpō'nĕ,* a. unpunished.
impunidad, *-pŭnĭdăd',* sf. impunity; guiltlessness.
impureza, *-pŭrĕ'thă,* sf. impurity.
impuro, ra, *ĭmpō'rŏ,* a. impure, foul.
imputable, *-pŭtă'blĕ,* a. imputable, charge-able. [able.
imputar, *-pŭtăr',* v. a. to impute.
inaccesible, *ĭnăkthĕsē'blĕ,* a. inaccessible; (fig.) incomprehensible. [labour.
inacción, *-ăkthĭŏn',* sf. cessation from
inadmisible, *-ădmĭsē'blĕ,* a. inadmissible.
inadvertencia, *ĭnădvĕrtĕn'thĭă,* sf. care-lessness, inattention. [inconsiderate.
inadvertido, da, *-tĭ'dŏ,* a. inadvertent,
inagotable, *ĭnăgŏtă'blĕ,* a. inexhaustible.
inaguantable, *-ăgŭă-tă'blĕ,* a. insupport-able, insufferable, intolerable.
inajenable, *-ă'hĕnă'blĕ,* a. inalienable.
inalterable, *-ăltĕră'blĕ,* a. unalterable.
inapelable, *-ăpĕlă'blĕ,* a. without appeal.
inapreciable, *-ăprĕthĭă'blĕ,* a. inappre-ciable, invaluable.
inaudito, ta, *-ăŭdĭ'tŏ,* a. unheard of.
inauguración, *-ăŭgŭrăthĭŏn',* sf. inaugu-ration, consecration.
inaugurar, *-ăŭgŭrăr',* v. a. to inaugurate.
incansable, *-kănsă'blĕ,* a. indefatigable.
incapacidad, *-kăpăthĭdăd',* sf. incapacity, inability; stupidity.
incapaz, *-kăpăth',* a. incapable, unable.
incauto, ta, *-kăŭ'tŏ,* a. incautious, un-wary, heedless. [set on fire.
incendiar, *-thĕndĭăr',* v. a. to kindle, to
incendiario, ria, *-thĕndĭă'rĭŏ,* sm. & a. incendiary. [tion; combustion.
incendio, *-thĕn'dĭŏ,* sm. fire, conflagra-
incensar, *-thĕnsăr',* v. a. to perfume, to incense. [censer.
incensario, *-thĕnsă'rĭŏ,* sm. incensory.
incentivo, *-thĕntē'vŏ,* sm. incitement, spur. [certitude, uncertainty.
incertidumbre, *-thĕrtĭdŭm'brĕ,* sf. in-
incesante, *-thĕsăn'tĕ,* a. incessant, con-tinual.
incesto, *-thĕs'tŏ,* sm. incest. [tinual.
incestuoso, sa, *-thĕstŭŏ'sŏ,* a. incestuous.
incidencia, *-thĭdĕn'thĭă,* sf. incidence; accident. [dent.
incidente, *-thĭdĕn'tĕ,* sm. incident, acci-
incidir, *-thĭdĭr',* v. n. to fall upon, to meet with.
incienso, *ĭnthĕn'sŏ,* sm. incense.
incierto, ta, *ĭnthĭĕr'tŏ,* a. uncertain, doubtful.
incisión, *-thĭsĭŏn',* sf. incision, cut.
incisivo, va, *-thĭsē'vŏ,* a. incisive.
inciso, *-thĭ'sŏ,* sm. (gr.) comma.
incitación, *-thĭtăthĭŏn',* sf. incitement.
incitar, *-thĭtăr',* v. a. to incite, to excite.
incitativo, va, *-thĭtătē'vŏ,* a. inciting.
incivil, *-thĭvĭl',* a. unpolished, incivil.
inclemencia, *-klĕmĕn'thĭă,* sf. inclemency, severity; á la —, openly, without shelter.
inclinación, *-klĭnăthĭŏn',* sf. inclination.

inclinar, –klīnâr´, v. a. to incline ; –, v. n. to resemble ; to incline ; to be favourably disposed to.
inclito, ta, ēn´klītō, a. famous, illustrious.
incluir, –klūīr´, v. a. to include, to comprise ; to allow one a share in a business.
inclusa, –klō´sã, sf. foundling-hospital.
inclusión, –klūsīōn´, sf. inclusion.
inclusive, –klūsē´vĕ, ad. inclusivy
incluso, sa, ēnklō´sã, a. inclosed.
incoativo, va, –kōātī´vō, a. inchoative, beginning.
incobrable, –kōbrã´blĕ, a. irrecoverable.
incógnito, ta, ēnkōg´nītō, a. unknown : de –, incognito.   [ence.
incoherencia, ēnkōĕrĕn´thīã, sf. incoherence.
incoherente, –tĕ, a. incoherent.
incombustible, ēnkōmbūstē´blĕ, a. incombustible.   [mode.
incomodar, –kōmōdâr´, v. a. to incommode.
incomodidad, –kōmōdīdâd´, sf. incommodity ; indisposition.
incómodo, da, ēnkōm´ōdō, a. incommodious, inconvenient.
incomparable, ēnkōmpārã´blĕ, a. incomparable, matchless.
incompatibilidad, –pātībīlīdâd´, sf. incompatibility.
incompatible, –pātē´blĕ, a. incompatible.
incompetencia, –pĕtĕn´thīã, sf. incompetency.
incompetente, –pĕtĕn´tĕ, a. incompetent.
incompleto, ta, –plĕ´tō, a. incomplete.
incomplexo, xa, –plĕk´sō, a. simple, simplex.   [hensible.
incomprensible, –prĕnsē´blĕ, a. incomprehensible.
incomunicación, ēnkōmūnīkāthīōn´, sf. want of communication.
incomunicado, da, –kā´dō, a. without communication.   [ceivable.
inconcebible, ēnkōnthĕbē´blĕ, a. inconceivable.
inconexo, xa, –kōnĕk´sō, a. unconnected, incoherent ; independent.
incongruencia, –kōngrūĕn´thīã, a. incongruity, incongruence.
incongruo, grua, ēnkōn´grūō, a. incongruous, disproportionate.
inconmensurable, ēnkōnmēnsūrã´blĕ, a. immeasurable.   [able.
inconmutable, –mūtã´blĕ, a. incommutable.
inconquistable, –kīstã´blĕ, a. unconquerable.   [sequence.
inconsecuencia, –sĕkūĕn´thīã, sf. inconsequence.
inconsiderado, da, –sīdĕrã´dō, a. inconsiderate, heedless.
inconsolable, –sōlã´blĕ, a. inconsolable.
inconstancia, –stãn´thīã, sf. inconstancy, unsteadiness, levity.   [able, fickle.
inconstante, –stãn´tĕ, a. inconstant, variable, fickle.
incontestable, –tēstã´blĕ, a. indisputable, incontrovertible, incontestable.
incontinencia, –tīnĕn´thīã, sf. incontinence, incontinency ; unchastity.
incontinente, –tīnĕn´tĕ, a. incontinent.
incontrastable, –trãstã´blĕ, a. insurmountable.
inconveniencia, –vĕnĕn´thīã, sf. inconvenience, incommodity ; unsuitableness.

inconveniente, –vĕnĕn´tĕ, a. inconvenient, incommodious.   [the groin).
incordio, ēnkōr´dīō, sm. bubo (tumour in
incorporación, –pōrāthīōn´, sf. incorporation, annexation.
incorporar, –pōrâr´, v. a. to incorporate ; –se, to become incorporated.
incorpóreo, rea, –pō´rĕō, a. incorporeal, immaterial.
incorrecto, ta, –rĕk´tō, a. incorrect.
incorregible, –rĕhē´blĕ, a. incorrigible.
incorruptible, –rūptē´blĕ, a. incorruptible.
increado, da, ēnkrĕā´dō, a. uncreated.
incredulidad, –krĕdūlīdâd´, sf. incredulity, incredulousness.
incrédulo, la, –krē´dūlō, a. incredulous.
increíble, –krĕē´blĕ, a. incredible.
incremento, –krĕmĕn´tō, sm. increment, increase ; growth ; cause of growth.
increpación, –krĕpāthīōn´, a. reprehension.   [hend, to scold.
increpar, –krĕpâr´, v. a. to chide, to reprehend, to scold.
incruento, ta, –krūĕn´tō, a. unstained with blood.
inculcar, –kūlkâr´, v. a. to inculcate.
inculpable, –kūlpā´blĕ, a. inculpable, unblamable.
inculpar, –kūlpâr´, v. a. to accuse, to blame.
inculto, ta, –kūl´tō, a. uncultivated, uneducated.   [bency ; duty.
incumbencia, –kūmbĕn´thīã, sf. incumbency ; duty.
incumbir, –kūmbīr´, v. n. to be incumbent upon one.   [diable.
incurable, –kūrã´blĕ, a. incurable ; irremediable.
incuria, –kō´rīã, sf. negligence.
incurrir, –kūrrīr´, v. n. to incur.
incursión, –kūrsīōn´, sf. incursion, incurring.   [quiry.
indagación, –dāgāthīōn´, sf. search, inquiry.
indagar, –dāgâr´, v. a. to search, to inquire.
indebido, da, –dĕbī´dō, a. undue, illegal, unlawful.
indecencia, –dĕthĕn´thīã, sf. indecency.
indecente, –dĕthĕn´tĕ, a. indecent.
indecible, –dĕthē´blĕ, a. inexpressible, unutterable.   [indecision.
indecisión, –dĕthīsīōn´, sf. irresolution, indecision.
indeciso, sa, –dĕthī´sō, a. irresolute ; undecided.
indeclinable, –dĕklīnã´blĕ, a. firm, unshaken ; (gr.) indeclinable.
indecoroso, sa, –dĕkōrō´sō, a. indecent, unbecoming, indecorous.
indefectible, –dĕfĕktē´blĕ, a. unfailing.
indefenso, sa, –dĕfĕn´sō, a. defenceless.
indefinible, –dĕfīnē´blĕ, a. indefinable.
indefinido, da, –dĕfīnī´dō, a. indefinite.
indeleble, –dĕlē´blĕ, a. indelible.
indeliberado, da, –dĕlībĕrã´dō, a. indeliberate, unpremeditated.
indemnización, –dĕmnīthāthīōn´, sf. indemnification.
indemnizar, –thâr´, v. a. to indemnify.
independencia, ēndĕpĕndĕn´thīã, sf. independence.
independiente, –dĕn´tĕ, a. independent.
indestructible, ēndĕstrūktē´blĕ, a. indestructible.

indeterminado, da, *–dĕtĕrmĭnã′dŏ,* a. indeterminate; indetermined, irresolute.

indevoto, ta, *–dĕvō′tŏ,* a. not devout, impious, irreligious.

indiana, *ĭndĭã′nă,* sf. chintz, printed cotton.

indiano, –nŏ, sm, Nabob.

indicación, *ĭndĭkãthŏn′,* sf. indication.

indicar, –kãr′, v. a. to indicate. [cative.

indicativo, va, *–kãtĭ′vŏ,* a. & sm. indi-

índice, *ĭn′dĭthĕ,* sm. mark, sign; hand of a watch or clock; index, table of contents; forefinger, index.

indicio, *ĭndĭ′thĭŏ,* sm. indication, mark; sign, token. [unconcern.

indiferencia, *ĭndĭfĕren′thĭă,* sf.indifference.

indiferente, –tĕ, a. indifferent.

indígena, *ĭndĭ′hĕnă,* a. indigenous, native.

indigencia, –dĭ′hen′thĭă, sf. indigence, poverty, need. [want.

indigente, –tĕ, a. indigent, poor, in

indigestión, *ĭndĭ′hestĭŏn′,* sf. indigestion.

indigesto, ta, –dĭ′hĕs′tŏ, a. undigested; indigestible; not properly thought or worked out. [anger.

indignación, –dĭgnãthĭŏn′, sf.indignation,

indignar, –dĭgnãr′, v. a. to irritate, to provoke, to tease. [meanness.

indignidad, –dĭgnĭdãd′, sf. indignity.

indigno, na, indĭg′nŏ, a. unworthy, in-dign, disgraceful.

índigo, ĭn′dĭgŏ, sm. indigo-plant; indigo.

indirecta, –dĭrĕk′tă, sf. innuendo, hint.

indirecto, ta, –tŏ, a. indirect. [cue.

indisciplinado, da, *ĭndĭsthĭplĭnã′dŏ,* a. undisciplined. [imprudence.

indiscreción, –krethĭŏn′, sf. indiscretion,

indiscreto, ta, –krĕ′tŏ, a. indiscreet, in-considerate.

indisculpable, –kŭlpã′blĕ, a. inexcusable.

indisoluble, *ĭndĭsŏlŏ′blĕ,* a. indissoluble.

indispensable, –dĭspensã′blĕ, a. indis-pensable. [indispose.

indisponer, –dĭspŏnĕr′, v. a. to disable; to indispose.

indisposición, –dĭspŏsĭthĭŏn′, sf. indis-position, slight disorder.

indispuesto, ta, –dĭspŭĕs′tŏ, a.indisposed.

indisputable, –dĭspŭtã′blĕ, a. indis-putable, incontrovertible.

indistinto, ta, –dĭstĭn′tŏ, a. indistinct.

individual, –dĭvĭdŭãl′, a. individual.

individualidad, –lĭdãd′, sf. indivi-duality. [individually.

individualizar, –lĭthãr′, v. a. to specify.

individuo, ĭndĭvĭ′dŭŏ, sm. individual.

indivisible, –dĭvĭsĭ′blĕ, a. indivisible.

indócil, ĭndŏ′thĭl, a. indocile; headstrong.

indocilidad, –thĭlĭdãd′, sf. indocility.

índole, ĭn′dŏlĕ, sf. disposition, temper, peculiar genius. [difference.

indolencia, –dŏlen′thĭă, sf. indolence, in-

indolente, –tĕ, a. indolent, indifferent.

indómito, ta, ĭndŏ′mĭtŏ, a. untamed, un-governed. [suasion.

inducción, –dŭkthĭŏn′, sf. induction, per-

inducir, –dŭthĭr′, v. a. to induce, to abet.

inductivo, va, –dŭktĭ′vŏ, a. inductive.

indulgencia, –dŭl′hen′thĭă, sf.indulgence, forgiveness.

indulgente, –tĕ, a. indulgent.

indultar, ĭndŭltãr′, v. a. to pardon; to exempt. [privilege, exemption.

indulto, ĭndŭl′tŏ, sm. pardon, amnesty;

industria, ĭndŭs′trĭă, sf. industry.

industrial, –dŭstrĭãl′, a. belonging to industry. [struct.

industriar, –trĭãr′, v. a. to teach, to in-

industrioso, sa, –trĭŏ′sŏ, a. industrious; ingenious. [unedited.

inédito, ta, ĭnĕ′dĭtŏ, a. not published,

inefable, ĭnĕfã′blĕ, a. ineffable, unspeak-able, unutterable.

ineficacia, –fĭkã′thĭă, sf. inefficacy.

ineficaz, –fĭkãth′, a. inefficacious.

ineptitud, –ĕptĭtŭd′, sf. inability, un-fitness, ineptitude.

inepto, ta, ĭnĕp′tŏ, a. inept, unfit, useless.

inercia, ĭnĕr′thĭă, sf. inertia; inactivity.

inerme, ĭnĕr′mĕ, a. disarmed, without arms.

inerte, ĭnĕr′tĕ, a. inert, dull, sluggish; unskilful, awkward.

inescrutable, –ĕskrŭtã′blĕ, a. unscrutable.

inesperado, da, –ĕspĕrã′dŏ, a.unexpected, unforeseen.

inestimable, –ĕstĭmã′blĕ, a. inestimable.

inevitable, –ĕvĭtã′blĕ, a. unavoidable.

inexactitud, –ĕksãktĭtŭd′, sf. inaccuracy, want of exactness.

inexacto, ta, –ĕksãk′tŏ, a. not exact.

inexorable, –ĕksŏrã′blĕ, a. inexorable.

infalibilidad, –fãlĭbĭlĭdãd′, sf. infalli-bility.

infalible, –fãlĭ′blĕ, a. infallible.

infamante, –fãmãn′tĕ, a. defamatory; opprobrious, disgraceful.

infamar, –fãmãr′, v. a. to defame.

infame, ĭnfã′mĕ, a. infamous.

infamia, ĭnfã′mĭă, sf. infamy.

infancia, ĭnfãn′thĭă, sf. infancy.

infando, da, ĭnfãn′dŏ, a. infamous, un-speakably abominable.

infanta, ĭnfãn′tă, sf. infanta (princess of the royal blood of Spain); infant (female child under seven years old).

infante, ĭnfãn′tĕ, sm. infant; infantryman, foot-soldier.

infantería, –tĕrĭ′ă, sf. infantry.

infanticida, –tĭthĭ′dă, sm. infanticide (person). [murder.

infanticidio, –tĭthĭ′dĭŏ, sm. infanticide

infantil, –fãntĭl′, a. infantile, infantine.

infanzón, –fãnthŏn′, sm. nobleman.

infatigable, –fãtĭgã′blĕ, a. indefatigable.

infausto, ta, –fã′ŭstŏ, a. unlucky, un-fortunate, luckless, fatal.

infección, –fĕkthĭŏn′, sf. infection.

infectar, –fĕktãr′, v. a. to infect.

infecto, ta, –fĕk′tŏ, a. infected.

infelicidad, –fĕlĭthĭdãd′, sf. misfortune, infelicity.

infeliz, –fĕlĭth′, a. unhappy, unfortunate.

inferior, –fĕrĭŏr′, a. inferior.

inferioridad, –fĕrĭŏrĭdãd′, sf. inferiority.

inferir, –fĕrĭr′, v. a. to infer.

infernal, –fĕrnãl′, a. infernal, hellish.

infestar, –fĕstãr′, v. a. to overrun, to harass, to annoy an enemy by incursions; to infect.

inficionar, *-fĭthĭŏnăr'*, v. a. to infect; to corrupt.

infidelidad, *-fĭdĕlĭdăd'*, sf. infidelity; treachery.   [godless.

infiel, *-fĭĕl'*, a. infidel; faithless; disloyal;

infierno, *-fĭĕr'nŏ*, sm. hell.   [filtration.

infiltración, *-fĭltrăthĭŏn'*, sf. (med.) in-

infiltrarse, *-fĭltrăr'sĕ*, v. r. to infiltrate.

ínfimo, ma, *ĭn'fĭmŏ*, a. lowest, lowermost.

infinidad, *-fĭnĭdăd'*, sf. infinity, immensity.

infinitivo, *-fĭnĭtĭvŏ*, sm. (gr.) infinitive.

infinito, ta, *-fĭnĭ'tŏ*, a. infinite, immense; —, ad. infinitely, immensely.

inflamable, *-flămă'blĕ*, a. inflammable.

inflamación, *-flămăthĭŏn'*, sf. inflammation; fervour.   [desires.

inflamar, *-măr'*, v. a. to inflame; to kindle

inflamatorio, ria, *-mătŏ'rĭŏ*, a. inflammatory.   [with wind.

inflar, *ĭnflăr'*, v. a. to inflate; to swell

inflexibilidad, *-flĕksĭbĭlĭdăd'*, sf. inflexibility.

inflexible, *-flĕksĭ'blĕ*, a. inflexible.

influencia, *-flŭĕn'thĭă*, sf. influence.

influir, *-flŭĭr'*, v. a. to influence, to prevail upon.

influjo, *ĭnflŭ'hŏ*, sm. influx, influence.

información, *-fŏrmăthĭŏn'*, sf. information; intelligence given; instruction, judicial inquiry.   [lished forms.

informal, *-fŏrmăl'*, a. contrary to established forms.

informalidad, *-mălĭdăd'*, sf. informality.

informar, *-măr'*, v. a. to inform.

informe, *ĭnfŏr'mĕ*, sm. information, account; —, a shapeless, formless.   [luck.

infortunio, *-fŏrtŭ'nĭŏ*, sm. misfortune, ill

infracción, *-frăkthĭŏn'*, sf. infraction; breach, contravention, violation, trespass.

infractor, *-făr'*, sm. violator.

infrascripto, *-frăskrĭp'tŏ*, a. underwritten, undersigned.

infructífero, ra, *-frŭktĭ'fĕrŏ*, a. unfruitful; useless.

infructuoso, sa, *-frŭktŭŏ'sŏ*, a. fruitless, unproductive, unprofitable.

infundado, da, *-fŭndă'dŏ*, a. groundless.

infundios, *-fŭn'dĭŏs*, sm. pl. jobbing in joint-stock companies.   [spire with.

infundir, *-fŭndĭr'*, v. a. to infuse, to in-

infusión, *-fŭsĭŏn'*, sf. infusion.

infuso, sa, *ĭnfŭ'sŏ*, a. infused, inspired.

ingeniar, *ĭn'hĕnĭăr'*, v. a. to conceive; to contrive; —se, to work in the mind; to endeavour to find out.

ingeniero, *-hĕnĭĕ'rŏ*, sm. engineer.

ingenio, *ĭn'hă'nĭŏ*, sm. genius; engine; means, expedient; — de azúcar, sugarmill.

ingenioso, sa, *-hĕnĭŏ'sŏ*, a. ingenious.

ingenuidad, *-hĕnŭĭdăd'*, sf. ingeniousness; candour, frankness.

ingenuo, nua, *ĭn'hă'nŭŏ*, a. ingenuous.

ingerir, *-hĕrĭr'*, v. a. to insert; to introduce, to inclose; —se, to interfere officiously.

ingle, *ĭn'glĕ*, sf. groin.   [ciously.

inglés, esa, *ĭnglĕs'*, a. English; English language.

ingratitud, *-grătĭtŭd'*, sf. ingratitude, unthankfulness.   [less; disagreeable.

ingrato, ta, *ĭngră'tŏ*, a. ungrateful, thankingredient, *-grĕdĭĕn'tĕ*, sm. ingredient.

inhábil, *ĭnă'bĭl*, a. unable, incapable; awkward.   [to disable.

inhabilitar, *-ăbĭlĭtăr'*, v. a. to disqualify,

inhabitable, *-ăbĭtă'blĕ*, a. uninhabitable.

inherente, *-hĕrĕn'tĕ*, a. inherent.

inhibición, *-ĭbĭthĭŏn'*, sf. inhibition, prohibition.

inhibir, *-ĭbĭr'*, v. a. to inhibit, to prohibit.

inhibitorio, ria, *-ĭbĭtŏ'rĭŏ*, a. prohibitory.

inhumanidad, *-ŭmănĭdăd'*, sf. inhumanity.

inhumano, na, *-ŭmă'nŏ*, a. inhuman.   [ity.

inicial, *-ĭthĭăl'*, a. initial.

iniciar, *-ĭthĭăr'*, v. a. to initiate; —se, to receive the first orders.   [tiatory.

iniciativa, va, *-ĭ'tĕ'vă*, a. initiating, in-

inicuo, cua, *ĭnĭ'kŭŏ*, a. iniquitous, unjust.

inimaginable, *-ĭmăhĭnă'blĕ*, a. unimaginable, inconceivable.

inimitable, *-ĭmĭtă'blĕ*, a. inimitable.

ininteligible, *-ĭntĕlĭ'hĕ'blĕ*, a. unintelligible.   [justice.

iniquidad, *-ĭkĭdăd'*, sf. iniquity, in-

injertar, *ĭnhĕrtăr'*, v. a. to ingraft a tree.

injerto, *-hĕr'tŏ*, sm. tree ingrafted.

injuria, *-hŏ'rĭă*, sf. injury.

injuriador, ra, *-'hŭrĭădŏr'*, sm. & f. injurer, wrong-doer.

injuriar, *-hŭrĭăr'*, v. a. to injure.   [sive.

injurioso, sa, *-rĭŏ'sŏ*, a. injurious; offen-

injusticia, *-hŭstĭ'thĭă*, sf. injustice.

injusto, ta, *-hŭs'tŏ*, a. unjust.

inmaculado, da, *-măkŭlă'dŏ*, a. immaculate.   [fading.

inmarcesible, *-mărthĕsĭ'blĕ*, a. never-

inmediatamente, *-mĕdĭătămĕn'tĕ*, ad. immediately, forthwith.

inmediato, ta, *-mĕdĭă'tŏ*, a. immediate.

inmemorial, *-mĕmŏrĭăl'*, a. immemorial, past time.

inmensidad, *-mĕnsĭdăd'*, sf. immensity.

inmenso, sa, *-mĕn'sŏ*, a. immense, infinite.   [surable.

inmensurable, *-mĕnsŭră'blĕ*, a. immen-

inminente, *-mĭnĕn'tĕ*, a. imminent.

inmoble, *ĭnmŏ'blĕ*, a. immovable; constant.   [derate.

inmoderado, da, *-mŏdĕră'dŏ*, a. immo-

inmodesto, ta, *-mŏdĕs'tŏ*, a. immodest.

inmolar, *-mŏlăr'*, v. a. to sacrifice.

inmortal, *-mŏrtăl'*, a. immortal.   [tality.

inmortalidad, *-mŏrtălĭdăd'*, sf. immor-

inmortalizar, *-lĭthăr'*, v. a. to immortalize.

inmóvil, *ĭnmŏ'vĭl*, a. immovable.

inmovilidad, *-mŏvĭlĭdăd'*, sf. immobility.

inmueble, *ĭnmŭĕ'blĕ*, a. immovable.

inmundicia, *-mŭndĭ'thĭă*, sf. nastiness, filth.   [obscene.

inmundo, da, *ĭnmŭn'dŏ*, a. filthy, dirty;

inmune, *ĭnmŏ'nĕ*, a. free, exempt.

inmunidad, *-mŭnĭdăd'*, sf. immunity, privilege.   [tability.

inmutabilidad, *-mŭtăbĭlĭdăd'*, sf. immu-

inmutable, *-tă'blĕ*, a. immutable.

inmutar, —*mûtấ*, v. a. to change, to alter.
innato, ta, —*nấ tố*, a. inborn, natural.
innegable, —*negấ blẽ*, a. incontestable, incontrovertible.
innoble, —*nố blẽ*, a. ignoble; mean of birth.
innovación, —*nôvãthiốn*, sf. innovation.
innovador, ra, —*dốr*, sm. & f. innovator.
innovar, —*vãr*, v. a. to innovate.
innumerable, —*nûmerã blẽ*, a. innumerable, numberless.   [dience.
inobediencia, —*ôbediẽn thĩã*, sf. disobedience.
inobediente, —*tẽ*, a. disobedient.
inobservancia, —*ôbservãn thĩã*, sf. inadvertency; inobservance.
inocencia, *inôthẽn thĩã*, sf. innocence.
inocentada, —*thẽn tã dã*, sf. harmless speech.
inocente, —*tẽ*, a. innocent.   [speech.
inoculación, —*ôkûlãthiốn*, sf. inoculation.
inocular, —*lãr*, v. a. to inoculate.
inoficioso, sa, —*ôfĩthiố số*, a. inofficious.
inopinado, da, —*ôpinã dố*, a. unexpected, unforeseen, sudden.   [disturb.
inquietar, —*kiẽtãr*, v. a. to disquiet, to disturb.
inquieto, ta, —*kiẽ tố*, a. restless, unquiet.
inquietud, —*kiẽtûd*, sf. inquietude, anxiety.
inquilino, na, —*kiliˈ nố*, sm. & f. tenant, lodger.
inquirir, —*kirĩr*, v. a. to inquire.
inquisición, —*kisĩthiốn*, sf. inquisition; judicial inquiry.
inquisidor, —*dốr*, sm. inquirer; inquisitor.
insaciable, —*sãthiã blẽ*, a. insatiable.
insalubre, —*sãlố brẽ*, a. insalubrious.
insalubridad, —*sãlûbridãd*, sf. insalubrity.
insano, na, *insã nố*, a. insane, mad.
inscribir, —*skribĩr*, v. a. to inscribe.
inscripción, —*skripthiốn*, sf. inscription.
insecto, *insẽk tố*, sm. insect.
insensatez, —*sensãtẽth*, sf. insensateness, stupidity, folly.   [mad.
insensato, sa, —*sã tố*, a. insensate, stupid, mad.
insensibilidad, —*sensĩbilidãd*, sf. insensibility.   [perceptible.
insensible, —*sensĩ blẽ*, a. insensible; imperceptible.
insensiblemente, —*mẽnˈ tẽ*, ad. by degrees.
inseparable, —*sepãrã blẽ*, a. inseparable.
inserción, —*serthiốn*, sf. insertion.
insertar, —*sertãr*, v. a. to insert.
inservible, —*servĩ blẽ*, a. unserviceable.
insidioso, sa, —*sidiố số*, a. insidious.
insigne, *insĩgˈ nẽ*, a. notable.   [signia.
insignia, *insĩgˈ niã*, sf. badge; —s, pl. insignia.
insinuación, —*sinuãthiốn*, sf. insinuation.
insinuar, —*sinuãr*, v. a. to insinuate; to steal into imperceptibly.
insipidez, —*sĩpidẽth*, sf. insipidity.
insípido, da, *insĩ pidố*, a. insipid.
insistencia, —*sistẽnˈ thĩã*, sf. persistence, steadiness.
insistir, —*sistĩr*, v. n. to insist.
insociable, —*sôthiã blẽ*, a. unsociable.
insoldable, —*sôldã blẽ*, a. that cannot be soldered; irreparable.
insolencia, —*sôlẽnˈ thĩã*, sf. insolence, impudence, effrontery.
insolente, —*tẽ*, a. insolent, impudent.
insólidum, *insố lĩdum*, ad. (law) jointly.
insolvencia, —*sôlvẽnˈ thĩã*, sf. insolvency.

insolvente, —*tẽ*, a. insolvent.
insondable, —*sôndấ blẽ*, a. unfathomable; inscrutable.   [able.
insoportable, —*sãpõrtã blẽ*, a. insupportable.
inspección, —*spẽkthiốn*, sf. inspection, survey, control.   [to oversee.
inspeccionar, —*thĩõnãr*, v. a. to inspect, to oversee.
inspector, —*tốr*, sm. inspector, superintendent.
inspiración, —*spĩrãthiốn*, sf. inspiration.
inspirar, —*spĩrãr*, v. a. to inspire.
instabilidad, —*stãbilidãd*, sf. instability, inconstancy, fickleness, mutability, fugitiveness, fugacity, fragility; giddiness.
instable, *instã blẽ*, a. instable, inconstant, changing, mutable, fickle, fugacious.
instalación, —*stãlãthiốn*, sf. installation.
instalar, —*lãr*, v. a. to install.
instancia, *instãnˈ thĩã*, sf. instance.
instantáneo, nea, —*iã nẽố*, a. instantaneous.   [mediately, instantly.
instante, *instãnˈ tẽ*, sm. instant; al —, immediately, instantly.
instar, *instãr*, v. a. to press, to urge a request or petition; to impugn the solution of a question; —, v. n. to be pressing or urgent; to be near (of danger, &c.); to argue necessity for prompt action.
instigación, —*stĩgãthiốn*, sf. incitement, impulse, instigation.
instigar, —*gãr*, v. a. to instigate.
instinto, *instĩnˈ tố*, sm. instinct.
institución, —*stĩtûthiốn*, sf. institution; —ones, pl. elements of a science; lessonbook.
instituir, —*stĩtûĩr*, v. a. to institute.
instituto, —*stĩtûˈ tố*, sm. institute.
instrucción, —*strũkthiốn*, sf. instruction.
instructivo, va, —*tĩˈ vố*, a. instructive, conveying knowledge.
instructor, —*tốr*, sm. instructor, teacher.
instruir, —*strũĩr*, v. a. to instruct, to teach.   [mental.
instrumental, —*strũmẽntãl*, a. instrumental.
instrumentista, —*tĩsˈ tã*, sm. musical player.   [machine; means, expedient.
instrumento, —*mẽnˈ tố*, sm. instrument;
insubsistencia, —*sũbsistẽnˈ thĩã*, sf. instability, inconstancy.   [unstable.
insubsistente, —*tẽ*, a. unable to subsist;
insuficiencia, —*sûfĩthiẽnˈ thĩã*, sf. insufficiency, inadequateness.   [quate.
insuficiente, —*tẽ*, a. insufficient, inadequate.
insufrible, —*sûfrĩ blẽ*, a. insufferable, insupportable.
insulsez, —*sũlsẽth*, sf. insipidity, flatness.
insulso, sa, —*sũlˈ số*, a. insipid; dull, heavy; flat; cold.
insultar, —*sũltãr*, v. a. to insult.
insulto, —*sũlˈ tố*, sm. insult; sudden and violent attack.   [insurmountable.
insuperable, —*sũperã blẽ*, a. insuperable, inexpugnable.
insurgente, —*sũrhẽnˈ tẽ*, sm. insurgent.
insurrección, —*sûrrẽkthiốn*, sf. insurrection.
intacto, ta, —*tãkˈ tố*, a. untouched; entire; intact.
integral, —*tegrãl*, a. integral, whole.
integridad, —*tegridãd*, sf. integrity; uncorruptedness.

integro, gra, *ín'tĕgrŏ,* a. integral, entire.
intelectual, *-tĕlĕktūäl',* a. intellectual.
inteligencia, *-tĕlĭ'hĕn'thĭä,* sf. intelligence; understanding.
inteligente, *-tĕ,* a. intelligent.
inteligible, *-tĕlĭ'hŭ'lĕ,* a. intelligible.
intemperancia, *-tĕmpĕrän'thĭä,* sf. intemperance. [ness.
intemperie, *-tĕmpĕ'rĭĕ,* sf. intemperateness. [view.
intempestivo, va, *-tĕmpĕstē'vŏ,* a. unseasonable. [sign, meaning, view.
intención, *-tĕnthĭŏn',* sf. intention, design. [clined, disposed.
intencionado, da, *-thĭŏnä'dŏ,* a. inclined, disposed.
intendencia, *-tĕndĕn'thĭä,* sf. administration; employment of an intendant.
intendente, *-tĕ,* sm. intendant.
intensión, *-tĕnsĭŏn',* sf. tension, ardency.
intenso, sa, *intĕn'sŏ,* a. intense, ardent.
intentar, *-tĕntär',* v. a. to try; to intend, to design. [sign.
intento, *intĕn'tŏ,* sm. intent, purpose, design. [sign; chimerical attempt.
intentona, *intĕntŏ'nä,* sf. extravagant design; chimerical attempt.
intercadencia, *intĕrkädĕn'thĭä,* sf. interruption; inconstancy; intermission of the pulse. [variable.
intercadente, *-kädĕn'tĕ,* a. changeable, variable.
intercalación, *-käläthĭŏn',* sf. intercalation, insertion. [to insert.
intercalar, *-kälär',* v. a. to intercalate.
interceder, *-thĕdĕr',* v. n. to intercede.
interceptar, *-thĕptär',* v. a. to intercept.
intercesión, *-thĕsĭŏn',* sf. intercession, mediation, entreaty. [cessor, mediator.
intercesor, ra, *-thĕsŏr',* sm. & f. intercessor, mediator.
interés, *intĕrĕs',* sm. interest; concern, advantage; profit.
interesado, da, *-sä'dŏ,* a. interested.
interesante, *-sän'tĕ,* a. interesting, useful, convenient.
interesar, *-sär',* v. n. & r. to be concerned or interested in; —, v. a. to interest; to concern, to give a share in. [mean time.
interin, *ĭn'tĕrĭn,* ad. in the interim, in the mean time.
interinidad, *-nĭdäd',* sf. temporary holding of office. [an employ or office.
interino, na, *intĕrē'nŏ,* a. provisional (of an employ or office).
interior, *-tĕrĭŏr',* a. interior, internal; —, sm. interior, inside; —es, pl. entrails, intestines.
interioridad, *-ĭdäd',* sf. inside, interior.
interjección, *-hĕkthĭŏn',* sf. (gr.) interjection.
interlineal, *-lĭnĕäl',* a. interlineal.
interlocución, *-lŏküthĭŏn',* sf. interlocution, dialogue. [locutory.
interlocutorio, ria, *-lŏkütŏ'rĭŏ,* a. interlocutory.
intermediar, *-mĕdĭär',* v. a. to interpose.
intermedio, dia, *-mä'dĭŏ,* a. intermediate, intermedial; —, sm. interval, intermedium; interlude. [endless.
interminable, *-mĭnä'blĕ,* a. interminable, endless.
intermisión, *-mĭsĭŏn',* sf. intermission, interruption.
intermitente, *-mĭtĕn'tĕ,* a. intermittent.
internar, *intĕrnär',* v. a. to pierce; to penetrate; —se, to insinuate; to wheedle.

interno, *intĕr'nŏ,* a. interior, internal.
interpelación, *intĕrpĕläthĭŏn',* sf. interpellation.
interpelar, *-pĕlär',* v. a. to appeal to.
interpolación, *-pŏläthĭŏn',* sf. interpolation; interruption. [to interrupt.
interpolar, *-pŏlär',* v. a. to interpolate;
interponer, *-pŏnĕr',* v. a. to interpose.
interposición, *-pŏsĭthĭŏn',* sf. interposition; mediation. [tation.
interpretación, *-prĕtäthĭŏn',* sf. interpretation.
interpretar, *-prĕtär',* v. a. to interpret, to explain; to translate.
intérprete, *intĕr'prĕtĕ,* sm. interpreter.
interregno, *intĕrrĕg'nŏ,* sm. interreign.
interrogación, *-rŏgäthĭŏn',* sf. interrogation, a question put.
interrogante, *-rŏgän'tĕ,* a. interrogative.
interrogar, *-rŏgär',* v. a. to interrogate.
interrogatorio, *-rŏgätŏ'rĭŏ,* sm. interrogatory.
interrumpir, *-rümpĭr',* v. a. to interrupt.
interrupción, *-rüpthĭŏn',* sf. interruption, discontinuance.
intersección, *-sĕkthĭŏn',* sf. intersection.
intervalo, *-vä'lŏ,* sm. interval.
intervención, *-vĕnthĭŏn',* sf. intervention, mediation. [mediate.
intervenir, *-vĕnĭr',* v. n. to intervene, to interpose.
interventor, ra, *-vĕntŏr',* sm. & f. intervener; controller.
intestado, da, *intĕstä'dŏ,* a. intestate.
intestino, na, *intĕstē'nŏ,* a. intestine, internal, interior. [hint.
intimación, *-tĭmäthĭŏn',* sf. intimation, hint.
intimar, *-tĭmär',* v. a. to intimate.
intimidad, *-tĭmĭdäd',* sf. intimacy.
intimidar, *-där',* v. a. to intimidate.
íntimo, ma, *ĭn'tĭmŏ,* a. internal, innermost; intimate, familiar.
intitular, *-tĭtülär',* v. a. to entitle.
intolerable, *-tŏlĕrä'blĕ,* a. intolerable, insufferable.
intolerancia, *-tŏlĕrän'thĭä,* sf. intolerance.
intolerante, *-tĕ,* a. intolerant.
intramuros, *inträmŏ'rŏs,* a. within the walls. [able, impenetrable.
intransitable, *intränsĭtä'blĕ,* a. impassable, impenetrable.
intransitivo, va, *-tränsĭtē'vŏ,* a. (gr.) intransitive. [governable.
intratable, *-trätä'blĕ,* a. intractable, ungovernable.
intrepidez, *-trĕpĭdĕth',* sf. intrepidity; temerity. [daring.
intrépido, da, *intrĕ'pĭdŏ,* a. intrepid, daring.
intriga, *intrē'gä,* sf. intrigue.
intrigante, *-trĭgän'tĕ,* sm. intriguer.
intrigar, *-trĭgär',* v. n. to intrigue.
intrincar, *-trĭnkär',* v. a. to intricate, to entangle, to involve; to confound.
intrínseco, ca, *-trēn'sĕkŏ,* a. intrinsic, internal; judicial. [duction.
introducción, *-trŏdükthĭŏn',* sf. introduction.
introducir, *-düthĭr',* v. a. to introduce; —se, to insinuate.
introductor, *-düktŏr',* sm. introducer.
introito, *intrŏ'ĭtŏ,* sm. entrance, entry.
intrusión, *-trüsĭŏn',* sf. intrusion, obtrusion.

intruso, sa, *întrŏ'sŏ*, a. intrusive, obtrusive.
intuición, *–tŭĭthĭŏn'*, sf. intuition.
intuitivo, va, *–tĭ'vŏ*, a. intuitive.
inundación, *–ăndăthĭŏn'*, sf. inundation, deluge.   [flow.
inundar, *–dăr'*, v. a. to inundate, to overmusitado, da, *–ăsĭ'tădŏ*, a. unusual.
inútil, *ĭnŏ'tĭl*, a. useless.
inutilidad, *–ŭtĭlĭdăd'*, sf. uselessness.
inutilizar, *–thăr'*, v. a. to render useless.
invadir, *–vădĭr'*, v. a. to invade, to attack a country.   [render null and void.
invalidar, *–vălĭdăr'*, v. a. to invalidate, to
inválido, da, *ĭnvă'lĭdŏ*, a. invalid, null; –, sm. (mil.) invalid.
invariable, *–vărĭă'blĕ*, a. invariable.
invasión, *–văsĭŏn'*, sf. invasion.
invasor, ra, *–văsŏr'*, sm. & f. invader.
invectiva, *–vĕktĭ'vă*, sf. invective.
invencible, *–vĕnthĭ'blĕ*, a. invincible.
invención, *–vĕnthĭŏn'*, sf. invention.
inventar, *–vĕntăr'*, v. a. to invent.
inventariar, *–tărĭăr'*, v. a. to make an inventory.
inventario, *–tă'rĭŏ*, sm. inventory.
invento, *ĭnvĕn'tŏ*, sm. invention.
inventor, *–vĕntŏr'*, sm. inventor.
inverisímil, *–vĕrĭsĕ'mĭl*, a. unlike, improbable.   [hood, improbability.
inverisimilitud, *–mĭlĭtŭd'*, sf. unlikeli-
invernadero, *–vĕrnădĕ'rŏ*, sm. (mil.) winter-quarters; green-house.
invernar, *–vĕrnăr'*, v. n. to pass the winter; to be the winter season.
invernizo, za, *–vĕrnĕ'thŏ*, a. winterly.
inversión, *–vĕrsĭŏn'*, sf. inversion.
inverso, sa, *ĭnvĕr'sŏ*, a. inverted, reciprocal.
invertir, *–vĕrtĭr'*, v. a. to invert.
investidura, *–vĕstĭdŭ'ră*, sf. investiture.
investigación, *–vĕstĭgăthĭŏn'*, sf. investigation, research; inquest.
investigar, *–vĕstĭgăr'*, v. a. to investigate, to search out.
investir, *–vĕstĭr'*, v. a. to invest.
inveterarse, *–vĕtĕrăr'sĕ*, v. r. to become antiquated, to grow old.
invicto, ta, *ĭnvĭk'tŏ*, a. unconquerable.
invierno, *ĭnvĭĕr'nŏ*, sm. winter.
inviolabilidad, *–vĭŏlăbĭlĭdăd'*, sf. inviolability.
inviolable, *–vĭŏlă'blĕ*, a. inviolable.
invisible, *–vĭsĕ'blĕ*, a. invisible.
invocación, *–vŏkăthĭŏn'*, sf. invocation.
invocar, *–vŏkăr'*, v. a. to invoke.
involuntario, ria, *–vŏlŏntă'rĭŏ*, a. involuntary.   [able.
invulnerable, *–vŭlnĕră'blĕ*, a. invulner-
ipso facto, *ĭp'sŏ făk'tŏ*, ad. (law) immediately, without delay.   [away, to depart.
ir, *ĭr*, v. n. to go, to walk; –se, to go
ira, *ĕ'ră*, sf. anger, wrath.   [enraged.
iracundo, da, *ĭrăkŭn'dŏ*, a. a passionate,
iris, *ĕ'rĭs*, sf. rainbow; iris (of the eye); water-lily, nenuphar; peace-maker.
ironía, *ĭrŏnĕ'ă*, sf. irony.
irónico, ca, *ĭrŏ'nĭkŏ*, a. ironical.
irracional, *ĭrrăthĭŏnăl'*, a. irrational.
irradiación, *–rădĭăthĭŏn'*, sf. irradiation.

irrazonable, *–răthŏnă'blĕ*, a. unreasonable.   [concileable.
irreconciliable, *–rĕkŏnthĭlĭă'blĕ*, a. irre-
irrecusable, *–rĕkŭsă'blĕ*, a. not to be refused; inevitable.   [consideration.
irreflexión, *–rĕflĕkthĭŏn'*, sf. rashness, in-
irrefragable, *–rĕfrăgă'blĕ*, a. irrefragable, irrefutable.   [normal.
irregular, *–rĕgŭlăr'*, a. irregular, ab-
irregularidad, *–rĕgŭlărĭdăd'*, sf. irregularity, anomaly.
irreligioso, sa, *–rĕlĭ'hĭŏ'sŏ*, a. irreligious, impious.   [able, helpless.
irremediable, *–rĕmĕdĭă'blĕ*, a. irremedi-
irremisible, *–rĕmĭsĕ'blĕ*, a. irremissible, unpardonable.   [irretrievable.
irreparable, *–rĕpără'blĕ*, a. irreparable,
irreprensible, *–rĕprĕnsĕ'blĕ*, a. irreprehensible.
irresistible, *–rĕsĭstă'blĕ*, a. irresistible.
irresolución, *–rĕsŏlŭthĭŏn'*, sf. irresolution.
irresoluto, ta, *–rĕsŏlŭ'tŏ*, a. irresolute.
irreverencia, *–rĕvĕrĕn'thĭă*, sf. irreverence, want of reverence, respect or veneration.
irreverente, *–rĕvĕrĕn'tĕ*, a. irreverent.
irrevocable, *–rĕvŏkă'blĕ*, a. irrevocable.
irrisible, *–rĭsĕ'blĕ*, a. laughable.
irrisión, *–rĭsĭŏn'*, sf. mockery, mocking laughter.   [able.
irrisorio, ria, *–rĭsŏ'rĭŏ*, a. risible, laugh-
irritación, *–rĭtăthĭŏn'*, sf. irritation; wrath.   [to exasperate.
irritar, *–rĭtăr'*, v. a. to annul; to irritate,
irrupción, *–rŭpthĭŏn'*, sf. irruption, in-
isla, *ĭs'lă*, sf. isle, island.   [road.
isleño, ña, *ĭslĕn'yŏ*, sm. & f. islander.
isleta, *ĭslĕ'tă*, sf. islet.
islote, *ĭslŏ'tĕ*, sm. small barren island.
israelita, *ĭsrăĕlĭ'tă*, sm. Israelite, Jew.
istmo, *ĭst'mŏ*, sm. isthmus.
italiano, *ĭtălĭă'nŏ*, sm. Italian language.
item, *ĕ'tĕm*, sm. item, another article; –, ad. also.
itinerario, *ĭtĭnĕră'rĭŏ*, a. & sm. itinerary.
izar, *ĭthăr'*, v. a. (mar.) to hoist.   [handed.
izquierdo, da, *ĭthkĭĕr'dŏ*, a. left; left-

J.

jabalí, *hăbălĭ'*, sm. wild boar.
jabalina, *–lĭ'nă*, sf. wild sow; javelin.
jabón, *hăbŏn'*, sm. soap.
jabonado, *hăbŏnă'dŏ*, sm. washing with soap; parcel of linen washed with soap.
jabonadura, *–nădŭ'ră*, sf. soap-suds.
jabonar, *–năr'*, v. a. to soap.   [lather.
jabonería, *–nĕrĭ'ă*, sf. soap-house.
jabonero, *–nĕ'rŏ*, sm. soap-boiler.
jaca, *hă'kă*, sf. nag, pony.
jácara, *hă'kără*, sf. country song or dance tune.
jacarear, *hăkărĕăr'*, v. n. to sing **jácaras.**
jacinto, *hăthĭn'tŏ*, sm. hyacinth.

Jaco, *'hắ kŏ,* sm. nag, pony; ash-coloured parrot.

Jactancia, *'hăktăn'thĭă,* sf. boasting.

Jactancioso, sa, *–thĭŏ'sŏ,* a. boastful, vain-glorious.

Jactarse, *'hăktăr'sĕ,* v. r. to boast.

Jaculatoria, *'hăkŭlătŏ'rĭă,* sf. ejaculatory prayer, short and hurried prayer.

Jaez, *'hăĕth',* sm. harness.

Jalapa, *'hălă'pă,* sf. jalap.

Jalea, *'hălĕ'ă,* sf. jelly. [the chase.

Jalear, *'hălĕăr',* v. a. to egg on hounds to

Jaleo, *'hălĕ'ŏ,* sm. halloo.

Jaletina, *'hălĕtĕ'nă,* sf. fruit jelly; gelatine.

Jamás, *'hămăs',* ad. never; **para siempre** –, for ever.

Jamón, *'hămŏn',* sm. ham, gammon.

Jándalo, la, *'hăn'dălŏ,* a. having the gait and dialect of an Andalusian.

Jaque, *'hă'kĕ,* sm. check (at the game of chess); – **y mate,** check-mate.

Jaquear, *'hăkĕăr',* v. a. to check.

Jaqueca, *'hăkĕ'kă,* sf. megrim.

Jarabe, *'hără'bĕ,* sm. syrup.

Jarana, *'hără'nă,* sf. merry clatter, outcry.

Jarcia, *'hăr'thĭă,* sf. bundle, packet; bundle or heap of odds and ends; (mar.)

Jardín, *'hărdĭn',* sm. garden. [tackle.

Jardinería, *'hărdĭnĕrĭ'ă,* sf. gardening.

Jardinero, ra, *–nĕ'rŏ,* sm. & f. gardener.

Jareta, *'hărĕ'tă,* sf. lacing-seam.

Jaropar, *'hărŏpăr',* v. a. to medicine.

Jarope, *'hărŏ'pĕ,* sm. medical draught.

Jarra, *'hăr'ră,* sf. jug, jar, pitcher; **en** –, **de** –**s,** with arms placed akimbo; with hands to the sides.

Jarrete, *'hăr'rĕ'tĕ,* sm. hock, hough.

Jarretera, *'hăr'rĕtĕ'ră,* sf. garter.

Jarro, *'hăr'rŏ,* sm. pot with one handle.

Jarrón, *'hărrŏn',* sm. large jug, urn.

Jaspe, *'hăs'pĕ,* sm. jasper. [speckle.

Jaspear, *'hăspĕăr',* v. a. to marble, to

Jaula, *'hă'ŭlă,* sf. cage; cell for mad persons; (rail.) cattle-van.

Jauría, *'hăŭrĭ'ă,* sf. pack of hounds.

Jazmín, *'hăthmĭn',* sm. jessamine.

Jefe, *'hĕ'fĕ,* sm. chief, head, leader; (rail.) – **de tren,** guard, conductor.

Jengibre, *'hĕn'hĭ'brĕ,* sm. (bot.) ginger.

Jerarquía, *'hĕrărkĭ'ă,* sf. hierarchy.

Jerárquico, *'hĕrăr'kĭkŏ,* a. hierarchical.

Jerga, *'hĕr'gă,* sf. coarse frieze, any coarse cloth; jargon; large sack.

Jergón, *'hĕrgŏn',* sm. coarse mattress.

Jerife, *'hĕrĕ'fĕ,* sm. Moorish title of honour.

Jerigonza, *'hĕrĭgŏn'thă,* sf. jargon, gibberish.

Jeringa, *'hĕrĭn'gă,* sf. syringe. [berish.

Jeringar, *–găr',* v. a. to syringe, to squirt.

Jeringazo, *–gă'thŏ,* sm. clyster.

Jeroglífico, ca, *–glĭ'fĭkŏ,* a. hieroglyphical; –, sm. hieroglyph, hieroglyphic.

Jesucristo, *'hĕsŭkrĭs'tŏ,* sm. Jesus Christ.

Jesuita, *'hĕsŭ'ĭtă,* sm. Jesuit.

Jesuítico, ca, *–sŭ'ĭtĭkŏ,* a. jesuitical.

Jiba, *'hĕ'bă,* sf. hump-back.

Jiboso, da, *'hĕbŏ'sŏ,* a. hump-backed.

Jibia, *'hĕ bĭă,* sf. cuttle-fish.

Jícara, *'hĕ'kără,* sf. chocolate-cup.

Jigote, *'hĭgŏ'tĕ,* sm. minced meat.

Jilguero, *'hĭlgĕ'rŏ,* sm. linnet.

Jinete, *'hĕnĕ'tĕ,* sm. cavalier.

Jocoserio, ria, *'hŏkŏsĕ'rĭŏ,* a. jocoserious.

Jocosidad, *–sĭdăd',* sf. jocosity.

Jocoso, sa, *'hŏkŏ'sŏ,* a. waggish, good-humoured.

Jornada, *'hŏrnă'dă,* sf. journey; military expedition; act (of a Spanish play); – **rompida,** fight, battle.

Jornal, *'hŏrnăl',* sm. day-work; journal; **á** –, by the day.

Jornalero, *–lă'rŏ,* sm. day-labourer.

Joroba, *'hŏrŏ'bă,* sf. hump.

Jorobado, da, *'hŏrŏbă'dŏ,* a. hump-backed.

Jorobar, *'hŏrŏbăr',* v. a. to importune, to tease.

Jota, *'hŏ'tă,* sf. jot, tittle; Spanish dance.

Joven, *'hŏ'vĕn,* a. young; –, sm. & f. youth; young woman.

Jovial, *'hŏvĭăl',* a. jovial, gay, merry.

Jovialidad, *–lĭdăd',* sf. joviality, gaiety.

Joya, *'hŏ'yă,* sf. jewel; present, gift.

Joyería, *'hŏyĕrĭ'ă,* sf. jeweller's shop.

Joyero, *'hŏyă'rŏ,* sm. jeweller.

Juanete, *'hăănĕ'tĕ,* sm. knuckle-bone of the great toe.

Jubilación, *'hŭbĭlăthĭŏn',* sf. festivity.

Jubilar, *'hŭbĭlăr',* v. a. to pension off; to superannuate; to lay aside as useless; –, v. n. to become a pensioner on retiring or leaving office.

Jubileo, *'hŭbĭlĕ'ŏ,* sm. jubilee.

Júbilo, *'hŏ'bĭlŏ,* sm. joy, merriment, festivity

Jubón, *'hŭbŏn',* sm. doublet, jacket.

Judaico, ca, *hŭdă'ĭkŏ,* a. Judaical, Jewish.

Judaísmo, *–ĭs'mŏ,* sm. Judaism, Jewish religion.

Judaizar, *–ĭthăr',* v. a. to judaize.

Judas, *'hŏ'dăs,* sm. (fig.) traitor.

Judía, *'hŭdĭ'ă,* sf. French bean, kidney-bean.

Judicatura, *'hŭdĭkătŭ'ră,* sf. judicature; dignity of a judge.

Judicial, *'hŭdĭthĭăl',* a. judicial, juridical.

Judío, día, *'hŭdĭ'ŏ,* a. Jewish; –, sm. Jew; word of contempt used in anger.

Juego, *'hŭĕ'gŏ,* sm. play, amusement, diversion, sport; game, gambling; –**s,** pl. public games of the ancients.

Jueves, *'hŭĕ'vĕs,* sm. Thursday.

Juez, *'hŭĕth',* sm. judge.

Jugada, *'hŭgă'dă,* sf. playing of a card.

Jugador, ra, *–dŏr',* sm. & f. player; gamester.

Jugar, *'hŭgăr',* v. a. & n. to play, to sport, to trifle, to toy; to gamble, to game; to intervene; to mock. [playing.

Jugarreta, *–ră'tă,* sf. bad play, unskilful

Jugo, *'hŏ'gŏ,* sm. sap, juice.

Jugoso, sa, *'hŏgŏ'sŏ,* a. juicy, succulent.

Juguete, *'hŭgĕ'tĕ,* sm. toy, play-thing, gew-gaw, trinket.

Juguetear, *–tĕăr',* v. n. to trifle, to fool.

Juguetón, ona, *–tŏn',* a. playful.

Juicio, *'hŭĭ'thĭŏ,* sm. judgment.

Juicioso, sa, *'hŭĭthĭŏ'sŏ,* a. judicious, prudent.

Julepe, *'hŭlĕ'pĕ,* sm. julap.

julio, 'hō'liō, sm. July (month).

jumenta, 'hūmĕn'tă, sf. female ass.

jumento, -tō, sm. beast of burden; ass; stupid person. [Chinese ship].

junco, 'hūn'kō, sm. (bot.) rush; junk (small

juncoso, sa, 'hūnkō'sō, a. full of rushes.

junio, 'hō'niō, sm. June (month).

junta, 'hūn'tă, sf. congress, assembly, council, meeting. [same time.

juntamente, -mĕn'tĕ, ad. jointly; at the

juntar, 'hūntär', v. a. to join, to unite; -se, to meet, to assemble; to be closely united.

junto, 'hūn'tō, ad. near, close to; (de) por -, by the bulk, in the lump.

juntura, 'hūntū'rä, sf. juncture; joint.

Júpiter, 'hū'pĭtĕr, sm. Jupiter (planet); (chem.) tin.

jura, 'hō'rä, sf. oath of allegiance.

jurado, 'hūrä'dō, sm. jury; juror, juryman; jurat.

jurador, ra, -dŏr', sm. & f. swearer.

juramentar, -mĕntär', v. a. to swear; -se, to bind oneself by an oath.

juramento, -mĕn'tō, sm. oath.

jurar, 'hūrär', v. a. to swear, to make oath; to curse.

jurídico, ca, 'hūrē'dĭkō, a. lawful, legal, juridical; done according to law.

jurisconsulto, 'hūrĭskōnsŭl'tō, sm. lawyer, jurist. [legal authority.

jurisdicción, -dĭkthĭōn', sf. jurisdiction.

jurisperito, -pĕrē'tō, sm. professor of jurisprudence. [prudence.

jurisprudencia, -prūdĕn'thĭä, sf. juris-

jurista, 'hūrĭs'tä, sm. jurist, lawyer.

juro, 'hō'rō, sm. right of perpetual property; de -, certainly.

justa, 'hūs'tä, sf. joust, tilt, tournament.

justamente, -mĕn'tĕ, ad. justly, just.

justicia, 'hūstē'thĭä, sf. justice; equity.

justiciero, ra, 'hūstĭthĭē'rō, sm. & f. administrator of justice.

justificación, -fĭkäthĭōn', sf. justification; adjustment of lines of type.

justificado, da, -fĭkä'dō, a. equal, justified; conformable to justice.

justificar, -fĭkär', v. a. to justify; to adjust lines of type. [ficatory.

justificativo, va, -fĭkätē'vō, a. justi-

justillo, 'hūstĭl'yō, sm. sleeveless jacket.

justipreciar, 'hūstĭprēthĭär', v. a. to estimate anything.

justo, ta, 'hūs'tō, a. just; lawful; honourable; -, sm. just and pious man; al -, ad. fitly, duly; punctually.

juvenil, 'hūvĕnĭl', a. juvenile, youthful.

juventud, 'hūvĕntūd', sf. youthfulness, youth. [cature.

juzgado, 'hūthgä'dō, sm. tribunal; judi-

juzgar, 'hūthgär', v. a. & n. to judge.

K.

kaleidoscopio, kälĕĭdŏskŏ'pĭō, sm. kaleidoscope.

kan, kän, sm. Khan, Khane, oriental

prince; call-house for journeymen in the Orient. [ingredients of china.

kaolín, käŏlĭn', sm. kaolin, one of the two

kepis, kĕ'pĭs, sm. military cap.

kermes, kĕr'mĕs, sm. church-ale, annual fair, fairing.

kilogramo, kĭlŏgrä'mō, sm. kilogram..

kilómetro, kĭlŏ'mĕtrō, sm. kilometre.

kiosco, kĭŏs'kō, sm. kiosk. [brandy.

kirs, kĭrs, kirsváser, -däs'ĕr, sm. cherry-

L.

la, lä, art. f. the.

laberinto, läbĕrĭn'tō, sm. labyrinth.

labia, lä'bĭä, sf. (fam.) winning eloquence.

labio, lä'bĭō, sm. lip; edge of anything.

labor, läbŏr', sf. labour, task; needlework; husbandry, tillage.

laboratorio, läbŏrätŏ'rĭō, sm. laboratory.

laboriosidad, läbŏrĭŏsĭdäd', sf. laboriousness, assiduity.

laborioso, sa, läbŏrĭō'sō, a. laborious.

labrado, da, läbrä'dō, a. worked (applied to figured cloth); -, sm. cultivated land.

labrador, ra, -dŏr', sm. & f. labourer; cultivator, farmer; peasant.

labrantío, tía, läbräntē'ō, a. arable.

labranza, läbrän'thä, sf. tillage; husbandry; tilled land.

labrar, läbrär', v. a. to work; to labour; to cultivate the ground; to build.

labriego, läbrĭē'gō, sm. peasant.

lacayo, läkä'yō, sm. lackey, foot-man.

lacerar, läthĕrär', v. a. to tear to pieces, to lacerate. [wretchedness.

lacería, läthĕrē'ä, sf. misery, poverty,

lacio, cia, lä'thĭō, a. faded, withered; languid. [cise.

lacónico, ca, läkŏ'nĭkō, a. laconic, con-

laconismo, läkŏnĭs'mō, sm. laconism.

lacra, lä'krä, sf. mark left by a wound; fault, vice. [to damage financially.

lacrar, läkrär', v. a. to injure one's health;

lacre, lä'krĕ, sm. sealing-wax. [suck.

lactancia, läktän'thĭä, sf. time of giving

lacticinio, läktĭthē'nĭō, sm. milk-pottage.

ladear, lädĕär', v. a. to move to one side; to incline; -, v. n. to incline to one side; -se, to incline to an opinion or party.

ladera, lädĕ'rä, sf. declivity.

ladilla, lädĭl'yä, sf. crablouse. [crafty.

ladino, na, lädĭ'nō, a. sagacious, cunning,

lado, lä'dō, sm. side; party; companion; ¡á un -! clear the way!

ladrar, lädrär', v. n. to bark. [tion.

ladrido, lädrĭ'dō, sm. barking; vocifera-

ladrillal, lädrĭlyäl', ladrillar, -yär', sm. brick-kiln.

ladrillo, lädrĭl'yō, sm. brick. [wayman.

ladrón, lädrŏn', sm. thief, robber, high-

ladronera, -nĕ'rä, sf. den of robbers.

ladronicio, -nĕ'thĭō, sm. larceny, theft, robbery. [ness.

lagaña, lägän'yä, sf. lippitude, bleared-

lagañoso, sa, –yō'sō, a. blear-eyed.
lagar, lágár', v. a. press-house; wine-press.
lagarero, lágárē'rō, sm. wine-presser; one employed in olive-pressing.
lagartija, lágártī'hǎ, sf. eft, newt.
lagarto, lágár'tō, sm. lizard; sly artful person; [of lions.
lago, lá'gō, sm. lake; – de leones, den
lágrima, lá'grēmǎ, sf. tear.
lagrimal, lágrēmál', sm. lachrymary bag.
lagrimoso, sa, –mō'sō, a. weeping, shedding tears. [ficiency.
laguna, lágō'nǎ, sf. lake; lagoon; de-
lagunoso, sa, lágōnō'sō, a. marshy, fenny.
laical, láíkál', a. lay, laical. [country.
lama, lá'má, sf. mud, slime, ooze; flat even
lamedor, ra, lámēdōr', sm. & f. licker; loch (medicine); enticement, allurement.
lamedura, lámēdō'rǎ, sf. act of licking.
lamentable, lámēntá'blě, a. lamentable, deplorable, pitiable.
lamentación, –táthiōn', sf. lamentation.
lamentar, –tár', v. a. to lament, to bewail; –, v. n. –se, to lament, to complain, to cry.
lamento, lámēn'tō, sm. lamentation.
lamer, lámēr', v. a. to lick, to lap.
lámina, lá'mínǎ, sf. plate, sheet of metal; copper-plate, engraving, print.
lámpara, lám'párǎ, sf. lamp.
lamparero, –párē'rō, sm. lamp-lighter.
lamparilla, –párī'lyǒ, sf. night-light.
lamparón, –párōn', sm. king's evil.
lampiño, ña, –pīn'yō, a. beardless.
lampión, lámpiōn', sm. large lantern.
lamprea, lámprē'á, sf. lamprey (fish).
lana, lá'ná, sf. wool.
lanar, lánár', a. woolly.
lance, lán'thě, sm. cast, throw; favourable opportunity; chance, hap-hazard; sudden quarrel; – de teatro, clap-trap.
lancear, lánthēár', v. a. to wound with a lance.
lancero, lánthē'rō, sm. pikeman, lancer.
lanceta, lánthē'tá, sf. lancet. [lancet.
lancetada, –tá'dǎ, sf. lancing, cut of a
lancha, lán'tshá, sf. barge, lighter; launch.
lanchón, lántshōn', sm. (mar.) lighter.
langosta, lángōs'tá, sf. locust; lobster; sharper, swindler.
langostin, lángōstīn', sm. small locust.
languidez, lángīdēth', sf. languidness.
lánguido, da, lán'gīdō, a. languid, faint, weak; languorous, languishing.
lanudo, da, lánō'dǎ, a. woolly, fleecy.
lanza, lán'thá, sf. lance, spear; pole of a coach; –s, pl. duty paid by the nobility of the realm (in lieu of military services).
lanzada, –thá'dǎ, sf. stroke with a lance.
lanzadera, –dē'rǎ, sf. shuttle.
lanzar, lánthár', v. a. to throw, to dart, to launch, to fling; (law) to eject.
lapicero, lápíthē'rō, sm. metal pencil-case.
lápida, lá'pídá, sf. flat stone, on which inscriptions are engraved. [dary.
lapidario, lápídá'ríō, sm. –, ria, a. lapi-
lápiz, lá'píth, sm. lead-pencil; black chalk used in drawing; black lead.

lapizar, lápíthár', v. a. to pencil.
lardar, lárdár', v. a. to baste; to beat with a stick.
lardoso, sa, lárdō'sō, a. greasy, fatty.
lares, lá'rēs, sm. pl. household-gods of the ancient Romans; home.
larga, lár'gá, sf. delay, adjournment.
largamente, –mēn'tě, ad. for a long time.
largar, lárgár', v. a. to loosen, to slacken; to let go; –se, to set sail.
largo, ga, lár'gō, a. long; large, generous, liberal; copious; a la –a, at length, extensively; –, ad. largely, profusely.
largueza, lárgē'thǎ, sf. length, largeness; liberality, generosity.
largura, lárgō'rǎ, sf. length, longitude.
lascivia, lásthē'vīá, sf. lasciviousness, lewdness.
lascivo, va, –vō, a. lascivious; lewd.
lasitud, lásītúd', sf. lassitude, weariness.
lástima, lás'tímǎ, sf. compassion, pity; object of pity.
lastimar, lástímár', v. a. to hurt; to wound; to move to compassion; –se, to be moved to compassion; to grieve.
lastimero, ra, –mē'rō, a. sad, mournful; lamentable. [mournful.
lastimoso, sa, –mō'sō, a. grievous, [ship.
lastrar, lástrár', v. a. to ballast a
lastre, lás'trě, sm. ballast; motive.
lateral, láterál', a. lateral.
latido, látī'dō, sm. pant, palpitation.
latigazo, látígá'thō, sm. lash, crack of a whip.
látigo, lá'tígō, sm. thong of a whip.
latin, látín', sm. Latin tongue.
latinajo, látíná'hō, sm. Latin jargon.
latinidad, látínídád', sf. Latinity, Latin tongue.
latinizar, –thár', v. a. to latinize.
latino, na, látī'nō, a. Latin.
latir, látír', v. n. to palpitate. [tude.
latitud, látítúd', sf. breadth; width; lati-
lato, ta, lá'tō, a. ample, large, diffuse, extensive.
latón, látōn', sm. brass, latten.
latonero, látōnē'rō, sm. brazier.
latría, látrī'á, sf. worship, adoration due to God only. [theft, robbery.
latrocinio, látrōthī'níō, sm. larceny,
laud, láúd', sf. lute (musical instrument).
laudable, láúdá'blě, a. laudable, praise-worthy.
láudano, lá'údánō, sm. laudanum.
lande, lá'dě, sf. tombstone with an epitaph engraved on it; –s, pl. Lauds.
laurear, láúrēár', v. a. to crown with laurel; to graduate; (fig.) to reward.
laurel, láúrēl', sm. (bot.) laurel; laurel-crown as a reward.
lauréola, láúrē'ōlá, sf. crown of laurel.
lavacaras, lávákǎ'rás, sm. (fig. & fam.) mean flatterer. [laundry.
lavadero, –dē'rō, sm. washing-place;
lavadura, –dō'rǎ, sf. wash, washing.
lavamanos, –má'nōs, sm. washing-stand (in a sacristy).
lavandera, lávándē'rǎ, sf. laundress.

lavar, *lăvăr′,* y. a. to wash; to whitewash.
lavativa, *lăvătĕ′yă,* sf. clyster.
lavatorio, *–tŏ′rĕŏ,* sm. act of washing; medicinal lotion; ceremony of washing the feet on Holy Thursday.
laxante, *lăksăn′tĕ,* sm. (med.) laxative.
laxar, *lăksăr′,* v. a. to loosen, to soften.
laxitud, *lăksĕtŭd′,* sf. laxity; laxness; weariness.
laxo, xa, *lăk′sŏ,* a. lax, slack; (fig.) vague.
layar, *lăyăr′,* v. a. to turn up the ground with a two-pronged instrument.
lazada, *lăthă′dă,* sf. running knot.
lazareto, *–rĕ′tŏ,* sm. lazaretto, lazaret.
lazarillo, *–rĕl′yŏ,* sm. boy who guides a blind man.   [tie; bond.
lazo, *lă′thŏ,* sm. slip-knot; snare, trick;
le, *lĕ,* pn. him, her; and dative of the feminine **ella,** she.
leal, *lĕăl′,* a. loyal; faithful.
lealtad, *lĕăltăd′,* sf. loyalty.   [pan.
lebrel, *lĕbrĕl′,* sm. greyhound.
lebrillo, *lĕbrĕl′yŏ,* sm. glazed earthen-ware
lección, *lĕkthŏn′,* sf. reading; lesson; lecture; lection.
lector, *lĕktŏr′,* sm. reader, lecturer.
lectoría, *lĕktŏrĕ′ă,* sf. lectureship.
lectura, *lĕktŏ′ră,* sf. reading, lecture.
leche, *lĕtshĕ,* sf. milk.   [maid.
lechera, *lĕtshĕ′ră,* sf. milkwoman, dairy-
lechería, *–rĕ′ă,* sf. cow-house, dairy.
lecho, *lĕtshŏ,* sm. bed; litter.   [fellow.
lechón, *lĕtshŏn′,* sm. sucking pig; dirty
lechuga, *lĕtshŏ′gă,* sf. lettuce.
lechugado, da, *–gă′dŏ,* a. having leaves like lettuce.   [lettuces.
lechuguino, *–gĕ′nŏ,* sm. bed of small
lechuza, *lĕtshŏ′thă,* sf. owl.
leer, *lĕĕr′,* v. a. to read; to lecture.
lega, *lĕ′gă,* sf. lay-sister.
legacía, *lĕgăthĕ′ă,* sf. embassy, legation.
legado, *lĕgă′dŏ,* sm. deputy, legate; legacy.
legajo, *lĕgă′hŏ,* sm. bundle of loose papers tied together.
legal, *lĕgăl′,* a. legal; loyal, faithful.
legalidad, *lĕgălĕdăd′,* sf. legality, fidelity.
legalización, *lĕgălĕthăthĕŏn′,* sf. legalization.
legalizar, *–thăr′,* v. a. to legalize.
legar, *lĕgăr′,* v. a. to depute; to bequeath.
legatario, *lĕgătă′rĕŏ,* sm. legatee.
legible, *lĕ′hĕblĕ,* a. legible.
legión, *lĕhĭŏn′,* sf. legion.
legionario, ria, *–nă′rĭŏ,* a. legionary.
legislación, *lĕhĭslăthĕŏn′,* sf. legislation.
legislador, *–dŏr′,* sm. legislator, lawgiver.
legislar, *lĕhĭslăr′,* v. a. to legislate.
legislativo, va, *–lătĕ′vŏ,* a. legislative, lawgiving.
legislatura, *–tŏ′ră,* sf. legislature.
legista, *lĕhĭs′tă,* sm. legist.
legítima, *lĕhĭ′tĭmă,* sf. (law) legitimate portion of the paternal or maternal estate.
legitimación, *–măthĕŏn′,* sf. legitimation.
legitimar, *–măr′,* v. a. to legitimate.
legitimidad, *–mĕdăd′,* sf. legitimacy.
legítimo, ma, *lĕhĭ′tĭmŏ,* a. legitimate, lawful.
lego, *lĕ′gŏ,* sm. lay-brother.

legua, *lĕ′gŭă,* sf. league.   [stuff.
legumbre, *lĕgŭm′brĕ,* sf.pot-herbs, garden-
leído, da, *lĕ′ĭ′dă,* a. well-read.
lejano, na, *lĕ′hă′nŏ,* a. distant, remote, far.
lejía, *lĕ′hĕ′ă,* sf. lie, lye.
lejos, *lĕ′hŏs,* ad. at a great distance, far off; –, sm. perspective, distant prospect.
lelo, la, *lĕ′lŏ,* a. stupid, ignorant.
lema, *lĕ′mă,* sm. argument of a poem explained in the title; lemma.
lencería, *lĕnthĕrĕ′ă,* sf. sortment of linen of different sorts; linen-draper's shop.
lendroso, sa, *lĕndrŏ′sŏ,* a. lousy, nitty.
lengua, *lĕn′gŭă,* sf. tongue; language, tongue.
lenguaje, *–gŭă′hĕ,* sm. language.
lenidad, *lĕnĭdăd′,* sf. lenity, mildness.
lenitivo, va, *–tĕ′vŏ,* a. lenient, mitigant; –, sm. emollient.
lente, *lĕn′tĕ,* sm.&f. lens. [–, sm. emollient.
lenteja, *lĕntĕ′hă′ă,* sf. (bot.) lentil.
lentitud, *lĕntĭtŭd′,* sf. slowness.
lento, ta, *lĕn′tŏ,* a. slow, tardy, lazy.
leña, *lĕn′yă,* sf. wood, timber.   [cutter.
leñador, *–yădŏr′,* sm. woodman, wood-
leñera, *–yĕ′ră,* sf. place for fire-wood.
leñero, *–yĕ′rŏ,* sm. timber-merchant.
leño, *lĕn′yŏ,* sm. block, log; crunk of a
leñoso, sa, *–yŏ′sŏ,* a. woody.   [tree.
Leo, *lă′ŏ,* Leo (sign of the zodiac).
león, *lĕŏn′,* sm. lion; beau, masher, dandy
leona, *lĕŏ′nă,* sf. lioness.
leonado, da, *–nă′dŏ,* a. lion-coloured, tawny; fallow.
leonera, *–nă′ră,* sf. lion-cage.
leonero, *–nă′rŏ,* sm. keeper of lions.
leopardo, *–păr′dŏ,* sm. leopard.
lepra, *lĕ′pră,* sf. leprosy.
leproso, sa, *lĕprŏ′sŏ,* a. leprous.
lerdo, da, *lĕr′dŏ,* a. slow, heavy; dull of comprehension.   [injury.
lesión, *lĕsĭŏn′,* sf. hurt, damage, wound;
lesna, *lĕs′nă,* sf. awl.
letal, *lĕtăl′,* a. mortal, deadly.
letanía, *lĕtănĕ′ă,* sf. litany; –s, pl. supplicatory processions.
letárgico, ca, *lĕtăr′hĭkŏ,* a. lethargic.
letargo, *lĕtăr′gŏ,* sm. lethargy.
letra, *lĕt′ră,* sf. letter; handwriting; printing-type; words of a song; bill of exchange; –s, pl. letters, learning.
letrado, da, *–ră′dŏ,* a. learned, lettered; –, sm. lawyer; professor of law.
letrero, *lĕtră′rŏ,* sm. inscription.
letrilla, *lĕtrĭl′yă,* sf. short poem, generally written to be sung to music.
letrina, *lĕtrĕ′nă,* sf. privy, W.C.
leva, *lĕ′vă,* sf. act of weighing anchor; (mil.) levy; (mar.) press.
levadizo, za, *lĕvădĕ′thŏ,* a. that can be lifted or raised; **puente** –, draw-bridge.
levantamiento, *lĕvăntămĭĕn′tŏ,* sm. elevation; insurrection.
levantar, *–tăr′,* v. a. to raise, to lift up, to heave; to build up; to impute falsely; to elevate, to promote; **–se,** to rise; to get up from bed; to stand up; to start.
levante, *–tĕ,* sm. Levant; east; east-wind.
leve, *lĕ′vĕ,* a. light; trifling.

levita, _lĕvĕ'tä_, sm. levite; —, sf. great-coat, frock-coat.
Levítico, _lĕvĕ'ĭkŏ_, sm. book of Leviticus.
ley, _lā'ĕ_, sf. law; loyalty; —es, pl. collection of laws.
leyenda, _lĕyĕn'dä_, sf. reading, lecture.
lía, _lĕ'ä_, sf. thin bass-rope.
liar, _lēăr'_, v. a. to tie, to bind, to fagot.
libación, _lĭbāthĭŏn'_, sf. libation.
libelo, _lĭbĕ'lŏ_, sm. petition; written charge against a prisoner; lampoon, libel.
liberal, _lĭbĕrăl'_, a. liberal, generous.
liberalidad, _—lĭdäd'_, sf. liberality, generosity. {independence; freeness.
libertad, _lĭbĕrtäd'_, sf. liberty, freedom;
libertador, ra, _—tädŏr'_, sm. & f. deliverer, liberator.
libertar, _—tär'_, v. a. to free, to set at liberty; to exempt, to clear from an obligation or debt. {licentiousness.
libertinaje, _—tĭnä'hĕ_, sm. libertinism,
libertino, na, _—tĕ'nŏ_, sm. & f. dissolute, licentious, lewd.
liberto, _lĭbĕr'tŏ_, sm. freed man.
libítum, _lĕ'bĭtŭm_, (ad —,) ad. at will.
libra, _lĕ'brä_, sf. pound; — carnicera, flesh-pound of thirty-six ounces; — esterlina, a pound sterling.
Libra, —, sf. Libra, Balance (sign of the zodiac).
librar, _lĭbrăr'_, v. a. to free, to deliver; to give an order for paying a certain sum; to dispatch, to expedite; — bien ó mal, to get over a thing well or ill; —se, to escape.
libre, _lĕ'brĕ_, a. free; exempt; innocent.
librea, _lĭbrĕ'ä_, sf. livery.
librejo, _lĭbrĕ'hŏ_, sm. little book, pamphlet.
libremente, _lĭbrĕmĕn'tĕ_, ad. freely; boldly; audaciously, impudently.
librería, _—rĕ'ä_, sf. book-seller's shop; library; — de alquiler, circulating-library. {tero, stationer.
librero, _lĭbrĕ'rŏ_, sm. book-seller; — pape-
libreta, _lĭbrĕ'tä_, sf. loaf of bread which weighs sixteen ounces; small memorandum-book. {memorandum-book.
libro, _lĕ'brŏ_, sm. book; — de memoria,
licencia, _lĭthĕn'thĭä_, sf. permission, license; licentiousness.
licenciado, _—thĭä'dŏ_, sm. licentiate.
licenciamiento, _—thĭämĭĕn'tŏ_, sm. taking of the degree of licentiate.
licenciar, _—thĭär'_, v. a. to permit, to allow; to license. {dissolute.
licencioso, sa, _—thĭŏ'sŏ_, a. licentious,
liceo, _lĭthĕ'ŏ_, sm. lyceum. {licitly.
lícitamente, _lĕ'thĭtämĕntĕ_, ad. lawfully,
lícito, ta, _lĕ'thĭtŏ_, a. lawful, licit.
licor, _lĭkŏr'_, sm. liquor.
lid, _lĭd_, sm. contest, fight; dispute.
lidiador, _lĭdĭädŏr'_, sm. combatant.
liebre, _lĭĕ'brĕ_, sf. hare.
liendre, _lĭĕn'drĕ_, sf. louse, nit.
lienzo, _lĭĕn'thŏ_, sf. linen; face or front of a building. {coalition; alloy.
liga, _lĕ'gä_, sf. garter; bird-lime; league;

ligadura, _lĭgädŏ'rä_, sf. ligature, binding.
ligar, _lĭgăr'_, v. a. to tie, to bind, to fasten; to allay; to confederate; —se, to league; to be allied; to bind oneself to the performance of a contract.
ligazón, _—thŏn'_, sf. union, connection.
ligereza, _lĭ'hĕrĕ'thä_, sf. lightness; levity.
ligero, ra, _lĭ'hĕ'rŏ_, a. light, swift, easy.
lija, _lĕ'hä_, sf. angel-fish; fish-skin.
lijar, _lĭhăr'_, v. a. to smooth, to polish.
lila, _lĕ'lä_, sf. lilac-tree; lilac-flower; came-
lima, _lĕ'mä_, sf. file. {lot of Lisle.
limadura, _lĭmädŏ'rä_, sf. filing.
limar, _lĭmăr'_, v. a. to file; to polish.
limbo, _lĭm'bŏ_, sm. limbo (a region assigned to the departed souls of children).
limitación, _lĭmĭtäthĭŏn'_, sf. limitation, restriction.
limitado, da, _—tä'dŏ_, a. limited.
limitar, _—tär'_, v. a. to limit; to restrain.
límite, _lĕ'mĭtĕ_, sm. limit, boundary.
limítrofe, _lĭmĕ'trŏfĕ_, a. limiting, border-
limo, _lĕ'mŏ_, sm. slime, mud. {ing.
limón, _lĭmŏn'_, sm. lemon.
limonada, _lĭmŏnä'dä_, sf. lemonade.
limonar, _—năr'_, sm. plantation of lime-trees.
limosna, _lĭmŏ'snä_, sf. alms, charity.
limosnero, _lĭmŏsnĕ'rŏ_, sm. almoner; —, ra, a. charitable. {pick.
limpiadientes, _lĭmpĭädĭĕn'tĕs_, sm. tooth-
limpiador, _—dŏr'_, sm. cleanser, scourer.
limpiar, _lĭmpĭăr'_, v. a. to scour, to cleanse, to clear, to purify.
limpieza, _lĭmpĭĕ'thä_, sf. cleanliness, neatness; chastity; integrity; purity of blood.
limpio, pia, _lĭm'pĭŏ_, a. clean; limpid, neat; pure.
limpión, _lĭmpĭŏn'_, sm. cleansing, cleaning.
linaje, _lĭnä'hĕ_, sm. lineage, race, descent.
linar, _lĭnăr'_, sm. flax-field.
linaza, _lĭnä'thä_, sf. linseed.
lince, _lĭn'thĕ_, sm. lynx.
lindar, _lĭndăr'_, v. n. to be contiguous.
linde, _lĭn'dĕ_, sm. landmark, boundary.
lindero, _lĭndĕ'rŏ_, sm. landmark, boundary.
lindeza, _lĭndĕ'thä_, sf. neatness, elegance.
lindo, da, _lĕn'dŏ_, a. neat, handsome, pretty.
línea, _lĕ'nĕä_, sf. line; boundary, limit.
lineal, _lĭnĕăl'_, a. lineal.
linear, _lĭnĕăr'_, v. a. to draw lines.
linfa, _lĭn'fä_, sf. lymph.
linfático, ca, _lĭnfä'tĭkŏ_, a. lymphatic.
lino, _lĕ'nŏ_, sm. flax.
linterna, _lĭntĕr'nä_, sf. lantern.
lío, _lĕ'ŏ_, sm. bundle, parcel.
liquidación, _lĭkĭdäthĭŏn'_, sf. liquidation.
liquidar, _lĭkĭdăr'_, v. a. to liquefy, to melt; to clear accounts.
líquido, da, _lĕ'kĭdŏ_, a. liquid.
lira, _lĕ'rä_, sf. lyre.
lirio, _lĕ'rĭŏ_, sm. (bot.) iris.
lis, _lĭs_, sf. fleur-de-lis.
lisiar, _lĭsĭăr'_, v. a. to lame; to hurt a limb.
liso, sa, _lĕ'sŏ_, a. plain, even, flat, smooth.
lisonja, _lĭsŏn'hä_, sf. adulation, flattery.

lisonjear, -heár', v. a. to flatter.
lisonjero, -hé'ró, sm. mean flatterer; —, ra, a. fawning; flattering; pleasing.
lista, lís'tä, sf. slip of paper, shred of linen; list, catalogue; — grande, list of drawers in a lottery; en —, en — de correos, "Post-office," "to be kept till called for" (address for letters where the private address is unknown).
listo, ta, lís'tö, a. ready, prompt, active.
listón, lïstón', sm. large shred; ferret (narrow silk riband). [candour.
lisura, lïsö'rä, sf. smoothness; sincerity,
litera, lïtē'rä, sf. litter.
literal, lïtērä'l, a. literal.
literario, ria, lïtērä'rïö, a. literary.
literato, ta, lïtērä'tö, a. learned, lettered; —, sm. literary man; —s, pl. literati, the learned.
literatura, lïtērätö'rä, sf. literature.
litigante, lïtïgän'tē, sm. litigant.
litigar, —gär', v. a. to litigate, to carry on
litigio, lïtï'h'ïö, sm. law-suit. [a cause.
litigioso, sa, lïtïhïö'sö, a. litigious.
litografía, lïtögräfï'ä, sf. lithography.
litográfico, ca, —gräf'ïkö, a. lithographic.
litografiar, —grïär', v. a. to lithograph.
litógrafo, lïtö'gräfö, sm. lithographer.
litoral, lïtörä'l, a. littoral.
litro, lï'trö, sm. litre (measure).
liturgia, lïtör'hïä, sf. liturgy.
litúrgico, ca, lïtör'hïkö, a. liturgical.
liviandad, lïvïändä'd, sf. lightness; levity, imprudence; incontinence.
liviano, na, lïvïä'nö, a. light; imprudent; unchaste; —s, sm. pl. lungs.
lívido, da, lï'vïdö, a. livid.
lo, lö, pn. it, a. neut. the.
loable, löä'blē, a. laudable.
loar, löär', v. a. to praise; to approve.
loba, lö'bä, sf. she-wolf.
lobanillo, löbänïl'yö, sm. wen, chafe.
lobato, löbä'tö, sm. young wolf.
lobo, lö'bö, sm. wolf. [sad.
lóbrego, ga, lö'brēgö, a. murky, obscure,
lobreguez, löbrēgēth', sf. obscurity, darkness.
lobuno, na, löbö'nö, a. wolfish.
local, lökä'l, a. local.
localidad, lökälïdä'd, sf. locality.
localizar, —thär', v. a. to localize.
loco, ca, lö'kö, a. mad, crack-brained.
locuacidad, lökäthïdä'd, sf. loquacity.
locuaz, lökäth', a. loquacious, garrulous.
locución, lökäthïón', sf. locution.
locura, lökö'rä, sf. madness, frenzy, folly; absurdity.
locutorio, lökätö'rïö, sm. parlour.
lodazal, lödäthä'l, sm. muddy place.
lodo, lö'dö, sm. mud, mire.
lodoso, sa, lödö'sö, a. muddy, miry; lutulent; luxurious.
logaritmo, lögärït'mö, sm. logarithm.
lógica, lö'hïkä, sf. logic. [logician.
lógico, ca, lö'hïkö, a. logical; —, sm.
lograr, lögrär', v. a. to gain, to obtain.
logrear, lögrēär', v. n. to lend on interest.
logrero, lögrä'rö, sm. usurer.

logro, lö'grö, sm. gain, benefit; interest; usury.
loma, lö'mä, sf. hillock.
lombarda, lömbär'dä, sf. red cabbage.
lombriz, lömbrïth', sf. dew-worm.
lomillo, lömïl'yö, sm. small loin; cross-stitch (needle-work).
lomo, lö'mö, sm. loin; back of a book; double of any cloth; ridge between two furrows; llevar ó traer —, to carry on the back.
lona, lö'nä, sf. canvas.
lóndiga, lön'dïgä, sf. lark.
longanimidad, löngänïmïdä'd, sf. long-sufferance, patience. [(best kind).
longaniza, —nï'thä, sf. German sausage
longitud, lönhïtö'd, sf. length; longitude.
lonja, lön'hä, sf. exchange; grocer's shop; warehouse; slice of ham.
lonjista, lönhïs'tä, sm. grocer who sells cocoa-nuts, spices, &c.
loor, löör', sf. (poet.) praise.
loquear, lökäär', v. n. to play the fool; to rejoice, to revel. [house.
loquero, lökä'rö, sm. keeper of a mad-house.
loro, lö'rö, sm. parrot.
lorri, lör'rï, sm. (rail.) lowry.
losa, lö'sä, sf. flag-stone.
lote, lö'tē, sm. lot.
lotería, lötērï'ä, sf. lottery.
loza, lö'thä, sf. delft, crockery.
lozanear, löthänäär', v. n. to act and speak in a pompous, ostentatious fashion.
lozanía, —nï'ä, sf. verdure, exuberant growth of plants; vigour; vivacity.
lozano, na, löthä'nö, a. luxuriant; sprightly.
lucero, löthä'rö, sm. morning-star, day-star.
lúcido, da, lö'thïdö, a. shining, magnificent; splendid.
luciérnaga, löthïär'nägä, sf. glow-worm.
lucimiento, löthïmïēn'tö, sm. splendour, lustre, applause; brightness.
lucio, cia, lö'thïö, a. lucid, bright.
lucir, löthïr', v. n., —se, to shine, to be brilliant; to dress to advantage; to out-shine.
lucrativo, ya, lökrätï'vä, a. lucrative.
lucro, lö'krö, sm. gain, profit, lucre.
lucha, löch'ä, sf. struggle, strife.
luchador, löchädör', sm. wrestler.
luchar, löchär', v. a. to wrestle, to struggle.
ludibrio, lüdïbrïö, sm. mockery, derision.
luego, löë'gö, ad. presently, immediately; soon afterwards.
lugar, lögär', sm. place, spot; village; employment, office; dignity; cause; motive; en — de, instead of, in lieu of.
lugareño, ña, lögärēn'yö, a. & sm. & f. belonging to a village; inhabitant of a village. [tenant.
lugarteniente, lögärtēnïēn'tē, sm. lieu-tenant.
lúgubre, lö'göbrē, a. sad, gloomy; lugubrious, dismal. [dresses, fare.
lujo, lä'h'ö, sm. profuseness in pomp,
lujoso, sa, lä'hö'sö, a. showy, profuse, lavish, sumptuous.
lujuria, lähö'rïä, sf. lewdness; luxury.
lujurioso, sa, —rïö'sö, a. luxurious, voluptuous, lewd.

lumbre, *lŭm'brĕ,* sf. fire; spark. [light.
lumbrera, *lŭmbrā'rā,* sf. luminary; sky-
luminaria, *lŭmīnā'rīä,* sf. illumination;
perpetual lamp in catholic churches.
luminoso, sa, *-nŏ'sŏ,* a. luminous, lucid.
luna, *lŏ'nä,* sf. moon; glass plate for mir-
rors. [-, a. lunar.
lunar, *lŭnär',* sm. mole; stain of infamy;
lunático, ca, *lŭnä'ťkŏ,* a. lunatic, moon-
lunes, *lŏ'nĕs,* sm. Monday. [struck.
luneta, *lŭnä'tä,* sf. stall (in a play-house);
eye-glass.
lupanar, *lŭpänär',* sm. brothel.
lupia, *lŏ'pīä,* sf. encysted tumour.
lustre, *lŭs'trĕ,* sm. gloss, lustre; splendour.
lustro, *lŭs'trŏ,* sm. lustrum (space of five
years).
lustroso, sa, *lŭstrŏ'sŏ,* a. bright, brilliant.
luteranismo, *lŭtĕränĭs'mŏ,* sm. Luther-
anism.
luterano, na, *-rä'nŏ,* sm. & f. Lutheran.
luto, *lŏ'tŏ,* sm. mourning (dress).
luz, *lŭth',* sf. light; candle; day; notice,
information, hint; **luces,** pl., windows;
lanterns; knowledge, science.

Ll.

llaga, *lyä'gä,* sf. wound, sore.
llagar, *lyägär',* v. a. to wound, to hurt.
llama, *lyä'mä,* sf. flame; lama (animal).
llamada, *lyämä'dä,* sf. call; (mil.) beat
of the drum to summon troops; (mil.)
chamade.
llamador, *lyämädŏr',* sm. door-knocker.
llamamiento, *-mĭĕn'tŏ,* sm. calling; convocation.
llamar, *lyämär',* v. a. to call; to summon,
to cite; to invoke; to knock at the door.
llamarada, *-rä'dä,* sf. sudden blaze of
fire; sudden burst of merriment.
llana, *lyä'nä,* sf. trowel; page (of a book, &c.).
llanada, *-nä'dä,* sf. wide tract of level
ground; plain.
llano, na, *lyä'nä,* a. plain, even, level,
smooth; meek, affable; plain, clear, evident; unmannerly; -, sm. level field.
llanto, *lyän'tŏ,* sm. flood of tears, cry.
llanura, *lyänŏ'rä,* sf. evenness, level;
vast tract of level ground.
llares, *lyä'rĕs,* sm. pl. pot-hanger. [key.
llave, *lyä'vĕ,* sf. key; =maestra, master-
llavero, *lyävä'rŏ,* sm. keeper of the keys
of a place; key-ring; bunch of keys.
llegada, *lyĕgä'dä,* sf. arrival, coming.
llegar, *lyĕgär',* v. a. to arrive, to reach;
-se, to proceed to some neighbouring
place; to unite.
llena, *lyä'nä,* sf. alluvion, overflow.
llenar, *lyĕnär',* v. a. to fill, to stuff, to
gorge; to overwhelm (with compliments,
kindness, &c.). -se, to feed gluttonously
to lose patience.
lleno, na, *lyä'nŏ,* a. full, replete; complete; **de -,** entirely, fully.

llevadero, ra, *lyĕvädä'rŏ,* a. tolerable.
llevar, *lyĕvär',* v. a. to carry, to convey,
to transport; to bear; to introduce.
lloraduelos, *lyŏrädŭĕ'lŏs,* sm. weeper.
llorar, *lyŏrär',* v. a. & n. to weep, to cry;
to bewail.
lloriquear, *lyŏrīkĕär',* v. n. to whine.
lloro, *lyŏ'rŏ,* sm. weeping, crying.
llorón, *lyŏrŏn',* sm. weeper. [tears.
lloroso, sa, *lyŏrŏ'sŏ,* a. mournful, full of
llovediza (agua -), *lyŏvĕdī'thä,* sf. rain-
llover, *lyŏvĕr',* v. imp. to rain. [water.
lloviznar, *lyŏvīthnär',* v. imp. to drizzle.
lluvia, *lyŏ'vĭä,* sf. rain.
lluvioso, sa, *lyŭvĭŏ'sŏ,* a. rainy.

M.

macareno, na, *mäkärä'nŏ,* a. bragging,
boasting. [roni.
macarrones, *mäkärrŏ'nĕs,* sm. pl. maca-
macarse, *mäkär'sĕ,* v. r. to rot (of fruit).
macear, *mäthĕär',* v. a. to pound with a
mallet; to knock. [soften.
macerar, *mäthĕrär',* v. a. to macerate, to
macero, *mäthä'rŏ,* sm. mace-bearer.
maceta, *mäthä'tä,* sf. flower-pot.
macilento, ta, *mäthĭlĕn'tŏ,* a. lean, extenuated; withered.
macizo, za, *mäthĕ'thŏ,* a. massive, solid.
machaca, *mätshä'kä,* sm. & f. ignorant,
tiresome person.
machacar, *mätshäkär',* v. a. to pound, to
crush; -, v. n. to importune, to molest.
machacón, ona, *-kŏn',* a. heavy, importunate, tedious. [stupidity.
machada, *mätshä'dä,* sf. flock of he-goats;
machete, *mätshä'tĕ,* sm. cutlass.
macho, *mätsh'ŏ,* sm. male animal; he-
mule; he-goat; pillar; hook to catch hold
in an eye; -, a. masculine, male; vigorous.
machón, *mätshŏn',* sm. buttress.
machorra, *mätshŏr'rä,* sf. barren woman.
machucadura, *mätshäkädŏ'rä,* sf. pounding, bruising.
machucar, *-kär',* v. a. to pound, to bruise.
machucho, cha, *mätshätsh'ŏ,* a. mature,
ripe; judicious.
madama, *mädä'mä,* sf. madam.
madeja, *mädĕ'hä,* sf. skein of thread;
lock of hair.
madera, *mädä'rä,* sf. timber, wood.
maderería, *-rĕrĭ'ä,* sf. timber-yard.
madero, *mädä'rŏ,* sm. beam of timber.
madrastra, *mädräs'trä,* sf. step-mother.
madraza, *mädrä'thä,* sf. very fond mother.
madre, *mä'drĕ,* sf. mother; womb, matrix;
bed of a river.
madreperla, *-pĕr'lä,* sf. mother of pearl.
madreselva, *-sĕl'vä,* sf. honey-suckle.
madrigal, *mädrīgäl',* sm. madrigal.
madriguera, *-gä'rä,* sf. burrow; den,
lurking-place.
madrina, *mädrē'nä,* sf. godmother.
madrona, *mädrŏ'nä,* sf. mother who spoils
her children by over-indulgence.

madroño, *mädrön'yŏ,* sm. strawberry, strawberry-plant. [at break of day.

madrugada, *mädrügä'dä,* sf. dawn; de –, [to anticipate, to be beforehand.

madrugador, ra, *–gädŏr',* sm. & f. early riser.

madrugar, *–gär',* v. n. to get up early; to ripen, to grow ripe; to arrive at maturity.

madurar, *mädürär',* v. a. to ripen; –, v. n. [wisdom.

madurativo, va, *mädürätē'vŏ,* a. maturative, ripening.

madurez, *–rĕth',* sf. maturity; prudence; prudent, judicious.

maduro, ra, *mädō'rŏ,* a. ripe, mature;

maestra, *mäës'trä,* sf. mistress; school-mistress; master's wife.

maestrante, *mäësträn'tĕ,* sm. academician.

maestranza, *–trän'thä,* sf. equestrian club; dock-yard; ship-building.

maestrazgo, *–träth'gŏ,* sm. grand-mastership of a military order.

maestre, *mäës'trĕ,* sm. grand-master of a military order; ship-master.

maestresala, *–sä'lä,* sm. chief waiter at a nobleman's table in Spain.

maestría, *mäëstrē'ä,* sf. mastership.

maestro, *mäës'trŏ,* sm. master; –, tra, a. masterly, principal.

magia, *mä'hïä,* sf. magic. [magician.

mágico, ca, *–hïkŏ,* a. magical; –, sm.

magisterio, *mä'hïstä'rïŏ,* sm. mastery; mastership. [magistracy.

magistrado, *–trä'dŏ,* sm. magistrate;

magistral, *–träl',* a. magisterial; –, sm. person who enjoys a prebend.

magistratura, *–trätō'rä,* sf. magistracy.

magnanimidad, *mägnänïmïdä',* sf. magnanimity. [nimous.

magnánimo, ma, *mägnä'nïmŏ,* a. magna-

magnate, *–tĕ,* sm. magnate.

magnesia, *mägnä'sïä,* sf. magnesia.

magnético, ca, *–tïkŏ,* a. magnetic.

magnetismo, *–tïs'mŏ,* sm. magnetism.

magnetizar, *–tïthär',* v. a. to magnetize.

magnificat, *mägnï'fïkät,* sf. the Magnificat.

magnificencia, *–fïthën'thïä,* sf. magnificence, splendour.

magnífico, ca, *mägnï'fïkŏ,* a. magnificent, splendid. [greatness, grandeur.

magnitud, *mägnïtōd',* sf. magnitude;

magno, na, *mäg'nŏ,* a. great.

mago, ga, *mä'gŏ,* sm. & f. magician.

magra, *mä'grä,* sf. rasher, slice of pork.

magro, gra, *–grŏ,* a. meagre.

magulladura, *mägülyädō'rä,* sf. bruise, contusion.

magullar, *–yär',* v. a. to bruise, to contuse.

mahometano, *mäömätä'nŏ,* s. & a. Mohammedan. [medanism.

mahometanismo, *–nïs'mŏ,* sm. Moham-

mahón, *mäön',* sm. nankeen.

maitines, *mäïtē'nĕs,* sm. pl. matins.

maíz, *mäïth',* sm. maize, Indian corn.

maizal, *–thäl',* sm. field sown with Indian corn. [corn.

majada, *mä'hä'dä,* sf. sheep-fold.

majaderia, *–dĕrē'ä,* sf. absurd speech; insult. [blockish; sm. gawk.

majadero, ra, *–dä'rŏ,* a. dull, silly,

majadura, *–dō'rä,* sf. pounding, bruising.

majar, *mä'här',* v. a. to pound.

majestad, *mä'hĕstäd',* sf. majesty.

majestuoso, *mä'hĕstüō'sŏ,* a. majestic(al).

majo, *mä'h'ŏ,* sm. boaster; gallant.

majuela, *mä'hüä'lä,* sf. fruit of the white hawthorn. [thorn.

majuelo, *–lŏ,* sm. vine newly planted; haw-

mal, *mäl,* sm. evil, hurt, injury; illness; –, a. (used only before masculine substantives) bad; –, malamente, ad. badly.

mala, *mä'lä,* sf. mail.

malandrín, *mäländrēn',* sm. highwayman; –, a. malign. [some.

malavenido, da, *–ävĕnē'dŏ,* a. quarrel-

malaventura, *–ävĕntō'rä,* sf. calamity, misfortune. [fortunate.

malaventurado, da, *–ävĕntürä'dŏ,* a. un-

malbaratador, ra, *–bärätädŏr',* sm. spend-thrift, lavisher.

malcontento, *–kŏntĕn'tŏ,* sm. game at cards; –, ta, a. discontented, malcontent.

malcriado, da, *–krïä'dŏ,* a. ill-bred, ill-behaved, unmannerly; naughty.

maldad, *mäldäd',* sf. wickedness.

maldición, *–dïthïōn',* sf. malediction, cursing. [damned, cursed.

maldito, ta, *mäl'dï'tŏ,* a. perverse, wicked

malear, *mälĕär',* v. a. to prevent, to corrupt. [calumny.

maledicencia, *mälĕdïthĕn'thïä,* sf. slander,

maleficiar, *–fïthïär',* v. a. to adulterate, to corrupt; to bewitch.

maleficio, *–fï'thïŏ,* sm. witchcraft, enchantment. [maleficent.

maléfico, ca, *mälĕ'fïkŏ,* a. mischievous,

maleta, *mälĕ'tä,* sf. portmanteau.

malevolencia, *–vŏlĕn'thïä,* sf. malevolence.

malévolo, la, *mälĕ'vŏlŏ,* a. malevolent.

maleza, *mälĕ'thä,* sf. wickedness, malice; brambles, briers, pl. [lavish.

malgastar, *–gästär',* v. a. to waste, to

malhablado, a, *–äblä'dŏ,* a. foul-mouthed.

malhecho, –ĕch'ŏ, sm. flagitious action, wrong. [factor.

malhechor, ra, *–ĕchŏr',* sm. & f. male-

malhumorado, da, *–ümŏrä'dŏ,* a. ill-humoured, peevish.

malicia, *mälē'thïä,* sf. malice, perversity; suspicion; cunning, artifice.

maliciar, *–thïär',* v. a. to corrupt, to adulterate; –, v. n. to suspect maliciously.

malicioso, sa, *–thïō'sŏ,* a. malicious, wicked, malign. [malice.

malignidad, *mälïgnïdä',* sf. malignity.

maligno, na, *mälïg'nŏ,* a. malignant, malicious. [cards like whist).

malilla, *mälïl'yä,* sf. manilla (game at

malmandado, da, *–mändä'dŏ,* a. disobedient. [1–lo so much the worse!

malo, la, *mä'lŏ,* a. bad, ill, wicked; sickly;

malograr, *mälŏgrär',* v. a. to disappoint; –se, to fail of success. [miscarriage.

malogro, *mälŏ'grŏ,* sm. disappointment,

malparado, da, *–pärä'dä,* a. ill conditioned, hurt. [had a miscarriage.

malparida, *–pärē'dä,* sf. woman who has

malparir, –*parir'*, v. n. to miscarry.
malparto, –*par'to*, sm. abortion.
malquistar, –*kistar'*, v. a. to excite quarrels.
malquisto, ta, –*kis'to*, a. hated, detested.
malrotar, –*rotar'*, v. a. to misspend, to lavish. [some.
malsano, na, –*sā'no*, a. sickly; unwhole-
maltratamiento, –*tratămien'to*, sm. ill treatment. [abuse, to maltreat.
maltratar, –*tratar'*, v. a. to treat ill, to
malva, *mäl'vä*, sf. (bot.) mallows.
malvabisco, –*bis'ko*, sm. marsh-mallows.
malvado, da, –*vä'do*, a. wicked, very perverse.
malvasía, –*väsĕ'ä*, sf. malmsey (wine).
malversación, –*versäthion'*, sf. malversa-tion. [son who misapplies property.
malversador, ra, –*versädor'*, sm. & f. per-
malversar, –*versär'*, v. a. to misapply.
malvís, *mälvis'*, sm. red-wing (pájaro).
malla, *mäl'yä*, sf. mesh, mash; coat of mail.
mallo, *mäl'yo*, sm. mall; mallet.
mama, *mämä'*, sf. mamma.
mamadera, –*dä'rä*, sf. breast-pump.
mamaluco, –*lū'ko*, sm. dolt, simpleton.
mamar, *mämär'*, v. a. to suck; to cram.
mamarrachada, –*rätshä'dä*, sf. collection of rude or ridiculous pictures; foolish ac-tion or speech.
mamarrachista, –*rätshis'tä*, sm. dauber.
mamarracho, –*rätsh'o*, sm. daub; gro-tesque ornament.
mameluco, *mämĕlū'ko*, sm. Mameluke.
mamola, *mämo'lä*, sf. chuck under the chin.
mamón, ona, *mämon'*, sm. & f. sucking animal; child who is suckled for a long time. [book.
mamotreto, –*trä'to*, sm. memorandum-
mampara, *mämpä'rä*, sf. screen.
mampostería, –*posterĕ'ä*, sf. rubble-work.
maná, *mänä'*, sm. manna.
manada, *mänä'dä*, sf. flock, drove of cattle; crowd, multitude. [origin.
manantial, *mänäntiäl'*, sm. source, spring;
manar, *mänär'*, v. n. to spring from; to distil from; to issue; to abound.
manceba, –*thä'bä*, sf. concubine.
mancebo, –*thä'bo*, sm. youth; companion.
mancilla, –*thil'yä*, sf. spot, blemish.
manco, ca, *män'ko*, a. handless; one-handed; maimed, faulty.
mancomún, –*kōmūn'*, de –, ad. jointly, by common consent.
mancomunar, –*kōmūnär'*, v. a. to associate, to unite; to make two or more persons pay jointly the costs of a law-suit; –se, to act together, to join in the execution of a thing. [fellowship.
mancomunidad, –*kōmūnĕdäd'*, sf. union,
mancha, *män'tshä*, sf. stain, spot.
manchado, da, –*tshä'do*, a. spotted.
manchar, –*tshär'*, v. a. to stain, to soil.
manda, *män'dä*, sf. offer, proposal; legacy.
mandado, da, –*dä'do*, sm. mandate; com-mand; errand, message.
mandamiento, –*mien'to*, sm. mandate; commandment.

mandar, *mändär'*, v. a. to command, to order; to offer; to bequeath; to send.
mandarín, *mändärin'*, sm. mandarin.
mandatario, –*tä'rio*, a. mandatory.
mandato, –*dä'to*, sm. mandate; order; ec-clesiastical ceremony of washing twelve persons' feet on Maundy Thursday.
mandíbula, *mändĭ'bülä*, sf. jaw-bone.
mandil, *mändil'*, sm. coarse apron.
mando, *män'do*, sm. command, authority, power; mandamus.
mandón, ona, –*don'*, a. imperious, domi-neering–, sm. imperious, haughty person.
manecilla, *mänĕthil'yä*, sf. small hand; book-clasp.
manejable, –*hä'blĕ*, a. manageable.
manejar, –*här'*, v. a. to manage; –se, to be able to move after having been de-prived of motion.
manejo, *mänĕh'o*, sm. managery, adminis tration; horsemanship, manège.
manera, *mänĕ'rä*, sf. manner, mode; kind.
manes, *mä'nes*, sm. pl. manes, pl. (souls of the dead).
manga, *män'gä*, sf. sleeve; hurricane; cloak-bag; straining-bag; body of troops in a line.
mango, *män'go*, sm. handle, haft.
mangonear, –*gönĕär'*, v. n. to rove idly.
mangote, *mängo'tĕ*, sm. wide sleeve.
manguito, *mängĕ'to*, sm. muff.
manía, *mänĕ'ä*, sf. frenzy, madness.
maniatar, *mäniätär'*, v. a. to manacle, to hand-cuff. [frantic.
maniático, ca, –*ä'tĭko*, a. maniac, mad,
manifactura, –*fäktö'rä*, sf. manufacture.
manifestación, –*festäthion'*, sf. manifes-tation. [declare.
manifestar, –*festär'*, v. a. to manifest, to
manifiesto, ta, –*fĭes'to*, a. manifest, open, clear; –, sm. act of exposing the Holy Sacrament to the public adoration; mani-festo. [manacle.
manilla, *mänil'yä*, sf. bracelet; hand-cuff.
maniobra, –*ö'brä*, sf. handiwork; hand-ling; cleverness in handling; (mil.) man-œuvre.
maniobrar, –*öbrär'*, v. a. to work with the hands; to work a ship; (mil.) to manœuvre troops; to intrigue.
maniota, –*ö'tä*, sf. shackles, hand-cuffs, pl.
manipulación, –*püläthion'*, sf. manipula-tion. [late
manipular, –*pülär'*, v.a.(fam.) to manipu-
manípulo, *mäni'pölo*, sm. maniple.
maniqueísmo, –*kĕis'mo*, sm. Manicheism.
maniqueo, a, *mänĭkĕ'o*, a. Manichean.
maniquí, *mänĭkĕ'*, sm. mannikin.
manir, *mänir'*, v. a. to keep meat until it grows tender. [liberal.
mapirrote, ta, –*rö'to*, a. wasteful, too
manjar, *mänhär'*, sm. food, victuals.
mano, *mä'no*, sf. hand; hand of a clock or watch; first hand at play; á –, at hand; with the hand; á –s llenas, liberally, abundantly; – á –, in company, familiarly.
manojo, *mäno'k'o*, sm. bundle of herbs, &c.

manopla, *mănŏ′plă*, sf. gauntlet; coach-man's whip.

manos ar, *mănŏsār′*, v. a. to handle.

manoseo, *sā′ŏ*, sm. handling.

manotada, *tă′dă*, sf. blow with the hand.

manoteo, *tā′ŏ*, sm. manual gesticulation.

mansedumbre, *mănsĕdŭm′brĕ*, sf. meekness, gentleness. [abode, home.

mansión, *mănsĭŏn′*, sf. sojourn, residence;

manso, sa, *măn′sŏ*, a. tame; gentle, soft; —, sm. leading male in a flock of goats, sheep or black-cattle. [drubbing.

manta, *măn′tă*, sf. blanket; thrashing,

manteamiento, *mănteămĭen′tŏ*, sm. tossing in a blanket.

mantear, *teār′*, v. a. to toss in a blanket.

manteca, *tĕ′kă*, sf. pomatum; butter.

mantecada, *tĕkă′dă*, sf. toast.

mantecado, *tĕkă′dŏ*, sm. butter-cake.

mantecoso, sa, *tĕkŏ′sŏ*, a. buttery.

mantel, *măntĕl′*, sm. table-cloth.

mantelería, *lĕrĕ′ă*, sf. table-linen.

manteleta, *lā′tă*, sf. mantelet.

mantellina, *măntĕllĕ′nă*, sf. woman's mantle.

mantener, *tĕnēr′*, v. a. to maintain, to support; to nourish; —se, to support oneself. [tenance; subsistence.

mantenimiento, *tĕnĭmĭen′tŏ*, sm. maintenance.

manteo, *măntā′ŏ*, sm. long cloak worn by priests and students.

mantequera, *măntĕkā′ră*, sf. churn.

mantequero, *rŏ*, sm. butter-man.

mantequilla, *măntĕkĭl′yă*, sf. butter-cake.

mantilla, *măntĭl′yă*, sf. head-covering for women; cloak; mantle of state; housing, horsecloth; —s, pl. swaddling-clothes.

manto, *măn′tŏ*, sm. mantle; cloak, robe.

mantón, *măntŏn′*, sm. large veil. [able.

manuable, *mănŭă′blĕ*, a. tractable, manageable.

manual, *mănŭăl′*, a. manual, handy; easily performed with the hand; —, sm. manual.

manufactura, *făktŏ′ră*, sf. manufacture.

manufacturar, *făktŏrār′*, v. a. to manufacture. [slavery.

manumitir, *mĭtĭr′*, v. a. to release from

manuscrito, *skrĭ′tŏ*, sm. manuscript; —, a. written. [maintenance.

manutención, *tĕnthĭŏn′*, sf. maintaining;

manzana, *mănthă′nă*, sf. apple.

manzanal, *thănăl′*, manzanar, *thă′năr*, sm. orchard. [chamomile.

manzanilla, *mănthănĭl′yă*, sf. common daisy; periwinkle.

manzano, *mănthă′nŏ*, sm. apple-tree.

maña, *măn′yă*, sf. handiness, dexterity, cleverness, cunning, artifice; evil habit or custom. [—, ad. to-morrow.

mañana, *yă′nă*, sf. morning, morrow;

mañoso, sa, *yŏ′sŏ*, a. skilful, handy;

mapa, *mă′pă*, sm. map. [cunning.

mapamundi, *măn′dĭ*, sf. map of the world.

maquilar, *mĭkĭlăr′*, v. a. to measure and take the miller's dues for grinding corn; to retrench, to clip.

máquina, *mă′kĭnă*, sf. machine. [tion.

maquinación, *măkĭnăthĭŏn′*, sf. machina-

maquinador, ra, *măkĭnădŏr′*, sm. & f. schemer, machinator. [nically.

maquinalmente, *—nălmĕn′tĕ*, ad. mecha-

maquinar, *—năr′*, v. a. to machinate; to conspire.

maquinaria, *mă′rĭă*, sf. mechanics.

maquinista, *—nĭs′tă*, sm. machinist, mechanician. [chanician.

mar, *măr*, sm. & f. sea.

maraña, *mărăn′yă*, sf. shrub, thicket; perplexity, puzzle; knot of a play [mus.

marasmo, *mărăs′mŏ*, sm. (med.) marasmus.

maravedí, *mărăvĕdĭ′*, sm. maravedi (smallest Spanish coin).

maravilla, *—vĭl′yă*, sf. wonder; & las —s, uncommonly well; exquisitely; á—, marvellously.

maravillar, *—vĭlyăr′*, v. a. to admire; —se, to wonder, to be astonished.

maravilloso, sa, *—vĭlyŏ′sŏ*, a. wonderful, marvellous.

marca, *măr′kă*, sf. frontier province; due measure or weight of anything; mark.

marcador, *—dŏr′*, sm. marker, assay-master.

marcar, *mărkăr′*, v. a. to mark; to observe, to note, to designate.

marcial, *mărthăl′*, a. martial, warlike.

marcialidad, *—lĭdăd′*, sf. freedom, assumed familiarity.

marco, *măr′kŏ*, sm. door-case, windowcase; picture-frame; mark (weight of eight ounces); branding-iron; measure of ground which may be sown with a fanega of grain.

márcola, *măr′kŏlă*, sf. pruning-hook.

marcha, *măr′tshă*, sf. march.

marchamar, *—măr′*, v. a. to put a mark on goods at the custom-house.

marchamo, *mărtshă′mŏ*, sm. mark put on goods at the custom-house. [to march.

marchar, *mărtshăr′*, v. n. to go; to go off; marchitable, *mărtshĭtă′blĕ*, a. perishable.

marchitar, *—tăr′*, v. a. to wither; to fade; to deprive of vigour.

marchito, ta, *mărchĭ′tŏ*, a. faded, withered.

marea, *mărā′ă*, sf. tide. [a ship.

mareaje, *mărĕă′h′ĕ*, sm. art of navigating

marear, *mărĕăr′*, v. a. to work a ship; to molest; —se, to be sea-sick.

marejada, *mărĕhă′dă*, sf. sea-swell, headsea, main, main-sea, surge.

mareo, *mără′ŏ*, sm. sea-sickness.

marfil, *mărfĭl′*, sm. ivory.

margarita, *mărgărĕ′tă*, sf. pearl; common daisy; periwinkle.

margen, *măr′hĕn*, sm. & f. margin; border.

marginal, *măr′hĭnăl′*, a. marginal.

marginar, *—năr′*, v. a. to make annotations on the margin.

margrave, *mărgră′vĕ*, sm. margrave.

marica, *mărĕ′kă*, sf. magpie; milksop.

maricón, *mărĭkŏn′*, sm. coward, poltroon.

maridable, *—blĕ*, a. matrimonial.

maridillo, *—dĭl′yŏ*, sm. small brazier, footbottle (for women).

marido, *măr′dŏ*, sm. husband.

marimacho, *—mătsh′ŏ*, sm. virago.

marimanta, *—măn′tă*, sf. bugbear.

marimorena, *—mŏră′nă*, sf. dispute, quarrel.

marina, *mắrĕ'nắ*, sf. navy. [sailors, pl.
marinaje, *mắrĭnắ'hĕ*, sm. seamanship;
marinar, *-nắr'*, v. a. to salt fish.
marinería, *-nĕrĕ'ă*, sf. seamanship; body
of seamen.
marinero, *-nắ'rŏ*, sm. mariner.
marinesco, ca, *-nĕs'kŏ*, a. nautical.
marino, na, *mắrĕ'nŏ*, a. marine; —, sm.
mariner, seaman. [light.
mariposa, *mắrĭpŏ'să*, sf. butterfly; rush-
mariscal, *mắrĭskắl'*, sm. marshal; farrier;
blacksmith.
marisco, *mắrĭs'kŏ*, sm. sea-shell.
marital, *mắrĭtắl'*, a. marital. [marine.
marítimo, ma, *mắrĭ'tĭmŏ*, a. maritime,
Maritornes, *-tŏr'nĕs*, sf. ill-shaped, awkward woman. [ridge-pot.
marmita, *mắrmĕ'tă*, sf. flesh-pot, por-
marmitón, *-mĭtŏn'*, sm. scullion.
mármol, *mắr'mŏl*, sm. marble.
marmolista, *-lĭs'tă*, sm. worker in marble.
marmóreo, ea, *mắrmŏ'rĕŏ*, a. marbled,
marmota, *-tă*, sf. marmot. [marble.
maroma, *mắrŏ'mă*, sf. rope.
marqués, *mắrkĕs'*, sm. marquis.
marquesa, *mắrkĕ'să*, sf. marchioness.
marquesado, *-să'dŏ*, sm. marquisate.
marrajo, *mắrrä'hŏ*, sm. white shark; —,
ja, a. sly, cunning.
marrana, *mắrră'nă*, sf. sow.
marrano, *-nŏ*, sm. pig, hog.
marras, *mắr'răs*, ad. long ago, long since.
marro, *mắr'rŏ*, sm. quoits (game); disappointment, failure.
marrón, *mắrrŏn'*, sm. quoit, pitcher.
marrullería, *mắrrŭlyĕrĕ'ă*, sf. knavery,
cunning; prank, trick.
marrullero, ra, *-yĕ'rŏ*, a. crafty, cunning.
marsellés, *mắrsĕlyĕs'*, sm. shooting-jacket.
marsopla, *mắrsŏ'plă*, sf. spermaceti-whale.
marta, *mắr'tă*, sf. marten, martern.
marte, *mắr'tĕ*, sm. iron.
martes, *mắr'tĕs*, sm. Tuesday.
martillada, *mắrtĭlyä'dă*, sf. blow with a
hammer.
martillar, *-yăr'*, v. a. to hammer.
martillo, *mắrtĭ'lyŏ*, sm. hammer.
martinete, *mắrtĭnĕ'tĕ*, sm. sand-martin;
hammer in copper-works; copper-mill.
mártir, *mắr'tĭr*, sm. & f. martyr.
martirio, *mắrtĕ'rĭŏ*, sm. martyrdom.
martirizar, *mắrtĭrĭthăr'*, v. a. to martyr.
martirologio, *-rŏlŏ'hĭŏ*, sm. martyrology.
marzo, *mắr'thŏ*, sm. March.
mas, *măs*, ad. but, yet.
más, *—s*, ad. more; besides, moreover; á —
tardar, at latest; de — á —, more and
more; sin — ni —, without more ado.
masa, *mă'să*, sf. dough, paste; mortar;
mass.
mascadura, *măskădŏ'ră*, sf. mastication.
mascar, *măskăr'*, v. a. to chew.
máscara, *măs'kără*, sm. & f. mask; masker,
masquerader; pretext.
mascarada, *măskără'dă*, sf. masquerade.
mascarilla, *-rĭ'lyă*, sf. small mask.
mascarón, *-rŏn'*, sm. carved satyr's faces
for fountains and buildings.

mascujar, *-kŭ'hăr'*, v. n. to masticate
with difficulty; to pronounce with difficulty.
masculino, *-kŭlĕ'nŏ*, a. masculine, male.
mascullar, *-kŭlyăr'*, v. a. to falter in
speaking.
masera, *măsĕ'ră*, sf. kneading-trough.
masticación, *măstĭkăthĭŏn'*, sf. mastication. [chew.
masticar, *-kăr'*, v. a. to masticate, to
mástil, *măs'tĭl*, sm. (mar.) top-mast.
mastín, *măstĭn'*, sm. mastiff. [cress.
mastuerzo, *-tŭĕr'thŏ*, sm. (bot.) common
mata, *mă'tă*, sf. shrub; sprig, blade; coppice; lock of matted hair. [guisher.
matacandelas, *mătăkăndĕ'lăs*, sf. extin-
matachín, *-tshĭn'*, sm. merry-Andrew;
dance performed by grotesque figures.
matadero, *-dă'rŏ*, sm. slaughter-house.
matador, *-dŏr'*, sm. murderer.
matadura, *-dŭ'ră*, sf. saddle-gall.
matanza, *mătăn'thă*, sf. slaughtering;
cattle to be slaughtered; massacre.
matar, *mătăr'*, v. a. to kill; to execute; to
murder; to quench, to extinguish fire; to
slack lime; to gall a horse; -se, to kill
oneself, to commit suicide.
matasanos, *mătăsä'nŏs*, sm. quack, charlatan, empiric.
matasiete, *-sĭĕ'tĕ*, sm. bully, braggadocio.
mate, *mă'tĕ*, sm. check-mate; —, a. unpolished.
matemática, *mătĕmä'tĭkă*, sf. mathematics.
matemático, ca, *-tĭkŏ*, a. mathematical;
—, sm. mathematician.
materia, *mătĕ'rĭă*, sm. matter, materials;
subject; matter (pus).
material, *mătĕrĭăl'*, a. material, corporal;
rude; uncouth; —, sm. ingredient, materials, pl. [rudeness, coarseness.
materialidad, *-lĭdăd'*, sf. materiality;
materialismo, *-lĭs'mŏ*, sm. materialism.
materialista, *-lĭs'tă*, sm. materialist.
maternal, *mătĕrnăl'*, a. maternal, motherly.
maternidad, *-nĭdăd'*, sf. motherhood,
motherliness. [motherly.
materno, na, *mătĕr'nŏ*, a. maternal,
matiz, *mătĭth'*, sm. shade of colour; shading.
matizar, *mătĭthăr'*, v. a. to mix colours
well; to beautify.
matón, *mătŏn'*, sm. bully.
matorral, *mătŏrrăl'*, sm. shrub, thicket.
matraca, *mătră'kă*, sf. wooden rattle; jest,
contemptuous joke; coxcomb.
matraquear, *-kĕăr'*, v. a. to jest, to scoff,
to mock, to ridicule.
matricida, *mătrĭthĕ'dă*, sm. & f. matricide
(person). [der).
matricidio, *-thĕ'dĭŏ*, sm. matricide (mur-
matrícula, *mătrĕ'kŭlă*, sf. register, list.
matricular, *mătrĕkŭlăr'*, v. a. to matriculate. [connubial.
matrimonial, *-mŏnĭăl'*, a. matrimonial,
matrimonio, *-mŏ'nĭŏ*, sm. marriage,
matrimony. [form.
matriz, *mătrĭth'*, sf. matrix, womb; mould;
matrona, *mătrŏ'nă*, sf. matron.
matutino, na, *mătŭtĕ'nŏ*, a. matutinal.

maula, *mā'ŭlă*, sf. object found in the street; deceitful tricks, imposition; —, sm. cheat, bad payer. [swindler.

maulero, *māŭlĕ'rŏ*, sm. impostor, cheat.

maullador, ra, *—yădŏr*, a. cat which is always mewing.

maullar, *—yŭr*, v. a. to mew.

maullido, *—yĕ'dŏ*, sm. mew, cry of a cat.

mauseolo, *māŭsĕŏ'lŏ*, mausoleo, *—sŏlĕ'ŏ*, sm. mausoleum.

máxima, *mŭx'sĭmă*, sf. maxim.

máxime, *—mĕ*, ad. principally.

máximo, ma, *—mŏ*, a. chief, principal; very great.

mayo, *mă'yŏ*, sm. May; May-pole.

mayor, *māyŏr*, a. greater, larger; elder; —, sm. superior; major; —, sf. first proposition in a syllogism; por—, wholesale; —as, sm. pl. forefathers.

mayoral, *—răl*, sm. head-shepherd; leader.

mayorazgo, *—rŭth'gŏ*, sm. first-born son with the right of primogeniture, son-and-heir; family estate entailed on the eldest son. [tration, stewardship.

mayordomía, *māyŏrdŏmē'ă*, sf. administration, stewardship.

mayordomo, *—dŏ'mŏ*, sm. steward.

mayoría, *māyŏrē'ă*, sf. advantage, excellence, superiority; majority.

mayorista, *—rĭs'tă*, sm. student of the highest classes in grammar-schools.

mayormente, *māyŏrmĕn'tĕ*, ad. principally, chiefly.

mayúscula, *māyŭs'kŭlă*, sf. capital letter.

maza, *mă'thă*, sf. club; mace; importunate, troublesome fellow.

mazada, *māthă'dă*, sf. blow with a mallet.

mazapán, *—pŭn'*, sm. marchpane.

mazmorra, *māthmŏr'ră*, sf. Moorish dungeon.

mazo, *mă'thŏ*, sm. mallet; bundle of ribands; importunate, tiresome person.

mazorca, *māthŏr'kă*, sf. spindle full of me, of me, pn. me. [thread; ear of corn.

mea, *mā'ă*, sf. term used by children to express their want to make water.

meada, *mĕă'dă*, sf. quantity of urine made at one time.

meadero, *—dĕ'rŏ*, sm. urinal.

meados, *mĕă'dŏs*, sm. pl. urine, piss.

mear, *mĕar'*, v. n. to make water; to pump ship.

mecánica, *mĕkă'nĭkă*, sf. mechanics; mean, despicable thing; management of soldiers, affairs. [mechanician.

mecánico, ca, *—kŏ*, a. mechanical; —, sm.

mecanismo, *mĕkănĭs'mŏ*, sm. mechanism.

mecer, *mĕthĕr'*, v. a. to stir, to agitate; to rock; to dandle a child to rest.

mecha, *mĕtsh'ă*, sf. wick; bacon with which fowls and meat are larded.

mechar, *mĕtshăr'*, v. a. to lard.

mechero, *mĕtshĕ'rŏ*, sm. nozzle of a lamp; socket of a candlestick; —de gas, burner.

mechinal, *mĕtshĭnăl'*, sm. square stones left projecting in a wall to be continued.

mechón, *mĕtshŏn'*, sm. large lock of hair; large bundle of threads or fibres.

medalla, *mĕdăl'yă*, sf. medal; gold coin weighing an ounce.

medallón, *—yŏn'*, sm. medallion.

media, *mă'dĭă*, sf. stocking.

mediación, *mĕdĭăthĭŏn'*, sf. mediation, intervention. [between.

mediador, *mĕdĭădŏr'*, sm. mediator; go-

medianería, *—nĕrĕ'ă*, sf. bounds or limits of contiguous things; partition-wall.

medianero, ra, *—nă'rŏ*, a. mediating, interceding. [crity.

medianía, *—nĕ'ă*, sf. moderation; medio-

medianista, *—nĭs'tă*, sm. student of the fourth class in grammar.

mediano, na, *mĕdĭă'nŏ*, a. moderate, middling; mediocre.

mediante, *mĕdĭăn'tĕ*, ad. by means of.

mediar, *mĕdĭăr'*, v. n. to be in the middle; to intercede for another; to mediate.

mediator, *mĕdĭătŏr'*, sm. ombre (game).

medicina, *mĕdĭthē'nă*, sf. physic; medicinal, *—thĭnăl'*, a. medicinal. [cine.

medicinar, *—thĭnăr'*, v. a. to medicine.

médico, *mĕ'dĭkŏ*, sm. physician; —, ca, a.

medida, *mĕdē'dă*, sf. measure. [medical.

medidor, *mĕdĭdŏr'*, sm. measurer.

mediero, *mĕdĭĕ'rŏ*, sm. hosier.

medio, dia, *mĕ'dĭă*, a. half; á medias, by halves; —, sm. middle; expedient; way, mean; medium; mexican coin.

mediocre, *mĕdĭŏ'krĕ*, a. middling, moderate, mediocre. [crity.

mediocridad, *mĕdĭŏkrĭdăd'*, sf. medio-

mediodía, *—dĭ'ă*, sm. noon, mid-day.

mediopaño, *—păn'yŏ*, sm. thin woollen cloth. [moderate.

medir, *mĕdĭr'*, v. a. to measure; —se, to be

meditación, *mĕdĭtăthĭŏn'*, sf. meditation.

meditar, *mĕdĭtăr'*, v. a. to meditate.

mediterráneo, nea, *—tărră'nĕŏ*, a. mediterranean. [improvement.

medra, *mĕ'dră*, sf. progress, melioration.

medrar, *mĕdrăr'*, v. n. to thrive, to prosper; to improve. [ous; terrible.

medroso, sa, *mĕdrŏ'sŏ*, a. fearful, timorous.

medula, *mĕdū'lă*, médula, *mĕ'dŭlă*, sf. marrow; principal substance; (fig.) pith.

meduloso, sa, *mĕdŭlŏ'sŏ*, a. full of marrow, marrowy.

mejido, da, *mĕhĕ'dŏ*, a. beaten up with sugar and water (of eggs).

mejilla, *mĕhĭl'yă*, sf. cheek.

mejor, *mĕhŏr'*, a. & ad. better.

mejora, *mĕhŏ'ră*, sf. improvement, melioration, growth.

mejorar, *mĕhŏrăr'*, v. a. to improve, to meliorate, to heighten; to cultivate; to mend; —, v. n. to recover, to grow well from a disease or calamity; —se, to improve, to grow better.

mejoría, *—rē'ă*, sf. improvement, melioration; mending; repairs; improvement in health; advantage; superiority.

melada, *mĕlă'dă*, sf. slice of toasted bread steeped in honey.

melancolía, *mĕlănkŏlē'ă*, sf. melancholy.

melancólico, ca, *—kŏ'lĭkŏ*, a. melancholy, sad, gloomy.

melena, *mělā'nă*, sf. dishevelled hair hanging loose over the eyes; fore-top hair or mane. [hair.

melenudo, da, *mělěnŏŏ'dŏ*, a. having bushy

melífero, ra, *mělē'fěrŏ*, a. productive of honey. [flowing with honey.

melifluo, flua, *-flŏŏ*, a. honey-mouthed;

melindre, *mělĭn'drě*, sf. fritters made of honey and flour; prudery.

melindrear, *-drěār'*, v. n. to act the prude.

melindroso, sa, *-drŏ'sŏ*, a. prudish, finical. [peach.

melocotón, *mělŏkŏtŏn'*, sm. (bot.) common

melodía, *mělŏdē'ă*, sf. melody.

melodioso, sa, *-dĭŏ'sŏ*, a. melodious.

melodrama, *-drā'mă*, sf. melodrama.

melón, *mělŏn'*, sm. melon.

melonar, *-năr'*, sm. bed of melons.

melosidad, *mělŏsĭdād'*, sf. sweetness.

meloso, sa, *mělŏ'sŏ*, a. honied; mellow.

melote, *-tě*, sm. molasses, treacle.

mella, *měl'yă*, sf. notch in edged tools; gap.

mellado, da, *-yā'dŏ*, a. gap-toothed.

mellar, *-yār'*, v. a. to notch; to deprive of lustre and splendour.

mellizo, za, *-yě'thŏ*, a. twin.

membrana, *měmbrā'nă*, sf. membrane.

membranoso, sa, *-nŏ'sŏ*, a. membranous, filmy.

membrete, *-brě'tě*, sm. memorandum, note; line of a letter containing the name of the addressee; invitation card.

membrillo, *-brĭl'yŏ*, sm. quince-tree; fruit of the quince-tree. [membered.

membrudo, da, *-brŏŏ'dŏ*, a. strong, robust;

mementos, *měměn'tŏs*, sm. pl. two prayers at mass for the quick and the dead.

memorable, *měmŏrā'blě*, a. memorable.

memoria, *měmŏ'rĭă*, sf. memory; memoir; -s, pl. compliments.

memorial, *měmŏrĭāl'*, sm. memorandum-book; memorial, brief.

memorialista, *-lĭs'tă*, sm. amanuensis; writer of petitions for others.

mención, *měnthĭŏn'*, sf. mention.

mencionar, *-năr'*, v. a. to mention.

mendicante, *měndĭkān'tě*, a. mendicant, begging; -, sm. mendicant. [to beg.

mendigar, *-găr'*, v. a. to ask charity.

mendigo, *měndē'gŏ*, sm. beggar.

mendiguez, *měndĭgěth'*, sf. beggary.

mendrugo, *-drŏ'gŏ*, sm. broken bread given to beggars.

menear, *měněār'*, v. a. to move from place to place; to manage; -se, to be brisk and active, to stir about. [body.

meneo, *měně'ŏ*, sm. waddling motion of the

menester, *měněstěr'*, sm. necessity, need, want; -es, pl. natural necessities, pl.

menesteroso, sa, *-rŏ'sŏ*, a. needy, necessitous. [different pulse and roots.

menestra, *měněs'tră*, sf. pottage made of

menestral, *-trāl'*, sm. tradesman, handicraftsman. [poverty; indigence.

mengua, *měn'gŭă*, sf. decay, decline;

menguado, da, *-gŭā'dŏ*, a. cowardly; foolish; avaricious; **hora -a,** fatal

moment; -s, sm. pl. stitches picked up in knitting, pl. [water; decline.

menguante, *-gŭān'tě*, sf. ebb-tide, low-

menguar, *-gŭār'*, v. n. to decay, to fall off; to fail, to diminish.

menjurje, *měn'hŭr'hě*, sm. hodge-podge.

menor, *měnŏr'*, sm. & f. minor (one under age); minor (second proposition in the syllogism); -, a. less, smaller, minor; **por -,** by retail, in small parts; minutely.

menoría, *-rē'ă*, sf. inferiority; nonage.

menorista, *-rĭs'tă*, sm. third-class student of grammar.

menos, *mā'nŏs*, ad. less; with exception of; **á lo -,** ó **por lo -,** at least, however. [terioration, loss.

menoscabar, *-kăbăr'*, v. a. to lessen; to make worse; to reduce.

menoscabo, *-kā'bŏ*, sm. diminution, de-

menospreciar, *-prěthĭăr'*, v. a. to undervalue; to despise, to contemn. [scorn.

menosprecio, *-prā'thĭŏ*, sm. contempt,

mensaje, *měnsā'h'ě*, sm. message, errand.

mensajero, *-'hā'rŏ*, sm. messenger.

menstruación, *měnstrŭāthĭŏn'*, sf. menstruation.

mensual, *měnsŭāl'*, a. monthly. [nowned.

mentado, da, *měntā'dŏ*, a. famous, re-

mental, *měntāl'*, a. mental, intellectual.

mentar, *měntăr'*, v. a. to mention.

mente, *měn'tě*, sf. mind, understanding, sense, meaning. [brained.

mentecato, ta, *-kā'tŏ*, a. silly, crack-

mentidero, *měntĭdā'rŏ*, sm. talking-corner.

mentir, *měntĭr'*, v. a. to lie.

mentira, *měntē'ră*, sf. lie, falsehood.

mentiroso, sa, *měntĭrŏ'sŏ*, a. lying.

mentís, *měntĭs'*, you lie.

menudear, *měnŭděār'*, v. a. to repeat, to detail minutely.

menudencia, *-děn'thĭă*, sf. trifle; minuteness; -s, pl. small matters. [fowls.

menudillos, *-dĭl'yŏs*, sm. pl. giblets of

menudo, da, *měnŏŏ'dŏ*, a. small; minute; of no moment; **á -,** repeatedly, often; **por -,** minutely; by retail; -s, sm. pl. copper coin.

meñique, *měnyě'kě*, sm. little finger.

meollo, *měŏl'yŏ*, sm. marrow.

meón, ona, *měŏn'*, a. continually making water. [noisy fellow.

mequetrefe, *měkětrě'fě*, sm. insignificant,

meramente, *měrăměn'tě*, ad. merely, solely.

mercader, *měrkăděr'*, sm. dealer, trader.

mercadería, *-děrē'ă*, sf. commodity, merchandise; trade. [place.

mercado, *měrkā'dŏ*, sm. market; market-

mercancía, *měrkănthē'ă*, sf. trade, traffic; saleable goods. [cantile.

mercantil, *-tĭl'*, a. commercial, mer-

merced, *měrthěd'*, sf. wages, favour, grace, mercy; will, pleasure; religious military order, whose chief object is to redeem captives; **estar á -,** to live at another's expense. [lab urer. [-, a. mercenary.

mercenario, *měrthěnā'rĭŏ*, sm. day-

mercería, *měrthěrē'ă*, sf. mercery.

Spanish and English.

11

mercero, *mĕrthā'rŏ*, sm. haberdasher.

mercurial, *merkŭrĭal'*, sm. (bot.) all-good, mercury goose-foot; —, a. mercurial.

mercurio, *mĕrkŏ'rĭŏ*, sm. mercury, quicksilver.

merecedor, ra, *mĕrĕthĕdŏr'*, a. deserving.

merecer, *–thĕr'*, v. n. to deserve, to merit.

merecido, da, *–thē'dŏ*, a. meritorious.

merendar, *mĕrĕndar'*, v. n. to take a collation between dinner and supper.

merengue, *mĕrĕn'gĕ*, sm. meringues, pl.

merge, *mĕr'gĕ*, sm. plungeon (bird).

meridiano, *mĕrĭdĭa'nŏ*, sm. meridian; —, a. meridional.

meridional, *–dĭŏnal'*, a. southern, meridional.

merienda, *mĕrĭĕn'dā*, sf. luncheon.

merino, *mĕrē'nŏ*, sm. royal judge and inspector of sheep-walks; shepherd of merino sheep; —, na, a moving from pasture to pasture.

mérito, *mā'rĭtŏ*, sm. merit, desert.

meritorio, ria, *mĕrĭtŏ'rĭŏ*, a. meritorious.

merluza, *mĕrlŏ'thā*, a. cod.

merma, *mĕr'mā*, sf. waste, leakage.

mermar, *mĕrmar'*, v. n. to waste, to diminish.

mermelada, *mĕrmĕla'dā*, sf. marmelade.

mero, *mā'rŏ*, sm. pollack; —, ra, a. mere, pure.

merodeador, *mĕrŏdĕadŏr'*, sm. (mil.) marauder.

merodear, *–dĕar'*, v. n. to pillage, to go *œs*, *mĕs*, sm. month.

mesa, *mā'sā*, sf. table; landing-place (of a stair-case); — redonda, table d'hôte, ordinary; — de trucos, Spanish trucktable.

mesada, *–sā'dā*, sf. monthly pay or wages.

mesana, *–sā'nā*, sf. (mar.) mizen-mast.

mesar, *–sar'*, v. a. to tear one's hair out.

meseta, *–sā'tā*, sf. landing (of a staircase).

Mesías, *mĕsē'ās*, sm. Messiah.

mesón, *mĕsŏn'*, sm. inn, hostelry.

mesonero, *–nā'rŏ*, sm. inn-keeper.

Mesta, *mĕs'tā*, sf. proprietors of black-cattle and sheep considered as a body; annual meeting of owners of flocks.

mestizo, za, *mĕstē'thŏ*, a. of a mongrel breed.

mesura, *mĕsŏ'rā*, sf. grave deportment; politeness; moderation.

mesurado, da, *–rā'dŏ*, a. moderate; modest; gentle; prudent

mesurar, *–rar'*, v. a. to assume a serious countenance.

metafísica, *mĕtāfē'sĭkā*, sf. metaphysics.

metafísico, ca, *–sĭkŏ*, a. metaphysical; —, sm. metaphysician.

metáfora, *mĕtā'fŏrā*, sf. metaphor.

metafórico, ca, *mĕtāfŏ'rĭkŏ*, a. metaphorical.

metal, *mĕtal'*, sm. metal; brass, latten; compass or strength of the voice.

metálico, ca, *mĕtā'lĭkŏ*, a. metallic.

metalurgia, *–lŭr'hĭā*, sf. metallurgy.

metamorfosis, *–mŏrfŏ'sĭs*, sf. metamorphosis, transformation.

metátesis, *mĕtā'tĕsĭs*, sf. metathesis, transposition.

metéoro, *mĕtā'ŏrŏ*, sm. meteor.

meteorología, *mĕtĕŏrŏlŏ'hĭā*, sf. meteorology.

meter, *mĕtĕr'*, v. a. to place, to put; to

smuggle goods into the country; to occasion; —se, to intermeddle, to interfere.

metódico, ca, *mĕtŏ'dĭkŏ*, a. methodical.

método, *mĕ'tŏdŏ*, sm. method.

metonimia, *mĕtŏnĭ'mĭā*, sf. metonymy.

metralla, *mĕtral'yā*, sf. grape-shot.

métrico, ca, *mā'trĭkŏ*, a. metrical.

metro, *mā'trŏ*, sm. metre; verse.

metrópoli, *mĕtrŏ'pŏlĭ*, sf. metropolis, the chief or principal city of a country; archiepiscopal church.

metropolitano, *mĕtrŏpŏlĭta'nŏ*, sm. metropolitan.

mezcla, *mĕth'klā*, sf. mixture, medley.

mezclar, *mĕthklar'*, v. a. to mix, to mingle; —se, to mix; to marry a person of inferior rank.

mezcolanza, *–kŏlan'thā*, sf. bad mixture of colours.

mezquindad, *–kĭndad'*, sf. penury, poverty; avarice.

mezquino, na, *–kē'nŏ*, a. poor, indigent; avaricious, covetous.

mezquita, *–kē'tā*, sf. mosque.

mi, *mē*, pn, oblique case of the pronoun yo; —, pn. my.

miaja, *mĭā'hā*, sf. crumb.

mico, *mē'kŏ*, sm. monkey.

microscópico, oa, *mĭkrŏskŏ'pĭkŏ*, a. microscopical.

microscopio, *–kŏ'pĭŏ*, sm. microscope.

miedo, *mĭā'dŏ*, sm. fear, dread.

miel, *mĭĕl'*, sf. honey. [dog-fish; rake.

mielga, *mĭĕl'gā*, sf. (bot.) lucern; small

miembro, *mĭĕm'brŏ*, sm. member.

mientras, *mĭĕn'trās*, ad. in the mean time.

miércoles, *mĭĕr'kŏlĕs*, sm. Wednesday.

mierda, *mĭĕr'dā*, sf. excrement, ordure.

mies, *mĭĕs'*, sf. harvest.

miga, *mē'gā*, sf. crumb; —s, pl. fried bread-crumbs. [particle.

migaja, *mĭgā'hā*, sf. scrap, crumb, small

migajón, *–hŏn'*, sm. crumb without crust.

migar, *mĭgar'*, v. a. to crumble.

mijo, *mē'hŏ*, sm. (bot.) millet.

mil, *mĭl*, sm. one thousand.

milagro, *mĭlā'grŏ*, sm. miracle, wonder; offering of wax or any other substance, hung up in churches in commemoration of a miracle.

milagroso, sa, *–grŏ'sŏ*, a. miraculous.

milano, *mĭlā'nŏ*, sm. kite, glede (bird).

milésimo, ma, *mĭlā'sĭmŏ*, a. thousandth.

milicia, *mĭlē'thĭā*, sf. militia.

miliciano, *mĭlĭthĭa'nŏ*, sm. militia-man; —, na, a. military. [serve in the army.

militar, *mĭlĭtar'*, a. military; —, v. n. to

milla, *mĭl'yā*, sf. mile.

millar, *mĭlyar'*, sm. thousand.

millón, *mĭlyŏn'*, sm. million.

millonario, *–nā'rĭŏ*, sm. millionaire.

mimar, *mĭmar'*, v. a. to coax, to wheedle, to flatter; to fondle, to caress.

mimbre, *mĭm'brĕ*, sm. twig of an osier.

mímico, ca, *mē'mĭkŏ*, a. mimic.

mimo, *mē'mŏ*, sm. buffoon, merry-Andrew; mime; prudery, delicacy.

mimoso, sa, *mĭmŏ'sŏ*, a. delicate, fond.

mina, *mē'nā*, sf. conduit, subterraneous canal; mine; source of water.

minador, *mĭnadŏr'*, sm. miner.

minar, *minár'*, v. a. to undermine, to mine.

mineral, *minérál'*, sm. mineral; spring of water; —, a. mineral.

mineralogía, *-lô'hê'á*, sf. mineralogy.

mineralógico, ca, *-lô'nikô*, a. belonging to mineralogy.

minero, *mind'rô*, sm. miner.

miniatura, *miniât'rá*, sf. miniature.

ínfima, *mé'nimá*, sf. (mus.) minim.

mínimo, ma, *-mô*, a. least, smallest; —s, sm. pl. second class in grammar-schools.

minio, *mé'niô*, sm. minium, red-lead.

ministerio, *ministê'riô*, sm. ministry (office).

ministril, *-trîl'*, sm. tipstaff; petty officer

ministro, *ministrô*, sm. minister of state; petty officer of justice. [diminish.

minorar, *minôrár'*, v. a. to lessen, to

minoridad, *minôrídád'*, sf. minority.

minucioso, sa, *minûthô'sô*, a. superfluously exact. [to letters).

minúscula, *minûs'kûlá*, a. small (applied

minuta, *minô'tá*, sf. minute, first draught of an agreement in writing.

minutero, *minûtê'rô*, sm. minute-hand of a watch or clock.

minuto, *minô'tô*, sm. minute.

mio, mia, *mê'á*, a. my, mine.

miope, *miô'pê*, sm. one near-sighted.

mira, *mê'rá*, sf. sight of a gun; needle or point in mathematical instruments for directing the sight; **estar á la —**, to be on the look-out.

mirada, *mirá'dá*, sf. glance; gaze.

mirador, ra, *-dôr'*, sm. & f. spectator, looker-on; belvedere, gazebo.

miramiento, *-miên'tô*, sm. consideration; circumspection.

mirar, *mirár'*, v. a. to behold, to look; to observe, to spy; —, v. imp. to concern; **por lo que mira á**, as to, concerning; **-se**, to look at oneself; to look at one

mirlo, *mir'lô*, sm. blackbird. [another.

mirón, ona, *mirôn'*, sm. & f. spectator, looker-on, by-stander; prier, one who inquires with too much curiosity and officiousness, gazer.

mirra, *mêr'rá*, sf. myrrh.

mirto, *mir'tô*, sm. myrtle.

misa, *mis'á*, sf. mass; **- del gallo**, midnight mass.

misal, *misál'*, sm. missal. [night mass.

misantropía, *misántrôpê'á*, sf. misanthropy. [thropist.

misántropo, *-án'trôpô*, sm. misan-

miscelánea, *-thêlâ'nêá*, sf. miscellany.

miserable, *misêrá'blê*, a. miserable, wretched, unhappy; exhausted; avaricious. [(med.) miserere.

miserere, *misêrê'rê*, sm. the Miserere;

miseria, *misê'riá*, sf. misery; niggardliness; trifle. [clemency.

misericordia, *misêríkôr'diá*, sf. mercy;

misericordioso, sa, *-kôrdiô'sô*, a. merciful, clement.

misión, *misiôn'*, sf. mission.

misionero, *-nê'rô*, sm. missionary.

mismo, ma, *mis'mô*, a. same, similar, equal.

misterio, *mistê'riô*, sm. mystery.

misterioso, sa, *-riô'sô*, a. mysterious, mystical.

mística, *mis'tiká*, sf. mysticalness.

místico, ca, *-tikô*, a. mystic, mystical.

mitad, *mitád'*, sf. moiety, half.

mitigación, *mitigâthiôn'*, sf. mitigation.

mitigar, *-gár'*, v. a. to mitigate.

mitología, *mitôlô'hê'á*, sf. mythology.

mitológico, ca, *-lô'hikô*, a. mythological.

mitones, *mitô'nês*, sm. pl. mittens.

mitra, *mê'trá*, sf. mitre.

mitrado, *mitrá'dô*, a. mitred.

mixtión, *mikstiôn'*, sf. mixing, mixture.

mixto, ta, *miks'tô*, misto, ta, *mis'tô*, a. mixed, mingled.

mixtura, *mikstô'rá*, sf. mixture.

mocadero, *môkádê'rô*, sm. pocket-handkerchief.

mocedad, *môthêdád'*, sf. youthfulness.

moción, *môthiôn'*, sf. motion.

moco, *mô'kô*, sm. snot; snuff of a candle.

mocosidad, *môkôsidád'*, sf. mucosity.

mocoso, sa, *môkô'sô*, a. snotty, snively; mucous.

mochila, *môtshê'lá*, sf. knapsack.

mocho, cha, *môtshô*, a. dishorned, having the horns cut off; cropped, shorn; lopped, having the branches cut off; maimed, mutilated.

mochuelo, *môtshûê'lô*, sm. red owl.

moda, *mô'dá*, sf. fashion, mode.

modelar, *môdêlár'*, v.a. to model, to form.

modelo, *môdê'lô*, sm. model, pattern.

moderación, *môdêrâthiôn'*, sf. moderation; temperance. [temperate.

moderado, da, *-rá'dô*, a. moderate,

moderar, *môdêrár'*, v. a. to moderate.

moderno, na, *môdêr'nô*, a. modern.

modestia, *môdês'tiá*, sf. modesty, decency

modesto, ta, *môdês'tô*, a. modest.

modificación, *môdifikâthiôn'*, sf. modification; limitation. [moderate.

modificar, *-kár'*, v. a. to modify; to

modificativo, va, *-kátê'vô*, sm. & a. modificative. [dress; —, sf. milliner.

modista, *môdis'tá*, s. a person fond of modo, *mô'dô*, sm. mode, method, manner; moderation; mood. [ness.

modorra, *môdôr'rá*, sf. drowsiness, doziness.

modorrar, *-rár'*, v. a. to render heavy with sleep; **-se**, to become flabby.

modorro, rra, *môdôr'rô*, a. drowsy, sleepy.

modrego, *môdrê'gô*, sm. dunce, dolt.

modulación, *môdûlâthiôn'*, sf. modulation.

modular, *môdûlár'*, v. a. to modulate.

mofa, *mô'fá*, sf. mockery. [scorner.

mofador, ra, *môfádôr'*, sm. & f. scoffer,

mofar, *-fár'*, v. a. & r. to deride; to mock; to scoff.

moflete, *-flê'tê*, sm. chub-cheek, blub-cheek.

mogollón, *-gôlyôn'*, sm. hanger-on, parasite, sponger. [with moss.

mohecer, *-êthêr'*, v. a. to moss, to cover

mohína, *-ê'ná*, sf. animosity, desire of revenge, resentment, grudge.

mohino, na, *-nô*, a. fretful, peevish.

moho, *mô'ô*, sm. (bot.) moss. [mossy.

mohoso, sa, *môô'sô*, a. mouldy, musty;

mojadura, *mŏ'hădŏ'ră,* sf. act of moistening *or* wetting. [meddle, to interfere.

mojar, *mŏ'hăr',* v. a. to wet, to moisten; to

moje, *mŏ'hĕ,* sm. fricassee, ragout.

mojicón, *mŏ'htkŏn',* sm. cuff, punch.

mojiganza, *—găn'thă,* sf. masquerade; mummery.

mojigato, *—gă'tŏ,* a. hypocritical.

mojón, *mŏ'hŏn',* sm. land-mark.

mola, *mŏ'lă,* sf. mole.

moldar, *mŏldăr',* v. a. to mould.

molde, *mŏl'dĕ,* sm. mould; model.

moldura, *mŏldŏ'ră,* sf. moulding.

mole, *mŏ'lĕ,* a. soft, mild; —, sf. vast size *or* quantity; massiness.

molécula, *mŏlĕ'kŭlă,* sf. molecule.

moledor, *mŏlĕdŏr',* sm. grinder; tiresome fellow, bore.

moler, *mŏlĕr',* v. a. to grind, to pound; to vex, to molest; to waste, to consume by use.

molestar, *mŏlĕstăr',* v. a. to vex, to molest, to trouble.

molestia, *mŏlĕs'tĭă,* sf. injury, molestation.

molesto, ta, *—tŏ,* a. molest, vexatious.

moletón, *mŏlĕtŏn',* sm. milled flannel.

molicie, *mŏlĭ'thĭĕ,* sf. tenderness, softness.

molienda, *mŏlĭĕn'dă,* sf. act of grinding *or* pounding; fatigue, lassitude.

molinero, *mŏlĭnĕ'rŏ,* sm. miller.

molinete, *—nĕ'tĕ,* sm. windlass; turnstile.

molinillo, *—nĭl'yŏ,* sm. hand-mill; chocomolino, *mŏlĭ'nŏ,* sm. mill. [late-mill.

mollar, *mŏlyăr',* a. soft, pappy, pulpous; credulous.

molleja, *mŏlyĕ'hă,* sf. gland; gizzard.

mollera, *—yĕ'ră,* sf. crown *or* top of the mollete, *—yĕ'tĕ,* sm. French roll. [head.

molletudo, da, *mŏlyĕtŏ'dŏ,* a. chub-faced.

momentáneo, nea, *mŏmĕntă'nĕŏ,* a. momentaneous.

momento, *mŏmĕn'tŏ,* sm. moment.

momería, *mŏmĕrĕ'ă,* sf. mummery.

momio, mia, *mŏ'mĭŏ,* a. meagre, lean.

momia, *mŏ'mĭă,* sf. mummy.

momo, *mŏ'mŏ,* sm. buffoonery, grimaces.

mona, *mŏ'nă,* sf. female monkey; ludicrous imitator; drunkenness; drunkard.

monacal, *mŏnăkăl',* a. monachal, monkish.

monacillo, *—thĭl'yŏ,* sm. acolyte.

monada, *mŏnă'dă,* sf. grimace.

monago, *mŏnă'gŏ,* **monaguillo,** *—gĭl'yŏ,* sm. acolyte.

monarca, *mŏnăr'kă,* sm. monarch.

monarquía, *—kĕ'ă,* sf. monarchy.

monárquico, ca, *mŏnăr'kĭkŏ,* a. monarchical. [cloister.

monasterio, *mŏnăstĕ'rĭŏ,* sm. monastery.

monástico, ca, *mŏnăs'tĭkŏ,* a. monastic.

monda, *mŏn'dă,* sf. pruning of trees

mondadientes, *—dĭĕn'tĕs,* sm. toothpick.

mondadura, *—dŏ'ră,* sf. cleaning, cleansing; —s, pl. parings, peelings.

mondar, *mŏndăr',* v. a. to clean, to cleanse; to husk, to peel; to deprive of money.

mondo, da, *mŏn'dŏ,* a. neat, clean, pure; — y lirondo, without any admixture.

mondongo, *—dŏn'gŏ,* sm. paunch, tripe.

moneda, *mŏnĕ'dă,* sf. money, coinage.

moned(e)ar, *mŏnĕd(ĕ)ăr',* v. a. to coin.

monedero, *mŏnĕdĕ'rŏ,* sm. coiner.

monería, *—rĕ'ă,* sf. grimace, mimicry; trifle, gewgaw. [coins.

monetario, *—tă'rĭŏ,* sm. cabinet of ancient

monición, *mŏnĭthĭŏn',* sf. admonition; publication of the banns (of marriage).

monises, *mŏnĭ'sĕs,* sm. pl. (vulg.) money.

monita, *mŏ'nĭtă,* sf. cunning, craft.

monitor, *mŏnĭtŏr',* sm. admonisher; (mar.) monitor, turret-ship. [nun.

monje, *mŏn'hĕ,* sm. **monja,** *—hă,* sf. monk;

mono, na, *mŏ'nŏ,* a. neat, pretty, nice; —, sm. monkey, ape.

monólogo, *mŏnŏ'lŏgŏ,* sm. monologue.

monopolio, *mŏnŏpŏ'lĭŏ,* sm. monopoly.

monopolista, *—pŏlĭs'tă,* sm. monopolist, monopoliser.

monosílabo, ba, *—sĭ'lăbŏ,* a. monosyllabical; —, sm. monosyllable.

monotonía, *—tŏnĕ'ă,* sf. monotony. [nous.

monótono, na, *mŏnŏ'tŏnŏ,* v. n. monoto

monstruo, *mŏn'strŭŏ,* sm. monster.

monstruosidad, *—sĭdăd',* sf. monstruosity.

monstruoso, sa, *—ŏ'sŏ,* a. monstrous.

monta, *mŏn'tă,* sf. amount, sum total.

montaje, *mŏntă'hĕ,* sm. mounting of artillery; —s, pl. carriage *or* bed of a cannon. [in fencing.

montante, *mŏntăn'tĕ,* sm. broadsword used

montaña, *mŏntăn'yă,* sf. mountain.

montañés, esa, *—yĕs',* a. pertaining to the mountains; mountainous; —, s. mountaineer.

montañoso, sa, *—yŏ'sŏ,* a. mountainous.

montar, *mŏntăr',* v. n. to mount (on horseback); to amount to. [untamed.

montaraz, *—răth',* a. mountainous; wild,

montazgo, *mŏntăth'gŏ,* sm. toll to be paid for cattle passing from one province into another.

monte, *mŏn'tĕ,* sm. mountain; wood, forest; difficulty; — alto, lofty grove; — bajo, copse, coppice, brush-wood.

montera, *mŏntĕ'ră,* sf. peasant's cap.

montería, *—rĕ'ă,* sf. hunting, chase.

montero, *mŏntĕ'rŏ,* sm. huntsman, hunter.

montés, esa, *mŏntĕs',* **montesino, na,** *—sĕ'nŏ,* a. bred *or* found in a forest *or* mountain.

montón, *mŏntŏn',* sm. heap, pile; mass, cluster; á —ones, abundantly, by heaps.

montuoso, sa, *mŏntŭŏ'sŏ,* a. mountainous, hilly. [intended for the saddle.

montura, *mŏntŏ'ră,* sf. horses and mules

monumento, *mŏnŭmĕn'tŏ,* sm. monument; altar raised in churches on Holy Thursday to resemble a sepulchre; —s, pl. monuments *or* remains of antiquity.

monzón, *mŏnthŏn',* sm. monsoon. [ness.

moña, *mŏn'yă,* sf. doll; (fam.) drunken

moño, *—yŏ,* sm. hair on the crown of the head tied together; tuft of feathers on the heads of some birds.

moquear, *mŏkĕăr',* v. n. to blow the nose.

moquero, *mŏkĕ'rŏ,* sm. pocket-handkerchief. [or nose.

moquete, *mŏkĕ'tĕ,* sm. blow on the face

moquillo, _-kĭl'yŏ_, sm. Np (disease in fowls).

moquita, _-kē'tă_, sf. snivel.

morada, _mŏră'dă_, sf. habitation, abode, residence.

morado, da, _-dŏ_, a. violet, mulberry-coloured.

morador, _-dŏr'_, sm. inhabitant, lodger.

moral, _mŏrăl'_, sm. mulberry-tree; —, sf. morals, ethics; —, a. moral.

moralidad, _mŏrălĭdăd'_, sf. morality.

moralista, _mŏrălĭs'tă_, sm. moralist.

moralizar, _mŏrălĭthăr'_, v. n. to moralise.

moralmente, _mŏrălmĕn'tĕ_, ad. morally.

morar, _mŏrăr'_, v. n. to inhabit, to dwell.

moratoria, _mŏrătŏ'rĭă_, sf. letter of license granted to a debtor.

mórbido, da, _mŏr'bĭdŏ_, a. morbid, diseased; [soft, mellow.

morboso, sa, _mŏrbŏ'sŏ_, a. diseased, morbid.

morcilla, _-thĭl'yă_, sf. black-pudding.

mordacidad, _-dăthĭdăd'_, sf. mordacity.

mordaz, _mŏrdăth'_, a. corrosive, biting; sarcastic; mordacious.

mordaza, _-dă'thă_, sf. gag.

mordedura, _-dĕdŏ'ră_, sf. bite.

morder, _mŏrdĕr'_, v. a. to bite.

mordiscar, _-dĭskăr'_, v. a. to gnaw, to nibble.

mordisco, _-dĭs'kŏ_, mordiscón, _-dĭskŏn'_, sm. bite.

morena, _mŏrĕ'nă_, sf. brown bread; sea-eel.

moreno, na, _-nŏ_, a. brown, swarthy.

morga, _mŏr'gă_, sf. dregs of oil.

moribundo, da, _mŏrĭbŏŏn'dŏ_, a. dying.

morigeración, _-hĕrăthĭŏn'_, sf. temperance.

morigerar, _mŏrĭhĕrăr'_, v. a. to moderate.

morillo, _mŏrĭl'yŏ_, sm. andiron.

morir, _mŏrĭr'_, v. n. to die, to expire; —se, to go out, to be extinguished; to be benumbed.

morisco, ca, _mŏrĭs'kŏ_, a. Moorish; —, sm. name given to the Moors who remained in Spain after its restoration.

morisma, _-mă_, sf. Mohammedan sect; multitude of Moors.

morisqueta, _-kĕ'tă_, sf. Moorish trick.

moriaco, ca, _mŏrĭă'kŏ_, a. affecting ignorance and stupidity.

moro, ra, _mŏ'rŏ_, a. Moorish. [podge.

morondanga, _mŏrŏndăn'gă_, sf. hodge-podge.

morondo, da, _mŏrŏn'dŏ_, a. bald; leafless.

morosidad, _mŏrŏsĭdăd'_, sf. slowness, delay, tardiness, dilatoriness.

moroso, sa, _mŏrŏ'sŏ_, a. slow, tardy, heavy.

morrada, _mŏrră'dă_, sf. butting with the heads between two people.

morral, _mŏrrăl'_, sm. fodder-bag, nose-bag; sportsman's-bag.

morralla, _mŏrrăl'yă_, sf. hotch-potch.

morrillo, _-rĭl'yŏ_, sm. pebble; fat of the nape of a sheep. [melancholy.

morriña, _-rĭn'yă_, sf. murrain; sadness, melancholy.

morrión, _mŏrrĭŏn'_, sm. morion, spike-helmet. [object; overhanging lip.

morro, _mŏr'rŏ_, sm. any round skull-like object; overhanging lip.

morrudo, da, _-rŏŏ'dŏ_, a. blubber-lipped.

mortaja, _mŏrtă'h'ă_, sf. shroud, winding-sheet; mortise.

mortal, _mŏrtăl'_, a. mortal; fatal, deadly.

mortalidad, _-lĭdăd'_, sf. mortality.

mortandad, _-tăndăd'_, sf. mortality, epidemic disease. [firing at festivities.

morterete, _-tĕrĕ'tĕ_, sm. small mortar for firing at festivities.

mortero, _mŏrtĕ'rŏ_, sm. mortar (cannon).

mortífero, ra, _mŏrtĭ'fĕrŏ_, a. mortiferous, fatal. [cation; yexation, trouble.

mortificación, _mŏrtĭfĭkăthĭŏn'_, sf. mortification; vexation, trouble.

mortificar, _-fĭkăr'_, v. a. to mortify; to afflict, to vex. [—, a. mortuary.

mortuorio, _mŏrtŏŏ'rĭŏ_, sm. burial, funeral; —, a. mortuary.

moruno, na, _mŏrŏŏ'nŏ_, a. Moorish.

mosaico, ca, _mŏsă'ĭkŏ_, a. Mosaic.

mosca, _mŏs'kă_, sf. fly.

moscardón, _mŏskărdŏn'_, sm. large gad-fly; importuning, sly fellow.

moscatel, _-kătĕl'_, a. muscadine or muscatel grape. [deceitful fellow.

moscón, _mŏskŏn'_, sm. large fly; crafty, deceitful fellow.

mosquero, _mŏskĕ'rŏ_, sm. fly-trap.

mosquetería, _mŏskĕtĕrĕ'ă_, sf. body of musketeers; musketry.

mosquetero, _-tĕ'rŏ_, sm. musketeer.

mosquitero, _mŏskĭtĕ'rŏ_, sm. mosquito-net.

mosquito, _mŏskē'tŏ_, sm. gnat, mosquito; tippler, toper, fuddler.

mostachón, _mŏstăchŏn'_, sm. marchpane.

mostaza, _mŏstă'thă_, sf. mustard; mustard-seed; hail-shot. [and mustard.

mostillo, _-tĭl'yŏ_, sm. sauce made of must and mustard.

mosto, _mŏs'tŏ_, sm. must, new wine.

mostrador, _-trădŏr'_, sm. counter; shop-front.

mostrar, _-trăr'_, v. a. to show, to exhibit; —se, to appear, to show oneself.

mostrenco, ca, _-trĕn'kŏ_, a. strayed, ownerless; vagabond, vagrant; ignorant, stupid.

mota, _mŏ'tă_, sf. bit of thread, &c. sticking to cloth; slight defect or fault.

mote, _mŏ'tĕ_, sm. nickname. [ridicule.

motejar, _mŏtĕhăr'_, v. a. to censure, to ridicule.

motilar, _mŏtĭlăr'_, v. a. to cut off the hair, to crop. [to crop.

motín, _mŏtĭn'_, sm. mutiny.

motivar, _mŏtĭvăr'_, v. a. to give a reason, to assign a motive.

motivo, _mŏtĕ'vŏ_, sm. motive, cause, reason.

motor, _mŏtŏr'_, sm. mover, motor; —, a. movable.

motriz, _mŏtrĭth'_, a. a motory, motive.

movedizo, za, _mŏvĕdĕ'thŏ_, a. movable; variable, inconstant.

mover, _mŏvĕr'_, v. a. to move; to touch pathetically; to stir up; to excite.

movible, _mŏvē'blĕ_, a. movable.

móvil, _mŏ'vĭl_, a. movable. [constancy.

movilidad, _mŏvĭlĭdăd'_, sf. mobility; inconstancy.

movimiento, _-mĭĕn'tŏ_, sm. movement, motion; sedition.

moza, _mŏ'thă_, sf. girl, lass; maid-servant; last or conquering game.

mozo, za, _-thŏ_, a. young; —, sm. youth, lad; man-servant. [officiating bishop.

muceta, _mŭthĕ'tă_, sf. mantlet worn by an officiating bishop.

muchacha, _mŭchă'chă_, sf. girl; lass.

muchachada, _-chă'dă_, sf. boyish trick.

muchacho, _-chŏ_, sm. boy; lad; —, cha, a. boyish, girlish. [tude, plenty.

muchedumbre, _mŭchĕdŏŏm'brĕ_, sf. multi-

mucho, cha, *mátsh'ŏ,* a. much, abundant, —, ad. much. [moulting.

muda, *mŏ dă,* sf. change, alteration; act of

mudable, *mŏdă blă,* a. changeable, variable, mutable. [tion; inconstancy.

mudanza, *mŏdăn'thă,* sf. change; muta-

mudar, *mŏdăr',* v. a. to change; to mew, to moult; to change one's voice; —se, to change; to change sentiments and manners; to shift; to change house.

mudez, *mŏdéth',* sf. dumbness.

mudo, da, *mŏ dŏ,* a. dumb; silent, mute.

mueca, *mŏĕ kă,* sf. grimace, wry face.

muela, *mŏĕ lă,* sf. upper mill-stone; grind-stone; mill-dam; hillock; —s, pl. grinders, molar-teeth.

muelle, *mŏĕľ ĕ,* a. tender, delicate, soft; —, sm. spring; regulator; quay, wharf.

muérdago, *mŏĕr dă gŏ,* sm. (bot.) mistletoe.

muermo, *mŏĕr mŏ,* sm. glanders.

muerte, *mŏĕr tă,* sf. death.

muerto, *—tŏ,* sm. corpse; —, ta, a. dead.

muesca, *mŏĕs kă,* sf. notch, groove.

muestra, *mŏĕs tră,* sf. pattern; fag-end of a piece of stuff; copy written to be imitated by boys; indicative sign; specimen, design, model; (mil.) muster-roll; dial, clock which does not strike; watch.

mugido, *mŏgĕ dŏ,* sm. lowing of an ox.

mugir, *mŏgĕr',* v. n. to low, to bellow.

mugre, *mŏ grĕ,* sm. dirt sticking to clothes, &c. [filthy.

mugriento, ta, *mŏgrĕăn'tŏ,* a. greasy, dirty,

mujer, *mŏhĕr',* sf. woman.

mujeril, *mŏhĕrĕl',* a. womanish, womanly.

mula, *mŏ lă,* sf. she-mule. [very dirty.

muladar, *mŏlădăr',* sm. laystall; anything

mular, *mŏlăr',* a. belonging to mules.

mulatero, *mŏlătĕ rŏ,* sm. muleteer.

mulato, *mŏlă tŏ,* a. mulatto.

muleta, *mŏlĕ tă,* sf. crutch.

mulo, *mŏ lŏ,* sm. mule.

multa, *mŏľ tă,* sf. mulct, fine, penalty.

multar, *mŏltăr',* v. a. to impose a pecuniary penalty. [tiplication.

multiplicación, *mŏltĕplĭkăthĭŏn',* sf. mul-

multiplicador, ra, *—kădŏr',* sm. & f. multiplier; (ar.) multiplicator. [plicand.

multiplicando, *—kăn'dŏ,* sm. (ar.) multi-

multiplicar, *—kăr',* v. a. to multiply.

multiplice, *mŏltĕ plĭthĕ,* a. multiple; mul-tiplicious. [plicity.

multiplicidad, *mŏltĕplĭthĭdăd',* sf. multi-

multitud, *mŏltĭtŭd',* sf. multitude, great number. [up.

mullir, *mŏľyĭr',* v. a. to beat up, to shake worldly.

mundano, na, *mŏndă nŏ,* a. mundane.

mundinovi, *mŏndĭnŏ vĕ,* **mundinuevo,** *—nă vŏ,* sm. raree-show, magic-lantern.

mundo, *mŏn'dŏ,* sm. world.

munición, *mŏnĭthĭŏn',* sf. ammunition.

municionar, *—năr',* v. a. to munition.

municipal, *mŏnĭthĭpăl',* a. municipal.

munificencia, *—thĕn'thĕă,* sf. munifi-cence, liberality.

muñeca, *mŏnyă kă,* sf. wrist; child's doll.

muñeco, *—kŏ,* sm. puppet; effeminate fellow. [poration; messenger.

muñidor, *mŏnyĭdŏr',* sm. beadle of a cor-

muñón, *mŏnyŏn',* sm. brawn; stump of an amputated limb.

muralla, *mŏrăľ yă,* sf. rampart, wall.

murciélago, *mŏrthĕă lăgŏ,* sm. bat.

murmullo, *mŏrmŭľ yŏ,* sm. murmur, mutter. [privy calumny.

murmuración, *—mŏrăthĭŏn',* sf.backbiting,

murmurador, ra, *—rădŏr',* sm. & f. de-tractor, backbiter.

murmurar, *—răr',* v. a. to murmur, to purl; to backbite. [stream.

murmurio, *mŏr'rĕŏ,* sm. murmuring of a

muro, *mŏ rŏ,* sm. wall.

murria, *mŏr'rĕă,* sf. heaviness of the head.

musa, *mŏ să,* sf. Muse.

musaraña, *mŏsărăn'yă,* sf. shrew-mouse; hobgoblin; vermin.

muscular, *mŏskŭlăr',* a. muscular.

músculo, *mŏs kŭlŏ,* sm. muscle.

muselina, *mŏsĕlĕ nă,* sf. muslin.

museo, *mŏsĕ ŏ,* sm. museum.

musgo, *mŏs gŏ,* sm. moss.

música, *mŏ sĭkă,* sf. music.

musical, *mŏsĭkăl',* a. musical. [musical.

músico, ca, *mŏ sĭkŏ,* s. musician; —, a.

muslo, *mŏs lŏ,* sm. thigh.

mustiamente, *mŏstĕămĕn'tĕ,* ad. sadly, in a melancholy manner.

mustio, tia, *mŏs'tĕŏ,* a. parched, withered; sad, sorrowful, musty. [inconstancy.

mutabilidad, *mŏtăbĭlĭdăd',* sf. mutability.

mutación, *—thĭŏn',* sf. mutation, change.

mutilación, *mŏtĭlăthĭŏn',* sf. mutilation.

mutilar, *—lăr',* v. a. to mutilate, to maim.

mutual, *mŏtŭăl',* **mutuo, tua,** *mŏ tŭŏ,* a. mutual, reciprocal. [most illustrious.

muy, *mŏ'ĕ,* ad. very; greatly; **– ilustre,**

N.

nabal, *năbăl',* **nabar,** *—băr'* sm. turnip-field; —a, made of turnips.

nabo, *nă bŏ,* sm. rape, colewort.

nácar, *nă kăr,* sm. mother of pearl, nacre.

nacarado, da, *—ră dŏ,* a. set with mother of pearl; pearl-coloured.

nacer, *năthĕr',* v. n. to be born, to bud, to shoot (of plants); to rise; to grow; —se, to be propagated by nature (as grass).

nacido, da, *năthĕ dŏ,* a. proper, apt, fit; inborn; —, sm. tumour, abscess; —s, pl. all men born. [ity.

nacimiento, *—mĕĕn'tŏ,* sm. birth; Nativ-

nación, *năthĭŏn',* sf. nation.

nacional, *—năl',* a. national.

nacionalidad, *—nălĭdăd',* sf. national customs, nationality. [by no means.

nada, *nă dă,* sf. nothing; —, ad. in no way,

nadaderas, *—dă răs,* sf. pl. swimming-bladders (for learning to swim).

nadadero, *—dĕ rŏ,* sm. swimming-place.

nadador, ra, *—dŏr',* sm. & f. swimmer.

nadar, *nădăr',* v. n. to swim.

nadie, *nä'dïë*, sm. nobody, no one.

nado, *nä'dö*, á —, ad. afloat.

naipe, *nä'ïpë*, sm. playing-card.

nalga, *näl'gä*, sf. buttock, rump.

nao, *nä'ö*, sf. ship, vessel.

naranja, *närän'hä*, sf. orange.

naranjada, *—hä'dä*, sf. conserve of oranges; orange-water.

naranjado, do, *—dö*, a. orange-coloured.

naranjal, *närän'häl'*, sm. orangery.

naranjazo, *'hä'thö*, sm. blow with an orange. [orange-tree.

naranjero, *—hä'rö*, sm. orange-seller.

naranjo, *närän'thö*, sm. orange-tree.

narciso, *närthï'sö*, sm. (bot.) daffodil; narcissus flower; precious stone of the colour of daffodil; fop, coxcomb.

narcótico, ca, *närkö'tïkö*, a. narcotic.

nardo, *när'dö*, sm. spikenard.

narigón, *närïgön'*, sm. large nose; —, ona, a. big-nosed.

narigudo, da, *—gö'dö*, a. big-nosed.

nariz, *närïth'*, sf. nose; sense of smelling.

narración, *närräthïön'*, sf. narration.

narrar, *närrär'*, v. a. to narrate, to tell.

narrativa, *närrätï'vä*, sf. narrative, relation; talent for narration.

nasa, *nä'sä*, sf. osier lobster-pot.

nata, *nä'tä*, sf. cream.

natal, *nätäl'*, a. natal, native.

natalicio, cia, *nätälï'thïö*, a. natal.

natillas, *nätïl'yäs*, sf. pl. cream made of boiled flour, eggs and sugar.

natividad, *nätïvïdäd'*, sf. nativity.

nativo, va, *nätï'vä*, a. native.

natural, *nätüräl'*, sm. temper, natural disposition; —, a. natural, native; common, usual; ingenuous, unaffected; al —, unaffectedly.

naturaleza, *—lë'thä*, sf. nature.

naturalidad, *—lïdäd'*, sf. birth-right; naturalness; ingenuity, candour.

naturalista, *—lïs'tä*, sm. naturalist.

naturalizar, *—lïthär'*, v. n. to naturalize; —se, to become accustomed.

naufragar, *näüfrägär'*, v. n. to be ship-wrecked, to suffer wreck; to suffer ruin in one's affairs.

naufragio, *näüfrä'hïö*, sm. shipwreck.

náufrago, ga, *nä'üfrägö*, a. relating to shipwreck.

náusea, *nä'üsëä*, sf. nauseousness, nausea.

náutica, *nä'ütïkä*, sf. art of navigating.

navaja, *nävä'hä*, sf. clasp-knife; razor.

navajada, *—hä'dä*, sf. gash given with a knife. [shaving-towel.

navajero, *—hä'rö*, sm. razor-case;

naval, *nävä'l*, a. naval.

nave, *nä'vë*, sf. ship; nave.

navegable, *nävëgä'blë*, a. navigable.

navegación, *—gäthïön'*, sf. navigation.

navegador, *—gädör'*, **navegante**, *—gän'të*, sm. navigator.

navegar, *nävëgär'*, v. n. to navigate.

naveta, *nävë'tä*, sf. cream.

navidad, *nävïdäd'*, sf. nativity.

navío, *nävï'ö*, sm. ship.

náyade, *nä'yädë*, sf. naiad, water-nymph.

neblina, *nëblï'nä*, sf. mist, fine rain, drizzle.

nebuloso, sa, *nëbülö'sö*, a. misty, cloudy, nebulous, foggy, hazy, drizzling.

necear, *nëthëär'*, v. n. to talk nonsense.

necedad, *—däd'*, sf. gross ignorance, stupidity; imprudence.

necesaria, *—sä'rïä*, sf. privy, water-closet.

necesario, ria, *—sä'rïö*, a. necessary.

necesidad, *—sïdäd'*, sf. necessity, need, want. [needy.

necesitado, da, *—sïtä'dö*, a. necessitous,

necesitar, *—sïtär'*, v. a. to necessitate; —, v. n. to want, to need.

necio, cia, *në'thïö*, a. ignorant, stupid, foolish; imprudent.

necrología, *nëkrölö'hë'ä*, sf. necrology, an account of persons deceased. [tuary.

necrologio, *—lö'hïö*, sm. necrology, mor-

néctar, *nëk'tär*, sm. nectar. [abominable.

nefando, da, *nëfän'dö*, a. base, nefarious,

nefario, ria, *nëfä'rïö*, a. nefarious, abominable. [or wrong.

nefas, *nä'fäs*, ad. por fas ó por —, right

negación, *nëgäthïön'*, sf. negation.

negado, *nëgä'dö*, a. incapable, unfit.

negar, *nëgär'*, v. a. to deny, to abnegate; to refuse; —se, to decline to do a thing.

negativa, *—tï'vä*, sf. negation; repulse; negative.

negativo, va, *—tï'vö*, a. negative.

negligencia, *nëglïhën'thïä*, sf. negligence.

negligente, *—hën'të*, a. negligent, careless, heedless.

negociación, *nëgöthïäthïön'*, sf. negotiation; commerce. [dealer.

negociante, *—thïän'të*, sm. & f. trader,

negociar, *—thïär'*, v. n. to negotiate (bills of exchange, political affairs).

negocio, *nëgö'thïö*, sm. business, affair; negotiation. [appear black.

negrear, *nëgrëär'*, v. n. to grow black, to

negrillo, *nëgrïl'yö*, sm. black poplar.

negro, gra, *nä'grö*, a. black; jetty; sm. negro, blackamoor.

negrura, *nëgrö'rä*, sf. blackness.

negruzco, ca, *nëgrüth'kö*, a. blackish.

némine discrepante, *në'mïnë dïskrë-pän'të*, ad. unanimously.

nene, *në'në*, sm., **nena**, *në'nä*, sf. baby.

neófito, *nëö'fïtö*, sm. neophyte.

nervio, *nër'vïö*, sm. nerve.

nervoso, sa, *nërvö'sö*, a. nervous.

nervudo, da, *—vö'dö*, a. nervous, vigorous.

nesga, *nës'gä*, sf. gore (of a gown).

neto, ta, *në'tö*, a. neat, pure, net.

neutral, *nëüträl'*, a. neutral, neuter.

neutralidad, *—lïdäd'*, sf. neutrality.

neutralizar, *—lïthär'*, v. a. (chem.) to neutralize.

neutro, tra, *në'üträ*, a. neutral, neuter.

nevada, *nëvä'dä*, sf. heavy fall of snow.

nevar, *nëvär'*, v. n. to snow.

nevera, *nëvë'rä*, **nevería**, *—rï'ä*, sf. [ice-house.

ni, *nï*, c. neither, nor.

nicho, *nĭtsh'ŏ*, sm, niche.

nido, *nĭ'dŏ*, sm. nest; habitation.

niebla, *nĭá'blă*, sf. fog, mist.

nieta, *nĭá'tă*, sf. granddaughter.

nieto, *nĭá'tŏ*, sm. grandson.

nieve, *nĭá'vĕ*, sf. snow.

nigromancia, *nĭgrŏmăn'thă̆*, sf. necro- [mancy.

nigromante, *–măn'tĕ*, sm. necromancer.

nigromántico, ca, *–măn'tĭkŏ*, a. necro- mantic.

nimiamente, *nĭ'mĭ̆mĕntĕ*, ad.excessively.

nimiedad, *nĭmĭĕdăd'*, sf. excess; extra- vagant nicety.

nimio, mia, *nĭ'mĭŏ*, a. excessive, too little.

ninfa, *nĭn'fă*, sf. nymph.

ningún, *nĭngūn'*, a, none, not one.

ninguno, na, *nĭngŏ'nŏ*, a. none, not one, neither,   [of the eye.

niña, *nĭn'yă̆*, sf. little girl; pupil, apple

niñada, *–yă̆'dă̆*, sf. puerility, childishness.

niñear, *–yĕăr'*, v. n. to act like a child.

niñera, *–yă̆'ră̆*, sf. nursemaid.   [action.

niñería, *–yĕrĭ'ă̆*, sf. puerility, childish

niñero, ra, *–yă̆'rŏ*, a. fond of children.

niñez, *–yĕth'*, sf. childhood.

niño, ña, *nĭn'yŏ*, a. childish; –, sm. child, infant; desde –, from infancy, from a child.

níspera, *nĭs'pĕră̆*, sf. medlar; –, sm. medlar- [child.

níspero, *nĭs'pĕrŏ*, sm. medlar-tree.

nitrato, *nĭtră̆'tŏ*, sm. (chem.) nitrate.

nitro, *nĕ'trŏ*, sm. nitre, saltpetre.

nivel, *nĭvĕl'*, sm. level, plane; á –, per- fectly level.

nivelador, *nĭvĕlădŏr'*, sm. leveller.

nivelar, *nĭvĕlăr'*, v. a. to level.

no, *nŏ*, ad. no; not.

noble, *nŏ'blĕ*, a. noble, illustrious, generous.

nobleza, *nŏblĕ'thă̆*, sf. nobleness, nobility.

noción, *nŏthĭŏn'*, sf. notion, idea.

nocivo, va, *nŏthĭ'vŏ*, a. noxious, hurtful.

nocturno, na, *nŏktŭr'nŏ*, a. nocturnal, nightly; –, sm. nocturn.

noche, *nŏtsh'ĕ*, sf. night; –buena, Christ- mas eve; ¡buenas –s! good night!

nodriza, *nŏdrĭ'thă̆*, sf. nurse.

nogal, *nŏgăl'*, sm. common walnut-tree.

nómade, *nŏ'mădĕ*, a, nomad, nomadic.

nombradía, *nŏmbrădĭ'ă̆*, sf. fame, repu- tation.   [tion; appointment.

nombramiento, *–mĭĕn'tŏ*, sm. nomina-

nombrar, *–brăr'*, v. a. to name; to nomi- nate, to appoint.   [tion.

nombre, *nŏm'brĕ*, sm. name; title; reputa-

nomenclatura, *nŏmĕnklătŏ'ră̆*, sf. nomen- clature; catalogue.

nómina, *nŏ'mĭnă̆*, sf. catalogue.

nominador, *–nădŏr'*, sm. nominator.

nominal, *–năl'*, a. nominal.   [native.

nominativo, *–nătĭ'vŏ*, sm. (gr.) nomi-

nomparelle, *nŏmpărĕl'yĕ*, sf. nonpareil [(type).

non, *nŏn'*, a. odd, uneven.

nona, *nŏ'nă̆*, sf. none.

nonada, *nŏnă̆'dă̆*, sf. trifle.

nonagenario, ria, *–'hĕnă̆'rĭŏ*, a. ninety years old; –, sm. & f. nonagenarian.

nonagésimo, ma, *–'hă̆'sĭmŏ*, a. ninetieth.

nonato, ta, *nŏnă̆'tŏ*, a. applied to one who has not been naturally born, but dragged

out of the mother's womb by means of the cesarean section.

nono, na, *nŏ'nŏ*, a. ninth.

no obstante, *nŏ ŏbstăn'tĕ*, ad. neverthe- less, notwithstanding.

nord, *nŏrd*, sm. north wind.

nordest(e), *–ĕs'tĕ*, sm. north-east.

noria, *nŏ'rĭă̆*, sf. chain-pump; draw-well.

norma, *nŏr'mă̆*, sf. square (tool); rule to guide and govern all operations.

norte, *nŏr'tĕ*, sm. north; rule, guide.

nos, *nŏs*, pn. we.

nosotros, tras, *–ŏ'trŏs*, pn. we, ourselves.

nostalgia, *nŏstăl'hĭă̆*, sf. home-sickness.

nota, *nŏ'tă̆*, sf. note, notice, remark.

notable, *nŏtă̆'blĕ*, a. notable, remarkable; –, sm. introductory observation.

notar, *nŏtăr'*, v. a. to note, to mark; to remark.   [tary; notary's office.

notaría, *nŏtă̆rĭ'ă̆*, sf. profession of a no-

notario, *nŏtă̆'rĭŏ*, sm. notary.

noticia, *nŏtĭ'thĭă̆*, sf. notice, knowledge, information, note; news.

noticiar, *nŏtĭthĭăr'*, v. a. to give notice.

noticioso, sa, *–thĭŏ'sŏ*, a. informed; learned.

notificación, *–fĭkă̆thĭŏn'*, sf. notification.

notificar, *–fĭkăr'*, v. a. to notify, to inform.

notoriedad, *nŏtŏrĭĕdăd'*, sf. notoriety.

notorio, ria, *nŏtŏ'rĭŏ*, a. notorious.

novación, *nŏvă̆thĭŏn'*, sf. renovation of an obligation formerly contracted.

noval, *nŏvăl'*, a. grown on newly broken up ground; newly broken up ground, and the fruits it produces.   [in anything.

novato, ta, *nŏvă̆'tŏ*, a. new, commencing

novator, *–tŏr'*, sm. innovator.

novecientos, tas, *nŏvĕthĭĕn'tŏs*, a. nine hundred.

novedad, *nŏvĕdăd'*, sf. novelty, modern- ness; admiration excited by novelties.

novela, *nŏvĕ'lă̆*, sf. novel, falsehood, fiction.

novelero, ra, *nŏvĕlĕ'rŏ*, a. fond of novels; fond of hearing and telling news; new- fangled; inconstant; –, sm. newsmonger.

novena, *nŏvĕ'nă̆*, sf. term of nine days ap- propriated to some special worship.

novenario, *nŏvĕnă̆'rĭŏ*, sm. novenary.

noveno, na, *nŏvĕ'nŏ*, a. ninth.

noventa, *nŏvĕn'tă̆*, sm. ninety.

novia, *nŏ'vĭă̆*, sf. bride; woman betrothed.

noviciado, *nŏvĭthĭă̆'dŏ*, sm. novitiate.

novicio, *nŏvĭ'thĭŏ*, sm. novice.

noviembre, *nŏvĭĕm'brĕ*, sm. November.

novilunio, *nŏvĭlŏ'nĭŏ*, sm. new-moon.

novilla, *nŏvĭl'yă̆*, sf. heifer.

novillada, *–yă̆'dă̆*, sf. drove of young bulls; fight of young bulls.

novillo, *nŏvĭl'yŏ*, sm. young bull or ox.

novio, *nŏ'vĭŏ*, sm. bridegroom.

novísimo, ma, *nŏvĭsĭmŏ*, a newest; –, sm. either of the four last events of man (death, judgment, heaven and hell).

nubada, *nŏbă̆'dă̆*, sf. shower of rain; plenty.

nubado, da, *–dŏ*, a. clouded (of stuffs).

nubarrón, *nŏbărrŏn'*, sm. heavy shower of rain, large cloud.

nube, *nŏ'bĕ*, sf. cloud; film.

nublado, *nōblă'dŏ,* sm. clouds announcing a storm.   [to be clouded.

nublarse, *nōblăr'sĕ,* v. r. to be afflicted.

nuca, *nō'kă,* sf. nape, scruff of the neck.

núcleo, *nō'klĕŏ,* sm. kernel of a nut.

nudillo, *nōdĭl'yŏ,* sm. knuckle; small knot made in stockings.

nudo, *nō'dŏ,* sm. knot; knuckle.

nudoso, sa, *nōdŏ'sŏ,* a. knotty.

nuera, *nŏā'ră,* sf. daughter-in-law.

nuestro, tra, *nŏĕs'trŏ,* a. our.

nueva, *nŏā'vă,* sf. news.

nueve, *nŏā'vĕ,* sm. & a. nine.

nuevo, va, –*vŏ,* a. new, modern, fresh; ¿qué hay de –? is there any news? what news?

nuez, *nŏĕth',* sf. walnut; Adam's apple; **apretará uno la –,** to strangle; **–moscada ó de especia,** nutmeg.

nulidad, *nōlĭdăd',* sf. nullity.

nulo, la, *nŏ'lŏ,* a. null.   [genius.

numen, *nō'mĕn,* sm. divinity; poetical

numeración, *nōmĕrăthĭŏn',* sf. numeration.

numerador, –*dŏr',* sm. numerator.

numeral, *nōmĕrăl',* a. numeral.

numerar, –*răr',* v. a. to number, **to numerate,** to count.

numerario, ria, *rā'rĭŏ,* a. numerary; **–,** sm. hard cash, coin.

numérico, ca, *nōmā'rĭkŏ,* a. numerical.

número, *nō'mĕrŏ,* sm. number; cipher.

Números, –s, sm. pl. the book of Numbers.

numeroso, sa, *nōmĕrŏ'sŏ,* a. numerous.

nunca, *nōn'kă,* ad. never.

nunciatura, *nōnthiătō'ră,* sf. nunciature.

nuncio, *nōn'thĭŏ,* sm. messenger; nuncio.

nuncupativa, va, *nōnkŏpătĭ'vŏ,* a. nominal; verbally pronounced.

nupcial, *nōpthĭăl',* a. nuptial.   [ding.

nupcias, *nōp'thĭăs,* sf. pl. nuptials, wed-

nutria, *nō'trĭă,* nutria, –*trĭă,* sf. otter.

nutrición, *nōtrĭthĭŏn',* sf. nutrition.

nutrimento, –*mĕn'tŏ,* sm. food, aliment, nourishment; nutrition.

nutrir, *nōtrĭr',* v. a. to nourish.

nutritivo, va, *nōtrĭtĭ'vŏ,* a. nutritive, [nourishing.

nutriz, *nōtrĭth',* sf. nurse.

N.

ñagaza, *nyăgă'thă,* sf. bird-call.

ñañaros, *nyănyă'rŏs,* sm. pl. speaking puppet-show.

ñaque, *nyă'kĕ,* sm. hodge-podge.

ñoclos, *nyŏ'klŏs,* sm. pl. kind of macaroons.

ñoño, ña, *nyŏ'nyŏ,* a. decrepit, impaired by age.

ñoñería, *nyŏnyĕrē'ă,* sf. dotage.

O.

ó, ŏ, c. or; either.

¡o! ŏ, interj. oh!

obcecación, *ŏbthĕkăthĭŏn',* sf. obduracy.

obcecar, *ŏbthĕkăr',* v. a. to blind, to darken.

obedecer, *ŏbĕdĕthĕr',* v. a. to obey.

obediencia, *ŏbĕdĭĕn'thĭă,* sf. obedience; **á la –,** at your service, your most obedient.

obediente, –*tĕ,* a. obedient.

obelisco, *ŏbĕlĭs'kŏ,* sm. obelisk.   [pl.

obenques, *ŏbĕn'kĕs,* sm. pl. (mar.) shrouds,

obertura, *ŏbĕrtō'ră,* sf. (mus.) overture.

obesidad, *ŏbĕsĭdăd',* sf. obesity.

obeso, sa, *ŏbā'sŏ,* a. obese, fat.

óbice, *ŏ'bĭthĕ,* sm. obstacle.   [copate.

obispado, *ŏbĭspă'dŏ,* sm. bishopric; epis-

obispillo, –*pĭl'yŏ,* sm. boy-bishop; large black-pudding; croup of a fowl.

obispo, *ŏbĭs'pŏ,* sm. bishop; **– de anillo,** bishop in partibus.

objeción, *ŏb'hĕthĭŏn',* sf. objection, opposition, exception.   [pose.

objetar, *ŏb'hĕtăr',* v. a. to object, to op-

objetivo, va, –*tĕ'vŏ,* a. objective.

objeto, *ŏb'hĕ'tŏ,* sm. object.

oblación, *ŏblăthĭŏn',* sf. oblation, offering.

oblada, *ŏblă'dă,* sf. funeral offering.

oblata, –*tă,* sf. money given to the church to defray the expenses of celebrating mass; host and chalice offered before being consecrated in the celebration of mass.

oblea, *ŏblā'ă,* sf. wafer.

oblicuidad, *ŏblĭkŭĭdăd',* sf. obliquity.

oblicuo, cua, *ŏblĭ'kŭŏ,* a. oblique.

obligación, *ŏblĭgăthĭŏn',* sf. obligation; **–ones,** pl. character and integrity.

obligado, –*gă'dŏ,* sm. public contractor; (law) obligee.

obligar, *ŏblĭgăr',* v. a. to oblige.

obligatorio, ria, –*tŏ'rĭŏ,* a. obligatory.

oblongo, ga, *ŏblŏn'gŏ,* a. oblong.

oboe, *ŏbŏ'ĕ,* sm. hautboy, oboe.

óbolo, *ŏ'bŏlŏ,* sm. obolus; obole.

obra, *ŏ'bră,* sf. work; means, virtue, power; toil, work, labour, employment; **poner por –,** to set to work.

obrada, *ŏbră'dă,* sf. as much ground as two mules or oxen can plough in a day.

obrador, ra, –*dŏr',* sm. & f. workman, workwoman; artificer; work-shop.

obrar, *ŏbrăr',* v. a. to work; to operate, **to** act; to put into practice.

obrepción, *ŏbrĕpthĭŏn',* sf. obreption.

obrepticio, cia, –*tĕ'thĭŏ,* a. obreptitious.

obrero, ra, *ŏbrā'rŏ,* sm. & f. workman, day-labourer.

obscenidad, *ŏbsthĕnĭdăd',* sf. obscenity.

obsceno, na, *ŏbthĕ'nŏ,* a. obscene.

obscurecer, *ŏbskŭrĕthĕr',* v. a. to obscure, to darken; **–,** v. imp. to grow dark; **–se,** to disappear.

obscuridad, *ŏbskŭrĭdăd',* sf. obscurity; darkness.

obscuro, ra, *ŏbskŭ'rŏ,* a. obscure, dark.

obsequiar, *ŏbsĕkĭăr',* v. a. to cour.

obsequio, –*sā'kĭŏ,* sm. obsequiousness, compliance.   [compliant, officious.

obsequioso, sa, –*sĕkĭŏ'sŏ,* a. obsequious,

observación, *ŏbsĕrvăthĭŏn',* sf. observation; remark.   [vor

observador, –*dŏr',* sm. observer, observa-

observancia, *ŏbsĕrvăn'thĭă,* sf. observance; ceremonial reverence.

observar, *ŏbsĕrvăr',* v. a. to observe.

observatorio, –sărvătŏ′riŏ, sm. observatory.   [pediment, hindrance.

obstáculo, ŏbstă′kŭlŏ, sm. obstacle, impediment, hindrance.

obstar, ŏbstăr′, v. n. to oppose, to obstruct, to hinder.   [stubbornness.

obstinación, ŏbstĭnăthĭŏn′, sf. obstinacy,

obstinado, –nă′dŏ, a. obstinate.

obstinarse, –năr′sĕ, v. r. to be obstinate.

obstrucción, ŏbstrŭkthĭŏn′, sf. (med.) obstruction.

obstruir, ŏbstrŭĭr′, v. a. to obstruct; –se, to be blocked up, to be obstructed.

obtener, ŏbtĕnĕr′, v. a. to obtain.

obtuso, sa, –tŏ′sŏ, a. obtuse, blunt.

obué, ŏbŏĕ′, sm. (mus.) hautboy.

obús, ŏbŭs′, sm. (mil.) howitzer.

obvención, ŏbvĕnthĭŏn′, sf. casual profit.

obviar, –vĭăr′, v. a. to obviate, to prevent.

obvio, via, ŏb′vĭŏ, a. obvious, evident.

ocasión, ŏkăsĭŏn′, sf. occasion, opportunity, danger, risk.

ocasional, ŏkăsĭŏnăl′, a. occasional.

ocasionar, –năr′, v. a. to cause, to occasion; to move, to excite.

ocaso, ŏkă′sŏ, sm. occident.   [western.

occidental, ŏkthĭdĕntăl′, a. occidental.

occidente, –dĕn′tĕ, sm. occident, west.

occipucio, –pŏ′thĭŏ, sm. occiput.

océano, ŏthă′ănŏ, sm. ocean.

ocio, ŏ′thĭŏ, sm. leisure; pastime.

ociosidad, ŏthĭŏsĭdăd′, sf. idleness, leisure.

ocioso, sa, ŏthĭŏ′sŏ, a. idle, vacant; procre, ŏ′krĕ, sm. ochre.   [fitable.

octava, ŏktă′vă, sf. octave.

octavario, –vă′rĭŏ, sm. eight days' festival.

octavo, va, ŏktă′vŏ, a. eight; libro en –, octavo volume.

octubre, ŏktŏ′brĕ, sm. October.

ocular, ŏkŭlăr′, a. ocular; –, sm. eye-glass.

oculista, –lĭs′tă, sm. oculist.

ocultación, ŏkŭltăthĭŏn′, sf. concealment.

ocultar, –tăr′, v. a. to hide, to conceal.

oculto, ta, ŏkŭl′tŏ, a. hidden, concealed, secret.   [business, employment.

ocupación, ŏkŭpăthĭŏn′, sf. occupation;

ocupar, –păr′, v. a. to occupy, to hold an office; –se, to occupy, to follow a business.

ocurrencia, ŏkŭrrĕn′thĭă, sf. occurrence, accident; idea occurring to the mind.

ocurrir, ŏkŭrrĭr′, v. n. to meet; to occur, to happen.   [eight-sided.

ochavado, da, ŏtshăvă′dŏ, a. octagonal,

ochavar, –văr′, v. a. to form an octagon.

ochavo, ŏtshă′vŏ, sm. small Spanish brass coin, valued at two maravedies.

ochenta, ŏtshĕn′tă, a. eighty.

ocho, ŏtshŏ′, sm. & a. eight.

ochocientos, –thĭĕn′tŏs, a. eight hundred.

oda, ŏ′dă, sf. ode.

odiar, ŏdĭăr′, v. a. to hate; –se, to hate one another.

odio, ŏ′dĭŏ, sm. hatred.   [one another.

odioso, sa, ŏdĭŏ′sŏ, a. odious, hateful.

odorífero, ra, ŏdŏrĕ′fĕrŏ, a. odoriferous, fragrant.

odre, ŏ′drĕ, sm. wine-bag; drunkard.

oeste, ŏĕs′tĕ, sm. west-wind.

ofender, ŏfĕndĕr′, v. a. to offend, to injure; –se, to be vexed; to take offence.

ofensa, ŏfĕn′să, sf. offence, injury.

ofensivo, va, –sĕ′vŏ, a. offensive, injurious.

ofensor, –sŏr′, sm. offender.

oferta, ŏfĕr′tă, sf. offer; offering.

ofertorio, –tŏ′rĭŏ, sm. offertory.

oficial, ŏfĭthĭăl′, sm. workman, artificer; officer; clerk in a public office.

oficiala, –thĭă′lă, sf. work-woman.

oficiar, –thĭăr′, v. a. to officiate, to minister (of clergymen, &c.).

oficina, –thĕ′nă, sf. work-shop; office, counting-house, business-room; –s, pl. lower apartments in houses.

oficio, ŏfĕ′thĭŏ, sm. office, employ, occupation, ministry; function; official letter; trade, business; notary's office; –s, pl. divine service.

oficiosidad, ŏfĭthĭŏsĭdăd′, sf. diligence; officiousness; importunity.

oficioso, sa, –thĭŏ′sŏ, a. officious, diligent; meddling.

ofrecer, ŏfrĕthĕr′, v. a. to offer; to present; to exhibit; –se, to offer, to occur, to present itself.   [promise.

ofrecimiento, –thĭmĭĕn′tŏ, sm. offer.

ofrenda, ŏfrĕn′dă, sf. offering, oblation.

ofrendar, –dăr′, v. a. to present offerings to God.   [sight; obfuscation.

ofuscación, ŏfŭskăthĭŏn′, sf. dimness of

ofuscar, –kăr′, v. a. to darken, to render obscure

oídas, ŏĭ′dăs, de ó por –, by hearsay.

oído, ŏĭ′dŏ, sm. hearing; ear; touch-hole.

oidor, ŏĭdŏr′, sm. hearer; judge appointed to hear pleadings and decide law-suits.

oir, ŏĭr′, v. a. to hear; to listen; to understand.   [stand.

ojal, ŏ′hăl′, sm. button-hole.

¡ojalá! ŏ′hălă′, would to God! God grant!

ojaladura, –dŏ′ră, sf. the set of button-holes in a suit of clothes.

ojalar, ŏ′hălăr′, v. a. to make button-holes.

ojeada, ŏ′hĕ′dă, sf. eye-glance, ogle.

ojear, ŏ′hĕăr′, v. a. to eye, to view; to glance; to rouse or put up game by hallooing.   [the chase by hallooing.

ojeo, ŏ′hĕ′ŏ, sm. putting up of game for

ojera, ŏ′hĕ′ră, sf. bluish circle under the lower eyelid, indicative of indisposition.

ojeriza, ŏ′hĕrĕ′thă, sf. spite, grudge, ill-will.   [(fam.) anus.

ojete, ŏ′hĕ′tĕ, sm. eyelet-hole in clothes;

ojimel, ŏ′hĕmĕl′, sm. oxymel.

ojo, ŏ′hŏ, sm. eye; sight; eye of a needle;

ola, ŏ′lă, sf. wave.   [arch of a bridge.

olaje, ŏlă′hĕ, sm. succession of waves, sea-swell.

oleada, ŏlĕă′dă, sf. surge; violent emotion.

olear, ŏlĕăr′, v. a. to administer extreme unction.   [oil.

óleo, ŏ′lĕŏ, sm. oil; extreme unction; holy

oler, ŏlĕr′, v. a. to smell, to scent; –, v. n. to smell; to smack of.

olfato, ŏlfă′tŏ, sm. odour; scent.

oligarquía, ŏlĭgărkĕ′ă, sf. oligarchy.

oligárquico, ca, –găr′kĭkŏ, a. oligarchical.

olímpico, ca, ŏlĕm′pĭkŏ, a. olympic.

Olimpo, *olím'pŏ*, sm. (poet.) heaven.

oliva, *ŏlē'vā*, sf. olive; olive-tree; owl.

olivar, *ŏlivār'*, sm. olive-grove.

olivo, *ŏlē'vŏ*, sm. olive-tree.

olmo, *ŏl'mŏ*, sm. elm-tree.

olor, *ŏlōr'*, sm. odour, scent.

oloroso, sa, *ŏlŏrō'sā*, a. fragrant, odorous.

olvidadizo, za, *ŏlvidādē'thŏ*, a. forgetful.

olvidar, *ŏlvidār'*, v. a. to forget.

olvido, *ŏl'vē'dŏ*, sm. forgetfulness.

olla, *ōl'yā*, sf. round earthen pot; oglio; — **podrida**, dish composed of different boiled meats and vegetables; **—s**, pl. gulf.

ollería, *ŏlyerē'ā*, sf. pottery.

ollero, *ŏlyē'rŏ*, sm. potter.

ombligo, *ŏmblē'gŏ*, sm. navel.

ominoso, sa, *ŏminō'sā*, a. ominous.

omisión, *ŏmisión'*, sf. omission.

omitir, *ŏmitir'*, v. a. to omit.

omnipotencia, *ŏmnipŏtén'thiā*, sf. omnipotence, almightiness.

omnipotente, *—pŏtén'tē*, a. omnipotent.

omniscio, scia, *ŏmnis'thiŏ*, a. all-knowing.

once, *ŏn'thē*, sm. & a. eleven.

onceno, na, *ŏnthē'nŏ*, a. eleventh.

onda, *ŏn'dā*, sf. wave.

ondear, *ŏndēar'*, v. a. to undulate; to fluctuate; **—se**, to see-saw.

oneroso, sa, *ŏnerō'sā*, a. burdensome.

ontología, *ŏntŏlŏ'hē'ā*, sf. ontology.

onza, *ŏn'thā*, sf. ounce; linx.

onzavo, va, *—thā'vŏ*, a. eleventh; **—**, sm. eleventh part.

opacidad, *ŏpāthidād'*, sf. opacity, gloom, darkness.

opaco, ca, *ŏpā'kŏ*, a. opaque; dark; melancholy, gloomy.

opción, *ŏpthión'*, sf. option, choice.

ópera, *ŏ'pērā*, sf. opera.

operación, *ŏpērāthión'*, sf. operation.

operar, *ŏpērār'*, v. n. to operate, to act.

operario, *—rā'riŏ*, sm. operator, labourer.

opiata, *ŏpiā'tā*, sf. opiate.

opilación, *ŏpilāthión'*, sf. obstruction of the body; stoppage of menstruation.

opilar, *ŏpilār'*, v. a. to oppilate, to obstruct.

ópimo, ma, *ŏ'pimŏ*, a. rich, fruitful.

opinable, *ŏpinā'blē*, a. problematical.

opinión, *ŏpinión'*, sf. opinion.

opio, *ŏ'piŏ*, sm. opium.

opíparo, ra, *ŏpē'pārŏ*, a. sumptuous.

oponer, *ŏpōnēr'*, v. a. to oppose; **—se**, to oppose, to be opposite.

oportunidad, *ŏpŏrtūnidād'*, sf. opportunity.

oportuno, na, *—tō'nŏ*, a. seasonable, opportune.

oposición, *ŏpŏsithión'*, sf. opposition; competition of skill.

opositor, *—tŏr'*, sm. opposer, opponent.

opresión, *ŏprēsión'*, sf. oppression.

opresivo, va, *—sē'vŏ*, a. oppressive.

opresor, *—sŏr'*, sm. oppressor.

oprimir, *ŏprimir'*, v. a. to oppress; to crush, to press, to squeeze.

oprobio, *ŏprŏ'biŏ*, sm. opprobrium, ignominy.

optar, *ŏptār'*, v. a. to choose, to elect.

optativo, *ŏptātē'vŏ*, a. (gr.) optative.

óptica, *ŏp'tikā*, sf. optics.

óptico, ca, *—tikŏ*, a. optical; **—**, sm. optician.

optimista, *—mis'tā*, sm. optimist.

óptimo, ma, *ŏp'timŏ*, a. best.

opuesto, ta, *ŏpŏés'tŏ*, a. opposite, contrary, adverse.

opulencia, *ŏpūlén'thiā*, sf. wealth, riches.

opulento, ta, *—lén'tŏ*, a. opulent, wealthy.

opúsculo, *ŏpŏs'kŭlŏ*, sm. opuscule.

oración, *ŏrāthión'*, sf. oration, speech; prayer; **—ones**, pl. prayers at sunset.

oráculo, *ŏrā'kŭlŏ*, sm. oracle.

orador, *ŏrādŏr'*, sm. orator.

orar, *ŏrār'*, v. n. to harangue; to pray.

orate, *ŏrā'tē*, sm. & f. lunatic, madcap.

oratoria, *ŏrātŏ'riā*, sf. oratory, rhetorical skill.

oratorio, *—riŏ*, sm. oratory; oratorio; **—**, ria, a. rhetorical.

orbe, *ŏr'bē*, sm. orb, sphere, the earth; celestial body.

órbita, *ŏr'bitā*, sf. orbit.

orden, *ŏr'dēn*, sm. & f. order (in all its meanings); **—del día**, order of the day.

ordenación, *—nāthión'*, sf. arrangement; ordination; edict, ordinance.

ordenando, *—nān'dŏ*, sm. candidate for holy orders; ordination.

ordenanza, *—nān'thā*, sf. order; statute, ordinance.

ordenar, *—nār'*, v. a. to arrange; to order; to ordain; **—se**, to take holy orders.

ordeñar, *—nyār'*, v. a. to milk.

ordinal, *ŏrdināl'*, a. ordinal.

ordinario, ria, *—nā'riŏ*, a. ordinary, common; **—**, sm. ordinary; established judge of ecclesiastical cases; carrier, carman; **de —**, regularly, commonly, ordinarily.

orear, *ŏrēār'*, v. a. to cool, to refresh; to air; **—se**, to take the air.

orégano, *ŏrā'gānŏ*, sm. wild marjoram.

oreja, *ŏrē'hā*, sf. ear; auricle.

orejera, *—hā'rā*, sf. covering for the ears to defend them from cold; pot-ear.

orejón, *—hŏn'*, sm. preserved peach; young nobleman of the ancient nobility of Peru.

oreo, *ŏrā'ŏ*, sm. breeze, fresh air.

orfandad, *ŏrfāndād'*, sf. orphanage.

organero, *ŏrgānē'rŏ*, sm. organ-builder.

orgánico, ca, *ŏrgā'nikŏ*, a. organic; harmonious.

organista, *—nis'tā*, sm. organist.

organización, *—nithāthión'*, sf. organization; arrangement.

organizar, *—nithār'*, v. a. to organize.

órgano, *ŏr'gānŏ*, sm. organ.

orgullo, *ŏrgŭl'yŏ*, sm. pride, haughtiness.

orgulloso, sa, *—yŏ'sŏ*, a. proud, haughty.

oriental, *ŏriéntāl'*, a. oriental, eastern.

oriente, *ŏrién'tē*, sm. orient; aperture.

orificio, *ŏrifē'thiŏ*, sm. orifice, mouth.

origen, *ŏrē'hēn*, sm. origin, source; natal country; family, extraction.

original, *ŏrihināl'*, a. original, primitive; **—**, sm. original, first copy.

originalidad, *—nālidād'*, sf. originality.

originar, *—nār'*, v. a. & n. to originate.

originario, ria, *—nā'riŏ*, a. originary.

orilla, *ŏrēl'yā*, sf. limit, border, margin; edge of cloth, foot-path in a street; shore.

orillar, *—yār'*, v. n. & a. to approach the shore; to arrange, to order.

orillo, *ŏrēl'yŏ*, sm. list, selvage.

orín, *orēn'*, sm. rust; urine.
orina, *ō-rē'nă*, sf. urine.
orinal, *ōrēnāl'*, sm. chamber-pot.
orinar, *-ār'*, v. n. to pass or make water.
oriundo, da, *ō-rēŏn'dŏ*, a. derived from.
orla, *ōr'lă*, sf. list, selvage, border.
orladura, *ŏrlādōō'ră*, sf. border, edging, list.
orlar, *ōrlär'*, v. a. to border, to edge.
ornamento, *ōrnāmĕn'tŏ*, sm. ornament, embellishment.   [decoration.
ornato, *ōrnä'tŏ*, sm. apparel, ornament.
oro, *ō'rŏ*, sm. gold; —s, pl. diamonds (at cards).
oropel, *ōrŏpĕl'*, sm. tinsel.
orquesta, *ōrkĕs'tă*, sf. orchestre, orchestra.
ortiga, *ōrtē'gă*, sf. (bot.) nettle.
ortodoxia, *ōrtŏdŏk'sēă*, sf. orthodoxy.
ortodoxo, xa, *-dŏk'sŏ*, a. orthodox.
ortografía, *-grăf ē'ă*, sf. orthography.
ortográfico, ca, *-grä'fēkŏ*, a. orthographical.
oruga, *ōrōō'gă*, sf. (bot.) rocket; caterpillar.
orujo, *ōrōō'hŏ*, sm. peel of pressed grapes.
orza, *ŏr'thă*, sf. gallipot, crock.
os, *ŏs*, pn. you.
osa, *ō'să*, sf. she-bear.   [daringly.
osadamente, *ŏsädämĕn'tĕ*, ad. boldly,
osadía, *-dē'ă*, sf. boldness, intrepidity; zeal, fervour.
osamenta, *-mĕn'tă*, sf. skeleton.
osar, *ŏsār'*, v. n. to dare, to venture.
osario, *ŏsä'rēŏ*, sm. charnel-house.
oscilación, *ŏsthēlāthiŏn'*, sf. oscillation.
oscilar, *-lär'*, v. n. to oscillate.
ósculo, *ŏs'kŏlŏ*, sm. kiss.
osificarse, *ŏsēfēkär'sĕ*, v. r. to ossify.
oso, *ō'sŏ*, sm. bear; —blanco, polar bear.
ostensible, *ŏstĕnsē'blĕ*, a. ostensible, apparent.   [manifestation.
ostensión, *-sēŏn'*, sf. show, exhibition,
ostensivo, va, *-sē'vŏ*, a. ostensive.
ostentación, *-tāthiŏn'*, sf. ostentation, ambitious display, vain show.
ostentar, *-tär'*, v. a. to show; —, v. n. to boast, to brag.   [stations.
ostentoso, sa, *-tō'sŏ*, a. sumptuous, ostenostiario, *ŏstēä'rēŏ*, sm. ostiary, door-keeper.
ostiatim, *ŏstēä'tēm*, ad. from door to door.
ostra, *ŏs'tră*, sf. oyster.   [woman.
ostrera, *ŏstrē'ră*, sf. oyster-bed; oysterostrogodo, da, *ŏstrŏgō'dŏ*, a. ostrogothic.
osudo, da, *ŏsōō'dŏ*, a. bony, full of bones.
otoñal, *ŏtŏnyäl'*, a. autumnal.
otoñar, *ŏtŏnyār'*, v. n. to spend the autumn-season; to grow in autumn; —se, to be seasoned, to be tempered (applied to earth in autumn).   [after rain).
otoño, *ŏtō'nyŏ*, sm. autumn.
otorgamiento, *ŏtŏrgämiĕn'tŏ*, sm. grant, licence, license; contract.
otorgar, *-gär'*, v. a. to consent, to stipulate.
otro, tra, *ō'trŏ*, a. another, other.
otrosí, *ŏtrŏsē'*, ad. besides, moreover; —, sm. item; (law) every petition made after the principal.
ovación, *ŏväthiŏn'*, sf. ovation.
ovalado, da, *ŏvälä'dŏ*, a. oval-formed.
óvalo, *ŏ'välŏ*, sm. oval.
ovar, *ŏvär'*, v. n. to lay eggs.
ovario, *ŏvä'rēŏ*, sm. ovary.

oveja, *ŏvē'hă*, sf. ewe; —s, pl. white spume or froth of waves which break against rocks.
ovejero, *-hä'rŏ*, sm. shepherd.   [rocks.
ovejuno, na, *-hō'nŏ*, a. relating to ewes.
ovillar, *ŏvēlyär'*, v. n. to wind off from a reel, to reel off; to coil up; —se, to double
ovillo, *ŏvē'lyŏ*, sm. clew.   [oneself up.
oviparo, ra, *ŏvē'pärŏ*, a. oviparous, egg-bearing.
ovoso, sa, *ŏvō'sŏ*, a. full of sea-weeds.
óxido, *ŏk'sēdŏ*, sf. (chem.) oxide.
oxígeno, *ŏksē'hĕnŏ*, sm. (chem.) oxygen.
¡oxte! *ŏks'tĕ*, keep off! begone!
oyente, *ŏyĕn'tĕ*, a. & sm. & f. hearing; auditor, hearer.

P.

pabellón, *pābĕlyŏn'*, sm. pavilion; summer-house.
pábilo, *pä'bēlŏ*, sm. wick; snuff of a candle.
pábulo, *pä'bŏlŏ*, sm. food, provender; aliment.   [bundle.
paca, *pä'kă*, sf. spotted agouti; bale,
pacato, ta, *pä-kä'tŏ*, a. pacific, quiet, mild, gentle, tender, peaceable.
pacer, *päthēr'*, v. a. to pasture, to graze.
paciencia, *päthiĕn'thiă*, sf. patience.
paciente, *-tĕ*, a. & sm. patient.
pacificación, *päthēfēkäthiŏn'*, sf. pacification; peace of mind.
pacificar, *päthēfēkär'*, v. a. to pacify, to appease; —, v. n. to treat for peace.   [ful.
pacífico, ca, *päthē'fēkŏ*, a. pacific, peacepacotilla, *päkŏtē'lyă*, sf. freight, portage; (mar.) adventure.   [to stipulate.
pactar, *päktär'*, v. a. to convent, to contract,
pacto, *päk'tŏ*, sm. contract, pact.
pachorra, *pächŏr'ră*, sf. sluggishness.
padecer, *pädĕthēr'*, v. a. to suffer any bodily affliction; to sustain an injury; to be liable to.
padecimiento, *-thēmiĕn'tŏ*, sm. suffering, sufferance.   [agnail (on the finger).
padecímiento, *-thēmiĕn'tŏ*, sm. step-father;
padrastro, *pädräs'trŏ*, sm. step-father; agnail (on the finger).
padrazo, *pädrä'thŏ*, sm. over-indulgent father.
padre, *pä'drĕ*, sm. father; —s, pl. parents, ancestors; all the members of a religious congregation taken as a body.   [nity.
padrinazgo, *pädrēnäth'gŏ*, sm. compaterpadrino, *pädrē'nŏ*, sm. god-father; second, protector, assistant.   [pattern, model.
padrón, *pädrŏn'*, sm. poll; indulgent parent.
paga, *pä'gă*, sf. payment, fee.
pagadero, ra, *pägädē'rŏ*, a. payable.
pagador, *-dŏr'*, sm. payer; paymaster.
pagaduría, *-dŏrē'ă*, sf. paymaster's office.
paganismo, *pägänēs'mŏ*, sm. paganism, heathenism.
pagano, *pägä'nŏ*, sm. heathen, pagan; one who pays or contributes his share; —, na, a. heathenish; pagan.
pagar, *pägär'*, v. a. to pay; to requite; —se, to be pleased with oneself.

pagaré, *pǎgǎrě',* sm. bond, note of hand, promissory note, I. O. U. (I owe you).

página, *pǎ'hǐnǎ,* sf. page of a book.

pago, *pǎ'gō,* sm. payment; reward.

país, *pǎís',* sm. country, region.

paisaje, *pǎísǎ'hě,* sm. landscape.

paisanaje, *–sǎnǎ'hě',* sm. peasantry, lay inhabitants of a country.

paisano, na, *–sǎ'nō,* a. of the same country; –, sm. countryman.

paja, *pǎ'hǎ,* sf. straw; echar –s, to draw lots with straws.

pajar, *pǎ'hǎr',* sm. straw-loft.

pajarear, *–rěǎr',* v. a. to go bird-catching; to loiter about.

pajarera, *–rě'rǎ,* sf. aviary.

pajarero, *–rě'rō,* sm. bird-catcher. [flow.

pájaro, *pǎ'hǎrō,* sm. bird; sly, acute fel-

pajarota, *–rō'tǎ,* pajarotada, *–rōtǎ'dǎ,* sf. false, idle report.

pajarraco, *–rǎ'kō,* pajarruco, *–rō'kō,* sm. large bird; cunning fellow.

paje, *pǎ'hě,* sm. page.

pajera, *pǎ'hǎ'rǎ,* sf. stack of straw.

pajero, *–rō,* sm. dealer in straw.

pajizo, za, *pǎ'hě'thō,* a. made of straw; thatched with straw; straw-coloured.

pajuela, *pǎ'hǔě'lǎ,* sf. match.

pala, *pǎ'lǎ,* sf. shovel; fire-shovel.

palabra, *pǎlǎ'brǎ,* sf. word; á media –, at the least hint; de –, by word of mouth.

palabrada, *–brǎ'dǎ,* sf. low language.

palabrita, *–brě'tǎ,* sf. short word; word full of meaning.

palaciego, ga, *–thǐā'gō,* a. pertaining or relating to the palace; –, sm. courtier.

palacio, *pǎlǎ'thǐō,* sm. palace.

palada, *–dǎ,* sf. a shovel-full.

paladar, *pǎlǎdǎr',* sm. palate; taste, relish.

paladín, *–dǐn',* sm. paladin.

paladino, na, *–dǐ'nō,* a. manifest, clear, public.

palafrén, *–frěn',* sm. palfrey. [public.

palafrenero, *–frěně'rō,* groom.

palanca, *pǎlǎn'kǎ,* sf. lever.

palancada, *–kǎ'dǎ,* sf. leverage.

palancana, *–kǎ'nǎ,* palangana, *–gǎ'nǎ,* sf. basin. [with stakes.

palanquera, *–kě'rǎ,* sf. enclosure made

palanqueta, *–kě'tǎ,* sf. bar-shot; small lever.

palatinado, *pǎlǎtǐnǎ'dō,* sm. palatinate.

palatino, na, *–tǐ'nō,* a. belonging to the palace or courtiers; –, sm. Palatin.

palco, *pǎl'kō,* sm. box in a play-house; – de proscenio, stage-box.

palenque, *pǎlěn'kě,* sm. passage from the pit to the stage in a play-house.

palestra, *pǎlěs'trǎ,* sf. inclosure, palisade; palestra; art of wrestling. [trowel.

paleta, *pǎlě'tǎ,* sf. fire-shovel; palette;

paletada, *pǎlětǎ'dǎ,* sf. trowel-full.

paleto, *pǎlě'tō,* sm. fallow deer; clown, rustic.

palia, *pǎ'lǐǎ,* sf. altar-cloth; square.

paliar, *pǎlǐǎr',* v. a. to palliate, to excuse; to cloak.

paliativo, va, *–tǐ'vō,* a. palliative.

palidez, *pǎlǐděth',* sf. paleness, wanness.

pálido, da, *pǎ'lǐdō,* a. pallid, pale.

palillero, *pǎlǐlyě'rō,* sm. one who makes or sells tooth-picks; tooth-pick case.

palillo, *pǎlǐl'yō,* sm. knitting-needle case; rolling-pin; tooth-pick; –s, pl. bobbins; drumsticks. [tation.

palinodia, *pǎlǐnō'dǐǎ,* sf. palinody, recan-

palio, *pǎ'lǐō,* sm. cloak; pall.

palique, *pǎlǐ'kě,* sm. trifling conversation.

palitroque, *pǎlǐtrō'kě,* sm. rough, ill-shaped stick. [with a stick.

paliza, *pǎlǐ'thǎ,* sf. cudgelling, drubbing

palizada, *pǎlǐthǎ'dǎ,* sf. palisade.

palma, *pǎl'mǎ,* sf. date palm-tree; palm of the hand; palm-leaf.

palmada, *pǎlmǎ'dǎ,* sf. slap given with the palm of the hand, clap; –s, pl. clapping of hands. [winder.

palmatoria, *–tō'rǐǎ,* sf. wax-stand, wax-

palmear, *pǎlměǎr',* v. a. to slap with the open hand; to clap.

palmera, *pǎlmě'rǎ,* sf. palm-tree.

palmeta, *–mě'tǎ,* sf. ferule.

palmito, *–mǐ'tō,* sm. dwarf fan-palm.

palmo, *pǎl'mō,* sm. palm. [the open hand.

palmotear, *pǎlmōtěǎr',* v. a. to slap with

palmoteo, *–tě'ō,* sm. clapping of hands.

palo, *pǎ'lō,* sm. stick; cudgel; blow given with a stick; execution on the gallows; suit at cards; –s, pl. masting.

paloma, *pǎlō'mǎ,* sf. pigeon, dove; – torcaz, ring-dove; – zorita, wood-pigeon.

palomar, *pǎlōmǎr',* sm. pigeon-house.

palomera, *–mě'rǎ,* sf. bleak place, much exposed to the wind.

palomilla, *–mǐl'yǎ,* sf. young pigeon; back-bone of a horse; chrysalis; horse of a milk-white colour. [fumitory.

palomina, *–mě'nǎ,* sf. pigeon-dung; (bot.)

palomino, *–nō,* sm. young pigeon; stain of excrement upon the tail of a shirt.

palomo, *pǎlō'mō,* sm. cock-pigeon.

palotada, *pǎlōtǎ'dǎ,* sf. stroke with a battledore.

palote, *pǎlō'tě,* sm. stick of a middling size; drum-stick; –s, pl. thick lines copied by children learning to write. [clash.

paloteo, *pǎlōtě'ō,* sm. fight with sticks;

palpable, *pǎlpǎ'blě,* a. palpable, evident.

palpar, *–pǎr',* v. a. to feel, to touch, to grope. [panting.

palpitación, *pǎlpǐtǎthǐōn',* sf. palpitation,

palpitar, *–pǐtǎr',* v. n. to palpitate.

palude, *pǎlō'dě,* sf. lake, pool. [rude.

palurdo, da, *pǎlōr'dō,* a. rustic, clownish,

pámpana, *pǎm'pǎnǎ,* sf. vine-leaf.

pampanilla, *pǎmpǎnǐl'yǎ,* sf. loin-cloth of leaves worn by the Indians.

pámpano, *pǎm'pǎnō,* sm. young vine-branch or tendril. [tendrils.

pampanoso, sa, *–pǎnō'sō,* a. abounding in

pampirolada, *–pǐrōlǎ'dǎ,* sf. (fig. & fam.) impertinence.

pamplina, *–plǐ'nǎ,* sf. toasted bread steeped in gravy; duck-weed; futility, trifle.

pampringada, *–pringå då,* sf. frivolous thing.   [wheat; gold-leaf, silver-leaf.

pan, *pån,* sm. bread; loaf; food in general;

pana, *pā´nå,* sf. velvet, plush. [medicine.

panacea, *pånåthå´å,* sf. panacea, universal

panadería, *–dērȳ å,* sf. trade of a baker; bakehouse.

panadero, *–dd´rŏ,* sm. baker.

panadizo, *–dȳ´thŏ,* sm. whitlow; pale-faced, sickly person.   [(in Havannah).

panal, *pånål´,* sm. honey-comb; sweet-rusk

panarra, *pånår´rå,* sm. dolt, simpleton.

pandero, *påndd´rŏ,* sm. timbrel.

pandilla, *–dȳ´yå,* sf. plot, league.

pando, *da, pån´dŏ,* a. bulging, convex.

pandorga, *–dŏr´gå,* sf. fat, bulky woman.

panegírico, *ca, pånŏ´hē´rĭkŏ,* a. pane-gyrical; **—,** sm. eulogy.

panegirista, *–hĭrĭs´tå,* sm. panegyrist.

panera, *pånd´rå,* sf. granary.

pánfilo, *pån´fĭlŏ,* sm. slow, sluggish, heavy person.

paniaguado, *pånĭågŭå´dŏ,* sm. table-fellow; comrade.

pánico, *ca, på´nĭkå,* a. panic.

paniego, *ga, pånĭā´gŏ,* a. eating or yield-ing much bread.

panilla, *pånĭl´yå,* sf. small measure of oil.

panizo, *pånĭ´thŏ,* sm. panic-grass.

panoja, *pånŏ´h´å,* sf. (bot.) pannicle.

panorama, *pånŏrā´må,* sm. panorama.

pantalón, *påntålŏn´,* sm. pantaloon; **— de media pierna,** breeches, small-clothes.

pantalla, *–tål´yå,* sf. candle-screen, lamp-shade; (fig.) man of straw.

pantano, *–tå´nŏ,* sm. pool of stagnant wa-ter; morass; obstacle, difficulty.

pantanoso, *sa, –tånŏ´sŏ,* a. marshy, fenny,

panteísta, *–tĕĭs´tå,* sf. pantheist. [boggy.

panteón, *–tĕŏn´,* sm. Pantheon.

pantera, *–tå´rå,* sf. panther.

pantomima, *–tŏmĭ´må,* sf. pantomime.

pantomímico, *ca, –tŏmĕ´mĭkŏ,* a. panto-mimical. [leg).

pantorilla, *–tŏrĭl´yå,* sf. calf (of the

pantorilludo, *da, –tŏrrĭlyŭ´dŏ,* a. hav-ing very large or thick calves.

pantuflo, *påntŭ´flŏ,* sm. slipper, shoe.

panza, *pån´thå,* sf. belly, paunch.

panzada, *pånthå´då,* sf. belly-full of food.

panzudo, *da, –thŭ´dŏ,* a. big-bellied.

pañal, *pånyål´,* sm. swaddling-cloth; cloth in which anything is wrapped up; tail of a shirt. [clothier.

pañero, *pånyd´rŏ,* sm. woollen-draper.

paño, *pån´yŏ,* sm. cloth; breadth of cloth.

pañuelo, *pånyŭå´lŏ,* sm. handkerchief.

papa, *på´på,* sm. pope; pap; **—s,** pl. pota-

papá, *påpå´,* sm. papa. [toes.

papada, *påpå´då,* sf. double-chin.

papadilla, *–dĭl´yå,* sf. the fleshy part under the chin.

papado, *påpå´dŏ,* sm. popedom, papacy.

papagayo, *–gå´yŏ,* sm. parrot.

papal, *påpål´,* a. papal, papistical.

papalina, *påpålĭ´nå,* sf. cap with ear-flaps.

papamoscas, *–mŏs´kås,* sm. gnat-snapper.

papanatas, *–nå´tås,* sm. oaf, simpleton, ninny. [tinence.

paparrucha, *–rūtsh´å,* sf. folly, imper-

papel, *påpĕl´,* sm. paper; writing; part acted in a play; **— de estraza,** brown paper; **— sellado,** stamped paper.

papelera, *–lå´rå,* sf. writing-desk, paper-case. [papers without order.

papelería, *–lĕrȳ å,* sf. large bundle of

papelero, *–lå´rŏ,* sm. paper-manufacturer.

papeleta, *–lå´tå,* sf. slip of paper on which something is written.

papelón, *–lŏn´,* sm. large piece of paper; prolix writing; cartoon; pamphlet.

papera, *påpå´rå,* sf. wen on the throat.

papilla, *påpĭl´yå,* sf. pap; guile, deceit.

papirotada, *påpĭrŏtå´då,* sf. fillip on the neck or face; rap on the nose.

papirote, *–rŏ´tĕ,* sm. fillip.

papista, *påpĭs´tå,* sm. papist.

papo, *på´pŏ,* sm. double-chin, under-chin.

papudo, *da, påpŏ´dŏ,* a. double-chinned.

paquebot, *påkĕbŏt´,* sm. packetboat.

paquete, *påkå´tĕ,* sm. small packet, bundle.

par, *pår´,* a. equal, alike, even; **sin —,** matchless; **—,** sm. pair; Peer.

para, *på´rå,* pr. for, to, in order to, towards, to the end that.

parabién, *påråbĭĕn´,* sm. congratulation; felicitation; event.

parábola, *pårå´bŏlå,* sf. parable; parabola.

parabólico, *ca, –bŏ´lĭkŏ,* a. parabolical.

paracleto, *–klĕ´tŏ,* sm. Paraclete (name given to the Holy Ghost). [suffers.

parachoques, *–tshŏ´kĕ,* sm. pl. (rail.)

parada, *pårå´då,* sf. halt; suspension; pause; relay; dam, bank; stake, set, bet; (mil.) parade. [end.

paradero, *–dd´rŏ,* sm. halting-place; term,

parado, *da, pårå´dŏ,* a. remiss, careless, in-

paradoja, *–dŏ´h´å,* sf. paradox. [dolent.

parador, *–dŏr´,* sm. one who stops or halts; inn.

parafrasear, *–fråsĕår´,* v.a. to paraphrase.

paráfrasi, *pårå´fråsĭ,* sf. paraphrase.

paragoge, *pårågŏ´h´ĕ,* sf. addition of a letter or syllable at the end of a word.

paraguas, *pårå´gŭås,* sm. umbrella.

paraíso, *pårå´ĭsŏ,* sm. Paradise.

paraje, *pårå´h´ĕ,* sm. place, residence; condition; disposition.

paralelo, la, *pårålĕ´lŏ,* a, & sm. & f. parallel.

paralelógramo, *–lĕlŏ´gråmŏ,* sm. paral-lelogram, oblong; **—, ma,** a. parallelo-grammic. [sied.

paralítico, *ca, –lĕ´tĭkŏ,* a. paralytic, pal-

paralogismo, *–lŏ´hĭs´mŏ,* sm. parslogism, false reasoning.

páramo, *på´råmŏ,* sm. desert, wilderness; any place extremely cold.

parangón, *pårångŏn´,* sm. paragon, model, comparison. [to parallel.

parangonar, *–gŏnår´,* v. a. to compare,

parapeto, *–på´tŏ,* sm. parapet, breast-work.

parar, *pårår´,* v. n. to stop, to halt; **—, v. a.** to stop, to detain; to treat ill; to stake at cards; — **en mal**, to have a bad end; **sin —**, instantly, without delay; **—se**, to stop, to halt; **—**, sm. lansquenet (game at cards). [conductor.

pararrayo, _–rä´yō_, sm. lightning-rod.

parasismo, _–sĭs´mō_, sm. paroxysm, fit.

parásito, _pärä´sĭtō_, sm. parasite, sponger.

parasol, _pärä´söl´_, sm. parasol.

parca, _pär´kä_, sf. (poet.) Fate, Fatal Sister. [given to grammar-scholars.

parce, _pär´thě_, sm. schedule of pardon

parcial, _pärthĭäl´_, a. partial.

parcialidad, _–ĭdäd´_, sf. partiality; sociability; party, faction.

parco, ca, _pär´kō_, a. sparing, scanty; sober, moderate. [(fig.) deception, jest.

parchazo, _pärtshä´thō_, sm. large plaster;

parche, _pär´tshě_, sm. plaster; drum-skin.

pardal, _pärdäl´_, a. clownish, rustic; cunning; —, sm. grey sand-piper.

pardear, _pärděär´_, v. n. to grow grey or brownish; to become dusky. [oath.

pardiez, _pärdĭě´th_, jocular affirmation or

pardillo, _pärdĭl´yō_, sm. linnet.

pardo, da, _pär´dō_, a. grey.

pardusco, ca, _–düs´kō_, a. grayish, grizzly.

parear, _pěär´_, v. a. to match, to pair, to couple.

parecer, _pärěthěr´_, sm. opinion, advice, counsel; countenance, air, mien; —, v. n. to appear; to seem; **—se**, to present oneself to view; to resemble.

parecido, da, _–thĭ´dō_, a. resembling, like.

pared, _pärěd´_, sf. wall; **— medianera**, party-wall.

paredón, _pärědōn´_, sm. thick wall.

pareja, _pärě´hä_, sf. pair, couple, brace; accouplement. [dred.

parentela, _pärentě´lä_, sf. parentage, kin-

parentesco, _–těs´kō_, sm. cognation, kindred; union, chain, link.

paréntesis, _pärěn´těsĭs_, sm. parenthesis.

pares y nones, _pä´rěs ĭ nō´něs_, sm. pl. even or odd. [in the East-Indies.

paria, _pä´rĭä_, sm. pariah, the lowest caste

parias, _pä´rĭäs_, sf. pl. tribute paid by one prince to another as an acknowledgment of superiority; placenta, after-birth.

parida, _pärĭ´dä_, sf. woman lately delivered.

paridad, _pärĭdäd´_, sf. parity, equality.

pariente, ta, _pärĭen´tě_, sm. & f. kinsman; kinswoman.

parihuela, _pärĭhuě´lä_, sf. barrow.

parir, _pärĭr´_, v. a. to bring forth; to produce; to lie in; to lay eggs. [gossip.

parla, _pär´lä_, sf. easy delivery, loquacity.

parlador, ra, _–dōr´_, sm. & f. prater.

parlamental, _–měntäl´_, a. parliamentary.

parlamentar, _–měntär´_, v. n. to talk, to converse, to parley.

parlamentario, _–měntä´rĭō_, sm. member of parliament; —, a. parliamentary.

parlamento, _–měn´tō_, sm. harangue delivered in a public assembly; parliament.

parlanchín, na, _pärläntshĭn´_, a. & sm. & f. chatterer, jabberer.

parlar, _pärlär´_, v. a. to chatter, to talk.

parleta, _pärlě´tä_, sf. conversation on trifling subjects. [chatter, to gossip.

parlotear, _pärlōtěär´_, v. n. to prate, to

Parnaso, _pärnä´sō_, sm. (poet.) Parnassus.

parodia, _pärō´dĭä_, sf. parody.

parola, _pärō´lä_, sf. eloquence; chatter.

parpadear, _pärpäděär´_, v. n. to twinkle.

párpado, _pär´pädō_, sm. eye-lid.

parque, _pär´kě_, sm. park; (mil.) park of artillery. [nailed to a wall.

parra, _pär´rä_, sf. vine raised on stakes or

párrafo, _pär´räfō_, sm. paragraph; a mark in printing. [earthen jar.

parral, _pärräl´_, sm. vine-arbour; a large

parricida, _pärrĭthĭ´dä_, sm. & f. parricide (person).

parricidio, _–thĭ´dĭō_, sm. parricide (murder).

parrillas, _pärrĭl´yäs_, sf. pl. gridiron.

parro, _pär´rō_, sm. gander, goose.

párroco, _pär´rōkō_, sm. parson.

parroquia, _pärrō´kĭä_, sf. parish.

parroquial, _pärrōkĭäl´_, a. parochial.

parroquiano, _–kĭä´nō_, sm. parishioner; customer; —, a. parochial.

parsimonia, _pärsĭmō´nĭä_, sf. parsimony.

parte, _pär´tě_, sf. part; side; party; **de ocho días á esta**, within these last eight days; **de —á —**, from side to side, through.

partear, _pärtěär´_, v. a. to deliver, to deliver a woman of a child.

partera, _pärtě´rä_, sf. midwife.

partero, _pärtě´rō_, sm. man-midwife.

partible, _pärtĭ´blě_, a. divisible, partible.

partición, _pärtĭthĭōn´_, sf. partition, division. [pation.

participación, _–thĭpäthĭōn´_, sf. partici-

participar, _–thĭpär´_, v. a. & n. to participate, to partake. [sharing.

participe, _pärtĭ´thĭpě_, a. participant.

participio, _pärtĭthĭ´pĭō_, sm. participle.

partícula, _pärtĭ´kŭlä_, sf. particle.

particular, _pärtĭkŭlär´_, a. particular, special; —, sm. private gentleman; peculiar matter or subject treated upon.

particularidad, _–lärĭdäd´_, sf. particularity; friendship, intimacy.

particularizar, _–lärĭthär´_, v. a. & r. to particularize.

partida, _pärtĭ´dä_, sf. departure; party of soldiers; item in an account; parcel; game at play; **—s**, pl. parts, talents, accomplishments; the laws of Castile.

partidario, _pärtĭdä´rĭō_, sm. partisan.

partido, _pärtĭ´dō_, sm. party; district.

partidor, _pärtĭdōr´_, sm. parter, divider.

partija, _pärtĭ´hä_, sf. partition, division.

partir, _pärtĭr´_, v. a. to part, to divide, to separate, to cut, to cleave; to break; —, v. n. to depart; **—se**, to differ in opinion.

partitivo, va, _pärtĭtĭ´vō_, a. (gr.) partitive.

parto, _pär´tō_, sm. child-birth.

parva, _pär´vä_, sf. unthrashed corn laid in heaps to be thrashed; multitude. [ness.

parvidad, _pärvĭdäd´_, sf. littleness, minute-

parvo, va, _pär´vō_, a. small, little.

párvulo, la, *pär'vŭlŏ,* a. very small; innocent; —, sm. child.

pasa, *päs'ä,* sf. raisin.

pasada, *päsä'dä,* sf. passage; pace, step; manner, behaviour; **de —,** on the way, in passing.

pasadera, *päsädĕ'rä,* sf. stepping-stone.

pasadero, ra, *—dĕ'rŏ,* a. supportable, sufferable; passable; —, sm. stepping-stone.

pasadizo, *päsädē'thŏ,* sm. narrow passage; narrow, covered way, subway.

pasado, *päsä'dŏ,* a. (gr.) past time; —s, pl. ancestors.

pasador, *päsädŏr',* sm. smuggler; sharp-pointed arrow from a crossbow; bolt of a lock; woman's brooch.

pasaje, *päsä'h'ĕ,* sm. passage.

pasajero, ra, *—hĕ'rŏ,* a. transient, transitory, fugitive; —, sm. & f. traveller, passenger.

pasalicor, *—lēkŏr',* sm. hydrometer, test-liquor.

pasamanería, *—mänĕrē'ä,* sf. lace-making.

pasamano, *—mä'nŏ,* sm. balustrade.

pasante, *päsän'tĕ,* sm. assistant of a physician or lawyer; student who acts the teacher or lecturer to beginners.

pasantía, *—tē'ä,* sf. profession of a law-student who practises under the direction of a professor of the faculty.

pasapasa, *päsäpä'sä,* sm. legerdemain.

pasaporte, *—pŏr'tĕ,* sm. passport; (mil.) furlough.

pasar, *päsär',* v. a. to pass; to surpass; to suffer; to strain; to dissemble; —, v. n. to pass; —, v. imp. to happen; **—se,** to go over to another party; to become corrupt or putrid.   [ment.

pasatiempo, *—tēĕm'pŏ,* sm. pastime, amusement.

pasavolante, *—vŏlän'tĕ,* sm. inconsiderate speech or action; seaman entered in the muster-book, but not actually existing.

Pascua, *päs'kŭä,* sf. Passover; Easter.

pascual, *päskŭäl',* a. paschal.

pase, *päs'ĕ,* sm. pass-bill; permit, cocket.

paseante, *päsĕän'tĕ,* sm. walker; **— en corte,** one who has neither office nor employ.

pasear, *päsĕär',* v. a. & n. to walk; to be at the walk; to walk about; **—se,** to walk for exercise or amusement; to loiter, to saunter.

paseo, *päsĕ'ŏ,* sm. walk.   [gape about.

pasibilidad, *päsĭbĭlĭdäd',* sf. passibleness.

pasible, *päsē'blĕ,* a. passible.

pasillo, *päsēl'yŏ,* sm. small narrow passage.

pasión, *päsŏn',* sf. passion.

pasionaria, *—nä'rĭä,* sf. passion-flower.

pasito, *päsē'tŏ,* ad. gently, softly.

pasiva, *päsē'vä,* sf. (gr.) passive.

pasivo, va, *päsē'vŏ,* a. passive.

pasmar, *päsmär',* v. a. to cause a spasm; to benumb; to chill; —, v. n. to marvel, to wonder; **—se,** to suffer spasms; to be astonished.   [astonishment, amazement.

pasmo, *päs'mŏ,* sm. spasm, convulsion.

pasmoso, sa, *päsmŏ'sŏ,* a. marvellous, wonderful.

paso, *pä'sŏ,* sm. pace, step; passage; man-

ner of walking; flight of steps; accident (rail.) **— á nivel,** railway-crossing; **al —,** on the way, in passing.

paspié, *päspĕ',* sm. a Breton merry dance.

pasquín, *päskĭn',* sm. pasquinade, pasquil, lampoon.   [or mildness.

pasta, *päs'tä,* sf. paste; excessive meekness

pastar, *pästär',* v. a. to pasture, to graze.

pastel, *pästĕl',* sm. pie; crayon for drawing.   [pastry.

pastelería, *—lĕrē'ä,* sf. pastrycook's shop.

pastelero, *—lĕ'rŏ,* sm. pastrycook.

pastilla, *pästēl'yä,* sf. lozenge.

pasto, *päs'tŏ,* sm. pasture; pasture-ground; **á —,** abundantly.

pastor, *pästŏr',* sm. shepherd; pastor.

pastoral, *—räl',* a. pastoral, rural.

pastorela, *—rä'lä,* sf. pastoral.

pastoril, *—rĭl',* a. pastoral.

pastoso, sa, *pästŏ'sŏ,* a. mellow, doughy.

pastura, *pästŏ'rä,* sf. pasture; pasture-ground.

pasturaje, *pästŏ'räh'ĕ,* sm. pasturage.

pata, *pä'tä,* sf. foot and leg of an animal; duck; **— de cabra,** unforeseen impediment; **á la — coja,** Scotch hoppers (children's play); **á —,** on foot.

patada, *pätä'dä,* sf. kick; step, pace; tract.

patagalana, *—gälä'nä,* sf. limping; halt.

patagón, *—gŏn',* sm. large clumsy foot.

patalear, *—lĕär',* v. n. to kick about violently.   [foot.

pataleo, *—lĕ'ŏ,* sm. act of stamping one's

pataleta, *—lĕ'tä,* sf. fainting-fit; swoon.

patán, *pätän',* sm. clown, churl, countryman,   [kickshaw.

patarata, *pätärä'tä,* sf. fiction, false story;

patata, *pätä'tä,* sf. potato.

patatús, *—tŭs',* sm. swoon, fainting-fit.

patear, *pätĕär',* v. a. to kick.

patena, *pätĕ'nä,* sf. patine.

patente, *pätĕn'tĕ,* a. patent, manifest, evident; —, sf. patent; warrant; letters of marque.

paternal, *pätĕrnäl',* a. paternal, fatherly.

paternidad, *—nĭdäd',* sf. paternity, fatherhood.

paterno, na, *pätĕr'nŏ,* a. paternal, fatherly.

pateta, *pätĕ'tä,* sm. nickname given to a lame person.

patético, ca, *pätĕ'tĭkŏ,* a. pathetic.

patíbulo, *pätē'bŭlŏ,* sm. gibbet, gallows.

paticojo, ja, *pätĭkŏ'h'ŏ,* a. lame, crippled.

patilla, *pätēl'yä,* sf. whiskers; **—s,** pl. (vulg.) devil.

patín, *pätĭn',* sm. skate, ice-spur.

patio, *pä'tĭŏ,* sm. court behind a house; pit in play-houses.   [prised.

patitieso, sa, *pätĭtĭä'sŏ,* a. stupefied, surprised.

patituerto, ta, *—tŭĕr'tŏ,* a. crook-legged.

patizambo, ba, *—thäm'bŏ,* a. bandy-legged.

pato, ta, *pä'tŏ,* a. equal, similar; —, sm. **—a, sf.** duck.   [sense, folly.

patochada, *—tshä'dä,* sf. blunder, non-

patología, *—lŏ'h'ĕ'ä,* sf. pathology.

patológico, ca, *—lŏ'h'ĭkŏ,* a. patologic.

patraña, *pâtrăn'yă*, sf. fabulous story.

patria, *pâ'triă*, sf. native country.

patriarca, *pâtriăr'kă*, sm. patriarch.

patriarcado, —*kă'dŏ*, sm. patriarchate.

patriarcal, —*kăl*, a. patriarchal.

patricio, *pâtrĕ'thiŏ*, sm. patrician; —, a. native, national.

patrimonial, *pâtrĭmŏniăl'*, a. patrimonial.

patrimonio, —*mŏ'niŏ*, sm. patrimony.

patrio, tria, *pâ'triŏ*, n. native, paternal.

patriota, *pâtriŏ'tă*, sm. & f. patriot.

patriótico, ca, *pâtriŏ'tĭkŏ*, a. patriotic.

patriotismo, —*tis'mŏ*, sm. patriotism.

patrocinar, *pâtrŏthĭnăr'*, v. a. to favour, to patronise, to protect. [tronage.

patrocinio, —*thĕ'niŏ*, sm. protection, patron, *pâtrŏn'*, sm. patron, protector; master of a trading vessel; landlord of a house or inn; guardian saint of a country, town, &c.

patrona, *pâtrŏ'nă*, sf. patroness.

patronado, da, *pâtrŏnă'dŏ*, a. having a patron. [sm. patronage.

patronato, —*nă'tŏ*, patronazgo, —*năth'gŏ*, patronímico, —*nĕ'mĭkŏ*, sm. patronymic.

patrono, *pâtrŏ'nŏ*, sm. lord of the manor.

patrulla, *pâtrŭl'yă*, sf. (mil.) patrol.

patrullar, —*yăr'*, v. n. to patrol, camp or garrison.

patudo, da, *pâtŭ'dŏ*, a. club-footed.

paulatina, na, *pâŭlătĭ'nă*, a. slowly, by degrees. [munication; reproof, chiding.

paulina, *pâŭlĭ'nă*, sf. decree of excommunication; pausa, *pâ'ŭsă*, sf. pause; repose; á —s, by intervals. [ate; calm, quiet, paused.

pausado, da, *pâŭsă'dŏ*, a. slow, deliberate.

pausar, *pâŭsăr'*, v. n. to pause.

pauta, *pâ'ŭtă*, sf. ruler made out of a board with cat-gut strings.

pava, *pâ'vă*, sf. turkey-hen; pea-hen.

pavero, *pâvĕ'rŏ*, sm. & f. one who feeds turkey-fowls. [remains, relics.

pavesa, *pâvĕ'să*, sf. embers, hot cinders; pavía, *pâvĕ'ă*, sf. peach with hard stones.

pávido, da, *pâ'vĭdŏ*, a. timid, fearful.

pavimento, *pâvĭmĕn'tŏ*, sm. pavement.

pavipollo, —*pŏl'yŏ*, sm. young turkey.

pavo, *pâ'vŏ*, sm. turkey; — real, peacock.

pavón, *pâvŏn'*, sm. peacock, peafowl.

pavonar, *pâvŏnăr'*, v. n. to give iron or steel a bluish colour.

pavonear, —*neăr'*, v. n. to strut, to walk with affected dignity. [able.

pavoroso, sa, —*rŏ'sŏ*, a. awful, formidpavura, *pâvŏ'ră*, sf. fear, dread, terror.

payo, *pâ'yŏ*, sm. clown, churl.

paz, *păth*, sf. peace; tranquillity, ease; ¡—! peace! hush! [ning to end.

pe, *pĕ*, ad. de — á —, entirely, from beginpeaje, *pĕă'h'ĕ*, sm. bridge-toll; ferriage.

peal, *pĕăl'*, sm. sock; worthless person.

peana, *pĕă'nă*, sf. pedestal; foot-stool, footboard.

peatón, *pĕătŏn'*, sm. rural postman.

peazgo, *pĕăth'gŏ*, sm. bridge-toll; ferriage.

pebete, *pĕbĕ'tĕ*, sf. pastil for fumigation; fusee, match.

pebetero, *pĕbĕtĕ'rŏ*, sm. censer.

peca, *pĕ'kă*, sf. freckle, spot.

pecado, *pĕkă'dŏ*, sm. sin.

pecador, ra, —*dŏr'*, sm. & f. sinner.

pecaminoso, sa, —*mĭnŏ'sŏ*, a. sinful.

pecar, *pĕkăr'*, v. n. to sin.

pecina, *pĕthĕ'nă*, sf. fish-pond. [knave.

pécora, *pĕ'kŏră*, sf. sheep; cunning fellow.

pecoso, sa, *pĕkŏ'sŏ*, a. freckled.

pectoral, *pĕktŏrăl'*, a. pectoral; —, sm. cross worn by bishops on the breast.

peculiar, *pĕkŭliăr'*, a. peculiar, special.

peculio, *pĕkŭ'liŏ*, sm. private fortune; capital allowed to a minor.

pecunia, *pĕkŭ'niă*, sf. hard cash, specie.

pecuniario, ria, —*niă'riŏ*, a. pecuniary.

pechar, *pĕtchăr'*, v. n. to pay taxes.

pechera, *pĕtchĕ'ră*, sf. stomacher; frill.

pechero, ra, —*rŏ*, a. liable to pay taxes; —, sm. commoner, plebeian; bib.

pecho, *pĕtchŏ'*, sm. breast; teat; bosom; courage, valour; tax, contribution; dar el —, to suckle; tener —, to have patience; tomar á —s, to take to heart.

pechuga, *pĕtchŏ'gă*, sf. breast of a fowl; bosom. [hoarseness.

pechuguera, *pĕtchŏgĕ'ră*, sf. cough.

pedagoga, *pĕdăgŏ'hiă*, sf. pedagogism.

pedagógico, ca, —*gŏ'hĭkŏ*, a. pedagogic.

pedagogo, —*gŏ'gŏ*, sm. pedagogue.

pedáneo, *pĕdă'nĕŏ*, a. petty, inferior (of law-courts).

pedante, *pĕdăn'tĕ*, sm. pedant.

pedantear, —*teăr'*, v. n. to play the pedant.

pedantería, —*tĕrĕ'ă*, sf. pedantry.

pedantesco, ca, —*tĕs'kŏ*, a. pedantic.

pedantismo, —*tĭs'mŏ*, sm. pedantry.

pedazo, *pĕdă'thŏ*, sm. piece, bit.

pedernal, *pĕdĕrnăl'*, sm. flint.

pedestal, *pĕdĕstăl'*, sm. pedestal, foot.

pedicular, *pĕdĭkŭlăr'*, a. lousy.

pedido, *pĕdĕ'dŏ*, sm. voluntary contribution, which is called for by government in urgent necessities of the State; request.

pedigüeña, —*güĕn'yă*, a. craving, demanding, beggary.

pediluvios, —*lŏ'viŏs*, sm. foot-bath.

pedimento, —*mĕn'tŏ*, sm. petition.

pedir, *pĕdĭr'*, v. a. to petition, to beg, to supplicate, to solicit.

pedo, *pĕ'dŏ*, sm. wind from the bowels.

pedorreras, *pĕdŏrrĕ'răs*, sf. flatulency.

pedorrero, ra, —*rŏ*, a. flatulent.

pedrada, *pĕdră'dă*, sf. throw of a stone.

pedrea, *pĕdrĕ'ă*, sf. conflict of boys belonging to different wards or districts fighting with stones; lapidation.

pedregal, *pĕdrĕgăl'*, sm. shingle; place full of stones.

pedregoso, sa, —*gŏ'sŏ*, a. stony.

pedrera, *pĕdrĕ'ră*, sf. quarry, stone-pit.

pedrería, *pĕdrĕrĕ'ă*, sf. collection of precious stones. [lapidary.

pedrero, *pĕdrĕ'rŏ*, sm. stone-cutter, slinger.

pedrisco, *pĕdrĭs'kŏ*, sm. hail-stone.

pedrusco, *pĕdrŭs'kŏ*, sm. rough piece of [marble.

peer, *pĕĕr'*, v. n. to break wind.

pega, *pā'gā,* sf. pitch; glue.

pegadizo, za, *pěgādē'thō,* a. clammy, viscous; contagious.   [plasm.

pegado, *pěgā'dō,* sm. sticking-plaster, cata-

pegadura, *-dō'rā,* sf. pitching.

pegajoso, sa, *-hō'sā,* a. sticky, viscous; contagious; attractive.

pegar, *pěgār',* v. a. to cement; to join, to unite; to beat; — **fuego,** to set fire to; —, v. n. to take root; —**se,** to intrude, to steal in.

Pegaso, *pěgā'sō,* sm. Pegasus.

peste, *pěgō'tě,* sm. pitch-plaster; impertinent intruder, hanger-on; sponger.

peguntar, *pěgŭn'tār',* v. a. to brand cattle with melted pitch.

peinado, *pěĭnā'dō,* sm. hair combed, dressed and curled.   [ing-gown.

peinador, *-dōr',* sm. hair-dresser; dress-

peinar, *pěĭnār',* v. a. to comb the hair.

peine, *pěĭ'ně,* sm. comb.

peineria, *pěĭněrē'ā,* sf. shop where combs are made and sold.

peinero, *-nā'rō,* sm. & f. comb-maker.

peineta, *-nā'tā,* sf. convex comb for women.

peladilla, *pělādēl'yā,* sf. sugared almond, burnt almond; small pebble.

peladura, *-dō'rā,* sf. plucking.

pelafustán, *-fŭstān',* sm. ragamuffin.

pelagallos, *-gāl'yōs,* sm. common people out of work.   [pocket.

pelagatos, *-gā'tōs,* sm. cutpurse, pick-

pelaje, *pělā'h'ě,* sm. colour or tint of animals' hair.

pelandusca, *pělāndŭs'kā,* sf. strumpet.

pelar, *pělār',* v. a. to pull out the hair; to strip off the feathers.   [of stairs.

peldaño, *pěldān'yō,* sm. step of a flight

pelea, *pělě'ā,* sf. battle, fight; quarrel.

pelear, *pělěār',* v. a. to fight, to combat; —**se,** to scuffle.   [ficant fellow.

pelele, *pělě'lě,* sm. man of straw; insigni-

peletería, *pělětěrē'ā,* sf. trade of a furrier; fellmonger's shop.

peletero, *-tā'rō,* sm. furrier.

peliagudo, da, *pělĭāgō'dō,* a. downy, furry; arduous, difficult; ingenious, dexterous.

pelicano, *pělĭkā'nō,* sm. pelican;   [hoary.

pelícano, *pělĭkā'nō,* a. gray-haired;

pelicorto, ta, *pělĭkōr'tā,* a. short-haired.

película, *pělĭkŭ'lā,* sf. pellicle.   [risk.

peligrar, *pělĭgrār',* v. n. to be in danger; to

peligro, *pělē'grō,* sm. danger, risk, peril.

peligroso, sa, *pělĭgrō'sō,* a. dangerous, perilous.   [trifle.

pelillo, *pělĭl'yō,* sm. short, tender hair;

pelma, *pěl'mā,* sf. pelmazo, *pělmā'thō,* sm. heavy paste or cake; food which lies heavy on the stomach.

pelo, *pā'lō,* sm. hair; pile; flaw (in precious stones); **á —,** to the purpose, timely.

pelón, ona, *pělōn',* a. hairless, bald.

pelota, *pělō'tā,* sf. ball; **— de viento,** foot-ball.

pelotazo, *pělōtā'thō,* sm. blow with a ball.

pelote, *pělō'tě,* sm. goat's hair.

pelotear, *pělōtěār',* v. n. to play at ball; to argue, to dispute.

pelotera, *-tā'rā,* sf. women's quarrel.

pelotero, *-tā'rō,* sm. ball-maker.

pelotón, *-tōn',* sm. large ball; (mil.) pla-   [toon.

peltre, *pěl'trě,* sm. pewter.

peltrero, *pěltrā'rō,* sm. pewterer.   [proof.

peluca, *pělū'kā,* sf. periwig, peruke; re-

peludo, da, *-dō,* a. hairy; —, sm. bass-mat of an oval shape.

peluquería, *-kěrē'ā,* sf. shop where wigs are made and sold.

peluquero, *-kā'rō,* sm. peruke-maker.

pelusa, *pělū'sā,* sf. bloom on fruit; fluff rubbed off from clothes in wear.

pella, *pěl'yā,* sf. ball; clew; mass of metal in its crude state; lard in the state in which it is taken from hogs; heron (bird).

pellada, *pělyā'dā,* sf. gentle blow.

pelleja, *pělyě'h'ā,* sf. skin stripped from an animal; female toper.

pellejería, *-hěrē'ā,* sf. fellmonger's shop.

pellejero, *-hā'rō,* sm. fellmonger, leather-dresser.

pellejo, *pělyā'h'ō,* sm. skin, hide; pelt; peel; wine-skin, leather-bag for wine; oil-skin; tippler, drunkard, fuddler.

pellejudo, da, *-hā'dō,* a. thick-skinned.

pellica, *pělyē'kā,* sf. coverlet of fine furs.

pellico, *-kō,* sm. dress made of skins or furs.

pelliza, *pělyē'thā,* sf. pelisse.   [furs.

pellizcar, *pělyĭthkār',* v. a. to pinch.

pellizco, *pělyĭth'kō,* sm. pinch; nip; small bit; (fig.) remorse.

pena, *pā'nā,* sf. punishment, pain; **á duras —s,** with great difficulty or trouble.

penacho, *pěnāsh'ō,* sm. tuft on the heads of some birds; crest; pride, haughtiness.

penal, *pěnāl',* a. penal.

penalidad, *-lĭdād',* sf. suffering, trouble; hardship; penalty; punishableness.

penar, *pěnār',* v. n. to suffer pain; —, v. a. to chastise; —**se,** to grieve, to mourn.

penates, *pěnā'těs,* sm. pl. Penates, household-gods, pl.

penca, *pěn'kā,* sf. prickly leaf of a plant; scourge, lash.

pendanga, *-dān'gā,* sf. common prostitute.

pendencia, *-děn'thĭā,* sf. quarrel, dispute.

pendenciero, ra, *pěndēnthĭā'rō,* a. quarrelsome.

pender, *pěndēr',* v. n. to impend, to hang over; to depend; to be irresolute.

pendiente, *-dĭěn'tě,* sm. & f. slope, declivity; **—s,** pl. ear-rings, ear-drops, pl.

péndola, *pěn'dōlā,* sf. pendulum.

pendolista, *-lĭs'tā,* sm. penman.

pendón, *pěndōn',* sm. standard; banner.

péndulo, la, *pěn'dŭlō,* a. pendent, hanging; —, sm. pendulum.

penetrable, *-pěnětrā'blě,* a. penetrable; comprehensible.   [complete intelligence.

penetración, *-thĭōn',* sf. penetration;

penetrar, *-trār',* v. a. to penetrate; —**se,** to coexist as two bodies in the same place.

península, *pěnīn'sŭlā,* sf. peninsula.

penitencia, *pěnĭtěn'thĭā,* sf. penitence; penalty, fine.

penitencial, _-thiãl'_, a. penitential.
penitenciar, _-thiãr'_, v. a. to impose a penance for a fault committed.
penitenciaría, _-thiãre̊ã'_, sf. office of a penitentiary.
penitenciario, _-thiãre̊ã'_, sm. penitentiary.
penitenta, _penitẽn'tã_, sf. female penitent.
penitente, _-tẽ_, a. penitent, repentant; _–_, sm. penitent.
penoso, sa, _penõ'so̊_, a. painful.
pensado, _pensã'do̊_, de _–_, sm. on purpose.
pensamiento, _-miẽn'to̊_, sm. thought.
pensar, _pensãr'_, v. n. to think. [thinking.
pensativo, va, _-tẽ'vo̊_, a. pensive, thoughtful.
pensión, _pensión'_, sf. pension; toil. [ful.
pensionado, da, _-nã'do̊_, sm. & f. pensioner, pensionary.
pensionar, _-nãr'_, v. a. to impose pensions.
pensionario, _-nã're̊ã'_, sm. pensionary.
pensionista, _-nis'tã_, sm. & f. pensioner, pensionary; boarder. [teuch.
Pentatéuco, _pentãtã'ko̊_, sm. the Penta-
Pentecostés, _pentẽkostẽs'_, sm. Pentecost, Whitsuntide. [last but one.
penúltimo, ma, _penãl'timo̊_, a. penultimate.
penuria, _penã're̊ã_, sf. penury, poverty, indigence, neediness, extreme want.
peña, _pẽn'yã_, sf. rock, large stone.
peñascal, _-yãskãl'_, sm. rocky hill or mountain. [rough cloth.
peñasco, _-yãs'ko̊_, sm. large rock; strong,
peñascoso, sa, _-yãskã'so̊_, a. rocky, mountainous.
peñón, _pẽnyón'_, sm. rocky mountain.
peón, _peón'_, sm. pedestrian; day-labourer; foot-soldier; gig, humming-top; pawn (at chess); hive of bees.
peonía, _peõnẽ'ã_, sf. (bot.) peony.
peonza, _peõn'thã_, sf. whip-top; noisy little fellow. [worse.
peor, _peõr'_, a. & ad. worse; worse and
peoría, _peõre̊ã'_, sf. deterioration, detriment.
pepinar, _pepinãr'_, sm. cucumber-field.
pepino, _pepẽ'no̊_, sm. cucumber.
pepita, _pepẽ'tã_, sf. kernel; pip.
pepitoria, _-tõ're̊ã_, sf. fricassee made of giblets, livers and lights.
pequeñez, _pẽkẽnyẽth'_, sf. littleness.
pequeño, ña, _pẽkẽn'yo̊_, a. little, small;
pera, _pã'rã_, sf. pear. [young.
perada, _perã'dã_, sf. conserve of pears.
peral, _perãl'_, sm. pear-tree.
percance, _pẽrkãn'thẽ_, sm. perquisite; bad luck, non-success.
percepción, _pẽrthẽpthión'_, sf. perception, notion. [ceivable.
perceptible, _-tẽ'blẽ_, a. perceptible, per-
percibir, _pẽrthibir'_, v. a. to receive; to perceive, to comprehend.
percusión, _-kũsión'_, sf. percussion.
percha, _pẽr'chã_, sf. perch.
perder, _pẽrdẽr'_, v. a. to lose; **-se**, to go astray; to be lost; to be spoiled.
perdición, _-dithión'_, sf. losing of a thing; perdition, ruin, loss. [lost.
pérdida, _pẽr'didã_, sf. loss, damage; object
perdidizo, za, _-didã'tho̊_, a. lost on purpose.

perdido, da, _pẽrdẽ'do̊_, a. lost, strayed.
perdigar, _-digãr'_, v. a. to broil partridges slightly before they are roasted; to stew larded meat in an earthen pan.
perdigón, _-digón'_, sm. partridge trained to decoy others; **-ones**, pl. hail-shot.
perdiguero, ra, _-digẽ'ro̊_, a. setting, pointing (of dogs).
perdiz, _pẽrdith'_, sf. partridge.
perdón, _pẽrdón'_, sm. pardon.
perdonable, _-donã'blẽ_, a. pardonable.
perdonar, _-donãr'_, v. a. to pardon, to forgive.
perdulario, ria, _-dũlã're̊ã_, a. extremely careless with regard to one's own interest.
perdurable, _-dũrã'blẽ_, a. perpetual, ever-lasting.
perecedero, ra, _pẽrethẽdã'ro̊_, a. perish-able; _–_, sm. misery, extreme want.
perecer, _pẽrethẽr'_, v. n. to perish, to die; to perish for want of the necessaries of life; **-se**, to die of love or envy. [age.
peregrinación, _-grinãthión'_, sf. pilgrim-
peregrinamente, _-mẽn'tẽ_, ad. rarely, curiously. [pilgrimage.
peregrinar, _peregrinãr'_, v. a. to go on a
peregrino, na, _-grẽ'no̊_, a. foreign, tra-velling; going on a pilgrimage; strange; _–_, sm. pilgrim.
perejil, _pẽrẽhil'_, sm. parsley.
perendengues, _pẽrẽndẽn'gẽs_, sm. pl. ear-drops, ear-rings, pl.
perenne, _pẽrẽn'nẽ_, a. perennial, perpetual.
perentorio, ria, _-tã're̊ã_, a. peremptory, decisive.
pereza, _pẽrẽ'thã_, sf. laziness, idleness.
perezoso, sa, _-tho̊'so̊_, a. lazy, idle.
perfección, _pẽrfẽkthión'_, sf. perfection.
perfeccionar, _-thionãr'_, v. a. to perfect, to complete, to finish.
perfecto, ta, _-fẽk'to̊_, a. perfect, complete
perfidia, _pẽrfĩ'diã_, sf. perfidy.
pérfido, da, _pẽr'fido̊_, a. perfidious.
perfil, _pẽrfil'_, sm. profile.
perfilado, da, _-lã'do̊_, a. well-formed, delicate (of features).
perfiladura, _-lãdũ'rã_, sf. art of profile-drawing; sketching of outlines.
perfilar, _-lãr'_, v. a. to draw profiles; to sketch outlines; **-se**, to incline.
perfumador, _pẽrfũmãdõr'_, sm. perfumer; perfuming-pan.
perfumar, _-fũmãr'_, v. a. to perfume.
perfume, _-fũ'mẽ_, sm. perfume.
perfumería, _-fũmẽrẽ'ã_, sf. perfumer's shop.
pergamino, _-gãmẽ'no̊_, sm. skin dressed for writing, parchment.
pericia, _pẽrẽ'thiã_, sf. skill, knowledge, connoisseurship.
pericón, _pẽrikón'_, sm. large fan.
perifollo, _-fõl'yo̊_, sm. common chervil; ribbon or other women's ornament.
perifrasear, _-frãsẽãr'_, v. a. to periphrase.
perífrasis, _pẽrẽ'frãsis_, sf. periphrasis, cir-cumlocution.
perigallo, _pẽrigãl'yo̊_, sm. little double-chin of lean persons; tall, lean, lank per-son; sling made of twine.

perihelio, –há'lið, sm. perihelium.

perilla, perïl'yä, sf. small pear; pear-shaped ornament; pommel; **de –s,** at the proper time. [vagrant.

perillán, ana, –yän', a. artful, knavish.

perímetro, perë'mëtrö, sm. circumference, compass. [neat little woman.

perinola, perïnö'lä, sf. die with four facets;

periódico, ca, perïó'dïkö, a. periodical; **–,** sm. newspaper. [periodical.

periodista, perïódïs'tä, sm. editor of a periodic, perë'ödö, sm. period.

peripatético, perïpätä'tïkö, sm. peripatetic. [drama).

peripecia, –pä'thïä, sf. peripetia (in a

peripuesto, ta, –püës'tö, a. tricked up, very spruce in dress.

periquito, –kï'tö, sm. parroquet.

peristilo, –stë'lö, sm. peristyle.

perito, ta, për'ï tö, a. skilful, experienced.

perjudicar, për'hüdïkär', v. a. to prejudice, to injure, to hurt, to damage.

perjudicial, –dïthïäl', a. prejudicial, damaging. [jury.

perjuicio, për'hüë'thïö, sm. prejudice injury.

perjurar, –hürär', v. n. to forswear, to swear falsely; to swear; **–se,** to perjure oneself.

perjurio, –hö'rïö, sm. perjury, false oath.

perjuro, ra, –hö'rö, a. perjured, forsworn.

perla, për'lä, sf. pearl; **de –s,** much to the purpose; eminently fine. [palsied.

perlático, ca, për'lä'tïkö, a. paralytic,

perlesía, përlës'ïä, sf. paralysis, palsy.

permanecer, përmänësër', v. n. to persist.

permanencia, –nën'thïä, sf. permanence, perseverance.

permanente, –nën'të, a. permanent.

permisión, përmïsïön', sf. permission, leave. [licence.

permiso, –më'sö, sm. permission, leave, leave.

permitir, –mïtïr', v. a. to permit, to give leave. [change.

permuta, –mö'tä, sf. permutation, exchange.

permutar, –mütär', v. a. to exchange, to permute.

pernada, –nä'dä, sf. kick with the foot.

pernear, përnëär', v. n. to kick, to shake the legs; to fret. [flegged.

pernetas (en –), përnë'täs, ad. barelegged.

pernicioso, sa, përnïthïö'sö, a. pernicious, destructive.

pernil, përnïl', sm. ham, gammon.

pernio, për'nïö, sm. hinge for doors and windows.

perniquebrar, përnïkëbrär', v. a. to break the legs; **–se,** to break one's leg.

pernoctar, –nöktär', v. n. to pass the night; to be awake the whole night. [can't.

pero, pä'rö, sm. kind of apple; **–,** c. but,

perogrullada, –grülyä'dä, sf. truth of no moment and universally known.

perol, përöl', sm. boiler, kettle.

peroración, përöräthïön', sf. peroration, the conclusion of an oration.

perorar, –rär', v. a. to put an end to a speech; to make an harangue.

perorata, –rä'tä, sf. harangue, speech.

perpendicular, përpëndïkülär', a. perpendicular. [plummet, pendulum.

perpendículo, –dï'külö, sm. plumb,

perpetrar, përpëträr', v. a. to perpetrate, to commit a crime. [xeranthemum.

perpetua, –pä'tüä, sf. everlasting flower,

perpetuar, –pëtüär', v. a. to perpetuate.

perpetuidad, –pëtüïdäd', sf. perpetuity.

perpetuo, tua, –pä'tüö, a. perpetual.

perplejidad, –plëhïdäd', sf. perple—

perplejo, ja, –plë'hö, a. perplexed.

perra, për'rä, sf. bitch; drunkenness, toxication. [master.

perrera, përrä'rä, sf. kennel; bad pay—

perrería, përrë'rïä, sf. pack of dogs; drudgery. [dogs out of the church.

perrero, përrä'rö, sm. beadle who drives

perrillo, –rïl'yö, sm. little dog; trigger; **– de falda,** lap-dog.

perro, për'rö, sm. dog; obstinate person; **– de aguas,** water-dog; **– de muestra,** pointer; **– de presa,** bull-dog; **– de ayuda,** Newfoundland-dog; **– lebrel,** greyhound.

persecución, përsëküthïön', sf. persecution; toil, trouble, fatigue.

perseguidor, –sëgïdör', sm. persecutor.

perseguir, –sëgïr', v. a. to pursue a fugitive; to dun; to persecute.

perseverancia, përsëvëränthïä, sf. perseverance, constancy.

perseverante, –të, a. perseverant.

perseverar, –përsëvërär', v. n. to persevere, to persist.

persiana, përsïä'nä, sf. Venetian blind.

persignarse, –sïgnär'së, v. r. to make the sign of the cross. [steadiness.

persistencia, –sïstën'thïä, sf. persistence,

persistir, –sïstïr', v. n. to persist.

persona, për'sö'nä, sf. person; **de á –,** from man to man; **hacer de –,** to boast, to brag.

personaje, –sönä'hë, sm. personage.

personal, –sönäl', a. personal.

personalidad, –sönälïdäd', sf. personality.

personero, –sönë'rö, sm. deputy, agent, attorney. [souify.

personificar, –sönïfïkär', v. a. to per—

perspectiva, –pëktï'vä, sf. perspective; false, deceitful appearance.

perspicacia, –spïkä'thïä, sf. perspicacity, clear-sightedness.

perspicaz, –spïkäth', a. perspicacious, quick-sighted; sagacious.

persuadir, –süädïr', v. a. to persuade; **–se,** to be persuaded.

persuasión, –süäsïön', sf. persuasion.

persuasiva, –süäsï'vä, sf. persuasiveness.

persuasivo, va, –süäsï'vö, a. persuasive.

pertenecer, –tënëhër', v. n. to belong to, to appertain, to concern.

pertenencia, –tënën'thïä, sf. right of property; appurtenance, dependence.

pértiga, për'tïgä, sf. long pole or rod.

pertiguería, –gërë'ä, sf. office or employment of a verger.

pertiguero, –gä'rö, sm. verger.

pertinacia, —*nä'thiä,* sf. pertinacity, obstinacy, stubbornness.

pertinaz, —*näth',* a. pertinacious, obstinate.

pertrechar, *pertréchär',* v. a. to supply a place with ammunition and other warlike stores; to dispose, to arrange, to prepare; —se, to be provided with the necessary defensive stores and arms.

pertrechos, —*tréch'ös,* sm. pl. tools, instruments; ammunition, warlike stores.

perturbación, —*türbäthiön',* sf. perturbation, disquiet of mind.

perturbador, —*türbädör',* sm. perturbator, disturb.

perturbar, —*türbär',* v. a. to perturb, to disturb.

perversidad, —*vérsidäd',* sf. perversity, malignity, depravation, corruption.

perversión, —*vérsiön',* sf. perversion; depravity.

perverso, sa, —*vér'sö,* a. perverse, extremely wicked, corrupt.

pervertir, —*vértir',* v. a. to pervert, to corrupt.

pesa, *pä'sä,* sf. weight.

pesadez, *pésädéth',* sf. heaviness; gravity, weight; slowness; peevishness, fretfulness; trouble, fatigue.

pesadilla, —*díl'yä,* sf. nightmare.

pesado, da, *pésä'dö,* a. peevish, troublesome, cumbersome; tedious, injurious; heavy, weighty.

pesadumbre, —*düm'bré,* sf. weightiness, gravity; quarrel, dispute; grief, trouble.

pésame, *pä'sämé,* sm. message of condolence.

pesantez, *pésäntéth',* sf. heaviness.

pesar, *pésär',* sm. sorrow, grief; repentance; á —, ad. in spite of, notwithstanding; —, v. n. to weigh, to be of weight; to repent; —, v. a. to weigh.

pesaroso, sa, *pésärö'sö,* a. sorrowful, full of repentance; restless, uneasy.

pesca, *pés'kä,* sf. fishing, fishery.

pescadería, —*derä'ä,* sf. fish-market.

pescado, *péskä'dö,* sm. fish (in general).

pescador, —*dör',* sm. fisher, fisherman.

pescante, *péskän'té,* sm. crane; coach-box.

pescar, —*kär',* v. a. to fish, to catch fish.

pescozón, —*köthön',* sm. slap on the neck with the open hand.

pescuezo, —*küä'thö,* sm. neck.

pesebre, *pésé'bré,* sm. crib, manger.

pesebrera, *pésébrä'rä,* sf. row of mangers in a stable.

pesebrón, —*brön',* sm. boot of a coach.

peseta, *pésä'tä,* sf. piece of two reales de plata, weighing eight gold or silver coin.

pesillo, *pésil'yö,* sm. small scales for pesimista, *pésimis'tä,* sm. pessimist.

pésimo, ma, *pés'imö,* a. very bad.

peso, *pä'sö,* sm. weight, heaviness; balance-scales; Spanish dollar, piaster.

pespuntar, *péspüntär',* v. a. to back-stitch.

pespunte, —*pün'té,* sm. back-stitching.

pesquera, *péskä'rä,* sf. fishery.

pesquisa, *péski'sä,* sf. inquiry, examination.

pesquisar, *péskisär',* v. a. to inquire.

pesquisidor, —*sidör',* sm. examiner, inquirer; magistrate appointed to inquire

into the causes and circumstances of a violent death.

pestaña, *péstän'yä,* sf. eye-lash.

pestañear, —*yär',* v. a. to move the eyelashes or eye-lids. lids or eye-lashes.

pestañeo, —*yd'ö,* sm. moving of the eyelids.

peste, *pés'té,* sf. pest, plague, pestilence.

pestífero, ra, *pésti'férö,* a. pestilential.

pestilencia, *péstilén'thiä,* sf. pestilence.

pestillo, *péstil'yö,* sm. bolt.

pesuña, *pésün'yä,* s. solid hoof.

petaca, *pétä'kä,* sf. covered hamper; tobacco-pouch.

petar, *pétär',* v. n. to please, to content.

petardear, *pétärdeär',* v. a. to beat down a door with petards; —, v. n. to cheat.

petardista, —*dis'tä,* sm. & f. deceiver, cheat. fraud, imposition.

petardo, *pétär'dö,* sm. petard; cheat.

petate, *pétä'té,* sm. straw-bed; (am.) sleeping-mat of the Indians; (mar.) sailors' beddings on board; (mar.) passengers' luggage; poor fellow.

petición, *pétithiön',* sf. petition, demand.

petimetre, —*mä'tré,* sm. fop, coxcomb, beau.

petitorio, ria, —*tö'riö,* a. petitory, petitionary; —, sm. impertinent and repeated petition.

peto, *pä'tö,* sm. breast-plate; plastron.

petrificación, *pétrifikäthiön',* sf. petrification, petrifaction.

petrificar, —*kär',* —se, v. r. to petrify.

petulancia, *pétülän'thiä,* sf. petulance, insolence.

petulante, —*län'té,* a. petulant, insolent.

pez, *péth,* sm. fish; —, sf. rosin, pitch; meconium; — griega, colophony.

pezón, *péthön',* sm. leaf-stalk; nipple.

pezonera, —*nä'rä,* sf. linch-pin; breast-glass, breast-pump; round piece of lead or pewter used by suckling women, to form the nipples.

pezuña, *péthün'yä,* sf. solid hoof.

piada, *piä'dä,* sf. chirping of birds; puling of chickens. merciful; moderate.

piadoso, sa, *piädö'sö,* a. pious, mild, pian piano, *piän piä'nö,* ad. gently, softly.

piar, *piär',* v. n. to squeak, to pule, to chirp. ewes.

piara, *piä'rä,* sf. herd of swine; flock of

piastra, *piäs'trä,* sf. piaster, Turkish silver coin.

pica, *pé'kä,* sf. pike.

picacho, *pikäsh'ö,* sm. sharp point.

picada, *pikä'dä,* sf. puncture.

picadero, —*dä'rö,* sm. riding-school; —s, pl. blocks of wood put under the keel of a ship, while she is building.

picadillo, —*dil'yö,* sm. minced meat, hash.

picador, —*dör',* sm. riding-master; pricker.

picadura, —*dö'rä,* sf. prick; puncture; gusset in clothes. quant.

picante, *pikän'té,* sm. piquancy; —, a. pi-picapedrero, —*pédrä'rö,* sm. stone-cutter.

picaporte, —*pör'té,* sm. picklock.

picar, *pikär',* v. a. to prick; to sting, to mince; to nibble; to pursue an enemy; to itch; —se, to be piqued; to be moth-eaten; to begin to rot.

picardear, –*deár*, v. n. to play the knave.

picardía, –*dí á*, sm. knavery, roguery; deceit, malice; lewdness.

picaresco, ca, –*pikáres kō*, a. roguish.

pícaro, ra, *pí kárō*, a. knavish, roguish; mischievous, malicious; sly; merry, gay; –, sm. & f. rogue, knave.

picarote, –*rō té*, sm. notorious villain, great impostor.　　　　　　[displeasure.

picazón, –*thōn'*, sf. itching, prurience;

pico, *pé kō*, sm. beak; bill, nib; peak; loquacity; perder por el –, to lose by too much chattering.　　　　[small pox.

picoso, sa, *pikō'sō*, a. pitted with the

picotazo, *pikōtá thō*, sm. peck of a bird.

picote, *pikō'té*, sm. coarse stuff made of goat's hair; glossy silk stuff.

picotear, –*teár'*, v. a. to peck (of birds); –, v. n. to prattle, to chatter; –se, to wrangle (applied to women).

picotero, ra, –*tá rō*, a. wrangling, chattering, prattling.　　　　　　[pointed.

picudo, da, *pikō'dō*, a. beaked; sharp-

pichón, *pitshōn'*, sm. young pigeon.

pie, *pié*, sm. foot; leg; basis; trunk (of trees); foundation; occasion; á –, on foot; á – enjuto, without labour or pain; dry-shod.

piedad, *piědád'*, sf. piety; mercy, pity.

piedra, *pié drá*, sf. stone; gravel; hail; –s, pl. playing-counters.

piel, *piél'*, sf. skin; hide; peel.

piélago, *pié lágō*, sm. high sea; great plenty, numberlessness.

pienso, *piěn'sō*, sm. common daily allowance given to horses or mules.

pierna, *piér'ná*, sf. leg; leg of mutton; stroke; hanger (in writing); cheek of a printing-press; – de sábana, one of the breadths of a sheet.

pieza, *pié thá*, sf. piece; piece of furniture.

pífano, *pí fánō*, sm. fife; fife-player, piper.

pifia, *pé fiá*, sf. sound of a rebounding billiard ball.　　　　　　　[dwarfish.

pigmeo, mea, *pígmá'ō*, sm. & a. dwarf;

pila, *pé lá*, sf. trough for water, in which cattle drink; font; pile, heap; holy-water basin; nombre de –, Christian name; sacar de –, to stand godfather or god-mother.　　　　　[at once; pile, heap.

pilada, *pilá dá*, sf. quantity of mortar made

pilar, *pilár'*, sm. large water-basin of a fountain; pillar.

pilastra, *pilás trá*, sf. pilaster.

píldora, *píl dōrá*, sf. pill.

pilón, *pilōn'*, sm. large water-basin, drinking-trough; loaf of sugar.

pilongo, ga, *pilōn'gō*, a. lean, meagre.

pilotaje, *pilótá'h'é*, sm. pilotage.

piloto, *pilō'tō*, sm. pilot; – práctico, coast-pilot.　　　　　is nearly all skin.

piltrafa, *piltrá'fá*, sf. piece of meat that

pillada, *pilyá dá*, sf. knavish trick.

pillaje, *pilyá'h'é*, sm. pillage, plunder.

pillar, *pilyár'*, v. a. to pillage, to plunder, to forey, to seize; to chop at.

pillería, –*yěrí á*, sf. gang of vagabonds or rogues; knavish trick or sham.

pillo, lla, *píl'yō*, a. marauding, good-for-nothing.　　　　　[ground.

pimental, *piměntál'*, sm. pepper-bearing

pimentero, –*tá rō*, sm. pepper-box; pepper-plant.　　　　　[pepper plant.

pimentón, –*tōn'*, sm. ground fruit of the

pimienta, *pimiěn'tá*, sf. pepper.

pimiento, –*tō*, sm. (bot.) capsicum.

pimpín, *pimpín'*, sm. children's play.

pimpollo, *pimpōl'yō*, sm. sucker; bud.

pina, *pé ná*, sf. landmark in the form of a cone; jaunt, felloe of a wheel.

pináculo, *piná kúlō*, sm. pinnacle.

pinar, *pinár'*, sm. grove of pines.

pincel, *pinthél'*, sm. pencil.　　　[touch.

pincelada, –*lá dá*, sf. dash with a pencil;

pinchadura, *pintshādō'rá*, sf. puncture.

pinchar, *pintshár'*, v. a. to prick.

pincho, *pin'tshō*, sm. thorn.　　　[about.

pindonguear, *pindōngeár'*, v. n. to gad

pingajo, –*gá'h'ō*, sm. rag, tatter.

pingüe, *pin'gué*, a. fat, greasy; fertile.

pino, *pé nō*, sm. (bot.) pine; á –, upright.

pinta, *pin'tá*, sf. spot, blemish, scar; mark on playing cards; pint.

pintado, da, *pintá'dō*, a. painted, mottled; venir –, to fit exactly.　　　[dauber.

pintamonas, –*mō'nás*, sm. bad painter.

pintar, *pintár'*, v. a. to paint, to picture; to limn, to describe; to exaggerate; –, v. n. to begin to ripen; to show, to give signs of; –se, to paint one's face.

pintarrajar, –*rá'hár'*, v. a. to variegate.

pintarrajo, –*rá'h'ō*, sm. daub.

pintiparado, da, *pintipárá dō*, a. exactly like, closely resembling.

pintiparar, –*párár'*, v. a. to compare.

pintor, *pintōr'*, sm. painter.

pintoresco, ca, –*rés'kō*, a. picturesque.

pintorrear, –*reár'*, v. a. to daub.

pintura, *pintō'rá*, sf. painting; picture.

pinzas, *pin'thás*, sf. pl. nippers, small pincers.

pinzón, *pinthōn'*, sm. chaffinch.

piña, *pin'yá*, sf. pine-apple; fir-cone; mass of silver in the shape of a pine-apple.

piñón, *pinyōn'*, sm. pine-apple seed; pinion; spring-nut of a gun.　　　　[monds.

piñonata, –*yōná'tá*, sf. conserve of al-

piñonate, –*ná'té*, sm. paste made of almonds and sugar.

pío, pía, *pé'ō*, a. pious, devout; mild, merciful; –, sm. cry of chickens.

piocha, *piō'tshá*, sf. ornament for women's head-dresses.

piojería, *piō'hěrí á*, sf. lousiness; misery.

piojo, *piō'h'ō*, sm. louse; troublesome hanger-on.　　　　　　[stingy.

piojoso, sa, –*hō'sō*, a. lousy; miserable;

pipa, *pé pá*, sf. wine-cask; pipe (liquid measure); tobacco-pipe; pipe which children make of the stalks of corn; reed of a clarion; fusee of a bomb.

pípero, *pípá'rō*, sm. cooper.

pipiar, *pipiár'*, v. n. to pule, to chirp.

pipote, *pipŏ'tĕ,* sm. keg.

pique, *pē'kĕ,* sm. pique, offence taken; echar á —, to sink a ship; á —, in danger, on the point of; steep (shore).

piquera, *pikĕ'rä,* sf. bung-hole of a barrel.

piquete, *pikĕ'tĕ,* sm. slight prick or sting; tracing-picket; (mil.) picket.

pira, *pē'rä,* sf. funeral pile.

piramidal, *pyramidäl',* a. pyramidal.

pirámide, *pyrä'midĕ,* sf. pyramid.

pirata, *pirä'tä,* sm. pirate; cruel wretch.

piratear, *–tĕär',* v. n. to pirate.

piratería, *–tĕrē'ä,* sf. piracy.

piropo, *pirŏ'pŏ,* sm. carbuncle; (fig.) affectation of purity in speech.

pirotécnica, *pirŏtĕk'nikä,* sf. pyrotechny.

pirueta, *pirŭä'tä,* sf. pirouette.

pisada, *pisä'dä,* sf. foot-step; kick.

pisar, *pisär',* v. a. to tread, to trample; to stamp on the ground; to hammer down paving-stones; to despise.

pisaverde, *pisävĕr'dĕ,* sm. fop, coxcomb, jackanapes.

piscina, *pisthē'nä,* sf. fish-pond.

Piscis, *pis'this,* sm. Piscis, Fishes (sign of the zodiac). [pavement; floor, storey.

piso, *pē'sŏ,* sm. tread, trampling; floor,

pisón, *pisŏn',* sm. rammer. [under foot.

pisotear, *pisŏtĕär',* v.a. to trample, to tread

pista, *pis'tä,* sf. trace, foot-print.

pisto, *pis'tŏ,* sm. thick broth; á –s, little

pistola, *pistŏ'lä,* sf. pistol. [by little.

pistolera, *pistŏlĕ'rä,* sf. pistol-holster.

pistoletazo, *–lĕtä'thŏ,* sm. pistol-shot.

pistolete, *–lĕ'tĕ,* sm. pocket-pistol.

pita, *pē'tä,* sf. (bot.) agave; term used to call hens.

pitagórico, ca, *pitägŏ'rikŏ,* a. Pythagorean.

pitanza, *pitän'thä,* sf. pittance, daily allowance; price.

pitirrojo, *pitirrŏ'h'ŏ,* sm. robin red-breast.

pito, *pē'tŏ,* sm. pipe; play among boys.

pitón, *pitŏn',* sm. tenderling; sprig, young shoot of a tree. [ress.

pitonisa, *pitŏnē'sä,* sf. sorceress, enchant-

pitorra, *pitŏr'rä,* sf. wood-cock.

pizarra, *pithär'rä,* sf. slate. [slate-pit.

pizarral, *pithärräl',* sm. slate-quarry,

pizca, *pith'kä,* sf. mite; pinch.

pizpereta, *–pĕrĕ'tä,* a. sharp, brisk, lively (applied to women).

pizpirigaña, *–pirigän'yä,* sf. play among boys, in which they pinch one another's hands.

placa, *plä'kä,* sf. clasp of a broadsword belt; star, insignia of an order of knighthood. [congratulation.

pláceme, *plä'thĕmĕ,* sm. compliment of

placentero, ra, *pläthĕntä'rŏ,* a. joyful, merry. [v. imp. to please.

placer, *pläthĕr',* sm. pleasure, delight; –,

plaga, *plä'gä,* sf. plague.

plagar, *plägär',* v. a. to plague, to torment.

plagiario, ria, *plä'hiä'riŏ,* a. & sm. plagiarising, plagiarist.

plagio, *plä'hiŏ,* sm. plagiarism.

plan, *plän,* sm. plan; design, plot.

plana, *plä'nä,* sf. trowel; page (of a book); level; –, mayor, (mil.) staff-office.

plancha, *plän'tshä,* sf. plate; ironing-iron.

planchar, *–tshär',* v. a. to iron linen.

planchoar, *–tshär',* v.a. to plate, to sheath.

planeta, *plänĕ'tä,* sm. planet.

planetario, *plänĕtä'riŏ,* a. planetary.

planisferio, *plänisfĕ'riŏ,* sm. planisphere.

plano, *plä'nŏ,* a. plain, level, flat; –, sm. plan, ground-plot; (rail.) – inclinado, dead level. [–s, pl. brag, boast.

planta, *plän'tä,* sf. plant; plantation;

plantación, *–täthiŏn',* sf. plantation.

plantador, *–dŏr',* sm. planter.

plántano, *plän'tänŏ,* sm. plantain-tree.

plantar, *pläntär',* v. a. to plant; to fix upright; to strike or hit a blow; to found, to establish; –se, to stand upright.

plantear, *–tĕär',* v. a. to plan, to trace.

plantel, *pläntĕl',* sm. nursery-garden.

plantificar, *–tifikär',* v. a. to plant; to beat; to box, to kick.

plantilla, *–til'yä,* sf. young plant; first sole of a shoe; vamp; plate of a gun-lock.

plantillar, *–tilyär',* v. a. to vamp or sole shoes or stockings.

plantío, tia, *pläntē'ŏ,* a. planted; ready to be planted; –, sm. planting, nursery.

plantón, *pläntŏn',* sm. scion, sprout; (mil.) sentry punished with extra duty.

plañidera, *plänyidä'rä,* sf. weeping-woman. [to bewail.

plañir, *plänyir',* v n. to lament, to grieve.

plasta, *pläs'tä,* sf. paste, soft clay.

plata, *plä'tä,* sf. silver; plate (wrought silver); en –, briefly.

plataforma, *–fŏr'mä,* sf. platform; (rail.) – giratoria, turn-plate, turn-table.

plátano, *plä'tänŏ,* sm. plane-tree.

plateado, da, *plätĕä'dŏ,* a. silvered; plated.

plateadura, *–dŏ'rä,* sf. silvering.

platear, *plätĕär',* v. a. to silver.

platería, *plätĕrē'ä,* sf. silversmith's shop; trade of a silversmith.

platero, *plätĕ'rŏ,* sm. silversmith.

plática, *plä'tikä,* sf. discourse, conversation. [practise.

platicar, *plätikär',* v. a. to converse, to

platillas, *plätil'yäs,* sf. pl. fine French [linen.

platina, *plätē'nä,* sf. platina.

plato, *plä'tŏ,* sm. dish; mess.

platónico, ca, *plätŏ'nikŏ,* a. platonic.

plausible, *pläûsē'blĕ,* a. plausible.

playa, *plä'yä,* sf. shore, strand.

plaza, *plä'thä,* sf. square, place; fortified place; office, public employment; enrolling of soldiers.

plazo, *plä'thŏ,* sm. term; tilt-yard.

pleamar, *plĕämär',* sf. (mar.) high water.

plebe, *plĕ'bĕ,* sf. common people, populace.

plebeyo, ya, *plĕbä'yŏ,* a. plebeian; –, sm. commoner.

plectro, *plĕk'trŏ,* sm. (poet.) plectrum.

plegable, *plĕgä'blĕ,* a. pliable.

plegadera, *–dä'rä,* sf. folding-stick.

plegador, *–dŏr',* sm. folding instrument; plaiter.

plegadura, *-dō'rā*, sf. fold, plaiting.

plegar, *plĕgār'*, v. a. to fold, to plait; —, v. imp. to please; **plegue á Dios que,** God grant that.

plegaria, *plĕgā'rīā*, sf. public prayer.

pleita, *plēĕ'tā*, sf. plaited strand of bass.

pleiteador, *-tĕādōr'*, sm. pleader; wrangler.

pleitear, *-tĕār'*, v. a. to plead, to litigate.

pleitista, *-tĭs'tā*, sm. litigious person.

pleito, *plā'tŏ*, sm. contract, bargain; dispute, controversy, debate; law-suit.

plenamente, *plĕnāmĕn'tĕ*, ad. fully, completely.

plenario, ria, *-nā'rĭŏ*, a. complete, full.

plenilunio, *plĕnīlū'nĭŏ*, sm. full-moon, full-faced moon. [plenipotentiary.

plenipotenciario, *-pŏtĕnthĭā'rĭŏ*, sm.

plenitud, *-tūd'*, sf. fulness, abundance.

pleonasmo, *plĕŏnās'mŏ*, sm. pleonasm.

pliego, *plĭā'gŏ*, sm. sheet of paper.

pliegue, *plĭā'gĕ*, sm. fold, plait; plight; ruff.

plomar, *plŏmār'*, v. a. to mark with a black-lead pencil; to stop teeth with lead.

plomero, *plŏmā'rŏ*, sm. plumber.

plomizo, za, *plŏmē'thŏ*, a. leaden.

plomo, *plŏ'mŏ*, sm. lead; **á —,** perpendicularly.

pluma, *plŏ'mā*, sf. feather, plume. [larly.

plumada, *plŏmā'dā*, sf. dash with a pen.

plumaje, *plŏmā'kĕ*, sm. plumage; plume.

plumero, *-mā'rŏ*, sm. bunch of feathers; feather-broom. [notary.

plumista, *-mĭs'tā*, sm. petty scrivener,

plural, *plŏrāl'*, a. (gr.) plural.

pluralidad, *-lĭdād'*, sf. plurality.

pluvial, *plŏvĭāl'*, a. rainy. [matic.

pneumático, ca, *pnĕŭmā'tĭkŏ*, a. pneu-

poblacho, *pŏblātsh'ŏ*, sm. populace, rabble.

población, ca, *-lā'dŏ*, sf. population.

poblado, *-lā'dŏ*, sm. town, village, inhabited place.

poblador, *-dōr'*, sm. populator, founder.

poblar, *pŏblār'*, v. a. to populate, to people; to fill, to occupy; to bud, to get leaves.

pobre, *pŏ'brĕ*, a. poor, indigent.

pobrete, *pŏbrā'tĕ*, sm. poor, unfortunate man; useless person. [avarice.

pobretería, *-tĕrē'ā*, sf. poor people;

pobreza, *pŏbrāth'ā*, sf. poverty, poorness.

pocero, *pŏthā'rŏ*, sm. well-digger; nightman. [dirty place.

pocilga, *pŏthĭl'gā*, sf. pig-sty; any nasty,

pócima, *pŏ'thĭmā*, sf. potion.

poco, ca, *pŏ'kŏ*, a. little, scanty; few; —, ad. little; **— ha que,** lately, latterly; **— á —,** gently; little by little; —, sm. a small part.

poda, *pŏ'dā*, sf. pruning of trees.

podadera, *pŏdādā'rā*, sf. pruning-knife.

podar, *pŏdār'*, v. a. to prune.

podenco, *pŏdĕn'kŏ*, sm. hound.

poder, *pŏdĕr'*, sm. power, authority; command; force; —, v. n. to be able; to possess the power of doing or performing; —, v. imp. to be possible.

poderhabiente, *-ābĭĕn'tĕ*, sm. attorney.

poderío, *pŏdĕrē'ŏ*, sm. power, authority; wealth, riches. [nent, excellent.

poderoso, sa, *-rŏ'sŏ*, a. powerful; emi-

podre, *pŏ'drĕ*, sf. pus, matter.

podredumbre, *pŏdrĕdŭm'brĕ*, sf. putrid matter; grief.

podrir, *pŏdrīr'*, v. n. to rot, to putrefy.

poema, *pŏā'mā*, sm. poem.

poesía, *pŏĕsē'ā*, sf. poetry; poesy.

poeta, *pŏā'tā*, sm. poet.

poética, *pŏā'tĭkā*, sf. poetry, poetics.

poético, ca, *-tĭkŏ*, a. poetical.

poetisa, *-tē'sā*, sf. poetess.

poetizar, *-tĭthār'*, v. a. to poetize.

polaca, *pŏlā'kā*, sf. tongue of a shoe.

polaina, *pŏlā'ĭnā*, sf. spatterdashes.

polar, *pŏlār'*, a. polar. [block.

polea, *pŏlā'ā*, sf. pulley; (mar.) tackle-

polémica, *pŏlā'mĭkā*, sf. polemics.

polémico, ca, *-mĭkŏ*, a. polemical.

policía, *pŏlĭthē'ā*, sf. police; politeness; neatness.

poligamia, *pŏlĭgā'mĭā*, sf. polygamy.

polígamo, *pŏlĭ'gāmŏ*, sm. polygamist.

polígono, *-gŏnŏ*, sm. polygon; —, na, a.

polilla, *pŏlĭl'yā*, sf. moth. [polygonal.

pólipo, *pŏ'lĭpŏ*, sm. polypus.

polisílabo, ba, *pŏlĭsē'lābŏ*, a. polysyllabic.

politécnico, *-tĕk'nĭkŏ*, a. polytechnical.

politeísmo, *-tĕĭs'mŏ*, sm. polytheism.

política, *pŏlĭ'tĭkā*, sf. politics; politeness.

político, ca, *-tĭkŏ*, a. political; polite; —, sm. politician.

póliza, *pŏlĭ'thā*, sf. written order to receive or recover a sum of money; policy; passport.

polo, *pŏ'lŏ*, sm. pole. [port.

poltrón, ona, *pŏltrŏn'*, a. idle, lazy; commodious, easy; **silla —ona,** elbowchair; —, sm. poltroon. [ness, indolence.

poltronería, *-nĕrē'ā*, sf. idleness, lazi-

polución, *pŏlŭthĭŏn'*, sf. pollution.

polvareda, *pŏlvārā'dā*, sf. cloud of dust.

polvo, *pŏl'vŏ*, sm. powder, dust; **un —,** a pinch of snuff. [fireworks, pl.

pólvora, *-vŏrā*, sf. gun-powder; artificial

polvorear, *pŏlvŏrĕār'*, v. a. to powder.

polvoriento, ta, *-rĭĕn'tŏ*, a. dusty.

polvorista, *-rĭs'tā*, sm. manufacturer of gun-powder. [to powder.

polvorizar, *-rĭthār'*, v. a. to pulverize;

polvoroso, sa, *-rŏ'sŏ*, a. dusty; **poner pies en —,** to scamper away.

polla, *pŏl'yā*, sf. pullet; money staked at cards; pool. [hatch, covey.

pollada, *-yā'dā*, sf. flock of young fowls;

pollera, *-yā'rā*, sf. hen-coop; go-cart.

pollería, *-yĕrē'ā*, sf. poultry-market.

pollero, *-yā'rŏ*, sm. poulterer.

pollino, *-yē'nŏ*, sm. young, untamed ass; dull, stupid, heavy fellow. [nestling.

pollo, *pŏl'yŏ*, sm. chicken just hatched,

pomada, *pŏmā'dā*, sf. pomatum, pomade.

pómez, *pŏ'mĕth*, sf. pumice-stone.

pomo, *pŏ'mŏ*, sm. fruit in general; apple; pommel.

pompa, *pŏm'pă*, sf. pomp; bubble.
pomposo, sa, *pŏmpŏ'sŏ*, a. pompous.
ponche, *pŏn'tshĕ*, sm. punch.
ponchera, *pŏntshā'ră*, sf. punchbowl.
poncho, cha, *pŏn'tshŏ*, a. soft, mild; —, sm. (am.) sleeveless frock.
poncil, *pŏntheil'*, a. bitter orange or lemon.
ponderable, *pŏndĕr'blĕ*, a. ponderable; measurable by scales; wonderful.
ponderación, *-dĕrăthŏn'*, sf. pondering, considering; exaggeration.
ponderar, *-dĕrár'*, v. a. to ponder, to weigh; to exaggerate, *fing.* hyperbolical.
ponderativo, va, *-dĕrătē'vŏ*, a. exaggerate.
ponedero, ra, *pŏnēdē'rŏ*, a. egg-laying; capable of being laid or placed; —, sm. nest; nest-egg; covey.
poner, *pŏnēr'*, v. a. to put, to place; to impose; to lay eggs; —se, to oppose; to set (of stars); to become.
poniente, *pŏnĭĕn'tĕ*, sm. west; west wind.
pontaje, *pŏntá'hĕ*, pontazgo, *-táth'gŏ*, sm. bridge-toll.
pontificado, *pŏntĭfĭkā'dŏ*, sm. pontificate.
pontifical, *-fĭkál'*, a. & sm. pontifical.
pontifice, *pŏntē'fĭthĕ*, sm. Pope, pontiff.
pontificio, cia, *-fē'thĭŏ*, a. pontifical.
pontón, *pŏntŏn'*, sm. pontoon.
ponzoña, *pŏnthŏn'yă*, sf. poison.
ponzoñoso, sa, *-thŏnyŏ'sŏ*, a. poisonous.
popa, *pŏ'pă*, sf. (mar.) poop, stern.
populacho, *pŏpŭlätsh'ŏ*, sm. populace, mob.
población, *-lăthŏn'*, sf. population.
popular, *-lár'*, a. popular.
popularidad, *-lărĭdăd'*, sf. popularity.
populoso, sa, *-lŏ'sŏ*, a. populous.
poquedad, *pŏkĕdăd'*, sf. paucity, littleness; cowardice. [through; on account of.
por, *pŏr'*, pr. for, by, about; by means of;
porcelana, *pŏrthĕlā'nă*, sf. porcelain, china.
porción, *pŏrthŏn'*, sf. part, portion; lot.
porciuncula, *-thĭŭn'kŭlă*, sf. small portion, *pŏrkŏ'nŏ*, a. hoggish. [tion.
porcuno, na, *pŏrkŏ'nŏ*, a. hoggish.
pordiosear, *-dĭŏsĕár'*, v. a. to beg alms.
pordiosería, *-sĕrē'ă*, sf. beggary.
pordiosero, ra, *-sĕrŏ'*, sm. & f. beggar.
porfía, *pŏrfē'ă*, sf. obstinate quarrel; stubbornness; importunity; á —, emulously; with strife and contention. [born.
porfiado, da, *-fĭă'dŏ*, a. obstinate, stubborn.
porfiador, ra, *-fĭădŏr'*, sm. & f. disputer, wrangler. [to persist in a pursuit.
porfiar, *-fĭár'*, v. a. to dispute obstinately;
pórfido, *pŏr'fĭdŏ*, sm. porphyry.
pormenor, *pŏrmĕnŏr'*, sf. detail.
poro, *pŏ'rŏ*, sm. pore.
porosidad, *pŏrŏsĭdăd'*, sf. porosity.
poroso, sa, *pŏrŏ'sŏ*, a. porous.
porque, *pŏrkĕ'*, c. because; why.
porqué, —, sm. cause, reason.
porquería, *pŏrkĕrē'ă*, sf. nastiness, foulness; brutishness, rudeness, trifle; dirty action.
porqueriza, *-rē'thă*, sf. pig-sty.
porquero, *pŏrkĕ'rŏ*, sm. swine-herd.
porra, *pŏr'ră*, sf. cudgel.

porrazo, *pŏr'ră'thŏ*, sm. blow with a cudgel.
porrería, *pŏrrĕrē'ă*, sf. stupidity, folly, silliness. [en —, stark-naked.
porreta, *pŏrrĕ'tă*, sf. green leaf of leek; porrillo, *-rĭl'yŏ*, (á —) ad. copiously, abundantly. [water.
porrón, *-rŏn'*, sm. earthen pitcher for
portabandera, *pŏrtăbăndē'ră*, sf. colour-sheath.
portacartas, *-kăr'tăs*, sm. mail; postman.
portada, *pŏrtă'dă*, sf. portal, porch; frontispiece.
portador, *-dŏr'*, sm. carrier, porter.
portaestandarte, *-ĕstăndár'tĕ*, sm. (mil.) standard-bearer; cornet. [musket.
portafusil, *-fŭsēl'*, sm. (mil.) sling of a
portaguión, *-gĭŏn'*, sm. standard-bearer of cavalry.
portal, *pŏrtál'*, sm. porch; portico, piazza.
portamanteo, *-măntē'ŏ*, sm. portmanteau, cloak-bag. [plate.
portapaz, *-páth'*, sm. & f. the image-
portarse, *pŏrtár'sĕ*, v. r. to behave, to comport.
portátil, *pŏrtá'tĭl*, a. portable. [comport.
portazgo, *-táth'gŏ*, sm. toll, turnpike-duty.
portazguero, *-táthgĕ'rŏ*, sm. toll-gatherer.
portazo, *pŏrtă'thŏ*, sm. bang of a door; banging a door in one's face.
porte, *pŏr'tĕ*, sm. porterage, portage; deportment, demeanour, conduct.
portento, *pŏrtĕn'tŏ*, sm. prodigy, portent.
portentoso, sa, *-tŏ'sŏ*, a. prodigious, marvellous, strange.
portería, *pŏrtĕrē'ă*, sf. principal door of a convent; porter's office.
portero, *pŏrtĕ'rŏ*, sm. porter, gate-keeper.
portezuela, *-thŭĕ'lă*, sf. little door.
pórtico, *pŏr'tĭkŏ*, sm. portico, porch, lobby.
portillo, *-tĭl'yŏ*, sm. aperture in a wall; gap, breach; —s, pl. small gates of a town, through which nothing dutiable is allowed to pass.
portón, *-tŏn'*, sm. inner door of a house.
¡porvida! *pŏrvē'dă*, sf. by the living God!
pos, *pŏs'*, en —, ad. after, behind; in pursuit of.
posa, *pŏ'să*, sf. passing-bell; stops made by the clergy who conduct a funeral, to sing a responsary.
posada, *pŏsă'dă*, sf. lodging-house, inn, hotel; pocket-case, containing a knife, spoon, and fork; —s, pl. apartments for the ladies in waiting in the royal palace.
posaderas, *-dĕ'răs*, sf. pl. buttocks.
posadero, *-dĕ'rŏ*, sm. inn-keeper; back-side, bottom.
posar, *pŏsár'*, v. n. to lodge; to sit down, to repose; —, v. a. to lay down a burden.
posdata, *pŏsdă'tă*, sf. postscript.
poseer, *pŏsĕĕr'*, v. a. to hold, to possess.
poseido, da, *pŏsĕē'dŏ*, a. possessed with the devil.
posesión, *pŏsĕsĭŏn'*, sf. possession.
posesivo, va, *-sē'vŏ*, a. (gr.) possessive.
posesor, ra, *-sŏr'*, sm. & f. possessor.
posesorio, ria, *-sŏ'rĭŏ*, a. possessory.

posibilidad, *pŏsĭbĭlĭdăd',* sf. possibility; wealth, riches.
posible, *pŏsē'blĕ,* a. possible.   [situation.
posición, *pŏsĭthĭŏn',* sf. position; posture;
positivo, va, *–tē'vŏ,* a. positive.
pósito, *pŏ'sĭtŏ,* sm. public granary; **– pío,** granary for charity.
poso, *pŏ'sŏ,* sm. sediment, dregs, lees,
posponer, *pŏspŏnēr',* v. a. to postpone.
posta, *pŏs'tä,* sf. post; post-house; post-stage; **–,** sm. person who travels post.
poste, *pŏs'tĕ,* sm. post, pillar.
poste restante, *– rĕstän'tĕ,* a. to be kept till called for (of letters).
postema, *pŏstē'mä,* sm. abscess, tumour; dull, troublesome person.
postergación, *pŏstĕrgäthĭŏn',* sf. missing out, putting back, passing over.
postergar, *–gär',* v. a. to leave behind.
posteridad, *pŏstĕrĭdăd',* sf. posterity.
posterior, *pŏstĕrĭŏr',* a. posterior.
posterioridad, *–rĭdăd',* sf. posteriority.
postigo, *pŏstē'gŏ,* sm. wicket; postern; pane or sash of a window.
postilón, *pŏstĭlyŏn',* sm. postilion.
postilloso, sa, *–yŏ'sŏ,* a. scabby, pustulous.   [natural.] **–,** sm. false hair.
postizo, za, *pŏstē'thŏ,* a. artificial (not
postor, *pŏstŏr',* sm. bidder at a public sale; bettor.
postración, *pŏstrāthĭŏn',* sf. prostration.
postrar, *pŏsträr',* v. a. to humble, to humiliate; **–se,** to prostrate oneself.
postre, *pŏs'trĕ,* a. last in order; **á la –,** at last; **–,** sm. dessert.
postrer, *pŏstrēr',* **postrero, ra,** *–rā'rŏ,* a. last in order, hindermost.
postrimería, *pŏstrĭmĕrē'ä,* sf. last portion or last years of life.
postrimero, ra, *–mā'rŏ,* a. hindermost.
póstumo, ma, *pŏs'tŭmŏ,* a. posthumous.
postura, *pŏstū'rä,* sf. posture, position; tax on eatables; price asked or offered; bet, wager; agreement, convention.
potable, *pŏtä'blĕ,* a. potable, drinkable.
potaje, *pŏtä'hĕ,* sm. pottage; drink made up of several ingredients; medley of various useless things.
potar, *pŏtär',* v. a. to equalize and mark weights and measures.
potasa, *pŏtä'sä,* sf. potash.
pote, *pŏ'tĕ,* sm. pot, jar; flower-pot; standard measure or weight.
potencia, *pŏtĕn'thĭä,* sf. power; mightiness.
potentado, *–tä'dŏ,* sm. potentate; prince.
potente, *pŏtĕn'tĕ,* a. potent, powerful, mighty.
poterna, *pŏtĕr'nä,* sf. postern, sally-port.
potestad, *pŏtĕstäd',* sf. power, dominion; jurisdiction.
potra, *pŏ'trä,* sf. rupture, hernia.
potro, ra, *pŏ'trŏ,* sm. & f. colt; foal.
potroso, sa, *pŏtrŏ'sŏ,* a. afflicted with a rupture; fortunate, lucky.   [door.]
poyo, *pŏ'yŏ,* sm. bench (near the street
poza, *pŏ'thä,* sf. puddle; hole.
pozal, *pŏthäl',* sm. bucket, pail.

pozo, *pŏ'thŏ,* sm. well; **– de nieve,** ice-house, ice-cellar; snow-pit.
práctica, *prăk'tĭkä,* sf. practice.
practicable, *–kä'blĕ,* a. practicable, feasible.
practicante, *–kän'tĕ,* sm. practiser; practitioner in surgery and medicine under a distinguished master.
practicar, *–kär',* v. a. to practise.
práctico, ca, *prăk'tĭkŏ,* a. practical; skilful, experienced; **–,** sm. practiser, practitioner.   [sf. meadow, mead.
pradera, *prädē'rä,* **pradería,** *prädĕrē'ä,*
prado, *prä'dŏ,* sm. lawn, meadow.
Prado, –, sm. a public walk in Madrid.
pragmática, *prägmä'tĭkä,* sf. royal edict.
prasio, *prä'sĭŏ,* sm. prase, a precious stone.
preámbulo, *prēäm'bŭlŏ,* sm. preamble; circumlocution.
prebenda, *–bĕn'dä,* sf. prebend.
prebendado, *–dä'dŏ,* sm. prebendary.
prebendar, *–där',* v. a. to give prebend.
preboste, *prĕbŏs'tĕ,* sm. provost.
precario, ria, *–kä'rĭŏ,* a. precarious.
precaución, *–käüthĭŏn',* sf. precaution.
precaver, *–kävēr',* v. a. to prevent, to guard against.   [preference; superiority.
precedencia, *–thĕdĕn'thĭä,* sf. precedence;
precedente, *–thĕdĕn'tĕ,* p. & a. precedent, foregoing.   [before.
preceder, *–thĕdēr',* v. a. to precede, to go
precepto, *prĕthĕp'tŏ,* sm. precept, order.
preceptor, *–thĕptŏr',* sm. master, teacher, preceptor.   [votions.
preces, *prĕ'thĕs,* sf. pl. prayers; de-
preciado, da, *prĕthĭä'dŏ,* a. proud, presumptuous.   [pride in.
preciarse, *–thĭär'sĕ,* v. a. to boast, to take
precio, *prĕ'thĭŏ,* sm. price, value.
preciosidad, *prĕthĭŏsĭdăd',* sf. excellence, preciousness.
precioso, sa, *–thĭŏ'sŏ,* a. precious.
precipicio, *–thĭpē'thĭŏ,* sm. precipice; violent, sudden fall; ruin, destruction.
precipitación, *–thĭpĭtäthĭŏn',* sf. precipitation, inconsiderate haste.
precipitado, da, *–tä'dŏ,* a. precipitate, headlong, hasty.
precipitar, *–tär',* v. a. to precipitate; **–se,** to run headlong to one's destruction.
precisar, *prĕthĭsär',* v. a. to compel, to oblige, to necessitate.
precisión, *–thĭsĭŏn',* sf. necessity, compulsion; preciseness.
preciso, sa, *prĕthē'sŏ,* a. necessary, requisite; precise, exact; abstracted.
precocidad, *–kŏthĭdăd',* sf. precocity.
preconizar, *–kŏnĭthär',* v. a. to proclaim.
precoz, *prĕkŏth',* a. precocious.
precursor, ra, *–kŭrsŏr',* sm. & f. harbinger, fore-runner.
predecesor, *–dĕthĕsŏr',* sm. & f. predecessor, antecessor, runner.
predecir, *–dĕthĭr',* v. a. to foretell.
predestinación, *–dĕstĭnäthĭŏn',* sf. predestination.
predestinar, *–dĕstĭnär',* v. a. to predestine.

predial, *prĕdiäl'*, a. consisting in landed property *or* relating to it.

predicable, *prĕdĭka'blĕ*, a. fit to be preached; predicable. [sermon.

predicación, *—kăthĭŏn'*, sf. preaching,

predicado, *—kä'dŏ*, sm. predicate.

predicador, *—kădŏr'*, sm. preacher.

predicamento, *—kämĕn'tŏ*, sm. predicament.

predicar, *—kär'*, v. a. to publish; to preach.

predicción, *—dĭkthĭŏn'*, sf. prediction.

predilección, *—lĕkthĭŏn'*, sf. predilection.

predilecto, ta, *—lĕk'tŏ*, a. darling, favourite.

predio, *prĕ'dĭŏ*, sm. landed property; farm; **- rústico,** piece of cultivated ground; **- urbano,** town- *or* country-house. [minate, to prevail; to command.

predominar, *prĕdŏmĭnär'*, v. a. to predo-

predominio, *—dŏmĕ'nĭŏ*, sm. predominant power, superiority.

preeminencia, *—ĕmĭnĕn'thĭă*, sf. pre-eminence, superiority of power.

preeminente, *—nĕn'tĕ*, a. pre-eminent, superior. [existence.

preexistencia, *—ĕksĭstĕn'thĭă*, sf. pre-

preexistente, *—tĕn'tĕ*, p. & a. pre-existent.

preexistir, *—ĭr'*, v. n. to pre-exist, to exist before.

prefacio, *prĕfä'thĭŏ*, sm. preface.

prefecto, *—fĕk'tŏ*, sm. prefect.

prefectura, *—fĕktŏ'rä*, sf. prefecture.

preferencia, *—fĕrĕn'thĭă*, sf. preference.

preferible, *—fĕrĕ'blĕ*, a. preferable.

preferir, *—fĕrĭr'*, v. a. to prefer.

prefijar, *—fĭhär'*, v. a. to prefix, to fix beforehand.

pregón, *prĕgŏn'*, sm. publication made in public places by the common crier, hue and cry. [public places.

pregonar, *—gŏnär'*, v. a. to proclaim in

pregonero, *—nĕ'rŏ*, sm. common crier; **-, ra,** a. publishing.

pregunta, *—gŭn'tä*, sf. question; inquiry.

preguntar, *—tär'*, v. a. to question, to demand; to inquire. [tive person.

preguntón, *—ŏn', tŏn'*, sm. & f. inquisi-

prelacia, *—lä'thĭä*, sf. prelacy.

prelada, *prĕlä'dä*, sf. abbess.

prelado, *—dŏ*, sm. prelate. [nary.

preliminar, *—lĭmĭnär'*, a. & sm. prelimi-

preludio, *—lŏ'dĭŏ*, sm. prelude.

prematuro, ra, *—mätŏ'rŏ*, a. premature, precocious. [ditation, forethought.

premeditación, *—mĕdĭtäthĭŏn'*, sf. preme-

premeditar, *—tär'*, v. a. to premeditate, to think out. [munerate.

premiar, *prĕmĭär'*, v. a. to reward, to re-

premio, *prĕ'mĭŏ*, sm. reward, recompense; premium.

premisa, *prĕmĭs'ä*, sf. premise.

premura, *—mŏ'rä*, sf. narrowness, pressure, haste, hurry.

prenda, *prĕn'dä*, sf. pledge; sweetheart; person *or* thing dearly loved; **-s,** pl. accomplishments, talents.

prendar, *—där'*, v. a. to pledge; to ingratiate oneself; **-se,** to take a fancy to oneself.

prender, *prĕndĕr'*, v. a. to seize, to catch, to lay hold of; to imprison; **-,** v. n. to take root; **-se,** to adorn oneself.

prendería, *—dĕrĭ'ä*, sf. pawnbroker's shop; frippery; [dawdler, slow-coach.

prendero, *prĕndĕ'rŏ*, sm. pawnbroker.

prendido, *—dĭ'dŏ*, sm. attire of women; pattern for bone-lace. [capture.

prendimiento, *—dĭmĭĕn'tŏ*, sm. seizure;

prensa, *prĕn'sä*, sf. press. [stuff).

prensado, *—sä'dŏ*, sm. lustre, gloss (of

prensadura, *—ĭŏ'rä*, sf. pressing, pressure.

prensar, *prĕnsär'*, v. a. to press.

prensista, *—sĭs'tä*, sm. pressman in a printing-office.

preñado, da, *prĕnyä'dŏ*, a. full, pregnant; big with child; **-,** sm. pregnancy.

preñez, *prĕnyĕth'*, sf. pregnancy.

preocupación, *prĕŏkŭpäthĭŏn'*, sf. preoccupation. [another; to preoccupy.

preocupar, *—pär'*, v. a. to occupy before

preparación, *—päräthĭŏn'*, sf. preparation.

preparar, *—pärär'*, v. a. to prepare; **-se,** to be prepared.

preparativo va, *—tĕ'vŏ*, a. preparative qualifying; **-,** sm. preparative.

preparatorio, ria, *—tŏ'rĭŏ*, a. preparatory. [ponderance.

preponderancia, *—pŏndĕrän'thĭă*, sf. pre-

preponderar, *—dĕrär'*, v. n. to preponderate, to prevail. [position.

preposición, *—prŏsĭthĭŏn'*, sf. (gr.) pre-

prepucio, *prĕpŏ'thĭŏ*, sm. prepuce, foreskin. [privilege.

prerrogativa, *—rŏgätĕ'vä*, sf. prerogative,

presa, *prĕ'sä*, sf. capture, seizure; carcass of a fowl; dike, dam, mole; **-s,** pl. tusks, fangs, claws. [forebode.

presagiar, *prĕsähĭär'*, v. a. to presage, to

presagio, *prĕsä'hĭŏ*, sm. presage.

presbiterado, *prĕsbĭtĕrä'dŏ*, **presbiterato,** *—rä'tŏ*, sm. priesthood.

presbiteral, *—räl'*, a. sacerdotal.

presbiterio, *—tĕ'rĭŏ*, sm. sanctuary.

presbítero, *prĕsbĕ'tĕrŏ*, sm. priest, clergyman. [foreknowledge.

presciencia, *—thĭĕn'thĭä*, sf. prescience.

prescindir, *prĕsthĭndĭr'*, v. a. to prescind, to cut off; to abstract.

prescribir, *prĕskrĭbĭr'*, v. a. to prescribe.

prescripción, *—skrĭpthĭŏn'*, sf. prescription.

prescriptible, *—skrĭptĕ'blĕ*, a. prescriptible.

prescripto, ta, *—skrĭp'tŏ*, a. & p. prescribed.

presea, *prĕsĕ'ä*, sf. jewel. [existence.

presencia, *prĕsĕn'thĭä*, sf. presence, co-

presenciar, *—thĭär'*, v. n. to assist, to be present.

presentación, *—täthĭŏn'*, sf. presentation.

presentar, *—tär'*, v. a. to present; **-se,** to present oneself. [present.

presente, *prĕsĕn'tĕ*, sm. present, gift; **-,** a.

presentemente, *—mĕn'tĕ*, ad. presently, now. [sentiment.

presentimiento, *—sĕntĭmĭĕn'tŏ*, sm. pre-

presentir, *—sĕntĭr'*, v. a. to have a presentiment. [tion.

preservación, *—sĕrväthĭŏn'*, sf. preserva-

preservador, ra, –*vådôr'*, sm. preserver.

preservar, –*vår'*, v. a. to preserve, to defend from evil.

preservativo, –*tê'võ*, sm. preservative.

presidencia, *presîdên'thîä*, sf. president-ship; presidency.

presidente, –*dên'tê*, sm. president.

presidiario, –*dîî'rîô*, sm. criminal condemned to hard labour or banishment in a garrison.

presidio, *presê'dîô*, sm. penitentiary, garrison of soldiers; Bridewell, house of correction in London.

presidir, *presîdîr'*, v. a. to preside.

presilla, *presîl'yä*, sf. small string; loop in clothes.

presión, *presîôn'*, sf. pressure, pressing.

preso, sa, *prê'sõ*, sm. & f. prisoner.

prestamero, *prestämê'rõ*, sm. incumbent of an ecclesiastical sinecure. [der.

prestamista, –*mîs'tä*, sm. borrower, lender.

préstamo, *prês'tämõ*, sm. loan.

prestar, *prestår'*, v. a. to lend.

preste, *prês'tê*, sm. priest who celebrates high mass. [speed.

presteza, *prestê'thä*, sf. quickness, haste, speed.

prestigiador, *prestîhîädôr'*, sm. cheat, juggler, impostor. [ture.

prestigio, *prestî'hîõ*, sm. prestige; imposture.

presto, ta, *prês'tä*, a. quick, prompt, ready; –, ad. soon, quickly.

presumible, *presümê'blê*, a. presumable.

presumido, da, –*sümî'dõ*, a. presumptuous, arrogant. [jecture.

presumir, –*sümîr'*, v. a. to presume, to conjecture; conceit.

presunción, –*sünthîôn'*, sf. presumption, conjecture; conceit.

presuntivo, va, –*tê'võ*, a. presumptive.

presuntuoso, sa, –*tüô'sõ*, a. presumptuous. [pose.

presuponer, –*süpõnêr'*, v. a. to presuppose.

presupuesto, –*püês'tõ*, sm. motive, pretext, pretence; presumed cost; budget.

presuroso, sa, –*sürô'sõ*, a. hasty, prompt, quick; nimble. [of a horse.

pretal, *prêtål'*, sm. poitrel, breast-leather

pretender, –*têndêr'*, v. a. to pretend, to claim; to try, to attempt.

pretendiente, –*dîên'tê*, a. pretender.

pretensión, –*sîôn'*, sf. pretension.

pretérito, ta, *prêtê'rîtõ*, a. preterite, past.

pretextar, –*têkstår'*, v. a. to find a pretext or pretence.

pretexto, –*têks'tõ*, sm. pretext, pretence.

pretil, *prêtîl'*, sm. battlement, breast-work.

pretina, *prêtê'nä*, sf. girdle, waistband.

pretor, *prêtôr'*, sm. pretor. [belt.

pretorial, –*tôrîäl'*, **pretoriano, na,** *prêtôrîä'nõ*, a. pretorian.

pretorio, *prêtô'rîõ*, sm. Pretorium.

pretura, –*tô'rä*, sf. pretorship.

prevalecer, –*vålêthêr'*, v. n. to prevail; to outshine; to take root. [cation.

prevaricación, –*vårîkäthîôn'*, sf. prevarication.

prevaricar, –*kår'*, v. a. to prevaricate; to fail in one's duty.

prevención, –*vênthîôn'*, sf. disposition,

preparation; supply of provisions; foresight; prevention; (mil.) police-guard.

prevenido, da, –*vênî'dõ*, a. prepared, provided; plentiful, abundant; provident, careful, cautious, foreseeing, forecasting.

prevenir, –*vênîr'*, v. a. to prepare; to foresee, to foreknow; to prevent; to advise; –se, to be prepared; to be predisposed.

preventivo, va, –*tê'võ*, a. preventive.

prever, *prêvêr'*, v. a. to foresee, to forecast.

previo, via, *prê'vîõ*, a. previous.

previsión, *prêvîsîôn'*, sf. foresight, prevision, forecast.

previsor, ra, –*vîsôr'*, a. foreseer.

priesa, *prîê'sä*, sf. haste, speed, hurry.

prieto, ta, *prîê'tõ*, a. blackish; narrowminded; indigent.

prima, *prê'mä*, sf. the first three hours of the day; prime; treble; female cousin.

primacía, *prîmäthê'ä*, sf. priority; primateship, primacy.

primado, –*mä'dõ*, sm. primeness; primate.

primavera, –*vê'rä*, sf. spring (the season).

primeramente, *prîmêrämên'tê*, ad. in the first place, mainly.

primeriza, –*rê'thä*, sf. woman who has borne her first child.

primero, ra, *prîmê'rõ*, a. first, prior, former; –, ad. first, rather, sooner.

primicia, *prîmê'thîä*, sf. first-fruits.

primitivo, va, *prîmîtê'võ*, a. primitive, original.

primo, ma, *prê'mõ*, a. first; –, sm. cousin.

primogénito, ta, *prîmõhê'nîtõ*, a. & sm. & sf. first-born; firstling. [geniture.

primogenitura, –*hênîtô'rä*, sf. primogeniture.

primor, *prîmôr'*, sm. beauty; dexterity, ability. [fine, excellent; handsome.

primoroso, sa, –*rô'sõ*, a. neat, elegant, fine, excellent; handsome.

princesa, *prînthê'sä*, sf. princess.

principado, –*thîpä'dõ*, sm. princedom.

principal, –*thîpäl'*, a. principal, chief.

príncipe, *prîn'thîpê*, sm. prince.

principiante, –*thîpîän'tê*, sm. beginner, learner. [to begin.

principiar, –*thîpîär'*, v. a. to commence, to begin.

principio, *prînthî'pîõ*, sm. beginning, commencement; principle.

pringada, –*gä'dä*, sf. slice of toasted bread steeped in gravy.

pringar, –*gär'*, v. a. to baste; to grease; to take a share in; to stain one's reputation; –se, to embezzle, to misappropriate, to defraud. [–, sm. grease-stain.

pringón, ona, –*gõn'*, a. dirty, greasy.

pringoso, sa, –*gô'sõ*, a. greasy, fat.

pringue, *prîn'gê*, sm. & f. grease, lard.

prior, *prîôr'*, sm. prior; –, a. prior, prioress, *prîõ'rä*, sf. prioress. [ceding.

prioral, *prîõräl'*, a. belonging to a prior.

priorato, –*rä'tõ*, sm. priorship.

prioridad, –*rîdäd'*, sf. priority. [hood.

prioste, *prîõs'tê*, sm. steward of a brotherhood.

prisa, *prê'sä*, sf. celerity, promptness.

prisión, *prîsîôn'*, sf. seizure, capture; prison; prey.

prisionero, –*nê'rõ*, sm. prisoner.

prisma, *prĕs'mä,* sm. prism.
privación, *priväthiŏn',* sf. privation, want.
privada, *vä'dä,* sf. filth or dirt thrown into the street. [—, sm. favourite.
privado, da, *vä'dŏ,* a. private; particular;
privanza, *vän'thä,* sf. familiar intercourse.
privar, *vär',* v. a. to deprive; to prohibit;
—se, to deprive oneself.
privativo, va, *tē'vŏ,* a. private, one's own; particular, peculiar.
privilegiar, *privilĕ'hēär',* v.a. to privilege.
privilegio, *lĕ'hĭŏ,* sm. privilege.
pro, *prŏ,* sm. & f. profit, benefit, advantage; **buena—,** much good may it do you.
proa, *prŏ'ä,* sf. (mar.) prow.
probabilidad, *prŏbäbĭlĭdäd',* sf. probability, likelihood.
probable, *prŏbä'blĕ,* a. probable, likely.
probado, da, *prŏbä'dŏ,* a. proved, tried.
probadura, *bädŏ'rä,* sf. trial.
probanza, *prŏbän'thä,* sf. proof, evidence.
probar, *bär',* v. a. to try; to prove; to taste; — v. n. to suit, to agree.
probatorio, ria, *tŏ'rĭŏ,* a. probatory.
probidad, *prŏbĭdäd',* sf. probity.
problema, *prŏblĕ'mä,* sm. problem.
problemático, ca, *blĕmä'tĭkŏ,* a. problematical.
probóscide, *prŏbŏs'thĭdĕ,* sm. proboscis.
procacidad, *käthĭdäd',* sf. impudence, petulance. [forward.
procaz, *prŏkäth',* a. impudent, petulant,
procedencia, *thĕdĕn'thĭä,* sf. derivation.
proceder, *thĕdĕr',* sm. procedure; —, v. n. to proceed, to go on; to issue; to prosecute any design. [ing; legal procedure.
procedimiento, *dĭmĭĕn'tŏ,* sm. proceed-
proceloso, sa, *thĕlŏ'sŏ,* a. tempestuous, stormy. [persons.
próceres, *prŏ'thĕrĕs,* sm. pl. the topping
procesado, *prŏthĕsä'dŏ,* a. prolix and circumstantial (of legal papers).
procesar, *thĕsär',* v. a. to inform against, to prosecute.
procesión, *thĕsĭŏn',* sf. procession.
proceso, *prŏthĕ'sŏ,* sm. process, law-suit.
proclama, *prŏklä'mä,* sf. proclamation, publication. [tion; acclamation.
proclamación, *mäthĭŏn',* sf. proclama-
proclamar, *mär',* v. a. to proclaim.
procónsul, *kŏn'sŭl,* sm. proconsul.
proconsulado, *sŭlä'dŏ,* sm. proconsulship.
proconsular, *kŏnsŭlär',* a. proconsular.
procreación, *krĕäthĭŏn',* sf. procreation, generation. [generate.
procrear, *krĕär',* v. a. to procreate, to
procuración, *kŭräthĭŏn',* sf. power of attorney; procurement.
procurador, *dŏr',* sm. procurer; attorney; proctor. [fice; proctorship.
procuraduría, *dürĕ'ä,* sf. attorney's of-
procurar, *rär',* v. a. to solicit; to act as an attorney.
prodigalidad, *dĭgälĭdäd',* sf. prodigality; plenty, abundance.
prodigar, *gär',* v. a. to waste, to lavish.

prodigio, *prŏdĭ'hĭŏ,* sm. prodigy, monster.
prodigioso, sa, *dĭ'hĭŏ'sŏ,* a. prodigious, monstrous; exquisite, excellent.
pródigo, ga, *prŏ'dĭgŏ,* a. prodigal.
producción, *prŏdŭkthĭŏn',* sf. production.
producible, *dŭthĭ'blĕ,* a. producible.
producir, *thĭr',* v. a. to produce; (law) to produce as evidence.
productivo, va, *dŭktĭ'vŏ,* a. productive.
producto, *prŏdŭk'tŏ,* sm. product.
proemio, *prŏĕ'mĭŏ,* sm. preface, introduction. [bravery.
proeza, *prŏĕ'thä,* sf. prowess, valour,
profanación, *fänäthĭŏn',* sf. profanation.
profanar, *fänär',* v. a. to profane.
profano, na, *prŏfä'nŏ,* a. profane.
profecía, *fĕthĕ'ä,* sf. prophecy.
profesar, *fĕsär',* v. a. to profess, to declare openly; to take the vows; to take the veil.
profesión, *fĕsĭŏn',* sf. profession.
profeso, sa, *fĕ'sŏ,* a. professed.
profesor, *fĕsŏr',* sm. professor.
profeta, *prŏfĕ'tä,* sm. prophet.
profético, ca, *fĕ'tĭkŏ,* a. prophetic.
profetisa, *fĕtĭ'sä,* sf. prophetess.
profetizar, *tĭthär',* v. a. to prophesy.
prófugo, ga, *prŏ'fŭgŏ,* a. fugitive.
profundidad, *fŭndĭdäd',* sf. profundity, profoundness; depth; grandeur.
profundizar, *fŭndĭthär',* v. a. to profound, to deepen; to penetrate.
profundo, da, *prŏfŭn'dŏ,* a. profound.
profusamente, *fŭsämĕn'tĕ,* ad. profusely.
profusión, *fŭsĭŏn',* sf. profusion, prodigality. [generation, off-spring, issue.
progenie, *prŏhĕ'nĭĕ,* sf. progeny, race,
progenitor, *hĕnĭtŏr',* sm. progenitor, ancestor, forefather.
progenitura, *hĕnĭtŏ'rä,* sf. progeny; primogeniture.
programa, *grä'mä,* sm. programme.
progresar, *grĕsär',* v. n. to progress.
progresión, *grĕsĭŏn',* sf. progression.
progresivo, va, *sē'vŏ,* a. progressive.
progreso, *prŏgrĕ'sŏ,* sm. progress.
prohibición, *hĭbĭthĭŏn',* sf. prohibition, forbiddance. [bid, to hinder.
prohibir, *hĭbĭr',* v. n. to prohibit, to for-
prohibitivo, va, *hĭbĭtĭ'vŏ,* a. prohibitory. [tion.
prohijamiento, *hĭhämĭĕn'tŏ,* sm. adop-
prohijar, *hĭ'här',* v. a. to adopt (a son).
prohombre, *ŏm'brĕ,* sm. topping man.
prójimo, *prŏ'hĭmŏ,* sm. fellow-creature; neighbour. [race.
prole, *prŏ'lĕ,* sf. issue, offspring, progeny,
proletario, ria, *prŏlĕtä'rĭŏ,* a. proletarian.
prolijidad, *lĭhĭdäd',* sf. prolixity; minute attention to trifles.
prolijo, ja, *prŏlĭ'hŏ,* a. prolix, tedious.
prólogo, *prŏ'lŏgŏ,* sm. prologue. [gation.
prolongación, *prŏlŏngäthĭŏn',* sf. prolon-
prolongar, *gär',* v. a. to prolong.
promediar, *mĕdĭär',* v. a. to share

equally; —, v. n. to interpose in a friendly manner. [offering.

promesa, *prŏmĕs'ā,* sf. promise; pious

prometer, *–mĕtĕr',* v. a. to promise, to asseverate, to assure; **–se,** v. r. to flatter oneself. [bidding.

prometido, *–tē'dŏ,* sm. promise; out-

prominencia, *–mĭnĕn'thĭā,* sf. protuberance, knob. [ting out.

prominente, *–nĕn'tĕ,* a. prominent, jutting out.

promiscuo, cua, *–mĭs'kŭŏ,* a. promiscuous, confusedly mingled; ambiguous.

promisión, *–mĭsĭŏn',* sf. promise.

promoción, *–mŏthĭŏn',* sf. promotion.

promontorio, *–mŏnĭd'rĭŏ,* sm. promontory, cape. [warder.

promotor, *–mŏtŏr',* sm. promoter, forwarder.

promover, *–mŏvĕr',* v. a. to promote, to advance. [mulgation.

promulgación, *–mŭlgāthĭŏn',* sf. promulgation.

promulgador, *–dŏr',* sm. publisher, promulgator. [to publish.

promulgar, *–gār',* v. a. to promulgate.

pronombre, *–nŏm'brĕ,* sm. pronoun.

pronosticación, *–nŏstĭkāthĭŏn',* sf. prognostication. [teller, prognosticator.

pronosticador, ra, *–dŏr',* sm. & f. fore-

pronosticar, *–kār',* v. a. to prognosticate, to predict, to foretell, to conjecture.

pronóstico, *–nŏs'tĭkŏ,* sm. prognostic, prediction; omen, foretoken; almanac published by astrologers. [promptness.

prontitud, *–prŏntĭtŭd',* sf. promptitude,

pronto, ta, *prŏn'tā,* a. prompt, ready; —, ad. promptly; —, sm. promptitude.

prontuario, *–tŭā'rĭŏ,* sm. memorandumbook. [nunciation.

pronunciación, *–nŭnthĭāthĭŏn',* sf. pronunciamiento, *–thĭāmĭēn'tŏ,* sm. (law) publication; insurrection, sedition.

pronunciar, *–thĭār',* v. a. to pronounce; **–se,** to rebel. [tion; extension.

propagación, *–pāgāthĭŏn',* sf. propaga-

propagador, ra, *–dŏr',* sm. & f. propagator.

propaganda, *–gān'dā,* sf. college at Rome, consisting of cardinals peculiarly charged with propagating the Roman catholic faith.

propagar, *–pāgār',* v. a. to propagate; to dilate, to increase. [divulge.

propalar, *–pālār',* v. a. to publish, to

propasar, *–pāsār',* v. a. to go beyond, to exceed.

propender, *–pĕndĕr',* v. n. to incline.

propensión, *–pĕnsĭŏn',* sf. propensity, inclination. [clined.

propenso, sa, *prŏpĕn'sŏ,* a. prone, in-

propiciación, *–pĭthĭāthĭŏn',* sf. propitiation, atonement.

propiciar, *–pĭthĭār',* v. a. to propitiate.

propiciatorio, ria, *–thĭātŏ'rĭŏ,* a. & sm. propitiatory.

propicio, cia, *prŏpē'thĭŏ,* a. propitious.

propiedad, *–pĭēdād',* sf. dominion, possession; right of property; propriety.

propietario, ria, *–tā'rĭŏ,* a. & sm. proprietor; **–s,** pl. proprietary.

propina, *prŏpē'nā,* sf. present, salary, pay; fees of office.

propinar, *–pĭnār',* v. a. to invite to drink.

propincuidad, *–pĭnkŭĭdād',* sf. propinquity. [tiguous.

propincuo, cua, *prŏpĕn'kŭŏ,* a. near, contiguous.

propio, pia, *prŏ'pĭŏ,* a. proper; —, sm. peculiar quality; **–s,** s. pl. lands, estates.

proponer, *–pŏnĕr',* v. a. to propose.

proporción, *–pŏrthĭŏn',* sf. proportion; symmetry.

proporcionado, da, *–thĭŏnā'dŏ,* a. proportionate, fit, comfortable.

proporcional, *–thĭŏnāl',* a. proportional.

proporcionar, *–thĭŏnār',* v. a. to proportion; to adjust, to adapt.

proposición, *–pŏsĭthĭŏn',* sf. proposition.

propósito, *prŏpŏ'sĭtŏ,* sm. purpose; **á –,** for the purpose; **de –,** on purpose, purposely; **fuera de –,** untimely, not to the purpose. [representation.

propuesta, *prŏpŭĕs'tā,* sf. proposal, offer;

prorrata, *prŏrrā'tā,* sf. quota.

prorratear, *–rātĕār',* v. a. to divide a quantity into certain shares.

prorrateo, *–rātĕ'ŏ,* sm. distribution.

prórroga, *prŏr'rŏgā,* sf. prolongation.

prorrogable, *–rŏgā'blĕ,* a. capable of being prorogued.

prorrogar, *–rŏgār',* v. a. to prorogue.

prorrumpir, *–rŭmpĭr',* v. n. to break forth, to burst forth.

prosa, *prŏ'sā,* sf. prose.

prosador, *prŏsādŏr',* sm. sarcastic speaker.

prosaico, ca, *prŏsā'ĭkŏ,* a. prosaic.

prosapia, *prŏsā'pĭā,* sf. race, generation.

proscenio, *prŏsthā'nĭŏ,* sm. proscenium.

proscribir, *–skrĭbĭr',* v. a. to proscribe, to outlaw. [tion.

proscripción, *–skrĭpthĭŏn',* sf. proscrip-

proscripto, *–skrĭp'tŏ,* sm. outlaw.

prosecución, *–sĕkŭthĭŏn',* sf. prosecution, pursuit.

proseguible, *–sĕgē'blĕ,* a. pursuable.

proseguir, *–sĕgĭr',* v. a. to pursue, to prosecute.

prosélito, *prŏsā'lĭtŏ,* sm. proselyte.

prosodia, *prŏsŏ'dĭā,* sf. prosody.

prosopopeya, *–sŏpŏpĕ'yā,* sf. prosopopœia, personification; splendour, pageantry.

prospecto, *prŏspĕk'tŏ,* sm. prospectus.

prosperar, *prŏspĕrār',* v. a. to make happy; to favour; —, v. n. to prosper, to thrive.

prosperidad, *–rĭdād',* sf. prosperity.

próspero, ra, *prŏs'pĕrŏ,* a. prosperous.

prostitución, *prŏstĭtŭthĭŏn',* sf. prostitution.

prostituir, *–tĭĭr',* v. a. to prostitute.

prostituta, *–tĭtŭ'tā,* sf. prostitute, woman of the town.

protección, *prŏtĕkthĭŏn',* sf. protection.

protector, *–tŏr',* sm. protector.

proteger, *–tĕhĕr',* v. a. to protect.

protervia, *prŏtĕr'vĭā,* sf. insolence.

protervo, va, -võ, a. stubborn, peevish, arrogant, insolent.

protesta, -tĕs'tä, sf. (law) protest.

protestación, -täthiŏn', sf. protestation.

protestante, -tän'tĕ, sm. Protestant.

protestar, -tär', v. a. to protest; to make public declaration of faith.

protoalbéitar, protŏälbĕ'itär, sm. chief veterinary surgeon.

protoalbeiterato, -älbĕïtĕrä'tŏ, sm. tribunal for examining veterinary surgeons previously to licensing them to practise.

protocolar, -kŏlär', protocolizar, -kŏlïthär', v. a. to place in the protocol.

protocolo, -kŏ'lŏ, sm. protocol. [tyr.

protomártir, -mär'tïr, sm. the first martyr.

protomedicato, -mĕdïkä'tŏ, sm. college of king's physicians, where students of medicine are examined and licensed.

protomédico, -mĕ'dïkŏ, sm. first physician (to the king). [notary.

protonotario, -nŏtä'rĭŏ, sm. protoprototipo, -tï'pŏ, sm. prototype.

provecho, prŏvĕtsh'ŏ, sm. profit.

provechoso, sa, -tshŏ'sŏ, a. profitable.

provecto, ta, -vĕk'tŏ, a. advanced in years or learning.

proveedor, ra, -vĕĕdŏr', sm.&f. purveyor.

proveeduría, -dürĕä', sf. store-house where provisions are kept and distributed; office of a purveyor.

proveer, -vĕĕr', v. a. to provide; to provision; to confer an employment; to decree; -se, to ease the body.

proveído, -vĕï'dŏ, sm. judgment, sentence, decree. [ing.

proveimiento, -mĭĕn'tŏ, sm. provision.

provenir, -vĕnïr', v. n. to arise, to proceed; to issue.

proverbial, -vĕrbĭäl', a. proverbial.

proverbio, prŏvĕr'bĭŏ, sm. proverb; -s, pl. Book of Proverbs.

providencia, prŏvïdĕn'thĭä, s. providence; foresight; divine providence. [tial.

providencial, -dĕnthĭäl', a. a providenciar, -thĭär', v. a. to ordain, to command.

próvido, da, prŏ'vïdŏ, a. provident.

provincia, prŏvïn'thĭä, sf. province.

provincial, -thĭäl', a. & sm. provincial; pasquinade, libel. [a provincial.

provincialato, -thĭälä'tŏ, sm. office of provinciano, na, -thĭä'nŏ, a. & sm. & f. native of Biscay. [visions; provender.

provisión, prŏvïsĭŏn', sf. store of provisional, -näl', a. provisional.

provisionalmente, -mĕn'tĕ, ad. provisionally. [vider; vicar-general.

provisor, ora, prŏvïsŏr', sm. & f. provocación, prŏvŏkäthĭŏn', sf. provocation.

provocador, ora, -dŏr', sm. & f. provoker. [cate.

provocar, -kär', v. a. to provoke, to exprovocativo, va, -tï'vŏ, a. provocative; quarrelsome. [kindred by birth.

proximidad, prŏksïmïdäd', sf. proximity.

próximo, ma, prŏk'sïmŏ, a. next, nearest.

proyección, prŏyĕkthĭŏn', sf. projection.

proyectar, -yĕktär', v. a. to project, to scheme.

proyecto, prŏyĕk'tŏ, sm. project. [dom.

prudencia, prüdĕn'thĭä, sf. prudence, wisprudente, prüdĕn'tĕ, a. prudent.

prueba, prü'bä, sf. proof, reason, argument; token; experiment, essay, attempt; relish, taste.

prurito, prürï'tŏ, sm. prurience, itching.

pu, pŏ, sf. excrements of children; 1—! fy! exclamation of disgust at a bad smell.

púa, pŏ'ä, sf. sharp point, prickle; shoot of a tree engrafted in another; weaver's reed; mental pain; sly person.

pubertad, pübĕrtäd', sf. puberty. [tion.

publicación, püblïkäthĭŏn', sf. publicacano, -kä'nŏ, sm. publican.

publicar, -kär', v. a. to publish, to proclaim. [cation.

publicata, -kä'tä, sf. certificate of publipublicidad, -thĭdäd', sf. publicity; en —, publicly.

público, ca, pŏ'blïkŏ, a. sm. public.

pucia, pŏ'thĭä, sf. chemist's jar, gallipot.

puchada, pütshä'dä, sf. poultice.

puchero, pütshĕ'rŏ, sm. glazed earthen pot; meat boiled in an earthen pot; grimace which precedes crying.

puches, pütsh'ĕs, sf. pl. pap, meal-pap.

pudicicia, püdïthĕ'thĭä, sf. pudicity, chastity, chasteness.

púdico, ca, pŏ'dïkŏ, a. chaste, pure.

pudiente, püdĭĕn'tĕ, a. rich, opulent.

pudingo, püdïn'gŏ, sm. pudding.

pudor, püdŏr', sm. bashfulness, shamefacedness.

pudrición, püdrïthĭŏn', sf. rottenness.

pudridero, -dă'rŏ, sm. rotting-place.

pudrimiento, -mĭĕn'tŏ, sm. rottenness.

pudrir, püdrïr', v. a. to make putrid; —, v. n. to rot, to be rotten.

pueblo, pü̆'blŏ, sm. town, village; population; populace. [bridge.

puente, pü̆ĕn'tĕ, sm. & f. bridge; (mus.)

puerca, pü̆ĕr'kä, sf. sow, female pig.

puerco, ca, pü̆ĕr'kŏ, a. nasty, filthy, dirty; rude, coarse; —, sm. hog; — espín, porcupine.

puericia, pü̆ĕrï'thĭä, sf. boyhood.

pueril, pü̆ĕrïl', a. boyish, childish.

puerilidad, -lïdäd', sf. puerility, boyishpuerro, pü̆ĕr'rŏ, sm. leek. [ness.

puerta, pü̆ĕr'tä, sf. door, doorway, gateway; duty paid at the entrance of the gates in towns; — trasera, back-door.

puerto, pü̆ĕr'tŏ, sm. port, harbour, haven; narrow pass, defile. [then.

pues, pü̆ĕs', ad. then, therefore; 1—! well, puesto, pü̆ĕs'tŏ, sm. place; particular spot; retail-shop; post, employment; barracks; stand, bushes to conceal sportsmen; put; —, ad. because; —que, —caso, although, puf! püf, fy! exclamation of disgust at a bad smell.

pugilato, pü̆'hïlä'tŏ, sm. pugilism.

pugna, püg'nä, sf. combat, battle.

pugnar, *pŭgnăr'*, v. n. to fight, to combat;
to solicit earnestly.　　[sale.

puja, *pŭ'hă*, sf. outbidding at a public

pujante, *–hăn'tĕ*, a. powerful, strong,
robust, stout, strapping.

pujanza, *–hăn'thă*, sf. power, strength.

pujar, *pŭ'hăr'*, v. a. to outbid.　　[tool.

pujavante, *pŭ'hăvăn'tĕ*, sm. parer(farrier's

pujo, *pŭ'h'ŏ*, sm. tenesmus; violent desire.

puloritud, *pŭlʹkrĭtŭd'*, sf. beauty.

puloro,cra, *pŭl'krŏ* a.beautiful; affectedly
nice in dress.

pulga, *pŭl'gă*, sf. flea; tener malas –s,
to be easily piqued; to be ill-tempered.

pulgada, *–gă'dă*, sf. inch.

pulgar, *pŭlgăr'*, sm. thumb.　　[tobacco).

pulgarada, *–ră'dă*, sf. fillip; pinch (of

pulgón, *pŭlgón'*, sm. vine-fretter, vine-

pulgoso, sa, *–gŏ'sŏ*, a. pulicose.　　[grub.

pulguera, *–gĕ'ră*, sf. place abounding with
fleas; (bot.) flea-wort.　　[instrument).

pulicán, *pŭlĭkăn'*, sm. pelican (surgical

pulidez, *pŭlĭdĕth'*, sf. neatness.

pulido, da, *pŭlĭ'dŏ*, a. neat, nice.

pulidor, *pŭlĭdŏr'*, sm. polisher; instrument used for polishing and burnishing.

pulimento, *–mĕn'tŏ*, sm. polish, glossiness.

pulir, *pŭlĭr'*, v. a. to polish; to burnish;
to put the last touches to; **–se**, to adorn
one'sclf; to become polished.

pulmón, *pŭlmón'*, sm. lungs.　　[lungs.

pulmonía, *–nĕ'ă*, sf. inflammation of the

púlpito, *pŭl'pĭtŏ*, sm. pulpit.

pulpo, *pŭl'pŏ*, sm. cuttle-fish; polypus.

pulposo, sa, *–pŏ'sŏ*, a. pulpous.

pulsación, *pŭlsăthĭón'*, sf. pulsation.

pulsar, *pŭlsăr'*, v. a. to touch; to feel the
pulse; to explore, to try; –, v. n. to pulse.

pulsera, *pŭlsĕ'ră*, sf. bandage applied to
the vein or artery of a sick person; –s, pl.
bracelets.

pulso, *pŭl'sŏ*, sm. pulse; firmness or steadiness of the hand; attention, care.

pulular, *pŭlŭlăr'*, v. n. to pullulate.

pulverización, *pŭlvĕrĭthăthĭón'*, sf. pulverization.

pulverizar, *–thăr'*, v. a. to pulverize.

pulla, *pŭl'yă*, sf. smart repartee; obscene
expression.

pundonor, *pŭndŏnŏr'*, sm. point of honour.

pundonoroso, sa, *–rŏ'sŏ*, a. having a
nice sense of honour, punctilious.

pungir, *pŭn'hĭr'*, v. a. to punch, to prick.

punición, *pŭnĭthĭón'*, sf. punishment.

punta, *pŭn'tă*, sf. point.　　[chastisement.

puntada, *–tă'dă*, sf. stitch made with a
needle and thread.

puntal, *pŭntăl'*, sm. prop, stay, buttress.

puntapié, *pŭntăpĭĕ'*, sm. kick.

puntear, *pŭntĕăr'*, v. a. to play the guitar;
to point out; to stiten; –, v. n. (mar.) to
tack.　　[glass.

puntel, *pŭntĕl'*, sm. iron tube for blowing

puntería, *–tĕrĕ'ă*, sf. aiming (of fire-arms).

puntero, *pŭntĕ'rŏ*, sm. fescue; –, ra, a.
aiming well (with fire-arms).　　[pointed.

puntiagudo, da, *pŭntĭăgŭ'dŏ*, a. sharp-

puntilla, *–tĭl'yă*, sf. narrow lace-edging;
de –s, on tiptoe.

puntillazo, *–yă'thŏ*, sm. kick.

puntillo, *pŭntĭl'yŏ*, sm. punctilio, trifling,
despicable thing.

punto, *pŭn'tŏ*, sm. point; end, design;
point of honour; aim, sight; stitch; mesh
of a net; **al –,** instantly.

puntuación, *–tŭăthĭón'*, sf. punctuation.

puntual, *pŭntŭăl'*, a. punctual, exact.

puntualidad, *–lĭdăd'*, sf. punctuality; certainty.　[mind or memory; to accomplish.

puntualizar, *–lĭthăr'*, v. a. to fix on the

puntuar, *pŭntŭăr'*, v. a. to punctuate, to
point.　　[compunction.

punzada, *–thă'dă*, sf. prick, sting; pain;

punzador, ora, *–thădŏr'*, sm. & f. pricker.

punzadura, *–dŏ'ră*, sf. puncture, prick.

punzar, *pŭnthăr'*, v. a. to punch, to prick,
to put the last touches to.　　[to sting.

punzón, *–thón'*, sm. punch.

puñada, *pŭnyă'dă*, sf. cuff, blow with the

puñado, *–dŏ*, sm. handful.　　[fist.

puñal, *pŭnyăl'*, sm. poniard, dagger.

puñalada, *pŭnyălă'dă*, sf. stab.

puñetazo, *–pŭnyĕtă'thŏ*, sm. blow with
the closed fist.　[band; hand-ruffle; hilt.

puño, *pŭn'yŏ*, sm. fist; handful; wrist-

pupila, *pŭpĭ'lă*, sf. eye-ball, pupil; orphan
girl.　　[house.

pupilaje, *–lă'hĕ*, sm. pupilage; boarding

pupilar, *–lăr'*, a. pupilary.

pupilo, *pŭpĭ'lŏ*, sm. pupil; scholar.

pureza, *pŭrĕ'thă*, sf. purity, chastity.

purga, *pŭr'gă*, sf. purging-draught.

purgación, *–găthĭón'*, sf. purgation.

purgante, *–găn'tĕ*, sm. purgative.

purgar, *–găr'*, v. a. to purge, to purify;
to atone, to expiate.　　[purging.

purgativo, va, *–gătĭ'vŏ*, a. purgative,

purgatorio, *–tŏ'rĭŏ*, sm. purgatory.

purificación, *pŭrĭfĭkăthĭón'* sf. purification.　　[purificatory.

purificador, ora, *–dŏr'*, sm. & f. purifier;

purificar, *–kăr'*, v. a. to purify; **–se**, to
be churched after lying-in.

purismo, *pŭrĭs'mŏ*, sm. purism, affectation of purity in verbal delivery.

purista, *pŭrĭs'tă*, sm. purist.

puritano, na, *pŭrĭtă'nŏ*, a. puritanical;
–, sm. & f. Puritan.

puro, ra, *pŏ'rŏ*, a. pure, unmingled, mere;
genuine; chaste, incorrupt.

púrpura, *pŭr'pŭră*, sf. purple-shell.

purpurado, *–ră'dŏ*, sm. cardinal.

purpurar, *–răr'*,v.a. to colour with purple.

purpurear, *–rĕăr'*, v. n. to grow purple.

purpúreo, rea, *pŭrpŏ'rĕŏ*, a. purple.

purulento, ta, *pŭrŭlĕn'tŏ*, a. purulent.

pus, *pŭs'*, sm. pus, matter, gleet.

pusilánime, *pŭsĭlă'nĭmĕ*, a. pusilanimous,
faint-hearted.　　[lanimity.

pusilanimidad, *–ănĭmĭdăd'*, sf. pusil-

pústula, *pŭs'tŭlă*, sf. pustule, pimple.

putativo, va, *pŭtătĭ'vŏ*, a. putative, supposed.　　[tion.

putrefacción, *pŭtrĕfăkthĭón'*, sf. putrefac-

pútrido, da, *pŏ'trĭdŏ*, a. putrid, rotten.

Q

que, *kē,* that; who; which; what.

quebrada, *kēbrā'dā,* sf. broken, uneven ground.

quebradero, *-dā'rō,* sm. breaker; — de cabeza, that which molests and importunes.

quebradizo, za, *-dē'thō,* a. brittle, flexible.

quebrado, *kēbrā'dō,* sm. (ar.) fraction.

quebradura, *-dō'rā,* sf. fracture; rupture, hernia.   [ture, rupture, bursting.

quebrantadura, *kēbrāntādō'rā,* sf. fracture.

quebrantamiento, *-mēēn'tō,* sm. fracture, rupture; breaking out of prison; weariness, fatigue; violation of the law.

quebrantar, *-tār',* v. a. to break, to crack, to burst; to pound, to grind; to violate; to fatigue; to weaken.

quebranto, *kēbrān'tō,* sm. weakness, lassitude; great loss, severe damage.

quebrar, *kēbrār',* v. a. to break, to transgress a law, to violate, —, v. n. to fail; —se, to break into pieces, to be ruptured.

quechemarín, *kētshēmārēn',* sm. (mar.) lugger.   [too.

queda, *kē'dā,* sf. resting-time; (mil.) last

quedar, *kēdār',* v. a. to stay; to be wanting; —se, to falter, to stop short.

quedito, *kēdē'tō,* ad. softly, gently.

quedo, da, *kē'dō,* a. quiet, still; —, ad. softly, gently.

quehacer, *kāāthēr',* sm. business.

queja, *kē'hā,* sf. complaint.

quejarse, *-hār'sā,* v. r. to complain of.

quejido, *-hē'dō,* sm. complaint.   [ous.

quejoso, sa, *-hō'sō,* a. plaintive, querulous.

quejumbroso, a, *-hāmbrō'sō,* a. complaining, plaintive.   [fire.

quema, *kā'mā,* sf. burning, combustion,

quemador, ra, *kēmādōr',* sm. & f. incendiary; burner.   [fire, burn.

quemadura, *-dō'rā,* sf. mark made by fire.

quemar, *-mār',* v. a. to burn; to kindle; —, v. n. to be too hot; —se, to be parched with heat; to burn oneself.

quemazón, *-thōn',* sf. burn.   [tation.

querella, *kērēl'yā,* sf. complaint, lamen-

querellarse, *-lyār'sā,* v. r. to lament, to complain; to lodge a complaint in a court of justice.

querelloso, sa, *-yō'sō,* a. querulous.

querer, *kērēr',* v. a. to wish, to desire; to will; —, sm. will, desire.

querido, da, *kērē'dō,* a. dear, beloved; —, sm. & f. darling, fondling, minion, lover; — mío ó —da mía, my dear, my love, my darling.

querubín, *kērōbēn',* sm. cherub.

quesera, *kēsā'rā,* sf. dairy.

quesero, *kēsā'rō,* sm. cheesemonger.

queso, *kē'sō,* sm. cheese.

quicial, *kēthiāl',* sf. side-post; jamb.

quicio, *kē'thiō,* sm. hook, hinge (of a door).

quídam, *kē'dām,* sm. someone, a certain person.

quiebra, *kiē'brā,* sf. crack, fracture; bankruptcy.

quiebro, *kiē'brō,* sm. (mus.) trill; inclination of the body.   [other.

quien, *kiēn',* pn. who, which; one or the

quienquiera, *-kiē'rā,* a. whosoever, whatever.

quieto, ta, *kiē'tō,* a. quiet, still, peaceable.

quietud, *kiētūd',* sf. quietness, peace, tranquillity, calmness.

quijada, *kī'hā'dā,* sf. jaw, jaw-bone.

quijotada, *kī'hōtā'dā,* sf. quixotic action.

quijote, *kī'hō'tā,* sm. cuish; a man who engages in quixotic enterprises.

quijotería, *-tērē'ā,* sf. quixotism, quixotry.

quijotesco, ca, *-tēs'kō,* a. quixotic.

quilatar, *kīlātār',* v. a. to assay.

quilate, *kīlā'tā,* sm. carat.

quilificar, *kīlēfikār',* v. a. to chylify.

quilla, *kīl'yā,* sf. keel.

quilma, *kīl'mā,* sf. large back, sack.

quilo, *kē'lō,* sm. (med.) chyle.

quiloso, sa, *kīlō'sō,* a. chylous.

quimera, *kīmā'rā,* sf. dispute, quarrel.

quimérico, ca, *kīmā'rīkō,* a. chimerical, fantastic.   [brawler.

quimerista, *kīmārīs'tā,* sm. wrangler,

química, *kē'mīkā,* sf. chemistry.

químico, *kē'mīkō,* sm. chemist; —, ca, a. chemical.

quina, *kē'nā,* sf. Peruvian bark.

quincalla, *kīnkāl'yā,* sf. hard-ware.

quince, *kēn'thā,* a. & sm. fifteen; fifteenth.

quinceno, na, *-thā'nō,* a. fifteenth.

Quincuagésima, *-kūā'hā'sīmā,* sf. Quinquagesima.   [years.

quindenio, *-dā'nīō,* sm. period of fifteen

quinientos, tas, *kīnīēn'tōs,* a. five hundred.

quinina, *-kē'nā,* sf. quinine.

quinquenal, *-kēnāl',* a. quinquennial.

quinquenio, *-kē'nīō,* sm. space of five years.

quinquillería, *-kīlyārē'ā,* sf. hard-ware.

quinquillero, *-kīlyā'rō,* sm. hawker, pedlar, hard-ware man.

quinta, *kīn'tā,* sf. country-seat, country-house; levy, drafting of soldiers; quint (mus. and piquet).

quintaesencia, *-āsēn'thiā,* sf. quintessence.

quintal, *kīntāl',* sm. quintal, hundred-weight.   [fjiye; to levy, to draft soldiers.

quintar, *kīntār',* v. a. to draw one out of

quintería, *-tērē'ā,* sf. farm; grange.

quintero, *-tā'rō,* sm. farmer; servant who takes care of a farm.   [of five verses.

quintilla, *-tīl'yā,* sf. metrical composition

quinto, *kīn'tō,* sm. fifth; share of a pasture-ground; drafted soldier; —, ta, a. fifth.

quintuplo, pla, *kīn'tūplō,* a. quintuple, fivefold.

quiñón, *kīnyōn',* sm. dividend.

quiñonero, *-yōnā'rō,* sm. part-owner.

quirite, *kīrē'tā,* sm. Roman citizen.

quiromancia, *kīrōmān'thiā,* sf. chiromancy.

quirúrgico, ca, *kīrūr'hīkō,* a. surgical.

quirurgo, *kīrūr'gō,* sm. surgeon.

quisicosa, *kĭsĭkŏ'sǎ,* sf. riddle; obscure question. [trifling dispute.
quisquilla, *kĭskĭl'yǎ,* sf. ridiculous nicety;
quisquilloso, sa, *—yŏ'sǎ,* a. nice, difficult, touchy, peevish, irritable.
quisto, ta, *kĭs'tŏ,* p. & a. only used with bien and mal; bien —, well received, generally beloved; mal —, ill received, hated. [away with you!
¡quita! *kĭ'tǎ,* God forbid! ¡ —de ahí!
quitamanchas, *kĭtǎmǎn'tshǎs,* sm. scourer of clothes.
quitapelillos, *—pēlĭl'yŏs,* sm. wheedler.
quitapesares, *—pēsǎ'rēs,* sm. & f. comfort, consolation.
quitapón, *—pŏn',* sm. ornament for the head-stall of draught-mules.
quitar, *kĭtǎr',* v. a. to take away, to remove; to fetch away; to redeem a pledge; to abrogate, to annul; to free from an obligation; to parry (in fencing); —se, to abstain; to get rid of.
quitasol, *kĭtǎsŏl',* sm. parasol.
quita y pon, (de), *kĭtǎ ĭ pŏn',* ad. that can be put on or off, as one likes.
quite, *kĭ'tē,* sm. obstacle, impediment.
quito, ta, *kĭ'tŏ,* a. free from an obligation, exempt. [haps.
quizá, *kĭthǎ',* quizás, *kĭthǎs',* ad. per-

R.

rabadán, *rǎbǎdǎn',* sm. head-shepherd.
rabadilla, *—dĭl'yǎ,* sf. rump, croup.
rabanero, ra, *—nǎ'rŏ,* sm. & f. seller of radishes.
rabaniza, *—nĭ'thǎ,* sf. radish-seed.
rábano, *rǎ'bǎnŏ,* sm. radish.
rabia, *rǎ'bĭǎ,* sf. rage, fury.
rabiar, *rǎbĭǎr',* v. n. to be furious, to rage.
rabicorto, ta, *—kŏr'tŏ,* a. short-tailed.
rabieta, *rǎbĭĕ'tǎ,* sf. touchiness, petulance, bad temper.
rabilargo, ga, *—lǎr'gŏ,* a. long-tailed.
rabino, *rǎbĭ'nŏ,* sm. rabbi, rabbin.
rabioso, sa, *rǎbĭŏ'sǎ,* a. rabid; furious.
rabisalsera, *—sǎlsǎ'rǎ,* a. petulant, saucy, impudent (applied to women).
rabo, *rǎ'bŏ,* sm. tail.
rabón, ona, *rǎbŏn',* a. docked, short-tailed.
rabosear, *rǎbŏsēǎr',* v. a. to spatter.
rabotear, *—tēǎr',* v. a. to cut or crop the tail.
rabudo, da, *rǎbŏ'dŏ,* a. long-tailed.
racimo, *rǎthĭ'mŏ,* sm. bunch of grapes.
racimoso, sa, *rǎthĭmŏ'sǎ,* a. grape-bearing.
raciocinar, *rǎthĭŏthĭnǎr',* v. n. to reason, to argue, to ratiocinate. [ment.
raciocinio, *—thĭ'nĭŏ,* sm. reasoning; argu-
ración, *rǎthŏn',* sf. ration; prebend so called in Spanish cathedrals.
racional, *—nǎl',* a. rational; reasonable.
racionalidad, *—nǎlĭdǎd',* sf. rationality.
racionero, *—nǎ'rŏ,* sm. prebendary.
rada, *rǎ'dǎ,* sf. anchoring-ground for ships at some distance from shore, roadstead.
radiacion, *rǎdĭǎthĭŏn',* sf. radiation.

radiante, *rǎdĭǎn'tē,* a. radiant.
radiar, *rǎdĭǎr',* v. n. (poet.) to radiate.
radicación, *rǎdĭkǎthĭŏn',* sf. taking root; becoming rooted (of a habit).
radical, *—kǎl',* a. radical.
radicarse, *—kǎr'sē,* v. r. to take root.
radio, *rǎ'dĭŏ,* sm. radius; ray.
radiómetro, *rǎdĭŏ'mētrŏ,* sm. forestaff.
radioso, sa, *rǎdĭŏ'sǎ,* a. radiant.
raedera, *rǎēdē'rǎ,* sf. scraper, raker.
raedura, *—dŭ'rǎ,* sf. erasure; scrapings.
raer, *rǎēr',* v. a. to scrape, to grate; to erase.
ráfaga, *rǎ'fǎgǎ,* sf. violent squall of wind.
raído, da, *rǎ'ĭdŏ,* a. scraped; worn out; impudent.
raíz, *rǎĭth',* sf. root; base, basis; origin; bienes raíces, pl. landed property.
raja, *rǎ'hǎ,* sf. splinter, chip of wood; chink, fissure; coarse cloth.
rajabroqueles, *—brŏkē'lēs,* sm. braggart, boasting fellow, bravado.
rajar, *rǎ'hǎr',* v. a. to split, to chop, to cleave; (fig. & fam.) to boast.
ralea, *rǎlē'ǎ,* sf. race, breed; species.
ralear, *rǎlēǎr',* v. n. to thin.
raleza, *rǎlē'thǎ,* sf. thinness; rarity.
ralo, la, *rǎ'lŏ,* a. thin, rare.
ralladura, *rǎlyǎdŏ'rǎ,* sf. mark left by the grater; small particles taken off by grating.
rallar, *rǎlyǎr',* v. a. to grate; to importune.
rallo, *rǎl'yŏ,* sm. grater.
rama, *rǎ'mǎ,* sf. branch (of a tree, of a family); printer's chase, form.
ramadán, *—dǎn',* sm. Mohammedan Lent.
ramaje, *rǎmǎ'hē,* sm. ramage; flowering branches designed in cloth.
ramal, *rǎmǎl',* sm. halter. [in a rock.
rambla, *rǎm'blǎ,* sf. sandy place; cavern
ramera, *rǎmē'rǎ,* sf. whore, prostitute.
ramificación, *rǎmĭfĭkǎthĭŏn',* sf. ramification.
ramificarse, *—fĭkǎr'sē,* v. r. to ramify.
ramillete, *rǎmĭlyē'tē,* sm. nosegay.
ramilletero, *—yētē'rŏ,* sm. vase with artificial flowers for ornamenting altars.
ramo, *rǎ'mŏ,* sm. branch of a tree.
ramonear, *—nēǎr',* v. n. to cut off the branches of trees.
ramoso, sa, *rǎmŏ'sŏ,* a. branchy.
rampante, *rǎmpǎn'tē,* a. rampant.
rampojo, *—pŏ'hŏ,* sm. rape.
rampollo, *—pŏl'yŏ,* sm. shoot, sprig, sucker.
rana, *rǎ'nǎ,* sf. frog.
rancio, cia, *rǎn'thĭŏ,* a. rank, rancid.
ranchear, *rǎntshēǎr',* v. a. to build huts.
ranchero, *—tshē'rŏ,* sm. steward of a mess.
rancho, *rǎn'tshŏ,* sm. mess; mess-room.
ranúnculo, *rǎnŭn'kŭlŏ,* sm. (bot.) crowfoot. [childish action.
rapacería, *rǎpǎthērē'ǎ,* sf. puerility.
rapacidad, *—thĭdǎd',* sf. rapacity.
rapadura, *—dŏ'rǎ,* sf. shaving; baldness.
rapar, *rǎpǎr',* v. a. to shave; to plunder.
rapaz, za, *rǎpǎth',* a. rapacious; —, za, sm. & f. young boy or girl. [speech.
rapazada, *—thǎ'dǎ,* sf. childish action or
rape, *rǎ'pē,* sm. shaving.

rapé, *răpĕ´*, sm. rappee.

rapidez, *răpĭdĕth´*, sf. rapidity.

rápido, da, *ră´pĭdŏ*, a. rapid, swift.

rapiña, *răpĭn´yă*, sf. rapine, robbery.

rapiñar, *–yăr´*, v. a. to plunder.

raposa, *răpŏ´să*, sf. female fox; cunning, deceitful person.

raposería, *–sĕrĕ´ă*, sf. trick, wile, cunning.

raposo, *răpŏ´sŏ*, sm. male fox.

rapto, *răp´tŏ*, sm. rapine, ecstasy, rapture; ravishment.

raptor, *răptŏr´*, sm. ravisher.

raqueta, *răkĕ´tă*, sf. racket, battledoor.

raquítico, ca, *răkĭ´tĭkŏ*, a. rickety.

raquitis, *răkĭ´tĭs*, sf. rickets.

rareza, *rărĕ´thă*, sf. rarity, rareness.

raridad, *rărĭdăd´*, sf. rarity.

raro, ra, *ră´rŏ*, a. rare, scarce, extraordinary; –, ad. rarely.

ras, *răs*, sm. level, even surface.

rasadura, *răsădŭ´ră*, sf. levelling with a strickle (in measuring grain).

rasar, *răsăr´*, v. a. to strike off with a strickle, or level a measure of grain.

rascador, *răskădŏr´*, sm. scraper, diamond head-pin, [scraping or rasping.

rascadura, *–dŭ´ră*, sf. act of scratching.

rascar, *răskăr´*, v. a. to scratch, to scrape.

rasero, *răsĕ´rŏ*, sm. strickle.

rasgar, *răsgăr´*, v. a. to tear, to rend.

rasgo, *răs´gŏ*, sm. dash, stroke, grand or magnanimous action.

rasgón, *răsgŏn´*, sm. rent, rag, tatter.

rasguear, *răsgĕăr´*, v. n. to form bold strokes with the pen; (mus.) to play arpeggios.

rasgueo, *răsgĕ´ŏ*, sm. arpeggio. [scrape.

rasguñar, *–gŭnyăr´*, v. a. to scratch, to

rasguño, *–gŭn´yŏ*, sm. scratch.

raso, *ră´sŏ*, sm. satin, glade, –, sa, a. plain; flat. al –, in the open air.

raspa, *răs´pă*, sf. beard of an ear of corn, back-bone of fish, stalk of grapes, rasp.

raspadera, *–dĕ´ră*, sf. raker.

raspador, *–dŏr´*, sm. rasp.

raspadura, *–dŭ´ră*, sf. filing, scraping; filings. [steal

raspar, *răspăr´*, v. a. to scrape, to rasp, to

raspear, *răspĕăr´*, v.n. to splutter (of pens)

rastra, *răs´tră*, sf. sledge. [a whip

rastrallar, *–trăl´yăr´*, v. n. to crack with

rastrear, *–trĕăr´*, v. a. to trace, to inquire into, –, v. n. to skim along close to the ground (of birds).

rastrero, ra, *–trĕ´rŏ*, a. creeping, low, humble, cringing, reptile; –, sm. inspector of a slaughterhouse.

rastrillador, *–trĭlyădŏr´*, sm. & f. hackler, flax-dresser, raker.

rastrillar, *–yăr´*, v. a. to hackle, to dress flax, to rake.

rastrillo, *răstrĭl´yŏ*, sm. hackle; flax-comb, portcullis, hammer of a gun-lock rake. [house, sign, token.

rastro, *răs´trŏ*, sm. track, sledge, slaughter-

rastrojera, *–hŏ´ră*, sf. stubble-ground.

rastrojo, *răstrŏ´hŏ*, sm. stubble.

rasurar, *răsŭrăr´*, v. a. to shave.

rata, *ră´tă*, sf. she-mouse, rat.

ratafia, *rătă´fĭă*, sf. ratafia (liquor).

ratear, *rătĕăr´*, v. a. to filch, to commit petty thefts, v. n. to creep.

ratería, *–rĕ´ă*, sf. larceny, petty theft.

ratero, ra, *rătĕ´rŏ*, a creeping, mean, vile.

ratificación, *rătĭfĭkăthĭŏn´*, sf. ratification. [of.

ratificar, *–kăr´*, v. a. to ratify, to approve

ratina, *rătĭ´nă*, sf. ratteen.

rato, *ră´tŏ*, sm. mouse, moment; á –s perdidos, in leisure-time.

ratón, *rătŏn´*, sm. mouse.

ratonar, *–năr´*, v. a. to gnaw (of animals).

ratonera, *–nĕ´ră*, sf. mouse-trap; wall where rats breed.

raudal, *răudăl´*, sm. torrent.

raya, *ră´yă*, sf. stroke, line; frontier, ray, roach (fish). [arms).

rayado, da, *răyă´dŏ*, a. rifled (of fire-

rayano, na, *răyă´nŏ*, a. neighbouring, contiguous. [gate, to rifle.

rayar, *răyăr´*, v. a. to draw lines; to varie-

rayo, *ră´yŏ*, sm. ray, beam of light, radius.

rayoso, sa, *răyŏ´sŏ*, a. radiating, striped.

raza, *ră´thă*, sf. race, lineage, quality.

razón, *răthŏn´*, sf. reason; ratiocination; reasonableness; account, calculation.

razonable, *–ná´blĕ*, a. reasonable.

razonado, da, *–ná´dŏ*, a. rational, prudent. [ing, discourse.

razonamiento, *–nămĭĕn´tŏ*, sm. reason-

razonar, *–năr´*, v. n. to reason, to discourse, to talk.

reacción, *rĕăkthĭŏn´*, sf. reaction.

reagravar, *rĕăgrăvăr´*, v. a. to aggravate anew. [camp, real (a Spanish coin).

real, *rĕăl´*, a. real, actual, royal, –, sm.

realce, *rĕăl´thĕ*, sm. embossment, flash; lustre, splendour.

realengo, ga, *–lĕn´gŏ*, a. royal, kingly.

realidad, *–lĭdăd´*, sf. reality, sincerity.

realista, *–lĭs´tă*, sm. royalist.

realizar, *–lĭthăr´*, v. a. to realize.

realzar, *rĕălthăr´*, v. a. to raise, to elevate, to emboss, to heighten.

reanimar, *–ănĭmăr´*, v. a. to cheer, to encourage, to reanimate. [resume.

reasumir, *–ăsŭmĭr´*, v. a. to retake, to

reata, *rĕă´tă*, sf. collar, leash; string of horses, leading mule, (fig.) submission to the opinion of others.

reato, *rĕă´tŏ*, sm. obligation of atonement for a sin which is unabsolved.

rebaja, *rĕbă´hă*, sf. abatement, deduction.

rebajar, *–bă´hăr´*, v. a. to abate, to lessen, to diminish.

rebalsa, *–băl´să*, sf. pool, puddle.

rebalsar, *–băl´săr´*, v. a. to dam a stream.

rebanada, *–bănă´dă*, sf. slice. [of cattle.

rebaño, *–băn´yŏ*, sm. flock of sheep, herd

rebatir, *–bătĭr´*, v. a. to resist, to parry, to ward off, to refute, to repress.

rebato, *–bă´tŏ*, sm. unexpected attack, surprise, alarm. [rebel, to resist.

rebelarse, *–bĕlăr´sĕ*, v. r. to revolt; to

rebelde, −*běl'dě*, sm. rebel; −, a. rebellious.

rebeldía, −*děě'ǎ*, sf. rebelliousness, contumaciousness, disobedience; (law) contumacy; en —, by default.

rebelión, *rěběliǒn'*, sf. rebellion, revolt.

rebenque, −*běn'kě*, sm. cat-o'-nine-tails.

rebollar, −*bǒlyǎr'*, sm. underwood.

rebollo, −*bǒl'yǒ*, sm. trunk of a tree.

rebollido, da, −*bǒlyě'dǒ*, a. thick-set.

rebosadura, −*bǒsǎdǒ'rǎ*, sf. overflow.

rebosar, −*bǒsǎr'*, v. a. to run over, to overflow; to abound.

rebotar, −*bǒtǎr'*, v. a. to clinch the point of a spike or nail; to repel; —, v. n. to rebound.

rebote, *rěbǒ'tě*, sm. rebound; de —, on a second thought.

rebotica, −*tǐkǎ*, sf. back-room behind an apothecary's shop; cistern.

rebozo, *rěbǒ'thǒ*, sm. muffling of oneself up; (fig.) pretext; cloak.   [move.

rebullir, −*bǔlyěr'*, v. n. to stir, to begin to

reburujar, −*bǔrǔ'hǎr'*, v. a. to wrap up, to pack up in bundles.

reburujón, −*hǒn'*, sm. bundle wrapped up carelessly and without order.

rebusca, *rěbǒs'kǎ* sf. research; refuge, remains.   [researcher.

rebuscador, ora, −*dǒr'*, sm. & f. gleaner;

rebuscar, *rěbǒskǎr'* v. a. to glean the remains of grapes left by the vintagers; to search, to inquire.

rebuznar, −*bǔthnǎr'*, v. n. to bray.

rebuzno, −*bǔth'nǒ*, sm. braying of an ass.

recabar, −*kǎbǎr'*, v. a. to obtain by entreaty.

recado, −*kǎ'dǒ*, sm. message; gift; compliments sent to an absent person.

recaer, −*kǎěr'*, v. n. to fall back.

recaída, −*kǎě'dǎ*, sf. relapse.

recalcar, −*kǎlkǎr'*, v. n. to squeeze; to stuff; −se, to utter repeatedly; to lean back in a chair.

recalcitrar, −*kǎlthětrǎr'*, v. n. to kick; to wince; to be recalcitrant.

recalentamiento, −*kǎlěntǎměěn'tǒ*, sm. incandescence.

recalentar, −*kǎlěntǎr'*, v. a. to heat again.

recalzar, −*kǎlthǎr'*, v. a. to pounce, to prick the outlines of a design on paper; to underwall.   [raised work.

recamar, −*kǎmǎr'*, v. a. to embroider with raised work.

recámara, *rěkǎ'mǎrǎ*, sf. wardrobe; chamber of a gun.

recantón, −*kǎntǒn'*, sm. corner-stone.

recapacitar, −*kǎpǎthětǎr'*, v. a. to call to recollection.   [capitulation.

recapitulación, −*kǎpǐtǔlǎthǐǒn'*, sf. recapitulation.

recapitular. −*kǎpǐtǔlǎr'*, v. a. to recapitulate.

recargar, −*kǎrgǎr'*, v. a. to recharge; to charge again; to remand to prison on a new charge.

recargo, *rěkǎr'gǒ*, sm. new charge or accusation; increase of a fever.

recatado, da, −*kǎtǎ'dǒ*, a. prudent, circumspect, modest.

recatar, −*kǎtǎr'*, v. a. to conceal carefully; −se, to take care.

recato, *rěkǎ'tǒ*, sm. prudence, circumspection; modesty; bashfulness.

recaudación, −*kǎǔdǎthǐǒn'*, sf. recovery of debts; collector's office.

recaudador, *rěkǎǔdǎdǒr'*, sm. tax-gatherer.

recaudar, −*dǎr'*, v. a. to gather; to obtain.   [a second time.

recavar, −*kǎvǎr'*, v. a. to dig the ground

recelar, −*thělǎr'*, v. a. to fear, to suspect, to misdoubt.   [trust.

recelo, −*thǎ'lǒ*, sm. dread, suspicion, mistrust.

receloso, sa, −*thělǒ'sǒ*, a. mistrustful, shy.

recentadura, −*thěntǎdǒ'rǎ*, sf. leaven preserved for the kneading and raising of bread.

recental, −*thěntǎl'*, a. sucking (of lambs).

recepción, −*thěpthǐǒn'*, sf. reception; acceptation.   [refuge, asylum.

receptáculo, −*thěptǎ'kǔlǒ*, sm. receptacle;

receptor, −*thěptǒr'*, sm. receiver, treasurer; investigating official.

receptoría, −*tǒrě'ǎ*, sf. receiver's or treasurer's office.   [account, list.

receta, −*thǎ'tǎ*, sf. recipe; prescription;

recetar, −*thětǎr'*, v. a. to prescribe medicines.

recetario, *rěthǎtǐ'rǐǒ*, sm. register of the prescriptions made by a physician; apothecary's file.

recibidor, −*thǐbǐdǒr'*, sm. receiver.

recibimiento, −*mǐěn'tǒ*, sm. reception; receipt; antechamber.

recibir, −*thǐbǐr'*, v. a. to accept, to receive; to let in; to go to meet; −se, to be admitted.

recibo, −*thǐ'bǒ*, sm. receipt, acquittance.

recién, −*thǐěn'*, ad. recently, lately.

reciente, −*thǐěn'tě*, ad. recent, new, fresh; modern.

recinto, −*thǐn'tǒ*, sm. precinct, district.

recio, cia, *rǎ'thǐǒ*, a. stout, strong, robust; coarse, thick; rude; arduous, rigid; −, ad. strongly, stoutly; hablar —, to talk loud.

récipe, *rǎ'thǐpě*, sm. prescription of a physician; (fig. & fam.) displeasure, disgust.

recipiente, −*thǐpǐěn'tě*, sm. (chem.) recipient.   [procity.

reciprocidad, −*thǐprǒthǐdǎd'*, sf. reciprocidad.

recíproco, ca, −*thǎ'prǒkǒ*, a. reciprocal, mutual.

recisión, −*thǐsǐǒn'*, sf. abrogation.

recitación, −*thǐtǎthǐǒn'*, sf. recitation.

recitar, −*thǐtǎr'*, v. a. to recite.

recitativo, va, −*thǐtǎtǐ'vǒ*, a. recitative.

reclamación, −*klǎmǎthǐǒn'*, sf. reclamation; remonstrance.

reclamar, −*klǎmǎr'*, v. a. to decoy birds with a call or whistle; to reclaim.

reclamo, −*klǎ'mǒ*, sm. decoy-bird; a bird trained to decoy others; call; an instrument for calling; allurement; reclamation; catch-word (in printing).

reclinación, −*klǐnǎthǐǒn'*, sf. reclining.

reclinar, −*klǐnǎr'*, v. a. & n. to recline, to lean back.

reclinatorio, −*klǐnǎtǒ'rǐǒ*, sm. couch.

recluir, −*klǔěr'*, v. a. to shut up.

reclusión, −*klǔsǐǒn'*, sf. reclusion; recess.

recluta, –klō'tā, sf. recruiting; –, sm. recruit. [ficer.

reclutador, –klōtādōr', sm. recruiting-of-

reclutar, –klōtār', v. a. to recruit.

recobrar, –kōbrār', v. a. to recover; –se, to recover from sickness; to recollect

recobro, –kō'brō, sm. recovery.

recocer, –kōthēr', v. a. to boil again; –se, to consume oneself with rage.

recocido, da, –kōthē'dō, a. skilful, clever.

recodar, –kōdār', v. n. to lean the elbow upon anything [out.

recodo, –kō'dō, sm. corner or angle jutting

recogedero, –kōʜhēdā'rō, sm. meeting-place, rendezvous ; collecting instrument

recogedor, –kōʜhēdōr', sm. harbourer, shelterer; gatherer; scraper (instrument).

recoger, –kōʜhēr', v. n. to retake, to take back; to gather; to shelter; to compile; to ask charity; –se, to take shelter or refuge; to retire to rest; to withdraw from the world. [cluded; stout.

recogido, da, –kōʜhē'dō, a. retired, se-

recogimiento, –ʜhēmēēn'tō, sm. collection, retreat, shelter; abstraction from all worldly concerns. [recollection.

recolección, –kōlēkthōn', sf. summary;

recoleto, ta, –kōlē'tō, sm. & f. Recollect (friar).

recomendación, –kōmēndāthōn', sf. recommendation. [to recommend.

recomendar, –kōmēndār', v. a. to charge;

recompensa, –kōmpēn'sā, sf. compensation; recompense, reward.

recompensar, –kōmpēnsār', v. a. to recompense, to reward. [compose.

recomponer, –kōmpōnēr', v. a. to re-

reconcentrar, –kōnthēntrār', v. a. to concentre; to dissemble. [conciliation.

reconciliación, –kōnthēlāthōn', sf. reconciliar, –kōnthēlēār', v. a. to reconcile; –se, to make one's peace for slight offences. [secret, concealed.

recóndito, ta, –kōn'dētō, a. recondite,

reconocedor, ra, –kōnōthēdōr', sm. & f. examiner, reviser.

reconocer, –kōnōthēr', v. a. to examine closely; to acknowledge favours received; to consider; (mil.) to reconnoitre; –se, to know oneself; to repent. [ful.

reconocido, da, –kōnōthē'dō, a. grate-

reconocimiento, –thēmēēn'tō, sm. recognition; acknowledgment; gratitude; confession; submission; inquiry.

reconquista, –kōnkēs'tā, sf. reconquest.

reconquistar, –kōnkēstār', v. a. to reconquer. [cover from sickness.

reconvalecer, –kōnvālēthēr', v. n. to re-

reconvención, –kōnvēnthōn', sf. recrimination. [to recriminate.

reconvenir, –kōnvēnēr', v. a. to retort,

recopilación, –kōpēlāthōn', sf. summary, abridgment.

recopilador, –kōpēlādōr', sm. compiler.

recopilar, –kōpēlār', v. a. to compile.

recordación, rēkōrdāthōn', sf. remembrance, memory, memento.

recordar, –kōrdār', v. a. to remind; –, v. n. to awake from sleep; to call to mind. [peruse; to mend, to repair.

recorrer, –kōrrēr', v. a. to run over, to

recortar, –kōrtār', v. a. to cut away, to pare off.

recorte, rēkōr'tā, sm. outline; shred.

recoser, –kōsēr', v. a. to sew again.

recostar, –kōstār', v. a. to lean against; to recline; –se, to go to rest.

recreación, –krēāthōn', sf. recreation, amusement. [to recreate.

recrear, –krēār', v. a. to amuse, to delight;

recreativo, va, –krēātē'vō, a. recreative, diverting.

recreo, rēkrē'ō, sm. recreation.

recriminación, –krēmēnāthōn', sf. recrimination. [minate.

recriminar, –krēmēnār', v. a. to recri-

rectángulo, la, rēktān'gūlō, a. rectangular; –, sm. rectangle. [fication.

rectificación, rēktēfēkāthōn', sf. recti-

rectificar, –fēkār', v. a. to rectify.

rectilíneo, nea, rēktēlē'nēō, a. rectilinear.

rectitud, –tūd', sf. straightness; rectitude; justness, honesty; exactitude.

recto, ta, rēk'tō, a. straight, right; just, honest.

rector, ra, rēktōr', sm. & f. superior of a community or establishment; rector (of a university); curate, rector.

rectorado, –rā'dō, sm. rectorship.

rectoral, –rāl', a. rectorial.

rectoría, –rē'ā, sf. rectory, curacy; rectorship. [burden.

recua, rā'kā, sf. drove of beasts of

recudimiento, rēkūdēmēēn'tō, sm. power vested in a person to gather rents or taxes.

recuento, –kēēn'tō, sm. inventory.

recuerdo, –kēēr'dō, sm. remembrance, memory. [descent.

recuesto, –kēēs'tō, sm. declivity, gradual

reculada, –kūlā'dā, sf. falling astern of a ship; recoil. [recoil.

recular, –kūlār', v. n. to fall back, to

reculones, –kūlō'nēs, á–, ad. backwards.

recuperable, –kūpērā'blā, a. recoverable.

recuperación, –rāthōn', sf. recovery.

recuperar, –pērār', v. a. to recover; –se, to recover from sickness.

recurrir, –kūrrēr', v. a. to recur.

recurso, –kūr'sō, sm. recourse.

recusación, –kūsāthōn', sf. refusal; recusation. [to admit.

recusar, –kūsār', v. a. to refuse; to refuse

rechazamiento, –tshāthāmēēn'tō, sf. repulsion. [pulse; to contradict.

rechazar, –tshāthār', v. a. to repel, to re-

rechazo, –tshā'thō, sm. rebound.

rechifla, –tshē'flā, sf. mockery, derision.

rechiflar, –tshēflār', v. a. to mock, to laugh.

rechinamiento, –tshēnāmēēn'tō, sm. creaking of a machine; gnashing of teeth.

rechinar, –tshēnār', v. n. to gnash the teeth. [teeth.

rechino, –tshē'nō, sm. creaking.

rechoncho, cha, –tshōn'tshō, a. chubby.

red, rēd', sf. net; grate through which fish

or bread are sold; snare, wile, fraud; silk coif.   [office.

redacción, *redăkthĭon'*, sf. editing; editor's

redactar, *—dăktăr'*, v. a. to edit a newspaper.   [paper.

redactor, *—tŏr'*, sm. editor.

redaño, *dăn'yŏ*, sm. caul, omentum.

redargüir, *—dărgür'*, v. a. to retort, to re-

redecilla, *—dĕthĭl'yă*, sf. hair-net.   [ply.

rededor, *—dĕdŏr'*, sm. environs; **al —,** round about.

redención, *—dĕnthĭon'*, sf. redemption; ransom; assistance, support.

redentor, ra, *—tŏr'*, sm. & f. redeemer.

redil, *rĕdĭl'*, sm. sheep-fold, sheep-cot.

redimible, *—dĭmě blĕ*, a. redeemable.

redimir, *—dĭmĭr'*, v. a. to redeem, to ransom; to succour.

redingote, *—ĭng'ŏ tĕ*, sm. riding-coat.

rédito, *rĕ'dĭtŏ*, sm. revenue, rent.   [rent.

reditüar, *—dĭtŭăr'*, v. a. to yield profit; to

redoblado, da, *—dŏblă'dŏ*, a. redoubled; stout and thick.   [rivet.

redoblar, *—dŏblăr'*, v. a. to redouble; to

redoble, *rĕdŏ'blĕ*, sm. doubling, repetition; (mus.) octave; (mil.) roll of a drum.

redoma, *—dŏ'mă*, sf. phial.

redondear, *—dŏndĕăr'*, v. a. to round; **—se,** to extricate oneself from a difficulty.

redondel, *—dŏndĕl'*, sm. round cloak; circle.   [lar form.

redondez, *—dŏndĕth'*, sf. roundness, circu-

redondilla, *—dŏndĭl'yă*, sf. roundel, roundelay.

redondo, da, *rĕdŏn'dŏ*, a. round.

redopelo, *—dŏp'lŏ*, sm. scuffle, affray; **al —,** against all rule and reason; **traer al —,** to vex, to drag about contemptuously.

reducción, *—dŭkthĭon'*, sf. reduction; mutation; dissolution, liquefaction; exchange, change of money.   [vertible.

reducible, *—dŭthĕ blĕ*, a. reducible, con-

reducir, *—dŭthĭr'*, v. a. to reduce; to exchange; to convert; **—se,** to cut down one's expenses, to economise.

reducto, *rĕdŭk'tŏ*, sm. (mil.) redoubt.

redundancia, *—dŭndăn'thĭă*, sf. superfluity, redundance, excess.

redundante, *—tĕ*, a. overflowing.

redundar, *—dŭndăr'*, v. n. to overflow, to be redundant; to contribute.   [ing.

reedificación, *—ĕdĭfĭkăthĭon'*, sf. rebuild-

reedificar, *—ĕdĭfĭkăr'*, v. a. to rebuild.

reelección, *—ĕlĕkthĭon'*, sf. re-election.

reelegir, *—ĕlĕhĭr'*, v. a. to re-elect, to elect again.   [money advanced; to reimburse.

reembolsar, *—ĕmbŏlsăr'*, v. a. to recover

reembolso, *—ĕmbŏl'sŏ*, sm. reimbursement; **contra —,** by reimbursement.

reemplazar, *—ĕmplăthăr'*, v. a. to replace, to restore.   [substitute in the militia.

reemplazo, *—ĕmplă'thŏ*, sm. replacing;

reencuentro, *—ĕnkŭĕn'trŏ*, sm. rencounter.

reenganchar, *—ĕngănchăr'*, v. a. (mil.) to re-enlist, **—se,** to enlist again.

reengendrar, *—ĕn'hĕndrăr'*, v. a. to regenerate, to reproduce.   [freshment.

refacción, *—făkthĭon'*, sf. refection, re-

refajo, *rĕfă'h'ŏ*, sm. short petticoat worn by mountaineers.

refectorio, *—fĕktŏ'rĭŏ*, sm. refectory.

referencia, *—fĕrĕn'thĭă*, sf. reference.

referendario, *—fĕrĕndă'rĭŏ*, sm. junior barrister.

referir, *—fĕrĭr'*, v. a. to refer, to relate, to report; **—se,** to refer to, to relate to.

refinadera, *—fĭnădă'ră*, sf. refiner (a long cylindrical stone).   [artful.

refinado, da, *—fĭnă'dŏ*, a. refined; subtle,

refinador, *—dŏr'*, sm. refiner.

refinadura, *—dŏ'ră*, sf. refining.

refinar, *—fĭnăr'*, v. a. to refine.

refitolero, *—fĭtŏlĕ'rŏ*, a. surveyor of the refectory.

reflectar, *—flĕktăr'*, v. a. to reflect (light).

reflejar, *—flĕ'hăr'*, v. n. to reflect the rays

reflejo, *rĕflĕ'h'ŏ*, sm. reflex.   [of light.

reflexión, *—flĕkthĭon'*, sf. reflexion; meditation, reflection.   [to meditate.

reflexionar, *—flĕkthĭonăr'*, v. n. to reflect,

reflexivo, va, *—flĕkthĭ vŏ*, a. reflexive; reflective.   [again.

reflorecer, *—flŏrĕthĕr'*, v. n. to blossom

refluir, *—flŭĭr'*, v. n. to flow back, to reflow.   [flujo **y —,** the tides.

reflujo, *rĕflŭ'h'ŏ*, sm. reflux, ebb-tide;

refocilación, *—fŏthĭlăthĭon'*, sf. restoration, refection.   [to revive.

refocilar, *—fŏthĭlăr'*, v. a. to strengthen,

reforma, *rĕfŏr'mă*, sf. reform; correction; dismissal from office.   [reform.

reformación, *—măthĭon'*, sf. reformation.

reformado, da, *—mă'dŏ*, sm. reformed officer.

reformar, *—măr'*, v. a. to reform; to correct, to restore; **—se,** to mend, to have one's manners reformed *or* corrected; to be prudent and moderate in speech and conduct.

reforzada, *—fŏrthă'dă*, sf. narrow taper.

reforzado, da, *—dŏ*, a. extra thick and strong at the breech (of fire-arms).

reforzar, *—fŏrthăr'*, v. a. to strengthen, to fortify; **—se,** to be strengthened and recovered.

refracción, *—frăkthĭon'*, sf. refraction.

refractario, ria, *—tă'rĭŏ*, a. refractory.

refrán, *rĕfrăn'*, sm. proverb.

refregar, *—frĕgăr'*, v. a. to rub one thing against another.

refregón, *—frĕgŏn'*, sm. friction, rubbing of one thing against another.

refrenamiento, *—frĕnămĭĕn'tŏ*, sm. curb, refraining.

refrenar, *—frĕnăr'*, v. a. to refrain.

refrendación, *—frĕndăthĭon'*, sf. countersigning.

refrendar, *—frĕndăr'*, v. a. to countersign.

refrendario, *—frĕndă'rĭŏ*, sm. officer appointed to countersign edicts, ordinances, or other public acts.   [ture.

refrendata, *—frĕndă'tă*, sf. counter-signa-

refrescar, *—frĕskăr'*, v. a. to refresh; **—,** v. n. to cool; to take the air.

refresco, *rĕfrĕs'kŏ*, sm. refreshment.

refriega, *—frĭĕ'gă*, sf. affray, skirmish, encounter, fray.

refrigerar, –*freˈheˈrâr*, v. a. to cool, to refresh, to comfort, to refrigerate.

refrigerio, –ˈhâˈreˈó, sm refrigeration, refreshment; consolation, comfort.

refuerzo, –*fooˈerˈthô*, sm. reinforcement.

refugiar, –*fooˈhârˈ*, v. a. to shelter; –se, to take refuge.

refugio, *reˈfooˈheˈô*, sm. refuge, asylum.

refulgente, –*foolˈhenˈteˈ*, a. refulgent.

refundición, –*foonˈdeˈtheˈón'*, sf. act of casting metals anew.

refundir, –*foonˈdêrˈ*, v. a. to melt metal again, –, v. n. to convert to.

refunfuñadura, –*foonˈfoonˈyâdoˈrâ*, sf. growling grumbling.   [to grumble.

refunfuñar, –*yârˈ*, v. n. to snarl, to growl,

refutación, –*foolˈtâˈtheˈón'*, sf refutation.

refutar, –*footârˈ*, v. a. to refute.

regadera, –*gâdáˈrâ*, sf watering-pot.

regadío, dia, *reˈgâˈdeˈô*, a. irrigated, watered.

regadizo, za, –*deˈthô*, a. that can be irrigated or watered.

regadura, –*dôˈrâ*, sf. irrigation, watering.

regalado, da, –*lâˈdô*, a. convenient, pleasant, delicate, dainty.

regalar, –*lârˈ*, v. a. to regale; to refresh; to caress –se, to feast, to regale oneself.

regalía, –*leˈâ*, s. sf. regalia, privilege.

regaliza, –*leˈthâ*, sf. licorice.

regalo, *reˈgâˈlô*, sm. present, gift, largess; regalement.

regalón, ona, –*lôn'*, a. delicate; pampered.

regañar, –*gânˈyârˈ*, v. n. to growl, to grumble, to quarrel.

regaño, *reˈgânˈyô*, sm. sourness of countenance, sternness of look.

regañón, ona, –*yôn'*, a snarling, growling, grumbling; troublesome.

regar, *reˈgârˈ*, v. a. to water, to irrigate.

regata, *reˈgâˈtâ*, sf. irrigating-ditch, regatta.

regatear, –*gâteˈârˈ*, v. n. to use evasions; –, v. a. to haggle, to higgle.

regateo, –*gâteˈô*, sm. act of haggling or bartering.   [ona, a retailing.

regatón, –*gâtôn'*, sm. socket, ferrule, –,

regazo, –*gâˈthô*, sm. lap of a woman.

regencia, *reˈhenˈtheˈâ*, sf. regency; regentship.   [generation.

regeneración, *reˈheˈneˈrâˈtheˈón'*, sf. regeneration.

regenerar, –ˈheˈnerârˈ, v. a. to regenerate.

regenta, *reˈhenˈtâ*, sf. wife of a regent.

regentar, –*târˈ*, v. a. to rule; to govern.

regente, *reˈhenˈteˈ*, sm. regent; manager (in printing-offices).

regiamente, *reˈheˈâmenˈteˈ*, ad. royally.

regidor, *reˈheˈdôrˈ*, sm. alderman; governor, prefect.   [ment; (gr.) rules of verbs.

régimen, *râˈheˈmen*, sm. regimen, management.

regimiento, –*meˈenˈtô*, sm. administration, government; regimen, diet; magistracy of a city, municipality; (mil.) regiment.

regio, gia, *reˈheˈô*, a. royal, kingly.

región, *reˈheˈón'*, sf. region, tract of country.

regir, *reˈhêrˈ*, v. a. to rule, to govern, to direct.   [controller.

registrador, *reˈheˈstrâdôrˈ*, sm. registrar;

registrar, –*trârˈ*, v. a. to survey, to inspect, to examine; to record, to enter in a register, –se, to be registered.

registro, *reˈhêsˈtrô*, sm. examining; enrolling office; register.

regla, *râˈglâ*, sf. rule, ruler.   [perate.

reglado, da, *reˈglâˈdô*, a. regulated, temperate.

reglamento, –*menˈtô*, sm. regulation; by-law.   [to regulate; –se, to reform.

reglar, *reˈglârˈ*, a. regular, –, v. a. to rule;

reglón, *reˈglôn'*, sm. level (used by masons).

regocijar, *reˈgôtheˈhârˈ*, v. a. to rejoice.

regocijo, –*theˈhˈô*, sm. joy, pleasure, merriment, rejoicing.

regodearse, –*deˈârˈseˈ*, v. r. to be merry, to be delighted, to dally, to trifle, to play the fool; to joke, to jest.   [sion.

regodeo, –*dâˈô*, sm. joy, merriment, diversion.

regojo, *reˈgôˈhˈô*, sm. crumb or piece of bread left on the table after meals.

regoldar, –*gôldârˈ*, v. n. to belch.

regolfar, –*gôlfârˈ*, v. n. to flow back.

regona, *reˈgôˈnâ*, sf irrigation-works, pl.

regordete, –*gôrdâˈteˈ*, a. chubby, plump.

regresar, –*gresârˈ*, v. n. to return to a place, to regress.

regreso, *reˈgrêsˈô*, sm. return, regression.

regüeldo, –*güelˈdô*, sm eructation, belch.

reguera, –*gâˈrâ*, sf. canal for watering lands or plants.

reguero, –*gâˈrô*, sm. small rivulet; trickling line of spilt liquid; drain, gutter.

regulación, –*gülâˈtheˈón'*, sf regulation; comparison, computation.

regulador, ra, –*dôrˈ*, sm. & f. regulator.

regular, –*lârˈ*, v. a. to regulate; to adjust; –, a. regular; ordinary.

regularidad, –*lâreˈdâˈd*, sf. regularity.

rehabilitación, –*âbilˈlitâˈtheˈón'*, sf. rehabilitation.

rehabilitar, –*târˈ*, v. a to rehabilitate.

rehacer, –*âˈthêrˈ*, v. a. to repair, to make again; –se, to regain strength and vigour; (mil.) to rally   [broad-shouldered.

rehecho, cha, *reˈêˈshˈô*, a. remade, squat,

rehén, *reˈên'*, sm. hostage.

rehilete, –*leˈâˈteˈ*, sm. shuttle-cock bearded with feathers.

rehogar, –*ôgârˈ*, v. a. to roast.

rehusar, –*âsârˈ*, v. a. to refuse, to decline.

reimpresión, –*impresˈeˈón'*, sf.reimpression.

reimprimir, –*imprimêrˈ*, v. a. to reimprint.

reina, *reˈeˈnâ*, sf. queen.

reinado, *reˈeˈnâˈdô*, sm. reign.

reinar, *reˈeˈnârˈ*, v. a. to reign, to govern.

reincidencia, –*inˈtheˈdenˈtheˈâ*, sf. reiteration, relapse.   [back.

reincidir, –*dêrˈ*, v. n. to relapse, to fall

reino, *reˈeˈnô*, sm. kingdom, reign.

reintegración, –*integrâˈtheˈón'*, sf. reintegration, restoration.

reintegrar, –*tegrârˈ*, v. a. to reintegrate, to restore; –se, to be reinstated or restored.

reintegro, –*dâˈgrô*, sm. reintegration.

reir, *reˈêrˈ*, v. n. to laugh.   [reiteration.

reiteración, –*iteˈrâˈtheˈón'*, sf. repetition,

reiterar, –*tĕrár',* v. a. to reiterate, to repeat.

reja, *rĕ'h'ă,* sf. plough-share; lattice, grating.

rejalgar, –*'hălgár',* sm. (chem.) realgar.

rejilla, –*'hĭl'ya,* sf. small lattice in confessionals.

rejo, *rĕ'k'ŏ,* sm. pointed iron bar or spike; [sting of an insect.

rejón, *rĕ'hŏn',* sm. dagger, poniard; spear used by bull-fighters; short broad knife with a sharp point.

rejonazo, –*nä'thŏ,* sm. dagger-thrust.

rejonear, –*hănăr',* v. a. to spear bulls.

rejuela, –*hŭĕ'lă,* sf. foot-stove, warming-pan. [young again, to be rejuvenated.

rejuvenecer, –*'hŭvĕnĕthĕr',* v. n. to grow young again, to be rejuvenated.

relación, –*lăthĭŏn',* sf. relation; report; account; romance; distant relation.

relacionar, –*năr',* v. a. to relate.

relajación, –*lă'hăthĭŏn',* sf. relaxation; remission; laxity; commutation of a vow; delivery of an offender by the ecclesiastical judge to a criminal court of justice, in cases of murder; hernia.

relajar, –*lă'hár',* v. a. to relax, to slacken, to remit; –**se,** to be relaxed; to labour under a hernia.

relamer, –*lămĕr',* v. a. to lick again; –**se,** to lick one's lips; to relish; to paint oneself to excess. [nice in dress.

relamido, da, –*lămĭ'dŏ, a.* affected, over-

relámpago, *rĕlăm'pägŏ,* sm. flash of lightning. [flash.

relampaguear, –*gĕár',* v. n. to lighten, to

relapso, sa, *rĕlăp'sŏ, a.* relapsed.

relatar, –*lătár',* v. a. to relate.

relativo, va, –*lătĭ'vŏ, a.* relative.

relato, *rĕlă'tŏ,* sm. recital.

relator, –*lătŏr',* sm. relater, narrator; (law) reporter.

relatoría, –*tŏrĕ'ă,* sf. office of a reporter of judicial causes in a court of justice.

releer, *rĕlĕĕr',* v. a. to read again.

relegación, –*lĕgăthĭŏn',* sf. relegation, exile. [to exile.

relegar, –*gár',* v. a. to relegate, to banish;

relente, *rĕlĕn'tĕ,* sm. evening-dew.

relentecer, –*tĕthĕr',* v. n. to be damp with dew.

relevación, –*lĕvăthĭŏn',* sf. relevation; alleviation, relief; remission, pardon.

relevante, –*văn'tĕ, a.* excellent, great, eminent.

relevar, –*văr',* v. a. to emboss, to work in relief; to exonerate, to disburden; to relieve from a burden or charge; to assist; to succour; to forgive, to pardon; to exalt, to aggrandize; (pict.) to paint an object to appear as if rising; to relieve (of soldiers).

relevo, *rĕlĕ'vŏ,* sm. (mil.) relief. [diers).

relicario, –*lĭkă'rĭŏ,* sm. reliquary.

relieve, *rĕlĭĕ'vĕ,* sm. relievo.

religión, *rĕlĭhĭŏn',* sf. religion.

religionario, –*nă'rĭŏ,* sm. & f. religionist; Reformist, Calvinist.

religiosidad, –*sĭdăd',* sf. religiousness.

religioso, sa, –*hĭŏ'sŏ, a.* a religious, pious.

relinchar, –*lĭntshár',* v. n. to neigh.

relincho, *rĕlĭn'tshŏ,* sm. neigh, neighing.

reliquia, *rĕlĭ'kĭă,* sf. residue, remains; saintly relic.

reloj, *rĕlŏ'h',* sm. clock, watch.

relojería, –*lŏ'hĕrĕ'ă,* sf. watch-making.

relojero, –*'hĕ'rŏ,* sm. watch-maker.

relucir, –*lŭthĭr',* v. n. to shine, to glitter; to excel, to be brilliant. [shine.

relumbrar, –*lŭmbrár',* v. n. to sparkle, to

relumbrón, –*brŏn',* sm. lustre.

rellenar, –*lyĕnár',* v. a. to fill again.

relleno, –*lyĕ'nŏ,* sm. forced meat; –, **na,** a. satiated.

remachar, –*mătshár',* v. a. to rivet.

remansarse, –*mănsár'sĕ,* v. r. to obstruct the course of a stream.

remanso, *rĕmăn'sŏ,* sm. stagnant water;

remar, *rĕmár',* v. n. to row. [tardiness.

rematadamente, –*mătădămĕn'tĕ, ad.* entirely, totally. [terly ruined.

rematado, da, –*tă'dŏ, a.* totally lost, ut-

rematar, –*mătár',* v. a. to terminate, to finish; to adjudge to the best bidder; –, v. n. to be at an end; –**se,** to be utterly ruined. [or best bid.

remate, *rĕmă'tĕ,* sm. end, conclusion; last

remedar, –*mĕdár',* v. a. to copy, to imitate, to mimic.

remediable, –*dĭă'blĕ, a.* remediable.

remediador, ra, –*dĭădŏr',* sm. & r. helper; curer.

remediar, –*dĭár',* v. a. to remedy; to assist, to help; to free from danger.

remedio, *rĕmĕ'dĭŏ,* sm. remedy, reparation; help; amendment, correction; resource; refuge.

remedo, *rĕmĕ'dŏ,* sm. imitation, copy.

remendar, *rĕmĕn'dăr',* v. a. to patch, to mend; to correct.

remendón, –*dŏn',* sm. botcher, cobbler.

remero, *rĕmĕ'rŏ,* sm. rower, oarsman.

remesa, *rĕmĕ'să,* sf. sending of goods; remittance of money.

remiendo, *rĕmĭĕn'dŏ,* sm. patch, clout.

remilgarse, *rĕmĭlgár'sĕ,* v. r. to be affectedly nice or grave. [gravity.

remilgo, *rĕmĭl'gŏ,* sm. affected nicety or

reminiscencia, *rĕmĭnĭsthĕn'thĭă,* sf. reminiscence, recollection. [tious.

remirado, da, *rĕmĭră'dŏ, a.* prudent, cau-

remirar, *rĕmĭrár',* v. a. to revise, to review; –**se,** to do very carefully; to consider.

remisible, *rĕmĭsĕ'blĕ, a.* remissible.

remisión, –*sĭŏn',* sf. act of sending back; remission, forgiveness. [indolent.

remiso, sa, *rĕmĭ'sŏ, a.* a remiss, careless,

remitir, –*mĭtĭr',* v. a. to remit, to transmit; to pardon a fault; to suspend, to put off; –, v. n., –**se,** to slacken.

remo, *ră'mŏ,* sm. oar; long and hard labour; –**s,** pl. limbs (of a person); legs (of an animal). [motion.

remoción, *rĕmŏthĭŏn',* sf. removal, re-

remojadero, –*hădă'rŏ,* sm. steeping-tub.

remojar, –*hár',* v. a. to steep; –**la palabra,** to go and drink liquor.

remojo, *rĕmŏ'h'ŏ,* sm. steeping, soaking.

remolacha, –*mŏlätsh'ă,* sf. beet-root.

remolcar, -mōlkär', v. a. (mar.) to tow.
remolinar, -mōlīnär', v. n. to spin round; —se. to collect together tumultuously (of a crowd). [pool.
remolino, -lē'nō, sm. whirlwind; whirl-
remolón, ona, -lōn', a. soft, lazy; —, sm. upper tusk of a wild boar.
remolonearse, -lōnĕär'sĕ, v. r. to refuse, to tarry, to delay.
remolque, rĕmōl'kĕ, sm. towing a ship.
remonta, rĕmōn'tä, sf. (mil.) remount, supply of cavalry-horses.
remontar, -tär', v. a. to frighten away; to remount cavalry; to repair saddles; —se, to tower, to soar.
remontista, -tĭs'tä, sm. commissioner for the purchase of cavalry horses.
remordedor, ra, -mōrdĕdōr', a. causing regret, disquieting, discomposing.
remorder, -dĕr', v. a. to cause remorse; —se, to manifest or express concern.
remordimiento, -dĭmĭen'tō, sm. remorse.
remoto, ta, rĕmō'tä, a. remote, distant, far.
remover, -mōvĕr', v. a. to remove; to excite an animal; to dismiss.
removimiento, -vĭmĭen'tō, sm. removal; restlessness.
remozar, -mōthär', v. a. to rejuvenate.
rempujar, rĕmpū'här', v. a. to push or shove a person out of his place. [thrust.
rempujón, -hōn', sm. impulse, push, [muneration, recompense. [munerator.
remuneración, rĕmŭnĕräthĭōn', sf. re-
remunerador, ra, -dōr', sm. & f. re-
remunerar, -rär', v. a. to reward, to remunerate. [to be new-born.
renacer, -näthĕr', v. n. to be born again; [thumb.
renacimiento, -thĭmĭen'tō, sm. regeneration; new birth.
renacuajo, -kŭä'hō, sm. hop o' my
rencilla, rĕnthĭl'yä, sf. slight grudge remaining after a quarrel. [quarrelsome.
rencilloso, sa, -yō'sō, a. peevish.
rencor, rĕnkōr', sm. rancour, grudge.
rencoroso, sa, -rō'sō, a. rancorous.
rendición, rĕndĭthĭōn', sf. rendition; profit.
rendidamente, -dĭdämĕn'tĕ, ad. humbly.
rendija, rĕndē'hä, sf. crevice, crack, cleft.
rendimiento, -dĭmĭen'tō, sm. rendition; weariness, submission; humbling compliance; rent, income.
rendir, rĕndĭr', v. a. to subject, to subdue; to surrender; —se, to be tired out.
renegado, rĕnĕgä'dō, sm. apostate; wicked person.
renegar, -gär', v. a. to deny, to disown; to detest, to abhor; —, v. n. to apostatize; to blaspheme, to curse.
renglón, rĕnglōn', sm. written or printed line; part of one's income; —ones, pl. writings. [or blasphemy.
reniego, rĕnĭĕ'gō, sm. kind of execration
renitencia, -tĕn'thĭä, sf. resistance, opposition, stubbornness.
renitente, -tĕn'tĕ, a. refractory, repugnant.
renombrado, da, -nōmbrä'dō, a. renowned.
renombre, rĕnōm'brĕ, sm. surname.

renovación, -nōväthĭōn', sf. renovation, renewal. [to reform.
renovar, -nōvär', v. a. to renew, to renovate.
renquear, rĕnkĕär', v. n. to limp, to halt.
renta, rĕn'tä, sf. rent, income.
rentero, rĕntĕ'rō, sm. renter, farmer.
rentilla, rĕntĭl'yä, sf. game at cards.
renuevo, rĕnŭĕ'vō, sm. sprout, shoot.
renuncia, -nän'thĭä, sf. renunciation; resignation. [be renounced.
renunciable, -thĭä'blĕ, a. that which can
renunciar, -thĭär', v. a. to renounce, to resign; [whom anything is resigned.
renunciatario, -thĭätä'rĭō, sm. he to
renuncio, rĕnŭn'thĭō, sm. renounce (at cards). [at odds.
reñido, da, rĕnyē'dō, a. at variance.
reñir, rĕnyĭr', v. a. & n. to wrangle, to quarrel; to scold, to chide.
reo, rä'ō, sm. offender, criminal.
reojo, rĕō'h'ō, sm. mirar de —, to look at furtively.
repanchigarse, -pänthĭgär'sĕ, **repantigarse,** -päntĭgär'sĕ, v. r. to stretch oneself out in a chair. [diable.
reparable, -pärä'blĕ, a. reparable, remediable.
reparación, -päräthĭōn', sf. reparation, repair. [a horse.
reparada, -pärä'dä, sf. sudden bound of
reparar, -pärär', v. a. to repair; to consider, to observe; to give heed; —, v. n. to parry; to pass (at cards).
reparativo, va, -tē'vō, a. reparative.
reparo, rĕpä'rō, sm. repair, reparation; notice; consideration; difficulty; cataplasm.
reparón, ona, -pärōn', a. too cautious.
repartición, -pärtĭthĭōn', sf. distribution.
repartidor, -dōr', sm. & f. distributer; assessor of taxes.
repartimiento, -mĭen'tō, sm. distribution; assessment of taxes.
repartir, -pärtĭr', v. a. to distribute.
repasadora, -päsädō'rä, sf. wool-comber.
repasar, -päsär', v. n. to repass; to revise.
repasata, -päsä'tä, sf. reprehension, censure.
repaso, rĕpä'sō, sm. revision. [sure.
repechar, -pĕtshär', v. a. & n. to ascend a declivity.
repecho, -pĕtsh'ō, sm. declivity, slope.
repeladura, -pĕlädō'rä, sf. second shearing. [one's hair.
repelar, -pĕlär', v. a. to tear out some-
repeler, -pĕlĕr', v. a. to repel; to refute, to reject.
repelón, -lōn', sm. tearing of hair; á —ones, by degrees, little by little; de —, by the way; in haste.
repente, -pĕn'tĕ, de —, ad. suddenly, on a sudden; off-hand.
repentino, na, -tē'nō, a. sudden, unforeseen. [tempore verses.
repentista, -tĭs'tä, sm. maker of ex-
repentón, -tōn', sm. unexpected event or incident. [tion.
repercusión, -pĕrkŭsĭōn', sf. reverbera-
repercutir, -kŭtĭr', v. n. to reverberate.
repertorio, -tō'rĭō, sm. repertory, index.

repetición, *–pĕtĭthĭŏn′*, sf. repetition; (mus.) repeat.

repetidor, **ra**, *–dŏr′*, sm. & f. repeater.

repetir, *–pĕtĭr′*, v. a. to repeat.

repicar, *–pĭkâr′*, v. a. to chime, to ring a merry peal; to count ninety before the other player counts one (at piquet); **–se**, to pique oneself in.

repique, *rĕpĭ′kĕ*, sm. chime; counting of ninety before the other player has counted one (at piquet).

repiquetear, *–tĕâr′*, v. a. to ring a merry peal on festive occasions; **–se**, to bicker, to wrangle.

repisa, *rĕpĭ′sä*, sf. pedestal *or* stand.

replegar, *rĕplĕ′gär*, v. a. to redouble; (mil.) to wheel round the wing of an army; **–se**, (mil.) to fall back.

repleto, **ta**, *–plĕ′tŏ*, a. replete, very full.

réplica, *rĕ′plĭkä*, sf. reply, answer; repartee.

replicar, *rĕplĭkâr′*, v.n. to reply. [arguer.

replicón, **ona**, *–kŏn′*, sm. & f. constant

repollo, *rĕpŏl′yŏ*, sm. white cabbage; head of lettuce; cabbage-head.

repolludo, **da**, *–yŏ′dŏ*, a. cabbage-headed; round-headed.

reponer, *–pŏnĕr′*, v. a. to replace; to restore a suit at law to its primitive state; **–se**, to recover lost health *or* property.

reportado, **da**, *–pŏrtä′dŏ*, a. moderate, temperate.

reportar, *–târ′*, v. a. to refrain; to obtain, to reach; to attain; to carry, to bring.

reportorio, *–tŏ′rĭŏ*, sm. repertory; almanac. [settled (wine).

reposado, **da**, *–pŏsä′dŏ*, a. quiet, peaceful.

reposar, *–pŏsâr′*, v. n. to rest, to repose.

reposición, *–pŏsĭthĭŏn′*, sf. restoring of a suit at law to its primitive state.

reposo, *rĕpŏ′sŏ*, sm. rest, repose.

repostería, *–pŏstĕrĭ′ä*, sf. repository in the royal palaces of Spain.

repostero, *–tĕ′rŏ*, sm. principal officer of the repostería. [to blame.

reprender, *–prĕndĕr′*, v. a. to reprehend.

reprensible, *–sĭ′blĕ*, a. reprehensible.

reprensión, *–sĭŏn′*, sf. reprehension, blame, blemish, reproach.

represa, *rĕprĕ′sä*, sf. stoppage, retention.

represalia, *–sä′lĭä*, sf. reprisal, reprise.

represar, *–sâr′*, v. a. to stop, to retain, to repress. [able.

representable, *–sĕntä′blĕ*, a. representable.

representación, *–täthĭŏn′*, sf. representation; authority.

representante, *–tän′tĕ*, sm. & f. representative; player; understudy (stage).

representar, *–târ′*, v. a. to represent; to play on the stage. [sentative.

representativo, **va**, *–tät′vŏ*, a. representative.

represión, *–prĕsĭŏn′*, sf. repression.

reprimenda, *–prĭmĕn′dä*, sf. reprimand.

reprimir, *–prĭmĭr′*, v. a. to repress, to refrain, to contain.

reprobable, *–prŏbä′blĕ*, a. reprehensible.

reprobación, *–thĭŏn′*, sf. reprobation, reproof. [demn, to upbraid.

reprobar, *–bâr′*, v. a. to reject, to con-

réprobo, **ba**, *rĕ′prŏbä*, a. reprobate.

reprochar, *rĕprŏtshâr′*, v. a. to reproach.

reproducción, *–prŏdŭkthĭŏn′*, sf. reproduction.

reproducir, *–thĭr′*, v. a. to reproduce.

reptil, *rĕptĭl′*, sm. reptile.

república, *rĕpŭ′blĭkä*, sf. republic.

republicano, **na**, *–kä′nŏ*, a. & sm. & f. republican.

repudiar, *–pŭdĭâr′*, v. a. to repudiate.

repudio, *rĕpŏ′dĭŏ*, sm. repudiation.

repuesto, *–pŭĕs′tŏ*, sm. store laid up against the future. [repugnance.

repugnancia, *–pŭgnän′thĭä*, sf. reluctance.

repugnante, *–tĕ*, a. repugnant.

repugnar, *–pŭgnâr′*, v. a. to oppose, to act with reluctance. [cast a seam.

repulgar, *–pŭlgâr′*, v. a. to hem; to over-

repulgo, *rĕpŏl′gŏ*, sm. hem.

repulsa, *rĕpŏl′sä*, sf. refusal. [to refuse.

repulsar, *–sâr′*, v. a. to reject, to decline,

repulsión, *–sĭŏn′*, sf. repulsion.

reputación, *–pŭtäthĭŏn′*, sf. reputation, renown.

reputar, *–târ′*, v. a. to repute, to estimate.

requebrar, *–kĕbrâr′*, v. a. to break to pieces; to woo, to court.

requerimiento, *–kĕrĭmĭĕn′tŏ*, sm. request, requisition; intimation.

requerir, *–kĕrĭr′*, v. a. to intimate, to notify; to request, to require, to need.

requesón, *–kĕsŏn′*, sm. cheese-curds.

requiebro, *–kĭĕ′brŏ*, sm. endearing expression; trill, quaver. [clarinet.

requinto, *rĕkĭn′tŏ*, sm. tithe of a tithe;

requisa, *rĕkĕ′sä*, sf. night and morning visit of a gaoler to his prisoners.

requisito, *–kĭsĭ′tŏ*, sm. requisite.

requisitorio, **ria**, *–tŏ′rĭŏ*, a. examinatory, requisitory; –, sm. (law) request, petition.

res, *rĕs*, sf. head of cattle.

resabiar, *rĕsäbĭâr′*, v. a. to contract evil habits; **–se**, to become vicious; to grumble.

resabio, *–sä′bĭŏ*, sm. unpleasant taste left on the palate; vicious habit, bad custom.

resaca, *–sä′kä*, sf. surge, surf.

resalado, **da**, *–sälä′dŏ*, a. very graceful.

resaltar, *–sältâr′*, v. n. to rebound; to jut out; to be evident.

resarcimiento, *–särthĭmĭĕn′tŏ*, sm. compensation, reparation.

resarcir, *–särthĭr′*, v. a. to compensate, to make amends. [place *or* road.

resbaladero, *rĕsbälädĕ′rŏ*, sm. slippery

resbaladizo, **za**, *–dĭ′thŏ*, sm. & f. slippery, glib. [backsliding.

resbaladura, *–dŏ′rä*, sf. slippery track;

resbalar, *–bälâr′*, v. n. & r. to slip, to slide.

resbalón, *–bälŏn′*, sm. slip, sliding.

rescatar, *–kätâr′*, v. a. to ransom, to rescate. [redeem.

rescate, *rĕskä′tĕ*, sm. ransom. [tion.

rescindir, *–thĭndĭr′*, v. a. to rescind, to annul.

rescisión, *–thĭsĭŏn′*, sf. rescission, revocation.

rescoldo, *–kŏl′dŏ*, sm. embers, cinders.

rescripto, *–skrĭp′tŏ*, sm. rescript.

resecar, *–sĕkâr′*, v. a. to dry again.

resellar, –sēlyăr', v. a. to coin again.
resello, –sĕl'yŏ, sm. recoinage.
resentimiento, –sĕntĭmĭĕn'tŏ, sm. resentment. [way; to resent.
resentirse, –tĕr'sĕ, v. r. to begin to give
reseña, –sĕn'yă, sf. review, muster; signal.
reseñar, –yăr', v. a. to describe from appearance.
reserva, –sĕr'vă, sf. reserve, reservation.
reservado, da, –vă'dŏ, a. reserved, cautious, circumspect.
reservar, –văr', v. a. to reserve; –se, to preserve oneself, to act with circumspection.
resfriado, –frĭă'dŏ, sm. cold, rheum.
resfriar, –frĭăr', v. n. to begin to be cold; –se, to catch cold.
resguardar, –gŭărdăr', v. a. to preserve, to defend, –se, to be on one's guard.
resguardo, –gŭăr'dŏ, sm. guard, security, safety, body of custom-house officers.
residencia, –sĭdĕn'thĭă, sf. residence.
residenciar, –thĭăr', v. a. to call a public officer to account for his administration.
residente, –dĕn'tĕ, p. & a. residing, –, sm. resident. [to assist personally.
residir, –sĭdĭr', v. n. to reside, to dwell;
residuo, –sĕ'dŭŏ, sm. residue, remainder.
resignación, –sĭgnăthĭŏn', sf. resignation.
resignadamente, –dămĕn'tĕ, ad. resignedly.
resignar, –năr', v. a. –se, to resign.
resina, –sĕ'nă, sf. resin, rosin.
resinoso, sa, –sĭnŏ'sŏ, a. resinous.
resisa, –sĕ'să, sf. extra collection of taxes.
resisar, –sĭsăr', v. r. to diminish any measures or things which have already been taxed. [opposition.
resistencia, –sĭstĕn'thĭă, sf. resistance,
resistero, –sĭstĕ'rŏ, sm. heat produced by the reflexion of the sun's rays.
resistir, –sĭstĭr', v. n. & a. to resist, to oppose, to gainsay.
resma, rĕs'mă, sf. ream (of paper).
resollar, rĕsŏlyăr', v. n. to respire, to talk; to take breath.
resolución, –sŏlŭthĭŏn', sf. resolution, boldness, decision, activity.
resolutivo, va, –tĕ'vŏ, a. (med.) resolutive; analytical.
resolver, –vĕr', v. a. to resolve, to decide, to analyze; –se, to resolve, to determine.
resonar, –sŏnăr', v. n. to resound.
resoplar, –sŏplăr', v. n. to snore, to snort; to huff. [breathing.
resoplido, –sŏplĕ'dŏ, sm. continued audible
resorte, –sŏr'tĕ, sm. spring (elastic body).
respaldar, –spăldăr', v. a. to endorse; –se, to recline against a chair or bench; –, sm. back (of seats).
respaldo, –spăl'dŏ, sm. back; endorsement; back of a seat.
respectivo, va, –spĕktĕ'vŏ, a. respective.
respecto, –spĕk'tŏ, sm. relation, respect; á –, al –, relatively, respectively.
respetable, –spĕtă'blĕ, a. respectable.

respetar, –spĕtăr', v. a. to respect; to revere. [sideration; homage.
respeto, –spĕ'tŏ, sm. respect, regard, conrespetoso, sa, –tŏ'sŏ, a. respectable, respectful.
respetuoso, sa, –tŭŏ'sŏ, a. respectful.
réspice, rĕs'pĭthĕ, sm. short reply.
respigar, –spĭgăr', v. a. to glean.
respigón, –spĭgŏn', sm. hag-nail; sty on the eyelid. [wince.
respingar, –spĭngăr', v. n. to kick, to
respingo, –spĭn'gŏ, sm. kick, yerk.
respiración, –spĭrăthĭŏn', sf. respiration, breathing. [hole; rest, repose.
respiradero, –dĕ'rŏ, sm. vent, breathingrespirar, –răr', v. n. to respire, to breathe.
resplandecer, –splăndĕthĕr', v. n. to emit rays of light, to glisten. [splendent.
resplandeciente, –thĭĕn'tĕ, p. & a. reresplandor, –dŏr', sm. splendour, brilliancy.
responder, –spŏndĕr', v. a. & n. to answer, to re-echo, to correspond, to be responsible for [reply.
respondón, ona, –dŏn', a. ever ready to
responsable, –să'blĕ, a. responsible, accountable, answerable. [sibility.
responsabilidad, –bĭlĭdăd', sf. responsoresponso, –spŏn'sŏ, sm. response for the dead.
responsorio, –sŏ'rĭŏ, sm. response.
respuesta, –pŭĕs'tă, sf. answer, reply.
resquicio, –kĕ'thĭŏ, sm. aperture between the jamb and leaf of a door, crack, cleft; subterfuge, evasion.
resta, rĕs'tă, sf. rest, residue, remainder.
restablecer, –stăblĕthĕr', v. a. to re-restablish, –se, to recover from a disease, &c.
restablecimiento, –thĭmĭĕn'tŏ, sm. reestablishment.
restallar, –stălyăr', v. n. to smack, to click.
restañar, –stănyăr', v. a. to stanch, to stop blood.
restar, rĕstăr', v. a. to subtract; –, v. n. to be left, to rest. [tion.
restauración, –stăŭrăthĭŏn', sf. restaurarestaurar, –stăŭrăr', v. a. to restore.
restitución, –stĭtŭthĭŏn', sf. restitution.
restituir, –tŭĭr', v. a. to restore; –se, to resto, rĕs'tŏ, sm. remainder, rest. [return.
restricción, –strĭkthĭŏn', sf. restriction, limitation.
restringir, –strĭn'hĭr', v. a. to restrain, to restrict, to limit. [tion.
restriñimiento, –yĭmĭĕn'tŏ, sm. restricrestriñir, –yĭr', v. a. to make costive, to restrain. [to revive, to renew.
resucitar, –sŭthĭtăr', v. a. to resuscitate.
resudar, –sŭdăr', v. n. to perspire, to transpire. [shortness of breath.
resuello, –sŭĕl'yŏ, sm. breath, breathing;
resuelto, ta, –sŭĕl'tŏ, a. resolute, determined, prompt. [sequence.
resultado, –sŭltă'dŏ, sm. result, conresultar, –sŭltăr', v. n. to result.
resumen, rĕsŭ'mĕn, sm. summary, recapitulation [marily.
resumidamente, –sŭmĭdămĕn'tĕ, ad. sum-

resumir, –*mir'*, v. a. to abridge; to resume.   [tion, revival.
resurrección, –*sŭrrĕkthiŏn'*, sf. resurrection.
retablo, –*tă'blŏ*, sm. picture drawn on a board; splendid altars-ornament.
retacar, –*tăkăr'*, v. a. to hit a ball twice at billiards.   [piece.
retaco, –*tă'kŏ*, sm. short, light fowling-piece.
retador, –*tădŏr'*, sm. challenger.
retaguardia, –*gŭăr'diă*, sf. rear-guard.
retahila, –*ĕ'lă*, sf. file, range, series.
retal, –*tăl'*, sm. remnant.
retar, –*tăr'*, v. a. to challenge, to call out.
retardar, –*tărdăr'*, v. a. to retard, to delay.
retardo, –*tăr'dŏ*, sm. delay, procrastination.
retazo, –*tă'thŏ*, sm. remnant; cutting.
retejar, –*tĕ'hăr'*, v. a. to repair the roof of a house.
retejo, –*tĕ'h'ŏ*, sm. repair of a roof.
retén, –*tĕn'*, sm. store, stock, reserve.
retención, –*thiŏn'*, sf. retention. [back.
retener, –*tĕnĕr'*, v. a. to retain, to keep
retentar, –*tĕntăr'*, v. a. to threaten with a relapse of a former disorder.   [dence.
retentiva, –*tĕ'vă*, sf. circumspection, prudence.
reticencia, –*ĭthĕn'thiă*, sf. reticence.
retina, –*tĕ'nă*, sf. retina.
retintín, –*tintin'*, sm. tingling sound; affected tone of voice.
retiñir, –*tĭnyir'*, v. n. to tingle, to resound.
retirada, –*tĭră'dă*, sf. (mil.) retreat.
retirar, –*tĭrăr'*, v. a. to withdraw, to retire; to print the back of a sheet; –se, to retire, to retreat.
retiro, –*tĕ'rŏ*, sm. retreat, retirement.
reto, –*rĕ'tŏ*, sm. challenge; threat, menace.
retocar, –*tŏkăr'*, v. a. to retouch a painting; to mend; to finish any work completely.
retoñar, –*tŏnyăr'*, v. a. to sprout again.
retoño, –*tĕn'yŏ*, sm. after-math.
retoque, –*tŏ'kĕ*, sm. finishing stroke; retouching.
retorcer, –*tŏrthĕr'*, v. a. to twist; to retort.
retorcimiento, –*thimiĕn'tŏ*, sm. twisting, contortion.
retórica, –*tŏ'rikă*, sf. rhetoric.
retórico, ca, –*rikŏ*, a. rhetorical; –, sm. rhetorician.
retornar, –*tŏrnăr'*, v. a. to return, to turn, to twist; –, v. n. to return.
retorno, –*tŏr'nŏ*, sm. return; barter, exchange.   [change.
retorta, –*tŏr'tă*, sf. retort.
retortero, –*tĕr'ŏ*, sm. twirl, rotation; andar al –, to hover about.
retortijón, –*tĭ'hŏn'*, sm. twisting; – de tripas, gripes.
retozar, –*tŏthăr'*, v. n. to frisk, to skip; to play the fool; –, v. a. to tickle; to amuse.
retozo, –*tŏ'thŏ*, sm. lascivious gaiety.
retozón, ona, –*thŏn'*, a.wanton,romping.
retracción, –*trăkthiŏn'*, sf. retraction.
retractación, –*tăthiŏn'*, sf. retractation, recantation.
retractar, –*tăr'*, v. a. to retract, to unsay.
retracto, –*trăk'tŏ*, sm. (law) retraction.

retraer, –*trăĕr'*, v. a. to draw back; to dissuade; –se, to take refuge; to flee.
retranca, –*trăn'kă*, sf. large crupper.
retrasar, –*trăsăr'*, v. a. to defer, to put off; –, v. n. to retrograde, to fall off.
retraso, –*trăs'ŏ*, sm. lateness; (rail.) el tren ha tenido –, the train is overdue or late.
retratar, –*trătăr'*, v. a. to portray.
retratista, –*tis'tă*, sm. portrait-painter.
retrato, –*tră'tŏ*, sm. portrait, effigy.
retreta, –*trĕ'tă*, sf. (mil.) retreat, tattoo.
retrete, –*trĕ'tĕ*, sm. closet; water-closet.
retribución, –*tributhiŏn'*, sf. retribution.
retribuir, –*buir'*, v. a. to repay.
retroacción, –*trŏăkthiŏn'*, sf. retroaction.
retroactivo, va, –*ăktĕ'vŏ*, a. retroactive.
retroceder, –*thĕdĕr'*, v. n. to go backward, to fly back.
retrocesión, –*tshĕsiŏn'*, sf. retrocession.
retrogradar, –*grădăr'*, v. n. to retrograde.
retrógrado, da, *rĕtrŏ'grădŏ*, a. retrograde.
retrucar, –*trŭkăr'*, v. n. to screw back (at billiards).   [upon words.
retruécano, –*trŏĕ'kănŏ*, sm. pun, play
retruque, –*trŏ'kĕ*, sm. screw-back, cannoning back of a ball at billiards; over-bid at cards.   [jingle.
retumbar, –*tŭmbăr'*, v. n. to resound, to
retumbo, –*tŭm'bŏ*, sm. resonance, echo.
reuma, *rĕ'ŭmă*, sf. rheum.
reumático, ca, *rĕŭmă'tikŏ*, a. rheumatic.
reumatismo, –*tis'mŏ*, sm. rheumatism.
reunión, –*ŭniŏn'*, sf. reunion, meeting.
reunir, –*ŭnir'*, v. a. to reunite, to unite.
revalidación, –*vălidăthiŏn'*, sf. confirmation, ratification.
revalidar, –*dăr'*, v. a. to ratify, to confirm; –se, to be admitted to a higher post or class.
revelación, –*vĕlăthiŏn'*, sf. revelation.
revelar, –*lăr'*, v. a. to reveal.
revendedor, –*vĕndĕdŏr'*, sm. retailer, huckster.
revendedora, –*dŏ'ră*, sf. hucksteress.
revender, –*dĕr'*, v. a. to retail.
revenirse, –*vĕnir'sĕ*, v. r. to be pricked, to grow sour (of wine and conserves).
reventadero, –*tădĕ'rŏ*, sm. rough, uneven ground; laborious work.
reventar, –*tăr'*, v. n. to burst, to crack; to toil, to drudge; –, v. a. to molest, to harass.
rever, –*vĕr'*, v. a. to review, to revise.
reverberación, –*vĕrbĕrăthiŏn'*, sf. reverberation.
reverberar, –*răr'*, v. a. to reverberate.
reverdecer, –*vĕrdĕthĕr'*, v. n. to grow green again.   [respect, veneration.
reverencia, –*vĕrĕn'thiă*, sf. reverence.
reverenciar, –*thiăr'*, v. a. to venerate, to revere.
reverendas, –*rĕn'dăs*, sf. pl. dimissory letters; qualities worthy of reverence.
reverendo, da, –*dŏ*, a. reverend.
reverente, –*tĕ*, a. respectful, reverent.
reversión, –*vĕrsiŏn'*, sf. reversion, return.
reverso, –*vĕr'sŏ*, sm. reverse.

revés, –vĕs', sm. back-side; disappointment. misadventure.

revesado, da, –sā'dŏ, a. obstinate; difficult, entangled, perplexed, obscure.

revesino, –sē'nŏ, sm. game at cards.

revestir, –tĕstir', v. a. to dress, to put on clerical robes.

revisar, –vĭsär', v. a. to revise, to review.

revisión, –vĭsĭŏn', sf. revision.

revisor, –sŏr', sm. reviser, corrector.

revista, vĭs'tä, sf. review, revision.

revistar, –vĭstär', v. a. to revise a suit at law; to review troops.

revocable, –vŏkä'blĕ, a. revocable.

revocación, –käthĭŏn', sf. revocation.

revocadura, –dŏ'rä, sf. rough-cast.

revocar, –kär', v. a. to revoke.

revocatorio, ria, –kätŏ'rĭŏ, a. revoking, annulling.

revolcadero, –vŏlkädĕ'rŏ, sm. wallow.

revolcarse, –kär'sĕ, v. r. to wallow.

revolotear, –vŏlŏtĕär', v. n. to flutter.

revolteo, –lŏtĕ'ŏ, sm. fluttering.

revoltillo, –vŏltĭl'yŏ, sm. confusion, disorder. [ditious.

revoltoso, sa, –tŏ'sŏ, a. turbulent, seditious.

revolución, –vŏlŭthĭŏn', sf. revolution; disturbance, sedition. [disturber.

revolvedor, ra, –vĕdŏr', sm. & f. revolter, disturber.

revolver, –vĕr', v. a. to return; to revolve; –se, to move to and fro; to change (of the weather).

revólver, –vŏl'vĕr, sm. revolver, m.

revoque, –vŏ'kĕ, sm. brick-work; rough-cast. [volution, revolt.

revuelta, –vŭĕl'tä, sf. second turn, rerey, rĕ't, sm. king; king (in cards or chess).

reyerta, rĕyĕr'tä, sf. dispute.

rezagar, –thägär', v. a. & n. to leave behind; to d r; to remain behind.

rezago, –thá gŏ, sm. remainder, residue.

rezar, rĕthär', v. a. to pray, to say one's prayers.

rezo, rā'thŏ, sm. prayer; divine office.

rezumarse, rĕthŭmär'sĕ, v. r. to ooze, to run gently, to leak.

ría, rĭ'ä, sf. mouth of a river.

riada, rĭä'dä, sf. inundation, overflow.

ribazo, rĭbä'thŏ, sm. hillock, ridge.

ribera, –bĕ'rä, sf. shore, strand.

ribereño, ña, –bĕrĕn'yŏ, a. belonging to the sea-shore or bank of a river.

ribete, –bĕ'tĕ, sm. trimming, seam, border.

ribetear, –bĕtĕär', v. a. to hem, to border.

ricacho, ch, –käтsh'ŏ, a. very rich.

rico, ca, rĭ'kŏ, a. n.ble, rich; delicious.

ricohombre, –ŏm'brĕ, ricohome, –ŏ'mĕ, sm. grandee. [ridicule.

ridículez, –dĭkŭlĕth', sf. ridiculous action; ridicule.

ridiculizar, –lĭthär', v. a. to ridicule.

ridículo, la, –dĭ kŭlŏ, a. ridiculous.

riego, rĭĕ'gŏ, sm. irrigation.

rienda, rĭĕn'dä, sf. rein of a bridle; á-suelta, loose-reined, swiftly.

riesgo, rĭĕs'gŏ, sm. danger, risk. [tery.

rifa, rĕ'fä, sf. scuffle, dispute; raffle, lottery.

rifar, rĭfär', v. a. to raffle.

rigidez, rĭ'hĭdĕth', sf. rigidity. [severe.

rígido, da, rĕ'hĭdŏ, a. rigid, rigorous,

rigor, rĭgŏr', sm. rigour, rigor.

riguroso, sa, –gŭrŏ'sŏ, a. rigorous.

rija, rĭ'hä, sf. lachrymal fistula; quarrel,

rima, rĕ'mä, sf. rhyme. [scuffle, dispute.

rimar, rĭmär', v. a. & n. to investigate; to rhyme.

rimero, –mĕ'rŏ, sm. collection of things placed regularly one over another.

rincón, rĭnkŏn', sm. inside corner.

rinconada, –nä'dä, sf. corner formed by two houses, streets, &c.

rinconera, –nĕ'rä, sf. small triangular table placed in a corner.

ringlera, rĭnglĕ'rä, sf. row, file.

ringorango, –gŏrän'gŏ, sm. flourish with a pen; extravagant nicety in dress.

rinoceronte, rĭnŏthĕrŏn'tĕ, sm. rhinoceros.

riña, rĭn'yä, sf. quarrel, dispute.

riñón, rĭnyŏn', sm. kidney.

río, rĕ'ŏ, sm. river, stream.

riolada, rĭŏlä'dä, sf. assemblage of many things at one time.

riqueza, rĭkĕ'thä, sf. riches, wealth.

risa, rĭ'sä, sf. laugh, laughter.

risada, –sä'dä, sf. horse-laugh.

risco, rĭs'kŏ, sm. steep rock.

riscoso, sa, –kŏ'sŏ, a. steep and rocky.

risible, rĭsĕ'blĕ, a. risible, laughable.

ristra, rĭs'trä, sf. string of onions; row, file.

ristre, –trĕ, sm. socket for a lance.

risueño, na, rĭsŭĕn'yŏ, a. smiling.

rítmico, ca, rĭt'mĭkŏ, a. rhythmical.

ritmo, rĭt'mŏ, sm. rhyme.

rito, rĕ'tŏ, sm. rite, ceremony.

ritual, rĭtŭäl', a. & sm. ritual.

rival, rĭväl', sm. rival, competitor.

rivalidad, –lĭdäd', sf. rivalry. [with.

rivalizar, –lĭthär', v. a. to rival, to vie

rizar, rĭthär', v. a. to curl hair; to plait.

rizo, rĕ'thŏ, sm. curl, frizzle; crimping; cut velvet; –s, pl. short pieces of braided cordage.

ro, rŏ, word used to lull children to sleep.

robador, ra, rŏbädŏr', sm. & f. robber.

robar, –bär', v. a. to rob, to plunder; to abduct a woman.

roble, rŏ'blĕ, sm. oak-tree.

robledal, –blĕdäl', sm. oak-grove.

robo, rŏ'bŏ, sm. robbery, theft.

roborar, –rär', v. a. to corroborate, to give strength.

robre, rŏ'brĕ, sm. rubber (at whist).

robustez, –bŭstĕth', sf. robustness.

robusto, ta, –bŭs'tŏ a. robust, vigorous.

roca, rŏ'kä, sf. rock, cliff; hard substance; –s, pl. precipice.

rocalla, –käl'yä, sf. pieces of rock-crystal.

roce, rŏ'thĕ, sm. familiarity; friction.

rociada, –thĭä'dä, sf. aspersion, sprinkling; dew-drops; malicious censure.

rociador, –thĭädŏr', sm. instrument for sprinkling cloth.

rociar, –thĭär', v. a. to sprinkle; to scatter about; –, v. n. to fall (of dew).

rocín, _–thĕn′,_ sm. hack; heavy, stupid person.

rocinal, _–nāl′,_ a. belonging to a hack.

rocinante, _–nän′tĕ,_ sm. miserable hack.

rocío, _rŏthē′ŏ,_ sm. dew.

rodada, _–dā′dä,_ sf. rut, track of a wheel.

rodadura, _–dō′rä,_ sf. act of rolling.

rodaja, _–dā′h′ä,_ sf. rowel of a spur; jagging-iron used by pastry-cooks.

rodaje, _–dā′h′ĕ,_ sm. wheelworks.

rodapié, _–dāpĕ′,_ sm. fringe round the foot of a bedstead. [of a key.

rodaplancha, _–plän′tshä,_ sf. main ward

rodar, _rŏdär′,_ v. a. to roll.

rodear, _–dĕār′,_ v. n. to encompass; to go a round-about way; –, v. a. to wrap up, to circle, to compass.

rodela, _–dā′lä,_ sf. shield, target.

rodeo, _–dĕ′ŏ,_ sm. act of going round; circuitous way; delay; subterfuge.

rodete, _–dā′tĕ,_ sm. large wheel, formed of many pieces; bolster; splinter-bar; ward of a key. [sisting of many pieces.

rodezno, _–dĕth′nŏ,_ sm. large wheel, con-

rodilla, _–dēl′yä,_ sf. knee; rubber, clout; de –s, on one's knees. [knee.

rodillazo, _–yā′thŏ,_ sm. push with the

rodillo, _–dēl′yŏ,_ sm. roller.

rodo, _rŏ′dŏ,_ sm. rolling-stone.

rodrigar, _–drēgär′,_ v. a. to prop up vines.

rodrigón, _–gŏn′,_ sm. prop for vines.

roedor, ra, _rŏĕdŏr′,_ sm. & f. gnawer; de-

roedura, _–dō′rä,_ sf. gnawing. [tractor.

roer, _rŏĕr′,_ v. n. to gnaw, to corrode.

rogación, _–gäthĕon′,_ sf. petition, supplication; **–ones,** pl. Rogation days.

rogar, _–gär′,_ v. a. to entreat; to pray.

rogativa, _–tē′vä,_ sf. supplication, prayer.

rojez, _rŏ′hĕth′,_ sf. redness.

rojizo, za, _–hē′thŏ,_ a. reddish.

rojo, ja, _rŏ′h′ŏ,_ a. red; ruddy.

rol, _rŏl,_ sm. list, roll, catalogue.

rollizo, za, _rŏlyĕ′thŏ,_ a. plump, robust, chopping.

rollo, _rŏl′yŏ,_ sm. roll; spiral.

romadizo, _rŏmädĕ′thŏ,_ sm. catarrh.

romana, _rŏmä′nä,_ sf. steelyard.

romanar, _–när′,_ v. a. to weigh with a steelyard. [language; romance.

romance, _rŏmän′thĕ,_ sm. common Spanish

romancero, ra, _–thā′rŏ,_ a. romancing; –, sm. collection of romances or ballads; romancer.

romancista, _–thĭs′tä,_ sm. author who writes in the vulgar Spanish language; surgeon practiser.

romano, na, _rŏmä′nŏ,_ a. Roman.

rombo, _rŏm′bŏ,_ sm. rhomb.

romboide, _–bŏĭ′dĕ,_ sm. rhomboid.

romería, _rŏmĕrē′ä,_ sf. pilgrimage.

romero, _rŏmā′rŏ,_ sm. (bot.) rosemary.

romo, ma, _rŏ′mŏ,_ a. blunt; flat-nosed.

romper, _rŏmpĕr′,_ v. a. & n. to break, to dash, to fracture; to break up land; to pierce; to begin.

rompimiento, _–pĭmĕĕn′tŏ,_ sm. rupture; crack, cleft; first ploughing of land.

ron, _rŏn,_ sm. rum.

ronca, _rŏn′kä,_ sf. menace; boast, brag.

roncar, _–kär′,_ v. n. to snore; to make a harsh noise; to roar; to threaten, to boast, to brag. [evasions.

roncear, _–thĕär′,_ v. n. to defer; to use flattery.

roncería, _–thĕrē′ä,_ sf. laziness, tardiness;

roncero, ra, _–thā′rŏ,_ a. snarling, growling, flattering; slow, tardy (applied to the sailing of a ship).

ronco, ca, _rŏn′kä,_ a. hoarse; husky; coarse.

roncón, _–kŏn′,_ sm. drone of a bag-pipe.

roncha, _rŏn′tshä,_ sf. wheal, pustule.

ronda, _rŏn′dä,_ sf. night-patrol. [guard.

rondador, _–dädŏr′,_ sm. watchman, night-

rondar, _–där′,_ v. a. & n. to patrol; to take walks by night about the streets; to go rondel, _–dĕl′,_ sm. roundelay. [round.

rondín, _–dĭn′,_ sm. rounds of an officer visiting sentinels.

ronquear, _–kĕär′,_ v. n. to be hoarse.

ronquera, _–kā′rä,_ sf. hoarseness.

ronquido, _–kē′dŏ,_ sm. snore; rough, harsh ronzal, _–thäl′,_ sm. halter. [sound.

ronzar, _–thär′,_ v. a. to chew, to munch, to grind.

roña, _rŏn′yä,_ sf. scab, mange; craft, fraud, cunning; nastiness, filth. [gardliness.

roñería, _–yĕrē′ä,_ sf. craft, cunning; nig-

roñoso, sa, _–yŏ′sŏ,_ a. scabby.

ropa, _rŏ′pä,_ sf. cloth; stuff; clothing, wearing-apparel; robe.

ropaje, _rŏpä′h′ĕ,_ sm. clothing, drapery.

ropavejería, _–vĕ′hĕrē′ä,_ sf. frippery.

ropavejero, _–hā′rŏ,_ sm. fripperer; old-clothes-man. [clothes-shop; wardrobe.

ropería, _rŏpĕrē′ä,_ sf. trade in old clothes;

ropero, _rŏpā′rŏ,_ sm. clothes-merchant.

ropón, _rŏpŏn′,_ sm. wide, loose gown worn over the rest of the clothes.

roque, _rŏ′kĕ,_ sm. rook (at chess).

roquete, _rŏkā′tĕ,_ sm. roquet.

ros, _rŏs,_ sm. (mil.) Spanish shako.

rosa, _rŏ′sä,_ sf. rose; red spot appearing in any part of the body. [rosy.

rosado, da, _rŏsä′dä,_ a. crimsoned, flushed.

rosal, _–säl′,_ sm. rose-bush, rosier.

rosario, _–sä′rĭŏ,_ sm. rosary.

rosca, _rŏs′kä,_ sf. screw; any thing round and spiral; sea-rusk (kind of biscuit).

roseta, _rŏsā′tä,_ sf. rosette. [tecture).

rosetón, _–sĕtŏn′,_ sm. carved rose (archi-

rosicler, _rŏsĭklĕr′,_ sm. bright rose colour.

rosoli, _rŏsŏ′lĭ,_ sm. rossolis.

rosquilla, _rŏskĭl′yä,_ sf. sweet spiral-shaped cake.

rostro, _rŏs′trŏ,_ sm. feature, human face.

rota, _rŏ′tä,_ sf. rout, defeat; ecclesiastical court in some Catholic countries.

rotación, _–täthĭon′,_ sf. rotation.

roto, ta, _rŏ′tŏ,_ a. broken, destroyed; leaky; debauched. [pan.

rótula, _rŏ′tūlä,_ sf. whirlbone of the knee-

rotular, _rŏtūlär′,_ v. a. to inscribe, to label.

rótulo, _rŏ′tūlŏ,_ sm. inscription put on books and papers, label; printed bill posted up in public places.

rotura, _rŏtō′rä,_ sf. rupture, crack, cleft.

roya, *rṓyä*, sf. rust, corn-blight; (bot.) madder.

rozadura, *rṓthädṓrä*, sf. graze, scratch.

rozagante, *–gän'tē*, a. trailing, sweeping (of gowns); splendid.

rozar, *–thär'*, v. a. to stub up; to nibble the grass; to scrape; to touch slightly; to cut each other; to falter, to stammer.

roznar, *rṓthnär'*, v. a. to chew, to nibble; to bray.

roznido, *–nēdṓ*, sm. noise made by the teeth in eating, smacking of the lips; braying of an ass. [weeding.

rozo, *rṓthṓ*, sm. chip of wood; stubbing.

rubf, *rṓbē'*, sm. ruby.

rubia, *rṓbēä*, sf. (bot.) madder.

rubicundo, **da**, *rṓbēkän'dṓ*, a. reddish, rubicund. [sm. red gurnard.

rubio, **bia**, *rṓbēō*, a. reddish, ruddy; –,

rublo, *rṓblṓ*, sm. rouble.

rubor, *rṓbōr'*, sm. blush; bashfulness.

rúbrica, *rṓbrēkä*, sf.bloodstone; red mark; flourish at the end of a signature; rubric.

rubricar, *rṓbrēkär'*, v. a. to mark with a red colour; to sign with one's peculiar flourish; to subscribe, sign and seal a writing.

rucio, **cia**, *rṓthēṓ*, a. light gray; grayhaired; **– rodado**, *–rōdädṓ*, dapple-grey.

ruda, *rṓdä*, sf. rue. [horses.

rudeza, *rṓdāthä*, sf. roughness, rudeness, stupidity.

rudimento, *rṓdēmēn'tṓ*, sm. principle; beginning; **–s**, pl. rudiments. [stupid.

rudo, **da**, *rṓdṓ*, a. rude, rough, coarse;

rueca, *rṓā'kä*, sf. distaff. [sun-fish.

rueda, *rṓā'dä*, sf. wheel; circle; crown;

ruedo, *rṓā'dṓ*, sm. rotation; circuit; border, selvage; round mat to sit upon.

ruego, *rṓā'gṓ*, sm. request, prayer, petition, entreaty, supplication.

rufián, *rṓfēän'*, sm. pimp, pander.

rufo, **fa**, *rṓfṓ*, a. red-haired; frizzled, curled. [the vapours, pl.

rugido, *rṓhē'dṓ*, sm. roaring of a lion;

rugir, *rṓhēr'*, v. n. to roar, to bellow; to

rugoso, **sa**, *rṓgṓsṓ*, a. wrinkled. [crack.

ruibarbo, *rṓēbär'bṓ*, sm. rhubarb.

ruido, *rṓē'dṓ*, sm. noise. [loud.

ruidoso, **sa**, *rṓēdṓsṓ*, a. noisy, clamorous, wicked; avaricious.

ruin, *rṓēn'*, a. mean, vile, despicable;

ruina, *rṓē'nä*, sf. ruin, downfall, destruction; **–**, pl. ruins of an edifice.

ruindad, *rṓēndäd'*, sf. meanness, baseness, avarice. [destructive.

ruinoso, **sa**, *rṓēnṓsṓ*, a. worthless, ruinous,

ruiseñor, *rṓēsēnyṓr'*, sm. nightingale.

rumbo, *rṓm'bṓ*, sm. point of the compass; road, route, way; pomp, ostentation.

rumboso, **sa**, *rṓmbṓsṓ*, a. pompous, liberal.

rumiar, *rṓmēär'*, v. a. to ruminate.

rumión, **ona**, *rṓmēṓn'*, a. ruminating much; (fig.) harping on a subject.

rumor, *rṓmōr'*, sm. rumour, report.

runrún, *rṓnrṓn'*, sm. rumour, report.

ruptura, *rṓptṓ'rä*, sf. rupture.

rural, *rṓräl'*, a. rural. [coarseness.

rusticidad, *rṓstēthēdäd'*, sf. rusticity;

rústico, **ca**, *rṓs'tēkṓ*, a. rustic; **–**, sm. peasant.

ruta, *rṓ'tä*, sf. route, itinerary.

rutilar, *rṓtēlär'*, v. n. (poet.) to radiate, to shine. [from custom.

rutina, *rṓtē'nä*, sf. routine, habit formed

rutinero, *rṓtēnē'rṓ*, a. of routine.

S.

sábado, *sä'bädṓ*, sm. Saturday; sabbath.

sábana, *sä'bänä*, sf. sheet; altar-cloth.

sabandija, *säbändē'h'ä*, sf. grub, beetle, insect.

sabañón, *säbänyṓn'*, sm. chilblain.

sabatina, *säbätē'nä*, sf. divine service on Saturday; literary exercise performed by students on Saturday evening.

sabedor, **ora**, *säbēdṓr'*, sm. & f. wellinformed person.

saber, *säbēr'*, v. a. to know; to experience; **–**, v. imp. to have a taste of; **–**, sm. learning, knowledge. [formed.

sabido, **da**, *säbē'dṓ*, a. learned, well in-

sabiduría, *säbēdṓrē'ä*, sf. learning, knowledge, wisdom; notice.

sabiendas, *säbēēn'däs*, **á –**, ad. knowingly.

sabina, *säbē'nä*, sf. (bot.) savin, sabine.

sabio, **bia**, *sä'bēṓ*, a. sage, wise; **–**, sm. f. sage, a wise person.

sabiondez, *säbēṓndēth'*, sf. sciolism.

sabiondo, **da**, *säbēṓn'dṓ*, a. sciolist.

sablazo, *säblä'thṓ*, sm. sabre-cut.

sable, *sä'blē*, sm. sabre, cutlass.

sabor, *säbṓr'*, sm. relish, taste, savour.

saborear, *säbṓrēär'*, v. a. to give a taste or zest; to engage one's affections; **–se**, to swallow slowly and with great enjoyment; to be pleased.

saboyana, *säbṓyä'nä*, sf. wide petticoat.

sabroso, **sa**, *säbrṓ'sṓ*, a. savoury; palatable; salted, saltish. [hound.

sabueso, *säbṓē'sṓ*, sm. blood-hound; lime-

saca, *sä'kä*, sf. exportation; saok.

sacabala, *–bä'lä*, sf. bullet-drawer (used by surgeons).

sacabocado(s), *–bṓkä'dṓ(s)*, sm. puncheon.

sacabotas, *–bṓ'täs*, sf. boot-jack.

sacabuche, *–bä'tsh'ē*, sf. sackbut.

sacacorchos, *–kṓr'tshṓs*, sm. cork-screw.

sacadinero(s), *–dēnē'rṓ(s)*, sm. catchpenny; tinsel finery.

sacadura, *–dṓ'rä*, sf. sloping cut by which tailors make clothes fit better.

sacaliña, *–lēn'yä*, sf. knack of tricking a person out of something with art and craft. [of clothes.

sacamanchas, *–män'tshäs*, sm. scourer

sacamuelas, *–mṓē'läs*, sm. tooth-drawer, dentist. [at cards).

sacanete, *–nē'tē*, sm. lansquenet (game

sacapotras, *–pṓ'träs*, sm. nickname for a bad surgeon.

sacar, sākăr´, v. a. to draw out; to except; to pull out; to draw lots; to bowl (at play).

sacatón, -tōn´, sm. cork-screw.

sacatrapos, -trā´pŏs, sm. worm of a ramrod.

sacerdocio, sātherdŏ´thĭŏ, sm. priesthood.

sacerdotal, -dŏtăl´, a. sacerdotal.

sacerdote, -dŏ´tĕ, sm. priest, clergyman.

sacerdotisa, -dŏtē´să, sf. priestess.

saciar, sāthĭăr´, v. a. to satiate.

saciedad, sāthĭĕdăd´, sf. satiety.

saco, sā´kŏ, sm. sack; sagum.

sacramental, sākrămĕntăl´, a. sacramental.

sacramentar, -mĕntăr´, v. a. to administer the sacraments.

sacramento, -mĕn´tŏ, sm. sacrament.

sacrificadero, sākrĭfĭkădă´rŏ, sm. place of sacrifice.

sacrificar, -kăr´, v. a. to sacrifice; -se, to devote oneself to religion.

sacrificio, -fē´thĭŏ, sm. sacrifice.

sacrilegio, -lĕ´hĭŏ, sm. sacrilege.

sacrilego, ga, sākrē´lĕgŏ, a. sacrilegious.

sacristán, sākrĭstăn´, sm. sacristan, sexton.

sacristana, -tă´nă, sf. nun sacristan.

sacristanía, -tănē´ă, sf. office of a sexton.

sacristía, -tē´ă, sf. sacristy, vestry.

sacro, cra, sā´krŏ, a. holy, sacred.

sacrosanto, ta, -sān´tŏ, a. very holy.

sacudida, sākūdē´dă, sf. shake, jerk.

sacudidura, -dĭdō´ră, sf. dusting, cleaning.

sacudimiento, -dĭmĭĕn´tŏ, sm. shaking off.

sacudir, -dĭr´, v. a. to shake, to jerk; to dart; to beat, to chastise with blows; -se, to reject with disdain.

saeta, sāĕ´tă, sf. arrow, dart.

saetar, sāĕtăr´, v. a. to wound with an arrow.

saetazo, sāĕtă´thŏ, a. arrow-wound.

saetín, sāĕtĭn´, sm. mill-trough; peg, pin, tack; satin.

sáfico, oa, sā´fĭkŏ, a. (poet.) sapphic.

sagacidad, sāgăthĭdăd´, sf. sagacity.

sagaz, sāgăth´, a. sagacious.

Sagitario, sāhĭtă´rĭŏ, Sagittarius, sā-hĭtă´rĭŭs, sm. Archer (sign of the zodiac).

sagrado, da, sāgră´dŏ, a. sacred, consecrated; —, sm. asylum.

sagrario, sāgră´rĭŏ, sm. place in a church wherein consecrated things are deposited; cibary.

sahumar, sāŭmăr´, v. a. to perfume; to smoke, to fume.

saín, sā´ĭn, sm. grease or fat of an animal; dirt on clothes.

sainete, -nā´tĕ, sm. farce; flavour, relish; delicate bit.

sajadura, sā´hădō´ră, sf. scarification.

sajar, sāhăr´, v. a. to scarify.

sal, săl, sf. salt.

sala, să´lă, sf. hall, saloon; council-room, session-room; guest-chamber.

saladero, -dā´rŏ, sm. salting-place; salting-tub.

salado, da, sălă´dŏ, a. salted; witty, facetious.

saladura, -dō´ră, sf. salting; saltness.

salamandra, -măn´dră, sf. salamander.

salar, sălăr´, v. a. to salt.

salario, sălă´rĭŏ, sm. salary.

salazón, sălăthŏn´, sf. seasoning, salting.

salcochar, sălkŏtshăr´, v. a. to dress meat, leaving it half raw and without salt.

salchicha, sāltshĭts´ă, sf. sausage.

salchichería, -tshĕrē´ă, sf. shop in which sausages are sold.

salchichero, -tshē´rŏ, a. maker or seller of sausages.

saledizo, za, sālĕdē´thŏ, a. salient.

salero, sālē´rŏ, sm. salt-cellar.

saleroso, sālĕrŏ´sŏ, a. graceful.

salida, sālē´dă, sf. outgoing; outlet; issue; result; (mil.) sally; —, a. in heat (or a bitch).

salina, sālē´nă, sf. salt-pit, salt-work, salt-mine.

salinero, sālĭnā´rŏ, sm. salter; salt-maker.

salino, na, sālē´nŏ, a. a saline.

salir, sālĭr´, v. n. ir. to go out of a place; to depart, to set out; to appear; to issue from; to cost; -se, to drop, to leak.

salitrado, da, sālĭtră´dŏ a. impregnated with saltpetre.

salitral, -trăl´, sm. saltpetre-works.

salitre, sālē´trĕ, sm. saltpetre.

salitrería, sālĭtrĕrē´ă, sf. saltpetre-work.

salitrero, -trā´rŏ, sm. saltpetre-refiner.

salitroso, sa, -trŏ´sŏ, a. nitrous.

saliva, sālē´vă, sf. saliva.

salivar, sālĭvăr´, v. n. to spit, to salivate.

salivoso, sa, -vŏ´sŏ, a. salivous.

salmear, sālmĕăr´, salmodiar, -mŏdĭăr´, v. a. to sing psalms.

salmista, -mĭs´tă, sm. psalmist.

salmo, sāl´mŏ, sm. psalm.

salmodia, sālmŏ´dĭă, sf. psalmody.

salmón, sālmŏn´, sm. salmon.

salmonado, da, -nā´dŏ, a. tasting like salmon.

salmonete, -nā´tĕ, sm. red-mullet.

salmuera, sālmŭā´ră, sf. brine.

salobre, sālŏ´brĕ, a. brackish, saltish.

salomar, sālŏmăr´, v. n. (mar.) to sing out.

salón, sālŏn´, sm. saloon.

salpicar, sālpĭkăr´, v. a. to bespatter.

salpicón, -pĭkŏn´, sm. salmagundy.

salpimentar, -pĭmĕn´tăr´, v. a. to season with pepper and salt.

salpimienta, -pĭmĭĕn´tă, sf. mixture of salt and pepper.

salpresar, -prĕsăr´, v. a. to salt.

salpullido, -pŭlyē´dŏ, sm. (med.) eruption, rash.

salpullir, -pŭlyĭr´, v. a. to break out in pustules or pimples on the skin.

salsa, săl´să, sf. sauce.

salsera, sālsē´ră, sf. saucer.

salserilla, -sĕrē´lyă, sf. small cup for colours.

salsero, -să´rŏ, a. (bot.) Spanish thyme.

saltabancos, sāltăbăn´kŏs, sm. saltinbanco, mountebank.

saltadero, -tādē´rŏ, sm. leaping-place; artificial fountain, jet.

saltador, da, -tă´dŏ, a. prominent, jutting.

saltador, -tādŏr´, sm. jumper, leaper.

saltar, -tăr´, v. n. to leap, to jump; to be irritated or agitated.

saltarín, ina, -tărĭn´, sm. & f. dancer; restless young rake.

saltatriz, -tărĭth´, sf. female rope-dancer.

salteador, -tĕădŏr´, sm. highwayman.

saltear, _–těǎr´,_ v. a. to rob on the highway.

salterio, _–tě´rǐǒ,_ sm. Psalter.

salto, _sǎl´tǒ,_ sm. leap, jump.

saltón, _sǎltǒn´,_ sm. grasshopper; **–, ona,** a. hopping or leaping much.

salubre, _sǎlǒ´brě,_ a. healthful.

salubridad, _sǎlǒbrǐdǎd´,_ sf. healthfulness.

salud, _sǎlǔd´,_ sf. health, sound state of the body. [some.

saludable, _–dǎ´blě,_ a. salubrious, wholesome.

saludador, _–dǎ´dǒr,_ sm. greeter; quack.

saludar, _–dǎr´,_ v. a. to greet, to salute.

saludo, _sǎlǒ´dǒ,_ sm. (mil.) salute.

salutación, _sǎlǒtǎthǒn´,_ sf. salutation, greeting; exordium. [arms.

salva, _sǎl´vǎ,_ sf. (mil.) salute with firearms.

salvación, _–vǎthǒn´,_ sf. salvation.

salvado, _–vǎ´dǒ,_ sm. bran.

Salvador, _–dǒr´,_ sm. Saviour.

salvaguardia, _–gǎr´dǐǎ,_ sf. safeguard.

salvaje, _sǎlvǎ´hě,_ a. savage. [manners.

salvajería, _–hěrǐ´ǎ,_ sf. rusticity, uncouth

salvam(i)ento, _–m(ǐ)ěn´tǒ,_ sm. safety; salvation; asylum. [escape from danger.

salvar, _sǎlvǎr´,_ v. a. to save; **–se,** so to [salve! _sǎl´vě,_ God bless you!

salvia, _sǎl´vǐǎ,_ sf. (bot.) sage.

salvilla, _–vǐl´yǎ,_ sf. salver. [excepting.

salvo, va, _sǎl´vǒ,_ a. saved, –, ad. saving.

salvoconducto, _–kǒndǔk´tǒ,_ sm. safeconduct. [conduct.

sallar, _sǎl´yǎr,_ v. a. to weed.

sallo, _sǎl´yǒ,_ sm. hoe.

sambenito, _sǎmběnǐ´tǒ,_ sm. garment, with a yellow cross at back and front, worn by penitents of the Inquisition; note [of infamy.

san, _sǎn,_ a. saint.

sanable, _sǎnǎ´blě,_ a. curable, healable.

sanalotodo, _–lǒtǒ´dǒ,_ sm. panacea, general remedy. [ably.

sanamente, _–měn´tě,_ ad. naturally; agreeably.

sanar, _sǎnǎr´,_ v. a. & n. to heal.

sanción, _sǎnthǒn´,_ sf. sanction.

sancionar, _–thǐǒnǎr´,_ v. a. to sanction.

sandalia, _–dǎ´lǐǎ,_ sf. sandal.

sándalo, _sǎn´dǎlǒ,_ sm. bergamot-mint; sandal-wood.

sandez, _sǎnděth´,_ sf. folly, stupidity.

sandio, dia, _sǎn´dǐǒ,_ a. foolish, nonsensical.

saneamiento, _sǎněǎmǐěn´tǒ,_ sm. surety, bail. [demnify.

sanear, _sǎněǎr´,_ v. a. to give bail; to insanedrín, _–drǐn´,_ sm. sanhedrim.

sangradera, _sǎngrǎdě´rǎ,_ sf. lancet.

sangrador, _–dǒr´,_ sm. blood-letter.

sangradura, _–dǒ´rǎ,_ sf. bleeding.

sangrar, _sǎngrǎr´,_ v. a. & n. to bleed; –, –se, to be bled.

sangre, _sǎn´grě,_ sf. blood; á – fria, in cool blood; á – y fuego, without mercy.

sangría, _–grě´ǎ,_ sf. bleeding; wound, incision.

sangriento, ta, _–grǐěn´tǒ,_ a. bloody, stained with blood, gory; blood-thirsty.

sanguijuela, _–gǐhǒě´lǎ,_ sf. leech; sharper.

sanguinaria, _–gǐnǎ´rǐǎ,_ sf. knot-grass; sanguine (a stone). [cruel, bloody.

sanguinario, ria, _–rǐǒ,_ a. sanguinary,

sanguíneo, nea, _–gǐ´něǒ,_ a. sanguine; sanguineous. [sacramental element.

sanguis, _sǎngǐs´,_ sm. blood of Christ, as

sanidad, _sǎnǐdǎd´,_ sf. soundness, health.

sanjuanista, _–hǒǎnǐs´tǎ,_ sm. knight of the order of St. John of Jerusalem.

sano, na, _sǎ´nǒ,_ a. sound, sane.

Santabárbara, _sǎntǎbǎr´bǎrǎ,_ sf. (mar.) powder-magazine. [tuary.

santasantórum, _–sǎntǒ´rǔm,_ sm. sanc-

santiaguista, _sǎntǐǎgǐs´tǎ,_ sm. knight of St. James. [ling of an eye.

santiamén, _–ǎměn´,_ sm. moment, twink-

santidad, _–dǎd´,_ sf. sanctity.

santificación, _–fǐkǎthǒn´,_ sf. sanctification.

santificador, _–fǐkǎdǒr´,_ sm. sanctifier.

santificar, _–fǐkǎr´,_ v. a. to sanctify; to justify.

santiguador, ra, _–gǐǎdǒr´,_ sm. & r. one who cures by making the sign of the cross.

santiguar, _–gǐǎr´,_ v. a. to make the sign of the cross over a sick person; to chastise, to punish. [moniousness.

santimonia, _–mǒ´nǐǎ,_ sf. sanctity; sancti-

santo, ta, _sǎn´tǒ,_ a. & sm. saint, holy; sacred; image of a saint; (mil.) watchword. [monk.

santón, _sǎntǒn´,_ sm. hypocrite; Moorish

santoral, _–tǒrǎl´,_ sm. lives of the saints; church-choir book, hymn-book.

santuario, _–tǒǎ´rǐǒ,_ sm. sanctuary.

santurrón, ona, _–tǔrrǒn´,_ sm. & f. & a. hypocrite pretending holiness.

santurronería, _–něrě´ǎ,_ sf. hypocrisy.

saña, _sǎn´yǎ,_ sf. anger, passion.

sañudo, da, _sǎnyǒ´dǒ,_ a. furious, enraged.

sapo, _sǎ´pǒ,_ sm. large toad.

saporífero, ra, _–rǐ´fěrǒ,_ a. saporific.

saque, _sǎ´kě,_ sm. striking out the ball.

saqueador, ra, _sǎkěǎdǒr´,_ sm. & f. ransacker, freebooter. [plunder.

saquear, _sǎkěǎr´,_ v. a. to ransack, to

saqueo, _sǎkě´ǒ,_ sm. pillage, freebooting.

sarampión, _sǎrǎmpǐǒn´,_ sm. measles, pl.

sarao, _sǎrǎ´ǒ,_ sm. ball, dance.

sarcasmo, _sǎrkǎs´mǒ,_ sm. sarcasm.

sarcástico, ca, _–kǎs´tǐkǒ,_ a. sarcastic.

sarcófago, _–kǒ´fǎgǒ,_ sm. sarcophagus.

sardina, _–dě´nǎ,_ sf. sardine, anchovy.

sardinero, ra, _–dǐně´rǒ,_ sm. & f. dealer in anchovies; –, a. belonging to anchovies.

sardio, _sǎr´dǐǒ,_ sardo, _–dǒ,_ sm. sardine (a stone). [cious stone).

sardónice, _–dǒ´nǐtsě,_ sf. sardonyx (pre-

sarga, _sǎr´gǎ,_ sf. serge.

sargento, _–hěn´tǒ,_ sm. serjeant.

sarmiento, _–mǐěn´tǒ,_ sm. vine shoot.

sarna, _sǎr´nǎ,_ sf. itch; mange; (fig) envy.

sarnoso, sa, _–nǒ´sǎ,_ a. itchy, scabby, mangy. [rescence.

sarpullido, _–pǔlyě´dǒ,_ sm. flea-bite, efflo-

sarpullir, _–pǔlyǐr´,_ v. n. to be flea-bitten; –, –se, to be full of flea-bites.

sarracina, _–rǎthě´nǎ,_ sf. tumultuous contest between a number of persons.

sarria, *sār'rĭä*, sf. wide net made of ropes, in which straw is carried.

sarro, *sār'rŏ*, sm. incrustation of the tongue in violent fevers; foulness of the teeth; sediment which adheres to vessels.

sarroso, **sa**, *–rŏ'sŏ*, a. incrusted.

sarta, *sār'tä*, sf. string of beads, pearls, &c.; string, row.

sartén, *sārtĕn'*, sf. frying-pan, saucepan.

sartenada, *–nä'dä*, sf. saucepan-full.

sartenazo, *–nä'thŏ*, sm. blow with a frying-pan; heavy blow.

sastre, *sās'trĕ*, sm. tailor.

sastrería, *–rē'ä*, sf. tailor's shop.

Satanás, *sätänäs'*, sm. Satan.

satélite, *sätē'lĭtĕ*, sm. bailiff, constable; satellite.

sátira, *sä'tĭrä*, sf. satire.

satírico, **ca**, *–tē'rĭkŏ*, a. satirical.

satirizar, *–tĭrĭthär'*, v. a. to satirize.

sátiro, *sä'tĭrŏ*, sm. satyr.

satisfacción, *sätĭsfäkthŏn'*, sf. satisfaction; presumption; confidence.

satisfacer, *–fäthĕr'*, v. a. to satisfy; to atone; **–se**, to satisfy oneself; to vindicate oneself.

satisfactorio, **ria**, *–fäktŏ'rĭŏ*, a. satisfactory.

satisfecho, **cha**, *–fĕtshŏ*, a. satisfied.

sátrapa, *sä'träpä*, sm. satrap; sly, crafty fellow.

saturación, *sätŭräthŏn'*, sf. (chem.) saturation.

saturnal, *sätŭrnäl'*, a. saturnalian.

Saturno, *sätŭr'nŏ*, sm. Saturn; (chem.) lead.

sauce, *sä'ŭthĕ*, sm. (bot.) willow.

saúco, *sä'ŭkŏ*, sf. (bot.) elder.

sauquillo, *säŭkēl'yŏ*, sm. (bot.) dwarf-elder.

savia, *sä'vĭä*, sf. sap.

saya, *sä'yä*, sf. skirt; ancient tunic or gown worn by men.

sayal, *säyäl'*, sm. sackcloth.

sayalete, *–lē'tĕ*, sm. thin or light stuff.

sayo, *sä'yŏ*, sm. large wide coat without buttons; any loose coat or dress.

sayón, *säyŏn'*, sm. corpulent, ill-looking fellow.

sayuelo, *säyŭē'lŏ*, sm. small jacket, little frock.

sazón, *säthŏn'*, sf. maturity; season, taste, flavour; opportunity; **en –**, seasonably, opportunely.

sazonadamente, *–nädämĕn'tĕ*, ad. maturely, seasonably.

sazonado, **da**, *–nä'dŏ*, a. witty.

sazonar, *–när'*, v. a. to season; to mature **–se**, to ripen.

se, *sĕ*, pn. (reflexive pronoun).

sebo, *sä'bŏ*, sm. suet; (fig.) large capital, great fortune.

seboso, **sa**, *sĕbŏ'sŏ*, a. fat, greasy.

seca, *sā'kä*, sf. drought, dry weather; inflammation and swelling in the glands.

secadera, *–dä'rä*, sm. place where fruit is dried.

secamente, *–mĕn'tĕ*, ad. drily, briefly.

secano, *sĕkä'nŏ*, sm. dry, arable land which is not irrigated.

secansa, *sĕkän'sä*, sf. game at cards.

secante, *–kän'tĕ*, sm. drying-oil used for painting; **–**, sf. (geom.) secant.

secar, *–kär'*, v. a. to dry; **–se**, to grow dry; to become meagre; to decay.

sección, *sĕkthŏn'*, sf. section.

seco, **ca**, *sā'kŏ*, a. dry; not rainy; arid, sapless; meagre; barren.

secreta, *sĕkrā'tä*, sf. privy, water-closet; **–s**, pl. private orisons said in a low voice by the priest at the beginning of the mass.

secretaria, *sĕkrĕtä'rĭä*, sf. secretary's wife; lady's secretary or amanuensis.

secretaría, *–tärē'ä*, sf. secretaryship.

secretario, *–tä'rĭŏ*, sm. confidant; secretary. **[–**, sm. secrecy.

secreto, **ta**, *sĕkrā'tŏ*, a. secret; hidden;

secta, *sĕk'tä*, sf. sect; doctrine.

sectario, **ria**, *–tä'rĭŏ*, a. & sm. & f. sectarian, sectary.

secuaz, *sĕkŭäth'*, a. & sm. sectary.

secuela, *–kŭā'lä*, sf. sequel, continuation.

secuencia, *–kŭĕn'thĭä*, sf. sequence in prose or verse said in mass after the epistles.

secuestrar, *–kŭĕsträr'*, v. a. to sequestrate.

secuestro, *–kŭĕs'trŏ*, sm. sequestration.

secular, *sĕkŭlär'*, a. secular; laical.

secularización, *–rĭthäthŏn'*, sf. secularization.

secularizar, *–thär'*, v. a. to secularize.

secundario, **ria**, *sĕkŭndä'rĭŏ*, a. secondary.

secura, *sĕkŭ'rä*, sf. dryness. **[dary.**

sed, *sĕd*, sf. thirst; eagerness.

seda, *sā'dä*, sf. silk; silk-stuff.

sedal, *sĕdäl'*, sm. fishing-line; seton.

sede, *sä'dĕ*, sf. see, seat of episcopal power. **[or silver.**

sedear, *sĕdĕär'*, v. a. to clean jewels, gold

sedentario, **ria**, *–dĕntä'rĭŏ*, a. sedentary.

sedería, *–dĕrē'ä*, sf. silk, silk-stuff; silk-mercer's shop.

sedero, *–dä'rŏ*, sm. silk-mercer.

sedición, *–dĭthŏn'*, sf. sedition, mutiny.

sedicioso, **sa**, *–thĭŏ'sŏ*, a. seditious, mutinous. **[desirous.**

sediento, **ta**, *–dĭĕn'tŏ*, a. thirsty; eagerly

seducción, *–dŭkthŏn'*, sf. seduction.

seducir, *–dŭthĭr'*, v. a. to seduce.

seductivo, **va**, *–dŭktĭ'vŏ*, a. seductive.

seductor, *–tŏr'*, sm. seducer.

segadera, *sĕgädä'rä*, sf. reaping-hook.

segador, **ra**, *–dŏr'*, sm. & f. reaper, harvester. **[harvest.**

segar, *sĕgär'*, v. a. to reap, to mow, to

seglar, *sĕglär'*, a. worldly; secular.

segmento, *sĕgmĕn'tŏ*, sm. segment.

segregación, *sĕgrĕgäthŏn'*, sf. segregation, separation. **[apart.**

segregar, *–gär'*, v. a. to separate, to set

seguida, *sĕgē'dä*, sf. following; succession; **de –**, successively.

seguidilla, *–dĭl'yä*, sf. merry Spanish tune and dance; **–s**, pl. diarrhoea.

seguido, **da**, *sĕgē'dŏ*, a. continued, successive, followed.

seguidor, **ra**, *–dŏr'*, sm. & f. follower; ruled paper for teaching to write straight.

seguimiento, *–mĭĕn'tŏ*, sm. pursuit.

seguir, *sĕgĭr'*, v. a. to follow, to pursue; **–se**, to ensue; to succeed.

según, *–gŭn'*, pr. according to.

segundar, –gŭndăr', v. a. to second ; –, v. n. to be second.

segundario, ria, –dắ'rĭŏ, a. secondary.

segundo, da, –gŭn'dŏ, a. second ; –, sm. second (of time).

segundón, –dŏn', sm. second son of a family.

segur, –gŭr', sf. axe, large hatchet.

seguridad, –rĭdăd', sf. security, surety, certainty, safety.

seguro, ra, –gō'rŏ, a. secure, sure, certain ; firm, constant ; –, sm. leave, license ; insurance of ships ; safe-conduct.

seis, sĕ'ĭs, a. six, sixth ; –, sm. six.

seiscientos, tas, –thĭĕn'tŏs, a. six hundred.

selección, sĕlĕk'thĭŏn', sf. selection, choice.

selecto, ta, –lĕk'tŏ, a. select, choice.

selva, sĕl'vă, sf. forest.

sellador, sĕlyădŏr', sm. sealer.

selladura, –dō'ră, sf. sealing.

sellar, –yăr', v. a. to seal, to finish.

sello, sĕl'yŏ, sm. seal ; stamp-office ; – de franqueo, postage-stamp.

semana, sĕmă'nă, sf. week.

semanal, –năl', a. weekly.

semanario, ria, –nă'rĭŏ, sm. weekly work.

semblante, sĕmblăn'tĕ, sm. face ; countenance.

sembradío, día, –brădĭ'ŏ, a. fit or prepared for sowing.

sembrado, –bră'dŏ, sm. corn-field.

sembrador, –dŏr', sm. sower, seedsman.

sembradura, –dō'ră, sf. sowing.

sembrar, –brăr', v. a. to sow.

semejante, sĕmĕhăn'tĕ, a. similar, like.

semejanza, –'hăn'thă, sf. resemblance, likeness.

semejar, –'hăr', v. n. to resemble.

semen, sĕ'mĕn, sm. semen, animal seed.

sementera, sĕmĕn'tĕ'ră, sf. sowing ; land sown with seed.

semi, sĕ'mĭ, sm. (in comp.) half.

semibreve, –bră'vĕ, sf. (mus.) semibreve.

semicircular, –thĭrkŭlăr', a. semicircular.

semicírculo, –thĭr'kŭlŏ, sm. semicircle.

semicorchea, –kŏrtshĕ'ă, sf. (mus.) semiquaver.

semidiós, –dĭŏs', sm. demigod.

semidoble, –dŏ'blĕ, a. semidouble (of Catholic church-feasts).

semidocto, –dŏk'tŏ, sm. sciolist.

semifusa, –fū'să, sf. (mus.) double demisemiquaver.

semilla, sĕmĭl'yă, sf. seed.

semillero, –yĕ'rŏ, sm. seed-plot.

seminario, ria, sĕmĭnă'rĭŏ, sm. seminary ; origin, course.

seminarista, –nărĭs'tă, sm. scholar who boards and is instructed in a seminary.

semínima, sĕmĕ'nĭmă, sf. (mus.) crotchet.

semiplena, sĕmĭplĕ'nă, sf. (law) imperfect proof, half-proof.

semitono, –tŏ'nŏ, sm. (mus.) semitone.

semivocal, –vŏkăl', a. semivowel.

sémola, sĕ'mŏlă, sf. groats, grits.

sempiterna, sĕmpĭtĕr'nă, sf. serge-cloth.

sempiterno, na, –tĕr'nŏ, a. everlasting, sempiternal.

senado, sĕnă'dŏ, sm. senate.

senadoconsulto, –kŏnsŭl'to, sm. decree

senador, sĕnădŏr', sm. senator.

senatorio, ria, –tŏ'rĭŏ, a. senatorial.

sencillez, sĕnthĭlyĕth', sf. slightness, simplicity, silliness.

sencillo, lla, –thĭl'yŏ, a. simple, light ; silly, harmless.

senda, sĕn'dă, sf. sendero, –dĕ'rŏ, sm. path, footpath.

senescal, sĕnĕskăl', sm. seneschal.

seno, sĕ'nŏ, sm. breast, bosom ; lap ; womb ; hole, cavity ; sinus ; asylum, refuge.

sensación, sĕnsăthĭŏn', sf. sensation, feeling.

sensato, ta, –să'tŏ, a. judicious, reasonable.

sensibilidad, –sĭbĭlĭdăd', sf. sensibility.

sensible, –sĕ'blĕ, a. sensible ; sensitive ; causing pain.

sensitiva, –sĭtĭ'vă, sf. sensitive plant.

sensitivo, va, –tĭ'vŏ, a. sensitive ; sensible.

sensual, sĕnsŭăl', a. sensive ; sensual, lewd.

sensualidad, –lĭdăd', sf. sensuality ; carnal desire.

sentado, ta, sĕntă'dŏ, a. sedate, judicious.

sentar, –tăr', v. a. to fit, to set up ; to seat ; –se, to sit down.

sentencia, –tĕn'thĭă, sf. sentence ; opinion.

sentenciar, –thĭăr', v. a. to sentence, to pass judgment, to give one's opinion.

sentencioso, sa, –thĭŏ'sŏ, a. sententious.

sentido, sĕntĭ'dŏ, sm. sense ; reason ; signification ; meaning ; –, da, a. sensible, feeling.

sentimental, –mĕntăl', a. sentimental.

sentimiento, –mĭĕn'tŏ, sm. sentiment ; grief ; chink ; resentment ; judgment, opinion.

sentina, sĕntĭ'nă, sf. sink, drain ; (mar.) well.

sentir, sĕntĭr', v. a. to feel ; to hear, to perceive, to suffer ; to grieve, to mourn ; to judge, to think ; to foresee ; –se, to find oneself ; to be moved, to feel pain ; to crack (of walls, &c.).

seña, sĕn'yă, sf. sign, mark, token ; signal ; (mil.) password.

señal, sĕnyăl', sf. sign, signature, token ; landmark, footstep ; earnest-money.

señaladamente, –lădămĕn'tĕ, ad. especially ; namely.

señalado, da, –lă'dŏ, a. famous, celebrated, noble.

señalamiento, –lămĭĕn'tŏ, sm. assignation.

señalar, –lăr', v. a. to stamp, to mark ; to sign decrees ; to signalize ; –se, to distinguish oneself, to excel.

Señor, sĕnyŏr', sm. Lord ; Sir ; sacrament of the Eucharist ; master ; governor.

Señora, –yŏ'ră, sf. lady ; mistress ; gentlewoman.

señorear, –rĕăr', v. a. to master, to domineer ; to govern one's passions ; –se, to affect a peculiar gravity in one's deportment.

Señoría, –rĭ'ă, sf. lordship ; person to whom this title is given.

señoril, –rĭl', a. lordly.

señorío, –rĕ'ŏ, sm. seigniory ; self-control in action.

señuelo, –yŭĕ'lŏ, sm. lure, enticement.

separable, sĕpără'blĕ, a. separable.

separación, –răthĭŏn', sf. separation.

separar, –răr', v. a. to separate, –se, to separate, to be disunited ; to withdraw,

septentrión, *sĕptĕntrĭŏn'*, sm. septentrion, north. [northern.
septentrional, *–trĭŏnăl'*, a. septentrional.
septiembre, *sĕptĭĕm'brĕ*, sm. September.
séptimo, ma, *sĕp'tĭmŏ*, a. seventh.
sepulcral, *sĕpŭlkrăl'*, a. sepulchral.
sepulcro, *–pŭl'krŏ*, sm. sepulchre, grave, tomb; **Santo –**, Holy Sepulchre.
sepultar, *–pŭltăr'*, v. a. to bury, to inter.
sepultura, *–tŏŏ'ră*, sf. sepulture, interment.
sepulturero, *–tŭrĕ'rŏ*, sm. grave-digger, sexton.
sequedad, *sĕkĕdăd'*, sf. aridity, dryness.
sequía, *sĕkĭ'ă*, sf. dryness; thirst; drought.
séquito, *sĕ'kĭtŏ*, sm. retinue, suite; public applause.
ser, *sĕr'*, v. n. to be; to exist; to fall out; to be useful, to serve; **–**, sm. being.
sera, *sĕ'ră*, sf. large pannier.
seráfico, ca, *sĕră'fĭkŏ*, a. seraphic.
serafín, *sĕrăfĭn'*, sm. seraph.
serenar, *sĕrĕnăr'*, v. a. & n. to clear up; to settle, to grow clear; to pacify, to tranquillize; to be serene.
serenata, *–nă'tă*, sf. (mus.) serenade.
sereni, *–nĭ'*, sm. (mar.) yawl, light boat.
serenidad, *–nĭdăd'*, sf. serenity.
sereno, *–rĕ'nŏ*, sm. evening-dew; night-watch; **–, na**, a. serene, calm, quiet.
serie, *sĕ'rĭĕ*, sf. series.
seriedad, *sĕrĭĕdăd'*, sf. seriousness; sternness of mien; sincerity.
serijo, *–rĭ'hŏ*, **serillo**, *–rĭl'yŏ*, sm. small basket made of palm leaves.
serio, ria, *sĕ'rĭŏ*, a. serious; severe.
sermón, *sĕrmŏn'*, sm. sermon.
sermonear, *–nĕăr'*, v. a. to lecture, to reprimand, [carry figs, raisins, &c.
serón, *sĕrŏn'*, sm. large pannier used to
serosidad, *sĕrŏsĭdăd'*, sf. serosity.
seroso, sa, *–rŏ'sŏ*, a. serous. [a serpent.
serpentear, *sĕrpĕntĕăr'*, v. n. to move like
serpentina, *–tĭ'nă*, sf. cock of a gun-lock; culverin. [strument.
serpentón, *–pĕntŏn'*, sm. serpent (musical in-
serpiente, *–pĭĕn'tĕ*, sf. serpent.
sérpol, *sĕr'pŏl*, sm. (bot.) wild thyme.
serrador, *sĕrrădŏr'*, sm. sawyer.
serraduras, *–dŏŏ'răs*, sf. pl. saw-dust.
serrallo, *–răl'yŏ*, sm. seraglio.
serranía, *–rănĭ'ă*, sf. range of mountains, mountainous country.
serrano, na, *–ră'nŏ*, sm. & sf. mountaineer.
serrar, *–răr'*, v. a. to saw.
serrín, *–rĭn'*, sm. saw-dust.
serrucho, *–rŭsh'ŏ*, sm. hand-saw with a small handle.
servible, *–vĕ'blĕ*, a. fit for service.
servicial, *–vĭthĭăl'*, a. obsequious, serviceable; **–**, sm, clyster.
servicio, *–vĭthĭŏ*, sm. service; attendance; good-turn; divine service; sum of money voluntarily offered to the king; utility; close-stool; service for the table.
servidero, ra, *–vĭdĕ'rŏ*, a. serviceable.
servidor, *–dŏr'*, sm. servant, waiter.
servidora, *–dŏ'ră*, sf. maid-servant.

servidumbre, *–dŭm'brĕ*, sf. attendance, servitude; slavery; servility; privy, common-sewer.
servil, *sĕrvĭl'*, a. servile. [mon-sewer.
servilleta, *–lyĕ'tă*, sf. napkin.
servir, *sĕrvĭr'*, v. a. to serve; to pay voluntarily a sum of money to the king; to wait at table; **–se**, to deign, to please; to make use of.
sesada, *sĕsă'dă*, sf. fried brains.
sesenta, *sĕsĕn'tă*, sm. sixty; **–**, a. sixtieth.
sesentón, ona, *–tŏn'*, sm. person over sixty years of age.
sesera, *sĕsĕ'ră*, sf. brain-pan; brain.
sesgadura, *sĕsgădŏŏ'ră*, sf. slope, sloping.
sesgar, *–găr'*, v. a. to slope, to cut slantwise.
sesgo, *sĕs'gŏ*, sm. slope; **–, ga**, a. sloping, oblique; grave; **al –**, obliquely.
sesión, *sĕsĭŏn'*, sf. session; conference.
seso, *sĕ'sŏ*, sm. brain. [dinner.
sestear, *sĕstĕăr'*, v. n. to take a nap after
sesudo, da, *sĕsŏŏ'dŏ*, a. judicious, discreet, prudent.
seta, *sĕ'tă*, sf. brittle; fungus (in general).
setecientos, tas, *sĕtĕthĭĕn'tŏs*, a. seven
setena, *sĕtĕ'nă*, sf. seven. [hundred.
setenario, ria, *–tĕnă'rĭŏ*, a. septenary.
setenta, *–tĕn'tă*, a. seventy.
setentón, ona, *–tŏn'*, a. turned of seventy.
setentrión, *–trĭŏn'*, a. septentrional.
setiembre, *sĕtĭĕm'brĕ*, sm. September.
sétimo, ma, *sĕ'tĭmŏ*, a. seventh.
seto, *sĕ'tŏ*, sm. fence, enclosure, hedge.
setuagenario, ria, *sĕtŭăhĕnă'rĭŏ*, a. seventy years old.
setuagésimo, ma, *–'hĕ'sĭmŏ*, **setuplo, pla**, *sĕtŭ'plă*, a. sevenfold.
seudo, *sĕ'ŭdŏ*, sm. pseudo, false.
severidad, *sĕvĕrĭdăd'*, sf. severity; punctuality, exactness.
severo, ra, *sĕvĕ'rŏ*, a. severe, rigorous; grave, serious; punctual, exact.
sexagenario, ria, *sĕksăhĕnă'rĭŏ*, a. sixty years old.
sexagésimo, ma, *–'hă'sĭmŏ*, a. sixtieth.
sexenio, *sĕksĕ'nĭŏ*, sm. space of six years.
sexo, *sĕk'sŏ*, sm. sex.
sexta, *sĕks'tă*, sf. sequence of six cards at piquet; sixth (minor canonical hour after tierce). [containing canonical decrees.
sexto, ta, *sĕks'tŏ*, a. sixth; **–**, sm. book
si, *sĭ*, sm. (mus.) B, seventh note of the gamut; **–**, c. if, when.
sí, *sĭ'*, ad. yes, without doubt; indeed; **–**, pn. himself: **de por –**, apart; **de –**, spontaneously. [luxurious.
sibarítico, ca, *sĭbără'tĭkŏ*, a. sybaritical.
sibila, *sĭbĭ'lă*, sf. prophetess; sibyl.
sicomoro, *sĭkŏmŏ'rŏ*, sm. (bot.) sycamore.
sidra, *sĭ'dră*, sf. cider.
siega, *sĭĕ'gă*, sf. harvest, mowing.
siembra, *sĭĕm'bră*, sf. seed-time.
siempre, *sĭĕm'prĕ*, ad. always; **– jamás**, for ever and ever.
siempreviva, *–vĕ'vă*, sf. (bot.) immortelle.
sien, *sĭĕn'*, sf. temple (of the head).
sierpe, *sĭĕr'pĕ*, sf. serpent.
sierra, *sĭĕr'ră*, sf. saw; range of mountains.

siervo, va, *sĭĕr'vŏ,* sm. & f. serf, slave; servant (by courtesy).

siesta, *sĭĕs'tă,* sf. siesta, after-dinner nap.

siete, *sĭĕ'tĕ,* a. & sm. seven.

sietemesino, na, *-mĕs'nŏ,* a. born seven months after conception.

sigilo, *sĭ'hĭ'lŏ,* sm seal, secret.

sigiloso, sa, *-lŏ'sŏ,* a. reserved; silent.

siglo, *sĕ'glŏ,* sm. century.

signar, *sĭgnär',* v. a. to sign, to seal; -se, to make the sign of the cross.

signatura, *-tŏ'rä,* sf. sign, mark, signature (in printing). [cation.

significación, *sĭgnĭfĭkăthĭŏn',* sf. signifi-

significado, *-fĭkä'dŏ,* sm. signification.

significar, *-fĭkär',* v. a, to signify.

significativo, va, *-fĭkătĭvŏ,* a. signifi-

signo, *sĭg'nŏ,* sm. sign, mark. [cant.

siguiente, *sĭgĭĕn'tĕ,* a. following, successive, sequent. [position.

sílaba, *sĭ'lăbă,* sf. syllable; metrical com-

silabario, *-bă'rĭŏ,* sm. primer.

silabear, *-bĕär',* v a. to spell.

silbar, *sĭlbär',* v a. to hiss; -, v. n. to whistle.

silbato, *sĭlbä'tŏ,* sm. whistle.

silbido, *sĭlbĭ'dŏ,* **silbo,** *sĭl'bŏ,* sm. hiss, whistling. [silence! hush!

silencio, *sĭlĕn'thĭŏ,* sm. silence; I-!

silencioso, sa, *-thĭŏ'sŏ,* a. silent.

silo, *sĕ'lŏ,* sm. subterranean granary for wheat.

silogismo, *sĭlŏ'hĭs'mŏ,* sm. syllogism.

silogizar, *sĭlŏ'hĭhär',* v. a. to reason, to argue.

silvestre, *sĭlvĕs'trĕ,* a. wild, uncultivated; savage.

silla, *sĭl'yă,* sf. chair; see; saddle; seat; - de manos, sedan-chair; - poltrona, elbow-chair; de - á -, face to face.

sillar, *sĭlyär',* sm. square hewn stone.

sillería, *-yĕrĕ'ä,* sf. set of chairs, saddler's shop; stalls about the choir of a church; building of hewn stone.

sillero, *sĭlyĕ'rŏ,* sm. saddler, chair-maker.

silleta, *sĭlyĕ'tă,* sf. close-stool. [maker.

silletero, *-yĕtĕ'rŏ,* sm. chairman; chair-

sillico, *sĭlyĕ'kŏ,* sm. basin of a close-stool.

sillón, *sĭlyŏn',* sm. large arm-chair; side-saddle for ladies.

sima, *sĕ'mă,* sf. deep and dark cavern.

simbólico, ca, *sĭmbŏ'lĭkŏ,* a. symbolical.

simbolizar, *sĭmbŏlĭthär',* v n. to symbolize.

símbolo, *sĭm'bŏlŏ,* sm. symbol; device.

simetría, *sĭmĕtrĕ'ä,* sf symmetry.

simétrico, ca, *sĭmĕ'trĭkŏ,* a. symmetrical.

simia, *sĕ'mĭă,* sf. she-ape.

simiente, *-mĭĕn'tĕ,* sf. seed. flar, like.

símil, *sĕ'mĭl,* sm resemblance; -, a. simi-

similitud, *sĭmĭlĭtŏd',* sf. similitude.

similor, *sĭmĭlŏr',* sm. pinchbeck.

simio, *sĕ'mĭŏ,* sm. male ape, monkey.

simón, *sĭmŏn',* sm. & f. hackney coachman in Madrid.

simonía, *sĭmŏnĕ'ä,* sf. simony. [simony.

simoníaco, ca, *-nĭ'ăkŏ,* sm. & f guilty of

simpatía, *sĭmpătĕ'ä,* sf. sympathy.

simpático, ca, *sĭmpä'tĭkŏ,* a. sympathetic.

simple, *sĭm'plĕ,* a. single, simple, silly; insipid; -, sm. simple (medicinal plant).

simpleza, *sĭmplĕ'thă,* sf. simpleness, silliness, rusticity.

simplicidad, *sĭmplĭthĭdăd',* sf. simplicity.

simplificar, *-fĭkär',* v. a. to simplify, to make simple.

simulación, *sĭmŭlăthĭŏn',* sf. simulation.

simulacro, *-lä'krŏ,* sm simulachrum, idol.

simuladamente, *-lädämen'tĕ,* ad. deceptively, hypocritically.

simular, *-lär',* v a. to simulate.

simultaneidad, *sĭmŭltănĕĭdăd',* sf. simultaneity. [neous.

simultáneo, nea, *-tă'nĕŏ,* a. simulta-

sin, *sĭn,* pr without, besides.

sinagoga, *sĭnăgŏ'gă,* sf. synagogue.

sincerar, *sĭnthĕrär',* v. a. to exculpate, to justify.

sinceridad, *-thĕrĭdăd',* sf. sincerity.

sincero, ra, *sĭnthä'rŏ,* a. sincere, ingenuous, honest.

síncopa, *sĭn'kŏpă,* sf. (gr mus.) syncope.

sincopar, *-kŏpär',* v. a. to syncopate.

síncope, *sĭn'kŏpĕ,* sf. (med.) syncope, fainting fit.

sindicado, *-dĭkä'dŏ,* sm. syndicate.

sindicar, *-dĭkär',* v. a. to lodge an information; to accuse.

síndico, *sĭn'dĭkŏ,* sm. syndic.

sinfonía, *-fŏnĕ'ä,* sf. symphony.

singular, *-gŭlär',* a. singular, particular.

singularidad, *-lărĭdăd',* sf. singularity.

singularizar, *-lărĭthär',* v. a. to distinguish, to singularize; -se, to distinguish oneself to be singular.

siniestra, *sĭnĭĕs'tră,* sf. left hand.

siniestro, tra, *-trŏ,* a. left, sinister; unhappy; -, sm. depravity, evil habit.

sino, *sĕ'nŏ,* c. if not; but, except, besides, only.

sinodal, *sĭnŏdäl',* a. synodic, synodal, -, sm. examiner of curates and confessors.

sínodo, *sĭ'nŏdŏ,* sm. synod; conjunction of the heavenly bodies.

sinónimo, ma, *sĭnŏ'nĭmŏ,* a. synonymous.

sinónimo, ma, *-nŏmŏ,* a. synonymous.

sinrazón, *-răhŏn',* sf injustice.

sinsabor, *-săbŏr',* sm displeasure, disgust.

sintaxis, *-tăk'sĭs,* sf syntax.

síntesis, *sĭn'tĕsĭs,* sf synthesis.

sintético, ca, *-tĕ'tĭkŏ,* a. synthetical.

síntoma, *sĭn'tŏmă,* sm symptom.

sinuosidad, *sĭnŭŏsĭdăd',* sf sinuosity.

sinuoso, sa, *sĭnŭŏ'sŏ,* a. sinuous.

siquiera, *sĭkĭĕ'ră,* c. at least, though, [although.

sirena, *sĭrĕ'nă,* sf. syren.

sirga, *sĭr'gă,* sf. tow-rope, tow-line.

sirgar, *sĭrgär',* v. a. to tow a vessel.

sirte, *sĭr'tĕ,* sf. moving sand bank

sirvienta, *-vĭĕn'tă,* sf female servant, serving-maid, maid-servant.

sirviente, *-tĕ,* sm. & f. a servant.

sisa, *sĕ'să,* sf. petty theft, clippings which tailors steal in cutting clothes, assize; excise. [cock.

sisón, *sĭsŏn',* sm. filcher, pilferer, mous-

sistema, *sīstā'mā*, sm. system, [matic.

sistemático, ca, *sīstēmā'tīkō*, a. syste-

sitiador, *sītīādōr'*, sm. besieger.

sitiar, *sītīār'*, v. a. to besiege.

sitio, *sē'tīō*, sm. place; situation (of a town, &c.); (mil.) siege, blockade.

sito, ta, *sē'tō*, a. situated.

situación, *sītūāthōn'*, sf. situation.

situado, –*tūā'dō*, sm. allowance.

situar, –*tūār'*, v. a. to place, to situate; to assign a fund; –se, to be established in place or business; to station oneself.

so, *sō*, pr. under; below (used in composition, it occasionally diminishes the import of the verb; ¡–! used to stop horses or cattle.

soba, *sō'bā*, sf. making soft; beating.

sobaco, *sōbā'kō*, sm. arm-pit, arm-hole.

sobadura, –*dō'rā*, sf. kneading, rubbing.

sobajar, –*hār'*, v. a. to scrub, to rub hard.

sobar, *sōbār'*, v. a. to handle, to soften; to pummel, to beat, to whip; to scrub, to rub hard; to rumple clothes.

sobarba, –*bār'bā*, sf. nose-band.

sobarbada, –*bārbā'dā*, sf. chuck under the chin; jerk; (fig.) reprimand, scolding.

soberanía, *sōbērānē'ā*, sf. sovereignty; pride, haughtiness.

soberano, na, –*rā'nō*, a. & sm. sovereign.

soberbia, –*bēr'bīā*, sf. pride, haughtiness; presumption.

soberbio, bia, –*bīō*, a. proud, haughty.

sobina, –*bē'nā*, sf. wooden pin or peg.

sobón, *sōbōn'*, sm. lazy fellow.

sobornador, ra, –*bōrnādōr'*, sm. & suborner, briber.

sobornar, –*nār'*, v. a. to suborn, to bribe.

soborno, *sōbōr'nō*, sm. subornation, bribe.

sobra, *sō'brā*, sf. overplus, surplus, excess; offence; de –, over and above.

sobradamente, *sōbrādāmēn'tē*, ad. super-abundantly.

sobradillo, –*dēl'yō*, sm. small granary; penthouse; shelter over a balcony.

sobrante, –*brān'tē*, sm. residue, super-fluity, surplus.

sobrar, –*brār'*, v. n. to have more than is necessary; to be more than enough; to remain, to be left.

sobre, *sō'brē*, pr. above, over; super; moreover; a little more; –, sm. direction and cover of a letter. [superabundance.

sobreabundancia, –*ābūndān'thīā*, sf.

sobreabundar, –*ābūndār'*, v. n. to super-abound. [treble.

sobreagudo, –*āgō'dō*, sm. (mus.) highest

sobrealzar, –*ālthār'*, v. a. to praise, to extol.

sobreasar, –*āsār'*, v. a. to roast again.

sobrecama, –*kā'mā*, sf. coverlet, quilt.

sobrecaña, –*kān'yā*, sf. tumour in a horse's leg.

sobrecarga, –*kār'gā*, sf. additional bundle thrown over a load; surcharge, over-burden.

sobrecargar, –*kārgār'*, v. a. to overload; to sew the whole night long.

sobrecargo, –*kār'gō*, sm. supercargo.

sobreceja, –*thē'h'ā*, sf. part of the fore-head over the eye-brows. [nyō, sm. frown.

sobrecejo, –*thē'h'ō*, sobreceño, –*thēn'*-

sobrecoger, –*kō'hēr'*, v. a. to surprise.

sobrecubierta, –*kūbīēr'tā*, sf. double cover. [mentioned.

sobredicho, cha, –*dīsh'ō*, a. above-

sobrediente, –*dīēn'tē*, sm. gag-tooth, projecting tooth. [palliate, to exculpate.

sobredorar, –*dōrār'*, v. a. to overgild; to

sobrehueso, –*hūē'sō*, sm. morbid swelling on the bones or joints; trouble, encum-brance. [human.

sobrehumano, na, –*āmā'nō*, a. super-

sobrellevar, –*lyēvār'*, v. a. to ease, to alleviate; to suffer, to tolerate.

sobremanera, –*mānē'rā*, ad. excessively.

sobremesa, –*mēs'ā*, sf. table-cover; des-sert; de –, immediately after dinner.

sobrenadar, –*nādār'*, v. a. to swim on the surface, to float.

sobrenatural, –*nātūrāl'*, a. supernatural.

sobrenaturalmente, –*mēn'tē*, ad. super-naturally. [nickname.

sobrenombre, –*nōm'brē*, sm. surname;

sobrentender, *sōbrēntēndēr'*, v. a. to under-stand. [augmentation of pay.

sobrepaga, *sōbrēpā'gā*, sf. increase or

sobreparto, –*pār'tō*, sm. time of lying-in.

sobrepelliz, –*pēlyēth'*, sf. surplice.

sobrepeso, –*pā'sō*, sm. overweight.

sobrepié, –*pīē'*, sm. osseous tumour at the top of horses' hoofs.

sobrepian, –*plān'*, sm. (mar.) rider.

sobreponer, –*pōnēr'*, v. a. to put one thing over or on another; –se, to put oneself out of reach of, to shew oneself superior to.

sobreprecio, –*prā'thīō*, sm. extra price.

sobrepujanza, –*pūhān'thā*, sf. excessive strength. [surpass, to excel.

sobrepujar, –*pūhār'*, v. a. to exceed, to

sobrerropa, –*rō'pā*, sf. long robe.

sobresaliente, –*sālīēn'tē*, a. (mil.) com-manding a picket; –, sm. substitute.

sobresalir, –*sālīr'*, v. a. to exceed in height, to surpass.

sobresaltar, –*sāltār'*, v. a. to make an unexpected attack; to frighten.

sobresalto, –*sāl'tō*, sm. sudden assault; sudden dread. [letter.

sobrescrito, –*skrē'tō*, sm. address of a

sobreseer, –*sēēr'*, v. n. to supersede; to overrule. [sion, suspension.

sobreseimiento, –*sēīmīēn'tō*, sm. omis-

sobresello, –*sēl'yō*, sm. double seal.

sobrestante, –*stān'tē*, sm. overseer; fore-man. [one's pay or allowance.

sobresueldo, –*sūēl'dō*, sm. addition to

sobretodo, –*tō'dō*, sm. surtout, great-coat.

sobrevenir, –*nēnīr'*, v. n. to happen, to come unexpectedly; to supervene.

sobrevivir, –*vīvīr'*, v. n. to survive.

sobriedad, *sōbrīēdād'*, sf. sobriety.

sobrina, *sōbrē'nā*, sf. niece.

sobrino, –*nō'*, sm. nephew.

sobrio, ria, *sō'brīō*, a. sober, frugal,

socaliña, *sōkālīn'yā*, sf. extortion. cheating, [cunning

socaliñar, *-līnyār'*, v. a. to extort by

socarrar, *sōkārrār'*, v. a. to half-roast.

socarrón, ona, *-ōn'*, a. cunning, sly, crafty [ning, artfulness

socarronería, *-nerīā*, sf craft, cunning.

socavar, *-kāvār'*, v. a. to undermine.

sociabilidad, *sōthīābīlīdād'*, sf. sociableness.

sociable, *-thīā'blē*, a. sociable. [ness.

social, *sōthīal'*, a social.

sociedad, *sōthīēdād'*, sf society

socio, *sō'thīō*, sm associate, companion.

socolor, *-kōlōr'*, sm pretext, pretence

socorredor, ra, *sōkōrrēdōr'*, sm. & f. succourer, helper

socorrer, *-kōrrēr'*, v. a. to succour.

socorrido, da, *-rī'dō*, a. furnished, supplied

socorro, *sōkōr'rō*, sm succour, help; part of a salary or allowance advanced or paid beforehand.

sochantre, *-tshān'trē*, sm sub-chanter.

sodomía, *sōdōmī'ā*, sf sodomy.

sodomita, *-mī'tā*, sm. sodomite.

soez, *sōēth'*, a. a mean, vile, lousy.

sofisma, *sōfīs'mā*, sm sophism.

sofista, *fīs'tā* sm sophister.

sofistería, *-tērī'ā*, sf sophistry.

sofisticar, *-tīkār'*, v. a. to sophisticate.

sofístico, ca, *sōfīs'tīkō* a. sophistical.

sofocar, *sōfōkār'*, v. a. to suffocate.

sofrenada, *-frēnā'dā*, sf. sudden check given to a horse with the bridle, severe reprimand.

sofrenar, *-frēnār'*, v. a. to check a horse by a violent pull of the bridle, to reprimand severely. [for shame!

soga, *sō'gā*, sf rope of bass-wood. [—! fy!

soguería, *sōgērī'ā*, sf. rope-walk, rope.

soguero, *-gā'rō*, sm rope maker. [yard.

sojuzgador, *sō'hūthgādōr'*, sm conqueror, subduer. [subdue

sojuzgar, *-hūthgār'*, v. a. to conquer, to

sol, *sōl*, sm sun; (mus) sol.

solamente, *-lāmēn'tē*, ad only, solely.

solana, *sōlā'nā*, sf. sunny place; open gallery for taking the sun.

solano, *-nō*, sm easterly wind.

solapa, *sōlā'pā*, sf lappet, pretence, pretext.

solapado, da, *-pā'dō*, a. cunning, crafty, [artful

solapar, *-pār'*, v. a. to button one's coat across to hide under a false pretence

solar, *sōlār'*, sm building-lot, real estate, ancestral mansion of a noble family; — a sola; —. v. a. to floor a room, to sole shoes or boots.

solariego, ga, *-rīā'gō*, a. belonging to the ancestral mansion of a noble family

solaz, *sōlath'*, sm solace, consolation, á —, pleasantly, agreeably.

solazar, *-thār'*, v a. to solace, to comfort.

solazo, *sōlā'thō*, sm scorching sun.

soldada, *sōldā'dā*, sf. wages

soldadesca, *-dēs'kā*, sf soldiery.

soldadesco, ca, *-kō*, a. soldierly. soldier-like.

soldado, *sōldā'dō*, sm soldier; — raso, common soldier, private

soldador, *-dōr'*, sm. solderer, soldering-iron [correction.

soldadura, *-dō'rā*, sf. soldering; solder;

soldar, *sōldār'*, v. a. to solder; to mend, to correct.

solecismo, *sōlēthīs'mō*, sm. solecism.

soledad, *-lēdād'*, sf solitude, solitariness; lonely place, desert.

solemne, *-lēm'nē*, a. solemn, celebrated; grand, high, gay, cheerful.

solemnidad, *-nīdād'*, sf. solemnity.

solemnizar, *-nīthār'*, v. a. to solemnize, to praise.

soler, *sōlēr'*, v. n. to be accustomed.

soleta, *sōlē'tā*, sf. linen sole put into stockings.

solfa, *sōl'fā*, sf. (mus) gamut, solmization, accordance, harmony, sound flogging

solfeador, *-fēādōr'*, sm. songster, music-master, dealer of blows.

solfear, *-fēār'*, v. n (mus.) to solfa.

solfeo, *-fā'ō*, sm. solfeggio

solfista, *-fīs'tā*, sm a f skilful musician.

solicitación, *sōlīthītāthīōn'*, sf. solicitation.

solicitar, *-tār'*, v. a. to solicit. [tation.

solicito, ta, *sōlī'thītō*, a. solicitous.

solicitud, *-thītūd'*, sf. solicitude.

solidar, *-dār'*, v. a. to consolidate.

solideo, *-dā'ō*, sm calotte.

solidez, *-dēth'*, sf solidity

sólido, da, *sō'līdō*, a. solid. [logue.

soliloquio, *sōlīlō'kīō*, sm soliloquy, mono-

solimán, *-mān'*, sm. (chem) corrosive

solio, *sō'līō*, sm. throne. [sublimate.

solitaria, *-tā'rīā*, sf solitaire.

solitario, ria, *-rīō*, a. solitary; —, sm. hermit.

solo, *sō'lō*, sm. (mus.) solo; —, la, a. alone, single, á solas, alone, unaided; á sus solas, quite alone, sólo, ad only.

solomillo, *sōlōmīl'yō*, solomo, *sōlō'mō*, sm loin, chine.

solsticio, *sōlstī'thīō*, sm. solstice.

soltar, *sōltār'*, v. a. to untie, to loosen; to set at liberty; —se, to get loose; to lose all decency and modesty. [woman.

soltera, *-tā'rā*, sf spinster, unmarried

soltería, *-tērī'ā*, sf celibacy.

soltero, *-tā'rō*, sm bachelor, unmarried man; —, a. unmarried.

soltura, *-tō'rā*, sf. liberation; release; agility, activity.

soluble, *sōlō'blē*, a. soluble, solvable.

solución, *sōlōthīōn'*, sf. solution, catastrophe of a drama

solutivo, va, *-tīvō*, a. solutive.

solvente, *sōlvēn'tē*, a. dissolvent, solvent

sollo, *sōl'yō*, sm. common pike.

sollozar, *-thār'*, v. a. to sob.

sollozo, *sōlyō'thō*, sm sob.

somanta, *sōmān'tā*, sf. beating, severe chastisement.

somatén, *sōmātēn'*, sm. armed corps destined for the defence of a city or province, one who serves in such a corps.

sombra, *sōm'brā*, sf. shade, shadow.

sombraje, –brá'h'ĕ, sm. hut covered with branches.

sombrear, –brĕár', v. a. to shade.

sombrerazo, –brĕrä'thŏ, sm. large hat; slap with a hat. [butter-bur.

sombrerera, –rá'rä, sf. hat-box: (bot.-

sombrerería, –rĕrë'ä, sf. hat-factory; hat-shop. [maker.

sombrerero, –rĕ'rŏ, sm. hatter, hat-

sombrerillo, –rĕl'yŏ, sm. (bot.) navel-wort.

sombrero, sŏmbrä'rŏ, sm. hat.

sombrío, bría, sŏmbrë'ŏ, a. shady, darksome, gloomy.

someter, sŏmĕtĕr', v. a. to submit; to subdue; –se, to humble oneself; to submit. [sion.

sometimiento, –tïmĕn'tŏ, sm. submis-

somnolencia, sŏmnŏlĕn'thïä, sf. sleepiness, drowsiness. [cloth; rudeness.

somonte, sŏmŏn'tĕ, sm. shaggy part of

somorgujar, sŏmŏrgu'här', v. a. to dive.

son, sŏn, sm. sound, report; á –, at the sound of. [generally reported.

sonado, da, –nä'dŏ, a. celebrated; famous;

sonaja, –nä'h'ä, sf. timbrel (musical instrument).

sonajero, –'hä'rŏ, sm. small timbrel.

sonámbulo, sŏnäm'bŭlŏ, a. & sm. sleep-walking; somnambulist.

sonar, sŏnár', v. a. to play upon a musical instrument; –, v. n. to sound; –se, to blow one's nose.

sonata, –nä'tä, sf. (mus.) sonata.

sonda, sŏn'dä, sf. sounding; catheter.

sondable, –dä'blĕ, a. that may be sounded.

sond(e)ar, –d(ĕ)är', v. a. (mar.) to sound.

sonecillo, sŏnĕthäl'yŏ, sm. short little tune.

soneto, sŏnä'tŏ, sm. sonnet.

sonido, sŏn'dŏ, sm. sound.

sonoro, ra, sŏnŏ'rŏ, a. sonorous.

sonreírse, sŏnrĕïr'sĕ, v. r. to smile.

sonrisa, –rĕ'sä, sf. smile.

sonroj(e)ar, –rŏ'h(ĕ)är', v. a. to make one blush with shame.

sonrojo, –rŏ'h'ŏ, sm. blush; offensive word which causes a blush.

sonros(e)ar, –rŏs(ĕ)är', v. a. to dye a rose colour; –se, to blush.

sonroseo, –rŏsä'ŏ, sm. blush. [wheedler.

sonsacador, ra, –säkädŏr', sm. & f.

sonsacamiento, –säkämĕn'tŏ, sm. wheedling, extortion. [out of a person.

sonsacar, –säkár', v. a. to pump a secret

sonsonete, –sŏnä'tĕ, sm. tapping noise; scornful, derisive tone.

soñador, ra, sŏnyädŏr', sm. & f. dreamer.

soñar, sŏnyár', v. a. to dream.

soñoliento, ta, sŏnyŏlĕn'tŏ, a. sleepy, drowsy; causing sleep; dull, lazy.

sopa, sŏ'pä, sf. sop; soup.

sopalanda, –län'dä, sf. ragged clothes worn by poor students.

sopapo, –pä'pŏ, sm. slap given with the hand; sucker of a pump.

sopera, –pä'rä, sf. soup-dish.

sopero, –pä'rŏ, sm. soup-plate.

sopetear, –pĕtĕár', v. a. to steep bread in sauce; to abuse with foul language.

sopetón, –tŏn', sm. hard box on the ears; de –, suddenly. [spruce.

soplado, da, sŏplä'dŏ, a. over-nice and

soplamocos, –mŏ'kŏs, sm. slap in the face.

soplar, sŏplár', v. n. & a. to blow; to blow bellows; to steal in an artful manner; to suggest; to inspire; to tipple, to drink much; to accuse, to denounce any one; –se, to dress in style.

soplete, sŏplä'tĕ, sm. blowing-pipe.

soplo, sŏ'plŏ, sm. blowing; puff of wind; advice given secretly; instant, moment.

soplón, ona, sŏplŏn', sm. & f. tale-bearer.

soponcio, sŏpŏn'thïŏ, sm. grief arising from disappointment.

sopor, sŏpŏr', sm. drowsiness, sleepiness.

soporífero, ra, –rĕ'fĕrŏ, a. soporific, soporiferous.

soporoso, sa, –rŏ'sŏ, a. soporiferous.

soportable, sŏpŏrtä'blĕ, a. tolerable, supportal. –tä'l, sm. portico. [portable.

soportar, –tär', v. a. to suffer, to tolerate; to support.

sor, sŏr, sister (used only to nuns).

sorber, –bär', v. a. to sip, to suck; to absorb; to swallow; to imbibe.

sorbete, –bä'tĕ, sm. sherbet.

sorbo, sŏr'bŏ, sm. sipping; a little; small quantity of anything.

sordera, sŏrdä'rä, sf. deafness, surdity.

sordidez, –dĭdĕth' sf. sordidness, nastiness, covetousness. [dirty; licentious.

sórdido, da, sŏr'dïdŏ, a. sordid; nasty,

sordina, –dĕ'nä, sf. damper.

sordo, da, sŏr'dŏ, a. deaf; silent, quiet; secret. [slowness.

sorna, sŏr'nä, sf. sluggishness, laziness;

sornavirón, –vïrŏn', sm. sudden stroke with the back of the open hand.

sorprender, –prĕndĕr', v. a. to surprise; to fall upon unexpectedly.

sorpresa, –prĕ'sä, sf. surprise.

sorteador, –tĕädŏr', sm. one who casts lots; dexterous bull-fighter.

sortear, –tĕár', v. n. to draw or cast lots; to fight bulls with skill and dexterity.

sorteo, sŏrtä'ŏ, sm. act of casting or drawing lots.

sortija, –tĕ'h'ä, sf. ring; hoop; buckle.

sortilegio, –tĭlä'hïŏ, sm. sortilege, sorcery.

sosegado, da, sŏsĕgä'dŏ, a. quiet, peaceful.

sosegar, –gär', v. a. to appease, to calm; –, v. n. to rest; to repose; to be calm or composed.

sosería, –sĕrĕ'ä, sf. insipidity.

sosiego, –sïä'gŏ, sm. tranquillity, calmness, heart's ease. [thing obliquely.

soslayar, –släyär', v. a. to do or place a

soslayo, –slä'yŏ, ad. obliquely; al ó de –, askew, sideways.

soso, sa, sŏ'sŏ, a. insipid, tasteless.

sospecha, sŏspĕtsh'ä, sf. suspicion, mistrust.

sospechar, –tshár', v. a. to suspect.

sospechoso, sa, –tshŏ'sŏ, a. suspicious, mistrustful.

sostén, *sôstěn'*, sm. support, steadiness of a ship in pursuing her course.

sostener, *-těněr'*, v. a. to sustain, to maintain, -se, to support or maintain oneself.

sostenido, *-těnī'dō*, sm. (mus.) sharp.

sostenimiento, *-měn'tō*, sm. sustenance.

sota, *sō'tá*, sf. knave (at cards). [bing.

sotana, *sōtá'ná*, sf. cassock; flogging, drub-

sotanilla, *-níl'yá*, sf. college gown.

sótano, *sō'táno*, sm. cellar under ground.

sotavento, *-věn'tō*, sm. (mar.) leeward, lee.

sotechado, *sōtěchá'dō*, sm. roofed or covered place. [growth.

soto, *sō'tō*, sm. grove, thicket; under-

su, *sú*, pn. his, her, its, one's; **sus**, theirs.

suave, *suá'vě*, a. smooth, soft, delicate; gentle, mild, meek. [ness; suavity.

suavidad, *-vīdá'*, sf. softness, sweet-

suavizar, *-vízár'*, v. a. to soften.

subalterno, na, *sūbáltěr'nō*, a. a subaltern, inferior. [under-tenant.

subarrendador, ra, *-árrěndádōr'*, sm. & f.

subarrendar, *-árrěndár'*, v. a. to sub-rent.

subarriendo, *-árrīěn'dō*, sm. sub-lease.

subasta, *-ás'tá*, **subastación**, *-ástā'thīōn'*, sf. judicial auction, open sale.

subastar, *-ástár'*, v. a. to sell by auction.

subdelegación, *-dělégáthīōn'*, sf. sub-delegation, substitution

subdelegado, *-děléga'dō*, sm. subdelegate.

subdelegar, *-dělégár'*, v. a. to subdelegate.

subdiaconato, *-dīákōná'tō*, sm. **subdia-conato**, *-ná'tō*, sm. subdeaconship.

subdiácono, *-dīá'kōnō*, sm. subdeacon.

súbdito, ta, *sūb'dītō*, a. subject.

subdividir, *sūbdīvīdīr'*, v. a. to subdivide.

subdivisión, *-dīvīsīōn'*, sf. subdivision.

subida, *sūbī'dá*, sf. mounting, ascent, activity, rise, enhancement, augmentation of value or price.

subido, da, *-dō*, a. deep-coloured; very fine, very excellent.

subir, *sūbīr'*, v. n. to mount, to ascend, to climb, to increase, to swell; to enter leaves (of silk-worms, in making their cocoons); to rise in dignity, fortune, &c., -, v. a. to ascend, to go up, to enhance.

súbito, ta, *sū'bītō*, a. sudden, hasty, un-foreseen. [junctive.

subjuntivo, *sūb'nán'tīvō*, sm. (gr.) sub-

sublevación, *-lěváthīōn'*, sf. sedition, revolt. [bellion, to rise in rebellion.

sublevar, *-lěvár'*, v. a. to excite a re-

sublimado, *sūblīmá'dō*, sm. sublimate.

sublime, *sūblī'mě*, a. sublime.

sublimidad, *sūblīmīdá'*, sf. sublimity.

subordinación, *-ōrdīnáthīōn'*, sf. sub-ordination.

subordinar, *-ōrdīnár'*, v. a. to sub-ordinate.

subrepción, *-rěpthīōn'*, sf. hidden action, underhand business, subreption.

subrepticio, cia, *-těthīō*, a. surrepti-tious, done in a clandestine manner.

subrogación, *-rōgáthīōn'*, sf. surroga-tion, subrogation, substitution.

subrogar, *-rōgár'*, v. a. to surrogate, to subrogate. [mend, to repair.

subsanar, *-sánár'*, v. a. to excuse; to

subsidio, *-sě'dīō*, sm. subsidy, aid.

subsistencia, *-sīstěn'thīá*, sf. subsistence; permanence, stability.

subsistir, *-sīstīr'*, v. n. to subsist.

substancia, *-stán'thīá*, sf. substance.

substancial, *-stánthīál'*, a. substantial.

substantialmente, *-měn'tě*, ad. sub-stantially. [to aver, to verify.

substanciar, *-stánthīár'*, v. a. to abridge;

substancioso, sa, *-thīō'sō*, a. substan-tial, nutritive, nutritious. [tion.

substracción, *-strákthīōn'*, sf. subtrac-

substraer, *-stráěr'*, v. a. to subtract; -se, to retire, to withdraw. [tenant.

subteniente, *-těnīěn'tě*, sm. sub-lieu-

subterfugio, *-těrfū'ǧīō*, sf. subterfuge, shift. [terraneous; -, sm. subterrane.

subterráneo, nea, *sūbtěrrá'něō*, a. sub-

subvenir, *-věnīr'*, v. a. to aid, to suc-cour. [overthrow.

subversión, *-věrsīōn'*, sf. subversion,

subversivo, va, *-věrsī'vō*, a. subversive.

subvertir, *-věrtīr'*, v. a. to subvert, to destroy, to ruin.

subyugar, *-yūgár'*, v. a. to subdue, to subjugate. [heirt.

suceder, *sūthěděr'*, v. n. to succeed, to in-

sucesión, *sūthě'sīōn'*, sf. succession; issue, offspring; hereditary succession.

sucesivo, va, *-sě'vō*, a. successive.

suceso, *sūthě'sō*, sm. success. [heir.

sucesor, *-sōr'*, sm. successor, succeeder;

suciedad, *sūthīědá'*, sf. nastiness, filthi-ness, dirt, mire

sucinto, ta, *-thīn'tō*, a. succinct, concise.

sucio, cia, *sū'thīō*, a. dirty, nasty, filthy; obscene, dishonest. [juicy.

suculento, ta, *sūkūlěn'tō*, a. succulent,

sucumbir, *-kūmbīr'*, v. n. to succumb.

sud, *sūd*, sm. south; south wind.

sudar, *sūdár'*, v. a. to sweat; to give with repugnance.

sudario, *-dá'rīō*, sm. sweat-cloth.

sudeste, *sūděst'*, sm. south-east.

sudoeste, *-ōěs'tě*, sm. south-west.

sudor, *sūdōr'*, sm. sweat. [sweat.

sudoriento, ta, *-rīěn'tō*, a. moist with

sudorifico, ca, *-rī'fīkō*, a. a sudorific.

sudoso, sa, *-dō'sō*, a. sweaty.

suegra, *sūě'grá*, sf. mother-in-law.

suegro, *-grō*, sm. father-in-law.

suela, *sūě'lá*, sf. sole of the shoe; sole-leather.

sueldo, *sūěl'dō*, sm. ancient Roman coin; sou (French halfpenny); wages, salary.

suelo, *sūě'lō*, sm. soil, surface, sole; district.

suelta, *sūěl'tá*, sf. loosening, loose, tethers; hobbl.s, **dar** -, to liberate for a short time.

suelto, ta, *sūěl'tō*, a. loose; expeditious, swift; -, sm. loose piece of metal found near mines.

sueño, *sūěn'yō*, sm. sleep; vision, dream.

suero, *sōō'rŏ,* sm. whey.
suerte, *sōōr'tĕ,* sf. chance, lot, fortune, good-luck, hap-hazard; kind, sort; species; manner.
suficiencia, *sōōfĭthĕn'thĭā,* sf. sufficiency; **á —,** sufficiently, enough. [capable.
suficiente, *—thĭĕn'tĕ,* a. sufficient; fit
sufocación, *sōōfŏkāthĭōn',* sf. suffocating.
sufocar, *—kār',* v. a. to suffocate, to choke; to quench.
sufragáneo, *sōōfrāgā'nĕŏ,* sm. suffragan; **—, ea,** a. belonging to a suffragan.
sufragar, *—frāgār',* v. a. to aid, to assist.
sufragio, *sōōfrā'hĭŏ,* sm. vote, suffrage; aid, assistance.
sufrible, *sōōfrē'blĕ,* a. sufferable.
sufrido, da, *sōōfrē'dŏ,* a. long suffering, patient. [patience.
sufrimiento, *—mĭĕn'tŏ,* sm. sufferance.
sufrir, *sōōfrēr',* v. a. to suffer, to bear with patience; to permit.
sugerir, *sōō'hĕrēr',* v. a. to suggest.
sugestión, *—hĕstĭōn',* sf. suggestion.
suicida, *sōōĭthē'dā,* sm. suicide, self-murderer.
suicidio, *—thē'dĭŏ,* sm. suicide, self-murder.
sujeción, *sōō'hĕthĭōn',* sf. subjection; argument. [ject.
sujetar, *—'hĕtār',* v. a. to subdue; to subject.
sujeto, *sōō'hĕ'tŏ,* a. subject, liable, exposed; **—,** sm. subject; matter under discussion.
sulfúreo, rea, *sōōlfō'rĕŏ,* a. sulphureous.
sulfúrico, *—rĭkŏ,* a. sulphuric.
sultán, *sōōltān',* sm. sultan.
sultana, *—tā'nā,* sf. sultana, sultaness.
suma, *sōō'mā,* sf. sum; substance.
sumar, *—mār',* v. a. to add, to sum up; **—,** v. n. to cast up accounts.
sumario, ria, *—mā'rĭŏ,* a. summary; **—,** sm. compendium, summary.
sumergir, *—mĕr'hēr',* v. a. to submerge.
sumersión, *—mĕrsĭōn',* sf. submersion, immersion.
sumidero, *—mĭdĕ'rŏ,* sm. sewer, drain.
sumiller, *—mĭlyĕr',* sm. chief of several offices in the king's household; **— de corps,** Lord Chamberlain.
suministración, *—mĭnĭstrāthĭōn',* sf. supply, furnishing.
suministrador, ra, *—trādŏr',* sm. & f. provider. [furnish.
suministrar, *—trār',* v. a. to supply, to
sumir, *sōōmĭr',* v. a. to take, to receive the chalice at mass; **—se,** to sink under ground; to be sunken (of one's features).
sumisión, *—mĭsĭōn',* sf. submission.
sumiso, sa, *—mĭs'ŏ,* a. submissive, humble.
sumo, ma, *sōō'mŏ,* a. highest, greatest; **á lo —,** at most; to the highest pitch.
súmulas, *sōō'mūlās,* sf. pl. synopsis of the first elements of logic.
sumulístico, ca, *sūmūlĭs'tĭkŏ,* a. belonging to summaries of logic. [ness.
suntuosidad, *sūntūŏsĭdād',* sf. sumptuousness.
suntuoso, sa, *—tūŏ'sŏ,* a. sumptuous.
supeditación, *sōōpĕdĭtāthĭōn',* sf. trampling under foot.

supeditar, *—tār',* v. a. to trample under foot.
superable, *sōōpĕrā'blĕ,* a. superable, conquerable. [superabundance.
superabundancia, *—ābūndān'thĭā,* sf.
superabundar, *—ābūndār',* v. n. to superabound.
superar, *sōōpĕrār',* v. a. to surpass.
superchería, *sōōpĕrchĕrē'ā,* sf. deceit, fraud. [smattering.
superficial, *—fĭthĭāl',* a. superficial;
superficie, *—fĭ'thĭĕ,* sf. superficies, surface.
superfino, na, *—fē'nŏ,* a. superfine.
superfluidad, *—flūĭdād',* sf. superfluity.
superfluo, ua, *sōōpĕr'flŏŏ,* a. superfluous, unnecessary. [superintendence.
superintendencia, *—ĭntĕndĕn'thĭā,* sf.
superintendente, *—dĕn'tĕ,* sm. superintendent, intendant.
superior, *sōōpĕrĭŏr',* a. superior; upper (in geography); **—,** sm. superior.
superioridad, *—rĭdād',* sf. superiority.
superlativa, va, *sōōpĕrlātē'vŏ,* a. & sm. (gr.) superlative. [supernumerary.
supernumerario, ria, *—nūmĕrā'rĭŏ,* a.
superstición, *—stĭthĭōn',* sf. superstition.
supersticioso, sa, *—stĭthĭŏ'sŏ,* a. superstitious.
supino, na, *sōōpē'nŏ,* a. supine, on one's back; **—,** sm. (gr.) supine.
suplantación, *sōōplāntāthĭōn',* sf. supplanting. [with a document.
suplantar, *—tār',* v. a. to falsify or tamper
suplefaltas, *sōōplĕfāl'tās,* sm. substitute.
suplemento, *—mĕn'tŏ,* sm. supplement.
súplica, *sōō'plĭkā,* sf. petition, request, supplication. [plicant.
suplicante, *sōōplĭkān'tĕ,* a. & sm. supplicar,
suplicar, *—kār',* v. a. to supplicate; to make a humble reply to a superior; to petition against a sentence. [rogatory.
suplicatorio, *—tŏ'rĭŏ,* sf. (law) letters
suplicio, *sōōplē'thĭŏ,* sm. capital punishment.
suplir, *sōōplēr',* v. a. to supply; to serve instead of, to perform another's functions; to disguise. [surmise.
suponer, *—pŏnĕr',* v. a. to suppose, to suposición,
suposición, *—pŏsĭthĭōn',* sf. supposition; authority.
supremo, ma, *sōōprĕ'mŏ,* a. supreme.
supresión, *—prĕsĭōn',* sf. suppression.
suprimir, *sōōprĭmēr',* v. a. to suppress.
supuesto, *—pōōĕs'tŏ,* sm. supposition; **—, ta,** a. supposititious, supposed; **— que,** allowing that, granting that.
supuración, *—pōōrāthĭōn',* sf. suppuration.
supurar, *—pōōrār',* v. a. to suppurate.
supurativo, va, *—rātē'vŏ,* a. promoting suppuration.
sur, *sōōr,* sm. south; south wind.
surcador, *—kādŏr',* sm. ploughman.
surcar, *—kār',* v. a. to furrow.
surco, *sōōr'kŏ,* sm. furrow.
surgidero, *—hĭdĕ'rŏ,* sm. anchoring-place.
surgir, *—'hēr',* v. a. to anchor; to surge.
surtido, *—tē'dŏ,* sm. assortment, supply.

surtidor, ra, –tēdŏr´, sm. & f. purveyor, caterer; water-spout. [to provide.
surtir, sŭrtir´, v. a. to supply; to furnish.
susceptible, sŭsthĕptē´blā, a. susceptible.
suscitar, –thētār´, v. a. to excite, to stir up.
suscribir, sŭskrībir´, v. a. to subscribe.
suscripción, –skrĭpthŏn´, sf. subscription; signature. [scriber.
suscriptor, ra, –skrĭptŏr´, sm. & f. subscriber, aforesaid.
susodicho, cha, sŭsŏdĭtsh´ō, a. fore-mentioned, aforesaid.
suspender, –pĕndĕr´, v. a. to suspend.
suspensión, –pĕnsŏn´, sf. suspension.
suspensivo, va, –sē´vŏ, a. suspensive.
suspenso, sa, –pĕn´sō, a. suspended, unfinished. [& f. suspensory.
suspensorio, ria, –pĕnsō´rĭō, a. & sm. suspensory.
suspicacia, sŭspĭkā´thĭā, sf. suspiciousness, jealousy.
suspicaz, –kāth´, a. suspicious, jealous.
suspirar, –spīrār´, v. n. to sigh.
suspiro, sŭspī´rō, sm. sigh; sugar sweetmeat. [jectives, &c. as substantives.
sustantivar, sŭstāntīvār´, v. a. to use adjectives, &c. as substantives.
sustantivo, va, –tē´vŏ, a. & sm. (gr.) substantive, noun.
sustentación, –tĕntāthŏn´, sf. sustentation, support. [support, to nourish.
sustentar, –tĕntār´, v. a. to sustain; to support, to nourish.
sustento, –tĕn´tō, sm. food, sustenance.
sustitución, –tĭtŭthŏn´, sf. substitution.
sustituir, –tĭtŭir´, v. a. to substitute.
sustituto, –tĭtō´tō, a. & sm. substitute.
susto, sŭs´tō, sm. fright, sudden terror.
susurrar, sŭsŭrrār´, v. n. to whisper, to divulge a secret; to murmur (of streams); –se, to be whispered about.
susurro, sŭsūr´rō, sm. whisper, murmur.
sútil, sū´tĭl, a. subtile; subtle.
sutileza, sŭtĭlē´thā, sf. subtlety.
sutilizar, –lĭthār´, v. a. to subtilize; to polish; to discuss profoundly.
suyo, ya, sū´yŏ, a. his, hers, theirs, one's; his, her, its own, one's own or their own; de –, spontaneously; –s, sm. pl. their own, near friends, relations, acquaintances, servants.

T.

taba, tā´bā, sf. bone of the knee-pan; small bone. [snuff.
tabaco, tābā´kō, sm. tobacco; – de polvo, snuff.
tábano, tā´bānŏ, sm. hornet.
tabaola, tābāō´lā, sf. noise, shouting.
tabaquera, –kē´rā, sf. snuff-box.
tabaquero, –kē´rō, sm. tobacconist.
tabardillo, tābārdĭl´yō, sm. burning fever.
taberna, tābĕr´nā, sf. tavern.
tabernáculo, –nā´kŭlō, sm. tabernacle.
tabernero, –nē´rō, sm. tavern-keeper.
tabicar, tābĭkār´, v. a. to wall up. [wall.
tabique, tābē´kē, sm. thin wall; partition.
tabla, tā´blā, sf. board; table; butcher's block; index of a book; bed of earth in a garden; –s, pl. tables containing the Decalogue; backgammon-board.
tablado, tāblā´dō, sm. scaffold; stage; frame of a bedstead; (mar.) platform.
tablajería, –´hērē´ā, sf. gaming, gambling.
tablajero, –´hā´rō, sm. gambler; butcher.
tablazo, –lā´thō, sm. blow with a board; arm of the sea or of a river.
tablazón, –thŏn´, sf. boarding, planking decks and sheathing of a ship.
tablero, tāblē´rō, sm. planed board; chessboard; draft-board; gambling-house; stock of a crossbow; tailor's shop-board.
tableta, –blā´tā, sf. tablet; cracknel.
tabletear, –blētēār´, v. n. to move boards noisily.
tablilla, –blĭl´yā, sf. list of persons excommunicated exhibited in churches; tablet of chocolate; – de mesón, sign of an inn.
tabuco, tābō´kō, sm. hut, small apartment.
taburete, –bŭrē´tē, sm. chair without arms.
taburón, –rŏn´, sm. shark (fish).
tacañería, tākānyē´rē´ā, sf. malicious cunning; niggardliness.
tacaño, ña, –kān´yŏ, a. artful, knavish; stingy, sordid.
tácito, ta, tā´thĭtō, a. tacit, silent; implied.
taciturno, na, tāthĭtūr´nō, a. tacit, silent; melancholy. [rammer; billiard-cue.
taco, tā´kō, sm. stopper, stopple; wad; taco.
tacón, tākŏn´, sm. heel-piece. [heels.
taconear, –nēār´, v. n. to walk on one's heels.
tacoñeo, –nē´ŏ, sm. clatter of the heels in dancing. [dancing.
táctica, tāk´tĭkā, sf. tactics. [dancing.
tacto, tāk´tō, sm. touch, feeling; tact.
tacha, tātsh´ā, sf. fault, defect; small nail.
tachar, tātshār´, v. a. to find fault with; to reprehend; to blot, to efface.
tachonar, tātshōnār´, v. a. to ornament with lace trimming; to stud with gilt-headed nails.
tachuela, tātshŭā´lā, sf. tack, nail.
tafanario, tāfānā´rĭō, sm. breeches, posterior, backside.
tafetán, tāfĕtān´, sm. taffety.
tafilete, tāfīlē´tē, sm. Morocco leather.
tahalí, tāālī´, sm. shoulder-belt.
tahona, tāō´nā, sf. horse-mill; crushing-mill; bakehouse. [mill).
tahonero, tāōnā´rō, sm. miller (of a horse-mill).
tahur, tāŭr´, sm. gambler, gamester.
tahurería, –rē´rē´ā, sf. gaming-house; fraudulent gambling. [crafty.
taimado, da, tāīmā´dō, a. sly, cunning, crafty.
taja, tā´hā, sf. cut, incision; dissection; tally. [ness.
tajada, tā´hā´dā, sf. slice; (fam.) hoarseness.
tajadera, –dā´rā, sf. chopping-knife.
tajador, ra, –dŏr´, sm. & f. chopper, cutter; chopping-block; trencher.
tajadura, –dō´rā, sf. cut, notch; section.
tajaplumas, –plō´mās, sm. pen-knife.
tajar, tāhār´, v. a. to cut, to chop; to hew; to cut a quill.
tajo, tā´hō, sm. cut, incision; cutting of a quill with a pen-knife; chopping-block.

tajuela, *tǎʰhǔǎʾlǎ*, sf., **tajuelo**, *—lŏ*, sm. low stool with four feet.

tal, *tǎl*, a. such; con —, provided that; **no hay —**, no such thing.

tala, *tǎʾlǎ*, sf. felling of trees.

talabera, *—bǎʾrǎ*, sf. kind of crockery.

talador, ra, *—ḡŏrʾ*, sm. & f. destroyer.

taladrar, *—drǎrʾ*, v. a. to bore, to pierce.

taladro, *tǎlǎʾdrŏ*, sm. borer, gimblet, auger

tálamo, *tǎʾlǎmŏ*, sm. bride-chamber; bridal bed.   [work.

talanquera, *tǎlǎnkǎʾrǎ*, sf. parapet, breast-

talante, *tǎlǎnʾtě*, sm. manner of performance; appearance, aspect; will, pleasure.

talar, *tǎlǎrʾ*, v. a. to fell trees; to desolate, to havoc; —, a. trailing, down to the heels (of clothes); —, sm. wing on the

talco, *tǎlʾkŏ*, sm. talk.   [heel of Mercury.

talega, *tǎlǎʾḡǎ*, sf. bag; bagful.

talego, *—ḡŏ*, sm. gunny-sack; clumsy, awkward fellow.

taleguilla, *tǎlěḡǐlʾyǎ*, sf. small bag.

talento, *tǎlěnʾtŏ*, sm. talent.

talión, *tǎlǐŏnʾ*, sf. retaliation, requital.

talismán, *tǎlǐsmǎnʾ*, sm. talisman.

talón, *tǎlŏnʾ*, sm. heel; heel-piece of a shoe; (rail.) luggage-ticket, receipt; (am.) duplicate-check.

talonear, *—nĕǎrʾ*, v. n. to walk fast.

talla, *tǎlʾyǎ*, sf. raised work; sculpture; stature, size; measure of any thing; hand, draw, turn (at cards); **media —**, half-relief.   [graved.

tallado, da, *tǎlyǎʾdŏ*, a. cut, carved, en-

tallador, *—ḡŏrʾ*, sm. engraver.

tallar, *tǎlyǎrʾ*, v. a. to cut, to chop; to carve in wood; to engrave; —, sm. forest of wood fit for cutting.   [waist.

talle, *tǎlʾyě*, sm. shape, size, proportion;

taller, *tǎlyěrʾ*, sm. workshop, laboratory.

tallista, *—yǐsʾtǎ*, sm. wood-carver, engraver.

tallo, *tǎlʾyŏ*, sm. shoot, sprout.

talludo, da, *—yŏʾdǎ*, a. thick-stalked.

tamañito, *tǎmǎnyǐʾtŏ*, a. fearful, intimidated.

tamaño, *tǎmǎnʾyŏ*, sm. size, shape, bulk; —, ña, a. showing the size, shape or bulk of anything.

tamarindo, *tǎmǎrǐnʾdŏ*, sm. tamarind-tree.

tamarisco, *—rǐsʾkŏ*, **tamariz**, *—rǐthʾ*, sm. tamarisk-shrub.   [ger, to waver.

tambalear, *—se*, *tǎmbǎlěǎrʾ*, v. n. to stagger.

tambaleo, *—bǎlěʾŏ*, sm. staggering, reeling.

también, *tǎmbǐěnʾ*, c. & ad. also, likewise; as well.

tambor, *tǎmbŏrʾ*, sm. drum; drummer; iron cylinder; small inclosure as a screen to the gates of a fortress; **— mayor**, (mil.) drum-major.

tamboril, *—bŏrǐlʾ*, sm. tabour, tabor.

tamborilada, *—bŏrǐlǎʾdǎ*, sf., **tamborilazo**, *—lǎʾthŏ*, sm. blow or fall on one's posterior.   [plane or level types.

tamborilear, *—rǐlěǎrʾ*, v. n. to tabour; to

tamborilero, *—lǎʾrŏ*, sm. tabourer.

tamborilete, *—lǎʾtě*, sm. planer (in printing).   [ing.

tamboritero, *—tǎʾrŏ*, sin. tabourer.

tamiz, *tǎmǐthʾ*, sm. fine sieve.

tamo, *tǎʾmŏ*, sm. fluff which falls from woollen or linen in weaving; corn-dust; dust under beds or behind furniture.

tamorlán, *tǎmŏrlǎnʾ*, sm. Tartar emperor.

tampoco, *tǎmpŏʾkŏ*, ad. neither, not either.

tan, *tǎn*, sm. sound of the tabour; —, ad. so, so much, as well, as much.

tanda, *tǎnʾdǎ*, sf. turn; rotation; task; gang; number of persons employed in a work; **en —**, number of lashes.

tanganillas, *tǎnḡǎnǐlʾyǎs*, ad. waveringly.

tanganillo, *—nǐlʾyŏ*, sm. small prop or stay.   [bone used at hob.

tángano, *tǎnʾḡǎnŏ*, sm. hob (boys' game).

tangente, *tǎnʾhěnʾtě*, sf. (geom.) tangent.

tangible, *—hěʾblě*, a. tangible.

tantarantán, *—tǎrǎntǎnʾ*, sm. roll of a drum; sounding blow.

tantear, *—těǎrʾ*, v. a. to measure, to proportion; to mark the game with counters; to consider; to examine; —se, to redeem a barony or lordship.

tanteo, *tǎntěʾŏ*, sm. computation, calculation; playing-counters; valuation.

tanto, *tǎnʾtŏ*, sm. certain sum or quantity; copy of a writing; —, ta, a. so much, as much; very great; —, ad. so, in such a manner; a long time.

tañedor, ra, *tǎnyědŏrʾ*, sm. & f. player on a musical instrument.

tañer, *tǎnyěrʾ*, v. imp. to concern.

tañido, *tǎnyěʾdŏ*, sm. tune; sound; clink.

tapa, *tǎʾpǎ*, sf. lid, cover; **— de los sesos**, top of the skull.

tapadera, *—dǎʾrǎ*, sf. lid of a pot, cover.

tapadero, *—dǎʾrŏ*, sm. large stopper.

tapadillo, *—dǐlʾyŏ*, sm. covercle; covered register in an organ-pipe.

tapadura, *—dŏʾrǎ*, sf. act of covering.

tapafunda, *—fǔnʾdǎ*, sf. holster-cover.

tapar, *tǎpǎrʾ*, v. a. to stop up, to cover; to conceal, to hide.

tapatán, *—tǎnʾ*, **taparatapán**, *—rǎtǎpǎnʾ*, sm. word indicating the sound of a drum.

tapete, *tǎpěʾtě*, sm. small floor-carpet.

tapia, *tǎʾpǐǎ*, sf. mud-wall.   [walls.

tapial, *tǎpǐǎlʾ*, sm. mould for making mud-

tapiar, *tǎpǐǎrʾ*, v. a. to brick up with a mud-wall; to stop up a passage.

tapicería, *tǎpǐthěrěʾǎ*, sf. tapestry.

tapicero, *—thǎʾrŏ*, sm. tapestry-maker.

tapiz, *tǎpǐthʾ*, sm. tapestry.   [pestry.

tapizar, *tǎpǐthǎrʾ*, v. a. to hang with ta-

tapón, *tǎpŏnʾ*, sm. cork, plug, bung.

tapujarse, *tǎpǔhǎrʾsě*, v. r. to muffle oneself up.   [writing.

taquigrafía, *tǎkǐḡrǎfěʾǎ*, sf. short-hand

taquígrafo, *tǎkěʾḡrǎfŏ*, sm. short-hand

tara, *tǎʾrǎ*, sf. tare.   [writer.

taracea, *—thǎʾǎ*, sf. marquetry, checkerwork.

taracear, *—thěǎrʾ*, v. a. to make inlaid work.

taragallo, *—ḡǎlʾyŏ*, sm. clog, piece of wood suspended from the neck of beasts.

tarambana, *tǎrǎmbǎʾnǎ*, sm. & f. giddy person of little stability or judgment.

tarantela, *tărăntă'lă,* sf. tarantella, Neapolitan peasant dance; its tune.

tarántula, *tărăn'tŭlă,* sf. tarantula.

tararira, *tără̆rē'ră,* sf. noisy mirth.

tarasca, *tără̆s'kă,* sf. figure of a serpent borne in processions, indicating the triumph of Christ over the devil; ugly, ill-natured woman. [answer.

tarascada, *–kă'dă,* sf. bite; pert, harsh

taravilla, *tără̆vĭl'yă,* sf. mill-clack; wooden latch; prattler, tattler.

taraxón, *–thŏn',* sm. large slice, especially of fish.

tardanza, *tărdăn'thă,* sf. slowness, delay.

tardar, *–dăr',* v. n. to delay, to put off, to tarry. [late.

tarde, *tăr'dĕ,* sf. afternoon; evening; –, ad.

tardepiache, *–pĭtsh'ă,* ad. very late.

tardío, dia, *tărdē'ō,* a. late; slow, tardy.

tardo, da, *tăr'dŏ,* a. sluggish, tardy.

tarea, *tără̆'ă,* sf. task.

tarifa, *tărē'fă,* sf. tariff. [tariff.

tarifar, *–făr',* v. a. to tariff, to set up a

tarima, *tărē'mă,* sf. window-ledge; step.

tarjeta, *tărʹhĕ'tă,* sf. visiting-card, card; – postal, post-card.

tarreñas, *tărrĕn'yăs,* sf. pl. rattle.

tarro, *tăr'rŏ,* sm. glazed earthen pan.

tarta, *tăr'tă,* sf. tart, pan for baking tarts.

tartalear, *tărtă̆lĕăr',* v. n. to reel, to stagger; to be perplexed. [to stammer.

tartamudear, *–mŭdĕăr',* v. n. to stutter,

tartamudo, da, *–mŏ'dŏ,* a. stammering.

tartana, *tărtă̆'nă,* sf. tartan.

Tártaro, *tăr'tă̆rŏ,* sm. Tartar; (poet.) hell.

tartera, *tărtĕ'ră,* sf. baking-pan (for tarts).

tarugo, *tărŭ'gŏ,* sm. wooden peg or pin.

tasa, *tăʹsă,* sf. rate, assize; measure, rule; valuation. [praisement.

tasación, *tăsăthĭŏn',* sf. valuation, appraisement.

tasador, *–dŏr',* sm. appraiser.

tasar, *tăsăr',* v. a. to appraise, to value.

tascar, *tăskăr',* v. a. to break flax or hemp; to nibble grass; to champ the bit.

tasco, *tăs'kŏ,* sm. refuse of flax or hemp; toppings of hemp.

tasto, *tăs'tŏ,* sm. nasty taste.

tatarabuelo, *tătără̆bŭĕ'lŏ,* sm. great-great-grandfather. [grandson.

tataranieto, *–nĭĕ'tŏ,* sm. great-great-tate ! *tă'tĕ,* take care! beware!

taumaturgo, *tăŭmătŭr'gŏ,* sm. miracle-worker. [zodiac)

Tauro, *tăŭ'rŏ,* sm. Taurus (sign of the

tautología, *tăŭtŏlō'hĕ'ă,* sf. tautology.

taza, *tă'thă,* sf. cup; basin of a fountain; (fig. & fam.) buttocks, breech.

tazmía, *tăthmē'ă,* sf. share of tithes.

te, *tĕ,* sm. (bot.) tea.

te, *tĕ,* pp. thee.

tea, *tĕ'ă,* sf. candle-wood; torch.

teatral, *tĕătrăl',* a. theatrical.

teatro, *tĕă'trŏ,* sm. theatre, playhouse.

tecla, *tĕk'lă,* sf. key of an organ or piano-forte.

teclado, *tĕklă'dŏ,* sm. key-board.

técnico, ca, *tĕk'nĭkŏ,* a. technical.

techo, *tĕtsh'ŏ,* sm. roof; dwelling-house.

techumbre, *–ŭm'brĕ,* sf. upper roof, ceiling.

Tedéum, *tĕdă'ŭm,* sm. Te Deum.

tedio, *tĕ'dĭŏ,* sm. disgust, dislike, abhorrence.

teja, *tĕ'h'ă,* sf. roof-tile. [rence.

tejado, *tĕhă'dŏ,* sm. roof covered with tiles. [tile.

tejar, *tĕhăr',* sm. tile-works; –, v. a. to

tejedor, *tĕhĕdŏr',* sm. weaver.

tejedura, *–dŏ'ră,* sf. texture, weaving; woven stuff. [cleverness; restlessness.

tejemaneje, *–mănĕ'h'ĕ,* sm. artfulness,

tejer, *tĕhĕr',* v. a. to weave. [kiln.

tejera, *–hă'ră,* tejería,* *–hĕr!'ă,* sf. tile-

tejero, *–'hĕ'rŏ,* sm. tile-maker.

tejido, *–hĕ'dŏ,* sm. texture, web.

tejo, *tĕ'h'ŏ,* sm. quoit; yew-tree.

tejón, *tĕhŏn',* sm. badger.

tela, *tĕ'lă,* sf. cloth; woven stuff.

telar, *tĕlăr',* sm. loom.

telaraña, *–răn'yă,* sf. cobweb.

telefonio, *tĕlĕfō'nĭŏ,* sm. telephon.

telegráfico, ca, *–gră'fĭkŏ,* a. telegraphic.

telégrafo, *tĕlĕ'gră̆fŏ,* sm. telegraph.

telescopio, *tĕlĕskō'pĭŏ,* sm. telescope.

telón, *tĕlŏn',* sm. drop-scene in a playhouse.

tema, *tĕ'mă,* sm. theme; –, sf. hobby.

temblar, *tĕmblăr',* v. n. to tremble.

tembleque, *–blĕ'kĕ,* sm. diamond pin, plume, or other ornament for ladies' head-dresses.

temblón, ona, *–blŏn',* a. tremulous.

temblor, *–blŏr',* sm. trembling.

temer, *tĕmĕr',* v. a. to fear, to doubt.

temerario, ria, *–ră'rĭŏ,* a. rash, temerarious. [prudence.

temeridad, *–rĭdăd',* sf. temerity, imtemeroso, sa,** *–rŏ'sŏ,* a. timid, timorous.

temible, *tĕmē'blĕ,* a. dreadful, terrible.

temor, *–mŏr',* sm. dread, fear.

témpano, *tĕm'pănŏ,* sm. tympanum.

temperamento, *–pĕrămĕn'tŏ,* sm. temperament.

temperar, *–pĕrăr',* v. a. to temperate.

temperatura, *–pĕrătŏ'ră,* sf. temperature.

tempestad, *–pĕstăd',* sf. tempest, storm; violent commotion.

tempestuoso, sa, *–tŏŏ'sŏ,* a. tempestuous, stormy. [perately, moderately.

templadamente, *–plădămĕn'tĕ,* ad. tem-

templado, da, *–plă'dŏ,* a. temperate, tempered.

templador, *–dŏr',* sm. & f. tuning-key.

templanza, *–plăn'thă,* sf. temperance, moderation; temperature.

templar, *–plăr',* v. a. to temper, to moderate, to cool; to tune; –se, to be moderate.

templario, *–plă'rĭŏ,* sm. templar.

temple, *tĕm'plĕ,* sm. temperature, temper, temperament; harmonious accordance of musical instruments; al –, painted in distemper.

templo, *tĕm'plŏ,* sm. temple. [distemper.

Témpora, *tĕm'pŏră,* sf. Ember-days.

temporada, *–ră'dă,* sf. certain space of time, epoch, period.

temporal, *–răl',* a. temporary, temporal; –, sm. season; tempest, storm

temporalidad, –lĭdăd̓, sf. temporality.
temporalizar, –lĭthăr, v. a. to make temporary what should be everlasting.
temprano, na, –prăˈnŏ, a. early, anticipated; –, ad. very early, prematurely.
tenacillas, tĕnăthĭlˈyăs, sf. pl. small tongs.
tenacidad, –thĭdăd̓, sf. tenacity; obstinacy.
tenada, tĕnăˈdă, sf. sheepfold.   [stinacy.
tenaz, –năthˈ, a. tenacious; stubborn.
tenaza, tĕnăˈthă, sf. tongs, pincers.
tenazada, –thăˈdă, sf. grip with pincers or tongs; act of biting strongly.
tenazmente, –mĕnˈtĕ, ad. tenaciously;
tenca, thĕnˈkă, sf. tench.   [obstinately.
ten con ten, tĕn kŏn tĕnˈ, sm. moderation, temperance; –, ad. equally.
tendedero, –dĕdĕˈrŏ, sm. drying-lines.
tendedor, –dŏrˈ, sm. stretcher.   [dency.
tendencia, –dĕnˈthĭă, sf. stretching; tendency.
tender, –dĕrˈ, v. a. to stretch out, to expand, to extend; –se, to stretch oneself at full length out.
ténder, tĕnˈdĕr, sm. (rail.) tender.
tendero, ra, dăˈrŏ, sm. & f. haberdasher.
tendido, –dĭˈdŏ, sm. row of seats for the spectators at a bull-fight.
tendinoso, sa, –nŏˈsŏ, a. sinewy, gristly.
tendón, –dŏnˈ, sm. tendon, sinew.
tenebrario, –tĕnĕbrăˈrĭŏ, sm. large candlestick with a triangular branch, holding 15 candles (in Roman Catholic churches).
tenebroso, sa, –brŏˈsŏ, a. dark, obscure.
tonedor, –dŏrˈ, sm. holder, keeper, tenant; fork.   [tenancy.
tenencia, tĕnĕnˈthĭă, sf. possession; lieutenancy.
tener, tĕnĕrˈ, v. a. to take, to hold, to possess; to have; –se, to take care not to fall; to stop, to halt; to resist; to adhere.
tenería, –rĕˈă, sf. tan-yard.
teniente, tĕnĭĕnˈtĕ, sm. lieutenant.
tenor, tĕnŏrˈ, sm. tenour; (mus.) tenor.
tensión, tĕnsĭŏnˈ, sf. tension.
tentación, –tăthĭŏnˈ, sf. temptation.
tentador, ra, –dŏrˈ, sm. & f. tempter.
tentar, –tărˈ, v. a. to touch; to try; to grope; to tempt; to attempt; to tent.
tentativa, –tĕˈvă, sf. attempt, trial.
tente bonete, tĕnˈtĕ bŏnĕˈtĕ, ad. abundantly.
tenue, tĕˈnŏĕ, a. thin, tenuous, slender.
tenuidad, tĕnŏĭdăd̓, sf. slenderness, weakness; trifle.
teñidura, tĕnyĭdŏˈră, sf. dyeing.
teñir, –yĭr, v. a. to tinge, to dye.
teologal, tĕŏlŏgălˈ, a. theological.
teología, –hĕˈă, sf. theology, divinity.
teológico, ca, –lŏˈhĭkŏ, a. theological.
teólogo, a, tĕŏˈlŏgŏ, sm. theologian, divine.
teorema, tĕŏrĕˈmă, sf. theorem.
teoría, tĕŏrĕˈă, **teórica**, tĕŏˈrĭkă, sf. theory.
teórico, ca, tĕŏˈrĭkŏ, a. theoretical.
tercena, tĕrthăˈnă, sf. wholesale tobacco warehouse.
tercenista, –thĕnĭsˈtă, sm. keeper of a wholesale tobacco warehouse.
tercería, –thĕrĕˈă, sf. mediation, arbitration; depositary.

tercero, –thăˈrŏ, sm. third person; pimp; mediator.
tercerola, –thĕrŏˈlă, sf. short carbine; tierce, terce.   [(mus.) trio.
terceto, –thĕˈtŏ, sm. terzarima, tiercet;
tercia, tĕrˈthĭă, sf. third; canonical hour falling at three o'clock; series of three
terciado, –thĭˈăd̓ŏ, sm. cutlass.   [cards.
terciana, –thĭăˈnă, sf. tertian-fever.
tercianario, ria, –năˈrĭŏ, sm. & f. person suffering from tertian-fever.
terciar, –thĭărˈ, v. a. to put on sideways; to divide into three parts; to plough the third time; –, v. n. to mediate.
terciero, –thĭăˈrŏ, sm. Spanish foot-soldier (16th and 17th centuries).
tercio, oia, tĕrˈthĭŏ, a. third; –, sm. third part; half a load; Spanish regiment (in the 16th century); **hacer bueno –**, to do good to.   [za, a. velvety.
terciopelado, –pĕlăˈd̓ŏ, sf. velveteen; –,
terciopelero, –pĕlĕˈrŏ, sm. velvet-weaver.
terciopelo, –pĕˈlŏ, sm. velvet.
terco, ca, tĕrˈkŏ, a. pertinacious, obstinate; hard as marble.   [yersation, evasion.
tergiversación, –hĭvĕrsăthĭŏnˈ, sf. tergiversation.
tergiversar, –sărˈ, v. a. to tergiversate.
teriaca, tĕrĭăˈkă, sf. treacle.
tericia, tĕrĭˈthĭă, sf. jaundice.
terliz, tĕrlĭthˈ, sm. tick, twilled stuff for
termal, –mălˈ, a. thermal.   [beds.
termas, tĕrˈmăs, sf. pl. thermal-waters, pl.
terminacho, –mĭnăˈtsh̓ŏ, sm. rude word or phrase.
terminación, –măthĭŏnˈ, sf. termination; conclusion; last syllable of a word.
terminante, –măn̓ˈtĕ, a. decisive.
terminar, –nărˈ, v. a. to terminate.
terminativo, va, –năˈtĕˈvŏ, a. terminative.   [dary; limit.
término, tĕrˈmĭnŏ, sm. term; end; boundary.
terminote, –nŏˈtĕ, sm. vulgar or affected expression.   [meter.
termómetro, –mŏˈmĕtrŏ, sm. thermo-
terna, terno, tĕrˈnă, sf. ternary number. [heffer.
ternezo, ra, –năˈrŏ, sm. & f. calf; veal;
terneza, –nĕˈthă, sf. softness, delicacy,
ternilla, –nĭlˈyă, sf. gristle.   [tenderness.
ternilloso, sa, –yŏˈsŏ, a. gristly, cartilaginous.
terno, tĕrˈnŏ, sf. ternary number; ornaments for celebrating high-mass.
ternura, –nŏˈră, sf. tenderness.
terquedad, –kĕdăd̓, **terquería**, –kĕrĕˈă,
terqueza, –kĕˈthă, sf. stubbornness, obterrado**, tĕrrăˈdŏ, sm. terrace.   [stinacy.
terraja, –răˈhˈă, sf. screw-plate.
terraplén, –plĕnˈ, sm. horizontal surface of a rampart; terrace, platform.
terraplenar, –plĕnărˈ, v. a. to make a platform or terrace.   [handles.
terraza, tĕrrăˈthă, sf. glazed jar with two
terremoto, –trĕmŏˈtŏ, sm. earthquake.
terrenal, –mălˈ, a. terrestrial, earthly.
terreno, na, tĕrrăˈnŏ, a. earthly, terrestrial; –, sm. land, ground, field.
terrestre, tĕrrĕsˈtrĕ, a. terrestrial.

terribilidad, *terrĭbĭlĭdăd'*, sf. roughness, ferocity. [ferocious.

terrible, *tĕr'rĭblĕ*, a. terrible, dreadful;

territorial, *tĕrrĭtōrĭăl'*, a. territorial.

territorio, *-tō'rĭŏ*, sm. territory.

terron, *tĕrrŏn'*, sm. clod of earth, glebe; lump; -ones, pl. landed property.

terror, *tĕrrŏr'*, sm. terror, dread.

terrorismo, *-rĭs'mŏ*, sm. terrorism.

terrorista, *-rĭs'tă*, sm. & f. terrorist.

tersar, *tĕrsăr'*, v. a. to smooth.

terso, sa, *tĕr'sŏ*, a. smooth, glossy.

tersura, *-sō'ră*, sf. smoothness, purity.

tertulia, *-tū'lĭă*, sf. club, assembly, circle.

tertuliano, *-lĭā'nŏ*, sm. member of a club.

tesauro, *tĕsă'ŭrŏ*, sm. polyglot dictionary.

tesis, *tĕ'sĭs*, sf. thesis.

tesón, *tĕsŏn'*, sm. tenacity, firmness.

tesorería, *-sōrĕrē'ă*, sf. treasury.

tesorero, *-rē'rŏ*, sm. treasurer.

tesoro, *-sō'rŏ*, sm. treasure; exchequer.

testa, *tĕs'tă*, sf. forehead; front, face.

testado, da, *-tā'dŏ*, a. leaving a will.

testador, *-tă'dŏr'*, sm. testator.

testadriz, *-dă'rĭz*, sf. testatrix.

testadura, *-dō'ră*, sf. erasure.

testamentaría, *-mĕntărē'ă*, sf. testamentary execution.

testamentario, *-mĕn'tō*, sm. executor of a will; -, ria, a. testamentary.

testamento, *-mĕn'tŏ*, sm. will, testament. [will; to bequeath; to scratch out.

testar, *tĕstăr'*, v. a. & n. to make one's

testarudo, da, *-rō'dŏ*, a. obstinate, wrong-headed. [seat of a carriage.

testera, *-tĕ'ră*, sf. front of anything; back

testerada, *-rā'dă*, sf. blow with the head; stubbornness. [genitals.

testículo, *-tĕ'kŭlŏ*, sm. testicle; -s, pl.

testificación, *-tĭfĭkăthŏn'*, sf. attestation.

testificar, *-kăr'*, v. a. to attest, to witness.

testificativo, va, *-kătĭ'vŏ*, a. that which testifies.

testigo, *-tĕ'gŏ*, sm. witness, deponent.

testimonial, *-tĭmōnĭăl'*, a. testimonial; -es, sf. pl. testimonials, pl.

testimoniar, *-mōnĭăr'*, v. a. to attest, to bear witness.

testimonio, *-mō'nĭŏ*, sm. testimony; instrument legalized by a notary.

testuz, *-tūth'*, sm. back of the head; poll.

tesura, *tĕsō'ră*, sf. stiffness, firmness; affected gravity.

teta, *tă'tă*, sf. dug, teat.

tetar, *tĕtăr'*, v. a. to suckle, to give suck.

tetera, *-tĕ'ră*, sf. tea-pot, tea-kettle.

tetilla, *-tū'yă*, sf. small teat.

tetrarca, *-trăr'kă*, sm. tetrarch. [surly.

tétrico, ca, *tĕ'trĭkŏ*, a. gloomy, sullen,

tetuda, *-tō'dă*, a. having large teats or nipples; -, sf. oblong olive. [type.

texto, *tĕks'tŏ*, sm. text; a certain size of

textual, *-tŭăl'*, a. textual.

textualista, *-lĭs'tă*, sm. he who adheres to the text. [hue.

tez, *tĕth*, sf. shining surface; complexion.

ti, *tĭ*, sm. & f. oblique case of tú.

tía, *tĭ'ă*, sf. aunt; good old woman.

tiara, *tĭă'ră*, sf. tiara.

tibieza, *-bĭĕ'thă*, sf. lukewarmness.

tibio, bia, *tĭ'bĭŏ*, a. lukewarm, careless.

tiburón, *tĭbărŏn'*, sm. shark.

tiempo, *tĭĕm'pŏ*, sm. time; term; occasion, opportunity; season.

tienda, *tĭĕn'dă*, sf. tent; awning; tilt; shop.

tienta, *tĭĕn'tă*, sf. probe (for surgeons).

tiento, *-tŏ*, sm. touch; circumspection; á -, gropingly.

tierno, na, *tĭĕr'nŏ*, a. tender.

tierra, *tĭĕr'ră*, sf. earth; land, ground; native country.

tieso, sa, *tĭĕ'sŏ*, a. stiff, hard, firm; robust; valiant; stubborn. [pot.

tiesto, *tĭĕs'tŏ*, sm. potsherd; large earthen

tigre, *tĕ'grĕ*, sm. tiger. [woodcatcher.

tijeras, *tĭ'hĕ'răs*, sf. scissors; drift-

tijeretada, *-hĕrĕtā'dă*, sf. cut with scissors, clip.

tijeretas, *-rĕ'tăs*, sf. pl. tendrils.

tijeretear, *-tĕăr'*, v. a. to cut with scissors; to dispose of other people's affairs at one's pleasure. [stigmatize.

tildar, *tĭldăr'*, v. a. to blot; to brand, to

tilde, *tĭl'dĕ*, sf. dot over a letter; iota, title; very small thing.

tilla, *tĭl'yă*, sf. midship, gangway.

tilo, *tĭ'lŏ*, sm. linden-tree, lime-tree.

timbal, *tĭmbăl'*, sm. kettle-drum.

timbalero, *-lĕ'rŏ*, sm. kettle-drummer.

timbre, *tĭm'brĕ*, sm. crest of a coat of arms.

timidez, *tĭmĭdĕth'*, sf. timidity.

tímido, da, *tĕ'mĭdŏ*, a. timid, cowardly.

timón, *-mŏn'*, sm. helm, rudder.

timorato, ta, *-mŏrā'tŏ*, a. full of the fear of God.

tímpano, *tĭm'pănŏ*, sm. kettle-drum; tympanum; tympan of a printing-press.

tina, *tĕ'nă*, sf. dyer's copper.

tinaja, *tĭnă'h'ă*, sf. large earthen jar.

tinajero, *-'hĕ'rŏ*, sm. water-jar maker.

tinajón, *-'hŏn'*, sm. small tub, kit.

tinelo, *-nĕ'lŏ*, sm. servants' dining-room.

tinglado, *tĭnglā'dŏ*, sm. shed, cart-house.

tiniebla, *-nĭă'blă*, sf. darkness, obscurity; -s, pl. utter darkness.

tino, *tĕ'nŏ*, sm. skill in discovering things by feel; judgment, prudence.

tinta, *tĭn'tă*, sf. tint, hue; ink.

tinte, *-tĕ*, sm. tint, dye.

tintero, *-tĕ'rŏ*, sm. inkhorn, inkstand.

tinto, ta, *tĭn'tŏ*, a. deep-coloured (of wine).

tintorería, *-rĕrē'ă*, sf. dyer's shop.

tintorero, *-rŏ'rŏ*, sm. dyer.

tintura, *-tŏ'ră*, sf. tincture. [tincture.

tinturar, *tŭrăr'*, v. a. to tinge, to dye, to

tiña, *tĭn'yă*, sf. scab. [niggardly.

tiñoso, sa, *tĭnyŏ'sŏ*, a. scabby, scurvy;

tío, *tĕ'ŏ*, sm. uncle; good old man.

tiple, *tĭ'plĕ*, sm. (mus.) treble; one who sings treble; small guitar.

tipo, *tĕ'pŏ*, sm. type.

tipografía, *tĭpŏgrăfĕ'ă*, sf. typography.

tipográfico, ca, *-grā'fĭkŏ*, a. typographical.

tipógrafo, *tĭpŏ'grăfŏ*, sm. printer.

tira, *tĕ'rä*, sf. long and narrow stripe; **—s**, pl. clerks' fees in appeal causes.

tirabraguero, *—brägä'rŏ*, sm. truss.

tirabuzón, *—bŭthŏn'*, sm. cork-screw.

tirada, *tĕrä'dä*, sf. cast, throw; distance from one place to another.

tirador, **ra**, *—dŏr'*, sm. & f. thrower; drawer; pressman; **— de oro**, gold-wire drawer.

tirana, *tĕrä'nä*, sf. female tyrant.

tiranía, *—nē'ä*, sf. tyranny.

tiránico, **ca**, *tĭrä'nĭkŏ*, a. tyrannical.

tiranizar, *—nĭthär'*, v. a. to tyrannize.

tirano, **na**, *tĕrä'nŏ*, a. tyrannical; **—**, sm. tyrant.

tirante, *tĕrän'tĕ*, sm. joist which runs across a beam; trace; gear; brace of a drum; **—**, a. taut, extended, drawn.

tirantez, *—tĕth'*, sf. span; tautness.

tirapié, *—pĭē'*, sm. stirrups, pl., strap.

tirar, *tĕrär'*, v. a. to throw, to cast; to pull; to draw; to fire off; to persuade; to draw metal into slender threads; to tend, to aim at.   [thing of little value.

tiritaña, *tĭrĭtä'nyä*, sf. thin woollen cloth;

tiritar, *—tär'*, v. n. to shiver.   [cold.

tiritona, *—tŏ'nä*, sf. shiver, shaking with

tiro, *tĕ'rŏ*, sm. cast, throw, shot; prank, imposition; set of coach-horses; trace (of harness); **—s**, pl. sword-belts; **errar el —**, to miss (at shooting).

tirón, *tĕrŏn'*, sm. pull, haul, tug.

tirotear, *tĕrŏtĕär'*, v. n. to shoot at random.

tiroteo, *—tä'ŏ*, sm. random-shooting, sharp-shooting.

tirria, *tĕr'rĭä*, sf. antipathy.

tirso, *tĕr'sŏ*, sm. thyrse, wand covered with ivy-leaves, used in sacrifices to Bacchus.

tisana, *tĭsä'nä*, sf. ptisan (a medical drink).

tísico, **ca**, *tĕ'sĭkŏ*, a. phthisical.

tisis, *tĕ'sĭs*, sf. phthisis.

tisú, *tĭsū'*, sm. tissue.   [fellow.

titere, *tĕ'tĕrĕ*, sm. puppet; ridiculous little

titiritaña, *tĭtĭrĭtä'ĭnä*, sf. noisy sport.

titiritero, *—tä'rŏ*, sm. puppet-player.

tito, *tĕ'tŏ*, sm. chick-pea; close-stool.

titubear, *tĕtŭbĕär'*, v. n. to threaten ruin; to stammer; to vacillate, to hesitate.

titubeo, *—bä'ŏ*, sm. vacillation.

titular, *—lär'*, v. a. to title; **—**, v. n. to obtain a title.   [pretence, under pretext.

título, *tĕ'tŭlŏ*, sm. title; name; **á —**, on

tiznar, *tĭthnär'*, v. a. to smut; to tarnish.

tizne, *tĕth'nĕ*, sm. soot, smut of coal.

tiznón, *—nŏn'*, sm. spot, stain.

tizo, *tĕ'thŏ*, sm. half-burnt charcoal.

tizón, *tĕthŏn'*, sm. half-burnt wood.

Tizona, *—thŏ'nä*, sf. sword (of the Cid Ruy Diaz).

tizonada, *—thŏnä'dä*, sf. **tizor.azo**, *—nä'thŏ*, sm. stroke with burning charred wood; (fam.) hell-fire.   [charcoal.

tizonera, *—nä'rä*, sf. heap of ill-burnt

¡to! *tŏ*, word used to call a dog; oh!

toalla, *tŏäl'yä*, sf. towel; **— rusa**, rough towel.

tobillo, *—bĭl'yŏ*, sm. ankle.   [towel.

toca, *tŏ'kä*, sf. hood; a thin stuff.

tocado, *tŏkä'dŏ*, sm. head-dress, head-gear.

tocador, *—dŏr'*, sm. one who touches; toilet, toilet-table.   [tact; inspiration.

tocamiento, *—mĭĕn'tŏ*, sm. touch, contact.

tocante (**á**), *—kän'tĕ*, pr. concerning, relating to.

tocar, *—kär'*, v. a. to touch; to attain, with the hand; (mus.) to play on; to ring a bell; to try metals on a touch-stone; to test; **—**, v. n. to belong; to concern; to be a duty or obligation; to import; to fall to one's share; **—se**, to put on one's hat.

tocayo, **ya**, *—kä'yŏ*, a. name-sake.

tocinero, *—thĕnä'rŏ*, sm. porkman.

tocino, *—thĕ'nŏ*, sm. bacon, salt pork; hog's lard; **hoja de —**, flitch.   [still.

todavía, *—dävĕ'ä*, ad. nevertheless; yet, still.

todo, **da**, *tŏ'dŏ*, a. all, entire; **—**, sm. whole.

todopoderoso, *—pŏdĕrŏ'sŏ*, a. almighty.

toesa, *tŏĕ'sä*, sf. toise, fathom (French measure).

toga, *tŏ'gä*, sf. toga; superior judgeship.

togado, **da**, *tŏgä'dŏ*, a. gowned.

Toisón, *tŏĭsŏn'*, sm. order of the Golden Fleece.

tolano, *—lä'nŏ*, sm. tumour in horses' gums; **—s**, pl. short hair on the neck.

toldillo, *tŏldĭl'yŏ*, sm. covered sedan-chair.

toldo, *tŏl'dŏ*, sm. awning; penthouse.

tolerable, *tŏlĕrä'blĕ*, a. tolerable, supportable.   [dulgence.

tolerancia, *—rän'thĭä*, sf. tolerance, indulgence.

tolerante, *—rän'tĕ*, a. tolerant.

tolerar, *—rär'*, v. n. to tolerate, to suffer.

tolondro, *tŏlŏn'drŏ*, **tolondrón**, *—drŏn'*, sm. contusion arising from a blow; **—ona**, a. giddy, hare-brained.

tolva, *tŏl'vä*, sf. mill-hopper.   [at once.

toma, *tŏ'mä*, sf. portion of any thing taken

tomar, *tŏmär'*, v. a. to take, to seize, to grasp; to understand, to interpret, to perceive; **— á cuestas**, to take upon one-self; **—se**, to get rusty, to rust.

tomate, *—mä'tĕ*, sm. (bot.) tomato.

tomatera, *—tä'rä*, sf. tomato-plant.

tomillar, *—mĭl'yär*, sm. bed of thyme.

tomillo, *—mĭl'yŏ*, sm. (bot.) thyme.

tomo, *tŏ'mŏ*, sm. bulk; tome; volume.

ton, *tŏn*, sm. tone; **sin - ni son**, without rhyme or reason.

tonada, *nä'dä*, sf. tune, melody.

tonadilla, *—dĭl'yä*, sf. interlude of music; short tune.

tonel, *tŏnĕl'*, sm. cask, barrel.

tonelada, *—lä'dä*, sf. tun; collection of casks in a ship; (mar.) tonnage-duty.

tonelería, *—lĕrĕ'ä*, sf. cooper's trade; cooper's workshop.

tonelero, *—lä'rŏ*, sm. cooper, hooper.

tonelete, *—lä'tĕ*, sm. little barrel.

tónico,ca, *tŏ'nĭkŏ*, a. tonic, strengthening.

tono, *tŏ'nŏ*, sm. tone.

tonsura, *tŏnsŏ'rä*, sf. tonsure.

tonsurar, *—sŭrär'*, v. a. to give the tonsure

tontada, *—tä'dä*, sf. nonsense.   [to.

tontear, *—tĕär'*, v. n. to talk nonsense, to act foolishly.

tontería, *—tĕrĕ'ä*, sf. foolery, nonsense.

tontillo, –_tīl'yŏ_, sm. farthingale.
tonto, ta, _tŏn'tŏ_, a. stupid, foolish.
topacio, _tŏpä'thĭŏ_, sm. topaz.
topar, _tŏpär'_, v. a. to run or strike against.
tope, _tŏ'pĕ_, sm. butt, rub; scuffle; –s, pl. (rail.) buffers.
topera, _tŏpā'rä_, sf. mole-hole.
topetada, –_pĕtä'dä_, sf. butt (by a horned animal).
topetar, –_tär'_, v. a. to butt. [animal].
topetón, –_tŏn'_, sm. collision, encounter, blow.
tópico, ca, _tŏ'pĭkŏ_, a. topical.
topinera, _tŏpĭnā'rä_, sf. mole-hill.
topo, _tŏ'pŏ_, sm. mole, molewarp; stumbler.
topografía, _tŏpŏgrăfē'ä_, sf. topography.
topográfico, ca, –_grä'fĭkŏ_, a. topographical.
toque, _tŏ'kĕ_, sm. touch; bell-ringing; crisis.
torada, _tŏrä'dä_, sf. drove of bulls.
torbellino, _tŏrbĕlyē'nŏ_, sm. whirlwind; lively, boisterous, restless person.
torcaz, –_käth'_, a., **paloma** –. ring-dove, wood-pigeon.
torcecuello, –_thĕkūĕl'yŏ_, sm. wry-neck.
torcedor, ra, –_thādŏr'_, sm. & f. twister (spindle); anything causing displeasure.
torcedura, –_dō'rä_, sf. twisting; light, paltry wine.
torcer, –_thĕr'_, v. a. to twist, to double, to curve, to distort; to refute an argument; –se, to change a resolution.
torcida, –_thī'dä_, sf. wick.
torcidillo, –_dĭl'yŏ_, sm. twisted silk.
torcido, da, –_thī'dŏ_, a. oblique, tortuous.
torcimiento, –_mĭĕn'tŏ_, sm. bending, deflection; circumlocution. [prints.
tórculo, _tŏr'kūlŏ_, sm. rolling press for
tordo, _tŏr'dŏ_, sm. thrush, throstle; –, da, a. speckled black and white. [horseback.
toreador, _tŏrĕädŏr'_, sm. bull-fighter on
torear, –_rār'_, v. n. to fight bulls
toreo, –_rā'ŏ_, sm. bull-fighting.
torero, –_rā'rŏ_, sm. bull-fighter on foot.
toril, –_rĭl'_, sm. place where bulls are shut up until brought out.
torillo, –_rĭl'yŏ_, sm. little or young bull.
tormenta, _tŏrmĕn'tä_, sf. storm, tempest.
tormento, –_tŏ_, sm. torment, pain, anguish; torture; tedious affliction. [wedding.
tornaboda, _tŏrnäbŏ'dä_, sf. day after a
tornaguía, –_gē'ä_, sf. debenture.
tornar, –_när'_, v. a. & n. to return; to restore; to repeat.
tornasol, –_sŏl'_, sm. (bot.) turnsol.
tornasolado, –_sŏlä'dŏ_, a. changing colours, chatoyant (of silk-stuff).
torneador, –_nĕä'dŏr_, sm. turner.
tornear, –_nĕär'_, v. a. & n. to turn (on a lathe); to turn; to tilt at tournaments.
torneo, –_nā'ŏ_, sm. tournament. [nery.
tornera, –_nā'rä_, sf. door-keeper of a nun-
tornero, –_rŏ_, sm. turner.
tornillo, –_nĭl'yŏ_, sm. male screw.
torniscón, –_nĭskŏn'_, sm. slap in the face.
torno, _tŏr'nŏ_, sm. wheel; revolution.
toro, _tŏ'rŏ_, sm. bull.
toronja, _tŏrŏn'hä_, sf. thick-peeled orange.
toronjil, _tŏrŏn'hīl'_, sm. (bot.) balm.

torozón, –_rŏthŏn'_, sm. gripes (among animals).
torpe, _tŏr'pĕ_, a. dull, heavy; torpid; stupid; unchaste, obscene; infamous.
torpeza, –_pĕ'thä_, sf. heaviness, dulness; torpor; obscenity; stupidity. [church.
torre, _tŏr'rĕ_, sf. tower; turret; steeple of a
torrejón, –_hŏn'_, sm. ill-shaped turret.
torrente, –_rĕn'tĕ_, sm. torrent.
torreznada, –_rĕthnä'dä_, sf. plentiful dish of rashers.
torrezno, –_rĕth'nŏ_, sm. rasher. [hot.
tórrido, da, _tŏr'rĭdŏ_, a. torrid, parched,
torrija, –_rī'hä_, sf. slice of bread, fried in white wine, eggs, and butter or oil.
torta, _tŏr'tä_, sf. tart.
tortada, –_tä'dä_, sf. meat-pie.
tortera, –_tā'rä_, sf. pan for baking tarts.
tortilla, –_tīl'yä_, sf. omelet, pancake.
tórtola, _tŏr'tŏlä_, sf. turtle-dove.
tortuga, –_tŏ'gä_, sf. tortoise. [cuitous.
tortuoso, sa, –_tŭō'sŏ_, a. tortuous, cir-
tortura, –_tŏ'rä_, sf. tortuosity, flexure; rack, torture.
torvo, va, _tŏr'vŏ_, a. stern, grim, torvid.
torzal, –_thäl'_, sm. cord, twist.
tos, _tŏs_, sf. cough. [grossly.
toscamente, –_kämĕn'tĕ_, ad. coarsely,
tosco, ca, _tŏs'kŏ_, a. coarse, ill-bred, clumsy.
toser, _tŏsĕr'_, v. n. to cough. [tree.
tósigo, _tŏ'sĭgŏ_, sm. poison (from the yew-
tostada, _tŏstä'dä_, sf. slice of toasted bread.
tostado, da, –_tä'dŏ_, a. parched, sun-burnt; light-yellow, light-brown. [toasting-fork.
tostador, ra, –_dŏr'_, sm. & f. toaster;
tostar, –_tär'_, v. a. to toast, to roast.
total, _tŏtäl'_, sm. whole, totality; –, a. total, entire.
totalidad, –_lĭdäd'_, sf. totality.
traba, _trä'bä_, sf. obstacle, impediment; trammel, fetter.
trabacuenta, –_kŭĕn'tä_, sf. error, mistake; dispute, controversy.
trabajador, ra, –_hädŏr'_, sm. & f. labourer, painstaker.
trabajar, –_här'_, v. a. to work, to labour.
trabajo, –_bä'hŏ_, sm. work, labour, toil; difficulty; –s, pl. troubles. [ful.
trabajoso, sa, –_hō'sŏ_, a. laborious, pain-
trabar, –_bär'_, v. a. to join, to unite; to dispute, to quarrel; to take hold of; to fetter, to shackle; to set the teeth of a saw.
trabazón, –_thŏn'_, sf. juncture, union.
trabilla, –_bĭl'yä_, sf. stitch dropped in knitting; strap (of trowsers). [mistake.
trabucación, –_bŭkäthĭŏn'_, sf. confusion,
trabucar, –_bŭkär'_, v. a. to derange, to confound; –se, to mistake.
trabucazo, –_kä'thŏ_, sm. shot with a blunderbuss; sudden fright.
trabuco, –_kŏ_, sm. catapult; blunderbuss.
tradición, –_dĭthĭŏn'_, sf. tradition.
traducción, –_dŭkthĭŏn'_, sf. version, translation.
traducir, –_dŭthĭr'_, v. a. to translate.
traductor, –_dŭktŏr'_, sm. translator.
traer, _trāĕr'_, v. a. to bring, to carry, to attract; to persuade; –se, to be dressed

in style; to have a graceful *or* ungainly deportment. [ful management of affairs.

tráfago, *trä'fägō,* sm. traffic, trade; care-

traficación, *–fĭkäthŏn',* sf. traffic, trade.

traficante, *–kän'tĕ,* sm. merchant, dealer.

traficar, *–kär',* v. n. to traffic, to commerce, to do business, to deal (in).

tráfico, *trä'fĭkō,* sm. traffic, trade.

tragadero, *–gädā'rō,* sm. œsophagus, gullet; gulph, abyss; **tener buenos –s ó buenas tragaderas,** to be very credulous. [gobbler.

tragador, ra, *–dōr',* sm. & f. glutton,

tragaldabas, *–gäld'bäs,* sm. glutton.

tragaleguas, *–gälā'gůäs,* sm. great walker.

tragaluz, *–lůth',* sm. sky-light.

tragantada, *–gäntä'dä,* sf. large draught of liquor. [–, a. gluttonous.

tragantón, ona, *–tōn',* sm. & f. glutton;

tragar, *–gär',* v. a. to swallow, to glut; to swallow up; **–se,** to dissemble.

tragedia, *trä'hā'dĭä,* sf. tragedy.

trágico, ça, *trä'hĭkō,* a. tragic, tragical.

trago, *trä'gō,* sm. draught of liquor; adversity, misfortune; **á –s,** by degrees.

tragón, ona, *–gōn',* a. gluttonous.

traición, *trä'ĭthŏn',* sf. treason.

traidor, ra, *–dōr',* sm. traitor; **–, ra,** a. treacherous.

trailla, *trä'lyä,* sf. leash, lash.

traillar, *–yär',* v. a. to level the ground.

traje, *trä'hĕ,* sm. complete dress of a woman; costume; fashion, mode.

trajinar, *–hĭnär',* v. a. to convey.

trajinero, *–hĭnā'rō,* sm. waggoner.

trama, *trä'mä,* sf. plot, complot.

tramador, ra, *–dōr',* sm. & f. plotter; artful contriver. [machinate.

tramar, *–mär',* v. a. to weave; to plot, to

trámite, *trä'mĭtĕ,* sm. path; (law) procedure.

tramo, *trä'mō,* sm. piece, morsel; piece of ground separated from another; flight of stairs. [vanity, pride.

tramontana, *–mŏntä'nä,* sf. north wind;

tramontano, na, *–nō,* a. tramontane.

tramontar, *–tär',* v. n. to cross the mountains; **–,** v. a. to assist, to relieve; **–se,** to fly, to escape.

tramoya, *–mŏ'yä,* sf. scene, theatrical decoration; craft, wile, artful trick.

tramoyista, *–yĭs'tä,* sm. scene-painter; swindler, diddler, humbug.

trampa, *trä m'pä,* sf. trap, snare; trap-door; fraud; debt fraudulently contracted.

trampantojo, *–päntŏ'hō,* sm. trick played before one's eyes.

trampear, *–pĕär',* v. n. & a. to swindle out of one's money; to impose upon, to deceive.

trampista, *–pĭs'tä,* sm. cheat, impostor, swindler, sharper, fourbe. [ling.

tramposo, sa, *–pŏ'sō,* a. deceitful, swind-

tramvía, *–vē'ä,* sm. tram-way.

tranca, *trän'kä,* sf. cross-bar, cross-beam.

trancar, *–kär',* v. a. to barricade.

trancazo, *–kä'thō,* sm. blow with a bar.

trance, *trän'thĕ,* sm. danger; last stage of life; sale of a debtor's property.

tranco, *trän'kō,* sm. long step *or* stride.

tranchete, *–tshä'tĕ,* sm. shoemaker's heel-knife. [repose, heart's ease.

tranquilidad, *–kĭlĭdäd',* sf. tranquillity;

tranquilizar, *–kĭlĭthär',* v. a. to tranquillize, to calm. [quiet.

tranquilo, la, *–kē'lō,* a. tranquil, calm,

transacción, *tränsäkthŏn',* sf. accommodation, adjustment. [to copy.

transcribir, *–skrĭbĭr',* v. a. to transcribe. **¡ tránseat! ** *träns'ĕät,* let it pass!

transeunte, *tränsĕůn'tĕ,* a. transitory; **–,** sm. passenger. [defer.

transferir, *–fĕrĭr',* v. a. to transfer; to

transfigurable, *–fĭgůrä'blĕ,* a. changeable.

transfiguración, *–fĭgůräthŏn',* sf. transformation, transfiguration.

transfigurarse, *–fĭgůrär'sĕ,* v. r. to be transfigured; to be metamorphosed.

transfixión, *–fĭksŏn',* sf. transfixing.

transflorear, *–flŏrĕär',* v. a. to enamel.

transformación, *–fŏrmäthŏn',* sf. transformation.

transformar, *–fŏrmär',* v. a. to transform; **–se,** to change one's sentiments *or* manners. [sm. deserter, fugitive.

tránsfuga, *träns'fůgä,* **tránsfugo,** *–fůgō,*

transfundir, *–fůndĭr',* v. a. to transfuse; to communicate.

transfusión, *–fůsŏn',* sf. transfusion.

transgresión, *–grĕsŏn',* sf. transgression.

transgresor, *–grĕsōr',* sm. transgressor, law-breaker.

transición, *–sĭthŏn',* sf. transition.

tránsido, da, *–sē'dō,* a. worn out with anguish; avaricious. [differences.

transigir, *–sĭhĭr',* v. a. to accommodate

transitar, *–sĭtär',* v. n. to travel, to pass by a place.

transitivo, va, *–sĭtē'vō,* a. transitive.

tránsito, *trän'sĭtō,* sm. passage; transition; road, way; change, removal; death of holy *or* virtuous persons.

transitorio, ria, *–sĭtō'rĭō,* a. transitory.

translación, *–läthŏn',* sf. translation.

transmarino, na, *–märē'nō,* a. transmarine. [migration.

transmigración, *–mĭgräthŏn',* sf. transmigrate.

transmigrar, *–mĭgrär',* v. a. to transmit;

transmitir, *–mĭtĭr',* v. a. to transmit.

transmutable, *–mŭtä'blĕ,* a. transmutable, changeable. [tation.

transmutación, *–mŭtäthŏn',* sf. transmu-

transmutar, *–mŭtär',* v. a. to transmute.

transparentarse, *–pärĕntär'sĕ,* v. r. to be transparent; to shine through.

transparente, *–pärĕn'tĕ,* a. transparent.

transpiración, *tränspĭräthŏn',* sf. transpiration.

transpirar, *–spĭrär',* v. a. to transpire.

transportación, *tränspŏrtäthŏn',* sf. transportamiento, *–mĭĕn'tō,* sm. transportation.

transportar, *–pŏrtär',* v. a. to transport, to convey; **–se,** to be in a transport.

transporte, –pŏr´tĕ, sm. transport, conveyance; transport-ship.

transposición, –pŏsĭthŏn´, sf. transposition, transposal.

transubstanciación, trănsŭbstănthĭăthĭŏn´, sf. transubstantiation.

transubstancial, –sŭbstănthĭăl´, a. converted into another substance.

transubstanciar, –sŭbstănthĭăr´, v. a. to transubstantiate.

transversal, –vĕrsăl´, a. transverse; collateral.

tranzadera, trănthădĕ´ră, sf. knot of plaited cords or ribbons.

trapacear, trăpăthĕăr´, v. n. to deceive, to defraud.

trapacería, –rĕ´ă, sf. fraud, deceit.

trapacero, ra, –thĕ´rŏ, a. deceitful.

trapacista, –thĭs´tă, sm. impostor, cheat.

trapajo, trăpă´h´ŏ, sm. rag, tatter.

trapajoso, sa, –´hŏ´sŏ, a. ragged, tattered.

trápala, tră´pălă, sf. stamping with the feet; bawling; babbler; garrulity.

trapalear, –lĕăr´, v. n. to babble.

trapalón, ona, –lŏn´, a. loquacious.

trapería, –pĕrĕ´ă, sf. frippery, rag-fair; woollen-draper's shop.

trapero, –pĕ´rŏ, sm. & f. dealer in rags.

trapisonda, –pĭsŏn´dă, sf. bustle, noise, confusion.

trapo, tră´pŏ, sm. rag, tatter.

traquear, trăkĕăr´, v. n. to crack; —, v. a. to shake, to agitate.

traqueo, –kĕ´ŏ, sm. noise of artificial fireworks; shaking; moving to and fro.

tras, trăs, pr. after, behind; —, sm. breach, bottom; blow attended with noise; —, —, bang, bang.

trascartarse, –kărtăr´sĕ, v. r. to remain (of a card which, had it come sooner, would have won the game).

trascartón, –kărtŏn´, sm. drawing of a winning card after the game is lost.

trascendencia, –thĕndĕn´thĭă, sf. transcendency; penetration.

trascendental, –thĕndĕntăl´, a. transcendental.

trascender, –thĕndĕr´, v. a. to go beyond; to rise above; —, v. n. to emit a strong smell.

trascolar, –kŏlăr´, v. a. (med.) to strain; to cross a mountain.

trascordarse, –kŏrdăr´sĕ, v. r. to forget.

trascoro, –kŏ´rŏ, sm. space of a church at the back of the choir.

trascurso, –kŭr´sŏ, sm. course of time.

trasegar, –sĕgăr´, v. a. to overset; to decant.

trasera, trăsĕ´ră, sf. back-part; croup.

trasero, ra, –rŏ, a. hind, hinder; —, sm. buttock.

trasgo, trăs´gŏ, sm. hobgoblin; lively, restless, noisy boy.

trashojar, –s´hăr´, v. a. to turn over the leaves, to skim a book.

trashumar, –ŭmăr´, v. a. to drive sheep to or from the common pasture-ground or the mountains in spring and autumn.

trasiego, –sĭĕ´gŏ, sm. removal; decanting of liquors.

trasladar, –lădăr´, v. a. to transport; to translate; to transcribe, to copy.

traslado, –lă´dŏ, sm. copy; image; resemblance; parent; to conjecture.

traslucirse, –lăthĭr´sĕ, v. r. to be translucent; to be transparent.

traslumbrarse, –lŭmbrăr´sĕ, v. r. to be dazzled with excessive light; to vanish.

trasluz, –lŭth´, sm. light which passes through a transparent body; transverse light.

trasmallo, –măl´yŏ, sm. trammel.

trasnochar, –nŏtshăr´, v. n. to watch, to sit up a whole night.

traspapelarse, –păpĕlăr´sĕ, v. r. to be mislaid among other papers.

traspasar, –păsăr´, v. n. to pass over; —, v. a. to remove; to transport; to transfix, to transpierce; to return, to repass; to exceed the proper bounds; to trespass; to transfer.

traspaso, –pă´sŏ, sm. conveyance; trespass.

traspié, –pĭĕ´, sm. trip; slip, stumble.

trasplantar, –plăntăr´, v. a. to transplant.

trasplante, –plăn´tĕ, sm. transplantation.

trasponer, –pŏnĕr´, v. a. to remove, to transport; to take a circuitous road in order to get out of sight; to conceal; –se, to be drowsy.

traspuesta, –pŭĕs´tă, sf. transport; hiding-place in a wood; flight.

traspuesto, ta, –tŏ, a. & p. transported.

traspunte, –pŭn´tĕ, sm. prompter.

trasquilador, –kĭlădŏr´, sm. shearer.

trasquiladura, –kĭlădŏ´ră, sf. shearing.

trasquilar, –kĭlăr´, v. a. to shear sheep; to clip; hair badly cut.

trasquilón, –kĭlŏn´, sm. cut of the shears; to shear.

traste, trăs´tĕ, sm. fret of a guitar.

trasteado, –tĕă´dŏ, sm. number of frets round a guitar's handle.

trasteador, ra, –tĕădŏr´, sm. & f. noisy fellow.

trastear, –tĕăr´, v. a. to put frets round the handle of a guitar; to move furniture.

trastejador, –tĕ´hădŏr´, sm. tiler.

trastejar, –tĕ´hăr´, v. a. to cover with tiles.

trastera, trăst´ă´ră, sf. lumber-room.

trastería, –tĕrĕ´ă, sf. heap of lumber; ridiculous or foolish action.

trastienda, –tĭĕn´dă, sf. back-room behind a shop; prudence, forecast.

trasto, trăs´tŏ, sm. furniture; useless person.

trastornador, –tŏrnădŏr´, sm. & f. disturber, turbulent person.

trastornar, –tŏrnăr´, v. a. to overthrow, to overturn; to perplex the mind.

trastorno, –tŏr´nŏ, sm. overthrow.

trastrocar, –trŏkăr´, v. a. to invert the order of things.

trasudar, –sŭdăr´, v. a. to sweat, to perspire.

trasudor, –sŭdŏr´, sm. gentle sweat.

trasvenarse, –vĕnăr´sĕ, v. r. to be spilled or lost by shedding.

tratable, trătă´blĕ, a. tractable; compliant.

tratado, –tă´dŏ, sm. treaty, convention; treatise; style of address.

tratamiento, –mĭĕn´tŏ, sm. treatment.

tratante, –tăn´tĕ, sm. dealer in provisions.

tratar, –tăr´, v. a. to treat on a subject; to traffic, to trade; to use, to treat; to be careful to attain an object; **–se**, to enter-tain a friendly intercourse; to live well or ill.

trato, *trä'tõ,* sm. treatment; manner, ad-dress; trade, traffic; conversation.

través, *trävés',* sm. bias; traverse of a fortress; **de ó al –,** across, athwart.

travesaño, *–sän'yõ,* sm. cross-timber; transom.

travesero, *–sä'rõ,* sm. transom; **–, ra,** a. [transverse, across.

travesía, *–sẽ'ä,* sf. transverse position or manner; trajectory; (mar.) side-wind.

travestido, da, *–vëst'dõ,* a. disguised.

travesura, *–sõ'rä,* sf. running to and fro in a restless manner; penetration; lively fancy; wickedness, knavery.

travieso, sa, *trävié'sõ,* a. restless, uneasy, fidgety; turbulent; lively; debauched.

traza, *trä'thä,* sf. first sketch; trace, out-line; project; manner; means; appear-ance.   [ject; to trace.

trazar, *–thär',* v. a. to plan out; to pro-

trazo, *trä'thõ,* sm. sketch, plan, design.

trébedes, *trä'bëdës,* sf. pl. trevet, tripod.

trébol, *trä'bõl,* sm. trefoil, clover.

trece, *trä'thë,* a. a thirteen; thirteenth.

trecho, *trëtsh'õ,* sm. space, distance of time or place; **á –s,** at intervals.

trecientos, tas, *trëthiën'tõs,* a. three hundred.   [hostilities.

tregua, *träˈgdä,* sf. truce, cessation of

treinta, *trä'intä,* a. thirty.

treinteno, na, *träintä'nõ,* a. thirtieth.

tremendo, da, *–mën'dõ,* a. terrible, for-midable; awful, grand.

trementina, *–mëntë'nä,* sf. turpentine.

tremés, tremesino, na, *–sẽ'nõ,* a. three months old.   [colours; to wave.

tremolar, *–mõlär',* v. a. to hoist the

tremolina, *–lẽ'nä,* sf. rustling of the wind; bustle, confused noise.   [bling.

trémulo, la, *trä'mulõ,* a. tremulous, trem-

tren, *trën,* sm. train, retinue; show, ostent-ation; (rail.) train; **– ordinario, – ómnibus,** parliamentary train, slow train; **–correo, –de gran velocidad,** fast or express train, mail-train; **– de mercancías,** goods train, luggage-train; **– ascendente,** up-train; **– descen-dente,** down-train.   [band.

trencilla, *–thĩl'yõ,* sm. gold or silver hat-

trenos, *trä'nõs,* sm. pl. lamentation.

trenza, *trën'thä,* sf. braided hair, plaited silk.

trenzado, *–thä'dõ,* sm. braided hair.

trenzar, *–thär',* v. a. to braid the hair.

trepar, *trëpär',* v. n. to climb, to crawl.

tres, *trës,* a. & s. three.   [wile.

treta, *trä'tä,* sf. thrust in fencing; trick,

triaca, *trä'kä,* sf. theriaca, treacle.

triangular, *triängdlär',* a. triangular.

triángulo, *triän'gulõ,* sm. triangle.

tribu, *trẽ'bä,* sm. & f. tribe.

tribulación, *–läthiõn',* sf. tribulation, affliction.

tribuna, *–bõ'nä,* sf. tribune.   [justice.

tribunal, *–bünäl',* sm. tribunal, court of

tribunali (pro –), *–nä'lï,* ad. in public courts; in a decisive tone.

tribuno, *–bõ'nõ,* sm. tribune.

tributar, *–bütär',* v. a. to pay tribute; **to** contribute to; to pay homage and respect.

tributario, ria, *–tä'riõ,* a. tributary.

tributo, *–bõ'tõ,* sm. tribute.

tricolor, *trïkölõr',* a. tricoloured.

tricorne, *–kõr'në,* a. three-horned.

tridente, *–dën'të,* a. three-pronged; **–, sm.** [trident.

trienal, *trïënäl',* a. triennial.

trienio, *trïë'niõ,* sm. space of three years.

trigaza, *–gä'thä,* a. short straw.

trigésimo, ma, *–hë'simõ,* a. thirtieth.

trigo, *trä'gõ,* sm. wheat; **–de las Indias,** maize.

trigueño, ña, *trïgën'yõ,* a. swarthy.

triguero, ra, *–gä'rõ,* a. growing among wheat; **–, sm.** winnowing-sieve, screen; corn-merchant.

trilingüe, *–lïn'gü,* a. a talking three, or relating to three languages.

trillado, *trïlyä'dõ,* a. beaten; trite, stale, hackneyed; **camino –,** common road.   [routine.

trillador, *–dõr',* sm. thrasher.

trilladura, *–dõ'rä,* sf. act of thrashing.

trillar, *–yär',* v. a. to thrash.

trillo, *trïl'yõ,* sm. flail.   [months.

trimestre, *trïmës'trë,* sm. space of three

trinado, *–nä'dõ,* sm. trill, quaver.

trinar, *–när',* v. n. to trill, to quaver.

trincar, *trënkär',* v. a. to break into small pieces; (mar.) to keep close to the wind; to fasten the rope-ends.   [knife.

trinchante, *–tshän'të,* sm. carver; carving-

trinchar, *–tshär',* v. a. to carve, to divide meat; to decide with an air of authority.

trinchera, *–tshä'rä,* sf. trench, entrench-

trinchero, *–tshä'rõ,* sm. trencher. [ment.

trinchete, *–tshë'të,* sm. paring-knife.

Trinidad, *trïnïdäd',* sf. Trinity.

trinitaria, *–tä'riä,* sf. three-coloured vio-let, heart's ease.

trino, na, *trä'nõ,* a. containing three dis-tinct things; **–, sm.** trill.   [quet; tennis.

trinquete, *trïnkë'të,* sm. foremast; trin-

trío, *trä'õ,* sm. (mus.) trio.

tripa, *trë'pä,* sf. gut, tripe, intestine; belly of a vessel; core.

tripe, *trë'pë,* sm. shag.

tripería, *trïpërë'ä,* sf. tripe-market, tripery.

tripero, *–pä'rõ,* **tripicallero, ra,** *–pï kälyä'rõ,* sm. & f. tripe-man.

triple, *trë'plë,* a. triple, treble.

triplicar, *trïplïkär',* v. a. to treble.

triplo, la, *trë'plõ,* a. treble, triplicate.

trípode, *trë'põdë,* sm. tripod, trivet.

triptongo, *trïptõn'gõ,* sm. triphthong.

tripudo, da, *–põ'dõ,* a. big-bellied.

tripulación, *–pülähiõn',* sf. crew of a ship.   [out.

tripular, *–lär',* v. n. to man ships; to fit

triquitraque, *trïkïträ'kë,* sm. clack, clatter, clashing.

tris, *trïs,* sm. noise made by the breaking of glass; trice, instant; **estar en un –,** to be on the point of.

trisagio, *–sä'hiõ,* sm. trisagion: holy, holy, holy is the Lord.

triscar, *trĭskăr'*, v. n. to make a noise with the feet; to frisk about.

trisilabo, ba, *-sē'lăbŏ*, a. trisyllabic.

triste, *trĭs'tĕ*, a. sad, mournful, melancholy. [ing.

tristeza, *-tĕ'thă*, sf. melancholy, mourning.

tritono, *trĭtŏ'nŏ*, sm. musical interval of three tones.

trituración, *-tŭrăthĭŏn'*, sf. pulverization.

triturar, *-răr'*, v. a. to reduce to powder, to grind, to pound.

triunfal, *trĭŭnfăl'* a. triumphal.

triunfar, *-făr'*, v. n. to triumph; to trump at cards. [(at cards).

triunfo, *trĭŭn'fŏ*, sm. triumph; trump

triunvirato, *-vĭrā'tŏ*, sm. triumvirate.

triunviro, *-vē'rŏ*, sm. triumvir.

trivial, *trĭvĭăl'*, a. frequented, beaten; vulgar, trivial.

trivialidad, *-lĭdăd'*, sf. vulgarity.

triza, *trĭ'thă*, sf. mite; cord, rope.

trobador, *trŏbădŏr'*, sm. troubadour.

trocable, *-kā'blĕ*, a. changeable.

trocar, *-kăr'*, v. a. to exchange, to barter; **-se**, to be changed or reformed.

trochemoche, *trŏtshĕmŏ'tshĕ*, (á —), ad. helter-skelter.

trofeo, *trŏfĕ'ŏ*, sm. trophy.

troj, *trŏ'h*, **troje**, *trŏ'h'ĕ*, sf. granary, fruit-loft. [large top.

trompa, *trŏm'pă*, sf. trumpet; proboscis.

trompada, *-pă'dă*, sf. blow with the nose or fist. [adverse accident.

trompazo, *-pă'thŏ*, sm. heavy blow.

trompeta, *-pĕ'tă*, sf. trumpet; —, sm. trumpeter. [trumpet.

trompetear, *-tĕăr'*, v. n. to sound the

trompetero, *-tĕ'rŏ*, sm. trumpeter; trumpet-maker.

trompetilla, *-tēl'yă*, sf. small trumpet; speaking-trumpet.

trompicar, *-pĭkăr'*, v. n. & a. to stumble frequently; to trip, to occasion stumbling.

trompicón, *-kŏn'*, sm. stumbling.

trompo, *trŏm'pŏ*, sm. whipping-top.

tronada, *trŏnă'dă*, sf. thunder-storm.

tronar, *-năr'*, v. n. to thunder.

troncar, *trŏnkăr'*, v. a. to truncate, to mutilate. [stock.

tronco, *trŏn'kŏ*, sm. trunk; log of wood;

tronchar, *-tshăr'*, v. a. to cut off at the stalk. [stalk.

troncho, *trŏn'tshŏ*, sm. sprig, stem or

tronchudo, *-tshŏ'dŏ*, a. having a long stem or stalk.

tronera, *trŏnĕ'ră*, sm. embrasure of a battery; loop-hole; dormer; hare-brained person; pocket of a billiard-table.

trono, *trŏ'nŏ*, sm. throne; **—s**, pl. seventh choir of angels.

tronzar, *trŏnthăr'*, v. a. to shatter, to break into pieces; to plait, to fold.

tropa, *trŏ'pă*, sf. troop.

tropel, *trŏpĕl'*, sm. confuse noise; hurry, bustle, confusion, heap of things; crowd; **de —**, in a tumultuous and confused manner.

tropelía, *-lĕ'ă*, sf. precipitation, hurry, confusion, vexation, oppression.

tropezadero, *-thădĕ'rŏ*, sm. any stumbling or slippery place.

tropezar, *-thăr'*, v. n. to stumble; to be detained or obstructed; to meet accidentally; to cut the feet in walking (horses).

tropezón, ona, *-thŏn'*, a. stumbling; **á -ones**, impeded and obstructed; —, sm. tripping. [tropical.

trópico, *trŏ'pĭkŏ*, sm. tropic; —, ca, a.

tropiezo, *trŏpĭĕ'thŏ*, sm. stumble, trip; obstacle; slip, fault; quarrel; dispute.

tropo, *trŏ'pŏ*, sm. trope.

troquel, *trŏkĕl'*, sm. solid piece of steel, in which a hollow figure is engraved.

trotador, ra, *trŏtădŏr'*, sm. & f. trotter.

trotar, *trŏtăr'*, v. n. to trot.

trote, *trŏ'tĕ*, sm. trot; **á —**, in haste.

trovador, ra, *trŏvădŏr'*, sm. & f. troubadour.

trovar, *-văr'*, v. a. to versify; to parody.

trozo, *trŏ'thŏ*, sm. piece cut off; (rail.) section of a line.

trucar, *trŭkăr'*, v. n. to lead (at cards).

truco, *trŏ'kŏ*, sm. skilful push at trucks; **—s**, pl. trucks, pl.

trucha, *trŭtsh'ă*, sf. trout; crane.

truchuela, *-tshŭĕ'lă*, sf. small cod-fish.

trueno, *trŭĕ'nŏ*, sm. thunder-clap.

trueque, *trŭĕ'kĕ*, sm. exchange, truck, barter. [barter.

truhán, *trŭăn'*, a. buffoon.

truhanear, *-nĕăr'*, v. n. to play the buffoon.

truhanería, *-nĕrĕ'ă*, sf. buffoonery.

truhanesco, ca, *-nĕs'kŏ*, a. belonging to a buffoon. [a buffoon.

trujal, *trŭhăl'*, sm. oil-mill.

truncado, da, *trŭnkă'dŏ*, a. truncated.

truncamiento, *-mĭĕn'tŏ*, sm. truncation.

truncar, *-kăr'*, v. a. to truncate, to maim.

truque, *trŭ'kĕ*, sm. a game at cards.

truquero, *-kĕ'rŏ*, sm. keeper of a truck. [table.

tu, *tŭ*, a. thy, thine.

tú, *tŭ*, pn. thou.

tuáutem, *tŭă'ŭtĕm*, sm. principal person; [essential point.

tubo, *tŏ'bŏ*, sm. tube.

tuerca, *tŭĕr'kă*, sf. female screw.

tuerto, ta, *tŭĕr'tŏ*, a. one-eyed; squint-eyed; —, sm. wrong, injury.

tuétano, *tŭĕ'tănŏ*, sm. marrow. [smell.

tufarada, *tŭfără'dă*, sf. strong scent or

tufo, *tŏ'fŏ*, sm. warm vapour arising from the earth; offensive smell; ear-lock.

tulipán, *tŭlĭpăn'*, sm. tulip.

tullido, da, *tŭlyĕ'dŏ*, a. a crippled, maimed.

tullimiento, *-mĭĕn'tŏ*, sm. maiming.

tullir, *-yĭr'*, v. n. to drop excrement (of birds), **-se**, to be crippled or maimed.

tumba, *tŭm'bă*, sf. tomb; roof of a coach'; tumble.

tumbaga, *-bă'gă*, sf. pinchbeck, tomback.

tumbar, *-băr'*, v. a. to tumble (to throw down); —, v. n. to tumble (to fall down); **-se**, to lie down to sleep. [ing.

tumor, *tŭmŏr'*, sm. tumour, morbid swelling.

túmulo, *tŏ'mŭlŏ*, sm. tomb, sepulchral monument.

tumulto, *tŭmŭl'tŏ*, sm. tumult, uproar.

tumultuoso, sa, *–tŏŏ´sŏ,* a. tumultuous.
tuna, *tŏ´nā,* sf. Indian fig; idle life.
tunante, *tŭnän´tĕ,* a. & p. cunning; leading a licentious life; —, sm. rake, lazy loiterer.
tunar, *–när´,* v.n. to lead a licentious life; to loiter.   [severe chastisement.
tunda, *tŭn´dā,* sf. act of shearing cloth;
tundidor, *–dīdŏr´,* sm. shearer of cloth.
tundir, *–dēr´,* v. a. to shear; to cudgel;
túnica, *tŏ´nīkā,* sf. tunic.   [to flog.
tuno, *tŏ´nŏ,* sm. truant, rake.
tupé, *tŭpĕ´,* sm. toupet, foretop.
tupir, *tŭpīr´,* v. a. to press close; **–se,** to stuff oneself with eating and drinking.
turba, *tŭr´bā,* sf. crowd; turf, sod.
turbación, *–thŏn´,* sf. perturbation, confusion, trouble, disorder.
turbador, ra, *–dŏr´,* sm. & f. disturber.
turbante, *–bän´tĕ,* sm. turban.
turbar, *–bār´,* v. a. to disturb, to trouble.
turbio, bia, *tŭr´bĭŏ,* a. muddy, troubled.
turbión, *–bĭŏn´,* sm. heavy shower of rain; hurricane.   [disturbance.
turbulencia, *–bŭlĕn´thĭā,* sf. turbulence.
turbulento, ta, *–lĕn´tŏ,* a. turbid, muddy; turbulent.
turnar, *tŭrnär´,* v. n. to alternate.
turno, *tŭr´nŏ,* sm. turn; vicissitude.
turquesa, *tŭrkĕs´ā,* sf. turquoise.
turquí, *tŭrkī´,* a. of a deep blue colour.
turrar, *tŭrrär´,* v. a. to toast, to roast.
turrón, *tŭrrŏn´,* sm. nougat (almond cake).
turronero, *–nŏ´rŏ,* sm. nougat-maker or seller.   [head.
turumbón, *–rŭmbŏn´,* sm. contusion on the
¡ tus ! *tŭs,* word used for calling dogs.
tuteamiento, *tŭtĕāmĭĕn´tŏ,* sm. thouing.
tutear, *–tĕār´,* v. a. to thou.
tutela, *–tŏ´lā,* sf. guardianship, tutelage.
tutelar, *–tĕlār´,* a. tutelar, tutelary.
tutor, *–tŏr´,* sm. guardian; tutor.
tutora, *–tŏ´rā,* sf. tutoress.
tutoría, *–tŏrē´ā,* sf. tutelage.
tuyo, ya, *tŏ´yŏ,* a. thine; **–s,** pl. friends and relations of the party addressed.

U.

ŭ, c. or (instead of ó, when the following word begins with an *o*); **¡ – ! ah !** alas!
ubre, *ŏ´brĕ,* sf. dug, teat, udder.
ufanamente, *ŭfānāmĕn´tĕ,* ad. ostentatiously, boastfully.
ufanarse, *–när´sĕ,* v. r. to boast.
ufanía, *–nē´ā,* sf. haughtiness.
ufano, na, *ŭfä´nŏ,* a. haughty, arrogant;   [gay, cheerful.
ujier, *ŭhĭĕr´,* sm. usher.
úlcera, *ŭl´thĕrā,* sf. ulcer.
ulceración, *–räthĭŏn´,* sf. ulceration.
ulcerar, *–rär´,* v. n. to ulcerate.
ulceroso, sa, *–rŏ´sŏ,* a. ulcerous.   [ther.
ulterior, *ŭltĕrĭŏr´,* a. ulterior, farther, fur-
ultimátum, *–ītmä´tŭm,* sm. ultimatum.
último, ma, *ŭl´tĭmŏ,* a. last, hindmost.
ultrajador, ra, *–trä´hādŏr´,* sm. & f. one who outrages *or* insults.

ultrajar, *–´här´,* v. a. to outrage; **to** despise, to depreciate; to abuse.
ultraje, *–trä´hĕ,* sm. outrage.
ultramar, *–trāmär´,* a. & sm. ultramarine.
ultramarino, na, *–mārē´nŏ,* a. ultramarine, oversea.   [montane.
ultramontano, na, *–mŏntä´nŏ,* a. ultra-
umbilical, *ŭmbīlīkäl´,* a. umbilical.
umbral, *–brāl´,* sm. threshold; architrave; beginning, rudiment.
un, *ŭn,* a. one (for uno).
unánime, *–ä´nĭmĕ,* a. unanimous.
unanimidad, *–mĭdäd´,* sf. unanimity.
unción, *ŭnthĭŏn´,* sf. unction; extreme *or* last unction; **–ones,** pl. course of salva-
uncir, *–thĭr´,* v. a. to yoke.   [tion.
undécimo, ma, *–dĕ´thĭmŏ,* a. eleventh.
undísono, na, *–dī´sŏnŏ,* a. billowy.
undoso, sa, *–dŏ´sŏ,* a. wavy, rising in waves.   [king, sovereign.
ungido, *–hē´dŏ,* sm. anointed of the Lord,
ungir, *–hēr´,* v. a. to anoint.
ungüento, *–gŭĕn´tŏ,* sm. unguent; ointment.   [simply.
únicamente, *ŭ´nĭkāmĕn´tĕ,* ad. only,
único, ca, *ŭ´nĭkŏ,* a. singular, unique.
unicornio, *–kŏr´nĭŏ,* sm. unicorn.
unidad, *–däd´,* sf. unity; conformity, union.
unidamente, *–dāmĕn´tĕ,* ad. jointly, un-
uniformar, *–fŏrmär´,* v. a. to make uniform.   [(mil.) uniform, regimentals.
uniforme, *–fŏr´mĕ,* a. uniform; **–,** sm.
uniformidad, *–mĭdäd´,* sf. uniformity.
unigénito, *–hä´nĭtŏ,* a. only-begotten.
unión, *ŭnĭŏn´,* sf. union.
unir, *ŭnĭr´,* v. a. to join, to unite; to **mingle,** to bind, to tie; **–se,** to associate.
unísono, na, *ŭnē´sŏnŏ,* a. unison.
unitivo, va, *–tē´vŏ,* a. unitive.
universal, *–vĕrsäl´,* a. universal.
universalidad, *–lĭdäd´,* sf. universality.
universidad, *–sĭdäd´,* sf. universality; university.
universo, *–vĕr´sŏ,* sm. universe.
uno, *ŭ´nŏ,* sm. one; **–,** na, a. one; sole, only; **– á otro,** one another; **– á –,** one by one; **á una,** jointly, together.
untar, *ŭntär´,* v. a. to anoint; to grease; **–se,** to be greased with unctuous matter.
unto, *ŭn´tŏ,* sm. grease; fat of animals.
untuoso, sa, *–tŭŏ´sŏ,* a. unctuous, greasy.
untura, *–tŏ´rā,* sf. unction; unguent.
uña, *ŭn´yā,* sf. nail; hoof; claw, talon; pointed book of instruments.
uñada, *–yä´dā,* uñarada, *–yärä´dā,* sf. scratch with the nail.
uñero, *–yä´rŏ,* sm. whitlow.
uñeta, *–yä´tā,* sf. sculptor's gouge; nail-claw; chuck-farthing (boys' game).
¡ upa ! *ŭ´pā,* up ! up ! up ! (to make children get up from the ground).
upar, *ŭpär´,* v. n. to endeavour to get up.
urbanidad, *ŭrbānĭdäd´,* sf. urbanity, politeness.
urbano, na, *–bä´nŏ,* a. polite, well-bred.
urdidor, ra, *–dīdŏr´,* sm. & f. warper; warping-mill.

urdidura, –dô'râ, sf. warping.

urdiembre, –dĭem'brĕ, urdimbre, –dĭm'brĕ, sf. chain, warp.

urdir, –dēr', v. a. to warp; to contrive.

urgencia, –hĕn'thĭä, sf. urgency, pressure of difficulty, need, necessity.

urgentemente, –tĕmĕn'tĕ, ad. urgently.

urgir, – hēr', v. n. to be urgent.

urinario, ria, ŭrĭnä'rĭō, a. urinary.

urna, ūr'nä, sf. urn; glass-case in which small statues or images are kept.

urraca, ŭrrä'kä, sf. magpie.

usado, da, ŭsä'dō, a. used; experienced.

usagre, ŭsä'grĕ, sm. milk-scab, kind of breaking out in the faces of children.

usanza, ŭsän'thä, sf. usage, use, custom.

usar, ŭsär', v. a. to use, to make use of; to accustom; –se, to be in use, to be wont. [Your Lordship.

Usía, ŭsĭ'ä (= Vuestra Señoría), sf.

uso, ū'sō, sm. use, service; custom; mode.

Usted, ŭstĕd', sm. & f. you (contraction of Vuestra Merced).

usuario, ria, ŭsŭä'rĭō, a. (law) having only the use of a thing.

usufructo, –frŭk'tō, sm. usufruct.

usufructuar, –frŭktŭär', v. a. to enjoy the usufruct of any thing; to render productive. [the usufruct of any thing.

usufructuario, ria, –tŭä'rĭō, a. possessing

usura, ŭsū'rä, sf. usury.

usurario, ria, –rä'rĭō, a. belonging to

usurero, –rĕ'rō, sm. usurer. [usury.

usurpación, ŭsŭrpäthĭōn', sf. usurpation.

usurpador, ra, –dōr', sm. & f. usurper.

usurpar, –pär', v. a. to usurp.

utensilio, ŭtĕnsĭ'lĭō, sm. utensil.

uterino, na, ŭtĕrĭ'nō, a. uterine.

útero, ū'tĕrō, sm. uterus, womb.

útil, ū'tĭl, a. useful, profitable; –, sm.

utilidad, –lĭdäd', sf. utility. [utility.

utilizar, –lĭthär', v. a. to make useful; to be useful; to yield profit; –se, to take advantage of.

ut supra, ŭt sū'prä, ad. as above.

uva, ū'vä, sf. grape; barberry.

V.

vaca, vä'kä, sf. cow; beef.

vacaciones, –thĭō'nĕs, sf. pl. holidays.

vacada, –kä'dä, sf. drove of cows.

vacante, –kän'tĕ, a. vacant; –, sf. vacancy.

vacar, –kär', v. n. to be vacant.

vaciadero, –thĭädĕ'rō, sm. drain, sink.

vaciador, –dōr', sm. moulder.

vaciar, –thĭär', v. a. to empty, to clear; to mould; –, v. n. to fall, to decrease (of waters); –se, to be spilt, to be emptied.

vacilación, –thĭläthĭōn', sf. vacillation; irresolution.

vacilar, –lär', v. n. to vacillate.

vacío, cia, väthĭ'ō, a. void, empty; unoccupied; concave; vain; presumptuous; unemployed; –, sm. vacuum; concavity.

vacuna, –kō'nä, sf. cow-pox, vaccine virus.

vacunar, –kŭnär', v. a. to vaccinate.

vacuno, na, väkō'nō, a. belonging to black cattle.

vade, vä'dĕ, sm. satchel.

vadeable, –dĕä'blĕ, a. fordable.

vadear, –dĕär', v. a. to wade, to ford.

vado, vä'dō, sm. ford.

vagabundo, da, –gäbŭn'dō, a. vagabond.

vagamundear, –mŭndĕär', v. n. to rove or loiter about.

vagamundo, da, –mŭn'dō, a. vagabond.

vagancia, –gän'thĭä, sf. vagrancy.

vagar, –gär', v. n. to rove or loiter about; to be loose and irregular; –, sm. leisure; slowness. [vulsive sob.

vagido, vähĭ'dō, sm. cry of a child; con-

vago, ga, vä'gō, a. vagrant; restless; vague; –, sm. vagabond; en –, in vain; unsteadily.

vagón, vägōn', sm. (rail.) waggon; –cama, sleeping-car; – cuadra, cattle-van; – freno, brake-van; –jaula, latticed waggon; – de mercancías, goods van; – de borde alto ó bajo, truck.

vaguear, –gĕär', v. n. to rove, to loiter.

vahido, vähĭ'dō, sm. vertigo, giddiness.

vaho, vä'ō, sm. steam, vapour.

vaina, vä'ĭnä, sf. scabbard of a sword; knife-case; pod, husk. [person.

vainazas, –näthäs, sm. humdrum, dull

vainilla, –nĭl'yä, sf. (bot.) vanilla.

vaivén, –vĕn', sm. fluctuation, vacillation, instability; giddiness; risk, danger.

vajilla, –hĭl'yä, sf. table-service.

vale, vä'lĕ, sm. farewell; promissory note, I.O.U.; note of pardon given to schoolboys by the master. [binding.

valedero, ra, –dĕ'rō, a. valid, efficacious,

valentía, –lĕntĭ'ä, sf. valour, courage; brag, boast; public place where mended old shoes are sold in Madrid.

valentón, –tōn', sm. braggadocio, hector.

valentonada, –nä'dä, sf. brag, boast.

valer, välĕr', v. n. to be valuable, to be deserving; to be marketable; to prevail; to avail; to serve as an asylum; to be valid; to have power, to be worth; to yield; to produce; to amount to; to have influence; to be equivalent to; to be current; –, v. a. to protect, to favour; –se, to employ, to make use of; to have recourse to. [strong, powerful.

valeroso, sa, –rō'sō, a. valiant; brave;

valetudinario, ria, –tŭdĭnä'rĭō, a. valetudinarian, sickly. [party.

valía, –lĭ'ä, sf. valuation; credit, favour;

validación, –lĭdäthĭōn', sf. validity.

validar, –där', v. a. to give validity.

validez, –dĕth', sf. validity, stability.

válido, välĭ'dō, sm. favourite.

válido, da, vä'lĭdō, a. valid; obligatory.

valiente, –lĭen'tĕ, a. robust, vigorous; valiant, brave; boasting.

valimiento, –mĭen'tō, sm. use, utility, advantage; contribution; favour, protection, support.

valiza, –lĭ'thä, sf. beacon.

valona, välō'nä, sf. tucker; cape, pelerine.

valor, *valór'*, sm. value, price; validity; force; power; courage, valour.

valor(e)ar, *-r(ē)ár'*, v. a. to value.

valuación, *-lūáthión'*, sf. valuation.

valuar, *-lūár'*, v. a. to value, to appraise.

valla, *vál'yä*, sf. intrenchment; barricade.

vallado, *-yá'dō*, sm. enclosure with stakes or palisades.

valle, *vál'yē*, sm. dale, valley.

vampiro, *vämpē'rō*, sm. vampire.

vanagloria, *vänäglō'rïä*, sf. vainglory.

vanagloriarse, *-glōrïár'sē*, v. r. to be vainglorious, to boast of; [glorious.

vanaglorioso, sa, *-glōrïō'sō*, a. vain-

vandalismo, *vändälīs'mō*, sm. vandalism.

vándalo, la, *-dä'lō*, sm. & a. vandal.

vanguardia, *-gǔär'dïä*, sf. vanguard, van.

vanidad, *vänïdád'*, sf. vanity; ostentation; futility; flirtation; illusion, phantom.

vanidoso, sa, *-dō'sō*, a. vain, showy; haughty, self-conceited.

vano, na, *vä'nō*, a. vain; useless; frivolous; arrogant; futile; en —, in vain.

vapor, *väpōr'*, sm. vapour, steam; breath.

vaporoso, sa, *-rō'sō*, a. vaporous.

vapular, *-pǔlár'*, v. a. to whip, to flog.

vaquerizo, za, *-kērē'thō*, a. relating to cows; —, sm. cow-herd.

vaquero, *-kā'rō*, sm. cow-herd; —, ra, a. belonging to cow-herds.

vaqueta, *-kā'tä*, sf. sole-leather; ramrod.

vara, *vä'rä*, sf. rod; pole, staff; verge; yard (measure); — alta, sway, high hand; —s, pl. shafts of a coach, pl. [person.

varal, *-rál'*, sm. long pole; tall, slender

varapalo, *-äpä'lō*, sm. long perch; blow with a pole; trouble, vexation.

varar, *-rár'*, v. a. to launch a new-built ship; —, v. n. to be stranded.

varchilla, *värtshēl'yä*, sf. measure of grain, containing the third part of a **fanega**.

vardasca, *-däs'kä*, sf. a thin twig.

vardascazo, *-kä'thō*, sm. stroke with a switch. [the yard.

vareaje, *värēä'h'ē*, sm. selling or measuring

varear, *-rēár'*, v. a. to knock the fruit off trees with a pole; to goad a bull; to measure or sell by the yard; **-se**, to grow thin or lean.

vareta, *-rē'tä*, sf. lime-twig for catching birds; stripe in any kind of stuff different in colour from the ground; **irse de —**, to suffer from diarrhœa.

variable, *-rïä'blē*, a. variable, changeable.

variación, *-rïäthïón'*, sf. variation.

variado, da, *-rïä'dō*, a. variegated.

variar, *-rïár'*, v. a. to change; —, v. n. to vary. [stancy.

variedad, *-rïēdád'*, sf. variety; incon-

varilla, *-rēl'yä*, sf. small rod; curtain-rod; spindle, pivot; —s, pl. jaw-bones; rib of a fan.

vario, ria, *vä'rïō*, a. various, different; vague; variegated; —s, pl. some.

varón, *-rón'*, sm. man, male human being; man of respectability. [cendants.

varonía, *-nē'ä*, sf. male issue; male des-

varonil, *-nēl'*, a. male, masculine; manful.

vasallaje, *väsälyä'h'ē*, sm. vassalage.

vasallo, *-säl'yō*, sm. vassal, liegeman.

vasar, *-sár'*, sm. buffet on which glasses or vessels are put.

vascuence, *väskŭën'thē*, sm. Biscay dialect.

vasija, *-sē'h'ä*, sf. vessel (in which liquors are kept).

vaso, *vä'sō*, sm. vessel; vase. [are kept.

vástago, *väs'tägō*, sm. bud, shoot.

vasto, ta, *-tō*, a. vast, huge. [diviner.

vaticinador, *vätïthïnädór'*, sm. prophet,

vaticinar, *-thïnár'*, v. a. to divine, to foretell.

vaticinio, *-thï'nïō*, sm. divination.

vecindad, *vëthïndád'*, sf. inhabitants of a place; neighbourhood.

vecindario, *-dä'rïō*, sm. number of inhabitants of a place.

vecino, na, *-thē'nō*, a. neighbouring; near; —, sm. neighbour, inhabitant.

veda, *vä'dä*, sf. prohibition. [to impede.

vedar, *vēdár'*, v. a. to prohibit, to forbid;

vedija, *-dē'h'ä*, sf. entangled lock of wool; flake; tuft of entangled hair, matted hair.

veedor, *vēēdór'*, sm. overseer, inspector.

veeduría, *-dērē'ä*, sf. inspector's office.

vega, *vä'gä*, sf. fruitful plain.

vegetación, *vēhētäthïón'*, sf. vegetation.

vegetal, *-täl'*, a. vegetable.

vegetar, *-tár'*, v. n. to vegetate. [force.

vehemencia, *vēēmën'thïä*, sf. vehemence,

vehemente, *-mën'tē*, a. vehement, violent.

vehículo, *vēē'kŭlō*, sm. vehicle.

veinte, *vä'ïntē*, a. & sm. twenty.

veintena, *-tä'nä*, sf. twentieth part; score.

veinteno, na, *-tä'nō*, a. twentieth.

vejación, *vēhäthïón'*, sf. vexation, molestation, oppression, cumber.

vejamen, *-hä'mën*, sm. taunt. [censure.

vejar, *-hár'*, v. a. to vex, to molest; to

vejestorio, *-hēstō'rïō*, sm. old trumpery; petulant old man.

vejete, *-hä'tē*, sm. ridiculous old man; actor of an old man.

vejez, *-hëth'*, sf. old age.

vejiga, *-hē'gä*, sf. bladder; blister.

vejigatorio, *-gätō'rïō*, sm. blistering-plaster; —, ria, a. raising blisters.

vela, *vä'lä*, sf. watch; watchfulness; night-guard; candle; a horse's ear; sail; ship; **hacerse á la —**, to set sail.

velación, *vēläthïón'*, sf. watching; **-ones**, pl. nuptial benedictions, pl.

velador, *-dór'*, sm. watchman; careful observer; large wooden candlestick.

velaje, *-lä'h'ē*, sm. sails, pl., sailwork.

velamen, *-lä'mën*, sm. set of sails.

velar, *-lár'*, v. n. to watch; to wake; to be attentive; (mar.) to appear; —, v. a. to guard, to watch; to marry.

veleidad, *-lēïdád'*, sf. lowest degree of desire; feeble will; inconstancy.

veleidoso, sa, *-dō'sō*, a. inconstant, fickle.

velero, ra, *-lä'rō*, a. swift sailing.

veleta, *-lä'tä*, sf. weather-cock.

velo, *vä'lō*, sm. veil; pretext.

velocidad, *vēlōthïdád'*, sf. velocity.

velón, *vēlón'*, sm. oil-lamp.

velonero, *–ná'rŏ*, sm. lamp-maker.
veloz(mente), *velóth' (mĕn'tĕ)*, a. (& ad.) swift(ly). [downy hair.
vello, *vĕl'yŏ*, sm. down; gossamer; short
vellón, *velyŏn'*, sm. fleece; lock of wool; copper coin of the province of Castile.
vellorí, *velyŏrí'*, sm. second-rate cloth.
velloso, sa, *–yŏ'sŏ*, a. downy, cottony.
velludo, da, *–yŏ'dŏ*, a. shaggy, woolly.
vena, *vá'ná*, sf. vein, blood-vessel.
venablo, *vená'blŏ*, sm. javelin.
venado, *–ná'dŏ*, sm. deer; venison.
venal, *–nál'*, a. belonging to the veins; saleable; mercenary.
venalidad, *–lidád'*, sf. venality.
venático, ca, *vená'tikŏ*, a. a little mad.
venatorio, ria, *–tŏ'riŏ*, a. used in hunting.
vencedor, ra, *vĕnthĕdŏr'*, sm. & f. conqueror, victor, foiler.
vencejo, *–thĕ'hŏ*, sm. martinet (bird).
vencer, *–thĕr'*, v. a. to conquer, to vanquish; **–se**, to govern one's desires and passions. [able.
vencible, *–thĕ'blĕ*, a. vincible, conquer-
vencido, da, *–thī'dŏ*, a. to be paid afterwards, due. [ing down.
vencimiento, *–mĭen'tŏ*, sm. victory; bend-
venda, *vĕn'dá*, sf. bandage; fillet; diadem.
vendaje, *–dá'hĕ*, sm. brokerage; bandage; dressing of wounds. [wink.
vendar, *–dár'*, v. a. to bandage; to hood-
vendaval, *–dávál'*, sm. a strong south-by-west wind.
vendedor, ra, *–dĕdŏr'*, sm. & f. seller.
vender, *vĕndĕr'*, v. a. to sell.
vendible, *–dĕ'blĕ*, a. saleable, vendible.
vendimia, *–dĕ'mĭá*, sf. vintage.
vendimiador, ra, *–dĭmĭádŏr'*, sm. & f. vintager. [vintage.
vendimiar, *–mĭár'*, v. a. to gather the
veneno, *vĕnĕ'nŏ*, sm. poison, venom.
venenoso, sa, *vĕnĕnŏ'sŏ*, a. venomous, poisonous.
venera, *–ná'rá*, sf. porcelain shell; badge worn by the knights of military orders.
venerable, *–nĕrá'blĕ*, a. venerable.
veneración, *–thĭŏn'*, sf. veneration, worship. [ship.
venerar, *–rár'*, v. a. to venerate, to wor-
venéreo, rea, *–ná'rĕŏ*, a. venereal.
venero, *–ná'rŏ*, sm. vein of metal in a mine; source of water. [geance.
venganza, *–gán'thá*, sf. revenge, ven-
vengar, *–gár'*, v. a. to revenge, to avenge; **–se**, to be revenged on.
vengativo, va, *–tĕ'vŏ*, a. revengeful.
venia, *vĕ'nĭá*, sf. pardon; leave, permission; bow. [sion; bow.
venial, *vĕnĭál'*, a. venial.
venida, *vĕnĭ'dá*, sf. arrival; return; overflow of a river. [pl. posterity.
venidero, ra, *–dĕ'rŏ*, a. future; **–s**, sm.
venir, *vĕnír'*, v. n. to come, to arrive; to follow, to succeed; to spring from; **–se**, to ferment.
venoso, sa, *–nŏ'sŏ*, a. veiny, veined.
venta, *vĕn'tá*, sf. sale; poor inn on roads.
ventaja, *–tá'há*, sf. advantage.
ventajoso, sa, *–hŏ'sŏ*, a. advantageous.

ventana, *–tá'ná*, sf. window; window-shutter; nostril. [dows in a building.
ventanaje, *–ná'hĕ*, sm. number of win-
ventanazo, *–ná'thŏ*, sm. banging off a window. [from the window.
ventanear, *–nĕár'*, v. n. to gaze repeatedly
ventarrón, *–rŏn'*, sm. violent wind.
ventear, *–tĕár'*, v. a. to smell, to scent; to investigate; to examine; to expose to the air; to be filled with wind; to break wind. [side inn.
ventero, *–tĕ'rŏ*, sm. & f. keeper of a road-
ventilación, *–tĭláthĭŏn'*, sf. ventilation; discussion. [to discuss.
ventilar, *–tĭlár'*, v. a. to ventilate; to fan;
ventisca, *–tĭs'ká*, sf. **ventisco**, *–kŏ*, sm. snow-storm. [drifts (snow).
ventiscar, *–kár'*, v. n. to drift, to lie in
ventisquero, *–tĭskĕ'rŏ*, sm. snow-drift; **–s**, pl. glaciers. [ness.
ventolera, *–tŏlĕ'rá*, sf. gust; pride, lofti-
ventor, *–tŏr'*, sm. setter. [house.
ventorrillo, *–tŏrrĭl'yŏ*, sm. roadside pot-
ventosa, *–tŏ'sá*, sf. cupping-glass.
ventosear, *–tŏsĕár'*, v. n. to break wind.
ventosidad, *–sĭdád'*, sf. flatulency.
ventoso, sa, *–tŏ'sŏ*, a. windy; flatulent.
ventrículo, *–trī'kŭlŏ*, sm. ventricle.
ventrílocuo, *–trĭlŏkŭŏ*, sm. ventriloquist.
ventrudo, da, *–trŏ'dŏ*, a. big-bellied.
ventura, *–tŏ'rá*, sf. luck, favourable chance, fortune; **por –**, by chance.
venturilla, *–tŏrĭl'yá*, sf. good luck.
venturina, *–tŏrĕ'ná*, sf. precious stone of a yellowish brown colour.
venturoso, sa, *–rŏ'sŏ*, a. lucky, fortunate, happy.
Venus, *vĕ'nŭs*, sf. evening-star.
ver, *vĕr'*, v. a. to see, to look; to observe; to visit; **–se**, to be seen; to be conspicuous; to find oneself; to have a bone to pick with someone; **–**, sm. sense of the sight; appearance.
veracidad, *vĕráthĭdád'*, sf. veracity.
veran(e)ar, *–rán(ĕ)ár'*, v. n. to pass the summer season.
verano, *–rá'nŏ*, sm. summer season.
veras, *vĕ'rás*, sf. pl. truth, sincerity; **de –**, in truth, really.
veraz, *vĕráth'*, a. veracious.
verbal, *vĕrbál'*, a. verbal.
verbena, *–bá'ná*, sf. (bot.) vervain.
verbigracia, *–bĭgrá'thĭá*, ad. for example.
verbo, *vĕr'bŏ*, sm. word, term; (gr.) verb.
verbosidad, *–sĭdád'*, sf. verbosity.
verboso, sa, *–bŏ'sŏ*, a. verbose.
verdacho, *vĕrdátsh'ŏ*, sm. green chalk.
verdad, *vĕrdád'*, sf. truth, veracity, reality; certain existence of things; **– de Perogrullo**, notorious truth. [in fact.
verdaderamente, *–dĕrámĕn'tĕ*, ad. truly.
verdadero, ra, *–dá'rŏ*, a. true, real; sincere. [sincere.
verde, *vĕr'dĕ*, sm. & a. green.
verdear, *vĕrdĕár'*, **verdecer**, *–dĕthĕr'*, v. n. to grow green.
verdecillo, *–dĕthĭl'yŏ*, sm. green-finch.
verdegay, *–gá'ĭ*, sm. parrot-green.
verdín, *vĕrdín'*, sm. verdure.

verdinegro, gra, –ná'grŏ, a. of a deep
green colour.

verdolaga, vĕrdŏlá'gä, sf. purslain.

verdor, vĕrdŏr', sm. verdure; vigour;
youth; –es, pl. age of vigour.

verdoso, sa, –dŏ'sŏ, a. greenish, greeny.

verdugo, ga, ––'gŏ, sm. young shoot of
a tree; hangman; very cruel person.

verduguillo, –dŭgĭl'yŏ, sm. small, narrow razor; long, narrow sword.

verdulero, –lä'rŏ, sf. green-grocer.

verdura, –dŏ'rä, sf. verdure; vegetables,
garden-stuff; vigour.

vereda, vĕrá'dä, sf. path; circular order
sent to several towns or places.

veredero, vĕrĕdá'rŏ, sm. messenger sent
with orders or despatches.　[(mar.) yard.

verga, vĕr'gä, sf. cord of the crossbow;

vergajo, –gä'h̄ŏ, sm. pizzle.

vergonzante, –gŏnthän'tĕ, a. bashful,
shamefaced.　[fulness; confusion.

vergüenza, –gŭĕn'thä, sf. shame; bash-

vericueto, vĕrĭkŭá'tŏ, sm. rough road.

veridico, ca, vĕr'dĭkŏ, a. veridical, truthful, worthy of faith.

verificación, –fĭkäthĭŏn', sf. verification.

verificar, –fĭkär', v. a. to verify; –se,
to be verified, to turn out true.

verificativo, va, –fĭkätĭ'vŏ, a. tending
to prove.　[lar.

verisimil, –sĭ'mĭl, a. probable, verisimi-

verisimilitud, –sĭmĭlĭtŭd', sf. probability, likelihood.　[bably.

verisimilmente, –sĭmĭlmĕn'tĕ, ad. pro-

verja, vĕr'h̄ä, sf. grate, lattice.

verjel, vĕr'h̄ĕl', sm. orchard; (fig.) thing
agreeable to the sight.

vermejo, vĕrmĕ'h̄ŏ, a. vermeil.

vermellón, –mĕlyŏn', sm. vermilion.

vermífugo, –mĕ'fŭgŏ, a. & sm. vermifuge.　[grubs.

verminoso, sa, –mĭnŏ'sŏ, a. full of

verónica, vĕrŏ'nĭkä, sf. (bot.) speedwell.

verosimil, vĕrŏsĭ'mĭl, a. verisimilar.

verosimilitud, –sĭmĭlĭtŭd', sf. verisimi-
litude.

verraco, vĕrrä'kŏ, sm. boar.　[lity.

verraquear, –kär', v. n. to grunt like a
boar.　[boar in rutting time.

verriondo, da, –rĭŏn'dŏ, a. foaming like a

verruga, –rŏ'gä, sf. wart, pimple.

verrugoso, sa, –rŭgŏ'sŏ, a. warty.

versado, da, –sä'dŏ, a. versed.

versal, –säl', a. capital (of letters).

versar, –sär', v. n. –se, to be versed; to
grow skilful.

versátil, –sä'tĭl, a. versatile.

versículo, –sĭ'kŭlŏ, sm. versicle; verse
of a chapter.　[tion.

versificación, –sĭfĭkäthĭŏn', sf. versifica-

versificador, –fĭkädŏr', sm. versifier.

versificar, –fĭkär', v. a. to versify.

versión, –sĭŏn', sf. translation, version.

verso, vĕr'sŏ, sm. verse.

vértebra, vĕr'tĕbrä, sf. vertebre.

vertedero, –tĕdä'rŏ, sm. sewer, drain.

vertedor, ra, –dŏr', sm. & f. nightman;
conduit, sewer; (mar.) scoop.　[empty.

verter, vĕrtĕr', v. a. to spill, to shed; to

vertical, –tĭkäl', a. vertical.

vértice, vĕr'tĭthĕ, sm. vertex, zenith;
crown of the head.

vertiente, –tĭĕn'tĕ, sm. waterfall, cascade.

vertiginoso, sa, –tĭ'hĭnŏ'sŏ, a. giddy.

vértigo, vĕr'tĭgŏ, sm. giddiness, vertigo.

Véspero, vĕs'pĕrŏ, sm. Vesper (evening-
star).

vespertino, na, –tĭ'nŏ, a. vespertine.

vestíbulo, vĕstĭ'bŭlŏ, sm. vestibule, lobby.

vestido, vĕstĭ'dŏ, sm. dress, suit of clothes.

vestidura, –dŏ'rä, sf. dress, wearing-apparel; robe of distinction.

vestigio, vĕstĭ'hĭŏ, sm. vestige, footstep.

vestiglo, –glŏ', sm. horrid monster.

vestir, vĕstĭr', v. a. to clothe, to dress; to
accoutre; to adorn; to cloak, to disguise;
–se, to dress.

vestuario, –tŭä'rĭŏ, sm. clothes; uniform;
vestry; green-room; vestiary.

veta, vá'tä, sf. vein (in mines, wood &c.);
stripe of a different colour in cloth.

vetado, da, vĕtä'dŏ, a. striped, veined.

veterano, na, vĕtĕrä'nŏ, a. experienced,
long practised; –, sm. veteran, old soldier

vez, vĕth, sf. turn, return; cada –, each
time; una–, once; á veces, sometimes,
by turns.

vía, vĭ'ä, sf. way, road, route; mode, manner, method; (rail.) railway, line.

viajar, vĭä'här', v. n. to travel.

viaje, vĭä'h̄ĕ, sm. journey, voyage, travel.

viajero, –h̄ä'rŏ, sm. traveller.

viático, vĭä'tĭkŏ, sm. viaticum.

víbora, vĭ'bŏrä, sf. viper.

viborezno, vĭbŏrĕth'nŏ, sm. young viper.

vibración, vĭbräthĭŏn', sf. vibration.

vibrar, vĭbrär', v. a. to vibrate, to brandish;
to throw, to dart; –, v. n. to vibrate.

vicaría, vĭkärĭ'ä, sf. vicarship; vicarage.

vicariato, vĭkärĭä'tŏ, sm. vicarage.

vicario, vĭkä'rĭŏ, sm. vicar; –, ría, a.

vice, –thĕ, (in comp.) vice.　[vicarial.

vicealmiranta, –älmĭrän'tä, sf. the galley
next in order to that of the admiral.

vicealmirante, –tĕ, sm. vice-admiral.

viceconsulado, –kŏnsŭlä'dŏ, sm. vice-
consulate.

viciar, vĭthĭär', v. n. to vitiate, to corrupt;
to annul; to deprave; –se, to become
vitiated; to deliver oneself up to vice.

vicio, vĭ'thĭŏ, sm. vice.

vicioso, sa, vĭthĭŏ'sŏ, a. vicious.

vicisitud, vĭthĭsĭtŭd', sf. vicissitude.

víctima, vĭk'tĭmä, sf. victim; sacrifice.

víctor, vĭk'tŏr', sm. shout, acclamation.

victorear, –rĕär', v. a. to shout, to huzza.

victoria, –tŏ'rĭä, sf. victory.

victorioso, sa, –rĭŏ'sŏ, a. victorious.

vid, vĭd, sf. (bot.) vine.

vida, vĭ'dä, sf. life.　[ware, crockery.

vidriado, vĭdrĭä'dŏ, sm. glazed earthen-

vidriar, –rĭär', v. a. to glaze earthenware.

vidriera, –rĭá'rä, sf. glass case.

vidriería, –rĭĕrĭ'ä, sf. glazier's shop; glass-

vidriero, –drĭä'rŏ, sm. glazier.　[house.

vidrio, vĭ'drĭŏ, sm. glass.

vidrioso, sa, vĭdrĭŏ'sŏ, a. glassy, brittle;
slippery; very delicate.

viejo,ja, *vĭē'h'ŏ,*a. old; ancient, antiquated.

viento, *vĭēn'tŏ,* sm. wind; air.

vientre, *vĭēn'trē,* sm. belly.

viernes, *vĭēr'nĕs,* sm. Friday; **— Santo,** Good-Friday.

viga, *vē'gä,* sf. beam (large and long piece [of timber).

vigente, *vĭ hĕn'tē,* a. in force.

vigésimo, ma, *vĭ hä'sĭmŏ,* a. twentieth.

vigía, *vĭ hē'ä,* sf. (mar.) look-out; —, sm. watchman. [watchfulness.

vigilancia, *vĭ hĭlän'thĭä,* sf. vigilance,

vigilante, *—län'tē,* a. watchful, vigilant.

vigilar, *—lär',* v. n. to watch over.

vigilia, *vĭ hē'lĭä,* sf. nocturnal study; vigil; watch.

vigor, *vĭgōr',* sm. vigour, strength.

vigoroso, sa, *—rŏ'sŏ,* a. vigorous.

vihuela, *vĭŭ ā'lä,* sf. guitar.

vihuelista, *—lĭs'tä,* sm. guitar-player.

vil, *vĭl,* a. mean, sordid, low; worthless; infamous; ungrateful. [abjectness.

vileza, *vĭlē'thä,* sf. meanness, lowness;

vilipendiar, *vĭlĭpĕndĭär',* v. a. to contemn, to revile. [dain.

vilipendio, *—pĕn'dĭŏ,* sm. contempt, dis-

vilmente, *vĭlmĕn'tē,* ad. vilely; abjectly.

vilordo, da, *vĭlōr'dŏ,* a. lazy, heavy.

vilorta, *vĭlōr'tä,* sf. ring made of twisted willow; cricket (in Old Castile).

villa, *vĭl'yä,* sf. town which enjoys peculiar privileges by charter; its magistracy.

Villadiego, *—dĭē'gŏ,* sm., **tomar las de —,** to run away.

villancico, *vĭlyänthē'kŏ,* sm. Christmas carol; hackneyed answers, pl.

villanesco, ca, *—nĕs'kŏ,* a. rustic.

villanía, *—nē'ä,* sf. lowness of birth; villany; indecorous word or act.

villano, na, *—yä'nŏ,* a. rustic, clownish; villanous; —, sm. villain; rustic.

villorín, *—yŏrín',* sm. second-rate cloth.

villorio, *—yŏ'rĭŏ,* sm. miserable little ham-

vinagre, *vĭnä'grē,* sm. vinegar. [let.

vinagrera, *—grā'rä,* sf. vinegar-cruet.

vinagrero, *—rŏ,* sm. vinegar-merchant.

vinajera, *—hā'rä,* sf. vinegar-cruet; flagon.

vinariego, *—rĭā'gŏ,* sm. vintager.

vinatería, *—tērē'ä,* sf. vintry; wine-trade.

vinatero, *—tā'rŏ,* sm. vintner. [entailed.

vinculable, *vĭnkŭlä'blē,* a. that may be

vinculación, *—läthĭŏn',* sf. entail.

vincular, *—lär',* v. a. to entail an estate; to perpetuate. [entail.

vínculo, *vĭn'kŭlŏ,* sm. tie, link, chain;

vindicación, *vĭndĭkäthĭŏn',* sf. revenge.

vindicar, *—kär',* v. a. to revenge.

vindicativo, va, *—kätē'vŏ,* a. vindictive.

vindicta, *vĭndĭk'tä,* sf. vengeance.

vino, *vē'nŏ,* sm. wine; **— tinto,** red wine; **— del reino,** home-grown wine.

vinolento, ta, *vĭnŏlĕn'tŏ,* a. inebriated.

vinoso, sa, *vĭnŏ'sŏ,* a. vinous, vinose.

viña, *vĭn'yä,* sf. vineyard.

viñador, *vĭnyädŏr',* sm. wine-grower.

viñedo, *vĭnyā'dŏ,* sm. vine-clad hills, pl.

viñero, *—nä'rŏ,* sm. wine-grower, vine-

viñeta, *—yä'tä,* sf. vignette. [dresser.

violación, *vĭŏläthĭŏn',* sf. violation.

violado, da, *—lä'dŏ,* a. violet-coloured; violated. [profaner.

violador, ra, *—lädŏr',* sm. & f. violator;

violar, *—lär',* v. a. to violate; to ravish; to profane a church.

violencia, *—lĕn'thĭä,* sf. violence.

violentar, *—tär',* v. a. to enforce by violent means. [absurd.

violento, ta, *—lĕn'tŏ,* a. violent, forced;

violeta, *—lā'tä,* sf. (bot.) violet.

violín, *vĭŏlín',* sm. violin, fiddle.

violinista, *—nĭs'tä,* sm. violinist.

violón, *vĭŏlōn',* sm. bass-viol.

violoncelo, *—thā'lŏ,* sm. violoncello.

viperino, na, *vĭpērē'nŏ,* a. viperine.

vira, *vē'rä,* sf. welt of a shoe.

virada, *vĭrä'dä,* sf. (mar.) tacking.

virar, *vĭrär',* v. a. to tack.

virgen, *vĭr'hĕn,* sm. & f. virgin.

virginal, *—hĭnäl',* a. virginal.

virginidad, *—hĭnĭdäd',* sf. virginity; maidenhood.

Virgo, *vĭr'gŏ,* sf. Virgo (sign of the zodiac).

virgulilla, *vĭrgŭlil'yä,* sf. comma.

viril, *vĭrĭl',* sm. clear and transparent glass; monstrance; —, a. virile, manly. [vigour.

virilidad, *—lĭdäd',* sf. virility, manhood;

virolento, ta, *vĭrōlĕn'tŏ,* a. diseased with the small-pox; pock-pitted.

virote, *vĭrō'tē,* sm. dart, arrow; showy, vain loiterer; conceited person.

virreinato, *vĭrrēnä'tŏ,* sm. viceroyship.

virrey, *—rā'ĭ,* sm. viceroy.

virtual, *vĭrtŭäl',* a. virtual.

virtud, *vĭrtŭd',* sf. virtue; efficacy, force; vigour, courage; **—es,** pl. the fifth of the nine celestial choirs.

virtuoso, sa, *—tŭŏ'sŏ,* a. virtuous.

viruela, *vĭrŭā'lä,* sf. small-pox.

virulencia, *—lĕn'thĭä,* sf. virulence.

virulento, ta, *—lĕn'tŏ,* a. virulent.

viruta, *vĭrō'tä,* sf. cuttings, pl.

visaje, *vĭsä'h'ē,* sm. grimace; visage.

víscera, *vĭs'thērä,* sf. vital organ.

viscosidad, *vĭskŏsĭdäd',* sf. viscosity.

viscoso, sa, *—kŏ'sŏ,* a. viscous, glutinous.

visera, *vĭsā'rä,* sf. visor.

visible, *vĭsē'blē,* a. visible; apparent.

visión, *vĭsĭŏn',* sf. sight, vision; frightful, ugly or ridiculous person; phantom.

visionario, ria, *—nä'rĭŏ,* a. visionary.

visir, *vĭsĭr',* sm. vizier.

visita, *vĭsē'tä,* sf. visit.

visitación, *vĭsĭtäthĭŏn',* sf. visitation.

visitador, ra, *—dŏr',* sm. & f. visitor; surveyor. [he on visiting terms, to visit

visitar, *vĭsĭtär',* v. a. to visit; **—se,** to

vislumbrar, *vĭslŭmbrär',* v. a. to catch a glimpse; to perceive indistinctly; to know imperfectly, to conjecture.

vislumbre, *—lŭm'brē,* sf. glimmering light, conjecture; imperfect knowledge; slight resemblance. [apparent likeness.

viso, *vē'sŏ,* sm. prospect; lustre, pretext.

víspera, *vĭs'pērä,* sf. evening before; evening before a festival; **—s,** pl. vespers.

vist, *vĭst,* sm. whist (juego de naipes de origen inglés).

vista, *vĭs′tă,* sf. sight, view; eye; appearance; prospect; intention, purpose; (law) **— de un pleito,** day of trial; **—,** sm. employment of a custom-house officer; **—s,** pl. presents made to a bride by a bridegroom the day preceding the nuptials; windows, pl.

vistazo, *vĭstă′thŏ,* sm. glance.

vistillas, *vĭstĭl′yăs,* sf. pl. height affording an extensive prospect.

visto, *vĭs′tŏ,* **— que,** c. considering that.

vistoso, sa, *vĭstŏ′sŏ,* a. beautiful, delightful.   [sight.

visual, *vĭsŭăl′,* a. visual, belonging to the

vital, *vĭtăl′,* a. vital.

vitalicio, cia, *vĭtălĭ′thĭŏ,* a. during life.

vitalidad, *vĭtălĭdăd′,* sf. vitality.

vitela, *vĭ′tĕ′lă,* sf. calf; vellum, calf-skin.

¡ vítor ! *vē′tŏr,* long life!   [plaud!

vitorear, *vĭtŏrĕăr′,* v. a. to shout, to applaud.

vitrificar, *vĭtrĭfĭkăr′,* v. a. to change into glass.

vitriolo, *vĭtrĕ′blŏ,* sm. vitriol.   [glass.

vitualla, *vĭtŭăl′yă,* sf. victuals, pl.

vituallado, da, *vĭtŭăl′dŏ,* a. victualled.

vituperable, *vĭtŭpĕră′blĕ,* a. blameable.

vituperación, *vĭtŭpĕrăthĭŏn′,* sf. blame.

vituperador, ra, *vĭtŭpĕrădŏr′,* sm. & f. blamer.

vituperar, *vĭtŭpĕrăr′,* v. a. to blame.

vituperio, *vĭtŭpĕ′rĭŏ,* sm. blame; infamy.

viuda, *vĭŭ′dă,* sf. widow; dowager.

viudedad, *vĭŭdĕdăd′,* sf. widowhood; dowry.

viudez, *vĭŭdĕth′,* sf. widowhood.

viudo, *vĭŭ′dŏ,* sm. widower; **—,** a. applied to pairing birds.   [liness.

vivacidad, *vĭvăthĭdăd′,* sf. vivacity, liveliness.

vivamente, *vĭvămĕn′tĕ,* ad. lively; to the life.

vivandero, *vĭvăndĕ′rŏ,* sm. (mil.) sutler.

vivaque, *vĭvă′kĕ,* sm. (mil.) bivouac.   **vivac,** *vĭvăk′,* sm.

vivaquear, *vĭvăkĕăr′,* v. n. (mil.) to bivouac.

vivar, *vĭvăr′,* sm. warren; vivary.

vivaracho, cha, *vĭvără′tʃŏ′,* a. lively, smart, sprightly.

vivera, *vĭvă′ră,* sf. **vivero,** *vĭvĕ′rŏ,* sm. warren; fish-pond; vivary.

víveres, *vĭ′vĕrĕs,* sm. pl. provisions, pl.

viveza, *vĭvĕ′thă,* sf. liveliness; strong resemblance.

vividero, ra, *vĭvĭdĕ′rŏ,* a. habitable.

vividor, ra, *vĭvĭdŏr′,* a. thrifty manager.

vivienda, *vĭvĭĕn′dă,* sf. dwelling-house.

vivificación, *vĭvĭfĭkăthĭŏn′,* sf. vivification.

vivificador, ra, *vĭvĭfĭkădŏr′,* sm. & f. one who vivifies, animates or enlivens; **—,** a. vivifying, animating.

vivificar, *vĭvĭfĭkăr′,* v. a. to vivify, to enliven.

vivificativo, va, *vĭvĭfĭkătĕ′vŏ,* a. animating, comforting.

vivíparo, ra, *vĭvĕ′pără,* a. viviparous.

vivir, *vĭvĭr′,* v. n. to live; to last.

vivo, va, *vĭ′vŏ,* a. living; lively; **al —,** to the life.   [ship.

vizcondado, *vĭthkŏndă′dŏ,* sm. viscountship.

vizconde, *vĭthkŏn′dĕ,* sm. viscount.

vizcondesa, *vĭthkŏndĕs′ă,* sf. viscountess.

vocablo, *vŏkă′blŏ,* sm. word, term, diction.

vocabulario, *vŏkăbŭlă′rĭŏ,* sm. vocabulary; (fig.) a mine of science.

vocación, *vŏkăthĭŏn′,* sf. vocation.

vocal, *vŏkăl′,* sf. vowel; **—,** sm. voter; **—** a. vocal, oral.

vocativo, va, *vŏkătĕ′vŏ,* sm. a. (gr.) vocative.

voceador, *vŏthĕădŏr′,* sm. vociferator.

vocear, *vŏthĕăr′,* v. n. to cry, to scream, to bawl, to shriek.

vocería, *vŏthĕrĭ′ă,* sf. vociferation.

vociferación, *vŏthĭfĕrăthĭŏn′,* sf. vociferation; praise.   [bragger.

vociferador, ra, *vŏthĭfĕrădŏr′,* sm. & f. boaster,

vociferar, *vŏthĭfĕrăr′,* v. n. to bawl, to proclaim in a loud voice.

vocinglería, *vŏthĭnglĕrĭ′ă,* sf. clamour, outcry; loquacity.   [prattling.

vocinglero, ra, *vŏthĭnglĕ′rŏ,* a. brawling.

volador, ra, *vŏlădŏr′,* a. flying; running fast; **—,** sm. flying-fish.

volandas, en, *vŏlăn′dăs,* ad. in the air.

volandera, *vŏlăndĕ′ră,* sf. runner (in oil-mills); movable ledge on a type-galley.

volandero, ra, *vŏlăndĕ′rŏ,* a. volatile; casual; unsettled.   [air.

volandillas, en, *vŏlăndĭl′yăs,* ad. in the air.

volante, *vŏlăn′tĕ,* sm. screen put before a candle; shuttle-cock; livery-servant, footman.

volar, *vŏlăr′,* v. n. to fly; to pass or to move swiftly; to execute with great promptitude and facility; **—,** v a. to rouse game; to blow up, to discharge a mine; to irritate.

volatería, *vŏlătĕrĭ′ă,* sf. fowling; fowls, pl.

volátil, *vŏlă′tĭl,* a. volatile; flying.

volatilizar, *vŏlătĭlĭthăr′,* v. a. to volatilize.

volatín, *vŏlătĭn′,* sm. rope-dancer.

volcán, *vŏlkăn′,* sm. volcano.

volcánico, *vŏlkă′nĭkŏ,* a. volcanic.

volcar, *vŏlkăr′,* v. a. to overset, to turn up; to make giddy; to tire out one's patience.

volear, *vŏlĕăr′,* v. n. to throw up in the air.

voleo, *vŏlĕ′ŏ,* sm. volley; step in a Spanish dance.   [inconstant.

voltario, ria, *vŏltă′rĭŏ,* a. fickle, variable,

volteador, ra, *vŏltĕădŏr′,* sm. tumbler.

voltear, *vŏltĕăr′,* v. a. to whirl, to overset; **—,** v. n. to tumble.

voltereta, *vŏltĕrĕ′tă,* **volteta,** *vŏltĕ′tă,* sf. light tumble in the air; turning up of a trump (at cards).

volubilidad, *vŏlŭbĭlĭdăd′,* sf. volubility.

voluble, *vŏlŭ′blĕ,* a. inconstant, fickle.

volumen, *vŏlŭmĕn′,* sm. volume; size.

voluminoso, sa, *vŏlŭmĭnŏ′să,* a. voluminous.   [ous.

voluntad, *vŏlŭntăd′,* sf. will.

voluntario, ria, *vŏlŭntă′rĭŏ,* a. voluntary; **—,** sm. volunteer.   [tuous.

voluptuoso, sa, *vŏlŭptŭŏ′sŏ,* a. voluptuous.

volver, *vŏlvĕr′,* v. a. & n. to return; to restore, to repay; to turn; to send back a present; to change a thing from one place to another; **—se,** to turn sour; to turn towards; to retract an opinion.

vómica, *vŏ′mĭkă,* sf. (med.) vomica.

vómico, ca, _–mĭkŏ,_ a. causing vomiting.
vomitar, _–tär′,_ v. a. to vomit. [emetic.
vomitivo, va, _–tē′vŏ,_ a. & sm. emetic.
vómito, _vŏ′mĭtŏ,_ sm. vomiting.
vomitón, ona, _–tŏn′,_ a. often throwing up milk from the stomach (of a sucking child).
vomitona, _–tŏ′nä,_ sf. violent vomiting after eating heartily.
voracidad, _vŏrăthĭdäd′,_ sf. voracity.
voraz(mente), _vŏräth′ (měn′tĕ),_ a. (& ad.) [voracious(ly).
vos, _vŏs,_ pn. you, ye.
vosotros, tras, _vŏsŏ′trŏs,_ pn. pl. you, ye.
votación, _vŏtäthĭŏn′,_ sf. voting.
votador, ra, _–dŏr′,_ sm. & f. vower; voter.
votar, _vŏtär′,_ v. n. to vow; to vote.
votivo, va, _–tē′vŏ,_ a. votive.
voto, _vŏ′tŏ,_ sm. vow; vote; opinion, advice; wish; supplication to God; execration.
voz, _vŏth,_ sf. voice; outcry; word, term.
Vuecelencia, _vŭĕthělĕn′thĭä,_ sf. contraction of **Vuestra Excelencia,** Your Excelency.
vuelco, _vŭĕl′kŏ,_ sm. overturning.
vuelo, _vŭĕ′lŏ,_ sm. flight; wing; part of a building which projects beyond the wall; width of clothes; ruffle, frill; space flown through at once; elevation in discoursing; **á –, al –,** flying, expeditiously.
vuelta, _vŭĕl′tä,_ sf. turn; circuit; return; petition; ruffle; excursion.
Vuesamerced, _vŭĕsämĕrthĕd′,_ sf. Your Worship, Your Honour (contraction of **Vuestra Merced**).
Vueseñoría, _–sěnyŏrē′ä,_ sf. My Lady (contraction of **Vuestra Señoría**).
vuestro, tra, _vŭĕs′trŏ,_ pn. your, yours.
vulgacho, _vŭlgätsh′ŏ,_ sm. mob, populace.
vulgar, _vŭlgär′,_ a. vulgar, common.
vulgaridad, _–rĭdäd′,_ sf. vulgarity; vulgata, _vŭlgä′tä,_ sf. vulgate. [garism.
vulgo, _vŭl′gŏ,_ sm. populace, mob.
vulneración, _vŭlněräthĭŏn′,_ sf. wounding.
vulnerar, _–rär′,_ v. a. to injure the character or reputation.
vulnerario, ria, _–rä′rĭŏ,_ a. vulnerary.
vulto, _vŭl′tŏ,_ sm. volume; bulk; face.

X.

xarro, _ksär′rŏ,_ sm. bawler. [helpless.
xaurado, da, _ksäŭrä′dŏ,_ a. abandoned.
xilografía, _ksĭlŏgräfē′ä,_ sf. xylography.
xilógrafo, _ksĭlŏ′gräfŏ,_ sm. xylographer.
xinglar, _ksĭnglär′,_ v. n. to cry joyfully.

Y.

y, ĕ, c. and.
ya, _yä,_ ad. already; presently; immediately; finally; – que, since, seeing that; – si, when, while, if; ¡ –! exclamation on being brought to recollect a thing.
yacer, _yäthĕr′,_ v. n. to lie, to lie down.
ya(o)te, _yä(k)′tĕ,_ sm. (mar.) yacht.

yámbico, ca, _yäm′bĭkŏ,_ a. iambic.
yambo, _–bŏ,_ sm. iambic foot (‿ –).
yedra, _yĕ′drä,_ sf. ivy; – terrestre, [ground-ivy.
yegua, _yĕ′gŭä,_ sf. mare.
yeguada, _–gŭä′dä,_ sf. stud.
yeguar, _yĕgŭär′,_ a. belonging to a mare.
yegüero, _–gŭĕ′rŏ,_ sm. keeper of breeding mares. [mares.
yelmo, _yĕl′mŏ,_ sm. helmet, helm. [mares.
yelo, _yä′lŏ,_ sm. frost; ice.
yema, _yä′mä,_ sf. bud, gem; yolk; – del dedo, tip of the finger.
yendo allá, _yĕn′dŏ älyä′,_ a. thitherward.
yerba, _yĕr′bä,_ sf. herb; – buena, mint; –s, pl. greens, vegetables, pl. [waste.
yermar, _–mär′,_ v. a. to depopulate, to lay
yermo, _yĕr′mŏ,_ sm. desert, wilderness; –, ma, a. waste, desert.
yerno, _yĕr′nŏ,_ sm. son-in-law.
yerro, _yĕr′rŏ,_ sm. error, mistake, fault.
yerto, ta, _yĕr′tŏ,_ a. a stiff, inflexible; rigid.
yesal, _yĕsäl′,_ **yesar,** _–sär′,_ sm. gypsum-**yesca,** _yĕs′kä,_ sf. spunk, tinder. [pit.
yesera, _yĕsĕ′rä,_ sf. kiln where gypsum is calcined.
yesería, _–sĕrē′ä,_ sf. building constructed with gypsum. [of gypsum.
yesero, _–sä′rŏ,_ sm. preparer or seller
yesizo, _–sē′thŏ,_ a. gypseous. [of Paris.
yeso, _yĕ′sŏ,_ sm. gypsum; – mate, plaster
yesón, _yĕsŏn′,_ sm. fragment of gypsum already used in building.
yesquero, _yĕskĕ′rŏ,_ sm. tinder-box.
yo, _ĭ′ŏ,_ pn. I; – mismo, I myself.
yugada, _yŭgä′dä,_ sf. yoke of land.
yugo, _yŏ′gŏ,_ sm. yoke.
yunque, _yŭn′kĕ,_ sm. anvil; constancy.
yunta, _yŭn′tä,_ sf. couple, pair, yoke.
yusera, _yŭsĕ′rä,_ sf. bedder, under mill-stone in oil-mills.

Z.

¡ za ! _thä,_ word used to frighten dogs.
zabordar, _thäbŏrdär′,_ v. n. (mar.) to get ashore, to be stranded. [agitate.
zabucar, _–bŭkär′,_ v. a. to shake, to
zabullidura, _–bŭlyĭdŏ′rä,_ sf. submersion, ducking.
zabullir, _–bŭlyĭr′,_ v. a. to plunge, to immerge; –se, to plunge suddenly under water; to lie concealed.
zacatín, _–kätĭn′,_ sm. clothes market.
zafar, _–fär′,_ v. a. to adorn, to embellish; to lighten a ship; –se, to escape; to avoid; to free oneself from trouble.
zafarancho, _–fěrän′tshŏ,_ sm. (mar.) clearing for action; hacer –, (mar.) to clear.
zafiedad, _–fĭĕdäd′,_ sf. clownishness, rusticity, awkwardness.
zafio, fia, _thä′fĭŏ,_ a. clownish, coarse.
zafir, _–fĭr′,_ **zafiro,** _–fē′rŏ,_ sm. sapphire.
zaga, _thä′gä,_ sf. load packed at the back of a carriage; –, sm. last player at a game of cards; –, ad. behind.
zagal, _–gäl′,_ sm. out-rider; swain.

zagala, *-gä'lä*, sf. shepherdess, lass, girl.

zagalejo, *-gälë'N'ö*, sm. under-petticoat.

zaguán, *-gään'*, sm. porch, hall.

zaheridor, ra, *-ërïdör'*, sm. & f. censurer.

zaherimiento, *-mïen'tö*, sm. censure, blame. [braid.

zaherir, *-ërër'*, v. a. to reproach; to up-

zahones, *-ä'nës*, sm. pl. overalls, pl.

zahorí, *-ër'ë*, sm. vulgar impostor pretending to see hidden things, although in the bowels of the earth.

zahurda, *-ûr'dä*, sf. hogsty; dirty hole.

zaino, na, *thä'ïnö*, a. of a chestnut colour; vicious (applied to animals); treacherous, wicked; mirar de ó á lo *-*, to look sideways.

zalagarda, *-lägär'dä*, sf. ambuscade, ambush; trap, snare; surprise; vulgar noise.

zalamería, *-lämër'ë'ä*, sf. flattery.

zalamero, ra, *-mër'ö*, sm. & f. wheedler.

zalea, *thälë'ä*, sf. undressed sheepskin.

zalear, *-lëär'*, v. a. to move any thing with care from one place to another.

zamacuco, *-mäkö'kö*, sm. dunce, dolt.

zamarra, *-mär'rä*, sf. dress made of undressed sheepskins.

zamarro, *-rö*, sm. shepherd's coat made of sheepskins; sheep *or* lambskin; stupid person.

zambo, ba, *thäm'bö*, a. bandy-legged.

zambomba, *-böm'bä*, sf. rural drum.

zambombo, *-bö*, sm. clown, lubber.

zambra, *thäm'brä*, sf. Moorish festival attended with dancing and music; noisy mirth. [mirth.

zambucar, *-bökär'*, v. a. to hide.

zambullida, *-bäjyä'dä*, sf. dipping, submersion. [into water, to dive.

zambullirse, *-bäjyër'së*, v. r. to plunge

zampar, *-pär'*, v. a. to devour eagerly; *-se*, to thrust oneself suddenly into any place. [clown, rustic.

zampatortas, *-pätör'täs*, sm. glutton;

zampear, *-pëär'*, v. a. to stake, to prop.

zampoña, *-pön'yä*, sf. shawm; inmate of a workhouse. [dive.

zampuzar, *-pûthär'*, v. a. to plunge, to

zampuzo, *-pö'thö*, sm. submersion.

zanahoria, *thänä'ö'rïä*, sf. (bot.) carrot.

zanca, *thän'kä*, sf. shank of a fowl; long

zancada, *-kä'dä*, sf. stride. [shank.

zancadilla, *-dïl'yä*, sf. trip; trick.

zancajear, *-hëär'*, v. a. to run about the streets bespattering the legs with dirt.

zancajo, *-kä'h'ö*, sm. heel-bone.

zancajoso, sa, *-kä'hö'sö*, a. bandy-legged.

zancarrón, *-rön'*, sm. heel-bone.

zanco, *thän'kö*, sm. stilt.

zancudo, da, *-kû'dä*, a. long-shanked.

zangandongo, *-gändön'gö*, sm. idler; dolt. [ness.

zanganear, *-gänëär'*, v. n. to live in idle-

zángano, *thän'gänö*, sm. drone; idler; sponger. [a guitar.

zangarrear, *-gärrëär'*, v. n. to scrape on

zangarullón, *-gärûlyön'*, sm. tall, lazy lad. [a violent yet ridiculous manner.

zangolotear, *-gölötëär'*, v. r. to move in

zangoloteo, *-lötë'ö*, sm. violent yet ridiculous waddling; wagging movement.

zanguayo, *-gää'yö*, sm. tall idler that pretends to be ill *or* silly.

zanja, *thän'hä*, sf. ditch, trench.

zanjar, *-'här'*, v. a. to open ditches; to lay a foundation. [much and fast.

zanquear, *-këär'*, v. n. to waddle, to walk

zanquilargo, ga, *-kïlär'gö*, a. long-shanked.

zapa, *thä'pä*, sf. spade; caminar á la *-*, (mil.) to advance by sap *or* mine.

zapador, *-dör'*, sm. (mil.) sapper.

zapar, *-pär'*, v. n. to sap, to mine.

zaparrastrar, *-rästrär'*, v. n. to trail, to drag along on the ground.

zaparrastroso, sa, *-räströ'sö*, a. dirty from trailing along on the ground.

zaparrazo, *-rä'thö*, sm. violent fall, attended with great noise; sudden calamity.

zapata, *-pä'tä*, sf. piece of sole-leather put on the hinge of a door to prevent its creaking. [shoe.

zapatazo, *-tä'thö*, sm. blow with a

zapatear, *-tëär'*, v. a. to strike with the shoe; to beat time with the sole of the shoe; *-se*, to resist in debating.

zapatera, *-tä'rä*, sf. shoemaker's wife; olive spoiled in the pickle.

zapatería, *-tër'ë'ä*, sf. trade of a shoemaker; shoemaker's shop.

zapatero, *-tä'rö*, sm. shoemaker; *- de viejo*, cobbler.

zapatilla, *-tïl'yä*, sf. pump(shoe); piece of shamois put behind the lock of a gun *or* pistol.

zapatillero, *-tïlyä'rö*, sm. shoemaker who makes pumps and children's shoes.

zapato, *-pä'tö*, sm, shoe.

¡ zape! *thä'pë*, word used to frighten cats away; God forbid!

zaque, *thä'kë*, sm. wine-bag; tippler.

zar, *thär*, sm, czar. [(dance).

zarabanda, *thäräbän'dä*, sf. saraband

zaragüelles, *-güël'yës*, sm. pl. wide breeches; overalls, pl.

zaramullo, *-mäl'yö*, sm. busybody.

zaranda, *thärän'dä*, sf. frame for sifting sand.

zarandajas, *-dä'h'äs*, sf. pl. trifles, pl.

zarandar, *-där'*, v. a. to winnow corn.

zarandillo, *-dïl'yö*, sm. frisker.

zaratán, *thärätän'*, sm. cancer in the breast.

zarcillo, *thärthïl'yö*, sm. ear-ring; tendril.

zarja, *thär'hä*, sf. reel.

zarpa, *-pä*, sf. dirt on clothes; claw.

zarpar, *-pär'*, v. a. to weigh anchor.

zarpazo, *-pä'thö*, sm. sound *or* thud of a body falling on the ground. [malion.

zarrapastrón, *-räpäströn'*, sm. tatterde-

zarrapastroso, sa, *-päströ'sö*, a. ragged.

zarza, *thär'thä*, sf. common bramble.

zarzal, *thärthäl'*, sm. briery. [bush.

zarzamora, *-thämö'rä*, sf. blackberry

zarzaparrilla, *-pärïl'yä*, sf. (bot.) sarsaparilla.

zarzo, *thär'thö*, sm. hurdle.

zarzoso, sa, *-thö'sö*, a. briery.

‖ **zas, zas!** *thắs'*, flap! slap!   [upstart.
zascandil, *–kåndil'*, sm. crafty swindler;
zequí, *thĕkĕ'*, sm. zechin (Arabic gold
coin).   [with blows.
zipizape, *thĭpĭthắ'pĕ*, sm. noisy scuffle
‖ **zis, zas!** *thĭs thắs*, flap! slap!
zizaña, *thĭthăn'yă*, sf. (bot.) darnel; disagreement; any thing injurious.
zizañar, *–yăr'* v. a. to sow discord.
zizañero, *–yă'rŏ*, sm. makebate.
zócalo, *thŏ'kălŏ*, sm. socle.
zoclo, *thŏ'klŏ*, sm. wooden shoe; golosh.
zodíaco, *thŏdĕ'ăkŏ*, sm. zodiac.
zona, *thŏ'nă*, sf. zone; girdle.
zonzo, *thŏn'thŏ*, a. insipid, tasteless.
zoología, *thŏŏlŏ·hĕ'ă*, sf. zoology.
zopenco, ca, *thŏpĕn'kŏ*, a. doltish, very
stupid.
zopo, pa, *thŏ'pŏ*, a. lame, maimed; –,
sm. clumsy, stupid fellow.
zoquete, *thŏkĕ'tĕ*, sm. block; morsel of
bread; blockhead.
zorra, *thŏr'ră*, sf. fox; prostitute, strumpet.
zorrastrón, ona, *–răstrŏn'*, sm. & f. cunning, roguish person.
zorrera, *–rĕ'ră*, sf. fox-hole.
zorrería, *–rĕrĕ'ă*, sf. artfulness of a fox;
cunning, craft.   [fellow.
zorro, *thŏr'rŏ*, sm. male fox; cunning
zorronglón, ona, *–rŏnglŏn'*, a. slow,
zorzal, *thŏrthăl'*, sm. thrush. [heavy, lazy.
zote, *thŏ'tĕ*, sm. stupid, lazy person.
zozobra, *thŏthŏ'pră*, sf. uneasiness, anxiety.
zozobrar, *–brăr'*, v. n. to be weather-
beaten; to be in great danger; to be afflicted; (mar.) to founder.
zueco, *thắĕ'kŏ*, sm. wooden shoe; golosh.
zullarse, *thắlyăr'sĕ*, v. r. to break wind.
zullón, *thắlyŏn'*, sm. flatulence.
zumacar, *thắmăkăr'*, v. a. to tan with
sumach.
zumaque, *thắmă'kĕ*, sm. sumach-tree.

zumba, *thắm'bă*, sf. large bell, used by
carriers; facetious raillery.
zumbar, *–băr'*, v. n. to resound, to hum;
–se, to jest, to joke.   [sound.
zumbido, *–bĕ'dŏ*, sm. humming, buzzing
zumbón, ona, *–bŏn'*, a. waggish.
zumo, *thŏ'mŏ*, sm. sap, juice; **– de cepas**
ó parras, juice of the grape, wine.
zumoso, sa, *thămŏ'sŏ*, a. juicy, succulent.
zupia, *thŏ'piă*, sf. wine which is turned;
liquor with a bad taste; refuse.   [darning.
zurcidura, *thărthĭdŏ'ră*, sf. fine-drawing;
zurcir, *–thĭr'*, v. a. to darn, to fine-draw;
to join, to unite; to hatch lies.
zurdo, da, *thŏr'dŏ*, a. left; left-handed.
zurra, *thŏr'ră*, sf. currying leathers;
flogging, drubbing; drudgery.   [currier.
zurrador, *–rădŏr'*, sm. leather-dresser,
zurrapa, *–ră'pă*, sf. lees, dregs; anything
vile or despicable.   [and dregs.
zurraposo, sa, *–pŏ'sŏ*, a. full of lees
zurrar, *–răr'*, v. a. to curry; to chastise
with a whip; –se, to have a sudden call
of nature; to dirty oneself.   [tops.
zurriaga, *–riă'gă*, sf. thong; whip for
zurriagar, *–găr'*, v. a. to flog, to whip.
zurriagazo, *–gă'thŏ*, sm. severe lash with
a whip; unfortunate calamity.
zurriago, *–riă'gŏ*, sm. whip for inflicting
punishment   [ging; noisy quarrel
zurribanda, *–băn'dă*, sf. repeated flog-
zurriburri, *–bŭr'rĕ*, sm. ragamuffin.
zurrido, *thărrĕ'dŏ*. sm. humming, buzzing;
confused noise.   [tinkle.
zurrir, *–rĭr'*, v. n. to hum, to buzz, to
zurrón, *–rŏn'*, sm. shepherd's pouch;
husks of grain.
zurruscarse, *–rŭskăr'sĕ*, v. r. to experience
a sudden call of nature; to dirty oneself.
zurrusco, *–rŭs'kŏ*, sm. overtoasted slice
of bread.
zutano, na, *thŭtă'nŏ*, a. such a one; **– y**
fulano, such and such a one, so and so.

Los más importantes nombres geográficos

Abisinia, *ăbĭsĕ'nĭă*, f. Abyssinia.

Adriático, *ădrĭă'tĭkŏ*, m. Adriatic, Adriatic Sea.

africano, a, *ăfrĭkă'nŏ*, m. & f. & a. African.

albanés, a, *ălbănĕs'*, m. & f. & a. Albanian.

alemán, a, *ălĕmăn'*, m. & f. & a. German. [many.

Alemania, —*nĭă*, f. Germany. [pl. alpines.

alpecienses, *ălpĕthĭĕn'sĕs*, m. pl. alpines.

Alpes, *ăl'pĕs*, m. pl. Alps.

alpino, a, *ălpĕ'nŏ*, a. alpine.

Alsacia, *ălsă'thĭă*, f. Alsace.

alsaciano, a, —*thĭă'nŏ*, m. & f. & a. Alsatian.

Amberes, *ămbă'rĕs*, m. Antwerp.

americano, a, *ămĕrĭkă'nŏ*, m. & f. & a. American.

Andalucía, *ăndălŭthĕ'ă*, f. Andalusia.

andaluz, a, *ăndălŭth'*, m. & f. & a. Andalusian.

Anseáticas, *ănsĕă'tĭkăs*, f. pl. Hanse Towns.

Apeninos, *ăpĕnĕ'nŏs*, m. pl. Apennines.

Apulia, *ăpŭ'lĭă*, f. Apulia.

Aquisgrán, *ăkĭsgrăn'*, sm. Aix la Chapelle.

árabe, *ă'răbĕ*, m. & f., arábico, *ără'bĭkŏ*, a. Arab.

aragonés, a, *ărăgŏnĕs'*, m. & f. & a. Aragonese.

Archipiélago, *ărtshĭpĭĕ'lăgŏ*, m. Archipelago.

Argel, *ăr'hĕl'*, m. Algiers.

armónico, a, armenio, a, *ărmă'nĭ(k)ŏ*, m. & f. & a. Armenian.

asiano, a, *ăsĭă'nŏ*, asiático, a, —*tĭkŏ*, m. & f. & a. Asiatic. [Athens.

Atenas, *ătĕ'năs*, f. pl.

ateniense, a, *ătĕnĭĕn'sĕ*, ateniense, —*ĕn'sĕ*, m. & f. & a. Athenian.

Atlántico, *ătlăn'tĭkŏ*, m. Atlantic. [Augsburg.

Ausburgo, *ăŭsbŭr'gŏ*, m.

australasino, a, *ăŭstrălă-sĕ'nŏ*, m. & f. & a. Australasian.

austriaco, a, *ăŭstrĭă'kŏ*, m. & f. & a. Austrian.

Báltico, *băl'tĭkŏ*, m. Baltic Sea. [Barbadoes.

Barbadas, *bărbă'dăs*, f. pl.

Basilea, *băsĭlĕ'ă*, f. Basle.

bátavo, a, *bă'tăvŏ*, m. & f. & a. Batavian.

bavario, a, *băvă'rĭŏ*, bávaro, a, *bă'vărŏ*, m. & f. & a. Bavarian. [varia.

Baviera, *băvĭĕ'ră*, f. Ba-Belén, *bĕlĕn'*, m. Bethlehem.

belga, *bĕl'gă*, m. & f., bélgico, a, —*hĭkŏ*, a. Belgian.

Bélgica, —*hĭkă*, f. Belgium.

Bengala, *bĕngă'lă*, f. Bengala. [bary.

Berbería, *bĕrbĕrĕ'ă*, f. Bar-Beocia, *bĕŏ'thĭă*, f. Bœotia.

beociano, a, *bĕŏthĭă'nŏ*, m. & f. & a. Bœotian.

berlinés, a, *bĕrlĭnĕs'*, m. & f. & a. Berlinian.

Bizancio, *bĭthăn'thĭŏ*, m. Byzantium.

bohémico, a, *bŏă'mĭkŏ*, a., bohemo, a, —*mŏ*, m. & f. Bohemian. [gundy.

Borgoña, *bŏrgŏn'yă*, f. Bur-borgonés, a, *bŏrgŏnyĕs'*, m. & f. & a. Burgundian.

Bósforo, *bŏs'fŏrŏ*, m. Bosphorus.

Brasil, *brăsĭl'*, m. Brazil.

brasileño, a, —*lĕn'yŏ*, m. & f. & a. Brazilian.

Bretaña, *brĕtăn'yă*, f. Britany; Gran —, Great Britain.

bretón, a, *brĕtŏn'*, m. & f. & a. British; Briton.

Brunswick, *brŭns'vĭk*, m. Brunswick. [Brussels.

Bruselas, *brŭsĕ'lăs*, f. pl.

búlgaro, a, *bŭl'gărŏ*, m. & f. & a. Bulgarian.

Burdeos, *bŭrdĕ'ŏs*, m. Bordeaux.

Cachemir, *kătshĕmĭr'*, m. Cashmere.

Cádiz, *kă'dĭth*, f. Cadiz.

Cafrería, *kăfrĕrĕ'ă*, f. Caffraria.

calabrés, a, *kălăbrĕs'*, m. & f. & a. Calabrian.

Caldea, *kăldĕ'ă*, f. Chaldea.

Calés, *kălĕs'*, m. Calais.

calmuco, a, *kălmŭ'kŏ*, m. Calmuck.

Cambrigia, *kămbrĭ'hĭă*, Cambrije, —*brĭ'hĕ*, f. Cambridge. [Campeachy.

Campeche, *kămpĕtsh'ĕ*, f.

Canarias, *kănă'rĭăs*, f. pl. Canaries, Canary-Islands.

candiote, *kăndĭŏ'tĕ*, m. & f. & a. Candian.

Cantórberi, *kăntŏr'bĕrĭ*, f. Canterbury. [rinthia.

Carintia, *kărĭn'tĭă*, f. Ca-Carpetanos, *kărpĕtă'nŏs*, m. pl. Carpathians. [Sea.

Caspio, *kăs'pĭŏ*, m. Caspian

castellano, a, *kăstĕlyă'nŏ*, m. & f. & a. Castilian.

Castilla, *kăstĭl'yă*, f. Castile.

catalán, a, *kătălăn'*, m. & f. & a. Catalonian.

Cataluña, *kătălŭn'yă*, f. Catalonia. [casus.

Cáucaso, *kă'ŭkăsŏ*, m. Cau-Ceilán, *thĕĭlăn'*, m. Ceylon.

Cerdeña, *thĕrdĕn'yă*, f. Sardinia. [f. Champagne.

Champaña, *tshămpăn'yă*,

chino, a, *tshĕ'nŏ*, m. & f. & a. Chinese.

Chipre, *tshĕ'prĕ*, m. Cyprus.

Circasia, *thĭrkă'sĭă*, f. Circassia.

circasiano, a, —*sĭă'nŏ*, m. & f. & a. Circassian.

Colonia, *kŏlŏ'nĭă*, f. Cologne.

Constantinopla, *kŏnstăn-tĭnŏ'plă*, f. Constantinople.

Copenaga, *kŏpĕnă'gă*, f. Copenhagen. [sica.

Córcega, *kŏr'thĕgă*, f. Cor-Corfú, *kŏrfŭ'*, m. Corfu.

Corinto, *kŏrĕn'tŏ*, m. Corinth. [Cornwall.
Cornualla, *kŏrnŭāl'yă*, f.
corsés, a, *kŏrsĕs'*, corso, a, *kŏr'sŏ*, m. & f. & a. Corsican. [sack.
cosaco, *kŏsā'kŏ*, m. Cos-
Cracovia, *krā̆kŏ'vĭă*, f. Cracow.
cretense, *krĕtĕn'sĕ*, cré-tico, a, *krā'tĭkŏ*, m. & f. & a. Cretan. [tia.
Croacia, *krŏā'thĭă*, f. Croa-croato, a, *—tŏ*, m. & f. & a. Croatian. [Corland.
Curlandia, *kŭrlăn'dĭă*, f.

Dalmacia, *dălmā'thĭă*, f. Dalmatia.
dalmático, a, *dălmāt'ĭkŏ*, m. & f. & a. Dalmatian.
Damasco, *dămăs'kŏ*, m. Damascus.
danés, a, *dănĕs'*, m. & f. & a. Dane; Danish.
Danubio, *dănŏ'bĭŏ*, m. Danube.
Delfinado, *dĕlfĭnā'dŏ*, m. Dauphinate, Dauphiny.
Delfos, *dĕl'fŏs*, f. Delphos.
Dinamarca, *dĭnămăr'kă*, f. Denmark. [Danish.
dinamarqués, a, *—kĕs'*, a,
Dovres, *dŏ'vrĕs*, m. Dover.
Dresde, *drĕs'dĕ*, f. Dresden.
Dunquerque, *dŭnkĕr'kĕ*, m. Dunkirk.
Duvre, *dŭ'vrĕ*, m. Dover.

Edimburgo, *ĕdĭmbŭr'gŏ*, m. Edinburgh.
Efeso, *ĕ'fĕsŏ*, m. Ephesus.
egipciaco, a, *ĕ'hĭpthĭā'kŏ*,
egipciano, a, *—thĭā'nŏ*,
egipcio, a, *ĕ'hĭp'thĭŏ*, m. & f. & a. Egyptian.
Egipto, *ĕ'hĭp'tŏ*, m. Egypt.
Epiro, *ĕp'rŏ*, m. Epirus.
Escafusa, *ĕskā̆fŭ'să*, f. Schaffhausen.
Escalda, *ĕskăl'dă*, m. Scheld.
Escandinavia, *ĕskăndĭ-nā'vĭă*, f. Scandinavia.
Esclavonia, *ĕsklăvŏ'nĭă*, f. Sclavonia.
esclavón, a, *ĕsklăvŏn'*,
esclavonio, a, *—vŏ'nĭŏ*, m. & f. & a. Sclavonian.
escocés, a, *ĕskŏthĕs'*, m. & f. & a. Scotsman, Scotch-woman; Scotch, Scottish.
Escocia, *ĕskŏ'thĭă*, f. Scotland. [Smyrna.
Esmirna, *ĕsmĭr'nă*, f.
España, *ĕspăn'yă*, f. Spain.
español, a, *ĕspănŏl'*, m. & f. & a. Spaniard; Spanish.
Esparta, *ĕspăr'tă*, f. Sparta.
Spanish and English

espartano, *—tă'nŏ*, m. & f. & a. Spartan.
esquimales, *ĕskĭmā'lĕs*, m. pl. Esquimaux.
Estiria, *ĕstĭ'rĭă*, f. Stiria.
estiriano, a, *—tĭā'nŏ*, m. & f. & a. Stirian.
Estocolmo, *ĕstŏkŏl'mŏ*, m. Stockholm.
Estrasburgo, *ĕstrăsbŭr'gŏ*, m. Strasburg.
Europa, *ĕŭrŏ'pă*, f. Europe.
europeo, a, *ĕŭrŏpĕ'ŏ*, m. & f. & a. European.

Fenicia, *fĕnĭ'thĭă*, f. Phe-nicia. [a, Phenician.
fenicio, a, *—thĭŏ*, m. & f. &
finlandés, a, *fĭnlăndĕs'*, m. & f. & a. Finlander.
Finlandia, *—lăn'dĭă*, f. Fiuland.
flamenco, a, *flămĕn'kŏ*, m. & f. Fleming, Flemish.
Flándes, *flăn'dĕs*, f. Flan-ders. [Flushing.
Flesinga, *flĕsĭn'gă*, f.
Florencia, *flŏrĕn'thĭă*, f. Florence.
florentin, a, *—tĭn'*, m. & f. & a. Florentine.
francés, a, *frănthĕs'*, m. & f. & a. Frenchman, French-woman; French; los franceses, the French (s. pl.).
Francfort del Mein, *frănk'fŏrt dĕl mĕĭn*, m. Frankfort on the Main.
Francoforte, *frănkŏfŏr'tĕ*, m. Frankfort. [Friburg.
Friburgo, *frĭbŭr'gŏ*, m. Friburg.
Frisia, *frē'sĭă*, f. Friesland.
frisón, a, *frĭsŏn'*, m. & f. & a. Frieslander.

Gáles, *gā'lĕs*, m. Wales.
galés, a, *gălĕs'*, m. & f. & a. Welsh, Gælic.
Galia, *gā'lĭă*, f. Gaul.
Galicia, *gălĭth'ĭă*, f. Galicia.
gálico, a, *gā'lĭkŏ*, m. & f. a. Gaul.
Galilea, *gălĭlĕ'ă*, f. Galilee.
Ganges, *găn'hĕs*, m. Ganges.
Gante, *găn'tĕ*, m. Ghent.
Gascuña, *găskŭn'yă*, f. Gascony. [Germany.
Germania, *hĕrmā'nĭă*, f.
Génova, *hĕ'nŏvă*, f. Genoa.
genovés, a, *—vĕs'*, m. & f. a. Genoese. [neva.
Ginebra, *hĭnĕ'bră*, f. Ge-ginebrés, a, *hĭnĕbrĕs'*, m. & f. & a. Genevese.
Grecia, *grā'thĭă*, f. Greece.

griego, a, *grā'gŏ*, m. & f. & a. Greek. [Grisons.
Grisones, *grĭsŏ'nĕs*, m. pl.
groenlandés, a, *grōĕn-lăndĕs'*, m. & f. & a. Green-lander. [Greenland.
Groenlandia, *—lăn'dĭă*, f.
Groninga, *grŏnĭn'gă*, f. Groningen. [Guelderland.
Guéldres, *gĕl'drĕs*, m.

Habana, *ăbā'nă*, f. Havan-nah. [Hamburg.
Hamburgo, *ămbŭr'gŏ*, m.
Haya, *ā'yă*, f. Hague.
Helvecia, *ĕlvĕ'thĭă*, f. Helve-tia. [Hessian.
hesés, a, *ĕsĕs'*, m. & f. & a.
Hesia, *ĕs'ĭă*, f. Hesse.
Holanda, *ŏlăn'dă*, f. Hol-land.
holandés, a, *—dĕs'*, m. & f. & a. Hollander, Dutch-man, Dutchwoman; Dutch.
húngaro, a, *ŭn'gărŏ*, m. & f. & a. Hungarian. [gary.
Hungria, *ŭngrĕ'ă*, f. Hun-

Iliria, *ĭlĭ'rĭă*, f. Illyria.
Indias, *ĭn'dĭăs*, f. pl. Indies; — orientales, East-In-dies; — occidentales, West-Indies. [a. Indian.
indio, a, *ĭn'dĭŏ*, m. & f. &
Inglaterra, *ĭnglătĕr'ră*, f. England.
inglés, a, *ĭnglĕs'*, m. & f & a. Englishman, English-woman; English; los in-gleses, the English (s. pl.).
Irlanda, *ĭrlăn'dă*, f. Ireland.
irlandés, a, *—dĕs'*, m. & f. & a. Irishman, Irish-woman; Irish. [land.
Islanda, *ĭslăn'dă*, f. Ice-islandés, a, *—dĕs'*, m. & f. & a. Icelander.
Italia, *ĭtā'lĭă*, f. Italy.
italiano, a, *—tĭā'nŏ*, m. & f. & a. Italian.

Japón, *hăpŏn'*, m. Japan.
japonés, a, *—nĕs'*, m. & f. & a. Japanese.
Jerusalén, *hĕrŭsălĕn'*, m. Jerusalem. [Jutland.
Jutlandia, *hŭtlăn'dĭă*, f.

laconio, a, *lăkŏ'nĭŏ*, m. & f. & a. Lacedæmonian.
lapón, a, *lăpŏn'*, m. & f. & a. Laplander. [land.
Laponia, *lăpŏ'nĭă*, f. Lap-
León, *lĕŏn'*, m. Lyons.
Líbano, *lĕ'bănŏ*, m. Leba-non.
Lieja, *lĭĕ'hă*, f. Liege.

Lila, *li'lǎ,* f. Lisle.
Liorna, *li̯or'nǎ,* f. Leghorn.
Lipsia, *lip'si̯ǎ,* f. Leipsic.
Lisboa, *lisbo'ǎ,* f. Lisbon.
Lituania, *litu̯ǎ'ni̯ǎ,* f. Lithuania.
lituánico, a.,–*nĭkǒ,* **lituaniense,** –*nĭen'sĕ,* m. & f. & a. Lithuanian.
livoniano, a. *livōnǐǎ'nǒ,* m. & f. & a. Livonian.
Lombardía, *lŏmbǎrdĭ'ǎ,* f. Lombardy.
lombárdico, a. –*bǎr'dĭkǒ,* a., **lombardo,** –*bǎr'dǒ,* m. & f. & a. Lombard.
Londres, *lŏn'dres,* m. London.
londrés, a, *lŏndres',* m. & f. & a. Londonian.
Lorena, *lōrē'nǎ,* f. Lorraine.
Lucemburgo, *lŭthēmbŭr'–gǒ,* **Lujemburgo,** *lŭ'hēm–bŭr'gǒ,* m. Luxemburg.
Lusacia, *lŭsǎ'thǐǎ,* f. Lusatia. [& f. & a. Lysatian.
lusaciano, a., –*thǐǎ'nǒ,* m.

macedónico, a., *mǎthēdǒ'–nǐkǒ,* m. & f. & a. Macedonian. [deira.
Madera, *mǎdē'rǎ,* f. Madrileño,** a, *mǎdrǐlēn'yǒ,* m. & f. & a. inhabitant of Madrid; from Madrid.
Maguncia, *mǎgŭn'thǐǎ,* f. Mentz.
Malina, *mǎlĭ'nǎ,* f. Malines.
maltés, a, a *mǎltes',* m. & f. & a. Maltese. [jorca.
Mallorca, *mǎlyǒr'kǎ,* f. Ma-
Marruecos, *mǎrrŭe'kǒs,* m. pl. Morocco. [Marseilles.
Marsella, *mǎrsel'yǎ,* f.
Meca, *mē'kǎ,* f. Mecca.
Mediterráneo, *mēdĭterrǎ'–nǒ,* m. Mediterranean.
mejicano, a., *mē'hĭkǎ'nǒ,* m. & f. & a. Mexican.
Méjico, *mē'hĭkǒ,* m. Mexico.
Menorca, *mēnǒr'kǎ,* f. Minorca. [sina.
Mesina, *mēsĭ'nǎ,* f. Mes-
Milano, *mĭlǎ'nǒ,* f. Milan.
Molucas, *mŏlŭ'kǎs,* f. pl. Moluccas.
moravo, a, *mōrǎ'vǒ,* m. & f. & a. Moravian.
moro, a, *mō'rǒ,* m. & f. & a. Moor; Moorish.
Mosa, *mō'sǎ,* m. Meuse.
Moscovia, *mŏskō'vǐǎ,* f. Moscovy.
Moscu, *mŏs'kŭ,* f. Moscow.
Mosela, *mŏsē'lǎ,* m. Moselle.
mulato, a, *mŭlǎ'tǒ,* m. & f. & a. Mulatto, Mulatress.

Munich, *mŭnĭk',* m. Munich.

Nápoles, *nǎ'pōles,* m. Naples.
napolitano, a, *nǎpōlĭtǎ'nǒ,* m. & f. & a. Neapolitan.
Neucastel, *nēŭkǎstel',* m. Neufchatel, Neuchatel.
Nilo, *nē'lǒ,* m. Nile. [guen.
Nimega, *nǐmē'gǎ,* f. Nime-
Niza, *nē'thǎ,* f. Nice.
Normandía, *nōrmǎndĭ'ǎ,* f. Normandy.
normando, a, –*mǎn'dǒ,* **normánico,** a, –*mǎ'nǐkǒ,* m. & f. & a. Norman.
Noruega, *nōrŭe'gǎ,* f. Norway. [& a. Norwegian.
noruego, a, –*gǒ,* m. & f.
nubio, a, *nŭ'bǐǒ,* m. & f. & a. Nubian. [f. New-York.
Nueva-York, *nŭe'vǎ̯yǒrk,*
Nuremberga, *nŭrember'–gǎ,* f. Nuremberg.

Olimpo, *ōlĭm'pǒ,* m. Olympus. [Orkneys.
Orcadas, *ŏrkǎ'dǎs,* f. pl.
Ostende, *ŏsten'dĕ,* f. Ostend.

Pacífico, *pǎthĭ'fĭkǒ,* m. Pacific. [m. Palatinate.
Palatinado, *pǎlǎtĭnǎ'dǒ,*
Palestina, *pǎlestĭ'nǎ,* f. Palestine.
parisiense, *pǎrĭsĭen'sĕ,* m. & f. & a. Parisian.
Parnaso, *pǎrnǎ'sǒ,* m. Parnassus. [m. Petersburg.
Pedroburgo, *pēdrōbŭr'gǒ,*
Peloponeso, *pēlōpōnē'sǒ,* m. Peloponnesus.
persa, *per'sǎ,* m. & f., **persiano,** a, –*sǐǎ'nǒ,* a. Persian.
Perú, *pērŭ',* m. Peru.
Piamonte, *pǐǎmŏn'tĕ,* m. Piedmont. [f. & a.
piamontés, a, –*tes',* m. & Piedmontese.
Pirineos, *pĭrĭnē'ōs,* m. pl. Pyrenees.
polaco, a, *pōlǎ'kǒ,* m. & f. & a. Pole; Polish.
Polonia, *pōlō'nǐǎ,* f. Poland.
Ponto, *pŏn'tǒ,* m. Pontus.
portugués, a, *pōrtŭges',* m. & f. & a. Portuguese.
Praga, *prǎ'gǎ,* f. Prague.
Provenza, *prōven'thǎ,* f. Provence.
Prusia, *prŭs'ǐǎ,* f. Prussia.
prusiano, a, –*sǐǎ'nǒ,* m. & f. & a. Prussian.
Puente Euxino, *pŭen'tĕ eŭksē'nǒ,* m. Euxine-Sea.

Puerta, *pŭer'tǎ,* f. Ottoman Empire.
Pulla, *pŭl'yǎ,* f. Apulia.

Ratisbona, *rǎtisbō'nǎ,* f. Ratisbon. [venna.
Ravena, *rǎvē'nǎ,* f. Ra-
Rin, Rhin, *rĭn,* m. Rhine.
Ródano, *rǒ'dǎnǒ,* m. Rhone.
Rodas, *rǒ'dǎs,* f. pl. Rhodes.
Roma, *rǒ'mǎ,* f. Roma.
Romania, *rōmǎ'nǐǎ,* f. Roumania. [f. & a. Roman.
romano, a, *rōmǎ'nǒ,* m. &
Rusia, *rŭs'ǐǎ,* f. Russia.
rusiano, a, –*sǐǎ'nǒ,* m. & f. & a. Russian.

Saboya, *sǎbǒ'yǎ,* f. Savoy.
saboyano, a, –*yǎ'nǒ,* m. & f. & a. Savoyard.
sajón, a, *sǎ'hǒn',* **sajono,** a, *sǎ'hǒ'nǒ,* m. & f. & a. Saxon. [Saxony.
Sajonia, *sǎ'hǒ'nǐǎ,* f.
samoyedo, a, *sǎmǒyē'dǒ,* m. & f. & a. Samoied. [n. Sardinian.
sardo, a, *sǎr'dǒ,* m. & f. &
Sena, *sē'nǎ,* m. Seine.
siberiano, a, *sǐbērǐǎ'nǒ,* m. & f. & a. Siberian.
Sicilia, *sǐthĭ'lǐǎ,* f. Sicily.
siciliano, a, –*lǐǎ'nǒ,* m. & f. & a. Sicilian.
silesio, a, *sǐlē'sǐǒ,* m. & f. & a. Silesian.
Suecia, *sŭe'thǐǎ,* f. Sweden.
sueco, a, –*kǒ,* m. & f. & a. Swede; Swedish.
Suiza, *sŭi'thǎ,* f. Switzerland. [Swiss.
suizo, a, –*thǒ,* m. & f. & a.
Sun, *sŭn,* m. the Sound.

Tajo, *tǎ'hǒ,* m. Tagus.
Támesis, *tǎ'mēsǐs,* m. Thames. [tary.
Tartaria, *tǎrtǎ'rǐǎ,* f. Tar-
tártaro, a, *tǎr'tǎrǒ,* m. & f. & a. Tartar.
Termópilas, *termǒ'pĭlǎs,* f. pl. Thermopylæ.
Terranova, *terrǎnǒ'vǎ,* f. Newfoundland. [saly.
Tesalia, *tēsǎ'lǐǎ,* f. Thes-
Tesalónica, *tēsǎlǒ'nǐkǎ,* f. Thessalonica.
tésalo, a, *tē'sǎlǒ,* m. & f. & a. Thessalian.
tirolés, a, *tǐrōles',* m. & f. & a. Tirolese.
Tolón, *tōlǒn',* m. Toulon.
Tolosa, *tōlǒ'sǎ,* f. Toulouse.
Toscana, *tōskǎ'nǎ,* f. Tuscany.
Tracia, *trǎ'thǐǎ,* f. Thracia.
Transilvania, *trǎnsǐlvǎ'–nǐǎ,* f. Transylvania.

Trento, *trĕn'tŏ*, m. Trent.
Tróveris, *trŏ'vĕrĭs*, m. Triers.
Troya, *trŏ'yă*, f. Troy.
troyano, a, *trŏyă'nŏ*, m. & f. & a. Trojan.
Túnez, *tŏ'nĕth*, f. Tunis.
turco, a, *tŭr'kŏ*, m. & f. & a. Turk; Turkish.
Turingia, *tŭrĭn'hĭă*, f. Thuringia.
turingio, a, *–hĭŏ*, m. & f. & a. Thuringian.

Turquía, *tŭrkē'ă*, f. Turkey.
Utreque, *ŭtrĕ'kĕ*, f. Utrecht.

valaco, a, *vălă'kŏ*, m. & f. & a. Wallachian.
Valaquia, *vălă'kĭă*, f. Wallachia.
Varsovia, *vărsŏ'vĭă*, f. Warsaw.
Venecia, *vĕnĕ'thĭă*, f. Venice.
veneciano, a, *vĕnĕthĭă'nŏ*, m. & f. & a. Venetian.

Versalles, *vĕrsăl'yĕz*, m. Versailles.
Vesuvio, *vĕsŏ'vĭŏ*, m. Vesuvius.
Viena, *vĭă'nă*, f. Vienna.
vienés, a, *–nĕs*, m. & f. & a. Viennese.
Vincenas, *vĭnthă'năs*, f. pl. Vincennes.
Virtembergo, *vĭrtĕmbĕr'gŏ*, m. Wurtemberg.

Zelandia, *thĕlăn'dĭă*, f. Zealand.
Zurico, *thŭrĭ'kŏ*, m. Zurich.

Los más comunes nombres de bautismo

Abrahán, *ăbrăăn'*, Abraham.
Adán, *ădăn'*, Adam.
Adelaida, *ădĕlă'dă*, Adelaide.
Adolfo, *ădŏl'fŏ*, Adolphus.
Agustín, *ăgŭstĭn'*, Austin.
Alejandro, *ălĕ'hăn'drŏ*, Alexander.
Alfonso, *ălfŏn'sŏ*, Alphonse.
Ambrosio, *ămbrŏ'sĭŏ*, Ambrose.
Amalia, *ămă'lĭă*, Amelia.
Amata, *ămă'tă*, Amy.
Ana, *ă'nă*, Ann.
Andreo, *ăndră'ŏ*, Andrés, *ăndrĕs'*, Andrew.
Anita, *ănĭ'tă*, Nan, Nancy, Jean, Janet.
Antonio, *ăntŏ'nĭŏ*, Anthony.
Augusto, *ăŭgŭs'tŏ*, Augustus.

Bártolo, *băr'tŏlŏ*, Bartolomé, *–mĕ*, Bartolomeo, *–mă'ŏ*, Bartholomew.
Beatriz, *bĕătrĭth'*, Beatrice.
Beltrán, *bĕltrăn'*, Bertram.
Benjaminito, *bĕn'hămĭnĭ'tŏ*, Ben. Bennet.
Benito, *bĕnĭ'tŏ*, Benedict.
Bianca, *bĭăn'kă*, Blanche.
Brígida, *brĭ'hĭdă*, Bridget.
Brigidita, *–dĭ'tă*, Biddy.

Carlos, *kăr'lŏs*, Charles.
Carlota, *kărlŏ'tă*, Charlotte.
Carolina, *kărŏlĭ'nă*, Caroline, Cary.
Catalina, *kătălĭ'nă*, Catharine, Kate. Cissy.
Cecilia, *thĕthĭ'lĭă*, Cecily.
Constancia, *kŏnstăn'thĭă*, Constance. stantine.
Constantino, *–tē'nŏ*, Constantine.
Cristo, *krĭs'tŏ*, Christ.
Cristóbal, *krĭstŏ'băl*, Christopher.

Chombo, *tshŏm'bŏ*, Jerónimo, *hĕrŏ'nĭmŏ*, Jerome.

Diego, *dĭĕ'gŏ*, James.
Dorotea, *dŏrŏtĕ'ă*, Dorothy.
Doroteita, *–tĕ'ĭtă*, Dolly.

Eduardo, *ĕdŭăr'dŏ*, Edward. nor.
Elena, *ĕlĕ'nă*, Ellen, Eleanor.
Emilia, *ĕmĭ'lĭă*, Emily.
Enrique, *ĕnrĭ'kĕ*, Henry.
Enriqueta, *–kĕ'tă*, Harriet.
Enriquito, *–kĭ'tŏ*, Harry, Hal.
Esteban, *ĕstĕ'băn*, Stephan.
Ester, *ĕstĕr'*, Esther.
Eugenio, *ĕŭhĕ'nĭŏ*, Eugene.
Eva, *ĕ'vă*, Eve.

Faquita, *făkĭ'tă*, Fanny.
Federico, *fĕdĕrĭ'kŏ*, Frederick.
Felipe, *fĕlĭ'pĕ*, Philip.
Fernando, *fĕrnăn'dŏ*, Ferdinand. Frances.
Francisca, *frănthĭs'kă*, Francisco, *–kŏ*, Francis, Frank.

Gaspar, *găspăr'*, Jasper.
Geofredo, *hĕŏfrĕ'dŏ*, Geoffrey, Jeffrey.
Gertrudis, *gĕrtrŏ'dĭs*, Tula, *tŏ'lă*, Gertrud, Gerty.
Gofredo, Godofredo, *gŏ(dŏ)frĕ'dŏ*, Godfrey.
Gregorio, *grĕgŏ'rĭŏ*, Gregory. ter.
Gualterio, *gŭăltĕ'rĭŏ*, Walter.
Guido, *gē'dŏ*, Guy.
Guillelma, *gĭlyĕl'mă*, Wilhelmine.
Guillermo, Guillermo, *gĭlyĕl'mŏ*, *–yĕr'mŏ*, William, Will, Willy, Billy. vus.
Gustavo, *gŭstă'vŏ*, Gustave.

Hedwigia, *ĕdwĭ'hĭă*, Edwiga.
Helena, *ĕlĕ'nă*, Helen.
Hilario, *ĭlă'rĭŏ*, Hilary.

16*

Hugo, *ŏ'gŏ,* Hugh.
Hunfredo, *ŭnfrā'dŏ,* Humphrey.

Ignacio, *ĭgnā'thĭŏ,* Ignacio. **Inés,** *ĭnĕs',* Agnes.   [tius.
Isabel, *ĭsăbĕl',* Elizabeth, Eliza, Lizzie.
Isabelita, —*lī'tă,* Bess, Betsy, Betty.

Jaime, *'hā'ĭmĕ,* James, Jem, Jemmy.
Jorge, *'hŏr'hĕ,* George.
José, *'hŏsĕ',* Joseph.
Juan, *'hŭăn',* John.
Juana, —*nă,* Jane.
Juanita, —*ē'tă,* Jenny.
Juanito, —*ē'tŏ,* Johnny, Jack.
Juliana, *'hŭlĭā'nă,* Julian.
Julio, *'hā'lĭŏ,* Julius.

Leonor, *lĕŏnŏr',* Eleanor.
Liseta, *lĭsĕ'tă,* Lizzie.
Lucas, *lŏ'kăs,* Luke.
Lucía, *lŭthĕ'ă,* Lucy.
Luis, *lŭĭs',* Lewis.
Luisa, *lŭĕ'să,* Louisa.

Magdalena, *măgdălĕ'nă,* Magdalen, Maud.
Manuel, *mănŏĕl',* Emanuel.
Marcos, *mār'kŏs,* Mark.
Margarita, *mărgărĭ'tă,* Margaret, Madge, Margery, Peggy.
María, *mărē'ă,* Mary.
Mariquita, *mărĭkē'tă,* **Maruja,** *mărū'h'ă,* Moll, Molly.   [Mat.
Mateo, *mătē'ŏ,* Matthew.
Mauricio, *maŭrē'thĭŏ,* Morris.
Miguel, *mēgĕl',* Michael.

Nicolas, *nĭkŏlăs',* Nicholas.

Pablo, *pă'blŏ,* Paul.
Patricio, *pătrē'thĭŏ,* Patrick, Paddy.
Pedro, *pā'drŏ,* Peter.
Pepe, *pĕ'pĕ,* **Pepillo,** —*pēl'-yŏ,* Joe.

Ramón, *rămŏn',* Raymund.
Reinaldo, *rēĭnăl'dŏ,* Reynald.   [Dicky.
Ricardito, *rĭkărdĭ'tŏ,* Dick,

Ricardo, *rĭkăr'dŏ,* Richard.
Roberto, *rŏbĕr'tŏ,* Robert, Bob, Robin.
Rogerio, *rŏ'hă'rĭŏ,* Roger.
Rodolfo, Rodulfo, *rŏdŭl'-fŏ,* Ralph.
Roldán, *rŏldăn',* **Rolando,** *rŏlăn'dŏ,* Rowland.

Sabedeo, *săbĕdē'ŏ,* Zebedee.
Salomón, *sălŏmŏn',* Solomon.   [Sam.
Samuel, *sămŭĕl',* Samuel.
Sara, *să'ră,* Sarah, Sally.
Sofía, *sŏfē'ă,* Sophia, Sophy.
Susana, *sŭsă'nă,* Susan, Sue, Suky.

Teresa, *tĕrĕ'să,* Theresa.
Timóteo, *tĭmŏ'tĕŏ,* Timothy.   [Tom.
Tomás, *tŏmăs',* Thomas,

Valentino, *vălĕntē'nŏ,* Valentine.

Zacarías, *thăkărē'ăs,* Zachary.

Las abreviaturas más comunes en castellano

Las palabras precedidas de asterisco han de llevar una raya, tilde ó rasgo encima, y á veces debajo, puesto á la larga, cruzando los trazos altos ó bajos de las letras.

A., Alteza; Aprobado (en examen).
a, área.
(a), *alias*.
(a), arroba.
(a)(a), arrobas.
A. A., Autores; Altezas.
ab., abad.
ab.l, abril.
Abs. gen., Absolución general.
A. C ó A. de C., Año de Cristo.
* admón, administración.
adm.or, administrador.
af.mo, afectísimo.
af.to, afecto.
Ag.n, Agustín.
ag.to, agosto.
alc.de, alcalde.
Alej.o, Alejandro.
Alf.o, Alfonso.
Al.o, Alonso.
Á L. R. P. de V. M., Á los reales pies de Vuestra Majestad.
Álv.o, Álvaro.
am.o, amigo.
* ana, antífona.
anac., anacoreta.
Ant.o, Antonio.
ap., aparte; apóstol.
ap.a, ap.o ó * aplica, aplico, apostólica; apostólico.
apóst., apóstol.
art ó art.o, artículo.
* arz. ó arzbpo., arzobispo.
Aud.a, Audiencia.

B., Beato; Bueno (en examen).
Bar.mé, Bartolomé.
Bern.o, Bernardo.
B. L. M. ó b. l. m., besa la mano.
B. L. P. ó b. l. p., beso los pies.
B.mo P.e, Beatísimo Padre.
B. p., Bendición papal.
Br. ó br., bachiller.

c.a, c.ía ó * comp., compañía.
c. ó cap., capítulo.

cap.n, capitán.
capp.n, capellán.
Card.l, Cardenal.
C. de J., Compañía de Jesús.
cénts., céntimos.
cf., conf. ó confr., confesor; confirma (en documentos antiguos).
cg., centigramo, centigramos.
cl., centilitro, centilitros.
Clem.te, Clemente.
* cllo, cuartillo.
cm., centímetro, centímetros.
C. M. B. ó c. m. b., cuyas manos beso.
col. ó col.a, columna; colonia.
comis., comisario.
cons.o, consejo.
Const., Constitución.
const., constitucional.
conv.te, conveniente.
corr.te, corriente.
C. P. B. ó c. p. b., cuyos pies beso.
cps., compañeros.
crec.te, creciente.
cs., cuartos; céntimos.

D. ó D.n, Don.
D.a, Doña.
D.D., doctores.
Dg., decagramo, decagramos.
* dha, dho, dhas, dhos, dicha, dicho, dichas, dichos.
dic.e, 10e ó 10bre, diciembre.
Dl., decalitro, decalitros.
dl., decilitro, decilitros.
Dm., decímetro.
dm., decímetro, decímetros; decigramo, decigramos.
Doct., D.r ó dr., doctor.
docum.to, documento.
D. O. M., *Deo Optimo Maximo*.
Dom.o, Domingo.
dom.o, domingo.
* dra, dro, dras, dros, derecha, derecho, derechas, derechos.
dup.do, duplicado.

E., este (oriental)

ec.ca, ec.co, eclesiástica, eclesiástico.
E. M., Estado Mayor.
Em.a, Eminencia.
E. M. G., Estado Mayor General.
Em.mo ó *Emmo, Eminentísimo.
ENE, estenordeste.
en.o, enero.
E. P. D., En paz descanse.
E. P. M., En propia mano.
ermit., ermitaño.
esc.o, escudo.
escrit.a, escritura.
*escrnía, escribanía.
*escrno, escribano.
escs, escudos.
ESE, estesudeste.
etc. ó &a., etcétera.
Eug.o, Eugenio.
Evang.o, Evangelio.
Evang.a, Evangelista.
Exc.a, Excelencia.
Exc.ma, Exc.mo ó *Excma, Excmo,
Excelentísima, Excelentísimo.

F., Fulano.
Fico ó Frano.o, Francisco.
Fl de T., Fulano de Tal.
feb.o, febrero.
Fern.do, Fernando.
*fha, fho, fecha, fecho.
f.o ó fol., folio.
Fr., Fray; Frey.
*Frnz ó *Fz, Fernandez.
fund., fundador.

G., gracia.
g., gramo, gramos.
g.de ó *gue, guarde.
Gen.l, general (dignidad).
G.o, Gonzalo.
gob.o, gobierno.
gob.r, gobernador.
*Gonz, González.
*gral, general.
Greg.o, Gregorio.
Guill.o, Guillermo.

hect., hectárea, hectáreas.
Hg., hectogramo, hectogramos.
Hl., hectolitro, hectolitros.
Hm., hectómetro, hectómetros.
hol., holandesa.

ib., ibidem.
id., idem.
i. e., id est (esto es).
*igl.a, iglesia.
Ign.o, Ignacio.
Ildef.o, Ildefonso.
Il.e, Ilustre.
Il.ma, Il.mo ó *Illma, Illmo, Ilustrísima, Ilustrísimo.
Indulg. plen. ó I. P., Indulgencia ple-
naria.
in p. inf., in pártibus infidélium.
inq.r, inquisidor.
intend.te, intendente.
it., ítem.

*izq.a, izq.o ó izq.da, izq.do, izquierda,
izquierdo.

Jac.to, Jacinto.
J. C., Jesucristo.
Jerón.o, Jerónimo.
*Jhs, Jesús.
J.o, Ju.o (ant.), Juan.
*Jph, José.
juev., jueves.
Jul.n, Julián.

kg., kilogramo, kilogramos.
kl., kilolitro, kilolitros.
km., kilómetro, kilómetros.

L., L.do ó l.do, Licenciado.
l., ley; libro; litro, litros.
*lbs, libras.
lín., línea.
Lor.zo, Lorenzo.
L. S., Locus sigilli (lugar del sello).
lun., lunes.

M., Madre (religiosa); Majestad; Merced;
Maestro; Mediano (en examen).
m., minuto, minutos; metro, metros; mañana.
Man.l, Manuel.
M.a, María.
Marg.ta, Margarita.
mart., martes.
márts ó mrs, mártires.
may.mo, mayordomo.
M.e, Madre (religiosa).
meng., menguante.
mg., miligramo, miligramos.
miérc., miércoles.
Mig.l, Miguel.
milés.s, milésimas.
min.o, ministro.
Mm., miriámetro, miriámetros.
mm., milímetro, milímetros.
monast.o, monasterio.
Mons., Monseñor.
M. P. S., Muy Poderoso Señor.
Mr, Monsieur; Míster.
mr, mártir.
mrd, merced.
*Mrn, Martín.
*Mrnz, Martínez.
*Mro, Maestro.
mrs, maravedises; mártires.
M. S., manuscrito.
m.s a.s, muchos años.
M. SS., manuscritos.

N., norte; Notablemente aprovechado (en
examen).
n., noche.
N.a S.a, Nuestra Señora.
N. B., Notabene.
NE, nordeste.
NNE, nornordeste.
NNO, nornoroeste.
NO, noroeste.
n.o, número (1. primero, 2. segundo etc.)
nov.e, 9e ó 9bre, noviembre.
Nov. Recop., Novísima Recopilación

N. Recop., Nueva Recopilación.
* nra, nro, nras, nros, ntra, ntro, ntras, ntros, nuestra, nuestro, nuestras, nuestros.
núm. ó núm.o, núms ó núm.s, número. números.
N. S., Nuestro Señor.
N. S. J. C., Nuestro Señor Jesucristo.

O, oeste.
ob. ú * obpo, obispo.
oct.e, 8e ú 8bre, octubre.
ONO, oestenoroeste.
onz., onza.
* orn, orden.
OSO, oessudoeste.

P., Papa; Padre; Pregunta.
P. A., Por ausencia; Por autorización.
p.a, para.
pág., págs, página, páginas.
Part., Partida.
Patr., Patriarca.
* pbro ó presb., presbítero.
P. D., Posdata.
P.e, Padre.
p. ej., por ejemplo
penit., penitente.
perg. ó pno, pergamino.
Pf., Pfs, peso fuerte, pesos fuertes.
P. M., Padre Maestro.
P. O., Por orden.
P.o, Pedro.
p.o, pero.
p°/o, por ciento.
P. P., Porte pagado; Por poder.
* p.p.do, próximo pasado.
p.r, por.
* pral, principal.
priv., privilegio.
proc., procesión.
prof., profeta.
pról., prólogo.
* pror, procurador.
prov.a, provincia.
prov.or, provisor.
P. S., Post scriptum (posdata).
P. S. M., Por su mandato.
ps, pesos.
pta, pasta.
ptas, pesetas.
p.te, parte.

Q. B. S. M. ó q. b. s. m., que besa su mano.
Q. B. S. P. ó q. b. s. p., que besa sus pies.
Q. D. G. ó q. D. g., que Dios guarde.
q.e, que.
q. e. g. e., que en gloria esté.

R., Reverendo; Reverencia; Respuesta; Reprobado (en examen).
R), Responde ó respuesta (en libros de rezo).
Raf., Rafael.
R.bí, Recibí.
R. D., Real Decreto.
Rda M. ó R. M., Reverenda Madre.
Rdo P. ó R. P., Reverendo Padre.
R.e, Récipe.

R. I. P., Requiescat in pace (en paz descanse).
r.l, real (moneda).
R.l, Real (del Rey).
* Rmrz, Ramírez.
R. O., Real Orden.
R. S., Real Servicio.
rs ó r.s, reales (moneda).
R.s, Reales (del rey).
rúst., rústica.

S., San ó Santo; sur; Sobresaliente (en) examen).
S.a, Señora.
S. A., Su Alteza.
sáb., sábado.
S. A. I., Su Alteza Imperial.
S. A. R., Su Alteza Real.
S. A. S., Su Alteza Serenísima.
Sb.n, Sebastián.
S. C. ó s. c., su casa.
S. C. M., Sacra, Católica Majestad.
S. C. C. R. M., Sacra, Cesárea, Católica, Real Majestad.
S. D., Se despide.
S. D. M., Su Divina Majestad.
SE, sudeste.
secret.a, secretaría.
s. e. ú o., salvo error ú omisión.
sept.e, 7e ó 7bre, septiembre.
Ser.ma, Ser.mo ó * Serma, Sermo, Serenísima, Serenísimo.
serv.o, servicio.
serv.or, servidor.
set.e, setiembre.
sig.te, siguiente.
S. M., Su Majestad.
S. M. A., Su Majestad Apostólica.
S. M. B., Su Majestad Británica.
S. M. C., Su Majestad Católica.
S. M. F., Su Majestad Fidelísima.
S. M. I., Su Majestad Imperial.
S.n, San.
S. N., Servicio Nacional.
SO, sudoeste.
* Sor, Señor.
* Sores, Señores.
* spre, siempre.
S.r ó Sr, Señor.
* Sra, Sras, Señora, Señoras.
Sres ó S.res, Señores.
* Sría, Secretaría.
s.ria, s.rio ó * sria, srio, secretaria, secretario.
S. R. M., Su Real Majestad.
Srta ó * Srta, Señorita.
S. S., Su Santidad.
S.a, Su Señoría.
SS. AA., Sus Altezas.
SSE, sudsudeste.
SS. MM., Sus Majestades.
SS.mo, Santísimo.
SS.mo P., Santísimo Padre.
SS.rio, escribano.
SSO, sudsudoeste.
S. S. S., su seguro servidor.
Sta, Santa.
Sto, Santo.
sup., súplica.

supert.te, superintendente.
supl.te, suplente.

t., tarde.
ten.te, teniente.
test.mto, testamento.)
test.o, testigo.
tít. ó tít.o, título.)
t.o ó tom., tomo. /
✻ **tpo**, tiempo.
trib.l, tribunal.

U. ó Ud, Usted.
Uds, Ustedes.

V., Usted; Venerable; Véase.)
V.ó Vers.o, Versículo.
V.a, Vigilia.
V. A., Vuestra Alteza.
V. A. R., Vuestra Alteza Real.
V. B.d, Vuestra Beatitud.
V. E., Vuestra Excelencia ó Vuecencia.)
vg., verbigracia; virgen.
v. g. ó v. gr., verbigracia.

vgs, vírgenes.
Vict.a, Victoria.
Vic.te, Vicente.
vier., viernes.
virg., **virgs**, virgen, vírgenes.)
V. M., Vuestra Majestad.
Vm. ó Vmd, Vuestra Merced ó Usted.
vn, vellón.
V.o B.o, Visto bueno.
vol., volumen; voluntad.
vols, volúmenes.
V. O. T., Venerable Orden Tercera.)
V. P., Vuestra Paternidad.
V. R., Vuestra Reverencia.
✻ **vra**, **vro**, **vras**, **vros**, vuestra, vuestro,
     vuestras, vuestros.
V. S., Vueseñoría ó Usía.
V. S. I., Vueseñoría, ó Usía, Ilustrísima.
v.ta, **v.to**, vuelta, vuelto.
V. V., Ustedes.

x.mo, diezmo.
✻ **xpiano**, **xptiano**, cristiano.[1])
✻ **Xpo**, **Xpto**, Cristo.[1])
✻ **Xptóbal**, Cristóbal.[1])

1) Los dos primeros caracteres de estas cinco últimas abreviaturas son las letras
griegas χ (ji) y ϱ (rho).

Direcciones de cartas

Uso comercial

Dirección: Bernard Newhouse and Company
Saludo: Gentlemen *or* Dear Sirs
Despedida: Very truly yours *or* Yours truly

Uso social

Señor
Dirección: Mister George Fuller
               (Mister is always abbreviated to Mr.)
Saludo: Dear Mr. Fuller *or* My dear Mr. Fuller
Despedida: Very truly yours *or* Sincerely yours *or* Respectfully yours

Señorita
Dirección: Miss Doris Richardson
Saludo: Dear Miss Richardson *or* My dear Miss Richardson
Despedida: Very truly yours *or* Sincerely yours

Señora
Dirección: Mrs. William B. Archer *or* Mrs. William Barth Archer
Saludo: Dear Mrs. Archer *or* My dear Mrs. Archer
Despedida: Very truly yours *or* Sincerely yours

Moneda, Pesos y Medidas españolas
(Spanish Currency, Weights and Measures)

Monedas (Currency).

Standard coin: la peseta = 100 céntimos.
Gold coins: pieces of 5, 10, 25 y 100 pesetas.
    la onza = 80 pesetas.
    la media onza = 40 pesetas.
    el doblón de oro = 20 pesetas.
Silver coins: el real = 25 céntimos.
    dos reales = 50 céntimos.
    cuatro reales = 100 céntimos = peseta.
    dos pesetas = 200 céntimos.
    el duro = 20 reales = 5 pesetas.
    el escudo = 2,50 pesetas.
    la peseta columniaria = 1,25 pesetas.
Copper coins: pieces of 1, 2, 5 céntimos
(vulg. perro chico), and of 10 céntimos
(vulg. perro grande).
Paper-money: Bank of Spain notes for 25,
50, 100, 500 and 1000 pesetas.

Pesos (Weights).

Kilogramo = 1000 gramos.
Hectogramo = 100 gramos.
Decagramo = 10 gramos.
Quintal métrico = 100 kilogramos.
Libra = 4 cuarterones = 16 onzas = 460
  gramos.
Cuarterón = 4 onzas = 115 gramos.
Onza = 16 adarmes = 287 decigramos.
Tomín = 6 centigramos.
Arroba = 4 cuartillas = 25 libras = 11,502
  kilogramos.   [kilogramos.
Cuartilla = ¹/₄ arroba = 6,25 libras = 2,875
Quintal = 4 arrobas = 46 kilogramos.

Medidas longitudinales (Linear Measure).

Standard: metro.
Pie = ¹/₃ vara = 12 pulgadas = 278 decímetros.

Medidas para áridos (Dry Measure)

Litro = 1 decímetro cubo.
Fanega = 12 celemines = 55,5 litros.
Celemín = 4 cuartillos = 4,625 litros.
Cuartillo = ¹/₄ celemín = 1,156 litros.
Cahiz = 12 fa egas = 6,66 hectolitros.

Medidas para líquidos (Liquid Measure).

Moyo = 16 cántaras = 2,58 hectolitros.
Cántara = 4 cuartillas = 16,133 litros.
Cuartilla = 2 azumbres = 4,023 litros.
Azumbre = 4 cuartillos = 2,016 litros.
Cuartillo = 5,04 decilitros.

Medidas agrarias (Square Measure).

Area = 100 metros cuadrados.
Hectárea = 100 áreas = 10,000 metros cua-
  drados.
Centiárea = 1 metro cuadrado.
Fanega de tierra = 576 estadales = 64,6 áreas.
Estadal = 1,12 deciáreas.
Aranzada = 400 estadales = 44,8 áreas.
Caballería = 60 fanegas = 3,8758 hectáreas.

Medidas cúbicas (Cubic Measure).

Estéreo = 1 metro cúbico.
Decastéreo = 10 metros cúbicos.
Decistéreo = ¹/₁₀ metro cúbico.

Irregular Verbs[1].

Infinitivo.	Presente del Indicativo.	Pretérito perfecto.	Futuro.	Imperativo.	Participio.
abastecer	*conjugated*	*as*	nacer		
aborrecer	*conjugated*	*as*	nacer		
abrir					abierto
absolver	yo absuelvó, tú absuelves, él absuelve, ellos absuelven			absuelve tú, absuelva él, absuelvan ellos	absuelto.
acertar	yo acierto, tú aciertas, él acierta, ellos aciertan			acierta tú, acierto él, acierten ellos	
acordar	*conjugated*	*as*	acostar		
acostar	yo acuesto, tú acuestas, él acuesta, ellos acuestan			acuesta tú, acueste él, acuesten ellos	
acrecentar	*conjugated*	*as*	acertar		
adestrar	*conjugated*	*as*	acertar		
adherir	*conjugated*	*as*	sentir		
adquirir	*conjugated*	*as*	sentir		
advertir	*conjugated*	*as*	sentir		
agorar	*conjugated*	*as*	acostar		
alentar	*conjugated*	*as*	acertar		
almorzar	*conjugated*	*as*	acostar		
amolar	*conjugated*	*as*	acostar		
andar	v. Ir.	yo anduve, tu anduviste &c.	yo iré &c. (v. Ir.)		
apacentar	*conjugated*	*as*	acertar		
aportar	*conjugated*	*as*	acostar		
apostar	*conjugated*	*as*	acostar		
apretar	*conjugated*	*as*	acertar		
aprobar	*conjugated*	*as*	acostar		
argüir	yo arguyo, tú arguyes, él arguye, ellos arguyen			arguye tú &c.	
arrendar	*conjugated*	*as*	acertar		
arrepentirse	*conjugated*	*as*	sentir		
ascender	yo asciendo, tú asciendes, él asciende, ellos ascienden			asciende tú, ascienda él, asciendan ellos	
asentar	*conjugated*	*as*	acertar		
asestar	*conjugated*	*as*	acertar		
asir	yo asgo			asga él, asgan ellos	
asolar	*conjugated*	*as*	acostar		
atender	*conjugated*	*as*	ascender		
aterrar	*conjugated*	*as*	acertar		
atestar	*conjugated*	*as*	acertar		
atravesar	*conjugated*	*as*	acertar		
atribuir	*conjugated*	*as*	argüir		
aventar	*conjugated*	*as*	acertar		
avergonzar	*conjugated*	*as*	acostar		
bendecir [2]	yo bendigo, tú bendices, él bendice, ellos bendicen	yo bendije, tú bendijiste &c.	yo bendeciré, tú bendecirás &c.	bendice tú, bendiga él, bendigan ellos	bendido (bendecido)

1) The persons *not* given in the tables, as well as the tenses in the columns of which a blank is left, are conjugated *regularly*. — 2) Gerundio: bendiciendo.

Infinitivo.	Presente del Indicativo.	Pretérito perfecto.	Futuro.	Imperativo.	Participio.
bregar	*conjugated*	*as*	acertar		
caber	yo quepo	yo cupe, tú cupiste &c.	yo cabré, tú cabrás &c.	quepa él, quepan ellos	
caer	yo caigo	él cayó, ellos cayeron		caigaél, caigamos nosotros, caigan ellos	
calentar	*conjugated*	*as*	acertar		
cegar	*conjugated*	*as*	acertar		
ceñir	*conjugated*	*as*	pedir		
cerner	*conjugated*	*as*	ascender		
cerrar	*conjugated*	*as*	acertar		
cimentar	*conjugated*	*as*	acertar		
cocer	*conjugated*	*as*	absolver		
colar	*conjugated*	*as*	acostar		
colegir	*conjugated*	*as*	pedir		
colgar	*conjugated*	*as*	acostar		
comenzar	*conjugated*	*as*	acertar		
compeler					cómpulso [(compelido)]
competir	*conjugated*	*as*	pedir		
concebir	*conjugated*	*as*	pedir		
concertar	*conjugated*	*as*	acertar		
concluir	*conjugated*	*as*	argüir		concluso (concluido)
condoler	*conjugated*	*as*	absolver		
conducir	yo conduzco	yo conduje, tú condujiste &c.		conduzca él, conduzcámos nosotros, conduzcan ellos	
conferir	*conjugated*	*as*	sentir		
confesar	*conjugated*	*as*	acertar		
confundir					confuso (confundido)
conmover	*conjugated*	*as*	absolver		
conocer	*conjugated*	*as*	nacer		
consolar	*conjugated*	*as*	acostar		
constituir	*conjugated*	*as*	argüir		
constreñir	*conjugated*	*as*	pedir		
contar	*conjugated*	*as*	acostar		
contener	*conjugated*	*as*	tener		
contradecir	*conjugated*	*as*	bendecir		
contribuir	*conjugated*	*as*	argüir		
controvertir	*conjugated*	*as*	sentir		
convencer					convicto (convencido)
convertir	*conjugated*	*as*	sentir		
costar	*conjugated*	*as*	acostar		
crecer	*conjugated*	*as*	nacer		
cubrir					cubierto
dar	yo doy	yo dí, tú diste, él dió &c.			
decentar	*conjugated*	*as*	acertar		
decir 1)	yo digo, tú dices, él dice, ellos dicen	yo dije, tú dijiste &c.	yo diré, tú dirás &c.	di tú, diga él, digamos nosotros, digan ellos	dicho.
deducir	*conjugated*	*as*	conducir		
defender	*conjugated*	*as*	ascender		
deferir	*conjugated*	*as*	sentir		
degollar	*conjugated*	*as*	acostar		
demoler	*conjugated*	*as*	absolver		
derrengar	*conjugated*	*as*	acertar		
derretir	*conjugated*	*as*	pedir		
derrocar	*conjugated*	*as*	acostar		
desasir	*conjugated*	*as*	asir		
descollar	*conjugated*	*as*	acostar		
descontar	*conjugated*	*as*	acostar		
desdecir	*conjugated*	*as*	bendecir		

1) Gerundio: diciendo.

Infinitivo.	Presente del Indicativo.	Pretérito perfecto.	Futuro.	Imperativo.	Participio.
desleir	*conjugated*	*as*	pedir		
desmembrar	*conjugated*	*as*	acertar		
desmentir	*conjugated*	*as*	sentir		
desolar	*conjugated*	*as*	acostar		
despedir	*conjugated*	*as*	pedir		
despernar	*conjugated*	*as*	acertar		
despertar					despierto (des-[pertado)
desterrar	*conjugated*	*as*	acertar		
destruir	*conjugated*	*as*	argüir		
detener	*conjugated*	*as*	tener		
dezmar	*conjugated*	*as*	acertar		
diferir	*conjugated*	*as*	sentir		
digerir	*conjugated*	*as*	sentir		
discernir	*conjugated*	*as*	sentir		
disolver	*conjugated*	*as*	absolver		
distribuir	*conjugated*	*as*	argüir		
divertir	*conjugated*	*as*	sentir		
doler	*conjugated*	*as*	absolver		
dormir 1)	yo duermo, tú duermes él duerme, ellos duermen	él durmió, ellos durmieron		duerme tú, duerma él, durmamos nosotros, duerman ellos	
elegir	*conjugatea*	*as*	pedir		electo (elegido.
empedrar	*conjugated*	*as*	acertar		
empezar	*conjugated*	*as*	acertar		
emporcar	*conjugated*	*as*	acostar		
encarecer	*conjugated*	*as*	nacer		
encender	*conjugated*	*as*	ascender		
encerrar	*conjugated*	*as*	acertar		
encomendar	*conjugated*	*as*	acertar		
encontrar	*conjugated*	*as*	acostar		
encordar	*conjugated*	*as*	acostar		
engreirse	*conjugated*	*as*	pedir		
engrosar	*conjugated*	*as*	acostar		
enjugar					enjuto (enju-[gado)
enmendar	*conjugated*	*as*	acertar		
entender	*conjugated*	*as*	ascender		
enterrar	*conjugated*	*as*	acertar		
envestir	*conjugated*	*as*	pedir		
errar	*conjugated*	*as*	acertar		
escarmentar	*conjugated*	*as*	acertar		
escribir					escrito
esforzar	*conjugated*	*as*	acostar		
estar	yo estoy	yo estuve, tú estuviste &c.			
estregar	*conjugated*	*as*	acèrtar		
excluir	*conjugated*	*as*	argüir		excluso (ex-[cluido)
expedir	*conjugated*	*as*	pedir		
expeler					expulso (expe-[lido)
exponer	*conjugated*	*as*	poner		
expresar					expreso (ex-[presado)
extender	*conjugated*	*as*	ascender		
extinguir					extinto (extin-[guido)
extraer	*conjugated*	*as*	traer		
fijar					fijo (fijado)
florecer	*conjugated*	*as*	nacer		
fluir	*conjugated*	*as*	argüir		
forzar	*conjugated*	*as*	acostar		
fregar	*conjugated*	*as*	acertar		
freir	*conjugated*	*as*	pedir		
gemir	*conjugated*	*as*	pedir		
gobernar	*conjugated*	*as*	acertar		
guarnecer	*conjugated*	*as*	nacer		

1) Gerundio: durmiendo.

Infinitivo.	Presente del Indicativo.	Pretérito perfecto.	Futuro.	Imperativo.	Participio.
haber 1)	yo he, tú has, él ha, nosotros hemos, vosotros habéis, [ellos han	yo hube, tú hubiste, él hubo &c.	yo habré, tú habrás &c.	haya él, hayamos nosotros, hayan ellos	habido
hacer	yo hago	yo hice, tú hiciste, él hizo &c.	yo haré, tú harás &c.	haz tú, haga él, hagamos nosotros, hagan ellos	hecho
hartar					harto (hartado)
heder	conjugated	es	ascender		
helar	conjugated	as	acertar		
henchir	conjugated	as	pedir		
hender	conjugated	as	ascender		
herir	conjugated	as	sentir		
herrar	conjugated	as	acertar		
hervir	conjugated	vs	sentir		
holgar	conjugated	as	acostar		
hollar	conjugated	as	acostar		
huir	conjugated	as	argüir		
imbuir	conjugated	as	argüir		[cluido]
incluir	conjugated	as	argüir		incluso (incluido)
incurrir					incurso (incurrido)
inducir	conjugated	as	conducir		
inferir	conjugated	as	sentir		
ingerir	conjugated	as	sentir		ingerto (ingerido)
inquirir	conjugated	as	sentir		
insertar					inserto (insertado)
instituir	conjugated	as	argüir		
instruir	conjugated	as	argüir		
introducir	conjugated	as	conducir		
invernar	conjugated	as	acertar		
invertir	conjugated	as	sentir		inverso (invertido)
ir 2)	yo voy, tú vas, él va, nosotros vamos, vosotros vais, ellos van	yo fui, tú fuiste, él fué &c.	yo iré, tú irás &c.	ve tú, vaya él, vayamos (vamos) nosotros, id vosotros, vayan ellos	
jugar	conjugated	as	acostar		
juntar					junto (juntado)
lucir	conjugated	as	nacer		
llover	conjugated	as	absolver		[décido]
maldecir	conjugated	as	bendecir		maldito (maldecido)
manifestar	conjugated	as	acertar		manifiesto [(manifestado)
mantener	conjugated	as	tener		
marchitar					marchito [(marchitado)
medir	conjugated	as	pedir		
mentar	conjugated	as	acertar		
mentir	conjugated	as	sentir		
merendar	conjugated	as	acertar		
moler	conjugated	as	absolver		
morder	conjugated	as	absolver		
morir	conjugated	as	dormir		muerto
mostrar	conjugated	as	acostar		
mover	conjugated	as	absolver		
nacer	yo nazco			nazca él, nazcan ellos	
negar	conjugated	as	acertar		
nevar	conjugated	as	acertar		
obscurecer	conjugated	as	nacer		
obstruir	conjugated	as	argüir		

1) Pres. del Subj.: yo haya &c. Imperf. del Ind.: yo había &c.; Imperf. del Subj.: yo hubiese &c. Condic. del Ind.: yo habría &c.; Cond. del Subj.: yo hubiera &c. Fut. del Subj.: yo hubiere &c. Gerundio: habiendo. — 2) Pres. del Subj.: yo vaya &c. Imperf. del Ind.: yo iba &c.; Imperf. del Subj.: yo fuese &c. Condic. del Indic.: yo iría &c.; Condic. del Subj.: yo fuera &c. Fut. del Subj.: yo fuere &c. Gerundio: yendo.

Infinitivo.	Presente del Indicativo.	Pretérito perfecto.	Futuro.	Imperativo.	Participio.
ofrecer	*conjugated*	*as*	nacer		
oir 1)	yo oigo, tú oyes &c.	yo oí, tú oiste, él oyó, ellos oyéron		oiga él, oigamos nosotros, oigan ellos	
oler	*conjugated*	*as*	absolver		[do]
omitir					omiso (omiti-
oprimir					opreso (opri-[mido)
pacer	*conjugated*	*as*	nacer		
parecer	*conjugated*	*as*	nacer		
pensar	*conjugated*	*as*	acertar		
pedir 2)	yo pido, tú pides, él pide, ellos piden	él pidió, ellos pidieron		pide tú, pida él, pidamos nosotros, pidan ellos.	
perder	*conjugated*	*as*	ascender		
perfeccionar					perfecto (per-[feccionado)
placer, v.def.3)	me (te, le) place	me &c. plugo			
plegar	*conjugated*	*as*	acertar		
poblar	*conjugated*	*as*	acostar		
poder 4)	yo puedo, tú puedes, él puede, ellos pueden	yo pude, tú pudiste &c.	yo podré, tú podrás &c.		
podrir	yo pudro, tú pudres, él pudre, ellos pudren	yo pudrí, pudriste &c.	yo pudriré, tú pudrirás &c.	pudre tú, pudra él, pudramos nosotros, pudran ellos	pudrido
poner	yo pongo	yo puse, tú pusiste &c.	yo pondré, tú pondrás &c.	pon tú, ponga él, pongamos nosotros, pongan ellos	
preferir	*conjugated*	*as*	sentir		[do]
prender					preso (prendi-
prescribir					prescrito (pre-[scribido)
probar	*conjugated*	*as*	acostar		
producir	*conjugated*	*as*	conducir		
prostituir	*conjugated*	*as*	argüir		
proveer					provisto (pro-[veído)
quebrar	*conjugated*	*as*	acertar		
querer	yo quiero, tú quieres, él quiere, ellos quieren	yo quise, tú quisiste &c.	yo querré, tú querrás &c.	quiere tú, quiera él, quieran ellos	
recluir	*conjugated*	*as*	argüir		recluso (reclu-[ido)
recomendar	*conjugated*	*as*	acertar		
reconocer	*conjugated*	*as*	nacer		
recordar	*conjugated*	*as*	acostar		
reducir	*conjugated*	*as*	conducir		
referir	*conjugated*	*as*	sentir		
regir	*conjugated*	*as*	pedir		
reir	*conjugated*	*as*	pedir		
renacer	*conjugated*	*as*	nacer		
rendir	*conjugated*	*as*	pedir		
renovar	*conjugated*	*as*	acostar		
reñir	*conjugated*	*as*	pedir		
reprobar	*conjugated*	*as*	acostar		
resentirse	*conjugated*	*as*	sentir		
retentar	*conjugated*	*as*	acertar		
retorcer	*conjugated*	*as*	absolver		
retribuir	*conjugated*	*as*	argüir		
reventar	*conjugated*	*as*	acertar		
revolcarse	*conjugated*	*as*	acostar		
rodar	*conjugated*	*as*	acostar		
romper					roto (rompido)

1) Gerundio: oyendo. — 2) Gerundio: pidiendo. — 3) Pres. del Subj.: plegue ó plazga (á Dios). Imperf. del Subj.: pluguiese (á Dios). Fut. del Subj.: si me pluguiere &c. Condic. del Subj.: pluguiera (á Dios). — 4) Gerundio:

Infinitivo.	Presente del Indicativo.	Pretérito perfecto.	Futuro.	Imperativo.	Participio.
saber	yo sé(Pres.delSubj. yo sepa &c.)	yo supe, tú supiste &c.	yo sabré, tú sabrás &c.	sepa él, sepan ellos	
salir	yo salgo		yo saldré, tú saldrás &c.	sal tú, salga él, salgamos nosotros, salgan ellos	
segar	conjugated	as	acertar		
seguir	conjugated	as	pedir		
sembrar	conjugated	as	acertar		
sentar	conjugated	as	acertar		
sentir	yo siento, tú sientes, él siente, ellos sienten	él sintió, ellos sintieron		siente tú, sienta él, sientan ellos	
ser 1)	yo soy, tú eres, él es, nosotros somos, vosotros sois, ellos son	yo fui,tú fuiste, él fué &c.	yo sere, tú serás &c.	se tú, sea él, seamos nosotros, sean ellos	sido
cerrar	conjugated	as	acertar		
servir	conjugated	as	pedir		
soldar	conjugated	as	acostar		
soler	conjugated	as	absolver		
soltar	conjugated	as	acostar		solto (soltado)
sonar	conjugated	as	acostar		
soñar	conjugated	as	acostar		
sostener	conjugated	as	tener		
substituir	conjugated	as	argüir		
sugerir	conjugated	as	sentir		
suprimir					supreso(suprimido)
temblar	conjugated	as	acertar		
tender	conjugated	as	ascender		
tener	yo tengo, tú tienes, él tiene, ellos tienen	yo tuve, tú tuviste &c.	yo tendré, tú tendrás &c.	ten tú, tenga él, tengamos nosotros, tengan ellos	
tentar	conjugated	as	acertar		
teñir	conjugated	as	pedir		
torcer	conjugated	as	absolver		
tostar	conjugated	as	acostar		
traducir	conjugated	as	conducir		
traer	yo traigo	yo traje, tu trajiste &c.			
tronar	conjugated	as	acostar		
trasferir	conjugated	as	sentir		
tropezar	conjugated	as	acertar		
valer	yo valgo		yo valdré, tú valdrás &c.	valga él, valgamos nosotros, valgan ellos	
venir 2)	yo vengo,tú vienes, él viene, ellos vienen	yo vine, tú viniste &c.	yo vendré, tú vendrás &c.	ven tú, venga él, vengan ellos	
ver					visto
verter	conjugated	as	ascender		
vestir	conjugated	as	pedir		
volar	conjugated	as	acostar		
volcar	conjugated	as	acostar		
volver	conjugated	as	absolver		vuelto
yacer, v. def.3)	(yago) él yace, ellos yacen				

1) Pres. del Subj.: yo sea &c. Imperf. del Ind.: yo era &c., nosotros éramos; Imperf. del Subj.: yo fuese &c. Condic. del Ind.: yo sería &c.; Condic. del Subj.: yo fuera &c. Futuro del Subj.: yo fuere &c. Gerundio: siendo. —2) Gerundio: viniendo. —3) Imperf.: él yacía, ellos yacían.

ENGLISH AND SPANISH.

A

a, â, art. un, uno, una; —, pr. **á,** al, en.

aback, *ăbăk′,* ad. detrás, atrás; (mar.) en facha; **to be taken —,** ser consternado.

abacus, *ăb′ăkŭs,* s. tabla aritmética, f.; ábaco, tablero de un capitel, m.

abaft, *ăbăft′,* ad. (mar.) á ó en popa.

abandon, *ăbăn′dŭn,* v. a. abandonar, dejar.

abandonment, *—mĕnt,* s. abandonamiento, abandono, m.; desamparo, m.

abase, *ăbās′,* v.a. abatir, humillar, envilecer.

abasement, *—mĕnt,* s. abatimiento, m.; humillación, f. [confusión, sonrojar.

abash, *ăbăsh′,* v. a. avergonzar, causar

abashment, *—mĕnt,* s. confusión, vergüenza, f.; rubor, m., consternación, f.

abate, *ăbāt′,* v. a. minorar, disminuir, rebajar; —, v. n. dismenuirse.

abatement, *—mĕnt,* s. rebaja, diminución, f.

abature, *ăb′ătūr,* s. pista, huella, f.

abb, *ăb,* s. urdi(e)mbre, f.

abbacy, *ăb′băse,* s. abadía, f.

abbess, *ăb′bĕs,* s. abadesa, f.

abb(e)y, *ăb′bĕ,* s. abadía, f.

abbot, *ăb′bŭt,* s. abad, m. [abadía, f.

abbotship, *—shĭp,* s. dignidad de abad, f.;

abbreviate, *ăbbrē′vĕāt,* v. a. abreviar, acortar, compendiar. [ción, f.

abbreviation, *ăbbrēvĕā′shŭn,* s. abreviación, f.

abdicate, *ăb′dĕkāt,* v. a. abdicar, renunciar.

abdication, *ăbdĕkā′shŭn,* s. abdicación, renuncia, f. [vientre, m.

abdomen, *ăbdō′mĕn,* s. abdomen, bajo vientre, m.

abdominal, *ăbdō′mĕnăl,* a. abdominal.

abduct, *ăbdŭkt′,* v. a. abducir; desviar, apartar, separar una cosa de otra.

abductor, *—ŭr,* s. músculo abductor, m.

abecedarian, *ăbēsēda′rĕăn,* s. maestro de primeras letras, m.

abed, *ăbĕd′,* ad. en (la) cama.

aberrance (—cy), *ăbĕr′răns(ĕ),* **aberration,** *ăbĕrā′shŭn,* s. error, desvío, m.; aberración, f. [viado.

aberrant, *—rănt,* p. & a. errante, extraviado.

abet, *ăbĕt′,* v. a. favorecer, patrocinar, sostener, excitar, animar. [f.

abetment, *—mĕnt,* s. apoyo, m.; instigación, f.

abetter, abettor, *—ŭr,* s. fautor, m.; instigador, m.

abeyance, *ăbā′ăns,* s. (law) expectativa, f.

abhor, *ăbhŏr′,* v. a. aborrecer, detestar.

abhorrence (—cy), —ĕns(ĕ), s. aborrecimiento, odio, m.

abhorrent,—rĕnt,a. horrorizado; contrario.

abide, *ăbīd′,* v. n. habitar, morar; continuar; —, v. a. soportar, sufrir, defender, sostener.

abigail, *ă′bĭgāl,* s. camarera, f.; mujer muy parlanchina, f.

ability, *ăbĭl′ĭtĕ,* s. potencia, habilidad, capacidad, aptitud, f.; **abilities,** pl., talento, m.; bienes, medios, m. pl.

abintestate, *ăbĭntĕs′tāt,* a. ab intestato, sin testamento.

abject, *ăb′jĕkt,* a. vil, despreciable, bajo.

abjection, *ăbjĕk′shŭn,* **abjectness,** *ăb′jĕktnĕs,* s. bajeza, vileza, f. [mente.

abjectly, *ăb′jĕktlĕ,* ad. vilmente, bajamente.

abjuration, *ăbjŭrā′shŭn,* s. abjuración, f.

abjure, *ăbjŭr′,* v. a. abjurar; renunciar.

ablactate, *ăblăk′tāt,* v. a. destetar.

ablactation, *ăblăktā′shŭn,* s. destete, m.

ablation, *ăblā′shŭn,* s. ablación, extirpación, f.

ablative, *ăb′lătĭv,* s. (gr.) ablativo, m.

ablaze, *ăblāz′,* a. en llamas.

able, *ā′bl,* a. fuerte, capaz, hábil; rico; **to be —,** poder. [roso.

able-bodied, *—bŏdĕd,* a. robusto, vigoroso.

ablegate, *ăb′lĕgāt,* v. a. enviar ó dar empleo á alguno en país extranjero; diputar.

ablegation, *ăblĕgā′shŭn,* s. misión, f.

ablocate, *ăb′lōkāt,* v. a. dar en arriendo.

ablocation, *ăblōkā′shŭn,* s. alquilamiento, arriendo, m.

ablution, *ăblū′shŭn,* s. ablución, f.

ably, *ā′blĕ,* ad. con habilidad.

abnegate, *ăb′nĕgāt,* v. a. negar, renunciar.

abnegation, *ăbnĕgā′shŭn,* s. abnegación, resignación, f.

abnormal, *ăbnŏr′măl,* a. irregular, deforme; fuera del modo acostumbrado.

abnormity, *ăbnŏr′mĭtĕ,* s. irregularidad, deformidad, f.

aboard, *ăbōrd′,* ad. abordo; **to fall — of a ship,** abordar un navío. [f.

abode, *ăbōd′,* s. domicilio, m., habitación, f.

abolish, *ăbŏl′ĭsh,* v. a. abolir, anular, destruir ó dar fin á alguna cosa, revocar.

abolishment, —mĕnt, abolition, *ăbŏlĭsh′ăn,* s. abolición, anulación, f.

abominable, *ăbŏm′mĕnăbl,* a. abominable, detestable, —bly, ad. abominablemente.

abominableness, —nĕs, s. calidad de lo que es abominable, f.; odiosidad, f.

abominate, *ăbŏm' mĕnăt,* **v. a.** abominar, detestar.   [nación, detestación, f.

abomination, *ăbŏmmĕnă' shŭn,* s. abomi-

aboriginal, *ăbŏrĭj' ĭnăl,* a. lo que pertenece á los habitantes primitivos de algún país.

aborigines, *ăbŏrĭj' jĕnēz,* s. pl. aborígenes, primeros habitantes de un país, m. pl.

abort, *ăbŏrt',* v. n. abortar, malparir. [m.

abortion, *ăbŏr' shŭn,* s. aborto, malparto.

abortive, *ăbŏr' tĭv,* a. abortivo; intempestivo; intempestivamente.

abortment, *ăbŏrt' mĕnt,* s. aborto, m.

abound, *ăbŏwnd',* v. n. abundar; **to —
with,** abundar de.

about, *ăbŏwt',* pr. cerca de, por ahí, hacia; acerca; tocante á. **I carry no money
— me,** no traigo dinero; —, ad. en contorno, aquí y allá; **to be — to,** estar para; **to
go —,** andar acá y acullá; **to go — a
thing,** emprender alguna cosa; **all —,** en todo lugar.

above, *ăbŭv',* pr. encima, sobre, superior, más alto (en cuanto á situación, dignidad, &c.); —, ad. arriba; **— all,** sobre todo, principalmente; **— mentioned,** ya mencionado.

abrade, *ăbrād',* v. a. raer.   [nado.

abrasion, *ăbrā' zhŭn,* s. raspadura, f.; lo que se quita de la superficie raspando.

abreast, *ăbrĕst',* ad. de costado.

abridge, *ăbrĭj',* v. a. abreviar, compendiar; acortar.

abridgment, *—mĕnt,* s. compendio, m.

abroach, *ăbrōtsh',* ad. para derramarse; **to set —,** barrenar.

abroad, *ăbrŏd',* ad. fuera de casa ó del país; en todas partes ó dirección; **to go —,** salir; **to set —,** divulgar, publicar.

abrogate, *ăb' rŏgāt,* v. a. abrogar, anular.

abrogation, *ăbrŏgā' shŭn,* s. abrogación, anulación, f.

abrupt, *ăbrŭpt',* a. quebrado, desigual; precipitado, repentino; bronco, rudo; **—ly,** ad. precipitadamente; bruscamente.

abruption, *ăbrŭp' shŭn,* s. separación repentina y violenta, rotura, f.

abruptness, *ăbrŭpt' nĕs,* s. precipitación, inconsideración, f.; descortesía, f.   [f.

abscess, *ăb' sĕs,* s. absceso, m., apostema, f.

abscind, *ăbsĭnd',* v. a. cortar, tajar, trinchar.

abscission, *ăbsĭsh' ŭn,* s. cortadura, f.

abscond, *ăbskŏnd',* v. n. esconderse; huirse.

absconder, *—ŭr,* s. la persona que se esconde; desertor, m.

absence, *ăb' sĕns,* s. ausencia, f.; distracción, f.; negligencia, f.

absent, *ăb' sĕnt,* a. ausente; fuera de sí; distraído; —, *ăbsĕnt',* v. a. ausentarse.

absentee, *ăbsĕntē',* s. el que está ausente de su empleo &c.

absenter, *ăbsĕnt' ŭr,* s. el que abandona su obligación ú oficio.

absinth, *ăbsĭnth',* s. ajenjo, m.

absolute, *ăb' sŏlūt,* a. absoluto; categórico; positivo; arbitrario; **—ly,** ad. absolutamente.

absoluteness, *—nĕs,* s. independencia, f.; despotismo, poder absoluto, m.

absolution, *ăbsŏlū' shŭn,* s. absolución, f.

absolutism, *ăb' sŏlŭtĭzm,* s. absolutismo, m.

absolutist, *ăb' sŏlŭtĭst,* s. absolutista, m.

absolutory, *ăbsŏl' ŭtărē,* a. absolutorio.

absolve, *ăbsŏlv',* v. a. absolver, dispensar, exentar.   [nante.

absonant, *ăb' sŏnănt,* a. absurdo; diso-

absorb, *ăbsŏrb',* v. a. absorber.   [cina).

absorbent, *—ĕnt,* s. & a. absorbente (medi-

absorption, *ăbsŏrp' shŭn,* s. absorción, f.

abstain, *ăbstān',* v. n. abstenerse, privarse.

abstemious, *ăbstē' mĕŭs,* a. abstemio, sobrio, moderado; **—ly,** ad. moderadamente.

abstemiousness, *—nĕs,* s. sobriedad, templanza, abstinencia, f.

abstention, *ăbstĕn' shŭn,* s. detención, f.

absterge, *ăbstĕrj',* v. a. absterger, limpiar.

abstergent, *—ĕnt,* a. abstersivo, lo que sirve para purificar, abstergente.

abstersion, *ăbstĕr' shŭn,* s. abstersión, purificación, f.   [templanza, f.

abstinence, *ăb' stĭnĕns,* s. abstinencia, f.;

abstinent, *ăb' stĭnĕnt,* a. abstinente, sobrio; **—ly,** ad. abstinentemente.

abstract, *ăb' străkt,* v. a. abstraer; compendiar; —, *ăb' străkt,* a. abstracto; —, s. extracto, m.; sumario, m.; **in the —,** de un modo abstracto.

abstracted, *ăbstrăkt' ĕd,* a. separado; abstraído; **—ly,** ad. abstractivamente.

abstracter, *ăbstrăkt' ŭr,* s. compendiador, extractor, m.

abstraction, *ăbstrăk' shŭn,* s. abstracción, f.; distracción, f.; destilación, f.

abstractive, *ăbstrăkt' ĭv,* a. abstractivo.

abstractly, *—lē,* ad. en abstracto.

abstruse, *ăbstrōs',* a. abstruso, recondito, obscuro; **—ly,** ad. obscuramente.

abstruseness, *—nĕs,* s. obscuridad, dificultad, f.; misterio, m.   ´

absurd, *ăbsŭrd',* a. absurdo, repugnante á la razón; **—ly,** ad. absurdamente.

absurdity, *—tē,* s. absurdidad, f.

abundance, *ăbŭn' dăns,* s. abundancia, copia, f.

abundant, *—dănt,* a. abundante; **—ly,** ad. abundantemente, en copia.

abuse, *ăbūz',* v. a. abusar; engañar; ultrajar, violar; —, *ăbūs',* s. abuso, engaño, m.; corruptela, seducción, f.; injuria, afrenta, f.

abusive, *ăbū' sĭv,* a. abusivo, injurioso; **—ly,** ad. abusivamente.

abusiveness, *—nĕs,* s. palabras injuriosas, f. pl.; propensión á injuriar á otro, f.

abut, *ăbŭt',* v. n. terminar, confinar.

abutment, *—mĕnt,* s. confín, límite, m.

abuttals, *—tălz,* s. pl. confines, m. pl.

abysmal, *ăbĭs' măl,* a. abismal; insondable.

abyss, *ăbĭss',* s. abismo, m.; golfo, m.; in-

acacia, *ăkā' shĭă,* s. acacia, f. [fierno, m.

academic(al), *ăkădĕm' mĭk(ăl),* a. académico.

academician, *ăkădĕmĭsh' ăn,* s. académico, el individuo *ăkăd' dĕmĭst,* s. académico, el individuo de alguna academia, m. [universidad, f.

academy, *ăkăd' dĕmē,* s. academia, f.;

accede, *ăksēd',* v. n. acceder, convenir en alguna cosa, asentir.

accedence, ăk'sēdĕns, s. asenso, m.

accelerate, ăksĕl'lărăt, v. a. acelerar.

acceleration, ăksĕllără'shŭn, s. aceleración, priesa, f.; apremio, m.

accelerative, ăksĕl'lărătĭvĕ, acceleratory, ăksĕl'lărătŭrĕ, a. acelerativo.

accent, ăk'sĕnt, s. acento, m., modulación, f., tono. m.; (poet.) lenguaje, m.; —, ăksĕnt', v. a. acentuar, colocar los acentos; (poet.) articular.

accentuate, ăksĕn'tjŭăt, v. a. acentuar.

accentuation, ăksĕntjŭá'shŭn, s. acentuación, f. [recibir cariñosamente.

accept, ăksĕpt', v. a. aceptar; admitir;

acceptable, -tăbl, a. aceptable, grato, digno de aceptación.

acceptableness, -nĕs, acceptability, ăksĕptăbĭl'lĕtĕ, s. aceptabilidad, f.

acceptably, -ē, ad. gustosamente, gratamente.

acceptance, -tăns, acceptation, ăksĕptá'shŭn, s. aceptación, recepción, f.; recibimiento, m.; acepción, f.

acception, -shŭn, s. sentido ó significado en que se toma alguna cosa, m.

access, ăksĕs', s. acceso, m.; entrada, f.; aumento, acceso periódico (de alguna enfermedad), m. [mente.

accessarily, ăk'sĕssărĕlĕ, ad. accessoria

accessariness, ăk'sĕssărĕnĕs, s. complicidad, f.; participación, f.

accessary, ăk'sĕssărĕ, s. cómplice, m.; —, a. accesorio; eventual, casual.

accessible, ăksĕs'sĭbl, a. accesible.

accession, ăksĕsh'ŭn, s. aumento, acrecentamiento, m.; advenimiento, m.; acceso, m.

accessory, ăk'sĕssŏrĕ, a. accesorio; confederado. [tos de la gramática, m.

accidence, ăk'sĭdĕns, s. libro de rudimen

accident, ăk'sĕdĕnt, s. accidente, m.; casualidad, f., suceso imprevisto, lance (funesto), m.

accidental, ăksĕdĕn'tăl, a. casual, contingente; -ly, ad. accidentalmente.

acclaim, ăkklăm', v. a. aclamar, aplaudir.

acclamation, ăkklămá'shŭn, s. aclamación, f.; aplauso, m.

acclimatise, ăkklĭ'mătĭz, v. a. aclimatar.

acclivity, ăkklĭv'ĭtĕ, s. cuesta, rampa, subida, ladera, f. [declive.

acclivous, ăkklĭ'vŭs, a. lo que sube en

accommodable, ăkkŏm'mŏdăbl, a. acomodable, acomodadizo.

accommodate, -mŏdăt, v. a. acomodar, ajustar; —, v. n. conformarse; —, a. acomodado; apto; -ly, ad. cómodamente, convenientemente. [vicial.

accommodating, ăkkŏm'mŏdătĭng, a. ser

accommodation, -dá'shŭn, s. comodidad, conveniencia, adaptación, f.; ajuste, m.; conciliación, f. [forma, f.

accommodation-bill, -bĭll, s. letra pro

accompaniment, ăkkŭm'pănĕmĕnt, s. (mus.) acompañamiento, m.

accompanist, -pănĭst, s. (mus.) acompañador, acompañante, m.

accompany, -pănĕ, v. a. acompañar.

accomplice, ăkkŏm'plĭs, s. cómplice, m.

accomplish, ăkkŏm'plĭsh, v. a. efectuar, completar; cumplir; adornar.

accomplished, -d, a. perfecto, completo, elegante, consumado.

accomplishment, -mĕnt, s. cumplimiento entero de alguna cosa, m.; perfección, f.; -s, pl. talentos, conocimientos, m. pl.

accord, ăkkŏrd', s. acuerdo, convenio, m.; armonía, f.; simetría, f.; with one –, unánimemente; of one's own –, espontáneamente; –, v. a. ajustar; –, v. n. acordar; convenir una cosa con otra.

accordance, -ăns, s. conformidad, f.; acuerdo, m. [veniente.

accordant, -ănt, a. acorde, conforme, con

according, -ĭng, pr. según, conforme; – as, según que, como; -ly, ad. en conformidad, de consiguiente, en efecto. [m.

accordion, ăkkŏr'dĭŏn, s. (mus.) acordeón,

accost, ăkkŏst', v. a. saludar á uno yendo hacia él; trabar conversación. [tero, m.

accoucheur, ăkkŏshŭr', s. comadrón, par

account, ăkkŏŭnt', s. cuenta, f., cálculo, m.; caso, m.; estimación, f.; aprecio, m.; narrativa de alguna cosa, f.; motivo, m.; on no –, de ninguna manera; por ningún título; on – of, por motivo de; to call to –, pedir cuenta; to turn to –, hacer provechoso; –, v. a. tener, reputar; contar, computar. [ponsabilidad, f.

accountability, ăkkŏŭntăbĭl'ĕtĕ, s. res

accountable, -ăbl, a. responsable.

accountant, -ănt, s. contador, m.; aritmético, m. [m.

account-book, -bŭk, s. libro de cuentas,

accoutre, ăkkŏ'tŭr, v. a. equipar, vestir.

accoutrement, -mĕnt, s. atavío, apresto, m.; vestidura, f.; ornamento, m. [cinar.

accredit, ăkkrĕd'ĭt, v. a. acreditar, patro

accrue, ăkkrŏ', v. n. resultar, provenir.

accumulate, ăkkŭ'mŭlăt, v. a. acumular; amontonar; –, v. n. crecer.

accumulation, ăkkŭmŭlá'shŭn, s. acumulación, f.; amontonamiento, m. [tivo.

accumulative, ăkkŭ'mŭlătĭv, a. acumula

accuracy, ăk'kŭrăsĕ, s. exactitud, diligencia, f., esmero, m.

accurate, ăk'kŭrăt, a. exacto, puntual; -ly, ad. exactamente.

accurateness, -nĕs, s. exactitud, puntualidad, precisión, f.

accursed, ăkkŭrsd', a. maldito, maldecido; execrable; excomulgado; fatal; – be I ¡mal haya!

accusation, ăkkŭzá'shŭn, s. acusación, f.

accusative, ăkkŭ'zătĭv, s. (gr.) acusativo,

accusatory, -zătŭrĕ, a. acusatorio. [m.

accuse, ăkkŭz', v. a. acusar; culpar.

accuser, -ŭr, s. acusador, m.; denunciador, m. [usar.

accustom, ăkkŭs'tŭm, v. a. acostumbrar,

accustomarily, -ărĕlĕ, ad. de costumbre, comúnmente, ordinariamente.

accustomary, -ărĕ, a. acostumbrado, usual, ordinario. [brado, habitual.

accustomed, ăkkŭs'tŭmd, a. acostum

ace, ăs, s. as; atomo, m.; migaja, partícula, f.; within an – of, casi, casi; por poco no . .

acerbity, ăsẽr'bĭtĕ, s. amargura, severidad, aspereza, dureza, acerbidad, f.

acetate, ắsẽtắt, s. (chem.) acetato, m.

acetous, ăsē'tŭs, a. acetoso. [doler.

ache, āk, s. dolor continuo, mal, m.; —, v. n.

achieve, ătshēv', v. a. ejecutar, perfeccionar; ganar, obtener, acabar.

achievement, —mĕnt, s. ejecución, f.; acción heroica, f.; hazaña, f.

achiever, —ẽr, s. hacedor, el que ejecuta, gana ó consigue. [f.

aching, ā'kĭng, s. dolor, m.; incomodidad, f.

achromatic, ăkrōmăt'ĭk, a. (opt.) acromático.

acid, ăs'ĭd, a. ácido, agrio, acedo.

acidify, ăsĭd'ĭfĭ, v. a. (chem.) acidificar.

acidity, —dĭtĕ, s. agrura, acedía, acidez, acritud, f.

acidulae, —dŭlā, s. pl. acídulas, f. pl.

acidulate, —dŭlāt, v. a. acidular; **—d drops,** pl. bombones de limón, m. pl.

acknowledge, ăknŏl'lĕj, v. a. reconocer, confesar. [decido.

acknowledging, —ĭng, a. reconocido, agradecido.

acknowledgment, —mĕnt, s. reconocimiento, m.; gratitud, f.; concesión, f.

acme, ăk'mē, s. crisis, f.; cima, f.; cenit, apogeo, m.

acolyte, ăk'ōlīt, s. acólito, m.

aconite, ăk'ōnīt, s. (bot.) acónito, m.

acorn, ā'kōrn, s. bellota, f.

acoustics, ăkŏŏs'tĭks, s. acústica, f.

acquaint, ăkkwānt', v. a. informar, advertir, avisar.

acquaintance, —ăns, s. conocimiento, m.; familiaridad, f.; conocido, m.

acquiesce, ăkkwĭĕs', v. n. someterse, consentir, asentir. [miento, m.

acquiescence, —sĕns, s. asenso, consentimiento, m.

acquiescent, —sĕnt, a. deferente.

acquirable, ăkkwī'răbl, a. adquirible, asequible.

acquire, ăkkwīr', v. a. adquirir, ganar, aprender. [adquirida, f.

acquirement, —mĕnt, s. adquisición, cosa adquirida, f.

acquisition, ăkkwēzĭsh'ăn, s. adquisición, obtención, f. [absolver.

acquit, ăkkwĭt', v. a. libertar, descargar, absolver.

acquitment, —mĕnt, s. acquittal, —tăl, s. absolución, f.; pago, pagamento, descargo, m. [cibo, finiquito, descargo, m.

acquittance, —tăns, s. carta de pago, f., recibo, finiquito, descargo, m.

acre, ā'kŭr, s. acre, m. (medida de tierra en Inglaterra que tiene 4840 varas cuadradas).

acrid, ā'krĭd, a. acre, mordaz. [das).

acridity, ăkrĭd'dĭtĕ, s. acidez, f. [sivo.

acrimonious, ăkrĭmō'nĕŭs, a. acre; corrosivo.

acrimony, ăk'krĭmōnĕ, s. acrity, ă'krĕtĕ, s. acrimonia, acritud, f.

across, ăkrŏs', ad. de través, de una parte á otra; **to come —,** sobrevenir algún impedimento ú obstáculo.

acrostic, ăkrŏs'tĭk, s. poema acróstico, m.

act, ăkt, v. a. representar; obrar; —, v. n. hacer; —, n. acto, hecho, m., acción, f.; efecto, m.; jornada (de una comedia), f.; **—s,** pl. actas, f. pl.; **—s of the apostles,** Actos, m. pl. [f.

acting, —ĭng, s. acción, f.; representación,

action, ăk'shăn, s. acción, operación, f.; batalla, f.; gesticulación, f.; proceso, m.; **—s,** pl. fondos públicos, m. pl.

actionable, —ăbl, a. acusable; punible.

actionary, —ărĕ, s. accionista, m.

action-taking, —tākĭng, a. litigioso, contencioso.

active, ăk'tĭv, a. activo; eficaz, ocupado; ágil; **—ly,** ad. activamente, ágilmente, eficazmente.

activeness, —nĕs, activity, ăktĭv'ĭtĕ, s. agilidad, actividad, f.; prontitud, f.; vivacidad, f. [(en los teatros) m.

actor, ăk'tŭr, s. agente, m.; cómico, actor

actress, ăk'trĕs, s. comedianta, actriz, f.

actual, ăk'tjăl, a. actual; cierto, real; efectivo; **—ly,** ad. en efecto, realmente.

actuality, ăktjăl'ĭtĕ, s. actualidad, f.

actuary, ăk'tjădrĕ, s. secretario, m.; registrador, m. [acción.

actuate, ăk'tjăt, v. a. excitar; poner en

aculeate, ăkū'lĕăt, a. punzante, puntiagudo, agudo.

acumen, ăkū'mĕn, s. punta aguzada, f.; agudeza, perspicacia, penetración, f.

acuminate, ăkū'mĕnăt, v. a. aguzar, afilar; —, v. n. terminar en punta.

acute, ăkūt', a. agudo; ingenioso; **— accent,** s. acento agudo, m.; **—angle,** s. ángulo agudo, m.; **—ly,** ad. con agudeza.

acuteness, —nĕs, s. agudeza, f.; perspicacia, sagacidad, f.

adage, ă'dĕj, s. proverbio, m. [titud, f.

adagio, ădă'jĭō, (mus.) s. adagio, m.; len-

adamant, ă'dămănt, s. diamante, m.

adamantine, ădămăn'tĭn, a. diamantino; (poet.) impenetrable.

adapt, ădăpt', v. a. adaptar, acomodar una cosa á otra; ajustar.

adaptability, ădăptăbĭl'ĭtĕ, s. facilidad de adaptarse, f.

adaptable, ădăpt'ăbl, a. adaptable.

adaptation, ădăptā'shŭn, adaptación, f.

add, ăd, v. a. aumentar; juntar; **to — up,** sumar.

addendum, ădĕn'dŭm, s. suplemento, m.

adder, ăd'dăr, s. culebra, f.; víbora, f.

addible, ăd'dĭbl, a. aumentable; sumable.

addict, ăd'dĭkt, v. a. dedicar; **to — one's self,** entregarse á. [f.

addictedness, —ĕdnĕs, addiction, ăd'dĭk'shăn, s. inclinación, propensión, dedicación, f.; devoción, afición, f., obsequio, m. [cación, f.

addition, ăddĭsh'ăn, s. adición, f. [m.

additional, —ăl, a. adicional; **—ly,** ad. en ó por adición.

addle, ăd'dl, a. vacío, vano, infecundo, estéril; —, v. a. hacer estéril.

addle-headed, —hĕdĕd, **-pated,** —pă'tĕd, a. totalmente inepto para alguna cosa.

address, ăddrĕs', v. a. hablar, interceder ó rogar; dirigir; —, s. petición, f.; memorial, m.; dedicatoria, f.; destreza, f.

adduce, ăddūs', v. a. alegar, aducir. [f.

ademption, ădĕm'shăn, s. (law) privación,

adept, ădĕpt', s. adepto, sabio, m.; alquimista, m.; —, a. adepto.

adequacy, ă'dĕkwăsĕ, s. suficiencia, f.; proporcionalidad, f.

adequate, *ă'dĕkwăt*, a. adecuado, proporcionado; suficiente; **-ly**, ad. adecuadamente.   [ción exacta, f.

adequateness,—*nĕs*, s. adecuación, proporción exacta, f.

adhere, *ădhēr'*, v. n. adherir; aficionarse.

adherence,—*ĕns*, s. viscosidad, f.; adherencia, f.

adherent,—*ĕnt*, a. pegajoso; tenaz; adherente; —, s. adherente, partidario, m.

adhesion, *ădhē'shăn*, s. adhesión, f.

adhesive,—*sĭv*, a. pegajoso, tenaz.

adhesiveness,—*nĕs*, s. adhesividad, f.

adieu, *ădū'*, ad, á Dios; —, s. despedida, f.

adipose, *ăd'ĕpōs*, a. adiposo.

adit, *ă'dĭt*, s. conducto subterráneo, m.; entrada de una mina, f.

adjacency, *ădjă'sĕnsĭ*, **adjacence**,—*sĕns*, s. contigüidad, vecindad, f.   [tiguo.

adjacent, *ădjă'sĕnt*, a. adyacente, contiguo.

adjectival, *ădjĕk'tĭvăl*, a. adjetivado; **-ly**, ad. adjetivamente.

adjective, *ăd'jĕktĭv*, s. adjetivo, m.; **-ly**, ad. como adjetivo.   [estar contiguo.

adjoin, *ădjŏin'*, v. a. juntar; unir; —, v. n.

adjourn, *ădjŭrn'* v. a. diferir, remitir.

adjournment,—*mĕnt*, s. prorroga, f.

adjudge, *ădjŭj'*, **adjudicate**, *ădjū'dĕkăt*, v. a. adjudicar; condenar; decretar.

adjunct, *ăd'jŭnkt*, s. adjunto, m.

adjuration, *ădjūrā'shŭn*, s. conjuro, m.; juramento, m.

adjure, *ădjūr'*, v. a. juramentar; conjurar.

adjust, *ădjŭst'*, v. a. ajustar, acomodar.

adjuster,—*ăr*, s. aforador, m.; mediador, m.

adjustment,—*mĕnt*, s. ajustamiento, arreglo, m.   [f.

adjutancy, *ăd'jŭtănsĭ*, s. (mil.) ayudantía, f.

adjutant, *ăd'jŭtănt*, s. (mil.) ayudante, m.

adjute, *ădjūt'*, v. a. ayudar.   [m.

admeasurement, *ădmĕzh'ŭrmĕnt*, s. reparto judicial, m.

administer, *ădmĭn'ĭstăr*, v. a. administrar; gobernar; contribuir; **to — an oath**, prestar juramento.

administration, *ădmĭnĭstrā'shŭn*, s. administración, f.; gobierno, m.

administrative, *ădmĭn'ĭstrātĭv*, a. administrativo.   [nistrador, m.

administrator, *ădmĭn'ĭstrātŭr*, s. administrador, m.

admirability, *ădmĭrăbĭl'tĭ*, s. excelencia de alguna cosa, f.

admirable,—*bl*, a. admirable; **-bly**, ad. admirablemente; á maravilla.

admiral, *ăd'mĕrăl*, s. almirante, m.; almiranta (nave), f.

admiralship,—*shĭp*, s. almirantía, f.

admiralty,—*tĭ*, s. almirantazgo, m.

admiration, *ădmĕrā'shŭn*, s. admiración, f., maravilla, f.

admire, *ădmīr'*, v. a. admirar; amar; —, v. n. admirarse de alguna cosa.   [m.

admirer,—*ăr*, s. admirador, m.; amante.

admiringly, *ădmī'rĭnglĭ*, ad. con admiración.

admissible, *ădmĭs'sĕbl*, a. admisible.

admission, *ădmĭsh'ăn*, s. admisión, recepción, entrada, f.

admit, *ădmĭt'*, v. a. admitir; dar entrada; recibir, conceder, permitir.

admittance,—*tăns*, s. entrada, admisión, f.

admittedly,—*tĕdlĭ*, a. perhisivamente.

admixture, *ădmĭks'tjŭr*, s. mistura, mezcla, f.   [reprender.

admonish, *ădmŏn'nĭsh*, v. a. amonestar.

admonishment,—*mĕnt*, s. amonestación, f.; consejo, aviso, m.   [nesta, exhortación.

admonition, *ădmŏnĭsh'ăn*, s. amonestación, f.; consejo, aviso, m.

admonitory, *ădmŏn'nĕtŭrĭ*, a. lo que amonesta, exhortación.

ado, *ădŏ'*, s. dificultad, f.; bullicio, tumulto, m.; fatiga, f.   [fiescencia, f.

adolescence (**-cy**), *ădŏlĕs'sĕns(ĭ)*, s. adolescencia, f.

adopt, *ădŏpt'*, v. a. adoptar, prohijar.

adoption, *ădŏp'shăn*, s. adopción, f.

adoptive,—*tĭv*, a. adoptivo.

adorable, *ădŏrā'bl*, a. adorable.

adorableness,—*nĕs*, s. excelencia, f.

adorably,—*ĭ*, ad. de un modo adorable.

adoration, *ădŏrā'shăn*, s. adoración, f.

adore, *ădŏr'*, v. a. adorar.   [nos, adornar.

adorn, *ădŏrn'*, v. a. hermosear con adornamiento.

adornment,—*mĕnt*, s. adorno, atavío, m.

adrift, *ădrĭft'*, ad. de flotando, á merced de las olas; á la ventura.

adroit, *ădrŏit'*, a. diestro, hábil, mañoso.

adroitness,—*nĕs*, s. destreza, f.

adulation, *ădŭlā'shăn*, s. adulación, lisonja, zalamería, f.

adulatory, *ă'dŭlătŏrĭ*, a. lisonjero.

adult, *ădŭlt'*, a. adulto; —, s. adulto, m.; adulta, f.

adulterate,—*ărăt*, v. a. adulterar, corromper, falcificar; —, a. adulterado, falsificado.   [corrupción, f.

adulteration,—*ărā'shăn*, s. adulteración, f.

adulterer,—*ărĭ*, s. adulterio, m.

adulteress,—*ărĕs*, s. adultera, f.

adulterine,—*ărĭn*, adulterous, —*ărăs*, a. adulterino; espurio.

adultery,—*ărĭ*, s. adulterio, m.

advance, *ădvăns'*, v. a. avanzar; promover; pagar adelantado; —, v. n. hacer progresos; —, s. avance, m.; paga adelantada, f.

advancement,—*mĕnt*, s. adelantamiento, m.; progreso, m.; promoción, f.

advantage, *ădvăn'tăj*, s. ventaja, superioridad, f.; provecho, m.; lucro, m.; ocasión favorable, f.; **to take — of**, sacar provecho de; —, v. a. ganar; remunerar; promover.   [ventajoso, m.

advantage-ground,—*grŏŭnd*, s. puesto ventajoso, m.

advantageous, *ădvăntă'jŭs*, a. ventajoso, útil; **-ly**, ad. ventajosamente.

advantageousness,—*nĕs*, s. ventaja, utilidad, f.   [Adviento, m.

advent, *ăd'vĕnt*, s. venida, f.; **Advent**, s.

adventitious, *ădvĕntĭsh'ŭs*, a. adventicio.

adventure, *ădvĕn'tjŭr*, s. aventura, casualidad, f.; riesgo, m.; **at all —s**, al acaso; —, v. n. osar, emprender; —, v. a. aventurar.

adventurer,—*ăr*, s. aventurero, m.

adventuresome,—*săm*, adventurous, *ădvĕn'tjărŭs*, a. intrépido; atrevido; valeroso; **-ly**, ad. arriesgadamente.

adventuress,—*ĕs*, s. aventurera, f.

adverb, *ăd'vĕrb*, s. adverbio, m.

adverbial, *ădvĕr'bĭăl*, a. adverbial; **-ly**, ad. adverbialmente.   [migo, m.

adversary, *ăd'vĕrsărĭ*, a. adversario, enemigo,

adversative, *ădvẽr´sătĭv,* a. adversativo, contrario.   [ad. al contrario.

adverse, *ăd´vẽrs,* a. adverso, contrario; **–ly,**

adversity, *ădvẽr´sĭtĕ,* s. adversidad, calamidad, f.; infortunio, m.   [atención.

advert, *ădvẽrt´,* v. n. advertir, considerar

advertence, *–ĕns,* s. atención, f.

advertise, *ădvẽrtĭz´,* y. a. avisar, advertir.

advertisement, *ădvẽr´tĭsmĕnt,* s. aviso, m.

advertising, *ădvẽrtĭ´zĭng,* s. anuncio, m.

advice, *ădvĭs´,* s. consejo, m.; aviso, m.

advice-boat, *–bōt,* s. (mar.) embarcación de aviso, f.   [conveniencia, f.

advisability, *ădvĭzăbĭl´ĭtĕ,* s. prudencia,

advisable, *– zăbl,* a. prudente, conveniente.

advise, *ădvĭz´* v. a. aconsejar; avisar; –,
v. n. considerar, deliberar.   [sadamente.

advisedly, *–dlĕ,* ad. prudentemente, avi-

advisedness, *–nĕs,* s. prudencia, f.

advocacy, *ăd´vŏkăsĕ,* s. vindicación, defensa, apología, f.

advocate, *ăd´vŏkăt,* s. abogado, m.; protector, m.; –, v. a. defender.

advocateship, *–shĭp,* s. abogacía, f.

advowee, *ădvŏŭ´,* s. patrono, m.

advowson, *ădvŏŭ´sŏn,* s. patronato, paadze, *ădz,* s. azuela, f.   [tronazgo, m.

ægis, *ē´jĭs,* s. egida, f., escudo, m.

æon, *ē´ŏn,* s. era, f. eternidad, f.

æra, *ē´ră,* s. era, época, data fija, f.

aerial, *ăē´rĭăl,* a. aéreo, puesto en el aire.

aerolite, *ă´rŏlĭt,* s. aerolito, m.

aerometer, *ăărŏ´mĕtăr,* s. aerómetro, m.

aeronaut, *ă´rŏnăt,* s. aeronauta, m.

aerostat, *ă´rŏstăt,* s. globo aerostático, m.

aerostatics, *ărŏstăt´ĭks,* **aerostation,** *ărŏstă´shŭn,* s. aerostación, f.

æruginous, *ērŏ´gĭnăs,* a. herrumbroso.

afar, *ăfăr´,* ad. lejos, distante; **from –,** de
algún lugar distante.

affability, *ăffăbĭl´ĭtĕ,* s. afabilidad, urbanidad, dulzura, f.

affable, *ăf´făbl,* a. afable, complaciente;
–bly, –ĕ, ad. afablemente.

affair, *ăfăr´,* s. asunto, m.; negocio, m.;
(mil.) acción, f.

affect, *ăfĕkt´,* v. a. conmover; afectar.

affectation, *–ă´shŭn,* s. afectación, f.;
pasión, f.

affected, *–ĕd,* p. & a. afectado, lleno de
afectación; inclinado; **–ly,** ad. con afectación.

affectingly, *–ĭnglĕ,* ad. con afecto.

affection, *ăfĕk´shŭn,* s. afección, f.; amor,
m.; afición, f.   [**–ly,** ad. cariñosamente.

affectionate, *–ăt,* a. afectuoso, benévolo;

affectionateness, *–nĕs,* s. afecto, m.;
benevolencia, f.

affiance, *ăfĭ´ăns,* s. confianza, f.; –, v. a.
contraer esponsales; inspirar confianza.

affidavit, *ăfĭdă´vĭt,* s. declaración jurada, f.

affiliate, *ăfĭl´ĭăt,* v. a. ahijar.

affiliation, *ăfĭlĭă´shŭn,* s. adopción, f.   [f.

affinity, *ăfĭn´nĭtĕ,* s. afinidad, atracción,

affirm, *ăfẽrm´,* v. a. afirmar, declarar,
confirmar, ratificar, aprobar.

affirmation, *–ă´shŭn,* s. afirmación, f.

affirmative, *–tĭv,* a. afirmativo; **–ly,**
ad. afirmativamente.

affix, *ăfĭks´,* v. a. anexar, añadir, fijar;
–, *ăf´fĭks,* s. (gr.) afijo, m.

afflict, *ăflĭkt´,* y. a. afligir; atormentar.

affliction, *ăflĭk´shŭn,* s. aflicción, f.;
dolor, m.

afflictive, *–tĭv,* a. aflictivo, penoso.

affluence, *ăf´flŭĕns,* s. copia, abundancia, f.

affluent, *ăf´flŭĕnt,* a. afluente, opulento.

afflux, *ăf´flŭks,* s. confluencia, afluencia, f.

afford, *ăfōrd´,* v. a. dar; proveer; producir.

affray, *ăfră´,* s. asalto, m.; tumulto, m.

affright, *ăfrĭt´,* v. a. espantar; –, s.
espanto, m.

affront, *ăfrŭnt´,* s. afrenta, injuria, f.; –,
v. a. afrentar, insultar, ultrajar.

affrontive, *–tĭv,* a. injurioso.

afield, *ăfēld´,* ad. en el campo.

afire, *ăfĭr´,* ad. en llamas.

aflame, *ăflăm´,* ad. en llamas.   [del suelo.

aflat, *ăflăt´,* ad. ras con la tierra, á nivel

afloat, *ăflōt´,* ad. flotante, á flote.

afoot, *ăfŭt´,* ad. á pie.

afore, *ăfōr´,* pr. antes; –, ad. primero.

afraid, *ăfrăd´,* a. espantado, tímido; **I am
–,** temo.

afresh, *ăfrĕsh´,* ad. de nuevo, otra vez.

aft, *ăft,* ad. (mar.) á popa.

after, *ăf´tăr,* pr. después; detrás; según;
–, ad. en seguida de; **– all,** en fin, en suma.

after-ages, *–ĕjĕs,* s.pl. tiempos venideros,
siglos venideros, m. pl.

after-birth, *–bĕrth,* s. secundinas, f. pl.

after-cost, *–kŏst,* s. gastos extraordinarios, m. pl.

after-crop, *–krŏp,* s. segunda cosecha, f.

after-days, *–dăz,* s. pl. tiempo venidero,
m.   [m.

after-game, *–găm,* s. juego de desquite

afterglow, *–glō,* s. reflejo del sol poniente
en el hielo, m.

after-hours, *–ŏŭrz,* s. pl. tiempo subsiguiente á una acción, m.

after-life, *–lĭf,* s. vida venidera, f.

aftermath, *–măth,* s. retoño, m., segunda hierba, f.

afternoon, *–nōn,* s. tarde, f.

after-pains, *–pănz,* s. pl. dolores de
sobreparto, m. pl.

after-part, *–părt,* s. parte posterior, f.

after-piece, *–pēs,* s. farsa, f.; intermedio,
m.   [escote, m.

after-reckoning, *–rĕkknĭng,* s. sobre-

after-taste, *–tăst,* s. resabio, m.

after-thought, *–thăt,* s. reflexión fuera
de tiempo, f.

afterward, *–wărd,* **afterwards,** *–wărds,*
ad. después, en seguida.

after-wit, *–wĭt,* s. entendimiento tardío,
m.; sabiduría, f.

again, *ăgĕn´,* ad. otra vez; **– and –,** muchas
veces; **as much –,** otra vez tanto.

against, *–st´,* pr. contra; enfrente; **– the
grain,** á contrapelo; de mala gana.

agape, *ăgăp´,* s. ágape, m.

agate, *ăgăt´,* s. ágata, f. **(piedra preciosa.**

age, *ăj´,* s. edad, f.; siglo, m.; vejez, f.;
under –, menor; –, v. a. envejecer.

aged, *–ĕd,* a. viejo, anciano; **–ly,** ad. á
manera de viejo.

agency, *d'jĕnsĕ,* s. agencia, f.
agent, *d'jĕnt,* a. operativo; —, s. agente; asistente, m. [merar; —, v. n. ovillarse.
agglomerate, *ăgglŏm'mĕrăt,* v. a. aglo-
agglomeration, *ăgglŏmmĕră'shŭn,* s. aglomeración, f.
agglutinate, *ăgglū'tĕnāt,* v. a. conglutinar, unir [clevar.
aggrandize, *ăg'grăndiz,* v. a. engrandecer
aggrandizement, *—mĕnt,* s. engrandecimiento, m. [agerar.
aggravate, *ăg'grăvāt,* v. a. agravar; ex-
aggravation, *ăggrăvă'shŭn,* s. agravación, f [unión, f.; —, v. a. agregar; reunir.
aggregate, *ăg'grĕgāt,* v. a. agregado, m.;
aggregation, *ăggrĕgă'shŭn,* s. agrega-
aggress, *ăggrĕs',* v. n. acometer. [ción, f.
aggress, — aggression, *—shŭn,* s. agresión, ofensa, f.; asalto, m.
aggressive, *—sĭv,* a. ofensivo.
aggressor, *—sŭr,* s. agresor, m.
aggrieve, *ăggrēv',* v. a. injuriar, gravar, dañar; apesadumbrar; —, v. n. lamentar.
aggroup, *ăggrōp',* v. a. agrupar.
aghast, *ăgăst',* a. horrorizado.
agile, *ă'jĭl,* a. ágil, vivo; diestro.
agility, *ăjĭl'ĭtĕ,* s. agilidad, f.; destreza, f.
agitate, *ă'jĭtāt,* v. a. agitar; discutir.
agitation, *ăjĭtă'shŭn,* s. agitación, f.; perturbación, f.
agitator, *—tŭr,* s. agitador, incitador, m.
agnail, *ăg'nāl,* s. uñero, panadizo, m.
agnate, *ăg'nāt,* a. agnado, m.; agnada, f.
agnation, *ăgnā'shŭn,* s. agnación, f.
ago, *ăgō',* ad. pasado, largo tiempo; después; **how long —?** ¿cuánto ha? [desear.
agog, *ăgŏg',* ad. con deseo; **to set —,** hacer
agoing, *ăgō'ĭng,* ad. en acción, en movimiento; dispuesto á.
agonising, *ăgŏnīs'ĭng,* a. agonizando.
agony, *ă'gŏnĕ,* s. agonía, f.; angustia extrema, f.
agrarian, *ăgrā'rĕăn,* a. agrario.
agree, *ăgrē',* v. n. concordar, convenir.
agreeable, *—ăbl,* a. conveniente, agradable; amable; **—bly,** ad. agradablemente; **— with,** según, conforme á.
agreeableness, *—ăblnĕs,* s. conformidad, f., amabilidad, gracia, f.
agreed, *ăgrēd',* a. establecido, convenido; **— I** ad. de acuerdo! [formidad, unión, f.
agreement, *—mĕnt,* s. concordia, f.; con-
agricultural, *ăgrĭkŭl'tŭrăl,* a. agrario.
agriculture, *—tŭr,* s. agricultura, f.
agriculturist, *—ĭst,* s. agricultor, m.
agrimony, *ă'grĭmŏnĕ,* s. (bot.) agrimonia, f. [pical.
aground, *ăgrŏŭnd',* ad. (mar.) barado, encallado. [tente, f.
ague, *ā'gū,* s. fiebre, calentura intermitente, f.
aguish, *ā'gŭĭsh,* a. febril.
ah! ¡ah! ¡ay!
ahead, *ăhĕd',* ad. más allá, delante de otro; (mar.) por la proa.
ahoy! *ăhŏĕ',* (mar.) ¡ohé! ¡ahupa!
ahull, *ăhŭl',* ad. (mar.) á palo seco.
aid, *ād,* v. a. ayudar, socorrer; —, s. ayuda, f.; auxilio, socorro, m.
aide-de-camp, *—dĕkăn(g),* s. (mil.) ayudante de campo, m.

aider, *—ăr,* s. auxiliador, m.; **— and abetter,** (law) cómplice, m.
ail, *āl,* v. a. afligir, molestar; **what —s you?** ¿qué te duele á U.?
ailing, *—ĭng,* a. doliente, valetudinario.
ailment, *—mĕnt,* s. dolencia, indisposición, f.
aim, *ām,* v. a. apuntar, dirigir el tiro con el ojo; aspirar á; intentar, —, s. designio, m.; mira, f.; puntería, f.; blanco, m.
aimless, *—lĕs,* a. sin designio, sin objeto.
ain't, *ānt,* ad. no es, no hay.
air, *ār,* s. aire, m.; aire de música; semblante, m., —, v. a. airear; secar; ventilar.
air-balloon, *—bălŏn,* s. globo aerostático, m. [nado de aire, m.
air-cushion, *—kŭshŭn,* s. cojinete relle-
air-gun, *—gŭn,* s. escopeta de viento, f.
air-hole, *—hōl,* s. respiradero, m.
airiness, *—ĕnĕs,* s. ventilación, f.
airing, *—ĭng,* s. caminata, f. [cado.
airless, *—lĕs,* a. falto de ventilación, sofo-
air-pump, *—pŭmp,* s. máquina neumática, f. [m.
air-shaft, *—shăft,* s. respiradero de mina,
air-tight, *—tĭt,* a. herméticamente cerrado.
air-trap, *—trăp,* s. ventilador, m.
air-vessel, *—vĕssl,* s. recipiente, m.
airy, *—ĕ,* a. aéreo.
aisle, *ĭl,* s. nave de una iglesia, f.
ajar, *ăjăr',* a. entreabierto.
akimbo, *ăkĭm'bŏ,* a. corvo.
akin, *ăkĭn',* a. consanguíneo, emparentado.
alabaster, *ăl'lăbăstăr,* s. alabastro, m.; —, a. alabastrino. [ción de dolor ó lástima.
alack-(a-day)! *ălăk' (dă),* ¡ay! (exclama-
alacrity, *ălă'krĭtĕ,* s. alegría, f.; buen humor, m. [v. a. alarmar; inquietar.
alarm, *ălărm',* s. alarma, f.; rebato, m.;
alarm-bell, *—bĕll,* s. campana de rebato, f.
alarmist, *—ĭst,* s. alarmista, m.
alarm-post, *—pŏst,* s. puesto de arma, m.
alarm-watch, *—wŏtsh,* s. reloj despertador, m. [dor, m.
alarum, *ălă'rŭm,* s. alarma, f.
alas, *ălăs',* ¡ay!
albeit, *ălb'ĭt,* s. alba, f.
albeit, *ălbĭt',* c. aunque. [los ojos), m.
albugo, *ălbū'gŏ,* s. albugo (enfermedad de
album, *ăl'bŭm,* s. álbum, m.
alchemical, *ălkĕm'mĕkăl,* a. alquímico.
alchemist, *ăl'kĕmĭst,* s. alquimista, m.
alchemy, *ăl'kĕmĕ,* s. alquimia, f.
alcohol, *ăl'kŏhŏl,* s. alcohol, espíritu rectificado de vino, m.
alcoholic, *ălkŏhŏl'lĭk,* a. alcohólico.
alcove, *ăl'kŏv,* s. alcoba, f.
alder, *ăl'dŭr,* s. aliso (árbol), m. [nicipal.
alderman, *—măn,* s. regidor, m. (oficial mu-
ale, *āl,* s. cerveza, f.
a-lee, *ălē',* ad. (mar.) á sotavento.
alehouse, *āl'hŏŭs,* s. cervecería, taberna, f.
alehouse-keeper, *—kēpăr,* s. cervecero, m.
alembic, *ălĕm'bĭk,* s. alambique, m. [m.
alert, *ălĕrt',* a. vigilante, vivo.
alertness, *—nĕs,* s. cuidado, m.; vigilancia, viveza á lo largo, actividad, f.
ale-silver, *āl'sĭlvăr,* s. derecho impuesto sobre la cerveza, m.
ale-stake, *—stăk,* s. muestra de taberna, f.
ale-wife, *—wĭf,* s. cervecera, f.

alga, *ăl'gă*, s. alga (planta que se cría en el mar), f.

algebra, *ăl'jĕbră*, s. álgebra, f.

algebraic(al), *ăljĕbrā'ĭk(ăl)*, a. algebraico.

algebraist, —*ĭst*, s. algebrista, m.

alias, *ā'lĭăs*, ad. de otra manera.

alibi, *ăl'ĭbī*, s. (law) coartada, f.

alien, *āl'yĕn*, s. & a. extraño; forastero(m.).

alienable, —*ăbl*, a. enajenable.

alienate, —*āt*, v. a. enajenar.

alienation, *ālyĕnā'shăn*, s. enajenación, f.; — of mind, devaneo, m.

alight, *ălīt'*, v. n. descender; apearse; —, s. encendido; ardiente, lo que arde.

alike, *ălīk'*, a. semejante, igual; —, ad. igualmente.

aliment, *ăl'ĭmĕnt*, s. alimento, m.

alimental, *ălĭmĕn'tăl*, alimentary, —*tărĭ*, a. alimentoso, nutritivo. [tación, f.

alimentation, *ălĭmĕntā'shăn*, s. alimentación, f.

alimony, *ăl'ĭmŭnĭ*, s. alimentos, m. pl.

aliquot part, *ă'lĭkwŏt pärt*, s. parte alícuota, f.

alive, *ălīv'*, a. vivo, viviente; activo.

alkali, *ăl'kălĭ*, s. álcali, m.

alkaline, *ăl'kălĭn*, a. alcalino.

all, *ăl*, a. todo; —, ad. enteramente; — at once, — of a sudden, de repente; — the same, absolutamente lo mismo; — the better, tanto mejor; not at —, no por cierto; once for —, una vez por todas, una buena y enmendarse; una que valga mil; —, s. todo, m.

allay, *ălā'*, v. a. aliviar, apaciguar.

allayment, —*mĕnt*, s. alivio, desahogo,m.; aligación, f. [disculpa, f.; cita,f.

allegation, *ălĕgā'shăn*, s. alegación, f.

allege, *ălĕj'*, v. a. alegar; declarar. [f.

allegiance, *ălē'jăns*, s. lealtad, fidelidad, f.

allegorical, *ălĕgŏ'rĭkăl*, a. alegórico; —ly, ad. alegóricamente.

allegorise, *ăl'lĕgŏrīz*, v. a. alegorizar.

allegory, *ăl'lĕgŏrĭ*, s. alegoría, f.

allegro, *ălē'grō*, s. (mus.) alegro, m.

alleviate, *ălē'vĭāt*, v. a. aliviar, aligerar.

alleviation, *ălēvĭā'shăn*, s. alivio, m.; mitigación, f. [juela, f.

alley, *ăl'ĭ*, s. paseo de árboles, m.; calle-

all-hallowmas, *ălhăl'lōmăs*, all-hallow-tide, —*tīd*, s. tiempo cercano al día de todos los santos, m.

alliance, *ălī'ăns*, s. alianza, f.; parentela, f.

allied, *ălīd'*, a. aliado, confederado.

alligate, *ăl'lĭgāt*, v. a. ligar, afianzar una cosa á otra. [ción, f.

alligation, *ălĭgā'shăn*, s. regla de aleaalligator, —*ŭr*, s. aligador, m. [f.

alliteration, *ălĭtŭrā'shăn*, s. aliteración, f.

allocation, *ălŏkā'shăn*, s. añadidura, f.

allocution, *ălŏkū'shăn*, s. alocución, f.

allodium, *ălō'dĕŭm*, s. alódio, m.

allopathy, *ăl'ōpăthĕ*, s. alopatía, f.

allot, *ălŏt'*, v. a. distribuir por suerte; asignar. [miento, m.

allotment, —*mĕnt*, s. asignación,f.; repartimiento, m.

allow, *ăllŏu'*, v. a. conceder, aprobar; permitir; dar, pagar. [justo.

allowable, —*ăbl*, a. admisible, permitido.

allowance, —*ăns*, s. concesión, f.; licencia, f.; (mar.) ración, f., alimentos, m. pl.

alloy, *ăllŏĭ'*, v. a. ligar, mezclar un metal con otro; quilatar oro; —, s.liga, mezcla,f.; quilate, m. [f. pl. (pimienta, clavos &c.).

allspice, *ăl'spĭs*, s. especerías, especias, f. pl. (pimienta, clavos &c.).

allude, *ăllūd'*, v. a. aludir.

allure, *ăllūr'*, v. a. alucinar, cebar.

alluring, —*rĭng*, s. poder de halagar, m.; —ly, ad. seductoramente.

alluringness, —*nĕs*, allurement, *ăllūr'mĕnt*, s. halago, cebo, aliciente, atractivo.

allusion, *ăllū'zhăn*, s. alusión, f. [m.

allusive, —*sĭv*, a. alusivo; —ly, ad. de un modo alusivo.

alluvial, —*vĭăl*, a. aluvial.

alluvion, —*vĕăn*, s. aluvión, f.; terrero, m.

ally, *ăllī'*, s. aliado, m.; pariente, m. (& f.); —, v. a. hacer alianza.

alwise, *ăl'wĭs*, a. omniscio.

almanac, *ăl'mănăk*, s. almanaque, m. [f.

almightiness, *ălmī'tĭnĕs*, s. omnipotencia, f.

almighty, —*tĕ*, a. omnipotente, todopoderoso. [gallas de la garganta, f. pl.

almond, *ă'mănd*, s. almendra, f.; —s, pl. [gallas de la garganta, f. pl.

almond-milk, —*mĭlk*, s. almendrada, f.

almond-tree, —*trē*, s. almendro, m.

almoner, *ăl'mănŭr*, s. limosnero, m.

almonry, —*rĕ*, s. hospicio para pobres, m.

almost, *ăl'mōst*, ad. casi, cerca de.

alms, *ămz*, s. limosna, f.

alms-house, —*hŏus*, s. hospicio para pobres, m.

alms-people, —*pēpl*, s. hospicianos, m.pl.

alnage, *ăl'nāj*, s. medición por anas, f.

alnight, *ăl'nĭt*, s. ambleo, m.

aloe, *ă'lō*, s. áloe, lináloe, m.

aloft, *ălŏft'*, pr. arriba, sobre.

alone, *ălōn'*, a.solo; —, ad. solamente, sólo; to let —, dejar en paz.

along, *ălŏng'*, ad. á lo largo; adelante; junto con; (mar.) al costado; —side, al lado.

aloof, *ălŏŏf'*, ad. lejos, de lejos, á lo largo.

aloud, *ălŏud'*, a. con voz fuerte, recio.

alphabet, *ăl'făbĕt*, s. alfabeto, m.

alphabetical, *ălfăbĕt'ĭkăl*, a. alfabético; —ly, ad. alfabéticamente.

alpine, *ăl'pĭn*, a. alpino. [antes de ahora.

already, *ălrĕd'ĭ*, ad. ya, á la hora de esta.

also, *ăl'sō*, ad. también, igualmente, además.

altar, *ăl'tŭr*, s. altar, m.

altar-piece, —*pēs*, s. retablo, m.

alter, *ăl'tŭr*, v. a. alterar, mudar.

alterable, —*ăbl*, a. alterable, mudable; —bly, ad.de una manera mudable.

alteration, *ăltŭrā'shăn*, s. alteración, f.

alterative, *ăl'tŭrătĭv*, a. alterativo. [f.

altercation, *ăltŭrkā'shăn*, s. altercación, f.

altercate, *ăl'tŭrkāt*, v. n. trabarse de palabras.

alternate, *ăltŭr'nāt*, a. alternativo, recíproco; —, v. a. alternar, variar; —ly, ad. alternativamente.

alternation, *ăltŭrnā'shăn*, s. alternación, f.

alternative, *ăltŭr'nătĭv*, s. alternativa, f.; —, a. alternativo; —ly, ad. alternativamente. [obstante, bien que.

although, *ăldhō'*, *ăldhō'*, c. aunque, no

altitude, *ăl'tĭtūd*, s. altitud, altura, f.

altogether, *ăltōgĕth'ŭr*, ad. del todo.

alum, *ăl'ŭm,* s. alumbre, m.   [minio, m.
aluminium, *ălŭmĭ'nĭŭm,* s. (chem.) alu-
aluminous, *ălŭ'mĭnŭs,* a. aluminoso.
alum-salt, *ăl'ŭmsălt,* s. sal mineral, f.
always, *ăl'wĕz,* ad. siempre, constantemente, en todo tiempo, sin cesar.
amain, *ămăn',* ad. con vehemencia, vigorosamente.   [diferentes metales, f.
amalgam(a), *ămăl'găm(ă),* s. mezcla de
amalgamate, –*āt,* v. a. & n. amalgamar.
amalgamation, *ămălgămā'shăn,* s. amalgamación, f.   [secretario, m.
amanuensis, *ămănŭĕn'sĭs,* s. amanuense.
amaranth, *ăm'ărănth,* s. (bot.) amaranto,
m.   [f.
amaryllis, *ămărĭl'lĭs,* s. (bot.) amarilis.
amass, *ămăs',* v. a. acumular, amontonar.
amateur, *ămătŭr',* s. aficionado, m.
amativeness, *ăm'ătĭvnĕs,* s. amatividad, f.
amatory, *ăm'ătŭrĕ,* a. amatorio; erótico.
amaze, *ămăz',* v. a. espantar; sorprender.
amazedly, –*ĕdlĕ,* ad. fuera de sí.
amazement, –*mĕnt,* s. espanto, pasmo, m.
amazing, *ămă'zĭng,* a. extraño, pasmoso;
–ly, ad. pasmosamente.
amazon, *ăm'ăzŭn,* s. amazona, f.
ambassador, *ămbăs'sădŭr,* s. embajador,
m.   [f.
ambassadress, –*sădrĕs,* s. embajadora.
amber, *ăm'bŭr,* s. ámbar, m.; –, a. ambarino.
ambidextrous, *ămbĕdĕks'trŭs,* a. ambi-
ambient, *ăm'bĭĕnt,* a. ambiente.   [dextro.
ambiguity, *ămbĕgŭ'ĕtĕ,* s. ambigüedad,
duda, f.; equívoco, m.
ambiguous, *ămbĭg'gŭŭs,* a. ambiguo; –ly,
ad. ambiguamente.   [cia, f.
ambit, *ăm'bĭt,* s. circuíto, m.; circunferen-
ambition, *ămbĭsh'ŭn,* s. ambición, f.
ambitious, –*ŭs,* a. ambicioso; –ly, ad.
ambiciosamente.
amble, *ăm'bl,* s. paso de andadura del caballo, m.; –, v. n. ambiar.   [andadura, f.
ambler, –*ŭr,* s. caballo que anda paso de
ambrosial, *ămbrō'zhĭă,* a. delicioso.
ambry, *ăm'brĕ,* s. armario, m.; despensa, f.
ambs-ace, *ămz'ăs,* s. parejas de ases en
algunos juegos, f. pl.   [de campaña, m.
ambulance, *ăm'bŭlăns,* s. (mil.) hospital
ambuscade, *ămbŭskād,* **ambush,** *ăm'-
bŭsh,* s. emboscada, celada, f.; sorpresa,
f.; to lie in –, estar emboscado.
ambush, *ăm'bŭsh,* v. a. emboscar.
ameliorate, *ămēl'yŏrāt,* v. a. mejorar.
amelioration, *ămēlyŏrā'shăn,* s. mejoramiento, m.
amenable, *ămē'năbl,* a. responsable.
amend, *ămĕnd',* v. a. enmendar; –, v. n.
enmendarse, reformarse, restablecerse.
amendable, –*ăbl,* a. reparable, corregible.
amendment, –*mĕnt,* s. enmienda, reforma, f.   [f.
amends, –*z',* s. recompensa, compensación,
amenity, *ămĕn'nĕtĕ,* s. amenidad, f.
amerce, *ămĕrs',* v. a. multar.
amercement, –*mĕnt,* s. multa, f.
amethyst, *ăm'mĕthĕst,* s. amatista, f.
amiability, *ămēbĭl'ĭtĕ,* s. amabilidad, f.
amiable, *ā'mĕăbl,* a. amable, amigable.
amiableness, –*nĕs,* s. amabilidad, gracia, f.

amiably, –*ĕ,* ad. amablemente.
amianthus, *ămĕăn'thŭs,* s. amianto, m.
amicable, *ăm'mĕkăbl,* a. amigable, amistoso;
–bly, ad. amigablemente.
amice, *ăm'mĭs,* s. amito, m., ornamento
sagrado.
amidst, *ămĭd'st,* pr. entre, en medio de.
amiss, *ămĭss',* ad. culpablemente, errada-
amity, *ăm'mĕtĕ,* s. amistad, f.   [mente, mal.
ammonia, *ămmō'nĕă,* s. amoníaco, m.
ammunition, *ămmŭnĭsh'ŭn,* s. munición,
f.   [general, m.
amnesty, *ăm'nĕstĕ,* s. amnistía, f.; olvido
among(st), *ămŭng'(st),* pr. entre, mezclado
con, en medio de.   [amorosamente.
amorous, *ăm'mŏrŭs,* a. amoroso; –ly, ad.
amorousness, –*nĕs,* s. cariño, m.; calidad
de ser amoroso, f.
amorphous, *ămŏr'fŭs,* a. informe.
amount, *ămŏunt',* s. importe, m.; –, v. n.
montar, importar, subir, ascender.
amour, *ămŏr',* s. intriga de amor, f.
amphibian, *ămfĭb'ĕăn,* s. anfibio, m.
amphibious, *ămfĭb'ĕŭs,* a. anfibio.   [m.
amphitheatre, *ămfĕthē'ătŭr,* s. anfiteatro,
ample, *ăm'pl,* a. amplio, largo.
ampleness, –*nĕs,* s. amplitud, abundancia, f.   [plificación, f.; extensión, f.
amplification, *ămplĕfĕkā'shŭn,* s. am-
amplify, *ăm'plĕfī,* v. a. ampliar, extender; –, v. n. extenderse.
amplitude, *ăm'plĕtūd,* s. amplitud, extensión, f.; abundancia, f.   [samente.
amply, *ăm'plĕ,* ad. ampliamente, copio-
amputate, *ăm'pŭtāt,* v. a. amputar.
amputation, *ămpŭtā'shŭn,* s. amputación,
f.; cortamiento, m.
amuck, *ămŭk',* ad. furiosamente.
amulet, *ăm'mŭlĕt,* s. amuleto, m.
amuse, *ămūz',* v. a. entretener, divertir.
amusement, –*mĕnt,* s. diversión, f., pasatiempo, entretenimiento, m.
amusing, *ămū'zĭng,* **amusive,** –*sĭv,* a.
divertido; –ly, ad. entretenidamente.
an, *ăn,* art. un, uno, una.   [anabaptistas, f.
anabaptism, *ănăbăp'tĭzm,* s. herejía de los
anabaptist, *ănăbăp'tĭst,* s. anabaptista,
m.   [mo, m.
anachronism, *ănăk'rŏnĭzm,* s. anacronis-
anemia, *ănĕ'mĕă,* s. anemia, f.
anemic, *ănĕ'mĭk,* a. anémico.
analogical, *ănălŏj'ĕkăl,* a. analógico;
–ly, ad. analógicamente.
analogous, *ănăl'ŏgŭs,* a. análogo.
analogy, *ănăl'ŏjĕ,* s. analogía, conformi-
analysis, *ănăl'ĕsĭs,* s. análisis, f.   [dad, f.
analyse, *ăn'ălĭz,* v. a. analizar.
analyst, *ăn'ălĭst,* s. analizador, m.
analytical, *ănălĭt'ĭkăl,* a. analítico; –ly,
ad. analíticamente.   [confuso.
anarchic(al), –*ĕ,* s. recompensa, compensación,
anarchy, *ăn'ărkĕ,* s. anarquía, f.
anathema, *ănă'thĕmă,* s. anatema, m. & f.,
excomunión, f.
anathematize, –*tīz,* v. a. anatematizar.
anatomical, *ănătŏm'ĕkăl,* a. anatómico;
–ly, ad. anatómicamente.
anatomist, *ănă'tŏmĭst,* s. anatomista, m.
anatomize, –*tŏmīz,* v. a. anatomizar.

anatomy, *tŏmĭ*. s. anatomía, f.
ancestor, *ăn'sĕstŭr*, s. abuelo, m.; **–s**, pl. antepasados, m, pl.
ancestral, *ăn'sĕstrăl*, a. hereditario.
ancestry, *ăn'sĕstrĭ*, s. linaje de antepasados, m.; raza, alcurnia, f.
anchor, *ăng'kŭr*, s. ancla, áncora, f.; **–**, v. n. ancorar, echar las anclas.
anchorage, *–ĕj*, s. anclaje, m.
anchorite, *ăng'kŏrīt*, s. anacoreta, m.
anchovy, *ăntshō'vĕ*, s. anchova, f.
ancient, *ān'shŭnt*, a. antiguo; **–ly**, ad. antiguamente.
ancientness, *–nĕs*, s. antigüedad, f.
ancientry, *–rĕ*, s. antigüedad de linaje, m.
and, *ănd*, c, y, é; aun. [hierro, m.
andiron, *ănd'īŭrn*, s. morillo, caballete de
anecdotal, *ă'nĕkdō'tăl*, a. anecdótico.
anecdote, *ă'nĕkdōt*, s. anécdota, f.
anemone, *ănĕm'mōnĕ*, s. (bot) anémona, f.
anent, *ănĕnt'*, pr. contra.
anew, *ănū'*, ad. de nuevo, nuevamente.
angel, *ān'jĕl*, s. ángel, m.
angelic(al), *ănjĕl'ĭk(ăl)*, a. angélico.
anger, *ăng'gŭr*, s. ira, cólera, f.; **–**, v. a. enojar, irritar, encolerizar.
angle, *ăng'gl*, s. ángulo, m.; caña de pescar, f.; **–**, v. a. pescar con caña; halagar.
angled, *–d*, a. anguloso.
angler, *–ŭr*, s. pescador de caña, m.
anglicism, *ăng'glĭsĭzm*, s. anglicismo, m.
angling-line, *ăng'glĭng līn*, s. sedal, m.
angling-rod, *–rŏd*, s. caña de pescar, f.
angrily, *ăng'grĭlĭ*, ad. coléricamente, con
angry, *ăng'grĕ*, a. colérico, irritado. [ira.
anguish, *ăng'gwĭsh*, s. ansia, pena, angustia, f.
angular, *ăng'gŭlăr*, a. angular.
angularity, *ăngŭlăr'ĭtĕ*, s. forma angular, f.
anigh, *ănī'*, pr. cerca. [lar, f.
anight(s), *ănīt'(s)*, ad. de noche, todas las
anil, *ăn'ĭl*, s. añil, m. [noches.
animadversion, *ănĕmădvŭr'shŭn*, s. animadversión, f.; advertencia, f.; reprensión, f. [observar; censurar; reprochar.
animadvert, *ănĕmădvŭrt'*, v.n.considerar,
animal, *ă'nĕmăl*, s. & a. animal (m.).
animalcule, *ănĕmăl'kŭl*, s. animalejo, m.
animality, *ănĕmăl'ĕtĕ*, s. vida animal, f.
animate, *ă'nĕmăt*, v. a. animar; **–**, a. viviente, animado.
animation, *ănĕmā'shŭn*, s. animación, f.
animosity, *ănĕmŏs'ĕtĕ*, s. animosidad, f.
animus, *ă'nĕmŭs*, s. voluntad, f.; intención, f.
anise, *ăn'nĭs*, s. anís, m. [ción, f.
aniseed, *ăn'nĭsĕd*, s. simiente de anís, f.
ankle, *ăng'kl*, s. maléolo, m.; **–bone**, hueso del tobillo, m.
annals, *ăn'nălz*, s. anales, m. pl.
anneal, *ănnēl'*, v. a. templar el vidrio.
annex, *ănnĕks'*, v. a. anejar; **–**, s. anejo, m.
annexation, *–d'shŭn*, s. anexión, f.
annibilable, *ănnī'hĕlăbl*, s. aniquilable.
annibilate, *ănnī'hĕlāt*, v. a. aniquilar.
annihilation, *ănnĕhĕlā'shŭn*, s. aniquilación, f. [rio, m.; **–s**, aniversario, m.
anniversary, *ănnĕvŭr'sărĕ*, s. aniversario, m.; **–s**, aniversario, m.
annotate, *ăn'nōtāt*, v. n. anotar.
annotation, *–d'shŭn*, s. anotación, f.

announce, *ănnŏuns'*, v. a. anunciar, publicar. [aviso, anuncio, m.
announcement, *–mĕnt*, s. advertencia, f.;
annoy, *ănnŏĕ'*, v. a. molestar, hacer mal; importuno.
annoyance, *–ăns*, s. molestia, f.
annoying, *ănnŏĕ'ĭng*, a. enfadoso, molesto, fastidioso, importuno.
annual, *ăn'nŭăl*, a.-anual; **–ly**, ad. anualmente, de año en año.
annuitant, *ănnū'ĭtănt*, s. proprietario de renta vitalicia, m.
annuity, *ănnū'ĭtĕ*, s. renta vitalicia, f.
annul, *ănnŭl'*, v. a. anular, aniquilar.
annular, *ăn'nŭlăr*, a. anular.
annulet, *ăn'nŭlĕt*, s. anillejo, m.
annulment, *ănnŭl'mĕnt*, s. anulación, f.
annunciate, *ănnŭn'shĕāt*, v. a. anunciar.
annunciation, *ănnŭnshĕā'shŭn*, s. anunciación, f.
anodyne, *ă'nōdīn*, a. (med.) anodino.
anoint, *ănŏĭnt'*, v. a. untar, ungir; (vulg.) apalear á uno.
anomalous, *ănŏm'ălŭs*, a. anómalo, irregular; **–ly**, ad. irregularmente.
anomaly, *ănŏm'ălĕ*, s. anomalía, irregularidad, f.
anon, *ănŏn'*, ad. presto, al instante, inmediatamente; **ever and**; bien á menudo.
anonymous, *ănŏn'nĕmŭs*, a. anónimo; **–ly**, ad. anónimamente. [**–**, uno á otro.
another, *ănŭ'thŭr*, a. otro, diferente; **one**
answer, *ăn'stŭr*, a. responder, replicar; corresponder; **–**, v. n. surtir efecto; **–**, s. respuesta, réplica, f.
answerable, *–ăbl*, a. responsable; conforme. [dad, f.; correspondencia, f.
answerableness, *–nĕs*, s. responsabilidad, f.
ant, *ănt*, s. hormiga, f.
antagonism, *ăntă'gŏnĭzm*, s. antagonismo, m., rivalidad, f.
antagonist, *–gŏnĭst*, s. antagonista, m.
antarctic, *ăntărk'tĭk*, a. antártico.
ant-bear, *ănt'bĕr*, **ant-eater**, *–ētŭr*, s. oso hormiguero, m. [f.
antecedence, *ăntĕsē'dĕns*, s. precedencia, f.
antecedent, *ăntĕsē'dĕnt*, a. antecedente; **–s**, s. pl. antecedentes, m. pl. [mara, f.
antechamber, *ăntĕtshăm'bŭr*, s. antecámara, f.
antedate, *ăn'tĕdāt*, v. a. antedatar.
antediluvian, *ăntĕdĭlū'vĭăn*, a. antediluviano.
antelope, *ăn'tĕlōp*, s. cabra líbica, f.
antemeridian, *ăntĕmĕrĭd'dĭăn*, a. antes de mediodía. [gunos insectos, f. pl.
antennae, *ăntĕn'nē*, s. pl. antenas de algunos insectos, f. pl.
antepenultimate, *ăntĕpĕnŭl'tĕmăt*, s. antepenúltima, f. [dente.
anterior, *ăntē'rĕŭr*, a. anterior, precedente.
anteriority, *ăntērĕ'ŏrĕtĕ*, s. anterioridad, precedencia, f.
anthem, *ăn'thĕm*, s. antífona, f.
anther, *ăn'thŭr*, s. (bot.) antera, f.
ant-hill, *ănt'hĭl*, s. hormiguero, m.
Anthony's fire, *ăn'tŏnĕstr*, s. (med.) fuego de San Antonio, m.
anthracite, *ăn'thrăsīt*, s. antracita, f.
anthropology, *ănthrŏpŏl'ŏjĕ*, s. antropología, f.

antic, *ăn'tĭk*, a. grotesco; —, s. bufón, m.
Antichrist, *ăn'tĭkrĭst*, s. Anticristo, m.
anticipate, *ăntĭs'ĕpāt*, v. a. anticipar, prevenir.
anticipation, *ăntĭssĕpā'shŭn*, s. anticipa- [ción, f.
anticipatory,*ăntĭs'ĕpātŏrĕ*,anticipant, *–sĕpănt*, a. anticipante. [neno, m.
antidote, *ăn'tĭdōt*, s. antídoto, contrave-
antimacassar, *ăntĭmăkăs'sŭr*, s. funda del reclinatorio de un sofá, f.
antimony, *ăn'tĭmonĕ*, s. antimonio, m.
antipathy, *ăntĭ'păthĕ*, s. antipatía, f.
antipodes, *ăn'tĭpōdz*,s.pl.antipodas,m.pl.
antiquarian, *ăntĭkwā'rĕăn*, antiquary, *ăn'tĭkwărĕ*, s. anticuario, m.
antiquated, *ăn'tĭkwātĕd*, a. anticuado.
antique, *ăntēk'*, a. antiguo; —, s. anti- gualla, f. [ancianidad, f.
antiquity, *ăntĭk'kwĕtĕ*, s. antigüedad, f.;
antiseptic, *ăntĭsĕp'tĭk*, a. antiséptico.
antithesis, *ăntĭ'thĕsĭs*, s. antítesis, contra- riedad, f.
antitype, *ăn'tĭtīp*, s. antitipo, m.
antler,*ănt'lŭr*,s. mogotes del ciervo, m.pl.
anvil, *ăn'vĭl*, s. yunque, m.; bigornia, f.
anxiety, *ăngzī'ĕtĕ*, s. ansiedad, ansia, f.; afán, m. [ansiosamente.
anxious, *ăngk'shŭs*, a. ansioso; –ly, ad.
any, *ĕn'nĕ*, a. & pn. cualquier, cualquiera, alguno, alguna, todo; –body, alguno, cualquiera; –how, de cualquier modo que sea; –more, más; –thing, algo; –where, en cualquier lugar.
apace, *ăpās'*, ad. apriesa, con presteza ó prontitud.
apart, *ăpărt'*, ad. aparte, separadamente.
apartment, *–mĕnt*, s. cuarto, m.
apathetic, *ăpăthĕt'ĭk*, a. apático.
apathy, *ă'păthĕ*, s. apatía, f.
ape, *āp*, s. mono (also fig.), m.; –, v. a. contrahacer, imitar. [(mar.) á pique.
apeak, *āpēk'*, ad. perpendicularmente;
aperient, *ăpē'rĕĕnt*, a. (med.) aperitivo.
aperture, *ă'pŭrtūr*, s. abertura, f.
apery, *āp'ŭrĕ*, s. monería, f.
apex, *ā'pĕks*, s. ápice, colmo, m.; cima, f.
aphorism, *ă'fŏrĭzm*, s. aforismo, m.; máxi- ma, f.
aphoristical, *ăfŏrĭs'tĕkăl*, a. aforístico.
apiary, *ā'pĕărĕ*, s. colmena, f.
apiece, *ăpēs'*, ad. por cabeza, por persona.
apish, *āp'ĭsh*, a. gestero, mímico, monero; –ly, ad. afectadamente.
apishness, *–nĕs*, s. monada, f.
Apocalypse, *ăpŏk'kălĭps*, s.Apocalipsis, f.
apocrypha, *ăpŏk'krĭfă*, s. pl. libros apó- crifos, m. pl. [nónico.
apocryphal, *–krĕfăl*, a. apócrifo, no ca-
apodictic, *ăpŏdĭk'tĭk*, a. apodíctico.
apologetical, *ăpŏlŏjĕt'ĭkăl*, a. apologético.
apologise, *ăpŏl'lŏjīz*, v. a. apologizar, de- fender, disculpar, excusar.
apologist, *–lŏjĭst*, s. apologista, m.
apology, *–lŏjĕ*, s. apología, defensa, f.
apophthegm, *ăp'ŏthĕm*, s. apotegma. m.
apoplectic(al), *ăpŏplĕk'tĭk(ăl)*, a. apoplé- tico.
apoplexy, *ăp'ŏplĕksĕ*, s. apoplejía, f.
apostasy, *ăpŏs'tăsĕ*, s. apostasía, f.

apostate, *ăpŏs'tāt*, s. apostata, m.
apostatise, *–tātĭz*, v. n. apostatar.
apostle, *ăpŏs'sl*, s. apóstol, m.
apostleship, *–shĭp*, s. apostolado. m.
apostolic(al), *ăpŏstŏl'ĭk(ăl)*, a. apostólico.
apostrophe, *ăpŏs'trŏfĕ*, s. apóstrofe, f.; (gr.) apóstrofo, m.
apostrophise, *–trŏfĭz*, v. a. apostrofar.
apothecary, *ăpŏth'ĕkărĕ*, s. boticario, m.; –'s shop, s. botica, f. [cación, f.
apotheosis, *ăpŏth'ĕōsĭs*, s. apoteosis, deifi-
appal, *ăppăl'*, v. a. espantar, aterrar.
appanage, *ăp'pănăj*, s. heredamiento, m.; infantazgo, m. [tren, m.
apparatus, *ăppără'tŭs*, s. aparato, aparejo,
apparel, *ăppăr'rĕl*, s. traje, vestido, m.; –, v. a. vestir, trajear; adornar.
apparent, *ăppā'rĕnt*, a. evidente, aparente; –ly, ad. claramente. [sión, f.
apparition, *ăppărĭsh'ŭn*, s. aparición, vi-
apparitor, *ăppăr'rĕtŭr*, s. ujier, m.; al- guacil (de corona ó de la curia eclesiás- tica), m.
appeal, *ăppēl'*, v. n. apelar, recurrir á un tribunal superior; llamar por testigo; –, s. (law) apelación, f. [ser evidente.
appear, *ăppēr'*, v. n. aparecer, manifestar
appearance, *–ăns*, s. apariencia, probabili- dad, f.; first–, primer paso en un negocio &c., m. [conciliable.
appeasable, *ăppē'zăbl*, a. aplacable, re-
appease, *ăppēz'*, v. a. aplacar, reconciliar.
appellant, *ăppĕl'lănt*, s. (law) apelante, m. [ción, f.
appellation, *ăppĕllā'shŭn*, s. (law) apela-
appellative,*ăppĕl'lātĭv*, s. (gr.) apelativo, m [mado, m.
appellee, *ăppĕllē'*, s. (law) apelado, inti-
append, *ăppĕnd'*, v. a anejar.
appendage, *–dj*, s. cosa accesoria, f.
appendix, *–ĭks*, s. apéndice, m. [s.
appertain, *ăppŭrtān'*, v.n. pertenecer, tocar
appetence, *ăp'pĕtĕns*, s. concupiscencia, f.
appetise, *ăp'pĕtīz*, v. a. excitar el apetito.
appetising, *ăp'pĕtīzĭng*, a. apetitivo.
appetite, *ăp'pĕtīt*, s. apetito, m.
applaud, *ăppląd'*, v. a. aplaudir; alabar, palmear; aclamar.
applauder, *–ŭr*, s. aclamador, m.
applause, *ăppląz'*, s. aplauso, m.
apple, *ăp'pl*, s. manzana, f.; pupila del ojo, f.; – of discord, manzana de la dis- cordia. [m.; in–order, en sumo orden.
apple-pie, *–pī*, s. pastelillo de manzanas.
apple-tree, *–trē*, s. manzano, m.
appliance, *ăpplī'ăns*, s. aplicación, f.; re- curso, m.
applicability, *ăpplĭkăbĭl'ĕtĕ*, s. aptitud, f.
applicable, *ăp'plĕkăbl*, a. aplicable, apto; conforme; –bly, ad. de un modo apli- cable.
applicant, *ăp'plĕkănt*, s. aspirante, m.
application, *ăpplĭkā'shŭn*, s. aplicación, f.
apply, *ăpplī'*, v. a. aplicar, acomodar; –, v. n. dirigirse ó recurrir á. [nar, decretar.
appoint, *ăppŏint'*, v. a. señalar, determi-
appointee, *–ē'*, s. funcionario, m.
appointment, *–mĕnt*, s. estipulación, f.; decreto, mandato, m.; sueldo, m.

apportion, ăppŏr′shŭn, v. a. proporcionar.

apportionment, —mĕnt, s. repartición, f.

appose, ăppōz′, y.a. cuestionar, examinar.

apposite, ăp′pŏzĭt, a. adaptado; propio; —ly, ad. convenientemente, á propósito.

appositeness, —nĕs, s. adaptación, f.; propiedad, f.; atributo, m.

apposition, ăppŏzĭsh′ăn, s. aposición, f.

appraise, ăpprāz′, v. a. apreciar; tasar; estimar. [mación, f.

appraisement, —mĕnt, s. aprecio, m., estimación, f.

appraiser, —ăr, s. apreciador, tasador, m.

appreciable, ăpprē′shĕăbl, a. apreciable.

appreciate, ăpprē′shĕăt, v. a. apreciar, estimar, valuar. [m.; tasa, f.

appreciation, ăpprēshĕă′shŭn, s. aprecio, m.

appreciative, —tĭv, a. apreciativo.

apprehend, ăpprēhĕnd′, v. a. aprehender, prender; concebir, comprender; temer.

apprehension, ăpprēhĕn′shŭn, s. aprehensión, f.; recelo, m.; presa, captura, f.

apprehensive, —sĭv, a. aprehensivo, tímido; perspicaz.

apprentice, ăpprĕn′tĭs, s. aprendiz, m.; —v. a. poner á alguno de aprendiz.

apprenticeship, —shĭp, s. aprendizaje, m.

apprise, ăpprīz′, v. a. informar, instruir.

approach, ăpprōtsh′, v. a. (& n.) aproximar(se); —, s. acceso, m.

approachable, —ăbl, a. accesible. [ción, f.

approbation, ăpprŏbă′shŭn, s. aprobación, f.

approbatory, ăp′prŏbătŏrē, a. aprobativo.

appropriate, ăpprō′prēăt, v. a. apropiar, adaptar; —, a. apropiado, particular, peculiar. [bación.

approvable, ăpprō′văbl, a. digno de aprobación.

approval, —văl, s. aprobación, f.

approve, ăpprōv′, v. a. aprobar.

approver, —ăr, s. aprobador, m.

approximate, ăpprŏk′sĕmăt, v. a. (& n.) acercar(se); —, a. aproximativo.

approximation, ăpprŏksēmă′shŭn, s. aproximación, f. [mativo.

approximative, ăpprŏk′sēmătĭv, a. aproximativo, f.

appurtenance, ăppŭr′tēnăns, s. (law) dependencia, pertenencia, f.

apricot, ā′prēkŏt, s. albaricoque, m.

April, ā′prĭl, s. abril, m. [de cañón, f.

apron, ā′pŭrn, s. delantal, m.; plomada

apsidal, ăp′sĭdăl, a. perteneciente al ápside.

apsis, ăp′sĭs, s. ápside. [mente.

apt, ăpt, a. apto, idóneo; —ly, ad. apta-

aptitude, ăp′tĭtŭd, **aptness,** ăpt′nĕs, s. aptitud, f.; disposición natural, f.

aqua fortis, ăk′kwă fōr′tĭs, s. agua fuerte, f.

Aquarius, ăkwā′rēŭs, s. Acuario, m. (signo del zodíaco).

aquatic, ăkwăt′ĭk, a. acuático, acuátil.

aqueduct, ăk′kwĕdŭkt, s. acueducto, m.

aqueus, ā′kwĕŭs, a. acuoso.

aquiline, ăk′kwēlĭn, a. aguileño.

arabesque, ăr′răbĕsk, s. arabesco, m.

arable, ă′răbl, a. labrantío.

arbalist, ăr′bălĭst, s. ballesta, f.

arbiter, ăr′bĭtăr, s. arbitrador, árbitro, m.

arbitrament, ărbĭt′rămĕnt, s. arbitrio, m.

arbitrarily, ăr′bĭtrărĭlē, ad. arbitraria-mente. [tismo, m.

arbitrariness, ăr′bĭtrărĭnĕs, s. despo-

arbitrary, —rĕ, a. arbitrario, despótico.

arbitrate, ăr′bĭtrăt, v. a. arbitrar, juzgar como árbitro.

arbitration, ărbĭtră′shŭn, **arbitrement,** ărbĭt′rĕmĕnt, s. arbitramento, arbitrio, m.

arbitrator, ăr′bĭtrătăr, s. arbitrador, árbitro, m.

arborescent, ărbŏrĕs′sĕnt, a. arborescente.

arbour, ăr′bŭr, s. emparrado, m.; enramada, f.

arbute, ăr′bŭt, s. (bot.) fresal, m. [f.

arcade, ărkād′, s. arcada, bóveda, f.

arcanum, ărkā′nŭm, s. arcano, m.

arch, ărtsh, s. arco (de círculo, de puente &c.), m.; —, v. a. cubrir con arcos; —, a. principal, insigne; grande; infame; artero, bellaco; (se usa en composición como aumentativo). [lógico.

archæological, ărkēŏlŏj′ĭkăl, a. arqueo-

archæology, ărkēŏl′ōjē, s. arqueología, f.

archaic, ărkā′ĭk, a. arcaico.

archangel, ărk′ănjĕl, s. arcángel, m.

archbishop, ărtshbĭsh′ăp, s. arzobispo, m.

archbishopric, —rĭk, s. arzobispado, m.

archduchess, ărtshdŭt′shĕs, s. archi-duquesa, f.

archduke, —dŭk′, s. archiduque, m.

archdukedom, —dăm′, s. archiducado, m.

archer, ărtsh′ăr, s. arquero, m.

archery, —ē, s. arte de tirar con arco y flecha, m.

archiepiscopacy, ărkēĕp′ĭs kŏpăsē, s. dignidad de arzobispo, f.

architect, ăr′kētĕkt, s. arquitecto, m.

architectural, ărkĕtĕk′tŭrăl, a. lo perteneciente á la arquitectura. [f.

architecture, ăr′kētĕktŭr, s. arquitectura, f.

archives, ăr′kīvz, s. pl. archivos, m. pl.

archivist, ăr′kĕvĭst, s. archivero, m.

archly, ărtsh′lē, ad. jocosamente; sutilmente; con ingenio.

archness, —nĕs, s. astucia, malignidad, f.; travesura, maula, f.

archpriest, —prēst′, s. arcipreste, m.

archway, —wā, s. arcada, bóveda, f.

arctic, ărk′tĭk, a. ártico, septentrional.

ardency, ăr′dĕnsē, **ardour,** ăr′dŭr, s. ardor, m.; vehemencia, f.; pasión, f.

ardent, ăr′dĕnt, a. ardiente; apasionado; —ly, ad. con pasión.

arduous, ăr′dūăs, a. arduo; laborioso; —ly, ad. laboriosamente. [difícil.

area, ā′rēă, s. área, f.; espacio, m.

arenaceous, ărĕnă′shăs, a. arenoso.

areometer, ărēŏm′mĕtăr, s. areómetro, m.

argentiferous, ărjĕntĭf′fĕrŭs, a. argentífero. [fero.

argil, ăr′jĭl, s. arcilla, f.

argillaceous, ărjĭllā′shăs, a. arcilloso.

argue, ăr′gū, v. n. disputar, discurrir; —, v. a. probar, con argumentos; acusar.

argument, ăr′gŭmĕnt, s. argumento, m., controversia, f. [mentación, f.

argumentation, ărgŭmĕntă′shŭn, s. argu-

argumentative, ărgŭmĕn′tētĭv, a. lo que contiene argumento, argumentoso.

argus-eyed, ăr′găs īd, a. que tiene vista de lince.

arid, ăr′rĭd, a. árido, seco, estéril.

aridity, ărĭd′ĭtē, s. sequedad, f.

Aries, ā′rēĭz, s. Aries, m. (signo del zodíaco).

aright, *ărīt'*, ad. rectamente, justamente, bien; **to set —**, rectificar. [venir.

arise, *ărīz'* s. n. levantarse; nacer; pro-

aristocracy, *ărīstō krăse*, s. aristocracia, f. [m.

aristocrat, *ărīs'tōkrăt*, s. aristócrata.

aristocratic, *ărīstōkrăt'ĭk*, a. aristocrático; **-ally**, ad. aristocráticamente

arithmetic, *ărĭth'mĕtĭk*, s. aritmética, f.

arithmetical, *-mĕt'ĭkăl*, a. aritmético; **-ly**, ad. aritméticamente

arithmetician, *ărĭthmĕtĭsh'ăn*, s. aritmético, m. [arca del testamento.

ark, *ărk*, s. arca, f.; **- of the covenant**,

arm, *ărm*, s. brazo, m.; rama del árbol, f.; poder, m.; arma, f.; **-**, v. a. (& n.) armar(se).

armament, *ăr'măment*, s. (mar.) arma-mento de navíos, m.; (mil.) armamento.

arm-chair, *ărm'chair*, s. silla de brazos, f.

armful, *-fŭl*, s. brazada, f.

arm-hole, *-hōl*, s. sobaco, m.

armistice, *ărm'ĭstĭs*, s. armisticio, m.

armlet, *ărm'lĕt*, s. brazuelo, m.; brazalete, m.; guardabrazo de la armadura, m. [m.

armorial, *ărmŏr'rĕăl*, s. libro de blasones,

armour, *ăr'mŭr*, s. armadura, f.

armour-bearer, *-băr'ĕr*, s. escudero, m.

armoury, *ăr'mŭrĭ*, s. armería, f.; insignias genealógicas, f. pl.

arm-pit, *ărm'pĭt*, s. sobaco, m.

army, *ăr'mĭ*, s. ejército, m., tropas, f. pl.

aroma, *ărō'mă*, s. aroma, m.

aromatic(al), *ărōmăt'ĭk(ăl)*, a. aromático.

aromatize, *ărō'mătĭz*, v. a. aromatizar.

around, *ărŏŭnd'*, pr. en, cerca; **-**, ad. al rededor. [sublevar.

arouse, *ărŏŭz'*, v. a. despertar; excitar;

arquebuse, *ăr'kĕbŏs*, s. arcabuz, m.

arrack, *ăr'răk*, s. aguardiente de arroz, m.

arraign, *ărrān'*, v. a. citar, delatar en justicia; acusar. [proceso criminal.

arraignment, *-mĕnt*, s. acusación, f.

arrange, *ărrānj'*, v. a. colocar, poner en orden. [orden, arreglo, m.

arrangement, *-mĕnt*, s. colocación, f.;

arrant, *ăr'rănt*, a. malo, perverso; infame; **-ly**, ad. corruptamente, vergonzosamente.

arras, *ăr'răz*, s. tapicerías tejidas, f. pl.

array, *ărră'*, s. adorno, vestido, m.; orden de batalla, f.; colocación de los jurados, f.; **-**, v. a. colocar; vestir, adornar; co-locar los jurados. [atraso, m.

arrear, *ărrēr'*, s. resto de una deuda, m.;

arrest, *ărrĕst'*, s. prisión, f.; arresto, m.; **-**, v. a. arrestar, embargar las cosas.

arrival, *ărrī'văl*, s. arribo, m.; llegada, venida, f.

arrive, *ărrīv'*, v. n. arribar; conseguir.

arrogance, *ăr'rōgăns*, s. arrogancia, pre-sunción, f.

arrogant, *ăr'rōgănt*, a. arrogante, presun-tuoso; **-ly**, ad. arrogantemente.

arrogate, *ăr'rōgāt*, v. a. arrogarse, presu-mir de sí.

arrogation, *ărrōgă'shŭn*, s. arrogación, f.

arrow, *ăr'rō*, s. flecha, saeta, f.

arsenal, *ăr'sĕnăl*, s. (mil.) arsenal, m.; (mar.) atarazana, armería, f.

arsenic, *ăr'sĕnĭk*, s. arsénico, m.

arson, *ăr'sŭn*, s. fuego incendiario, delito de incendiar, m. [ciencia, f.

art, *ărt*, s. arte, m. & f.; industria, f.;

arterial, *ărtē'rĕăl*, a. arterial, arterioso.

artesian well, *ărtē'zhăn wĕll*, s. pozo ar-tesiano, m.

artery, *ăr'tărĭ*, s. arteria, f. [tesiano, m.

artful, *ărt'fŭl*, a. artificioso; diestro; **-ly**, ad. artificiosamente, diestramente [f.

artfulness, *-fŭlnĕs*, s. astucia, habilidad,

artichoke, *ăr'tĭshōk*, s. alcachofa, f.

article, *ăr'tĭkl*, s. artículo, m.; **-**, v. n. capitular, contratar mutuamente.

articulate, *ărtĭk'kŭlāt*, a. articulado, claro, distinto; **-ly**, ad. distintamente; **-**, v. a. articular, pronunciar distintamente

articulation, *ărtĭkŭlă'shŭn*, s. articula-ción, f.; (bot.) nudo en las plantas, m.

artifice, *ăr'tĭfĭs*, s. artificio, fraude, m.

artificer, *ărtĭf'fĭsĕr*, s. artesano, m.

artificial, *ărtĕfĭsh'ăl*, a. artificial; artifi-cioso; **-ly**, ad. artificialmente; artificiosa-mente. [cia, f.; destreza, f.

artificiality, *ărtĕfĭshălĭt'tĭ*, s. arte, astu-

artillery, *ărtĭl'lărĭ*, s. artillería, f.

artillery-man, *-măn*, s. artillero, m. [m.

artillery-practice, *-prăktĭs*, s. cañoneo,

artisan, *ăr'tĭzăn*, s. artista, artesano, m.

artist, *ăr'tĭst*, s. artista, m.

artistic, *ărtĭs'tĭk*, a. artístico.

artless, *ărt'lĕs*, a. sencillo, simple; **-ly**, ad. sencillamente, naturalmente.

artlessness, *-nĕs*, s. sencillez, f.

as, *ăs*, c. como; mientras; también; visto que, pues que; **- for**, **- to**, en cuanto á.

asbestos, *ăsbĕs'tŏs*, s. asbesto, amianto, m.

ascend, *ăssĕnd'*, v. n. ascender, subir.

ascendant, *-ănt*, s. ascendiente, m.; **-**, a. superior, predominante.

ascendency, *-ĕnsĕ*, s. influjo, poder, m.

ascension, *ăssĕn'shŭn*, s. ascensión, f.

ascent, *ăssĕnt'*, s. subida, f.; eminencia, f.; altura, f. [establecer; reglar el precio.

ascertain, *ăssĕrtān'*, v. a. asegurar, fijar;

ascetic, *ăssĕt'ĭk*, a. ascético; **-**, s. asceta, m. [adjudicar.

ascribe, *ăskrīb'*, v. a. adscribir; atribuir;

ash, *ăsh*, s. (bot.) fresno, m.; **-es**, *-ĕz*, pl. ceniza, f., reliquias de un cadáver, f. pl.

ashamed, *ăshāmd'*, a. avergonzado.

ash-coloured, *ăsh'kŭllŭrd*, a. ceniciento.

ashen, *ăsh'n*, a. hecho de fresno.

ash-hole, *ăsh'-hōl*, **—pan**, **—păn**, **—pit**, **—pĭt**, s. cenicero, cenizal, m.

ashore, *ăshōr'*, ad. en tierra, á tierra; **to get —**, desembarcar. [coles de ceniza, m.

Ash-Wednesday, *ăsh'wĕnzdă*, s. miér-coles de ceniza, m.

ashy, *ăsh'ĭ*, a. cenizoso, ceniciento.

aside, *ăsīd'*, ad. al lado, á parte.

ask, *ăsk*, v. a. pedir, rogar, interrogar; **to - out**, convidar.

askance, *ăskăns'*, **askant**, *ăskănt'*, ad. al sesgo, oblicuamente. [con desdén.

askew, *ăskū'*, ad. al lado, de lado; de través;

aslant, *ăslănt'*, ad. oblicuamente.

asleep, *ăslēp'*, a. dormido, **to fall —**, dor-asp, *ăsp*, s. áspid, m. [mirse.

asparagus, *ăspăr'ăgŭs*, s. espárrago, m.

aspect, *ăs'pĕkt*, s. aspecto, m.; vista, f.; aire, m.; semblante, m.

aspen(-tree), äs'pĕn(trē), s. álamo temblón, m.; –, a. de álamo temblón.

asperity, äspĕr'itĕ, s. aspereza, rudeza, f.

asperse, äspĕrs', y. a. calumniar, infamar.

aspersion, äspĕr'shän, s. aspersión, f.; defamación, calumnia, f.

asphalt, äs'fält', s. asfalto, m.

asphyxia, äsfïk'sĕä, s. (med.) asfixia, f.

asphyxiate, äsfïk'sĕät, v. a. asfixiar.

aspirant, äspī'ränt, s. aspirante, m.

aspirate, äs'pĕrät, v. a. aspirar, pronunciar con aspiración; –, s. sonido aspirado, m.

aspiration, äspĕrä'shän, s. aspiración, f.

aspire, äspīr', y. n. aspirar, desear.

asquint, äskwïnt', ad. de través. [f.

ass, äss, s. borrico, asno, m.; –, borrica,

assail, ässāl', v. a. asaltar, atacar.

assailable, –äbl, a. lo que puede ser asaltado. [tador, agresor, m.

assailant, –änt, **assailer,** –ŭr, s. asal-

assassin, ässä'sïn, s. asesino, matador, m.

assassinate, –ät, v. a. asesinar, matar.

assassination, ässässinä'shän, s. asesinato, m. [–, v. a. acometer, asaltar.

assault, ässält', s. asalto, m.; insulto, m.;

assay, ässā', s. ensayo, f.; prueba, f.; experimento, m.; –, v. a. tentar; probar.

assayer, –ŭr, s. ensayador, m. [ensayar.

assemblage, ässĕm'blĕj, s. agregado, m.; multitud, f. [–, v. n. juntarse.

assemble, –bl, v. a. congregar, convocar;

assembly, –blĕ, s. asamblea, junta, f.; congreso, m.

assent, ässĕnt', s. asenso, m.; aprobación, f.; –, v. n. asentir, aprobar.

assert, ässĕrt', v. a. sostener, mantener; afirmar; asegurar.

assertion, ässĕr'shän, s. aserción, f.

assertive, ässĕr'tïv, a. perentorio.

assess, ässĕs', v. a. amillarar.

assessable, –äbl, a. el que puedo ser amillarado. [m.; catastro, m.

assessment, –mĕnt, s. amillaramiento,

assets, ässĕts', s. pl. bienes de un difunto, m. pl. [v. a. aseverar, afirmar.

assever, ässĕv'ĕr, v. a. **asseverate,** –ärät,

asseveration, ässĕvĕrä'shän, s. aseveración, afirmación, f.

assiduity, ässïdū'ïtĕ, s. asiduidad, aplicación, f.; constancia, f.

assiduous, ässïd'ūs, a. asiduo, aplicado; –ly, ad. constantemente; diligentemente.

assign, ässīn', v. a. asignar; disputar; transferir algún derecho á otro.

assignable, –äbl, a. asignable.

assignation, ässïgnä'shän, s. asignación, f.; cesión f.; cita, f.

assignee, ässïnē', s. síndico, apoderado, m.; cesionario, m.

assignment, ässïn'mĕnt, s. asignación, f.; cesión, f.; señalamiento, m. [asemejar.

assimilate, ässïm'mĕlät, v. a. asimilar,

assimilation, ässïmĕlä'shän, s. asimilación, f. [rrer.

assist, ässïst', v. a. asistir, ayudar, soco-

assistance, –äns, s. asistencia, f.; socorro, m. [m.

assistant, –änt, s. asistente, ayudante,

assize, ässīz', s. tribunal que entiende en los asuntos criminales, m.; tasa del pan, f.

associate, ässō'shĕät, v. a. asociar; acompañar; frecuentar; –, a. asociado; –, s. socio, compañero, m.

association, ässŏshĕä'shän, s. asociación, unión, sociedad, f.

assonance, äs'sŏnäns, s. asonancia, f.

assort, ässŏrt', v. a. clasificar, adecuar.

assortment, –mĕnt, s. surtido, m.

assuage, ässwāj' v. a. mitigar, suavizar; –, v. n. disminuir; apaciguarse. [f.

assuagement, –mĕnt, s. mitigación, calma,

assume, ässūm', v. a. arrogar, apropiar, presumir; –, v. n. arrogarse.

assumption, ässŭm'shän, s. presunción, f.; postulado, m.; **Assumption,** s. Asunción de la bienaventurada Virgen María, f.

assurance, äshō'räns, s. seguridad, certeza, f.; fianza, f.

assure, äshōr', v. a. asegurar, afirmar.

assuredly, –ĕdlĕ, ad. ciertamente, f.

asterisk, äs'tĕrïsk, s. asterisco, m. [duda.

astern, ästĕrn', ad. (mar.) por la popa.

asthma, äst'mä, s. asma, f.

asthmatic, ästmăt'ïk, a. asmático.

astir, ästïr' ad. agitado, en turbación.

astonish, ästŏn'ïsh, v. a. pasmar, sorprender. [–ly, ad. asombrosamente.

astonishing, ästŏn'ïshïng, a. asombroso;

astonishment, –mĕnt, s. espanto, pasmo, asombro, m.; sorpresa, f.

astound, ästŏûnd', v. a. consternar, aterrar, pasmar, conturbar.

astounding, –ïng, a. consternativo.

astraddle, ästräd'dl, ad. á horcajadas.

astral, äs'träl, a. astral, de los astros.

astray, ästrä', ad. extraviado, descaminado; **to lead** –, desviar, seducir.

astriction, ästrïk'shän, s. astricción, f.

astride, ästrïd', ad. á horcajadas.

astringent, ästrïn'jĕnt, a. astringente.

astrolabe, äs'trŏläb, s. astrolabio, m.

astrologer, ästrŏl'ŏjŭr, s. astrólogo.

astrological, ästrŏlŏj'ïkäl, a. astrológico, m. [v. a. aseverar, afirmar.

astrology, ästrŏl'ŏjĕ, s. astrología, f. [m.

astronomer, ästrŏn'ŏmŭr, s. astrónomo,

astronomical, ästrŏnŏm'ïkäl, a. astronómico.

astronomy, ästrŏn'ŏmĕ, s. astronomía, f.

astute, ästūt', a. astuto; aleve. [parte.

asunder, äsŭn'dŭr, ad. separadamente, á

asylum, äsī'lŭm, s. asilo, refugio, m.

at, ät, pr. á, en; – **once,** al instante, de un golpe; – **all,** generalmente; – **all events,** á todo trance; – **first,** en el principio; – **large,** ampliamente, á larga; á la inclemencia; – **last,** por último; **his honour is** – **stake,** le va en ello de su honor.

atheism, ä'thĕïzm, s. ateísmo, m.

atheist, ä'thĕïst, s. ateísta, ateo, m.

atheistic(al), äthĕïst'ïk(äl), a. impío.

athirst, äthŭrst', ad. sediento, con gana [de beber.

athlete, äth'lēt, s. atleta, m.

athletic, äthlĕt'ïk, a. atlético, vigoroso:

athwart, äthwärt', pr. al través.

atilt, ätïlt', ad. en ademán de dar una estocada.

atlas, ät'läs, s. atlas, m.; atlante, m. [cada.

atmosphere, ăt'mŏsfẽr, s. atmósfera, f.

atmospherical, ătmŏsfẽr'ĭkăl, a. atmos-

atom, ă'tŭm, s. átomo, m.   [férico.

atomic(al), ătŏm'ĭk(ăl), a. atómico.

atone, ătōn', v. a. expiar, aplacar.

atonement, –mĕnt, s. expiación, propiciación, f.

atop, ătŏp', ad. encima, en la punta ó
parte superior de alguna cosa.

atrabilious, ătrăbĭl'ĕăs, a. atrabiliario,
melancólico.

atrocious, ătrō'shăs, a. atroz; enorme;
odioso; –ly, ad. atrozmente.   [dad, f.

atrocity, ătrŏs'ĕtĕ, s. atrocidad, enormi-

atrophy, ăt'rŏfĕ, s. (med.) atrofia, f.

attach, ăttătsh', v. a. prender, pillar, asir,
coger; ganar, adquirir, atraer á sí.

attaché, ătăshā', s. agregado á alguna
legación, m.

attachment, ăttătsh'mĕnt, s. adherencia,
f.; afecto, m.; secuestro, m.   [ataque, m.

attack, ăttăk', v. a. atacar; acometer; –, s.

attain, ăttăn', v. a. ganar, conseguir, obtainable, –ăbl, a. asequible.   [tener.

attainder, –dẽr, s. imputación de algún
delito, tacha, deshonra, infamia, f.

attainment, –mĕnt, s. logro, m.; consecución de lo que se pretende, f.; –s, pl. conocimientos, m. pl.

attaint, –t', v. a. convencer de algún delito;
corromper, viciar, manchar; –, s. mácula,
f.; auto jurídico, m.

attar, ăt'tăr, s. aceite rosado ó de rosas, m.

attempt, ăttĕmt', v. a. tentar; probar, experimentar; –, s. empresa, f.; experimento
(peligroso), m.; tentativa, f.

attend, ăttĕnd', v. a. servir, asistir, acompañar; –, v. n. prestar atención; considerar.

attendance, –ăns, s. corte, f.; tren, séquito, m.; servicio, m.; cuidado, m.   [m.

attendant, –ănt, s. sirviente, m.; cortejo,

attention, ăttĕn'shăn, s. atención, f.; cuidado, m.   [–ly, ad. con atención.

attentive, –tĭv, a. atento; cuidadoso;

attenuate, ăttĕn'ŭăt, v. a. atenuar, disminuir.

attenuation, ăttĕnŭā'shăn, s. atenuación, f.

attest, ăttĕst', v. a. atestiguar.

attestation, –tā'shăn, s. atestación, f.; testimonio, m.

attic, ăt'tĭk, s. desván, m.; guardilla, f.;
–, a. ático, juicioso, picante (aplícase al
estilo).   [nar, ataviar.

attire, ăttīr', s. atavío, m.; –, v. a. ador-

attitude, ăt'tĕtūd, s. actitud, postura, f.

attitudinarian, ătĭtūdĭnā'rĭăn, s. asentador, m.   [actitud.

attitudinise, ăttĭtū'dĭnĭz, v. n. tomar cierta

attorney, ăttŭr'nĕ, s. procurador, poderhabiente, m.; –general, fiscal, m.

attract, ăttrăkt', v. a. atraer, persuadir.

attraction, ăttrăk'shăn, s. atracción, f.;
atractivo, m.

attractive, –tĭv, a. atractivo, halagüeño;
–ly, ad. por atracción.

attributable, ăttrĭb'ŭtăbl, a. imputable.

attribute, ăttrĭb'ŭt, v. a. atribuir, imputar; –, s. ăt'trĕbŭt, atributo, m.

attribution, ăttrĭbū'shăn, s. atributo, m.;
reputación, f.   [atricion, f.

attrition, ăttrĭsh'ăn, s. trituración, f.;

attune, ăttūn', v. a. acordar; armonizar.

auburn, ă'bŭrn, s. moreno, castaño.   [f.

auction, ăk'shăn, s. venta pública, subasta,

auctioneer, –ẽr', s. corredor de almoneda,
vendutero, m.   [–ly, ad. atrevidamente.

audacious, ădā'shăs, a. audaz, temerario;

audacity, ădăs'ĕtĕ, s. audacia, osadía, f.

audible, ă'dĭbl, a. perceptible al oido;
–ly, ad. de modo que se pueda oir, alto.

audience, ă'dĕĕns, s. audiencia, f.; auditorio, m.

audit, ă'dĭt, s. remate de una cuenta, m.;
–, v. a. rematar una cuenta, examinar.

auditor, ă'dĭtŏr, s. oidor, m.   [tivo.

auditory, –ĕ, s. auditorio, m.; –, a. audi-

auger, ă'gŭr, s. barrena, f.

aught, ăt, pn. algo, alguna cosa.

augment, ăgmĕnt', v. a. aumentar, ácre-
centar; –, v. n. crecer.   [f.; aumento, m.

augmentation, –ā'shăn, s. aumentación, f.

augur, ă'gŭr, v. n. augurar, adivinar por
conjeturas.

augury, ă'gŭrĕ, s. agüero, presagio, m.

August, ă'gŭst, s. agosto, m. (mes).

august, ăgŭst', a. augusto; majestuoso.

augustness, –nĕs, s. grandeza, f.

aulic, ă'lĭk, a. aulico.

aunt, ănt, s. tia, f.

aureola, ărē'ŏlă, s. auréola, f.

auricular, ărĭk'dlăr, aural, ă'răl, a.
dicho al oido; lo que se sabe por tradición; –ly, ad. al oido; secretamente.

auriferous, ărĭfĕrŭs, a. aurifero.

aurora, ărō'ră, s. aurora, f.; –borealis,
aurora boreal, f.

ausculation, ăskŭltā'shăn, s. ausculta-
ción, f.   [lección, f.

auspices, ă'spĭsĕz, s. pl. auspicio, m.; pro-

auspicious, ăspĭsh'ŭs, a. próspero, favorable; propicio; –ly, ad. prósperamente.

austere, ăstēr', a. austero, severo, rígido;
–ly, ad. austeramente.   [ficación, f.

austerity, ăstĕr'ĕtĕ, s. austeridad; morti-

austral, ăs'trăl, a. austral, austrino.

authentic(al), ăthĕn'tĭk(ăl), a. auténtico;
–ly, ad. auténticamente.

authenticate, –āt, v. a. autenticar.

authenticity, ăthĕnŭs'ĕtĕ, s. autenticidad, f.

author, ă'thŭr, s. autor, m.; escritor, m.

authoress, –ĕs, s. autora, escritora, f.

authorisation, ăthărĕzā'shăn, s. autorización, f.

authorise, ă'thŏrĭz, v. a. autorizar.

authoritative, ăthŏr'ĭtătĭv, a. autoritativo; –ly, ad. autoritativamente, con autoridad.   [apariencia autoritativa, f.

authoritativeness, –nĕs, s. presunción, f.

authority, ăthŏr'ĕtĕ, s. autoridad, f.

authorship, ă'thŭrshĭp, a. calidad de autor,
f.

autocracy, ătŏk'răsĕ, s. autocracia, f.   [f.

autocrat, ă'tŏkrăt, s. autócrata, m.   [tico.

autocratic(al), ătŏkrăt'ĭk(ăl), a. autocrá-

autograph, ă'tŏgrăf, s. autógrafo, m.

autography, ătŏg'răfĕ, s. autografía, f.

automatic, ătŏmă'tĭk, a. automático.

automaton, ătŏ´mătŏn, s. automato, m.
autonomy, ătŏn´ŏmĕ, s. autonomía, f.
autopsy, â´tŏpsĕ, s. autopsia, f.
autumn, â´tŭm, s. otoño, m.
autumnal, ătăm´năl, a. otoñal.
auxiliary, ăgzĭl´yărĕ, a. auxiliar, asistente.
auxiliaries, –z, s.pl. tropas auxiliares, f.pl.
avail, ăvāl´, v. a. aprovechar; –, v. n. servir, ser ventajoso; –, s. provecho, m.; ventaja, f.
available, –ĭbl, a. útil, ventajoso.
avalanche, ăv´ălăntsh, s. alud, lurte, m.
avarice, ăv´ărĭs, s. avaricia, f.
avaricious, ăvărĭsh´ŭs, a. avaro; –ly, ad. avaramente.
avaunt, ăvânt´ ¡fuera! ¡quita!
avenge, ăvĕnj´, v. a. vengarse, castigar.
avenue, ăv´ĕnū, s. calle de árboles, f.; avenida, f.
aver, ăvĕr´, a. v. afirmar, verificar, declarar.
average, ăv´ărĕj, v. a. tomar un termino medio; –, s. precio medio, m.; (mar.) avería, f.; –ly, ad. con equidad.
averse, ăvĕrs´, a. contrario, repugnante;
aversion, ăvĕr´shŭn, aversation, ăvĕrsā´shăn, s. aversión, f., disgusto, m.
avert, ăvĕrt´, v. a. desviar, apartar.
aviary, â´vĕărĕ, s. pajarera, f.
avidity, ăvĭd´ĭtĕ, s. codicia, avidez, f.
avocation, ăvŏkā´shŭn, s. ocupación, f.; estorbo, m.   [(law) anular.
avoid, ăvŏĭd´, v. a. evitar, escapar, huir;
avoidable, –ĭbl, a. evitable.   [fuga, f.
avoidance, –ăns, s. vacación, f.; evitación,
avoirdupois, ăv´ărdăpŏz´, s. peso inglés de diez y seis onzas, m.   [sostener.
avouch, ăvŏtsh´, v. a. afirmar, justificar.
avow, ăvŏ´, v. a. confesar, declarar.
avowal, –ăl, s. declaración justificativa, confesión, f.   [abiertamente.
avowedly, –ĕdlĕ, ad. declaradamente,
await, ăvāt´, v. a. aguardar; –, v. n. estar.
awake, ăwāk´, v. a. & n. despertar; dejar de dormir; –, a. despierto.
awaken, –n, v. n. despertar.
awaking, –ĭng, s. despertamiento, m.
award, ăwârd´, v. a. juzgar, sentenciar; –, v. n. determinar; –, s. sentencia, decisión, f.   [¡dado! ¡mira!
aware, ăwăr´, a. cauto, vigilante; –! ¡cuiaway, ăwā´, ad. ausente, fuera; –! ¡fuera, quita de ahí, marcha! far and –, de mucho, con mucho.
awe, ă´, s. miedo, temor reverencial, m.; –, v. a. infundir miedo ó temor reverencial.
awful, –fŭl, a. tremendo; funesto; horroroso; –ly, ad. con respeto y veneración.
awfulness, –nĕs, s. veneración, f.; horror, m.
awhile, ăhwĭl´, ad. un rato, algún tiempo.
awkward, ăk´wărd, a. tosco, inculto, rudo, poco diestro; –ly, ad. groseramente, toscamente.   [poca habilidad, f.
awkwardness, –nĕs, s. tosquedad, grosería,
awl, ăl, s. lesna, f.
awning, ă´nĭng, s. (mar.) toldo (para guardarse del sol), m.   [al través, m.
awry, ărĭ´, ad. oblicuamente, torcidamente,
axe, ăks, s. segur, f.; hacha, f.

axiom, ăk´sĭŭm (ăk´shŭm), s. axioma, m.
axis, ăk´sĭs, s. eje, m.
axle(–tree), ăk´sl(trē), s. eje de una rueda, ay, ăĭ, ad. sí; –! ¡ay de mí!   [m.
azalea, ăzăl´ā, s. (bot.) azalea, f. [leo, m.
azure, ā´zhŭr, a. azulado; –, s. color cerú-

B.

baa, bā´, s. balido, m.; –, v. n. balar.
babble, băb´bl, v. n. charlar, parlotear; –, babbling, –ĭng, s. charla, cháchara, f., flujo de hablar, m.
babbler, –ăr, s. charlador, charlatán, m.
babe, băb, baby, bă´bĕ, s. niño pequeño, nene, m.; infante, m.   [grande.
baboon, băbŏn´, s. cinocéfalo, m., mono
babyhood, bă´bĕhŭd, s. niñez, f.
babyish, –ĭsh, a. niñero; pueril.
baby-linen, –lĭnĕn, s. envoltura de una criatura recién nacida, f.
bacchanalian, băkkănā´lĕăn, a. disipado, licencioso, disoluto.   [m.
bachelor, bătsh´ĕlăr, s. soltero, m.; bachiller.
bachelorship, –shĭp, s. soltería, f.; bachillerato, m.
back, băk, s. dorso, m.; revés de la mano, m.; recazo, m.; –, ad. atrás, detrás; otra ó segunda vez; – of, detrás; a few years –, algunos años ha; –, v. a. montar á caballo; sostener, apoyar, favorecer.
backbite, –bĭt´, v. a. hablar mal del que está ausente; difamar.
backbiter, –bĭtăr, s. detractor, m.
back-board, –bōrd, s. respaldo de bote, m.
backbone, –bōn, s. hueso dorsal, espinazo,
backdoor, –dōr, s. puerta trasera, f.   [m.
backer, –ăr, s. partidario, m.
backfriend, –frĕnd, s. amigo falso, m.
backgammon, –găm´mŭn, s. juego de chaquete ó tablas, m.
background, –grŏŭnd, s. fondo, m.; hondo (de una perspectiva, &c.), m.
back-number, –năm´băr, s. número atrasado de algún periódico, m.   [sada, f.
back-payment, –pām´ĕnt, s. paga atrabacksight, –sĭt, s. mira (de una escopeta), f.   [versar.
backslide, –slĭd, v. n. apostatar; tergibackstairs, –stărs, s.pl. escalera secreta, f.
backward, –wărd, a. opuesto, enemigo; tardo, lento; –, –s, –ly, ad. preposteramente; con repugnancia.
backwardness, –wărdnĕs, s. torpeza, tardanza, f.; repugnancia, f.
backwoods, –wŭdz, s. pl. bosques del bacon, bā´kn, s. tocino, m.   [Misuri, m.pl.
bad, băd, a. mal, malo; perverso; infeliz; dañoso; indispuesto; –ly, ad. malamente.
badge, băj, s. señal, f.; símbolo, m.; divisa, f.; –, v. a. divisar.
badger, –ăr, s. tejón, m.; –, v. a. fatigar; cansar, atormentar.   [f.
badness, băd´nĕs, s. maldad, mala calidad,
baffle, băf´fl, v. a. eludir; confundir, hun- dir; acosar.   [v. a. entalegar.
bag, băg, s. saco, m.; talega, f.; bolsa, f.;

baggage, *băg'gij,* s. bagaje, equipaje, m.

bagging, *băg'ging,* s. tela basta, f.

bagman, *băg'măn,* s. comisionista viajante de una casa de comercio, m.

bagnio, *băn'yŏ,* s. estufa, f. burdel, m.

bagpipe, *băg'pīp,* s. gaita, f.

bail, *băl,* s. fianza, caución (juratoria),f.; fiador, m.; —, v. a. caucionar, fiar.

bailable, *–ăbl,* a. caucionable.

bailee, *–ē,* s. (law) depositario, m. [m.

bailiff, *bāʾlif,* s. alguacil, m.; mayordomo,

bait, *băt,* v. a. cebar; azuzar; atraer; —, v. n. tomar el refrigerio; —, s. cebo, m.; anzuelo, m.; refrigerio, m.

baize, *băz,* s. bayeta, f.

bake, *băk,* v. a. cocer en horno. [dería, f.

bakehouse, *–hŏŭs,* **bakery,** *–rē,* s. pana-

baker, *–ăr,* s. hornero, panadero, m.; **–'s dozen,** trece piezas.

balance, *băl'lăns,* s. balanza, f., equilibrio, m., volante de reloj, m., saldo de una cuenta, m.; **to lose one's —,** caerse, dar en tierra; —, v. a. pesar en balanza, contrapesar; saldar; considerar; examinar; —, v. n. dudar, fluctuar.

balance-sheet, *–shēt,* s. bilance, m.

balancing-pole, *băl'lănsĭngpōl,* s. balan- [cín, m.

balcony, *băl'kŏnĭ,* s. balcón, m.

bald, *bâld,* a. calvo, desabrido.

baldness, *–nĕs,* s. calvez, f., desnudez, f.

bale, *băl,* s. bala, f.; fardo de mercaderías, m., —, v. a. embalar, tirar el agua del bote.

baleful, *–fŭl,* a. triste, funesto; **–ly,** ad. tristemente, miserablemente.

balk, *băk,* s. viga, f.; contratiempo, m.; agravio, perjuicio, m.; —, v. a. frustrar; faltar á la palabra, pasar, omitir. [m.

ball, *băl,* s. bola, f., pelota, f.; bala, f., baile.

ballad, *băl'lăd,* s. balada ó balata, f.

ballad-singer, *–sĭngăr,* s. jucarero, m.

ballast, *băl'lăst,* s. lastre, m., –, v. a. lastrar.

ballet, *băl'lĕt,* s. baileto, m.

balloon, *băllŏn',* s. globo, m.; máquina aerostática, f.

ballot, *băl'lŏt,* s. bolilla para votar f.; escrutinio, m.; —, v. n. votar con balotas.

balm, *băm,* **balsam,** *băl'săm,* s. bálsamo, m.; —, v. a. untar con bálsamo, suavizar.

balmy, *–ĕ,* **balsamic,** *bălsăm'ĭk,* a. balsámico, fragante, lo que mitiga y suaviza.

baluster, *băl'ŭstăr,* s. balaustre, m.

balustrade, *bălŭstrād',* s. balaustrada, f.

bamboo, *bămbŏ',* s. bambúa, f.

bamboozle, *bămbŏ'zl,* v. a.(vulg.) engañar; causar, burlar.

ban, *băn,* s. bando, anuncio, m.; excomunión, f.; proclama, f.; —, v. a. excomulgar; maldecir.

band, *bănd,* s. venda, faja, unión, f.; cuadrilla, f., banda (de soldados), f.; orquesta, capilla, f.; —, v. a. unir, juntar, vendar.

bandage, *–ĕj,* s. venda, faja, f.; vendaje, m., —, v. a. vendar, fajar. [sombrerera, f.

bandbox, *–bŏks,* s. caja para cintas, f.]

bandit, *băn'dĭt,* s. bandido, m.

band-master, *bănd'măstăr,* s. (mus.) maestro de capilla, m.

bandy, *băn'dĭ,* v. a. pelotear; discutir.

bandy-legged, *–lĕggĕd,* a. patizambo.

bane, *băn,* s. veneno, m; ruina, f., **rat's –** arsénico, m. –, v. a. envenenar.

baneful, *–fŭl,* a. venenoso, destructivo.

bang, *băng,* s. puñada, f; golpe, m.; –, v. a. dar puñadas, sacudir; cerrar con violencia. [las indias, m.

bangle, *băng'gl,* s. brazalete delgado de

banish, *băn'nĭsh,* v a. desterrar, echar fuera, proscribir, expatriar.

banishment, *–mĕnt,* s. destierro, m

banjo, *băn'jŏ,* s. banjo, m., guitarra de los negros.

bank, *băngk,* s. orilla (de río), f., montón de tierra, f.; banco, m.; dique, m., escollo, m.; –, v. a. poner dinero en un banco; detener el agua con diques.

banker, *–ăr,* s. banquero, cambista, m.

bank-note, *–nŏt,* s. billete de banco, m.

bankrupt, *–răpt,* a. insolvente, —, s. fallido, quebrado, m. [bra, f.,

bankruptcy, *–răptsĕ,* s. bancarrota, quie-

banner, *băn'năr,* s. bandera, f., estandarte, m.

banneret, *–nărĕt,* s. ricohombre de pendón y caldera, m., bandereta, f.

bannister, *–nĭstĕr,* balaustre m.

banquet, *băng'kwĕt,* s. banquete, m.; –, v. a. banquetear.

bantam, *băn'tăm,* s. bantama, f (ave).

banter, *băn'tăr,* v. a. zumbar; divertirse á costa de alguno –, s. zumba, burla, f.

bantling, *bănt'lĭng,* s. chicuelo, m., chicuela, f.

baptise, *băp'tīz,* v. a. bautizar.

baptism, *băp'tĭzm,* s. bautismo, m.

baptismal, *băptĭz'măl,* a. bautismal.

baptistery, *băp'tĭstărĕ,* s. bautisterio, m.

bar, *băr,* s. barra, f.; tranca, f.; obstáculo, m.; (law) estrados, m. pl.; aparador, m.; –, v. a. cerrar con barras, impedir, prohibir; excluir.

barb, *bărb,* s. barba, f.; caballo de Berbería, m.; –, v. a. hacer la barba, guarnecer á un caballo con barda; armar flechas con lengüetas. [m.; –, a. bárbaro, cruel.

barbarian, *bărbăʾrĭăn,* s. hombre bárbaro.

barbarism, *băr'bărĭzm,* s. (gr.) barbarismo, m., crueldad, f. [humanidad, f.

barbarity, *bărbărʾtĭ,* s. barbaridad, in-

barbarous, *băr'bărŭs,* a. bárbaro, cruel; **–ly,** ad. bárbaramente, cruelmente.

barber, *băr'băr,* s. barbero, m.

bard, *bărd,* s. bardo, m., poeta, m.

bare, *băr,* a. desnudo, descubierto; simple; público; pobre, puro; –, v. a. desnudar, descubrir, privar. [muy flaca, f.

barebone, *–bŏn,* s. esqueleto, m.; persona

barefaced, *–făsd,* a. desvergonzado, impudente. [pos.

barefooted, *–fŭt(ĕd),* a. descalzo, sin za-

bareheaded, *–hĕd,* a. descubierto, con la cabeza al aire. [desnudas.

barelegged, *–lĕggĕd,* a. con las piernas

barely, *–lĕ,* ad. apenas, solamente, pobremente.

bareness, *–nĕs,* s. desnudez, f., pobreza, f.

bargain, *băr'gĕn,* s. contrato, pacto, m.; compra ó venta, f.; **a –! 'tis a –! ¡seal!** –, v. n. pactar, negociar.

barge, *bārj*, s. falúa, chalupa, f.

bargeman, *—măn*, **bargee**, *bārjē*, s. barquero, m.

bar-iron, *bār'īrn*, s. hierro en barras, m.

baritone, *bār'i tōn*, s. (mus.) baritono, m.

bark, *bārk*, s. corteza; ladra, f. (del perro); —, v. a. descortezar; —, v. n. ladrar.

barley, *bār'lĭ*, s. cebada, f.

barmaid, *bār'mād*, s. moza de taberna, f.

barn, *bārn*, s. granero, henil, pajar, m.

barnacles, *bār'năklz*, s. pl. acial, m.

barn-floor, *bārn'flōr*, s. era, f.; pajar, m.

barometer, *bărŏ'mĕtŭr*, s. barómetro, m.

baron, *bār'ŭn*, s. barón, m.; juez de la

baronage, *—dj*, s. baronía, f. [tesorería,m.

baroness, *—ĕs*, s. baronesa, f.

baronet, *—ĕt*, s. título de honor inferior al de barón y superior al de caballero, m.

baronial, *băr'nēąl*, a. de barón.

barony, *băr'rŭnĕ*, s. baronía, f.

barrack, *băr'răk*, s. cuartel, m. [m.

barratry, *băr'rătrē*, s. baratería, f.; engaño,

barrel, *băr'rĕl*, s. barril, m.; cañón de escopeta; cilindro, m.; —, v.a. embarrilar.

barrelled, *—d*, a. (of fire-arms) con ... cañones; (of roads) encorvado.

barrel-organ, *—ŏr'găn*, s. gaita, f.; organillo de cilindro, m.

barren, *băr'rĕn*, a. estéril, infructuoso; —ly, ad. infructuosamente, sin fruto.

barrenness, *—nĕs*, s. esterilidad, infecundidad, f.; falta de ingenio, f.; tibieza, f.

barricade, *băr'rĕkād*, s. barricada, f.; estacada, f.; barrera, f.; —, v. a. cerrar con barreras, empalizar; atrincherar. [m.

barrier, *băr'rēŭr*, s. barrera, f.; obstáculo,

barring, *băr'rĭng*, ad. excepto, fuera de.

barrister, *băr'rĭstŭr*, s. abogado, m.

bar-room, *băr'rōm*, s. taberna, f. [m.

barrow, *băr'rō*, s. angarillas, f. pl.; puerco,

barter, *băr'tŭr*, v. n. baratar, traficar; —, v. a. cambiar, trocar.

basaltes, *băsăl'tĭz*, s. basalto, m.

base, *băs*, s. fondo, m.; basa, f.; pedestal, m.; contrabajo, m.; —, v. a. apoyar; —, a. bajo, vil; —ly, ad. bajamente.

baseless, *—lĕs*, a. sin fondo ó base.

basement, *—mĕnt*, s. basamento, m.

baseness, *—nĕs*, s. bajeza, vileza, f.; ilegitimidad de nacimiento, f.; mezquinería, f.

bashaw, *băshă'*, s. bajá, m.

bashful, *băsh'fŭl*, a. vergonzoso, modesto, tímido; —ly, ad. vergonzosamente.

basilisk, *băz'zĭlĭsk*, s. basilisco, m.

basin, *bā'sn*, s. jofaina, bacía, f.

basis, *bā'sĭs*, s. base, f.; fundamento, m.

bask, *băsk*, v. n. ponerse á tomar el sol.

basket, *băs'kĕt*, s. cesta, canasta, f.

bass, *băss*, s. estera, f.; —, *băs*, (mus.) contrabajo, m.

bassoon, *băssŏŏn'*, s. bajón, m.

bass-viol, *băsvī'ŏl*, s. viola, f.

bass-voice, *băs'vŏĭs*, s. bajo cantante, m.

bastard, *băs'tărd*, s. & a. bastardo (m.).

bastardy, *—ĕ*, s. bastardía, f.

baste, *băst*, v. a. dar golpes con un bastón; pringar la carne en el asador; hilvanar.

bastinado, *băstĭnā'dŏ*, s. bastonada, f.; —, v. a. dar golpes con un bastón.

basting, *băs'tĭng*, s. hilván, m.; apaleamiento, m., paliza, f.

bastion, *băs'yŏn*, s. (mil.) bastión, m.

bat, *băt*, s. garrote, m.; murciélago, m.

batch, *bătsh*, s. cochura, hornada, f.

bate, *băt*, v. a. minorar; bajar el precio.

bat-fowling, *băt'fŏŭlĭng*, s. caza de pájaros

bath, *băth*, s. baño, m. [por la noche, f.

bathe, *băth*, v. a. (& n.) bañar(se). [m.

bathing-gown, *bā'thĭnggŏŭn*, s. peinador,

bath-keeper, *băth'kēpŭr*, s. bañero, m.

bathos, *bā'thŏs*, s. estilo bajo en la poesía, m.

bath-tub, *băth'tŭb*, s. baño, m. (la cuba).

battalion, *băttăl'yăn*, s. (mil.) batallón, m.

batten, *băt'tn*, s. astilla, f.; —, v. a. cebar; —, v. n. engordar.

batter, *băt'tŭr*, v. a. apalear; batir, cañonear; demoler; —, s. batido, m.

battering-ram, *—ĭngrăm*, s. (mil.) ariete,

battery, *—ē*, s. batería, f. [m.

battle, *băt'tl*, s. combate, m.; batalla, f.; —, v. n. batallar, combatir.

battle-array, *—ărrā*, s. orden de batalla, f.

battledore, *—dŏr*, s. raqueta, f.

battlement, *—mĕnt*, s. muralla almenada, f.

bauble, *bă'bl*, s. chuchería, cosa de poca importancia, pero pulida y delicada, f.

bawl, *băl*, v. n. gritar, vocear; ladrar.

bay, *bā*, s. puerto donde se abrigan las embarcaciones, m.; bahía, f.; laurel, lauro, m.; —, v. n. ladrar; balar; —, a. bayo.

bayonet, *bā'ŏnĕt*, s. bayoneta, f.; —, v.a. traspasar con la bayoneta.

bay-window, *bā'wĭndŏ*, s. ventana sale-

be, *bē*, v. n. ser; estar. [diza, f.

beach, *bētsh*, s. costa, ribera, orilla, f.; cabo, m.; —, v. a. (mar.) encallar.

beacon, *bēk'n*, s. valiza, almenara, f.

bead, *bēd*, s. cuenta, f.; —s, s. pl. rosario, m.

beadle, *bē'dl*, s. macero, m.; bedel (en las universidades), m.; alguacil, ministril, m. (en los tribunales).

beagle, *bē'gl*, s. sabueso, m.

beak, *bēk*, s. pico; espolón de navío, m.

beaker, *—ŭr*, s. taza con pico, f.

beam, *bēm*, s. lanza de coche, f.; rayo de luz, m.; volante, m.; brazos de balanza, m. pl.; —, v. n. emitir rayos, brillar. [m.

bean, *bēn*, s. haba, f.; French —, faséolo,

bear, *băr*, v. a. llevar alguna cosa como carga; sostener, apoyar; soportar; producir; parir; —, v. n. sufrir (algún dolor); pasar á algún paraje.

bear, *—*, s. oso, m.; she —, osa, f.

bearable, *—ăbl*, a. soportable.

beard, *bērd*, s. barba, f.; arista de espiga, f.; —, v. a. insultar á uno.

bearded, *—ĕd*, a. barbado.

beardless, *—lĕs*, a. desbarbado, joven.

bearer, *băr'ŭr*, s. portador, m.; árbol fructífero.

bearing, *băr'ĭng*, s. situación, f.; modo de portarse en lo exterior, m.; dolor, m.

beast, *bēst*, s. bestia, f.; hombre brutal, m.; — of burden, acémila, f.

beastliness, *—lĭnĕs*, s. bestialidad, brutalidad, f. [inente.

beastly, *—lĭ*, a. bestial, brutal; —, ad. bestial-

beat, *bēt*, v. a. golpear; batir; tocar (un

tambor); pisar, abatir; —, v. n. pulsar,
palpitar; —, s. golpe, m.; pulsación, f.
beatific, *bēătĭf'ĭk*, a. beatífico.
beatify, *bē'ăt'ĭfī*, v. a. beatificar, santificar.
beating, *bēt'ĭng*, s. paliza, zurra, f.; pulsación, f.   [f.
beatitude, *bēăt'ĭtŭd*, s. beatitud, felicidad,
beau, *bō*, s. petimetre, currutaco, m.
beauteous, *bū'tĭŭs*, a. bello, hermoso.
beautiful, *bū'tĭfŭl*, a. hermoso, bello; **-ly**,
ad. con belleza ó perfección.
beautify, *bū'tĭfī*, v. a. hermosear; embellecer; adornar; —, v. n. hermosearse.
beauty, *bū'tĕ*, s. hermosura, belleza, f.
--spot, s. lunar, m.
beaver, *bē'vûr*, s. castor, m.; sombrero
de pelo de castor, m.
becalm, *bĕkäm'*, v. a. serenar, calmar alguna tempestad; sosegar.
because, *bĕkăz'*, c. porque, á causa de.
beck, *bĕk*, s. seña, indicación muda, f.
beckon, *bĕk'n*, v. n. hacer seña con la
cabeza, ó la mano.
become, *bĕkŭm'*, v. a. convenir, estar bien;
—, v. n. hacerse, convertirse, venir á parar.
becoming, *bĕkŭm'ĭng*, a. decente, conveniente; **-ly**, ad. decentemente.
becomingness, *-nĕs*, s. decencia, elegancia, propiedad, f.   [cama, acostar.
bed, *bĕd*, s. cama, f.; —, v. a. meter en la
bedaub, *bĕdăb'*, v. a. salpicar; ensuciar.
bed-chamber, *bĕd'tshämbûr*, s. dormitorio, m.   [mantas ó colchas, pl.
bed-clothes, *-klōz*, s. pl. cobertores,
bedding, *-ĭng*, s. ropa de cama, f.
bedecked, *bĕdĕk'd*, a. adornado.
bedew, *bĕdū'*, v. a. rociar; regar.
bedim, *bĕdĭm'*, v. a. obscurecer.
bedizen, *bĕdī'zn*, v. a. ataviar, perifollar.
bedlam, *bĕd'lăm*, s. manicomio, m.
bedlamite, *-īt*, s. loco, orate, m.
bed-post, *bĕd'pōst*, s. pilar de cama, m.
bedraggle, *bĕdrăg'gl*, v. a. vulg. enlodar.
bedridden, *bĕd'rĭdn*, a. postrado en cama
(sea por vejez ó enfermedad).
bedstead, *-stĕd*, s. armazón de cama, f.
bed-time, *-tĭm*, s. hora de irse á la cama, f.
bee, *bē*, s. abeja, f.
beech, *bētsh*, s. haya, f.
beechen, *-n*, a. de haya.
beech-nut, *-nŭt*, s. hayuco, m.
beef, *bēf*, s. buey (toro ó vaca), m.; **beeves,**
bēvz, pl., ganado vacuno, m.
beef-eater, *-tûr*, s. alabardero real, m.
beef-fork, *-fôrk*, s. tenedor de cocina, m.
beef-steak, *-stăk*, s. lonja de carne de
beef-tea, *-tē*, s. caldo, m.   [vaca, f.
bee-hive, *bē'hĭv*, s. colmena, f.
bee-line, *-lĭn*, s. línea recta, f. [floja, f.
beer, *bēr*, s. cerveza, f.; **small** —, cerveza
beeswax, *bēs'wăks*, s. cera, f.
beet, *bēt*, s. acelga, f.
beetle, *-l*, s. escarabajo, m.; pisón, m.
beet-root, *-rōt*, s. betarraga, f. [venir.
befall, *bĕfăl'*, v. n. suceder, acontecer, sobre-
befit, *bĕfĭt'*, v. a. convenir, acomodarse á.
befool, *bĕfōl'*, v. a. infatuar.
before, *bĕfōr'*, ad. & pr. más adelante; delante, enfrente, ante, antes de.

beforehand, *-hănd*, ad. de antemano,
anticipadamente.   [tiempo atrás.
beforetime, *-tĭm*, ad. en tiempo pasado,
befoul, *bĕfŏul'*, v. a. ensuciar, emporcar.
befriend, *bĕfrĕnd'*, v. a. favorecer, proteger, amparar.
beg, *bĕg*, v. a. mendigar, rogar; suplicar;
suponer; —, v. n. vivir de limosna.
beget, *bĕgĕt'*, v. a. engendrar.   [pobrecer.
beggar, *bĕg'gûr*, s. mendigo, m.; —, v. a. em-
beggarliness, *-lĭnĕs*, s. miseria, mezquindad, pobreza, miseria, f.
beggarly, *-lĕ*, a. pobre, miserable; —, ad.
mezquinamente, pobremente.
beggary, *-ĕ*, s. mendicidad, mendiguez, f.
begin, *bĕgĭn'*, v. a. & n. comenzar, principiar.
beginner, *-nûr*, s. principiante, m.; novicio, m.   [-s, pl. rudimentos, m. pl.
beginning, *-nĭng*, s. principio, origen, m.
begone, *bĕgŏn'*! ¡fuera, apártate de ahí!
begrime, *bĕgrīm'*, v. a. encenagar, ennegrecer, embarrar, manchar.
begrudge, *bĕgrŭj'*, v. a. envidiar.
beguile, *bĕgīl'*, v. a. engañar.
behalf, *bĕhăf'*, s. favor, patrocinio, m.;
consideración, f.   [bien ó mal.
behave, *bĕhāv'*, v. n. comportarse, portarse
behaviour, *bĕhāv'yûr*, s. conducta, f.;
modo de portarse, m.   [cabeza.
behead, *bĕhĕd'*, v. a. decapitar, cortar la
behest, *bĕhĕst'*, s. mandato, precepto, m.
behind, *bĕhīnd'*, pr. detrás; atrás; inferior
á; —, ad. atrasadamente; fuera de la vista.
behindhand, *-hănd*, ad. con atraso.
behold, *bĕhōld'*, v. a. ver, contemplar, observar; —! ¡he aquí! ¡vele ahí!
beholden, *-n*, a. obligado (por gratitud).
behoof, *bĕhōf'*, s. provecho, m.; utilidad,
ventaja, f.   [ó necesario.
behove, *bĕhōv'*, v. n. importar, ser útil
being, *bē'ĭng*, s. existencia, f.; estado, m.,
ente, m.; persona (que existe), f.; —, c. ya
que, puesto que.   [das.
belabour, *bĕlā'bûr*, v. n. apalear, dar puña-
belated, *bĕlā'tĕd*, a. trasnochado.
belch, *bĕlsh*, v. n. eructar, vomitar; —, s.
eructo, m.; eructación, f.
beldam, *bĕl'dăm*, s. vejezuela, f.; bruja, f.
beleaguer, *bĕlē'gûr*, v. a. sitiar, bloquear.
belfry, *bĕl'frĕ*, s. campanario, m.
belie, *bĕlī'*, v. a. contrahacer, desmentir,
calumniar.   [f.; credo, m.
belief, *bĕlēf'*, s. fe, creencia, f.; opinión,
believable, *bĕlēv'ăbl*, a. creíble.
believe, *bĕlēv'*, v. a. creer; —, v. n. pensar,
imaginar.   [m.
believer, *-ûr*, s. creyente, fiel, cristiano,
bell, *bĕl*, s. campana, f.: **to bear the —,** ser
el primero; —, v. n. crecer una planta en
figura de campana; gritar (como los
ciervos).
bellicose, *bĕl'lĕkōs*, a. belicoso.
belligerent, *bĕl'lĭj'ûrĕnt*, a. beligerante.
bellman, *bĕl'măn*, s. pregonero, m.
bellow, *bĕl'lō*, v. n. bramar; rugir; vociferar, —, s. bramido, m.
bellows, *bĕl'lōz* (vulg. *bĕl'lŭs*), s. fuelle, m.
bell-pull, *bĕl'pŭl*, **bell-rope,** *-rōp*, s.
conductor de una campanilla, m.

bell-ringer, -ríngŭr, s. campanero, m.

belly, bĕl'lĭ, s. vientre, m.; panza, f.

bellyful, -fŭl, s. panzada, f.; hartura, f.

belong, bĕlóng', v. n. pertenecer, tocar á, concernir.

belongings, -ĭngs, s. pl. calidades, f. pl.

beloved, bĕlŭvd', a. querido, amado.

below, bĕlō', ad. & pr. debajo, inferior;

belt, bĕlt, s. cinturón, cinto, m.　　　[abajo.

bemoan, bĕmōn', v. a. deplorar, lamentar.

bench, bĕnsh, s. banco, m.; **King's—**, tribunal principal de justicia, m.; una prisión

bencher, -ŭr, s. asesor, m.　　[de Londres.

bend, bĕnd, v. a. encorvar, inclinar, plegar; hacer una reverencia; —, v. n. encorvarse, inclinarse; —, s. comba, encorvadura, f.

beneath, bĕnēth', ad. & pr. debajo, abajo; de lo más hondo.　　　　　　　　　　[f.

benediction, bĕnĕdĭk'shŭn, s. bendición, f.

benefaction, bĕnĕfăk'shŭn, s. beneficio, m.; gracia, f.

benefactor, -tŭr, s. bienhechor, m.

benefactress, -trĕs, s. bienhechora, f.

benefice, bĕn'nĕfĭs, s. beneficio, m.; beneficio eclesiástico.

beneficence, bĕnĕf'ĭsĕns, s. beneficencia, liberalidad, f.　　　　　　　　[benéficamente.

beneficent, -fĭsĕnt, a. benéfico; -ly, ad.

beneficial, bĕnĕfĭsh'ăl, a. beneficioso, provechoso, útil · -ly, ad. provechosamente, ventajosamente.

beneficiary, -fĭĭrĕ, s. beneficiario, m.

benefit, bĕn'nĕfĭt, s. beneficio, m.; utilidad, f.; provecho, m.; —, v. a. beneficiar; —, v. n. utilizarse; prevalerse.

benefit-night, -nīt, s. representacion dramática al beneficio de un actor ó de una actriz, f.

benevolence, bĕnĕv'ŏlĕns, s. benevolencia, f.; donativo gratuito, m.

benevolent, -ŏlĕnt, a. benévolo.

benighted, bĕnīt'ĕd, (p. &) a. anochecido.

benign, bĕnīn', a. benigno; afable; liberal; -ly, ad. benignamente.

benignant, bĕnĭg'nănt, a. bondadoso.

benignity, -nĭtĕ, s. benignidad, bondad, dulzura, f.

bent, bĕnt, s. encorvadura, f.; inclinación, f.

benumb, bĕnŭm', v. a. entorpecer.　　[f.

benzine, bĕn'zĕn, s. (chem.) benzina, f.

benzoin, bĕn'zŏĭn, s. benjuí, m.　　[camente.

bepraise, bĕprās', v. a. lisonjear hiperbóli-

bequeath, bĕkwēth', v. a. legar en testa-

bequeather, -ŭr, s. testador, m.　　[mento.

bequest, bĕkwĕst', s. legado, m.

bereave, bĕrēv', v. a. despojar, privar.

bereavement, -mĕnt, s. despojo, m.

berlin, bĕr'lĭn, s. berlina, f. (coche).

berry, bĕr'rĕ, s. baya, f.　　　　　[navío, m.

berth, bŭrth, s. (mar.) alojamiento de un

beseech, bĕsēch', v. a. suplicar, implorar, conjurar, rogar.

beseem, bĕsēm', v. n. convenir, parecer bien.

beseeming, -ĭng, s. gracia, decencia, f.

beset, bĕsĕt', v. a. sitiar; cercar; perseguir.

besetting, -tĭng, a. habitual.

beside(s), bĕsīd(s)', pr. al lado de ; excepto ; sobre; fuera de ; —, ad. por otra parte, aun.

besiege, bĕsēj', v. a. sitiar, bloquear.

besmear, bĕsmēr', v. a. salpicar, ensuciar.

besot, bĕsŏt', v. a. infatuar; embrutecer.

bespatter, bĕspăt'tŭr, v. a. manchar con porquería; disfamar.　　　　　[alguna cosa.

bespeak, bĕspēk', v. a. ordenar, apalabrar

besprinkle, bĕsprĭng'kl, v. a. rociar, esparcir sobre.　　　　　　　　　　　　[lo mejor.

best, bĕst. a. mejor; —, ad. más bien ; —, s.

bestial, bĕst'yăl, a. bestial, brutal; -ly, ad. bestialmente.　　　　　　[brutalidad, f.

bestiality, bĕstyăl'ĭtĕ, s. bestialidad,

bestir, bĕstŭr', v. n. removerse, intrigar.

bestow, bĕstō' v. a. dar, conferir; otorgar; dar en matrimonio; regalar.

bestowal, -ăl, s. donativo, m.

bestrew, bĕstrē', v. a. esparcir ó derramar sobre; polvorear, salpicar.

bet, bĕt, s. apuesta, f.; —, v. a. apostar.

betake, bĕtāk', v. a. recurrir, acudir; — one's self to, aplicarse.

bethink, bĕthĭnk', v. a. recordar algo; —, v. n. considerar, pensar.

betide, bĕtīd', v. n. acaecer, suceder.

betoken, bĕtō'kn, v. a. anunciar; denotar.

betime(s), bĕtīm(z)', ad. con tiempo, en sazón; pronto.　　　　[gar algún secreto.

betray, bĕtrā', v. a. hacer traición; divulgar algún secreto.

betrayal, -ăl, s. traición, f.

betroth, bĕtrŏth', v. a. contraer esponsales.

betrothal, -ăl, s. esponsales, m. pl.

better, bĕt'tŭr, a. & ad. mejor; mejor, más bien; **so much the—**, tanto mejor; **—s**, s. pl. superiores, m. pl.; —, v. a. mejorar, reformar.

bettor, bĕt'tŭr, s. apostador, m.

between, bĕtwēn', **betwixt**, bĕtwĭkst', pr. entre, en medio de; **—whiles**, (vulg.) á ratos, mientras tanto.

bevel, bĕv'ĕl, s. cartabón, m.; —, v. a. cortar un ángulo al sesgo.　　　　　　　[m.

beverage, bĕv'ŭrăj, s. bebida, f.; trago,

bevy, bĕv'ĕ, s. bandada (de aves), f.

bewail, bĕwāl', v. a. lamentar, deplorar.

beware, bĕwār', v. n. guardarse.

bewilder, bĕwĭl'dŭr, v. a. descaminar; embarazar; pasmar; —, v. n. extraviarse.

bewilderment, -mĕnt, s. extravío, m.; embarazo, m.

bewitch, bĕwĭtsh', v. a. encantar, hechizar.

bewitchingly, -ĭnglĕ, ad. halagüeñamente.　　　　　　　　　[lante, fuera de.

beyond, bĕyŏnd', pr. más allá, más ade-

bezel, bĕz'ĕl, s. chatón, m.

bezoar, bĕz'ōr, s. bezar, m.

bias, bī'ăs, s. propensión, inclinación, f.; sesgo, m.; objeto, fin, m.; —, v. a. inclinar; preocupar; ganar.

bib, bĭb, s. babador, m.

bibber, -bŭr, s. bebedor, borrachón, m.

Bible, bī'bl. s. Biblia (la sagrada escritura), f.

biblical, bĭb'lĭkăl, a. bíblico.　　　　[f.

bibliography, bĭblĕŏg'răfĕ, s. bibliografía,

bicker, bĭk'kŭr, v. n. escaramucear, reñir, disputar.

bickern, -n, s. pico de bigornia, m.

bid, bĭd, v. a. convidar; mandar, ordenar; ofrecer; **— adieu to**, despedirse.

bidding, -dĭng, s. orden, f., mandato, m.; ofrecimiento m.

bide, *bīd,* v. a. sufrir, aguantar; —, v. n.
biennial, *bīén'niäl,* a. bienal. [residir.
bier, *bér,* s. féretro, ataúd, m.
biffin, *bĭf'fīn,* s. manzana cocida en el horno, f. [puntas ó dientes.
bifurcated, *bĭfŭr'kātéd,* a. dividido en dos
big, *bĭg,* a. grande, lleno; inflado.
bigamist, *bĭg'ămĭst,* s. bígamo, m.
bigamy, *bĭg'ăme,* s. bigamia, f.
bight, *bīt,* s. bahía, f. [bulto, m.
bigness, *bĭg'nĕs,* s. grandeza, f.; tamaño,
bigot, *bĭg'ŏt,* s. beatón, m.; hipócrita, m.
bigoted, *—ĕd,* a. santurrón, beatón; —ly, ad. como un santurrón.
bilander, *bĭl'ăndăr,* s. balandra, f.
bilberry, *bĭl'bĕrrĕ,* s. arándano, f.
bilbo, *bĭl'bō,* s. estoque, m.; —es, s. pl. cepo con grillos, m.
bile, *bīl,* s. bilis, f.; cólera, f. [hacer agua.
bilge, *bĭlj,* s. pantoque, m.; —, v. a. (mar.)
bilious, *bĭl'yŭs,* a. bilioso.
bilk, *bĭlk,* v. a. engañar, defraudar.
bill, *bĭll,* s. pico de ave, m.; honcejo, m.; papel, billete, m.; cédula, f.; cuenta, f.; — of exchange, letra de cambio, f.; doctor's —, receta de médico, f.; - of lading, conocimiento, m.; - of fare, minuta ó lista de una comida, f.; —s, pl. letras de cambio, cartas de pago, f. pl.; —s-payable, s. letras pagaderas; —s-receivable, s. letras aceptables; —, v. n. arrullar, acariciar. [dor, m.
bill-broker, *—brōkăr,* s. agiotador, corre-
billet, *bĭl'lĕt,* s. billete, m.; zoquete de leña, m.; —, v. a. alojar soldados.
billiard-ball, *bĭl'yărdbŏl,* s. bola de billar, f.
billiard-pocket, *—pŏkkĕt,* s. bolsa en las mesas de billar, f.
billiards, *—z,* s. billar, m.
billiard-table, *—tábl,* s. mesa de billar, f.
Billingsgate, *bĭl'ĭngsgāt,* s. pescadería en Londres, f.; lenguaje bajo, m.
billion, *bĭl'yŭn,* s. millón de millones, m.
billow, *bĭl'ō,* s. ola grande, f.
billowy, *—ē,* a. hinchado como las olas.
bill-poster, *bĭl'pōstăr,* **bill-sticker,** *—stĭkkăr,* s. fijacarteles, m.
bin, *bĭn,* s. artesón, cofre, m.; armario, m.; despensa, f.
bind, *bīnd,* v. a. atar; unir; encuadernar; obligar, constreñir; impedir; poner á uno á servir; —, v. n. ser obligatorio.
binder, *—ăr,* s. encuadernador, m.
binding, *—ĭng,* s. venda, faja, f.
binnacle, *bĭn'ăkl,* s. (mar.) bitácora, f.
binocular, *bĭnŏk'ŭlăr,* a. (opt.) binocular.
biographer, *bīŏg'răfăr,* s. biógrafo, m.
biographical, *bīŏgrăf'ĭkăl,* a. biográfico.
biography, *bīŏg'răfē,* s. biografía, f.
biped, *bī'pĕd,* s. bípede, m.
birch, *bŭrtsh,* s. abedul, m.; —, v. a. varear.
birchen, *—n,* a. de abedul.
bird, *bŭrd,* s. ave, f.; pájaro, m.; —, v. n. cazar ó coger pájaros.
bird-lime, *—līm,* s. liga, f. [jaro, f.
bird's eye-view, *—s'ī vū,* s. vista de pá-
birth, *bŭrth,* s. nacimiento, m.; origen, m.; parto, m.; puesto, m.; alojamiento de un navío, m.

birth-day, *—dā,* s. cumpleaños, m.
birth-place, *—plās,* s. suelo nativo, m.
birth-right, *—rīt,* s. derechos de nacimiento, m. pl.; primogenitura, f.
biscuit, *bĭs'kĭt,* s. bizcocho, m.
bisect, *bĭsĕkt',* v. a. dividir en dos partes.
bishop, *bĭsh'ŭp,* s. obispo, m.
bishopric, *—rĭk,* s. obispado, m.
bismuth, *bĭz'măth,* s. bismuto, m.
bison, *bī'zŏn,* s. bisonte, m.
bit, *bĭt,* s. bocado, m.; pedacito, m.; - of a bridle, bocado del freno, m.; - of a key, paletón de llave, m.; —, v. a. enfrenar.
bitch, *bĭtsh,* s. perra, f.; (fig.) zorra, f.
bite, *bīt,* v. a. morder; punzar, picar; satirizar; engañar; —the dust, fam. morder la tierra, morir; —, s. mordedura, f.; engañador, impostor, ladrón, m.
bitter, *bĭt'tăr,* a. amargo, áspero; mordaz, satírico; penoso; —ly, ad. amargamente; con pena; severamente.
bittern, *—n,* s. alcaraván, bitor, m.
bitterness, *—nĕs,* s. amargor, m.; rencor, m.; pena, f.; dolor, m.
bitumen, *bĭtŭ'mĕn,* s. betún, m.
bituminous, *—mĭnŭs,* a. bituminoso.
bivouac, *bĭv'ăk,* s. (mil.) vivac, vivaque, m.; —, v. n. vivaquear.
bizarre, *bĭzăr',* a. raro, extravagante.
blab, *blăb,* v. a. parlar, charlar, divulgar; —, v n. chismear; —s. chismoso, soplón, m.
black, *blăk,* a. negro, obscuro; tétrico, malvado; funesto; —, s. color negro, m.; —, v. a. teñir de negro, negrecer; limpiar (las botas).
blackamoor, *—ămōr,* s. negro, m.
black-art, *—ărt,* s. nigromancia, f.
black-ball, *—bŏl,* v. a. excluir á uno votando con una bolita negra. [sano).
black-beetle, *—bētl,* s. farinal, m. (gu-
blackberry, *—bĕrrĕ,* s. zarzamora, f.
blackbird, *—bŭrd,* s. merla, f. [f.
black-board, *—bōrd,* s. tabla, plancha,
black-book, *—bŭk,* s. libro de nigromancia, m.; (mil.) lista de castigos, f. [m.
black-cattle, *—kăttl,* s. ganado vacuno,
black-draught, *—drắft,* s. infusión de sene, f. [grecer.
blacken, *—n,* v. a. teñir de negro; enne-
blackfriar, *—frī ăr,* s. dominicano, m.
blackguard, *—gărd,* s. hombre soez, galopín, m.
black-lead, *—lĕd,* s. lápiz-plomo, m.
blackleg, *—lĕg,* s. bribón, m.
black-letter, *—lĕttăr,* s. letra gótica, f.
blackmail, *—māl,* s. tributo ó rascate que los viajeros pagan á los salteadores, m.
blackness, *—nĕs,* s. negrura, f.
black-pudding, *—pŭddĭng,* s. morcilla, f.
black-sheep, *—shēp,* s. oveja sarnosa, f.
blacksmith, *—smĭth,* s. herrero, m.
black-thorn, *—thŏrn,* s. endrino, m.
bladder, *blăd'dăr,* s. vejiga, f.
blade, *blād,* s. brizna, f.; hoja, f.; pala (de remo), f.; jaquetón, m.
blamable, *blā'măbl,* a. culpable; vituperable; —bly, ad. culpablemente.
blame, *blām,* v. a. vituperar; —, s. culpa, f.; vituperación, imputación, f.

blameless, -*lĕs*, a. inocente, irreprensible, puro; -**ly,** ad. inocentemente.

blanch, *blănsh*, v. a. blanquear; mondar, pelar; hacer pálido. [cible.

bland, *blănd*, a. blando, suave, dulce, apa-

blandishment, -*ĭshmĕnt*, s. halago, m.; zalamería, f.; caricia, f.

blank, *blăngk*, a. blanco; pálido; (poet.) sin rima; confuso; —, s. blanco, m.; carta blanca, f. [quilla, f. (especie de pera).

blanket, -*ĕt*, s. cubierta de cama; blan-

blaspheme, *blăsfēm'*, v.a.blasfemar, jurar, decir blasfemias.

blasphemous, *blăs'fēmŭs*, a. blasfematorio; -**ly,** ad. blasfemamente.

blasphemy, *blăs'fēmĕ*, s. blasfemia, f.

blast, *blăst*, s. soplo de aire, m.; influjo de astro maligno, m.; anublo, m.; —, v. a. marchitar, secar; arruinar; infamar; volar por medio de pólvora. [m.

blast-furnace, -*fŭrnăs*, s. horno soplante.

blatant, *blă'tănt*, a. vocinglero.

blaze, *blāz*, s. llama, f.; rumor, m.; estrella, f.; —, v. n. encenderse en llama; brillar, resplandecer; —, v. a. inflamar; divulgar.

blazon, *blā'zn*, v. a. blasonar; decorar; blazonry, -*rĕ*, s. blasón, m. [publicar.

bleach, *blētsh*, v.a. blanquear al sol; —, v. n. blanquear. [helado.

bleak, *blēk*, a. pálido, descolorido; frío; **bleakness,** -*nĕs*, s. frialdad, f.; palidez, f.

blear(-eyed), *blēr'(ĭd)*, a. lagañoso.

blearedness, -*ĕdnĕs*, s. lagaña, f.

bleat, *blēt*, s. balido, m.; —, v. n. balar.

bleed, *blēd*, v. n. sacar sangre; —, v. a. **bleeding,** -*ĭng*, s. sangría, f. [sangrar.

blemish, *blĕm'ĭsh*, v. a. manchar, ensuciar; infamar; —, s. tacha, f.; deshonra, infamia, f. [brarse.

blench, *blĕnsh*, v. a. obstar; —, v. n. asom-

blend, *blĕnd*, v. a. mezclar, confundir

bless, *blĕs*, v. a. bendecir, alabar; - me! buen Dios! [santidad, beatitud, f.

blessedness, -*ĕdnĕs*, s. felicidad, f.;

blessing, -*ĭng*, s. bendición, f.; favores del cielo, m. pl.

blight, *blīt*, s. tizón, m.; pulgón, m.; alheña, f.; —, v. a. añeblar las mieses.

blind, *blīnd*, a. ciego; oculto; obscuro; - **alley,** s. callejón sin salida, m.; —, v. a. cegar; deslumbrar; -, s. velo, m.; (**Venetian** -,) persiana, f.

blindfold, -*fōld*, v. a. vendar los ojos; —, a. con los ojos vendados.

blindly, -*lĕ*, ad. ciegamente á ciegas.

blindman's-buff, -*mănsbŭf*, s. gallina ciega, f. (un juego). [f.

blindness, -*nĕs*, s. ceguedad, alucinación,

blind-side, -*sīd*, s. el flaco de alguna persona, f.

blind-worm, -*wŭrm*, s. cecilia, f.

blink, *blĭngk*, v. n. guiñar, cerrar los ojos; echar llama; —, v. ojeada, f.

blinker, -*ŭr*, s. antojera, f.

bliss, *blĭs*, s. felicidad (eterna), f.

blissful, -*fŭl*, a. feliz en sumo grado; beato, bienaventurado; -**ly,** ad. felizmente. [dad, f.

blissfulness, -*fŭlnĕs*, s. suprema felici-

blister, *blĭs'tŭr*, s. vejiga, ampolla, f.; vejigatorio, m.; —, v n. ampollarse; —, v. a. aplicar un vejigatorio.

blithe, *blĭth*, a. alegre, contento, gozoso.

blizzard, *blĭz'zărd*, -s. (am.) huracán, m.

bloat, *blōt*, v. a. hinchar; —, v. n. entumecerse; —, a. hinchado, turgente.

bloatedness, -*ĕdnĕs*, s. turgencia, f.

bloater, -*ŭr*, s. arenque ahumado, m.

block, *blŏk*, s. zoquete, m.; horma (de sombrero), f.; tajo de cocina, m.; obstáculo, m.; —(**up**), v. a. bloquear.

blockade, -*kād'*, s. bloqueo, m.; —, v. a. bloquear. [m.

blockhead, -*hĕd*, s. bruto, necio, zopenco,

blockship, -*shĭp*, s. barco costeño, m.

block-system, -*sĭstĕm*, s. (rail.) sistema de cobertura de una vía, m.

block-up, -*ŭp*, s. embarazo, m.

blond, *blŏnd*, s. blonda, f.

blood, *blŭd*, s. sangre, f.; linaje, parentesco, m.; ira, cólera, f.; —, v. a. ensangrentar; exasperar.

blood-guiltiness, -*gĭltĕnĕs*,s. homicidio, asesinato, m.

blood-hound, -*hŏŭnd*, s. sabueso, m.

bloodily, -*ĭlĕ* ad. cruelmente, inhumanamente.

bloodiness, -*ĭnĕs*, s. (fig.) crueldad, f.

bloodless, -*lĕs*, a. exangüe; sin efusión de sangre; muerto. [botomísta, m.

blood-letter, -*lĕttŭr*, s. sangrador, fle-

blood-letting, -*lĕttĭng*, s. sangría, f.

bloodshed, -*shĕd*, s. efusión de sangre, f.; matanza, f.

bloodshot, -*shŏt*, a. ensangrentado.

blood-sucker, -*sŭkkŭr*, s. sanguijuela, f.; (fig.) desollador, m.

blood-vessel, -*vĕssl*, s. vena, f.; canal de la sangre, m.

bloody, -*ĕ*, a. sangriento, ensangrentado; cruel; -**flux,** s. disentería, f.; --**minded,** a. sanguinario.

bloom, *blōm*, s. flor, f.; (also fig.); —, v. n. florecer.

blossom, *blŏs'sŭm*, s. flor, f.

blot, *blŏt*, v. a. manchar (lo escrito); cancelar; denigrar; —, s. canceladura; mancha,f.

blotch, *blŏtsh*, s. roncha, f.

blotting-case, *blŏt'tĭngkăs*, -**pad,** -*păd*, s. papelera, f.

blotting-paper, -*păpŭr*, s. papel de secar, m.; teleta, f.

blouse, *blŏŭs*, s. blusa, f., sobretodo de tela, en forma de camisa.

blow, *blō*, v. n. soplar; sonar; florecer; —, v. a. soplar; inflar; calentar algo con el aliento; **to - up,** volar(se) por medio de pólvora; -, s. golpe, m.

blow-pipe, -*pīp*, s. soplete, m.

blubber, *blŭb'bŭr*, s. grasa de ballena, f. —, v. n. & a: llorar hasta hincharse los carrillos. [guíes, m. pl.

bluchers, *blō'tshŭrz*, s. pl. botines, borce-

bludgeon, *blŭj'ŭn*, s. cachiporra, f.; palocorto, m.

blue, *blū*, a. azul; —, v. a. teñir de azul.

blue-bottle, -*bŏttl*, s. (bot.) campanilla, f.; coróni da, f. (mosca).

blue-devils, *–dĕvlz,* blues, *blűz,* s. pl. mal de bazo, m.; hipocondría, f.

blue-eyed, *–īd,* a. ojizarco.

blueness, *–nĕs,* s. color azul, m.

blue-peter, *–pētăr,* s. (mar.) pabellón de partida, m. [f.

blue-stocking, *–stŏkking,* s. mujer docta.

bluff, *blŭf,* a. rústico; rudo; –, v. a. vendar los ojos.

bluffness, *–nĕs,* s. asperidad, rusticidad, f.

bluish, *blűīsh,* a. azulado.

blunder, *blăn'dŭr,* s. desatino, m.; error craso, m.; atolondramiento, m.; –, v. a. & n. confundir; desatinar. [corta).

blunderbuss, *–bŭss,* s. trabuco, m. (escopeta

blunt, *blŭnt,* a. obtuso; lerdo; bronco; grosero; –, v. a. embotar; enervar; calmar (un dolor). [obtusamente.

bluntly, *–lĕ,* ad. sin artificio; claramente;

bluntness, *–nĕs,* s. embotadura, grosería, f.

blur, *blŭr,* s. mancha, f.; –, v. a. manchar; defamar. [y á locas.

blurt(out), *blŭrt(ŏŭt),* v.a. hablar á tontas

blush, *blŭsh,* s. rubor, m.; sonrojo, m.; –, v. n. ponerse colorado (de vergüenza).

bluster, *blŭs'tŭr,* s. ruido, tumulto, m.; jactancia, f.; –, v. n. hacer ruido tempestuoso.

blusterous, *–ŭs,* a. tumultuoso, tempestuoso; violento.

boa, *bŏă,* s. boá, f. (serpiente); pelerina, f. (vestido de mujeres).

boar, *bōr,* s. verraco, m.; **wild** –, jabalí, m.

board, *bōrd,* s. tabla, f.; mesa, f.; tribunal, consejo, m.; (mar.) puente, m.; –, v. a. abordar; entablar; –, v. n. estar á pupilaje; tomar pupilos.

boarder, *–ăr,* s. pensionista, pupilo, m.

boarding-house, *–ĭnghŏŭs,* s. casa de pupilos, f.; casa de huéspedes.

boarding-school, *–ĭngskōl,* s. casapensión, f.

board-wages, *–wājĕz,* s. ración en dinero que se da á los criados para mantenerse, f.

boast, *bōst,* v. n. jactarse; –, s. jactancia, f.; ostentación, f.

boastful, *–fŭl,* a. jactancioso.

boat, *bōt,* s. bote, m.; barca, chalupa, f.

boathook, *–hōk,* s. (mar.) cloque, bichero, m.

boatman, *–măn,* s. barquero, m. [m.

boating, *bōt'ĭng,* s. barcaje, m.; paseo en barquilla, m.; regata, f.

boatswain, *bō'sn,* s. contramaestre, m.

bob, *bŏb,* s. pinzajo, m.; pendiente de oreja, m.; pulla, chufleta, f.; (cant) chelín, m.; –, v.a. apalear; engañar; –, v.n.bambolear.

bobbin, *–bĭn,* s. canilla, broca, f.

bobtail, *–tāl,* s. rabón, f.; cola cortada, f.

bode, *bōd,* v. a. presagiar, pronosticar.

bodice, *bŏd'īs,* s. corsé, m.; cotilla, f.

bodied, *bŏd'īd,* a. corpóreo.

bodiless, *bŏd'īlĕs,* a. incorpóreo.

bodiliness, *bŏd'īlīnĕs,* a. corporeidad.

bodily, *bŏd'īlĕ,* a. & ad. corpóreo; corporalmente. [aguja de jareta, f.

bodkin, *bŏd'kĭn,* s. punzón de sastre, m.;

body, *bŏd'ĕ,* s. cuerpo, m.; individuo, m.; gremio, m.; **any** –, cualquier; **every** –, cada uno.

body-clothes, *–klōz,* s. pl. caparazón, m.

body-colour, *–kŭllŭr,* s. primera mano de color, f. [corps, f.

body-guard, *–gărd,* s. (mil.) guardia de

body-snatcher, *–snătshŭr,* s. resurreccionista, m. (en Inglaterra).

bog, *bŏg,* s. pantano, m.

bogey, *–ĕ* s. duende, m. [cear.

boggle, *–gl,* v. n. titubear, vacilar, balan-

boggy, *–ĕ,* a. pantanoso, palustre.

bogus, *bŏ'gŭs,* a. postizo.

bohea, *bŏhĕ',* s. te negro de la China.

boil, *bŏĭl,* v. n. hervir; bullir; hervirle á uno la sangre; –, v. a. cocer; –, s. furúnculo, m.

boiler, *–ăr,* s. marmita, f.; caldero, m.

boisterous, *bŏĭs'tŭrŭs,*a. borrascoso, tempestuoso; violento; **-ly,** ad. tumultuosamente, furiosamente.

bold, *bōld,* a. ardiente, valiente; audaz; temerario; impudente; **-ly,** ad. descaradamente. [osadía, f.

boldness, *–nĕs,* s. intrepidez, f.; valentía, f.

bole, *bōl,* s. tronco, m.; bolo, m.; medida de grano de seis fanegas, f.

bolster, *bŏl'stŭr,* s. travesero, m.; cabezal, m.; –, v. a. recostar la cabeza en el travesero; apoyar.

bolt, *bōlt,* s. dardo, m.; flecha, f.; cerrojo, m.; –, v. a. cerrar con cerrojo; examinar, amarrar con grillos; cribar.

bolter, *–ăr,* s. cedazo, m. [colar, m.

bolting-cloth, *–ĭngklŏth,* s. tamiz para

bolting-house, *–ĭnghŏŭs,* s. cernedero, m.

bolus, *bŏ'lŭs,* s. bola, bolilla, f. [m.

bomb, *bŏm,* s. (mil.) bomba, f.

bombard, *–bărd,* v. a. bombardear.

bombardier, *–bărdĕr',* s. bombardero, m.

bombardment, *–bărd'mĕnt,* s. bombardeo, m.

bombast, *băm'băst,* s. hinchazón, f. [m.

bombastic, *bămbăst'ĭk,* a. pomposo, hinchado, ampuloso.

bond, *bŏnd,* s. ligadura, f.; vínculo, m.; vale, m.; obligación, f.; –, v. a. poner en depósito. [f.

bondage, *–āj,* s. esclavitud, servidumbre,

bond-holder, *–hōldŭr,* s. tenedor de unos vales, m. [almacén de la aduana.

bonding-warehouse, *–ĭngwărhŏŭs,* s.

bond(s)man, *–măn,* s. esclavo, siervo, m., (law) fiador, m.

bone, *bōn,* s. hueso, m.; –, v. a. desosar.

bonelace, *–lās,* s. encaje de hilo, m.

boneless, *–lĕs,* a. sin huesos; desosado.

bonesetter, *–sĕttŭr,* s. algebrista, m.

bonfire, *bŏn'fĭr,* s. fuego de regocijo, m.

bonnet, *bŏn'nĕt,* s. gorra, f.; bonete, m.

bonny, *bŏn'nĕ,* a. bonito, galán, gentil.

bonus, *bŏ'nŭs,* s. cuota, prima, f.

bony, *bŏ'nĕ,* a. osudo.

booby, *bŏ'bĕ,* s. zote, hombre bobo, m.

book, *bŭk,* s. libro, m.; **to bring to** –, v. a. pedir cuenta; asentar en un libro.

book-binder, *–bĭndăr,* s. encuadernador de libros.

book-case, *–kās,* s. armario para libros, m

book-keeper, *–kēpŭr,* s. tenedor de libros, m. [libros, f.

book-keeping, *–kēpĭng,* s. teneduría de

book-making, *—mákǐng,* s. apuesta en las corridas de caballos, f.

book-marker, *—márkǔr,* s. registro de un libro, m.

book-post, *—pōst,* s., **by —,** bajo faja.

book-seller, *—sěllǔr,* s. librero, m.

book-worm, *—wǔrm,* s. polilla que roe los libros, f.; hombre del todo aficionado á los libros, m.

boom, *bōm,* s. (mar.) botalón, m.; cadena para cerrar un puerto, f.; —, v. n. zumbar.

boon, *bōn,* s. presente, regalo, m.; favor, m.; gracia, f.; —, a. alegre, festivo; generoso.

boor, *bōr,* s. patán, villano, m.

boorish, *—ǐsh,* a. rústico, agreste; **-ly,** ad. rústicamente.   [sería, f.

boorishness, *—ǐshněs,* s. rusticidad, gro-

boot, *bōt,* s. ganancia, f.; provecho, m.; bota, f.; **to —,** ad. además.

booted, *—ěd,* a. calzado con botas.

booth, *bōth,* s. barraca, cabaña, f.

boot-jack, *bōt' jǎk,* s. sacabotas, m.

bootless, *—lěs,* a. inútil, sin provecho, vano.

boot-tree, *—trē,* s. ensanchador, m.

boots, *—s,* s. limpiabotas, m.

booty, *—ě,* s. botín, m.; presa, f.; saqueo, m.

booze, *bōz,* v. n. emborracharse.

borax, *bō'rǎks,* s. borraj, m.

border, *bōr'dǎr,* s. orilla, f.; borde, m., margen, f.; frontera, f.; —, v. n. confinar; —, v. a. ribetear; limitar.

borderer, *—ǎr,* s. confinante, m.

bore, *bōr,* v. a. taladrar; barrenar; fastidiar; —, s. taladro, m.; calibre, m.; hombre enfadoso, m.

boreal, *bō'rěǎl,* a. septentrional, boreal.

Boreas, *bō'rěǎs,* s. viento del septentrión, m.

boredom, *bōr'dǎm,* s. incomodidad, f.

born, *bōrn,* a. nacido; destinado.

borough, *bǔr'rǒ,* s. villa, f.; burgo, m.

borrow, *bǒr'rǒ,* v. a. tomar fiado; pedir prestado.

borrower, *—ǎr,* s. prestamista, m.

boscage, *bǒs'kǎj,* s. boscaje, m.; arboleda, f.

bosh, *bǒsh,* s. galimatías, n

bosom, *bǔm,* s. seno, pech   m.; amor, m.; cariño, m.; **— of a shirt,** guirindola, f.; —, v. a. guardar en el pecho.

bosom-friend, *—frěnd,* s. amigo íntimo, m.

boss, *bǒs,* s. clavo, m.; jiba, joroba, f.; —, *bǎs,* (am.) patrón, maestro, m.

botanic(al), *bǒtǎn'ǐk(ǎl),* a. botánico.

botanise, *bǒt'ǎnǐz,* v. a. herborizar.

botanist, *bǒt'ǎnǐst,* s. botánico m.

botany, *bǒt'ǎně,* s. botánica, f.

botch, *bǒtsh,* s. remiendo, m.; roncha, f.; úlcera, f.; —, v. a. remendar; chapuzar.

botcher, *—ǎr,* s. sastre remendón, m.

both, *bōth,* a. ambos, entrambos; ambas, entrambas; —, c. tanto como.

bother, *bǒ'thǎr,* v. a. aturrullar; confundir; —, s. terquería, terqueza, importunidad, f.

bottle, *bǒt'tl,* s. botella, f.; gavilla de heno, f.; —, v. a. embotellar.

bottle-holder, *—hōldǎr,* s. partidario, m.; segundo (en duelo), m.

bottom, *bǒt'tǔm,* s. fondo, m.; fundamento, m.; valle, m.; buque, m.; fin, designio, m.; —, a. inferior, de debajo, —, v. a. ovillar,

devanar un ovillo; —, v. n. apoyarse; **— upwards,** ad. lo de arriba abajo.

bottomless, *—lěs,* a. insondable, excesivo; impenetrable.

bottomry, *—rě,* s. (mar.) casco y quilla, m.

bough, *bǒǔ,* s. brazo del árbol; ramo, m.

bounce, *bǒǔns,* v. n. arremeter, brincar; jactarse; —, s. golpazo, brinco, m.; bravata, f.

bouncer, *—ǎr,* s. fanfarrón, m.; mentira, f.

bound, *bǒǔnd,* s. límite, m.; salto, m.; repercusión, f.; —, v. a. confinar, limitar; destinar; obligar; reprimir; —, v. n. resaltar; —, a. destinado.   [f.

boundary, *bǒǔn'dǎrě,* s. límite, m.; frontera,

bounden, *bǒǔn'dn,* a. obligado; obligatorio.

boundless, *—lěs,* a. ilimitado, infinito.

bounteous, *bǒǔn'tǔs,* **bountiful,** *bǒǔn'těfǔl,* a. liberal, generoso, bienhechor **-ly,** ad. generosamente, liberalmente.

bounty, *—tě,* s. liberalidad, bondad, f.

bouquet, *bō'kā,* s. ramillete de flores, m.

bourn, *bōrn,* s. distrito, m.; confín, m.

bout, *bǒǔt,* s. vez, f.; experimento, rato, m.

bovine, *bō'vǐn,* a. bovino.

bow, *bǒǔ,* v. a. encorvar, doblar, oprimir; —, v. n. encorvarse; hacer reverencia; —, s. reverencia, inclinación, f.   [f.; nudo, m.

bow, *bō,* s. arco, m.; arco de violín; corbata,

bowels, *bǒǔ'ělz,* s. pl. intestinos, m. pl.; entrañas, f. pl.; ternura, compasión, f.

bower, *bǒǔ'ǎr,* s. enramada de jardín; bóveda, f.; aposento retirado, m.

bowie-knife, *bō'nǐf,* s. puñal, largo y ancho, m.   [á las bochas.

bowl, *bōl,* s. taza; bola, f.; —, v. n. jugar

bowlder, *bōl'dǎr,* s. guijarro, m.

bowline, *bō'lǐn,* s. (mar.) bolina, f.

bowling-green, *bōl'ǐnggrēn,* s. bolingrín, m.; boleo, plano para jugar á las bochas, m.

bowsprit, *bō'sprǐt,* s. (mar.) bauprés, m.

bowstring, *—strǐng,* s. cuerda del arco, f.

bow-window, *—wǐndō,* s. ventana arqueada, f.

box, *bǒks,* s. boj (árbol), m.; caja, cajita, f.; palco de teatro, m.; **— on the ear,** bofetada, f.; —, v. a. meter alguna cosa en una caja; apuñetear; —, v. n. combatir á puñadas.

boxen, *—n,* a. hecho de boj.

boxer, *—ǎr,* s. púgil, m.

boxing-day, *—ǐngdā,* **--night,** *—nǐt,* s. el segundo día de Navidad.

box-keeper, *bǒks'kēpǔr,* s. portero de los palcos, m. (en el teatro).

box-maker, *—mǎkǔr,* s. cofrero, m.

box-seat, *—sēt,* s. pescante, m.

boy, *bǒě,* s. muchacho, m.; niño, m.; criado, lacayo, m.

boycot, *—kǒt,* v. a. desacreditar, echar fuera; —, s. terrorismo que consiste en declarar por desechado á los propietarios de tierras en Irlanda, m.

boyhood, *—hǒd,* s. muchachez, f.

boyish, *—ǐsh,* a. pueril; frívolo; **-ly,** ad. puerilmente.   [muchachería, f.

boyishness, *—ǐshněs,* s. puerilidad,

brace, *brás*, s. abrazadera, f.; sopanda de coche, f.; par, m.; –s, pl. tirantes para sostener los pantalones, m. pl.; –, v. a. ligar, amarrar; (mar.) bracear.

bracelet, –*lêt*, s. brazalete, m.

bracken, *brák kn*, s. (bot.) helecho, m.

bracket, *brák kêt*, s. puntal, m.; listón, m.; **to – with**, v. a. unir, ligar.

brackish, *brák ish*, a. salobre.

bracing, *brás ing*, a. confortante.

brad, *brád*, s. tachuela, punta, f.

brad-awl, –*ál*, s. lesna, f.

brag, *brág*, s. jactancia, f.; –, v. n. jactarse, fanfarronear. [m.

braggadocio, –*gádó shêô*, s. fanfarrón.

braggart, –*gárt*, a. & s. jactancioso; fanfarrón, m.

braid, *brád*, s. trenza, f.; –, v. a. trenzar.

brain, *brán*, s. cerebro, m.; seso, juicio, m.; –, v. a. descerebrar; matar á uno.

brain-fever, –*fē vur*, s. cerebritis, f.

brainless, –*lês*, a. tonto, insensato.

brain-pan, –*pŏn*, s. cráneo, m.

brain-sick, –*sik*, a. frenético.

brake, *brák*, s. helechal, m.; agramadera, f.; amasadera, f.; palanca, f.; (rail.) freno, f. [frenos, m.

brakesman, *brá kemŏn*, s. (rail.) guardafreno, m.

brake-van, *brák vŏn*, s. (rail.) vagón-freno, m.

bramble, *brám bl*, s. zarza, espina, f.

bran, *brŏn*, s. salvado, m.

branch, *brŏnch*, s. ramo, m.; rama, f.; –, v. a. (& n.) ramificar(se).

branch-house, –*hóes*, s. comandita, f.

branch-line, –*lln*, s. (rail.) empalme, ramal, m.; hijuela de ferrocarril, f.

brand, *brŏnd*, s. tizón, m.; nota de infamia, f.; –, v. a marcar con un hierro ardiente; infamar.

brandish, –*ish*, v. n. blandir, ondear.

bran(d)new, –*nú*, a. flamante.

brandy, *brŏn dé*, s. aguardiente, m.

brangle, *brŏng gl*, s. quimera, disputa, f.; –, v. a. reñir, disputar.

brass, *brás*, s. bronce, m.; desvergüenza, f.; **red –**, tumbaga, f.

brass-founder, –*fŏndur*, s. fundidor de bronce, m.

brat, *brát*, s. rapaz; chulo, m.

bravado, *brává dô*, s. baladronada, f.

brave, *bráv*, a. bravo, valiente, atrevido; –, v. a bravear; – s. bravo, m.; **–ly**, ad. bravamente.

bravery, –*árê*, s. valor, m.; magnificencia, f.; bravata, f.

brawl, *brál*, s. quimera, disputa, camorra, f.; –, v. n. alborotar, vociglerar.

brawn, *brán*, s. pulpa, f.; carne de verraco.

brawny, –*é*, a. carnoso, musculoso.

bray, *brá*, v. a. triturar; –, v. n. rebuznar; –, s. rebuzno (del asno), m.; ruido bronco, m. [broncear.

braze, *bráz*, v. a. soldar con latón.

brazen, –n, a. de bronce; desvergonzado; impudente; –, v. n. hacerse descarado.

brazier, *brá zúr*, s. latonero, m.; brasero, m. [violación, f.

breach, *brétsh*, s. rotura, f.; brecha, f.;

bread, *brêd*, s. pan, m. (fig.) sustento, m.; **brown –**, pan moreno.

breadstuffs, –*stŏfz*, s. pl. granos, m. pl.

breadth, *brêdth*, s. anchura, f.

break, *brák*, v. n. romper; vencer; quebrantar; violar; domar; arruinar; interrumpir; –, v. n. romperse; reventarse algún tumor; separarse; (com.) quebrar; **to – out**, abrirse salida; derramarse, desaguar; –, s. rotura, abertura, f.; interrupción, f.; **– of day**, despuntar del día, m., aurora, f.

breakdown, –*dŏŏn*, s. descalabro, m.

breakfast, *brêk fást*, s. almuerzo, desayuno, m.; –, v. n. almorzar.

breaking, *brák ing*, s. rompimiento, m.; principio de las vacaciones en las escuelas, m.; fractura, f. [picio, m.

breakneck, –*nêk*, s. derrumbadero, preci-

breakwater, –*wátur*, s. muelle, m.

breast, *brêst*, s. pecho, seno, m.; tetas, f. pl.; corazón, m.; –, v. a. acometer; resistir; –, v. n. bruscar (los caballos).

breast-bone, –*bôn*, s. esternón, m.

breast-high, –*hi*, a. alto hasta el pecho.

breast-plate, –*plát*, s. peto, m.; pectoral, m.; coraza, f.

breast-work, –*wúrk*, s. parapeto, m.

breath, *brêth*, s. aliento, m., respiración, f.; soplo de aire, m.; momento, m.

breathe, *brêth*, v. a. & n. respirar; exhalar; **to – after**, desear, ansiar.

breathing, –*ing*, s. aspiración, f.; respiración, f.; aliento, m. [poso, m.

breathing-time, –*tlm*, s. descanso, reposo, m.

breathless, *brêth lês*, a. falto de aliento; desalentado. [cañón ó fusil, f.

breech, *brêch*, s. trasero, m.; culata de

breeches, –*êz*, s. pl. calzones, f. pl.

breed, *brêd*, s. casta, raza, f.; –, v. a. procrear; engendrar; producir; educar; –, v. n. parir; multiplicarse.

breeder, –*úr*, s. criador, m.; yegua de cría ó vientre, f. [cación, f.

breeding, –*ing*, s. crianza, f.; buena edu-

breeze, *brêz*, s. brisa, f.; tábano, m.

breezy, *brê zé*, a. refrescado con brisas.

brethren, *brêth rên*, s. pl. (de *brother*) hermanos, m. pl. (en estilo grave).

brevet, *brêv ĕt*, s. despacho, título, m.

breviary, *brê vĭárê*, s. epítome, compendio, m.; breviario, m.

brevity, *brêv ĭtê*, s. brevedad, concisión, f.

brew, *brô*, v. a. tramar, maquinar; mezclar; –, v. n. hacer cerveza; –, s. calderada de cerveza, f.

brewer, –*úr*, s. cervecero, m.

brewery, –*úr*, s. cervecería, f.

briar, brier, *brĭ úr*, s. zarza, f., espino, m.

bribe, *brĭb*, s. cohecho, soborno, m.; –, v. a. cohechar, corromper, sobornar.

bribery, –*árê*, s. cohecho, soborno, m.

brick, *brĭk*, s. ladrillo, m.; ladrillo de pan, hombre alegre, m.; –, v. a. enladrillar.

brick-bat, –*bát*, s. pedazo de ladrillo, m.

brick-layer, –*láúr*, s. albañil, m.

bridal, *brĭ dál*, a. nupcial; –, s. boda, f.

bride, *brĭd*, s. novia, f.

bridegroom, –*grôm*, s. novio, m.

bridesmaid, –s'mäd, s. madrina de boda, f.

bridge, brĭj, s. puente, m. & f.; caballete de la nariz, m.; puente de violin, m.; **to – (over),** v. a. construir un puente.

bridle, brī'dl, s. brida, f., freno, m.; –, v. a. embridar; reprimir, refrenar.

brief, bref, a. breve, conciso, sucinto; –, s. compendio, m.; breve, m.

briefly, –lĕ, ad. brevemente, en pocas palabras.

brig, brĭg, brigantine, –änten, s. (mar.) bergantin, m.

brigade, brĭgäd', s. (mil.) brigada, f.

brigadier, –ér', s. (mil.) general de brigada, m.

brigand, brĭg'änd, s. bandido, m.

bright, brĭt, a. claro, luciente, brillante; – v, ad. esplendidamente.

brighten, –n, v. a. pulir, dar lustre; ilustrar; –, v. n. aclarar.

brightness, –nĕs, s. esplendor, m., brillantez, f.; agudeza, f.; claridad, f.

brilliancy, brĭl'yänsĕ, s. brillantez, f.

brilliant, brĭl'yänt, a. brillante; –ly, ad. esplendidamente; –, s. brillante (diamante abrillantado), m.

brim, brĭm, s. borde extremo, m.; orilla, f.; –, v. a. llenar hasta el borde; –, v. n. estar lleno.

brimful, –fŭl, a. lleno hasta el borde.

brimstone, –stōn, s. azufre, m.

brindled, brĭn'dld, a. abigarrado.

brine, brīn, s. salmuera, f.; (fig.) lágrimas, f. pl.

bring, brĭng, v. a. llevar, traer; conducir; inducir, persuadir; **to – about,** efectuar; **to – forth,** producir; parir; **to – up,** educar;   [borde, m.

brink, brĭngk, s. orilla, f.; margen, m. & f.,

briny, brī'nĕ, s. salado.

brisk, brĭsk, a. vivo, alegre, jovial; fresco.

brisket, –ĕt, s. pecho (de un animal), m.

briskly, –lĕ, ad. vigorosamente; alegremente; vivamente.

brisknes, –nĕs, s. vivacidad, alegría, f.

bristle, brĭs'sl, s. cerda, seta, f.; –, v. n. erizarse.

bristly, brĭs'slĕ, a. cerdoso, lleno de cerdas.

brittle, brĭt'tl, a. quebradizo, frágil.

brittleness, –nĕs, s. fragilidad, f.

broach, brōtsh, s. asador, m.; –, v. a. espetar; divulgar; propagar mentiras; barrenar.

broad, brăd, a. ancho; abierto; grosero; **at – noon,** al medio día.   [f. pl.

broadbeans, –bēns, s. pl. habas de laguna.

broadcloth, –klŏth, s. paño fino, m.

broaden, –n, v. n. ensancharse.

broadly, –lĕ, ad. anchamente.

broadness, –nĕs, s. ancho, m.; anchura, f.; grosería, f.   [m.; andanada, f.

broadside, –sīd, s. costado de navío.

broadsword, –sōrd, s. espada ancha, f.; alfanje, m.   [lo ancho.

broadwise, –wīs, ad. á lo ancho, por

brocade, brŏkäd', s. brocado, m.

brogue, brŏg, s. abarca, f.; idioma corrompido, m.

broider, brōi'där, v. a. bordar.

broil, brŏil, s. tumulto, m.; riña, f.; –, v. a. asar (carne); –, v. n. padecer calor.

broken, brō'kn, p. roto, interrumpido; **– english,** inglés mal articulado, m.; **–meat,** carne cortada, f.; **– week,** s. una semana que tiene días de fiesta, f.

broker, brō'kär, s. corredor, m.; chamarillero, chamarilero, chalán, m.

brokerage, –ĭj, s. corretaje, m.

bronchial, brŏng'kĕäl, a. bronquial.

bronchitis, brŏngkī'tĭs, s. bronquitis, f.

bronze, brŏnz, s. bronce, m.; –, v. a. broncear.   [adornar con joyas.

brooch, brōtsh, s. broche, m.; –, v. a.

brood, brōd, v. n. cobijar; pensar alguna cosa con cuidado; madurar; –, s. raza, f.; nidada, f.

brood-hen, –hĕn, s. empolladora, f.

brook, brŏk, s. arroyo, m.; –, v. n. sufrir, tolerar.   [hiniesta, f.

broom, brōm, s. hiniesta, f.; escoba de

broom-stick, –stĭk, s. palo de escoba, m.

broth, brŏth, s. caldo, m.

brothel, brŏth'ĕl, s. burdel, m.

brother, brŭth'är, s. hermano, m.

brotherhood, –hŭd, s. hermandad, f.; fraternidad, f.

brother-in-law, –ĭnlä, s. cuñado, m.

brotherly, –lĕ, a. & ad. fraternal; fraternalmente.

Brougham, brō'äm, s. coche cerrado que anda en cuatro ruedas, m.

brow, brŏu, s. ceja, f.; frente, f.; cima, f.

browbeat, –bēt, v. a. mirar con ceño.

brown, brŏun, a. bruno, moreno; **to be in a – study,** estar melancólico; **– paper,** s. papel de estraza, m.; **–sugar,** s. azúcar terciado, m.; –, s. color moreno, m.; –, v. a. volver moreno ó bruno.

browse, brŏuz, v. a. ramonear; –, v. n. pacer la hierba; –, s. (bot.) pimpollos, renuevos, vástagos, m. pl.

bruin, brū'ĭn, s. oso, m.

bruise, brūz, v. a. magullar, machacar, abollar, majar; pulverizar; –, s. magulladura, contusión, f.

bruit, brŏt, v. a. echar voz, dar fama.

brunt, brŭnt, s. choque, m.; esfuerzo, m.; desastre, m.

brush, brŭsh, s. bruza, f.; escobilla, f.; asalto, m.; combate, m.; –, v. a. acepillar; **to – off,** huir; –, v. n. mover apresuradamente; pasar ligeramente.

brushwood, –wŭd, s. breñal, zarzal, m.

brushy, –ĕ, a. cerdoso; velludo.   [mente.

brutal, brō'täl, a. brutal; –ly, ad. brutalmente.

brutality, brŏtäl'ĭtĕ, s. brutalidad, f.

brutalize, brō'tälīz, v. a. (& n.) embrutecer(se).   [irracional.

brute, brōt, s. bruto, m.; –, a. feroz, bestial;

brutish, brō'tĭsh, a. brutal, bestial; feroz; –ly, ad. brutalmente.

bubble, bŭb'bl, s. burbuja, f.; bagatela, f.; engañifa, f.; –, v. n. burbujear, bullir; –, v. a. engañar.   [cano), m.

buccanier, bŭkkänér', s. corsario (americano), m.

buck, bŭk, s. gamo, m.; macho (de algunos animales), m.; lejía, f.

bucket, –ĕt, s. cubo, pozal, m.

buckle, –*l,* s. hebilla, f.; –, v. a. hebillar; afianzar; –, v. n. encorvarse.

buckler, –*lär,* s. escudo, m.; adarga, f.

buckram, –*räm,* s. bocací, m. [tido, m.

buckskin, –*skin,* s. cuero de gamo cur-

buckwheat, –*hwēt,* s. trigo negro, m.

bucolic, *bŭkŏl'ĭk,* a. bucólico.

bud, *bŭd,* s. pimpollo, botón, m.; –, v. a. & n. inocular; abotonar. [m.

budding-knife, –*dĭng nĭf,* s. injertador, m.

budge, *bŭj,* v. n. moverse, menearse.

budget, *bŭj'ĕt,* s. presupuesto de los gastos del Estado, m., mochila, f.

buff, *bŭf,* s ante, m.; búfalo, m.; color de amarillo ligero, m.; –, a. de ante; –s, s. pl. correaje de un soldado, m.

buffalo, *bŭf'fălō,* s búfalo, m.

buffer(-head), *bŭf'fär(hĕd),* s. (rail.) acolchado de la fricción, m. [topes, m. pl.

buffers, *bŭf'färz,* s. pl. (rail.) parachoques,

buffet, *bŭf'fĕt,* s. puñada, f.; aparador, m.; –, v. n. combatir á puñadas.

buffoon, *bŭfōn',* s. bufón, chocarrero, m.

buffoonery, –*ärē,* s. bufonada, bufonería,

bug, *bŭg,* s. chinche, f. [f.

bugbear, –*bär,* s. espantajo, coco, m.

buggy, –*gē,* a. chinchero.

bugle(horn), *bū'gl(hörn),* s. trompa de caza, f.

buhl, *bōl,* s. taracea, f. [caza, f.

build, *bĭld,* v. a. edificar; construir; –, v.n. fiarse. [obras, m.

builder, –*är,* s. arquitecto, m.; maestro de

building, –*ĭng,* s. fábrica, f.; edificio, m.; construcción, f.

bulb, *bŭlb,* s. bulbo, m.; cebolla, f.

bulbous, –*ŭs,* a. bulboso.

bulge, *bŭlj,* v. n. hacer agua; combarse.

bulk, *bŭlk,* s. masa, f.; volumen, m.; grosura, f.; mayor parte, f ; capacidad de un buque, f.; **in** –, en grueso. [tud, f.

bulkiness, –*ĭnēs,* s. bulto, m.; masa, magni-

bulky, –*ē,* a. macizo, grueso, grande.

bull, *bŭl,* s. toro, m.; descuido, m., bula, f., breve pontificio, m.; dicho absurdo, m.

bull-baiting, –*bāting,* s. combate de toros y perros, m.

bull-dog, –*dŏg,* s. perro de presa, m.

bullet, *bŭl'lĭt,* s. bala, f

bull-finch, *bŭl'fĭnĭsh,* s. pinzón real, m.

bullion, *bŭl'yĭn,* s. oro ó plata en barras.

bullock, *bŭl'lŏk,* s. novillo capado, m.

bully, *bŭl'lē,* s. espadachín, m.; –, v. n. fanfarronear.

bulrush, *bŭl'rŭsh,* s. junco, m.

bulwark, *bŭl'wärk,* s. baluarte, m.; –, v. a. fortificar con baluartes.

bumble-bee, *bŭm'blē,* s. abejarrón, abejón, abejorro, zángaro, m.

bumboat, –*bōt,* s. bote vivandero, m.

bump, *bŭmp,* s. hinchazón, f.; jiba, f.; bollo, m.; barriga, f.; –, v. a estrellarse.

bumper, –*är,* s. copa, f.; vaso lleno, m.

bumpkin, –*kĭn,* s. patán, m.; villano, m.

bumptious, *bŭm'shŭs,* a. presumido.

bun, *bŭn,* s. cañamiza, f.

bunch, *bŭnsh,* s. tumor, m.; jiba, f.; nudo, m.; –, v. n. formar corcova.

bunch-backed, –*bäkd,* a. jorobado.

bunchy, –*ē,* a. racimoso; jiboso.

bundle, *bŭn'dl,* s. atado, furdillo, m., haz, m. (de leña &c.); paquete, m.; rollo, m.; –, v. a. atar, hacer un lío.

bung, *bŭng,* s. tapón, m.; –, v a. atarugar.

bungalow, *bŭng'gălō,* s. quinta de piso bajo en las Indias, f. [licores), f.

bung-hole, –*hōl,* s. boca (para envasar

bungle, *bŭng'gl,* v.a. chapucear, chafallar; –, v. n. hacer algo chabacanamente; –, s. yerro, m.; obra mal hecha, f.

bunion, *bŭn'yŭn,* s. juanete, m., callosidad que se forma en los pies.

bunting, *bŭn'tĭng,* s. lanilla para banderas, f. [boyar.

buoy, *bŭŏĕ,* s. (mar.) boya, f.; –, v. a.

buoyancy, –*änsē,* s. fluctuación, f.

buoyant, –*änt,* a. boyante.

bur, *bŭr,* s. (bot.) bardana, f.

burden, *bŭr'dn,* s. carga, f.; estrambote, m.; –, v. a. cargar; embarazar.

burdensome, –*săm,* a. gravoso, molesto, incómodo.

burdock, *bŭr'dŏk,* s. bardana (planta), f.

bureau, *bū'rō,* s. armario, m.; escritorio, m.

bureaucrat, –*krăt,* s. burócrata. m. [m.

burgess, *bŭr'jĕs,* s. ciudadano, m.

burgher, *bŭr'gär,* s. ciudadano, vecino, m.

burglar, *bŭr'glär,* s. salteador de noche en poblado, m. [de una casa, m.

burglary, –*ē,* s. asalto y robo nocturno

burgomaster, *bŭr'gōmăstär,* s. burgomaestre, m. [quias, f. pl.

burial, *bĕr'ĭäl,* s. enterramiento, m.; exe-

burial-place, –*plăs,* s. cimenterio, m.

burlesque, *bŭrlĕsk',* s. & a. lengua burlesca, f.; burlesco, m.; –, v. a. burlar, zumbar.

burly, *bŭr'lē,* a. voluminoso, turbulento.

burn, *bŭrn,* v. a. quemar, abrasar ó herir, incendiar; –, v. n. arder; –, s. quemadura, f.

burner, –*är,* s. quemador, m.; mechero,m.

burning-glass, –*ĭnggläs,* s. espejo ó vidrio ustorio, m. [–, v. n. tomar lustre.

burnish, *bŭr'nĭsh,* v. a. bruñir, dar lustre;

burnisher, –*är,* s. bruñidor, m.

burr, *bŭr,* s. lóbulo de la oreja, m.; (bot.) bardana, f.

burrow, *bŭr'rō,* s. conejera, f.; –, v. n. esconderse en la conejera.

bursar, *bŭr'sär,* s. tesorero, m.

burse, *bŭrs,* s. bolsa, lonja, f.

burst, *bŭrst,* v. n. reventar; abrirse; **to — into tears,** prorrumpir en lágrimas; **to — with laughing,** descoyuntarse de risa; –, s. reventón, m.; rebosadura, f. [der.

bury, *bĕr'ē,* v. a. enterrar, sepultar; escon-

burying-ground, –*ĭnggröünd,* s. cimenterio, m.

bus, *bŭs,* s. ómnibus, m.

busby, *bŭs'bē,* s. gorra de húsar, f.

bush, *bŭsh,* s. arbusto, espinal, m.; cola de zorra, f.

bushel, –*ĭl,* s. fanega, f. [lanudo.

bushy, –*ē,* a espeso, lleno de arbustos;

busily, *bĭz'ĕlē,* ad. solícitamente, diligentemente, apresuradamente.

business, *bĭz'nĕs,* s. empleo, m.; ocupación, f.; negocio, m.

busk, *băsk,* s. ballena de corsé, f.   [m.
buskin, *băs'kĭn,* s. borceguí, m.; coturno,
buss, *băs,* s. beso, m.; (mar.) neura, f.
bust, *băst,* s. busto, m.
bustard, *băs'tărd,* s. abutarda, f.
bustle, *băs'sl,* v. n. hacer ruido; entremeterse; —, s. baraúnda, f.; ruido, m.
busy, *bĭz'ĭ,* a. ocupado; entremetido; —,
   v. a. ocupar.
busybody, *—bŏdĭ,* s. entremetido, m.
but, *băt,* c. excepto, menos; pero; solamente.
butcher, *băt'shăr,* s. carnicero, m.; —, v. a.
   matar atrozmente.
butcherly, *—lĭ,* a. sanguinario, cruel.
butcher's shop, *—s shŏp,* s. tienda del
butchery, *—ĭ,* s. matadero, m. [carnicero, f.
butler, *băt'lăr,* s. despensero, m.
butt, *bătt,* s. terrero, m.; blanco, hito, m.;
   bota, f.; —, v. a. topar.
butter, *băt'tăr,* s. manteca, f.; —, v. a.
   batir la leche; untar con manteca; doblar
   las puestas (en el juego).
butter-cup, *—kŭp,* s. (bot.) amargón,
   diente de león, m.
butterfly, *—flĭ,* s. mariposa, f.
butter-milk, *—mĭlk,* s. suero de manteca, m.
buttery, *—ĭ,* s. despensa, f.; —, a. mantecoso.   [charros, m. pl.
buttock, *băt'tŏk,* s. anca, f.; (mar.) cu-
button, *băt'n,* s. botón, m.; —, v. a. abo-
button-hole, *—hŏl,* s. ojal, m.   [tonar.
button-hook, *—hŏk,* s. abotonador, m.
buttress, *băt'trĕs,* s. estribo, m.; apoyo,
   m.; —, v. a. estribar.
buxom, *băk'sŭm,* a. obediente; vivo, alegre, jovial; —ly, ad. jovialmente; amo-
buy, *bĭ,* v. a. comprar.   [rosamente.
buzz, *băz,* s. susurro, soplo, m.; —, v. n.
   zumbar; cuchuchear.
buzzard, *băz'zărd,* s. modrego, buaro, m.
by, *bĭ,* pr. por; á, en; de; cerca, al lado
   de; — and —, de aquí á poco, ahora; —
   the —, de paso; — much, con mucho; —
   all means, cueste lo que cueste.
bygone, *—gŏn,* a. pasado.
by-lane, *—lăn,* s. contracalle, f.
by-law, *—lă,* s. ley local, f.
by-name, *—năm,* s. apodo, m.
by-path, *—păth,* s. atajo, m., trocha, f.
by-place, *—plăs,* s. lugar oculto, m.
by-road, *—rŏd,* s. camino descarriado, m.
bystander, *—stăndăr,* s. mirador, m.;
   uno que está presente, m.
by-street, *—strĕt,* s. calle extraviada, f.
by-word, *—wŭrd,* s. proverbio, refrán, m.

C.

cab, *kăb,* s. coche de plaza, m.
cabalistic, *kăbălĭs'tĭk,* a. cabalístico.
cabbage, *kăb'ădj,* s. berza, col, f.; —, v. a.
   hurtar retazos.   [menca, f.
cabbage-lettuce, *—lĕttĭs,* s. lechuga fla-
cabin, *kăb'ĭn,* s. cabaña, cámara de navío, f.; —, v. a. & n. encerrar en cabaña;
   vivir en cabaña.   [capitán, m.
cabin-boy, *—bŏĭ,* s. paje de la cámara del

cabinet, *kăb'ĭnĕt,* s. gabinete, m.; escritorio, m.   [ministros, m.
cabinet-council, *—kŏŭnsĭl,* s. consejo de
cabinet-maker, *—măkăr,* s. ebanista, m.
cable, *kă'bl,* s. (mar.) cable, m.; —'s
   length, medida de 120 brazas, f.   [m.
cabman, *kăb'măn,* s. calesero, m.; simón,
caboose, *kăbŏz',* s. (mar.) cocina, f.
cabstand, *kăb'stănd,* s. punto de los
   coches de plaza, m.
cache, *kăsh,* s. (am.) silo, m.
cackle, *kăk'kl,* v. n. cacarear ó graznar;
   —, s. cacareo, m.; charla, f.   [m.
cackler, *—ăr,* s. cacareador, m.; parlanchín,
cadaverous, *kădăv'ărăs,* a. cadavérico.
caddy, *kăd'dĭ,* s. caja para el te, f.
cade, *kăd,* s. barril, m.; banasta, f.
cadence, *kă'dĕns,* s. (mus.) cadencia, f.
cadet, *kădĕt',* s. cadete, m.; hermano menor, m.   [enjaular.
cage, *kădj,* s. jaula, f.; prisión, f.; —, v. a.
cairn, *kărn,* s. galgal, m.
cajole, *kăjŏl',* v. a. lisonjear, adular.
cajolery, *—ărĭ,* s. adulación, lisonja, f.;
   zalamería, f.
cake, *kăk,* s. bollo, m.; tortita, f.; —, v. n.
   endurecerse (como el pan en el horno).
calamitous, *kălăm'ĭtăs,* a. calamitoso.
calamity, *—ĕtĭ,* s. calamidad, miseria, f.
calcareous, *kălkă'rĕăs,* a. calcáreo.
calcine, *kăl'sĭn,* v. a. calcinar.
calculable, *kăl'kălăbl,* a. calculable.
calculate, *—kălăt,* v. a. calcular, contar.
calculation, *kălkălă'shăn,* s. calculación,
   f.; cálculo, m.
calculus, *kăl'kălăs,* s. cálculo, m.
caldron, *kăl'drăn,* s. caldera, f.
calendar, *kăl'ĕndăr,* s. calendario, almanaque, m.   [sar con calandria.
calender, *—,* s. calandria, f.; —, v. a. pren-
calf, *kăf,* s. ternero, m.; ternera, f.; carne
   de ternero, f.
calibre, *kăl'ĭbăr,* s. calibre, m.
calico, *kăl'ĭkŏ,* s. calicó, m.
caligraphy, *kălĭg'răfĭ,* s. caligrafía, f.
calisthenics, *kălĭsthĕn'ĭks,* s. pl. ejerci-
   cios gimnásticos, m. pl.
calk, *kăk,* v. a. (mar.) calafatear un navío.
call, *kăl,* v. a. llamar, nombrar; convocar,
   citar; apelar; **to — for,** preguntar por alguno, ir á buscarle; **to — attention,** llamar la atención; **to — names,** injuriar;
   to — upon, visitar; —, s. llamada, f.; instancia, f.; invitación, f.; urgencia, f.;
   vocación, f.; profesión, f.; empleo, m.;
   (mar.) pito, m.
call-boy, *—bŏĭ,* s. mozo, sirviente, m.
caller, *—ăr,* s. visitador, m.
calligraphy, *kălĭg'răfĭ,* s. caligrafía, f.
calling, *kăl'lĭng,* s. profesión, vocación, f.
callosity, *kăllŏs'ĭtĭ,* s. callosidad, dureza
   de la especie del callo, f.   [sensible.
callous, *kăl'lăs,* a. calloso, endurecido; in-
callow, *kăl'lŏ,* a. pelado, desplumado.
calm, *kăm,* s. calma, tranquilidad, f.; —, a.
   quieto, tranquilo; —, v. a. calmar; aplacar, aquietar; **—ly,** ad. tranquilamente,
   quieta y sosegadamente.

calmness, —*nĕs*, s. tranquilidad, calma, f.
calomel, *kăl'ŏmĕl*, s. calomel, m.
caloric, *kălŏr'ik*, s. calórico, m.
calumet, *kăl'ŭmĕt*, s. cañutillo de una pipa de fumar, m.
calumniation, *kălŭmnĕă'shŭn*, **calumny,** *kăl'ŭmnĕ*, s. calumnia, f.
calumniate, *kălŭm'nĕăt*, v. a. calumniar.
calumnious, —*ŭs*, a. calumnioso.
Calvary, *kăl'vărĕ*, s. calvario, m.
calve, *kăv*, v. n. parir, producir la vaca.
Calvinist, *kăl'vĭnĭst*, s. calvinista, f.
cambric, *kăm'brĭk*, s. batista, f.
camel, *kăm'ĕl*, s. camello, m.
camelopard, *kămĕl'ŏpărd*, s. camellopardal, m.
cameo, *kăm'ĕŏ*, s. camafeo, m. [dal, m.
camera, *kăm'ĕră*, s. aparato para fotografiar, m.
camlet, *kăm'lĕt*, s. camelote, m.
camomile, *kăm'ŏmĭl*, s. manzanilla, f.
camp, *kămp*, s. (mil.) campo, m.; —, v. n. acampar.
campaign, *kămpān'*, s. campaña, f.; —, v.n. servir en campaña.
campaigner, —*ŭr*, s. campeador, m.
camp-follower, *kămp'fŏl'lŏŭr*, s. (mil.) mozo de campaña, m.
camping-out, *kămpĭng'ŏŭt*, s. (am.) dormir á campo raso, m.
camphor, *kăm'fŭr*, s. alcanfor, m.
camp-meeting, *kămp'mētĭng*, s. oficio divino de campaña, m.
camp-stool, —*stŏl*, s. silla de tijera, f.
can, *kăn*, v. n. ir. poder; —, s. jarro, m.
canal, *kănăl'*, s. estanque, m.; canal, m.
canary-bird, *kănā'rēbŭrd*, s. canario, m.
cancel, *kăn'sĕl*, v. a. cancelar, borrar; anular, invalidar. [m.
cancer, *kăn'sŭr*, s. cangrejo, m.; cáncer, m.
Cancer, —, s. Cáncer, m. (signo del zodíaco).
cancerous, —*ŭs*, a. canceroso.
candid, *kăn'dĭd*, a. cándido, sencillo, ingenuo, sincero; —*ly*, ad. cándidamente, francamente. [pretendiente, m.
candidate, *kăn'dĭdăt*, s. candidato, m.;
candied, *kăn'dĭd*, a. bañado de azúcar.
candle, *kăn'dl*, s. candela, f.; vela, f.
candle-light, —*lĭt*, s. luz de candela, f.
Candlemas, —*măs*, s. Candelaria, f.
candle-snuffers, —*snŭf'ŭrz*, s. despabiladeras, f. pl. [branched —, araña, f.
candlestick, —*stĭk*, s. candelero, m.;
candle-waster, —*wăstŭr*, s. ladrón (en la vela), m.; gastador, m.
cando(u)r, *kăn'dŭr*, s. candor, m.; sinceridad, jugenuidad, f. [m. pl.
candy, *kăn'dĕ*, v.a. confitar; s. confites, m.
cane, *kăn*, s. caña, f.; bastón, m.; —, v. n. apalear con un bastón ó caña.
cane-bottom(ed) chair, —*bŏttăm(d) tshăr*, s. silla de caña, f.
cane-mill, —*mĭl*, s. fábrica de azúcar, f.
canicular, *kănĭk'ŭlăr*, a. perteneciente á la canícula.
canine, *kănīn'*, a. canino, perruno.
caning, *kăn'ĭng*, s. aporreo, m.
canister, *kăn'ĭstŭr*, s. canastillo, m.; vasija (para tener te, tabaco, &c.), f.
canister-shot, —*shŏt*, s. metralla, f.

canker, *kăng'kŭr*, s. gangrena, f.; cáncer, m.; —, v. a. roer, corromper; —, v. n. corromperse, roerse. [tropófago, m.
cannibal, *kăn'nĕbăl*, s. caníbal, m.; an-
cannibalism, —*ĭsm*, s. canibalismo, m.
cannie, *kăn'nĕ*, a. cuerdo, discreto.
cannon, *kăn'nŭn*, s. cañón, m.
cannonade, —*dă'*, s. cañoneo, m.; —, v. a. cañonear.
cannon-ball, —*băl*, s. bala de artillería, f.
cannonier, —*ŭr*, s. cañonero, artillero, m.
canoe, *kănŏ'*, s. canoa, f.
canon, *kăn'ŭn*, s. canon, m., regla, f.; —-law, derecho canónico, m.
canoness, —*ĕs*, s. cayonesa, f.
canonical, *kănŏn'ĭkăl*, a. canónico; —*s,* s. pl. vestidos clericales, m. pl.
canonization, *kănŏnĕză'shŭn*, s. canonización, f.
canonize, *kăn'ŏnīz*, v. a. canonizar.
canonry, *kăn'ŭnrĕ*, s. canonicato, m.
canopy, *kăn'ŏpĕ*, s. dosel, pabellón, m.
cant, *kănt*, s. jerigonza, f.; almoneda pública, f.; —, v. n. hablar en jerigonza.
cantalupe, *kăn'tălŭp*, s. cantalú, m. (melón.)
cantankerous, *kăntăng'kŭrŭz*, a. áspero, fastidioso.
canteen, *kăntēn'*, s. cantina, f.
canter, *kăn'tŭr*, s. hipócrita, f.; galope corto, m. [das, f. pl.
cantharides, *kănthăr'ĭdēz*, s. pl. cantári-
canticle, *kăn'tĭkl*, s. cántico, salmo, m.
canton, *kăn'tŏn*, s. cantón, m.; —, v. a. acantonar. [m.
cantonment, —*mĕnt*, s. acantonamiento, m.
canvas, *kăn'văs*, s. cañamazo, m.; el acto de solicitar votos (parar lograr algún destino); —, v. a. escudriñar, examinar; controvertir; —, v. n. solicitar votos; pretender.
canvasser, —*ŭr*, s. solicitador, m.
caoutchouc, *kŏ'tshŭk*, s. cautchuc, m., goma elástica, f.
cap, *kăp*, s. gorra, f., birreta, f.; reverencia hecha con la gorra, f.; —, v. a. cubrir la cabeza. [titud, inteligencia, f.
capability, *kăpăbĭl'ĭtĕ*, s. capacidad, ap-
capable, *kā'păbl*, a. capaz, idóneo. [vasto.
capacious, *kăpā'shŭs*, a. capaz, espacioso,
capacitate, *kăpăs'ĕtăt*, v. a. hacer capaz.
capacity, *kăpăs'ĕtĕ*, s. capacidad, f.; inteligencia, habilidad, f.; calidad, f.
caparison, *kăpăr'ĭsŭn*, s. caparazón, m.; —, v. a. enjaezar un caballo.
cape, *kăp*, s. cabo, promontorio, m.
caper, *kā'pŭr*, s. cabriola, f.; alcaparra, f.; corsario, m.; to cut a —, cabriolar; —, v. n. hacer cabriolas.
capillary, *kăp'ĭllărĕ*, a. capilar.
capital, *kăp'ĭtăl*, a. capital, excelente; principal; —, s. capitel, m.; capital f. (la ciudad principal); capital, fondo, m.; mayúscula, f.; —*ly*, ad. superiormente, admirablemente, capitalmente; con pena de muerte.
capitalise, —*īz*, v. a. capitalizar.
capitalist, —*ĭst*, s. capitalista, m.
capitation, *kăpĕtā'shŭn*, s. capitación, f.

Capitol, *kăp'ĕtŏl*, s. Capitolio, m.

capitulary, *kăpi'tŭlărĕ*, s. capitular (individuo de algún capítulo), m.

capitulate, *-tŭlāt*, v. n. (mil.) capitular.

capitulation, *kăpĭtŭlā'shăn*, s. capitulación, f.

capon, *kā'pn*, s. capón (pollo castrado), m.

capote, *kăpōt'*, s. capote, levitón, m.

caprice, *kăprēs'*, s. capricho, m.; extravagancia, f. [—ly, ad. caprichosamente.

capricious, *kăprish'ŭs*, a. caprichoso;

capricorn, *kăp'rĭkŏrn*, s. capricornio, m.

Capricorn, —, s. Capricornio, m. (signo del zodíaco). [zozobrar.

capsize, *kăpsīz'*, v. a. (mar.) trabucar,

capstan, *kăp'stăn*, s. (mar.) cabrestante,m.

capsule, *kăp'sŭl*, s. cápsula, f.

captain, *kăp'tĭn*, s. capitán, m.; —of foot, capitán de infantería, m. [capitanía, f.

captaincy, *-sĕ*, captainship, *-shĭp*, s.

caption, *kăp'shăn*, s. presa, captura, f.

captious, *kăp'shŭs*, a. sofístico, insidioso, engañoso, caviloso; —ly, ad. cavilosamente.

captiousness, *-nĕs*, s. cavilación, trapacería, f.; engaño, fraude, m. [clavizar.

captivate, *kăp'tĭvāt*, v. a. cautivar; esclavizar.

captivation, *kăptĭvā'shăn*, s. atractivo, m.

captive, *kăp'tĭv*, s. cautivo, esclavo, m.

captivity, *kăptĭv'ĭtĕ*, s. cautividad, esclavitud, f.; cautiverio, m.

captor, *kăp'tŭr*, s. apresador, pirata, m.

capture, *kăp'tŭr*, s. captura, f.; presa,f.; —, v. a. apresar, capturar. [capucha, f.

capuchin, *kăpŭshēn'*, s. capuchino, m.;

car, *kăr*, s. carreta, f.; carro, m.

carabine, *kăr'bĭn*, s. carabina, f.

carabinier, *kărbēnēr'*, s. carabinero, m.

caracole, *kăr'ăkŏl*, s. vuelta que hace el caballo de una ó dos pistas, f.

caramel, *kăr'ămĕl*, s. caramelo, m.

caravan, *kăr'ăvăn'*, s. caravana, f.

caravansary, *-sărĕ*, s. caravanera, f.

caraway, *kăr'ăwă*, s. (bot.) alcaravea, f.

carbolic acid, *kărbōl'ĭk ăs'ĭd*, s. ácido carbólico, m.

carbon, *kăr'bŏn*, s. carbón dulce, m.

carboniferous, *kărbōnĭf'ĕrŭs*, a. carbonífero.

carbonize, *kăr'bŏnīz*, v. a. carbonizar.

carbuncle, *kăr'bŭng'kl*, s. carbúnculo, rubí, m.; carbunco, tumor maligno, m.

carcass, *kăr'kăs*, s. (mil.) carcasa, f.; cadáver, m.

card, *kărd*, s. naipe, m.; carta, f.; cardencha, f.; pack of —s, baraja de naipes, f.; —, v. a. cardar lana.

card-board, *-bŏrd*, s. cartón, m.

cardiac, *kăr'dĕăk*, a. cardíaco.

cardinal, *kăr'dĕnăl*, s. cardinal, principal; —, s. cardenal, m.

card-table, *kărd'tăbl*, s. mesa para jugar,f.

care, *kăr*, s. cuidado, m.; solicitud, f.; —, v. n. cuidar, tener cuidado ó pena, inquietarse; estimar, apreciar; what—I? ¿á mí qué me importa?

careen, *kărēn'*, v. a. carenar.

career, *kărēr'*, s. carrera, f.; curso, m.; —, v. n. correr á carrera tendida.

careful, *kăr'fŭl*, a. cuidadoso, ansioso, diligente, prudente; —ly, ad. cuidadosamente.

carefulness, *-nĕs*, s. cuidado, m., cautela, atención, diligencia, f.

careless, *kăr'lĕs*, a. descuidado, negligente, indolente; —ly, ad. descuidadamente.

carelessness, *-nĕs*, s. negligencia, indiferencia, f. [ciar, alhagar.

caress, *kărĕs'*, s. caricia, f.; —, v. a. acariciar,

caressing, *-sĭng*, a. cariñoso; —ly, ad. con cariño.

cargo, *kăr'gŏ*, s. cargamento de navío, m.

caricature, *kăr'ĭkătŭr*, s. caricatura, f.; —, v. a. hacer caricaturas, ridiculizar.

caricaturist, *kărĕkătŭ'rĭst*, s. el que hace caricaturas.

caries, *kăr'rĕz*, s. caries, m.

cark, *kărk*, v. a. rascar, arañar; to—and care, tener cuidado.

carman, *kăr'măn*, s. carretero, m.

Carmelite, *kărmĕlīt'*, s. carmelita, m.

carminative, *kărmĭn'ătĭv*, a. carminante, carminativo.

carmine, *kăr'mĭn*, s. carmín, m.

carnage, *kăr'nāj*, s. carnicería, matanza, f.

carnal, *kăr'năl*, a. carnal; sensual; —ly, ad. carnalmente. [sualidad, f.

carnality, *kărnăl'ĭtĕ*, s. carnalidad, sensualidad, f.

carnation, *kărnā'shăn*, s. encarnación, f.; clavel, m. (flor)

carnival, *kăr'nĭvăl*, s. carnaval, m.

carnivorous, *kărnĭv'ŏrŭs*, a. carnívoro.

carol, *kăr'ăl*, s. villancico, m., canción de alegría ó piedad, f.; —, v. a. celebrar con villancicos.

carotic, *kărŏt'ĭk*, a. comatoso; —state, s. sueño letárgico, m.

carotid, *kărŏt'ĭd*, a. carotídeo; —artery, s. carótida, f.

carousal, *kărŏū'zăl*, s. cachiboda, f.

carouse, *kărŏūz'*, v. a. beber excesivamente.

carp, *kărp*, s. carpa, f.; —, v. n. censurar, criticar, reprobar.

carpenter, *kăr'pĕntăr*, s. carpintero, m.; —'s bench, banco de carpintero, m.

carpentry, *kăr'pĕntrĕ*, s. carpintería, f.

carper, *kăr'pŭr*, s. criticón, censurador, m.

carpet, *kăr'pĕt*, s. tapete de mesa, m.; tapiz, m.; —, v. a. cubrir con alfombras.

carpet-bag, *-băg*, s. baulillo de viandante, m.

carpeting, *-ĭng*, s. tapiz en piezas, m.

carpet-knight, *-nīt*, s. caballerete, m.

carping, *kăr'pĭng*, a. capcioso, caviloso; —ly, ad. malignamente.

carriage, *kăr'rĭj*, s. porte, talante, m.; coche, m., carroza, f.; vehículo, m.; carga, f.; cureña de cañón, f.; a—and four, carroza con cuatro caballos, f.

carriage-free (—paid), *-frĕ(păd)*, a. franco de porte.

carriage-house, *-hŏūs*, s. cochera, f.

carrier, *kăr'rēăr*, s. portador, carretero, m.

carrier-pigeon, *-pĭj'ŭn*, s. paloma correo ó mensajera, f.

carrion, *kăr'rĭŭn*, s. carroña, f.

carronade, *kăr'rŏnād*, s. carronada, f.

carrot, *kăr'rŏt*, s. chirivía, f.

carroty, *-ĕ*, a. pelirrojo.

carry, *kăr'rĕ*, v. a. llevar, conducir; lograr; —, v. n. portarse; to — the day, quedar victorioso; to — it high, afectar grandeza; to — on, conducir.

carry-all, *—ăl*, s. ómnibus, m.

carrying-business, *—ĭngbĭznĕs*, s. negocio de expedición, m.

cart, *kărt*, s. carro, m.; carreta, f.; —, v. a. & n. carretear; usar carretas ó carros.

cartage, *—dj*, **carting**, *—ĭng*, s. carretaje, m.

cartel, *kăr'tĕl*, s. cartel, m. [m.

carter, *kăr'ăr*, s. carretero, m.

cart-horse, *kărt'hŏrs*, s. caballo de tiro, m.; caballo de coche.

Carthusian, *kărthū'zhŭan*, s. cartujo (monje), m. [nilla, f.

cartilage, *kăr'tĭlăj*, s. cartílago, m.; ter-

cart-load, *kărt'lŏd*, s. carretada, f.

cartoon, *kărtōn'*, s. cartón, m.

cartouch, *kărtōsh'*, **cartridge**, *kăr'trĭj*, s. cartucho, m.; **ball**—, cartucho con bala; **blank**—, cartucho sin bala.

cartridge-box, *kăr'trĭjbŏks*, s. cartuchera, f. [tero de prieto, m.

cartwright, *kăr'rĭt*, s. carretero, carpin-

carve, *kărv*, v. a. cincelar; trinchar; grabar; —, v. n. esculpir. [m.

carver, *—ăr*, s. escultor, m.; trinchante.

carving, *kărv'ĭng*, s. escultura, f.

carving-knife, *—nĭf*, s. cuchillo grande de mesa, m.

case, *kās*, s. estado, m.; situación, f.; caso, m.; estuche, m.; vaina, f.; **in**—, si acaso.

case-hardened, *—hărdnd*, a. acerado.

case-knife, *—nĭf*, s. cuchillo grande de cocina, m.

casemate, *—māt*, s. (mil.) casamata, f.

casement, *—mĕnt*, s. puerta ventana, f.

case-shot, *—shŏt*, s. balas encajonadas, f. pl. [—, v. a. cobrar dineros.

cash, *kăsh*, s. dinero contante, m.; caja, f.;

cashier, *kăshēr'*, s. cajero, m.; —, v. a. privar á uno de su empleo.

cashmire, *kăsh'mēr*, s. cachemira, f.

casing, *kā'sĭng*, s. forro, m.; cubierta, f.

cask, *kăsk*, s. barril, tonel, m.; —, v. a. entonelar. [poner en cajita.

casket, *—ĕt*, s. cajita para joyas, f.; —, v. a.

cassation, *kăssā'shŭn*, s. (law) casación, f.; **court of** —, tribunal que anula ó confirma las sentencias de los tribunales inferiores, m.

cassock, *kăs'sŏk*, s. sotana, f.

cassowary, *kăs'sŏwărĕ*, s. casoar, m.

cast, *kăst*, v. a. tirar, lanzar; ganar; modelar; imponer una pena; to — an account, ajustar una cuenta; to — lots, echar suertes; —, v. n. maquinar alguna cosa; —, s. tiro, golpe, m.; forma, f.; aire, m.; echamiento, m.; apariencia exterior, f.; (of the eyes) ojeada, f. [f. pl.

castanets, *kăs'tănĕts*, s. pl. castañetas, f.

castaway, *kăst'ăwā*, s. réprobo, m.

cast-down, *—dŏĕn*, a. humillado.

caste, *kăst*, s. casta, corporación, f.

castellan, *kăs'tĕllăn*, s. castellano, m.

caster, *kăst'ăr*, s. calculador, m.; pimentero, m.; tirador, m.; adivino, m.; ruedecita, f.

castigate, *kăs'tĭgāt*, v. a. castigar.

castigation, *kăstĭgā'shŭn*, s. castigo, m.; pena, f.

casting-voice(-vote), *kăst'ĭngvŏĭs(vōt)*, s. voto decisivo, m.

castings, *—z*, s. pl. obras de fundición, f. pl.

cast-iron, *kăst'ărn*, s. hierro colado, m.

castle, *kăs'sl*, s. castillo, m.; fortaleza, f.; —, v. a. to — one's king, enrocar (en el juego de ajedrez).

castled, *—d*, a. fortificado con castillo.

castor, *kăs'tăr*, s. castor, m.; sombrero fino hecho del pelo de castor, m.

castoreum, *kăstō'rĕm*, s. castóreo, m.

castor-oil, *kăs'tărŏĭl*, s. aceite de ricino ó de palmacristi, m.

castration, *kăstrā'shŭn*, s. capadura, f.

cast steel, *kăst'stēl*, s. acero fundido, m.

casual, *kăzh'ŭăl*, a. casual, fortuito; **-ly**, ad. casualmente, fortuitamente.

casualty, *—tĕ*, s. casualidad, f.; acaso, accidente, m.

casuist, *kăzh'ŭĭst*, s. casuísta, m.

casuistical, *kăzhŭĭst'ĭkăl*, a. casuístico.

cat, *kăt*, s. gato, m.; gata, f.; — o' nine tails, s. (mar.) azote con nueve cordeles, m.; -'s paw (mar.), soplo, m.; (fig.) engañado. m. [vío, m.

cataclysm, *kăt'tăklĭzm*, s. cataclismo, dilu-

catacombs, *kă'tăkōmz*, s. pl. catacumbas, f. pl.

catalepsy, *kăt'ălĕpsĕ*, s. catalepsis, f.

catalogue, *kăt'ălŏg*, s. catálogo, m.

catamount, *kăt'ămŏĕnt*, s. gato montaraz, m.

cataplasm, *kăt'ăplăsm*, s. cataplasma, f.

catapult, *kăt'ăpŭlt*, s. catapulta, f.

cataract, *kăt'ărăkt*, s. cascada, f.; catarata, f.; **to couch the** —, operar la catarata, f.

catarrh, *kătăr'*, s. catarro, m.; reuma, f.

catarrhal, *—răl*, a. catarral.

catastrophe, *kătăs'trŏfĕ*, s. catástrofe, f.

cat-call, *kăt'kăl*, s. silbido, m.; reclamo, m.

catch, *kătsh*, v. a. coger, agarrar, asir; atrapar; pillar; sorprender; —, v. n. pegarse, ser contagioso; to — cold, resfriarse; to — fire, encenderse; —, s. presa, f.; captura, f.; idea, f.; (mus.) repetición, f.; provecho, m.; trampa, f.

catcher, *—ăr*, s. cogedor, m.; engañador, m.

catching, *—ĭng*, a. contagioso.

catchword, *—wŭrd*, s. reclamo, m.

catechise, *kăt'ĕkĭz*, v. a. catequizar, examinar.

catechism, *kăt'ĕkĭzm*, s. catecismo, m.

catechist, *kăt'ĕkĭst*, s. catequista, m.

categorical, *kătĕgŏr'ĭkăl*, a. categórico; **-ly**, ad. categóricamente.

category, *kăt'ĕgŏrĕ*, s. categoría, f.

cater, *kā'tăr*, v. n. abastecer, proveer.

caterer, *—ăr*, s. proveedor, abastecedor, m.

caterpillar, *kăt'ărpĭlăr*, s. oruga, f.

caterwaul, *kăt'ărwăl*, v. n. maullar; encerrar; —, s. maullido, maúllo, m.; encerrada, f.

cat-gut, *kăt'gŭt*, s. cuerda de violón, f.

cathedral, *kăthē'drăl*, s. catedral, f.

cat-hole, *kăt'hŏl*, s. gatera, f.

catholic, *kắth'ŏlĭk*, a. & s. católico (m.).
catholicism, *kăthŏl'ĭsĭzm*, s. catolicismo, m.   [les), f.
batkin, *kắt'kĭn*, s. candeda (de los árbo-
cattle, *kắt'tl*, s. ganado, m.; black —,
ganado vacuno, m.
cattle-plague, —*plăg*, s. epizootia, f.
cattle-show, —*shô*, s. exposición de ganados, f.   [s, (rail.) vagón cuadra, m.
cattle-van, —*văn*, cattle-box, —*bŏks*,
caucus, *kă'kŭs*, s. (am.) junta electoral, f.
caul, *kăl*, s. cofia, redecilla, f.
cauliflower, *kŏl'ĭflŏŭr*, s. coliflor, f.
cause, *kăz*, s. causa, f.; razón, f.; motivo,
m.; proceso, m.; —, v. a. causar, hacer.
causeless, —*lĕs*, a. infundado, sin razón.
causeway, —*wâ*, s. arrecife, m.
caustic, *kă'stĭk*, a. & s. cáustico (m.);
lunar —, s. piedra infernal, f.
cauterise, *kă'tŭrīz*, v. a. cauterizar.
caution, *kă'shŭn*, s. prudencia, precaución, f.; aviso, m.; —, v. a. avisar; amonestar; advertir.
cautionary, —*ărĭ*, a. dado á fianzas.
cautious, *kă'shŭs*, a. prudente, circunspecto, cauto.   [gata, cabalgada, f.
cavalcade, *kăv'ălkād*, *kăvălkād'*, s. cabal-
cavalier, *kăvălēr'*, s. jinete, m.; caballero.
cavalry, *kăv'ălrĭ*, s. caballería, f.   [m.
cave, *kāv*, s. caverna, f.; bodega, f.
caveat, *kā'vĭăt*, s. aviso, m.; advertencia, f.; (law) notificación, f.
cavern, *kăv'ŭrn*, s. caverna, f.; bodega, f.
cavernous, —*ŭs*, a. cavernoso.
caviar, *kăvĭăr'*, s. cabial, m.
cavil, *kăv'ĭl*, s. cavilación, sofistería, f.;
—, v. n. cavilar; criticar.
caviller, —*lŭr*, s. sofista, enredador, m.
cavity, *kăv'ĭtĭ*, s. hueco, m.
caw, *kă*, v. n. graznar, crascitar.
cease, *sēs*, v. a. parar, suspender; —, v. n.
desistir.   —*lĭ*, ad. perpetuamente.
ceaseless, —*lĕs*, a. incesante, continuo;
cedar, *sē'dŭr*, s. cedro, m.
cede, *sēd*, v. a. ceder, transferir.
ceil, *sēl*, v. a. techar.   [habitación, m.
ceiling, —*ĭng*, s. techo ó cielo raso de una
celebrate, *sĕl'ĕbrāt*, v. a. celebrar; elogiar.
celebration, *sĕlĕbrā'shŭn*, s. celebración,
f.; alabanza, f.
celebrity, *sĕlĕb'rĭtĭ*, s. celebridad, fama, f.
celerity, *sĕlĕr'ĭtĭ*, s. celeridad, velocidad, f.
celery, *sĕl'ŭrĭ*, s. apio, m.
celestial, *sĕlĕs'tyăl*, a. celeste, divino;
s. celícola, m.   [tería, f.
celibacy, *sĕl'ĭbăsĭ*, s. celibato, m.; sol-
celibate, *sĕl'ĭbăt*, a. soltero; soltera.
cell, *sĕl*, s. celdilla, f.; alvéolo, m.; cueva,
cellar, —*lŭr*, s. sótano, m.; bodega, f.   [f.
cellarage, —*lŭrĭj*, s. cueva, f.
cellaret, —*lŭrĕt*, s. cantina, frasquera, f.
cellarist, —*lĭrĭst*, s. cillerero, m.
cellular, —*lŭlŭr*, a. celular.
cellule, —*lŭl*, s. celdita, f.
cellulose, —*lŭlōs*, s. (chem.) celulosa, f.
cement, *sĕmĕnt'*, s. argamasa, f.; cimento,
(fig.) vínculo, m.; —, v. a. pegar con cimento; —, v. n. unirse.
cemetery, *sĕm'ĕtŭrĭ*, s. cimenterio, m.

cenotaph, *sĕn'ŏtăf*, s. cenotafio, m.
censer, *sĕn'sŭr*, s. incensario, m.
censor, *sĕn'sŏr*, s. censor, m.; crítico, m.
censorious, *sĕnsō'rĭŭs*, a. severo, crítico;
—ly, ad. severamente.
censorship, *sĕn'sŏrshĭp*, s. censura, f.
(oficio).   [sura.
censurable, *sĕn'shŭrăbl*, a. digno de cen-
censure, *sĕn'shŭr*, s. censura, reprensión,
f.; —, v. a. censurar, reprender; criticar.
census, *sĕn'sŭs*, s. censo, encabezamiento,
cent, *sĕnt*, s. ciento, m.   [m.
centenarian, *sĕntĭnā'rĭăn*, s. centenario,
m.; centenaria, f.   [centenario.
centenary, *sĕn'tĭnărĭ*, s. centena, f.; —, a.
centennial, *sĕntĕn'nĭăl*, a. centenario.
centimeter, *sĕn'tĭmĕtŭr*, s. centímetro, m.
centipede, *sĕn'tĭpēd*, s. escolopendra, f.
central, *sĕn'trăl*, a. central; —ly, ad. cen-
tralmente, en el centro.
centralize, *—līz*, v. a. centralizar.
centre, *sĕn'tŭr*, s. centro, m.; —, v. a. colocar en un centro; reconcentrar; —, v. n.
colocarse en el centro; reconcentrarse.
centrifugal, *sĕntrĭf'ŭgăl*, a. centrífugo.
centripetal, *sĕntrĭp'ĕtăl*, a. centrípeto.
centuple, *sĕn'tŭpl*, a. céntuplo; —, v. a.
centuplicar.
century, *sĕn'tŭrĭ*, s. centuria, f.; siglo, m.
cereals, *sēr'rĕălz*, s. pl. cereales, f. pl.
cerecloth, *sēr'klŏth*, cerement, —*mĕnt*,
s. encerado, hule, m.
ceremonial, *sĕrĕmō'nĭăl*, a. & s. ceremonial, m.; rito externo, m.
ceremonious, *sĕrĕmō'nĕŭs*, a. ceremonioso; —ly, ad. ceremoniosamente.
ceremony, *sĕr'ĕmŏnĭ*, s. ceremonia, f.;
fórmulas exteriores, f. pl.
certain, *sŭr'tĭn*, a. cierto, evidente; seguro;
—ly, ad. ciertamente; sin duda.
certainty, —*tĭ*, certitude, *sŭr'tĭtūd*, s.
certeza, f.; seguridad, f.
certificate, *sŭrtĭf'ĭkăt*, s. certificado, testimonio, m.   [cado, m.
certification, *sŭrtĭfĭkā'shŭn*, s. certifi-
certify, *sŭr'tĭfī*, v. a. certificar, afirmar.
cerulean, *sĕrū'lĕăn*, a. cerúleo, azulado.
cerumen, *sĕrō'mĕn*, s. cera de los oídos, m.
cesarean section, - operation, *sĕzā'-
rĭăn sĕk'shŭn* ú *ŏpĕrā'shŭn*, s. (med.)
operación cesárea, f.
cessation, *sĕssā'shŭn*, s. cesación, f.; - of
arms, suspensión de armas, f.
cession, *sĕsh'ŭn*, s. cesión, f.   [m.
cesspool, *sĕs'pōl*, s. cloaca, f.; sumidero,
chafe, *tshāf*, v. a. frotar, enojar, irritar;
—, v. n. acalorarse; —, s. cólera, f.; ardor,
chafer, —*ŭr*, s. escarabajo, m.   [m.
chaff, *tshăf*, s. zurrón, hollejo, m.; paja
menuda, f.; (fig.) paja.
chaff-cutter, —*kŭtŭr*, s. tajador, m.
chaffer, —*fŭr*, v. n. regatear, baratear.
chaffinch, —*fĭntsh*, s. pinzón, m.
chagrin, *shăgrĕn'*, s. zapa, f.
chain, *tshān*, s. cadena, f.; serie, sucesión,
f.; —s, pl. esclavitud, f.; —, v. a. encadenar, atar con cadena.
chain-bridge, —*brĭj*, s. puente colgante,

chain-gang, *-găng,* s. gavilla de malhechores encadenados juntos, f.

chain-shot, *-shŏt,* s. balas encadenadas, f. pl [m.; —, v. a. llevar en triunfo.

chair, *tshăr,* s. silla, f.; asiento portátil,

chair-bottomer, *-bŏtŏmăr,* s.sillero,m.

chair-man, *-măn,* s. presidente, m.; silletero, m. [coche, m.

chaise, *shās,* s. silla volante, f.; calesín

chalice, *tshălĭz,* s. cáliz, m.

chalk, *tshăk,* s. greda, f.; marga, f.; **French —,** espuma de mar, f.; —, v. a. dibujar con yeso; lapizar, lapizar.

chalk-pit, *-pĭt,* s. gredera, f.; marguera,

chalky, *-ĕ,* a. gredoso. [f.

challenge, *tshălĕnj,* s. desafío, cartel, m.; pretensión, f.; recusación, f.; —, v. a. desafiar; provocar; reclamar; (mil.) llamar ¿quién vive?

challenger, *-ăr,* s. desafiador, m.

chalybeate, *kălĭbĭăt,* a. ferruginoso.

chamber, *tshămbăr,* s. cámara, f.; aposento, m.; (mil.) cámara de mina.

chamber-counsel, *-kŏŭnsĕl,* s. jurisconsulto, m.

chamberlain, *-lăn,* s. camarero, m. [f.

chamberlainship, *-lănshĭp,* s.camarería,

chamber-maid, *-mād,* s. moza de cámara,

chamber-pot, *-pŏt,* s. orinal, m. [f.

chameleon, *kămĭlĕăn,* s. camaleón, m.

chamois-leather, *shăm'wălĕthăr,* s. gamuza, f. [— up, devorar.

champ, *tshămp,* v. a. morder, mascar; to

champagne, *shămpān',* s. vino de Champaña, m. [nura, f.

champaign, *shăm'pān,* s. campiña, llanura, f.

champion, *tshăm'pĭŏn,* s. campeón, m.; —, v. a. desafiar, retar.

championship, *-shĭp,* s. campeonaje, m

chance, *tshăns,* s. ventura, suerte, f.; acaso, m.; riesgo, m.; by —, por acaso; —, v. n. suceder, acontecer. [la iglesia)

chancel, *tshăn'sĕl,* s. presbiterio, m. (en

chancellor, *-lăr,* s. cancelario, m.; **lord high —,** ministro de justicia, gran canciller, m. [f.

chancellorship, *-lărshĭp,* s. cancillería,

chancery, *tshăn'sărĕ,* s. chancillería, f.

chancre, *shăng'kăr,* s. úlcera venérea, f.; cáncer, m. [f.; candelero, m.

chandelier, *shăndĕlēr',* s. araña de luces, f.

chandler, *tshănd'lăr,* s. cerero, m.; lonjista, m.; regatón, m.

change, *tshānj,* v. a. cambiar; trasmutar; —, v. n. variar, alterarse; —, s. mudanza, variedad, f.; vicisitud, f.; cambio, m.; —, a. fortuito.

changeable, *-ăbl,* **changeful,** *-fŭl,* a. variable, inconstante; mudable.

changeableness, *-ăblnĕs,* s. mutabilidad, inconstancia, f.

changeless, *-lĕs,* a. constante, inmutable.

changeling, *-lĭng,* s. niño cambiado (por otro), hijo supuesto, m.; veleidoso, m.; inconstante, m.

channel, *tshăn'nĕl,* s. canal, álveo, m.; —, v. a. acanalar, estriar.

chant, *tshănt,* s. canto (llano), m.; —, v. a. cantar.

chanticleer, *-ĭklēr',* s. gallo, m.; cantor sonoro, m.

chantry, *-rĕ,* s. chantría, f.

chaos, *kā'ŏs,* s. caos, m.; confusión, f.

chaotic, *kāŏt'ĭk,* a. confuso.

chap, *tshăp,* v. n. rajarse, henderse; —, s. hendrija, rendija, f.; mandíbula, f.

chape, *tshăp,* s. chapa de cinturón, f.; charnela de hebilla, f.

chapel, *tshăp'ĕl,* s. capilla, f.

chap-fallen, *tshăp'făln,* a. boquihundido.

chapiter, *tshăp'ĕtăr,* s. capitel, m.

chaplain, *tshăp'lĭn,* s. capellán, m.; limosnero, m. [m.

chaplet, *tshăp'lĕt,* s. guirnalda, f.; rosario,

chapman, *tshăp'măn,* s. comprador, m.; vendedor, m.; traficante, m. [m.

chapter, *tshăp'tăr,* s. capítulo, m.; cabildo,

char, *tshăr,* v. a. hacer carbón de leña; —, v. n. trabajar á jornal; —, s. (trabajo á) jornal, m.

character, *kăr'ăktăr,* s. carácter, m.; señal, f.; forma de la letra, f.; calidad, f.; —, v. a. esculpir, grabar.

characteristic(al), *kărăktărĭst'ĭk(ăl),* a. característico; **-ally,** ad. característicamente. [zar, imprimir.

characterize, *kăr'ăktărīz,* v. a. caracterizar.

characterless, *kăr'ăktărlĕs,* a. sin carácter.

charade, *shărād',* s. charada, f.

charcoal, *tshăr'kōl,* s. carbón de leña, m.

charcoal-pencil, *-pĕn'sĭl,* s. carboncillo para bosquejar, m.

charge, *tshărj,* v. a. encargar, comisionar; cargar; acusar, imputar; —, s. cargo, cuidado, m.; mandato, m.; acusación, f.; (mil.) ataque, m.; depósito, m.; carga, f.

chargeable, *-ăbl,* a. dispendioso; imputable. [caballo de guerra, m.

charger, *-ăr,* s. fuente, f.; plato grande, m.;

chariness, *tshăr'ĭnĕs,* s. circunspección, cordura, f. [militar, m.

chariot, *tshăr'ĭŏt,* s. faetonte, m.; carro

charioteer, *-ēr',* s. cochero, m.

charitable, *tshăr'ĭtăbl,* a. caritativo; benigno, clemente; **-bly,** ad. caritativamente.

charitableness, *-nĕs,* s. caridad, f.

charity, *tshăr'ĭtĕ,* s. caridad, benevolencia, f.; limosna, f. [f.

charity-school, *-skōl,* s. escuela gratuita,

charlatan, *shăr'lătăn,* s. charlatán, m.

charlatanry, *-rĕ,* s. charlatanería, f.

Charles's-Wain, *tshărlz'ĕzwān,* s. Osa Mayor, f. [amarillo, m.

charlock, *tshăr'lŏk,* s. alhaceña, f.; alhelí

charm, *tshărm,* s. encanto, m.; atractivo, m.; —, v. a. encantar, embelesar, atraer.

charmingly, *-ĭnglĕ,* ad. agradablemente, deleitosamente.

charnel-house, *tshăr'nĕlhŏŭs,* s. carnero, m.

chart, *tshărt,* s. carta de navegar, f. [m.

charter, *tshăr'tăr,* s. letra patente, f.; privilegio, m.; —, v. a. fletar un buque.

charter-party, *-părtĕ,* s. (mar.) contrato de fletamento, f. [f.

char-woman, *tshăr'wŭmăn,* s. jornalera,

chary, *tshă'rĕ,* a. circunspecto; frugal.

chase, *tshâs*, v. a. cazar; perseguir; cincelar; —, s. caza, f.

chasing, *tshâsïng*, s. cinceladura, f.

chasm, *kâzm*, s. hendidura, f.; vacío, m.

chaste, *tshâst*, a. casto; puro; honesto; púdico.

chasten, *tshâsn*, v. a. corregir, castigar.

chastisement, *tshâstïzment*, s. castigo, m. [mar, corregir.

chastise, *tshâstïz'*, v. a. castigar, reformar.

chastity, *tshâstïtä*, s. castidad, pureza, f.

chat, *tshât*, v. n. charlar; —, s. charla, cháchara, f.; garrulidad, f.; astilla, f.

chattel, *tll*, s. bienes muebles, m. pl.

chatter, *târ*, v. n. cotorrear; rechinar; charlar; —, s. chirrido, m.; charla, f.

chatter-box, *túrbôks*, **chatterer**, *túrâr*, s. parlero, hablador, gárrulo, m.

chatty, *tä*, a. locuaz, parlanchín.

chaw, *tshâ*, v. a. mascar, masticar.

cheap, *tshëp*, a. barato; —ly, ad. á poco precio.

cheapen, *n*, v. a. regatear; abaratar.

cheapness, *nës*, s. baratura, f.; bajo precio, m.

cheat, *tshët*, v. a. engañar, defraudar; trampear; —, s. trampa, f.; fraude, engaño, m.; trampista, m.

check, *tshëk*, v. a. reprimir, refrenar; regañar; registrar; —, s. restricción, f.; freno, m.; represión, f.; jaque, m.; pagaré, m.

checker, *âr*, v. a. taracear.

checker-board, *bôrd*, s. tablero de ajedrez, m.

checker-work, *wûrk*, s. taracea, f.

check-mate, *tshëk'mât*, s. mate, m.

cheek, *tshëk*, s. carrillo, m.; mejilla f.; (fam.) desvergüenza, f.; atrevimiento, m.; — by jowl, cara á cara.

cheek-bone, *bôn*, s. hueso del carrillo, m.

cheer, *tshër*, s. banquete, m.; alegría, f.; aplauso, m.; buen humor, m.; vigor, m.; —, v. a. animar, alentar; —, v. n. alegrarse.

cheerful, *fúl*, a. alegre, vivo, jovial; —ly, ad. alegremente.

cheerfulness, *fúlnës*, **cheeriness**, *ïnës*, s. alegría, f.; buen humor, júbilo, m.

cheerings, *ïngz*, s. pl. aplauso, m.

cheerless, *lës*, a. triste, melancólico.

cheese, *tshëz*, s. queso, m.

cheese-dairy, *ddrë*, s. quesera, f.

cheese-hopper, *hôppûr*, s. arador, m.

cheese-monger, *mûngûr*, s. quesero, el que hace ó vende queso, m. [queso.

cheese-paring, *pâring*, s. raedura de queso, f.

chemical, *këm'ïkâl*, a. químico.

chemist, *këm'ïst*, s. químico, m.

chemistry, *rä*, s. química, f.

cherish, *tshër-ïsh*, v. a. mantener, fomentar, proteger. [cigarro).

cheroot, *shëröt'*, s. manilla, f. (especie de cigarro).

cherry, *tshër'rë*, s. cereza, f.; —, a. bermejo.

cherry-stone, *stôn*, s. cuesco de cereza, m.

cherry-tree, *trë*, s. cerezo, m. [m.

cherub, *tshër'âb*, s. querubín, m.

chess, *tshës*, s. juego del ajedrez, m.

chess-board, *bôrd*, s. tablero (para jugar al ajedrez), m.

chess-man, *mân*, s. pieza de ajedrez, f.

chest, *tshëst*, s. pecho, m.; arca, f.; — of drawers, cómoda, f.

chestnut, *nût*, s. castaña, f.; color de castaña, m.

chestnut-tree, *nûttrë*, s. castaño, m.

chetah, *tshë'tä*, s. lobo-tigre, m.

cheval-glass, *shëvâl'glâs*, s. espejo que gira, m.

chew, *tshû*, v. a. mascar, masticar; rumiar, meditar, reflexionar.

chicane, *shëkân'*, s. cavilación, trampa, f.; —, v. n. cavilar, sofisticar.

chicaner, *ûr*, s. sofista, trampista, m.

chicanery, *ärë*, s. sofistería, quisquilla, f.

chick(en), *tshïk(ân)*, s. polluelo, m.; (fig.) joven, m. & f.

chicken-hearted, *knhârtëd*, a. cobarde, tímido, gallina. [f. pl.

chicken-pox, *knpôks*, s. viruelas locas, f. pl.

chick-pea, *pë*, s. garbanzo, m.

chicory, *tshïk'örë*, s. achicoria, f.

chide, *tshïd*, v. a. reprobar, regañar; —, v. n. reñir, alborotar.

chider, *ûr*, s. regañón, m.

chief, *tshëf*, a. principal, capital; —ly, ad. principalmente; —, s. jefe, principal, m.

chieftain, *tïn*, s. jefe, comandante, m.

chilblain, *tshïl'bldn*, s. sabañón, m.

child, *tshïld*, s. infante, m.; hijo, m.; hija, f.; from a —, desde niño; with —, preñada, embarazada.

child-bed, *bëd*, s. sobreparto, m.

childhood, *hûd*, s. infancia, niñez, f.

childish, *ïsh*, a. frívolo, pueril; —ly, ad. puerilmente.

childishness, *ïshnës*, s. puerilidad, f.

childless, *lës*, a. sin hijos.

childlike, *lïk*, a. pueril. [m. pl

children, *tshïl'drën*, s. pl. de child; niños, m.

chill, *tshïl*, a. frío, friolero; —, s. frío, m.; —, v. a. enfriar; helar. [f.

chilliness, *tïnës*, s. calofrío, m.; tiritona, f.

chilly, *tä*, a. friolero, friolento.

chime, *tshïm*, s. armonía, f.; clave, m.; —, v. n. sonar con armonía; concordar.

chimera, *këm'râ*, s. quimera, f.

chimerical, *këmër'ïkâl*, a. quimérico; —ly, ad. quiméricamente.

chimney, *tshïm'në*, s. chimenea, f.

chimney-corner, *kôrnûr*, s. rincón de chimenea, m.

chimney-doctor, *dôktûr*, s. fumista, f.

chimney-piece, *pës*, s. dintel que adorna la chimenea, m. [chimeneas, m.

chimney-sweeper, *swëpûr*, s. limpia-chimeneas, m.

chin, *tshïn*, s. barba, f. [loza de China, f.

china-(ware), *tshï'nd(wâr)*, s. porcelana, f.

chine, *tshïn*, s. espinazo, m.; solomo, m.

chink, *tshïnk*, s. grieta, hendedura, f.; —, v. n. henderse; resonar.

chints, *tshïnts*, s. zaraza, f.

chip, *tshïp*, v. a. desmenuzar, picar; —, v. n. reventarse; —, s. brizna, astilla, f.; raspaduras de la corteza del pan, f. pl.

chirographer, *kïrög'râfûr*, s. quirógrafo, m.; quirografario, m.

chirography, *râfä*, s. quirografía, f.

chiromancy, *kï'römânsë*, s. quiromancia, f.

chiropodist, *kĭróp´ŏdĭst*, s. pedicuro, m.
chirp, *tshärp*, v.n. chirriar, gorjear; —, s. gorjeo, chirrido, m.
chirping, *-ĭng*, s. canto de las aves, m.
chisel, *tshĭz´ĕl*, s. escoplo, cincel, m.; —, v. a. escoplear, cincelar, grabar.
chit, *tshĭt*, s. niño, m.; tallo (del grano), m.
chit-chat, *-tshăt*, s. charla, parlería, f.
chitterlings, *-tŭrlĭngz*, s. embuchado de tripas, m.
chivalrous, *shĭv´ălrŭs*, chivalric, *-rĭk*, a. caballeresco.
chivalry, *shĭv´ălrĕ*, s. caballería, f.; hachives, *tshlyz*, s. pl. cebolleta, f. [zaña,f.
choral, *klōr´ăl*, a. (chem.) cloral, m.
chloroform, *klōr´ŏfŏrm*, s. cloroformo, m.
chlorosis, *klōrŏ´sĭs*, s. (med.) clorosis, f.
chock-full, *tshŏk´fŭl*, choke-full, *tshŏk´fŭl*, a. de bote en bote, completamente lleno.
chocolate, *tshŏ´kŏlăt*, s. chocolate, m.
chocolate-drop, *-drŏp*, s. pastilla de chocolate, f.
chocolate-pot, *-pŏt*, s. chocolatera, f.
chocolate-stick, *-stĭk*, s. molinillo, m.
choice, *tshŏĭs*, s. elección, preferencia, f.; selecto, m.; —, a. selecto, exquisito, excelente; —ly, ad. escogidamente, primorosamente.
choiceless, *-lĕs*, a. sin poder elegir.
choiceness, *-nĕs*, s. delicadeza f.; discernimiento, m.
choir, *kwīr*, s. coro, m.
choke, *tshŏk*, v. a. sufocar; oprimir; tapar.
choker, *-ŭr*, s. (fam.) cravata, f.
choky, *tshŏ´kĕ*, a. sufocante.
choler, *kŏl´ŭr*, s. cólera,f.; bilis, f.; ira, f.
cholera, *kŏl´ŭrā*, s. cólera, m.
choleric, *kŏl´ŭrĭk*, a. colérico.
choose, *tshŏŏz*, v. a. escoger, elegir; —, v. n. tener facultad para elegir.
chop, *tshŏp*, v. a. tajar, cortar; picar; —, v n. girar, mudar; trocar; —, s. tajada de carne, f.; costilla de ternera, f.; raja, f.; —s, pl. (vulg.) quijadas, f. pl.
chopper, *-ŭr*, s. cuchillo de carnicero, m.
chopping-block, *-pĭngblŏk*, s. tajo de cocina, m.
chopping-knife, *-pĭngnĭf*, s. machete, m.
choral, *kŏ´răl*, a. coral.
chord, *kŏrd*, s. cuerda, f.; —, v. a. encordar.
chorist, *kŏ´rĭst*, chorister, *kŏr´ĭstŭr*, s coro m.
chorus, *kŏ´rŭs*, s. coro, m. [corista, m.
chouse, *tshŏŭs*, v. a. engañar, engatusar.
chrism, *krĭzm*, s. crisma, m. & f.
Christ, *krĭst*, s. Jesucristo, m.
christen, *krĭs´n*, v. a. cristianar, bautizar.
christendom, *-dŭm*, s. cristianismo, m.; cristiandad, f.
christening, *-ĭng*, s. bautismo, m.
Christian, *krĭst´yăn*, a. & s. cristiano (m.); —name, nombre de bautismo, m.
christianise, *krĭst´yănĭz*,v. a. cristianizar.
Christianity, *krĭstyăn´ĭtĕ*,s.cristianismo, m.; cristiandad, f. [mente.
christianly, *krĭst´yănlĕ*, ad. cristianamente.
Christmas, *krĭs´măs*, s. Natividad, f.
Christmas-box, *-bŏks*, s. aguinaldo, m.
Christmas-eve, *-ĕv*, s. víspera de Natividad, f.
chromatic, *krŏmăt´ĭk*, a. cromático.

chromo, *krō´mŏ*, chromolithography, *-lĭth´ŏgrăfĕ*, s. cromolitografía, f.
chronic(al), *krŏn´ĭk(ăl)*, a. crónico.
chronicle, *-ĭkl*, s. crónica, f.; —, v. a. formar una crónica.
chronicler, *-ŭr*, s. cronista, m.
chronological, *krŏnŏlŏj´ĭkăl*, a. cronológico; -ly, ad. cronológicamente.
chronology, *krŏnŏl´ŏjĕ*, s. cronología, f.
chronometer, *krŏnŏm´ĕtŭr*, s.cronómetro, m.
chrysalis, *krĭs´ălĭs*, s. crisálida, f. [m.
chub, *tshŭb*, s. gobio, m. (pez).
chubby, *-bĕ*, a. gordo, cariancho.
chuck, *tshŭk*, v. n. cloquear; —, v. a. dar una sobarbada; —, s. cloqueo, m.; sobarbada, f. [v. n. reirse á carcajadas.
chuckle, *-kl*, v. a. cloquear, acariciar; —,
chum, *tshŭm*, s. compañero de cuarto (entre estudiantes), m. [tronco, m.
chump, *-p*, chunk, *tshŭngk*, s. tajo,
church, *tshŭrtsh*, s. iglesia, f.; —, v. a. ir á misa; —, v. n. ejecutar las ceremonias de la purificación con alguna mujer recién parida.
church-ale, *-ăl*, s. fiesta del lugar, f.
churching, *-ĭng*, s. ceremonia de la purificación, f.
church-law, *-lă*, s. derecho canónico, m.
churchman, *-măn*, s. sacerdote, eclesiástico, m. [de la iglesia, m.
church-warden, *-wărdn*, s. mayordomo.
churchyard, *-yărd*, s. cementerio, m.
churl, *tshŭrl*, s. patán, rústico, m.
churlish, *-ĭsh*, a. rústico, grosero; tacaño; -ly, ad. rudamente, brutalmente.
churn, *tshŭrn*, s. mantequera, f.; —, v. a. mazar, batir la leche para hacer manteca.
churn-staff, *-stăf*, s. batidera, f.
cicatrice, *sĭk´ătrĭs*, s. cicatriz, f.
cider, *sī´dŭr*, s. sidra, f.
cigar, *sĕgăr´*, s. cigarro, m. [m.
cigar-divan, *-dĭvăn*, s. salón para fumar,
cigarette, *sĕg´ărĕt*, s. cigarrito, m.
cigar-holder, *-hŏldŭr*, cigar-tip, *-tĭp*, s. boquilla, f.; portacigarros, m.
cimeter, *sĭm´ĕtŭr*, s. cimitarra, f.
cincture, *sĭngk´tshŭr*, s. cinto, ceñidor, m., cinta, pretinilla, f. [f.
cinder, *sĭn´dŭr*, s. ceniza gruesa y caliente,
cinnabar, *sĭn´năbăr*, s. cinabrio, m.
cinnamon, *sĭn´nămŏn*, s. canela, f.
cipher, *sī´fŭr*, s. cifra, f.; —, v. n. numerar, calcular.
circle, *sŭr´kl*, s. círculo, m.; corrillo, m.; asamblea, f.; —, v. a. circundar; cercar, ceñir; —, v. n. circular.
circlet, *-klĕt*, s. círculo pequeño, m.
circuit, *-kĭt*, s. circuito, m.; recinto, m.
circuitous, *sŭrkū´ĭtŭs*, a. circular.
circular, *sŭr´kŭlăr*, a. circular, redondo; —. s. carta circular, f. [al rededor.
circulate, *-kŭlăt*, v. n. circular; moverse
circulating-library, *-kŭlātĭnglĭbrărĕ*, s. gabinete de lectura, m.
circulation, *sŭrkŭlā´shŭn*,s. circulación,f.
circumcise, *sŭr´kŭmsīz*, v. a. circuncidar.
circumcision, *sŭrkŭmsĭzh´ŭn*, s. circuncisión, f. [ferencia, f.; circuito, m.
circumference, *sŭrkŭm´fĕrĕns*, s circun-

circumflex, –*flĕks*, s.acento circunflejo, m.
circumjacent, –*jā'sĕnt*, a. convecino, contiguo.
circumlocution, –*lŏk'shŭn*, s. circunlocución, f.
circumlocutory, –*lŏk'ūtŭrĕ*, a. con perifrasis.
circumnavigate, –*năv'ĭgāt*, v. a, circumnavegar.
circumnavigation, –*năvĕgā'shŭn*, s. circumnavegación, f.
circumscribe, –*skrīb'*, v. a. circunscribir.
circumscription, –*skrĭp'shŭn*, s. circunscripción, f.
circumspect, *sŭr'kŭmspĕkt*, a. circunspecto, prudente, reservado; –, v. a. examinar con atención.
circumspection, –*spĕk'shŭn*, s. circunspección, prudencia, f.
circumstance, –*stăns*, s. circunstancia, condición, f.; incidente, m.
circumstanced, –*stănsd*, a. en condición, circunstanciado.
circumstantial, –*stăn'shăl*, a. accidental; accesorio; –ly, ad. circunstanciadamente, exactamente. [cunstanciar, detallar.
circumstantiate, –*stăn'shĭāt*, v. a. circumvent, –*vĕnt*, v. a. circumvenir.
circumvention, –*vĕn'shŭn*, s. engaño, m.; trampa, f.; embrollo, m.
circus, *sŭr'kŭs*, s. circo, m.
cistern, *sis'tŭrn*, s. cisterna, f.
citadel, *sĭt'ădĕl*, s. ciudadela, fortaleza, f.
citation, *sītā'shŭn*, s. citación, cita, f.
cite, *sīt*, v. a. citar (á juicio); alegar; referirse á.
citizen, *sĭt'ĭzĕn*, s. ciudadano, m.
citizenship, –*shĭp*, s. ciudadanía, f.
citron, *sĭt'rŏn*, cidra, f.
citron-tree, –*trĕ*, s. cidro, m.
cittern, *sĭt'tŭrn*, **cithern**, *sĭth'ŭrn*, s. [cítara, f.
city, *sĭt'ĕ*, s. ciudad, f.
civet, *sĭv'ĕt*, s. gato de algalia, m.; algalia, f.
civic, *sĭv'ĭk*, a. cívico. [f.
civil, *sĭv'ĭl*, a. civil, cortés; –ly, ad. civilmente. [consulto, m.
civilian, *sĕvĭl'yăn*, s. paisano, m.; jurisconsulto, m.
civilisation, *sĭvĭlĭzā'shŭn*, s. civilización, f.
civilise, *sĭv'ĭlĭz*, v. a. civilizar. [f.
civility, *sĕvĭl'ĭtĕ*, s. civilidad y urbanidad, cortesía, f.
clack, *klăk*, s. ruido continuo, estrépito, m.; cítola de molino, f.; –, v. n. cencerrear.
clad, *klăd*, a. vestido, cubierto.
claim, *klām*, v. a. pedir en juicio, reclamar, pretender como cosa debida; –, s. pretensión, f.; derecho, m. [dador, m.
claimant, –*ănt*, s. reclamante, m.; demandador, m.
clam, *klăm*, v. a. empastar, pegar.
clamber, –*bŭr*, v. n. gatear, trepar.
clamminess, –*minĕs*, s. viscosidad, f.
clammy, –*mĕ*, a. viscoso, tenaz.
clamorous, *klăm'ărŭs*, a. clamoroso, tumultuoso, estrepitoso; –ly, ad. clamorosamente. [v. n. vociferar, gritar.
clamour, *klăm'ŭr*, s. clamor, grito, m.; –, clamp, *klămp*, s. empalmadura; laña, f.; –, v. a. empalmar.
clan, *klăn*, s. familia, tribu, raza, f.
clandestine, *klăndĕs'tĭn*, a. clandestino, oculto; –ly, a. clandestinamente.

clang, *klăng*, s. rechino, sonido desapacible, m.; –, v. n. rechinar.
clangorous, –*gărŭs*, a. ruidoso.
clangour, –*gŭr*, s. rechinamiento, m.
clank, *klăngk*, v.n. chillar; –, s. chischás, retintín, m.
clap, *klăp*, v. a. batir; aplicar; palmear; –, s. estrépito, m.; golpe, m.; trueno, m.; palmoteo, m.
clapper, –*pŭr*, s. palmoteador, m.; badajo de campana, m.; cítola de molino, f.; llamador (de una puerta), m.
clapping, –*pĭng*, s. palmada, f.; aplauso, palmoteo, m. [engañabobos, m.
clap-trap, –*trăp*, s. lance de teatro, m.; clare-obscure, *klărŏbskŭr'*, s. claroscuro, m.
claret, *klă'rĕt*, s. clarete, m. (vino).
clarification, *klărĭfĭkā'shŭn*, s. clarificación, f.
clarify, *klăr'ĭfĭ*, v. a. clarificar, aclarar, –, v. n. ponerse claro.
clarinet, *klăr'ĭnĕt*, s. clarinete, m.
clarion, *klăr'ĭŏn*, s. clarín, m.
clash, *klăsh*, v. n. rechinar, encontrarse contradecir; –, s. rechino, crujido, m.; estrépito, m.; disputa, f.; choque, m.
clasp, *klăsp*, s. broche, m.; hebilla, f.; abrazo, m.; –, v. a. abrochar; abrazar.
clasp-knife, –*nĭf*, s. navaja, f.
class, *klăs*, s. clase, f.; orden, f.; –, v. a. clasificar, coordinar. [clásico, m.
classic(al), –*sĭk(ăl)*, a. clásico; –, s. autor
classification, –*sĭfĭkā'shŭn*, s. clasificación, f.
classify, –*sĭfĭ*, v. a. clasificar. [ción, f.
clatter, *klăt'ŭr*, v.n. resonar; hacer ruido; –, s. ruido, fracaso, m. [estipulación, f.
clause, *klăz*, s. cláusula, f.; artículo, m.;
claustral, *klăs'trăl*, a. claustral.
clavicle, *klăv'ĭkl*, s. clavícula, f.
claw, *klă*, s. garra, f.; garfa, f.; –, v. a. desgarrar, arañar; lisonjear.
clawed, –*d'*, a. armado de garras.
clay, *klā*, s. arcilla, f.
clayey, –*ĕ*, **clayish**, –*ĭsh*, a. arcilloso.
clay-pit, –*pĭt*, s. barrizal, m.
clean, *klēn*, a. limpio; casto; –, ad. enteramente; –, v. a. limpiar.
cleanliness, –*lĭnĕs*, s. limpieza, f.; curiosidad en el vestir, f.
cleanly, –*lĕ*, a. limpio; puro, delicado; –, ad. primorosamente, ascadamente.
cleanness, –*nĕs*, s. limpieza, f.; pureza, f.
cleanse, *klĕnz*, v. a. limpiar, purificar; purgar.
clear, *klēr*, a. claro; neto; diáfano; sereno; evidente; inocente; –, ad. claramente; enteramente; –.v.a. clarificar, aclarar; justificar, absolver; **to – accounts**, liquidar cuentas; –, v. n. aclararse.
clearage, –*rădj*, s. despejo, m.
clearance, –*ăns*, s. albalá de pago y finiquito, m. & f.
clearly, –*lĕ*, ad. claramente, evidentemente.
clearness, –*nĕs*, s. claridad, transparencia, f.; esplendor, m.; perspicacia, f.; sinceridad, f. [cioso.
clear-sighted, –*sĭtĕd*, a. perspicaz, jui-
clearstarch, –*stărtsh*, v. a. almidonar.

cleave, *klēv,* v. a. & n. hender; partir; dividir; pegarse.

cleaver, *–ăr,* s. cuchillo de carnicero, m.

cleft, *klĕft,* s. hendedura, abertura, f.

clematis, *klĕm'ătĭs,* s. clemátita, f.

clemency, *klĕm'ĕnsĕ,* s. clemencia, f.

clement, *klĕm'ĕnt,* a. clemente, benigno.

clenched, *klĕnshd,* a. cerrado (dícese de la mano ó del puño).

clergy, *klŭr'jĕ,* s. clero, m.

clergyman, *–măn,* s. eclesiástico, m.; little –, aprendiz de un deshollinador, m.

clerical, *klĕr'ĭkăl,* a. clerical, eclesiástico.

clerk, *klărk,* s. eclesiástico, clérigo, m.; estudiante, m.; amanuense, escribiente, m.; – of a parish, sacristán, m.

clerkship, *–shĭp,* s. educación literaria, f.; empleo de clérigo ó escribiente, m.

clever, *klĕv'ăr,* a. diestro, hábil, mañoso; propio; **–ly,** ad. diestramente, hábilmente. [f.

cleverness, *–nĕs,* s. destreza, habilidad, f.

clew, *klū,* s. ovillo de hilo, m.; – (up), v. a. (mar.) cargar las velas.

click, *klĭk,* v. n. retiñir.

client, *klī'ĕnt,* s. cliente, m. [f.

cliff, *klĭf,* s. peñasco, m.; roca escarpada.

climacteric, *klĭmăk'tărĭk,* a. climactérico. [tura, f.

climate, *klĭ'măt,* s. clima, m.; temperatura, f.

climatic, *klĭmă'tĭk,* a. climatérico.

climax, *klĭ'măks,* s. clímax, m.

climb, *klĭm,* v. a. escalar, trepar, ç, v. n. subir.

clinch, *klĭnsh,* v. a. empuñar, cerrar el puño; remachar un clavo; –, s. pulla; f.; equívoco, m.

clincher, *–ăr,* s. laña, f.

cling, *klĭng,* v. n. colgar, adherirse, pegarse.

clinic(al), *klĭn'ĭk(ăl),* a. clínico.

clink, *klĭngk,* v. a. hacer resonar; –, v. n. retiñir, resonar; –, s. retintín, m.

clinker, *–ăr,* s. cagafierro, m.; ladrillo refractor, m. [timar.

clip, *klĭp,* v. a. abrazar; cortar á raíz; escamondar.

clipper, *–păr,* s. cercenador de monedas, m.; (mar.) navío velero, m.

clippings, *–pĭngz,* s. pl. tundizno, m.

clique, *klĕk,* s. gatería, f.

cloak, *klōk,* s. capa, f.; pretexto, m.; –, v. n. encapotar; paliar.

cloak-room, *–rōm,* s. (rail.) factoría, f., equipajes, mpl. [st? ¿qué hora es?

clock, *klŏk,* s. reloj, m.; what o'clock is

clock-dial, *–dĭăl,* s. muestra de un reloj, f.

clock-maker, *–măkăr,* s. relojero, m. [f.

clock-work, *–wŭrk,* s. mecanismo de un reloj, m.; –, a. sumamente exacto y puntual. [m.; –, v. n. coagularse.

clod, *klŏd,* s. terrón, m.; césped, m.; zoquete.

clog, *klŏg,* s. obstáculo, m.; galocha, f.; –, v. a. cargar, embarazar; –, v. n. coagularse; unirse. [sculo, m.

clogginess, *–gĭnĕs,* s. embarazo, obstáculo.

cloister, *klŏĭs'tăr,* s. claustro, monasterio, m.

close, *klōz,* v. a. cerrar; concluir, terminar; –, v. n. cerrarse, unirse; convenirse; –, s. cercado, m.; fin, m.; conclusión, f.; –, a.

cerrado; preso; estrecho, angosto; ajustado; secreto; avaro; retirado; obscuro; denso; secreto; – fight, s. viva pelea, f.; –, ad. de cerca; – by, muy arrimado; junto. [tado.

close-fisted, *–fĭstĕd,* a. mezquino, apretadamente.

closely, *–lĕ,* ad. estrechamente; secretamente. [reclusión, f.

closeness, *–nĕs,* s. estrechez, espesura, f.

closet, *–ĕt,* s. retrete, m.; gabinete, m.; –, v. a. encerrar en un retrete ó gabinete.

closure, *klō'zhŭr,* s. cerradura, f.; conclusión, f. [v. n. engrumecerse.

clot, *klŏt,* s. grumo, m.; zoquete, m.; –,

cloth, *klŏth,* s. paño, m.; mantel, m.; vestido, m.; lienzo, m.

clothe, *klōth,* v. a. vestir, cubrir.

clothes, *klōthz,* s. pl. vestidura, f.; ropaje, m.; ropa de cama, f.; suit of –, s. vestido completo, m.; bed–, cobertores, m. pl.

clothes-basket, *–băskĕt,* s. cesta grande, f.

clothes-horse, *–hŏrs,* s. enjugador, m.

clothes-peg, *–pĕg,* s. percha, f.

clothes-press, *–prĕs,* s. guardarropa, f.

clothier, *klŏth'tăr,* s. pañero, m.

clothing, *–ĭng,* s. vestidos, m. pl.

cloud, *klŏŭd,* s. nube, f.; nublado, m.; manchita, f.; (fig.) adversidad, f.; –, v. a. anublar; obscurecer; –, v. n. anublarse; obscurecerse.

cloudily, *–ĭlĭ,* ad. obscuramente.

cloudiness, *–ĭnĕs,* s. nublosidad, f.; obscuridad, f.

cloudless, *–lĕs,* a. sin nubes, claro, sereno.

cloudy, *–ĭ,* a. nublado, nubloso; obscuro; sombrío, melancólico.

clout, *klŏŭt,* s. rodilla, f.; remiendo, m.; –, v. a. remendar; chapucear.

clove, *klōv,* s. clavo, m. (flor).

clover, *–ăr,* s. trébol, m.; to live in –, vivir lujosamente. [m.

clown, *klŏŭn,* s. patán, rústico, m.; payaso.

clownish, *–ĭsh,* a. rústico; grosero; **–ly,** ad. toscamente, groseramente.

cloy, *klŏĭ,* v. a. saciar, hartar; clavar.

club, *klŭb,* s. clava, cachiporra, f.; escote, m.; club, m.; –, v. n. contribuir; unirse.

club-law, *–lă,* s. la ley del más fuerte, f.

clue, *klū,* s. ovillo de hilo, m.; seña, idea, guía, norma, f.; vestigio, indicio, apoyo, m.

clump, *klŭmp,* s. trozo sin forma; bosquecillo, m.

clump-soles, *–sōlz,* s. pl. suelas dobladas, f. pl. [ramente.

clumsily, *klŭm'zĭlĕ,* ad. zafiamente, groseramente.

clumsiness, *klŭm'zĭnĕs,* s. zafiedad, rustiquez, grosería, f. [arte.

clumsy, *klŭm'zĕ,* a. tosco, pesado; sin

cluster, *klŭs'tăr,* s. racimo, m.; manada, f.; pelotón, m.; –, v. a. agrupar; –, v. n. arracimarse.

clutch, *klŭtsh,* s. garra, f.; presa, f.; –, v. a. empuñar.

coach, *kŏtsh,* s. coche, m.; carroza, f.; – (up) v. a. infundir, inculcar.

coach-box, *–bŏks,* s. pescante de coche, m.

coach-hire, *–hĭr,* s. alquiler de coche, m.

coach-house, *–hŏŭs,* s. cochera, f.

coachman, *–măn,* s. cochero, m.

coaction, kŏăk'shăn, s. coacción, necesidad, fuerza, f. [pañero, m.

coadjutor, kŏădjŏ'tŭr, s. coadjutor, compañero, m.

coagulate, kŏăg'ŭlāt, s. a. coagular, cuajar, condensar lo que es líquido; –, v. n. coagularse, cuajarse, espesarse.

coagulation, kŏăgŭlā'shăn, s. coagulación, f.

coal, kōl, s. carbón de piedra, m. [ción, f.

coalesce, kŏălĕs', v. n. juntarse, incorporarse.

coalescence, –sĕns, s. coalescencia, f.

coal-heaver, kōl'hĕvŭr, s. mozo de barco de carbonero, m.

coal-hole, –hōl, s. carbonera, f.

coalition, kŏălĭsh'ŭn, s. coalición, confederación, f.

coal-mine, kōl'mĭn, **coal-pit,** –pĭt, s. mina de carbón, carbonería, f.

coarse, kōrs, a. basto, rústico, grosero; –ly, ad. groseramente. [f.

coarseness, –nĕs, s. tosquedad, grosería, f.

coast, kōst, s. costa, f.; –, v. n. costear.

coaster, –ŭr, s. piloto, m.; buque costacoasting, –ĭng, s. cabotaje, m. [nero, m.

coat, kōt, casaca, f.; frac, m.; hábito, m.; saya, f.; – of mail, – of arms, cota de malla, f.; –, v. a. cubrir, vestir.

coating, –ĭng, s. revestimiento, m.

coax, kōks, v. a. lisonjear, acariciar.

coaxer, –ŭr, s. adulador, mimador, m.

cob, kŏb, s. gaviota, f.; mazorca de maíz, f.; caballo doble, m. [zapatos.]

cobble, –bl, v. a. chapucear; remendar

cobbler, –blŭr, s. chapucero, m.

cobweb, –wĕb, s. telaraña, f.; (fig.) trama, f.

cochineal, kŏtsh'ĕnil, s. cochinilla, f.

cock, kŏk, s. gallo, m.; macho, m.; giraldilla, f.; llave, f.; montoncillo de heno, m.; pie de gato de escopeta, m.; gnómon de reloj de sol, m.; armadura de sombrero, f.; aguja de romana, f.; at half–, desamartillado (escopeta); at full –, amartillado, montado (escopeta); –, v. a. armar el sombrero; amartillar, montar una escopeta; amontonar heno.

cockade, –kād', s. cucarda, f.

cock-a-doodle-doo, –dūdŭldū, s. canto del gallo, m.

cockatoo, –tū', s. cacatoy, m.

cockatrice, kŏk'ătrĭs, s. basilisco, m.

cock-chafer, –tshāfŭr, s. saltón, m. (insecto.)

cock-crow, –krō, s. canto del gallo, m.

cocker, –ŭr, v. a. acariciar.

cockerel, –ĕrĕl, s. gallipollo, m.

cocket, –ĕt, s. sello de la aduana, m.; albalá de pago, m. & f. [gallos, f.

cock-fighting, –fĭtĭng, s. riña de

cockle, –kl, s. caracol de mar, m.; (bot.) zizaña, f.; –, v. a. arrugar; doblar; –, v. n. plegarse, doblarse.

cock-loft, –lŏft, s. desván, zaquizamí, m.

cockney, –nĕ, s. pazguato de Londres, m.; hombre afeminado, m.

cockpit, –pĭt, s. reñidero de gallos, m.; (mar.) entarimado del sollado, m.

cock's comb, kŏks'kŏm, s. cresta de gallo, f.; (fig.) currutaco, m. [trón de bote, m.

cockswain, coxwain, kŏk'sn, s. pa-

cocoa, kō'kō, s. coco, m.; cacao, m.

cocoon, kōkōn', s. capullo del gusano de seda, m. [(bot.) vaina, f.

cod, kŏd, s. bacalao, m.; merluza, f.

coddle, –dl, v. a. medio cocer; acariciar; afeminar.

code, kōd, s. código, m.

codicil, kŏd'ĭsĭl, s. (law) codicilo, m.

codify, kō'dĭfī, v. a. hacer un código. [f.

codling, kŏd'lĭng, s. manzana medio cocida,

cod-liver oil, kŏd'lĭvŭrŏĭl, s. aceite de merluza, m. [m.

coefficient, kōĕffĭsh'ĕnt, s. coeficiente,

coequal, kōĕ'kwŏl, a. igual.

coerce, kōărs', v. a. contener, refrenar; restringir. [f.

coercion, kōăr'shŭn, s. coerción, opresión,

coercive, kōăr'sĭv, a. coercitivo. [(m.).

coeval, kōĕ'vŏl, a. & s. coevo; contemporáneo

coexistence, kōĕgzĭs'tĕns, s. coexistencia,

coffee, kŏf'fē, s. café, m. [f.

coffee-berry, –bĕrrē, s. fruto del café, m.

coffee-house, –hōŭs, s. café, m.

coffee-pot, –pŏt, s. cafetera, f.

coffee-set, –sĕt, s. servicio para el café.

coffee-tree, –trē, s. cafeto, m. [m.

coffer, kŏf'fŭr, s. cofre, m.; caja, f.

coffin, kŏf'fĭn, s. féretro, ataúd, m.; –, v. a. meter en un ataúd.

cog, kŏg, s. diente (de rueda), m.; –, v. a. adular, lisonjear; to – a die, cargar un dado (con plomo).

cogency, kō'jĕnsē, s. fuerza, urgencia, f.

cogent, kō'jĕnt, a. convincente, urgente; –ly, ad. de un modo convincente.

cogitate, kŏj'ĭtāt, v. n. pensar, meditar.

cogitation, kŏjĭtā'shŭn, s. meditación, f.

cognate, kŏg'nāt, a. cognado.

cognation, kŏgnā'shŭn, s. cognación, f.

cognition, kŏgnĭsh'ŭn, s. conocimiento, m.; convicción, f.

cognizance, kŏg'nĭzăns, s. conocimiento, m.; divisa, f.; competencia, f.

cognizant, kŏg'nĭzănt, a. informado; (law) competente.

cog-wheel, kŏg'hwēl, s. rueda dentada, f.

cohabit, kōhăb'ĭt, v. n. cohabitar.

cohabitation, –tā'shăn, s. cohabitación, f.

coheir, kōăr', s. coheredero, m.

coheiress, –ĕs, s. coheredera, f.

cohere, kōhăr', v. n. pegarse; unirse; convenir, conformarse. [f.

coherence, –ĕns, s. coherencia, conexión, f.

coherent, –ĕnt, a. coherente; consiguiente.

cohesion, kōhē'zhŭn, s. coherencia, f.

cohesive, kōhē'sĭv, a. coherente.

coif, kŏĭf, s. cofia, redecilla, f.

coil, kŏĭl, v. a. recoger; to – a cable, (mar.) adujar un cable; –, s. barahúnda, f.; fracaso, m.; (mar.) adujada, f.

coin, kŏĭn, s. rincón, m.; moneda acuñada, f.; dinero, m.; –, v. a. acuñar moneda; falsificar; inventar.

coinage, –dj, s. acuñación, f.; braceaje, m.; falsificación, f.; invención, f.

coincide, kōĭnsīd', v. n. coincidir, concurrir, convenir. [f.

coincidence, kōĭn'sĭdĕns, s. coincidencia,

coincident, kōĭn'sĭdĕnt, a. coincidente.

coiner, *kõin'ũr*, s. acuñador de moneda. monedero falso, m.; inventor, m.

coke, *kõk*, s. cok, m.

colander, *kŭl'ãndẽr*, s. **coladera**, f.; colador, pasador, m.

cold, *kõld*, a. frío; indiferente, insensible; reservado; **-ly**, ad. fríamente; indiferentemente; **—**, s. frío, m.; frialdad, f.

cold-blooded, *-blŭdĕd*, a. impasible.

coldness, *-nĕs*, s. frialdad, f.; indiferencia, insensibilidad, apatía, f.

cole-wort, *kõl'wŭrt*, s. berza verde, f.

colic, *kõl'ĭk*, s. cólico, m.

collaborate, *kõllãb'õrãt*, v. a. cooperar.

collaboration, *kõllãbõrã'shũn*, s. cooperación, f.

collapse, *kõllãps'*, v. n. descaecer; **—**, s. hundimiento; (med.) colapso, m.

collar, *kõl'ũr*, s. collar, m.; collera, f.; **—**, v. a. agarrar á uno de los cabezones; arrollar.

collar-bone, *-bõn*, s. clavícula, f.

collate, *kõllãt'*, v. a. comparar, confrontar.

collateral, *kõllãt'ũrãl*, a. colateral; indirecto; **-ly**, ad. colateralmente; indirectamente.

collation, *kõllã'shũn*, s. colación; colección, f.

colleague, *kõl'lēg*, s. colega, compañero, m.

collect, *kõllĕkt'*, v. a. recoger, colegir; **—**, *kõl'lĕkt*, s. colecta, f.

collection, *kõllĕk'shũn*, s. compilación, f.; colección, f.

collective, *kõllĕk'tĭv*, a. colectivo, congregado; **-ly**, ad. colectivamente.

college, *kõl'lĕj*, s. colegio, m.

collegian, *kõllē'jĭan*, s. miembro de un colegio, m.

collegiate, *kõllē'jĭāt*, a. colegiado.

collide, *kõllīd'*, v. n. colidir.

collier, *kõl'yũr*, s. carbonero, m.; barco carbonero, m.

colliery, *-ē*, s. carbonera, f.

collision, *kõllĭzh'ũn*, s. colisión, f.; ludimiento, m.

collop, *kõl'lõp*, s. tajada (pequeña) de carne, f.

colloquial, *kõllõ'kwĭal*, a. dialogal; íntimo; **-ly**, ad. familiarmente.

colloquialism, *-ĭsm*, s. lengua usual, f.

colloquy, *kõl'lõkwē*, s. coloquio, m.; conversación, plática, f.

collusion, *kõllū'zhũn*, s. colusión, f.

collusive, *kõllū'sĭv*, a. colusorio; **-ly**, ad. colusoriamente.

colon, *kõ'lõn*, s. colon perfecto, m.; (:).

colonel, *kũr'nĕl*, s. (mil.) coronel, m.

colonelcy, *-sē*, s. coronelía, f.

colonial, *kõlõ'nĭal*, a. colonial.

colonise, *kõl'õnĭz*, v. a. colonizar.

colonist, *-õnĭst*, s. colono.

colony, *-õnē*, s. colonia, f.

colophony, *-õfõnē*, s. colofonía, f.

colossal, *kõlõs'sãl*, a. colosal.

colossus, *-sũs*, s. coloso, m.

colour, *kũl'ũr*, s. color, m.; pretexto, m.; **-s**, pl. bandera, f.; **—**, v. a. colorar; paliar; **—**, v. n. ponerse colorado.

colourable, *-ãbl*, a. especioso, plausible.

colourably, *-ãblĕ*, ad. plausiblemente.

colour-blind, *-blĭnd*, a. que tiene daltonismo.

colouring, *-ĭng*, s. colorido, m.

colourist, *-ĭst*, s. colorista, m.

colourless, *-lĕs*, a. descolorido, sin color.

colt, *kõlt*, s. potro, m.; mozuelo sin juicio.

colter, *-ũr*, s. reja de arado, f.

columbine, *kõl'ũmbĭn*, s. (bot.) aguileña, f.; **—**, a. violado.

column, *kõl'ũm*, s. columna, f.

columnar, *kõlũm'nũr*, a. columnario.

coma, *kõ'mã*, s. coma, letargo, m.

comatose, *kõ'mãtõs*, a. comatoso, f.

comb, *kõm*, s. peine, m; almohaza, f.; **—**, v. a. peinar; almohazar; cardar la lana.

combat, *kũm'bãt*, s. combate, m.; batalla, f.; **single —**, duelo, m.; **—**, v. n. combatir; **—**, v. a. resistir.

combatant, *-ãnt*, s. combatiente, m.

combative, *kũm'bãtĭv*, a. quisquilloso.

comber, *kõm'ũr*, s. cardador, m.

combination, *kõmbĭnã'shũn*, s. combinación, coordinación, f.; [unirse.

combine, *-bīn'*, v. a. combinar; **—**, v. n.

combing-cloth, *kõm'ĭngklõth*, s. peinador, m. [bustible.

combustible, *kõmbŭs'tĭbl*, a. & s. combustible.

combustion, *-bŭs'tyũn*, s. combustión, f.; incendio, m.

come, *kũm*, v. n. venir; acontecer; proceder; **— ! ¡sus! ¡ánimo!** [mico, m.

comedian, *kõmē'dĭan*, s. comediante, cómico, m.

comedy, *kõm'ĕdē*, s. comedia, f. [m.

comeliness, *kũm'lĭnĕs*, s. gracia, f.; garbo, m.

comely, *kũm'lĕ*, a. garboso, decente; **—**, ad. decentemente.

comestible, *kõmĕs'tĭbl*, a. comestible.

comet, *kõm'ĕt*, s. cometa, f.

comfit, *kũm'fĭt*, s. confite, m.

comfort, *kũm'fũrt*, s. confortación, f.; ayuda, f.; consuelo, m.; comodidad, f.; **—**, v. a. confortar; alentar, consolar.

comfortable, *-ãbl*, a. cómodo, consolatorio. [agrado, m.; comodidad, f.

comfortableness, *-ãblnĕs*, s. consuelo, f.

comfortably, *-ãblĕ*, ad. agradablemente, cómodamente. [da, f.

comforter, *-ũr*, s. consolador, m.; bufanda, f.

comfortless, *-lĕs*, a. desconsolado; desagradable. [-ly, ad. cómicamente.

comic, *kõm'ĭk(al)*, a. cómico, burlesco;

comical, *kõm'ĭk(al)*, a. cómico, burlesco; **-ly**, ad. cómicamente.

comicalness, *-ãlnĕs*, s. facecia, f.; gracejo, chiste, m. [**—**, a. venidero, viniente.

coming, *kũm'ĭng*, s. venida, llegada, f.

comma, *kõm'mã*, s. (gr.) coma, f.

command, *kõmmãnd'*, v. a. comandar; ordenar; **—**, v. n. gobernar; **—**, s. orden, f., comando, m.

commander, *-ũr*, s. comandante, m.

commandment, *-mĕnt*, s. mandato, precepto, m. [conmemorar; celebrar.

commemorate, *kõmmĕm'õrãt*, v. a.

commemoration, *-mĕmõrã'shũn*, s. conmemoración, f.

commence, *-mĕns'*, v. a. & n. comenzar.

commencement, *-mĕnt*, s. principio, m.; comienzo, m.

commend, *-mĕnd'*, v. a. encomendar; alabar; enviar.

commendable, *-ãbl*, a. recomendable.

commendably, *-ãblĕ*, ad. loablemente.

commendation, *-dã'shũn*, s. recomendación, f. [comendatorio.

commendatory, *kõmmĕn'dãtũrē*, a. re-

commensurability, *kŏmmĕnsŭrăbĭl'ĭtĕ,* s. conmensurabilidad, f.   [mensurable.

commensurable, *–mĕn'sŭrăbl,* a. conmensurar; –, a. conmensurativo, proporcionado.

commensurate, *–mĕn'sŭrăt,* v. a. conmensurar; –, a. conmensurativo, proporcionado.

comment, *kŏm'mĕnt,* s. comento, m.; gloss, f.; –, v. a. comentar, glosar.

commentary, *–tărĕ,* s. comentario, m.; interpretación, f.

commentator, *–tā'tŭr,* s. comentador, m.

commerce, *kŏm'mŭrs,* s. comercio, tráfico, trato, negocio, m.

commercial, *–mŭr'shăl,* a. comercial; – directory, s. almanaque de negocio. m.

comminatory, *–mĭn'ătŭrĕ,* a. conminatorio, conminatio.   [clar(se).

commingle, *–mĭng'gl,* v. a. (& n.) mezclar(se).

comminute, *–mĭz'ŭrdt,* v. a. compadecer, tener compasión.

commiseration, *–mĭzŭrd'shŭn,* s. conmiseración, piedad, f.

commissariat, *–mĭsăr'răt,* s. comisaría, f.; comisariato, m.   [m.

commissary, *kŏm'mĭssărĕ,* s. comisario.

commission, *kŏmmĭsh'ŭn,* s. comisión, f.; patente, f.; –, v. a. comisionar; encargar, apoderar.   [gado, m.

commissioner, *–ŭr,* s. comisionado, delegado.

commit, *kŏmmĭt',* v. a. cometer; depositar; encargar.   [s. auto de prisión, m.

commitment, *–mĕnt,* s. commital, –tăl.

committee, *–tĕ,* s. comité, m.

commodious, *kŏmmō'dĭŭs,* a. cómodo, conveniente; –, ad. cómodamente.

commodity, *–mŏd'ĭtĕ,* s. ventaja, utilidad, f.; provecho, m.; comodidad, f.; mercaderías, f. pl.   [escuadra, m.

commodore, *kŏm'mŏdōr,* s. (mar.) jefe de escuadra, m.

common, *kŏm'mŏn,* a. común; bajo; in –, comunmente; – prayer, s. liturgia de la Iglesia anglicana, f.; –, s. pastos comunales, m. pl.

commonage, *–ăj,* s. derecho de pastar ganados en algún común, m.

commonalty, *–ăltĕ,* s. populacho, m.; sociedad, comunidad, f.; [municipal, m.

common-council, *–kŏŭnsĭl,* s. concejo

commoner, *–ŭr,* s. plebeyo, m.; miembro de la cámara baja (en Inglaterra), m. [f.

common-hall, *–hăl,* s. casa consistorial.

common-law, *–lă,* s. ley municipal, f.; costumbre que tiene fuerza de ley, f.

commonly, *–lĕ,* ad. comunmente, frecuentemente.   [cuencia, f.

commonness, *–nĕs,* s. comunidad, f.; frecuencia, f.

common-place, *–plăs,* s. lugares comunes, m. pl.; a. trivial.

commons, *–z,* s. pl. pueblo bajo, m.; cámara baja (en Inglaterra), f.

commonwealth, *–wĕlth,* s. república, f.

commotion, *kŏmmō'shŭn,* s. tumulto, m.; perturbación del ánimo, f.

commune, *–mŭn',* v. n. conversar, conferir.

communicable, *–mŭ'nĭkăbl,* a. comunicable, impartible.   [cante, m.

communicant, *–mŭ'nĭkănt,* s. comunicante.

communicate, *–mŭ'nĭkăt,* v. a. comunicar, participar; –, v. n. comunicarse.

communication, *–mŭnĭkă'shŭn,* s. comunicación, f.; participación, f.; comercio, m.

communicative, *–mŭ'nĭkătĭv,* a. comunicativo.   [conunicativo, m.

communicativeness, *–nĕs,* s. carácter

communion, *kŏmmŭn'yŭn,* s. comunidad, f.; comunión, f.

communist, *kŏm'mŭnĭst,* s. comunista, m.

community, *–mŭ'nĭtĕ,* s. comunidad, f.; república, f.

commutable, *–mŭ'tăbl,* a. conmutable, cambiable.   [conmutación, f.

commutation, *–mŭtă'shŭn,* s. mudanza, f.;

commute, *–mŭt',* v. a. conmutar.

compact, *–păkt',* a. compacto, sólido, denso; –, *kŏm'păkt,* s. pacto, convenio, m.; **–ly,** *kŏmpăkt'lĕ,* ad. estrechamente; en pocas palabras.

compactness, *–nĕs,* s. solidez, densidad, f.

companion, *kŏmpăn'yŭn,* s. compañero, socio, compinche, m.

companionable, *–ăbl,* a. sociable.

companionship, *–shĭp,* s. sociedad, compañía, f.

company, *kŭm'pănĕ,* s. compañía, sociedad, f.; compañía de comercio.

comparable, *kŏm'părăbl,* a. comparable.

comparative, *kŏmpăr'ătĭv,* a. comparativo; – degree, s. (gr.) comparativo, m.; **–ly,** ad. comparativamente.

compare, *–păr',* v. a. comparar, colacionar; –, s. comparación, f.; semejanza, f.

comparison, *–păr'ĭsn,* s. comparación, f.; símil, m.   [miento, m.

compartment, *–părt'mĕnt,* s. compartimiento, m.

compass, *kŭm'păs,* s. círcuito, alcance, m.; circunferencia, f.; compás de la voz, m.; compás; –, v. a. circundar; conseguir; acabar.   [tica, f.

compass-card, *–kărd,* s. (mar.) rosa náutica, f.

compasses, *–ĭz,* s. pl. compás, m.

compassion, *kŏmpăsh'ŭn,* s. compasión, piedad, f.   [alguno; –, a. compasivo.

compassionate, *–ăt,* v. a. compadecer á

compatibility, *kŏmpătĭbĭl'ĭtĕ,* s. compatibilidad, f.

compatible, *–păt'ĭbl,* a. compatible.

compatriot, *–pā'trĭŏt,* s. compatriota, m.

compeer, *–pēr',* s. compañero, colega, m.

compel, *–pĕl',* v. a. compeler, obligar, constreñir.   [tome, m.

compend, *kŏm'pĕnd,* s. compendio, epítome, m.

compendious, *kŏmpĕn'dĭŭs,* a. compendioso, sucinto; **–ly,** ad. compendiosamente.

compensate, *–pĕn'săt,* v. a. compensar.

compensation, *–pĕnsă'shŭn,* s. compensación, f.; resarcimiento, f.

compete, *–pēt',* v. n. concurrir, competir.

competence, *kŏm'pĕtĕns,* s. competencia, f.; suficiencia, f.

competent, *–pĕtĕnt,* a. competente, bastante; **–ly,** ad. competentemente.

competition, *kŏmpĕtĭsh'ŭn,* s. competencia, f.; concurrencia, f.

competitive, *–pĕt'ĭtĭv,* a. que compete. [m.

competitor, *–pĕt'ĭtŭr,* s. competidor, rival.

compilation, *–pĭlă'shŭn,* s. compilación, f.

compile, *–pīl',* v. a. compilar.   [f.

complacence, _–plā´sĕns_, s. complacencia,
deferencia, f.   [cortés.
complacent, _–plā´sĕnt_, a. complaciente,
complain, _–plān´_, v. n. quejarse, lamen-
tarse, lastimarse, dolerse.
complaint, _–t´_, s. queja, pena, f.; lamento,
llanto, quejido, m.   [dad, f.
complaisance, _kŏmplāzäns´_, s. oficiosi-
complaisant, _kŏmplāzänt´_, a. oficioso.
complement, _kŏm´plĕmĕnt_, s. complemento, m.
complete, _kŏmplēt´_, a. completo, perfecto;
–ly, ad. completamente; –. v. a. completar, acabar.   [colmo, f.
completion, _–plē´shŭn_, s. complemento
complex, _kŏm´plĕks_, a. complexo, compuesto.   [m.; complexión, f.; tez, f.
complexion, _kŏmplĕk´shŭn_, s. complexo,
complexioned, _–d_, a. complexionado.
complexity, _–plĕk´stĭ_, s. complexo, m.
compliance, _–plī´ăns_, s. complacencia,
sumisión, condescendencia, f.   [cioso.
compliant, _–plī´ănt_, a. complaciente, ofi-
complicate, _kŏm´plĭkāt_, v. a. complicar.
complication, _kŏmplĭkā´shŭn_, s. compli-
cación, f.
complier, _–plī´ĕr_, s. consentidor, m.
compliment, _kŏm´plĭmĕnt_, s. cumplimiento, m.; –, v. a. cumplimentar; hacer
ceremonias.   [plimento, ceremonioso.
complimentary, _kŏmplĭmĕn´tărĭ_, a. cum-
compline, _kŏm´plĭn_, s. completas, f. pl.
(vísperas).   [cender, conformarse.
comply, _kŏmplī´_, v. n. cumplir; condes-
component, _–pō´nĕnt_, a. componente.
comport, _–pōrt´_, v. a. & n. sufrir; comportarse.   [concertar, reglar, ordenar.
compose, _–pōz´_, v. a. componer; sosegar;
composed, _–d_, a. compuesto, moderato;
–ly, ad. tranquilamente, serenamente.
composer, _–ĕr_, s. autor, m.; compositor,
m.; cajista, m.   [ponedor, m.
composing-stick, _–pōz´ĭng stĭk_, s. com-
composition, _–pŏzĭ´shŭn_, s. composición,
f.; compuesto, m.; acomodamiento, m.
compositor, _–pŏz´ĭtŭr_, s. cajista, m.
compost, _kŏm´pŏst_, s. abono, estiércol, m.
composure, _kŏmpō´zhŭr_, s. composición,
f.; tranquilidad, sangre fría, f.
compound, _–pŏŭnd´_, v. a. componer, combinar; –, v. n. concertarse; ajustar; –, a.
& s. compuesto, (m.).
comprehend, _–prĕhĕnd´_, v. a. comprender, contener; entender.
comprehensible, _–prĕhĕn´sĭbl_, a. comprensible; –ly, ad. comprensiblemente.
comprehension, _–shŭn_, s. comprensión,
f.; inteligencia, f.
comprehensive, _–sĭv_, a. comprensivo,
corto; –ly, ad. comprensivamente.
comprehensiveness, _–nĕs_, s. concisión,
precisión, f.
compress, _kŏmprĕs´_, v. a. comprimir, estrechar; –, _kŏm´prĕs_, s. cabezal, m.
compression, _–prĕsh´ŭn_, s. compresión, f.
comprise, _–prīz´_, v. a. comprender, incluir.   [m.; –, v. a. comprometer.
compromise, _kŏm´prŏmīz_, s. compromiso,

compulsion, _kŏmpŭl´shŭn_, s. compulsión,
f.; apremio, m.
compulsive, _–pŭl´sĭv_, compulsory, _–_
pŭl´sŭrĭ, a. compulsivo; –ly, ad. por
fuerza.   [ción, contrición, f.
compunction, _–pŭngk´shŭn_, s. compun-
computable, _–pū´tăbl_, a. computable, calculable.   [cuenta hecha, f.
computation, _–pūtā´shŭn_, s. computación,
compute, _–pūt´_, v. a. computar, calcular.
comrade, _kŏm´răd_, s. camarada, compañero, m.   [estudiar, reflexionar.
con, _kŏn_, pr. contra; –, v. a. meditar,
concatenation, _kŏnkătĕnā´shŭn_, s. encadenamiento, m.; serie, f.
concave, _kŏn´kăv_, a. cóncavo.
concavity, _kŏnkăv´ĭtĭ_, s. concavidad, f.
conceal, _kŏnsēl´_, v. a. ocultar, esconder.
concealment, _–mĕnt_, s. ocultación, f.; encubrimiento, m.
concede, _–sēd´_, v. a. conceder, asentir.
conceit, _–sēt´_, s. concepción, f.; capricho,
m.; pensamiento, m.; presunción, f.; –, v.
n. imaginar, creer.
conceited, _–ĕd_, a. afectado, vano, presumido; –ly, ad. fantásticamente.
conceivable, _kŏnsē´văbl_, a. concebible,
inteligible.
conceive, _–sēv´_, v. a. concebir, comprender; –, v. n. imaginar, pensar.
concentrate, _–sĕn´trāt_, v. a. concentrar.
concentration, _–sĕntrā´shŭn_, s. concentración, f.
concentric(al), _–sĕn´trĭk(ăl)_, a. concéntrico.   [sentimiento, m.
conception, _–sĕp´shŭn_, s. concepción, f.;
concern, _–sŭrn´_, v. a. concernir, importar,
pertenecer; –, s. negocio, m.; interés, m.;
importancia, consecuencia, f.; afecto, m.
concerning, _–ĭng_, pr. tocante á.
concert, _kŏn´sŭrt_, s. concierto, m.; convenio, m.; –, _kŏnsŭrt´_, v. a. (& n.) con-
certar(se).   [privilegio, m.
concession, _kŏnsĕsh´ŭn_, s. concesión, f.;
conch, _kŏngk_, s. concha, f.
conciliate, _kŏnsĭl´ĭāt_, v. a. conciliar; atraer.
conciliation, _–sĭlĭā´shŭn_, s. conciliación, f.
conciliator, _–sĭl´ĭātŭr_, s. conciliador, m.
conciliatory, _–ē_, a. conciliativo.
concise, _kŏnsīs´_, a. conciso, sucinto; –ly,
ad. concisamente.   [nismo, m.
conciseness, _–nĕs_, s. concisión, f.; laco-
conclude, _kŏnklūd´_, v. a. concluir; decidir; determinar.
conclusion, _–klū´zhŭn_, s. conclusión, determinación, f.; fin, m.
conclusive, _–klū´sĭv_, a. decisivo, conclu-
sivo; –ly, ad. concluyentemente. [durar.
concoct, _–kŏkt´_, v. a. cocer, digerir; ma-
concoction, _–kŏk´shŭn_, s. digestión, f.;
cocción, maduración, f.
concomitant, _–kŏm´ĭtăn.._, a. concomitante; –, s. compañero, m.
concord, _kŏng´kŏrd_, s. concordia, armonía, f.; buena inteligencia, f.   [cia, f.
concordance, _kŏnkŏr´dăns_, s. concordan-
concordant, _–dănt_, a. concordante, conforme.   [venio, m.
concordat, _–dăt_, s. concordato, m.; con-

concourse, kŏng'kŏrs, s. concurso, m.; multitud, f., gentío, m.

concrete, kŏng'krēt, s. concreto, m.; -, kŏngkrēt', v. n. concretar. [agregado, m.

concretion, kŏnkrē'shŭn, s. concreción, f.

concubinage, -kū'bĭnāj, s.concubinato, m.

concubine, kŏng'kūbĭn, s. concubina, f.

concupiscence, kŏnkū'pĭssĕns, s. concupiscencia, codicia, f.

concur, -kŭr', v. n. concurrir; juntarse.

concurrence, -rĕns, s. concurrencia, f.; unión, f.; asistencia, f.

concussion, kŏnkŭsh'ŭn, s. concusión, f.

condemn, -dĕm', v.a. condenar; desaprobar; vituperar. [f.

condemnation, -nā'shŭn, s. condenación, f.

condemnatory, kŏndĕm'nātŭrĕ, a. condenatorio. [sación, f.

condensation, kŏndĕnsā'shŭn, s. condensación, f.

condense, -dĕns', v. a. condensar.

condescend, -dĕsĕnd', v. n. condescender; consentir. [cendencia, f.

condescension, -dĕsĕn'shŭn, s. condescendencia, f.

condign, -dīn', a. condigno, merecido.

condiment, kŏn'dĭment, s. condimento, m.; salsa, f.

condition, kŏndĭsh'ŭn, s. situación, condición, calidad, f.; estado, m.; esfera, f.

conditional, -ăl, a. condicional, hipotético; -ly, ad. condicionalmente.

conditioned, -d, a. hecho de natura.

condole, kŏndōl', v. a. lamentar (con otro); -, v. n. condolerse.

condolence, -ĕns, s. compasión, lástima.

condonation, kŏndŏnā'shŭn, s. pardón, m.

condone, -dōn', v. a. perdonar.

conduce, -dūs', v. a. conducir, concurrir.

conducive, -dū'sĭv, a. conducente, oportuno.

conduct, kŏn'dŭkt, s. conducta, f.; manejo, proceder, m.; conducción (de tropas), f.; -, kŏndŭkt', v. a. conducir, guiar.

conduction, kŏndŭk'shŭn, s. conducta, conducción, f.

conductor, -dŭkt'ŭr, s. conductor, m.; guía, director, m.; conductor de electricidad. [m.

conduit, kŏn'dĭt, s. conducto, m.; caño, m.

cone, kōn, s. cono, m.

confabulate, kŏnfăb'ūlāt, v. n. platicar.

confection, kŏnfĕk'shŭn, s. confitura, f.; confección, f.

confectioner, -ŭr, s. confitero, m.

confederacy, kŏnfĕd'ŭrāsĕ, s. confederación, f.

confederate, -fĕd'ŭrāt, v.n. confederarse; -, a. & s. confederado (m.).

confer, -fŭr', v. n. conferenciar; -, v. a. conferir, comparar.

conference, kŏn'fĕrĕns, s. conferencia, f.

confess, kŏnfĕs', v. a. (& n.) confesar(se).

confessedly, -fĕs'sĕdlĕ, ad. conocidamente, infaliblemente.

confession, -fĕsh'ŭn, s. confesión, f.

confessional, -ăl, s. confesionario, m.

confessor, -ŭr, s. confesor, m.

confidant, kŏn'fĭdănt (kŏnfĭdănt'), s. confidente, amigo íntimo, m.

confide, kŏnfīd', v. a. & n. confiar; fiarse.

confidence, kŏn'fĭdĕns, s. confianza, seguridad, f.

confident, kŏn'fĭdĕnt, a. cierto, seguro; confiado; atrevido; -, s. confidente, m.

confidential, kŏnfĭdĕn'shăl, a. confidencial. [figuración, f.

configuration, -fĭgŭrā'shŭn, s.

confine, kŏn'fīn, s. confín, límite, m.; -, kŏnfīn', v. a. limitar; aprisionar; -, v. n. confinar. [estreñimiento, m.

confinement, kŏnfīn'mĕnt, s. prisión, f.

confirm, kŏnfŭrm', v. a. confirmar; ratificar. [ratificación, f.; prueba, f.

confirmation, -d'shŭn, s.confirmación, f.

confirmative, kŏnfŭrm'ātĭv, confirmatory, kŏnfŭrm'ātŭrĕ, a. confirmatorio.

confiscate, kŏnfĭs'kāt, v.a. confiscar. [f.

confiscation, -fĭskā'shŭn, s. confiscación, f.; incendio general, m.

conflagration, -flăgrā'shŭn, s. conflagración, f.; incendio general, m.

conflict, kŏn'flĭkt, s. conflicto, m.; combate, m.; pelea, f.; -, kŏnflĭkt', v. a. contender; combatir. [concurso, l.l.

confluence, kŏn'flōĕns, s. confluencia, f.;

confluent, kŏn'flōĕnt, a. confluente.

conform, kŏnfŏrm', v. a. (& n.) conformar(se).

conformable, -ăbl, a. conforme, semejante; -bly, ad. conformemente.

conformation, -d'shŭn, s. conformación, f.

conformity, -ĭtĕ, s. conformidad, conveniencia, f. [fundir; destruir.

confound, kŏnfŏŭnd', v. a. turbar, confundir; destruir.

confront, -frŏnt', v. a. afrontar; confrontar; comparar.

confuse, -fūz', v.a. confundir; desordenar.

confusedly, -ĕdlĕ, ad. confusamente.

confusion, kŏnfū'zhŭn, s. confusión, f.; perturbación, f.; desorden, m.

confute, -fūt', v. a. confutar, refutar.

congeal, -jēl', v. a. (& n.) helar, congelar(se).

congelation, -jēlā'shŭn, s. congelación, f.

congenial, -jē'nĭăl, a. congenial.

congeniality, -jēnĭăl'ĭtĕ, s. semejanza de genio, f. [genio, m.

congenital, kŏn'jĕ gĕr, s. congrio, m.

congestion, kŏnjĕs'tshŭn, s. congestión, f.; formación de una masa, acumulación, f.

conglomerate, -glŏm'ŭrāt, v. a. conglomerar, aglomerar; -, a. aglomerado.

conglomeration, -glŏmŭrā'shŭn, s. aglomeración, f. [lar, felicitar.

congratulate, -grăt'ūlāt, v. a. congratular, felicitar.

congratulation, -grătūlā'shŭn, s. congratulación, f. [tulatorio.

congratulatory, -grăt'ūlātŭrĕ, a. congratulatorio.

congregate, kŏng'grēgāt, v.a. congregar, reunir. [gación, reunión, f.

congregation, kŏnggrēgā'shŭn, s. congregación, f.

congress, kŏng'grĕs, s. congreso, m.; conferencia, f.

congruity, kŏngrō'ĭtĕ, s. congruencia, f.

congruous, kŏn'grōŭs, a. idóneo, congruo, apto; -ly, ad. oportunamente.

conic(al), kŏn'ĭk(ăl), a. cónico; -ally, ad. en forma cónica.

coniferous, kŏnĭf'ŭrŭs, a. (bot.) conífero.

conjectural, kŏnjĕk'tŭrăl, a. conjetural; -ly, ad. conjeturalmente.

conjecture, *–jĕk'tŭr,* s. conjetura, apariencia, f.; –, v. a. conjeturar; pronosticar.

conjoin, *–jŏin',* v. a. juntar; asociar; –, v. n. unirse, ligarse.

conjoint, *–t,* a. asociado, confederado.

conjugal, *kŏn'jŭgăl,* a. conyugal, matrimonial; –ly, ad. conyugalmente.

conjugate, *kŏn'jŭgāt,* v. a. (gr.) conjugar.

conjugation, *kŏnjŭgā'shŭn,* s. conjugación, f.   [f.; unión, f.

conjunction, *–jŭnk'shŭn,* s. conjunción, f.

conjunctive, *–jŭnk'tĭv,* a. conjunto; conjuntivo.   [ocasión, f.; tiempo crítico, m.

conjuncture, *–jŭnk'tŭr,* s. coyuntura, f.;

conjuration, *–jŭrā'shŭn,* s. súplica ardiente, f.; conspiración, f.

conjure, *–jūr',* v. a. rogar, pedir con instancia; –, *kŏn'jŭr,* v. n. conjurar, exorcizar; encantar; hechizar.

conjurer, *kŏn'jŭrŭr,* s. conjurador, encantador, m.

connate, *kŏn'nāt,* a. innato.   [lazar.

connect, *kŏnnĕkt',* v. a. juntar, unir, enlazar.

connexion, *–nĕk'shŭn,* s. conexión, f.

connivance, *–nīvāns,* s. convivencia, f.

connive, *–nīv',* v. n. guiñar el ojo; tolerar.

connoisseur, *kŏnĕssŭr'* (*kŏn'ĭssŭr*), s. conocedor, m.   [trimonial.

connubial, *kŏnnū'bĭăl,* a. conyugal, matrimonial.

conquer, *kŏng'kŭr,* v. a. conquistar; vencer.   [dor, m.

conqueror, *–ŭr,* s. vencedor, conquistador, m.

conquest, *kŏng'kwĕst,* s. conquista, f.

consanguineous, *kŏnsănggwĭn'ĕŭs,* a. consanguíneo.

consanguinity, *–sănggwĭn'ĭtĭ,* s. consanguinidad, f.   [escrúpulo, m.

conscience, *kŏn'shĕns,* s. conciencia, f.;

conscientious, *kŏnshĭĕn'shŭs,* a. concienzudo, escrupuloso; –ly, ad. según conciencia.   [cido; –ly, ad. á sabiendas.

conscious, *kŏn'shŭs,* a. sabedor, convencido.

conscript, *kŏn'skrĭpt,* a. conscripto.

conscription, *kŏnskrĭp'shŭn,* s. asiento en algún registro, m.; reclutamiento, f.

consecrate, *kŏn'sĕkrāt,* v. a. consagrar; dedicar.   [ción, f.

consecration, *kŏnsĕkrā'shŭn,* s. consagración, f.

consecutive, *–sĕk'ŭtĭv,* a. consecutivo; –ly, ad. consecutivamente.

consent, *–sĕnt',* s. consentimiento, asenso, m.; aprobación, f.; –, v. n. consentir; aprobar.   [cia, f.; importancia, f.

consequence, *kŏn'sĕkwĕns,* s. consecuencia, f.

consequent, *–sĕkwĕnt,* a. consecutivo, concluyente; –ly, ad. consiguientemente.

consequential, *kŏnsĕkwĕn'shăl,* a. presumido.   [ción, f.

conservation, *–sĕrvā'shŭn,* s. conservación, f.

conservative, *–sĕr'vătĭv,* a. conservativo.

conservator, *–sĕrvā'tŭr,* s. conservador, m.; defensor, m.   [vatorio (m.).

conservatory, *–sĕr'vătŭrĕ,* a. & s. conservatorio (m.).

consider, *–sĭd'ŭr,* v. a. considerar, examinar; –, v. n. pensar, deliberar.

considerable, *–ăbl,* a. considerable; importante; **–bly,** ad. considerablemente.

considerate, *–ăt,* a. considerado, prudente, discreto; **–ly,** ad. juiciosamente; prudentemente.

consideration, *–ā'shŭn,* s. consideración, f.; deliberación, f.; importancia, f.; valor, mérito, m.

considering, *–ĭng,* c. en atención á; – that, á causa de; visto que, en razón á.

consign, *kŏnsīn',* v. a. consignar.

consignee, *–ē',* s. agente, m.

consignment, *–mĕnt,* s. consignación, f.

consist, *kŏnsĭst',* v. n. consistir; acordarse.   [f.

consistence(cy), *–ĕns(sĕ),* s. consistencia,

consistent, *–ĕnt,* a. consistente; conveniente, conforme; sólido, estable; **–ly,** ad. conformemente.

consistory, *kŏnsĭs'tŭrĕ,* s. consistorio, m.

consolable, *–sō'lăbl,* a. consolable.

consolation, *–sōlā'shŭn,* s. consolación, f.; consuelo, m.

consolatory, *–sōl'ătŭrĕ,* a. consolatorio.

console, *–sōl',* v. a. consolar; –, *kŏn'sōl,* s. cartela, f.   [solidar(se).

consolidate, *–sōl'ĭdāt,* v. a. (& n.) consolidar.   [dos], m. pl.

consolidation, *–sōlĭdā'shŭn,* s. consolidación, f.

consols, *kŏn'sōls,* s. pl, consolidados (fondos), m. pl.

consonance, *kŏn'sōnăns,* s. consonancia, f.; armonía, f.

consonant, *kŏn'sōnănt,* a. consonante, conforme; –, s. (gr.) consonante, f.

consort, *kŏn'sōrt,* s. consorte, socio, m.; esposo, m.; esposa, f.; –, *kŏnsōrt',* v. n. asociarse.

conspicuous, *kŏnspĭk'ūŭs,* a. conspicuo, aparente; notable; **–ly,** ad. claramente, insignemente.

conspiracy, *–spĭr'ăsĕ,* s. conspiración, f.

conspirator, *–spĭr'ătŭr,* s. conspirador, m.

conspire, *–spīr',* v. n. conspirar, maquinar.

constable, *kŏn'stăbl,* s. condestable, m.

constabulary, *kŏnstăb'ŭlărĕ,* s. policía, f.

constancy, *kŏn'stănsĕ,* s. constancia, perseverancia, persistencia, f.

constant, *kŏn'stănt,* a. constante; perseverante; **–ly,** ad. constantemente.

constellation, *kŏnstĕllā'shŭn,* s. constelación, f.; conjunto de circunstancias, m.

consternation, *–stĕrnā'shŭn,* s. consternación, f.; terror, m.

constipate, *kŏn'stĭpāt,* v. a. espesar, condensar; obstruir.

constituency, *kŏnstĭt'ūĕnsĕ,* s. junta electoral, f.   [–, a. constituyente.

constituent, *–ĕnt,* s. constitutivo, m.;

constitute, *kŏn'stĭtūt,* v. a. constituir; establecer; diputar.

constitution, *kŏnstĭtū'shŭn,* s. constitución, f.; estado, m.; temperamento, m.

constitutional, *–ăl,* a. constitucional, legal.   [restringir.

constrain, *–strān',* v. a. constreñir, forzar.

constrainable, *–ăbl,* a. constreñible.

constrainedly, *–ĕdlĕ,* ad. por fuerza.

constraint, *–t',* s. constreñimiento, m.; fuerza, violencia, f.   [char.

constrict, *kŏnstrĭkt',* v. a. constreñir, estre-

constringent, *kŏnstrĭn'jĕnt*, a. constrictivo.   [ficar.

construct, *–strŭkt'*, v. a. construir, edificar.

construction, *–strŭk'shŭn*, s. construcción, f.; interpretación, f.

construe, *–strō'*, v. a. construir; interpretar.   [pretar.

consul, *kŏn'sŭl*, s. cónsul, m.

consular, *kŏn'sŭlăr*, a. consular.

consulate, *kŏn'sŭlăt*, **consulship**, *kŏn'sŭlshĭp*, s. consulado, m.   [aconsejar(se).

consult, *kŏnsŭlt'*, v. a. & n. consultar(se).

consultation, *–sŭltā'shŭn*, s. consulta, deliberación, f.   [destruible.

consumable, *–sū'măbl*, a. consumible.

consume, *kŏnsūm'*, v. a. consumir; disipar; –, v. n. consumirse.   [quiano, m.

consumer, *–ŭr*, s. consumidor, parro-

consummate, *kŏn'sŭmmăt*, v. a. consumar, acabar, perfeccionar; –, *kŏnsŭm'măt*, a. cumplido, consumado.

consummation, *kŏnsŭmmā'shŭn*, s. consumación, perfección, f.

consumption, *–sŭm'shŭn*, s. consunción, f.; disipación, f.; tisis, f.   [tísico, ético.

consumptive, *–sŭm'tĭv*, a. consuntivo.

contact, *kŏn'tăkt*, s. contacto, tocamiento, m.   [inficion, infección, f.

contagion, *–tā'jŭn*, s. contagio, m.;

contagious, *–tā'jŭs*, a. contagioso.

contain, *–tān'*, v. a. contener, comprender; caber; reprimir, refrenar.

contaminate, *–tăm'ĭnăt*, v. a. contaminar; corromper; –, a. contaminado, corrompido.   [minación, f.

contamination, *–tămĭnā'shŭn*, s. conta-

contemn, *–tĕm'*, v. a. despreciar, menospreciar, desestimar; desdeñar.

contemplate, *kŏntĕm'plăt (kŏn'tĕmplăt)*, v. a. contemplar.   [plación, f.

contemplation, *–tĕmplā'shŭn*, s. contem-

contemplative, *–tĕm'plătĭv*, a. contemplativo; –ly, ad. con atención y estudio.

contemporaneous, *–tĕmpŏrā'nĭŭs*, **contemporary**, *kŏntĕm'pŏrărĕ*, a. contemporáneo.

contempt, *–tĕmt'*, s. desprecio, desdén, m.

contemptible, *–ĭbl*, a. despreciable, vil; –bly, ad. vilmente.

contemptuous, *–tĕm'tŭŭs*, a. desdeñoso, insolente; –ly, ad. con desdén.

contend, *–tĕnd'*, v. n. contender, disputar, afirmar.

content, *–tĕnt'*, a. contento, satisfecho; –, v. a. contentar, satisfacer; –, s. contento, m.; satisfacción, f.; –s, pl. contenido, m.; tabla de materias, f.

contentedly, *–ĕdlĕ*, ad. de un modo satisfecho; con paciencia.

contentedness, *–ĕdnĕs*, s. contento, m., satisfacción, f.   [altercación, f.

contention, *kŏntĕn'shŭn*, s. contención, f.

contentious, *–tĕn'shŭs*, a. contencioso, litigioso; –ly, ad. contenciosamente.

contentment, *–tĕnt'mĕnt*, s. contentamiento, placer, m.

contest, *–tĕst'*, v. a. contestar, disputar, litigar; –, *kŏn'tĕst*, s. disputa, contestación, altercación, f.

contestant, *kŏntĕs'tănt*, s. contestante.

context, *kŏn'tĕkst*, s. contexto, m.; contextura, f.   [tejido, m.

contexture, *kŏntĕks'tŭr*, s. contextura, f.;

contiguity, *–tĭgū'ĭtĕ*, s. contigüidad, f.

contiguous, *–tĭg'ŭŭs*, a. contiguo, vecino.

continence(y), *kŏn'tĭnĕns(sĕ)*, s. continencia, f.; castidad, f.

continent, *kŏn'tĭnĕnt*, a. continente; –ly, ad. castamente; –, s. continente, m.

continental, *kŏntĭnĕn'tăl*, a. continental.

contingency, *–tĭn'jĕnsĕ*, s. contingencia, f.; acontecimiento, m.; eventualidad, f.

contingent, *–tĭn'jĕnt*, s. contingente, m.; cuota, f.; –, a. contingente, casual; –ly, ad. casualmente.   [continuamente.

continual, *–tĭn'ŭăl*, a. continuo; –ly, ad.

continuance, *–tĭn'ŭăns*, s. continuación, permanencia, f.; duración, f.

continuation, *–tĭnŭā'shŭn*, s. continuación, serie, f.

continue, *–tĭn'ŭ*, v. a. continuar; –, v. n. durar, perseverar, persistir.

continuedly, *–ĕdlĕ*, ad. continuadamente.

continuity, *kŏntĭnū'ĭtĕ*, s. continuidad, f.

continuous, *–tĭn'ŭŭs*, a. continuo, unido.

contort, *–tŏrt'*, v. a. torcer.

contortion, *–tŏr'shŭn*, s. contorsión, f.

contour, *–tŏr'*, s. contorno, m.

contraband, *kŏn'trăbănd*, s. contrabando, m.; –, a. prohibido, ilegal.

contrabandist, *–ĭst*, s. contrabandista, m.

contract, *–trăkt'*, v. a. contraer; abreviar; contratar; –, v. n. contraerse; –, *kŏn'trăkt*, s. contrato, pacto, m.

contraction, *kŏntrăk'shŭn*, s. contracción, f.; abreviatura, f.

contractor, *–trăk'tŭr*, s. contratante, m.

contradict, *kŏntrădĭkt'*, v. a. contradecir.

contradiction, *–dĭk'shŭn*, s. contradicción, oposición, f.

contradictoriness, *–dĭk'tŭrĕnĕs*, s. oposición en sumo grado, f.   [torio.

contradictory, *–dĭk'tŭrĕ*, a. contradic-

contrariety, *–rī'ĕtĕ*, **contrariness**, *kŏn'trărĕnĕs*, s. contrariedad, oposición, f.

contrary, *kŏn'trărĕ*, a. contrario, opuesto; –, s. contrario, m.; on the –, al contrario.

contrast, *–trăst'*, s. contraste, m.; oposición, f.; –, *kŏn'trăst*, v. a. contrastar, oponer.   [vención, f.

contravention, *kŏntrăvĕn'shŭn*, s. contra-

contributary, *–trĭb'ŭtărĕ*, a. contributario.

contribute, *–trĭb'ŭt*, v. a. contribuir, ayudar.   [ción, f.; tributo, m.

contribution, *–trĭbū'shŭn*, s. contribu-

contributor, *–trĭb'ŭtŭr*, s. contribuidor, m.

contributory, *–ĕ*, a. **contributive**, *–trĭb'ŭtĭv*, a. contribuyente; tributario.

contrite, *kŏn'trīt*, a. contrito, arrepentido.

contrition, *kŏntrĭsh'ŭn*, s. penitencia, contrición, f.   [invención, f.; concepto, m.

contrivance, *–trī'văns*, s. designio, m.;

contrive, *–trīv'*, v. a. inventar, trazar, maquinar; manejar; combinar.

control, *kŏntrōl'*, s. contrarregistro, m.; inspección, f.; –, v. a. restringir; gobernar; refutar; registrar; criticar.   [m.

controller, *–tŭr*, s. contralor, registrador,

controversial, *kŏntrōvär'shăl,* a. polémico, f. [f.

controversy, *kŏn'trŏvŭrsĕ,* s. controversia.

controvert, *kŏn'trŏvŭrt,* v.a. controvertir, disputar.

contumacious, *kŏntŭmā'shŭs,* a. contumaz; **-ly,** ad. contumazmente.

contumacy, *kŏn'tŭmăsĕ,* s. contumacia, resistencia, f.

contumelious, *kŏntŭmē'lŭs,* a. contumelioso, injurioso; **-ly,** ad. contumeliosamente. [juria, f.

contumely, *kŏn'tŭmēlĕ,* s. contumelia, in-

contusion, *kŏntū'zhŭn,* s. contusión, f., magullamiento, m.

conundrum, *kŏnŭn'drŭm,* s. pulla, f.

convalescence, *kŏnvălĕs'sĕns,* s. convalecencia, f.

convalescent, *-sĕnt,* a. convaleciente.

convene, *kŏnvēn',* v.a. convocar; juntar, unir; **-,** v. n. convenir, juntarse.

convenience, *-vē'nĭĕns,* s. conveniencia, comodidad, conformidad, f.

convenient, *-vē'nĭĕnt,* a. conveniente, apto, cómodo, propio; **-ly,** ad. cómodamente, oportunamente. [monasterio, m.

convent, *kŏn'vĕnt,* s. convento, claustro, culo, m.

conventicle, *kŏnvĕn'tĭkl,* s. conventí-

convention, *-vĕn'shŭn,* s. convención, f.; contrato, tratado, m. [pulado.

conventional, *-ăl,* a. convencional, esti-

conventual, *kŏnvĕn'tŭăl,* a. conventual.

converge, *-vĕrj',* v. n. convergir.

convergence, *-vĕr'jĕns,* s. convergencia, f.

convergent, *-vĕr'jĕnt,* a. convergente.

conversable, *-vĕr'săbl,* a. conversable, sociable. [timo.

conversant, *-vĕr'sănt,* a. versado en; ín-

conversation, *-vĕrsā'shŭn,* s. conversación, familiaridad, f. [divertido, m.

conversationalist, *-ălĭst,* s. hombre

converse, *-vĕrs',* v. n. conversar; platicar; **-,** *kŏn'vĕrs,* s. conversación, plática, f.; familiaridad, f.; comercio, m.

conversely, *kŏnvĕrs'lĕ,* ad. mutuamente, recíprocamente. [transmutación, f.

conversion, *-vĕr'shŭn,* s. conversión,

convert, *-vĕrt',* v. a. (& n.) convertir(se); **-,** *kŏn'vĕrt,* s. converso, convertido, m.

convertible, *kŏnvĕr'tĭbl,* a. convertible, transmutable.

convex, *kŏn'vĕks,* a. convexo.

convexity, *kŏnvĕk'sĭtĕ,* s. convexidad, f.

convey, *-vā',* v. a. transportar; transmitir, trasferir, transferir.

conveyance, *-āns,* s. transporte, m.; conducción, f.; escritura de traspaso, f.

conveyancer, *-ănsŭr,* s. notario, m.

convict, *kŏnvĭkt',* v.a. convencer, probar un delito; **-,** *kŏn'vĭkt,* s. convicto, m.

conviction, *-vĭk'shŭn,* s. convicción, f.; refutación, f.

convince, *-vĭns',* v. a. convencer, poner en evidencia. [modo convincente.

convincingly, *-vĭn'sĭnglĕ,* ad. de un

convivial, *-vĭ'vĭăl,* a. sociable; hospitalario.

conviviality, *-ĭtĕ,* s. sociabilidad, f.

convocation, *kŏnvŏkā'shŭn,* s. convocación, f.; sínodo, m.

convoke, *-vōk',* v. a. convocar, reunir.

convolvulus, *-vŏl'vŭlŭs,* s. (bot.) albohol, m., bigorda, f.

convoy, *-vŏĭ',* v. a. convoyar; **-,** *kŏn'vŏĭ,* s. convoy, m.; conserva, f.; escolta, f.

convulse, *-vŭls',* v. a. conmover, trastornar. [conmoción, f.; tumulto, m.

convulsion, *-vŭl'shŭn,* s. convulsión, f.;

convulsive, *-vŭl'sĭv,* a. convulsivo; **-ly,** ad. convulsivamente.

cony, *kō'nĕ,* s. conejo, m.

coo, *kō,* v. n. arrullar. [halago, m.

cooing, *kō'ĭng,* s. arrullo de palomas, m.;

cook, *kŏk,* s. cocinero, m.; cocinera, f.; **-,** v. a. aderezar las viandas; **-,** v. n. cocinar; guisar.

cookery, *-ărĕ,* s. arte culinaria, f.

cool, *kōl,* a. fresco; indiferente; **-,** s. frescura, f.; **-,** v. a. enfriar, refrescar, atemperar. [frigerante, m.

cooler, *-ŭr,* s. enfriadera, f.; (med.) re-

coolly, *-lĕ,* ad. frescamente; indiferentemente. [frescura, f.

coolness, *-nĕs,* s. fresco, m.; frialdad,

coom, *kŏm,* s. unto de coche, m.

coop, *kŏp,* s. caponera, f.; redil, m.; **-,** v. a. enjaular, encarcelar.

cooper, *-ŭr,* s. cubero, tonelero, m.

cooperate, *kŏŏp'ărāt,* v. n. cooperar.

cooperation, *kŏŏpărā'shŭn,* s. cooperación, f. [cooperante.

cooperative, *kŏŏp'ărătĭv,* a. cooperativo;

coordination, *kŏŏrdĭnā'shŭn,* s. coordinación, elección, f. [socio, m.

copartner, *kŏpärt'nŭr,* s. compañero,

cope, *kŏp,* s. capa pluvial, f.; cualquier cobertura, f.; **-,** v. n. competir, lidiar con

copier, *kŏp'ĭŭr,* s. copista, m. [otro.

coping, *kō'pĭng,* s. cumbre de edificio, f.

copious, *kō'pĭŭs,* a. copioso, abundante; **-ly,** ad. en abundancia.

copiousness, *-nĕs,* s. abundancia, copia, f.

copper, *kŏp'pŭr,* s. cobre, m.; calderón, m.; moneda de cobre, f.

copperas, *-ăs,* s. caparrosa, f.

copper-plate, *-plăt,* s. lámina de cobre, f.; estampa, f.

coppersmith, *-smĭth,* s. calderero, m. [f.

copper-work, *-wŭrk,* s. fábrica de cobre,

coppery, *-ĕ,* a. cobrizo. [bajo, m.

coppice, *kŏp'pĭs,* copse, *kŏps,* s. monte

copy, *kŏp'ĕ,* s. copia, f.; original, m.; ejemplar de algún libro, m.; **-,** v. a. copiar; imitar.

copy-book, *-bŭk,* s. copiador de cartas (libro), m. [nero, m.

copying-clerk, *-ĭngklărk,* s. expedicio-

copying-machine, *-ĭngmăshēn,* s. pantó-

copyist, *-ĭst,* s. copista, m. [grafo, m.

copyright, *-rĭt,* s. propiedad de una obra literaria, f.; derechos de autor, m. pl.

coquet, *kŏkĕt',* v. n. cocar, cortejar.

coquetry, *kŏ'kĕtrĕ,* s. coquetería, f.

coquettish, *kŏkĕt'tĭsh,* a. pisaverde, coral, *kŏr'ăl,* s. coral, m. [queta.

coralline, *-ĭn,* s. coralina, f.

cord, *kŏrd,* s. cuerda, f.; cordel, m.; montón de leña, m.; –, v. a. encordelar.

cordage, *kŏr´dáj,* s. cordaje, m.

cordial, *kŏr´dĭál,* a. cordial, de corazón, amistoso; –ly, ad. cordialmente; –, s. remedio confortativo, m.

cordiality, *kŏrdĭál´tĭ,* s. cordialidad, f.

corduroy, *kŏrdúrŏĭ´,* s. terciopelo cruzado, m.

core, *kŏr,* s. cuesco, m.; interior, centro, corazón, m.; pus, m.; materia, f.

cork, *kŏrk,* s. alcornoque, m.; corcho, m.; –, v. a. tapar botellas con corchos.

cork-screw, *–skrŏ,* s. tirabuzón, m.

corky, *–ĭ,* a. de corcho.

cormorant, *kŏr´mŏránt,* s. corvejón, m.; [glotón, m.

corn, *kŏrn,* s. grano, m.; callo, m.; –, v. a. salar; granular.

corn-cob, *–kŏb,* s. (am.) mazorca, f.

cornelian, *kŏrnĕ´lĭán,* (tree), s. cornejo, m.; (stone), cornerina, f.

corner, *kŏr´nŭr,* s. ángulo, m.; rincón, m.; extremidad, f.; remate, m.

corner-house, *–hŏûs,* s. casa esquina, f.

corner-stone, *–stŏn,* s. piedra angular, f.; mocheta, f. [darte, m.

cornet, *kŏr´nĕt,* s. corneta, f.; portaestandarte, m.

cornetoy, *–sĕ,* s. grado de portaestandarte, m. [de granos, m.

corn-exchange, *kŏrn´ĕkstshánj,* s. lonja

corn-field, *–fĭld,* s. sembrado, m.

corn-flower, *–flŏŭr,* s. azulejo, aciano, m.

cornice, *kŏr´nĭs,* s. cornisa, f. [m.

corn-rose, *kŏrn´rŏs,* s. ababa, amapola, f.

corn-salad, *–sálád,* s. macha, valerianilla, f.

corny, *kŏr´nĭ,* a. lo que produce ó contiene grano; de pan llevar; calloso.

corollary, *kŏr´ŏllrĕ,* s. corolario, m.

coronation, *kŏrŏná´shún,* s. coronación, f.

coroner, *kŏr´ŏnŭr,* s. oficial que hace la inspección jurídica de los cadáveres, m.

coronet, *kŏr´ŏnĕt,* s. corona pequeña, f.

corporal, *kŏr´pŏrál,* s. caporal, m.; –, a. corpóreo; material; –ly, ad. corporalmente.

corporate, *kŏr´pŏrát,* a. formado en cuerpo ó en comunidad. [ción, f.; gremio, m.

corporation, *ŏrpŏrá´shún,* s. corporación.

corporeal, *kŏrpŏ´rĭál,* a. corpóreo.

corps, *kŏr,* s. cuerpo de ejército, m.; regimiento, m.

corpse, *kŏrps,* s. cadáver, m. [lencia, f.

corpulence(cy), *kŏr´pŭlĕns(ĕ),* s. corpulencia.

corpulent, *kŏr´pŭlĕnt,* a. corpulento, grordo.

Corpus-Christi-Day, *kŏr´pŭskrĭstĭád,* s. día de Corpus, m.

corpuscle, *kŏr´pŭskl,* s. corpúsculo, átomo.

correct, *kŏrĕkt´,* v. a. corregir, reprender, castigar; enmendar, amonestar; –, a. correcto, revisto; –ly, ad. correctamente.

correction, *kŏrĕk´shún,* s. corrección, f.; castigo, m.; enmienda, f.; censura, f.

corrective, *kŏrĕk´tĭv,* a. correctivo; –, s. correctivo, m.; restricción, f.

correctness, *kŏrĕkt´nĕs,* s. exactitud, f.

correlative, *kŏrĕl´átĭv,* a. correlativo.

correspond, *kŏrrĕspŏnd´,* v. n. corresponder; corresponderse.

correspondence, *–ĕns,* s. correspondencia, f.; inteligencia, f.

correspondent, *–ĕnt,* a. correspondiente, conforme; –, s. corresponsal, m.

corrigible, *kŏr´rĭjĭbl,* a. corregible.

corroborate, *kŏrrŏb´ŏrát,* v. a. corroborar.

corroboration, *kŏrrŏbŏrá´shún,* s. corroboración, f. [borativo.

corroborative, *kŏrrŏb´ŏrátĭv,* a. corro-

corrode, *kŏrrŏd´,* v. a. corroer.

corrosion, *kŏrrŏ´shún,* s. corrosión, f.

corrosive, *kŏrrŏ´sĭv,* a. & s. corrosivo (m.).

corrupt, *kŏrrŭpt´,* v. a. corromper; sobornar; infectar; –, v. n. corromperse, pudrirse; –, a. corrompido; depravado.

corruptible, *–ĭbl,* a. corruptible.

corruption, *kŏrrŭp´shún,* s. corrupción, f.; depravación, f.; alteración, f.; pus, m.

corruptive, *–ĭtv,* a. corruptivo.

corruptness, *–nĕs,* s. corruptela, corrupción, f. [forbante, m.

corsair, *kŏr´sár,* s. corsario, pirata, m.;

corset, *kŏr´sĕt,* s. corsé, corpiño, m.

coruscation, *kŏrúská´shún,* s. resplandor, m. [beta, m.

corvette, *kŏrvĕt´, kŏr´vĕt,* s. (mar.) corbeta, m.

cosily, *kŏ´sĭlĭ,* ad. cómodamente, con facilidad.

cosmetic, *kŏzmĕt´ĭk,* a. & s. cosmético(m.).

cosmopolitan, *kŏzmŏpŏl´ĭtán,* cosmopolite, *kŏzmŏp´ŏlĭt,* a. & s. cosmopolita (m.).

cosset, *kŏs´sĕt,* v. a. mimar. [(m.).

cost, *kŏst,* s. coste, precio, m.; expensas, f. pl.; –, v. n. costar. [gŭr, s. frutero, m.

coster, *kŏs´tŭr,* **coster-monger,** *–mŭn´gŭr,* s. frutero, m.

costive, *kŏs´tĭv,* a. restriñente.

costiveness, *–nĕs,* s. constipación, f.

costliness, *kŏst´lĭnĕs,* s. suntuosidad, f.

costly, *kŏst´lĭ,* a. costoso, suntuoso, caro; espléndido, suntuoso.

costume, *kŏstŭm´,* s. traje, m.

cosy, *kŏ´sĭ,* a. cómodo.

cot, *kŏt,* s. cabaña, f.; barquillo, m.

cotillion, *kŏtĭl´yŭn,* s. cotillón, m.

cotrustee, *kŏtrŭstĕ´,* s. curador, m.

cottage, *kŏt´tĭj,* s. cabaña, casucha, f.

cottager, *kŏt´tĭjŭr,* s. aldeano, lugareño, m.

cotton, *kŏt´tn,* s. algodón, m.; cotonía, f.; –, v. n. cubrirse de pelusa; acordarse.

cotton-mill, *–mĭl,* s. hilandería de algodón

cotton-tree, *–trĕ,* s. algodonero, m.

cotton-wool, *–wŭl,* s. algodón basto, m.

couch, *kŏûtsh,* v. n. echarse; agobiarse; –, v. a. acostar; extender; esconder; bajar (los ojos); (in writing) componer; –, s. cama, f., lecho, m.; canapé, m.

cough, *kŏf,* s. tos, f.; –, v. n. toser.

councillor, *kŏûn´sĭlŭr,* s. concejal, individuo del concejo, m.

council, *kŏûn´sĭl,* s. concilio, consejo, m.; sínodo, m. [consejo, m.

council-board, *–bŏrd,* s. reunión del

counsel, *kŏûn´sĕl,* s. consejo, aviso, m.; abogado, m. [gado, m.

counsellor, *–lŭr,* s. consejero, m.; abo-

count, *kŏûnt,* v. a. contar, numerar; calcular, reputar; –, s. cuenta, f.; cálculo, m.; conde, m.

countenance, *kŏŭn'tĕnăns*, s. rostro, m.;
aspecto, m.; (buena ó mala) cara, f.; protección, f.; favor, m.; aire, m.; —, v. a.
proteger, favorecer.

counter, *kŏŭn'tăr*, s. contador, m.; ficha,
f.; —, ad. contra, al contrario, al revés.

counteract, —*ăkt*, v.a. contrariar, impedir,
estorbar; frustrar.

counteraction, —*ăk'shŭn*, s. oposición, f.

counterbalance, —*băl'ăns*, v. a. contrapesar; igualar, compensar; —, —*băl'ăns*,
s. contrapeso, m.

counterfeit, —*fĭt*, v.a. contrahacer, imitar,
falsear; —, s. contrahacedor, impostor, m.;
falsificación, f.; —, s. falsificado; fingido.

counterfeiter, —*fĭt'ăr*, s. contrahacedor,
falsario, m.; — of coin, monedero falso, m.

counter-foil, —*fŏĭl*, s. contramarca, f.

counterjumper, —*jŭmpăr*, s. hortera, m.

countermand, —*mănd'*, v. a. contramandar; revocar.

counterpane, —*păn*, s. colcha de cama, f.;
cobertor, s. [diente, f.

counterpart, —*părt*, s. parte correspondiente, f.

counterplot, —*plŏt*, s. contratreta, f.

counterpoise, —*pŏĭz'*, v.a. contrapesar; —,
kŏŭn'tărpŏĭz, s. contrapeso, m.

counterscarp, —*skărp*, s. contraescarpa, f.

countersign, —*sĭn*, v.a. refrendar; firmar
un decreto. [trarrestar.

countervail, —*văl*, v. a. contrapesar, contarrestar.

countess, *kŏŭn'tĕs*, s. condesa, f.

counting-house, *kŏŭnt'ĭnghŏŭs*, s. despacho, escritorio, m.

countless, *kŏŭnt'lĕs*, a. innumerable.

countrified, *kŭn'trĭfĭd*, a. rústico; tosco,
rudo.

country, *kŭn'trĕ*, s. país, f.; campo, m.;
región, f.; patria, f.; —, a. rústico; campestre, rural.

country-dance, —*dăns*, s. contradanza, f.

country-house, —*hŏŭs*, s. casa de campo,
granja, f. [patriota, m.

countryman, —*măn*, s.· paisano, m.; —

country-squire, —*skwĭr*, s. caballero de
provincia, hidalgo de aldea, m.

county, *kŏŭn'tĕ*, s. condado, m.

couple, *kŭp'l*, s. par, m.; lazo, m.; —, v.
a. unir, parear; casar; —, v. n. juntarse
carnalmente.

couplet, *kŭp'lĕt*, s. copla, f.; par, m.

couplings, *kŭp'lĭngz*, s. pl. (rail.) locomotoras acopladas, f. pl.

courage, *kăr'ăj*, s. coraje, valor, f.

courageous, *kărā'jŭs*, a. corajudo, valeroso; —ly, ad. valerosamente. [preso, m.

courier, *kŏr'tăr*, s. correo, mensajero, expreso, m.

course, *kōrs*, s. curso, m.; carrera, f.; camino, m.; ruta, f.; viaje de comidas, m.;
curso, m.; método, m.; entrada, f.; servicio, m.; regularidad, orden, f.; —s, pl.
menstruación, f.; —, v. a. & n. cazar; corretear; of —, por supuesto, sin duda.

courser, —*ăr*, s. corcel, corredor, m.

court, *kōrt*, s. corte, f.; palacio, m.; tribunal de justicia, m.; cortejo, m.; patio, m.;
—, v. a. cortejar; solicitar, adular.

court-day, —*dă*, s. día de besamanos, m.

court-dresser,—*drĕssăr*,s. lisonjeador, m.

courteous, *kăr'tyŭs*, a. cortés; benévolo;
—ly, ad. cortésmente.

courter, *kōr'tăr*, s. cortejador, amante, m.

courtesan, *kăr'tĕzăn*, s. cortesana, f.

courtesy, *kăr'tĕsĕ*, s. cortesía, f.; benignidad, f.; —, v. n. hacer la reverencia.

court-house, *kōrt'hŏŭs*, s. foro, tribunal,
m. [m.; cortejo, m.

courtier, *kōrt'yĕr*, s. cortesano, palaciego,

courtliness, *kōrt'lĭnĕs*, s. cortesía, urbanidad, política, f.; elegancia, f.

courtly, —*lĕ*, a. cortesano, elegante.

court-martial, —*mărshăl*, s. (mil.) corte
marcial, f.; consejo militar, m. [m.

court-plaster, —*plăstăr*, s. tafetán inglés,

courtship, —*shĭp*, s. cortejo, m.; galanteria, f. [s. patio, m.

court-yard, —*yărd*, s. patio, m.

cousin, *kŭz'n*, s. primo, m.; prima, f.;
first —, primo hermano, m. [picaro, m.

cove, *kōv*, s. (mar.) ensenada, caleta, f.;

covenant, *kŭv'ĕnănt*, s. contrato, m.; convención, f.; —, v. n. pactar, estipular.

cover, *kŭv'ăr*, s. cubierta, f.; abrigo, m.;
pretexto, m.; under open —, bajo faja;
—, v. a. cubrir; tapar; ocultar; proteger,
paliar, honestar.

covering, —*ĭng*, s. ropa, f.; vestido, m.

coverlet, —*lĕt* coverlid, —*lĭd*, s. colcha, f.

covert, —*t*, s. cubierto, m.; refugio, m.; —,
a. cubierto; oculto, secreto; —ly, ad.
secretamente.

covertnre, —*tăr*, s. abrigo, refugio, m.

covet, *kŭv'ĕt*, v.a. codiciar, desear con ansia.

covetous, —*ŭs*, a. avariento, sórdido; —ly,
ad. codiciosamente. [mezquindad, f.

covetousness, —*ĕsnĕs*, s. codicia, avaricia,

covey, *kŭv'ĕ*, s. nidada, pollada, f.

cow, *kŏŭ*, s. vaca, f.; —, v. a. acobardar, intimidar.

coward, —*ărd*, s. cobarde, medroso, m.

cowardice, —*ărdĭs*, s. cobardía, timidez, f.

cowardly, —*ărdlĕ*, a. & ad. cobarde; pusilánime; cobardemente.

cower, —*ăr*, v. n. agacharse.

cow-herd, —*hĕrd*, s. vaquero, m.

cow-house, —*hŏŭs*, s. boyera, f.

cowl, *kŏŭl*, s. capuz, m.

cowslip, *kŏŭ'slĭp*, s. prímula, primavera, f.

coxcomb, *kŏks'kŏm*, s. petimetre, m.

coy, *kŏĭ*, a. recatado, modesto; esquivo;
—ly, ad. con esquivez.

coyness, —*nĕs*, s. esquivez, modestia, f.

coz, *kŭz*, s. (fam.) primo, m.; prima, f.

cozen, —*n*, v. a. engañar, defraudar.

cozenage, —*n'ĕj*, s. engaño, m.; trampa, f.

crab, *krăb*, s. cangrejo, m.; manzana silvestre, f.

crab-apple, —*ăp'pl*, s. manzana silvestre,
f.; crab-apple-tree, —*trĕ*, s. manzano
silvestre, m.

crabbed, —*bĕd*, a. áspero, austero, bronco,
tosco; —ly, ad. de mal humor; ásperamente.

crabbedness, —*bĕdnĕs*, s. aspereza, rigideza, f.; austeridad, f.; dificultad, f.

crack, *krăk*, s. crujido, m.; hendedura,
quebraja, f.; fanfarrón, m.; —, v. a. hender,
rajar; romper; —, v. n. reventar; jactarse;
—, a. raro, fino. [estúpido.

crack-brained, —*brănd*, a. alocado.

cracker, -ăr, s. fanfarrón, m.; pastillita de chocolate, f.; cohete, m.

crackle, -kl, y. n. crujir, chillar.

crackling, -ling, s. estallido, crujido, m.

cracknel, -nĕl, s. hojuela, f.   [cuna.

cradle, krd'dl, s. cuna, f.; -, v. a. mecer la

craft, krăft, s. arte, m.; artificio, m.; astucia, f.

craftily, -lĭli, ad. astutamente.   [f.

craftiness, -ĭnĕs, s. astucia, estratagema, f.

craftsman, -s'măn, s. artífice, artesano, m.

crafty, -ē, a. astuto, artificioso.

crag, krăg, s. despeñadero, m.; nuca, f.

cragged, -gĕd, a. escabroso, áspero.

cragginess, -gĭnĕs, s. escabrosidad, aspereza, f.

craggy, -gē, a. escabroso, áspero.

cram, krăm, v. a. embutir; engordar; empujar; -, y. n. atracarse de comida.

cramp, krămp, s. calambre, m.; laña, f.; -, v. a. lañar; constreñir.   [ga, f. (pez).

cramp-fish, -fĭsh, s. torpedo, m., tremielcramp-iron, -īrn, s. laña, f.

cranberry, krăn'bĕrrē, s. arandilla, f.

crane, krān, s. grulla, f.; grúa, f.; pescante, m.; sifón, m.; -, v. a. guindar.

crank, krăngk, s. manecilla, f.; sinuosidad, f.; -, a. sano, alegre; vigoroso.

crannied, krăn'nĕd, a. hendido.

cranny, krăn'nē, s. grieta, hendedura, f.

crape, krāp, s. crespón, m.

crash, krăsh, v. n. estallar, rechinar; -, s. estallido, fracaso, m.

crass, krăs, s. craso, grueso, basto, tosco, grosero.   [lozas, f.

crate, krāt, s. cesta grande para embalar

crater, krā'tăr, s. cráter, m.; boca de volcán, m.

cravat, krăvăt', s. corbata, f.   [f.

crave, krāv, v. a. rogar, suplicar.

craven, -n, s. gallo vencido, m.; cobarde.

craving, krā'ving, a. insaciable, pedigüeño; -, s. deseo ardiente, m.

craw, krā, s. buche de ave, m.   [m.

crawfish, -fĭsh, s. cangrejo de agua dulce.

crawl, krăl, v. n. arrastrar; to - with, hormiguear.

crayfish, krā'fĭsh, s. cangrejo de río, m.

crayon, krā'ŏn, s. lápiz, m.

craze, krāz, v. a. quebrantar; romper. [f.

craziness, krā'zĭnĕs, s. debilidad, f.; locura, f.

crazy, krā'zē, a. decrépito; caduco; fatuo.

creak, krēk, v. n. crujir, estallar.   [simple.

cream, krēm, s. crema, f.; -, v. a. desnatar; -, v. n. criar nata.

creamy, -ē, a. lleno de crema.

crease, krēs, s. pliegue, m.; -, v. a. plegar.

create, krēāt', v. a. crear; causar.   [ción, f.

creation, krēā'shŭn, s. creación, f.; electivo.

creative, krēā'tĭv, a. creativo.

creator, krēā'tăr, s. criador, m.

creature, krē'tjŭr, s. criatura, f.

credence, krē'dĕns, s. creencia, fe, f.; renombre, m.   [credenciales, f. pl.

credentials, krēdĕn'shăls, s. pl. cartas credenciales, f. pl.

credibility, krēdĭbĭl'ĭtĕ, s. credibilidad, f.

credible, krēd'ĭbl, a. creíble; -bly, ad. creíblemente; según se cree.

credit, krēd'ĭt, s. crédito, m.; creencia, fe, f.; reputación, f.; autoridad, f.; -, v. a. creer, fiar, acreditar.

creditable, -ăbl, a. estimable, honorífico; -bly, ad. honorablemente.

creditableness, -ăblnĕs, s. reputación, estimación, f.

creditor, -ăr, s. acreedor, m.

credulity, krēdū'lĭtĕ, s. credulidad, f.

credulous, krēd'ŭlŭs, a. crédulo; -ly, ad

creed, krēd, s. credo, m.   [con credulidad.

creek, krēk, s. bahía pequeña, f.; (am.) arroyo, m.   [placer bajamente.

creep, krēp, v. n. arrastrar, serpear; com-

creeper, -ăr, s. solano trepador; reptil, m.

creep-hole, -hōl, s. huronera, f.; subterfugio, m.; escapatoria, f.   [res.

cremate, krēmāt', v. a. incinerar cadáve-

cremation, krēmā'shŭn, s. cremación, f.

crenellated, krĕn'ĕlātĕd, a. dentado.

crescent, krĕs'sĕnt, a. creciente; -, s. creciente, f. (fase de la luna).

cress, krĕs, s. lepidio, mastuerzo, m. [m.

crest, krĕst, s. cresta, f.; copete, m.; orgullo,

crested, -ĕd, a. crestado.   [de espíritu.

crest-fallen, -fāln, a. acobardado, abatido

cretaceous, krētā'shŭs, a. cretáceo.

crevice, krĕv'ĭs, s. raja, hendedura, f.

crew, krō, s. banda, tropa, f.; (mar.) tripulación, f.

crewel, -ĕl, s. ovillo de estambre, m.

crib, krĭb, s. pesebre, m.; casucha, f.

crick, krĭk, s. chirrido, m.

cricket, -ĕt, s. grillo, m.; bilorta, f. (juego).

crier, krī'ăr, s. pregonero, m.

crime, krĭm, s. crimen, m.; culpa, f.

criminal, krĭm'ĭnăl, a. criminal, reo; -ly, ad. criminalmente; -, s. reo convicto, m.

criminality, krĭmĭnăl'ĭtĕ, s. criminalidad, f.

criminate, krĭm'ĭnăt, v. a. acriminar.

crimination, krĭmĭnā'shŭn, s. criminación, f.

crimp, krĭmp, s. comisionista, m.; (mil.) enganchador, m.; -, v. a. rizar, encrespar.

crimson, krĭm'zn, a. & s. carmesí (m.)

cringe, krĭnj, s. bajeza, f.; -, v. n. incensar, adular con bajeza.   [a. serpentear.

crinkle, krĭng'kl, s. sinuosidad, f.; -, v.

crinoline, krĭn'ŏlĭn, s. crinolina, f.

cripple, krĭp'l, s. & a. estropeado (m.); -, v. a. derrengar, estropear.

crisis, krī'sĭs, s. crisis, f.; esfuerzo, m.

crisp, krĭsp, a. crespo; -, v. a. crespar, rizar.

crispness, -nĕs, s. encrespadura, f.

criterion, krītē'rŏn, s. criterio, m.

critic, krĭt'ĭk, s. crítico, m.; crítica, f.

critic(al), -(ăl), a. crítico; exacto; delicado; -ally, ad. exactamente, rigurosamente.

criticise, krĭt'ĭsĭz, v. a. criticar, censurar.

criticism, krĭt'ĭsĭzm, s. crítica, f.

croak, krōk, v. n. graznar, crocitar.

crockery, krŏk'ărĕ, s. loza, f.; vasijas de barro, f. pl.; vidriado, m.

crocodile, krŏk'ŏdĭl, s. cocodrilo, m.

crone, krōn, s. anciana, vieja, f.

crony, krō'nĕ, s. amigo (ó conocido) antiguo, m.

crook, krŏk, s. gancho, m.; artificio, m.; -, v. a. encorvar, torcer; pervertir.

crooked, *krŭk'ĕd*, a. torcido, corvo; perverso; **-ly**, ad. torcidamente; de mala gana.

croon, *krōn*, v. n. zumbir; arrullar.

crop, *krŏp*, s. buche de ave, m.; caballo desorejado, m.; corbacho, m.; cosecha, f.; **—**, v. a. segar las mieses; pacer la hierba; cortar las orejas.

croquet, *krōkā'*, s. juego de pelota cerrado y de poca extensión para el boleo, m.

crosier, *krō'zhŭr*, s. cayado pastoral de obispo, m.

cross, *krŏs*, s. cruz, f.; carga, f.; trabajo, m.; pena, aflicción, f.; tormento, m.; **—**, a. contrario, opuesto, atravesado; mal humorado; **—**, pr. al través; **—**, v. a. atravesar, cruzar; **to — over**, traspasar.

cross-bar, *-bär*, **--beam**, *-bēm*, s. travesaño, m.

cross-breed, *-brēd*, s. raza cruzada, f.

cross-examine, *-ĕgzăm'īn*, v. a. preguntar á un testigo. [tratable.

cross-grained, *-grānd*, a. perverso, intratable.

crossing, *-sing*, **cross-line**, *-līn*, s. (rail.) cruzamiento de dos vías, m.

crossing-sweeper, *-swēpŭr*, s. barrendero de las encrucijadas, m.

crossly, *-lĕ*, ad. contrariamente, desgraciadamente.

crossness, *-nĕs*, s. espíritu de contradicción, m.; malicia, travesía, f.

cross-purpose, *-pŭrpŭs*, s. disposición contraria, f.; contradicción, f. [m.

cross-road, *-rŏd*, s. (rail.) paso á nivel, m.

cross-way, *-wā*, s. camino de travesía, m.

crotch, *krŏtsh*, s. gancho, corchete, m.

crotchet, *-ĕt*, s. corchea, f.; capricho, m.; corchete, m.

crouch, *krŏutsh*, v. n. agacharse, bajarse.

croup, *krŏp*, s. obispillo, m.; grupa (de caballo), f.; coqueluche, m.

crow, *krō*, s. cuervo, m.; barra, f.; canto del gallo, m.; **—**, v. n. cantar el gallo.

crowd, *krŏud*, s. tropel, m.; turba, muchedumbre, f.; **—**, v. a. amontonar; **to — sail**, hacer fuerza de vela; **—**, v. n. estrecharse.

crown, *krŏun*, s. corona, f.; guirnalda de flores, f.; moneda de plata del valor de cinco chelines, f.; complemento, colmo, m.; **—**, v. a. coronar; recompensar; dar cima; cubrir el peón que ha llegado á ser dama.

crown-glass, *-glăs*, s. vidrio fino, m.

crown-lands, *-lănds*, s. pl. dominios de la corona, m. pl. [m.

crown-prince, *-prins*, s. príncipe real, m.

crucial, *krō'shŭl*, a. en forma de cruz, crucial.

crucible, *krō'sĭbl*, s. crisol, m.

crucifix, *krō'sĭfĭks*, s. crucifijo, m.

crucify, *krō'sĭfī*, v. a. crucificar; atormentar. [ciecto; **-ly**, ad. crudamente.

crude, *krōd*, a. crudo, indigesto, imperfecto; **-ly**, ad. crudamente.

crudity, *krō'dĭtĕ*, s. crudeza, f.; indigestión, f. [cruelmente.

cruel, *krō'ĕl*, a. cruel, inhumano; **-ly**, ad.

cruelty, *krō'ĕltĕ*, s. crueldad, f.

cruet, *krō'ĕt*, s. vinagrera, f.

cruet-stand, *-stănd*, s. angarillas, f. pl.

English and Spanish.

cruise, *krōz*, s. jícara, f.; (mar.) corso, m.; **—**, v. n. (mar.) andar en corso. [m.

cruiser, *krō'zŭr*, s. crucero, m.; corsario, crumb, *krŭm*, s. miga, f.

crumble, *-bl*, v. a. desmigajar, desmenuzar; **—**, v. n. desmigajarse.

crummy, *-mĕ*, a. blando, tierno.

crumple, *krŭm'pl*, v. a. arrugar.

crusade, *krōsād'*, s. cruzada, f.

crush, *krŭsh*, v. a. apretar, oprimir; amilanar; **—**, s. choque, m.

crushing-mill, *-ĭngmĭl*, s. bocarte, m.

crust, *krŭst*, s. costra, f.; corteza, f.; **—**, v. a. (& n.) encostrar(se). [chado.

crustaceous, *-d'shŭs*, a. crustáceo; concustily, *-tĭlē*, ad. enojadamente, broncamente. [f.; mal genio, m.

crustiness, *-ĭnĕs*, s. dureza de la costra, f.

crusty, *-tĕ*, a. costroso; bronco, áspero.

crutch, *krŭtsh*, s. muleta, f.

cry, *krī*, v. a. & n. gritar; pregonar; exclamar; llorar; **—**, s. grito, m.; lloro, m.; clamor, m. [nea, f.

crypt, *krĭpt*, s. cripta (bóveda subterránea), f.

crystal, *krĭs'tăl*, s. cristal, m.

crystalline, *-lĭn*, a. cristalino; transparente. [talización, f.

crystallisation, *krĭstăllīză'shŭn*, s. cristalización, f.

crystallise, *krĭs'tăllīz*, v. a. (& n.) cristalizar(se). [(la osa ó zorra).

cub, *kŭb*, s. cachorro, m.; **—**, v. n. parir.

cube, *kŭb*, s. cubo, m.

cubic(al), *kū'bĭk(ăl)*, a. cúbico.

cubiform, *kū'bĭfŏrm*, a. cúbico.

cubit, *kū'bĭt*, s. codo, m. (medida).

cuckoo, *kŭk'ō*, s. cuclillo, cuco, m.

cucumber, *kū'kŭmbŭr*, s. cohombro, pepino, m.

cud, *kŭd*, s. panza, f.; primer estómago de los rumiantes; pasto contenido en la panza, m.; **to chew the —**, rumiar; fig. reflexionar.

cuddle, *-l*, v. n. agacharse, agazaparse.

cuddy, *kŭd'dĕ*, s. camarote de proa, m. (mar.)

cudgel, *kŭd'jĕl*, s. garrote, palo, m.; **—**, v. a. apalear.

cudgelling, *-lĭng*, s. bastonada, f.

cue, *kū*, s. cola, f.; apunte de comedia, m.; humor, m.; taco (de billar), m.

cuff, *kŭf*, s. puñada, f.; vuelta de manga de vestido, f.

cuirass, *kwĕrăs'*, s. coraza, f.

cuirassier, *-sēr'*, s. coracero, m.

culinary, *kū'lĭnărĕ*, a. culinario, de la cocina.

cull, *kŭll*, v. a. escoger, elegir. [f.

culminate, *kŭl'mĭnăt*, v. n. culminar.

culpability, *kŭlpăbĭl'ĭtĕ*, s. culpabilidad, f.

culpable, *kŭl'păbl*, a. culpable, criminal; **-bly**, ad. culpablemente, criminalmente, por la vía criminal.

culprit, *kŭl'prĭt*, s. reo acusado, m.

cultivate, *kŭl'tĭvāt*, v. n. cultivar, mejorar; perfeccionar. [f.; cultivo, m.

cultivation, *kŭltĭvā'shŭn*, s. cultivación, f.

culture, *kŭl'tjŭr*, s. cultura, f.

culverin, *kŭl'vărĭn*, s. (mil.) culebrina, f.

cumber, *kŭm'bŭr*, v. a. embarazar, embrollar.

cumbersome, *–săm,* **cumbrous,** *kăm'-brăs,* a. engorroso, pesado, confuso.

cumulative, *kămŭlă'tĭv,* a. cumulativo.

cunning, *kăn'nĭng,* a. experto; artificioso, astuto; intrigante; *–ly,* ad. astutamente; expertamente; **–,** s. astucia, sutileza, f.

cup, *kăp,* s. copa, taza, jícara, f.; (bot.) cáliz, m.; **– and ball,** boliche, m.; **–,** v. a. aplicar ventosas.

cupboard, *–bŏrd,* s. armario, m.

cupidity, *kŭpĭd'ĭtĕ,* s. concupiscencia, f.

cupola, *kŭ'pŏlă,* s. cúpola, f.

cupping-glass, *kăp'pĭnggläs,* s. ventosa, f.

cup-shot, *kăp'shŏt,* a. embriagado.

cur, *kăr,* s. perro de mala ralea, m.; vil.

curable, *kŭ'răbl,* a. curable. [llano, m.

curacy, *kŭ'răsĕ,* s. tenencia, f.; vicariato, m. [párroco, m.

curate, *kŭ'răt,* s. teniente de cura, m.

curative, *kŭ'rătĭv,* a. curativo. [m.

curator, *kŭrā'tŭr,* s. curador, m.; guardián, m.; **–,** v. a. refrenar, contener, moderar. [coagular.

curb, *kărb,* s. barbada, f.; freno, m.; restricción, f.; **–,** v. a. refrenar, contener, moderar. [coagular.

curd, *kŭrd,* s. cuajada, f.; **–,** v. a. cuajar.

curdle, *–l,* v. a. (& n.) cuajar(se), coagular(se).

cure, *kŭr,* s. cura, f.; remedio, m.; **–,** v. a. curar, sanar; **to –skins;** curar con sal las pieles. [chimenea, f.

curfew, *kŭr'fŭ,* s. guardafuego, tapador de curing, *kŭ'rĭng,* s. curación, f.

curiosity, *kŭriŏs'ĭtĕ,* s. curiosidad, f.; rareza, f.

curious, *kŭ'rŭs,* a. curioso, exacto, delicado; exquisito; *–ly,* ad. curiosamente, elegantemente.

curl, *kărl,* s. rizo de pelo, m.; tortuosidad, f.; **–,** v. a. encrespar el pelo; ondear; **–,** v. n. rizarse.

curling-iron, *–ĭngĭrn,* s., **curling-tongs,** *–ĭngtŏngz,* s. pl. encrespador, m.

curling-paper, *–ĭngpāpŭr,* s. papel á propósito para hacer los rizos, m.

curly, *kŭr'lĕ,* a. rizado. [tacaño, m.

curmudgeon, *kărmŭj'ŭn,* s. hombre currant, *kŭr'rănt,* s. grosella, f.; uva de Corinto, f.; **rough–,** grosella espinosa, f.

currency, *kŭr'rĕnsĕ,* s. circulación, f.; valor corriente de alguna cosa, m.; duración, f.

current, *kŭr'rĕnt,* a. corriente, común; **–,** s. curso, progreso, m., marcha, f.; corriente, f., fluido (eléctrico), m.; **alternant –,** corriente eléctrica inversa. [moda.

currently, *–lĕ,* ad. corrientemente; á la currier, *kŭr'tŭr,* s. curtidor, m.

currish, *kŭr'rĭsh,* a. perruno, brutal, regañón; *–ly,* ad. brutalmente.

curry, *kŭr'rĕ,* v. a. zurrar; almohazar; **–,** s. especería anglo-india, compuesta de varios ingredientes, f.

currycomb, *–kŏm,* s. almohaza, f.

curse, *kŭrs,* v. a. maldecir; **–,** v. n. imprecar; blasfemar; **–,** s. maldición, f.; imprecación, f. [minablemente.

cursedly, *–ĕdlĕ,* ad. miserablemente, abo-

cursive, *kŭr'sĭv,* a. cursivo.

cursorily, *kŭr'sŏrĭlĕ,* ad. precipitadamente, de paso. [siderado.

cursory, *kŭr'sŏrĕ,* a. precipitado, inconsiderado.

curt, *kŭrt,* a. sucinto.

curtail, *kŭrtāl',* v. a. cortar; mutilar.

curtain, *kŭr'tĭn,* s. cortina, f.; telón en los teatros, m.; **–,** v. a. proveer con cortinas.

curtain-lecture, *–lĕktŭr,* s. reconvención conyugal, f. [f.

curtain-rod, *–rŏd,* s. varilla de cortinaje, curtsy, *kŭrt'sĕ,* s. saludo á una mujer, m.

curvated, *kŭr'vātĕd,* a. corvo, encorvado.

curvature, *kŭr'vātŭr,* s. curvatura, f.

curve, *kŭrv,* v. a. encorvar; **–,** a. corvo, torcido; **–,** s. corva, combadura, f.

curvet, *kŭr'vĕt,* s. corveta, f.; **–,** v. n. corcovear; saltar de alegría. [f.

cushion, *kŭsh'ŭn,* s. cojín, m., almohada, cusp, *kŭsp,* s. cuerno de la luna, m.

custard, *kăs'tărd,* s. natillas, f. pl.

custodian, *kŭstō'dĭăn,* s. custodio, m.

custody, *kŭs'tŏdĕ,* s. custodia, f.; prisión, f.

custom, *kăs'tăm,* s. costumbre, f., uso, m.; despacho, m.; derechos de aduana, m. pl. [nariamente.

customarily, *–ărĭlĕ,* ad. comunmente, ordi-customary, *–ărĕ,* a. usual, acostumbrado, ordinario.

customer, *–ăr,* s. parroquiano, m.

custom-free, *–frē,* a. exento de derechos.

custom-house, *–hŏŭs,* s. aduana, f.

custom-house duty, *–dū'tĕ,* s. derechos de aduana, m. pl. [aduanero, m.

custom-house officer, *–ŏf'fĭsŭr,* s. out, *kăt,* v. a. cortar; separar; herir; dividir; alzar los naipes; **to – short,** interrumpir, cortar la palabra; **to – capers,** cabriolar; **to – teeth,** nacerle los dientes (á un niño); **–,** v. n. traspasar; cruzarse; **–,** s. cortadura, f.; estampa, f; grabado, m.; hechura, figura, f.; lonja, f.; herida, f.; **– and dry,** a. pronto.

cut-away, *–ăwā,* s. frac, m.

cuticle, *kŭ'tĭkl,* s. epidermis, f.; lapa, f.

cutlass, *kăt'lăs,* s. espada ancha, f.; alcutler, *kăt'lăr,* s. cuchillero, m. [fanje, f.

cutlery, *–s,* s. cuchillería, f.

cutlet, *kăt'lĕt,* s. costilla asada de carnero, f.

cutter, *kăt'tŭr,* s. cortador, m.; (mar.) cúter, m.

cut-throat, *kăt'thrŏt,* s. asesino, m.

cutting, *kăt'tĭng,* s. cortadura, f.; incisión, f.; alce de naipes, m.; trinchado, m.

cutting-nippers, *–nĭppŭrz,* s. pl. pinzas, tenacillas, f. pl. [del timón, m.

cutwater, *kăt'wătŭr,* s. (mar.) azafrán cycle, *sĭ'kl,* s. ciclo, m. [f.

cyclopædia, *sĭklŏpē'dĭă,* s. enciclopedia, cygnet, *sĭg'nĕt,* s. pollo del cisne, m. [m.

cylinder, *sĭl'ĭndŭr,* s. cilindro, m.; rollo, cylindric(al), *sĭlĭn'drĭk(ăl),* a. cilíndrico.

cymbal, *sĭm'băl,* s. címbalo, m.

cynic(al), *sĭn'ĭk(ăl),* a. cínico; obsceno; **–,** s. cínico, m. (filósofo).

Cynosure, *sĭ'nŏzhŭr,* s. Cinosura, f.

cypress, *sĭ'prĕs,* s. ciprés, m.

czar, *zăr,* s. Zar, m.

czarina, *zărē'nă,* s. Zarina, f.

D.

dab, *dăb,* v. a. rociar; empapar; —, s. pedazo pequeño, m.; salpicadura, f.; golpe blando, m.; barbada, f. (pez).

dabble, *–bl,* v. a. rociar, salpicar; —, v. n. chapotear.

dabbler, *–blăr,* s. chisgaravís, m.

dace, *dās,* s. albur, gobio, yáculo, m. (pez).

dad(dy), *dăd('dé),* s. papá, m.; [cudo, m.

daddy-longlegs, *–dăng'lĕgs,* s. zandaffodil, *dăf'fŏdíl,* s. narciso, m.

dagger, *dăg'găr,* s. puñal, m.

daily, *dā'lĕ,* a. diario, cotidiano; —, ad. diariamente, cada día.

daintily, *dăn'tĭlĕ,* ad. delicadamente.

daintiness, *dăn'tĭnĕs,* s. elegancia, f.; delicadeza, f. [s. bocado exquisito, m.

dainty, *dăn'tĕ,* a. delicado; elegante; —,

dairy, *dā'rĕ,* s. lechería, quesera, f.

dairy-maid, *–mād,* s. lechera, mantequera, f.

daisy, *dā'sĕ,* s. margarita, maya, f.

dale, *dāl,* s. cañada, f.; valle, m.

dalliance, *dăl'lĭăns,* s. diversión, f.; juguete, m.; dilación, f.

dally, *dăl'lĕ,* v. n. juguetear, divertirse; burlarse; tardar; —, v. a. dilatar, suspender; hacer pasar el tiempo con gusto.

dam, *dăm,* s. madre, f. (en los animales); dique, m.; azud, presa, f.; —, v. a. represar; tapar.

damage, *dăm'ĕj,* s. daño, detrimento, m.; resarcimiento de daño, m.; —, v. a. dañar.

damageable, *–ăbl,* a. perjudicial; nocivo.

damask, *dăm'ăsk,* s. damasco, m.; —, a. de damasco; —, v. a. adamascar.

damaskeen, *–ĭn,* v. a. ataujiar.

dame, *dām,* s. dama, señora, f.

damn, *dăm,* v. a. condenar; silbar.

damnable, *–năbl,* a. condenable; *–bly,* ad. de un modo condenable; horriblemente, detestablemente.

damnation, *–nā'shŭn,* s. condenación, f.

damp, *dămp,* a. húmedo; triste, abatido; —, s. aire húmedo, m.; aflicción, f.; —, v. a. humedecer; desanimar, abatir.

dampen, *–n,* v. a. humedecer.

damper, *–ăr,* s. sordina, f.; apagador, m.; tarasca, m.

dampness, *–nĕs,* s. humedad, f.

damsel, *dăm'zĕl,* s. damisela, señorita, f.

damson, *dăm'zn,* s. damascena, f. (ciruela).

dance, *dăns,* s. danza, f.; baile, m.; —, v. n. bailar; **to — attendance,** servir con prontitud y atención.

dancer, *–ăr,* s. danzarín, bailarín, m.

dancing-master, *–dăns'ĭngmăstăr,* s. maestro de baile ó danza, m.

dandle, *dăn'dl,* v. a. mecer; halagar, acariciar.

dandruff, *dăn'drŭf,* s. caspa, f. [ciar.

dandy, *dăn'dĕ,* s. petimetre, currutaco, m.

danger, *dăn'jăr,* s. peligro, riesgo, m.

dangerous, *–ăs,* a. peligroso; *–ly,* ad. peligrosamente. [estar colgado en el aire.

dangle, *dăng'gl,* v. n. temblar, fluctuar;

dangler, *–ăr,* s. Juan de las damas, m.

dank, *dăngk,* a. húmedo.

dapper, *dăp'păr,* a. activo, vivaz, despierto.

dapple, *dăp'pl,* v. a. abigarrar; —, a. vareteado; rayado; **—grey horse,** s. caballo tordo, m.

dare, *dăr,* v. n. osar, atreverse, arriesgarse; —, v. a. desafiar, provocar.

daring, *dăr'ĭng,* s. osadía, f.; —, a. osado, temerario; emprendedor; *–ly,* ad. atrevidamente, osadamente.

dark, *dărk,* a. obscuro; opaco; ciego; ignorante; *–ly,* ad. obscuramente, secretamente; —, s. obscuridad, f., ignorancia, f.

darken, *–n,* v. a. (& n.) obscurecer(se).

dark-lantern, *–lăn'tărn,* s. linterna sorda, f. [blas, f. pl.

darkness, *–nĕs,* s. obscuridad, f.; tinieblas, f. pl.

darksome, *–sŭm,* a. obscuro, opaco, sombrío. [m.; —, a. querido, amado.

darling, *dăr'lĭng,* s. predilecto, favorito,

darn, *dărn,* v. a. zurcir.

darnel, *dăr'nĕl,* s. zizaña, f. [dora, f.

darner, *dăr'năr,* s. zurcidor, m.; zurcidart, *dărt,* s. dardo, m.; —, v. a. lanzar, tirar; —, v. n. volar como dardo.

dash, *dăsh,* v. a. arrojar, chocar, romper; salpicar; borrar; confundir; —, v. n. saltar, zambullirse en el agua de golpe; —, s. colisión, f.; choque, m., golpe, m.; **— of a pen,** rasgo de pluma, m.; **at one —,** de un golpe.

dash-board, *–bŏrd,* s. paralodo, m.

dashing, *–ĭng,* a. vistoso, brillante.

dastard, *dăs'tărd,* s. collón, m.

dastardly, *–lĕ,* a. cobarde, tímido.

date, *dāt,* s. data, fecha, f.; conclusión, f.; (bot.) dátil, m.; —, v. a. datar.

dative, *dā'tĭv,* s. dativo, m.; —, a. dado, dativo. [manchar, ensuciar.

daub, *dăb,* v. a. pintorrear; untar; pintar.

dauber, *–ăr,* s. pintor tosco, m.

daughter, *dă'tăr,* s. hija, f.; **—in-law,** nuera, f.

daunt, *dănt,* v. a. intimidar, espantar.

dauntless, *–lĕs,* a. intrépido, arrojado.

Dauphin, *dă'fĭn,* s. delfín, m. (de Francia).

davenport, *dăv'ĕnpŏrt,* s. papelera para daw, *dă,* s. corneja, f. [señoras, f.

dawdle, *dă'dl,* v. n. gastar tiempo.

dawdler, *–ăr,* s. bausán, bodoque, m.

dawn, *dăn,* s. alba, f.; albor, m.; —, v. n. amanecer.

day, *dă,* s. día, m.; luz, f.; **by —,** de día; **— by —,** de día en día; **—s,** pl. tiempo, m., vida, f. [nista, m.

day-boarder, *–bŏrdăr,* s. semipensionista, m.

day-book, *–bŭk,* s. diario, m.

day-break, *–brăk,* s. alba, f.

day-labourer, *–lăbărăr,* s. jornalero, m.

day-light, *–lĭt,* s. luz del día, luz natural, f.

day-scholar, *–skŏlăr,* s. externo, m.

day-spring, *–sprĭng,* s. alba, f.

day-star, *–stăr,* s. lucero del alba, m.

daytime, *–tĭm,* s. tiempo del día, m.

dazed, *dāz'd,* a. achacoso.

dazzle, *dăz'zl,* **daze,** *dăz,* v. a. deslumbrar, ofuscar.

deacon, *dē'kn,* s. diácono, m.

dead, dĕd, a. muerto; flojo, entorpecido; vacío, inútil, triste; apagado, sin espíritu; despoblado; evaporado; marchito; devuelto (hablando de cartas); **— bargain,** s. precio muy bajo, m.; **— water,** s. agua muerta, f.; **— wood,** s. leña seca, f.; **— silence,** s. silencio profundo, m.; **the,—,** pl. los finados.

dead-drunk, —drăngk, a. hecho un cuero.

deaden, —n, v. a. amortecer.

deadhead, —hĕd, s. cero, hombre que vale para nada, m.; (am.) plaza supuesta, f.

dead-heat, —hēt, s. corrida indecisa, f.

dead-house, —hŏus, s. sitio público en donde se exponen los cadáveres encontrados, m.

deadly, —lĕ, a. mortal; terrible, implacable; **—, ad.** mortalmente. [f.

dead-march, —mârtsh, marcha fúnebre.

deadness, —nĕs, s. flojedad, inercia, f.; amortiguamiento, m. [m.

dead-nettle, —nĕt'tl, s. cáñamo bastardo.

deaf, dĕf, a. sordo; estéril.

deafen, —n, v. a. ensordar; causar sordera. [ción á oír, f.

deafness, —nĕs, s. sordera, f.; desinclinación

deal, dĕl, s. parte, f.; cantidad, f.; madera de pino, f.; **a great —,** mucho; **a good —,** bastante; **—,** v. a. distribuir; dar; **—,** v. n. traficar, repartir; **to — with,** tratar con; contender con.

dealer, —ăr, s. mercader, traficante, m.; el que da las cartas en el juego de naipes.

dealing, —ĭng, s. conducta, f.; trato, m.; tráfico, comercio, m.

dean, dēn, s. deán, m.

deanery, —ărĕ, s. deanato, m.

dear, dēr, a. predilecto, amado; caro, costoso; **-ly,** ad. caramente, tiernamente.

dearness, —nĕs, s. cariño, amor, m.; carestía, f.

dearth, dărth, s. carestía, f.; esterilidad, f.

death, dĕth, s. muerte, f. [f.; agonía, f.

death-bed, —bĕd, s. cama del moribundo.

death-bell, —bĕl, s. toque de agonía, m.

death-blow, —blō, s. golpe mortal, m.

death-dealing, —dēl'ĭng, a. mortífero.

deathlike, —līk, a. quedo; letárgico.

death-penalty, —pĕnltĕ, s. pena de muerte.

death-throe, —thrō, s. agonía, f.

death-warrant, —wŏrrănt, s. sentencia de muerte, f.

death-watch, —wŏtsh, s. grillo, m.

debar, dēbâr', v. a. excluir, no admitir.

debarkation, dĕbărkā'shăn, s. desembarco, m.

debase, dēbās', v. a. humillar, envilecer; falsificar. [envilecimiento, m.

debasement, —mĕnt, s. abatimiento, m.

debatable, dēbāt'ăbl, a. disputable.

debate, dēbāt', s. debate, m.; riña, disputa, f.; **—,** v. a. discutir; examinar; **—,** v. n. deliberar; disputar.

debater, —ăr, s. controversista, m.

debauch, dēbŏtsh', s. vida disoluta, f.; exceso, m.; **—,** v. a. & n. corromper; hacer excesos. [disolución, f.

debauchery, —ărĕ, s. desarreglo, m.;

debenture, dēbĕn'tŭr, s. vale, m.; draucbăc, m.

debilitate, dēbĭl'ĭtăt, v. a. debilitar, enervar. [f.

debility, dēbĭl'ĭtĕ, s. debilidad, languidez.

debit, dĕb'ĭt, s. debe, m.; **—,** v. a. (com.) adeudar, cargar en una cuenta.

debouch, dēbŏsh', v. n. (mil.) desfilar; desembocar un río.

debt, dĕt, s. deuda, f.; débito, m.; obligación, f.; **to run into —s,** adeudar(se).

debtor, —tăr, s. deudor, m.

decade, dĕk'ād, s. década, f.

decadence, dĕkā'dĕns, s. decadencia, f.

Decalogue, dĕk'ălŏg, s. Decálogo, m.

decamp, dēkămp', v. n. (mil.) decampar, levantar el campo; escapar.

decampment, —mĕnt, s. (mil.) levantamiento de un campamento, m.

decant, dēkănt', v. a. decantar; trasegar.

decanter, —ăr, s. garrafa, f.

decapitate, dēkăp'ĭtăt, v. a. decapitar, degollar. [ción, f.

decapitation, dēkăpĭtā'shăn, s. decapita-

decay, dēkā', v. n. decaer, descaecer, declinar; degenerar; **—,** s. descaecimiento, m.; decadencia, declinación, diminución, f.

decease, dēsēs', s. muerte, f. [postura, f.

deceit, dēsēt', s. engaño, fraude, m.; impostura, f.

deceitful, —fŭl, a. fraudulento, engañoso; falaz; **-ly,** ad. fraudulentamente, falsamente.

deceive, dēsēv', v. a. engañar, defraudar.

December, dēsĕm'bĕr, s. diciembre, m.

decency, dē'sĕnsĕ, s. decencia, f.; modestia,

decennial, dēsĕn'nĭăl, a. decenal. [f.

decent, dē'sĕnt, a. decente, razonable; propio, conveniente; **-ly,** ad. decentemente.

deception, dēsĕp'shăn, s. decepción, impostura, f.; engaño, m.

deceptive, dēsĕp'tĭv, a. falso, engañoso.

decide, dēsīd', v. a. & n. decidir, determinar, resolver, juzgar.

decidedly, —ĕdlĕ, ad. determinadamente.

decidence, dĕs'ĭdĕns, s. (bot.) caída de las hojas, f.

decider, —ăr, s. árbitro, juez, m.

deciduous, dēsĭd'ūăs, a. perecedero; (bot.) decedente.

decimal, dĕs'ĭmăl, a. decimal.

decimate, dĕs'ĭmăt, v. a. diezmar.

decimation, dĕsĭmā'shăn, s. diezmo, m.

decipher, dēsī'fŭr, v. a. descifrar.

decision, dēsĭzh'ăn, s. decisión, determinación, resolución, f. [decisivamente

decisive, dēsī'sĭv, a. decisivo; **-ly,** ad.

deck, dĕk, s. (mar.) bordo, m.; cubierta, f.; **—,** v. a. adornar.

deck-hand, —hănd, s. marinero de río, m.

declaim, dēklām', v. n. declamar, perorar.

declamation, dĕklămā'shăn, s. declamación, arenga, f. [torio.

declamatory, dēklăm'ătŭrĕ, a. declama-

declaration, dĕklără'shăn, s. declaración, publicación, f.; explicación, f.

declare, dēklâr', v. a. declarar, manifestar.

declension, dēklĕn'shăn, s. declinación, f.; declivio, m.

declination, *dĕklĭnā'shŭn,* s. declinación, f.; decremento, m.

decline, *dĕklīn',* v. a. (gr.) declinar; huir, evitar; —, v. n. decaer, desmejorar; inclinarse; —, s. declinación, decadencia, f.; consunción, f.

declivity, *dĕklĭv'ĭtĭ,* s. declividad, f.; pendiente (de algún terreno), m. & f.

declivous, *dĕklī'vŭs,* a. en declive, pendiente.

decoction, *dĕkŏk'shŭn,* s. cocción, f.; (med.) cocimiento, m.

decompose, *dĕkŏmpōz',* v. a. descomponer.

decomposition, *dĕkŏmpŏzĭsh'ŭn,* s. descomposición, f.

decorate, *dĕk'ōrāt,* v. a. decorar, adornar.

decoration, *dĕkōrā'shŭn,* s. decoración, f.

decorative, *dĕk'ōrātĭv,* a. decorativo.

decorator, *dĕk'ōrātŭr,* s. adornista, m.; guarnecedor, m.; tapicero, m.; el sujeto en general de los negocios y dependencias de alguna casa; intendente de las decoraciones de un teatro, m.

decorous, *dĕk'ōrŭs,* a. decente, decoroso; —ly, ad. decorosamente.

decorum, *dĕkō'rŭm,* s. decoro, garbo, m.; decencia, f.; conveniencia, f.

decoy, *dĕkŏĭ',* v. a. atraer (algún pájaro) embaucar, engañar; —, s. seducción, f.; cazadero con señuelo, m.

decoy-bird, *-bŭrd,* s. pájaro de reclamo, m.

decrease, *dĕkrēs',* v. a. disminuir, minorar; —, s. decremento; descaecimiento, m.; diminución, f. [v. a. decretar; ordenar.

decree, *dĕkrē',* s. decreto, edicto, m.; —,

decrepit, *dĕkrep'ĭt,* a. decrépito. [m.

decrial, *dĕkrī'al,* s. gritería, f.; insulto,

decrier, *dĕkrī'ŭr,* s. difamador, m.

decry, *dĕkrī',* v. a. desacreditar, censurar públicamente, disfamar.

decuple, *dĕk'ŭpl,* v. a. multiplicar por diez; —, a. décuplo. [grar.

dedicate, *dĕd'ĭkāt,* v. a. dedicar; consagrar.

dedication, *dĕdĭkā'shŭn,* s. dedicación, f.; dedicatoria, f.

dedicatory, *dĕd'ĭkātŭrĭ,* a. dedicatorio.

deduce, *dĕdūs',* v. a. deducir; concluir, inferir.

deduct, *dĕdŭkt',* v. a. deducir, sustraer.

deduction, *dĕdŭk'shŭn,* s. deducción, consecuencia, f.; descuento, m.

deductively, *-tĭvlĕ,* ad. por ilación ó consecuencia.

deed, *dēd,* s. acción, f.; hecho, m.; hazaña, f.; instrumento auténtico, m.

deem, *dēm,* v. n. juzgar, pensar, estimar.

deep, *dēp,* a. profundo; sagaz; artificioso; grave; obscuro; taciturno; —, s. el piélago, la mar. [cer.

deepen, *-n,* v. a. profundizar; obscurecer.

deep-laid, *-lād,* a. profundo, infernal.

deeply, *-lĕ,* ad. profundamente; astutamente; tristemente; obscuramente.

deepness, *-nĕs,* s. profundidad, f.

deer, *dēr,* s. ciervo, venado, m.

deface, *dĕfās',* v. a. borrar, destruir; desfigurar, afear.

defacement, *-mĕnt,* s. desfiguración, f.

defalcate, *dĕfăl'kāt,* v. a. desfalcar, deducir.

defamation, *dĕfămā'shŭn,* s. difamación, calumnia, f. [difamatorio.

defamatory, *dĕfăm'ătŭrĕ,* a. calumnioso,

defame, *dĕfām',* v. a. disfamar; calumniar.

default, *dĕfawlt',* s. culpa, f.; delito, m.; defecto, m.; falta, f.; —, v. a. & n. faltar, ofender.

defaulter, *-ŭr,* s. (law) contumaz, m.

defeat, *dĕfēt',* s. derrota, f.; vencimiento, m.; —, v. a. derrotar; frustrar.

defect, *dĕfĕkt',* s. defecto, m.; falta, f.

defection, *dĕfĕk'shŭn,* s. defección, f.

defective, *-tĭv,* a. defectivo, imperfecto.

defence, *dĕfĕns',* s. defensa, f.; protección, f.; amparo, m. [tente.

defenceless, *-lĕs,* a. indefenso; impotente.

defend, *dĕfĕnd',* v. a. defender; proteger; prohibir. [mandado, m.

defendant, *-ănt,* s. defensor, m.; reo defensivo.

defensive, *-sĭv,* a. defensivo; —, a. de un modo defensivo; —, s. estado de defensa, m. [v. n. deferir.

defer, *dĕfŭr',* v. a. diferir, retardar; —,

deference, *dĕf'ŭrĕns,* s. deferencia, f.; respeto, m.; consideración, f.

deferential, *dĕfŭrĕn'shĭal,* a. respetoso.

defiance, *dĕfī'ăns,* s. desafío, cartel, m.

defiant, *-t,* a. desconfiado.

deficiency, *dĕfĭsh'ĕnsĕ,* s. defecto, m.; imperfección, f. falta, f.; insolvencia, f.

deficient, *dĕfĭsh'ĕnt,* a. deficiente.

deficit, *dĕf'ĭsĭt,* s. déficit, descubierto, m.

defile, *dĕfĭl',* s. desfiladero, m.; —, v. a. ensuciar. [minable.

definable, *dĕfī'năbl,* a. definible; determinable.

define, *dĕfīn',* v. a. definir; limitar, determinar; —,v. n. decidir, juzgar.

definite, *dĕf'ĭnĭt,* a. definido, exacto, preciso, limitado, cierto.

definition, *dĕfĭnĭsh'ŭn,* s. definición, f.

definitive, *dĕfĭn'ĭtĭv,* a. definitivo; —ly, ad. definitivamente.

deflect, *dĕflĕkt',* v. n. desviarse; ladearse.

deflection, *dĕflĕk'shŭn,* s. desvío, rodeo, m. [florar, estuprar.

deflower, deflower, *dĕflŏŭr',* v. a. desflorar, estuprar.

defoliation, *dĕfōlĭā'shŭn,* s. caída de las hojas, m. [figurar.

deform, *dĕfŏrm',* v. a. desformar, desfigurar.

deformity, *dĕfŏrm'ĭtĭ,* s. deformidad, f.

defraud, *dĕfrăd',* v. a. defraudar; frustrar.

defray, *dĕfrā',* v. a. costear.

deft, *dĕft,* a. despierto, despejado, diestro; —ly, ad. con ingenio y viveza.

defunct, *dĕfŭnkt',* a. difunto, muerto; —, s. difunto, m. [deñar, negar.

defy, *dĕfī',* v. a. desafiar; despreciar; desdeñar.

degeneracy, *dĕjĕn'ŭrăsĕ,* s. degeneración, bajeza, depravación, f.

degenerate, *dĕjĕn'ŭrāt,* v. n. degenerar; —, a. degenerado. [ción, f.

degeneration, *dĕjĕnŭrā'shŭn,* s. degeneración, f.

degradation, *dĕgrădā'shŭn,* s. degradación, f.; degeneración, f.

degrade, *dĕgrād',* v. a. degradar; deshonrar, envilecer.

degree, *dĕgrē'*, s. grado, m.; rango, m.; condición, f.; **by —s,** gradualmente.

deification, *dēĭfĭkā'shŭn*, s. apoteosis, f.

deify, *dē'ĭfĭ*, v. a. deificar; divinizar.

deign, *dān*, v. n. dignarse.

deism, *dē'ĭzm*, s. deísmo, m.

deist, *dē'ĭst*, s. deísta, m.

deity, *dē'ĭtĭ*, s. deidad, divinidad, f.

deject, *dĕjĕkt'*, v. a. abatir, desanimar.

dejection, *dĕjĕk'shŭn*, s. tristeza, aflicción, f.; (med.) cámara, f.

delay, *dĕlā'*, v. a. diferir; retardar; —, s. dilación, f.; retardo, m.

delectable, *dĕlĕk'tăbl*, a. deleitoso; **-bly,** ad. deleitosamente; con gusto.

delegate, *dĕl'ĕgāt*, v. a. delegar, diputar; —, s. delegado, diputado, m.

delegation, *dĕlĕgā'shŭn*, s. delegación, diputación, comisión, f.

delf(t), *dĕlf*, s. loza vidriada, f.

deliberate, *dĕlĭb'ŭrāt*, v.a. deliberar, considerar; —, a. cauto; avisado; **-ly,** ad. deliberadamente.

deliberateness, *-nĕs*, **deliberation,** *dĕlĭbŭrā'shŭn*, s. deliberación, circunspección, f., miramiento, m.

deliberative, *dĕlĭb'ŭrātĭv*, a. deliberativo.

delicacy, *dĕl'ĭkăsĭ*, s. delicadeza, f.; tenuidad, f.

delicate, *dĕl'ĭkăt*, a. delicado; exquisito; afeminado; **—,** ad. delicadamente; afeminadamente.

delicious, *dĕlĭsh'ŭs*, a. delicioso; exquisito; **-ly,** ad. deliciosamente. [m.

deliciousness, *-nĕs*, s. delicia, f.; gusto.

delight, *dĕlīt'*, s. delicia, f.; placer, gozo, encanto, m.; —, v. a. (& n.) deleitar(se).

delightful, *-fŭl*, a. delicioso; deleitable; **-ly,** ad. deliciosamente. [miento, m.

delimitation, *dĕlĭmĭtā'shŭn*, s. amojonamiento, m.

delineate, *dĕlĭn'ĕāt*, v. a. delinear, diseñar.

delineation, *dĕlĭnĕā'shŭn*, s. delineación, f.; delineamento, m. [culpa, f.

delinquency, *dĕlĭng'kwĕnsĭ*, s. delito, m.;

delinquent, *-kwĕnt*, s. delincuente, m.

delirious, *dĕlĭr'ĭŭs*, a. delirante, desvaríado.

delirium, *-rĭŭm*, s. delirio, m. [ríado.

deliver, *dĕlĭv'ŭr*, v. a. dar; rendir; libertar; recitar, relatar; partear.

deliverance, *-ăns*, s. libramiento, m.

delivery, *-ŭrĭ*, s. entrega, f.; libramiento, m.; parto, m.

dell, *dĕl*, s. valle hondo, m.; hondonada, f.

delude, *dĕlūd'*, v. a. engañar.

deluge, *dĕl'ūj*, s. inundación, f.; diluvio, m.; —, v. a. diluviar. [sión, f.

delusion, *dĕlū'zhŭn*, s. engaño, m.; ilusión, f.

delusive, *-sĭv*, a. engañoso, falaz.

delve, *dĕlv'*, s. foso, m.; hoyo, m.; mina, f.

demagogue, *dĕm'ăgŏg*, s. demagogo, m.

demand, *dĕmānd'*, s. demanda, f.; petición jurídica (de una deuda), f.; venta continuada, f.; —, v. a. demandar, reclamar.

demarcate, *dĕmārkāt'*, v. a. amojonar.

demarcation, *dĕmārkā'shŭn*, s. demarcación, f.; límite, m.

demean, *dĕmēn'*, v. n. portarse.

demeanour, *-ŭr*, s. porte, el modo de gobernarse ó portarse en la conducta.

demented, *dĕmĕn'tĕd*, a. demente, loco.

demerit, *dĕmĕr'ĭt*, v. a. desmerecer.

demesnes, *dĕmēns'*, s. pl. posesión 'de bienes raíces, f. [mento; —, s. muerte, f.

demise, *dĕmīz'*, v. a. legar, dejar en testa-

demisemiquaver, *dĕ'mĭsĕmĭkwāvŭr*, s. (mus.) semicorchea, f.

demission, *dĕmĭsh'ŭn*, s. aflojamiento, m.

democracy, *dĕmŏk'răsĕ*, s. democracia, f.

democrat, *dĕm'ŏkrăt*, s. demócrata, m.

democratio(al), *dĕmŏkrăt'ĭk(ăl)*, a. democrático. [nar; arrasar.

demolish, *dĕmŏl'ĭsh*, v. a. demoler, arrui-

demolition, *dĕmŏlĭsh'ŭn*, s. demolición, f.

demon, *dē'mŏn*, s. demonio, diablo, m.

demoniac, *dĕmō'nĭăk*, a. demoniaco; endemoniado; —, s. energúmeno, m.

demonstrable, *dĕmŏn'străbl*, a. demostrable; **-bly,** ad. demostrablemente, ostensiblemente.

demonstrate, *dĕmŏn'strāt*, v. a. demostrar, probar. [mostración, f.

demonstration, *dĕmŏnstrā'shŭn*, s. de-

demonstrative, *dĕmŏn'strātĭv*, a. demostrativo; **-ly,** ad. demostrativamente.

demoralization, *dĕmŏrălĭzā'shŭn*, s. desmoralización, f.

demoralize, *dĕmŏr'ălĭz*, v. a. desmoralizar.

demur, *dĕmŭr'*, v. n. objetar; suspender; vacilar, fluctuar; —, v. a. dudar; —, s. duda, f.

demure, *dĕmŭr'*, a. reservado; decente; grave, serio; **-ly,** ad. modestamente.

demureness, *-nĕs*, s. seriedad, gravedad de aspecto, f. [prorroga, f.

demurrer, *dĕmŭr'rŭr*, s. (law) demora,

den, *dĕn*, s. caverna, f.; antro, m.

deniable, *dĕnī'ăbl*, a. negable, recusable.

denial, *dĕnī'ăl*, s. denegación, repulsa, f.

denizen, *dĕn'ĭzn*, s. extranjero naturalizado, m.; —, v. a. naturalizar.

denominate, *dĕnŏm'ĭnāt*, v. a. denominar, nombrar.

denomination, *dĕnŏmĭnā'shŭn*, s. denominación, f.; título, nombre, apelativo, m. [nominador, m.

denominator, *dĕnŏm'ĭnātŭr*, s. (ar.) de-

denote, *dĕnōt'*, v. a. denotar, indicar.

denounce, *dĕnŏuns'*, v. a. denunciar; promulgar; declarar.

dense, *dĕns*, a. denso, espeso.

density, *dĕn'sĭtĕ*, s. densidad, solidez, f.

dent, *dĕnt*, s. muesca, f.; —, v. a. abollar.

dental, *-ăl*, a. dental; —, s. letra dental, f.

dentifrice, *dĕn'tĭfrĭs*, s. dentrífico, m.

dentist, *dĕn'tĭst*, s. dentista, m.

dentistry, *-rē*, s. arte del dentista, m.

denudation, *dĕnūdā'shŭn*, s. despojo de ropa, m.

denude, *dĕnūd'*, v. a. desnudar, despojar.

denunciate, *dĕnŭn'sĭăt*, v. a. denunciar, delatar. [ciación, f.; publicación, f.

denunciation, *dĕnŭnsĭā'shŭn*, s. denuncia-

deny, *dĕnī'*, v. a. negar, rehusar; renunciar; abjurar.

deodorize, *dē'ōdŭrĭz*, v. a. desinficionar.

depart, *dĕpārt'*, v. n. partir(se); morir; desistir. [trito, m.

department, *-mĕnt*, s. departamento, dis-

departure, -ár, s. partida, f.; abandono, m.

depend, depénd' v. n. depender, estar dependiente; - on ó upon, confiar.

dependant, -ánt, dependent, -ént, a. & s. dependiente (m.).

dependence(cy), -ens(sé), s. dependencia f.; confianza, f.; foreign -, colonia, f.

depict, depíkt', v. a. pintar, retratar; describir.

depilation, depilá shŭn, s. caída del pelo, f.

depletion, depli shŭn, s. (med.) deplección, f.

deplorable, depló rábl, a. deplorable, lamentable; -bly, ad. deplorablemente.

deplore, deplór', v. a. deplorar, lamentar.

deploy, deplóȳ', v. a. (mil.) desplegar.

deponent, depó nênt, s. (law) testigo, m.

depopulate, depóp úlát, v. a. despoblar; devastar. [ción, f.; devastación, f.

depopulation, depópúlá shŭn, s. despoblación, f.; despoblado.

deportation, depórtá shŭn, s. deportación, f.; destierro, m.

deport, depórt' mênt, s. conducta, f.; porte, manejo, m. [testificar.

depose, depóz', v. a. deponer; destronar.

deposit, depóz ít, v. a. depositar; -, s. depósito, m.

deposition, depózísh' ŭn, s. deposición, f.; testimonio, m.; destitución, f.

depository, depóz ĭtúré, s. depositaría, f.

deprave, deprāv', v. a. depravar, corromper.

depraved, deprāv'd, a. depravado.

depravity, deprāv íté, s. depravación, f.

deprecate, dep rékát, v. a. suplicar con instancia, deprecar.

deprecation, deprékā shŭn, s. súplica para conjurar los males, f.; [suplicante.

deprecatory, dep rékátúré, s. deprecativo.

depreciate, deprí shíát, v. a. rebajar el precio; despreciar, deprimir.

depreciation, deprēshíā shŭn, s. descrédito, m.; desestimación, f. [quear.

depredate, dep réddt, v. a. depredar, saquear.

depredation, deprédá shŭn, s. depredación, f.; pillaje, m.

depress, deprés', v. a. deprimir, humillar.

depressed, deprés'd, a. desgraciado.

depression, deprésh'ŭn, s. depresión, f.; abatimiento, m. [pérdida, f.

deprivation, deprivá shŭn, s. privación, f.

deprive, deprív', v. a. privar, despojar.

depth, depth, s. hondura, profundidad, f.; abismo, m.; (fig.) rigor, m.; obscuridad, f.

deputation, depútá shŭn, s. diputación, f.

depute, depút', v. a. diputar, delegar.

deputy, dep úté, s. diputado, delegado, m.

derange, derānj', v. a. desarreglar, desordenar. [orden, m.

derangement, -mênt, s. desarreglo, desorden, m.

derelict, der élikt, a. (mar.) abandonado en alta mar.

dereliction, derélik shŭn, s. desamparo, abandono, m.; (law) dejación de bienes, f.

deride, derīd', v. a. burlar, mofar.

derision, derízh ŭn, s. irrisión, mofa, f.; escarnio, m.; burla, chulada, f.

derisive, der ĭsīv, a. irrisorio. [cible.

derivable, der ĭvábl, a. derivable, deducible.

derivation, derívá shŭn, s. derivación, f.

derive, derív', v. a. (& n.) derivar(se); descender, proceder.

derogate, der ógát, v. n. derogar.

derogation, derógá shŭn, s. derogación, f.

derogatory, deróg ĭtúré, a. derogatorio.

derrick, der rĭk, s. máquina para levantar pesos, f.

dervish, der vĭsh, s. derviche, m.

descant, des kánt, v. n. discantar; discurrir; -, s. (mus.) discante, m.

descend, desénd', v. n. descender.

descendent, -ént, a. descendiente.

descent, desént', s. descenso, m.; pendiente, m.; invasión, f.; descendencia, posteridad, f.

describe, deskrīb', v. a. describir, delinear. [f.

description, deskríp shŭn, s. descripción, f.

descriptive, deskríp tĭv, a. descriptivo.

descry, deskrī', v. a. espiar; observar; describir.

desecrate, des ékrát, v. a. profanar.

desecration, desékrá shŭn, s. profanación, f. [-, a. desierto, solitario.

desert, dez ŭrt, s. desierto, m.; soledad, f.;

desert, dezŭrt', v. a. abandonar; desertar; -, s. mérito, m. [m.

deserter, dezŭr tŭr, s. desertor, tránsfuga, m.

desertion, dezŭr shŭn, s. deserción, f.

deserve, dezŭrv', v. a. merecer; ser digno.

deservedly, -ĕdlé, ad. merecidamente, dignamente.

deserving, dezŭr ving, a. meritorio.

deshabille, dézábél', s. paños menores, m. pl. [se desea, m.; lo que falta.

desideratum, desídárá tŭm, s. objeto que

design, dezīn', v. a. designar, proyectar; tramar; diseñar, -, s. designio, intento, m.; empresa, f.; diseño, m.

designate, des ĭgnát, v. a. apuntar, señalar; distinguir. [f.

designation, desĭgná shŭn, s. designación, f.

designatory, des ĭgnátúré, a. designativo.

designedly, dezī nédlé, ad. de propósito, de intento.

designing, dezīn ĭng, a. insidioso, astuto.

desirability, dezīrábíl ĭté, s. apetencia, ansia, f.

desirable, dezīr ábl, a. deseable.

desire, dezīr', s. deseo, m.; apetencia, f.; -, v. a. desear, apetecer.

desirous, dezī rŭs, a. deseoso, ansioso; -ly, ad. ansiosamente.

desist, dezíst', v. n. desistir.

desk, desk, s. escritorio, m.; papelera, f.; bufete, m.; atril (de coro), m.

desolate, des ólát, v. a. desolar; devastar; -, a. desolado; solitario.

desolation, desólá shŭn, s. desolación, ruina, destrucción, f. [v. n. desesperar.

despair, despár', s. desesperación, f.; -,

despairingly, -íngle, ad. desesperadamente. [despacho, m.; expreso, m.

despatch, despátsh', v. a. despachar; -, s.

despatch-boat, -bót, s. (mar.) aviso, m.

despatch-box, -bóks, s. escritorio portátil, m. [vido, m.

desperado, despér dó, s. hombre atre-

desperate, *dĕs'pŭrăt,* a. desesperado; furioso; **-ly,** ad. desesperadamente, furiosamente; sumamente;   [ción, f.
desperation, *dĕspŭrā'shŭn,* s. desesperación, f.
despicable, *dĕs'pĭkăbl,* a. despreciable, bajo; **-bly,** ad. despreciablemente.
despise, *dĕspīz',* v.a. despreciar; desdeñar.
despite, *dĕspīt',* s. despecho, m.; despique, m.; malicia, f.; **in — of,** á despecho de.
despoil, *dĕspŏĭl',* v. a. despojar; privar.
despond, *dĕspŏnd',* v. n. descomulgar, abatirse; desesperar.   [abatimiento, m.
despondency, *—ĕnsĕ,* s. desesperación, f.
despot, *dĕs'pŏt,* s. déspota, m.
despotic(al), *dĕspŏt'ĭk(ăl),* a. despótico, absoluto; **-ally,** ad. despóticamente.
despotism, *dĕs'pŏtĭzm,* s. despotismo, m.
dessert, *dĕzzŭrt',* s. postres, m. pl.   [f.
destination, *dĕstĭnā'shŭn,* s. destinación, f.
destine, *dĕs'tĭn,* v. a. destinar, señalar.
destiny, *dĕs'tĭnĕ,* s. destino, hado, m.; suerte, f.   [nado, privado.
destitute, *dĕs'tĭtūt,* a. destituído, abandonado.
destitution, *dĕstĭtū'shŭn,* s. destitución, privación, f.; abandono, m.
destroy, *dĕstrŏĭ',* v. a. destruir, arruinar.
destruction, *dĕstrŭk'shŭn,* s. destrucción, ruina f.
destructive, *dĕstrŭk'tĭv,* a. destructivo, ruinoso; **-ly,** ad. destructivamente.
desultoriness, *dĕs'ŭltŏrĭnĕs,* s. instabilidad, falta de método, f.
desultory, *dĕs'ŭltŭrĕ,* a. irregular, inconstante, sin método.
detach, *dĕtătsh',* y. a. (mil.) destacar.
detachment, *—mĕnt,* s. (mil.) destacamento, m.
detail, *dĕtāl',* s. detalle, m.; (am.) recluta, f.; **in —,** al por menor; **—,** v. a. detallar; referir por menor.   [pedir.
detain, *dĕtān',* v. a. retener, detener; impedir.
detect, *dĕtĕkt',* v. a. descubrir, revelar.
detector, *—ŭr,* s.descubridor, m.; delator, m.
detection, *dĕtĕk'shŭn,* s. descubrimiento, m.; revelación, f.   [secreta, m.
detective, *dĕtĕk'tĭv,* s. oficial de policía
detention, *dĕtĕn'shŭn,* s. detención, retención, f.; cautividad, f.; cautiverio, m.
deter, *dĕtŭr',* v. a. desanimar; disuadir.
deterge, *dĕtŭrj',* v. a. deterger, limpiar, bañar una llaga.
deteriorate, *dĕtē'rĕŏrāt,* v. a. deteriorar.
deterioration, *dĕtērĕŏrā'shŭn,* s. deterioración, f.   [nable.
determinable, *dĕtŭr'mĭnăbl,* a. determinable.
determinate, *dĕtŭr'mĭnăt,* a.determinado, decidido; **-ly,** ad. determinadamente.
determination, *dĕtŭrmĭnā'shŭn,* s. determinación, f.; decisión, f.
determine, *dĕtŭr'mĭn,* v. a. determinar, decidir; **—,** v. n. terminar, concluir.
detest, *dĕtĕst',* v. a. detestar, aborrecer.
detestable, *—ăbl,* a.detestable, abominable; **-bly,** ad. detestablemente.
detestation, *dĕtĕstā'shŭn,* s. detestación, f.; aborrecimiento, m.
dethrone, *dĕthrōn',* v. a. destronar.   [m.
dethronement, *—mĕnt,* s. destronamiento, m.
detonate, *dĕt'ŏnāt,* v. n. (chem.) detonar.

detonation, *dĕtŏnā'shŭn,* s. detonación, f.
detract, *dĕtrăkt',* v.a.detractar; disminuir.
detraction, *dĕtrăk'shŭn,* s. detracción, f.
detriment, *dĕt'rĭmĕnt,* s.detrimento, daño, perjuicio, m.
detrimental, *dĕtrĭmĕn'tăl,* a. perjudicial.
deuce, *dūs,* s. dos (en los juegos), m.; diantre, m.
devastate, *dĕv'ăstāt,* v. a. devastar; robar.
devastation, *dĕvăstā'shŭn,*s.devastación, f.   [arrollar.
develop, *dĕvĕl'ŏp,* v. a. desenvolver; desarrollar.
development, *dĕvĕl'ŏpmĕnt,* s. desarrollo, m.
deviate, *dē'vĭāt,* v. n. desviarse.   [llo, m.
deviation, *dēvĭā'shŭn,* s.desvío,m.; deviación, f.
device, *dĕvīs',* s. proyecto, expediente, m.; invención, f.; divisa, f.
devil, *dĕv'l,* s. diablo, demonio, m.
devilish, *—ĭsh,* a. diabólico; **-ly,** ad. diabólicamente.
devilkin, *—kĭn,* s. diablillo, m.
devilment, *—mĕnt,* s. diablería, f.
devilry, *—rĕ,* s. diablura, f.; maleficio, m.
devious, *dē'vĭŭs,* a. desviado; errante.
devise, *dĕvīz',* v. a. trazar; inventar; idear; legar; **—,** s. legado, m., donación testamentaria, f.
deviser, *—ŭr,* s. inventor, m.   [mentaria, f.
devisor, *dĕv'ĭsŭr,* s. testador, m.
devoid, *dĕvŏĭd',* a. vacío; privado.
devolve, *dĕvŏlv',* v. a. rodar abajo; trasmitir, transmitir, m.
devote, *dĕvōt',* v. a. dedicar; consagrar.
devotedness, *—ĕdnĕs,* s. devoción, f.
devotee, *dĕv'ŏtē,* s. santurrón, m.
devotion, *dĕvō'shŭn,* s. devoción, f.; oración, f.; rezo, m.; afición, f.
devotional, *—ăl,* a. devoto, religioso.
devour, *dĕvŏŭr',* v. a. devorar; echar á perder.
devout, *dĕvŏŭt',* a. devoto, piadoso; **-ly,** ad. devotamente.
dew, *dū,* s. rocío, m.; **—,** v. a. rociar.
dewlap, *—lăp,* s. papada del buey, f.
dew-worm, *—wŭrm,* s. lombriz, f.
dewy, *—ĕ,* a. rociado.
dexterity, *dĕkstĕr'ĭtĕ,* s. destreza, f.
dexterous, *dĕks'tŭrŭs,* a. diestro, hábil; **-ly,** ad. diestramente.
diabetes, *dīăbē'tĕz,* s. diabetes, m.
diabolic(al), *dīăbŏl'ĭk(ăl),* a. diabólico; **-ally,** ad. diabólicamente.
diadem, *dī'ădĕm,* s. diadema, m. & f.
diagnosis, *dīăgnō'sĭs,*s.(med.)diagnosis, f.
diagnostic, *dīăgnŏs'tĭk,* s. diagnóstico; **-s,** pl. diagnóstica, f.   [diagonalmente.
diagonal, *dīăg'ŏnăl,* s. diagonal; **-ly,** ad.
diagram, *dī'ăgrăm,* s. diagrama, m.
dial, *dī'ăl,* s. reloj de sol, m.; cuadrante, m.
dialect, *dī'ălĕkt,* s. dialecto, m.
dialogue, *dī'ălŏg,* s. diálogo, m.
diameter, *dīăm'ĕtŭr,* s. diámetro, m.
diametrical, *dīămĕt'rĭkăl,* a. diametral; **-ly,** ad. diametralmente.
diamond, *dī'ămŏnd,* s. diamante, m.; (at cards) oros, m.pl.; **— cut into angles,** diamante abrillantado, brillante, m.
diamond-cutter, *—kŭttŭr,* s. diamantista, m.

diamond-letter, –lĕttăr, s. corpus cuatro, m. [–, v. a. matizar; adamascar.
diaper, dī'ăpăr, s. lienzo adamascado, m.
diapason, dīăpā'zŏn, s.(mus.)diapasón, m.
diaphragm, dī'ăfrăm, s. diafragma, m.
diarrhœa, dīărrē'ă, s. diarrea, f.
diary, dī'ărĭ, s. diario, m.
dibble, dĭb'l, v. a. plantar con plantador.
dice, dīs, s. pl, dados, m. pl.
dice-box, –bŏks, s. cubilete de dados, m.
dickens, dĭk'nz, s. (vulg.) diablo, m.
dictate, dĭk'tăt, v.a.dictar; –, s. dictamen, m.; lección, f.
dictation, dĭktā'shŭn, s. dictado, m.
dictatorial, dĭktătō'rĭăl, a. autoritativo; magistral. [f.; dictatura,f.
dictatorship, dĭktā'tărshĭp, s. dictadura,
diction, dĭk'shŭn, s. dicción, f.; estilo, m.
dictionary, –ărĕ, s. diccionario, m.
didactic(al), dĭdăk'tĭk(ăl), a. didáctico.
diddle, dĭd'l, v. n. vacilar; anadear.
die, dī, v. n. morir, expirar; evaporarse; desvanecerse; marchitarse.
die, dī, s, dado, m.; cuño, m.; (fig.) suerte,f.
diet, dī'ĕt, s. dieta, f.; régimen, m.; asamblea, f.; –, v. a. alimentar; –, v. n. estar á dieta. [cinal, f.
dietary, –ărĕ, a. dietético; –, s. dieta medi-
differ, dĭf'făr, v. n. diferenciarse; contradecir. [f.
difference, –ĕns, s. diferencia, disparidad,
different, –ĕnt, a. diferente; desemejante; –ly, ad. diferentemente. [renciar.
differentiate, dĭffărĕn'shĭăt, v. a. dife-
difficult, dĭf'fĭkŭlt, a. difícil, áspero; –ly, ad. difícilmente. [m.; duda, f.
difficulty, –ĕ, s. dificultad, f.; obstáculo,
diffidence, dĭf'fĭdĕns, s. difidencia, f.
diffident, dĭf'fĭdĕnt, a. desconfiado; –ly, ad. desconfiadamente.
diffraction, dĭffrăk'shŭn, s. (opt.) difracción de los rayos luminosos, f.
diffuse, dĭffūs', v. a. difundir, esparcir; –, a. difundido,esparcido; prolijo; –ly,ad. copiosamente. [dad,f.; esparcimiento, m.
diffusion, dĭffū'zhŭn, s. difusión, proliji-
diffusive, dĭffū'sĭv, a. diffusivo; prolijo.
dig, dĭg, v. a. cavar, ahondar, azadonar; –, s. empujo, m.
digest, dĭjĕst', v. a. digerir, ordenar; rumiar; –, v. n. supurar; –, s. (law) digesto, m.; –of the case, resumen del pleito, m.
digestible, –ĭbl, a. digerible.
digestion, dĭjĕst'tŭn, s. digestión, f.
digestive, dĭjĕs'tĭv, a. medicamento digestivo.
digger, dĭg'găr, s. cavador, m. [tivo, m.
digit, dĭj'ĭt,s.dígito (medida longitudinal), m.
dignified, dĭg'nĭfīd, a. altivo. [m.
dignify, dĭg'nĭft, v. a. exaltar, elevar.
dignitary, dĭg'nĭtărĕ, s. dignitario, m.
dignity, dĭg'nĭtĕ, s. dignidad, f.; rango, m.; aire noble, m.
digress, dĭgrĕs', v. n. hacer digresión.
digression, dĭgrĕsh'ăn, s. digresión, f.; desvío, m. [lijo.
digressive, dĭgrĕs'ĭv, a. digresivo, pro-
dike, dīk, s. dique, canal, m.

dilapidated, dĭlăp'ĭdātĕd, a. malgastado.
dilapidation, dĭlăpĭdā'shăn, s. dilapidación, f.; ruina, f.
dilate, dīlāt', v. a. (& n.) dilatar(se), extender(se).
dilatory, dĭl'ătărĕ, a. tardo, dilatorio.
dilemma, dĭlĕm'mă, s. dilema, m.
diligence, dĭl'ĭjĕns, s. diligencia, f.; exactitud, f. [–ly, ad. diligentemente.
diligent, dĭl'ĭjĕnt, a. diligente, asiduo;
dilly-dally, dĭl'ĭdăl'lĕ, v. n. entretenerse con pataratas.
dilucid, dĭlū'sĭd, a. lúcido, claro.
diluent, dĭl'ĕnt, a. diluente.
dilution, dĭlū'shăn, s. dilución, f.
diluvial, dĭlū'vĭăl, a. diluviano.
dim, dĭm, a. turbio de vista, lerdo; obscuro; –, v. a. ofuscar, obscurecer; eclipsar.
dimension, dĭmĕn'shăn, s. dimensión, medida, extensión, f.
diminish, dĭmĭn'ĭsh, v. a. (& n.) decrecer, disminuir(se). [f.; descrédito, m.
diminution, dĭmĭnū'shăn, s. diminución,
diminutive, dĭmĭn'ŭtĭv, s. & a. diminutivo; –ly, ad. diminutivamente.
dimissory, dĭmĭs'sărĕ, a. dimisorio.
dimity, dĭm'ĭtĕ, s. fustán, bombasí, m.
dimly, dĭm'lĕ, ad. obscuramente.
dimness, dĭm'nĕs, s. ofuscamiento, m.; estupidez, f.
dimple, dĭm'pl, s.hoyuelo de la mejilla, m.
din, dĭn, s. ruido violento, alboroto, m.; –, v. a. atolondrar.
dine, dīn, v. a. dar de comer; –, v.n. comer.
diner-out, –ărŏŭt, s. el que toma la comida en el mesón, m.; mogollón, m.
dingy, dĭn'jĕ, a. moreno, obscuro.
dining-hall, dī'nĭnghăl, **dining-room**, –rŏm, s. comedor, m.; refectorio, m.
dinner, dĭn'năr, s. comida, f.
dinner-time, –tĭm, s. hora de comer, f.
dinner-waggon, –wăggŏn,s. (fam.) marmitón, m. [de.
dint, dĭnt, s. golpe, m.; by–of, en fuerza
diocese, dī'ŏsĕs, s. diócesis, diócesi, f.
diorama, dīŏrā'mă, s. diorama, m.
dip, dĭp, v. a. remojar, sumergir; repasar ligeramente; –, v.n. sumergirse; penetrar; –, s. (of the horizon) depresión, f.; (of the needle) inclinación, f.; plumada de tinta, f.; inmersión, f.
diphtheria, dĭf'rĭă, s. difteritis, f.
diphthong, dĭp'thŏng, s. diptongo, f.
diploma, dĭplō'mă, s. diploma, m.; letra real, f.
diplomacy, dĭplō'măsĕ, s. diplomática, f.
diplomatic, dĭplōmăt'ĭk, a. diplomático; –s, pl. diplomacia, f. [tico, m.
diplomat(ist), dĭplō'măt(ĭst), s. diploma-
dipsomania, dĭpsōmā'nĭă,s.dipsomanía,f.
dire, dīr, a. horrendo; cruel.
direct, dĭrĕkt', a. directo, derecho; claro; –, v. a. dirigir, enderezar; reglar, ordenar.
direction, dĭrĕk'shăn, s. dirección, f.; in strucción, f.; mandado, m.
directly, dĭrĕkt'lĕ, ad. directamente, inmediatamente.
director, dĭrĕk'tăr, s. director, m.
directory, –ĕ, s. directorio, m.

dirge, *dŭrj*, s. canción lúgubre, f.

dirigent, *dir'ĭjĕnt*, s. dirigente, director, m.

dirt, *dŭrt*, s. lodo, m.; porquería, f.; —, v. a. ensuciar, emporcar.

dirtily, *-ĭlĭ*, ad. puercamente; vilmente.

dirtiness, *-ĭnĕs*, s. suciedad, f.; bajeza, f.

dirty, *-ĭ*, a. puerco, sucio; vil, bajo.

disability, *dĭsăbĭl'ĭtĭ*, s. impotencia, f.; inhabilidad, incapacidad, f.

disable, *dĭsā'bl*, v. a. hacer incapaz; (mar.) desaparejar un navío.

disablement, *-mĕnt*, s. (law) impedimento legal, m.; (mar.) desaparejo de una nave de resultas de algún combate, m.

disabuse, *dĭsăbūz'*, v. a. desengañar.

disaccustom, *dĭsăkkŭs'tŭm*, v. a. desacostumbrar.   [desconocer.

disacknowledge, *dĭsăknŏl'ĕj*, v. a. negar.

disadvantage, *dĭsădvăn'tĕj*, s. desventaja, f.; daño, m.; —, v. a. dañar, perjudicar.

disadvantageous, *dĭsădvăntā'jŭs*, a. desventajoso; **-ly**, ad. desventajosamente.

disaffect, *dĭsăffĕkt'*, v. a. descontentar; indisponer.   [m.; desamor, m.

disaffection, *dĭsăffĕk'shŭn*, s. desafecto.

disagree, *dĭsăgrē'*, v. n. desconvenir, discordar.

disagreeable, *-ăbl*, a. desagradable, contrario; **-bly**, ad. desagradablemente.

disagreeableness, *-nĕs*, s. desavenencia, f.; contradicción, f.

disagreement, *-mĕnt*, s. diferencia, f.; discordia, f.   [n. negar, prohibir.

disallow, *dĭsăllŏ'*, v. a. desaprobar; —, v.

disappear, *dĭsăppēr'*, v. n. desaparecer; ausentarse.   [m.

disappearance, *-ăns*, s. desaparecimiento, f.

disappoint, *dĭsăppŏĭnt'*, v. a. frustrar, faltar á la palabra; engañar.

disappointment, *-mĕnt*, s. chasco, m.; contratiempo, m.

disapprobation, *dĭsăpprŏbā'shŭn*, **disapproval**, *dĭsăpprō'văl*, s. desaprobación, censura, f.

disapprove, *dĭsăpprōv'*, v. a. desaprobar.

disarm, *dĭsărm'*, v. a. desarmar, privar de armas.   [armamiento, m.

disarmament, *dĭsărm'ămĕnt*, s. desarray, *dĭsărrā'*, s. desarreglo, m.; —, v. a. desnudar; desarreglar.

disaster, *dĭzăs'tĕr*, s. desastre, m.; infortunio, m.

disastrous, *dĭzăs'trŭs*, a. desastroso, infeliz; calamitoso; **-ly**, ad. desastradamente.   [cer.

disavow, *dĭsăvŏ'*, v. a. negar; desconocer.

disavowal, *-ăl*, s. denegación, f.

disband, *dĭsbănd'*, v. a. descartar, despedir.   [confianza, f.

disbelief, *dĭsbĕlēf'*, s. incredulidad, desconfianza.

disbelieve, *dĭsbĕlēv'*, v. a. descreer, desconfiar.   [m.

disbeliever, *-ĕr*, s. descreído, incrédulo.

disburden, *dĭsbŭr'dn*, v. a. descargar.

disburse, *dĭsbŭrs'*, v. a. desembolsar, pagar.

disbursement, *-mĕnt*, s. desembolso, m.

disc, disk, *dĭsk*, s. disco, tejo, m.; (rail.) disco de señales.

discard, *dĭskărd'*, v. a. descartar, licenciar.

---

discern, *dĭzŭrn'*, v. a. discernir, percibir, distinguir.

discernible, *-ĭbl*, a. perceptible; sensible.

discerning, *-ĭng*, a. juicioso, perspicaz; **-ly**, ad. juiciosamente.

discharge, *dĭstshărj'*, v. a. descargar, pagar (una deuda); dispensar; ejecutar; cumplir: descartar; —, v. n. descargarse; despedir; cumplir con su obligación; —, s. descarga, f.; descargo, m.; finiquito, m.; dimisión, f.; absolución, f.

disciple, *dĭssī'pl*, s. discípulo, m.

disciplinarian, *dĭssĭplĭnā'rĭăn*, a. disciplinario; —, s. dómine, m.; presbiteriano, m.

discipline, *dĭs'sĭplĭn*, s. disciplina, f.; enseñanza, f.; ciencia, f.; rigor, m.; —, v. a. disciplinar, instruir.

disclaim, *dĭsklām'*, v. a. negar, renunciar.

disclaimer, *-ĕr*, s. denegación, f.

disclose, *dĭsklōz'*, v. n. descubrir; revelar.

disclosure, *dĭsklō'zhŭr*, s. descubrimiento, m.; revelación, f.

discoloration, *dĭskŭlărā'shăn*, s. descoloramiento, m.; tinte, m.

discolour, *dĭskŭl'ŭr*, v. a. descolorar.

discomfit, *dĭskŭm'fĭt*, v. a. derrotar, vencer, deshacer.   [miento, m.

discomfiture, *-ŭr*, s. derrota, f.; vencimiento, m.

discomfort, *dĭskŭm'fŭrt*, s. desconsuelo m.; aflicción, f.   [dar, molestar.

discommode, *dĭskŏmmōd'*, v. a. incomodar.

discompose, *dĭskŏmpōz'*, v. a. descomponer; desordenar; turbar.

discomposure, *dĭskŏmpō'zhŭr*, s. descomposición, f.; confusión, f.

disconcert, *dĭskŏnsŭrt'*, v. a. desconcertar, confundir, turbar.

disconnect, *dĭskŏnnĕkt'*, v. a. desunir.

disconnection, *dĭskŏnnĕk'shŭn*, s. desunión, f.

disconsolate, *dĭskŏn'sōlăt*, a. inconsolable; **-ly**, ad. desconsoladamente.

discontent, *dĭskŏntĕnt'*, s. descontento, m.; —, a. malcontento: —, v. a. descontentar.

discontinuation, *dĭskŏntĭnŭā'shŭn*, s. descontinuación, cesación, interrupción, f.

discontinue, *dĭskŏntĭn'ŭ*, v. n. descontinuar, interrumpir; cesar.

discord, *dĭs'kŏrd*, discordance, *dĭskŏr'dăns*, s. discordia, f.; discordancia, disensión, f.

discordant, *dĭskŏr'dănt*, a. discorde; incongruo; **-ly**, ad. con discordancia.

discount, *dĭs'kŏŭnt*, s. descuento, m.; rebaja, f.; —, *dĭskŏŭnt'*, v. a. descontar.

discountenance, *dĭskŏŭn'tĕnăns*, v. a. aturdir, inmutar; desaprobar.

discourage, *dĭskŭr'ĭj*, v. a. desalentar, desanimar.   [m.

discouragement, *-mĕnt*, s. desaliento, f.

discourse, *dĭskŏrs'*, s. discurso, m.; tratado, m.; —, v. n. conversar, discurrir, tratar (de).

discursive, *dĭskŏr'sĭv*, a. discursivo.

discourteous, *dĭskŭr'tyŭs*, a. descortés, grosero; **-ly**, ad. descortesmente.

discourtesy, *dĭskŭr'tĕsĭ*, s. descortesía, grosería, f.   [lar; manifestar.

discover, *dĭskŭv'ŭr*, v. a. descubrir; reve-

discoverable, _-ăbl,_ a. descubrible.
discovery, _-ĕ,_ s. descubrimiento, m.;
revelación, f.
discredit, _dĭskrĕd'ĭt,_ s. discrédito, deshonor, m.; —, v. a. desacreditar, deshonrar.
discreditable, _-ăbl,_ a. ignominioso.
discreet, _dĭskrēt',_ a. discreto; circunspecto;
-ly, ad. discretamente.
discrepancy, _dĭskrĕp'ănsĭ,_ s. discrepancia, diferencia, f.
discretion, _dĭskrĕsh'ŭn,_ s. discreción, f.
discretionary, _-ārĕ,_ a. ilimitado.
discriminate, _dĭskrĭm'ĭnāt,_ v. a. distinguir; señalar; **-ly,** ad. distintamente.
discrimination, _dĭskrĭmĭnā'shŭn,_ s. distinción, f.; distintivo, m.
discursive, _dĭskŭr'sĭv,_ a. inconstante;
discursivo; **-ly,** ad. de un modo argu
discuss, _dĭskŭs',_ v. a. discutir. [mentoso.
discussion, _dĭskŭsh'ŭn,_ s. discusión, f.
disdain, _dĭsdān',_ v.a. desdeñar, despreciar;
—, s. desdén, desprecio, m.
disdainful, _-fŭl,_ a. desdeñoso; **-ly,** ad.
desdeñosamente.
disease, _dĭzēz',_ s. mal, m.; enfermedad, f.
diseased, _-d',_ a. enfermo.
disembarcation, _dĭsĕmbārkā'shŭn,_ s.
(mil.) desembarco de tropas.
disembark, _dĭsĕmbārk'_ v. a. & n. desembarcar.
disembarrass, _dĭsĕmbăr'răs,_ **disencumber,** _dĭsĕnkŭm'bŭr,_ v. a. desembarazar. [lizado.
disembodied, _dĭsĕmbŏd'ĭd,_ a. inmateria
disembogue, _dĭsĕmbōg',_ v. n. desembocar.
disenchant, _dĭsĕnshănt',_ v. a. desencantar. [m.
disenchantment, _-mĕnt,_ s. desencanto,
disencumbrance, _dĭsĕnkŭm'brăns,_ s.
desembarazo, m.
disengage, _dĭsĕngāj',_ v. a. desenredar,
librar; —, v. n. libertarse de, desembarazarse. [dar, separar; desembarazar.
disentangle, _dĭsĕntăng'gl,_ v. a. desenre
disentanglement, _-mĕnt,_ s. desenredo, m.
disentomb, _dĭsĕntōm',_ v. a. exhumar.
disestablish, _dĭsĕstăb'lĭsh,_ v. a. expeler,
desalojar.
disfavour, _dĭsfā'vŭr,_ v. a. desfavorecer;
—, s. disfavor, disgusto, m.
disfiguration, _dĭsfĭgūrā'shŭn,_ **disfigurement,** _dĭsfĭg'ŭrmĕnt,_ s. deformidad, f.
disfigure, _dĭsfĭg'ŭr,_ v. a. desfigurar,
afear. [franquicias.
disfranchise, _dĭsfrăn'tshĭz,_ v. a. quitar
disgorge, _dĭsgŏrj',_ v. a. vomitar.
disgrace, _dĭsgrās',_ s. deshonra, f.; desgracia, f.; disfavor, m.; —, v. a. deshonrar; hacer caer en desgracia.
disgraceful, _-fŭl,_ a. deshonroso, ignominioso; **-ly,** ad. vergonzosamente.
disguise, _dĭsgīz',_ v. a. disfrazar, enmascarar; simular; —, s. disfraz, m.; máscara, f.
disgust, _dĭsgŭst',_ s. disgusto, m.; aversión,
f.; —, v. a. disgustar.
dish, _dĭsh,_ s. fuente, f., plato, m.; taza, f.;
—, v. a. poner la vianda en fuente; **to-
up,** servir la comida.
dish-clout, _-klŏt,_ s. rodilla, f.

dishearten, _dĭshār'tn,_ v. a. desalentar,
decorazonar.
dishevel, _dĭshĕv'l,_ v. a. desgreñar.
dishonest, _dĭsŏn'ĕst,_ a. deshonesto; ignominioso; **-ly,** ad. deshonestamente. [f.
dishonesty, _-ĕ,_ deshonestidad, impureza,
dishonour, _dĭsŏn'ŭr,_ s. deshonra, ignominia, f.; —, v. a. deshonrar, infamar.
dishonourable, _-ăbl,_ a. deshonroso,
afrentoso, indecoroso; **-bly,** ad. ignominisamente. [dor, m.
dish-warmer, _dĭsh'wărmŭr,_ s. escalfa
dish-water, _-wătŭr,_ s. lavazas, f. pl.
disillusion, _dĭsĭl'ūshŭn,_ s. desengaño, m.
disinclination, _dĭsĭnklĭnā'shŭn,_ s. desafecto, m., aversión, f.
disincline, _dĭsĭnklīn',_ v. a. desinclinar.
disinfect, _dĭsĭnfĕkt',_ v. a. desinficionar.
disingenuous, _dĭsĭnjĕn'ūŭs,_ a. falso,
disimulado.
disinherit, _dĭsĭnhĕr'ĭt,_ v. a. desheredar.
disinter, _dĭsĭntŭr',_ v. a. desenterrar.
disinterested, _dĭzĭn'tŭrĕstĕd,_ a. desinteresado; **-ly,** ad. desinteresadamente.
disinterestedness, _-nĕs,_ s. desinterés, m.
disinterment, _dĭsĭntŭr'mĕnt,_ s. desenterramiento, m.
disjoint, _dĭsjŏĭnt',_ v. a. dislocar, desmembrar; —, v. n. desmembrarse.
dislike, _dĭslīk',_ s. aversión, f.; disgusto,
m.; —, v. a. disgustar; desaprobar.
dislocate, _dĭs'lŏkāt,_ v. a. dislocar, descoyuntar. [f.; descoyuntamiento, m.
dislocation, _dĭslŏkā'shŭn,_ s. dislocación.
dislodge, _dĭslŏj',_ v. a. & n. desalojar.
disloyal, _dĭslŏĭ'ăl,_ a. desleal; infiel; **-ly,**
ad. deslealmente. [dad, perfidia, f.
disloyalty, _-tĕ,_ s. deslealtad, infideli
dismal, _dĭs'măl,_ a. triste, funesto; horrendo; **-s,** s. pl. hipocondría, f.
dismantle, _dĭsmăn'tl,_ v. a. (mil.) desmantelar (una plaza); (mar.) desaparejar.
dismast, _dĭsmăst',_ v. a. desarbolar (un
navío). [—, v. a. & n. desmayar(se).
dismay, _dĭsmā',_ s. desmayo, m.; terror, m.;
dismember, _dĭsmĕm'bŭr,_ v. a. desmembrar, despedazar. [descartar.
dismiss, _dĭsmĭs',_ v. a. despedir; echar;
dismissal, _-ăl,_ **dismission,** _dĭsmĭsh'ŭn,_
despedida, f.; dimisión, f.
dismount, _dĭsmŏunt',_ v. a. desmontar,
apearse del caballo; —, v. n. desmontar,
descender. [diencia, f.
disobedience, _dĭsŏbē'dĭĕns,_ s. desobe
disobedient, _dĭsŏbē'dĭĕnt,_ a. desobediente.
disobey, _dĭsŏbā',_ v. a. desobedecer.
disobliging, _dĭsŏblī'jĭng,_ a. desagradable.
disorder, _dĭsŏr'dŭr,_ s. desorden, m.; confusión, f.; indisposición, f.; —, v. a. desordenar, confundir, perturbar.
disorderly, _-lĕ,_ a. desarreglado, confuso;
ad. desordenadamente, ilegalmente.
disorganization, _dĭsŏrgănĭzā'shŭn,_ s.
desorganización, f. [zar.
disorganize, _dĭsŏr'gănĭz,_ v. a. desorgani
disown, _dĭsōn',_ v. a. negar, desconocer,
renunciar.
disparage, _dĭspăr'āj,_ v. a. envilecer,
mofar, desdorar.

disparagement, *—mĕnt,* s. desdoro, m.; casamiento desigual, m.; censura, f.; desprecio, m.; insulto, m.

disparity, *dĭspăr'ĭtĕ,* s. disparidad, f.

dispassionate, *dĭspăsh'ŭnăt,* a. sereno, desapasionado; templado.

dispel, *dĭspĕl',* y. a. expeler.

dispensary, *dĭspĕn'sărĕ,* s. dispensario, m.   [ción, f.; dispensa, f.

dispensation, *dĭspĕnsā'shŭn,* s. distribu-

dispensatory, *dĭspĕn'sătŭrĕ,* s. farmacopea, f.   [tribuir.

dispense, *dĭspĕns',* v. a. dispensar; dis-

disperse, *dĭspĕrs',* v. a. esparcir, disipar; distribuir.   [separación, f.

dispersion, *dĭspĕr'shŭn,* s. dispersión, f.

dispirit, *dĭspĭr'ĭt,* v. a. desalentar, desanimar.   [nar.

displace, *dĭsplās',* v. a. dislocar, desordenar.

displant, *dĭsplănt',* v. a. trasplantar.

display, *dĭsplā',* v. a. desplegar; explicar; exponer; ostentar; —, s. ostentación, f.; despliegue, m.   [gustar; ofender.

displease, *dĭsplēz',* v. a. desplacer, ofender.

displeasure, *dĭsplĕzh'ŭr,* s. desplacer, disgusto, m.; indignación, f.

disport, *dĭspōrt',* v. a. juguetear; —, v. n. divertirse.

disposal, *dĭspō'zăl,* s. disposición, f.

dispose, *dĭspōz',* v. a. disponer, dar; arreglar; —, v. n. vender; transferir.

disposed, *—d,* a. (& p.) dispuesto, inclinado, —of, vendido.

disposition, *dĭspŏzĭsh'ŭn,* s. disposición, f.; orden, m.; índole, f.; inclinación, f.

dispossess, *dĭspŏzĕs',* v. a. desposeer.

dispraise, *dĭsprāz',* v. a. vituperar.

disproportion, *dĭsprŏpŏr'shŭn,* s. desproporción, f.   [nado.

disproportionate, *—ăt,* a. desproporcionado.

disprove, *dĭsprōv',* v. a. confutar; desaprobar.   [testable.

disputable, *dĭspū'tăbl,* a. disputable, contestable.

disputant, *dĭs'pŭtănt,* s. disputador, m.

disputation, *dĭspŭtā'shŭn,* s. disputa, controversia, f.   [quisquilloso.

disputatious, *dĭspŭtā'shŭs,* a. disputador,

dispute, *dĭspūt',* s. disputa, controversia, f.; —, v. a. & n. disputar, controvertir, argüir.   [inhabilidad, f.

disqualification, *dĭskwŏlĭfĭkā'shŭn,* s.

disqualify, *dĭskwŏl'ĭfĭ,* v. n. hacer inhábil.

disquiet, *dĭskwī'ĕt,* s. inquietud, perturbación, f.; —, v. a. inquietar, turbar.

disquietude, *—ūd,* s. inquietud, f.

disquisition, *dĭskwĭzĭsh'ŭn,* s. disquisición, f.; examen, m.

disregard, *dĭsrēgărd',* v. a. desatender, desdeñar; —, s. desatención, f.; desdén, m.

disregardful, *—fŭl,* a. desatento, negligente; —ly, ad. desatentamente.

disrelish, *dĭsrĕl'ĭsh,* s. disgusto, tedio, hastío, m.; —, v. a. desaprobar; tener tedio.   [de la memoria.

disremember, *dĭsrĕmĕm'bĕr,* v. a. irse

disrepair, *dĭsrēpăr',* s. destrozo, m.

disreputable, *dĭsrĕp'ūtăbl,* a. deshonroso; —bly, ad. deshonrosamente.

disrespect, *dĭsrēspĕkt',* s. irreverencia, f.

disrespectful, *—fŭl,* a. irreverente, descortés; —ly, ad. irreverentemente.

disrobe, *dĭsrōb',* v. a. desnudar, despojar.

disruption, *dĭsrŭp'shŭn,* s. rompimiento, m.; fractura, f.   [contento, disgusto, m.

dissatisfaction, *dĭssătĭsfăk'shŭn,* s. des-

dissatisfy, *dĭssăt'ĭsfĭ,* v. a. descontentar, desagradar.

dissect, *dĭssĕkt',* v. a. disecar.

dissecting-room, *—ĭngrŏm,* s. sala de anatomía, f.

dissection, *dĭssĕk'shŭn,* s. disección, anatomía, f.; examen minucioso, m.

dissemble, *dĭssĕm'bl,* v. a. disimular; —, v. n. hacer el papel de hipócrita.

disseminate, *dĭssĕm'ĭnăt,* v. a. diseminar, sembrar, esparcir.   [cordia, f.

dissension, *dĭssĕn'shŭn,* s. disensión, dis-

dissent, *dĭssĕnt',* v. n. disentir, diferenciarse; —, s. disensión, contrariedad de opinión, f.   [formista, m.

dissenter, *dĭssĕn'tĕr,* s. disidente, m.; no con-

dissentient, *dĭssĕn'shĭĕnt,* a. discrepante.

dissertation, *dĭssĕrtā'shŭn,* s. disertación, f.   [separar.

dissever, *dĭssĕv'ĕr,* v. a. partir, dividir,

dissimilar, *dĭssĭm'ĭlăr,* a. desemejante, heterogéneo.   [neidad, f.

dissimilarity, *dĭssĭmĭlăr'ĭtĕ,* s. heteroge-

dissimulate, *dĭssĭm'ūlăt,* v. a. disimular.

dissimulation, *dĭssĭmūlā'shŭn,* s. disimulación.

dissipate, *dĭs'ĭpăt,* v. a. disipar.

dissipation, *dĭsĭpā'shŭn,* s. disipación, f.; dispersión, f.

dissociate, *dĭssō'shĭăt,* v. a. disociar.

dissoluble, *dĭs'sŏlŭbl,* a. disoluble.

dissolute, *dĭs'sŏlŭt,* a. disoluto, libertino.

dissolution, *dĭssŏlū'shŭn,* s. disolución, f.; muerte, f.   [disolverse, derretirse

dissolve, *dĭzzŏlv',* v. a. disolver; —, v. n.

dissolving scenes, *dĭzzŏl'vĭngsĕns,* **dissolving views,** *—văz,* s. pl. cromotropos, m. pl.   [desconcierto, f.

dissonance, *dĭs'sŏnăns,* s. disonancia, f.;

dissonant, *dĭs'sŏnănt,* a. disonante; discordante; diferente.

dissuade, *dĭsswād',* v. a. disuadir.

dissuasion, *dĭsswā'shŭn,* s. disuasión, f.

dissuasive, *dĭsswā'sĭv,* a. disuasivo.

dissyllable, *dĭssĭl'lăbl,* s. disílabo, m.

distaff, *dĭs'tăf,* s. rueca, f.

distance, *dĭs'tăns,* s. distancia, f.; respeto, m.; esquivez, f.; at a —, de lejos; out of —, fuera de vista; —, v. a. apartar; sobrepasar; espaciar.

distant, *dĭs'tănt,* a. distante; esquivo.

distaste, *dĭstāst',* s. hastío, disgusto, tedio, m.   [dable; chocante; maligno.

distasteful, *—fŭl,* a. desabrido, desagra-

distemper, *dĭstĕm'pĕr,* s. indisposición, enfermedad, f.; desasosiego, m.; desorden tumultuoso, m.; —, v. a. perturbar; causar una enfermedad.

distend, *dĭstĕnd',* v. a. extender, ensanchar.

distension, *dĭstĕn'shŭn,* s. dilatación, m.

distich, *dĭs'tĭk,* s. dístico, m.   [chura, f.

distil, *dĭstĭl',* v. a. & n. destilar; gotear.

distillation, *—lā'shŭn,* s. destilación, f.

distillery, -lărĕ, s. destilatorio, m.

distinct, distingkt', a. distinto, diferente, diverso; claro, formal; —ly, ad. distintamente. [diferencia, f.

distinction, distingk'shăn, s. distinción, distintivo, a. distintivo;

distinctive, distingk'tiv, a. distintivo; —ly, ad. distintamente, claramente.

distinctness, distingkt'něs, s. distinción, claridad, f. [guir; discernir.

distinguish, disting'gwish, v. a. distinguishable, —ăbl, a. distinguible, notable.

distort, distŏrt', v. a. retorcer; desviar.

distortion, distŏr'shăn, s. contorsión, f.; torcimiento, m.

distract, distrăkt', v. a. distraer; separar; perturbar. [ad. locamente.

distracted, —ĕd, a. loco, perturbado; —ly, **distraction,** distrăk'shăn, s. distracción, f.; confusión, f.; frenesí, m. [trar.

distrain, distrăn', v. a. embargar, secues-**distraint,** distrănt', s. (law) secuestro, m.

distress, distrěs', s. secuestro, m.; calamidad, miseria, f.; —, v. a. secuestrar; angustiar, congojar. [turbativo.

distressing, distrěs'sing, a. penoso, con-**distribute,** distrib'ut, v. a. distribuir, dividir, repartir. [f.

distribution, distribū'shăn, s. distribución, **district,** dis'trikt, s. distrito, m.; región, f.; jurisdicción, f.

distrust, distrŭst', v. a. desconfiar; —, s. desconfianza, sospecha, f.

distrustful, —fŭl, a. desconfiado; sospechoso; —ly, ad. desconfiadamente.

disturb, distŭrb', v. a. perturbar, estorbar.

disturbance, —ăns, s. disturbio, m.; confusión, f.; tumulto, m. [dia, f.

disunion, disū'niăn, s. desunión, discor-**disunite,** disūnīt', v. a. (& n.) desunir(se), separar(se).

disuse, disūs', s. desuso, m.; —, v. a. desusar, desacostumbrar, cesar.

ditch, dich, s. zanja, f.; foso, m.; —, v. a. abrir zanjas ó fosos.

ditty, dit'tĕ, s. canción, jácara, f.

diuretic, diŭrĕt'ik, a. (med.) diuretico.

diurnal, diŭr'năl, a. diurno, cotidiano; —, s. diario, jornal, m.

dive, div, v. n. sumergirse; bucear.

diver, —ăr, s. buzo, m.; colimbo, m. (ave); cortabolsas, m.

diverge, divŭrj', v. n. divergir(se).

divergence, —ăns, s. divergencia, f.

divergent, —ĕnt, a. divergente. [m. pl.

divers, di'vărz, a. varios, diversos, muchos, **diverse,** di'vŭrs, a. diverso, diferente; variado; —ly, ad. diversamente.

diversion, divŭr'shăn, s. diversión, f.; pasatiempo, m. [riegación, f.

diversity, divŭr'sitĕ, s. diversidad, f.; va-**divert,** divŭrt', v. a. desviar; divertir; recrear. [despojar.

divest, divĕst', v. a. desnudar; privar.

divestiture, divĕs'titūr, s. desarropamiento, m.

divide, divīd', v. a. dividir, distribuir; desunir; —, v. n. desunirse, dividirse.

dividend, div'idĕnd, s. dividendo, m.

divider, divīd'ăr, s. (ar.) divisor, m.; distribuidor, m.

divination, divină'shăn, s. divinación, f.

divine, divīn', a. divino, sublime, excelente; —, s. teólogo, m.; —, v. a. adivinar; —, v. n. presentir.

divinely, —lĕ, ad. divinamente.

diving-bell, div'ingbĕl, s. campana de buzo, f. [natoria, f.

diving-rod, div'ingrŏd, s. vara divi-**divinity,** divin'itĕ, s. divinidad, f.; deidad, f.; teología, f. [f.

divisibility, divizibil'itĕ, s. divisibilidad, **divisible,** diviz'ibl, a. divisible.

division, diviz'hăn, s. (ar.) división, f.; desunión, f.

divisor, divi'zŭr, s. (ar.) divisor, m.

divorce, divŏrs', s. divorcio, m.; —, v. a. divorciar.

divulge, divŭlj', v. a. divulgar, publicar.

dizziness, diz'zinĕs, s. vértigo, m.; ligereza, f.

dizzy, diz'zĕ, a. vertiginoso; ligero.

do, dŏ, v. a. hacer, ejecutar, obrar; finalizar; despachar; dejar algún empeño; cocer; —, v. n. comportarse; estar; —i ¡de gracia! [apacible.

docile, dŏs'ibl, **docile,** dŏs'il, a. dócil.

docility, dŏsil'itĕ, s. docilidad, f.

dock, dŏk, s. bardana, f.; lampazo, m.; trozo, m.; (rail.) dock, m.; (mar.) dique, m.; atarazana, f.; —, v. a. descolar; cortar. [—, v. a. rotular.

docket, —ĕt, s. rótulo, m.; extracto, m.;

dockyard, —yărd, s. (mar.) astillero, m.

doctor, dŏk'tăr, s. doctor, m.; médico, m.; —, v. a. medicinar.

doctoress, —ĕs, s. doctora, f. [mático.

doctrinal, dŏk'trinăl, a. doctrinal, dog-**doctrine,** dŏk'trin, s. doctrina, erudición, f.; ciencia, f. [precepto, m.

document, dŏk'ūmĕnt, s. documento, m.;

documentary, dŏkūmĕn'tărĕ, a. documental.

dodge, dŏj, v. a. trampear, entrampar.

dodger, —ăr, s. trampista, m.

doe, dŏ, s. gama, f.; —rabbit, coneja, f.

dog, dŏg, s. perro, m.; —, v. a. cazar con perros; espiar.

dog-cheap, —chēp, a. muy barato.

dog-days, —dăz, s. pl. días caniculares, m. pl. [m.

doge, dŏj, s. dux (de Venecia y Génova),

dog-fish, dŏg'fish, s. tiburón, m.

dogged, dŏg'gĕd, a. ceñudo, intratable, áspero, brutal; —ly, ad. con ceño.

doggedness, —nĕs, s. ceño, m.; mohina, bronquedad, f. [de versos).

doggerel, dŏg'grĕl, a. vil, bajo (hablando **dog-hole,** dŏg'hŏl, **dog-kennel,** —kĕnnĕl, s. perrera, f.

dog-latin, —lătin, s. latin bárbaro, m.

dogmatic(al), dŏgmăt'ik(ăl), a. dogmático; —ly, ad. dogmáticamente.

dog-rose, dŏg'rŏs, s. rosa silvestre, f.

dog's-ear, —s ēr, s. pliegue en los ángulos de la hoja de un libro, m.

Dog-star, —stăr, s. Sirio, m.; canícula, f.

doings, *dŏ´ings,* s. pl. hechos, m. pl.; acciones, f. pl.; eventos, m. pl.

doldrums, *dŏl´drắms,* s. pl. mal humor, m.; vientos bonancibles del Ecuador, m. pl. (mar.)

dole, *dŏl,* s. distribución, f.; porción, f.; limosna, f.; —, v. a. repartir, distribuir.

doleful, *–fŭl,* a. doloroso, lúgubre, triste.

doll, *dŏll,* s. muñeca, f.

dollar, *dŏl´lar,* s. escudo americano, m.; peso, m. (moneda de España).

dollman, *dŏl´mắn,* s. dolimán, m.

dolomite, *dŏl´ŏmīt,* s. dolomita, f. (min.)

dolour, *dŏ´lur,* s. dolor, pesar, m., dolencia, f.

dolphin, *dŏl´fĭn,* s. delfin, m. [cia, f.

dolt, *dŏlt,* s. hombre bobo, m.

domain, *dŏmān´,* s. dominio, m.

dome, *dŏm,* s. cúpula, f.

domestic, *dŏmĕs´tĭk,* a. doméstico, intestino.

domesticate, *–āt,* v. a. domesticar.

domestication, *dŏmĕstĭkā´shăn,* s. domesticación, f. [f.

domesticity, *dŏmĕs´tĭs´ĭtĭ,* s. domesticidad, f.

domicile, *dŏm´ĭsĭl,* s. domicilio, m.

domiciliary, *dŏmĭsĭl´tărŏ,* a. domiciliario; – visit, *vĭzĭt,* s. (law) visita judicial de la habitación de alguno como indagación, f.

dominate, *dŏm´ĭnāt,* v. n. dominar, predominar. [f.; imperio, m.

domination, *dŏmĭnā´shăn,* s. dominación, f.

domineer, *dŏmĭnēr´,* v. n. dominar, señorear.

dominie, *dŏm´ĭnē,* s. (vulg.) cura, m.

dominion, *dŏmĭn´yăn,* s. dominio, territorio, m.; soberanía, f.

domino, *dŏm´ĭnō,* s. dominó, m., traje de máscara; –es, pl. dominó (juego).

don, *dŏn,* v. a. meter el vestido.

donate, *dŏnāt´,* v. a. donar.

donation, *dŏnā´shăn,* s. donación, f.

done, *dŭn,* p. & a. hecho; cocido, asado.

donkey, *dŏng´kĕ,* s. asno, borrico, m.; –engine, *ĕnjĭn,* s. secunda máquina de los vapores, f.

donor, *dŏ´nur,* s. donador, m. [m.

doodle, *dŏ´dl,* s. (vulg.) haragán, holgazán.

doom, *dŏm,* s. sentencia, f.; condena, f.; suerte, f.; –, v. a. sentenciar, juzgar, condenar. [sal, m.

doomsday, *–sdā,* s. día del juicio universal.

door, *dŏr,* s. puerta, f.; within –s, en casa.

door-keeper, *–kēpŭr,* s. portero, m.

door-plate, *–plŭt,* s. planchuela, f.

door-way, *–wū,* s. portada, f.

dormant, *dŏr´mănt,* a. durmiente; secreto, m.

dormer-window, *dŏr´mŭrwĭndō,* s. lumbrera, f.

dormitory, *dŏr´mĭtŭrĕ,* s. dormitorio, m.

dormouse, *dŏr´mŏŭs,* s. lirón, m.

dorsal, *dŏr´sắl,* a. dorsal.

dose, *dŏs,* s. dosis, porción, f.; –, v. a. disponer la dosis de un remedio.

dot, *dŏt,* s. tilde, m.; –, v. a. tildar.

dotage, *dŏ´tŭj,* s. chochera, chochez, cariño excesivo, m.

dotard, *dŏ´tărd,* s. viejo que chochea, m.

dotation, *dŏtā´shăn,* s. dotación, f.

dote, *dŏt,* v. n. chochear.

dotingly, *dŏ´tĭnglĕ,* ad. con cariño excesivo.

double, *dŭb´l,* a. doble, duplicado; falso; –, v. a. doblar; plegar; disimular; –, s. duplo, m.; engaño, m.; artificio, m.

double-chin, *–tshĭn,* s. papada, f.

double-dealing, *–dēlĭng,* s. duplicidad, f.

double-edged, *–ĕjd,* a. con dos filas.

double-entry, *–ĕntrĕ,* s. (com.) partida doble, f.

double-faced, *–fāsd,* a. disimulado.

double-lock, *–lŏk,* v. a. echar segunda vuelta á la llave. [doblado.

double-quick, *–kwĭk,* a. (mil.) á paso redoblado.

doublet, *dŭb´lĕt,* s. justillo, m.

double-tongued, *–tắngd,* a. falso.

doubloon, *dŭblŏn´,* s. doblón, m.

doubly, *dŭb´lĕ,* ad. doblemente.

doubt, *dŏŭt,* s. duda, sospecha, f.; –, v. a. & n. dudar; sospechar.

doubtful, *–fŭl,* a. dudoso, dudable; incierto; –ly, ad. dudosamente. [sin duda.

doubtless, *–lĕs,* a. indubitable; –ly, ad.

dough, *dŏ,* s. masa, f.

doughty, *dŏŭ´tĕ,* a. bravo, valeroso.

douse, *dŏŭs,* v. a. (& n.) zabullir(se).

dove, *dŭv,* s. paloma, f. [palomar, m.

dove-cot, *–kŏt,* dove-house, *–hŏŭs,* s.

dovelike, *–lĭk,* a. columbino, inocente.

dove-tail, *–tāl,* s. cola de milano, f.

dowager, *dŏ´ăjŭr,* s. viuda de calidad que goza viudedad de su marido, f.

dowdy, *dŏŭ´dĕ,* s. mujer desaliñada, f.

dower, *dŏŭ´ŭr,* s. dote, viudedad, f.; dotación, f.

dowered, *–d,* a. dotado. [ción, f.

down, *dŏŭn,* s. plumón, m.; flojel, m.; –, pr. abajo; en el suelo; to sit –, sentarse; upside –, lo de arriba abajo; up and –, acá y acullá. [bajo.

downcast, *–kăst,* a. apesadumbrado, cabizbajo.

downfall, *–fŭl,* s. ruina, decadencia, f.

down-hill, *–hĭll,* s. declivio, m.

downright, *–rĭt,* a. patente, manifiesto; –, ad. á plomo.

down-train, *–trăn,* s. (rail.) tren descendente, m., el que desde la capital marcha en dirección de otro punto lejano.

downward, *–wŭrd,* a. inclinado; cabizbajo, triste; –(s), ad. hacia abajo.

downy, *–ĕ,* a. velloso; suave. [dormitar.

doze, *dŏz,* s. atontar, entorpecer; –, v. n.

dozen, *dŭz´n,* s. docena, f.

doziness, *dŏ´zĭnĕs,* s. somnolencia, f.

dozy, *dŏ´zĕ,* a. soñoliente.

drab, *drăb,* s. paño castaño, m.; mujercilla, f.; –, a. de color entre gris y moreno.

drachm, *drắm,* s. dracma, f.

draft, *drăft,* s. dibujo, m.; letra de cambio, f.; –, v. a. dibujar; (mil.) destacar.

drag, *drắg,* v. a. arrastrar; tirar con fuerza; –, v. n. arrastrar por el suelo; –, s. carretilla, f.; instrumento con garfio ó gancho, m.

draggle, *–gl,* v. a. emporcar alguna cosa arrastrándola por el suelo; –, v. n. ensuciarse alguna cosa por llevarla arrastrando.

drag-net, *–nĕt,* s. red barredera, f.

dragoman, *drắ´gŏmăn,* s. dragomán, m.

dragon, _drăg'ŏn_, s. dragón, m.
dragon-fly, _-flī_, s. libélula, f.
dragoon, _drăgŏn'_, s. (mil.) dragón, m.
drain, _drān_, v. a. desaguar; secar; —, s. desaguadero, m.; (mar.) colador, m.
drainage, _-dj_, s. desagüe, m.; derramamiento, m.
drake, _drāk_, s. ánade macho, m.
dram, _drăm_, s. dracma, f.; porción de licor que se bebe de una vez, f.; —, v. n. beber aguardiente.
drama, _drā'mă_, s. drama, m.
dramatic(al), _drămăt'ĭc(ăl)_, a. dramático; -ally, ad. dramáticamente.
dramatist, _drăm'ătĭst_, s. dramático, m.
dramatize, _drăm'ătīz_, v. a. dramatizar.
drape, _drāp_, v. a. trapear.
draper, _-ăr_, s. pañero, m.
drapery, _-ĕ_, s. manufactura de paños, f.; ropaje, m.
drastic, _drăs'tĭk_, a. (med.) drástico.
draught, _drăft_, s. trago, m.; porción de cualquier licor que se bebe de una vez, f.; bebida medicinal, f.; dibujo, m.; letra de cambio, f.
draught-board, _-bōrd_, s. tablero, m.
draught-horse, _-hŏrs_, s. caballo de tiro, m. [m.
draughts, _-s_, s. pl. juego de las damas,
draughty, _drăf'tĕ_, a. expuesto al aire colado.
draw, _drā_, v. a. tirar, traer; atraer; arrastrar; dibujar; librar una letra de cambio; **to — nigh**, acercarse; —, v. n. tirar; encogerse; moverse.
drawback, _-băk_, s. draubac, m., restitución de los derechos al tiempo de exportar los géneros. [m.
draw-bridge, _-brĕj_, s. puente levadizo,
drawer, _-ăr_, s. aguador, m.; mozo de taberna, m.; gaveta, f.; -s, pl. calzoncillos,
drawing, _-ĭng_, s. dibujo, m. [m. pl.
drawing-board, _-ĭngbōrd_, s. tabla para dibujar, f.
drawing-room, _-ĭngrŏm_, s. sala de palacio, f.; sala principal de alguna casa, f.; recepción en la corte, f.
drawl, _drāl_, v. n. hablar con pesadez.
draw-well, _-wĕl_, s. pozo hondo, m.
dray-(cart), _drā'(kărt)_, s. carromato, m.
dray-man, _-măn_, s. carromatero, m.
dread, _drĕd_, s. miedo, terror, espanto, m.; -, terrible; —, v. a. & n. espantar; temer.
dreadful, _-fŭl_, a. terrible, espantoso; -ly, ad. terriblemente.
dream, _drēm_, s. sueño, m.; fantasía, f.; -, v. n. soñar; imaginar. [m.
dreaminess, _drē'mĭnĕs_, s. sopor, letargo,
dreamy, _-ĕ_, a. quimérico, fabuloso.
drearily, _drē'rĭlĕ_, ad. espantosamente, tristemente.
dreary, _drē'rĕ_, a. espantoso, triste.
dredge, _drĕj_, v. a. (mar.) rastrear con el rezón.
dredger, _-ăr_, s. pescador de ostras, m.
dredging-machine, _drĕj'ĭngmăshēn_, s. máquina para limpiar un río, estanque &c., f.
dregs, _drĕgz_, s. pl. hez, f.; morralla, f.

drench, _drĕnsh_, v. a. empapar, humedecer; abrevar; —, s. bebida purgante (para ciertos animales), f.
dress, _drĕs_, v. a. vestir, ataviar; curar las heridas; almohazar; ajustar; cocinar; podar las vides; —, v. n. vestirse; —, s. vestido, m.; atavío, tocado, m.
dresser, _-sŭr_, s. mozo de cámara, m.; mesa de cocina, f.; aparador, m.
dressing, _-sĭng_, s. curación, f.; adorno, m.; cultivo de tierra labrantía, m.
dressing-gown, _-sĭnggŏŭn_, s. peinador, m.; bata, f. [tocador, m.
dressing-room, _-sĭngrŏm_, s. gabinete-
dressing-table, _-sĭngtābl_, s. tocador, m.
dressy, _-sĕ_, a. aficionado á ataviarse.
dribble, _drĭb'bl_, v. a. hacer caer gota á gota; —, v. n. gotear.
dribblet, _drĭb'lĕt_, s. deuda pequeña, f.
drift, _drĭft_, s. impulso, m.; tempestad, f.; montón, m.; objeto de discurso, m.; designio, m.; manejo, m.; (mar.) deriva, f.; **— of ice**, hielo flotante, m.; **— of sand**, arena movediza, f.; **— of snow**, nevada con ventisca, f.; —, v. n. impeler; amontonar; —, v. n. formar en montones.
drift-wood, _-wŭd_, s. leña acarreada por el agua, f.
drill, _drĭl_, s. taladro, m.; terraja, f.; (mil.) instrucción de reclutas, f.; —, v. a. taladrar; (mil.) disciplinar reclutas.
drink, _drĭngk_, v. a. & n. beber, embeber, absorber; embriagarse; —, s. bebida, f.
drinkable, _-ăbl_, a. potable.
drinking-bout, _-ĭngbŏŭt_, s. borrachera, f.
drip, _drĭp_, v. a. despedir algún líquido á gotas; —, v. n. gotear, destilar; —, s. gotilla, f.
dripping, _-pĭng_, s. pringue, m. & f.
dripping-pan, _-pĭngpăn_, s. grasera, f.
drive, _drĭv_, v. a. & n. impeler; guiar, conducir (algún carruaje); llevar, forzar á; reducir á; andar en coche; **to — at**, tener puesta la mira en; —, s. paseo en coche, m.
drivel, _drĭv'l_, s. baba, f.; —, v. n. babear.
driver, _drĭ'vĕr_, s. empujador, m.; cochero, m.; carretero, m.; boyero &c., m.; (am.) inspector de esclavos, m.
drizzle, _drĭz'l_, v. n. gotear; lloviznar. [f.
drizzling-rain, _drĭz'lĭngrān_, s. llovizna,
droll, _drŏl_, a. jocoso, facecioso; gracioso; -, s. bufón, m.; -ly, ad. jocosamente.
drollery, _-ŭrĕ_, s. bufonería, bufonada, fursa, f.
dromedary, _drŏm'ĕdārĕ_, s. dromedario, m.; (cant) ladrón desmañado, m.
drone, _drŏn_, s. zángano de colmena, m.; haragán, m.; —, v. n. holgazanear; dar un sonido sordo. [zumirse; desfallecer.
droop, _drŏp_, v. n. descaecer; penar, con-
drooping, _-ĭng_, a. lánguido.
drop, _drŏp_, s. gota, f.; pendiente con diamantes pequeños, m.; **by -s**, gota á gota; —, v. a. destilar; soltar; cesar; dejar; —, v. n. gotear; morir de repente; desvanecerse; sobrevenir.
drops, _drŏps_, s. (mil.) plano inclinado, m.
drop-scene, _drŏp'sĕn_, s. telón de foro, m.
dropsical, _-sĭkăl_, a. hidrópico.

dropsy, _–sĕ_, s. hidropesía, f.

dross, _drŏs_, s. escoria de metales, f.; hez, f.

drought, _drŏŭt_, s. seca, f.; sequedad, f.; sed, f.

drove, _drŏv_, s. manada, f.; hato, m.; muchedumbre de gente, f.

drover, _–ŭr_, s. ganadero, m.

drown, _drŏŭn_, v. a. anegar; sumergir; —, v. n. anegarse. [lentamente.

drowsily, _drŏŭ'zĭlĭ_, ad. soñolientamente.

drowsiness, _drŏŭ'zĭnĕs_, s. somnolencia, pereza, indolencia, f.

drowsy, _drŏŭ'zĕ_, a. soñoliento; estúpido.

drub, _drŭb_, s. golpe, m., puñada, f.; —, v. a. apalear, sacudir.

drudge, _drŭj_, v. n. afanarse; —, s. ganapán, m.; yunque, esclavo, m.

drudgery, _–ĕrĕ_, s. trabajo vil, m.

drudgingly, _–ĭnglĕ_, ad. trabajosamente.

drug, _drŭg_, s. droga, f.; frusleria, f.; —, v. a. sazonar ó mezclar con drogas.

drugget, _–gĕt_, s. droguete, m.

druggist, _–gĭst_, s. droguero, m.

drum, _drŭm_, s. tambor, m.; tímpano (del oido), m.; —, v. n. tocar el tambor; (am.) atraer parroquianos. [m.

drum-head, _–hĕd_, s. parche del tambor.

drum-major, _–mȧjŭr_, s. tambor mayor, m.

drummer, _–mĕr_, s. tambor, m.; (am.) el que atrae parroquianos.

drumming, _–mĭng_, s. toque del tambor, m.

drum-stick, _–stĭk_, s. palillo de tambor, m.

drunk, _drŭngk_, a. borracho, ebrio, embriagado. [el que bebe mucho.

drunkard, _–ŭrd_, s. borrachón, cuero, m.; borracho, a. ebrio.

drunken, _–n_, a. ebrio. [borrachera, f.

drunkenness, _–n'nĕs_, s. embriaguez, f.;

dry, _drĭ_, a. árido, seco; sediento; frío; insípido; —, v. a. secar; enjugar; —, v. n. secarse, enjuagarse.

dry-goods, _–gŭds_, s. pl. géneros que se venden al ana ó al corte, m. pl. [m.

drying-lines, _–ĭnglĭnz_, s. pl. tendedero.

dryly, _–lĕ_, ad. secamente, friamente; estérilmente. [estilo, f.

dryness, _–nĕs_, s. sequedad, f.; aridez de

dry-nurse, _–nŭrs_, s. ama que alimenta á un niño sin darle de mamar, f.; —, v. a. criar á un niño sin darle de mamar.

dry-rot, _–rŏt_, s. podre, m. & f., podredumbre, f. [pies secos.

dry-shod, _–shŏd_, a. á pie enjuto, con los

dual, _dŭ'ăl_, a. binario, m.

dub, _dŭb_, v. a. armar á alguno caballero.

dubious, _dŭ'bĭăs_, a. dudoso; –ly, ad. dudosamente.

ducal, _dŭ'kăl_, a. ducal. [dosamente.

ducat, _dŭk'ăt_, s. ducado, m.

duchess, _dŭtsh'ĕs_, s. duquesa, f.

duchy, _dŭtsh'ĕ_, s. ducado, m.

duck, _dŭk_, s. ánade, m. & f.; tela para velas, f.; mona, querida, f. (voz de cariño); —, v. a. (& n.) zabullir(se).

duckling, _–lĭng_, s. anadeja, f.

duckweed, _–wĕd_, s. lenteja acuática, f.

ductile, _dŭk'tĭl_, a. dúctil, flexible; tratable.

ductility, _dŭktĭl'ĭtĕ_, s. ductilidad, f.; docilidad, f.

dudgeon, _dŭj'ŭn_, s. ojeriza, malicia, f.

duds, _dŭdz_, s. pl. atavío m.

due, _dŭ_, a. debido, apto; —, ad. exactamente; —, s. derecho, m.; tributo, impuesto, m. [en duelo

duel, _dŭ'ĕl_, s. duelo, m.; —, v. n. combatir

duellist, _–lĭst_, s. duelista, m.

duet, _dŭ'ĕt_, s. (mus.) dúo, m.

duffer, _dŭf'fŭr_, s. (vulg.) ropavejero, m.;

dug, _dŭg_, s. teta, f. [embustero, m.

dug-out, _–ŏŭt_, s. (am.) piragua, f.

duke, _dŭk_, s. duque, m.

dukedom, _–dŏm_, s. ducado, m.

dulcimer, _dŭl'sĭmĕr_, s. (mus.) tímpano, m.

dull, _dŭl_, a. lerdo, estúpido; insípido; obtuso; tosco; triste, murrio; opaco; — of hearing, algo sordo; —, v. a. entontecer; obstruir; contristar; ofuscar; –y, ad. estúpidamente; lentamente.

dullard, _–lărd_, s. estólido, m.

dulness, _–nĕs_, s. estupidez, torpeza, f.; somnolencia, f.; pereza, f.; pesadez, f.

duly, _dŭ'lĕ_, ad. debidamente; puntualmente.

dumb, _dŭm_, a. mudo, m.; –ly, ad. sin chistar.

dumb-bell, _–bĕl_, s. halterio, m.

dumbfound, _–fŏŭnd_, v. a. confundir; enmudecer.

dumbness, _–nĕs_, s. mudez, f.; silencio, m.

dumb-show, _–tshŏ_, s. pantomimo, m.

dumb-waiter, _–wātŭr_, s. mesita giratoria, mesa de servicio, f.

dummy, _dŭm'mĕ_, s. (vulg.) mudo, m.; espantajo, m.; maniquí, m.

dump, _dŭmp_, s. murria, tristeza, f.

dumpling, _–lĭng_, s. bola de pasta, f.

dumpy, _–ĕ_, a. gordo, rollizo.

dun, _dŭn_, a. bruno; sombrío; —, s. acreedor importuno, m.; —, v. a. pedir un acreedor á su deudor con importunidad.

dunce, _dŭns_, s. zote, zopenco, m.

dune, _dŭn_, s. mégano, m., duna, f.

dung, _dŭng_, s. estiércol, m.; —, v. a. estercolar.

dungeon, _dŭn'jŭn_, s. calabozo, m.

dung-hill, _dŭng'hĭl_, s. estercolero, m.

duodecimo, _dŭŏdĕs'ĭmŏ_, s. libro en dozavo, m. [embaucar.

dupe, _dŭp_, s. bobo, m.; —, v. a. engañar.

duplicate, _dŭ'plĭkăt_, s. duplicado, m.; copia, f.; —check, _tshĕk_, s. (rail.) talón, m.

duplicity, _dŭplĭs'ĭtĕ_, s. doblez, duplicidad, f. [f.

durability, _dŭrăbĭl'ĭtĕ_, s. dura, duración, f.

durable, _dŭ'răbl_, a. durable, duradero; –bly, ad. duraderamente.

durance, _dŭ'răns_, s. cautividad, f.

duration, _dŭrā'shŭn_, s. duración, f.

during, _dŭ'rĭng_, pr. mientras, durante el tiempo que.

dusk, _dŭsk_, a. obscurecido, fusco; —, s. color fusco, m.; crepúsculo, m.; —, v. a. obscurecer; —, v. n. hacerse noche.

duskily, _dŭsk'ĭlĕ_, ad. obscuramente.

duskiness, _–ĭnĕs_, s. principio de la obscuridad, m.

dusky, _dŭsk'ĕ_, a. obscuro. [curidad, m.

dust, _dŭst_, s. polvo, m.; —, v. a. despolvorear; llenar de polvo.

dust-cart, _–kărt_, s. carro de basura, m.

duster, _–ŭr_, s. rodilla, f.

dustman, _–măn_, s. basurero, m.

dust-shot, *-shŏt,* s. cendra, escoria de
dusty, *-ĭ,* a. polvoriento. [plomo, f.
dutch courage, *dătsh kŭr'ĕj,* s. valor
fingido, s.
duteous, *dū'tĭăs,* a. fiel, leal.
dutiful, *dū'tĭfŭl,* a. obediente, sumiso;
respetoso; **-ly,** ad. obedientemente, respe-
tosamente. [peto, m.
dutifulness, *-nĕs,* s. obediencia, f.; res-
duty, *dū'tĭ,* s. deber, m.; obligación, f.;
respeto, homenaje, m.; (mil.) facción, f.;
aduana, f., derechos de aduanas, m. pl.
dwarf, *dwărf,* s. enano, m.; enana, f.; **—,**
v. a. impedir que alguna cosa llegue á su
tamaño natural.
dwarfish, *-ĭsh,* a. enano, pequeño.
dwell, *dwĕl,* v. n. habitar, morar; dilatarse.
dwelling, *-ĭng,* s. habitación, f.; domicilio,
m. [nuirse; degenerar; consumirse.
dwindle, *dwĭn'dl,* v. n. mermar, dismi-
dye, *dī,* v. a. teñir; **—,** s. tinte, m.
dyer, *-ăr,* s. tintorero, m.
dy(e)ing, *-ĭng,* s. tintorería, f.; tintura, f.
dye-works, *-wărks,* s. pl. taller del tintorero, m. [bundo; **—,** s. muerte, f.
dying, *-ĭng,* p. y a. agonizante, mori-
dynamics, *dĭnăm'ĭks,* s. dinámica, f.
dynamite, *dĭn'ămĭt,* s. dinamita, f.
dynamiter, *-tăr,* s. dinamitista, f.
dynamo, *dĭnăm'ō,* s. dinamo, m., máquina
generatriz de las corrientes eléctricas, f.
dynasty, *dĭn'ăstĭ,* s. dinastía, f.
dysentery, *dĭs'ĕntărĭ,* s. disentería, f.
dyspepsia, *dĭspĕp'sĭă,* s. (med.) dispepsia,
dyspeptic, *dĭspĕp'tĭk,* a. dispéptico. [f.

E.

each, *ĕtsh,* pn. cualquiera; cada uno; **—
other,** unos á otros, mutuamente.
eager, *ē'găr,* a. deseoso; fogoso; ardiente,
vehemente; **-ly,** ad. vehementemente, ardientemente. [hemencia, f.; ardor, m.
eagerness, *-nĕs,* s. ansia, f.; anhelo, m.; ve-
eagle, *ē'gl,* s. águila; moneda de oro
(= 10 dollars), f.
eagle-eyed, *-īd,* a. de vista lince.
eaglet, *ē'glĕt,* s. aguilucho, m.
ear, *ĕr,* s. oreja, f.; oído, m.; asa, f.; espiga,
f.; by **—** de oreja; **—,** v. n. espigar.
ear-ache, *-āk,* s. dolor de oídos, m.
earl, *ărl,* s. conde, m.
ear-lap, *ĕr'lăp,* s. punta de la oreja, f.
earldom, *ărl'dăm,* s. condado, m.
earliness, *ăr'lĭnĕs,* s. precocidad, f.; pre-
teza, prontitud, f. [prano.
early, *ăr'lĭ,* a. temprano, presto; **—,** ad. tem-
earn, *ărn,* v. a. ganar, obtener, conseguir.
earnest, *ăr'nĕst,* a. ardiente, fervoroso,
serio, importante; **—,** s. seriedad, f.; estrena, f.; señal, f.; esperanza, f.; prueba,
f.; **in good —** de buena fe; **-ly,** ad.
seriamente; ansiosamente.
earnest-money, *-mănĕ,* s. caparra, f.
earnestness, *-nĕs,* s. ansia, f.; ardor, celo,
m.; seriedad, vehemencia, f.
ear-ring, *ĕr'ring,* s. zarcillo, pendiente, m.

earth, *ărth,* s. tierra, f.; terrestre, m.; **—,** v. a.
enterrar; **—,** v. n. retirarse debajo de tierra.
earth-born, *-bŏrn,* a. de bajo nacimiento;
terrestre.
earthen, *-n,* a. terreno; hecho de tierra.
earthenware, *-nwăr,* s. loza de barro, f.
earthiness, *-ĭnĕs,* s. terrenidad; grosería, f.
earthliness, *-lĭnĕs,* s. vanidad mundana, f.
earthly, *-lĭ,* a. terrestre, mundano; sensual.
earthquake, *-kwăk,* s. terremoto, m.
earthwork, *-wărk,* s. (mil.) fuerte de
tierra, m.
earth-worm, *-wŭrm,* s. lombriz, f.
ear-trumpet, *ĕr'trŭmpĕt,* s. trompetilla, f.
ear-wig, *-wĭg,* s. goplón, m. [m.
ear-witness, *-wĭtnĕs,* s. testigo de oídos,
ease, *ēz,* s. quietud, f.; reposo, ocio, m.;
comodidad, f.; facilidad, f.; **at —,** con desahogo; **—,** v. a. aliviar; mitigar.
easel, *ē'zl,* s. caballete (de los pintores), m.
casement, *ēz'mĕnt,* s. alivio, apoyo, m.;
ventaja, f.
easily, *ē'zĭlĭ,* ad. fácilmente; quietamente.
easiness, *ē'zĭnĕs,* s. condescendencia, f.
east, *ēst,* s. oriente, m.; este, m.
Easter, *-ăr,* s. Pascua de resurrección, f.;
— Eve, Sábado santo, m.
easterly, *-ărlĭ,* **eastern,** *-ărn,* a. oriental.
eastward, *-wŭrd,* ad. hacia el oriente.
easy, *ē'zĭ,* a. fácil; cortés, sociable; cómodo;
pronto; libre; tranquilo, aliviado; **—going,** inalterable, sereno.
eat, *ēt,* v. a. comer; roer; **—,** v. n. alimentarse.
eatable, *-ăbl,* a. comestible; **-s,** pl. víveres, m. pl. [tible, f.
eatableness, *-nĕs,* s. calidad de lo comes-
eating-house, *-ĭnghŏŭs,* s. bodegón, m.;
fonda, f. [hostería, f.
eaves, *ēvz,* s. pl. socarrén, m. [hostería, f.
eaves-drop, *-drŏp,* v. a. escuchar á la ventana lo que se habla dentro de la casa.
ebb, *ĕb,* s. menguante, m.; decremento, m.;
—, v. n. menguar; decaer, disminuir.
ebon, *ĕb'ŏn,* a. de ébano; negro.
ebony, *ĕb'ŏnĕ,* s. ébano, m.; **to deal in —**
comerciar en negros. [mentación, f.
ebullition, *ĕbŭlĭsh'ŭn,* s. ebullición, fer-
eccentric(al), *ĕksĕn'trĭk(ăl),* a. excéntrico.
eccentricity, *ĕksĕntrĭs'ĭtĭ,* s. excentricidad, f. [tico, m.
ecclesiastic, *ĕkklēzĭăs'tĭk,* a. & s. eclesiás-
echo, *ĕk'ō,* s. eco, m.; **—,** v. n. resonar;
—, v. a. repercutir (la voz).
eclectic, *ĕklĕk'tĭk,* a. ecléctico.
eclipse, *ĕklĭps',* s. eclipse, m.; **—,** v. a.
eclipsar.
ecliptic, *ĕklĭp'tĭk,* s. eclíptica, f.
economic(al), *ĕkŏnŏm'ĭk(ăl),* a. económico,
frugal, parco, moderado.
economist, *ĕkŏn'ŏmĭst,* s. economista, m.
economise, *ĕkŏn'ŏmĭz,* v. a. economizar.
economy, *ĕkŏn'ŏmĕ,* s. economía, f.; frugalidad, f.
ecstasy, *ĕk'stăsĕ,* s. éxtasi, éxtasis, m.
ecstatic(al), *ĕkstăt'ĭk(ăl),* a. extático;
-ally, ad. en éxtasis.
eddy, *ĕd'dĕ,* s. reflujo de agua, m.; remolino,
m.; **—,** v. n. remolinar.

edge, *ĕj*, s. filo, m.; punta, f.; esquina, f.; margen, m. & f.; acrimonia, f.; –, v. a. afilar, ribetear; introducir; –, v. n. oponerse.

edge-tool, –*tōl*, s. herramienta cortante, f.

edge-ways, –*wāz*, ad. de filo, de lado.

edging, *ĕj'ĭng*, s. orla, orilla, f.

edible, *ĕd'ĭbl*, a. comedero, comestible.

edict, *ē'dĭkt*, s. edicto, mandato, m.   [f.

edification, *ĕdĭfĭkā'shŭn*, s. edificación,

edifice, *ĕd'ĭfĭs*, s. edificio, m.; fábrica, f.

edify, *ĕd'ĭfī*, v. a. edificar; fabricar; instruir.

edit, *ĕd'ĭt*, v. a. publicar alguna obra ajena ó ser su editor.   [ción, f.; impresión, f.

edition, *ĕdĭsh'ŭn*, s. edición, f.; publica-

editor, *ĕd'ĭtŭr*, s. editor, m.

editorial, *ĕdĭtō'rĭăl*, a. editorial.

educate, *ĕd'ūkāt*, v. a. educar; enseñar.

education, *ĕdūkā'shŭn*, s. educación, f.

eel, *ēl*, s. anguila, f.   [crianza, f.

eel-pout, –*pōŭt*, s. lamprea de río, f.

eerie, *ē'rĭ*, a. adundeado.

efface, *ĕfās'*, v. a. borrar, destruir.

effect, *ĕfĕkt'* s. efecto, m.; realidad, f.; –s, s. pl. efectos, bienes, m. pl.; –, v. a. efectuar, ejecutar.

effective, –*tĭv*, a. eficaz; efectivo; real; –ly, ad. efectivamente, en efecto; –s, s. pl. gente de guerra, f.

effectual, *ĕfĕk'tūăl*, a. eficiente, eficaz; –ly, ad. eficazmente   [f.

effeminacy, *ĕfĕm'ĭnăsē*, s. afeminación, f.

effeminate, –*mĭnăt*, v. a. afeminar, debilitar; –, v. n. afeminarse, enervarse; –, a. afeminado; –ly, ad. con afeminación.

effervesce, *ĕfŭrvĕs'*, v. n. hervir, fermentar.   [hervor, f.

effervescence, –*sĕns*, s. efervescencia, f.;

effete, *ĕffēt'*, a. estéril.   [ad. eficazmente

efficacious, *ĕfĭkā'shŭs*, a. eficaz; –ly,

efficacy, *ĕf'ĭkāsē*, s. eficacia, f.   [tud, f.

efficiency, *ĕfĭsh'ĭĕnsē*, s. eficiencia, vir-

efficient, *ĕfĭsh'ĭĕnt*, a. eficaz.   [m.

effigy, *ĕf'ĭjē*, s. efigie, imagen, f., retrato,

efflorescence, *ĕfflōrĕs'ĕns*, s. eflorescencia, f.; excrecencia, f.   [nación, f.

effluvium, *ĕfflū'vĭŭm*, s. efluvio, m.; ema-

effort, *ĕf'fŏrt*, s. esfuerzo, empeño, m.

effrontery, *ĕffrŭn'tŭrē*, s. descaro, m.; impudencia, desvergüenza, f.   [m.

effulgence, *ĕffŭl'jĕns*, s. esplendor, fulgor,

effulgent, –*jĕnt*, a. resplandeciente.

effusion, *ĕffū'zhŭn*, s. efusión, f.; flujo de palabras, m.

eft, *ĕft*, s. lagartija, f.

egg, *ĕg*, s. huevo, m.; to – on, v. a. airar.

egg-cup, –*kŭp*, s. huevera, f.

egg-flip, –*flĭp*, –nog, –*nŏg*, s. leche de gallina, f.

egg-shell, –*shĕl*, s. cáscara de huevo, f.

eglantine, *ĕg'lăntīn*, s. agabanzo, m.

egotism, *ĕg'ōtĭzm*, s. egoísmo, m.

egotist, *ĕg'ōtĭst*, s. egoísta, m.

egotistical, *ĕgōtĭs'tĭkăl*, a. egoístico.

egregious, *ĕgrē'jŭs*, a. egregio, famoso, excelente; –ly, ad. egregiamente.

egress, *ē'grĕs*, egression, *ĕgrĕsh'ăn*, s. salida, f.

eiderdown, *ī'dŭrdŏŭn*, s. edredón, m.; emplumado, cubrepiés, m.

eight, *āt*, a. ocho; pieces of –, s. pl. escudos de España, m. pl.

eighteen, *ā'tēn*, a. diez y ocho.

eighteenth, –*th*, a. décimoctavo.

eighth, *ātth*, a. octavo; –ly, ad. en el octavo lugar.

eightieth, *ā'tĭĕth*, a. octogésimo.

eighty, *ā'tĭ*, a. ochenta.

either, *ē'thŭr*, pn. cualquiera, uno de dos; –, c. ó, sea, ya.   [pedir.

ejaculate, *ĕjăk'ūlāt*, v. a. arrojar, des-

ejaculation, *ĕjăkūlā'shŭn*, s. ejaculatoria, f.

eject, *ĕjĕkt'*, v. a. expeler, desechar.   [f.

ejection, *ĕjĕk'shŭn*, s. expulsión, f.; (med.) evacuación, f.   [hacer crecer.

eke, *ēk*, v. a. aumentar; alargar; prolongar.

elaborate, *ĕlăb'ōrăt*, v. a. elaborar; –, a. elaborado, primoroso; –ly, ad. cuidadosamente.

elapse, *ĕlăps'*, v. n. pasar, correr (el tiempo).   [cursivo.

elastic(al), *ĕlăs'tĭk(ăl)*, a. elástico; reper-

elasticity, *ĕlăstĭs'tĭē*, s. elasticidad, f.

elate, *ĕlāt'*, a. altivo, orgulloso; –, v. a. ensoberbecer; exaltar, elevar.

elation, *ĕlā'shŭn*, s. altivez, soberbia, f.

elbow, *ĕl'bō*, s. codo; –, v. a. codear; –, v. n. formar recodos.

elbow-chair, –*tshār*, s. silla de brazos, f.

elbow-room, –*rōm*, s. anchura, f.; espacio suficiente, m.; (fig.) libertad, latitud, f.

eld, *ĕld*, s. los ancianos.   [mayor.

elder, *ĕl'dŭr*, saúco, m. (árbol); –, a.

elderly, –*lē*, a. de edad ya madura.

elders, –*z*, s. pl. ancianos, antepasados, m. pl.   [genitura, f.

eldership, –*shĭp*, s. ancianidad, f.; pri-

eldest, *ĕl'dĕst*, a. el, la ó lo más anciano.

eldritch, *ĕl'drĭtsh*, a. adundeado.

elect, *ĕlĕkt'*, v. a. elegir; –, a. elegido, escogido.

election, *ĕlĕk'shŭn*, s. elección, f.

electioneering, –*ĕr'ĭng*, s. maniobras secretas en la elección de parlamentario, m.

elective, *ĕlĕk'tĭv*, a. electivo; – attraction, afinidad química, f.; –ly, ad. electivamente.

elector, *ĕlĕk'tŭr*, s. elector, m.

electoral, –*tŏrăl*, a. electoral.

electorate, –*tŏrăt*, s. electorado, m.

electric(al), –*trĭk(ăl)*, a. eléctrico.

electrician, *ĕlĕktrĭsh'ăn*, s. persona versada en la electricidad, f.

electricity, *ĕlĕktrĭs'tĭē*, s. electricidad, f.

electrify, *ĕlĕk'trĭfī*, v. a. electrizar.

electro-gilding, –*trōgĭldĭng*, –plating, –*plātĭng*, s. doradura galvánica, f.

electrolize, –*līz*, v. a. descomponer por electricidad.

electuary, *ĕlĕk'tūărē*, s. electuario, m.

eleemosinary, *ĕlēmōz'ĭnārē*, a. pobre que vive de limosna, m.

elegance, *ĕl'ĕgăns*, s. elegancia, f.

elegant, *ĕl'ĕgănt*, a. elegante, delicado; –ly, ad. elegantemente.

elegiac(al), ĕlĕjĭ'ăk(ăl), a. elegiaco.

elegy, ĕl'ĕjĭ, s. elegía, f.

element, ĕl'ĕmĕnt, s. elemento, m.; fundamento, m.

elemental, ĕlĕmĕn'tăl, **elementary**, -tărĭ, a. elemental, simple, inicial.

elephant, ĕl'ĕfănt, s. elefante, m.

elephantine, ĕlĕfăn'tĭn, a. inmenso.

elevate, ĕl'ĕvāt, v. a. elevar, alzar, exaltar.

elevation, ĕlĕvā'shăn, s. elevación, f.; altura, f.; alteza (de pensamientos), f.

eleven, ĕlĕv'n, a. once.

eleventh, -th, a. onceno, undécimo.

elf, ĕlf, s. duende, m.; —, v. a. enmarañar el pelo.

elfin, -ĭn, a. lo perteneciente á duendes.

elicit, ĕlĭs'ĭt, v. a. ejecutar lo ideado; sacar de; atraer.

eligibility, ĕlĭjĭbĭl'ĭtĭ, s. elegibilidad, f.

eligible, ĕl'ĭjĭbl, a. elegible; deseable.

eliminate, ĕlĭm'ĭnāt, v. a. eliminar, desechar. [cartar.

elk, ĕlk, s. alce, m.

ell, ĕl, s. ana, f.

ellipse, ĕllĭps', s. (gr.) elipsis, f.; (geom.)

elliptic(al), -tĭk(ăl), a. elíptico. [elipse, f.

elm, ĕlm, s. olmo, m. [habla, f.

elocution, ĕlŏkū'shăn, s. elocución, f.;

elocutionist, -ĭst, s. profesor de declamación, m.

elongate, ĕlŏn'gāt, v. a. alargar, apartar, alejar; —, v. n. alejarse, desviarse.

elope, ĕlōp', v. n. escapar, huir, evadirse.

elopement, -mĕnt, s. fuga, huída, evasión, f.

eloquence, ĕl'ōkwĕns, s. elocuencia, f.

eloquent, ĕl'ōkwĕnt, a. elocuente; -ly, ad. elocuentemente.

else, ĕls, pn. otro; —, c. de otro modo ó manera; sino.

elsewhere, -hwār, ad. en otra parte.

elucidate, ĕlū'sĭdāt, v. a. dilucidar, explicar.

elucidation, ĕlūsĭdā'shăn, s. elucidación, explicación, f.

elude, ĕlūd', v. a. eludir, evitar.

elusion, ĕlū'zhăn, s. escaparia, f.; fraude, artificio, m.

elusive, -ĭv, **elusory**, -sŭrĭ, a. artificioso, falaz.

emaciate, ĕmāsh'ĭāt, v. a. extenuar, adelgazar; —, v. n enflaquecer.

emaciation, ĕmāshĭā'shăn, s. emaciación, f.; enflaquecimiento, m.

emanate (from), ĕm'ănāt, v. n. emanar.

emanation, ĕmănā'shăn, s. emanación, f.; origen, m. [dar libertad.

emancipate, ĕmăn'sĭpāt, v. a. emancipar;

emancipation, ĕmănsĭpā'shăn, s. emancipación, f.

embalm, ĕmbām', v. a. embalsamar.

embank, ĕmbăngk', v. a. terraplenar.

embankment, -mĕnt, s. allanamiento de algún terreno añadiéndole vezones &c. m.; encajonamiento, m. [de buques), m.

embargo, ĕmbăr'gō, s. embargo (detención

embark, ĕmbărk', v. a. embarcar.

embarkation, ĕmbărkā'shăn, s. embarcación, f. [redar.

embarrass, ĕmbăr'răs, v. a. embarazar, en-

embarrassment, -mĕnt, s. embarazo, enredo, m.

embassy, ĕm'băssĭ, s. embajada, f.

embattle, ĕmbăt'l, v. a. formar en orden de batalla. [nar.

embellish, ĕmbĕl'ĭsh, v. a. hermosear, ador-

embellishment, -mĕnt, s. adorno, m.

ember-days, ĕm'bŭrdāz, s. pl. Témpora, f.

embers, ĕm'bŭrz, s. pl. rescoldo, m.

embezzle, ĕmbĕz'l, v. a. apropiarse alguna cosa ilícitamente; malgastar.

embezzlement, -mĕnt, s. hurto, m.

embitter, ĕmbĭt'ŭr, v. a. hacer amargo.

emblazon, ĕmblā'zn, v. a. blasonar. [m.

emblem, ĕm'blĕm, s. emblema, m.; esmalte,

emblematic(al), ĕmblĕmăt'ĭk(ăl), a. emblemático, simbólico. [ción, f.

embodiment, ĕmbŏd'ĭmĕnt, s. incorpora-

embody, ĕmbŏd'ĭ, v. a. incorporar.

embolden, ĕmbōl'dn, v. a. animar.

emboss, ĕmbŏs', v. a. formar alguna cosa en relieve. [—, s. abrazo, m.

embrace, ĕmbrās', v a. abrazar; contener;

embrasure, ĕmbrā'zhŭr, s. tronera, f.

embrocation, ĕmbrōkā'shăn, s. (med.) embrocación, f.

embroider, ĕmbrŏĭ'dŭr, v. a. bordar.

embroidery, -ĭ, s. bordado, m.; bordadura, f. [fundir.

embroil, ĕmbrŏĭl', v. a. embrollar; con-

embryo, ĕm'brĭō, s. embrión, m.

emendation, ĕmĕndā'shăn, s. enmienda, corrección, f.

emerald, ĕm'ĕrăld, s. esmeralda, f.

emerge, ĕmĕrj', v. n. salir, proceder.

emergency, -ĕnsĭ, s. emersión, f.; emergencia; necesidad urgente, f.

emery, ĕm'ĕrĭ, s. esmeril, m.

emetic, ĕmĕt'ĭk, s. emético, vomitivo, m.

emigrant, ĕm'ĭgrănt, s. emigrado, m.

emigrate, ĕm'ĭgrāt, v. n. emigrar.

emigration, ĕmĭgrā'shăn, s. emigración, f.

eminence, ĕm'ĭnĕns, s. altura, sumidad, f.; eminencia, excelencia, f.

eminent, ĕm'ĭnĕnt, a. eminente, elevado; distinguido; -ly, ad. eminentemente.

emissary, ĕm'ĭssărĭ, s. emisario, m.; espía,

emission, ĕmĭsh'ăn, s. emisión, f. [m.

emit, ĕmĭt', v. a. emitir, echar de sí; arrojar, despedir.

emmet, ĕm'mĕt, s. hormiga, f.

emollient, ĕmŏl'lĭĕnt, a. emoliente; —, s. emolientes (medicamentos), m. pl.

emolument, ĕmŏl'ūmĕnt, s. emolumento, provecho, m. [conmoción, f.

emotion, ĕmō'shăn, s. agitación del ánimo,

emotional, ĕmō'shănăl, a. concitativo.

emperor, ĕm'pĕrŭr, s. emperador, m.

emphasis, ĕm'făsĭs, s. énfasis, m. & f.

emphasise, ĕm'făsĭz, v. a. hablar con énfasis. [—, ally, ad. enfáticamente.

emphatic(al), ĕmfăt'ĭk(ăl), a. enfático;

empire, ĕm'pĭr, s. imperio, m.

empiric, ĕmpĭr'ĭk, s. empírico, medicastro, m.; -al, a. empírico; -ally, ad. como un empírico.

5*

employ, *ĕmplŏĭ'*, v. a. emplear, ocupar; –, s. empleo, m.; ocupación, f.; oficio público, m. [m.

employee, *ĕmplŏĭ'ăr*, s. amo, dueño.

employment, *–mĕnt*, s. empleo, m.; ocupación, f.

emporium, *ĕmpŏ'rĭŭm*, s. emporio, m.

empower, *ĕmpŏ'ăr*, v. a. autorizar, dar poder.

empress, *ĕm'prĕs*, s. emperatriz, f.

emptiness, *ĕm'tĭnĕs*, s. vaciedad, f.; vacuo, m.; futilidad, f.

empty, *ĕm'tĕ*, a. vacío; vano; ignorante; –, v. a. vaciar, evacuar.

empyrean, *ĕmpĭrē'ăn*, a. empíreo, celestial.

emulate, *ĕm'ŭlăt*, v. a. emular, competir; imitar.

emulation, *ĕmŭlă'shŭn*, s. emulación, f.; rivalidad, f.

emulgent, *ĕmŭl'jĕnt*, a. emulgente.

emulous, *ĕm'ŭlŭs*, a. émulo; –ly, ad. á competencia.

emulsion, *ĕmŭl'shŭn*, s. emulsión, f.

enable, *ĕnā'bl*, v. n. habilitar; poner en estado de.

enact, *ĕnăkt'*, v. a. establecer, decretar.

enactment, *–mĕnt*, s. decreto, dictamen, m.

enamel, *ĕnăm'ĕl*, s. esmalte, m.; –, v. a. esmaltar.

enamour, *ĕnăm'ăr*, v. a. enamorar.

encage, *ĕnkāj'*, v. a. enjaular, encerrar.

encamp, *ĕnkămp'*, v. n. acamparse.

encampment, *–mĕnt*, s. campamento, m.

encase, *ĕnkās'*, v. a. encajar, encajonar.

encaustic, *ĕnkăs'tĭk*, a. encáustico; – painting, s. pintura encáustica, f.

enchain, *ĕntshān'*, v. a. encadenar.

enchant, *ĕntshănt'*, v. a. encantar.

enchantingly, *–tĭnglĕ*, ad. de un modo deleitoso.

enchantment, *–mĕnt*, s. encanto, m.

enchantress, *–rĕs*, s. encantadora, f.

encircle, *ĕnsŭr'kl*, v. a. cercar, circundar.

enclose, *ĕnklŏz'*; v. a. cercar, circunvalar, circundar; incluir. [cercado, m.

enclosure, *ĕnklŏ'zhŭr*, s. cercamiento, m.

encomium, *ĕnkŏ'mĭŭm*, s. encomio, elogio, m. [cercar; circuir.

encompass, *ĕnkŭm'păs*, v. a. circundar;

encore, *ăngkŏr'*, ad. otra vez, de nuevo; –, v. a. pedir que un actor repita segunda vez lo que ha cantado.

encounter, *ĕnkŏun'tăr*, s. encuentro, m.; duelo, m.; pelea, f.; –, v. a. encontrar; –, v. b. encontrarse; combatir.

encourage, *ĕnkŭr'ĕj*, v. a. animar, alentar.

encouragement, *–mĕnt*, s. estímulo, patrocinio, m. [zar gradualmente.

encroach, *ĕnkrŏtsh'*, v. a. usurpar, avanzar.

encroachment, *–mĕnt*, s. usurpación, intrusión, f.

encrusted, *ĕnkrŭst'ĕd*, a. incrustado.

encumber, *ĕnkŭm'bŭr*, v. a. embarazar, cargar. [pedimento, m.

encumbrance, *–brăns*, s. embarazo, impedimento, m.

encyclical, *ĕnsĭk'lĭkăl*, a. encíclico, circular.

end, *ĕnd*, s. fin, m.; extremidad, f.; término, m.; resolución, f.; intento, m.; to the – that, para que; to no –, en vano; on –, en pie, de pie; –, v. a. matar; concluir, fenecer; –, v. n. acabarse, terminarse. [gar.

endanger, *ĕndăn'jăr*, v. a. peligrar, arriesgar.

endear, *ĕndēr'*, v. a. encarecer.

endearment, *–mĕnt*, s. encarecimiento, m.

endeavour, *ĕndĕv'ăr*, v. n. esforzarse; intentar; –, v. a. tentar; –, s. esfuerzo, m.

endemic(al), *ĕndĕm'ĭk(ăl)*, a. endémico.

ending, *ĕnd'ĭng*, s. conclusión, cesación, f.; muerte, f.

endive, *ĕn'dĭv*, s. (bot.) endibia, f.

endless, *ĕnd'lĕs*, a. infinito, perpetuo; –ly, ad. sin fin, perpetuamente.

endorse, *ĕndŏrs'*, v. a. endosar una letra de cambio.

endorsee, *ĕndŏrsē'*, s. endosatario, m.

endorsement, *–mĕnt*, s. endoso, m. [m.

endorser, *–ŭr*, s. endosador, endosante.

endow, *ĕndŏu'*, v. a. dotar á una mujer.

endowment, *–mĕnt*, s. dote, dotación, f.

endurable, *ĕndū'răbl*, a. sufrible, tolerable.

endurance, *–răns*, s. duración, f.; paciencia, f.; sufrimiento, m. [v. n. durar.

endure, *ĕndūr'*, v. a. sufrir, soportar; –,

endways, *ĕnd'wāz*, **endwise,** *–wīz*, ad. de punta, derecho. [m.; diablo, m.

enemy, *ĕn'ĕmĕ*, s. enemigo, antagonista.

energetic, *ĕnărjĕt'ĭk*, a. enérgico, vigoroso.

energy, *ĕn'ărjĕ*, s. energía, fuerza, f.

enervate, *ĕnŭr'vāt*, v. a. enervar, debilitar, quitar las fuerzas.

enfeeble, *ĕnfē'bl*, v. a. debilitar, enervar.

enfilade, *ĕnfĭlād'*, s. hila, hilera, f.; –, v. a. (mil.) enfilar. [rodear.

enfold, *ĕnfŏld'*, v. a. envolver, arrollar.

enforce, *ĕnfŏrs'*, v. a. esforzar; violentar; compeler.

enforcement, *–mĕnt*, s. compulsión, coacción, f.; fuerza, f.; sanción, f.; aprieto, m.

enfranchise, *ĕnfrăn'tshĭz*, v. a. franquear; naturalizar.

engage, *ĕngāj'*, v. a. empeñar, obligar; halagar; ocupar; –, v. n. pelear, empeñarse.

engagement, *–mĕnt*, s. empeño, m.; combate, m.; pelea, f.; obligación, f.

engagingly, *–lĕ*, ad. de un modo halagüeño.

engender, *ĕnjĕn'dăr*, v. a. engendrar; producir; –, v. n. producirse.

engine, *ĕn'jĭn*, s. ingenio, m.; máquina, f.; locomotora, f.; instrumento, m.

engine-driver, *–drīvăr*, s. conductor de una locomotora, m. [nista, m.

engineer, *–ēr'*, s. ingeniero, m.; maquinista, m.

engineering, *–ĭng*, s. arte del ingeniero, f. [tallar.

engrave, *ĕngrāv'*, v. a. grabar; esculpir;

engraving, *ĕngrā'vĭng*, s. grabado, m.; estampa, f. [monopolizar.

engross, *ĕngrŏs'*, v. a. engordar, engrosar.

engulf, *ĕngŭlf'*, v. a. engolfar; engullir.

enhance, *ĕnhăns'*, v. a. encarecer, levantar en alto; agravar.

enigma, *ěnĭg'mâ*, s. enigma, m.

enigmatical, *ěnĭgmăt'ĭkâl*, a. enigmático; **-ly**, ad. enigmáticamente.

enjoin, *ěnjŏĭn'*, v. a. ordenar, prescribir; advertir.

enjoy, *ěnjŏĭ'*, v. a. gozar; poseer; –, v. n. vivir felizmente.

enjoyment, *–měnt*, s. goce, disfrute, m.; placer, m., fruición, f.

enlarge, *ěnlârj'*, v. a. engrandecer, dilatar, extender; desapricionar; –, v. n. extenderse, dilatarse.

enlargement, *–měnt*, s. aumento, m.; ampliación, f. soltura, f. [nar; instruir.

enlighten, *ěnlī'tn*, v. a. alumbrar; iluminar.

enlightenment, *–měnt*, s. luces, f. pl.

enlist, *ěnlĭst'*, v. a. alistar.

enlistment, *–měnt*, s. alistamiento, m.

enliven, *ěnlĭv'n*, v. a. animar; avivar; alegrar. [de improviso.

enmesh, *ěnměsh'*, v. a. coger con arte ó alevosía.

enmity, *ěn'mĭtĕ*, s. enemistad, f.; odio, m.

ennoble, *ěnnō'bl*, v. a. ennoblecer.

enormity, *ěnôr'mĭtĕ*, s. enormidad, f.; atrocidad, f. [enormemente.

enormous, *–mûs*, a. enorme; **-ly**, ad.

enough, *ěnŭf'*, ad. bastantemente; basta; –, s. bastante, m.

enounce, *ěnŏuns'*, v. a. declarar.

enquire, *ěnkwīr'*, v. a. informarse, tomar informes, averiguar, inquirir.

enquiry, *ěnkwī'rĕ*, s. indagación, f.

enrage, *ěnrāj'*, v. a. enfurecer, irritar.

enrapture, *ěnrăp'tūr*, v. a. arrebatar, entusiasmar; encantar.

enrich, *ěnrĭtsh'*, v. a. enriquecer; adornar.

enrichment, *–měnt*, s. enriquecimiento, m.

enrol, *ěnrōl'*, v. a. registrar; arrollar.

enrolment, *–měnt*, s. alistamiento, m.

ensconce, *ěnskŏns'*, v. a. (mil.) resguardar con un fortín. [reliquia.

enshrine, *ěnshrīn'*, v. a. guardar para

ensign, *ěn'sīn*, s. (mil.) bandera, f.; abanderado, m.; (mar.) alférez, m. [m.

ensign-bearer, *–bārâr*, s. abanderado.

enslave, *ěnslāv'*, v. a. esclavizar, cautivar.

ensnare, *ěnsnâr'*, v. a. entrampar; engañar.

ensue, *ěnsū'*, v. n. seguirse; suceder.

entablature, *ěntăb'lâtūr*, s. entablamento, m. [m.; –, v. a. vincular.

entail, *ěntāl'*, s. (law) vínculo, mayorazgo.

entangle, *ěntăng'gl*, v. a. enmarañar, embrollar, embarazar. [m.

entanglement, *–měnt*, s. enredo, embarazo.

enter, *ěn'târ*, v. a. entrar; admitir; registrar; empezar; –, v. n. entrar; empeñarse en algo; emprender, aventurar.

enterprise, *–prīz*, s. empresa, f.

entertain, *–tān'*, v. a. conversar; tratar; hospedar; mantener; entretener.

entertainer, *–tān'âr*, s. huésped, m.

entertainment, *–tān'měnt*, s. conversación, f.; festejo, m.; mantenimiento, m.; entretenimiento, pasatiempo, m.

enthral, *ěnthrăl'*, v. a. oprimir, esclavizar.

enthralling, *–ĭng*, a. opresivo.

enthrone, *ěnthrōn'*, v. a. entronizar.

enthusiasm, *ěnthū'zĭăsm*, s. entusiasmo.

enthusiast, *–zĭăst*, s. entusiasta, m. [m.

enthusiastic(al), *ěnthūzĭăs'tĭk(âl)*, a. entusiasmado. [tar, inducir.

entice, *ěntīs'*, v. a. halagar, acariciar, excitar.

entire, *ěntīr'*, a. entero, cumplido, completo, perfecto; **-ly**, ad. enteramente.

entirety, *–tĕ*, s. entereza, integridad, f.

entitle, *ěntī'tl*, v. a. intitular; conferir algún derecho.

entity, *ěn'tĭtĕ*, s. entidad, existencia, f.

entomb, *ěntōm'*, v. a. sepultar. [logo, m.

entomologist, *ěntōmŏl'ōgĭst*, s. entomólogo.

entomology, *–ōjē*, s. entomología, f.

entrails, *ěn'trālz*, s. pl. entrañas, f. pl.

entrance, *ěn'trăns*, s. entrada, f.; admisión, f.; principio, m. [bulo.

entrance-hall, *–hăl*, s. pórtico, vestíbulo.

entrance-money, *–mŭnĕ*, s. entrada, f.

entrap, *ěntrăp'*, v. a. entrampar; enredar; engañar.

entreat, *ěntrēt'*, v. a. rogar, suplicar. [f.

entreaty, *–ĕ*, s. petición, súplica, instancia.

entrust, *ěntrŭst'*, v. a. confiar.

entry, *ěn'trĕ*, s. entrada, f. [torcer.

entwine, *ěntwīn'*, v. a. entrelazar, enroscar.

enumerate, *ěnū'mērāt*, v. a. enumerar, numerar, contar uno á uno. [ción, f.

enumeration, *ěnūmērā'shûn*, s. enumeración, f. [ciar, f.

enunciate, *ěnŭn'sĭāt*, v. a. enunciar, declarar. [ción, f.

enunciation, *ěnŭnsĭā'shûn*, s. enunciación.

envelop, *ěnvěl'ŏp*, v. a. envolver, aforrar.

envelope, *ěnvěl'ōp*, s. envolvedero, m.; cubierta, f. [sigar.

envenom, *ěnvěn'ōm*, v. a. envenenar, atosigar.

enviable, *ěn'vĭăbl*, a. envidiable.

envious, *ěn'vĭûs*, a. envidioso; **-ly**, ad. envidiosamente. [contornos, m. pl.

environs, *ěnvī'rōnz*, s. pl. ciudad, f.; contornos.

envoy, *ěn'vŏĭ*, s. enviado, m.; mensajero, m.

envy, *ěn'vĕ*, s. envidia, malicia, f. –, v. a. envidiar.

epaulet, *ěp'ālět*, s. (mil.) charretera, f.

ephemeral, *ěfěm'ěrâl*, a. efímero.

epic, *ěp'ĭk*, s. épico.

Epicure, *ěp'ĭkūr*, s. hombre voluptuoso, m.

epicurean, *ěpĭkūrē'ân*, a. epicúreo.

epidemic(al), *ěpĭděm'ĭk(âl)*, a. epidémico; –, s. epidemia, f.

epigram, *ěp'ĭgrăm*, s. epigrama, m. & f.

epigrammatic, *ěpĭgrămmăt'ĭk*, a. epigramático.

epilepsy, *ěp'ĭlěpsĕ*, s. epilepsia, f.

epileptic(al), *ěpĭlěp'tĭk(âl)*, a. epiléptico.

epilogue, *ěp'ĭlŏg*, s. epílogo, m.

Epiphany, *ěpĭf'ânĕ*, s. Epifanía, f.

episcopacy, *ěpĭs'kōpâsĕ*, s. episcopado, m.

episcopal, *ěpĭs'kōpâl*, a. episcopal.

episcopalian, *ěpĭskōpā'lĭân*, s. anglicano, m.

episode, *ěp'ĭsōd*, s. episodio, m. [m.

epistle, *ěpĭs'l*, s. epístola, f.

epistolary, *ěpĭs'tōlârĕ*, a. epistolar.

epitaph, *ěp'ĭtâf*, s. epicafio, m.

epithet, *ěp'ĭthĕt*, s. epíteto, m. [m.

epitome, *ěpĭt'ōmĕ*, s. epítome, compendio.

epitomize, *ěpĭt'ōmīz*, v. a. epitomar, abreviar. [viar.

epoch, *ěp'ŏk*, s. época, f.

equable, *ěk'wâbl*, a. uniforme; **-bly**, ad. uniformemente.

equal, *ĕ'kwŏl*, a. igual; justo; semejante; imparcial; —, *s.* igualdad, f.; compañero, m.; —, v. a. igualar; compensar.

equalisation, *ĕkwŏlĭzā'shŭn*, s. igualamiento, m.

equalise, *-īz*, v. a. igualar. [dad, f.

equality, *ĕkwŏl'tĭĕ*, s. igualdad, uniformidad, f.

equally, *ĕ'kwŏllĕ*, ad. igualmente. [f.

equanimity, *ĕkwănĭm'ĭtĕ*, s. ecuanimidad, f.

equation, *ĕkwā'shŭn*, s. ecuación, f.

equator, *ĕkwā'tŭr*, s. ecuador, m.

equatorial, *ĕkwătō'rĭăl*, a. ecuatorial, ecuatorio. [m.; establo, m.

equerry, *ĕk'wĕrrĕ*, s. caballerizo del rey, m.

equestrian, *ĕkwĕs'trĭăn*, a. ecuestre; — performer, s. diestro en caballos, m.

equilateral, *ĕkwĭlăt'ĕrăl*, a. equilátero.

equilibrist, *ĕkwĭl'ĭbrĭst*, s. equilibrista, m.

equilibrium, *ĕkwĭlĭb'rĭŭm*, s. equilibrio, m.

equine, *ĕ'kwĭn*, a. caballar. [m.

equinoctial, *ĕkwĭnŏk'shăl*, a. equinoccial.

equinox, *ĕ'kwĭnŏks*, s. equinoccio, m.

equip, *ĕkwĭp'*, v. a. equipar, pertrechar; aprestar un navío. [carroza, f.

equipage, *ĕk'wĭpāj*, s. equipaje, tren, m.;

equipment, *ĕkwĭp'mĕnt*, s. equipaje, m.; apresto, m.

equipoise, *ĕ'kwĭpŏiz*, s. equilibrio, m.

equitable, *ĕk'wĭtăbl*, a. equitativo, imparcial; —bly, ad. equitativamente.

equity, *ĕk'wĭtĕ*, s. equidad, justicia, imparcialidad, f. [lente (m.).

equivalent, *ĕkwĭv'ălĕnt*, a. & s. equivalente (m.).

equivocal, *-ōkăl*, a. equívoco, ambiguo; —ly, ad. equivocadamente, ambiguamente.

equivocate, *-ōkāt*, v. a. equivocar, usar equívocos. [m.; anfibología, f.

equivocation, *ĕkwĭvōkā'shŭn*, s. equívoco,

era, *ĕ'rā*, s. era, data eterminada, f.

eradicate, *ĕrād'ĭkāt*, v. a. desarraigar, extirpar. [f.

eradication, *ĕrādĭkā'shŭn*, s. extirpación,

erase, *ĕrāz'*, v. a. cancelar, rayar.

eraser, *-ĕr*, s. raspador, m.; rascador, m.

erasure, *ĕrā'zhŭr*, s. rascadura, f.

ere, *ār*, ad. antes, más, pronto, antes que.

erect, *ĕrĕkt'*, v. a. erigir; establecer; —, a. derecho, levantado hacia arriba.

erection, *ĕrĕk'shŭn*, s. establecimiento, m.; estructura, f.

ermine, *ŭr'mĭn*, s. armiño, m.

erotic, *ĕrŏt'ĭk*, a. erótico.

err, *ŭr*, v. n. vagar, errar; desviarse.

errand, *ĕr'rănd*, s. recado, mensaje, m..

errand-boy, *-bŏĭ*, s. mozo de mandados, m.

errant, *ĕr'rănt*, a. errante; vagabundo.

errantry, *-rĕ*, s. vida errante, f.; caballería andante, f.

errata, *ĕrrā'tă*, s. pl. fe de erratas, f.

erratic, *ĕrrăt'ĭk*, a. errático, errante; irre-

erring, *ŭr'rĭng*, a. errado, errante. [gular.

erroneous, *ĕrrō'nĭăs*, a. erróneo; falso; —ly, ad. erróneamente. [errada, f.

error, *ĕr'rŭr*, s. error, yerro, m.; dirección

eructation, *ĕrăktā'shŭn*, s. eructación, f.;

erudite, *ĕr'ŭdĭt*, a. erudito. [eructo, ru.

erudition, *ĕrŭdĭsh'ŭn*, s. erudición, f.; doctrina, f.

eruption, *ĕrŭp'shŭn*, s. erupción, f.; excursión hostil, f.

erysipelas, *ĕrĭsĭp'ĕlăs*, s. erisipela, f.

escalade, *ĕskălād'*, s. escalada, f.

escape, *ĕskāp'*, v. a. evitar; escapar; —, v. n. evadirse, salvarse; —, s. escapada, huída, fuga, f.; inadvertencia, f.; to make one's — poner pies en polvorosa. [m.

escarpment, *ĕskărp'mĕnt*, s.(mil.) escarpe,

eschalot, *ĕshălŏt'*, s. (bot.) chalote, m.

escheat, *ĕstshēt'*, s. desherencia, f.; provecho inesperado, m.; —, v. n. caer en devolución, devolverse.

eschew, *ĕstshū'*, v. a. huir, evitar, evadir.

escort, *ĕs'kŏrt*, s. escolta, f.; —, *ĕskŏrt'*, v. a. escoltar, convoyar. [medero, (m.)

esculent, *ĕs'kŭlĕnt*, a. & s. comestible; co-

escutcheon, *ĕskŭtsh'ăn*, s. escudo, m.

esoteric, *ĕsŏtĕr'ĭk*, a. esotérico.

especial, *ĕspĕsh'ăl*, a. especial; —ly, ad. especialmente.

espial, *ĕspī'ăl*, s. espía, m.

espionage, *ĕspī'ŏnāj*, s. espionaje, m. [f.

esplanade, *ĕsplănād'*, s. (mil.) esplanada,

espousals, *ĕspŏu'zăls*, s. pl. esponsales, m. pl.

espouse, *ĕspŏuz'*, v. a. desposar. [brir.

espy, *ĕspī'*, v. a. espiar; percibir; descu-

Esquire, *ĕskwīr'*, s. Señor, m. (título).

essay, *ĕssā'*, v. a. ensayar, tentar, probar; —, *ĕs'sā*, s. conato, ensayo, m.; tentativa, f.; prueba, experiencia, f.

essayist, *ĕs'sāĭst*, s. tratadista, m.

essence, *ĕs'sĕns*, s. esencia, f.; perfume, m.

essential, *ĕssĕn'shăl*, s. esencia, f.; —, a. esendial substancial, principal; —ly, ad. esencialmente. [dar, fijar; confirmar.

establish, *ĕstăb'lĭsh*, v. a. establecer, fundar.

establishment, *-mĕnt*, s.establecimiento, m.; estatuto, m.; fundación, f.; institución, f. [hacienda, f.; bienes, m. pl.

estate, *ĕstāt'*, s. estado, m.; rango, m.;

esteem, *ĕstēm'*, v. a. estimar, apreciar; pensar; —, s. estima, f.; consideración, f.

esthetic(al), *ĕsthĕt'ĭk(ăl)*, a. estético; —s, s. pl. estética, f.

estimable, *ĕs'tĭmăbl*, a. estimable.

estimate, *ĕs'tĭmāt*, v. a. estimar, apreciar, tasar. [valuación, f.; opinión, f.

estimation, *ĕstĭmā'shŭn*, s. estimación, f.

estrange, *ĕstrānj'*, v. a. extrañar, apartar, enajenar.

estrangement, *-mĕnt*, s. enajenamiento, m.; extrañeza, distancia, f.

estuary, *ĕs'tūărĕ*, s. estuario, brazo de mar, m.; desembocadura de lago ó río, f.

etch, *ĕtsh*, v. a. grabar al agua fuerte.

etching, *-ĭng*, s. grabado al agua fuerte, m.

eternal, *ĕtŭr'năl*, a. eterno, perpetuo, inmortal; —ly, ad. eternamente.

eternity, *ĕtŭr'nĭtĕ*, s. eternidad, f.

ether, *ē'thŭr*, s. éter, m.

ethereal, *ĕthē'rĭăl*, a. etéreo, celeste.

etherealise, *-īz*, v. a. eterificar.

ethic(al), *ĕth'ĭk(ăl)*, a. ético; —ly, ad. moralmente; —s, s. pl. ética, f.

etymological, ĕtĭmŏlŏj'ĭkăl, a. etimológico. [m.
etymologist, ĕtĭmŏl'ŏjĕst, s. etimologista.
etymology, ĕtĭmŏl'ŏjē, s. etimología, f.
Eucharist, ū'kărĭst, s. Eucaristía, f.
eulogise, ū'lŏjĭz, v. a. elogiar.
eulogy, ū'lŏjĭ, s. elogio, encomio, m.; alabanza, f.
eunuch, ū'nŭk, s. eunuco, m. [banza, f.
euphemism, ū'fĕmĭzm, s. eufemismo, m.
euphony, ū'fŏnĕ, s. eufonía, f.
evacuate, ĕvăk'ūāt, v. a. evacuar. [ción.
evacuation, ĕvăkūā'shŭn, s. evacuación, f.
evade, ĕvād', v. a. evadir, escapar, evitar.
evanescent, ĕvănĕs'ĕnt, a. fugitivo; imperceptible.
evangelic(al), ĕvănjĕl'ĭk(ăl), a. evangélico; -ally, ad, evangélicamente.
evangelist, ĕvăn'jĕlĭst, s. evangelista, m.
evaporate, ĕvăp'ŏrāt, v. a. despedir vapores; -, v. n. evaporarse; disiparse.
evaporation, ĕvăp...., s. evaporación, f. [refugio, m.
evasion, ĕ...shŭn, s. evasión, f.; escape,
evasive, ĕvā'sĭv, a. evasivo; sofístico; -ly, ad. sofísticamente.
eve, ĕv, s. tardecita, f.; vigilia, víspera, f.
even, ē'vn, a. llano, igual; par, semejante; -, ad. aun; aun cuando, supuesto que; no obstante; - as, como; - now, ahora mismo; - on, derechamente; - so, lo mismo, de veras; - or odd, pares ó nones; -, v. a. igualar, allanar.
even-handed, -hăndĕd, a. imparcial, equitativo.
evening, -ĭng, s. tardecita, f.
evenly, -lĕ, ad. igualmente, llanamente.
evenness, -nĕs, s. igualdad, f.; uniformidad, f.; llanura, f.; imparcialidadf, f.
event, ĕvĕnt', s. evento, acontecimiento, m.; éxito, m.
eventful, -fŭl, a. lleno de acontecimientos.
eventual, ĕvĕn'tŭăl, a. eventual, fortuito; -ly, ad. por acaso. [f.
eventuality, -tŭăl'ĭtĕ, s. eventualidad,
ever, ĕv'ŭr, ad. siempre; for - and -, siempre jamás, eternamente; - since, después; - and anon, de cuando en cuando.
evergreen, -grēn, a. siempre verde; -, s. siemprepreviva (planta), f. [nidad, f.
everlasting, -lăst'ĭng, a. eterno; -, s., eternamente, para siempre jamás.
evermore, -mōr', ad. eternamente, para siempre jamás.
every, -ĕ, a, cada uno ó cada una; - where, en ó por todas partes; -thing, todo; -one, -body, cada uno, cada una.
evict, ĕvĭkt', v. a. despojar jurídicamente.
eviction, ĕvĭk'shŭn, s. evicción, f., despojo jurídico, m.
evidence, ĕv'ĭdĕns, s. evidencia, f.; testimonio, m., prueba, f.; -, v. a. evidenciar.
evident, ĕv'ĭdĕnt, a. evidente; patente, manifiesto; -ly, ad. evidentemente.
evil, ĕv'ĭl, a. malo, depravado, pernicioso; dañoso; -, s. maldad, f.; daño, m.; calamidad, f.
evil-doer, -dŏŭr, s. malhechor, m.
evilly, -lĕ, ad. malamente.

evil-minded, -mĭndĕd, a. malicioso, mal intencionado.
evil-speaking, -spēkĭng, s. maledicencia, murmuración, calumnia, f.
evince, ĕvĭns', v. a. probar, justificar, demostrar.
evocation, ĕvŏkā'shŭn, s. evocación, f.
evoke, ĕvōk', v. a. evocar.
evolution, ĕvŏlū'shŭn, s. desplegadura, f.; evolución, f.
evolve, ĕvŏlv', v. a. & n. desenvolver; desplegarse; extraer.
ewe, ū, s. oveja, f. (hembra del carnero).
ewer, -ŭr, s. palancana ó palangana, f.
exacerbate, ĕksăsĕr'bāt, v. a. exasperar.
exact, ĕgzăkt', a. exacto, puntual; cuidadoso; -, v. a. exigir. [sión, f.
exaction, ĕgzăk'shŭn, s. exacción, extorsión, f.
exactly, ĕgzăkt'lĕ, a. exactamente, puntualmente. [exactitud, f.
exactness, -nĕs, **exactitude**, s. -itud, s.
exaggerate, ĕgzăj'ŏrāt, v. a. exagerar.
exaggeration, ĕgzăjŭrā'shŭn, s. exageración, f. [bar; realzar.
exalt, ĕgzălt', v. a. exaltar, elevar; alabar; realzar.
exaltation, -tā'shŭn, s. exaltación, elevación, f. [m.
examination, ĕgzămĭnā'shŭn, s. examen,
examine, ĕgzăm'ĭn, v. a. examinar; escudriñar. [plo, m.
example, ĕgzăm'pl, s. ejemplar, m.; ejemplo, m.
exasperate, ĕgzăs'pĕrāt, v. a. exasperar, irritar, enojar, provocar; agravar, amargar. [peración, irritación, f.
exasperation, ĕgzăspŭrā'shŭn, s. exasperación, irritación, f.
excavate, ĕks'kăvāt, v. a. excavar, ahondar. [f.; cavidad, f.; excava, f.
excavation, ĕkskăvā'shŭn, s. excavación, f.
exceed, ĕksēd', v. a. exceder; sobrepujar; -, v. n. excederse.
exceeding, -ĭng, a. excesivo; -ly, ad. extremamente, en sumo grado.
excel, ĕksĕl', v. a. sobresalir, exceder.
excellence, ĕk'sĕlĕns, s. excelencia, f.; preeminencia, f. [tulo), f.
Excellency, ĕk'sĕlĕnsĕ, s. Excelencia (título), f.
excellent, ĕk'sĕlĕnt, a. excelente; -ly, ad. excelentemente.
except, ĕksĕpt', v. a. exceptuar, excluir; -, v. n. recusar; -(ing), pr. excepto, á excepción de. [clusión, f.
exception, ĕksĕp'shŭn, s. excepción, exclusión, f.
exceptionable, -ăbl, a. recusable, expuesto á reparos y contradicciones.
exceptional, -ăl, a. excepcional.
excerpt, ĕksĕrpt', v. a. extraer.
excess, ĕksĕs', s. exceso, m.; intemperancia, f. [cesivamente.
excessive, -sĭv, a. excesivo; -ly, ad. excesivamente.
exchange, ĕkstshānj', v. a. cambiar; trocar, permutar; -, s. cambio, m.; bolsa, lonja, f.
exchangeable, -ăbl, a. cambiable.
exchequer, ĕkstshĕk'ŭr, s. fisco, m.; tesorería, f.
exchequer-bill, -bĭl, **exchequer-bond**, -bŏnd, s. vale real, m.

excise, *ĕksīz',* s. sisa, f.

exciseman, *–măn,* s. sisero, m. [f.

excitability, *ĕksītăbĭl'ĭtē,* s. excitabilidad,

excitable, *ĕkst'tăbl,* a. excitable.

excite, *ĕksīt',* v. a. excitar; estimular.

excitement, *–mĕnt,* s. estímulo, incita-
miento, m. [mucho.

Exolaim, *ĕksklām',* v. n. exclamar, clamar

exclamation, *–klămā'shŭn,* s. exclamación, f.; clamor, m. [torio.

exclamatory, *ĕksklăm'ătărĕ,* a. exclama-

exclude, *ĕksklūd',* v. a. excluir; exceptuar.

exclusion, *–klū'shŭn,* s. exclusión, f.
clusiva, excepción, f.

exclusive, *–klū'sĭv,* a. exclusivo; **–ly,**
ad. exclusivamente. [excomulgar.

excommunicate, *ĕkskŏmmū'nĭkāt,* v.a.

excommunication, *–kā'shŭn,* s. excomunión, f. [f.

excoriation, *ĕkskōrē'ā'shŭn,* s. excoriación,

excrement, *ĕks'krēmĕnt,* s. excremento,
m., materias fecales, f. pl. [cia, f.

excrescence, *ĕkskrĕs'sĕns,* s. excrescen-

excruciating, *ĕkskrō'shĭātĭng,* a. atroz,
enorme, grave. [justificar.

exculpate, *ĕkskŭl'pāt,* v. a. disculpar;

exculpation, *–pā'shŭn,* s. disculpa, f.

exculpatory, *–pătărĕ,* a. justificativo.

excursion, *ĕkskŭr'shŭn,* s. excursión, f.;
digresión, f. [siones.

excursionist, *–ĭst,* s. el que hace excur-

excusable, *ĕkskū'zăbl,* a. excusable.

excuse, *ĕkskūz',* v. a. excusar; perdonar;
–, s. excusa, f. [testable.

execrable, *ĕks'ēkrăbl,* a. execrable, de-

execrably, *–ē,* ad. execrablemente.

execrate, *–ēkrāt,* v. a. execrar, maldecir.

execration, *–krā'shŭn,* s. execración,
maldición, f. [ciar.

execute, *ĕks'ēkūt,* v. a. ejecutar; ajusti-

execution, *–kū'shŭn,* s. ejecución, f.

executioner, *–ăr,* s. ejecutor, m.; verdugo, m.

executive, *ĕgzĕk'ūtĭv,* a. ejecutivo.

executor, *–ătăr,* s. testamentario, m.

executrix, *–ătrĭks,* s. (law) albacea, eje-
cutora testamentaria, f.

exemplar, *ĕgzĕm'plăr,* s. ejemplar, original, modelo, m.

exemplary, *ĕgzĕm'plărĕ,* a. ejemplar.

exemplify, *ĕgzĕm'plĭfī,* v.a. ejemplificar.

exempt, *ĕgzĕmt',* a. exento, libre por privilegio. [quicia, f.

exemption, *ĕgzĕm'shŭn,* s. exención, fran-

exercise, *ĕk'sŭrsĭz,* s. ejercicio, m.; ensayo, m.; tarea, f.; práctica, f.; **–,** v. n.
hacer ejercicio; **–,** v. a. ejercitar; atarear.

exert, *ĕgzŭrt',* v. a. emplear; **to –one's
self,** esforzarse.

exertion, *ĕgzŭr'shŭn,* s. esfuerzo, m.

exfoliate, *ĕksfō'lĭāt,* v. n. exfoliarse.

exfoliation, *ĕksfōlĭā'shŭn,* s. exfoliación,f.

exhalation, *ĕgzhălā'shŭn,* s. exhalación,
f.; vapor, m.

exhale, *ĕgzhāl',* v. a. exhalar.

exhaust, *ĕgzhăst',* v. a. apurar, agotar.

Exhaustion, *ĕgzhăs'tyŭn,* s. agotamiento,
m., extenuación, f.

exhaustive, *–ĭv,* a. agotable.

exhibit, *ĕgzhĭb'ĭt,* v. a. exhibir; mostrar;
–, s. (law) memorial, libelo, m.

exhibition, *ĕgzhĭbĭsh'ŭn,* s. exhibición,
presentación, f.; beca, f.; espectáculo, m.

exhibitioner, *–ăr,* s. beca, f., colegial
prebendado, m. [público, m.

exhibitor, *ĕgzhĭb'ĭtăr,* s. ostentador en

exhilarate, *ĕgzhĭl'ărāt,* v. a. alegrar,
causar alegría.

exhilaration, *–rā'shŭn,* s. alegría, f.;
buen humor, regocijo, m.

exhort, *ĕgzhŏrt',* v. a. exhortar, excitar.

exhortation, *–tā'shŭn,* s. exhortación, f.

exhume, *ĕks hūm',* v. a. exhumar, desenterrar. [dad, urgencia, f.

exigency, *ĕks'ĭjĕnsē,* s. exigencia, necesi-

exile, *ĕg'zĭl,* s. destierro, m.; **–,** v. a.
desterrar, deportar.

exist, *ĕgzĭst',* v. n. existir.

existence, *–ĕns,* s. existencia, f.

existent, *–ĕnt,* a. existente.

existing, *–ĭng,* a. actual, presente.

exit, *ĕks'ĭt,* s. partida, salida, f.; éxito, m.

exonerate, *ĕgzŏn'ărāt,* v. a. exonerar,
descargar.

exoneration, *–rā'shŭn,* s. exoneración, f.

exorbitance, *ĕgzŏr'bĭtăns,* s. exorbitancia,
enormidad, f. [cesivo.

exorbitant, *–bĭtănt,* a. exorbitante, ex-

exorcise, *ĕks'ŏrsīz,* v. a. exorcizar, conjurar.

exorcism, *–ŏrsĭzm,* s. exorcismo, m.

exordium, *ĕgzŏr'dĭŭm,* s. exordio, m.

exotic, *ĕgzŏt'ĭk,* a. exótico, extranjero; **–,**
s. planta exótica, f.

expand, *ĕkspănd',* v. a. extender, dilatar.

expanse, *ĕkspăns',* s. extensión de lugar, f.

expansion, *–shŭn,* s. expansión, f.

expansive, *–sĭv,* a. expansivo.

expatiate, *ĕkspā'shĭāt,* v. n. espaciarse.

expatriate, *–trĭāt,* v. a. expatriar.

expect, *ĕkspĕkt',* v. a. esperar, aguardar.

expectance, *–ăns,* **expectancy,** *–ē,* s.
expectación, esperanza, f.

expectant, *–ănt,* s. esperador, m.

expectation, *–tā'shŭn,* s. expectación,
expectativa, f. [torar.

expectorate, *ĕkspĕk'tŏrāt,* v. a. expec-

expectoration, *–rā'shŭn,* s. expectoración, f. [conveniencia, oportunidad, f.

expediency, *ĕkspē'dĭĕnsē,* s. propiedad, f.

expedient, *–dĭĕnt,* a. oportuno, conveniente; **–,** s. expediente, medio, m.; **–ly,**
ad. convenientemente. [dir.

expedite, *ĕks'pēdīt,* v. a. acelerar; expe-

expedition, *–dĭsh'ŭn,* s. expedición,
priesa, f. [–ly, ad. prontamente.

expeditious, *–ŭs,* a. pronto, expedito;

expel, *ĕkspĕl',* v. a. expeler, desterrar.

expend, *ĕkspĕnd',* v. a. expender; desembolsar. [embolso, m.

expenditure, *ĕkspĕn'dĭtăr,* s. gasto, des-

expense, *ĕkspĕns',* s. expensas, f. pl.;
coste, m.

expensive, *ĕkspĕn'sĭv,* a. pródigo; costoso; **–ly,** ad. costosamente.

experience, *ĕkspē'rĭĕns,* s. experiencia, f.;
práctica, f.; **–,** v. a. experimentar.

experiment, *ĕkspĕr'ĭmĕnt,* s. experimento,
m.; **–,** v. a. experimentar.

experimental, ĕkspĕrĭmĕn'tắl, a. experimental; –ly, ad. experimentalmente.

expert, ĕkspŭrt', a. experto, práctico, diestro; –ly, ad. diestramente.

expertness, –nĕs, s. maña, destreza, habilidad, f. [daño.

expiate, ĕks'pĭất, v. a. expiar; reparar un

expiation, ĕkspĭ ăshŭn, s. expiación, f.

expiatory, –tŭrĕ, a. expiatorio.

expiration, ĕkspĭră shŭn, s. expiración, f.; muerte, f.; vapor, vaho, m.

expire, ĕkspīr', v. n. expirar.

explain, ĕksplăn', v. a. explanar, explicar.

explanation, ĕksplắnă shŭn, s. explanación, explicación, f.

explanatory, ĕkplăn'ătărĕ, a. explicativo.

expletive, ĕks'plĕtĭv, a. expletivo.

explicable, ĕks'plĭkăbl, a. explicable. [f.

explication, ĕksplĭkắ shŭn, s. explicación, f.

explicit, ĕksplĭs'ĭt, a. explícito; –ly, ad. explícitamente.

explode, ĕksplōd', v. a. & n. disparar con estallido; reprobar; condenar.

exploit, ĕksplŏĭt', s. hazaña, f.; hecho heroico, m. [ción, f.; examen, m.

exploration, ĕksplŏră shŭn, s. exploración.

explore, ĕksplŏr', v. a. explorar, examinar; sondear.

explosion, ĕksplŏ zhŭn, s. explosión, f.

explosive, –sĭv, a. explosivo; – cotton, s. piróxilo, m. [m.

exponent, ĕkspŏ'nĕnt, s. (ar.) exponente.

export, ĕkspŏrt', v. a. exportar.

export, ĕks'pŏrt, exportation, ĕkspŏr tă'shŭn, s. exportación, f.

expose, ĕkspŏz', v. a. exponer; mostrar; descubrir; poner en peligro.

exposition, ĕkspŏzĭsh'ŭn, s. exposición, f.; interpretación, f. [contender.

expostulate, ĕkspŏs'tŭlăt, v. n. debatir.

expostulation, ĕkspŏstŭlă shŭn, s. debate, m.; disputa, f.

exposure, ĕkspŏ'zhŭr, s. situación peligrosa, f.; exposición, f. [pretar.

expound, ĕkspŏŭnd', v. a. exponer; inter-

express, ĕksprĕs', v. a. exprimir; representar; –, a. expreso, claro; á propósito; –, s. expreso, correo, m.; (rail.) tren expreso, m.

expression, ĕksprĕsh'ŭn, s. expresión, f.; locución, f.; animación del rostro, f.

expressionless, –lĕs, a. sin expresión (cara). [expresivamente.

expressive, –sĭv, a. expresivo; –ly, ad.

expressly, –lĕ, ad. expresamente.

expropriate, ĕksprŏ'prĭất, v. a. expropiar (por causa de utilidad pública).

expropriation, ĕksprŏprĭă shŭn, s. (law) expropiación, f.

expulsion, ĕkspŭl'shŭn, s. expulsión, f.

expunge, ĕkspŭnj', v. a. borrar, cancelar.

expurgate, ĕkspŭr'găt, v. a. expurgar.

expurgation, –gă'shŭn, s. purificación, f.; expurgo, m.

exquisite, ĕks'kwĭzĭt, a. exquisito, perfecto, excelente; –ly, ad. exquisitamente.

exquisiteness, –nĕs, s. primor, m., excelencia, f.

extant, ĕks'tănt, s. estante, existente.

extemporaneous, ĕkstĕmpŏră nŭs, extemporary, ĕkstĕm'pŏrărĕ, a. extemporáneo, improviso. [in promptu.

extempore, ĕkstĕm'pŏrĕ, ad. de improviso.

extemporize, –pŏrĭz, v. n. improvisar.

extend, ĕkstĕnd', v. a. extender; amplificar; –, v. n. extenderse.

extension, ĕkstĕn'shŭn, s. extensión, f.

extensive, –sĭv, a. extenso, dilatado; –ly, ad. extensivamente.

extent, ĕkstĕnt', s. extensión, f.

extenuate, ĕkstĕn'ŭăt, v. a. extenuar, disminuir, atenuar. [mitigación, f.

extenuation, –ă'shŭn, s. extenuación, f.; exterior, ĕkstĕ'rĭŭr, a. & s. exterior (m.).

exteriority, ĕkstĕrĭŏr'ĭtĕ, s. exterioridad, f. [nar; extirpar.

exterminate, ĕkstŭr'mĭnăt, v. a. extermi-

extermination, –nă'shŭn, s. exterminación, extirpación, f.

external, ĕkstŭr'năl, a. externo; –ly, ad. exteriormente; –s, s. pl. exterior, m.

extinct, ĕkstĭngkt', a. extinto; abolido.

extinction, ĕkstĭngk'shŭn, s. extinción, f.; abolición, f. [guir; suprimir.

extinguish, ĕkstĭng'gwĭsh, v. a. extin-

extinguisher, –ŭr, s. matacandelas, m.

extirpate, ĕkstŭr'păt, v. a. extirpar.

extirpation, –pă'shŭn, s. extirpación, f.; exterminio, m. [zar, exaltar.

extol, ĕkstŏl', v. a. alabar, magnificar, al-

extort, ĕkstŏrt', v. a. sacar por fuerza; adquirir por violencia.

extortion, ĕkstŏr'shŭn, s. extorsión, f.

extortionate, –ăt, a. violento.

extortioner, –ŭr, s. exactor, m.

extra, ĕks'tră, ad. extra; –, –special, s. suplemento extraordinario de un periódico, m.

extract, ĕkstrăkt', v. a. extraer; extractar; –, ĕks'trăkt, s. extracto, m.; compendio, m.

extraction, ĕkstrăk'shŭn, s. extracción, f.; descendencia, f. [dición, f.

extradition, ĕkstrădĭsh'ŭn, s. (law) extra-

extraneous, ĕkstră'nŭs, a. extraño, exótico. [extraordinariamente.

extraordinarily, ĕkstrăŏr'dĭnărĭlĕ, ad.

extraordinary, –dĭnărĕ, a. extraordinario.

extravagance, ĕkstrăv'ăgăns, s. extravagancia, f.; gastos excesivos, m. pl.

extravagant, –ăgănt, a. extravagante, singular, exorbitante; pródigo; –ly, ad. extravagantemente.

extreme, ĕkstrĕm', a. extremo, supremo; último; –, s. extremo, m.; –ly, ad. extremamente.

extremity, ĕkstrĕm'ĭtĕ, s. extremidad, f.

extricate, ĕks'trĭkăt, v. a. desembarazar, desenredar. [zo, desempeño, m.

extrication, ĕkstrĭkă shŭn, s. desembar-

extrinsic(al), ĕkstrĭn'sĭk(ăl), a. extrínseco, exterior. [tuberancia, f.

exuberance, ĕkstŭ'bŭrăns, s. (med.) protuberancia, f.

exuberancy, ĕgzŭ'bŭrăns, s. exuberancia, suma abundancia, f.

exuberant, –bŭrănt, a. exuberante, abundantísimo; –ly, ad. abundantemente.

exude, ĕksŭd', v. n. transpirar. [triunfar.

exult, ĕgzŭlt', v. a. exultar, regocijarse

exultation, –tĕ'shŭn, s. exultación, f.; regocijo, m.

eye, s. ojo, m.; corcheta, f.; (bot.) yema, f., botón, m.; –, v. a. ojear, contemplar, observar.

eye-ball, –bŏl, s. niña del ojo, f.

eye-brow, –brŏw, s. ceja, f. [ocular, f.

eye-glass, –glŭs, s. anteojo, m.; lente

eye-lash, –lŭsh, s. pestaña, f.

eyeless, –lĕs, a. ciego; sin ojos.

eyelet, –lĕt, s. resquicio, m.; ojete, m.

eye-lid, –lĭd, s. párpado, m. [vista, f.

eye-sight, –sĭt, s. potencia visiva, f.;

eye-sore, –sŏr, s. mal de ojos, m.

eye-tooth, –tŏth, s. colmillo, m.

eye-wash, –wŏsh, s. colirio, m.

eye-witness, –wĭtnĕs, s. testigo ocular, m.

eyry, eyrie, ā'rĕ, s. nido de ave de rapiña, m.

fail, fāl, v. a. & n. omitir, abandonar; descuidar; faltar; perecer; perderse; –, s. desgracia, f.; omisión, f.

failing, –ĭng, s. falta, f.; defecto, m.

failure, –ŭr, s. falta, f.; culpa, f.; descuido, m.; quiebra, bancarrota, f.

fain, fān, a. obligado, estrechado; –, ad. de buena gana.

faint, fānt, v. n. desmayarse, debilitarse; –, s. deliquio, m.; –, a. lánguido; cobarde; –ly, ad. desmayadamente, débilmente.

faint-hearted, –hārtĕd, a. cobarde, medroso, pusilánime; –ly, ad. medrosamente.

faintness, –nĕs, s. languidez, flaqueza, f.; timidez, f.

fair, fār, a. hermoso, bello; blanco; rubio; claro, sereno; favorable; recto, justo; franco; –, ad. cortésmente; con buena armonía; –, s. feria, f.; belleza, f.

fairing, –ĭng, s. ferias, f. pl.

fairly, –lĭ, ad. bellamente; agradablemente, ingenuamente. [f.; candor, m.

fairness, –nĕs, s. hermosura, f.; honradez,

fair-spoken, –spŏkn, a. bien hablado, cortés.

F.

fable, fā'bl, s. fábula, f.; ficción, f.

fabric, făb'rĭk, s. fábrica, f.; edificio, m.; manufactura, f.; tejido, m.

fabricate, –rĭkāt, v. a. fabricar, edificar.

fabrication, –kā'shŭn, s. fabricación, f.

fabulous, făb'ŭlŭs, a. fabuloso; –ly, ad. fabulosamente.

face, fās, s. cara, faz, f.; haz, f.; superficie, f.; fachada, f.; frente, f.; aspecto, m.; apariencia, f.; atrevimiento, m.; in my –, á mi presencia; –, v. a. encararse; hacer frente; volver un naipe.

face-ache, –āk, s. nevralgia facial, f.

faced, –d, a. con cara (in comp.).

facet, fās'ĕt, s. faceta, f.

facetious, fāsē'shŭs, a. chistoso, alegre, gracioso; –ly, ad. chistosamente.

facial, fā'shĭăl, a. facial.

facile, fās'ĭl, a. fácil, afable.

facilitate, fāsĭl'ĭtāt, v. a. facilitar.

facility, –tĭ, s. facilidad, ligereza, f.; afabilidad, f. [frente.

facing, fā'sĭng, s. paramento, m.; –, pr. en

fac-simile, făksĭm'ĭlē, s. facsímile, m.

fact, făkt, s. hecho, m.; realidad, f.; in –, con ó en efecto; in the –, en el acto.

faction, făk'shŭn, s. facción, f.; disensión, f.

factionist, –ĭst, s. faccioso, inquieto, m.

factious, făk'shŭs, a. faccioso; –ly, ad. sediciosamente. [m.

factiousness, –nĕs, s. espíritu de facción, f.

factitious, făktĭsh'ŭs, a. facticio.

factor, făk'tŭr, s. factor (agente), m.; (ar.)

factory, –ĕ, s. factoría, f. [factor.

factotum, făktŏ'tŭm, s. criado que hace de todo, m. [privilegio, m.

faculty, făk'ŭltĭ, s. facultad, f.; poder,

fad, făd, s. fruslería, niñería, f.

fade, fād, v. n. decaer, marchitarse, fallecer.

fag, făg, s. trabajador, m.; esclavo, m.; nudo en el paño, m.; –, v. n. desmayarse.

fag-end, –ĕnd, s. cadillos, m. pl.

fagot, făg'ŏt, s. haz, m., gavilla de leña, f.

fairy, –ĭ, s. duende, m.; bruja, encantadora, f.; –, a. lo que pertenece á los duendes.

faith, fāth, s. fe, f.; dogma de fe, m.; fidelidad, sinceridad, f. [mente.

faithful, –fŭl, a. fiel, leal; –ly, ad. fielmente.

faithfulness, –nĕs, s. fidelidad, lealtad, f.

faithless, –lĕs, a. infiel, pérfido, desleal.

falchion, făl'shŭn, s. cimitarra, f. (espada corta).

falcon, fŏl'kn, s. halcón, m. [corta).

falconer, –ĕr, s. halconero, m.

falconry, –rĕ, s. halconería, f.

fall, fŏl, v. n. caer(se); perder el poder; disminuir, decrecer en precio; to – asleep, dormirse; to – short, faltar, chasquear; to – sick, enfermar; to – in love, enamorarse; to – off, desaparecer, disolverse; separarse; apostatar; to – out, reñir, disputar; acaecer, acontecer; to – upon, atacar, asaltar; –, s. caída, f.; declive, m.; catarata, f.

fallacious, fălā'shŭs, a. falaz, fraudulento; –ly, ad. falazmente. [engaño, m.

fallacy, făl'lăsĕ, s. falacia, sofistería, f.

fallibility, fălĭbĭl'ĭtĕ, s. falibilidad, f.

fallible, făl'ĭbl, a. falible. [lepsia, f.

falling-sickness, fŏl'ĭngsĭknĕs, s. epi-

fallow, făl'lŏ, a. flavo; – deer, s. corzo, m.; corza, f. [terreno, f.

fallowness, –nĕs, s. esterilidad de algún terreno, f.

false, fŏls, a. falso, pérfido; –ly, ad. falsamente; pérfidamente.

falsehood, –hŭd, s. falsedad, falseness, –nĕs, s. falsedad, f.; perfidia, f.

falsify, fŏl'sĭfī, v. a. falsificar.

falsity, –sĭtĕ, s. falsedad, mentira, f.

falter, fŏl'tĕr, v. n. tartamudear; faltar.

faltering, –ĭng, s. debilidad, f.; defecto, m.; –ly, ad. balbuciente, tartamudo; con lengua tropezosa.

fame, fām, s. fama, f.; renombre, m.

famed, –d, a. celebrado, famoso.

familiar, fămĭl'yăr, a. familiar; casero; –ly, ad. familiarmente; –, s. amigo íntimo, m.

familiarity, *familiär'ĭtĕ,* s. familiaridad, f.

familiarize, *fămĭl'yärĭz,* v.a. familiarizar.

family, *făm'ĭlĕ,* s. familia, f.; linaje, m.; clase, especie, f.

famine, *făm'ĭn,* s. hambre, f.; carestía, f.

famish, *—ĭsh,* v. a. hambrear; —, v. n. morirse de hambre.   [ad. famosamente.

famous, *fā'mŭs,* a. famoso, afamado; —ly, ad.

fan, *făn,* s. abanico, m.; aventador, m.; —, v. a. abanicar; aventar.

fanatic, *fănăt'ĭk,* a. & s. fanático (m.).

fanaticism, *—ĭsĭzm,* s. fanatismo, m.

fanciful, *făn'sĭfŭl,* a. imaginativo, caprichoso; —ly, ad. caprichosamente.

fancifulness, *—nĕs,* s. antojo, capricho, m.

fancy, *făn'sĕ,* s. fantasía, imaginación, f.; capricho, m.; —, v. a. imaginar; amar; —, v. n. apasionarse, figurarse; fantasear.

fancy-articles, *—ärtĭkls,* fancy-goods, *—gŭds,* s. pl. novedades, modas, f. pl.

fancy-ball, *—băl,* s. baile de máscaras, m.

fancy-fair, *—fār,* s. bazar, m.

fancy-sick, *—sĭk,* a. enfermo imaginario.

fanfare, *făn'fār,* s. (mus.) charanga, f.

fang, *făng,* s. colmillo, m.; garra, uña, f.

fanged, *—d,* a. colmilludo.

fantastic(al), *făntăs'tĭk(ăl),* a. fantástico; caprichoso; —ally, ad. fantásticamente.

fantasticalness, *—dĭnĕs,* s. fantasía, f.; capricho, m.

fantasy, *făn'tăsĕ,* s. fantasía, f.

far, *fär,* ad. lejos, á una gran distancia; —, a. lejano, distante, remoto; — and away, con mucho, de mucho; — off, lejano.

farce, *färs,* s. farsa, f.   [lejano.

farcical, *fär'sĭkăl,* a. burlesco.

farcy, *fär'sĕ,* s. lamparones, m. pl.

fardel, *fär'dĕl,* s. fardel, fardillo, m.

fare, *fār,* s. comida, f.; viajero, m.; pasaje, m.; —, v. n. viajar; encontrarse.

farewell, *—wĕl',* s. despedida, f.; —! ad. ¡á Dios! ¡siga U. bueno!   [farináceo.

farinaceous, *fărĭnā'shŭs,* a. harináceo.

farm, *färm,* s. tierra arrendada, f.; arquería, f.; —, v. a. arrendar; tomar en arriendo; cultivar.

farmer, *—ăr,* s. arrendatario de tierra labrantía, m.; labrador, m.

farming, *—ĭng,* s. agricultura, f.

farm-yard, *—yärd,* s. corral, m.

farrago, *fărrā'gō,* s. fárrago, m.; broza, f.

farrier, *fär'rĭĕr,* s. herrador, m.

farriery, *—ĕ,* s. albeitería, f.

farrow, *fär'rō,* s. lechigada de puercos, f.; —, v. a. parir la puerca.

far-seeing, *fär'sēĭng,* a. perspicaz.

farther, *fär'thŭr,* ad. más lejos; más adelante; —, a. más lejos, ulterior.

farthest, *fär'thĕst,* ad. lo más lejos; lo más tarde; á lo más.   [m.; ardite, m.

farthing, *fär'thĭng,* s. cuarto de penique.

fascinate, *făs'ĭnāt,* v. a. fascinar, encantar.

fascination, *—nā'shŭn,* s. fascinación, f.; encanto, m.

fascine, *făssēn',* s. fagina, haz, f.

fashion, *făsh'ŭn,* s. forma, figura, f.; moda, f.; uso, m.; condición (de nacimiento), f.;

people of —, gente de tono, f.; —, v. a, formar, amoldar.

fashionable, *—ăbl,* a. hecho á la moda; elegante; the — world, el gran mundo; —bly, ad. á ó según la moda.

fashionableness, *—nĕs,* s. moda, elegancia, f.

fast, *făst,* v. n. ayunar; —, s. ayuno, m.; —, a. firme, estable; veloz, pronto; —, ad. firmemente; estrechamente; de priesa; á menudo.

fast-day, *—dā,* s. día de ayuno, m.

fasten, *făs'n,* v.a. afirmar, asegurar, atar; fijar; —, v. n. fijarse, establecerse.

faster, *făst'ăr,* s. ayunador, m.

fastidious, *făstĭd'ĭŭs,* a. fastidioso, desdeñoso; —ly, ad. fastidiosamente.

fastness, *făst'nĕs,* s. prontitud, f.; firmeza, f.; fortaleza, f.   [grasa, f.

fat, *făt,* a. gordo, pingüe; —, s. gordo, m.; —, v. a. engordar.

fatal, *fā'tăl,* a. fatal; funesto; —ly, ad.

fatalist, *—ĭst,* s. fatalista, m.   [fatalmente.

fatality, *fătăl'ĭtĕ,* s. fatalidad, predestinación, f.   [Parcas, f. pl.

fate, *fāt,* s. hado, destino, m.; —s, pl. (poet.)

fated, *—ĕd,* a. lo que está decretado por los hados.

fateful, *fāt'fŭl,* a. fatídico.   [hados.

father, *fä'thŭr,* s. padre, m.

fatherhood, *—hŭd,* s. paternidad, f.

father-in-law, *—ĭnlä,* s. suegro, m.

fatherland, *—lănd,* s. patria, f.

fatherless, *—lĕs,* a. huérfano de padre.

fatherly, *—lĕ,* a. (& ad.) paternal(mente).

fathom, *făth'ŭm,* s. braza (medida), f.; —, v. a. abrazar; sondar; penetrar.

fathomless, *—lĕs,* a. insondable.   [cansar.

fatigue, *fătēg',* s. fatiga, f.; —, v. a. fatigar,

fatigue-party, *—pärtĕ,* s. (mil.) servicio, m.; función, f.

fatling, *făt'lĭng,* s. cebón, m.

fatness, *făt'nĕs,* s. gordura, pinguosidad, f.

fatten, *făt'n,* v. a. cebar, engordar; —, v. n. engrosarse.

fattening, *—ĭng,* s. cebadura, f.

fatty, *făt'ĕ,* a. untoso, craso, pingüe.

fatuity, *fătū'ĭtĕ,* s. fatuidad, simpleza, f.

fatuous, *făt'ŭŭs,* a. fatuo, tonto, imbécil.

fault, *fält,* s. falta, culpa, f.; delito, m.; defecto, m.

fault-finder, *—fĭndăr,* s. censurador, m.

faultily, *—tĭlĕ,* ad. defectuosamente.   [m.

faultiness, *—tĭnĕs,* s. culpa, f.; defecto,

faultless, *—lĕs,* a. perfecto, cumplido.

faulty, *—ĕ,* a. culpable, defectuoso.

faun, *fän,* s. fauno, m.

favour, *fā'vŭr,* s. favor, beneficio, m.; patrocinio, m.; blandura, f.; with (ó under) your —, con licencia ó permiso de U.; —, v. a. favorecer, proteger.

favourable, *—ăbl,* a. favorable, propicio; —bly, ad. favorablemente.

favoured, *—d,* a. favorecido.   [cido.

favourite, *—ĭt,* s. favorito, m.; —, a. favore-

fawn, *fän,* s. cervato, m.; —, v. n. parir la cierva; adular servilmente.

fawningly, *—ĭnglĕ,* ad. lisonjeramente, con adulación servil.   [con otra.

fay, *fā,* v. n. cuadrar, venir bien una cosa

realty, *rĕ′ălti,* s. homenaje, m.; fidelidad, lealtad, f. [miedo, m.

fear, *fēr,* v. a. espantar; —, v. n. temer; —, s.

fearful, *fēr′fŭl,* a. medroso, temeroso; tímido; **-ly,** ad. medrosamente, temerosamente.

fearless, *-lĕs,* a. intrépido, atrevido; **-ly,** ad. sin miedo.

fearlessness, *-nĕs,* s. intrepidez, f.

feasibility, *fēzibĭl′ĭtĭ,* s. posibilidad, f.

feasible, *fē′zŏbl,* a. factible, hacedero.

feast, *fēst,* s. banquete, festín, m.; fiesta, f.; —, v. a. festejar, regalar; —, v. n. comer opíparamente.

feaster, *-ŭr,* s. goloso, m.; anfitrión, m.

feat, *fēt,* s. hecho, m.; acción, hazaña, f.

feather, *fĕth′ŭr,* s. pluma, f.; (fig.) bagatela, f.; —, v. a. emplumar; enriquecer.

feather-bed, *-bĕd,* s. plumón, m.; colcedra, f. [plumita.

feathery, *-ĭ,* a. plumado; ligero como una pluma.

feature, *fē′tŭr,* s. rostro, m.; facción del rostro, f.; forma, f.

febrile, *fēb′rĭl,* a. febril.

February, *fĕb′rŏŏrĭ,* s. febrero, m.

fecula, *fĕk′ūlă,* s. fécula, f.

fecund, *fĕk′ŭnd,* a. fecundo, fértil.

fecundity, *fēkŭn′dĭtĭ,* s. fecundidad, fertilidad, f.; abundancia, f.

federal, *fĕd′ĕrăl,* a. federal.

federalist, *-ĭst,* s. federalista, m.

federate, *fĕd′ĕrăt,* a. confederado, m.

federation, *-ā′shŭn,* s. confederación, f.

fee, *fē,* s. feudo, m.; paga, gratificación, f.; salario, m.; —, v. a. pagar; premiar; sobornar.

feeble, *fē′bl,* a. flaco, débil. [bornar.

feebleness, *-nĕs,* s. debilidad, f.

feebly, *-blĕ,* ad. débilmente.

feed, *fēd,* v. a. pacer; nutrir; alimentar; —, v. n. nutrirse; engordar; —, s. alimento, m.; pasto, m.

feeder, *-ŭr,* s. el que da de comer, m.; glotón, m.; babadero, m.; tolva de molino, f.

feeding-bottle, *-ĭngbŏt′l,* s. bebedero, m.

feel, *fēl,* v. a. sentir; palpar; —, v. n. tener sensibilidad; —, s. tacto, sentido, m.

feeler, *-ŭr,* s. antenas, f. pl.; (fig.) tentativa, m.; —, s. tacto, m.; sensibilidad, f.

feelingly, *-ĭnglĕ,* ad. sensiblemente. [f.

feeling, *-ĭng,* s. tacto, m.; sensibilidad,

feet, *fēt,* s. pl. (de foot) (anat.) infantería, f.

feign, *fān,* a. inventar; fingir; disimular; —, v. n. referir falsedades imaginadas.

feignedly, *-ĕdlĕ,* ad. fingidamente.

feint, *fānt,* s. ficción, f.; finta, f.

felicitate, *fēlĭs′ĭtăt,* v. a. felicitar; congratularse (con otro). [gratulación, f.

felicitation, *-ā′shŭn,* s. felicitación, con-

felicitous, *fēlĭs′ĭtŭs,* a. feliz, dichoso.

felicity, *-ĭtĭ,* s. felicidad, dicha, f.

feline, *fē′lĭn,* a. gatuno.

fell, *fĕl,* a. cruel, bárbaro; —, s. cuero, m.; piel, f.; pellejo, m.; —, v. a. matar las reses; cortar árboles.

fellow, *fĕl′ō,* s. compañero, camarada, m.; socio de algún colegio, m. [m.

fellow-citizen, *-sĭtĭzn,* s. conciudadano,

fellow-creature, *-krē′tŭr,* s. prójimo, m.

fellow-feeling, *-fēlĭng,* s. simpatía, f.

fellow-prisoner, *-prĭz′ōnŭr,* s. compañero de prisión, m.

fellowship, *-shĭp,* s. compañía, sociedad, f.; beca, (en un colegio) f.

fellow-soldier, *-sōl′jŭr,* s. conmilitón, m.

fellow-student, *-stūdĕnt,* s. condiscípulo, m. [de infortunio, m.

fellow-sufferer, *-sŭf′ŭrŭr,* s. compañero

fellow-traveller, *-trăv′ĕlŭr,* s. compañero de viaje, m.

felly, *fĕl′lĭ,* s. pina de una rueda, f.

felon, *fĕl′ŏn,* s. reo de un delito capital, m.; —, a. cruel, traidor.

felonious, *fēlō′nĭŭs,* a. traidor, pérfido; **-ly,** ad. traidoramente.

felony, *fĕl′ŏnĭ,* s. felonía, f.

felt, *fĕlt,* s. fieltro, m.; pellejo, m.

felucca, *fēlŭk′kă,* s. faluca, f.

female, *fē′măl,* s. hembra, f.; —, a. femenino. [terno; afeminado, amujerado.

feminine, *fĕm′ĭnĭn,* a. femenino; femenil,

fen, *fĕn,* s. marjal, pantano, m.

fence, *fĕns,* s. cerca, palizada, f.; defensa, f.; —, v. a. cercar; defender, preservar; —, v. n. esgrimir. [cercado.

fenceless, *-lĕs,* a. abierto, lo que no está

fencing, *fĕn′sĭng,* s. esgrima, f.

fencing-master, *-măstŭr,* s. maestro de armas, m. [defenderse.

fend, *fĕnd,* v. a. parar; rechazar; —, v. n.

fender, *-ŭr,* s. barandilla que se pone delante del hogar, f.

fennel, *fĕn′nĕl,* s. (bot.) hinojo, m.

ferment, *fŭr′mĕnt,* s. fermento m.; —, *fŭrmĕnt′,* v. a. & n. hacer fermentar; fermentar.

fermentation, *fŭrmĕntā′shŭn,* s. fermentación, f.

fern, *fŭrn,* s. (bot.) helecho, m.

fernery, *-ŭrĭ,* s. lechar, m.

ferocious, *fērō′shŭs,* a. feroz; fiero; **-ly,** ad. ferozmente.

ferocity, *fērŏs′ĭtĭ,* s. ferocidad, fiereza, f.

ferret, *fĕr′ĕt,* s. hurón, m.; —, v. a. hacer near; **to — out,** descubrir, echar fuera.

ferreter, *-ŭr,* s. (fig.) espía, m.

ferruginous, *fērō′jĭnŭs,* a. ferruginoso.

ferry, *fĕr′rĭ,* s. barca de transporte, f.; —, v. a. llevar en barca.

ferryman, *-măn,* s. barquero, m.

fertile, *fŭr′tĭl,* a. fértil, fecundo.

fertilise, *fŭr′tĭlīz,* v. a. fertilizar. [f.

fertility, *fŭrtĭl′ĭtĭ,* s. fertilidad, fecundidad,

ferule, *fĕr′ūl,* s. férula, palmeta, f.

fervency, *fŭr′vĕnsĭ,* s. fervor, celo, m.

fervent, *fŭr′vĕnt,* a. ferviente; fervoroso; **-ly,** ad. con fervor.

fervid, *fŭr′vĭd,* a. ardiente, vehemente.

fervour, *fŭr′vŭr,* s. fervor, ardor, m.

fescue, *fĕs′kū,* s. puntero, m.

festal, *fĕs′tăl,* a. festivo, de fiesta.

fester, *fĕs′tŭr,* v. n. enconarse, inflamarse.

festival, *fĕs′tĭvăl,* a. festivo; —, s. día festivo, m.

festive, *fĕs′tĭv,* a. festivo.

festivity, *fĕstĭv′ĭtĭ,* s. festividad, f. [near.

festoon, *fĕstōn′,* s. festón, m.; —, v. a. festo-

fetch, *fĕtsh,* v. a. ir á traer algo; producir; llevar; arrebatar; —, s. estratagema, f.; artificio, ardid, m.

fetid, *fĕt′ĭd,* a. fétido, hediondo.

fetidness, *-nĕs,* s. fetor, m.

fetlock, _fĕt´lŏk_, s. cerneja, f.
fetter, _fĕt´tår_ v. a. atar con cadenas.
fetters, _-z_, s. pl. grillos, m. pl.
feud, _fūd_, s. riña, contienda, f.; feudo, m.
feudal, _-dl_, a. feudal.
feudalism, _-dlĭzm_, s. feudalismo, m.
feudatory, _-dtŭrĕ_, s. feudatario, m.
fever, _fĕ´vŭr_, s. fiebre, f.; yellow –, vómito
feverish, _-ĭsh_, a. febricitante. [negro, m.
few, _fū_, a. poco; a –, algunos; – and far
  between, lo que ocurre rara vez.
fewer, _-ŭr_, a. menor; –, ad. menos.
fewness, _-nĕs_, s. poquedad, f.; corto
  número, m.
fiat, _fī´åt_, s. mandato absoluto, m.
fib, _fĭb_, s. mentira, f.; –, v. n. mentir.
fibre, _fī´bŭr_, s. fibra, hebra, f.
fibrin, _-brĭn_, s. fibrina, f.
fibrous, _-brŭs_, a. fibroso, f. [dable.ligero.
fickle, _fĭk´l_, a. voluble, inconstante, mu-
fickleness, _-nĕs_, s. volubilidad, inconstancia, f.   [f.
fiction, _fĭk´shŭn_, s. ficción, f.; invención,
fictitious, _fĭktĭsh´ŭs_, a. ficticio; fingido;
  _-ly_, ad. fingidamente.
fiddle, _fĭd´l_, s. violín, m.; –, v. n. tocar
  el violín; chocarrear.
fiddler, _-ŭr_, s. violinista, m.
fiddlesticks! _-stĭks´_, s.pl.; ¡nini naná!m.
fiddle-string, _-strĭng_, s. cuerda de violín, f.
fidelity, _fĭdĕl´ĭtĕ_, s. fidelidad, lealtad, f.
fidget, _fĭj´ĕt_, v. n. (vulg.) contonearse; –,
  s. agitación inquieta, f.; hombre azogado,
  azogue, m.
fidgety, _-ĕ_, a. (fam.) inquieto, impaciente.
fie, _fī_, ¡vaya!
fief, _fēf_, s. feudo, m.
field, _fēld_, s. campo, m.; campaña, f.; espacio, m.; to take the –, (mil.) salir á cam-
field-book, _-bŭk_, s. catastro,m. [paña.
field-day, _-dā_, s. (mil.) día de la revista, m.
fieldfare, _-får_, s. zorzal, m. (pájaro).
field-marshal, _-mårshål_, s. feldmariscal,
  m.; general en jefe de un ejército, m.
field-mouse, _-mŏŭs_, s. turón, m.
field-officer, _-ŏf´ĭsŭr_, s. (mil.) oficial
  del estado mayor, m.   [paña, f.
field-piece, _-pēs_, s. artillería de cam-
field-practice, _-pråktĭs_, s. (mil.) maniobras grandes, f. pl.
field-sports, _-spŏrts_, s.pl. entretenimien-
  tos de la caza, m. pl.
field-work, _-wŭrk_, s. (mil.) fortín, m.;
  –, s. pl. (mil.) obras de campaña, f. pl.
fiend, _fēnd_, s. enemigo, m.; demonio, m.
fiendish, _-ĭsh_, a. demoníaco.
fierce, _fērs_, a. fiero, feroz; cruel, furioso;
  _-ly_, ad. furiosamente.
fierceness, _-nĕs_, s. fiereza, ferocidad, f.
fieriness, _fī´rĭnĕs_, s. ardor, m.; fogosidad, f.
fiery, _fī´ŭrĕ_, a. ígneo; fogoso, colérico.
fife, _fīf_, s. pífano, m.
fifteen, _fīf´tēn_, a. quince.
fifteenth, _-th_, a. décimoquinto.   [lugar.
fifth, _fĭfth_, a. quinto; _-ly_, ad. en quinto
fiftieth, _fĭf´tĭĕth_, a. quincuagésimo.

fifty, _fĭf´tĕ_, a. cincuenta.
fig, _fĭg_, s. higo, m.; (fig.) bagatela, f.
fight, _fīt_, v. a. & n. reñir; batallar; combatir; –, s. batalla, f.; combate, m.; pelea.
fig-leaf, _-lēf_, s. hoja de higuera, f. [f.
fig-pecker, _-pĕkkŭr_, s. becafigo, m.
fig-tree, _-trē_, s. higuera, f.
figurative, _fĭg´ŭrdtĭv_, a. figurativo; _-ly_,
  ad. figuradamente.
figure, _fĭg´ŭr_, s. figura, forma, hechura,
  f.; imagen, f.; cifra, f.; –, v. a. figurar.
figure-head, _-hĕd_, s. (mar.) león, m.;
  figura de proa, f.   [fibra, f.
filament, _fĭl´åmĕnt_, s. filamento, m.;
filbert, _fĭl´bŭrt_, s. avellana de cáscara
filch, _fĭltsh_, v. n. ratear.   [delgada, f.
filcher, _-ŭr_, s. ratero, ladroncillo, m.
file, _fīl_, s. hilo, m.; lista, f.; (mil.) fila, hilera, f.; lima, f.; –, v. a. enhilar; limar;
  pulir; to – off, (mil.) desfilar.   [m.
file-cutter, _-kŭttŭr_, s. picador de limas,
filial, _fĭl´ĭål_, a. de hijo, filial.
filibuster, _fĭl´ŏbŭstŭr_, s. pirata, filibustero,
filigree, _fĭl´ĭgrē_, s. filigrana, f.   [m.
filings, _fī´lĭngz_, s. pl. limaduras, f. pl.
fill, _fĭl_, v. a. llenar, henchir; hartar; –,
  v. n. hartarse; –, s. hartura, abundancia, f.   [nera, f.
fillet, _fĭl´lĕt_, s. venda, faja, f.; tapa de ter-
fillip, _fĭl´lĭp_, s. papirote, m.
filly, _fĭl´lĕ_, s. potranca, f.
film, _fĭlm_, s. película, membrana, f.
filter, _fĭl´tŭr_, s. filtro, m.; –, v. a. filtrar.
filthiness, _fĭlth´ĭnĕs_, s. inmundicia, porquería, f.; fango, lodo, m.
filthily, _-lĕ_, ad. puercamente.
filthy, _-ĕ_, a. sucio, puerco.
filtration, _fĭltrā´shŭn_, s. filtración, f.
fin, _fĭn_, s. aleta, f. (de pez).   [mente.
final, _fī´nål_, a. final, último; _-ly_, ad. final-
finance, _fĭnåns´_, s. renta, f.
financial, _fĭnån´shål_, a. rentístico.
financier, _fĭnånsēr´_, s. rentista, hacendista,
finch, _fĭnsh_, s. pinzón, m.   [m.
find, _fīnd_, v. a. hallar, descubrir; proveer;
  to – one's self, hallarse, estar; –, s.
  hallazgo, m.
fine, _fīn_, a. fino; agudo, cortante; claro,
  trasparente; delicado; astuto; diestro; galán, lindo; elegante; bello; bien criado;
  –, s. multa, f.; in –, finalmente, por fin;
  –, v. a. afinar, refinar; multar.
fine-draw, _-drå_, v. a. zurcir.
finely, _-lĕ_, ad. con elegancia.   [mosura, f.
fineness, _-nĕs_, s. fineza, delicadeza, her-
finery, _-årĕ_, s. adorno, atavío, m.
fine-spun, _-spŭn_, a. (fig.) ingeniosamente
  ideado.   [manosear; manejar.
finger, _fĭng´gŭr_, s. dedo, m.; –, v. a. tocar,
finger-board, _-bŏrd_,s. teclado, m.; teclas.
finger-glass, _-glås_, s. enjuague, m. [f.pl.
fingering, _-ĭng_, s. tecleo, m.; modo de
  tocar un instrumento de música, m.
finger-post, _-pŏst_, s. columna miliaria, f.
finger-stall, _-stål_, s. dedal, m.
finical, _fĭn´ĭkål_, a. afectado.
finish, _fĭn´ĭsh_, v. a. acabar, terminar; concluir.   [cluir.
finite, _fī´nĭt_, a. finito.

finny, *fĭn'nĕ*, a. armado de aletas.

fir (-tree), *fŭr'trē*, s. abeto, m.

fire, *fīr*, s. fuego, m.; incendio, m.; —, v. a. quemar, inflamar; —, v. n. encenderse; (mil.) tirar, hacer fuego. [f. pl.

fire-arms, *-ārms*, s. pl. armas de fuego,

fire-ball, *-bāl*, s. granada real ó de mano, f.; meteoro, meteoro, m. [rio, m.

fire-brand, *-brānd*, s. tizón, m.; incendia-

fire-brigade, *-brĭgād*, s. bomberos, m. pl.

fire-damp, *-dāmp*, s. aire inflamable, m.

fire-eater, *-ētĕr*, s. fanfarrón, m.

fire-engine, *-ĕnjĭn*, s. bomba de apagar los incendios, f.

fire-escape, *-ĕskāp*, s. aparato de salva-mento para incendios, m.

fire-fly, *-flī*, s. luciérnaga, f.

fire-man, *-măn*, s. bombero, m.; (rail.) fuellero, m.

fire-place, *-plās*, s. hogar, fogón, m.

fire-policy, *-pŏlĭsē*, s. carta de seguro contra los incendios, f.

fire-proof, *-prōf*, a. spiro, macizo.

fire-screen, *-skrēn*, s. pantalla de chime-nea, f. [m.

fire-shovel, *-shŭvl*, s. paleta, f.; badil,

fire-side, *-sīd*, s. fogón de chimenea, m.

fire-water, *-wātĕr*, s. aguardiente, m.

fire-wood, *-wŭd*, s. leña para la lumbre, f.

firing, *fī'rĭng*, s. leña, f.; (mil.) descarga, f.

firkin, *fŭr'kĭn*, s. cuarteruola, f. (medida inglesa = ¼ barrel).

firm, *fŭrm*, a. firme, estable, constante; —, s. (com.) razón, firma, f.; —ly, ad. fir-memente.

firmament, *fŭr'mămĕnt*, s. firmamento, m.

firmness, *-nĕs*, s. firmeza, f.; constancia, f.

first, *fŭrst*, a. primero; —, ad. primera-mente; at — al principio; —ly, ad. en primer lugar.

firstling, *-lĭng*, s. primogénito, m.

fisc, *fĭsk*, s. fisco, m., la Hacienda pública.

fiscal, *fĭs'kăl*, a. fiscal.

fish, *fĭsh*, s. pez, m.; —, v. n. pescar.

fish-bone, *-bōn*, s. espina, f. [nes, m.

fish-day, *-dā*, s. día de abstinencia de car-

fisher, *-ĕr*, fisherman, *-ărmăn*, s. pescador, m.

fishery, *-ărē*, s. pesca, f.; pesquera, f.

fish-hook, *-hōk*, s. anzuelo, m.

fishing, *-ĭng*, s. pesca, f.

fishing-line, *-ĭnglĭn*, s. sedal, m.

fishing-rod, *-ĭngrŏd*, s. caña de pescar, f.

fish-market, *-mărkĕt*, s. pescadería, f.

fish-monger, *-mănggăr*, s. pescadero, f.

fish-pond, *-pŏnd*, s. estanque de peces, m.

fish-wife, *-wĭf*, s. pescadera, f.

fishy, *-ĕ*, a. abundante de pescado.

fissure, *fĭsh'ŭr*, s. grieta, hendedura, f.

fist, *fĭst*, s. puño, m.

fistula, *fĭs'tŭlă*, s. fístula, fístola, f.

fit, *fĭt*, s. paroxismo, m.; convulsión, f.; capricho, m.; ataque repentino de algún mal ó de alguna pasión de ánimo, m.; —, a. apto, idóneo, capaz; cómodo; justo; —, v. a. ajustar, acomodar, adaptar; to — out, proveer; —, v. n. convenir.

fitful, *-fŭl*, a. alternado con paroxismos.

fitly, *-lĕ*, ad. aptamente, justamente.

fitness, *-nĕs*, s. aptitud, conveniencia, f.; proporción, f.; oportunidad, f.

fitting, *-tĭng*,a. conveniente, idóneo, justo; —, s. conveniencia, f.; —s, pl. guarnición, f.

five, *fīv*, a. cinco.

fiver, *fī'vĕr*, s. billete de cinco libras ester-linas. [lfn, m.

fives, *-z*, s. pl. juego de pelota, m.

fix, *fĭks*, v. a. fijar, establecer; —, v. n. fijarse, determinarse.

fixedly, *-sĕdlĕ*, ad. fijamente, ciertamente.

fixedness, *-sĕdnĕs*, fixity, *-tĭ*, s. firmeza, f.; constancia, f.

fixings, *-ĭngz*, s. pl. equipajes, m. pl.; pertrechos, m. pl.; ajuar, m.

fixture, *-tŭr*, s. mueble fijo de una casa, f.

fizz(le), *fĭz'(l)*, v. n. silbar.

flabby, *flăb'bĕ*, a. blando, flojo, lacio.

flaccid, *flăk'sĭd*, a. flojo, flaco; flácido.

flag, *flăg*, s. bandera, f.; (mar.) pabellón, m.; (bot.) gladiolo, m.; —, v. a. (with stones) ensolar; —, v. n. pender; debili-tarse.

flagellate, *flăj'ĕlāt*, v. a. azotar. [tarse.

flageolet, *flăj'ŏlĕt*, s. flajolé, m. [vado.

flagitious, *flăjĭsh'ŭs*, a. facineroso, mal-vado.

flag-man, *flăg'măn*, s. (rail.) guardavía, m.

flag-officer, *-ŏf'ĭsĕr*, s. (mar.) jefe de una escuadra, m.

flagon, *flăg'ŏn*, s. frasco, m. [midad, f.

flagrancy, *flă'grănsē*, s. escándalo, m.; enor-

flagrant, *-grănt*, a. flagrante; notorio.

flag-ship, *flăg'shĭp*, s. navío almirante, m.

flag-staff, *-stăf*, s. asta del pabellón, m.

flail, *flāl*, s. mayal, m.

flake, *flāk*, s. copo, m.; lámina, f.; (of fire), centella, f.; (of ice), carámbano, m.; —, v. n. romperse en láminas.

flaky, *flā'kĕ*, a. vedijoso; roto en pequeñas laminillas. [m.; —, v. n. arder; brillar.

flame, *flām*, s. llama, f.; fuego (del amor),

flaming, *flā'mĭng*, a. inflamado, com-puesto de llamas.

flange, *flănj*, s. listón, bocel, m.

flank, *flăngk*, s. ijada, f.; (mil.) flanco, m.; —, v. a. atacar el flanco; flanquear.

flannel, *flăn'nĕl*, s. franela, flanela, f.

flap, *flăp*, s. falda, faldilla, f.; válvula, f.; oreja (de los zapatos), f.; golpe ligero, m.; —, v. a. mosquear; —, v. n. aletear. [f.

flare, *flăr*, v. n. lucir, brillar; —, s. llama,

flash, *flăsh*, s. relámpago, m.; llamarada, f.; borbollón, m.; — of wit, agudeza, f.; rasgo, m.; —, v. a. despedir agua á bor-bollones; —, v. n. relampaguear, brillar; —, a. falso, contrahecho.

flashy, *-ĕ*, a. superficial; insulso, desabrido.

flask, *flăsk*, s. frasco, m.; botella, f.

flat, *flăt*, a. llano, plano; insípido; —, s. llanura, f.; plano, m.; (mar.) bajío, m.; (mus.) bemol, m.; —ly, ad. horizontal-mente; llanamente; enteramente; de plano, de nivel; francamente.

flatness, *-nĕs*, s. llanura, f.; insipidez, f.

flatten, *-n*, v. a. allanar; aplastar; —, v. n. aplanarse; atontarse. [allanador, m.

flatter, *flăt'tĕr*, v. a. adular, lisonjear; —, s.

flattery, *-ĕ*, s. adulación, lisonja, f. [m.

flatting-mill, *flăt'tĭngmĭl*, s. laminador,

flatulence, *flăt'dlĕns,* s. (med.) flatulencia, f.; vano, fútil, frívolo, caduco.

flatulent, *-dĕnt,* a. flatulento; hinchado.

flatwise, *-wiz,* ad. de llano.   [f.

flaunt, *flănt,* v. n. pavonearse; —, s. borla.

flavour, *flā'vŭr,* s. sainete, perfume, m.; —, v. a. dar un olor suave.

flavourless, *-lĕs,* a. desabrido, soso.

flaw, *flă,* s. resquebradura, hendedura, f.; falta, tacha, f.; ráfaga, f.; —, v. a. rajar.

flawless, *-lĕs,* a. sin defecto.   [hender.

flax, *flăks,* s. lino, m.; **to dress -.** rastrillar lino.

flaxen, *-n,* **flaxy,** *-ĕ,* a. de lino; blondo.

flay, *flā,* v. a. desollar, descortezar.

flea, *flĕ,* s. pulga, f.

flea-bite, *-bīt,* s. picadura de pulga, f.

fledge, *flĕj,* v. a. dar alas ó plumas.

flee, *flē,* v. n. escapar; huir.

fleece, *flēs,* s. vellón, m.; —, v. a. esquilar; desnudar, despojar.

fleecy, *flē'sĕ,* a. lanudo.   [ligero.

fleet, *flēt,* s. flota, f.; —, a. veloz, acelerado.

fleeting, *-ĭng,* a. pasajero, fugitivo.

fleetness, *-nĕs,* s. velocidad, ligereza, f.

flesh, *flĕsh,* s. carne, f.; —, v. a. hartar, saciar.   [m.

flesh-broth, *-brŏth,* s. caldo (de carne).

flesh-brush, *-brŭsh,* s. cepillo de dar friegas, m.

fleshiness, *-ĭnĕs,* s. gordura extremada, f.

fleshings, *-ĭngz,* s. pl. fajos, m. pl.

fleshless, *-lĕs,* a. flaco; descarnado.

fleshy, *-ĕ,* a. carnoso, pulposo.

flexibility, *flĕksĭbĭl'ĭtĭ,* s. flexibilidad, f.

flexible, *flĕks'ĭbl,* **flexile,** *-ĭl,* a. flexible.

flexion, *flĕk'shŭn,* s. flexión, corvadura, f.

flick, *flĭk,* v. a. robar, hurtar con ligereza.

flicker, *-kŭr,* v. a. aletear; fluctuar.

flier, *flī'ŭr,* s. fugitivo, m.; volante de unas máquinas, m.

flight, *flīt,* s. huída, fuga, f.; vuelo, m.; bandada (de pájaros), f.; (fig.) elevación, f.

flighty, *-ĕ,* a. veloz, inconstante.

flimsiness, *flĭm'zĭnĕs,* s. textura débil, f.

flimsy, *-zĕ,* a. débil; fútil.   [ligera, f.

flinch, *flĭnsh,* v. n. echarse con la carga, desistir, faltar; retirarse.

fling, *flĭng,* v. a. lanzar, echar; —, v. n. brincar, resentirse; —, s. tiro, m.; burla, f.

flint, *flĭnt,* s. pedernal, m.   [chuleta, f.

flint-glass, *-glăs,* s. cristal de piedra, m.

flinty, *-ĕ,* a. roqueño; pedregoso; inexorable.

flip, *flĭp,* v. a. arrojar, lanzar.

flippancy, *-pănsĕ,* s. volubilidad, f.; petulancia, f.; impertinencia, f.

flippant, *-pănt,* a. ligero, veloz; petulante, locuaz.

flirt, *flŭrt,* v. a. arrojar, lanzar; —, v. n. mofar; coquetear; —, s. coqueta, f.

flirtation, *flŭrtā'shŭn,* s. coquetería, f.

flit, *flĭt,* v. n. volar, huir; aletear.

flitch, *flĭtsh,* s. hoja de tocino, f.

float, *flōt,* v. a. inundar; —, v. n. flotar; fluctuar; —, s. cosa que flota, f.

floating-bridge, *-ĭngbrĕj,* s. pontón, m.

floating-capital, *-kăp'ĭtăl,* s. capital en circulación, f.

floating-debt, *-dĕt,* s. deuda flotante, f.

flock, *flŏk,* s. manada, f.; rebaño, m.; gentío, m.; vedija de lana, f.; —, v. n. congregarse.

floe, *flō,* s. carámbano, m.

flog, *flŏg,* v. a. azotar.

flogging, *-gĭng,* s. tunda, zurra, f.

flood, *flŭd,* s. diluvio, m.; inundación, f.; flujo, m.; —, v. a. inundar.

floor, *flōr,* s. pavimento, suelo, piso, m.; piso de una casa; —, v. a. solar.

flooring, *-ĭng,* s. estrado, m.; ensamblaje de madera para suelos, m.

floral, *flō'răl,* a. floral.

florescence, *flōrĕs'ĕns,* s. florescencia, f.

florid, *flŏr'ĭd,* a. florido.

florin, *flŏr'ĭn,* s. florín, m.

florist, *flŏr'ĭst,* s. florista, m.

floss-silk, *flŏs'sĭlk,* s. filadiz, m.

flossy, *-sĕ,* a. blando como la seda.

flotilla, *flōtĭl'lă,* s. (mar.) flotilla, f.

flounce, *flŏuns,* s. farfalá, m.; —, v. a. guarnecer con falbalás; —, v. n. revolcarse en agua ó cieno.

flounder, *flŏun'dŭr,* s. acedía, platija (pez de mar), f.; —, v. n. patear, brincar.

flour, *flŏur,* s. harina, f.

flourish, *flŭr'ĭsh,* v. a. exornar con flores retóricas; adornar; vibrar (una espada); —, v. n. florecer; gozar de prosperidad; jactarse; escribir haciendo lazos con la pluma; amplificar; (mus.) preludiar, florear; —, s. belleza, f.; floreo de palabras, m.; lazo, m.; (mus.) floreo, preludio, m.   [mofa, burla, f.

flout, *flŏut,* v. a. mofar, burlarse; —, s.

flow, *flō,* v. n. fluir, manar; crecer la marea; ondear; —, s. creciente de la marea, f.; abundancia, f.; flujo, m.

flower, *flŏu'r,* s. flor, f.; harina, f.; (fig.) lo mejor; —, v. a. & n. florear; florecer.

flower-bed, *-bĕa,* s. cuadro (en un jardín), m.

flower-girl, *-gŭrl,* s. florera, f.

floweret, *-ĕt,* s. florecilla, florecita, f.

flower-pot, *-pŏt,* s. tiesto de flores, m.

flowery, *-ĕ,* a. florido.

flower-show, *-shō,* s. exposición de flores, f.   [suspenso.

fluctuate, *flŭk'tūāt,* v. n. fluctuar; estar

fluctuation, *flŭktūā'shŭn,* s. fluctuación, f.

flue, *flū,* s. humero, m.; pelusa, f.   [f.

fluency, *-ĕnsĕ,* s. fluidez, f.; volubilidad, f.

fluent, *-ĕnt,* a. fluido; fluente; fácil; **-ly.** ad. con facundia.

fluid, *-ĭd,* a. & s. fluido (m.).

fluidity, *flūĭd'ĭtĕ,* s. fluidez, f.

fluke, *flōk,* s. lengüeta de áncora, f.; acedía, f. (pez).

flummery, *flŭm'ărĕ,* s. gachas de harina de avena, f. pl.; lisonja grosera, f.   [m.

flunkey, *flŭn'kĕ,* s. lacayo, m.; estafero.

flurry, *flŭr'rĕ,* s. ráfaga, f.; priesa, agitación, f.; —, v. a. confundir; alarmar.

flush, *flŭsh,* v. a. sonrojar; exaltar; —, v. n. fluir con violencia; ponerse colorado; —, s. flujo rápido, m.; (at cards) flux, m.

rubor suelto, m.; —, a. fresco, robusto, opulento; pródigo.

fluster, *flŭs'tŭr,* v. a. confundir, desordenar;   [estriar.

flute, *flōt,* s. flauta, f.; estría, f.; —, v. a.

flutist, *–tĭst,* s. flautista, m.

flutter, *flŭt'tŭr,* v. a. turbar, desordenar; —, v. n. revolotear; estar en agitación; s. confusión, f.; agitación, f.; undulación, f.   [disenteria, f.

flux, *flŭks,* s. flujo, m.; concurso, m.;

fly, *flī,* v. a. & n. volar; pasar ligeramente; saltar, reventar; huir, escapar; —, s. mosca, f.; volante, m.; diligencia, f. (coche); Spanish —, cantárida, f.

fly-blow, *–blō,* s. cresa, f.

fly-catcher, *–kătshŭr,* s. papamoscas, m.

fly-fish, *–fĭsh,* v. a. pescar con moscas.

fly-flap, *–flăp,* s. mosqueador, m.

flying-fish, *flī'ĭngfĭsh,* s. volador, pez volante, m.

fly-man, *–măn,* s. caleséro, m.

foal, *fōl,* s. potro, m., potra, f.; buche, m.; —, v. a. parir una yegua.

foam, *fōm,* s. espuma, f.; —, v. n. espumar.

foamy, *–ĭ,* a. espumoso.   [m.

fob, *fŏb,* s. faltriquera pequeña, f.; engaño,

focus, *fō'kŭs,* s. foco, m., el punto céntrico.

fodder, *fŏd'dŭr,* s. forraje, m.

foe, *fō,* s. adversario, enemigo, m.

fog, *fŏg,* s. niebla, f.

fogey, *fō'gĕ,* s. patán, zompo, m.

foggy, *fŏg'gĕ,* a. nebuloso, brumoso.

foible, *fŏi'bl,* s. debilidad, parte flaca, f.

foil, *fŏil,* v. a. vencer; frustrar; —, s. desventaja, desgracia, f.; chasco, m.; hoja (de estaño), f.; florete, m.

foist, *fŏist,* v.a. insertar (subrepticiamente).

fold, *fōld,* s. redil, aprisco, m.; plegadura, f.; hoja de una puerta, f.; —, v. a. apriscar el ganado; plegar.

folder, *–ŭr,* s. plegador, m., plegadera, f.

folding, *–ĭng,* s. plegadura, f.

folding-bed, *–ĭngbĕd,* s. catre de tijera ó de campaña, f.

folding-chair, *–ĭngtshŭr,* s. silla de tijera, f.   [f.

folding-door, *–ĭngdōr,* s. media puerta,

folding-screen, *–ĭngskrēn,* s. biombo, m.

foliage, *fō'lĭăj,* s. follaje, m.   [m.

foliation, *fōlĭā'shŭn,* s. (bot.) foliación, f.; azogamiento de los espejos, m.

folio, *fō'lĭō,* s. infolio, libro en folio, m.

folk, *fōk,* s. gente, f., mundo, m.

follow, *fŏl'lō,* v. a. seguir; acompañar; imitar; —, v.n. seguirse, resultar, provenir.

follower, *–ŭr,* s. seguidor, m.; imitador, m.; secuaz, partidario, m.; adherente, m.; compañero, m.

folly, *fŏl'lĕ,* s. extravagancia, bobería, f.

foment, *fōmĕnt',* v. a. fomentar; proteger.

fomentation, *–ā'shŭn,* s. fomentación, f.; fomento, m.

fond, *fŏnd,* a. loco, enamorado (por) apasionado, demasiado indulgente; **–ly,** ad. locamente, cariñosamente.

fondle, *–l,* v. a. mimar, hacer caricias.

fondling, *–lĭng,* s. favorito, niño mimado, m.   [pasión loca, f.; indulgencia, f.

fondness, *–nĕs,* s. debilidad, f.; terneza, f.

font, *fŏnt,* s. pila bautismal, f.

food, *fōd,* s. alimento, m.; comida, f.

fool, *fōl,* s. loco, tonto, m.; bufón, m.; —, v. a. engañar; infatuar; —, v. n. tontear.

foolery, *–ărĕ,* s. tonteria, boberia; f.

foolhardiness, *–hărdĭnĕs,* s. temeridad, locura, f.

foolhardy, *–hărdĕ,* a. temerario.

foolish, *–ĭsh,* a. bobo, tonto; **–ly,** ad. bobamente, sin juicio.

foolscap, *–s'kăp,* s. papel grifón, m.

foot, *fŭt,* s. pie, m.; base, f.; infantería, f.; estado, m.; sistema, m.; paso, m.; **– by –,** paso entre paso; **on ó by –,** á pie; —, v. n. bailar, saltar, brincar; ir á pie; —, v. a. patear, pisotear; rechazar con el pie; remontar botas.   [los pies, m.

foot-ball, *–băl,* s. balón para jugar con

foot-bath, *–băth,* s. pediluvio, m.

foot-board, *–bōrd,* s. estribo, m.

foot-bridge, *–brĭj,* s. puentecilla, f.

foot-guards, *–gărds,* s. pl. guardias del rey que sirven á pie, f. pl.   [el pie, m.

foot-hold, *–hōld,* s. espacio en que cabe

footing, *–ĭng,* s. base, f.; piso, paso, m.; estado, m.; condición, f.; fundamento, m.

foot-lights, *–lĭts,* s. pl. lámparas del proscenio, f. pl.   [infantería.

footman, *–măn,* s. lacayo, m.; soldado de

foot-muff, *–mŭf,* s. folgo, m.

foot-note, *–nōt,* s. anotación debajo de un escrito, f.

foot-pace, *–pās,* s. paso lento ó corto, m.

foot-pad, *–păd,* s. salteador á pie, m.

foot-path, *–păth,* s. senda, f.

foot-pavement, *–pāvment,* s. acera, f.

foot-post, *–pōst,* s. peatón, m.

foot-print, *–prĭnt,* s. huella, pisada, f.

foot-step, *–stĕp,* s. vestigio, m.; huella, f.

foot-stool, *–stōl,* s. escabelo, m.

foot-warmer, *–wŭrmŭr,* s. estufilla, f.

foot-way, *–wā,* s. sendero, m.

fop, *fŏp,* s. petimetre, pisaverde, m.

foppery, *–pŭrĕ,* s. tontería, f.; afectación (en el vestirse), f.

foppish, *–pĭsh,* vanidoso; afectado.

for, *fōr,* pr. por, á causa de; para; á pesar de; —, c. porque, para que; por cuánto; **as – me,** tocante á mí; **– as much,** respecto á, por lo tocante á; **what – ?** ¿á qué? ¿á qué fin? ¿para qué?

forage, *fōr'dj,* s. forraje, m.; —, v. a. forrajear; saquear.

forager, *–ŭr,* s. forrajero, m.

forbear, *fōrbār',* v. n. cesar, detenerse, abstenerse; —, v. a. omitir; soportar.

forbearance, *–ăns,* s. paciencia, indulgencia, f.

forbid, *fōrbĭd',* v. a. prohibir, vedar; impedir; **God – !** ¡Dios no quiera!

force, *fōrs,* s. fuerza, f.; poder, vigor, m.; violencia, f.; necesidad, f.; **–s,** pl. tropas, f. pl.; —, v. a. forzar, violentar; esforzar; constreñir; —, v. n. esforzarse.   [fuerza.

forcedly, *–ĕdlĕ,* ad. forzosamente, por

forced march, *fōrs'd mārtsh*, s. (mil.) marcha forzada, f. [de comadrón, f.

forceps, *fōr'sĕps*, s. fórceps, m., tenaza

forcible, *fōr'sĭbl*, a. fuerte, eficaz, poderoso, prevaleciente; -bly, ad. fuertemente, forzadamente. [dero, m.

forcing-house, *fōr'sĭnghōŭs*, s. invernadero, m.

ford, *fōrd*, s. vado, m.; -, v. a. vadear.

fordable, *-ĭbl*, a. vadeable.

fore, *fōr*, a. anterior; -, ad. delante, antes.

forebode, *-bōd'*, v. n. pronosticar, presagiar.

forecast, *-kāst'*, v. n. proyectar, prever; conjeturar de antemano; -, *fōr'kāst*, s. previsión, f.; proyecto, m. [el paso.

foreclose, *-klōz'*, v. a. excluir; impedir

foreclosure, *-klō'shŭr*, s. exclusión, f.; impedimento, m.

foredoom, *-dōm'*, v. a. predestinar.

forefather, *-fäther*, s. abuelo, antecesor, m.

forefend, *-fĕnd'*, v. a. prohibir, vedar.

forefinger, *-fĭnggŭr*, s. índice, m. [der.

forego, *-gō'*, v. a. ceder, abandonar; preceder.

foregone, *-gōn'*, a. pasado; anticipado.

foreground, *-grōŭnd*, s. delantera, f.

forehead, *-hĕd*, s. frente, f.; insolencia, f.

foreign, *fōr'ĭn*, a. extranjero; extraño.

foreigner, *-ŭr*, s. extranjero, forastero, m. [f.

foreknowledge, *fōrnōl'ĕj*, s. presciencia,

foreland, *-lănd*, s. cabo, promontorio, m.

forelock, *-lŏk*, s. melena, f., copete, m.

foreman, *-măn*, s. presidente del jurado, m.; primer mancebo en las tiendas ó talleres, m. [quete, m.

foremast, *-māst*, s. (mar.) palo de trinquete, m.

forementioned, *-mĕn'shŭnd*, a. ya citado, arriba citado.

foremost, *-mōst'*, a. delantero.

forenoon, *-nōn*, s. mañana, f.

forensic, *fōrĕn'sĭk*, a. forense.

forepart, *fōr'pärt*, s. delantera, f.

forerunner, *-rŭnnŭr*, s. precursor, m.; predecesor, m.

foresail, *-săl*, s. (mar.) vela de trinquete, f.

foresee, *-sē'*, v. a. prever. [f.

foreshadow, *-shăd'ō*, v. a. pronosticar; simbolizar.

foreshorten, *-shōr'tn*, v. a. recortar. [f.

foresight, *-sīt*, s. previsión, f.; presciencia.

forest, *fōr'ĕst*, s. bosque, m.; selva, f.

forestall, *fōrstăl'*, v. a. anticipar; preocupar, prevenir; monopolizar.

forester, *fōr'ĕstŭr*, s. guardabosque, m.

foretaste, *fōrtāst'*, v. a. tener presciencia; catar ó gustar antes que; -, *fōr'tāst*, s. goce anticipado.

foretell, *fōrtĕl'*, v. a. predecir, profetizar.

foreteller, *-lŭr*, s. profeta, m.

forethought, *-thăt*, s. providencia, f.; premeditación, f.

fore-top, *-tŏp*, s. tupé, m. [mano.

forewarn, *-wărn'*, v. a. prevenir de antemano.

forfeit, *fōr'fĕt*, s. multa, f., confiscación, f.; confiscado, m.; -, v. a. confiscar; perder; pagar una multa, f.

forfeiture, *-ŭr*, s. confiscación, f.; multa,

forge, *fōrj*, s. fragua, f.; fábrica de metales, f.; -, v. a. forjar; contrahacer; inventar.

forger, *-ŭr*, s. forjador, m.; falsario, m.

forgery, *-ŭrĕ*, s. falsificación, f.; forjadura, f.

forget, *fŏrgĕt'*, v. a. olvidar; descuidar.

forgetful, *-fŭl*, a. olvidadizo; descuidado.

forgetfulness, *-fŭlnĕs*, s. olvido, m.; negligencia, f. [silla, f.

forget-me-not, *-mĕnŏt*, s. (bot.) vellorita, f.

forgive, *fŏrgĭv'*, v. a. perdonar, remitir.

forgiveness, *-nĕs*, s. perdón, m.; remisión, f.

fork, *fōrk*, s. tenedor, m.; horca, f.; -, v. n. bifurcarse; -, v. a. ahorquillar.

forked, *-ĕd*, forky, *-ĕ*, a. horcado.

forlorn, *fŏrlōrn'*, a. abandonado, perdido; - hope, (mil.) centinela perdida, f.

forlornness, *-nĕs*, s. miseria, f.; soledad, f.; abandono, desamparo, m.

form, *fōrm*, s. forma, f.; modelo, m.; modo, m.; formalidad, f.; método, m.; banco, m.; molde, m. -, v. a. formar.

formal, *fōr'măl*, a. formal, metódico; ceremonioso; -ly, ad. formalmente.

formality, *fōrmăl'ĭtĕ*, s. formalidad, f.; ceremonia, f.

formation, *fōrmā'shŭn*, s. formación, f.

former, *fōr'mŭr*, a. precedente; anterior, pasado; -ly, ad. antiguamente, en tiempos pasados. [terrible.

formidable, *fōr'mĭdăbl*, a. formidable.

formula, *fōr'mŭlă*, s. fórmula, f.

formulary, *fōr'mŭlārĕ*, s. formulario, m.

formulate, *fōr'mŭlāt*, v. a. formular, articular.

forsake, *fŏrsāk'*, v. a. dejar, abandonar.

forsooth, *fŏrsōth'*, ad. en verdad, ciertamente. [juramento; perjurar.

forswear, *-swăr'*, v. a. renunciar con

fort, *fōrt*, s. castillo, m.; fortaleza, f.

forth, *fōrth*, ad. en adelante; fuera; hasta lo último; and so -, y así de lo demás, et cetera. [parecer.

forthcoming, *-kŭmĭng*, a. pronto á comparecer.

forthwith, *-wĭth'*, a. inmediatamente, sin tardanza.

fortieth, *fōr'tĭĕth*, s. cuadragésimo, m.

fortification, *fōrtĭfĭkā'shŭn*, s. fortificación, f.

fortify, *fōr'tĭfī*, v. a. fortificar; corroborar.

fortitude, *fōr'tĭtūd*, s. fortaleza, f.; valor, m.

fortnight, *fōrt'nĭt*, s. quince días, m. pl.; dos semanas, f. pl.; -ly, a. & ad. cada quince días.

fortress, *fōr'trĕs*, s. (mil.) fortaleza, f.

fortuitous, *fōrtū'ĭtŭs*, a. impensado; casual; -ly, ad. fortuitamente.

fortunate, *fōr'tūnăt*, a. afortunado; -ly, ad. felizmente.

fortune, *fōr'tūn*, s. fortuna, suerte, f.; estado, m., condición, f.; bienes de fortuna, m. pl.; hacienda, dote, f.

fortune-hunter, *-hăntŭr*, s. aventurero, m.; el que va en busca de esposa rica.

fortune-teller, *-tĕllŭr*, s. sortílego, adi.

forty, *fōr'tĕ*, a. cuarenta. [vino, m.]

forward, *fŏr´wŭrd,* a. apresurado; presumido; anterior; pronto, activo, dispuesto; —, ad. adelante, más allá; **-ly,** ad. apresuradamente; atrevidamente; —, v. a. acelerar; promover, patrocinar.

forwarder, *–ŭr,* s. promotor, m.; (am.) comisionista.

forwardness, *–nĕs,* s. prontitud, f.; progreso, m.; precocidad, f.; audacia, f.

forwards, *–z,* ad. adelante.

foss, *fŏs,* s. foso, m., zanca f.

fossil, *fŏs´sĭl,* a. & s. fósil (m.).

foster, *fŏs´tŭr,* v. a. criar, nutrir.

foster-brother, *–brŭttŭr,* s. hermano de leche, m.

foster-child, *–tshĭld,* s. alumno, m.

foster-father, *–fāttŭr,* s. el que cría y enseña á un hijo ajeno, m.

foster-mother, *–mŭttŭr,* s. ama de leche, f.

foster-son, *–sŭn,* s. hijo de leche, m.

foul, *fŏul,* a. sucio, puerco; impuro, detestable; **– copy,** s. borrador, m.; **-ly,** ad. suciamente; ilegítimamente; —, v. a. ensuciar.

foulness, *–nĕs,* s. porquería, f.; deformidad, f.

found, *fŏund,* v. a. fundar, establecer; edificar; fundir.

foundation, *fŏundā´shŭn,* s. fundación, f.; fundamento, m.

foundation-stone, *–stōn,* s. piedra fundamental, f.

founder, *fŏund´ŭr,* s. fundador, m.; fundidor, m.; —, v. n. (mar.) irse á pique.

foundery, *–ĭ,* s. fundería, f.

foundling, *fŏund´lĭng,* s. niño expósito, m.

fount, *fŏunt,* **fountain,** *–ĭn,* s. fuente, f.; **–s,** pl. artificio de una fuente, m.

fountain-head, *–inhĕd,* s. origen de fuente, f.

four, *fōr,* a. cuatro.

fourfold, *–fōld,* a. cuádruplo.

four-footed, *–fūtĕd,* a. cuadrúpedo.

fourscore, *–skōr,* a. ochenta.

fourteen, *–tēn,* a. catorce.

fourteenth, *–tēnth,* a. décimocuarto.

fourth, *fōrth,* a. cuarto; **-ly,** ad. en cuarto lugar.

fowl, *fŏul,* s. ave, f.; volatería, f.

fowler, *–ŭr,* s. pajarero, m.

fowling, *–ĭng,* s. cetrería, caza de aves, f.

fowling-piece, *–pēs,* s. escopeta de pajarero, f.

fox, *fŏks,* s. zorra, f.; (fig.) zorro, m.

fox-glove, *–glŭv,* s. (bot.) dedalera, f.

fraction, *frăk´shŭn,* a. fracción, f.

fractional, *–ăl,* a. fraccionario.

fractious, *frăk´shŭs,* a. regañón, enojadizo.

fracture, *frăk´tŭr,* s. fractura, f.; —, v. a. fracturar, romper.

fragile, *frăj´ĭl,* a. frágil; débil.

fragility, *frăjĭl´ĭtĕ,* s. fragilidad, f.; debilidad, flaqueza, f.

fragment, *frăg´mĕnt,* s. fragmento, m.

fragmentary, *–tărĕ,* a. fragmentario.

fragrance, *frā´grăns,* s. fragancia, f.

fragrant, *frā´grănt,* a. fragante, oloroso; **-ly,** ad. con fragancia.

frail, *frāl,* a. frágil, débil.

frailty, *–tĕ,* s. fragilidad, f.; debilidad, f.

frame, *frām,* s. fábrica, f.; marco, cerco, m.; bastidor, m.; telar, m.; cuadro de vidriera, m.; estructura, f.; sistema, m.; organización, orden, disposición, f.; figura, forma, f., cuerpo, m.; forjadura, f.; —, v. a. fabricar, componer, construir, formar; ajustar; idear; poner en bastidor; telar.

frame-work, *–wŭrk,* s. labor hecha en el bastidor ó telar, f.; armazón, f.

franchise, *frăn´tshĭz,* s. franquicia, inmunidad, f.; privilegio, m.

frank, *frăngk,* a. franco, liberal; —, s. carta franca, f.; franco, m. (moneda); —, v. a. franquear una carta.

frankincense, *–ĭnsĕns,* s. incienso, m.

frankly, *–lĕ,* ad. francamente.

frankness, *–nĕs,* s. franqueza, ingenuidad, f.

frantic, *frăn´tĭk,* a. frenético, furioso.

fraternal, *frătŭr´năl,* a., **-ly,** ad. fraternal(mente).

fraternity, *frătŭr´nĭtĕ,* s. fraternidad, f.

fraternize, *frăt´ŭrnĭz,* v. n. hermanarse.

fratricide, *frăt´rĭsĭd,* s. fratricidio, m.; fratricida, m.

fraud, *frăd,* s. fraude, engaño, m.

fraudulence, *frŭ´dŭlĕns,* s. fraudulencia, f.

fraudulent, *frŭ´dŭlĕnt,* a. fraudulento; **-ly,** ad. fraudulentamente.

fraught, *frăt,* a. cargado, lleno.

fray, *frā,* s. riña, disputa, querella, f.; —, v. a. estregar; espantar.

freak, *frēk,* s. fantasía, f.; capricho, m.

freckle, *frĕk´l,* s. peca, f.

freckled, *–d,* a. pecoso.

free, *frē,* a. libre; liberal; franco, ingenuo; exento, dispensado, privilegiado; —, v. a. libertar; librar; eximir.

freebooter, *–bōtŭr,* s. filibustero, forbante.

freedman, *–d´măn,* s. esclavo manumiso, m.

freedom, *–dŭm,* s. libertad, f.; inmunidad, f.

free-hearted, *–hărtĕd,* a. liberal, generoso.

freehold, *–hōld,* s. feudo franco, m.

freely, *–lĕ,* ad. libremente; espontáneamente; liberalmente.

freeman, *–măn,* s. hombre libre, m.; ciudadano, m.

freemason, *–māsn,* s. francmasón, m.

freemasonry, *–māsnrĕ,* s. francmasonería, f.

freeness, *–nĕs,* s. libertad, f.; sinceridad, f.; liberalidad, f.

free-school, *–skōl,* s. escuela gratuita, f.

free-spoken, *–spōkn,* a. dicho sin reserva.

free-thinker, *–thĭngkŭr,* s. libertino, m.

free-thinking, *–thĭnkĭng,* s. incredulidad, f.

free-trade, *–trād,* s. libre cambio, m.

free-will, *–wĭl,* s. libre albedrío, m.; voluntariedad, f.

freeze, *frēz,* v. n. helar(se); —, v. a. congelar.

freight, *frāt,* s. carga, f.; flete, m.; —, v. a. (mar.) fletar; cargar.

freighter, *–ŭr,* s. fletador, m.

frenchify, *frĕnsh´ĭfĭ,* v. a. afrancesarse.

frenzied, *frĕn´zĭd,* a. loco, delirante.

frenzy, *frĕn´zĕ,* s. frenesí, m.; locura, f.

frequency, *frē´kwĕnsĕ,* s. frecuencia, f.; multitud, f.

frequent, *frē´kwĕnt,* a., **-ly,** ad. frecuente(mente); —, *frĕkwĕnt´,* v. a. frecuentar.

frequentative, frĕkwĕn'tătĭv, a. frecuentativo. [m.

frequenter, frĕkwĕnt'ẽr, s. frecuentador,

fresco, frĕs'kō, s. pintura al fresco, f.

fresh, frĕsh, a. fresco; nuevo, reciente; – water, s. agua dulce, f.

freshen, –n, v. a. (& n.) refrescar(se).

freshet, –ĕt, s. arroyo de agua dulce, m.

freshly, –lĕ, ad. frescamente; reciente-

freshman, –măn, s. novicio, m. [mente.

freshness, –nĕs, s. frescura, f.; fresco, m.

freshwater, –wătẽr, s. (mar.) fig. zapatero, marinero inexperimentado, m.

fret, frĕt, s. (mar.) estrecho, m.; enojo, m.; –, v. a. frotar; corroer; cincelar; irritar; agitar, enojar; –, v. n. agitarse, enojarse.

fretful, –fŭl, a. enojadizo, colérico; –ly, ad. de mala gana. [humor, m.

fretfulness, –fŭlnĕs, s. mal genio, mal

fret-saw, –sǟ, s. serrucho, m.

fretting, –tĭng, s. agitación, f.

friability, frīăbĭl'ĭtĕ, s. friabilidad, f.

friable, frī'ăbl, a. friable, desmenuzable.

friar, frī'ẽr, s. fraile, m.; –'s lantern, s. fuego fatuo, m.

friary, –ĕ, s. convento de frailes, m.

Friday, frī'dă, s. viernes, m.; good –, Viernes Santo, m. [pl. parientes, m. pl.

friend, frĕnd, s. amigo, m.; amiga, f.; –s,

friendless, –lĕs, a. sin amigos.

friendliness, –lĭnĕs, s. amistad, benevolencia, bondad, f.

friendly, –lĕ, a. amigable, amistoso.

friendship, –shĭp, s. amistad, f.

frieze, frēz, s. friso m.

frigate, frĭg'ăt, s. (mar.) fragata, f.

fright, frīt, s. espanto, terror, m.

frighten, –n, v. a. espantar.

frightful, –fŭl, a. espantoso, horrible; –ly, ad. espantosamente, terriblemente.

frigid, frĭj'ĭd, a. frío, frígido; –ly, ad. friamente. [rencia, f.; impotencia, f.

frigidity, frĭjĭd'ĭtĕ, s. frialdad, f.; indife-

frill, frĭl, s. escote, vuelo, m.

fringe, frĭnj, s. franja, f.; –, v. a. guarnecer con franjas. [vieja, f.

frippery, frĭp'pără, s. ropavejería, f.; ropa

frisk, frĭsk, v. n. saltar, cabriolar; –, s. gambeta, f.; brinco, m.

frisky, –ĕ, a. alegre, placentero.

frith, frĭth, s. estrecho, brazo de mar, m.

fritter, frĭt'tẽr, s. fritilla, f.; –, v. a. tajar carne; desmenuzar.

frivolity, frĭvŏl'ĭtĕ, s. frivolidad, f.

frivolous, frĭv'ŏlŭs, a. frívolo, vano; –ly, ad. frívolamente, sin substancia.

frizz(le), frĭz'(l), v. a. frisar; rizar.

fro, frō, ad. atrás; to go to and –, ir y venir. [sayo, m.; túnica, f.

frock, frŏk, s. blusa, f.; bata de niño, f.;

frog, frŏg, s. rana, f.

frolic(k), frŏl'ĭk, a. alegre, vivo; –, s. fantasía, f.; capricho, m.; –, v. n. loquear, juguetear, triscar.

frolicsome, –sŭm, a. juguetón, travieso.

from, frŏm, pr. de; después; desde.

frond, frŏnd, s. rama verde, f.

front, frŭnt, s. frente, f.; frontispicio, m.; –, v. a. hacer frente,

frontal, –tăl, s. frontero, m.; venda, f.

frontier, frŏn'tĭẽr, s. frontera, f.

frontispiece, frŏn'tĭspēs, s. frontispicio, m.; frontis grabado de un libro, m.

frontlet, frŏnt'lĕt, s. frontal, m.; venda para la frente, f.

frost, frŏst, s. helada, f.; hielo, m.

frost-bitten, –bĭttn, a. helado, quemado del hielo.

frosty, –ĕ, a. helado, frío como el hielo.

froth, frŏth, s. espuma (de algún líquido), f.; –, v. n. espumar.

frothy, –ĕ, a. espumoso; frívolo, vano.

froward, frō'wŭrd, a. incorregible; impertinente; –ly, ad. insolentemente.

frowardness, –nĕs, s. mal genio, m.; petulancia, f. [ceño, m.; enojo, m.

frown, frŏŭn, v. a. mirar con ceño; –, s.

frozen, frō'zn, a. helado.

frugal, frō'găl, a. frugal; económico; sobrio; –ly, ad. frugalmente. [ción, f.

frugality, frŏgăl'ĭtĕ, s. frugalidad, modera-

fruit, frŏt, s. fruto, m.; producto, m.

fruiterer, –ẽrẽr, s. frutero, m.

fruitful, –fŭl, a. fructífero, fértil; proveechoso, útil; –ly, ad, con fertilidad.

fruitfulness, –fŭlnĕs, s. fertilidad, f.

fruitless, –lĕs, a. estéril; inútil; –ly, ad. vanamente, inútilmente.

fruit-tree, –trē, s. frutal, m.

frump, frŭmp, s. vieja cotorrera, f.

frustrate, frŭs'trăt, v. a. frustrar; anular; chasco, m.

frustration, frŭstră'shŭn, s. contratiempo,

fry, frī, s. freza, f.; fritura, f.; enjambre, m.; montón, m.; hígado, m.; –, v. a. freir.

frying-pan, –ĭngpăn, s. sartén, f.

fuchsia, fū'shĭă, s. (bot.) fuchsia, f.

fuddle, fŭd'l, v. a. (& n.) emborrachar(se).

fudge, fŭj, ¡quita de ahí!, ¡vete allá!

fuel, fū'ĕl, s. combustible, m.

fugitive, fū'jĭtĭv, a. & s. fugitivo (m.).

fugue, fŭg, s. (mus.) fuga, f.

fulcrum, fŭl'krŭm, s. apoyo de palanca ó alzaprima, m.

fulfil, fŭlfĭl', v. a. colmar; cumplir.

fulfilment, –mĕnt, s. cumplimiento, m.

full, fŭl, a. lleno, repleto, completo; todo; perfecto; –, s. total, m.; complemento, m.; –, ad. enteramente, del todo; –, v. a. batanar el paño.

full-blown, –blōn, a. desplegado completamente (hablando de las flores).

full-cock, –kŏk, a. montado, amartillado (dícese de una escopeta).

full-compass, –kămpăs, a. (mus.) con siete octavas. [m.

full-cry, –krī, s. grito agudo y penetrante,

full-dress, –drĕs, s. vestido de gala, m.

fuller, –lẽr, s. batanero, m. [f.

full-length, –lĕngth, s. grandeza natural,

fulling-mill, –ĭngmĭl, s. batán, m.

full-moon, –mōn, s. plenilunio, m.; luna llena, f. [pliamente.

fully, –lĕ, ad. llenamente, enteramente, am-

fulminant, fŭl'mĭnănt, a. fulminante.

fulminate, fŭl'mĭnăt, v. a. & n. fulminar.

fulmination, fŭlmĭnă'shŭn, s. fulminación, f.

fulness, *fŭl'nĕs,* s. plenitud, llenura, abundancia, f.
fulsome, *fŭl'sŭm,* a. rancio; impuro.
fumble, *fŭm'bl,* v. a. & n. tartamudear; chapucear, muchachear; andar á tientas.
fume, *fūm,* s. humo, vapor, m.; cólera, f.; vanidad, f.; —, v. a. ahumar, —, v. n. humear, exhalar; encolerizarse. [mar.
fumigate, *fū'mĭgāt,* v. a. perfumar, sahumar.
fumigation, *fūmĭgā'shŭn,* s. sahumerio, m.; fumigación, f. [toria, f.
fumigator, *fū'mĭgātŭr,* s. máquina fumigatoria.
fun, *fŭn,* s. chanza, burla, f. [pleo, m.
function, *fŭngk'shŭn,* s. función, f.; empleo, m.
functionary, *—ārĕ,* s. empleado, m.
fund, *fŭnd,* s. fondo, m.; fondos públicos, m. pl.; —, v. a. poner dinero en los fondos públicos.
fundament, *—ămĕnt,* s. fundamento, m.
fundamental, *—ămĕn'tăl,* a. fundamental; **—ly,** ad. fundamentalmente.
funeral, *fū'nĕrăl,* s. funeral, m.; —, **funereal,** *fūnē'rĭăl,* a. funeral, fúnebre.
fungosity, *fŭnggŏs'ĭtĕ,* s. fungosidad, f.
fungous, *fŭng'gŭs,* a. fungoso; esponjoso.
fungus, *—,* s. hongo, m.; seta, f.
funk, *fŭngk,* s. (vulg.) hedor, m.
funnel, *fŭn'nĕl,* s. embudo, m.; cañón (de chimenea), m.
funny, *fŭn'nĕ,* a. burlesco, bufón.
fur, *fŭr,* s. forro de pieles, m.; pelo, m.; —, v. a. aforrar con pieles.
furbelow, *fŭr'bēlō,* s. falbalá, m.
furbish, *fŭr'bĭsh,* v. a. acicalar, pulir.
furious, *fū'rĭŭs,* a. furioso, frenético; **—ly,** ad. con furia. [las velas.
furl, *fŭrl,* v. a. desdoblar; (mar.) aferrar
furlong, *fŭr'lŏng,* s. estadio, m. (octava parte de una milla). [miso, m.
furlough, *fŭr'lō,* s. (mil.) licencia, f.; permiso.
furnace, *fŭr'nās,* s. horno, m.; hornaza, f.
furnish, *fŭr'nĭsh,* v. a. suplir, proveer; equipar; (a house) amueblar una casa.
furnisher, *—ŭr,* s. proveedor, m.
furniture, *fŭr'nĭtūr,* s. ajuar, m.; aparejo, m. [chero de alhajas (&c.), m.
furniture-broker, *—brōkŭr,* s. cambalachero.
furrier, *fŭr'rĭŭr,* s. peletero, m.
furrow, *fŭr'rō,* s. surco, m.; —, v. a. surcar; estriar. [pieles.
furry, *fŭr'rĕ,* a. hecho ó guarnecido de
further, *fŭr'thŭr,* a. ulterior, más distante; —, ad. más lejos, más allá; aun; además de eso; —, v. a. adelantar, promover, ayudar.
furtherance, *—ăns,* s. adelantamiento, m.; progreso, m.; ayuda, asistencia, f.
furthermore, *—mōr,* ad. además.
furthest, *fŭr'thĕst,* ad. lo más lejos, lo más remoto. [ad. furtivamente.
furtive, *fŭr'tĭv,* a. furtivo; secreto; **—ly,**
fury, *fū'rĕ,* s. furor, m.; furia, f.; ira, f.
furze, *fŭrz,* s. (bot.) tojo, m.
fuse, *fūz,* v. a. & n. fundir; derretirse.
fusee, *—ē,* s. huso, m.; fusil, m.; espoleta, f.
fusible, *fū'zĭbl,* a. fusible, fundible.
fusilier, *fūzĭlēr',* s. fusilero, m.
fusion, *fū'zhŭn,* s. fusión, licuación, f.
fuss, *fŭs,* s. (vulg.) alboroto, tumulto, m.

fussy, *fŭs'ĕ,* a. jactancioso. [sonante, m.
fustian, *fŭs'tĭăn,* s. fustán, m.; estilo altisonante.
fustiness, *fŭs'tĭnĕs,* s. enmohecimiento, m.;
fusty, *fŭs'tĕ,* a. mohoso. [hedor, m.
futile, *fū'tĭl,* a. fútil, frívolo.
futility, *fūtĭl'ĭtĕ,* s. futilidad, vanidad, f.
future, *fū'tŭr,* a. futuro; —, s. lo futuro, el tiempo venidero. [venideros, m. pl.
futurity, *fūtūr'ĭtĕ,* s. futuro, m.; sucesos
fy, *fī!* ¡vaya! — **for shame,** ¡qué vergüenza!

G.

gab, *găb,* s. (fam.) locuacidad, f.
gabble, *—bl,* v. n. charlar, parlotear; —, s. algarabía, f.
gable-end, *gā'bl ĕnd,* s. socarrén, alero, m.
gaby, *gā'bĕ,* s. papanatas, m.
gad, *găd,* v. n. tunar, corretear, andorrear.
gad-fly, *—flī,* s. tábano, m.
gaff, *găf,* s. (mar.) cangreja, f.
gag, *găg,* s. mordaza, f.; —, v. a. tapar la boca con mordaza.
gage, *gāj,* s. prenda, f.
gaiety, *gā'ĕtĕ,* s. alegría, f.
gaily, *gā'lĕ,* ad. alegremente.
gain, *gān,* s. ganancia, f.; interés, provecho, m.; —, v. a. ganar; conseguir; —, v. n. enriquecerse; prevalecer, obtener
gainer, *—ŭr,* s. ganador, m. [influjo.
gainings, *—ĭngz,* s. pl. ganancia, f.; provecho, m. [tuoso.
gainless, *—lĕs,* a. desventajoso, infructuoso.
gainsay, *—sā,* v. a. contradecir; negar; contrariar.
gait, *gāt,* s. marcha, f.; porte, m.
gaiter, *—ŭr,* s. polaina, f.; botín, m.
galaxy, *găl'ăksē,* s. galaxia, vía láctea, f.
gale, *gāl,* s. (mar.) viento fresco, m.
galiot, *găl'ĭŏt,* s. (mar.) galeota, f.
gall, *găl,* s. hiel, f.; rencor, odio, m.; —, v. a. desollar; acibarar.
gallant, *găl'lănt,* a. galante, elegante; valeroso; **—ly,** ad. galantemente; bravamente; —, s. galán, cortejo, m. [f.
gallantry, *—rē,* s. galantería, f.; bravura,
galleon, *găl'lĕŏn,* s. (mar.) galeón, m.
gallery, *găl'lŭrē,* s. galería, f.; corredor, m.
galley, *găl'lē,* s. (mar.) galera, f.
galley-slave, *—slāv,* s. galeote, m.
gallinaceous, *găllĭnā'shŭs,* a. galináceo.
gallipot, *găl'lĭpŏt,* s. orza, f.
gall-nut, *găl'nŭt,* s. agalla, f.
gallon, *găl'lŏn,* s. galón, m. (medida). [pear.
gallop, *găl'lŭp,* s. galope, m.; —, v. n. galo-
galloshes, *gălŏsh'ĕz,* s. pl. chanclos, zuecos, m. pl.
gallows, *găl'lōz,* s. horca, f. [cos, m. pl.
galvanic, *gălvăn'ĭk,* a. galvánico.
galvanise, *găl'vănīz,* v. a. galvanizar.
galvanism, *găl'vănĭzm,* s. galvanismo, m.
gambit, *găm'bĭt,* s. gambit, gambis, m. (jugada de ajedrez).
gamble, *găm'bl,* v. n. jugar con exceso.
gambler, *—ŭr,* s. tahur, gariotero, fullero, m.

gambling-house, –blínghǒǔs, s. garito, m.; casa de juego, f.   [gamba, f.
gamboge, gámbój, s. gomaguta, guta-
gambol, gám'bŏl, s. cabriola, f.; –, v. n. brincar, saltar.
game, gám, s. juego, m.; pasatiempo, m.; burla, f.; caza, f.; –, v. n. jugar.   [dor, f.
game-bag, –bág, s. mochila de un caza-
game-cock, –kŏk, s. gallo de riña, m.
game-keeper, –kēpǎr, s. guarda de coto, m.
gamesome, –sŭm, a. juguetón, retozón; –ly, ad. alegremente.
gamester, –stǎr, tahur, jugador, m.
gaming, gá'mĭng, s. juego, m.; juego. [duría, f.
gammon, gám'mŭn, s. jamón, m.; habla-
gamut, gám'ǎt, s. (mus.) gama, f.
gander, gán'dǎr, s. ánsar, ganso, m.
gang, gáng, s. cuadrilla, banda, f.
gangrene, gáng'grēn, s. gangrena, f.
gangway, –wá, s. pasamano de un navío.
gaol, jál, s. cárcel, prisión, f.   [portalón, m.
gaoler, –ǎr, s. carcelero, m.
gap, gáp, s. boquete, m.; brecha, f.
gape, gáp, v. n. bostezar, boquear; ansiar, hendirse; estar con la boca abierta.
gaping, gá'pĭng, s. bostezo, m.
garb, gárb, s. vestidura, f.; traje, m.; apariencia exterior, f.
garbage, gár'bǐj, s. tripas, f. pl.
garble, gár'bl, v. a. entresacar; garbillar.
garden, gár'dn, s. huerto, m.; jardín, m.; –, v. n. cultivar un jardín ó un huerto.
garden-engine, –engĭn, **garden-hose,** –hŏz, s. regadera, f.   [f.
gardener, –ǎr, s. jardinero, m.; jardinera, f.
gardening, –ĭng, s. jardinería, f.
gargle, gár'gl, v. a. & n. gargarizar; –, s. gargarismo, m.
gargoyle, gár'gŏĭl, s. gárgola, f.
garish, gár'ĭsh, a. pomposo, ostentoso.
garland, gár'lánd, s. guirnalda, f.
garlic, gár'lĭk, s. (bot.) ajo, m.
garment, gár'ment, s. vestidura, f.
garner, gár'nǎr, s. granero, m.
garnet, gár'nĕt, s. granate, m.; (mar.) candeletón, m.
garnish, gár'nĭsh, v. a. guarnecer, ador-nar; –, s. guarnición, f.; adorno, m.
garret, gár'rĕt, s. guardilla, f.; desván, m.
garrison, gár'rĭsn, s. (mil.) guarnición, f.; –, v. a. (mil.) guarnecer.
garrote, gárŏt', v. a. estrangular.
garroter, –ǎr, s. estrangulador, m.
garrulity, gárrŭ'ltĭ, s. garrulidad, locua-cidad, charladuría, f.   [charlador.
garrulous, gár'rŏlŭs, a. gárrulo, locuaz.
garter, gár'tǎr, s. cenojil, m.; jarretera, f.
gas, gás, s. gas, m.
gasalier, –lēr', s. candil de gas, m.
gas-burner, –bǔrnǎr, s. mechero de gas.
gaseous, gá'zěǔs, a. gaseoso, m.
gash, gásh, s. cuchillada, f.; cicatriz, f.; –, v. a. dar una cuchillada.
gas-holder, gás'hŏldǎr, **gasometer,** gásŏm'ǎtǎr, s. gasómetro, m.
gas-jets, –jĕtz, s. pl. gasíferos, m. pl.
gas-lighting, –líing, s. alumbramiento de gas, m.

gasp, gásp, v. n. boquear; anhelar; –, s. respiración difícil, f.
gastric, gás'trĭk, a. gástrico.   [mico.
gastronomic, gástrŏnŏm'ĭk, a. gastronó-
gastronomy-works, gás'wǔrks, s. pl. fábrica de gas, f.
gate, gát, s. puerta, f.; puerta de cercado.
gate-way, –wá, s. puerta cochera, f.
gather, gáth'ǎr, v. a. recoger, amontonar; fruncir; inferir; arrugar, plegar; –, v. n. condensarse, aumentarse, juntarse; su-purar.   [lecta.
gathering, –ĭng, s. acumulación, f.; co-
gaudily, gá'dĭlě, ad. ostentosamente, fasto-samente.   [clón, f.
gaudiness, gá'dĭnĕs, s. pompa, f.; ostenta-
gaudy, –ě, a. fastoso; pomposo; –, s. fiesta, f.; festín, m.
gauge, gádj, s. aforo, m.; –, v. a. aforar.
gauger, –ǎr, s. aforador, m.
gaunt, gánt, a. & s. flaco, delgado (m.).
gauntlet, gánt'lĕt, s. guantelete, m.; mano-
gauze, gáz, s. gasa, f.   [pla, f.
gawky, gá'kě, a. bobo, tonto, rudo.
gay, gá, a. gayo, alegre.   [mirada, f.
gaze, gáz, v. n. contemplar, considerar; –, s.
gazelle, gázĕll', s. gacela, f.
gazer, gá'zǎr, s. mirón, m.
gazette, gázĕt', s. gaceta, f.
gazetteer, gázĕtēr', s. gacetero, m.; dic-cionario geográfico, m.
gear, gēr, s. atavío, m.; vestido, m.; apa-rejo, m.; tirantes, m. pl.
gelatin(e), jĕl'ǎtĭn, s. jaletina, jalea, f.
gelatinous, jĕlát'ĭnŭs, a. gelatinoso.
geld, gĕld, v. a. castrar, capar.
gelding, –ĭng, s. caballo capón, m.
gem, jĕm, s. joya, f.; yema, f.; –, v. a. ador-nar con piedras preciosas; –, v. n. abotonar.
Gemini, jĕm'ĭnē, s. Géminis, m. (signo del
gender, jĕn'dǎr, s. género, m. [zodíaco).
genealogical, gĕnĕǎlŏj'ĭkǎl, a. genealógico.
genealogy, jĕnĕǎl'ǒjě, s. genealogía, f.
general, jĕn'ĕrǎl, a. general, común, usual; in –, por lo común; –ly, ad. general-mente; –, s. general, m.; generala, f.
generalisation, jĕnĕrǎlĭzá'shǔn, s. gene-ralización, f.
generalise, jĕn'ĕrǎlīz, v. a. generalizar.
generality, jĕnĕrǎl'ĭtě, s. generalidad, mayor parte, f.   [m.
generalship, jĕn'ĕrǎlshĭp, s. generalato, s.
generate, jĕn'ĕrǎt, v. a. engendrar; pro-ducir; causar.
generation, –rǎ'shŭn, s. generación, f.
generator, –tǎr, s. engendrador, m.
generic, jĕnĕr'ĭk, a. genérico.   [ralidad, f.
generosity, jĕnĕrŏs'ĭtě, s. generosidad, libe-
generous, jĕn'ĕrŭs, a. generoso; –ly, ad. magnánimamente.   [f.
genet, jĕn'ĕt, s. jaca de España, f.; jinete,
genial, jē'nĭǎl, a. genial, natural; alegre; –ly, ad. genialmente.   [gría, f.
geniality, jĕnĭǎl'ĭtě, s. ingenuidad, f.; ale-
genitive, jĕn'ĭtĭv, s. genitivo, m.
genius, jē'nĭŭs, s. genio, m.
genteel, jĕntēl', a. gentil, lindo, galán, elegante; –ly, ad. gentilmente.

gentian, *jĕn'shăn*, s. (bot.) genciana, f.
gentile, *jĕn'til*, s. gentil, pagano, m.
gentility, *jĕntīl'tĭ*, s. gentileza, f.; gentilidad, f.; nobleza de sangre, f.
gentle, *jĕn'tl*, a. suave, dócil, manso, moderado; benigno.   [f.
gentlefolks, —*fōkz*, s. pl. gente bien nacida, f.
gentleman, —*măn*, s. gentilhombre, caballero, m.   [urbano.
gentlemanlike, —*mănlĭk*, a. caballeroso,
gentleness, —*nĕs*, s. dulzura, suavidad de carácter, f.; nobleza, f.
gentlewoman, —*wŭmăn*, a. señora, dama, f.
gently, *jĕn'tlĭ*, ad. gentilmente.   [m. pl.
gentry, *jĕn'trĭ*, s. ciudadanos distinguidos,
genuflexion, *jĕnūflĕk'shŭn*, s. genuflexión, f.   [ad. puramente, naturalmente.
genuine, *jĕn'ūĭn*, a. genuino, puro; —ly,
genuiness, —*nĕs*, s. pureza, f.
genus, *jē'nŭs*, s. género, m.
geographer, *jĕŏg'răfŭr*, s. geógrafo, m.
geographical, *jĕŏgrăf'ĭkăl*, a. geográfico.
geography, *jĕŏg'răfĭ*, s. geografía, f.
geological, *jĕŏlŏj'ĭkăl*, a. geológico.
geologist, *jĕŏl'ŏjĭst*, s. geólogo, m.
geology, *jĕŏl'ŏjĭ*, s. geología, f.   [trico.
geometric(al), *jĕŏmĕt'rĭk(ăl)*, a. geomé-
geometrician, *jĕŏmĕtrĭsh'ăn*, s. geómetra.
geometry, *jĕŏm'ĕtrĭ*, s. geometría, f. [m.
geranium, *jĕrā'nĭŭm*, s. (bot.) geranio, m.
germ, *jŭrm*, s. (bot.) germen, m.
german, *jŭr'măn*, a. alemán; pariente.
germinal, *jŭr'mĭnăl*, a. germinativo.
germinate, *jŭr'mĭnăt*, v. n. brotar.
gesticulate, *jĕstĭk'ūlăt*, v. n. gesticular.
gesticulation, —*lā'shŭn*, s. gesticulación, f.
gesture, *jĕs'tūr*, s. gesto, movimiento expresivo, m.
get, *gĕt*, v. a. granjear, ganar; conseguir, obtener, alcanzar; coger; agarrar, robar; persuadir; —, v. n. alcanzar; llegar, venir; hacerse, ponerse; prevalecer; introducirse;
to — by heart, aprender de memoria;
to — the better, salir vencedor, sobrepujar; **to — with child**, poner encinta á una mujer.
getter-up, —*tŭrŭp*, s. promotor, m. [m.
gewgaw, *gū'gŏ*, s.chuchería,f.; miriñaque,
Geyser, *gī'sŭr*, s. Géiser, m.; fuente caliente en Islandia, f.   [davérica, f.
ghastliness, *găst'lĭnĕs*, s. palidez, cara ca-
ghastly, —*lĭ*, a. pálido, espantoso. [m.
gherkin, *gŭr'kĭn*, s. pepinillo, cohombrillo,
ghost, *gŏst*, s. alma racional, f.; espectro, m.
ghostly, —*lĭ*, a. espiritual.   [m.
giant, *jī'ănt*, s. gigante, m.
giantess, —*ĕs*, s. giganta, f.
gibberish, *gĭb'bărĭsh*, s. jerigonza, f.
gibbet, *jĭb'bĕt*, s. horca, f.; —, v. a. ahorcar.
gibe, *jĭb*, v. n. escarnecer, burlarse, mofar; —, s. mofa, burla, f.   [(de aves), m. pl.
giblets, *jĭb'lĕts*, s. pl.despojos y menudillos
giddily, *gĭd'dĭlĭ*, ad. con vértigos; descuidadamente.   [tancia, f.
giddiness, —*dĭnĕs*, s. vértigo, m.; incons-
giddy, —*dĭ*, a. vertiginoso; inconstante.
gift, *gĭft*, s. don, m.; dádiva, f.; talento, m.

gig, *gĭg*, s. tílburi, calesín, m.; trompo, m.
gigantic(al), *jĭgănt'ĭk(ăl)*, a. gigantesco.
   perínola, f.; esquife, m.   [gigantesco.
giggle, *gĭg'gl*, v. n. fisgarse sonriéndose.
gild, *gĭld*, v. a. dorar.
gilding, —*ĭng*, gilt, *gĭlt*, s. doradura, f.
gill, *jĭl*, s. cuarta parte de pinta, f.; hiedra terrestre, f.; torrentera, f.; —s, pl. barbas del gallo, f. pl.; agallas de los peces, f. pl.
gillyflower, —*flŏŭr*, s. (bot.) alelí, m.
gimcrack, *jĭm'krăk*, s. carraca, f.
gimlet, *jĭm'lĕt*, s. barrena pequeña, f.
gimp, *gĭmp*, s. encaje de hilo ó seda, m.
gin, *jĭn*, s. trampa, f.; cabria, f.; aguardiente de nebrina, m.
ginger, *jĭr'*, s. jengibre, m.
gingerbread, —*brĕd*, s. pan de jengibre, m.
gipsy, *jĭp'sĭ*, s. gitano, m.
giraffe, *jĭrăf'*, s. jirafa, f.   [farse.
gird, *gŭrd*, v. a. ceñir; cercar; —, v. n. mo-
girder, —*ŭr*, s. cuartón, m.
girdle, —*l*, s. cinturón, m.; —, v. a. ceñir.
girl, *gŭrl*, s. muchacha, doncellita, f.
girlhood, —*hŭd*, s. doncellez, soltería, f.
girlish, —*ĭsh*, a. juvenil.
girth, *gŭrth*, s. cincha, f.; circunferencia, f.
gist, *jĭst*, s. punto principal de una acusación, f.
give, *gĭv*, v. a. & n. dar, donar; conceder; renunciar; abandonar; pronunciar; aplicarse, dedicarse.
gizzard, *gĭz'zŭrd*, s. molleja, f.
glacial, *glā'shăl*, a. glacial.   [m.
glacier, *glā'shŭr* (*glăs'*), s. ventisquero,
glad, *glăd*, a. alegre, contento, agradable;
   I am — to see, me alegro de; —ly, ad. alegremente.
gladden, —*n*, v. a. alegrar, recrear.
glade, *glād*, s. cañada, f.; (am.) nevisca, f.
gladiator, *glăd'ĭā'tŭr*, s. gladiator, m.
gladness, *găd'nĕs*, s. alegría, f.
gladsome, —*sŭm*, a. alegre, contento.
glair, *glăr*, s. claro de huevo, m.
glamour, *glăm'ŭr*, s. ilusión óptica, f.
glance, *glăns*, s. vislumbre, f.; relámpago; m.; ojeada, f.; —, v. a. lanzar miradas; raspar; pasar ligeramente; —, v. n. centellar; hojear.
gland, *glănd*, s. glándula, f.
glanders, *glănd'ŭrz*, s. muermo, m.
glare, *glăr*, s.deslumbramiento, m.; mirada feroz y penetrante, f.; —, v. n. relumbrar, brillar; echar miradas de indignación.
glaring, —*ĭng*,a.deslumbrante; manifiesto; que clama al cielo.
glass, *glăs*, s. vidrio, m.; telescopio, m.; vaso para beber, m.; espejo, m.; reloj de arena, m.; barómetro, m.; —es, pl. anteojo, m.; —, a. vítreo.   [vidrio, m.;
glass-blower, —*blŏŭr*, s. soplador de
glass-door, —*dŏr*, s.puerta con vidrieras, f.
glass-work, —*wŭrk*, s. fábrica de vidrio ó cristales, f.
glassy, —*ĭ*, a. vítreo, cristalino, vidrioso.
glaze, *glāz*, v. a. vidriar; embarnizar.
glazier, *glā'zhŭr*, s. vidriero, m.
glazing, —*zĭng*, s. conjunto de vidrios, m.
gleam, *glēm*, s. relámpago, rayo, m.; —, v. n. relampaguear, brillar.

glean, _glēn,_ v. a. espigar; recoger.

glebe, _glēb,_ s. gleba, f.; terrón, m.

glee, _glē,_ s. alegría, f.; gozo, m.; jovialidad, f.; canción jovial, f.

gleeful, _–fūl,_ a. alegre, gozoso.

gleet, _glēt,_ s. gonorrea, f.; podre, m.

glen, _glēn,_ s. valle, m.; llanura, f.

glib, _glib,_ a. liso, resbaladizo; **–ly,** ad. corrientemente, volublemente.

glide, _glīd,_ v. n. resbalar; pasar ligeramente.

glim, _glim,_ s. farol de ronda, m.; linterna sorda, f. [vislumbrarse.

glimmer, _–mŭr,_ s. vislumbre, f.; **–,** v. n.

glimpse, _glimps,_ s. vislumbre, f.; relámpago, m.; ojeada, f.; **–,** v. a. (am.) descubrir, percibir. [lucir, brillar.

glisten, _glis'n,_ **glitter,** _glit'tŭr,_ v. n. relumbrar.

gloaming, _glōm'ing,_ s. crepúsculo, m.

gloat, _glōt,_ v. n. ojear con admiración.

globe, _glōb,_ s. globo, m.; esfera, f.

globular, _glob'ŭlăr,_ a. globoso.

globule, _glob'ŭl,_ s. glóbulo, m.

gloom, _glōm,_ **gloominess,** _–inĕs,_ s. obscuridad, f.; melancolía, tristeza, f.; **–ly,** ad. obscuramente o tristemente.

gloomy, _–ĭ,_ a. sombrío, obscuro; cubierto de nubes; triste, melancólico.

glorification, _glōrĭfĭkā'shŭn,_ s. glorificación, alabanza, f.

glorify, _glō'rĭfī,_ v. a. glorificar, celebrar.

glorious, _glō'rĭŭs,_ a. glorioso, ilustre; **–ly,** ad. gloriosamente.

glory, _glō'rĭ,_ s. gloria, fama, celebridad, f.; aureola, f.; **–,** v. n. gloriarse, jactarse.

gloss, _glŏs,_ s. glosa, f.; escolio, m.; lustre, m.; **–,** v. a. glosar, interpretar; notar.

glossary, _–ărĭ,_ s. glosario, m. [barnizar.

glosser, _–ŭr,_ s. comentador, m.

glossy, _–sĭ,_ a. lustroso, brillante.

glove, _glŭv,_ s. guante, m.

glover, _–ŭr,_ s. guantero, m.

glow, _glō,_ v. n. arder; inflamarse; relucir; **–,** s. color vivo, m.; viveza de color, f.; vehemencia de una pasión, f.

glower, _glō'ŭr,_ v. n. mirar con ceño.

glow-worm, _–wŭrm,_ s. luciérnaga, f.

gloze, _glōz,_ v. n. adular, lisonjear.

glue, _glū,_ s. cola, f.; visco, m.; **–,** v. a. encolar, pegar.

gluey, _–ĭ,_ a. viscoso, pegajoso.

glum, _glŭm,_ a. tétrico, triste.

glut, _glŭt,_ v. a. engullir, tragar, devorar; saciar; **–,** s. hartura, abundancia, f.

gluten, _glū'tĕn,_ s. gluten, m.

glutinous, _glū'tĭnŭs,_ a. glutinoso, viscoso.

glutton, _glŭt'n,_ s. glotón, tragón, m.

gluttony, _–ĭ,_ s. glotonería, f.

glycerine, _glis'ărĭn,_ s. glicerina, f.

gnarled, _nār'ld,_ a. nudoso. [dientes.

gnash, _nāsh,_ v. a. & n. chocar; crujir los

gnat, _nāt,_ s. mosquito, m.

gnaw, _nȧ,_ v. a. roer; mordicar.

gnome, _nōm,_ s. gnomo, m.

go, _gō,_ v. n. ir, irse, andar, caminar; partir(se), marchar; huir; pasar; **– to** ¡vamos!, ¡á ello! [aguijar; estimular, incitar.

goad, _gōd,_ s. aguijada, aijada, f.; **–,** v. a.

goal, _gōl,_ s. meta, f.; fin, m. [m.

goat, _gōt,_ s. cabra, chiva, f.; **he––,** cabrón,

goat-herd, _–hĕrd,_ s. cabrero, m.

gobble, _gŏb'bl,_ v. a. engullir, tragar; **–,** v. n. gorgorear como los gallipavos.

gobbler, _–ŭr,_ s. glotón, m.

go-between, _gō bĕtwēn,_ s. mediador, m.; entremetido, m.

goblet, _gŏb'lĕt,_ s. copa, f. [duende, m.

goblin, _gŏb'lĭn,_ s. espíritu ambulante

God, _gŏd,_ s. Dios, m. [m.

god-child, _–tshīld,_ s. ahijado, hijo de pila.

god-daughter, _–dȧtŭr,_ s. ahijada, hija

goddess, _–dĕs,_ s. diosa, f. [de pila.

god-father, _–fȧthŭr,_ s. padrino, m.

godhead, _–hĕd,_ s. deidad, divinidad, f.

godless, _–lĕs,_ a. infiel, impío, sin Dios.

godlike, _–līk,_ a. divino. [ateo.

godliness, _–lĭnĕs,_ s. piedad, devoción, santidad, f.

godly, _–lĭ,_ a. piadoso, devoto, religioso; recto, justificado; **–,** ad. piadosamente, justamente.

god-mother, _–mŭthŭr,_ s. madrina, f.

god-son, _–sŭn,_ s. ahijado, m.

goer, _gō'ŭr,_ s. andador, paseante, m.

goggle, _gŏg'gl,_ v. n. volver los ojos.

goggle-eyed, _–īd,_ a. bisojo, bizco.

going, _gō'ĭng,_ s. paso, m.; andadura, f.; partida, f.; progreso, m.

gold, _gōld,_ s. oro, m. [batihoja, m.

gold-beater, _–bētŭr,_ s. batidor de oro,

gold-bound, _–bŏund,_ a. guarnecido de oro.

golden, _–n,_ a. áureo, de oro; excelente; **– rule,** s. (ar.) regla de tres, f.

gold-fish, _–fĭsh,_ s. dorado, m.

gold-leaf, _–lēf,_ s. hoja de oro batido, f.

goldsmith, _–smĭth,_ s. orifice, m.

golf, _gŏlf,_ s. juego de pelota escocés, m.

golosh, _gŏlŏsh,_ s. galocho, m.

gondolier, _gŏndŏlēr,_ s. gondolero, m.

gone, _gŏn,_ a. ido; perdido; pasado; gastado; muerto.

gong, _gŏng,_ s. atabal chino, m.

good, _gŭd,_ a. bueno, benévolo, cariñoso; conveniente, apto; **–,** ad. bien; **–,** s. bien, m. prosperidad, ventaja, f.; **–s,** pl. bienes muebles, m. pl.; mercaderías, f. pl.

good-bye, _–bī!_ [¡á Dios!

goodies, _–ĭz,_ s. pl. golosinas, f. pl.

goodliness, _–lĭnĕs,_ s. hermosura, elegancia, gracia, f.

goodly, _–lĭ,_ a. hermoso, espléndido; alegre.

good-nature, _–nā'tŭr,_ s. bondad, f.

good-natured, _–nā'tŭrd,_ a. bondadoso.

goodness, _–nĕs,_ s. bondad, f.

goodwill, _–wĭl,_ s. benevolencia, bondad, f.

goose, _gōs,_ s. ganso, m.; oca, f.; plancha de sastre, f.

gooseberry, _–bĕrĭ,_ s. uva espina, f.

goose-step, _–stĕp,_ s. (mil.) desfilada, f.

gopher, _gō'fŭr,_ s. turón, m.

gore, _gōr,_ s. sangre cuajada, f.; **–,** v. a. punzar; herir con puñal; herir un animal con sus cuernos á otro.

gorge, _gŏrj,_ s. gorja, garganta, f.; **–,** v. a. engullir, tragar.

gorgeous, *gŏr'jŭs*, a. primoroso, brillante, vistoso; **-ly**, ad. con esplendor y magnificencia.

gorget, *gŏr'jĕt*, s. gola, f.

Gorgon, *gŏr'gŏn*, s. Gorgona, f.

gormandize, *gŏr'mändiz*, v. n. glotonear.

gormandizer, *-ăr*, s. golosazo, m.

gory, *gŏ'rĕ*, a. cubierto de sangre grumosa.

goshawk, *gŏs'hăk*, s. azor, halcón palumbario, m.

gosling, *gŏz'lĭng*, s. gansarón, m.

gospel, *gŏs'pĕl*, s. evangelio, m.

gossamer, *gŏs'sămăr*, s. vello, m.; pelusa (de frutas), f.

gossip, *gŏs'sĭp*, s. compadre, m.; comadre, f.; charla, f.; —, v. n. charlar.

gothic, *gŏth'ĭk*, a. gótico.

gouge, *gŏj*, s. gubia, f.; escoplo, m.

gourd, *gŏrd*, s. (bot.) calabaza, f.

gout, *gŏŭt*, s. gota, f. (enfermedad).

gouty, *-ĭ*, a. gotoso.

govern, *gŭv'ărn*, v. a. gobernar, dirigir, regir.

governable, *ăbl*, a. dócil, manejable.

governess, *-es*, s. gobernadora, f.

government, *-mĕnt*, **governance**, *-ăns*, s. gobierno, m.; administración pública, f.

governor, *-ăr*, s. gobernador, m.

gown, *gŏŭn*, s. talar, m.; toga, f.; vestido de mujer, m.; bata, f.; camiseta, f.

gownsman, *-s'măn*, s. estudiante de alguna universidad, m.

grabble, *grăb'bl*, grab, grăb, v. a. tentar, palpar.

grace, *grās*, s. gracia, f.; favor, m.; merced, f.; perdón, m.; gracias, f. pl.; to say —, bendecir la mesa; —, v. a. adornar; agraciar.

Grace, —, s. Alteza (título), f.

graceful, *-fŭl*, a. graciosa, primoroso; **-ly**, ad. elegantemente, con gracia.

graceless, *-lĕs*, a. desagraciado; réprobo, malvado; **-ly**, ad. graciosamente.

gracious, *grā'shŭs*, a. gracioso; favorable; **-ly**, ad. graciosamente.

graciousness, *-nĕs*, s. gracia, bondad, f.

gradation, *grădā'shŭn*, s. graduación, f.

grade, *grād*, s. grado, m.

gradient, *grā'dĭĕnt*, s. (rail.) pendiente y contrapendiente, m. &f.; **falling**—, (rail.) declive, m.

gradual, *grăd'ŭăl*, a. gradual; **-ly**, ad. gradualmente.

graduate, *grăd'ŭăt*, v. a. graduar; adelantar.

graduation, *grădŭă'shŭn*, s. graduación, f.

graft, *grăft*, s. injerto, m.; —, v. a. injertar, ingerir.

grafting-knife, *-ĭngnĭf*, s. ingeridor, m.

grain, *grān*, s. grano, m.; semilla, f.; grana, f.; disposición, índole, f.; **-s**, pl. orujo, m. buruja, m.; **against the**—, contra pelo; con repugnancia; **crudo**.

grained, *-d'*, a. granado; áspero; teñido en grana.

gram, *grăm*, s. gramo, m. (peso).

grammar, *grăm'măr*, s. gramática, f. [m.

grammarian, *grămmā'rĭăn*, s. gramático, m.

grammatic(al), *grămmăt'ĭk(ăl)*, a. **-ally**, ad. gramatical(mente).

grampus, *grăm'pŭs*, s. marsopa, f. (pez).

granary, *grăn'ărĕ*, s. granero, m.

grand, *grănd*, a. grande, ilustre.

grandchild, *-tshĭld*, s. nieto, m.; nieta, f.

granddaughter, *-ădŭăr*, s. nieta, f.; **great**—, biznieta, f.

grandee, *-ē*, s. grande (de España), m.

grandeur, *grănd'yŭr*, s. grandeza, f.; pompa, f. [—, bisabuelo, m.

grandfather, *-fădŭăr*, s. abuelo, m.; **great**

grandiloquent, *grănd'ĭlŏkwĕnt*, a. grandílocuo.

grandiose, *grănd'ĭōs*, a. grandioso.

grandly, *grănd'lĕ*, ad. grandemente, sublimemente. [great—, bisabuela, f.

grandmother, *-mŭdăr*, s. abuela, f.;

grand-sire, *-sĭr*, s. abuelo, m.

grandson, *-sŭn*, s. nieto, m.; great—, [bisnieto, m.

grange, *grānj*, s. granja, f.

granite, *grăn'ĭt*, s. granito, m.

grant, *grănt*, v. a. conceder; **to take for** —**ed**, presuponer; —, s. concesión, f.

granulate, *grăn'ŭlāt*, v. a. granular.

grape, *grāp*, s. uva, f.; **bunch of** —**s**, racimo de uvas, m.

grape-shot, *-shŏt*, s. (mil.) metralla, f.

grape-stone, *-stōn*, s. granuja, f.

graphic(al), *grăf'ĭk(ăl)*, a. gráfico; pintoresco; **-ally**, ad. gráficamente.

grapnel, *grăp'nĕl*, s. (mar.) arpeo, m.

grapple, *grăp'pl*, v. a. (& n.) agarrar(se); —**s**, s. arpeo, m.

grasp, *grăsp*, v. a. empuñar, asir, agarrar; —, v. n. esforzarse á agarrar; —, s. puño, puñado, m.; poder, m.

grass, *grăs*, s. hierba, f.; herbaje, m.

grass-hopper, *-hŏppăr*, s. cigarrón, m.

grass-plot, *-plŏt*, s. césped, m.

grass-widow, *-wĭdō*, s. (am.) mujer cuyo marido está ausente, f.

grassy, *-sĕ*, a. herboso.

grate, *grāt*, s. reja, verja, rejilla, f.; —, v. a. rallar; rechinar (los dientes); enrejar; ofender. [ad. agradecidamente.

grateful, *-fŭl*, a. grato, agradecido; **-ly**,

gratefulness, *-fŭlnĕs*, s. gratitud, f.

grater, *-ăr*, s. rallo, m. [ción, f.

gratification, *grătĭfĭkā'shăn*, s. gratificación, f.

gratify, *grăt'ĭfĭ*, v. a. contentar; gratificar.

grating, *grā'tĭng*, s. rejado, m.; —, a. áspero; ofensivo.

gratis, *grā'tĭs*, ad. gratis, de balde.

gratitude, *grăt'ĭtŭd*, s. gratitud, f.

gratuitous, *grătū'ĭtŭs*, a. gratuito, voluntario; **-ly**, ad. gratuitamente.

gratuity, *grătū'ĭtĕ*, s. gratificación, recompensa, f.

gratulate, *grăt'ŭlāt*, v. a. congratular.

gratulation, *grătŭlā'shŭn*, s. congratulación, f.

grave, *grāv*, s. sepultura, f.; —, v. a. grabar, esculpir; —, a. grave, serio; **-ly**, ad. con gravedad, seriamente.

grave-clothes, *-klōtŭz*, s. pl. mortaja, f.

grave-digger, *-dĭggăr*, s. sepulturero, m.

gravel, *grăv'ĕl*, s. cascajo, m.; mal de piedra, m.; —, v. a. cubrir con cascajo; embarazar.

graveless, *grăv'lĕs*, a. insepulto.

gravelly, *grăv'ĕllĕ*, a. arenisco, cascajoso.

gravel-pit, *grăv'ĕlpĭt*, s. arenaria, f.

gravel-walk,—wắk, s. camino empedrado.
graven, grắvᵔn, a. grabado. [m.
graver, grắvᵔr, s, grabador, m.; buril, m.
grave-stone, grắv stŏn, s. piedra sepulcral, f.
gravitate, grắvᵔĭdt, v. n. gravitar. [f.
gravitation, grắvᵔtắshᵔn, s. gravitación.
gravity, grắvᵔtĕ, s. gravedad, f.
gravy, grắvĕ, s. jugo de la carne, f.; salsa,
gray, grắ, a. gris; cano; –, s. gris, m.
gray-beard,—bĕrd, s. barbicano, m.
grayish,—ᵔ̆sh, a. pardusco; entrecano.
grayling,—lᵔ̆ng, s. tímalo, m. (pez).
grayness,—nĕs, s. color gris, m.
graze, grắz, v. a. pastorear; tocar ligeramente; –, v. n. rozar; pacer.
grazier, grắ zhᵔr, s. ganadero, m.
grease, grēs, s. grasa, f.; –, v. a. untar.
greasiness,—ĭnĕs, s. grasa, f., pringue,
m. & f.; porquería, f.
greasy,—ĕ̆, a. grasiento, craso, gordo.
great, grắt, a. gran, grande; principal;
ilustre; noble, magnánimo; –ly, ad. muy,
mucho; grandemente.
great-coat,—kŏt, s. sobretodo, m.
greatness,—nĕs, s. grandeza, f.; dignidad,
f.; poder, m.; magnanimidad, f.
greedily, grē dᵔlĕ, ad. vorazmente, ansiosamente.
greediness, grē dᵔnĕs greed, grēc, s.
voracidad, f.; gula, f.; codicia, f.
greedy, grē dĕ, a. voraz, hambrient^; ansioso, deseoso; insaciable.
Greek, grēk, s. griego (idioma), m.
green, grēn, a. verde, fresco, reciente; no
maduro; –, s. verde, m.; llanura verde,
f.; –s, pl. verduras, f. pl.
greenback,—bắk, s. rana de zarzal, f.;
–s, pl. (am.) papel moneda, m.
green-gage,—gắj, s. ciruela verdal, f.
green-grocer,—grŏsᵔr, s. verdulero, m.
green-horn,—hŏrn, s. (vulg.) joven sin
experiencia, m.
green-house,—hŏᵔs, s. invernáculo, m.
greenish,—ᵔ̆sh, a. verdoso.
greenness,—nĕs, s. verdín, verdor, vigor,
m.; frescura, falta de experiencia,f.; novedad, f. [descanso, m. (en los teatros).
green-room,—rŏm, s. hogar, salón de
green-sickness,—sĭknĕs, s. opilación,
clorosis, f. [frutas y verduras, m.
green-stall,—stắl, s. puesto para vender
green-sward,—swắrd, s. césped, m.
green-wood,—wᵔld, s. bosque verde, m.
green-yard,—yắrd, s. lefiera, f.
greet, grēt, v. a. saludar, congratular; –,
v. n. encontrarse y saludarse.
greeting,—ᵔ̆ng, s. salutación, f.
gregarious, grĕgắrᵔᵔs, a. gregal.
grenade, grĕnắd, s. (mil.) granada, f.
grenadier, grĕnᵔdēr, s. granadero, m.
grey, grắ, a. gris, pardo.
greyhound,—hŏᵔnd, s. galgo, m.
gridiron, grᵔd ᵔrn, s. parrillas, f. pl.
grief, grēf, s. dolor, m.; aflicción, pena, f.
grievance, grē vᵔns, s. pesar, m.; molestia, f.; agravio, m.; injusticia, f.; perjuicio, m. [afligirse; llorar.
grieve, grēv, v. a. agraviar, afligir; –, v. n.

grievous, grē vᵔs, a. doloroso; enorme,
atroz; –ly, ad. penosamente; cruelmente.
griffin, grᵔ̆f fᵔ̆n, s. grifo, m. [rero, m.
grig, grᵔ̆g, s. anguila pequeña, f.; chora-
grill, grᵔ̆l, v. a. asar en parrillas.
grim, grĭm, s. feo; horrendo; ceñudo.
grimace, grĭmắs, s. visaje, m.; mueca, f.
grimalkin, grĭmắl kᵔ̆n, s. gatazo, m.
grime, grĭm, s. porquería, f.; –, v. n. ensuciar. [m.
grimness, grĭm nĕs, s. grima, f.; horror,
grimy, grᵔ̆ mĕ, a. ensuciado.
grin, grᵔ̆n, s. mueca, f.; rechino de los
dientes, m.; –, v.n. hacer visajes; rechinar
los dientes.
grind, grᵔ̆nd, v. a. moler; pulverizar;
afilar; estregar; mascar; rechinar los
dientes; (– students) preparar.
grinder,—ᵔ̆r, s. molinero, m.; molinillo,
m.; amolador, m.; preparador, m.; muela,
piedra molar, f. [f.
grindstone,—stŏn, s. piedra amoladera,
grip, grᵔ̆p, v. a. desaguar; –, s. caz, m.
gripe, grᵔ̆p, v. a. asir, empuñar; dar
cólico; –, v. n. padecer cólico; –, s.
toma, f.; presa, f.; opresión, f; tenedor,
m.; –s, pl. dolor cólico, m.
griper,—ᵔ̆r, s. usurero, m.
griskin, grᵔ̆s kᵔ̆n, s. costilla de tocino, f.
grisly, grᵔ̆z lĕ, grisled,—ld, a. horroroso.
grist, grᵔ̆st, s. molienda, f.; provisión, f.
gristle, grᵔ̆s l, s. tendón, nervio, m.
gristly, grᵔ̆s lĕ, a. tendinoso, nervioso.
grit, grᵔ̆t, s. moyuelo, m.; avena mondada
y medio molida, f.; arena, f.
gritty, grᵔ̆t tĕ, a. arenoso.
grizzle, grᵔ̆z l, s. gris, m.
grizzled,—d, grizzly, grᵔ̆z lĕ, a. mezclado
con gris, pardusco. [gemido, suspiro, m.
groan, grŏn, v. n. gemir, suspirar; –, s.
groat, grŏt, s. moneda del valor de cuatro
peniques, f.; –s, pl. avena mondada y
medio molida, f.
grocer, grŏ sᵔr, s. especiero, abacero, m.
grocery,—ĕ, s. especería, abacería, f.
grog, grŏg, s. grog, ponche, m.
groggy,—gĕ, a. medio borracho.
groin, grŏᵔn, s. ingle, f.
groom, grŏm, s. establero, m.; criado, m.;
novio, m.; –, v. a. cuidar los caballos.
groomsman,—smᵔn, s. padrino, m., el
que conduce el novio.
groove, grŏv, s. cavidad profunda, f;
muesca, f.; –, v. a. acanalar.
grope, grŏp, v. a. & n. tentar, buscar á
obscuras; andar á tientas.
gross, grŏs, a. grueso, corpulento, espeso;
grosero; estúpido; –ly, ad. groseramente;
en bruto; –, s. grueso, m.; todo, m.
grossness,—nĕs, s. rudeza, grosería, f.
grot(to), grŏt(ᵔ), s. gruta, f.
grotesque, grŏtĕsk, s. grotesco.
ground, grŏᵔnd, s. tierra, f.; país, m.;
terreno, suelo, pavimento, m.; fundamento, m.; razón fundamental, f.; campo
(de batalla), m.; fondo, m.; –s, pl. hez,
f.; poso, m.; –, v. a. establecer; (mar.)
varar.

ground-floor, *—flôr,* s. entresuelo, m.
ground-ivy, *—ivĕ,* s. hiedra terrestre, f.
groundless, *—lĕs,* a. infundado; **—ly,** ad. sin fundamento, sin razón ó motivo.
groundlessness, *—lĕsnĕs,* s. falta ó razón ó fundamento, f.
ground-plot, *—plôt,* s. solar, terreno, m.; (fig.) fundamento, m.   [raíz, f.
ground-rent, *—rĕnt,* s. renta de un bien
groundsel, *—sĕl,* s. hierba caña, f.
ground-work, *—wûrk,* s. plan, fundamento, m,
group, *grôp,* s. grupo, m. ; **—,** v. a. agrupar.
grouse, *grŏŭs,* s. gallina silvestre, f.
grout, *grŏŭt,* s. harina basta, f.; hez, f.; borras, f. pl.
grove, *grōv,* s. arboleda, f.; boscaje, m.
grovel, *grŏv'l,* v. n. serpear; bajarse.
grow, *grō,* v. a. cultivar; — v. n. crecer, aumentarse; nacer; vegetar; adelantar; hacerse, ponerse ó volverse; — **up,** crecer.
grower, *—ûr,* s. arrendador, m.
growl, *grŏŭl,* v. n. regañar, gruñir, rezongar; —, s. gruñido, m.
growth, *grōth,* s. vegetación, f.; crecimiento, m.; producto, m.; aumento, m.; progreso, adelanto, m.
grub, *grŭb,* s. hombre pequeño, m.; gorgojo, m.; —, v. a. desarraigar; desmontar, rozar.
grudge, *grŭj,* s. rencor, odio, m.; envidia, f.; —, v. a. & n. envidiar; repugnar.
grudgingly, *grŭj'ĭnglĕ,* ad. con repugnancia, de mala gana;
gruel, *grō'ĕl,* s. harina de avena mondada, f.   [ásperamente.
gruff, *grŭf,* a. ceñudo, grosero; **—ly,** ad.
gruffness, *—nĕs,* s. aspereza, severidad, f.
grumble, *grŭm'bl,* v. n. gruñir; murmurar.
grumpy, *—pĕ,* a. regañón.   [rar.
Grundy, Mrs. —, *mis'trĕs grŭn'dĕ,* s. moralista mimosa, f.
grunt, *grŭnt,* v. n. gruñir; gemir.
guarantee, *gârântē',* s. garante, fiador, m.; garantía, f.; —, v. a. garantir.
guaranty, —, *gâr'ântĕ,* s. garante, m.; garantía, f.
guard, *gârd,* s. guarda, guardia, f.; (rail.) conductor, m.; —, v. a. guardar; defender; —, v. n. guardarse; prevenirse.
guarded, *—ĕd,* a. mesurado, circunspecto.
guard-house, *—hŏŭs,* s. **guard-room,** *—rōm,* s. (mil.) cuerpo de guardia, m.
guardian, *gâr'dĭân,* s. tutor, m.; curador, m.; guardián (prelado), m.; —, a. tutelar.
guardianship, *—shĭp,* s. tutela, f.; guardianía, f.   [ó de ronda, f.
guard-ship,*gârd'shĭp,* s. navío de guardia
gudgeon, *gŭj'ûn,*s.gobio,m.(pez); bobo, m.
guerdon, *gûr'dn,* s. galardón, m.
guess, *gĕs,* v. a. & n. conjeturar; adivinar; —, s. conjetura, f.   [forastero, m.
guest, *gĕst,* s. huésped, convidado, m.;
guffaw, *gŭfâ',* s. carcajada, f.   [ción, f.
guidance, *gĭ'dâns,* s. gobierno, m.; dirección, f.
guide, *gĭd,* v.a. guiar, dirigir; —, s. guía, m.
guide-book, *—bŭk,* s. itinerario, f.
guild, *gĭld,* s. gremio, m.; corporación, f.

guild-hall, *—hâl,* s. casa consistorial, f.
guile, *gĭl,* s. engaño, fraude, m.
guileful, *—fûl,* a. engañoso, impostor.
guileless, *—lĕs,* a. cándido, sincero.
guillotine, *gĭl'ōtēn,* s. guillotina, f.; —, v. a. guillotinar.
guilt, *gĭlt,* s. delito, m. ; culpa, f.
guiltless, *—lĕs,* a. inocente, libre de culpa,
guilty, *—ĕ,* a. reo, culpable.
guinea, *gĭn'ĕ,* s. guinea, f. (moneda).   [f.
guinea-hen, *—hĕn,* s. gallinaza de Indias,
guise, *gĭz,* s. modo, m.; manera, f.; práctica, f.   [úca, f.
guitar, *gĭtâr',* s. guitarra, f.
gulch, *gûltsh,* s. glotón, m.
gulf, *gûlf,* s. golfo, m.; abismo, m.
gull, *gûl,* s. gaviota, f.; engaño, m.; bobo, m.; impostor, m.; —, v. a. engañar.
gullet, *—lĕt,* s. gaznate, m.; gola, f.
gullibility *—lĭbil'ĭtĕ,* s. credulidad, f.
gullible, *—lĭbl,* a. crédulo.
gully, *—lĕ,* s. v. n. fluir murmurando.
gully-hole, *—hōl,* s. sumidero, albañal, m.
gulp, *gûlp,* s. trago, m.; —, v. n. engullir, tragar.   [engomar.
gum, *gûm,* s. goma, f.; encía, f.; —, v. a.
gummy, *—mĕ,* a. gomoso.   [f.; juicio, m.
gumption, *gûm'shûn,*s.(fam.) inteligencia,
gum-tree, *gûm'trĕ,* s. árbol gomífero, m.
gun, *gûn,* s. arma de fuego, f.; cañón, m.
gun-boat, *—bōt,* s. cañonera, f.
gun-carriage, *—kârrĭj,* s. afuste, m.
gun-metal, *—mĕtâl,* s. bronce de cañones,
gunnel, *—nĕl,* s. (mar.) borda, f.   [m.
gunner, *—nâr,* s. artillero, m.
gunnery, *—nârĕ,* s. artillería, f.
gunpowder, *—pŏŭdûr,* s. pólvora, f.
gun-room, *—rōm,* s. (mar.) Santabárbara, f.
gun-shot, *—shôt,* s. tiro de escopeta, m.; alcance de unas armas, m.   [m.
gunsmith, *—smĭth,* s. arcabucero, armero,
gun-stock, *—stôk,* s. caja de escopeta, f.
gurgle, *gûr'gl,* v. n. salir con ruido.
gush, *gûsh,* v. n. brotar; chorrear; —, s. chorro, m.
gushing, *—ĭng,* a. superabundante.
gusset, *gûs'ĕt,* s. cuadrado, m.
gust, *gûst,* s. gusto, m.; soplo de aire, m.
gusty, *—ĕ,* a. tempestuoso.
gut, *gût,* s. intestino, m.; glotonería, f.; —, v. a. desventrar, destripar.
gutter, *—tûr,* s. gotera, f.; —, v. a. & n. acanalar; caer en gotas.
guttural, *—tûrâl,* a. gutural.
guy, *gĭ,* s. (mar.) retenida, f.; Juan de las Viñas, m.   [glotonería.
guzzle, *gûz'zl,* v. a. & n. beber ó comer con
gymnasium, *jĭmnā'zĭŭm,* s. gimnasio, m.
gymnast, *jĭm'nâst,* s. gimnasta, m.
gymnastic(al), *jĭmnâs'tĭk(âl),* a. gimnástico; —s, s. gimnástica, f.
gyrate, *jĭrāt',* v. n. girar.

H.

haberdasher, *hâb'ûrdâshûr,* s. tendero,
haberdashery, *—ĕ,* s. mercería, f.   [m.
habiliment, *hâbĭl'ĭmĕnt,* s. vestido, m.; compostura, f.

habilitate, _–tāt_, v. a. habilitar.

habit, _hăb'it_, s. hábito, vestido, m.; uso, m., costumbre, f.; complexión, f.

habitable, _–dbl_, a. habitable.

habitation, _hăbitā'shŭn_, s. habitación, f.; domicilio, m. [habitualmente.

habitual, _hăb'ū'ăl_, a. habitual; –ly, ad.

habituate, _–āt_, v. a. habituar, acostumbrarse.

habitude, _hăb'itūd_, s. costumbre, f.

hack, _hăk_, s. caballo de alquiler, rocín, m.; muesca, f.; –, v. a. tajar, cortar; hablar mal una lengua. [f.; –, v. a. rastrillar.

hackle, _–l_, s. rastrillo, m.; seda cruda,

hackney, _–nė_, s. caballo de alquiler, m.; –, a. alquilado.

hackneyed, _–nēd_, a. trillado, trivial.

haddock, _hăd'dŏk_, s. egrefín, gado, m. (pez).

haft, _hăft_, s. mango, m.; asa, f.; –, v. a. poner mango á alguna cosa.

hag, _hăg_, s. bruja, hechicera, f.

haggard, _–gărd_, a. feroz, huraño.

haggle, _–gl_, v. a. cortar en tajadas; –, v.n.

haggler, _–glăr_, s. regatón, m. [regatear.

ha-ha, _hă hă_, s. salto de lobo, m.

hail, _hăl_, s. granizo, m.; saludo, m.; –, v. a. saludar; (mar.) venir á la voz; –, v. imp. granizar; –, ¡salve! [m.

hail-fellow, _–fĕllō_, s. compañero íntimo,

hail-stone, _–stōn_, s. piedra de granizo, f.

hair, _hăr_, s. pelo; (of the head) cabello, m. [m.; casi nada, f.

hair-breadth, _–brĕdth_, s. ancho de un pelo,

hair-cloth, _–klōth_, s. cilicio, m.

hair-dresser, _–drĕssăr_, s. peluquero,

hairless, _–lĕs_, a. calvo [peinador, m.

hair-pin, _–pin_, s. alfiler para afianzar los cabellos, m.

hair-powder, _–pŏddăr_, s. polvos de peinar ó para el pelo, m. pl.

hair-sieve, _–sĕv_, s. tamiz para colar, m.

hair-splitting, _–splitting_, s.quisquilla,f.

hairy, _–ė_, a. peludo, velludo, cabelludo.

halberd, _hăl'bŭrd_, s. alabarda, f.

halberdier, _–ĕr_, s. alabardero, m.

halcyon, _hăl'sŏn_, a. quieto, tranquilo; –, s. alcedón, alción, m. (ave).

hale, _hăl_, a. sano, vigoroso; ileso.

half, _hăf_, s. mitad, f.; –, a. medio.

half-blood, _–blŭd_, s. medio hermano, m.; media hermana, f. [mestizo.

half-bred, _–brĕd_, **half-caste**, _–kăst_, a.

half-caste, _–kăst_, s. casta cruzada, f.

half-cock, _–kŏk_, a. desmontado (escopeta)

half-moon, _–mōn_, s. semilunio, m.

half-penny, _hă'pĕnnė_, s.medio penique, m.

halfway, _hăf'wă_, ad. á medio camino.

hall, _hăl_, s. vestíbulo, m.; salón, colegio, m.

halliards, _hăl'yŭrdz_, s. pl. (mar.) driza, f.

halloo, _hăllō'_, ¡hola!; ¡ea! – v. n. azuzar (á los perros en la caza); llamar á uno gritando.

hallow, _hăl'lō_, v. a. consagrar, santificar.

hallucination, _hălōsinā'shŭn_, s. alucinación, f.

halo, _hăl'lō_, s. halón, m. [ción, f.

halt, _hălt_, v. n. cojear; parar; dudar; –, s. cojera, f.; parada, f.; alto, m.

halter, _–ăr_, s. soga, f.; cuerda, f.

halve, _hăv_, v. a. partir en dos mitades.

ham, _hăm_, s. corva, f.; jamón, m.

hamlet, _hăm'lĕt_, s. villorro, m.

hammer, _hăm'măr_, s. martillo, m.; serpentín de fusil, m.; subasta, f.; –, v. a. martillar; forjar; –, v. n. trabajar.

hammer-cloth, _–klōth_, s. paño del pescante de un coche, m.

hammock, _hăm'mŏk_, s. hamaca, f.

hamper, _hăm'păr_, s. cuévano, m.; –, v. a. embarazar; entrampar.

hamstring, _hăm'string_, s. tendón de la corva, m.; –, v. a. desjarretar.

hand, _hănd_, s. mano, f.; palmo, m. (medida); carácter de escritura, m.; poder, m.; talento, m.; (mar.) marinero, m.; obrero, m.; mano de un reloj; at –, á la mano, al lado; – in –, de acuerdo; –, v. a. alargar; guiar por la mano; echar la mano; manejar.

hand-barrow, _–bărrō_, s. angarillas, f.pl

hand-bell, _–bĕl_, s. campanilla, f.

hand-bill, _–bil_, s. cartel, m.

hand-book, _–bŭk_, s. manual, m.

hand-cuff, _–kŭf_, s. manilla, f.

handed, _–ĕd_, a. transmitido, pasado de uno á otro.

handful, _–fŭl_, s. manojo, puñado, m.

hand-gallop, _–găllŏp_, s. galope corto, m.

handicap, _hăn'dikăp_, s. carrera ciega con caballos de peso igualado, f.

handicapper, _–păr_, s. arbitrador en las carreras ciegas, m. [f.

handicraft, _hăn'dikrăft_, s. arte mecánica,

handicraftsman, _–'măn_, s. artesano, m.

handily, _hăn'dilė_, ad. mañosamente.

handiness, _hăn'dinĕs_, s. maña, habilidad, f. [f.

handiwork, _hăn'diwŭrk_, s. obra manual,

handkerchief, _hăn'kŭrtshif_, s. pañuelo, m. [manija, f.; –, v. a. manejar; tratar.

handle, _hăn'dl_, s. mango, puño, m.; asa,

handling, _hănd'ling_, s. manejo, m.; toque,

hand-mill, _–mil_, s. molinillo, m.

hand-rail, _–rāl_, s. guardalado, m.

handsel, _hăn'sĕl_, s. estreno, m.; –, v. a. estrenar alguna cosa.

handsome, _hăn'sŭm_, a. hermoso, bello, gentil; –ly, ad. hermosamente, primorosamente.

hand-spike, _hănd'spik_, s. palanca, f.

hand-writing, _–riting_, s. carácter de escritura, m.

handy, _hăn'dė_, a. manual; diestro, mañoso.

hang, _hăng_, v. a. colgar, suspender; ahorcar; entapizar; –, v. n. colgar; ser ahorcado; pegarse; quedarse suspenso; depender. [f.

hanger, _–ăr_, s. alfanje, m.; espada ancha,

hanger-on, _–ăr ŏn_, s. dependiente, m.; mogollón, m.

hangings, _–ĭngz_, s. pl. tapicería, f.

hangman, _–măn_, s. verdugo, m.

hank, _hăngk_, s. madeja de hilo, f.

hanker, _–ăr_, v. n. ansiar, apetecer.

hansom, _hăn'sŭm_, s. cabriolé, m.

hap-hazard, _hăp'hăzărd_, s. accidente, lance, m. [rado.

hapless, _–lĕs_, a. desgraciado, desventu-

haply, _–lė_, ad. por casualidad.

happen, –pn, v. n. acontecer, acaecer.

happily, –pilé, ad. felizmente.

happiness, –pinés, s. felicidad, dicha, f.

happy, –pé, a. feliz, bienaventurado.

harangue, háráng, s. arenga, f.; –, v. n. arengar. [matar de cansancio.

harass, hár'ds, v. a. cansar, fatigar; –out,

harbinger, hár'binjár, s. precursor, m.

harbour, hár'búr, s. albergue, m.; puerto, m.; asilo, m.; –, v. a. albergar; hospedar; –, v. n. tomar albergue.

hard, hárd, a. duro, firme; difícil; penoso; cruel, severo, rígido; – of hearing, medio sordo; –, ad. cerca, á la mano; difícilmente; – by, muy cerca.

harden, –n, v. a. (& n.) endurecer(se).

hard-hearted, –hárted, a. duro de corazón, insensible. [valor, m.

hardihood, hár'dihûd, s. atrevimiento,

hardiness, hár'dinés, s. fatiga, f.; intrepidez, f.; atrevimiento.

hardly, hárd'lé, ad. apenas; severamente.

hardness, –nés, s. dureza, f.; dificultad, f.; inhumanidad, f.; severidad, f.

hardship, –ship, s. injuria, opresión, f.; injusticia, f.; penalidad, f.; trabajo, m.; molestia, fatiga, f.

hardware, –wár, s. quincallería, f.

hardy, hár'dé, a. atrevido, bravo, intrépido; fuerte, robusto.

hare, hár, s. liebre, f. [foliada, f.

harebell, –bél, s. campánula rotundi-

hare-brained, –brānd, a. aturdido, atolondrado.

hare-lipped, –lipped, a. labihendido.

hark, hárk, i¡he! ¡oye! ¡mira! m.

harlequin, hár'lékwin, s. arlequín, bufón,

harlot, hár'lát, s. puta, meretriz, f.

harm, hárm, s. mal, daño, m.; desgracia, f.; perjuicio, m.; –, v. a. dañar, injuriar, ofender. [–ly, ad. dañosamente.

harmful, –fûl, a. dañoso; perjudicial;

harmless, –lés, a. sencillo, inocente; –ly, ad. inocentemente; sin daño.

harmonic(al), hármón'ik(ál), a. armónico.

harmonious, hármō'niûs, a. armonioso; –ly, ad. armoniosamente.

harmonise, hár'mónīz, v. a. ajustar; concertar; –, v. n. convenir, corresponder.

harmony, hár'móné, s. armonía, f.

harness, hár'nés, s. arreos de un caballo, m. pl.; –, v. a. enjaezar.

harp, hárp, s. arpa, f.; –, v. a. & n. tocar el arpa; machacar.

harpist, –ist, s. arpista, m.

harpoon, hárpón', s. arpón, m.

harpsichord, hárp'síkórd, s. clavicordio,

harpy, hár'pé, s. arpía, f. [m.

harridan, hár'ridán, s. rocín, m.

harrier, hár'riúr, s. galgo, m.

harrow, hár'ró, s. grada, f.; rastro, m.; –, v. a. gradar.

harry, hár'ré, v. a. tormentar.

harsh, hársh, a. áspero, agrio, rígido, duro, austero, –ly, ad. ásperamente, severamente. [deza, austeridad, severidad, f.

harshness, –nés, s. aspereza, dureza, ru-

hart, hárt, s. ciervo, m.

harum-scarum, hár'rúm skár'rúm, ad. cochite hervite.

harvest, hár'vést, s. cosecha, f.; agosto, m.; –, v. a. recoger las mieses.

harvester, –ár, s. agostero, m.

harvest-home, –hóm, s. fiesta al acabar la siega, f.

hash, hásh, s. jigote, m.; –, v. a. picar.

hasp, hásp, s. aldaba de candado, f.; broche, m.; –, v. a. abrochar; cerrar con aldaba.

hassock, hás'sók, s. cojín de paja, m.

haste, hást, s. priesa, f.; presteza, f.; to be in –, estar de priesa.

hasten, hás'n, v. a. acelerar, apresurar; –, v. n. estar de priesa. [airadamente.

hastily, hás'tilé, ad. precipitadamente;

hastiness, hás'tinés, s. precipitación, f.

hasty, hás'té, a. pronto, apresurado; colérico; temprano.

hasty-pudding, –pûdding, s. papilla hecha con leche y harina, f.

hat, hát, s. sombrero, m.; –s off! ¡quítense el sombrero!

hat-band, –bánd, s. cinta del sombrero, f.

hat-box, –bóks, **hat-case,** –kás, s. sombrerera, f.

hatch, hátsh, v. a. criar pollos; empollar; tramar; –, s. pollada, nidada, f.; media puerta, f.

hatchet, –ét, s. destral, m.; hacha pequeña,

hatchment, –mént, s. escudo fúnebre, m.

hatchway, –wá, s. (mar.) escotilla, f.

hate, hát, s. odio, aborrecimiento, m.; –, v. a. odiar, detestar.

hateful, –fûl, a. odioso, detestable; –ly, ad. detestablemente, con tirria.

hatred, hát'réd, s. odio, aborrecimiento, m.

hatter, hát'tár, s. sombrerero, m.

haughtily, hát'tilé, ad. fieramente, orgullosamente. [vez, f.

haughtiness, hát'tinés, s. orgullo, m.; alti-

haughty, hát'té, a. altanero, altivo, orgulloso. [m.

haul, hál, v. a. tirar, halar; –, s. estirón,

haunch, hánsh, s. anca, f.

haunt, hánt, v. a. frecuentar, rondar; –, s. guarida, f.; costumbre, f.

hautboy, hó'bói, s. (mus.) oboe, m.

have, háv, v. a. ir, haber, tener; poseer; to – rather, querer más, preferir. [m.

haven, hā'vn, s. puerto, m.; abrigo, asilo,

havoc, háv'ók, s. estrago, m.; ruina, f.

haw, há, s. cañada, cerca, f.; –, v. n. tartamudear.

hawk, hák, s. halcón, m.; –, v. n. cazar con halcón; llevar y vender mercaderías por las calles. [buhonero, m.

hawker, –ár, s. mercachiste, mercachifle,

hawser, há'sár, s. (mar.) garlín, m.; (mar.) remolque, m.

haw-thorn, há'thórn, s. espino blanco, m.

hay, há, s. heno, m.

hay-cock, –kók, s. pila de heno, f.

hay-loft, –lóft, s. henil, m.

hay-making, –máking, s. henaje, m.

hay-rick, –rik, **hay-stack,** –sták, s. niara, f.

hazard, *hǎz'ŭrd,* s. acaso, accidente, m.; riesgo, m.; juego de azar á los dados, m.; —, v. a. arriesgar; aventurar.

hazardous, *—ŭs,* a. arriesgado, **peligroso; -ly,** ad. peligrosamente.

haze, *hāz,* s. niebla, f.

hazel, *hā'zĕl,* s. avellano, m.

hazel(ly), *—(lĕ),* a. castaño.

hazel-nut, *—nŭt,* s. avellana, f.

hazy, *hā'zĕ,* a. anieblado; obscuro.

he, *hē,* pn. él.

head, *hĕd,* s. cabeza, f.; jefe, m.; juicio, m.; talento, m.; título (de un libro), m.; puño (de bastón), m.; fuente, f.; nacimiento de un río, m.; cabeza de jabalí, f.; —, v. a. gobernar, dirigir; degollar; podar los árboles.

head-ache, *—āk,* s. dolor de cabeza, m.

head-dress, *—drĕs,* s. cofia, f.; tocado, m.

headiness, *—ĭnĕs,* s. precipitación, obstinación, f.

head-land, *—lǎnd,* s. promontorio, m.

headless, *—lĕs,* a. inconsiderado.

headlong, *—lŏng,* a. & ad. temerario, inconsiderado; temerariamente; precipitadamente. [las clases superiores, m.

head-master, *—mǎstŭr,* s. profesor de

headmost, *—mōst,* a. primero.

head-piece, *—pēs,* s. casco, yelmo, m.; entendimiento, m. [cuartel general, m.

head-quarters, *—kwǎrtŭrz,* s. (mil.)

headship, *—shĭp,* s. primado, m.; autoridad, f. [m.

headsman, *—s'mǎn,* s. degollador, verdugo,

headstall, *—stǎl,* s. cabezada del freno, testera, f. [zudo, obstinado.

headstrong, *—strŏng,* a. testarudo, cabe-

head-way, *—wā,* s. buen éxito, m.

heady, *—ĕ,* a. temerario; obstinado; vio-

heal, *—hēl,* v. a. & n. curar; sanar. [lento.

health, *hĕlth,* s. salud, sanidad, f.; brin-

healthiness, *—ĭnĕs,* s. sanidad, f. [dis, m.

healthy, *—ĕ,* a. sano; sanativo.

heap, *hēp,* s. montón, m.; turba, f.; —, v. a. amontonar, acumular.

hear, *hēr,* v. a. oir; entender; obedecer; —, v. n. oir; escuchar.

hearer, *—ŭr,* s. oyente, oidor, m.

hearing, *—ĭng,* s. oído, m.; audiencia, f.

hearken, *hǎr'kn,* v. n. escuchar, atender.

hearsay, *hēr'sā,* s. rumor, m.; fama, f.

hearse, *hŭrs,* s. ataúd, féretro, m.

heart, *hǎrt,* s. corazón, m.; interior, centro, m.; ánimo, valor, m.; amor, m.; **by —,** de memoria; **with all my —,** con toda mi alma. [—, s. congoja, f.

heart-breaking, *—brāking,* a. congojoso;

heart-burning, *—bŭrning,* s. cardialgia, f.

heart-felt, *—fĕlt,* a. sentido en el fondo del corazón.

hearth, *hǎrth,* s. hogar, fogón, m.

heartily, *hǎr'tĭlĕ,* ad. sinceramente, cordialmente. [ceridad, f.

heartiness, *hǎr'tĭnĕs,* s. cordialidad, sin-

heartless, *hǎrt'lĕs,* a. tímido; inclemente; **-ly,** ad. tímidamente. [m.; trinitaria, f.

heart's-ease, *—s'ēz,* s. (bot.) pensamiento,

heart-sick, *—sĭk,* a. dolorido, afligido.

heart-whole, *—hōl,* a. que tiene aun libre su corazón.

hearty, *—ĕ,* a. sincero; sano; vigoroso.

heat, *hĕt,* s. ardor, calor, m., vehemencia, f.; animosidad, f.; —, v. a. calentar, en-

heater, *—ŭr,* s. escalfador, m. [cender.

heath, *hĕth,* **heather,** *hĕth'ŭr,* s. (bot.) brezo, m.; brezal, matorral, m.

heathen, *hē'thn,* s. gentil, pagano, m.; **-ish,** a. gentílico; salvaje; **-ishly,** ad. á la manera de los paganos.

heathenism, *—ĭzm,* s. paganismo, m.

heave, *hēv,* v. a. alzar; elevar; hincharse; (mar.) birar para proa; —, v. n. palpitar; respirar trabajosamente; tener náuseas; —, s. esfuerzo para levantarse, m.; suspiro de congoja, m.

heaven, *hĕv'n,* s. cielo, m.; firmamento, m.

heavenly, *—lĕ,* a. & ad. celeste, divino; divinamente.

heavily, *hĕv'ĭlĕ,* ad. pesadamente.

heaviness, *hĕv'ĭnĕs,* s. pesadez, f.; aflicción, f.; opresión, f.

heavy, *hĕv'ĕ,* a. grave, pesado; opresivo, penoso, molesto; triste; tardo, soñoliento.

hebrew, *hē'brō,* s. hebreo, judío, m.

hecatomb, *hĕk'ătōm,* s. hecatomba, f.

hectic(al), *hĕk'tĭk(ăl),* a. hético.

hector, *hĕk'tŭr,* s. matasiete, fanfarrón, m.; —, v. n. baladronear, bravear.

hedge, *hĕj,* s. seto, m.; —, v. a. cercar con

hedge-hog, *—hŏg,* s. erizo, m. [un seto.

hedger, *—ŭr,* s. cercador, m.

hedge-row, *—rō,* s. serie de árboles en los cercados, f.

heed, *hēd,* v. a. atender, observar; —, s. cuidado, m.; atención, precaución, f.

heedful, *—fŭl,* a. vigilante, atento; circunspecto; **-ly,** ad. cautelosamente.

heedless, *—lĕs,* a. descuidado, negligente; **-ly,** ad. negligentemente.

heel, *hēl,* s. talón, m.; **to take to one's —s,** apretar los talones, huir; —, v. a. taconear. [mahometanos.

Hegira, *hĕj'ĭrā,* s. egira, f.; era de los

heifer, *hĕf'ŭr,* s. becerra, vaquilla, ternera, f. [f.; sublimidad, f.

height, *hīt,* s. altura, elevación, sumidad,

heighten, *—n,* v. a. realzar; adelantar; mejorar; exaltar.

heinous, *hā'nŭs,* a. atroz, odioso; **-ly,** ad. atrozmente, horriblemente.

heir, *ār,* s. heredero, m.; **— apparent,** heredero forzoso, m.

heirdom, *—dŭm,* **heirship,** *—shĭp,* s. herencia, heredad, f.

heiress, *—ĕs,* s. heredera, f. [muebles, m.

heirloom, *—lōm,* s. vínculo de bienes

heliograph, *hē'lĭōgrăf,* s. heliografía, f.

hell, *hĕl,* s. infierno, m.

hell-bred, *—brĕd,* a. producido en los in-

hell-cat, *—kăt,* s. bruja, f. [fiernos.

hellenism, *hĕl'ĕnĭzm,* s. helenismo, m.

hellenist, *hĕl'ĕnĭst,* s. helenista, m.

hell-hound, *hĕl'hōŭnd,* s. Cerbero, m.; pícaro, m. [ad. diabólicamente.

hellish, *hĕl'ĭsh,* a. infernal, malvado; **-ly,**

helm, *hĕlm,* s. (mar.) timón, gobernalle. [m.
helmet, *-ĕt,* s. yelmo, m.
help, *hĕlp,* v. a. (& n.) ayudar, asistir, socorrer; servir á la mesa; aliviar, remediar, reparar; evitar; I cannot - it, no puedo remediarlo; I puedo dejarlo de hacer; -, s. ayuda, f.; socorro, remedio, m.
helper, *-ŭr,* **helpmate,** *-māt,* **helpmeet,** *-mēt,* s. auxiliador, socorredor, m.; esposa, f.
helpful, *-fŭl,* a. útil; saludable.
helpless, *-lĕs,* a. abandonado; irremediable; **-ly,** ad. irremediablemente, sin recurso. [trochemoche, en desorden.
helter-skelter, *hĕl'tŭrskĕl'tŭr,* ad. á
helve, *hĕlv,* s. mango, m.; astil de hacha, m.
hem, *hĕm,* s. ribete, m.; -, v. a. ribetear; repular; -! ¡ho! ¡he!
hemisphere, *hĕm'isfēr,* s. hemisferio, m.
hemlock, *hĕm'lŏk,* s. cicuta, f.
hemorrhage, *hĕm'ŏrrāj,* s. hemorragia, f.
hemorrhoids, *hĕm'ŏrrŏīdz,* s.pl. hemorroides, m. pl.
hemp, *hĕmp,* s. cáñamo, m. [des, m. pl.
hempen, *-n,* a. cañameño.
hen, *hĕn,* s. gallina, f.
hence, *hĕns,* ad. de aquí; por esto.
henceforth, *-fŏrth,* **henceforward,** *-fŏr'wŭrd,* ad. de aquí en adelante; en lo venidero; para siempre. [s. gallinero, m.
hen-coop, *hĕn'kūp,* **hen-house,** *-hŏūs,*
hen-pecked, *-pĕkt,* a. maricón, m.
hen-roost, *-rōst,* s. gallinero, m.
her, *hŭr,* pn. su, ella, de ella, á ella.
herald, *hĕr'ăld,* s. heraldo, m.
heraldic, *hĕr'ăl'dĭk,* a. heráldico.
heraldry, *hĕr'ăldrĕ,* s. heráldica, f.
herb, *hŭrb,* s. yerba, f.; **-s,** pl. legumbre, hortaliza, f.
herbaceous, *hŭrbā'shŭs,* a. herbáceo.
herbage, *hŭr'bāj,* s. herbaje, m.
herbalist, *-ĭst,* s. herbolario, m.
herbivorous, *hŭrbĭv'ŏrŭs,* a. herbívoro.
herd, *hĕrd,* s. hato, rebaño, m.; manada, f.; grey, f.; -, v. n. ir en hatos; asociarse.
herdsman, *-s'măn,* s.guarda de ganado, m.
here, *hĕr,* ad. aquí, acá. [dor.
hereabout(s), *-ābŏūt' (z),* ad. aquí al rededor.
hereafter, *-āf'tŭr,* ad. en el tiempo venidero, en lo futuro; -, s. estado venidero, m.
hereby, *-bī',* ad. por esto. [m.
hereditary, *hĕrĕd'ĭtārĕ,* a. hereditario.
heredity, *-tĕ,* s. derecho de sucesión, f.
herefrom, *hĕrfrŏm',* ad. de aquí.
herein, *-ĭn',* ad. en esto, aquí dentro.
hereof, *-ŏf',* ad. de esto, de aquí.
heresy, *hĕr'rĕsĕ,* s. herejía, f. [tico.
heretic, *hĕr'ĕtĭk,* s. hereje, m.; -, a. herético.
hereto, *hĕrtō',* ad. á esto, para esto.
heretofore, *hĕrtŏfŏr',* ad. antes, en tiempos pasados.
hereupon, *-ăpŏn',* ad. sobre esto.
herewith, *-wĭth',* ad. con esto.
heritance, *hĕr'ĭtăns,* s. herencia, f.
hermetic(al), *hŭrmĕt'ĭk(ăl),* a. hermético; **-ly,** ad. herméticamente.
hermit, *hŭr'mĭt,* s. ermitaño, eremita, m.
hermitage, *hŭr'mĭtăj,* s. ermita, f.
hernia, *hŭr'nĭa,* s. hernia, rotura, f.

hero, *hē'rō,* s. héroe, m. [heroicamente.
heroic(al), *hĕrō'ĭk(ăl),* a. heroico; **-ally,** ad.
heroine, *hĕr'ōĭn,* s. heroína, f.
heroism, *hĕr'ōĭzm,* s. heroísmo m.
heron, *hĕr'ŭn,* s. garza, f. [zas, m.
heronry, *-rĕ,* s. lugar para criar las gar-
herring, *hĕr'rĭng,* s. arenque, m.
hers, *hŭrz,* pn. suyo, de ella.
herself, *hŭrsĕlf',* pn. ella misma.
hesitate, *hĕz'ĭtāt,* v. a. dudar; tardar.
hesitation, *hĕzĭtā'shŭn,* s. hesitación, duda, irresolución, f.
heterodox, *hĕt'ĕrŏdŏks,* a. heterodoxo.
heterogeneous, *hĕtĕrōjē'nŭs,* a. heterogeneo.
hew, *hū,* v. a. leñar; tajar; cortar, picar.
hewer, *-ŭr,* s. leñador, m.
hey, *hā,* ¡he! [be.
heyday, *-dā,* s. alegría, f.; gozo, m.; -í
hiatus, *hĭā'tŭs,* s. abertura, Hendedura, f.; (gr.) hiato, m.
hibernate, *hĭbĕr'nāt,* v. n. invernar.
hiccough, *hĭk'ŭp,* s. hipo, m.; -, v. n. tener hipo.
hickory, *hĭk'ŏrĕ,* s. noguera americana, f.
hide, *hĭd,* v. a. esconder; (vulg.) apalear; -, s. cuero, m.; piel, f. [riblemente.
hideous, *hĭd'ĕŭs,* a. horrible; **-ly,** ad. hor-
hiding-place, *hī'dĭngplās,* s. escondite, escondrijo, m.
hierarchy, *hī'ŭrărkĕ,* s. jerarquía, f.
hieroglyphic, *hīĕrōglĭf'ĭk,* a. & s. jero-
higgle, *hĭg'l,* v. n. regatear. [glífico, m.
higglody-piggledy, *-dĕpĭgldĕ,* ad. (vulg.) confusamente.
higgler, *-ŭr,* s. revendedor, m.
high, *hī,* a. alto, elevado; arduo; altivo; noble, ilustre; sublime; violento; solemne; caro.
high-altar, *-ăltŭr,* s. altar mayor, m.
high-born, *-bŏrn,* a. noble, ilustre por nacimiento. [color.
high-coloured, *-kŭlŭrd,* a. subido de
high-flown, *-flōn,* a. altivo, orgulloso.
highland, *-lănd,* s. tierras montañosas, f.
highlander, *-lăndŭr,* s. montañés, m. [pl.
highly, *-lĕ,* ad. altamente; en sumo grado; arrogantemente; ambiciosamente. [nimo.
high-minded, *-mĭndĕd,* a. fiero, magná-
highness, *-nĕs,* s. altura, f.; alteza, f.
high-water, *-wătŭr,* s. marea alta, f.
highway, *-wā,* s. camino real, m.
highwayman, *-wămăn,* s. salteador de caminos, m.
hilarious, *hĭlā'rĕŭs,* a. alegre.
hilarity, *hĭlăr'ĭtĕ,* s. alegría, f.; regocijo, m.
hill, *hĭl,* s. collado, m.
hillock, *-lŏk,* s. colina, f.; otero, m.
hilly, *-lĕ,* a. montañoso.
hilt, *hĭlt,* s. puño de espada, m.
him, *hĭm,* pn. le, á él.
himself, *-sĕlf',* pn. á él mismo.
hind, *hĭnd,* a. trasero, posterior; -, s. cierva, f. (hembra del ciervo); criado, m.; patán, m.
hinder, *hĭn'dŭr,* v. a. impedir, embarazar.
hinder, *hĭn'dŭr,* a. trasero.
hind(e)rance, *hĭn'd(ŭ)răns,* s. impedimento, obstáculo, m.

hind(er)most, *hĭnd'(ẽr)mŏst*, a. postrero.
hind-quarter, *-kwártãr*, s. pie trasero, m.
hinge, *hĭnj*, s. charnela, bisagra, f.; razón principal, f.; –, v. a. engoznar.
hint, *hĭnt*, s. seña, f.; sugestión, insinuación, f.; luz, f.; aviso, m.; –, v. a. apuntar, insinuar; sugerir; hacer señas.
hip, *hĭp*, cadera, f.
hip-bath, *-báth*, s. baño inglés, m. [m.
hippodrome, *hĭp'pŏdrŏm*, s. hipódromo,
hippopotamus, *hĭppŏpŏt'ãmŭs*, s. hipopótamo, m. [quiler, m.; salario, m.
hire, *hĭr*, v. a. alquilar; arrendar; –, s. alquiler
hireling, *-lĭng*, s. jornalero, m.; hombre mercenario, m.; –, a. mercenario, venal.
hirsute, *hãrsút'*, a. hirsuto, velludo, áspero.
his, *hĭs*, pn. su, suyo, de él.
hiss, *hĭs*, v. a. & n. silbar.
hist, *hĭst*, ¡chito! ¡chitón!
historian, *hĭstŏ'rĭan*, s. historiador, m.
historic(al), *hĭstŏr'ĭk(ãl)*, a. histórico; –ally, ad. históricamente.
history, *hĭs'tŏrẽ*, s. historia, narración, f.
histrionic, *hĭstrĭŏn'ĭk*, a. estudiado, gestero.
hit, *hĭt*, v. a. golpear; atinar; –, v. n. acaecer, acontecer (felizmente); salir bien; encontrar(se); –, s. golpe, m.; suerte feliz, f.; alcance, m.
hitch, *hĭtsh*, v. n. menearse; engancharse; –, s. impedimento, m.; (mar.) vuelta de cabo, f.
hither, *hĭth'ãr*, ad. acá; á este fin; –, a. citerior; –to, hasta ahora, hasta aquí.
hive, *hĭv*, s. colmena, f.; –, v. a. enjambrar; –, v. n. vivir muchos en un mismo lugar.
hoar, *hŏr*, a. blanco, cano. [lugar.
hoard, *hŏrd*, s. montón, m.; tesoro escondido, m.; –, v. a. atesorar, acumular.
hoar-frost, *hŏr'frŏst*, s. escarcha, f.
hoariness, *hŏ'rĭnĕs*, s. blancura, f.; canas de viejo, f. pl. [mente.
hoarse, *hŏrs*, a. ronco; –ly, ad. roncamente.
hoarseness, *-nĕs*, s. ronquera, carraspera, f.
hoary, *hŏ'rĕ*, a. blanquecino, cano. [f.
hoax, *hŏks*, s. burla, f.; petardo, m.; –, v. a. engañar, burlar.
hob, *hŏb*, s. patán, m.
hobble, *hŏb'l*, v. a. cojear; –, v. a. enredar; –, s. dificultad, f.; cojera, f.
hobby, *-bĕ*, s. caballico, m.; zoquete, m.
hobby-horse, *-bĕhŏrs*, s. objeto predilecto, m.; caballico en que corren los niños.
hobgoblin, *-gŏb'lĭn*, s. duende, m. [m.
hobnail, *-ndl*, s. clavo de herradura, m.
hob-nob, *-nŏb*, v. n. hermanarse con otro.
Hobson's choice, *-sŭns tshŏĭs*, s. alternativa entre eso ó nada, f.
hock, *hŏk*, s. vino añejo del Rin, m.; jarrete, m.; –(le), v. a. desjarretar.
hockey, *hŏk'ĕ*, s. juego de pelota inglés, [m.
hocus, *hŏ'kŭs*, v. a. engañar.
hocus-pocus, *-pŏkŭs*, s. pasapasa, f.
hodge-podge, *hŏj'pŏj*, s. almodrote, m.
hodman, *hŏd'mãn*, s. peón de albañil, m.
hoe, *hŏ*, s. azada, f.; –, v. a. cavar la tierra con azada.
hog, *hŏg*, s. cerdo, puerco, m.

hoggish, *-gĭsh*, a. porcuno; –ly, ad. puercamente; vorazmente. [m.
hogshead, *-z'hĕd*, s. oxoft (barril grande).
hoiden, hoyden, *hŏĭd'n*, s. payo, m.; paya.
hoist, *hŏĭst*, v. a. alzar; (mar.) izar. [f.
hold, *hŏld*, v. a. tener, asir; detener; sostener; mantener; juzgar, reputar; poseer; continuar, proseguir; contener; celebrar; apostar; –, v.n. valer; mantenerse; durar; abstenerse; adherirse á depender; – ¡tente! ¡para! éstate quieto; –, s. presa, f.; mango, m.; asa, f.; prisión, f.; custodia, f.; (mar.) bodega, f.; apoyo, m.; poder,
holdfast, *-fãst*, s. grapa, laña, f. [m.
holding, *-ĭng*, s. tenencia, posesión, f.; influencia, f. [m.
hole, *hŏl*, s. agujero, m.; cueva, f.; hoyo,
holiday, *hŏl'ĭdã*, s. día de fiesta, m.; aniversario, m.; –s, pl. vacaciones, f. pl.
holiness, *hŏ'lĭnĕs*, s. santidad, f.
hollow, *hŏl'lŏ*, a. hueco; disimulado; –, s. cavidad, caverna, f.; –, v. a. excavar, ahuecar. [ción, f.
hollowness, *-nĕs*, s. cavidad, f.; simulación
holly, *hŏl'lĕ*, s. (bot.) acebo, m.
holly-hock, *-hŏk*, s. malva hortense, f.
holocaust, *hŏl'ŏkãst*, s. holocausto, m.
holster, *hŏl'stãr*, s. funda de pistola, f.
holy, *hŏ'lĕ*, a. santo, pío; consagrado.
holy-water, *-wãtãr*, s. agua bendita, f.
holy-week, *-wĕk*, s. semana santa, f.
homage, *hŏm'ãj*, s. homenaje, m.; –, v. a. reverenciar.
home, *hŏm*, s. casa propia, morada, f.; patria, f.; domicilio, m.; –ly, ad. á su propia casa; á su país.
home-bred, *-brĕd*, a. nativo; casero.
home-keeping, *-kēpĭng*, a. apoltronado en su casa.
homeless, *-lĕs*, a. sin casa ni hogar.
homeliness, *-lĭnĕs*, s. simpleza, f.; grosería, f. [sería, f.
homely, *-lĕ*, a. casero, grosero.
home-made, *-mãd*, a. hecho en casa.
home-rule, *-rōl*, s. proyecto de ley acerca de la autonomía de Irlanda, m.
home-ruler, *-dr*, s. individuo del partido irlandés que quiere la autonomía por su país. [isla, m.
home-sick, *-sĭk*, a. nostálgico.
home-sickness, *-sĭknĕs*, s. mal del país, m., nostalgia, f. [basto.
home-spun, *-spŭn*, a. casero; grosero,
homeward, *-wãrd*, a. hacia casa, hacia su país.
homicidal, *hŏm'ĭs'ĭdãl*, a. homicida.
homicide, *hŏm'ĭsĭd*, s. homicidio, m.; homicida, m.
homily, *hŏm'ĭlĕ*, s. homilía, f.
homoeopathist, *hŏmĕŏpãth'ĭst*, s. homeopatista, m. [patía, f.
homoeopathy, *hŏmĕŏp'ãthĕ*, s. homeopatía, f.
homogeneous, *hŏmŏjē'nĭŭs*, a. homogéneo.
hone, *hŏn*, s. piedra amoladera, f. [géneo.
honest, *ŏn'ĕst*, a. honesto; justo; casto; –ly, ad. honestamente.
honesty, *-ĕ*, s. honestidad, justicia, f.
honey, *hŭn'ĕ*, s. miel, f.; dulzura, f.; my, –, querida mía, f.
honey-comb, *-kŏm*, s. panal, m.

honey-dew, –dū, s. rocío dulce, m.

honeymoon, –mōn, s. luna de miel, f.,
primer mes de casados, m.　　[selva, f.

honey-suckle, –sǔkl, s. (bot.) madre-
honied, hǔn'td, a. dulce, meloso, enmelado.

honorary, ǒn'ǔrǎrě, a. honorario.

honour, ǒn'ǔr, s. honra, f.; honor, m.;
v. a. honrar; hacer honor á una letra de
cambio.　　[la gallina ciega, m.

honourable, –ǎbl, a. honorable; ilustre.

honourably, –ǎblě, ad. honorablemente.

hood, hǔd, s. caperuza, f.; capirote (de
graduados), m.; capucha (de religioso), f.;
–, v. a. cubrir con caperuza delante de los
ojos.　　[la gallina ciega, m.

hoodman-blind, –mǎnblǐnd, s. juego de

hoodwink, –wǐnk, v. a. vendar ó uno
los ojos; engañar.　　[m.

hoof, hōf, s. casco de las bestias caballares.

hoof-bound, –bōǔnd, a. estrecho de cascos.

hook, hōk, s. gancho, m.; anzuelo, m.; by
– or crook, de un modo ú otro; –, v. a.
enganchar.

hooked, –d, a. enganchado, encorvado.

hook-nosed, –nōsd, a. cariaguileño.

hoop, hōp, s. cerco de barril, m.; tontillo,
m.; –, v. a. cercar; –, v. n. gritar.

hooper, –ǔr, s. tonelero, m.　　[siva, f.

hooping-cough, –ǐngkǒf, s. tos convul-

hoopoo, hō'pō, s. abubilla, f. (ave).

hoot, hōt, v. n. gritar; –, s. grito, m.

hop, hōp, s. (bot.) lúpulo, m.; salto, m.;
to –(beer), v. a. echar lúpulo en la cerveza; –, v. n. saltar, brincar.

hope, hōp, s. esperanza, f.; –, v.n. esperar.

hopeful, –fūl, a. lleno de buenas calidades;
esperanzado; –ly, ad. con esperanza.

hopefulness, –fǔlněs, s. buena esperanza,
f.　　[sin esperanza.

hopeless, –lěs, a. desesperado; –ly, ad.

hop-garden, hǒp'gǎrdn, s. plantío de lú-
pulos, m.　　[en los molinos.]

hopper, hǒp'pǔr, s. saltador, m.; tolva, f.

hop-pole, hǒp'pōl, s. estaca de hoblón, f.

horary, hǒ'rǎrě, a. horario.

horde, hǒrd, s. horda, f.

horizon, hǒrī'zǔn, s. horizonte, m.

horizontal, hǒrǐzǒn'tǎl, a. horizontal;
–ly, ad. horizontalmente.　　[f.

horn, hǒrn, s. cuerno, m.; corneta de monte,
f.; (mar.) ampolleta, f.

horn-beetle, –bětl, s. escarabajo, m.

horn-blower, –blōǔr, s. trompetero.

horned, –d, a. cornudo.　　[bocinero, m.

hornet, hǒr'nět, s. tábano, m.; abejón, m.

horn-owl, hǒrn'ōǔl, s. buho cornudo, m.

horn-pipe, –pīp, s. gaita, f.

horny, –ě, a. hecho de cuerno; calloso.

horrible, hǒr'rǐbl, a. horrible, terrible.

horribly, –ě, ad. horriblemente; enormemente.

horrid, hǒr'rǐd, a. hórrido, horrible.

horrific, hǒrrǐf'ǐk, a. horrífico; horroroso.

horror, hǒr'rǔr, s. horror, terror, m.

horse, hǒrs, s. caballo, m.; caballería, f.;
caballete, m.; –, v. a. cabalgar.

horseback, –bǎk, ad. on –, á caballo.

horse-block, –blǒk, s. montadero, m.

horse-breaker, –brǎkǔr, s. picador, ó
domador de caballos, m.

horse-chesnut, –tshěsnǔt, s. castaño de
Indias, m.　　[ballo, f.

horse-cloth, –klǒth, s. mantilla de ca-

horse-fly, –flī, s. moscarda, f., moscardón, m.　　[á caballo, f.

horse-guards, –gǎrds, s. pl. guardias de

horse-hair, –hǎr, s. crin de caballo, f.

horse-laugh, –lǎf, s. carcajada, f.

horse-leech, –lětsh, s. sanguijuela, f.;
albeitar, m.

horseman, –mǎn, s. jinete, m.　　[f.

horsemanship, –mǎnshǐp, s. equitación,

horseplay, –plǎ, s. chanza pesada, f.

horsepond, –pǒnd, s. vado, m.; vadera, f.

horse-race, –rǎs, s. carrera ó corrida de
caballos, f.　　[m.

horse-radish, –rǎdǐsh, s. rábano silvestre,

horse-shoe, –shō, s. herradura de caballo,
f.; –, v. a. azotar.

horsewhip, –hwǐp, s. látigo, m.; fusta,
f.

horsewoman, –wǔmǎn, s. caballera, f.

horticulture, hǒrtǐkǔl'tǔr, s. horticultura,
jardinería, f.　　[dinero, m.

horticulturist, –tǔrǐst, s. hortelano, jar-

hose, hōz, s. bragas, f. pl.; calzones, m. pl.

hosier, hǒ'zhǔr, s. bonetero, m.

hosiery, –ě, s. bonetería, f.

hospitable, hǒs'pǐtǎbl, a. hospital.

hospitably, –ě, ad. con hospitalidad.

hospital, hǒs'pǐtǎl, s. hospital, m.

hospitality, hǒspǐtǎl'ǐtě, s. hospitalidad, f.

host, hǒst, s. huésped, m.; mesonero, m.;
ejército, m.; hostia, f.

hostage, hǒs'tǎj, s. rehén, m.

hostess, hǒst'ěs, s. posadera, mesonera, f.

hostile, hǒs'tǐl, a. hostil.

hostility, hǒstǐl'ǐtě, s. hostilidad, f.

hot, hǒt, a. cálido, ardiente; fervoroso; violento.　　[estufas, m.

hot-bed, –běd, s. era, f.; invernadero (con

hotch-potch, hǒtsh'pǒtsh, s.almodrote, m.

hotel, hǒtěl', s. posada, fonda, f.

hot-house, hǒt'hōǔs, s. estufa, f.

hotly, –lě, ad. con calor; violentamente.

hotspur, –spǔr, s. colérico, exaltado, m.

hough, hǒk, s. jarrete, m.; –, v. a. des-
hound, hōǔnd, s. sabueso, m.　　[jarretar.

hour, ōǔr, s. hora, f. (mar.) ampolleta, f.

hour-glass, –glǎs, s.reloj de arena, m.;

hour-hand, –hǎnd, s. mano del reloj que
señala las horas, f.

hourly, –lě, ad. á cada hora.

hour-plate, –plǎt, s. muestra de reloj, f.

house, hǒǔs, s. casa, f.; familia, f.; linaje,
m.; cámara (del parlamento), f.; –, v. a.
& n. albergar; residir.

house-breaker, –brǎkǔr, s. ladrón que
fuerza las puertas de una casa para ro-
barla, m.

house-dog, –děg, s. mastín, m.

household, –hōld, s. familia, f.; manejo
doméstico, m.; –bread, pan casero ó bazo,
m.　　[padre de familia, m.

householder, –hōldǔr, s. amo de casa;

housekeeper, –kěpǔr, s. amo de casa,
jefe de familia, m.; ama de llaves, f.

housekeeping, –*kêping*, s. gobierno doméstico, m.

houseless, –*lês*, a. sin habitación ó sin casa.

house-maid, –*mâd*, s. criada de casa, f.

house-warming, –*wârming*, s. convite que se da al tiempo de estrenar una casa nueva, m.

housewife, –*wîf*, s. ama de una casa, f.; ama de gobierno, mujer económica, f.; –, *hâz zîf*, bolsillo de señora, m. [f.

housewifery, –*rê*, s. economía doméstica,

housing, *hôâz'ing*, s. almacenaje, m.; –s, pl. gualdrapa, f.

hovel, *hôv'êl*, s. choza, cabaña, f.

hover, *hôv'âr*, v. n. colgar; dudar; rondar.

how, *hôâ*, ad. como, cuanto; – **do you do?** ¿cómo le va á U.? – **so?** ¿por qué? ¿cómo así?

how(so)ever, –*(sô)êv'âr*, ad. como quiera, como quiera que sea; aunque; no obstante.

howitzer, *hôâ'îtsâr*, s. (mil.) obús, m. (mortero para arrojar granadas.)

howl, *hôâl*, v. n. aullar; –, s. aullo, m.

hubbub, *hâb'bâb*, s. (vulg.) grito, ruido, m.; alboroto, tumulto, m.

huckaback, *hûk'âbâk*, s. alemanisco, m.

huckle, *hûk'êl*, s. codera, f.

huckster, *hûk'stâr*, s. revendedor, m.

huddle, *hûd'dl*, v. a. tapujar, confundir; –, s. confusión, barafunda, f.

hue, *hû*, s. color, m.; tez del rostro, f.; matiz, m.; – **and cry,** alarma que se da contra un criminal, f.

huff, *hûf*, s. arrebato, m.; cólera, f.; – v. a. bufar, brayear; –, v. n. patear de enfado.

huffish, –*fîsh*, a. arrogante, insolente; –**ly,** ad. con arrogancia, insolentemente.

hug, *hûg*, v. a. abrazar, acariciar; –, s. abrazo apretado, m.

huge, *hûj*, a. vasto, enorme; –**ly,** ad. inmensamente. [mesurada, f.

hugeness, –*nês*, s. grandeza enorme ó desmesurada.

hulk, *hûlk*, s. (mar.) casco de la embarcación, m.; armatoste, m. [buque, m.

hull, *hûl*, s. cáscara, f.; (mar.) casco de un

hum, *hûm*, v. n. zumbar, susurrar; murmurar; –, s. zumbido, m.; chasco, m.; –!

human, *hû'mân*, a. humano. [¡ya!

humane, *hûmân'*, a. humano; benigno; –**ly,** ad. humanamente.

humanise, *hû'mânîz*, v. a. humanizar.

humanist, *hû'mânîst*, s. humanista, m.

humanity, *hûmân'itê*, s. humanidad, f.

humankind, *hû'mânkînd*, s. el género ó linaje humano.

humanly, –*lê*, ad. humanamente.

humble, *hâm'bl*, a. humilde, modesto; –, v. a. humillar, postrar.

humble-bee, –*bê*, s. zángano, m.

humbleness, –*nês*, s. humildad, f.

humbly, *hâm'blê*, ad. con humildad.

humbug, *hâm'bûg*, s. engaño, m.; trampa, f.; –, v. a. engañar, chasquear.

humdrum, *hâm'drûm*, a. lerdo, estúpido, monótono.

humid, *hû'mîd*, a. húmedo, algo mojado.

humidity, *hûmîd'itê*, s. humedad, f.

humiliate, *hûmîl'iât*, v. a. humillar.

humiliation, *hûmîlîâ'shân*, s. humillación, mortificación, f.

humility, *hûmîl'itê*, s. humildad, f.

humming-bird, *hâm'mingbûrd*, s. guainambí, colibrí, m. (pajarito).

humming-top, –*tôp*, s. trompo, peón, m.

humorist, *hû'mûrist*, s. hombre caprichoso ó fantástico; bufón, m.

humorous, *hû'mûrûs*, a. caprichoso, chistoso, placentero; –**ly,** ad. de buen humor; caprichosamente. [prichoso.

humorsome, *hû'mûrsûm*, a. petulante, caprichoso.

humour, *hû'mûr*, s. humor, m.; humorada, fantasía, f.; capricho, m.; – v. a. complacer, dar gusto; ejecutar lo que á uno se le manda.

hump, *hâmp*, s. jiba, joroba, f.

humpbacked, –*bâkd*, a. jorobado, jiboso.

hunch, *hûnsh*, s. puñada, f.; codazo, m.; jiba, f.; –**backed,** a. jorobado, jiboso.

hundred, *hûn'drêd*, a. ciento; –, s. centenar, m.; un ciento.

hundredfold, –*fôld*, a. céntuplo.

hundredth, –*th*, a. centésimo.

hundred-weight, –*wât*, s. quintal, m.

hung-beef, *hâng'bêf*, s. carne ahumada, f.

hunger, *hâng'gûr*, s. hambre, f.; –, v. n. hambrear. [mente.

hungrily, *hâng'grilê*, ad. hambrientamente.

hungry, *hâng'grê*, a. hambriento; voraz.

hunk, *hângk*, s. pedazo grande, m.

hunks, –*s*, s. hombre sórdido, m.

hunt, *hûnt*, v. a. montear, cazar; perseguir; buscar; –, v. n. andar á caza; –, s. caza, f.

hunter, –*âr*, s. cazador, m.; caballo de caza, m.; perro de monte, perro braco, m.

hunting, –*îng*, s. montería, caza, f. [f.

hunting-box, –*îngbôks*, s. casa de campo.

hunting-crop, –*krôp*, s. corbacho, m.

hunting-horn, –*înghôrn*, s. corneta de caza, f. [caza, m.

hunting-watch, –*îngwôtsh*, s. reloj de

huntress, –*rês*, s. cazadora, f.

huntsman, –*s'mân*, s. cazador, montero, m.

hurdle, *hûr'dl*, s. zarzo, m. [rana, f.

hurdy-gurdy, *hûr'digûrdê*, s. gaita zamorana, f.

hurl, *hûrl*, v. a. tirar con violencia; arrojar.

hurly-burly, *hûr'libûr'lê*, s. alboroto, m.; confusión, babilonia, f.

hurricane, *hûr'rikân*, s. huracán, m.

hurry, *hûr'rê*, v. a. acelerar, apresurar, precipitar; –, v. n. atropellarse, apresurarse; –, s. precipitación, f.; confusión, f.

hurt, *hûrt*, v. a. dañar; herir; ofender; –, s. mal, daño, perjuicio, m.; golpe, m.; herida, f. [–**ly,** ad. dañosamente.

hurtful, –*fûl*, a. dañoso, nocivo; injurioso;

hurtfulness, –*nês*, s. lo nocivo de una cosa.

husband, *hûz'bând*, s. marido, m.; labrador, m., **ship's** –, armador de navío, m.; –, v. a. gobernar con economía; labrar la tierra. [m.

husbandman, –*mân*, s. labrador, viñador,

husbandry, –*rê*, s. agricultura, f.; economía, f.

hush! *hâsh*, ¡chitón!, ¡silencio! –, v. a. aquietar; acallar; –, v. n. estar quieto.

hush-money, –*mûnê*, s. cohecho que se da á alguno para que calle, m.

husk, *hŭsk*, s. cáscara, f.; pellejo, m.; –, v. a. descascarar, mondar.
huskiness, *–nĕs*, s. ronquedad, f.
husky, *–ĕ*, a. lleno de cáscaras; ronco.
hussar, *hăzzăr'*, s. húsar, m. (soldado de á.
hussy, *hăz'zĕ*, s. mujercilla, f. (caballo).
hustings, *hŭs'tĭngz*, s. tribuna para las elecciones, f. [con fuerza.
hustle, *hŭs'l*, v. a. escaramuzar; empujar
hut, *hŭt*, s. cabaña, barraca, f.
hutch, *hŭtsh*, s. arca, f.; cofre, m.; madriguera de conejos, m.
hyacinth, *hī'ăsĭnth*, s. jacinto, m. [f.
hydrant, *hī'drănt*, s. llave de un encañado.
hydraulic(al), *hīdrăl'ĭk(ăl)*, a. hidráulico; –s, s. pl. hidráulica, f.
hydrophobia, *hīdrŏf'bĕă*, s. hidrofobia, f.
hydrostatic(al), *hīdrŏstăt'ĭks*, s. pl. hidrostática, f.
hyena, *hī'nă*, s. hiena, f. [estática, f.
hygiene, *hī'jĕn*, s. higiena, f.
hymen, *hī'mĕn*, s. himeneo, m.
hymeneal, *hĭmĕnē'ăl*, a. nupcial.
hymn, *hĭm*, s. himno, m. [ageración, f.
hyperbole, *hīpŭr'bŏlē*, s. hipérbole, m.; exhyperbolic(al), *hīpărbŏl'ĭk(ăl)*, a. hiperbólico; –ally, ad. hiperbólicamente.
hypercritic, *hīpŭrkrĭt'ĭk*, s. rigorista, crítico austero, m.
hyphen, *hī'fĕn*, s. (gr.) división, f.
hypochondria, *hīpŏkŏndrī'ă*, s. hipocondría, f. [pocondríaco (m.).
hypochondriac, *hīpŏkŏn'drĭăk*, a. & s. hipocrisy, *hĭpŏk'rĭsē*, s. hipocresía, f.
hypocrite, *hĭp'ŏkrĭt*, s. hipócrita, m.
hypocritic(al), *hĭpŏkrĭt'ĭk(ăl)*, a. hipócrita, disimulado,
hypothesis, *hīpŏth'ĕsĭs*, s. hipótesis, f.
hypothetic(al), *hīpŏthĕt'ĭk(ăl)*, a. hipotético; –ly, ad. condicionalmente.
hyssop, *hĭs'săp*, s. hisopo, f.
hysteric(al), *hĭstĕr'ĭk(ăl)*, a. histérico.
hysterics, *hĭstĕr'ĭks*, s. pl. paroxismo histérico, m.

I.

I, *ī*, pn. yo.
ice, *īs*, hielo, m.; –, v. a. helar.
ice-bound, *–boŭnd*, a. rodeado de hielos.
ice-box, *–bŏks*, ice-cellar, *–sĕllăr*, ice-house, *–hoŭs*, ice-safe, *–săf*, s. nevera.
icicle, *ī'sĭkl*, s. cerrión, m. [ría, f.
iciness, *ī'sĭnĕs*, s. congelación, f.; congelamiento, m.
iconoclast, *īkŏn'ŏklăst*, s. iconoclasta, m.
icy, *ī'sĕ*, a. helado; frío.
idea, *īdē'ă*, s. idea, imagen mental, f.
ideal, *–ăl*, a. ideal, intelectual; –ly, ad. idealmente.
identic(al), *īdĕn'tĭk(ăl)*, a. idéntico.
identify, *–tĭfī*, v. a. identificar.
identity, *–ĭtē*, s. identidad, f.
idiocy, *ĭd'ĭŏsē*, s. idiotismo, m.
idiom, *ĭd'ĭŭm*, s. idioma, m.
idiomatic(al), *ĭdĭŏmăt'ĭk(ăl)*, a. peculiar á alguna lengua.

idiosyncrasy, *ĭdĭŏsĭng'krăsĕ*, s. idiosincrasia, f.
idiot, *ĭd'ĭŏt*, s. idiota, necio, m.
idiotic(al), *ĭdĭŏt'ĭk(ăl)*, a. tonto, bobo.
idle, *ī'dl*, a. ocioso; perezoso, desocupado; holgazán; inútil, vano, frívolo; –, v. n. holgazanear; estar ocioso.
idleness, *–nĕs*, s. ociosidad, pereza, f.; negligencia, f.; frivolidad, f.
idler, *ī'dlăr*, s. holgazán, hombre poltrón, m.
idly, *ī'dlē*, ad. ociosamente; vanamente.
idol, *ī'dŏl*, s. ídolo, m.; imagen, f.
idolater, *īdŏl'ătŭr*, s. idólatra, m.
idolatrous, *–ătrŭs*, a. idolátrico.
idolatry, *–ătrē*, s. idolatría, f.
idolise, *ī'dŏlīz*, v. a. idolatrar.
idyl, *ī'dĭl*, s. idilio, m.
idyllic, *īdĭl'ĭk*, a. idílico. [sino.
if, *ĭf*, c. si; aunque, supuesto que; – not,
igneous, *ĭg'nĕŭs*, a. ígneo, de fuego. [m.
ignis-fatuus, *ĭg'nĭs făt'ūăs*, s. fuego fatuo,
ignite, *ĭgnīt'*, v. a. encender, abrasar.
ignition, *ĭgnĭsh'ăn*, s. (chem.) ignición, m.
ignoble, *ĭgnō'bl*, a. innoble; bajo.
ignobly, *–ĕ*, ad. vilmente, bajamente.
ignominious, *ĭgnŏmĭn'ĭŭs*, a. ignominioso; –ly, ad. ignominiosamente. [famia, f.
ignominy, *ĭg'nŏmĭnē*, s. ignominia, inignoramus, *ĭgnŏră'mŭs*, s. ignorante, tonto,
ignorance, *ĭg'nŏrăns*, s. ignorancia, f. [m.
ignorant, *ĭg'nŏrănt*, a. ignorante: –ly, ad. ignorantemente.
ignore, *ĭgnōr'*, v. a. ignorar.
ill, *ĭl*, a. malo, enfermo, doliente; –, s. mal, infortunio, m.; –, ad. mal, malamente.
illegal, *ĭllē'găl*, a. –ly, ad. ilegal(mente).
illegality, *ĭllēgăl'ĭtē*, s. ilegalidad, f.
illegible, *ĭllĕj'ĭbl*, a. ilegible.
illegibly, *–ĕ*, ad. de un modo ilegible. [f.
illegitimacy, *ĭllĕjĭt'ĭmăsē*, s. ilegitimidad, f.
illegitimate, *ĭllĕjĭt'ĭmăt*, a. ilegítimo; –ly, ad. ilegítimamente. [feo.
ill-favoured, *ĭll-făvărd*, a. mal carado;
illiberal, *ĭllĭb'ărăl*, a. innoble; mezquino; –ly, ad. sin libertad; mesquinamente.
illiberality, *ĭllĭbără'lĭtē*, s. cortedad de ánimo, f.; tacañería, f.
illicit, *ĭllĭs'ĭt*, a. ilícito.
illimitable, *ĭllĭm'ĭtăbl*, a. ilimitado.
illiterate, *ĭllĭt'ărăt*, a. indocto, iliterato.
illness, *ĭl'nĕs*, s. enfermedad, f.; maldad, f.
illogical, *ĭllŏj'ĭkăl*, a. no conforme á las reglas de la lógica. [hecho.
ill-shaped, *ĭll-shăpt*, a. disforme; mal
ill-timed, *ĭll'tĭmd*, a. intempestivo, á deshora. [tratar.
ill-treat, *ĭll'trēt*, ill-use, *–ăz*, v. a. maltratar.
illuminate, *ĭllū'mĭnăt*, v. a. iluminar.
illumination, *ĭllūmĭnā'shăn*, s. iluminación, f.
illumine, *ĭllū'mĭn*, v. a. iluminar.
illusion, *ĭllū'zhăn*, s. ilusión, f.
illusive, *ĭllū'sĭv*, illusory, *ĭllū'sărĕ*, a. ilusivo, ilusorio.
illustrate, *ĭllŭs'trăt*, v. a. ilustrar; explicar.
illustration, *ĭllŭstrā'shăn*, s. ilustración, f.; elucidación, f.
illustrative, *ĭllŭs'trătĭv*, a. explicativo.

illustrious, *ĭllŭs'trĭŭs,* a. ilustre, insigne, célebre; **-ly,** ad. ilustremente.

ill-will, *ĭl'wĭl,* s. malquerencia, f.

image, *ĭm'ĭj,* s. imagen, estatua, f.; **-, v. a.** imaginar.

imagery, *ĭmĭj'ŭrĕ,* s. imagen, pintura, f.; vuelos de la fantasía, m. pl. [cebible.

imaginable, *ĭmăj'ĭnăbl,* a. imaginable, concebible.

imaginary, *ĭmăj'ĭnărĕ,* a. imaginario.

imagination, *ĭmăjĭnā'shŭn,* s. imaginación, f.; idea fantástica, f.

imaginative, *ĭmăj'ĭnătĭv,* a. imaginativo.

imagine, *ĭmăj'ĭn,* v. a. imaginar; idear, inventar.

imbecile, *ĭm'bĕsĭl,* a. imbécil, necio.

imbecility, *ĭmbĕsĭl'ĭtĕ,* s. imbecilidad, mentecatez, f.; idiotismo, m.

imbedded, *ĭmbĕd'ĕd,* a. incrustado.

imbibe, *ĭmbīb',* v. a. embeber; chupar.

imbroglio, *ĭmbrōl'yō,* s. embrollo, m.; maraña, f.

imbrue, *ĭmbrō',* v. a. remojar.

imbue, *ĭmbū',* v. a. imbuir, infundir.

imbursement, *ĭmbŭrs'mĕnt,* s.pagamento.

imitable, *ĭm'ĭtăbl,* a. imitable. [m.

imitate, *ĭm'ĭtāt,* v. a. imitar, copiar. [f.

imitation, *ĭmĭtā'shŭn,* s. imitación, copia.

imitative, *ĭm'ĭtătĭv,* a, imitativo, imitado.

immaculate, *ĭmmăk'dlăt,* a. inmaculado, puro. [poco importante.

immaterial, *ĭmmătē'rĭăl,* a. inmaterial;

immature, *ĭmmătūr',* a. inmaduro.

immeasurable, *ĭmmĕzh'ŭrăbl,* a. inmensurable, inmenso. [inmensurablemente.

immeasurably, *-ĕ,* ad. inmensamente.

immediate, *ĭmmē'dĭăt,* a. inmediato; **-ly,** ad. inmediatamente.

immemorial, *ĭmmĕmō'rĭăl,* a. inmemorial.

immense, *ĭmmĕns',* a. inmenso; vasto; **-ly,** ad. inmensamente. [dumbre, f.

immensity, *-sĭtĕ,* s. inmensidad, muchedumbre, f.

immerge, *ĭmmŭrj',* **immerse,** *ĭmmŭrs',* v. a. sumergir, zambullir.

immersion, *ĭmmŭr'shŭn,* s. inmersión, f.

immigrant, *ĭm'mĭgrănt,* s. inmigrante, m.

imminent, *ĭm'mĭnĕnt,* a. inminente.

immobile, *ĭmmō'bĭl,* a. inmóvil. [f.

immobility, *ĭmmōbĭl'ĭtĕ,* s. inmovilidad.

immoderate, *ĭmmŏd'ŭrăt,* a. inmoderado, excesivo; **-ly,** ad. inmoderadamente.

immodest, *ĭmmŏd'ĕst,* a. inmodesto; **-ly,** ad. inmodestamente.

immodesty, *-ĕ,* s. inmodestia, f.

immolate, *ĭm'mōlăt,* v. a. inmolar, sacrificar. [f.

immolation, *ĭmmōlā'shŭn,* s. inmolación.

immoral, *ĭmmŏr'ăl,* a. inmoral, depravado.

immorality, *ĭmmōrăl'ĭtĕ,* s. pravedad, corrupción de costumbres, f. [(mente).

immortal, *ĭmmŏr'tăl,* a. **-ly,** ad. inmortal.

immortalise, *ĭmmŏr'tălĭz,* v. a. inmortalizar, eternizar. [dad, f.

immortality, *ĭmmŏrtăl'ĭtĕ,* s. inmortalidad.

immovable, *ĭmmōv'ăbl,* a. inmoble; inmovible; **-s,** s. pl. bienes raíces, m. pl.

immovably, *-ĕ,* a. inmoblemente.

immunity, *ĭmmū'nĭtĕ,* s. inmunidad, franquicia, f.; privilegio, m.

immure, *ĭmmūr',* v. a. emparedar.

immutability, *ĭmmŭtăbĭl'ĭtĕ,* s. inmutabilidad, f.

immutable, *ĭmmū'tăbl,* a. inmutable.

immutably, *-ĕ,* ad. inmutablemente.

imp, *ĭmp,* s. diablillo, duende, m.; injerto, m.; vástago, m.

impact, *ĭm'păkt,* s. impulso, m.

impair, *ĭmpār',* v. a. empeorar, deteriorar; disminuir.

impale, *ĭmpăl',* v. a. empalar á un reo.

impalpable, *ĭmpăl'păbl,* a. impalpable.

impannel, *ĭmpăn'nĕl,* v. a. (law) inscribir á los jurados sobre la lista.

impart, *ĭmpărt',* v. a. comunicar, dar parte.

impartial, *ĭmpăr'shăl,* a. **-ly,** ad. imparcial(mente). [dad, f.

impartiality, *ĭmpărshăl'ĭtĕ,* s. imparcialidad, f.

impassable, *ĭmpăs'ăbl,* a. intransitable, impracticable. [bilidad, f.

impassibility, *ĭmpăssĭbĭl'ĭtĕ,* s. impasibilidad, f.

impassion, *ĭmpăsh'ŭn,* v. a. mover las pasiones.

impassive, *ĭmpăs'sĭv,* a. impasible.

impatience, *ĭmpā'shĕns,* s. impaciencia, f.

impatient, *ĭmpā'shĕnt,* a. **-ly,** ad. impaciente(mente).

impeach, *ĭmpētsh',* v. a. acusar, denunciar.

impeachable, *-ăbl,* a. delatable. [f.

impeachment, *-mĕnt,* s.acusación pública.

impecunious, *ĭmpĕkū'nĭŭs,* a. indigente.

impede, *ĭmpēd',* v. a. impedir, embarazar.

impediment, *ĭmpĕd'ĭmĕnt,* s. impedimento, obstáculo, m.

impel, *ĭmpĕl',* v. a. impeler.

impend, *ĭmpĕnd',* v. n. amenazar, aproximarse un peligro &c.

impenetrability, *ĭmpĕnĕtrăbĭl'ĭtĕ,* s. impenetrabilidad, f. [trable.

impenetrable, *ĭmpĕn'ĕtrăbl,* a. impenetrable; **impenetrably,** *-ĕ,* ad. impenetrablemente.

impenitence, *ĭmpĕn'ĭtĕns,* s. impenitencia, f. [**-ly,** ad. sin penitencia.

impenitent, *ĭmpĕn'ĭtĕnt,* a. impenitente;

imperative, *ĭmpĕr'ătĭv,* a. imperativo; **-ly,** ad. imperativamente. [ceptible.

imperceptible, *ĭmpŭrsĕp'tĭbl,* a. imperceptible; **imperceptibly,** *-ĕ,* ad.imperceptiblemente.

imperfect, *ĭmpŭr'fĕkt,* a. imperfecto, defectuoso; **-ly,** ad. imperfectamente; **-,** s. (gr.) pretérito imperfecto, m.

imperfection, *ĭmpŭrfĕk'shŭn,* s. imperfección, f. defecto, m.

imperial, *ĭmpē'rĭăl,* a. imperial; **-,** s. imperial, cielo, m.; mostacho, m.

imperialists, *-ĭsts,* s. pl. tropas del antiguo emperador de Alemania, f. pl.

imperil, *ĭmpĕr'ĭl,* v. a. arriesgar.

imperious, *ĭmpē'rĭŭs,* a. imperioso; arrogante; **-ly,** ad. imperiosamente, arrogantemente. [tible; eterno.

imperishable, *ĭmpĕr'ĭshăbl,* a. indestructible.

impermeable, *ĭmpŭr'mĭăbl,* a. impermeable. [personal(mente).

impersonal, *ĭmpŭr'sŏnăl,* a. **-ly,** ad. impersonate,** *ĭmpŭr'sŏnăt,* v. a. personalizar. [sentación (de un actor), f.

impersonation, *ĭmpŭrsŏnā'shŭn,* s.repre-

impertinence, *ĭmpŭr´tĭnĕns,* s. impertinencia, f.; descaro, m.

impertinent, *ĭmpŭr´tĭnĕnt,* a. impertinente; **-ly,** ad. impertinentemente; fuera de propósito.

imperturbable, *ĭmpŭrtŭrb´ăbl,* a. imperturbable; **-bly,** ad. sin perturbación.

impervious, *ĭmpŭr´vĭŭs,* a. impenetrable.

impetuosity, *ĭmpĕtŭôs´ĭtĭ,* s. impetuosidad, f., ímpetu, m. [ad. impetuosamente.

impetuous, *ĭmpĕt´ŭŭs,* a. impetuoso; **-ly,**

impetus, *ĭm´pĕtŭs,* s. ímpetu, m. [f.

impiety, *ĭmpī´ĕtĭ,* s. impiedad, irreligión, f.

impinge (on), *ĭmpĭnj´ (ŏn),* v. a. tener influjo en.   **-ly,** ad. impíamente.

impious, *ĭm´pĭŭs,* a. impío, irreligioso;

implacable, *ĭmplā´kăbl,* a. implacable, irreconciliable.   [irreconciliablemente.

implacably, *-ĭ,* ad. implacablemente,

implant, *ĭmplănt´,* v. a. plantar; injertar; imprimir.   [f.; utensilio, m.; mueble, m.

implement, *ĭm´plĕmĕnt,* s. herramienta,

implicate, *ĭm´plĭkāt,* v. a. implicar, envolver.   [f.

implication, *ĭmplĭkā´shŭn,* s. implicación.

implicit, *ĭmplĭs´ĭt,* a. implícito; **-ly,** ad. implícitamente.

implore, *ĭmplōr´,* v. a. implorar, suplicar.

imply, *ĭmplī´,* v. a. implicar; comprender.

impolite, *ĭmpōlīt´,* a. descortés, impolítico.

impoliteness, *-nĕs,* s. falta de cortesía, f.

impolitic(al), *ĭmpŏl´ĭtĭk, ĭmpōlĭt´ĭkăl,* a. imprudente; impolítico.

import, *ĭmpōrt´,* v. a. importar; significar; **-,** *ĭm´pōrt,* s. importancia, f.; importe, m.; sentido, m.; significación, f.; **-duty,** derechos de entrada, m. pl.

importance, *ĭmpōr´tăns,* s. importancia, f.

important, *-tănt,* a. importante.

importation, *ĭmpōrtā´shŭn,* s. importación, f.   [géneros extranjeros, m.

importer, *ĭmpōr´tŭr,* s. introductor de

importunate, *ĭmpōr´tŭnăt,* a. importuno; **-ly,** ad. importunamente.

importune, *ĭmpōrtūn´,* v. a. importunar.

importunity, *-tĭ,* s. importunidad, f.

impose, *ĭmpōz´,* v. a. imponer; engañar.

imposing, *-ĭng,* a. imponente, que infunde respeto.

imposition, *ĭmpōzĭzh´ŭn,* s. imposición, carga, f.; impostura, f.   [bilidad, f.

impossibility, *ĭmpŏssĭbĭl´ĭtĭ,* s. imposi-

impossible, *ĭmpŏs´sĭbl,* a. imposible.

impost, *ĭm´pōst,* s. impuesto, tributo, m.

impostor, *ĭmpŏs´tŭr,* s. impostor, m.

imposture, *-tŭr,* s. impostura, f.; engaño, m.   [capacidad, f.

impotence, *ĭm´pōtĕns,* s. impotencia; in-

impotent, *ĭm´pōtĕnt,* a. impotente; incapaz; **-ly,** ad. sin poder.   [rralar.

impound, *ĭmpŏŭnd´,* v. a. encerrar, aco-

impoverish, *ĭmpŏv´ărĭsh,* v.a.empobrecer.

impoverishment, *-mĕnt,* s. empobrecimiento, m.   [imposibilidad, f.

impracticability, *ĭmprăktĭkăbĭl´ĭtĭ,* s.

impracticable, *ĭmprăk´tĭkăbl,* a. impracticable, imposible.

imprecate, *ĭm´prĕkāt,* v. a. maldecir.

imprecation, *ĭmprĕkā´shŭn,* s. imprecación, maldición, f.

impregnable, *ĭmprĕg´năbl,* a. inexpugnable.   [pregnar.

impregnate, *-nāt,* v. a. empreñar; im-

impregnation, *ĭmprĕgnā´shŭn,* s. fecundación, f.; impregnación, f.

impress, *ĭmprĕs´,* v. a. imprimir, estampar; hacer una leva; **-,** *ĭm´prĕs,* s. impresión, f.; empresa, f.; divisa, f.

impressible, *ĭmprĕs´sĭbl,* **impressionable** *-shŭnăbl,* a. impresionable.

impression, *ĭmprĕsh´ŭn,* s. impresión, f.; edición, f.

impressive, *ĭmprĕs´sĭv,* a. penetrante; impresionable; **-ly,** ad. de un modo eficaz.

imprint, *ĭmprĭnt´,* v.a.imprimir; estampar.

imprison, *ĭmprĭz´n,* v. a. aprisionar.

imprisonment, *-mĕnt,* s. prisión, f.; encierro, m.   [babilidad, f.

improbability, *ĭmprŏbăbĭl´ĭtĭ,* s. impro-

improbable, *ĭmprŏb´ăbl,* a. improbable.

improbably, *-ĭ,* ad. improbablemente.

improbity, *ĭmprŏb´ĭtĭ,* s. falta de probidad, f.   [mente.

impromptu, *ĭmprŏm´tū,* a. extemporánea-

improper, *ĭmprŏp´ŭr,* a. impropio, indecente; **-ly,** ad. impropiamente.

impropriety, *ĭmprōprī´ĕtĭ,* s. impropiedad, incongruencia, f.

improve, *ĭmprŏŏv´,* v. a. & n. mejorar, perfeccionar; mejorar; hacer progresos.

improvement, *-mĕnt,* s. progreso, mejoramiento, m.   [cia, falta de previsión, f.

improvidence, *ĭmprŏv´ĭdĕns,* s. impruden-

improvident, *-ĭĕnt,* a. impróvido; **-ly,** ad. impróvidamente.

improvise, *ĭmprŏvīz´,* v. a. improvisar.

imprudence, *ĭmprŏŏ´dĕns,* s. imprudencia, f.

imprudent, *-dĕnt,* a. imprudente; **-ly,** ad. imprudentemente.

impudence, *ĭm´pūdĕns,* s. impudencia, f.

impudent, *ĭm´pūdĕnt,* a. impudente; **-ly,** ad. desvergonzadamente; impúdicamente.

impugn, *ĭmpūn´,* v. a. impugnar.

impulse, *ĭm´pŭls,* **impulsion,** *ĭmpŭl´shŭn,* s. impulsión, f.; impulso, m.

impulsive, *ĭmpŭl´sĭv,* a. impulsivo.

impunity, *ĭmpū´nĭtĭ,* s. impunidad, f.

impure, *ĭmpūr´,* a. impuro; impúdico, sucio; **-ly,** ad. impuramente.   [pureza, f.

impurity, *ĭmpū´rĭtĭ,* s. impuridad, in-

imputation, *ĭmpūtā´shŭn,* s. imputación, f.

impute, *ĭmpūt´,* v. a. imputar.   [f.

in, *ĭn,* pr. ú, en, por, á, de, mientras, bajo, con, para.   [pacidad, f.

inability, *ĭnăbĭl´ĭtĭ,* s. inhabilidad, inca-

inaccessible, *ĭnăksĕs´sĭbl,* a. inaccesible.

inaccuracy, *ĭnăk´kŭrăsĭ,* s. incuria, negligencia, f.; incorrección, f.

inaccurate, *ĭnăk´kŭrăt,* a. inexacto.

inaction, *ĭnăk´shŭn,* s. inacción, holgazanería, f.

inactive, *ĭnăk´tĭv,* a. flojo, perezoso, negligente.   [día, f.

inactivity, *ĭnăktĭv´ĭtĭ,* s. ociosidad, desi-

inadequate, *ĭnăd´ĕkwăt,* a. inadecuado; defectuoso; imperfecto, insuficiente.

inadmissible, *ĭnădmĭs'sĭbl,* a. inadmisible. [f.

inadvertence, *–vŭr'tĕns,* s inadvertencia.

inadvertently, *–vŭr'tĕntlĕ,* ad. inadvertidamente. [inalienable.

inalienable, *ĭnāl'yĕnăbl,* a. inajenable.

inanimate, *ĭnăn'ĭmăt* a inánime, m. inanimado.

inanition, *ĭnănĭsh'ŭn,* s. inanición, f.

inanity, *ĭnăn'ĭtĕ,* s. vacuidad, f.; nulidad, f.

inapplicable, *ĭnăpp'plĭkăbl,* a. inaplicable.

inapposite, *ĭnăp'pŏzĭt,* a. mal puesto, mal colocado. [apreciable, inestimable.

inappreciable, *ĭnăpprē'shĭăbl,* a. inapreciable.

inappropriate, *ĭnăpprō'prĭăt,* a. impropio.

inaptitude, *ĭnăp'tĭtūd,* s. ineptitud, f.

inarticulate, *ĭnartĭk'ūlăt,* a. inarticulado; *–ly,* ad. indistintamente. [que.

inasmuch, *ĭnăzmŭtsh',* ad. visto ó puesto

inattention, *ĭnăttĕn'shŭn,* s. desatención, f.; descuido, m. [dado.

inattentive, *–tĭv,* a. desatento, descuidado; *–ly,* ad. desatentamente.

inaudible, *ĭnă'dĭbl,* a. inaudible, lo que no se puede oir.

inaugural, *ĭnă'gŭrăl,* a. inaugural.

inaugurate, *ĭnă'gŭrāt,* v. a. inaugurar.

inauguration, *ĭnăgŭrā'shŭn,* s. inauguración, f.

inauspicious, *ĭnăspĭsh'ŭs,* a. malaventurado; *–ly,* ad. desgraciadamente.

inborn, *ĭn'bŏrn,* inbred, *ĭn'brĕd,* a. innato, insito. [lable.

incalculable, *ĭnkăl'kŭlăbl,* a. incalculable.

incandescent, *ĭnkăndĕs'sĕnt,* a. incandescente; *–light,* s. luz eléctrica incandescente. f. [miento, m.

incantation, *ĭnkăntā'shŭn,* s. encantación, f.

incapability, *ĭnkăpăbĭl'ĭtĕ.* s. incapacidad, f.

incapable, *ĭnkā'păbl,* a. incapaz, inhábil.

incapacitate, *ĭnkăpăs'ĭtăt,* v. a. inhabilitar.

incapacity, *–ĭtĕ,* s. incapacidad, f.

incarcerate, *ĭnkar'sărăt,* v. a. encarcelar, aprisionar.

incarnate, *ĭnkar'năt,* a. encarnado.

incarnation, *ĭnkarnā'shŭn,* s. encarnación, encarnadura, f.

incase, *ĭnkās',* v. a. encajar, incluir.

incautious, *ĭnkă'shŭs,* a. incauto; *–ly,* ad. incautamente.

incendiary, *ĭnsĕn'dĭărĕ,* s. incendiario, m.

incense, *ĭn'sĕns,* s. incienso, m.; *– ĭnsĕns'* v. a. exasperar, irritar, provocar.

incentive, *ĭnsĕn'tĭv,* s. estímulo, m.

inception, *ĭnsĕp'shŭn,* s. principio, m.

incertitude, *ĭnsŭr'tĭtūd,* s. incertidumbre, f.

incessant, *ĭnsĕs'sănt,* a. incesante, constante; *–ly,* ad. continuamente.

incest, *ĭn'sĕst,* s. incesto, m.

incestuous, *ĭnsĕs'tūŭs,* a. incestuoso.

inch, *ĭnsh,* s. pulgada, f. (duodécima parte de un pie), *–by –,* palmo á palmo.

incidence, *ĭn'sĭdĕns,* s. incidencia, f.; accidente, m.

incident, *ĭn'sĭdĕnt,* a. incidente; dependiente; *–,* s. incidente. m.

incidental, *ĭnsĭdĕn'tăl,* a. accidental, casual; *–,* ad. incidentemente.

incipient, *ĭnsĭp'ĭĕnt,* a. incipiente.

incise, *ĭnsīz',* v. a. tajar, cortar, grabar.

incision, *ĭnsĭzh'ŭn,* s. incisión, f.

incisivo, *ĭnsī'sĭv,* a. incisivo, incisorio.

incisor, *–zŭr,* s. incisivos, m. pl.

incite, *ĭnsīt',* v. a. incitar, estimular.

incivility, *ĭnsĭvĭl'ĭtĕ,* s. incivilidad, descortesía, f. [severidad, f.

inclemency, *ĭnklĕm'ĕnsĕ,* s. inclemencia,

inclement, *–ĕnt,* a. inclemente, verso.

inclination, *ĭnklĭnā'shŭn,* s. inclinación, propensión, f.; declive, m.

incline, *ĭnklīn',* v. a. & n. inclinar(se).

include, *ĭnklōd',* v. a. incluir, comprender.

inclusive, *ĭnklō'sĭv,* a. inclusivo; *–ly,* ad. inclusivamente.

incognito, *ĭnkŏg'nĭtō,* ad. de incógnito.

incoherence, *ĭnkōhē'rĕns,* s. incoherencia, f.

incoherent, *–rĕnt,* a. incoherente, inconsecuente; *–ly,* ad. incongruamente.

incombustible, *ĭnkŏmbŭs'tĭbl,* a. incombustible. [anual, m.

income, *ĭn'kŭm,* s. renta, f.; beneficio

incommensurable, *ĭnkŏmmen'shŭrăbl,* inconmensurable.

incommode, *ĭnkŏmmōd',* v. a. incomodar.

incommodious, *ĭnkŏmmō'dĭŭs,* a. incómodo, molesto. [parable, excelente.

incomparable, *ĭnkŏm'părăbl,* a. incomparable; *–,* ad. incomparablemente. [compatibilidad, f.

incompatibility, *ĭnkŏmpătĭbĭl'ĭtĕ,* s. incompatibilidad, f.

incompatible, *ĭnkŏmpăt'ĭbl,* a. incompatible, opuesto. [petencia, f.

incompetency, *ĭnkŏm'pĕtĕnsĕ,* s. incompetencia, f.

incompetent, *–pĕtĕnt,* a., *–ly,* ad. incompetente(mente). [falto, imperfecto.

incomplete, *ĭnkŏmplēt',* a. incompleto,

incomprehensibility, *ĭnkŏmprēhĕnsĭbĭl'ĭtĕ,* s. incomprehensibilidad, f.

incomprehensible, *ĭnkŏmprēhĕn'sĭbl,* a. incomprehensible.

inconceivable, *ĭnkŏnsē'văbl,* a. incomprehensible, inconcebible.

inconclusive, *–klō'sĭv,* a. no concluyente; *–,* ad. sin conclusión. [incongruidad, f.

incongruity, *–grōō'ĭtĕ,* s. incongruencia,

incongruous, *ĭnkŏn'grŭŭs,* a. incongruo; *–ly,* ad. incongruamente.

inconsequent, *ĭnkŏn'sĕkwĕnt,* a. inconsecuente. [frívolo, poco considerable.

inconsiderable, *ĭnkŏnsĭd'ărăbl,* a.

inconsiderate, *–sĭd'ărăt,* a. inconsiderado; *–ly,* ad. inconsideradamente.

inconsistency, *–sĭs'tĕnsĕ,* s. incompatibilidad, incongruencia, f.

inconsistent, *–sĭs'tĕnt,* a. inconsistente; *–ly,* ad. incongruamente.

inconsolable, *–sō'lăbl,* a. inconsolable.

inconstancy, *ĭnkŏn'stănsĕ,* s. inconstancia, f. [dable.

inconstant, *–stănt,* a. inconstante mudable.

incontestable, *ĭnkŏntĕs'tăbl,* a. incontestable, incontrastable. [mente.

incontestably, *–ĕ,* ad. incontestable-

incontinence, ĭnkŏn'tĭnĕns, s. incontinencia, f.   [ad. incontinentemente.
incontinent, —tĭnĕnt, a. incontinente; —ly.
incontrovertible, ĭnkŏntrŏvŭr'tĭbl, a.
incontrovertible.
inconvenience, ĭnkŏnvē'nĭĕns, s. inconveniencia, incomodidad, f.; —, v. a. incomodar.
inconvenient, —nĭĕnt, a. incómodo, inconveniente; —ly, ad. incómodamente.
inconvertible, —vŭr'tĭbl, a. inconvertible.
incorporate, ĭnkŏr'pŏrāt, v. a. (& n.) in-
corporar(se); —, a. incorporado.
incorporation, —rā'shŭn, s. incorporación, f.
incorporeal, ĭnkŏrpō'rēăl, a. incorpóreo,
incorporal. [ad. de un modo incorrecto.
incorrect, ĭnkŏrrĕkt', a. incorrecto; —ly.
incorrigible, ĭnkŏr'rĭjĭbl, a. incorregible.
incorrupt, ĭnkŏrrŭpt', a. incorrupto.
incorruptibility, —rŭptĭbĭl'ĭtĭ, s. incor-
ruptibilidad, f.
incorruptible, —rŭp'tĭbl, a. incorruptible.
increase, ĭnkrēs', v. a. acrecentar, aumentar; —, v. n. crecer, tomar aumento; —,
ĭn'krēs, s. aumento, acrecentamiento, m.
incredibility, ĭnkrĕdĭbĭl'ĭtĭ, s. incredibi-
lidad, f.
incredible, ĭnkrĕd'ĭbl, a. increíble.
incredibly, —ĭ, a. increíblemente.   [f.
incredulity, ĭnkrĕdū'lĭtĭ, s. incredulidad,
incredulous, ĭnkrĕd'ūlŭs, a. incrédulo.
increment, ĭn'krĕmĕnt, s. incremento, m.
incriminate, ĭnkrĭm'ĭnāt, v. a. acriminar, acusar de algún crimen.
incrust, ĭnkrŭst', v. a. incrustar.
incubate, ĭn'kūbāt, v. n. empollar.
incubator, ĭn'kūbātŭr, s. horno para empollar, m.
incubus, ĭn'kūbŭs, s. íncubo, m.
inculcate, ĭnkŭl'kāt, v. a. inculcar.
inculpate, ĭnkŭl'pāt, v. a. inculpar.
incumbency, ĭnkŭm'bĕnsĭ, s. posesión
de un beneficio eclesiástico, f.
incumbent, ĭnkŭm'bĕnt, a. echado; obligatorio; —, s. beneficiado, m.
incur, ĭnkŭr', v. a. incurrir; ocurrir.
incurability, ĭnkŭrăbĭl'ĭtĭ, s. incurabili-
dad, f., estado incurable, m.
incurable, ĭnkū'răbl, a. incurable.
incurably, —ĭ, ad. de un modo incurable.
incursion, ĭnkŭr'shŭn, s. incursión, invasión, f.   [peñado.
indebted, ĭndĕt'ĕd, a. endeudado, em-
indecency, ĭndē'sĕnsĕ, s. indecencia,
mala crianza, f.   [ad. indecentemente.
indecent, ĭndē'sĕnt, a. indecente; —ly.
indecision, ĭndēsĭzh'ŭn, s. irresolución, f.
indecisive, ĭndēsī'sĭv, a. indeciso.
indecorous, ĭndēkō'rŭs, a. indecoroso, indecente.   [veras.
indeed, ĭndēd', ad. verdaderamente, de
indefatigable, ĭndēfăt'ĭgăbl, a. infatigable.
indefinite, ĭndĕf'ĭnĭt, a. indefinido, indeterminado; —ly, ad. indefinidamente.
indelible, ĭndĕl'ĭbl, a. indeleble.
indelicacy, ĭndĕl'ĭkăsĕ, s. falta de delicadeza, grosería, indecencia, f.

indelicate, ĭndĕl'ĭkăt, a. poco delicado.
indemnification, ĭndĕmnĭfĭkā'shŭn, s. indemnización, f.; resarcimiento de daño, m.
indemnify, ĭndĕm'nĭfī, v. a. indemnizar.
indemnity, —nĭtĕ, s. indemnidad, f.
indent, ĭndĕnt', v. a. dentar.   [tada, f.
indentation, —tā'shŭn, s. recortadura den-
indenture, ĭndĕn'tŭr, s. contrato de un
aprendiz, m.   [dencia, f.
independence, ĭndĕpĕn'dĕns, s. indepen-
independent, —dĕnt a. independiente;
—ly, ad. independientemente.
indescribable, ĭndĕskrī'băbl, a. indescri-
bible, indescriptible.
indestructible, ĭndĕstrŭk'tĭbl, a. indestructible.
indeterminate, ĭndētŭr'mĭnăt, a. indeterminado; —ly, ad. indeterminada-
mente.
index, ĭn'dĕks, s. indicio, m.; índice, m.,
tabla de un libro, f.; manecilla de reloj, f.
India-man, ĭn'dĭămăn, s. nave índica, f.
India-rubber, —rŭbbŭr, s. goma elástica,
f.   [verano tardío, m.
indian-summer, ĭn'dĭănsŭmmŭr, s. (am.)
indicate, ĭn'dĭkāt, v. a. indicar.
indication, ĭndĭkā'shŭn, s. indicación, f.;
indicio, m.; señal, f.   [cativo (m.)
indicative, ĭndĭk'ătĭv, a. & s. (gr.) indi-
indicator, ĭn'dĭkātŭr, s. indicador, apuntador, m.
indictment, ĭndīt'mĕnt, s. acusación ante
el jurado, f.   [imparcialidad, f.
indifference, ĭndĭf'fĕrĕns, s. indiferencia,
indifferent, —fĕrĕnt, a. indiferente; —ly,
ad. indiferentemente.   [breza, f.
indigence, ĭn'dĭjĕns, s. indigencia, po-
indigenous, ĭndĭj'ĕnŭs, a. indígena.
indigent, ĭn'dĭjĕnt, a. indigente, pobre.
indigestible, ĭndĭjĕs'tĭbl, a. indigestible.
indigestion, —tshŭn, s. indigestión, f.
indignant, ĭndĭg'nănt, a. airado.
indignation, ĭndĭgnā'shŭn, s. indignación, f.; despecho, m.
indignity, ĭndĭg'nĭtĭ, s. indignidad, f.
indigo, ĭn'dĭgŏ, s. añil, m.
indirect, ĭndĭrĕkt', a. indirecto; —ly, ad.
indirectamente.
indiscreet, ĭndĭskrēt', a. indiscreto, inconsiderado; —ly, ad. indiscretamente.
indiscretion, ĭndĭskrĕsh'ŭn, s. indiscreción, imprudencia, inconsideración, f.
indiscriminate, ĭndĭskrĭm'ĭnăt, a. indistinto; —ly, ad. sin distinción. [pensable.
indispensable, ĭndĭspĕn'săbl, a. indis-
indispensably, —ĕ, ad. indispensable-
mente.
indispose, ĭndĭspōz', v. a. indisponer.
indisposed, —d', a. indispuesto, achacoso.
indisposition, ĭndĭspŏzĭsh'ăn, s. indisposición, f.; mala gana, f.   [table.
indisputable, ĭndĭspū'tăbl, a. indispu-
indisputably, —ĭ, ad. indisputablemente.
indissoluble, ĭndĭs'sŏlŭbl, a. indisoluble.
indistinct, ĭndĭstĭngkt', a. indistinto, confuso; —ly, ad. indistintamente.
indistinguishable, ĭndĭstĭng'gwĭshăbl,
a. indistinguible.

indite, *ĭndīt'*, v. a. redactar.

individual, *ĭndĭvĭd'dŭl*, a. individual, individuo; **-ly**, ad. individualmente; **-**, s. individuo, m. [dualidad, f.

individuality, *ĭndĭvĭdŭăl'ĭtĭ*, s. indivi-

indivisible, *ĭndĭvĭz'ĭbl*, ad. indivisible; **-bly**, ad. indivisiblemente.

indocil, *ĭndŏs'ĭl*, a. indócil, cerril.

indocility, *ĭndŏsĭl'ĭtĭ*, s. indocilidad, pertinacia, f. [f.

indolence, *ĭn'dŏlĕns*, s. indolencia, pereza,

indolent, *ĭn'dŏlĕnt*, a. indolente; **-ly**, ad. con negligencia.

indomitable, *ĭndŏm'ĭtăbl*, a. indomable.

indorse, *ĭndōrs'*, v. a. endosar una letra, vale, ú otro documento.

indubitable, *ĭndū'bĭtăbl*, a. indubitable.

indubitably, *-ĭ*, ad. indubitablemente.

induce, *ĭndūs'*, v. a. inducir, persuadir; causar. [tivo, m.

inducement, *-mĕnt*, s. inducimiento, mo-

induction, *ĭndŭk'shŭn*, s. inducción, deducción, f.; ilación, f.

inductive, *-tĭv*, a. inductivo; ilativo.

indue, *ĭndū'*, v. a. vestir; dotar; proveer.

indulge, *ĭndŭlj'*, v. a. & n. favorecer; conceder; ser indulgente.

indulgence, *-ĕns*, s. indulgencia, f.

indulgent, *-ĕnt*, a. indulgente; **-ly**, ad. de un modo indulgente.

induration, *ĭndŭrā'shŭn*, s. endurecimiento, m.; dureza de corazón, f.

industrial, *ĭndŭs'trĭăl*, a. industrial.

industrious, *ĭndŭs'trĭŭs*, a. industrioso; laborioso, **-ly**, ad. industriosamente.

industry, *ĭn'dŭstrĭ*, s. industria, f.

inebriate, *ĭnē'brĭăt*, v. a. embriagar.

inebriation, *ĭnēbrĭā'shŭn*, inebriety, *ĭnēbrī'ĕtĭ*, s. embriaguez, f.

ineffable, *ĭnĕf'ăbl*, a. inefable.

ineffective, *ĭnĕffĕk'tĭv*, ineffectual, *-tŭăl*, a. ineficaz; **-ly**, ad. sin efecto.

inefficacious, *ĭnĕffĭkā'shŭs*, a. ineficaz.

inefficiency, *ĭnĕffĭsh'ĕnsĭ*, s. ineficacia, f.

inefficient, *ĭnĕffĭsh'ĕnt*, a. ineficaz.

inelegant, *ĭnĕl'ĕgănt*, a. inelegante; sin pulimento. [excluye elección, f.

ineligibility, *ĭnĕlĭjĭbĭl'ĭtĭ*, s. calidad que

ineptitude, *ĭnĕp'tĭtūd*, s. ineptitud, f.

inequality, *ĭnēkwŏl'ĭtĭ*, s. desigualdad, disparidad, diferencia, f.

inert, *ĭnĕrt'*, a. inerte, perezoso; **-ly**, ad. indolentemente.

inertness, *-nĕs*, inertia, f. [inapreciable.

inestimable, *ĭnĕs'tĭmăbl*, a. inestimable.

inevitable, *ĭnĕv'ĭtăbl*, a. inevitable.

inexcusable, *ĭnĕkskū'zăbl*, a. inexcusable.

inexcusably, *-ĭ*, ad. inexcusablemente.

inexhaustible, *ĭnĕgzhăs'tĭbl*, a. inexhausto, inagotable. [flexible, duro.

inexorable, *ĭnĕks'ŏrăbl*, a. inexorable, in-

inexpediency, *ĭnĕkspē'dĭĕnsĭ*, s. inconveniencia, falta de oportunidad, f.

inexpedient, *-dĕnt*, a. impropio.

inexpensive, *ĭnĕkspĕn'sĭv*, a. de poco gasto. [encia, impericia, f.

inexperience, *ĭnĕkspē'rĭĕns*, s. inexperi-

inexpert, *ĭnĕkspŭrt'*, a. inexperto.

inexpiable, *ĭnĕks'pĭăbl*, a. inexpiable.

inexplicable, *ĭnĕks'plĭkăbl*, a. inexplicable.

inexpressible, *-prĕs'ĭbl*, a. indecible; **-s**, s. pl. pantalones, m. pl.

inexpressibly, *-ĭ*, ad. de una manera indecible. [enmarañado.

inextricable, *ĭnĕks'trĭkăbl*, a. intrincado;

infallibility, *ĭnfălĭbĭl'ĭtĭ*, s. infalibilidad, f.

infallible, *ĭnfăl'ĭbl*, a. infalible. [f.

infallibly, *-ĭ*, ad. infaliblemente.

infamous, *ĭn'fămŭs*, a. vil, infame; **-ly**, ad. infamemente.

infamy, *-fămĭ*, s. infamia, f.

infancy, *-fănsĭ*, s. infancia, f.

infant, *-fănt*, s. infante, m.; niño, m.

infanta, *ĭnfăn'tă*, s. infanta, f.

infanticide, *ĭnfăn'tĭsīd*, s. infanticidio, m.; infanticida, m. & f. [pueril, infantil.

infantile, *ĭn'făntīl*, infantine, *-tĭn*, a.

infantry, *-făntrĭ*, s. infantería, f. [bobar.

infatuate, *ĭnfăt'ŭāt*, v. a. infatuar, em-

infatuation, *-tŭā'shŭn*, s. infatuación, f.

infect, *ĭnfĕkt'*, v. a. infectar.

infection, *ĭnfĕk'shŭn*, s. infección, f.

infectious, *-shŭs*, a. infecto, inficionado; **-ly**, ad. por infección.

infer, *ĭnfŭr'*, v. a. inferir. [f.

inference, *ĭn'fĕrĕns*, s. inferencia, ilación,

inferior, *ĭnfē'rĭŭr*, a. inferior; **-**, s. oficial subordinado, m.

inferiority, *ĭnfērĭŏr'ĭtĭ*, s. inferioridad, f.

infernal, *ĭnfŭr'năl*, a. infernal; **-stone**, s. piedra infernal, f.

infest, *ĭnfĕst'*, v. a. infestar, incomodar.

infidel, *ĭn'fĭdĕl*, s. infiel, pagano, m.

infidelity, *ĭnfĭdĕl'ĭtĭ*, s. infidelidad, f., perfidia, f. [-ly, ad. infinitamente.

infinite, *ĭn'fĭnĭt*, a. infinito, innumerable;

infinitive, *ĭnfĭn'ĭtĭv*, s. infinitivo, m.

infirm, *ĭnfŭrm'*, a. enfermo, débil.

infirmary, *-ărĭ*, s. enfermería, f. [f.

infirmity, *-ĭtĭ*, s. fragilidad, enfermedad,

inflame, *ĭnflām'*, v. a. (& n.) inflamar(se).

inflammable, *ĭnflăm'ăbl*, a. inflamable.

inflammation, *-mā'shŭn*, s. inflamación, f.

inflammatory, *ĭnflăm'mătŭrĭ*, a. inflamatorio.

inflate, *ĭnflāt'*, v. a. inflar, hinchar.

inflation, *ĭnflā'shŭn*, s. inflación, f.; hinchazón, f.; acumulación excesiva de oro ó plata, f. [modulación de la voz, f.

inflection, *ĭnflĕk'shŭn*, s. inflexión, f.;

inflexibility, *ĭnflĕksĭbĭl'ĭtĭ*, s. inflexibilidad, f. [flexible.

inflexible, *ĭnflĕks'ĭbl*, a. inmoble, in-

inflexibly, *-ĭ*, ad. inflexiblemente.

inflict, *ĭnflĭkt'*, v. a. castigar; imponer penas corporales. [pena corporal, f.

infliction, *ĭnflĭk'shŭn*, s. imposición de

influence, *ĭn'flŭĕns*, s. influencia, f.; **-**, v. a. influir.

influential, *ĭnflŭĕn'shăl*, a. influente.

influenza, *-ză*, s. influenza, gripa, f.

influx, *ĭn'flŭks*, s. influjo, m.; infusión, f.

inform, *ĭnfŏrm'*, v. a. informar, enseñar.

informal, *-ăl*, a. informal, irregular.

informality, *-ăl'ĭtĭ*, s. informalidad, f.

informant, ĭnför'mănt, s. denunciador, acusador, m. [instrucción, f.

information, —mā'shŭn, s. información, f.

infraction, ĭnfrăk'shŭn, s. infracción, f.

infrangible, ĭnfrăn'jĭbl, a. infrangible.

infrequent, ĭnfrē'kwĕnt, a. raro, insólito; —ly, ad. raramente.

infringe, ĭnfrĭnj', v. a. violar (una ley ó pacto), contravenir á. [m.

infringer, —ŭr, s. violador, contraventor,

infuriate, ĭnfū'rĭăt, v. a. irritar, provocar, enfurecer.

infuse, ĭnfūz', v. a. infundir. [ción, f.

infusion, ĭnfū'zhŭn, s. infusión, f.; inspira-

ingathering, ĭngăth'ŭrĭng, s. cosecha, f.

ingenious, ĭnjē'nĭŭs, a. ingenioso; —ly, ad. ingeniosamente.

ingenuity, ĭnjĕnū'ĭtĕ, s. ingeniosidad, f.; ingenuidad, f.; destreza, f.

ingenuous, ĭnjĕn'ŭĭs, a. ingenuo, sincero; —ly, ad. ingenuamente.

ingle, ĭng'gl, s. chimenea, f.

inglorious, ĭnglō'rĭŭs, a. ignominioso, vergonzoso; —ly, ad. ignominiosamente.

ingot, ĭn'gŏt, s. barra de metal (sin labrar).

ingraft, ĭngrăft', v. a. injertar. [f.

ingrained, ĭngrānd', a. inveterado.

ingrate, ĭngrāt', a. ingrato.

ingratiate, ĭngrā'shĭăt, v. n. insinuarse; congraciarse.

ingratitude, ĭngrăt'ĭtūd, s. ingratitud, f.

ingredient, ĭngrē'dĭĕnt, s. ingrediente, m.

ingress, ĭn'grĕs, s. entrada, f.

ingulf, ĭngŭlf', v. a. engolfar, tragar, sumir.

inhabit, ĭnhăb'ĭt, v. a. & n. habitar; vivir, residir.

inhabitable, —ăbl, a. habitable. [m.

inhabitant, —ănt, s. habitador, habitante,

inhale, ĭnhāl', v. a. inspirar.

inharmonious, ĭnhărmō'nĭŭs, a. disonante, discordante.

inherent, ĭnhē'rĕnt, a. inherente.

inherit, ĭnhĕr'ĭt, v. a. heredar.

inheritance, —ăns, s. herencia, f.

inheritor, —ŭr, s. heredero, m.

inhospitable, ĭnhŏs'pĭtăbl, a. inhospitable, inhospedable. [lidad, f.

inhospitality, ĭnhŏspĭtăl'ĭtĕ, s. inhospita-

inhuman, ĭnhū'măn, a. inhumano, cruel; —ly, ad. inhumanamente. [crueldad, f.

inhumanity, ĭnhūmăn'ĭtĕ, s. inhumanidad, f.

inhume, ĭnhūm', v. a. enterrar, sepultar.

inimical, ĭnĭm'ĭkăl, a. enemigo.

inimitable, ĭnĭm'ĭtăbl, a. inimitable. [m.

iniquitous, ĭnĭk'wĭtŭs, a. inicuo, injusto.

iniquity, ĭnĭk'wĭtĕ, s. iniquidad, injusticia, f. [cial, f.

initial, ĭnĭsh'ăl, a. inicial; —s, letra ini-

initiate, ĭnĭsh'ĭăt, v. a. principiar, iniciar.

initiation, ĭnĭshĭā'shŭn, s. principio, m.; iniciación, f.

inject, ĭnjĕkt', v. a. inyectar.

injection, ĭnjĕk'shŭn, s. inyección, f.

injudicious, ĭnjūdĭsh'ŭs, a. poco juicioso; —ly, ad. sin juicio.

injunction, ĭnjŭngk'shŭn, s. mandato, precepto, m.

injure, ĭn'jŭr, v. a. injuriar, ofender.

injurious, ĭnjū'rĭŭs, a. injurioso, injusto; —ly, ad. injuriosamente. [daño, m.

injury, ĭn'jŭrē, s. injuria, afrenta, f.;

injustice, ĭnjŭs'tĭs, s. injusticia, f.; agravio, m. [tinta.

ink, ĭngk, s. tinta, f.; —, v. a. linear con

ink-horn, —hōrn, s. tintero (de faltriquera),

inkling, ĭng'klĭng, s. aviso secreto, m. [m.

ink-stand, —stănd, s. tintero, m.

inky, —ĕ, a. de tinta; semejante á la tinta.

inlaid, ĭnlād', a. ataraceado.

inland, ĭn'lănd, a. interior; —, ĭnlănd', ad. dentro de un país.

inlay, ĭnlā', v. a. ataracear; —, ĭn'lā, s.

inlet, ĭn'lĕt, s. entrada, f. [ataracea, f.

inmate, ĭn'māt, s. inquilino, m.

inmost, ĭn'mōst, a. íntimo.

inn, ĭn, s. posada, f.; mesón, m.

innate, ĭn'nāt, a. innato, natural, ínsito.

inner, ĭn'nŭr, a. interior.

innermost, —mōst, a. íntimo.

inning, ĭn'nĭng, s. mano en los naipes, f.; —s, pl. tierras aluviales cerradas con diques, f. pl. [nero, m.

inn-keeper, ĭnn'kēpŭr, s. posadero, mesonero.

innocence, ĭn'nŏsĕns, s. inocencia, f.

innocent, —nŏsĕnt, a. inocente; —ly, ad. inocentemente.

innocuous, ĭnnŏk'ŭŭs, a. innocuo, inocente; —ly, ad. inocentemente.

innovate, ĭn'nŏvăt, v. a. innovar.

innovation, ĭnnŏvā'shŭn, s. innovación, f.

innoxious, ĭnnŏk'shŭs, a. inocente; no nocivo; —ly, ad. sin hacer daño.

innuendo, ĭnnŭĕn'dŏ, s. indirecta, insinuación, f. [rabie.

innumerable, ĭnnū'mŭrăbl, a. innume-

inoculate, ĭnŏk'ŭlăt, v. a. inocular; injertar. [f.

inoculation, ĭnŏkŭlā'shŭn, s. inoculación,

inoffensive, ĭnŏffĕn'sĭv, a. pacífico; inofensivo. [niente, no oportuno.

inopportune, ĭnŏppŏrtūn', a. inconve-

inordinate, ĭnŏr'dĭnăt, a. desordenado; —ly, ad. desordenadamente. [nico.

inorganic(al), ĭnŏrgăn'ĭk(ăl), a. inorgá-

inquest, ĭn'kwĕst, s. pesquisa, f.

inquire, ĭnkwīr', v. a. preguntar alguna cosa; —, v. n. inquirir, examinar.

inquiry, ĭnkwī'rē, s. interrogación, f.; pesquisa, f. [escudriñamiento, m.

inquisition, ĭnkwĭzĭsh'ŭn, s. inquisición, f.

inquisitive, ĭnkwĭz'ĭtĭv, a. curioso; —ly, ad. inquisitivamente. [inquisidor, m.

inquisitor, —ŭr, s. juez pesquisidor, m.;

inroad, ĭn'rŏd, s. incursión, invasión, f.

insane, ĭnsān', a. insano, loco, demente.

insanity, ĭnsăn'ĭtĕ, s. insania, f.; locura, f.

insatiable, ĭnsā'shĭăbl, a. insaciable, inhartable; deseoso.

inscribe, ĭnskrīb', v. a. inscribir; dedicar.

inscription, ĭnskrĭp'shŭn, s. inscripción; dedicación, f.

inscrutable, ĭnskrō'tăbl, a. inescrutable.

insect, ĭn'sĕkt, s. insecto, m. [guro.

insecure, ĭnsēkūr', a. desconfiado; no se-

insecurity, ĭnsēkū'rĭtĕ, s. peligro, riesgo, m. [to.

insensate, ĭnsĕn'sāt, a. insensato.

insense, *ĭnsĕns'*, v. a. enojar á uno.

insensibility, *ĭnsĕnsĭbĭl'ĭtĭ*, s. insensibi- lidad, f.; estupidez, f.   [perceptible.

insensible, *ĭnsĕn'sĭbl*, a. insensible; im- insensibly, *—ĭ*, ad. insensiblemente.

inseparable, *ĭnsĕp'ărăbl*, a. inseparable.

inseparably, *—ĭ*, ad. inseparablemente.

insert, *ĭnsûrt'*, v. a. insertar, ingerir una cosa en otra.

insertion, *ĭnsûr'shŭn*, s. inserción, f.

inside, *ĭn'sīd*, s. interior, m.; —, ad. adentro, dentro.   [insidiosamente.

insidious, *ĭnsĭd'ĭŭs*, a. insidioso; —ly, ad.

insight, *ĭn'sīt*, s. conocimiento profundo, m.   [estandartes, m. pl.

insignia, *ĭnsĭg'nĭ*, s. pl. insignias, f. pl.

insignificance, *ĭnsĭgnĭf'ĭkăns*, s. insigni- ficación, f.; nulidad, f.

insignificant, *—ĭkănt*, ad. insignificativo, frívolo; —ly, ad. sin significación.

insincere, *ĭnsĭnsēr'*, a. poco sincero.

insincerity, *—sēr'ĭtĭ*, s. disimulación, f.

insinuate, *ĭnsĭn'ūāt*, v. a. insinuar.

insinuation, *ĭnsĭnūā'shŭn*, s. insinua- ción, f.

insipid, *ĭnsĭp'ĭd*, a. insípido; insulso; —ly, ad. insulsamente.   [sez, f.

insipidity, *ĭnsĭpĭd'ĭtĭ*, s. insipidez, insul-

insist, *ĭnsĭst'*, v. n. insistir, persistir.

insistance, *—ăns*, s. insistencia, f.

insolence, *ĭn'sŏlĕns*, s. insolencia, f.

insolent, *ĭn'sŏlĕnt*, a. insolente; —ly, ad. insolentemente.   [luble.

insoluble, *ĭnsŏl'ūbl*, a. insoluble; indiso-

insolvency, *ĭnsŏl'vĕnsĕ*, s. insolvencia, f.

insolvent, *ĭnsŏl'vĕnt*, a. insolvente.

insomuch, *ĭnsŏmŭtsh'*, c. de manera que.

inspect, *ĭnspĕkt'*, v.a. reconocer, examinar, inspeccionar.

inspection, *ĭnspĕk'shŭn*, s. inspección, f.

inspector, *—tŭr*, s. inspector, superinten- dente, m.

inspiration, *ĭnspĭrā'shŭn*, s. inspiración, f.

inspire, *ĭnspīr'*, v. a. inspirar (el aire); ins- pirar, sugerir.   [dar vigor.

inspirit, *ĭnspĭr'ĭt*, v. a. alentar, animar;

instability, *ĭnstăbĭl'ĭtĭ*, s. instabilidad, inconstancia, f.

instal, *ĭnstăl'*, v. a. instalar.   [f.

installation, *ĭnstăllā'shŭn*, s. instalación,

instalment, *ĭnstăl'mĕnt*, s. instalación, f.; pago parcial, m.

instance, *ĭn'stăns*, s. instancia, f.; solici- tación, f.; ejemplo, documento, m.; prueba, f.; for —, por ejemplo; —, v. n. alegar ejemplos.

instant, *ĭn'stănt*, a. instante, urgente; —ly, ad. en un instante; —, s. instante, mo- mento, m.

instantaneous, *ĭnstăntā'nĭŭs*, a. instan- táneo; —ly, ad. instantáneamente.

instead, (of), *ĭnstĕd'*, pr. cor, en lugar de, en vez de.

instep, *ĭn'stĕp*, s. empeine del pie, m.

instigate, *ĭn'stĭgāt*, v. a. instigar, mover.

instigation, *ĭnstĭgā'shŭn*, s. instigación, sugestión, provocación á hacer daño, f.

instil, *ĭnstĭl'*, v. a. insinuar, instilar.

instinct, *ĭn'stĭngkt*, s. instinto, m.; —, a. vivo, despabilado.

instinctive, *ĭnstĭngk'tĭv*, a. instintivo; —ly, ad. por instinto.

institute, *ĭn'stĭtūt*, v. a. instituir, estable- cer; —, s. instituto, m.; principio, m.

institution, *—tū'shŭn*, s. institución, f.

instruct, *ĭnstrŭkt'*, v. a. instruir, enseñar.

instruction, *ĭnstrŭk'shŭn*, s. instrucción, enseñanza, f.

instructive, *ĭnstrŭk'tĭv*, a. instructivo.

instructor, *—tŭr*, s. instructor, m.

instrument, *ĭn'strŭmĕnt*, s. instrumento; contrato, m.

instrumental, *—mĕn'tăl*, a. instrumental.

insubordinate, *ĭnsŭbŏr'dĭnăt*, a. insub- ordinado.   [dinación, f.

insubordination, *—nā'shŭn*, s. insubor-

insufferable, *ĭnsŭf'ărăbl*, a. insufrible, insoportable.   [de un modo insoportable.

insufferably, *—ĭ*, ad. inaguantablemente.

insufficiency, *ĭnsŭffĭsh'ĕnsĭ*, s. insuficien- cia, f.   [insuficientemente.

insufficient, *—ĕnt*, a. insuficiente; —ly, ad.

insular, *ĭn'sŭlăr*, a. insular, isleño.

insulate, *ĭn'sŭlāt*, v. a. aislar (las co- rrientes eléctricas).   [insulto, m.

insult, *ĭnsŭlt'*, v. a. insultar; —, *ĭn'sŭlt*, s.

insulter, *ĭnsŭl'tŭr*, s. insultador, m.

insultingly, *—ĭnglĭ*, ad. con insolencia.

insuperable, *ĭnsū'părăbl*, a. insuperable.

insuperably, *—ĭ*, ad. invenciblemente.

insupportable, *ĭnsŭppŏr'tăbl*, a. inso- portable, inaguantable.

insupportably, *—ĭ*, ad. intolerablemente, insoportablemente.   [m.; seguridad, f.

insurance, *ĭnshō'răns*, s. (com.) seguro,

insure, *ĭnshōr'*, v. a. asegurar.

insurgent, *ĭnsŭr'jĕnt*, s. insurgente, re- belde, m.   [perable.

insurmountable, *ĭnsŭrmŏn'tăbl*, a.insu-

insurrection, *ĭnsŭrrĕk'shŭn*, s. insurrec- ción, sedición, f.   [nal.

insurrectionary, *—shŭnărĭ*, a.insurrecio-

intact, *ĭntăkt'*, a. salvo, sano, entero.

intaker, *ĭn'tākĭr*, s. recaudador, m.

integral, *ĭn'tĕgrăl*, a. íntegro; (chem.) in- tegrante; —, s. todo, m.   [f.

integrity, *ĭntĕg'rĭtĭ*, s. integridad; pureza,

intellect, *ĭn'tĕllĕkt*, s. entendimiento, m.

intellectual, *ĭntĕllĕk'tŭăl*, a. intelectual, mental.

intelligence, *ĭntĕl'ĭjĕns*, s. inteligencia, f.; conocimiento, m.; correspondencia, f.; nueva, f.; concierto, m.

intelligencer, *—ljĕnsĭr*, s. novelero, m.

intelligent, *—ljĕnt*, a. inteligente.

intelligible, *—ljĭbl*, a. inteligible.

intelligibly, *—ĭ*, ad. inteligiblemente.

intemperance, *ĭntĕm'pŭrăns*, s. intem- perancia, f.

intemperate, *—pŭrāt*, a. destemplado; inmoderado; —ly, ad. destempladamente, inmoderadamente.

intend, *ĭntĕnd'*, v. a. intentar.

intendant, *—ănt*, s. intendente, m.

intense, *ĭntĕns'*, a. intenso; vehemente; —ly, ad. intensamente.

intensity, -ĭtĕ, s. intensidad, f.; exceso, m.
intent, ĭntĕnt', a. atento, cuidadoso; **-ly,** ad. con aplicación; **-,** s. intento, designio, m. [signio, m.
intention, ĭntĕn'shŭn, s. intención, f.; de
intentional, -ăl, a. intencional; **-ly,** ad. de intento.
inter, ĭntŭr', v. a. enterrar, soterrar.
intercede, ĭntŭrsēd', v. n. interceder, mediar. [pedir.
intercept, -sĕpt', v. a. interceptar; **intercession,** -sĕsh'ŭn, s. intercesión, mediación, f. [diador, m.
intercessor, -sĕs'sŭr, s. intercesor, me-
interchange, ĭn'tŭrtshānj, v. a. alternar, trocar; **-,** s. comercio, m.; permuta de géneros, f. [comunicación, f.
intercourse, ĭn'tŭrkōrs, s. comercio, m.;
interdict, ĭn'tŭrdĭkt, s. entredicho, m.; **-,** ĭntŭrdĭkt', v. a. interdecir; entredecir
interdiction, ĭntŭrdĭk'shŭn, s. interdicción, prohibición, f.
interest, ĭn'tŭrĕst, v. a. interesar; empeñar; **-,** s. interés, provecho, m.; influjo, empeño, m.; **compound -,** interés de interés. [mezclarse.
interfere, ĭntŭrfēr', v. n. entremeterse, **interference,** -ĕns, s. interposición, mediación, f. [entre tanto; en el interín.
interim, ĭn'tŭrĭm, s. intermedio, m.; **ad-,**
interior, ĭntē'rĭŭr, a. interior, interno.
interjection, ĭntŭrjĕk'shŭn, s. (gr.) interjección, f.
interlace, -lās', v. a. entretejer.
interlard, -lärd', v. a. mechar.
interleave, -lēv', v. a. interpolar hojas blancas entre las impresas de un libro.
interline, -līn', v. a. interlinear.
interlocution, -lōkū'shŭn, s. interlocución, f.
interlocutor, -lōk'ūtŭr, s. interlocutor, m.
interlope, -lōp', v. n. entremeterse; traficar sin licencia. [bandista, m.
interloper, -lō'pŭr, s. entremetido; contra-
intermarriage, -măr'rĭj, s. doble casamiento entre dos familias, m.
intermarry, -măr'rē, v. n. unirse por un doble casamiento.
intermediate, -mē'dĭăt, a. intermedio.
interment, ĭntŭr'mĕnt, s. entierro, m.; sepultura, f. [nable, ilimitado.
interminable, ĭntŭr'mĭnăbl, a. intermi-
intermingle, ĭntŭrmĭng'gl, v. a. & n. entremezclar; mezclarse. [interrupción, f.
intermission, -mĭsh'ŭn, s. intermisión, f.
intermit, -mĭt', v. a. intermitir; **-,** v. n. descontinuar, cesar. [ternamente.
internal, ĭntŭr'năl, a. interno; **-ly,** ad. in-
international, ĭntŭrnă'shŭnăl, a. internacional.
interpellation, -pĕllā'shŭn, s. interpelación, f.
interpolate, ĭntŭr'pōlāt, v. a. interpolar.
interpolation, -pōlā'shŭn, s. interpolación, f.
interpose, -pōz', v. a. interponer, entreponer; **-,** v. n. interponerse.
interposer, -ŭr, s. mediador, m. [ción, f.
interposition, -pōzĭsh'ŭn, s. interposi-

interpret, ĭntŭr'prĕt, v. a. interpretar.
interpretation, ĭntŭrprĕtā'shŭn, s. interpretación, f.
interpreter, ĭntŭr'prĕtŭr, s. intérprete, m. [examinar.
interregnum, ĭntĕrrĕg'nŭm, s. interregno, m.
interrogate, ĭntĕr'rōgāt, v. a. interrogar,
interrogation, ĭntĕrrōgā'shŭn, s. interrogación, pregunta, f.
interrogatory, -rŏg'ătŭrē, a. interrogativo.
interrupt, -rŭpt', v. a. interrumpir.
interruptedly, -ĕdlē, ad. con interrupción.
interruption, -rŭp'shŭn, s. interrupción, f. [v. n. intersecarse.
intersect, ĭntŭrsĕkt', v. a. entrecortar; **-,**
intersection, -sĕk'shŭn, s. intersección, f. [cosa entre otras.
intersperse, -spŭrs', v. a. esparcir una
interstice, ĭn'tŭrstĭs, (ĭntŭr'stĭs), s. intersticio, intervalo, m.
intertwine, ĭntŭrtwīn', v. a. entretejer.
interval, ĭn'tŭrvăl, s. intervalo, m.
intervene, ĭntŭrvēn', v. n. intervenir; ocurrir. [interposición, f.
intervention, -vĕn'shŭn, s. intervención, f.
interview, ĭn'tŭrvū, s. entrevista, f.; **-,** v. a. pescudar á los políticos (dícese de periodistas).
interviewer, -ŭr, s. periodista que va pescudando á los hombres de Estado, m
interweave, ĭntŭrwēv', v. a. entretejer enlazar.
intestate, ĭntĕs'tāt, a. intestado.
intestinal, -tĭnăl, a. intestinal.
intestine, -tĭn, a. intestino, doméstico; **-s,** s. pl. intestinos, m. pl.
inthral, ĭnthrăl', v. a. esclavizar.
inthralment, -mĕnt, s. esclavitud, f.
intimacy, ĭn'tĭmăsē, s. intimidad, confianza, f.
intimate, ĭn'tĭmāt, s. amigo íntimo, m.; **-,** a. íntimo, familiar; **-ly,** ad. intimamente; **-,** ĭn'tĭmāt, v. a. insinuar, dar á entender. [directa, f.
intimation, -mā'shŭn, s. insinuación, f.
intimidate, ĭntĭm'ĭdāt, v. a. intimidar.
into, ĭn'tō, pr. en, dentro, adentro.
intolerable, ĭntŏl'ărăbl, a. intolerable.
intolerably, -ĭ, ad. intolerablemente.
intolerance, -ărăns, s. intolerancia, f.
intolerant, -ărănt, a. intolerante.
intonation, ĭntōnā'shŭn, s. entonación, f.
intoxicate, ĭntŏks'ĭkāt, v. a. embriagar.
intoxication, -kā'shŭn, s. embriaguez, f.
intractable, ĭntrăk'tăbl, a. intratable.
intransitive, ĭntrăn'sĭtĭv, a. (gr.) intransitivo. [v. n. usurpar, invadir.
intrench, ĭntrĕnsh', v. a. atrincherar; **-,**
intrepid, ĭntrĕp'ĭd, a. arrojado; intrépido; **-ly,** ad. intrépidamente.
intrepidity, ĭntrĕpĭd'ĭtē, s. intrepidez, f.
intricacy, ĭn'trĭkăsē, s. embrollo, embarazo, m.; dificultad, f.
intricate, ĭn'trĭkāt, a. intricado, complicado; **-ly,** ad. intricadamente.
intrigue, ĭntrēg', s. intriga, f.; **-,** v. n. intrigar.

intrinsic(al), *intrĕn'sik(ăl),* a. intrínseco, interno; –ally, ad. intrínsecamente.
introduce, *intrōdūs',* v. a. introducir. [f.
introduction, *–dŭk'shŭn,* s. introducción.
introductory, *–dŭk'tǒr,* **introductory,** *–dŭk'tŭré,* a. previo, preliminar.
introspection, *–spek'shŭn,* s. examen interior, m, [ducirse.
intrude, *intrōd',* v. n. entremeterse, introducirse.
intruder, *–ăr,* s. intruso, entremetido, m.
intrusion, *intrō'shun,* s. intrusión, f.; entremetimiento, m.
intrust, *intrŭst',* v. a. confiar.
intuition, *intūish'ŭn,* s. intuición, f.
intuitive, *intū'tiv,* a. evidente; intuitivo.
inundate, *inăn'dāt,* v. a. inundar.
inundation, *inŭndā'shŭn,* s. inundación, f.
inure, *inūr',* v. a. acostumbrar, habituar.
inurement, *–mĕnt,* s. hábito, m., costumbre, f.
inutility, *inūtil'itē,* s. inutilidad, f. [f.
invade, *invād',* v. a. invadir, asaltar.
invader, *–ăr,* s. usurpador, invasor, m.
invalid, *invăl'id,* a. inválido, nulo; –, *invălēd',* s. inválido, m.
invalidate, *–lĭdāt,* v. a. invalidar, anular.
invalidity, *invălĭd'itē,* s. invalidación, nulidad, f.; debilidad, f.
invaluable, *invăl'ūăbl,* a. inapreciable.
invariable, *invā'rĭăbl,* a. invariable.
invariably, *–ĕ,* ad. invariablemente.
invasion, *invā'zhŭn,* s. invasión, f.
invective, *invĕk'tiv,* s. invectiva, f.
inveigh, *invā',* v. n. escribir ó decir invectivas.
inveigle, *invē'gl,* v. a. seducir, persuadir.
invent, *invĕnt',* v. a. inventar.
invention, *invĕn'shŭn,* s. invención, f.
inventive, *–tiv,* a. inventivo. [m.
inventor, *–tŭr,* s. inventor, m.; forjador.
inventory, *in'vĕntŭré,* s. inventario, m.
inverse, *invŭrs',* a. inverso, trastornado.
inversion, *invŭr'shŭn,* a. inversión, f.
invert, *invŭrt',* v. a. invertir, trastrocar.
invest, *invĕst',* v. a. investir.
investigate, *invĕs'tigāt,* v. a. investigar.
investigation, *invĕstigā'shŭn,* s. investigación, pesquisa, f.
investiture, *invĕs'titŭr,* s. investidura, f.
investment, *invĕst'mĕnt,* s. vestido, m., vestidura, f.
inveterate, *invĕt'ĕrāt,* a. inveterado.
invidious, *invid'ĭŭs,* a. envidioso; –ly, ad. envidiosamente. [vigor.
invigorate, *invig'ŏrāt,* v. a. vigorar, dar
invincible, *invin'sĭbl,* a. invencible.
invincibly, *–ĕ,* ad. invenciblemente.
inviolable, *invī'ŏlăbl,* a. inviolable; invulnerable.
inviolate, *invī'ŏlāt,* a. ileso.
invisibility, *invĭzĭbil'itē,* s. invisibilidad, f.
invisible, *invĭz'ĭbl,* a. invisible.
invisibly, *–ĕ,* ad. invisiblemente.
invitation, *invĭtā'shŭn,* s. convite, m.
invite, *invīt',* v. a. convidar.
invocation, *invŏkā'shŭn,* s. invocación, f. (la acción de invocar y la fórmula con que se invoca).
invoice, *in'vŏis,* s. (com.) factura, f.

invoke, *invōk',* v. a. invocar.
involuntarily, *invŏl'ŭntărilĕ,* ad. involuntariamente.
involuntary, *–ăntărĕ,* a. involuntario.
involve, *invŏlv',* v. a. envolver, implicar.
invulnerable, *invŭl'nĕrăbl,* a. invulnerable.
inward, *in'wărd,* a. interior; interno; –, –s, –ly, ad. interiormente; internamente, hacia dentro.
iodine, *ī'ŏdin,* s. (chem.) iodo, m.
I. O. U. (I owe you), *ī ō yō,* vale, m.
irascible, *irăs'sĭbl,* a. irascible.
irate, *īrāt,* **ireful,** *īr'fŭl,* a.irato,iracundo.
ire, *īr,* s. ira, iracundia, f.
iridescent, *iridĕs'sĕnt,* a. iridescente.
iris, *ī'ris,* s. arco iris, m.
irksome, *irk'săm,* a. tedioso, fastidioso.
iron, *ī'rn,* s. hierro, m.; –, a. férreo; –, v. a. aplanchar; poner en grillos.
iron-dust, *–dăst,* s. limadura de hierro, f.
ironic(al), *irŏn'ik(ăl),* a. irónico; –ly, ad. con ironía.
ironing, *ī'rning,* s. planchado, m.
iron-monger, *ī'rnmŭngăr,* s. traficante de hierro, m.
iron-)mould, *–mōld,* s. robín, m.
iron-ware, *–wār,* s. ferretería, f.; quincallería, f. [herrería, f.
iron-work, *–wărk,* s. herraje, m.; –s, pl.
irony, *ī'rŏnĕ,* s. ironía, f.
irradiate, *irrā'dĭāt,* v. a. irradiar, brillar.
irrational, *irrăsh'ănăl,* a. irracional.
irreclaimable, *irrēklām'ăbl,* a. incorregible. [ciable, implacable.
irreconcilable, *–kŏnsī'lăbl,* s. irreconciliable; irremediable. [tizable (deuda).
irrecoverable, *–kŭv'ărăbl,* a. irrecuperable; irremediable.
irredeemable, *irrēdēm'ăbl,* a. no amortizable. [rable.
irrefragable, *irrĕf'răgăbl,* a. irrefragable.
irregular, *irrĕg'ŭlăr,* a. –ly, ad. irregular(mente). [f.
irregularity, *–gătăr'itē,* s. irregularidad.
irrelevant, *irrĕl'ĕvănt,* a. no aplicable; lo que no prueba nada; no concluyente.
irreligion, *irrēlĭj'ăn,* s. irreligión, impiedad, f. [irreligiosamente.
irreligious, *–ăs,* a. irreligioso; –ly, ad.
irremediable, *irrēmē'dĭăbl,* a. irremediable.
irreparable, *irrĕp'ărăbl,* a. irreparable.
irreproachable, *irrēprōtsh'ăbl,* a. irreprensible.
irresistible, *–zĭst'ĭbl,* a. irresistible.
irresolute, *irrĕz'ŏlūt,* a. irresoluto; –ly, ad. irresolutamente.
irresolution, *–lū'shăn,* s. irresolución, f.
irrespective, *–spĕk'tiv,* a. inconsiderado.
irresponsible, *–spŏn'sĭbl,* a. no responsable. [irreparable.
irretrievable, *–trē'văbl,* a. irrecuperable, irreparable.
irretrievably, *–ĕ,* ad. irreparablemente.
irreverence, *irrĕv'ărĕns,* s. irreverencia, f.
irreverent, *–ărĕnt,* a. irreverente; –ly, ad. irreverentemente.
irrevocable, *irrĕv'ŏkăbl,* a. irrevocable.
irrigate, *ir'rigāt,* v. a. regar, mojar.
irrigation, *–gā'shăn,* s. regamiento, m.
irritability, *irrĭtăbil'itē,* s. irritabilidad, f.

irritable, ĭr'rĭtăbl, a. irritable. [m.
irritant, ĭr'rĭtănt, s, (med.) estimulante,
irruption, ĭrrŭp'shŭn, s. irrupción, entrada forzada, f.
isinglass, ĭ'zĭngglăs, s. cola de pescado, f.
Islamism, ĭz'lămĭzm, s. islamismo, m.
island, ī'lănd, s. isla, f.
islander, –ăr, s. isleño, m.
isle, ĭl, islet, ī'lĕt, s. islote, m., isleta, f.
isolate, ī'sōlăt, v. a. aislar.
issue, ĭsh'shū, s. salida, f.; evento, m.; resulta, f.; fin, término, m.; cauterio, m.; prole, progenie, f; —, v. n. salir, prorrumpir, brotar; venir, proceder, provenir; —, v. a. echar; expedir, despachar; publicar; emitir.
isthmus, ĭst'mŭs, s. istmo, m.
it, ĭt, pn. él, ella, ello, lo, la, le.
italic, ĭtăl'ĭk, s. letra cursiva, f.
itch, ĭtsh, s. sarna, f.; picazón, f.; prurito, m.; –, v. n. picar.   [s. artículo, m.
item, ī'tĕm, ad. ítem, otro sí, aun más; –,
iteration, ĭtŭră'shŭn, s. reiteración, f.
itinerant, ĭtĭn'ĕrănt, a. ambulante, errante.
itinerary, –ărărĕ, s. itinerario, m.
its, ĭts, pn. su, suyo.   [mismo.
itself, ĭtsĕlf, pn. el mismo, la misma, lo
ivory, ī'vŏrĕ, s. marfil, m.
ivy, ī'vĕ, s. hiedra, f.

J.

jabber, jăb'băr, v. n. charlar, farfullar.
jabberer, –ăr, s. farfullador, parlanchín, m.
jack, jăk, s. sacabotas, m.; martinete, m.; torno de asador, m.; jarro de cuero encerado, m.; cota de malla, f.; boliche, m.; macho, m.; burro, m.; lucio, m.; –o'lantern, fuego fatuo, m.; to be – of all trades, meterse en todo.
jackal, –ăl, s. adiva, f, adive, m.
jackanapes, –ănăps, s. pisaverde, mequetrefe, m.
jack-ass, –ăs, s. garañón, burro, m.
jack-boots, –bŏts, s. pl. botas grandes y fuertes, f. pl.
jack-daw, –dă, s. grajo, m.
jacket, –ĕt, s. chaqueta, jaqueta, f.
jade, jăd, s. rocín, m.; –, v. a. cansar.
jag, jăg, s. diente de sierra, m.; mella, f.; –, v. a. dentar.
jagged, –gĕd, a. desigual, dentado.
jaguar, jăg'ŭăr, s. jaguar, m.
jail, jăl, s. cárcel, f.
jail-bird, –bŭrd, s. preso, m.
jailer, –ăr, s. carcelero, m.
jam, jăm, s. conserva, f.; mermelada de frutas, f.; –, v. a. acuñar estrechamente.
jamb, jăm, s. quicial, m.
jangle, jăng'gl, v. n. reñir, altercar.
janitor, jăn'ĭtăr, s. sujier, portero, m.
Janizary, jăn'ĭzăre, s. jenízaro, m.
jant, jănt, s. pina de la rueda, f.
January, jăn'ŭărĕ, s. enero, m.   [rolar.
Japan, jăpăn', s. charol, m.; –, v. a. chaJapanner, –năr, s. charolista, m.
jar, jăr, v. n. chocar, (mus.) discordar;

reñir; –, s. jarro, m.; tinaja, f.; riña, f.; sonido desapacible, m.
jargon, jăr'gŏn, s. jerga, jerigonza, f.
jasper, jăs'păr, s. jaspe, m.
jaundice, jăn'dĭs, s. ictericia, f.
jaundiced, –d, a. ictérico.
jaunt, jănt, s. excursión, f.
jaunty, –ĕ, a. alegre, festivo.
jaw, jă, s. quijada, f.; boca, f.
jay, jă, s. picaza, urraca, marica, f. (ave).
jealous, jĕl'ŭs, a. celoso; envidioso.
jealousy, –ĕ, s. celos, m. pl.
jeer, jĕr, v. n. befar, mofar, escarnecer; –, s. befa, mofa, burla, f.
Jehu, jē'hū, s. cochero arrojado, m.
jelly, jĕl'lĕ, s. jalea, gelatina, f.
jelly-broth, –brŏth, s. consumado, m.
jelly-fish, –fĭsh, s. aguamar, m.; medusa, f.
jeopard(ise), jĕp'ărd(ĭz), v. a. arriesgar, poner en riesgo.   [dar latigazos, azotar.
jerk, jŭrk, s. sacudida, sobarbada, f.; –, v. a.
jessamine, jĕs'sămĭn, s. jazmín, m.
jest, jĕst, s. chanza, burla, f.
jester, –ăr, s. mofador, bufón, m.
jestingly, –ĭnglĕ, ad. de burlas.
Jesuit, jĕz'ŭĭt, s. jesuita, m.; –'s bark, quina, cascarilla, f.
Jesuitic(al), jĕzŭĭt'ĭk(ăl), a. jesuítico.
jet, jĕt, s. azabache, m.; surtidor, m.
jetty, –tĕ, a. hecho de azabache; –, s
Jew, jō, s. judío, m.   [muelle, m.
jewel, jō'ĕl, s. joya, f.
jeweller, –lăr, s. joyero, m.
jewelry, –rĕ, s. joyería, f.
Jewess, jō'ĕs, s. judía, f.
jewish, –ĭsh, a. judaico, judío.
jewry, –rĕ, s. judería, f.
Jews'harp, jōz'hărp, s. birimbao, m.
jib, jĭb, s. (mar.) maraguto, foque, m.
jig, jĭg, s. baile alegre, m.
jilt, jĭlt, s. coqueta, f.; –, v. n. coquetear.
jingle, jĭng'gl, v. n. retiñir, resonar; –, s. retintín, resonido, m.
job, jŏb, s. friolera, f.; destajo, m.; engañifa, f.; cucaña, f.; –, v. a. & n. dar una mojada; cambalachar.
jobation, jŏbă'shŭn, s. paulina, f.
jobber, jŏb'băr, s. agiotista, m.; destajero, m.; usurero, m.
jobbing, –bĭng, s, infundios, m. pl.
job-master, –măstăr, s. alquilador de caballos, m.
jockey, jŏk'ĕ, s. jinete, chalán, m.; persona apasionada por los caballos, f.; engañabobos, m.; –, v. a. trampear, engañar.
jocose, jŏkŏs', a. jocoso, burlesco; –ly, ad. jocosamente.
jocosity, jŏkŏs'ĭtĕ, s. jocosidad, chanza, f.
jocular, jŏk'ŭlăr, jocund, –ănd, a. jocoso, alegre.
jog, jŏg, v. a. empujar; dar un golpe suave; –, v. n. bambolearse; andar á saltos; –, s. empellón, m.; traqueo, m.   [tina, f.
jog-trot, –trŏt, s., trote de perro, m.; ru-
John Bull, jŏn'bŭl, s. apodo de los ingleses.   [juntarse, asociarse.
join, jŏĭn, v. a. juntar, unir, –, v. n. unirse
joiner, –ăr, s. carpintero de taller, m.

joinery, *-ărĕ*, s. carpintería, f.
joint, *jŏint*, s. coyuntura, articulación, f.; charnela, f.; cuarto, m.; nudo (de una planta), m.; –, a. unido; participante; – heir, s. coheredero, m.; –, v. a. juntar; descuartizar.
jointly, *-lĭ*, ad. juntamente.
joint-stock-company, *-stŏk kŭm' pănĕ*, s. (com.) sociedad por acciones, f.
jointure, *jŏin' tūr*, s. viudedad, f.
joist, *jŏist*, s. viga de bovedilla ó suelo, f.
joke, *jŏk*, s. chanza, burla, f.; –, v. n. chancear.
jollity, *jŏl' lĭtĕ*, s. alegría, f.; regocijo, m.
jolly, *jŏl' lĕ*, a. alegre, gallardo.
jolly-boat, *-bŏt*, s. botequín, m.
jolt, *jŏlt*, v. a. traquear, sacudir; –, s. traqueo, m.
Jonathan, Brother —, *brŏth' ăr jŏn' ēthăn*, s. apodo de los americanos del norte.
jostle, *jŏs' l*, v. rempujar.
jot, *jŏt*, s. jota, f.; punto, m.
journal, *jŭr' năl*, s. jornal, diario, m.
journalism, *-ĭzm*, s. periodismo, m.
journalist, *-ĭst*, s. periodista, m.
journey, *jŭr' nĕ*, s. jornada, f.; viaje, m.; –, v. a. viajar.
journeyman, *-măn*, s. jornalero, m.
journey-work, *-wărk*, s. jornal, m.
joust, *jŭst* (*jŏst*), s. torneo, m.; justa, f.; –, v. n. justar.
jovial, *jŏ' vĭăl*, a. jovial, alegre; -ly, ad. con jovialidad.
joviality, *jŏvĭăl' ĭtĕ*, s. jovialidad, f.
joy, *jŏi*, s. alegría, f.; júbilo, m.; to give or wish —, congratular.
joyful, *-fŭl*, a. joyous, *-ăs*, s. alegre, gozoso; -ly, ad. alegremente.
joyless, *-lĕs*, a. triste, sin alegría.
jubilant, *jŏ' bĭlănt*, a. lleno de júbilo.
jubilation, *-lā' shŭn*, s. júbilo, regocijo, m.
jubilee, *jŏ' bĭlĕ*, s. jubileo, m.
Judaism, *jŏ' dāĭzm*, s. judaísmo, m.
judge, *jŭj*, s. juez, m.; –, v. n. juzgar; inferir; [opinión, decisión, f.
judgment, *-mĕnt*, s. juicio, m.; sentir, m.;
judicature, *jŏ' dĭkātŭr*, s. judicatura, f.
judicial, *jŏdĭsh' ăl*, a. –ly, ad. judicial(mente). [-ly, ad. juiciosamente.
judicious, *jŏdĭsh' ăs*, a. juicioso, prudente;
jug, *jŭg*, s. jarro, m.
juggle, *-gl*, s. juego de manos, m.; –, v. n. hacer juegos de manos.
juggler, *-glăr*, s. juglar, m.
juice, *jŏis*, s. zumo, jugo, m.; suco, m.
juicy, *-ĕ*, a. jugoso.
July, *jŏlĕ'*, s. julio, m. (mes).
jumble, *jŭm' bl*, v. a. mezclar confusamente; –, s. mezcla, confusión, f.
jump, *jŭmp*, v. n. saltar, brincar; convenir, concordar; –, s. salto, m.
junction, *jŭngk' shŭn*, s. junta, unión, f.
juncture, *-tŭr*, s. juntura, coyuntura, f.
June, *jŏn*, s. junio, m. (mes).
jungle, *jŭn' gl*, s. matorral, m.
junior, *jŏ' nŭr*, a. más joven.
juniper, *jŏ' nĭpŭr*, s. (bot.) enebro, m.

junket, *jŭng' kĕt*, s. dulce seco; convite familiar, m.; –, v. n. dar un cónvite en secreto. [asamblea, f.; reunión, f.
junta, *jŭn' tă*, junto, *jŭn' tŏ*, s. junta.
juridic(al), *jŏrĭd' ĭk(ăl)*, a. jurídico, judicial; -ly, ad. jurídicamente.
jurisdiction, *jŏrĭsdĭk' shăn*, s. jurisdicción, f. [dencia, f.
jurisprudence, *-prŏ' dĕns*, s. jurispru-
jurist, *jŏ' rĭst*, s. jurista, m. [rado, m.
juror, *jŏ' rŭr*, juryman, *jŏ' rĭmăn*, s. jury, *jŏ' rĕ*, s. junta de jurados, f.; jurado, m.
just, *jŭst*, a. justo, honrado, virtuoso; –, ad. justamente, exactamente; – as, como; – now, ahora mismo.
justice, *jŭs' tĭs*, s. justicia, f.; juez, m.; –, v. a. administrar justicia.
justifiable, *jŭstĭf' ăbl*, a. conforme á razón, según justicia.
justifiably, *-ē*, ad. con justicia y rectitud.
justification, *jŭstĭfĭkā' shăn*, s. justificación, f.; defensa, f.
justify, *jŭs' tĭfĕ*, v. a. justificar.
justle, *jŭs' l*, v. a. & n. rempujar; chocar.
justly, *jŭst' lĕ*, ad. justamente; exactamente. [tud, f.
justness, *-nĕs*, s. justicia, equidad, exacti-
jut, *jŭt*, v. n. chocar en algo cuando se va corriendo; to – out, sobresalir.
jute, *jŏt*, s. jute, m.
juvenile, *jŏ' vĕnĭl*, a. juvenil.
juxtaposition, *jŭkstăpŏzĭsh' ăn*, s. yuxtaposición, f.

K.

kale, *kăl*, s. col, berza, f. [pio, m.
kaleidoscope, *kălĭ' dŏskŏp*, s. kaleidosco-
kangaroo, *kăng' gărŏ*, s. canguro, f.
keel, *kĕl*, s. (mar.) quilla, f.
keen, *kĕn*, a. afilado, agudo; penetrante, sútil, vivo; vehemente; satírico, picante; -ly, ad. agudamente; sútilmente; agriamente. [spicacia, f.; aspereza, f.
keenness, *-nĕs*, s. agudeza, sutileza, per-
keen-sighted, *-sĭtĕd*, a. perspicaz.
keep, *kĕp*, v. a. tener, mantener, retener; preservar, guardar; proteger; detener; conservar; reservar; sostener; observar; solemnizar; –, v. n. perseverar; soler; mantenerse; quedar; vivir, residir; tener cuidado; –, s. torre, f.; guardia, f.; sustentación, f. [prison, carcelero, m.
keeper, *-ăr*, s. guardián, m.; – of a
keeping, *-ĭng*, s. custodia, f.; guarda, f.
keepsake, *-săk*, s. dádiva en memoria.
keg, *kĕg*, s. barrica, f. [f.; regalo, m.
ken, *kĕn*, s. vista, f. [rrera, f.
kennel, *-nĕl*, s. perrera, f.; jauría, f.; zo-
kerb-stone, *kărb' stŏn*, s. brocal de pozo, m.; guardacantón, m.
kerchief, *kŭr' tshĭf*, s. pañuelo, m.
kernel, *kŭr' nĕl*, s. almendra, pepita, f.; meollo, m.
ketch, *kĕtsh*, s. quaiche, queche, m.
kettle, *kĕt' tl*, s. caldera, f.

kettle-drum, –drŭm, s. timbal, atabal, m.
key, kē, s. llave, f.; (mus.) clave, f.; tecla, f.
key-board, –bōrd, s. teclado de órgano, m.
key-hole, –hōl, s. agujero de la llave, m.
key-note, –nōt, s. (mus.) tónica, f.
key-ring, –rĭng, s. colgajo de llaves, m.
key-stone, –stōn, s. llave de un arco ó bóveda, f. [–, s. puntapié, m.; patada, f.
kick, kĭk, v. a. acocear; –, v. n. patear;
kickshaw, kĭkshā, s. patarada, fruslería.
kid, kĭd, s. cabrito, m. [bagatela, f.
kidnap, –năp, v. a. robar niños ú hombres.
kidney, –nē, s. riñón, m.; (fig.) especie, f.
kilderkin, kĭl'dûrkĭn, s. medio barril, m.
kill, kĭl, v. a. matar, asesinar.
kiln, kĭl, s. horno, m. [orno.
kiln-dry, –drī, v. a. secar ó quemar en
kilt, kĭlt, s. saya de los escoceses serranos, f.
kimbo, kĭm'bō, a. encorvado, torcido; to
set one's arms a –, ponerse en asas.
kin, kĭn, s. parentesco, m.; afinidad, f.;
next of –, pariente próximo, m.
kind, kīnd, a. benévolo, benigno, afable,
cariñoso; –, s. género, m.; especie, naturaleza, manera, f.; calidad, f.
kindle, kĭn'dl, v. a. & n. encender; arder.
kindliness, kīnd'lĭnĕs, s. benevolencia, f.
kindly, –lē, a. blando, suave, tratable;
–, ad. benignamente. [beneficio, m.
kindness, –nĕs, s. benevolencia, f.; favor,
kindred, kĭn'drĕd, s. parentesco, m.; parentela, casta, f.; –, a. emparentado.
king, kĭng, s. rey, m.
kingdom, –dŭm, s. reino, m. [m. (ave).
king-fisher, –fĭshûr, s. martín pescador,
kinglike, –līk, kingly, –lē, a. real; regio;
–, ad. como de rey.
king's evil, –s' ēvĭl, s. escrófula, f.
kinsfolk, kĭnz'fōk, s. parientes, m. pl.
kinship, kĭn'shĭp, s. parentela, f.
kinsman, kĭnz'măn, s. pariente, m.
kinswoman, –wŭmăn, s. parienta, f.
kirtle, kûr'tl, s. sobretodo, m.
kiss, kĭs, s. beso, ósculo, m.; –, v. a. besar.
kissing, –ĭng, s. beso, m.; – of hand,
besamano, m. [m.
kissing-crust, –ĭngkrŭst, s. beso del pan.
kit, kĭt, s. botellón, m.; violín pequeño, m.;
vasija para salmón, f.; colodra, f.
kitchen, kĭtsh'ĕn, s. cocina, f. [cocina, f.
kitchen-dresser, –drĕssûr, s. mesa de
kitchen-garden, –gārdn, s. huerta, f.
kitchen-maid, –mād, s. cocinera, f.
kitchen-range, –rānj, s. cocina inglesa, f.
kite, kĭt, s. milano, m.; cometa, birlocha, f.
kitten, kĭt'tn, s. gatillo, m.; –, v. n. parir
(la gata). [f.
knack, năk, s. chuchería, f.; maña, destreza.
knacker, –ûr, s. cordelero, suguero, m.
knapsack, năp'săk, s. mochila, f.
knave, năv, s. bribón, pícaro, m.; (at
cards) sota, f.
knavery, –ûrĭ, s. picardía, bribonada, f.
knavish, nă'vĭsh, a. fraudulento, pícaro, m.; –ly, ad. picaramente.
knead, nēd, v. a. amasar.
kneading-trough, –ĭngtrŏf, s. amasadera, f.

knee, nē, s. rodilla, f.; (mar.) curva, f.;
ángulo, m.
kneed, –d, a. lo que tiene rodillas.
knee-deep, –dēp, a. metido ó subido hasta
las rodillas.
kneel, nēl, v. n. arrodillarse.
knee-pan, nē'păn, s. rótula, f.
knell, nĕl, s. clamoreo, m.
knickerbockers, nĭk'ûrbŏk'ûrz, s. pl.
calzones de cazador, m. pl. [juguete, m.
knick-knacks, nĭk'năks, s. pl. bujería, f.;
knife, nīf, s. cuchillo, m.
knight, nīt, s. caballero, m.; –, v. a. crear
á uno caballero. [dante, m.
knight-errant, –ĕrrănt, s. caballero-an-
knighthood, –hŭd, s. caballería, f. (dignidad de caballero). [llero.
knightly, –lē, a. propio ó digno de caba-
knit, nĭt, v. a. & n. enlazar; atar, unir;
trabajar á punto de aguja; to – the
brows, fruncir las cejas.
knitter, –tûr, s. calcetero, mediero, m.
knitting-needle, –tĭngnēdl, s. aguja de
hacer media, f.
knob, nŏb, s. bulto, m.; nudo en la madera,
m.; botón de las flores, m.
knobby, –bē, a. lleno de nudos.
knock, nŏk, v. a. & n. chochar; golpear,
tocar; pagar; to – down, derribar; –, s.
golpe, m.; llamada, f.
knocker, –ûr, s. llamador, m.; aldaba, f.
knoll, nŏl, s. cima de una colina, f.
knot, nŏt, s. nudo, m.; lazo, m.; maraña,
f.; dificultad, f.; confederación, f.; –, v. a.
enredar, juntar; –, v. n. hechar nudos las
plantas.
knotty, –tē, a. nudoso; dificultoso.
knout, nŏŭt, s. knut, m.; bastonada rusa, f.
know, nō, v. a. & n. conocer, saber; tener
noticia de.
knowing, –ĭng, a. instruído, inteligente,
entendido; –ly, ad. hábilmente, á sabiendas; á propósito.
knowledge, nŏl'ĕj, s. conocimiento, m.;
ciencia, f.; inteligencia, habilidad, f.
knuckle, nŭk'l, s. nudillo, m.; jarrete de
ternero, m.

L.

la, lā, [he aquí!, ved aquí!
label, lā'bĕl, s. esquela, f.; marbete, m.;
rótulo, m.; –, v. a. rotular ó señalar alguna cosa con un rótulo.
labial, lā'bĭăl, a. labial.
laboratory, lăb'ŏrătûrē, s. laboratorio, m.
laborious, lăbō'rĭŭs, a. laborioso; difícil;
–ly, ad. laboriosamente.
labour, lā'bûr, s. trabajo, m.; labor, f.;
fatiga, f.; to be in –, estar de parto;
–, v. a. trabajar; afanarse; estar con dolores de parto. [dor, m.
labourer, –ûr, s. labrador, m.; trabaja-
labyrinth, lăb'ĭrĭnth, s. laberinto, m.
lac, lăk, s. laca, goma laca, f.
lace, lās, s. lazo, cordón, m.; encaje, m.;
randa, f.; galón, m.; –, v. a. abrochar,
encordonar; galonear.

lacerate, *lás'ărăt,* a. lacerar, rasgar.
lachrymose, *lăk'rimōs,* a. lloroso.
lack, *lăk,* v. a. & n. carecer, necesitar; faltar algo; —, s. falta, f.; menester, m.
lackey, *lăk'ĕ,* s. lacayo, m.
laconic(al), *lăkŏn'ĭk(ăl),* a. lacónico.

lacquer, *lăk'ŭr,* s. laca, f.
lad, *lăd,* s. mozo, muchacho, m.
ladder, *lăd'dŭr,* s. escala ó escalera portátil, f.
lade, *lăd,* v. a. cargar.
lading, *lă'dĭng,* s. carga, f.; cargamento, m.
ladle, *lă'dl,* s. cucharón, m.
ladleful, *-fŭl,* s. cucharada, f.
lady, *lă'dĕ,* s. señora, señorita, dama, f.
lady-bird, *-bŭrd,* s. vaquilla de Dios (insecto), f.
Lady-day, *-dā,* s. día de la Anunciación de nuestra Señora, m.
lady-killer, *-kĭllăr,* s. favorito de las mujeres, m.
ladylike, *-lĭk,* a. afeminado; elegante.
lady-love, *-lŭv,* s. dama, querida, f.
ladyship, *-shĭp,* s. señoría, f.
lag, *lăg,* v. n. moverse lentamente; quedarse atrás.
laggard, *-gărd,* **lagger,** *-gŭr,* s. haragán, holgazán, m.
lagoon, *lăgŏn',* s. laguna, f.
lair, *lăr,* s. cubil, m.; pastura, f.
laity, *lă'ĭtĕ,* s. estado seglar, m.
lake, *lăk,* s. lago, m.; laguna, f.
lamb, *lăm,* s. cordero, m.; —, v. n. parir corderos.
lambent, *lăm'bĕnt,* a. centelleante.
lambkin, *-kĭn,* s. corderito, m.
lame, *lăm,* a. lisiado, estropeado; imperfecto; -ly, ad. con cojera; imperfectamente; —, v. a. lisiar, estropear.
lameness, *-nĕs,* s. cojera, f.; imperfección, f.; estado de una persona estropeada, m.
lament, *lămĕnt',* v. a. (& n.) lamentar(se); —, s. lamento, m. [deplorable.
lamentable, *lăm'ĕntăbl,* a. lamentable.
lamentation, *lăm'ĕntā'shŭn,* s. lamentación, f.
lamp, *lămp,* s. lámpara, f. [ción, f.
lamp-black, *-blăk,* s. negro de humo, m.
lampoon, *lămpōn',* s. sátira, f.; libelo, m.; —, v. a. escribir sátiras.
lamp-post, *lămp'pōst,* s. candelabro, m.
lamprey, *lăm'prĕ,* s. lamprea, f. (pez).
lance, *lăns,* s. lanza, f.; —, v. a. dar un lancetazo; hacer una operación quirúrgica con lanceta.
lancer, *-ŭr,* s. (mil.) lancero, m.
lancet, *lăn'sĕt,* s. lanceta, f.
land, *lănd,* s. país, m.; región, f.; territorio, m.; tierra, f.; —, v. a. & n. desembarcar; saltar en tierra.
landau, *lăndŏ',* s. landó, m. (coche).
landed, *lănd'ĕd,* a. hacendado.
land-forces, *-fōrsĕz,* s. pl. tropas de tierra, f. pl.
land-holder, *-hōldŭr,* s. hacendado, m.
landing, *-ĭng,* s. desembarco, m.
landing-(place), *-ĭng(plăs),* s. desembarcadero, m. [marina, posadera, f.
landlady, *-lădĕ,* s. propietaria, f.; mesolandlord,** *-lōrd,* s. propietario, m.; huésped, posadero, m. [m.
land-lubber, *-lŭbbŭr,* s. marinero de río,

land-mark, *-mărk,* s. mojón, m.; marca, f.
landscape, *-skăp,* s. paisaje, m. [f.
land-slip, *-slĭp,* s. hundimiento, desplomamiento de un terreno, m. [m.
land-tax, *-tăks,* s. tributo sobre tierras, f.
landward, *-wărd,* ad. hacia la tierra.
lane, *lăn,* s. callejuela, f. [guaje, m.
language, *lăng'gwĭj,* s. lengua, f.: lenguaguid,** *lăng'gwĭd,* a. lánguido, débil; -ly, ad. lánguidamente, débilmente.
languish, *-gwĭsh,* v. n. entristecerse, afligirse
languor, *-gwŭr,* s. languidez, f. [girse
lank(y), *lăngk(ĕ),* a. alto y delgado. [m.
lansquenet, *lăn'skĕnĕt,* s. soldado de á pie,
lantern, *lăn'tŭrn,* s. linterna, f.; farol, m.; dark —, linterna sorda, f.
lap, *lăp,* s. faltas, f. pl.; regazo, m.; —, v. a. arrollar, envolver; lamer.
lap-dog, *-dŏg,* s. perro de faldas, m.
lapidary, *lăp'ĭdărĕ,* s. lapidario, m.
lappet, *lăp'pĕt,* s. falda, f.
lapse, *lăps,* s. caída, f.; falta ligera, f.; traslación de derecho ó dominio, f.; lapso, m.; —, v. n. escurrir, manar; deslizarse.
lapwing, *lăp'wĭng,* s. avefría, f.
larboard, *lăr'bōrd,* s. (mar.) babor, m. (lado izquierdo del navío).
larceny, *lăr'sĕnĕ,* s. ratería, f.
larch, *lărtsh,* s. alerce, lárice, m. (árbol).
lard, *lărd,* s. lardo, tocino gordo, m.; —, v. a. mechar.
larder, *-dr,* s. despensa, f.
larding-pin, *-ĭngpĭn,* s. mechera, f.
large, *lărj,* a. amplio, vasto; largo, liberal; at —, á lo largo; -ly, ad. largamente, copiosamente, liberalmente.
largeness, *-nĕs,* s. grandor, m.; anchura, amplitud, f.
largess, *lăr'jĕs,* s. liberalidad, f.
lark, *lărk,* s. alondra, f.
larva, *lăr'vă,* s. larva, oruga, f.
lascivious, *lăssĭv'ĭŭs,* a. lascivo; -ly, ad. lascivamente.
lash, *lăsh,* s. latigazo, m.; punta del látigo, f.; pihuela, f.; sarcasmo, m.; —, v. a. dar latigazos; atar; satirizar.
lass, *lăs,* s. doncella, moza, f.
lassitude, *lăs'ĭtŭd,* s. lasitud, fatiga, f.
last, *lăst,* a. último, postrero, pasado; at —, últimamente; al fin; -ly, ad. la última vez; al fin; finalmente; —, s. horma de zapatero, f.; (mar.) carga de un navío, f.; —, v. n. durar.
lasting, *-ĭng,* a. duradero, permanente; -ly, ad. perpetuamente; —, s. lastén, m. (tela). [a. cerrar con aldaba.
latch, *lătsh,* s. aldaba de puerta, f.; —, v.
latch-key, *-kĕ,* s. llave maestra, f.
late, *lăt,* a. tardío; tarde, lento; difunto; (rail.) the train is ten minutes —, el tren ha sufrido retraso de diez minutos; —, ad. tarde; of —, de poco tiempo acá; -ly, ad. poco ha, recientemente.
lateness, *-nĕs,* s. tiempo avanzado, m.
latent, *lă'tĕnt,* a. escondido, oculto.
lateral, *lăt'ĕrăl,* a. -ly, ad. lateral(mente).
lath, *lăth,* s. listón, m.; —, v. a. poner latas en los techumbres.
lathe, *lădh,* s. torno, m.

lather, *lăth'ăr,* s. jabonaduras, f. pl.; —, v. a. & n. bañar con espuma de jabón.

latten, *lăt'tn,* s. latón, m. [espumar.

latter, *lăt'tăr,* a. posterior, último; —ly, ad. últimamente, recientemente.

lattice, *lăt'tĭs,* s. celosía, f.; —, v. a. enrejar.

laudable, *lăd'ăbl,* a. laudable, loable.

laudably, —ĕ, ad. laudablemente, loablemente.

laugh, *lăf,* v. n. reir; —, s. risa, risada, f.

laughable, —ăbl, a. risible. [risa.

laughingly, —ĭnglĕ, ad. alegremente, con risa.

laughing-stock, —ĭngstŏk, s. hazmerreir, m.

laughter, —tăr, s. risa, risada, f.

launch, *lănsh,* v. a. (& n.) lanzar(se); —, s. (mar.) lancha, f.

laundress, *lăn'drĕs,* s. lavandera, f.

laundry, *lăn'drĕ,* s. lavadero, m.

laureate, *lă'rĕăt,* a. laureado.

laurel, *lŏr'ĕl,* s. laurel guindo ó regio, m.

laurelled, —d, a. laureado.

lava, *lă'vă,* s. lava, f.

lavender, *lăv'ĕndăr,* s. (bot.) espliego, m., lavándula, f.

lavish, *lăv'ĭsh,* a. pródigo; —ly, ad. pródigamente; —, v. a. disipar.

law, *lă,* s. ley, f.; derecho, m.; litigio judicial, m.; jurisprudencia, f.

lawful, —fŭl, a. legal; legítimo; —ly, ad. legalmente.

law-giver, —gĭvăr, s. legislador, m.

lawless, —lĕs, a. ilegal; anárquico.

lawlessness, —nĕs, s. anarquía, f.

law-maker, —măkăr, s. legislador, m.

lawn, *lăn,* s. prado, m.; linón, m.

law-suit, *lă'sŭt,* s. proceso, lite, m.

lawyer, *lă'yăr,* s. abogado, jurisperito, m.

lax, *lăks,* a. laxo, flojo.

laxity, —ĭtĕ, s. laxitud, flojedad, f.

lay, *lă,* v. a. poner, colocar, extender; calmar, sosegar; imputar; apostar; exhibir; **to-claim,** reclamar, pretender; —, v. n. aovar, poner huevos las aves; tramar.

layer, —ăr, s. lecho, m.; cama, f.; pimpollo, m.; gallina que pone, f.

layman, —măn, s. lego, seglar, m.; maniquí, m.

lazaretto, *lăzărĕt'tō,* **lazar-house,** *lă'zărhŏŭs,* s. lazareto, m.

lazily, *lă'zĭlĕ,* ad. perezosamente; lentamente.

laziness, —zĭnĕs, s. pereza, f. [mente.

lazy, —zĕ, a. perezoso, tardo, pesado.

lea, *lĕ,* s. prado, m., pradera, f.

lead, *lĕd,* s. plomo, m.; —s, pl. techo emplomado, m.; —, *lĕd,* v. a. conducir, guiar; gobernar; emplear; —, v. n. mandar en jefe; ser mano (en el juego de naipes); —, s. conducta; **(at cards)** mano, f. [estípulo.

leaden, *lĕd'n,* a. hecho de plomo; pesado; estúpido.

leader, *lĕd'ăr,* s. guia, conductor, m.; jefe, general, m.

leading, —ĭng, a. principal; capital; **—article,** s. artículo de fondo de una gaceta, m.; **—hand,** s. el que juega primero en las partidas de naipes; **—horse,** s. caballo de silla, m. [res, m. pl.; trailla, f.

leading-strings, —strĭngz, s. pl. andado-

leaf, *lĕf,* s. hoja, f.; hoja de un libro; hoja de puerta.

leafy, —ĕ, a. frondoso, hojudo.

league, *lĕg,* s. liga, alianza, f.; legua, f.; —, v. n. confederarse.

leaguer, —ăr, s. confederado, m.

leak, *lĕk,* s. (mar.) via de agua, f.; —, v. n. (mar.) hacer agua.

leakage, —āj, s. derrame, m., merma, f.

leaky, —ĕ, a. roto, agujereado.

lean, *lĕn,* v. a. & n. ladear, inclinar; apoyarse; —, a. magro. [f.

leanings, —ĭngz, s. ladeo, m.; inclinación, f.

leanness, —nĕs, s. magrura, f.

leap, *lĕp,* v. n. saltar, brincar; salir con ímpetu; palpitar; —, s. salto, m.

leap-year, —yĕr, s. año bisiesto ó intercalar, m. [aprender.

learn, *lărn,* v. a. & n. instruir, enseñar;

learned, —d, a. docto; **the —,** s. pl. literatos, m. pl.; —ly, ad. doctamente.

learner, —ăr, s. tirón, m.; escolar, m.; aprendiz, m. [erudición, f.

learning, —ĭng, s. literatura, ciencia, f.

lease, *lĕs,* s. arriendo, m.; —, v. a. arrendar.

leasehold, —hōld, s. arriendo, m.

leash, *lĕsh,* s. pihuela, correa, f.; —, v. a. atar con correa.

least, *lĕst,* a. mínimo; —ly, ad. lo menos; **at —,** á lo menos; **not in the —,** ni en lo más mínimo.

leather, *lĕth'ăr,* s. cuero, pellejo, m.

leathern, —n, a. (hecho) de cuero.

leathery, —ĕ, a. correoso.

leave, *lĕv,* s. licencia, f.; permiso, m.; despedida, f.; **to take —,** despedirse; —, v. a. & n. dejar, abandonar; ceder; cesar.

leaven, *lĕ'vn,* s. levadura, f.; fermento, m.; —, v. a. fermentar. [relieves, m. pl.

leavings, *lĕ'vĭngz,* s. pl. sobras, f. pl.

lection, *lĕk'shăn,* s. lección, lectura, f.

lecture, *lĕk'tăr (lĕk'tshŭr),* s. lectura, leyenda, f.; corrección, f.; reprensión, f.; —, v. a. enseñar; censurar.

lecturer, —ăr, s. lector, instructor, m.

ledge, *lĕj,* s. capa, tonga, f.; borde, m.

ledger, *lĕj'ăr,* s. (com.) libro mayor, m.

led-horse, *lĕd'hŏrs,* s. caballo de mano, m. [ventado.

lee, *lĕ,* s. (mar.) sotavento, m.; —, a. sota-

leech, *lĕtsh,* s. sanguijuela, f.; médico, m.

leek, *lĕk,* s. (bot.) puerro, m.

leer, *lĕr,* s. ojeada, f.; —, v. n. ojear al través. [poso, m.

lees, *lĕs,* s. pl. heces, f. pl.; sedimento, m.

lee-side, *lĕ'sĭd,* s. (mar.) banda de sotavento, f.

leeward, —wărd, a. (mar.) sotavento.

left, *lĕft,* a. siniestro, izquierdo; **on the —,** á la izquierda.

left-handed, —hăndĕd, a. zurdo; morga [nático.

leg, *lĕg,* s. pierna, f., pie, m.

legacy, *lĕg'ăsĕ,* s. legado, m.; manda, f.

legal, *lĕ'găl,* a. legal, legítimo; —ly, ad. legalmente. [dad, f.

legality, *lĕgăl'ĭtĕ,* s. legalidad, legitimi-

legalize, *lĕ'gălĭz,* v. a. legalizar, autorizar, legitimar.

legate, *lĕg'ăt,* s. legado, diputado, m.

legatee, lĕg'ătĭ, s. legatario, f.
legation, lĕgā'shăn, s. legación, emba-jada, f.
legend, lĕj'ĕnd, s. leyenda, legenda, f.
legendary, —āri, a. fabuloso, quijotesco.
legerdemain, lĕj'ărdĕmān, s. juego de manos, m. [italiano, m.
leghorn, lĕg'hŏrn, s. sombrero de paja
legible, lĕj'ĭbl, a. legible, que puede leerse.
legibly, —ĭ, ad. legiblemente.
legion, lē'jŭn, s. legión, f.
legislate, lĕj'ĭslăt, v. a. legislar.
legislation, lĕjĭslā'shăn, s. legislación, f.
legislative, —ĭtv, a. legislativo.
legislator, —tăr, s. legislador, m.
legislature, lĕj'ĭslātūr, s. legislatura, f.
legitimacy, lĕjĭt'ĭmăsĭ, s. legitimidad, f.
legitimate, —ĭmăt, a. legítimo; —ly, ad.
legtimamente; —, v. a. legitimar.
leisure, lē'zhăr, s. desocupación, f.; ocio, m.; comodidad, f.; at —, leisurely, ad. cómodamente, con sosiego.
lemon, lĕm'ŏn, s. limón, f.
lemonade, —dd, s. limonada, f.
lemon-tree, —trē, s. limonero, m.
lend, lĕnd, v. a. prestar.
length, lĕngth, s. longitud, f.; duración, f.; distancia, f.; at —, finalmente.
lengthen, —n, v. a. alargar; —, v. n. alar-garse, dilatarse.
lengthy, —ĭ, a. largo; fastidioso.
leniency, lē'nĭĕnsĭ, s. benignidad, f. [(m).
lenient, lē'nĭĕnt, a. & s. leniente; lenitivo.
lenitive, lĕn'ĭtĭv, a. & s. lenitivo, (m.).
lenity, lĕn'ĭtĭ, s. lenidad, benignidad, f.
lens, lĕns, s. lente, m. & f. (vidrio convexo).
lent, lĕnt, s. cuaresma, f.
lentil, lĕn'tĭl, s. lenteja, f.
leonine, lē'ŏnĭn, a. leonino.
leopard, lĕp'ărd, s. leopardo, m.
leper, lĕp'ăr, s. leproso, m.
leprosy, lĕp'rŏsē, s. lepra, f.
leprous, lĕp'rŭs, a. leproso.
less, lĕs, a. menor; —, ad. menos.
lessee, lĕssē', s. arrendatario, m.
lessen, lĕs'ĕn, v. a. minorar, disminuir; —, v. n. disminuirse.
lesser, —săr, a. más pequeño. [sión, f.
lesson, lĕs'ĕn, s. lección, f.; fraterna, repren-
lessor, lĕs'săr, s. arrendador, m.
lest, lĕst, c. para que no, de miedo que.
let, lĕt, v. a. dejar, permitir; arrendar; im-
lethal, lē'thăl, a. letal. [pedir.
lethargic(al), lĕthăr'jĭk(ăl), a. letárgico.
lethargy, lĕth'ărjē, s. letargo, m.
letter, lĕt'tăr, s. letra, f.; carta, f.
letter-box, —bŏks, s. buzón para las car-
letter-case, —kăs, s. cartera, f. [tas, m.
lettered, —d, a. letrado, docto.
letter-press, —prĕs, s. impresión, obra
lettuce, lĕt'tĭs, s. lechuga, f. [impresa, f.
levant, lĕvănt', s. levante, oriente, m.
levee, lĕv'ē, s. tiempo de levantarse por la mañana, m.: corte, f.; besamanos, m.
level, lĕv'ĕl, a. llano, igual; nivelado; alla-nado; —, s. llanura, f.; plano, m.; nivel, m.; —, v. a. allanar; nivelar.
lever, lē'văr, s. palanca, f.
leverage, lē'ărăj, s. momento estático, m.

leveret, lĕv'ărĕt, s. lebratillo, m.
levite, lē'vĭt, s. levita, m.
levity, lĕv'ĭtĭ, s. levedad, ligereza, f.; in-constancia, veledad, f. [hacer leva.
levy, lĕv'ĭ, s. leva (de tropas), f.; —, v. a.
lewd, lōd, a. lascivo, disoluto.
lewdness, —nĕs, s. lascivia, disolución, f.
lexicographer, lĕksĭkŏg'răfăr, s. lexicó-grafo, m.
lexicon, lĕks'ĭkŏn, s. diccionario, m.
liability, līăbĭl'ĭtĭ, s. responsabilidad, f.
liable, lī'ăbl, a. sujeto, expuesto á; res-
liar, lī'ăr, s. embustero, f. [ponsable.
libation, lĭbā'shăn, s. libación, f.
libel, lī'bĕl, s. libelo, m.; —, v. a. difamar.
libeller, —lăr, s. libelista, m.
libellous, —lăs, a. difamatorio.
liberal, lĭb'ărăl, a. liberal, generoso; —ly, ad. liberalmente. [rosidad, f.
liberality, lĭbărăl'ĭtĭ, s. liberalidad, gene-
liberate, lĭb'ărăt, v. a. libertar.
liberation, lĭbără'shăn, s. liberación, f.
libertine, lĭb'ărtĭn, s. libertino, m.; —, a. disoluto. [m.
liberty, lĭb'ărtĭ, s. libertad, f.; privilegio,
Libra, lī'bră, s. Libra, f.(signo del zodíaco).
librarian, lībrā'rĭăn, s. bibliotecario, m.
library, lī'brărē, s. librería, f.; biblioteca, f.
licence, lī'sĕns, s. licencia, f.; permiso, m.
licentious, līsĕn'shŭs, a. licencioso; —ly, ad. licenciosamente.
lichen, lī'kĕn, (lĭtsh'ĕn), s. (bot.) liquen, m.
lick, lĭk, v. a. lamer, chupar; (vulg.) gol-
licking, —ĭng, s. paliza, f. [pear.
lid, lĭd, s. tapa, f.; párpado, m.
lie, lī, s. mentira, f.; —, v. n. ir. mentir; echarse; reposar, acostarse; yacer.
lief, lēf, ad. de buena gana.
liege, lēj, a. ligio; súbdito. [m.
lien, lī'ĕn, (lēn), s. derecho de retención,
lieu, lū, s. lugar, m.; in—of, en vez de.
lieutenancy, lĕftĕn'ănsĭ, s. lugartenencia, f.
lieutenant, —ănt, s. lugarteniente, m. [f.
life, līf, s. vida, f.; conducta, f.; vivaci-dad, f.; mundo, m.; high—, el gran mundo; for —, por toda la vida; to the —, al natural.
life-belt, —bĕlt, s. ceñidor para nadar, m.
life-guard, —gărd, s. guardia de corps, f.
lifeless, —lĕs, a. muerto, inanimado; sin vivacidad. [de la vida, m.
life-office, —ŏffĭs, s. oficio de aseguración
life-preserver, —prĕzărvăr, s. macana, f.
life-size, —sīz, s. grandeza natural, f.
life-time, —tīm, s. duración de la vida, f.
lift, lĭft, v. a. alzar, elevar, levantar; hur-tar, robar; —, s. esfuerzo para levantar al-guna cosa pesada, m.; alzamiento, f.; alza, f.; ayuda, f.; ascensor (hidráulico), m.; at one—, de un golpe; to give one a —, ayudar á uno.
ligament, lĭg'ămĕnt, ligature, lĭg'ătŭr, s. ligamento, m.; ligadura, f.
light, lĭt, s. luz, f.; claridad, f.; conoci-miento, m.; día, m.; —, a. ligero, leve, fácil; frívolo; superficial; ágil; inconstante; claro; blondo; —, v. a. encender; alum-brar; —, v. n. hallar, encontrar; desmon-tarse; desembarcar.

lighten, *–n,* v. n. relampaguear ; **–,** v. a. iluminar, aligerar.

lighter, *–ûr,* s. (mar.) alijador, m.   [m.

lighterman, *–ârmän,* s. (mar.) lanchonero, considerado.   [m.

light-hearted, *–hârtéd,* a. ligero, inconsiderado.

light-house, *–hoûs,* s. (mar.) faro, fanal.

lighting, *–ȋng,* s. iluminación, f.

lightly, *–lé,* ad. ligeramente ; fácilmente ; alegremente.   [velocidad, f.

lightness, *–nés,* s. ligereza, f.; agilidad, f.

lightning, *–nȋng,* s. relámpago, m.

lightning-rod, *–nȋngród,* s. pararrayos, m.

lights, *–z,* s. pl. bofes, m. pl.   [alegre.

lightsome, *–sûm,* a. luminoso, claro ;

ligneous, *lȋg´néüs,* a. leñoso.

like, *lȋk,* a. semejante ; igual ; verosímil ; **–,** s. semejante, m., semejanza, f.; **–,** ad. como, del mismo modo que; **–,** v. a. & n. querer, amar ; gustar, agradar alguna cosa; **as you - it,** como quisiere.

likelihood, *–lȋhúd,* s. apariencia, f.; probabilidad, f.   [probablemente.

likely, *–lé,* a. probable, verosímil ; **–,** ad.

liken, *–n,* v. a. asemejar ; comparar.

likeness, *–nés,* s. semejanza, f.; igualdad, f.; retrato fiel, m.

likewise, *–wȋs,* ad. también ; igualmente.

liking, *lȋ´kȋng,* s. robustez, f.; gusto, agrado.

lilac, *lȋ´lâk,* s. lila, f.; lilas, m.   [m.

lily, *lȋl´é,* s. lirio, m.; **- of the valley,** lirio de los valles.

limb, *lȋm,* s. miembro, m.   [avantrén, m.

limber, *–bûr,* a. manejable, flexible ; **–,** s.

lime, *lȋm,* s. cal, f.; liga, f.; lima, f. (especie de limón); **(-tree)** tilo, m.; **–,** v. a. untar con liga.

lime-stone, *–stón,* s. piedra de cal, f.   [f.

lime-pit, *–pȋt,* s. cantera de piedra caliza.

limit, *lȋm´ȋt,* s. límite, término, m.; **–,** v. a. restringir.   [restricción, f.

limitation, *lȋmȋtä´shûn,* s. limitación, f.;

limitless, *lȋm´ȋtlés,* a. inmenso.

limn, *lȋm,* v. a. pintar ; dibujar ; retratar.

limner, *–nûr,* s. pintor, m., retratista, m.

limp, *lȋmp,* v. n. cojear ; **–,** s. cojera, f.; **–,** a. débil, flaco.   [parente.

limpid, *lȋm´pȋd,* a. limpio, claro, trans-

linch-pin, *lȋnsh´pȋn,* s. pezonera, f.

linden-(tree, *lȋn´dn(tré)* s. tilo, m.

line, *lȋn,* s. línea, f.; (mil.) línea de batalla, f.; raya, f.; esquicio, contorno, m.; ecuador, m., ferrocarril, m., vía, f.; renglón, m.; verso, m.; linaje, m.; cordón (muy delgado), m.; **–,** v. a. forrar ; revestir.

lineage, *lȋn´éâj,* s. linaje, m.; descendencia, f.   [recta.

lineal, *lȋn´éâl,* a. lineal; **-ly,** ad. en línea

lineament, *lȋn´éäment,* s. lineamiento, m.

linear, *lȋn´éâr,* a. lineal.   [m. pl.

line-keeper, *lȋn´képûr,* s. (rail.) guardavía, guardabarreras, m.

line-keeper's lodge, *–s lój,* s. (rail.) casilla de guarda, f.   [de lienzo.

linen, *lȋn´én,* s. lienzo, lino, m.; **–,** a. hecho

linen-draper, *–drápûr,* s. lencero, m.

linger, *lȋng´gûr,* v. n. consumirse, penar; tardar.

lingering, *–ȋng,* s. tardanza, dilación, f.; **-ly,** ad. lentamente ; lánguidamente.

linguist, *lȋng´gvȋst,* s. lingüista, m.

liniment, *lȋn´ȋmént,* s. linimento, m.

link, *lȋngk,* s. anillo de cadena, m.; cadena, f.; (mar.) hacha de viento, f.; **–,** v. a. juntar ; encadenar.

link-boy, *–bói,* s. paje de hacha, m.

linnet, *lȋn´nét,* s. pardillo, m.

linseed, *lȋn´séd,* s. linaza, f.

linsey-woolsey, *lȋn´zȋwûl´zé,* s. tejido de lana grosero y con mezcla de hilo, m.

lint, *lȋnt,* s. lino, m.; hilas, f. pl.

lintel, *lȋn´tél,* s. dintel, tranquero, m.

lion, *lȋ´ûn,* s. león, m.

lioness, *–nés,* s. leona, f.   [á la moda.

lionize, *lȋ´ónȋz,* v. a. poner á uno el hombre

lip, *lȋp,* s. labio, borde, m.

liquefy, *lȋk´wéfȋ,* v. a. licuar, liquidar, **–,** v. n. liquidarse.

liqueur, *lȋkûr´,* s. aguardiente, m.

liquid, *lȋk´wȋd,* a. líquido ; **–,** s. licor, m.

liquidate, *lȋk´wȋdät,* v. a. liquidar.   [f.

liquidation, *lȋkwȋdä´shûn,* s. liquidación, f.

liquor, *lȋk´ûr,* s. licor, m.

liquorice, *–ȋs,* s. orozuz, m., regaliza, f.

lisp, *lȋsp,* v. n. tartamudear, cecear ; **–,** s. tartamudeo, ceceo, m.

list, *lȋst,* s. lista, f.; gana, f.; voluntad, f.; cenefa, f.; **–,** v. n. querer, desear ; **–,** v. a. registrar ; (mil.) alistar.

listen, *lȋs´n,* v. n. escuchar, atender.

listless, *lȋst´lés,* a. indiferente, descuidado; **-ly,** ad. negligentemente.

listlessness, *–nés,* s. descuido m.

litany, *lȋt´âné,* s. letanía, f.

literal, *lȋt´érâl,* a. **-ly,** ad. literal(mente).

literary, *lȋt´érâré,* a. literario.

literature, *lȋt´érâtûr,* s. literatura, f.

lithe, *lȋth,* a. flexible, manejable.

lithograph, *lȋth´ógrâf,* s. litografía, f.; **–,** v. a. litografiar.

lithographer, *lȋthóg´râfûr,* s. litógrafo, m.

lithography, *–râfé,* s. litografía, f.

litigant, *lȋt´ȋgânt,* s. litigante. m.

litigate, *–ȋgât,* v. a. litigar, pleitear.

litigation, *lȋtȋgä´shûn,* s. litigio, m.

litigious, *lȋtȋj´ûs,* a. litigioso.

litter, *lȋt´ûr,* s. litera, cama portátil, f.; lechigada, ventregada, f.; **–,** v. a. parir los animales; desordenar.

little, *lȋt´tl,* a. pequeño, poco ; **by - and -,** poco á poco ; **–,** s. poco, m.; parte pequeña, f.   [queña, f.

littleness, *–nés,* s. pequeñez, f.

liturgy, *lȋt´ûrjé,* s. liturgia, f.

live, *lȋv,* v. n. vivir ; mantenerse ; habitar, **–,** *lȋv,* a. vivo.   [cia, f.

livelihood, *lȋv´lȋhúd,* s. vida, f.; subsistencia, f.

liveliness, *–lȋnés,* s. vivacidad, f.

lively, *–lé,* a. vivo, brioso, gallardo.

liver, *lȋv´ûr,* s. viviente, m.; hígado, m.

livery, *–é,* s. librea, f.; **the Livery,** cuerpo de ciudadanos de Londres, m.

livid, *lȋv´ȋd,* a. lívido, cárdeno.

living, *lȋv´ȋng,* s. modo de vivir, m.; subsistencia, f.; **–,** a. vivo.

lizard, *lȋz´ârd,* s. lagarto, m.

lo, lō, ¡he aquí!, ¡ved aquí!
load, lōd, v. a. cargar; —, s. carga, f. [f.
loadstar, lodestar, —*stär,* s. estrella polar.
loadstone, —*stōn,* s. imán, m. [azúcar, m.
loaf, lōf, s. pan, m.; (of sugar) pilón de
loafer, *lō'fŭr,* s. holgazán, gandul, m.
loam, lōm, s. marga, f.
loan, lōn, s. préstamo, empréstito, m.
loathe, lōth, v. a. aborrecer; tener hastío
— , v. n. fastidiar.
loathing, —*ing,* s. disgusto, m., aversión, f.
loathly, —*lē,* **loathsome,** *lōth'sŭm,* a.
detestable, fastidioso.
lobby, *lŏb'bē,* s. vestíbulo, m.
lobe, lōb, s. lóbulo, m.
lobster, *lŏb'stŭr,* s. langosta, f.
local, lō'kăl, a. local.
locality, *lōkăl'itē,* s. localidad, f.
localize, *lō'kălīz,* v. a. localizar.
loch, lŏk, s. lago, m. (en Escocia).
lock, lŏk, s. cerradura, cerraja, f.; llave (de
arma de fuego), f.; cerca, f.; vedija de
lana, f.; —, v. a. cerrar; estar una cosa
cerrada; **to — one out,** cerrar la puerta á
uno para que no entre.
locker, —*ŭr,* s. armario, m. [dallón, m.
locket, —*ĕt,* s. broche, corchete, m.; me-
lock-jaw, —*jä,* s. trismo, m.
lock-out, —*ōŭt,* s. cesación del trabajo, f.
locksmith, —*smith,* s. cerrajero, m.
locomotion, *lōkōmō'shŭn,* s. locomoción, f.
locomotive, *lōkōmō'tiv,* a. movible; —, s.
locomotora, f.
locust, lō'kŭst, s. langosta, f.
lodge, lŏj, s. casa de guarda en el bosque,
f.; casita pequeña, f.; —, v. a. alojar; fijar
en la memoria; —, v. n. residir, habitar.
lodger, —*ŭr,* s. huésped, inquilino, m.
lodging, *lŏj'ing,* s. yáciga, f.; —s, pl. casa,
habitación, f.
lodging-house, —*hōŭs,* s. posada, f.
loft, lŏft, s. piso, m.; desván, m.
loftiness, —*inēs,* s. altura, f.; sublimidad,
f.; soberbia, f.
lofty, —*ē,* a. alto; sublime; altivo.
log, lŏg, s. leño, trozo de árbol, m.; (mar.)
barquilla, f. [gación, m.
log-book, —*bŭk,* s. (mar.) diario de navi-
loggerhead, —*gŭrhĕd,* s. zote, m.
logic, lŏj'ik, s. lógica, f.
logical, —*ăl,* a. lógico.
logician, *lōjish'ăn,* s. lógico, m.
log-line, *lŏg'līn,* s. (mar.) corredera, f.
logwood, —*wŭd,* s. palo de Campeche, m.
loin, lŏin, s. lomo, m.; —s, pl. lomos, m. pl.
loiter, *lŏi'tŭr,* v. n. haraganear.
loiterer, —*ŭr,* s. haragán, holgazán, m.
loll, lŏl, v. a. tender; —, v. n. apoyarse,
recostarse. [solitario; solo.
lone(ly), lōn'(lē), **lonesome,** *lōn'sŭm,* a.
loneliness, —*linēs,* s. soledad, f.]
long, lŏng, a. largo; —, ad. á una gran distancia; mucho; —, v. n. desear con vehemencia, anhelar.
longevity, *lŏnjĕv'itē,* s. longevidad, duración larga de la vida. [helo, m.
longing, *lŏng'ing,* s. deseo vehemente, an-
longitude, *lŏn'jitūd,* s. longitud, f. [nal.
longitudinal, *lŏnjitū'dinăl,* a. longitudi-

loo, lō, s. especie de juego de naipes.
look, lŭk, v. a. & n. mirar, considerar,
pensar, contemplar; esperar; parecer;
tener traza de; buscar; —, s. aspecto, m.;
mirada, f.
looking-glass, —*inglăs,* s. espejo, m.
look-out, —*ōŭt,* s. (mil.) centinela, f.;
(mar.) vigía, f. [mar.
loom, lōm, s. telar, m.; —, v. n. (mar.) aso-
loop, lōp, s. ojal, m.; presilla, f. [f.
loop-hole, —*hōl,* s. tronera, f.; escapatoria,
loose, lōs, a. suelto, desatado; flojo; suelto
de vientre; vago, relajado; disoluto; des-
enredado; descuidado; —ly, ad. suelta-
mente; —, **loosen,** —*n,* v. a. aflojar,
laxar, desliar. [f.; flujo de vientre, m.
looseness, —*nēs,* s. flojedad, f.; relajación,
loot, lōt, v. a. saquear.
loo-table, —*tābl,* s. velador, m.
lop, lŏp, v. a. desmochar.
lop-eared, —*ērd,* a. con las orejas caídas.
lop-sided, —*sidĕd,* a. (vulg.) ladeado, sesgado. [dor.
loquacious, *lōkwā'shŭs,* a. locuaz, charla-
loquacity, *lōkwăs'itē,* s. locuacidad, charla, garrulidad, f.
Lord, lŏrd, s. señor, m.; Dios, m.; amo,
dueño, m.; Lord, m.; — Mayor, Corregidor de Londres, m.; —, v. n. señorear, dominar. [f.; orgullo, m.
lordliness, —*inēs,* s. señorío, m.; altivez,
lordling, —*ling,* s. lord pequeño, m.
lordly, —*lē,* a. señoril; orgulloso, imperioso; —, ad. imperiosamente, altivamente.
Lordship, —*ship,* s. Excelencia, Señoría, f.
lore, lŏr, s. lección, doctrina, instrucción, f.
lose, lōz, v. a. perder; disipar, malgastar;
—, v. n. perderse, decaer.
loss, lŏs, s. pérdida, f.; daño, m.; **to be**
at a —, desatinar. [porción, f.
lot, lŏt, s. suerte, f.; lote, m.; cuota, f.;
loth, lōth, a. repugnante, disgustado.
lotion, lō'shŭn, s. loción, ablución, f.
lottery, *lŏt'tŭrē,* s. lotería, rifa, f.
loud, lŏŭd, a. ruidoso, alto; clamoroso;
—ly, ad. altamente. [m.
loudness, —*nēs,* s. tono elevado, m.; ruido,
lounge, lŏŭnj, v. n. haraganear.
louse, lŏŭs, (pl. **lice),** s. piojo, m.
lousy, *lŏŭ'zē,* a. piojoso; miserable, vil.
lout, lŏŭt, s. patán, rústico, zafio, m.
loutish, —*ish,* a. rústico, tosco.
lovable, *lŭv'ăbl,* a. amable.
love, lŭv, s. amor, cariño, m.; galanteo,
m.; **to fall in —,** enamorarse; —, v. a.
amar; gustar. [amorosa, f.
love-letter, —*lĕttŭr,* s. esquela, carta
loveliness, —*linēs,* s. amabilidad, f.;
agrado, m.; belleza, f.
lovely, —*lē,* a. amable, hermoso.
lover, —*ŭr,* s. amante, galán, cortejo, m.
love-sick, —*sik,* a. enamorado; herido de
amor. [afectuosamente.
loving, —*ing,* p. & a. aficionado; —ly, ad.
loving-kindness, —*kindnēs,* s. gracia,
f., afecto, m.
low, lō, a. bajo, pequeño; hondo; abatido;
vil; —, ad. á precio bajo; vilmente.

low, *ló*, v. n. mugir.

lower, *ló'ár*, a. más bajo; —, v. a. abajar, humillar, disminuir; —, v. n. disminuirse; encapotarse.

lowering, *ló'áring*, a. sombrío.

lowermost, *ló'ármóst*, **lowest**, *ló'ést*, a. más bajo, ínfimo.

lowing, *ló'ing*, s. mugido, m.

lowland, *-lánd*, s. tierra baja, f. [f.

lowliness, *-línés*, s. bajeza, f.; humildad,

lowly, *-lé*, a. humilde; vil; —, ad. humildemente; vilmente.

lowness, *-nés*, s. bajeza, f.

lowry, *-ré*, s. (rail.) lorri, truck, m.

low-water, *-wátár*, s. baja mar, f.

loyal, *ló'ál*, a. leal, fiel; **-ly**, ad. lealmente.

loyalty, *-té*, s. lealdad, f.; fidelidad, f.

lozenge, *lóz'énj*, s. rombo, m.; pastilla de boca, f.

lubber, *láb'bár*, s. bobo, m.; bigardo, m.

lubberly, *-lé*, a. perezoso, bigardo.

lubricate, *ló'brikát*, v. a. untar con materias crasas.

lucid, *ló'sid*, a. luciente, luminoso.

lucidity, *lósid'ité*, s. esplendor, resplandor, m. [pajuela química, f.

Lucifer, *ló'sifár*, s. Lucero, m.; -(-match),

luck, *lák*, s. acaso, m.; fortuna, f.

luckily, *-ilé*, ad. por fortuna, afortunadamente.

luckless, *-lés*, a. infeliz, desventurado.

lucky, *-é*, a. afortunado, feliz, venturoso.

lucrative, *ló'krátiv*, a. lucrativo.

lucre, *ló'kár*, s. lucro, m.; ganancia, f.

lucubration, *lókúbrá'shán*, s. lucubración, f. [burlescamente.

ludicrous, *ló'dikrás*, a. burlesco; **-ly**, ad.

luff, *láf*, v. a. (mar.) ceñir el viento.

lug, *lág*, v. a. tirar; (mar.) halar.

luggage, *lág'gáj*, s. baggage, m.; (rail.) bulto, equipaje, m.; **small —**, (rail.) bultos á la mano, m. pl.

luggage-office, *-óffis*, s. (rail.) factoría, f.; equipajes, m. pl. [m.

luggage-ticket, *-tikkét*, s. (rail.) talón,

luggage-train, *-trán*, s. (rail.) tren de mercancías, f.

luggage-van, *-ván*, **luggage-waggon**, *-vágón*, s. (rail.) vagón completo, vagón de mercancías, m.

luger, *lág'gár*, s. lugre, m.

lugubrious, *lógú'briás*, a. lúgubre, triste.

lukewarm, *lók'wárm*, a. tibio; **-ly**, ad. tibiamente. [tar.

lull, *lál*, v. a. arrullar; adormecer; aquietar.

lullaby, *-lábi*, s. arrullo, m.

lumbago, *lámbá'gó*, s. lumbago, m.

lumber-room, *lám'bárróm*, s. trastera, f.

luminary, *ló'minárė*, s. luminar, m.; lumbrera, f. [ciente.

luminous, *-nás*, a. luminoso, resplandeciente.

lump, *lámp*, s. masa informe, f.; **by the —**, por grueso ó por junto; —, v. a. tomar alguna cosa por junto ó por mayor.

lunacy, *ló'násé*, s. locura, f., frenesí, m.

lunar, *-nár*, a. lunar; **- caustic**, s. nitrato de plata, m. [tástico.

lunatic, *-nátik*, a. lunático, frenético; fan-

lunch, *lánsh*, **luncheon**, *lánsh'án*, s. merienda, f.

lunette, *lánét'*, s. (mil.)media luna, f.

lung, *láng*, **lungs**, *lángz*, pl. pulmones, m.

lurch, *lártsh*, s. abandono, m. [m. pl.

lure, *lór*, s. señuelo, m., añagaza, f.; cebo, m.; —, v. a. atraer, inducir.

lurk, *lárk*, v. n. espiar, ponerse en acecho.

lurking-place, *-ingplás*, s. escondrijo, m.; guarida, f.

luscious, *lásh'ás*, a. dulzazo; delicioso.

lust, *lást*, s. lujuria, sensualidad, f.; concupiscencia, f.; —, v. n. lujuriar.

lustful, *-fúl*, a. lujurioso, voluptuoso; **-ly**, ad. lujuriosamente.

lustily, *lás'tilé*, ad. vigorosamente.

lustiness, *-tinés*, s. vigor, m.; robustez, f.

lustre, *-tár*, s. lustre, m.; brillantez, f.

lustring, *-tring*, s. lustrina, f. (tela).

lusty, *-té*, a. fuerte, vigoroso.

lute, *lót*, s. laúd, m.; luten, m.

Lutheran, *ló'thárán*, s. luterano, m.

luxuriance, *lágzú'riáns*, s. exuberancia, superabundancia, f. [abundante.

luxuriant, *-riánt*, a. exuberante, super-

luxuriate, *-riát*, v. n. crecer con exuberancia. [te; **-ly**, ad. voluptuosamente.

luxurious, *-riás*, a. lujurioso; exuberan-

luxury, *láks'úrė*, s. lujuria, voluptuosidad, f.; exuberancia, f.

lyceum, *lisé'ám*, s. liceo, m.

lye(-washing), *li('wóshing*), s. lejía, f.

lying, *li'ing*, s. acto de mentir, m.; mentira, f. [tira, f.

lying-in, *-in*, s. parto, m.

lymph, *limf*, s. linfa, f.

lymphatic, *limfát'ik*, a. linfático.

lynch, *lintsh*, v. a. ajusticiar al reo en el acto el populacho (am.).

lynx, *lingks*, s. lince, m.

lyre, *lir*, s. lira, f.

lyric(al), *lir'ik(ál*), a. lírico.

M.

macadamize, *mákád'ámiz*, v. a. empedrar un camino al estilo de MacAdam.

macaroni, *mákáró'né*, s. macarones, m.pl.

macaroon, *mákáró'n*, s. almendrado, m.

mace, *más*, s. maza, f.; macis, f.

macerate, *más'árát*, v.a. macerar; mortificar el cuerpo.

machinate, *mák'inát*, v. n. maquinar.

machination, *mákiná'shán*, s. maquinación, trama, f.

machine, *máshén'*, s. máquina, f.

machinery, *-árė*, s. maquinaria, mecánica, f.

machinist, *-ist*, s. maquinista, m.

mackerel, *mák'árél*, s. escombro, m. (pez).

mackintosh, *mák'intósh*, s. sobretodo impermeable, m. [sato.

mad, *mád*, a. loco, furioso, rabioso, insensato.

mad-cap, *mád'káp*, s. locarias, orate, m.

madden, *-dn*, v. a. enloquecer.

madder, *-dár*, s. (bot.) rubia, f.

mad-house, *–hŏŭs,* s. casa de locos, f.

madly, *–lĭ,* ad. furiosamente; como un loco.

madman, *–măn,* s. loco, maniático, m.

madness, *–nĕs,* s. locura, manía, f.; furor, m. [(mar.) Santabárbara, f.

magazine, *măgăzēn´,* s. almacén, m.;

maggot, *măg´gŏt,* s. gusano, m.; capricho, m.

magic, *măj´ĭk,* s. magia negra, f.; –, a. mágico; –ally, ad. mágicamente.

magician, *măjĭsh´ăn,* s. mago, nigromante, m.

magisterial, *măjĭstē´rĭăl,* a. magistral; imperioso; –ly, ad. magistralmente.

magistracy, *măj´ĭstrăsĭ,* s. magistratura, f.

magistrate, *–strāt,* s. magistrado, m.

magnanimity, *măgnănĭm´ĭtĭ,* s. magnanimidad, f.

magnanimous, *măgnăn´ĭmŭs,* a. magnánimo; –ly, ad. magnánimamente. [f.

magnet, *măg´nĕt,* s. imán, m., piedra imán.

magnetic(al), *măgnĕt´ĭk(ăl),* a. magnético.

magnetism, *măg´nĕtĭzm,* s. magnetismo, m. [cencia, f.

magnificence, *măgnĭf´ĭsĕns,* s. magnifi-

magnificent, *–ĭsĕnt,* a. magnífico; –ly, ad. pomposamente. [altar, exagerar.

magnify, *măg´nĭfī,* v. a. magnificar; ex-

magnitude, *–nĭtūd,* s. magnitud, grandeza, f.

magpie, *măg´pī,* s. urraca, picaza, f.

mahogany, *măhŏg´ănĭ,* s. caoba, caobana, f. [moza, criada, f.

maid(en), *mād´(n),* s. doncella, joven, f.;

maiden, *–n,* a. virgíneo, virginal; nuevo, intacto. [dad, f.

maidenhood, *–hŭd,* s. doncellez, virgini-

maidenly, *–lĭ,* a. virginal, púdico.

maiden-speech, *–spētsh,* s. primer discurso de un diputado en el parlamento, m.

mail, *māl,* s. cota de malla, f.; mala, balija, f.

mail-coach, *–kōtsh,* s. diligencia, f.

mail-train, *–trān,* s. (rail.) tren correo, m.

maim, *mām,* v. a. mutilar; estropear; –, s. mutilación, f.

main, *mān,* a. principal; esencial; –, s. grueso, m.; océano, m., alta mar, f.; fuerza, f.; in the –, en general.

mainland, *–lănd,* s. continente, m.

main-line, *–lĭn,* s. (rail.) línea principal, f., tronco, m. [todo.

mainly, *–lĭ,* ad. principalmente, sobre

main-mast, *–măst,* s. palo mayor de un navío, m. [sostener.

maintain, *māntān´,* v. a. & n. mantener,

maintenance, *mān´tĕnăns,* s. mantenimiento, m.; protección, f.; sustento, m.

maize, *māz,* s. maíz, trigo de las Indias ó de la Turquía, m.

majestic(al), *măjĕs´tĭk(ăl),* a. majestuoso; grande; –ally, ad. majestuosamente.

majesty, *măj´ĕstĭ,* s. majestad, f.

major, *mā´jŭr,* a. mayor; –, s. (mil.) sargento mayor, m.; primera proposición de un silogismo, f.

majority, *măjŏr´ĭtĭ,* s. mayoría, f.; pluralidad, f.; (mil.) sargentía mayor, f.

make, *māk,* v. a. hacer, crear, producir; formar, fabricar; ejecutar; obligar, forzar; –, v. n. hacerse; ir, encaminarse; –, s. hechura, forma, figura, f.

make-believe, *–bēlēv´,* s. disimulo, m.; pretexto, m. [dor, m.

makepeace, *–pēs,* s. pacificador, conciliador, m.

makeshift, *–shĭft,* s. expediente, m.; lo pésimo. [peso, m.

make-weight, *–wāt,* s. complemento de

making, *–ĭng,* s. composición, f.; estructura, hechura, f.

malady, *măl´ădĭ,* s. enfermedad, f.

malapert, *măl´ăpĕrt,* a. desvergonzado.

malaria, *mălā´rĭă,* s. aire infecto, m.

malcontent, *măl´kŏntĕnt,* a. & s. malcontento (m.).

male, *māl,* a. masculino; –, s. macho, m.

malediction, *mălĕdĭk´shŭn,* s. maldición, f.

malefactor, *–făk´tŭr,* s. malhechor, m.

maleficent, *–f´ĭsĕnt,* a. maléfico, maligno.

malevolence, *mălĕv´ŏlĕns,* s. malevolencia, f. [malignamente.

malevolent, *–ŏlĕnt,* a. malévolo; –ly, ad.

malice, *măl´ĭs,* s. malicia, f.

malicious, *mălĭsh´ŭs,* a. malicioso; –ly, ad. maliciosamente.

malign, *mălīn´,* a. maligno; contagioso; –, v. a. envidiar; dañar.

malignant, *mălĭg´nănt,* a. maligno; –ly, ad. malignamente.

malignity, *–nĭtĭ,* s. malignidad, f.

malleable, *măl´lĕăbl,* a. maleable.

mallet, *măl´ĕt,* s. mazo, m.

mallows, *măl´lōz,* s. (bot.) malva, f.

malmsey, *măm´zĕ,* s. malvasía, f.

malpractice, *mălprăk´tĭs,* s. malversación, f.; maltrato, m. [la cerveza, f.

malt, *mălt,* s. cebada preparada para hacer

maltreat, *măltrēt´,* v. a. maltratar.

maltster, *mălt´stŭr,* s. obrero que prepara la cebada para hacer cerveza, m.

mam(ma), *măm(mä),* s. mamá, f.

man, *măn,* s. hombre, m.; marido, m.; criado, m.; peón, m.; –of war, navío de guerra, m.; –to–, el uno como el otro; –, v. a. (mar.) tripular, armar.

manacle, *măn´ăkl,* s. manilla, f.; –s, pl. esposas, f. pl.; –, v. a. maniatar.

manage, *măn´dj,* v. a. & n. manejar, gobernar, administrar; tomar sus disposiciones.

manageable, *–ăbl,* a. manejable; dócil, tratable. [ministración, f.; conducta, f.

management, *–mĕnt,* s. manejo, m.; ad-

manager, *–ŭr,* s. administrador, director, m.; hombre económico, m. [sión, f.

mandate, *măn´dāt,* s. mandato, m.; com-

mandatory, *măn´dătŭrĭ,* s. mandatario, m.

mandrake, *măn´drāk,* s. (bot.) mandrágora, f.

mane, *mān,* s. crines del caballo, f. pl.

man-eater, *măn´ētĕr,* s. caribe, antropófago, m. [valerosamente.

manful, *–fŭl,* a. bravo, valiente; –ly, ad.

mange, *mănj,* s. roña, sarna perruna, f.

manger, *măn´jŭr,* s. pesebre, m.

mangle, *măng´gl,* s. calandria, f.; –, v. a. pasar por la calandria; mutilar.

mangy, *măn'jĭ*, a. sarnoso. [m.

manhood, *măn'hŭd*, s. edad viril, f.; valor

mania, *mā'nĭă*, s. manía, f. [maniaco.

maniac(al), *mā'nĭăk(ăl)*, a. maniático,

manifest, *măn'ĭfĕst*, a. manifiesto, patente;
—, s. manifiesto, m.; —, v. a. manifestar.

manifestation, *măn'ĭfĕstā'shŭn*, s. manifestación, f.

manifold, *măn'ĭfŏld*, a. muchos, varios.

manikin, *măn'ĭkĭn*, s. hombrecillo, m.

manipulate, *mănĭp'ŭlāt*, v. a. manejar.

manipulation, *mănĭpŭlā'shŭn*, s. manipulación, f. [humano, m.

mankind, *măn'kīnd*, s. género ó linaje

manlike, *—līk*, a. varonil.

manliness, *—lĭnĕs*, s. valentía, f.; valor, m.

manly, *—lĭ*, a. varonil, valeroso.

man-midwife, *—mĭdwīf*, s. comadrón, partero, m.

manner, *măn'nĕr*, s. manera, f.; modo, m.; forma, f.; método, m.; maña, f.; hábito, m.; moda, f.; especie, f.; —s, pl. modales, m. pl.; urbanidad, crianza, f.

manœuvre, *mănöö'vŭr*, s. maniobra, f.; —, v. n. maniobrar.

manor, *măn'ŭr*, s. señorío, m.; feudo, m.

manorial, *mănō'rĭăl*, a. señorial.

mansion, *măn'shŭn*, s. mansión, morada, residencia, f. [sin premeditación), m.

manslaughter, *măn'slătĕr*, s. homicidio

mantle, *măn'tl*, s. campana de chimenea, f.

mantle-piece, *—pēs*, s. repisa de chimenea.

manual, *măn'ŭăl*, a. & s. manual (m.). [f.

manufactory, *mănŭfăk'tŭrĕ*, s. fábrica, manufactura, f.

manufacture, *—tŭr*, s. manufactura, f.; artefacto, m.; —, v. a. fabricar, manufacturar.

manufacturer, *—ŭr*, s. fabricante, m.

manumission, *mănŭmĭsh'ŭn*, s. manumisión, f.

manure, *mănūr'*, s. abono, m.; estiércol, m.; fiemo, m.; —, v. a. abonar, estercolar, cultivar. [m.

manuscript, *măn'ŭskrĭpt*, s. manuscrito,

many, *mĕn'ĭ*, a. muchos, muchas; — a time, muchas veces; how —? ¿ cuántos ? as — as, tantos como.

map, *măp*, s. mapa, f. (carta geográfica); —, v. a. delinear mapas.

maple, *mā'pl*, s. arce, m. (plátano falso).

mar, *mār*, v. a. dañar, corromper.

marauder, *mărăw'dŭr*, s. merodeador, m.

marble, *mār'bl*, s. mármol, m.; bolilla de mármol, f., —, a. marmóreo; —, v. a. jaspear.

March, *mārtsh*, s. marzo, m. (mes).

march, —, s. marcha, f.; —, v. n. marchar, caminar. [f.

marchioness, *mār'tshŏnĕs*, s. marquesa,

mare, *mār*, s. yegua, f.

margin, *mār'jĭn*, s. margen, m. & f., borde, m.; orilla, f.; —, v. a. marginar.

marginal, *—ăl*, a. marginal.

marigold, *măr'ĭgŏld*, s. (bot.) caléndula, f.

marine, *mărēn'*, a. marino; —, s. marina, f.; soldado de marina, m.

mariner, *măr'ĭnĕr*, s. marinero, m.

marital, *măr'ĭtăl*, a. marital.

maritime, *măr'ĭtĭm*, a. marítimo, naval.

marjoram, *mār'jŏrăm*, s. mejorana, f.

mar-joy, *mār'jŏĭ*, s. derramasolaces, m.

mark, *mārk*, s. marca, f.; señal, nota, f.; blanco, m.; —, v. a. marcar; —, v. n. advertir. [compra, f.

market, *mār'kĕt*, s. mercado, m.; venta,

marketable, *—bl*, a. común, corriente.

marksman, *mārks'măn*, s. tirador, m.

marl, *mārl*, s. marga, f.; —, v. a. margar.

marl-pit, *—pĭt*, s. marguera, f.

marly, *—ĭ*, a. margoso.

marmalade, *mār'mălād*, s. mermelada, f.

marmoset, *mār'mŏzĕt*, s. mico pequeño, m.

marmot, *mār'mŏt*, s. marmota, f.

maroon, *mărōn'*, s. castaña, f.

mar-plot, *mār'plŏt*, s. travieso, m.

marquee, *mārkēe'*, s. marquesina, f.

marquess, *mār'kwĕs*, s. marqués, f.

marquetry, *—kĕtrĕ*, s. marquetería, f.

marquis, *—kwĭs*, s. marqués, m. [tea, f.

marquisate, *—kwĭzăt*, s. marquesado, m.

marriage, *măr'rĭj*, s. maridaje, m.; matrimonio, m.; casamiento, m.

marriageable, *—ăbl*, a. casadero, núbil.

marriage-articles, *—ār'tĭklz*, s. pl., —settlement, *—sĕt'tlmĕnt*, s. contrato matrimonial, m.

married, *măr'rĭd*, a. casado, conyugal.

narrow, *măr'rō*, s. caña, m.; medula, f.

marry, *măr'rĭ*, v. n. casar(se).

marsh, *mārsh*, s. pantano, m.; laguna, f.

marshal, *mār'shăl*, s. mariscal, m.

marshy, *mār'shĭ*, a. pantanoso.

mart, *mārt*, s. emporio, m.; comercio, m.;

marten, *mār'tĕn*, s. marta, f. [feria, f.

martial, *mār'shăl*, a. marcial, guerrero; — law, s. derecho militar, m. [ún, m.

Martinmas, *mār'tĭnmăs*, s. día de S. Martín, m.

martyr, *mār'tŭr*, s. mártir, m.

martyrdom, *—dăm*, s. martirio, m.

marvel, *mār'vĕl*, s. maravilla, f.; —, v. n. maravillar(se). [maravillosamente.

marvellous, *—lŭs*, a. maravilloso; —ly, ad.

masculine, *măs'kŭlĭn*, a. masculino, varonil. [v. a. amasar; mezclar.

mash, *măsh*, s. mezcla, f.; fárrago, m.; —;

mask, *măsk*, s. máscara, f.; pretexto, color, m.; —, v. a. enmascarar; disimular, ocultar; —, v. n. andar enmascarado.

masker, *—ŭr*, s. el ó la que se enmascara.

mason, *mā'sn*, s. albañil, m.

masonry, *—rĕ*, s. albañilería, f.

masquerade, *măskĕrād'*, s. mascarada, f.

masquerader, *—ŭr*, s. máscara, m. & f.

mass, *măs*, s. masa, f.; misa, f.; montón, m.

massacre, *măs'săkŭr*, s. carnicería, matanza, f.; —, v. a. matar atrozmente, hacer una carnicería.

massive, *măs'sĭv*, a. macizo, sólido.

mast, *măst*, s. árbol de navío, palo, m.; fabuco, m.; —, v. a. arbolar un palo.

master, *măs'tŭr*, s. amo, dueño, m.; maestro, m.; señor, m.; señorito, m.; (mar.) maestre, patrón, m.; —, v. a. domar, domeñar; gobernar, dominar.

master-hand, *—hănd*, s. mano maestra, maestría, f.

masterly, *—lĭ*, a. imperioso, despótico; —, ad. con maestría.

master-piece, -pés, s. obra ó pieza maestra, f.

master-stroke, -strók, master-touch, -tútsh, s. golpe de maestro ó diestro, m.

mastery, -i, s. superioridad, maestría, f.

masticate, más'tikát, v. a. mascar, masticar.

mastiff, más'tif, s. mastín, m. [car.

mat, mát, s. estera, esterilla, f.; (mar.) palleta, f.; —, v. a. esterar.

match, mátsh, s. mecha, pajuela, f.; fósforo, m.; partido, m.; contrincante, m.; pareja, f.; casamiento, m.; combate, m.; —, v. a. igualar; aparear; casar; —, v. n. hermanarse.

match-box, -bóks, s. cajita de fósforos, f.

matchless, -lés, a. incomparable, sin par.

match-maker, -mákdr, s. casamentero, m.

mate, mát, s. consorte, m.; compañero, m.; compañera, f.; (mar.) piloto, m.; —, v. a. desposar; igualar. [mente).

material, máti'ridl, a. -ly, ad. material.

materialism, -lizm, s. materialismo, m.

maternal, mátúr'ndl, a. maternal, materno.

maternity, -nitē, s. maternidad, f.

mathematic(al), máthēmát'ik(dl), a. matemático; -ly, ad. matemáticamente.

mathematician, máthēmátish'dn, s. matemático, m. [máticas, f. pl.

mathematics, máthēmát'iks, s. pl. matemáticas.

matins, mát'inz, s. pl. maitines, m. pl.

matricide, mát'risid, s. matricidio, m.; matricida, m.

matriculate, mátrik'ûlát, v. a. matricular.

matriculation, mátrikûlá'shûn, s. matriculación, f. [nial, marital.

matrimonial, mátrimō'nidl, a. matrimonial.

matrimony, mát'rimone, s. matrimonio, casamiento, m.

matron, má'trón, s. matrona, f. [grave.

matronly, -lē, a. como matrona, seria.

matter, mát'tär, s. materia, substancia material, f.; asunto, objeto, m.; cuestión, importancia, f.; it is no —, no importa; what is the —? ¿de qué se trata? a — of fact, un hecho; —, v. n. importar.

mattings, mát'tings, s. pl. esteras, f. pl.

mattock, -tūk, s. azadón de peto, m.

mattress, -trés, s. colchón, m.

mature, mátúr, a. maduro; juicioso; —, v. a. madurar.

maturity, mátú'ritē, s. madurez, f.

maul, mól, v. a. apalear, maltratar á golpes.

maul-stick, -stík, s. tiento, m.

Maundy-Thursday, mán'delhúrz'dá, s. Jueves Santo, m.

mausoleum, másolē'ûm, s. mausoleo, m.

maw, má, s. cuajar, m.; molleja de las aves, f. [bundo.

mawkish, -kish, a. fastidioso, nauseabundo.

may, má, v. n. ir. poder; —be, acaso, quizá.

May, -, s. mayo, m. (mes).

May-day, -dá, s. día primero de mayo, m.

May-pole, -pól, s. mayo (árbol), m.

mayor, má'ūr, s. corregidor, m.

mayoralty, -áltē, s. corregimiento, m.

mayoress, -ēs, s. corregidora, f.

maze, máz, s. laberinto, m.; perplejidad, f.

mazy, má'zē, a. confuso, embrollado.

me, mē, pn. me.

mead, mēd, s. aguamiel, f.

meadow, mēd'ō, s. pradería, f.; prado, m.

meagre, mē'gūr, a. magro; flaco; -ly, ad. pobremente, estérilmente. [f.

meagreness, -nēs, s. flaqueza, f.; escasez.

meal, mēl, s. comida, f.; harina, f.

mealy, -ē, a. harinoso.

mean, mēn, s. bajo, vil, despreciable; abatido; mediocre; in the —time, —while, ínterin, mientras tanto; —, s. medio, m.; expediente, m.; —s, pl. medios, m. pl.; caudal, m.; —, v. a. & n. significar; hacer intención, pensar. [tortuoso, m.

meander, mēán'dūr, s. laberinto, camino

meaning, mēn'ing, s. intención, f.; inteligencia, f.; sentido, significado, m.

meanly, mēn'lē, ad. mediocremente; pobremente; vilmente.

meanness, -nēs, s. bajeza, f.; pobreza, f.; mezquindad, f.; mediocridad, f.

measles, mē'zlz, s. pl. sarampión, m.

measurable, mēzh'ûrdbl, a. mensurable.

measure, mēzh'ûr, s. medida, f.; (mus.) compás, m.; —, v. a. medir; ajustar.

measurement, -mēnt, s. medición, f.

measurer, -ūr, s. medidor, m.

meat, mēt, s. carne, f.; vianda, f.

mechanic, mēkán'ik, s. mecánico, m.

mechanical, -dl, a. mecánico; servil, bajo; -ly, ad. mecánicamente.

mechanician, mēkánish'dn, mechanist, mēk'ánist, s. mecánico, maquinista, m.

mechanics, mēkán'iks, s. pl. mecánica, f.

mechanism, mēk'ánizm, s. mecanismo, m.

medal, mēd'dl, s. medalla, f.; moneda antigua, f.

medallion, mēdál'yûn, s. medallón, m.

meddle, mēd'l, v. n. entremeterse.

meddler, -ūr, s. entremetido, m.

mediate, mē'diát, v. n. mediar.

mediation, mēdiá'shûn, s. mediación, interposición, f.

medical, mēd'ikdl, a. médico. [m.

medicament, -ikámēnt, s. medicamento, m.

medicate, -ikát, v. a. medicinar.

medicinal, mēdis'indl, a. medicinal.

medicine, mēd'isin, s. medicina, f.; medicamento, m. [f.

mediocrity, mēdiōk'ritē, s. mediocridad, f.

meditate, mēd'itát, v. a. meditar; idear.

meditation, mēditá'shûn, s. meditación, f.

meditative, mēd'itátiv, a. meditativo, contemplativo. [terráneo.

mediterranean, mēditērrá'nēân, a. mediterráneo.

medium, mē'diûm, s. medio, m.; expediente, m.; moderación, f.

medlar, mēd'lär, s. níspero, m.; níspola, f.

medley, mēd'lē, s. miscelánea, mezcla, m.

meek, mēk, a. mego, apacible; dulce; -ly, ad. suavemente.

meekness, -nēs, s. suavidad, f.; modestia, f.; dulzura, f. [f.

meerschaum, mär'shâum, s. piedra loca, f.

meet, mēt, v. a. encontrar; convocar; —, v. n. encontrarse; juntarse; —, a. idóneo, propio.

meeting, -ing, s. asamblea, f.; congreso, m.; entrevista, f.; conventículo, m.

melancholy, *mĕl'ăngkŏlĕ,* s. melancolía, f.; –, a. melancólico.

mellifluous, *mĕllĭf'lŭăs,* a. melifluo.

mellow, *mĕl'lō,* a. maduro, meloso; tierno; –, v. a. (& n.) madurar(se).

mellowness, *–nĕs,* s. madurez, f.

melodious, *mĕlō'dĭŭs,* a. melodioso **-ly,** ad. melodiosamente.

melody, *mĕl'ŏdĕ,* s. melodía, f.

melon, *mĕl'ŏn,* s. melón, m.

melt, *mĕlt,* v. a. derretir, fundir; liquidar; enternecer; –, v. n. derretirse, liquidarse.

member, *mĕm'bŭr,* s. miembro, m.; parte, f.; individuo, m.

membrane, *mĕm'brăn,* s. membrana, f.

memento, *mĕmĕn'tō,* s. memento, m.

memoir, *mĕm'wŏir,* s. memoria, relación narrativa, f. [memorando.

memorable, *mĕm'ŏrăbl,* a. memorable,

memorably, *–lĕ,* ad. memorablemente.

memorandum, *mĕmŏrăn'dŭm,* memorándum, m. [morial, m.

memorial, *mĕmō'rĭăl,* s. memoria, f.;

memory, *mĕm'ŏrĕ,* s. memoria, f.; recuerdo, m. [amenazar.

menace, *mĕn'ăs,* s. amenaza, f.; –, v. a.

menagery, *mĕnăzh'ŭrĕ,* s. casa de fieras ó animales raros, f.

mend, *mĕnd,* v. a. reparar, remendar, retocar; mejorar; corregir.

mendacious, *mĕndā'shŭs,* a. mendoso.

mendacity, *mĕndăs'ĭtĕ,* s. falsedad, mentira, f.

mendicancy, *mĕn'dĭkănsĕ,* **mendicity,** *mĕndĭs'ĭtĕ,* s. mendiguez, mendicidad, f.

mendicant, *–dĭkănt,* a. & s. mendicante

mendicate, *–dĭkāt,* v. a. mendigar. [(m.).

menial, *mē'nĭăl,* a. servil, doméstico.

menstruation, *mĕnstrŭā'shŭn,* s. menstruo, m. [f.

mensuration, *mĕnsŭrā'shŭn,* s. medición,

mental, *mĕn'tăl,* a. mental, intelectual; **-ly,** ad. mentalmente, intelectualmente.

mention, *mĕn'shŭn,* s. mención, f., –, v. a. mencionar.

Mentor, *mĕn'tŏr,* s. ayo, guía, m.

mephitic(al), *mĕfĭt'ĭk(ăl),* a. mefítico.

mercantile, *mŭr'kăntĭl,* a. mercantil.

mercenary, *mŭr'sĕnărĕ,* a. & s. mercenario (m.).

mercer, *mŭr'sŭr,* s. mercero, sedero, m.

mercery, *–ĕ,* s. mercería, sedería, f.

merchandise, *mŭr'tshăndĭz,* s. mercancía, f.

merchant, *mŭr'tshănt,* s. comerciante, m.

merchantman, *–măn,* s. navío mercantil, m. [-ly, ad. misericordiosamente.

merciful, *mŭr'sĭfŭl,* a. misericordioso;

merciless, *–lĕs,* a. duro de corazón, inhumano; **-ly,** ad. cruelmente.

mercurial, *mŭrkū'rĭăl,* a. vivo, activo; mercurial.

mercury, *mŭr'kŭrĕ,* s. mercurio, m.

mercy, *mŭr'sĕ,* s. misericordia, piedad, f.; perdón, m. [mente; puramente.

mere, *mēr,* a. mero, puro, **-ly,** ad. simple-

meretricious, *mĕrĕtrĭsh'ŭs,* a. meretricio.

merge, *mŭrj,* v. a. sumergir. [cio.

meridian, *mĕrĭd'ĭăn,* s. mediodía, m., meridiano, m.

meridional, *–ĭōnăl,* a. meridional.

merit, *mĕr'ĭt,* s. mérito, m.; –, v. a. merecer.

meritorious, *mĕrĭtō'rĭŭs,* a. meritorio; **-ly,** ad. meritoriamente.

mermaid, *mŭr'mād,* s. sirena, f.

merrily, *mĕr'rĭlĕ,* ad. alegremente.

merriment, *mĕr'rĭmĕnt,* s. diversión, f.; regocijo, m.

merry, *mĕr'rĕ,* a. alegre, jovial, festivo.

Merry-Andrew, *–ăn'drō,* s. bufón, chulo, m.

mesh, *mĕsh,* s. malla, f. [chulo, m.

Mesmerism, *mĕs'mŭrĭzm,* s. mesmerismo, f. [ción, f.

mess, *mĕs,* s. plato, m.; rancho, m.; por-

message, *–sāj,* s. mensaje, m.

messenger, *–sĕnjŭr,* s. mensajero, m.

mess-mate, *–māt,* s. comensal, m.

messuage, *–swĕj,* s. menaje, ajuar de casa, m.; habitación, f. [espíritu, m.

metal, *mĕt'ăl,* s. metal, m.; (fig.) coraje;

metallic(al), *mĕtăl'ĭk(ăl),* a. metálico.

metallurgy, *mĕt'ălŭrjĕ,* s. metalurgia, f.

metamorphose, *mĕtămōr'fōs,* v. a. transformar. [morfosis, f.

metamorphosis, *mĕtămōr'fōsĭs,* s. meta-

metaphor, *mĕt'ăfŏr,* s. metáfora, f.

metaphoric(al), *mĕtăfŏr'ĭk(ăl),* a. metafórico. [sico; **-ly,** ad. metafísicamente.

metaphysic(al), *mĕtăfĭz'ĭk(ăl),* a. metafí-

metaphysics, *–ĭks,* s. pl. metafísica, f.

mete, *mēt,* v. a. medir.

meteor, *mē'tĕŭr,* s. metéoro, meteoro, m.

meteorological, *mētĕŏrŏlŏj'ĭkăl,* a. meteorológico. [gía, f.

meteorology, *mētĕŏrŏl'ōjĕ,* s. meteorolo-

meter, *mē'tŭr,* s. medidor, m.

methinks, *mĕthĭnks',* v. imp. me parece, creo, pienso.

method, *mĕth'ŏd,* s. método, m.

methodic(al), *mĕthŏd'ĭk(ăl),* a. metódico; **-ly,** ad. metódicamente.

methodist, *mĕth'ŏdĭst,* m. metodista, m.

metre, *mē'tŭr,* s. metro, m.

metrical, *mĕt'rĭkăl,* a. métrico.

metropolis, *mĕtrŏp'ŏlĭs,* s. metrópoli, f.

metropolitan, *mĕtrŏpŏl'ĭtăn,* s. metropolitano, m. [m.

mettle, *mĕt'l,* s. brío, valor, coraje, ardor,

mettled, *–d,* **mettlesome,** *–săm,* a. brioso, vivo, ardiente.

mew, *mū,* s. jaula, f.; gaviota, f.; caballeriza, f.; –, v. a. enjaular; –, v. n. maullar (como el gato).

microscope, *mī'krōskōp,* s. microscopio, m.

microscopic(al), *mīkrōskŏp'ĭk(ăl),* m. microscópico.

mid, *mĭd,* a. medio.

mid-course, *–kŏrs,* s. media carrera, f.; medio camino, m.

mid-day, *–dā,* s. mediodía, m.

middle, *–dl,* s. medio, intermedio; mediocre; –, s. medio, centro, m.

middling, *–dlĭng,* a. mediano, mediocre.

midland, *–lănd,* a. mediterráneo.

midnight, *–nĭt,* s. media noche, f. [f.

midshipman, *–shĭpmăn,* s. guardia marina,

midst, *mĭdst,* s. medio, centro, m.

midsummer, *–mĕr,* s. **solsticio** estival, m.; rigor del estío, m.

midway, *—wā,* s. medio camino, m.; —, ad. á medio camino.

midwife, *—wíf,* s. comadre, partera, f.

midwifery, *—wīfrē,* s. obstetricia, f.

mien, *mēn,* s. semblante, m.

night, *mīt,* s. poder, m.; fuerza, f.; — **and main,** suma fuerza, f.   [mente.

mightily, *—tīl,* ad. poderosamente, suma-

mightiness, *—īnēs,* s. poder, m.; potencia, f.

mighty, *—ē,* a. fuerte, potente.   [f.

mignonette, *mēn'yónét,* s. (bot.) reseda, f.

migrate, *mī'grāt,* v. n. emigrar.

migration, *mīgrā'shán,* s. emigración, f.

migratory, *mī'grātārē,* a. migratorio.

milch, *miltsh,* a. lactífero.

mild, *mīld,* a. indulgente, blando, dulce, apacible, suave, moderado; —ly, ad. suave-mente, con blandura.

mildew, *mīl'dū,* s. tizón, tizoncillo, m.

mildness, *mīld'nēs,* s. clemencia, dulzura, f.

mile, *mīl,* s. milla, f.   [f.

mileage, *—dj,* s. indemnización kilométrica.

mile-stone, *—stōn,* s. mijero, m.   [f.

milfoil, *mīl'fóil,* s.(bot.) milenrama, f.

militant, *mīl'ídnt,* a. militante.

military, *mīl'ītárē,* a. & s. militar (m.).

militate, *mīl'ītát,* v. n. militar.

militia, *mīlish'á,* s. milicia, f.

milk, *mīlk,* s. leche, f.; —, v. a. ordeñar.

milk-maid, *—mād,* s. lechera, f.

milk-sop, *—sóp,* s. marica, f.

milky, *—ē,* s. lácteo, lactífero; lechal; — **way,** s. galaxia, vía láctea, f.

mill, *mīl,* s. molino, m.; —, v. a. moler; batir con el molinillo; estampar.

mill-dam, *—dám,* s. esclusa de molino, f.

millennium, *mīlén'nīúm,* s. espacio de mil años, m.

miller, *mīl'ár,* s. molinero, m.

millet, *mīl'lēt,* s. (bot.) mijo, m.

milliner, *mīl'línár,* s. modista, m. & f.

millinery, *—ē,* s. modas, f. pl.   [vulgo, m.

million, *mīl'yán,* s. millón, m.; **the —,** el —.

millionth, *—th,* a. millonésimo.

mill-stone, *—stōn,* s. muela, f.

mime, *mīm,* s. mimo, bufón, m.

mimic, *mīm'ik,* v. a. imitar, contrahacer; —(al), a. burlesco.

mimicry, *—ē,* s. mímica, f.; bufonería, f.

mince, *mīns,* v. a. picar la carne; —, v. n. hablar con afectación; andar muy poco á poco afectadamente.   [afectación.

mincingly, *mīn'sínglé,*ad. á pedacitos; con

mind, *mīnd,* s. mente, f.; entendimiento, m.; gusto, afecto, m.; voluntad, intención, f.; pensamiento, m.; opinión, f.; ánimo, m.; —, v. a. notar, observar, considerar; pensar; —, v. n. inclinarse; estar dispuesto.

minded, *—ēd,* a. inclinado, dispuesto.

mindful, *—fúl,* a. atento, diligente; —ly, ad. atentamente.

mindless, *mīnd'lés,* a. descuidado, negligente.

mine, *mīn,* pn. mío, mía, mi; —, s. mina; —, v. n. minar, cavar.

miner, *—ár,* s. minador, m.

mineral, *mīn'árál,* a. & s. mineral (m.).

mineralogy, *mīnárál'djē,* s. mineralogía, f.

mingle, *mīng'gl,* v. a. mezclar.

miniature, *mīn'ītár,* s. miniatura, f.

minim, *mīn'ím,* s. (mus.) mínima, f.

minimise, *mīn'īmīz,* v. a. reducir á un mínimum.

minimum, *mīn'īmúm,* s. mínimum, m.

minion, *mīn'yán,* s. favorito, m.

minister, *mīn'īstár,* s. ministro, m.; —, v. a. ministrar; servir; suministrar; pro-veer; socorrer.

ministerial, *mīnīstē'rīál,* a. ministerial.

ministration, *mīnīstrā'shán,* s. agencia, f.; ministerio, m.

ministry, *mīn'īstrē,* s. ministerio, m.

minnow, *mīn'nō,* s. vario, m. (pez).

minor, *mī'nár,* a. menor, pequeño; infe-rior; —, s. menor (de edad), m.   [ría, f.

minority, *mīnór'ítē,* s. minoridad,f.; mino-

minster, *mīn'stár,* s. iglesia catedral, f.

minstrel, *mīn'strēl,* s. ministril, m.

mint, *mīnt,* s. (bot.) menta, f.; ceca, casa de moneda, f.; —, v. a. acuñar.

mintage, *—dj,* s. derechos de cuño, m. pl.

minuet, *mīn'úēt,* s. minuete, minué, m.

minus, *mī'nás,* ad. menos.

minute, *mīnút',* a. menudo, pequeño; —ly, ad. exactamente.

minute, *mīn'ít,* s. minuto, m.; momento, instante, m.; minuta, f.

minute-book, *—púk,* s. libro de minutas, m.

minuteness, *mīnút'nēs,* s. minucia, pe-queñez, f.

minutiae, *mīnú'shīē,* s. pl. minucias, f. pl.

minx, *mīngks,* s. moza atrevida y libre, f.

miracle, *mīr'ákl,* s. milagro, m.; mara-villa, f.   [—ly, ad. maravillosamente.

miraculous, *mīrák'úlús,* a. milagroso;

mirage, *mīráj (mīrázh'),* s. espejismo, m.

mire, *mīr,* s. fango, limo, m.   [pañado.

mirky, *már'kē,* a. sombrío; turbio; em-

mirror, *mīr'rár,* s. espejo, m.

mirth, *mǔrth,* s. alegría, f.; regocijo, m.

mirthful, *—fúl,* a. alegre, jovial.

miry, *mī'rē,* a. cenagoso, lodoso.

misadventure, *mīsádvén'túr,* s. desven-tura, f.; infortunio, m.

misalliance, *—dlī'áns,* s. mal matrimo-nio, m.   [m.

misanthrope, *mīs'ánthróp,*s. misántropo,

misanthropy, *mīsán'thrópē,* s. misan-tropía, f.   [aplicación, f.

misapplication, *—ápplīkā'shán,* s. mala

misapply, *—ápplī',* v. a. usar de alguna cosa impropiamente.

misapprehend, *—ápprēhénd',* v. a. en-tender mal.   [error, yerro, m.

misapprehension, *—ápprēhén'shán,* s.

misbehave, *—bēháv',* v. n. portarse mal.

misbehaviour, *—bēháv'yúr,* s. mala con-ducta, f.   [heterodoxia, f.

misbelief, *—bēlēf',* s. opinión falsa, f.;

misbeliever, *—bēlē'vúr,* s. incrédulo, m.

miscalculate, *—kál'kúlát,* v. a. calcular mal.

miscarriage, *—kár'ráj,* s. éxito infeliz de alguna empresa, m.; mala conducta, f.; aborto, m.   [grarse; abortar.

miscarry, *—kár'rē,* v. n. frustrarse, malo-

miscellaneous, *misséllá néus,* a. mezclado. [miscelánea, f.
miscellany, *misséll'lánd* (*mis séllánd*), s.
mischance, *mistsháns,* s. desventura; infortunio, mal] suceso, m. [m.
mischief, *-tshíf,* s. mal, daño, infortunio.
mischief-maker, *-mákár,* s. derramasolaces, destripameriendas, m.
mischievous, *-tshíu is,* a. dañoso, malicioso, malévolo; **-ly,** ad. malignamente.
misconceive, *-kónsév,* v. a. concebir una idea falsa. [cación, f.
misconception, *-kónsép'shán,* s. equivocación, interpretación siniestra, f.
misconduct, *-kón'dúkt,* s. mala conducta, f.; **-,** **-,** v. a. portarse mal.
misconstruction, *-kónstrúk'shán,* s. mala construcción, interpretación siniestra, f.
misconstrue, *-kón'strö,* v. a. interpretar mal. [m., malvado, malhechor, m.
miscreant, *mís'kréánt,* s. infiel, incrédulo,
misdeed, *misdéd',* s. mal hecho, delito, m.
misdemeanour, *-démén'ár,* s. mala conducta, f. [mente.
misdirect, *-dîrékt',* v. a. dirigir erradamente.
misdoubt, *-dödt',* v. a. recelar, sospechar.
miser, *mí'zár,* s. hombre tacaño y avariento, m. [pobre; mezquino.
miserable, *míz'árábl,* a. miserable, infeliz;
miserably, *-é,* ad.miserablemente; avaramente.
miserly, *mí'zúrlá,* a. mezquino, tacaño.
misery, *míz'úré,* s. miseria, f.; infortunio, m. [que cae mal, f.
misfit, *misfít',* s. condición de un vestido
misfortune, *misfór'tán,* s. infortunio, m.; calamidad, f. [cer temer.
misgive, *-gív',* v. a. llenar de dudas; ha-
misgiving, *-gív'ing,* s. recelo, m.; duda, f.; presentimiento, m.
misgovern, *-gúv'árn,* v. a. gobernar mal.
misguide, *-gíd',* v. a. guiar mal. [m.
mishap, *-háp',* s. desventura, f.; desastre.
misinform, *-ínfórm',* v. a. informar mal.
misinterpret, *-íntár'prét,* v.a. interpretar tar mal.
misjudge, *-fúj',* v. n. juzgar mal.
mislay, *-lá',* v. a. colocar mal, extraviar.
mislead, *-léd',* v. a. extraviar, descaminar; seducir.
mismanage, *-mán'áj,* v. a. manejar mal.
mismanagement, *-mént,* s. mala administración, f.; desarreglo, m.
misname, *-nám',* v. a.dar un nombre falso.
misnomer, *-nó'már,* s. nombre ó título falso, m.
misogynist, *mísóg'ínist,* s. misógino, m.
misplace, *-plás',* v. a. colocar mal; sacar algo de su quicio.
misprint, *-prínt',* v. a. imprimir mal; **-,** s. errata en un libro, f.
misrepresent, *-réprézént',* v.a. representar mal. [tación falsa, f.
misrepresentation, *-tá'shán,*s.represen-
misrule, *mísról',* s. tumulto, m.; confusión, f.
miss, *mís,* s. señorita, f.; pérdida, falta, f.; **-,** **-,** v. a. errar, perder; omitir; **-,** v. n. frustrarse; faltar.

missal, *mís'ál,* s. misal, m. [gurar.
misshape, *missháp',* v. a. deformar, desfi-
missile, *mís'íl,* s. proyectil, m.
missing, *mís'sing,* a. lo que falta; perdido.
mission, *mísh'án,* s. misión, comisión, f.
missionary, *-áré,* s. misionero, m.
missive, *mís'siv,* s. carta misiva, f.; **-,** a.
mist, *míst,* s. niebla, f. [místivo.
mistake, *mistéd',* v. a. equivocar; **-,** v. n. equivocarse; engañarse; **to be mistaken,** haberse equivocado; **-,** s. equivocación, f.; yerro, engaño, m.
Mister, *mís'túr,* s. Señor (título), m.
mistiness, *mís'tínés,* s. nebulosidad, f.
mistletoe, *mís'ltó,* s. (bot.) muérdago, m.; liga, f. [**-,** (mís'ets), señora, doña, f.
mistress, *mís'trés,* s. ama, f.; concubina, f.
mistrust, *mistrúst',* v. a. desconfiar; sospechar; **-,** s. desconfianza, sospecha, f.
mistrustful, *-fúl,* a. desconfiado, sospechoso, m. [pechoso.
misty, *mís'tá,* a. nebuloso;
misunderstand, *misúndárstánd',* v. a. entender mal una cosa.
misusage, *-ú'zdj,* s. abuso, m. [algo.
misuse, *-ús',* v. a. maltratar; abusar de
mite, *mít,* s. cresa, f.; pizca, f.
mitigate, *mít'igát,* v. a. mitigar, calmar.
mitigation, *mítigá'shán,* s. mitigación, f.;
mitre, *mí'túr,* s. mitra, f. [alivio, m.
mittens, *mít'ns,* s. pl. mitones, m. pl.
mix, *míks,* v. a. mezclar. [mezcla, f.
mixture, *míks'tjúr,* s. mistura, mixtura, f.
mizzen, *míz'n,* s. (mar.) mesana, f.
mizzle, *míz'l,* v. n. molliznar, lloviznar.
moan, *món,* s. lamento, gemido, m.; **-,** v. a. lamentar, gemir, **-,** v. n. afligirse.
moanful, *-fúl,* a. **-ly,** ad. lamentable (mente). [canales de agua.
moat, *mót,* s. mota, f.; **-,** v. a. rodear con
mob, *mób,* s. populacho, m., canalla, f.; **-,** v. a. tumultuar.
mobilise, *mób'ilíz,* v. a. (mil.) movilizar.
mobility, *móbí'lít,* s.movilidad,f.; (vulg.) populacho, m. [de los indianos, m.
moccasin, *mó'kássin,* s. zapato ramplón
mock, *mók,* v.a. mofar, burlar; **-,** s. mofa, burla, f.; **-,** a. ficticio, falso.
mockery, *-áré,* s. mofa, burla, zumba, f.
mocking-bird, *-íngbárd,* s. burlón, m. (ave). [nera, f.; costumbre, f.
mode, *mód,* s. modo, m.; forma, f.; ma-
model, *mód'él,* s. modelo, m.; **-,** v. a. modelar.
modeller, *-ár,* s. trazador, dibujador, m.
moderate, *mód'árát,* a. moderado; mediocre; **-ly,** ad. moderadamente; **-,** v. a. moderar. [f.
moderation, *módárá'shán,* s. moderación,
modern, *mód'árn,* a. moderno, reciente.
modernize, *mód'árníz,* v. a. modernizar.
modest, *mód'ést,* a. modesto; **-ly,** ad. modestamente.
modesty, *-é,* s. modestia, decencia, f.
modification, *módífíká'shán,* s. modifica-
modify, *mód'ífí,* v. a. modificar. [ción,f.
modulate, *mód'úlát,* v. a. modular.
modulation, *módúlá'shán,* s. (mus.) modulación, f.

mohair, *mō´hår*, s. tela hecha de pelo de camello, f.

moiety, *mōt´iẽ*, s. mitad, f. [camello, f.

moist, *mōist*, a. húmedo, mojado.

moisten, *mōs´sn*, v. a. humedecer.

moisture, *mōis´tūr*, s. humedad, f.; jugo, m. [muelas, f. pl.

molar, *mō´lår*, a. molar; – teeth, s. pl.

molasses, *mōlás´sẽz*, s. pl. melaza, f.

mole, *mōl*, s. mola, f.; muelle, dique, m.; mole-hill, –*hil*, s. topinera, f. [topo, m.]

molest, *mōlẽst´*, v. a. molestar, atormentar.

molestation, *mōlẽstā´shån*, s. molestia, f.; enfado, m.

mollify, *mōl´lifī*, v. a. ablandar.

mollusk, *mōl´lŭsk*, s. molusco, m.

molten, *mōl´tn*, a. derretido; the – calf, el becerro de fundición. (Exod. 32, 8.)

moment, *mō´mẽnt*, s. momento, m.; importancia, f.

momentarily, *–ãrilı*, ad. á cada momento.

momentary, *–ãrẽ*, a. momentáneo.

momentous, *mōmẽn´tŭs*, a. importante.

momentum, *–tŭm*, s. fuerza de impulsión de un cuerpo, f.

monarch, *mōn´årk*, s. monarca, m.

monarchic(al), *mōnårk´ik(ăl)*, a. monárquico.

monarchy, *mōn´årkẽ*, s. monarquía, f.

monastery, *mōn´åstũrẽ*, s. monasterio, m.

monastic(al), *mōnås´tik(ăl)*, a. monástico.

Monday, *mŭn´dẽ*, s. lunes, m.

monetary, *mŭn´ẽtårẽ*, a. monetario.

money, *mŭn´ẽ*, s. moneda, f.; dinero, m.; ready –, – in hand, dinero contante.

moneyed, *monied*, –ẽd, a. adinerado, rico.

monger, *mŭng´gŭr*, s. tratante, traficante, m.

mongrel, *mŭng´grẽl*, a. & s. mestizo (m.)

monition, *mōnish´ẽn*, s. amonestación, f.

monitor, *mōn´itŭr*, s. admonitor, m.; (mar.) monitor, m.

monitory, *mōn´itŏrẽ*, a. monitorio.

monk, *mŭngk*, s. monje, m. [lada, f.

monkery, *–ẽ*, s. vida monástica, f.; frailmonkey, –*ẽ*, s. mono, m.

monkish, *–ish*, a. monástico. [niaco.

monomaniac, *mōnomā´niăk*, a. monomanomonopolist, *mŏnŏp´ŏlist*, s. monopolista,

monopolize, *–ōlīz*, v.a. monopolizar. [m.

monopoly, *–ōlẽ*, s. monopolio, m.

monosyllabic, *mŏnŏsillăb´ik*, a. monosílabo

monosyllable, *–síl´lăbl*, s. monosílabo, m.

monotonous, *mōnŏt´ŏnŭs*, a. monótono.

monotony, *–ōnẽ*, s. monotonía, f.

monsoon, *mōnsōn´*, s. (mar.) monzón, m.

monster, *mōn´stŭr*, s. monstruo, m.

monstrosity, *mōnstrŏs´itẽ*, s. monstruosidad, f. [ad. monstruosamente.

monstrous, *mōn´strŭs*, a. monstruoso; –ly,

month, *mŭnth*, s. mes, m.

monthly, *–lẽ*, a. (& ad.) mensual(mente).

monument, *mōn´ūmẽnt*, s. monumento, m.

monumental, *mōnūmẽn´tăl*, a. hecho en memoria. [pricho, m.

mood, *mōd*, s. (gr.) modo, m.; humor, camoodiness, *–inẽs*, s. capricho, m.; extramoody, –*ẽ*, a. caprichoso. [vagancia, f.

moon, *mōn*, s. luna, f.

moon-beam, –*bēm*, s. rayos lunares, m. pl.

moon-light, –*lit*, s. luz de la luna, f.

moon-shine, –*shin*, s. claridad de la luna, f.; (fig.) ilusión, f.

moon-struck, –*strŭk*, a. lunático, loco.

moor, *mōr*, s. pantano, marjal, m.; moro negro, m.; – v. a. (mar.) amarrar.

moot, *mōt*, v. a. debatir materias de ley.

mop, *mōp*, s. estropajo, m.; – v. a. aljofifar. [estar triste.

mope, *mōp*, v. n. dormitar, entontecerse,

moral, *mōr´ăl*, a. –ly, ad. moral(mente); –, s. moralidad, f.; –s, s. pl. costumbres, f. pl., usanza general, f.

moralise, *mōr´ăliz*, v. a. & n. moralizar.

moralist, *–ist*, s. moralista, m.

morality, *mōrăl´itẽ*, s. ética, moralidad, f.

morass, *mōrás´*, s. lavajo, pantano, m.

morbid, *mōr´bid*, a. enfermo, morboso.

more, *mōr*, a. & ad. más; never –, nunca más, jamás; once –, otra vez; – and –, más y más ó cada vez más; so much the –, cuanto más. [también.

moreover, *mōr´ŏvãr*, ad. además; –, c.

morning, *mōr´ning*, (poet.) morn, mōrn, s. mañana, f.; good –, buenos días, m. pl.

morning-gown, –*gōūn*, s. bata, f.

morning-star, –*står*, s. lucero de la mañana, m. [marroquí, m.

morocco(-leather), *mōrŏk´kō (lẽthår)*, s.

morose, *mōrōs´*, a. moroso; cabezudo; –ly, ad. morosamente.

morrow, *mōr´rō*, s. mañana, f.

morse, *mōrs*, s. manatí, m., vaca marina, f.

morsel, *mōr´sẽl*, s. bocado, m.

mortal, *mōr´tăl*, a. mortal; humano; –ly, ad. mortalmente; –, s. mortal, m. (el hombre ó la mujer).

mortality, *mōrtăl´itẽ*, s. mortalidad, f.

mortar, *mōr´tăr*, s. mortero, m.

mortgage, *mōr´gãj*, s. hipoteca, f.; –, v. a. hipotecar.

mortgagee, –*ẽ*, s. acreedor hipotecario, m.

mortgager, –*ũr*, s. deudor hipotecario, m.

mortification, *mōrtifikā´shån*, s. mortificación, f.; gangrena, f.

mortify, *mōr´tifī*, v. a. (&n.) mortificar(se).

mortmain, *mōr´mãn*, s. mano muerta, f.

mortuary, *mōr´tūărẽ*, a. funeral.

mosaic, *mōzā´ik*, s. obra mosaica, f.; –, a.

mosque, *mōsk*, s. mezquita, f. [mosaico.

mosquito, *mōskē´tō*, s. mosquito, m.

moss, *mōs*, s. (bot.) musgo, m.; moho, m.

mossy, *–ẽ*, a. musgoso.

most, *mōst*, a. los, las ó lo más; –, ad. sumamente, en sumo grado; –, s. los más; mayor número, m.; mayor valor, m.; at –, á lo más; –ly, ad. por lo común.

mote, *mōt*, s. mota, f.; átomo, m.

moth, *mōth*, s. polilla, f.

mother, *mŭth´ũr*, s. madre, f.; –of pearl, madreperla, f.

motherhood, *–hŭd*, s. maternidad, f.

mother-in-law, *–ĭnlā*, s. suegra, f.

motherless, *–lẽs*, a. sin madre.

motherly, *–lẽ*, a. maternal, materno.

mothy, *mŏth´ẽ*, a. apolillado.

motion, *mō'shăn,* s. movimiento, m., moción, f.; proposición, f.; —, v. a. proponer.

motionless, *–lĕs,* a. inmoble, inmóvil.

motive, *mō'tiv,* a. & s. razón, f.; motivo, (m.). [garrado, gayado, barajado.

motley, *mŏt'lĕ,* mottled, *mŏt'tld,* a. abigarrado, gayado, barajado.

motto, *mŏt'tō,* s. mote, m.; divisa, f.

mould, *mōld,* s. moho, m.; tierra, f.; suelo, m.; molde, m.; matriz, f.; —, v. a. enmohecer, moldar; formar; —, v. n. enmohecerse. [n.) convertir(se) en polvo.

moulder, *–ăr,* s. moldeador, m.; —, v. a. (& n.) convertir(se) en polvo.

mouldiness, *–nĕs,* s. moho, m.

moulding, *–ĭng,* s. moldura, f. pl., cornisamiento, m.

mouldy, *–ĕ,* a. mohoso, lleno de moho.

moult, *mōlt,* v. n. mudar, estar de muda las aves. [m.

mound, *mŏŭnd,* s. terraplén, baluarte, dique, (m.).

mount, *mŏŭnt,* s. monte, m.; montaña, f., —, v. a. subir, levantar. [f., monte, m.

mountain, *mŏŭn'tĭn,* s. montaña, sierra, (f.).

mountaineer, *–ēr',* s. montañés, m.

mountainous, *–ăs,* a. montañoso.

mountebank, *mŏŭn'tĕbăngk,* s. saltimbanco, charlatán, m.

mourn, *mōrn,* v. a. deplorar; —, v. n. lamentar; llevar luto.

mourner, *–ăr,* s. lamentador, m.; llorón, (m.). [mente.

mournful, *–fŭl,* a. triste; **-ly,** ad. tristemente.

mourning, *–ĭng,* s. lamento, m.; luto, m.

mourningly, *–ĭnglĕ,* ad. tristemente.

mouse, *mŏŭs,* s. (mice, pl.) ratón, m.

moustache, *mŭstăsh',* s. bigotes, m. pl.

mouth, *mŏŭth,* s. boca, f.; entrada, f.; embocadura, f.; —, *mŏŭth,* v. a. & n. mascar; hablar á gritos.

mouthful, *mŏŭth'fŭl,* s. bocado, m.

mouth-piece, *–pēs,* s. boquilla de un instrumento de música, f.

move, *mōv,* v. a. mover; proponer; excitar; persuadir, mover á piedad, —, v. n. moverse, menearse; andar, marchar un ejército; —, s. movimiento, m.; movimiento (en el juego de ajedrez).

moveable, *–ăbl,* a. movible, movedizo; **-s,** s. pl. muebles, m. pl. [moción, f.

movement, *–mĕnt,* s. movimiento, m.;

mover, *–ăr,* s. motor, m.

moving, *–ĭng,* s. movimiento, m., —, a. patético, persuasivo; **-ly,** ad. patéticamente.

mow, *mō,* v. a. guadañar, segar. [mente.

mower, *–ăr,* s. guadañero, m.

much, *mŭtsh,* a. & ad. mucho, con mucho.

mucilage, *mū'sĭlăj,* s. mucílago, m.

mucous, *mū'kŭs,* a. mocoso, viscoso.

mud, *mŭd,* s. fango, limo, m.

muddle, *mŭd'l,* v. a. enturbiar, embriagar.

muddy, *–dĕ,* a. cenagoso; turbio.

mud-wall, *–wâl,* s. tapia, f.

muff, *mŭf,* s. manguito, m.

muffle, *–l,* v. a. embozar; envolver.

mug, *mŭg,* s. cubilete, m.

muggy, *–gĕ,* a. húmedo. [morera, f.

mulberry, *mŭl'bĕrrĕ,* s. mora, f.; **–tree,** s. moral, m.

mulct, *mŭlkt,* v. a. multar; —, s. multa, f.

mule, *mūl,* s. mulo, m.; mula, f.

mule-driver, *–drīvăr,* **muleteer,** *mū'lĕtēr',* s. mulero, m. [quier licor.

mull, *mŭl,* v. a. entibiar, calentar cualquier licor.

mullet, *mŭl'lĕt,* s. mágil, sargo, m. (pez)

multifarious, *mŭltĭfā'rĭăs,* a. vario, diferente. [múltiplo, m.

multiple, *mŭl'tĭpl,* a. multíplice; —, s. múltiplo, m.

multiplicand, *mŭltĭplĭkănd',* s. (ar.) multiplicando, m.

multiplication, *mŭltĭplĭkā'shăn,* s. multiplicación, f.; **–table,** tabla de multiplicar, f. [dor, m.

multiplicator, *–tăr,* s. (ar.) multiplicador, m.

multiplicity, *mŭltĭplĭs'ĭtĕ,* s. multiplicidad, f.

multiply, *mŭl'tĭplĕ,* v. a. multiplicar.

multitude, *mŭl'tĭtūd,* s. multitud, f.; vulgo, m. [roso.

multitudinous, *mŭltĭtū'dĭnăs,* a. numeroso.

mum, *mŭm,* ¡chito!, ¡silencio!

mumble, *mŭm'bl,* v. a. barbotar; —, v. n. gruñir, mormullar.

mummer, *mŭm'măr,* s. máscara, m. & f.

mummery, *–mărĕ,* s. momería, f.

mummy, *–mĕ,* s. momia, f.

mumps, *mŭmps,* s. pl. murria, f.; angina, f.

munch, *mŭntsh,* v. a. masticar á bocados grandes.

mundane, *mŭn'dān,* a. mundano.

municipal, *mŭnĭs'ĭpăl,* a. municipal.

municipality, *mŭnĭsĭpăl'ĭtĕ,* s. municipalidad, f. [liberalidad, f.

munificence, *mŭnĭf'ĭsĕns,* s. munificencia, f.

munificent, *–ĭsĕnt,* a. munífico, liberal.

muniment, *mū'nĭmĕnt,* s. (law) título, documento, m.

muniment-house, *–hōs,* s. archivo, m.

munition, *mŭnĭsh'ăn,* s. pl. municiones, f. pl. [corona mural, f.

mural, *mū'răl,* a. mural; **–crown,** s. corona mural, f.

murder, *mŭr'dăr,* s. asesinato, homicidio, m., —, v. a. asesinar, cometer homicidio.

murderer, *–ăr,* s. asesino, m.

murderess, *–ĕs,* s. matadora, f.

murderous, *–ăs,* a. sanguinario, cruel.

murky, *mŭr'kĕ,* a. obscuro, lóbrego.

murmur, *mŭr'măr,* s. murmullo, murmurio, m., —, v. n. murmurar.

murmuringly, *–ĭnglĕ,* ad. con murmullo.

murrain, *mŭr'răn,* s. morriña, f.

muscle, *mŭs'l,* s. músculo, m.

muscular, *mŭs'kūlăr,* a. muscular.

muse, *mūz,* s. musa, f.; meditación profunda, f.; —, v. r. meditar, pensar profundamente.

museum, *mūzĕ'ŭm,* s. museo, m.

mushroom, *mŭsh'rōm,* s. (bot.) seta, f.

music, *mū'zĭk,* s. música, f.

musical, *–ăl,* a. musical, melodioso; **-ly,** ad. con armonía.

music-hall, *–hâl,* s. sala de concierto, f.

musician, *mūzĭsh'ăn,* s. músico, m.

musing, *mū'zĭng,* s. meditación, f.

musk, *mŭsk,* s. musco, m.

musket, *mŭs'kĕt,* s. mosquete, m.

musketeer, *–ēr',* s. mosquetero, m.

musketry, *–rĕ,* s. mosquetería, f.

musky, *mŭs'kĕ,* a. almizcleño.

muslin, *mŭz'lĭn*, s. muselina, f.

mussel, *mŭs'ĕl*, s. marisco, m.

must, *mŭst*, v. imp. & def. estar obligado; ser menester, ser necesario, convenir.

mustard, *mŭs'tărd*, s. mostaza, f. [f.

mustard-seed, *—sēd*, s.simiente de jenabe.

muster, *mŭs'tĕr*, v. a. pasar revista de tropa; agregar; —, s. (mil.) revista, f.

musty, *mŭs'tĭ*, a. moboso, añejo.

mutability, *mūtăbĭl'ĭtĕ*, s. mutabilidad, inconstancia, f. [mutación, f.

mutation, *mūtā'shăn*, s. mudanza, f.

mute, *mūt*, a. mudo, silencioso; -ly, ad. mudamente, sin chistar.

mutilate, *mū'tĭlăt*, v. a. mutilar.

mutilation, *mūtĭlā'shăn*, s. mutilación, f. [sórdido.

mutineer, *mūtĭnēr'*, s. amotinador, sedicioso, m. [amotinadamente.

mutinous, *mū'tĭnŭs*, a.sedicioso; -ly, ad.

mutiny, *mū'tĭnĕ*, s. motín, tumulto, m. —, v. n. amotinarse, rebelarse

mutter, *mŭt'tĕr*, v. a. & n. murmurar, musitar; —, s. murmuración, f.

mutton, *mŭt'n*, s. carnero, m.

mutual, *mū'tŭăl*, a. mutuo, mutual, recíproco; -ly, ad. mutuamente, recíprocamente.

muzzle, *mŭz'l*, s. bozal, frenillo, m.; hocico, m.; jeta, f.; —, v. a. embozar.

my, *mī*, pn. mi, mis; mío, mía; míos, mías.

myriad, *mĭr'ĭăd*, s. miríada, f.; gran número, m.

myrrh, *mĭr*, s. mirra, f. [mero, m.

myrtle, *mĭr'tl*, s. mirto, arrayán, m.

myself, *mīsĕlf'*, pn. yo mismo.

mysterious, *mĭstē'rĭŭs*, a. misterioso; -ly, ad. misteriosamente.

mystery, *mĭs'tărĕ*, s. misterio, m.

mystic(al), *mĭs'tĭk(ăl)*, a. místico; -ally, ad. místicamente. [m.; burla, f.

mystification, *mĭstĭfĭkā'shăn*, s. chasco,

mystify, *mĭs'tĭfī*, v. a. chasquear, burlar.

myth, *mĭth*, s. fábula mitológica, f.

mythologic(al), *mĭthŏlŏj'ĭk(ăl)*, a. mitológico.

mythology, *mĭthŏl'ōjĕ*, s. mitología, f.

N.

nab, *năb*, v. a. atrapar, apiolar.

nag, *năg*, s. haca, jaca, f. [—, v. a. clavar.

nail, *nāl*, s. uña, f.; garra, f.; clavo, m.;

nailery, *—ĕrĕ*, s. fábrica de clavos, f.

naked, *nā'kĕd*, a. desnudo; evidente; puro, simple; -ly, ad. desnudamente; claramente, patentemente. [f.

nakedness, *—nĕs*,s. desnudez, f.; claridad,

name, *nām*, s. nombre, m.; fama, reputación, f.; —, v. n. nombrar; mencionar.

nameless, *—lĕs*, a. anónimo.

namely, *—lĕ*, ad. particularmente; á saber.

namesake, *—sāk*, s. tocayo, colombroño, m.

nankeen, *năngkēn'*, s. mahón, m. [m.

nap, *năp*, s. sueño ligero, m.; lanilla, f.

nape, *nāp*, s. nuca, f.

naphtha, *năp'thă*, s. nafta, f.

napkin, *năp'kĭn*, s. servilleta, f.

narcissus, *nărsĭs'sŭs*, s. (bot.) narciso, m.

narcotic(al), *nărkŏt'ĭk(ăl)*, a. narcótico.

narrate, *năr'răt*, v. a. narrar, relatar.

narration, *nărrā'shăn*, s. narración, relación de alguna cosa, f.

narrative, *năr'ătĭv*, a. narrativo.

narrow, *năr'rō*, a. angosto, estrecho; avariento; próximo; escrupuloso; -ly, ad. estrechamente; —. v. a. estrechar; limitar.

narrowness, *năr'rōnĕs*, s. angostura, estrechez,

nasal, *nā'săl*, a. nasal; [f.; pobreza, f.

nascent, *năs'sĕnt*, a. naciente.

nastily, *năs'tĭlĕ*, ad. suciamente.

nastiness, *năs'tĭnĕs*, s. porquería, obscenidad, f. [sórdido.

nasty, *năs'tĕ*, a. sucio, puerco; obsceno; natal, *nā'tăl*, a. nativo; natal.

nation, *nā'shăn*, s. nación, f. [(mente.

national, *năsh'ŭnăl*, a. -ly, ad. nacional,

nationalise, *năsh'ŭnălīz*, v. a. hacer nacional. [f.

nationality, *năshŭnăl'ĭtĕ*, s. nacionalidad, f.

native, *nā'tĭv*, a. nativo; —, s. natural, m.

nativity, *nătĭv'ĭtĕ*, s. nacimiento, m.; origen, m.; horóscopo, m.

natural, *năt'ŭrăl*, a. natural; sencillo; ilegítimo; -ly, ad. naturalmente; —, s. (mus.) becuadro, m.

naturalist, *—ĭst*, s. naturalista, m.

naturalise, *năt'ŭrălīz*, v. a. naturalizar.

nature, *nāt'ŭr (nā'tshŭr)*, s. naturaleza, f.; índole, f. [verso, indigno.

naught, *nŏt*, s. nada, f.; —, a. malo, perverso,

naughtily, *—tĭlĕ*, ad. malvadamente.

naughtiness, *—nĕs*, s. maldad, malignidad, f.

naughty, *—ĕ*, a. malo, malvado [dad, f.

nausea, *nŏ'shĭă*, s. náusea, gana de vomitar, f. [sear, tener disgusto.

nauseate, *—shĭāt*, v. a. dar disgusto; nau-

nauseous, *nŏ'shŭs*, a. fastidioso; -ly, ad. con náusea. [náutico, naval.

nautic(al), *nŏ'tĭk(ăl)*, a. naval, *nā'văl*, a.

nave, *nāv*, s. cubo, m.; nave (de la iglesia), f.

navel, *nā'vĕl*, s. ombligo, m.

navigable, *năv'ĭgăbl*, a. navegable.

navigate, *năv'ĭgăt*, v. n. navegar. [f.

navigation, *năvĭgā'shăn*, s. navigación,

navvy, *năv'vĕ*, s. quebrantaterrones, m.

navy, *nā'vĕ*, s. marina, f.; armada, f.

nay, *nā*, ad. no; y aun, aun más.

near, *nēr*, pr. cerca de, junto á; —, ad. casi; cerca, cerca de; —, a. cercano, próximo, inmediato; allegado. [mente.

nearly, *—lĕ*, ad. á poca distancia; estrechamente.

nearness, *—nĕs*, s. proximidad, f.; mezquindad, f.

near-sighted, *nēr'sĭtĕd*, a. miope.

neat, *nēt*, a. hermoso, pulido; puro; neto; -ly, ad. elegantemente; —, s. ganado vacuno, m.

neatness, *—nĕs*, s. pulidez, elegancia, f.

nebulous, *nĕb'ŭlŭs*, a. nebuloso.

necessaries, *nĕs'ĕsărĕz*, s.pl. necesario, m.

necessarily, *nĕs'ĕsărĭlĕ*, ad. necesariamente.

necessary, *nĕs'ĕsărĕ*, a. necesario.

necessitate, *nĕsĕs'ĭtāt*, v. a. necesitar.

necessitous, *—tŭs*, a. indigente, pobre.

necessity, -ĭtĕ, s. necesidad, f.

neck, nĕk, s. cuello, m.; - of land, lengua de tierra entre dos mares, f.

neckerchief, -ărtshĭf, s. corbata, f.; pañuelo de cuello, m.

necklace, -lās, s. collar, m. [f.

necromancy, nĕk'rōmănsĕ, s. necromancia, f.

nectar, nĕk'tăr, s. néctar, m.

need, nēd, s. necesidad, f.; pobreza, f.; -, v. a. & n. pedir; necesitar.

needful, -fŭl, a. necesario, indispensable; -ly, ad. necesariamente. [f.

neediness, -ĭnĕs, s. indigencia, pobreza, f.

needle, nē'dl, s. aguja, f. [m.

needle-case, -kās, s. alfiletero, palillero, m.

needless, nēd'lĕs, a. superfluo, inútil.

needle-work, nē'dlwŭrk, s. costura, f.; bordado de aguja, m.; obra de punto, m.

needs, nēdz, ad. necesariamente. [pobre.

needy, nē'dĕ, a. indigente, necesitado, m.

nefarious, nĕfā'rĭŭs, a. nefario.

negation, nĕgā'shŭn, s. negación, f.

negative, nĕg'ătĭv, a. negativo; -ly, ad. negativamente; -, s. negativa, f.

neglect, nĕglĕkt', v. a. descuidar, desatender; -, s. negligencia, f. [descuido, f.

negligence, nĕg'lĭjĕns, s. negligencia, f.;

negligent, nĕg'lĭjĕnt, a. negligente, descuidado; -ly, ad. negligentemente.

negotiable, nĕgō'shăbl, a. negociable.

negotiate, nĕgō'shĭāt, v. n. negociar, comerciar. [ción, f.; negocio, m.

negotiation, nĕgōshĭā'shŭn, s. negociación, f.

negress, nē'grĕs, s. negra, f.

negro, nē'grō, s. negro, etíope, m. [m.

negro, nā, v. n. relinchar; -, s. relincho, m.

neighbour, nā'băr, s. vecino, m., -, v. a. confinar. [vecindario, m.

neighbourhood, -hŭd, s. vecindad, f.

neighbourly, -lĕ, a. sociable.

neither, nē'thăr c. ni; -, pn. ninguno, uno ni otro.

neophyte, nē'ōfīt, s. neófito, novicio, m.

nephew, nĕv'ū, s. sobrino, m.

nepotism, nĕp'ōtĭzm, s. nepotismo, m.

nerve, nărv, s. nervio, m.; vigor, m.

nerveless, -lĕs, a. enervado; débil.

nervous, năr'vŭs, a. nervoso; nervudo.

nest, nĕst, s. nido, m.; nidada, f.

nestle, nĕs'l, v. a. anidarse.

nestling, nĕs'tĭng, s. pollo, m.

net, nĕt, s. red, f.

nether, nĕth'ăr, a. inferior, más bajo.

netting, nĕt'ĭng, s. mallado, m.

nettle, nĕt'tl, s. ortiga, f.; -, v. a. picar como ortiga; irritar. [(gr.) neutro.

neuter, nē'tŭr, a. neutral, indiferente;

neutral, nē'trăl, a. neutral; -ly, ad. neutralmente.

neutrality, nētrăl'ĭtĕ, s. neutralidad, f.

neutralize, nē'trălīz, v. a. neutralizar.

never, nĕv'ăr, ad. nunca, jamás; - mind, no importa; - a whit, ni una pizca.

nevertheless, -thĕlĕs, ad. no obstante que.

new, nū, a. nuevo, fresco, reciente; -, -ly, ad. nuevamente.

new-comer, -kŭmăr, s. recién llegado, m.

new-fangled, -fănglĕd, a. inventado por

newness, -nĕs, s. novedad, f. [novedad.

news, năz, s. pl. novedad, nuevas, f. pl.

news-monger, -mŭngăr, s. novelero, m.

newspaper, -pāpăr, s. gaceta, f.

next, nĕkst, a. próximo; the - day, el día siguiente; -, ad. luego, inmediatamente

nib, nĭb, s. pico, m.; punta, f. [después.

nibble, -bl, v. a. picar; -, v. n. mordiscar; criticar.

nice, nīs, a. delicado, exacto, solícito; circunspecto; tierno; fino; elegante; escrupuloso; -ly, ad. primorosamente.

niceness, -nĕs, nicety, -ĭtĕ, s. exactitud, f., esmero, m.; delicadeza, f.; niceties.

niche, nĭtsh, s. nicho, m. [pl. golosina, f.

nick, nĭk, s. punto crítico, m.; ocasión oportuna, f.; old -, el diablo; -, v. a. dar en el hito; llegar á tiempo.

nickel, nĭk'kl, s. níquel, m.

nickname, -nām, s. mote, apodo, m.; -, v. a. poner apodos.

niece, nēs, s. sobrina, f.

niggard, nĭg'gărd, s. hombre avaro y mezquino, m. [sería, f.

niggardliness, -lĭnĕs, s. tacañería, miniggardly, -lĕ, a. avaro, sórdido; -, ad. tacañamente, miserablemente.

niggor, nĭg'gŭr, s. negro, m. -s, pl. recortadores de piezas de moneda, m. pl.

nigh, nī, pr. cerca, no lejos; -, ad. cerca, inmediato; -, a. cercano; -ly, ad. cercanamente. [good - buenas noches.

night, nīt, s. noche, f.; by -, de noche;

night-fall, -făl, s. anochecer, m.

nightingale, -ĭngāl, s. ruiseñor, m.

night-light, -līt, s. vela de noche, f.; lamparillas para luz, f. pl.

nightly, -lĕ, ad. por las noches, todas las noches; -, a. nocturno.

night-mare, -măr, s. pesadilla, f. [f.

night-shade, -shăd, s. (bot.) hierbamora,

nihilist, nī'hĭlĭst, s. nihilista, m.

nimble, nĭm'bl, a. ligero, activo, listo, ágil;

nimbly, -ĕ, ad. ágilmente.

nimbus, nĭm'bŭs, s. auréola, f.

nine, nīn, a. nueve.

nine-pins, -pĭnz, s. juego de bolos, m.

nineteen, -tēn, a. diez y nueve.

nineteenth, -tēnth, a. décimonono.

ninetieth, -tĭĕth, a. nonagésimo.

ninety, -tĕ, a. noventa.

ninny, nĭn'nĕ, s. badulaque, bobo, m.

ninth, nĭnth, a. noveno, nono; -ly, ad. en nono lugar.

nip, nĭp, v. a. arañar, rasguñar; morder.

nippers, -părz, s. pl. alicates, m. pl.

nipping, -pĭng, a. sensible (frío).

nipple, -pl, s. pezón, m.

nit, nĭt, s. liendre, f.

nitre, nē'tăr, s. nitro, m.

no, nō, ad no; -, a. ningún, ninguno.

nobility, nōbĭl'ĭtĕ, s. nobleza, f.

noble, nō'bl, a. noble; insigne; generoso; -, s. noble, m.

nobleman, -măn, s. noble, m.

nobleness, -nĕs, s. nobleza, f.

nobly, nō'blĕ, ad. noblemente.

nobody, nō'bŏdĕ, s. nadie, ninguna persona, f. [turno,

nocturnal, nŏktŭr'năl, a. nocturnal, noc-

nod, *nŏd,* s. cabeceo, m.; señal, f.; —, v. n. cabecear; amodorrarse.

node, *nŏd,* s. nudo, m.; nodo, tumor, m.

noise, *nŏiz,* s. ruido, estruendo, m.; rumor, m.; —, v. a. divulgar alguna noticia.

noiseless, *—lĕs,* a. atentado, sin ruido.

noisily, *—lĕ,* ad, con ruido.

noisiness, *—nĕs,* s. estrépito, ruido, tumulto, alboroto, m. [asqueroso.

noisome, *nŏi'sŭm,* a. nocivo, malsano;

noisy, *nŏi'zĕ,* a. ruidoso, turbulento.

nomadic, *nŏmăd'ĭk,* a. á modo de nómadas. [clatura, f.

nomenclature, *nŏmĕnklā'tŭr,* s. nomenclatura, f.

nominal, *nŏm'ĭnăl,* a. **-ly,** ad. nominal (mente).

nominate, *nŏm'ĭnāt,* v. a. nombrar. [f.

nomination, *nŏmĭnā'shŭn,* s. nominación, f.

nominative, *nŏm'ĭnătĭv,* s. (gr.) nominativo, m. [f.

non-age, *nŏn'āj,* s. minoridad, menoredad.

non-attendance, *nŏndŭĕn'dăns,* s. falta de asistencia, f.

non-descript, *—dĕskrĭpt',* a. no descrito.

none, *nŭn,* a. nadie, ninguno.

nonentity, *nŏnĕn'ĭtĕ,* s. nada, falta de existencia, f. [falta de ejecución, f.

non-performance, *nŏnpŭrfŏrm'ăns,* s.

nonplus, *nŏn'plŭs,* s. embarazo, m.; perplejidad, f.; —, v.a. confundir, embarazar.

non-resistance, *nŏnrĕzĭs'tăns,* s. obediencia pasiva, f. [m.

nonsense, *nŏn'sĕns,* s. disparate, absurdo,

nonsensical, *nŏnsĕn'sĭkăl,* a. absurdo.

nonsuit, *nŏn'sūt,* s. desistimiento de un proceso, m.; —, v. a. absolver de la instancia. [—s, pl. (am.) fideos, m. pl.

noodle, *nŏŏ'dl,* s. simplón, mentecato, m.;

nook, *nŏk,* s. rincón, ángulo, m.

noon, *nŏŏn,* s. mediodía, m.

noontide, *—tīd,* s. tiempo del mediodía, m.

noose, *nŏŏz,* s. lazo corredizo, m.; —, v. a. [enlazar.

nor, *nŏr,* c, ni.

normal, *nŏr'măl,* a. normal. [nal.

north, *nŏrth,* s. norte, m.; —, a. septentrional.

northerly, *nŏr'thŭrlĕ,* **northern,** *nŏr'thŭrn,* a. septentrional.

north-pole, *(nŏrth'pōl,* s. polo ártico, m.

northward(s), *—wŭrd(z),* ad. hacia el norte.

nose, *nŏz,* s. nariz, f.; olfato, m. sagacidad. [dad, f.

nose-bag, *—băg,* s. morral, m.

nosegay, *—gā,* s. ramillete, m.

nostril, *nŏs'trĭl,* s. ventana de la nariz.

nostrum, *nŏs'trŭm,* s. arcano, m.

not, *nŏt,* ad, no.

notable, *nŏ'tăbl,* a. notable; memorable.

notably, *—ĕ,* ad. notablemente.

notary, *nŏ'tărĕ,* s. notario, m. [muescas.

notch, *nŏtsh,* s. muesca, f.; —, v. a. hacer

note, *nŏt,* s. nota, marca, f.; señal, f.; aprecio, m.; billete, m.; consecuencia, f.; noticia, f.; indirecta, f.; —, v. a. notar, marcar; observar.

note-book, *—bŏk,* s. librito de apuntes, m.

noted, *—ĕd,* a. afamado, célebre.

nothing, *nŭth'ĭng,* s. nada, f.; **good for —,** lo que sirve para nada.

notice, *nŏ'tĭs,* s. noticia, f.; aviso, m.; —, v. a. observar.

noticeable, *—ăbl,* a. notable, reparable.

notification, *nŏtĭfĭkā'shŭn,* s. notificación, f.

notify, *nŏ'tĭfī,* v. a. notificar. [f.

notion, *nŏ'shŭn,* s. noción, f.; opinión, f.; idea, f.

notoriety, *nŏtŏrī'ĕtĕ,* s. notoriedad, f.

notorious, *nŏtŏ'rĭŭs,* a. notorio; **-ly,** ad. notoriamente. [obstante, aunque.

notwithstanding, *nŏtwĭthstănd'ĭng,* c. no

nought, *năt,* s. nada, f.

noun, *nŏŭn,* s. (gr.) nombre, sustantivo, m.

nourish, *nŭr'ĭsh,* v. a. nutrir, alimentar.

nourishment, *—mĕnt,* s. nutrimiento, alimento, m. [mento, m.

novel, *nŏv'ĕl,* s. novela, f.

novelist, *—ĭst,* s. novelador, m.

novelty, *—tĕ,* s. novedad, f.

November, *nŏvĕm'bŭr,* s. noviembre, m.

novice, *nŏv'ĭs,* s. novicio, m.

noviciate, *nŏvĭsh'ĭăt,* s. noviciado, m.

now, *nŏŭ,* ad. ahora, en el tiempo presente; **— and then,** de cuando en cuando.

nowadays, *—ddz,* ad. al presente.

nowhere, *nŏ'hwār,* ad. en ninguna parte.

nowise, *nŏ'wīz,* ad. de ningún modo.

noxious, *nŏk'shŭs,* a. nocivo, dañoso; **-ly,** ad. ad. perniciosamente.

nucleus, *nū'klĕŭs,* s. núcleo, m.

nude, *nŭd,* a. desnudo, en carnes, en cueros, sin vestido; (law) nulo.

nudge, *nŭdj,* v. a. dar del codo á uno para avisarle secretamente.

nudity, *nū'dĭtĕ,* s. desnudez, f.

nugatory, *nū'gătŏrĕ,* a. nugatorio, frívolo.

nuisance, *nū'săns,* s. daño, perjuicio, m.; incomodidad, f.

null, *nŭl,* a. nulo, inválido.

nullify, *nŭl'ĭfī,* v. a. anular, invalidar.

nullity, *nŭl'ĭtĕ,* s. nulidad, f. [pecer.

numb, *nŭm,* a. entorpecido; —, v. a. entorpecer.

number, *nŭm'bŭr,* s. número, m.; cantidad, f.; —, v. a. numerar. [mero.

numberless, *—lĕs,* a. innumerable, sin número.

numbness, *nŭm'nĕs,* s. torpor, m.

numeral, *nū'mŭrăl,* a. numeral. [f.

numeration, *nūmŭrā'shŭn,* s. numeración, f.

numerator, *nū'mŭrātŭr,* s. (ar.) numerador, m.

numerical, *nūmĕr'ĭkăl,* a. numérico.

numerous, *nū'mŭrŭs,* a. numeroso.

numismatics, *nūmĭsmăt'ĭks,* s. pl. numismática, f.

numskull, *nŭm'skŭl,* s. zote, m.

nun, *nŭn,* s. monja, religiosa, f. [m.

nunnery, *nŭn'nŭrĕ,* s. convento de monjas.

nuptial, *nŭp'shăl,* a. nupcial; **-s,** pl. nupcias, f. pl.

nurse, *nŭrs,* s. ama de cría, f.; enfermera, —, v. a. criar criaturas; alimentar.

nursery, *—ŭrĕ,* s. crianza, f.; plantel, m.

nursling, *nŭrs'ĭng,* s. niño de teta, m.

nurture, *nŭr'tŭr,* s. crianza, f.; —, v. a. criar, educar.

nut, *nŭt,* s. nuez, f. [ces, m.

nut-crackers, *—krăkŭrz,* s. pl. cascanueces, m.

nut-gall, *—gŏl,* s. agalla de monte, f.

nutmeg, *—mĕg,* s. nuez moscada, f.

nutriment, *nū'trĭmĕnt,* s. nutrimento, alimento, m. [trimento, m.

nutrition, *nūtrĭsh'ŭn,* s. nutrición, f.; nu-

nutritious, nŭt'rĭsh'ŭs, nutritive, nā'-
    trĭtĭv, a. nutritivo, nutricio.
nut-shell, nŭt'shĕl, s. cáscara de nuez, f.
nut-tree, —trē, s. avellano, m.
nymph, nĭmf, s. ninfa, f.

O.

oaf, ōf, s. idiota, zoquete, m.
oak, ōk, s. roble, m.
oak-apple, —ăppl, s. agalla, f.
oaken, —n, a. (hecho) de roble.
oakum, ō'kŭm, s. (mar.) estopa, f.
oar, ōr, s. remo, m.
oarsman, ōrz'măn, s. remero, m.
oasis, ōā'sĭs, s. oasis, f.
oat, ōt, s. avena, f.
oath, ōth, s. juramento, m.
obduracy, ŏb'dūrăsĭ, s. endurecimiento,
    m.; dureza de corazón, f.
obdurate, ŏb'dūrăt, a. endurecido, duro;
    —ly, ad. tercamente, ásperamente.
obedience, ŏbē'dĭĕns, s. obediencia, f.
obedient, ŏbē'dĭĕnt, a. —ly, a. obediente-
    (mente).   [cia, f.
obeisance, ŏbā'săns, s. cortesía, reveren-
obelisk, ŏb'ĕlĭsk, s. obelisco, m.
obese, ŏbēs', a. obeso, gordo.
obesity, ŏbēs'ĭtĕ, s. obesidad, crasitud, f.
obey, ŏbā', v. a. obedecer.
obituary, ŏbĭt'ūărĕ, s. necrología, f.
object, ŏb'jĕkt, s. objeto, m.; —, ŏbjĕkt',
    v. a. objetar.   [ción, réplica, f.
objection, ŏbjĕk'shŭn, s. oposición, obje-
objectionable, —ăbl, a. capaz de objeción.
objective, ŏbjĕk'tĭv, a. objetivo.   [f.
oblation, ŏblā'shŭn, s. oblación, ofrenda.
obligation, ŏblĭgā'shŭn, s. obligación, f.
obligatory, ŏb'lĭgătŭrĕ, a. obligatorio.
oblige, ŏblīj', v. a. obligar; complacer,
    favorecer.   [cortesmente.
obliging, ŏblī'jĭng, a. servicial; —ly, ad.
oblique, ŏblēk', a. oblicuo; indirecto;
    —ly, ad. oblicuamente.
obliquity, ŏblĭk'wĭtĕ, s. oblicuidad, f.
obliterate, ŏblĭt'ŭrāt, v. a. borrar.
oblivion, ŏblĭv'ŭn, s. olvido, m.
oblivious, —ŭs, a. olvidadizo.
oblong, ŏb'lŏng, a. oblongo.
obloquy, ŏb'lōkwĕ, s. maledicencia, f.; des-
    honra, f.   [pable.
obnoxious, ŏbnŏk'shŭs, a. sujeto; cul-
obscene, ŏbsēn', a. obsceno, impúdico.
obscenity, ŏbsĕn'ĭtĕ, s. obscenidad, f.
obscure, ŏbskūr', a. obscuro; —ly, ad. ob-
    scuramente; —, v. a. obscurecer.
obscurity, ŏbskū'rĭtĕ, s. obscuridad, f.
obsequies, ŏb'sĕkwĭz, s. pl. exequias,
    honras funerales, f. pl.
obsequious, ŏbsē'kwĭŭs, a. obsequioso;
    —ly, ad. obsequiosamente.   [spicuo.
observable, ŏbzŭr'văbl, a. notable, con-
observance, —văns, s. observancia, f.;
    veréncia, f.   [tuoso.
observant, —vănt, a. observante, respe-

observation, ŏbzŭrvā'shăn, a. observa-
    ción, f.   [rio, m.
observatory, ŏbzŭr'vătŭrĕ, s. observato-
observe, ŏbzŭrv', v. a. observar, mirar;
    —, v. n. ser circumspecto.
observer, —ŭr, s. observador, m.
observingly, ŏbzŭr'vĭnglĕ, ad. cuidado-
    samente, atentamente.
obsolete, ŏb'sŏlĕt, a. obsoleto.
obstacle, ŏb'stăkl, s. obstáculo, m.
obstinacy, ŏb'stĭnăsĕ, s. obstinación, f.
obstinate, ŏb'stĭnăt, a. obstinado; —ly,
    ad. obstinadamente.
obstreperous, ŏbstrĕp'ŭrŭs, a. estrepitoso,
    turbulento.   [pedir.
obstruct, ŏbstrŭkt', v. a. obstruir; im-
obstruction, ŏbstrŭk'shŭn, s. obstrucción,
    f.; impedimento, m.; obstrucción de los
    debates parlamentarios.
obtain, ŏbtān', v. a. obtener, adquirir; —,
    v. n. estar establecido.
obtainable, —ăbl, a. asequible.   [lencia.
obtrude, ŏbtrŏd', v. a. introducir con vio-
obtrusive, ŏbtrŏ'sĭv, a. intruso, impor-
    tuno.   [torpe.
obtuse, ŏbtūs', a. obtuso, sin punta; lerdo,
obviate, ŏb'vĭāt, v. a. obviar, evitar.
obvious, ŏb'vĭŭs, a. obvio, evidente; —ly,
    ad. patentemente.
occasion, ŏkkā'zhŭn, s. ocasión, ocurren-
    cia, f.; tiempo oportuno, m.; —, v. a. oca-
    sionar, causar.   [ad. ocasionalmente.
occasional, —ăl, a. ocasional, casual; —ly.
occidental, ŏksĭdĕn'tăl, a. occidental.
occult, ŏkkŭlt', a. oculto, escondido.
occupancy, ŏk'kŭpănsĕ, s. toma de pose
    sión, f.
occupant, ŏk'kŭpănt, occupier, ŏk'kŭ-
    pīŭr, s. ocupador, m.; poseedor, m.; in-
    quilino, m.   [f.; empleo, m.
occupation, ŏkkŭpā'shŭn, s. ocupación,
occupy, ŏk'kŭpĭ, v. a. ocupar, emplear.
occur, ŏkkŭr', v. n. ocurrir; encontrarse.
occurrence, —rĕns, s. ocurrencia, f.; luci-
    miento, m.
ocean, ō'shăn, s. océano, m.; alta mar, f.
oceanic, ŏshēăn'ĭk, a. oceánico; inmenso.
ochre, ō'kŭr, s. ocra, f.   [octavo.
octave, ŏk'tăv, s. octava, f.   [octavo.
octavo, ŏktā'vō, s. libro en octavo, m.; —, a.
October, ŏktō'bŭr, s. octubre, m.
ocular, ŏk'ūlăr, a. ocular.
oculist, ŏk'ūlĭst, s. oculista, m.
odd, ŏd, a. impar; particular; extrava-
    gante; extraño; tonto; —ly, ad. extraña-
    mente.   [dad, rareza, f.
oddity, —dĭtĕ, s. singularidad, particulari-
oddness, —nĕs, s. disparidad, desigual-
    dad, f.; singularidad, f.
odds, —z, s. diferencia, disparidad, f.; ven-
    taja, superioridad, f.   [mente.
odious, ō'dĭŭs, a. odioso; —ly, ad. odiosa-
odium, ō'dĭŭm, s. odiosidad, f.; odio, m.
odorous, ō'dŭrŭs, a. odorífero.
odour, ō'dŭr, s. olor, m.; fragancia, f.
of, ŏv, pr. de; tocante; según.
off, ŏf, ad. lejos, á distancia; —hand, de.
    repente; —! ¡fuera!, ¡abajo!

offal, *ŏf'făl*, s. sobras, f. pl.; desecho, m.
offence, *ŏffĕnß'*, s. ofensa, f.; injuria, f.
offend, *ŏffĕnd'*, v. a. ofender, irritar; injuriar; —, v. n. pecar.
offender, *-ûr*, s. delincuente, ofensor, m.
offensive, *ŏffĕn'ßiv*, a. ofensivo; injurioso; —ly, ad. ofensivamente.
offer, *ŏf'fûr*, v. a. ofrecer; inmolar; atentar; —, v. n. ofrecerse; —, s. oferta, f.
offering, *-ing*, s. sacrificio, m.; oferta, f.
offertory, *-tûrĭ*, s. ofertorio, m. [cio, m.
office, *ŏf'fiß*, s. oficio, empleo, m.; servicio; —, v. a. ofrecer.
officer, *-ûr*, s. oficial, empleado, m.
official, *ŏffish'ăl*, a. oficial; —ly, ad. de oficio; —, s. empleado, m.
officiate, *-ĭāt*, v. a. hacer alguna cosa de oficio; —, v. n. oficiar. [ciosamente.
officious, *-ûs*, a. oficioso; —ly, ad. oficiosamente.
offing, *ŏf'ing*, s. pleamar, f.
offscouring, *ŏf'skŏûring*, s. basura, f.; lavaduras, f. pl.
offset, *-sĕt*, s. pimpollo, m.
offspring, *-spring*, s. prole, f.; linaje, m.; descendencia, f. [ad. muchas veces.
oft, *ŏft*, often, *ŏf'n*, oftentimes, *-tīmz*, ad. muchas veces.
ogle, *ŏ'gl*, v. a. mirar al soslayo; guiñar.
ogre, *ŏ'gr*, s. ogro, m. [aceitar.
oil, *ŏĭl*, s. aceite, m.; óleo, m.; —, v. a. aceitar.
oil-cloth, *-klŏth*, s. encerado, hule, m.
oil-colour, *-kŭlûr*, s. color preparado con aceite.
oilman, *-măn*, s. aceitero, m. [aceite, m.
oil-painting, *-pānting*, s. pintura al óleo, f. [rado, hule, m.
oil-silk, *-ßilk*, oil-skin, *-skin*, s. encerado, hule, m.
oily, *-ĭ*, a. aceitoso, oleaginoso.
ointment, *ŏint'mĕnt*, s. ungüento, m.
old, *ōld*, olden, *ōl'dĕn*, a. viejo; antiguo; of —, antiguamente.
oleaginous, *ŏlĕăj'ĭnŭs*, a. oleaginoso.
oleander, *ŏlĕăn'dûr*, s. adelfa, f.; baladre, m.
olfactory, *ŏlfăk'tûrĭ*, s. olfatorio. [m.
olive, *ŏl'iv*, s. olivo, m.; oliva, f.
olive-grove, *-grōv*, s. olivar, m.
olive-oil, *-ŏĭl*, s. aceite de olivas, m.
olive-tree, *-trē*, s. olivo, m.
omelet, *ŏm'lĕt*, s. tortilla de huevos, f.
omen, *ŏ'mĕn*, s. agüero, presagio, m.
omened, *-d*, a. fatídico, augural.
ominous, *ŏm'ĭnŭs*, a. ominoso; —ly, ad. ominosamente, [cuido, m.
omission, *ŏmĭsh'ăn*, s. omisión, f.; descuido, m.
omit, *ŏmĭt'*, v. a. omitir.
omnibus, *ŏm'nĭbŭs*, s. ómnibus, m.
omnipotence, *ŏmnĭp'ŏtĕnß*, s. omnipotencia, f. [dopoderoso.
omnipotent, *-tĕnt*, a. omnipotente, todopoderoso.
omniscience, *ŏmnĭsh'iĕnß*, s. omnisciencia, f.
on, *ŏn*, pr. sobre, encima, en; de; á; —, ad. adelante, sin cesar; — ! ¡vamos !, ¡adelante !
once, *wŭnß*, ad. una vez; for all, una vez por todas; at —, de un golpe; all at —, de una vez, de seguida; — more, más todavía, otra vez. [uno por uno.
one, *wŭn*, a. un, uno; —, s. uno ó uno, — by —, uno á uno.
onerous, *ŏn'ărŭs*, a. oneroso, molesto.
oneself, *wŭnßĕlf'*, pn. sí mismo.

onion, *ăn'yŭn*, s. cebolla, f.
only, *ŏn'lĕ*, a. único, solo; —, ad. solamente.
onset, *ŏn'sĕt*, onslaught, *ŏn'slăt*, s. primer ímpetu, m.; ataque, m.
onward(s), *ŏn'wărd(z)*, ad. adelante.
ooze, *ŏz*, s. fango, m.; —, v. n. manar ó correr algún líquido suavemente.
opacity, *ŏpăs'ĭtĭ*, s. opacidad, f.
opal, *ŏ'păl*, s. ópalo, m.
opaque, *ŏpāk'*, a. opaco.
open, *ŏ'pn*, a. abierto; patente, evidente; sincero, franco; —ly, ad. con franqueza; —, v. a. (& n.) abrir(se); descubrir(se).
open-handed, *-hănded*, a. dadivoso, liberal. [sencillo.
open-hearted, *-hărtĕd*, a. franco, sincero, sencillo.
opening, *-ing*, s. abertura, f.; (com.) salida, f.; principio, m. [sinceridad, f.
openness, *-nĕs*, s. claridad, f.; franqueza, f.; sinceridad, f.
open-work, *-wŭrk*, s. obra á claros, f.
opera, *ŏp'ără*, s. ópera, f.
opera-glass, *-glăs*, s. anteojo de ópera, m.
opera-hat, *-hăt*, s. clac, m.
operate, *ŏp'ărāt*, v. n. obrar, operar.
operatical, *ŏpărăt'ĭkăl*, a. de ópera.
operation, *ŏpără'shăn*, s. operación, f.; efecto, m.
operative, *ŏp'ărătĭv*, a. operativo.
operator, *ŏp'ărā'tûr*, s. operario, m.; (med.) operador, m.
ophthalmy, *ŏf'thălmĕ*, s. oftalmía, f. [a opiate, *ŏ'pĭāt*, s. opiata, f.
opine, *ŏpīn'*, v. n. opinar, juzgar.
opinion, *ŏpĭn'yŭn*, s. opinión, f.; juicio, m.
opinionative, *-ătĭv*, a. obstinado, pertinaz. [arguyente, m.
opponent, *ŏppŏ'nĕnt*, s. antagonista, m.
opportune, *ŏppŏrtūn'*, a. oportuno; —ly, ad. oportunamente. [f.
opportunity, *-ĭtĕ*, s. oportunidad, sazón, f.
oppose, *ŏppōz'*, v. n. oponer(se).
opposite, *ŏp'rŏ-zĭt*, a. fronterizo, opuesto; contrario; —ly, ad. enfrente; —, s. antagonista, adversario, m.
opposition, *ŏppŏzĭsh'ăn*, s. oposición, f.; resistencia, f.; impedimento, m.
oppress, *ŏpprĕs'*, v. a. oprimir. [ción, f.
oppression, *ŏpprĕsh'ăn*, s. opresión, f.
oppressive, *ŏpprĕs'ĭv*, a. opresivo, cruel.
oppressor, *ŏpprĕs'ûr*, s. opresor, m.
opprobrious, *ŏpprŏ'brĭŭs*, a. oprobioso, ignominioso.
opprobrium, *-brĭăm*, s. ignominia, f.; [óptica, f.
optic(al), *ŏp'tĭk(ăl)*, a. óptico; —s, s. pl. óptica, f.
optician, *ŏptĭsh'ăn*, s. óptico, m.
optimist, *ŏp'tĭmĭst*, s. optimista, m.
option, *ŏp'shăn*, s. opción, f.; deseo, m.
optional, *-ăl*, a. facultativo. [f.
opulence, *ŏp'ūlĕnß*, s. opulencia, riqueza, f.
opulent, *ŏp'ūlĕnt*, a. opulento; —ly, ad.
or, *ŏr*, ó, ú. [opulentamente.
oracle, *ŏr'ăkl*, s. oráculo, m.
oracular, *ŏrăk'ūlăr*, a. obscuro, ambiguo.
oral, *ŏ'răl*, a. oral, vocal; —ly, ad. verbalmente, de palabra.
orange, *ŏr'ĕnj*, s. naranja, f.
orange-tree, *--trē*, s. naranjo, m.

oration, *ŏrá'shŭn*, s. oración, arenga, f.
orator, *ŏr'átŭr*, s, orador, m.   [rio.
oratorio(al), *ŏrátŏ'rĭk(ăl)*, a. retórico, orato-
oratory, *ŏr'átŭrĕ*, s. oratoria, f.; oratorio,
m.; elocuencia, arte oratoria, f.
orb, *ŏrb*, s. orbe, m.; esfera, f.; globo, m.
orbit, *ŏr'bĭt*, s. órbita, f.
orchard, *ŏr'tshŭrd*, s. pomar, verjel, m.
orchestra, *ŏr'kĕstrá*, s. orquesta, f.
ordain, *ŏrdán'*, v. a. ordenar; establecer.
ordeal, *ŏr'dēăl*, s. ordalía, f.
order, *ŏr'dŭr*, s. orden, m. & f.; regla, f.;
mandato, m.; serie, clase, f.; —, v. a. ordenar, arreglar; mandar. [disposición, f.
ordering, —ĭng, s. manejo, m.; dirección,
orderly, —lĕ, a. ordenado, regular.
ordinance, *ŏr'dĭnáns*, s. ordenanza, f.
ordinarily, *ŏr'dĭnárĭlĕ*, ad. ordinariamente.   [dinario, m.; hostería, f.
ordinary, *ŏr'dĭnárĕ*, a. ordinario; —, s. or-
ordination, *ŏr'dĭná'shŭn*, s. ordenación, f.
ordnance, *ŏr'dnáns*, s. artillería, f.; caño-
ore, *ŏr*, s. mineral, m.   [nes, m. pl.
organ, *ŏr'gán*, s. órgano, m.
organic(al), *ŏrgăn'ĭk(ăl)*, a. orgánico.
organisation, *ŏrgănĭzá'shŭn*, s. organización, f.
organise, *ŏr'gănĭz*, v. a. organizar.
organism, *ŏr'gănĭzm*, s. organismo, m.
organist, *ŏr'gănĭst*, s. organista, m.
organ-pipe, *ŏr'gánpĭp*, s. fístula de órgano, f.   [gano, m.
organ-stop, —stŏp, s. registro de un ór-
oriental, *ŏrĭĕn'tăl*, a. oriental.
orifice, *ŏr'ĭfĭs*, s. orificio, m.
origin, *ŏr'ĭjĭn*, s. origen, principio, m.
original, *ŏrĭj'ĭnăl*, a. original, primitivo;
—ly, ad. originalmente.
originality, *ŏrĭjĭnăl'ĭtĕ*, s. originalidad, f.
originate, *ŏrĭj'ĭnát*, v.a.(& n.) originar(se).
orison, *ŏr'ĭzŏn*, s. oración, f.; rezo, m.
ormolu, *ŏr'mŏlŭ*, s. oro molido, m.
ornament, *ŏr'nămĕnt*, s. ornamento, m.;
—, v. a. ornamentar, adornar. [adorno.
ornamental, —mĕn'tăl, a. lo que sirve de
ornate, *ŏr'nát*, a. adornado, ataviado.
orphan, *ŏr'fán*, a. & s. huérfano (m.).
orphanage, —éj, s. orfandad, f.
orphan-asylum, —ásĭlŭm, s. casa de
huérfanos, f., orfanotrofio, m.
orthodox, *ŏr'thŏdŏks*, a. ortodoxo.
orthodoxy, —ĕ, s. ortodoxia, f.
orthographical, *ŏrthŏgráf'ĭkăl*, a. ortográfico; —ly, ad. ortográficamente.
orthography, *ŏrthŏg'răfĕ*, s. ortografía, f.
oscillate, *ŏs'ĭlát*, v. n. oscilar, vibrar.
oscillation, *ŏsĕllá'shŭn*, s. oscilación, f.
vibración, f.
osier, *ō'zhĭŭr*, s. (bot.) mimbrera, f.
osprey, *ŏs'prá*, s. águila marina, f.
ossification, *ŏssĭfĭká'shŭn*, s. osificación, f.
ossify, *ŏs'ĭfĭ*, v. a. & n. osificar(se).   [f.
ostensible, *ŏstĕn'stbl*, a. ostensible, mani-
festable.
ostensibly, —stbly, ad. ostensiblemente.
ostentation, *ŏstĕntá'shŭn*, s. ostentación, f.
ostentatious, —shăs, a. ostentoso, fas-
tuoso; —ly, ad. pomposamente.

ostler, *ŏs'lŭr*, s. mozo de caballos, m.
ostracise, *ŏs'trásĭz*, v. a. desterrar por
medio del ostracismo.
ostrich, *ŏs'trĭtsh*, s. avestruz, m.
other, *ŭth'ŭr*, pn. otro.   [otra parte.
otherwise, —wĭz, ad. de otra manera, por
otter, *ŏt'tŭr*, s. nutria, nutria, f.
ottoman, *ŏt'tŏmăn*, s. otomana, f.; sofá, m.
ought, *ăt*, v. imp. & def. deber, ser menes-
ounce, *ŏŭns*, s. onza, f.   [ter.
our, *ŏŭr*, ours, *ŏŭrz*, pn. nuestro, nuestra,
nuestros, nuestras.   [mos.
ourselves, —sĕlvz, pn. pl. nosotros mis-
oust, *ŏŭst*, v. a. quitar; desposeer.
out, *ŏŭt*, ad, fuera, afuera; —, v. a. expeler,
outbid, —bĭd', v. a. pujar.   [desposeer.
outbreak, *ŏŭt'brák*, s. erupción, f.
outburst, —bŭrst', s. explosión, f.
outcast, *ŏŭt'kăst*, a. desechado; desterra-
do, expulso.   [venta pública, f.
outcry, —krĭ, s. clamor, m.; gritería, f.;
outdo, —dŭ', v. a. exceder á otro, sobre-
outer, *ŏŭt'ŭr*, a. exterior.   [pujar.
outermost, —mŏst, a. extremo; lo más
exterior.
outfit, *ŏŭt'fĭt*, s. vestidos, m. pl.; ropa, f.
outfitter, —fĭttŭr, s. confeccionador, m.
outgoing, —gŏĭng, s. salida, f.; —s, pl.
gasto, m.   [en vegetación.
outgrow, —grŏ', v. a. sobrecrecer; exceder
outhouse, *ŏŭt'hŏŭs*, s. dependencia de una
casa, f.
outlandish, —lănd'ĭsh, a. extranjero.
outlast, —lăst', v. a. exceder en duración.
outlaw, *ŏŭt'lá*, s. proscripto, m.; bandido,
m.; —, v. a. proscribir.
outlawry, —lărĕ, s. proscripción, f.
outlay, —lá, s. despensa, f., gastos, m. pl.
outlet, —lĕt', s. salida, f.   [m.
outline, —lĭn, s. contorno, m.; bosquejo,
outlive, —lĭv', v. a. sobrevivir.
outlying, —lĭĭng, a. distante de, lejos de.
outnumber, —nŭm'bŭr, v. a. exceder en
número.
out of doors, *ŏŭt'ŏvdŏrs*, ad. fuera de casa.
outpost, *ŏŭt'pŏst*, s. puesto avanzado, m.
outrage, —rá́j, s.ultraje, m.; —,v.a. ultrajar.
outrageous, —rá'jŭs, a. ultrajoso; atroz;
—ly, ad. injuriosamente; enormemente.
outrider, —rĭdŭr, s. palafrenero, m.
outright, —rĭt', ad. cumplidamente, luego.
outrun, —rŭn', v. a. correr más que otro.
outset, *ŏŭt'sĕt*, s. principio, m.
outshine, —shĭn', v. a. exceder en brillantez, eclipsar.   [m.; apariencia, f.
outside, *ŏŭt'sĭd*, s. superficie, f.; exterior,
outsiders, —ŭrz, s. pl. público, m.
outskirt, —skŭrt, s. parte exterior, f.;
suburbio, m.   [alargar.
outstretch, —strĕtsh', v. a. extenderse.
outstrip, —strĭp', v. a. dejar atrás; sobrepujar.
outwall, *ŏŭt'wál*, s. antemural, m.
outward, —wŭrd, a. exterior, externo; —ly,
ad. fuera; exteriormente.
outweigh, —wá', v. a. preponderar.
outwit, —wĭt', v. a. engañar á uno á fuerza
de tretas.

outworks, *ŏät'wŭrkz,* s. pl. (mil.) obras avanzadas, f. pl.

oval, *ŏ'vŭl,* s. óvalo, m.; –, a. oval.

ovary, *ŏ'vări,* s. ovario, m.

ovation, *ŏvā'shŭn,* s. ovación, f.

oven, *ŭv'n,* s. horno, m.

over, *ŏ'vŭr,* pr. sobre, encima; all –, por todos lados –; ad. más, demás; – again, otra vez; – against, enfrente; – and –, repetidas veces.

overall, *–ŭl',* s. sobretodo, m.

overawe, *–ä',* v. a. tener á freno; imponer respeto. [rar; –, s. preponderancia, f.

overbalance, *–băl'läns,* v. a. preponderar.

overbear, *–băr',* v. a. sujetar, oprimir.

overbearing, *–băr'ing,* a. ultrajoso, despótico.

overboard, *–bōrd,* ad. (mar.) encima de [bordo, al mar.

overburden, *–bŭr'dn,* v. a. sobrecargar.

overcast, *–kāst',* v. a. anublar, obscurecer; repulgar; valuar demasiado.

overcharge, *–tshärj',* v. a. sobrecargar; poner alguna cosa á precio muy subido.

overcloud, *–klŏŭd',* v. a. cubrir de nubes.

overcome, *–kŭm',* v. a. vencer; superar.

over-confident, *kŏn'fident,* a. demasiado atrevido. [sario.

overdo, *–dō',* v. n. hacer más de lo necesario.

overdrafts, *–drăfts,* s.pl. adelantos, m. pl.

overdress, *–drĕs',* v. a. engalanar con exceso.

overeat, *–ĕt',* v. n. tupirse. [exceso.

overflow, *–flō',* v. a. & n. inundar; salir de madre; rebosar; –, *ŏ'vĕrflō,* s. inundación, f.; superabundancia, f.

overfond, *–fŏnd',* a. el que quiere ó gusta demasiado de alguna cosa.

overgrow, *–grō',* v. n. crecer demasiado.

overgrowth, *ŏ'vŭrgrōth,* s. vegetación exuberante, f.

overhang, *ŏvŭrhăng',* v. a. estar colgando sobre alguna cosa; salir algo fuera del nivel de un edificio. [lo alto.

overhead, *–hĕd',* ad. sobre la cabeza, en

overhear, *–hĕr',* v. a. oir algo por casualidad.

overheat, *–hĕt',* v. a. acalorar. [lidad.

overjoyed, *–jŏid',* a. muy gozoso.

overlay, *–lă',* v. a. abrumar.

overlook, *–lŏk',* v. a. mirar desde lo alto; examinar; rever; repasar; pasar por alto, tolerar; descuidar; desdeñar.

overmuch, *–mŭtsh',* a. demasiado. [omitir.

overpass, *–pās',* v. a. pasar por alto.

overplus, *ŏ'vŭrplŭs,* s. sobrante, m.

overpower, *ŏvŭrpŏä'ŭr,* v. a. predominar, oprimir.

overrate, *ŏvärrāt',* v. a. apreciar ó valuar alguna cosa en más de lo que vale.

overreach, *–rĕtsh',* v. a. sobresalir, exceder en altura; engañar. [con exceso.

override, *–rīd',* v. a. fatigar un caballo

overrule, *–rōl',* v. a. predominar, dominar.

overrun, *–rŭn',* v. a. hacer correrías; cubrir enteramente; inundar; infestar; repasar; –, v. n. rebosar. [omitir.

oversee, *–sĕ',* v. a. inspeccionar; pasar.

overseer, *–ŭr',* s. superintendente, m.

overset, *–sĕt',* v. a. volcar; trastornar; –, v. n. volcarse, caerse. [obscurecer.

overshadow, *–shăd'ŏ,* v. a. asombrar.

overshoe, *ŏ'vŭrshŏ,* s. galocha, f.

overshoot, *ŏvŭrshŏt',* v. a. tirar más allá del blanco; –, v. n. pasar de raya.

oversight, *ŏ'vŭrsīt,* s. yerro, m.; equivocación, f. [siado.

oversleep, *ŏvŭrslĕp',* v. n. dormir demasiado.

overspread, *–sprĕd',* v. a. desparramar.

overstate, *–stāt',* v. n. exagerar. [cubrir.

overstep, *–stĕp',* v. a. pasar más allá.

overt, *ŏ'vŭrt,* a. abierto; público; –ly, ad. abiertamente [en el hecho.

overtake, *ŏvŭrtāk',* v. a. alcanzar; coger

overtax, *–tăks',* v. a. oprimir con tributos.

overthrow, *–thrō',* v. a. trastornar; demoler; destruir; –, *ŏ'vŭrthrō,* s. trastorno, m.; ruina, derrota, f.

overture, *ŏ'vŭrtūr,* s. abertura, f.; (mus.) obertura, f. [tornar.

overturn, *ŏvŭrtŭrn',* v. a. subvertir, trastornar.

overweening, *–wĕn'ing,* a. presuntuoso.

overweight, *ŏ'vŭrwāt,* s. preponderancia, f.; exceso en el peso, m.

overwhelm, *ŏvŭrhwĕlm',* v. a. abrumar; oprimir; sumergir. [siado.

overwork, *–wŭrk',* v. a. trabajar demasiado.

oviparous, *ŏvīp'ărŭs,* a. ovíparo.

owe, *ō,* v. a. deber; tener deudas; estar obligado. [causa de.

owing, *ō'ing,* a. que es debido; – to, por

owl, *ŏŭl,* **owlet,** *–ĕt,* s. lechuza, f.

own, *ōn,* a. propio; my –, mío, mía; –, v. a. reconocer; poseer; confesar.

owner, *–ŭr,* s. dueño, propietario, m.; – of a ship, naviero, m. [piedad, f.

ownership, *–ship,* s. dominio, m.; propiedad, f.

ox, *ŏks,* s. buey, m.; –, pl. oxen, ganado vacuno, m.

oxidize, *ŏks'idīz,* v. a. oxidar.

oxygen, *ŏks'jĕn,* s. oxígeno, m.

oyster, *ŏis'tŭr,* s. ostra, f.

P.

pace, *pās,* s. paso, m.; –, v. a. medir á pasos; –, v. n. pasear. [dura, m.

pacer, *–ŭr,* s. caballo de paso de andadura, m.

pacific(al), *păsīf'ik(ăl),* a. pacífico.

pacification, *păsīfikā'shŭn,* s. pacificación, f.

pacify, *păs'ifī,* v. a. pacificar. [ción, f.

pack, *păk,* s. lío, fardo, m.; baraja de naipes, f.; muta, perrada, f.; cuadrilla, f.; –, v. a. enfardelar, embalar; empaquetar; empadillar el naipe.

package, *–āj,* s. fardo, m.; embalaje, m.

pack-cloth, *–klōth,* s. arpillera, f.

packet, *–ĕt,* s. paquete, m.

packet-boat, *–bōt,* s. paquebote, f.

pack-horse, *–hŏrs,* s. caballo de carga, m.

packing, *–ing,* s. embalaje, m. [guita, f.

pack-thread, *–thrĕd,* s. bramante, m.

pad, *păd,* s. senda, f.; haca, f.; salteador de caminos á pie, m.; silla de montar baja y blanda, f.; –, v. a. acolchar con algodón.

paddle, *–dl,* v. n. remar; chapotear; –, s. canalete, m. (especie de remo).

9*

paddock, *–ŏk,* s. escuerzo, sapo, m. ; parpadlock, *–lŏk,* s. candado, m. [que, m.
pagan, *pā'găn,* a. & s. pagano (m.).
paganism, *–ĭsm,* s. paganismo, m.
page, *pāj,* s. página, f.; paje, m.; —, v. a. foliar.   [m.
pageant, *pāj'ĕnt,* s. espectáculo público,
pageantry, *–rē,* s. fasto, m.; pompa, f.
pail, *pāl,* s. colodra, f.; cubo, pozal, m.
pain, *pān,* s. pena, f.; castigo, m.; dolor, m.; —, v. a. afligir.
painful, *–fŭl,* a. dolorido; penoso; –ly, ad. dolorosamente, con pena.
painless, *–lĕs,* a. sin pena; sin dolor.
painstaking, *pānz'tāking,* a. laborioso, incansado.
paint, *pānt,* v. a. & n. pintar; afeitarse.
painter, *–ŭr,* s. pintor, m.
painting, *–ĭng,* s. pintura, f.
pair, *pār,* s. par, m.; —, v. a. (& n.) parear
palace, *pāl'ăs,* s. palacio, m.   [(se).
palatable, *pāl'ătŏbl,* a. sabroso.
palate, *pāl'ăt,* s. paladar, m.; gusto, m.
palatial, *pălā'schŭl,* a. palatino.
palatinate, *pălăt'ĭnāt,* s. palatinado, m.
palatine, *pāl'ătēn,* a. palatino.
palaver, *pălā'vŭr,* s. charla, f.; fruslería, f.; zalamería, f.; —, v. n. & n. congraciarse con zalamerías; charlar.
pale, *pāl,* a. pálido; claro; —, s. palidez, f.; palizada, f.; —, v. a. empalizar.
paleness, *–nĕs,* s. palidez, f.
palfrey, *pāl'frē,* s. palfrén, m.
paling, *pā'lĭng,* palisade, *pālĭsād',* s. estacada, palizada, f.
pall, *pāl,* s. paño de tumba, m.; palio de arzobispo, m.; —, v. n. desvanecerse; —, v. a. evaporar; condecorar con palio.
pallet, *pāl'lĕt,* s. camilla, f., cama pequeña
palliate, *pāl'lĭāt,* v. a. paliar.   [y pobre.
palliation, *pāllĭā'shŭn,* s. paliación, f.
palliative, *pāl'lĭătĭv,* a. & s. paliativo (m.).
pallid, *pāl'lĭd,* a. pálido.
pallor, *pāl'lŏr,* s. palidez, f.
palm, *pām,* s. (bot.) palma, f.; victoria, f.; palma (de la mano); —, v. a. escamotar; manosear.
palmated, *pālmā'tĕd,* a. palmeado.
palmistry, *pāl'mĭstrē,* s. quiromancia, f.
Palm-Sunday, *pām'sŭndā,* s. domingo de ramos, m.
palpable, *pāl'pŏbl,* a. palpable; evidente.
palpably, *–ē,* ad. palpablemente; clara-
palpitate, *pāl'pĭtāt,* v.n. palpitar. [mente.
palpitation, *–ā'shŭn,* s. palpitación, f.
palsied, *pāl'zēd,* a. paralítico.
palsy, *pāl'zē,* s. parálisis, perlesía, f.
paltry, *pāl'trē,* a. vil; mezquino.
pamper, *pām'pŭr,* v. a. atracar, engordar.
pamphlet, *pām'flĕt,* s. folleto, librejo, m.
pamphleteer, *–ēr',* s. folletista, m.
pan, *pān,* s. cazuela, f.
panacea, *pănăsē'ă,* s. panacea, f.
pancake, *pān'kăk,* s. buñuelo, m.
pander, *pān'dăr,* s. alcahuete, m.; —, v. a. alcahuear.
pane, *pān,* s. cuadro de vidrio, m.

panegyric, *pănĕjir'ĭk,* s. panegírico, m.
panel, *pān'ĕl,* s. entrepaño, m.; (law) lista de jurados, f.
pang, *păng,* s. angustia, congoja, f.
panic, *pān'ĭk,* a. & s. pánico; terror pánico
pannier, *pān'nŭr,* s. cuévano, m.   [(m.).
panoply, *pān'ŏplē,* s. panoplia, f.
pansy, *pān'sē,* s. (bot.) trinitaria, f.
pant, *pānt,* v. n. palpitar; jadear; to–for or after, suspirar por.
pantaloon, *pāntălōn',* s. Pantalón, bufón, m.; –s, pl. pantalones, m. pl.   [f.
pantechnicon, *pāntĕk'nĭkŏn,* s. trastera,
panther, *pān'thŭr,* s. pantera, f.
pantomime, *pān'tŏmĭm,* s. pantomimo, m.; pantomima, f.
pantry, *pān'trē,* s. despensa, f.; oficio en una casa principal, m.
pap, *păp,* s. pezón, m.; papa, papilla, f.; carne (de la fruta), f.
papacy, *pā'păsē,* s. papado, m.
papal, *pā'păl,* a. papal.
paper, *pā'pŭr,* s. papel, m.; jornal, m.; –s, pl. escrituras, f. pl.; (com.) fondos, m. pl.; —, de papel; —, v. a. entapizar con papel.   [papel moneda. m.
paper-credit, *–krĕdĭt,* (– currency), s,
paper-weight, *–wāt,* s. sujetapapeles, m.
papist, *pā'pĭst,* s. papista, m.
pappy, *pāp'pē,* a. mollar, jugoso.
par, *pār,* s. equivalencia, f.; igualdad, f.; at –, (com.) á la par.
parable, *pār'ăbl,* s. parábola, f.
parade, *pārād',* s. ostentación, pompa, f.; (mil.) parada, f.; —, v. a. & n. formar parada; pasear; hacer gala.
paradise, *pār'ădĭs,* s. paraíso.   [paradojo.
paradoxical, *părădŏks'ĭkăl,* a. paradójico,
paragon, *pār'ăgŏn,* s. modelo perfecto, m.
paragraph, *pār'ăgrăf,* s. párrafo, m.
parallel, *pār'ălĕl,* a. paralelo; —, s. línea paralela, f.; —, v. a. paralelizar; parangonar.   [nar.
paralyse, *pār'ălĭz,* v. a. paralizar. [nar.
paralysis, *pārāl'ĭsĭs,* s. parálisis, f.
paralytic(al), *părălĭt'ĭk(ăl),* a. paralítico.
paramount, *pār'ămŏunt,* a. supremo, superior; —, s. jefe, superior, m.
paramour, *pārămōr',* s. cortejo, m.
parasite, *pār'ăsĭt,* s. gorrista, m.   [lison-
parasitic, *părăsĭt'ĭk,* a. adulatorio, [Jero.
parasol, *pārăsŏl',* s. parasol, quitasol, m.
parboil, *pār'bŏil,* v. a. medio cocer.
parcel, *pār'sĕl,* s. paquete, m.; porción, cantidad, f.; equipajes, bultos, m. pl.; –'s post, *–zpŏst,* s. diligencia, f.; –'s delivery office, *–z dĕlĭv'ŭrē ŏffĭs,* s. entrega de equipajes, f.; —, v. a. partir.
parch, *pārtsh,* v. a. tostar.   [dividir.
parchment, *–mĕnt,* s. pergamino, m.
pardon, *pār'dn,* s. perdón, m.; —, v. a. perdonar; **pardonable,** *–ăbl,* a. perdonable. [donar.
pare, *pār,* v. a. recortar.
parent, *pā'rĕnt,* s. padre, m.; madre, f.
parentage, *–ĕntăj,* s. parentela, f.; extracción, f.
parental, *părĕn'tăl,* a. paternal.   [m.
parenthesis, *pārĕn'thĕsĭs,* s. paréntesis,

parish, *pắr'ĭsh,* s. parroquia, f.; -, a. parroquial. [m.	**party-wall,** *-wăl,* s. pared medianera, f.
parishioner, *pắrĭsh'ŭnẽr,* s. parroquiano.	**paschal,** *pắs'kăl,* a. pascual.
park, *pắrk,* s. parque, m.; -, v. a. cerrar un coto. [entretenimiento, m.	**pass,** *pắs,* v. a. pasar; traspasar; transferir; -, v. n. pasar, ocurrir; -s. pasillo, m.; paso, camino, m.; pase, m.; estado, m.; condición, f.; estocada, f.
parlance, *pắr'lăns,* s. conversación, f.;	**passable,** *-săbl,* a. pasadero, transitable.
parley, *pắr'lĕ,* s. conferencia, plática, f.	**passage,** *-sāj,* s. pasaje, m.; travesía, f.; pasadizo, m.; acontecimiento, m.
parliament, *pắr'lĭmĕnt,* s. parlamento, m.	**passenger,** *-sẽnjẽr,* s. pasajero, m.
parliamentary, *-lĭmĕnt'ărĕ,* a. parlamentario; - train, s. (rail.) tren ordinario, tren ómnibus, m. [recibimiento, f.	**passer-by,** -, s. el que pasa.
parlour, *pắr'lŭr,* s. parlatorio, m., sala de	**passing,** *-sĭng,* a. sobresaliente, eminente; -, ad. eminentemente. [á muerto, f.
parochial, *pắr'kĭăl,* a. parroquial.	**passing-bell,** *-bĕl,* s. campana que toca
parody, *pắr'ŏdĕ,* s. parodia, f.; -, v. a. parodiar. [m.	**passion,** *pắsh'ŭn,* s. pasión, f.; amor, m.; celo, ardor, m.
paroquet, *pắr'ŏkĕt,* s. papagayo pequeño	**passionate,** *-ăt,* a. apasionado; colérico; -ly, ad. apasionadamente; ardientemente.
parricide, *pắr'rĭsĭd,* s. parricidio, m.; parricida, m.	**passion-flower,** *-flŏwr,* s. pasionaria, f.
parrot, *pắr'rŏt,* s. papagayo, m.	**Passion-week,** *-wĕk,* s. semana de Pasión, f. [mente.
parry, *pắr'rĕ,* v. n. parar, rechazar.	**passive,** *pắs'ĭv,* a. pasivo; -ly, ad. pasiva-
parse, *pắrs,* v. a. (gr.) construir.	**pass-key,** *pắs'kĕ,* s. llave maestra, f.
parsimonious, *pắrsĭmō'nĭŭs,* a. económico, moderado en sus gastos; -ly, ad. con parsimonia.	**Passover,** *pắs'ŏvẽr,* s. Pascua, f.
parsimony, *pắr'sĭmōnĕ,* s. parsimonia, f.	**passport,** *-pōrt,* s. pasaporte, m.
parsley, *pắr'slĕ,* s. (bot.) perejil, m.	**pass-word,** *-wărd,* s. (mil.) pase de la palabra, m.
parsnip, *pắr'snĭp,* s. (bot.) chirivía, f.	**past,** *pắst,* a. pasado; gastado; -, s. (gr.) pretérito, m.; -, pr. más; fuera.
parson, *pắr'sn,* s. párroco, m.	**paste,** *pắst,* s. pasta, f.; engrudo, m.; -, v. a. engrudar.
parsonage, *-ăj,* s. beneficio, curado, m.	**pasteboard,** *-bŏrd,* s. cartón fuerte, m.
part, *pắrt,* s. parte, f.; partido, m.; oficio, m.; papel (de un actor), m.; obligación, f.; -s, pl. partes, f. pl. paraje, distrito, m.; -, v. a. partir, separar, desunir; -, v. n. partirse, separarse; -ly, ad. en parte. [tomar parte en.	**pastel,** *pắs'tĕl,* s. hierba pastel, f.; glasto, m.
partake, *pắrtāk',* v. a. & n. participar;	**pastern,** *pắs'tẽrn,* s. cuartilla del caballo, f. [versión, f.
partaker, *-ẽr,* s. partícipante, m.	**pastime,** *pắs'tĭm,* s. pasatiempo, m.; di-
partial, *pắr'shăl,* a. -ly, ad. parcial-(mente)	**pastor,** *pắs'tŏr,* s. pastor, m.
partiality, *pắrshăl'ĭtĕ,* s. parcialidad, f.	**pastoral,** *-ăl,* a. pastoril; pastoral.
participant, *pắrtĭs'ĭpănt,* a. participante, partícipe.	**pastry,** *pắs'trĕ,* s. pastelería, f.
participate, *-pāt,* v. a. participar.	**pasturage,** *pắs'tŭrăj,* s. pasturaje, m.
participation, *pắrtĭsĭpā'shŭn,* s. participación, f. [m.	**pasture,** *pắs'tŭr,* s. pastura, f.; -, v. a. pastar, apacentar; -, v. n. pastar, pacer.
participle, *pắr'tĭsĭpl,* s. (gr.) participio,	**pasty,** *pắs'tĕ,* s. pastel, borrón, m.
particle, *pắr'tĭkl,* s. partícula, f.	**pat,** *pắt,* a. apto, conveniente, propio; -, s. golpecillo, m.; -, v. a. dar golpecillos.
particular, *pắrtĭk'ŭlăr,* a. particular, singular; -ly, ad. particularmente; -, s. particular, m.; particularidad, f.	**patch,** *pắtsh,* s. remiendo, m.; lunar, m.; -, v. a. remendar; adornar al rostro con lunares. [f.; chapucería, f.
particularise, *pắrtĭk'ŭlărĭz,* s. particularizar. [laridad, circunstancia, f.	**patch-work,** *-wărk,* s. obra de retacitos.
particularity, *pắrtĭkŭlăr'ĭtĕ,* s. particu-	**pate,** *pắt,* s. (fam.) cabeza, f.
parting, *pắrt'ĭng,* s. separación, partida, f.; raya (en los cabellos).	**paten,** *pắt'n,* s. patena de cáliz, f.
partisan, *pắr'tĭzăn,* s. partidario, m.	**patent,** *pắ'tĕnt,* a. patente; privilegiado; -, s. patente, f.; -, v. a. privilegiar.
partition, *pắrtĭsh'ŭn,* s. partición, separación, f.; -, v. a. partir, dividir en varias partes. [f.	**patentee,** *-ĕ',* s. el que posee un privilegio de invención. [embar-
partition-wall, *-wăl,* s. pared medianera,	**patent-leather,** *-lĕthẽr,* s. cuero embar-
partner, *pắrt'nẽr,* s. socio, compañero, m. [de comercio, f.	**paternal,** *pắtẽr'năl,* a. paternal.
partnership, *-shĭp,* s. compañía, sociedad	**paternity,** *pắtẽr'nĭtĕ,* s. paternidad, f.
partridge, *pắr'trĭj,* s. perdiz, f.	**path,** *pắth,* s. senda, f.
party, *pắr'tĕ,* s. partido, m.; parte, f.; función, f.; (mil.) partida, f.	**pathetic(al),** *pắthĕt'ĭk(ăl),* a. patético; -ally, ad. patéticamente. [table.
party-coloured, *-kŭlŭrd,* a. abigarrado.	**pathless,** *pắth'lĕs,* a. sin senda, intransi-
party-man, *-măn,* s. partidario, m.	**pathological,** *pắthŏlŏj'ĭkăl,* a. patológico.
	pathology, *pắthŏl'ŏjĕ,* s. patología, f.
	patience, *pắ'shĕns,* s. paciencia, f.
	patient, *-shĕnt,* a. paciente, sufrido; -ly, ad. con paciencia; -, s. enfermo, m.

patriarch, *pā'trīärk,* s. patriarca, m.

patrimony, *păt' rĭmŏnĕ,* s. patrimonio, m.

patriot, *pā'trĭŏt,* s. patriota, m.

patriotic, *pătrĭŏt'ĭk,* a. patriótico. [m.

patriotism, *pā'trĭŏtĭzm,* s. patriotismo, m.

patrol, *pătrōl',* s. patrulla, f.; —, v. n. patrullar.

patron, *pā'trŏn,* s. patrón, protector, m.

patronage, —*dj,* s. patrocinio, m.; patronato, patronazgo, m.

patroness, *pā'trŏnĕs,* s. patrona, f.

patronise, *pā'trŏnīz,* v. a. patrocinar, proteger.   [lumna, f.

patten, *păt'tĕn,* s. galocha, f.; base de columna, f.

patter, *păt'tĕr,* v. n. patalear, patear.

pattern, —*n,* s. modelo, f.; ejemplar, m.

patty, *păt'tĭ,* s. pastelillo, m.   [tidad, f.

paucity, *pŏ'sĭtĕ,* s. poquedad, pequeña cantidad, f.

paunch, *pŏnsh,* s. panza, f.; vientre, m.

pauper, *pā'pŭr,* s. pobre, m.

pauperism, —*ĭzm,* s. pauperismo, m.

pause, *pāz,* s. pausa, f.; —, v. a. pausar; deliberar.   [dosar.

pave, *pāv,* v. a. empedrar; enlosar, embaldosar.

pavement, —*mĕnt,* s. pavimento, empedrado de calle, m.

pavilion, *pāvĭl'yŏn,* s. (mar.) pabellón, (tienda), m.; pabellón (bandera). [losa, f.

paving-stone, *pā'vĭngstōn,* s. ladrillo, m.

paw, *pā,* s. garra, f.; —, v. a. herir con el pie delantero; manosear alguna cosa con poca maña.   [empeñar.

pa'wn, *pān,* s. prenda, f.; peón, m.; —, v. a.

pawn-broker, —*brōkŭr,* s. prendero, m.

pay, *pā,* v. a. pagar; sufrir por; —, s. paga, f.; salario, m.

payable, —*dbl,* a. pagadero.

pay-day, —*dā,* s. día de paga, m.   [m.

payee, —*ē',* s. portador de una libranza, m.

pay-master, —*māstŭr,* s. pagador, m.

payment, —*mĕnt,* s. paga, f.; pagamento, pago, m.

pea, *pē,* s. (pease, pl.) guisante, m.

peace, *pēs,* s. paz, f.; — ! [paz !, ¡silencio !

peaceable, —*ŭbl,* **peaceful,** —*fŭl,* a. tranquilo, pacífico.

peach, *pēsh,* s. melocotón, durazno, m.

peach-tree, —*trē,* s. melocotonero, m.

peacock, *pē'kŏk,* s. pavón, pavo real, m.

peahen, —*hĕn,* s. pava real, f.

peak, *pēk,* s. cima, f.

peal, *pēl,* s. campaneo, m.; estruendo, m.; —, v. a. & n. hacer resonar; devolver el eco los sonidos.

pear, *pār,* s. pera, f.

pearl, *pŭrl,* s. perla, f.; catarata en el ojo, m.

pearled, —*d,* a. guarnecido de perlas. [f.

pearly, —*ĕ,* a. lo que tiene perlas ó es semejante á ellas.

pear-tree, *pār'trē,* s. peral, m.

peasant, *pĕz'ănt,* s. labriego, patán, m.

pea-shooter, *pē'shŏtŭr,* s. cerbatana, f.

peat, *pēt,* s. turba, f.; césped de tierra, m.

pebble, *pĕb'bl,* s. guija, f.; guijarro, m.

pebbly, *pĕb'blĕ,* a. guijarroso.

peccadillo, *pĕkkădĭl'lō,* s. pecadillo, m.

peck, *pĕk,* s. picotazo, m.; celemín, m. (medida de granos); —, v. a. picotear; picar.

pectoral, *pĕk'tŏrăl,* a. pectoral; —, s. medicamento pectoral, m.

peculate, *pĕk'ŭlāt,* v. n. robar al público.

peculation, *pĕkŭlā'shăn,* s. peculado, m.

peculiar, *pĕkŭ'lĭăr,* a. peculiar, particular, singular; —ly, ad. peculiarmente.

peculiarity, *pĕkŭlĭăr'ĭtĭ,* s. particularidad, singularidad, f.

pecuniary, *pĕkŭ'nĭărĕ,* a. pecuniario.

pedagogue, *pĕd'ăgŏg,* s. pedagogo, m.; pedante, m.   [órganos, m.

pedal, *pē'dăl* (*pĕd'ăl*), s. pedales de los órganos, m.

pedant, *pĕd'ănt,* s. pedante, m.

pedantic(al), *pĕdănt'tĭk(ăl),* s. pedantesco.

pedantry, *pĕd'ăntrĕ,* s. pedantería, f.

peddle, *pĕd'dl,* v. n. ocuparse en frioleras.

peddling, *pĕd'dĭng, a.* fútil, frívolo.

pedestal, *pĕd'ĕstăl,* s. pedestal, m.

pedestrian, *pĕdĕs'trĭăn,* s. andador, peón, m.; —, a. pedestre.

pedigree, *pĕd'ĭgrē,* s. genealogía, f.

pediment, *pĕd'ĭmĕnt,* s. frontis, m.

pedlar, *pĕd'lăr,* s. buhonero, m.

peel, *pēl,* v. a. descortezar; —, s. corteza, f.; pellejo (de frutas), m.; pala de horno, f.

peep, *pēp,* v. n. asomar; atisbar; piar los pollos; —, s. asomo, m.; alba, f.; ojeada.

peep-hole, —*hōl,* s. atisbadero, m.   [f.

peer, *pēr,* s. compañero, m. | Par, m. (grande de Inglaterra).

peerage, —*dj,* s. dignidad de Par, f.

peeress, —*ĕs,* s. mujer de un Par, f.; señora noble, f.

peerless, —*lĕs,* a. incomparable.

peevish, *pē'vĭsh,* a. regañón, bronco; enojadizo; —ly, ad. con impertinencia.

peevishness, —*nĕs,* s. mal humor, m.

peg, *pĕg,* s. clavija, espita, f.; —, v. a. clavar.   [var.

pelf, *pĕlf,* s. riquezas, f. pl.

pelican, *pĕl'ĭkăn,* s. pelícano, m.

pelisse, *pĕlēs',* s. ropón, m.

pell, *pĕl,* s. pellejo, cuero, m.

pellet, *pĕl'lĕt,* s. pelotilla, f.

pellicle, *pĕl'lĭkl,* s. película, f.

pell-mell, *pĕlmĕl',* ad. á trochemoche.

pelt, *pĕlt,* s. pellejo, cuero, m.; pelta, f.

pen, *pĕn,* s. pluma, f.; caponera, f.; —, v. a. enjaular, encerrar; escribir.

penal, *pē'năl,* a. penal.   [multa, f.

penalty, *pĕn'ăltĕ,* s. pena, f., castigo, m.;

penance, *pĕn'ăns,* s. penitencia, f.

pence, *pĕns,* s. pl. de penny.

pencil, *pĕn'sĭl,* s. pincel, m.; lápiz, m.; —, v. a. pintar; escribir con lápiz.

pencil-case, —*kās,* s. lapicero, m.

pendant, *pĕn'dănt,* s. pendiente, m.; (mar.) gallardete, m.

pendent, —*dĕnt,* a. pendiente.

pending, —*dĭng,* a. pendiente, indeciso.

pendulum, —*dŭlăm,* s. péndulo, m.

penetrate, *pĕn'ĕtrăt,* v. a. & n. penetrar.

penetration, *pĕnĕtrā'shăn,* s. penetración, sagacidad, f.   [m.

pen-holder, —*hōldŭr,* s. portapluma.

peninsula, *pĕnĭn'sŭlă,* s. península, f.

penitence, *pĕn'ĭtĕns,* s. penitencia, f.

penitent, *–tĕnt*, a. & s. penitente (m.); **–ly**, ad. con arrepentimiento.

penitential, *pĕnĭtĕn'shăl*, s. penitencial.

penitentiary, *–shărĕ*, s. penitenciario, m.

pen-knife, *pĕn'nĭf*, s. cortaplumas, m.

penman, *–măn*, s. pendolista m.; autor, escritor, m.   [fesión de escritor, f.

penmanship, *–shĭp*, s. caligrafía, f.; pro-

pennant, *pĕn'nănt*, pennon, *pĕn'nŏn*, s. (mar.) flámula, banderola, f.

penniless, *pĕn'nĭlĕs*, a. falto de dinero.

penny, *pĕn'nĕ*, s. penique, m.; dinero, m.

penny-a-liner, *–līnŭr*, s. gacetista que recibe un penique por cada línea, m.

penny-post, *–pōst*, s. correo interior, m.

pennyweight, *–wāt*, s. peso de 20 granos tory, m.

penny-wise, *–wĭz*, a. económico de manera falsa; – and **pound-foolish**, ganador en los gastos menores, gastador en los mayores.   [nique, m.

penny-worth, *–wŭrth*, s. valor de un pe-

pension, *pĕn'shŭn*, s. pensión, f.; –, v. a. dar alguna pensión.

pensionary, *–ŭrĕ*, **pensioner**, *–ŭr*, s. pensionista, pensionado, m.

pensive, *pĕn'sĭv*, a. pensativo; **–ly**, ad. melancólicamente.

Pentecost, *pĕn'tĕkŏst*, s. Pentecostés, m.

penthouse, *pĕnt'hŏus*, s. cobertizo, tejadillo, m.

penultimate, *pĕnŭl'tĭmăt*, a. penúltimo.

penurious, *pĕnū'rŭs*, a. tacaño, avaro.

penury, *pĕn'ŭrĕ*, s. penuria, carestía, f.

peony, *pē'ŏnĕ*, s. peonía, f.

people, *pē'pl*, s. pueblo, m.; nación, f.; vulgo, m.; gente, f.; –, v. a. poblar.

pepper, *pĕp'pŭr*, s. pimienta, f.; –, v. a. sazonar con pimienta; golpear.

pepper-box, *–bŏks*, s. pimentero, m.

pepper-corn, *–kŏrn*, s. semilla de pimienta, f.; pr. por.   [mienta, f.

peradventure, *–ădvĕn'tŭr*, ad. por acaso.

perambulate, *–ăm'bŭlāt*, v. a. transitar, recorrer algún territorio.   [para niños, m.

perambulator, *–ăm'bŭlātŭr*, s. cochecito

perceivable, *–sē'văbl*, a. perceptible.

perceive, *–sēv*, v. a. percibir, comprender.

percentage, *–sĕnt'dj*, s. tasa del por ciento, f.   [bilidad, f.

perceptibility, *–sĕptĭbĭl'tĕ*, s. percepti-

perceptible, *–sĕp'tĭbl*, a. perceptible.

perceptibly, *–ĕ*, ad. perceptiblemente.

perception, *–sĕp'shŭn*, s. percepción, idea, noción, f.   [perchar.

perch, *pŭrtsh*, s. pértiga, f.; –, v. a. em-

perchance, *pŭrtshăns'*, ad. acaso, quizá.

percolate, *pŭr'kōlāt*, v. a. colar; filtrar.

percussion, *pŭrkŭsh'ŭn*, s. percusión, f.; golpe, m.

percussion-cap, *–kăp*, s. pistón, m.

perdition, *pŭrdĭsh'ŭn*, s. pérdida, ruina, f.

peregrination, *pĕrĕgrĭnā'shŭn*, s. peregrinación, f.   [mente; definitivamente.

peremptorily, *pĕr'ĕmtărĭlĕ*, ad. perentoria-

peremptoriness, *–ĕmtărĕnĕs*, s. decisión absoluta, f.

peremptory, *–ĕmtărĕ*, a. perentorio; decisivo.

perennial, *–ĕn'nĭăl*, a. perenne; perpetuo.

perfect, *–fĕkt*, a. perfecto, acabado; puro; **–ly**, ad. perfectamente; –, v. a. perficionar, acabar.

perfection, *pŭrfĕk'shŭn*, s. perfección, f.

perfidious, *–fĭd'yŭs*, a. pérfido, desleal; **–ly**, ad. pérfidamente.

perfidy, *–fĭdĕ*, s. perfidia, f.

perforate, *–fōrāt*, v. a. horadar.

perforation, *–fōrā'shŭn*, s. perforación, f.

perforce, *–fōrs'*, ad. forzosamente.

perform, *pŭrfŏrm'*, v. a. ejecutar; efectuar; –, v. n. representar, hacer papel.

performance, *–ăns*, s. ejecución, f.; cumplimiento, m.; obra, f.; representación teatral, función, f.

performer, *–ŭr*, s. ejecutor, m.; actor, m.

perfume, *pŭr'fūm*, s. perfume, m.; fragancia, f.; –, *pŭrfūm'*, v. a. perfumar.

perfumer, *–ŭr*, s. perfumero, perfumista, m.

perfunctory, *pŭrfŭngk'tŭrĕ*, a. descuidado, superficial, negligente.

perhaps, *–hăps'*, ad. quizá, quizás.

peril, *pĕr'ĭl*, s. peligro, riesgo, m.

perilous, *–ŭs*, a. peligroso; **–ly**, ad. peligrosamente.

period, *pē'rĭŏd*, s. período, m.

periodic(al), *pērĭŏd'ĭk(ăl)*, a. periódico; **–ly**, ad. periódicamente; –, s. jornal, periódico, m.   [peripatético (m).

peripatetic(al), *pĕrĭpătĕt'ĭk(ăl)*, a. & s.

periphrase, *pĕ'rĭfrāz*, s. perífrasis, circunlocución, f.

perish, *pĕr'ĭsh*, v. n. perecer.

perishable, *–ăbl*, a. perecedero.

peristyle, *pĕr'ĭstĭl*, s. peristilo, m.

periwig, *pĕr'ĭwĭg*, s. peluca, f.

periwinkle, *pĕr'ĭwĭngkl*, s. caracol marino, m.; (bot.) vincapervinca, f.

perjure, *pŭr'jŭr*, v. a. perjurar.

perjury, *–ĕ*, s. perjurio, m.

perk, *pŭrk*, v. n. pavonearse.   [f.

permanence, *pŭr'mănĕns*, s. permanencia,

permanent, *–mănĕnt*, a. **–ly**, ad. permanente(mente).

permeate, *–mĕāt*, v. a. penetrar, atravesar.

permissible, *–mĭs'sĭbl*, a. lícito, permiso.

permission, *–mĭsh'ăn*, s. permisión, licencia, f.

permissive, *–mĭs'sĭv*, a. admisible.

permit, *–mĭt'*, v. a. permitir; –, *pŭr'mĭt*, s. guía, f.; permiso, m.   [f.

permutation, *–mŭtā'shŭn*, s. permutación,

pernicious, *–nĭsh'ŭs*, a. pernicioso; perjudicial; **–ly**, ad. perniciosamente.

peroration, *pĕrōrā'shŭn*, s. peroración, f.

perpendicular, *pŭrpĕndĭk'ŭlăr*, a. **–ly**, ad. perpendicular(mente); –, s. línea perpendicular, f.   [meter algún delito.

perpetrate, *–pĕtrăt*, v. a. perpetrar, co-

perpetration, *–pĕtrā'shŭn*, s. perpetración, f.   [perpetuamente.

perpetual, *–pĕt'ŭăl*, a. perpetuo; **–ly**, ad.

perpetuate, *–pĕt'ŭăt*, v. a. perpetuar, eternizar.

perpetuation, *-pĕtúá'shŭn,* s. perpetuación, f.

perpetuity, *-pĕtú'ŭtĕ,* s. perpetuidad, f.

perplex, *-plĕks',* v.a.confundir, embrollar.

perplexity, *-plĕks'ŭtĕ,* s. perplejidad, f.

perquisite, *-kwĭzĭt,* s. percance, emolumento, gaje, m.

perry, *pĕr'rĕ,* s. cidra de peras, f.

persecute, *pŭr'sĕkút,* v. a. perseguir, importunar.　　　　　　　[f.

persecution, *-sĕkú'shŭn,* s. persecución, f.

perseverance, *-sĕvē'rãns,* s. perseverancia, f.

persevere, *pŭrsĕvēr',* v. n. perseverar.

perseveringly, *-ĭnglĕ,* ad. con perseverancia.　　　　　　　　[rancia.

persist, *pŭrsĭst',* v. n. persistir.

persistency, *-ĕnsĕ,* s. persistencia, f.

persistent, *-ĕnt,* a. persistente.

person, *pŭr'sŏn,* s. persona, f.

personage, *-ĕj,* s. personaje, m.

personal, *-ăl,* a. -ly, ad. personal(mente); - estate, - goods, bienes muebles, m.pl.

personality, *-ăl'ŭtĕ,* s. personalidad, f.

personalty, *-ăltĕ,* s. (law) bienes muebles, m.

personate, *-ăt,* v. a. representar. [m. pl.

personation, *-ā'shŭn,* s. disfraz, m.

personification, *-ĭfĭkā'shŭn,* s. prosopopeya, f.

personify, *-ĭfĭ,* v. a. personificar.

perspective, *pŭrspĕk'tĭv,* s. perspectiva, f.; -, a. perspectivo.　　　　　[penetrante.

perspicacious, *-spĭkā'shŭs,* a. perspicaz.

perspicacity, *-spĭkă'ŭtĕ,* a. perspicacia, f.

perspicuity, *-spĭkú'ŭtĕ,* s. perspicuidad, f.

perspiration, *-spīrā'shŭn,* s. transpiración, f.

perspire, *-pīr',* v. n. transpirar.

persuade, *-swād',* v. a. persuadir.

persuasion, *-swā'zhŭn,* s. persuasión, f.

persuasive, *-swā'sĭv,* a. persuasivo; -ly, ad. de un modo persuasivo.

pert, *pŭrt,* a. listo, vivo; petulante.

pertain, *pŭrtān',* v. n. pertenecer.

pertinacious, *-tĭnā'shŭs,* a. pertinaz, obstinado; -ly, ad. pertinazmente.

pertinacity, *-tĭnăs'ŭtĕ,* s. pertinacia, f.

pertinence, *pŭr'tĭnĕns,* s. conexión, relación de una cosa con otra, f.

pertinent, *-tĭnĕnt,* a. pertinente; perteneciente; -ly, ad. oportunamente.

pertness, *pŭrt'nĕs,* s. impertinencia, f.; vivacidad, f.

perturb, *pŭrtŭrb',* v. a. perturbar.

perturbation, *-tŭrbā'shŭn,* s. perturbación, agitación de ánimo, f.

peruke, *pĕrŏk',* s. peluca, f.

perusal, *pĕrŏ'zăl,* s. lectura, lección, f.

peruse, *pĕrŏz',* v. a. leer; examinar atentamente.

peruser, *-ŭr,* s. lector, m.; revisor, m.

Peruvian-bark, *pĕrŏ vĭănbárk,* s.quina, f.

pervade, *pŭrvād',* v.a. atravesar, penetrar.

perverse, *-vŭrs',* a. perverso, depravado; -ly, ad. perversamente.

perversion, *-vŭr'shŭn,* s. perversión, f.

perversity, *-vŭr'sĭtĕ,* s. perversidad, f.

pervert, *-vŭrt',* v.a. pervertir, corromper

pervious, *pŭr'vĭŭs,* a. penetrable; penetrante.

pessimist, *pĕs'sĭmĭst,* s. pesimista, m.

pest, *pĕst,* s. peste, pestilencia, f.

pester, *pĕs'tŭr,* v. a. molestar, cansar.

pest-house, *pĕst'hŏŭs,* s. lazareto, m

pestilence, *pĕs'tĭlĕns,* s. pestilencia, f.

pestilent, *pĕs'tĭlĕnt,* pestilential, *pĕstĭlĕn'shăl,* a. pestilente, pestilencial.

pestle, *pĕs'l,* s. mano de almirez, f.; majadero de mortero, m.　[-, v. a. mimar.

pet, *pĕt,* s. enojo, enfado, m.; favorito, m.;

petal, *pĕt'ăl,* s. (bot.) pétalo, m.

petard, *pĕtárd',* s. petardo, m.

petition, *pĕtĭsh'ŭn,* s. memorial, m.; representación, petición, súplica, f.; -, v. a. suplicar; requerir en justicia.

petitioner, *-ŭr,* s. suplicante, m.

petrel, *pĕt'rĕl,* s. petrel, m., procelaria, f. (ave).　　　　　　　　[ción, f.

petrification, *pĕtrĭfĭkā'shŭn,* s. petrificación, f.

petrify, *pĕt'rĭfĭ,* -, v. a. & n. petrificar.

petroleum, *pĕtrō'lĕŭm,* s. petróleo, m.

petticoat, *pĕt'ĭkŏt,* s. guardapiés, zagalejo, m., basquiña, f.　　　[guardilla, m.

pettifogger, *pĕt'ĭfŏggŭr,* s. abogado de pettifogging, *-fŏggĭng,* s. embrollos de los malos abogados, m. pl.

pettiness, *-nĕs,* s. pequeñez, f.

pettish, *pĕt'ĭsh,* a. caprichudo, regañón.

pettitoes, *pĕt'ĭtōz,* s. pl. (vulg.) los pies.

petty, *pĕt'ĕ,* a. pequeño, corto.

petulance, *pĕt'ŭlăns,* s. petulancia, f.

petulant, *pĕt'ŭlănt,* a. petulante; -ly, ad. con petulancia.

pew, *pā,* s. banco cerrado de iglesia, m.

pewter, *pū'tŭr,* s. peltre, m.

phaeton, *fā'ĕtŏn,* s. faetón, faetonte, m.

phalanx, *făl'ăngks,* s. falange, f.

phantasm, *făn'tăzm,* phantom, *făn'tŏm,* s. fantasma, f.

phare, *fār,* s. faro, m.　[s. fantasma, f.

pharisaic(al), *fărĭsā'ĭk(ăl),* a. farisaico.

pharisee, *făr'ĭsĕ,* s. fariseo, m.

pharmaceutic(al), *fármăsū'tĭk(ăl),* a. farmacéutico.　　　　　　　[copea, f.

pharmacopoeia, *fármăkōpē'ă,* s. farmacopea, f.

pharmacy, *fár'măsĕ,* s. farmacia, f.

phase, *fās,* phasis, *fā'sĭs,* s. fase, f.

pheasant, *fĕz'ănt,* s. faisán, m.

phenomenal, *fĕnŏm'ĕnăl,* a. prominente.

phenomenon, *fĕnŏm'ĕnŏn,* s. fenómeno, m.

phial, *fī'ăl,* s. redomilla, f.　[lantrópico.

philanthropic(al), *fĭlănthrŏp'ĭk(ăl),* a. filantrópico.

philanthropist, *fĭlăn'thrŏpĭst,* s. filántropo, m.

philanthropy, *-thrŏpĕ,* s. filantropía, f.

philological, *fĭlŏlŏj'ĭkăl,* a. filológico.

philologist, *fĭlŏl'ŏjĭst,* s. filólogo, m.

philology, *fĭlŏl'ŏjĕ,* s. filología, m.

philosopher, *fĭlŏs'ŏfŭr,* s. filósofo, m.; natural -, físico, m.

philosophic(al), *fĭlŏsŏf'ĭk(ăl),* a. filosófico; -ally, ad. filosóficamente.

philosophise, *fĭlŏs'ŏfīz,* v. n. filosofar.

philosophy, *fĭlŏs'ŏfĕ,* s. filosofía, f.; natural -, física, f.

philter, *fĭl'tur,* s. filtro, m.
phiz, *fĭz,* s. (vulg.) facha, cara, f.
phlegm, *flĕm,* s. flema, f. [tico.
phlegmatic(al), *flĕgmăt'ĭk(ăl),* a. flemá-
phosphoric, *fŏsfŏr'ĭk,* a. fosfórico.
phosphorus, *fŏs'fŭrŭs,* s. fósforo, m.
photograph, *fō'tŏgrăf,* s. fotografía, f.; —, v. a. fotografiar. [m.
photographer, *fŏtŏg'răfŭr,* s. fotógrafo,
photographic(al), *fōtŏgrăf'ĭk(ăl),* a. foto-gráfico.
photography, *fŏtŏg'răfē,* s. fotografía, f.
phrase, *frāz,* s. frase, f.; estilo, m.; —, v. a. nombrar; expresar. [m.
phraseology, *frāzĕŏl'ŏjĭ,* s. libro de frases,
phrenology, *frĕnŏl'ŏjē,* s. frenología, f.
phthisis, *tī'sĭs,* s. tisis, f.
physic, *fĭz'ĭk,* s. medicina, f., medica-mento, m.; —s, s. pl. física, f.; —, v. a. medicamentar. [mente.
physical, *—ăl,* a. físico; —ly, ad. física-
physician, *fĭzĭsh'ăn,* s. médico, m.
physiognomist, *fĭzĭŏg'nŏmĭst,* s. fisono-mista, fisónomo, m. [f.
physiognomy, *fĭzĭŏg'nŏmē,* s. fisonomía,
physiological, *fĭzĭŏlŏj'ĭkăl,* a. fisiológico.
physiologist, *fĭzĭŏl'ŏjĕ,* s. fisiologista, fisiólogo, m.
physiology, *fĭzĭŏl'ŏjē,* s. fisiología, f.
pianist, *pĭăn'ĭst,* s. pianista, m. & f.
piano, *pĭā'nō,* s. piano-forte, m.
piaster, *pĭăs'tŭr,* s. escudo, m. (moneda italiana); peso, m. (moneda española).
picaroon, *pĭkărōn',* s. pícaron, m.; la-drón, m.
pick, *pĭk,* v. a. escoger, elegir; recoger; mondar, limpiar; —, v. n. mascullar, roer; —, s. pico, m.; lo escogido.
pick-axe, *—ăks,* s. pico, m.
pickerel, *—ĕrĕl,* s. sollito, m. (pez).
picket, *—ĕt,* s. (mil.) piquete, m. [bechar.
pickle, *—l,* s. salmuera, f.; —, v. a. esca-
picklock, *—lŏk,* s. ganzúa, f.
pickpocket, *—pŏkĕt,* **pickpurse,** *—pŭrs,* s. cortabolsas, m. [se paga entre muchos, f.
picnic, *pĭk'nĭk,* s. comida, merienda, que
pictorial, *pĭktō'rĭăl,* a. pictórico.
picture, *pĭk'tŭr (pĭk'tshŭr),* s. pintura, f.; retrato, m.; —, v. a. pintar; figurar.
picturesque, *—ĕsk',* a. pintoresco.
pie, *pĭ,* s. pastel, m.; marica, f. [colores.
piebald, *—bāld',* a. manchado de varios
piece, *pēs,* s. pedazo, m.; pieza, obra, f.; cañón ó fusil, m.; a —, cada uno; —, v. a. remendar. [dividido.
piecemeal, *—mēl,* ad. en pedazos; —, a.
pied, *pĭd,* a. variegado, manchado.
pier, *pēr,* s. estribo de puente, m.; muelle, m. [ladrar; excitar.
pierce, *pērs,* v. a. penetrar, agujerear, ta-
piercingly, *—ĭnglĭ,* ad. agudamente.
pier-glass, *pēr'glăs,* s. trumó, m.
pier-table, *—tābl,* s. repisa, f.
piety, *pĭ'ĕtĭ,* s. piedad, devoción, f.
pig, *pĭg,* s. cochinillo, lechón, m.; lingote, m.; —, v. n. parir la puerca.
pigeon, *pĭj'ŭn,* s. palomo, m.; paloma, f.

pigeon-hole, *—hōl,* s. mechinal, m.; ca-silla para guardar cartas, f.
pigeon-house, *—hŏus,* s. palomar, m.
pig-headed, *pĭg'hĕdĕd,* a. estúpido.
pigment, *—mĕnt,* s. pigmento, m.; afeite, m.
pigmy, *—mē,* s. pigmeo, m.
pig-sty, *—stĭ,* s. zahurda, f.
pike, *pĭk,* s. lucio, m.; pica, f.
pilaster, *pĭlăs'tŭr,* s. pilastra, f.
pile, *pĭl,* s. estaca, f.; pila, f.; montón, m.; pira, f.; edificio grande y macizo, m.; pelo, m.; pelillo (en las telas de lana), m.; —s, pl. almorranas, f. pl.; —, v. a. amon-tonar, apilar.
pilfer, *pĭl'fŭr,* v. a. ratear.
pilgrim, *pĭl'grĭm,* s. peregrino, romero, m.
pilgrimage, *—dĭj,* s. peregrinación, f.
pill, *pĭl,* s. píldora, f.
pillage, *—lăj,* s. pillaje, botín, saqueo, m.; —, v. a. pillar, hurtar.
pillar, *pĭl'lŭr,* s. pilar, m.
pillion, *—yŭn,* s. jalma, enjalma, f.
pillory, *—lŭrē,* s. argolla, f.; cepo, m.; —, v. a. empicotar, poner á un malhechor á la vergüenza en alguna picota ó argolla.
pillow, *pĭl'lō,* s. almohada, f.
pillow-case, *—kās,* s. funda, f.
pilot, *pĭ'lŏt,* s. piloto, m.; —, v. a. guiar un navío en su navegación.
pilotage, *—dĭj,* s. pilotaje, m.
pimp, *pĭmp,* s. alcahuete, m.
pimpernel, *pĭm'pŭrnĕl,* s. pimpinela, f.
pimple, *pĭm'pl,* s. postilla, pupa, buba, f.
pimpled, *—d,* a. empurpurado.
pin, *pĭn,* s. alfiler, m.; cavilla, f.; —, v. a. prender con alfileres; fijar con clavija.
pinafore, *—fōr,* s. delantal, m.
pin-case, *—kās,* s. alfiletero, m. [pl.
pincers, *pĭn'zŭrs,* s. pinzas, tenazuelas, f.
pinch, *pĭnsh,* v. a. pellizcar, apretar con pinzas; estrechar á alguno persiguiéndole; —, v. n. ser frugal, excusar gastos; —, s. pellizco, m.; pulgarada, f.; aprieto, m.
pinch-beck, *—bĕk,* s. crisocálico, m.
pin-cushion, *pĭn'kŭshŭn,* s. acerico, m.
pine, *pĭn,* s. (bot.) pino, m.; —, v. n. estar lánguido; ansiar alguna cosa.
pine-apple, *—ăppl,* s. ananas, piña, f.
pinion, *pĭn'yŭn,* s. piñón, m.; ala, f.; —, v. a. atar las alas; maniatar.
pink, *pĭngk,* s. (bot.) clavel, m.; (mar.) pingüe, m.; a. rojizo; pequeño.
pin-money, *pĭn'mŭnē,* s. alfileres, m. pl.
pinnace, *pĭn'năs,* s. (mar.) pinaza, f.
pinnacle, *pĭn'năkl,* s. pináculo, chapitel, m.
pint, *pĭnt,* s. pinta, f. (medida de líquidos).
pioneer, *pĭōnēr',* s. (mil.) zapador, m.
pious, *pĭ'ŭs,* a. pío, devoto; —ly, ad. pia-dosamente. [aves.
pip, *pĭp,* s. pepita, f.; —, v. n. piar ciertas
pipe, *pĭp,* s. tubo, cañón, conducto, caño, m.; pipa para fumar, f.; churumbela, f.; —, v. n. tocar la flauta; graznar.
pipe-clay, *—klā,* s. arcilla refractaria, f.
piper, *—ŭr,* s. flautero, flautista, m.
piping, *—ĭng,* a. enfermizo; hirviente.
pipkin, *pĭp'kĭn,* s. pucherito, m.
pippin, *pĭp'pĭn,* s. (bot.) esperiega, f.

piquancy, *pĕ'kănsĕ,* s. picante, m.; acrimonia, f. [ad. agriamente.

piquant, —*kănt,* a. punzante, picante; —ly,

pique, *pēk,* s. pique, m.; desazón, f.; ojeriza,f.; pundonor, m.; —, v.a. picar; irritar.

piquet, *pĕkĕt',* s. juego de los cientos, m.

piracy, *pī'răsĕ,* s. piratería, f.

pirate, *pī'rdt,* s. pirata, forbante, m.; —, v. n. & a. piratear; robar.

piratical, *pīrăt'ĭkăl,* a. pirático.

Pisces, *pĭs'sēz,* s. Piscis, m. (signo del zodíaco).

pish! *pĭsh,* ¡quita allá! [zodíaco).

pistachio, *pĭstă'shŏ,* s. (bot.) alfónsigo,

pistol, *pĭs'tŏl,* s. pistola. [pistacho, m.

pistol-shot, —*shŏt,* s. pistoletazo, m.

piston, *pĭs'tŏn,* s. émbolo, m.

pit, *pĭt,* s. hoyo, m.; sepultura, f.; patio,m.; —, v. n. azuzar á uno para que riña. [f.

pit-a-pat, —*ăpăt',* s.palpitacion de corazón.

pitch, *pĭtsh,* s. pez, f.; cima, f.; grado de elevación, m.; —, v. a. fijar, plantar; colocar, ordenar; tirar, arrojar; embrear; obscurecer; —, v.n.caerse alguna cosa hacia abajo; caer de cabeza; escoger.

pitch-dark, —*dărk,* a. negro como la pez.

pitcher, —*ŭr,* s. cántaro, m. [pasón, m.

pitchfork, —*fŏrk,* s. horca, f.; (mus.) diapasón, m.

piteous, *pĭt'ĕŭs,* a. lastimoso; compasivo, tierno; miserable; —ly, ad. lastimosamente.

pitfall, *pĭt'făl,* s. trampa, f. [mente.

pith, *pĭth,* s. meollo, m.; médula, f.; energía, f.

pithily, —*ĭlĕ,* ad. vigorosamente. [gía, f.

pithy, —*ĕ,* a. enérgico; meduloso.

pitiable, *pĭt'ĭăbl,* a. lastimoso.

pitiful, *pĭt'ĭfŭl,* a. lastimoso, compasivo; —ly, ad. lastimosamente. [misericordia, f.

pitifulness, —*nĕs,* s. compasión, piedad,

pitiless, *pĭt'ĭlĕs,* a. desapiadado, cruel; —ly, ad. cruelmente. [porcioncilla, f.

pittance, *pĭt'tăns,* s. pitanza, ración, f.;

pitted, *pĭt'tĕd,* a. cavado, picado,

pity, *pĭt'ĕ,* s. piedad, compasión, f.; —, v. a. compadecer; —, v. n. lastimarse.

pivot, *pĭv'ŏt,* s. espigón, quicio, m.

pix, *pĭks,* s. píxide, f.

placable, *plăk'ăbl,* a. aplacable.

placard, *plăk'ărd,* s. placarte m.

place, *plās,* s. lugar, sitio, m.; (mil.) plaza, fortaleza, f.; rango, empleo, m.; —, v. a. colocar; poner dinero á ganancias.

placid, *plăs'ĭd,* a. plácido, quieto; —ly, ad. apaciblemente.

plagiarism, *plā'jărĭzm,* s. plagio, m.

plagiarist, —*jărĭst,* **plagiary,** —*jărĕ,* s. plagiario, m.

plague, *plāg,* s. peste, plaga, f.; —, v. a. atormentar; infestar, apestar.

plaguily, *plā'gĭlĕ,* ad. molestamente.

plaice, *plās,* s. platija, f. (pez).

plaid, *plăd,* s. capa suelta de sarga listada que usan los montañeses de Escocia, f.

plain, *plăn,* a. liso, llano, abierto; sincero; puro, simple, común; claro, evidente, distinto; —, v. a. allanar, alisar; —ly, ad. llanamente; claramente; —, s. llano, m.; llanada, f.

plain-dealing, —*dēlĭng,* s. buena fe, f.

plainness, —*nĕs,* s. llanura, igualdad f.; sinceridad, f.; claridad, f.

plain-speaking, —*spēkĭng,* a. franco.

plaint, *plănt,* s. queja, f.; lamento, m.

plaintiff, *plăn'tĭf,* s. (law) demandador, m.

plaintive, —*tĭv,* a. lamentoso, lastimoso; —ly, ad. de un modo lastimoso.

plait, *plăt,* s. pliegue, m.; trenza, f.; —, v. a. plegar; trenzar; rizar; tejer.

plan, *plăn,* s. plano, m.; delineación (de un edificio), f.; —, v. a. proyectar.

plane, *plăn,* s. plano; cepillo, m.; —, v. a. allanar; acepillar.

planet, *plăn'ĕt,* s. planeta, m.

planetary, *plăn'ĕtărĕ,* a. planetario.

plane-tree, *plăn'trē,* s. plátano, m.

plank, *plăngk,* s. tablón, f. (mar.) tablaje, m.; —, v. a. entablar.

plant, *plănt,* s. planta, f.; planta (asiento del pie); —, v. a. plantar.

plantain, *plăn'tān,* s. (bot.) llantén, m.

plantation, *plăntă'shŭn,* s. plantación, f.; colonia, f. [m.

planter, *plănt'ŭr,* s. plantador, m.; colono,

plant-louse, —*lŏus,* s. pulgón, m.

plash, *plăsh,* s. charquillo, lagunajo, m.

plaster, *plăs'tŭr,* s. yeso, m.; emplasto, m.; —, v. a. enyesar; emplastar.

plastic(al), *plăs'tĭk(ăl),* a. plástico.

plat, *plăt,* s. pedazo de tierra, m.; cintilla de paja, f.; etcetera, f.; —, v. a. entretejer.

plate, *plāt,* s. plancha ó lámina de metal, f.; plata labrada, f.; vajilla, f.; plato, m.; —, v. a. planchear; batir hoja. [vía, m.

plate-layer, —*lā'ŭr,* s. (rail.) asentador de

platform, *plăt'fŏrm,* s. plataforma, f.

platinum, *plăt'ĭnŭm,* s. platina, f.

platoon, *plătŏŏn',* s. (mil.) pelotón, m. [m.

platter, *plăt'tŭr,* s. fuente, f.; plato grande,

plaudit, *plă'dĭt,* s. aplauso, m. [dad, f.

plausibility, *plă'zĭbĭl'ĭtĕ,* s. plausibilidad, f.

plausible, *plă'zĭbl,* a. plausible.

plausibly, —*ĕ,* ad. plausiblemente.

play, *plā,* s. juego, m.; representación dramática, f.; —, v. a. & n. jugar; juguetear; burlarse; representar; (mus.) tocar. [m.

play-bill, —*bĭl,* s.programa de espectáculo.

player, —*ŭr,* s. jugador, m.; comediante, actor, m.; tocador m.

play-fellow, —*fĕllŏ,* **play-mate,** —*māt,* s. camarada, m.

playful, —*fŭl,* a. juguetón, travieso; —ly, ad. juguetonamente, retozando.

playfulness, —*nĕs,* s. jovialidad, f.

play-house, —*hŏus,* s. teatro, m.

plaything, —*thĭng,* s. juguete, m.

play-wright, —*rĭt,* s. poeta dramático, m.

plea, *plē,* s. defensa, f.; excusa, f.; pretexto, socolor, refugio, m. [gar.

plead, *plēd,* v. a. defender en juicio; alegar.

pleadable, —*ăbl,* a. pleiteable.

pleader, —*ŭr,* s. abogado, m.; defensor, m.

pleading, —*ĭng,* s. acto de abogar, m.

pleasant, *plĕz'ănt,* a. agradable; placentero, alegre; —ly, ad. alegremente, placenteramente. [recreo, m.

pleasantness, —*nĕs,* s. alegría, f.; placer,

pleasantry, —*rĕ,* s. chocarrería, chanza, f.

please, *plēz,* v. a. agradar, contar, complacer. [tero.

pleasing, *plē'zĭng,* a. agradable, placentero-

pleasurable, *plĕzh'ūrăbl,* a. deleitante, divertido, alegre, [arbitrio, m.
pleasure, *plĕzh'ŭr,* s. gusto, placer, m.;
pleasure-ground, *-grŏŭnd,* s. parque de recreo, jardín, m. [plebeyo (m.).
plebeian, *plĕbē'ăn,* a. & s. vulgar, bajo;
pledge, *plĕj,* s. prenda, f.; fianza, f.; —, v. a. empeñar, dar fianzas.
plenary, *plē'nărē,* a. plenario, entero.
plenipotentiary, *plĕnĭpōtĕn'shiărē,* s. & a. plenipotenciario (m.). [dancia, f.
plenitude, *plĕn'ĭtūd,* s. plenitud, abun-
plenteous, *plĕn'tŭs,* **plentiful,** *plĕn'tĭfŭl,* a. copioso, abundante; **-ly,** ad. con abundancia.
plenty, *plĕn'tē,* s. copia, abundancia, f.
plethora, *plĕth'ōră,* s. plétora, repleción, f.
plethoric, *plĕthŏr'ĭk,* a. pletórico, repleto.
pleurisy, *plō'rĭsē,* s. pleuresía, f. [dócil.
pliable, *plī'ăbl,* **pliant,** *-ănt,* a. flexible,
pliancy, *-ănsē,* s. flexibilidad, f.
plight, *plīt,* v. a. empeñar; —, s. estado, m.; condición, f. [trearse.
plod, *plŏd,* v. n. afanarse mucho, aje-
plodding, *-ding,* s. trabajo improbo, m.
plot, *plŏt,* s. pedazo pequeño de terreno, m.; plano, m.; conspiración, trama, f.; estratagema, f.; —, v. a. & n. trazar; conspirar; tramar.
plotter, *-tŭr,* s. conspirador, m.
plough, *plŏŭ,* s. arado, m.; —, v. a. arar, labrar la tierra.
plough-boy, *-bŏĭ,* s. arador, m.
plough-share, *-shār,* s. reja de arado, f.
plover, *plŏ'vŭr,* s. frailecillo, m. (ave).
pluck, *plŭk,* v. a. tirar con fuerza; arrancar; desplumar; —, s.asadura, f.; arranque, tirón, m.
plucky, *-ē,* a. guapo, gallardo. [rugar.
plug, *plŭg,* s. tapón, tarugo, m.; —, v.a. ata-
plum, *plŭm,* s. ciruela, f.
plumage, *plŏm'āj,* s. plumaje, m.
plumb, *plŭm,* s. plomada, f.; —, ad. á plomo; —, v. a. aplomar.
plumbago, *plŭmbā'gō,* s. lápiz plomo, m.
plumber, *plŭm'ŭr,* s. plomero, m.
plumb-line, *-lĭn,* s. cuerda de plomada, f.; nivel, m.
plume, *plŏm,* s. pluma, f.; plumaje, penacho, m.; —, v. a. desplumar; adornar con plumas.
plummet, *plŭm'mĕt,* s. plomada, f.
plump, *plŭmp,* a. gordo, rollizo; —, ad. de repente; —, v.a. & n. hinchar; caer á plomo.
plumpness, *-nĕs,* s. gordura, corpulencia, obesidad, f. [m.
plum-pudding, *plŭm'pŭdĭng,* s. pudín,
plum-tree, *-trē,* s. ciruelo, m.
plunder, *plŭn'dŭr,* v. a. saquear, pillar, robar; —, s. pillaje, botín, m.; (am.) bagaje, m. [cipitarse.
plunge, *plŭnj,* v. a. & n. sumergir(se), pre-
plunger, *-ŭr,* s. buzo, somorgujador, m.
plural, *plŏ'răl,* a. & s. plural (m.).
plurality, *plŏrăl'ĭtē,* s. pluralidad, f.
plush, *plŭsh,* s. tripe, m. (tela felpada).
ply, *plī,* v. a. trabajar con ahinco; importunar, solicitar; —, v. n. afanarse; aplicarse; (mar.) barloventear.

pneumatic(al), *nūmăt'ĭk(ăl),* a. neumático.
pneumonia, *nūmō'nĭă,* s. neumonía, f.
poach, *pōtsh,* v. a. medio cocer (huevos); —, v. n. cazar en vedado.
poacher, *-ŭr,* s. cazador furtivo, m.
pock, *pŏk,* s. viruela, pústula, f.
pocket, *pŏk'ĕt,* s. bolsillo, m.; faltriquera, f.; —, v. a. embolsar; **to — an affront,** tragarse una injuria.
pocket-book, *-bŭk,* s. librito de memoria, m.; cartera, f. [gastos menudos, m.
pocket-money, *-mŭnē,* s. dinero para los
pod, *pŏd,* s. vaina, f.
poem, *pō'ĕm,* s. poema, m.
poesy, *pō'ĕsē,* s. poesía, f.
poet, *pō'ĕt,* s. poeta, m.
poetaster, *pōĕtăs'tŭr,* s. poetastro, m.
poetess, *pō'ĕtĕs,* s. poetisa, f.
poetic(al), *pōĕt'ĭk(ăl),* a. poético; **-ly,** ad. poéticamente.
poetics, *pōĕt'ĭks,* s. poética, f.
poetise, *pō'ĕtīz,* v. n. poetizar.
poetry, *pō'ĕtrē,* s. poesía, f.
poignancy, *pŏĭ'nănsē,* s. **picante, m.;** acrimonia, f.
poignant, *-nănt,* a. picante; punzante; satírico; **-ly,** ad. con satirización.
point, *pŏĭnt,* s. punta, f.; punto, m.; promontorio, m.; puntillo, m.; estado, m.; —, v. a. apuntar; aguzar; puntuar.
point-blank, *-blăngk,* ad. directamente.
pointed, *-ĕd,* a. puntiagudo; epigramático; **-ly,** ad. sútilmente.
pointer, *-ŭr,* s. apuntador, m.; perro de punta y vuelta, m.
pointless, *-lĕs,* a. obtuso, sin punta.
pointsman, *-s'măn,* s. (rail.) guarda-aguja, m.; **-'s lodge,** s. garita, f.
poise, *pŏĭz,* s. peso, m.; equilibrio, m.; —, v. a. pesar, equilibrar.
poison, *-n,* s. veneno, m.; —, v. a. envenenar, atosigar. [rruptor, m.
poisoner, *-nŭr,* s. envenenador, m.; co-
poisonous, *-nŭs,* a. venenoso.
poke, *pōk,* s. barjuleta, bolsa, f.; —, v. a. andar á tientas; hurgar la lumbre.
poker, *-ŭr,* s. hurgón, m.; (am.) coco, m.
polar, *pō'lŭr,* a. polar.
pole, *pōl,* s. polo, m.; (mar.) palo, m.; pértiga, f.; lanza de coche, f.; percha, f.
pole-axe, *-ăks,* s. hachuela de mano, f.
pole-cat, *-kăt,* s. gato montés, m.
polemic, *pōlĕm'ĭk,* a. & s. polémico (m.); controversista (m.); **-s,** s. pl. polémica, f.
pole-star, *-stăr,* s. Cinosura, f.
police, *pōlēs',* s. policía, f. [m.
police-court, *-kōrt,* s. tribunal de policía,
policeman, *-măn,* s. oficial de policía, m.
policy, *pŏl'ĭsē,* s. política de estado, f.; astucia, f.
polish, *pŏl'ĭsh,* v. a. pulir, alisar; limar; —, v. n. recibir pulimento; —, s. pulimento, m.
polished, *-d,* a. elegante, pulido.
polite, *pōlīt',* a. pulido, cortés; **-ly,** ad. urbanamente.
politeness, *-nĕs,* s. cortesía, f.
politic, *pŏl'ĭtĭk,* a. político; astuto.

political, *polit'ikal,* a. político; —ly, ad. según reglas de política.

politician, *politish'an,* s. político, m.

politics, *pol'itiks,* s. pl. política, f.

poll, *pol,* s. cabeza, f.; lista de los que votan en alguna elección, f.; voto, m.; —, v. a. descabezar; desmochar; —, v. n. dar voto en las elecciones.

pollard, *pol'lard,* s. árbol desmochado, m.

pollen, *pol'len,* s. (bot.) polen, m.

poll-tax, *pol'taks,* s. capitación, f.

pollute, *pollöt',* v.a. ensuciar; corromper.

polluter, *—ûr,* s. corruptor, m.

pollution, *pollö'shûn,* s. polución, contaminación, f.

poltroon, *poltrön',* s. collón, m.

polygamist, *polig'amist,* s. polígamo, m.

polygamy, *—me,* s. poligamia, f.

polyglot, *pol'iglot,* a. & s. polígloto (m.).

polygon, *pol'igon,* s. polígono, m.

polypus, *pol'ipûs,* s. pólipo, m.

polysyllable, *pol'isilabl,* s. polisílabo, m.

polytechnic, *politek'nik,* a. politécnico.

pomade, *pomäd',* **pomatum,** *pomä'tûm,* s. pomada, f.   [nado, m.; granada, f.

pomegranate, *pôm'granät,* s. (bot.) gra-

pommel, *pôm'mel,* s. pomo de espada, m.; —, v. a. cascar.

pomp, *pomp,* s. pompa, f.; esplendor, m.

pomposity, *pompos'ite,* s. ostentación, f.; énfasis, m. & f.   [pomposamente.

pompous, *pom'pûs,* a. pomposo; —ly, ad.

pond, *pond,* s. estanque de agua, m.

ponder, *pon'dûr,* v.a. ponderar, considerar.

ponderous, *—ûs,* a. ponderoso, pesado; —ly, ad. pesadamente.   [herir con puñal.

poniard, *pon'yard,* s. puñal, m.; —, v. a.

pontiff, *pon'tif,* s. pontífice, papa, m.

pontifical, *pontif'ikal,* a. & s. pontifical (libro) (m.).   [m.

pontificate, *—ikät,* s. pontificado, papado,

pontoon, *pontön',* s. pontón, m.

pony, *po'ne,* s. haca, f.; jaco, m.

poodle, *pö'dl,* s. perro de aguas, m.

pool, *pöl,* s. charco, m.; lago, m.

poop, *pöp,* s. (mar.) popa, f.; toldilla, f.

poor, *pör,* a. pobre; humilde, de poco valor; estéril; —ly, ad. pobremente; the —, s. los pobres, m. pl.   [m.

poor-box, *—böks,* s. tronco de los pobres,

poor-house, *—hous,* s. casa de caridad, f.

poor-law, *—lä,* s. ley de asistencia pública.

poorness, *—nes,* s. pobreza, f.

poor-rate, *—rät,* s. contribución al provecho de los pobres, f.

pop, *pop,* s. chasquido, m.; —, v. a. & n. entrar ó salir de sopetón; meter alguna cosa repentinamente.

Pope, *pöp,* s. papa, m.

Popedom, *—dôm,* s. papado, m.

popery, *—ûre,* s. papismo, m.

pop-gun, *pop'gûn,* s. escopetilla con que juegan los muchachos, f.   [verde, m.

popinjay, *—injä,* s. papagayo, m.; pisa-

popish, *po'pish,* a. papal, romano; —ly, ad. á la manera de los papistas.

poplar, *pop'lûr,* s. álamo temblón, m.

poplin, *—lin,* s. popelina, moselina de lana y seda, f.   [pola, f.

poppy, *—pe,* s. (bot.) adormidera, amapola, f.

populace, *—läs,* s. populacho, m.

popular, *—lûr,* a. —ly, ad. popular(mente).

popularity, *popûlär'ite,* s. popularidad, f.

popularize, *pop'ûlariz,* v. a. popularizar.

populate, *—lät,* v. n. poblar.

population, *popûlä'shûn,* s. población, f.

populous, *pop'ûlûs,* a. populoso.

populousness, *—nes,* s. abundancia de habitantes, f.   [loza fina, f.

porcelain, *pors'lân,* s. porcelana, china,

porch, *portsh,* s. pórtico, vestíbulo, m.

porcupine, *por'kûpin,* s. puerco espín, m.

pore, *por,* s. poro, m.

pork, *pork,* s. carne de puerco, f.

porker, *—ûr,* s. porcino, cochino, m.

porosity, *poros'ite,* s. porosidad, f.

porous, *po'rûs,* a. poroso.

porphyry, *por'fire,* s. pórfido, m.

porpoise, *—pûs,* s. puerco marino, m.

porridge, *—rij,* s. potaje, m.; sopa, f.

porringer, *—rinjûr,* s. escudilla, f.

port, *port,* s. puerto, m.; (mar.) babor, m.; vino de Oporto, m.

portable, *—abl,* a. portátil.

portal, *—al,* s. portal, m.; portada, f.

portend, *portend',* v. a. pronosticar.

portent, *portent',* s. portento, prodigio, m.

portentous, *—ûs,* a. portentoso.

porter, *por'tûr,* s. portero, m.; mozo, m.; cerveza fuerte (en Londres), f.

porterage, *—ij,* s. porte, m.   [m.

portfire, *port'fir,* s. lanzafuego, botafuego,

portfolio, *portfo'lio,* s. cartera, f.

portico, *por'tiko,* s. pórtico, portal, m.

portion, *por'shûn,* s. porción, parte, f.; dote, m. & f.; —, v. a. partir, dividir; dotar.

portliness, *port'lines,* s. porte majestuoso,

portly, *port'le,* a. majestuoso; rollizo, m.

portmanteau, *portman'to,* s. portamanteo,

portrait(ure), *por'trät(ûr),* s. retrato, m.

portray, *porträ',* v. a. retratar.

portrayer, *—ûr,* s. retratista, m.

pose, *poz,* v. a. parar; confundir; preguntar, interrogar.   [que confunde, f.

poser, *—ûr,* s. examinador, m.; pregunta

position, *pozish'ûn,* s. posición, situación, f.; proposición, f.

positive, *poz'itiv,* a. positivo, real, verdadero; —ly, ad. positivamente; ciertamente; perentoriamente.

positiveness, *—nes,* s. carácter positivo, m.; realidad, f.; determinación, f.; obstinación, f.

posse, *pos'se,* s. la fuerza armada,

possess, *pozzes',* v. a. poseer; gozar.

possession, *pozzesh'ûn,* s. posesión, f.

possessive, *pozzes'iv,* a. posesivo.

posset, *pos'set,* s. suero, m., agua de leche, f.   [f.

possibility, *possibil'ite,* s. posibilidad,

possible, *pos'sibl,* a. posible; —ly, ad. quizá, quizás.

post, *post,* s. posta, estafeta, f.; correo, m.; puesto, m.; empleo, m.; poste, m.;

—, v. a. apostar; —, v. n. ir en posta, correr la posta.

postage, -dj, s. porte de carta, m.

postage-stamp, -stámp, s. sello, sello de correo ó de franqueo, m.

post-boy, -bŏi, s. postillón, m.

post-captain, -káptin, s. capitán de navío, m.

post-card, -kárd, s. tarjeta postal, f.

post-chaise, -shds, s. silla de posta, f.

posterior, postẽ'rĭŭr, s. posterior, trasero.

posterity, postēr'ĭtĕ, s. posteridad, f.

postern, pŏst'ŭrn, s. postigo, m.; poterna, f.

post-haste, -hdst, ad, á rienda suelta.

posthumous, pŏst'ŭmŭs, a. póstumo.

postillion, postĭl'yŭn, s. postillón, m.

posting, pōst'ĭng, s. viaje con el correo, m. [rural —, peatón, m.

postman, -mắn, s. cartero, m.; correo, m.

post-mark, -márk, s. timbre de posta, m.

post-master, -mástŭr, s. administrador de correos, m.

post-office, -ŏffĭs, s. administración de correos, f.; **a letter under address "Post-office"**, carta en lista de correos, f. [rreos, f.

post-paid, -pâd, a. franco.

postpone, pŏstpōn', v. a. diferir, suspender; posponer.

postscript, pŏst'skrĭpt, s. posdata, f.

posture, pŏs'tŭr [pŏs'tshŭr], s. postura, f.; positura, f. [m.

posy, pō'zĕ, s. mote, m.; ramillete de flores, m.

pot, pŏt, s. marmita, f.; olla, f.; —, v. a. preservar en marmitas.

potable, pō'tăbl, a. potable.

potash, pŏt'ăsh, s. potasa, f.

potation, pŏtă'shŭn, s. trago, m.

potato, pŏtă'tō, s. patata, f.

pot-bellied, -pŏt bĕllĭd, a. panzudo.

pot-boy, -bŏĭ, s. mozo de cervecero, m.

potent, pō'tĕnt, a. potente, poderoso, eficaz.

potentate, pō'tĕntăt, s. potentado, m.

potential, pŏtĕn'shăl, a. potencial, poderoso.

pot-hanger, pŏt'hăngŭr, s. llares, m. pl.

pother, pŏth'ŭr, s. baraúnda, f.; alboroto, bullicio, m.

pot-herb, pŏt'hĕrb, s. hortaliza, f.

pot-hook, -hŏk, s. asa de caldera, f.

pot-house, -hŏŭs, s. ventorrillo, m.

potion, pō'shŭn, s. poción, bebida medicinal, f. [f.

pot-luck, pŏt'lŭk, s. comida ordinaria, f.

potter, pŏt'tŭr, s. alfarero, m.; -'s ware, m.

pottery, -ĕ, s. alfar, m. [vidriado, m.

pouch, pŏŭtsh, s. bolsillo, m.; faltriquera, f. [m.

poulterer, pōl'tŭrŭr, s. pollero, gallinero, m.

poultice, pōl'tĭs, s. cataplasma, f.

poultry, pōl'trĕ, s. aves caseras, f. pl.

poultry-yard, -yärd, s. corral donde se crian las aves caseras, m.

pounce, pŏŭns, s. garra, f.; grasilla, f.; cisquero, m.; —, v. a. apomazar.

pound, pŏŭnd, s. libra, f.; libra esterlina, f.; corral de concejo, m.; —, v. a. machacar.

pounder, -ŭr, s. pera de á libra, f.; cañón

de á tantas libras de bala, m.; mano de almirez, f.; embargador de bestias, m.

pour, pōr, v. a. echar ó vaciar líquidos de una parte en otra; arrojar alguna cosa continuadamente; —, v. n. fluir con rapidez; llover á cántaros.

pout, pŏŭt, v. n. ponerse ceñudo.

poverty, pŏv'ŭrtĕ, s. pobreza, f.

powder, pŏŭ'dŭr, s. polvo, m.; pólvora, f.; —, v. a. pulverizar; salar.

powder-chest, -tshĕst, s. pl. (mar.) caja de fuego, fph. [pólvora, m.

powder-horn, -hŏrn, s. frasco para pólvora, m.

powdery, -ĕ, a. polvoriento.

power, pŏŭ'ŭr, s. poder, m.; potestad, f.; imperio, m.; potencia, f.; autoridad, f.; fuerzas militares, f. pl.

powerful, -fŭl, a. poderoso; **-ly**, ad. poderosamente, con mucha fuerza.

powerless, -lĕs, a. impotente.

pox, pŏks, s. viruelas, f. pl.; **chicken--**, viruelas locas, f. pl.; **cow--**, vacuna, f.

practicability, prăktĭkăbĭl'ĭtĕ, s. posibilidad de hacer una cosa, f. [hacedero.

practicable, prăk'tĭkăbl, a. practicable;

practically, -ĕ, ad. posiblemente.

practical, prăk'tĭkăl, a. práctico; **-ly**, ad. prácticamente.

practice, prăk'tĭs, s. práctica, f.; uso, m.; costumbre, f.; -s, pl. intrigas, f. pl.

practise, —, v. a. & n. practicar, ejercer.

practitioner, prăktĭsh'ŭnŭr, s. práctico (médico), m.

pragmatic(al), prăgmăt'ĕk(ăl), a. pragmático; entremetido; **-ally**, ad. impertinentemente.

prairie, prā'rĕ, s. pradería, f.

praise, prāz, s. fama, f.; renombre, m.; alabanza, f.; —, v. a. celebrar, alabar.

praiseworthy, -wŭrthĕ, a. digno de alabanza. [banza.

prance, prăns, v. n. cabriolar.

prank, prăngk, s. travesura, extravagancia, f.

prate, prāt, v. a. charlar; —, s. charla, f.

prattle, prăt'tl, v. n. charlar; —, s. parlería, charla, f.

pray, prā, v. a. & n. suplicar, rogar; orar.

prayer, -ŭr, s. oración, súplica, f.; **Lord's —**, oración dominical, f.; Padre nuestro, m.

prayer-book, -bŭk, s. libro de devociones, m.

preach, prĕtsh, v. a. & n. predicar. [m.

preacher, -ŭr, s. predicador, m.

preaching, -ĭng, s. predicación, f.

preamble, prĕăm'bl, s. preámbulo, m.

prebend, prĕb'ĕnd, s. prebenda, f.

prebendary, -ărĕ, s. prebendado, m.

precarious, prĕkă'rĭŭs, a. precario, incierto; **-ly**, ad. precariamente, f.

precariousness, -nĕs, s. incertidumbre, f.

precaution, prĕkă'shŭn, s. precaución, f.

precautionary, -ărĕ, a. preventivo.

precede, prĕsēd', v. a. anteceder, preceder.

precedence, -sē'dĕns, s. precedencia, f.

precedent, -sē'dĕnt, a. & s. precedente (m).

precentor, -sĕn'tŭr, s. chantre, m.

precept, prē'sĕpt, s. precepto, m.

preceptor, prĕsĕp'tŭr, s. preceptor, m.

precinct, prē'sĭngkt, s. limite, lindero, m.

precious, *prĕsh' ŭs,* a. precioso; **—ly,** ad. preciosamente.

preciousness, *—nĕs,* s. preciosidad, f.

precipice, *prĕ sĭpĭs,* s. precipicio, m.

precipitate, *prĕsĭp' ĭtāt,* v. a. & n. precipitar(se); **—,** s. precipitado, m.; **—ly,** ad. precipitadamente; **—,** s. precipitado, m.

precipitation, *—tātĭd shūn,* s. precipitación, inconsideración, f.

precipitous, *—stĭp' ĭtŭs,* a. precipitoso.

precise, *—sīs',* a. preciso, exacto; **—ly,** ad. precisamente, exactamente.

precision, *—sĭzh' ŭn,* s. precisión, limitación exacta, f.

preclude, *—klōd',* v. a. prevenir, impedir.

precocious, *—kō' shŭs,* a. precoz, temprano, prematuro.

precocity, *—kŏs' ĭtĭ,* s. precocidad, f.

preconceive, *prēkŏnsēv',* v. a. opinar ó imaginar con antelación; ocupación, f.

preconception, *—kŏnsĕp' shŭn,* s. preocupación, f.

preconcert, *—kŏnsŭrt',* v. a. concertar, convenir ó estipular de antemano.

precursor, *prēkŭr' sŭr,* s. precursor, m.

predatory, *prĕd' ătŭrĭ,* a. rapaz, voraz.

predecessor, *prĕdĕsĕs' sŭr,* s. predecesor, antecesor, m.; destinación, f.

predestination, *prĕdĕstĭnā shŭn,* s. predestinación, f.

predestine, *—dĕs' tĭn,* v. a. predestinar.

predicament, *—dĭk' ămĕnt,* s. predicamento, m.; categoría, f.

predicate, *prĕd' ĭkāt,* v. a. afirmar; **—,** s. predicado, m.; f.

predication, *prĕdĭkā' shŭn,* s. afirmación, f.

predict, *prĕdĭkt',* v. a. predecir.

prediction, *—dĭk' shŭn,* s. predicción, f.

predictor, *—dĭk' tŭr,* a. adivino, m.

predilection, *prĕdĭlĕk' shŭn,* s. predilección, f.

predispose, *—dĭspōz',* v. a. predisponer.

predisposition, *—dĭspŏzĭsh' ŭn,* s. predisposición, f.; nio, m.

predominance, *prēdŏm' ĭnăns,* s. predominio, m.; predominancia, f.

predominant, *—ĭnĕnt,* a. predominante.

predominate, *—ĭnāt,* v. a. predominar.

pre-eminence, *prēĕm' ĭnĕns,* s. preeminencia, f.

pre-eminent, *—ĭnĕnt,* a. preeminente.

pre-emption, *—ĕm' shŭn,* s. compra de antemano, f.; peño anterior, m.

pre-engagement, *—ĭngādjʹ mĕnt,* s. empeño anterior, m.

pre-existence, *—ĕgzĭs' tĕns,* s. preexistencia, f.; hacer un prólogo á un libro.

preface, *prĕf' ăs,* s. prefación, f.; **—,** v. a.

prefatory, *prĕf' ătŭrĭ,* a. preliminar.

prefect, *prē fĕkt,* s. prefecto, m.

prefecture, *—fĕktŭr,* s. prefectura, f.

prefer, *prĕfŭr',* v. a. preferir, proponer en público; exhibir.

preferable, *prĕf' ŭrăbl,* a. preferible.

preference, *—ŭrĕns,* s. preferencia, f.

preferment, *prĕfŭr' mĕnt,* s. promoción, f.; preferencia, f.

prefix, *prĕfĭks',* v. a. prefijar; **—,** *prē fĭks,* s. (gr.) prefijo, m.

pregnancy, *prĕg' nănsĭ,* s. preñez, f.

pregnant, *—nănt,* a. a preñada; fértil.

prejudge, *prĕjŭj',* v. a. juzgar provisionalmente.

prejudice, *prĕj' ŭdĭs,* s. perjuicio, daño, m.; **—,** v. a. perjudicar, hacer daño.

prejudicial, *—dĭsh' ăl,* a. perjudicial, dañoso.

prelacy, *prĕl' ăsĭ,* s. prelacía, f.; ñoso.

prelate, *—āt,* s. prelado, m.

preliminary, *prĕlĭm' ĭnărĭ,* a. preliminar.

prelude, *prĕl' ūd,* s. preludio, m.; **—,** *prĕlūd',* v. a. (mus.) florear.

premature, *prĕmătūr',* a. prematuro; **—ly,** ad. anticipadamente.

prematureness, *—nĕs,* s. madurez ó sazón anticipada, f.; meditación, f.

premeditation, *prĕmĕdĭtā shŭn,* s. premeditación, f.

premier, *prĕm' ĭŭr,* s. primer ministro, m.

premise, *prĕmīz',* v. a. exponer premisas.

premises, *prĕm' ĭsĕz,* s. pl. premisas, f. pl.; predio rústico, m.

premium, *prē mĭŭm,* s. premio, m.; remuneración, f.; prima, f.; tivo.

premonitory, *prĕmŏn' ĭtŭrĭ,* a. preven

preoccupation, *prĕŏkkūpā' shŭn,* s. anticipación de la adquisición, f.; preocupación (del ánimo), f.

preparation, *prĕpără' shŭn,* s. preparación, f.; cosa preparada, f.; rio.

preparatory, *prĕpăr' ătŭrĭ,* a. preparatorio.

prepare, *—pār',* v. a. (& n.) preparar(se).

prepay, *prĕpā',* v. a. franquear una carta.

prepense, *prĕpĕns',* a. (law) premeditado.

preponderance, *prĕpŏn dŭrăns,* s. preponderancia, f.; derar.

preponderate, *—dŭrāt,* v. a. & n. prepon

preposition, *prĕpŏzĭsh' ŭn,* s. preposición, f.

prepossessing, *prĕpŏzĕs' sĭng,* a. atractivo; ción, f.; prevención, f.

prepossession, *—pŏzzĕsh' ŭn,* s. preocupa

preposterous, *prĕpŏs' tŭrŭs,* a. preposotero; absurdo; **—ly,** ad. al revés, sin razón, f.

prerogative, *prĕrŏg' ătĭv,* s. prerrogativa, f.

presage, *prĕs' āj,* s. presagio, pronóstico, m.; **—,** *prĕsāj',* v. a. presagiar.

prescience, *prĕ shăns,* s. presciencia, f.

prescient, *—shĕnt,* a. profético.

prescribe, *prēskrīb',* v. a. & n. prescribir, ordenar; recetar.

prescription, *—skrĭp' shŭn,* s. prescripción, f.; receta medicinal, f.; m.

presence, *prĕz' ĕns,* s. presencia, f.; talle.

presence-chamber, *—tshāmbŭr,* presence-room, *—rōm,* s. sala de recibimiento, f.

present, *prĕz' ĕnt,* s. presente, regalo, m.; **—,** a. presente; **—ly,** ad. al presente; **—,** *prĕsĕnt',* v. a. ofrecer, presentar; regalar; (am.) acusar; coroso.

presentable, *prĕzĕnt' ăbl,* a. decente, de

presentation, *prĕzĕntā' shŭn,* s. presentación, f.; regalado, m.

presentation-copy, *—kŏpĭ,* s. ejemplar

presentiment, *prĕsĕn' tĭmĕnt,* s. presentimiento, m.; ción, f.

presentment, *prĕsĕnt' mĕnt,* s. presenta

preservation, *prĕzŭrvā' shŭn,* s. preservación, f.; m.

preservative, *—zŭr vătĭv,* s. preservativo,

preserve, -zûrv', v. a. preservar, conservar; hacer conservas de frutas; -, s. conserva, confitura, f.
preside, prĕzĭd', v. n. presidir; dirigir.
presidency, prĕz'ĭdĕnsĕ, s. presidencia, f.
president, -dĕnt, s. presidente, m.
press, prĕs, v. a. apresar, apretar; oprimir, angustiar; compeler; importunar; estrechar; hacer levas; -, v. n. apresurarse; agolparse la gente al rededor de una persona ó cosa; -, s. prensa, turba, f.; armario, m. [matrícula, f.
press-gang, -găng, s. (mar.) ronda de
pressing, -ĭng, p. & a. -ly, ad. urgente(mente). [sĭón, f.; opresión, f.
pressure, prĕsh'ûr, s. prensadura, f.; pre-
presumable, prĕzŭm'ābl, a. presumible, f.
presume, prĕzŭm', v.n. presumir, suponer.
presumption, prĕzŭm'shŭn, s. presunción, f. [-ly, ad. presuntuosamente.
presumptuous, -tŭûs, a. presuntuoso;
presuppose, prĕsŭppōz', v.a. presuponer.
presupposition, prĕsŭppōzĭsh'ŭn, s. presuposición, f. [sĭón, f.
pretence, prĕtĕns', s. pretexto, m.; preten-
pretend, -tĕnd', v. a. & n. pretender; presumir.
pretender, -ûr, s. pretendiente, m.
pretendingly, -ĭnglĕ, ad. presuntuosamente.
pretension, -shŭn, s. pretensión, f.
preterite, prĕt'ĕrĭt, s. pretérito, m.
preternatural, prĕtûrnăt'ûrăl, s. sobrenatural.
pretext, prĕ'tĕkst, s. pretexto, socolor, m.
prettily, prĭt'ĭlĕ, ad. lindamente; agradablemente. [f.
prettiness, -tĭnĕs, s. lindeza, f.; belleza,
pretty, -tĕ, a. lindo, bien parecido; hermoso; -, ad. algo, un poco. [minar.
prevail, prĕvāl', v. n. prevalecer, predo-
prevailing, -ĭng, a. dominante (uso, costumbre). [superioridad, f.
prevalence, prĕv'ālĕns, s. predominio,m.;
prevalent, -ălĕnt, a. predominante, eficaz.
prevaricate, prĕvăr'ĭkăt, v.n. prevaricar; transgredir. [ción, transgresión, f.
prevarication, -kā'shŭn, s. prevarica-
prevent, prĕvĕnt', v. a. prevenir; impedir.
prevention, -vĕn'shŭn, s. prevención, preocupación, f. [servativo, m.
preventive, -tĭv, a. preventivo; -, s. pre-
previous, prĕ'vĭûs, a. previo; antecedente; -ly, ad. de antemano.
prey, prā, s. botín, m.; rapiña, f.; -, v. a. rapiñar, pillar, robar.
price, prĭs, s. precio, m.; premio, m.
priceless, -lĕs, a. inapreciable.
prick, prĭk, v. a. punzar, picar; apuntar; excitar, estimar; poner en música una canción; -, s. puntura, f.; picadura, f.; punzada, f.; pista, f. [f.
pricking, -ĭng, s. picadura, f.; punzada,
prickle, -l, s. pincho, m.; espina, f.
prickly, -lĕ, a. espinoso.
pride, prĭd, s. orgullo, m.; vanidad, f.; jactancia, f.; -, v. n. jactarse.

priest, prēst, s. sacerdote, presbítero, m.
priestess, -ĕs, s. sacerdotisa, f.
priesthood, -hŭd, s. clerecía, f.; sacer-
priestly, -lĕ, a. sacerdotal. [docio, m.
priest-ridden, -rĭddn, a. gobernado por sacerdotes. [verde, m.
prig, prĭg, v. n. hurtar, ratear; -, s. pisa-
priggish, -gĭsh, a. afectado.
prim, prĭm, a. peripuesto, afectado.
primacy, prĭ'māsĕ, s. primacía, f.
primarily, prĭ'mărĭlĕ, ad. primariamente, sobre todo. [primero.
primary, prĭ'mărĕ, a. primario, principal,
primate, prĭ'māt, s. primado, m.
prime, prĭm, s. madrugada, alba, f.; (fig.) flor, nata, f.; primavera, f.; principio, m.; -, a. primero; primoroso, excelente; -, v. a. cebar; imprimir. [f.
primer, prĭm'ûr, s. cartilla para los niños,
primeval, prĭmē'văl, a. primitivo.
priming, prĭ'mĭng, s. cebo, m.; imprimación, f. [primitivamente.
primitive, prĭm'ĭtĭv, a.primitivo; -ly,ad.
primness, prĭm'nĕs, s. afectación, f.
primogeniture, prĭmōjĕn'ĭtûr, s. primogenitura, f.
primrose, prĭm'rōz, s. (bot.) prímula, f.
prince, prĭns, s. príncipe, soberano, m.
princedom, -dŭm, s. principado, m.
princely, -lĕ, a. semejante ó correspondiente á un príncipe; -, ad. como un príncipe. [príncipe.
princess, -ĕs, s. princesa, f.
principal, prĭn'sĭpăl, a. -ly, ad. principal(mente); -, s. principal, jefe, m.; capital, m. [m.
principality, prĭnsĭpăl'ĭtĕ, s. principado,
principle, prĭn'sĭpl, s. principio, m.; causa primitiva, f.; fundamento, motivo, m.
print, prĭnt, v. a. estampar, imprimir; -, s. impresión, estampa, edición, f.; impreso, m.; out of -, vendido, agotado (libros).
printer, -ûr, s. impresor, m.; indianero, m.; -'s reader, corrector, m.
printing-house, -ĭng hŏŭs, **printing-office**, -ŏfĭs, s. imprenta, f.
prior, prī'ûr, a. anterior, precedente; -, s. prior (prelado), m.
prioress, -ĕs, s. priora, f.
priority, prīŏr'ĭtĕ, s. prioridad, f.
priory, prī'ŏrĕ, s. priorato, m.
prism, prĭzm, s. prisma, f.
prison, prĭz'n, s. prisión, cárcel, f.
prisoner, -ûr, s. prisionero, m.
pristine, prĭs'tĭn, a. prístino, antiguo.
privacy, prĭ'vāsĕ, s. secreto, m.; retiro, m.
private, prĭ'vāt, a. secreto, privado; particular; - **soldier**, s. soldado raso, m.; -ly, ad. en secreto, en particular.
privateer, -vātēr', s. corsario, m.
privation, prĭvā'shŭn, s. privación, f.
privilege, prĭv'ĭlĕj, s. privilegio, m.; -, v. a. privilegiar.
privily, prĭv'ĭlĕ, a. secretamente.
privity, prĭv'ĭtĕ, s. confianza, f.; consentimiento, m.
privy, prĭv'ĕ, a. privado, secreto; confidente; -, s. secreta, letrina, f.

prize, *priz*, s. premio, m.; precio, m.; presa, f.; –, v. a. apreciar, valuar.

pro, *pró*, pr. para.   [verisimilitud, f.

probability, *probábil'ité*, s. probabilidad,

probable, *prób'ábl*, a. probable, verisímil; –bly, ad. probablemente.

probate, *pró'bát*, s. verificación de los testamentos, f.   [men, m.; noviciado, m.

probation, *bá'shän*, s. prueba, f., exa-

probationary, *–áré*, a. probatorio.

probationer, *–är*, s. novicio, m.

probe, *prób*, s. (med.) tienta, f.; –, v. a. tentar (alguna herida).   [f.

probity, *prób'ité*, s. probidad, sinceridad,

problem, *prób'lêm*, s. problema, m.

problematical, *problémät'ikäl*, a. problemático; –ly, ad. problemáticamente.

proboscis, *próbós'sis*, s. probóscide, m.

procedure, *prósed'úr*, s. procedimiento, m.; progreso, proceso, m.

proceed, *proséd'*, v. n. proceder; provenir; portarse; originarse; –s, *pró'séds*, s. pl. producto, m.; rédito, m.; gross –s, producto íntegro; net –s, producto neto.

proceeding, *–ing*, s. procedimiento, m.; proceso, m.; conducta f.   [m.

process, *pró'sés*, s. proceso, m.; progreso,

procession, *sésh'än*, s. procesión, f.

proclaim, *próklám'*, v. a. proclamar, promulgar; publicar.

proclamation, *próklámá'shän*, s. proclamación, f.; decreto, bando, m.

proclivity, *próklív'ité*, s. propensión, inclinación, f.

proconsul, *prókón'sül*, s. procónsul, m.

procrastinate, *prókräs'tinát*, v. a. diferir, retardar.   [ción, tardanza, f.

procrastination, *–krästiná'shän*, s. dila-

procrastinator, *–krästiná'tär*, s. pelmazo, m.   [escolástico, m.

proctor, *prók'tär*, s. procurador, m.; juez

proctorship, *–ship*, s. procuraduría, f.

procurable, *prókú'rábl*, a. asequible.

procuration, *prókúrá'shän*, s. procuración, f.

procurator, *–á'tär*, s. procurador, m.

procure, *prókúr'*, v. a. procurar.

procurement, *–mént*, s. procuración, f.

procurer, *–är*, s. entremetido, m.

prodigal, *pród'igäl*, a. pródigo; –ly, ad. pródigamente; –s, disipador, m.   [f.

prodigality, *pródigäl'ité*, s. prodigalidad,

prodigious, *pródij'üs*, a. prodigioso; –ly, ad. prodigiosamente.

prodigy, *pród'éjé*, s. prodigio, m.

produce, *pródús'*, v. a. producir, criar; causar; –, *pród'üs*, s. producto, m.

producer, *pródú'sär*, s. producente, m.

product, *pród'ükt*, s. producto, m.; obra, f.; efecto, m.   [f.; producto, m.

production, *pródük'shän*, s. producción,

productive, *pródük'tiv*, a. productivo.

productiveness, *–nés*, s. producibilidad, f.

profanation, *prófäná'shän*, s. profanación, f.   [fanamente; –, v. a. profanar.

profane, *prófán'*, a. profano; –ly, ad. pro-

profess, *prófés'*, v. a. profesar; ejercer; declarar.

professedly, *–édlé*, ad. declaradamente; públicamente.

profession, *prófésh'än*, s. profesión, f.

professional, *–äl*, a. lo que tiene relación con una profesión particular.

professor, *prófés'sär*, s. profesor, catedrático, m.   [f.

professorship, *–ship*, s. profesorado, m.; cátedra, f.   [–, s. oferta, f.

proffer, *próf'fär*, v. a. proponer, ofrecer;

proficiency, *prófish'énsé*, s. aprovechamiento, m.

proficient, *–ént*, a. proficiente, adelantado.   [tado.

profile, *pró'fél*, s. perfil, m.

profit, *próf'it*, s. ganancia, f.; provecho, m.; ventaja, f.; –, v. a. & n. aprovechar, servir; ser útil; adelantar; aprovecharse.

profitable, *–äbl*, a. provechoso, ventajoso; –bly, ad. provechosamente.

profitableness, *–äblnés*, s. ganancia, f.; provecho, m.

profitless, *–lés*, a. inútil, sin provecho.

profligacy, *próf'ligäsé*, s. perversidad, disolución, f.; desarreglo, m.

profligate, *próf'ligát*, a. licencioso, perdido; –ly, ad. disolutamente.

profound, *prófóünd'*, a. profundo; –ly, ad. profundamente.

profundity, *–fünd'ité*, s. profundidad, f.

profuse, *prófús'*, a. profuso, pródigo; –ly, ad. profusamente.   [abundancia, f.

profusion, *–fú'zhän*, s. prodigalidad, f.;

progenitor, *prójén'itär*, s. progenitor, m.

progeny, *prój'éné*, s. progenie, casta, f.

prognostic, *prógnós'tik*, s. pronóstico, m.

prognosticate, *–tikát*, v. a. pronosticar.

prognostication, *–tiká'shän*, s. pronosticación, f.; pronóstico, m.

programme, *pró'grám*, s. programa, m.

progress, *pró'grés*, s. progreso, m.; viaje, curso, m.; –, *prógrés'*, v. n. hacer progresos.   [adelantamiento, m.

progression, *prógrésh'än*, s. progresión, f.;

progressive, *prógrés'siv*, a. progresivo; –ly, ad. progresivamente.   [impedir.

prohibit, *próhib'it*, v. a. prohibir, vedar;

prohibition, *próhibish'än*, s. prohibición, f.; auto prohibitorio, m.

prohibitory, *próhib'itäré*, a. prohibitivo.

project, *prójékt'*, v. a. proyectar, trazar; –, *pró'jékt*, s. proyecto, m.

projectile, *prójék'til*, s. proyectil, m.

projection, *–shän*, s. proyección, f.; proyectura, f.

projector, *–tär*, s. proyectista, m.

proletarian, *prólétá'riän*, a. proletario, vulgar.   [cundo.

prolific(al), *prólif'ik(äl)*, a. prolífico, fe-

prolix, *pró'liks*, a. prolijo, difuso.

prolixity, *próliks'ité*, s. prolijidad, f.

prologue, *pró'lóg*, s. prólogo, m.

prolong, *prólóng'*, v. a. prolongar; diferir.   [dilatación, f.

prolongation, *–gá'shän*, s. prolongación, f.

promenade, *próm'énád*, v. n. pasearse; –, *próménád'*, s. paseo, m.   [f.

prominence, *próm'inéns*, s. prominencia,

prominent,-ĭnĕnt, a. prominente, saledizo.

promiscuous, prŏmĭs'kūŭs, a. promiscuo; -ly, ad. promiscuamente. [prometer.

promise, prŏm'ĭs, s. promesa, f.; -, v. a.

promissory, -ĭssŭrĕ, a. promisorio. [m.

promontory, prŏm'ŏntŭrĕ, s. promontorio.

promote, prŏmōt', v. a. promover.

promoter, -ŭr, s. promotor, promovedor, m.; -of a joint-stock-company, fillibustero de banco, m.

promotion, prŏmō'shŭn, s. promoción, f.

prompt, prŏmt, a. pronto; constante; -ly, ad. prontamente; -, v. a. sugerir, insinuar; apuntar (en el teatro).

prompter, -ŭr, s. apuntador de teatro, m.

promptitude, -tĭūd, promptness,-nĕs, s. prontitud, presteza,f. [publicar.

promulgate, prŏmŭl'gāt, v.a. promulgar.

promulgation, -mŭlgā'shŭn, s. promulgación, f.

prone, prōn, a. prono, inclinado.

proneness,-nĕs, s. inclinación, propensión,f. [labrador, m. pl.

prong, prŏng, s. dientes de una horca de

pronominal, prŏnŏm'ĭnăl, a. pronominal.

pronoun, prō'nŏŭn, s. pronombre, m.

pronounce, prŏnŏŭns', v. a. pronunciar; recitar. [nunciación, f.

pronunciation, prŏnŭnsĭā'shŭn, s. pro-

proof, prōf, s. prueba, f.; -, a. impenetrable; de prueba.

proof-sheets, -shēts, s. pl. pruebas, primeras muestras de la composición tipográfica, f. pl.

prop, prŏp, v. a. sostener; apuntalar; -, s. apoyo, puntal, m.; sostén, m. [f.

propaganda, prŏpăgăn'dă, s. propaganda,

propagate, prŏp'ăgāt, v. a. (& n.) propagar(se). [ción, f.

propagation, prŏpăgā'shŭn, s. propaga-

propel, prŏpĕl', v. a. impeler.

propeller, -ŭr, s. navío ó hélice, m.

propensity, prŏpĕn'sĭtĕ, s. propensión, tendencia, f.

proper, prŏp'ŭr, a. propio; conveniente; exacto; bien parecido; -ly, ad. propiamente, justamente.

property, -tĕ, s. propiedad, calidad, f.

prophecy, prŏf'ĕsĕ, s. profecía, f.

prophesy, prŏf'ĕsī, v. a. profetizar; predecir.

prophet, prŏf'ĕt, s. profeta, m. [dicar.

prophetess, -ĕs, s. profetisa, f.

prophetic(al), prŏfĕt'ĭk(ăl), a. profético; -ally, ad. proféticamente.

propinquity, prŏpĭng'kwĭtĕ, s. propincuidad, proximidad, f.; parentesco, m.

propitiate, prŏpĭsh'ĭāt, v. n. propiciar.

propitiation, prŏpĭshĭā'shŭn, s. propiciación, acción agradable á Dios, f.

propitiatory, -ĭātŭrĕ, a. propiciatorio.

propitious,-ŭs, a. propicio, favorable; -ly, ad. propiciamente.

proportion, prŏpōr'shŭn, s. proporción, f.; simetría, f.; -, v. n. proporcionar.

proportionable, -ăbl, proportional, -ăl, a. proporcional, proporcionable.

proposal, prŏpōz'ăl, s. propuesta, proposición, f.; oferta, f.

propose, prŏpōz', v. a. proponer.

proposition, prŏpŏzĭsh'ŭn, s. proposición, propuesta, f. [sentar una proposición.

propound, prŏpŏŭnd', v. a. proponer;

proprietary, prŏprī'ĕtărĕ, a. propio.

proprietor, -ĕtŭr, s. propietario, m.

proprietress, -ĕtrĕs, s. propietaria, f.

propriety, -tĕ, s. propiedad, f. [ción, f.

prorogation, prŏrŏgā'shŭn, s. prorroga-

prorogue, prŏrōg', v. a. prorrogar.

prosaic, prōzā'ĭk, a. prosaico, en prosa.

proscenium, prŏsē'nĭŭm, s. proscenio, m.

proscribe, prŏskrīb', v. a. proscribir.

proscription, prŏskrĭp'shŭn, s. proscripción, f.

prosecute, prŏs'ĕkūt, v. a. proseguir.

prosecution, -kū'shŭn, s. prosecución, f.; seguimiento de una causa criminal, m.

prosecutor, -kūtŭr, s. acusador, m.

proselyte, prŏs'ĕlīt, s. prosélito, m.

prosody, prŏs'ŏdĕ, s. prosodia, f.

prospect, prŏs'pĕkt, s. perspectiva, f.; esperanza, f. [lejos; próvido.

prospective, prŏspĕk'tĭv, a. lo que mira de

prospectus, prŏspĕk'tŭs, s. prospecto, m.

prosper, prŏs'pŭr, v. a. & n. prosperar.

prosperity, prŏspĕr'ĭtĕ, s. prosperidad, f.

prosperous, -pŭrŭs, a. próspero, feliz; -ly, ad. prósperamente. [s. prostituta, f.

prostitute, prŏs'tĭtūt, v. a. prostituir; -,

prostitution, -tū'shŭn, s. prostitución, f.

prostrate, prŏs'trāt, a. prosternado; -, v. a. postrar.

prostration, prŏstrā'shŭn, s. postración, f.

protect, prŏtĕkt', v. a. proteger; amparar.

protection, prŏtĕk'shŭn, s. protección, f.

protective, -tĭv, a. protectorio.

protector, -tŭr, s. protector, patrono, m.

protest, prŏtĕst', v. n. protestar; -, prō'tĕst, s. protesta, f., protesto, m.

protestant, prŏt'ĕstănt, s. protestante, m.

protestantism, -ĭzm, s. protestantismo, m.

protestation, prŏtĕstā'shŭn, s. protestación, f.; protesta.

protocol, prŏt'ŏkŏl, s. protocolo, m.

prototype, prō'tŏtīp, s. prototipo, m.

protract, prŏtrăkt', v. a. prolongar, dilatar. [ción, dilatación, f.

protraction, prŏtrăk'shŭn, s. prolonga-

protrude, prŏtrōōd', v. a. empujar; impeler; -, v. n. empujarse. [rancia, f.

protuberance, prŏtū'bŭrăns, s. protube-

protuberant, -bŭrănt, a. prominente, saliente. [ad. soberbiamente.

proud, prŏŭd, a. soberbio, orgulloso; -ly,

prove, prōv, v. a. probar, justificar; experimentar; -, v. n. resultar; salir (bien ó mal).

provender, prŏv'ĕndŭr, s. forraje, m.

proverb, prŏv'ŭrb, s. proverbio, m.

proverbial, prŏvŭr'bĭăl, a. -ly, ad. proverbial(mente).

provide, prŏvīd', v. a. proveer.

provided, -ĕd (- that), c. con tal que.

providence, prŏvĭdĕns, s. providencia, f.; economía, f.

provident, prŏv'ĭdĕnt, a. próvido; providente; -ly, ad. próvidamente.

providential, *prŏvĭdĕn'shăl,* a. -ly, ad. providencial(mente)

province, *prŏv'ĭns,* s. provincia, f.; obligación particular, f.   [(m.)

provincial, *prŏvĭn'shăl,* a. & s. provincial

provision, *prŏvĭzh'ŭn,* s. provisión, f.; precaución, f.   [(mente).

provisional, *—ăl,* a. -ly, ad. provisional

proviso, *prŏvĭ'zō,* s. estipulación, f.

provisory, *prŏv'ĭzărĕ,* a. provisorio.

provocation, *prŏvŏkă'shŭn,* s. provocación, f.; apelación, f.

provoke, *prŏvōk',* v. a. provocar; apelar.

provokingly, *—ĭnglĕ,* ad. de un modo provocativo.

provost, *prŏv'ŏst,* s. preboste, m.

prow, *prŏ̄,* s. (mar.) proa, f.

prowess, *—ĕs,* s. proeza, valentía, f.

prowl, *prŏl,* v. n. andar en busca de pillaje; rondar, vagar; rastrear.

prowler, *—ăr,* s. ladrón, estafador, m.

proximate, *prŏks'ĭmăt,* a. próximo; -ly, ad. próximamente.

proximity, *prŏksĭm'ĭtĕ,* s. proximidad, f.

proxy, *prŏks'ĕ,* s. procuración, f.; procurador, m.

prude, *prŏd,* s. mojigata, f.   [dor, m.

prudence, *—ĕns,* s. prudencia, f.

prudent, *—ĕnt,* a. prudente, circunspecto; -ly, ad. con juicio.

prudential, *prŏdĕn'shăl,* a. juicioso.

prudentials, *—z,* s. pl. máximas de prudencia, f.   [gatez, f.

prudery, *prŏd'ărĕ,* s. gazmoñería, mojigatería, f.

prudish, *prŏd'ĭsh,* a. gazmoño, mojigato.

prune, *prŏn,* v. a. podar; escamondar los árboles; —, s. ciruela pasa, f.

prunello, *prŏnĕl'lŏ,* s. ciruelita, f.; cerro de oro, m. (tela de lana).

pruning-hook, *prŏn'ĭnghŏk,* s.

pruning-knife, *—nĭf,* s. podadera, f.   [rito, m.

pruriency, *prŏ'rĭĕnsĕ,* s. comezón, f.; prurito, m.

prurient, *—rĭĕnt,* a. lo que padece prurito.

prussic acid, *prŭs'ĭk ăs'ĭd,* s. ácido prúsico.

pry, *prĭ,* v. n. espiar, acechar.   [azul, m.

psalm, *săm,* s. salmo, m.   [m.

psalter, *săl'tăr,* s. salterio, libro de salmos.

pseudonym, *sū'dŏnĭm,* s. seudónimo, m.

pshaw! *shă,* ¡vaya!, ¡fuera!, ¡quita!, ¡malhaya!   [lógico.

psychologic(al), *sĭkŏlŏj'ĭk(ăl),* a. sicológico.

psychology, *sĭkŏl'ŏjĕ,* s. sicología, f.

puberty, *pū'bărtĕ,* s. pubertad, f.

public, *pŭb'lĭk,* a. público; común; notorio; -ly, ad. públicamente; —, s. público, m.

publican, *—ăn,* s. publicano, m.; tabernero, m.   [f.; edición, f.

publication, *pŭblĭkă'shŭn,* s. publicación, f.

publicist, *pŭb'lĭsĭst,* s. publicista, m.

publicity, *pŭblĭs'ĭtĕ,* s. publicidad, f.

publish, *pŭb'lĭsh,* v. a. publicar.

publisher, *—ăr,* s. publicador, editor, m.

pucker, *pŭk'ŭr,* v. a. arrugar; hacer pliegues.   [morcilla, f.

pudding, *pŭd'ĭng,* s. pudín, pudingo, m.;

puddle, *pŭd'dl,* s. lodazal, cenagal, m.; —, v. a. enlodar; enturbiar el agua con lodo.

pudenda, *pŭdĕn'dă,* s. partes vergonzosas, f. pl.

pudicity, *pŭdĭs'ĭtĕ,* s. pudor, recato, m.

pudor, *pū'dŏr,* s. pudor, m.; modestia, f.

puerile, *pū'ărĭl,* a. pueril.

puff, *pŭf,* s. bufido, soplo, m.; bejín, m.; borla para empolvar, f.; rizado, m.; —, v. a. hinchar; soplar; ensoberbecer; —, v. n. inflarse; bufar; resollar.

puffiness, *—ĭnĕs,* s. hinchazón, f.   [soplar.

puffing, *—ĭng,* s. reclamo, m.

puff-paste, *—pāst,* s. hojaldre, m.

puffy, *—ĕ,* a. hinchado, entumecido.

pug, *pŭg,* s. perrillo fino, m.

pugilism, *pū'jĭlĭzm,* s. pugilato, m.

pugilist, *pū'jĭlĭst,* s. pugil, m.

pugnacious, *pŭgnă'shŭs,* a. pugnaz; -ly, ad. con valor.   [f.

pug-nose, *pŭg'nŏz,* s. nariz roma ó chata.

puisne, *pū'nĕ,* a. inferior; pequeño; segundón.   [m.

puling, *pūl'ĭng,* s. gemido, m.; piamiento, m.

pull, *pŭl,* v. a. tirar; coger; rasgar, desgarrar; **to — off,** arrancar; —, s. tirón, m.; sacudida, f.

pull-back, *—băk,* s. obstáculo, m.

pullet, *—lĕt,* s. polla, f.

pulley, *pŭl'ĕ,* s. polea, garrucha, f.

pulmonary, *pŭl'mŏnărĕ,* **pulmonic(al),** *pŭlmŏn'ĭk(ăl),* a. pulmoníaco.

pulp, *pŭlp,* s. pulpa, f.

pulpit, *pŭl'pĭt,* s. púlpito, m.

pulpy, *pŭlp'ĕ,* s. pulposo.

pulsate, *pŭl'sāt,* v. n. pulsar, latir.

pulsation, *pŭlsă'shŭn,* s. pulsación, f.

pulse, *pŭls,* s. pulso, m.; legumbres, f. pl.

pulverization, *pŭlvărĭză'shŭn,* s. pulverización, f.

pulverize, *pŭl'vărĭz,* v. a. pulverizar.

pumice, *pū'mĭs,* s. piedra pómez, f.

pump, *pŭmp,* s. bomba, f.; escarpín, m.; —, v. a. dar á la bomba; sondear; sonsacar.

pumpkin, *pŭm'kĭn,* s. calabaza, f.

pump-room, *—rŏm,* s. pabellón para beber termas, m.

pun, *pŭn,* s. equívoco, chiste, m.; —, v. n. jugar del vocablo, decir equívocos.

punch, *pŭnsh,* s. punzón, m.; ponche, m. (bebida); arlequín, m.

puncheon, *—ŭn,* s. punzón, m.; cuño, m.; medida de veinte arrobas, f.   [fón, m.

punchinello, *—ĭnĕl'lŏ,* s. polichinela, bufón, m.

punctilio, *pŭngktĭl'ĭŏ,* s. puntillo, m.

punctilious, *—ăs,* a. puntoso.

punctual, *pŭngk'tŭăl,* a. puntual, exacto; -ly, ad. puntualmente.   [tualidad, f.

punctuality, *—tŭăl'ĭtĕ,* s. exactitud, puntualidad, f.

punctuate, *—tŭăt,* v. n. puntuar.

punctuation, *—tŭă'shŭn,* s. puntuación, f.

puncture, *—tŭr,* s. puntura, f.

pungency, *pŭn'jĕnsĕ,* s. acrimonia, f.; picante, m.

pungent, *—jĕnt,* a. picante, acre, mordaz.

punic, *pū'nĭk,* a. púnico, pérfido.

puniness, *pū'nĭnĕs,* s. pequeñez, f.

punish, *pŭn'ĭsh,* v. a. castigar, penar.

punishable, *—ăbl,* a. punible.

punishment, *—mĕnt,* s. castigo, m.; pena, f.

punster, *pŭns'tăr,* s. truhán, m.; dichero, m.

punt, *pănt,* v. a. apuntar, parar (poner el dinero á las cartas); —, s. barco llano, m.
punter, *–ăr,* s. apuntador, m. (en el juego de faraon).
puny, *pū'ně,* a. joven, pequeño; inferior.
pup, *pŭp,* s. cachorrillo, m.; —, v. n. parir la perra.
pupil, *pū'pĭl,* s. pupila, f.; pupilo, m.; discípulo, m.
pupilage, *–lĭj,* s. pupilaje, m.
pupillary, *–ărĕ,* a. pupilar.
puppet, *pŭp'pĕt,* s. títere, muñeco, m.
puppet-show, *–shō,* s. representación de títeres, f.
puppy, *pŭp'pĕ,* s. perrillo, trasto, m.
puppyism, *–ĭzm,* s. fatuidad, f.
purblind, *pŭr'blīnd,* a. miope, cegato.
purchase, *pŭr'tshăs,* v. a. comprar; mercar; —, s. compra, f.; adquisición, f.
purchaser, *–ăr,* s. comprador, m.
pure, *pūr,* a. —puro; —ly, ad. puramente.
purgation, *pŭrgā'shŭn,* s. purgación, f.
purgative, *pŭr'gătĭv,* a. purgativo.
purgatory, *pŭr'gătărĕ,* s. purgatorio, m.
purge, *pŭrj,* v. a. purgar. [ción, f.
purification, *pŭrĭfĭkā'shŭn,* s. purificación, f.
purify, *pū'rĭfī,* v. a. (& n.) purificar(se).
purist, *pū'rĭst,* s. purista, m.
puritan, *pū'rĭtăn,* s. puritano, m.
purity, *pū'rĭtĕ,* s. pureza, f.
purl, *pŭrl,* s. cerveza de ajenjos, f.; murmullo, m.; —, v. n. murmurar.
purlieu, *pŭr'lū,* s. comarca, f.
purloin, *pŭrlŏin',* v. a. hurtar, robar.
purple, *pŭr'pl,* a. purpúreo; —, s. púrpura, f.; –s, s. pl. (med.) tabardillo pintado, m.; —, v. a. purpurar.
purplish, *–plĭsh,* a. purpurino.
purport, *pŭr'pōrt,* s. designio, m.; contenido, m.; —, v. a. significar, designar.
purpose, *pŭr'pŭs,* s. intención, f.; designio, proyecto, m.; **to the —,** al propósito; **to no —,** inútilmente; **on —,** de propósito; —, v. n. proponer. [son contentos.
purr, *pŭr,* v. n. roncar los gatos cuando están contentos.
purse, *pŭrs,* s. bolsa, f.; —, v. a. embolsar.
purse-proud, *–prŏŭd,* a. plutocrático.
purslain, *pŭrs'lăn,* s. (bot.) verdolaga, f.
pursuance, *pŭrsū'ăns,* s. prosecución, f.
pursuant, *–ănt,* a. hecho en consecuencia de . . [acosar; continuar.
pursue, *pŭrsū',* v. a. & n. perseguir; seguir.
pursuit, *pŭrsūt',* s. perseguimiento, m.;
pursy, *pŭr'sĕ,* a. asmático. [ocupación, f.
purulence, *pū'rŏlĕns,* s. purulencia, f.
purulent, *–lĕnt,* a. purulento.
purvey, *pŭrvā',* v. a. & n. proveer; procurar. [sión, f.
purveyance, *–ăns,* s. abasto m.; provisión, f.
purveyor, *–ăr,* s. abastecedor, m.
push, *pŭsh,* v. a. empujar; estrechar; apretar; —, v. n. hacer esfuerzos; —, s. impulso, m.; empujón, m.; momento crítico, m.; esfuerzo, m.; asalto, m.
pushing, *–ĭng,* a. emprendedor.
pusillanimity, *pŭsĭllănĭm'ĭtĕ,* s. pusilanimidad, f. [ánime.
pusillanimous, *pŭsĭllăn'ĕmŭs,* a. pusi-

puss, *pŏs,* s. miz, m. (voz de cariño para [el gato).
pustule, *pŭs'tŭl,* s. pústula, f.
put, *pŭt,* v. a. poner, colocar; proponer; imponer, obligar; —, v. n. brotar, germinar.
putative, *pū'tătĭv,* a. putativo, reputado.
put-off, *pŭt'ŏf,* s. retardo, m.; dilatación, f.
put-on, *–ŏn,* s. engaño, m. [f.
putrefaction, *pūtrĕfăk'shŭn,* s. putrefacción, f.
putrefy, *pū'trĕfī,* v. n. pudrirse. [ción, f.
putrescence, *pūtrĕs'sĕns,* s. pudrición, f.
putrescent, *–sĕnt,* **putrid,** *pū'trĭd,* a. podrido, pútrido. [ción, f.
putridness, *–nĕs,* s. podredumbre, pudrición, f.
putty, *pŭt'tĕ,* s. almáciga, f.
puzzle, *pŭz'zl,* s. embarazo, m.; perplejidad, f.; —, v. a. embrollar; —, v. n. confundirse.
pyramid, *pĭr'ămĭd,* s. pirámide, f.
pyramidal, *pĭrăm'ĭdăl,* a. piramidal.
pyre, *pīr,* s. pira, hoguera, f. [técnica, f.
pyrotechnics, *pĭrōtĕk'nĭks,* s. pl. pirotécnica, f.
python, *pĭth'ŏn,* s. pitón atigrado, m.
pythoness, *pĭ'thŏnĕs,* s. pitonisa, f.
pyx, *pĭks,* s. pixide, copón, m.

Q.

quack, *kwăk,* v. n. graznar (como un pato); —, s. charlatán, m.
quackery, *–ărĕ,* s. charlatanería, f.
quadragésima, *kwŏdrăjĕs'ĕmă,* s. cuadragésima, m. [m.
quadrangle, *kwŏd'răngl,* s. cuadrángulo.
quadrant, *–rănt,* s. cuarto, m.; cuadrante, m.; (mar.) octante, m.
quadrennial, *kwŏdrĕn'nĭăl,* a. cuadrienal.
quadrilateral, *kwŏdrĭlăt'ărăl,* a. cuadrilátero.
quadrille, *kădrĭl',* s. contradanza, f.
quadroon, *kwŏdrōn',* s. cuarterón, m.
quadruped, *kwŏd'rŭpĕd,* s. cuadrúpedo, m.
quadruple, *kwŏd'rŭpl,* a. cuádruplo.
quaff, *kwăf,* v. a. beber á grandes tragos; —, v. n. beber demasiado.
quaffer, *–ăr,* s. borracho, m.
quagmire, *kwăg'mīr,* s. tremedal, m.
quail, *kwăl,* s. codorniz, f.
quaint, *kwănt,* a. nimiamente exacto; pulido; exquisito; —ly, ad. pulidamente.
quaintness, *–nĕs,* s. elegancia, f.; delicadeza, f.
quake, *kwăk,* v. n. temblar; tiritar.
quaker, *–ăr,* s. cuácaro, m. (sectario).
qualification, *kwŏlĭfĭkā'shŭn,* s. calificación, f.; prendas, f. pl.
qualify, *kwŏl'ĭfī,* v. a. calificar; modificar; (am.) afirmar con juramento; templar.
qualitative, *kwŏl'ĭtātĭv,* a. cualitativo.
quality, *kwŏl'ĭtĕ,* s. calidad, f.
qualm, *kwăm,* s. deliquio, desmayo, m.
qualmish, *–ĭsh,* a. desfallecido, lánguido.
quandary, *kwŏndā'rĕ,* s. incertidumbre, duda, f. [tivo.
quantitative, *kwŏn'tĭtātĭv,* a. cuantitativo.
quantity, *kwŏn'tĭtĕ,* s. cantidad, f.
quantum, *kwŏn'tŭm,* s. tanto, m.
quarantine, *kwŏr'ăntēn,* s. cuarentena, f.

quarrel, *kwŏr'rĕl,* s. quimera, riña, **con-**
  tienda, f.; —, v. n. reñir, disputar.
quarreller, *—lăr,* s. querellista, m.
quarrelsome, *—sŭm,* a. pendenciero, qui-
quarry, *kwŏr'rĕ,* s. cantera, f. [merista.
quarryman, *—măn,* s. cavador de cantera,
  m. [cientos); media azumbre, f.
quart, *kwărt,* s. cuarta, f. (en el juego de los
quartan, *kwăr'tăn,* s. cuartana, f.
quarter, *—tăr,* s. cuarto, m.; cuarta parte,
  f.; cuartel, m.; barriada, f.;—**of an hour,**
  un cuarto de hora; —, v. a. cuartear;
  acuartelar.
quarter-deck, *—dĕk,* s. (mar.) alcázar, m.
quarterly, *—lĕ,* a. lo que se hace cada tres
  meses; —, ad. una vez cada trimestre.
quartern, *—tŭrn,* s. cuarta parte de un
  cuartillo, f.
quartet, *kwărtĕt',* s. (mus.) cuarteto, m.
quarto, *kwŏr'tŏ,* s. libro en cuarto, m.
quartz, *kwŏrts,* s. (min.) cuarzo, m.
quash, *kwŏsh,* v. a. fracasar; cascar; anular, abrogar. [v. n. gorgoritear; trinar.
quaver, *kwā'văr,* s. (mus.) corchea, f.; —,
quay, *kĕ,* s. muelle, m.
quean, *kwĕn,* s. mujercilla, f.
queasiness, *kwē'zĭnĕs,* s. hastío, m.
queasy, *kwē'zĕ,* a. nauseabundo; fastidioso.
queen, *kwĕn,* s. reina, f.; dama, f. (en el
  juego de damas y en el ajedrez). [reina.
queen-like, *—lĭk,* **queenly,** *—lĕ,* a. á lo
queer, *kwĕr,* a. estraño; ridículo; **-ly,** ad.
  ridículamente.
queerness, *—nĕs,* s. rareza, ridiculez, f.
quell, *kwĕl,* v. a. subyugar, postrar, avasallar.
quench, *kwĕnsh,* v. a. apagar; extinguir.
querist, *kwē'rĭst,* s. inquisidor, pregunta-
  dor, m. [quejosamente.
querulous, *kwĕr'ŭlŭs,* a. quejoso; **-ly,** ad.
querulousness, *—nĕs,* s. la disposición ó
  costumbre de quejarse.
query, *kwē'rĕ,* s. cuestión, pregunta, f.;
  —, v. a. preguntar. [busca, f.
quest, *kwĕst,* s. pesquisa, inquisición, f.
question, *kwĕst'yăn,* s. cuestión, f.; disquisición, f.; asunto, m.; duda, f.; cuestión de tormento; —, v. a. cuestionar,
  preguntar; —, v. n. dudar, desconfiar.
questionable, *—dŏl,* a. cuestionable, dudoso. [dor, m.
questioner, *—ăr,* s. inquiridor, pregunta-
questor, *kwĕst'ăr,* s. cuestor, m.
quibble, *kwĭb'bl,* s. juguete de vocablo, m.;
  —, v. n. jugar del vocablo, decir equívocos.
quick, *kwĭk,* a. vivo, viviente; veloz; ligero,
  pronto; ágil, ardiente, penetrante; **-ly,**
  ad. con presteza; —, s. carne viva, f.
quicken, *—n,* v. a. vivificar; acelerar; ani-
quick-lime, *—lĭm,* s. cal viva, f. [mar.
quickness, *—nĕs,* s. presteza, f.; actividad,
  f.; viveza, penetración, f.
quick-sand, *—sănd,* s. arena movediza, f.
quickset, *—sĕt,* s. plantón, m.; **—hedge,**
  seto vivo, m.
quick-sighted, *—sītĕd,* a. perspicaz. [m.
quick-silver, *—sĭlvăr,* s. azogue, mercurio,
quick-silvered, *—sĭlvărd,* a. azogado.

quick-witted, *—wĭttĕd,* a. agudo, perspicaz.
quid, *kwĭd,* s. pedazo de tabaco que mascan
  los marineros, m. [f.
quiddity, *—tĕ,* s. cavilación, trampa legal,
quidnunc, *—nŭngk,* s. fanfarrón. m.
quiescent, *kwīĕs'sĕnt,* a. quieto, descansado. [**-ly,** ad. quietamente.
quiet, *kwī'ĕt,* a. quieto, quieto, tranquilo;
quietism, *—ĭzm,* s. tranquilidad de ánimo, f.
quietness, *—nĕs,* **quietude,** *—ŭd,* s. quietud,
  tranquilidad, f. [f.
quietus, *kwī'ĕtŭs,* s. finiquito, m.; muerte,
quill, *kwĭl,* s. pluma (para escribir), f.;
  canilla, f.
quill-driver, *—drĭvăr,* s. cagatinta, m.
quilt, *kwĭlt,* s. colcha, f. [brillo, m.
quince, *kwĭns,* s. (bot.) membrillero, mem-
quincunx, *kwĭng'kăngks,* s. quincunce,
quinine, *kwĭn'ĭn,* s. quinina, f. [m.
quinquennial, *kwĭnkwĕn'nĭal,* a. lo que
  dura un quinquenio ó sucede una vez en
  cinco años.
quinsy, *kwĭn'zĕ,* s. esquinancia, f.
quint, *kwĭnt,* s. quinta, f. (en algunos juegos
  de naipes).
quintal, *kwĭn'tăl,* s. quintal, m. [cia, f.
quintessence, *kwĭntĕs'sĕns,* s. quinta esen-
quintet, *kwĭntĕt',* s. (mus.) quinteto, m.
quintuple, *kwĭn'tŭpl,* a. quíntuplo.
quip, *kwĭp,* s. indirecta, f.; —, v. a. echar
quire, *kwīr,* s. mano de papel, f. [pullas.
quirk, *kwŭrk,* s. pulla, f.; sutileza, f.
quit, *kwĭt,* v. a. descargar; desempeñar;
  absolver; —, a. libre, descargado.
quite, *kwĭt,* ad. totalmente, enteramente,
  absolutamente.
quits, *kwĭts,* ¡en paz! [peño, m.
quittance, *kwĭt'tăns,* s. finiquito, desem-
quiver, *kwĭv'ăr,* s. aljaba, f.; —, v. n.
  temblar; **-ed,** a. armado con aljaba.
quixotic, *kwĭksŏt'ĭk,* a. quijotesco.
quiz, *kwĭz,* v. a. burlar, chulear.
quizzing-glass, *kwĭz'ĭngglăs,* s. **anteojo**
  de puño, m.; lágrima jocosa, f.
quoit, *k(w)ŏĭt,* s. tejo, m.
quondam, *kwŏn'dăm,* a. antiguo.
quorum, *kwŏr'ăm,* s. número competente
quota, *kwŏ'tă,* s. cuota, f. [de jueces, m.
quotation, *kwŏtā'shăn,* s. citación, cita, f.
quote, *kwŏt,* v. a. citar. [**— he,** él dijo.
quoth, *kwăth* (kwŏth), v. imp. — **I,** dije yo;
quotidian, *kwŏtĭd'tăn,* s. calentura coti-
  diana, f.
quotient, *kwŏ'shĕnt,* s. cociente, m.

R.

rabbet, *răb'bĕt,* s. ranura, f.
rabbi, *răb'bĕ,* s. rabí, rabino, m.
rabbit, *răb'bĭt,* s. conejo, m.
rabble, *răb'bl,* s. gentuza, canalluza, f.
rabid, *răb'ĭd,* a. rabioso, furioso.
race, *rās,* s. raza, casta, f.; carrera, f.; sabor rancio del vino, m.; —, v. n. correr
  con mucha ligereza.

racer, *-ŭr,* s. caballo de carrera, m.
raciness, *rā'sĭnĕs,* s. calidad rancia del vino, f. [carrera ciega, f.
racing, *rās'ĭng,* s. corrida de caballos,
rack, *răk,* s. tormento, m.; rueca, f.; morillos de asador, m. pl.; pesebre, m.; —, v. n. atormentar; trasegar. [queta, f.
racket, *-ĕt,* s. baraúnda, confusión, f.; raqueta.
rack-rent, *-rĕnt,* s. arriendo exorbitante,
racy, *rā'sĭ,* a. rancio, espirituoso. [m.
radiance, *rā'dĭăns,* s. brillo, esplendor, m.
radiant, *-dĭănt,* a. radiante, brillante.
radiate, *-dĭāt,* v. n. echar rayos, centellear.
radiation, *rādĭā'shŭn,* s. irradiación, f.
radical, *rā'dĭkăl,* a. **-ly,** ad. radical-
(mente).
radicalism, *-ĭzm,* s. radicalismo, m.
radish, *rā'dĭsh,* s. rábano, m.
radius, *rā'dĭŭs,* s. radio; semidiámetro, m.
raffle, *răf'fl,* s. rifa, f. (juego); —, v. n. rifar.
raft, *răft,* s. balsa, almadía, f.; jangada, f.
rafter, *-ŭr,* s. cabrio, m.; viga, f.
rag, *răg,* s. trapo, andrajo, girón, m.
ragamuffin, *-ămŭf'fĭn,* s. andrajo, mendigo, pordiosero, m.; bribón, m.
rage, *rāj,* s. rabia, f.; furor, m.; —, v. n. rabiar; encolerizarse.
rag-gatherer, *răg'găthŭrŭr,* s. (--man, --picker), s. trapero, m.
ragged, *răg'gĕd,* a. andrajoso.
raging, *rāj'ĭng,* s. furia, rabia, f.; **-ly,** ad.
raid, *rād,* s. invasión, f. [rabiosamente.
raider, *-ŭr,* s. merodeador, m.
rail, *rāl,* s. baranda, barrera, f.; balaustrada, f.; (rail.) raíl, carril de los caminos de hierro, m.; —, v. a. cercar con balaustradas; —, v. n. injuriar de palabra. [m.
railer, *-ŭr,* s. maldiciente, murmurador,
raillery, *rāl'ŭrĕ,* s. chocarrería, burla, f.
railroad, *rāl'rōd,* **railway,** *-wā,* s. ferrocarril, m.
raiment, *rā'mĕnt,* s. ropa, f.; vestido, m.
rain, *rān,* s. lluvia, f.; —, v. n. llover.
rainbow, *-bō,* s. arco iris, arco celeste, m.
rain-water, *-wātŭr,* s. agua llovediza, f.
rainy, *rā'nĕ,* a. lluvioso.
raise, *rāz,* v. a. levantar, alzar; fabricar, edificar; engrandecer, elevar; excitar, causar.
raisin, *rā'zn,* s. pasa, f. (uva seca). [sar.
rake, *rāk,* s. rastro, rastrillo, m.; tunante, hombre perdulario, m.; —, v. a. rastrillar; raer; rebuscar.
rakish, *rāk'ĭsh,* a. libertino, disoluto.
rally, *răl'lĕ,* v. a. (mil.) reunir; ridiculizar; —, v. n. reunirse; burlarse de alguno.
ram, *răm,* s. morueco, m.; ariete, m.; —, v. a. impeler con violencia.
ramble, *răm'bl,* v. n. vagar; callejear; —, s. correría, f.
rambler, *-ŭr,* s. vagabundo, callejero, m.
ramification, *rămĭfĭkā'shŭn,* s. ramificación, f.
ramify, *răm'ĭfĭ,* v. n. ramificarse. [ción, f.
rammer, *răm'mŭr,* s. maza, f.; baqueta de escopeta, f.
rampant, *rămp'ănt,* a. exuberante.
rampart, *răm'pārt,* s. plataforma, f.; terraplén, m.; (mil.) muralla, f. [dor, m.
ramrod, *răm'rŏd,* s. baqueta, f.; ataca-

ramshackle, *răm'shăkl,* a. en ruina.
rancid, *răn'sĭd,* a. rancio.
rancidity, *rănsĭd'ĭtĭ,* s. rancidez, f.
rancour, *răng'kŭr,* s. rencor, m.
random, *răn'dŭm,* s. ventura, casualidad, f.; **at —,** á trochemoche.
range, *rānj,* v. a. colocar, ordenar; cerner; —, v. n. vagar; —, s. clase, f.; orden, m.; hilera, f.; correría, f.; línea de un tiro de artillería, f.; reja de cocina, f.; lanza de coche, f.
rank, *răngk,* a. exuberante; rancio; fétido; —, s. fila, hilera, clase, f.; grado de dignidad, m.
rankle, *-l,* v. n. enconarse, inflamarse.
rankness, *-nĕs,* s. exuberancia, f.; olor ó gusto rancio, m.; fuerza, f., vigor, m.
ransack, *răn'săk,* v. a. saquear, pillar.
ransom, *răn'sŭm,* v. a. saquear, pillar.
rant, *rănt,* v. n. decir disparates.
ranter, *-ŭr,* s. declamador, m.
rap, *răp,* v. a. & n. dar un golpe vivo y repentino; arrebatar; —, s. golpe ligero y vivo, m. [con rapacidad.
rapacious, *răpā'shŭs,* a. rapaz; **-ly,** ad.
rapacity, *răpăs'ĭtĭ,* s. rapacidad, f.
rape, *răp,* s. fuerza, f.; estupro, m.; (bot.) nabo silvestre, m. [mente.
rapid, *răp'ĭd,* a. rápido; **-ly,** ad. rápidamente.
rapidity, *răpĭd'ĭtĭ,* s. rapidez, f.
rapier, *rā'pĭŭr,* s. espadín, m.
rapine, *răp'ĭn,* s. rapiña, f.
rapper, *răp'pŭr,* s. llamador ó aldabón de puerta, m.; mentira grosera, f.
rapt, *răpt,* a. encantado, enajenado.
rapture, *răp'tshŭr,* s. rapto, m.; éxtasis, m.
rapturous, *-ŭs,* a. maravilloso.
rare, *rār,* a. raro, extraordinario; ralo; **-ly,** ad. raramente. [de nuevo, m.
rareeshow, *rā'rēshō,* s. mundinovi, mundi
rarefaction, *rārĕfăk'shŭn,* s. rarefacción, f.
rarefy, *rā'rĕfĭ,* v. a. rarificar.
rarity, *rā'rĭtĭ,* s. raridad, rareza, f.
rascal, *răs'kăl,* s. pícaro, bribón, m.
rascality, *răskăl'ĭtĭ,* s. pillada, f.
rascallion, *răskăl'yŭn,* s. villano, m.
rash, *răsh,* a. precipitado, temerario; **-ly,** ad. temerariamente; —, s. roncha, f.
rasher, *-ŭr,* s. torrezno, m.
rashness, *-nĕs,* s. temeridad, f.; arrojo, m.
rasp, *răsp,* s. raspador, m.; —, v. a. raspar; escofinar. [frambueso, f.
raspberry, *-bĕrĭ,* s. frambuesa, f.; --bush,
rat, *răt,* s. rata, f.
rate, *rāt,* s. tasa, f.; precio, valor, m.; grado, m.; manera, f.; —, v. a. tasar, apreciar; reñir á uno. [bien; antes.
rather, *răth'ŭr,* ad. de mejor gana; más
ratification, *rătĭfĭkā'shŭn,* s. ratificación, f.
ratify, *răt'ĭfĭ,* v. a. ratificar. [ción, f.
ratio, *rā'shĭō,* s. razón, f. [porción, f.
ration, *rā'shŭn,* s. (mil.) ración, f.; proporción.
rational, *răsh'ŭnăl,* a. racional; razonable; **-ly,** ad. racionalmente. [natural, f.
rationality, *răshŭnăl'ĭtĭ,* s. razón, luz
rat's-bane, *răts'bān,* s. arsénico, m.
rattan, *răttăn',* s. (bot.) rotén, m.

ratteen, *rắttĕn'*, s. ratina (tela de lana), f.

rattle, *rắt'tl*, v. a. & n. hacer ruido; regañar; zumbar; zurrir; to — in the throat, resollar con fuerza agonizando; —, s. sonido rechino; sonajero, m. [bel, f.

rattle-snake, *-snăk*, s. culebra de cascaravage, *răv'dj*, v. a. saquear, pillar; asolar; —, s. saqueo, m.

rave, *răv*, v. n. delirar; enfurecerse.

ravel, *răv'l*, v. a. embrollar; —, v. n. enraven, *răv'vn*, s. cuervo, m.   [redarse.

ravenous, *-ăs*, a. -ly, ad. voraz(mente).

ravine, *răvēn'*, s. barranca, f.

raving, *răv'ĭng*, a furioso, frenético; -ly, ad. como un loco furioso.

ravish, *răv'ĭsh*, v. a. estuprar; arrebatar.

ravisher, *-ăr*, s. estuprador, forzador, m.

ravishingly, *-ĭnglĕ*, ad. de un modo encantador.   [m.

ravishment, *-mĕnt*, s. rapto, m.; éxtasis.

raw, *ră*, a. crudo; puro; nuevo; novato, m.

raw-boned, *-bōnd*, a. huesudo; magro.

rawness, *-nĕs*, s. crudeza, f.; falta de experiencia, f.

ray, *ră*, s. rayo de luz, m.; raya, f. (pez).

rayless, *-lĕs*, a. sin brillo, apagado.

raze, *răz*, v. a. arrasar, extirpar; borrar.

razor, *ră'zŭr*, s. navaja de barbero, m.

reach, *rēch*, v. a. alcanzar; llegar hasta; —, v. n. extenderse, llegar; alcanzar, penetrar; esforzarse; —, s. alcance, poder, m.; capacidad, f.; astucia, f.

react, *rēăkt'*, v. a. rechazar; obrar recíprocamente.

reaction, *rēăk'shăn*, s. reacción, f.

read, *rēd*, v. a. leer; enseñar en público; —, v. n. estudiar; saber; —, *rĕd*, [erudito. [ad. pretérito.

readable, *-ăbl*, a. legible.

reader, *-ăr*, s. lector, m.   [gana.

readily, *rĕd'ĭlĕ*, ad. prontamente; de buena

readiness, *rĕd'ĭnĕs*, s. facilidad, f.; vivacidad del ingenio, f.; voluntad, gana, f.; prontitud, f.

reading, *rēd'ĭng*, s. lectura, f.

reading-room, *-rōm*, s. gabinete de lectura, m.

re-adjust, *rēădjăst'*, v. a. recomponer.

ready, *rĕd'ĕ*, a. listo, pronto; inclinado; fácil; ligero; —, ad. prontamente, presto.

real, *rē'ăl*, a. real, verdadero, efectivo; inmoble; -ly, ad. realmente.

reality, *rēăl'ĭtĕ*, s. realidad, entidad, f.

realization, *rēălĭzā'shăn*, s. realización, f.

realize, *rē'ălĭz*, v. a. realizar.   [ción.

realm, *rĕlm*, s. reino, m.

ream, *rēm*, s. resma, f.

re-animate, *rēăn'ĭmăt*, s. a. reanimar.

reap, *rēp*, v. a. segar.

reaper, *-ăr*, s. segador, m.

reaping-hook, *-ĭnghŏk*, s. hoz, f.

re-appear, *rēăppēr'*, v. n. parecer de nuevo.   [m. levantar, alzar.

rear, *rēr*, s. retaguardia, f.; última clase, re-ascend, *rēăssĕnd'*, v. a. & n. subir otra vez.   [& n. razonar, raciocinar.

reason, *rē'zn*, s. razón, f.; causa, f.; —, v. a.

reasonable, *-ăbl*, a. razonable.

reasonableness, *-nĕs*, s. razón, f.; racionalidad, f.

reasonably, *-ĕ*, ad. razonablemente.

reasoner, *-ăr*, s. razonador, m.

reasoning, *-ĭng*, s. raciocinio, m.

re-assure, *rēăshōr'*, v. a. volver á asegurar; (com.) dar un nuevo seguro.

rebel, *rĕb'ĕl*, s. rebelde, m.; —, *rĕbĕl'*, v. n. rebelarse.

rebellion, *rĕbĕl'yăn*, s. rebelión, f.

rebellious, *-yăs*, a. rebelde.   [repercutir.

rebound, *rĕbōnd'*, v. a. & n. rechazar;

rebuff, *rĕbăf'*, s. repercusión, f.; —, v. a. rechazar.

rebuild, *rĕbĭld'*, v. a. reedificar.

rebuke, *rĕbūk'*, v. a. reprender, regañar; —, s. reprensión, f.

robus, *rē'băs*, s. pl. equivoquillos, m. pl.

rebut, *rĕbăt'*, v. n. repercutir.

recalcitrant, *rĕkăl'sĭtrănt*, a. recalcitrante.   [ción.

recall, *rĕkăl'*, v. a. revocar; —, s. revoca-

recant, *rĕkănt'*, v.a. retractarse, desdecirse.

recantation, *-d'shăn*, s. retractación, f.

recapitulate, *rĕkăpĭt'ŭlăt*, v.a. recapitular.

recapitulation, *rĕkăpĭtŭlā'shăn*, s. recapitulación, f.   [navío, f.

recapture, *rĕkăp'tăr*, s. represa de un

recede, *rĕsēd'*, v. n. retroceder; desistir.

receipt, *rĕsēt'*, s. recibo, m.; receta, f.; (rail.) talón, m.; —, v. pl. abastos, m. pl.

receivable, *rĕsēv'ăbl*, a. recibidero, misible.

receive, *rĕsēv'*, v. a. recibir; aceptar, admitir; -ly, ad. recientemente.

recent, *rē'sĕnt*, a. reciente, nuevo; fresco;

receptacle, *rĕsĕp'tăkl*, s. receptáculo, m.

reception, *rĕsĕp'shăn*, s. acogida, f.

recess, *rĕsĕs'*, s. retiro, m.; fondo, m.

recession, *rĕsĕsh'ăn*, s. retirada, f.

recipe, *rĕs'ĭpĕ*, s. receta de médico, f.

recipient, *rĕsĭp'ĭĕnt*, s. recipiente. m.

reciprocal, *rĕsĭp'rŏkăl*, a. recíproco; -ly, ad. recíprocamente.

reciprocate, *-rŏkăt*, v. n. reciprocar.   [f.

reciprocity, *rĕsĭprŏs'ĭtĕ*, s. reciprocidad, f.

recital, *rĕsī'tăl*, recitation, *rĕsĭtā'shăn*, s. recitación, f.

recitative, *rĕsĭtătĕv'*, s. (mus.) recitativo,

recite, *rĕsīt'*, v. a. recitar; referir, relatar.

reck, *rĕk*, v. a. & n. cuidar.

reckless, *-lĕs*, a. descuidado, omiso; -ly, ad. con descuido.

reckon, *rĕk'n*, v. a. contar, numerar; —, v. n. computar, calcular.   [f.

reckoning, *-ĭng*, s. cuenta, f.; calculación,

reclaim, *rĕklām'*, v. a. reformar, corregir; reclamar.

reclaimable, *-ăbl*, a. redimible.

recline, *rĕklīn'*, v. a. & n. reclinar; reposar.

recluse, *rĕklōs'*, a. recluso, retirado; —, s. persona retirada del mundo, f.

reclusion, *rĕklō'zhăn*, s. reclusión, f.

recognisance, *rĕkŏg'nĭzăns*, s. reconocimiento; m.; obligación, f.

recognise, *rĕk'ŏgnīz*, v. a. reconocer.

recognition, *rĕkŏgnĭsh'ăn*, s. reconocimiento, recuerdo, m.

recoil, *rĕkŏĭl'*, v. n. recular.

recollect, rĕkŏllĕkt', v. a. acordarse; recobrarse [m.; reminiscencia, f.

recollection, rĕkŏllĕk'shŭn, s. recuerdo,

recommence, rĕkŏmmĕns', v. a. empezar de nuevo. [dar.

recommend, rĕkŏmmĕnd', v. a. recomen-

recommendation, rĕk'ŏmmĕn'dā'shŭn, s. recomendación, f. [datorio.

recommendatory, rĕk'ŏmmĕn'dātŭrē, a. recomen-

recompense, rĕk'ŏmpĕns, s. recompensa, f.; —, v. a. recompensar.

recompose, rĕkŏmpōz', v. a. volver á componer; tranquilizar de nuevo.

reconcilable, rĕk'ŏnsīlābl, a. reconciliable.

reconcile, rĕk'ŏnsīl, v. a. reconciliar.

reconciliation, rĕk'ŏnsīlīā'shŭn, s. reconciliación, f. [vado.

recondite, rĕk'ŏndīt, a. recóndito, reser-

reconnoitre, rĕkŏnnŏi'tŭr, v. a. (mil.) reconocer. [de nuevo.

reconsider, rĕkŏnsĭd'ŭr, v. a. considerar

reconstruct, rĕkŏnstrŭkt', v. a. reedificar.

record, rĕkŏrd', v. a. registrar; protocolar; —, rĕk'ŏrd, s. registro, archivo, m.; —s, pl. anales, m. pl.

recorder, rĕkŏrd'ŭr, s. registrador, archivero, m. [de nuevo.

recount, rĕkŏŭnt', v. a. referir; contar

recourse, rĕkŏrs', s. recurso, retorno, m.

recover, rĕkŭv'ŭr, v. a. recobrar; reparar; restablecer; —, v. n. convalecer, restablecerse; **to — one's self**, volver en sí

recoverable, -ābl, a. recuperable. [m.

recovery, -ē, s. convalecencia, f.; recobro,

recreant, rĕk'rĕănt, a. & s. cobarde, m.; apóstata, m. [divertir.

recreate, rĕk'rĕāt, v. a. recrear, deleitar,

recreation, rĕkrĕā'shŭn, s. recreación, f.

recreative, rĕk'rĕātīv, s. recreativo, m.

recriminate, rĕkrĭm'ĭnāt, v. a. & n. recriminar, acusar al acusador. [minación, f.

recrimination, rĕkrĭmĭnā'shŭn, s. recri-

recruit, rĕkrŏt', v. a. reclutar; **to — one's self**, restablecerse; —, s. (mil.) recluta, m.

recruiting, -ĭng, s. recluta, f.

rectangle, rĕk'tănggl, s. rectángulo, m.

rectangular, rĕktăng'gŭlŭr, a. rectangular.

rectification, rĕktĭfīkā'shŭn, s. rectificación, f.

rectify, rĕk'tĭfī, v. a. rectificar.

rectilinear, rĕktĭlĭn'ĕŭr, a. rectilíneo

rectitude, rĕk'tĭtŭd, s. rectitud, derechura, f. [fete, m.

rector, rĕk'tŭr, s. rector, m.; párroco, m.;

rectorship, -shĭp, s. rectorado, m.

rectory, -ē, s. rectoría, f. [clinado.

recumbent, rĕkŭm'bĕnt, a. recostado, re-

recuperative, rĕkū'pŭrātĭv, a. recuperativo.

recur, rĕkŭr', v. n. recurrir. [tivo.

recurrence, -rĕns, s. retorno, m.; vuelta,

recurrent, -rĕnt, a. periódico. [f.

recusant, rĕk'ūzănt, s. nonconformista, m.

red, rĕd, a. rojo; rubio; —, s. rojez, f.

red-breast, -brĕst, s. pitirrojo, m.

redcoat, -kōt, s. soldado inglés, m.

redden, -n, v. a. teñir de color rojo; —, v. n. ponerse colorado.

reddish, -ĭsh, a. rojizo.

redeem, rĕdēm', v. a. redimir, rescatar.

redeemable, -ābl, a. redimible.

redeemer, -ŭr, s. redentor, m.

redemption, rĕdĕm'shŭn, s. redención, f.

redhanded, rĕd'hănded, a. en fraganti, en el acto.

redhot, -hŏt, a. candente, ardiente.

red-lead, -lĕd, s. minio, bermellón, m.

red-letter day, -lĕtŭrdā, s. día colendo.

redness, -nĕs, s. rojez, bermejura, f. [m.

redolence, rĕd'ŏlĕns, v. n. resaltar, fragar,

redolent, rĕd'ŏlĕnt, a. fragante, fragrante, oloroso.

redouble, rĕdŭb'l, v. a. (& n.) redoblar(se).

redoubt, rĕdŏŭt', s. (mil.) reducto, m.

redoubtable, -ābl, a. formidable, terrible.

redound, rĕdŏŭnd', v. n. resaltar, rebotar; redundar.

redress, rĕdrĕs', v. a. enderezar; corregir; reformar; rectificar; —, s. reforma, corrección, f.

redresser, -ŭr, s. reformador, m.

red-tapist, rĕd'tăpĭst, s. burócrata, m.

reduce, rĕdūs', v. a. reducir; disminuir; sujetar.

reducible, rĕdū'sĭbl, a. reducible.

reduction, rĕdŭk'shŭn, s. reducción, f.

reductively, -tĭvlē, ad. por reducción.

redundancy, rĕdŭn'dănsē, s. redundancia, f. [fluo.

redundant, -dănt, a. redundante, super-

reduplicate, rĕdū'plĭkāt, v. a. reduplicar.

reduplication, rĕdūplĭkā'shŭn, s. reduplicación, f.

re-echo, rĕĕk'ō, v. n. resonar el eco.

reed, rēd, s. caña, f.; flecha, f.

reedy, -ē, a. lleno de cañas.

reef, rēf, v. a. (mar.) tomar rizos á las velas.

reek, rēk, s. humo, vapor, m.; —, v. n. humear; vahear.

reel, rēl, s. aspa, devanadera, f.; un baile, m.; —, v. a. aspar; —, v. n. vacilar al andar.

re-election, rĕēlĕk'shŭn, s. reelección, f.

re-engage, rĕĕngāj', v. a. empeñar de nuevo. [vado, m.

re-engagement, -mĕnt, s. empeño reno-

re-enter, rĕĕn'tŭr, v. a. volver á entrar.

re-establish, rĕĕstăb'lĭsh, v. a. restablecer, volver á establecer una cosa.

re-establishment, -mĕnt, s. restablecimiento, m.; restauración, f.

refection, rĕfĕk'shŭn, s. refección, f.

refectory, rĕfĕk'tŭrē, s. refectorio, m.

refer, rĕfŭr', v. a. & n. referir, remitir; referirse.

referee, rĕfŭrē', s. arbitrador, árbitro, m.; (com.) en caso necesario á . . . .

reference, rĕf'ŭrĕns, s. referencia, relación, f. [v. n. purificarse.

refine, rĕfīn', v. a. refinar, purificar; —,

refinement, -mĕnt, s. refinación, f.; refinadura, f.; elegancia afectada, f.

refinery, -ŭrē, s. refinadura, f.

refit, rĕfĭt', v. a. reparar; (mar.) embonar.

reflect, rĕflĕkt', v. a. & n. reflejar, repercutir; reflectar; reflexionar; recaer, refluir en. [tación, f.

reflection, rĕflĕk'shŭn, s. reflexión, medi-

reflective, -tĭv, a. reflexivo.

reflector, *-tūr*, s. telescopio de reflexión.
reflex, *rḗ fleks*, a. reflejo. [m.
reform, *rēfōrm'*, v. a. (& n.) v. a. reformar(se). [*shūn*, s. reformación, f.
reforma, *rēfōrm'*, reformation, *rēfōrmā́-*
reformer, *rēfōrm' ēr*, s. reformador, m.
reformist, *rēf' ōrmist*, s. religioso reformado. m.
refract, *rēfrákt'*, v. a. refringir.
refraction, *rēfrák shūn*, s. refracción, f.
refractoriness, *-tūriness*, s. obstinación, terqueza, f. [tinado.
refractory, *-tūrē*, a. refractario, obstinado.
refrain, *rēfrān'*, v. a. refrenar, reprimir.
refresh, *rēfresh'*, v. a. refrigerar, [rio, m.
refreshment, *-mēnt*, s. refresco, refrigerio.
refreshment-bar, *-bār*, s. pabellón en la calle para beber, m.
refrigerator, *rēfrij' ūrātūr*, s. enfriadera.
refuge, *rēf' ūj*, s. refugio, asilo, m.   [f.
refugee, *rēfūjē'*, s. refugiado, m.
refund, *rēfūnd'*, v. a. restituir; volver á pagar.   [f.
refusal, *rēfū́ zūl*, s. repulsa, denegación.
refuse, *rēfū́ z*, v. a. rehusar, repulsar;
—s, *rēf' ūs*, desecho, m., zupia, sobra, f.
refutation, *rēfūtā́ sh' ūn*, s. refutación, f.
refute, *rēfūt'*, v. a. refutar.
regain, *rēgān'*, v. a. recobrar, **recuperar.**
regal, *rē' gāl*, a. real.
regale, *rēgāl'*, v. a. regalar.
regalia, *rēgā́ li ā*, s. insignias, f. pl.
regard, *rēgārd'*, v. a. estimar; considerar;
—s, consideración, f.; respeto, m. [mente.
regardful, *-fūl*, a. atento; —ly, ad. atentamente.
regarding, *-ing*, pr. concerniente á.
regardless, *-lēs*, a. descuidado, negligente; descacatado.
regatta, *rēgát' tā*, s. regata, f.   [m.
regency, *rē' jensē*, s. regencia, f.; gobierno.
regenerate, *rējen' ūrāt*, v. a. regenerar;
—, a. regenerado. [ción, f.
regeneration, *rējēnūrā́ shūn*, s. regeneración.
regent, *rē' jēnt*, s. regente, m.   [dio, m.
regicide, *rē' jisīd*, s. regicida, m.; regicidio.
regimen, *rēj' ēmen*, s. régimen, m.; dieta, f.
regiment, *-t*, s. regimiento, m.   [m.
regimentals, *rējimen' tālz*, s.pl. uniforme.
region, *rē' jūn*, s. región, f.; distrito, m.
register, *rēj' istūr*, s. registro, m.; —, v. a.
registrar, encabezar, empadronar; —ed
letter, s. carta certificada, f.
registrar, *rēj' istrār*, s. registrador, m.
registration, *rējistrā́ shūn*, s. registro, m.;
empadronamiento, m.
registry, *rēj' istrē*, s. asiento, registro, m.
regressive, *rēgrēs' siv*, a. retrógrado.
regret, *rēgrēt'*, s. arrepentimiento, m.; —,
v. a. sentir pena ó dolor.
regretful, *-fūl*, a. pesaroso.
regular, *rēg' ūlūr*, a. regular; ordinario;
—ly, ad. regularmente; —s, regular, m.
regularity, *rēgūlār' itē*, s. regularidad, f.
regulate, *rēg' ūlāt*, v. a. regular, ordenar.
regulation, *rēgūlā́ shūn*, s. regulación, f.;
arreglo, m.   [registro de reloj, m.
regulator, *rēg' ūlātūr*, s. regulador, m.;

rregulus, *rēg' ūlūs*, s. régulo, m.
rehabilitate, *rēhābil' itāt*, v. a. rehabilitar.
rehabilitation, *rēhābilitā́ shūn*, s. rehabilitación, f.
rehearsal, *rēhūrs' āl*, s. repetición, f.; relación, f.; prueba, f. (de una pieza de teatro).
rehearse, *rēhūrs'*, v. a. repetir, recitar.
reign, *rān*, s. reinado, reino, m.; —, v. n. reinar, prevalecer.
reimburse, *rēimbūrs'*, v. a. reembolsar, m.
reimbursement, *-mēnt*, s. reembolso, m.
rein, *rān*, s. rienda, f.; —, v. a. refrenar.
reindeer, *-dēr*, s. reno, rangífero, m.
re-insert, *rēinsūrt'*, v. a. insertar de nuevo.
re-instate, *rēinstāt'*, v. a. instalar de nuevo; restablecer;   [gurar; refirmar.
re-insure, *rēinshōr'*, v. a. (com.) reasegurar.
re-issue, *rēish' shā*, s. nueva edición, f.
reiterate, *rēit' ūrāt*, v. a. reiterar.
reiteration, *rēitūrā́ shūn*, s. reiteración, repetición, f.
reject, *rējekt'*, v. a. rechazar, rebatir.
rejection, *rējek' shūn*, s. desecho, m.
rejoice, *rējōis'*, v. a (& n.) regocijar(se).
rejoicing, *-ing*, s. regocijo, m.
rejoin, *rējōin'*, v. n. volver á juntarse; —,
v. a. replicar.
rejoinder, *-dūr*, s. contrarréplica, f.
relapse, *rēlaps'*, v. n. recaer; —, s. reincidencia, f.
relate, *rēlāt'*, v. a. & n. relatar, referirse.
related, *-ēd*, a. emparentado.
relater, *-ūr*, s. relator, m.
relation, *rēlā́ shūn*, s. relación, f.; parentesco, m.; pariente, m.
relationship, *-ship*, s. parentesco, m.
relative, *rēl' ātiv*, a. relativo; —ly, ad. relativamente; —, s. pariente, m.
relax, *rēlaks'*, v. a. & n. relajar, aflojar.
relaxation, *rēlaksā́ shūn*, s. relajación, f.
relay, *rēlā'*, s. parada ó posta, f.
release, *rēlēs'*, v. a. soltar, libertar; relejar; —, s. soltura, f.; descargo, m.
relegate, *rēl' ēgāt*, v. a. desterrar, relegar.
relegation, *rēlēgā́ shūn*, s. relegación, f.;
destierro, m.
relent, *rēlent'*, v. n. relentecer, ablandarse.
relentless, *-lēs*, a. empedernido, inflexible.
relevant, *rēl' evūnt*, a. lo que alivia ó auxilia.   [fiar.
reliable, *rēlī' ābl*, a. en quien se puede
reliance, *rēlī' āns*, s. confianza, f.
relic, *rēl' ik*, s. reliquia, f.
relict, *rēl' ikt*, s. viuda, f.   [suelo, m.
relief, *rēlēf'*, s. relieve, m.; alivio, consuelo, m.
relieve, *rēlēv'*, v. a. aliviar, consolar; socorrer.   [limosnero, m.
relieving-officer, *rēlēv' ing ōf' isūr*, s.
religion, *rēlij' ūn*, s. religión, f.
religious, *rēlij' ūs*, a. religioso; —ly, ad. religiosamente.
religiousness, *-nēs*, s. religiosidad, f.
relinquish, *rēling' kwish*, v. a. abandonar, dejar.
relinquishment, *-mēnt*, s. abandono, m.
reliquary, *rēl' ikwārē*, s. relicario, m.

relish, *rĕl'ĭsh*, s. sainete, sabor, m.; gusto, deleite, m.; —, v. a. tener buen gusto; gustar, agradar.

reluctance, *rĕlŭk'tăns*, s. repugnancia, f.

reluctant, *—tănt*, a. repugnante.

rely, *rĕlī'*, v. n. confiar en; contar con.

remain, *rĕmān'*, v. n. quedar, restar, permanecer, durar.

remainder, *—dŭr*, s. resto, residuo, m.

remains, *rĕmānz'*, s. pl. restos, residuos, m. pl.; sobras, f. pl.

remand, *rĕmănd'*, v. a. enviar á alguno al paraje donde había estado antes.

remark, *rĕmärk'*, s. observación, nota, f.; —, v. a. notar, observar.

remarkable, *—ăbl*, a. notable, interesante.

remarkably, *—ăblĭ*, ad. notablemente.

remediable, *rĕmē'dĭăbl*, a. remediable.

remedial, *rĕmē'dĭăl*, a. curativo.

remedy, *rĕm'ĕdĭ*, s. remedio, medicamento, m.; —, v. a. remediar. [mentar; recordar.

remember, *rĕmĕm'bŭr*, v. a. acordarse,

remembrance, *rĕmĕm'brăns*, s. memoria, f.; recuerdo, m.

remind, *rĕmīnd'*, v. a. acordar, recordar.

reminiscence, *rĕmĭnĭs'sĕns*, s. reminiscencia, f.

remiss, *rĕmĭs'*, a. remiso, flojo, perezoso, negligente; —ly, ad. negligentemente.

remissible, *—ĭbl*, a. remisible, perdonable.

remission, *rĕmĭsh'ŭn*, s. remisión, f.; perdón, m. [siencia, f.

remissness, *rĕmĭs'nĕs*, s. incuria, indolencia, f.

remit, *rĕmĭt'*, v. a. & n. remitir, perdonar; disminuir, debilitarse.

remittance, *—tăns*, s. remesa, f.

remnant, *rĕm'nănt*, s. resto, residuo, m.

remodel, *rĕmŏd'ĕl*, v. a. reformar.

remonstrance, *rĕmŏn'străns*, s. súplica motivada. [tar á lo vivo.

remonstrate, *rĕmŏn'strāt*, v. n. representar á lo vivo.

remorse, *rĕmŏrs'*, s. remordimiento, m.; compunción, f. [mordimientos.

remorseless, *—lĕs*, a. insensible á los remordimientos.

remote, *rĕmōt'*, a. remoto, lejano; —ly, ad. remotamente, lejos. [tancia, f.

remoteness, *—nĕs*, s. alejamiento, m.; distancia, f.

remount, *rĕmŏunt'*, v. a. & n. remontar; volver á subir.

removable, *rĕmŏo'ăbl*, a. amovible. [f.

removal, *rĕmŏo'ăl*, s. remoción, deposición, f.

remove, *rĕmŏo'*, v. a. remover, alejar; deponer del empleo; —, v. n. mudarse; —, s. cambio de puesto, m.; partida, f.

remunerate, *rĕmū'nŭrāt*, v. a. remunerar.

remuneration, *rĕmūnŭrā'shŭn*, s. remuneración, f. [ratorio.

remunerative, *rĕmū'nŭrātĭv*, a. remuneratorio.

rencounter, *rĕnkŏun'tŭr*, s. encuentro, m.; (mil.) refriega, f. [rasgar.

rend, *rĕnd*, v. a. lacerar, hacer pedazos,

render, *rĕn'dŭr*, v. a. volver, restituir; traducir; rendir.

rendezvous, *rĕn'dĕvŏo*, s. cita, f.; lugar señalado para encontrarse, m. [m.

renegade, *rĕn'ĕgăd*, s. renegado, apóstata.

renew, *rĕnū'*, v. a. renovar, restablecer.

renewal, *—ăl*, s. renovación, f.

rennet, *rĕn'nĕt*, s. cuajo, m.

renounce, *rĕnŏuns'*, v. a. renunciar

renovate, *rĕn'ŏvāt*, v. a. renovar.

renovation, *rĕnŏvā'shŭn*, s. renovación, f.

renown, *rĕnŏun'*, s. renombre, m.; celebridad, f.

renowned, *—d*, a. célebre. [dad, f.

rent, *rĕnt*, s. renta, f.; arrendamiento, m.; alquiler, m.; rasgón, m.; cisma, f.; —, v. a. arrendar, alquilar.

rental, *—ăl*, s. lista de arriendos, f.

renter, *—ŭr*, s. rentero, arrendador, m.

renunciation, *rĕnŭnsĭā'shŭn*, s. renuncia, renunciación, f.

reopen, *rĕō'pn*, v. a. abrir de nuevo.

reorganization, *rĕŏrgănĭzā'shŭn*, s. reorganización, f.

reorganize, *rĕŏr'gănĭz*, v. a. reorganizar.

repair, *rĕpār'*, v. a. reparar; resarcir; —, v. n. ir; —, s. reparo, m.

reparable, *rĕp'ărăbl*, a. reparable.

reparation, *rĕpărā'shŭn*, s. reparación, f.

repartee, *rĕpärtē'*, s. réplica aguda ó picante, f.

repast, *rĕpăst'*, s. comida, colación, f.

repay, *rĕpā'*, v. a. volver á pagar, restituir.

repayment, *—mĕnt*, s. pago, m.

repeal, *rĕpēl'*, v. a. abrogar, revocar; —, s. revocación, anulación, f.

repealable, *—ăbl*, a. capaz de ser abrogado.

repeat, *rĕpēt'*, v. a. repetir.

repeatedly, *—ĕdlĭ*, ad. repetidamente.

repeater, *—ŭr*, s. reloj de repetición, m.

repel, *rĕpĕl'*, v. a. repeler, rechazar.

repent, *rĕpĕnt'*, v. n. arrepentirse.

repentance, *—ăns*, s. arrepentimiento, m.

repentant, *—ănt*, a. arrepentido.

repeople, *rĕpē'pl*, v. a. poblar de nuevo.

repertory, *rĕp'ĕrtărĭ*, s. repertorio, m.

repetition, *rĕpĕtĭsh'ŭn*, s. repetición, reiteración, f.

repine, *rĕpīn'*, v. n. afligirse, arrepentirse.

repining, *—ĭng*, s. pesar, m.

replace, *rĕplās'*, v. a. reemplazar; reponer.

replant, *rĕplănt'*, v. a. trasplantar. [m.

replantation, *rĕplăntā'shŭn*, s. trasplante.

replenish, *rĕplĕn'ĭsh*, v. a. llenar, surtir.

replete, *rĕplēt'*, a. repleto, lleno.

repletion, *rĕplē'shŭn*, s. repleción, plenitud, f. [v. a. replicar.

reply, *rĕplī'*, s. réplica, respuesta, f.; —,

report, *rĕpōrt'*, v. a. referir, contar; dar cuenta; —, s. voz, f.; rumor, m.; fama, f.; relación, f. [m.

reporter, *—ŭr*, s. relator, m.; estenógrafo,

repose, *rĕpōz'*, v. a. fiar, confiar; —, v. n. reposar; fiarse de; —, s. reposo, m.

reposite, *rĕpŏz'ĭt*, v. a. depositar.

repository, *rĕpŏz'ĭtărĭ*, s. depósito, m.

repossess, *rĕpŏzzĕs'*, v. a. recuperar lo perdido.

reprehend, *rĕprĕhĕnd'*, v. a. reprender.

reprehensible, *rĕprĕhĕn'sĭbl*, a. reprensible. [sión, fraterna, f.

reprehension, *rĕprĕhĕnsh'ŭn*, s. reprensión, fraterna, f.

represent, *rĕprĕzĕnt'*, v. a. representar.

representation, *rĕprĕzĕntā'shŭn*, s. representación, f.

representative, *rĕp'rĕzĕnt'ătĭv,* a. representativo; —, s. representante, m.

repress, *rĕprĕs',* v. a. reprimir, domar.

repression, *rĕprĕsh'ŭn,* s. represión, f.

repressive, *rĕprĕs'sĭv,* a. represivo.

reprieve, *rĕprēv',* v. a. suspender una ejecución; dar espera; —, s. dilación, f. (de algún castigo)

reprimand, *rĕp'rĭmănd,* v. a. reprender, corregir; —, s. reprensión, f.; reprimenda, f.

reprint, *rĕprĭnt',* v. a. reimprimir.

reprisal, *rĕprī'zăl,* s. represalia, f.

reproach, *rĕprōtsh',* s. improperio, oprobio, m.; —, v. a. improperar; vituperar.

reproachful, *-fŭl,* a. ignominioso; —ly, ad. ignominiosamente.

reprobate, *rĕp'rŏbāt,* v. a. reprobar; —, s. réprobo, malvado, m.

reprobation, *rĕprŏbā'shŭn,* s. reprobación, f.

reproduce, *rĕprŏdūs',* v. a. reproducir.

reproduction, *rĕprŏdŭk'shŭn,* s. reproducción, f.

reproof, *rĕprōf',* s. reprensión, f.

reprove, *rĕprōv',* v. a. censurar; improbar.

reptile, *rĕp'tĭl,* a. reptil, m.; —, s. reptil, m.

republic, *rĕpŭb'lĭk,* s. república, f.

republican, *rĕpŭb'lĭkăn,* a. & s. republicano (m.).

republicanism, *-ănĭzm,* s. republicanismo, m.

repudiate, *rĕpū'dĭāt,* v. a. repudiar.

repugnance, *rĕpŭg'năns,* s. repugnancia, desgana, f.

repugnant, *-nănt,* a. repugnante; —ly, ad. de muy mala gana.

repulse, *rĕpŭls',* v. a. repulsar, desechar; —, s. repulsa, f.; rechazo, m.

repulsion, *rĕpŭl'shŭn,* s. repulsión, repulsa, f.

repulsive, *rĕpŭl'sĭv,* a. repulsivo.

repurchase, *rĕpŭr'tshăs,* v. a. recomprar.

reputable, *rĕp'ūtăbl,* a. honroso.

reputably, *-ī,* ad. honrosamente.

reputation, *rĕpūtā'shŭn,* s. reputación, f.

repute, *rĕpūt',* v. a. reputar.

request, *rĕkwĕst',* s. petición, súplica, f.; —, v. a. rogar, suplicar.

require, *rĕkwīr',* v. a. requerir, demandar.

requirement, *-mĕnt,* s. requisito, m.; exigencia, f.

requisite, *rĕk'wĭzĭt,* a. necesario, indispensable; —, s. requisito, m.

requisition, *rĕkwĭzĭsh'ŭn,* s. pedimento, m.; petición, demanda, f.

requital, *rĕkwīt'ăl,* s. retorno, m.; recompensa, f.

requite, *rĕkwīt',* v. a. recompensar.

rescind, *rĕsĭnd',* v. a. rescindir, abrogar.

rescript, *rĕs'krĭpt,* s. rescripto, edicto, m.

rescue, *rĕs'kū,* v. a. librar, rescatar; —, s. libramiento, recobro, m.

research, *rĕsŭrtsh',* s. escudriñamiento, m.

reseat, *rĕsēt',* v. a. asentar de nuevo.

resemblance, *rĕzĕm'blăns,* s. semejanza, f.

resemble, *rĕzĕm'bl,* v. n. asemejarse.

resent, *rĕzĕnt',* v. a. resentirse.

resenter, *-ŭr,* s. el que se resiente de un agravio.

resentful, *-fŭl,* a. resentido; vengativo; —ly, ad. con resentimiento.

resentment, *-mĕnt,* s. resentimiento, m.

reservation, *rĕzŭrvā'shŭn,* s. reservación, reserva, f.; restricción mental, f.

reserve, *rĕzŭrv',* v. a. reservar; —, s. reserva, f.

reservedly, *-ĕdlī,* ad. con reserva.

reset, *rĕsĕt',* v. a. recibir géneros hurtados.

reside, *rĕzīd',* v. n. residir, morar.

residence, *rĕz'ĭdĕns,* s. residencia, morada, f.

resident, *rĕz'ĭdĕnt,* a. residente; —, s. (law) legatario universal, m.

residuary, *rĕzĭd'ūārē,* a. sobrado; — legatee, s. (law) legatario universal, m.

residue, *rĕz'ĭdū,* s. residuo, resto, m.

residuum, *rĕzĭd'ūăm,* s. (chem.) residuo, m.

resign, *rĕzīn',* v. a. & n. resignar, renunciar, ceder; resignarse, rendirse.

resignation, *rĕzĭgnā'shŭn,* s. resignación, f.

resin, *rĕz'ĭn,* s. resina, f.

resinous, *-ŭs,* a. resinoso.

resist, *rĕzĭst',* v. a. resistir, oponerse.

resistance, *-ăns,* s. resistencia, f.

resolute, *rĕz'ŏlūt,* a. resuelto; —ly, ad. resueltamente.

resolution, *rĕzŏlū'shŭn,* s. resolución, f.

resolve, *rĕzŏlv',* v. a. & n. resolver(se).

resonance, *rĕz'ŏnăns,* s. resonancia, f.

resonant, *rĕz'ŏnănt,* a. resonante.

resort, *rĕzŏrt',* v. n. recurrir, frecuentar; —, s. concurso, m.; resorte, m.

resound, *rĕzŏwnd',* v. n. resonar.

resource, *rĕsŏrs',* s. recurso, m.; expediente, m.

respect, *rĕspĕkt',* s. respecto, m.; respeto, m.; motivo, m.; —s, pl. enhorabuena, f.; —, v. a. apreciar; respetar; venerar.

respectability, *rĕspĕktăbĭl'ĭtĭ,* s. consideración, f.; carácter respetable, m.

respectable, *rĕspĕkt'ăbl,* a. respetable; considerable; respetuoso.

respectful, *-fŭl,* a. respetuoso; —ly, ad. respetuosamente.

respecting, *-ĭng,* pr. con respecto á.

respective, *-tĭv,* a. respectivo, relativo; —ly, ad. respectivamente.

respirator, *rĕs'pĭrātŭr,* s. respirador, m.

respiratory, *rĕspĭ'rātŭrē,* a. respirable.

respite, *rĕs'pĭt,* s. suspensión, f.; respiro, m.; —, v. a. suspender, diferir.

resplendence, *rĕsplĕn'dĕns,* s. resplandor, brillo, m.

resplendent, *-dĕnt,* a. resplandeciente.

respond, *rĕspŏnd',* v. a. responder; corresponder.

respondent, *-ĕnt,* s. (law) defensor, m.

response, *rĕspŏns',* s. respuesta, réplica, f.

responsibility, *rĕspŏnsĭbĭl'ĭtĭ,* s. responsabilidad, f.

responsible, *rĕspŏn'sĭbl,* a. responsable.

responsive, *-sĭv,* a. conforme.

rest, *rĕst,* s. reposo, m.; sueño, m.; quietud, f.; (mus.) pausa, f.; resto, residuo, m.; —, v. a. poner á descansar; apoyar; —, v. n. dormir, reposar.

resting-place, *-ĭngplās,* s. descansadero, m.

restitution, *rĕstĭtū'shŭn,* s. restitución, f.

restive, *rĕs'tĭv,* a. repropio; obstinado.

restless, *rĕst'lĕs,* a. insomne; inquieto.

restoration, *rĕstŏrā'shŭn,* s. restauración, f.

restorative, *rĕstŏr'ătĭv,* a. restaurativo; —, s. medicamento restaurativo, m.

restore, *rĕstŏr',* v. a. restaurar, restituir.

restrain, *rĕstrán'*, v.a. restringir, restriñir.
restraint, *-t*, s. refrenamiento, constreñimiento, m.
restrict, *rĕstríkt'*, v. a. restringir, limitar.
restriction, *rĕstrík'shŭn*, s. restricción, f.
restrictive, *rĕstríkt'ĭv*, a. restricto.
result, *rĕzúlt'*, v. n. resultar; -, s. resulta, f. [nuevo.
resume, *rĕzúm'*, v. a. resumir; empezar de nuevo.
resumption, *rĕzŭm'shŭn*, s. reasunción, f.
resurrection, *rĕsŭrrĕk'shŭn*, s. resurrección, f.; --pie, s. fajardo, m.
resurrectionist, *-ĭst*, s. resurreccionista, m. (en Inglaterra, el que desentierra los muertos para vender sus cadáveres á los disectores).
resuscitate, *rĕsŭs'sĭtát*, v. a. resucitar.
retail, *rĕtál'*, v. a. revender, regatonear; -, s. venta por menor, f.
retain, *rĕtán'*, v. a. retener, guardar.
retainer, *-ŭr*, s. adherente, partidario, m.; -s, pl. comitiva, f.; seguito, m.
retake, *rĕták'*, v. a. volver á tomar.
retaliate, *rĕtál'ĭát*, v. a. talionar.
retaliation, *rĕtálĭá'shŭn*, s. talión, m.
retard, *rĕtárd'*, v. a. retardar.
retardation, *-á'shŭn*, s. retardación, f.
retch, *rĕtsh*, v. n. esforzarse á vomitar.
retention, *rĕtĕnsh'ŭn*, s. retención, f.
retentive, *rĕtĕn'tĭv*, a. retentivo.
reticence, *rĕt'ĭsens*, s. reticencia, f.
reticle, *rĕt'ĭkl*, s. redecilla, f. [mujeres.
reticule, *rĕt'ĭkŭl*, s. saquita, f. (entre las
retina, *rĕt'ĭná*, s. retícula, f. (del ojo).
retine, *rĕt'ĭne*, s. retina, f. (túnica del ojo).
retire, *rĕtír'*, v. a. (& n.) retirar(se).
retired, *-d*, a. apartado, retirado. [m.
retirement, *-mĕnt*, s. retiro, retiramiento.
retort, *rĕtórt'*, v. a. redargüir, retorcer (un argumento); -, s. redargución, f.; (chem.) retorta, f.
retouch, *rĕtŭtsh'*, v. a. retocar.
retrace, *rĕtrás'*, v. a. volver á trazar.
retract, *rĕtrákt'*, v. a. retraer; retractar.
retreat, *rĕtrét'*, s. retirada, f.; -, v. n. retirarse.
retrench, *rĕtrĕnsh'*, v. a. cercenar; (mil.) atrincherar; -, v. n. cercenar sus gastos.
retrenchment, *-mĕnt*, s. atrincheramiento, m.; trinchera, f.
retribution, *rĕtrĭbú'shŭn*, s. retribución, recompensa, f. [reparable.
retrievable, *rĕtrĕv'ăbl*, a. recuperable;
retrieve, *rĕtrēv'*, v. a. recuperar, recobrar.
retriever, *-ŭr*, s. sabueso, m.
retrograde, *rĕt'rógrád*, a. retrógrado; v. n. retrogradar. [gradación, f.
retrogression, *rĕtrógrĕsh'ŭn*, s. retrogradación, f.
retrospect, *rĕ'tróspĕkt*, **retrospection**, *rĕt'róspĕk'shŭn*, s. retrospección de las cosas pasadas, f.
retrospective, *-spĕk'tĭv*, a. retrospectivo.
return, *rĕtŭrn'*, v. a. retribuir; restituir; volver; -, s. retorno, m.; vuelta, f.; recompensa, retribución, f.; vicisitud, f.; recaída, f.
reunion, *rĕún'yŭn*, s. reunión, f.
reunite, *rĕúnít'*, v. a (& n.) reunir(se).
reveal, *rĕvēl'*, v. a. revelar.

revel, *rĕv'ĕl*, v. n. andar en borracheras; -, s. borrachera, f. [divina, f.
revelation, *rĕvĕlá'shŭn*, s. revelación
reveller, *rĕv'ĕlŭr*, s. vividor, novillero, m.
revelry, *rĕv'ĕlrĕ*, s. borrachera, f.
revenge, *rĕvĕnj'*, v. a. vengar; -, s. venganza, f. [con venganza.
revengeful, *-fŭl*, a. vengativo; -ly, ad.
revenue, *rĕv'ĕnú*, s. renta, f.; rédito, m.
reverberate, *rĕvŭr'bŭrát*, v. a. & n. reverberar; resonar, retumbar.
reverberation, *rĕvŭrbŭrá'shŭn*, s. rechazo, m.; reverberación, f.
revere, *rĕvēr'*, v. a. reverenciar, venerar.
reverence, *rĕv'ĕrens*, s. reverencia, f.; -, v. a. reverenciar.
reverend, *rĕv'ĕrĕnd*, a. reverendo; venerable; -, s. abad, m.; pastor, m.
reverent, *rĕv'ĕrĕnt*, **reverential**, *rĕvŭrĕn'shăl*, a. reverencial, respetuoso; -ly, ad. reverencialmente.
reversal, *rĕvŭr'săl*, s. revocación de una sentencia, f.
reverse, *rĕvŭrs'*, v. a. trastrocar; abolir; -, s. vicisitud, f.; contrario, m.; reverso, m. (de una moneda).
reversible, *-ĭbl*, a. revocable.
reversion, *rĕvŭr'shŭn*, s. futura, f.; reversión f.
reversionary, *-ărĕ*, a. reversible.
revert, *rĕvŭrt'*, v. a. & n. trastrocar; volverse atrás.
revertible, *-ĭbl*, a. reversible.
revictual, *rĕvít'l*, v. a. volver á proveer de víveres. [-, s. revista, f.; reseña, f.
review, *rĕvú'*, v. a. rever; (mil.) revistar;
reviewer, *-ŭr*, s. revisor, m.; redactor de una revista.
revile, *rĕvíl'*, v. a. ultrajar; disfamar.
revise, *rĕvíz'*, v. a. reyer; -, s. revista, f.; segunda prueba de un pliego, f.
reviser, *-ŭr*, s. revisor, m.
revision, *rĕvízh'ŭn*, s. revisión, f.
revisit, *rĕvíz'ĭt*, v. a. volver á visitar.
revival, *rĕvī'văl*, s. restauración, f.
revive, *rĕvív'*, v. a. avivar; restablecer; -, v. n. revivir, m.
reviver, *-ŭr*, s. vivificador, m.
revocable, *rĕv'ókăbl*, a. revocable.
revocation, *rĕvókă'shŭn*, s. revocación, f.
revoke, *rĕvók'*, v. a. revocar, anular.
revolt, *rĕvólt'*, v. n. rebelarse; -, s. rebelión, f.
revolting, *-ĭng*, a. escandaloso.
revolution, *rĕvólŭ'shŭn*, s. revolución, f.
revolutionary, *-ărĕ*, a. revolucionario.
revolutionist, *-ĭst*, s. revolucionario, m.
revolve, *rĕvólv'*, v. a. revolver; meditar; -, v. n. girar.
revolver, *-ŭr*, s. revolvedor, m. (pistola).
revolving, *-ĭng*, a. periódico.
revulsion, *rĕvŭl'shŭn*, s. (med.) revulsión, f. [recompensar.
reward, *rĕwárd'*, s. recompensa, f.; -, v.a.
rewarder, *-ŭr*, s. remunerador, m.
rhapsody, *răp'sódĕ*, s. rapsódia, f.
rhetoric, *rĕt'órĭk*, s. retórica, f.
rhetorical, *rĕtór'ĭkăl*, a. retórico.

rhetorician, *rĕtŏrĭsh'ăn*, s. retórico, m.
rheum, *rŏm*, s. reuma, m.
rheumatic, *rŏmăt'ĭk*, a. reumático. [m.
rheumatism, *rŏ'mătĭzm*, s. reumatismo, m.
rhinoceros, *rĭnŏs'ĕrŏs*, s. rinoceronte, m.
rhomb, *rŏm*, s. rombo, m.
rhomboid, *−bŏĭd*, s. romboide, m.
rhubarb, *rŏ'bărb*, s. ruibarbo, m.
rhyme, *rĭm*, s. rima, f.; poema, m.; −, v.
  n. rimar.
rhym(ster, *−(st)ŭr*, s. versista, m.
rhythm, *rĭthm*, s. ritmo, m.
rhythmical, *rĭth'mĭkăl*, a. rítmico.
rib, *rĭb*, s. costilla, f.
ribald, *rĭb'ăld*, s. hombre lascivo, m.
ribaldry, *−rĕ*, s. lenguaje obsceno, m.
ribband, *rĭb'ănd*, ribbon, *−ŏn*, s. listón,
rice, *rĭs*, s. arroz, m. [m., cinta, f.
rich, *rĭtsh*, a. rico; opulento; abundante;
  −ly, ad. ricamente.
riches, *−ĕz*, s. pl. riqueza, f.
richness, *−nĕs*, s. riqueza, f.; abundancia.
rick, *rĭk*, s. niara, pila de cereal, f. [f.
rickets, *−ĕts*, s. raquitis, f.
rickety, *−ĕtĕ*, a. raquítico. [franco.
rid, *rĭd*, v. a. librar, desembarazar; −, a.
riddance, *−dăns*, s. libramiento, m.; za-
  fada, f. [cribar.
riddle, *−dl*, s. enigma, m.; criba, f.; −, v. a.
ride, *rĭd*, v. n. cabalgar; andar en coche;
  −, s. paseo á caballo ó en coche, m.
rider, *−ŭr*, s. caballero, cabalgador, m.
ridge, *rĭdj*, s. espinazo, lomo, m.; cumbre,
  f.; −, v. a. formar lomos ó surcos.
ridicule, *rĭd'ĭkŭl*, s. ridículez, f.; ridículo,
  m.; −, v. a. ridiculizar.
ridiculous, *rĭdĭk'ŭlŭs*, a. ridiculoso; **−ly**,
  ad. ridiculamente. [f.
ridiculousness, *−nĕs*, s. calidad ridícula.
riding, *rĭ'dĭng*, s. acción de andar á caballo ó en coche, f.; paseo á caballo ó en
  coche, m. [jana, m.
riding-habit, *−hăbĭt*, s. traje de ama-
riding-hood, *−hŏd*, s. capirote gabán, m.
riding-school, *−skŏl*, s. picadero, m.
rife, *rĭf*, a. común, frecuente. [m.
riff-raff, *rĭf'răf*, s. desecho, desperdicio,
rifle, *rĭ'fl*, v. a. robar, pillar; estriar,
  rayar; −, s. carabina rayada, f.
rifle-man, *−măn*, s. escopetero, m.
rig, *rĭg*, v. a. ataviar; (mar.) aparejar; −,
  s. burla, f.
rigging, *−ĭng*, s. (mar.) aparejo, m.
right, *rĭt*, a. derecho, recto; justo; honesto;
  − I ¡bien!, ¡bueno! **−ly,** ad. rectamente,
  justamente; −, s. justicia, f.; razón, f.;
  derecho, m.; mano derecha, f.; −, v. a.
  hacer justicia.
righteous, *rĭt'yŭs*, a. justo, honrado; **−ly**,
  ad. justamente. [radez, f.
righteousness, *−nĕs*, s. equidad, f.; hon-
rigid, *rĭj'ĭd*, a. rígido; austero; severo;
  −ly, ad. con rigidez.
rigidity, *rĭjĭd'ĭtĕ*, s. rigidez, austeridad, f.
rigmarole, *rĭg'mărŏl*, s. galimatías, m.
rigorous, *rĭg'ŭrŭs*, a. rigoroso; **−ly,** ad.
  rigorosamente.
rigour, *rĭg'ŭr*, s. rigor, m.; severidad, f.

rill, *rĭl*, s. riachuelo, m.
rim, *rĭm*, s. margen, m. & f.; orilla, f.
rime, *rĭm*, s. escarcha, f.
rimy, *rĭ'mĕ*, a. nebuloso, húmedo.
rind, *rĭnd*, s. corteza, f.; hollejo, m.
ring, *rĭng*, s. círculo, cerco, m.; anillo, m.;
  campaneo, m.; −, v. a. sonar; −, v. n.
  retiñir, retumbar; **to − the bell,** tirar de
  la campanilla.
ringer, *−ŭr*, s. campanero, m.
ring-finger, *−fĭng'gur*, s. dedo anular, m.
ringleader, *−lĕdur*, s. cabeza de partido
  ó bando, f.
ringlet, *−lĕt*, s. anillejo, m.
ring-worm, *−wŭrm*, s. (med.) tiña favosa,
rinse, *rĭns*, v. a. lavar, limpiar. [f.
riot, *rĭ'ŏt*, s. tumulto, bullicio, m.; borrachera, f.; −, v. n. andar en borracheras;
  causar alborotos. [m.
rioter, *−ŭr*, s. hombre disoluto ó sedicioso,
riotous, *−ŭs*, a. bullicioso, sedicioso; disoluto; **−ly,** ad. disolutamente.
rip, *rĭp*, v. a. rasgar, lacerar; descoser.
ripe, *rĭp*, a. maduro, sazonado; **−ly,** ad.
  maduramente.
ripen, *−n*, v. a. & n. madurar.
ripeness, *−nĕs*, s. madurez, f.
ripple, *rĭp'pl*, v. n. manar ó hervir el
  agua á borbotones. [s. borbollones, m.
rippling, *rĭp'lĭng*, s. movimiento del agua
rise, *rĭz*, v. n. levantarse; nacer, salir (hablando de los astros); rebelarse; ascender;
  hincharse; elevarse; resucitar; −, s. levantamiento, m.; elevación, f.; subida, f.;
  salida (del sol), f.; causa, f.
risible, *rĭz'ĭbl*, a. risible.
rising, *rĭz'ĭng*, s. salida del sol, f.; fin de
  una junta ó sesión, m. [riesgar.
risk, *rĭsk*, s. riesgo, peligro, m.; −, v. a. ar-
risky, *−ĕ*, a. (am.) peligroso.
rite, *rĭt*, s. rito, m.
ritual, *rĭt'ŭăl*, a. & s. ritual (m.).
rival, *rĭ'văl*, a. émulo; −, s. rival, m.; −,
  v. a. competir, emular.
rivalry, *−rĕ*, s. rivalidad, f.
rive, *rĭv*, v. a. (& n.) hender(se).
river, *rĭv'ŭr*, s. río, m. [machar, roblar.
rivet, *rĭv'ĕt*, s. remache, m.; −, v. a. re-
rivulet, *rĭv'ŭlĕt*, s. riachuelo, m.
roach, *rŏtsh*, s. raya, f.; **as sound as a**
  −, en perfecta salud.
road, *rŏd*, s. camino real, m.
roadstead, *−stĕd*, s. (mar.) rada, f.
roadster, *−stŭr*, s. (mar.) buque anclado
  en la rada, m.; caballo de viaje, m.
roam, *rŏm*, v. a. (& n.) corretear; tunar.
roan, *rŏn*, a. roano, ruano.
roar, *rŏr*, v. n. rugir; aullar; bramar; −,
  s. rugido, m.; bramido, truendo, m.; mu-
roast, *rŏst*, v. a. asar; tostar. [gido, m.
roastbeef, *−bĕf*, s. asado de vaca, m.
roaster, *−ŭr*, s. asador, m.
rob, *rŏb*, v. a. robar, hurtar.
robber, *−bŭr*, s. robador, ladrón, m.
robbery, *−bărĕ*, s. robo, m.
robe, *rŏb*, s. manto, m.; toga, f.; −, v. a.
  vestir de gala. [s. petirrojo, m.
robin(−redbreast), *rŏb'ĭn(rĕdbrĕst),* s.
robust, *rŏbŭst'*, a. robusto.

robustness, *—nĕs,* s. robustez, f.

rock, *rŏk,* s. roca, f.; escollo, m.; rueca, f.; —, v. a. mecer; arrullar; (am.) apedrear; —, v. n. bambolear.

rock-crystal, *—kristdl,* s. cuarzo,. m.

rocker, *—ĕr,* s. cunera, f.

rocket, *—ĕt,* s. roquete, m.

rock-oil, *—ŏil,* s. petróleo, m.

rock-salt, *—sŏlt,* s. sal gema, f.

rock-work, *—wŭrk,* s. grotesco, m.

rocky, *—ĕ,* a. peñascoso.

rod, *rŏd,* s. varilla, verga, caña, f.

rodents, *rŏ'dĕntz,* s. pl. roedores, m. pl.

rodomontade, *rŏdŏmŏntdd',* s. fanfarria, f.

roe, *rŏ,* s. corzo, m.; hueva, f.   [f.

roebuck, *—bŭk,* s. corzo, m.

rogation, *rŏgd'shŭn,* s. rogaciones, f. pl.

rogue, *rŏg,* s. bribón, pícaro, villano, m.

roguery, *rŏ'gĕrĕ,* s. picardía, f

roguish, *rŏ'gĭsh,* a. pícaro.

roister, *rŏĭs'tŭr,* v.n. bravear, fanfarronear.

roll, *rŏl,* v. a. rodar; volver; arrollar; —, v. n. rodar; girar; —, s. rodadura, f.; rollo, m.; lista, f.; catálogo, m.; rasero, m.; roleo, m.; voluta, f.; bollo, m.; panecillo, m.

roller, *—ĕr,* s. rodillo, cilindro, m.

rollicking, *rŏl'ĭkĭng,* a. ruidoso.

rolling-pin, *rŏl'ĭngpĭn,* s. rodillo de pastelero, m.   [f.; cuento, m.; fábula, f.

romance, *rŏmăns',* s. romance, m.; ficción, f.

romancist, *rŏmăn'sĭst,* s. romancero, m.

romantic(al), *—tĭk(ăl),* a. quijotesco.

romish, *rŏ'mĭsh,* a. romano.

romp, *rŏmp,* s. muchacha retozona, f.; —, v. n. retozar.

rood, *rŏd,* s. pértiga para medir, f.

roof, *rŏf,* s. tejado, m.; paladar, m.; imperial de un coche, f.; —, v. a. techar.

roofing, *—ĭng,* s. techado, tejo de bóveda, m.

rook, *rŏk,* s. corneja de pico blanco, f.; roque, m. (en el juego de ajedrez); trampista, m.; —, v. n. trampear.

rookery, *—ĕrĕ,* s. árboles donde hacen sus nidos muchas cornejas, m. pl.; lugar sospechoso, m.   [m.; cámara, f.

room, *rŏm,* s. lugar, espacio, m.; aposento, m.

roominess, *—ĭnĕs,* s. espaciosidad, capacidad, f.

roomy, *—ĕ,* a. espacioso.   [cidad, f.

roost, *rŏst,* s. pértiga del gallinero, f.; —, v. n. dormir las aves en una pértiga.

root, *rŏt,* s. raíz, f.; origen, m.; —, v. a. & n. (- out) desarraigar; arraigar.

rooted, *—ĕd,* a. inveterado.

rope, *rŏp,* s. cuerda, f.; cordel, m.; —, v. n. hacer hebras.   [de cuerda, m.

rope-dancer, *—dănsŭr,* s. volatín, bailarín

rope-maker, *—mdkĕr,* s. cordelero, m.

rope-walk, *—wdk,* **rope-yard,** *—ydrd,* s. cordelería, f.

rosary, *rŏ'zdrĕ,* s. rosario, m.

rose, *rŏz,* s. rosa, f.

roseate, *rŏ'zĕĕt,* a. róseo.

rose-bed, *—bĕd,* s. campo de rosales, m.

rose-bud, *—bŭd,* s. capullo de rosa, m.

rosemary, *—mdrĕ,* s. (bot.) romero, m.

rose-tree, *—trĕ,* s. rosal, m.

rosette, *rŏzĕt',* s. roseta, f.

rosewood, *—wŭd,* s. palo de rosa, m.

rosin, *rŏz'ĕn,* s. trementina, f.

rosiness, *rŏ'zĭnĕs,* s. color róseo, m.

rosy, *rŏ'zĕ,* a. róseo.   [putrefacción, f.

rot, *rŏt,* v. n. pudrirse; s. morriña, f.

rotate, *rŏ'tdt,* v. a. & n. girar.

rotation, *rŏtd'shŭn,* s. rotación, f.

rotatory, *rŏ'tdtdrĕ,* a. lo que rueda.

rote, *rŏt,* s. uso, m.; práctica, f.

rotgut, *rŏt'gŭt,* s. (vulg.) mala cerveza, f.

rotten, *rŏt'n,* a. podrido, corrompido.

rottenness, *—nĕs,* s. podredumbre, putrefacción, f.   [cular, esférico.

rotund, *rŏtŭnd',* a. rotundo, redondo, circular.

rotundity, *—tĭt,* s. rotundidad, redondez, f.

rouble, *rŏ'bl,* s. rublo, m.

rouge, *rŏzh,* s. arrebol, colorete, m.

rough, *rŭf,* a. áspero, tosco; bronco, bruto, brusco; tempestuoso; —ly, ad. rudamente.

rough-cast, *—kăst,* v. a. bosquejar una figura ó cuadro; —, s. modelo en bruto, m.

rough-draw, *—drd,* v. a. bosquejar.

roughen, *—n,* v. a. poner áspero.

rough-hew, *—hd,* v. a. formar el modelo tosco de alguna cosa.

roughness, *—nĕs,* s. aspereza, f.; rudeza, tosquedad, f.; tempestad, f.   [bruto.

roughwork, *—wŭrk,* v. a. trabajar en

round, *rŏŭnd,* a. redondo; cabal; franco, sincero; —, s. círculo, m.; redondez, f.; vuelta, f.; giro, m.; escalón, m.; (mil.) ronda, f.; andanada de cañones, f.; descarga, f.; —, ad. redondamente; por todos lados; —ly, ad. redondamente; francamente; —, v. a. cercar, rodear; redondear.

roundabout, *— băŭt,* a. amplio, indirecto, vago; —, s. (am.) jubón, m.

roundelay, *rŏŭn'dĕld,* s. coplas que se cantan en rueda, f. pl.   [sivo, m.

roundhand, *rŏŭnd'hănd,* s. carácter cursivo, m.

roundly, *—lĕ,* ad. redondamente; francamente.

roundness, *—nĕs,* s. redondez, f.   [menta.

rouse, *rŏŭz,* v. a. despertar; excitar.

rout, *rŏŭt,* s. rota, derrota, f.; —, v. a. derrotar.

route, *rŏt,* s. ruta, f.; camino, m.   [trotar.

rove, *rŏv,* v. n. vagar, vaguear.

rover, *—ŭr,* s. vagamundo, m.; pirata, m.

row, *rŏū,* (rŏ), s. camorra, f.; zipizape, m.

row, *rŏ,* s. hilera, fila, f.; —, v. a. & n. (mar.) remar, bogar.   [llanguero, m.

rowdy, *rŏŭdĕ,* s. (am.) alborotador, buscarruidos, m.

rowel, *rŏŭĕl,* s. estrella de espuela, f.

rower, *rŏŭĕr,* s. remero, m.   [ceras, f. pl.

row-locks, *rŏ'lŏkz,* s. pl. (mar.) chumaceras, f. pl.

royal, *rŏ'ăl,* a. real; regio; —ly, ad. regiamente.

royalist, *—ĭst,* s. realista, m.   [mente.

royalty, *—tĕ,* s. realeza, dignidad real, f.; navío real, m.; honorarios que paga el editor al autor por cada ejemplar vendido de su obra, m. pl.; **royalties,** pl. regalías, f. pl.; insignias de la corona, f. pl.

rub, *rŭb,* v. a. estregar, fregar, frotar; raspar; —, s. frotamiento, m.; (fig.) embarazo, m.; dificultad, f.

rubber, *—băr,* s. estropajo, m.; escofina, f.

rubber-ball, *—băl,* s. goma elástica, f.

rubbish, *răb'bĭsh,* s. escombro, m.; ruinas, f. pl.; andrajos, m. pl.

rubicund, *rŏ'bĭkŭnd,* a. rubicundo.

rubric, *rȭ'brĭk,* s. rúbrica, f.

ruby, *rȭ'bĭ,* s. rubí, m.

rudder, *rŭd'dŭr,* s. timón, m. [cendida,f.

ruddiness, *rŭd'dĭnĕs,* s. tez lustrosa y encendida, f.

ruddy, *rŭd'dĭ,* a. colorado, rubio.

rude, *rȭd,* a. rudo, brutal, rústico, grosero; tosco; **—ly,** ad. rudamente, groseramente.

rudeness, *—nĕs,* s. descortesía, f.; rudeza, insolencia, f.

rudiment, *rȭ'dĭmĕnt,* s. rudimentos, m. pl.

rue, *rȭ,* v. n. compadecerse; **—, s.** (bot.) ruda, f.

rueful, *—fŭl,* a. lamentable, triste.

ruff, *rŭf,* s. lechuguilla, f.   [—, a. brutal.

ruffian, *—fĭăn,* s. malhechor, bandolero, m.;

ruffianly, *—lĕ,* a. malvado, perverso.

ruffle, *rŭf'fl,* v. a. desordenar, desazonar; rizar; **—, s.** vuelo de las mangas de mujer, m.; tumulto, m.

rug, *rŭg,* s. paño burdo, m.; frazada, f.

rugged, *—gĕd,* a. áspero, tosco; brutal; peludo.

ruin, *rȭ'ĭn,* s. ruina, f.; perdición, f.; escombros, m. pl.; **—,** v.a. arruinar; destruir.

ruinous, *—ŭs,* a. ruinoso; **—ly,** ad. ruinosamente.

rule, *rȭl,* s. mando, m.; regla, f.; regularidad, f.; **—,** v. a. & n. gobernar; reglar, arreglar, dirigir.

ruler, *—ŭr,* s. gobernador, m.; regla, f.

rum, *rŭm,* s. ron, m.; **—, a.** (vulg.) extraño.

rumble, *—bl,* v. n. crujir, rugir.   [singular.

ruminate, *rȭ'mĭnāt,* v. a. rumiar.   [f.

rumination, *rȭmĭnā'shŭn,* s. meditación, f.

rummage, *rŭm'mădj,* v. a. trastornar; **—,** s. tumulto, m.

rummer, *rŭm'mŭr,* s. vaso para beber, m.

rumour, *rȭ'mŭr,* s. rumor, m.; **—,** v. a. divulgar alguna noticia.

rump, *rŭmp,* s. obispillo de ave, m.

rumple, *rŭm'pl,* s. arruga, f.

run, *rŭn,* v. a. arrojar con violencia; traspasar; **to — the risk,** aventurar, arriesgar; **—,** v. n. correr; fluir, manar; pasar rápidamente; proceder; **—, s.** corrida, carrera, f.; curso, m.; serie, f.; moda, f.; ataque, m.

runaway, *—ăwă,* s. fugitivo, desertor, m.

run(d)let, *rŭn(d)'lĕt,* s. barrilejo, m.

rung, *rŭng,* s. escalón, peldaño, m. (de escalera de mano).   [mensajero, m.

runner, *rŭn'nŭr,* s. corredor, m.; correo

running, *rŭn'nĭng,* s. carrera, corrida, f.; curso, m.

running-ice, *—ĭs,* s. hielo movedizo, m.

rupture, *rŭp'tshŭr,* s. rotura, f.; hernia, quebradura, f.; **—,** v. a. reventar, romper.

rural, *rȭ'răl,* a. rural, campestre, rústico.

ruse, *rȭz,* s. astucia, maña, artería, f.

rush, *rŭsh,* s. junco, m.; (fig.) bledo, ardite, m.; ímpetu, m.; **—,** v. n. abalanzarse, tirarse.   [noche, f.

rush-light, *—lĭt,* s. vela ó lamparilla de

rusk, *rŭsk,* s. galleta, f.

russet, *rŭs'sĕt,* a. bermejizo.

Russia-leather, *rŭsh'ă lĕthŭr,* s. cuero de Moscovia, m.   [v. n. enmohecerse.

rust, *rŭst,* s. herrumbre, f.; robín, m.; **—,**

rustic(al), *rŭs'tĭk(ăl),* a. rústico; **—, s.** patán, rústico, m.

rusticate, *—āt,* v. n. vivir en el campo; **—,** v. a. desterrar al campo.   [pestre, f.

rustication, *rŭstĭkā'shŭn,* s. vida campestre, f.

rusticity, *rŭstĭs'ĭtĭ,* s. rusticidad, f.

rustiness, *rŭs'tĭnĕs,* s. herrumbre, f.

rustle, *rŭs'l,* v. n. crujir, rechinar.   [m.

rustling, *rŭs'lĭng,* s.estruendo,m.; crujido,

rusty, *rŭs'tĭ,* a. oriniento, mohoso; rancio.

rut, *rŭt,* v. n. bramar los venados y ciervos cuando están en celo; **—,** s. brama, f.; carril, m.   [—ly, ad. inhumanamente.

ruthless, *rȭth'lĕs,* a. cruel, insensible;

rye, *rĭ,* s. (bot.) centeno, m.

S.

sabbath, *săb'băth,* s. sábado, m.

sable, *sā'bl,* s. cebellina, f.   [con sable.

sabre, *sā'bŭr,* s. sable, m.; **—,** v. a. matar

sacerdotal, *săsŭrdō'tăl,* a. sacerdotal.

sack, *săk,* s. saco, m.; vino dulce de Canarias, m.; **—,** v. a. meter en sacos; saquear.   [Eucaristía, f.

sacrament, *săk'rămĕnt,* s. sacramento,m.;

sacramental, *săkrămĕn'tăl,* a. **—ly,** ad. sacramental(mente).

sacred, *sā'krĕd,* a. sagrado, sacro; inviolable; **—ly,** ad. sagradamente, inviolable

sacredness, *—nĕs,* s. santidad, f.   [mente.

sacrifice, *săk'rĭfĭz,* s. sacrificio, m.; **—,** v. a. & n. sacrificar.   [los sacrificios.

sacrificial, *săkrĭfĭsh'ăl,* a. perteneciente á

sacrilege, *săk'rĭlĕj,* s. sacrilegio, m.

sacrilegious, *săkrĭlē'jŭs,* a. sacrílego.

sad, *săd,* a. triste, melancólico; infausto; obscuro; **—ly,** ad. tristemente.

sadden, *—n,* v. a. entristecer.

saddle, *săd'l,* s. silla, f.; **—,** v. a. ensillar.

saddle-bag, *—băg,* s. saco para dinero, m.

saddle-cloth, *—klŏth,* s. mantilla de silla,f.

saddle-horse, *—hŏrs,* s. caballo de montar.

saddler, *—ŭr,* s. sillero, m.

saddlery, *—ŭrĭ,* s. guarnicionería, f.

sadness, *săd'nĕs,* s. tristeza, f.; aspecto tétrico, m.

safe, *sāf,* a. seguro; **—ly,** ad. á salvo; **— and sound,** sano y salvo; **—, s.** despensa, f.   [ducto, m.

safe-conduct, *—kŏn'dŭkt,* s. salvoconducto, m.

safe-guard, *—gărd,* s. salvaguardia, f.

safety, *—tĭ,* s. seguridad, f.; salvamento.

saffron, *săf'rŏn,* s. azafrán, m.   [m.

sagacious, *săgā'shŭs,* a. sagaz, sutil; **—ly,** ad. sagazmente.   [f.

sagacity, *săgăs'ĭtĭ,* s. sagacidad, astucia,

sage, *sāj,* s. (bot.) salvia, f.; sabio, m.; **—, a.** sabio; **—ly,** ad. sabiamente.

Sagittarian, *săjĭttā'rĭăn,* s. Sagitario, m. (signo del zodíaco).

sago, *sā'gō,* s. (bot.) zagú, m.

sail, *sāl,* s. vela, f.; **—,** v. n. dar á la vela,

sailer, *—ŭr,* s. navío, buque, m.   [navegar.

sailing, *—ĭng,* s. navegación, f.

sailor, -úr, s. marinero, m.

saint, sánt, s. santo, m.; santa, f.

saint, sánt, **sainted,** -ĕd, **saintly,** -lĕ, a. santo; **saintly,** ad. santamente.

sake, sák, s. causa, razón, f.; **for God's** —, por amor de Dios.

salad, sál'ŭd, s. ensalada, f.

salad-bowl, -bōl, s. ensaladera, f.

salad-oil, -ŏil, s. aceite de olivas, m.

salamander, sál'ămăndŭr, s. salamandra, f.

salary, sál'ărĕ, s. salario, m.

sale, sál, s. venta, f.

saleable, sá'lăbl, a. vendible.

sale-goods, -gŭdz, s. pl. mercancías para vender, f. pl.

salesman, -z'măn, s. ropero, m.

salient, sá'lĭĕnt, a. saliente, saledizo.

saline, sálĭn', a. salino.

saliva, sálí'vă, s. saliva, f.

sallow, sál'lō, a. cetrino, pálido.

sally, sál'lĕ, s. (mil.) salida, surtida, f.; —, v. n. salir.

salmon, săm'ŭn, s. salmón, m.

salmon-trout, -trŏŭt, s. trucha salmonada, f.

saloon, sálŏn', s. salón, m. [nada, f.

salt, sált, s. sal, f.; (fig.) sabor, m.; agudeza, f.; —, a. salado; —, v. a. salar.

salt-cellar, -sĕllŭr, s. salero, m. (en la mesa).

salter, -ŭr, s. salinero, m.

salting-tub, -ĭngtŭb, s. saladero, m.

saltness, -nĕs, s. saladura, f.

saltpetre, -pétŭr, s. nitro, salitre, m.

salt-works, -wŭrks, s. pl. salina, f.

salubrious, sálŏ'brĭŭs, a. salubre, saludable.

salubrity, sálŏ'brĭtĕ, s. salubridad, f.

salutary, sál'ŭtărĕ, a. salubre, salutífero.

salutation, sálŭtá'shŭn, s. salutación, f.

salute, sálŏt', v. a. saludar; —, s. salutación, f. [salvamento, m.

salvage, sál'vădj, s. (mar.) s. derecho de salvación, f.

salvation, sálvá'shŭn, s. salvación, f.

salve, sáv, s. emplasto, ungüento, m.

salver, sál'vŭr, s. salvilla, bandeja, f.

salvo, sál'vō, s. reservación, excusa, f.

same, sám, a. mismo, idéntico.

sameness, -nĕs, s. identidad, f.

sample, săm'pl, s. muestra, f.; ejemplo, m.; —, v. a. ejemplificar. [delo, m.

sampler, -ŭr, s. muestra, f.; dechado, modelo, m.

sanctification, săngktĭfĭká'shŭn, s. santificación, f.; consagración, f.

sanctify, săngk'tĭfĭ, v. a. santificar.

sanctimonious, săngktĭmō'nĭŭs, a. semejante á santo. [santidad, f.

sanctimony, săngk'tĭmŏnĕ, s. santimonia, f.

sanction, săngk'shŭn, s. sanción, f.; —, v. a. sancionar.

sanctity, săngk'tĭtĕ, s. santidad, f.

sanctuary, săngk'tŭărĕ, s. santuario, m.; asilo, m.

sand, sánd, s. arena, f.; —, v. a. enarenar.

sandal, sán'dăl, s. sandalia, f.

sand-bags, sánd'bágz, s. pl. (mil.) sacos de tierra, m. pl. [salvadera, f.

sand-box, -bŏks, s. banco de arena, m.;

sanded, -ĕd, a. arenoso.

sand-pit, -pĭt, s. arenal, m.

sandstone, -stōn, s. piedra arenisca, f.

sandy, -ĕ, a. arenoso, arenisco.

sane, sán, a. sano.

sanguinary, sáng'gwĭnărĕ, a. sanguinario.

sanguine, sáng'gwĭn, a. sanguíneo. [f.

sanguineness, -nĕs, s. anhelo, m.; ansia, f.

sanguineous, sănggwĭn'ĕŭs, a. sanguino; sanguíneo. [inún, m.

sanity, sán'ĭtĕ, s. juicio sano, sentido común, m.

sap, sáp, s. savia, f.; (mil.) zapa, f.; —, v. a. zapar.

sapient, sá'pĭĕnt, a. sabio, cuerdo.

sapling, sáp'lĭng, s. renuevo, m.

sapper, -pŭr, s. (mil.) zapador, m.

sapphire, sáf'fŭr, s. zafir, zafiro, m.

sarcasm, sár'kăzm, s. sarcasmo, m.

sarcastic(al), sárkás'tĭk(ăl), a. mordaz, cáustico; -ally, ad. mordazmente. [m.

sarcenet, sárs'nĕt, s. tafetán de Florencia, m.

sarcophagus, sárkŏf'ăgŭs, s. sarcófago, sepulcro, m.

sardine, sár'dĭn, s. sardina, f.

sash, sásh, s. cíngulo, m., cinta, f.

sash-window, -wĭndō, s. ventana o vidriera corrediza, f.

Satan, sá'tăn, s. Sátanas, m.

satanic(al), sátán'ĭk(ăl), a. diabólico.

satchel, sátsh'ĕl, s. recado, quillo, m.

satellite, sát'ĕlĭt, s. satélite, m. [hartar.

satiate, sá'shĭát, sate, sát, v. a. saciar,

satiety, sátí'ĕtĕ, s. saciedad, hartura, f.

satin, sát'ĕn, s. raso, m.

satinet, -ĕt, s. rasete, m.

satire, sát'ĭr, s. sátira, f.

satiric(al), sátĭr'ĭk(ăl), a. satírico; -ly, ad. satíricamente.

satirist, sát'ĭrĭst, s. autor satírico, m.

satirize, sát'ĭrĭz, v. a. satirizar. [f.

satisfaction, sátĭsfák'shŭn, s. satisfacción, f.

satisfactorily, -tărĭlĕ, ad. satisfactoriamente.

satisfactory, -tărĕ, a. satisfactorio.

satisfy, sát'ĭsfĭ, v. a. satisfacer.

satrap, sá'trăp, s. sátrapa, m.

saturate, sát'ŭrát, v. a. saturar.

saturday, sát'ŭrdá, s. sábado, m.

saturnine, sát'ŭrnĭn, a. saturnino, melancólico. [cólico.

satyr, sát'ŭr, s. sátiro, m.

sauce, sás, s. salsa, f.; (am.) legumbre, f.; —, v. a. condimentar.

saucepan, -pán, s. cazo para estofar, m.

saucer, -ŭr, s. salsera, f.; platillo, m.

saucily, sá'sĭlĕ, ad. desvergonzadamente.

sauciness, sá'sĭnĕs, s. insolencia, impudencia, f.

saucy, sá'sĕ, a. insolente. [dencia, f.

saunter, sán'tŭr, v. n. callejear, corretear.

sausage, sá'sădj, s. salchicha, f.

savage, sáv'ădj, a. salvaje, bárbaro; -ly, ad. bárbaramente [s. salvaje, m.

savageness, -nĕs, s. salvajería, f.; crueldad, f.

savagery, -ŭrĕ, s. yermo, m.; crueldad, f.

savannah, sávăn'nă, s. sábana, f.

save, sáv, v. a. salvar; economizar; con servar: —, ad. salvo, excepto.

save-all, -ál, s. cañón de candelero, m.

saveloy, *săv'ĕlŏĭ,* s. chorizo, m.   [m.
saver, *sā'vŭr,* s. libertador, m.; ahorrador,
saving, *sā'ving,* a. frugal, económico; —,
  pr. fuera de, excepto; **-ly,** ad. económi-
  camente, parcamente; —, s. salvamiento,
  m.; **-s,** pl. ahorro, m., economía, f.
Saviour, *sā'vyŭr,* s. Redentor, m.
savour, *sā'vŭr,* s. olor, m.; sabor, m.; —,
  v. a. gustar, saborear.   [grancia, f.
savouriness, *—ĭnĕs,* s. paladar, m.; fra-
savoury, *—ĕ,* a. gustoso.
saw, *sā,* s. sierra, f.; —, v. a. serrar.
saw-dust, *—dŭst,* s. aserraduras, f. pl.
saw-fish, *—fĭsh,* s. priste, m.
saw-mill, *—mĭl,* s. molino de aserrar, m.
saw-pit, *—pĭt,* s. fosa de los serraderos de
sawyer, *—yŭr,* s. aserrador, m.   [madera.
say, *sā,* v. a. decir, hablar; —, s. habla, f.
saying, *—ĭng,* s. dicho, proverbio, m.
scab, *skăb,* s. roña, f.; roñoso, m.
scabbard, *—bărd,* s. vaina de espada, f.;
  cobertura, f.
scabbiness, *—bĭnĕs,* s. estado roñoso, m.
scabby, *—bĕ,* **scabious,** *skā'bĭŭs,* a. sarnoso.   [m.
scaffold, *skăf'fŏld,* s. tablado, m.; cadalso,
scaffolding, *—ĭng,* s. construcción de tabla-
  dos ó andamios, f.
scald, *skăld,* v. a. escaldar; —, s. tiña, f.
scale, *skāl,* s. balanza, f.; escama, f.; escala,
  f.; gama, f.; laminita, f.; **pair of—s,** peso
  de cruz, m.; —, v. a. & n. escalar; descostrarse.
Scales, *skālz,* s. pl. Libra, f. (signo del zodíaco.)   [de sitio, f.
scaling-ladder, *skā'lĭnglăddŭr,* s. escala
scallion, *skăl'yŭn,* s. ascalonia, cebolleta,
  f.   [festonear.
scallop, *skăl'lŏp,* s. pelne, m.; —, v. a.
scalp, *skălp,* s. cráneo, m.; —, v. a. levantar los tegumentos que cubren el cráneo.
scamp, *skămp,* s. bribón, ladrón, m.
scamper, *—ŭr,* v. n. escapar, huir.
scan, *skăn,* v. a. escudriñar; medir las
  sílabas de un verso.   [f.
scandal, *—dăl,* s. escándalo, m.; infamia,
scandalize, *—dălīz,* v. a. escandalizar.
scandalous, *—dălŭs,* a. escandaloso; **-ly,**
  ad. escandalosamente.   [sórdido.
scant, *skănt,* **scanty,** *—ĕ,* a. escaso, parco;
scantily, *skănt'ĭlĕ,* ad. escasamente, estrechamente.
scantiness, *skănt'ĭnĕs,* s. estrechez, escasez, f.   [f.
scantling, *skănt'lĭng,* s. cantidad pequeña,
scape-goat, *skāp'gŏt,* s. chivo emisario.
scape-grace, *—grās,* s. pícaro, m.   [m.
scar, *skăr,* s. cicatriz, f.; —, v. a. hacer
  alguna cicatriz.
scarce, *skărs,* a. raro; **-ly,** ad. apenas.
scarcity, *skărs'ĭtĕ,* s. escasez, f.; raridad, f.
scare, *skăr,* v. a. espantar.
scarecrow, *—krŏ,* s. espantajo, m.
scarf, *skărf,* s. trena, f.
scarify, *skăr'ĭfī,* v. a. sajar.
scarlatina, *skărlătē'nă,* s. escarlatina, f.
scarlet, *skăr'lĕt,* s. escarlata, f.; —, a. de
  color de escarlata ó grana.
scarp, *skărp,* s. escarpa, f.

soat, *skăt,* s. chaparrón, m.
scatter, *skăt'tŭr,* v. a. esparcir; disipar.
scavenger, *skăv'ĕnjŭr,* s. basurero, m.
scene, *sēn,* s. escena, f.   [(teatro), f.
scenery, *—ĕrē,* s. vista, f.; decoración (de
scenic(al), *sēn'ĭk(ăl),* a. escénico.
scent, *sĕnt,* s. olfato, m.; olor, m.; rastro,
  m.; —, v. a. oler.   [de olor, m.]
scent-bottle, *—bŏttl,* s. frasquito con agua
scentless, *—lĕs,* a. sin olfato; inodoro.
sceptic, *skĕp'tĭk,* s. escéptico, m.
sceptic(al), *—tĭk(ăl),* a. escéptico.
scepticism, *—tĭsĭzm,* s. escepticismo, m.
sceptre, *sĕp'tŭr,* s. cetro, m.
schedule, *shĕd'ūl, (sĕd'jūl),* s. esquela, f.;
  cédula, f.
scheme, *skēm,* s. proyecto, designio, m.;
  plan, modelo, m.; —, v. a. proyectar.
schemer, *—ŭr,* s. proyectista, invencionero,
schism, *sĭzm,* s. cisma, m. & f.   [m.
schismatic(al), *sĭzmăt'ĭk(ăl),* a. cismático,
  [literato, m.
scholar, *skŏl'ŭr,* s. escolar, estudiante, m.
scholarship, *—shĭp,* s. ciencia, f.; educación literaria, f.
scholastic, *skŏlăs'tĭk,* a. escolástico.
school, *skōl,* s. escuela, f.; —, v. a. enseñar.
school-boy, *—bŏĭ,* s. niño de escuela, m.
schooling, *—ĭng,* s. instrucción, f.
school-master, *—măstŭr,* s. maestro de
  escuela, m.   [de niños ó niñas, f.
school-mistress, *—mĭstrĕs,* s. maestra
schooner, *skōn'ŭr,* s. (mar.) goleta, f.
sciatica, *sīăt'ĭkă,* s. ciática, f.
science, *sī'ĕns,* s. ciencia, f.
scientific(al), *sīĕntĭf'ĭk(ăl),* a. científico;
  -ally, ad. científicamente.
scimitar, *sĭm'ĭtăr,* s. cimitarra, f.
scintillate, *sĭn'tĭlăt,* v. n. chispear, centellar.   [m.
scintillation, *sĭntĭlā'shŭn,* s. chispazo,
sciolist, *sī'ŏlĭst,* s. semisabio, m.   [m.
scion, *sī'ŏn,* s. verduguillo, m.; vástago,
scission, *sĭzh'ŭn,* s. separación, partición,
scissors, *sĭz'zŭrs,* s. pl. tijeras, f. pl.   [f.
scoff, *skŏf,* v. n. mofarse, burlarse; —, s.
  mofa, burla, f.
scoffer, *—fŭr,* s. mofador, m.   [nio.
scoffingly, *—fĭnglĕ,* ad. con mofa y escar-
scold, *skōld,* v. a. & n. reñir, reñir, refunfuñar; —, s. regañona, f.
sconce, *skŏns,* s. cornucopia, f.
scoop, *skōp,* s. cucharón; (mar.) achicador, m.; —, v. a. cavar, socavar.
scope, *skōp,* s. objeto, intento, designio,
  blanco, espacio, m.; libertad, f.
scorbutic, *skŏrbū'tĭk,* a. escorbútico.
scorch, *skŏrtsh,* v. a. quemar por encima;
  tostar; —, v. n. quemarse, secarse.
score, *skŏr,* s. muesca, canalita, f.; consideración, f.; cuenta, f.; escote, m.;
  razón, f.; motivo, m.; ventena, f.; —, v. a.
  sentar alguna deuda; imputar; señalar
  con una línea.
scoria, *skŏ'rĭă,* s. escoria, hez, f.
scorn, *skŏrn,* v. a. & n. despreciar; mofar,
  —, s. desdén, menosprecio, m.
scorner, *—ŭr,* s. desdeñador, m.   [desdén.
scornful, *—fŭl,* a. desdeñoso; **-ly,** ad. con

scorpion, *skór piän,* s. escorpión, m.

Scorpion, –, s. Escorpión, m. (signo del

scot, *skót,* s. escote, m. [zodíaco).

scotch, *skótsh,* s. cortadura, incisión, f.; –, v. a. escoplear. [m.

scoundrel, *skóŭn drĕl,* s. belitre, pícaro.

scoundrelly, –*lĕ,* a. ruin, de pícaro.

scour, *skóŭr,* v. a. fregar, estregar; limpiar; –, v. n. corretear.

scourge, *skŭrj,* s. azote, m.; castigo, m.; –, v. a. azotar, castigar.

scout, *skóŭt,* s. (mil.) batidor de la campaña, m.; centinela avanzada, f.; espía, m.; –, v. n. reconocer secretamente los movimientos del enemigo.

scowl, *skóŭl,* v. n. mirar con ceño; –, s. ceño, semblante ceñudo, m.

scowlingly, –*ĭnglĕ,* ad. con ceño.

scragginess, *skrăg' gĭnĕs,* s. flaqueza, extenuación, f.; aspereza, f.

scraggy, *skrăg' gĕ,* a. áspero; macilento.

scramble, *skrăm' bl,* v. n. arrapar; trepar; disputar; –, s. disputa, f.; juego de muchachos, m. [pedacito, m.

scrap, *skrăp,* s. migaja, f.; sobras, f. pl.;

scrape, *skrăp,* v. a. & n. raer, raspar; arañar; tocar mal un instrumento; –, s. embarazo, m.; dificultad, f.

scraper, –*ŭr,* s. rascador, m.; aprendiz de violín, m.

scratch, *skrătsh,* v. a. rascar, raspar; raer, garrapatear; –, s. rascadura, f.

scrawl, *skrăl,* v. a. & n. garrapatear; –, s. garabatos, m. pl.

scream, *skrēm,* screech, *skrētsh,* v. n. chillar, dar alaridos; –, s. chillido, grito, alarido, m.

screech-owl, –*ôl,* s. zumaya, f.

screen, *skrēn,* s. biombo, m.; mámpara, f.; abanico de chimenea, m.; harnero, m.; –, v. a. abrigar, esconder; cribar, cerner.

screw, *skrö,* s. tornillo, m.; female –, tuerca, f.; –, v. a. torcer con tornillo; forzar, apretar, estrechar.

screw-driver, –*drīvăr,* s. destornillador.

screw-nut, –*nŭt,* s. tuerca, f. [m.

screw-steamer, –*stēmăr,* s. navío á hélice, m. [escrito de poco mérito, m.

scribble, *skrĭb' bl,* v. a. escarabajear; –, s.

scribe, *skrĭb,* s. escritor, m.; escriba, m.

scrimmage, *skrĭm' mädj,* s. turbamulta, f.

scrip, *skrĭp,* s. bolsa, taleguilla, f.; cédula,

scriptural, *skrĭp' tŭrăl,* a. bíblico. [f.

Scripture, *skrĭp' tŭr* (*skrĭp' tshŭr*), s. Escritura sagrada, f. [público, m.

scrivener, *skrĭv' ĕnŭr,* s. escribano, notario

scrofula, *skrŏf' ŭlă,* s. escrófula, f.

scrofulous, *skrŏf' ŭlŭs,* a. escrofuloso. [m.

scroll, *skrōl,* s. rollo (de papel ó pergamino),

scrub, *skrŭb,* v. a. estregar con un estropajo; –, s. belitre, m.; estropajo, m.

scruple, *skrö' pl,* s. escrúpulo, m.; –, v. n. escrupulizar, tener duda. [sidad, f.

scrupulosity, *skrö' pŭlŏs' ĭtĕ,* s. escrupulo-

scrupulous, *skrö' pŭlŭs,* a. escrupuloso; –ly, ad. escrupulosamente.

scrutinize, *skrö' tĭnīz,* v. a. escudriñar, examinar.

scrutiny, *skrö' tĭnĕ,* s. escrutinio, examen,

soud, *skŭd,* v. n. huirse, escaparse. [m.

scuffle, *skŭf' fl,* s. quimera, riña, f.; –, v. n. reñir, pelear.

scull, *skŭl,* s. cráneo, m.; barquillo, m.

scullery, –*lărĕ,* s. espetera, f.; fregadero, m. [gona, f.

scullion, *skŭl' yŭn,* s. marmitón, m.; fre-

sculptor, *skŭlp' tŭr,* s. escultor, m.

sculpture, *skŭlp' tŭr* (*skŭlp' tshŭr*), s. escultura, f.; –, v. a. esculpir.

scum, *skŭm,* s. nata, f.; espuma, f.; escoria, f.; –, v. a. espumar.

scurf, *skŭrf,* s. tiña, f.; costra de una herida, f. [nada, f.

scurrility, *skŭrrĭl' ĭtĕ,* s. bufonería, bufos-

scurrilous, *skŭr' rĭlŭs,* a. vil, bajo; injurioso; –ly, ad. injuriosamente.

scurvily, *skŭr' vĭlĕ,* ad. vilmente.

scurviness, *skŭr' vĭnĕs,* s. ruindad, f.; malignidad, f.

scurvy, *skŭr' vĕ,* s. escorbuto, m.; –, a. escorbútico; vil, despreciable. [m.

scutcheon, *skŭtsh' ŭn,* s. escudo de armas,

scuttle, *skŭt' tl,* s. banasta, f.; –, v. n. apretar á correr.

scythe, *sĭth,* s. guadaña, f. [f.

sea, *sĕ,* s. mar, m. & f.; **heavy** –, oleada,

seaboard, –*bôrd,* s. (mar.) mar adentro, al largo.

sea-breeze, –*brēz,* s. viento de mar, m.

sea-coast, –*kôst,* s. costa marítima, f.

sea-fight, –*fīt,* s. combate naval, m.

sea-green, –*grēn,* a. verdemar.

sea-gull, –*gŭl,* s. gaviota, f.

sea-horse, –*hŏrs,* s. morso, m.

seal, *sēl,* s. sello, m.; –, v. a. sellar.

sealing-wax, –*ĭngwăks,* s. lacre, m.

seam, *sēm,* s. costura, f.; cicatriz, f.; –, v. a.

seaman, *sē' măn,* s. marinero, m. [coser.

seamanship, –*shĭp,* s. pericia en la navegación, m.

seamstress, *sēm' strĕs,* s. costurera, f.

seamy, *sēm' ĕ,* a. lo que tiene costuras.

sea-piece, *sē' pēs,* s. pintura marítima, f.

sea-port, –*pôrt,* s. puerto de mar, m.

sear, *sēr,* v. a. cauterizar.

search, *sŭrtsh,* v. a. examinar; escudriñar; inquirir, tentar; investigar, buscar; –, s. pesquisa, f.; busca, f.; buscada, f.

search-light, –*lĭt,* s. reflector eléctrico, m.

sea-shore, *sē' shŏr,* s. ribera, f., litoral, m.

sea-sick, –*sĭk,* a. mareado. [mareo, m.

sea-sickness, –*sĭknĕs,* s. mareamiento, m.

sea-side, –*sĭd,* s. orilla ó ribera del mar, f.

season, *sē' zn,* s. estación, f.; tiempo oportuno, m.; sazón, f.; –, v. a. sazonar; imbuir; –, v. n. sazonarse.

seasonable, –*ăbl,* a. oportuno, á propósito.

seasonably, –*ăblĕ,* ad. en sazón.

seasoning, –*ĭng,* s. condimento, m.

season-ticket, –*tĭkĕt,* s. (rall.) abono de pasaje, m.

seat, *sēt,* s. silla, morada, f.; domicilio, m.; situación, f.; –, v. a. situar; colocar; asentar.

sea-term, *sē' tŭrm,* s. término naval, m.

seaward, –*wŭrd,* a. del litoral; –, **seawards.** hacia el mar.

sea-weed, —*wéd*, s. alga marina, f.

sea-worthy, —*wûrthé*, a. á propósito para

secant, *sé kánt,* s. secante, f. [navegar.

secede, *séséd,* v. n. apartarse, separarse.

secession, *sésésh án,* s. apartamiento, m.; separación, f.

seclude, *séklód,* v. a. apartar, excluir.

seclusion, *séklo shán,* [s. separación, f.; exclusión, f.

second, *sék ánd,* a. segundo; —ly, ad. en segundo lugar; —, s. padrino, m.; defensor, m.; segundo, m.; (mus.) segunda, f.; —, v. a. ayudar; segundar.

secondary, —*árë,* a. secundario.

secondhand, —*hánd,* s. segunda mano, f. (en las compras).

secrecy, *sé kresé,* s. secreto, silencio cuidadoso, m. [ad. secretamente.

secret, *sé krét,* a. & s. secreto (m.); —ly,

secretary, *sék rétárë,* s. secretario, m.

secretaryship, —*ship,* s. secretaría, f.

secrete, *sékrét',* v. a. esconder; (med.) secretar.

secretion, *sékré shán,* s. secreción, f.

secretive, *sékré tiv,* a. misterioso.

sect, *sékt,* s. secta, f. [s. sectario, m.

sectarian, *séktá rián,* **sectary,** *sék tárë,*

section, *sék shán,* s. sección, f.

sector, *sék tûr,* s. sector, m.

secular, *sék úlûr,* a. secular, seglar.

secularity, *sékúlár tté,* s. apego á las cosas mundanas, m.

secularize, *sék úláriz,* v. a. secularizar.

secure, *sékúr,* a. seguro; salvo; —ly, ad. seguramente; —, v. a. asegurar; salvar.

security, *sékúr tté,* s. seguridad, f.; defensa, f.; confianza, f.; fianza, f.

sedan, *sédán',* s. silla de manos, f.

sedate, *sédát',* a. sosegado, tranquilo; —ly, ad. tranquilamente.

sedateness, —*nés,* s. tranquilidad, f.

sedative, *séd' átiv,* a. sedativo.

sedentary, *séd' éntûrë,* a. sedentario.

sederunt, *sédé rûnt,* s. (law)estrados, m.pl

sedge, *séj,* s. (bot.) lirio espadañal, m.

sediment, *séd'ément,* s. sedimento, m.; hez, f.; poso, m.

sedition, *sédish'án,* s.sedición,f.; tumulto, alboroto, motín, m.; revuelta, f.

seditious, *sédish'ûs,* a. sedicioso; —ly, ad. sediciosamente.

seditiousness, —*nés,* s. turbulencia, f.

seduce, *sédús',* v. a. seducir; engañar.

seducer, —*ûr,* s. seductor, m.

seduction, *sédûk'shán,* s. seducción, f.

seductive, *sédúk'tiv,* a. seductivo.

sedulous, *séd'úlús,* a. asiduo; —ly, ad. diligentemente.

see, *sé,* v. a. & n. ver, observar, descubrir; advertir; conocer; juzgar; comprender; —, ¡mira! —, s. silla episcopal, f.

seed, *séd,* s. semilla, simiente, f.; —, v. n. granar. [f.

seedling, —*ling,* s. planta de semillero, f.

seed-plot, —*plót,* s. semillero, plantel, m.

seedsman, —*z' mán,* s. tratante en semillas, m.

seed-time, —*tím,* s. sementera, siembra, f.

seedy, —*ë,* a. granado, lleno de granos.

seeing, *sé'ing,* s. vista, f.; acto de ver m.; —that, visto que.

seek, *sék,* v. a. & n. buscar; pretender.

seem, *sém,* v. n. parecer, semejarse.

seeming, —*ing,* s. apariencia, f.; —ly, ad. al parecer.

seemliness, —*lines,* s. decencia, f.

seemly, —*lé,* a. decente, propio.

seer, *sé úr,* s. profeta, m. [lancear.

seesaw, *sé sâ,* s. vaivén, m.; —, v. n. balancear.

seethe, *séth,* v. n. hervir, bullir.

seether, —*ûr,* s. caldera, marmita, f.

segment, *ség' ment,* s. segmento de un círculo, m. [(bienes ó efectos).

seize, *séz,* v. a. asir, agarrar; secuestrar

seizure, *sé zhúr,* s. captura,f.; secuestro,m.

seldom, *sél' dûm,* ad. raramente, rara vez.

select, *sélékt',* v. a. elegir, escoger; —, a. selecto, escogido.

selection, *sélék shán,* s. selección, f.

self, *sélf,* pr. mismo, propio.

self-command, —*kômmánd,* s. imperio sobre sí mismo, m.

self-conceit, —*kônsét,* s. presunción, f.

self-confident, —*kônfîdênt,* a. que tiene confianza en sí mismo. [f.

self-defence, —*déféns,* s. defensa propia,

self-denial, —*dénîâl,* s. abnegación de sí mismo, f.

self-evident, —*évîdênt,* a. natural. [m

self-interest, —*întêrêst,* s. propio interés,

selfish, —*ish,* a. egoísta; —ly, ad. interesadamente.

selfishness, —*îshnés,* s. egoísmo, m.

self-possession, —*pôzzésh'án,* s. sangre fría, tranquilidad de ánimo, f.

self-respect, —*réspékt,* s. estima de sí mismo, f. [lo mismo exactamente.

self-same, —*sám,* a. idéntico, el mismo ó

self-seeking, —*séking,* s. egoístico.

self-styled, —*sttld,* a. titulado.

self-taught, —*tât,* a. autodidacto..

self-willed, —*wíld,* a. obstinado.

sell, *sél,* v. a. & n. vender; traficar; —, s.

seller, —*lûr,* s. vendedor, m. [engaño, m.

selling-off, —*ling ôf,* s. venta pública, f.

selvage, *sél'váj,* s. orilla del paño, f.

semblance, *sém' blâns,* s. semejanza, apariencia, f. [f.

semibreve, *sém' îbrêv,* s. (mus.) semibreve,

semicircle, —*sûrkl,* s. semicírculo, m.

semicircular, —*sûr' kûlûr,* a. semicircular.

semicolon, —*kô' lôn,* s. punto y coma, m.

seminary, *sém'înârë,* s. seminario, m.

semiquaver, *sém'îkwâvûr,* s. (mus.) semicorchea, f.

semitone, —*tôn,* s. (mus.) semitono, m..

sempstress, *sém'strês,* s. costurera, f.

senate, *sén'ât,* s. senado, m.

senate-house, —*hôûs,* s. senado, m.; casa de ayuntamiento, f.

senator, *sén'âtûr,* s. senador, m.

senatorial, *sénât'ôrâl,* a. senatorio.

send, *sénd,* v. a. enviar, despachar, mandar; enviar; producir.

sender, —*ûr,* s. comisionista, f.

seneschal, *sén'êshâl,* s. senescal, m.

senile, *sé'nil,* a. senil.

senility, *sĕnĭl'ĭtĭ*, s. senectud; vejez, f.
senior, *sēn'yŭr*, s. anciano, m.
seniority, *sēnĭŏr'ĭtĭ*, s. antigüedad, ancianidad, f.
senna, *sĕn'nä*, s. (bot.) sen ó sena, f.
sennight, *sĕn'nĭt*, s. ocho días, m. pl.; semana, f.
sensation, *sĕnsā'shŭn*, s. sensación, f.
sense, *sĕns*, s. sentido, m.; entendimiento, m.; razón, f.; juicio, s.; sentimiento, m.
senseless, *—lĕs*, a. insensible, insensato; —ly, ad. insensatamente. [sensatez, f.
senselessness, *—lĕsnĕs*, s. tontería, insensibility, *sĕnsĭbĭl'ĭtĭ*, s. sensibilidad, f.
sensible, *sĕn'sĭbl*, a. sensible, sensitivo; juicioso.
sensibly, *—ĭ*, ad. sensiblemente.
sensitive, *sĕn'sĭtĭv*, a. sensitivo; —ly, ad. sensitiva, f.; —ly, ad. sensual(mente).
sensual, *sĕn'shŭăl*, a. sensuoso, —shŭăs, a.
sensualist, *—ĭst*, s. persona sensual, f.
sensuality, *sĕnshŭăl'ĭtĭ*, s. sensualidad, f.
sentence, *sĕn'tĕns*, s. sentencia, f.; —, v. a. sentenciar, condenar.
sententious, *sĕntĕn'shŭs*, a. sentencioso; —ly, ad. sentenciosamente.
sentient, *sĕn'shĭĕnt*, a. sensitivo.
sentiment, *sĕn'tĭmĕnt*, s. sentimiento, m.; opinión, f.
sentimental, *sĕntĭmĕn'tăl*, a. sentimental.
sentinel, *sĕn'tĭnĕl*, sentry, *sĕn'trĭ*, s. centinela, f. [f.
sentry-box, *—bŏks*, s. garita de centinela.
separable, *sĕp'ărăbl*, a. separable.
separate, *sĕp'ărāt*, v. a. (& n.) separar(se); —, a. separado; —ly, ad. separadamente.
separation, *sĕpărā'shŭn*, s. separación, f.
sepoy, *sē'pŏĭ*, s. soldado natural de las Indias orientales, m.
September, *sĕptĕm'bŭr*, s. setiembre, m.
septennial, *sĕptĕn'nĭăl*, a. sieteñal.
septuagenarian, *sĕptŭăjĕnā'rĭăn*, s. septuagenario, m. [nebre.
sepulchral, *sĕpŭl'krăl*, a. sepulcral, fúsepulchre, *sĕp'ŭlkŭr*, s. sepulcro, m.
sepulture, *sĕp'ŭltŭr*, s. sepultura, f.
sequel, *sē'kwĕl*, s. secuela, consecuencia, f.
sequence, *sē'kwĕns*, s. continuación, f.
sequester, *sĕkwĕs'tŭr*, sequestrate, *sĕkwĕs'trāt*, v. a. secuestrar. [cuestro, m.
sequestration, *sĕkwĕstrā'shŭn*, s. seseraglio, *sĕr'ăl'yŏ*, s. serallo, m.
seraph, *sĕr'ăf*, s. serafín, m.
serenade, *sĕrĕnād'*, s. serenata, f.; —, v. a. dar serenatas. [mente.
serene, *sĕrēn'*, a. sereno; —ly, ad. serenaserenity, *sĕrĕn'ĭtĭ*, s. serenidad, f.
serf, *sŭrf*, s. siervo, esclavo, m.
serge, *sŭrj*, s. sarga, f. (tela de lana fina).
sergeant, serjeant, *sär'jĕnt*, s. sargento, m.; alguacil, m.; abogado de primera clase, m.
serial, *sē'rĭăl*, a. que sale á luz en series; —, s. publicación en cuadernos periódicos, f.
series, *sē'rĭēs*, s. serie, f.
serious, *sē'rĭŭs*, a. serio, grave; —ly, ad. seriamente.

sermon, *sĕr'mŏn*, s. sermón, f.; oración evangélica, f.
sermonise, *—ĭz*, v. a. sermonear.
serous, *sē'rŭs*, a. seroso, acuoso.
serpent, *sŭr'pĕnt*, s. serpiente, sierpe, f.
serpentine, *—ĭn*, a. serpentino; —, s. (chem.) serpentina, f.
serrated, *sĕr'rātĕd*, a. serratiforme.
serum, *sē'rŭm*, s. suero, m.
servant, *sŭr'vănt*, s. criado, m.; criada, f.
servant-girl, *—gŭrl*, servant-maid, *—mād*, s. criada, f.
serve, *sŭrv*, v. a. & n. servir; asistir (á la mesa); ser á propósito; to— a warrant, ejecutar un auto de prisión.
service, *sŭr'vĭs*, s. servicio, m.; servidumbre, utilidad, f.; culto divino, m.; acomodo, m.
serviceable, *—ăbl*, a. servicial; oficioso.
servile, *sŭr'vĭl*, a. —ly, ad. servil(mente).
servility, *sŭrvĭl'ĭtĭ*, s. bajeza, vileza de ánimo, f. [vitud, f.
servitude, *sŭr'vĭtŭd*, s. servidumbre, esclasession, *sĕsh'ŭn*, s. junta, f.; sesión, f.
set, *sĕt*, v. a. poner, colocar, fijar; establecer, determinar; parar (en el juego); —, v. n. ponerse (el sol ó los astros); cuajarse; aplicarse; —, s. juego, conjunto de buenas cartas, m.; servicio (de plata), m.; conjunto ó agregado de muchas cosas, m.; cuadrilla, bandada, f.; —, a. puesto, fijo.
set-off, *—ŏf*, s. adorno, m.; guarnición, f.
set-out, *—ŏut*, s. festejo, m.
settee, *—tē'*, s. canapé pequeño, m.
setter, *—tŭr*, s. perro de muestra, m.; espía, m.; el que compone música.
setter-on, *—tŭrŏn*, s. instigador, m.
setting, *—tĭng*, s. establecimiento, m.; — of the sun, puesta del sol, f.
settle, *sĕt'l*, v. a. colocar, fijar, afirmar; arreglar; calmar; —, v. n. reposarse; establecerse; sosegarse; —, s. asiento, m.
settlement, *—mĕnt*, s. establecimiento, m.; domicilio, m.; contrato, m.; empleo, m.; poso, m.; colonia, f.
settler, *—ŭr*, s. colono, m.
set-to, *sĕt'tŏ'*, s. riña, f.; combate, m.
seven, *sĕv'n*, a. siete.
sevenfold, *—fōld*, a. séptuplo.
seventeen, *—tēn*, a. diez y siete.
seventeenth, *—tēnth*, a. décimoséptimo.
seventh, *—th*, a. séptimo; —ly, ad. en séptimo lugar.
seventieth, *—tĭĕth*, a. septuagésimo.
seventy, *—tĭ*, a. setenta.
sever, *sĕv'ŭr*, v. a. & n. separar.
several, *—ăl*, a. diversos, muchos; particular; —ly, ad. separadamente.
severance, *—ăns*, s. separación, f.
severe, *sĕvēr'*, a. severo, riguroso, áspero, duro; —ly, ad. severamente.
severity, *sĕvĕr'ĭtĭ*, s. severidad, f. [que.
sew, *sŏ*, v. a. & n. coser; desaguar un estansewer, *sŭ'ŭr*, s. albañal, m.; —, *sŏ'ŭr*, costurera, f.
sewerage, *sŭ'ŭrăj*, s. construcción de albañales, f.; agua de sumidero, f.
sex, *sĕks*, s. sexo, m.

11 *

sexennial, *sĕksĕn'nĭăl,* a. lo que dura ó acontece en seis años.

sextant, *sĕks'tănt,* s. sextante, m.

sexton, *sĕks'tŏn,* s. sepulturero, m.

sextuple, *sĕks'tŭpl,* a. séxtuplo.

sexual, *sĕks'ŭăl,* a. sexual. [namente.

shabbily, *shăb'bĭlĭ,* ad. vilmente, mezqui-

shabbiness, *shăb'bĭnĕs,* s. vileza, bajeza, miseria, f. [pado; tacaño.

shabby, *shăb'bĕ,* a. vil, bajo; desharra-

shackle, *shăk'l,* v. a. encadenar; -s, s. pl.

shad, *shăd,* s. alosa, f. [grillos, m. pl.

shade, *shād,* s. sombra, obscuridad, f.; matiz, m.; sombrilla, f.; -, v. a. asombrar; abrigar; proteger. [umbría, f.

shadiness, *shā'dĭnĕs,* s. sombraje, m.

shadow, *shăd'ō,* s. sombra; f. protección, f.

shadowy, *-ĕ,* a. umbroso; obscuro; quimérico.

shady, *shā'dĕ,* a. opaco, obscuro, sombrío.

shaft, *shăft,* s. flecha, saeta, f.; fuste de columna, m.; lanza de los coches, f.

shag, *shăg,* s. pelo áspero y lanudo, m.; felpa, f.

shagged, *-gĕd,* shaggy, *-gĕ,* a. afelpado.

shagreen, *shăgrēn',* s. zapa, lija, f.

shake, *shāk,* v. a. sacudir; agitar; -, v. n. vacilar; temblar; to — hands, darse las manos mutuamente en señal de amistad; -, s. concusión, sacudida, f.; vibración, f.

shaking, *shā'kĭng,* s. sacudimiento; temblor, m.

shaky, *shā'kĕ,* a. titubeante. [bror, m.

shall, *shăl,* v. n. def. deber.

shallop, *shăl'lŏp,* s. (mar.) chalupa, f.

shallow, *shăl'lō,* a. somero, superficial; trivial; -, s. bajío, m. (banco de arena).

shallowness, *-nĕs,* s. poca profundidad, f.; necedad, f.

sham, *shăm,* v. a. engañar, chasquear; -, s. socolor, m.; fingimiento, m.; impostura, f.; -, a. fingido, disimulado.

shambles, *shăm'blz,* s. pl. carnicería, f.

shambling, *shăm'blĭng,* a. lo que se mueve toscamente.

shame, *shām,* s. vergüenza, f.; deshonra, f.; -, v. a. avergonzar, deshonrar. [roso.

shamefaced, *-fāsd,* a. vergonzoso, pudo-

shameful, *-fŭl,* a. vergonzoso; deshonroso; -ly, ad. ignominiosamente.

shameless, *-lĕs,* a. desvergonzado; -ly, ad. desvergonzadamente. [impudencia, f.

shamelessness, *-lĕsnĕs,* s. desvergüenza, f.

shamois, *shăm'ĕ̄,* s. gamuza, f.

shampoo, *shămpō',* v. a. dar las friegas.

shampooing, *-ĭng,* s. friega, f.; friegas, pl.

shamrock, *shăm'rŏk,* s. trébol, m.

shank, *shăngk,* s. pierna, f.; asta, f.; asta de ancla; cañón de pipa, m.

shanty, *shăn'tĕ,* s. cabaña, f.

shape, *shāp,* v. a. & n. formar; proporcionar; concebir; -, s. forma, figura, f.; modelo, m.

shapeless, *-lĕs,* a. informe. [delo, m.

shapely, *-lĕ,* a. bien hecho.

share, *shăr,* s. parte, porción, f.; (com.) acción, f.; reja del arado, f.; -, v. a. & n. repartir; participar. [m.

shareholder, *-hōldăr,* s. (com.) accionista, m.

sharer, *-ăr,* s. partícipe, m.

shark, *shărk,* s. tiburón, m.; petardista, m.

sharp, *shărp,* a. agudo, aguzado; astuto; perspicaz; penetrante; acre, mordaz, severo, rígido; vivo, violento; -, s. (mus.) becuadro, m.

sharpen, *-n,* v. a. afilar, aguzar.

sharper, *-ăr,* s. petardista, estafador, m.

sharply, *-lĕ,* ad. con filo; severamente, agudamente; ingeniosamente.

sharpness, *-nĕs,* s. agudeza, f.; sutileza, perspicacia, f.; acrimonia, f.

shatter, *shăt'tăr,* v. a. destrozar, estrellar; -, v. n. hacerse pedazos; -, s. pedazo, m.

shave, *shāv,* v. a. rasurar; raspar; rozar; (fig.) escatimar.

shaver, *-ăr,* s. barbero, m.; usurero, m.

shaving, *-ĭng,* s. raedura, f.; rasura, f.

shawl, *shăl,* s. chal, m.

she, *shē,* pn. ella.

sheaf, *shēf,* s. gavilla, f.; -, v. a. agavillar.

shear, *shēr,* v. a. atusar; tundir; -s, s. pl. tijeras grandes, f. pl.

sheath, *shēth,* s. vaina, f.; -, *shēth,* v. a. envainar; (mar.) aforrar el fondo de un navío.

shed, *shĕd,* v. a. verter, derramar; esparcir; -, s. sotechado, tejadillo, m.; cabaña, f.

sheen, *shēn,* s. resplandor, m.

sheep, *shēp,* s. oveja, f.; carnero, m.; papanatas, m. [redil, m.

sheep-cot, *-kŏt,* sheep-fold, *-fōld,* s. aprisco, m.

sheepish, *-ĭsh,* a. vergonzoso; tímido.

sheepishness, *-ĭshnĕs,* s. timidez, cortedad de genio, f. [ojeada modesta, f.

sheep's-eye, *-z'ī,* s. mirada al soslayo, f.

sheepskin, *-skĭn,* s. piel de carnero, m.

sheep-walk, *-wăk,* s. dehesa, f.; carnefil, pasto de ovejas, m.

sheer, *shēr,* a. puro, claro, sin mezcla; -, ad. de un golpe; -, v. n. alargarse, escaparse.

sheet, *shēt,* s. sábana, f.; pliego de papel, m.; (mar.) escota, f.; book in -s, libro no encuadernado, m. [de un navío, f.

sheet-anchor, *-ăngkăr,* s. áncora mayor

sheeting, *-ĭng,* s. tela para sábanas, f.

sheet-iron, *-ĭrn,* s. plancha de hierro batido, f. [gueamiento, m.

sheet-lightning, *-lĭtnĭng,* s. relampa-

shelf, *shĕlf,* s. anaquel, m.; (mar.) arrecife, m.; escollera, f.; on the -, desecho.

shell, *shĕl,* s. cáscara, f.; silicua, f.; concha, f.; corteza, f.; -, v. a. descascarar, descortezar; -, v. n. descascararse.

shelter, *shĕl'tăr,* s. guarida, f.; amparo, abrigo, m.; asilo, refugio, m.; -, v. a. guarecer, abrigar; acoger.

shelterless, *-lĕs,* a. sin asilo. [conar.

shelve, *shĕlv,* v. a. echar á un lado, arrin-

shelving, *shĕl'vĭng,* a. inclinado, en declive; -, a. lleno de escollos. [clive.

shelvy, *-ĕ,* a. lleno de escollos.

shepherd, *shĕp'ărd,* s. pastor, m.; zagal, m.

shepherdess, *-ĕs,* s. pastora, f.; zagala, f.

sherbet, *shăr'bĕt,* s. sorbete, m.

sheriff, *shĕr'ĭf,* s. jerif, m.

sherry, *shĕr'rĕ,* s. vino de Jerez, m.

shield, *shēld,* s. escudo, m.; patrocinio, m.; -, v. a. defender.

shift, *shĭft*, v. n. cambiarse; mudarse el vestido; ingeniarse; trampear; —, v. a. mudar, cambiar; transportar; —, s. último recurso, m.; artificio, m.; astucia, f.; efugio, m.; camisa de mujer, f.

shifter, *—ẽr*, s. tramoyista, m.

shillelagh, *shĭllẽ′lâ*, s. macana, f.

shilling, *shĭl′lĭng*, s. chelín, m.

shin(-bone), *shĭn(′bōn)*, s. espinilla, f.

shine, *shĭn*, v. n. lucir, brillar, resplandecer. [herpes, m. & f. pl.

shingle, *shĭng′gl*, s. ripia, f.; —s, pl. (med.)

shining, *shĭ′nĭng*, a. resplandeciente; —, s. esplendor, m.

shiny, *shĭ′nĭ*, a. brillante, luciente.

ship, *shĭp*, s. nave, f.; bajel, navío, buque, m.; —, v. a. embarcar. [on —, á bordo.

ship-board, *—bōrd*, s. tablón de navío, m.;

ship-boy, *—bōĭ*, s. grumete, m.

ship-building, *—bĭlding*, s. arquitectura naval, f.

shipmate, *—māt*, s. (mar.) ayudante, m.

shipment, *—mênt*, s. cargazón, f.

ship-owner, *—ōnẽr*, s. naviero, m.

shipwreck, *—rēk*, s. naufragio, m.

shire, *shĭr* (in comp. *shẽr*), s. condado (de Inglaterra), m.

shirt, *shẽrt*, s. camisa de hombre, f. [f.

shirting, *—ĭng*, s. indiana para camisas.

shiver, *shĭv′ẽr*, s. cacho, pedazo, fragmento, m.; —, v. n. tiritar de frío; —, v. a. estrellar. [plor, m.

shivering, *—ĭng*, s. horripilación, f.; temblor.

shoal, *shōl*, s. multitud, muchedumbre, f.; bajío, m.; —, a. lleno de bajíos; —, v. n. atroparse; estar lleno de bajíos.

shoaly, *—ĭ*, a. lleno de bajíos.

shock, *shŏk*, s. choque, encuentro, m.; combate, m.; ofensa, f.; hacina, f.; —, v. a. sacudir; ofender.

shoddy, *shŏd′dĭ*, s. caedura, f.

shoe, *shō*, s. zapato, m.; herradura de caballo, f.; —, v. a. calzar; herrar un caballo.

shoe-black, *—blăk*, **shoe-boy**, *—bōĭ*, s. limpiabotas, m.

shoeing, *—ĭng*, s. acto de herrar, m.

shoeing-horn, *—ĭnghōrn*, s. calzador, m.

shoelace, *—lās*, s. correa de zapato, f.

shoemaker, *—mākẽr*, s. zapatero, m. [m.

shoe-string, *—strĭng*, s. lazo de zapato.

shoot, *shōt*, v. a. tirar, arrojar, lanzar, disparar; —, v. n. brotar, germinar; sobresalir; lanzarse; —, s. tiro, m.; vástago, m.

shooter, *—ẽr*, s. tirador, m. [tiro, m.

shooting, *—ĭng*, s. caza con escopeta, f.;

shop, *shŏp*, s. tienda, f.; taller, m.

shop-bill, *—bĭl*, s. señal, f.

shop-front, *—frŏnt*, s. escaparate, m. [m.

shop-keeper, *—kēpẽr*, s. tendero, mercader.

shop-lifter, *—lĭftẽr*, s. ladrón de tiendas, m.

shop-man, *—măn*, s. hortera, mancebo de tienda, m. [tienda, m.

shop-walker, *—wâkẽr*, s. celador de

shop-woman, *—wûmăn*, s. tendera, f.

shore, *shōr*, s. costa, ribera, playa, f.

short, *shŏrt*, a. corto breve, sucinto, conciso; **-ly**, ad. brevemente; presto; en pocas palabras.

shortcoming, *—kŭmĭng*, s. insuficiencia, f.; déficit, m.

shorten, *—n*, v. a. acortar; abreviar.

shorthand, *—hănd*, s. taquigrafía, estenografía, f.

shorthand-writer, *—hăndrĭtẽr*, s. taquígrafo, estenógrafo, m. [f.

shortness, *—nẽs*, s. cortedad, f.; brevedad.

short-sighted, *—sĭtẽd*, a. corto de vista.

short-sightedness, *—sĭtẽdnẽs*, s. cortedad de vista, f.

shot, *shŏt*, s. tiro, m.; alcance, m.; perdigones, m. pl.; escote, m.

shoulder, *shōl′dẽr*, s. hombro, m.; brazuelo, m.; —, v. a. cargar al hombro.

shout, *shōŭt*, v. n. dar vivas, aclamar; reprobar con gritos; —, s. aclamación, gritería, f.

shouting, *—ĭng*, s. gritos de alegría, m. pl.

shove, *shŭv*, v. a. & n. empujar; impeler; —, s. empujón, m.

shovel, *shŭv′l*, s. pala, f.; —, v. a. traspalar.

show, *shō*, v. a. mostrar; descubrir, manifestar; probar; enseñar, explicar; —, v. n. parecer; —, s. espectáculo, m.; muestra, f.; exposición, parada, f.

shower, *shō′ẽr*, s. nubada, f.; llovizna, f.; (fig.) abundancia, f.; —, v. n. llover.

showery, *—ĭ*, a. lluvioso.

showful, *shō′fûl*, s. moneda falsa, f.

showy, *shō′ĭ*, a. ostentoso, suntuoso.

shred, *shrĕd*, s. cacho, pedazo pequeño, m.; —, v. a. picar. [musaraña, m.

shrew, *shrō*, s. mujer de mal genio, f.;

shrewd, *shrōd*, a. astuto; maligno; **-ly**, ad. astutamente.

shrewdness, *—nẽs*, s. astucia, f.

shrewish, *shrō′ĭsh*, a. regañón; **-ly**, ad. con mal humor. [musaraña, f.

shrewmouse, *—mōŭs*, s. musgaño, m.

shriek, *shrēk*, v. n. chillar; —, s. chillido, m.

shrill, *shrĭl*, a. agudo, penetrante. [m.

shrillness, *—nẽs*, s. aspereza del sonido ó de la voz, f. [hombrecillo, m.

shrimp, *shrĭmp*, s. camarón, m.; enano.

shrine, *shrĭn*, s. relicario, m.

shrink, *shrĭngk*, v. n. encogerse; angostarse, acortarse. [—, v. a. arrugar.

shrivel, *shrĭv′l*, v. n. arrugarse, encogerse;

shroud, *shrōŭd*, s. cubierta, f.; mortaja, f.; —s, pl. (mar.) obenques, m. pl.; —, v. a. cubrir, defender; amortajar; proteger; —, v. n. guarecerse, refugiarse.

shrovetide, *shrōv′tĭd*, s. martes de carnaval, m.

shrub, *shrŭb*, s. arbusto, m. [m.

shrubbery, *—bẽrĭ*, s. plantío de arbustos.

shrug, *shrŭg*, v. a. encoger de hombros; —, s. encogimiento de hombros, m.

shudder, *shŭd′dẽr*, v. n. estremecerse, despeluzarse; —, s. despeluzamiento, temblor, m.

shuffle, *shŭf′fl*, v. a. & n. poner en confusión, desordenar; barajar los naipes; trampear; tergiversar; hacer esfuerzos; —, s. barajadura, f.; treta, f.

shuffling, *shŭf′flĭng*, s. tramoya, f.

shun, *shŭn*, v. a. huir, evitar.

shunt, *shŭnt,* s. (rail.) bifurcación, f.; cambio de vía, m.

shut, *shŭt,* v. a. cerrar, encerrar.

shutter, *-ar,* s. postigo de ventana, m.

shuttle, *-tl,* s. lanzadera, f. [m.

shuttle-cock, *-tlkŏk,* s. volante, rehilete.

shy, *shî,* a. tímido; reservado; vergonzoso, contenido; **-ly,** ad. tímidamente.

shyness, *-nĕs,* s. timidez, f.

sibyl, *sĭb'ŭl,* s. sibila, profetisa, f.

sick, *sĭk,* a. malo, enfermo; disgustado.

sicken, *-n,* v. a. enfermar; **—,** v. n. caer enfermo.

sickle, *sĭk'kl,* s. hoz, f. [enfermo.

sickliness, *-lĭnĕs,* s. indisposición habitual.

sickly, *-lĕ,* a. enfermizo. [tual.

sickness, *-nĕs,* s. enfermedad, f.

side, *sîd,* s. lado, m.; costado, m.; facción, f.; partido, m.; **—,** a. lateral; oblicuo; **—,** v. a. unirse con alguno.

sideboard, *-bôrd,* s. aparador, m.; alacena.

sideface, *-fās,* s. cabeza en perfil, f.

sidelong, *-lŏng,* a. lateral; **-ly,** ad. de lado. [m. pl.

side-scene, *-sēn,* s. bastidores de un teatro,

sideways, *-wāz,* ad. de lado, al través.

siding, *sî'dĭng,* s. toma de partido, f.; (rail.) aguja, f. [de lado.

sidle, *sî'dl,* v. n. estar echado de lado, ir

siege, *sēj,* s. (mil.) sitio, m.

sieve, *sĭv,* s. tamiz, m.; criba, f.; cribo, m.

sift, *sĭft,* v. a. cerner; cribar; examinar; investigar.

siftings, *-ĭngz,* s. pl. granzas, f. pl.

sigh, *sî,* v. n. suspirar, gemir; **—,** s. suspiro.

sight, *sît,* s. vista, f.; mira, f. [m.

sightless, *-lĕs,* a. ciego.

sightly, *-lĕ,* a. vistoso, hermoso.

sight-seeing, *-sēĭng,* s. curiosidad, f.

sign, *sîn,* s. señal, f., indicio, m.; tablilla, f.; signo, m.; firma, f.; seña, f.; **—,** v. a. señalar; hacer señas. [insigne, señalado.

signal, *sĭg'năl,* s. señal, f., aviso, m.; **—,** a.

signalize, *-îz,* v. a. señalar.

signal-light, *-lît,* s. (rail.) farol, m. (de mano ó de disco).

signal-man, *-măn,* s. (rail.) guardavía, m.

signature, *sĭg'nătŭr,* s. marca, f.; seña, f.; signatura, f.

signet, *sĭg'nĕt,* s. sello (del rey), m. [f.

significance, *sĭgnĭf'ĭkăns,* s. importancia, f.

significant, *sĭgnĭf'ĭkănt,* a. significante.

signification, *sĭgnĭfĭkā'shŭn,* s. significación, f.; sentido, m. [tener energía.

signify, *sĭg'nĭfî,* v. a. significar; **—,** v. n.

sign-post, *sîn'pōst,* s. pilar de anuncio, m.

silence, *sî'lĕns,* s. silencio, m.; **—,** v. a. imponer silencio. [ciosamente.

silent, *sî'lĕnt,* a. silencioso; **-ly,** ad. silen-

silex, *sî'lĕks,* s. guijarro, m.

silk, *sĭlk,* s. seda, f.

silken, *-n,* a. hecho de seda; sedeño.

silkiness, *-ĭnĕs,* s. blandura, molicie, f.

silk-man, *-măn,* s. mercader de seda, m.

silk-pod, *-pŏd,* s. capullo del gusano de seda, m.

silk-worm, *-wŭrm,* s. gusano de seda, m.

silky, *-ĕ,* a. hecho de seda; sedeño.

sill, *sĭl,* s. umbral de puerta, m.

sillily, *sĭl'ĭlĕ,* ad. tontamente.

silliness, *sĭl'lĭnĕs,* s. simpleza, **bobería,** tontería, necedad, f.

silly, *sĭl'lĕ,* a. tonto, mentecato, imbécil.

silver, *sĭl'vär,* s. plata, f.; **—,** a. de plata; **—,** v. a. platear. [platero, m.

silverer, *-är,* s. silversmith, *-smĭth,* a.

silvery, *-ĕ,* a. plateado.

similar, *sĭm'ĭlär,* a. similar; semejante; **-ly,** ad. similitudinariamente.

similarity, *sĭmĭlăr'ĭtĕ,* similitude, *sĭmĭl'ĭtŭd,* s. semejanza, f.

smile, *sĭm'îl,* s. semejanza, similitud, f.

simmer, *sĭm'är,* v. n. hervir á fuego lento.

simony, *sĭm'ŏnĕ,* s. simonía, f. [risa, f.

simper, *sĭm'pär,* v. n. sonreírse; **—,** s. sonrisa, f.

simple, *sĭm'pl,* a. simple, puro, sencillo.

simpleness, *-nĕs,* s. simplicidad, f.

simpleton, *-tŏn,* s. simplón, simplonazo, m.

simplicity, *sĭmplĭs'ĭtĕ,* s. simplicidad, f.; simpleza, f. [plicación, f.

simplification, *sĭmplĭfĭkā'shŭn,* s. sim-

simplify, *sĭm'plĭfî,* v. a. simplificar.

simply, *sĭm'plĕ,* ad. simplemente.

simulate, *sĭm'ŭlāt,* v. a. simular, fingir.

simulation, *sĭmŭlā'shŭn,* s. simulación, f.

simultaneous, *sĭmŭltā'nĕŭs,* a. simultáneo. [faltar.

sin, *sĭn,* s. pecado, m.; **—,** v. n. pecar.

since, *sĭns,* ad. ya que; desde que; pues que; **—,** pr. desde, después.

sincere, *sĭnsēr',* a. sencillo; sincero; **-ly,** ad. sinceramente; **— yours** (ending to a letter), de U., S.S.S. (su segurísimo servidor); quedo de U. su at° y S.S. (su atento y seguro servidor).

sincerity, *sĭnsĕr'ĭtĕ,* s. sinceridad, f.

sinecure, *sĭ'nĕkŭr,* s. sueldo sin empleo, m.

sinew, *sĭn'ŭ,* s. tendón, m.; nervio, m.

sinewy, *-ĕ,* a. nervoso; robusto.

sinful, *sĭn'fŭl,* a. pecaminoso, malvado; **-ly,** ad. malvadamente.

sinfulness, *-nĕs,* s. corrupción, f.

sing, *sĭng,* v. n. & a. cantar; gorjear los pájaros; (poet.) celebrar.

singe, *sĭnj,* v. a. chamuscar.

singer, *sĭng'är,* s. cantor, m.; cantora, f.

singing, *sĭng'ĭng,* s. canto, m.

single, *sĭng'gl,* a. sencillo, simple, solo; soltero, soltera; **—,** v. a. singularizar; separar.

singleness, *-nĕs,* s. sencillez, sinceridad, f.

singly, *sĭng'glĕ,* ad. separadamente.

singular, *sĭng'gŭlär,* a. singular, peculiar; **-ly,** ad. singularmente. [f.

singularity, *sĭnggŭlăr'ĭtĕ,* s. singularidad,

sinister, *sĭn'ĭstär,* a. siniestro, izquierdo; viciado; infeliz, funesto.

sink, *sĭngk,* v. n. hundirse; sumergirse; bajarse; penetrar; arruinarse, decaer; **—,** v. a. hundir, echar á lo hondo; deprimir, destruir; **—,** s. alcantarilla, f.; sentina, f.

sinking-fund, *-ĭngfŭnd,* s. caja de amortización, f.

sinner, *sĭn'när,* s. pecador, m.; pecadora, f.

sin-offering, *sĭn'ŏffŭrĭng,* s. sacrificio propiciatorio, m.

sinuosity, *sĭnŭŏs'ĭtĕ,* s. sinuosidad, f.

sinuous, *sĭn'ŭŭs*, a. sinuoso.
sinus, *sī'nŭs*, s. seno, m.; bahía, f.
sip, *sĭp*, v. a. beborrotear, echar sorbitos; —, s. sorbo, m.
siphon, *sī'făn*, s. sifón, m. [tada, f.
sippet, *sĭp'pĕt*, s. rebanada de pan; tos-
Sir, *sŭr*, s. Señor, m.
sire, *sīr*, s. caballero, m.; (poet.) padre, m.
siren, *sī'rĕn*, s. sirena, f.
sirloin, *sŭr'lŏĭn*, s. lomo de buey ó vaca, m.
sister, *sĭs'tŭr*, s. hermana, f.; religiosa, f.
sister-in-law, *—ĭnlä*, s. cuñada, f.
sisterhood, *—hŏd*, s. hermandad, f.
sisterly, *—lĕ*, a. con hermandad.
sit, *sĭt*, v. n. sentarse; estar situado.
site, *sīt*, s. sitio, m.; situación, f. [f.
sitting, *sĭt'tĭng*, s. sesión, junta, f.; sentada,
situate, *sĭt'ŭāt*, a. situado.
situation, *sĭtŭā'shŭn*, s. situación, f.
six, *sĭks*, a. seis. [chelín), m. pl.
sixpence, *—pĕns*, s. seis peniques (medio
sixteen, *—tēn*, a. diez y seis.
sixteenth, *—tēnth*, a. décimosexto.
sixth, *—th*, a. sexto; —ly, ad. en sexto lugar.
sixtieth, *—tĭĕth*, a. sexagésimo.
sixty, *—tĕ*, a. sesenta.
size, *sīz*, s. tamaño, talle, m.; calibre, m.; dimensión, f.; estatura, f.; condición, f.; cola de retazo, f.; —, v. a. encolar.
sized, *—d*, a. lo que pertenece al tamaño ó grandor de las cosas.
skate, *skāt*, s. patín, m.; —, v. n. correr sobre el hielo con patines.
skating, *—ĭng*, s. el ejercicio de correr patines sobre el hielo.
skating-rink, *—rĭngk*, s. camino trillado para patinar, m.
skein, *skān*, s. madeja, f.
skeleton, *skĕl'ĕtŭn*, s. esqueleto, m.
skeleton-key, *—kē*, s. llave maestra, f.
sketch, *skĕtsh*, s. esbozo, m.; esquicio, m.; —, v. a. esquiciar, bosquejar.
skew, *skū*, a. oblicuo.
skewer, *—ŭr*, s. aguja de lardear, f.; espetón, m.; —, v. a. espetar.
skid, *skĭd*, s. arrastradera de un carruaje, f.; —, v. a. enrayar.
skiff, *skĭf*, s. esquife, m. [diestramente.
skilful, *skĭl'fŭl*, a. práctico, diestro; —ly, ad.
skilfulness, *—nĕs*, s. destreza, f.
skill, *skĭl*, s. destreza, arte, pericia, f.
skilled, *—lĕd*, a. práctico, instruido.
skillet, *skĭl'lĕt*, s. marmita pequeña, f.
skim, *skĭm*, v. a. espumar; tratar superficialmente; —, s. espuma, f.
skimmer, *—mŭr*, s. espumadera, f.
skin, *skĭn*, s. cutis, m. & f.; —, v. a. desollar.
skinned, *—d*, a. desollado.
skinner, *—nŭr*, s. pellejero, m.; peletero, m.
skinny, *—nĕ*, a. flaco, macilento.
skip, *skĭp*, v. n. saltar, brincar; —, v. a. pasar, omitir; —, s. salto, brinco, m.
skirmish, *skŭr'mĭsh*, s. escaramuza, f.; —, v. n. escaramuzar.
skirmisher, *—ŭr*, s. escaramuzador, m.
skirt, *skŭrt*, s. falda, orla, f.; —, v. a. orillar.
skit, *skĭt*, s. burla, zumba, f.

skittish, *skĭt'tĭsh*, a. espantadizo, retozón; terco; inconstante; —ly, ad. caprichosa-
skittle, *skĭt'tl*, s. bolo, m. [mente.
skulk, *skŭlk*, v. n. escuchar, acechar.
skull, *skŭl*, skulk, *skŭlk*, s. cráneo, m.
skull-cap, *—kăp*, s. gorro, m.
sky, *skī*, s. cielo, firmamento, m.
sky-light, *—lĭt*, s. claraboya, f.
sky-rocket, *—rŏkĕt*, s. cohete, m.
slab, *slăb*, s. losa, f.
slabber, *—bŭr*, v. n. babear; ensuciar.
slack, *slăk*, a. flojo, perezoso, negligente, lento.
slack(en), *—(n)*, v. a. & n. aflojar; ablandar; entibiarse; decaer; relajar; aliviar.
slackness, *—nĕs*, s. flojedad, remisión, f.
slag, *slăg*, s. escoria, f. [descuido, m.
slake, *slāk*, v. a. extinguir.
slam, *slăm*, s. capote, m. (en los juegos de naipes); —, v. a. dar capote; empujar con violencia. [—, s. calumnia, f.
slander, *slăn'dŭr*, v. a. calumniar, infamar;
slanderer, *—dŭrŭr*, s. calumniador, maldiciente, m. [ad. calumniosamente.
slanderous, *—dŭrŭs*, a. calumnioso; —ly,
slang, *slăng*, s. jerigonza, f.
slant, *slănt*, v. n. pender oblicuamente.
slanting, *—ĭng*, a. sesgado, oblicuo.
slap, *slăp*, s. manotada, f.; (on the face), bofetada, f.; —, ad. de sopetón; —, v. a. golpear, dar una bofetada. [llada, f.
slash, *slăsh*, v. a. acuchillar; —, s. cuchi-
slate, *slāt*, s. pizarra, f.; —, v. a. empizarrar.
slate-pencil, *—pĕnsĭl*, s. lápiz de pizarra, f. [m.
slater, *—ŭr*, s. pizarrero, m.
slating, *slā'tĭng*, s. techo de pizarras, m.
slattern, *slăt'tŭrn*, s. mujer desaliñada, f.
slatternly, *—lĕ*, ad. desaliñadamente.
slaughter, *slä'tŭr*, s. carnicería, matanza, f.; —, v. a. matar atrozmente; matar en la carnicería. [tadero, m.
slaughter-house, *—hŏs*, s. rastro, ma-
slaughterer, *—ŭr*, s. matador, asesino, m.
slave, *slāv*, s. esclavo, m.; esclava, f.; —, v. n. trabajar como esclavo. [m. (navío).
slaver, *—ŭr*, slave-ship, *—shĭp*,s. negrero,
slaver, *slăv'ŭr*, s. baba, f.; —, v. n. babosear.
slavery, *slā'vŭrĕ*, s. esclavitud, f.
slavish, *slā'vĭsh*, a. servil, humilde; —ly, ad. servilmente. [f.
slavishness, *—nĕs*, s. bajeza, servidumbre,
slay, *slā*, v. a. matar, quitar la vida.
slayer, *—ŭr*, s. matador, m.
sled, *slĕd*, sledge, *slĕj*, sleigh, *slā*, s. rastra, narria, f.; trineo, m. [m.
sledge-hammer, *slĕj'hămmŭr*, s. macho,
sleek, *slēk*, a. liso, bruñido; —, v. a. alisar, pulir.
sleep, *slēp*, v. n. dormir; —, s. sueño, m.
sleeper, *—ŭr*, s. zángano, m.; travesaño, m.
sleepily, *—lĕ*, ad. con somnolencia ó torpeza.
sleepiness, *—ĭnĕs*, s. adormecimiento, m.
sleeping-room, *—ĭngrŏm*, s. dormitorio, m.
sleepless, *—lĕs*, a. desvelado. [m.
sleep-walking, *—wäkĭng*, s. sonambulis-
sleepy, *—ĕ*, a. soñoliento. [mo, m.
sleet, *slēt*, s. aguanieve, f.; —, v. n. caer
sleeve, *slēv*, s. manga, f. [aguanieve,

sleight, *slīt,* s. astucia, maña, f.
slender, *slĕn'dạr,* a. delgado, sútil, débil, pequeño, escaso; **—ly,** ad. delgadamente.
slenderness, *—nĕs,* s. delgadez, f.; tenuidad, f.; pequeñez, f. [f.; **—** v. a. rebanar.
slice, *slīs,* s. rebanada, longa, f.; espátula,
slide, *slīd,* v. n. resbalar, deslizarse; correr por encima del hielo; **—,** s. resbalón, m.; resbaladero, m.; corredera, f.
sliding, *slīd'ĭng,* s. deslizamiento, m.
slight, *slīt,* a. ligero, leve, pequeño **;—,** s. descuido, m.; **—,** v. a. despreciar.
slightingly, *—inglĕ,* ad. con desprecio.
slightly, *—lĕ,* ligeramente.   [gencia, f.
slightness, *—nĕs,* s. debilidad, f.; negli-
slim, *slĭm,* a. delgado, sútil.
slime, *slīm,* s. lodo, m.; substancia viscosa.
sliminess, *slī'mĭnĕs,* s. viscosidad, f.   [f.
slimy, *slī'mĕ,* a. viscoso, pegajoso.
sling, *slĭng,* s. honda, f.; hondazo, m.; **—,** v. a. tirar con honda.
slink, *slĭngk,* v. n. escaparse; esconderse.
slip, *slĭp,* v. n. resbalar; escapar, huirse; **—,** v. a. meter ó introducir secretamente; dejar; **—,** s. resbalón, m.; tropiezo, m.; escapada, f.
slipper, *—pạr,* s. chinela, f.   [diza, f.
slipperiness, *—pạrĭnĕs,* s. calidad resbala-
slippery, *—pạrĕ,* a. resbaladizo.
slip-shod, *—shŏd,* a. en chancletas.
slip-slop, *—slŏp,* s. aguachirle, f.
slit, *slĭt,* v. a. rajar, hender; **—,** s. raja, hendedura, f.
slobber, *slŏb'bạr,* s. baba, f.   [dedura, f.
sloe, *slō,* s. endrina, f.
sloop, *slōp,* s. (mar.) balandra, f.
slop, *slŏp,* s. aguachirle, f.; lodazal, m.; **—s,** pl. gregüescos, m. pl.
slope, *slōp,* s. sesgo, m.; declivio, m.; escarpa, f.; **—,** v. a. sesgar.
sloping, *slō'pĭng,* a. oblicuo; declive.
slop-pail, *slŏp'pál,* s. cubeta, f.
sloppy, *slŏp'pĕ,* a. lodoso.
sloth, *slōth,* s. pereza, f.; perezoso, m. (animal de América).
slothful, *—fŭl,* a. perezoso.
slouch, *slŏutsh,* v. a. & n. estar cabizbajo (como un patán); bambolearse pesadamente.
slough, *slŏ,* s. lodazal, m.; **—,** *slŏff,* pellejo de serpiente, m.; escara, f. (de una llaga, etc.)
sloughy, *slŏ'ĕ,* a. lodoso.   [herida].
sloven, *slŭv'ĕn,* s. hombre desaliñado, m.
slovenliness, *—lĭnĕs,* s. desaliño, m.; porquería, f.
slovenly, *—lĕ,* a. desaliñado, puerco, sucio.
slow, *slō,* a. tardío, lento, torpe, perezoso; **—ly** ad. lentamente.   [dez, f.
slowness, *—nĕs,* s. lentitud, tardanza, pesa-
slow-worm, *—wărm,* s. cecilia, f.
slug, *slŭg,* s. holgazán, zángano, m.; babosa, f.; pedazo de metal, m.
sluggard, *—gạrd,* s. haragán, holgazán, m.
sluggish, *—gĭsh,* a. perezoso; lento; **—ly,** ad. perezosamente.
sluggishness, *—nĕs,* s. pereza, f.
sluice, *slōs,* s. compuerta, f.; **—,** v. a. soltar la compuerta de un canal etc.

slum, *slŭm,* s. garito, m.; callejuela, f.; (vulg.) carta, f.   [sueño ligero, m.
slumber, *slŭm'bạr,* v. n. dormitar; **—,** s.
slur, *slạr,* v. a. ensuciar; pasar ligeramente; **—,** s. (mus.) ligado, m.
slush, *slŭsh,* s. lodo, barro, cieno, m.
slut, *slŭt,* mujer sucia, f.
sly, *slī,* a. astuto; **—ly,** ad. astutamente.
slyness, *—nĕs,* s. astucia, maña, f.
smack, *smăk,* s. sabor, gusto, m.; beso fuerte (que se oye), m.; chasquido de látigo, m.; **—,** v. n. saber; besar con ruido.
small, *smăl,* a. pequeño, menudo; **—,** s. parte estrecha de cualquiera cosa, f.
smallish, *—ĭsh,* a. algo pequeño.
smallness, *—nĕs,* s. pequeñez, f.
small-pox, *—pŏks,* s. viruelas, f. pl.
small-talk, *—tāk,* s. charla, prosa, f.
smalt, *smălt,* s. esmalte, m.
smart, *smărt,* s. escozor, m.; **—,** a. punzante, agudo, agrio; ingenioso; mordaz; doloroso; **—,** v. n. escocer.
smartly, *—lĕ,* ad. agudamente, vivamente.
smartness, *—nĕs,* s. agudeza, viveza, sutileza, f.   [**—,** s. fracaso, m.
smash, *smăsh,* v. a. romper, quebrantar;
smatterer, *smăt'ạrạr,* s. erudito á la violeta, m.   [superficial, m.
smattering, *smăt'tạrĭng,* s. conocimiento
smear, *smēr,* v. a. untar; emporcar.
smell, *smĕl,* v. a. & n. oler; percibir; **—,** s. olfato, m.; olor, m.; hediondez, f.
smelling-bottle, *—ĭngbŏttl,* s. pomito de olor, m.   [v. a. fundir (el metal).
smelt, *smĕlt,* s. espirenque de mar, m.; **—,**
smelter, *—ạr,* s. fundidor, m.
smile, *smīl,* v. n. sonreirse; **—,** s. sonrisa, f.
smirk, *smạrk,* v. n. sonreirse.
smite, *smīt,* v. a. herir, golpear.
smith, *smĭth,* s. forjador de metales, m.
smithery, *—ạrĕ,* s. smithy, *—ĕ,* s. herrería, f.
smock, *smŏk,* s. camisa de mujer, f.
smock-frock, *—frŏk,* s. blusa, f.
smoke, *smŏk,* s. humo, m.; vapor, m.; **—,** v. a. & n. ahumar; humear; fumar (tobacco).
smoke-consumer, *—kŏnsūmạr,* s. locomotora fumívora, f.   [humo.
smoke-dry, *—drī,* v. a. ahumar; secar al
smokeless, *—lĕs,* a. sin humo.
smoker, *—ạr,* s. fumador, m.
smoky, *smŏ'kĕ,* a. humeante; humoso.
smooth, *smŏth,* a. liso, pulido, llano; suave; afable; **—,** s. (am.) pradería, f.; **—,** v. a. allanar; alisar; lisonjear.   [dura.
smoothly, *—lĕ,* ad. llanamente; con blan-
smoothness, *—nĕs,* s. lisura; llanura; suavidad, f.   [mir; **—,** s. humareda, f.
smother, *smăth'ạr,* v. a. sufocar; supri-
smoulder, *smōl'dạr,* v. n. aclocarse; arder debajo la ceniza.   [graba, mugre, f.
smudge, *smŭj,* v. a. ahogar, asfixiar; **—,** s.
smug, *smŭg,* a. atildado, nimiamente compuesto.   [matutear.
smuggle, *—gl,* v. a. hacer el contrabando,
smuggler, *—glạr,* s. contrabandista, m.
smuggling, *—glĭng,* s. contrabando, m.
smut, *smŭt,* s. tizñon, m.; suciedad, f.; **—,** v. a. tizñar; ensuciar.

smuttily, –*tĭlĕ*, ad. suciamente.　[dad, f.
smuttiness, –*tĭnĕs*, s. tizne, m.; obsceni-
smutty, –*tĕ*,a.tiznado ; anieblado; obsceno.
snack, *snăk*, s. parte, porción, f.
snaffle, *snăf'fl*, s. brida con muserola, f.
snag, *snăg*, s. dentadura, f.; coreova, f.;
　nudo en la madera, m.
snail, *snāl*, s. caracol, m.
snake, *snāk*, s. culebra, f.
snaky, *sad'kĕ*, a. serpentino.
snap, *snăp*, v. a. & n. romper ; agarrar;
　morder; insultar; (one's fingers) cas-
　tañetear; –, s. estallido, m.　　　　[m.
snapdragon, –*drăgon*, s. (bot.) antirrino,
snappers, –*pŭrz*, s. pl. castañetas, f. pl.
snappish, –*pĭsh*, a. mordaz; regañón;
　–ly, ad. agriamente.　　　　　[el truto, m.
snappishness, –*pĭshnĕs*, s. despego en
snare, *snār*, s. lazo, m.; trampa, f.
snarl, *snärl*, v. n. regañar, gruñir.
snarler, –*ăr*, s. regañón, m.
snast, *snăst*, s. pábilo de una vela, m.
snatch, *snătsh*, v. a. arrebatar; agarrar;
　–, s. arrebatamiento, m.; arrebatiña, f.
　bocado, m.　　　　　　　　　[servil, m.
sneak, *snēk*, v. n. arrastrar; –, s. hombre
sneer, *snēr*, v. n. hablar con desprecio;
　fisgarse; –, s. fisga, f.
sneeringly, –*ĭnglĕ*, ad. con desprecio.
sneeze, *snēz*, v. n. estornudar.　　[arriba.
sniff, *snĭf*, v. n. resollar con fuerza hacia
snigger, *snĭg'gŭr*, v. n. reir á menudo.
snip, *snĭp*, v. a. tijeretear ; –, s. tijeretada,
　f., pedazo pequeño, m.; porción, f.
snipe, *snĭp*, s. agachadiza, f.; zopenco, m.
snivel, *snĭv'l*, s. moquita, f.; – v. n. mo-
sniveller, –*ŭr*, s. lloraduelos, m.　　[quear.
snob, *snŏb*, s. medrado, m.; galopín, m.
snobbish, –*bĭsh*, a. á manera de medrado.
snood, *snŏd*, a. peripuesto; liso.
snooze, *snŏz*, s. sueño ligero, m.
snore, *snōr*, v. n. roncar; –, s. ronquido, m.
snort, *snŏrt*, v. n. resoplar (bufar como
　un caballo fogoso).　　　　　　　[fante, f.
snout, *snŏŭt*, s. hocico, m.; trompa de ele-
snow, *snō*, s. nieve, f.; – v. n. nevar.
snow-ball, –*băl*, s. pelota de nieve, f.
snow-drop, –*drŏp*, s. (bot.) campanilla
snow-slip, –*slĭp*, s. alud, m.　　[blanca, f.
snowy, –*ĕ*, a. nevoso; nevado.
snub, *snŭb*, v. a. reprender; regañar.
snub-nosed, –*nŏzd*, a. romo.
snuff, *snŭf*, s. moco de candela, m.; pábilo,
　m.; tabaco de polvo, m.; – v. a. atraer en
　la nariz con el aliento; despabilar; oler.
snuff-box, –*bŏks*, s. tabaquera, f.
snuffers, –*ŭrz*, s. pl. despabiladeras, f. pl.
snuffle, –*fl*, v.n.ganguear, hablar gangoso.
snuff-taker, –*tăkŭr*, s. tabaquista, m.
snug, *snŭg*, a. abrigado ; conveniente,
　cómodo, agradable, grato.
so, *sō*, ad. así ; tal ; de modo que; **and—
　forth,** y así de lo demás.
soak, *sōk*, v. n. & a. remojarse; calarse;
　empapar, remojar.
soaker, –*ŭr*, s. beberrón, m.
soap, *sōp*, s. jabón, m.; – v. a. jabonar.

soap-ball, –*băl*, s. bola de jabón, f.
soap-boiler, –*bōilŭr*, s. jabonero, m.
soap-bubble, –*băbl*, s.ampolla de jabón,f.
soap-suds, –*sŭdz*, s. jabonaduras, f. pl.
soapy, –*ĕ*, a. jabonoso.
soar, *sōr*, v. n. remontarse, sublimarse.
soaring, –*ĭng*, s. vuelo muy alto, m.
sob, *sŏb*, s. sollozo, m.; – v. n. sollozar.
sober, *sō'bŭr*, a. sobrio; serio; –ly, ad.
　sobriamente ; juiciosamente.
sobriety, *sōbrī'ĕtĕ*, s. sobriedad, f.; serie-
　dad, sangre fría, f.
sociability, *sōshăbĭl'ĭtĕ*, s. sociabilidad, f.
sociable, *sō'shăbl*, a. sociable, comuni-
sociably, –*ĕ*, ad. sociablemente.　[cativo.
social, *sō'shăl*, a. social, sociable; –ly, ad.
　sociablemente.
society, *sōsī'ĕtĕ*, s. sociedad, f.; compañía,
sock, *sŏk*, s. escarpín, m.; zueco, m.　[f.
socket, –*ĕt*, s. cañón del candelero, m.;
　cuenca del ojo, f.; alvéolo de un diente, m.
socle, *sō'kl*, s. zócalo, plinto, m.
sod, *sŏd*, s. césped, m.; turba, f.
soda, *sō'dă*, s. sosa, f.
soever, *sōĕv'ŭr*, c. que sea.
sofa, *sō'fă*, s. sofá, m.
soft, *sŏft*, a. blando, mole, suavecito; be-
　nigno, tierno ; jugoso ; afeminado ; –ly,
　ad. suavemente ; paso á paso.　[necer.
soften, *sŏf'n*, v.a.ablandar, mitigar; enter-
soft-hearted, *sŏft'härtĕd*, a. compasivo.
softness, *sŏf'nĕs*, s. blandura, dulzura, f.
soft-spoken, –*spŏkn*, a. afable.
soil, *sŏil*, v. a. ensuciar, emporcar; –, s.
　mancha, porquería, f.; terreno, m.; estiér-
　col, m.　　　　　[morada, f.; residencia, f.
sojourn, *sō'jŭrn*, v. n. residir, morar; –, s.
solace, *sŏl'ăs*, v. a. solazar, consolar; –,
solar, *sō'lŭr*, a. solar.　　[s. consuelo, m.
sold, *sŏld*, s. sueldo, estipendio, m.　[f.
solder, *sŏl'dŭr*, v. a. soldar; –, s.soldadura,
soldier, *sŏl'jŭr*, s. soldado, m.　[dadesco.
soldierlike, –*lĭk*, soldierly, –*lĕ*, a. sol-
soldiery, –*ĕ*, s. soldadesca, f.
sole, *sōl*, s. planta del pie, f.; suela del za-
　pato, f.; –, a. único, solo; – v. a. solar.
solecism, *sŏl'ĕsĭzm*, s. (gr.) solecismo, m.
solemn, *sŏl'ĕm*, a. –ly, ad. solemne(mente).
solemnity, *sōlĕm'nĭtĕ*, s. solemnidad, f.
solemnization, *sōlĕmnĭzā'shăn*, s. solem-
　nización, f.
solemnize, *sŏl'ĕmnĭz*, v. a. solemnizar.
solicit, *sōlĭs'ĭt*, v. a. solicitar; implorar.
solicitation, *sōlĭsĭtā'shăn*, s. solicitación,
　f.　　　　　　　　　　　　　　[tador, m.
solicitor, *sōlĭs'ĭtŭr*, s. procurador, solici-
solicitous, *sōlĭs'ĭtŭs*, a. solícito, diligente;
　–ly, ad. solícitamente.
solicitude, *sōlĭs'ĭtŭd*, s. solicitud, f.
solid, *sŏl'ĭd*, a. sólido, compacto; –ly, ad.
　sólidamente.
solidify, *sōlĭd'ĭfī*, v. a. solidificar.
solidity, *sōlĭd'ĭtĕ*, s. solidez, f.　　[solas.
soliloquize, *sōlĭl'ōkwĭz*, v. n. hablar á
soliloquy, *sōlĭl'ōkwĕ*, s. soliloquio, m.
solitaire, *sŏlĭtār'*, s. solitario, m., grueso
　diamante.
solitarily, *sŏl'ĭtărĭlĕ*, ad. solitariamente.

solitariness, *sŏl'ĭtărĭnĕs,* s. soledad, f.; retiro, m. [—, s. ermitaño, m.

solitary, *sŏl'ĭtărĭ,* a. solitario, retirado;

solitude, *sŏl'ĭtūd,* s. soledad, f.; vida solisolo, *sŏ'lŏ,* s. (mus.) solo, m. [taria, f.

solstice, *sŏl'stĭs,* s. solsticio, m.

soluble, *sŏl'ŭbl,* a. soluble.

solution, *sŏlū'shŭn,* s. solución, f.

solve, *sŏlv,* v. a. solver, disolver.

solvency, *sŏl'vĕnsĕ,* s. solvencia, f.

solvent, *—vĕnt,* a. solvente.

some, *sŭm,* a. algo de, un poco, algún, alguno, alguna, unos, pocos, ciertos.

somebody, *—bŏdĭ,* s. alguien, m.

somehow, *—hŏu,* ad. de algún modo.

somerset, *sŭm'ĕrsĕt,* **somersault,** *—sŏlt,* s. salto mortal, m.

something, *sŭm'thĭng,* s. alguna cosa, algo; —, ad. algún tanto. [guamente.

sometimes, *—tĭm,* ad. en algún tiempo, antisometimes, *—tĭmz,* ad. algunas veces.

somewhat, *—whŏt,* s. alguna cosa, algo; —, ad. algún tanto, un poco. [lugar.

somewhere, *—hwăr,* ad. en cualquier

somnambulism, *sŏmnăm'būlĭzm,* s. somnambulismo, m. [bulo, m.

somnambulist, *sŏmnăm'būlĭst,* s. sonámsomnolence, *sŏm'nŏlĕns,* s. somnolencia, f.

somnolent, *—lĕnt,* a. somnolente.

son, *sŭn,* s. hijo, m.

sonata, *sŏnä'tä,* s. (mus.) sonata, f.

song, *sŏng,* s. canción, f.; old —, cantinela.

songster, *—stăr,* s. cantor, m. [f.

songstress, *—strĕs,* s. cantatriz, f.

son-in-law, *—ĭnlŏ,* s. yerno, m.

sonnet, *sŏn'nĕt,* s. soneto, m.

sonorous, *sŏnō'rŭs,* a. sonoro; **-ly,** ad. sonoramente.

soon, *sŏn,* ad. presto, pronto; **as — as,** luego

sooner, *—ŭr,* ad. más pronto, primero que.

soonest, *—ĕst,* ad. cuanto antes.

soot, *sŭt,* s. hollín, m. [daderamente.

sooth, *sŏth,* s. verdad, f.; **in good —,** ver-

soothe, *sŏth,* v. a. adular; calmar.

soothsayer, *sŏth'sŭr,* s. adivino, m.

sooty, *sŭt'ĕ,* a. holliniento, fuliginoso.

sop, *sŏp,* s. sopa, f.

sophism, *sŏf'ĭzm,* s. sofisma, m.

sophist, *sŏf'ĭst,* s. sofista.

sophistic(al), *sŏfĭs'tĭk(ăl),* a. sofístico; falsificar.

sophisticate, *sŏfĭs'tĭkāt,* v. a. sofisticar;

sophistry, *sŏf'ĭstrĭ,* s. sofistería, f.

soporific, *sŏpŏrĭf'ĭk,* a. soporífero.

sorcerer, *sŏr'sŭrŭr,* s. hechicero, f.

sorceress, *sŏr'sŭrĕs,* s. hechicera, f.

sorcery, *sŏr'sŭrĕ,* s. hechizo, encanto, m.

sordid, *sŏr'dĭd,* a. sórdido, sucio; avariento; **-ly,** ad. codiciosamente. [dad, f.

sordidness, *—nĕs,* s. sordidez, mezquin-

sore, *sŏr,* s. llaga, úlcera, f.; —, a. doloroso, penoso; **-ly,** ad. penosamente.

soreness, *—nĕs,* s. dolencia, f.; mal, m.

sorrel, *sŏr'ĕl,* s. (bot.) acedera, f.; —, a. alazán rojo. [mente.

sorrily, *sŏr'rĭlĭ,* ad. malamente, pobre-

sorrow, *sŏr'rŏ,* s. pesar, m.; tristeza, f.; —, v. n. entristecerse.

sorrowful, *—fŭl,* a. pesaroso, afligido; **-ly,** ad. con aflicción. [for it, lo siento.

sorry, *sŏr'rĕ,* a. triste, afligido; **I am —**

sort, *sŏrt,* s. suerte, f.; género, m.; especie, f.; calidad, f.; manera, f.; —, v. a. separar en distintas clases; escoger, elegir.

sot, *sŏt,* s. zote, m. [pemente.

sottish, *—tĭsh,* a. torpe, rudo; **-ly,** ad. tor-

soul, *sōl,* s. alma, f.; esencia, f.; persona, f.

soul-bell, *—bĕl,* s. toque á agonía, m.

sound, *sŏund,* a. sano; entero; puro; firme; **-ly,** ad. sanamente, vigorosamente; —, s. tienta, sonda, f.; sonido, ruido, m.; —, v. a. sondar; tocar; celebrar; —, v. n. sonar, resonar.

sound(ing)-board, *—(ĭng) bŏrd,* s. diapasón, m.; sombrero de púlpito, m.

sounding-lead, *—(ĭng)lĕd,* s. escandallo, m.

sounding-line, *—lĭng,* s. sondalesa, f.

soundings, *—z,* s. pl. (mar.) sondeo, m.; (mar.) surgidero profundo, m. [lidez, f.

soundness, *—nĕs,* s. sanidad, f.; fuerza, so-

soup, *sŏp,* s. sopa, f.

sour, *sŏur,* a. agrio, ácido; áspero; **-ly,** ad. agriamente; —, v. a. & n. agriar, acedar; agriarse. [m.

source, *sŏrs,* s. manantial, m.; principio,

sourness, *sŏur'nĕs,* s. acedía, agrura, f.; acrimonia, f.

souse, *sŏus,* s. salmuera, f.; —, ad. (vulg.) zas, con violencia; —, v. a. escabechar; chapuzar.

south, *sŏuth,* s. mediodía, sud, sur, m.

southerly, *sŭ'thŭrlĭ,* **southern,** *sŭth'ŭrn,* a. meridional. [sudoeste.

southernmost, *—ŭrnmŏst,* a. sur cuarta al

southward, *sŏuthwŭrd,* ad. hacia el mediodía.

southwester, *sŏuthwĕst'ŭr,* s. (mar.) viento de sudoeste, m.; sombrero grande de los marineros, m.

sovereign, *sŏv'ŭrĭn,* a. & s. soberano (m.).

sovereignly, *—lĭ,* ad. soberanamente.

sovereignty, *—tĭ,* s. soberanía, f.

sow, *sŏ,* s. puerca, marrana, f.

sow, *sŏ,* v. a. sembrar; esparcir.

sowing-time, *—ĭng tĭm,* s. sementera, siembra, f.

space, *spăs,* s. espacio, m.; intersticio, m.

spacious, *spā'shŭs,* a. espacioso, amplio; **-ly,** ad. con bastante espacio.

spaciousness, *—nĕs,* s. espaciosidad, f.

spade, *spād,* s. laya, azada, f.; espadas, f. pl. (en los naipes). [palinos.

span, *spăn,* s. palmo, m.; —, v. a. medir á

spangle, *spăng'gl,* s. lentejuela, f.; —, v. a. adornar con lentejuelas.

spaniel, *spăn'yĕl,* s. sabueso, m.

Spanish fly, *spăn'ĭsh flī,* s. cantárida, f.

Spanish leather, *—lĕth'ŭr,* s. cordobán, m.

spar, *spăr,* s. espato, m.; —, v. n. fingir un combate á puñadas.

spare, *spăr,* v. a. & n. ahorrar, economizar; perdonar; vivir con economía; —, a. escaso, económico; **-ly,** ad. escasamente; **-ly built,** a. magro.

sparing, *spā'rĭng,* a. escaso, raro, económico; **-ly,** ad. parcamente, frugalmente.

sparingness, *–nĕs,* s. economía, f.

spark, *spärk,* s. chispa, f.; (poet.) centella, f.; pisaverde, m. [chispear; espumar.

sparkle, *–l,* s. centella, chispa, f.; –, v. n.

sparrow, *spăr'rŏ,* s. gorrión, pardal, m.

sparrow-hawk, *–hăk,* s. hembra del gavilán, f. [tenuemente.

sparse, *spärs,* a. delgado; tenue; **–ly,** ad.

spasm, *spăzm,* s. espasmo, m.

spasmodic, *spăzmŏd'ĭk,* a. espasmódico.

spatter, *spăt'tăr,* v. a. salpicar, manchar.

spatterdashes, *–dăshĕz,* s. pl. polainas.

spatula, *spăt'ŭlă,* s. espátula, f. [f. pl.

spavin, *spăv'ĭn,* s. esparaván, m.

spawn, *spăn,* s. freza, f.; –, v. a. & n. desovar; engendrar.

spawner, *–ăr,* s. hembra en los peces, f.

spawning, *–ing,* s. freza, f.

speak, *spēk,* v. a. & n. hablar; decir; arengar; conversar; pronunciar.

speaker, *–ăr,* s. el que habla; orador, m.

speaking-trumpet, *–ing trŭmpĕt,* s. bocina, f. [herir con lanza.

spear, *spēr,* s. lanza, f.; arpón, m.; –, v. a.

special, *spĕsh'ăl,* a. especial, particular; **–ly,** ad. especialmente. [cialidad, f.

specialty, *–tĕ,* **speciality,** *–ĭtĕ,* s. especie, f.

specie, *spĕsh'ĕ,* s. dinero contante, m.

species, *spē'shĕz,* s. especie, f.

specific(al), *spĕsĭf'ĭk(ăl),* a. específico; –, s. específico, m.

specifically, *–ăllĕ,* ad. en especie.

specification, *spĕsĭfĭkă'shŭn,* s. especificación, f.

specify, *spĕs'ĭfῑ,* v. a. especificar.

specimen, *spĕs'ĭmĕn,* s. muestra, f.; prueba, f. [**–ly,** ad. especiosamente.

specious, *spē'shăs,* a. especioso, hermoso;

speck(le), *spĕk(l),* s. mácula, tacha, f.; –, v. a. abigarrar, manchar.

spectacle, *spĕk'tăkl,* s. espectáculo, m.; **–s,** pl. anteojos, m. pl.

spectator, *spĕktā'tăr,* s. espectador, m.

spectral, *spĕk'trăl,* a. aduendado; espectométrico; **– analysis,** s. análisis del espectro solar, f.

spectre, *spĕk'tăr,* s. espectro, m.

speculate, *spĕk'ŭlāt,* v. n. especular; reflexionar.

speculation, *spĕkŭlā'shŭn,* s. especulación, f.; especulativa, f.; meditación, f.

speculative, *spĕk'ŭlātĭv,* a. especulativo, teórico.

speculum, *spĕk'ŭlŭm,* s. espejo, m.

speech, *spētsh,* s. habla, m.; arenga, f.; conversación, f.

speechify, *–ĭfῑ,* v. n. arengar.

speechless, *–lĕs,* a. mudo.

speed, *spēd,* s. priesa, f.; celeridad, f.; suceso, m.; –, v. a. apresurar; despachar; ayudar; –, v. n. darse priesa; salir bien.

speedily, *–ĭlĕ,* ad. aceleradamente, de priesa. [precipitación, f.

speediness, *–ĭnĕs,* s. celeridad, prontitud,

speedy, *–ĕ,* a. veloz, pronto, diligente.

spell, *spĕl,* s. hechizo, encanto, m.; –, v. a. & n. escribir correctamente; deletrear; hechizar, encantar.

spelling-book, *–ing bŭk,* s. silabario, m.

spelter, *spĕl'tăr,* s. zinc, m.

spend, *spĕnd,* v. a. gastar; disipar; consumir; –, v. n. hacer gastos; consumirse.

spendthrift, *–thrῑft,* s. pródigo, m.

spent, *spĕnt,* a. alcanzado de fuerzas.

sperm, *spŭrm,* s. esperma, m.

spermaceti, *spŭrmăsē'tĕ,* s. espermaceti, m.

spew, *spū,* v. n. (vulg.) vomitar.

sphere, *sfēr,* s. esfera, f.

spheric(al), *sfĕr'ĭk(ăl),* a. esférico; **–ly,** ad. en forma esférica. [a. especiar.

spice, *spῑs,* s. especia, f.; migaja, f.; –, v. a.

spick-and-span, *spĭk'ănd spăn',* a. flamante.

spicy, *spῑ'sĕ,* a. aromático.

spider, *spῑ'dăr,* s. araña, f.

spigot, *spĭg'ŏt,* s. llave de fuente, f.

spike, *spῑk,* s. espiga de grano, f.; espigón, m.; –, v. n. clavar con espigones.

spill, *spῑl,* v. a. derramar, verter; –, s. clavija, espiga, f.

spin, *spĭn,* v. a. hilar; alargar, prolongar; –, v. n. hilar; correr hilo á hilo.

spinach, spinage, *spĭn'āj,* s. espinaca, f.

spinal, *spῑ'năl,* a. espinal.

spindle, *spĭn'dl,* s. huso, m.; quicio, m.

spindle-legged, *–lĕggĕd,* **––shanked,** *–shănkă,* a. zanquivano.

spine, *spῑn,* s. espinazo, m. espina, f.

spinet, *spĭn'nĕt,* s. (mus.) espineta, f.

spinner, *spĭn'năr,* s. hilador, m.; hilandera, f.

spinney, *spĭn'nĕ,* s. maleza, f. [dera, f.

spinning-jenny, *spĭn'ning jĕnnĕ,* s. máquina de hilar, f. [de hilar.

spinning-wheel, *–hwĕl,* s. torno de hilar,

spinster, *spĭn'stăr,* s. hilandera, f.; doncella, soltera, f. [de espiral.

spiral, *spῑ'răl,* a. espiral; **–ly,** ad. en figura

spire, *spῑr,* s. espira, f.; pirámide, m.; aguja, f. (de una torre)

spirit, *spĭr'ĭt,* s. aliento, m.; espíritu, m.; ánimo, valor, m.; brío, m.; humor, m.; fantasma, m.; –, v. a. incitar, animar; **to – away,** quitar secretamente.

spirited, *–ĕd,* a. vivo, brioso; **–ly,** ad. con espíritu.

spirit-lamp, *–lămp,* s. velón ó quinqué alimentado con alcohol, m.

spiritless, *–lĕs,* a. abatido, sin espíritu.

spiritual, *–ŭăl,* a. **–ly,** ad. espiritual(mente).

spiritualist, *–ădĭst,* s. espiritualista, m.

spirituality, *spῑrĭtŭăl'ĭtĕ,* s. espiritualidad, inmaterialidad, f.

spirituous, *spĭr'ĭtŭăs,* a. espirit(u)oso.

spirt, *spŭrt,* v. a. & n. arrojar un líquido en un chorro; jeringar. [tar; escupir.

spit, *spĭt,* s. asador, m.; –, v. a. & n. asaespit,

spite, *spῑt,* s. rencor, m.; malevolencia, f.; **in – of,** á pesar de, á despecho; –, v. a. dar pesar.

spiteful, *–fŭl,* a. rencoroso, malicioso; **–ly,** ad. malignamente, con tirria. [m.

spitefulness, *–fŭlnĕs,* s. malicia, f., rencor,

spitfire, *spĭt'fῑr,* s. locarias, m.

spittle, *spĭt'tl,* s. saliva, f.; esputo, m.

spittoon, *spĭttŏn',* s. escupidera, f.

splash, *splăsh,* v. a. salpicar, enlodar.

splash-board, -*bôrd*, s. mantelete, m.
splay, *splâ*, v. a. despaldar á un caballo.
splay-footed, -*fútéd*, a. patiestevado.
spleen, *splén*, s. bazo, m.; esplin, m.
splendid, *splén'dúd*, a. espléndido, magnífico; -ly, ad. espléndidamente.
splendour, *splén'dúr*, s. esplendor, m.; pompa, f.
splenetic(al), *splénét'ĭk(ăl)*, a. atrabiliario.
splice, *splīs*, v. a. (mar.) empalmar, empleitar.   [zales, m. pl.
splint, *splĭnt*, s. astilla, f.; -s, pl. brasinter, *splĭn'tăr*, s. cacho, m.; astilla, f.;
splinter, *splĭn'tăr*, s. cacho, m.; astilla, f.; brisna, f.; -, v. a. (& n.) hender(se).
split, *splĭt*, v. a. hender, rajar; -, v. n. henderse.
spoil, *spŏil*, v. a. pillar, robar; despojar; arruinar; -, v. n. corromperse, dañarse; -, s. despojo, botín, m.; ruina, f.
spoiler, -*ăr*, s. corruptor, robador, m.
spoke, *spŏk*, s. rayo de la rueda, m.
spokesman, *spŏks'măn*, s. interlocutor, m.
spoliate, *spŏ'lĭât*, v. a. robar, pillar.
spoliation, *spŏlĭă'shăn*, s. despojo, m.; espoliación de bienes, f.
sponge, *spŭnj*, s. esponja, f.; -, v. a. limpiar con esponja; -, v. n. meterse de mogollón.
sponge-bath, -*băth*, s. baño inglés, m.
sponger, -*ăr*, s. pegote, mogollón, m.
sponginess, *spŭnj'ĭnés*, s. calidad esponjosa, f.
sponging-house, *spŭnj'ĭnghŏŭs*, s. casa adonde llevan á los deudores insolventes antes de ponerlos en la cárcel, f.
spongy, *spŭnj'ĭ*, a. esponjoso.
sponsor, *spŏn'săr*, s. fiador, m.; padrino, m.; madrina, f.   [dad, voluntariedad, f.
spontaneity, *spŏntănĕ'ĭtĭ*, s. espontaneidad, f.
spontaneous, *spŏntă'nĕăs*, a. espontáneo; -ly, ad. espontáneamente.
spool, *spŏl*, s. canilla, broca, f.
spoon, *spŏn*, s. cuchara, f.
spoonful, -*fúl*, s. cucharada, f.
sporadic(al), *spŏrăd'ĭk(ăl)*, a. esporádico.
sport, *sport*, s. juego, retozo, m.; juguete, divertimiento, recreo, pasatiempo, m.; -, v. a. divertirse; -, v. n. chancear, juguetear.
sportive, -*ĭv*, a. festivo, juguetón.   [tear.
sportiveness, -*ĭvnés*, s. festividad, holganza, f.   [á la pesca &c., m.
sportsman, -*s'măn*, s. aficionado á la caza, m.
spot, *spŏt*, s. mancha, f.; borrón, m.; sitio, lugar, m.; -, v. a. abigarrar; manchar.
spotless, -*lés*, a. limpio, inmaculado.
spotted, -*téd*, spotty, -*tĭ*, a. lleno de manchas, sucio.   [matrimonial, nupcial.
spousal, *spŏu'zăl*, s. nupcias, f. pl.; -, a.
spouse, *spŏŭz*, s. esposo, m.; esposa, f.
spout, *spŏut*, v. a. & n. arrojar agua con mucho ímpetu; borbotar; chorrear; estar de hocico; -, s. llave de fuente, f.; gárgola, f.; bomba marina, f.   [locación, f.
sprain, *sprân*, a. descoyuntar; -, s. dislocación.
sprat, *sprăt*, v. n. bregar; revolcarse.
sprawl, *sprăl*, v. n. bregar; revolcarse.
spray, *sprâ*, s. leña menuda, f.; vástago, m.; espuma de la mar, f.

spread, *sprĕd*, v. a. extender, desplegar; esparcir, divulgar; -, v. n. extenderse, desplegarse; -, s. extensión, dilatación, f.
spree, *sprē*, s. fiesta, f., festín, m.
sprig, *sprĭg*, s. ramito.   [cidad, f.
sprightliness, *sprīt'lĭnés*, s. alegría, vivacidad, f.
sprightly, *sprīt'lĭ*, a. alegre, despierto; vivaracho.
spring, *sprĭng*, v. n. brotar, arrojar; nacer, provenir; dimanar, originarse; saltar, brincar; -, v. a. ojear la caza; hacer volar; -, s. primavera, f.; elasticidad, f.; muelle, resorte, m.; salto, m.; manantial, m.; hendidura, f.
springe, *sprĭnj*, s. lazo de cazador, m.
springiness, *sprĭng'ĭnés*, s. elasticidad, f.
spring-tide, *sprĭng'tĭd*, s. marea viva, f.
spring-water, -*wătăr*, s. agua de fuente, f.
springy, *sprĭng'ĭ*, a. elástico.   [f.
sprinkle, *sprĭng'kl*, v. a. rociar; hisopear; salpimentar.
sprinkling, -*ĭng*, s. viso, tinte, m.; brizna, f.
sprite, *sprĭt*, s. espíritu, m.; fantasma, f.
sprout, *sprŏut*, s. vástago, renuevo, m.; -s, pl. bretones, m. pl.; -, v. n. brosar.
spruce, *sprŏs*, a. pulido, gentil; -ly, ad. bellamente, lindamente; -, v. n. vestirse con afectación.   [f.
spruceness, -*nés*, s. lindeza, hermosura, f.
spume, *spăm*, s. espuma, f.; -, v. n. espumar.
spur, *spăr*, s. espuela, f.; espolón (del gallo), m.; estímulo, m.; -, v. a. espolear; estimular.   [trabecho; supuesto; bastardo.
spurious, *spă'rĭăs*, a. espurio, falso; contrahecho; supuesto; bastardo.
spurn, *spărn*, v. a. acocear; despreciar.
sputter, *spăt'tăr*, v. n. escupir con frecuencia; babosear; barbotar.
sputterer, -*ăr*, s. faramallón, m.
spy, *spī*, s. espía, m.; -, v. a. & n. espiar; -, v. n. espiar.   [m.
spy-glass, -*glăs*, s. anteojo de larga vista, m.
squab, *skwŏb*, a. implume; cachigordo, regordete; -, s. canapé, m.; cojín, m.; pichón, m.   [riña, disputa, f.
squabble, -*bl*, v. n. reñir, disputar; -, s. riña, disputa, f.
squabbler, -*blăr*, s. pendenciero, m.
squad, *skwŏd*, s. escuadra de soldados, f.
squadron, -*rŏn*, s. (mil.) escuadrón, m.
squalid, *skwŏl'ĭd*, a. sucio, puerco.
squall, *skwăl*, s. fugada, f.; chubasco, m.; -, v. n. chillar.
squally, -*ĭ*, a. borrascoso.
squalor, *skwŏl'lăr*, s. porquería, suciedad, f.
squander, *skwŏn'dăr*, v. a. malgastar, disipar.
square, *skwăr*, a. cuadrado, cuadrángulo; exacto; cabal; -, s. cuadro, m.; plaza, f.; escuadra, f.; -, v. a. cuadrar; ajustar, arreglar; -, v. n. ajustarse.
squareness, -*nés*, s. cuadratura, f.
squash, *skwŏsh*, v. a. aplastar.
squat, *skwŏt*, v. n. agacharse; -, a. agachado; rechoncho.   [m.
squatter, -*tăr*, s. (am.) colono usurpador, m.
squaw, *skwă*, s. hembra de un indiano, f.
squeak, *skwēk*, v. n. plañir, chillar; -, s. grito, plañido, m.
squeal, *skwēl*, v. n. plañir, gritar.

squeamish — statue

squeamish, *skwēm'ĭsh*, a. fastidioso; demasiado delicado.

squeeze, *skwēz*, v. a. apretar, comprimir; estrechar; —, s. compresión, f.

squib, *skwĭb*, s. cohete, m.

squint, *skwĭnt*, a. ojizaino; bizco; —, v. n. bizquear. [de cortesía]

Squire, *skwīr*, s. Caballero, m. (tratamiento

squirrel, *skwĭr'rĭl*, s. ardilla, f.

squirt, *skwŭrt*, v. a. jeringar; —, s. jeringa, f.; chorro, m.; (am.) pisaverde, m.

stab, *stăb*, v. a. matar á puñaladas; —, s. puñalada, f. [f.

stability, *stăbĭl'ĭtē*, s. estabilidad, solidez,

stable, *stā'bl*, s. establo, m.; —, v. a. poner en el establo; —, a. estable.

stabling, *stā'blĭng*, s. caballerizas, f. pl.

stack, *stăk*, s. niara, f.; —, v. a. hacinar.

staff, *stăf*, s. báculo, palo, m.; apoyo, m.; (mil.) estado mayor, m.

stag, *stăg*, s. ciervo, m.

stage, *stāj*, s. tablado, m.; teatro, m.; parada, f.; escalón, m. [perimentado, m.

stager, *stā'jâr*, s. cómico, m.; hombre ex-

stagger, *stăg'gâr*, v. n. vacilar, titubear; estar incierto; —, v. a. asustar; hacer vacilar. [nd'shăn, s. estagnación, f.

stagnancy, *stăg'nănsē*, **stagnation**, *stăg-*

stagnant, *stăg'nănt*, a. estancado.

stagnate, *–ndt*, v. n. estancarse.

staid, *stăd*, a. grave, serio.

staidness, *–nĕs*, s. gravedad, f.

stain, *stăn*, v. a. manchar; empañar la reputación; —, s. mancha, f.; deshonra, f.

stainer, *–âr*, s. tintorero, m.

stainless, *lĕs*, a. limpio; inmaculado.

stair, *stăr*, s. escalón, m.; —s, pl. escalera.

staircase, *–kās*, s. escalera, f. [f.

stake, *stāk*, s. estaca, f.; posta, f. (en el juego); —, v. a. estacar; poner en el juego.

stale, *stāl*, a. añejo, viejo, rancio; —, s. orina, f.; —, v. n. orinar.

staleness, *–nĕs*, s. vejez, f.; rancidez, f.

stalk, *stăk*, v. n. andar con paso majestuoso; —, s. paso orgulloso, m.; tallo, pie, tronco, m.; troncho, m. (de ciertas hortalizas).

stalking-horse, *–ĭnghŏrs*, s. caballo verdadero ó figurado que sirve á los cazadores para ocultarse y cazar, m.; máscara, f.; disfraz, m.

stall, *stăl*, s. pesebre, m.; tienda portátil, f.; tabanco, m.; silla, f. (de coro); butaca en el teatro, f.; —, v. a. meter en el establo.

stallion, *stăl'yăn*, s. caballo padre, m.

stalwart, *–wŭrt*, a. robusto, vigoroso.

stamen, *stăm'ĕn*, s. estambre, m.; fundamento, m. [m. pl.

stamina, *stăm'ĭnă*, s. pl. (bot.) estambres,

stammer, *stăm'mĭr*, v. n. tartamudear.

stammerer, *–âr*, s. tartamudo, m.

stamp, *stămp*, v. a. patear; moler, majar; estampar, imprimir; acuñar; andar con mucha pesadez; —, s. cuño, m.; sello, m.; impresión, f.; estampa, f. [pánico, m.

stampede, *stămpēd'*, s. (am.) susto, terror

stanch, *stănsh*, v. a. (& n.) estancar(se); —, a. sano; firme, seguro, zeloso.

stand, *stănd*, v. n. estar en pie ó derecho; sostenerse; resistir; permanecer; pararse; hacer alto, estar situado; hallarse; erizarse el pelo; —, v. a. sostener, defender; —, s. puesto, sitio, m.; posición, situación, f.; parada, f.; embarazo, m.; estado, m. (fijo); velador para poner la luz, m.; estante, vasar, m.

standard, *–ârd*, s. estandarte, m.; modelo, m.; precio ordinario, m.; norma, f.

standing, *–ĭng*, a. permanente, fijado; establecido; estancado; —, s. duración, f.; posición, f.; puesto, m.

stand-still, *–stĭl*, s. pausa, f.; alto, m.

staple, *stā'pl*, s. emporio de comercio, m.; escala de depósito, f.; cerradero, m.; —, a. ajustado, establecido.

star, *stär*, s. estrella, f.; asterisco, m.

starboard, *–bôrd*, s. estribor, m. [donar.

starch, *stärtsh*, s. almidón, m.; —, v. a. almi-

stare, *stär*, v. a. clavar la vista; —, s. mirada fija, f.

staringly, *stär'ĭnglē*, ad. brillantemente.

stark, *stärk*, a. fuerte, áspero; puro; —, ad. del todo.

starless, *stär'lĕs*, a. sin estrellas.

starling, *stär'lĭng*, s. estornino, m.; esquina del estribo de un puente, f.

starred, *stärd*, **starry**, *stär'rē*, a. estrellado.

start, *stärt*, v. n. sobrecogerse, sobresaltarse, estremecerse; levantarse de repente; salir los caballos en las carreras; —, v. a. sobrecoger; suscitar; descubrir; —, s. sobresalto, m.; ímpetu, m.; paso primero, m.

starter, *–âr*, s. el oficial que da la salida en las carreras; hombre pavorido, m.

starting-point, *–ĭngpŏĭnt*, s. poste de salida, m. (en las carreras).

startle, *stär'tl*, v. n. sobresaltarse, estremecerse de repente; —, s. espanto, susto repentino, m. [brē, inanición, f.

starvation, *stärvā'shăn*, s. muerte de ham-

starve, *stärv*, v. n. perecer de hambre. [m.

starveling, *–lĭng*, s. hombre hambriento,

state, *stāt*, s. estado, m.; condición, f.; Estado (político); pompa, grandeza, f.; —, v. a. ajustar, arreglar. [f.

stateliness, *–lĭnĕs*, s. grandeza, pompa,

stately, *–lē*, a. augusto, majestuoso.

statement, *–mĕnt*, s. relación, cuenta, f.

statesman, *–s'măn*, s. estadista, político,

statesmanship, *–shĭp*, s. política, f. [m.

statics, *stăt'ĭks*, s. estática, f.

station, *stā'shăn*, s. estación, f.; empleo, puesto, m.; situación, postura, f.; grado, m.; condición, f.; (rail.) estación, f.; **intermediate—**, estación auxiliar de señales; —, v. a. apostar.

stationary, *–ârē*, a. estacionario, fijo.

stationer, *–âr*, s. librero-papelero, m.

stationery, *–ârē*, s. toda especie de papel y demás cosas necesarias para escribir, f.

statist, *stā'tĭst*, s. estadista, m.

statistic(al), *stătĭs'tĭk(ăl)*, a. estadístico.

statistics, *stătĭs'tĭks*, s. pl. estadística, f.

statuary, *stăt'ūârē*, s. estatuario, escultor, m.

statue, *stăt'ū*, s. estatua, f. [m.

stature, *stăt'ŭr*, s. estatura, talla, f. |m.
statute, *stăt'ŭt*, s. estatuto, m.; reglamento
stave, *stāv*, v. a. descabezar algún barril;
   —s, s. pl. duelas de barril, f. pl.
stay, *stā*, s. estancia, mansión, f.; —s, s. pl.
   corsé, justillo, m.; —, v. n. quedarse,
   estarse; tardar, detenerse; aguardarse, es-
   perarse; —, v. a. detener; contener; apoyar.
stead, *stĕd*, s. lugar, sitio, paraje, m.
steadfast, *–făst*, a. firme, estable, sólido;
   –ly, ad. firmemente, con constancia.
steadfastness, *–făstnĕs*, s. firmeza, constancia, f.   [mente.
steadily, *–ĭlĭ*, ad. firmemente; invariable-
steadiness, *–ĭnĕs*, s. firmeza, estabilidad, f.   [firme.
steady, *–ĭ*, a. firme, fijo; —, v. a. hacer
steak, *stāk*, s. tajada de carne cocida ó
   asada, f.
steal, *stēl*, v. a. & n. hurtar, robar; introducirse clandestinamente; escapar sin ser
   visto.   [dillas.
stealth, *stĕlth*, s. hurto, m.; **by —**, á hurta-
stealthily, *–ĭlĭ*, ad. furtivamente.
stealthy, *–ĭ*, a. furtivo.
steam, *stēm*, s. vapor, m.; —, v. n. vahear;
   to — it, viajar ó navegar á vapor.
steam-bath, *–băth*, s. baño de vapor, m.
steam-boiler, *–bŏilŭr*, s. caldera de una
   máquina de vapor, f.
steam-carriage, *–kărrĭj*, s. (rail.) locomotora, f.; (rail.) vagón, m.   [vapor, f.
steam-engine, *–ĕnjĭn*, s. máquina de
steamer, *stēm'ŭr*, **steam-boat**, *–bŏt*,
   steam-vessel, *–vĕsl*, s. vapor, buque
   de vapor, m.
steed, *stēd*, s. caballo de regalo, m.
steel, *stēl*, s. acero, m.; eslabón, m.; —,
   v. a. acerar; fortalecer, endurecer.
steelyard, *–yărd*, s. romana, f.
steep, *stēp*, a. escarpado; —, s. precipicio,
   m.; —, v. a. empapar.
steeple, *–l*, s. torre, f.; campanario, m.
steeple-chase, *–tshās*, s. carrera ciega, f.
steepness, *–nĕs*, s. precipicio, m.; escarpa,
   f.   [nar.
steer, *stēr*, s. novillo, m.; —, v. a. gober-
steerage, *–ĭj*, s. gobierno, m.; (mar.) antecámara de un navío, f.
steerage-way, *–wā*, s. (mar.) estela, f.
stellar, *stĕl'lŭr*, a. estrellado.
stem, *stĕm*, s. vástago, tallo, m.; estirpe,
   f.; (mar.) branque, m.; —, v. a. cortar la
stench, *stĕnsh*, s. hedor, m.   [corriente.
stencil, *stĕn'sĭl*, s. patrón, dechado, m.
stenographer, *stĕnŏg'răfŭr*, s. estenógrafo, m.
stenographic(al), *stĕnŏgrăf'ĭk(ăl)*, a.
   estenográfico.   [f.
stenography, *stĕnŏg'răfĭ*, s. estenografía,
step, *stĕp*, s. paso, escalón, m.; huella, f.;
   —, v. n. dar un paso; andar.
step-brother, *–brŭthŭr*, s. medio hermano
step-daughter, *–dătŭr*, s. hijastra, f. |m.
step-father, *–făthŭr*, s. padrastro, m.
step-mother, *–mŭthŭr*, s. madrastra, f.
stepping-stone, *–pĭngstōn*, s. pasadera, f.
step-sister, *–sĭstŭr*, s. media hermana, f.

step-son, *–sŭn*, s. hijastro, m.
stereotype, *stĕr'ĕŏtĭp*, s. estereotipía, f.;
   —, v. a. estereotipar.
sterile, *stĕr'ĭl*, a. estéril.
sterility, *stĕrĭl'ĭtĭ*, s. esterilidad, f.
sterling, *stŭr'lĭng*, a. esterlín, genuino,
   verdadero; —, s. moneda esterlina, f.
stern, *stŭrn*, a. austero, rígido, severo;
   —, s. (mar.) popa, f.; -ly, ad. austeramente.
stertorous, *stŭr'tŏrŭs*, a. roncador.
stethoscope, *stĕth'ŏskōp*, s. (med.) este-
   toscopio, m.   [m.
stevedore, *stĕv'ĕdōr*, s. (mar.) estivador,
stew, *stū*, v. a. estofar; —, s. estufa, f.
steward, *–ŭrd*, s. mayordomo, m.; (mar.)
   despensero, m.
stewardship, *–shĭp*, s. mayordomía, f.
stew-pan, *–păn*, s. cazuela, f.
stick, *stĭk*, s. palo, palillo, bastón, m.;
   vara, f.; —, v. a. pegar, hincar; picar,
   punzar; —, v. n. pegarse; detenerse; perseverar; dudar.
stickiness, *–nĕs*, s. viscosidad, f.
stickle, *–l*, v. n. tomar partido; disputar.
stickler, *–lŭr*, s. padrino en un duelo,
   m.; partidario, m.
sticky, *–ĭ*, a. viscoso, tenaz.
stiff, *stĭf*, a. tieso; duro, torpe; rígido;
   obstinado; -ly, ad. obstinadamente.
stiffen, *stĭf'fn*, v. a. atiesar, endurecer; —,
   v. n. endurecerse.   [tuerto, m.
stiff-neck, *–nĕk*, s. torticolí, m.; cabiz-
stiffness, *–nĕs*, s. tesura, rigidez, f.; obstina-
stifle, *stĭ'fl*, v. a. sufocar.   [ción, f.
stigma, *stĭg'mă*, s. nota de infamia, f.
stigmatize, *–tīz*, v. a. infamar, manchar.
stile, *stīl*, s. portillo con escalones, m. (para-
   pasar de un cercado á otro); gnomon, m.;
   estilo, m.
stiletto, *stĭlĕt'tŏ*, s. verduguillo, m.
still, *stĭl*, v. a. aquietar, aplacar; destilar;
   —, a. silencioso, tranquilo; —, s. silencio,
   m.; alambique, m.; —, ad. todavía; siempre, hasta ahora; no obstante.
still-born, *–bŏrn*, a. nacido muerto.
stillness, *–nĕs*, s. calma, quietud, f.
stilts, *stĭlts*, s. pl. zancos, m. pl.
stimulant, *stĭm'ŭlănt*, s. estimulante, m.
stimulate, *–ŭlāt*, v. a. estimular, aguijonear.
stimulation, *stĭmŭlā'shŭn*, s. estímulo,
   m.; estimulación, f.
stimulative, *stĭm'ŭlātĭv*, a. estimulante.
stimulus, *–ŭlŭs*, s. estímulo, m.
sting, *stĭng*, v. a. picar ó morder (un insecto); —, s. aguijón, m.; punzada, picadura, picada, f.; remordimiento de conciencia, m.
stingily, *stĭn'jĭlĭ*, ad. avaramente. [f.
stinginess, *–nĕs*, s. tacañería, avaricia,
stinging-nettle, *stĭng'ĭngnĕtl*, s. ortiga, f.
stingy, *stĭn'jĭ*, a. mezquino, tacaño, avaro.
stink, *stĭngk*, v. n. heder; —, s. hedor, m.
stint, *stĭnt*, v. a. limitar; —, s. límite, m.;
   restricción, f.   [salario, m.
stipend, *stĭ'pĕnd*, s. estipendio, m.; sueldo,
stipendiary, *stĭpĕn'dĭărĭ*, s. estipendiario.
stipulate, *stĭp'ŭlāt*, v. n. estipular.

stipulation, *stĭpŭlă'shăn,* s. estipulación, f.; contrato mutuo, m.

stir, *stŭr,* v. a. remover; agitar; incitar; —, v. n. moverse; —, s. tumulto, m.; turbulencia, f.

stirrer, *—rŭr,* s. instigador, m.

stirrup, *stĭr'răp,* s. estribo, m.

stirrup-leather, *—lĕthăr,* s. ación, f.

stitch, *stĭtsh,* v. a. coser; —, s. puntada, f.

stoat, *stōt,* s. comadreja, f. (f.; punto, m.

stock, *stŏk,* s. tronco, m.; injerto, m.; zoquete, estólido, m.; mango, m.; corbatín, m.; estirpe, f., linaje, m.; capital, principal, m.; fondo, m.; —s, pl. acciones en los fondos públicos, f. pl.; —, v. a. proveer, abastecer.

stockade, *stŏkkād',* s. palizada, f.; estocada, f.

stock-fish, *stŏk'fĭsh,* s. bacalao seco, m.

stock-holder, *—hōldăr,* s. accionista, f.

stocking, *—ĭng,* s. media, f.

stock-jobber, *—jŏbbăr,* s. agiotador, m.

stock-still, *—stĭl,* a. inmoble, inmóvil.

stoic, *stō'ĭk,* s. estoico, m. [mente.

stoical, *—ăl,* a. estoico; **—ly,** ad. estoicamente.

stoicism, *stō'ĭsĭzm,* s. estoicismo, m.

stoker, *stō'kĕr,* s. fuellero, m.

stole, *stōl,* s. estola, f.

stomach, *stŭm'ăk,* s. estómago, m.; apetito, m.; —, v. n. enojarse.

stomacher, *—ăr,* s. peto, m.

stomachic(al), *stŏmăk'ĭk(ăl),* a. estomático; —, s. medicamento estomacal, m.

stone, *stōn,* s. piedra, f.; cálculo, cuesco, m.; pepita, f.; testículo, m.; hueso de fruta, m.; peso de catorce libras, m.; —, a. de piedra; —, v. a. apedrear; quitar los huesos de las frutas; empedrar; trabajar de albañilería.

stone-blind, *—blīnd,* a. enteramente ciego.

stone-cutter, *—kŭttăr,* s. picapedrero, m.

stone-dead, *—dĕd,* a. muerto.

stone-fruit, *—frōt,* s. fruta de hueso, f.

stone-horse, *—hŏrs,* s. caballo entero, m.

stone-pit, *—pĭt,* s. cantera, f.

stone-ware, *—wăr,* s. loza de piedra, f.

stoning, *stōn'ĭng,* s. apedreamiento, m.

stony, *—ĭ,* a. de piedra, pétreo; duro.

stool, *stōl,* s. banquillo, taburete, m.; cámara, evacuación, f.

stoop, *stōp,* v. n. encorvarse, inclinarse; bajarse; —, s. inclinación hacia abajo, f.; abatimiento, m. [hacia abajo.

stoopingly, *—ĭnglĭ,* ad. con inclinación

stop, *stŏp,* v. a. detener, parar, diferir; tapar; —, v. n. pararse, hacer alto; —, s. pausa, f.; obstáculo, m.

stoppage, *—pĕj,* s. **stopping,** *—pĭng,* s. obstrucción, f.; impedimento, m.; (rail.) alto, m.

stopple, *—pl,* s. tapón, m. [m.

stop-watch, *—wŏtsh,* s. reloj que da los segundos, m. [almacenaje, m.

storage, *stō'rŏj,* s. almacenamiento, m.;

store, *stōr,* s. abundancia, f.; provisión, f.; almacén, m.; —, v. a. surtir, proveer, abastecer. [m.

store-keeper, *—kēpăr,* s. guardaalmacén, m.

storey, *stōrĕ,* s. piso de una casa, f.

storied, *stō'rĭd,* a. historiado; **(of houses)** con pisos.

stork, *stŏrk,* s. cigüeña, f.

storm, *stŏrm,* s. tempestad, borrasca, f.; asalto, m.; —, v. a. tomar por asalto; —, v. n. tempestar.

stormily, *—ĭlĕ,* a. violentamente.

stormy, *—ĭ,* a. tempestuoso; violento.

story, *stō'rĕ,* s. historia, f.; fábula, f.; piso, m. (de una casa).

stout, *stŏŭt,* a. robusto, corpulento, vigoroso; terco; **—ly,** ad. valientemente, obstinadamente; —, s. cerveza fuerte, f.

stoutness, *—nĕs,* s. valor, m.; fuerza, f.; corpulencia, f.

stove, *stōv,* s. estufa, f. [estivar.

stow, *stō,* v. a. ordenar, colocar; (mar.)

stowage, *—ŏj,* s. almacenaje, m.; (mar.) arrumaje, m.

straggle, *străg'gl,* v. n. vagar.

straggler, *—ăr,* s. soldado rezagado; vagamundo, m. [luego; directamente.

straight, *strāt,* a. derecho; estrecho; —, ad.

straighten, *—n,* v. a. enderezar.

straightforward, *—fŏr'wărd,* a. derecho; franco; leal. [chura, f.

straightforwardness, *—nĕs,* s. derechura, f.

straightway, *strāt'wā,* ad. inmediatamente, luego.

strain, *strān,* v. a. colar, filtrar; apretar (á uno contra sí); forzar, violentar; —, v. n. esforzarse; —, s. retorcimiento, m.; raza, f.; linaje, m.; estilo, m.; sonido, m.; armonía, f.

strainer, *—ăr,* s. colador, m.; coladera, f.

strait, *strāt,* a. estrecho, angosto; íntimo; rígido, exacto; escaso; **—ly,** ad. estrechamente; —, s. estrecho, m.; aprieto, peligro, m.; penuria, f.

straiten, *—n,* v. a. acortar, estrechar.

straitness, *—nĕs,* s. estrechez, f.; penuria, f.; severidad, f. [& m. (mar.) encallar.

strand, *strănd,* s. costa, playa, f.; —, v. a.

strange, *strānj,* a. extranjero; extraño; **—ly,** ad. extrañamente, extraordinariamente. [trañeza, f.

strangeness, *—nĕs,* s. extranjería, f.; ex-

stranger, *—ăr,* s. extranjero, m.

strangle, *străng'gl,* v. a. ahogar.

strangulation, *stranggŭlā'shăn,* s. ahogamiento, m. [tirante de bota, m.

strap, *străp,* s. correa, tira de cuero, f.;

strapping, *—pĭng,* a. abultado, corpulento.

stratagem, *străt'ăjĕm,* s. estratagema, f.; astucia, f.

strategic, *stratĕj'ĭk,* a. estratégico, m.

strategy, *străt'ĕjĕ,* s. estrategia, f.

stratum, *strā'tŭm,* s. lecho, m.; bancal, m.

straw, *strā,* s. paja, m.; bagatela, f.

straw-bed, *—bĕd,* s. jergón, m.

strawberry, *—bĕrrĕ,* s. fresa, f.

strawberry-tree, *—bĕrrĕtrē,* s. madroño, m.

straw-cutter, *—kăttăr,* s. tajador, m. (máquina).

stray, *strā,* v. n. extraviarse; perder el camino; —, s. descarriamiento, m.; —, a. extraviado.

streak, *strēk,* s. raya, lista, f.; —, v. a. rayar.

stream, *strēm,* s. arroyo, río, torrente, m.; —, v. n. correr; echar rayos.

streamer, *–ăr*, s. (mar.) flámula, f.
streamlet, *–lĕt*, s. arroyo, arroyuelo, m.
street, *strĕt*, s. calle, f.
strength, *strĕngth*, s. fuerza, robustez, f.;
vigor, m.; fortaleza, f.
strengthen, *–n*, v.a. fortificar; corroborar.
strenuous, *strĕn'ŭús*, a. estrenuo, valeroso;
ágil; **–ly,** ad. acérrimamente; valerosamente.   [m.; vigor, m.
strenuousness, *–nĕs*, s. valor, esfuerzo,
stress, *strĕs*, s. fuerza, f.; peso, m.; importancia, f.; acento, m.; **– syllable,** s.
sílaba acentuada, f.
stretch, *strĕtsh*, v.a. & n. extender, alargar;
estirar; extenderse; esforzarse; **–,** s. extensión, f.; esfuerzo, m.; estirón, m.
stretcher, *–ăr*, s. cualquier cosa que sirve
para alargar ó estirar á otra, f.
strew, *strŏ*, v.a. esparcir; sembrar.
striated, *strī'ātĕd*, a. estriado.
strict, *strĭkt*, a. estricto, estrecho; exacto,
riguroso, severo; **–ly,** ad. exactamente,
con severidad.   [dad, f.
strictness, *–nĕs*, s. exactitud, f.; severi-
stricture, *strĭk'tŭr*, s. sello, m.; marca, f.;
contracción, f.
stride, *strīd*, s. tranco, m.; **–,** v.n. atrancar.
strife, *strīf*, s. contienda, disputa, f.
strike, *strīk*, v.a. & n. golpear; herir;
castigar; tocar; amedrentar; chocar; sonar; cesar de trabajar; **–,** s. rasero, m.;
cesación de trabajadores, huelga, f.
striking, *strī'king*, a. lo que sorprende;
–ly, ad. de un modo sorprendente.
string, *string*, s. cordón, m.; hilo, m.;
cuerda, f.; hilera, f.; fibra, f.; **–,** v.a. encordar; enhilar; estirar.
stringent, *strĭn'jĕnt*, a. astringente.
stringy, *string'ĕ*, a. fibroso.   [tira, f.
strip, *strĭp*, v.a. desnudar, despojar; **–,** s.
stripe, *strĭp*, s. raya, lista, f.; azote, m.;
–, v.a. rayar.   [bete, m.
stripling, *strĭp'lĭng*, s. mozuelo, mozal-
strive, *strīv*, v.n. esforzarse; empeñarse;
disputar, contender; oponerse.
stroke, *strōk*, s. golpe, m.; toque (en la
pintura), m.; sonido (del reloj), m.; plumada, f.; **–,** v.a. acariciar.
stroll, *strōl*, v.n. tunar, vagar.
strong, *strong*, a. fuerte, vigoroso, robusto;
poderoso; violento; **–ly,** ad. fuertemente,
con violencia.
strong-box, *–bŏks*, s. cofre fuerte, m.
stronghold, *–hōld*, s. plaza fuerte, f.
strop, *strŏp*, s. cuero á navajas, suaviza-
strophe, *strŏf'ĕ*, s. estrofa, f.   [dor, m.
structure, *strŭk'tŭr*, (*strŭk'tshŭr*), s. estructura, f.; edificio, m.
struggle, *strŭg'gl*, v.n. esforzarse; luchar;
agitarse.   [tienda, lucha, f.
struggling, *strŭg'lĭng*, s. esfuerzo, m.; con-
strum, *strŭm*, v.a. (mus.) tocar malísi-
mamente.
strumpet, *strŭm'pĕt*, s. ramera, puta, f.
strut, *strŭt*, v.n. pavonearse; **–,** s. con-
stub, *stŭb*, s. tronco, m.   [toneo, m.
stubble, *–bl*, s. rastrojo, m.
stubborn, *–ŭrn*, a. obstinado, testarudo;
–ly, ad. obstinadamente.

stubbornness, *–bŭrnnĕs*, s. obstinación,
pertinacia, f.
stubby, *–bĕ*, a. cachigordete; gordo.
stucco, *stŭk'kō*, s. estuco, m.
stud, *stŭd*, s. estaca, f.; tachón, m.; **–,** v.
a. tachonar.
student, *stū'dĕnt*, s. estudiante, m.
stud-horse, *stŭd'hŏrs*, s. caballo entero, m.
studied, *stŭd'ĭd*, a. docto, leído, versado.
studio, *stŭd'ĭō*, s. estudio de un artista, m.
studious, *stū'dĭŭs*, a. estudioso; diligente;
–ly, ad. estudiosamente, diligentemente.
study, *stŭd'ĕ*, s. estudio, m.; aplicación,
f.; meditación profunda, f.; **–,** v.a. estudiar; observar; **–,** v.n. estudiar; aplicarse.
stuff, *stŭf*, s. materia, f.; material, m.;
jarope, m.; estofa, f.; **– !** ¡ bagatela !, ¡niñería !; **–,** v.a. henchir, llenar; **–,** v. n.
atracarse; tragar.
stuffing, *–ĭng*, s. relleno, m.
stuffy, *–fĕ*, a. agdaz, resuelto.
stultify, *stŭl'tĭfī*, v.a. bobear, atontar.
stumble, *stŭm'bl*, v.n. tropezar; **–,** s. traspié, tropiezo, m.
stumbling-block, *stŭm'blĭngblŏk*, s.
tropezadero, m.; piedra de escándalo, f.
stump, *stŭmp*, s. tronco, m.; tocón, m.; **–,**
v.a. esfumar.
stun, *stŭn*, v.a. aturdir, ensordecer.
stunner, *–năr*, s. cualquier cosa qué sor-
stunt, *–t*, v.a. no dejar crecer.   [prende, f.
stupefaction, *stūpĕfăk'shŭn*, s. aturdimiento, estupor, m.
stupefy, *stū'pĕfī*, v.a. atontar, atolondrar.
stupendous, *stūpĕn'dŭs*, a. estupendo,
maravilloso.   [pidamente.
stupid, *stū'pĭd*, a. estúpido; **–ly,** ad. estú-
stupidity, *stūpĭd'tĕ*, s. estupidez, f.
stupor, *stū'pŏr*, s. estupor, m.
sturdily, *stŭr'dĭlĕ*, ad. insolentemente,
obstinadamente.   [f.; obstinación, f.
sturdiness, *stŭr'dĭnĕs*, s. fuerza, fortaleza,
sturdy, *stŭr'dĕ*, a. fuerte, tieso, robusto;
bronco, insolente.
sturgeon, *stŭr'jŏn*, s. esturión, m.
stutter, *stŭt'tŭr*, v.n. tartamudear.
sty, *stī*, s. zahurda, f.; pocilga, f.
stye, *–*, s. orzuelo, m.
style, *stĭl*, s. estilo, m.; título, m.; gnomon, m.; modo, m.; **–,** v.a. intitular,
nombrar.   [galancete.
stylish, *stĭk'lĭsh*, a. elegante, en buen estilo;
suave, *swäv*, a. suave; **–ly,** ad. suavemente.
suavity, *swäv'ĭtĕ*, s. suavidad, dulzura, f.
subaltern, *sŭb'ăltŭrn*, a. subalterno.
subdivide, *–dĭvīd'*, v.a. subdividir.
subdivision, *–dĭvĭzh'ăn*, s. subdivisión, f.
subdual, *–dū'ăl*, s. sujeción, f.
subdue, *–dū'*, v.a. sojuzgar, sujetar; conquistar; mortificar.
subject, *sŭb'jĕkt*, a. sujeto; sometido á;
–, s. sujeto, m.; **–** *subjĕkt'*, v.a. sujetar;
exponer.
subjection, *–jĕk'shăn*, s. sujeción, f.
subjoin, *–jŏĭn'*, v.a. sobreañadir.
subjugate, *–jŭgāt'*, v.a. sojuzgar, sujetar.
subjugation, *–jŭgā'shăn*, s. sujeción, f.

subjunctive, –jŭngk'tĭv, s. subjuntivo.
sublet, sŭblĕt', v. a. subarrendar.   [m.
sublimate, –lĭmāt, s. sublimado, m.; –,
v. a. sublimar.
sublime, –lĭm', a. sublime, excelso; –ly,
ad. de un modo sublime; –, s. sublime, m.
sublimity, –lĭm'tĭ, s. sublimidad, f.
sublunar(y), –lō'nǎr(ĕ), a. sublunar; terrestre.
submarine, –mārēn', a. submarino.
submerge, –mŭrj', v. a. sumergir.
submersion, –mŭr'shǔn, s. sumersión, f.
submission, –mĭsh'ǔn, s. sumisión, f.
submissive, –mĭs'sĭv, a. sumiso, obsequioso; –ly, ad. con sumisión.
submissiveness, –nĕs, s. obsequio, m.;
sumisión, f.
submit, sŭbmĭt', v. a. (& n.) someter(se).
sub-officer, –ŏf'fĭsǎr, s. sargento, m.
subordinate, –ŏr'dĭnāt, a. subordinado,
inferior; –, v. a. subordinar.   [nación, f.
subordination, –ŏrdĭnā'shǔn, s. subordi-
suborn, –ŏrn', v. a. sobornar, cohechar.
subornation, –ŏrnā'shǔn, s. soborno, m.
subpoena, –pē'nǎ, s. comparendo, m.
subscribe, –skrĭb', v. a. & n. suscribir,
certificar con su firma; consentir.
subscriber, –ǎr, s. suscriptor, m.
subscription, sŭbskrĭp'shǔn, s. suscripción, f.   [siguiente(mente).
subsequent, sŭb'sĕkwĕnt, a. –ly, ad. sub-
subserve, –sǔrv', v. a. servir, estar subordinado.
subserviency, –sǔr'vĭĕnsĕ, s. servicio,
m.; utilidad, f.; concurso, m.; ayuda, f.
subservient, –sǔr'vĭĕnt, a. subordinado;
útil.   [fondo.
subside, –sīd', v. n. sumergirse, irse al
subsidence, –sĭ'dĕns, s. derrumbamiento.
subsidiary, –sĭd'ĭǎrĕ, a. subsidiario.   [m.
subsidize, –sĭd'sĭz, v. a. dar subsidios.
subsidy, –sĭdĕ, s. subsidio, socorro, m.
subsist, sŭbsĭst', v. n. subsistir; existir.
subsistence, –sĭs'tĕns, s. existencia, f.;
subsistencia, f.   [dad, f.; esencia, f.
substance, sŭb'stǎns, s. substancia, f.; enti-
substantial, sŭbstǎn'shǎl, a. substancial;
real, material; substancioso; fuerte; –ly,
ad. substancialmente.
substantiality, –stǎnshĭǎl'ĭtĕ, s. existencia, material, f.; solidez, f.   [existir.
substantiate, –stǎn'shĭāt, v. a. hacer
substantive, sŭb'stǎntĭv, s. sustantivo, m.
substitute, –stĭtāt, v. a. sustituir.
substitution, sŭbstĭtū'shǔn, s. sustitución,
substratum, –strā'tǔm, s. lecho, m.   [f.
subterfuge, sŭb'tǎrfūj, s. subterfugio, m.;
evasión, f.   [neo.
subterranean, sŭbtĕrrā'nĕǎn, a. subterrá-
subtile, sŭb'tĭl (sŭt'l), a. sútil, delicado,
tenue; penetrante, agudo; –ly, ad. sútilmente.
subtility, sŭbtĭl'ĭtĕ, s. sutilidad, f.   [ción, f.
subtilization, –tĭlĭzā'shǔn, s. sutiliza-
subtilize, sŭb'tĭlĭz, v. a. sutilizar.
subtle, sŭt'l, a. sútil, astuto.
subtlety, –tĕ, s. sutileza, astucia, f.
subtly, sŭt'lĕ, ad. sútilmente.

subtract, sŭbtrăkt', v. a. (ar.) sustraer.
suburb, sŭb'ǔrb, s. suburbio, m.
suburban, sŭbǔr'bǎn, a. suburbano.
subversion, –vǔr'shǔn, s. subversión, f.
subversive, –vǔr'sĭv, a. subversivo.
subvert, –vǔrt', v. a. subvertir, destruir.
subway, sŭb'wā, s. túnel, m.
succeed, sŭksēd', v. n. & a. suceder,
seguir; conseguir, lograr, tener suceso.
success, sŭksĕs', s. suceso, éxito m.
successful, –fūl, a. próspero, dichoso;
–ly, ad. prósperamente.
succession, sŭksĕsh'ǔn, s. sucesión, f.;
descendencia, f.; herencia, f.
successive, sŭksĕs'sĭv, a. sucesivo; –ly,
ad. sucesivamente.
successor, sŭksĕs'sǔr, s. sucesor, m.
succinct, sŭksĭngkt', a. sucinto, compendioso; –ly, ad. con brevedad.
succour, sŭk'kǔr, v. a. socorrer, ayudar;
–, s. socorro, m.; ayuda, asistencia, f.
succulence, sŭk'kǔlĕns, s. jugosidad, f.
succulent, sŭk'kǔlĕnt, a. suculento, jugoso.
succumb, sǔkkǔm', v. n. sucumbir.
such, sǔtsh, pn. tal, semejante; – as, el
que, los que, las que, lo que.
suck, sǔk, v. a. & n. chupar; mamar.
sucking-pig, –ĭngpĭg, s. lechoncillo, m.
suckle, –l, v. a. amamantar.
suckling, –lĭng, s. mamantón, m.
suction, sǔk'shǔn, s. (med.) succión, f.
sudden, sǔd'dn, a. repentino, no prevenido; –ly, ad. de repente, súbitamente.
suddenness, –nĕs, s. precipitación, f.
sudorific, sūdǒrĭf'ĭk, a.&s. sudorífico(m.).
suds, sǔdz, s. lejía de agua y jabón, f.
sue, sū, v. a. & n. poner por justicia; supli-
suet, sū'ĕt, s. sebo, m.   [car.
suffer, sǔf'fǎr, v. a. & n. sufrir, padecer;
tolerar, permitir.
sufferable, –ǎbl, a. sufrible, soportable.
sufferance, –ǎns, s. sufrimiento, m.;
tolerancia, f.
suffering, –ĭng, s. pena, f.; dolor, m.
suffice, sǔfĭs', v. n. bastar, ser suficiente.
sufficiency, sǔffĭsh'ĕnsĕ, s. suficiencia, f.;
capacidad, f.   [ad. bastante.
sufficient, sǔffĭsh'ĕnt, a. suficiente; –ly,
suffocate, sǔf'fōkāt, v. a. sufocar.
suffocation, sǔffōkā'shǔn, s. sufocación, f.
suffragan, sǔf'frǎgǎn, s. sufragáneo, m.
suffrage, sǔf'frǎj, s. sufragio, voto, m.
suffuse, sǔf'jūz', v. a. difundir, derramar.
suffusion, sǔffū'zhǔn, s. (med.) sufusión, f.
sugar, shūg'ǎr, s. azúcar, m.; –, v. a.
azucarar.
sugar-basin, –bāsn, s. azucarero, m.
sugar-cane, –kān, s. caña de azúcar, f.
sugar-loaf, –lōf, s. pan de azúcar, m.
sugar-plum, –plǔm, s. confite, m.
sugary, –ĕ, a. azucarado.
suggest, sǔjjĕst' (sǔdjĕst'), v. a. sugerir.
suggestion, sǔjjĕs'tshǔn, s. sugestión, f.
suicidal, sǔ'ĭsīdǎl, a. de suicida.
suicide, sǔ'ĭsīd, s. suicidio, m.; suicida, m.
suit, sūt, s. vestido (entero), m.; galanteo,
m.; petición, f.; pleito, m.; surtido, m.;

—, v. a. & n. adaptar; surtir; ajustarse, acomodarse.

suitable, –*ăbl*, a. conforme, conveniente.

suitableness –*ăblnĕs*, s. conformidad, conveniencia, f.

suitably, –*ăblĕ*, ad. según, conforme.

suite, *swēt*, s. serie, f.; tren, m., comitiva, f. [cortejo, m.: pleiteante, m.

suitor, *sū'tŭr*, s. suplicante, m.; amante

sulkiness, *sŭl'kĭnĕs*, s. mal humor, m.

sulky, *sŭl'kĕ*, a. regañón, vinagre; terco.

sullen, *sŭl'lĕn*, a. malcontento; intratable; –ly, ad. de mal humor; tercamente.

sullenness –*nĕs*, s. mal humor, m.; obstinación, pertinacia, terquedad, f.

sully, *sŭl'lĕ*, v. a. manchar, ensuciar.

sulphur, *sŭl'fŭr*, s. azufre, m.

sulphurous –*ŭs*, a. sulfúreo, azufroso.

sultan, *sŭl'tăn*, s. sultán, m.

sultana, *sŭltă'nă*, s. sultana, f.

sultriness, *sŭl'trĭnĕs*, s. bochorno, m.

sultry, *sŭl'trĕ*, a. caluroso; sofocante.

sum, *sŭm*, s. suma, f.; –, v. a. sumar; recopilar.

summarily, –*mărĭlĕ*, ad. sumariamente.

summary –*mărĭ*, a. & s. sumario (m.).

summer, *sŭm'mŭr*, s. verano, estío, m.

summer-house –*hŏŭs*, s. glorieta de jardín, f.

summit, *sŭm'mĭt*, s. ápice, m.; cima, f.

summon, *sŭm'mŭn*, v. a. citar, requerir por auto de juez; convocar, convidar; (mil.) intimar la rendición.

summoner –*nŭr*, s. convidador, m.

summons –*z*, s. citación, f.; requerimiento, m.

sumptuary, *sŭm'tūŭrĕ*, s. suntuario. [m.

sumptuous, *sŭm'tŭŭs*, a. suntuoso; –ly, ad. suntuosamente.

sumptuousness –*nĕs*, s. suntuosidad, f.

sun, *sŭn*, s. sol, m.

sun-beam –*bēm*, s. rayo del sol, m.

sun-burnt –*bŭrnt*, a. tostado por el sol,

Sunday, –*dă*, s. domingo, m. [asoleado.

sunder, *sŭn'dŭr*, v. a. separar, apartar.

sun-dial –*dĭăl*, s. reloj de sol, cuadrante, m.

sundry, –*drĕ*, a. varios, muchos, diversos.

sunflower –*flŏŭr*, s. girasol, m.

sun-glass –*glăs*, s. espejo ustorio, m.

sunless –*lĕs*, a. sin sol; sin luz.

sun-light –*lĭt*, s. luz del sol, f.

sunny, –*nĕ*, a. semejante al sol; asoleado; brillante.

sun-rise –*rĭz*, **sun-rising**, –*rĭzĭng*, s. salida del sol, f., nacer del sol, m.

sunset –*sĕt*, s. puesta del sol, f.

sun-shade –*shăd*, s. quitasol, m.

sun-shine –*shĭn*, s. solana, f.; claridad, del sol, f. [el sol.

sunshiny, –*shĭnĕ*, a. resplandeciente como

sun-stroke –*strŏk*, s. insolación, f.

sup, *sŭp*, v. a. sorber, beber á sorbos; v. n. cenar; –, s. sorbo, m.

super, *sū'pŭr*, s. comparsa, m. & f.

superabound, *sūpŭrăbŏŭnd'*, v. n. super-abundar. [abundancia, f.; lo superfluo.

superabundance, –*ăbŭn'dăns*, s. super-

superabundant, –*ăbŭn'dănt*, a. –ly, ad. superabundante(mente).

superadd, –*ădd'*, v. a. sobreañadir.

superaddition, –*ădĭsh'ŭn*, s. sobreañadidura, f. [pensionado.

superannuated, –*ăn'nŭătĕd*, a. afiejado;

superannuation, –*ănnŭă'shŭn*, s. pensión, jubilación, f.; retiro, m.

superb, *sūpŭrb'*, a. soberbio; –ly, ad. soberbiamente. [cargo, m.

supercargo, *sūpŭrkăr'gō*, s. (mar.) sobre-

supercilious, –*sĭl'ŭs*, a. arrogante, altanero; –ly, ad. con altivez. [erogación, f.

supererogation, –*ĕrŏgă'shŭn*, s. super-

supererogatory, –*ĕrŏg'ătŭrĕ*, a. super-erogatorio. [ficial(mente).

superficial, –*fĭsh'ăl*, a. –ly, ad. super-

superficies, –*fĭsh'ĭĕz*, s. superficie, f.

superfine, –*fĭn'*, a. superfino.

superfluity, –*flŏ'ĭtĭ*, s. superfluidad, f.

superfluous, *sūpŭr'flŭŭs*, a. superfluo.

superhuman, *sūpŭrhū'măn*, a. sobrehumano. [vigilar.

superintend, –*ĭntĕnd'*, v. a. inspeccionar,

superintendence, –*ĕns*, s. superintendencia, f. [dente, m.

superintendent, –*ĕnt*, s. superintendente,

superior, *sūpē'rĭŭr*, a. & s. superior (m.).

superiority, *sūpērĭŏr'ĭtĭ*, s. superioridad, f.

superlative, *sūpŭr'lătĭv*, a. & s. superlativo, m.; –ly, ad. superlativamente, en sumo grado. [natural.

supernatural, *sūpŭrnăt'ŭrăl*, s. sobre-

supernumerary, –*nū'mŭrărĕ*, a. super-numerario.

superscribe, –*skrĭb'*, v. a. sobreescribir.

superscription, –*skrĭp'shŭn*, s. sobreescrito, m. [invalidar.

supersede, –*sēd'*, v. a. sobreseer; diferir;

superstition, –*stĭsh'ŭn*, s. superstición, f.

superstitious, –*stĭsh'ŭs*, a. supersticioso; –ly, ad. supersticiosamente.

superstructure, –*strŭk'tshŭr*, s. edificio levantado sobre otra fábrica, m.

supervene, –*vēn'*, v. n. sobrevenir.

supervise, –*vīz'*, v. a. inspeccionar, revistar. [cia, f.

supervision, –*vĭzh'ŭn*, s. superintenden-

supervisor, –*vī'zŭr*, s. superintendente, m. [ad. descuidadamente.

supine, *sūpīn'*, a. supino; negligente; –ly,

supineness, –*nĕs*, s. negligencia, f.

supper, *sŭp'pŭr*, s. cena, f.; Lord's –, institución de la Eucaristía, f.

supperless, –*lĕs*, a. sin haber cenado.

supplant, *sŭpplănt'*, v. a. suplantar.

supple, *sŭp'pl*, a. flexible, manejable; blando; –, v. a. hacer flexible. [m.

supplement, *sŭp'plĕmĕnt*, s. suplemento,

supplemental, *sŭpplĕmĕn'tăl*, supplementary, *sŭpplĕmĕn'tŭrĕ*, a. adicional.

suppleness, *sŭp'plnĕs*, s. flexibilidad, f.

suppli(o)ant, *sŭp'plĭ(k)ănt*, s. suplicante,

supplicate, *sŭp'plĭkăt*, v. a. suplicar. [m.

supplication, *sŭpplĭkă'shŭn*, s. súplica, suplicación, f.

supplicatory, *săp'plĭkătărĭ,* a. lo que suplica.

supply, *săpplī',* v. a. suplir, completar; surtir; —, s. socorro, refuerzo, m.

support, *săppōrt',* v. a. sostener; soportar, asistir.

supportable, *-ăbl,* a. soportable.

supporter, *-ăr,* s. sustentáculo, m.; apoyo, m.; protector, m.

suppose, *săppōz',* v. a. suponer.

supposition, *săppŏzĭsh'ăn,* s. suposición, f.

suppositious, *săppŏzĭtsh'ŭs,* a. supuesto, falso, fingido.

suppress, *săpprĕs',* v. a. suprimir.

suppression, *săpprĕsh'ăn,* s. supresión, f.

suppurate, *săp'pŭrāt,* v. n. supurar.

suppuration, *săppŭrā'shăn,* s. supuración, f.

supremacy, *săprĕm'ăsĭ,* s. supremacía, f.

supreme, *săprēm',* a. supremo; **-ly,** ad. supremamente.

surcease, *sŭrsēs',* s. cesación, parada, f.

surcharge, *sŭrtshärj',* v. a. sobrecargar.

surcingle, *sŭrsĭng'gl,* s. sobrecincha, f.

surcoat, *sŭr'kōt,* s. sobretodo, gabán, m.

sure, *shōr,* a. seguro, cierto; firme; estable; **to be —,** sin duda; ya se ve; **-ly,** ad. ciertamente, seguramente, sin duda.

sureness, *-nĕs,* s. certeza, seguridad, f.

surety, *-tĭ,* s. seguridad, f.; fiador, m.

surf, *sŭrf,* s. (mar.) resaca, f.

surface, *sŭr'fās,* s. superficie, sobrefaz, f.

surfeit, *sŭr'fĭt,* v. a. & n. hartar, saciar; ahitarse, saciarse; —, s. ahíto, empacho, m.; indigestión, f.

surge, *sŭrj,* s. ola, onda, f.; —, v. n. embravecerse el mar.

surgeon, *sŭr'jŭn,* s. cirujano, m.

surgery, *sŭr'jărĭ,* s. cirugía, f.

surgical, *sŭr'jĭkăl,* a. quirúrgico.

surlily, *sŭr'lĭlĭ,* ad. con mal humor.

surliness, *sŭr'lĭnĕs,* s. mal humor, m.

surly, *sŭr'lĭ,* a. áspero de genio.

surmise, *sŭrmīz',* v. a. sospechar; —, s. sospecha, f.

surmount, *sŭrmōŭnt',* v. a. sobrepujar.

surmountable, *-ăbl,* a. superable.

surname, *sŭr'nām,* s. apellido, sobrenombre, m.; —, *sŭrnām',* v. a. apellidar.

surpass, *sŭrpăs',* v. a. sobresalir, sobrepujar, exceder, aventajar.

surpassing, *-ĭng,* a. sobresaliente.

surplice, *sŭr'plĭs,* s. sobrepelliz, m.

surplus(age), *sŭr'plŭs(ĭj),* s. sobrante, f.

surprise, *sŭrprīz',* v. a. sorprender; —, s. sorpresa, f.

surprising, *sŭrprī'zĭng,* a. maravilloso.

surrender, *sŭrrĕn'dăr,* v. a. & n. rendir; ceder; rendirse; —, s. rendición, f.

surreptitious, *sŭrrĕptĭsh'ŭs,* a. subreptício; **-ly,** ad. subrepticiamente.

surrogate, *sŭr'rŏgāt,* v. a. subrogar; —, s. subrogado, m.

surround, *sŭrrōŭnd',* v. a. circundar, cercar, rodear.

survey, *sŭrvā',* v. a. inspeccionar, examinar; apear; —, *sŭr'vā,* s. inspección, f.; apeo (de tierras), m.

surveyor, *-ăr,* s. sobrestante, m.; agri-

surveyorship, *-shĭp,* s. empleo de sobrestante, m.

survive, *sŭrvīv',* v. n. sobrevivir.

survivor, *sŭrvī'văr,* s. sobreviviente, m.

susceptibility, *sŭssĕptĭbĭl'ĭtĭ,* s. susceptibilidad, f.

susceptible, *sŭssĕp'tĭbl,* a. susceptible.

suspect, *sŭspĕkt',* v. a. & n. sospechar.

suspend, *sŭspĕnd',* v. a. suspender.

suspense, *sŭspĕns',* s. suspensión, f.; detención, f.; incertidumbre, f.

suspension, *sŭspĕn'shŭn,* s. suspensión, f.; **— of arms,** tregua, f.

suspension-bridge, *-brĭj,* s. puente colgante o colgado, m.

suspensor(y), *sŭspĕn'sŭr(ĭ),* s. braguero, m.

suspicion, *sŭspĭsh'ŭn,* s. sospecha, f.

suspicious, *sŭspĭsh'ŭs,* a. suspicaz; **-ly,** ad. sospechosamente.

suspiciousness, *-nĕs,* s. suspicacia, f.

sustain, *sŭstān',* v. a. sostener, sustentar, mantener; apoyar; sufrir.

sustainable, *-ăbl,* a. sustentable.

sustainer, *-ăr,* s. apoyo, sostén, m.

sustenance, *sŭs'tĕnăns,* s. sostenimiento, sustento, m.

sutler, *sŭt'lăr,* s. vivandero, m.

sutling-booth, *sŭt'lĭngbōŭth,* s. cantina, f.

suture, *sŭ'tăr,* s. sutura, costura, f.

swab, *swŏb,* s. lampazo, m.

swaddle, *swŏd'dl,* v. a. fajar.

swaddling-clothes, *-ĭngklōthz,* s. pl. pañales, m. pl.

swagger, *swăg'găr,* v. n. baladronear.

swaggerer, *-ăr,* s. fanfarrón, baladrón, m.

swain, *swān,* s. zagal, joven aldeano, pastorcillo, m.

swallow, *swăl'lō,* s. golondrina, f.; gula, f.; —, v. a. tragar, engullir.

swamp, *swŏmp,* s. pantano, m.

swampy, *-ĕ,* a. pantanoso.

swan, *swŏn,* s. cisne, m.

swanskin, *-skĭn,* s. moletón, m.

swap, *swŏp,* v. a. cambalachear.

sward, *swărd,* s. césped, m.

swarm, *swărm,* s. enjambre, m.; gentío, m.; hormiguero, m.; —, v. n. enjambrar; hormiguear de gente; abundar.

swart, *swărt,* **swarthy,** *swărth'ĕ,* a. atezado.

swarthiness, *swărth'ĭnĕs,* s. tez morena, f.

swash-buckler, *swŏsh'bŭklăr,* s. fanfarrón.

swath, *swŏth,* s. tranco, m. [rrón, m.

swathe, *swāth,* v. a. fajar; —, s. faja, f.

sway, *swā,* v. a. empuñar; dominar, gobernar; —, v. n. ladearse, inclinarse; tener influjo; —, s. bamboneo, m.; poder, imperio, influjo, m.

swear, *swăr,* v. a. & n. jurar; hacer jurar.

sweat, *swĕt,* s. sudor, m.; —, v. n. sudar; trabajar con fatiga. [juramento, m.

sweep, *swēp,* v. a. & n. barrer; arrebatar; deshollinar; pasar o tocar ligeramente; oscilar; —, s. barredura, f.; vuelta, f.; giro, m. [duras, f. pl.

sweeping, *-ĭng,* a. rápido; **-s,** pl. barreduras.

sweep-stakes, *-stāks,* s. pl. el que gana todo cuanto se apuesta o se juega.

sweet, *swĕt,* a. dulce, grato, gustoso; suave; oloroso; melodioso; hermoso; amable; —, ad. dulcemente, suavemente; —, s. dulzura; querida, f. [f. pl.

sweet-bread,—*brĕd,* s.mellejas de ternera.

sweeten,—*n,* v. a. endulzar; suavizar; aplacar; perfumar.

sweetener,—*nŭr,* s. calmante, m.

sweetheart,—*härt,* s. galanteador, m.; querida, f. [m. pl.

sweetmeats,—*mēts,* s. pl. dulces secos.

sweetness,—*nĕs,* s. dulzura, suavidad, f.

sweet-scented,—*sĕntĕd,* a. perfumado.

sweet-william,—*wĭlyăm,* s.(bot.) dianto, clavel, m.

swell, *swĕl,* v. n. hincharse; ensoberbecerse; embravecerse; —, v. a. hinchar, inflar, agravar; —, s. hinchazón, f.; bulto, m.; petimetre, m.; mar de leva, m.; —, a. á la moda.

swelling,—*ĭng,* s. hinchazón, f., tumor, m.

swelter, *swĕl´tŭr,* v. a. & n. ahogar(se) de calor.

swerve, *swŭrv,* v. n. vagar; desviarse.

swift, *swĭft,* a. veloz, ligero, rápido; —, s. vencejo, m.

swiftly,—*lĭ,* ad. velozmente.

swiftness,—*nĕs,* s. velocidad, rapidez, f.

swill, *swĭl,* v. a. beber con exceso; —, s. bazofia, f.

swim, *swĭm,* v. n. nadar; abundar en; ser vertiginoso; —, v. a. pasar á nado; —, s. nadadera de pez, f.

swimming,—*mĭng,* s. natación, f.; vértigo, m.; —*ĭy,* ad. lisamente, sin dificultad.

swindle, *swĭn´dl,* v. a. petardear, estafar.

swindler,—*ŭr,* s. petardista, trampista, m.

swine, *swĭn,* s. puerco, cochino, m.

swine-herd,—*härd,* s. porquero, m.

swing, *swĭng,* v.n. balancear, columpiarse; vibrar; agitarse; —, v. a. vibrar; —, s. vibración. f.; balanceo, m.; columpio, m.

swing-door,—*dŏr,* s. puerta con un peso colgante, f.

swinging,—*ĭng,* a. (vulg.) grande, monstruoso; —*lĭy,* ad. monstruosamente.

swinish, *swĭn´nĭsh,* a. porcuno, cochino; grosero.

swirl, *swŭrl,* s. hacer remolinos el agua.

switch, *swĭtsh,* s. varilla, f.; (rail.) aguja, f.; —, v. a. varear. [baladero, f.

switchback railway,—*băk rālwā,* s. res-

switchman,—*măn,* s. (rail.) guardaaguja,

swivel, *swĭv´l,* s. alacrán, m. [m.

swoon, *swōn,* v. n. desmayarse; —, s. desmayo, deliquio, pasmo, m.

swoop, *swōp,* v. a. coger, agarrar; —, s. acto de echarse una ave de rapiña sobre su presa, m.; **at one**—, de un golpe.

sword, *sŏrd,* s. espada, f.

sword-arm,—*ärm,* s. brazo derecho, m.

sword-cutler,—*kŭtlŭr,* s. espadero, m.

sword-fish,—*fĭsh,* s. pez espada, f. [m.

swordsman,—*z´măn,* s. guerrero, soldado,

sybaritic, *sĭbărĭt´ĭk,* a. sibarítico.

sycamore, *sĭk´āmor,* s.sicomoro, m. (árbol).

sycophant, *sĭk´ŏfănt,* s. sicofante, m.

syllabic(al), *sĭllăb´ĭk(ăl),* a. silábico.

syllable, *sĭl´lābl,* s. sílaba, f. [m.

syllabus, *sĭl´lābŭs,* s. extracto, resumen,

syllogism, *sĭl´lŏjĭzm,* s. silogismo, m.

sylph, *sĭlf,* s. silfio, m.; sílfida, f.

symbol, *sĭm´bŏl,* s. símbolo, m.

symbolic(al), *sĭmbŏl´ĭk(ăl),* a. simbólico.

symbolise, *sĭm´bŏlz,* v. a. simbolizar.

symmetrical, *sĭmmĕt´rĭkăl,* a. simétrico; —*lĭy,* ad. con simetría.

symmetry, *sĭm´mĕtrĭ,* s. simetría, f.

sympathetic(al), *sĭmpăthĕt´ĭk(ăl),* a. simpático; —*ally,* ad. simpáticamente.

sympathize, *sĭm´păthĭz,* v. n. compadecerse.

sympathy, *sĭm´păthĭ,* s. simpatía, f.

symphony, *sĭm´fŏnĕ,* s. sinfonía, f.

symptom, *sĭm´tŭm,* s. síntoma, m.

synagogue, *sĭn´ăgŏg,* s. sinagoga, f.

synchronism, *sĭn´krŏnĭzm,* s. sincro- [nismo, m.

syndic, *sĭn´dĭk,* s. síndico, m.

syndicate, *sĭn´dĭkăt,* s. sindicato, f.

synod, *sĭn´ŏd,* s. sínodo, m.

synonyme, *sĭn´ŏnĭm,* s. sinónimo, m.

synonymous, *sĭnŏn´ĭmŭs,* a. sinónimo; —*lĭy,* ad. con sinonimia. [rio, m.

synopsis, *sĭnŏp´sĭs,* s. sinopsis, f., suma-

synoptical, *sĭnŏp´tĭkăl,* a. sinóptico.

syntax, *sĭn´tăks,* s. sintaxis, f.

synthesis, *sĭn´thĕsĭs,* s. síntesis, f.

syringe, *sĭr´ĭnj,* s. jeringa, lavativa, f.; —, v. a. jeringar.

system, *sĭs´tĕm,* s. sistema, m.

systematic(al), *sĭstĕmăt´ĭk(ăl),* a. sistemático; —*ally,* ad. sistemáticamente.

T.

tabby, *tăb´bĕ,* s. tabí, m.

tabernacle, *tăb´ärnăkl,* s. tabernáculo, m.

tablature, *tăb´lătŭr,* s. pentagrama, m.

table, *tā´bl,* s. mesa, f.; tabla, f.; —, v. a. apuntar en forma sinóptica; poner sobre la mesa; —**d'hôte,** mesa redonda.

table-cloth,—*klŏth,* s. mantel, m.

table-land,—*lănd,* s. meseta, f. [f.

table-spoon,—*spōn,* s. cuchara para comer.

tablet, *tăb´lĕt,* s. tableta, f.; plancha (grabada ó pintada), f.

taboo, *tăbō´,* v. a. interdecir.

tabular, *tăb´ŭlăr,* a. reducido á índices.

tacit, *tăs´ĭt,* a. tácito; —*lĭy,* ad. tácitamente.

taciturn, *tăs´ĭtŭrn,* a. taciturno, callado.

taciturnity, *tăsĭtŭrn´ĭtĕ,* s. taciturnidad, f.

tack, *tăk,* s. tachuela, f., bordo, m.; —, v. a. atar; pegar; —, v. n. virar.

tackle,—*kl,* s. todo género de instrumentos ó aparejos, m.; (mar.) cordaje, m., jarcia,

tact, *tăkt,* s. tacto, m. [f.

tactician, *tăktĭsh´ăn,* s. táctico, m.

tactics, *tăk´tĭks,* s. pl. táctica, f.

tadpole, *tăd´pŏl,* s. ranilla, f.; sapillo, m.

taffeta, *tăf´fĕtă,* s. tafetán, m.

tag, *tăg,* s. herrete, m.; —, v. a. herretear,

tagrag,—*răg,* s. canalla, f. [f.

tail, *tāl,* s. cola, f., rabo, m.

tailor, *tǎl'ǎr,* s. sastre, m.

taint, *tānt,* v. a. tinturar, manchar; inficionar; viciar; —, s. mácula, mancha, f.

taintless, *—lĕs,* a. incorrupto, incontaminado, sin tacha.

take, *tāk,* v. a. tomar, coger, asir; recibir, aceptar; hurtar, pillar; prender; admitir; entender; —, v. n. encaminarse, dirigirse; salir bien, efectuarse una cosa; arraigarse; prender el fuego; —, s. toma, f.; presa, f.

take-in, *—ĭn',* s. engaño, m.

take-off, *—ŏf',* s. caricatura, f.

taker, *—ǎr,* s. tomador, m.

taking, *tā'kĭng,* a. agradable, manso; —, s. presa, f.; secuestro, m.

tale, *tāl,* s. cuento, m.; fábula, f.

tale-bearer, *—bārǎr,* s. soplón, f. [f.

talent, *tǎl'ĕnt,* s. talento, m.; capacidad, f.

talented, *—ĕd,* a. talentoso.

talisman, *tǎl'ĭsmǎn,* s. talismán, m.

talk, *tǎk,* v. n. hablar, conversar; charlar; —, s. plática, habla, f.; charla, f.; fama, f.

talkative, *tǎk'ǎtĭv,* a. gárrulo, locuaz.

talkativeness, *—nĕs,* s. locuacidad, f.

tall, *tǎl,* a. alto, elevado; robusto.

tallness, *—nĕs,* s. talle, cuerpo, m.

tallow, *tǎl'lō,* s. sebo, m.; —, v. a. ensebar.

tallowy, *—ĕ,* a. seboso.

tally, *tǎl'lĕ,* v. a. ajustar; tarjar.

talon, *tǎl'ŏn,* s. garra del ave de rapiña, f.

tamable, *tā'mǎb',* a. domable.

tamarind, *tǎm'ǎrĭnd,* s. tamarindo, m.

tamarisk, *tǎm'ǎrĭsk,* s. tamarisco, m.

tambourine, *tǎmbǎrēn',* s. tamboril, m.

tame, *tǎm,* a. amansado, domado, domesticado; abatido; sumiso; —ly, ad. mansamente; bajamente; —, v. a. domar, domesticar.

tameness, *—nĕs,* s. domesticidad, f.; sumisión, f.; carácter apocado, m.

tamper, *tǎm'pǎr,* v. n. jaroparse.

tan, *tǎn,* v. a. curtir, zurrar; —, s. casca, f.

tandem, *tǎn'dĕm,* ad. á lo largo; **to drive —,** conducir un coche con caballo de guía.

tangent, *tǎn'jĕnt,* s. tangente, f.

tangible, *tǎn'jĭbl,* a. tangible.

tangle, *tǎng'gl,* v. a. enredar, embrollar.

tank, *tǎngk,* s. cisterna, f.; aljibe, m.

tankard, *tǎng'kǎrd,* s. cántaro con tapadera, m.

tanner, *tǎn'nǎr,* s. curtidor, m. [dera, m.

tantalize, *tǎn'tǎlĭz,* v. a. atormentar á alguno mostrándole placeres que no puede alcanzar.

tantamount, *tǎn'tǎmŏnt,* a. equivalente.

tantivy, *tǎn'tĭvĕ,* ad. á rienda suelta, á [escape.

tan-yard, *tǎn'yǎrd,* s. tenería, f.

tap, *tǎp,* v. a. tocar ligeramente; barrenar; extraer el jugo de un árbol por incisión; sacar agua del cuerpo humano; —, s. palmada suave, f.; toque ligero, m.; espita, f.

tape, *tǎp,* s. cinta, f.; galón, m.; —s, pl. tiras de papel del telégrafo que contienen los telegramas, f. pl. [v. n. rematar en punta.

taper, *—ǎr,* s. cirio, m.; —, a. cónico; —, v. n. rematar en punta.

tapestry, *tǎp'ĕstrĕ,* s. tapiz, m.; tapicería, f.

tape-worm, *tǎp'wǔrm,* s. tenia, f. [f.

tap-house, *tǎp'hŏŭs,* s. taberna, f.

tar, *tǎr,* s. brea, f.; (vulg.) marinero, m.; —, v. a. embrear.

tardily, *tǎr'dĭlĕ,* ad. lentamente.

tardiness, *tǎr'dĭnĕs,* s. lentitud, tardanza, f.

tardy, *tǎr'dĕ,* a. tardo, lento. [f.

tare, *tǎr,* s. (bot.) zizaña, f.; tara, f.

target, *tǎr'gĕt,* s. rodela, f.; [lanco, m.

tariff, *tǎr'ĭf,* s. tarifa, f. [(para tirar).

tarlatan, *tǎr'lǎtǎn,* s. tarlatana, f.

tarn, *tǎrn,* s. aguazal, m., laguna, f.

tarnish, *tǎr'nĭsh,* v. a. (& n.) deslustrar(se).

tarpaulin, *tǎrpǎ'lĭn,* s. tela embreada, f.

tarragon, *tǎr'rǎgŏn,* s. (bot.) estragón, m.

tarry, *tǎr'rĕ,* v. n. tardar, pararse; —, *tǎr'rĕ,* a. embreado. [mente.

tart, *tǎrt,* a. acedo, acre; —ly, ad. agriamente.

tart, *tǎrt,* tartlet, s. tarta, torta, f.

tartar, *tǎr'tǎr,* s. tártaro, f.

tartness, *tǎrt'nĕs,* s. agrura, acedía, f.

task, *tǎsk,* s. tarea, f.; —, v. a. atarear.

tassel, *tǎs'sĕl,* s. registro de un libro, m.; borlita, f.; —s, pl. capotas, f. pl.

taste, *tǎst,* s. gustadura, f.; gusto, m.; sabor, m.; saboreo, m.; ensayo, m.; —, v. a. & n. gustar; probar; experimentar; agradar; tener sabor. [samente.

tasteful, *—fǔl,* a. sabroso; —ly, ad. sabrosamente.

tasteless, *—lĕs,* a. insípido, sin sabor.

taster, *—ǎr,* s. catador, m.

tastily, *—tĭlĕ,* ad. con gusto.

tasty, *tǎst'ĕ,* a. hecho ó expresado con gusto.

tatter, *tǎt'ǎr,* s. andrajo, arrapiezo, m.

tatterdemalion, *—dĕmǎl'yǎn,* s. pobre andrajoso, m.

Tattersall, *—sǎl,* s. grandes caballerizas en Londres en donde se venden caballos de corrida, f. pl. [charla, f.

tattle, *tǎt'tl,* v. n. charlar, parlotear; —, s.

tattoo, *tǎttō',* s. (mil.) retreta, queda, f.; picadura y pintura del cuerpo, f.; —, v. a. pintarse el cuerpo los salvajes.

taunt, *tānt,* v. a. mofar; ridiculizar; **dar chanza;** —, s. mofa, burla, chanza, f.

tauntingly, *—ĭnglĕ,* ad. con mofa.

Taurus, *tǎ'rǔs,* s. Tauro, m. (signo del zodíaco).

taut, *tǎt,* a. tieso, terco. [zodíaco).

tautological, *tǎtŏlŏj'ĭkǎl,* a. tautológico.

tautology, *tǎtŏl'ŏjĕ,* s. tautología, f.

tavern, *tǎv'ǎrn,* s. taberna, f.

tavern-keeper, *—kēpǎr,* s. tabernero, m.

taw, *tǎ,* v. a. ablandar pieles; —, s. bolita de mármol, f.

tawdriness, *tǎ'drĭnĕs,* s. oropel, m.

tawdry, *tǎ'drĕ,* a. jarifo, vistoso, chabacano.

tawer, *tǎ'ǎr,* s. curtidor (con alumbre), m.

tawny, *tǎn'ĕ,* a. curtido, moreno.

tax, *tǎks,* s. impuesto, m.; contribución, f.; —, v. a. imponer tributos; acusar.

taxable, *—ǎbl,* a. sujeto á impuestos.

taxation, *—shǎn,* s. imposición de impuestos, f. [impuestos, m.

tax-gatherer, *—gǎthǎrǎr,* s. colector de impuestos, m.

taxing-master, *—ĭngmǎstǎr,* s. tasador, m.

tea, *tē,* s. té, m.

teach, *tētsh,* v. a. enseñar, instruir; —, v. n. tener por oficio la enseñanza pública ó particular.

teachable, –ăbl, a. dócil.
teacher, –ăr, s. preceptor, enseñador, m.
tea-garden, –gärdn, s. café cantante, m.
teak, têk, s. teca, f. (árbol).
tea-kettle, tê kêtl, s. tetera, f.
teal, têl, s. cerceta, zarcela, f.
team, têm, s. tiro de caballos, m.
teamster, –stăr, s. galerero, m.
tear, tăr, v. a. despedazar, lacerar; ras-
tear, têr, s. lágrima, f; gota, f. [gañar.
tearful, têr făl, a. lloroso; –ly, ad. con
tearless, –lês, a. sin lágrimas. [lloro.
tease, têz, v. a. cardar (lana ó lino); im-
teasel, tê zl, s. capota, f. [portunar.
tea-service, –sărvis, tea-set, –sêt,
    tea-things, –thingz, s. pl. servicio para
teat, têt, s. ubre, teta, f. [el te, m.
techiness, têtsh inês, s. caprichos, m. pl.
technical, têk nikăl, a. técnico.
technicalities, têknikăl tiz, s. pl. térmi-
    nos técnicos, m. pl.
technology, têknŏl ŏjê, s. tecnología, f.
techy, têtsh ê, a. caprichoso.
tedious, tê dĭŭs, a. tedioso, fastidioso;
    –ly, ad. fastidiosamente.
tediousness, –nês, tedium, tê dĭŭm, s.
    tedio, fastidio, m.
teem, têm, v. a. & n. parir; estar en cinta.
teens, tênz, s. pl. años desde 13 hasta 20
    años. [dentecer.
teeth, têth, s. pl. de tooth; –, v. n. en-
teetotal, têtô tăl, a. moderado, sobrio.
teetotaller, –ăr, s. hombre sobrio, m.
teetotalism, –izm, s. sobriedad, f.
teetotally, –lê, ad. (am.) totalmente.
teetotum, têtô tŭm, s. perinela, f.
telegram, têl êgrăm, s. telegrama, m.
telegraph, têl êgrăf, s. telégrafo, m.
telegraphic, têlêgrăf ĭk, a. telegráfico.
telegraphy, têlêg răfê, s. telegrafía, f.
telephone, têl êfôn, s. teléfono, m.
telescope, têl êskôp, s. telescopio, m.
telescopic(al), têlêskŏp ĭk(ăl), a. teles-
    cópico. [numerar, relevar.
tell, têl, v. a. & n. decir; informar, contar,
teller, –ăr, s. relator, m.; computista, f.
telling, –ĭng, a. que hace impresión.
tell-tale, –tâl, s. soplón, m.
temerity, têmêr ĭtê, s. temeridad, f.
temper, têm păr, v. a. templar, moderar;
    atemperar; –, s. temperamento, m. [m.
temperament, –ăment, s. temperamento.
temperance, –ăns, s. templanza, modera-
    ción, f.
temperate, –ăt, a. templado, moderado,
    sobrio; –ly, ad. templadamente. [perie, f.
temperature, –ătŭr, s. temperatura, tem-
tempered, –ĕrd, a. templado, acondicionado.
tempest, têm pêst, s. tempestad, f.
tempestuous, têmpês tŭŭs, a. tempestuoso,
    proceloso. [m.
templar, têm plăr, s. estudiante de leyes,
temple, têmpl, s. templo, m.; sien, f.
temporal, têm pŏrăl, a. –ly, ad. temporal-
    (mente). [mente.
temporarily, têm pŏrărĭlŭ, ad. temporal-
temporary, têm pŏrărê, a. temporario.
temporise, têm pŏrĭz, v. n. temporizar.

tempt, têmt, v. a. tentar; provocar.
temptation, têm tăshŭn, s. tentación, f.
ten, tên, a. diez.
tenable, tên ăbl, a. defendible. [(mente).
tenacious, tênâ shŭs, a. –ly, ad. tenaz-
tenacity, tênăs ĭtê, s. tenacidad, f.; porfía,
tenancy, tên ănsê, s. tenencia, f. [f.
tenant, tên ănt, s. arrendador, inquilino,
    m.; –, v. n. arrendar.
tenantless, –lês, a. sin inquilinos.
tenantry, –rê, s. arriendo, m.; conjunto
    de los arrendatarios, m.
tench, tênsh, s. tenca, f. (pez).
tend, tênd, v. a. guardar, velar; –, v. n.
    tirar, dirigirse.
tendency, tênd ênsê, s. tendencia, f.
tender, tên dăr, a. tierno, delicado; sen-
    sible; –ly, ad. tiernamente; –, s. oferta,
    f., patache, m.; (rail.) tender de una loco-
    motora, m.; –, v. a. ofrecer; estimar.
tenderness, –nês, s. terneza, delicadeza, f.
tendon, tên dŏn, s. tendón, m.
tendril, tên dril, s. zarcillo, m.
tenement, tên êment, s. tenencia, f.
tenet, tên êt, s. dogma, m.; aserción, f.
tenfold, tên fŏld, a. décuplo.
tennis, tên nĭs, s. raqueta, f. (juego).
tennis-court, –kôrt, s. sitio en que se
    juega la raqueta, m. [m.; substancia, f.
tenor, tên ăr, s. (mus.) tenor, m.; contenido.
tense, tênz, a. tieso, tenso; –, s. (gr.)
    tiempo, f.
tension, tên shŭn, s. tensión, tirantez, f.
tent, tênt, s. (mil.) tienda de campaña, f.;
    –, v. n. alojarse en tienda.
tentacle, tên tăkl, s. tentáculo, m.
tentative, tên tătĭv, a. de ensayo, de
    prueba; –ly, ad. como prueba.
tenter, –ăr, s. rama, f.
tenter-hook, –hŏk, s. clavija de rama, f.
tenth, tênth, a. décimo; –ly, ad. en dé-
    cimo lugar.
tenuity, tênŭ ĭtê, s. tenuidad, f.
tenure, tên ăr, s. tenencia, f.
tepid, têp ĭd, a. tibio. [versación, f.
tergiversation, tărjĭvŭrsâ shŭn, s. tergi-
term, tărm, s. término, confín, m.; dicción,
    f.; vocablo, m.; condición, estipulación,
    f.; –, v. a. nombrar, llamar.
termagant, tăr măgănt, s. diabla, f.
terminate, tăr mĭnât, v. a. n. terminar,
    limitar. [conclusión, f.
termination, tărmĭnâ shŭn, s. terminación,
terminus, tăr mĭnŭs, s. (rail.) última esta-
    ción de ferrocarril, f.
terrace, têr răs, s. terrado, m.; terraplén,
    m.; –, v. a. terraplenar.
terrestrial, têrrês trĭăl, a. terrestre, terreno.
terrible, têr rĭbl, a. terrible.
terribly, –ê, ad. terriblemente.
terrier, têr rĭăr, s. zorrero, m.
terrific, têr rĭf ĭk, a. terrífico.
terrify, têr rĭfĭ, v. a. aterrar, espantar.
territorial, têrrĭtô rĭăl, a. territorial. [m.
territory, têr rĭtŏrê, s. territorio, distrito,
terror, têr răr, s. terror, pavor, m.
terrorist, –ĭst, s. terrorista, m. [pulidez.
terse, tărs, a. terso, pulido; –ly, ad. con

terseness, *-nĕs*, s. elegancia, f.
tertian, *tŭr'shän*, s. terciana, f.   [logía).
tertiary, *tŭr'shū'rĕ*, a. terciario (en geo-
tesselate, *tĕs'sĕlāt*, v. a. taracear.
test, *tĕst*, s. copela, f.; piedra de toque, f.;
   prueba, f.
testaceous, *tĕstā'shŭs*, a. testáceo.
testament, *tĕs'tăment*, s. testamento, m.
testamentary, *tĕstăment'ărĕ*, a. testamen-
testator, *tĕstā'tŭr*, s. testador, m. |tario.
testatrix, *tĕstā'triks*, s. testadora, f.
tester, *tĕs'tŭr*, s. cielo de cama, m.
testicles, *tĕs'tĭkls*, s. pl. testículos, m. pl.
testifier, *tĕs'tĭflŭr*, s. testificante, m.
testify, *tĕs'tĭfī*, v. a. testificar, atestiguar.
testily, *tĕs'tĭlĕ*, ad. con morosidad.
testimonial, *tĕstĭmō'nĭăl*, s. atestación, f.
testimony, *tĕs'tĭmŏnĕ*, s. testimonio, m.
testiness, *tĕs'tĭnĕs*, s. mal humor, m.
testy, *tĕs'tĭ*, a. tétrico.
tether, *tĕth'ŭr*, s. traba, f.; maniota, f.
text, *tĕkst*, s. texto, m.   [gordo, m.
text-hand, *-hănd*, s. carácter de letra muy
textile, *tĕks'tĭl*, a. hilable.
textual, *tĕks'tŭăl*, a. textual.
texture, *tĕks'tŭr*, s. textura, f.; tejido, m.
than, *thăn*, ad. que, de.   [cias.
thank, *thăngk*, v. a. agradecer, dar gra-
thankful, *-fŭl*, a. grato, agradecido; -ly,
   ad. con gratitud.
thankfulness, *-fŭlnĕs*, s. gratitud, f.
thankless, *-lĕs*, a. ingrato.
thank-offering, *-ŏffŭrĭng*, s. ofrecimiento
   en acción de gracias, m.
thanks, *-s*, s. pl. gracias, f. pl.
thanks-giving, *-s'gĭvĭng*, s. acción de
   gracias, f.; fiesta nacional americana del
   4 de julio, n.
that, *thăt*, pn. aquel, aquello, aquella;
   que; este; – c. porque; para que; so –,
   de modo que.   [v. a. techar con paja.
thatch, *thătsh*, s. techo de paja, m.; –,
thaw, *thă*, s. deshielo, m.; –, v. n. deshe-
   larse.
the, *thĕ*, (*thē*), art. el, la, lo; los, las.
theatre, *thĕ'ătŭr*, s. teatro, m.
theatrical, *thĕā'trĭkăl*, a. teatral; -ly, ad.
   según las reglas del teatro.
thee, *thē*, pn. te, á ti.
theft, *thĕft*, s. hurto, m.
their, *thār*, pn. su, sus; suyo, suya; de ellos, de
   ellas; –s, el suyo, la suya, los suyos, las
   suyas; de ellos, de ellas.
theism, *thĕ'ĭzm*, s. teísmo, deísmo, m.
theist, *thĕ'ĭst*, s. teísta, deísta, m.
them, *thĕm*, pn. los, las, les; ellos, ellas;
   á aquellos, á aquellas.
theme, *thēm*, s. tema, m.
themselves, *thĕmsĕlvs'*, pn. pl. ellos mismos, ellas mismas; sí mismos.
then, *thĕn*, ad. entonces, después; en tal
   caso; now and –, de cuando en cuando.
thence, *thĕns*, ad. desde allí, de ahí, por eso.
thenceforth, *-fŏrth*, ad. desde entonces.
theocracy, *thĕŏk'răsĕ*, s. teocracia, f.
theocratic(al), *thĕŏkrăt'ĭk(ăl)*, a. teocrá-
   tico.
theologic(al), *thĕŏlŏj'ĭk(ăl)*, a. teológico.

theologian, *thĕŏlō'jĭăn*, s. teólogo, m.
theology, *thĕŏl'ŏjĕ*, s. teología, f.
theorem, *thĕ'ŏrĕm*, s. teorema, m.
theoretic(al), *thĕŏrĕt'ĭk(ăl)*, a. teórico; -ly,
   ad. teóricamente.
theorise, *thĕ'ŏrīz*, v. a. teorizar.
theorist, *thĕ'ŏrĭst*, s. teórico, m.
theory, *thĕ'ŏrĕ*, s. teoría, f.   [f.
therapeutics, *thĕrăpū'tĭks*, s. terapéutica.
there, *thār*, ad. allí, allá.   [acerca de.
thereabout(s), *thār'ăbŏŭt(s)*, ad. por ahí,
thereafter, *thārăf'tŭr*, ad. después; según.
thereat, *-ăt'*, ad. por eso, á causa de eso;
   allá.   [eso.
thereby, *-bī'*, ad. con eso; por medio de
therefore, *thār'fŏr*, ad. por esto, por esta
   razón; á consecuencia de eso.
therefrom, *thārfrŏm'*, ad. de allí, de allá;
   de eso, de aquello.
therein(to), *-ĭn'(tō')*, ad. en aquello, en
   eso; dentro de aquello.   [ello.
thereof, *-ŏf'*, ad. de esto, de aquello, de
thereon, *-ŏn'*, ad. en eso, sobre eso.
thereunder, *-ŭn'dŭr*, ad. debajo de eso.
there(un)to, *-(ŭn)tō'*, a. á eso, á ello.
thereupon, *-ăpŏn'*, ad. en consecuencia
   de eso.   [lo; luego, inmediatamente.
therewith, *-wĭth'*, ad. con eso ó con aque-
therewithal, *-wĭthăl'*, ad. además, á más.
thermal waters, *thŭr'măl wăłŭrz*, s. pl.
   termas, f. pl.   [metro, m.
thermometer, *thŭrmŏm'ĕtŭr*, s. termó-
these, *thēz*, pn. pl. estos, estas.
thesis, *thĕ'sĭs*, s. tesis, f.
they, *thā*, pn. pl. ellos, ellas.
thick, *thĭk*, a. espeso, denso, turbio; grueso;
   frecuente; grosero; to speak –, hablar
   con media lengua; –, s. grueso, m.; -ly,
   ad. frecuentemente, continuadamente.
chicken, *-n*, v. a. & n. espesar, condensar;
   condensarse.
thicket, *-ĕt*, s. espesura de un bosque, f.
thick-head(ed), *-hĕd(ĕd)*, a. estúpido.
thickness, *-nĕs*, s. espesura, densidad, f.;
   grosería, f.   [rechoncho.
thick-set, *-sĕt*, a. plantado muy espeso;
thief, *thēf*, s. ladrón, m.; moco de una luz, m.
thief-catcher, *-kătshŭr*, s. alguacil, m.
thieve, *thēv*, v. n. hurtar, robar.
thievish, *thēv'ĭsh*, a. inclinado á hurtar;
   -ly, ad. como ladrón.
thievishness, *-nĕs*, s. ladronicio, m.
thigh, *thī*, s. muslo, m.
thill, *thĭl*, s. vara de un carro, f.
thiller, *-ŭr*, thill-horse, *-hŏrs*, s. caballo de varas, m.
thimble, *thĭmbl*, s. dedal, m.
thin, *thĭn*, a. delgado, delicado, sútil, flaco;
   claro; ralo; –, v. a, enrarecer, atenuar;
   adelgazar; aclarar.
thine, *thīn*, pn. tuyo, tuya, tuyos, tuyas.
thing, *thĭng*, s. cosa, f.; criatura, f.
think, *thĭngk*, v. a. & n. pensar, imaginar,
   meditar, considerar; creer, juzgar.
thinker, *-ŭr*, s. pensador, m.
thinking, *-ĭng*, s. pensamiento, m.; juicio,
   m.; opinión, f.   [número.
thinly, *thĭn'lĕ*, ad. delgadamente; en corto

thinness, —*nĕs,* s. tenuidad, delgadez, raleza, f. [—ly, ad. en tercer lugar.
third, *thĕrd,* a. tercero; —, s. tercio, m.
thirst, *thărst,* s. sed, f.; —, v. n. tener ó padecer sed.
thirstily, —*tlĭ,* a. con anhelo.
thirsty, —*tĭ,* a. sediento.
thirteen, *thăr'tēn,* a. trece.
thirteenth, —*th,* a. décimotercio.
thirtieth, *thăr'tĭĭth,* a. trigésimo.
thirty, *thăr'tĭ,* a. treinta.
this, *thĭs,* pn. este, esta, esto; aqueste, aquesta, aquesto.
thistle, *thĭs'l,* s. cardo silvestre, m.
thither, *thĭth'ăr,* ad. allá, á aquel lugar.
thong, *thŏng,* s. correa, correhuela, f.
thorn, *thŏrn,* s. espino, m.; espina, f.
thorny, —*ĭ,* a. espinoso; arduo.
thorough, *thăr'ō,* pr. por, por medio; —, a. entero, cabal, perfecto; —ly, ad. enteramente, cabalmente.
(**thoroughbred,** —*brĕd,* a. de sangre, de casta (hablando de caballos).
thoroughfaro, —*fār,* s. paso, tránsito, m.
thorough-paced, —*pāst,* a. cabal, perfecto.
those, *thōz,* pn. pl. aquellos, aquellas.
thou, *thŏu,* pn. tú. [que, como sí.
though, *thō,* c. aunque, no obstante; como
thought, *thăt,* s. pensamiento, juicio, m.; opinión, f.; cuidado, m.
thoughtful, —*fŭl,* a. pensativo, meditabundo; —ly, ad. de un modo muy pensativo. [profunda, f.
thoughtfulness, —*fŭlnĕs,* s. meditación
thoughtless, —*lĕs,* a. descuidado; insensato; —ly, ad. descuidadamente, sin reflexión. [inadvertencia, f.
thoughtlessness, —*lĕsnĕs,* s. descuido, m.;
thousand, *thŏu'zănd,* a. mil.
thousandfold, —*fōld,* a. mil veces otro tanto.
thousandth, —*th,* a. milésimo.
thraldom, *thrăl'dăm,* s. esclavitud, f.
thrall, *thrăl,* s. esclavo, m.; esclava, f.
thrash, *thrăsh,* v. a. trillar (grano); golpear; —, v. n. trabajar.
thrasher, —*ăr,* s. trillador, m.
thrashing-floor, —*ĭngflōr,* s. era, f.
thread, *thrĕd,* s. hilo, m.; —, v. a. enhebrar; atravesar.
threadbare, —*băr,* a. raído, muy usado.
threat, *thrĕt,* s. amenaza, f.
threaten, —*n,* v. a. amenazar.
threatening, —*nĭng,* s. amenaza, f.; —ly, [ad. con amenazas.
three, *thrē,* a. tres.
three-cornered, —*kŏrnărd,* a. triangular.
threefold, —*fōld,* a. tríplice, triplo.
three-master, —*māstăr,* s. (mar.) buque de tres palos.
threshold, *thrĕsh'ōld,* s. umbral, m.
thrice, *thrĭs,* ad. tres veces.
thrift, *thrĭft,* s. ganancia, utilidad, f.; economía, frugalidad, f.
thriftily, —*tlĭ,* ad. frugalmente. [monía, f.
thriftiness, —*ĭnĕs,* s. frugalidad, parsi-
thriftless, —*lĕs,* a. manirroto, pródigo.
thrifty, —*ĭ,* a. frugal, económico.
thrill, *thrĭl,* v. a. taladrar, horadar; —, v. n. estremecerse; —, s. estremecimiento, m.

thrive, *thrĭv,* v. n. prosperar, adelantar, aprovechar.
thrivingly, *thrĭ'vĭnglĕ,* ad. prósperamente.
throat, *thrōt,* s. garganta, f.
throat-band, —*bănd,* s. ahogadero, m.
throb, *thrŏb,* v. n. palpitar; —, s. palpitación, f. [agonía, f.
throe, *thrō,* s. dolores de parto, m. pl.;
throne, *thrōn,* s. trono, m.
throng, *thrŏng,* s. tropel de gente, m.; —, v. a. & n. venir de tropel; estrujar á uno la concurrencia muy numerosa y apiñada de gente. [—, v. a. ahogar.
throttle, *thrŏt'tl,* s. gaznate, garguero, m.;
through, *thrō,* pr. de medio á medio; por medio de; — and —, de un lado á otro.
throughout, —*ŏŭt,* pr. por todo; —, ad. en todas partes.
throw, *thrō,* v. a. & n. echar(se), arrojar(se), tirar, lanzar; —, s. tiro, m.; golpe, m.
thrum, *thrŭm,* v. a. rascar las cuerdas de un instrumento.
thrush, *thrŭsh,* s. tordo, m. (ave).
thrust, *thrŭst,* v. a. & n. empujar, impeler; estrechar; entremeterse, introducirse; —, s. estocada, f.; puñalada, f.; lanzada, f.
thud, *thŭd,* s. estrépito, m.; ráfaga, f.
thumb, *thŭm,* s. pulgar, m.; —, v. a. manosear con poca destreza; emporcar con los dedos.
thumbscrew, —*skrō,* s. pulgueras, f. pl.
thump, *thŭmp,* s. porrazo, golpe, m.; —, v. a. aporrear, apuñetear.
thumping, —*ĭng,* a. grueso, pesado.
thunder, *thŭn'dăr,* s. trueno, m.; —, v. a. & n. tronar; atronar; fulminar.
thunder-bolt, —*bōlt,* s. rayo, m.
thunder-clap, —*klăp,* s. tronada, tempestad de truenos, f.
thunder-storm, —*stŏrm,* s. temporal, m.
Thursday, *thărz'dă,* s. jueves, m.
thus, *thŭs,* ad. así, de este modo.
thwack, *thwăk,* v. a. aporrear, apuñear.
thwart, *thwărt,* v. a. cruzar, atravesar; contradecir; —, s. banco de remero, m.
thy, *thĭ,* pn. tu, tus.
thyme, *tĭm,* s. (bot.) tomillo, m.
thyself, *thĭsĕlf',* pn. tí mismo.
tiara, *tĭă'ră,* s. tiara, f.
tick, *tĭk,* s. crédito, m.; garrapata (insecto, f.; funda de almohada, f. [billete, m.
ticket, —*ĕt,* s. boleta, f.; cédula, f.; (rail.)
ticket-collector, —*kŏllĕktăr,* s. ticket-holder, —*hōldăr,* s. (rail.) expendedor de billetes, m.
ticket-office, —*ŏffĭs,* s. (rail.) despacho, m.
ticket-porter, —*pŏrtăr,* s. (rail.) encomendero, comisionista, m.
ticking, *tĭk'ĭng,* s. terliz, m.; tíc-tac, m.
tickle, *tĭk'l,* v. a. hacer cosquillas á alguno; —, v. n. tener cosquillas.
tickling, —*ĭng,* s. cosquillas, f. pl.
ticklish, —*lĭsh,* a. cosquilloso.
ticklishness, —*lĭshnĕs,* s. propiedad de ser cosquilloso, f.
tidal, *tĭ'dăl,* a. (mar.) de la marea.
tide, *tĭd,* s. tiempo, m.; estación, f.; marea, f.; —, v. n. (mar.) andar con la marea.

tide-waiter, *—wātăr,* s. aduanero en el litoral, m.

tidily, *tīd′ĭlĭ,* ad. mañosamente. [aseo,m.

tidiness, *tīd′ĭnĕs,* s. maña, prontitud, f.

tidings, *tī′dĭngz,* s. pl. nuevas, noticias, f.

tidy, *tīd′ĕ,* a. airoso, aseado; diestro. [pl.

tie, *tī,* v. a. anudar, atar; —, s. nudo, m.; atadura, f.; lazo, m.

tier, *—ăr,* s. fila, hilera, f.

tiff, *tĭf,* s. bebida, f.; pique, disgusto, m.

tiffany, *tĭf′ănĕ,* s. tafetán sencillo, m.

tiger, *tī′găr,* s. tigre, m.; lacayo, m.

tight, *tīt,* a. tirante, tieso, tenso; aseado.

tighten, *—n,* v. a. tirar, estirar.

tightly, *—lĕ,* ad. bien apretado; con aseo.

tightness, *—nĕs,* s. tensión, tirantez, f.

tigress, *tī′grĕs,* s. tigra, f.

tile, *tīl,* s. teja, f.; —, v. a. tejar.

tiling, *—ĭng,* s. tejado, m.

till, *tĭl,* pr. & c. hasta que, hasta; —, s. cajón, m.; gaveta, f.; —, v. a. cultivar, labrar.

tillage, *—ĭdj,* s. labranza, f. [del timón, f.

tiller, *—lăr,* s. agricultor, m.; (mar.) caña

tilling, *—lĭng,* s. labranza, f.

tilt, *tĭlt,* s. tienda, cubierta, f.; justa, f.; torneo, m.; —, v. a. entoldar; apuntar la lanza; empinar; —, v. n. justar.

tilth, *tĭlth,* s. labranza, f.

timber, *tĭm′băr,* s. madera de construcción, f.; vigas maestras, f. pl.; —, v.a. enmaderar.

timber-work, *—wărk,* s. maderaje, m.

timber-yard, *—yărd,* s. astillero, m.

timbrel, *tĭm′brĕl,* s. pandero, m.

time, *tīm,* s. tiempo; (mus.) compás, m.; in —, á tiempo; from — to —, de cuando en cuando; —, v. a. adaptar al tiempo.

time-keeper, *—kēpăr,* s.reloj astronómico, m.

timeliness, *—lĭnĕs,* s. oportunidad, f.

timely, *—lĕ,* ad. con tiempo; á propósito; —, a. oportuno.

time-piece, *—pēs,* s. reloj astronómico, m.

time-server, *—sărvăr,* s. (fig.) veleta, f.

time-serving, *—sărvĭng,* s. servilismo, m.

time-worn, *—wŏrn,* a. usado, deslustrado.

timid, *tĭm′ĭd,* a. tímido, temeroso; —ly, ad. con timidez.

timidity, *tĭmĭd′ĭtĕ,* s. timidez, f.

timorous, *tĭm′ărŭs,* a. temeroso; —ly, ad. temerosamente.

tin, *tĭn,* s. estaño, m.; —, v. a. estañar.

tincture, *tĭngk′tŭr,* s. tintura, f.; tinte, m.; —, v. a. teñir, tinturar.

tinder, *tĭn′dăr,* s. yesca, f.

tinge, *tĭnj,* v. a. tinturar, teñir.

tingle, *tĭng′gl,* v. n. zumbar los oídos; latir, punzar. [m.; latido, m.

tingling, *tĭng′glĭng,* s. zumbido de oídos.

tinker, *tĭngk′ăr,* s. latonero, m.; calderero remendón, m. [bar los oídos.

tinkle, *tĭng′kl,* v. a. & n. cencerrear; zum-

tinman, *tĭn′măn,* s. hojalatero, m.

tinner, *tĭn′năr,* s. minero de estaño, m.

tin-plate, *tĭn′plăt,* s. hoja de lata, f.

tinsel, *tĭn′sĕl,* s. brocadillo, m.; oropel, m.

tint, *tĭnt,* s. tinte, m.; —, v. a. teñir.

tin-tack, *tĭn′tăk,* s. tachuela de estaño, f.

tiny, *tī′nĕ,* a. (vulg.) pequeño, chico.

tip, *tĭp,* s. punta, extremidad, f.; —, v. a. herretear; golpear ligeramente.

tippet, *—pĕt,* s. palatina, f.

tipple, *—pl,* v. n. beber con exceso; —, s. bebida, f. [f.

tipsiness, *—sĭnĕs,* s. pequeña embriaguez.

tipstaff, *—stăf,* s. alguacil de vara, m.

tipsy, *—sĕ,* a. borrachuelo, entre dos vinos.

tiptoe, *—tō,* s. punta del pie, f.

tiptop, *—tŏp,* a. excelente, el ó lo mejor; —, s. cumbre, f. [dencia, f.

tirade, *tĭrād′,* s. invectiva, f.; (mus.) ca-

tire, *tīr,* s. fila, hilera, f.; atavío, m.; —, v. a. cansar, fatigar; —, v. n. cansarse; fastidiarse.

tiresome, *tīr′sŭm,* a. tedioso, molesto.

tiresomeness, *—nĕs,* s. tedio, fastidio, m.

tiring-room, *tī′rĭngrŏm,* s. vestuario, m.

tit, *tĭt,* s. haca, f.; paro, m.; — for tat, ad. taz á taz.

titbit, *—bĭt,* s. bocado regalado, m.

tithe, *tĭth,* s. diezmo, m.

titillate, *tĭt′ĭlăt,* v. n. titilar.

title, *tī′tl,* s. título, m.; —, v. a. titular.

title-deed, *—dēd,* s. derecho de propiedad, [m.

title-page, *—pādj,* s. frontispicio de un libro,

titmouse, *tĭt′mŏŭs,* s. paro, m. (pájaro).

titter, *tĭt′tăr,* v. n. sonreírse; —, s. sonrisa

tittle, *tĭt′tl,* s. tilde, m.; mínima, f. [f.

tittle-tattle, *—tăt′tl,* s. charla, f.

titular(y), *tĭt′ŭlăr(ĕ),* a. titular.

to, *tō (tŏ),* pr. á, al, á la, á los, á las; para; por; de; hasta; en; con; que; delante de un verbo, indica sólo el infinitivo y no se usa.

toad, *tōd,* s. sapo, escuerzo, m. [traduce.

toad-stool, *—stŏl,* s. (bot.) hongovejín, m.

toady, *—ĕ,* v. n. andar de gorra.

toadyism, *—ĭzm,* s. servilismo, m.

toast, *tōst,* v. a. tostar; brindar; —, s. tos- tada, f.; brindis, m.

toaster, *—ăr,* s. parrillas, f. pl.

tobacco, *tŏbăk′kō,* s. tabaco, m.

tobacco-box, *—bŏks,* s. tabaquera, f.

tobacconist, *—nĭst,* s. tabaquero, m.

tobacco-pouch, *—pŏŭtsh,* s. petaca, f.

tocsin, *tŏk′sĭn,* s. campana á rebato, f.

to-day, *tŏdā′,* ad. hoy.

toddle, *tŏd′dl,* v. n. trotar.

toddy, *tŏd′dĕ,* s. grog, m.

toe, *tō,* s. dedo del pie, m.

together, *tŏgĕth′ăr,* ad. juntamente, en compañía de otro; al mismo tiempo.

toggery, *tŏg′gărĕ,* s. fruslería, f.; ropave- jería, f.

toil, *tŏĭl,* v. n. fatigarse, trabajar mucho; afanarse; —, s. trabajo, m.; fatiga, f.; afán, f.

toilet, *tŏĭl′ĕt,* s. tocador, m. [m.

toilsome, *tŏĭl′sŭm,* a. trabajoso; fatigoso.

token, *tō′kn,* s. señal, f.; memoria, f.; re- cuerdo, m.

tolerable, *tŏl′ărăbl,* a. tolerable; mediocre.

tolerably, *—ĕ,* ad. tolerablemente, así así.

tolerance, *tŏl′ărăns,* s. toleration, f.; *tŏlără- shŭn,* s. tolerancia, f.

tolerant, *tŏl′ărănt,* a. tolerante.

tolerate, *tŏl′ărăt,* v. a. tolerar.

toll, *tōl,* s. peaje, m.; —, v. a. tocar una campana. [m.

toll-gatherer, *—gădhărŭr,* s. portazguero.

tomahawk, *tŏm'ăhăk,* s. hacha de armas de los indios americanos, f.

tomato, *tŏmā'tŏ,* s. tomate, m.

tomb, *tōm,* s. tumba, f.; sepulcro, m.

tomboy, *tŏm'bŏi,* s. villano, m.; doncella pizpireta y respingona, f. [cral, f.

tomb-stone, *tōm'stŏn,* s. piedra sepul-

tom-cat, *tŏm'kăt,* s. gato entero, m.

tomfoolery, *tŏmfōō'ărĕ,* s. pataratas, frioleras, f. pl.

to-morrow, *tŏmŏr'rō,* ad. mañana.

tomtit, *tŏm'tĭt,* s. paro, m. (pájaro).

ton, *tŭn,* s. tonelada, f.

tone, *tōn,* s. tono de la voz, m.; acento, m.

tongs, *tŏngz,* s. pl. tenaza, f.

tongue, *tăng,* s. lengua, f.; habla, f.; bahía, f.; (of a balance) lengua en el peso; to hold the —, callar.

tongueless, *—lĕs,* a. mudo.

tonic, *tŏn'ĭk,* a. (med.) tónico.

to-night, *tŏnīt',* ad. esta tarde.

tonnage, *tŏn'ăj,* s. porte de un buque, m.

tonsil, *tŏn'sĭl,* s. agallas, f. pl.

tonsure, *tŏn'shŭr,* s. tonsura, f.

too, *tōō,* ad. demasiado; así mismo, aun.

tool, *tōl,* s. herramienta, f.; utensilio, m.

tooth, *tōōth,* s. diente, m.; gusto, m.; —, v. a. dentar; encajar unos dientes en otros.

tooth-ache, *—āk,* s. dolor de muelas, m.

toothless, *—lĕs,* a. desdentado.

toothpick, *—pĭk,* s. mondadientes, m.

toothpowder, *—pŏdŭr,* s. dentrífico, m.

toothsome, *—sŭm,* a. sabroso; comedero.

top, *tŏp,* s. cima, cumbre, f.; último grado, m.; tupé, m.; trompo, m.; (mar.) cofa, f.; —, v. a. & n. elevarse por encima; sobrepujar, exceder; cubrir el mango, el cabo; descabezar los árboles.

topaz, *tŏ'păz,* s. topacio, m.

toper, *tŏ'pŭr,* s. borrachón, bebedor, m.

topic, *tŏp'ĭk,* s. principio general, m.; remedio tópico, m.

topmost, *tŏp'mōst,* a. lo más alto.

topographic(al), *tŏpŏgrăf'ĭk(ăl),* a. topográfico.

topography, *tŏpŏg'răfĕ,* s. topografía, f.

topple, *tŏp'pl,* v. n. volcarse.

topsy-turvy, *tŏp'sĕtŭr'vĕ,* ad. al revés.

torch, *tŏrtsh,* s. antorcha, hacha, f.

torch-bearer, *—bărŭr,* s. hachero, m.

torch-light, *—lĭt,* s. luz de antorcha, f.; —procession, procesión con antorchas, f.

torment, *tŏr'mĕnt,* s. tormento, m. [cán, m.

torment, *tŏrmĕnt',* v. a. atormentar; —

tornado, *tŏrnā'dŏ,* s. turbonada, f.; huracán, m.

torpedo, *tŏrpē'dŏ,* s. tremielga, f. (pez).

torpid, *tŏr'pĭd,* a. entorpecido. [m.

torpor, *tŏr'pŭr,* s. entorpecimiento, estupor, m.

torrent, *tŏr'rĕnt,* s. torrente, m.

torrid, *tŏr'rĭd,* a. tórrido, tostado.

tortoise, *tŏr'tĭs,* s. tortuga, f. [f.

tortoise-shell, *—shĕl,* s. concha de tortuga,

tortuous, *tŏr'tŭăs,* a. tortuoso, sinuoso.

torture, *tŏr'tŭr,* s. tortura, f.; —, v. a. atormentar.

Tory, *tŏ'rĕ,* s. tory, m. (partido conservativo de Inglaterra).

toss, *tŏs,* v. a. tirar, lanzar, arrojar; agitar, sacudir; (in a blanket) mantear; —, s. sacudida, f.; cabezada, f. [mente.

total, *tŏ'tăl,* a. total, entero; —ly, ad. totalmente.

totality, *tŏtăl'ĭtĕ,* s. totalidad, f.

totter, *tŏt'tŭr,* v. n. bambolear; vacilar.

touch, *tŭtsh,* v. a. & n. tocar, palpar; —, s. tocamiento, m.; contacto, m.; tacto, m.; toque, m.; prueba, f.

touch-hole, *—hōl,* s. fogón, m.

touchiness, *—ĭnĕs,* s. susceptibilidad, f.

touching, *—ĭng,* a. patético, conmovedor; —, pr. por lo que toca á. [rial, m.

touch-me-not, *—mĕnŏt,* s. (bot.) mercu-

touch-stone, *—stŏn,* s. piedra de toque, f.

touch-wood, *—wŭd,* s. yesca, f.

touchy, *—ĕ,* a. cosquilloso, vidrioso.

tough, *tŭf,* a. correoso; tieso; viscoso.

toughen, *—n,* v. n. hacerse correosa alguna cosa. [dad, f.; tesura, f.

toughness, *—nĕs,* s. tenacidad, f.; viscosidad, f.

tour, *tŏr,* s. viaje, m.; peregrinación, f. [m.

tourist, *—ĕst,* s. viajero, m.; escritor de viajes, m.

tournament, *—nămĕnt,* s. torneo, m.; justa, f.

tout, *tŏt,* s. el todo; trasero, m.; otero, m.

tow, *tō,* s. copa, f.; remolque, m.; —, v. a. (mar.) remolcar, atoar. [m.

towage, *—ăj,* s. (mar.) remolque, atoaje, m.

toward(s), *tŏ'ărd(z),* pr. & ad. hacia, con dirección á; cerca de, con respecto á.

towel, *tŏw'ĕl,* s. toalla, f.

towel-horse, *—hŏrs,* s. enjugador, m.

tower, *tŏw'ŭr,* s. torre, f.; ciudadela, f.; —, v. n. remontarse; elevarse á una altura. [desmesurada.

town, *tŏwn,* s. ciudad, f.

town-councillor, *—kŏŭnsĭlŭr,* s. concejal, concejil, m.

town-crier, *—krĭŭr,* s. pregonero, m.

town-hall, *—hăl,* **town-house,** *—hŏŭs,* s. casa consistorial, f. [dad, f.

townsfolk, *—zfŏk,* s. pl. gente de la ciudad, f.

township, *—shĭp,* s. ayuntamiento, m.

townsman, *—zmăn,* s. conciudadano, m.

toy, *tŏĭ,* s. chuchería, f.; mirifaque, juguete, m.; —, v. n. jugar, divertirse.

trace, *trăs,* s. huella, pisada, f.; —, v. a. trazar, delinear.

track, *trăk,* s. vestigio, m.; huella, f.; rodada, f.; estola, f.; —, v. a. rastrear.

trackless, *—lĕs,* a. lo que no presenta vestigio de que hayan andado por encima.

tract, *trăkt,* s. trecho, m.; región, comarca, f.; serie, f.; tratado, m.

tractable, *trăk'tăbl,* a. tratable, afable.

tractableness, *—nĕs,* s. afabilidad, docilidad, f.

tractably, *—ĕ,* ad. dócilmente. [dad, f.

traction, *trăk'shŭn,* s. acarreo, m.

trade, *trăd,* s. comercio, tráfico, m.; negocio, trato, m.; ocupación, f.; —, v. n. comerciar, traficar. [navío mercante, m.

trader, *—ŭr,* s. comerciante, traficante, m.

tradesman, *—zmăn,* s. tendero, mercader, m. [los artesanos, f.

trades-union, *—zŭnyăn,* s. asociación de

trade-winds, *—wĭndz,* s. pl. (mar.) monzón, m. [comercial

trading, *trā'dĭng,* s. comercio, m.; —, a

tradition, *trădĭsh'ŭn,* s. tradición, f.
traditional, *–ăl,* a. tradicional; **-ly,** ad.
por tradición. [niar; acusar; propagar.
traduce, *trădūs',* v. a. vituperar; calum-
traffic, *trăf'ĭk,* s. tráfico, m.; mercaderías, f. pl.; **–,** v. n. traficar, comerciar.
trafficker, *–ăr,* s. traficante, comerciante,
negociante, mercader, m.
tragedian, *trăjē'dĭăn,* s. actor trágico, m.
tragedy, *trăj'ĕdĕ,* s. tragedia, f.
tragic(al), *trăj'ĭk(ăl),* a. trágico; **-ally,**
ad. trágicamente. [dad.
tragicalness, *–ălnĕs,* s. tristeza, calami-
tragicomedy, *trăjĭkŏm'ĕdĕ,* s. tragicome-
dia, f. [cómico.
tragi-comical, *trăjĭkŏm'ĭkăl,* a. tragi-
trail, *trāl,* v. a. & n. rastrear; arrastrar;
–, s. rastro, m.; pisada, f.; cola, f.
train, *trān,* v. a. arrastrar, amaestrar, enseñar, criar, adiestrar; disciplinar; **–,** s.
estratagema, f., engaño, m.; serie, f.; séquito, tren, m.; cebo, m.; (rail.) tren.
train-bands, *–băndz,* s. pl. milicias, f. pl.
trainer, *–ăr,* s. maestro, enseñador, m.
training, *–ĭng,* s. educación, disciplina, f.
train-oil, *–ŏĭl,* s. aceite de ballena, m.
trait, *trā,* s. rasgo de carácter, m.
traitor, *trā'tăr,* s. traidor, m.
traitorous, *–ŭs,* a. pérfido, traidor; **-ly,**
ad. traidoramente.
traitress, *trā'trĕs,* s. traidora, f.
trammel, *trăm'mĕl,* s. trasmallo, m.; **–,**
v. a. coger, interceptar. [en el suelo, f.
tramp, *trămp,* s. vagabundo, m.; patada
trample, *trăm'pl,* v. n. pisar muy fuerte.
trampling, *trăm'plĭng,* s. pataleo, m.
tram-way, *–wā,* s. tranvía, m.
trance, *trăns,* s. rapto, m.; éxtasi, m.
tranquil, *trăn'kwĭl,* a. tranquilo; **-ly,** ad.
tranquilamente. [f.
tranquillity, *trănkwĭl'ĭtĕ,* s. tranquilidad,
tranquillize, *trăn'kwĭlĭz,* v. a. tranquilizar.
transact, *trănsăkt',* v. a. negociar; transigir.
transaction, *–ăk'shŭn,* s. transacción, f.;
negociación, f.; **–s,** pl. memorias, f. pl.
transactor, *–ăk'tăr,* s. negociador, m.
transatlantic, *–ătlăn'tĭk,* a. transatlántico.
transcend, *trănsĕnd',* v. a. trascender, pasar; exceder.
transcendency, *–ĕnsĕ,* s. excelencia, f.
transcendent, *–sĕn'dĕnt,* a. sobresaliente;
-ly, ad. excelentemente.
transcribe, *trănskrīb',* v. a. trascribir, copiar.
transcriber, *–ăr,* s. copiante, m.
transcript, *trăn'skrĭpt,* s. trasunto, f.
transcription, *trănskrĭp'shŭn,* s. traslado,
m.; copia, f. [una iglesia, f.
transept, *trăn'sĕpt,* s. nave transversal de
transfer, *trănsfŭr',* v. a. transferir, transportar; **–,** *trăns'fŭr,* s. cesión, f.
transferable, *–făr'ăbl,* a. transferible.
transfiguration, *trănsfĭgūrā'shŭn,* s.
transfiguración, f.
transfigure, *–fĭg'ūr,* v. a. transformar.
transfix, *–fĭks',* v. a. traspasar.
transform, *–fŏrm',* v. a. (& n.) transformarse). [mación, f.
transformation, *–fŏrmā'shŭn,* s. transfor-

transgress, *–grĕs',* v. a. & n. transgredir,
violar. [f.
transgression, *–grĕsh'ŭn,* s. transgresión.
transgressor, *–grĕs'ŏr,* s. transgresor, m.
transient, *trăn'shĕnt,* a. pasajero, transitorio; **-ly,** ad. de un modo transitorio.
transit, *trăns'ĭt,* s. tránsito, m.
transition, *trănzĭsh'ăn,* s. tránsito, m.;
transición, f. [uno á otro.
transitional, *–ăl,* a. que se transfiere de
transitive, *trăns'ĭtĕv,* a. transitivo.
transitoriness, *–ŭărĭnĕs,* s. brevedad, f.
transitory, *–ĭtŭrĕ,* a. transitorio.
translate, *trănslāt',* v. a. trasladar, traducir. [traducción, f.
translation, *–lā'shŭn,* s. translación, f.;
translator, *–lā'tŭr,* s. traductor, m.
translucent, *–lō'sĕnt,* a. trasluciente,
diáfano.
transmarine, *–mărēn',* a. trasmarino.
transmigration, *–mĭgrā'shŭn,* a. transmigración, f. [f.
transmission, *–mĭsh'ŭn,* s. transmisión,
transmit, *–mĭt',* v. a. transmitir.
transmutation, *–mŭtā'shŭn,* s. transmutación, f.
transom, *trăn'sŏm,* s. travesaño, m.
transparency, *trănspā'rĕnsĕ,* s. transparencia, f. [diáfano.
transparent, *–pā'rĕnt,* a. transparente,
transpire, *trănspīr',* v. a. transpirar.
transplant, *trănsplănt',* v. a. trasplantar.
transplantation, *–plăntā'shŭn,* s. tras-
plantación, f., trasplante, m.
transport, *trănspŏrt',* v. a. transportar
deportar, **–,** *trăns'pŏrt,* s. transportación,
f.; (mar.) transporte, m.; criminal conde-
nado á la deportación, m.
transportation, *–pŏrtā'shŭn,* s. transportación, f., transportamiento, m.
transporting, *–pŏr'tĭng,* a. embelesador.
transpose, *–pōz',* v. a. transponer.
transposition, *–pŏzĭsh'ŭn,* s. transposición, f. [shăn, s. transubstanciación, f.
transubstantiation, *trănsŭbstănshā'-*
transverse, *trănsvŭrs',* a. transverso;
-ly, ad. transversalmente.
trap, *trăp,* s. trampa, f.; **–,** v. a. hacer
caer en la trampa. [escotillón, m.
trap-door, *–dŏr,* s. puerta disimulada, f.;
trapeze, *trăpēz',* s. trapecio, m.
trapper, *–pŭr,* s. (am.) cazador de animales peliferos, m.
trappings, *–pĭngz,* s. pl. jaeces, m. pl.
trash, *trăsh,* s. heces, f. pl., desecho, m.;
zupia, f. [valor.
trashy, *–ĕ,* a. vil, despreciable, de ningún
travail, *trăv'ĕl,* s. dolores de parto, m.
travel, *trăv'ĕl,* v. n. viajar; **–,** s. viaje, m.
traveller, *–ăr,* s. viajante, viajero, m.
travelling, *–ĭng,* s. viajes, m. pl.
traverse, *trăv'ŭrs,* v. a. atravesar, cruzar.
travesty, *trăv'ĕstĕ,* s. disfraz, m.; **–,** a.
disfrazado; **–,** v. a. disfrazar.
trawl, *trăl,* v. n. pescar con red rastrera.
tray, *trā,* s. salvilla, batea, f.; artesa, f.

treacherous, *trĕtsh'ắrŭs*, a. traidor, pérfido; **-ly**, ad, traidoramente.

treachery, *trĕtsh'ắrĕ*, s. perfidia, deslealtad, traición, f.

treacle, *trē'kl*, s. triaca, f.

tread, *trĕd*, v. a. & n. pisar, hollar, apretar con el pie; pisotear; patalear; caminar con majestad; **–**, s. piso, f.; pisada,
f.; galladura, f.

treadle, *–l*, s. cárcola, f.; galladura, f.

treason, *trē'zn*, s. traición, f.; **high –**,
delito de lesa majestad, f.　　[á traición.

treasonable, *–ắbl*, a. traidor; **-bly**, ad.

treasure, *trĕzh'ŭr*, s. tesoro, m.; **–**, v. a.

treasurer, *–ŭr*, s. tesorero, m.　　[atesorar.

treasurership, *–ŭrshĭp*, s. tesorería, f.
(empleo).

treasury, *–ĕ*, s. tesorería, f. (oficina).

treat, *trēt*, v. a. & n. tratar; regalar; **–**, s.
trato, banquete, festín, m.

treatise, *–ĭz*, s. tratado, m.

treatment, *–mĕnt*, s. trato, m.

treaty, *–ĕ*, s. tratado, m.

treble, *trĕb'l*, a. tríplice; **–**, v. a. & n.
triplicar(se); **–**, s. (mus.) tiple, m.

trebly, *trĕb'lĕ*, ad. triplicadamente.

tree, *trē*, s. árbol, m.; cepo, m., asta, f.

trefoil, *trē'fŏĭl*, s. trébol, m.

trellis, *trĕl'lĭs*, s. enrejado, m.

tremble, *trĕm'bl*, v. n. temblar.

trembling, *–blĭng*, s. temor, m.; trino, m.

tremblingly, *–lĕ*, ad. trémulamente.

tremendous, *trĕmĕn'dŭs*, a. tremendo;
-ly, ad. de un modo tremendo.

tremor, *trĕm'ŏr*, s. tremor, temblor, m.

tremulous, *trĕm'ūlŭs*, a. trémulo.

tremulousness, *–ŭlŭsnĕs*, s. temblor, m.

trench, *trĕnsh*, v. a. cortar; atrincherar;
–, s. foso, m.; (mil.) trinchera, f.

trenchant, *trĕn'shănt*, a. afilado, cortante.

trencher, *trĕnsh'ŭr*, s. trinchero, m.; mesa,

trencher-man, *–ŭrmăn*, s. comedor, m. [f.

trepan, *trĕpăn'*, s. trépano, m.; **–**, v. a.
trepanar.

trespass, *trĕs'pŭs*, v. a. quebrantar, trans-
pasar, violar; **–**, s. transgresión, violación,

trespasser, *–ŭr*, s. transgresor, m.　　[f.

tress, *trĕs*, s. trenza, f.; rizo de pelo, m.

trestle, *trĕs'sl*, s. armazón de la mesa, f.;
caballete de serrador, m.

trial, *trī'ăl*, s. prueba, f.; ensayo, m.;
examen (judicial), m.

triangle, *trī'ăngl*, s. triángulo, m.

triangular, *trī'ăng'gŭlŭr*, a. triangular.

tribal, *trī'băl*, a. perteneciente á una tribu.

tribe, *trīb*, s. tribu, m. (& f.); raza, casta, f.

tribulation, *trĭbŭlā'shŭn*, s. tribulación, f.

tribunal, *trĭbū'năl*, s. tribunal, m.

tribune, *trĭb'ūn*, s. tribuno, m.; tribuna, f.

tributary, *trĭb'ūtărĕ*, a. & s. tributario (m.).

tribute, *trĭb'ūt*, s. tributo, m.

trice, *trĭs*, s. momento, tris, m.

trick, *trĭk*, s. engaño, fraude, m.; superchería, astucia, f.; burla, f.; maña, f.; baza,
f. (en el juego de naipes); **–**, v. a. engañar;
ataviar; hacer juegos de manos.

trickery, *–ŭrĕ*, s. engaño, dolo, m.

trickster, *–stŭr*, s. engañador, m.

trickle, *–l*, v. n. gotear.

tricky, *–ĕ*, a. astuto, artificioso.

trident, *trī'dĕnt*, s. tridente, m. (cetro).

triennial, *trĭĕn'nĭăl*, a. trienal.

trifle, *trī'fl*, s. bagatela, niñería, f.; **–**, v. n.
bobear; chancear, juguetear.

trifler, *–ŭr*, s. necio, m.; tararira, m.

trifling, *trī'flĭng*, a. frívolo, inútil; **-ly**,
ad. frívolmente, sin consecuencia.

trigger, *trĭg'gŭr*, s. gatillo de escopeta (ó
pistola), m.; pararruedas, m.　[metría, f.

trigonometry, *trĭgŏnŏm'ĕtrĕ*, s. trigono-

trilateral, *trĭlăt'ŭrăl*, a. trilátero.

trill, *trĭl*, s. trino, m.; **–**, v. a. trinar.

trim, *trĭm*, a. compuesto, ataviado; **–**, v. a.
aparejar, preparar; acomodar; adornar;
podar; (mar.) rasurar; orientar (las velas); **–**, v. n. balancear, vacilar; **–**, s.
atavío, adorno, aderezo, m.

trimly, *–lĕ*, ad. lindamente, con primor.

trimming, *–mĭng*, s. guarnición de vestido.

Trinity, *trĭn'ĭtĕ*, s. Trinidad, f.　　　[f.

trinket, *trĭng'kĕt*, s. joya, alhaja, f.;
adorno, m.; bujería, f.; juguetes, m.

trio, *trī'ŏ*, s. (mus.) trío, m.

trip, *trĭp*, v. a. hacer caer á uno echándole
la zancadilla; **–**, v. n. tropezar; resbalar;
hacer un viaje corto; **–**, s. zancadilla, f.;
resbalón, m.; viaje corto, m.

tripartite, *trĭpăr'tĭt*, a. tripartito.

tripe, *trĭp*, s. tripa, f.; intestino, m.

triple, *trĭp'l*, a. tríplice; triple; **–**, v. a.
triplicar.　　　　　　[pl. trigemelos, m. pl.

triplet, *trĭp'lĕt*, s. (poet.) tercerilla, f.; **-s**,

tripod, *trī'pŏd*, s. trípode, m.

tripping, *trĭp'pĭng*, a. veloz, ligero, ágil;
–, s. baile ligero, m.; tropiezo, m.; **-ly**,
ad. velozmente.

trireme, *trī'rēm*, s. trirreme, m.

trisect, *trĭsĕkt'*, v. a. tripartir.　　[f.

trisyllable, *trĭsŭl'ăbl*, s. palabra trisilábica.

trite, *trīt*, a. trivial; usado; **-ly**, ad. vulgarmente.

triteness, *–nĕs*, s. trivialidad, f.

triturate, *trĭt'ŭrāt*, v. a. triturar.

triumph, *trī'ŭmf*, s. triunfo, m.; **–**, v. n.)
triunfar.

triumphal, *trĭŭm'făl*, a. triunfal.

triumphant, *trĭŭm'fănt*, a. triunfante;
victorioso; **-ly**, ad. en triunfo.

triumvirate, *trĭŭm'vĭrăt*, s. triunvirato,
m.　　　　　　　　　　　[trivialmente.

trivial, *trĭv'ĭăl*, a. trivial, vulgar; **-ly**, ad.

triviality, *trĭvĭăl'ĭtĕ*, s. trivialidad, f.

troat, *trōt*, v. n. bramar.　　　　[andorrear.

troll, *trōl*, v. a. voltear; **–**, v. n. girar;

trolley, *trŏl'ĭĕ*, s. (rail.) lorri, truck, m.

trollop, *trŏl'ŭp*, s. gorrona, f.

troop, *trŏp*, s. tropa, f.; cuadrilla, turba,
f.; **–**, v. n. atroparse.

trooper, *–ŭr*, s. soldado á caballo, m.

trophy, *trō'fĕ*, s. trofeo, m.; (poet.) triunfo

tropics, *trŏp'ĭkz*, s. pl. trópico, m.　　[m.

tropical, *–ăl*, a. trópico.

trot, *trŏt*, s. trote, m.; **–**, v. n. trotar.

trotter, *–tŭr*, s. caballo trotón, m.

trouble, *trŭb'l*, v. a. disturbar; afligir;

, s. turbación, f.; disturbio, m.; inquietud, f.; aflicción, pena, f.; congoja, f.

troublesome, *–săm,* a. penoso, fatigoso; importuno [dad, molestia, f.

troublesomeness, *–sămnĕs,* s. incomodi-

troublous, *trăb'lăs,* a. turbulento, confuso.

trough, *trŏf,* s. artesa, gamella, f.; dornajo, m. [talones.

trousering, *trŏá'zŭrĭng,* s. paño para pan-

trousers, *trŏá'zŭrz,* s. pl. calzones largos,

trout, *trŏŭt,* s. trucha, f. (pez). [m. pl.

trowel, *trŏá'ĕl,* s. trulla, llana, f. [(m.).

truant, *trŏá'ănt,* a. & s. holgazán, haragán

truce, *trŏs,* s. tregua, suspensión de armas, f.

truck, *trŭk,* v. n. trocar, cambiar; –, s. cambio, trueque, m.; rueda de cureña, f. (rail.) truck, lorri, m. [cita, f.

truckle, *–l,* v. n. someterse; –, s. ruede-

truckle-bed, *–bĕd,* s. carriola, f.

truck-system, *trŭk'sĭstĕm,* s. paga de los obreros en especie, en ser, f. [f.

truculence, *trŭk'ălĕns,* s. fiereza, crueldad,

truculent, *–ălĕnt,* a. truculento, cruel.

trudge, *trăj,* v. n. andar con afán; afanarse. [exacto.

true, *trŏ,* a. verdadero, cierto; sincero;

true-born, *–bŏrn,* a. legítimo.

true-bred, *–brĕd,* a. de casta legítima.

true-hearted, *–hărtĕd,* a. leal, sincero, franco, fiel.

true-love, *–lăv,* a. (bot.) uva de oso, f.

truffle, *trăf'fl,* s. criadilla de tierra, f.

truism, *trŏ'ĭzm,* s. verdad indubitable f.

truly, *trŏ'lĕ,* ad. en verdad; sinceramente.

trump, *trămp,* s. trompeta, f.; triunfo (en el juego de naipes), m.; –, v. a. ganar con el triunfo; to – up, forjar; inventar.

trumpery, *–ărĕ,* s. hojarasca, f.; bujería, baratija, f. [trompetear; divulgar.

trumpet, *trăm'pĕt,* s. trompeta, f.; –, v. a.

trumpeter, *–ăr,* s. trompetero, m.

truncate, *trăng'kăt,* v. a. truncar; troncar.

truncheon, *trăn'shŭn,* s. cachiporra, f.

trundle, *trăn'dl,* s. rueda baja, f.; carreta de ruedas bajas, f.; rodillo, m.; –, v. a. rodar. [trompa, f.

trunk, *trăngk,* s. tronco, baúl, cofre, m.;

trunk-line, *–lĭn,* **trunk-road,** *–rŏd,* (rail.) tronco, m., línea principal, f.

trunk-maker, *–măkŭr,* s. cofrero, m.

trunnion, *trăn'yŭn,* s. muñón, m.

truss, *trăs,* s. braguero, m.; haz, f.; atado, m.; –, v. a. empaquetar; arremangar.

trust, *trăst,* s. confianza, f.; cargo, depósito, m.; crédito, m.; asociación comercial para monopolizar la venta de algún género, f.; –, v. a. & n. confiar; encargar y fiar; confiarse, fiarse; dar crédito; esperar.

trustee, *trăstĕ',* s. fideicomisario, curador, m.

trustful, *trăst'fŭl,* a. fiel; confiado.

trustily, *–ĭlĕ,* a. fielmente.

trustiness, *–ĭnĕs,* s. fidelidad, probidad, f.

trustworthy, *–wărthĕ,* a. digno de confianza.

trusty, *–ĕ,* a. fiel, leal; seguro. [fianza.

truth, *trŏth,* s. verdad, f.; fidelidad, f.; realidad, f.; **in –,** en verdad.

truthful, *–fŭl,* a. verídico.

truthfulness, *–fŭlnĕs,* s. veracidad, f.

try, *trī,* v. a. & n. examinar, ensayar, probar; experimentar; tentar; intentar; juzgar; purificar, refinar.

trying, *–ĭng,* a. crítico; penoso; cruel.

tub, *tŭb,* s. cubo, m.; tina de madera, f.

tube, *tŭb,* s. tubo, cañón, cañuto, m.

tubercle, *tŭ'bărkl,* s. (med.) tubérculo, m.

tuberose, *tŭ'bărŏz,* s. (bot.) tuberosa, f.

tubular, *tŭ'bŭlăr,* a. tubular.

tuck, *tŭk,* s. estoque, m.; alforza, f.; pliegue; m.; –, v. a. arremangar, recoger.

tucker, *–ăr,* s. gargantilla, f.

Tuesday, *tŭz'dă,* s. martes, m.

tuft, *tŭft,* s. borla, f.; penacho, m.; mazorca de flores, f.; grupo, m.; moño, m.

tufted, *–ĕd,* a. frondoso, velludo. [m.

tug, *tŭg,* v. a. tirar con fuerza; arrancar; –, v. n. esforzarse; –, s. tirada, f.; esfuerzo, m.; (mar.) remolcador, m.

tuition, *tŭĭsh'ăn,* s. tutoría, tutela, f.

tulip, *tŭ'lĭp,* s. tulipa, f.; tulipán, m.

tumble, *tăm'bl,* v. n. caer, hundirse, voltear; revolcarse; –, v. a. revolver; rodar; volcar; –, s. caída, f.; vuelco, m.

tumbler, *–ăr,* s. volteador, m.; vaso (sin pie) para beber, m.

tumbrel, *tăm'brĕl,* s. (mil.) caja de municiones, f.; chirrión, m.

tumbril, *tăm'brĭl,* s. pesebre hecho de esteras de mimbre, m.

tumefy, *tŭ'mĕfĭ,* v. a. hacer entumecerse.

tumor, *tŭ'mŏr,* s. tumor, m., hinchazón, f.

tumult, *tŭ'mŭlt,* s. tumulto, m.

tumultuous, *tŭmŭl'tŭăs,* a. tumultuoso; **–ly,** ad. tumultuariamente [lada, f.

tun, *tŭn,* s. tonel, m.; (fam.) cuero, m.; tonetune, *tăn,* s. tono, m.; armonía, f.; aria, f.; humor, m.; –, v. a. templar un instrumento músico. [dioso.

tuneful, *–fŭl,* a. armonioso, acorde, melo-

tuneless, *–lĕs,* a. disonante.

tunic, *tŭ'nĭk,* s. túnica, f. [quilla tónica, f.

tuning-fork, *tŭ'nĭngfŏrk,* s. (mus.) hor-

tunnel, *tăn'nĕl,* s. cañón de chimenea, m.; túnel, m.; –, v. a. hacer una cosa en forma de embudo. [f.

tunnelling, *–ĭng,* s. abertura de un túnel.

tunny, *tăn'nĕ,* s. atún, m. (pez).

turban, *tŭr'băn,* s. turbante, m.

turbid, *tŭr'bĭd,* a. turbio, cenagoso.

turbot, *tŭr'bŏt,* s. rodaballo, rombo, m. (pez). [confusión, f.

turbulence, *tŭr'bălĕns,* s. turbulencia,

turbulent, *tŭr'bălĕnt,* a. turbulento, tumultuoso; **–ly,** ad. tumultuariamente.

tureen, *tŭrĕn',* s. sopera, f.

turf, *tŭrf,* s. césped, m.; turba, f.; hipódromo, m.; corrida de caballos, f.; –, v. s. cubrir con céspedes.

turgid, *tŭr'jĭd,* a. túmido, inflado.

turkey, *tŭr'kĕ,* s. pavo, m.; pava, f.

turmoil, *tŭr'mŏĭl,* s. disturbio, m.; barahúnda, f.

turn, *tŭrn,* v. a. volver, trocar; verter, traducir; cambiar; tornear; –, v. n. volver, girar, rodar; voltear; dar vueltas; volverse á, mudarse, transformarse; volver casaca; —, s. vuelta, f.; giro, m.; rodeo, m.; turno, m.; vez, f.; procedimiento, modo de portarse, m.; inclinación, f.; servicio, m.; forma, figura, hechura, f.

turncoat, —*kōt,* s. desertor, renegado, m.

turncock, —*kŏk,* s. fontanero, m.

turner, —*ẽr,* s. torneador, tornero, m.

turning, —*ŭng,* s. vuelta, f.; rodeo, m.

turning-in, —*ŭng ĭn,* s. pliegue, m.

turning-lathe, —*ŭng lātk,* s. torno, m.

turnip, *tẽr'nĭp,* s. (bot.) nabo, m.

turnkey, *tẽrn'kē,* s. demandadero de una cárcel, m.

turn-off, *tẽrn'ŏf,* s. encrucijada, f.

turn-out, —*ŏŭt,* s. cesación del trabajo, f.; (rail.) aguja, f.; coche y demás aparejo, m.; producto limpio ó neto, m.

turnpike, —*pīk,* s. molinete, m.; barrera, f.

turn-plate, —*plāt,* **turn-rail,** —*rāl,* **turn-table,** —*tābl,* s. (rail.) plataforma giratoria, tornavía, f.

turnscrew, —*skrō,* s. destornillador, m.

turnspit, —*spĭt,* s. galopín de cocina que da vueltas al asador de mano, m.

turnstile, —*stīl,* s. molinete, m.

turpentine, *tẽr'pẽntīn,* s. trementina, f.

turpitude, *tẽr'pĭtūd,* s. torpeza, infamia, f.

turquoise, *tẽrkōiz',* s. turquesa, f.

turret, *tẽr'rĕt,* s. torrecilla, f.

turreted, —*ĕd,* a. armado con torrecillas.

turtle, *tẽr'tl,* s. tórtola, f.; tortuga de mar, f.

turtle-dove, —*dŭv,* s. tórtola, f.

tush! *tŭsh,* **tut!** *tŭt,* tararira!

tusk, *tŭsk,* s. colmillo, m.

tusked, —*ĕd,* a. colmilludo.

tussle, *tŭs'l,* s. alboroto, m.; grita, f.

tutelage, *tū'tĭlāj,* s. tutela, tutoría, f.

tutelar, *tū'tĕlẽr,* a. tutelar.

tutor, *tū'tẽr,* s. tutor, m.; preceptor, m.; —, v. a. enseñar, instruir; señorear.

tutoress, —*ĕs,* s. tutriz, aya, f.

twaddle, *twŏd'dl,* v. n. charlar.

twain, *twān,* a. dos.

twang, *twāng,* v. a. & n. producir un sonido agudo; restallar; —, s. gangueo, m.; sonido agudo, m.

tweezers, *twē'zẽrs,* s. pl. tenacillas, f. pl.

twelfth, *twĕlfth,* a. duodécimo.

Twelfth-day, —*dā,* **Twelfth-night,** —*nīt,* s. día de reyes, m.; Epifanía, f.

twelve, *twĕlv,* a. doce.

twelvemonth, —*mŭnth,* s. año, m. (doce meses).

twentieth, *twĕn'tĭĕth,* a. vigésimo.

twenty, *twĕn'tē,* a. veinte.

twice, *twīs,* ad. dos veces; al doble.

twig, *twĭg,* s. vareta, varilla, f.; vástago, m.

twilight, *twī'līt,* s. crepúsculo, m.

twill, *twĭl,* s. crucero, m.

twin, *twĭn,* s. gemelo, m.

twine, *twīn,* v. a. torcer; enroscar; —, v. n. entrelazarse; caracolear; —, s. guita, f.; abrazo, m.

twinge, *twĭnj,* v. a. punzar, pellizcar; —, s. dolor agudo ó punzante, m.

twinkle, *twĭng'kl,* v. n. centellear; parpadear.

twinkling, *twĭng'klĭng,* s. vislumbre, f.; guiñada, f.; pestañeo, m.

twirl, *twẽrl,* v. a. voltear; —, s. rotación, f.

twist, *twĭst,* v. a. & n. torcer, retorcer; entretejer; retortijarse; —, s. trenza, f.; cordón, m.; hilo de algodón, m.; torcedura, f.

twit, *twĭt,* v. a. regañar.

twitch, *twĭtsh,* v. a. pellizcar; —, s. pellizco, m.

twitter, *twĭt'tẽr,* v. n. gorjear; —, s. gorjeo, m.

two, *tō,* a. dos.   [ad. al doble.

twofold, —*fōld,* a. doble, duplicado; —, tympan(um), *tĭm'păn(ăm),* s. tímpano, m.

type, *tĭp,* s. tipo, m.; letra, f.

typhoid, *tĭ'foĭd,* a. tifoídeo.

typhus, *tĭ'fŭs,* s. tifo, m.

typic(al), *tĭp'ĭk(ăl),* a. típico; **-ly,** ad. simbólicamente.

typographer, *tĭpŏg'răfẽr,* s. tipógrafo, m.

typographic(al), *tĭpŏgrăf'ĭk(ăl),* a. tipográfico.

typography, *tĭpŏg'răfĕ,* s. tipografía, f.

tyrannic(al), *tĭrăn'nĭk(ăl),* a. tiránico; **-ly,** ad. tiránicamente.

tyrannize, *tĭr'ănīz,* v. a. tiranizar.

tyranny, *tĭr'ănĕ,* s. tiranía, f.; crueldad, f.

tyrant, *tĭ'rănt,* s. tirano, m.

tyro, *tĭ'rō,* s. tirón, bisoño, m.

U.

ubiquitous, *ŭbĭk'wĭtŭs,* a. ubicuo.

ubiquity, *ŭbĭk'wĭtĕ,* s. ubicuidad, f.

udder, *ŭd'dẽr,* s. ubre, f.   [f.

ugliness, *ŭg'lĭnĕs,* s. fealdad, deformidad,

ugly, *ŭg'lĕ,* a. feo, disforme.

ulcer, *ŭl'sẽr,* s. úlcera, f.

ulcerate, —*āt,* v. a. ulcerar.

ulceration, *ŭlsẽrā'shŭn,* s. ulceración, f.

ulterior, *ŭltē'rẽr,* a. ulterior.

ultimate, *ŭl'tĭmāt,* a. último; **-ly,** ad. últimamente.

ultimatum, *ŭltĭmā'tŭm,* s. ultimátum, m.; última condición irrevocable, f.

ultramarine, *ŭltrămărēn',* s. ultramar, m.; —, a. ultramarino.   [tano.

ultramontane, —*mŏn'tān,* s. ultramon-

umber, *ŭm'bẽr,* s. tierra de sombras, f.

umbrage, *ŭm'brāj,* s. sombra, f.; umbría, f.; pretexto, m.; **take—,** tener sospecha.

umbrageous, *ŭmbrā'jŭs,* a. sombrío, umbrío, sombroso.   [m.

umbrella, *ŭmbrĕl'lă,* s. parasol, quitasol,

umpire, *ŭm'pīr,* s. árbitro, m.

unabashed, *ŭnăbăsht',* v. a. descocado.

unabated, *ŭnăbā'tĕd,* a. no disminuído; —, cabal.   [cabal.

unable, *ŭnă'bl,* a. incapaz.

unaccommodating, *ŭnăkkŏm'mŏdātĭng,* a. inconveniente.   [sin acompañamiento.

unaccompanied, *ŭnăkkŏm'pănĭd,* a. solo,

unaccomplished, *ŭnăkkŏm'plĭsht,* a. incompleto, no acabado.

unaccountable, *ŭnăkkŏŭnt'ăbl,* a. inexplicable, extraño.

unaccountably, —*ĕ,* ad. extrañamente.

unaccustomed, *ănăkkăs'tŭmd,* a. desacostumbrado, desusado.

unacknowledged, *ănăknŏl'ĕjd,* a. desconocido; negado.   [cido; ignorado.

unacquainted, *ănăkkwănt'ĕd,* a. desconocido.

unadorned, *ănădôrnd',* a. sin adorno.

unadulterated, *ănădŭl'tŭrătĕd,* a. genuino, puro; sin mezcla.

unaffected, *ănăfĕkt'ĕd,* a. sincero, sin afectación; -ly, ad. naturalmente.

unaided, *ănăd'ĕd,* a. sin ayuda.

unaltered, *ănăl'tŭrd,* a. invariado.

unambitious, *ănămbish'ŭs,* a. no ambicioso.   [f.

unanimity, *ănănĭm'ĭtĕ,* s. unanimidad.

unanimous, *ănăn'ĭmŭs,* a. unánime; -ly, ad. unánimemente.

unanswerable, *ănăn'sŭrăbl,* a. incontrovertible, incontestable.

unanswered, *ănăn'sŭrd,* a. no respondido.

unapproachable, *ănăpprŏtsh'ăbl,* a. inaccesible.

unarmed, *ănărmd',* a. inerme, desarmado.

unasked, *ănăskt',* a. no llamado, no convidado.   [ser asaltado.

unassailable, *ănăssăl'ăbl,* a. incapaz de ser asaltado.

unassisted, *ănăssĕst'ĕd,* a. sin socorro, sin auxilio, sin ayuda.

unassuming, *ănăssŭm'ĭng,* a. nada presuntuoso, modesto.   [disponible.

unattached, *ănătătsht',* a. independiente.

unattainable, *ănăttăn'ăbl,* a. inasequible.

unattempted, *ănăttĕm'tĕd,* a. no experimentado; no intentado.

unattended, *ănăttĕnd'ĕd,* a. sin comitiva.

unavailing, *ănăvăl'ĭng,* a. inútil, vano, infructuoso.

unavoidable, *ănăvŏĭd'ăbl,* a. inevitable.

unavoidably, *-ĕ,* ad. inevitablemente.

unaware, *ănăwăr',* a. desatento.

unawares, *-z,* ad. inadvertidamente; de improviso.

unbar, *ănbăr',* v. a. desatrancar.

unbearable, *ănbăr'ăbl,* a. intolerable.

unbecoming, *ănbĕkŭm'ĭng,* a. indecente, indecoroso; -ly, ad. indecentemente.

unbelief, *ănbĕlĕf',* s. incredulidad, f.

unbeliever, *ănbĕlĕv'ŭr,* s. incrédulo, infiel.

unbend, *ănbĕnd',* v. a. aflojar.   [fiel, m.

unbending, *-ĭng,* a. inflexible.

unbiassed, *ănbĕ'ăst,* a. exento de preocupaciones.   [pontáneo.

unbidden, *ănbĭd'dn,* a. no convidado; espontáneo.

unbind, *ănbĭnd',* v. a. desatar.

unbleached, *ănblĕtsht',* a. no blanqueado.

unblemished, *ănblĕm'ĭsht,* a. sin mancha, sin tacha, irreprensible.

unblushing, *ănblŭsh'ĭng,* a. impudente.

unbolt, *ănbŏlt',* v. a. desatrancar.

unborn, *ănbŏrn',* a. que no ha nacido aun.

unbosom, *ănbŏz'ŭm,* v. a. abrir su pecho á alguno.   [desatado.

unbound, *ănbŏŭnd',* a. no encuadernado.

unbounded, *-ĕd,* a. infinito; ilimitado; -ly, ad. ilimitadamente.

unbred, *ănbrĕd',* a. descortés, impolítico.

unbridle, *ănbrī'dl,* v. a. desenfrenar; -d, a. desenfrenado, licencioso.

unbroken, *ănbrō'kn,* a. indómito; entero.

unbuckle, *ănbŭk'kl,* v. a. deshebillar.

unburden, *ănbŭr'dn,* v. a. descargar, aliunburied, *ănbĕr'ĕd,* a. insepulto.   [viar.

unbutton, *ănbŭt'tn,* v. a. desabotonar.

uncalled for, *ănkâld' fôr,* a. de por su propia voluntad.

uncared for, *ănkărd' fôr,* a. descuidado.

unceasing, *ănsēs'ĭng,* a. sin cesar, continuo.

uncertain, *ănsŭr'tĭn,* a. incierto, dudoso.

uncertainty, *-tĕ,* s. incertidumbre, f.

unchangeable, *ăntshănj'ăbl,* a. inmutable.   [dad, f.

unchangeableness, *-nĕs,* s. inmutabilidad, f.

unchangeably, *-ĕ,* ad. inmutablemente.

unchanged, *ăntshănjd',* a. no alterado.

unchanging, *ăntshănj'ĭng,* a. inalterable, inmutable.   [tativo, etc.

uncharitable, *ăntshăr'ĭtăbl,* a. nada caritativo.

uncharitableness, *-nĕs,* s. falta de caridad, dureza, f.

unchecked, *ăntshĕkt',* a. desenfrenado.

unchristian, *ănkrĭst'yăn,* a. indigno de un cristiano.

uncivil, *ănsĭv'ĕl,* a. grosero, descortés.

uncivilized, *-ĭzd,* a. tosco, salvaje, no civilizado.

unclad, *ănklăd',* a. sin vestido, desnudo.

unclaimed, *ănklāmd',* a. sin reclamación.

uncle, *ăng'kl,* s. tío; (cant) prendero, m.

unclean, *ănklēn',* a. inmundo, puerco, sucio.   [-lĭnĕs, s. suciedad, f.; impureza, f.

uncleanness, *-nĕs,* **uncleanliness,**

unclose, *ănklōz',* v. a. abrir; descubrir, revelar.   [sereno.

unclouded, *ănklŏŭd'ĕd,* a. libre de nubes.

uncock, *ănkŏk',* v. a. desarmar una escopeta.

uncoil, *ănkŏĭl',* v. a. desarrollar.

uncombed, *ănkōmd',* a. no peinado.

uncomely, *ănkŭm'lĕ,* a. indecente; feo; desagradable.

uncomfortable, *ănkŭm'fŭrtăbl,* a. desconsolado; desagradable, descómodo.

uncomfortableness, *-nĕs,* s. descomodidad, f.; desconsuelo, m.

uncomfortably, *-ĕ,* ad. desconsoladamente, incómodamente; tristemente.

uncommon, *ănkŏm'mŏn,* a. raro, extraordinario; -ly, ad. extraordinariamente; raramente.

uncommonness, *-nĕs,* s. raridad, f.

uncompromising, *ănkŏm'prŏmĭzĭng,* a. irreconciliable.   [descuido, m.

unconcern, *ănkŏnsŭrn',* s. indiferencia, f.;

unconcerned, *-d,* a. indiferente; -ly, ad. con indiferencia.   [condiciones, absoluto.

unconditional, *ănkŏndĭsh'ănăl,* a. sin condiciones.

unconfined, *ănkŏnfīnd',* a. libre, ilimitado.

unconfirmed, *ănkŏnfŭrmd',* a. irresoluto, sin resolución, indeciso.

unconnected, *ănkŏnnĕk'tĕd,* a. inconexo.

unconquerable, *ănkŏng'kŭrăbl,* a. invencible, insuperable.

unconscionable, *ănkŏn'shŭnăbl,* a. desrazonable; -bly, ad. sin razón.

unconscious, ănkŏn′shŭs, a. inconsciente; –ly, ad. sin conocimiento ó conciencia de las cosas. [luntario.

unconstrained, ănkŏnstrānd′, a. libre, vo-

uncontrolled, ănkŏntrōld′, a. desenfrenado, irresistible. [vincente.

unconvincing, ănkŏnvĭn′sĭng, a. no convincente. [cork, ănkŏrk′, v. a. destapar.

uncork, ănkŏrk′, v. a. destapar.

uncorrected, ănkŏrrĕk′tĕd, a. incorrecto, no corregido. [íntegro.

uncorrupted, ănkŏrrŭp′tĕd, a. incorrupto.

uncouple, ănkŭp′l, v. a. desatraillar.

uncouth, ănkŭth′, a. extraño; grosero; –ly, ad. groseramente.

uncouthness, –nĕs, s. extrañeza, rareza, f.

uncover, ănkŭv′ŭr, v. a. descubrir.

uncrown, ănkrŏūn′, v. a. destronar.

unction, ăngk′shŭn, s. unción, f.

unctuous, ăngk′tŭŭs, a. untuoso.

uncultivated, ănkŭl′tĭvātĕd, a. inculto.

uncurl, ănkŭrl′, v. a. desenrizar el pelo.

uncut, ănkŭt′, a. no cortado, entero.

undamaged, ăndăm′ăjd, a. ileso, libre de daño.

undaunted, ăndănt′ĕd, a. intrépido.

undeceive, ăndĕsēv′, v. a. desengañar.

undecided, ăndĕsī′dĕd, a. indeciso.

undefiled, ăndĕfīld′, a. impoluto, puro.

undeniable, ăndĕnī′ăbl, a. innegable, incontestable; –bly, ad. indubitablemente.

under, ăn′dŭr, pr. & ad. debajo, inferior á; soto; menos que.

underbid, –bĭd′, v. a. ofrecer por alguna cosa menos de lo que vale.

under-clerk, –klŭrk, s. sotosecretario, m.

underclothing, –klŏthĭng, s. vestido de debajo, m.

undercut, –kŭt′, s. solomo, m. [debajo, m.

underdone, –dŭn′, a. poco cocido.

undergo, –gō′, v. a. sufrir; sostener.

undergraduate, –grăd′ŭăt, s. estudiante que no ha recibido ningún grado, m.

underground, –grŏūnd, s. soterráneo, m.

undergrowth, –grŏth, s. soto, monte tallar, m. [–, s. secreto, clandestino.

underhand, –hănd′, ad. clandestinamente.

underlet, –lĕt′, v. a. subarrendar.

underlie, –lī′, v. n. estar debajo.

underline, –līn′, v. a. rayar las palabras.

underling, –lĭng′, s. agente inferior, m.; hombre vil, m. [brevil, m.

undermine, –mīn′, v. a. minar.

undermost, –mōst, a. ínfimo.

underneath, –nēth, ad. debajo.

under-part, –părt, s. parte inferior, f.

underrate, –rāt′, v. a. desapreciar.

under-secretary, –sĕkrĕtărĕ, s. subsecretario, m. [(que otro).

undersell, –sĕl′, v. a. vender por menos

understand, –stănd′, v. a. entender, comprender.

understanding, –stănd′ĭng, s. entendimiento, m.; inteligencia, f.; conocimiento, m.; correspondencia, f.; –, a. inteligente, perito. [ponder.

undertake, –tāk′, v. a. & n. emprender, resolver, intentar; osar; obligarse á; responder.

undertaker, –tāk′ŭr, s. empresario, m.; asentista, m. [peño, m.

undertaking, –tāk′ĭng, s. empresa, f.; empeño, m.

undertone, –tōn, s. ton bajo, m.

undervalue, –văl′ū, v. a. desapreciar; apreciar en menos. [m.

undervaluer, –văl′ūŭr, s. menospreciador.

underwood, –wŏd, s. monte bajo, m.

underwork, –wŭrk′, v. a. suplantar; –, ăn′dŭrwŭrk, s. menudencias, f. pl.

underwrite, –rīt′, v. a. suscribir; asegurar contra los riesgos del mar.

undeserved, ăndĕzĕrvd′, a. no merecido; –ly, ad. sin haberlo merecido.

undeserving, ăndĕzĕr′vĭng, a. indigno de.

undesigned, ăndĕzīnd′, a. involuntario, hecho sin intención. [cillo.

undesigning, ăndĕzīn′ĭng, a. sincero, sencillo.

undesirable, ăndĕzī′răbl, a. lo que no es deseable. [minado, indeciso.

undetermined, ăndĕtĕr′mĭnd, a. indeterminado, indeciso.

undeviating, ăndē′vĭātĭng, a. regular, firme, estable.

undigested, ăndĭjĕs′tĕd, a. indigesto.

undiminished, ăndĭmĭn′ĭsht, a. entero, no disminuído.

undiscerning, ăndĭzzŭrn′ĭng, a. falto de discernimiento. [plinado.

undisciplined, ăndĭs′sĭplĭnd, a. indisciplinado.

undisguised, ăndĭsgīzd′, a. sin disfraz, cándido, sincero.

undismayed, ăndĭsmād′, a. intrépido.

undisputed, ăndĭspū′tĕd, a. incontestable.

undisturbed, ăndĭstŭrbt′, a. quieto, tranquilo.

undivided, ăndĭvī′dĕd, a. indiviso, entero.

undo, ăndō′, v. a. deshacer, desatar.

undoubted, ăndŏūt′ĕd, a. indubitado, evidente; –ly, ad. indubitablemente.

undress, ăndrĕs′, v. a. desnudar; –, ăn′drĕs, s. paños menores, m. pl., ropa de casa, f. [casa, f.

undried, ăndrīd′, a. mojado.

undue, ăndū′, a. indebido; injusto.

undulate, ăn′dŭlāt, v. n. ondear. [f.

undulation, ăndŭlā′shŭn, s. undulación, f.

unduly, ăndū′lĕ, ad. indebidamente; ilícitamente.

undutiful, ăndū′tĭfŭl, a. desobediente; –ly, ad. inobedientemente. [falta de respeto, f.

undutifulness, –nĕs, s. desobediencia, f.

undying, ăndī′ĭng, a. inmortal.

unearth, ănŭrth′, v. a. desenterrar.

unearthly, –lĕ, a. celeste.

uneasily, ănē′zĭlĕ, ad. inquietamente, incómodamente. [incómodo.

uneasy, ănē′zĕ, a. inquieto, desasosegado.

unedifying, ănēd′ĭfīĭng, a. lo que no edifica con su ejemplo. [ocioso.

unemployed, ănĕmplŏīd′, a. desocupado.

unenlightened, ănĕnlīt′nd, a. no iluminado. [nótono, insípido.

unentertaining, ănĕntŭrtān′ĭng, a. monótono, insípido.

unenviable, ănĕn′vĭăbl, a. lo que no debe envidiarse. [(mente).

unequal, ănē′kwŏl, a. –ly, ad. desigual.

unequalled, –d, a. incomparable.

unerring, ănŭr′rĭng, a. –ly, ad. infalible(mente).

uneven, ănē′vn, a. desigual; barrancoso; impar; –ly, ad. desigualmente.

unevenness, –nĕs, s. desigualdad.

unexampled, *ănĕgzăm' pld,* a. sin ejemplo, único. [irreprensible; irrecusable.

unexceptionable, *–nĕs,* a. [irreprensible; irrecusable.

unexpected, *ănĕkspĕk' tĕd,* a. inesperado; inopinado; *–ly,* ad. de repente; inopinadamente.

unexpectedness, *–nĕs,* s. repentón, m.

unexplored, *ănĕksplŏrd',* a. ignorado, no descubierto.

unfading, *ănfā' dĭng,* a. inmarcesible.

unfailing, *ănfāl' ĭng,* a. infalible, seguro.

unfair, *ănfār',* a. doble, falso; injusto; *–ly,* ad. injustamente.

unfaithful, *ănfăth' fŭl,* a. infiel, pérfido.

unfaithfulness, *–nĕs,* s. infidelidad, perfidia, f. [rado.

unfaltering, *ănfăl' tărĭng,* a. firme, aseguunfamiliar, *ănfămĭl' yăr,* a. desacostumbrado, poco común.

unfashionable, *ănfăsh' ănăbl,* a. opuesto á la moda; *–bly,* ad. contra la moda.

unfasten, *ănfăs' n,* v. a. desatar, soltar, aflojar. [dable, impenetrable.

unfathomable, *ănfăth' ămăbl,* a. insonunfavourable, *ănfā' vărăbl,* a. no favorable. [poco favorable.

unfavourably, *–ĭ,* ad. de una manera unfed, *ănfĕd',* a. falto de alimento.

unfeeling, *ănfēl' ĭng,* a. insensible, duro de corazón.

unfeigned, *ănfānd',* a. verdadero, genuino; *–ly,* ad. sinceramente.

unfelt, *ănfĕlt',* a. no sentido.

unfilial, *ănfĭl' ĭăl,* a. indigno de un hijo.

unfinished, *ănfĭn' ĭsht,* a. imperfecto, no acabado.

unfit, *ănfĭt',* a. desconveniente, inepto, incapaz; *–ly,* ad. impropiamente; *–v,* a. inhabilitar. [dad, f.

unfitness, *–nĕs,* s. ineptitud, f.; impropieunfitting, *–tĭng,* a. desconvenible. [dar.

unfix, *ănfĭks',* v. a. soltar, aflojar; liquiunfixed, *–ĕd,* a. errante, vacilante.

unfledged, *ănflĕjd',* a. implume.

unfold, *ănfōld',* v. a. desplegar; revelar; desencerrar.

unforeseen, *ănfŏrsēn',* a. imprevisto.

unforgiving, *ănfŏrgĭv' ĭng,* a. implacable.

unfortunate, *ănfŏr' tănăt,* a. desafortunado, infeliz; *–ly,* ad. por desgracia, infelizmente. [mento.

unfounded, *ănfŏŭnd' ĕd,* a. sin fundaunframed, *ănfrāmd',* a. sin forma ó figura.

unfrequent, *ănfrē' kwĕnt,* a. raro, nada frecuente; *–ly,* ad. raramente.

unfrequented, *ănfrēkwĕnt' ĕd,* a. nada frecuentado. [benevolencia, f.

unfriendliness, *ănfrĕnd' lĭnĕs,* s. falta de unfriendly, *ănfrĕnd' lĭ,* a. nada afable.

unfruitful, *ănfrŏŏt' fŭl,* a. estéril; infructuoso. [fecundidad, f., infructuosidad, f.

unfruitfulness, *–nĕs,* s. esterilidad, inunfurl, *ănfŭrl',* v. a. desplegar, extender.

unfurnished, *ănfŭr' nĭsht,* a. sin muebles; desprovisto.

ungainly, *ăngān' lĭ,* a. zafio, desmañado.

ungenerous, *ănjĕn' ărŭs,* a. ignoble, bajo.

ungentlemanly, *ănjĕn' tlmănlĭ,* a. indigno de un hombre bien criado.

unglazed, *ănglāzd',* a. que no tiene vidrieras; que está sin vidriar.

ungodliness, *ăngŏd' lĭnĕs,* s. impiedad, f.

ungodly, *ăngŏd' lĭ,* a. impío.

ungovernable, *ăngŭv' ărnăbl,* a. indomable, ingobernable.

ungoverned, *ăngŭv' ărnd,* a. desgobernado, desenfrenado.

ungrammatical, *ăngrămmăt' ĭkăl,* a. contrario á las reglas de la gramática.

ungrateful, *ăngrāt' fŭl,* a. ingrato; desagradable; *–ly,* ad. ingratamente.

ungratefulness, *–nĕs,* s. ingratitud, f.

ungrounded, *ăngrŏŭnd' ĕd,* a. infundado.

ungrudgingly, *ăngrŭj' ĭnglĭ,* ad. de buena gana. [defensa; negligente.

unguarded, *ăngărd' ĕd,* a. sin guarda ó unhallowed, *ănhăl' lōd,* a. profano.

unhand, *ănhănd',* v. a. soltar las manos.

unhandsome, *–săm,* a. feo, falto de gracia; *–ly,* ad. sin gracia; feamente.

unhandy, *ănhănd' ĭ,* a. desmañado.

unhappily, *ănhăp' pĭlĭ,* ad. infelizmente.

unhappiness, *ănhăp' pĭnĕs,* s. infelicidad.

unhappy, *ănhăp' pĕ,* a. infeliz. [f.

unharmed, *ănhărmd',* a. ileso, sano y salvo.

unhealthiness, *ănhĕlth' ĭnĕs,* s. insalubridad, f.; falta de salud, f.

unhealthy, *ănhĕlth' ĕ,* a. enfermizo.

unheard (of), *ănhărd' (ŏf),* a. inaudito, extraño, sin ejemplo. [preciado.

unheeded, *ănhēd' ĕd,* a. no atendido, desunheedful, *ănhēd' fŭl,* unheeding, *ănhēd' ĭng,* a. negligente; distraído.

unhinge, *ănhĭnj',* v. a. desquiciar; desordenar.

unholy, *ănhōl' ĕ,* a. profano, impío.

unhonoured, *ănŏn' ărd,* a. despreciado, no venerado.

unhook, *ănhŏŏk',* v. a. desganchar.

unhoped (for), *ănhōpd' (fŏr),* a. inesperado.

unhorse, *ănhŏrs',* v. a. botar de la silla al jinete.

unhurt, *ănhŭrt',* a. ileso.

unicorn, *ū' nĭkŏrn,* s. unicornio, m.

uniform, *ū' nĭfŏrm,* a. *–ly,* ad. uniforme(mente); *–,* s. uniforme, m.

uniformity, *ūnĭfŏr' mĭtĕ,* s. uniformidad, f.

unimaginable, *ŭnĭmăj' ĭnăbl,* a. inimaginable. [no alterado.

unimpaired, *ŭnĭmpārd',* a. no disminuído, unimpeachable, *ŭnĭmpētsh' ăbl,* a. incontestable. [portante.

unimportant, *ŭnĭmpŏr' tănt,* a. nada importante.

uninformed, *ŭnĭnfŏrmd',* a. ignorante.

uninhabitable, *ŭnĭnhăb' ĭtăbl,* a. uninhabitable. [desierto.

uninhabited, *ŭnĭnhăb' ĭtĕd,* a. inhabitado.

uninjured, *ŭnĭn' jŭrd,* a. ileso, no dañado.

uninstructed, *ŭnĭnstrăk' tĕd,* a. ignorante, sin educación. [es instructivo.

uninstructive, *ŭnĭnstrăk' tĭv,* a. lo que no unintelligible, *ŭnĭntĕl' ĭjĭbl,* a. ininteligible. [telligible.

unintelligibly, *–ĭ,* a. de un modo inin-

unintentional, ănĕntĕn'shŭndl, a. lo que se hace sin intención. [sado.

uninterested, ănĭn'tŭrĕstĕd, a. desinteresado.

uninteresting, ănĭn'tŭrĕstĭng, a. poco interesante.

uninterrupted, ănĭntŭrrŭp'tĕd, a. sin interrupción, continuo; -ly, ad. continuamente.

uninvited, ănĭnvĭ'tĕd, a. no convidado.

union, ūn'ĭŭn (ūn'yŭn), s. unión, f.

unionist, ūn'yŭnĭst, s. unitario m.

unique, yūn'ĕk, a. único, uno, singular.

unison, ūn'ĭsŭn, s. unisonancia, f.; unisón, m. [m.

unit, ū'nĭt, s, unidad, f.

unitarian, ūnĭtā'rĭăn, s. unitario m.

unite, ūnĭt', v. a. & n. unir(se), juntarse

unitedly, ūnĭ'tĕdlĭ, ad. unidamente, de acuerdo. [formidad, f.

unity, ū'nĭtĭ, s. unidad, concordia, con-

universal, ūnĭvŭr'săl, a. -ly, ad. universal(mente). [lidad, f.

universality, ūnĭvŭrsăl'ĭtĭ, a. universa-

universe, ū'nĭvŭrs, s. universo, m.

university, ūnĭvŭr'sĭtĭ, s. universidad, f.

unjust, ŭnjŭst', a. injusto; -ly, ad. injustamente.

unjustifiable, ŭnjŭs'tĭfĭăbl, a. indisculpable; -bly, ad. inexcusablemente.

unkempt, ŭnkĕmt',a. (fig.) tosco, impolítico.

unkind, ŭnkĭnd', a. nada cortés; -ly, a. & ad. poco favorable; ásperamente.

unkindness, -nĕs, s. desafecto, m.; malignidad, f.

unknowingly, ŭnnō'ĭnglĭ, ad. sin saberlo.

unknown, ŭnnōn', a. incógnito. [lazar.

unlace, ŭnlās', v. a. desabrochar; desenlazar.

unlawful, ŭnlâ'fŭl, a. ilegítimo, ilícito; -ly, ad. ilegítimamente.

unlawfulness, -nĕs, s. ilegalidad, f.

unlearn, ŭnlŭrn', v. a. desaprender.

unlearned, -ĕd, a. indocto.

unleavened, ŭnlĕv'nd, a. ázimo.

unless, ŭnlĕs', c. á menos que, si no.

unlettered, ŭnlĕt'tŭrd, a. iliterato.

unlicensed, ŭnlĭ'sĕnst, a. sin licencia.

unlike, ŭnlĭk', unlikely, -lĭ, a. diferente, disímil; improbable; inverosímil; -ly, ad. improbablemente. [f.

unlikelihood, -lĭhŭd, s. inverisimilitud,

unlimited, ŭnlĭm'ĭtĕd, á. ilimitado; -ly, ad. ilimitadamente.

unload, ŭnlōd', v. a. descargar. [dura.

unlock, ŭnlŏk', v. a. abrir alguna cerra-

unlooked (for), ŭnlŏkt' (fŏr), a. inopinado.

unloose, ŭnlŏs', v. a. desatar. [mente.

unluckily, ŭnlŭk'ĭlĭ, ad. desafortunada-

unlucky, ŭnlŭk'ĭ, a. desafortunado; siniestro.

unmake, ŭnmāk', v. a. deshacer. [niestro.

unman, ŭnmăn', v. a. afeminar; castrar, capar; desarmar. [jable, intratable.

unmanageable, ŭnmăn'ājăbl, a. inmane-

unmanly, ŭnmăn'lĭ, a. inhumano; afeminado. [tal, grosero.

unmannered, ŭnmăn'nŭrd, a. rudo, bru-

unmannerliness, ŭnmăn'nŭrlĭnĕs, s. mala crianza, descortesía, f.

unmannerly, ŭnmăn'nŭrlĭ, a. malcriado, descortés.

unmarried, ŭnmăr'rĭd, a. soltero; soltera.

unmarry, ŭnmăr'rĭ, v. a. divorciar, descasar.

unmask, ŭnmăsk', v. a. quitar la máscara.

unmeaning, ŭnmēn'ĭng, a. insignificativo.

unmentionable, ŭnmĕn'shŭndbl, a. que no se puede mencionar.

unmerited, ŭnmĕr'ĭtĕd, a. desmerecido.

unmindful, ŭnmĭnd'fŭl, a. olvidadizo, negligente. [-bly, ad. con evidencia.

unmistakable, ŭnmĭstāk'ăbl, a. evidente;

unmoved, ŭnmŏvd', a. inmoto, firme.

unnatural, ŭnnă'tŭrăl, a. contrario á las leyes de la naturaleza; -ly, ad. contra la naturaleza. [cesidad; inútilmente.

unnecessarily, ŭnnĕs'sĕsărĭlĭ, ad. sin ne-

unnecessary, ŭnnĕs'sĕsărĭ, a. inútil, no necesario. [con sus vecinos; descortés.

unneighbourly, ŭnnā'bŭrlĭ,a. poco atento

unnerve, ŭnnŭrv', v. a. enervar.

unnoticed, ŭnnō'tĭst, a. no observado.

unnumbered, ŭnnŭm'bŭrd, a. innumerable.

unobserved, ŭnŏbzŭrvd', a. no observado.

unobtainable, ŭnŏbtān'ăbl, a. lo que no puede obtenerse.

unobtrusive, ŭnŏbtrŏ'sĭv, a. modesto.

unoccupied, ŭnŏk'kŭpĭd, a. desocupado.

unoffending, ŭnŏffĕnd'ĭng, a. sencillo, inocente.

unorthodox, ŭnŏr'thŏdŏks, a. heterodoxo.

unpack, ŭnpăk', v. a. desempaquetar; desenvolver.

unpaid, ŭnpād', a. no pagado.

unpalatable, ŭnpăl'ătăbl, a. desabrido.

unparalleled, ŭnpăr'ălĕld, a. sin paralelo; no par. [sible.

unpardonable, ŭnpăr'dnăbl, a. irremi-

unpardonably, -ĭ, ad. sin perdón.

unparliamentary, ŭnpărlĭmĕn'tări, a. contrario á las reglas del parlamento.

unpeople, ŭnpē'plĭ, v. a. despoblar.

unperceived, ŭnpŭrsēvd', a. no percibido.

unpitying, ŭnpĭt'ĭng, a. incompasivo.

unpleasant, ŭnplĕz'ănt, a. -ly, ad. desagradable(mente).

unpleasantness, -nĕs, s. desagrado, m.

unpolished, ŭnpŏl'ĭsht, a. que no está pulido; rudo, grosero. [maculado.

unpolluted, ŭnpŏllŏ'tĕd, a. impoluto, inmaculado.

unpopular, ŭnpŏp'ŭlăr, a. no popular.

unpractised, ŭnprăk'tĭst, a. inexperto, no versado. [ejemplo.

unprecedented, ŭnprĕs'ĕdĕntĕd, a. sin ejemplo.

unprejudiced, ŭnprĕj'ŭdĭst, a. no preocupado.

unpremeditated, ŭnprĕmĕd'ĭtātĕd, a. inopinado; no premeditado, no pensado con anterioridad.

unprepared, ŭnprĕpārd', a. no preparado.

unpretending, ŭnprĕtĕnd'ĭng, a. el que no tiene pretensiones.

unprincipled, ŭnprĭn'sĭpld, a. el que no tiene principios.

unproductive, ŭnprŏdŭk'tĭv, a. estéril.

unprofitable, ŭnprŏf'ĭtăbl, a. inútil, vano, que para nada sirve.

unprofitableness, *–nēs,* s. inutilidad, f.
unprofitably, *–ĕ,* ad. inútilmente, sin provecho. [no favorable.
unpropitious, *ănprŏpísh'ŭs,* a. infausto.
unprotected, *ănprŏtĕkt'ĕd,* a. desvalido, sin protección.
unprovided, *ănprŏv'ĭdĕd,* a. desprovisto.
unpublished, *ănpŭb'lĭsht,* a. secreto, oculto, no publicado; inédito.
unpunctual, *ănpŭngk'tŭăl,* a. inexacto.
unpunished, *ănpŭn'ĭsht,* a. impune.
unquenchable, *ănkwĕnsh'ăbl,* a. inextinguible.
unquestionable, *ănkwĕst'yănăbl,* a. indubitable, indisputable; **–bly,** ad. sin duda, sin disputa.
unquestioned, *ănkwĕst'yănd,* a. incontestable, no preguntado.
unquiet, *ănkwī'ĕt,* a. inquieto, agitado.
unravel, *ănrăv'l,* v. a. desenredar; desbastar.
unread, *ănrĕd',* a. no leído; ignorante.
unready, *–ĕ,* a. desprevenido, no preparado; pesado.
unreal, *ănrē'ăl,* a. sin realidad.
unreasonable, *ănrē'znăbl,* a. desrazonable.
unreasonableness, *–nēs,* s. sinrazón, f.
unreasonably, *–ĕ,* ad. irracionable.
unregarded, *ănrĕgärd'ĕd,* a. descuidado; despreciado. [inflexible.
unrelenting, *ănrĕlĕnt'ĭng,* a. incompasivo.
unremitting, *ănrĕmĭt'ĭng,* a. constante, incansable.
unrepentant, *ănrĕpĕnt'ănt,* **unrepenting,** *ănrĕpĕnt'ĭng,* a. impenitente.
unreserved, *ănrēzûrvd',* a. sin restricción; franco; **–ly,** ad. abiertamente. [cia.
unresisting, *ănrēzĭst'ĭng,* a. sin resistencia.
unrestrained, *ănrēstrānd',* a. desenfrenado; ilimitado.
unriddle, *ănrĭd'dl,* v. a. desatar un enigma.
unrighteous, *ănrīt'yŭs,* a. injusto; **–ly,** ad. inicuamente. [justicia, f.
unrighteousness, *–nēs,* s. iniquidad, injusticia, f.
unripe(ned), *ănrīp'(nd),* a. inmaturo.
unripeness, *–nēs,* s. falta de madurez, f.
unrival, *ănrī'văl,* a. sin rival, sin igual.
unroll, *ănrōl',* v. a. desarrollar. [igual.
unroof, *ănrōf',* v. a. destechar.
unruffle, *ănrŭf'l,* v. n. calmar.
unruliness, *ănrŏ'lĭnĕs,* s. turbulencia, f.; desenfreno, m. [glado.
unruly, *ănrŏ'lĕ,* a. desenfrenado, desarreglado.
unsaddle, *ănsăd'dl,* v. a. desensillar.
unsafe, *ănsăf',* a. no seguro, peligroso; **–ly,** ad. peligrosamente.
unsaleable, *ănsăl'ăbl,* a. invendible.
unsatisfactory, *ănsătĭsfăk'tŭrĕ,* a. lo que no satisface ó no convence. [harto.
unsatisfied, *ănsăt'ĭsfīd,* a. descontento; no
unsavouriness, *ănsā'vŭrĭnĕs,* s. insipidez, f. [sípido.
unsavoury, *ănsā'yŭrĕ,* a. desabrido, insípido.
unschooled, *ănskŏld',* a. indocto.
unscrew, *ănskrō',* v. a. desentornillar.
unseasonable, *ănsē'znăbl,* a. intempestivo, fuera de propósito. [m.
unseasonableness, *–nēs,* s. despropósito,

unseasonably, *–ĕ,* ad. fuera de sazón.
unseat, *ănsēt',* v. a. tomar el asiento de otra persona. [f.
unseemliness, *ănsēm'lĭnĕs,* s. indecencia.
unseemly, *ănsēm'lĕ,* a. indecente. [visto.
unseen, *ănsēn',* a. invisible; que no se ha
unselfish, *ănsĕlf'ĭsh,* a. desinteresado.
unsettle, *ănsĕt'tl,* v. a. perturbar; hacer incierta alguna cosa.
unsettled, *–d,* a. voluble, inconstante, irresuelto; sin residencia fija. [moble.
unshaken, *ănshā'kn,* a. firme, estable, in-
unsheath, *ănshēth',* v. a. desenvainar.
unsheltered, *ănshĕl'tŭrd,* a. desvalido.
unship, *ănshĭp',* v. a. desembarcar.
unshod, *ănshŏd',* a. descalzo; desherrado.
unshorn, *ănshŏrn',* a. que no ha sido esquilado.
unshrinking, *ănshrĭngk'ĭng,* a. intrépido.
unsightliness, *ănsīt'lĭnĕs,* s. fealdad, deformidad, f. [vista.
unsightly, *ănsīt'lĕ,* a. desagradable á la
unskilful, *ănskĭl'fŭl,* a. inhábil, poco mañoso; **–ly,** ad. con poca maña.
unskilfulness, *–nēs,* s. falta de maña, f.
unskilled, *ănskĭld',* a. inhábil.
unsociable, *ănsō'shăbl,* a. insociable, intratable, huraño.
unsold, *ănsōld',* a. no vendido.
unsoldierlike, *ănsōl'jŭrlīk,* **unsoldierly,** *–lĕ,* a. indigno de un soldado.
unsought, *ănsăt',* a. hallado sin buscarlo.
unsound, *ănsăănd',* a. falto de salud; erróneo; podrido. [de solidez, f.
unsoundness, *–nēs,* s. heterodoxia, f.; falta
unsparing, *ănspăr'ĭng,* a. liberal, generoso. [decible.
unspeakable, *ănspēk'ăbl,* a. inefable, in-
unspeakably, *–ĕ,* ad. indeciblemente.
unstable, *ănstā'bl,* a. instable, inconstante.
unsteadily, *ănstĕd'ĭlĕ,* ad. ligeramente, inconstantemente. [inconstancia, f.
unsteadiness, *ănstĕd'ĭnĕs,* s. ligereza,
unsteady, *ănstĕd'ĕ,* a. voluble, inconstante.
unstruck, *ănstrŭk',* a. impávido.
unstudied, *ănstŭd'ĕd,* a. no estudiado; no premeditado.
unsubdued, *ănsŭbdūd',* a. indomado.
unsubstantial, *ănsŭbstăn'shăl,* a. imaginario; impalpable.
unsuccessful, *ănsŭksĕs'fŭl,* a. infeliz, desafortunado; **–ly,** ad. infelizmente.
unsuitable, *ănsū'tăbl,* a. desproporcionado, incongruente.
unsullied, *ănsŭl'ĭd,* a. inmaculado, puro.
untamable, *ăntā'măbl,* a. indomable.
untamed, *ăntāmd',* a. indómito, indomado, no domado.
untaught, *ăntăt',* a. ignorante; novato.
unteachable, *ăntētsh'ăbl,* a. incapaz de ser enseñado.
untenable, *ăntĕn'ăbl,* a. insostenible.
untenanted, *ăntĕn'ăntĕd,* a. desarrendado.
unthankful, *ănthănk'fŭl,* a. ingrato; **–ly,** ad. ingratamente.
unthankfulness, *–nēs,* s. ingratitud, f.
unthinking, *ănthĭngk'ĭng,* a. desatento, indiscreto.

13 *

unthought(of), *ănthắt' (ŏf)*, a. impensado.

untidiness, *ănti' dĭnĕs*, s. desaliño, m.

untidy, *ănti' dĕ*, a. sucio.

untie, *ănti'*, v. a. desatar, deshacer, soltar.

until, *ăntil'*, ad. hasta; hasta que.

untimely, *ăntim' lĕ*, a. intempestivo, que no está en sazón; —ly, ad. intempestivamente.

untiring, *ăntir' ĭng*, a. incansable.

unto, *ăn' tŏ*, pr. á, para en.

untold, *ăntōld'*, a. que no se ha referido, que no se ha dicho.   [sido tocado.

untouched, *ăntŭtsht'*, a. intacto, que no ha

untoward, *ăntō'ărd*, a. testarudo, desmandiado; siniestro, adverso; —ly, ad. indócilmente; con poca maña; fatalmente.

untravelled, *ăntrăv'ĕld*, a. no frecuentado de pasajeros.

untried, *ăntrīd'*, a. no ensayado ó probado.

untrod(den), *ăntrŏd'(n)*, a. lo que no ha sido pisado.   [tranquilo.

untroubled, *ăntrŭb'ld*, a. no perturbado,

untrue, *ăntrŏ'*, a. falso; pérfido.

untruly, *ăntrŏ'lĭ*, ad. falsamente.

untrustworthy, *ăntrŭst'wŭrthĕ*, a. indigno de la confianza.

untruth, *ăntrŏth'*, s. falsedad, mentira, f.

untutored, *ăntū'tŭrd*, a. mal educado; no instruído.   [sólito.

unused, *ănūzd'*, a. inusitado, no usado; inusual, *ăn'zhăl*, a. inusitado, raro; —ly, ad. inusitadamente, raramente.

unutterable, *ănŭt'tŭrăbl*, a. inefable.

unvaried, *ănvā'rĭd*, a. invariado.

unvarying, *ănvā'rĭing*, a. lo que no varía.

unveil, *ănvā'l*, v. n. quitar el velo, descubrir.   [sado.

unversed, *ănvŭrst'*, a. inexperto, no versado.

unwarrantable, *ănwŏr'răntăbl*, a. indisculpable.   [no asegurado.

unwarranted, *ănwŏr'răntĕd*, a. incierto, no

unwary, *ănwā'rĕ*, a. incauto, imprudente.

unwelcome, *ănwĕl'kăm*, a. desagradable, importuno.

unwell, *ănwĕl'*, a. enfermizo, malo.

unwholesome, *ănhōl'săm*, a. malsano, insalubre.

unwieldy, *ănwēl'dĕ*, a. pesado.

unwilling, *ănwil'ĭng*, a. desinclinado; —ly, ad. de mala gana.   [nancia, f.

unwillingness, *—nĕs*, s. mala gana, repugunwind, *ănwīnd'*, v. a. desenredar, desenmarañar.

unwise, *ănwīz'*, a. imprudente.

unwittingly, *ănwit'tĭnglĕ*, ad. sin saber.

unwonted, *ănwŏn'tĕd*, a. insólito.

unworthily, *ănwŭr'thĭlĕ*, ad. indignamente.   [dad, bajeza, f.

unworthiness, *ănwŭr'thĭnĕs*, s. indignidad, unworthy, *ănwŭr'thĕ*, a. indigno; vil.

unyielding, *ănyēld'ĭng*, a. inflexible.

unyoke, *ănyōk'*, v. a. desuncir.   [reacio.

up, *ăp*, ad. arriba, en lo alto; levantado; —, pr. hacia; hasta; —! ¡arriba! — and down, acá y allá, arriba y abajo.

upbear, *—bār'*, v. a. sostener en alto.

upbraid, *—brād'*, v. a. echar en cara, vituperar.   [convención.

upbraidingly, *—ĭnglĕ*, ad. por vía de re-

upheaval, *ăphē' văl*, s. alzamiento, m.

uphill, *—hĭl*, a. difícil, penoso; —, s. subida, f.   [tener, apoyar, proteger.

uphold, *—hōld'*, v. n. levantar en alto; sosupholder, *—ăr*, s. fautor, m.; sustentáculo, apoyo, m.

upholsterer, *—hōl'stŭrăr*, s. tapicero, m.

upholstery, *—hōl'stŭrĕ*, s. país montañoso, m.; —, a. alto, elevado.

upland, *ăp'lănd*, s. país montañoso, m.; —, a. alto, elevado.

uplift, *—lĭft'*, v. a. levantar en alto.

upon, *ăpŏn'*, pr. sobre, encima, f, por.

upper, *ăp'păr*, a. superior; más elevado.

upper-hand, (fig.) *—hănd*, s. superioridad, f.   [preme; to be —, predominar.

uppermost, *—mŏst*, a. lo más alto, supuppish, *ăp'pĭsh*, a. engreído, altivo.

upright, *ăp'rĭt*, a. derecho, perpendicular, recto; puesto en pie; equitativo; —ly, ad. perpendicularmente; derechamente, rectamente; sinceramente.

uprightness, *—rĭtnĕs*, s. elevación perpendicular, f.; rectitud, probidad, f.

uproar, *ăp'rōr*, s. tumulto, alboroto, m.

uproot, *—rŏt'*, v. a. desarraigar.

upset, *—sĕt'*, v. a. (vulg.) trastornar.

upshot, *ăp'shŏt*, s. remate, m.; fin, m.; conclusión, f.   [abajo.

upside-down, *—sīddŏŭn*, ad. de arriba

upstart, *—stărt*, s. medrado, m.

upward, *—wărd*, a. lo que se dirige hacia arriba; —s, ad. hacia arriba.

uptrain, *ăp' trăn*, s. (rail.) tren ascendente, m., el que marcha al interior en dirección de la capital.

urban, *ăr'băn*, a. urbano.

urbanity, *ŭrbăn'ĭtĕ*, s. urbanidad, f.

urchin, *ŭr'tshĭn*, s. erizo, m.

urethra, *ŭrē'thră*, s. uretra, f.

urge, *ŭrj*, v. a. & n. incitar, hurgar; activar; irritar; urgir.

urgency, *—ĕnsĕ*, s. urgencia, f.

urgent, *—ĕnt*, a. urgente; —ly, ad. instantemente.   [mente.

urinal, *ū'rĭnăl*, s. orinal, m.

urinary, *ū'rĭnŭrĕ*, a. urinario.

urine, *ū'rĭn*, s. orina, f.

urn, *ŭrn*, s. urna, f.

us, *ŭs*, pn. nos; nosotros.

usable, *ūz'ăbl*, a. apto, hábil.

usage, *ū'zăj*, s. tratamiento, m.; uso, m.; usance, *ū'zăns*, s. uso, m.

use, *ūs*, s. uso, m.; servicio, m.; utilidad, práctica, f.; —, v. a. & n. usar, emplear, servirse; acostumbrar; tratar; practicar, soler.

useful, *—fŭl*, a. —ly, ad. útil(mente).

usefulness, *—fŭlnĕs*, s. utilidad, f.

useless, *—lĕs*, a. inútil; —ly, ad. inútilmente.

uselessness, *—lĕsnĕs*, s. inutilidad, f.

usher, *ŭsh'ăr*, s. ujier, m.; sotomaestro, m.; —, v. a. introducir; anunciar.

usual, *ū'zhŭăl*, a. usual, común, usado; —ly, ad. usualmente, ordinariamente.

usurer, *ū'zhŭrăr*, s. usurero, m.

usurious, *ŭzhŏ'rŭs*, a. usurario.

usurp, *ŭzŭrp'*, v. a. usurpar.

usurpation, *ŭzŭrpă'shăn*, s. usurpación, f.

usury, *ú'zhŏrĕ,* s. usura, f.
utensil, *ŭtĕn'sĭl,* s. utensilio, ඕ.
uterine, *ú'tŭrĭn,* a. uterino.
utilise, *ú'tĭlĭz,* v. a. utilizar.
utility, *ŭtĭ'lĭtĕ,* s. utilidad, f.
utmost, *ŭt'mŏst,* a. extremo, sumo; último.
utter, *ŭt'tŭr,* a. exterior; todo; extremo; entero; —, v. a. proferir; expresar; publicar. [presión, f.; venta, f.
utterance, *-ăns,* s. prolación, habla, ext, f.
utterly, *-lĭ,* ad. enteramente, del todo.
uvula, *ú'vŭlă,* s. gallillo, m.
uxorious, *ŭgzŏ'rĭŭs,* a. gurrumino; **-ly,** ad. con gurrumina.

V.

vacancy, *vā'kănsĕ,* s. vacío, m.; vacante, m.; vacación, f. [vacante.
vacant, *vā'kănt,* a. vacío; desocupado;
vacate, *vākāt',* v. a. anular, invalidar.
vacation, *vākā'shŭn,* s. vacación, f.
vaccinate, *văk'sĭnăt,* v. a. vacunar.
vaccination, *văksĭnā'shŭn,* s. vacunación, f.
vacillate, *văs'ĭllăt,* v. n. vacilar. [f.
vacillation, *văsĭllā'shŭn,* s. vaivén, m.
vacuity, *văkū'ĭtĕ,* s. vacuidad, f.
vacuous, *văk'ūŭs,* a. vacío.
vacuum, *văk'ūŭm,* s. vacuo, m.
vagabond, *văg'ăbŏnd,* a. vagabundo; —, s. vagamundo, m. [vagancia, f.
vagary, *văgā'rĕ,* s. capricho, m.; extra-
vagrancy, *vā'grănsĕ,* s. tuna, f.
vagrant, *vā'grănt,* a. vagabundo.
vague, *văg,* a. vago; **-ly,** ad. vagamente.
vails, *vālz,* s. pl. propina, f.
vain, *văn,* a. vano, inútil; vanidoso.
vainglorious, *-glŏ'rĭŭs,* a. vanaglorioso.
vainglory, *-glŏ'rĕ,* s. vanagloria, f.
vainly, *-lĭ,* ad. vanamente. [gada, f.
valance, *văl'ăns,* s. cenefada de cama col-
vale, *vāl,* s. (poet.) valle, m. [vale, m.
valediction, *vălĕdĭk'shŭn,* s. despedida, f.
valedictory, *-tŭrĕ,* a. haciendo despedida.
valentine, *văl'ĕntĭn,* s. filipina, f. apuesta amorosa que hacen en Inglaterra, el día de 14 febrero, los jóvenes y las jóvenes entre sí.
valerian, *vălē'rĭăn,* s. (bot.) valeriana, f.
valet, *văl'ĕt,* s. criado, m.
valetudinarian, *vălĕtūdĭnā'rĭăn,* a. valetudinario, enfermizo.
valiant, *văl'yănt,* a. valiente, valeroso; **-ly,** ad. valientemente.
valid, *văl'ĭd,* a. valido, fuerte.
validity, *vălĭd'ĭtĕ,* s. validación, fuerza, f.
valley, *văl'lĕ,* s. valle, m. [con valor.
valorous, *văl'ŭrŭs,* a. valeroso; **-ly,** ad.
valour, *văl'ŭr,* s. valor, aliento, brío, esfuerzo, m.; fortaleza, f.
valuable, *văl'ūăbl,* a. precioso; **-s,** s. pl. cosas preciosas, f. [f.
valuation, *vălūā'shŭn,* s. tasa, valuación, f.
value, *văl'ū,* s. valor, precio, m.; —, v. a. valuar; estimar, apreciar.

valueless, *-lĕs,* a. que no vale nada.
valve, *vălv,* s. válvula, f.
vamose, *vāmŏs'* (*vā'mŏs*), v. n. (am.) escaparse.
vamp, *vămp,* v. a. remendar. [parse.
vampire, *văm'pĭr,* s. vampiro, m.
van, *văn,* s. vanguardia, f.; abanico, m.; bieldo, m.
vandalism, *văn'dălĭzm,* s. vandalismo, m.
vane, *văn,* s. veleta, f.; (mar.) grímpola, f.
vanguard, *văn'gărd,* s. vanguardia, f.
vanilla, *vănĭl'lă,* s. vainilla, f. [aparecer.
vanish, *văn'ĭsh,* v. n. desvanecerse, des-
vanity, *văn'ĭtĕ,* s. vanidad, f. [quistar.
vanquish, *văng'kwĭsh,* v. a. vencer, con-
vanquisher, *-ŭr,* s. vencedor, m.
vantage(-ground), *văn'tăjgrŏund,* s. ventaja, f.; provecho, m.; oportunidad, f.; superioridad, f. [sípido.
vapid, *văp'ĭd,* a. exhalado, evaporado; in-
vapidness, *-nĕs,* s. insipidez, f.
vaporous, *vā'pŏrŭs,* a. vaporoso. [f.
vapour, *vā'pŭr,* s. vapor, m.; exhalación, f.
variable, *vā'rĭăbl,* a. variable.
variableness, *-nĕs,* s. instabilidad, inconstancia, f.
variably, *-ĕ,* ad. variablemente.
variance, *vā'rĭăns,* s. discordia, desavenencia, f. [danza, f.
variation, *vārĭā'shŭn,* s. variación, mu-
varicose vein, *vā'rĭkōs vĕn,* s. variz, f.
variegated, *vā'rĭĕgātĕd,* a. abigarrado.
variegation, *vārĭĕgā'shŭn,* s. variedad de colores, f.
variety, *vārĭ'ĕtĕ,* s. variedad, f.
various, *vā'rĭŭs,* a. vario, diverso, diferente; **-ly,** ad. variamente. [barnizar.
varnish, *vār'nĭsh,* s. barniz, m.; —, v. a.
varnisher, *-ŭr,* s. embarnizador, m.
vary, *vā'rĕ,* v. a. & n. variar, diferenciar; cambiar, mudarse, discrepar.
vase, *văs,* s. vaso, m.
vassal, *văs'ĕl,* s. vasallo, m.
vassalage, *-ăj,* s. vasallaje, m.
vast, *văst,* a. vasto; inmenso; **-ly,** ad. excesivamente.
vastness, *-nĕs,* s. vastedad, inmensidad, f.
vat, *văt,* s. tina, f.
vault, *vălt,* s. bóveda, f.; cueva, f.; caverna, f.; —, v. a. abovedar; —, v. n. voltear.
vaunt, *vănt,* v. n. jactarse, vanagloriarse.
vaunter, *-ŭr,* s. baladrón, fanfarrón, m.
veal, *vĕl,* s. ternera, f.; ternero, m.
veer, *vĕr,* v. n. (mar.) virar.
vegetable, *vĕj'ĕtăbl,* a. vegetable; —, s. vegetal, m.; **-s,** pl. legumbre, f.
vegetable-garden, *-gărdn,* s. huerta, f.
vegetarian, *vĕjĕtā'rĭăn,* s. vegetariano, m.
vegetate, *vĕj'ĕtăt,* v. n. vegetar.
vegetation, *vĕjĕtā'shŭn,* s. vegetación, f.
vegetative, *vĕj'ĕtătĭv,* a. vegetativo.
vehemence(cy), *vē'ĕmĕns(sĕ),* s. vehemencia, violencia, f.
vehement, *vē'ĕmĕnt,* a. vehemente, violento; **-ly,** ad. vehementemente, patéticamente.
vehicle, *vē'ĭkl,* s. vehículo, m.; carruaje, m.

veil, *vāl,* s. velo, m.; disfraz, m.; –, v. a. encubrir, ocultar.

vein, *vān,* s. vena, f.; cavidad, f.; inclinación del ingenio, f.; humor, m.

veined, *–d,* **veiny,** *–ē,* a. venoso; vetado.

vellum, *vĕl'lŭm,* s. vitela, f.

velocity, *yĕlŏs'ĭtĕ,* s. velocidad, f.

velvet, *vĕl'vĕt,* s. terciopelo, m.; –, a. hecho de terciopelo; terciopelado.

velveteen, *velvētēn',* s. felpa, f.; velludo, m.

velvet-pile, *–pīl,* s. moqueta, f.   [m.

venal, *vē'nāl,* a. venal, mercenario.

venality, *vēnăl'ĭtĕ,* s. venalidad, f.

vend, *vĕnd,* v. a. vender por menor.

veneer, *vēnēr',* v. a. taracear.

venerable, *vĕn'ŭrăbl,* a. venerable.

venerably, *–ē,* ad. venerablemente.

venerate, *vĕn'ŭrāt,* v. a. venerar, honrar.

veneration, *vĕnŭrā'shŭn,* s. veneración, f.

venereal, *vĕnē'rēāl,* a. venéreo.

vengeance, *vĕn'jāns,* s. venganza, f.

venial, *vē'nĭāl,* a. venial.

venison, *vĕn'zn,* s. (carne de) venado, f.

venom, *vĕn'ŏm,* s. veneno, m.

venomous, *–ŭs,* a. venenoso; **–ly,** ad. venenosamente.

venomousness, *–ŭsnĕs,* s. venenosidad, f.

vent, *vĕnt,* s. respiradero, m.; salida, f.; venta, f.; –, v. a. dar salida; echar fuera; divulgar (un proyecto &c.); ventear.

vent-hole, *–hōl,* s. respiradero, m.

ventilate, *vĕn'tĭlāt,* v. a. ventilar; aventar; discutir.   [f.

ventilation, *vĕntĭlā'shŭn,* s. ventilación, f.

ventricle, *vĕn'trĭkl,* s. ventrículo, m.

ventriloquist, *vĕntrĭl'ŏkwĭst,* s. ventrílocuo, m.

venture, *vĕn'tŭr (vĕn'tshŭr),* s. riesgo, m.; ventura, f.; at a –, á la aventura; –, v. n. osar, aventurarse; –, v. a. aventurar, arriesgar.

venturesome, *vĕn'tŭrsŭm,* **venturous,** *–ŭs,* a. osado, atrevido; **–ly,** ad. osadamente.

venturousness, *–nĕs,* s. temeridad, f.

veracious, *vĕrā'shŭs,* a. veraz.

veracity, *vĕrăs'ĭtĕ,* s. veracidad, f.

verb, *vŭrb,* s. (gr.) verbo, m.

verbal, *–āl,* a. verbal, literal; **–ly,** ad. verbalmente.   [palabra.

verbatim, *vŭrbā'tĭm,* ad. palabra por palabra.

verbose, *vŭrbōs',* a. verboso.

verbosity, *vŭrbŏs'ĭtĕ,* s. verbosidad, f.

verdant, *vŭr'dănt,* a. verde.

verdict, *vŭr'dĭkt,* s. (law) veredicto, m.; dictamen, m.

verdigris, *vŭr'dĕgrĭs,* s. cardenillo, verdín, f.

verdure, *vŭr'dŭr,* s. verdura, f.   [m.

verge, *vŭrj,* s. vara, f.; maza, f.; borde, m.; margen, m. & f.; –, v. n. inclinarse ó doblarse hacia abajo.   [dral, m.

verger, *–ŭr,* s. pertiguero de una catedral.   [ción, f.

verification, *vărĭfĭkā'shŭn,* s. verificación, f.

verify, *vĕr'ĭfī,* v. a. verificar.

verily, *vĕr'ĭlĕ,* ad. en verdad.

verjuice, *vŭr'jŏs,* s. agraz, m.

vermicelli, *vŭrmĭtshĕl'lē,* s. pl. fideos, m.pl.

vermicular, *vŭrmĭk'ūlăr,* a. vermicular.

vermifuge, *vŭr'mĭfūj,* s. vermífugo, m.

vermilion, *vŭrmĭl'yăn,* s. bermellón, m.; –, v. a. teñir de cinabrio.

vermin, *vŭr'mĭn,* s. bichos, m. pl.

vernacular, *vŭrnăk'ūlăr,* a. nativo.

vernal, *vŭr'năl,* a. vernal.

versatile, *vŭr'sătĭl,* a. versátil, voluble.

versatility, *vŭrsătĭl'ĭtĕ,* s. veleidad, f.

verse, *vŭrs,* s. verso, m.; versículo, m.

versed, *–d,* a. versado.

version, *vŭr'shŭn,* s. versión, traducción, f.

versus, *vŭr'sŭs,* pr. contra.

vertebra, *vŭr'tĕbrā,* s. vértebra, f.

vertebral, *vŭr'tĕbrăl,* **vertebrate,** *vŭr'tĕbrāt,* a. vertebral.

vertex, *vŭr'tĕks,* s. cenit, vértice, m.

vertical, *vŭr'tĭkāl,* a. –ly, ad. vertical.

vertigo, *vŭrtĭ'gō,* s. vértigo, m. [(mente).

very, *vĕr'ĕ,* a. verdadero, real; idéntico, mismo; –, ad. muy, mucho, sumamente.

vesicle, *vĕs'ĭkl,* s. vejiguela, f.

vespers, *vĕs'pŭrz,* s. pl. vísperas, f. pl.

vessel, *vĕs'sĕl,* s. vasija, f.; vaso, m.; buque, bajel, m.   [investir.

vest, *vĕst,* s. chaleco, m.; –, v. a. vestir.

vestal, *vĕs'tăl,* s. vestal, f. (virgen).

vested, *vĕs'tĕd,* a. vestido, envestido.

vestige, *vĕs'tĭj,* s. vestigio, m.   [dura, f.

vestment, *vĕst'mĕnt,* s. vestido, m.; vestidura, f.

vestry, *vĕs'trĕ,* s. sacristía, f.; concejo abierto, m.   [vestidura, f.

vesture, *vĕs'tŭr (vĕs'tshŭr),* s. vestido, m.;

vetch, *vĕtsh,* s. (bot.) alverjana, f.

veteran, *vĕt'ĕrăn,* a. & s. veterano (m.).

veterinary, *vĕt'ĕrĭnărĕ,* a. lo que pertenece á la veterinaria.

veto, *vē'tō,* s. veto, m.   [á la veterinaria.

vex, *vĕks,* v. a. vejar, molestar.

vexation, *–d'shŭn,* s. vejación, molestia, f.

vexatious, *–d'shŭs,* a. penoso, molesto, enfadoso; **–ly,** ad. penosamente.

viaduct, *vī'ădŭkt,* s. viaducto, m.

vial, *vī'āl,* s. redoma, ampolleta, f.

viand, *vī'ănd,* s. vianda, f.

viaticum, *vīăt'ĭkŭm,* a. viático, m.

vibrate, *vī'brāt,* v. a. vibrar.

vibration, *vībrā'shŭn,* s. vibración, f.

vicar, *vĭk'ăr,* s. vicario, m.

vicarage, *adj.* s. vicaría, f.

vicarious, *vĭkā'rĕŭs,* a. sustituto.

vice, *vīs,* s. vicio, m.; culpa, f.; tornillo, m.; garra, f.; –, ad. (in comp.) vice.

viceroy, *vĭs'rŏĕ,* s. virrey, m.   [dad, f.

vicinity, *vĭsĭn'ĭtĕ,* s. vecindad, proximidad, f.

vicious, *vĭsh'ŭs,* a. vicioso; **–ly,** ad. de una manera viciosa.

vicissitude, *vĭsĭs'ĭtūd,* s. vicisitud, f.

victim, *vĭk'tĭm,* s. víctima, f.

victimize, *–īz,* v. a. sacrificar.

victor, *vĭk'tŭr,* s. vencedor, m.

victorious, *vĭktō'rĕŭs,* a. victorioso; **–ly,** ad. victoriosamente.

victory, *vĭk'tŭrĕ,* s. victoria, f.

victual, *vĭt'l,* v. a. abastecer.   [m.

victualler, *–lăr,* s. abastecedor, proveedor,

victuals, *vĭt'lz,* s. pl. vituallas, f. pl.

videlicet, *vĕdĕl'ĭsĕt,* ad. á saber.

vie, *vī*, v. n. competir.

view, *vū*, s. vista, f.; perspectiva, f.; aspecto, m.; examen, m.; apariencia, f.; –, v. mirar, ver; examinar.

vigil, *vij'il*, s. vela, f.; vigilia, f.

vigilance, *–áns*, s. vigilancia, f.

vigilant, *–ánt*, a. vigilante, atento; –ly, ad. con vigilancia.

vigorous, *vig'ŭrŭs*, a. vigoroso; –ly, ad. vigorosamente.

vigour, *vig'ŭr*, s. vigor, m.; robustez, f.; energía, f.

vile, *vīl*, a. vil, bajo; –ly, ad. vilmente.

vileness, *–nés*, s. vileza, bajeza, f.

vilify, *vil'ifī*, v. a. envilecer.

villa, *vil'lä*, s. quinta, casa de campo, f.

village, *vil'idj*, s. aldea, f.

villager, *–ŭr*, s. aldeano, m.

villainy, *vil'läně*, s. villanía, vileza, f.

villanous, *vil'länŭs*, a. bellaco, vil, ruin; villano; –ly, ad. vilmente.

vindicate, *vin'dikät*, v. a. vindicar, defender; justificación, f.

vindication, *vindikä'shŭn*, s. vindicación, f.

vindictive, *vindik'tiv*, a. vengativo; –ly, ad. por medio de vindicación.

vine, *vīn*, s. vid, f. [rrado, m.

vine-arbour, *–ärbŭr*, s. parral, emparrado, m.

vine-branch, *–bränsh*, s. sarmiento, m.

vine-dresser, *–dressŭr*, s. viñador, m.

vine-estate, *–éstāt*, s. viñedo, m.

vinegar, *vin'égŭr*, s. vinagre, m. [f.

vine-growing, *vīn'grōing*, s. viticultura,

vine-stick, *–stik*, s. rodrigón, m.

vine-stock, *–stŏk*, s. cepa, f.

vineyard, *vin'yärd*, s. viña, f.

vinous, *vīn'ŭs*, a. vinoso.

vintage, *vin'tidj*, s. vendimia, f.

vintager, *–ŭr*, s. vendimiador, m.

vintner, *vint'nŭr*, s. vinatero, m.

viol, *vī'ŏl*, s. (mus.) viola, f.

violate, *vī'ŏlät*, v. a. violar.

violation, *vīŏlä'shŭn*, s. violación, f.

violator, *vī'ŏlätŭr*, s. violador, m.

violence, *vī'ŏléns*, s. violencia, f.

violent, *vī'ŏlént*, a. violento; –ly, ad. violentamente.

violet, *vī'ŏlét*, s. (bot.) violeta, f.

violin, *vī'ŏlín*, s. (mus.) violín, m.

violinist, *–ist*, s. violinista, m.

violoncello, *vīŏlóntshel'lō*, s. (mus.) violón, violoncello, m.

viper, *vī'pŭr*, s. víbora, f.

viperine, *–ín*, **viperous**, *–ŭs*, s. viperino.

virago, *vīrā'gō*, s. marimacho, m.

virgin, *vŭr'jin*, s. virgen, f.; –, a. virginal.

virginal, *–ál*, a. virginal.

virginity, *vŭrjin'itě*, s. virginidad, f.

Virgo, *vŭr'gō*, s. Virgo, f. (signo del zodíaco.

virile, *vir'il* (*vī'ril*), a. viril. [díaco.

virility, *vĭril'itě*, s. virilidad, f. [artes.

virtu, *vŭr'tō*, s. gusto, m. (en las bellas

virtual, *vŭr'tŭäl*, a. –ly, ad. virtual(mente).

virtue, *vŭr'tū*, s. virtud, f.

virtuous, *vŭr'tŭŭs*, a. virtuoso; –ly, ad. virtuosamente.

virulence, *vir'ŭléns*, s. virulencia, f.

virulent, *vir'ŭlént*, a. virulento; –ly, ad. malignamente.

virus, *vī'rŭs*, s. virus, m.

visage, *viz'ādj*, s. rostro, m.; cara, f.

viscera, *vis'sérä*, s. pl. intestinos, m. pl.

viscosity, *viskŏs'itě*, s. viscosidad, f.

viscount, *vī'kŏunt*, s. vizconde, m.

viscountess, *–és*, s. vizcondesa, f.

viscous, *vis'kŭs*, a. viscoso, glutinoso.

visibility, *vizibil'itě*, s. visibilidad, f.

visible, *viz'ibl*, a. visible.

visibly, *–ě*, ad. visiblemente.

vision, *vizh'ŭn*, s. visión, f., fantasma, m.

visionary, *–rě*, a. & s. visionario (m.).

visit, *viz'it*, v. a. (& n.) visitar(se); –, s. visita, f.

visitant, *–ánt*, s. visitador, m.

visitation, *–äshŭn*, s. visitación, visita, f.

visitor, *–ŭr*, s. visitador, m.

visor, *vīz'ŭr*, s. visera, f.; máscara, f.

visored, *–d*, a. enmascarado, disfrazado.

vista, *vis'tä*, s. vista, perspectiva, f.

vital, *vī'tŭl*, a. vital; –ly, ad. vitalmente; –s, s. pl. partes vitales, f. pl.

vitality, *vītäl'itě*, s. vitalidad, f.

vitiate, *vish'iät*, v. a. viciar, corromper.

vitiation, *vishiä'shŭn*, s. depravación, f.

vitreous, *vit'rŭs*, a. vítreo, de vidrio.

vitrify, *vit'rifī*, v. a. (& n.) vitrificar(se).

vitriol, *vit'riŏl*, s. vitriolo, m.

vituperate, *vitū'pŭrät*, v. a. vituperar.

vivacious, *vivā'shŭs*, a. vivaz, despejado.

vivacity, *vivăs'itě*, s. vivacidad, f.

vivid, *viv'id*, a. vivo; –ly, ad. vivamente.

vividness, *–nés*, s. vivacidad, f.

vivification, *vivifikä'shŭn*, s. vivificación,

vivify, *viv'ifī*, v. a. vivificar. [f.

viviparous, *vivip'ărŭs*, a. vivíparo.

vivisection, *vivisek'shŭn*, s. vivisección, f.

vivisectionist, *–ist*, s. partidario de la vivisección, m.

vivisector, *–tŭr*, s. vivisector, m.

vixen, *viks'n*, s. zorra, raposa, f.; mujer vocinglera, f.

vixenish, *–ish*, a. quimerista.

viz, *viz*, ad. á saber.

vizier, *viz'yŭr*, s. visir, m. [m.

vocabulary, *vōkăb'ūlărě*, s. vocabulario,

vocal, *vō'kăl*, a. vocal. [tatriz, f.

vocalist, *vō'kălist*, s. cantador, m.; can-

vocation, *vōkā'shŭn*, s. vocación, f.; oficio, m.; carrera, profesión, f.

vocative, *vōk'ătiv*, s. vocativo, m.

vociferate, *vōsif'ărät*, v. n. vociferar.

vociferation, *vōsifără'shŭn*, s. vocería, grita, f.

vociferous, *vōsif'ărŭs*, a. vocinglero, clamoroso; –ly, ad. de una manera clamorosa.

vogue, *vōg*, s. moda, f.; boga, f. [rosa.

voice, *vŏis*, s. voz, f.; sufragio, m.

void, *vŏid*, a. vacío, desocupado, nulo; falto, privado; –, s. vacuo, m.; –, v. a. vaciar, desocupar.

volatile, *vŏl'ătil*, a. volátil; voluble

volatility, *vŏlătil'itě*, s. volatilidad, f.

volcanic, *vŏlkăn'ik*, a. volcánico.

volcano, *vŏlkā'nŏ*, s. volcán, m.

volition, *vōlish'ŭn*, s. voluntad, f.

volley, *vŏl′lĕ*, s. descarga de armas de fuego, f.; salva, f.; rociada de insultos &c., f.
volt, *vōlt*, s. vuelta, f. (entre jinetes).
volubility, *vŏlŭbĭl′ĭtĭ*, s. volubilidad, f.
voluble, *vŏl′ŭbl*, a. voluble; ligero, veloz.
volume, *vŏl′ŭm*, s. volumen, m.; libro, m. (encuadernado).
voluminous, *vŏlŭ′mĭnŭs*, a. voluminoso.
voluntarily, *vŏl′ŭntărĭlĕ*, ad. voluntariamente.   [(mus.) capricho, m.
voluntary, *vŏl′ŭntărĕ*, a. voluntario; —, s.
volunteer, *vŏlăntēr′*, s. (mil.) voluntario, m.; —, v. n. servir como voluntario.
voluptuous, *vŏlŭp′tūărĕ*, s. hombre voluptuoso, m.
voluptuous, *vŏlŭp′tūăs*, a. voluptuoso; —ly, ad. voluptuosamente.
voluptuousness, *—nĕs*, s. sensualidad, f.
volute, *vŏlūt′*, s. voluta, f. (roleo de columna).
vomica, *vŏm′ĭkă*, s. (med.) vómica, f.
vomit, *vŏm′ĭt*, v. a. vomitar; —, s. vómito, m.; vomitivo, m.   [(mente).
voracious, *vŏrā′shŭs*, a. —ly, ad. voraz.
voracity, *vŏrăs′ĭtĭ*, s. voracidad, f.
vortex, *vŏr′tĕks*, s. remolino, torbellino, m.
votary, *vō′tărĕ*, s. el que ama apasionadamente alguna cosa.
vote, *vōt*, s. voto, sufragio, m.; —, v. a.
voter, *—ăr*, s. votante, m.   [votar.
votive, *vō′tĭv*, a. votivo.   [afirmar.
vouch, *vŏŭtsh*, v. a. atestiguar, certificar,
voucher, *—ăr*, s. testigo, m.; documento justificativo, m.   [dignarse.
vouchsafe, *—sāf′*, v. a. conceder; —, v. n.
vow, *vŏŭ*, s. voto, m.; —, v. a. & n. dedicar, consagrar; votar.
vowel, *—ĕl*, s. vocal, f.
voyage, *vŏŭ′ăj*, s. viaje por mar, m.; —, v. n. hacer un viaje por mar.
voyager, *vŏŭ′ăjŭr*, s. navegador, m.
vulcano, *vŭlkā′nō*, s. volcán, m.
vulgar, *vŭl′gŭr*, a. —ly, ad. vulgar(mente); —, s. vulgo, populacho, m.
vulgarism, *—ĭzm*, s. palabrota, f.
vulgarity, *vŭlgăr′ĭtĭ*, s. vulgaridad, f.; bajeza, f.
vulgarize, *—ĭz*, v. a. vulgarizar.
vulnerable, *vŭl′nărăbl*, a. vulnerable.
vulnerary, *vŭl′nărărĕ*, a. vulnerario.
vulpine, *vŭl′pĭn*, a. zorruno, vulpino.
vulture, *vŭl′tŭr* (*vŭl′tshŭr*), s. buitre, m.
vying, *vī′ĭng*, s. emulación, f.

W.

wad, *wŏd*, s. atado de paja, m.; borra, f.; taco, m.; —, v. a. acolchar.
wadding, *—dĭng*, s. entretela, f.; taco, m.
waddle, *wŏd′dl*, v. n. anadear.
wade, *wād*, v. n. vadear.
wafer, *wā′făr*, s. hostia, f.; oblea, f.
waffle, *wăf′fl*, s. hojuela, f.
waft, *wăft*, v. a. llevar por el aire ó por encima del agua; —, v. n. flotar; —, s. bandería, m.

wag, *wăg*, v. a. mover ligeramente; —, s. persona chocarrera, f.
wage, *wăj*, v. a. hacer guerra.
wager, *—ăr*, s. apuesta, f.; —, v. a. apostar.
wages, *—ĕz*, s. pl. salario, m.   [nada, f.
waggery, *wăg′gărĕ*, s. chocarrería, bufonada, f.
waggish, *wăg′gĭsh*, a. chocarrero.
waggishness, *—nĕs*, s. juguete, m.; chocarrería, f.
waggle, *wăg′gl*, v. n. anadear; menearse.
waggon, *wăg′gŏn*, s. carro grande para llevar géneros ó equipajes, m.; (rail.) vagón, f.
waggoner, *—ăr*, s. carretero, m.   [m.
wagtail, *wăg′tăl*, s. motolita, nevatilla, f.
waif, *wăf*, s. bienes mostrencos, m. pl.
wail, *wăl*, s. lamento, gemido, m.
wain, *wăn*, s. carruaje, m.
wainscot, *wăn′skŏt*, s. enmaderamiento de ensambladura, m.; —, v. a. entablar.
waist, *wăst*, s. cintura, f. (parte inferior del talle).   [m.
waistcoat, *wăst′kŏt* (*wĕs′kŏt*) s. chaleco,
wait, *wăt*, v. a. & n. esperar, aguardar, asechar; quedarse; —, s. asechanza, celada, f.
waiter, *—ăr*, s. mozo de café, sirviente, m.
waiting, *—ĭng*, s. espera, f.; servicio, m.
waiting-maid, (**—woman**), *—ĭngmăd*, (*wŭmăn*), s. doncella, f.
waits, *—s*, s. pl. murga, f., músicos que tocan de noche por las calles en ciertas épocas del año y especialmente por Navidad.
waive, *wăv*, v. a. abandonar.
wake, *wăk*, v. n. velar; despertarse; —, v. a. despertar; —, s. vela, f.; vigilia, f.; (mar.) estela, f.
wakeful, *—fŭl*, a. vigilante; despierto.
wakefulness, *—nĕs*, s. vigilancia, f.; insomnia, f.
waken, *wā′kn*, v. a. (& n.) despertar(se).
waking, *—kĭng*, s. vela, f.
wale, *wăl*, s. (mar.) cinta, f.
walk, *wăk*, v. a. & n. pasear, ir; andar, caminar; —, s. paseo, m.; sitio para pasearse, m.
walker, *—ăr*, s. paseador, andador, m.
walking, *—ĭng*, s. paseo, m.
wall, *wăl*, s. pared, f.; muralla, f.; muro, m.; —, v. a. cercar con muros.
wall-creeper, *—krēpăr*, s. pico murario, m.
wallet, *wŏl′lĕt*, s. mochila, f.; morral de viandante, m.   [m.
wall-flower, *wăl′flŏŭr*, s.(bot.) alelí doble.
wall-fruit, *—frōt*, s. fruta de espalera, f.
wallow, *wŏl′lō*, v. n. encenagarse.
walnut, *wăl′nŭt*, s. nogal, m.; nuez, f.
walrus, *wăl′răs*, s. caballo marino, m.
waltz, *wălts*, s. vals, m. (baile).
wan, *wŏn*, a. pálido.
wand, *wŏnd*, s. vara, f.; vara divinatoria.
wander, *wŏn′dăr*, v. a. & n. errar; vagar;
wanderer, *—ăr*, s. vagamundo, m.   [rodar.
wandering, *—ĭng*, s. paseos, m. pl.; extravío, m.
wane, *wăn*, v. n. disminuir; decaer; —, s. decadencia, f.; (**of the moon**) menguante de la luna, f.

wanness, *wŏn'nĕs,* s. palidez, f.; languidez, f.

want, *wŏnt,* v. a. & n. haber menester; necesitar; faltar; —, s. necesidad, f.; indigencia, f.; falta, f.

wanting, *-ĭng,* a. falto, defectuoso.

wanton, *wŏn'tŏn,* a. lascivo, licencioso; juguetón; —, s. hombre ó mujer lasciva, m.; —, v. n. retozar, juguetear. [mente.

wantonly, *-lĕ,* ad. lascivamente; alegre-

wantonness, *nĕs,* s. lascivia, impudicia, f.; juguete, m.; chanza, f.

war, *wâr,* s. guerra, f.; —, v. n. guerrear.

warble, *wâr'bl,* v. n. trinar; gorjear.

ward, *wârd,* v. a. guardar, defender; (off), evitar; —, s. guarda, defensa, f.; cuartel, m.; tutela, f.; pupilo, m.

warden, *-n,* s. custodio, guardián, m.; alcaide de una cárcel, m.; bedel, m.; gobernador, m.

warder, *-ûr,* s. guarda, guardia, m.

wardmote, *-mōt,* s. junta de barrio, f.

wardrobe, *-rōb,* s. guardarropa, f.

wardship, *-shĭp,* s. tutela, f.

ware, *wâr,* s. mercadería, f.

warehouse, *-hōûs,* s. almacén, m.

warehouse-keeper, *-hōûs kēpûr,* **warehouse-man,** *-hōûsmăn,* s. guarda-almacén, almacenero, m. [dado, f.

warfare, *wâr'fâr,* s. guerra, f.; vida del soldado, f.

warily, *wâ'rĭlĕ,* ad. prudentemente. [f.

wariness, *wâr'ĭnĕs,* s. cautela, prudencia, f.

warlike, *wâr'lĭk,* a. guerrero, belicoso.

warlock, *-lŏk,* s. brujo, hechicero, m.

warm, *wârm,* a. cálido; caliente; furioso, celoso; —, v. a. calentar.

warming-pan, *-ĭngpăn,* s. calentador, m.

warmly, *-lĕ,* ad. con calor, ardientemente.

warmth, *wârmth,* s. calor (moderado), m.; celo, m.

warn, *wârn,* v. a. avisar; advertir, precaver.

warp, *wârp,* s. urdimbre, f.; —, v. n. torcerse, alabearse; —, v. a. torcer; urdir.

warrant, *wŏr'rănt,* v. a. autorizar; privilegiar; garantir, asegurar; —, s. testimonio, m.; justificación, f.; decreto de prisión, m.; autorización, f. [ficable.

warrantable, *-ăbl,* a. abonable, justi-

warranter, *-ûr,* s. garante, fiador, m.

warranty, *-ĕ,* s. garantía, seguridad, f

warren, *wŏr'rĕn,* s. conejero, m.

warrior, *wŏr'rûr,* s. guerrero, soldado, m.

wart, *wârt,* s. verruga, f.

warty, *-ĕ,* a. verrugoso.

vary, *wâ'rĕ,* a. cauto, prudente.

wash, *wŏsh,* v. a. lavar; bañar; —, v. n. lavarse; —, s. lavadura, f.; loción, ablución, f.; pantano, m.; bazofia, f. [dera, f.

washer-woman, *-ûrwûmăn,* s. lavan-

washhand-basin, *-hănd băsn,* s. balangana, f.

wash-house, *-hōûs,* s. lavadero, m.

washing, *-ĭng,* s. lavadura, f.

washy, *-ĕ,* a. húmedo, mojado.

wasp, *wŏsp,* s. avispa, f.

waspish, *-ĭsh,* a. enojadizo, caprichudo.

wassail, *wŏs'sĕl,* s. orgía, orgia, f.

waste, *wâst,* v. a. disminuir; malgastar, disipar; destruir, arruinar, asolar; —, v. n. gastarse; —, s. desperdicio, m.; destrucción, f.; despilfarro, m.; baldío, m.

wasteful, *-fŭl,* a. destructivo; pródigo; -ly, ad. pródigamente.

wastefulness, *-fŭlnĕs,* s. prodigalidad, f.

waste-paper, *-pāpûr,* s. papel de desecho, m.

waster, *-ûr,* s. disipador, gastador, m.

watch, *wŏtsh,* s. desvelo, m.; vigilia, f.; vela, f.; centinela, f.; reloj de faltriquera, m.; -es, s. pl. desvelo, m.; —, v. a. & n. velar, guardar, custodiar; espiar, observar.

watcher, *-ûr,* s. observador, espía, m.

watch-fire, *-fĭr,* s. fuego de bivac, m.

watchful, *-fŭl,* a. vigilante; -ly, ad. cuidadosamente.

watchfulness, *-fŭlnĕs,* s. vigilancia, f.

watch-light, *-lĭt,* s. farol, m.

watch-maker, *-mākûr,* s. relojero, m.

watch-man, *-măn,* s. sereno, m. [f.

watch-tower, *-tŏûûr,* s. atalaya, garita, f.

watch-word, *-wûrd,* s. (mil.) santo, m.; seña, f.

water, *wâ'tûr,* s. agua, f.; marea, f.; —, v. a. regar, humedecer, mojar, bañar; —, v. n. chorrear agua.

waterage, *-āj,* s. barcaje, m.

water-closet, *-klŏzĕt,* s. común á la inglesa, m. [f. pl.

water-colours, *-kŭlûrz,* s. pl. aguadas,

water-course, *-kŏrs,* s. corriente de las aguas, f. [m. pl.

water-cresses, *-krĕsĕz,* s. (bot.) berros,

water-cure, *-kûr,* s. hidropatía, f.

water-dog, *-dŏg,* s. perro de aguas, m.

water-fall, *-făl,* s. cascada, f.

watering, *-ĭng,* s. riego, m.; abrevadura, f.; prensado, m. [m.

watering-place, *-ĭngplās,* s. abrevadero,

watering-pot, *-ĭngpŏt,* s. regadera, f.

water-lily, *-lĭlĕ,* s. ninfea, f.

water-line, *-lĭn,* s. (mar.) flotación, f.

water-man, *-măn,* s. barquero, m.

water-melon, *-mĕl'ŏn,* s. zandía, f.

water-shed, *-shĕd,* s. cumbre de las vertientes de las aguas, f. [marina, f.

water-spout, *-spŏût,* s. manga, bomba

water-tight, *-tĭt,* a. impermeable.

watery, *-ĕ,* a. acuoso, acueo.

wattle, *wŏt'tl,* s. zarco, m.; barbas de gallo, f. pl.; —, v. a. enzarzar. [fluctuar.

wave, *wâv,* s. ola, onda, f.; —, v. n. ondear;

waver, *wâ'vûr,* v. n. vacilar; balancear; estar suspenso. [solución, f.

wavering, *-ĭng,* a. inconstante; —, s. irre-

wavy, *wâ'vĕ,* a. ondeado, undoso.

wax, *wŏks,* s. cera, f.; —, v. a. encerar; —, v. n. crecer; hacerse.

waxen, *-n,* a. de cera.

wax-taper, *-tāpûr,* s. cerilla, f.

wax-work, *-wûrk,* a. figura de cera, f.

waxy, *-ĕ,* a. ceroso.

way, *wĕ,* s. camino, m.; vía, f.; ruta, f.; modo, m.; expediente, m.; **to give —,** ceder; **—s and means,** s. pl. posibles, términos, m. pl.

wayfarer, *–fārdr,* s. pasajero, viajador, m.

waylay, *–lá,* v. a. insidiar.

wayside, *–síd,* s. acera, f.

wayward, *–wûrd,* a. caprichoso, cabe- we, *wê,* pn. nosotros, nosotras.   [zudo.

weak, *wêk,* a. *–ly,* ad. débil(mente.)

weaken, *–n,* v. a. debilitar.

weakling, *–lîng,* s. alfeñique, m.; persona muy delicada, f.

weakness, *–nês,* s. debilidad, f.; parte flaca de una persona, f.

weal, *wêl,* s. prosperidad, f.; bien, m.

wealth, *wêlth,* s. riqueza, f.; bienes, m. pl.

wealthily, *–îlê,* ad. ricamente, opulentamente.

wealthiness, *–nês,* s. opulencia, f.

wealthy, *–ê,* a. rico, opulento.

wean, *wên,* v. a. destetar.   [destetado, m.

weanling, *–lîng,* s. niño ó animal recién

weapon, *wêp'n,* s. arma, f.

wear, *wâr,* v. a. gastar, consumir; usar, llevar; –, v. n. consumirse; –, s. uso, m.

wearable, *–âbl,* a. lo que se puede traer.

weariness, *wêr'inês,* s. cansancio, m.; fatiga, f.; enfado, m.   [enfadosamente.

wearisome, *wêr'tsûm,* a. tedioso; –ly, ad.

weary, *wêr'ê,* v. a. cansar, fatigar; molestar; –, a. cansado, fatigado, tedioso.

weasel, *wê'zl,* s. comadreja, f.

weather, *wêth'ûr,* s. tiempo, m., temperatura, f.; tempestad, f.; –, v. a. doblar; (out), sufrir, superar.   [la intemperie.

weather-beaten, *–bêtn,* a. endurecido á

weather-cock, *–kôk,* s. gallo de campanario, m., giraldilla, veleta, f.

weather-glass, *–glâs,* s. barómetro, m.

weatherwise, *–wîz,* s. vaticinador de las mudanzas del tiempo, m.

weave, *wêv,* v. a. tejer; trenzar.

weaver, *–âr,* s. tejedor, m.

weaving, *wêv'îng,* s. tejido, m.

web, *wêb,* s. tela, f.; tejido, m.

webbed, *–bd,* a. lo que está unido por medio de una telilla.

wed, *wêd,* v. a. (& n.) casar(se).

wedding, *–dîng,* s. nupcias, f. pl.; casamiento, m.   [–, v. a. acuñar; apretar.

wedge, *wêj,* s. cuña, f. (para partir leña);

wedlock, *wêd'lôk,* s. matrimonio, m.

Wednesday, *wênz'dâ,* s. miércoles, m.

wee, *wê,* a. pequeñito.

weed, *wêd,* s. mala hierba, f.; vestido de luto, m.; –, v. a. escardar.

weedy, *–ê,* a. lleno de malas hierbas.

week, *wêk,* s. semana, f.; to–morrow –, mañana en una semana; yesterday, –, ayer hace ocho días.

week-day, *–dâ,* s. día de trabajo, m.

weekly, *–lê,* a. semanal; –, ad. semanalmente, por semana.

weep, *wêp,* v. a. & n. llorar; lamentar.

weeping-willow, *–îngwîlló,* s. sauce de Babilonia, m.

weevil, *wê'vl,* s. gorgojo, m. (insecto).

weft, *wêft,* s. trama, f.; tejido, m.   [siderar.

weigh, *wâ,* v. a. & n. pesar; examinar, con-

weight, *wât,* s. peso, m.; pesadez, f.

weightily, *–îlê,* ad. pesadamente.

weightiness, *–înês,* s. ponderosidad, pesadez, f.; importancia, f.

weighty, *–ê,* a. ponderoso; importante.

weir, *wêr,* s. azud, pesquera, f.

welcome, *wêl'kûm,* a. recibido con agrado; – I ; bien venido! ; –, s. bienvenida, f.; –, v. a. dar la bienvenida á alguno

weld, *wêld,* v. a. soldar el hierro.   [tar, m.

welfare, *wêl'fâr,* s. prosperidad, f.; bienes-

well, *wêl,* s. fuente, f.; manantial, m.; pozo (para sacar agua), m.; –, a. bueno, sano ; –, ad. bien, felizmente; favorablemente; suficientemente; convenientemente; as–as, así como, también como, lo mismo que.

well-being, *–bêîng,* s. felicidad, prosperidad, f.   [educado.

well-bred, *–brêd,* a. bien criado, bien

well-doing, *–dôîng,* s. beneficio, m.

well-met ! *–mêt,* ! bien hallado!

well-to-do, *–tôdô,* a. contento, gozoso.

well-wisher, *–wîshûr,* s. amigo, partidario, m.

welt, *wêlt,* s. ribete, m.; –, v. a. ribetear.

welter, *–ûr,* v. n. revolcarse en lodo.

wen, *wên,* s. lobanillo, m., lupia, f.

wench, *wênsh,* s. moquela, cantonera, f.

wend, *wênd,* v. a. ir; rodear.

west, *wêst,* s. poniente, occidente, m.; –, a. occidental.

westerly, *–ûrlê,* **western,** *–ûrn,* a. occidental.   [occidente.

westward, *–wûrd,* ad. á poniente, hacia occidente.

wet, *wêt,* a. húmedo, mojado; –, s. humedad, f.; –, v. a. mojar, humedecer.

wether, *wêth'ûr,* s. carnero llano, m. .

wetness, *wêt'nês,* s. humedad, f.

wetnurse, *wêt'nûrs,* s. ama de leche, f.

whack, *hwâk,* v. a. aporrear; –, s. golpe, m.

whale, *hwêl,* s. ballena, f.   [m.]

whale-bone, *–bôn,* s. ballena, f.

whaler, *–ûr,* s. pescador de ballena, m.

wharf, *hwôrf,* s. muelle, m.

wharfage, *–âj,* s. muellaje, m.

wharfinger, *–înjûr,* s. fiel de muelle, m.

what, *hwôt,* pn. que, el que, la que, lo que.

what(so)ever, *–(sô)êv'ûr,* pn. cualquier ó cualquiera cosa que, que sea.

wheat, *hwêt,* s. trigo, m.

wheaten, *–n,* a. hecho de trigo.

wheedle, *hwêdl,* v. a. halagar, engañar con lisonjas.

wheel, *hwêl,* s. rueda, f.; –, v. a. (hacer) rodar; volver, girar; –, v. n. rodar.

wheel-barrow, *–bârró,* s. carretón de una rueda, m.

wheeler, *–ûr,* **wheel-horse,** *–hôrs,* s. s. caballo de tronco, m.   [m.

wheel-wright, *–rît,* s. carpintero de prieto.

wheeze, *hwêz,* v. n. jadear.

whelm, *hwêlm,* v. a. cubrir; oprimir.

whelp, *hwêlp,* s. cachorro, m.; –, v. n. parir (a perra).

when, *hwên,* ad. cuando; mientras que.

whence, *hwêns,* ad. de donde; de que.

whence(so)ever, *–(sô)êv'ûr,* ad. de donde quiera.   [quiera que, siempre que.

when(so)ever, *hwên(sô)êv'ûr,* ad. cuando.

where, *hwâr,* ad. donde; **any –,** en cualquier parte; **every –,** en todas partes.

whereabout(s), *–hwŏŭt(s),* ad. hacia donde.

whereas, *–âs',* ad. por cuanto, mientras que; pues que, ya que.

whereat, *–ât',* ad. á lo cual.

whereby, *–bî',* ad. por lo cual, con lo cual, por donde, de que. [cuyo motivo.

wherefore, *whâr'fôr,* ad. por lo que, por

wherefrom, *whârfrôm',* ad. de donde.

wherein, *–în',* ad. en donde, en lo cual, en que.

whereinto, *–în'tŏ,* ad. dentro de lo que.

whereof, *–ôf',* ad. de la cual, de que.

whereon, *–ôn',* ad. sobre lo cual, sobre que. [en cualquiera parte que.

wheresoever, *–sŏĕv' âr,* ad. donde quiera,

where(un)to, *–(ăn)tŏ',* ad. á lo que, á que.

wherever, *–ĕv'âr,* ad. donde quiera que.

whereupon, *–ăpŏn',* ad. sobre que; entonces. [con lo cual.

wherewith(al), *–with(âl)',* ad. con que,

wherry, *hwĕr'rĕ,* s. esquife, m.; barca, f.

whet, *hwĕt,* v. a. afilar, amolar; excitar.

whether, *hwĕth'âr,* ad. si, sea, sea que; –, pn. cual, cual de los dos.

whetstone, *hwĕt'stŏn,* s. aguzadera, f.

whey, *hwâ,* s. suero, m.

which, *hwĭtsh,* pn. que, el, cual, la cual, los cuales, las cuales.

which(so)ever, *–(sŏ)ĕv'âr,* pn. cualquiera.

whiff, *hwĭf,* s. vaharada, f.; bocanada de humo, fumada, f. [terra, m.

Whig, *hwĭg,* s. partido liberal en Inglaterra.

while, *hwîl,* s. rato, m.; vez, f.; **a – ago,** rato ha.

while, *hwîl,* **whilst,** *hwîlst,* ad. mientras.

whim, *hwîm,* s. antojo, capricho, m.

whimper, *–pâr,* v. n. sollozar, gemir.

whimsical, *–sĭkâl,* a. caprichoso, fantástico. [quejido, lamento, m.

whine, *hwîn,* v. n. llorar, lamentar; –, s.

whinny, *hwĭn'nĕ,* v. n. relinchar los caballos. [a. & n. azotar; andar de priesa.

whip, *hwĭp,* s. azote, m.; látigo, m.; –, v.

whip-hand, *–hănd,* s. ventaja, f.

whipper-in, *–pâr'în,* s. cabo de hilera, m. (en el Parlamento de Londres).

whipple-tree, *–pl trē,* s. balancín, m. (de coche &c.).

whirl, *hwârl,* v. a. & n. girar; hacer girar; mover(se) rápidamente; –, s. giro muy rápido, m.

whirligig, *hwâr'lĭgĭg,* s. perinola, f.

whirlpool, *–pŏl,* s. vórtice, m.

whirlwind, *–wĭnd,* s. torbellino, m.

whisk, *hwĭsk,* s. escobilla, f.; cepillo, m.

whisker, *–âr,* s. mostacho, m.; patilla, f.

whisky, *–ĕ,* s. aguardiente de grano, m.; calesín, m. [surrar.

whisper, *hwĭs'pâr,* v. n. cuchichear; su-

whispering, *–îng,* s. cuchicheo, m.; susurro, m.

whist, *hwĭst,* s. wist, m. (juego de naipes).

whistle, *hwĭs'sl,* v. a. & n. silbar; chiflar; –, s. silbo, silbido, m.

whit, *hwĭt,* s. algo, m.; **not a –,** nada.

white, *hwît,* a. blanco, pálido; cano; puro; –, s. color blanco, m.; clara del huevo, f.; –, bn., breca, f. (pez).

whitebait, *–bât,* s. albur, alburno, gobio, f.

white-lead, *–lĕd,* s. albayalde, m. (cal de plomo).

white-heat, *–hĕt,* s. incandescencia, f.

white-hot, *–hŏt,* a. incandescente.

whiten, *–n,* v. a. & n. blanquear; emblanquecerse. [f.

whiteness, *–nĕs,* s. blancura, f.; palidez.

white-wash, *–wŏsh,* s. blanquete, m.; enlucimiento, m.; –, v. a. encalar; jalbegar.

whither, *hwĭth'âr,* ad. adonde, donde.

whithersoever, *–sŏĕv'âr,* ad. adonde quiera. [(pez).

whiting, *hwî'tĭng,* s. albur, cadoce, m.

whitish, *hwî'tĭsh,* a. blanquizco, blanquecino.

whitlow, *hwît'lŏ,* s. panadizo, panarizo, m.

Whitsuntide, *hwĭt'sûntîd,* s. Pentecostés, m., fiesta judaica y cristiana.

whittle, *hwĭt'tl,* v. a. cortar con navaja.

whiz, *hwĭz,* v. n. zumbar, silbar.

who, *hŏ,* pn. quien, que.

who(so)ever, *–(sŏ)ĕv'âr,* pn. quienquiera que, cualquiera que. [–, s. total, m.

whole, *hŏl,* a. todo, total; sano, entero;

wholesale, *–sâl,* s. venta por mayor, f.

wholesome, *–sûm,* a. sano, saludable; **–ly,** ad. saludablemente. [f.

wholesomeness, *–sûmnĕs,* s. salubridad,

wholly, *hŏl'lĕ,* ad. enteramente.

whom, *hŏm,* pn. acusativo de **who.**

whomsoever, *–sŏĕv'âr,* pn. acusativo de **whosoever.** [chear, gritar.

whoop, *hŏp,* s. gritería, f.; –, v. n. hu-

whooping-cough, *–îng kôf,* s. pertusis, f.

whore, *hŏr,* s. puta, f.

why, *hwî,* ad. porque.

wick, *wĭk,* s. torcida f.; pábilo, m.

wicked, *wĭk'ĕd,* a. malvado, perverso; **–ly,** ad. malamente. [nidad, f.

wickedness, *–nĕs,* s. perversidad, malig-

wicker, *wĭk'âr,* s. mimbre, m.; –, a. tejido de mimbres.

wicket, *wĭk'ĕt,* s. postigo, m.; portezuela, f.

wide, *wîd,* a. ancho, vasto, remoto; **–ly,** ad. lejos; anchamente; **far and –,** por todos lados.

wide-awake, *–âwâk,* a. despierto.

widen, *–n,* v. a. ensanchar, extender.

wideness, *–nĕs,* s. anchura, extensión, f.

widgeon, *wĭj'ân,* s. ayucasta, avutarda, f.

widow, *wĭd'ŏ,* s. viuda, f.; –, v. a. privar á una mujer de su marido.

widower, *–âr,* s. viudo, m.

widowhood, *–hŏd,* s. viudez, viudedad, f.

width, *wĭdth,* s. anchura, f. [f.

wield, *wēld,* v. a. manejar, empuñar.

wife, *wîf,* s. esposa, consorte, f.; mujer, f.

wifely, *–lĕ,* a. lo que conviene á una esposa. [esposa

wig, *wĭg,* s. peluca, f.

wig-block, *–blŏk,* s. cabeza de madera, f.

wight, *wît,* s. persona, criatura racional, f.

wig-maker, *wĭg'mâkâr,* s. peluquero, m.

wigwam, *wĭg'wăm,* s. cabaña de los indios, f. [salvaje; –, s. yermo, desierto, m.

wild, *wîld,* a. silvestre, feroz; desierto;

wilderness, *wĭl′ dŭrnĕs,* s. desierto, m.
wildfire, *wĭld′ fĭr,* s. fuego griego, m.; erisipela, f.
wilding, *wĭld′ ĭng,* s. manzana silvestre, f.
wildly, *wĭld′ lĕ,* ad. sin cultivo; desatinadamente. [brutalidad, f.
wildness, *wĭld′ nĕs,* s. selvatiquez, f.;
wile, *wĭl,* s. dolo, engaño, m.; astucia, f.
wilful, *wĭl′ fŭl,* a. voluntarioso, temoso; **—ly,** ad. obstinadamente.
wilfulness, *—nĕs,* s. obstinación, f.
wiliness, *wĭl′ lĭnĕs* s. fraude, engaño, m.
will, *wĭl,* s. voluntad, f.; testamento, m.; **—,** v. a. querer, desear.
willing, *—lĭng,* a. inclinado, pronto; **—ly,** ad. de buena gana. [buena gana, f.
willingness, *—lĭngnĕs,* s. buena voluntad,
willow, *wĭl′ lŏ,* s. sauce, m. (árbol.)
wily, *wĭl′ lĕ,* a. astuto, insidioso.
wimble, *wĭm′ bl,* s. berbiquí, m.
wimple, *wĭm′ pl,* s. velo, m.; (mar.) gallardete, m. [lograr.
win, *wĭn,* v. a. ganar, conquistar; alcanzar;
wince, *wĭns,* v. n. cocear.
winch, *wĭnsh,* s. cigüeña de torno, f.
wind, *wĭnd,* s. viento, m.; aliento, m.; pedo, m.
wind, *wĭnd,* v. a. & n. soplar; dar vuelta; torcer; ventear; serpentear; mudar, cambiar; envolver; volverse, cambiarse.
winded, *wĭnd′ ĕd,* a. desalentado.
winder, *wĭn′ dŭr,* s. argadillo, m.
windiness, *wĭn′ dĭnĕs,* s. ventosidad, flatulencia, f.
winding, *wĭnd′ ĭng,* s. vuelta, revuelta, f.
winding-sheet, *—shĕt,* s. mortaja, f.
windlass, *wĭnd′ lăs,* s. árgano, m.
wind-mill, *wĭnd′ mĭl,* s. molino de viento,
window, *wĭn′ dŏ,* s. ventana, f. [m.
wind-pipe, *wĭnd′ pĭp,* s. traquea, f.
windward, *wĭnd′ wărd,* ad. (mar.) á barlovento. [lovento.
windy, *wĭn′ dĕ,* a. ventoso. [lovento.
wine, *wĭn,* s. vino, m.
wine-bibber, *—bĭbbăr,* s. borracho, m.
wine-press, *—prĕs,* s. prensa, f.; lagar, m.
wine-taster, *—tăstăr,* s. piloto, m.
wing, *wĭng,* s. ala, f., aventador, m.; **—,** v. a. dar alas; mover las alas.
winged, *—d,* a. alado.
wink, *wĭngk,* v. n. cerrar los ojos; guiñar; **—,** s. pestañeo, m.; guiño, m.
winner, *wĭn′ năr,* s. ganador, vencedor, m.
winning, *wĭn′ nĭng,* s. ganancia, f.; lucro, m.; **—,** a. atractivo, encantador.
winnow, *wĭn′ nŏ,* v. a. aventar.
winsome, *wĭn′ sŭm,* a. alegre, jovial.
winter, *wĭn′ tŭr,* s. invierno, m.; **—,** v. n. invernar.
wintry, *wĭn′ trĕ,* a. brumal, invernal.
wipe, *wĭp,* v. a. limpiar; borrar; **—,** s. limpiadura, f.; limpión, m.; pulla, f.
wire, *wĭr,* s. alambre, m.
wiredraw, *—dră,* v. a. tirar á hilo algunos metales; prolongar. [trigante, m.
wire-puller, *—pŭl′ lăr,* s. tiritero, m.; intrigante, m.
wire-pulling, *—pŭl′ lĭng,* s. maquinaciones secretas, f. pl.
wiry, *wĭr′ rĕ,* a. hecho de alambre.

wisdom, *wĭz′ dŭm,* s. sabiduría, prudencia, f. [juicio, f. pl.
wisdom-teeth, *—tĕth,* s. pl. muelas del
wise, *wĭz,* a. sabio, docto, juicioso, prudente; **—,** s. modo, m., manera, f.
wiseacre, *—ăkŭr,* s. necio, tonto, m.
wisely, *—lĕ,* ad. sabiamente, con prudencia.
wish, *wĭsh,* v. a. desear, anhelar, ansiar; **—,** s. anhelo, deseo, m. [anhelo.
wishful, *—fŭl,* a. deseoso; **—ly,** ad. con
wisp, *wĭsp,* s. manojo de heno &c., m.
wistful, *wĭst′ fŭl,* a. pensativo, atento; **—ly,** ad. atentamente.
wit, *wĭt,* s. entendimiento, ingenio, m.; **to —,** ad. es á saber.
witch, *wĭtsh,* s. bruja, hechicera, f.
witchcraft, *—krăft,* s. brujería, f.; sortilegio, m.
witchery, *—ărĕ,* s. hechicería, f.
with, *wĭth,* pr. con; por, de, á. [también.
withal, *wĭthăl′,* ad. además, á más de esto;
withdraw, *wĭthdră′,* v. a. quitar; privar; retirar; **—,** v. n. retirarse, apartarse.
withe, *wĭth,* s. mimbre, m.
wither, *wĭth′ ŭr,* v. n. marchitarse, secarse; **—,** v. a. marchitar. [dir, retener.
withhold, *wĭthhŏld′,* v. a. detener, impe-
withholder, *—ăr,* s. detentador, m.
within, *wĭthĭn′,* pr. dentro, adentro; **—,** ad. interiormente; en casa.
without, *wĭthŏŭt′,* pr. sin, con falta de; fuera, afuera; **—,** ad. exteriormente; **—,** c. si no, sin que, á menos que.
withstand, *wĭthstănd′,* v. a. resistir.
withy, *wĭth′ ĕ (wĭth′ ĕ),* s. mimbre, m.
witless, *wĭt′ lĕs,* a. necio, tonto, falto de ingenio.
witling, *wĭt′ lĭng,* s. truhán, chocarrero, m.
witness, *wĭt′ nĕs,* s. testimonio, m.; testigo, m.; **—,** v. a. atestiguar, testificar; **—,** v. n. servir de testigo.
witted, *wĭt′ tĕd,* a. ingenioso.
wittily, *wĭt′ tĭlĕ,* ad. ingeniosamente.
wittiness, *wĭt′ tĭnĕs,* s. agudeza, f.; chiste ingenioso, m.; viveza de ingenio, f. [sito.
wittingly, *wĭt′ tĭnglĕ,* ad. adrede, de propó-
witty, *wĭt′ tĕ,* a. ingenioso, agudo, chistoso.
wizard, *wĭz′ ărd,* s. brujo, hechicero, m.
woad, *wŏd,* s. hierba pastel, gualda, f.
woe, *wŏ,* s. dolor, m.; miseria, f.
woeful, *—fŭl,* a. triste, funesto; **—ly,** ad. tristemente.
wolf, *wŭlf,* s. lobo, m.; **she —,** loba, f.
wolfish, *—ĭsh,* a. lobero.
woman, *wŭm′ ăn,* s. mujer, f.; **— of the town,** dama cortesana, f.
woman-hater, *—hătŭr,* s. aborrecedor de las mujeres, m. [m.
womanhood, *—hŭd,* s. estado de mujer,
womanish, *—ĭsh,* a. mujeril.
womankind, *—kĭnd,* s. mujeriego, m.
womanly, *—lĕ,* a. mujeril, mujeriego.
womb, *wŏm,* s. útero, m.
wonder, *wŭn′ dŭr,* s. milagro, m.; maravilla, f.; **—,** v. n. maravillarse de.
wonderful, *—fŭl,* a. maravilloso; **—ly,** ad. maravillosamente.

wondrous, *wŭn´drŭs,* a. maravilloso.

won't, *wónt,* abrev. de **will not.**

wont, *wŭnt,* s. uso, m., costumbre, f.

wonted, *—ĕd,* a. acostumbrado, usual.

woo, *wŏ,* v. a. cortejar, requerir de amores.

wood, *wŭd,* s. bosque, m.; selva, f.; madera, f.; leña, f.

wood-bine, *—bīn,* s. (bot.) madreselva, f.

wood-cock, *—kŏk,* s. chocha, becada, f.

wood-cut, *—kŭt,* s. estampa de madera, f.

wood-cutter, *—kŭttŭr,* s. grabador en láminas de madera, xilógrafo, m.

wooded, *—ĕd,* a. arbolado.

wooden, *—n,* a. hecho de madera.

wood-land, *—lănd,* s. arbolado, m.

wood-louse, *—lŏŭs,* s. cucaracha, f.

woodman, *—măn,* s. cazador, m.; guardabosque. m. [m.

wood-pecker, *—pĕkŭr,* s. picamaderos,

wooer, *wŏ´ŭr,* s. galanteador, m.

woof, *wŏf,* s. trama, f.; textura, f.

wool, *wŭl,* s. lana, f.

wool-gathering, *—găthŭring,* a. **his wits have gone —,** tiene distracciones.

woolly, *—lĕ,* a. lanudo, lanoso.

word, *wŭrd,* s. palabra, voz, f.; —, v. a. expresar; componer en escritura; —, v. n. disputar, trabarse de palabras.

wordiness, *—inĕs,* s. verbosidad, f.

wordy, *—ĕ,* a. verboso.

work, *wŭrk,* v. n. trabajar; obrar; estar en movimiento ó en acción; fermentar; —, v. a. trabajar, labrar; fabricar, manufacturar; —, s. trabajo, m.; fábrica, f.; obra (de manos), f.; fatiga, f.

worker, *—ŭr,* s. trabajador, obrero, m.

work-house, *—hŏŭs,* s. fábrica, f.; obrador, taller, m. [m.

working-day, *—ĭngdā,* s. día de trabajo,

workman, *—măn,* s. artífice, labrador, m.

workmanship, *—mănship,* s. manufactura, f.; destreza del artífice, f.

workshop, *—shŏp,* s. taller, obrador, m.

work-woman, *—wŭmăn,* s. costurera, f.; obrera, f.

world, *wŭrld,* s. mundo, m.; universo, m.; modo de vida, m.; gente, f.; gentío, m.; cantidad, f.: **—to-be,** el otro mundo.

worldliness, *—linĕs,* s. vanidad mundana, f.; profanidad, f.; avaricia, f.

worldling, *—ling,* s. hombre mundano, m.

worldly, *—lĕ,* a. mundano, terreno.

worm, *wŭrm,* s. gusano, gorgojo, m.; (of a screw) rosca de tornillo, f.; —, v. n. trabajar ú obrar lentamente y debajo de mano; —, v. a. suplantar por medios secretos. [llado.

worm-eaten, *—ĕtn,* a. carcomido, apoli-

wormwood, *—wŭd,* s. (bot.) ajenjo, m.

worry, *wŭr´rĕ,* v. a. molestar, atormentar.

worse, *wŭrs,* a. & ad. peor; de un modo más malo.

worship, *wŭr´ship,* s. culto, m.; adoración, f.; **your —,** Usía, f.; Vuestra Merced, f.; —, v. a. adorar, venerar.

worshipful, *—fŭl,* a. venerable.

worshipping, *—ping,* s. adoración, f.

worst, *wŭrst,* a. pésimo, malísimo, —, s. lo peor, lo más malo, m.; —, v. a. vencer, sujetar.

worsted, *wŭr´stĕd,* s. estambre, m. [sujetar.

wort, *wŭrt,* s. hierba, f.; cerveza nueva, f.

worth, *wŭrth,* s. valor, precio, m.; mérito, m.; —, a. digno, benemérito; que vale.

worthily, *wŭr´thĭlĕ,* ad. dignamente, convenientemente. [mérito, m.

worthiness, *wŭr´thinĕs,* s. dignidad, f.;

worthless, *wŭrth´lĕs,* a. indigno.

worthlessness, *—nĕs,* s. indignidad, vileza, f. [s. varón ilustre, m.

worthy, *wŭr´thĕ,* a. digno, benemérito; —,

would-be, *wŭd´bĕ,* a. titulado, llamado.

wound, *wŭnd,* s. herida, llaga, f.; —, v. a. herir, llagar.

wove(n), *wŏv(´n),* a. semejante á la vitela.

wraith, *rāth,* s. fantasma, m.

wrangle, *răng´gl,* v. n. pelotear, reñir; —, s. pelotera, riña, f. [m.

wrangler, *—ŭr,* s. pendenciero, disputador,

wrap, *răp,* v. a. arrollar; envolver.

wrapper, *—pŭr,* s. envolvedero, m.; ropa de casa, f.; chal pequeño, m.

wrath, *răth,* s. ira, rabia, cólera, f.

wrathful, *—fŭl,* a. furioso, irritado.

wreak, *rēk,* v. a. vengar; **to — one's anger,** descargar la cólera.

wreath, *rēth,* s. corona, guirnalda, f.; —, v. a. coronar; enroscar, torcer.

wreck, *rĕk,* s. naufragio, m.; destrucción, f.; navío naufragado, m.; —, v. a. & n. naufragar; arruinar; salir mal de algún negocio.

wren, *rĕn,* s. reyezuelo, m. (avecilla).

wrench, *rĕnsh,* v. a. arrancar; dislocar; torcer; —, s. torcedura del pie, f.; destornillador, m. [arrebatar.

wrest, *rĕst,* v. a. arrancar, quitar á fuerza.

wrestle, *rĕs´l,* v. n. luchar; disputar.

wrestling, *rĕs´ling,* s. lucha, f.

wretch, *rĕtsh,* s. pobre infeliz, hombre muy miserable, m.; **poor —!** ¡pobre diablo!

wretched, *—ĕd,* a. infeliz, miserable; mezquino; **—ly,** ad. miserablemente.

wretchedness, *—ĕdnĕs,* s. miseria, f.; vileza, bajeza, f.

wriggle, *rig´gl,* v. n. menearse, agitarse.

wright, *rīt,* s. artesano, obrero, m. [jar.

wring, *ring,* v. a. torcer; arrancar; estru-

wrinkle, *ring´kl,* s. arruga (de la cara, del paño), f.; —, v. a. arrugar.

wrist, *rist,* s. muñeca, f.

wrist-band, *—bănd,* s. puño de camisa, m.

writ, *rit,* s. escrito, m.; escritura, f.; orden, f.

write, *rīt,* v. a. escribir; componer. [m.

writer, *—ŭr,* s. escritor, autor, m.

writhe, *rīth,* v. a. torcer; —, v. n. acongojarse. [m.; manuscrito, m.

writing, *rt´ing,* s. escritura, f.; escrito,

writing-book, *—bŭk,* s. cuaderno, m.

writing-desk, *—dĕsk,* s. escritorio, m.

writing-master, *—măstŭr,* s. maestro de escribir, m. [escribir, m.

writing-paper, *—păpŭr,* s. papel para

wrong, *rŏng,* s. injuria, f.; injusticia, f.;

perjuicio, m.; error, m.; –, a. errado, falso; –, ad. mal, injustamente; al revés; –, v. a. agraviar, injuriar.

wrongful, *–fŭl,* a. injusto, inicuo; **-ly,** ad. injustamente.

wroth, *rŏth,* a. encoleradizo.

wrought, *rŏt,* a. hermoseado.

wry, *rī,* a. torcido, tuerto, no derecho.

wry-face, *–făs,* s. mueca, f.

wry-neck, *–něk,* s. torcecuello, m. (ave).

X.

xebec, *zě běk,* s. (mar.) jabeque, m.

Xmas, *krĭs măs,* s. Natividad, f.

xylography, *zīlŏg`răfĭ,* s. arte de grabar en láminas de madera, f.

Y.

yacht, *yŏt,* s. (mar.) yacte, yac, m.

yam, *yăm,* s. (bot.) batata, f.

Yankee, *yăng`kĕ,* s. indígena de los Estados Unidos, m.

yard, *yărd,* s. corral, m.; yarda (medida), f.; (mar.) verga, f. [m.

yarn, *yărn,* s. estambre, m.; hilo de lino,

yarrow, *yăr`rŏ,* s. (bot.) milhojas, f.

yawl, *yăl,* s. (mar.) serení, m.

yawn, *yăn,* v. n. bostezar.

yclept, *ěklěpt´,* a. nombrado, llamado.

ye, *yě,* pn. vos.

yea, *yā,* ad. sí, verdaderamente.

yean, *yěn,* v. n. parir la oveja.

year, *yēr,* s. año, m.

year-book, *–bŏŏk,* s. anales, m. pl.

yearling, *–lĭng,* s. animal que tiene un año, m. [todos los años.

yearly, *–lĭ,* a. anual; –, ad. anualmente,

yearn, *yărn,* v. n. compadecerse; afligirse interiormente.

yearning, *–ĭng,* s. compasión, f.

yeast, *yěst,* s. jiste, m.

yell, *yěl,* v. n. aullar; –, s aullido, m.

yellow, *yěl`lŏ,* a. amarillo; –, s. color amarillo, m.

yellow-boy, *–bŏĭ,* s. (vulg.) guinea, f.

yellowish, *–ĭsh,* a. amarillento.

yellowness, *–něs,* s. amarillez, f.

yelp, *yělp,* v. n. latir, gañir.

yelping, *–ĭng,* s. gañido, m.

yeoman, *yŏ`măn,* s. hacendado, m.; ciertos guardias del rey de Inglaterra, m. pl.

yeomanry, *–rĕ,* s. conjunto de los hacendados de alguna provincia, m.; uno de los cuerpos de guardias del rey de Inglaterra. [ballerías; –, s. embuje, m.

yerk, *yărk,* v. a. golpear; cocear las cayes, *yěs* (vulg. *yĭs*), ad. sí.

yesterday, *yěs´tŭrdă,* ad. ayer.

yet, *yět,* c. sin embargo; pero; –, ad. adeyew, *yŏ,* s. tejo, m. (árbol). [más; aun.

yield, *yěld,* v. a. dar, producir; ceder, admitir; conceder; –, v. n. rendirse, someterse; asentir.

yielding, *–ĭng,* a. condescendiente.

yoke, *yŏk,* s. yugo, m.; yunta, f.; –, v. a. uncir; sojuzgar. [(árbol).

yoke-elm, *–ělm,* s. carpe, ojaranzo, m.

yolk, *yŏk,* **yelk,** *yělk,* s. yema de huevo, f.

yon(der), *yŏn(´dĕr),* ad. allí, allá.

yore, *yŏr,* ad. tiempo hace, en los tiempos de entonces.

you, *yŏ,* pn. vosotros, U., Vd., Uds., Vds.

young, *yăng,* a. joven, mozo.

youngish, *–gĭsh,* a. mozuelo, jovencillo.

youngster, *–stŭr,* s. jovencito, joven, m.

your(s), *yŏr(z),* pn. vuestro, de U(ds).; **sincerely -s,** de U. S.S.S. (su seguro servidor).

yourself, *–sělf´,* Ud. mismo. [dor).

youth, *yŏth,* s. juventud, adolescencia, f.; joven, m. [modo juvenil.

youthful, *–fŭl,* a. juvenil; **-ly,** ad. de un

youthfulness, *–něs,* s. juventud, f.

Z.

zany, *ză`ně,* s. gracioso (de las comedias italianas), m.; bufón, m.

zeal, *zěl,* s. celo, m.; ardor, m.

zealot, *zěl`ŏt,* s. celador, m.

zealotry, *zěl`ŭtrě,* **zealousness,** *–ăsněs,* s. fanatismo, m. [celo.

zealous, *zěl`ăs,* a. celoso; **-ly,** ad. con zenith, *zěn`ĭth,* s. zenit, cenit, m.

zephyr, *zěf`ŭr,* s. céfiro, m.

zero, *zě`rŏ,* s. zero, cero, m. [na, f.

zest, *zěst,* s. luquete, m.; sainete, m.; biz,

zigzag, *zĭg`zăg,* s. ese, f.; ziczag, m.

zinc, *zĭngk,* s. zinc, m. (metal).

zodiac, *zŏ`dĭăk,* s. zodíaco, m.

zone, *zŏn,* s. banda, faja, f.; zona, f.

zoological, *zŏŏlŏj`ĭkăl,* a. zoológico.

zoologist, *zŏŏl`ŏjĭst,* s. zoólogo, m.

zoology, *zŏŏ`lŏjě,* s. zoología, f.

zoophyte, *zŏ`ŏfīt,* s. zoofito, m.

zounds, *zŏŭnds,* i ¡cáscaras!

List of the most important geographical names

Abruzzi, ăbrŏt' sē, Abruzos, m. pl. [sinia, f.
Abyssinia, ăbĭssĭn' yă, Abi-
Adriatic, ădrĭăt' ĭk, s. (Mar) Adriático, m.
African, ăf' rĭkăn, s. & a. africano. [a. albanés.
Albanian, ălbā' nĭăn, s. & a.
Algiers, ăljērz', s. Argel, m.
Alpine, ăl' pĭn (ăl' pĭn), a. alpino, a.; -s, s. pl. alpecienses, m. pl.
Alps, ălps, s. pl. Alpes, m. pl.
Alsace, ălsăs', Alsacia, f.
Alsatian, ălsā' shĭăn, s. & a. alsaciano.
American, ămer' ĭkăn, s. & a. americano.
Andalusia, ăndălō' zhă, Andalucía, f.
Andalusian, ăndălō' zhăn, s. & a. andaluz.
Antwerp, ănt' wŭrp, Amberes, m.
Apennines, ăp' pĕnnīnz, Apeninos, m. pl.
Apulia, ăpō' lĭă, Apulia, Pulla, f.
Arab, ăr' ăb, **Arabian,** ărā' bĭăn, s. & a. árabe, arábigo.
Arabia, ărā' bĭă, Arabia, f.
Aragonese, ărăgŏnēz', s. & a. aragonés.
Archipelago, ărkĭpĕl' ăgŏ, Archipiélago, m.
Armenian, ărmē' nĭăn, s. & a. armenio, arménico.
Asia, ā' zhă (ā' shĭă), Asia, f.
Asiatic, ăzhĭăt' ĭk, s. & a. asiático, asiano.
Athenian, ăthē' nĭăn, s. & a. ateniense. [f. pl.
Athens, ă' thĕnz, Atenas,
Atlantic, ătlăn' tĭk, (Mar) Atlántico, m. [burgo, m.
Augsburg, ăgs' bŭrg, Aus-
Australian, ăstrā' lĭăn, s. & a. australasino.
Austrian, ăs' trĭăn, s & a. austriaco.

Baltic, băl' tĭk, Mar Báltico, m. [badas, f. pl.
Barbadoes, bărbā' dōz, Bar-
Barbary, băr' bări, Berbería, f. [f.
Basle, bā' zĕl (băl), Basilea,
Batavian, bătā' vĭăn, s. & a. bátavo. [f.
Bavaria, băvā' rĭă, Baviera,
Bavarian, -n, s. & a. bavario, bávaro.
Belgian, bĕl' jĭăn, s. & a. belga, m.; bélgico. [f.
Belgium, bĕl' jŭm, Bélgica,
Bengal, bĕngăl', Bengala, f.
Bengalese, bĕngălēz', s. & a. bengalés.
Berlin, bŭr' lĭn (bŭrlĭn'), Berlín, m. [Belén, m.
Bethlehem, bĕth' lĕhĕm,
Biscay, bĭs' kē, Vizcaya, f.
Black Forest, blăk fŏr' ĕst, Selva Negra, f.
Bœotia, bēŏ' shĭă, Beocia, f.
Bœotian, -n, s. & a. beociano.
Bohemian, bŏhē' mĭăn, s. & a. bohemo, m.; bohémico.
Bordeaux, bŏr' dō, Burdeos, m. [foro, m.
Bosphorus, bŏs' fŏrŭs, Bós-
Brazil, brăzĭl', Brasil, m.
Brazilian, -yăn, s. & a. brasileño. [m.
Breton, brĕt' ŏn, s. bretón,
Britain, brĭt' ĕn, (Great-) Gran Bretaña, f.
Briton, brĭt' ŏn, s. bretón, m. & f. [f.
Brittany, brĭt' ăni, Bretaña,
Brittish, brĭt' ĭsh, a. bretón; - Channel, la Mancha, [Brunswick, m.
Brunswic(k), brŭnz' wĭk,
Brussels, brŭs' sĕlz, Bruselas, f. pl.
Bulgarian, bŭlgā' rĭăn, s. & a. búlgaro.
Burgundian, bŭrgŭn' dĭăn, s. & a. borgoñón, borgoñés.

Burgundy, bŭr' gŭndĭ, Borgoña, f. [Bizancio, m.
Byzantium, bĭzăn' shĭŭm,

Cadiz, kā' dĭz, Cádiz, f.
Caffraria, kăfrā' rĭă, Cafrería, f.
Calabrian, kălā' brĭăn, s. & a. calabrés.
Calais, kăl' ĭs, Celés, m.
Calmuck, kăl' mŏk, calmuco, m.
Cambridge, kăm' brĭj, Cambrije, Cambrigia, f.
Campeachy, kămpē' tshĕ, Campeche, f.
Canaries, kănā' rĭz, Canary-Islands, kănā' rĭ ĭlănds, Canarias, f. pl.
Candian, kăn' dĭăn, s. & a. candiote.
Canterbury, kăn' tŭrbĕrĭ, Cantórberi, f. [rintĭa, f.
Carinthia, kărĭn' thĭă, Ca-
Carpathians, kărpā' thĭănz, Montes Carpetanos, m. pl. [chemir, m.
Cashmere, kăshmēr', Ca-
Caspian Sea, kăs' pĭăn sē, (Mar) Caspio, m.
Castile, kăstēl', Castilla, f.
Castilian, kăstĭl' yăn, s. & a. castellano.
Catalonia, kătălō' nĭă, Cataluña, f. [talán.
Catalonian, -n, s. & a. ca-
Caucasus, kă' kăsŭs, Cáucaso, m.
Ceylon, sĕ' lŏn, Ceilán, m.
Chaldea, kăldē' ă, Caldea, f.
Champagne, shămpān', Champaña, f.
China, tshī' nă, China, f.
Chinese, tshīnēz', s. & a. chino. [casĭa, f.
Circassia, sŭrkā' shĭă, Cir-
Circassian, -stăn, s. & a. circasiano.
Cologne, kŏlōn', Colonia, f.
Constantinople, kŏnstăn' tĭnō' pl, Constantinopla, f.

Copenhagen, *köpĕnhā'gĕn*, Copenaga, f.

Corfu, *kŏrfö'*, Corfú, f.

Corinth, *kŏr'ĭnth*, Corinto, m.   [nualla, f.

Cornwall, *kŏrn'wŏl*, Cor-

Corsica, *kŏr'sĭkă*, Córcega, f.   [corso.

Corsican, —*n*, s. &a. corsés,

Cossack, *kŏs'sŭk*, cosaco, m.   [landia, f.

Courland, *kŏr'lănd*, Cur-

Cracow, *krā'kŏ*, Cracovia, f.

Cretan, *krē'tăn*, s. & a. cretense, m.; crético.

Crimea, *krimē'ă*, Crimea, f.

Croatia, *krŏā'shĭă*, Croacia, f.   [a.

Croatian, —*n*, s. & a. croato.

Cyprus, *sī'prŭs*, Chipre, f.

Dalmatia, *dălmā'shĭă*, Dalmacia, f.   [mático.

Dalmatian, —*n*, s. & a. dal-

Damascus, *dămăs'kŭs*, Damasco, m.   [m. & f.

Dane, *dān*, s. dinamarqués.

Danish, *dā'nĭsh*, a. danés, dinamarqués.

Danube, *dăn'ŭb*, Danubio,

Dauphinate, *dā'fĭnāt*, Dauphiny, *dā'fĭnē*, Delfinado, m.

Delphos, *dĕl'fŏs*, Delfos, f.

Denmark, *dĕn'mărk*, Dinamarca, f.   [Dovres, f.

Dover, *dō'vŭr*, Duvre, m.,

Dresden, *drĕs'dn*, Dresde, Dresda, f.   [querque, m.

Dunkirk, *dŭn'kŭrk*, Dun-

Dutch, *dŭtsh*, a. Dutchman, —*măn*, s. Dutchwoman, —*wŏmăn*, s. holandés, m., holandesa, f.

East-Indies, *ēst ĭn'dĭz*, Indias orientales, f. pl.

Edinburgh, *ĕd'ĭnbŭrrŏ*, Edimburgo, m.

Egypt, *ē'jĭpt*, Egipto, m.

Egyptian, *ē'jĭp'shăn*, s. & a. egipciaco, egipciano, egipcio.   [terra, f.

England, *ĭng'glănd*, Ingla-

English, *ĭng'glĭsh*, a. inglés, a; - Channel, la Mancha.

Englishman, —*măn*, Englishwoman, —*wŭlmăn*, inglés, m., inglesa, f.

Ephesus, *ĕf'ĕsŭs*, Efeso, m.

Epiros, *ĭpī'rŭs*, Epiro, m.

Esquimaux, *ĕs'kĭmō*, esquimales, m. pl.

Europe, *ū'rŏp*, Europa, f.

European, *ūrŏpē'ăn*, s. & a. europeo.

Euxine, *ū'ksĭn*, Mar Negro, Puente-Euxino, m.

Finland, *fĭn'lănd*, Finlandia, f.   [landés.

Finlander, —*ŭr*, s. & a. finlandés.   [flamenco.

Flanders, *flăn'dŭrz*, Flandes, f.

Fleming, *flĕm'ĭng*, s. & a.

Flemish, *flĕm'ĭsh*, a. flamenco.   [cia, f.

Florence, *flŏr'ĕns*, Floren-

Florentine, *flŏr'ĕntĭn*, s. & a. florentino.

Flushing, *flŭsh'ĭng*, Flesinga, f.

France, *frăns*, Francia, f.

Frankfort, *frănk'fŏrt*, Francoforte, m.

French, *frĕnsh*, a. francés, a; the —, s. pl. los franceses.

Frenchman, —*măn*, s. Frenchwoman, —*wŭman*, francés, m., francesa, f.   [m.

Friburg, *frī'bŭrg*, Friburgo,

Friesland, *frēz'lănd*, Frisia, f.   [frisón.

Frieslander, —*ŭr*, s. & a.

Frozen Ocean, *frō'zn ō'shăn*, Mar Glacial, Mar Helado, m.

Gaelic, *gā'lĭk*, s. & a. galés.

Galicia, *gălĭsh'ĭă*, Galicia, f.

Galilee, *găl'ĭlē*, Galilea, f.

Ganges, *găn'jēz*, Ganges, m.   [cuña, f.

Gascony, *găs'kŏnē*, Gascólico.

Gaul, *găl*, s. & a. Galia, f.; gálico.

Geneva, *jĕnē'vă*, Ginebra, f.

Genevese, *jĕnĕvēz'*, s. & a. ginebrés, ginebrino, a.

Genoa, *jĕn'ŏă*, Génova, f.

Genoese, *jĕnŏēz'*, s. & a. genovés.

German, *jŭr'măn*, s. & a. alemán.   [Germania, f.

Germany, —*ē*, Alemania, f.

Ghent, *gĕnt*, Gante, m.

Grecian, *grē'shăn*, s. & a. griego.

Greece, *grēs*, Grecia, f.

Greek, *grēk*, s. & a. griego.

Greenland, *grēn'lănd*, Groenlandia, f.

Greenlander, —*ŭr*, s. & a. groenlandés.

Grisons, *grē'sŏnz*, Grisones, m. pl.

Groningen, *grō'nĭngĕn*, Groninga, f.

Guelderland, *gĕl'dŭrlănd*, Gueldres, m.

Hague, *hāg*, Haya, f.

Hamburg, *hăm'bŭrg*, Hamburgo, m.

Hanse Towns, *hăns' tōŭns*, Ciudades Anseáticas, f. pl.

Havannah, *hăvăn'nă*, Habana, f.   [vecia, f.

Helvetia, *hĕlvē'shĭă*, Hel-

Hercynian Forest, *hĕr'sĭn'yăn fŏr'ĕst*, Harz, harts, el bosque de Harz.

Hesse, *hĕs*, Hesia, f.   [m.

Hessian, *hĕsh'ăn*, s. & a. hesés.   [da, f.

Holland, *hŏl'lănd*, Holan-

Hollander, —*ŭr*, holandés, m.   [Hungria, f.

Hungaria, *hănggā'rĕă*,

Hungarian, —*n*, s. & a. húngaro.   [gris, f.

Hungary, *hŭng'gărĕ*, Hun-

Iceland, *īs'lănd*, Islanda, f.

Icelander, —*ŭr*, s. & a. islandés, m.; islándico.

Illyria, *ĭllĭr'ĭă*, Iliria, f.

Indian, *ĭn'dĭăn*, s. & a. indiano; indio.

Indies, *ĭn'dĕz*, las Indias.

Ireland, *ī'rlănd*, Irlanda, f.

Irish, *ī'rĭsh*, a. irlandés.

Irishman, —*măn*, Irishwoman, —*wŏmăn*, irlandés, m., irlandesa, f.

Italian, *ĭtăl'ĭăn*, s. & a. italiano.

Italy, *ĭt'ălē*, Italia, f.

Japan, *jăpăn'*, Japón, m.

Japanese, *jăpănēz'*, s. & a. japonés.   [rusalén, m.

Jerusalem, *jĕrö'sălĕm*, Je-

Jutland, *jŭt'lănd*, Jutlandia, f.

Lacedæmonian, *lăsĕdēmō'nĭăn*, s. & a. laconio.

Lapland, *lăp'lănd*, Laponia, f.   [lapón.

Laplander, —*ŭr*, s. & a.

Lebanon, *lĕb'ănŏn*, Líbano, m.   [f.

Leghorn, *lĕg'ŏrn*, Liorna,

Leipsic, *lĭp'sĭk*, Lipsia, f.

Liege, *lĕj*, Lieja, f.

Lisbon, *lĭz'bŏn*, Lisboa, f.

Lisle, *līl*, Lila, f.

Lithuania, *lĭthā'nĭă*, Lituania, f.

Lithuanian, —*n*, s. & a. lituaniense, m.; lituáni(c)o.

Livonian, *lĭvō'nĭăn*, s. & a. livoniano.

Lombard, *lŏm'bŭrd*, s. & a. lombardo, m.; lombárdico.

Lombardy, —*ē*, Lombardía, f.   [m.

London, *lŏn'dn*, Londres, f.

Lorraine, *lŏrrān'*, Lorena, f.

Low-Countries, lŏ' kŭn-triz, Países Bajos, m. pl.

Lusatia, lūsā' shĭā, Lusacia, f.

Lusatian, —n, s. & a. lusaciano.

Luxemburg, lŭks' embŭrg, Lucemburgo, Lujemburgo, m.

Lyons, lī' ŭnz, León, m.

Macedonian, măsedō' nĭăn, s. & a. macedónio, m.; macedónico, f.

Madeira, mădā' rā, Madera, f.

Maese, māz, Mosa, f.

Majorca, mājōr' kā, Mallorca, f.

Malines, mălēn', Malina, f.

Maltese, măltēz', s. & a. maltés.

Marseilles, mărsālz', Marsella, f.

Mecca, mĕk' kā, Meca, f.

Mediterranean, mĕdĭtĕr-rā' nĭăn, Mediterráneo, m.

Mentz, mĕnts, Maguncia, f.

Messina, mĕssī' nā, Mesina, f.; mejicano.

Mexican, mĕks' ĭkăn, s. & a.

Mexico, mĕks' ĭkō, Méjico, m.

Milan, mĭl' ăn, Milano, m.

Minorca, mĭnōr' kā, Menorca, f.; lucas, f. pl.

Moluccas, mōlŭk' kăz, Moluccas, f.

Moor, mōr, s. Moorish, —ish, a. moro.

Moravian, mōrā' vĭăn, s. & a. moravo.

Morocco, mōrŏk' kō, Marruecos, m. pl.

Moscow, mŏs' kō, Moscú, f.

Moselle, mōzĕl', Mosela, f.

Mulatto, mŭlăt' ō, mulato, m., Mulattress, mŭlăt'-rĕs, mulata, f.

Munich, mū' nĭk, Monaco, Munich, m.; moscovita.

Muscovite, mŏs' kŏvīt, a.

Muscovy, mŏs' kŏvē, Moscovia, f.

Naples, nā' plz, Nápoles, m.

Neapolitan, nēăpŏl' ĭtăn, s. & a. napolitano.

Netherlands, nĕ' thărlăndz, Países Bajos, m. pl.

Neufchatel, nāshătĕl', Neucastel, m.

New-Foundland, nū'-făndlănd, Terranova, f.

New York, nū yŏrk', Nueva York, f.

Nice, nēs, Niza, f.

Nile, nīl, Nilo, m.

Nimeguen, nĭmā' gĕn, Nimega, f.

Norman, nŏr' măn, s. & a. normando, m.; normánico.

Normandy, —dē, Normandia, f.

North America, nŏrth' amĕr' ĭkā, América del Norte, f.; f.

Norway, nŏr' wē, Noruega, f.

Norwegian, nŏrwē' jĭăn, s. & a. noruego.

Nubian, nū' bĭăn, s. & a. nubio.

Nuremberg, nū' rĕmbŭrg, Nuremberga, f.

Olympus, ōlĭm' pŭs, Olimpo, m.; f. pl.

Orkneys, ŏrk' nĭz, Orcadas, f.

Ostend, ŏstĕnd', Ostende, f.

Ottoman Empire, ŏt' ōmăn ĕm' pīr, la Puerta.

Pacific, păsĭf' ĭk, (Mar) Pacífico, m.; latinado, m.

Palatinate, pălăt' ĭnăt, Palatinado, m.

Palestine, păl' ĕstīn, Palestina, f.; parisiense.

Parisian, părĭs' ĭăn, s. & a.

Parnassus, părnăs' sŭs, Parnaso, m.

Peloponnesus, pĕlōpŏn-nē' sŭs, Peloponeso, m.

Persian, pĕr' shăn, s. & a. persa, m.; persiano.

Peru, pĕrō', Perú, m.

Petersburg, pē' tŭrzbŭrg, Pedroburgo, m.

Phenicia, fĕnē' shĭā, Fenicia, f.; nicio.

Phenician, —n, s. & a. fe-

Piedmont, pēd' mŏnt, Piamonte, m.

Piedmontese, pēdmŏntēz', s. & a. piamontés.

Poland, pō' lănd, Polonia, f.

Pole, pōl, m., Polish, pō' lĭsh, a. polaco.

Pontus, pŏn' tŭs, Ponto, m.

Portuguese, pŏrtūgēz', s. & a. portugués.

Prague, prāg, Praga, f.

Provence, prŏvăns', Provenza, f.; f.

Prussia, prŭs' shĭā, Prusia, f.

Prussian, prŭsh' ăn, s. & a. prusiano.

Pyrenean Mountains, pĭrēnē' ăn mŏũn' tĭnz, Pyrenees, pĭr' ĕnēz, Pirineos, m. pl.

Ratisbon, răt' ĭzbŏn, Ratisbona, f.; vena, f.

Ravenna, răvĕn' nā, Ra-

Rhenish, rĕn' ĭsh, a. del Rin ó del Rhin.

Rhine, rīn, Rin ó Rhin, m.

Rhinelander, —lăndŭr, habitante del Rhin, m.

Rhodes, rō' dĭz, Rodas, f. pl.

Rhone, rōn, Ródano, m.

Roman, rō' măn, s. & a. romano.

Rome, rōm, Roma, f.

Roumania, rōmā' nĭā, Romania, f.

Russia, rŭs' shĭā, Rusia, f.

Russian, rŭsh' ăn, s. & a. ruso, m.; rusiano.

Samoied, sămō' yĕd, Samoyedo, m.; deña, f.

Sardinia, sărdĭn' ĭā, Cerdeña, f.

Sardinian, —ăn, s. & a. sardo.

Savoy, săvŏĭ', Saboya, f.

Savoyard, —ărd', s. saboyano, a., m. & f.

Saxon, săks' ŏn, s. & a. sajon, m.; sajonio, a.

Saxony, —nē, Sajonia, f.

Scandinavia, skăndĭnā' vĭā, Escandinavia, f.

Schaffhausen, shăfhŏů' ĕn, Escafusa, f.

Scheldt, skĕlt, Escalda, f.

Sclavonia, sklăvō' nĭā, Esclavonia, f.

Sclavonian, —n, s. & a. esclavón, m.; esclavonio.

Scotch, skŏtsh, a. escocés; —man, —măn, s. escocés, m.; —woman, —wŭmăn, s. escocesa, f.; cia, f.

Scotland, skŏt' lănd, Esco-

Scottish, skŏt' tĭsh, a. escocés.

Seine, sān, Sena, m.

Servian, sŭr' vĭăn, s. & a. servio.

Siberia, sībē' rĭā, Siberia, f.

Siberian, —n, s. & a. siberiano.; siciliano.

Sicilian, sĭsĭl' ĭăn, s. & a.

Sicily, sĭs' ĭlē, Sicilia, f.

Silesian, sĭlē' shĭăn, s. & a. silesiano, m.; silesio.

Smyrna, smŭr' nā, Esmirna, f.; da, f.

Sound, sŏůnd, Sunda, Son-

South Sea, sŏůth sē, Mar Austral, m.

Spain, spān, España, f.

Spaniard, spăn' yărd, s. español, a. m. & f.

Spanish, spăn' ĭsh, a. español.

Sparta, spăr' tā, Esparta, f.

Spartan, —n, s. & a. espartano.

Stiria, stŭr' ĭā, Estiria, f.

Stirian, —n, s. & a. estiriano.; colino, m.

Stockholm, stŏk' ōlm, Esto-

Strasburg, străs' bŭrg, Estrasburgo, m.; gardo, m.

Stutgart, stŭt' gărt, Estu-

Suabia, *swð bèå*, Suabia, f.
Suabian, *—n*, s. & a. suabo.
Swede, *swêd*, s. sueco, m. & f.
Sweden, *swê' dèn*, Suecia, f.
Swedish, *swê' dïsh*, a. sueco.
Swiss, *swïs*, s. & a. suizo.
Switzerland, *swït' zär-länd*, Suiza, f. [cusa, f.
Syracuse, *sïr' äkûs*, Sira-

Tagus, *tä' gŭs*, Tajo, m.
Tartar, *tär' tär*, s. & a. tártaro. [f.
Tartary, *tär' tŭrě*, Tartaria,
Thames, *těmz*, Támesis, m.
Thermopylae, *thärmŏp' ïlē*, Termópilas, f. pl.
Thessalonica, *thěssālŏn' ïkä*, Tesalónica, f.
Thessalian, *thěssā' lïăn*, s. & a. tesaliense, tésalo.
Thessaly, *thěs' sălě*, Tesalia, f. [f.
Thracia, *thrā' shïă*, Tracia,
Thuringia, *thŭrïn' jïă*, Turingia, f.

Thuringian, *—n*, s. & a. turingiano, turingio.
Toulon, *tŏlŏn'*, Tolón, m.
Toulouse, *tŏlôs'*, Tolosa, f.
Transylvania, *trănsïlvā'-nïă*, Transilvania, f.
Trent, *trěnt*, Trento, m.
Treves, *trěvz*, Tréveris, m.
Trojan, *trō' ăn*, s. & a. troyano, a.
Troy, *trŏï*, Troya, f.
Tunis, *tū' nïs*, Túnez, m. & f.
Turk, *tŭrk*, s. turco, a, m.
Turkey, *tŭr' kě*, Turquía, f.
Turkish, *—ïsh*, a, turco, a.
Tuscany, *tŭs' kăně*, Toscana, f.
Tyrol, *tïr' ŏl*, el Tirol.
Tyrolese, *tïrŏlēz'*, s. & a. tirolés.

the United States (of North America), *thě ûnī' těd stäts*, Estados Unidos, m. pl.
Utrecht, *ū' rěkt*, Utreque, m.

Venetian, *věně' shïăn*, s. & a. veneciano.
Venice, *věn' ïs*, Venecia, f.
Versailles, *věrsālz'*, Versalles, m. [suyio, m.
Vesuvius, *vězū' vïŭs*, Ve-
Vienna, *vïěn' nä*, Viena, f.
Viennese, *vïěnněz'*, s. & a. vienés.
Vincennes, *vïnsěnz'*, Vincenas, f. pl.

Wales, *wālz*, Gales, m.
Wallachia, *wŏlā' kïă*, Valaquia, f. [valaquo.
Wallachian, *—n*, s. & a.
Warsaw, *wŏr' sä*, Varsovia, f. [Vallés.
Welsh, *wělsh*, s. natural de West-Indies, *wěst ïn' děz*, Indias occidentales, f. pl.
Wurtemberg, *wŭr' těm-bŭrg*, Vurtembergo, m.

Zealand, *zě' länd*, Zelanda, f.
Zurich, *zū' rïk*, Zurico, m.

List of the most usual Christian names

Abraham, *ā' brăhăm*, Abrahán.
Adam, *ăd' ăm*, Adán. [da.
Adelaide, *ăd' ĕlădd*, Adelai-
Adolphus, *ădŏl' fŭs*, Adolfo.
Alexander, *ălĕgzăn' dŭr*, Alejandro. [so.
Alphonso, *ălfŏn' zō*, Alfonso.
Ambrose, *ăm' brōz*, Ambrosio.
Amelia, *ămē' lïă*, Amalia.
Amy, *ā' mě*, Amita.
Andrew, *ăn' drō*, Andreo, a. [Andrés.
Ann, *ăn*, Ana.
Anthony, *ăn' tŏně*, Antonio.
Augustus, *ăgŭs' tŭs*, Augusto.
Austin, *ăs' tïn*, Agustín.

Bartholomew, *bärthŏl' ō-mă*, Bartolomé, Bartolomeo, Bártolo.

Beatrice, *bě' ătrïs*, Beatriz.
Ben, *běn*, Benjaminito.
Benedict, *běn' ĕdïkt*, Benito.
Bernard, *bŭr' nărd*, Bernardo. [Berta. [do.
Bertha, *bŭr' thă*, Berta.
Bertie, *bŭr' tě*, abreviatura de: Bertram, *bŭr' trăm*, Beltrán.
Bess, *běs*, Bessy, *—ě*, Betsey, *běť sě*, Isabelita.
Biddy, *bïd' dě*, Brigidita.
Bill, Billy, *bïl(' lě*), abreviatura de: William.
Blanche, *blănsh*, Bianca.
Bob, Bobby, *bŏb(' bě*), abreviatura de: Robert.
Bridget, *brï' jět*, Brígida.

Carry, *kăr' ě*, abreviatura de: Caroline, Carolina.
Catherine, *kă' thĕrïn*, Catalina.

Cecily, *sĕs' sïlě*, Cecilia.
Charles, *tshärlz*, Carlos.
Charlotte, *shăr' lŏt*, Carlota.
Christ, *krïst*, Cristo. [lota.
Christopher, *krïs' tŏfŭr*, Cristóbal.
Constance, *kŏn' stăns*, Constanza. [Constantino.
Constantine, *kŏn' stăntïn*,

Dan, *dăn*, abreviatura de: Daniel.
Dick, *dïk*, Ricardito.
Doll, *dŏl*, Doroteita.
Dorothy, *dŏr' ŏthě*, Dorotea.

Edward, *ĕd' wărd*, Eduardo.
Edwiga, *ĕdwě' gă*, Hedvigis.
Effie, *ĕf' fě*, abreviatura de: Euphemia.
Eleanor, *ĕl' ĕnŏr*, Leonor.

Elizabeth, ĕlĭz'ăbĕth, Isabella, ĕl'lĕn, Elena. [bel.
Ellen, ĕl'lĕn, Elena. [bel.
Ellie, ĕl'lĭ, abreviatura de: Eleanor.
Emily, ĕm'ĭlĭ, Emilia.
Essie, ĕs'sĭ, abreviatura de: Esther, Ester.
Eugene, ĕu'jĕn, Eugenio.
Eva, ĕ'vă, Eve, ĕv, Eva.

Fanny, făn'nĕ, Faquita.
Ferdinand, făr'dĭnănd, Fernando. [cisca.
Frances, frăn'sĕs, Frau-
Francis, frăn'sĭs, Frank, frănk, Francisco.
Frederica, frĕdĕrĭk'ă, Federica. [derico.
Frederic(k), frĕd'ĕrĭk, Fe-

Geoffr(e)y, jĕf'frĕ, Geofre-
George, jŏrj, Jorge. [do.
Giles, jĭlz, Julio.
Gillian, jĭl'ĭăn, Juliana.
Godfrey, gŏd'frĕ, Gofredo, Godofredo. [rio.
Gregory, grĕg'ŏrĕ, Grego-
Gustavus, gŭstă'vŭs, Gustavo.
Guy, gĭ, Guido. [tavo.

Hal, hăl, Enriquito.
Hannah, hăn'nă, Ana.
Harriet, hăr'ĭĕt, Enriqueta.
Harry, hăr'rĕ, por: Henry.
Helen, hĕl'lĕn, Helena.
Henry, hĕn'rĕ, Enrique.
Hilary, hĭl'ărĕ, Hilario.
Hodge, hŏj, abreviatura de: Roger.
Hugh, hū, Hugo. [Roger.
Humphrey, hŭm'frĕ, Hunfredo.

Ignatius, ĭgnă'shŭs, Ignacio.
Isabel, ĭz'ăbĕl, Elizabeth.

Jack, jăk, por: John, Juanillo, Juanito.
James, jāmz, Diego, Jaime.
Jane, jān, Juana.
Jasper, jăs'păr, Gaspar.
Jeffry, jĕf'rĕ, Geofredo.
Jemmy, jĕm'mĕ, abreviatura de: James.
Jenny, jĕn'nĕ, Juanita.
Jeremy, jĕr'ĕmĕ, Jeremías.
Jerry, jĕr'rĕ, abreviatura de Jeremy.
Jessie, jĕs'sĕ.

Jim, jĭm, abreviatura de: James.
Joan, jōn (jō'ăn), Juana.
Joe, jō, Pepe, Pepillo.
John, jŏn, Juan.
Johnny, -nĕ, Juanito.
Joseph, jō'zĕf, José, Pepe.

Kate, kāt, Kit, Kitty, kĭt'tĕ, abreviatura de: Catherine.
Kit, kĭt, abreviatura de Christopher.

Laurence, lă'rĕns, Lorenzo.
Lewis, lō'ĭs, Luis.
Lizzie, Lizz(e)y, lĭz'zĕ, Lizeta.
Lola, lō'lă, Dolores.
Loo, lō, abreviatura de: Louisa, lō'ĭză, Luisa.
Lucretia, lōkrē'shĭă, Lu-
Lucy, lō'sĕ, Lucía. [crecia.

Mabel, mā'bĕl.
Madeline, măd'lĭn, Magdalen, măg'dălĕn, Magdalena.
Madge, măj, Margery, măr'jărĕ, abreviatura de: Margaret. [Margarita.
Margaret, măr'gărĕt,
Mark, mărk, Marcos.
Martha, măr'thă, Marta.
Mary, mā'rĕ, María.
Mat, măt, abreviatura de: Matthew, măt'thū, Mateo.
Matilda, mătĭl'dă, Matilde.
Maud, mŏd, abreviatura de: Magdalen.
Meg, mĕg, abreviatura de: Margaret.
Michael, mā'kĕl, Miguel.
Moll, Molly, mŏl'(lĕ), (por: Mary), Mariquita, Maruja.
Morris, mŏr'rĭs, Mauricio.

Nan, năn, abreviatura de: Anna.
Nancy, năn'sĕ, Anita.
Ned, nĕd, abreviatura de: Edward.
Nell, Nelly, nĕl'(lĕ), abreviatura de: Eleanor.
Nick, nĭk, abreviatura de: Nicholas, Nicolás.
Noll, nŏl, abreviatura de: Oliver, ŏl'ĭvăr, Oliveros.

Patty, păt'tĕ, por: Matilda. [da.
Paul, pŏl, Pablo.
Peg, Peggy, pĕg'(gĕ), por: Margaret.
Peter, pē'tăr, Pedro.
Phil, fĭl, abreviatura de: Philip, fĭl'ĭp, Felipe.
Poll, Polly, pŏl'(lĕ), Maruja.

Ralph, rălf (rāf), Rodolfo, Rodulfo.
Raymond, rā'mănd, Raimundo, Ramón.
Reynold, rĕn'ŏld, Reinaldo.
Richard, rĭtsh'ărd, Ricardo. [rō'bĕrt, Roberto.
Robin, rŏb'ĭn, por: Robert,
Roger, rŏj'ăr, Rogerio.
Rose, rōz, Rosie, rō'sĕ, Rosa. [Rolando.
Rowland, rō'lănd, Roldán,

Sal, Sally, săl'(lĕ), por: Sarah, Sara.
Sam, săm, abreviatura de: Samuel, Samuel.
Sandy, săn'dĕ, abreviatura de: Alexander.
Solomon, sŏl'ŏmŏn, Salomón. [sŏfē, Sofía.
Sophia, sŏfē'ă, Sophy,
Stephen, stē'vĕn, Esteban.
Susan, sū'zăn, Susannah, sūzăn'nă, Susana.

Ted, Teddy, tĕd'(dĕ), por: Edward.
Theresa, tĕrē'ză, Teresa.
Tim, tĭm, abreviatura de: Timothy. [teo.
Timothy, tĭm'ŏthĕ, Timo-
Tobias, tŏbī'ăs, Toby, tō'bĕ, Tobías.
Tom, Tommy, tŏm'(mĕ), por: Thomas, tŏm'ăs, Tomás. Anthony.
Tony, tō'nĕ, abreviatura de:

Valentine, văl'ĕntīn, Valentino.
Violet, vī'ŏlĕt, Violeta.

Walter, wăl'tăr, Gualterio.
Will, wĭl, abreviatura de: William, wĭl'yăm, Guillelmo, Guillermo.

Zachary, zăk'ărĕ, Zacarías.

A List of the most usual Abbreviations in Writing and Printing.

A. B., *artium baccalaureus*, Bachelor of Arts = B.A.

A. B., able-bodied seaman.

Abp., Archbishop.

A. C., *ante Christum*, before Christ.

a c., account.

A. D., *anno Domini*, in the year of our Lord.

A. D. C., aide-de-camp.

ad lib., ad libit., *ad libitum*, at pleasure.

Æ, Æt., *ætatis*, aged.

A. G., adjutant-general.

a. m., *ante meridiem*, before noon.

A. M., *artium magister*, Master of Arts = M. A.

Anon., anonymous.

A. R. A., Associate of the Royal Academy.

A. S., AS., Anglo-Saxon.

A. V., Authorized Version.

avdp., avoirdupois.

b., born.

B. A., Bachelor of Arts.

Bart., Bt., Baronet.

B. C., before Christ.

B. C. L., Bachelor of Civil Law.

B. D., Bachelor of Divinity.

bd., bound (of books).

bds., boards (of books).

B. I., British India.

B. L., Bachelor of Law.

Bp., Bishop.

Bros., Brothers.

B. S. L., Botanical Society of London.

Cam., Camb., Cambridge.

Cantab., *Cantabrigiensis*, Cambridge student.

Cantuar., *Cantuariensis*, Canterbury student.

Cap., *caput*, chapter.

Caps., capitals, capital letters.

Capt., captain.

C. B., Companion of the Bath.

C. C. C., Corpus Christi College, Cambridge.

C. E., Civil Engineer

cf., *confer*, compare.

C. G., Consul-General.

Ch. Ch., Christ Church, Oxford.

chap., chapter.

Chas., Charles.

C. I., Order of the Crown of India.

cif., cost; insurance.

C. J., Chief Justice.

cl., cloth (of books).

Co., Company; county.

Col., Colonel.

Coll., College.

coll., colloq., colloquial.

con., *contra*, against.

C. P. S., *custos privati sigilli*, Keeper of the Privy Seal.

crim. con., criminal conversation.

C. S. I., Companion of the Star of India.

C. T., Certificated Teacher.

cwt., hundredweight.

d., died; *denarius*, penny.

D. C. L., Doctor of Civil Law.

D. D., Doctor of Divinity.

dep., deputy.

dept., department.

D. G., *Dei gratia*, by the grace of God.

D. L., Deputy Lieutenant.

do., Do., ditto, the same.

doz., dozen.

Dr., Doctor.

D. V., *Deo volente*, God willing.

dwt., pennyweight.

E. C., East Central postal district of London.

Ed., editor.

E. E., errors excepted.

e. g., *exempli gratia*, for instance.

E. I., East India.

E. I. C., East India Company.

E. I. C. S., East India Company's Service.

E. long., eastern longitude.

E. N. E., east-north-east.

E. S. E., east-south-east.

Esq., Esqr., Esquire.

etc., &c., *et cetera*, and so on.

et seq., *et sequentes*, and the following.

ex., example; **exx.**, examples.

Exch., Exchequer.

E. & O. E., errors and omissions excepted.

F., Fellow; Fahrenheit; folio.

fo., fol., folio.

Fahr., Fahrenheit (thermometer).

F. A. S., Fellow of the Antiquarian Society

F. B. S., Fellow of the Botanical Society.

fcp., fcap., foolscap.

F. D., *fidei defensor*, Defender of the Faith.

fec., *fecit*, he did it.

F. G. S., Fellow of the Geological Society.

F.H.S., Fellow of the Horticultural Society.
F. M., Field-marshal.
F. O. B., fob., free on board.
F. P., fire-plug.
F. R. A. S., Fellow of the Royal Astronomical Society.
F. R. C. P., Fellow of the Royal College of Physicians.
F. R. C. S., Fellow of the Royal College of Surgeons.
F R. G. S., Fellow of the Royal Geographical Society.
F. R. Hist. S., Fellow of the Royal Historical Society.
F. R. S., Fellow of the Royal Society.
F. R. S. L., Fellow of the Royal Society of Literature.
F.S.A., Fellow of the Society of Antiquaries.
F. S. S., Fellow of the Statistical Society.
ft., foot, feet.
F. Z. S., Fellow of the Zoological Society.

gal., gallon, gallons = 4.54 lit.
G. B. and I., Great Britain and Ireland.
G. C. B., Grand Cross of the Bath.
G. C. S. I., Grand Commander of the Star of India.
G. D., Grand Duke; Grand Duchess.
gent., gentleman (as title).
Geo., George.
gm., grammes.
G. M., Grand Master.
G. M. S. I., Grand Master of the Star of India.
Gov.-Gen., Governor-General.
G. P. O., General Post-Office.
gu., guinea; **gs.**, guineas.

H. B. C., Hudson Bay Company.
H. B. M., Her or His Britannic Majesty.
H. C., Herald's College.
H. E. I. C., Honourable East India Company.
hf.-bd., half-bound (of books).
H. G., Horse Guards.
H. H., His or Her Highness; His Holiness (the Pope).
hhd., hogshead.
H. I. H., His or Her Imperial Highness.
H. M., His or Her Majesty.
H. M. S., His or Her Majesty's service, ship, steamer.
Hon., Honourable.
H. P., horse-power; half-pay.
H. R. H., His or Her Royal Highness.
H. S. H., His or Her Serene Highness.

I., **Id.**, **Ids.**, island, islands.
ib., *ibid.*, *ibidem.*
id., *idem.*
i. e., *id est*, that is.
Ill., Illinois.
imp., imperial; imperative; imperfect tense.
in., inch, inches.
incog., incognito.
inst., instant.
int., interjection.
I. O. U., I owe you.
i. q., *idem quod*, the same as.

I. R. O., Inland Revenue Office.
I. W., Isle of Wight.

Jas., James.
J. C., Jesus Christ.
Jno., John.
Jos., Joseph.
Josh., Joshua.
J. P., Justice of the Peace.
jr., **junr.**, junior.

K. B., Knight of the Bath; King's Bench.
K. C. B., Knight Commander of the Bath.
K. C. S. I., Knight Commander of the Star of India.
K. G., Knight of the Garter.
K. M., Knight of Malta.
Knt., Knight.
Ky., Kentucky.

L., **l.**, £, pound sterling.
La., Louisiana.
lat., latitude.
lb., *libra*, pound in weight.
L. B., Bachelor of Law.
L. C., Lord Chancellor; Lord Chamberlain; Lower Canada.
L. C. J., Lord Chief Justice.
L. D., Lady-Day, Annunciation-Day.
L. G., Life-Guards.
Lieut., **Lt.**, Lieutenant.
LL. B., *legum baccalaureus*, Bachelor of Laws.
LL. D., *legum doctor*, Doctor of Laws.
L. L., Lord-Lieutenant.
loc. cit., **l. c.**, *loco citato*, in the place quoted.
long., longitude.
loq., *loquitur*, he or she speaks.
L. S., *locus sigilli*, the place of the seal.
L. S. D., £ s. d., *libra, solidi, denarii*, pounds, shillings, pence.

M., Monsieur.
M. A., *magister artium*, Master of Arts.
Maj., major.
Mass., Massachusetts.
M. B., *medicinæ baccalaureus*, Bachelor of Medicine.
M. C., Member of Congress.
M. D., *medicinæ doctor*, Doctor of Medicine.
Md., Maryland.
Me., Maine.
M. E., Mining Engineer; Military Engineer; Mechanical Engineer.
mem., memorandum.
Messrs., Messieurs.
M. F. H., Master of Fox Hounds.
M. G., Major-General.
Mgr., Monsignor.
M. Hon., Most Honourable.
Mi., Mississippi.
Mich., Michigan; Michaelmas.
Miss., Mississippi.
Minn., Minnesota.
M. L. C., Member of Legislative Council.
Mn., Michigan.
Mo., Missouri.
M. P., Member of Parliament.
Mr., Mister (title).

M. R. A. S., Member of the Royal Academy of Science.
M. R. C. S., Member of the Royal College of Surgeons.
M. R. G. S., Member of the Royal Geographical Society.
Mrs., mistress (title).
M. R. S. L., Member of the Royal Society of Literature.
Ms., manuscript; **Mss.,** manuscripts.
Mus. Doc., *musicæ doctor,* Doctor of Music.

N., north; northern postal district.
N. A., North America.
N. B., *nota bene,* note well, take notice; North Britain, Scotland; New Brunswick.
N. E., New England, United States of America; north-eastern postal district.
nem. con., *nemine contradicente,* no one opposing.
N. H., New Hampshire.
N. J., New Jersey.
N. lat., north latitude.
N. N. E., north-north-east.
N. N. W., north-north-west.
No., *numero,* number; **Nos.,** numbers.
N. O., New Orleans.
N. S., Nova Scotia; New Style (of the calendar).
N. T., New Testament.
N. W., north-west; north-western postal district.
N. Y., New York.
N. Z., **N. Zeal.,** New Zealand.

O., Ohio.
ob., *obiit,* he *or* she died.
obs., obsolete.
obt., obdt., obedient.
O. H. M. S., on her Majesty's Service.
O. S., Old Style (of the calendar); on service.
O. T., Old Testament.
Oxon., *Oxonia,* Oxford; Oxford student.
oz., ounce, ounces.

p., page; pint; pipe; **pp.,** pages.
Pa., Pennsylvania.
par., paragraph.
payt., payment.
p. c., *per cent.,* *per centum.*
P. C., Privy Council; Privy Councillor; Police Constable.
pd., paid.
Penn., Pennsylvania.
Ph. D., *philosophiæ doctor,* Doctor of Philosophy.
P. L., Poet Laureate.
p. m., *post meridiem,* after noon.
P. M., Postmaster.
P. M. G., Postmaster-General.
P. O., Post-office; to be kept till called for.
P. O. O., Post-office Order.
P. & O. C., Peninsular and Oriental Steam-Navigation Company.
P. P., parish-priest.
P. P. C., *pour prendre congé,* for bidding adieu.
P. R. A., President of the Royal Academy.

Prof., Professor.
pron., pronounced; pronoun.
prox., *proximo,* of the next month.
P. R. S., President of the Royal Society.
Ps., Psalm.
P. S., post-script; permanent Secretary; Privy Seal.
P. T. O., please turn over.
pwt, pennyweight.
px., *pinxit,* painted by . . .

Q., Qy., query.
Q. B., Queen's Bench.
Q. C., Queen's Counsel.
q. e., *quod est,* which is.
Q. E. D., *quod erat demonstrandum.*
q. l., *quantum libet,* as much as you like.
qr., quarter; **qrs.,** quarters.
Q. S., *quantum sufficit,* as much as is necessary.
qt., quart; **qts.,** quarts.
q. v., *quod vide,* which see.

R., Réaumur (thermometer); Rex; Regina.
R. A., Royal Academy; Royal Artillery; Rear-Admiral.
R. C., Roman Catholic.
R. E., Royal Engineers.
recd., received.
Reg. Prof., Regius Professor, Royal Professor.
Rev., Revd., Reverend.
R. H. S., Royal Human Society.
R. I. P., *requiescat in pace.*
R. M. S., Royal Mail Steamer.
R. N., Royal Navy.
R. R., Right Reverend.
R. S., Royal Society of London.
Rs., rupees.
R. S. A., Royal Society of Antiquaries.
R. S. V. P., *répondez s'il vous plaît,* please to answer.
Rt., Right; **Rt. Hon.,** Right Honourable; **Rt. Rev.,** Right Reverend; **Rt. Wpful,** Right Worshipful.
R. T. S., Religious Tract Society.
Ry., railway.

s., shilling.
S. A., South America; South Africa.
sc., *sculpsit,* sculpted by . . .
sc., scil., *scilicet,* that's to say.
S. C., South Carolina.
Sc. B., Bachelor of Science.
scr., scruple (weight).
S. E., south-east; south-eastern postal district.
sec., secretary.
serv., servt., servant.
S. G., Solicitor-General.
sh., shilling.
S. J., Society of Jesus.
S. lat., south latitude.
S. P. C. K., Society for Promoting Christian Knowledge.
sq., square.
s. s., steam-ship.
S. S. E., south-south-east.
S. S. W., south-south-west.
St., Saint.

s. v., *sub voce.*
S. W., south-west.

Thos., Thomas.
Tim., Timothy.
Trin., Trinity.

U. C., Upper Canada.
U. K., United Kingdom.
ult., ultimo.
U. S., United States.

V., Victoria.
v., *versus,* against; *vide,* see.
Va., Virginia.
V. A., Vice-Admiral; Apostolical Vicar.
V. C., Victoria Cross; Vice-Chancellor.
Ven., Venerable (title).
V. G., Vicar-General.
viz., *vidilicet.*
vol., volume; **vols.,** volumes.
V. P., Vice-President.
V. R., Victoria Regina.

V. S., Veterinary Surgeon.
Vt., Vermont.

W., west; western postal district.
W. C., Western Central postal district;
    water-closet.
W. I., West-Indies.
W. long., western longitude.
W. N. W., west-north-west.
Wp., Worship (title of a judge)
Wpful., Worshipful (title).
W. S., writer of the signet.
W. S. W., west-south-west.
wt., weight.

X., Xt., Christ.
Xmas., Christmas.

Y. C., Yacht-Club.
yd., yard; **yds.,** yards.
yr., your; year; **yrs.,** yours.

Z. G., Zoological Gardens.

Forms of Address

Business Usage

Address: Señores Bernardo Villanova y Cía. *or*
    Sres. Bernardo Villanova y Cía.
Salutation: Muy señores nuestros:
Complimentary close: Muy attos. y as. s.s.,

Social Usage

Gentleman
Address: Señor Miguel Sandoval *or* Señor Sandoval.
    (Señor may be abbreviated to Sr.)
Salutation: Muy señor mío:
Complimentary close: Muy atentamente,

Unmarried woman
Address: Señorita Doña Dolores Rodríguez, *or* Señorita Dolores
    Rodríguez.
    (Señorita may be abbreviated to Srta., and Doña
    may be abbreviated to Da.)
Salutation: Muy distinguida señorita:
Complimentary close: De Vd. afma. amiga.

Married woman
Address: Señora Doña Pepita de Gómez, *or* Señora de Gómez,
    (Señora may be abbreviated to Sra.)
Salutation: Muy estimada señora:
Complimentary close: Soy de Vd. s.s.,

Present.	Imperfect.	Participle.	Present.	Imperfect.	Participle.
abide	abode	abode	drink	drank	drunk
am	was	been	drive	drove	driven
arise	arose	arisen	dwell	dwelt ❋	dwelt ❋
awake	awoke ❋	awaked	eat	ate, eat	eaten
backbite	backbit	backbitten	engrave	engraved	engraven ❋
bear	bore, bare	borne, born	fall	fell	fallen
beat	beat	beat, beaten	feed	fed	fed
become	became	become	feel	felt	felt
it befalls	it befell	befallen	fight	fought	fought
beget	begot, be-gotten	find	found	found
begin	began	begun	flee	fled	fled
begird	begirt ❋	begirt ❋	fling	flung	flung
behold	beheld	beheld	fly	flew	flown
bend	bent ❋	bent ❋	forbear	forbore	forborne
bereave	bereft ❋	bereft ❋	forbid	forbade	forbidden
beseech	besought	besought	forecast	forecast	forecast
beset	beset	beset	forego	forewent	foregone
bestride	bestrode	bestrid, be-stridden	foresee	foresaw	foreseen
			foretell	foretold	foretold
betake	betook	betaken	forget	forgot	forgot, gotten
bid	bid, bade	bid, bidden	forgive	forgave	forgiven
bind	bound	bound	forsake	forsook	forsaken
bite	bit	bit, bitten	forswear	forswore	forsworn
bleed	bled	bled	freeze	froze	frozen
blow	blew	blown	freight	fraught ❋	fraught ❋
break	broke	broken	geld	gelt ❋	gelt ❋
breed	bred	bred	get	got	got, gotten
bring	brought	brought	gild	gilt ❋	gilt ❋
build	built ❋	built ❋	gird	girt ❋	girt ❋
burn	burnt ❋	burnt ❋	give	gave	given
burst	burst	burst	go	went	gone
buy	bought	bought	grave	graved	graven ❋
can	could	—	grind	ground	ground
cast	cast	cast	grow	grew	grown
catch	caught	caught	hang	hung ❋	hung ❋
chide	chid	chid, chidden	have	had	had
choose	chose	chosen	hear	heard	heard
cleave	cleft, clove ❋	cleft, cloven ❋	heave	hove ❋	hove ❋
cling	clung	clung	hew	hewed	hewn ❋
clothe	clad ❋	clad ❋	hide	hid	hid, hidden
come	came	come	hit	hit	hit
cost	cost	cost	hold	held	held, holden
creep	crept	crept	hurt	hurt	hurt
crow	crew ❋	crowed	inlay	inlaid	inlaid
cut	cut	cut	interweave	interwove	interwoven
dare	durst ❋	durst ❋	inweave	inwove	inwoven
deal	dealt	dealt	keep	kept	kept
dig	dug ❋	dug ❋	kneel	knelt ❋	knelt ❋
dip	dipt ❋	dipt ❋	knit	knit ❋	knit ❋
distract	distracted	distraught ❋	know	knew	known
do	did	done	lade	laded	laden ❋
draw	drew	drawn	lay	laid	laid
dream	dreamt ❋	dreamt ❋	lead	led	led

*) Significa que este verbo se conjuga también regularmente.

89